LOCOMOTIVE ALLOCATIONS :

BR : SOUTHERN REGION

C000212074

Xpress PUBLISHING

37 Rhyd Fadog,
Caernarvon.
Gwynedd. LL55 3HL
(01286-870817. Fax 01286-870071)

Printed by W.O. Jones (Printers) Ltd

Copyright : Xpress Publishing 1998

Containing something like two hundred thousand separate items of information this book may constitute something of a record in terms of railway history. More importantly it should also provide the reader with a useful source of research by listing the movements of all mainland Southern Region locomotives during the 1950's. (To allow a 'buffer zone' the decade has been stretched by almost a year in each direction.)

In addition to Southern Railway classes the tables also include BR main line diesel and electric engines, standard locomotives, LMS classes produced and used by the SR, Austerity 2-8-0 and others brought under SR control during the period.

Because of the difficulties imposed by the SR numbering system, entries have been ordered by wheel arrangement; the general principle being that smaller locomotives are listed towards the front of the book with the larger further back.. BR and LMS locomotives are given in the rear together with a summary of diesel shunting engines.

Whilst every attention has been given to the accuracy of the contents - the information has been derived from data issued to the writers at the time of reallocation - the publishers would deem it a favour to be advised, with supporting evidence, of any errors so that amendments can be issued should the need arise.

loco	May-49	Jun-49	Aug-49	Sep-49	Dec-49	Feb-50	Mar-50
B4 0-4-0T (1891)							
30082	EASTLEIGH - 71A	EASTLEIGH - 71A	EASTLEIGH - 71A	EASTLEIGH - 71A	EASTLEIGH - 71A	EASTLEIGH - 71A	EASTLEIGH - 71A
30083	EASTLEIGH - 71A	EASTLEIGH - 71A	EASTLEIGH - 71A	EASTLEIGH - 71A	EASTLEIGH - 71A	EASTLEIGH - 71A	EASTLEIGH - 71A
30084	PLYMOUTH - 72D	PLYMOUTH - 72D	PLYMOUTH - 72D	PLYMOUTH - 72D	PLYMOUTH - 72D	PLYMOUTH - 72D	PLYMOUTH - 72D
30086	BOURNEMOUTH - 71B	BOURNEMOUTH - 71B	BOURNEMOUTH - 71B	BOURNEMOUTH - 71B	BOURNEMOUTH - 71B	BOURNEMOUTH - 71B	BOURNEMOUTH - 71B
30087	EASTLEIGH - 71A	EASTLEIGH - 71A	BOURNEMOUTH - 71B	BOURNEMOUTH - 71B	BOURNEMOUTH - 71B	BOURNEMOUTH - 71B	BOURNEMOUTH - 71B
30088	PLYMOUTH - 72D	PLYMOUTH - 72D	PLYMOUTH - 72D	PLYMOUTH - 72D	PLYMOUTH - 72D	PLYMOUTH - 72D	PLYMOUTH - 72D
30089	STEWARTS LANE - 73A	STEWARTS LANE - 73A	STEWARTS LANE - 73A	EASTLEIGH - 71A	EASTLEIGH - 71A	EASTLEIGH - 71A	EASTLEIGH - 71A
30093	BOURNEMOUTH - 71B	BOURNEMOUTH - 71B	BOURNEMOUTH - 71B	BOURNEMOUTH - 71B	BOURNEMOUTH - 71B	BOURNEMOUTH - 71B	BOURNEMOUTH - 71B
30094	PLYMOUTH - 72D	PLYMOUTH - 72D	PLYMOUTH - 72D	PLYMOUTH - 72D	PLYMOUTH - 72D	PLYMOUTH - 72D	PLYMOUTH - 72D
30096	EASTLEIGH - 71A	EASTLEIGH - 71A	EASTLEIGH - 71A	ASHFORD - 74A	ASHFORD - 74A	ASHFORD - 74A	ASHFORD - 74A
30102	PLYMOUTH - 72D	PLYMOUTH - 72D	PLYMOUTH - 72D	PLYMOUTH - 72D	PLYMOUTH - 72D	PLYMOUTH - 72D	PLYMOUTH - 72D
C14 0-4-0T (1906)							
30588	EASTLEIGH - 71A	EASTLEIGH - 71A	EASTLEIGH - 71A	EASTLEIGH - 71A	EASTLEIGH - 71A	EASTLEIGH - 71A	EASTLEIGH - 71A
30589	EASTLEIGH - 71A	EASTLEIGH - 71A	EASTLEIGH - 71A	EASTLEIGH - 71A	EASTLEIGH - 71A	EASTLEIGH - 71A	EASTLEIGH - 71A
'0458' 0-4-0ST (1890)							
30458	GUILDFORD - 70C	GUILDFORD - 70C	GUILDFORD - 70C	GUILDFORD - 70C	GUILDFORD - 70C	GUILDFORD - 70C	GUILDFORD - 70C
'1302' 0-4-0CT							
31302	STEWARTS LANE - 73A	STEWARTS LANE - 73A	W/D	W/D	W/D	W/D	W/D
D1 0-4-2T (1873)							
32215	EASTBOURNE - 75G	EASTBOURNE - 75G	EASTBOURNE - 75G	EASTBOURNE - 75G	EASTBOURNE - 75G	EASTBOURNE - 75G	W/D
32234	EASTBOURNE - 75G	EASTBOURNE - 75G	EASTBOURNE - 75G	EASTBOURNE - 75G	EASTBOURNE - 75G	EASTBOURNE - 75G	W/D
32252	HORSHAM - 75D	HORSHAM - 75D	HORSHAM - 75D	HORSHAM - 75D	HORSHAM - 75D	HORSHAM - 75D	HORSHAM - 75D
32253	BRIGHTON - 75A	BRIGHTON - 75A	BRIGHTON - 75A	W/D	W/D	W/D	W/D
32274	EASTBOURNE - 75G	EASTBOURNE - 75G	EASTBOURNE - 75G	EASTBOURNE - 75G	EASTBOURNE - 75G	EASTBOURNE - 75G	W/D
32359	DOVER - 74C	DOVER - 74C	DOVER - 74C	DOVER - 74C	DOVER - 74C	DOVER - 74C	DOVER - 74C
'0756' 0-6-0T (1907)							
30756	STEWARTS LANE - 73A	STEWARTS LANE - 73A	STEWARTS LANE - 73A	STEWARTS LANE - 73A	STEWARTS LANE - 73A	STEWARTS LANE - 73A	STEWARTS LANE - 73A
0757' 0-6-2T (1907)							
30757	PLYMOUTH - 72D	PLYMOUTH - 72D	PLYMOUTH - 72D	PLYMOUTH - 72D	PLYMOUTH - 72D	PLYMOUTH - 72D	PLYMOUTH - 72D
30758	PLYMOUTH - 72D	PLYMOUTH - 72D	PLYMOUTH - 72D	PLYMOUTH - 72D	PLYMOUTH - 72D	PLYMOUTH - 72D	PLYMOUTH - 72D
A1X 0-6-0T (1872)							
32635	DEPARTMENTAL	DEPARTMENTAL	DEPARTMENTAL	DEPARTMENTAL	DEPARTMENTAL	DEPARTMENTAL	DEPARTMENTAL
32636	BRIGHTON - 75A(N)	BRIGHTON - 75A(N)	BRIGHTON - 75A(N)	BRIGHTON - 75A(N)	BRIGHTON - 75A(N)	BRIGHTON - 75A(N)	BRIGHTON - 75A(N)
32640	ASHFORD - 74A	ASHFORD - 74A	ASHFORD - 74A	ASHFORD - 74A	ASHFORD - 74A	ASHFORD - 74A	ASHFORD - 74A
32644	ASHFORD - 74A	ASHFORD - 74A	ASHFORD - 74A	ASHFORD - 74A	ASHFORD - 74A	ASHFORD - 74A	ASHFORD - 74A
32646	FRATTON - 71D	FRATTON - 71D	FRATTON - 71D	FRATTON - 71D	FRATTON - 71D	FRATTON - 71D	FRATTON - 71D
32647	BRIGHTON - 75A(N)	BRIGHTON - 75A(N)	BRIGHTON - 75A(N)	BRIGHTON - 75A(N)	BRIGHTON - 75A(N)	BRIGHTON - 75A(N)	BRIGHTON - 75A(N)
32650	LANCING-75A	LANCING-75A	LANCING-75A	LANCING-75A	LANCING-75A	LANCING-75A	LANCING-75A
32655	FRATTON - 71D	FRATTON - 71D	FRATTON - 71D	FRATTON - 71D	FRATTON - 71D	FRATTON - 71D	FRATTON - 71D
32659	FRATTON - 71D	FRATTON - 71D	FRATTON - 71D	ASHFORD - 74A	ASHFORD - 74A	ASHFORD - 74A	ASHFORD - 74A
32661	FRATTON - 71D	FRATTON - 71D	FRATTON - 71D	FRATTON - 71D	FRATTON - 71D	FRATTON - 71D	FRATTON - 71D
32662	FRATTON - 71D	FRATTON - 71D	FRATTON - 71D	FRATTON - 71D	FRATTON - 71D	FRATTON - 71D	FRATTON - 71D
32670	ASHFORD - 74A	ASHFORD - 74A	ASHFORD - 74A	ASHFORD - 74A	ASHFORD - 74A	ASHFORD - 74A	ASHFORD - 74A
32677	FRATTON - 71D	FRATTON - 71D	FRATTON - 71D	FRATTON - 71D	FRATTON - 71D	FRATTON - 71D	FRATTON - 71D
32678	ASHFORD - 74A	ASHFORD - 74A	ASHFORD - 74A	ASHFORD - 74A	ASHFORD - 74A	ASHFORD - 74A	ASHFORD - 74A
E1 0-6-0T (1874)							
32097	NINE ELMS - 70A	NINE ELMS - 70A	NINE ELMS - 70A	NINE ELMS - 70A	W/D	W/D	W/D
32112	BOURNEMOUTH - 71B	BOURNEMOUTH - 71B	BOURNEMOUTH - 71B	BOURNEMOUTH - 71B	W/D	W/D	W/D
32113	TONBRIDGE - 74D	TONBRIDGE - 74D	TONBRIDGE - 74D	TONBRIDGE - 74D	TONBRIDGE - 74D	B ARMS - 73B	B ARMS - 73B
32127	BRIGHTON - 75A	BRIGHTON - 75A	BRIGHTON - 75A	BRIGHTON - 75A	W/D	W/D	W/D
32128	B ARMS - 73B	B ARMS - 73B	B ARMS - 73B	B ARMS - 73B	STEWARTS LANE - 73A	STEWARTS LANE - 73A	STEWARTS LANE - 73A
32129	NINE ELMS - 70A	NINE ELMS - 70A	FRATTON - 71D	FRATTON - 71D	FRATTON - 71D	FRATTON - 71D	FRATTON - 71D
32133	EASTLEIGH - 71A	EASTLEIGH - 71A	EASTLEIGH - 71A	EASTLEIGH - 71A	EASTLEIGH - 71A	EASTLEIGH - 71A	EASTLEIGH - 71A
32138	NINE ELMS - 70A	NINE ELMS - 70A	NINE ELMS - 70A	NINE ELMS - 70A	NINE ELMS - 70A	NINE ELMS - 70A	NINE ELMS - 70A
32139	BRIGHTON - 75A	BRIGHTON - 75A	BRIGHTON - 75A	BRIGHTON - 75A	BRIGHTON - 75A	BRIGHTON - 75A	BRIGHTON - 75A
32141	B ARMS - 73B	B ARMS - 73B	B ARMS - 73B	B ARMS - 73B	W/D	W/D	W/D
32142	B ARMS - 73B	B ARMS - 73B	B ARMS - 73B	B ARMS - 73B	B ARMS - 73B	B ARMS - 73B	B ARMS - 73B
32145	TONBRIDGE - 74D	TONBRIDGE - 74D	TONBRIDGE - 74D	TONBRIDGE - 74D	TONBRIDGE - 74D	TONBRIDGE - 74D	TONBRIDGE - 74D
32147	EASTLEIGH - 71A	EASTLEIGH - 71A	EASTLEIGH - 71A	EASTLEIGH - 71A	EASTLEIGH - 71A	EASTLEIGH - 71A	EASTLEIGH - 71A
32151	B ARMS - 73B	B ARMS - 73B	B ARMS - 73B	B ARMS - 73B	B ARMS - 73B	B ARMS - 73B	B ARMS - 73B
32153	FRATTON - 71D	FRATTON - 71D	FRATTON - 71D	FRATTON - 71D	FRATTON - 71D	FRATTON - 71D	FRATTON - 71D
32156	SOUTHAMPTON - 71I	SOUTHAMPTON - 71I	SOUTHAMPTON - 71I	SOUTHAMPTON - 71I	SOUTHAMPTON - 71I	SOUTHAMPTON - 71I	SOUTHAMPTON - 71I
32160	BASINGSTOKE - 70D	BASINGSTOKE - 70D	BASINGSTOKE - 70D	BASINGSTOKE - 70D	BASINGSTOKE - 70D	BASINGSTOKE - 70D	BASINGSTOKE - 70D
32162	BASINGSTOKE - 70D	BASINGSTOKE - 70D	BASINGSTOKE - 70D	BASINGSTOKE - 70D	W/D	W/D	W/D
32606	BRIGHTON - 75A	BRIGHTON - 75A	BRIGHTON - 75A	BRIGHTON - 75A	BRIGHTON - 75A	BRIGHTON - 75A	BRIGHTON - 75A
32689	SOUTHAMPTON - 71I	SOUTHAMPTON - 71I	SOUTHAMPTON - 71I	SOUTHAMPTON - 71I	SOUTHAMPTON - 71I	SOUTHAMPTON - 71I	SOUTHAMPTON - 71I
32690	FRATTON - 71D	FRATTON - 71D	FRATTON - 71D	FRATTON - 71D	FRATTON - 71D	W/D	W/D
32691	FRATTON - 71D	FRATTON - 71D	FRATTON - 71D	FRATTON - 71D	FRATTON - 71D	FRATTON - 71D	FRATTON - 71D
32694	FRATTON - 71D	FRATTON - 71D	FRATTON - 71D	FRATTON - 71D	FRATTON - 71D	FRATTON - 71D	FRATTON - 71D
E2 0-6-0T (1913)							
32100	STEWARTS LANE - 73A	STEWARTS LANE - 73A	STEWARTS LANE - 73A	STEWARTS LANE - 73A	STEWARTS LANE - 73A	STEWARTS LANE - 73A	STEWARTS LANE - 73A
32101	STEWARTS LANE - 73A	STEWARTS LANE - 73A	STEWARTS LANE - 73A	STEWARTS LANE - 73A	STEWARTS LANE - 73A	STEWARTS LANE - 73A	STEWARTS LANE - 73A
32102	STEWARTS LANE - 73A	STEWARTS LANE - 73A	STEWARTS LANE - 73A	STEWARTS LANE - 73A	STEWARTS LANE - 73A	STEWARTS LANE - 73A	STEWARTS LANE - 73A
32103	STEWARTS LANE - 73A	STEWARTS LANE - 73A	STEWARTS LANE - 73A	STEWARTS LANE - 73A	STEWARTS LANE - 73A	STEWARTS LANE - 73A	STEWARTS LANE - 73A
32104	STEWARTS LANE - 73A	STEWARTS LANE - 73A	STEWARTS LANE - 73A	STEWARTS LANE - 73A	STEWARTS LANE - 73A	STEWARTS LANE - 73A	STEWARTS LANE - 73A
32105	STEWARTS LANE - 73A	STEWARTS LANE - 73A	STEWARTS LANE - 73A	STEWARTS LANE - 73A	STEWARTS LANE - 73A	STEWARTS LANE - 73A	STEWARTS LANE - 73A
32106	STEWARTS LANE - 73A	STEWARTS LANE - 73A	STEWARTS LANE - 73A	STEWARTS LANE - 73A	STEWARTS LANE - 73A	STEWARTS LANE - 73A	STEWARTS LANE - 73A
32107	STEWARTS LANE - 73A	STEWARTS LANE - 73A	STEWARTS LANE - 73A	STEWARTS LANE - 73A	STEWARTS LANE - 73A	STEWARTS LANE - 73A	STEWARTS LANE - 73A
32108	DOVER - 74C	DOVER - 74C	DOVER - 74C	DOVER - 74C	DOVER - 74C	DOVER - 74C	DOVER - 74C
32109	DOVER - 74C	DOVER - 74C	DOVER - 74C	DOVER - 74C	DOVER - 74C	DOVER - 74C	DOVER - 74C

The survival of the smaller and older shunting engines depended on the need to send locomotives with light axle-loadings to remote sidings where the volume of traffic was minimal. Several classes remained at work until the 1960's for such duties although their numbers were gradually diluted by the general acceptance of diesel shunting engines which for much of the decade had been employed in the larger marshalling yards and not on the main line. The greatest blow came in 1959 with the Kent coast electrification which saw the near-elimination of steam on the LCDR lines and the transfer of survivors to steam worked constituents of the SR

loco	Apr-50	Sep-50	Oct-50	Nov-50	Dec-50	Mar-51	Apr-51
B4 0-4-0T (1891)							
30082	EASTLEIGH - 71A	EASTLEIGH - 71A	EASTLEIGH - 71A	EASTLEIGH - 71A	EASTLEIGH - 71A	EASTLEIGH - 71A	EASTLEIGH - 71A
30083	EASTLEIGH - 71A	EASTLEIGH - 71A	ASHFORD - 74A	ASHFORD - 74A	ASHFORD - 74A	ASHFORD - 74A	ASHFORD - 74A
30084	PLYMOUTH - 72D	PLYMOUTH - 72D	PLYMOUTH - 72D	PLYMOUTH - 72D	PLYMOUTH - 72D	PLYMOUTH - 72D	PLYMOUTH - 72D
30086	BOURNEMOUTH - 71B	BOURNEMOUTH - 71B	BOURNEMOUTH - 71B	BOURNEMOUTH - 71B	BOURNEMOUTH - 71B	BOURNEMOUTH - 71B	BOURNEMOUTH - 71B
30087	BOURNEMOUTH - 71B	BOURNEMOUTH - 71B	BOURNEMOUTH - 71B	BOURNEMOUTH - 71B	BOURNEMOUTH - 71B	BOURNEMOUTH - 71B	BOURNEMOUTH - 71B
30088	PLYMOUTH - 72D	PLYMOUTH - 72D	PLYMOUTH - 72D	PLYMOUTH - 72D	PLYMOUTH - 72D	PLYMOUTH - 72D	PLYMOUTH - 72D
30089	EASTLEIGH - 71A	EASTLEIGH - 71A	EASTLEIGH - 71A	EASTLEIGH - 71A	EASTLEIGH - 71A	EASTLEIGH - 71A	EASTLEIGH - 71A
30093	BOURNEMOUTH - 71B	BOURNEMOUTH - 71B	BOURNEMOUTH - 71B	BOURNEMOUTH - 71B	BOURNEMOUTH - 71B	BOURNEMOUTH - 71B	BOURNEMOUTH - 71B
30094	PLYMOUTH - 72D	PLYMOUTH - 72D	PLYMOUTH - 72D	PLYMOUTH - 72D	PLYMOUTH - 72D	PLYMOUTH - 72D	PLYMOUTH - 72D
30096	ASHFORD - 74A	ASHFORD - 74A	EASTLEIGH - 71A	EASTLEIGH - 71A	EASTLEIGH - 71A	EASTLEIGH - 71A	EASTLEIGH - 71A
30102	PLYMOUTH - 72D	FRATTON - 71D	FRATTON - 71D	FRATTON - 71D	FRATTON - 71D	FRATTON - 71D	FRATTON - 71D
C14 0-4-0T (1906)							
30588	EASTLEIGH - 71A	EASTLEIGH - 71A	EASTLEIGH - 71A	EASTLEIGH - 71A	EASTLEIGH - 71A	EASTLEIGH - 71A	EASTLEIGH - 71A
30589	EASTLEIGH - 71A	EASTLEIGH - 71A	EASTLEIGH - 71A	EASTLEIGH - 71A	EASTLEIGH - 71A	EASTLEIGH - 71A	EASTLEIGH - 71A
'0458' 0-4-0ST (1890)							
30458	GUILDFORD - 70C	GUILDFORD - 70C	GUILDFORD - 70C	GUILDFORD - 70C	GUILDFORD - 70C	GUILDFORD - 70C	GUILDFORD - 70C
D1 0-4-2T (1873)							
32252	HORSHAM - 75D	W/D					
32359	DOVER - 74C	DOVER - 74C	DOVER - 74C	DOVER - 74C	DOVER - 74C	DOVER - 74C	DOVER - 74C
'0756' 0-6-0T (1907)							
30756	STEWARTS LANE - 73A	STEWARTS LANE - 73A	STEWARTS LANE - 73A	STEWARTS LANE - 73A	STEWARTS LANE - 73A	STEWARTS LANE - 73A	STEWARTS LANE - 73A
0757' 0-6-2T (1907)							
30757	PLYMOUTH - 72D	PLYMOUTH - 72D	PLYMOUTH - 72D	PLYMOUTH - 72D	PLYMOUTH - 72D	PLYMOUTH - 72D	PLYMOUTH - 72D
30758	PLYMOUTH - 72D	PLYMOUTH - 72D	PLYMOUTH - 72D	PLYMOUTH - 72D	PLYMOUTH - 72D	PLYMOUTH - 72D	PLYMOUTH - 72D
A1X 0-6-0T (1872)							
32635	DEPARTMENTAL	DEPARTMENTAL	DEPARTMENTAL	DEPARTMENTAL	DEPARTMENTAL	DEPARTMENTAL	DEPARTMENTAL
32636	BRIGHTON - 75A(N)	BRIGHTON - 75A(N)	BRIGHTON - 75A(N)	BRIGHTON - 75A(N)	BRIGHTON - 75A(N)	BRIGHTON - 75A(N)	BRIGHTON - 75A(N)
32640	ASHFORD - 74A	ASHFORD - 74A	ASHFORD - 74A	ASHFORD - 74A	ASHFORD - 74A	BRIGHTON - 75A	BRIGHTON - 75A
32644	ASHFORD - 74A	ASHFORD - 74A	ASHFORD - 74A	ASHFORD - 74A	ASHFORD - 74A	ASHFORD - 74A	W/D
32646	FRATTON - 71D	FRATTON - 71D	FRATTON - 71D	FRATTON - 71D	FRATTON - 71D	FRATTON - 71D	FRATTON - 71D
32647	BRIGHTON - 75A(N)	BRIGHTON - 75A(N)	BRIGHTON - 75A(N)	BRIGHTON - 75A(N)	BRIGHTON - 75A(N)	BRIGHTON - 75A(N)	FRATTON - 71D
32650	LANCING - 75A	LANCING - 75A	LANCING - 75A	LANCING - 75A	LANCING - 75A	LANCING - 75A	LANCING - 75A
32655	FRATTON - 71D	FRATTON - 71D	FRATTON - 71D	FRATTON - 71D	FRATTON - 71D	FRATTON - 71D	FRATTON - 71D
32659	ASHFORD - 74A	ASHFORD - 74A	ASHFORD - 74A	ASHFORD - 74A	ASHFORD - 74A	ASHFORD - 74A	ASHFORD - 74A
32661	FRATTON - 71D	FRATTON - 71D	FRATTON - 71D	FRATTON - 71D	FRATTON - 71D	FRATTON - 71D	FRATTON - 71D
32662	FRATTON - 71D	FRATTON - 71D	FRATTON - 71D	FRATTON - 71D	FRATTON - 71D	FRATTON - 71D	FRATTON - 71D
32670	ASHFORD - 74A	ASHFORD - 74A	ASHFORD - 74A	ASHFORD - 74A	ASHFORD - 74A	ASHFORD - 74A	ASHFORD - 74A
32677	FRATTON - 71D	FRATTON - 71D	FRATTON - 71D	FRATTON - 71D	FRATTON - 71D	FRATTON - 71D	FRATTON - 71D
32678	ASHFORD - 74A	ASHFORD - 74A	ASHFORD - 74A	ASHFORD - 74A	ASHFORD - 74A	ASHFORD - 74A	ASHFORD - 74A
E1 0-6-0T (1874)							
32113	B ARMS - 73B	B ARMS - 73B	B ARMS - 73B	B ARMS - 73B	B ARMS - 73B	B ARMS - 73B	B ARMS - 73B
32128	STEWARTS LANE - 73A	STEWARTS LANE - 73A	STEWARTS LANE - 73A	STEWARTS LANE - 73A	STEWARTS LANE - 73A	SOUTHAMPTON - 71I	B ARMS - 73B
32129	FRATTON - 71D	FRATTON - 71D	FRATTON - 71D	FRATTON - 71D	FRATTON - 71D	FRATTON - 71D	FRATTON - 71D
32133	EASTLEIGH - 71A	EASTLEIGH - 71A	EASTLEIGH - 71A	EASTLEIGH - 71A	EASTLEIGH - 71A	SOUTHAMPTON - 71I	SOUTHAMPTON - 71I
32138	NINE ELMS - 70A	NINE ELMS - 70A	NINE ELMS - 70A	NINE ELMS - 70A	NINE ELMS - 70A	NINE ELMS - 70A	NINE ELMS - 70A
32139	BRIGHTON - 75A	BRIGHTON - 75A	BRIGHTON - 75A	FRATTON - 71D	FRATTON - 71D	FRATTON - 71D	FRATTON - 71D
32142	B ARMS - 73B	BRIGHTON - 75A	BRIGHTON - 75A	W/D	W/D	W/D	W/D
32145	TONBRIDGE - 74D	TONBRIDGE - 74D	TONBRIDGE - 74D	BRIGHTON - 75A	BRIGHTON - 75A	BRIGHTON - 75A	BRIGHTON - 75A
32147	EASTLEIGH - 71A	EASTLEIGH - 71A	EASTLEIGH - 71A	EASTLEIGH - 71A	BRIGHTON - 75A	BRIGHTON - 75A	BRIGHTON - 75A
32151	B ARMS - 73B	B ARMS - 73B	B ARMS - 73B	B ARMS - 73B	EASTLEIGH - 71A	EASTLEIGH - 71A	EASTLEIGH - 71A
32156	SOUTHAMPTON - 71I	SOUTHAMPTON - 71I	SOUTHAMPTON - 71I	SOUTHAMPTON - 71I	SOUTHAMPTON - 71I	SOUTHAMPTON - 71I	W/D
32160	BASINGSTOKE - 70D	BASINGSTOKE - 70D	BASINGSTOKE - 70D	GUILDFORD - 70C	BASINGSTOKE - 70D	BASINGSTOKE - 70D	GUILDFORD - 70C
32606	SOUTHAMPTON - 71I	SOUTHAMPTON - 71I	SOUTHAMPTON - 71I	SOUTHAMPTON - 71I	SOUTHAMPTON - 71I	SOUTHAMPTON - 71I	SOUTHAMPTON - 71I
32689	BRIGHTON - 75A	BRIGHTON - 75A	BRIGHTON - 75A	BRIGHTON - 75A	BRIGHTON - 75A	SOUTHAMPTON - 71I	SOUTHAMPTON - 71I
32691	FRATTON - 71D	FRATTON - 71D	FRATTON - 71D	FRATTON - 71D	FRATTON - 71D	FRATTON - 71D	FRATTON - 71D
32694	FRATTON - 71D	FRATTON - 71D	FRATTON - 71D	FRATTON - 71D	FRATTON - 71D	FRATTON - 71D	FRATTON - 71D
E2 0-6-0T (1913)							
32100	STEWARTS LANE - 73A	STEWARTS LANE - 73A	STEWARTS LANE - 73A	STEWARTS LANE - 73A	STEWARTS LANE - 73A	STEWARTS LANE - 73A	STEWARTS LANE - 73A
32101	STEWARTS LANE - 73A	STEWARTS LANE - 73A	STEWARTS LANE - 73A	STEWARTS LANE - 73A	STEWARTS LANE - 73A	STEWARTS LANE - 73A	STEWARTS LANE - 73A
32102	STEWARTS LANE - 73A	STEWARTS LANE - 73A	STEWARTS LANE - 73A	STEWARTS LANE - 73A	STEWARTS LANE - 73A	STEWARTS LANE - 73A	STEWARTS LANE - 73A
32103	STEWARTS LANE - 73A	STEWARTS LANE - 73A	STEWARTS LANE - 73A	STEWARTS LANE - 73A	STEWARTS LANE - 73A	STEWARTS LANE - 73A	STEWARTS LANE - 73A
32104	STEWARTS LANE - 73A	STEWARTS LANE - 73A	STEWARTS LANE - 73A	STEWARTS LANE - 73A	STEWARTS LANE - 73A	STEWARTS LANE - 73A	STEWARTS LANE - 73A
32105	STEWARTS LANE - 73A	STEWARTS LANE - 73A	STEWARTS LANE - 73A	STEWARTS LANE - 73A	STEWARTS LANE - 73A	STEWARTS LANE - 73A	STEWARTS LANE - 73A
32106	STEWARTS LANE - 73A	STEWARTS LANE - 73A	STEWARTS LANE - 73A	STEWARTS LANE - 73A	STEWARTS LANE - 73A	STEWARTS LANE - 73A	STEWARTS LANE - 73A
32107	STEWARTS LANE - 73A	STEWARTS LANE - 73A	STEWARTS LANE - 73A	STEWARTS LANE - 73A	STEWARTS LANE - 73A	STEWARTS LANE - 73A	STEWARTS LANE - 73A
32108	DOVER - 74C	DOVER - 74C	DOVER - 74C	DOVER - 74C	DOVER - 74C	DOVER - 74C	DOVER - 74C
32109	DOVER - 74C	DOVER - 74C	DOVER - 74C	DOVER - 74C	DOVER - 74C	DOVER - 74C	DOVER - 74C

The A1X 0-6-0T of the LBSCR was probably one of the most versatile small engines ever produced, spending a long career on local goods and passenger work. 32655 was for many years a Portsmouth (Fratton) engine, moving to Ashford in 1953, Hastings (St Leonards) the years afterwards and in 1955 to Brighton, where it is pictured above. It remained at Brighton for five years before being transferred to Eastleigh for preservation.

loco	Jun-51	Jul-51	Sep-51	Dec-51	Jan-52	Mar-52	Jun-52
B4 0-4-0T (1891)							
30082	EASTLEIGH - 71A	EASTLEIGH - 71A	EASTLEIGH - 71A	EASTLEIGH - 71A	EASTLEIGH - 71A	EASTLEIGH - 71A	EASTLEIGH - 71A
30083	ASHFORD - 74A	ASHFORD - 74A	PLYMOUTH - 72D	PLYMOUTH - 72D	PLYMOUTH - 72D	PLYMOUTH - 72D	PLYMOUTH - 72D
30084	PLYMOUTH - 72D	PLYMOUTH - 72D	PLYMOUTH - 72D	DOVER - 74C	DOVER - 74C	DOVER - 74C	DOVER - 74C
30086	BOURNEMOUTH - 71B	BOURNEMOUTH - 71B	BOURNEMOUTH - 71B	BOURNEMOUTH - 71B	BOURNEMOUTH - 71B	BOURNEMOUTH - 71B	BOURNEMOUTH - 71B
30087	BOURNEMOUTH - 71B	BOURNEMOUTH - 71B	BOURNEMOUTH - 71B	BOURNEMOUTH - 71B	BOURNEMOUTH - 71B	BOURNEMOUTH - 71B	BOURNEMOUTH - 71B
30088	PLYMOUTH - 72D	PLYMOUTH - 72D	PLYMOUTH - 72D	PLYMOUTH - 72D	PLYMOUTH - 72D	PLYMOUTH - 72D	EASTLEIGH - 71A
30089	EASTLEIGH - 71A	EASTLEIGH - 71A	EASTLEIGH - 71A	EASTLEIGH - 71A	EASTLEIGH - 71A	PLYMOUTH - 72D	PLYMOUTH - 72D
30093	BOURNEMOUTH - 71B	BOURNEMOUTH - 71B	BOURNEMOUTH - 71B	BOURNEMOUTH - 71B	BOURNEMOUTH - 71B	BOURNEMOUTH - 71B	BOURNEMOUTH - 71B
30094	PLYMOUTH - 72D	PLYMOUTH - 72D	PLYMOUTH - 72D	PLYMOUTH - 72D	PLYMOUTH - 72D	PLYMOUTH - 72D	PLYMOUTH - 72D
30096	EASTLEIGH - 71A	EASTLEIGH - 71A	EASTLEIGH - 71A	EASTLEIGH - 71A	EASTLEIGH - 71A	EASTLEIGH - 71A	EASTLEIGH - 71A
30102	FRATTON - 71D	FRATTON - 71D	FRATTON - 71D	FRATTON - 71D	FRATTON - 71D	FRATTON - 71D	FRATTON - 71D
C14 0-4-0T (1906)							
30588	EASTLEIGH - 71A	EASTLEIGH - 71A	EASTLEIGH - 71A	EASTLEIGH - 71A	EASTLEIGH - 71A	EASTLEIGH - 71A	EASTLEIGH - 71A
30589	EASTLEIGH - 71A	EASTLEIGH - 71A	EASTLEIGH - 71A	EASTLEIGH - 71A	EASTLEIGH - 71A	EASTLEIGH - 71A	EASTLEIGH - 71A
'0458' 0-4-0ST (1890)							
30458	GUILDFORD - 70C	GUILDFORD - 70C	GUILDFORD - 70C	GUILDFORD - 70C	GUILDFORD - 70C	GUILDFORD - 70C	GUILDFORD - 70C
D1 0-4-2T (1873)							
32359	DOVER - 74C	W/D	W/D	W/D	W/D	W/D	W/D
'0756' 0-6-0T (1907)							
30756	STEWARTS LANE - 73A	STEWARTS LANE - 73A	STEWARTS LANE - 73A	W/D	W/D	W/D	W/D
0757 0-6-2T (1907)							
30757	PLYMOUTH - 72D	PLYMOUTH - 72D	PLYMOUTH - 72D	PLYMOUTH - 72D	PLYMOUTH - 72D	PLYMOUTH - 72D	PLYMOUTH - 72D
30758	PLYMOUTH - 72D	PLYMOUTH - 72D	PLYMOUTH - 72D	PLYMOUTH - 72D	PLYMOUTH - 72D	PLYMOUTH - 72D	PLYMOUTH - 72D
A1X 0-6-0T (1872)							
32635	DEPARTMENTAL	DEPARTMENTAL	DEPARTMENTAL		DEPARTMENTAL	DEPARTMENTAL	DEPARTMENTAL
32636	BRIGHTON - 75A(N)	BRIGHTON - 75A(N)	BRIGHTON - 75A(N)	BRIGHTON - 75A(N)	BRIGHTON - 75A(N)	BRIGHTON - 75A(N)	BRIGHTON - 75A(N)
32640	BRIGHTON - 75A	BRIGHTON - 75A	EASTLEIGH - 71A	EASTLEIGH - 71A	EASTLEIGH - 71A	EASTLEIGH - 71A	FRATTON - 71D
32646	FRATTON - 71D	FRATTON - 71D	BRIGHTON - 75A(N)	BRIGHTON - 75A(N)	BRIGHTON - 75A(N)	BRIGHTON - 75A(N)	BRIGHTON - 75A(N)
32647	FRATTON - 71D	FRATTON - 71D	W/D	W/D	W/D	W/D	W/D
32650	LANCING - 75A	LANCING - 75A	LANCING - 75A	LANCING - 75A	LANCING - 75A	LANCING - 75A	LANCING - 75A
32655	FRATTON - 71D	FRATTON - 71D	FRATTON - 71D	FRATTON - 71D	FRATTON - 71D	FRATTON - 71D	FRATTON - 71D
32659	ASHFORD - 74A	ASHFORD - 74A	ASHFORD - 74A	ASHFORD - 74A	ASHFORD - 74A	ASHFORD - 74A	ASHFORD - 74A
32661	FRATTON - 71D	FRATTON - 71D	FRATTON - 71D	FRATTON - 71D	FRATTON - 71D	FRATTON - 71D	FRATTON - 71D
32662	FRATTON - 71D	FRATTON - 71D	FRATTON - 71D	FRATTON - 71D	FRATTON - 71D	FRATTON - 71D	FRATTON - 71D
32670	ASHFORD - 74A	ASHFORD - 74A	ASHFORD - 74A	ASHFORD - 74A	ASHFORD - 74A	ASHFORD - 74A	ASHFORD - 74A
32677	FRATTON - 71D	FRATTON - 71D	ASHFORD - 74A	ASHFORD - 74A	ASHFORD - 74A	ASHFORD - 74A	ASHFORD - 74A
32678	ASHFORD - 74A	ASHFORD - 74A	ASHFORD - 74A	ASHFORD - 74A	ASHFORD - 74A	ASHFORD - 74A	ASHFORD - 74A
E1 0-6-0T (1874)							
32113	B ARMS - 73B	B ARMS - 73B	B ARMS - 73B	B ARMS - 73B	B ARMS - 73B	B ARMS - 73B	B ARMS - 73B
32128	B ARMS - 73B	B ARMS - 73B	B ARMS - 73B	B ARMS - 73B	B ARMS - 73B	W/D	W/D
32133	SOUTHAMPTON - 71I	SOUTHAMPTON - 71I	SOUTHAMPTON - 71I	SOUTHAMPTON - 71I	SOUTHAMPTON - 71I	SOUTHAMPTON - 71I	SOUTHAMPTON - 71I
32138	NINE ELMS - 70A	NINE ELMS - 70A	SOUTHAMPTON - 71I	SOUTHAMPTON - 71I	SOUTHAMPTON - 71I	SOUTHAMPTON - 71I	SOUTHAMPTON - 71I
32139	FRATTON - 71D	FRATTON - 71D	FRATTON - 71D	FRATTON - 71D	FRATTON - 71D	FRATTON - 71D	FRATTON - 71D
32147	B ARMS - 73B	B ARMS - 73B	B ARMS - 73B	W/D	W/D	W/D	W/D
32151	EASTLEIGH - 71A	EASTLEIGH - 71A	EASTLEIGH - 71A	EASTLEIGH - 71A	EASTLEIGH - 71A	EASTLEIGH - 71A	EASTLEIGH - 71A
32160	FRATTON - 71D	FRATTON - 71D	FRATTON - 71D	W/D	W/D	W/D	W/D
32606	SOUTHAMPTON - 71I	SOUTHAMPTON - 71I	SOUTHAMPTON - 71I	SOUTHAMPTON - 71I	SOUTHAMPTON - 71I	SOUTHAMPTON - 71I	SOUTHAMPTON - 71I
32689	SOUTHAMPTON - 71I	SOUTHAMPTON - 71I	SOUTHAMPTON - 71I	SOUTHAMPTON - 71I	SOUTHAMPTON - 71I	SOUTHAMPTON - 71I	SOUTHAMPTON - 71I
32691	FRATTON - 71D	FRATTON - 71D	FRATTON - 71D	W/D	W/D	W/D	W/D
32694	FRATTON - 71D	FRATTON - 71D	FRATTON - 71D	FRATTON - 71D	FRATTON - 71D	FRATTON - 71D	FRATTON - 71D
E2 0-6-0T (1913)							
32100	STEWARTS LANE - 73A	STEWARTS LANE - 73A	STEWARTS LANE - 73A	STEWARTS LANE - 73A	STEWARTS LANE - 73A	STEWARTS LANE - 73A	STEWARTS LANE - 73A
32101	STEWARTS LANE - 73A	STEWARTS LANE - 73A	STEWARTS LANE - 73A	STEWARTS LANE - 73A	STEWARTS LANE - 73A	STEWARTS LANE - 73A	STEWARTS LANE - 73A
32102	STEWARTS LANE - 73A	STEWARTS LANE - 73A	STEWARTS LANE - 73A	STEWARTS LANE - 73A	STEWARTS LANE - 73A	STEWARTS LANE - 73A	STEWARTS LANE - 73A
32103	STEWARTS LANE - 73A	STEWARTS LANE - 73A	STEWARTS LANE - 73A	STEWARTS LANE - 73A	STEWARTS LANE - 73A	STEWARTS LANE - 73A	STEWARTS LANE - 73A
32104	STEWARTS LANE - 73A	STEWARTS LANE - 73A	STEWARTS LANE - 73A	STEWARTS LANE - 73A	STEWARTS LANE - 73A	STEWARTS LANE - 73A	STEWARTS LANE - 73A
32105	STEWARTS LANE - 73A	STEWARTS LANE - 73A	STEWARTS LANE - 73A	STEWARTS LANE - 73A	STEWARTS LANE - 73A	STEWARTS LANE - 73A	STEWARTS LANE - 73A
32106	STEWARTS LANE - 73A	STEWARTS LANE - 73A	STEWARTS LANE - 73A	STEWARTS LANE - 73A	STEWARTS LANE - 73A	STEWARTS LANE - 73A	STEWARTS LANE - 73A
32107	STEWARTS LANE - 73A	STEWARTS LANE - 73A	STEWARTS LANE - 73A	STEWARTS LANE - 73A	STEWARTS LANE - 73A	STEWARTS LANE - 73A	STEWARTS LANE - 73A
32108	DOVER - 74C	DOVER - 74C	DOVER - 74C	DOVER - 74C	DOVER - 74C	DOVER - 74C	DOVER - 74C
32109	DOVER - 74C	DOVER - 74C	DOVER - 74C	DOVER - 74C	DOVER - 74C	DOVER - 74C	DOVER - 74C

Although slated for replacement in the 1910's, the wide availability of the LBSCR E1 0-6-0T's ensured their continued survival especially after the electrification of the Brighton section when many of the class were transferred across to the LSWR, saving the Southern Railway the expense of producing a new class for sidings over which larger engines were prohibited. 32147 is seen at Eastleigh where it worked as a shed pilot, shunting the loco coal sidings from 07.30 to 17.00 each day for many years. Another of the class could be seen daily in Southampton New Docks where it spent sixteen hours a day carriage shunting boat train stock.

loco	Sep-52	Dec-52	Mar-53	May-53	Jul-53	Sep-53	Nov-53
B4 0-4-0T (1891)							
30082 EASTLEIGH - 71A	EASTLEIGH - 71A	EASTLEIGH - 71A	EASTLEIGH - 71A	EASTLEIGH - 71A	EASTLEIGH - 71A	EASTLEIGH - 71A
30083 PLYMOUTH - 72D	PLYMOUTH - 72D	PLYMOUTH - 72D	PLYMOUTH - 72D	PLYMOUTH - 72D	PLYMOUTH - 72D	EASTLEIGH - 71A
30084 DOVER - 74C	DOVER - 74C	DOVER - 74C	DOVER - 74C	DOVER - 74C	DOVER - 74C	DOVER - 74C
30086 BOURNEMOUTH - 71B	BOURNEMOUTH - 71B	BOURNEMOUTH - 71B	BOURNEMOUTH - 71B	BOURNEMOUTH - 71B	BOURNEMOUTH - 71B	BOURNEMOUTH - 71B
30087 BOURNEMOUTH - 71B	BOURNEMOUTH - 71B	BOURNEMOUTH - 71B	BOURNEMOUTH - 71B	BOURNEMOUTH - 71B	BOURNEMOUTH - 71B	BOURNEMOUTH - 71B
30088 EASTLEIGH - 71A	EASTLEIGH - 71A	EASTLEIGH - 71A	EASTLEIGH - 71A	EASTLEIGH - 71A	PLYMOUTH - 72D	PLYMOUTH - 72D
30089 PLYMOUTH - 72D	PLYMOUTH - 72D	PLYMOUTH - 72D	PLYMOUTH - 72D	PLYMOUTH - 72D	PLYMOUTH - 72D	PLYMOUTH - 72D
30093 BOURNEMOUTH - 71B	BOURNEMOUTH - 71B	BOURNEMOUTH - 71B	BOURNEMOUTH - 71B	BOURNEMOUTH - 71B	BOURNEMOUTH - 71B	BOURNEMOUTH - 71B
30094 PLYMOUTH - 72D	PLYMOUTH - 72D	PLYMOUTH - 72D	PLYMOUTH - 72D	PLYMOUTH - 72D	PLYMOUTH - 72D	PLYMOUTH - 72D
30096 EASTLEIGH - 71A	EASTLEIGH - 71A	EASTLEIGH - 71A	EASTLEIGH - 71A	EASTLEIGH - 71A	EASTLEIGH - 71A	EASTLEIGH - 71A
30102 FRATTON - 71D	FRATTON - 71D	FRATTON - 71D	FRATTON - 71D	FRATTON - 71D	FRATTON - 71D	FRATTON - 71D
C14 0-4-0T (1906)							
30588 EASTLEIGH - 71A	EASTLEIGH - 71A	EASTLEIGH - 71A	EASTLEIGH - 71A	EASTLEIGH - 71A	EASTLEIGH - 71A	EASTLEIGH - 71A
30589 EASTLEIGH - 71A	EASTLEIGH - 71A	EASTLEIGH - 71A	EASTLEIGH - 71A	EASTLEIGH - 71A	EASTLEIGH - 71A	EASTLEIGH - 71A
'0458' 0-4-0ST (1890)							
30458 GUILDFORD - 70C	GUILDFORD - 70C	GUILDFORD - 70C	GUILDFORD - 70C	GUILDFORD - 70C	GUILDFORD - 70C	GUILDFORD - 70C
0757' 0-6-2T (1907)							
30757 PLYMOUTH - 72D	PLYMOUTH - 72D	PLYMOUTH - 72D	PLYMOUTH - 72D	PLYMOUTH - 72D	PLYMOUTH - 72D	PLYMOUTH - 72D
30758 PLYMOUTH - 72D	PLYMOUTH - 72D	PLYMOUTH - 72D	PLYMOUTH - 72D	PLYMOUTH - 72D	PLYMOUTH - 72D	PLYMOUTH - 72D
A1X 0-6-0T (1872)							
32635 DEPARTMENTAL	DEPARTMENTAL	DEPARTMENTAL	DEPARTMENTAL	DEPARTMENTAL	DEPARTMENTAL	DEPARTMENTAL
32636 BRIGHTON - 75A(N)	BRIGHTON - 75A(N)	BRIGHTON - 75A(N)	BRIGHTON - 75A	BRIGHTON - 75A (N)	BRIGHTON - 75A (N)	BRIGHTON - 75A (N)
32640 BRIGHTON - 75A(N)	BRIGHTON - 75A(N)	BRIGHTON - 75A(N)	BRIGHTON - 75A(N)	BRIGHTON - 75A(N)	BRIGHTON - 75A(N)	BRIGHTON - 75A(N)
32646 BRIGHTON - 75A(N)	BRIGHTON - 75A(N)	BRIGHTON - 75A(N)	BRIGHTON - 75A(N)	FRATTON - 71D	FRATTON - 71D	FRATTON - 71D
32650 LANCING-75A	LANCING-75A	LANCING-75A	LANCING-75A	FRATTON - 71D	FRATTON - 71D	FRATTON - 71D
32655 FRATTON - 71D	FRATTON - 71D	FRATTON - 71D	ASHFORD - 74A	ASHFORD - 74A	ASHFORD - 74A	ASHFORD - 74A
32659 ASHFORD - 74A	ASHFORD - 74A	ASHFORD - 74A	ASHFORD - 74A	ASHFORD - 74A	ASHFORD - 74A	ASHFORD - 74A
32661 FRATTON - 71D	FRATTON - 71D	FRATTON - 71D	FRATTON - 71D	FRATTON - 71D	FRATTON - 71D	FRATTON - 71D
32662 FRATTON - 71D	FRATTON - 71D	FRATTON - 71D	FRATTON - 71D	FRATTON - 71D	ST LEONARDS - 74E	BRIGHTON - 75A(N)
32670 ASHFORD - 74A	ASHFORD - 74A	ASHFORD - 74A	ASHFORD - 74A	ASHFORD - 74A	ASHFORD - 74A	ASHFORD - 74A
32677 ASHFORD - 74A	ASHFORD - 74A	FRATTON - 71D	FRATTON - 71D	FRATTON - 71D	FRATTON - 71D	FRATTON - 71D
32678 ASHFORD - 74A	ASHFORD - 74A	ASHFORD - 74A	ASHFORD - 74A	ASHFORD - 74A	ASHFORD - 74A	ASHFORD - 74A
E1 0-6-0T (1874)							
32113 B ARMS - 73B	B ARMS - 73B	EASTLEIGH - 71A	EASTLEIGH - 71A	EASTLEIGH - 71A	EASTLEIGH - 71A	EASTLEIGH - 71A
32133 SOUTHAMPTON - 71I	W/D	W/D	W/D	W/D	W/D	W/D
32138 FRATTON - 71D	FRATTON - 71D	FRATTON - 71D	FRATTON - 71D	FRATTON - 71D	FRATTON - 71D	FRATTON - 71D
32139 FRATTON - 71D	FRATTON - 71D	FRATTON - 71D	FRATTON - 71D	FRATTON - 71D	FRATTON - 71D	FRATTON - 71D
32151 EASTLEIGH - 71A	EASTLEIGH - 71A	EASTLEIGH - 71A	EASTLEIGH - 71A	EASTLEIGH - 71A	EASTLEIGH - 71A	EASTLEIGH - 71A
32606 SOUTHAMPTON - 71I	SOUTHAMPTON - 71I	SOUTHAMPTON - 71I	SOUTHAMPTON - 71I	SOUTHAMPTON - 71I	SOUTHAMPTON - 71I	SOUTHAMPTON - 71I
32689 SOUTHAMPTON - 71I	SOUTHAMPTON - 71I	SOUTHAMPTON - 71I	SOUTHAMPTON - 71I	SOUTHAMPTON - 71I	SOUTHAMPTON - 71I	SOUTHAMPTON - 71I
32694 FRATTON - 71D	FRATTON - 71D	FRATTON - 71D	FRATTON - 71D	FRATTON - 71D	FRATTON - 71D	FRATTON - 71D
E2 0-6-0T (1913)							
32100 STEWARTS LANE - 73A	STEWARTS LANE - 73A	STEWARTS LANE - 73A	STEWARTS LANE - 73A	STEWARTS LANE - 73A	STEWARTS LANE - 73A	STEWARTS LANE - 73A
32101 STEWARTS LANE - 73A	STEWARTS LANE - 73A	STEWARTS LANE - 73A	STEWARTS LANE - 73A	STEWARTS LANE - 73A	STEWARTS LANE - 73A	STEWARTS LANE - 73A
32102 STEWARTS LANE - 73A	STEWARTS LANE - 73A	STEWARTS LANE - 73A	STEWARTS LANE - 73A	STEWARTS LANE - 73A	STEWARTS LANE - 73A	STEWARTS LANE - 73A
32103 STEWARTS LANE - 73A	STEWARTS LANE - 73A	STEWARTS LANE - 73A	STEWARTS LANE - 73A	STEWARTS LANE - 73A	STEWARTS LANE - 73A	STEWARTS LANE - 73A
32104 STEWARTS LANE - 73A	STEWARTS LANE - 73A	STEWARTS LANE - 73A	STEWARTS LANE - 73A	STEWARTS LANE - 73A	STEWARTS LANE - 73A	STEWARTS LANE - 73A
32105 STEWARTS LANE - 73A	STEWARTS LANE - 73A	STEWARTS LANE - 73A	STEWARTS LANE - 73A	STEWARTS LANE - 73A	STEWARTS LANE - 73A	STEWARTS LANE - 73A
32106 STEWARTS LANE - 73A	STEWARTS LANE - 73A	STEWARTS LANE - 73A	STEWARTS LANE - 73A	STEWARTS LANE - 73A	STEWARTS LANE - 73A	STEWARTS LANE - 73A
32107 STEWARTS LANE - 73A	STEWARTS LANE - 73A	STEWARTS LANE - 73A	STEWARTS LANE - 73A	STEWARTS LANE - 73A	STEWARTS LANE - 73A	STEWARTS LANE - 73A
32108 DOVER - 74C	DOVER - 74C	DOVER - 74C	DOVER - 74C	DOVER - 74C	DOVER - 74C	DOVER - 74C
32109 DOVER - 74C	DOVER - 74C	DOVER - 74C	DOVER - 74C	DOVER - 74C	DOVER - 74C	DOVER - 74C

Until 1956, when they were moved to Eastleigh, the two Plymouth, Devonport & South Western 0-6-2T's spent a quiet life in the backwaters of Plymouth and were regarded by observers of the day as rarities. After the grouping some thought was given to developing the class as the standard passenger tank for general service in the west of England but eventually the choice was changed in favour of the E1/R class.

B4 0-4-0T (1891)

loco	Jan-54	Mar-54	May-54	Jun-54	Aug-54	Oct-54	Dec-54
30082	EASTLEIGH - 71A	EASTLEIGH - 71A	EASTLEIGH - 71A	EASTLEIGH - 71A	EASTLEIGH - 71A	EASTLEIGH - 71A	EASTLEIGH - 71A
30083	EASTLEIGH - 71A	EASTLEIGH - 71A	EASTLEIGH - 71A	EASTLEIGH - 71A	EASTLEIGH - 71A	EASTLEIGH - 71A	EASTLEIGH - 71A
30084	DOVER - 74C	DOVER - 74C	DOVER - 74C	DOVER - 74C	DOVER - 74C	DOVER - 74C	DOVER - 74C
30086	BOURNEMOUTH - 71B	BOURNEMOUTH - 71B	DOVER - 74C	DOVER - 74C	DOVER - 74C	DOVER - 74C	DOVER - 74C
30087	BOURNEMOUTH - 71B	BOURNEMOUTH - 71B	BOURNEMOUTH - 71B	BOURNEMOUTH - 71B	BOURNEMOUTH - 71B	BOURNEMOUTH - 71B	BOURNEMOUTH - 71B
30088	PLYMOUTH - 72D	PLYMOUTH - 72D	PLYMOUTH - 72D	PLYMOUTH - 72D	PLYMOUTH - 72D	PLYMOUTH - 72D	PLYMOUTH - 72D
30089	PLYMOUTH - 72D	PLYMOUTH - 72D	PLYMOUTH - 72D	PLYMOUTH - 72D	PLYMOUTH - 72D	PLYMOUTH - 72D	PLYMOUTH - 72D
30093	BOURNEMOUTH - 71B	BOURNEMOUTH - 71B	BOURNEMOUTH - 71B	BOURNEMOUTH - 71B	BOURNEMOUTH - 71B	BOURNEMOUTH - 71B	BOURNEMOUTH - 71B
30094	PLYMOUTH - 72D	PLYMOUTH - 72D	PLYMOUTH - 72D	PLYMOUTH - 72D	PLYMOUTH - 72D	PLYMOUTH - 72D	PLYMOUTH - 72D
30096	EASTLEIGH - 71A	EASTLEIGH - 71A	EASTLEIGH - 71A	EASTLEIGH - 71A	EASTLEIGH - 71A	EASTLEIGH - 71A	EASTLEIGH - 71A
30102	FRATTON - 71D	FRATTON - 71D	FRATTON - 71D	FRATTON - 71D	FRATTON - 71D	FRATTON - 70F	FRATTON - 70F

C14 0-4-0T (1906)

loco	Jan-54	Mar-54	May-54	Jun-54	Aug-54	Oct-54	Dec-54
30588	EASTLEIGH - 71A	EASTLEIGH - 71A	EASTLEIGH - 71A	EASTLEIGH - 71A	EASTLEIGH - 71A	EASTLEIGH - 71A	EASTLEIGH - 71A
30589	EASTLEIGH - 71A	EASTLEIGH - 71A	EASTLEIGH - 71A	EASTLEIGH - 71A	EASTLEIGH - 71A	EASTLEIGH - 71A	EASTLEIGH - 71A

'0458' 0-4-0ST (1890)

loco	Jan-54	Mar-54	May-54	Jun-54	Aug-54	Oct-54	Dec-54
30458	GUILDFORD - 70C	GUILDFORD - 70C	GUILDFORD - 70C	W/D	W/D	W/D	W/D

0757' 0-6-2T (1907)

loco	Jan-54	Mar-54	May-54	Jun-54	Aug-54	Oct-54	Dec-54
30757	PLYMOUTH - 72D	PLYMOUTH - 72D	PLYMOUTH - 72D	PLYMOUTH - 72D	PLYMOUTH - 72D	PLYMOUTH - 72D	PLYMOUTH - 72D
30758	PLYMOUTH - 72D	PLYMOUTH - 72D	PLYMOUTH - 72D	PLYMOUTH - 72D	PLYMOUTH - 72D	PLYMOUTH - 72D	PLYMOUTH - 72D

A1X 0-6-0T (1872)

loco	Jan-54	Mar-54	May-54	Jun-54	Aug-54	Oct-54	Dec-54
32635	DEPARTMENTAL	DEPARTMENTAL	DEPARTMENTAL	DEPARTMENTAL	DEPARTMENTAL	DEPARTMENTAL	DEPARTMENTAL
32636	BRIGHTON - 75A (N)	BRIGHTON - 75A(N)	BRIGHTON - 75A (N)	BRIGHTON - 75A (N)	BRIGHTON - 75A (N)	BRIGHTON - 75A (N)	BRIGHTON - 75A (N)
32640	BRIGHTON - 75A(N)	BRIGHTON - 75A(N)	FRATTON - 71D	FRATTON - 71D	FRATTON - 71D	FRATTON - 70F	FRATTON - 70F
32646	FRATTON - 71D	FRATTON - 71D	BRIGHTON - 75A (N)	BRIGHTON - 75A (N)	BRIGHTON - 75A (N)	BRIGHTON - 75A (N)	BRIGHTON - 75A (N)
32650	FRATTON - 71D	FRATTON - 71D	FRATTON - 71D	FRATTON - 71D	FRATTON - 71D	FRATTON - 71D	FRATTON - 71D
32655	ST LEONARDS - 74E	ST LEONARDS - 74E	ST LEONARDS - 74E	ST LEONARDS - 74E	ST LEONARDS - 74E	ST LEONARDS - 74E	ST LEONARDS - 74E
32659	ASHFORD - 74A	ASHFORD - 74A	ASHFORD - 74A	ASHFORD - 74A	ASHFORD - 74A	ASHFORD - 74A	ASHFORD - 74A
32661	FRATTON - 71D	FRATTON - 71D	FRATTON - 71D	FRATTON - 71D	FRATTON - 71D	FRATTON - 70F	FRATTON - 70F
32662	BRIGHTON - 75A(N)	BRIGHTON - 75A(N)	BRIGHTON - 75A(N)	BRIGHTON - 75A(N)	BRIGHTON - 75A(N)	BRIGHTON - 75A(N)	BRIGHTON - 75A(N)
32670	ASHFORD - 74A	ASHFORD - 74A	ASHFORD - 74A	ASHFORD - 74A	ST LEONARDS - 74E	ST LEONARDS - 74E	ST LEONARDS - 74E
32677	FRATTON - 71D	FRATTON - 71D	FRATTON - 71D	FRATTON - 71D	FRATTON - 71D	FRATTON - 70F	FRATTON - 70F
32678	ST LEONARDS - 74E	ST LEONARDS - 74E	ST LEONARDS - 74E	ST LEONARDS - 74E	ST LEONARDS - 74E	ST LEONARDS - 74E	ST LEONARDS - 74E

E1 0-6-0T (1874)

loco	Jan-54	Mar-54	May-54	Jun-54	Aug-54	Oct-54	Dec-54
32113	EASTLEIGH - 71A	EASTLEIGH - 71A	EASTLEIGH - 71A	EASTLEIGH - 71A	EASTLEIGH - 71A	EASTLEIGH - 71A	EASTLEIGH - 71A
32138	FRATTON - 71D	FRATTON - 71D	FRATTON - 71D	FRATTON - 71D	FRATTON - 71D	FRATTON - 70F	FRATTON - 70F
32139	FRATTON - 71D	FRATTON - 71D	FRATTON - 71D	FRATTON - 71D	FRATTON - 71D	FRATTON - 71D	FRATTON - 70F
32151	EASTLEIGH - 71A	EASTLEIGH - 71A	EASTLEIGH - 71A	EASTLEIGH - 71A	EASTLEIGH - 71A	EASTLEIGH - 71A	EASTLEIGH - 71A
32606	SOUTHAMPTON - 71I	SOUTHAMPTON - 71I	SOUTHAMPTON - 71I	SOUTHAMPTON - 71I	SOUTHAMPTON - 71I	SOUTHAMPTON - 71I	SOUTHAMPTON - 71I
32689	SOUTHAMPTON - 71I	SOUTHAMPTON - 71I	SOUTHAMPTON - 71I	SOUTHAMPTON - 71I	SOUTHAMPTON - 71I	SOUTHAMPTON - 71I	SOUTHAMPTON - 71I
32694	FRATTON - 71D	FRATTON - 71D	FRATTON - 71D	FRATTON - 71D	FRATTON - 71D	FRATTON - 70F	FRATTON - 70F

E2 0-6-0T (1913)

loco	Jan-54	Mar-54	May-54	Jun-54	Aug-54	Oct-54	Dec-54
32100	STEWARTS LANE - 73A	STEWARTS LANE - 73A	STEWARTS LANE - 73A	STEWARTS LANE - 73A	STEWARTS LANE - 73A	STEWARTS LANE - 73A	STEWARTS LANE - 73A
32101	STEWARTS LANE - 73A	STEWARTS LANE - 73A	STEWARTS LANE - 73A	STEWARTS LANE - 73A	STEWARTS LANE - 73A	STEWARTS LANE - 73A	STEWARTS LANE - 73A
32102	STEWARTS LANE - 73A	STEWARTS LANE - 73A	STEWARTS LANE - 73A	STEWARTS LANE - 73A	STEWARTS LANE - 73A	STEWARTS LANE - 73A	STEWARTS LANE - 73A
32103	STEWARTS LANE - 73A	STEWARTS LANE - 73A	STEWARTS LANE - 73A	STEWARTS LANE - 73A	STEWARTS LANE - 73A	STEWARTS LANE - 73A	STEWARTS LANE - 73A
32104	STEWARTS LANE - 73A	STEWARTS LANE - 73A	STEWARTS LANE - 73A	STEWARTS LANE - 73A	STEWARTS LANE - 73A	STEWARTS LANE - 73A	STEWARTS LANE - 73A
32105	STEWARTS LANE - 73A	STEWARTS LANE - 73A	STEWARTS LANE - 73A	STEWARTS LANE - 73A	STEWARTS LANE - 73A	STEWARTS LANE - 73A	STEWARTS LANE - 73A
32106	STEWARTS LANE - 73A	STEWARTS LANE - 73A	STEWARTS LANE - 73A	STEWARTS LANE - 73A	STEWARTS LANE - 73A	STEWARTS LANE - 73A	STEWARTS LANE - 73A
32107	STEWARTS LANE - 73A	STEWARTS LANE - 73A	STEWARTS LANE - 73A	STEWARTS LANE - 73A	STEWARTS LANE - 73A	STEWARTS LANE - 73A	STEWARTS LANE - 73A
32108	DOVER - 74C	DOVER - 74C	DOVER - 74C	DOVER - 74C	DOVER - 74C	DOVER - 74C	DOVER - 74C
32109	DOVER - 74C	DOVER - 74C	DOVER - 74C	DOVER - 74C	DOVER - 74C	DOVER - 74C	DOVER - 74C

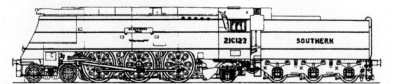

loco	Feb-55	Apr-55	Jun-55	Aug-55	Sep-55	Nov-55	Dec-55
B4 0-4-0T (1891)							
30082 EASTLEIGH - 71A	EASTLEIGH - 71A	EASTLEIGH - 71A	EASTLEIGH - 71A	EASTLEIGH - 71A	EASTLEIGH - 71A	EASTLEIGH - 71A
30083 EASTLEIGH - 71A	EASTLEIGH - 71A	EASTLEIGH - 71A	EASTLEIGH - 71A	EASTLEIGH - 71A	EASTLEIGH - 71A	EASTLEIGH - 71A
30084 DOVER - 74C	DOVER - 74C	DOVER - 74C	DOVER - 74C	DOVER - 74C	DOVER - 74C	DOVER - 74C
30086 DOVER - 74C	DOVER - 74C	DOVER - 74C	DOVER - 74C	GUILDFORD - 70C	GUILDFORD - 70C	GUILDFORD - 70C
30087 BOURNEMOUTH - 71B	BOURNEMOUTH - 71B	BOURNEMOUTH - 71B	BOURNEMOUTH - 71B	BOURNEMOUTH - 71B	BOURNEMOUTH - 71B	BOURNEMOUTH - 71B
30088 PLYMOUTH - 72D	PLYMOUTH - 72D	PLYMOUTH - 72D	PLYMOUTH - 72D	PLYMOUTH - 72D	PLYMOUTH - 72D	PLYMOUTH - 72D
30089 PLYMOUTH - 72D	PLYMOUTH - 72D	PLYMOUTH - 72D	PLYMOUTH - 72D	PLYMOUTH - 72D	PLYMOUTH - 72D	PLYMOUTH - 72D
30093 BOURNEMOUTH - 71B	BOURNEMOUTH - 71B	BOURNEMOUTH - 71B	BOURNEMOUTH - 71B	BOURNEMOUTH - 71B	BOURNEMOUTH - 71B	BOURNEMOUTH - 71B
30094 PLYMOUTH - 72D	PLYMOUTH - 72D	PLYMOUTH - 72D	PLYMOUTH - 72D	PLYMOUTH - 72D	PLYMOUTH - 72D	PLYMOUTH - 72D
30096 EASTLEIGH - 71A	EASTLEIGH - 71A	EASTLEIGH - 71A	EASTLEIGH - 71A	EASTLEIGH - 71A	EASTLEIGH - 71A	EASTLEIGH - 71A
30102 FRATTON - 70F	FRATTON - 70F	FRATTON - 70F	FRATTON - 70F	FRATTON - 70F	FRATTON - 70F	FRATTON - 70F
C14 0-4-0T (1906)							
30588 EASTLEIGH - 71A	EASTLEIGH - 71A	EASTLEIGH - 71A	EASTLEIGH - 71A	EASTLEIGH - 71A	EASTLEIGH - 71A	EASTLEIGH - 71A
30589 EASTLEIGH - 71A	EASTLEIGH - 71A	EASTLEIGH - 71A	EASTLEIGH - 71A	EASTLEIGH - 71A	EASTLEIGH - 71A	EASTLEIGH - 71A
0757' 0-6-2T (1907)							
30757 PLYMOUTH - 72D	PLYMOUTH - 72D	PLYMOUTH - 72D	PLYMOUTH - 72D	PLYMOUTH - 72D	PLYMOUTH - 72D	PLYMOUTH - 72D
30758 PLYMOUTH - 72D	PLYMOUTH - 72D	PLYMOUTH - 72D	PLYMOUTH - 72D	PLYMOUTH - 72D	PLYMOUTH - 72D	PLYMOUTH - 72D
A1X 0-6-0T (1872)							
32635 DEPARTMENTAL	DEPARTMENTAL	DEPARTMENTAL	DEPARTMENTAL	DEPARTMENTAL	DEPARTMENTAL	DEPARTMENTAL
32636 BRIGHTON - 75A (N)	BRIGHTON - 75A (N)	BRIGHTON - 75A (N)	BRIGHTON - 75A (N)	BRIGHTON - 75A	ST LEONARDS - 74E	ST LEONARDS - 74E
32640 FRATTON - 70F	FRATTON - 70F	FRATTON - 70F	FRATTON - 70F	BRIGHTON - 75A	BRIGHTON - 75A	BRIGHTON - 75A
32646 BRIGHTON - 75A (N)	BRIGHTON - 75A (N)	BRIGHTON - 75A (N)	BRIGHTON - 75A (N)	BRIGHTON - 75A	BRIGHTON - 75A	BRIGHTON - 75A
32650 FRATTON - 70F	FRATTON - 70F	FRATTON - 70F	FRATTON - 70F	FRATTON - 70F	FRATTON - 70F	FRATTON - 70F
32655 ST LEONARDS - 74E	ST LEONARDS - 74E	ST LEONARDS - 74E	ST LEONARDS - 74E	ST LEONARDS - 74E	BRIGHTON - 75A	BRIGHTON - 75A
32659 ASHFORD - 74A	ASHFORD - 74A	ASHFORD - 74A	ASHFORD - 74A	ASHFORD - 74A	ASHFORD - 74A	ASHFORD - 74A
32661 FRATTON - 70F	FRATTON - 70F	FRATTON - 70F	FRATTON - 70F	FRATTON - 70F	FRATTON - 70F	FRATTON - 70F
32662 BRIGHTON - 75A(N)	BRIGHTON - 75A(N)	BRIGHTON - 75A(N)	BRIGHTON - 75A(N)	BRIGHTON - 75A	BRIGHTON - 75A	BRIGHTON - 75A
32670 ST LEONARDS - 74E	ST LEONARDS - 74E	ST LEONARDS - 74E	ST LEONARDS - 74E	ST LEONARDS - 74E	ST LEONARDS - 74E	ST LEONARDS - 74E
32677 FRATTON - 70F	FRATTON - 70F	FRATTON - 70F	FRATTON - 70F	FRATTON - 70F	FRATTON - 70F	FRATTON - 70F
32678 ST LEONARDS - 74E	ST LEONARDS - 74E	ST LEONARDS - 74E	ST LEONARDS - 74E	ST LEONARDS - 74E	ST LEONARDS - 74E	ST LEONARDS - 74E
E1 0-6-0T (1874)							
32113 EASTLEIGH - 71A	EASTLEIGH - 71A	EASTLEIGH - 71A	EASTLEIGH - 71A	EASTLEIGH - 71A	SOUTHAMPTON - 71I	SOUTHAMPTON - 71I
32138 FRATTON - 70F	FRATTON - 70F	FRATTON - 70F	FRATTON - 70F	FRATTON - 70F	FRATTON - 70F	FRATTON - 70F
32139 FRATTON - 70F	FRATTON - 70F	FRATTON - 70F	FRATTON - 70F	FRATTON - 70F	FRATTON - 70F	FRATTON - 70F
32151 EASTLEIGH - 71A	EASTLEIGH - 71A	EASTLEIGH - 71A	EASTLEIGH - 71A	EASTLEIGH - 71A	EASTLEIGH - 71A	EASTLEIGH - 71A
32606 SOUTHAMPTON - 71I	SOUTHAMPTON - 71I	SOUTHAMPTON - 71I	SOUTHAMPTON - 71I	SOUTHAMPTON - 71I	SOUTHAMPTON - 71I	SOUTHAMPTON - 71I
32689 SOUTHAMPTON - 71I	SOUTHAMPTON - 71I	SOUTHAMPTON - 71I	SOUTHAMPTON - 71I	SOUTHAMPTON - 71I	SOUTHAMPTON - 71I	SOUTHAMPTON - 71I
32694 FRATTON - 70F	FRATTON - 70F	FRATTON - 70F	FRATTON - 70F	FRATTON - 70F	FRATTON - 70F	FRATTON - 70F
E2 0-6-0T (1913)							
32100 STEWARTS LANE - 73A	STEWARTS LANE - 73A	STEWARTS LANE - 73A	STEWARTS LANE - 73A	STEWARTS LANE - 73A	STEWARTS LANE - 73A	STEWARTS LANE - 73A
32101 STEWARTS LANE - 73A	STEWARTS LANE - 73A	STEWARTS LANE - 73A	STEWARTS LANE - 73A	STEWARTS LANE - 73A	STEWARTS LANE - 73A	STEWARTS LANE - 73A
32102 STEWARTS LANE - 73A	STEWARTS LANE - 73A	STEWARTS LANE - 73A	STEWARTS LANE - 73A	STEWARTS LANE - 73A	STEWARTS LANE - 73A	STEWARTS LANE - 73A
32103 STEWARTS LANE - 73A	STEWARTS LANE - 73A	STEWARTS LANE - 73A	STEWARTS LANE - 73A	STEWARTS LANE - 73A	STEWARTS LANE - 73A	STEWARTS LANE - 73A
32104 STEWARTS LANE - 73A	STEWARTS LANE - 73A	STEWARTS LANE - 73A	STEWARTS LANE - 73A	STEWARTS LANE - 73A	STEWARTS LANE - 73A	STEWARTS LANE - 73A
32105 STEWARTS LANE - 73A	STEWARTS LANE - 73A	STEWARTS LANE - 73A	STEWARTS LANE - 73A	STEWARTS LANE - 73A	STEWARTS LANE - 73A	STEWARTS LANE - 73A
32106 STEWARTS LANE - 73A	STEWARTS LANE - 73A	STEWARTS LANE - 73A	STEWARTS LANE - 73A	STEWARTS LANE - 73A	STEWARTS LANE - 73A	STEWARTS LANE - 73A
32107 STEWARTS LANE - 73A	STEWARTS LANE - 73A	STEWARTS LANE - 73A	STEWARTS LANE - 73A	STEWARTS LANE - 73A	STEWARTS LANE - 73A	STEWARTS LANE - 73A
32108 DOVER - 74C	DOVER - 74C	DOVER - 74C	DOVER - 74C	DOVER - 74C	DOVER - 74C	DOVER - 74C
32109 DOVER - 74C	DOVER - 74C	DOVER - 74C	DOVER - 74C	DOVER - 74C	DOVER - 74C	DOVER - 74C

Introduced in 1891 with a further batch being added in 1908, the LSWR B4 0-4-0T's were for many years the standard dock shunters at Dover, Southampton and Plymouth. Whilst those at Southampton were superseded by USA 0-6-0T's after the war, one B4 working was retained for shunting at Southampton Terminus and working occasional trips of vans to the docks. Another was located at Winchester, a sub-shed of Eastleigh, where it shunted the LSWR station yard from 07.45 to 17.15 each day.

30089, one of the 1891 engines, was a well travelled member of the class and was photographed at Eastleigh - from where it took its turn on the Winchester shunt - in 1950 a few months after arriving from Stewarts Lane. In early 1952 it transferred to Plymouth remaining there until late 1958 when it returned to Eastleigh.

loco	Jan-56	Apr-56	May-56	Aug-56	Oct-56	Nov-56	Jan-57
B4 0-4-0T (1891)							
30082	EASTLEIGH - 71A	EASTLEIGH - 71A	EASTLEIGH - 71A	EASTLEIGH - 71A	EASTLEIGH - 71A	EASTLEIGH - 71A	EASTLEIGH - 71A
30083	EASTLEIGH - 71A	EASTLEIGH - 71A	EASTLEIGH - 71A	EASTLEIGH - 71A	EASTLEIGH - 71A	EASTLEIGH - 71A	EASTLEIGH - 71A
30084	DOVER - 74C	DOVER - 74C	DOVER - 74C	DOVER - 74C	DOVER - 74C	DOVER - 74C	DOVER - 74C
30086	GUILDFORD - 70C	GUILDFORD - 70C	GUILDFORD - 70C	GUILDFORD - 70C	GUILDFORD - 70C	GUILDFORD - 70C	GUILDFORD - 70C
30087	BOURNEMOUTH - 71B	BOURNEMOUTH - 71B	BOURNEMOUTH - 71B	BOURNEMOUTH - 71B	BOURNEMOUTH - 71B	BOURNEMOUTH - 71B	BOURNEMOUTH - 71B
30088	PLYMOUTH - 72D	PLYMOUTH - 72D	PLYMOUTH - 72D	PLYMOUTH - 72D	PLYMOUTH - 72D	PLYMOUTH - 72D	PLYMOUTH - 72D
30089	PLYMOUTH - 72D	PLYMOUTH - 72D	PLYMOUTH - 72D	PLYMOUTH - 72D	PLYMOUTH - 72D	PLYMOUTH - 72D	PLYMOUTH - 72D
30093	BOURNEMOUTH - 71B	BOURNEMOUTH - 71B	BOURNEMOUTH - 71B	BOURNEMOUTH - 71B	BOURNEMOUTH - 71B	BOURNEMOUTH - 71B	BOURNEMOUTH - 71B
30094	PLYMOUTH - 72D	PLYMOUTH - 72D	PLYMOUTH - 72D	PLYMOUTH - 72D	PLYMOUTH - 72D	PLYMOUTH - 72D	PLYMOUTH - 72D
30096	EASTLEIGH - 71A	EASTLEIGH - 71A	EASTLEIGH - 71A	EASTLEIGH - 71A	EASTLEIGH - 71A	EASTLEIGH - 71A	EASTLEIGH - 71A
30102	FRATTON - 70F	FRATTON - 70F	FRATTON - 70F	FRATTON - 70F	FRATTON - 70F	FRATTON - 70F	FRATTON - 70F
C14 0-4-0T (1906)							
30588	EASTLEIGH - 71A	EASTLEIGH - 71A	EASTLEIGH - 71A	EASTLEIGH - 71A	EASTLEIGH - 71A	EASTLEIGH - 71A	EASTLEIGH - 71A
30589	EASTLEIGH - 71A	EASTLEIGH - 71A	EASTLEIGH - 71A	EASTLEIGH - 71A	EASTLEIGH - 71A	EASTLEIGH - 71A	EASTLEIGH - 71A
0757' 0-6-2T (1907)							
30757	PLYMOUTH - 72D	PLYMOUTH - 72D	EASTLEIGH - 71A	EASTLEIGH - 71A	EASTLEIGH - 71A	EASTLEIGH - 71A	EASTLEIGH - 71A
30758	PLYMOUTH - 72D	PLYMOUTH - 72D	EASTLEIGH - 71A	EASTLEIGH - 71A	EASTLEIGH - 71A	EASTLEIGH - 71A	W/D
A1X 0-6-0T (1872)							
32635	DEPARTMENTAL	DEPARTMENTAL	DEPARTMENTAL	DEPARTMENTAL	DEPARTMENTAL	DEPARTMENTAL	DEPARTMENTAL
32636	ST LEONARDS - 74E	ST LEONARDS - 74E	ST LEONARDS - 74E	ST LEONARDS - 74E	ST LEONARDS - 74E	ST LEONARDS - 74E	ST LEONARDS - 74E
32640	BRIGHTON - 75A	BRIGHTON - 75A	FRATTON - 70F	FRATTON - 70F	FRATTON - 70F	FRATTON - 70F	FRATTON - 70F
32646	BRIGHTON - 75A	BRIGHTON - 75A	FRATTON - 70F	FRATTON - 70F	FRATTON - 70F	FRATTON - 70F	FRATTON - 70F
32650	FRATTON - 70F	FRATTON - 70F	FRATTON - 70F	FRATTON - 70F	FRATTON - 70F	FRATTON - 70F	FRATTON - 70F
32655	BRIGHTON - 75A	BRIGHTON - 75A	BRIGHTON - 75A	BRIGHTON - 75A	BRIGHTON - 75A	BRIGHTON - 75A	BRIGHTON - 75A
32659	ASHFORD - 74A	ASHFORD - 74A	ASHFORD - 74A	ASHFORD - 74A	ASHFORD - 74A	ASHFORD - 74A	ASHFORD - 74A
32661	FRATTON - 70F	FRATTON - 70F	FRATTON - 70F	FRATTON - 70F	FRATTON - 70F	FRATTON - 70F	FRATTON - 70F
32662	BRIGHTON - 75A	BRIGHTON - 75A	BRIGHTON - 75A	BRIGHTON - 75A	BRIGHTON - 75A	BRIGHTON - 75A	BRIGHTON - 75A
32670	ST LEONARDS - 74E	ST LEONARDS - 74E	ST LEONARDS - 74E	ST LEONARDS - 74E	ST LEONARDS - 74E	ST LEONARDS - 74E	ST LEONARDS - 74E
32677	FRATTON - 70F	FRATTON - 70F	FRATTON - 70F	FRATTON - 70F	FRATTON - 70F	FRATTON - 70F	FRATTON - 70F
32678	ST LEONARDS - 74E	ST LEONARDS - 74E	ST LEONARDS - 74E	ST LEONARDS - 74E	ST LEONARDS - 74E	ST LEONARDS - 74E	ST LEONARDS - 74E
E1 0-6-0T (1874)							
32113	SOUTHAMPTON - 71I	SOUTHAMPTON - 71I	SOUTHAMPTON - 71I	SOUTHAMPTON - 71I	SOUTHAMPTON - 71I	SOUTHAMPTON - 71I	SOUTHAMPTON - 71I
32138	FRATTON - 70F	FRATTON - 70F	FRATTON - 70F	FRATTON - 70F	FRATTON - 70F	W/D	W/D
32139	FRATTON - 70F	FRATTON - 70F	FRATTON - 70F	FRATTON - 70F	FRATTON - 70F	FRATTON - 70F	FRATTON - 70F
32151	EASTLEIGH - 71A	EASTLEIGH - 71A	EASTLEIGH - 71A	EASTLEIGH - 71A	EASTLEIGH - 71A	SOUTHAMPTON - 71I	SOUTHAMPTON - 71I
32606	SOUTHAMPTON - 71I	SOUTHAMPTON - 71I	SOUTHAMPTON - 71I	W/D	W/D	W/D	W/D
32689	SOUTHAMPTON - 71I	SOUTHAMPTON - 71I	SOUTHAMPTON - 71I	SOUTHAMPTON - 71I	SOUTHAMPTON - 71I	SOUTHAMPTON - 71I	SOUTHAMPTON - 71I
32694	FRATTON - 70F	FRATTON - 70F	FRATTON - 70F	SOUTHAMPTON - 71I	SOUTHAMPTON - 71I	FRATTON - 70F	FRATTON - 70F
E2 0-6-0T (1913)							
32100	STEWARTS LANE - 73A	STEWARTS LANE - 73A	STEWARTS LANE - 73A	STEWARTS LANE - 73A	STEWARTS LANE - 73A	STEWARTS LANE - 73A	STEWARTS LANE - 73A
32101	STEWARTS LANE - 73A	STEWARTS LANE - 73A	STEWARTS LANE - 73A	STEWARTS LANE - 73A	STEWARTS LANE - 73A	STEWARTS LANE - 73A	SOUTHAMPTON - 71I
32102	STEWARTS LANE - 73A	STEWARTS LANE - 73A	STEWARTS LANE - 73A	STEWARTS LANE - 73A	STEWARTS LANE - 73A	STEWARTS LANE - 73A	STEWARTS LANE - 73A
32103	STEWARTS LANE - 73A	STEWARTS LANE - 73A	STEWARTS LANE - 73A	STEWARTS LANE - 73A	STEWARTS LANE - 73A	STEWARTS LANE - 73A	STEWARTS LANE - 73A
32104	STEWARTS LANE - 73A	STEWARTS LANE - 73A	STEWARTS LANE - 73A	STEWARTS LANE - 73A	STEWARTS LANE - 73A	STEWARTS LANE - 73A	STEWARTS LANE - 73A
32105	STEWARTS LANE - 73A	STEWARTS LANE - 73A	STEWARTS LANE - 73A	STEWARTS LANE - 73A	STEWARTS LANE - 73A	STEWARTS LANE - 73A	STEWARTS LANE - 73A
32106	STEWARTS LANE - 73A	STEWARTS LANE - 73A	STEWARTS LANE - 73A	STEWARTS LANE - 73A	STEWARTS LANE - 73A	STEWARTS LANE - 73A	STEWARTS LANE - 73A
32107	STEWARTS LANE - 73A	STEWARTS LANE - 73A	STEWARTS LANE - 73A	STEWARTS LANE - 73A	STEWARTS LANE - 73A	STEWARTS LANE - 73A	STEWARTS LANE - 73A
32108	DOVER - 74C	DOVER - 74C	DOVER - 74C	DOVER - 74C	DOVER - 74C	EASTLEIGH - 71A	SOUTHAMPTON - 71I
32109	DOVER - 74C	DOVER - 74C	DOVER - 74C	DOVER - 74C	DOVER - 74C	EASTLEIGH - 71A	SOUTHAMPTON - 71I

Built in 1906 as 2-2-0T one-coach push & pull railcar replacements, the C14 tanks were rebuilt as 0-4-0T shunters in 1912, two of the original five engines surviving until 1957 after spending their last years at Southampton shed (although nominally allocated to Eastleigh). The normal duty in the 1950's was for one of the pair to shunt Southampton Town Quay between 05.30 and 14.45 whilst the second engine remained spare. 30589 is pictured at Eastleigh in 1950.

loco	Mar-57	Jun-57	Jul-57	Oct-57	Jan-58	Feb-58	Mar-58
				B4 0-4-0T (1891)			
30082	EASTLEIGH - 71A	W/D	W/D	W/D	W/D	W/D	W/D
30083	EASTLEIGH - 71A	EASTLEIGH - 71A	EASTLEIGH - 71A	EASTLEIGH - 71A	EASTLEIGH - 71A	EASTLEIGH - 71A	EASTLEIGH - 71A
30084	DOVER - 74C	DOVER - 74C	DOVER - 74C	DOVER - 74C	DOVER - 74C	DOVER - 74C	DOVER - 74C
30086	GUILDFORD - 70C	GUILDFORD - 70C	GUILDFORD - 70C	GUILDFORD - 70C	GUILDFORD - 70C	GUILDFORD - 70C	GUILDFORD - 70C
30087	BOURNEMOUTH - 71B	BOURNEMOUTH - 71B	BOURNEMOUTH - 71B	BOURNEMOUTH - 71B	BOURNEMOUTH - 71B	BOURNEMOUTH - 71B	BOURNEMOUTH - 71B
30088	PLYMOUTH - 72D	PLYMOUTH - 72D	PLYMOUTH - 72D	PLYMOUTH - 72D	PLYMOUTH - 72D	PLYMOUTH - 83H	PLYMOUTH - 83H
30089	PLYMOUTH - 72D	PLYMOUTH - 72D	PLYMOUTH - 72D	PLYMOUTH - 72D	PLYMOUTH - 72D	PLYMOUTH - 83H	PLYMOUTH - 83H
30093	BOURNEMOUTH - 71B	BOURNEMOUTH - 71B	BOURNEMOUTH - 71B	BOURNEMOUTH - 71B	BOURNEMOUTH - 71B	BOURNEMOUTH - 71B	BOURNEMOUTH - 71B
30096	EASTLEIGH - 71A	EASTLEIGH - 71A	EASTLEIGH - 71A	EASTLEIGH - 71A	EASTLEIGH - 71A	EASTLEIGH - 71A	EASTLEIGH - 71A
30102	FRATTON - 70F	FRATTON - 70F	FRATTON - 70F	FRATTON - 70F	FRATTON - 70F	FRATTON - 70F	FRATTON - 70F
				C14 0-4-0T (1906)			
30588	EASTLEIGH - 71A	EASTLEIGH - 71A	EASTLEIGH - 71A	EASTLEIGH - 71A	W/D	W/D	W/D
30589	EASTLEIGH - 71A	W/D	W/D	W/D	W/D	W/D	W/D
				0757' 0-6-2T (1907)			
30757	EASTLEIGH - 71A	EASTLEIGH - 71A	EASTLEIGH - 71A	EASTLEIGH - 71A	W/D	W/D	W/D
				A1X 0-6-0T (1872)			
32635	DEPARTMENTAL	DEPARTMENTAL	DEPARTMENTAL	DEPARTMENTAL	DEPARTMENTAL	DEPARTMENTAL	DEPARTMENTAL
32636	ST LEONARDS - 74E	ST LEONARDS - 74E	ST LEONARDS - 74E	ST LEONARDS - 74E	ST LEONARDS - 74E	ST LEONARDS - 74E	ST LEONARDS - 74E
32640	FRATTON - 70F	FRATTON - 70F	FRATTON - 70F	FRATTON - 70F	FRATTON - 70F	FRATTON - 70F	FRATTON - 70F
32646	FRATTON - 70F	FRATTON - 70F	FRATTON - 70F	FRATTON - 70F	FRATTON - 70F	FRATTON - 70F	FRATTON - 70F
32650	FRATTON - 70F	FRATTON - 70F	FRATTON - 70F	FRATTON - 70F	FRATTON - 70F	FRATTON - 70F	FRATTON - 70F
32655	BRIGHTON - 75A	BRIGHTON - 75A	BRIGHTON - 75A	BRIGHTON - 75A	BRIGHTON - 75A	BRIGHTON - 75A	BRIGHTON - 75A
32659	ASHFORD - 74A	ASHFORD - 74A	ASHFORD - 74A	ASHFORD - 74A	ASHFORD - 74A	ASHFORD - 74A	ASHFORD - 74A
32661	FRATTON - 70F	FRATTON - 70F	FRATTON - 70F	FRATTON - 70F	FRATTON - 70F	FRATTON - 70F	FRATTON - 70F
32662	BRIGHTON - 75A	BRIGHTON - 75A	BRIGHTON - 75A	BRIGHTON - 75A	BRIGHTON - 75A	BRIGHTON - 75A	BRIGHTON - 75A
32670	ST LEONARDS - 74E	ST LEONARDS - 74E	ST LEONARDS - 74E	ST LEONARDS - 74E	BRIGHTON - 75A	BRIGHTON - 75A	BRIGHTON - 75A
32677	FRATTON - 70F	FRATTON - 70F	FRATTON - 70F	FRATTON - 70F	FRATTON - 70F	FRATTON - 70F	FRATTON - 70F
32678	ST LEONARDS - 74E	ST LEONARDS - 74E	ST LEONARDS - 74E	ST LEONARDS - 74E	ST LEONARDS - 74E	ST LEONARDS - 74E	ST LEONARDS - 74E
				E1 0-6-0T (1874)			
32113	SOUTHAMPTON - 71I	SOUTHAMPTON - 71I	SOUTHAMPTON - 71I	SOUTHAMPTON - 71I	SOUTHAMPTON - 71I	SOUTHAMPTON - 71I	SOUTHAMPTON - 71I
32139	FRATTON - 70F	FRATTON - 70F	FRATTON - 70F	FRATTON - 70F	FRATTON - 70F	FRATTON - 70F	FRATTON - 70F
32151	SOUTHAMPTON - 71I	SOUTHAMPTON - 71I	SOUTHAMPTON - 71I	SOUTHAMPTON - 71I	SOUTHAMPTON - 71I	SOUTHAMPTON - 71I	SOUTHAMPTON - 71I
32689	SOUTHAMPTON - 71I	SOUTHAMPTON - 71I	SOUTHAMPTON - 71I	SOUTHAMPTON - 71I	SOUTHAMPTON - 71I	SOUTHAMPTON - 71I	SOUTHAMPTON - 71I
32694	FRATTON - 70F	FRATTON - 70F	FRATTON - 70F	FRATTON - 70F	FRATTON - 70F		
				E2 0-6-0T (1913)			
32100	STEWARTS LANE - 73A	STEWARTS LANE - 73A	STEWARTS LANE - 73A	STEWARTS LANE - 73A	STEWARTS LANE - 73A	STEWARTS LANE - 73A	STEWARTS LANE - 73A
32101	SOUTHAMPTON - 71I	SOUTHAMPTON - 71I	SOUTHAMPTON - 71I	SOUTHAMPTON - 71I	SOUTHAMPTON - 71I	SOUTHAMPTON - 71I	SOUTHAMPTON - 71I
32102	STEWARTS LANE - 73A	STEWARTS LANE - 73A	STEWARTS LANE - 73A	STEWARTS LANE - 73A	STEWARTS LANE - 73A	STEWARTS LANE - 73A	STEWARTS LANE - 73A
32103	STEWARTS LANE - 73A	STEWARTS LANE - 73A	STEWARTS LANE - 73A	STEWARTS LANE - 73A	STEWARTS LANE - 73A	STEWARTS LANE - 73A	STEWARTS LANE - 73A
32104	STEWARTS LANE - 73A	B ARMS - 73B	B ARMS - 73B	B ARMS - 73B	B ARMS - 73B	B ARMS - 73B	B ARMS - 73B
32105	STEWARTS LANE - 73A	B ARMS - 73B	B ARMS - 73B	B ARMS - 73B	B ARMS - 73B	B ARMS - 73B	B ARMS - 73B
32106	STEWARTS LANE - 73A	STEWARTS LANE - 73A	STEWARTS LANE - 73A	STEWARTS LANE - 73A	STEWARTS LANE - 73A	STEWARTS LANE - 73A	STEWARTS LANE - 73A
32107	STEWARTS LANE - 73A	B ARMS - 73B	B ARMS - 73B	B ARMS - 73B	B ARMS - 73B	B ARMS - 73B	B ARMS - 73B
32108	SOUTHAMPTON - 71I	SOUTHAMPTON - 71I	SOUTHAMPTON - 71I	SOUTHAMPTON - 71I	SOUTHAMPTON - 71I	SOUTHAMPTON - 71I	SOUTHAMPTON - 71I
32109	SOUTHAMPTON - 71I	SOUTHAMPTON - 71I	SOUTHAMPTON - 71I	SOUTHAMPTON - 71I	SOUTHAMPTON - 71I	SOUTHAMPTON - 71I	SOUTHAMPTON - 71I

loco	May-58	Oct-58	Mar-59	Jun-59	Jul-59	Aug-59	Oct-59
				B4 0-4-0T (1891)			
30083	EASTLEIGH - 71A	EASTLEIGH - 71A	EASTLEIGH - 71A	EASTLEIGH - 71A	EASTLEIGH - 71A	EASTLEIGH - 71A	EASTLEIGH - 71A
30084	DOVER - 74C	DOVER - 73H	DOVER - 73H	DOVER - 73H	DOVER - 73H	DOVER - 73H	W/D
30086	GUILDFORD - 70C	GUILDFORD - 70C	W/D	W/D	W/D	W/D	W/D
30087	BOURNEMOUTH - 71B	BOURNEMOUTH - 71B	W/D	W/D	W/D	W/D	W/D
30088	PLYMOUTH - 83H	EASTLEIGH - 71A	EASTLEIGH - 71A	EASTLEIGH - 71A	W/D	W/D	W/D
30089	PLYMOUTH - 83H	EASTLEIGH - 71A	GUILDFORD - 70C	GUILDFORD - 70C	GUILDFORD - 70C	GUILDFORD - 70C	GUILDFORD - 70C
30093	BOURNEMOUTH - 71B	BOURNEMOUTH - 71B	BOURNEMOUTH - 71B	BOURNEMOUTH - 71B	BOURNEMOUTH - 71B	BOURNEMOUTH - 71B	BOURNEMOUTH - 71B
30096	EASTLEIGH - 71A	EASTLEIGH - 71A	EASTLEIGH - 71A	EASTLEIGH - 71A	EASTLEIGH - 71A	EASTLEIGH - 71A	EASTLEIGH - 71A
30102	FRATTON - 70F	EASTLEIGH - 71A	BOURNEMOUTH - 71B	BOURNEMOUTH - 71B	BOURNEMOUTH - 71B	BOURNEMOUTH - 71B	BOURNEMOUTH - 71B
				A1X 0-6-0T (1872)			
32635	DEPARTMENTAL	RESTORED TO TFC	BRIGHTON - 75A	BRIGHTON - 75A	BRIGHTON - 75A	BRIGHTON - 75A	BRIGHTON - 75A
32636	ASHFORD - 74A	ASHFORD - 73F	ASHFORD - 73F	ASHFORD - 73F	ASHFORD - 73F	ASHFORD - 73F	FRATTON - 70F
32640	FRATTON - 70F	FRATTON - 70F	FRATTON - 70F	FRATTON - 70F	FRATTON - 70F	FRATTON - 70F	FRATTON - 70F
32646	FRATTON - 70F	FRATTON - 70F	FRATTON - 70F	FRATTON - 70F	FRATTON - 70F	FRATTON - 70F	FRATTON - 70F
32650	FRATTON - 70F	FRATTON - 70F	FRATTON - 70F	FRATTON - 70F	FRATTON - 70F	FRATTON - 70F	FRATTON - 70F
32655	BRIGHTON - 75A	BRIGHTON - 75A	BRIGHTON - 75A	BRIGHTON - 75A	BRIGHTON - 75A	BRIGHTON - 75A	BRIGHTON - 75A
32659	ASHFORD - 74A	ASHFORD - 73F	ASHFORD - 73F	ASHFORD - 73F	ASHFORD - 73F	ASHFORD - 73F	ASHFORD - 73F
32661	FRATTON - 70F	FRATTON - 70F	FRATTON - 70F	FRATTON - 70F	FRATTON - 70F	FRATTON - 70F	FRATTON - 70F
32662	BRIGHTON - 75A	BRIGHTON - 75A	BRIGHTON - 75A	BRIGHTON - 75A	BRIGHTON - 75A	BRIGHTON - 75A	BRIGHTON - 75A
32670	BRIGHTON - 75A	BRIGHTON - 75A	BRIGHTON - 75A	BRIGHTON - 75A	BRIGHTON - 75A	BRIGHTON - 75A	BRIGHTON - 75A
32677	FRATTON - 70F	FRATTON - 70F	FRATTON - 70F	FRATTON - 70F	FRATTON - 70F	FRATTON - 70F	W/D
32678	FRATTON - 70F	FRATTON - 70F	FRATTON - 70F	FRATTON - 70F	FRATTON - 70F	FRATTON - 70F	FRATTON - 70F
				E1 0-6-0T (1874)			
32113	SOUTHAMPTON - 71I	W/D	W/D	W/D	W/D	W/D	W/D
32139	FRATTON - 70F	FRATTON - 70F	W/D	W/D	W/D	W/D	W/D
32151	SOUTHAMPTON - 71I	SOUTHAMPTON - 71I	SOUTHAMPTON - 71I	SOUTHAMPTON - 71I	SOUTHAMPTON - 71I	SOUTHAMPTON - 71I	SOUTHAMPTON - 71I
32689	SOUTHAMPTON - 71I	SOUTHAMPTON - 71I	SOUTHAMPTON - 71I	SOUTHAMPTON - 71I	SOUTHAMPTON - 71I	SOUTHAMPTON - 71I	SOUTHAMPTON - 71I
32694	FRATTON - 70F	FRATTON - 70F	FRATTON - 70F	FRATTON - 70F	FRATTON - 70F	FRATTON - 70F	FRATTON - 70F
				E2 0-6-0T (1913)			
32100	STEWARTS LANE - 73A	STEWARTS LANE - 73A	STEWARTS LANE - 73A	STEWARTS LANE - 73A	STEWARTS LANE - 73A	STEWARTS LANE - 73A	STEWARTS LANE - 73A
32101	SOUTHAMPTON - 71I	SOUTHAMPTON - 71I	SOUTHAMPTON - 71I	SOUTHAMPTON - 71I	SOUTHAMPTON - 71I	SOUTHAMPTON - 71I	SOUTHAMPTON - 71I
32102	STEWARTS LANE - 73A	STEWARTS LANE - 73A	STEWARTS LANE - 73A	STEWARTS LANE - 73A	STEWARTS LANE - 73A	STEWARTS LANE - 73A	STEWARTS LANE - 73A
32103	STEWARTS LANE - 73A	STEWARTS LANE - 73A	STEWARTS LANE - 73A	STEWARTS LANE - 73A	STEWARTS LANE - 73A	STEWARTS LANE - 73A	STEWARTS LANE - 73A
32104	B ARMS - 73B	B ARMS - 73B	B ARMS - 73B	B ARMS - 73B	B ARMS - 73B	B ARMS - 73B	NORWOOD JCN - 75C
32105	B ARMS - 73B	B ARMS - 73B	B ARMS - 73B	B ARMS - 73B	B ARMS - 73B	B ARMS - 73B	NORWOOD JCN - 75C
32106	STEWARTS LANE - 73A	STEWARTS LANE - 73A	STEWARTS LANE - 73A	STEWARTS LANE - 73A	STEWARTS LANE - 73A	STEWARTS LANE - 73A	STEWARTS LANE - 73A
32107	B ARMS - 73B	B ARMS - 73B	B ARMS - 73B	B ARMS - 73B	B ARMS - 73B	B ARMS - 73B	THREE BRIDGES - 75E
32108	SOUTHAMPTON - 71I	SOUTHAMPTON - 71I	SOUTHAMPTON - 71I	SOUTHAMPTON - 71I	SOUTHAMPTON - 71I	SOUTHAMPTON - 71I	SOUTHAMPTON - 71I
32109	SOUTHAMPTON - 71I	SOUTHAMPTON - 71I	SOUTHAMPTON - 71I	SOUTHAMPTON - 71I	SOUTHAMPTON - 71I	SOUTHAMPTON - 71I	SOUTHAMPTON - 71I

loco	Dec-59	Feb-60	Mar-60	Apr-60	Jul-60	Aug-60	Sep-60	Nov-60
			B4 0-4-0T (1891)					
30089	GUILDFORD-70C	GUILDFORD-70C	GUILDFORD-70C	GUILDFORD-70C	GUILDFORD-70C	GUILDFORD-70C	GUILDFORD-70C	GUILDFORD-70C
30093	BOURNEMOUTH-71B	BOURNEMOUTH-71B	BOURNEMOUTH-71B	WD	WD	WD	WD	WD
30096	EASTLEIGH-71A	EASTLEIGH-71A	EASTLEIGH-71A	EASTLEIGH-71A	EASTLEIGH-71A	EASTLEIGH-71A	EASTLEIGH-71A	EASTLEIGH-71A
30102	BOURNEMOUTH-71B	BOURNEMOUTH-71B	BOURNEMOUTH-71B	BOURNEMOUTH-71B	BOURNEMOUTH-71B	BOURNEMOUTH-71B	BOURNEMOUTH-71B	BOURNEMOUTH-71B
			A1X 0-6-0T (1872)					
32635	BRIGHTON-75A	BRIGHTON-75A	BRIGHTON-75A	BRIGHTON-75A	BRIGHTON-75A	BRIGHTON-75A	BRIGHTON-75A	BRIGHTON-75A
32636	EASTLEIGH-71A	BRIGHTON-75A	BRIGHTON-75A	BRIGHTON-75A	BRIGHTON-75A	BRIGHTON-75A	BRIGHTON-75A	BRIGHTON-75A
32640	EASTLEIGH-71A	EASTLEIGH-71A	EASTLEIGH-71A	EASTLEIGH-71A	EASTLEIGH-71A	EASTLEIGH-71A	EASTLEIGH-71A	EASTLEIGH-71A
32646	EASTLEIGH-71A	EASTLEIGH-71A	EASTLEIGH-71A	EASTLEIGH-71A	EASTLEIGH-71A	EASTLEIGH-71A	EASTLEIGH-71A	EASTLEIGH-71A
32650	FRATTON-70F	FRATTON-70F	FRATTON-70F	FRATTON-70F	FRATTON-70F	FRATTON-70F	FRATTON-70F	FRATTON-70F
32655	BRIGHTON-75A	EASTLEIGH-71A	EASTLEIGH-71A	EASTLEIGH-71A	PRESERVED	PRESERVED	PRESERVED	PRESERVED
32659	ASHFORD-73F	ASHFORD-73F	ASHFORD-73F	ASHFORD-73F	ASHFORD-73F	ASHFORD-73F	ASHFORD-73F	ASHFORD-73F
32661	EASTLEIGH-71A	EASTLEIGH-71A	EASTLEIGH-71A	EASTLEIGH-71A	EASTLEIGH-71A	EASTLEIGH-71A	EASTLEIGH-71A	EASTLEIGH-71A
32662	BRIGHTON-75A	BRIGHTON-75A	BRIGHTON-75A	BRIGHTON-75A	BRIGHTON-75A	BRIGHTON-75A	BRIGHTON-75A	BRIGHTON-75A
32670	BRIGHTON-75A	BRIGHTON-75A	BRIGHTON-75A	BRIGHTON-75A	BRIGHTON-75A	BRIGHTON-75A	BRIGHTON-75A	BRIGHTON-75A
32678	EASTLEIGH-71A	EASTLEIGH-71A	EASTLEIGH-71A	EASTLEIGH-71A	EASTLEIGH-71A	EASTLEIGH-71A	EASTLEIGH-71A	EASTLEIGH-71A
			E1 0-6-0T (1874)					
32151	SOUTHAMPTON-71I	WD	WD	WD	WD	WD	WD	WD
32689	SOUTHAMPTON-71I	WD	WD	WD	WD	WD	WD	WD
32694	SOUTHAMPTON-71I	SOUTHAMPTON-71I	SOUTHAMPTON-71I	SOUTHAMPTON-71I	SOUTHAMPTON-71I	SOUTHAMPTON-71I	SOUTHAMPTON-71I	SOUTHAMPTON-71I
			E2 0-6-0T (1913)					
32100	STEWARTS LANE-73A	STEWARTS LANE-73A	STEWARTS LANE-73A	STEWARTS LANE-73A	STEWARTS LANE-73A	STEWARTS LANE-73A	STEWARTS LANE-73A	STEWARTS LANE-73A
32101	SOUTHAMPTON-71I	SOUTHAMPTON-71I	SOUTHAMPTON-71I	SOUTHAMPTON-71I	SOUTHAMPTON-71I	SOUTHAMPTON-71I	SOUTHAMPTON-71I	SOUTHAMPTON-71I
32102	STEWARTS LANE-73A	STEWARTS LANE-73A	STEWARTS LANE-73A	STEWARTS LANE-73A	STEWARTS LANE-73A	STEWARTS LANE-73A	STEWARTS LANE-73A	STEWARTS LANE-73A
32103	STEWARTS LANE-73A	STEWARTS LANE-73A	STEWARTS LANE-73A	STEWARTS LANE-73A	STEWARTS LANE-73A	STEWARTS LANE-73A	STEWARTS LANE-73A	STEWARTS LANE-73A
32104	NORWOOD JCN-75C	NORWOOD JCN-75C	NORWOOD JCN-75C	NORWOOD JCN-75C	NORWOOD JCN-75C	NORWOOD JCN-75C	NORWOOD JCN-75C	NORWOOD JCN-75C
32105	NORWOOD JCN-75C	NORWOOD JCN-75C	NORWOOD JCN-75C	NORWOOD JCN-75C	NORWOOD JCN-75C	NORWOOD JCN-75C	NORWOOD JCN-75C	NORWOOD JCN-75C
32106	STEWARTS LANE-73A	STEWARTS LANE-73A	STEWARTS LANE-73A	STEWARTS LANE-73A	STEWARTS LANE-73A	STEWARTS LANE-73A	STEWARTS LANE-73A	STEWARTS LANE-73A
32107	THREE BRIDGES-75E	SOUTHAMPTON-71I	SOUTHAMPTON-71I	SOUTHAMPTON-71I	SOUTHAMPTON-71I	SOUTHAMPTON-71I	SOUTHAMPTON-71I	SOUTHAMPTON-71I
32108	SOUTHAMPTON-71I	SOUTHAMPTON-71I	SOUTHAMPTON-71I	SOUTHAMPTON-71I	SOUTHAMPTON-71I	SOUTHAMPTON-71I	SOUTHAMPTON-71I	SOUTHAMPTON-71I
32109	SOUTHAMPTON-71I	SOUTHAMPTON-71I	SOUTHAMPTON-71I	SOUTHAMPTON-71I	SOUTHAMPTON-71I	SOUTHAMPTON-71I	SOUTHAMPTON-71I	SOUTHAMPTON-71I

loco	May-49	Jun-49	Aug-49	Sep-49	Dec-49	Feb-50	Mar-50
				G6 0-6-0T (1894)			
30160	NINE ELMS - 70A	NINE ELMS - 70A	NINE ELMS - 70A	NINE ELMS - 70A	NINE ELMS - 70A	NINE ELMS - 70A	NINE ELMS - 70A
30162	DORCHESTER - 71C	DORCHESTER - 71C	DORCHESTER - 71C	DORCHESTER - 71C	DORCHESTER - 71C	DORCHESTER - 71C	DORCHESTER - 71C
30238	SALISBURY - 72B	SALISBURY - 72B	SALISBURY - 72B	SALISBURY - 72B	SALISBURY - 72B	SALISBURY - 72B	SALISBURY - 72B
30258	READING (SR) - 70E	READING (SR) - 70E	READING (SR) - 70E	READING (SR) - 70E	READING (SR) - 70E	BASINGSTOKE - 70D	BASINGSTOKE - 70D
30259	NINE ELMS - 70A	NINE ELMS - 70A	NINE ELMS - 70A	NINE ELMS - 70A	NINE ELMS - 70A	NINE ELMS - 70A	NINE ELMS - 70A
30260	BOURNEMOUTH - 71B	BOURNEMOUTH - 71B	BOURNEMOUTH - 71B	BOURNEMOUTH - 71B	BOURNEMOUTH - 71B	BOURNEMOUTH - 71B	BOURNEMOUTH - 71B
30262	GUILDFORD - 70C	GUILDFORD - 70C	GUILDFORD - 70C	GUILDFORD - 70C	W/D	W/D	W/D
30263	NINE ELMS - 70A	NINE ELMS - 70A	NINE ELMS - 70A	W/D	W/D	W/D	W/D
30265	BASINGSTOKE - 70D	BASINGSTOKE - 70D	W/D	W/D	W/D	W/D	W/D
30266	NINE ELMS - 70A	NINE ELMS - 70A	NINE ELMS - 70A	NINE ELMS - 70A	NINE ELMS - 70A	NINE ELMS - 70A	NINE ELMS - 70A
30268	GUILDFORD - 70C	GUILDFORD - 70C	GUILDFORD - 70C	GUILDFORD - 70C	GUILDFORD - 70C	GUILDFORD - 70C	GUILDFORD - 70C
30269	GUILDFORD - 70C	GUILDFORD - 70C	GUILDFORD - 70C	GUILDFORD - 70C	W/D	W/D	W/D
30270	GUILDFORD - 70C	GUILDFORD - 70C	GUILDFORD - 70C	GUILDFORD - 70C	GUILDFORD - 70C	GUILDFORD - 70C	GUILDFORD - 70C
30272	EASTLEIGH - 71A	EASTLEIGH - 71A	EASTLEIGH - 71A	EASTLEIGH - 71A	BASINGSTOKE - 70D	BASINGSTOKE - 70D	BASINGSTOKE - 70D
30274	SALISBURY - 72B	SALISBURY - 72B	SALISBURY - 72B	SALISBURY - 72B	YEOVIL - 72C	YEOVIL - 72C	YEOVIL - 72C
30275	EASTLEIGH - 71A	EASTLEIGH - 71A	EASTLEIGH - 71A	EASTLEIGH - 71A	W/D	W/D	W/D
30276	YEOVIL - 72C	YEOVIL - 72C	YEOVIL - 72C	YEOVIL - 72C	W/D	W/D	W/D
30277	EASTLEIGH - 71A	EASTLEIGH - 71A	EASTLEIGH - 71A	EASTLEIGH - 71A	EASTLEIGH - 71A	EASTLEIGH - 71A	EASTLEIGH - 71A
30349	GUILDFORD - 70C	GUILDFORD - 70C	GUILDFORD - 70C	GUILDFORD - 70C	GUILDFORD - 70C	GUILDFORD - 70C	GUILDFORD - 70C
30353	GUILDFORD - 70C	GUILDFORD - 70C	GUILDFORD - 70C	GUILDFORD - 70C	GUILDFORD - 70C	GUILDFORD - 70C	GUILDFORD - 70C
30354	GUILDFORD - 70C	GUILDFORD - 70C	GUILDFORD - 70C	GUILDFORD - 70C	W/D	W/D	W/D
				P 0-6-0T (1909)			
31027	DOVER - 74C	DOVER - 74C	DOVER - 74C	DOVER - 74C	DOVER - 74C	DOVER - 74C	DOVER - 74C
31178	BRIGHTON - 75A	BRIGHTON - 75A	BRIGHTON - 75A	BRIGHTON - 75A	BRIGHTON - 75A	BRIGHTON - 75A	BRIGHTON - 75A
31323	DOVER - 74C(F)	DOVER - 74C(F)	DOVER - 74C(F)	DOVER - 74C(F)	DOVER - 74C(F)	DOVER - 74C(F)	DOVER - 74C(F)
31325	BRIGHTON - 75A	BRIGHTON - 75A	BRIGHTON - 75A	EASTLEIGH - 71A	EASTLEIGH - 71A	EASTLEIGH - 71A	EASTLEIGH - 71A
31555	DOVER - 74C(F)	DOVER - 74C(F)	STEWARTS LANE - 73A	STEWARTS LANE - 73A	STEWARTS LANE - 73A	STEWARTS LANE - 73A	STEWARTS LANE - 73A
31556	DOVER - 74C	DOVER - 74C	DOVER - 74C	DOVER - 74C	DOVER - 74C	DOVER - 74C	DOVER - 74C
31557	BRIGHTON - 75A	BRIGHTON - 75A	BRIGHTON - 75A	BRIGHTON - 75A	BRIGHTON - 75A	BRIGHTON - 75A	BRIGHTON - 75A
31558	DOVER - 74C(F)	DOVER - 74C(F)	DOVER - 74C(F)	DOVER - 74C(F)	DOVER - 74C(F)	DOVER - 74C(F)	DOVER - 74C(F)
				R1 0-6-0T (1888/1910)			
31010	ASHFORD - 74A	ASHFORD - 74A	ASHFORD - 74A	ASHFORD - 74A	ASHFORD - 74A	ASHFORD - 74A	ASHFORD - 74A
31047	DOVER - 74C(F)	DOVER - 74C(F)	DOVER - 74C(F)	DOVER - 74C(F)	DOVER - 74C(F)	DOVER - 74C(F)	DOVER - 74C(F)
31069	ASHFORD - 74A	ASHFORD - 74A	ASHFORD - 74A	ASHFORD - 74A	ASHFORD - 74A	ASHFORD - 74A	ASHFORD - 74A
31107	DOVER - 74C(F)	DOVER - 74C(F)	DOVER - 74C(F)	DOVER - 74C(F)	DOVER - 74C(F)	DOVER - 74C(F)	DOVER - 74C(F)
31128	DOVER - 74C(F)	DOVER - 74C(F)	DOVER - 74C(F)	DOVER - 74C(F)	DOVER - 74C(F)	DOVER - 74C(F)	DOVER - 74C(F)
31147	DOVER - 74C(F)	DOVER - 74C(F)	DOVER - 74C(F)	DOVER - 74C(F)	DOVER - 74C(F)	DOVER - 74C(F)	DOVER - 74C(F)
31154	DOVER - 74C(F)	DOVER - 74C(F)	DOVER - 74C(F)	DOVER - 74C(F)	DOVER - 74C(F)	DOVER - 74C(F)	DOVER - 74C(F)
31174	ST LEONARDS - 74E	ST LEONARDS - 74E	ST LEONARDS - 74E	ST LEONARDS - 74E	ST LEONARDS - 74E	ST LEONARDS - 74E	ST LEONARDS - 74E
31335	ST LEONARDS - 74E	ST LEONARDS - 74E	ST LEONARDS - 74E	ST LEONARDS - 74E	ST LEONARDS - 74E	ST LEONARDS - 74E	ST LEONARDS - 74E
31337	DOVER - 74C(F)	DOVER - 74C(F)	DOVER - 74C(F)	DOVER - 74C(F)	DOVER - 74C(F)	DOVER - 74C(F)	DOVER - 74C(F)
31339	ASHFORD - 74A	ASHFORD - 74A	ASHFORD - 74A	ASHFORD - 74A	ASHFORD - 74A	ASHFORD - 74A	ASHFORD - 74A
31340	DOVER - 74C(F)	DOVER - 74C(F)	DOVER - 74C(F)	DOVER - 74C(F)	DOVER - 74C(F)	DOVER - 74C(F)	DOVER - 74C(F)
				S 0-6-0ST (1917)			
31685	B.ARMS - 73B	B.ARMS - 73B	B.ARMS - 73B	B.ARMS - 73B	B.ARMS - 73B	B.ARMS - 73B	B.ARMS - 73B
				T 0-6-0T (1879)			
31602	STEWARTS LANE - 73A	STEWARTS LANE - 73A	STEWARTS LANE - 73A	STEWARTS LANE - 73A	STEWARTS LANE - 73A	READING (SR) - 70E	READING (SR) - 70E
31604	STEWARTS LANE - 73A	STEWARTS LANE - 73A	STEWARTS LANE - 73A	STEWARTS LANE - 73A	STEWARTS LANE - 73A	READING (SR) - 70E	READING (SR) - 70E
				U.S.A. 0-6-0T (1942)			
30061	SOUTHAMPTON - 71I	SOUTHAMPTON - 71I	SOUTHAMPTON - 71I	SOUTHAMPTON - 71I	SOUTHAMPTON - 71I	SOUTHAMPTON - 71I	SOUTHAMPTON - 71I
30062	SOUTHAMPTON - 71I	SOUTHAMPTON - 71I	SOUTHAMPTON - 71I	SOUTHAMPTON - 71I	SOUTHAMPTON - 71I	SOUTHAMPTON - 71I	SOUTHAMPTON - 71I
30063	SOUTHAMPTON - 71I	SOUTHAMPTON - 71I	SOUTHAMPTON - 71I	SOUTHAMPTON - 71I	SOUTHAMPTON - 71I	SOUTHAMPTON - 71I	SOUTHAMPTON - 71I
30064	SOUTHAMPTON - 71I	SOUTHAMPTON - 71I	SOUTHAMPTON - 71I	SOUTHAMPTON - 71I	SOUTHAMPTON - 71I	SOUTHAMPTON - 71I	SOUTHAMPTON - 71I
30065	SOUTHAMPTON - 71I	SOUTHAMPTON - 71I	SOUTHAMPTON - 71I	SOUTHAMPTON - 71I	SOUTHAMPTON - 71I	SOUTHAMPTON - 71I	SOUTHAMPTON - 71I
30066	SOUTHAMPTON - 71I	SOUTHAMPTON - 71I	SOUTHAMPTON - 71I	SOUTHAMPTON - 71I	SOUTHAMPTON - 71I	SOUTHAMPTON - 71I	SOUTHAMPTON - 71I
30067	SOUTHAMPTON - 71I	SOUTHAMPTON - 71I	SOUTHAMPTON - 71I	SOUTHAMPTON - 71I	SOUTHAMPTON - 71I	SOUTHAMPTON - 71I	SOUTHAMPTON - 71I
30068	SOUTHAMPTON - 71I	SOUTHAMPTON - 71I	SOUTHAMPTON - 71I	SOUTHAMPTON - 71I	SOUTHAMPTON - 71I	SOUTHAMPTON - 71I	SOUTHAMPTON - 71I
30069	SOUTHAMPTON - 71I	SOUTHAMPTON - 71I	SOUTHAMPTON - 71I	SOUTHAMPTON - 71I	SOUTHAMPTON - 71I	SOUTHAMPTON - 71I	SOUTHAMPTON - 71I
30070	SOUTHAMPTON - 71I	SOUTHAMPTON - 71I	SOUTHAMPTON - 71I	SOUTHAMPTON - 71I	SOUTHAMPTON - 71I	SOUTHAMPTON - 71I	SOUTHAMPTON - 71I
30071	SOUTHAMPTON - 71I	SOUTHAMPTON - 71I	SOUTHAMPTON - 71I	SOUTHAMPTON - 71I	SOUTHAMPTON - 71I	SOUTHAMPTON - 71I	SOUTHAMPTON - 71I
30072	SOUTHAMPTON - 71I	SOUTHAMPTON - 71I	SOUTHAMPTON - 71I	SOUTHAMPTON - 71I	SOUTHAMPTON - 71I	SOUTHAMPTON - 71I	SOUTHAMPTON - 71I
30073	SOUTHAMPTON - 71I	SOUTHAMPTON - 71I	SOUTHAMPTON - 71I	SOUTHAMPTON - 71I	SOUTHAMPTON - 71I	SOUTHAMPTON - 71I	SOUTHAMPTON - 71I
30074	SOUTHAMPTON - 71I	SOUTHAMPTON - 71I	SOUTHAMPTON - 71I	SOUTHAMPTON - 71I	SOUTHAMPTON - 71I	SOUTHAMPTON - 71I	SOUTHAMPTON - 71I
				D3 0-4-4T (1892)			
32364	T.WELLS - 75F	T.WELLS - 75F	HORSHAM - 75D	HORSHAM - 75D	HORSHAM - 75D	HORSHAM - 75D	HORSHAM - 75D
32365	ASHFORD - 74A	ASHFORD - 74A	ASHFORD - 74A	ASHFORD - 74A	ASHFORD - 74A	ASHFORD - 74A	ASHFORD - 74A
32368	BRIGHTON - 75A	BRIGHTON - 75A	BRIGHTON - 75A	BRIGHTON - 75A	BRIGHTON - 75A	BRIGHTON - 75A	BRIGHTON - 75A
32372	BRIGHTON - 75A	BRIGHTON - 75A	BRIGHTON - 75A	BRIGHTON - 75A	BRIGHTON - 75A	BRIGHTON - 75A	BRIGHTON - 75A
32376	BRIGHTON - 75A	BRIGHTON - 75A	BRIGHTON - 75A	BRIGHTON - 75A	BRIGHTON - 75A	BRIGHTON - 75A	BRIGHTON - 75A
32378	ST LEONARDS - 74E	ST LEONARDS - 74E	ST LEONARDS - 74E	ST LEONARDS - 74E	ST LEONARDS - 74E	ST LEONARDS - 74E	ST LEONARDS - 74E
32379	ST LEONARDS - 74E	ST LEONARDS - 74E	ST LEONARDS - 74E	ST LEONARDS - 74E	ST LEONARDS - 74E	ST LEONARDS - 74E	ST LEONARDS - 74E
32380	ASHFORD - 74A	ASHFORD - 74A	ASHFORD - 74A	ASHFORD - 74A	ASHFORD - 74A	ASHFORD - 74A	ASHFORD - 74A
32384	HORSHAM - 75D	HORSHAM - 75D	HORSHAM - 75D	HORSHAM - 75D	HORSHAM - 75D	HORSHAM - 75D	HORSHAM - 75D
32385	EASTBOURNE - 75G	EASTBOURNE - 75G	EASTBOURNE - 75G	EASTBOURNE - 75G	EASTBOURNE - 75G	EASTBOURNE - 75G	EASTBOURNE - 75G
32386	BRIGHTON - 75A	BRIGHTON - 75A	BRIGHTON - 75A	BRIGHTON - 75A	BRIGHTON - 75A	BRIGHTON - 75A	BRIGHTON - 75A
32388	ASHFORD - 74A	ASHFORD - 74A	ASHFORD - 74A	ST LEONARDS - 74E	ST LEONARDS - 74E	ST LEONARDS - 74E	ST LEONARDS - 74E
32390	T.WELLS - 75F	T.WELLS - 75F	T.WELLS - 75F	T.WELLS - 75F	T.WELLS - 75F	T.WELLS - 75F	T.WELLS - 75F
32391	ST LEONARDS - 74E	ST LEONARDS - 74E	ST LEONARDS - 74E	ST LEONARDS - 74E	ST LEONARDS - 74E	ST LEONARDS - 74E	ST LEONARDS - 74E
32393	T.WELLS - 75F	T.WELLS - 75F	BRIGHTON - 75A	BRIGHTON - 75A	BRIGHTON - 75A	BRIGHTON - 75A	BRIGHTON - 75A
32394	T.WELLS - 75F	T.WELLS - 75F	T.WELLS - 75F	T.WELLS - 75F	EASTBOURNE - 75G	EASTBOURNE - 75G	EASTBOURNE - 75G
32395	EASTBOURNE - 75G	W/D	W/D	W/D	W/D	W/D	W/D
				T1 0-4-4T (1888)			
30001	EASTLEIGH - 71A	EASTLEIGH - 71A	W/D	W/D	W/D	W/D	W/D
30005	EASTLEIGH - 71A	EASTLEIGH - 71A	EASTLEIGH - 71A	EASTLEIGH - 71A	EASTLEIGH - 71A	W/D	W/D
30007	PLYMOUTH - 72D	PLYMOUTH - 72D	PLYMOUTH - 72D	PLYMOUTH - 72D	PLYMOUTH - 72D	PLYMOUTH - 72D	PLYMOUTH - 72D
30020	FRATTON - 71D	FRATTON - 71D	FRATTON - 71D	FRATTON - 71D	FRATTON - 71D	FRATTON - 71D	FRATTON - 71D
30367	EASTLEIGH - 71A	EASTLEIGH - 71A	EASTLEIGH - 71A	EASTLEIGH - 71A	EASTLEIGH - 71A	EASTLEIGH - 71A	EASTLEIGH - 71A
				R1 0-4-4T (1900)			
31696	FAVERSHAM - 73E	FAVERSHAM - 73E	FAVERSHAM - 73E	FAVERSHAM - 73E	FAVERSHAM - 73E	FAVERSHAM - 73E	FAVERSHAM - 73E
31697	GILLINGHAM - 73D	GILLINGHAM - 73D	GILLINGHAM - 73D	GILLINGHAM - 73D	GILLINGHAM - 73D	GILLINGHAM - 73D	GILLINGHAM - 73D
31698	FAVERSHAM - 73E	FAVERSHAM - 73E	FAVERSHAM - 73E	FAVERSHAM - 73E	FAVERSHAM - 73E	FAVERSHAM - 73E	FAVERSHAM - 73E
31699	FAVERSHAM - 73E	FAVERSHAM - 73E	FAVERSHAM - 73E	FAVERSHAM - 73E	FAVERSHAM - 73E	W/D	W/D
31700	TONBRIDGE - 74D	TONBRIDGE - 74D	TONBRIDGE - 74D	TONBRIDGE - 74D	TONBRIDGE - 74D	TONBRIDGE - 74D	TONBRIDGE - 74D
31703	TONBRIDGE - 74D	TONBRIDGE - 74D	TONBRIDGE - 74D	TONBRIDGE - 74D	TONBRIDGE - 74D	TONBRIDGE - 74D	TONBRIDGE - 74D
31704	TONBRIDGE - 74D	TONBRIDGE - 74D	TONBRIDGE - 74D	TONBRIDGE - 74D	TONBRIDGE - 74D	TONBRIDGE - 74D	TONBRIDGE - 74D
31705	FAVERSHAM - 73E	FAVERSHAM - 73E	FAVERSHAM - 73E	FAVERSHAM - 73E	FAVERSHAM - 73E	FAVERSHAM - 73E	FAVERSHAM - 73E
31706	STEWARTS LANE - 73A	STEWARTS LANE - 73A	STEWARTS LANE - 73A	STEWARTS LANE - 73A	STEWARTS LANE - 73A	STEWARTS LANE - 73A	STEWARTS LANE - 73A
31708	DOVER - 74C	DOVER - 74C	DOVER - 74C	DOVER - 74C	DOVER - 74C	DOVER - 74C	DOVER - 74C
31709	FAVERSHAM - 73E	FAVERSHAM - 73E	FAVERSHAM - 73E	FAVERSHAM - 73E	W/D	W/D	W/D
31710	STEWARTS LANE - 73A	STEWARTS LANE - 73A	STEWARTS LANE - 73A	STEWARTS LANE - 73A	STEWARTS LANE - 73A	STEWARTS LANE - 73A	STEWARTS LANE - 73A

loco	Apr-50	Sep-50	Oct-50	Nov-50	Dec-50	Mar-51	Apr-51
G6 0-6-0T (1894)							
30160	NINE ELMS - 70A	NINE ELMS - 70A	NINE ELMS - 70A	NINE ELMS - 70A	NINE ELMS - 70A	NINE ELMS - 70A	NINE ELMS - 70A
30162	DORCHESTER - 71C	DORCHESTER - 71C	DORCHESTER - 71C	DORCHESTER - 71C	DORCHESTER - 71C	DORCHESTER - 71C	DORCHESTER - 71C
30238	SALISBURY - 72B	SALISBURY - 72B	READING (SR) - 70E	GUILDFORD - 70C	GUILDFORD - 70C	GUILDFORD - 70C	GUILDFORD - 70C
30258	BASINGSTOKE - 70D	BASINGSTOKE - 70D	BASINGSTOKE - 70D	BASINGSTOKE - 70D	GUILDFORD - 70C	GUILDFORD - 70C	BASINGSTOKE - 70D
30259	NINE ELMS - 70A	NINE ELMS - 70A	NINE ELMS - 70A	W/D	W/D	W/D	W/D
30260	BOURNEMOUTH - 71B	BOURNEMOUTH - 71B	BOURNEMOUTH - 71B	BOURNEMOUTH - 71B	BOURNEMOUTH - 71B	BOURNEMOUTH - 71B	BOURNEMOUTH - 71B
30266	NINE ELMS - 70A	BASINGSTOKE - 70D	BASINGSTOKE - 70D	BASINGSTOKE - 70D	NINE ELMS - 70A	NINE ELMS - 70A	BASINGSTOKE - 70D
30268	GUILDFORD - 70C	GUILDFORD - 70C	GUILDFORD - 70C	W/D	W/D	W/D	W/D
30270	GUILDFORD - 70C	GUILDFORD - 70C	GUILDFORD - 70C	READING (SR) - 70E	READING (SR) - 70E	READING (SR) - 70E	READING (SR) - 70E
30272	BASINGSTOKE - 70D	W/D					
30274	YEOVIL - 72C	TEMPLECOMBE - 71H	TEMPLECOMBE - 71H	TEMPLECOMBE - 71H	TEMPLECOMBE - 71H	TEMPLECOMBE - 71H	TEMPLECOMBE - 71H
30277	EASTLEIGH - 71A	TEMPLECOMBE - 71H	TEMPLECOMBE - 71H	TEMPLECOMBE - 71H	BASINGSTOKE - 70D	BASINGSTOKE - 70D	NINE ELMS - 70A
30349	GUILDFORD - 70C	GUILDFORD - 70C	GUILDFORD - 70C	GUILDFORD - 70C	NINE ELMS - 70A	NINE ELMS - 70A	GUILDFORD - 70C
30353	NINE ELMS - 70A	NINE ELMS - 70A	NINE ELMS - 70A	NINE ELMS - 70A	NINE ELMS - 70A	W/D	W/D
P 0-6-0T (1909)							
31027	DOVER - 74C	DOVER - 74C	DOVER - 74C	DOVER - 74C	DOVER - 74C	DOVER - 74C	DOVER - 74C
31178	BRIGHTON - 75A	BRIGHTON - 75A	BRIGHTON - 75A	BRIGHTON - 75A	DOVER - 74C	DOVER - 74C	DOVER - 74C
31323	DOVER - 74C	DOVER - 74C	DOVER - 74C	DOVER - 74C	DOVER - 74C	DOVER - 74C	DOVER - 74C
31325	EASTLEIGH - 71A	EASTLEIGH - 71A	EASTLEIGH - 71A	EASTLEIGH - 71A	BRIGHTON - 75A	BRIGHTON - 75A	BRIGHTON - 75A
31555	STEWARTS LANE - 73A	STEWARTS LANE - 73A	DOVER - 74C	DOVER - 74C	DOVER - 74C	DOVER - 74C	DOVER - 74C
31556	BRIGHTON - 75A	BRIGHTON - 75A	BRIGHTON - 75A	BRIGHTON - 75A	BRIGHTON - 75A	BRIGHTON - 75A	BRIGHTON - 75A
31557	DOVER - 74C	DOVER - 74C	DOVER - 74C	DOVER - 74C	DOVER - 74C	DOVER - 74C	DOVER - 74C
31558	DOVER - 74C	DOVER - 74C	STEWARTS LANE - 73A	STEWARTS LANE - 73A	STEWARTS LANE - 73A	STEWARTS LANE - 73A	STEWARTS LANE - 73A
R1 0-6-0T (1888/1910)							
31010	ASHFORD - 74A	ASHFORD - 74A	ASHFORD - 74A	ASHFORD - 74A	ASHFORD - 74A	ASHFORD - 74A	ASHFORD - 74A
31047	DOVER - 74C(F)	DOVER - 74C(F)	DOVER - 74C(F)	DOVER - 74C(F)	DOVER - 74C(F)	DOVER - 74C(F)	DOVER - 74C(F)
31069	ASHFORD - 74A	ASHFORD - 74A	ASHFORD - 74A	ASHFORD - 74A	ASHFORD - 74A	ASHFORD - 74A	ASHFORD - 74A
31107	DOVER - 74C(F)	DOVER - 74C(F)	DOVER - 74C(F)	DOVER - 74C(F)	DOVER - 74C(F)	DOVER - 74C(F)	DOVER - 74C(F)
31128	DOVER - 74C(F)	DOVER - 74C(F)	DOVER - 74C(F)	DOVER - 74C(F)	DOVER - 74C(F)	DOVER - 74C(F)	DOVER - 74C(F)
31147	DOVER - 74C(F)	DOVER - 74C(F)	DOVER - 74C(F)	DOVER - 74C(F)	DOVER - 74C(F)	DOVER - 74C(F)	DOVER - 74C(F)
31154	DOVER - 74C(F)	DOVER - 74C(F)	DOVER - 74C(F)	DOVER - 74C(F)	DOVER - 74C(F)	DOVER - 74C(F)	DOVER - 74C(F)
31174	ST LEONARDS - 74E	ST LEONARDS - 74E	ST LEONARDS - 74E	ST LEONARDS - 74E	ST LEONARDS - 74E	ST LEONARDS - 74E	ST LEONARDS - 74E
31335	ST LEONARDS - 74E	ST LEONARDS - 74E	ST LEONARDS - 74E	ST LEONARDS - 74E	ST LEONARDS - 74E	ST LEONARDS - 74E	ST LEONARDS - 74E
31337	DOVER - 74C(F)	DOVER - 74C(F)	DOVER - 74C(F)	DOVER - 74C(F)	DOVER - 74C(F)	DOVER - 74C(F)	DOVER - 74C(F)
31339	ASHFORD - 74A	ASHFORD - 74A	ASHFORD - 74A	ASHFORD - 74A	ASHFORD - 74A	ASHFORD - 74A	ASHFORD - 74A
31340	DOVER - 74C(F)	DOVER - 74C(F)	DOVER - 74C(F)	DOVER - 74C(F)	DOVER - 74C(F)	DOVER - 74C(F)	DOVER - 74C(F)
S 0-6-0ST (1917)							
31685	B ARMS - 73B	ASHFORD - 74A	ASHFORD - 74A	ASHFORD - 74A	ASHFORD - 74A	ASHFORD - 74A	ASHFORD - 74A
T 0-6-0T (1879)							
31602	READING (SR) - 70E	READING (SR) - 70E	READING (SR) - 70E	READING (SR) - 70E	READING (SR) - 70E	READING (SR) - 70E	READING (SR) - 70E
31604	READING (SR) - 70E	READING (SR) - 70E	READING (SR) - 70E	W/D	W/D	W/D	W/D
U.S.A. 0-6-0T (1942)							
30061	SOUTHAMPTON - 71I	SOUTHAMPTON - 71I	SOUTHAMPTON - 71I	SOUTHAMPTON - 71I	SOUTHAMPTON - 71I	SOUTHAMPTON - 71I	SOUTHAMPTON - 71I
30062	SOUTHAMPTON - 71I	SOUTHAMPTON - 71I	SOUTHAMPTON - 71I	SOUTHAMPTON - 71I	SOUTHAMPTON - 71I	SOUTHAMPTON - 71I	SOUTHAMPTON - 71I
30063	SOUTHAMPTON - 71I	SOUTHAMPTON - 71I	SOUTHAMPTON - 71I	SOUTHAMPTON - 71I	SOUTHAMPTON - 71I	SOUTHAMPTON - 71I	SOUTHAMPTON - 71I
30064	SOUTHAMPTON - 71I	SOUTHAMPTON - 71I	SOUTHAMPTON - 71I	SOUTHAMPTON - 71I	SOUTHAMPTON - 71I	SOUTHAMPTON - 71I	SOUTHAMPTON - 71I
30065	SOUTHAMPTON - 71I	SOUTHAMPTON - 71I	SOUTHAMPTON - 71I	SOUTHAMPTON - 71I	SOUTHAMPTON - 71I	SOUTHAMPTON - 71I	SOUTHAMPTON - 71I
30066	SOUTHAMPTON - 71I	SOUTHAMPTON - 71I	SOUTHAMPTON - 71I	SOUTHAMPTON - 71I	SOUTHAMPTON - 71I	SOUTHAMPTON - 71I	SOUTHAMPTON - 71I
30067	SOUTHAMPTON - 71I	SOUTHAMPTON - 71I	SOUTHAMPTON - 71I	SOUTHAMPTON - 71I	SOUTHAMPTON - 71I	SOUTHAMPTON - 71I	SOUTHAMPTON - 71I
30068	SOUTHAMPTON - 71I	SOUTHAMPTON - 71I	SOUTHAMPTON - 71I	SOUTHAMPTON - 71I	SOUTHAMPTON - 71I	SOUTHAMPTON - 71I	SOUTHAMPTON - 71I
30069	SOUTHAMPTON - 71I	SOUTHAMPTON - 71I	SOUTHAMPTON - 71I	SOUTHAMPTON - 71I	SOUTHAMPTON - 71I	SOUTHAMPTON - 71I	SOUTHAMPTON - 71I
30070	SOUTHAMPTON - 71I	SOUTHAMPTON - 71I	SOUTHAMPTON - 71I	SOUTHAMPTON - 71I	SOUTHAMPTON - 71I	SOUTHAMPTON - 71I	SOUTHAMPTON - 71I
30071	SOUTHAMPTON - 71I	SOUTHAMPTON - 71I	SOUTHAMPTON - 71I	SOUTHAMPTON - 71I	SOUTHAMPTON - 71I	SOUTHAMPTON - 71I	SOUTHAMPTON - 71I
30072	SOUTHAMPTON - 71I	SOUTHAMPTON - 71I	SOUTHAMPTON - 71I	SOUTHAMPTON - 71I	SOUTHAMPTON - 71I	SOUTHAMPTON - 71I	SOUTHAMPTON - 71I
30073	SOUTHAMPTON - 71I	SOUTHAMPTON - 71I	SOUTHAMPTON - 71I	SOUTHAMPTON - 71I	SOUTHAMPTON - 71I	SOUTHAMPTON - 71I	SOUTHAMPTON - 71I
30074	SOUTHAMPTON - 71I	SOUTHAMPTON - 71I	SOUTHAMPTON - 71I	SOUTHAMPTON - 71I	SOUTHAMPTON - 71I	SOUTHAMPTON - 71I	SOUTHAMPTON - 71I
D3 0-4-4T (1892)							
32364	HORSHAM - 75D	HORSHAM - 75D	HORSHAM - 75D	HORSHAM - 75D	HORSHAM - 75D	HORSHAM - 75D	HORSHAM - 75D
32365	ASHFORD - 74A	HORSHAM - 75D	HORSHAM - 75D	HORSHAM - 75D	HORSHAM - 75D	HORSHAM - 75D	HORSHAM - 75D
32368	BRIGHTON - 75A	BRIGHTON - 75A	BRIGHTON - 75A	BRIGHTON - 75A	BRIGHTON - 75A	BRIGHTON - 75A	BRIGHTON - 75A
32372	BRIGHTON - 75A	BRIGHTON - 75A	BRIGHTON - 75A	BRIGHTON - 75A	BRIGHTON - 75A	BRIGHTON - 75A	BRIGHTON - 75A
32376	BRIGHTON - 75A	BRIGHTON - 75A	BRIGHTON - 75A	BRIGHTON - 75A	BRIGHTON - 75A	BRIGHTON - 75A	BRIGHTON - 75A
32378	ST LEONARDS - 74E	ST LEONARDS - 74E	ST LEONARDS - 74E	ST LEONARDS - 74E	ST LEONARDS - 74E	BRIGHTON - 75A(N)	BRIGHTON - 75A(N)
32379	ST LEONARDS - 74E	HORSHAM - 75D	HORSHAM - 75D	HORSHAM - 75D	HORSHAM - 75D	HORSHAM - 75D	HORSHAM - 75D
32380	HORSHAM - 75D	HORSHAM - 75D	HORSHAM - 75D	HORSHAM - 75D	HORSHAM - 75D	HORSHAM - 75D	HORSHAM - 75D
32384	HORSHAM - 75D	HORSHAM - 75D	HORSHAM - 75D	HORSHAM - 75D	HORSHAM - 75D	HORSHAM - 75D	HORSHAM - 75D
32385	EASTBOURNE - 75G	EASTBOURNE - 75G	EASTBOURNE - 75G	EASTBOURNE - 75G	EASTBOURNE - 75G	EASTBOURNE - 75G	EASTBOURNE - 75G
32386	BRIGHTON - 75A	BRIGHTON - 75A	BRIGHTON - 75A	BRIGHTON - 75A	BRIGHTON - 75A	BRIGHTON - 75A	BRIGHTON - 75A
32388	ST LEONARDS - 74E	ST LEONARDS - 74E	ST LEONARDS - 74E	ST LEONARDS - 74E	ST LEONARDS - 74E	EASTBOURNE - 75G	EASTBOURNE - 75G
32390	T.WELLS - 75F	T.WELLS - 75F	T.WELLS - 75F	ST LEONARDS - 74E	ST LEONARDS - 74E	ST LEONARDS - 74E	ST LEONARDS - 74E
32391	ST LEONARDS - 74E	ST LEONARDS - 74E	ST LEONARDS - 74E	ST LEONARDS - 74E	ST LEONARDS - 74E	ST LEONARDS - 74E	ST LEONARDS - 74E
32393	BRIGHTON - 75A	BRIGHTON - 75A	BRIGHTON - 75A	BRIGHTON - 75A	BRIGHTON - 75A	ST LEONARDS - 74E	ST LEONARDS - 74E
32394	EASTBOURNE - 75G	EASTBOURNE - 75G	EASTBOURNE - 75G	EASTBOURNE - 75G	EASTBOURNE - 75G	ST LEONARDS - 74E	ST LEONARDS - 74E
T1 0-4-4T (1888)							
30007	PLYMOUTH - 72D	PLYMOUTH - 72D	PLYMOUTH - 72D	PLYMOUTH - 72D	PLYMOUTH - 72D	PLYMOUTH - 72D	PLYMOUTH - 72D
30020	FRATTON - 71D	FRATTON - 71D	FRATTON - 71D	FRATTON - 71D	FRATTON - 71D	FRATTON - 71D	FRATTON - 71D
30367	EASTLEIGH - 71A	EASTLEIGH - 71A	EASTLEIGH - 71A	EASTLEIGH - 71A	EASTLEIGH - 71A	EASTLEIGH - 71A	EASTLEIGH - 71A
R1 0-4-4T (1900)							
31696	FAVERSHAM - 73E	FAVERSHAM - 73E	FAVERSHAM - 73E	FAVERSHAM - 73E	FAVERSHAM - 73E	W/D	W/D
31697	GILLINGHAM - 73D	GILLINGHAM - 73D	GILLINGHAM - 73D	GILLINGHAM - 73D	GILLINGHAM - 73D	GILLINGHAM - 73D	GILLINGHAM - 73D
31698	FAVERSHAM - 73E	FAVERSHAM - 73E	FAVERSHAM - 73E	FAVERSHAM - 73E	FAVERSHAM - 73E	FAVERSHAM - 73E	FAVERSHAM - 73E
31700	TONBRIDGE - 74D	TONBRIDGE - 74D	TONBRIDGE - 74D	TONBRIDGE - 74D	TONBRIDGE - 74D	TONBRIDGE - 74D	TONBRIDGE - 74D
31703	TONBRIDGE - 74D	TONBRIDGE - 74D	TONBRIDGE - 74D	TONBRIDGE - 74D	TONBRIDGE - 74D	TONBRIDGE - 74D	TONBRIDGE - 74D
31704	TONBRIDGE - 74D	TONBRIDGE - 74D	TONBRIDGE - 74D	TONBRIDGE - 74D	TONBRIDGE - 74D	TONBRIDGE - 74D	TONBRIDGE - 74D
31705	FAVERSHAM - 73E	FAVERSHAM - 73E	FAVERSHAM - 73E	FAVERSHAM - 73E	FAVERSHAM - 73E	FAVERSHAM - 73E	FAVERSHAM - 73E
31706	STEWARTS LANE - 73A	STEWARTS LANE - 73A	ST LEONARDS - 74E	TONBRIDGE - 74D	TONBRIDGE - 74D	TONBRIDGE - 74D	TONBRIDGE - 74D
31708	DOVER - 74C	DOVER - 74C	DOVER - 74C	DOVER - 74C	DOVER - 74C	DOVER - 74C	DOVER - 74C
31710	STEWARTS LANE - 73A	ASHFORD - 74A	ASHFORD - 74A	ASHFORD - 74A	ASHFORD - 74A	ASHFORD - 74A	ASHFORD - 74A

loco	Jun-51	Jul-51	Sep-51	Dec-51	Jan-52	Mar-52	Jun-52
				G6 0-6-0T (1894)			
30160	NINE ELMS - 70A	NINE ELMS - 70A	NINE ELMS - 70A	NINE ELMS - 70A	NINE ELMS - 70A	NINE ELMS - 70A	READING (SR) - 70E
30162	DORCHESTER - 71C	DORCHESTER - 71C	DORCHESTER - 71C	DORCHESTER - 71C	DORCHESTER - 71C	DORCHESTER - 71C	DORCHESTER - 71C
30238	GUILDFORD - 70C	GUILDFORD - 70C	GUILDFORD - 70C	GUILDFORD - 70C	GUILDFORD - 70C	GUILDFORD - 70C	GUILDFORD - 70C
30258	BASINGSTOKE - 70D	BASINGSTOKE - 70D	BASINGSTOKE - 70D	BASINGSTOKE - 70D	BASINGSTOKE - 70D	BASINGSTOKE - 70D	BASINGSTOKE - 70D
30260	BOURNEMOUTH - 71B	BOURNEMOUTH - 71B	BOURNEMOUTH - 71B	BOURNEMOUTH - 71B	BOURNEMOUTH - 71B	BOURNEMOUTH - 71B	BOURNEMOUTH - 71B
30266	BASINGSTOKE - 70D	BASINGSTOKE - 70D	BASINGSTOKE - 70D	BASINGSTOKE - 70D	BASINGSTOKE - 70D	BASINGSTOKE - 70D	BASINGSTOKE - 70D
30270	READING (SR) - 70E	READING (SR) - 70E	READING (SR) - 70E	READING (SR) - 70E	READING (SR) - 70E	READING (SR) - 70E	READING (SR) - 70E
30274	TEMPLECOMBE - 71H	TEMPLECOMBE - 71H	TEMPLECOMBE - 71H	TEMPLECOMBE - 71H	TEMPLECOMBE - 71H	TEMPLECOMBE - 71H	TEMPLECOMBE - 71H
30277	NINE ELMS - 70A	NINE ELMS - 70A	NINE ELMS - 70A	NINE ELMS - 70A	NINE ELMS - 70A	GUILDFORD - 70C	GUILDFORD - 70C
30349	GUILDFORD - 70C	GUILDFORD - 70C	GUILDFORD - 70C	GUILDFORD - 70C	GUILDFORD - 70C	GUILDFORD - 70C	GUILDFORD - 70C
				P 0-6-0T (1909)			
31027	DOVER - 74C	DOVER - 74C	DOVER - 74C	DOVER - 74C	DOVER - 74C	EASTLEIGH - 71A	FRATTON - 71D
31178	DOVER - 74C	DOVER - 74C	DOVER - 74C	DOVER - 74C	DOVER - 74C	DOVER - 74C	DOVER - 74C
31323	DOVER - 74C	DOVER - 74C	DOVER - 74C	DOVER - 74C	DOVER - 74C	DOVER - 74C	DOVER - 74C
31325	BRIGHTON - 75A	BRIGHTON - 75A	BRIGHTON - 75A	BRIGHTON - 75A	BRIGHTON - 75A	BRIGHTON - 75A	BRIGHTON - 75A
31555	DOVER - 74C	DOVER - 74C	DOVER - 74C	DOVER - 74C	DOVER - 74C	DOVER - 74C	DOVER - 74C
31556	BRIGHTON - 75A	BRIGHTON - 75A	BRIGHTON - 75A	BRIGHTON - 75A	BRIGHTON - 75A	BRIGHTON - 75A	BRIGHTON - 75A
31557	DOVER - 74C	DOVER - 74C	DOVER - 74C	STEWARTS LANE - 73A	STEWARTS LANE - 73A	STEWARTS LANE - 73A	STEWARTS LANE - 73A
31558	STEWARTS LANE - 73A	STEWARTS LANE - 73A	STEWARTS LANE - 73A	STEWARTS LANE - 73A	STEWARTS LANE - 73A	STEWARTS LANE - 73A	STEWARTS LANE - 73A
				R1 0-6-0T (1888/1910)			
31010	ASHFORD - 74A	ASHFORD - 74A	ASHFORD - 74A	ASHFORD - 74A	ASHFORD - 74A	ASHFORD - 74A	ASHFORD - 74A
31047	DOVER - 74C(F)	DOVER - 74C(F)	DOVER - 74C(F)	DOVER - 74C(F)	DOVER - 74C(F)	DOVER - 74C(F)	DOVER - 74C(F)
31069	ASHFORD - 74A	ASHFORD - 74A	ASHFORD - 74A	ASHFORD - 74A	ASHFORD - 74A	ASHFORD - 74A	DOVER - 74C(F)
31107	DOVER - 74C(F)	DOVER - 74C(F)	DOVER - 74C(F)	DOVER - 74C(F)	DOVER - 74C(F)	DOVER - 74C(F)	DOVER - 74C(F)
31128	DOVER - 74C(F)	DOVER - 74C(F)	DOVER - 74C(F)	DOVER - 74C(F)	DOVER - 74C(F)	DOVER - 74C(F)	DOVER - 74C(F)
31147	DOVER - 74C(F)	DOVER - 74C(F)	DOVER - 74C(F)	DOVER - 74C(F)	DOVER - 74C(F)	DOVER - 74C(F)	ASHFORD - 74A
31154	DOVER - 74C(F)	DOVER - 74C(F)	DOVER - 74C(F)	DOVER - 74C(F)	DOVER - 74C(F)	DOVER - 74C(F)	DOVER - 74C(F)
31174	ST LEONARDS - 74E	ST LEONARDS - 74E	ST LEONARDS - 74E	ST LEONARDS - 74E	ST LEONARDS - 74E	ST LEONARDS - 74E	ST LEONARDS - 74E
31335	ST LEONARDS - 74E	ST LEONARDS - 74E	ST LEONARDS - 74E	ST LEONARDS - 74E	ST LEONARDS - 74E	ST LEONARDS - 74E	ST LEONARDS - 74E
31337	DOVER - 74C(F)	DOVER - 74C(F)	DOVER - 74C(F)	DOVER - 74C(F)	DOVER - 74C(F)	DOVER - 74C(F)	DOVER - 74C(F)
31339	ASHFORD - 74A	ASHFORD - 74A	ASHFORD - 74A	ASHFORD - 74A	ASHFORD - 74A	ASHFORD - 74A	ASHFORD - 74A
31340	DOVER - 74C(F)	DOVER - 74C(F)	DOVER - 74C(F)	DOVER - 74C(F)	DOVER - 74C(F)	DOVER - 74C(F)	DOVER - 74C(F)
				S 0-6-0ST (1917)			
31685	ASHFORD - 74A	ASHFORD - 74A	W/D		W/D	W/D	W/D
				T 0-6-0T (1879)			
31602	READING (SR) - 70E	W/D	W/D	W/D	W/D	W/D	W/D
				U.S.A. 0-6-0T (1942)			
30061	SOUTHAMPTON - 71I	SOUTHAMPTON - 71I	SOUTHAMPTON - 71I	SOUTHAMPTON - 71I	SOUTHAMPTON - 71I	SOUTHAMPTON - 71I	SOUTHAMPTON - 71I
30062	SOUTHAMPTON - 71I	SOUTHAMPTON - 71I	SOUTHAMPTON - 71I	SOUTHAMPTON - 71I	SOUTHAMPTON - 71I	SOUTHAMPTON - 71I	SOUTHAMPTON - 71I
30063	SOUTHAMPTON - 71I	SOUTHAMPTON - 71I	SOUTHAMPTON - 71I	SOUTHAMPTON - 71I	SOUTHAMPTON - 71I	SOUTHAMPTON - 71I	SOUTHAMPTON - 71I
30064	SOUTHAMPTON - 71I	SOUTHAMPTON - 71I	SOUTHAMPTON - 71I	SOUTHAMPTON - 71I	SOUTHAMPTON - 71I	SOUTHAMPTON - 71I	SOUTHAMPTON - 71I
30065	SOUTHAMPTON - 71I	SOUTHAMPTON - 71I	SOUTHAMPTON - 71I	SOUTHAMPTON - 71I	SOUTHAMPTON - 71I	SOUTHAMPTON - 71I	SOUTHAMPTON - 71I
30066	SOUTHAMPTON - 71I	SOUTHAMPTON - 71I	SOUTHAMPTON - 71I	SOUTHAMPTON - 71I	SOUTHAMPTON - 71I	SOUTHAMPTON - 71I	SOUTHAMPTON - 71I
30067	SOUTHAMPTON - 71I	SOUTHAMPTON - 71I	SOUTHAMPTON - 71I	SOUTHAMPTON - 71I	SOUTHAMPTON - 71I	SOUTHAMPTON - 71I	SOUTHAMPTON - 71I
30068	SOUTHAMPTON - 71I	SOUTHAMPTON - 71I	SOUTHAMPTON - 71I	SOUTHAMPTON - 71I	SOUTHAMPTON - 71I	SOUTHAMPTON - 71I	SOUTHAMPTON - 71I
30069	SOUTHAMPTON - 71I	SOUTHAMPTON - 71I	SOUTHAMPTON - 71I	SOUTHAMPTON - 71I	SOUTHAMPTON - 71I	SOUTHAMPTON - 71I	SOUTHAMPTON - 71I
30070	SOUTHAMPTON - 71I	SOUTHAMPTON - 71I	SOUTHAMPTON - 71I	SOUTHAMPTON - 71I	SOUTHAMPTON - 71I	SOUTHAMPTON - 71I	SOUTHAMPTON - 71I
30071	SOUTHAMPTON - 71I	SOUTHAMPTON - 71I	SOUTHAMPTON - 71I	SOUTHAMPTON - 71I	SOUTHAMPTON - 71I	SOUTHAMPTON - 71I	SOUTHAMPTON - 71I
30072	SOUTHAMPTON - 71I	SOUTHAMPTON - 71I	SOUTHAMPTON - 71I	SOUTHAMPTON - 71I	SOUTHAMPTON - 71I	SOUTHAMPTON - 71I	SOUTHAMPTON - 71I
30073	SOUTHAMPTON - 71I	SOUTHAMPTON - 71I	SOUTHAMPTON - 71I	SOUTHAMPTON - 71I	SOUTHAMPTON - 71I	SOUTHAMPTON - 71I	SOUTHAMPTON - 71I
30074	SOUTHAMPTON - 71I	SOUTHAMPTON - 71I	SOUTHAMPTON - 71I	SOUTHAMPTON - 71I	SOUTHAMPTON - 71I	SOUTHAMPTON - 71I	SOUTHAMPTON - 71I
				D3 0-4-4T (1892)			
32364	HORSHAM - 75D	HORSHAM - 75D	HORSHAM - 75D	HORSHAM - 75D	HORSHAM - 75D	HORSHAM - 75D	HORSHAM - 75D
32365	HORSHAM - 75D	HORSHAM - 75D	HORSHAM - 75D	BRIGHTON - 75A	BRIGHTON - 75A	BRIGHTON - 75A	BRIGHTON - 75A
32368	BRIGHTON - 75A	BRIGHTON - 75A	BRIGHTON - 75A	BRIGHTON - 75A	BRIGHTON - 75A	BRIGHTON - 75A	BRIGHTON - 75A
32372	BRIGHTON - 75A	BRIGHTON - 75A	BRIGHTON - 75A	BRIGHTON - 75A	BRIGHTON - 75A	BRIGHTON - 75A	BRIGHTON - 75A
32376	BRIGHTON - 75A	BRIGHTON - 75A	BRIGHTON - 75A	BRIGHTON - 75A	BRIGHTON - 75A	BRIGHTON - 75A	BRIGHTON - 75A
32378	BRIGHTON - 75A(N)	BRIGHTON - 75A(N)	BRIGHTON - 75A(N)	BRIGHTON - 75A(N)	BRIGHTON - 75A(N)	BRIGHTON - 75A(N)	BRIGHTON - 75A(N)
32379	HORSHAM - 75D	HORSHAM - 75D	HORSHAM - 75D	HORSHAM - 75D	HORSHAM - 75D	HORSHAM - 75D	HORSHAM - 75D
32380	HORSHAM - 75D	HORSHAM - 75D	HORSHAM - 75D	HORSHAM - 75D	HORSHAM - 75D	HORSHAM - 75D	HORSHAM - 75D
32384	HORSHAM - 75D	HORSHAM - 75D	EASTBOURNE - 75G	EASTBOURNE - 75G	EASTBOURNE - 75G	EASTBOURNE - 75G	EASTBOURNE - 75G
32385	EASTBOURNE - 75G	EASTBOURNE - 75G	EASTBOURNE - 75G	EASTBOURNE - 75G	EASTBOURNE - 75G	EASTBOURNE - 75G	EASTBOURNE - 75G
32386	BRIGHTON - 75A	BRIGHTON - 75A	BRIGHTON - 75A	EASTBOURNE - 75G	ST LEONARDS - 74E	ST LEONARDS - 74E	W/D
32388	EASTBOURNE - 75G	EASTBOURNE - 75G	ST LEONARDS - 74E	W/D	W/D	W/D	W/D
32390	ST LEONARDS - 74E	ST LEONARDS - 74E	ST LEONARDS - 74E	ST LEONARDS - 74E	ST LEONARDS - 74E	ST LEONARDS - 74E	ST LEONARDS - 74E
32391	ST LEONARDS - 74E	ST LEONARDS - 74E	ST LEONARDS - 74E	ST LEONARDS - 74E	ST LEONARDS - 74E	ST LEONARDS - 74E	ST LEONARDS - 74E
32393	ST LEONARDS - 74E	ST LEONARDS - 74E	W/D	W/D	W/D	W/D	W/D
32394	ST LEONARDS - 74E	ST LEONARDS - 74E	ST LEONARDS - 74E	W/D	W/D	W/D	W/D
				R1 0-4-4T (1900)			
31697	GILLINGHAM - 73D	GILLINGHAM - 73D	GILLINGHAM - 73D	GILLINGHAM - 73D	GILLINGHAM - 73D	GILLINGHAM - 73D	GILLINGHAM - 73D
31698	FAVERSHAM - 73E	FAVERSHAM - 73E	FAVERSHAM - 73E	FAVERSHAM - 73E	FAVERSHAM - 73E	FAVERSHAM - 73E	FAVERSHAM - 73E
31700	TONBRIDGE - 74D	TONBRIDGE - 74D	TONBRIDGE - 74D	TONBRIDGE - 74D	TONBRIDGE - 74D	TONBRIDGE - 74D	TONBRIDGE - 74D
31703	TONBRIDGE - 74D	TONBRIDGE - 74D	TONBRIDGE - 74D	TONBRIDGE - 74D	TONBRIDGE - 74D	TONBRIDGE - 74D	TONBRIDGE - 74D
31704	TONBRIDGE - 74D	TONBRIDGE - 74D	TONBRIDGE - 74D	TONBRIDGE - 74D	TONBRIDGE - 74D	TONBRIDGE - 74D	TONBRIDGE - 74D
31706	TONBRIDGE - 74D	TONBRIDGE - 74D	TONBRIDGE - 74D	TONBRIDGE - 74D	TONBRIDGE - 74D	TONBRIDGE - 74D	TONBRIDGE - 74D
31708	DOVER - 74C	DOVER - 74C	DOVER - 74C	DOVER - 74C	DOVER - 74C	DOVER - 74C	FAVERSHAM - 73E

The most celebrated of the small miscellaneous classes was probably the USA 0-6-0 class - the only remaining examples of American wartime influence on British Railways - which handled almost all the dock shunting at Southampton. Apart from two examples which went on loan to the Midland Region in 1955 the USA tanks remained at Southampton and were rarely seen anywhere else, a parochialism similar to that of the R1 0-6-0T's which were generally confined to the extremities of Kent, the class being used on the Canterbury & Whitstable and the Folkestone Harbour branches. The 0-4-4 tanks in this section rapidly succumbed to the new LM 2MT 2-6-2T locomotives which took over many secondary services in East Sussex and Kent.

loco	Sep-52	Dec-52	Mar-53	May-53	Jul-53	Sep-53	Nov-53
G6 0-6-0T (1894)							
30160	READING (SR) - 70E	READING (SR) - 70E	READING (SR) - 70E	READING (SR) - 70E	READING (SR) - 70E	READING (SR) - 70E	READING (SR) - 70E
30162	DORCHESTER - 71C	DORCHESTER - 71C	DORCHESTER - 71C	DORCHESTER - 71C	DORCHESTER - 71C	DORCHESTER - 71C	DORCHESTER - 71C
30238	GUILDFORD - 70C	GUILDFORD - 70C	GUILDFORD - 70C	GUILDFORD - 70C	GUILDFORD - 70C	GUILDFORD - 70C	GUILDFORD - 70C
30258	BASINGSTOKE - 70D	BASINGSTOKE - 70D	BASINGSTOKE - 70D	BASINGSTOKE - 70D	BASINGSTOKE - 70D	BASINGSTOKE - 70D	BASINGSTOKE - 70D
30260	BOURNEMOUTH - 71B	BOURNEMOUTH - 71B	BOURNEMOUTH - 71B	BOURNEMOUTH - 71B	BOURNEMOUTH - 71B	BOURNEMOUTH - 71B	BOURNEMOUTH - 71B
30266	BASINGSTOKE - 70D	BASINGSTOKE - 70D	BASINGSTOKE - 70D	BASINGSTOKE - 70D	BASINGSTOKE - 70D	BASINGSTOKE - 70D	BASINGSTOKE - 70D
30270	READING (SR) - 70E	READING (SR) - 70E	READING (SR) - 70E	READING (SR) - 70E	READING (SR) - 70E	READING (SR) - 70E	SALISBURY - 72B
30274	TEMPLECOMBE - 71H	TEMPLECOMBE - 71H	TEMPLECOMBE - 71H	TEMPLECOMBE - 71H	TEMPLECOMBE - 71H	TEMPLECOMBE - 71H	TEMPLECOMBE - 71H
30277	GUILDFORD - 70C	GUILDFORD - 70C	GUILDFORD - 70C	GUILDFORD - 70C	GUILDFORD - 70C	GUILDFORD - 70C	GUILDFORD - 70C
30349	GUILDFORD - 70C	GUILDFORD - 70C	GUILDFORD - 70C	GUILDFORD - 70C	GUILDFORD - 70C	GUILDFORD - 70C	GUILDFORD - 70C
P 0-6-0T (1909)							
31027	FRATTON - 71D	ASHFORD - 74A	ASHFORD - 74A	ASHFORD - 74A	DOVER - 74C	DOVER - 74C	DOVER - 74C
31178	DOVER - 74C	DOVER - 74C	DOVER - 74C	DOVER - 74C	BOWATERS	BOWATERS	DOVER - 74C
31323	DOVER - 74C	DOVER - 74C	DOVER - 74C	DOVER - 74C	DOVER - 74C	SNOWDOWN	SNOWDOWN
31325	BRIGHTON - 75A	BRIGHTON - 75A	BRIGHTON - 75A	BRIGHTON - 75A	BRIGHTON - 75A	BRIGHTON - 75A	BRIGHTON - 75A
31555	DOVER - 74C	STEWARTS LANE - 73A	STEWARTS LANE - 73A	STEWARTS LANE - 73A	STEWARTS LANE - 73A	STEWARTS LANE - 73A	STEWARTS LANE - 73A
31556	BRIGHTON - 75A	BRIGHTON - 75A	BRIGHTON - 75A	BRIGHTON - 75A	BRIGHTON - 75A	BRIGHTON - 75A	BRIGHTON - 75A
31557	STEWARTS LANE - 73A	STEWARTS LANE - 73A	STEWARTS LANE - 73A	STEWARTS LANE - 73A	STEWARTS LANE - 73A	STEWARTS LANE - 73A	STEWARTS LANE - 73A
31558	STEWARTS LANE - 73A	STEWARTS LANE - 73A	EASTLEIGH - 71A	EASTLEIGH - 71A	EASTLEIGH - 71A	EASTLEIGH - 71A	EASTLEIGH - 71A
R1 0-6-0T (1888/1910)							
31010	ASHFORD - 74A	ASHFORD - 74A	ASHFORD - 74A	ASHFORD - 74A	ASHFORD - 74A	ASHFORD - 74A	ASHFORD - 74A
31047	DOVER - 74C(F)	DOVER - 74C(F)	DOVER - 74C(F)	DOVER - 74C(F)	DOVER - 74C(F)	DOVER - 74C(F)	DOVER - 74C(F)
31069	DOVER - 74C(F)	DOVER - 74C(F)	DOVER - 74C(F)	DOVER - 74C(F)	DOVER - 74C(F)	DOVER - 74C(F)	DOVER - 74C(F)
31107	DOVER - 74C(F)	DOVER - 74C(F)	DOVER - 74C(F)	DOVER - 74C(F)	DOVER - 74C(F)	DOVER - 74C(F)	DOVER - 74C(F)
31128	DOVER - 74C(F)	DOVER - 74C(F)	DOVER - 74C(F)	DOVER - 74C(F)	DOVER - 74C(F)	DOVER - 74C(F)	DOVER - 74C(F)
31147	ASHFORD - 74A	ASHFORD - 74A	ASHFORD - 74A	ASHFORD - 74A	ASHFORD - 74A	ASHFORD - 74A	ASHFORD - 74A
31154	DOVER - 74C(F)	DOVER - 74C(F)	DOVER - 74C(F)	DOVER - 74C(F)	DOVER - 74C(F)	DOVER - 74C(F)	DOVER - 74C(F)
31174	ST LEONARDS - 74E	ST LEONARDS - 74E	ST LEONARDS - 74E	ST LEONARDS - 74E	ST LEONARDS - 74E	ST LEONARDS - 74E	ST LEONARDS - 74E
31335	ST LEONARDS - 74E	ST LEONARDS - 74E	ST LEONARDS - 74E	ST LEONARDS - 74E	ST LEONARDS - 74E	ST LEONARDS - 74E	ST LEONARDS - 74E
31337	DOVER - 74C(F)	DOVER - 74C(F)	DOVER - 74C(F)	DOVER - 74C(F)	DOVER - 74C(F)	DOVER - 74C(F)	DOVER - 74C(F)
31339	ASHFORD - 74A	ASHFORD - 74A	ASHFORD - 74A	ASHFORD - 74A	ASHFORD - 74A	ASHFORD - 74A	ASHFORD - 74A
31340	DOVER - 74C(F)	DOVER - 74C(F)	DOVER - 74C(F)	DOVER - 74C(F)	DOVER - 74C(F)	DOVER - 74C(F)	DOVER - 74C(F)
U.S.A. 0-6-0T (1942)							
30061	SOUTHAMPTON - 71I	SOUTHAMPTON - 71I	SOUTHAMPTON - 71I	SOUTHAMPTON - 71I	SOUTHAMPTON - 71I	SOUTHAMPTON - 71I	SOUTHAMPTON - 71I
30062	SOUTHAMPTON - 71I	SOUTHAMPTON - 71I	SOUTHAMPTON - 71I	SOUTHAMPTON - 71I	SOUTHAMPTON - 71I	SOUTHAMPTON - 71I	SOUTHAMPTON - 71I
30063	SOUTHAMPTON - 71I	SOUTHAMPTON - 71I	SOUTHAMPTON - 71I	SOUTHAMPTON - 71I	SOUTHAMPTON - 71I	SOUTHAMPTON - 71I	SOUTHAMPTON - 71I
30064	SOUTHAMPTON - 71I	SOUTHAMPTON - 71I	SOUTHAMPTON - 71I	SOUTHAMPTON - 71I	SOUTHAMPTON - 71I	SOUTHAMPTON - 71I	SOUTHAMPTON - 71I
30065	SOUTHAMPTON - 71I	SOUTHAMPTON - 71I	SOUTHAMPTON - 71I	SOUTHAMPTON - 71I	SOUTHAMPTON - 71I	SOUTHAMPTON - 71I	SOUTHAMPTON - 71I
30066	SOUTHAMPTON - 71I	SOUTHAMPTON - 71I	SOUTHAMPTON - 71I	SOUTHAMPTON - 71I	SOUTHAMPTON - 71I	SOUTHAMPTON - 71I	SOUTHAMPTON - 71I
30067	SOUTHAMPTON - 71I	SOUTHAMPTON - 71I	SOUTHAMPTON - 71I	SOUTHAMPTON - 71I	SOUTHAMPTON - 71I	SOUTHAMPTON - 71I	SOUTHAMPTON - 71I
30068	SOUTHAMPTON - 71I	SOUTHAMPTON - 71I	SOUTHAMPTON - 71I	SOUTHAMPTON - 71I	SOUTHAMPTON - 71I	SOUTHAMPTON - 71I	SOUTHAMPTON - 71I
30069	SOUTHAMPTON - 71I	SOUTHAMPTON - 71I	SOUTHAMPTON - 71I	SOUTHAMPTON - 71I	SOUTHAMPTON - 71I	SOUTHAMPTON - 71I	SOUTHAMPTON - 71I
30070	SOUTHAMPTON - 71I	SOUTHAMPTON - 71I	SOUTHAMPTON - 71I	SOUTHAMPTON - 71I	SOUTHAMPTON - 71I	SOUTHAMPTON - 71I	SOUTHAMPTON - 71I
30071	SOUTHAMPTON - 71I	SOUTHAMPTON - 71I	SOUTHAMPTON - 71I	SOUTHAMPTON - 71I	SOUTHAMPTON - 71I	SOUTHAMPTON - 71I	SOUTHAMPTON - 71I
30072	SOUTHAMPTON - 71I	SOUTHAMPTON - 71I	SOUTHAMPTON - 71I	SOUTHAMPTON - 71I	SOUTHAMPTON - 71I	SOUTHAMPTON - 71I	SOUTHAMPTON - 71I
30073	SOUTHAMPTON - 71I	SOUTHAMPTON - 71I	SOUTHAMPTON - 71I	SOUTHAMPTON - 71I	SOUTHAMPTON - 71I	SOUTHAMPTON - 71I	SOUTHAMPTON - 71I
30074	SOUTHAMPTON - 71I	SOUTHAMPTON - 71I	SOUTHAMPTON - 71I	SOUTHAMPTON - 71I	SOUTHAMPTON - 71I	SOUTHAMPTON - 71I	SOUTHAMPTON - 71I
D3 0-4-4T (1892)							
32365	BRIGHTON - 75A	W/D	W/D	W/D	W/D	W/D	W/D
32368	BRIGHTON - 75A	BRIGHTON - 75A	W/D	W/D	W/D	W/D	W/D
32372	BRIGHTON - 75A	BRIGHTON - 75A	BRIGHTON - 75A	W/D	W/D	W/D	W/D
32376	BRIGHTON - 75A	BRIGHTON - 75A	BRIGHTON - 75A	W/D	W/D	W/D	W/D
32379	HORSHAM - 75D	W/D	W/D	W/D	W/D	W/D	W/D
32380	HORSHAM - 75D	HORSHAM - 75D	HORSHAM - 75D	W/D	W/D	W/D	W/D
32384	ST LEONARDS - 74E	ST LEONARDS - 74E	ST LEONARDS - 74E	ST LEONARDS - 74E	ST LEONARDS - 74E	ST LEONARDS - 74E	W/D
32385	ST LEONARDS - 74E	ST LEONARDS - 74E	ST LEONARDS - 74E	ASHFORD - 74A	W/D	W/D	W/D
32390	ST LEONARDS - 74E	ST LEONARDS - 74E	BRIGHTON - 75A	BRIGHTON - 75A	BRIGHTON - 75A	BRIGHTON - 75A	BRIGHTON - 75A
32391	ST LEONARDS - 74E	W/D	W/D	W/D	W/D	W/D	W/D
R1 0-4-4T (1900)							
31697	GILLINGHAM - 73D	GILLINGHAM - 73D	W/D	W/D	W/D	W/D	W/D
31698	FAVERSHAM - 73E	FAVERSHAM - 73E	TONBRIDGE - 74D	TONBRIDGE - 74D	TONBRIDGE - 74D	TONBRIDGE - 74D	TONBRIDGE - 74D
31703	TONBRIDGE - 74D	TONBRIDGE - 74D	TONBRIDGE - 74D	TONBRIDGE - 74D	TONBRIDGE - 74D	TONBRIDGE - 74D	TONBRIDGE - 74D
31704	TONBRIDGE - 74D	TONBRIDGE - 74D	TONBRIDGE - 74D	TONBRIDGE - 74D	TONBRIDGE - 74D	TONBRIDGE - 74D	TONBRIDGE - 74D
31706	TONBRIDGE - 74D	W/D	W/D	W/D	W/D	W/D	W/D

Southampton being the principal port for transatlantic sailings, it was unconsciously appropriate that Britain's only American locomotives should shunt the docks: someone suggested their presence was to make arriving Americans feel at home. They performed the duties quietly and efficiently from their introduction at the end of the war until being replaced by diesel shunters in the mid-1960's. Two of the class were tried out at sheds on the Midland Region in 1955 but quickly returned to Southampton. 30067 reverses during a shunting movement at Eastleigh.

loco	Jan-54	Mar-54	May-54	Jun-54	Aug-54	Oct-54	Dec-54
G6 0-6-0T (1894)							
30160	READING (SR) - 70E	READING (SR) - 70E	READING (SR) - 70E	READING (SR) - 70E	READING (SR) - 70E	READING (SR) - 70E	READING (SR) - 70E
30162	DORCHESTER - 71C	DORCHESTER - 71C	BOURNEMOUTH - 71B	BOURNEMOUTH - 71B	BOURNEMOUTH - 71B	BOURNEMOUTH - 71B	BOURNEMOUTH - 71B
30238	GUILDFORD - 70C	GUILDFORD - 70C	GUILDFORD - 70C	GUILDFORD - 70C	GUILDFORD - 70C	GUILDFORD - 70C	GUILDFORD - 70C
30258	BASINGSTOKE - 70D	BASINGSTOKE - 70D	BASINGSTOKE - 70D	BASINGSTOKE - 70D	BASINGSTOKE - 70D	BASINGSTOKE - 70D	BASINGSTOKE - 70D
30260	BOURNEMOUTH - 71B	BOURNEMOUTH - 71B	BOURNEMOUTH - 71B	BOURNEMOUTH - 71B	BOURNEMOUTH - 71B	BOURNEMOUTH - 71B	BOURNEMOUTH - 71B
30266	BASINGSTOKE - 70D	BASINGSTOKE - 70D	SALISBURY - 72B	SALISBURY - 72B	SALISBURY - 72B	SALISBURY - 72B	SALISBURY - 72B
30270	SALISBURY - 72B	SALISBURY - 72B	SALISBURY - 72B	SALISBURY - 72B	SALISBURY - 72B	SALISBURY - 72B	SALISBURY - 72B
30274	TEMPLECOMBE - 71H	TEMPLECOMBE - 71H	TEMPLECOMBE - 71H	TEMPLECOMBE - 71H	TEMPLECOMBE - 71H	TEMPLECOMBE - 71H	TEMPLECOMBE - 71H
30277	GUILDFORD - 70C	GUILDFORD - 70C	GUILDFORD - 70C	GUILDFORD - 70C	GUILDFORD - 70C	GUILDFORD - 70C	GUILDFORD - 70C
30349	GUILDFORD - 70C	GUILDFORD - 70C	GUILDFORD - 70C	GUILDFORD - 70C	GUILDFORD - 70C	GUILDFORD - 70C	GUILDFORD - 70C
P 0-6-0T (1909)							
31027	DOVER - 74C	DOVER - 74C	DOVER - 74C	DOVER - 74C	DOVER - 74C	DOVER - 74C	DOVER - 74C
31178	DOVER - 74C	DOVER - 74C	DOVER - 74C	DOVER - 74C	DOVER - 74C	DOVER - 74C	DOVER - 74C
31323	SNOWDOWN	SNOWDOWN	SNOWDOWN	DOVER - 74C	DOVER - 74C	DOVER - 74C	DOVER - 74C
31325	BRIGHTON - 75A	BRIGHTON - 75A	BRIGHTON - 75A	BRIGHTON - 75A	BRIGHTON - 75A	BRIGHTON - 75A	BRIGHTON - 75A
31555	STEWARTS LANE - 73A	STEWARTS LANE - 73A	STEWARTS LANE - 73A	STEWARTS LANE - 73A	STEWARTS LANE - 73A	STEWARTS LANE - 73A	STEWARTS LANE - 73A
31556	BRIGHTON - 75A	BRIGHTON - 75A	BRIGHTON - 75A	BRIGHTON - 75A	BRIGHTON - 75A	BRIGHTON - 75A	BRIGHTON - 75A
31557	STEWARTS LANE - 73A	STEWARTS LANE - 73A	STEWARTS LANE - 73A	STEWARTS LANE - 73A	STEWARTS LANE - 73A	STEWARTS LANE - 73A	STEWARTS LANE - 73A
31558	EASTLEIGH - 71A	EASTLEIGH - 71A	BRIGHTON - 75A	BRIGHTON - 75A	BRIGHTON - 75A	BRIGHTON - 75A	BRIGHTON - 75A
R1 0-6-0T (1888/1910)							
31010	ASHFORD - 74A	ASHFORD - 74A	ASHFORD - 74A	ASHFORD - 74A	ASHFORD - 74A	ASHFORD - 74A	ASHFORD - 74A
31047	DOVER - 74C(F)	DOVER - 74C(F)	DOVER - 74C(F)	DOVER - 74C(F)	DOVER - 74C(F)	DOVER - 74C(F)	DOVER - 74C(F)
31069	DOVER - 74C(F)	DOVER - 74C(F)	DOVER - 74C(F)	DOVER - 74C(F)	DOVER - 74C(F)	DOVER - 74C(F)	DOVER - 74C(F)
31107	DOVER - 74C(F)	DOVER - 74C(F)	DOVER - 74C(F)	DOVER - 74C(F)	DOVER - 74C(F)	DOVER - 74C(F)	DOVER - 74C(F)
31128	DOVER - 74C(F)	DOVER - 74C(F)	DOVER - 74C(F)	DOVER - 74C(F)	DOVER - 74C(F)	DOVER - 74C(F)	DOVER - 74C(F)
31147	ASHFORD - 74A	ASHFORD - 74A	ASHFORD - 74A	ASHFORD - 74A	ASHFORD - 74A	ASHFORD - 74A	ASHFORD - 74A
31154	DOVER - 74C(F)	DOVER - 74C(F)	DOVER - 74C(F)	DOVER - 74C(F)	DOVER - 74C(F)	DOVER - 74C(F)	DOVER - 74C(F)
31174	ST LEONARDS - 74E	ST LEONARDS - 74E	ST LEONARDS - 74E	ST LEONARDS - 74E	ST LEONARDS - 74E	ST LEONARDS - 74E	ST LEONARDS - 74E
31335	ST LEONARDS - 74E	ST LEONARDS - 74E	ST LEONARDS - 74E	ST LEONARDS - 74E	ST LEONARDS - 74E	ST LEONARDS - 74E	ST LEONARDS - 74E
31337	DOVER - 74C(F)	DOVER - 74C(F)	DOVER - 74C(F)	DOVER - 74C(F)	DOVER - 74C(F)	DOVER - 74C(F)	DOVER - 74C(F)
31339	ASHFORD - 74A	ASHFORD - 74A	ASHFORD - 74A	ASHFORD - 74A	ASHFORD - 74A	ASHFORD - 74A	DOVER - 74C(F)
31340	DOVER - 74C(F)	DOVER - 74C(F)	DOVER - 74C(F)	DOVER - 74C(F)	DOVER - 74C(F)	DOVER - 74C(F)	DOVER - 74C(F)
U.S.A. 0-6-0T (1942)							
30061	SOUTHAMPTON - 71I	SOUTHAMPTON - 71I	SOUTHAMPTON - 71I	SOUTHAMPTON - 71I	SOUTHAMPTON - 71I	SOUTHAMPTON - 71I	SOUTHAMPTON - 71I
30062	SOUTHAMPTON - 71I	SOUTHAMPTON - 71I	SOUTHAMPTON - 71I	SOUTHAMPTON - 71I	SOUTHAMPTON - 71I	SOUTHAMPTON - 71I	SOUTHAMPTON - 71I
30063	SOUTHAMPTON - 71I	SOUTHAMPTON - 71I	SOUTHAMPTON - 71I	SOUTHAMPTON - 71I	SOUTHAMPTON - 71I	SOUTHAMPTON - 71I	SOUTHAMPTON - 71I
30064	SOUTHAMPTON - 71I	SOUTHAMPTON - 71I	SOUTHAMPTON - 71I	SOUTHAMPTON - 71I	SOUTHAMPTON - 71I	SOUTHAMPTON - 71I	SOUTHAMPTON - 71I
30065	SOUTHAMPTON - 71I	SOUTHAMPTON - 71I	SOUTHAMPTON - 71I	SOUTHAMPTON - 71I	SOUTHAMPTON - 71I	SOUTHAMPTON - 71I	SOUTHAMPTON - 71I
30066	SOUTHAMPTON - 71I	SOUTHAMPTON - 71I	SOUTHAMPTON - 71I	SOUTHAMPTON - 71I	SOUTHAMPTON - 71I	SOUTHAMPTON - 71I	SOUTHAMPTON - 71I
30067	SOUTHAMPTON - 71I	SOUTHAMPTON - 71I	SOUTHAMPTON - 71I	SOUTHAMPTON - 71I	SOUTHAMPTON - 71I	SOUTHAMPTON - 71I	SOUTHAMPTON - 71I
30068	SOUTHAMPTON - 71I	SOUTHAMPTON - 71I	SOUTHAMPTON - 71I	SOUTHAMPTON - 71I	SOUTHAMPTON - 71I	SOUTHAMPTON - 71I	SOUTHAMPTON - 71I
30069	SOUTHAMPTON - 71I	SOUTHAMPTON - 71I	SOUTHAMPTON - 71I	SOUTHAMPTON - 71I	SOUTHAMPTON - 71I	SOUTHAMPTON - 71I	SOUTHAMPTON - 71I
30070	SOUTHAMPTON - 71I	SOUTHAMPTON - 71I	SOUTHAMPTON - 71I	SOUTHAMPTON - 71I	SOUTHAMPTON - 71I	SOUTHAMPTON - 71I	SOUTHAMPTON - 71I
30071	SOUTHAMPTON - 71I	SOUTHAMPTON - 71I	SOUTHAMPTON - 71I	SOUTHAMPTON - 71I	SOUTHAMPTON - 71I	SOUTHAMPTON - 71I	SOUTHAMPTON - 71I
30072	SOUTHAMPTON - 71I	SOUTHAMPTON - 71I	SOUTHAMPTON - 71I	SOUTHAMPTON - 71I	SOUTHAMPTON - 71I	SOUTHAMPTON - 71I	SOUTHAMPTON - 71I
30073	SOUTHAMPTON - 71I	SOUTHAMPTON - 71I	SOUTHAMPTON - 71I	SOUTHAMPTON - 71I	SOUTHAMPTON - 71I	SOUTHAMPTON - 71I	SOUTHAMPTON - 71I
30074	SOUTHAMPTON - 71I	SOUTHAMPTON - 71I	SOUTHAMPTON - 71I	SOUTHAMPTON - 71I	SOUTHAMPTON - 71I	SOUTHAMPTON - 71I	SOUTHAMPTON - 71I
D3 0-4-4T (1892)							
32390	BRIGHTON - 75A	BRIGHTON - 75A	BRIGHTON - 75A	BRIGHTON - 75A	BRIGHTON - 75A	BRIGHTON - 75A	BRIGHTON - 75A
R1 0-4-4T (1900)							
31698	TONBRIDGE - 74D	TONBRIDGE - 74D	TONBRIDGE - 74D	TONBRIDGE - 74D	TONBRIDGE - 74D	TONBRIDGE - 74D	TONBRIDGE - 74D
31703	TONBRIDGE - 74D	W/D	W/D	W/D	W/D	W/D	W/D
31704	TONBRIDGE - 74D	TONBRIDGE - 74D	TONBRIDGE - 74D	TONBRIDGE - 74D	TONBRIDGE - 74D	TONBRIDGE - 74D	TONBRIDGE - 74D

A journey into deepest Kent was usually necessary to find the dozen-strong class of R1 0-6-0T's most of which were allocated to Dover (sub-shedded at Folkestone) for duties on the Folkestone Harbour branch where, on the heavier trains, triple heading was a regular feature of operations.

loco	Feb-55	Apr-55	Jun-55	Aug-55	Sep-55	Nov-55	Dec-55
			G6 0-6-0T (1894)				
30160	READING (SR) - 70E	READING (SR) - 70E	READING (SR) - 70E	READING (SR) - 70E	READING (SR) - 70E	READING (SR) - 70E	READING (SR) - 70E
30162	BOURNEMOUTH - 71B	BOURNEMOUTH - 71B	BOURNEMOUTH - 71B	EASTLEIGH - 71A	EASTLEIGH - 71A	EASTLEIGH - 71A	EASTLEIGH - 71A
30238	GUILDFORD - 70C	GUILDFORD - 70C	GUILDFORD - 70C	GUILDFORD - 70C	GUILDFORD - 70C	GUILDFORD - 70C	GUILDFORD - 70C
30258	BASINGSTOKE - 70D	BASINGSTOKE - 70D	BASINGSTOKE - 70D	BASINGSTOKE - 70D	BASINGSTOKE - 70D	BASINGSTOKE - 70D	BASINGSTOKE - 70D
30260	BOURNEMOUTH - 71B	BOURNEMOUTH - 71B	BOURNEMOUTH - 71B	BOURNEMOUTH - 71B	BOURNEMOUTH - 71B	BOURNEMOUTH - 71B	BOURNEMOUTH - 71B
30266	SALISBURY - 72B	SALISBURY - 72B	SALISBURY - 72B	SALISBURY - 72B	SALISBURY - 72B	SALISBURY - 72B	SALISBURY - 72B
30270	SALISBURY - 72B	SALISBURY - 72B	SALISBURY - 72B	SALISBURY - 72B	SALISBURY - 72B	SALISBURY - 72B	SALISBURY - 72B
30274	TEMPLECOMBE - 71H	TEMPLECOMBE - 71H	TEMPLECOMBE - 71H	TEMPLECOMBE - 71H	TEMPLECOMBE - 71H	TEMPLECOMBE - 71H	TEMPLECOMBE - 71H
30277	GUILDFORD - 70C	GUILDFORD - 70C	GUILDFORD - 70C	GUILDFORD - 70C	GUILDFORD - 70C	GUILDFORD - 70C	GUILDFORD - 70C
30349	GUILDFORD - 70C	GUILDFORD - 70C	GUILDFORD - 70C	GUILDFORD - 70C	GUILDFORD - 70C	GUILDFORD - 70C	GUILDFORD - 70C
			P 0-6-0T (1909)				
31027	DOVER - 74C	DOVER - 74C	DOVER - 74C	DOVER - 74C	DOVER - 74C	DOVER - 74C	DOVER - 74C
31178	DOVER - 74C	DOVER - 74C	DOVER - 74C	DOVER - 74C	DOVER - 74C	DOVER - 74C	DOVER - 74C
31323	DOVER - 74C	DOVER - 74C	DOVER - 74C	DOVER - 74C	DOVER - 74C	DOVER - 74C	DOVER - 74C
31325	BRIGHTON - 75A	BRIGHTON - 75A	BRIGHTON - 75A	BRIGHTON - 75A	BRIGHTON - 75A	BRIGHTON - 75A	BRIGHTON - 75A
31556	BRIGHTON - 75A	BRIGHTON - 75A	BRIGHTON - 75A	BRIGHTON - 75A	BRIGHTON - 75A	BRIGHTON - 75A	BRIGHTON - 75A
31557	STEWARTS LANE - 73A	STEWARTS LANE - 73A	STEWARTS LANE - 73A	STEWARTS LANE - 73A	STEWARTS LANE - 73A	STEWARTS LANE - 73A	STEWARTS LANE - 73A
31558	BRIGHTON - 75A	BRIGHTON - 75A	STEWARTS LANE - 73A	STEWARTS LANE - 73A	STEWARTS LANE - 73A	STEWARTS LANE - 73A	STEWARTS LANE - 73A
			R1 0-6-0T (1888/1910)				
31010	ASHFORD - 74A	ASHFORD - 74A	ASHFORD - 74A	ST LEONARDS - 74E	ST LEONARDS - 74E	ST LEONARDS - 74E	ST LEONARDS - 74E
31047	DOVER - 74C(F)	DOVER - 74C(F)	DOVER - 74C(F)	DOVER - 74C(F)	DOVER - 74C(F)	DOVER - 74C(F)	DOVER - 74C(F)
31069	DOVER - 74C(F)	DOVER - 74C(F)	DOVER - 74C(F)	DOVER - 74C(F)	DOVER - 74C(F)	DOVER - 74C(F)	DOVER - 74C(F)
31107	DOVER - 74C(F)	DOVER - 74C(F)	DOVER - 74C(F)	DOVER - 74C(F)	DOVER - 74C(F)	DOVER - 74C(F)	DOVER - 74C(F)
31128	DOVER - 74C(F)	DOVER - 74C(F)	DOVER - 74C(F)	DOVER - 74C(F)	DOVER - 74C(F)	DOVER - 74C(F)	DOVER - 74C(F)
31147	ASHFORD - 74A	ASHFORD - 74A	ASHFORD - 74A	ASHFORD - 74A	DOVER - 74C(F)	DOVER - 74C(F)	DOVER - 74C(F)
31154	DOVER - 74C(F)	DOVER - 74C(F)	DOVER - 74C(F)	W/D	W/D	W/D	W/D
31174	ST LEONARDS - 74E	ST LEONARDS - 74E	ST LEONARDS - 74E	ST LEONARDS - 74E	ST LEONARDS - 74E	ST LEONARDS - 74E	ST LEONARDS - 74E
31335	ST LEONARDS - 74E	ST LEONARDS - 74E	W/D	W/D	W/D	W/D	W/D
31337	DOVER - 74C(F)	DOVER - 74C(F)	DOVER - 74C(F)	DOVER - 74C(F)	DOVER - 74C(F)	DOVER - 74C(F)	DOVER - 74C(F)
31339	ASHFORD - 74A	ASHFORD - 74A	ASHFORD - 74A	ASHFORD - 74A	DOVER - 74C(F)	DOVER - 74C(F)	DOVER - 74C(F)
31340	DOVER - 74C(F)	DOVER - 74C(F)	DOVER - 74C(F)	DOVER - 74C(F)	DOVER - 74C(F)	DOVER - 74C(F)	DOVER - 74C(F)
			U.S.A. 0-6-0T (1942)				
30061	SOUTHAMPTON - 71I	SOUTHAMPTON - 71I	SOUTHAMPTON - 71I	KENTISH TOWN (LM)	KENTISH TOWN (LM)	SOUTHAMPTON - 71I	SOUTHAMPTON - 71I
30062	SOUTHAMPTON - 71I	SOUTHAMPTON - 71I	SOUTHAMPTON - 71I	SOUTHAMPTON - 71I	SOUTHAMPTON - 71I	SOUTHAMPTON - 71I	SOUTHAMPTON - 71I
30063	SOUTHAMPTON - 71I	SOUTHAMPTON - 71I	SOUTHAMPTON - 71I	SOUTHAMPTON - 71I	SOUTHAMPTON - 71I	SOUTHAMPTON - 71I	SOUTHAMPTON - 71I
30064	SOUTHAMPTON - 71I	SOUTHAMPTON - 71I	SOUTHAMPTON - 71I	SOUTHAMPTON - 71I	SOUTHAMPTON - 71I	SOUTHAMPTON - 71I	SOUTHAMPTON - 71I
30065	SOUTHAMPTON - 71I	SOUTHAMPTON - 71I	SOUTHAMPTON - 71I	SOUTHAMPTON - 71I	SOUTHAMPTON - 71I	SOUTHAMPTON - 71I	SOUTHAMPTON - 71I
30066	SOUTHAMPTON - 71I	SOUTHAMPTON - 71I	SOUTHAMPTON - 71I	BANKHALL (LM)	BANKHALL (LM)	SOUTHAMPTON - 71I	SOUTHAMPTON - 71I
30067	SOUTHAMPTON - 71I	SOUTHAMPTON - 71I	SOUTHAMPTON - 71I	SOUTHAMPTON - 71I	SOUTHAMPTON - 71I	SOUTHAMPTON - 71I	SOUTHAMPTON - 71I
30068	SOUTHAMPTON - 71I	SOUTHAMPTON - 71I	SOUTHAMPTON - 71I	SOUTHAMPTON - 71I	SOUTHAMPTON - 71I	SOUTHAMPTON - 71I	SOUTHAMPTON - 71I
30069	SOUTHAMPTON - 71I	SOUTHAMPTON - 71I	SOUTHAMPTON - 71I	SOUTHAMPTON - 71I	SOUTHAMPTON - 71I	SOUTHAMPTON - 71I	SOUTHAMPTON - 71I
30070	SOUTHAMPTON - 71I	SOUTHAMPTON - 71I	SOUTHAMPTON - 71I	SOUTHAMPTON - 71I	SOUTHAMPTON - 71I	SOUTHAMPTON - 71I	SOUTHAMPTON - 71I
30071	SOUTHAMPTON - 71I	SOUTHAMPTON - 71I	SOUTHAMPTON - 71I	SOUTHAMPTON - 71I	SOUTHAMPTON - 71I	SOUTHAMPTON - 71I	SOUTHAMPTON - 71I
30072	SOUTHAMPTON - 71I	SOUTHAMPTON - 71I	SOUTHAMPTON - 71I	SOUTHAMPTON - 71I	SOUTHAMPTON - 71I	SOUTHAMPTON - 71I	SOUTHAMPTON - 71I
30073	SOUTHAMPTON - 71I	SOUTHAMPTON - 71I	SOUTHAMPTON - 71I	SOUTHAMPTON - 71I	SOUTHAMPTON - 71I	SOUTHAMPTON - 71I	SOUTHAMPTON - 71I
30074	SOUTHAMPTON - 71I	SOUTHAMPTON - 71I	SOUTHAMPTON - 71I	SOUTHAMPTON - 71I	SOUTHAMPTON - 71I	SOUTHAMPTON - 71I	SOUTHAMPTON - 71I
			D3 0-4-4T (1892)				
32390	BRIGHTON - 75A	BRIGHTON - 75A	BRIGHTON - 75A	BRIGHTON - 75A	W/D	W/D	W/D
			R1 0-4-4T (1900)				
31698	TONBRIDGE - 74D	TONBRIDGE - 74D	TONBRIDGE - 74D	TONBRIDGE - 74D	W/D	W/D	W/D
31704	TONBRIDGE - 74D	TONBRIDGE - 74D	TONBRIDGE - 74D	TONBRIDGE - 74D	TONBRIDGE - 74D	TONBRIDGE - 74D	TONBRIDGE - 74D

Having experimented with railcars in the early years of the century, the SECR extended the idea by producing small 0-6-0 tank engines designed to operate single coach push and pull services. Eight P class engines, one of which became 31557, were introduced from 1909 and although rather underpowered, worked a variety of branch services until being replaced by more powerful 0-4-4T's around the time of the grouping. From that time the 0-6-0T's were used for shunting in sidings restricted to larger engines, 31557 spending many years at Dover and, from 1938, Brighton, for shunting at Shoreham. In early 1950 it was moved to Dover and a year later to Stewarts Lane where it worked the Stewarts Lane carriage siding pilot from 03.00 to 15.35 each day. The view above shows 31557 at Stewarts Lane in 1954.

loco	Jan-56	Apr-56	May-56	Aug-56	Oct-56	Nov-56	Jan-57
				G6 0-6-0T (1894)			
30160	READING (SR)-70E	READING (SR)-70E	READING (SR)-70E	READING (SR)-70E	READING (SR)-70E	BASINGSTOKE-70D	BASINGSTOKE-70D
30162	EASTLEIGH-71A	EASTLEIGH-71A	EASTLEIGH-71A	PLYMOUTH-72D	PLYMOUTH-72D	PLYMOUTH-72D	PLYMOUTH-72D
30238	GUILDFORD-70C	GUILDFORD-70C	GUILDFORD-70C	GUILDFORD-70C	GUILDFORD-70C	GUILDFORD-70C	GUILDFORD-70C
30258	GUILDFORD-70C	BASINGSTOKE-70D	BASINGSTOKE-70D	BASINGSTOKE-70D	BASINGSTOKE-70D	BASINGSTOKE-70D	BASINGSTOKE-70D
30260	BOURNEMOUTH-71B	BOURNEMOUTH-71B	BOURNEMOUTH-71B	BOURNEMOUTH-71B	BOURNEMOUTH-71B	BOURNEMOUTH-71B	BOURNEMOUTH-71B
30266	SALISBURY-72B	SALISBURY-72B	SALISBURY-72B	SALISBURY-72B	SALISBURY-72B	SALISBURY-72B	SALISBURY-72B
30270	SALISBURY-72B	SALISBURY-72B	SALISBURY-72B	SALISBURY-72B	SALISBURY-72B	SALISBURY-72B	SALISBURY-72B
30274	TEMPLECOMBE-71H	TEMPLECOMBE-71H	TEMPLECOMBE-71H	TEMPLECOMBE-71H	TEMPLECOMBE-71H	TEMPLECOMBE-71H	TEMPLECOMBE-71H
30277	GUILDFORD-70C	GUILDFORD-70C	GUILDFORD-70C	GUILDFORD-70C	GUILDFORD-70C	GUILDFORD-70C	GUILDFORD-70C
30349	GUILDFORD-70C	GUILDFORD-70C	GUILDFORD-70C	GUILDFORD-70C	GUILDFORD-70C	GUILDFORD-70C	GUILDFORD-70C
				P 0-6-0T (1909)			
31027	DOVER-74C	DOVER-74C	DOVER-74C	DOVER-74C	DOVER-74C	DOVER-74C	DOVER-74C
31178	DOVER-74C	DOVER-74C	DOVER-74C	DOVER-74C	DOVER-74C	DOVER-74C	DOVER-74C
31323	DOVER-74C	DOVER-74C	DOVER-74C	DOVER-74C	DOVER-74C	DOVER-74C	DOVER-74C
31325	BRIGHTON-75A	BRIGHTON-75A	BRIGHTON-75A	BRIGHTON-75A	BRIGHTON-75A	BRIGHTON-75A	BRIGHTON-75A
31556	BRIGHTON-75A	BRIGHTON-75A	BRIGHTON-75A	BRIGHTON-75A	BRIGHTON-75A	BRIGHTON-75A	BRIGHTON-75A
31557	STEWARTS LANE-73A	STEWARTS LANE-73A	STEWARTS LANE-73A	STEWARTS LANE-73A	STEWARTS LANE-73A	STEWARTS LANE-73A	STEWARTS LANE-73A
31558	STEWARTS LANE-73A	STEWARTS LANE-73A	STEWARTS LANE-73A	STEWARTS LANE-73A	STEWARTS LANE-73A	STEWARTS LANE-73A	STEWARTS LANE-73A
				R1 0-6-0T (1888/1910)			
31010	ST LEONARDS-74E	ST LEONARDS-74E	ST LEONARDS-74E	ST LEONARDS-74E	ST LEONARDS-74E	ST LEONARDS-74E	ST LEONARDS-74E
31047	DOVER-74C(F)	DOVER-74C(F)	DOVER-74C(F)	DOVER-74C(F)	DOVER-74C(F)	DOVER-74C(F)	DOVER-74C(F)
31069	DOVER-74C(F)	DOVER-74C(F)	DOVER-74C(F)	DOVER-74C(F)	DOVER-74C(F)	DOVER-74C(F)	DOVER-74C(F)
31107	DOVER-74C(F)	DOVER-74C(F)	DOVER-74C(F)	DOVER-74C(F)	DOVER-74C(F)	DOVER-74C(F)	DOVER-74C(F)
31128	DOVER-74C(F)	DOVER-74C(F)	DOVER-74C(F)	DOVER-74C(F)	DOVER-74C(F)	DOVER-74C(F)	DOVER-74C(F)
31147	DOVER-74C(F)	DOVER-74C(F)	DOVER-74C(F)	DOVER-74C(F)	DOVER-74C(F)	DOVER-74C(F)	DOVER-74C(F)
31174	ST LEONARDS-74E	ST LEONARDS-74E	ST LEONARDS-74E	ST LEONARDS-74E	ST LEONARDS-74E	ST LEONARDS-74E	ST LEONARDS-74E
31337	DOVER-74C(F)	DOVER-74C(F)	DOVER-74C(F)	DOVER-74C(F)	DOVER-74C(F)	DOVER-74C(F)	DOVER-74C(F)
31339	DOVER-74C(F)	DOVER-74C(F)	DOVER-74C(F)	DOVER-74C(F)	DOVER-74C(F)	DOVER-74C(F)	DOVER-74C(F)
31340	DOVER-74C(F)	DOVER-74C(F)	DOVER-74C(F)	DOVER-74C(F)	DOVER-74C(F)	DOVER-74C(F)	DOVER-74C(F)
				U.S.A. 0-6-0T (1942)			
30061	SOUTHAMPTON-71I	SOUTHAMPTON-71I	SOUTHAMPTON-71I	SOUTHAMPTON-71I	SOUTHAMPTON-71I	SOUTHAMPTON-71I	SOUTHAMPTON-71I
30062	SOUTHAMPTON-71I	SOUTHAMPTON-71I	SOUTHAMPTON-71I	SOUTHAMPTON-71I	SOUTHAMPTON-71I	SOUTHAMPTON-71I	SOUTHAMPTON-71I
30063	SOUTHAMPTON-71I	SOUTHAMPTON-71I	SOUTHAMPTON-71I	SOUTHAMPTON-71I	SOUTHAMPTON-71I	SOUTHAMPTON-71I	SOUTHAMPTON-71I
30064	SOUTHAMPTON-71I	SOUTHAMPTON-71I	SOUTHAMPTON-71I	SOUTHAMPTON-71I	SOUTHAMPTON-71I	SOUTHAMPTON-71I	SOUTHAMPTON-71I
30065	SOUTHAMPTON-71I	SOUTHAMPTON-71I	SOUTHAMPTON-71I	SOUTHAMPTON-71I	SOUTHAMPTON-71I	SOUTHAMPTON-71I	SOUTHAMPTON-71I
30066	SOUTHAMPTON-71I	SOUTHAMPTON-71I	SOUTHAMPTON-71I	SOUTHAMPTON-71I	SOUTHAMPTON-71I	SOUTHAMPTON-71I	SOUTHAMPTON-71I
30067	SOUTHAMPTON-71I	SOUTHAMPTON-71I	SOUTHAMPTON-71I	SOUTHAMPTON-71I	SOUTHAMPTON-71I	SOUTHAMPTON-71I	SOUTHAMPTON-71I
30068	SOUTHAMPTON-71I	SOUTHAMPTON-71I	SOUTHAMPTON-71I	SOUTHAMPTON-71I	SOUTHAMPTON-71I	SOUTHAMPTON-71I	SOUTHAMPTON-71I
30069	SOUTHAMPTON-71I	SOUTHAMPTON-71I	SOUTHAMPTON-71I	SOUTHAMPTON-71I	SOUTHAMPTON-71I	SOUTHAMPTON-71I	SOUTHAMPTON-71I
30070	SOUTHAMPTON-71I	SOUTHAMPTON-71I	SOUTHAMPTON-71I	SOUTHAMPTON-71I	SOUTHAMPTON-71I	SOUTHAMPTON-71I	SOUTHAMPTON-71I
30071	SOUTHAMPTON-71I	SOUTHAMPTON-71I	SOUTHAMPTON-71I	SOUTHAMPTON-71I	SOUTHAMPTON-71I	SOUTHAMPTON-71I	SOUTHAMPTON-71I
30072	SOUTHAMPTON-71I	SOUTHAMPTON-71I	SOUTHAMPTON-71I	SOUTHAMPTON-71I	SOUTHAMPTON-71I	SOUTHAMPTON-71I	SOUTHAMPTON-71I
30073	SOUTHAMPTON-71I	SOUTHAMPTON-71I	SOUTHAMPTON-71I	SOUTHAMPTON-71I	SOUTHAMPTON-71I	SOUTHAMPTON-71I	SOUTHAMPTON-71I
30074	SOUTHAMPTON-71I	SOUTHAMPTON-71I	SOUTHAMPTON-71I	SOUTHAMPTON-71I	SOUTHAMPTON-71I	SOUTHAMPTON-71I	SOUTHAMPTON-71I
				R1 0-4-4T (1900)			
31704	TONBRIDGE-74D	W/D	W/D	W/D	W/D	W/D	W/D

loco	Mar-57	Jun-57	Jul-57	Oct-57	Jan-58	Feb-58	Mar-58
				G6 0-6-0T (1894)			
30160	BASINGSTOKE-70D	BASINGSTOKE-70D	BASINGSTOKE-70D	BASINGSTOKE-70D	BASINGSTOKE-70D	BASINGSTOKE-70D	BASINGSTOKE-70D
30162	PLYMOUTH-72D	PLYMOUTH-72D	PLYMOUTH-72D	PLYMOUTH-72D	PLYMOUTH-72D	PLYMOUTH-83H	W/D
30238	GUILDFORD-70C	GUILDFORD-70C	GUILDFORD-70C	GUILDFORD-70C	GUILDFORD-70C	GUILDFORD-70C	GUILDFORD-70C
30258	BASINGSTOKE-70D	BASINGSTOKE-70D	BASINGSTOKE-70D	BASINGSTOKE-70D	BASINGSTOKE-70D	BASINGSTOKE-70D	BASINGSTOKE-70D
30260	BOURNEMOUTH-71B	BOURNEMOUTH-71B	BOURNEMOUTH-71B	BOURNEMOUTH-71B	BOURNEMOUTH-71B	BOURNEMOUTH-71B	BOURNEMOUTH-71B
30266	SALISBURY-72B	SALISBURY-72B	SALISBURY-72B	SALISBURY-72B	SALISBURY-72B	SALISBURY-72B	SALISBURY-72B
30270	SALISBURY-72B	SALISBURY-72B	SALISBURY-72B	SALISBURY-72B	SALISBURY-72B	SALISBURY-72B	SALISBURY-72B
30274	TEMPLECOMBE-71H	TEMPLECOMBE-71H	TEMPLECOMBE-71H	TEMPLECOMBE-71H	TEMPLECOMBE-71H	TEMPLECOMBE-82G	TEMPLECOMBE-82G
30277	READING (SR)-70E	READING (SR)-70E	READING (SR)-70E	READING (SR)-70E	READING (SR)-70E	READING (SR)-70E	READING (SR)-70E
30349	GUILDFORD-70C	GUILDFORD-70C	GUILDFORD-70C	GUILDFORD-70C	GUILDFORD-70C	GUILDFORD-70C	GUILDFORD-70C
				P 0-6-0T (1909)			
31027	DOVER-74C	DOVER-74C	DOVER-74C	DOVER-74C	DOVER-74C	DOVER-74C	DOVER-74C
31178	DOVER-74C	DOVER-74C	DOVER-74C	STEWARTS LANE-73A	STEWARTS LANE-73A	STEWARTS LANE-73A	STEWARTS LANE-73A
31323	DOVER-74C	DOVER-74C	DOVER-74C	DOVER-74C	DOVER-74C	DOVER-74C	DOVER-74C
31325	DOVER-74C	EASTLEIGH-71A	EASTLEIGH-71A	EASTLEIGH-71A	EASTLEIGH-71A	EASTLEIGH-71A	EASTLEIGH-71A
31556	BRIGHTON-75A	BRIGHTON-75A	BRIGHTON-75A	BRIGHTON-75A	BRIGHTON-75A	BRIGHTON-75A	BRIGHTON-75A
31557	STEWARTS LANE-73A	STEWARTS LANE-73A	STEWARTS LANE-73A	W/D	W/D	W/D	W/D
31558	STEWARTS LANE-73A	STEWARTS LANE-73A	STEWARTS LANE-73A	STEWARTS LANE-73A	STEWARTS LANE-73A	STEWARTS LANE-73A	STEWARTS LANE-73A
				R1 0-6-0T (1888/1910)			
31010	ST LEONARDS-74E	ST LEONARDS-74E	ST LEONARDS-74E	DOVER-74C	DOVER-74C	DOVER-74C	DOVER-74C
31047	DOVER-74C(F)	DOVER-74C(F)	DOVER-74C(F)	DOVER-74C(F)	DOVER-74C(F)	DOVER-74C(F)	DOVER-74C(F)
31069	DOVER-74C(F)	DOVER-74C(F)	DOVER-74C(F)	DOVER-74C(F)	DOVER-74C(F)	DOVER-74C(F)	DOVER-74C(F)
31107	DOVER-74C(F)	DOVER-74C(F)	DOVER-74C(F)	DOVER-74C(F)	DOVER-74C(F)	DOVER-74C(F)	DOVER-74C(F)
31128	DOVER-74C(F)	DOVER-74C(F)	DOVER-74C(F)	DOVER-74C(F)	DOVER-74C(F)	DOVER-74C(F)	DOVER-74C(F)
31147	DOVER-74C(F)	DOVER-74C(F)	DOVER-74C(F)	DOVER-74C(F)	DOVER-74C(F)	DOVER-74C(F)	DOVER-74C(F)
31174	ST LEONARDS-74E	ST LEONARDS-74E	ST LEONARDS-74E	DOVER-74C	DOVER-74C	DOVER-74C	DOVER-74C
31337	DOVER-74C(F)	DOVER-74C(F)	DOVER-74C(F)	DOVER-74C(F)	DOVER-74C(F)	DOVER-74C(F)	DOVER-74C(F)
31339	DOVER-74C(F)	DOVER-74C(F)	DOVER-74C(F)	DOVER-74C(F)	DOVER-74C(F)	DOVER-74C(F)	DOVER-74C(F)
31340	DOVER-74C(F)	DOVER-74C(F)	DOVER-74C(F)	DOVER-74C(F)	DOVER-74C(F)	DOVER-74C(F)	DOVER-74C(F)
				U.S.A. 0-6-0T (1942)			
30061	SOUTHAMPTON-71I	SOUTHAMPTON-71I	SOUTHAMPTON-71I	SOUTHAMPTON-71I	SOUTHAMPTON-71I	SOUTHAMPTON-71I	SOUTHAMPTON-71I
30062	SOUTHAMPTON-71I	SOUTHAMPTON-71I	SOUTHAMPTON-71I	SOUTHAMPTON-71I	SOUTHAMPTON-71I	SOUTHAMPTON-71I	SOUTHAMPTON-71I
30063	SOUTHAMPTON-71I	SOUTHAMPTON-71I	SOUTHAMPTON-71I	SOUTHAMPTON-71I	SOUTHAMPTON-71I	SOUTHAMPTON-71I	SOUTHAMPTON-71I
30064	SOUTHAMPTON-71I	SOUTHAMPTON-71I	SOUTHAMPTON-71I	SOUTHAMPTON-71I	SOUTHAMPTON-71I	SOUTHAMPTON-71I	SOUTHAMPTON-71I
30065	SOUTHAMPTON-71I	SOUTHAMPTON-71I	SOUTHAMPTON-71I	SOUTHAMPTON-71I	SOUTHAMPTON-71I	SOUTHAMPTON-71I	SOUTHAMPTON-71I
30066	SOUTHAMPTON-71I	SOUTHAMPTON-71I	SOUTHAMPTON-71I	SOUTHAMPTON-71I	SOUTHAMPTON-71I	SOUTHAMPTON-71I	SOUTHAMPTON-71I
30067	SOUTHAMPTON-71I	SOUTHAMPTON-71I	SOUTHAMPTON-71I	SOUTHAMPTON-71I	SOUTHAMPTON-71I	SOUTHAMPTON-71I	SOUTHAMPTON-71I
30068	SOUTHAMPTON-71I	SOUTHAMPTON-71I	SOUTHAMPTON-71I	SOUTHAMPTON-71I	SOUTHAMPTON-71I	SOUTHAMPTON-71I	SOUTHAMPTON-71I
30069	SOUTHAMPTON-71I	SOUTHAMPTON-71I	SOUTHAMPTON-71I	SOUTHAMPTON-71I	SOUTHAMPTON-71I	SOUTHAMPTON-71I	SOUTHAMPTON-71I
30070	BOURNEMOUTH-71B	SOUTHAMPTON-71I	SOUTHAMPTON-71I	SOUTHAMPTON-71I	SOUTHAMPTON-71I	SOUTHAMPTON-71I	SOUTHAMPTON-71I
30071	SOUTHAMPTON-71I	SOUTHAMPTON-71I	SOUTHAMPTON-71I	SOUTHAMPTON-71I	SOUTHAMPTON-71I	SOUTHAMPTON-71I	SOUTHAMPTON-71I
30072	SOUTHAMPTON-71I	SOUTHAMPTON-71I	SOUTHAMPTON-71I	SOUTHAMPTON-71I	SOUTHAMPTON-71I	SOUTHAMPTON-71I	SOUTHAMPTON-71I
30073	SOUTHAMPTON-71I	SOUTHAMPTON-71I	SOUTHAMPTON-71I	SOUTHAMPTON-71I	SOUTHAMPTON-71I	SOUTHAMPTON-71I	SOUTHAMPTON-71I
30074	SOUTHAMPTON-71I	SOUTHAMPTON-71I	SOUTHAMPTON-71I	SOUTHAMPTON-71I	SOUTHAMPTON-71I	SOUTHAMPTON-71I	SOUTHAMPTON-71I

			G6 0-6-0T (1894)				
30160	BASINGSTOKE-70D	BASINGSTOKE-70D	BASINGSTOKE-70D	BASINGSTOKE-70D	BASINGSTOKE-70D	BASINGSTOKE-70D	BASINGSTOKE-70D
30238	GUILDFORD-70C	GUILDFORD-70C	GUILDFORD-70C	GUILDFORD-70C	GUILDFORD-70C	GUILDFORD-70C	GUILDFORD-70C
30258	BASINGSTOKE-70D	BASINGSTOKE-70D	BASINGSTOKE-70D	BASINGSTOKE-70D	BASINGSTOKE-70D	BASINGSTOKE-70D	BASINGSTOKE-70D
30260	BOURNEMOUTH-71B	BOURNEMOUTH-71B	W/D	W/D	W/D	W/D	W/D
30266	SALISBURY-72B	SALISBURY-72B	SALISBURY-72B	SALISBURY-72B	SALISBURY-72B	SALISBURY-72B	SALISBURY-72B
30270	SALISBURY-72B	SALISBURY-72B	W/D	W/D	W/D	W/D	W/D
30274	TEMPLECOMBE-82G	TEMPLECOMBE-82G	BOURNEMOUTH-71B	BOURNEMOUTH-71B	BOURNEMOUTH-71B	BOURNEMOUTH-71B	BOURNEMOUTH-71B
30277	READING (SR)-70E	READING (SR)-70E	READING (SR)-70E	READING (SR)-70E	READING (SR)-70E	READING (SR)-70E	READING (SR)-70E
30349	GUILDFORD-70C	GUILDFORD-70C	GUILDFORD-70C	GUILDFORD-70C	GUILDFORD-70C	GUILDFORD-70C	GUILDFORD-70C
			P 0-6-0T (1909)				
31027	DOVER-74C	DOVER-73H	DOVER-73H	DOVER-73H	DOVER-73H	DOVER-73H	DOVER-73H
31323	DOVER-74C	DOVER-73H	DOVER-73H	DOVER-73H	DOVER-73H	DOVER-73H	DOVER-73H
31325	EASTLEIGH-71A	BRIGHTON-75A	BRIGHTON-75A	BRIGHTON-75A	BRIGHTON-75A	BRIGHTON-75A	BRIGHTON-75A
31556	BRIGHTON-75A	BRIGHTON-75A	BRIGHTON-75A	BRIGHTON-75A	BRIGHTON-75A	BRIGHTON-75A	BRIGHTON-75A
31558	STEWARTS LANE-73A	STEWARTS LANE-73A	STEWARTS LANE-73A	STEWARTS LANE-73A	STEWARTS LANE-73A	STEWARTS LANE-73A	STEWARTS LANE-73A
			R1 0-6-0T (1888/1910)				
31010	DOVER-74C	DOVER-73H	DOVER-73H	NINE ELMS-70A	NINE ELMS-70A	W/D	W/D
31047	DOVER-74C(F)	DOVER-73H(F)	DOVER-73H(F)	NINE ELMS-70A	NINE ELMS-70A	NINE ELMS-70A	NINE ELMS-70A
31107	DOVER-74C(F)	DOVER-73H(F)	DOVER-73H(F)	NINE ELMS-70A	NINE ELMS-70A	W/D	W/D
31128	DOVER-74C(F)	DOVER-73H(F)	DOVER-73H(F)	NINE ELMS-70A	NINE ELMS-70A	NINE ELMS-70A	W/D
31147	DOVER-74C(F)	W/D	W/D	W/D	W/D	W/D	W/D
31174	DOVER-74C	DOVER-73H	DOVER-73H	NINE ELMS-70A	NINE ELMS-70A	W/D	W/D
31337	DOVER-74C(F)	DOVER-73H(F)	DOVER-73H(F)	NINE ELMS-70A	NINE ELMS-70A	NINE ELMS-70A	NINE ELMS-70A
31340	DOVER-74C(F)	DOVER-73H(F)	DOVER-73H(F)	NINE ELMS-70A	W/D	W/D	W/D
			U.S.A. 0-6-0T (1942)				
30061	SOUTHAMPTON-71I	SOUTHAMPTON-71I	SOUTHAMPTON-71I	SOUTHAMPTON-71I	SOUTHAMPTON-71I	SOUTHAMPTON-71I	SOUTHAMPTON-71I
30062	SOUTHAMPTON-71I	SOUTHAMPTON-71I	SOUTHAMPTON-71I	SOUTHAMPTON-71I	SOUTHAMPTON-71I	SOUTHAMPTON-71I	SOUTHAMPTON-71I
30063	SOUTHAMPTON-71I	SOUTHAMPTON-71I	SOUTHAMPTON-71I	SOUTHAMPTON-71I	SOUTHAMPTON-71I	SOUTHAMPTON-71I	SOUTHAMPTON-71I
30064	SOUTHAMPTON-71I	SOUTHAMPTON-71I	SOUTHAMPTON-71I	SOUTHAMPTON-71I	SOUTHAMPTON-71I	SOUTHAMPTON-71I	SOUTHAMPTON-71I
30065	SOUTHAMPTON-71I	SOUTHAMPTON-71I	SOUTHAMPTON-71I	SOUTHAMPTON-71I	SOUTHAMPTON-71I	SOUTHAMPTON-71I	SOUTHAMPTON-71I
30066	SOUTHAMPTON-71I	SOUTHAMPTON-71I	SOUTHAMPTON-71I	SOUTHAMPTON-71I	SOUTHAMPTON-71I	SOUTHAMPTON-71I	SOUTHAMPTON-71I
30067	SOUTHAMPTON-71I	SOUTHAMPTON-71I	SOUTHAMPTON-71I	SOUTHAMPTON-71I	SOUTHAMPTON-71I	SOUTHAMPTON-71I	SOUTHAMPTON-71I
30068	SOUTHAMPTON-71I	SOUTHAMPTON-71I	SOUTHAMPTON-71I	SOUTHAMPTON-71I	SOUTHAMPTON-71I	SOUTHAMPTON-71I	SOUTHAMPTON-71I
30069	SOUTHAMPTON-71I	SOUTHAMPTON-71I	SOUTHAMPTON-71I	SOUTHAMPTON-71I	SOUTHAMPTON-71I	SOUTHAMPTON-71I	SOUTHAMPTON-71I
30070	SOUTHAMPTON-71I	SOUTHAMPTON-71I	SOUTHAMPTON-71I	SOUTHAMPTON-71I	SOUTHAMPTON-71I	SOUTHAMPTON-71I	SOUTHAMPTON-71I
30071	SOUTHAMPTON-71I	SOUTHAMPTON-71I	SOUTHAMPTON-71I	SOUTHAMPTON-71I	SOUTHAMPTON-71I	SOUTHAMPTON-71I	SOUTHAMPTON-71I
30072	SOUTHAMPTON-71I	SOUTHAMPTON-71I	SOUTHAMPTON-71I	SOUTHAMPTON-71I	SOUTHAMPTON-71I	SOUTHAMPTON-71I	SOUTHAMPTON-71I
30073	SOUTHAMPTON-71I	SOUTHAMPTON-71I	SOUTHAMPTON-71I	SOUTHAMPTON-71I	SOUTHAMPTON-71I	SOUTHAMPTON-71I	SOUTHAMPTON-71I
30074	SOUTHAMPTON-71I	SOUTHAMPTON-71I	SOUTHAMPTON-71I	SOUTHAMPTON-71I	SOUTHAMPTON-71I	SOUTHAMPTON-71I	SOUTHAMPTON-71I

loco	Dec-59	Feb-60	Mar-60	Apr-60	Jul-60	Aug-60	Sep-60	Nov-60
				G6 0-6-0T (1894)				
30160	BASINGSTOKE-70D	BASINGSTOKE-70D	BASINGSTOKE-70D	BASINGSTOKE-70D	BASINGSTOKE-70D	BASINGSTOKE-70D	BASINGSTOKE-70D	BASINGSTOKE-70D
30238	GUILDFORD-70C	GUILDFORD-70C	GUILDFORD-70C	GUILDFORD-70C	GUILDFORD-70C	GUILDFORD-70C	GUILDFORD-70C	GUILDFORD-70C
30258	BASINGSTOKE-70D	BASINGSTOKE-70D	BASINGSTOKE-70D	BASINGSTOKE-70D	BASINGSTOKE-70D	BASINGSTOKE-70D	BASINGSTOKE-70D	BASINGSTOKE-70D
30266	SALISBURY-72B	SALISBURY-72B	SALISBURY-72B	SALISBURY-72B	SALISBURY-72B	W/D	W/D	W/D
30274	BOURNEMOUTH-71B	BOURNEMOUTH-71B	BOURNEMOUTH-71B	BOURNEMOUTH-71B	BOURNEMOUTH-71B	BOURNEMOUTH-71B	BOURNEMOUTH-71B	W/D
30277	READING (SR)-70E	READING (SR)-70E	READING (SR)-70E	READING (SR)-70E	READING (SR)-70E	READING (SR)-70E	READING (SR)-70E	READING (SR)-70E
30349	GUILDFORD-70C	FELTHAM-70B	FELTHAM-70B	FELTHAM-70B	FELTHAM-70B	FELTHAM-70B	FELTHAM-70B	FELTHAM-70B
				P 0-6-0T (1909)				
31027	DOVER-73H	DOVER-73H	DOVER-73H	DOVER-73H	DOVER-73H	DOVER-73H	DOVER-73H	DOVER-73H
31323	DOVER-73H	DOVER-73H	DOVER-73H	DOVER-73H	W/D	W/D	W/D	W/D
31325	BRIGHTON-75A	BRIGHTON-75A	W/D	W/D	W/D	W/D	W/D	W/D
31556	BRIGHTON-75A	BRIGHTON-75A	BRIGHTON-75A	BRIGHTON-75A	BRIGHTON-75A	BRIGHTON-75A	BRIGHTON-75A	BRIGHTON-75A
31558	STEWARTS LANE-73A	W/D	W/D	W/D	W/D	W/D	W/D	W/D
				R1 0-6-0T (1888/1910)				
31047	NINE ELMS-70A	NINE ELMS-70A	W/D	W/D	W/D	W/D	W/D	W/D
31337	NINE ELMS-70A	W/D	W/D	W/D	W/D	W/D	W/D	W/D
				U.S.A. 0-6-0T (1942)				
30061	SOUTHAMPTON-71I	SOUTHAMPTON-71I	SOUTHAMPTON-71I	SOUTHAMPTON-71I	SOUTHAMPTON-71I	SOUTHAMPTON-71I	SOUTHAMPTON-71I	SOUTHAMPTON-71I
30062	SOUTHAMPTON-71I	SOUTHAMPTON-71I	SOUTHAMPTON-71I	SOUTHAMPTON-71I	SOUTHAMPTON-71I	SOUTHAMPTON-71I	SOUTHAMPTON-71I	SOUTHAMPTON-71I
30063	SOUTHAMPTON-71I	SOUTHAMPTON-71I	SOUTHAMPTON-71I	SOUTHAMPTON-71I	SOUTHAMPTON-71I	SOUTHAMPTON-71I	SOUTHAMPTON-71I	SOUTHAMPTON-71I
30064	SOUTHAMPTON-71I	SOUTHAMPTON-71I	SOUTHAMPTON-71I	SOUTHAMPTON-71I	SOUTHAMPTON-71I	SOUTHAMPTON-71I	SOUTHAMPTON-71I	SOUTHAMPTON-71I
30065	SOUTHAMPTON-71I	SOUTHAMPTON-71I	SOUTHAMPTON-71I	SOUTHAMPTON-71I	SOUTHAMPTON-71I	SOUTHAMPTON-71I	SOUTHAMPTON-71I	SOUTHAMPTON-71I
30066	SOUTHAMPTON-71I	SOUTHAMPTON-71I	SOUTHAMPTON-71I	SOUTHAMPTON-71I	SOUTHAMPTON-71I	SOUTHAMPTON-71I	SOUTHAMPTON-71I	SOUTHAMPTON-71I
30067	SOUTHAMPTON-71I	SOUTHAMPTON-71I	SOUTHAMPTON-71I	SOUTHAMPTON-71I	SOUTHAMPTON-71I	SOUTHAMPTON-71I	SOUTHAMPTON-71I	SOUTHAMPTON-71I
30068	SOUTHAMPTON-71I	SOUTHAMPTON-71I	SOUTHAMPTON-71I	SOUTHAMPTON-71I	SOUTHAMPTON-71I	SOUTHAMPTON-71I	SOUTHAMPTON-71I	SOUTHAMPTON-71I
30069	SOUTHAMPTON-71I	SOUTHAMPTON-71I	SOUTHAMPTON-71I	SOUTHAMPTON-71I	SOUTHAMPTON-71I	SOUTHAMPTON-71I	SOUTHAMPTON-71I	SOUTHAMPTON-71I
30070	SOUTHAMPTON-71I	SOUTHAMPTON-71I	SOUTHAMPTON-71I	SOUTHAMPTON-71I	SOUTHAMPTON-71I	SOUTHAMPTON-71I	SOUTHAMPTON-71I	SOUTHAMPTON-71I
30071	SOUTHAMPTON-71I	SOUTHAMPTON-71I	SOUTHAMPTON-71I	SOUTHAMPTON-71I	SOUTHAMPTON-71I	SOUTHAMPTON-71I	SOUTHAMPTON-71I	SOUTHAMPTON-71I
30072	SOUTHAMPTON-71I	SOUTHAMPTON-71I	SOUTHAMPTON-71I	SOUTHAMPTON-71I	SOUTHAMPTON-71I	SOUTHAMPTON-71I	SOUTHAMPTON-71I	SOUTHAMPTON-71I
30073	SOUTHAMPTON-71I	SOUTHAMPTON-71I	SOUTHAMPTON-71I	SOUTHAMPTON-71I	SOUTHAMPTON-71I	SOUTHAMPTON-71I	SOUTHAMPTON-71I	SOUTHAMPTON-71I
30074	SOUTHAMPTON-71I	SOUTHAMPTON-71I	SOUTHAMPTON-71I	SOUTHAMPTON-71I	SOUTHAMPTON-71I	SOUTHAMPTON-71I	SOUTHAMPTON-71I	SOUTHAMPTON-71I

loco	May-49	Jun-49	Aug-49	Sep-49	Dec-49	Feb-50	Mar-50
				H 0-4-4T (1904)			
31005	STEWARTS LANE - 73A	STEWARTS LANE - 73A	STEWARTS LANE - 73A	STEWARTS LANE - 73A	STEWARTS LANE - 73A	STEWARTS LANE - 73A	STEWARTS LANE - 73A
31016	STEWARTS LANE - 73A	STEWARTS LANE - 73A	T.WELLS - 75F	T.WELLS - 75F	T.WELLS - 75F	T.WELLS - 75F	T.WELLS - 75F
31158	ASHFORD - 74A	ASHFORD - 74A	ASHFORD - 74A	ASHFORD - 74A	ASHFORD - 74A	ASHFORD - 74A	ASHFORD - 74A
31161	DOVER - 74C	DOVER - 74C	DOVER - 74C	DOVER - 74C	DOVER - 74C	DOVER - 74C	DOVER - 74C
31162	B ARMS - 73B	B ARMS - 73B	B ARMS - 73B	B ARMS - 73B	B ARMS - 73B	B ARMS - 73B	B ARMS - 73B
31164	RAMSGATE - 74B	RAMSGATE - 74B	RAMSGATE - 74B	TONBRIDGE - 74D	TONBRIDGE - 74D	TONBRIDGE - 74D	TONBRIDGE - 74D
31177	STEWARTS LANE - 73A	STEWARTS LANE - 73A	STEWARTS LANE - 73A	STEWARTS LANE - 73A	STEWARTS LANE - 73A	STEWARTS LANE - 73A	STEWARTS LANE - 73A
31182	RAMSGATE - 74B	RAMSGATE - 74B	T.WELLS - 75F	T.WELLS - 75F	T.WELLS - 75F	T.WELLS - 75F	T.WELLS - 75F
31184	STEWARTS LANE - 73A	STEWARTS LANE - 73A	STEWARTS LANE - 73A	STEWARTS LANE - 73A	STEWARTS LANE - 73A	STEWARTS LANE - 73A	STEWARTS LANE - 73A
31193	TONBRIDGE - 74D	TONBRIDGE - 74D	TONBRIDGE - 74D	TONBRIDGE - 74D	TONBRIDGE - 74D	TONBRIDGE - 74D	TONBRIDGE - 74D
31239	ASHFORD - 74A	ASHFORD - 74A	ASHFORD - 74A	ASHFORD - 74A	ASHFORD - 74A	ASHFORD - 74A	ASHFORD - 74A
31259	RAMSGATE - 74B	RAMSGATE - 74B	RAMSGATE - 74B	RAMSGATE - 74B	RAMSGATE - 74B	RAMSGATE - 74B	RAMSGATE - 74B
31261	ASHFORD - 74A	ASHFORD - 74A	ASHFORD - 74A	ASHFORD - 74A	ASHFORD - 74A	ASHFORD - 74A	ASHFORD - 74A
31263	STEWARTS LANE - 73A	STEWARTS LANE - 73A	STEWARTS LANE - 73A	STEWARTS LANE - 73A	STEWARTS LANE - 73A	STEWARTS LANE - 73A	STEWARTS LANE - 73A
31265	RAMSGATE - 74B	RAMSGATE - 74B	RAMSGATE - 74B	RAMSGATE - 74B	RAMSGATE - 74B	RAMSGATE - 74B	RAMSGATE - 74B
31266	STEWARTS LANE - 73A	STEWARTS LANE - 73A	STEWARTS LANE - 73A	STEWARTS LANE - 73A	STEWARTS LANE - 73A	STEWARTS LANE - 73A	STEWARTS LANE - 73A
31269	ASHFORD - 74A	ASHFORD - 74A	ASHFORD - 74A	ASHFORD - 74A	ASHFORD - 74A	ASHFORD - 74A	ASHFORD - 74A
31274	ASHFORD - 74A	ASHFORD - 74A	ASHFORD - 74A	ASHFORD - 74A	ASHFORD - 74A	ASHFORD - 74A	ASHFORD - 74A
31276	DOVER - 74C	DOVER - 74C	DOVER - 74C	DOVER - 74C	DOVER - 74C	DOVER - 74C	DOVER - 74C
31278	GILLINGHAM - 73D	GILLINGHAM - 73D	GILLINGHAM - 73D	GILLINGHAM - 73D	GILLINGHAM - 73D	GILLINGHAM - 73D	GILLINGHAM - 73D
31279	ST LEONARDS - 74E	ST LEONARDS - 74E	ST LEONARDS - 74E	ST LEONARDS - 74E	ST LEONARDS - 74E	ST LEONARDS - 74E	ST LEONARDS - 74E
31295	STEWARTS LANE - 73A	STEWARTS LANE - 73A	STEWARTS LANE - 73A	STEWARTS LANE - 73A	STEWARTS LANE - 73A	STEWARTS LANE - 73A	STEWARTS LANE - 73A
31305	ASHFORD - 74A	ASHFORD - 74A	ASHFORD - 74A	ASHFORD - 74A	ASHFORD - 74A	ASHFORD - 74A	ASHFORD - 74A
31306	ASHFORD - 74A	ASHFORD - 74A	ASHFORD - 74A	ASHFORD - 74A	ASHFORD - 74A	ASHFORD - 74A	ASHFORD - 74A
31307	STEWARTS LANE - 73A	STEWARTS LANE - 73A	STEWARTS LANE - 73A	STEWARTS LANE - 73A	STEWARTS LANE - 73A	STEWARTS LANE - 73A	STEWARTS LANE - 73A
31308	GILLINGHAM - 73D	GILLINGHAM - 73D	GILLINGHAM - 73D	GILLINGHAM - 73D	GILLINGHAM - 73D	GILLINGHAM - 73D	GILLINGHAM - 73D
31309	ST LEONARDS - 74E	ST LEONARDS - 74E	ST LEONARDS - 74E	ST LEONARDS - 74E	ST LEONARDS - 74E	ST LEONARDS - 74E	ST LEONARDS - 74E
31310	ST LEONARDS - 74E	ST LEONARDS - 74E	ST LEONARDS - 74E	ST LEONARDS - 74E	ST LEONARDS - 74E	ST LEONARDS - 74E	ST LEONARDS - 74E
31311	STEWARTS LANE - 73A	STEWARTS LANE - 73A	STEWARTS LANE - 73A	STEWARTS LANE - 73A	STEWARTS LANE - 73A	STEWARTS LANE - 73A	STEWARTS LANE - 73A
31319	STEWARTS LANE - 73A	STEWARTS LANE - 73A	STEWARTS LANE - 73A	STEWARTS LANE - 73A	STEWARTS LANE - 73A	STEWARTS LANE - 73A	STEWARTS LANE - 73A
31320	TONBRIDGE - 74D	TONBRIDGE - 74D	TONBRIDGE - 74D	TONBRIDGE - 74D	TONBRIDGE - 74D	TONBRIDGE - 74D	TONBRIDGE - 74D
31321	STEWARTS LANE - 73A	STEWARTS LANE - 73A	STEWARTS LANE - 73A	STEWARTS LANE - 73A	STEWARTS LANE - 73A	STEWARTS LANE - 73A	STEWARTS LANE - 73A
31322	ASHFORD - 74A	ASHFORD - 74A	ASHFORD - 74A	ASHFORD - 74A	ASHFORD - 74A	ASHFORD - 74A	ASHFORD - 74A
31324	B ARMS - 73B	B ARMS - 73B	B ARMS - 73B	B ARMS - 73B	B ARMS - 73B	B ARMS - 73B	B ARMS - 73B
31326	B ARMS - 73B	B ARMS - 73B	B ARMS - 73B	B ARMS - 73B	B ARMS - 73B	B ARMS - 73B	B ARMS - 73B
31327	TONBRIDGE - 74D	TONBRIDGE - 74D	TONBRIDGE - 74D	TONBRIDGE - 74D	TONBRIDGE - 74D	TONBRIDGE - 74D	TONBRIDGE - 74D
31328	B ARMS - 73B	B ARMS - 73B	B ARMS - 73B	B ARMS - 73B	B ARMS - 73B	ST LEONARDS - 74E	ST LEONARDS - 74E
31329	STEWARTS LANE - 73A	STEWARTS LANE - 73A	STEWARTS LANE - 73A	STEWARTS LANE - 73A	STEWARTS LANE - 73A	STEWARTS LANE - 73A	STEWARTS LANE - 73A
31500	B ARMS - 73B	B ARMS - 73B	B ARMS - 73B	B ARMS - 73B	B ARMS - 73B	B ARMS - 73B	B ARMS - 73B
31503	TONBRIDGE - 74D	TONBRIDGE - 74D	TONBRIDGE - 74D	TONBRIDGE - 74D	TONBRIDGE - 74D	DOVER - 74C	DOVER - 74C
31512	DOVER - 74C	DOVER - 74C	DOVER - 74C	DOVER - 74C	DOVER - 74C	DOVER - 74C	DOVER - 74C
31517	DOVER - 74C	DOVER - 74C	DOVER - 74C	DOVER - 74C	DOVER - 74C	TONBRIDGE - 74D	TONBRIDGE - 74D
31518	TONBRIDGE - 74D	TONBRIDGE - 74D	RAMSGATE - 74B	RAMSGATE - 74B	RAMSGATE - 74B	RAMSGATE - 74B	RAMSGATE - 74B
31519	TONBRIDGE - 74D	TONBRIDGE - 74D	TONBRIDGE - 74D	RAMSGATE - 74B	RAMSGATE - 74B	RAMSGATE - 74B	RAMSGATE - 74B
31520	DOVER - 74C	DOVER - 74C	TONBRIDGE - 74D	TONBRIDGE - 74D	TONBRIDGE - 74D	TONBRIDGE - 74D	TONBRIDGE - 74D
31521	RAMSGATE - 74B	RAMSGATE - 74B	RAMSGATE - 74B	RAMSGATE - 74B	RAMSGATE - 74B	RAMSGATE - 74B	RAMSGATE - 74B
31522	RAMSGATE - 74B	RAMSGATE - 74B	RAMSGATE - 74B	RAMSGATE - 74B	RAMSGATE - 74B	RAMSGATE - 74B	RAMSGATE - 74B
31523	RAMSGATE - 74B	RAMSGATE - 74B	RAMSGATE - 74B	TONBRIDGE - 74D	TONBRIDGE - 74D	TONBRIDGE - 74D	TONBRIDGE - 74D
31530	DOVER - 74C	DOVER - 74C	DOVER - 74C	DOVER - 74C	DOVER - 74C	DOVER - 74C	DOVER - 74C
31531	DOVER - 74C	DOVER - 74C	DOVER - 74C	DOVER - 74C	DOVER - 74C	DOVER - 74C	DOVER - 74C
31532	DOVER - 74C	DOVER - 74C	DOVER - 74C	DOVER - 74C	DOVER - 74C	DOVER - 74C	DOVER - 74C
31533	B ARMS - 73B	B ARMS - 73B	B ARMS - 73B	B ARMS - 73B	B ARMS - 73B	B ARMS - 73B	B ARMS - 73B
31540	TONBRIDGE - 74D	TONBRIDGE - 74D	TONBRIDGE - 74D	TONBRIDGE - 74D	TONBRIDGE - 74D	DOVER - 74C	DOVER - 74C
31541	B ARMS - 73B	B ARMS - 73B	B ARMS - 73B	B ARMS - 73B	B ARMS - 73B	B ARMS - 73B	B ARMS - 73B
31542	B ARMS - 73B	B ARMS - 73B	B ARMS - 73B	B ARMS - 73B	B ARMS - 73B	B ARMS - 73B	B ARMS - 73B
31543	TONBRIDGE - 74D	TONBRIDGE - 74D	TONBRIDGE - 74D	RAMSGATE - 74B	RAMSGATE - 74B	RAMSGATE - 74B	RAMSGATE - 74B
31544	NINE ELMS - 70A	NINE ELMS - 70A	NINE ELMS - 70A	NINE ELMS - 70A	NINE ELMS - 70A	NINE ELMS - 70A	NINE ELMS - 70A
31546	B ARMS - 73B	B ARMS - 73B	B ARMS - 73B	B ARMS - 73B	B ARMS - 73B	B ARMS - 73B	B ARMS - 73B
31548	DOVER - 74C	DOVER - 74C	DOVER - 74C	DOVER - 74C	DOVER - 74C	TONBRIDGE - 74D	TONBRIDGE - 74D
31550	B ARMS - 73B	B ARMS - 73B	B ARMS - 73B	B ARMS - 73B	B ARMS - 73B	B ARMS - 73B	B ARMS - 73B
31551	NINE ELMS - 70A	NINE ELMS - 70A	NINE ELMS - 70A	NINE ELMS - 70A	NINE ELMS - 70A	NINE ELMS - 70A	NINE ELMS - 70A
31552	NINE ELMS - 70A	NINE ELMS - 70A	NINE ELMS - 70A	NINE ELMS - 70A	NINE ELMS - 70A	NINE ELMS - 70A	NINE ELMS - 70A
31553	NINE ELMS - 70A	NINE ELMS - 70A	NINE ELMS - 70A	NINE ELMS - 70A	NINE ELMS - 70A	NINE ELMS - 70A	NINE ELMS - 70A
31554	STEWARTS LANE - 73A	STEWARTS LANE - 73A	STEWARTS LANE - 73A	STEWARTS LANE - 73A	STEWARTS LANE - 73A	STEWARTS LANE - 73A	STEWARTS LANE - 73A
				O2 0-4-4T (1889)			
30177	DORCHESTER - 71C	DORCHESTER - 71C	DORCHESTER - 71C	DORCHESTER - 71C	DORCHESTER - 71C	DORCHESTER - 71C	DORCHESTER - 71C
30179	DORCHESTER - 71C	DORCHESTER - 71C	DORCHESTER - 71C	DORCHESTER - 71C	DORCHESTER - 71C	DORCHESTER - 71C	DORCHESTER - 71C
30182	P LYMOUTH - 72D	P LYMOUTH - 72D	P LYMOUTH - 72D	P LYMOUTH - 72D	P LYMOUTH - 72D	P LYMOUTH - 72D	P LYMOUTH - 72D
30183	P LYMOUTH - 72D	P LYMOUTH - 72D	P LYMOUTH - 72D	P LYMOUTH - 72D	P LYMOUTH - 72D	P LYMOUTH - 72D	P LYMOUTH - 72D
30192	EXMOUTH J CN - 72A	EXMOUTH J CN - 72A	EXMOUTH J CN - 72A	EXMOUTH J CN - 72A	EXMOUTH J CN - 72A	EXMOUTH J CN - 72A	EXMOUTH J CN - 72A
30193	EXMOUTH J CN - 72A	EXMOUTH J CN - 72A	EXMOUTH J CN - 72A	EXMOUTH J CN - 72A	EXMOUTH J CN - 72A	EXMOUTH J CN - 72A	EXMOUTH J CN - 72A
30197	P LYMOUTH - 72D	P LYMOUTH - 72D	DORCHESTER - 71C	DORCHESTER - 71C	DORCHESTER - 71C	DORCHESTER - 71C	DORCHESTER - 71C
30199	EXMOUTH J CN - 72A	EXMOUTH J CN - 72A	EXMOUTH J CN - 72A	EXMOUTH J CN - 72A	EXMOUTH J CN - 72A	EXMOUTH J CN - 72A	EXMOUTH J CN - 72A
30200	WADEBRIDGE - 72F	WADEBRIDGE - 72F	WADEBRIDGE - 72F	WADEBRIDGE - 72F	WADEBRIDGE - 72F	WADEBRIDGE - 72F	WADEBRIDGE - 72F
30203	WADEBRIDGE - 72F	WADEBRIDGE - 72F	WADEBRIDGE - 72F	WADEBRIDGE - 72F	WADEBRIDGE - 72F	WADEBRIDGE - 72F	WADEBRIDGE - 72F
30204	BOURNEMOUTH - 71B	BOURNEMOUTH - 71B	BOURNEMOUTH - 71B	BOURNEMOUTH - 71B	BOURNEMOUTH - 71B	BOURNEMOUTH - 71B	BOURNEMOUTH - 71B
30207	P LYMOUTH - 72D	P LYMOUTH - 72D	P LYMOUTH - 72D	P LYMOUTH - 72D	P LYMOUTH - 72D	P LYMOUTH - 72D	P LYMOUTH - 72D
30212	BOURNEMOUTH - 71B	BOURNEMOUTH - 71B	BOURNEMOUTH - 71B	BOURNEMOUTH - 71B	BOURNEMOUTH - 71B	BOURNEMOUTH - 71B	BOURNEMOUTH - 71B
30213	EASTLEIGH - 71A	EASTLEIGH - 71A	EASTLEIGH - 71A	EASTLEIGH - 71A	EASTLEIGH - 71A	EASTLEIGH - 71A	EASTLEIGH - 71A
30216	P LYMOUTH - 72D	P LYMOUTH - 72D	P LYMOUTH - 72D	P LYMOUTH - 72D	P LYMOUTH - 72D	P LYMOUTH - 72D	P LYMOUTH - 72D
30221	NINE ELMS - 70A	NINE ELMS - 70A	NINE ELMS - 70A	NINE ELMS - 70A	NINE ELMS - 70A	NINE ELMS - 70A	NINE ELMS - 70A
30223	DORCHESTER - 71C	DORCHESTER - 71C	DORCHESTER - 71C	DORCHESTER - 71C	DORCHESTER - 71C	DORCHESTER - 71C	DORCHESTER - 71C
30224	EXMOUTH J CN - 72A	EXMOUTH J CN - 72A	EXMOUTH J CN - 72A	EXMOUTH J CN - 72A	EXMOUTH J CN - 72A	EXMOUTH J CN - 72A	EXMOUTH J CN - 72A
30225	EASTLEIGH - 71A	EASTLEIGH - 71A	EASTLEIGH - 71A	EASTLEIGH - 71A	EASTLEIGH - 71A	EASTLEIGH - 71A	EASTLEIGH - 71A
30229	DORCHESTER - 71C	DORCHESTER - 71C	DORCHESTER - 71C	DORCHESTER - 71C	DORCHESTER - 71C	DORCHESTER - 71C	DORCHESTER - 71C
30230	EXMOUTH J CN - 72A	EXMOUTH J CN - 72A	EXMOUTH J CN - 72A	EXMOUTH J CN - 72A	EXMOUTH J CN - 72A	EXMOUTH J CN - 72A	EXMOUTH J CN - 72A
30231	EASTLEIGH - 71A	EASTLEIGH - 71A	EASTLEIGH - 71A	EASTLEIGH - 71A	EASTLEIGH - 71A	EASTLEIGH - 71A	EASTLEIGH - 71A
30232	EXMOUTH J CN - 72A	EXMOUTH J CN - 72A	EXMOUTH J CN - 72A	EXMOUTH J CN - 72A	EXMOUTH J CN - 72A	EXMOUTH J CN - 72A	EXMOUTH J CN - 72A
30233	DORCHESTER - 71C	DORCHESTER - 71C	P LYMOUTH - 72D	P LYMOUTH - 72D	EXMOUTH J CN - 72A	EASTLEIGH - 71A	EASTLEIGH - 71A
30236	P LYMOUTH - 72D	P LYMOUTH - 72D	P LYMOUTH - 72D	P LYMOUTH - 72D	P LYMOUTH - 72D	P LYMOUTH - 72D	P LYMOUTH - 72D

loco	Apr-50	Sep-50	Oct-50	Nov-50	Dec-50	Mar-51	Apr-51
				H 0-4-4T (1904)			
31005	STEWARTS LANE - 73A	STEWARTS LANE - 73A	STEWARTS LANE - 73A	STEWARTS LANE - 73A	STEWARTS LANE - 73A	STEWARTS LANE - 73A	STEWARTS LANE - 73A
31016	T.WELLS - 75F	T.WELLS - 75F	T.WELLS - 75F	T.WELLS - 75F	T.WELLS - 75F	T.WELLS - 75F	T.WELLS - 75F
31158	ASHFORD - 74A	ASHFORD - 74A	ASHFORD - 74A	T.WELLS - 75F	ASHFORD - 74A	ASHFORD - 74A	ASHFORD - 74A
31161	DOVER - 74C	ASHFORD - 74A	ASHFORD - 74A	ASHFORD - 74A	ASHFORD - 74A	ASHFORD - 74A	ASHFORD - 74A
31162	B.ARMS - 73B	B.ARMS - 73B	B.ARMS - 73B	B.ARMS - 73B	B.ARMS - 73B	B.ARMS - 73B	B.ARMS - 73B
31164	TONBRIDGE - 74D	TONBRIDGE - 74D	TONBRIDGE - 74D	ST LEONARDS - 74E	ST LEONARDS - 74E	ST LEONARDS - 74E	ST LEONARDS - 74E
31177	STEWARTS LANE - 73A	STEWARTS LANE - 73A	STEWARTS LANE - 73A	STEWARTS LANE - 73A	STEWARTS LANE - 73A	STEWARTS LANE - 73A	TONBRIDGE - 74D
31182	T.WELLS - 75F	T.WELLS - 75F	T.WELLS - 75F	T.WELLS - 75F	T.WELLS - 75F	T.WELLS - 75F	T.WELLS - 75F
31184	STEWARTS LANE - 73A	STEWARTS LANE - 73A	STEWARTS LANE - 73A	STEWARTS LANE - 73A	STEWARTS LANE - 73A	STEWARTS LANE - 73A	STEWARTS LANE - 73A
31193	TONBRIDGE - 74D	TONBRIDGE - 74D	TONBRIDGE - 74D	TONBRIDGE - 74D	TONBRIDGE - 74D	TONBRIDGE - 74D	TONBRIDGE - 74D
31239	ASHFORD - 74A	ASHFORD - 74A	ASHFORD - 74A	ASHFORD - 74A	ASHFORD - 74A	ASHFORD - 74A	ASHFORD - 74A
31259	RAMSGATE - 74B	RAMSGATE - 74B	RAMSGATE - 74B	FAVERSHAM - 73E	FAVERSHAM - 73E	FAVERSHAM - 73E	FAVERSHAM - 73E
31261	ASHFORD - 74A	STEWARTS LANE - 73A	STEWARTS LANE - 73A	STEWARTS LANE - 73A	STEWARTS LANE - 73A	STEWARTS LANE - 73A	STEWARTS LANE - 73A
31263	STEWARTS LANE - 73A	STEWARTS LANE - 73A	STEWARTS LANE - 73A	STEWARTS LANE - 73A	STEWARTS LANE - 73A	STEWARTS LANE - 73A	STEWARTS LANE - 73A
31265	RAMSGATE - 74B	RAMSGATE - 74B	RAMSGATE - 74B	RAMSGATE - 74B	RAMSGATE - 74B	RAMSGATE - 74B	RAMSGATE - 74B
31266	STEWARTS LANE - 73A	STEWARTS LANE - 73A	STEWARTS LANE - 73A	STEWARTS LANE - 73A	STEWARTS LANE - 73A	STEWARTS LANE - 73A	STEWARTS LANE - 73A
31269	ASHFORD - 74A	ASHFORD - 74A	ASHFORD - 74A	ASHFORD - 74A	ASHFORD - 74A	ASHFORD - 74A	ASHFORD - 74A
31274	ASHFORD - 74A	ASHFORD - 74A	ASHFORD - 74A	ASHFORD - 74A	ASHFORD - 74A	ASHFORD - 74A	ASHFORD - 74A
31276	DOVER - 74C	DOVER - 74C	DOVER - 74C	DOVER - 74C	DOVER - 74C	DOVER - 74C	DOVER - 74C
31278	B.ARMS - 73B	B.ARMS - 73B	B.ARMS - 73B	B.ARMS - 73B	B.ARMS - 73B	B.ARMS - 73B	B.ARMS - 73B
31279	ST LEONARDS - 74E	ST LEONARDS - 74E	ST LEONARDS - 74E	ST LEONARDS - 74E	ST LEONARDS - 74E	ST LEONARDS - 74E	ST LEONARDS - 74E
31295	STEWARTS LANE - 73A	STEWARTS LANE - 73A	STEWARTS LANE - 73A	STEWARTS LANE - 73A	STEWARTS LANE - 73A	STEWARTS LANE - 73A	STEWARTS LANE - 73A
31305	ASHFORD - 74A	ASHFORD - 74A	ASHFORD - 74A	ASHFORD - 74A	ASHFORD - 74A	ASHFORD - 74A	ASHFORD - 74A
31306	ASHFORD - 74A	DOVER - 74C	DOVER - 74C	DOVER - 74C	DOVER - 74C	DOVER - 74C	DOVER - 74C
31307	STEWARTS LANE - 73A	STEWARTS LANE - 73A	STEWARTS LANE - 73A	STEWARTS LANE - 73A	STEWARTS LANE - 73A	STEWARTS LANE - 73A	STEWARTS LANE - 73A
31308	GILLINGHAM - 73D	GILLINGHAM - 73D	GILLINGHAM - 73D	GILLINGHAM - 73D	GILLINGHAM - 73D	GILLINGHAM - 73D	GILLINGHAM - 73D
31309	B.ARMS - 73B	B.ARMS - 73B	B.ARMS - 73B	B.ARMS - 73B	RAMSGATE - 74B	RAMSGATE - 74B	RAMSGATE - 74B
31310	ST LEONARDS - 74E	ST LEONARDS - 74E	ST LEONARDS - 74E	ST LEONARDS - 74E	RAMSGATE - 74B	RAMSGATE - 74B	RAMSGATE - 74B
31311	STEWARTS LANE - 73A	STEWARTS LANE - 73A	STEWARTS LANE - 73A	STEWARTS LANE - 73A	STEWARTS LANE - 73A	STEWARTS LANE - 73A	STEWARTS LANE - 73A
31319	STEWARTS LANE - 73A	ST LEONARDS - 74E	ST LEONARDS - 74E	ST LEONARDS - 74E	ST LEONARDS - 74E	ST LEONARDS - 74E	ST LEONARDS - 74E
31320	TONBRIDGE - 74D	TONBRIDGE - 74D	TONBRIDGE - 74D	TONBRIDGE - 74D	TONBRIDGE - 74D	TONBRIDGE - 74D	STEWARTS LANE - 73A
31321	STEWARTS LANE - 73A	STEWARTS LANE - 73A	STEWARTS LANE - 73A	STEWARTS LANE - 73A	STEWARTS LANE - 73A	STEWARTS LANE - 73A	STEWARTS LANE - 73A
31322	ASHFORD - 74A	ASHFORD - 74A	ASHFORD - 74A	ASHFORD - 74A	ASHFORD - 74A	ASHFORD - 74A	ASHFORD - 74A
31324	B.ARMS - 73B	B.ARMS - 73B	B.ARMS - 73B	B.ARMS - 73B	B.ARMS - 73B	B.ARMS - 73B	B.ARMS - 73B
31326	B.ARMS - 73B	B.ARMS - 73B	B.ARMS - 73B	B.ARMS - 73B	B.ARMS - 73B	B.ARMS - 73B	B.ARMS - 73B
31327	TONBRIDGE - 74D	TONBRIDGE - 74D	TONBRIDGE - 74D	TONBRIDGE - 74D	TONBRIDGE - 74D	TONBRIDGE - 74D	TONBRIDGE - 74D
31328	ST LEONARDS - 74E	ST LEONARDS - 74E	ST LEONARDS - 74E	ST LEONARDS - 74E	ST LEONARDS - 74E	ST LEONARDS - 74E	ST LEONARDS - 74E
31329	STEWARTS LANE - 73A	STEWARTS LANE - 73A	STEWARTS LANE - 73A	STEWARTS LANE - 73A	STEWARTS LANE - 73A	STEWARTS LANE - 73A	STEWARTS LANE - 73A
31500	B.ARMS - 73B	B.ARMS - 73B	B.ARMS - 73B	B.ARMS - 73B	B.ARMS - 73B	B.ARMS - 73B	B.ARMS - 73B
31503	DOVER - 74C	DOVER - 74C	DOVER - 74C	DOVER - 74C	DOVER - 74C	DOVER - 74C	DOVER - 74C
31512	DOVER - 74C	DOVER - 74C	DOVER - 74C	DOVER - 74C	DOVER - 74C	DOVER - 74C	DOVER - 74C
31517	TONBRIDGE - 74D	TONBRIDGE - 74D	TONBRIDGE - 74D	TONBRIDGE - 74D	TONBRIDGE - 74D	TONBRIDGE - 74D	TONBRIDGE - 74D
31518	RAMSGATE - 74B	DOVER - 74C	DOVER - 74C	DOVER - 74C	DOVER - 74C	DOVER - 74C	DOVER - 74C
31519	RAMSGATE - 74B	RAMSGATE - 74B	RAMSGATE - 74B	RAMSGATE - 74B	RAMSGATE - 74B	RAMSGATE - 74B	RAMSGATE - 74B
31520	ASHFORD - 74A	ASHFORD - 74A	ASHFORD - 74A	ASHFORD - 74A	ASHFORD - 74A	T.WELLS - 75F	T.WELLS - 75F
31521	RAMSGATE - 74B	RAMSGATE - 74B	RAMSGATE - 74B	RAMSGATE - 74B	RAMSGATE - 74B	RAMSGATE - 74B	RAMSGATE - 74B
31522	RAMSGATE - 74B	RAMSGATE - 74B	RAMSGATE - 74B	RAMSGATE - 74B	RAMSGATE - 74B	RAMSGATE - 74B	RAMSGATE - 74B
31523	TONBRIDGE - 74D	TONBRIDGE - 74D	TONBRIDGE - 74D	TONBRIDGE - 74D	TONBRIDGE - 74D	TONBRIDGE - 74D	TONBRIDGE - 74D
31530	DOVER - 74C	DOVER - 74C	DOVER - 74C	DOVER - 74C	DOVER - 74C	DOVER - 74C	DOVER - 74C
31531	DOVER - 74C	DOVER - 74C	DOVER - 74C	DOVER - 74C	DOVER - 74C	DOVER - 74C	DOVER - 74C
31532	RAMSGATE - 74B	RAMSGATE - 74B	RAMSGATE - 74B	FAVERSHAM - 73E	FAVERSHAM - 73E	W/D	W/D
31533	B.ARMS - 73B	B.ARMS - 73B	B.ARMS - 73B	B.ARMS - 73B	B.ARMS - 73B	B.ARMS - 73B	B.ARMS - 73B
31540	DOVER - 74C	DOVER - 74C	DOVER - 74C	DOVER - 74C	DOVER - 74C	DOVER - 74C	DOVER - 74C
31541	B.ARMS - 73B	B.ARMS - 73B	B.ARMS - 73B	B.ARMS - 73B	B.ARMS - 73B	B.ARMS - 73B	W/D
31542	B.ARMS - 73B	B.ARMS - 73B	B.ARMS - 73B	B.ARMS - 73B	B.ARMS - 73B	B.ARMS - 73B	B.ARMS - 73B
31543	RAMSGATE - 74B	RAMSGATE - 74B	RAMSGATE - 74B	B.ARMS - 73B	B.ARMS - 73B	B.ARMS - 73B	B.ARMS - 73B
31544	NINE ELMS - 70A	B.ARMS - 73B	B.ARMS - 73B	B.ARMS - 73B	B.ARMS - 73B	B.ARMS - 73B	B.ARMS - 73B
31546	B.ARMS - 73B	B.ARMS - 73B	B.ARMS - 73B	B.ARMS - 73B	W/D	W/D	W/D
31548	TONBRIDGE - 74D	TONBRIDGE - 74D	TONBRIDGE - 74D	TONBRIDGE - 74D	TONBRIDGE - 74D	TONBRIDGE - 74D	TONBRIDGE - 74D
31550	TONBRIDGE - 74D	TONBRIDGE - 74D	TONBRIDGE - 74D	TONBRIDGE - 74D	TONBRIDGE - 74D	TONBRIDGE - 74D	TONBRIDGE - 74D
31551	NINE ELMS - 70A	NINE ELMS - 70A	NINE ELMS - 70A	NINE ELMS - 70A	NINE ELMS - 70A	NINE ELMS - 70A	NINE ELMS - 70A
31552	NINE ELMS - 70A	NINE ELMS - 70A	NINE ELMS - 70A	NINE ELMS - 70A	NINE ELMS - 70A	NINE ELMS - 70A	NINE ELMS - 70A
31553	NINE ELMS - 70A	NINE ELMS - 70A	NINE ELMS - 70A	NINE ELMS - 70A	NINE ELMS - 70A	NINE ELMS - 70A	NINE ELMS - 70A
31554	NINE ELMS - 70A	NINE ELMS - 70A	NINE ELMS - 70A	NINE ELMS - 70A	NINE ELMS - 70A	NINE ELMS - 70A	NINE ELMS - 70A
				O2 0-4-4T (1889)			
30177	DORCHESTER - 71C	DORCHESTER - 71C	DORCHESTER - 71C	DORCHESTER - 71C	DORCHESTER - 71C	DORCHESTER - 71C	DORCHESTER - 71C
30179	DORCHESTER - 71C	DORCHESTER - 71C	DORCHESTER - 71C	DORCHESTER - 71C	DORCHESTER - 71C	DORCHESTER - 71C	DORCHESTER - 71C
30182	P.LYMOUTH - 72D	P.LYMOUTH - 72D	P.LYMOUTH - 72D	P.LYMOUTH - 72D	P.LYMOUTH - 72D	P.LYMOUTH - 72D	P.LYMOUTH - 72D
30183	P.LYMOUTH - 72D	P.LYMOUTH - 72D	P.LYMOUTH - 72D	P.LYMOUTH - 72D	P.LYMOUTH - 72D	P.LYMOUTH - 72D	P.LYMOUTH - 72D
30192	EXMOUTH JCN - 72A	EXMOUTH JCN - 72A	EXMOUTH JCN - 72A	EXMOUTH JCN - 72A	EXMOUTH JCN - 72A	EXMOUTH JCN - 72A	EXMOUTH JCN - 72A
30193	EXMOUTH JCN - 72A	EXMOUTH JCN - 72A	EXMOUTH JCN - 72A	EXMOUTH JCN - 72A	EXMOUTH JCN - 72A	EXMOUTH JCN - 72A	EXMOUTH JCN - 72A
30197	DORCHESTER - 71C	DORCHESTER - 71C	DORCHESTER - 71C	DORCHESTER - 71C	DORCHESTER - 71C	DORCHESTER - 71C	DORCHESTER - 71C
30199	EXMOUTH JCN - 72A	EXMOUTH JCN - 72A	EXMOUTH JCN - 72A	EXMOUTH JCN - 72A	EXMOUTH JCN - 72A	EXMOUTH JCN - 72A	EXMOUTH JCN - 72A
30200	WADEBRIDGE - 72F	WADEBRIDGE - 72F	WADEBRIDGE - 72F	WADEBRIDGE - 72F	WADEBRIDGE - 72F	WADEBRIDGE - 72F	WADEBRIDGE - 72F
30203	WADEBRIDGE - 72F	WADEBRIDGE - 72F	WADEBRIDGE - 72F	WADEBRIDGE - 72F	WADEBRIDGE - 72F	WADEBRIDGE - 72F	WADEBRIDGE - 72F
30204	BOURNEMOUTH - 71B	BOURNEMOUTH - 71B	BOURNEMOUTH - 71B	BOURNEMOUTH - 71B	BOURNEMOUTH - 71B	BOURNEMOUTH - 71B	BOURNEMOUTH - 71B
30207	P.LYMOUTH - 72D	P.LYMOUTH - 72D	P.LYMOUTH - 72D	P.LYMOUTH - 72D	P.LYMOUTH - 72D	P.LYMOUTH - 72D	P.LYMOUTH - 72D
30212	BOURNEMOUTH - 71B	BOURNEMOUTH - 71B	BOURNEMOUTH - 71B	BOURNEMOUTH - 71B	BOURNEMOUTH - 71B	BOURNEMOUTH - 71B	BOURNEMOUTH - 71B
30213	EASTLEIGH - 71A	EASTLEIGH - 71A	EASTLEIGH - 71A	EASTLEIGH - 71A	EASTLEIGH - 71A	EASTLEIGH - 71A	EASTLEIGH - 71A
30216	P.LYMOUTH - 72D	P.LYMOUTH - 72D	P.LYMOUTH - 72D	P.LYMOUTH - 72D	P.LYMOUTH - 72D	P.LYMOUTH - 72D	P.LYMOUTH - 72D
30221	NINE ELMS - 70A	NINE ELMS - 70A	NINE ELMS - 70A	NINE ELMS - 70A	NINE ELMS - 70A	NINE ELMS - 70A	NINE ELMS - 70A
30223	DORCHESTER - 71C	DORCHESTER - 71C	DORCHESTER - 71C	DORCHESTER - 71C	DORCHESTER - 71C	DORCHESTER - 71C	DORCHESTER - 71C
30224	EXMOUTH JCN - 72A	EXMOUTH JCN - 72A	EXMOUTH JCN - 72A	EXMOUTH JCN - 72A	EXMOUTH JCN - 72A	EXMOUTH JCN - 72A	EXMOUTH JCN - 72A
30225	EASTLEIGH - 71A	EASTLEIGH - 71A	EASTLEIGH - 71A	EASTLEIGH - 71A	EASTLEIGH - 71A	EASTLEIGH - 71A	EASTLEIGH - 71A
30229	DORCHESTER - 71C	DORCHESTER - 71C	DORCHESTER - 71C	DORCHESTER - 71C	DORCHESTER - 71C	DORCHESTER - 71C	DORCHESTER - 71C
30230	EXMOUTH JCN - 72A	EXMOUTH JCN - 72A	EXMOUTH JCN - 72A	EXMOUTH JCN - 72A	EXMOUTH JCN - 72A	EXMOUTH JCN - 72A	EXMOUTH JCN - 72A
30231	EASTLEIGH - 71A	DORCHESTER - 71C	DORCHESTER - 71C	DORCHESTER - 71C	DORCHESTER - 71C	DORCHESTER - 71C	DORCHESTER - 71C
30232	EXMOUTH JCN - 72A	EXMOUTH JCN - 72A	EXMOUTH JCN - 72A	EXMOUTH JCN - 72A	EXMOUTH JCN - 72A	EXMOUTH JCN - 72A	EXMOUTH JCN - 72A
30233	EASTLEIGH - 71A	EASTLEIGH - 71A	EASTLEIGH - 71A	EASTLEIGH - 71A	EASTLEIGH - 71A	EASTLEIGH - 71A	EASTLEIGH - 71A
30236	P.LYMOUTH - 72D	P.LYMOUTH - 72D	P.LYMOUTH - 72D	P.LYMOUTH - 72D	P.LYMOUTH - 72D	P.LYMOUTH - 72D	P.LYMOUTH - 72D

H 0-4-4T (1904)

loco	Jun-51	Jul-51	Sep-51	Dec-51	Jan-52	Mar-52	Jun-52
31005	STEWARTS LANE - 73A	STEWARTS LANE - 73A	STEWARTS LANE - 73A	STEWARTS LANE - 73A	STEWARTS LANE - 73A	STEWARTS LANE - 73A	STEWARTS LANE - 73A
31016	T.WELLS - 75F	W/D	W/D	W/D	W/D	W/D	W/D
31158	ASHFORD - 74A	ASHFORD - 74A	ASHFORD - 74A	STEWARTS LANE - 73A	STEWARTS LANE - 73A	STEWARTS LANE - 73A	STEWARTS LANE - 73A
31161	ASHFORD - 74A	ASHFORD - 74A	ASHFORD - 74A	ASHFORD - 74A	ASHFORD - 74A	ASHFORD - 74A	ASHFORD - 74A
31162	FAVERSHAM - 73E	FAVERSHAM - 73E	FAVERSHAM - 73E	FAVERSHAM - 73E	FAVERSHAM - 73E	FAVERSHAM - 73E	FAVERSHAM - 73E
31164	ST LEONARDS - 74E	ST LEONARDS - 74E	TONBRIDGE - 74D	TONBRIDGE - 74D	TONBRIDGE - 74D	TONBRIDGE - 74D	TONBRIDGE - 74D
31177	TONBRIDGE - 74D	TONBRIDGE - 74D	TONBRIDGE - 74D	TONBRIDGE - 74D	TONBRIDGE - 74D	TONBRIDGE - 74D	TONBRIDGE - 74D
31182	T.WELLS - 75F	W/D	W/D	W/D	W/D	W/D	W/D
31184	STEWARTS LANE - 73A	STEWARTS LANE - 73A	STEWARTS LANE - 73A	STEWARTS LANE - 73A	STEWARTS LANE - 73A	STEWARTS LANE - 73A	STEWARTS LANE - 73A
31193	TONBRIDGE - 74D	TONBRIDGE - 74D	TONBRIDGE - 74D	TONBRIDGE - 74D	TONBRIDGE - 74D	TONBRIDGE - 74D	TONBRIDGE - 74D
31239	ASHFORD - 74A	ASHFORD - 74A	ASHFORD - 74A	ASHFORD - 74A	ASHFORD - 74A	ASHFORD - 74A	ASHFORD - 74A
31259	FAVERSHAM - 73E	FAVERSHAM - 73E	FAVERSHAM - 73E	FAVERSHAM - 73E	FAVERSHAM - 73E	FAVERSHAM - 73E	FAVERSHAM - 73E
31261	STEWARTS LANE - 73A	STEWARTS LANE - 73A	STEWARTS LANE - 73A	STEWARTS LANE - 73A	STEWARTS LANE - 73A	STEWARTS LANE - 73A	STEWARTS LANE - 73A
31263	STEWARTS LANE - 73A	STEWARTS LANE - 73A	STEWARTS LANE - 73A	STEWARTS LANE - 73A	STEWARTS LANE - 73A	STEWARTS LANE - 73A	STEWARTS LANE - 73A
31265	RAMSGATE - 74B	RAMSGATE - 74B	RAMSGATE - 74B	RAMSGATE - 74B	RAMSGATE - 74B	RAMSGATE - 74B	RAMSGATE - 74B
31266	STEWARTS LANE - 73A	STEWARTS LANE - 73A	STEWARTS LANE - 73A	STEWARTS LANE - 73A	STEWARTS LANE - 73A	STEWARTS LANE - 73A	STEWARTS LANE - 73A
31269	ASHFORD - 74A	ASHFORD - 74A	ASHFORD - 74A	ASHFORD - 74A	ASHFORD - 74A	ASHFORD - 74A	ASHFORD - 74A
31274	ASHFORD - 74A	ASHFORD - 74A	ASHFORD - 74A	DOVER - 74C	DOVER - 74C	DOVER - 74C	DOVER - 74C
31276	DOVER - 74C	DOVER - 74C	DOVER - 74C	DOVER - 74C	DOVER - 74C	RAMSGATE - 74B	RAMSGATE - 74B
31278	B.ARMS - 73B	B.ARMS - 73B	B.ARMS - 73B	B.ARMS - 73B	B.ARMS - 73B	B.ARMS - 73B	B.ARMS - 73B
31279	ST LEONARDS - 74E	ST LEONARDS - 74E	ST LEONARDS - 74E	ST LEONARDS - 74E	ST LEONARDS - 74E	ST LEONARDS - 74E	ST LEONARDS - 74E
31295	STEWARTS LANE - 73A	FAVERSHAM - 73E	FAVERSHAM - 73E	FAVERSHAM - 73E	FAVERSHAM - 73E	FAVERSHAM - 73E	GILLINGHAM - 73D
31305	FAVERSHAM - 73E	FAVERSHAM - 73E	FAVERSHAM - 73E	FAVERSHAM - 73E	FAVERSHAM - 73E	FAVERSHAM - 73E	GILLINGHAM - 73D
31306	GILLINGHAM - 73D	GILLINGHAM - 73D	GILLINGHAM - 73D	GILLINGHAM - 73D	GILLINGHAM - 73D	GILLINGHAM - 73D	GILLINGHAM - 73D
31307	STEWARTS LANE - 73A	STEWARTS LANE - 73A	STEWARTS LANE - 73A	STEWARTS LANE - 73A	STEWARTS LANE - 73A	STEWARTS LANE - 73A	STEWARTS LANE - 73A
31308	GILLINGHAM - 73D	GILLINGHAM - 73D	GILLINGHAM - 73D	GILLINGHAM - 73D	GILLINGHAM - 73D	GILLINGHAM - 73D	GILLINGHAM - 73D
31309	RAMSGATE - 74B	RAMSGATE - 74B	RAMSGATE - 74B	RAMSGATE - 74B	RAMSGATE - 74B	RAMSGATE - 74B	RAMSGATE - 74B
31310	RAMSGATE - 74B	RAMSGATE - 74B	RAMSGATE - 74B	RAMSGATE - 74B	RAMSGATE - 74B	RAMSGATE - 74B	RAMSGATE - 74B
31311	STEWARTS LANE - 73A	STEWARTS LANE - 73A	STEWARTS LANE - 73A	STEWARTS LANE - 73A	STEWARTS LANE - 73A	STEWARTS LANE - 73A	REDHILL - 75B
31319	ST LEONARDS - 74E	ST LEONARDS - 74E	ST LEONARDS - 74E	ST LEONARDS - 74E	ST LEONARDS - 74E	ST LEONARDS - 74E	ST LEONARDS - 74E
31320	STEWARTS LANE - 73A	STEWARTS LANE - 73A	STEWARTS LANE - 73A	STEWARTS LANE - 73A	STEWARTS LANE - 73A	STEWARTS LANE - 73A	STEWARTS LANE - 73A
31321	STEWARTS LANE - 73A	STEWARTS LANE - 73A	STEWARTS LANE - 73A	STEWARTS LANE - 73A	STEWARTS LANE - 73A	STEWARTS LANE - 73A	STEWARTS LANE - 73A
31322	ASHFORD - 74A	T.WELLS - 75F	T.WELLS - 75F	T.WELLS - 75F	T.WELLS - 75F	T.WELLS - 75F	T.WELLS - 75F
31324	B.ARMS - 73B	B.ARMS - 73B	B.ARMS - 73B	FAVERSHAM - 73E	FAVERSHAM - 73E	FAVERSHAM - 73E	RAMSGATE - 74B
31326	B.ARMS - 73B	FAVERSHAM - 73E	FAVERSHAM - 73E	FAVERSHAM - 73E	FAVERSHAM - 73E	FAVERSHAM - 73E	RAMSGATE - 74B
31327	TONBRIDGE - 74D	FAVERSHAM - 73E	FAVERSHAM - 73E	FAVERSHAM - 73E	ASHFORD - 74A	ASHFORD - 74A	ASHFORD - 74A
31328	ST LEONARDS - 74E	ST LEONARDS - 74E	ST LEONARDS - 74E	ST LEONARDS - 74E	ST LEONARDS - 74E	DOVER - 74C	DOVER - 74C
31329	STEWARTS LANE - 73A	STEWARTS LANE - 73A	STEWARTS LANE - 73A	ST LEONARDS - 74E	ST LEONARDS - 74E	ST LEONARDS - 74E	ST LEONARDS - 74E
31500	B.ARMS - 73B	B.ARMS - 73B	B.ARMS - 73B	FAVERSHAM - 73E	FAVERSHAM - 73E	FAVERSHAM - 73E	FAVERSHAM - 73E
31503	DOVER - 74C	B.ARMS - 73B	B.ARMS - 73B	FAVERSHAM - 73E	FAVERSHAM - 73E	FAVERSHAM - 73E	FAVERSHAM - 73E
31512	DOVER - 74C	DOVER - 74C	DOVER - 74C	ASHFORD - 74A	ASHFORD - 74A	ASHFORD - 74A	ASHFORD - 74A
31517	TONBRIDGE - 74D	TONBRIDGE - 74D	T.WELLS - 75F	T.WELLS - 75F	T.WELLS - 75F	T.WELLS - 75F	T.WELLS - 75F
31518	DOVER - 74C	DOVER - 74C	DOVER - 74C	DOVER - 74C	DOVER - 74C	ST LEONARDS - 74E	ST LEONARDS - 74E
31519	RAMSGATE - 74B	RAMSGATE - 74B	RAMSGATE - 74B	RAMSGATE - 74B	RAMSGATE - 74B	RAMSGATE - 74B	ST LEONARDS - 74E
31520	T.WELLS - 75F	T.WELLS - 75F	T.WELLS - 75F	T.WELLS - 75F	T.WELLS - 75F	T.WELLS - 75F	T.WELLS - 75F
31521	RAMSGATE - 74B	RAMSGATE - 74B	RAMSGATE - 74B	RAMSGATE - 74B	RAMSGATE - 74B	RAMSGATE - 74B	DOVER - 74C
31522	RAMSGATE - 74B	RAMSGATE - 74B	RAMSGATE - 74B	RAMSGATE - 74B	RAMSGATE - 74B	ASHFORD - 74A	ASHFORD - 74A
31523	TONBRIDGE - 74D	TONBRIDGE - 74D	TONBRIDGE - 74D	TONBRIDGE - 74D	TONBRIDGE - 74D	TONBRIDGE - 74D	TONBRIDGE - 74D
31530	DOVER - 74C	DOVER - 74C	DOVER - 74C	DOVER - 74C	DOVER - 74C	DOVER - 74C	DOVER - 74C
31531	DOVER - 74C	DOVER - 74C	DOVER - 74C	DOVER - 74C	DOVER - 74C	DOVER - 74C	DOVER - 74C
31533	B.ARMS - 73B	B.ARMS - 73B	B.ARMS - 73B	B.ARMS - 73B	B.ARMS - 73B	B.ARMS - 73B	B.ARMS - 73B
31540	DOVER - 74C	DOVER - 74C	DOVER - 74C	DOVER - 74C	DOVER - 74C	DOVER - 74C	DOVER - 74C
31542	B.ARMS - 73B	B.ARMS - 73B	B.ARMS - 73B	B.ARMS - 73B	B.ARMS - 73B	B.ARMS - 73B	B.ARMS - 73B
31543	B.ARMS - 73B	B.ARMS - 73B	B.ARMS - 73B	B.ARMS - 73B	B.ARMS - 73B	B.ARMS - 73B	B.ARMS - 73B
31544	B.ARMS - 73B	B.ARMS - 73B	B.ARMS - 73B	B.ARMS - 73B	B.ARMS - 73B	B.ARMS - 73B	B.ARMS - 73B
31548	TONBRIDGE - 74D	TONBRIDGE - 74D	TONBRIDGE - 74D	TONBRIDGE - 74D	TONBRIDGE - 74D	TONBRIDGE - 74D	TONBRIDGE - 74D
31550	TONBRIDGE - 74D	TONBRIDGE - 74D	TONBRIDGE - 74D	TONBRIDGE - 74D	TONBRIDGE - 74D	TONBRIDGE - 74D	NINE ELMS - 70A
31551	NINE ELMS - 70A	NINE ELMS - 70A	NINE ELMS - 70A	NINE ELMS - 70A	NINE ELMS - 70A	NINE ELMS - 70A	NINE ELMS - 70A
31552	NINE ELMS - 70A	NINE ELMS - 70A	NINE ELMS - 70A	NINE ELMS - 70A	NINE ELMS - 70A	NINE ELMS - 70A	NINE ELMS - 70A
31553	NINE ELMS - 70A	NINE ELMS - 70A	NINE ELMS - 70A	NINE ELMS - 70A	NINE ELMS - 70A	NINE ELMS - 70A	NINE ELMS - 70A
31554	NINE ELMS - 70A	NINE ELMS - 70A	NINE ELMS - 70A	NINE ELMS - 70A	NINE ELMS - 70A	NINE ELMS - 70A	TONBRIDGE - 74D

O2 0-4-4T (1889)

loco	Jun-51	Jul-51	Sep-51	Dec-51	Jan-52	Mar-52	Jun-52
30177	DORCHESTER - 71C	DORCHESTER - 71C	DORCHESTER - 71C	DORCHESTER - 71C	DORCHESTER - 71C	DORCHESTER - 71C	DORCHESTER - 71C
30179	DORCHESTER - 71C	DORCHESTER - 71C	DORCHESTER - 71C	DORCHESTER - 71C	DORCHESTER - 71C	DORCHESTER - 71C	DORCHESTER - 71C
30182	PLYMOUTH - 72D	PLYMOUTH - 72D	PLYMOUTH - 72D	PLYMOUTH - 72D	PLYMOUTH - 72D	PLYMOUTH - 72D	PLYMOUTH - 72D
30183	PLYMOUTH - 72D	PLYMOUTH - 72D	PLYMOUTH - 72D	PLYMOUTH - 72D	PLYMOUTH - 72D	PLYMOUTH - 72D	PLYMOUTH - 72D
30192	EXMOUTH JCN - 72A	EXMOUTH JCN - 72A	WADEBRIDGE - 72F	WADEBRIDGE - 72F	WADEBRIDGE - 72F	WADEBRIDGE - 72F	WADEBRIDGE - 72F
30193	EXMOUTH JCN - 72A	EXMOUTH JCN - 72A	EXMOUTH JCN - 72A	EXMOUTH JCN - 72A	EXMOUTH JCN - 72A	EXMOUTH JCN - 72A	EXMOUTH JCN - 72A
30197	DORCHESTER - 71C	DORCHESTER - 71C	DORCHESTER - 71C	DORCHESTER - 71C	DORCHESTER - 71C	DORCHESTER - 71C	DORCHESTER - 71C
30199	EXMOUTH JCN - 72A	EXMOUTH JCN - 72A	EXMOUTH JCN - 72A	EXMOUTH JCN - 72A	EXMOUTH JCN - 72A	EXMOUTH JCN - 72A	EXMOUTH JCN - 72A
30200	WADEBRIDGE - 72F	WADEBRIDGE - 72F	WADEBRIDGE - 72F	WADEBRIDGE - 72F	WADEBRIDGE - 72F	WADEBRIDGE - 72F	WADEBRIDGE - 72F
30203	WADEBRIDGE - 72F	WADEBRIDGE - 72F	WADEBRIDGE - 72F	WADEBRIDGE - 72F	WADEBRIDGE - 72F	WADEBRIDGE - 72F	WADEBRIDGE - 72F
30204	BOURNEMOUTH - 71B	BOURNEMOUTH - 71B	BOURNEMOUTH - 71B	BOURNEMOUTH - 71B	BOURNEMOUTH - 71B	BOURNEMOUTH - 71B	BOURNEMOUTH - 71B
30207	PLYMOUTH - 72D	PLYMOUTH - 72D	PLYMOUTH - 72D	PLYMOUTH - 72D	PLYMOUTH - 72D	PLYMOUTH - 72D	PLYMOUTH - 72D
30212	BOURNEMOUTH - 71B	BOURNEMOUTH - 71B	BOURNEMOUTH - 71B	BOURNEMOUTH - 71B	BOURNEMOUTH - 71B	BOURNEMOUTH - 71B	BOURNEMOUTH - 71B
30213	EASTLEIGH - 71A	EASTLEIGH - 71A	EASTLEIGH - 71A	EASTLEIGH - 71A	EASTLEIGH - 71A	EASTLEIGH - 71A	EASTLEIGH - 71A
30216	PLYMOUTH - 72D	PLYMOUTH - 72D	PLYMOUTH - 72D	PLYMOUTH - 72D	PLYMOUTH - 72D	PLYMOUTH - 72D	PLYMOUTH - 72D
30221	NINE ELMS - 70A	NINE ELMS - 70A	NINE ELMS - 70A	NINE ELMS - 70A	NINE ELMS - 70A	NINE ELMS - 70A	NINE ELMS - 70A
30223	DORCHESTER - 71C	DORCHESTER - 71C	DORCHESTER - 71C	DORCHESTER - 71C	DORCHESTER - 71C	DORCHESTER - 71C	BOURNEMOUTH - 71B
30224	EXMOUTH JCN - 72A	EXMOUTH JCN - 72A	EXMOUTH JCN - 72A	EXMOUTH JCN - 72A	EXMOUTH JCN - 72A	EXMOUTH JCN - 72A	EXMOUTH JCN - 72A
30225	EASTLEIGH - 71A	EASTLEIGH - 71A	EASTLEIGH - 71A	EASTLEIGH - 71A	EASTLEIGH - 71A	EASTLEIGH - 71A	EASTLEIGH - 71A
30229	DORCHESTER - 71C	DORCHESTER - 71C	DORCHESTER - 71C	DORCHESTER - 71C	DORCHESTER - 71C	DORCHESTER - 71C	DORCHESTER - 71C
30230	EXMOUTH JCN - 72A	EXMOUTH JCN - 72A	DORCHESTER - 71C	DORCHESTER - 71C	DORCHESTER - 71C	FELTHAM - 70B	FELTHAM - 70B
30231	DORCHESTER - 71C	DORCHESTER - 71C	DORCHESTER - 71C	DORCHESTER - 71C	DORCHESTER - 71C	DORCHESTER - 71C	DORCHESTER - 71C
30232	EXMOUTH JCN - 72A	EXMOUTH JCN - 72A	EXMOUTH JCN - 72A	EXMOUTH JCN - 72A	EXMOUTH JCN - 72A	EXMOUTH JCN - 72A	EXMOUTH JCN - 72A
30233	EASTLEIGH - 71A	EASTLEIGH - 71A	EASTLEIGH - 71A	EASTLEIGH - 71A	EASTLEIGH - 71A	EASTLEIGH - 71A	EASTLEIGH - 71A
30236	PLYMOUTH - 72D	PLYMOUTH - 72D	PLYMOUTH - 72D	PLYMOUTH - 72D	PLYMOUTH - 72D	PLYMOUTH - 72D	PLYMOUTH - 72D

loco	Sep-52	Dec-52	Mar-53	May-53	Jul-53	Sep-53	Nov-53
				H 0-4-4T (1904)			
31005	STEWARTS LANE - 73A	STEWARTS LANE - 73A	STEWARTS LANE - 73A	STEWARTS LANE - 73A	STEWARTS LANE - 73A	STEWARTS LANE - 73A	STEWARTS LANE - 73A
31158	STEWARTS LANE - 73A	STEWARTS LANE - 73A	STEWARTS LANE - 73A	STEWARTS LANE - 73A	STEWARTS LANE - 73A	STEWARTS LANE - 73A	GILLINGHAM - 73D
31161	ASHFORD - 74A	ASHFORD - 74A	GILLINGHAM - 73D	GILLINGHAM - 73D	GILLINGHAM - 73D	GILLINGHAM - 73D	GILLINGHAM - 73D
31162	FAVERSHAM - 73E	FAVERSHAM - 73E	ST LEONARDS - 74E	ST LEONARDS - 74E	ST LEONARDS - 74E	ST LEONARDS - 74E	ST LEONARDS - 74E
31164	TONBRIDGE - 74D	TONBRIDGE - 74D	TONBRIDGE - 74D	TONBRIDGE - 74D	TONBRIDGE - 74D	TONBRIDGE - 74D	TONBRIDGE - 74D
31177	TONBRIDGE - 74D	TONBRIDGE - 74D	TONBRIDGE - 74D	TONBRIDGE - 74D	TONBRIDGE - 74D	TONBRIDGE - 74D	TONBRIDGE - 74D
31184	STEWARTS LANE - 73A	STEWARTS LANE - 73A	STEWARTS LANE - 73A	STEWARTS LANE - 73A	STEWARTS LANE - 73A	STEWARTS LANE - 73A	STEWARTS LANE - 73A
31193	TONBRIDGE - 74D	TONBRIDGE - 74D	TONBRIDGE - 74D	TONBRIDGE - 74D	TONBRIDGE - 74D	TONBRIDGE - 74D	TONBRIDGE - 74D
31239	ASHFORD - 74A	ASHFORD - 74A	ASHFORD - 74A	ASHFORD - 74A	ASHFORD - 74A	ASHFORD - 74A	ASHFORD - 74A
31259	FAVERSHAM - 73E	FAVERSHAM - 73E	FAVERSHAM - 73E	FAVERSHAM - 73E	FAVERSHAM - 73E	FAVERSHAM - 73E	FAVERSHAM - 73E
31261	STEWARTS LANE - 73A	STEWARTS LANE - 73A	STEWARTS LANE - 73A	STEWARTS LANE - 73A	STEWARTS LANE - 73A	STEWARTS LANE - 73A	STEWARTS LANE - 73A
31263	STEWARTS LANE - 73A	STEWARTS LANE - 73A	STEWARTS LANE - 73A	STEWARTS LANE - 73A	STEWARTS LANE - 73A	STEWARTS LANE - 73A	STEWARTS LANE - 73A
31265	RAMSGATE - 74B	RAMSGATE - 74B	RAMSGATE - 74B	RAMSGATE - 74B	RAMSGATE - 74B	RAMSGATE - 74B	RAMSGATE - 74B
31266	STEWARTS LANE - 73A	STEWARTS LANE - 73A	STEWARTS LANE - 73A	STEWARTS LANE - 73A	STEWARTS LANE - 73A	STEWARTS LANE - 73A	STEWARTS LANE - 73A
31269	ASHFORD - 74A	ASHFORD - 74A	ASHFORD - 74A	ASHFORD - 74A	STEWARTS LANE - 73A	STEWARTS LANE - 73A	ST LEONARDS - 74E
31274	DOVER - 74C	ST LEONARDS - 74E	ST LEONARDS - 74E	ST LEONARDS - 74E	ST LEONARDS - 74E	ST LEONARDS - 74E	ST LEONARDS - 74E
31276	RAMSGATE - 74B	RAMSGATE - 74B	RAMSGATE - 74B	RAMSGATE - 74B	RAMSGATE - 74B	ASHFORD - 74A	ASHFORD - 74A
31278	B.ARMS - 73B	B.ARMS - 73B	B.ARMS - 73B	DOVER - 74C	DOVER - 74C	DOVER - 74C	DOVER - 74C
31279	ST LEONARDS - 74E	ST LEONARDS - 74E	ST LEONARDS - 74E	ST LEONARDS - 74E	ST LEONARDS - 74E	ST LEONARDS - 74E	ST LEONARDS - 74E
31295	GILLINGHAM - 73D	GILLINGHAM - 73D	GILLINGHAM - 73D	GILLINGHAM - 73D	ST LEONARDS - 74E	ST LEONARDS - 74E	ST LEONARDS - 74E
31305	GILLINGHAM - 73D	GILLINGHAM - 73D	GILLINGHAM - 73D	GILLINGHAM - 73D	GILLINGHAM - 73D	GILLINGHAM - 73D	GILLINGHAM - 73D
31306	GILLINGHAM - 73D	GILLINGHAM - 73D	GILLINGHAM - 73D	GILLINGHAM - 73D	GILLINGHAM - 73D	GILLINGHAM - 73D	GILLINGHAM - 73D
31307	STEWARTS LANE - 73A	GILLINGHAM - 73D	GILLINGHAM - 73D	GILLINGHAM - 73D	GILLINGHAM - 73D	GILLINGHAM - 73D	GILLINGHAM - 73D
31308	GILLINGHAM - 73D	GILLINGHAM - 73D	GILLINGHAM - 73D	GILLINGHAM - 73D	GILLINGHAM - 73D	GILLINGHAM - 73D	GILLINGHAM - 73D
31309	RAMSGATE - 74B	RAMSGATE - 74B	RAMSGATE - 74B	RAMSGATE - 74B	RAMSGATE - 74B	RAMSGATE - 74B	RAMSGATE - 74B
31310	RAMSGATE - 74B	RAMSGATE - 74B	RAMSGATE - 74B	RAMSGATE - 74B	RAMSGATE - 74B	BRIGHTON - 75A	BRIGHTON - 75A
31311	REDHILL - 75B	REDHILL - 75B	REDHILL - 75B	REDHILL - 75B	REDHILL - 75B	REDHILL - 75B	REDHILL - 75B
31319	ST LEONARDS - 74E	ST LEONARDS - 74E	ST LEONARDS - 74E	ST LEONARDS - 74E	BRIGHTON - 75A	BRIGHTON - 75A	BRIGHTON - 75A
31320	STEWARTS LANE - 73A	STEWARTS LANE - 73A	STEWARTS LANE - 73A	STEWARTS LANE - 73A	STEWARTS LANE - 73A	STEWARTS LANE - 73A	BRIGHTON - 75A
31321	STEWARTS LANE - 73A	STEWARTS LANE - 73A	STEWARTS LANE - 73A	STEWARTS LANE - 73A	STEWARTS LANE - 73A	STEWARTS LANE - 73A	STEWARTS LANE - 73A
31322	T.WELLS - 75F	T.WELLS - 75F	T.WELLS - 75F	T.WELLS - 75F	T.WELLS - 75F	T.WELLS - 75F	T.WELLS - 75F
31324	RAMSGATE - 74B	RAMSGATE - 74B	RAMSGATE - 74B	RAMSGATE - 74B	RAMSGATE - 74B	RAMSGATE - 74B	RAMSGATE - 74B
31326	RAMSGATE - 74B	RAMSGATE - 74B	RAMSGATE - 74B	RAMSGATE - 74B	RAMSGATE - 74B	RAMSGATE - 74B	RAMSGATE - 74B
31327	ASHFORD - 74A	ASHFORD - 74A	ASHFORD - 74A	ASHFORD - 74A	ASHFORD - 74A	ASHFORD - 74A	ASHFORD - 74A
31328	DOVER - 74C	DOVER - 74C	DOVER - 74C	DOVER - 74C	DOVER - 74C	DOVER - 74C	DOVER - 74C
31329	ST LEONARDS - 74E	ST LEONARDS - 74E	ST LEONARDS - 74E	ST LEONARDS - 74E	DOVER - 74C	DOVER - 74C	DOVER - 74C
31500	FAVERSHAM - 73E	FAVERSHAM - 73E	ASHFORD - 74A	ASHFORD - 74A	ASHFORD - 74A	ASHFORD - 74A	ASHFORD - 74A
31503	FAVERSHAM - 73E	FAVERSHAM - 73E	FAVERSHAM - 73E	FAVERSHAM - 73E	FAVERSHAM - 73E	FAVERSHAM - 73E	FAVERSHAM - 73E
31512	ASHFORD - 74A	ASHFORD - 74A	ASHFORD - 74A	ASHFORD - 74A	ASHFORD - 74A	ASHFORD - 74A	ASHFORD - 74A
31517	T.WELLS - 75F	T.WELLS - 75F	T.WELLS - 75F	T.WELLS - 75F	T.WELLS - 75F	T.WELLS - 75F	T.WELLS - 75F
31518	ST LEONARDS - 74E	ST LEONARDS - 74E	GILLINGHAM - 73D	GILLINGHAM - 73D	GILLINGHAM - 73D	GILLINGHAM - 73D	GILLINGHAM - 73D
31519	ST LEONARDS - 74E	ST LEONARDS - 74E	FAVERSHAM - 73E	FAVERSHAM - 73E	ST LEONARDS - 74E	ST LEONARDS - 74E	ST LEONARDS - 74E
31520	T.WELLS - 75F	T.WELLS - 75F	T.WELLS - 75F	T.WELLS - 75F	T.WELLS - 75F	T.WELLS - 75F	T.WELLS - 75F
31521	DOVER - 74C	DOVER - 74C	DOVER - 74C	ASHFORD - 74A	ASHFORD - 74A	ASHFORD - 74A	ASHFORD - 74A
31522	ASHFORD - 74A	ASHFORD - 74A	ASHFORD - 74A	ASHFORD - 74A	ASHFORD - 74A	ASHFORD - 74A	ASHFORD - 74A
31523	TONBRIDGE - 74D	TONBRIDGE - 74D	TONBRIDGE - 74D	TONBRIDGE - 74D	TONBRIDGE - 74D	TONBRIDGE - 74D	TONBRIDGE - 74D
31530	DOVER - 74C	DOVER - 74C	DOVER - 74C	DOVER - 74C	TONBRIDGE - 74D	TONBRIDGE - 74D	TONBRIDGE - 74D
31531	DOVER - 74C	DOVER - 74C	DOVER - 74C	DOVER - 74C	DOVER - 74C	DOVER - 74C	DOVER - 74C
31533	B.ARMS - 73B	B.ARMS - 73B	B.ARMS - 73B	B.ARMS - 73B	B.ARMS - 73B	B.ARMS - 73B	B.ARMS - 73B
31540	DOVER - 74C	DOVER - 74C	DOVER - 74C	DOVER - 74C	DOVER - 74C	DOVER - 74C	DOVER - 74C
31542	B.ARMS - 73B	B.ARMS - 73B	B.ARMS - 73B	B.ARMS - 73B	B.ARMS - 73B	B.ARMS - 73B	B.ARMS - 73B
31543	B.ARMS - 73B	B.ARMS - 73B	B.ARMS - 73B	B.ARMS - 73B	B.ARMS - 73B	B.ARMS - 73B	TONBRIDGE - 74D
31544	B.ARMS - 73B	B.ARMS - 73B	B.ARMS - 73B	B.ARMS - 73B	B.ARMS - 73B	B.ARMS - 73B	B.ARMS - 73B
31548	TONBRIDGE - 74D	TONBRIDGE - 74D	TONBRIDGE - 74D	TONBRIDGE - 74D	TONBRIDGE - 74D	TONBRIDGE - 74D	TONBRIDGE - 74D
31550	NINE ELMS - 70A	NINE ELMS - 70A	NINE ELMS - 70A	NINE ELMS - 70A	NINE ELMS - 70A	REDHILL - 75B	REDHILL - 75B
31551	NINE ELMS - 70A	NINE ELMS - 70A	NINE ELMS - 70A	NINE ELMS - 70A	NINE ELMS - 70A	REDHILL - 75B	NINE ELMS - 70A
31552	NINE ELMS - 70A	NINE ELMS - 70A	NINE ELMS - 70A	NINE ELMS - 70A	NINE ELMS - 70A	TONBRIDGE - 74D	TONBRIDGE - 74D
31553	NINE ELMS - 70A	NINE ELMS - 70A	NINE ELMS - 70A	NINE ELMS - 70A	NINE ELMS - 70A	TONBRIDGE - 74D	B.ARMS - 73B
31554	TONBRIDGE - 74D	TONBRIDGE - 74D	TONBRIDGE - 74D	TONBRIDGE - 74D	TONBRIDGE - 74D	TONBRIDGE - 74D	TONBRIDGE - 74D
				O2 0-4-4T (1889)			
30177	DORCHESTER - 71C	DORCHESTER - 71C	DORCHESTER - 71C	EASTLEIGH - 71A	EASTLEIGH - 71A	EASTLEIGH - 71A	EASTLEIGH - 71A
30179	DORCHESTER - 71C	DORCHESTER - 71C	DORCHESTER - 71C	DORCHESTER - 71C	DORCHESTER - 71C	DORCHESTER - 71C	DORCHESTER - 71C
30182	PLYMOUTH - 72D	PLYMOUTH - 72D	YEOVIL - 72C	YEOVIL - 72C	YEOVIL - 72C	YEOVIL - 72C	YEOVIL - 72C
30183	PLYMOUTH - 72D	PLYMOUTH - 72D	PLYMOUTH - 72D	PLYMOUTH - 72D	FRATTON - 71D	FRATTON - 71D	PLYMOUTH - 72D
30192	WADEBRIDGE - 72F	WADEBRIDGE - 72F	PLYMOUTH - 72D	PLYMOUTH - 72D	PLYMOUTH - 72D	PLYMOUTH - 72D	PLYMOUTH - 72D
30193	EXMOUTH JCN - 72A	EXMOUTH JCN - 72A	EXMOUTH JCN - 72A	EXMOUTH JCN - 72A	WADEBRIDGE - 72F	EXMOUTH JCN - 72A	EXMOUTH JCN - 72A
30197	DORCHESTER - 71C	DORCHESTER - 71C	W/D	W/D	W/D	W/D	W/D
30199	EXMOUTH JCN - 72A	EXMOUTH JCN - 72A	EXMOUTH JCN - 72A	EXMOUTH JCN - 72A	EXMOUTH JCN - 72A	EXMOUTH JCN - 72A	EXMOUTH JCN - 72A
30200	WADEBRIDGE - 72F	WADEBRIDGE - 72F	WADEBRIDGE - 72F	WADEBRIDGE - 72F	WADEBRIDGE - 72F	WADEBRIDGE - 72F	WADEBRIDGE - 72F
30203	WADEBRIDGE - 72F	WADEBRIDGE - 72F	WADEBRIDGE - 72F	WADEBRIDGE - 72F	WADEBRIDGE - 72F	WADEBRIDGE - 72F	WADEBRIDGE - 72F
30204	BOURNEMOUTH - 71B	BOURNEMOUTH - 71B	W/D	W/D	W/D	W/D	W/D
30207	PLYMOUTH - 72D	PLYMOUTH - 72D	FRATTON - 71D	FRATTON - 71D	FRATTON - 71D	FRATTON - 71D	FRATTON - 71D
30212	BOURNEMOUTH - 71B	BOURNEMOUTH - 71B	BOURNEMOUTH - 71B	BOURNEMOUTH - 71B	BOURNEMOUTH - 71B	BOURNEMOUTH - 71B	BOURNEMOUTH - 71B
30213	EASTLEIGH - 71A	EASTLEIGH - 71A	W/D	W/D	W/D	W/D	W/D
30216	PLYMOUTH - 72D	PLYMOUTH - 72D	PLYMOUTH - 72D	PLYMOUTH - 72D	PLYMOUTH - 72D	PLYMOUTH - 72D	PLYMOUTH - 72D
30221	NINE ELMS - 70A	NINE ELMS - 70A	NINE ELMS - 70A	NINE ELMS - 70A	W/D	W/D	W/D
30223	BOURNEMOUTH - 71B	BOURNEMOUTH - 71B	BOURNEMOUTH - 71B	BOURNEMOUTH - 71B	BOURNEMOUTH - 71B	BOURNEMOUTH - 71B	BOURNEMOUTH - 71B
30224	EXMOUTH JCN - 72A	EXMOUTH JCN - 72A	EXMOUTH JCN - 72A	EXMOUTH JCN - 72A	NINE ELMS - 70A	NINE ELMS - 70A	NINE ELMS - 70A
30225	EASTLEIGH - 71A	EASTLEIGH - 71A	EASTLEIGH - 71A	EASTLEIGH - 71A	EASTLEIGH - 71A	EASTLEIGH - 71A	EASTLEIGH - 71A
30229	DORCHESTER - 71C	DORCHESTER - 71C	DORCHESTER - 71C	DORCHESTER - 71C	DORCHESTER - 71C	DORCHESTER - 71C	DORCHESTER - 71C
30230	FELTHAM - 70B	FELTHAM - 70B	FELTHAM - 70B	FELTHAM - 70B	FELTHAM - 70B	FELTHAM - 70B	FELTHAM - 70B
30231	DORCHESTER - 71C	DORCHESTER - 71C	W/D	W/D	W/D	W/D	W/D
30232	EXMOUTH JCN - 72A	EXMOUTH JCN - 72A	EXMOUTH JCN - 72A	EXMOUTH JCN - 72A	EXMOUTH JCN - 72A	EXMOUTH JCN - 72A	EXMOUTH JCN - 72A
30233	EASTLEIGH - 71A	EASTLEIGH - 71A	EASTLEIGH - 71A	EASTLEIGH - 71A	EASTLEIGH - 71A	EASTLEIGH - 71A	EASTLEIGH - 71A
30236	PLYMOUTH - 72D	PLYMOUTH - 72D	PLYMOUTH - 72D	PLYMOUTH - 72D	PLYMOUTH - 72D	PLYMOUTH - 72D	PLYMOUTH - 72D

loco	Jan-54	Mar-54	May-54	Jun-54	Aug-54	Oct-54	Dec-54
				H 0-4-4T (1904)			
31005	STEWARTS LANE - 73A	STEWARTS LANE - 73A	STEWARTS LANE - 73A	STEWARTS LANE - 73A	STEWARTS LANE - 73A	STEWARTS LANE - 73A	STEWARTS LANE - 73A
31158	GILLINGHAM - 73D	GILLINGHAM - 73D	GILLINGHAM - 73D	GILLINGHAM - 73D	GILLINGHAM - 73D	GILLINGHAM - 73D	GILLINGHAM - 73D
31161	GILLINGHAM - 73D	GILLINGHAM - 73D	GILLINGHAM - 73D	GILLINGHAM - 73D	GILLINGHAM - 73D	GILLINGHAM - 73D	GILLINGHAM - 73D
31162	ST LEONARDS - 74E	ST LEONARDS - 74E	ST LEONARDS - 74E	ST LEONARDS - 74E	ST LEONARDS - 74E	ST LEONARDS - 74E	ST LEONARDS - 74E
31164	TONBRIDGE - 74D	TONBRIDGE - 74D	TONBRIDGE - 74D	TONBRIDGE - 74D	TONBRIDGE - 74D	TONBRIDGE - 74D	TONBRIDGE - 74D
31177	TONBRIDGE - 74D	TONBRIDGE - 74D	TONBRIDGE - 74D	TONBRIDGE - 74D	TONBRIDGE - 74D	TONBRIDGE - 74D	TONBRIDGE - 74D
31184	STEWARTS LANE - 73A	STEWARTS LANE - 73A	STEWARTS LANE - 73A	STEWARTS LANE - 73A	STEWARTS LANE - 73A	STEWARTS LANE - 73A	STEWARTS LANE - 73A
31193	TONBRIDGE - 74D	TONBRIDGE - 74D	TONBRIDGE - 74D	TONBRIDGE - 74D	TONBRIDGE - 74D	TONBRIDGE - 74D	TONBRIDGE - 74D
31239	ASHFORD - 74A	ASHFORD - 74A	ASHFORD - 74A	ASHFORD - 74A	ASHFORD - 74A	ASHFORD - 74A	ASHFORD - 74A
31259	FAVERSHAM - 73E	FAVERSHAM - 73E	FAVERSHAM - 73E	FAVERSHAM - 73E	FAVERSHAM - 73E	FAVERSHAM - 73E	FAVERSHAM - 73E
31261	STEWARTS LANE - 73A	STEWARTS LANE - 73A	STEWARTS LANE - 73A	STEWARTS LANE - 73A	STEWARTS LANE - 73A	STEWARTS LANE - 73A	STEWARTS LANE - 73A
31263	STEWARTS LANE - 73A	STEWARTS LANE - 73A	STEWARTS LANE - 73A	STEWARTS LANE - 73A	STEWARTS LANE - 73A	STEWARTS LANE - 73A	STEWARTS LANE - 73A
31265	RAMSGATE - 74B	RAMSGATE - 74B	RAMSGATE - 74B	RAMSGATE - 74B	RAMSGATE - 74B	RAMSGATE - 74B	RAMSGATE - 74B
31266	STEWARTS LANE - 73A	STEWARTS LANE - 73A	STEWARTS LANE - 73A	STEWARTS LANE - 73A	STEWARTS LANE - 73A	STEWARTS LANE - 73A	STEWARTS LANE - 73A
31269	ST LEONARDS - 74E	ST LEONARDS - 74E	ST LEONARDS - 74E	ST LEONARDS - 74E	ST LEONARDS - 74E	ST LEONARDS - 74E	ST LEONARDS - 74E
31274	ST LEONARDS - 74E	ST LEONARDS - 74E	ST LEONARDS - 74E	ST LEONARDS - 74E	ST LEONARDS - 74E	ST LEONARDS - 74E	ST LEONARDS - 74E
31276	ASHFORD - 74A	ASHFORD - 74A	ASHFORD - 74A	ASHFORD - 74A	ASHFORD - 74A	ASHFORD - 74A	ASHFORD - 74A
31278	DOVER - 74C	DOVER - 74C	DOVER - 74C	DOVER - 74C	DOVER - 74C	DOVER - 74C	DOVER - 74C
31279	ST LEONARDS - 74E	ST LEONARDS - 74E	ST LEONARDS - 74E	ST LEONARDS - 74E	ST LEONARDS - 74E	ST LEONARDS - 74E	ST LEONARDS - 74E
31295	ST LEONARDS - 74E	ST LEONARDS - 74E	ST LEONARDS - 74E	ST LEONARDS - 74E	ST LEONARDS - 74E	ST LEONARDS - 74E	ST LEONARDS - 74E
31305	GILLINGHAM - 73D	GILLINGHAM - 73D	GILLINGHAM - 73D	GILLINGHAM - 73D	GILLINGHAM - 73D	GILLINGHAM - 73D	FAVERSHAM - 73E
31306	GILLINGHAM - 73D	GILLINGHAM - 73D	GILLINGHAM - 73D	GILLINGHAM - 73D	GILLINGHAM - 73D	GILLINGHAM - 73D	B.ARMS - 73B
31307	GILLINGHAM - 73D	GILLINGHAM - 73D	GILLINGHAM - 73D	GILLINGHAM - 73D	GILLINGHAM - 73D	GILLINGHAM - 73D	GILLINGHAM - 73D
31308	GILLINGHAM - 73D	GILLINGHAM - 73D	GILLINGHAM - 73D	GILLINGHAM - 73D	GILLINGHAM - 73D	GILLINGHAM - 73D	GILLINGHAM - 73D
31309	RAMSGATE - 74B	RAMSGATE - 74B	REDHILL - 75B	REDHILL - 75B	REDHILL - 75B	REDHILL - 75B	REDHILL - 75B
31310	BRIGHTON - 75A	BRIGHTON - 75A	BRIGHTON - 75A	BRIGHTON - 75A	BRIGHTON - 75A	BRIGHTON - 75A	BRIGHTON - 75A
31311	REDHILL - 75B	REDHILL - 75B	REDHILL - 75B	REDHILL - 75B	REDHILL - 75B	REDHILL - 75B	W/D
31319	BRIGHTON - 75A	BRIGHTON - 75A	BRIGHTON - 75A	BRIGHTON - 75A	BRIGHTON - 75A	BRIGHTON - 75A	BRIGHTON - 75A
31320	BRIGHTON - 75A	BRIGHTON - 75A	BRIGHTON - 75A	BRIGHTON - 75A	BRIGHTON - 75A	BRIGHTON - 75A	BRIGHTON - 75A
31321	STEWARTS LANE - 73A	STEWARTS LANE - 73A	STEWARTS LANE - 73A	STEWARTS LANE - 73A	STEWARTS LANE - 73A	STEWARTS LANE - 73A	STEWARTS LANE - 73A
31322	T.WELLS - 75F	T.WELLS - 75F	T.WELLS - 75F	T.WELLS - 75F	T.WELLS - 75F	T.WELLS - 75F	T.WELLS - 75F
31324	RAMSGATE - 74B	RAMSGATE - 74B	RAMSGATE - 74B	RAMSGATE - 74B	RAMSGATE - 74B	RAMSGATE - 74B	RAMSGATE - 74B
31326	RAMSGATE - 74B	RAMSGATE - 74B	RAMSGATE - 74B	RAMSGATE - 74B	RAMSGATE - 74B	RAMSGATE - 74B	RAMSGATE - 74B
31327	ASHFORD - 74A	ASHFORD - 74A	ASHFORD - 74A	ASHFORD - 74A	ASHFORD - 74A	ASHFORD - 74A	ASHFORD - 74A
31328	DOVER - 74C	DOVER - 74C	DOVER - 74C	DOVER - 74C	DOVER - 74C	DOVER - 74C	DOVER - 74C
31329	DOVER - 74C	DOVER - 74C	DOVER - 74C	DOVER - 74C	DOVER - 74C	DOVER - 74C	DOVER - 74C
31500	ASHFORD - 74A	ASHFORD - 74A	ASHFORD - 74A	ASHFORD - 74A	ASHFORD - 74A	ASHFORD - 74A	ASHFORD - 74A
31503	FAVERSHAM - 73E	FAVERSHAM - 73E	FAVERSHAM - 73E	FAVERSHAM - 73E	FAVERSHAM - 73E	FAVERSHAM - 73E	FAVERSHAM - 73E
31512	ASHFORD - 74A	ASHFORD - 74A	ASHFORD - 74A	ASHFORD - 74A	ASHFORD - 74A	ASHFORD - 74A	ASHFORD - 74A
31517	T.WELLS - 75F	T.WELLS - 75F	T.WELLS - 75F	T.WELLS - 75F	T.WELLS - 75F	T.WELLS - 75F	T.WELLS - 75F
31518	GILLINGHAM - 73D	GILLINGHAM - 73D	GILLINGHAM - 73D	GILLINGHAM - 73D	GILLINGHAM - 73D	GILLINGHAM - 73D	GILLINGHAM - 73D
31519	ST LEONARDS - 74E	ST LEONARDS - 74E	ST LEONARDS - 74E	ST LEONARDS - 74E	ST LEONARDS - 74E	ST LEONARDS - 74E	ST LEONARDS - 74E
31520	T.WELLS - 75F	T.WELLS - 75F	T.WELLS - 75F	T.WELLS - 75F	T.WELLS - 75F	T.WELLS - 75F	T.WELLS - 75F
31521	ASHFORD - 74A	ASHFORD - 74A	ASHFORD - 74A	ASHFORD - 74A	ASHFORD - 74A	ASHFORD - 74A	ASHFORD - 74A
31522	ASHFORD - 74A	ASHFORD - 74A	ASHFORD - 74A	ASHFORD - 74A	ASHFORD - 74A	ASHFORD - 74A	ASHFORD - 74A
31523	TONBRIDGE - 74D	TONBRIDGE - 74D	TONBRIDGE - 74D	TONBRIDGE - 74D	TONBRIDGE - 74D	TONBRIDGE - 74D	TONBRIDGE - 74D
31530	TONBRIDGE - 74D	TONBRIDGE - 74D	TONBRIDGE - 74D	TONBRIDGE - 74D	TONBRIDGE - 74D	TONBRIDGE - 74D	TONBRIDGE - 74D
31531	DOVER - 74C	DOVER - 74C	DOVER - 74C	DOVER - 74C	DOVER - 74C	DOVER - 74C	DOVER - 74C
31533	B.ARMS - 73B	B.ARMS - 73B	B.ARMS - 73B	B.ARMS - 73B	B.ARMS - 73B	B.ARMS - 73B	B.ARMS - 73B
31540	DOVER - 74C	DOVER - 74C	DOVER - 74C	DOVER - 74C	DOVER - 74C	DOVER - 74C	DOVER - 74C
31542	B.ARMS - 73B	B.ARMS - 73B	B.ARMS - 73B	B.ARMS - 73B	B.ARMS - 73B	B.ARMS - 73B	B.ARMS - 73B
31543	TONBRIDGE - 74D	TONBRIDGE - 74D	TONBRIDGE - 74D	TONBRIDGE - 74D	TONBRIDGE - 74D	TONBRIDGE - 74D	TONBRIDGE - 74D
31544	B.ARMS - 73B	B.ARMS - 73B	B.ARMS - 73B	TONBRIDGE - 74D	TONBRIDGE - 74D	TONBRIDGE - 74D	TONBRIDGE - 74D
31548	TONBRIDGE - 74D	TONBRIDGE - 74D	TONBRIDGE - 74D	TONBRIDGE - 74D	TONBRIDGE - 74D	TONBRIDGE - 74D	TONBRIDGE - 74D
31550	REDHILL - 75B	REDHILL - 75B	REDHILL - 75B	STEWARTS LANE - 73A	STEWARTS LANE - 73A	STEWARTS LANE - 73A	STEWARTS LANE - 73A
31551	REDHILL - 75B	REDHILL - 75B	STEWARTS LANE - 73A	STEWARTS LANE - 73A	STEWARTS LANE - 73A	STEWARTS LANE - 73A	STEWARTS LANE - 73A
31552	TONBRIDGE - 74D	TONBRIDGE - 74D	TONBRIDGE - 74D	STEWARTS LANE - 73A	STEWARTS LANE - 73A	STEWARTS LANE - 73A	STEWARTS LANE - 73A
31553	B.ARMS - 73B	B.ARMS - 73B	B.ARMS - 73B	B.ARMS - 73B	B.ARMS - 73B	B.ARMS - 73B	B.ARMS - 73B
31554	TONBRIDGE - 74D	TONBRIDGE - 74D	TONBRIDGE - 74D	TONBRIDGE - 74D	TONBRIDGE - 74D	TONBRIDGE - 74D	TONBRIDGE - 74D
				O2 0-4-4T (1889)			
30177	EASTLEIGH - 71A	EASTLEIGH - 71A	EASTLEIGH - 71A	EASTLEIGH - 71A	EASTLEIGH - 71A	EASTLEIGH - 71A	EASTLEIGH - 71A
30179	EASTLEIGH - 71A	EASTLEIGH - 71A	EASTLEIGH - 71A	EASTLEIGH - 71A	EASTLEIGH - 71A	EASTLEIGH - 71A	EASTLEIGH - 71A
30182	YEOVIL - 72C	YEOVIL - 72C	YEOVIL - 72C	YEOVIL - 72C	YEOVIL - 72C	YEOVIL - 72C	YEOVIL - 72C
30183	PLYMOUTH - 72D	PLYMOUTH - 72D	PLYMOUTH - 72D	PLYMOUTH - 72D	PLYMOUTH - 72D	PLYMOUTH - 72D	PLYMOUTH - 72D
30192	PLYMOUTH - 72D	PLYMOUTH - 72D	PLYMOUTH - 72D	PLYMOUTH - 72D	PLYMOUTH - 72D	PLYMOUTH - 72D	PLYMOUTH - 72D
30193	EXMOUTH JCN - 72A	EXMOUTH JCN - 72A	EXMOUTH JCN - 72A	EXMOUTH JCN - 72A	EXMOUTH JCN - 72A	EXMOUTH JCN - 72A	EXMOUTH JCN - 72A
30199	EXMOUTH JCN - 72A	EXMOUTH JCN - 72A	EXMOUTH JCN - 72A	EXMOUTH JCN - 72A	EXMOUTH JCN - 72A	EXMOUTH JCN - 72A	EXMOUTH JCN - 72A
30200	WADEBRIDGE - 72F	WADEBRIDGE - 72F	WADEBRIDGE - 72F	WADEBRIDGE - 72F	WADEBRIDGE - 72F	WADEBRIDGE - 72F	WADEBRIDGE - 72F
30203	WADEBRIDGE - 72F	WADEBRIDGE - 72F	WADEBRIDGE - 72F	WADEBRIDGE - 72F	WADEBRIDGE - 72F	WADEBRIDGE - 72F	WADEBRIDGE - 72F
30207	FRATTON - 71D	FRATTON - 71D	FRATTON - 71D	FRATTON - 71D	FRATTON - 71D	FRATTON - 70F	FRATTON - 70F
30212	BOURNEMOUTH - 71B	BOURNEMOUTH - 71B	BOURNEMOUTH - 71B	BOURNEMOUTH - 71B	BOURNEMOUTH - 71B	BOURNEMOUTH - 71B	BOURNEMOUTH - 71B
30216	PLYMOUTH - 72D	PLYMOUTH - 72D	PLYMOUTH - 72D	PLYMOUTH - 72D	PLYMOUTH - 72D	PLYMOUTH - 72D	PLYMOUTH - 72D
30223	BOURNEMOUTH - 71B	BOURNEMOUTH - 71B	BOURNEMOUTH - 71B	BOURNEMOUTH - 71B	BOURNEMOUTH - 71B	BOURNEMOUTH - 71B	BOURNEMOUTH - 71B
30224	NINE ELMS - 70A	NINE ELMS - 70A	NINE ELMS - 70A	NINE ELMS - 70A	NINE ELMS - 70A	NINE ELMS - 70A	NINE ELMS - 70A
30225	EASTLEIGH - 71A	EASTLEIGH - 71A	PLYMOUTH - 72D	PLYMOUTH - 72D	PLYMOUTH - 72D	PLYMOUTH - 72D	PLYMOUTH - 72D
30229	DORCHESTER - 71C	DORCHESTER - 71C	DORCHESTER - 71C	DORCHESTER - 71C	DORCHESTER - 71C	DORCHESTER - 71C	DORCHESTER - 71C
30230	FELTHAM - 70B	FELTHAM - 70B	FELTHAM - 70B	FELTHAM - 70B	FELTHAM - 70B	FELTHAM - 70B	FELTHAM - 70B
30232	EXMOUTH JCN - 72A	EXMOUTH JCN - 72A	EXMOUTH JCN - 72A	EXMOUTH JCN - 72A	EXMOUTH JCN - 72A	EXMOUTH JCN - 72A	EXMOUTH JCN - 72A
30233	EASTLEIGH - 71A	EASTLEIGH - 71A	EASTLEIGH - 71A	EASTLEIGH - 71A	EASTLEIGH - 71A	EASTLEIGH - 71A	EASTLEIGH - 71A
30236	PLYMOUTH - 72D	PLYMOUTH - 72D	PLYMOUTH - 72D	PLYMOUTH - 72D	PLYMOUTH - 72D	PLYMOUTH - 72D	PLYMOUTH - 72D

loco	Feb-55	Apr-55	Jun-55	Aug-55	Sep-55	Nov-55	Dec-55
				H 0-4-4T (1904)			
31005	STEWARTS LANE - 73A	STEWARTS LANE - 73A	ASHFORD - 74A	ASHFORD - 74A	ASHFORD - 74A	ASHFORD - 74A	ASHFORD - 74A
31158	GILLINGHAM - 73D	W/D	W/D	W/D	W/D	W/D	W/D
31161	GILLINGHAM - 73D	GILLINGHAM - 73D	GILLINGHAM - 73D	GILLINGHAM - 73D	GILLINGHAM - 73D	GILLINGHAM - 73D	GILLINGHAM - 73D
31162	ST LEONARDS - 74E	ST LEONARDS - 74E	ST LEONARDS - 74E	ST LEONARDS - 74E	ST LEONARDS - 74E	ST LEONARDS - 74E	ST LEONARDS - 74E
31164	TONBRIDGE - 74D	TONBRIDGE - 74D	TONBRIDGE - 74D	TONBRIDGE - 74D	TONBRIDGE - 74D	TONBRIDGE - 74D	TONBRIDGE - 74D
31177	TONBRIDGE - 74D	TONBRIDGE - 74D	TONBRIDGE - 74D	TONBRIDGE - 74D	TONBRIDGE - 74D	TONBRIDGE - 74D	TONBRIDGE - 74D
31184	STEWARTS LANE - 73A	STEWARTS LANE - 73A	STEWARTS LANE - 73A	STEWARTS LANE - 73A	STEWARTS LANE - 73A	STEWARTS LANE - 73A	STEWARTS LANE - 73A
31193	TONBRIDGE - 74D	TONBRIDGE - 74D	TONBRIDGE - 74D	TONBRIDGE - 74D	TONBRIDGE - 74D	TONBRIDGE - 74D	TONBRIDGE - 74D
31239	ASHFORD - 74A	ASHFORD - 74A	ASHFORD - 74A	ASHFORD - 74A	ASHFORD - 74A	ASHFORD - 74A	ASHFORD - 74A
31259	FAVERSHAM - 73E	FAVERSHAM - 73E	FAVERSHAM - 73E	FAVERSHAM - 73E	FAVERSHAM - 73E	FAVERSHAM - 73E	FAVERSHAM - 73E
31261	STEWARTS LANE - 73A	STEWARTS LANE - 73A	STEWARTS LANE - 73A	STEWARTS LANE - 73A	STEWARTS LANE - 73A	STEWARTS LANE - 73A	STEWARTS LANE - 73A
31263	STEWARTS LANE - 73A	STEWARTS LANE - 73A	REDHILL - 75B	REDHILL - 75B	REDHILL - 75B	REDHILL - 75B	REDHILL - 75B
31265	RAMSGATE - 74B	RAMSGATE - 74B	RAMSGATE - 74B	RAMSGATE - 74B	RAMSGATE - 74B	RAMSGATE - 74B	RAMSGATE - 74B
31266	STEWARTS LANE - 73A	STEWARTS LANE - 73A	STEWARTS LANE - 73A	STEWARTS LANE - 73A	STEWARTS LANE - 73A	STEWARTS LANE - 73A	STEWARTS LANE - 73A
31269	ST LEONARDS - 74E	ST LEONARDS - 74E	ST LEONARDS - 74E	ST LEONARDS - 74E	ST LEONARDS - 74E	ST LEONARDS - 74E	ST LEONARDS - 74E
31274	ST LEONARDS - 74E	ST LEONARDS - 74E	ST LEONARDS - 74E	ST LEONARDS - 74E	ST LEONARDS - 74E	ST LEONARDS - 74E	ST LEONARDS - 74E
31276	ASHFORD - 74A	ASHFORD - 74A	ASHFORD - 74A	ASHFORD - 74A	ASHFORD - 74A	ASHFORD - 74A	ASHFORD - 74A
31278	DOVER - 74C	DOVER - 74C	DOVER - 74C	DOVER - 74C	DOVER - 74C	DOVER - 74C	DOVER - 74C
31279	ST LEONARDS - 74E	ST LEONARDS - 74E	ST LEONARDS - 74E	ST LEONARDS - 74E	ST LEONARDS - 74E	ST LEONARDS - 74E	ST LEONARDS - 74E
31295	ST LEONARDS - 74E	ST LEONARDS - 74E	ST LEONARDS - 74E	ST LEONARDS - 74E	ST LEONARDS - 74E	ST LEONARDS - 74E	ST LEONARDS - 74E
31305	FAVERSHAM - 73E	FAVERSHAM - 73E	FAVERSHAM - 73E	FAVERSHAM - 73E	B.ARMS - 73B	B.ARMS - 73B	B.ARMS - 73B
31306	B.ARMS - 73B	B.ARMS - 73B	B.ARMS - 73B	B.ARMS - 73B	B.ARMS - 73B	B.ARMS - 73B	B.ARMS - 73B
31307	GILLINGHAM - 73D	GILLINGHAM - 73D	GILLINGHAM - 73D	GILLINGHAM - 73D	GILLINGHAM - 73D	GILLINGHAM - 73D	ASHFORD - 74A
31308	GILLINGHAM - 73D	GILLINGHAM - 73D	GILLINGHAM - 73D	GILLINGHAM - 73D	GILLINGHAM - 73D	GILLINGHAM - 73D	GILLINGHAM - 73D
31309	REDHILL - 75B	REDHILL - 75B	W/D	W/D	W/D	W/D	W/D
31310	BRIGHTON - 75A	BRIGHTON - 75A	RAMSGATE - 74B	RAMSGATE - 74B	ASHFORD - 74A	ASHFORD - 74A	ASHFORD - 74A
31319	BRIGHTON - 75A	BRIGHTON - 75A	REDHILL - 75B	REDHILL - 75B	BRIGHTON - 75A	BRIGHTON - 75A	BRIGHTON - 75A
31320	BRIGHTON - 75A	BRIGHTON - 75A	GILLINGHAM - 73D	GILLINGHAM - 73D	GILLINGHAM - 73D	GILLINGHAM - 73D	GILLINGHAM - 73D
31321	STEWARTS LANE - 73A	STEWARTS LANE - 73A	STEWARTS LANE - 73A	STEWARTS LANE - 73A	STEWARTS LANE - 73A	STEWARTS LANE - 73A	STEWARTS LANE - 73A
31322	T.WELLS - 75F	T.WELLS - 75F	GILLINGHAM - 73D	GILLINGHAM - 73D	GILLINGHAM - 73D	GILLINGHAM - 73D	GILLINGHAM - 73D
31324	RAMSGATE - 74B	RAMSGATE - 74B	RAMSGATE - 74B	RAMSGATE - 74B	RAMSGATE - 74B	RAMSGATE - 74B	RAMSGATE - 74B
31326	RAMSGATE - 74B	RAMSGATE - 74B	RAMSGATE - 74B	RAMSGATE - 74B	RAMSGATE - 74B	RAMSGATE - 74B	RAMSGATE - 74B
31327	ASHFORD - 74A	ASHFORD - 74A	ASHFORD - 74A	ASHFORD - 74A	ASHFORD - 74A	ASHFORD - 74A	ASHFORD - 74A
31328	DOVER - 74C	DOVER - 74C	DOVER - 74C	DOVER - 74C	DOVER - 74C	DOVER - 74C	DOVER - 74C
31329	DOVER - 74C	DOVER - 74C	DOVER - 74C	DOVER - 74C	DOVER - 74C	DOVER - 74C	DOVER - 74C
31500	ASHFORD - 74A	ASHFORD - 74A	ASHFORD - 74A	ASHFORD - 74A	RAMSGATE - 74B	RAMSGATE - 74B	RAMSGATE - 74B
31503	FAVERSHAM - 73E	FAVERSHAM - 73E	FAVERSHAM - 73E	FAVERSHAM - 73E	FAVERSHAM - 73E	FAVERSHAM - 73E	FAVERSHAM - 73E
31512	ASHFORD - 74A	ASHFORD - 74A	ASHFORD - 74A	ASHFORD - 74A	ASHFORD - 74A	ASHFORD - 74A	GILLINGHAM - 73D
31517	T.WELLS - 75F	T.WELLS - 75F	TONBRIDGE - 74D	TONBRIDGE - 74D	TONBRIDGE - 74D	TONBRIDGE - 74D	TONBRIDGE - 74D
31518	GILLINGHAM - 73D	GILLINGHAM - 73D	GILLINGHAM - 73D	GILLINGHAM - 73D	GILLINGHAM - 73D	GILLINGHAM - 73D	GILLINGHAM - 73D
31519	ST LEONARDS - 74E	ST LEONARDS - 74E	ST LEONARDS - 74E	ST LEONARDS - 74E	ST LEONARDS - 74E	ST LEONARDS - 74E	ST LEONARDS - 74E
31520	T.WELLS - 75F	T.WELLS - 75F	ST LEONARDS - 74E	ST LEONARDS - 74E	ST LEONARDS - 74E	ST LEONARDS - 74E	ST LEONARDS - 74E
31521	ASHFORD - 74A	ASHFORD - 74A	ASHFORD - 74A	ASHFORD - 74A	ASHFORD - 74A	ASHFORD - 74A	ASHFORD - 74A
31522	ASHFORD - 74A	ASHFORD - 74A	ASHFORD - 74A	ASHFORD - 74A	ASHFORD - 74A	ASHFORD - 74A	ASHFORD - 74A
31523	TONBRIDGE - 74D	TONBRIDGE - 74D	TONBRIDGE - 74D	TONBRIDGE - 74D	TONBRIDGE - 74D	TONBRIDGE - 74D	TONBRIDGE - 74D
31530	TONBRIDGE - 74D	TONBRIDGE - 74D	TONBRIDGE - 74D	TONBRIDGE - 74D	TONBRIDGE - 74D	TONBRIDGE - 74D	TONBRIDGE - 74D
31531	DOVER - 74C	W/D	W/D	W/D	W/D	W/D	W/D
31533	B.ARMS - 73B	B.ARMS - 73B	B.ARMS - 73B	B.ARMS - 73B	B.ARMS - 73B	B.ARMS - 73B	B.ARMS - 73B
31540	DOVER - 74C	DOVER - 74C	DOVER - 74C	DOVER - 74C	B.ARMS - 73B	B.ARMS - 73B	B.ARMS - 73B
31542	B.ARMS - 73B	B.ARMS - 73B	B.ARMS - 73B	B.ARMS - 73B	B.ARMS - 73B	B.ARMS - 73B	B.ARMS - 73B
31543	TONBRIDGE - 74D	TONBRIDGE - 74D	TONBRIDGE - 74D	TONBRIDGE - 74D	TONBRIDGE - 74D	TONBRIDGE - 74D	TONBRIDGE - 74D
31544	TONBRIDGE - 74D	TONBRIDGE - 74D	TONBRIDGE - 74D	TONBRIDGE - 74D	TONBRIDGE - 74D	TONBRIDGE - 74D	TONBRIDGE - 74D
31548	TONBRIDGE - 74D	TONBRIDGE - 74D	TONBRIDGE - 74D	TONBRIDGE - 74D	TONBRIDGE - 74D	TONBRIDGE - 74D	TONBRIDGE - 74D
31550	STEWARTS LANE - 73A	STEWARTS LANE - 73A	STEWARTS LANE - 73A	STEWARTS LANE - 73A	STEWARTS LANE - 73A	STEWARTS LANE - 73A	STEWARTS LANE - 73A
31551	STEWARTS LANE - 73A	STEWARTS LANE - 73A	STEWARTS LANE - 73A	STEWARTS LANE - 73A	STEWARTS LANE - 73A	STEWARTS LANE - 73A	STEWARTS LANE - 73A
31552	STEWARTS LANE - 73A	STEWARTS LANE - 73A	STEWARTS LANE - 73A	STEWARTS LANE - 73A	STEWARTS LANE - 73A	STEWARTS LANE - 73A	STEWARTS LANE - 73A
31553	B.ARMS - 73B	B.ARMS - 73B	B.ARMS - 73B	B.ARMS - 73B	B.ARMS - 73B	B.ARMS - 73B	B.ARMS - 73B
31554	TONBRIDGE - 74D	TONBRIDGE - 74D	TONBRIDGE - 74D	TONBRIDGE - 74D	TONBRIDGE - 74D	TONBRIDGE - 74D	TONBRIDGE - 74D
				O2 0-4-4T (1889)			
30177	EASTLEIGH - 71A	EASTLEIGH - 71A	EASTLEIGH - 71A	EASTLEIGH - 71A	EASTLEIGH - 71A	EASTLEIGH - 71A	EASTLEIGH - 71A
30179	EASTLEIGH - 71A	EASTLEIGH - 71A	EASTLEIGH - 71A	EASTLEIGH - 71A	EASTLEIGH - 71A	EASTLEIGH - 71A	EASTLEIGH - 71A
30182	YEOVIL - 72C	YEOVIL - 72C	YEOVIL - 72C	YEOVIL - 72C	YEOVIL - 72C	YEOVIL - 72C	YEOVIL - 72C
30183	PLYMOUTH - 72D	PLYMOUTH - 72D	PLYMOUTH - 72D	PLYMOUTH - 72D	PLYMOUTH - 72D	PLYMOUTH - 72D	PLYMOUTH - 72D
30192	PLYMOUTH - 72D	PLYMOUTH - 72D	PLYMOUTH - 72D	PLYMOUTH - 72D	PLYMOUTH - 72D	PLYMOUTH - 72D	PLYMOUTH - 72D
30193	EXMOUTH JCN - 72A	EXMOUTH JCN - 72A	EXMOUTH JCN - 72A	EXMOUTH JCN - 72A	EXMOUTH JCN - 72A	EXMOUTH JCN - 72A	EXMOUTH JCN - 72A
30199	EXMOUTH JCN - 72A	EXMOUTH JCN - 72A	EXMOUTH JCN - 72A	EXMOUTH JCN - 72A	EXMOUTH JCN - 72A	EXMOUTH JCN - 72A	EXMOUTH JCN - 72A
30200	WADEBRIDGE - 72F	WADEBRIDGE - 72F	WADEBRIDGE - 72F	WADEBRIDGE - 72F	WADEBRIDGE - 72F	WADEBRIDGE - 72F	WADEBRIDGE - 72F
30203	WADEBRIDGE - 72F	WADEBRIDGE - 72F	WADEBRIDGE - 72F	WADEBRIDGE - 72F	WADEBRIDGE - 72F	WADEBRIDGE - 72F	WADEBRIDGE - 72F
30207	FRATTON - 70F	FRATTON - 70F	FRATTON - 70F	FRATTON - 70F	FRATTON - 70F	FRATTON - 70F	FRATTON - 70F
30212	BOURNEMOUTH - 71B	BOURNEMOUTH - 71B	BOURNEMOUTH - 71B	BOURNEMOUTH - 71B	BOURNEMOUTH - 71B	BOURNEMOUTH - 71B	BOURNEMOUTH - 71B
30216	PLYMOUTH - 72D	PLYMOUTH - 72D	PLYMOUTH - 72D	PLYMOUTH - 72D	PLYMOUTH - 72D	PLYMOUTH - 72D	PLYMOUTH - 72D
30223	BOURNEMOUTH - 71B	BOURNEMOUTH - 71B	BOURNEMOUTH - 71B	BOURNEMOUTH - 71B	BOURNEMOUTH - 71B	BOURNEMOUTH - 71B	BOURNEMOUTH - 71B
30224	NINE ELMS - 70A	NINE ELMS - 70A	NINE ELMS - 70A	NINE ELMS - 70A	NINE ELMS - 70A	NINE ELMS - 70A	NINE ELMS - 70A
30225	PLYMOUTH - 72D	PLYMOUTH - 72D	PLYMOUTH - 72D	PLYMOUTH - 72D	PLYMOUTH - 72D	PLYMOUTH - 72D	PLYMOUTH - 72D
30229	DORCHESTER - 71C	DORCHESTER - 71C	DORCHESTER - 71C	DORCHESTER - 71C	DORCHESTER - 71C	DORCHESTER - 71C	DORCHESTER - 71C
30230	FELTHAM - 70B	FELTHAM - 70B	FELTHAM - 70B	FELTHAM - 70B	FELTHAM - 70B	FELTHAM - 70B	FELTHAM - 70B
30232	EXMOUTH JCN - 72A	EXMOUTH JCN - 72A	EXMOUTH JCN - 72A	EXMOUTH JCN - 72A	EXMOUTH JCN - 72A	EXMOUTH JCN - 72A	EXMOUTH JCN - 72A
30233	EASTLEIGH - 71A	EASTLEIGH - 71A	EASTLEIGH - 71A	EASTLEIGH - 71A	EASTLEIGH - 71A	EASTLEIGH - 71A	EASTLEIGH - 71A
30236	PLYMOUTH - 72D	PLYMOUTH - 72D	PLYMOUTH - 72D	PLYMOUTH - 72D	PLYMOUTH - 72D	PLYMOUTH - 72D	WADEBRIDGE - 72F

				H 0-4-4T (1904)			
31005	ASHFORD - 74A	ASHFORD - 74A	ASHFORD - 74A	ASHFORD - 74A	ASHFORD - 74A	ASHFORD - 74A	ASHFORD - 74A
31161	GILLINGHAM - 73D	GILLINGHAM - 73D	GILLINGHAM - 73D	GILLINGHAM - 73D	GILLINGHAM - 73D	GILLINGHAM - 73D	GILLINGHAM - 73D
31162	ST LEONARDS - 74E	ST LEONARDS - 74E	ST LEONARDS - 74E	ST LEONARDS - 74E	ST LEONARDS - 74E	ST LEONARDS - 74E	ST LEONARDS - 74E
31164	TONBRIDGE - 74D	TONBRIDGE - 74D	TONBRIDGE - 74D	TONBRIDGE - 74D	TONBRIDGE - 74D	TONBRIDGE - 74D	TONBRIDGE - 74D
31177	TONBRIDGE - 74D	TONBRIDGE - 74D	TONBRIDGE - 74D	TONBRIDGE - 74D	TONBRIDGE - 74D	TONBRIDGE - 74D	TONBRIDGE - 74D
31184	STEWARTS LANE - 73A	STEWARTS LANE - 73A	STEWARTS LANE - 73A	STEWARTS LANE - 73A	STEWARTS LANE - 73A	STEWARTS LANE - 73A	STEWARTS LANE - 73A
31193	TONBRIDGE - 74D	TONBRIDGE - 74D	TONBRIDGE - 74D	TONBRIDGE - 74D	TONBRIDGE - 74D	TONBRIDGE - 74D	TONBRIDGE - 74D
31239	ASHFORD - 74A	ASHFORD - 74A	ASHFORD - 74A	ASHFORD - 74A	ASHFORD - 74A	ASHFORD - 74A	ASHFORD - 74A
31259	FAVERSHAM - 73E	FAVERSHAM - 73E	FAVERSHAM - 73E	FAVERSHAM - 73E	FAVERSHAM - 73E	FAVERSHAM - 73E	FAVERSHAM - 73E
31261	STEWARTS LANE - 73A	STEWARTS LANE - 73A	STEWARTS LANE - 73A	STEWARTS LANE - 73A	STEWARTS LANE - 73A	STEWARTS LANE - 73A	STEWARTS LANE - 73A
31263	REDHILL - 75B	REDHILL - 75B	ASHFORD - 74A	ASHFORD - 74A	ASHFORD - 74A	ASHFORD - 74A	ASHFORD - 74A
31265	RAMSGATE - 74B	RAMSGATE - 74B	RAMSGATE - 74B	RAMSGATE - 74B	RAMSGATE - 74B	RAMSGATE - 74B	RAMSGATE - 74B
31266	STEWARTS LANE - 73A	STEWARTS LANE - 73A	STEWARTS LANE - 73A	STEWARTS LANE - 73A	STEWARTS LANE - 73A	STEWARTS LANE - 73A	STEWARTS LANE - 73A
31269	ST LEONARDS - 74E	ST LEONARDS - 74E	ST LEONARDS - 74E	ST LEONARDS - 74E	ST LEONARDS - 74E	ST LEONARDS - 74E	ST LEONARDS - 74E
31274	ST LEONARDS - 74E	ST LEONARDS - 74E	ST LEONARDS - 74E	ST LEONARDS - 74E	ST LEONARDS - 74E	ST LEONARDS - 74E	ST LEONARDS - 74E
31276	ASHFORD - 74A	ASHFORD - 74A	ASHFORD - 74A	ASHFORD - 74A	ASHFORD - 74A	ASHFORD - 74A	ASHFORD - 74A
31278	DOVER - 74C	T.WELLS - 75F	T.WELLS - 75F	T.WELLS - 75F	T.WELLS - 75F	T.WELLS - 75F	T.WELLS - 75F
31279	ST LEONARDS - 74E	ST LEONARDS - 74E	ST LEONARDS - 74E	ST LEONARDS - 74E	ST LEONARDS - 74E	ST LEONARDS - 74E	ST LEONARDS - 74E
31295	ST LEONARDS - 74E	ST LEONARDS - 74E	ST LEONARDS - 74E	ST LEONARDS - 74E	ST LEONARDS - 74E	ST LEONARDS - 74E	ST LEONARDS - 74E
31305	B.ARMS - 73B	B.ARMS - 73B	B.ARMS - 73B	B.ARMS - 73B	B.ARMS - 73B	B.ARMS - 73B	B.ARMS - 73B
31306	B.ARMS - 73B	B.ARMS - 73B	B.ARMS - 73B	B.ARMS - 73B	B.ARMS - 73B	B.ARMS - 73B	B.ARMS - 73B
31307	ASHFORD - 74A	ASHFORD - 74A	ASHFORD - 74A	ASHFORD - 74A	ASHFORD - 74A	ASHFORD - 74A	ASHFORD - 74A
31308	GILLINGHAM - 73D	GILLINGHAM - 73D	GILLINGHAM - 73D	GILLINGHAM - 73D	GILLINGHAM - 73D	GILLINGHAM - 73D	GILLINGHAM - 73D
31310	ASHFORD - 74A	ASHFORD - 74A	T.WELLS - 75F	T.WELLS - 75F	T.WELLS - 75F	T.WELLS - 75F	T.WELLS - 75F
31319	BRIGHTON - 75A	ASHFORD - 74A	ASHFORD - 74A	ASHFORD - 74A	ASHFORD - 74A	ASHFORD - 74A	ASHFORD - 74A
31321	STEWARTS LANE - 73A	STEWARTS LANE - 73A	STEWARTS LANE - 73A	STEWARTS LANE - 73A	STEWARTS LANE - 73A	STEWARTS LANE - 73A	STEWARTS LANE - 73A
31322	GILLINGHAM - 73D	GILLINGHAM - 73D	GILLINGHAM - 73D	GILLINGHAM - 73D	GILLINGHAM - 73D	GILLINGHAM - 73D	GILLINGHAM - 73D
31324	RAMSGATE - 74B	RAMSGATE - 74B	RAMSGATE - 74B	RAMSGATE - 74B	RAMSGATE - 74B	RAMSGATE - 74B	RAMSGATE - 74B
31326	RAMSGATE - 74B	RAMSGATE - 74B	RAMSGATE - 74B	RAMSGATE - 74B	RAMSGATE - 74B	RAMSGATE - 74B	RAMSGATE - 74B
31327	ASHFORD - 74A	ASHFORD - 74A	T.WELLS - 75F	T.WELLS - 75F	T.WELLS - 75F	T.WELLS - 75F	T.WELLS - 75F
31328	DOVER - 74C	DOVER - 74C	DOVER - 74C	DOVER - 74C	DOVER - 74C	DOVER - 74C	DOVER - 74C
31329	DOVER - 74C	T.WELLS - 75F	T.WELLS - 75F	T.WELLS - 75F	T.WELLS - 75F	T.WELLS - 75F	T.WELLS - 75F
31500	RAMSGATE - 74B	RAMSGATE - 74B	RAMSGATE - 74B	RAMSGATE - 74B	RAMSGATE - 74B	RAMSGATE - 74B	RAMSGATE - 74B
31503	FAVERSHAM - 73E	FAVERSHAM - 73E	FAVERSHAM - 73E	FAVERSHAM - 73E	FAVERSHAM - 73E	FAVERSHAM - 73E	FAVERSHAM - 73E
31512	GILLINGHAM - 73D	GILLINGHAM - 73D	GILLINGHAM - 73D	GILLINGHAM - 73D	GILLINGHAM - 73D	GILLINGHAM - 73D	GILLINGHAM - 73D
31517	TONBRIDGE - 74D	TONBRIDGE - 74D	TONBRIDGE - 74D	TONBRIDGE - 74D	TONBRIDGE - 74D	TONBRIDGE - 74D	TONBRIDGE - 74D
31518	GILLINGHAM - 73D	GILLINGHAM - 73D	GILLINGHAM - 73D	GILLINGHAM - 73D	GILLINGHAM - 73D	GILLINGHAM - 73D	GILLINGHAM - 73D
31519	ST LEONARDS - 74E	ST LEONARDS - 74E	ST LEONARDS - 74E	ST LEONARDS - 74E	ST LEONARDS - 74E	ST LEONARDS - 74E	ST LEONARDS - 74E
31520	ST LEONARDS - 74E	ST LEONARDS - 74E	ST LEONARDS - 74E	ST LEONARDS - 74E	ST LEONARDS - 74E	ST LEONARDS - 74E	ST LEONARDS - 74E
31521	ASHFORD - 74A	ASHFORD - 74A	THREE BRIDGES - 75E	THREE BRIDGES - 75E	THREE BRIDGES - 75E	THREE BRIDGES - 75E	THREE BRIDGES - 75E
31522	ASHFORD - 74A	ASHFORD - 74A	ASHFORD - 74A	ASHFORD - 74A	ASHFORD - 74A	ASHFORD - 74A	ASHFORD - 74A
31523	TONBRIDGE - 74D	TONBRIDGE - 74D	TONBRIDGE - 74D	TONBRIDGE - 74D	TONBRIDGE - 74D	TONBRIDGE - 74D	TONBRIDGE - 74D
31530	TONBRIDGE - 74D	TONBRIDGE - 74D	THREE BRIDGES - 75E	THREE BRIDGES - 75E	THREE BRIDGES - 75E	THREE BRIDGES - 75E	THREE BRIDGES - 75E
31533	B.ARMS - 73B	B.ARMS - 73B	B.ARMS - 73B	B.ARMS - 73B	B.ARMS - 73B	B.ARMS - 73B	B.ARMS - 73B
31540	B.ARMS - 73B	B.ARMS - 73B	B.ARMS - 73B	B.ARMS - 73B	B.ARMS - 73B	B.ARMS - 73B	B.ARMS - 73B
31542	B.ARMS - 73B	B.ARMS - 73B	B.ARMS - 73B	B.ARMS - 73B	B.ARMS - 73B	DOVER - 74C	DOVER - 74C
31543	TONBRIDGE - 74D	TONBRIDGE - 74D	TONBRIDGE - 74D	TONBRIDGE - 74D	TONBRIDGE - 74D	TONBRIDGE - 74D	TONBRIDGE - 74D
31544	TONBRIDGE - 74D	TONBRIDGE - 74D	T.WELLS - 75F	T.WELLS - 75F	T.WELLS - 75F	T.WELLS - 75F	T.WELLS - 75F
31548	TONBRIDGE - 74D	TONBRIDGE - 74D	TONBRIDGE - 74D	TONBRIDGE - 74D	TONBRIDGE - 74D	TONBRIDGE - 74D	TONBRIDGE - 74D
31550	STEWARTS LANE - 73A	STEWARTS LANE - 73A	STEWARTS LANE - 73A	STEWARTS LANE - 73A	STEWARTS LANE - 73A	STEWARTS LANE - 73A	STEWARTS LANE - 73A
31551	STEWARTS LANE - 73A	STEWARTS LANE - 73A	STEWARTS LANE - 73A	STEWARTS LANE - 73A	STEWARTS LANE - 73A	STEWARTS LANE - 73A	STEWARTS LANE - 73A
31552	STEWARTS LANE - 73A	STEWARTS LANE - 73A	STEWARTS LANE - 73A	STEWARTS LANE - 73A	STEWARTS LANE - 73A	STEWARTS LANE - 73A	STEWARTS LANE - 73A
31553	B.ARMS - 73B	B.ARMS - 73B	B.ARMS - 73B	B.ARMS - 73B	B.ARMS - 73B	B.ARMS - 73B	B.ARMS - 73B
31554	TONBRIDGE - 74D	TONBRIDGE - 74D	TONBRIDGE - 74D	TONBRIDGE - 74D	TONBRIDGE - 74D	TONBRIDGE - 74D	TONBRIDGE - 74D
				O2 0-4-4T (1889)			
30177	EASTLEIGH - 71A	EASTLEIGH - 71A	EASTLEIGH - 71A	EASTLEIGH - 71A	EASTLEIGH - 71A	FELTHAM - 70B	FELTHAM - 70B
30179	EASTLEIGH - 71A	EASTLEIGH - 71A	EASTLEIGH - 71A	EASTLEIGH - 71A	EASTLEIGH - 71A	FELTHAM - 70B	FELTHAM - 70B
30182	YEOVIL - 72C	YEOVIL - 72C	YEOVIL - 72C	YEOVIL - 72C	YEOVIL - 72C	YEOVIL - 72C	YEOVIL - 72C
30183	P.LYMOUTH - 72D	P.LYMOUTH - 72D	EXMOUTH JCN - 72A	EXMOUTH JCN - 72A	EXMOUTH JCN - 72A	EXMOUTH JCN - 72A	EXMOUTH JCN - 72A
30192	P.LYMOUTH - 72D	P.LYMOUTH - 72D	P.LYMOUTH - 72D	P.LYMOUTH - 72D	P.LYMOUTH - 72D	P.LYMOUTH - 72D	P.LYMOUTH - 72D
30193	EXMOUTH JCN - 72A	EXMOUTH JCN - 72A	EXMOUTH JCN - 72A	EXMOUTH JCN - 72A	EXMOUTH JCN - 72A	EXMOUTH JCN - 72A	EXMOUTH JCN - 72A
30199	EXMOUTH JCN - 72A	EXMOUTH JCN - 72A	EXMOUTH JCN - 72A	EXMOUTH JCN - 72A	EXMOUTH JCN - 72A	EXMOUTH JCN - 72A	EXMOUTH JCN - 72A
30200	WADEBRIDGE - 72F	WADEBRIDGE - 72F	WADEBRIDGE - 72F	WADEBRIDGE - 72F	WADEBRIDGE - 72F	WADEBRIDGE - 72F	WADEBRIDGE - 72F
30207	FRATTON - 70F	FRATTON - 70F	FRATTON - 70F	FRATTON - 70F	FRATTON - 70F	FRATTON - 70F	FRATTON - 70F
30212	BOURNEMOUTH - 71B	BOURNEMOUTH - 71B	BOURNEMOUTH - 71B	BOURNEMOUTH - 71B	BOURNEMOUTH - 71B	EASTLEIGH - 71A	EASTLEIGH - 71A
30216	P.LYMOUTH - 72D	P.LYMOUTH - 72D	P.LYMOUTH - 72D	P.LYMOUTH - 72D	P.LYMOUTH - 72D	P.LYMOUTH - 72D	P.LYMOUTH - 72D
30223	BOURNEMOUTH - 71B	BOURNEMOUTH - 71B	BOURNEMOUTH - 71B	BOURNEMOUTH - 71B	BOURNEMOUTH - 71B	EASTLEIGH - 71A	EASTLEIGH - 71A
30224	NINE ELMS - 70A	NINE ELMS - 70A	NINE ELMS - 70A	NINE ELMS - 70A	NINE ELMS - 70A	NINE ELMS - 70A	NINE ELMS - 70A
30225	P.LYMOUTH - 72D	P.LYMOUTH - 72D	P.LYMOUTH - 72D	P.LYMOUTH - 72D	P.LYMOUTH - 72D	P.LYMOUTH - 72D	P.LYMOUTH - 72D
30229	DORCHESTER - 71C	DORCHESTER - 71C	DORCHESTER - 71C	DORCHESTER - 71C	DORCHESTER - 71C	DORCHESTER - 71C	DORCHESTER - 71C
30230	FELTHAM - 70B	FELTHAM - 70B	FELTHAM - 70B	W/D	W/D	W/D	W/D
30232	EXMOUTH JCN - 72A	EXMOUTH JCN - 72A	EXMOUTH JCN - 72A	EXMOUTH JCN - 72A	EXMOUTH JCN - 72A	EXMOUTH JCN - 72A	EXMOUTH JCN - 72A
30233	EASTLEIGH - 71A	EASTLEIGH - 71A	EASTLEIGH - 71A	EASTLEIGH - 71A	EASTLEIGH - 71A	EASTLEIGH - 71A	EASTLEIGH - 71A
30236	WADEBRIDGE - 72F	WADEBRIDGE - 72F	WADEBRIDGE - 72F	WADEBRIDGE - 72F	WADEBRIDGE - 72F	WADEBRIDGE - 72F	WADEBRIDGE - 72F

Designed for the intensive suburban services from Victoria and Charing Cross, the H 0-4-4T's were effectively made redundant as electrification spread to Chatham and Sevenoaks during the 1920's and 30's, but were given a fresh lease of life by being moved to a number of country sheds as replacements for older locomotives; all but two of the class entering service with British Railways in 1948. In early 1949 twenty-nine of the class were equipped with push & pull apparatus removed from older 0-4-4 locomotives, many being transferred to the Central Division for work in the Brighton and Tunbridge Wells areas. The arrival of the large standard and LMS classes did not have a marked effect on the H class and a considerable number survived into the 1960's. (The move of some engines away from SECR metals was by no means their farthest jaunt: three of the class 31174,31184 and 31259 spent eighteen months of the war operating from Forfar due to a shortage of motive power in Scotland.)

The older LSWR O2 tanks also survived into the 1960's although in much smaller numbers than the H class, most of their final duties being carried out in the Plymouth (LSW) area.

loco	Mar-57	Jun-57	Jul-57	Oct-57	Jan-58	Feb-58	Mar-58
				H 0-4-4T (1904)			
31005	ASHFORD - 74A	ASHFORD - 74A	ASHFORD - 74A	ASHFORD - 74A	ASHFORD - 74A	ASHFORD - 74A	ASHFORD - 74A
31161	GILLINGHAM - 73D	GILLINGHAM - 73D	GILLINGHAM - 73D	GILLINGHAM - 73D	GILLINGHAM - 73D	GILLINGHAM - 73D	GILLINGHAM - 73D
31162	ST LEONARDS - 74E	ST LEONARDS - 74E	ST LEONARDS - 74E	ST LEONARDS - 74E	ST LEONARDS - 74E	ST LEONARDS - 74E	ST LEONARDS - 74E
31164	TONBRIDGE - 74D	TONBRIDGE - 74D	TONBRIDGE - 74D	TONBRIDGE - 74D	TONBRIDGE - 74D	TONBRIDGE - 74D	TONBRIDGE - 74D
31177	TONBRIDGE - 74D	TONBRIDGE - 74D	TONBRIDGE - 74D	TONBRIDGE - 74D	TONBRIDGE - 74D	TONBRIDGE - 74D	TONBRIDGE - 74D
31184	STEWARTS LANE - 73A	STEWARTS LANE - 73A	STEWARTS LANE - 73A	STEWARTS LANE - 73A	STEWARTS LANE - 73A	STEWARTS LANE - 73A	W/D
31193	TONBRIDGE - 74D	TONBRIDGE - 74D	TONBRIDGE - 74D	TONBRIDGE - 74D	TONBRIDGE - 74D	TONBRIDGE - 74D	TONBRIDGE - 74D
31239	ASHFORD - 74A	ASHFORD - 74A	ASHFORD - 74A	ASHFORD - 74A	ASHFORD - 74A	ASHFORD - 74A	ASHFORD - 74A
31259	FAVERSHAM - 73E	FAVERSHAM - 73E	FAVERSHAM - 73E	FAVERSHAM - 73E	FAVERSHAM - 73E	FAVERSHAM - 73E	FAVERSHAM - 73E
31261	STEWARTS LANE - 73A	STEWARTS LANE - 73A	STEWARTS LANE - 73A	STEWARTS LANE - 73A	STEWARTS LANE - 73A	STEWARTS LANE - 73A	STEWARTS LANE - 73A
31263	ASHFORD - 74A	ASHFORD - 74A	ASHFORD - 74A	ASHFORD - 74A	ASHFORD - 74A	ASHFORD - 74A	ASHFORD - 74A
31265	RAMSGATE - 74B	RAMSGATE - 74B	RAMSGATE - 74B	RAMSGATE - 74B	RAMSGATE - 74B	RAMSGATE - 74B	RAMSGATE - 74B
31266	STEWARTS LANE - 73A	STEWARTS LANE - 73A	STEWARTS LANE - 73A	STEWARTS LANE - 73A	STEWARTS LANE - 73A	STEWARTS LANE - 73A	STEWARTS LANE - 73A
31269	ST LEONARDS - 74E	ST LEONARDS - 74E	ST LEONARDS - 74E	ST LEONARDS - 74E	ST LEONARDS - 74E	ST LEONARDS - 74E	ST LEONARDS - 74E
31274	ST LEONARDS - 74E	ST LEONARDS - 74E	ST LEONARDS - 74E	ST LEONARDS - 74E	W/D	W/D	W/D
31276	ASHFORD - 74A	ASHFORD - 74A	ASHFORD - 74A	ASHFORD - 74A	ASHFORD - 74A	ASHFORD - 74A	ASHFORD - 74A
31278	T.WELLS - 75F	T.WELLS - 75F	T.WELLS - 75F	T.WELLS - 75F	T.WELLS - 75F	T.WELLS - 75F	T.WELLS - 75F
31279	ST LEONARDS - 74E	ST LEONARDS - 74E	ST LEONARDS - 74E	ST LEONARDS - 74E	ST LEONARDS - 74E	ST LEONARDS - 74E	ST LEONARDS - 74E
31295	ST LEONARDS - 74E	ST LEONARDS - 74E	ST LEONARDS - 74E	ST LEONARDS - 74E	ST LEONARDS - 74E	ST LEONARDS - 74E	ST LEONARDS - 74E
31305	B.ARMS - 73B	B.ARMS - 73B	B.ARMS - 73B	B.ARMS - 73B	B.ARMS - 73B	B.ARMS - 73B	B.ARMS - 73B
31306	B.ARMS - 73B	B.ARMS - 73B	B.ARMS - 73B	B.ARMS - 73B	B.ARMS - 73B	B.ARMS - 73B	B.ARMS - 73B
31307	ASHFORD - 74A	ASHFORD - 74A	ASHFORD - 74A	ASHFORD - 74A	ASHFORD - 74A	ASHFORD - 74A	ASHFORD - 74A
31308	T.WELLS - 75F	GILLINGHAM - 73D	GILLINGHAM - 73D	GILLINGHAM - 73D	GILLINGHAM - 73D	GILLINGHAM - 73D	GILLINGHAM - 73D
31310	T.WELLS - 75F	T.WELLS - 75F	T.WELLS - 75F	T.WELLS - 75F	T.WELLS - 75F	T.WELLS - 75F	T.WELLS - 75F
31319	ASHFORD - 74A	ASHFORD - 74A	ASHFORD - 74A	ASHFORD - 74A	ASHFORD - 74A	ASHFORD - 74A	ASHFORD - 74A
31321	STEWARTS LANE - 73A	STEWARTS LANE - 73A	STEWARTS LANE - 73A	STEWARTS LANE - 73A	W/D	W/D	W/D
31322	GILLINGHAM - 73D	GILLINGHAM - 73D	GILLINGHAM - 73D	GILLINGHAM - 73D	GILLINGHAM - 73D	GILLINGHAM - 73D	GILLINGHAM - 73D
31324	RAMSGATE - 74B	RAMSGATE - 74B	RAMSGATE - 74B	RAMSGATE - 74B	RAMSGATE - 74B	RAMSGATE - 74B	RAMSGATE - 74B
31326	RAMSGATE - 74B	RAMSGATE - 74B	RAMSGATE - 74B	RAMSGATE - 74B	RAMSGATE - 74B	RAMSGATE - 74B	RAMSGATE - 74B
31327	T.WELLS - 75F	T.WELLS - 75F	T.WELLS - 75F	T.WELLS - 75F	T.WELLS - 75F	T.WELLS - 75F	T.WELLS - 75F
31328	DOVER - 74C	DOVER - 74C	DOVER - 74C	DOVER - 74C	DOVER - 74C	DOVER - 74C	DOVER - 74C
31329	T.WELLS - 75F	T.WELLS - 75F	T.WELLS - 75F	T.WELLS - 75F	T.WELLS - 75F	T.WELLS - 75F	T.WELLS - 75F
31500	RAMSGATE - 74B	RAMSGATE - 74B	RAMSGATE - 74B	RAMSGATE - 74B	RAMSGATE - 74B	RAMSGATE - 74B	RAMSGATE - 74B
31503	FAVERSHAM - 73E	FAVERSHAM - 73E	FAVERSHAM - 73E	FAVERSHAM - 73E	FAVERSHAM - 73E	FAVERSHAM - 73E	FAVERSHAM - 73E
31512	GILLINGHAM - 73D	GILLINGHAM - 73D	GILLINGHAM - 73D	GILLINGHAM - 73D	GILLINGHAM - 73D	GILLINGHAM - 73D	GILLINGHAM - 73D
31517	TONBRIDGE - 74D	TONBRIDGE - 74D	TONBRIDGE - 74D	TONBRIDGE - 74D	TONBRIDGE - 74D	TONBRIDGE - 74D	TONBRIDGE - 74D
31518	GILLINGHAM - 73D	GILLINGHAM - 73D	GILLINGHAM - 73D	GILLINGHAM - 73D	GILLINGHAM - 73D	GILLINGHAM - 73D	GILLINGHAM - 73D
31519	ST LEONARDS - 74E	ST LEONARDS - 74E	ST LEONARDS - 74E	ST LEONARDS - 74E	ST LEONARDS - 74E	ST LEONARDS - 74E	ST LEONARDS - 74E
31520	ST LEONARDS - 74E	ST LEONARDS - 74E	ST LEONARDS - 74E	ST LEONARDS - 74E	ST LEONARDS - 74E	ST LEONARDS - 74E	ST LEONARDS - 74E
31521	THREE BRIDGES - 75E	THREE BRIDGES - 75E	THREE BRIDGES - 75E	THREE BRIDGES - 75E	THREE BRIDGES - 75E	THREE BRIDGES - 75E	THREE BRIDGES - 75E
31522	ASHFORD - 74A	ASHFORD - 74A	ASHFORD - 74A	ASHFORD - 74A	ASHFORD - 74A	ASHFORD - 74A	ASHFORD - 74A
31523	TONBRIDGE - 74D	TONBRIDGE - 74D	TONBRIDGE - 74D	TONBRIDGE - 74D	TONBRIDGE - 74D	TONBRIDGE - 74D	TONBRIDGE - 74D
31530	THREE BRIDGES - 75E	THREE BRIDGES - 75E	THREE BRIDGES - 75E	THREE BRIDGES - 75E	THREE BRIDGES - 75E	THREE BRIDGES - 75E	THREE BRIDGES - 75E
31533	B.ARMS - 73B	B.ARMS - 73B	B.ARMS - 73B	B.ARMS - 73B	B.ARMS - 73B	B.ARMS - 73B	B.ARMS - 73B
31540	B.ARMS - 73B	B.ARMS - 73B	B.ARMS - 73B	B.ARMS - 73B	B.ARMS - 73B	B.ARMS - 73B	B.ARMS - 73B
31542	DOVER - 74C	DOVER - 74C	DOVER - 74C	DOVER - 74C	DOVER - 74C	DOVER - 74C	DOVER - 74C
31543	TONBRIDGE - 74D	TONBRIDGE - 74D	TONBRIDGE - 74D	TONBRIDGE - 74D	TONBRIDGE - 74D	TONBRIDGE - 74D	TONBRIDGE - 74D
31544	T.WELLS - 75F	T.WELLS - 75F	T.WELLS - 75F	T.WELLS - 75F	T.WELLS - 75F	T.WELLS - 75F	T.WELLS - 75F
31548	TONBRIDGE - 74D	TONBRIDGE - 74D	TONBRIDGE - 74D	TONBRIDGE - 74D	TONBRIDGE - 74D	TONBRIDGE - 74D	TONBRIDGE - 74D
31550	STEWARTS LANE - 73A	STEWARTS LANE - 73A	STEWARTS LANE - 73A	STEWARTS LANE - 73A	STEWARTS LANE - 73A	STEWARTS LANE - 73A	STEWARTS LANE - 73A
31551	STEWARTS LANE - 73A	STEWARTS LANE - 73A	STEWARTS LANE - 73A	STEWARTS LANE - 73A	STEWARTS LANE - 73A	STEWARTS LANE - 73A	STEWARTS LANE - 73A
31552	STEWARTS LANE - 73A	STEWARTS LANE - 73A	STEWARTS LANE - 73A	STEWARTS LANE - 73A	STEWARTS LANE - 73A	STEWARTS LANE - 73A	STEWARTS LANE - 73A
31553	B.ARMS - 73B	B.ARMS - 73B	B.ARMS - 73B	B.ARMS - 73B	B.ARMS - 73B	B.ARMS - 73B	B.ARMS - 73B
31554	T.WELLS - 75F	T.WELLS - 75F	T.WELLS - 75F	T.WELLS - 75F	T.WELLS - 75F	T.WELLS - 75F	T.WELLS - 75F
				O2 0-4-4T (1889)			
30177	FELTHAM - 70B	FELTHAM - 70B	FELTHAM - 70B	FELTHAM - 70B	FELTHAM - 70B	FELTHAM - 70B	FELTHAM - 70B
30179	FELTHAM - 70B	FELTHAM - 70B	FELTHAM - 70B	FELTHAM - 70B	FELTHAM - 70B	FELTHAM - 70B	FELTHAM - 70B
30182	YEOVIL - 72C	YEOVIL - 72C	YEOVIL - 72C	YEOVIL - 72C	YEOVIL - 72C	YEOVIL - 72C	YEOVIL - 72C
30183	EXMOUTH JCN - 72A	EXMOUTH JCN - 72A	PLYMOUTH - 72D	PLYMOUTH - 72D	PLYMOUTH - 72D	PLYMOUTH - 83H	PLYMOUTH - 83H
30192	PLYMOUTH - 72D	PLYMOUTH - 72D	PLYMOUTH - 72D	PLYMOUTH - 72D	PLYMOUTH - 72D	PLYMOUTH - 83H	PLYMOUTH - 83H
30193	EXMOUTH JCN - 72A	PLYMOUTH - 72D	PLYMOUTH - 72D	PLYMOUTH - 72D	PLYMOUTH - 72D	PLYMOUTH - 83H	PLYMOUTH - 83H
30199	EXMOUTH JCN - 72A	PLYMOUTH - 72D	EXMOUTH JCN - 72A	EXMOUTH JCN - 72A	EXMOUTH JCN - 72A	EXMOUTH JCN - 72A	EXMOUTH JCN - 72A
30200	WADEBRIDGE - 72F	WADEBRIDGE - 72F	WADEBRIDGE - 72F	WADEBRIDGE - 72F	WADEBRIDGE - 72F	WADEBRIDGE - 72F	WADEBRIDGE - 72F
30207	FRATTON - 70F	W/D	W/D	W/D	W/D	W/D	W/D
30212	EASTLEIGH - 71A	EASTLEIGH - 71A	EASTLEIGH - 71A	EASTLEIGH - 71A	EASTLEIGH - 71A	EASTLEIGH - 71A	EASTLEIGH - 71A
30216	PLYMOUTH - 72D	PLYMOUTH - 72D	PLYMOUTH - 72D	PLYMOUTH - 72D	W/D	W/D	W/D
30223	EASTLEIGH - 71A	EASTLEIGH - 71A	EASTLEIGH - 71A	EASTLEIGH - 71A	EASTLEIGH - 71A	EASTLEIGH - 71A	EASTLEIGH - 71A
30224	NINE ELMS - 70A	NINE ELMS - 70A	NINE ELMS - 70A	NINE ELMS - 70A	NINE ELMS - 70A	W/D	W/D
30225	PLYMOUTH - 72D	PLYMOUTH - 72D	PLYMOUTH - 72D	PLYMOUTH - 72D	PLYMOUTH - 72D	PLYMOUTH - 83H	PLYMOUTH - 83H
30229	DORCHESTER - 71C	DORCHESTER - 71C	DORCHESTER - 71C	DORCHESTER - 71C	DORCHESTER - 71C	DORCHESTER - 71C	DORCHESTER - 71C
30232	EXMOUTH JCN - 72A	EXMOUTH JCN - 72A	EXMOUTH JCN - 72A	EXMOUTH JCN - 72A	EXMOUTH JCN - 72A	EXMOUTH JCN - 72A	EXMOUTH JCN - 72A
30233	EASTLEIGH - 71A	EASTLEIGH - 71A	EASTLEIGH - 71A	EASTLEIGH - 71A	EASTLEIGH - 71A	W/D	W/D
30236	WADEBRIDGE - 72F	WADEBRIDGE - 72F	WADEBRIDGE - 72F	WADEBRIDGE - 72F	WADEBRIDGE - 72F	WADEBRIDGE - 72F	WADEBRIDGE - 72F

loco	May-58	Oct-58	Mar-59	Jun-59	Jul-59	Aug-59	Oct-59
			H 0-4-4T (1904)				
31005	ASHFORD - 74A	ASHFORD - 73F	ASHFORD - 73F	ASHFORD - 73F	ASHFORD - 73F	ASHFORD - 73F	ASHFORD - 73F
31161	GILLINGHAM - 73D	GILLINGHAM - 73D	GILLINGHAM - 73D	THREE BRIDGES - 75E	THREE BRIDGES - 75E	THREE BRIDGES - 75E	THREE BRIDGES - 75E
31162	T.WELLS - 75F	THREE BRIDGES - 75E	THREE BRIDGES - 75E	THREE BRIDGES - 75E	THREE BRIDGES - 75E	THREE BRIDGES - 75E	THREE BRIDGES - 75E
31164	TONBRIDGE - 74D	TONBRIDGE - 73J	TONBRIDGE - 73J	TONBRIDGE - 73J	TONBRIDGE - 73J	TONBRIDGE - 73J	TONBRIDGE - 73J
31177	TONBRIDGE - 74D	TONBRIDGE - 73J	TONBRIDGE - 73J	TONBRIDGE - 73J	TONBRIDGE - 73J	TONBRIDGE - 73J	TONBRIDGE - 73J
31193	TONBRIDGE - 74D	TONBRIDGE - 73J	TONBRIDGE - 73J	TONBRIDGE - 73J	TONBRIDGE - 73J	TONBRIDGE - 73J	TONBRIDGE - 73J
31239	ASHFORD - 74A	ASHFORD - 73F	ASHFORD - 73F	ASHFORD - 73F	ASHFORD - 73F	ASHFORD - 73F	ASHFORD - 73F
31259	FAVERSHAM - 73E	FAVERSHAM - 73E	FAVERSHAM - 73E	FAVERSHAM - 73E	FAVERSHAM - 73E	FAVERSHAM - 73E	FAVERSHAM - 73E
31261	STEWARTS LANE - 73A	STEWARTS LANE - 73A	STEWARTS LANE - 73A	STEWARTS LANE - 73A	STEWARTS LANE - 73A	STEWARTS LANE - 73A	STEWARTS LANE - 73A
31263	ASHFORD - 74A	ASHFORD - 73F	ASHFORD - 73F	ASHFORD - 73F	ASHFORD - 73F	ASHFORD - 73F	ASHFORD - 73F
31265	RAMSGATE - 74B	RAMSGATE - 73G	RAMSGATE - 73G	RAMSGATE - 73G	RAMSGATE - 73G	RAMSGATE - 73G	RAMSGATE - 73G
31266	TONBRIDGE - 74D	TONBRIDGE - 73J	TONBRIDGE - 73J	NINE ELMS - 70A	NINE ELMS - 70A	NINE ELMS - 70A	T.WELLS - 75F
31269	T.WELLS - 75F	THREE BRIDGES - 75E	THREE BRIDGES - 75E	BRIGHTON - 75A	BRIGHTON - 75A	BRIGHTON - 75A	BRIGHTON - 75A
31276	ASHFORD - 74A	ASHFORD - 73F	ASHFORD - 73F	BRIGHTON - 75A	BRIGHTON - 75A	BRIGHTON - 75A	BRIGHTON - 75A
31278	T.WELLS - 75F	T.WELLS - 75F	T.WELLS - 75F	T.WELLS - 75F	T.WELLS - 75F	T.WELLS - 75F	T.WELLS - 75F
31279	TONBRIDGE - 74D	TONBRIDGE - 73J	TONBRIDGE - 73J	BRIGHTON - 75A	BRIGHTON - 75A	BRIGHTON - 75A	W/D
31295	TONBRIDGE - 74D	TONBRIDGE - 73J	TONBRIDGE - 73J	W/D	W/D	W/D	W/D
31305	B ARMS - 73B	B ARMS - 73B	B ARMS - 73B	B ARMS - 73B	B ARMS - 73B	B ARMS - 73B	B ARMS - 73B
31306	B ARMS - 73B	B ARMS - 73B	B ARMS - 73B	B ARMS - 73B	B ARMS - 73B	B ARMS - 73B	B ARMS - 73B
31307	ASHFORD - 74A	ASHFORD - 73F	ASHFORD - 73F	ASHFORD - 73F	ASHFORD - 73F	ASHFORD - 73F	ASHFORD - 73F
31308	GILLINGHAM - 73D	GILLINGHAM - 73D	GILLINGHAM - 73D	BRIGHTON - 75A	BRIGHTON - 75A	BRIGHTON - 75A	BRIGHTON - 75A
31310	T.WELLS - 75F	T.WELLS - 75F	T.WELLS - 75F	T.WELLS - 75F	T.WELLS - 75F	T.WELLS - 75F	T.WELLS - 75F
31319	ASHFORD - 74A	ASHFORD - 73F	ASHFORD - 73F	TONBRIDGE - 73J	TONBRIDGE - 73J	TONBRIDGE - 73J	TONBRIDGE - 73J
31322	GILLINGHAM - 73D	GILLINGHAM - 73D	GILLINGHAM - 73D	TONBRIDGE - 73J	TONBRIDGE - 73J	TONBRIDGE - 73J	TONBRIDGE - 73J
31324	RAMSGATE - 74B	RAMSGATE - 73G	RAMSGATE - 73G	NINE ELMS - 70A	NINE ELMS - 70A	NINE ELMS - 70A	NINE ELMS - 70A
31326	RAMSGATE - 74B	RAMSGATE - 73G	RAMSGATE - 73G	NINE ELMS - 70A	NINE ELMS - 70A	DOVER - 73H	DOVER - 73H
31327	T.WELLS - 75F	T.WELLS - 75F	T.WELLS - 75F	T.WELLS - 75F	T.WELLS - 75F	T.WELLS - 75F	T.WELLS - 75F
31328	DOVER - 74C	DOVER - 73H	DOVER - 73H	DOVER - 73H	DOVER - 73H	DOVER - 73H	DOVER - 73H
31329	T.WELLS - 75F	T.WELLS - 75F	T.WELLS - 75F	T.WELLS - 75F	T.WELLS - 75F	T.WELLS - 75F	T.WELLS - 75F
31500	RAMSGATE - 74B	RAMSGATE - 73G	RAMSGATE - 73G	NINE ELMS - 70A	NINE ELMS - 70A	NINE ELMS - 70A	NINE ELMS - 70A
31503	FAVERSHAM - 73E	FAVERSHAM - 73E	FAVERSHAM - 73E	NINE ELMS - 70A	NINE ELMS - 70A	W/D	W/D
31512	GILLINGHAM - 73D	GILLINGHAM - 73D	GILLINGHAM - 73D	TONBRIDGE - 73J	TONBRIDGE - 73J	TONBRIDGE - 73J	TONBRIDGE - 73J
31517	TONBRIDGE - 74D	TONBRIDGE - 73J	TONBRIDGE - 73J	TONBRIDGE - 73J	TONBRIDGE - 73J	TONBRIDGE - 73J	TONBRIDGE - 73J
31518	GILLINGHAM - 73D	GILLINGHAM - 73D	GILLINGHAM - 73D	TONBRIDGE - 73J	TONBRIDGE - 73J	TONBRIDGE - 73J	TONBRIDGE - 73J
31519	ASHFORD - 74A	ASHFORD - 73F	ASHFORD - 73F	TONBRIDGE - 73J	TONBRIDGE - 73J	TONBRIDGE - 73J	TONBRIDGE - 73J
31520	ASHFORD - 74A	ASHFORD - 73F	ASHFORD - 73F	TONBRIDGE - 73J	TONBRIDGE - 73J	TONBRIDGE - 73J	TONBRIDGE - 73J
31521	THREE BRIDGES - 75E	THREE BRIDGES - 75E	THREE BRIDGES - 75E	THREE BRIDGES - 75E	THREE BRIDGES - 75E	THREE BRIDGES - 75E	THREE BRIDGES - 75E
31522	ASHFORD - 74A	ASHFORD - 73F	ASHFORD - 73F	THREE BRIDGES - 75E	THREE BRIDGES - 75E	THREE BRIDGES - 75E	THREE BRIDGES - 75E
31523	TONBRIDGE - 74D	TONBRIDGE - 73J	W/D	W/D	W/D	W/D	W/D
31530	T.WELLS - 75F	T.WELLS - 75F	T.WELLS - 75F	BRIGHTON - 75A	BRIGHTON - 75A	BRIGHTON - 75A	BRIGHTON - 75A
31533	B ARMS - 73B	B ARMS - 73B	B ARMS - 73B	B ARMS - 73B	B ARMS - 73B	B ARMS - 73B	B ARMS - 73B
31540	B ARMS - 73B	B ARMS - 73B	B ARMS - 73B	B ARMS - 73B	B ARMS - 73B	B ARMS - 73B	B ARMS - 73B
31542	DOVER - 74C	DOVER - 73H	DOVER - 73H	DOVER - 73H	DOVER - 73H	DOVER - 73H	DOVER - 73H
31543	TONBRIDGE - 74D	TONBRIDGE - 73J	TONBRIDGE - 73J	BRIGHTON - 75A	BRIGHTON - 75A	BRIGHTON - 75A	BRIGHTON - 75A
31544	T.WELLS - 75F	T.WELLS - 75F	T.WELLS - 75F	T.WELLS - 75F	T.WELLS - 75F	T.WELLS - 75F	T.WELLS - 75F
31548	GILLINGHAM - 73D	GILLINGHAM - 73D	GILLINGHAM - 73D	BRIGHTON - 75A	BRIGHTON - 75A	W/D	W/D
31550	STEWARTS LANE - 73A	STEWARTS LANE - 73A	STEWARTS LANE - 73A	STEWARTS LANE - 73A	STEWARTS LANE - 73A	STEWARTS LANE - 73A	STEWARTS LANE - 73A
31551	STEWARTS LANE - 73A	STEWARTS LANE - 73A	STEWARTS LANE - 73A	STEWARTS LANE - 73A	STEWARTS LANE - 73A	STEWARTS LANE - 73A	STEWARTS LANE - 73A
31552	STEWARTS LANE - 73A	STEWARTS LANE - 73A	STEWARTS LANE - 73A	NINE ELMS - 70A	NINE ELMS - 70A	NINE ELMS - 70A	NINE ELMS - 70A
31553	B ARMS - 73B	B ARMS - 73B	B ARMS - 73B	NINE ELMS - 70A	NINE ELMS - 70A	NINE ELMS - 70A	NINE ELMS - 70A
31554	T.WELLS - 75F	BRIGHTON - 75A	BRIGHTON - 75A	W/D	W/D	W/D	W/D
			O2 0-4-4T (1889)				
30177	FELTHAM - 70B	FELTHAM - 70B	FELTHAM - 70B	FELTHAM - 70B	FELTHAM - 70B	FELTHAM - 70B	W/D
30179	FELTHAM - 70B	FELTHAM - 70B	FELTHAM - 70B	FELTHAM - 70B	FELTHAM - 70B	FELTHAM - 70B	FELTHAM - 70B
30182	YEOVIL - 72C	EXMOUTH JCN - 72A	EXMOUTH JCN - 72A	EXMOUTH JCN - 72A	EXMOUTH JCN - 72A	EXMOUTH JCN - 72A	EXMOUTH JCN - 72A
30183	PLYMOUTH - 83H	PLYMOUTH - 83H	PLYMOUTH - 83H	PLYMOUTH - 83H	PLYMOUTH - 83H	PLYMOUTH - 83H	PLYMOUTH - 83H
30192	PLYMOUTH - 83H	PLYMOUTH - 83H	PLYMOUTH - 83H	PLYMOUTH - 83H	PLYMOUTH - 83H	PLYMOUTH - 83H	PLYMOUTH - 83H
30193	PLYMOUTH - 83H	PLYMOUTH - 83H	PLYMOUTH - 83H	PLYMOUTH - 83H	PLYMOUTH - 83H	PLYMOUTH - 83H	PLYMOUTH - 83H
30199	EXMOUTH JCN - 72A	EXMOUTH JCN - 72A	EXMOUTH JCN - 72A	EXMOUTH JCN - 72A	EXMOUTH JCN - 72A	EXMOUTH JCN - 72A	EXMOUTH JCN - 72A
30200	WADEBRIDGE - 72F	WADEBRIDGE - 72F	WADEBRIDGE - 72F	WADEBRIDGE - 72F	WADEBRIDGE - 72F	WADEBRIDGE - 72F	WADEBRIDGE - 72F
30212	EASTLEIGH - 71A	EASTLEIGH - 71A	EASTLEIGH - 71A	EASTLEIGH - 71A	EASTLEIGH - 71A	EASTLEIGH - 71A	EASTLEIGH - 71A
30223	EASTLEIGH - 71A	EASTLEIGH - 71A	EASTLEIGH - 71A	EASTLEIGH - 71A	EASTLEIGH - 71A	EASTLEIGH - 71A	EASTLEIGH - 71A
30225	PLYMOUTH - 83H	PLYMOUTH - 83H	PLYMOUTH - 83H	PLYMOUTH - 83H	PLYMOUTH - 83H	PLYMOUTH - 83H	PLYMOUTH - 83H
30229	DORCHESTER - 71C	DORCHESTER - 71C	DORCHESTER - 71C	DORCHESTER - 71C	DORCHESTER - 71C	DORCHESTER - 71C	DORCHESTER - 71C
30232	EXMOUTH JCN - 72A	EXMOUTH JCN - 72A	EXMOUTH JCN - 72A	EXMOUTH JCN - 72A	EXMOUTH JCN - 72A	EXMOUTH JCN - 72A	W/D
30236	WADEBRIDGE - 72F	WADEBRIDGE - 72F	WADEBRIDGE - 72F	WADEBRIDGE - 72F	WADEBRIDGE - 72F	WADEBRIDGE - 72F	WADEBRIDGE - 72F

One of the Plymouth-based O2 0-4-4T's continued to work a regular passenger service until 1960 and 30192 is seen at Bere Alston with the 12.50 local service to Plymouth (North Road) in that year. Most of the survivors were to be found at work on the Isle of Wight.

loco	Dec-59	Feb-60	Mar-60	Apr-60	Jul-60	Aug-60	Sep-60	Nov-60
H 0-4-4T (1904)								
31005 ASHFORD - 73F	ASHFORD - 73F	ASHFORD - 73F	ASHFORD - 73F	ASHFORD - 73F	ASHFORD - 73F	NORWOOD JCN - 75C	BRIGHTON - 75A
31161 THREE BRIDGES - 75E	THREE BRIDGES - 75E	THREE BRIDGES - 75E	THREE BRIDGES - 75E	T.WELLS - 75F	T.WELLS - 75F	T.WELLS - 75F	T.WELLS - 75F
31162 T.WELLS - 75F	T.WELLS - 75F	T.WELLS - 75F	T.WELLS - 75F	T.WELLS - 75F	T.WELLS - 75F	T.WELLS - 75F	T.WELLS - 75F
31177 TONBRIDGE - 73J	TONBRIDGE - 73J	TONBRIDGE - 73J	TONBRIDGE - 73J	TONBRIDGE - 73J	TONBRIDGE - 73J	TONBRIDGE - 73J	TONBRIDGE - 73J
31193 TONBRIDGE - 73J	TONBRIDGE - 73J	TONBRIDGE - 73J	TONBRIDGE - 73J	TONBRIDGE - 73J	TONBRIDGE - 73J	TONBRIDGE - 73J	TONBRIDGE - 73J
31239 ASHFORD - 73F	W/D	W/D	W/D	W/D	W/D	W/D	W/D
31261 STEWARTS LANE - 73A	STEWARTS LANE - 73A	STEWARTS LANE - 73A	STEWARTS LANE - 73A	STEWARTS LANE - 73A	STEWARTS LANE - 73A	STEWARTS LANE - 73A	STEWARTS LANE - 73A
31263 ASHFORD - 73F	ASHFORD - 73F	TONBRIDGE - 73J	TONBRIDGE - 73J	TONBRIDGE - 73J	TONBRIDGE - 73J	TONBRIDGE - 73J	TONBRIDGE - 73J
31265 RAMSGATE - 73G	RAMSGATE - 73G	RAMSGATE - 73G	RAMSGATE - 73G	RAMSGATE - 73G	W/D	W/D	W/D
31266 T.WELLS - 75F	T.WELLS - 75F	T.WELLS - 75F	T.WELLS - 75F	T.WELLS - 75F	T.WELLS - 75F	T.WELLS - 75F	W/D
31276 BRIGHTON - 75A	BRIGHTON - 75A	BRIGHTON - 75A	BRIGHTON - 75A	BRIGHTON - 75A	BRIGHTON - 75A	BRIGHTON - 75A	BRIGHTON - 75A
31278 T.WELLS - 75F	T.WELLS - 75F	T.WELLS - 75F	T.WELLS - 75F	T.WELLS - 75F	T.WELLS - 75F	T.WELLS - 75F	T.WELLS - 75F
31305 B.ARMS - 73B	B.ARMS - 73B	B.ARMS - 73B	B.ARMS - 73B	B.ARMS - 73B	B.ARMS - 73B	B.ARMS - 73B	B.ARMS - 73B
31306 T.WELLS - 75F	T.WELLS - 75F	T.WELLS - 75F	T.WELLS - 75F	THREE BRIDGES - 75E	THREE BRIDGES - 75E	THREE BRIDGES - 75E	THREE BRIDGES - 75E
31307 ASHFORD - 73F	ASHFORD - 73F	ASHFORD - 73F	ASHFORD - 73F	ASHFORD - 73F	ASHFORD - 73F	ASHFORD - 73F	ASHFORD - 73F
31308 BRIGHTON - 75A	BRIGHTON - 75A	BRIGHTON - 75A	BRIGHTON - 75A	BRIGHTON - 75A	BRIGHTON - 75A	BRIGHTON - 75A	BRIGHTON - 75A
31310 T.WELLS - 75F	T.WELLS - 75F	T.WELLS - 75F	T.WELLS - 75F	W/D	W/D	W/D	W/D
31319 TONBRIDGE - 73J	W/D	W/D	W/D	W/D	W/D	W/D	W/D
31322 TONBRIDGE - 73J	TONBRIDGE - 73J	ASHFORD - 73F	BRIGHTON - 75A	BRIGHTON - 75A	BRIGHTON - 75A	BRIGHTON - 75A	BRIGHTON - 75A
31324 NINE ELMS - 70A	TONBRIDGE - 73J	ASHFORD - 73F	ASHFORD - 73F	ASHFORD - 73F	ASHFORD - 73F	ASHFORD - 73F	ASHFORD - 73F
31326 DOVER - 73H	DOVER - 73H	DOVER - 73H	DOVER - 73H	NINE ELMS - 70A	NINE ELMS - 70A	NINE ELMS - 70A	NINE ELMS - 70A
31328 DOVER - 73H	DOVER - 73H	DOVER - 73H	DOVER - 73H	NINE ELMS - 70A	NINE ELMS - 70A	NINE ELMS - 70A	NINE ELMS - 70A
31500 TONBRIDGE - 73J	TONBRIDGE - 73J	TONBRIDGE - 73J	TONBRIDGE - 73J	TONBRIDGE - 73J	TONBRIDGE - 73J	TONBRIDGE - 73J	TONBRIDGE - 73J
31512 TONBRIDGE - 73J	TONBRIDGE - 73J	TONBRIDGE - 73J	TONBRIDGE - 73J	TONBRIDGE - 73J	TONBRIDGE - 73J	TONBRIDGE - 73J	TONBRIDGE - 73J
31517 TONBRIDGE - 73J	TONBRIDGE - 73J	TONBRIDGE - 73J	TONBRIDGE - 73J	TONBRIDGE - 73J	TONBRIDGE - 73J	TONBRIDGE - 73J	TONBRIDGE - 73J
31518 TONBRIDGE - 73J	TONBRIDGE - 73J	TONBRIDGE - 73J	TONBRIDGE - 73J	TONBRIDGE - 73J	TONBRIDGE - 73J	TONBRIDGE - 73J	TONBRIDGE - 73J
31519 TONBRIDGE - 73J	TONBRIDGE - 73J	TONBRIDGE - 73J	TONBRIDGE - 73J	TONBRIDGE - 73J	TONBRIDGE - 73J	TONBRIDGE - 73J	TONBRIDGE - 73J
31520 TONBRIDGE - 73J	TONBRIDGE - 73J	TONBRIDGE - 73J	TONBRIDGE - 73J	TONBRIDGE - 73J	TONBRIDGE - 73J	W/D	TONBRIDGE - 73J
31521 THREE BRIDGES - 75E	THREE BRIDGES - 75E	THREE BRIDGES - 75E	THREE BRIDGES - 75E	THREE BRIDGES - 75E	THREE BRIDGES - 75E	THREE BRIDGES - 75E	THREE BRIDGES - 75E
31522 T.WELLS - 75F	T.WELLS - 75F	T.WELLS - 75F	T.WELLS - 75F	T.WELLS - 75F	T.WELLS - 75F	T.WELLS - 75F	T.WELLS - 75F
31530 BRIGHTON - 75A	BRIGHTON - 75A	BRIGHTON - 75A	BRIGHTON - 75A	BRIGHTON - 75A	BRIGHTON - 75A	BRIGHTON - 75A	BRIGHTON - 75A
31533 B.ARMS - 73B	B.ARMS - 73B	B.ARMS - 73B	TONBRIDGE - 73J	TONBRIDGE - 73J	TONBRIDGE - 73J	TONBRIDGE - 73J	TONBRIDGE - 73J
31540 B.ARMS - 73B	W/D	W/D	W/D	W/D	W/D	W/D	W/D
31542 DOVER - 73H	DOVER - 73H	DOVER - 73H	DOVER - 73H	NINE ELMS - 70A	NINE ELMS - 70A	NINE ELMS - 70A	NINE ELMS - 70A
31543 BRIGHTON - 75A	BRIGHTON - 75A	BRIGHTON - 75A	BRIGHTON - 75A	BRIGHTON - 75A	BRIGHTON - 75A	TONBRIDGE - 73J	TONBRIDGE - 73J
31544 T.WELLS - 75F	T.WELLS - 75F	T.WELLS - 75F	T.WELLS - 75F	T.WELLS - 75F	T.WELLS - 75F	T.WELLS - 75F	T.WELLS - 75F
31550 STEWARTS LANE - 73A	STEWARTS LANE - 73A	STEWARTS LANE - 73A	STEWARTS LANE - 73A	STEWARTS LANE - 73A	STEWARTS LANE - 73A	STEWARTS LANE - 73A	STEWARTS LANE - 73A
31551 STEWARTS LANE - 73A	STEWARTS LANE - 73A	STEWARTS LANE - 73A	STEWARTS LANE - 73A	STEWARTS LANE - 73A	STEWARTS LANE - 73A	TONBRIDGE - 73J	TONBRIDGE - 73J
31552 NINE ELMS - 70A	ASHFORD - 73F	ASHFORD - 73F	ASHFORD - 73F	ASHFORD - 73F	ASHFORD - 73F	ASHFORD - 73F	ASHFORD - 73F
31553 NINE ELMS - 70A	TONBRIDGE - 73J	TONBRIDGE - 73J	TONBRIDGE - 73J	TONBRIDGE - 73J	TONBRIDGE - 73J	TONBRIDGE - 73J	TONBRIDGE - 73J
O2 0-4-4T (1889)								
30182 EXMOUTH JCN - 72A	W/D	W/D	W/D	W/D	W/D	W/D	W/D
30183 PLYMOUTH - 83H	PLYMOUTH - 83H	PLYMOUTH - 83H	PLYMOUTH - 83H	PLYMOUTH - 83H	PLYMOUTH - 83H	PLYMOUTH - 83H	PLYMOUTH - 83H
30192 PLYMOUTH - 83H	PLYMOUTH - 83H	PLYMOUTH - 83H	PLYMOUTH - 83H	PLYMOUTH - 83H	PLYMOUTH - 83H	PLYMOUTH - 83H	PLYMOUTH - 83H
30193 PLYMOUTH - 83H	PLYMOUTH - 83H	PLYMOUTH - 83H	PLYMOUTH - 83H	PLYMOUTH - 83H	PLYMOUTH - 83H	PLYMOUTH - 83H	PLYMOUTH - 83H
30199 EXMOUTH JCN - 72A	EXMOUTH JCN - 72A	EXMOUTH JCN - 72A	EXMOUTH JCN - 72A	EXMOUTH JCN - 72A	EXMOUTH JCN - 72A	EXMOUTH JCN - 72A	EXMOUTH JCN - 72A
30200 WADEBRIDGE - 72F	WADEBRIDGE - 72F	WADEBRIDGE - 72F	WADEBRIDGE - 72F	WADEBRIDGE - 72F	WADEBRIDGE - 72F	WADEBRIDGE - 72F	WADEBRIDGE - 72F
30223 EASTLEIGH - 71A	EASTLEIGH - 71A	EASTLEIGH - 71A	EASTLEIGH - 71A	EASTLEIGH - 71A	EASTLEIGH - 71A	EASTLEIGH - 71A	EASTLEIGH - 71A
30225 PLYMOUTH - 83H	PLYMOUTH - 83H	PLYMOUTH - 83H	PLYMOUTH - 83H	PLYMOUTH - 83H	PLYMOUTH - 83H	PLYMOUTH - 83H	PLYMOUTH - 83H
30229 DORCHESTER - 71C	DORCHESTER - 71C	DORCHESTER - 71C	DORCHESTER - 71C	DORCHESTER - 71C	DORCHESTER - 71C	DORCHESTER - 71C	DORCHESTER - 71C
30236 WADEBRIDGE - 72F	W/D	W/D	W/D	W/D	W/D	W/D	W/D

The withdrawal during the early 1950's of the R1 0-4-4T class gave some of the H class 0-4-4T's a number of additional duties for which were fitted with push & pull apparatus between 1949 and 1961. H 0-4-4T 31543 of Tonbridge is seen in 1955 with the Paddock Wood - Hawkhurst push and pull, one of the workings taken over from an R1. 31543 had an active life of fifty-four years, its earlier years being spent at Orpington on the London suburban workings. After the electrification of the inner-suburban lines, it was transferred to Ramsgate, where it remained - apart from a short stay at Tonbridge - until 1950 when it returned to the London area, working ECS duties based at Bricklayers Arms for three years until being fitted with push & pull equipment and being sent to Tonbridge. In 1959 it was moved to Brighton for a short period but returned to Tonbridge a year later to finish its final three years of service.

loco	May-49	Jun-49	Aug-49	Sep-49	Dec-49	Feb-50	Mar-50
			M7 0-4-4T (1897)				
30021	HORSHAM - 75D	HORSHAM - 75D	HORSHAM - 75D	HORSHAM - 75D	HORSHAM - 75D	HORSHAM - 75D	HORSHAM - 75D
30022	GUILDFORD - 70C	GUILDFORD - 70C	GUILDFORD - 70C	GUILDFORD - 70C	GUILDFORD - 70C	GUILDFORD - 70C	GUILDFORD - 70C
30023	SALISBURY - 72B	SALISBURY - 72B	SALISBURY - 72B	SALISBURY - 72B	SALISBURY - 72B	SALISBURY - 72B	SALISBURY - 72B
30024	EXMOUTH JCN - 72A	EXMOUTH JCN - 72A	EXMOUTH JCN - 72A	EXMOUTH JCN - 72A	EXMOUTH JCN - 72A	EXMOUTH JCN - 72A	EXMOUTH JCN - 72A
30025	EXMOUTH JCN - 72A	EXMOUTH JCN - 72A	EXMOUTH JCN - 72A	EXMOUTH JCN - 72A	EXMOUTH JCN - 72A	EXMOUTH JCN - 72A	EXMOUTH JCN - 72A
30026	GUILDFORD - 70C	GUILDFORD - 70C	GUILDFORD - 70C	GUILDFORD - 70C	GUILDFORD - 70C	GUILDFORD - 70C	GUILDFORD - 70C
30027	HORSHAM - 75D	HORSHAM - 75D	HORSHAM - 75D	HORSHAM - 75D	HORSHAM - 75D	HORSHAM - 75D	HORSHAM - 75D
30028	BOURNEMOUTH - 71B	BOURNEMOUTH - 71B	BOURNEMOUTH - 71B	BOURNEMOUTH - 71B	BOURNEMOUTH - 71B	BOURNEMOUTH - 71B	BOURNEMOUTH - 71B
30029	EASTLEIGH - 71A	EASTLEIGH - 71A	EASTLEIGH - 71A	EASTLEIGH - 71A	EASTLEIGH - 71A	EASTLEIGH - 71A	EASTLEIGH - 71A
30030	EXMOUTH JCN - 72A	EXMOUTH JCN - 72A	EXMOUTH JCN - 72A	EXMOUTH JCN - 72A	EXMOUTH JCN - 72A	EXMOUTH JCN - 72A	EXMOUTH JCN - 72A
30031	FELTHAM - 70B	FELTHAM - 70B	FELTHAM - 70B	FELTHAM - 70B	FELTHAM - 70B	FELTHAM - 70B	FELTHAM - 70B
30032	EXMOUTH JCN - 72A	EXMOUTH JCN - 72A	EXMOUTH JCN - 72A	EXMOUTH JCN - 72A	EXMOUTH JCN - 72A	EXMOUTH JCN - 72A	EXMOUTH JCN - 72A
30033	NINE ELMS - 70A	NINE ELMS - 70A	NINE ELMS - 70A	NINE ELMS - 70A	NINE ELMS - 70A	NINE ELMS - 70A	NINE ELMS - 70A
30034	EXMOUTH JCN - 72A	EXMOUTH JCN - 72A	EXMOUTH JCN - 72A	EXMOUTH JCN - 72A	EXMOUTH JCN - 72A	EXMOUTH JCN - 72A	EXMOUTH JCN - 72A
30035	PLYMOUTH - 72D	PLYMOUTH - 72D	PLYMOUTH - 72D	PLYMOUTH - 72D	PLYMOUTH - 72D	PLYMOUTH - 72D	PLYMOUTH - 72D
30036	BARNSTAPLE - 72E	BARNSTAPLE - 72E	BARNSTAPLE - 72E	BARNSTAPLE - 72E	BARNSTAPLE - 72E	BARNSTAPLE - 72E	BARNSTAPLE - 72E
30037	PLYMOUTH - 72D	PLYMOUTH - 72D	PLYMOUTH - 72D	PLYMOUTH - 72D	PLYMOUTH - 72D	PLYMOUTH - 72D	PLYMOUTH - 72D
30038	NINE ELMS - 70A	NINE ELMS - 70A	NINE ELMS - 70A	NINE ELMS - 70A	NINE ELMS - 70A	NINE ELMS - 70A	NINE ELMS - 70A
30039	EXMOUTH JCN - 72A	EXMOUTH JCN - 72A	EXMOUTH JCN - 72A	EXMOUTH JCN - 72A	EXMOUTH JCN - 72A	EXMOUTH JCN - 72A	EXMOUTH JCN - 72A
30040	BOURNEMOUTH - 71B	BOURNEMOUTH - 71B	BOURNEMOUTH - 71B	BOURNEMOUTH - 71B	BOURNEMOUTH - 71B	BOURNEMOUTH - 71B	BOURNEMOUTH - 71B
30041	SALISBURY - 72B	SALISBURY - 72B	SALISBURY - 72B	SALISBURY - 72B	SALISBURY - 72B	SALISBURY - 72B	SALISBURY - 72B
30042	BARNSTAPLE - 72E	BARNSTAPLE - 72E	BARNSTAPLE - 72E	BARNSTAPLE - 72E	BARNSTAPLE - 72E	BARNSTAPLE - 72E	BARNSTAPLE - 72E
30043	FELTHAM - 70B	FELTHAM - 70B	FELTHAM - 70B	FELTHAM - 70B	FELTHAM - 70B	FELTHAM - 70B	FELTHAM - 70B
30044	BARNSTAPLE - 72E	BARNSTAPLE - 72E	BARNSTAPLE - 72E	BARNSTAPLE - 72E	BARNSTAPLE - 72E	BARNSTAPLE - 72E	BARNSTAPLE - 72E
30045	FRATTON - 71D	FRATTON - 71D	FRATTON - 71D	FRATTON - 71D	FRATTON - 71D	FRATTON - 71D	FRATTON - 71D
30046	EXMOUTH JCN - 72A	EXMOUTH JCN - 72A	EXMOUTH JCN - 72A	EXMOUTH JCN - 72A	EXMOUTH JCN - 72A	EXMOUTH JCN - 72A	EXMOUTH JCN - 72A
30047	HORSHAM - 75D	HORSHAM - 75D	HORSHAM - 75D	HORSHAM - 75D	HORSHAM - 75D	HORSHAM - 75D	HORSHAM - 75D
30048	EASTLEIGH - 71A	EASTLEIGH - 71A	EASTLEIGH - 71A	EASTLEIGH - 71A	EASTLEIGH - 71A	EASTLEIGH - 71A	EASTLEIGH - 71A
30049	EXMOUTH JCN - 72A	EXMOUTH JCN - 72A	EXMOUTH JCN - 72A	EXMOUTH JCN - 72A	EXMOUTH JCN - 72A	EXMOUTH JCN - 72A	EXMOUTH JCN - 72A
30050	HORSHAM - 75D	HORSHAM - 75D	HORSHAM - 75D	HORSHAM - 75D	HORSHAM - 75D	HORSHAM - 75D	HORSHAM - 75D
30051	BOURNEMOUTH - 71B	BOURNEMOUTH - 71B	BOURNEMOUTH - 71B	BOURNEMOUTH - 71B	BOURNEMOUTH - 71B	BOURNEMOUTH - 71B	BOURNEMOUTH - 71B
30052	BOURNEMOUTH - 71B	BOURNEMOUTH - 71B	BOURNEMOUTH - 71B	BOURNEMOUTH - 71B	BOURNEMOUTH - 71B	BOURNEMOUTH - 71B	BOURNEMOUTH - 71B
30053	EASTLEIGH - 71A	EASTLEIGH - 71A	EASTLEIGH - 71A	EASTLEIGH - 71A	EASTLEIGH - 71A	EASTLEIGH - 71A	EASTLEIGH - 71A
30054	FRATTON - 71D	FRATTON - 71D	FRATTON - 71D	FRATTON - 71D	FRATTON - 71D	FRATTON - 71D	FRATTON - 71D
30055	EXMOUTH JCN - 72A	EXMOUTH JCN - 72A	EXMOUTH JCN - 72A	EXMOUTH JCN - 72A	EXMOUTH JCN - 72A	EXMOUTH JCN - 72A	EXMOUTH JCN - 72A
30056	GUILDFORD - 70C	GUILDFORD - 70C	GUILDFORD - 70C	GUILDFORD - 70C	GUILDFORD - 70C	GUILDFORD - 70C	GUILDFORD - 70C
30057	BOURNEMOUTH - 71B	BOURNEMOUTH - 71B	BOURNEMOUTH - 71B	BOURNEMOUTH - 71B	BOURNEMOUTH - 71B	BOURNEMOUTH - 71B	BOURNEMOUTH - 71B
30058	YEOVIL - 72C	YEOVIL - 72C	YEOVIL - 72C	YEOVIL - 72C	YEOVIL - 72C	YEOVIL - 72C	YEOVIL - 72C
30059	BOURNEMOUTH - 71B	BOURNEMOUTH - 71B	BOURNEMOUTH - 71B	BOURNEMOUTH - 71B	BOURNEMOUTH - 71B	BOURNEMOUTH - 71B	BOURNEMOUTH - 71B
30060	GUILDFORD - 70C	GUILDFORD - 70C	GUILDFORD - 70C	GUILDFORD - 70C	GUILDFORD - 70C	GUILDFORD - 70C	GUILDFORD - 70C
30104	BOURNEMOUTH - 71B	BOURNEMOUTH - 71B	BOURNEMOUTH - 71B	BOURNEMOUTH - 71B	BOURNEMOUTH - 71B	BOURNEMOUTH - 71B	BOURNEMOUTH - 71B
30105	EXMOUTH JCN - 72A	EXMOUTH JCN - 72A	EXMOUTH JCN - 72A	EXMOUTH JCN - 72A	EXMOUTH JCN - 72A	EXMOUTH JCN - 72A	EXMOUTH JCN - 72A
30106	BOURNEMOUTH - 71B	BOURNEMOUTH - 71B	BOURNEMOUTH - 71B	BOURNEMOUTH - 71B	BOURNEMOUTH - 71B	BOURNEMOUTH - 71B	BOURNEMOUTH - 71B
30107	PLYMOUTH - 72D	PLYMOUTH - 72D	PLYMOUTH - 72D	PLYMOUTH - 72D	PLYMOUTH - 72D	PLYMOUTH - 72D	PLYMOUTH - 72D
30108	GUILDFORD - 70C	GUILDFORD - 70C	GUILDFORD - 70C	GUILDFORD - 70C	GUILDFORD - 70C	GUILDFORD - 70C	GUILDFORD - 70C
30109	EASTLEIGH - 71A	EASTLEIGH - 71A	EASTLEIGH - 71A	EASTLEIGH - 71A	EASTLEIGH - 71A	EASTLEIGH - 71A	EASTLEIGH - 71A
30110	GUILDFORD - 70C	GUILDFORD - 70C	GUILDFORD - 70C	GUILDFORD - 70C	GUILDFORD - 70C	GUILDFORD - 70C	GUILDFORD - 70C
30111	BOURNEMOUTH - 71B	BOURNEMOUTH - 71B	BOURNEMOUTH - 71B	BOURNEMOUTH - 71B	BOURNEMOUTH - 71B	BOURNEMOUTH - 71B	BOURNEMOUTH - 71B
30112	BOURNEMOUTH - 71B	BOURNEMOUTH - 71B	BOURNEMOUTH - 71B	BOURNEMOUTH - 71B	BOURNEMOUTH - 71B	BOURNEMOUTH - 71B	BOURNEMOUTH - 71B
30123	NINE ELMS - 70A	NINE ELMS - 70A	NINE ELMS - 70A	NINE ELMS - 70A	NINE ELMS - 70A	NINE ELMS - 70A	NINE ELMS - 70A
30124	EXMOUTH JCN - 72A	EXMOUTH JCN - 72A	EXMOUTH JCN - 72A	EXMOUTH JCN - 72A	EXMOUTH JCN - 72A	EXMOUTH JCN - 72A	EXMOUTH JCN - 72A
30125	EASTLEIGH - 71A	EASTLEIGH - 71A	EASTLEIGH - 71A	EASTLEIGH - 71A	EASTLEIGH - 71A	EASTLEIGH - 71A	EASTLEIGH - 71A
30127	SALISBURY - 72B	SALISBURY - 72B	SALISBURY - 72B	SALISBURY - 72B	SALISBURY - 72B	SALISBURY - 72B	SALISBURY - 72B
30128	EASTLEIGH - 71A	EASTLEIGH - 71A	EASTLEIGH - 71A	EASTLEIGH - 71A	EASTLEIGH - 71A	EASTLEIGH - 71A	EASTLEIGH - 71A
30129	YEOVIL - 72C	YEOVIL - 72C	YEOVIL - 72C	YEOVIL - 72C	YEOVIL - 72C	YEOVIL - 72C	YEOVIL - 72C
30130	NINE ELMS - 70A	NINE ELMS - 70A	NINE ELMS - 70A	NINE ELMS - 70A	NINE ELMS - 70A	NINE ELMS - 70A	NINE ELMS - 70A
30131	BOURNEMOUTH - 71B	BOURNEMOUTH - 71B	BOURNEMOUTH - 71B	BOURNEMOUTH - 71B	BOURNEMOUTH - 71B	BOURNEMOUTH - 71B	BOURNEMOUTH - 71B
30132	NINE ELMS - 70A	NINE ELMS - 70A	NINE ELMS - 70A	NINE ELMS - 70A	NINE ELMS - 70A	NINE ELMS - 70A	NINE ELMS - 70A
30133	EXMOUTH JCN - 72A	EXMOUTH JCN - 72A	EXMOUTH JCN - 72A	EXMOUTH JCN - 72A	EXMOUTH JCN - 72A	EXMOUTH JCN - 72A	EXMOUTH JCN - 72A
30241	NINE ELMS - 70A	NINE ELMS - 70A	NINE ELMS - 70A	NINE ELMS - 70A	NINE ELMS - 70A	NINE ELMS - 70A	NINE ELMS - 70A
30242	EASTLEIGH - 71A	EASTLEIGH - 71A	EASTLEIGH - 71A	EASTLEIGH - 71A	EASTLEIGH - 71A	EASTLEIGH - 71A	EASTLEIGH - 71A
30243	SALISBURY - 72B	SALISBURY - 72B	SALISBURY - 72B	SALISBURY - 72B	SALISBURY - 72B	SALISBURY - 72B	SALISBURY - 72B
30244	NINE ELMS - 70A	NINE ELMS - 70A	NINE ELMS - 70A	NINE ELMS - 70A	NINE ELMS - 70A	NINE ELMS - 70A	NINE ELMS - 70A
30245	EXMOUTH JCN - 72A	EXMOUTH JCN - 72A	EXMOUTH JCN - 72A	EXMOUTH JCN - 72A	EXMOUTH JCN - 72A	EXMOUTH JCN - 72A	EXMOUTH JCN - 72A
30246	GUILDFORD - 70C	GUILDFORD - 70C	GUILDFORD - 70C	GUILDFORD - 70C	GUILDFORD - 70C	GUILDFORD - 70C	GUILDFORD - 70C
30247	BARNSTAPLE - 72E	BARNSTAPLE - 72E	BARNSTAPLE - 72E	BARNSTAPLE - 72E	BARNSTAPLE - 72E	BARNSTAPLE - 72E	BARNSTAPLE - 72E
30248	NINE ELMS - 70A	NINE ELMS - 70A	NINE ELMS - 70A	NINE ELMS - 70A	NINE ELMS - 70A	NINE ELMS - 70A	NINE ELMS - 70A
30249	NINE ELMS - 70A	NINE ELMS - 70A	NINE ELMS - 70A	NINE ELMS - 70A	NINE ELMS - 70A	NINE ELMS - 70A	NINE ELMS - 70A
30250	BARNSTAPLE - 72E	BARNSTAPLE - 72E	BARNSTAPLE - 72E	BARNSTAPLE - 72E	BARNSTAPLE - 72E	BARNSTAPLE - 72E	BARNSTAPLE - 72E
30251	BOURNEMOUTH - 71B	BOURNEMOUTH - 71B	BOURNEMOUTH - 71B	BOURNEMOUTH - 71B	BOURNEMOUTH - 71B	BOURNEMOUTH - 71B	BOURNEMOUTH - 71B
30252	EXMOUTH JCN - 72A	EXMOUTH JCN - 72A	EXMOUTH JCN - 72A	EXMOUTH JCN - 72A	EXMOUTH JCN - 72A	EXMOUTH JCN - 72A	EXMOUTH JCN - 72A
30253	EXMOUTH JCN - 72A	EXMOUTH JCN - 72A	EXMOUTH JCN - 72A	EXMOUTH JCN - 72A	EXMOUTH JCN - 72A	EXMOUTH JCN - 72A	EXMOUTH JCN - 72A
30254	FELTHAM - 70B	FELTHAM - 70B	FELTHAM - 70B	FELTHAM - 70B	FELTHAM - 70B	FELTHAM - 70B	FELTHAM - 70B
30255	EXMOUTH JCN - 72A	EXMOUTH JCN - 72A	EXMOUTH JCN - 72A	EXMOUTH JCN - 72A	EXMOUTH JCN - 72A	EXMOUTH JCN - 72A	EXMOUTH JCN - 72A
30256	EXMOUTH JCN - 72A	EXMOUTH JCN - 72A	EXMOUTH JCN - 72A	EXMOUTH JCN - 72A	EXMOUTH JCN - 72A	EXMOUTH JCN - 72A	EXMOUTH JCN - 72A
30318	BOURNEMOUTH - 71B	BOURNEMOUTH - 71B	BOURNEMOUTH - 71B	BOURNEMOUTH - 71B	BOURNEMOUTH - 71B	BOURNEMOUTH - 71B	BOURNEMOUTH - 71B
30319	NINE ELMS - 70A	NINE ELMS - 70A	NINE ELMS - 70A	NINE ELMS - 70A	NINE ELMS - 70A	NINE ELMS - 70A	NINE ELMS - 70A
30320	EXMOUTH JCN - 72A	EXMOUTH JCN - 72A	EXMOUTH JCN - 72A	EXMOUTH JCN - 72A	EXMOUTH JCN - 72A	EXMOUTH JCN - 72A	EXMOUTH JCN - 72A
30321	BARNSTAPLE - 72E	BARNSTAPLE - 72E	BARNSTAPLE - 72E	BARNSTAPLE - 72E	BARNSTAPLE - 72E	BARNSTAPLE - 72E	BARNSTAPLE - 72E
30322	NINE ELMS - 70A	NINE ELMS - 70A	NINE ELMS - 70A	NINE ELMS - 70A	NINE ELMS - 70A	NINE ELMS - 70A	NINE ELMS - 70A
30323	EXMOUTH JCN - 72A	EXMOUTH JCN - 72A	EXMOUTH JCN - 72A	EXMOUTH JCN - 72A	EXMOUTH JCN - 72A	EXMOUTH JCN - 72A	EXMOUTH JCN - 72A
30324	GUILDFORD - 70C	GUILDFORD - 70C	GUILDFORD - 70C	GUILDFORD - 70C	GUILDFORD - 70C	GUILDFORD - 70C	GUILDFORD - 70C
30328	GUILDFORD - 70C	GUILDFORD - 70C	GUILDFORD - 70C	GUILDFORD - 70C	GUILDFORD - 70C	GUILDFORD - 70C	GUILDFORD - 70C
30356	PLYMOUTH - 72D	PLYMOUTH - 72D	PLYMOUTH - 72D	PLYMOUTH - 72D	PLYMOUTH - 72D	PLYMOUTH - 72D	PLYMOUTH - 72D
30357	EASTLEIGH - 71A	EASTLEIGH - 71A	EASTLEIGH - 71A	EASTLEIGH - 71A	EASTLEIGH - 71A	EASTLEIGH - 71A	EASTLEIGH - 71A
30374	EXMOUTH JCN - 72A	EXMOUTH JCN - 72A	EXMOUTH JCN - 72A	EXMOUTH JCN - 72A	EXMOUTH JCN - 72A	EXMOUTH JCN - 72A	EXMOUTH JCN - 72A
30375	PLYMOUTH - 72D	PLYMOUTH - 72D	PLYMOUTH - 72D	PLYMOUTH - 72D	PLYMOUTH - 72D	PLYMOUTH - 72D	PLYMOUTH - 72D
30376	EXMOUTH JCN - 72A	EXMOUTH JCN - 72A	EXMOUTH JCN - 72A	EXMOUTH JCN - 72A	EXMOUTH JCN - 72A	EXMOUTH JCN - 72A	EXMOUTH JCN - 72A
30377	EXMOUTH JCN - 72A	EXMOUTH JCN - 72A	EXMOUTH JCN - 72A	EXMOUTH JCN - 72A	EXMOUTH JCN - 72A	EXMOUTH JCN - 72A	EXMOUTH JCN - 72A
30378	GUILDFORD - 70C	GUILDFORD - 70C	EASTLEIGH - 71A	EASTLEIGH - 71A	EASTLEIGH - 71A	EASTLEIGH - 71A	EASTLEIGH - 71A
30379	BOURNEMOUTH - 71B	BOURNEMOUTH - 71B	BOURNEMOUTH - 71B	BOURNEMOUTH - 71B	BOURNEMOUTH - 71B	BOURNEMOUTH - 71B	BOURNEMOUTH - 71B
30479	EASTLEIGH - 71A	EASTLEIGH - 71A	EASTLEIGH - 71A	EASTLEIGH - 71A	EASTLEIGH - 71A	EASTLEIGH - 71A	EASTLEIGH - 71A
30480	FRATTON - 71D	FRATTON - 71D	FRATTON - 71D	FRATTON - 71D	FRATTON - 71D	FRATTON - 71D	FRATTON - 71D
30481	GUILDFORD - 70C	GUILDFORD - 70C	GUILDFORD - 70C	GUILDFORD - 70C	GUILDFORD - 70C	GUILDFORD - 70C	GUILDFORD - 70C
30667	NINE ELMS - 70A	NINE ELMS - 70A	NINE ELMS - 70A	NINE ELMS - 70A	NINE ELMS - 70A	NINE ELMS - 70A	NINE ELMS - 70A
30668	EXMOUTH JCN - 72A	EXMOUTH JCN - 72A	EXMOUTH JCN - 72A	EXMOUTH JCN - 72A	EXMOUTH JCN - 72A	EXMOUTH JCN - 72A	EXMOUTH JCN - 72A
30669	EXMOUTH JCN - 72A	EXMOUTH JCN - 72A	EXMOUTH JCN - 72A	EXMOUTH JCN - 72A	EXMOUTH JCN - 72A	EXMOUTH JCN - 72A	EXMOUTH JCN - 72A
30670	BARNSTAPLE - 72E	BARNSTAPLE - 72E	BARNSTAPLE - 72E	BARNSTAPLE - 72E	BARNSTAPLE - 72E	BARNSTAPLE - 72E	BARNSTAPLE - 72E
30671	EXMOUTH JCN - 72A	EXMOUTH JCN - 72A	EXMOUTH JCN - 72A	EXMOUTH JCN - 72A	EXMOUTH JCN - 72A	EXMOUTH JCN - 72A	EXMOUTH JCN - 72A
30673	EASTLEIGH - 71A	EASTLEIGH - 71A	EASTLEIGH - 71A	EASTLEIGH - 71A	EASTLEIGH - 71A	EASTLEIGH - 71A	EASTLEIGH - 71A
30674	EASTLEIGH - 71A	EASTLEIGH - 71A	EASTLEIGH - 71A	EASTLEIGH - 71A	EASTLEIGH - 71A	EASTLEIGH - 71A	EASTLEIGH - 71A
30675	SALISBURY - 72B	SALISBURY - 72B	SALISBURY - 72B	SALISBURY - 72B	SALISBURY - 72B	SALISBURY - 72B	SALISBURY - 72B
30676	NINE ELMS - 70A	NINE ELMS - 70A	NINE ELMS - 70A	NINE ELMS - 70A	NINE ELMS - 70A	NINE ELMS - 70A	NINE ELMS - 70A

loco	Apr-50	Sep-50	Oct-50	Nov-50	Dec-50	Mar-51	Apr-51
				M7 0-4-4T (1897)			
30021	HORSHAM - 75D	GUILDFORD - 70C	GUILDFORD - 70C	GUILDFORD - 70C	GUILDFORD - 70C	EXMOUTHJCN - 72A	EXMOUTHJCN - 72A
30022	GUILDFORD - 70C	GUILDFORD - 70C	GUILDFORD - 70C	GUILDFORD - 70C	GUILDFORD - 70C	GUILDFORD - 70C	GUILDFORD - 70C
30023	SALISBURY - 72B	SALISBURY - 72B	SALISBURY - 72B	SALISBURY - 72B	SALISBURY - 72B	EXMOUTHJCN - 72A	EXMOUTHJCN - 72A
30024	EXMOUTHJCN - 72A	EXMOUTHJCN - 72A	EXMOUTHJCN - 72A	EXMOUTHJCN - 72A	EXMOUTHJCN - 72A	EXMOUTHJCN - 72A	EXMOUTHJCN - 72A
30025	EXMOUTHJCN - 72A	EXMOUTHJCN - 72A	EXMOUTHJCN - 72A	EXMOUTHJCN - 72A	EXMOUTHJCN - 72A	EXMOUTHJCN - 72A	EXMOUTHJCN - 72A
30026	GUILDFORD - 70C	GUILDFORD - 70C	GUILDFORD - 70C	GUILDFORD - 70C	GUILDFORD - 70C	GUILDFORD - 70C	GUILDFORD - 70C
30027	HORSHAM - 75D	HORSHAM - 75D	HORSHAM - 75D	HORSHAM - 75D	HORSHAM - 75D	HORSHAM - 75D	GUILDFORD - 70C
30028	BOURNEMOUTH - 71B	BOURNEMOUTH - 71B	BOURNEMOUTH - 71B	BOURNEMOUTH - 71B	BOURNEMOUTH - 71B	BOURNEMOUTH - 71B	BOURNEMOUTH - 71B
30029	EASTLEIGH - 71A	EASTLEIGH - 71A	EASTLEIGH - 71A	EASTLEIGH - 71A	EASTLEIGH - 71A	EASTLEIGH - 71A	EASTLEIGH - 71A
30030	EXMOUTHJCN - 72A	EXMOUTHJCN - 72A	EXMOUTHJCN - 72A	EXMOUTHJCN - 72A	EXMOUTHJCN - 72A	EXMOUTHJCN - 72A	EXMOUTHJCN - 72A
30031	FELTHAM - 70B	EASTLEIGH - 71A	EASTLEIGH - 71A	EASTLEIGH - 71A	EASTLEIGH - 71A	EASTLEIGH - 71A	EASTLEIGH - 71A
30032	EASTLEIGH - 71A	EASTLEIGH - 71A	EASTLEIGH - 71A	EASTLEIGH - 71A	EASTLEIGH - 71A	EASTLEIGH - 71A	EASTLEIGH - 71A
30033	EASTLEIGH - 71A	EASTLEIGH - 71A	EASTLEIGH - 71A	EASTLEIGH - 71A	EASTLEIGH - 71A	EASTLEIGH - 71A	EASTLEIGH - 71A
30034	EXMOUTHJCN - 72A	EXMOUTHJCN - 72A	EXMOUTHJCN - 72A	EXMOUTHJCN - 72A	EXMOUTHJCN - 72A	YEOVIL - 72C	YEOVIL - 72C
30035	PLYMOUTH - 72D	PLYMOUTH - 72D	PLYMOUTH - 72D	PLYMOUTH - 72D	PLYMOUTH - 72D	PLYMOUTH - 72D	PLYMOUTH - 72D
30036	BARNSTAPLE - 72E	BARNSTAPLE - 72E	BARNSTAPLE - 72E	BARNSTAPLE - 72E	BARNSTAPLE - 72E	YEOVIL - 72C	YEOVIL - 72C
30037	PLYMOUTH - 72D	PLYMOUTH - 72D	PLYMOUTH - 72D	PLYMOUTH - 72D	PLYMOUTH - 72D	PLYMOUTH - 72D	PLYMOUTH - 72D
30038	NINE ELMS - 70A	NINE ELMS - 70A	NINE ELMS - 70A	NINE ELMS - 70A	NINE ELMS - 70A	NINE ELMS - 70A	FELTHAM - 70B
30039	EXMOUTHJCN - 72A	EXMOUTHJCN - 72A	EXMOUTHJCN - 72A	EXMOUTHJCN - 72A	EXMOUTHJCN - 72A	EXMOUTHJCN - 72A	EXMOUTHJCN - 72A
30040	BOURNEMOUTH - 71B	BOURNEMOUTH - 71B	BOURNEMOUTH - 71B	BOURNEMOUTH - 71B	BOURNEMOUTH - 71B	BOURNEMOUTH - 71B	BOURNEMOUTH - 71B
30041	SALISBURY - 72B	SALISBURY - 72B	SALISBURY - 72B	SALISBURY - 72B	SALISBURY - 72B	SALISBURY - 72B	EXMOUTHJCN - 72A
30042	BARNSTAPLE - 72E	BARNSTAPLE - 72E	BARNSTAPLE - 72E	BARNSTAPLE - 72E	BARNSTAPLE - 72E	BARNSTAPLE - 72E	BARNSTAPLE - 72E
30043	FELTHAM - 70B	FELTHAM - 70B	FELTHAM - 70B	FELTHAM - 70B	FELTHAM - 70B	FELTHAM - 70B	FELTHAM - 70B
30044	BARNSTAPLE - 72E	BARNSTAPLE - 72E	BARNSTAPLE - 72E	BARNSTAPLE - 72E	BARNSTAPLE - 72E	BARNSTAPLE - 72E	BARNSTAPLE - 72E
30045	FRATTON - 71D	FRATTON - 71D	FRATTON - 71D	FRATTON - 71D	FRATTON - 71D	FRATTON - 71D	FRATTON - 71D
30046	EXMOUTHJCN - 72A	EXMOUTHJCN - 72A	EXMOUTHJCN - 72A	EXMOUTHJCN - 72A	EXMOUTHJCN - 72A	EXMOUTHJCN - 72A	EXMOUTHJCN - 72A
30047	HORSHAM - 75D	HORSHAM - 75D	HORSHAM - 75D	HORSHAM - 75D	HORSHAM - 75D	HORSHAM - 75D	HORSHAM - 75D
30048	EASTLEIGH - 71A	EASTLEIGH - 71A	EASTLEIGH - 71A	EASTLEIGH - 71A	EASTLEIGH - 71A	EASTLEIGH - 71A	EASTLEIGH - 71A
30049	EXMOUTHJCN - 72A	EXMOUTHJCN - 72A	EXMOUTHJCN - 72A	EXMOUTHJCN - 72A	EXMOUTHJCN - 72A	EXMOUTHJCN - 72A	HORSHAM - 75D
30050	FRATTON - 71D	FRATTON - 71D	FRATTON - 71D	FRATTON - 71D	FRATTON - 71D	FRATTON - 71D	FRATTON - 71D
30051	BOURNEMOUTH - 71B	BOURNEMOUTH - 71B	BOURNEMOUTH - 71B	BOURNEMOUTH - 71B	BOURNEMOUTH - 71B	BOURNEMOUTH - 71B	BOURNEMOUTH - 71B
30052	BOURNEMOUTH - 71B	BOURNEMOUTH - 71B	BOURNEMOUTH - 71B	BOURNEMOUTH - 71B	BOURNEMOUTH - 71B	BOURNEMOUTH - 71B	BOURNEMOUTH - 71B
30053	EASTLEIGH - 71A	EASTLEIGH - 71A	EASTLEIGH - 71A	FRATTON - 71D	FRATTON - 71D	FRATTON - 71D	FRATTON - 71D
30054	FRATTON - 71D	FRATTON - 71D	FRATTON - 71D	FRATTON - 71D	FRATTON - 71D	FRATTON - 71D	FRATTON - 71D
30055	EXMOUTHJCN - 72A	EXMOUTHJCN - 72A	EXMOUTHJCN - 72A	EXMOUTHJCN - 72A	EXMOUTHJCN - 72A	EXMOUTHJCN - 72A	EXMOUTHJCN - 72A
30056	GUILDFORD - 70C	GUILDFORD - 70C	GUILDFORD - 70C	GUILDFORD - 70C	GUILDFORD - 70C	GUILDFORD - 70C	GUILDFORD - 70C
30057	BOURNEMOUTH - 71B	BOURNEMOUTH - 71B	BOURNEMOUTH - 71B	BOURNEMOUTH - 71B	BOURNEMOUTH - 71B	BOURNEMOUTH - 71B	BOURNEMOUTH - 71B
30058	YEOVIL - 72C	YEOVIL - 72C	YEOVIL - 72C	YEOVIL - 72C	YEOVIL - 72C	YEOVIL - 72C	YEOVIL - 72C
30059	BOURNEMOUTH - 71B	BOURNEMOUTH - 71B	BOURNEMOUTH - 71B	BOURNEMOUTH - 71B	BOURNEMOUTH - 71B	BOURNEMOUTH - 71B	BOURNEMOUTH - 71B
30060	GUILDFORD - 70C	GUILDFORD - 70C	GUILDFORD - 70C	GUILDFORD - 70C	GUILDFORD - 70C	GUILDFORD - 70C	GUILDFORD - 70C
30104	BOURNEMOUTH - 71B	BOURNEMOUTH - 71B	BOURNEMOUTH - 71B	BOURNEMOUTH - 71B	BOURNEMOUTH - 71B	BOURNEMOUTH - 71B	BOURNEMOUTH - 71B
30105	EXMOUTHJCN - 72A	EXMOUTHJCN - 72A	EXMOUTHJCN - 72A	EXMOUTHJCN - 72A	EXMOUTHJCN - 72A	EXMOUTHJCN - 72A	EXMOUTHJCN - 72A
30106	BOURNEMOUTH - 71B	BOURNEMOUTH - 71B	BOURNEMOUTH - 71B	BOURNEMOUTH - 71B	BOURNEMOUTH - 71B	BOURNEMOUTH - 71B	BOURNEMOUTH - 71B
30107	PLYMOUTH - 72D	PLYMOUTH - 72D	PLYMOUTH - 72D	PLYMOUTH - 72D	PLYMOUTH - 72D	PLYMOUTH - 72D	PLYMOUTH - 72D
30108	GUILDFORD - 70C	GUILDFORD - 70C	GUILDFORD - 70C	GUILDFORD - 70C	GUILDFORD - 70C	GUILDFORD - 70C	GUILDFORD - 70C
30109	EASTLEIGH - 71A	EASTLEIGH - 71A	EASTLEIGH - 71A	EASTLEIGH - 71A	EASTLEIGH - 71A	GUILDFORD - 70C	GUILDFORD - 70C
30110	GUILDFORD - 70C	GUILDFORD - 70C	GUILDFORD - 70C	GUILDFORD - 70C	GUILDFORD - 70C	GUILDFORD - 70C	GUILDFORD - 70C
30111	BOURNEMOUTH - 71B	BOURNEMOUTH - 71B	BOURNEMOUTH - 71B	BOURNEMOUTH - 71B	BOURNEMOUTH - 71B	BOURNEMOUTH - 71B	BOURNEMOUTH - 71B
30112	BOURNEMOUTH - 71B	BOURNEMOUTH - 71B	BOURNEMOUTH - 71B	BOURNEMOUTH - 71B	BOURNEMOUTH - 71B	BOURNEMOUTH - 71B	BOURNEMOUTH - 71B
30123	NINE ELMS - 70A	NINE ELMS - 70A	NINE ELMS - 70A	NINE ELMS - 70A	NINE ELMS - 70A	NINE ELMS - 70A	NINE ELMS - 70A
30124	EXMOUTHJCN - 72A	EXMOUTHJCN - 72A	EXMOUTHJCN - 72A	EXMOUTHJCN - 72A	EXMOUTHJCN - 72A	EXMOUTHJCN - 72A	EXMOUTHJCN - 72A
30125	EASTLEIGH - 71A	EASTLEIGH - 71A	EASTLEIGH - 71A	EASTLEIGH - 71A	EASTLEIGH - 71A	EASTLEIGH - 71A	EASTLEIGH - 71A
30127	SALISBURY - 72B	BOURNEMOUTH - 71B	BOURNEMOUTH - 71B	EASTLEIGH - 71A	EASTLEIGH - 71A	EASTLEIGH - 71A	EASTLEIGH - 71A
30128	EASTLEIGH - 71A	EASTLEIGH - 71A	EASTLEIGH - 71A	EASTLEIGH - 71A	EASTLEIGH - 71A	EASTLEIGH - 71A	EASTLEIGH - 71A
30129	YEOVIL - 72C	YEOVIL - 72C	YEOVIL - 72C	YEOVIL - 72C	YEOVIL - 72C	YEOVIL - 72C	YEOVIL - 72C
30130	NINE ELMS - 70A	NINE ELMS - 70A	NINE ELMS - 70A	NINE ELMS - 70A	NINE ELMS - 70A	NINE ELMS - 70A	NINE ELMS - 70A
30131	BOURNEMOUTH - 71B	BOURNEMOUTH - 71B	BOURNEMOUTH - 71B	BOURNEMOUTH - 71B	BOURNEMOUTH - 71B	BOURNEMOUTH - 71B	BOURNEMOUTH - 71B
30132	NINE ELMS - 70A	NINE ELMS - 70A	NINE ELMS - 70A	NINE ELMS - 70A	NINE ELMS - 70A	NINE ELMS - 70A	NINE ELMS - 70A
30133	EXMOUTHJCN - 72A	EXMOUTHJCN - 72A	EXMOUTHJCN - 72A	EXMOUTHJCN - 72A	EXMOUTHJCN - 72A	EXMOUTHJCN - 72A	EXMOUTHJCN - 72A
30241	NINE ELMS - 70A	NINE ELMS - 70A	NINE ELMS - 70A	NINE ELMS - 70A	NINE ELMS - 70A	NINE ELMS - 70A	NINE ELMS - 70A
30242	EASTLEIGH - 71A	EASTLEIGH - 71A	EASTLEIGH - 71A	EASTLEIGH - 71A	EASTLEIGH - 71A	EASTLEIGH - 71A	EASTLEIGH - 71A
30243	SALISBURY - 72B	SALISBURY - 72B	SALISBURY - 72B	EASTLEIGH - 71A	EASTLEIGH - 71A	EASTLEIGH - 71A	EASTLEIGH - 71A
30244	NINE ELMS - 70A	NINE ELMS - 70A	NINE ELMS - 70A	NINE ELMS - 70A	NINE ELMS - 70A	NINE ELMS - 70A	NINE ELMS - 70A
30245	EXMOUTHJCN - 72A	EXMOUTHJCN - 72A	EXMOUTHJCN - 72A	EXMOUTHJCN - 72A	EXMOUTHJCN - 72A	EXMOUTHJCN - 72A	EXMOUTHJCN - 72A
30246	GUILDFORD - 70C	GUILDFORD - 70C	GUILDFORD - 70C	GUILDFORD - 70C	GUILDFORD - 70C	GUILDFORD - 70C	GUILDFORD - 70C
30247	BARNSTAPLE - 72E	BARNSTAPLE - 72E	BARNSTAPLE - 72E	BARNSTAPLE - 72E	BARNSTAPLE - 72E	BARNSTAPLE - 72E	BARNSTAPLE - 72E
30248	NINE ELMS - 70A	NINE ELMS - 70A	NINE ELMS - 70A	NINE ELMS - 70A	NINE ELMS - 70A	NINE ELMS - 70A	NINE ELMS - 70A
30249	NINE ELMS - 70A	NINE ELMS - 70A	NINE ELMS - 70A	FELTHAM - 70B	FELTHAM - 70B	FELTHAM - 70B	NINE ELMS - 70A
30250	BARNSTAPLE - 72E	BARNSTAPLE - 72E	BARNSTAPLE - 72E	BARNSTAPLE - 72E	BARNSTAPLE - 72E	BARNSTAPLE - 72E	BARNSTAPLE - 72E
30251	BOURNEMOUTH - 71B	BOURNEMOUTH - 71B	BOURNEMOUTH - 71B	BOURNEMOUTH - 71B	BOURNEMOUTH - 71B	BARNSTAPLE - 72E	BARNSTAPLE - 72E
30252	EXMOUTHJCN - 72A	EXMOUTHJCN - 72A	EXMOUTHJCN - 72A	EXMOUTHJCN - 72A	EXMOUTHJCN - 72A	BARNSTAPLE - 72E	BARNSTAPLE - 72E
30253	EXMOUTHJCN - 72A	EASTLEIGH - 71A	EASTLEIGH - 71A	EASTLEIGH - 71A	EASTLEIGH - 71A	BARNSTAPLE - 72E	BARNSTAPLE - 72E
30254	FELTHAM - 70B	FELTHAM - 70B	FELTHAM - 70B	FELTHAM - 70B	FELTHAM - 70B	FELTHAM - 70B	FELTHAM - 70B
30255	EXMOUTHJCN - 72A	EXMOUTHJCN - 72A	EXMOUTHJCN - 72A	EXMOUTHJCN - 72A	EXMOUTHJCN - 72A	EXMOUTHJCN - 72A	EXMOUTHJCN - 72A
30256	EXMOUTHJCN - 72A	EXMOUTHJCN - 72A	EXMOUTHJCN - 72A	EXMOUTHJCN - 72A	EXMOUTHJCN - 72A	EXMOUTHJCN - 72A	EXMOUTHJCN - 72A
30318	BOURNEMOUTH - 71B	BOURNEMOUTH - 71B	BOURNEMOUTH - 71B	BOURNEMOUTH - 71B	BOURNEMOUTH - 71B	BOURNEMOUTH - 71B	BOURNEMOUTH - 71B
30319	NINE ELMS - 70A	NINE ELMS - 70A	NINE ELMS - 70A	NINE ELMS - 70A	NINE ELMS - 70A	NINE ELMS - 70A	BOURNEMOUTH - 71B
30320	EXMOUTHJCN - 72A	EXMOUTHJCN - 72A	EXMOUTHJCN - 72A	EXMOUTHJCN - 72A	EXMOUTHJCN - 72A	EXMOUTHJCN - 72A	BOURNEMOUTH - 71B
30321	BARNSTAPLE - 72E	BARNSTAPLE - 72E	BARNSTAPLE - 72E	BARNSTAPLE - 72E	BARNSTAPLE - 72E	BARNSTAPLE - 72E	BOURNEMOUTH - 71B
30322	NINE ELMS - 70A	NINE ELMS - 70A	NINE ELMS - 70A	NINE ELMS - 70A	NINE ELMS - 70A	NINE ELMS - 70A	EASTLEIGH - 71A
30323	EXMOUTHJCN - 72A	EXMOUTHJCN - 72A	EXMOUTHJCN - 72A	EXMOUTHJCN - 72A	EXMOUTHJCN - 72A	EXMOUTHJCN - 72A	EASTLEIGH - 71A
30324	GUILDFORD - 70C	GUILDFORD - 70C	GUILDFORD - 70C	GUILDFORD - 70C	GUILDFORD - 70C	GUILDFORD - 70C	EASTLEIGH - 71A
30328	GUILDFORD - 70C	GUILDFORD - 70C	GUILDFORD - 70C	GUILDFORD - 70C	GUILDFORD - 70C	GUILDFORD - 70C	EASTLEIGH - 71A
30356	PLYMOUTH - 72D	PLYMOUTH - 72D	PLYMOUTH - 72D	PLYMOUTH - 72D	PLYMOUTH - 72D	EXMOUTHJCN - 72A	EXMOUTHJCN - 72A
30357	EASTLEIGH - 71A	EASTLEIGH - 71A	EASTLEIGH - 71A	EASTLEIGH - 71A	EASTLEIGH - 71A	EASTLEIGH - 71A	EASTLEIGH - 71A
30374	EXMOUTHJCN - 72A	EXMOUTHJCN - 72A	EXMOUTHJCN - 72A	EXMOUTHJCN - 72A	PLYMOUTH - 72D	EXMOUTHJCN - 72A	EXMOUTHJCN - 72A
30375	PLYMOUTH - 72D	PLYMOUTH - 72D	PLYMOUTH - 72D	PLYMOUTH - 72D	PLYMOUTH - 72D	EXMOUTHJCN - 72A	EXMOUTHJCN - 72A
30376	EXMOUTHJCN - 72A	EXMOUTHJCN - 72A	EXMOUTHJCN - 72A	EXMOUTHJCN - 72A	EXMOUTHJCN - 72A	EXMOUTHJCN - 72A	EXMOUTHJCN - 72A
30377	EXMOUTHJCN - 72A	EXMOUTHJCN - 72A	EXMOUTHJCN - 72A	EXMOUTHJCN - 72A	EXMOUTHJCN - 72A	EXMOUTHJCN - 72A	EXMOUTHJCN - 72A
30378	EASTLEIGH - 71A	EASTLEIGH - 71A	EASTLEIGH - 71A	EASTLEIGH - 71A	EASTLEIGH - 71A	EASTLEIGH - 71A	EXMOUTHJCN - 72A
30379	BOURNEMOUTH - 71B	BOURNEMOUTH - 71B	BOURNEMOUTH - 71B	BOURNEMOUTH - 71B	BOURNEMOUTH - 71B	BOURNEMOUTH - 71B	EXMOUTHJCN - 72A
30479	EASTLEIGH - 71A	EASTLEIGH - 71A	EASTLEIGH - 71A	EASTLEIGH - 71A	EASTLEIGH - 71A	EASTLEIGH - 71A	EASTLEIGH - 71A
30480	FRATTON - 71D	FRATTON - 71D	FRATTON - 71D	FRATTON - 71D	FRATTON - 71D	EASTLEIGH - 71A	EASTLEIGH - 71A
30481	GUILDFORD - 70C	GUILDFORD - 70C	GUILDFORD - 70C	GUILDFORD - 70C	GUILDFORD - 70C	GUILDFORD - 70C	GUILDFORD - 70C
30667	NINE ELMS - 70A	NINE ELMS - 70A	NINE ELMS - 70A	EASTLEIGH - 71A	EASTLEIGH - 71A	EASTLEIGH - 71A	EXMOUTHJCN - 72A
30668	EXMOUTHJCN - 72A	EXMOUTHJCN - 72A	EXMOUTHJCN - 72A	EXMOUTHJCN - 72A	EXMOUTHJCN - 72A	EXMOUTHJCN - 72A	EXMOUTHJCN - 72A
30669	EXMOUTHJCN - 72A	EXMOUTHJCN - 72A	EXMOUTHJCN - 72A	EXMOUTHJCN - 72A	EXMOUTHJCN - 72A	EXMOUTHJCN - 72A	EXMOUTHJCN - 72A
30670	BARNSTAPLE - 72E	BARNSTAPLE - 72E	BARNSTAPLE - 72E	BARNSTAPLE - 72E	BARNSTAPLE - 72E	EXMOUTHJCN - 72A	EXMOUTHJCN - 72A
30671	EXMOUTHJCN - 72A	EXMOUTHJCN - 72A	EXMOUTHJCN - 72A	EXMOUTHJCN - 72A	EXMOUTHJCN - 72A	EXMOUTHJCN - 72A	EXMOUTHJCN - 72A
30673	EASTLEIGH - 71A	EASTLEIGH - 71A	EASTLEIGH - 71A	EASTLEIGH - 71A	EASTLEIGH - 71A	SALISBURY - 72B	SALISBURY - 72B
30674	EASTLEIGH - 71A	EASTLEIGH - 71A	EASTLEIGH - 71A	EASTLEIGH - 71A	EASTLEIGH - 71A	SALISBURY - 72B	SALISBURY - 72B
30675	SALISBURY - 72B	SALISBURY - 72B	SALISBURY - 72B	SALISBURY - 72B	SALISBURY - 72B	SALISBURY - 72B	SALISBURY - 72B
30676	NINE ELMS - 70A	NINE ELMS - 70A	NINE ELMS - 70A	NINE ELMS - 70A	NINE ELMS - 70A	NINE ELMS - 70A	NINE ELMS - 70A

loco	Jun-51	Jul-51	Sep-51	Dec-51	Jan-52	Mar-52	Jun-52
				M7 0-4-4T (1897)			
30021	EXMOUTHJCN - 72A	EXMOUTHJCN - 72A	EXMOUTHJCN - 72A	EXMOUTHJCN - 72A	EXMOUTHJCN - 72A	EXMOUTHJCN - 72A	EXMOUTHJCN - 72A
30022	GUILDFORD - 70C	GUILDFORD - 70C	GUILDFORD - 70C	GUILDFORD - 70C	GUILDFORD - 70C	GUILDFORD - 70C	GUILDFORD - 70C
30023	EXMOUTHJCN - 72A	EXMOUTHJCN - 72A	EXMOUTHJCN - 72A	EXMOUTHJCN - 72A	EXMOUTHJCN - 72A	EXMOUTHJCN - 72A	EXMOUTHJCN - 72A
30024	EXMOUTHJCN - 72A	EXMOUTHJCN - 72A	EXMOUTHJCN - 72A	EXMOUTHJCN - 72A	EXMOUTHJCN - 72A	EXMOUTHJCN - 72A	EXMOUTHJCN - 72A
30025	EXMOUTHJCN - 72A	EXMOUTHJCN - 72A	EXMOUTHJCN - 72A	EXMOUTHJCN - 72A	EXMOUTHJCN - 72A	EXMOUTHJCN - 72A	EXMOUTHJCN - 72A
30026	GUILDFORD - 70C	GUILDFORD - 70C	GUILDFORD - 70C	GUILDFORD - 70C	GUILDFORD - 70C	GUILDFORD - 70C	GUILDFORD - 70C
30027	GUILDFORD - 70C	GUILDFORD - 70C	GUILDFORD - 70C	GUILDFORD - 70C	GUILDFORD - 70C	GUILDFORD - 70C	GUILDFORD - 70C
30028	GUILDFORD - 70C	GUILDFORD - 70C	GUILDFORD - 70C	GUILDFORD - 70C	GUILDFORD - 70C	GUILDFORD - 70C	GUILDFORD - 70C
30029	EASTLEIGH - 71A	EASTLEIGH - 71A	EASTLEIGH - 71A	EASTLEIGH - 71A	EASTLEIGH - 71A	EASTLEIGH - 71A	EASTLEIGH - 71A
30030	EXMOUTHJCN - 72A	EXMOUTHJCN - 72A	EXMOUTHJCN - 72A	EXMOUTHJCN - 72A	EXMOUTHJCN - 72A	EASTLEIGH - 71A	EASTLEIGH - 71A
30031	EASTLEIGH - 71A	EASTLEIGH - 71A	EASTLEIGH - 71A	EASTLEIGH - 71A	EASTLEIGH - 71A	EASTLEIGH - 71A	EASTLEIGH - 71A
30032	EASTLEIGH - 71A	EASTLEIGH - 71A	EASTLEIGH - 71A	EASTLEIGH - 71A	EASTLEIGH - 71A	EASTLEIGH - 71A	EASTLEIGH - 71A
30033	EASTLEIGH - 71A	EASTLEIGH - 71A	EASTLEIGH - 71A	EASTLEIGH - 71A	EASTLEIGH - 71A	EASTLEIGH - 71A	EASTLEIGH - 71A
30034	YEOVIL - 72C	YEOVIL - 72C	YEOVIL - 72C	YEOVIL - 72C	YEOVIL - 72C	YEOVIL - 72C	YEOVIL - 72C
30035	PLYMOUTH - 72D	PLYMOUTH - 72D	PLYMOUTH - 72D	PLYMOUTH - 72D	PLYMOUTH - 72D	PLYMOUTH - 72D	PLYMOUTH - 72D
30036	YEOVIL - 72C	YEOVIL - 72C	YEOVIL - 72C	YEOVIL - 72C	YEOVIL - 72C	YEOVIL - 72C	YEOVIL - 72C
30037	PLYMOUTH - 72D	PLYMOUTH - 72D	PLYMOUTH - 72D	PLYMOUTH - 72D	PLYMOUTH - 72D	PLYMOUTH - 72D	PLYMOUTH - 72D
30038	FELTHAM - 70B	FELTHAM - 70B	FELTHAM - 70B	FELTHAM - 70B	FELTHAM - 70B	FELTHAM - 70B	FELTHAM - 70B
30039	EXMOUTHJCN - 72A	EXMOUTHJCN - 72A	EXMOUTHJCN - 72A	EXMOUTHJCN - 72A	EXMOUTHJCN - 72A	EXMOUTHJCN - 72A	EXMOUTHJCN - 72A
30040	EXMOUTHJCN - 72A	EXMOUTHJCN - 72A	EXMOUTHJCN - 72A	EXMOUTHJCN - 72A	EXMOUTHJCN - 72A	EXMOUTHJCN - 72A	EXMOUTHJCN - 72A
30041	EXMOUTHJCN - 72A	EXMOUTHJCN - 72A	EXMOUTHJCN - 72A	EXMOUTHJCN - 72A	EXMOUTHJCN - 72A	EXMOUTHJCN - 72A	EXMOUTHJCN - 72A
30042	BARNSTAPLE - 72E	BARNSTAPLE - 72E	BARNSTAPLE - 72E	BARNSTAPLE - 72E	BARNSTAPLE - 72E	BARNSTAPLE - 72E	BARNSTAPLE - 72E
30043	FELTHAM - 70B	FELTHAM - 70B	FELTHAM - 70B	FELTHAM - 70B	FELTHAM - 70B	FELTHAM - 70B	FELTHAM - 70B
30044	BARNSTAPLE - 72E	BARNSTAPLE - 72E	BARNSTAPLE - 72E	BARNSTAPLE - 72E	BARNSTAPLE - 72E	BARNSTAPLE - 72E	BARNSTAPLE - 72E
30045	FRATTON - 71D	FRATTON - 71D	EXMOUTHJCN - 72A	EXMOUTHJCN - 72A	EXMOUTHJCN - 72A	EXMOUTHJCN - 72A	EXMOUTHJCN - 72A
30046	EXMOUTHJCN - 72A	EXMOUTHJCN - 72A	EXMOUTHJCN - 72A	EXMOUTHJCN - 72A	EXMOUTHJCN - 72A	EXMOUTHJCN - 72A	EXMOUTHJCN - 72A
30047	HORSHAM - 75D	HORSHAM - 75D	HORSHAM - 75D	HORSHAM - 75D	HORSHAM - 75D	HORSHAM - 75D	HORSHAM - 75D
30048	HORSHAM - 75D	HORSHAM - 75D	HORSHAM - 75D	HORSHAM - 75D	HORSHAM - 75D	HORSHAM - 75D	HORSHAM - 75D
30049	HORSHAM - 75D	HORSHAM - 75D	HORSHAM - 75D	HORSHAM - 75D	HORSHAM - 75D	HORSHAM - 75D	HORSHAM - 75D
30050	FRATTON - 71D	FRATTON - 71D	FRATTON - 71D	HORSHAM - 75D	HORSHAM - 75D	HORSHAM - 75D	HORSHAM - 75D
30051	FRATTON - 71D	FRATTON - 71D	FRATTON - 71D	FRATTON - 71D	FRATTON - 71D	FRATTON - 71D	FRATTON - 71D
30052	BOURNEMOUTH - 71B	BOURNEMOUTH - 71B	BOURNEMOUTH - 71B	FRATTON - 71D	FRATTON - 71D	FRATTON - 71D	FRATTON - 71D
30053	FRATTON - 71D	FRATTON - 71D	FRATTON - 71D	FRATTON - 71D	FRATTON - 71D	FRATTON - 71D	FRATTON - 71D
30054	FRATTON - 71D	FRATTON - 71D	BOURNEMOUTH - 71B	FRATTON - 71D	FRATTON - 71D	FRATTON - 71D	FRATTON - 71D
30055	BOURNEMOUTH - 71B	BOURNEMOUTH - 71B	BOURNEMOUTH - 71B	BOURNEMOUTH - 71B	BOURNEMOUTH - 71B	BOURNEMOUTH - 71B	BOURNEMOUTH - 71B
30056	BOURNEMOUTH - 71B	BOURNEMOUTH - 71B	BOURNEMOUTH - 71B	BOURNEMOUTH - 71B	BOURNEMOUTH - 71B	BOURNEMOUTH - 71B	BOURNEMOUTH - 71B
30057	BOURNEMOUTH - 71B	BOURNEMOUTH - 71B	BOURNEMOUTH - 71B	BOURNEMOUTH - 71B	BOURNEMOUTH - 71B	BOURNEMOUTH - 71B	BOURNEMOUTH - 71B
30058	YEOVIL - 72C	YEOVIL - 72C	BOURNEMOUTH - 71B	BOURNEMOUTH - 71B	BOURNEMOUTH - 71B	BOURNEMOUTH - 71B	BOURNEMOUTH - 71B
30059	BOURNEMOUTH - 71B	BOURNEMOUTH - 71B	BOURNEMOUTH - 71B	BOURNEMOUTH - 71B	BOURNEMOUTH - 71B	BOURNEMOUTH - 71B	BOURNEMOUTH - 71B
30060	BOURNEMOUTH - 71B	BOURNEMOUTH - 71B	BOURNEMOUTH - 71B	BOURNEMOUTH - 71B	BOURNEMOUTH - 71B	BOURNEMOUTH - 71B	BOURNEMOUTH - 71B
30104	BOURNEMOUTH - 71B	BOURNEMOUTH - 71B	BOURNEMOUTH - 71B	BOURNEMOUTH - 71B	BOURNEMOUTH - 71B	BOURNEMOUTH - 71B	BOURNEMOUTH - 71B
30105	BOURNEMOUTH - 71B	BOURNEMOUTH - 71B	BOURNEMOUTH - 71B	BOURNEMOUTH - 71B	BOURNEMOUTH - 71B	BOURNEMOUTH - 71B	BOURNEMOUTH - 71B
30106	BOURNEMOUTH - 71B	BOURNEMOUTH - 71B	BOURNEMOUTH - 71B	BOURNEMOUTH - 71B	BOURNEMOUTH - 71B	BOURNEMOUTH - 71B	BOURNEMOUTH - 71B
30107	PLYMOUTH - 72D	PLYMOUTH - 72D	BOURNEMOUTH - 71B	BOURNEMOUTH - 71B	BOURNEMOUTH - 71B	BOURNEMOUTH - 71B	BOURNEMOUTH - 71B
30108	GUILDFORD - 70C	GUILDFORD - 70C	GUILDFORD - 70C	GUILDFORD - 70C	GUILDFORD - 70C	GUILDFORD - 70C	GUILDFORD - 70C
30109	GUILDFORD - 70C	GUILDFORD - 70C	GUILDFORD - 70C	GUILDFORD - 70C	GUILDFORD - 70C	GUILDFORD - 70C	GUILDFORD - 70C
30110	GUILDFORD - 70C	GUILDFORD - 70C	GUILDFORD - 70C	GUILDFORD - 70C	GUILDFORD - 70C	GUILDFORD - 70C	GUILDFORD - 70C
30111	BOURNEMOUTH - 71B	BOURNEMOUTH - 71B	BOURNEMOUTH - 71B	BOURNEMOUTH - 71B	BOURNEMOUTH - 71B	BOURNEMOUTH - 71B	BOURNEMOUTH - 71B
30112	BOURNEMOUTH - 71B	BOURNEMOUTH - 71B	BOURNEMOUTH - 71B	BOURNEMOUTH - 71B	BOURNEMOUTH - 71B	BOURNEMOUTH - 71B	BOURNEMOUTH - 71B
30123	NINE ELMS - 70A	NINE ELMS - 70A	NINE ELMS - 70A	NINE ELMS - 70A	NINE ELMS - 70A	NINE ELMS - 70A	NINE ELMS - 70A
30124	EXMOUTHJCN - 72A	EXMOUTHJCN - 72A	EXMOUTHJCN - 72A	EXMOUTHJCN - 72A	EXMOUTHJCN - 72A	NINE ELMS - 70A	NINE ELMS - 70A
30125	EASTLEIGH - 71A	EASTLEIGH - 71A	EASTLEIGH - 71A	EASTLEIGH - 71A	EASTLEIGH - 71A	EASTLEIGH - 71A	EASTLEIGH - 71A
30127	EASTLEIGH - 71A	EASTLEIGH - 71A	EASTLEIGH - 71A	EASTLEIGH - 71A	EASTLEIGH - 71A	EASTLEIGH - 71A	EASTLEIGH - 71A
30128	EASTLEIGH - 71A	EASTLEIGH - 71A	YEOVIL - 72C	BOURNEMOUTH - 71B	BOURNEMOUTH - 71B	BOURNEMOUTH - 71B	BOURNEMOUTH - 71B
30129	YEOVIL - 72C	YEOVIL - 72C	YEOVIL - 72C	YEOVIL - 72C	YEOVIL - 72C	YEOVIL - 72C	YEOVIL - 72C
30130	NINE ELMS - 70A	NINE ELMS - 70A	NINE ELMS - 70A	NINE ELMS - 70A	NINE ELMS - 70A	NINE ELMS - 70A	NINE ELMS - 70A
30131	BOURNEMOUTH - 71B	BOURNEMOUTH - 71B	YEOVIL - 72C	YEOVIL - 72C	YEOVIL - 72C	YEOVIL - 72C	YEOVIL - 72C
30132	NINE ELMS - 70A	NINE ELMS - 70A	NINE ELMS - 70A	NINE ELMS - 70A	NINE ELMS - 70A	NINE ELMS - 70A	NINE ELMS - 70A
30133	EXMOUTHJCN - 72A	EXMOUTHJCN - 72A	EXMOUTHJCN - 72A	EXMOUTHJCN - 72A	EXMOUTHJCN - 72A	EXMOUTHJCN - 72A	EXMOUTHJCN - 72A
30241	NINE ELMS - 70A	NINE ELMS - 70A	NINE ELMS - 70A	NINE ELMS - 70A	NINE ELMS - 70A	NINE ELMS - 70A	NINE ELMS - 70A
30242	EASTLEIGH - 71A	EASTLEIGH - 71A	EASTLEIGH - 71A	EASTLEIGH - 71A	EASTLEIGH - 71A	EASTLEIGH - 71A	NINE ELMS - 70A
30243	EASTLEIGH - 71A	EASTLEIGH - 71A	EASTLEIGH - 71A	EASTLEIGH - 71A	EASTLEIGH - 71A	EASTLEIGH - 71A	NINE ELMS - 70A
30244	NINE ELMS - 70A	NINE ELMS - 70A	NINE ELMS - 70A	NINE ELMS - 70A	NINE ELMS - 70A	NINE ELMS - 70A	NINE ELMS - 70A
30245	EXMOUTHJCN - 72A	EXMOUTHJCN - 72A	EXMOUTHJCN - 72A	EXMOUTHJCN - 72A	EXMOUTHJCN - 72A	EXMOUTHJCN - 72A	BARNSTAPLE - 72E
30246	GUILDFORD - 70C	GUILDFORD - 70C	GUILDFORD - 70C	GUILDFORD - 70C	GUILDFORD - 70C	GUILDFORD - 70C	GUILDFORD - 70C
30247	BARNSTAPLE - 72E	BARNSTAPLE - 72E	BARNSTAPLE - 72E	BARNSTAPLE - 72E	BARNSTAPLE - 72E	BARNSTAPLE - 72E	BARNSTAPLE - 72E
30248	NINE ELMS - 70A	NINE ELMS - 70A	NINE ELMS - 70A	NINE ELMS - 70A	NINE ELMS - 70A	NINE ELMS - 70A	NINE ELMS - 70A
30249	NINE ELMS - 70A	NINE ELMS - 70A	NINE ELMS - 70A	NINE ELMS - 70A	NINE ELMS - 70A	NINE ELMS - 70A	NINE ELMS - 70A
30250	BARNSTAPLE - 72E	BARNSTAPLE - 72E	BARNSTAPLE - 72E	BARNSTAPLE - 72E	BARNSTAPLE - 72E	BARNSTAPLE - 72E	BARNSTAPLE - 72E
30251	BARNSTAPLE - 72E	BARNSTAPLE - 72E	BARNSTAPLE - 72E	BARNSTAPLE - 72E	BARNSTAPLE - 72E	BARNSTAPLE - 72E	BARNSTAPLE - 72E
30252	BARNSTAPLE - 72E	BARNSTAPLE - 72E	BARNSTAPLE - 72E	BARNSTAPLE - 72E	BARNSTAPLE - 72E	BARNSTAPLE - 72E	BARNSTAPLE - 72E
30253	BARNSTAPLE - 72E	BARNSTAPLE - 72E	BARNSTAPLE - 72E	BARNSTAPLE - 72E	BARNSTAPLE - 72E	BARNSTAPLE - 72E	BARNSTAPLE - 72E
30254	FELTHAM - 70B	FELTHAM - 70B	FELTHAM - 70B	FELTHAM - 70B	FELTHAM - 70B	FELTHAM - 70B	FELTHAM - 70B
30255	EXMOUTHJCN - 72A	EXMOUTHJCN - 72A	EXMOUTHJCN - 72A	EXMOUTHJCN - 72A	EXMOUTHJCN - 72A	EXMOUTHJCN - 72A	EXMOUTHJCN - 72A
30256	EXMOUTHJCN - 72A	EXMOUTHJCN - 72A	EXMOUTHJCN - 72A	EXMOUTHJCN - 72A	EXMOUTHJCN - 72A	EXMOUTHJCN - 72A	EXMOUTHJCN - 72A
30318	BOURNEMOUTH - 71B	BOURNEMOUTH - 71B	BOURNEMOUTH - 71B	BOURNEMOUTH - 71B	BOURNEMOUTH - 71B	BOURNEMOUTH - 71B	BOURNEMOUTH - 71B
30319	BOURNEMOUTH - 71B	BOURNEMOUTH - 71B	BOURNEMOUTH - 71B	BOURNEMOUTH - 71B	BOURNEMOUTH - 71B	BOURNEMOUTH - 71B	BOURNEMOUTH - 71B
30320	BOURNEMOUTH - 71B	BOURNEMOUTH - 71B	BOURNEMOUTH - 71B	BOURNEMOUTH - 71B	BOURNEMOUTH - 71B	BOURNEMOUTH - 71B	BOURNEMOUTH - 71B
30321	BOURNEMOUTH - 71B	BOURNEMOUTH - 71B	BOURNEMOUTH - 71B	BOURNEMOUTH - 71B	BOURNEMOUTH - 71B	BOURNEMOUTH - 71B	BOURNEMOUTH - 71B
30322	EASTLEIGH - 71A	EASTLEIGH - 71A	EASTLEIGH - 71A	EASTLEIGH - 71A	EASTLEIGH - 71A	EASTLEIGH - 71A	EASTLEIGH - 71A
30323	EASTLEIGH - 71A	EASTLEIGH - 71A	EASTLEIGH - 71A	EASTLEIGH - 71A	EASTLEIGH - 71A	EASTLEIGH - 71A	EASTLEIGH - 71A
30324	EASTLEIGH - 71A	EASTLEIGH - 71A	EASTLEIGH - 71A	EASTLEIGH - 71A	EASTLEIGH - 71A	EASTLEIGH - 71A	EASTLEIGH - 71A
30328	EASTLEIGH - 71A	EASTLEIGH - 71A	EASTLEIGH - 71A	EASTLEIGH - 71A	EASTLEIGH - 71A	EASTLEIGH - 71A	EASTLEIGH - 71A
30356	EXMOUTHJCN - 72A	EXMOUTHJCN - 72A	EXMOUTHJCN - 72A	EXMOUTHJCN - 72A	EXMOUTHJCN - 72A	EXMOUTHJCN - 72A	EXMOUTHJCN - 72A
30357	EXMOUTHJCN - 72A	EXMOUTHJCN - 72A	EXMOUTHJCN - 72A	EXMOUTHJCN - 72A	EXMOUTHJCN - 72A	EXMOUTHJCN - 72A	EXMOUTHJCN - 72A
30374	EXMOUTHJCN - 72A	EXMOUTHJCN - 72A	EXMOUTHJCN - 72A	EXMOUTHJCN - 72A	EXMOUTHJCN - 72A	EXMOUTHJCN - 72A	EXMOUTHJCN - 72A
30375	EXMOUTHJCN - 72A	EXMOUTHJCN - 72A	EXMOUTHJCN - 72A	EXMOUTHJCN - 72A	EXMOUTHJCN - 72A	EXMOUTHJCN - 72A	EXMOUTHJCN - 72A
30376	EXMOUTHJCN - 72A	EXMOUTHJCN - 72A	EXMOUTHJCN - 72A	EXMOUTHJCN - 72A	EXMOUTHJCN - 72A	EXMOUTHJCN - 72A	EXMOUTHJCN - 72A
30377	EXMOUTHJCN - 72A	EXMOUTHJCN - 72A	EXMOUTHJCN - 72A	EXMOUTHJCN - 72A	EXMOUTHJCN - 72A	EXMOUTHJCN - 72A	EXMOUTHJCN - 72A
30378	EXMOUTHJCN - 72A	EXMOUTHJCN - 72A	EXMOUTHJCN - 72A	EXMOUTHJCN - 72A	EXMOUTHJCN - 72A	EXMOUTHJCN - 72A	EXMOUTHJCN - 72A
30379	EASTLEIGH - 71A	EASTLEIGH - 71A	EASTLEIGH - 71A	EASTLEIGH - 71A	EASTLEIGH - 71A	EASTLEIGH - 71A	EASTLEIGH - 71A
30479	EASTLEIGH - 71A	EASTLEIGH - 71A	EASTLEIGH - 71A	EASTLEIGH - 71A	EASTLEIGH - 71A	EASTLEIGH - 71A	EASTLEIGH - 71A
30480	EASTLEIGH - 71A	EASTLEIGH - 71A	EASTLEIGH - 71A	EASTLEIGH - 71A	EASTLEIGH - 71A	EASTLEIGH - 71A	EASTLEIGH - 71A
30481	EASTLEIGH - 71A	EASTLEIGH - 71A	EASTLEIGH - 71A	EASTLEIGH - 71A	EASTLEIGH - 71A	EASTLEIGH - 71A	EASTLEIGH - 71A
30667	EXMOUTHJCN - 72A	EXMOUTHJCN - 72A	EXMOUTHJCN - 72A	EXMOUTHJCN - 72A	EXMOUTHJCN - 72A	EXMOUTHJCN - 72A	EXMOUTHJCN - 72A
30668	EXMOUTHJCN - 72A	EXMOUTHJCN - 72A	EXMOUTHJCN - 72A	EXMOUTHJCN - 72A	EXMOUTHJCN - 72A	EXMOUTHJCN - 72A	EXMOUTHJCN - 72A
30669	EXMOUTHJCN - 72A	EXMOUTHJCN - 72A	EXMOUTHJCN - 72A	EXMOUTHJCN - 72A	EXMOUTHJCN - 72A	EXMOUTHJCN - 72A	EXMOUTHJCN - 72A
30670	EXMOUTHJCN - 72A	EXMOUTHJCN - 72A	EXMOUTHJCN - 72A	EXMOUTHJCN - 72A	EXMOUTHJCN - 72A	EXMOUTHJCN - 72A	EXMOUTHJCN - 72A
30671	EXMOUTHJCN - 72A	EXMOUTHJCN - 72A	EXMOUTHJCN - 72A	EXMOUTHJCN - 72A	EXMOUTHJCN - 72A	EXMOUTHJCN - 72A	EXMOUTHJCN - 72A
30673	SALISBURY - 72B	SALISBURY - 72B	SALISBURY - 72B	SALISBURY - 72B	SALISBURY - 72B	SALISBURY - 72B	SALISBURY - 72B
30674	SALISBURY - 72B	SALISBURY - 72B	SALISBURY - 72B	SALISBURY - 72B	SALISBURY - 72B	SALISBURY - 72B	SALISBURY - 72B
30675	SALISBURY - 72B	SALISBURY - 72B	SALISBURY - 72B	SALISBURY - 72B	SALISBURY - 72B	SALISBURY - 72B	SALISBURY - 72B
30676	NINE ELMS - 70A	NINE ELMS - 70A	NINE ELMS - 70A	NINE ELMS - 70A	NINE ELMS - 70A	EXMOUTHJCN - 72A	EXMOUTHJCN - 72A

loco	Sep-52	Dec-52	Mar-53	May-53	Jul-53	Sep-53	Nov-53
				M7 0-4-4T (1897)			
30021	EXMOUTHJCN - 72A	EXMOUTHJCN - 72A	EXMOUTHJCN - 72A	EXMOUTHJCN - 72A	EXMOUTHJCN - 72A	EXMOUTHJCN - 72A	EXMOUTHJCN - 72A
30022	GUILDFORD - 70C	GUILDFORD - 70C	GUILDFORD - 70C	GUILDFORD - 70C	GUILDFORD - 70C	GUILDFORD - 70C	READING (SR) - 70E
30023	EXMOUTHJCN - 72A	EXMOUTHJCN - 72A	FRATTON - 71D	FRATTON - 71D	FRATTON - 71D	FRATTON - 71D	FRATTON - 71D
30024	EXMOUTHJCN - 72A	EXMOUTHJCN - 72A	EXMOUTHJCN - 72A	EXMOUTHJCN - 72A	EXMOUTHJCN - 72A	EXMOUTHJCN - 72A	EXMOUTHJCN - 72A
30025	EXMOUTHJCN - 72A	EXMOUTHJCN - 72A	EXMOUTHJCN - 72A	EXMOUTHJCN - 72A	EXMOUTHJCN - 72A	EXMOUTHJCN - 72A	EXMOUTHJCN - 72A
30026	GUILDFORD - 70C	GUILDFORD - 70C	GUILDFORD - 70C	GUILDFORD - 70C	GUILDFORD - 70C	GUILDFORD - 70C	GUILDFORD - 70C
30027	GUILDFORD - 70C	GUILDFORD - 70C	GUILDFORD - 70C	GUILDFORD - 70C	GUILDFORD - 70C	GUILDFORD - 70C	GUILDFORD - 70C
30028	GUILDFORD - 70C	GUILDFORD - 70C	GUILDFORD - 70C	GUILDFORD - 70C	GUILDFORD - 70C	GUILDFORD - 70C	GUILDFORD - 70C
30029	EASTLEIGH - 71A	EASTLEIGH - 71A	EASTLEIGH - 71A	EASTLEIGH - 71A	EASTLEIGH - 71A	EASTLEIGH - 71A	EASTLEIGH - 71A
30030	EASTLEIGH - 71A	EASTLEIGH - 71A	EASTLEIGH - 71A	EASTLEIGH - 71A	EASTLEIGH - 71A	EASTLEIGH - 71A	EASTLEIGH - 71A
30031	EASTLEIGH - 71A	EASTLEIGH - 71A	EASTLEIGH - 71A	EASTLEIGH - 71A	EASTLEIGH - 71A	EASTLEIGH - 71A	EASTLEIGH - 71A
30032	EASTLEIGH - 71A	EASTLEIGH - 71A	EASTLEIGH - 71A	EASTLEIGH - 71A	EASTLEIGH - 71A	EASTLEIGH - 71A	EASTLEIGH - 71A
30033	EASTLEIGH - 71A	EASTLEIGH - 71A	EASTLEIGH - 71A	EASTLEIGH - 71A	EASTLEIGH - 71A	EASTLEIGH - 71A	EASTLEIGH - 71A
30034	YEOVIL - 72C	YEOVIL - 72C	YEOVIL - 72C	YEOVIL - 72C	YEOVIL - 72C	YEOVIL - 72C	YEOVIL - 72C
30035	PLYMOUTH - 72D	PLYMOUTH - 72D	PLYMOUTH - 72D	PLYMOUTH - 72D	PLYMOUTH - 72D	PLYMOUTH - 72D	PLYMOUTH - 72D
30036	YEOVIL - 72C	YEOVIL - 72C	YEOVIL - 72C	YEOVIL - 72C	YEOVIL - 72C	YEOVIL - 72C	YEOVIL - 72C
30037	PLYMOUTH - 72D	PLYMOUTH - 72D	PLYMOUTH - 72D	PLYMOUTH - 72D	PLYMOUTH - 72D	PLYMOUTH - 72D	PLYMOUTH - 72D
30038	FELTHAM - 70B	FELTHAM - 70B	FELTHAM - 70B	FELTHAM - 70B	FELTHAM - 70B	FELTHAM - 70B	FELTHAM - 70B
30039	EXMOUTHJCN - 72A	EXMOUTHJCN - 72A	EXMOUTHJCN - 72A	EXMOUTHJCN - 72A	EXMOUTHJCN - 72A	EXMOUTHJCN - 72A	EXMOUTHJCN - 72A
30040	PLYMOUTH - 72D	PLYMOUTH - 72D	PLYMOUTH - 72D	PLYMOUTH - 72D	PLYMOUTH - 72D	PLYMOUTH - 72D	PLYMOUTH - 72D
30041	EXMOUTHJCN - 72A	EXMOUTHJCN - 72A	EXMOUTHJCN - 72A	EXMOUTHJCN - 72A	EXMOUTHJCN - 72A	EXMOUTHJCN - 72A	EXMOUTHJCN - 72A
30042	BARNSTAPLE - 72E	BARNSTAPLE - 72E	BARNSTAPLE - 72E	BARNSTAPLE - 72E	EXMOUTHJCN - 72A	EXMOUTHJCN - 72A	EXMOUTHJCN - 72A
30043	FELTHAM - 70B	FELTHAM - 70B	FELTHAM - 70B	FELTHAM - 70B	FELTHAM - 70B	FELTHAM - 70B	FELTHAM - 70B
30044	BARNSTAPLE - 72E	BARNSTAPLE - 72E	BARNSTAPLE - 72E	EXMOUTHJCN - 72A	EXMOUTHJCN - 72A	EXMOUTHJCN - 72A	EXMOUTHJCN - 72A
30045	EXMOUTHJCN - 72A	EXMOUTHJCN - 72A	EXMOUTHJCN - 72A	EXMOUTHJCN - 72A	EXMOUTHJCN - 72A	EXMOUTHJCN - 72A	EXMOUTHJCN - 72A
30046	EXMOUTHJCN - 72A	EXMOUTHJCN - 72A	EXMOUTHJCN - 72A	EXMOUTHJCN - 72A	EXMOUTHJCN - 72A	EXMOUTHJCN - 72A	EXMOUTHJCN - 72A
30047	HORSHAM - 75D	HORSHAM - 75D	HORSHAM - 75D	HORSHAM - 75D	HORSHAM - 75D	HORSHAM - 75D	HORSHAM - 75D
30048	HORSHAM - 75D	HORSHAM - 75D	HORSHAM - 75D	HORSHAM - 75D	HORSHAM - 75D	HORSHAM - 75D	HORSHAM - 75D
30049	HORSHAM - 75D	HORSHAM - 75D	HORSHAM - 75D	HORSHAM - 75D	HORSHAM - 75D	HORSHAM - 75D	HORSHAM - 75D
30050	HORSHAM - 75D	HORSHAM - 75D	HORSHAM - 75D	HORSHAM - 75D	HORSHAM - 75D	HORSHAM - 75D	HORSHAM - 75D
30051	FRATTON - 71D	FRATTON - 71D	FRATTON - 71D	FRATTON - 71D	BRIGHTON - 75A	HORSHAM - 75D	HORSHAM - 75D
30052	FRATTON - 71D	FRATTON - 71D	FAVERSHAM - 73E	FAVERSHAM - 73E	FAVERSHAM - 73E	FAVERSHAM - 73E	FAVERSHAM - 73E
30053	FRATTON - 71D	FRATTON - 71D	FAVERSHAM - 73E	FAVERSHAM - 73E	FAVERSHAM - 73E	FAVERSHAM - 73E	FAVERSHAM - 73E
30054	FRATTON - 71D	FRATTON - 71D	FRATTON - 71D	FRATTON - 71D	FRATTON - 71D	FRATTON - 71D	FRATTON - 71D
30055	BOURNEMOUTH - 71B	BOURNEMOUTH - 71B	BOURNEMOUTH - 71B	BOURNEMOUTH - 71B	FRATTON - 71D	FRATTON - 71D	FRATTON - 71D
30056	BOURNEMOUTH - 71B	BOURNEMOUTH - 71B	BOURNEMOUTH - 71B	BOURNEMOUTH - 71B	BOURNEMOUTH - 71B	BOURNEMOUTH - 71B	BOURNEMOUTH - 71B
30057	BOURNEMOUTH - 71B	BOURNEMOUTH - 71B	BOURNEMOUTH - 71B	BOURNEMOUTH - 71B	BOURNEMOUTH - 71B	BOURNEMOUTH - 71B	BOURNEMOUTH - 71B
30058	BOURNEMOUTH - 71B	BOURNEMOUTH - 71B	BOURNEMOUTH - 71B	BOURNEMOUTH - 71B	BOURNEMOUTH - 71B	BOURNEMOUTH - 71B	BOURNEMOUTH - 71B
30059	BOURNEMOUTH - 71B	BOURNEMOUTH - 71B	BOURNEMOUTH - 71B	BOURNEMOUTH - 71B	BOURNEMOUTH - 71B	BOURNEMOUTH - 71B	BOURNEMOUTH - 71B
30060	BOURNEMOUTH - 71B	BOURNEMOUTH - 71B	BOURNEMOUTH - 71B	BOURNEMOUTH - 71B	BOURNEMOUTH - 71B	BOURNEMOUTH - 71B	BOURNEMOUTH - 71B
30104	BOURNEMOUTH - 71B	BOURNEMOUTH - 71B	BOURNEMOUTH - 71B	BOURNEMOUTH - 71B	BOURNEMOUTH - 71B	BOURNEMOUTH - 71B	READING (SR) - 70E
30105	BOURNEMOUTH - 71B	BOURNEMOUTH - 71B	BOURNEMOUTH - 71B	BOURNEMOUTH - 71B	BOURNEMOUTH - 71B	BOURNEMOUTH - 71B	BOURNEMOUTH - 71B
30106	BOURNEMOUTH - 71B	BOURNEMOUTH - 71B	BOURNEMOUTH - 71B	BOURNEMOUTH - 71B	BOURNEMOUTH - 71B	BOURNEMOUTH - 71B	BOURNEMOUTH - 71B
30107	BOURNEMOUTH - 71B	BOURNEMOUTH - 71B	BOURNEMOUTH - 71B	BOURNEMOUTH - 71B	BOURNEMOUTH - 71B	BOURNEMOUTH - 71B	BOURNEMOUTH - 71B
30108	GUILDFORD - 70C	GUILDFORD - 70C	HORSHAM - 75D	HORSHAM - 75D	HORSHAM - 75D	HORSHAM - 75D	HORSHAM - 75D
30109	GUILDFORD - 70C	GUILDFORD - 70C	GUILDFORD - 70C	GUILDFORD - 70C	GUILDFORD - 70C	GUILDFORD - 70C	GUILDFORD - 70C
30110	GUILDFORD - 70C	GUILDFORD - 70C	GUILDFORD - 70C	GUILDFORD - 70C	GUILDFORD - 70C	GUILDFORD - 70C	GUILDFORD - 70C
30111	BOURNEMOUTH - 71B	BOURNEMOUTH - 71B	BOURNEMOUTH - 71B	BOURNEMOUTH - 71B	BOURNEMOUTH - 71B	BOURNEMOUTH - 71B	BOURNEMOUTH - 71B
30112	BOURNEMOUTH - 71B	BOURNEMOUTH - 71B	BOURNEMOUTH - 71B	BOURNEMOUTH - 71B	BOURNEMOUTH - 71B	BOURNEMOUTH - 71B	BOURNEMOUTH - 71B
30123	NINE ELMS - 70A	NINE ELMS - 70A	NINE ELMS - 70A	NINE ELMS - 70A	NINE ELMS - 70A	NINE ELMS - 70A	REDHILL - 75B
30124	NINE ELMS - 70A	NINE ELMS - 70A	NINE ELMS - 70A	NINE ELMS - 70A	NINE ELMS - 70A	NINE ELMS - 70A	NINE ELMS - 70A
30125	EASTLEIGH - 71A	EASTLEIGH - 71A	EASTLEIGH - 71A	EASTLEIGH - 71A	EASTLEIGH - 71A	EASTLEIGH - 71A	EASTLEIGH - 71A
30127	EASTLEIGH - 71A	EASTLEIGH - 71A	EASTLEIGH - 71A	EASTLEIGH - 71A	EASTLEIGH - 71A	EASTLEIGH - 71A	EASTLEIGH - 71A
30128	BOURNEMOUTH - 71B	BOURNEMOUTH - 71B	BOURNEMOUTH - 71B	BOURNEMOUTH - 71B	BOURNEMOUTH - 71B	BOURNEMOUTH - 71B	BOURNEMOUTH - 71B
30129	YEOVIL - 72C	YEOVIL - 72C	FAVERSHAM - 73E	FAVERSHAM - 73E	FAVERSHAM - 73E	FAVERSHAM - 73E	FAVERSHAM - 73E
30130	NINE ELMS - 70A	NINE ELMS - 70A	NINE ELMS - 70A	NINE ELMS - 70A	NINE ELMS - 70A	NINE ELMS - 70A	NINE ELMS - 70A
30131	YEOVIL - 72C	YEOVIL - 72C	YEOVIL - 72C	YEOVIL - 72C	YEOVIL - 72C	YEOVIL - 72C	YEOVIL - 72C
30132	NINE ELMS - 70A	NINE ELMS - 70A	NINE ELMS - 70A	NINE ELMS - 70A	NINE ELMS - 70A	NINE ELMS - 70A	NINE ELMS - 70A
30133	EASTLEIGH - 71A	NINE ELMS - 70A	EASTLEIGH - 71A	EASTLEIGH - 71A	EASTLEIGH - 71A	EASTLEIGH - 71A	EASTLEIGH - 71A
30241	NINE ELMS - 70A	NINE ELMS - 70A	NINE ELMS - 70A	NINE ELMS - 70A	NINE ELMS - 70A	NINE ELMS - 70A	NINE ELMS - 70A
30242	NINE ELMS - 70A	NINE ELMS - 70A	NINE ELMS - 70A	NINE ELMS - 70A	NINE ELMS - 70A	NINE ELMS - 70A	NINE ELMS - 70A
30243	NINE ELMS - 70A	NINE ELMS - 70A	NINE ELMS - 70A	NINE ELMS - 70A	NINE ELMS - 70A	NINE ELMS - 70A	NINE ELMS - 70A
30244	NINE ELMS - 70A	NINE ELMS - 70A	NINE ELMS - 70A	NINE ELMS - 70A	NINE ELMS - 70A	NINE ELMS - 70A	NINE ELMS - 70A
30245	BARNSTAPLE - 72E	NINE ELMS - 70A	NINE ELMS - 70A	NINE ELMS - 70A	NINE ELMS - 70A	NINE ELMS - 70A	REDHILL - 75B
30246	GUILDFORD - 70C	GUILDFORD - 70C	GUILDFORD - 70C	GUILDFORD - 70C	GUILDFORD - 70C	GUILDFORD - 70C	GUILDFORD - 70C
30247	NINE ELMS - 70A	BARNSTAPLE - 72E	BARNSTAPLE - 72E	BARNSTAPLE - 72E	BARNSTAPLE - 72E	BARNSTAPLE - 72E	BARNSTAPLE - 72E
30248	NINE ELMS - 70A	NINE ELMS - 70A	NINE ELMS - 70A	NINE ELMS - 70A	NINE ELMS - 70A	NINE ELMS - 70A	NINE ELMS - 70A
30249	NINE ELMS - 70A	NINE ELMS - 70A	NINE ELMS - 70A	NINE ELMS - 70A	NINE ELMS - 70A	NINE ELMS - 70A	NINE ELMS - 70A
30250	BARNSTAPLE - 72E	BARNSTAPLE - 72E	BARNSTAPLE - 72E	BARNSTAPLE - 72E	BARNSTAPLE - 72E	BARNSTAPLE - 72E	BARNSTAPLE - 72E
30251	BARNSTAPLE - 72E	BARNSTAPLE - 72E	BARNSTAPLE - 72E	BARNSTAPLE - 72E	BARNSTAPLE - 72E	BARNSTAPLE - 72E	BARNSTAPLE - 72E
30252	BARNSTAPLE - 72E	BARNSTAPLE - 72E	BARNSTAPLE - 72E	BARNSTAPLE - 72E	BARNSTAPLE - 72E	BARNSTAPLE - 72E	BARNSTAPLE - 72E
30253	BARNSTAPLE - 72E	BARNSTAPLE - 72E	BARNSTAPLE - 72E	BARNSTAPLE - 72E	BARNSTAPLE - 72E	BARNSTAPLE - 72E	FELTHAM - 70B
30254	BARNSTAPLE - 72E	BARNSTAPLE - 72E	BARNSTAPLE - 72E	BARNSTAPLE - 72E	BARNSTAPLE - 72E	BARNSTAPLE - 72E	BARNSTAPLE - 72E
30255	EXMOUTHJCN - 72A	EXMOUTHJCN - 72A	EXMOUTHJCN - 72A	EXMOUTHJCN - 72A	EXMOUTHJCN - 72A	EXMOUTHJCN - 72A	EXMOUTHJCN - 72A
30256	EXMOUTHJCN - 72A	EXMOUTHJCN - 72A	EXMOUTHJCN - 72A	EXMOUTHJCN - 72A	EXMOUTHJCN - 72A	EXMOUTHJCN - 72A	EXMOUTHJCN - 72A
30318	BOURNEMOUTH - 71B	BOURNEMOUTH - 71B	BOURNEMOUTH - 71B	BOURNEMOUTH - 71B	BOURNEMOUTH - 71B	BOURNEMOUTH - 71B	BOURNEMOUTH - 71B
30319	BOURNEMOUTH - 71B	BOURNEMOUTH - 71B	BOURNEMOUTH - 71B	BOURNEMOUTH - 71B	BOURNEMOUTH - 71B	BOURNEMOUTH - 71B	BOURNEMOUTH - 71B
30320	NINE ELMS - 70A	NINE ELMS - 70A	NINE ELMS - 70A	NINE ELMS - 70A	NINE ELMS - 70A	NINE ELMS - 70A	NINE ELMS - 70A
30321	NINE ELMS - 70A	NINE ELMS - 70A	NINE ELMS - 70A	NINE ELMS - 70A	NINE ELMS - 70A	NINE ELMS - 70A	NINE ELMS - 70A
30322	EASTLEIGH - 71A	EASTLEIGH - 71A	EASTLEIGH - 71A	EASTLEIGH - 71A	EASTLEIGH - 71A	EASTLEIGH - 71A	EASTLEIGH - 71A
30323	EASTLEIGH - 71A	EASTLEIGH - 71A	EASTLEIGH - 71A	EASTLEIGH - 71A	EASTLEIGH - 71A	EASTLEIGH - 71A	EASTLEIGH - 71A
30324	EASTLEIGH - 71A	EASTLEIGH - 71A	EASTLEIGH - 71A	EASTLEIGH - 71A	EASTLEIGH - 71A	EASTLEIGH - 71A	EASTLEIGH - 71A
30328	EASTLEIGH - 71A	EASTLEIGH - 71A	EASTLEIGH - 71A	EASTLEIGH - 71A	EASTLEIGH - 71A	EASTLEIGH - 71A	EASTLEIGH - 71A
30356	EXMOUTHJCN - 72A	EXMOUTHJCN - 72A	EXMOUTHJCN - 72A	EXMOUTHJCN - 72A	FRATTON - 71D	FRATTON - 71D	FRATTON - 71D
30357	EXMOUTHJCN - 72A	EXMOUTHJCN - 72A	EXMOUTHJCN - 72A	EXMOUTHJCN - 72A	FRATTON - 71D	FRATTON - 71D	FRATTON - 71D
30374	EXMOUTHJCN - 72A	EXMOUTHJCN - 72A	EXMOUTHJCN - 72A	EXMOUTHJCN - 72A	EXMOUTHJCN - 72A	EXMOUTHJCN - 72A	READING (SR) - 70E
30375	EXMOUTHJCN - 72A	EXMOUTHJCN - 72A	EXMOUTHJCN - 72A	EXMOUTHJCN - 72A	EASTLEIGH - 71A	EASTLEIGH - 71A	EASTLEIGH - 71A
30376	EASTLEIGH - 71A	EASTLEIGH - 71A	EASTLEIGH - 71A	EASTLEIGH - 71A	EASTLEIGH - 71A	EASTLEIGH - 71A	EASTLEIGH - 71A
30377	EASTLEIGH - 71A	EASTLEIGH - 71A	EASTLEIGH - 71A	EASTLEIGH - 71A	EASTLEIGH - 71A	EASTLEIGH - 71A	REDHILL - 75B
30378	EXMOUTHJCN - 72A	EXMOUTHJCN - 72A	EXMOUTHJCN - 72A	EXMOUTHJCN - 72A	EXMOUTHJCN - 72A	EXMOUTHJCN - 72A	EXMOUTHJCN - 72A
30379	EASTLEIGH - 71A	EASTLEIGH - 71A	EASTLEIGH - 71A	EASTLEIGH - 71A	EASTLEIGH - 71A	EASTLEIGH - 71A	EASTLEIGH - 71A
30479	EASTLEIGH - 71A	EASTLEIGH - 71A	EASTLEIGH - 71A	EASTLEIGH - 71A	EASTLEIGH - 71A	EASTLEIGH - 71A	EASTLEIGH - 71A
30480	EASTLEIGH - 71A	EASTLEIGH - 71A	EASTLEIGH - 71A	EASTLEIGH - 71A	EASTLEIGH - 71A	EASTLEIGH - 71A	EASTLEIGH - 71A
30481	EASTLEIGH - 71A	EASTLEIGH - 71A	EASTLEIGH - 71A	EASTLEIGH - 71A	EASTLEIGH - 71A	EASTLEIGH - 71A	EASTLEIGH - 71A
30667	EXMOUTHJCN - 72A	EXMOUTHJCN - 72A	EXMOUTHJCN - 72A	EXMOUTHJCN - 72A	EXMOUTHJCN - 72A	EXMOUTHJCN - 72A	READING (SR) - 70E
30668	EXMOUTHJCN - 72A	EXMOUTHJCN - 72A	EXMOUTHJCN - 72A	EXMOUTHJCN - 72A	EXMOUTHJCN - 72A	EXMOUTHJCN - 72A	EXMOUTHJCN - 72A
30669	EXMOUTHJCN - 72A	EXMOUTHJCN - 72A	EXMOUTHJCN - 72A	EXMOUTHJCN - 72A	EXMOUTHJCN - 72A	EXMOUTHJCN - 72A	EXMOUTHJCN - 72A
30670	EXMOUTHJCN - 72A	EXMOUTHJCN - 72A	EXMOUTHJCN - 72A	EXMOUTHJCN - 72A	EXMOUTHJCN - 72A	EXMOUTHJCN - 72A	EXMOUTHJCN - 72A
30671	EXMOUTHJCN - 72A	EXMOUTHJCN - 72A	EXMOUTHJCN - 72A	EXMOUTHJCN - 72A	EXMOUTHJCN - 72A	EXMOUTHJCN - 72A	EXMOUTHJCN - 72A
30673	SALISBURY - 72B	SALISBURY - 72B	SALISBURY - 72B	SALISBURY - 72B	SALISBURY - 72B	SALISBURY - 72B	SALISBURY - 72B
30674	SALISBURY - 72B	SALISBURY - 72B	SALISBURY - 72B	SALISBURY - 72B	SALISBURY - 72B	SALISBURY - 72B	SALISBURY - 72B
30675	SALISBURY - 72B	GUILDFORD - 70C	GUILDFORD - 70C	GUILDFORD - 70C	GUILDFORD - 70C	GUILDFORD - 70C	GUILDFORD - 70C
30676	EXMOUTHJCN - 72A	EXMOUTHJCN - 72A	EXMOUTHJCN - 72A	EXMOUTHJCN - 72A	EXMOUTHJCN - 72A	EXMOUTHJCN - 72A	EXMOUTHJCN - 72A

M7 0-4-4T (1897)

loco	Jan-54	Mar-54	May-54	Jun-54	Aug-54	Oct-54	Dec-54
30021	EXMOUTHJCN - 72A	EXMOUTHJCN - 72A	EXMOUTHJCN - 72A	EXMOUTHJCN - 72A	EXMOUTHJCN - 72A	EXMOUTHJCN - 72A	EXMOUTHJCN - 72A
30022	GUILDFORD - 70C	GUILDFORD - 70C	GUILDFORD - 70C	GUILDFORD - 70C	GUILDFORD - 70C	GUILDFORD - 70C	GUILDFORD - 70C
30023	FRATTON - 71D	FRATTON - 71D	FRATTON - 71D	FRATTON - 71D	FRATTON - 71D	FRATTON - 70F	FRATTON - 70F
30024	EXMOUTHJCN - 72A	EXMOUTHJCN - 72A	EXMOUTHJCN - 72A	EXMOUTHJCN - 72A	EXMOUTHJCN - 72A	EXMOUTHJCN - 72A	EXMOUTHJCN - 72A
30025	EXMOUTHJCN - 72A	EXMOUTHJCN - 72A	EXMOUTHJCN - 72A	EXMOUTHJCN - 72A	EXMOUTHJCN - 72A	EXMOUTHJCN - 72A	EXMOUTHJCN - 72A
30026	GUILDFORD - 70C	GUILDFORD - 70C	GUILDFORD - 70C	GUILDFORD - 70C	GUILDFORD - 70C	GUILDFORD - 70C	GUILDFORD - 70C
30027	GUILDFORD - 70C	GUILDFORD - 70C	GUILDFORD - 70C	GUILDFORD - 70C	GUILDFORD - 70C	GUILDFORD - 70C	GUILDFORD - 70C
30028	GUILDFORD - 70C	GUILDFORD - 70C	GUILDFORD - 70C	GUILDFORD - 70C	GUILDFORD - 70C	GUILDFORD - 70C	GUILDFORD - 70C
30029	EASTLEIGH - 71A	EASTLEIGH - 71A	EASTLEIGH - 71A	EASTLEIGH - 71A	EASTLEIGH - 71A	EASTLEIGH - 71A	EASTLEIGH - 71A
30030	EASTLEIGH - 71A	EASTLEIGH - 71A	EASTLEIGH - 71A	EASTLEIGH - 71A	EASTLEIGH - 71A	EASTLEIGH - 71A	EASTLEIGH - 71A
30031	EASTLEIGH - 71A	EASTLEIGH - 71A	EASTLEIGH - 71A	EASTLEIGH - 71A	EASTLEIGH - 71A	EASTLEIGH - 71A	EASTLEIGH - 71A
30032	EASTLEIGH - 71A	EASTLEIGH - 71A	EASTLEIGH - 71A	EASTLEIGH - 71A	EASTLEIGH - 71A	EASTLEIGH - 71A	EASTLEIGH - 71A
30033	EASTLEIGH - 71A	EASTLEIGH - 71A	EASTLEIGH - 71A	EASTLEIGH - 71A	EASTLEIGH - 71A	EASTLEIGH - 71A	EASTLEIGH - 71A
30034	YEOVIL - 72C	YEOVIL - 72C	YEOVIL - 72C	YEOVIL - 72C	YEOVIL - 72C	YEOVIL - 72C	YEOVIL - 72C
30035	PLYMOUTH - 72D	PLYMOUTH - 72D	PLYMOUTH - 72D	PLYMOUTH - 72D	PLYMOUTH - 72D	PLYMOUTH - 72D	PLYMOUTH - 72D
30036	PLYMOUTH - 72D	PLYMOUTH - 72D	PLYMOUTH - 72D	PLYMOUTH - 72D	PLYMOUTH - 72D	PLYMOUTH - 72D	PLYMOUTH - 72D
30037	PLYMOUTH - 72D	PLYMOUTH - 72D	PLYMOUTH - 72D	PLYMOUTH - 72D	PLYMOUTH - 72D	PLYMOUTH - 72D	PLYMOUTH - 72D
30038	FELTHAM - 70B	FELTHAM - 70B	FELTHAM - 70B	FELTHAM - 70B	FELTHAM - 70B	FELTHAM - 70B	FELTHAM - 70B
30039	EXMOUTHJCN - 72A	EXMOUTHJCN - 72A	EXMOUTHJCN - 72A	EXMOUTHJCN - 72A	EXMOUTHJCN - 72A	PLYMOUTH - 72D	PLYMOUTH - 72D
30040	PLYMOUTH - 72D	PLYMOUTH - 72D	PLYMOUTH - 72D	PLYMOUTH - 72D	PLYMOUTH - 72D	PLYMOUTH - 72D	PLYMOUTH - 72D
30041	EXMOUTHJCN - 72A	EXMOUTHJCN - 72A	EXMOUTHJCN - 72A	FELTHAM - 70B	FELTHAM - 70B	FELTHAM - 70B	FELTHAM - 70B
30042	EXMOUTHJCN - 72A	EXMOUTHJCN - 72A	EXMOUTHJCN - 72A	FELTHAM - 70B	FELTHAM - 70B	FELTHAM - 70B	FELTHAM - 70B
30043	FELTHAM - 70B	FELTHAM - 70B	FELTHAM - 70B	FELTHAM - 70B	FELTHAM - 70B	FELTHAM - 70B	FELTHAM - 70B
30044	EXMOUTHJCN - 72A	EXMOUTHJCN - 72A	EXMOUTHJCN - 72A	EXMOUTHJCN - 72A	EXMOUTHJCN - 72A	EXMOUTHJCN - 72A	EXMOUTHJCN - 72A
30045	EXMOUTHJCN - 72A	EXMOUTHJCN - 72A	EXMOUTHJCN - 72A	EXMOUTHJCN - 72A	EXMOUTHJCN - 72A	EXMOUTHJCN - 72A	EXMOUTHJCN - 72A
30046	EXMOUTHJCN - 72A	EXMOUTHJCN - 72A	EXMOUTHJCN - 72A	EXMOUTHJCN - 72A	EXMOUTHJCN - 72A	EXMOUTHJCN - 72A	EXMOUTHJCN - 72A
30047	HORSHAM - 75D	HORSHAM - 75D	HORSHAM - 75D	HORSHAM - 75D	HORSHAM - 75D	HORSHAM - 75D	HORSHAM - 75D
30048	HORSHAM - 75D	HORSHAM - 75D	HORSHAM - 75D	HORSHAM - 75D	HORSHAM - 75D	HORSHAM - 75D	HORSHAM - 75D
30049	HORSHAM - 75D	HORSHAM - 75D	HORSHAM - 75D	HORSHAM - 75D	HORSHAM - 75D	HORSHAM - 75D	HORSHAM - 75D
30050	HORSHAM - 75D	HORSHAM - 75D	HORSHAM - 75D	HORSHAM - 75D	HORSHAM - 75D	HORSHAM - 75D	HORSHAM - 75D
30051	HORSHAM - 75D	HORSHAM - 75D	HORSHAM - 75D	HORSHAM - 75D	HORSHAM - 75D	HORSHAM - 75D	HORSHAM - 75D
30052	FAVERSHAM - 73E	FAVERSHAM - 73E	FAVERSHAM - 73E	FAVERSHAM - 73E	FAVERSHAM - 73E	FAVERSHAM - 73E	FAVERSHAM - 73E
30053	FAVERSHAM - 73E	FAVERSHAM - 73E	FAVERSHAM - 73E	FAVERSHAM - 73E	FAVERSHAM - 73E	FAVERSHAM - 73E	FAVERSHAM - 73E
30054	FRATTON - 71D	FRATTON - 71D	FRATTON - 71D	FRATTON - 71D	FRATTON - 71D	FRATTON - 70F	FRATTON - 70F
30055	FRATTON - 71D	FRATTON - 71D	FRATTON - 71D	FRATTON - 71D	FRATTON - 71D	FRATTON - 70F	FRATTON - 70F
30056	BOURNEMOUTH - 71B	BOURNEMOUTH - 71B	BOURNEMOUTH - 71B	BOURNEMOUTH - 71B	BOURNEMOUTH - 71B	BOURNEMOUTH - 71B	BOURNEMOUTH - 71B
30057	BOURNEMOUTH - 71B	BOURNEMOUTH - 71B	BOURNEMOUTH - 71B	BOURNEMOUTH - 71B	BOURNEMOUTH - 71B	BOURNEMOUTH - 71B	BOURNEMOUTH - 71B
30058	BOURNEMOUTH - 71B	BOURNEMOUTH - 71B	BOURNEMOUTH - 71B	BOURNEMOUTH - 71B	BOURNEMOUTH - 71B	BOURNEMOUTH - 71B	BOURNEMOUTH - 71B
30059	BOURNEMOUTH - 71B	BOURNEMOUTH - 71B	BOURNEMOUTH - 71B	BOURNEMOUTH - 71B	BOURNEMOUTH - 71B	BOURNEMOUTH - 71B	BOURNEMOUTH - 71B
30060	BOURNEMOUTH - 71B	BOURNEMOUTH - 71B	BOURNEMOUTH - 71B	BOURNEMOUTH - 71B	BOURNEMOUTH - 71B	BOURNEMOUTH - 71B	BOURNEMOUTH - 71B
30104	BOURNEMOUTH - 71B	BOURNEMOUTH - 71B	BOURNEMOUTH - 71B	BOURNEMOUTH - 71B	BOURNEMOUTH - 71B	BOURNEMOUTH - 71B	BOURNEMOUTH - 71B
30105	BOURNEMOUTH - 71B	BOURNEMOUTH - 71B	BOURNEMOUTH - 71B	BOURNEMOUTH - 71B	BOURNEMOUTH - 71B	BOURNEMOUTH - 71B	BOURNEMOUTH - 71B
30106	BOURNEMOUTH - 71B	BOURNEMOUTH - 71B	BOURNEMOUTH - 71B	BOURNEMOUTH - 71B	BOURNEMOUTH - 71B	BOURNEMOUTH - 71B	BOURNEMOUTH - 71B
30107	BOURNEMOUTH - 71B	BOURNEMOUTH - 71B	BOURNEMOUTH - 71B	BOURNEMOUTH - 71B	BOURNEMOUTH - 71B	BOURNEMOUTH - 71B	BOURNEMOUTH - 71B
30108	HORSHAM - 75D	HORSHAM - 75D	HORSHAM - 75D	HORSHAM - 75D	HORSHAM - 75D	HORSHAM - 75D	HORSHAM - 75D
30109	GUILDFORD - 70C	GUILDFORD - 70C	GUILDFORD - 70C	GUILDFORD - 70C	GUILDFORD - 70C	GUILDFORD - 70C	GUILDFORD - 70C
30110	GUILDFORD - 70C	GUILDFORD - 70C	GUILDFORD - 70C	GUILDFORD - 70C	GUILDFORD - 70C	GUILDFORD - 70C	GUILDFORD - 70C
30111	BOURNEMOUTH - 71B	BOURNEMOUTH - 71B	BOURNEMOUTH - 71B	BOURNEMOUTH - 71B	BOURNEMOUTH - 71B	BOURNEMOUTH - 71B	BOURNEMOUTH - 71B
30112	BOURNEMOUTH - 71B	BOURNEMOUTH - 71B	BOURNEMOUTH - 71B	BOURNEMOUTH - 71B	BOURNEMOUTH - 71B	BOURNEMOUTH - 71B	BOURNEMOUTH - 71B
30123	NINE ELMS - 70A	NINE ELMS - 70A	NINE ELMS - 70A	NINE ELMS - 70A	NINE ELMS - 70A	NINE ELMS - 70A	NINE ELMS - 70A
30124	NINE ELMS - 70A	NINE ELMS - 70A	NINE ELMS - 70A	NINE ELMS - 70A	NINE ELMS - 70A	NINE ELMS - 70A	NINE ELMS - 70A
30125	EASTLEIGH - 71A	EASTLEIGH - 71A	EASTLEIGH - 71A	EASTLEIGH - 71A	EASTLEIGH - 71A	EASTLEIGH - 71A	EASTLEIGH - 71A
30127	EASTLEIGH - 71A	EASTLEIGH - 71A	EASTLEIGH - 71A	EASTLEIGH - 71A	EASTLEIGH - 71A	EASTLEIGH - 71A	EASTLEIGH - 71A
30128	BOURNEMOUTH - 71B	BOURNEMOUTH - 71B	BOURNEMOUTH - 71B	BOURNEMOUTH - 71B	BOURNEMOUTH - 71B	BOURNEMOUTH - 71B	BOURNEMOUTH - 71B
30129	FAVERSHAM - 73E	FAVERSHAM - 73E	FAVERSHAM - 73E	FAVERSHAM - 73E	FAVERSHAM - 73E	FAVERSHAM - 73E	FAVERSHAM - 73E
30130	NINE ELMS - 70A	NINE ELMS - 70A	NINE ELMS - 70A	NINE ELMS - 70A	EASTLEIGH - 71A	EASTLEIGH - 71A	EASTLEIGH - 71A
30131	YEOVIL - 72C	YEOVIL - 72C	YEOVIL - 72C	YEOVIL - 72C	YEOVIL - 72C	YEOVIL - 72C	YEOVIL - 72C
30132	NINE ELMS - 70A	NINE ELMS - 70A	NINE ELMS - 70A	NINE ELMS - 70A	NINE ELMS - 70A	NINE ELMS - 70A	NINE ELMS - 70A
30133	EASTLEIGH - 71A	EASTLEIGH - 71A	EASTLEIGH - 71A	EASTLEIGH - 71A	NINE ELMS - 70A	NINE ELMS - 70A	NINE ELMS - 70A
30241	NINE ELMS - 70A	NINE ELMS - 70A	NINE ELMS - 70A	NINE ELMS - 70A	NINE ELMS - 70A	NINE ELMS - 70A	NINE ELMS - 70A
30242	NINE ELMS - 70A	NINE ELMS - 70A	NINE ELMS - 70A	NINE ELMS - 70A	NINE ELMS - 70A	NINE ELMS - 70A	NINE ELMS - 70A
30243	NINE ELMS - 70A	NINE ELMS - 70A	NINE ELMS - 70A	NINE ELMS - 70A	NINE ELMS - 70A	NINE ELMS - 70A	NINE ELMS - 70A
30244	NINE ELMS - 70A	NINE ELMS - 70A	NINE ELMS - 70A	NINE ELMS - 70A	NINE ELMS - 70A	NINE ELMS - 70A	NINE ELMS - 70A
30245	NINE ELMS - 70A	NINE ELMS - 70A	NINE ELMS - 70A	NINE ELMS - 70A	NINE ELMS - 70A	NINE ELMS - 70A	NINE ELMS - 70A
30246	GUILDFORD - 70C	GUILDFORD - 70C	GUILDFORD - 70C	GUILDFORD - 70C	GUILDFORD - 70C	GUILDFORD - 70C	GUILDFORD - 70C
30247	BARNSTAPLE - 72E	BARNSTAPLE - 72E	BARNSTAPLE - 72E	BARNSTAPLE - 72E	BARNSTAPLE - 72E	BARNSTAPLE - 72E	BARNSTAPLE - 72E
30248	NINE ELMS - 70A	NINE ELMS - 70A	NINE ELMS - 70A	NINE ELMS - 70A	NINE ELMS - 70A	NINE ELMS - 70A	NINE ELMS - 70A
30249	NINE ELMS - 70A	NINE ELMS - 70A	NINE ELMS - 70A	NINE ELMS - 70A	NINE ELMS - 70A	NINE ELMS - 70A	NINE ELMS - 70A
30250	BARNSTAPLE - 72E	BARNSTAPLE - 72E	BARNSTAPLE - 72E	BARNSTAPLE - 72E	BARNSTAPLE - 72E	BARNSTAPLE - 72E	BARNSTAPLE - 72E
30251	BARNSTAPLE - 72E	BARNSTAPLE - 72E	BARNSTAPLE - 72E	BARNSTAPLE - 72E	BARNSTAPLE - 72E	BARNSTAPLE - 72E	BARNSTAPLE - 72E
30252	BARNSTAPLE - 72E	BARNSTAPLE - 72E	BARNSTAPLE - 72E	BARNSTAPLE - 72E	BARNSTAPLE - 72E	BARNSTAPLE - 72E	BARNSTAPLE - 72E
30253	BARNSTAPLE - 72E	BARNSTAPLE - 72E	BARNSTAPLE - 72E	BARNSTAPLE - 72E	BARNSTAPLE - 72E	BARNSTAPLE - 72E	BARNSTAPLE - 72E
30254	BARNSTAPLE - 72E	BARNSTAPLE - 72E	BARNSTAPLE - 72E	BARNSTAPLE - 72E	BARNSTAPLE - 72E	BARNSTAPLE - 72E	BARNSTAPLE - 72E
30255	EXMOUTHJCN - 72A	EXMOUTHJCN - 72A	EXMOUTHJCN - 72A	EXMOUTHJCN - 72A	EXMOUTHJCN - 72A	EXMOUTHJCN - 72A	EXMOUTHJCN - 72A
30256	EXMOUTHJCN - 72A	EXMOUTHJCN - 72A	EXMOUTHJCN - 72A	EXMOUTHJCN - 72A	EXMOUTHJCN - 72A	EXMOUTHJCN - 72A	EXMOUTHJCN - 72A
30318	BOURNEMOUTH - 71B	BOURNEMOUTH - 71B	BOURNEMOUTH - 71B	BOURNEMOUTH - 71B	BOURNEMOUTH - 71B	BOURNEMOUTH - 71B	BOURNEMOUTH - 71B
30319	BOURNEMOUTH - 71B	BOURNEMOUTH - 71B	BOURNEMOUTH - 71B	BOURNEMOUTH - 71B	BOURNEMOUTH - 71B	BOURNEMOUTH - 71B	BOURNEMOUTH - 71B
30320	NINE ELMS - 70A	NINE ELMS - 70A	NINE ELMS - 70A	NINE ELMS - 70A	NINE ELMS - 70A	NINE ELMS - 70A	NINE ELMS - 70A
30321	NINE ELMS - 70A	NINE ELMS - 70A	NINE ELMS - 70A	NINE ELMS - 70A	NINE ELMS - 70A	NINE ELMS - 70A	NINE ELMS - 70A
30322	EASTLEIGH - 71A	EASTLEIGH - 71A	EASTLEIGH - 71A	EASTLEIGH - 71A	EASTLEIGH - 71A	EASTLEIGH - 71A	EASTLEIGH - 71A
30323	EASTLEIGH - 71A	EASTLEIGH - 71A	EASTLEIGH - 71A	EASTLEIGH - 71A	EASTLEIGH - 71A	EASTLEIGH - 71A	EASTLEIGH - 71A
30324	EASTLEIGH - 71A	EASTLEIGH - 71A	EASTLEIGH - 71A	EASTLEIGH - 71A	EASTLEIGH - 71A	EASTLEIGH - 71A	EASTLEIGH - 71A
30328	EASTLEIGH - 71A	EASTLEIGH - 71A	EASTLEIGH - 71A	EASTLEIGH - 71A	EASTLEIGH - 71A	EASTLEIGH - 71A	EASTLEIGH - 71A
30356	FRATTON - 71D	FRATTON - 71D	FRATTON - 71D	FRATTON - 71D	FRATTON - 71D	FRATTON - 70F	FRATTON - 70F
30357	FRATTON - 71D	FRATTON - 71D	FRATTON - 71D	FRATTON - 71D	FRATTON - 71D	FRATTON - 70F	FRATTON - 70F
30374	EXMOUTHJCN - 72A	EXMOUTHJCN - 72A	EXMOUTHJCN - 72A	EXMOUTHJCN - 72A	EXMOUTHJCN - 72A	EXMOUTHJCN - 72A	EXMOUTHJCN - 72A
30375	EASTLEIGH - 71A	EASTLEIGH - 71A	EASTLEIGH - 71A	EASTLEIGH - 71A	EASTLEIGH - 71A	EASTLEIGH - 71A	EASTLEIGH - 71A
30376	EASTLEIGH - 71A	EASTLEIGH - 71A	EASTLEIGH - 71A	EASTLEIGH - 71A	EASTLEIGH - 71A	EASTLEIGH - 71A	EASTLEIGH - 71A
30377	EASTLEIGH - 71A	EASTLEIGH - 71A	EASTLEIGH - 71A	EASTLEIGH - 71A	EASTLEIGH - 71A	EASTLEIGH - 71A	EASTLEIGH - 71A
30378	EXMOUTHJCN - 72A	EXMOUTHJCN - 72A	EXMOUTHJCN - 72A	EXMOUTHJCN - 72A	EXMOUTHJCN - 72A	EXMOUTHJCN - 72A	EXMOUTHJCN - 72A
30379	EASTLEIGH - 71A	EASTLEIGH - 71A	EASTLEIGH - 71A	EASTLEIGH - 71A	EASTLEIGH - 71A	EASTLEIGH - 71A	EASTLEIGH - 71A
30479	EASTLEIGH - 71A	EASTLEIGH - 71A	EASTLEIGH - 71A	EASTLEIGH - 71A	EASTLEIGH - 71A	EASTLEIGH - 71A	EASTLEIGH - 71A
30480	EASTLEIGH - 71A	EASTLEIGH - 71A	EASTLEIGH - 71A	EASTLEIGH - 71A	EASTLEIGH - 71A	EASTLEIGH - 71A	EASTLEIGH - 71A
30481	EASTLEIGH - 71A	EASTLEIGH - 71A	EASTLEIGH - 71A	EASTLEIGH - 71A	EASTLEIGH - 71A	EASTLEIGH - 71A	EASTLEIGH - 71A
30667	EXMOUTHJCN - 72A	EXMOUTHJCN - 72A	EXMOUTHJCN - 72A	EXMOUTHJCN - 72A	EXMOUTHJCN - 72A	EXMOUTHJCN - 72A	EXMOUTHJCN - 72A
30668	EXMOUTHJCN - 72A	EXMOUTHJCN - 72A	EXMOUTHJCN - 72A	EXMOUTHJCN - 72A	EXMOUTHJCN - 72A	EXMOUTHJCN - 72A	EXMOUTHJCN - 72A
30669	EXMOUTHJCN - 72A	EXMOUTHJCN - 72A	EXMOUTHJCN - 72A	EXMOUTHJCN - 72A	EXMOUTHJCN - 72A	EXMOUTHJCN - 72A	EXMOUTHJCN - 72A
30670	EXMOUTHJCN - 72A	EXMOUTHJCN - 72A	EXMOUTHJCN - 72A	EXMOUTHJCN - 72A	EXMOUTHJCN - 72A	EXMOUTHJCN - 72A	EXMOUTHJCN - 72A
30671	EXMOUTHJCN - 72A	EXMOUTHJCN - 72A	EXMOUTHJCN - 72A	EXMOUTHJCN - 72A	EXMOUTHJCN - 72A	EXMOUTHJCN - 72A	EXMOUTHJCN - 72A
30673	SALISBURY - 72B	SALISBURY - 72B	SALISBURY - 72B	SALISBURY - 72B	SALISBURY - 72B	SALISBURY - 72B	SALISBURY - 72B
30674	SALISBURY - 72B	SALISBURY - 72B	SALISBURY - 72B	SALISBURY - 72B	SALISBURY - 72B	SALISBURY - 72B	SALISBURY - 72B
30675	GUILDFORD - 70C	GUILDFORD - 70C	GUILDFORD - 70C	GUILDFORD - 70C	GUILDFORD - 70C	GUILDFORD - 70C	GUILDFORD - 70C
30676	EXMOUTHJCN - 72A	EXMOUTHJCN - 72A	EXMOUTHJCN - 72A	EXMOUTHJCN - 72A	EXMOUTHJCN - 72A	EXMOUTHJCN - 72A	EXMOUTHJCN - 72A

loco	Feb-55	Apr-55	Jun-55	Aug-55	Sep-55	Nov-55	Dec-55
				M7 0-4-4T (1897)			
30021	EXMOUTHJCN - 72A	EXMOUTHJCN - 72A	EXMOUTHJCN - 72A	EXMOUTHJCN - 72A	EXMOUTHJCN - 72A	EXMOUTHJCN - 72A	EXMOUTHJCN - 72A
30022	GUILDFORD - 70C	GUILDFORD - 70C	FRATTON - 70F	FRATTON - 70F	FRATTON - 70F	FRATTON - 70F	FRATTON - 70F
30023	FRATTON - 70F	FRATTON - 70F	FRATTON - 70F	FRATTON - 70F	FRATTON - 70F	FRATTON - 70F	FRATTON - 70F
30024	EXMOUTHJCN - 72A	EXMOUTHJCN - 72A	EXMOUTHJCN - 72A	EXMOUTHJCN - 72A	EXMOUTHJCN - 72A	EXMOUTHJCN - 72A	EXMOUTHJCN - 72A
30025	EXMOUTHJCN - 72A	EXMOUTHJCN - 72A	EXMOUTHJCN - 72A	EXMOUTHJCN - 72A	EXMOUTHJCN - 72A	EXMOUTHJCN - 72A	EXMOUTHJCN - 72A
30026	GUILDFORD - 70C	GUILDFORD - 70C	GUILDFORD - 70C	GUILDFORD - 70C	GUILDFORD - 70C	GUILDFORD - 70C	GUILDFORD - 70C
30027	GUILDFORD - 70C	GUILDFORD - 70C	GUILDFORD - 70C	GUILDFORD - 70C	GUILDFORD - 70C	GUILDFORD - 70C	GUILDFORD - 70C
30028	GUILDFORD - 70C	GUILDFORD - 70C	THREE BRIDGES - 75E	THREE BRIDGES - 75E	THREE BRIDGES - 75E	THREE BRIDGES - 75E	THREE BRIDGES - 75E
30029	EASTLEIGH - 71A	EASTLEIGH - 71A	EASTLEIGH - 71A	EASTLEIGH - 71A	EASTLEIGH - 71A	EASTLEIGH - 71A	EASTLEIGH - 71A
30030	EASTLEIGH - 71A	EASTLEIGH - 71A	EASTLEIGH - 71A	EASTLEIGH - 71A	EASTLEIGH - 71A	EASTLEIGH - 71A	EASTLEIGH - 71A
30031	EASTLEIGH - 71A	EASTLEIGH - 71A	BRIGHTON - 75A	BRIGHTON - 75A	BRIGHTON - 75A	BRIGHTON - 75A	BRIGHTON - 75A
30032	EASTLEIGH - 71A	EASTLEIGH - 71A	EASTLEIGH - 71A	EASTLEIGH - 71A	EASTLEIGH - 71A	EASTLEIGH - 71A	EASTLEIGH - 71A
30033	EASTLEIGH - 71A	EASTLEIGH - 71A	EASTLEIGH - 71A	EASTLEIGH - 71A	EASTLEIGH - 71A	EASTLEIGH - 71A	EASTLEIGH - 71A
30034	PLYMOUTH - 72D	PLYMOUTH - 72D	PLYMOUTH - 72D	PLYMOUTH - 72D	PLYMOUTH - 72D	PLYMOUTH - 72D	PLYMOUTH - 72D
30035	PLYMOUTH - 72D	PLYMOUTH - 72D	PLYMOUTH - 72D	PLYMOUTH - 72D	PLYMOUTH - 72D	PLYMOUTH - 72D	PLYMOUTH - 72D
30036	PLYMOUTH - 72D	PLYMOUTH - 72D	PLYMOUTH - 72D	PLYMOUTH - 72D	PLYMOUTH - 72D	PLYMOUTH - 72D	PLYMOUTH - 72D
30037	PLYMOUTH - 72D	PLYMOUTH - 72D	PLYMOUTH - 72D	PLYMOUTH - 72D	PLYMOUTH - 72D	PLYMOUTH - 72D	PLYMOUTH - 72D
30038	FELTHAM - 70B	FELTHAM - 70B	FELTHAM - 70B	FELTHAM - 70B	FELTHAM - 70B	FELTHAM - 70B	FELTHAM - 70B
30039	PLYMOUTH - 72D	PLYMOUTH - 72D	FRATTON - 70F	FRATTON - 70F	FRATTON - 70F	FRATTON - 70F	FRATTON - 70F
30040	PLYMOUTH - 72D	PLYMOUTH - 72D	BOURNEMOUTH - 71B	BOURNEMOUTH - 71B	BOURNEMOUTH - 71B	BOURNEMOUTH - 71B	BOURNEMOUTH - 71B
30041	FELTHAM - 70B	FELTHAM - 70B	FELTHAM - 70B	FELTHAM - 70B	FELTHAM - 70B	FELTHAM - 70B	FELTHAM - 70B
30042	FELTHAM - 70B	FELTHAM - 70B	FELTHAM - 70B	FELTHAM - 70B	FELTHAM - 70B	FELTHAM - 70B	FELTHAM - 70B
30043	FELTHAM - 70B	FELTHAM - 70B	FELTHAM - 70B	FELTHAM - 70B	FELTHAM - 70B	FELTHAM - 70B	FELTHAM - 70B
30044	EXMOUTHJCN - 72A	EXMOUTHJCN - 72A	EXMOUTHJCN - 72A	EXMOUTHJCN - 72A	EXMOUTHJCN - 72A	EXMOUTHJCN - 72A	EXMOUTHJCN - 72A
30045	EXMOUTHJCN - 72A	EXMOUTHJCN - 72A	EXMOUTHJCN - 72A	EXMOUTHJCN - 72A	EXMOUTHJCN - 72A	EXMOUTHJCN - 72A	EXMOUTHJCN - 72A
30046	EXMOUTHJCN - 72A	EXMOUTHJCN - 72A	EXMOUTHJCN - 72A	EXMOUTHJCN - 72A	EXMOUTHJCN - 72A	EXMOUTHJCN - 72A	EXMOUTHJCN - 72A
30047	HORSHAM - 75D	HORSHAM - 75D	HORSHAM - 75D	HORSHAM - 75D	HORSHAM - 75D	HORSHAM - 75D	HORSHAM - 75D
30048	HORSHAM - 75D	HORSHAM - 75D	HORSHAM - 75D	HORSHAM - 75D	HORSHAM - 75D	HORSHAM - 75D	HORSHAM - 75D
30049	HORSHAM - 75D	HORSHAM - 75D	HORSHAM - 75D	HORSHAM - 75D	HORSHAM - 75D	HORSHAM - 75D	HORSHAM - 75D
30050	HORSHAM - 75D	HORSHAM - 75D	HORSHAM - 75D	HORSHAM - 75D	HORSHAM - 75D	HORSHAM - 75D	HORSHAM - 75D
30051	HORSHAM - 75D	HORSHAM - 75D	HORSHAM - 75D	HORSHAM - 75D	HORSHAM - 75D	HORSHAM - 75D	HORSHAM - 75D
30052	FAVERSHAM - 73E	FAVERSHAM - 73E	THREE BRIDGES - 75E	THREE BRIDGES - 75E	THREE BRIDGES - 75E	THREE BRIDGES - 75E	THREE BRIDGES - 75E
30053	FAVERSHAM - 73E	FAVERSHAM - 73E	FAVERSHAM - 73E	FAVERSHAM - 73E	FAVERSHAM - 73E	FAVERSHAM - 73E	FAVERSHAM - 73E
30054	FRATTON - 70F	FRATTON - 70F	T.WELLS - 75F	T.WELLS - 75F	T.WELLS - 75F	T.WELLS - 75F	T.WELLS - 75F
30055	FRATTON - 70F	FRATTON - 70F	T.WELLS - 75F	T.WELLS - 75F	T.WELLS - 75F	T.WELLS - 75F	T.WELLS - 75F
30056	BOURNEMOUTH - 71B	BOURNEMOUTH - 71B	T.WELLS - 75F	T.WELLS - 75F	T.WELLS - 75F	T.WELLS - 75F	T.WELLS - 75F
30057	BOURNEMOUTH - 71B	BOURNEMOUTH - 71B	T.WELLS - 75F	T.WELLS - 75F	T.WELLS - 75F	T.WELLS - 75F	T.WELLS - 75F
30058	BOURNEMOUTH - 71B	BOURNEMOUTH - 71B	T.WELLS - 75F	T.WELLS - 75F	T.WELLS - 75F	T.WELLS - 75F	T.WELLS - 75F
30059	BOURNEMOUTH - 71B	BOURNEMOUTH - 71B	T.WELLS - 75F	T.WELLS - 75F	T.WELLS - 75F	T.WELLS - 75F	T.WELLS - 75F
30060	BOURNEMOUTH - 71B	BOURNEMOUTH - 71B	BOURNEMOUTH - 71B	BOURNEMOUTH - 71B	BOURNEMOUTH - 71B	BOURNEMOUTH - 71B	BOURNEMOUTH - 71B
30104	BOURNEMOUTH - 71B	BOURNEMOUTH - 71B	BOURNEMOUTH - 71B	BOURNEMOUTH - 71B	BOURNEMOUTH - 71B	BOURNEMOUTH - 71B	BOURNEMOUTH - 71B
30105	BOURNEMOUTH - 71B	BOURNEMOUTH - 71B	BOURNEMOUTH - 71B	BOURNEMOUTH - 71B	BOURNEMOUTH - 71B	BOURNEMOUTH - 71B	BOURNEMOUTH - 71B
30106	BOURNEMOUTH - 71B	BOURNEMOUTH - 71B	BOURNEMOUTH - 71B	BOURNEMOUTH - 71B	BOURNEMOUTH - 71B	BOURNEMOUTH - 71B	BOURNEMOUTH - 71B
30107	BOURNEMOUTH - 71B	BOURNEMOUTH - 71B	BOURNEMOUTH - 71B	BOURNEMOUTH - 71B	BOURNEMOUTH - 71B	BOURNEMOUTH - 71B	BOURNEMOUTH - 71B
30108	HORSHAM - 75D	HORSHAM - 75D	HORSHAM - 75D	HORSHAM - 75D	HORSHAM - 75D	BRIGHTON - 75A	BRIGHTON - 75A
30109	GUILDFORD - 70C	GUILDFORD - 70C	GUILDFORD - 70C	GUILDFORD - 70C	GUILDFORD - 70C	GUILDFORD - 70C	GUILDFORD - 70C
30110	GUILDFORD - 70C	GUILDFORD - 70C	GUILDFORD - 70C	GUILDFORD - 70C	GUILDFORD - 70C	GUILDFORD - 70C	GUILDFORD - 70C
30111	BOURNEMOUTH - 71B	BOURNEMOUTH - 71B	BOURNEMOUTH - 71B	BOURNEMOUTH - 71B	BOURNEMOUTH - 71B	BOURNEMOUTH - 71B	BOURNEMOUTH - 71B
30112	BOURNEMOUTH - 71B	BOURNEMOUTH - 71B	BOURNEMOUTH - 71B	BOURNEMOUTH - 71B	BOURNEMOUTH - 71B	BOURNEMOUTH - 71B	BOURNEMOUTH - 71B
30123	NINE ELMS - 70A	NINE ELMS - 70A	NINE ELMS - 70A	NINE ELMS - 70A	NINE ELMS - 70A	NINE ELMS - 70A	NINE ELMS - 70A
30124	NINE ELMS - 70A	NINE ELMS - 70A	NINE ELMS - 70A	NINE ELMS - 70A	NINE ELMS - 70A	NINE ELMS - 70A	NINE ELMS - 70A
30125	EASTLEIGH - 71A	EASTLEIGH - 71A	EASTLEIGH - 71A	EASTLEIGH - 71A	EASTLEIGH - 71A	EASTLEIGH - 71A	EASTLEIGH - 71A
30127	BOURNEMOUTH - 71B	BOURNEMOUTH - 71B	BOURNEMOUTH - 71B	BOURNEMOUTH - 71B	BOURNEMOUTH - 71B	BOURNEMOUTH - 71B	BOURNEMOUTH - 71B
30128	BOURNEMOUTH - 71B	BOURNEMOUTH - 71B	BOURNEMOUTH - 71B	BOURNEMOUTH - 71B	BOURNEMOUTH - 71B	BOURNEMOUTH - 71B	BOURNEMOUTH - 71B
30129	FAVERSHAM - 73E	FAVERSHAM - 73E	FAVERSHAM - 73E	FAVERSHAM - 73E	FAVERSHAM - 73E	FAVERSHAM - 73E	FAVERSHAM - 73E
30130	EASTLEIGH - 71A	EASTLEIGH - 71A	EASTLEIGH - 71A	EASTLEIGH - 71A	EASTLEIGH - 71A	EASTLEIGH - 71A	EASTLEIGH - 71A
30131	YEOVIL - 72C	YEOVIL - 72C	YEOVIL - 72C	YEOVIL - 72C	YEOVIL - 72C	YEOVIL - 72C	YEOVIL - 72C
30132	NINE ELMS - 70A	NINE ELMS - 70A	NINE ELMS - 70A	NINE ELMS - 70A	NINE ELMS - 70A	NINE ELMS - 70A	NINE ELMS - 70A
30133	NINE ELMS - 70A	NINE ELMS - 70A	NINE ELMS - 70A	NINE ELMS - 70A	NINE ELMS - 70A	NINE ELMS - 70A	NINE ELMS - 70A
30241	NINE ELMS - 70A	NINE ELMS - 70A	NINE ELMS - 70A	NINE ELMS - 70A	NINE ELMS - 70A	NINE ELMS - 70A	NINE ELMS - 70A
30242	NINE ELMS - 70A	NINE ELMS - 70A	NINE ELMS - 70A	NINE ELMS - 70A	NINE ELMS - 70A	NINE ELMS - 70A	NINE ELMS - 70A
30243	NINE ELMS - 70A	NINE ELMS - 70A	NINE ELMS - 70A	NINE ELMS - 70A	NINE ELMS - 70A	NINE ELMS - 70A	NINE ELMS - 70A
30244	NINE ELMS - 70A	NINE ELMS - 70A	NINE ELMS - 70A	NINE ELMS - 70A	NINE ELMS - 70A	NINE ELMS - 70A	NINE ELMS - 70A
30245	NINE ELMS - 70A	NINE ELMS - 70A	NINE ELMS - 70A	NINE ELMS - 70A	NINE ELMS - 70A	NINE ELMS - 70A	NINE ELMS - 70A
30246	GUILDFORD - 70C	GUILDFORD - 70C	GUILDFORD - 70C	GUILDFORD - 70C	GUILDFORD - 70C	GUILDFORD - 70C	GUILDFORD - 70C
30247	BARNSTAPLE - 72E	BARNSTAPLE - 72E	BARNSTAPLE - 72E	BARNSTAPLE - 72E	BARNSTAPLE - 72E	BARNSTAPLE - 72E	BARNSTAPLE - 72E
30248	NINE ELMS - 70A	NINE ELMS - 70A	NINE ELMS - 70A	NINE ELMS - 70A	NINE ELMS - 70A	NINE ELMS - 70A	NINE ELMS - 70A
30249	NINE ELMS - 70A	NINE ELMS - 70A	NINE ELMS - 70A	NINE ELMS - 70A	NINE ELMS - 70A	NINE ELMS - 70A	NINE ELMS - 70A
30250	BARNSTAPLE - 72E	BARNSTAPLE - 72E	BARNSTAPLE - 72E	BARNSTAPLE - 72E	BARNSTAPLE - 72E	BARNSTAPLE - 72E	BARNSTAPLE - 72E
30251	BARNSTAPLE - 72E	BARNSTAPLE - 72E	BARNSTAPLE - 72E	BARNSTAPLE - 72E	BARNSTAPLE - 72E	BARNSTAPLE - 72E	BARNSTAPLE - 72E
30252	BARNSTAPLE - 72E	BARNSTAPLE - 72E	BARNSTAPLE - 72E	BARNSTAPLE - 72E	BARNSTAPLE - 72E	BARNSTAPLE - 72E	BARNSTAPLE - 72E
30253	BARNSTAPLE - 72E	BARNSTAPLE - 72E	BARNSTAPLE - 72E	BARNSTAPLE - 72E	BARNSTAPLE - 72E	BARNSTAPLE - 72E	BARNSTAPLE - 72E
30254	BARNSTAPLE - 72E	BARNSTAPLE - 72E	BARNSTAPLE - 72E	BARNSTAPLE - 72E	BARNSTAPLE - 72E	BARNSTAPLE - 72E	BARNSTAPLE - 72E
30255	EXMOUTHJCN - 72A	EXMOUTHJCN - 72A	EXMOUTHJCN - 72A	EXMOUTHJCN - 72A	BARNSTAPLE - 72E	BARNSTAPLE - 72E	BARNSTAPLE - 72E
30256	EXMOUTHJCN - 72A	EXMOUTHJCN - 72A	EXMOUTHJCN - 72A	EXMOUTHJCN - 72A	EXMOUTHJCN - 72A	EXMOUTHJCN - 72A	EXMOUTHJCN - 72A
30318	BOURNEMOUTH - 71B	BOURNEMOUTH - 71B	BOURNEMOUTH - 71B	BOURNEMOUTH - 71B	BOURNEMOUTH - 71B	BOURNEMOUTH - 71B	BOURNEMOUTH - 71B
30319	BOURNEMOUTH - 71B	BOURNEMOUTH - 71B	BOURNEMOUTH - 71B	BOURNEMOUTH - 71B	BOURNEMOUTH - 71B	BOURNEMOUTH - 71B	BOURNEMOUTH - 71B
30320	NINE ELMS - 70A	NINE ELMS - 70A	NINE ELMS - 70A	NINE ELMS - 70A	NINE ELMS - 70A	NINE ELMS - 70A	NINE ELMS - 70A
30321	NINE ELMS - 70A	NINE ELMS - 70A	NINE ELMS - 70A	NINE ELMS - 70A	NINE ELMS - 70A	NINE ELMS - 70A	NINE ELMS - 70A
30322	EASTLEIGH - 71A	EASTLEIGH - 71A	EASTLEIGH - 71A	EASTLEIGH - 71A	EASTLEIGH - 71A	EASTLEIGH - 71A	EASTLEIGH - 71A
30323	EASTLEIGH - 71A	EASTLEIGH - 71A	EASTLEIGH - 71A	EASTLEIGH - 71A	EASTLEIGH - 71A	EASTLEIGH - 71A	EASTLEIGH - 71A
30324	EASTLEIGH - 71A	EASTLEIGH - 71A	EASTLEIGH - 71A	EASTLEIGH - 71A	EASTLEIGH - 71A	EASTLEIGH - 71A	BOURNEMOUTH - 71B
30328	EASTLEIGH - 71A	EASTLEIGH - 71A	BOURNEMOUTH - 71B	BOURNEMOUTH - 71B	BOURNEMOUTH - 71B	BOURNEMOUTH - 71B	THREE BRIDGES - 75E
30356	EASTLEIGH - 71A	EASTLEIGH - 71A	EASTLEIGH - 71A	EASTLEIGH - 71A	EASTLEIGH - 71A	EASTLEIGH - 71A	EASTLEIGH - 71A
30357	FRATTON - 70F	FRATTON - 70F	FRATTON - 70F	FRATTON - 70F	FRATTON - 70F	FRATTON - 70F	FRATTON - 70F
30374	EXMOUTHJCN - 72A	EXMOUTHJCN - 72A	EXMOUTHJCN - 72A	EXMOUTHJCN - 72A	EXMOUTHJCN - 72A	EXMOUTHJCN - 72A	EXMOUTHJCN - 72A
30375	EASTLEIGH - 71A	EASTLEIGH - 71A	EASTLEIGH - 71A	EASTLEIGH - 71A	EASTLEIGH - 71A	EASTLEIGH - 71A	EASTLEIGH - 71A
30376	EASTLEIGH - 71A	EASTLEIGH - 71A	EASTLEIGH - 71A	EASTLEIGH - 71A	EASTLEIGH - 71A	EASTLEIGH - 71A	EASTLEIGH - 71A
30377	EASTLEIGH - 71A	EASTLEIGH - 71A	EASTLEIGH - 71A	EASTLEIGH - 71A	EASTLEIGH - 71A	EASTLEIGH - 71A	EASTLEIGH - 71A
30378	EXMOUTHJCN - 72A	EXMOUTHJCN - 72A	EXMOUTHJCN - 72A	EXMOUTHJCN - 72A	EXMOUTHJCN - 72A	EXMOUTHJCN - 72A	EXMOUTHJCN - 72A
30379	EASTLEIGH - 71A	EASTLEIGH - 71A	THREE BRIDGES - 75E	THREE BRIDGES - 75E	THREE BRIDGES - 75E	THREE BRIDGES - 75E	EASTLEIGH - 71A
30479	EASTLEIGH - 71A	EASTLEIGH - 71A	EASTLEIGH - 71A	EASTLEIGH - 71A	EASTLEIGH - 71A	EASTLEIGH - 71A	EASTLEIGH - 71A
30480	EASTLEIGH - 71A	EASTLEIGH - 71A	EASTLEIGH - 71A	EASTLEIGH - 71A	EASTLEIGH - 71A	EASTLEIGH - 71A	EASTLEIGH - 71A
30481	EASTLEIGH - 71A	EASTLEIGH - 71A	EASTLEIGH - 71A	EASTLEIGH - 71A	EASTLEIGH - 71A	EASTLEIGH - 71A	EASTLEIGH - 71A
30667	EXMOUTHJCN - 72A	EXMOUTHJCN - 72A	EXMOUTHJCN - 72A	EXMOUTHJCN - 72A	EXMOUTHJCN - 72A	EXMOUTHJCN - 72A	EXMOUTHJCN - 72A
30668	EXMOUTHJCN - 72A	EXMOUTHJCN - 72A	EXMOUTHJCN - 72A	EXMOUTHJCN - 72A	EXMOUTHJCN - 72A	EXMOUTHJCN - 72A	EXMOUTHJCN - 72A
30669	EXMOUTHJCN - 72A	EXMOUTHJCN - 72A	EXMOUTHJCN - 72A	EXMOUTHJCN - 72A	EXMOUTHJCN - 72A	EXMOUTHJCN - 72A	EXMOUTHJCN - 72A
30670	EXMOUTHJCN - 72A	EXMOUTHJCN - 72A	EXMOUTHJCN - 72A	EXMOUTHJCN - 72A	EXMOUTHJCN - 72A	EXMOUTHJCN - 72A	EXMOUTHJCN - 72A
30671	EXMOUTHJCN - 72A	EXMOUTHJCN - 72A	EXMOUTHJCN - 72A	EXMOUTHJCN - 72A	EXMOUTHJCN - 72A	EXMOUTHJCN - 72A	EXMOUTHJCN - 72A
30673	SALISBURY - 72B	SALISBURY - 72B	SALISBURY - 72B	SALISBURY - 72B	SALISBURY - 72B	SALISBURY - 72B	SALISBURY - 72B
30674	SALISBURY - 72B	SALISBURY - 72B	SALISBURY - 72B	SALISBURY - 72B	SALISBURY - 72B	SALISBURY - 72B	SALISBURY - 72B
30675	GUILDFORD - 70C	GUILDFORD - 70C	GUILDFORD - 70C	GUILDFORD - 70C	GUILDFORD - 70C	GUILDFORD - 70C	GUILDFORD - 70C
30676	EXMOUTHJCN - 72A	EXMOUTHJCN - 72A	EXMOUTHJCN - 72A	EXMOUTHJCN - 72A	EXMOUTHJCN - 72A	EXMOUTHJCN - 72A	EXMOUTHJCN - 72A

loco	Jan-56	Apr-56	May-56	Aug-56	Oct-56	Nov-56	Jan-57
			M7 0-4-4T (1897)				
30021	EXMOUTH JCN - 72A	EXMOUTH JCN - 72A	EXMOUTH JCN - 72A	EXMOUTH JCN - 72A	EXMOUTH JCN - 72A	EXMOUTH JCN - 72A	EXMOUTH JCN - 72A
30022	FRATTON - 70F	FRATTON - 70F	FRATTON - 70F	FRATTON - 70F	FRATTON - 70F	FRATTON - 70F	FRATTON - 70F
30023	FRATTON - 70F	FRATTON - 70F	FRATTON - 70F	FRATTON - 70F	FRATTON - 70F	FRATTON - 70F	FRATTON - 70F
30024	EXMOUTH JCN - 72A	EXMOUTH JCN - 72A	EXMOUTH JCN - 72A	EXMOUTH JCN - 72A	EXMOUTH JCN - 72A	EXMOUTH JCN - 72A	EXMOUTH JCN - 72A
30025	EXMOUTH JCN - 72A	EXMOUTH JCN - 72A	EXMOUTH JCN - 72A	EXMOUTH JCN - 72A	EXMOUTH JCN - 72A	SALISBURY - 72B	SALISBURY - 72B
30026	GUILDFORD - 70C	GUILDFORD - 70C	GUILDFORD - 70C	GUILDFORD - 70C	GUILDFORD - 70C	GUILDFORD - 70C	GUILDFORD - 70C
30027	GUILDFORD - 70C	GUILDFORD - 70C	GUILDFORD - 70C	GUILDFORD - 70C	GUILDFORD - 70C	GUILDFORD - 70C	GUILDFORD - 70C
30028	THREE BRIDGES - 75E	THREE BRIDGES - 75E	EASTLEIGH - 71A	EASTLEIGH - 71A	EASTLEIGH - 71A	EASTLEIGH - 71A	EASTLEIGH - 71A
30029	EASTLEIGH - 71A	EASTLEIGH - 71A	EASTLEIGH - 71A	EASTLEIGH - 71A	EASTLEIGH - 71A	EASTLEIGH - 71A	EASTLEIGH - 71A
30030	EASTLEIGH - 71A	EASTLEIGH - 71A	EASTLEIGH - 71A	EASTLEIGH - 71A	EASTLEIGH - 71A	EASTLEIGH - 71A	EASTLEIGH - 71A
30031	BRIGHTON - 75A	BRIGHTON - 75A	BRIGHTON - 75A	BRIGHTON - 75A	BRIGHTON - 75A	BRIGHTON - 75A	BRIGHTON - 75A
30032	EASTLEIGH - 71A	EASTLEIGH - 71A	EASTLEIGH - 71A	EASTLEIGH - 71A	EASTLEIGH - 71A	EASTLEIGH - 71A	EASTLEIGH - 71A
30033	EASTLEIGH - 71A	EASTLEIGH - 71A	EASTLEIGH - 71A	EASTLEIGH - 71A	EASTLEIGH - 71A	EASTLEIGH - 71A	EASTLEIGH - 71A
30034	PLYMOUTH - 72D	PLYMOUTH - 72D	PLYMOUTH - 72D	PLYMOUTH - 72D	PLYMOUTH - 72D	PLYMOUTH - 72D	PLYMOUTH - 72D
30035	PLYMOUTH - 72D	PLYMOUTH - 72D	PLYMOUTH - 72D	PLYMOUTH - 72D	PLYMOUTH - 72D	PLYMOUTH - 72D	PLYMOUTH - 72D
30036	PLYMOUTH - 72D	PLYMOUTH - 72D	PLYMOUTH - 72D	PLYMOUTH - 72D	PLYMOUTH - 72D	PLYMOUTH - 72D	PLYMOUTH - 72D
30037	PLYMOUTH - 72D	PLYMOUTH - 72D	PLYMOUTH - 72D	PLYMOUTH - 72D	PLYMOUTH - 72D	PLYMOUTH - 72D	PLYMOUTH - 72D
30038	FELTHAM - 70B	FELTHAM - 70B	FELTHAM - 70B	FELTHAM - 70B	FELTHAM - 70B	FELTHAM - 70B	FELTHAM - 70B
30039	FRATTON - 70F	FRATTON - 70F	FRATTON - 70F	FRATTON - 70F	FRATTON - 70F	FRATTON - 70F	FRATTON - 70F
30040	BOURNEMOUTH - 71B	BOURNEMOUTH - 71B	BOURNEMOUTH - 71B	BOURNEMOUTH - 71B	BOURNEMOUTH - 71B	BOURNEMOUTH - 71B	BOURNEMOUTH - 71B
30041	FELTHAM - 70B	FELTHAM - 70B	FELTHAM - 70B	FELTHAM - 70B	FELTHAM - 70B	FELTHAM - 70B	FELTHAM - 70B
30042	FELTHAM - 70B	FELTHAM - 70B	FELTHAM - 70B	FELTHAM - 70B	FELTHAM - 70B	FELTHAM - 70B	FELTHAM - 70B
30043	FELTHAM - 70B	FELTHAM - 70B	FELTHAM - 70B	FELTHAM - 70B	FELTHAM - 70B	FELTHAM - 70B	FELTHAM - 70B
30044	EXMOUTH JCN - 72A	EXMOUTH JCN - 72A	EXMOUTH JCN - 72A	EXMOUTH JCN - 72A	EXMOUTH JCN - 72A	EXMOUTH JCN - 72A	EXMOUTH JCN - 72A
30045	EXMOUTH JCN - 72A	EXMOUTH JCN - 72A	EXMOUTH JCN - 72A	EXMOUTH JCN - 72A	EXMOUTH JCN - 72A	EXMOUTH JCN - 72A	EXMOUTH JCN - 72A
30046	EXMOUTH JCN - 72A	EXMOUTH JCN - 72A	EXMOUTH JCN - 72A	EXMOUTH JCN - 72A	EXMOUTH JCN - 72A	EXMOUTH JCN - 72A	EXMOUTH JCN - 72A
30047	HORSHAM - 75D	HORSHAM - 75D	HORSHAM - 75D	HORSHAM - 75D	HORSHAM - 75D	HORSHAM - 75D	HORSHAM - 75D
30048	HORSHAM - 75D	HORSHAM - 75D	HORSHAM - 75D	HORSHAM - 75D	HORSHAM - 75D	HORSHAM - 75D	HORSHAM - 75D
30049	HORSHAM - 75D	HORSHAM - 75D	HORSHAM - 75D	HORSHAM - 75D	HORSHAM - 75D	HORSHAM - 75D	HORSHAM - 75D
30050	HORSHAM - 75D	HORSHAM - 75D	HORSHAM - 75D	HORSHAM - 75D	HORSHAM - 75D	HORSHAM - 75D	HORSHAM - 75D
30051	HORSHAM - 75D	HORSHAM - 75D	HORSHAM - 75D	HORSHAM - 75D	HORSHAM - 75D	HORSHAM - 75D	HORSHAM - 75D
30052	THREE BRIDGES - 75E	THREE BRIDGES - 75E	BRIGHTON - 75A	BRIGHTON - 75A	BRIGHTON - 75A	BRIGHTON - 75A	BRIGHTON - 75A
30053	FAVERSHAM - 73E	FAVERSHAM - 73E	FAVERSHAM - 73E	FAVERSHAM - 73E	FAVERSHAM - 73E	FAVERSHAM - 73E	FAVERSHAM - 73E
30054	T.WELLS - 75F	T.WELLS - 75F	BRIGHTON - 75A	BRIGHTON - 75A	BRIGHTON - 75A	BRIGHTON - 75A	BRIGHTON - 75A
30055	T.WELLS - 75F	BRIGHTON - 75A	BRIGHTON - 75A	BRIGHTON - 75A	BRIGHTON - 75A	BRIGHTON - 75A	BRIGHTON - 75A
30056	T.WELLS - 75F	T.WELLS - 75F	BRIGHTON - 75A	BRIGHTON - 75A	BRIGHTON - 75A	BRIGHTON - 75A	BRIGHTON - 75A
30057	T.WELLS - 75F	T.WELLS - 75F	BOURNEMOUTH - 71B	BOURNEMOUTH - 71B	BOURNEMOUTH - 71B	BOURNEMOUTH - 71B	BOURNEMOUTH - 71B
30058	T.WELLS - 75F	T.WELLS - 75F	BOURNEMOUTH - 71B	BOURNEMOUTH - 71B	BOURNEMOUTH - 71B	BOURNEMOUTH - 71B	BOURNEMOUTH - 71B
30059	T.WELLS - 75F	BOURNEMOUTH - 71B	BOURNEMOUTH - 71B	BOURNEMOUTH - 71B	BOURNEMOUTH - 71B	BOURNEMOUTH - 71B	BOURNEMOUTH - 71B
30060	BOURNEMOUTH - 71B	BOURNEMOUTH - 71B	BOURNEMOUTH - 71B	BOURNEMOUTH - 71B	BOURNEMOUTH - 71B	BOURNEMOUTH - 71B	BOURNEMOUTH - 71B
30104	BOURNEMOUTH - 71B	BOURNEMOUTH - 71B	BOURNEMOUTH - 71B	BOURNEMOUTH - 71B	BOURNEMOUTH - 71B	BOURNEMOUTH - 71B	BOURNEMOUTH - 71B
30105	BOURNEMOUTH - 71B	BOURNEMOUTH - 71B	BOURNEMOUTH - 71B	BOURNEMOUTH - 71B	BOURNEMOUTH - 71B	BOURNEMOUTH - 71B	BOURNEMOUTH - 71B
30106	BOURNEMOUTH - 71B	BOURNEMOUTH - 71B	BOURNEMOUTH - 71B	BOURNEMOUTH - 71B	BOURNEMOUTH - 71B	BOURNEMOUTH - 71B	BOURNEMOUTH - 71B
30107	BOURNEMOUTH - 71B	BOURNEMOUTH - 71B	BOURNEMOUTH - 71B	BOURNEMOUTH - 71B	BOURNEMOUTH - 71B	BOURNEMOUTH - 71B	BOURNEMOUTH - 71B
30108	BRIGHTON - 75A	BRIGHTON - 75A	BOURNEMOUTH - 71B	BOURNEMOUTH - 71B	BOURNEMOUTH - 71B	BOURNEMOUTH - 71B	BOURNEMOUTH - 71B
30109	GUILDFORD - 70C	GUILDFORD - 70C	GUILDFORD - 70C	GUILDFORD - 70C	GUILDFORD - 70C	GUILDFORD - 70C	GUILDFORD - 70C
30110	GUILDFORD - 70C	GUILDFORD - 70C	GUILDFORD - 70C	GUILDFORD - 70C	GUILDFORD - 70C	GUILDFORD - 70C	GUILDFORD - 70C
30111	BOURNEMOUTH - 71B	BOURNEMOUTH - 71B	BOURNEMOUTH - 71B	BOURNEMOUTH - 71B	BOURNEMOUTH - 71B	BOURNEMOUTH - 71B	BOURNEMOUTH - 71B
30112	BOURNEMOUTH - 71B	BOURNEMOUTH - 71B	BOURNEMOUTH - 71B	BOURNEMOUTH - 71B	BOURNEMOUTH - 71B	BOURNEMOUTH - 71B	BOURNEMOUTH - 71B
30123	NINE ELMS - 70A	NINE ELMS - 70A	NINE ELMS - 70A	NINE ELMS - 70A	NINE ELMS - 70A	NINE ELMS - 70A	NINE ELMS - 70A
30124	NINE ELMS - 70A	NINE ELMS - 70A	NINE ELMS - 70A	NINE ELMS - 70A	NINE ELMS - 70A	GUILDFORD - 70C	GUILDFORD - 70C
30125	EASTLEIGH - 71A	EASTLEIGH - 71A	EASTLEIGH - 71A	EASTLEIGH - 71A	EASTLEIGH - 71A	EASTLEIGH - 71A	EASTLEIGH - 71A
30127	BOURNEMOUTH - 71B	BOURNEMOUTH - 71B	BOURNEMOUTH - 71B	BOURNEMOUTH - 71B	BOURNEMOUTH - 71B	BOURNEMOUTH - 71B	BOURNEMOUTH - 71B
30128	BOURNEMOUTH - 71B	BOURNEMOUTH - 71B	BOURNEMOUTH - 71B	BOURNEMOUTH - 71B	BOURNEMOUTH - 71B	BOURNEMOUTH - 71B	BOURNEMOUTH - 71B
30129	FAVERSHAM - 73E	FAVERSHAM - 73E	YEOVIL - 72C	YEOVIL - 72C	YEOVIL - 72C	YEOVIL - 72C	YEOVIL - 72C
30130	EASTLEIGH - 71A	EASTLEIGH - 71A	EASTLEIGH - 71A	EASTLEIGH - 71A	EASTLEIGH - 71A	EASTLEIGH - 71A	EASTLEIGH - 71A
30131	YEOVIL - 72C	YEOVIL - 72C	YEOVIL - 72C	YEOVIL - 72C	YEOVIL - 72C	YEOVIL - 72C	YEOVIL - 72C
30132	NINE ELMS - 70A	NINE ELMS - 70A	NINE ELMS - 70A	NINE ELMS - 70A	NINE ELMS - 70A	NINE ELMS - 70A	NINE ELMS - 70A
30133	NINE ELMS - 70A	NINE ELMS - 70A	NINE ELMS - 70A	NINE ELMS - 70A	NINE ELMS - 70A	NINE ELMS - 70A	NINE ELMS - 70A
30241	NINE ELMS - 70A	NINE ELMS - 70A	NINE ELMS - 70A	NINE ELMS - 70A	NINE ELMS - 70A	NINE ELMS - 70A	NINE ELMS - 70A
30242	NINE ELMS - 70A	NINE ELMS - 70A	NINE ELMS - 70A	NINE ELMS - 70A	NINE ELMS - 70A	NINE ELMS - 70A	NINE ELMS - 70A
30243	NINE ELMS - 70A	NINE ELMS - 70A	NINE ELMS - 70A	NINE ELMS - 70A	NINE ELMS - 70A	NINE ELMS - 70A	NINE ELMS - 70A
30244	NINE ELMS - 70A	NINE ELMS - 70A	NINE ELMS - 70A	NINE ELMS - 70A	NINE ELMS - 70A	NINE ELMS - 70A	NINE ELMS - 70A
30245	NINE ELMS - 70A	NINE ELMS - 70A	NINE ELMS - 70A	NINE ELMS - 70A	NINE ELMS - 70A	NINE ELMS - 70A	NINE ELMS - 70A
30246	GUILDFORD - 70C	GUILDFORD - 70C	GUILDFORD - 70C	GUILDFORD - 70C	GUILDFORD - 70C	GUILDFORD - 70C	GUILDFORD - 70C
30247	BARNSTAPLE - 72E	BARNSTAPLE - 72E	BARNSTAPLE - 72E	BARNSTAPLE - 72E	BARNSTAPLE - 72E	BARNSTAPLE - 72E	BARNSTAPLE - 72E
30248	NINE ELMS - 70A	NINE ELMS - 70A	NINE ELMS - 70A	NINE ELMS - 70A	NINE ELMS - 70A	NINE ELMS - 70A	NINE ELMS - 70A
30249	NINE ELMS - 70A	NINE ELMS - 70A	NINE ELMS - 70A	NINE ELMS - 70A	NINE ELMS - 70A	NINE ELMS - 70A	NINE ELMS - 70A
30250	BARNSTAPLE - 72E	BARNSTAPLE - 72E	BARNSTAPLE - 72E	BARNSTAPLE - 72E	BARNSTAPLE - 72E	BARNSTAPLE - 72E	BARNSTAPLE - 72E
30251	BARNSTAPLE - 72E	BARNSTAPLE - 72E	BARNSTAPLE - 72E	BARNSTAPLE - 72E	BARNSTAPLE - 72E	BARNSTAPLE - 72E	BARNSTAPLE - 72E
30252	BARNSTAPLE - 72E	BARNSTAPLE - 72E	BARNSTAPLE - 72E	BARNSTAPLE - 72E	BARNSTAPLE - 72E	BARNSTAPLE - 72E	BARNSTAPLE - 72E
30253	BARNSTAPLE - 72E	BARNSTAPLE - 72E	BARNSTAPLE - 72E	BARNSTAPLE - 72E	BARNSTAPLE - 72E	BARNSTAPLE - 72E	BARNSTAPLE - 72E
30254	BARNSTAPLE - 72E	BARNSTAPLE - 72E	BARNSTAPLE - 72E	BARNSTAPLE - 72E	BARNSTAPLE - 72E	BARNSTAPLE - 72E	BARNSTAPLE - 72E
30255	BARNSTAPLE - 72E	BARNSTAPLE - 72E	BARNSTAPLE - 72E	BARNSTAPLE - 72E	BARNSTAPLE - 72E	BARNSTAPLE - 72E	BARNSTAPLE - 72E
30256	EXMOUTH JCN - 72A	EXMOUTH JCN - 72A	EXMOUTH JCN - 72A	EXMOUTH JCN - 72A	EXMOUTH JCN - 72A	EXMOUTH JCN - 72A	EXMOUTH JCN - 72A
30318	BOURNEMOUTH - 71B	BOURNEMOUTH - 71B	BOURNEMOUTH - 71B	BOURNEMOUTH - 71B	BOURNEMOUTH - 71B	BOURNEMOUTH - 71B	BOURNEMOUTH - 71B
30319	BOURNEMOUTH - 71B	BOURNEMOUTH - 71B	BOURNEMOUTH - 71B	BOURNEMOUTH - 71B	BOURNEMOUTH - 71B	BOURNEMOUTH - 71B	BOURNEMOUTH - 71B
30320	NINE ELMS - 70A	NINE ELMS - 70A	NINE ELMS - 70A	NINE ELMS - 70A	NINE ELMS - 70A	NINE ELMS - 70A	NINE ELMS - 70A
30321	NINE ELMS - 70A	NINE ELMS - 70A	NINE ELMS - 70A	NINE ELMS - 70A	NINE ELMS - 70A	NINE ELMS - 70A	NINE ELMS - 70A
30322	EASTLEIGH - 71A	EASTLEIGH - 71A	EASTLEIGH - 71A	EASTLEIGH - 71A	EASTLEIGH - 71A	EASTLEIGH - 71A	EASTLEIGH - 71A
30323	EASTLEIGH - 71A	EASTLEIGH - 71A	EASTLEIGH - 71A	EASTLEIGH - 71A	EASTLEIGH - 71A	EASTLEIGH - 71A	EASTLEIGH - 71A
30324	BOURNEMOUTH - 71B	BOURNEMOUTH - 71B	BOURNEMOUTH - 71B	BOURNEMOUTH - 71B	BOURNEMOUTH - 71B	BOURNEMOUTH - 71B	BOURNEMOUTH - 71B
30328	THREE BRIDGES - 75E	THREE BRIDGES - 75E	EASTLEIGH - 71A	EASTLEIGH - 71A	EASTLEIGH - 71A	EASTLEIGH - 71A	EASTLEIGH - 71A
30356	EASTLEIGH - 71A	EASTLEIGH - 71A	EASTLEIGH - 71A	EASTLEIGH - 71A	EASTLEIGH - 71A	EASTLEIGH - 71A	EASTLEIGH - 71A
30357	FRATTON - 70F	FRATTON - 70F	FRATTON - 70F	FRATTON - 70F	FRATTON - 70F	FRATTON - 70F	FRATTON - 70F
30374	EXMOUTH JCN - 72A	EXMOUTH JCN - 72A	EXMOUTH JCN - 72A	EXMOUTH JCN - 72A	EXMOUTH JCN - 72A	SALISBURY - 72B	SALISBURY - 72B
30375	EASTLEIGH - 71A	EASTLEIGH - 71A	EASTLEIGH - 71A	EASTLEIGH - 71A	EASTLEIGH - 71A	EASTLEIGH - 71A	EASTLEIGH - 71A
30376	EASTLEIGH - 71A	EASTLEIGH - 71A	EASTLEIGH - 71A	EASTLEIGH - 71A	EASTLEIGH - 71A	EASTLEIGH - 71A	EASTLEIGH - 71A
30377	EASTLEIGH - 71A	EASTLEIGH - 71A	EASTLEIGH - 71A	EASTLEIGH - 71A	EASTLEIGH - 71A	EASTLEIGH - 71A	EASTLEIGH - 71A
30378	EXMOUTH JCN - 72A	EXMOUTH JCN - 72A	EXMOUTH JCN - 72A	EXMOUTH JCN - 72A	EXMOUTH JCN - 72A	EXMOUTH JCN - 72A	EXMOUTH JCN - 72A
30379	EASTLEIGH - 71A	EASTLEIGH - 71A	EASTLEIGH - 71A	EASTLEIGH - 71A	EASTLEIGH - 71A	EASTLEIGH - 71A	EASTLEIGH - 71A
30479	EASTLEIGH - 71A	EASTLEIGH - 71A	EASTLEIGH - 71A	EASTLEIGH - 71A	EASTLEIGH - 71A	EASTLEIGH - 71A	EASTLEIGH - 71A
30480	EASTLEIGH - 71A	EASTLEIGH - 71A	EASTLEIGH - 71A	EASTLEIGH - 71A	EASTLEIGH - 71A	EASTLEIGH - 71A	EASTLEIGH - 71A
30481	EASTLEIGH - 71A	EASTLEIGH - 71A	EASTLEIGH - 71A	EASTLEIGH - 71A	EASTLEIGH - 71A	EASTLEIGH - 71A	EASTLEIGH - 71A
30667	EXMOUTH JCN - 72A	EXMOUTH JCN - 72A	EXMOUTH JCN - 72A	EXMOUTH JCN - 72A	EXMOUTH JCN - 72A	EXMOUTH JCN - 72A	EXMOUTH JCN - 72A
30668	EXMOUTH JCN - 72A	EXMOUTH JCN - 72A	EXMOUTH JCN - 72A	EXMOUTH JCN - 72A	EXMOUTH JCN - 72A	EXMOUTH JCN - 72A	EXMOUTH JCN - 72A
30669	EXMOUTH JCN - 72A	EXMOUTH JCN - 72A	EXMOUTH JCN - 72A	EXMOUTH JCN - 72A	EXMOUTH JCN - 72A	EXMOUTH JCN - 72A	EXMOUTH JCN - 72A
30670	EXMOUTH JCN - 72A	EXMOUTH JCN - 72A	EXMOUTH JCN - 72A	EXMOUTH JCN - 72A	EXMOUTH JCN - 72A	EXMOUTH JCN - 72A	EXMOUTH JCN - 72A
30671	EXMOUTH JCN - 72A	EXMOUTH JCN - 72A	BARNSTAPLE - 72E	BARNSTAPLE - 72E	BARNSTAPLE - 72E	BARNSTAPLE - 72E	BARNSTAPLE - 72E
30673	SALISBURY - 72B	SALISBURY - 72B	SALISBURY - 72B	SALISBURY - 72B	SALISBURY - 72B	SALISBURY - 72B	SALISBURY - 72B
30674	SALISBURY - 72B	SALISBURY - 72B	SALISBURY - 72B	SALISBURY - 72B	SALISBURY - 72B	SALISBURY - 72B	SALISBURY - 72B
30675	GUILDFORD - 70C	GUILDFORD - 70C	GUILDFORD - 70C	GUILDFORD - 70C	GUILDFORD - 70C	GUILDFORD - 70C	GUILDFORD - 70C
30676	EXMOUTH JCN - 72A	EXMOUTH JCN - 72A	EXMOUTH JCN - 72A	EXMOUTH JCN - 72A	EXMOUTH JCN - 72A	EXMOUTH JCN - 72A	EXMOUTH JCN - 72A

loco	Mar-57	Jun-57	Jul-57	Oct-57	Jan-58	Feb-58	Mar-58
				M7 0-4-4T (1897)			
30021	EXMOUTHJCN - 72A	EXMOUTHJCN - 72A	EXMOUTHJCN - 72A	EXMOUTHJCN - 72A	EXMOUTHJCN - 72A	EXMOUTHJCN - 72A	EXMOUTHJCN - 72A
30022	FRATTON - 70F	FRATTON - 70F	FRATTON - 70F	FRATTON - 70F	FRATTON - 70F	FRATTON - 70F	FRATTON - 70F
30023	FRATTON - 70F	FRATTON - 70F	FRATTON - 70F	FRATTON - 70F	FRATTON - 70F	FRATTON - 70F	FRATTON - 70F
30024	EXMOUTHJCN - 72A	EXMOUTHJCN - 72A	EXMOUTHJCN - 72A	EXMOUTHJCN - 72A	EXMOUTHJCN - 72A	EXMOUTHJCN - 72A	EXMOUTHJCN - 72A
30025	SALISBURY - 72B	SALISBURY - 72B	SALISBURY - 72B	SALISBURY - 72B	SALISBURY - 72B	SALISBURY - 72B	SALISBURY - 72B
30026	GUILDFORD - 70C	GUILDFORD - 70C	GUILDFORD - 70C	GUILDFORD - 70C	GUILDFORD - 70C	GUILDFORD - 70C	GUILDFORD - 70C
30027	GUILDFORD - 70C	GUILDFORD - 70C	GUILDFORD - 70C	GUILDFORD - 70C	GUILDFORD - 70C	GUILDFORD - 70C	GUILDFORD - 70C
30028	EASTLEIGH - 71A	EASTLEIGH - 71A	EASTLEIGH - 71A	EASTLEIGH - 71A	EASTLEIGH - 71A	EASTLEIGH - 71A	EASTLEIGH - 71A
30029	EASTLEIGH - 71A	EASTLEIGH - 71A	EASTLEIGH - 71A	EASTLEIGH - 71A	EASTLEIGH - 71A	EASTLEIGH - 71A	EASTLEIGH - 71A
30030	EASTLEIGH - 71A	EASTLEIGH - 71A	EASTLEIGH - 71A	EASTLEIGH - 71A	EASTLEIGH - 71A	EASTLEIGH - 71A	EASTLEIGH - 71A
30031	BRIGHTON - 75A	BRIGHTON - 75A	BRIGHTON - 75A	BRIGHTON - 75A	BRIGHTON - 75A	BRIGHTON - 75A	BRIGHTON - 75A
30032	EASTLEIGH - 71A	EASTLEIGH - 71A	EASTLEIGH - 71A	EASTLEIGH - 71A	EASTLEIGH - 71A	EASTLEIGH - 71A	EASTLEIGH - 71A
30033	EASTLEIGH - 71A	EASTLEIGH - 71A	EASTLEIGH - 71A	EASTLEIGH - 71A	EASTLEIGH - 71A	EASTLEIGH - 71A	EASTLEIGH - 71A
30034	PLYMOUTH - 72D	PLYMOUTH - 72D	PLYMOUTH - 72D	PLYMOUTH - 72D	PLYMOUTH - 72D	PLYMOUTH - 83H	PLYMOUTH - 83H
30035	PLYMOUTH - 72D	PLYMOUTH - 72D	PLYMOUTH - 72D	PLYMOUTH - 72D	PLYMOUTH - 72D	PLYMOUTH - 83H	PLYMOUTH - 83H
30036	PLYMOUTH - 72D	PLYMOUTH - 72D	PLYMOUTH - 72D	PLYMOUTH - 72D	PLYMOUTH - 72D	PLYMOUTH - 83H	PLYMOUTH - 83H
30037	PLYMOUTH - 72D	PLYMOUTH - 72D	PLYMOUTH - 72D	PLYMOUTH - 72D	PLYMOUTH - 72D	PLYMOUTH - 83H	PLYMOUTH - 83H
30038	FELTHAM - 70B	FELTHAM - 70B	FELTHAM - 70B	FELTHAM - 70B	FELTHAM - 70B	W/D	W/D
30039	FRATTON - 70F	FRATTON - 70F	FRATTON - 70F	FRATTON - 70F	FRATTON - 70F	FRATTON - 70F	FRATTON - 70F
30040	BOURNEMOUTH - 71B	BOURNEMOUTH - 71B	BOURNEMOUTH - 71B	BOURNEMOUTH - 71B	BOURNEMOUTH - 71B	BOURNEMOUTH - 71B	BOURNEMOUTH - 71B
30041	FELTHAM - 70B	FELTHAM - 70B	FELTHAM - 70B	W/D	W/D	W/D	W/D
30042	FELTHAM - 70B	FELTHAM - 70B	W/D	W/D	W/D	W/D	W/D
30043	FELTHAM - 70B	FELTHAM - 70B	FELTHAM - 70B	FELTHAM - 70B	FELTHAM - 70B	FELTHAM - 70B	FELTHAM - 70B
30044	EXMOUTHJCN - 72A	EXMOUTHJCN - 72A	EXMOUTHJCN - 72A	EXMOUTHJCN - 72A	EXMOUTHJCN - 72A	EXMOUTHJCN - 72A	EXMOUTHJCN - 72A
30045	EXMOUTHJCN - 72A	EXMOUTHJCN - 72A	EXMOUTHJCN - 72A	EXMOUTHJCN - 72A	EXMOUTHJCN - 72A	EXMOUTHJCN - 72A	EXMOUTHJCN - 72A
30046	EXMOUTHJCN - 72A	EXMOUTHJCN - 72A	EXMOUTHJCN - 72A	EXMOUTHJCN - 72A	EXMOUTHJCN - 72A	EXMOUTHJCN - 72A	EXMOUTHJCN - 72A
30047	HORSHAM - 75D	HORSHAM - 75D	HORSHAM - 75D	HORSHAM - 75D	HORSHAM - 75D	HORSHAM - 75D	HORSHAM - 75D
30048	HORSHAM - 75D	HORSHAM - 75D	HORSHAM - 75D	HORSHAM - 75D	HORSHAM - 75D	HORSHAM - 75D	HORSHAM - 75D
30049	HORSHAM - 75D	HORSHAM - 75D	HORSHAM - 75D	HORSHAM - 75D	HORSHAM - 75D	HORSHAM - 75D	HORSHAM - 75D
30050	HORSHAM - 75D	HORSHAM - 75D	HORSHAM - 75D	HORSHAM - 75D	HORSHAM - 75D	HORSHAM - 75D	HORSHAM - 75D
30051	HORSHAM - 75D	HORSHAM - 75D	HORSHAM - 75D	HORSHAM - 75D	HORSHAM - 75D	HORSHAM - 75D	HORSHAM - 75D
30052	BRIGHTON - 75A	BRIGHTON - 75A	BRIGHTON - 75A	THREE BRIDGES - 75E	THREE BRIDGES - 75E	THREE BRIDGES - 75E	THREE BRIDGES - 75E
30053	FAVERSHAM - 73E	FAVERSHAM - 73E	FAVERSHAM - 73E	FAVERSHAM - 73E	FAVERSHAM - 73E	FAVERSHAM - 73E	FAVERSHAM - 73E
30054	BRIGHTON - 75A	BRIGHTON - 75A	BRIGHTON - 75A	BRIGHTON - 75A	BRIGHTON - 75A	BRIGHTON - 75A	BRIGHTON - 75A
30055	BRIGHTON - 75A	BRIGHTON - 75A	BRIGHTON - 75A	BRIGHTON - 75A	BRIGHTON - 75A	BRIGHTON - 75A	BRIGHTON - 75A
30056	BRIGHTON - 75A	BRIGHTON - 75A	BRIGHTON - 75A	THREE BRIDGES - 75E	THREE BRIDGES - 75E	THREE BRIDGES - 75E	THREE BRIDGES - 75E
30057	BOURNEMOUTH - 71B	BOURNEMOUTH - 71B	BOURNEMOUTH - 71B	BOURNEMOUTH - 71B	BOURNEMOUTH - 71B	BOURNEMOUTH - 71B	BOURNEMOUTH - 71B
30058	BOURNEMOUTH - 71B	BOURNEMOUTH - 71B	BOURNEMOUTH - 71B	BOURNEMOUTH - 71B	BOURNEMOUTH - 71B	BOURNEMOUTH - 71B	BOURNEMOUTH - 71B
30059	BOURNEMOUTH - 71B	BOURNEMOUTH - 71B	BOURNEMOUTH - 71B	BOURNEMOUTH - 71B	BOURNEMOUTH - 71B	BOURNEMOUTH - 71B	BOURNEMOUTH - 71B
30060	BOURNEMOUTH - 71B	BOURNEMOUTH - 71B	BOURNEMOUTH - 71B	BOURNEMOUTH - 71B	BOURNEMOUTH - 71B	BOURNEMOUTH - 71B	BOURNEMOUTH - 71B
30104	BOURNEMOUTH - 71B	BOURNEMOUTH - 71B	BOURNEMOUTH - 71B	BOURNEMOUTH - 71B	BOURNEMOUTH - 71B	BOURNEMOUTH - 71B	BOURNEMOUTH - 71B
30105	BOURNEMOUTH - 71B	BOURNEMOUTH - 71B	BOURNEMOUTH - 71B	BOURNEMOUTH - 71B	BOURNEMOUTH - 71B	BOURNEMOUTH - 71B	BOURNEMOUTH - 71B
30106	BOURNEMOUTH - 71B	BOURNEMOUTH - 71B	BOURNEMOUTH - 71B	BOURNEMOUTH - 71B	BOURNEMOUTH - 71B	BOURNEMOUTH - 71B	BOURNEMOUTH - 71B
30107	BOURNEMOUTH - 71B	BOURNEMOUTH - 71B	BOURNEMOUTH - 71B	BOURNEMOUTH - 71B	BOURNEMOUTH - 71B	BOURNEMOUTH - 71B	BOURNEMOUTH - 71B
30108	BOURNEMOUTH - 71B	BOURNEMOUTH - 71B	BOURNEMOUTH - 71B	BOURNEMOUTH - 71B	BOURNEMOUTH - 71B	BOURNEMOUTH - 71B	BOURNEMOUTH - 71B
30109	GUILDFORD - 70C	GUILDFORD - 70C	GUILDFORD - 70C	GUILDFORD - 70C	GUILDFORD - 70C	GUILDFORD - 70C	GUILDFORD - 70C
30110	GUILDFORD - 70C	GUILDFORD - 70C	GUILDFORD - 70C	GUILDFORD - 70C	GUILDFORD - 70C	GUILDFORD - 70C	GUILDFORD - 70C
30111	BOURNEMOUTH - 71B	BOURNEMOUTH - 71B	BOURNEMOUTH - 71B	BOURNEMOUTH - 71B	BOURNEMOUTH - 71B	BOURNEMOUTH - 71B	BOURNEMOUTH - 71B
30112	BOURNEMOUTH - 71B	BOURNEMOUTH - 71B	BOURNEMOUTH - 71B	BOURNEMOUTH - 71B	BOURNEMOUTH - 71B	BOURNEMOUTH - 71B	BOURNEMOUTH - 71B
30123	NINE ELMS - 70A	NINE ELMS - 70A	NINE ELMS - 70A	NINE ELMS - 70A	NINE ELMS - 70A	NINE ELMS - 70A	NINE ELMS - 70A
30124	GUILDFORD - 70C	GUILDFORD - 70C	GUILDFORD - 70C	GUILDFORD - 70C	GUILDFORD - 70C	GUILDFORD - 70C	GUILDFORD - 70C
30125	EASTLEIGH - 71A	EASTLEIGH - 71A	EASTLEIGH - 71A	EASTLEIGH - 71A	EASTLEIGH - 71A	EASTLEIGH - 71A	EASTLEIGH - 71A
30127	BOURNEMOUTH - 71B	BOURNEMOUTH - 71B	BOURNEMOUTH - 71B	BOURNEMOUTH - 71B	BOURNEMOUTH - 71B	BOURNEMOUTH - 71B	BOURNEMOUTH - 71B
30128	BOURNEMOUTH - 71B	BOURNEMOUTH - 71B	BOURNEMOUTH - 71B	BOURNEMOUTH - 71B	BOURNEMOUTH - 71B	BOURNEMOUTH - 71B	BOURNEMOUTH - 71B
30129	YEOVIL - 72C	YEOVIL - 72C	YEOVIL - 72C	YEOVIL - 72C	YEOVIL - 72C	YEOVIL - 72C	YEOVIL - 72C
30130	EASTLEIGH - 71A	EASTLEIGH - 71A	EASTLEIGH - 71A	EASTLEIGH - 71A	EASTLEIGH - 71A	EASTLEIGH - 71A	EASTLEIGH - 71A
30131	YEOVIL - 72C	YEOVIL - 72C	YEOVIL - 72C	YEOVIL - 72C	YEOVIL - 72C	YEOVIL - 72C	YEOVIL - 72C
30132	NINE ELMS - 70A	NINE ELMS - 70A	NINE ELMS - 70A	NINE ELMS - 70A	NINE ELMS - 70A	NINE ELMS - 70A	NINE ELMS - 70A
30133	NINE ELMS - 70A	NINE ELMS - 70A	NINE ELMS - 70A	NINE ELMS - 70A	NINE ELMS - 70A	NINE ELMS - 70A	NINE ELMS - 70A
30241	NINE ELMS - 70A	NINE ELMS - 70A	NINE ELMS - 70A	NINE ELMS - 70A	NINE ELMS - 70A	NINE ELMS - 70A	NINE ELMS - 70A
30242	NINE ELMS - 70A	NINE ELMS - 70A	NINE ELMS - 70A	NINE ELMS - 70A	NINE ELMS - 70A	NINE ELMS - 70A	NINE ELMS - 70A
30243	NINE ELMS - 70A	NINE ELMS - 70A	NINE ELMS - 70A	FELTHAM - 70B	FELTHAM - 70B	FELTHAM - 70B	FELTHAM - 70B
30244	NINE ELMS - 70A	NINE ELMS - 70A	NINE ELMS - 70A	NINE ELMS - 70A	W/D	W/D	W/D
30245	NINE ELMS - 70A	NINE ELMS - 70A	NINE ELMS - 70A	NINE ELMS - 70A	NINE ELMS - 70A	NINE ELMS - 70A	NINE ELMS - 70A
30246	GUILDFORD - 70C	GUILDFORD - 70C	GUILDFORD - 70C	GUILDFORD - 70C	GUILDFORD - 70C	GUILDFORD - 70C	GUILDFORD - 70C
30247	BARNSTAPLE - 72E	BARNSTAPLE - 72E	BARNSTAPLE - 72E	BARNSTAPLE - 72E	BARNSTAPLE - 72E	BARNSTAPLE - 72E	BARNSTAPLE - 72E
30248	NINE ELMS - 70A	NINE ELMS - 70A	NINE ELMS - 70A	NINE ELMS - 70A	NINE ELMS - 70A	NINE ELMS - 70A	NINE ELMS - 70A
30249	NINE ELMS - 70A	NINE ELMS - 70A	NINE ELMS - 70A	NINE ELMS - 70A	NINE ELMS - 70A	NINE ELMS - 70A	NINE ELMS - 70A
30250	BARNSTAPLE - 72E	BARNSTAPLE - 72E	BARNSTAPLE - 72E	W/D	W/D	W/D	W/D
30251	BARNSTAPLE - 72E	BARNSTAPLE - 72E	BARNSTAPLE - 72E	BARNSTAPLE - 72E	BARNSTAPLE - 72E	BARNSTAPLE - 72E	BARNSTAPLE - 72E
30252	BARNSTAPLE - 72E	BARNSTAPLE - 72E	BARNSTAPLE - 72E	BARNSTAPLE - 72E	BARNSTAPLE - 72E	BARNSTAPLE - 72E	BARNSTAPLE - 72E
30253	BARNSTAPLE - 72E	BARNSTAPLE - 72E	BARNSTAPLE - 72E	BARNSTAPLE - 72E	BARNSTAPLE - 72E	BARNSTAPLE - 72E	BARNSTAPLE - 72E
30254	BARNSTAPLE - 72E	BARNSTAPLE - 72E	BARNSTAPLE - 72E	BARNSTAPLE - 72E	BARNSTAPLE - 72E	BARNSTAPLE - 72E	BARNSTAPLE - 72E
30255	BARNSTAPLE - 72E	BARNSTAPLE - 72E	BARNSTAPLE - 72E	BARNSTAPLE - 72E	BARNSTAPLE - 72E	BARNSTAPLE - 72E	BARNSTAPLE - 72E
30256	EXMOUTHJCN - 72A	EXMOUTHJCN - 72A	EXMOUTHJCN - 72A	EXMOUTHJCN - 72A	EXMOUTHJCN - 72A	EXMOUTHJCN - 72A	EXMOUTHJCN - 72A
30318	BOURNEMOUTH - 71B	BOURNEMOUTH - 71B	BOURNEMOUTH - 71B	BOURNEMOUTH - 71B	BOURNEMOUTH - 71B	BOURNEMOUTH - 71B	BOURNEMOUTH - 71B
30319	BOURNEMOUTH - 71B	BOURNEMOUTH - 71B	BOURNEMOUTH - 71B	BOURNEMOUTH - 71B	BOURNEMOUTH - 71B	BOURNEMOUTH - 71B	BOURNEMOUTH - 71B
30320	NINE ELMS - 70A	NINE ELMS - 70A	NINE ELMS - 70A	NINE ELMS - 70A	NINE ELMS - 70A	NINE ELMS - 70A	NINE ELMS - 70A
30321	NINE ELMS - 70A	NINE ELMS - 70A	NINE ELMS - 70A	NINE ELMS - 70A	NINE ELMS - 70A	NINE ELMS - 70A	NINE ELMS - 70A
30322	EASTLEIGH - 71A	EASTLEIGH - 71A	EASTLEIGH - 71A	EASTLEIGH - 71A	EASTLEIGH - 71A	EASTLEIGH - 71A	EASTLEIGH - 71A
30323	EASTLEIGH - 71A	EASTLEIGH - 71A	EASTLEIGH - 71A	EASTLEIGH - 71A	EASTLEIGH - 71A	EASTLEIGH - 71A	EASTLEIGH - 71A
30324	BOURNEMOUTH - 71B	BOURNEMOUTH - 71B	BOURNEMOUTH - 71B	BOURNEMOUTH - 71B	BOURNEMOUTH - 71B	BOURNEMOUTH - 71B	BOURNEMOUTH - 71B
30328	EASTLEIGH - 71A	EASTLEIGH - 71A	EASTLEIGH - 71A	EASTLEIGH - 71A	EASTLEIGH - 71A	EASTLEIGH - 71A	EASTLEIGH - 71A
30356	EASTLEIGH - 71A	EASTLEIGH - 71A	EASTLEIGH - 71A	EASTLEIGH - 71A	EASTLEIGH - 71A	EASTLEIGH - 71A	EASTLEIGH - 71A
30357	FRATTON - 70F	FRATTON - 70F	FRATTON - 70F	FRATTON - 70F	FRATTON - 70F	FRATTON - 70F	FRATTON - 70F
30374	SALISBURY - 72B	EXMOUTHJCN - 72A	EXMOUTHJCN - 72A	EXMOUTHJCN - 72A	EXMOUTHJCN - 72A	EXMOUTHJCN - 72A	EXMOUTHJCN - 72A
30375	EASTLEIGH - 71A	EASTLEIGH - 71A	EASTLEIGH - 71A	EASTLEIGH - 71A	EASTLEIGH - 71A	EASTLEIGH - 71A	EASTLEIGH - 71A
30376	EASTLEIGH - 71A	EASTLEIGH - 71A	EASTLEIGH - 71A	EASTLEIGH - 71A	EASTLEIGH - 71A	EASTLEIGH - 71A	EASTLEIGH - 71A
30377	EASTLEIGH - 71A	EASTLEIGH - 71A	EASTLEIGH - 71A	EASTLEIGH - 71A	EASTLEIGH - 71A	EASTLEIGH - 71A	EASTLEIGH - 71A
30378	EXMOUTHJCN - 72A	EXMOUTHJCN - 72A	EXMOUTHJCN - 72A	EXMOUTHJCN - 72A	EXMOUTHJCN - 72A	EXMOUTHJCN - 72A	EXMOUTHJCN - 72A
30379	EASTLEIGH - 71A	EASTLEIGH - 71A	EASTLEIGH - 71A	EASTLEIGH - 71A	EASTLEIGH - 71A	EASTLEIGH - 71A	EASTLEIGH - 71A
30479	EASTLEIGH - 71A	EASTLEIGH - 71A	EASTLEIGH - 71A	EASTLEIGH - 71A	EASTLEIGH - 71A	EASTLEIGH - 71A	EASTLEIGH - 71A
30480	EASTLEIGH - 71A	EASTLEIGH - 71A	EASTLEIGH - 71A	EASTLEIGH - 71A	EASTLEIGH - 71A	EASTLEIGH - 71A	EASTLEIGH - 71A
30481	EASTLEIGH - 71A	EASTLEIGH - 71A	EASTLEIGH - 71A	EASTLEIGH - 71A	EASTLEIGH - 71A	EASTLEIGH - 71A	EASTLEIGH - 71A
30667	EXMOUTHJCN - 72A	EXMOUTHJCN - 72A	EXMOUTHJCN - 72A	EXMOUTHJCN - 72A	EXMOUTHJCN - 72A	EXMOUTHJCN - 72A	EXMOUTHJCN - 72A
30668	EXMOUTHJCN - 72A	EXMOUTHJCN - 72A	EXMOUTHJCN - 72A	EXMOUTHJCN - 72A	EXMOUTHJCN - 72A	EXMOUTHJCN - 72A	EXMOUTHJCN - 72A
30669	EXMOUTHJCN - 72A	EXMOUTHJCN - 72A	EXMOUTHJCN - 72A	EXMOUTHJCN - 72A	EXMOUTHJCN - 72A	EXMOUTHJCN - 72A	EXMOUTHJCN - 72A
30670	EXMOUTHJCN - 72A	EXMOUTHJCN - 72A	EXMOUTHJCN - 72A	EXMOUTHJCN - 72A	EXMOUTHJCN - 72A	EXMOUTHJCN - 72A	EXMOUTHJCN - 72A
30671	BARNSTAPLE - 72E	BARNSTAPLE - 72E	BARNSTAPLE - 72E	BARNSTAPLE - 72E	BARNSTAPLE - 72E	BARNSTAPLE - 72E	BARNSTAPLE - 72E
30673	SALISBURY - 72B	SALISBURY - 72B	SALISBURY - 72B	SALISBURY - 72B	SALISBURY - 72B	SALISBURY - 72B	SALISBURY - 72B
30674	SALISBURY - 72B	SALISBURY - 72B	SALISBURY - 72B	SALISBURY - 72B	SALISBURY - 72B	SALISBURY - 72B	SALISBURY - 72B
30675	GUILDFORD - 70C	GUILDFORD - 70C	GUILDFORD - 70C	GUILDFORD - 70C	GUILDFORD - 70C	GUILDFORD - 70C	W/D
30676	EXMOUTHJCN - 72A	EXMOUTHJCN - 72A	EXMOUTHJCN - 72A	EXMOUTHJCN - 72A	EXMOUTHJCN - 72A	EXMOUTHJCN - 72A	EXMOUTHJCN - 72A

loco	May-58	Oct-58	Mar-59	Jun-59	Jul-59	Aug-59	Oct-59
				M7 0-4-4T (1897)			
30021	EXMOUTHJCN - 72A	EXMOUTHJCN - 72A	EXMOUTHJCN - 72A	EXMOUTHJCN - 72A	EXMOUTHJCN - 72A	EXMOUTHJCN - 72A	EXMOUTHJCN - 72A
30023	FRATTON - 70F	FRATTON - 70F	FRATTON - 70F	FRATTON - 70F	FRATTON - 70F	FRATTON - 70F	FRATTON - 70F
30024	EXMOUTHJCN - 72A	EXMOUTHJCN - 72A	EXMOUTHJCN - 72A	EXMOUTHJCN - 72A	EXMOUTHJCN - 72A	EXMOUTHJCN - 72A	EXMOUTHJCN - 72A
30025	SALISBURY - 72B	SALISBURY - 72B	SALISBURY - 72B	SALISBURY - 72B	SALISBURY - 72B	SALISBURY - 72B	SALISBURY - 72B
30026	GUILDFORD - 70C	GUILDFORD - 70C	GUILDFORD - 70C	W/D	W/D	W/D	W/D
30027	GUILDFORD - 70C	GUILDFORD - 70C	EXMOUTHJCN - 72A	EXMOUTHJCN - 72A	EXMOUTHJCN - 72A	EXMOUTHJCN - 72A	EXMOUTHJCN - 72A
30028	EASTLEIGH - 71A	EASTLEIGH - 71A	EASTLEIGH - 71A	EASTLEIGH - 71A	EASTLEIGH - 71A	EASTLEIGH - 71A	EASTLEIGH - 71A
30029	EASTLEIGH - 71A	EASTLEIGH - 71A	EASTLEIGH - 71A	EASTLEIGH - 71A	EASTLEIGH - 71A	EASTLEIGH - 71A	EASTLEIGH - 71A
30030	EASTLEIGH - 71A	EASTLEIGH - 71A	EASTLEIGH - 71A	EASTLEIGH - 71A	EASTLEIGH - 71A	EASTLEIGH - 71A	W/D
30031	BRIGHTON - 75A	BRIGHTON - 75A	BRIGHTON - 75A	FELTHAM - 70B	FELTHAM - 70B	FELTHAM - 70B	FELTHAM - 70B
30032	EASTLEIGH - 71A	EASTLEIGH - 71A	FELTHAM - 70B	FELTHAM - 70B	FELTHAM - 70B	FELTHAM - 70B	FELTHAM - 70B
30033	EASTLEIGH - 71A	EASTLEIGH - 71A	EASTLEIGH - 71A	BARNSTAPLE - 72E	BARNSTAPLE - 72E	BARNSTAPLE - 72E	BARNSTAPLE - 72E
30034	PLYMOUTH - 83H	PLYMOUTH - 83H	PLYMOUTH - 83H	PLYMOUTH - 83H	PLYMOUTH - 83H	PLYMOUTH - 83H	PLYMOUTH - 83H
30035	PLYMOUTH - 83H	PLYMOUTH - 83H	PLYMOUTH - 83H	PLYMOUTH - 83H	PLYMOUTH - 83H	PLYMOUTH - 83H	PLYMOUTH - 83H
30036	PLYMOUTH - 83H	PLYMOUTH - 83H	PLYMOUTH - 83H	PLYMOUTH - 83H	PLYMOUTH - 83H	PLYMOUTH - 83H	PLYMOUTH - 83H
30039	FRATTON - 70F	FRATTON - 70F	FRATTON - 70F	FRATTON - 70F	FRATTON - 70F	FRATTON - 70F	FRATTON - 70F
30040	BOURNEMOUTH - 71B	BOURNEMOUTH - 71B	BOURNEMOUTH - 71B	BOURNEMOUTH - 71B	BOURNEMOUTH - 71B	BOURNEMOUTH - 71B	BOURNEMOUTH - 71B
30043	FELTHAM - 70B	FELTHAM - 70B	FELTHAM - 70B	FELTHAM - 70B	FELTHAM - 70B	FELTHAM - 70B	FELTHAM - 70B
30044	EXMOUTHJCN - 72A	EXMOUTHJCN - 72A	EXMOUTHJCN - 72A	EXMOUTHJCN - 72A	EXMOUTHJCN - 72A	EXMOUTHJCN - 72A	EXMOUTHJCN - 72A
30045	EXMOUTHJCN - 72A	EXMOUTHJCN - 72A	EXMOUTHJCN - 72A	EXMOUTHJCN - 72A	EXMOUTHJCN - 72A	EXMOUTHJCN - 72A	EXMOUTHJCN - 72A
30046	EXMOUTHJCN - 72A	EXMOUTHJCN - 72A	W/D	W/D	W/D	W/D	W/D
30047	HORSHAM - 75D	HORSHAM - 75D	HORSHAM - 75D	HORSHAM - 75D	BRIGHTON - 75A	BRIGHTON - 75A	BRIGHTON - 75A
30048	HORSHAM - 75D	HORSHAM - 75D	HORSHAM - 75D	HORSHAM - 75D	BRIGHTON - 75A	EXMOUTHJCN - 72A	EXMOUTHJCN - 72A
30049	HORSHAM - 75D	HORSHAM - 75D	HORSHAM - 75D	HORSHAM - 75D	BRIGHTON - 75A	BRIGHTON - 75A	BRIGHTON - 75A
30050	HORSHAM - 75D	HORSHAM - 75D	HORSHAM - 75D	HORSHAM - 75D	BRIGHTON - 75A	BRIGHTON - 75A	BRIGHTON - 75A
30051	HORSHAM - 75D	HORSHAM - 75D	HORSHAM - 75D	HORSHAM - 75D	BRIGHTON - 75A	BRIGHTON - 75A	BRIGHTON - 75A
30052	THREE BRIDGES - 75E	BRIGHTON - 75A	BRIGHTON - 75A	EASTLEIGH - 71A	EASTLEIGH - 71A	EASTLEIGH - 71A	EASTLEIGH - 71A
30053	FAVERSHAM - 73E	FAVERSHAM - 73E	FAVERSHAM - 73E	EASTLEIGH - 71A	EASTLEIGH - 71A	EASTLEIGH - 71A	EASTLEIGH - 71A
30054	BRIGHTON - 75A	BRIGHTON - 75A	W/D	W/D	W/D	W/D	W/D
30055	BRIGHTON - 75A	BRIGHTON - 75A	BRIGHTON - 75A	BRIGHTON - 75A	BRIGHTON - 75A	BRIGHTON - 75A	BRIGHTON - 75A
30056	THREE BRIDGES - 75E	BRIGHTON - 75A	BRIGHTON - 75A	EASTLEIGH - 71A	EASTLEIGH - 71A	EASTLEIGH - 71A	BRIGHTON - 75A
30057	BOURNEMOUTH - 71B	BOURNEMOUTH - 71B	BOURNEMOUTH - 71B	EASTLEIGH - 71A	EASTLEIGH - 71A	EASTLEIGH - 71A	EASTLEIGH - 71A
30058	BOURNEMOUTH - 71B	BOURNEMOUTH - 71B	BOURNEMOUTH - 71B	BOURNEMOUTH - 71B	BOURNEMOUTH - 71B	BOURNEMOUTH - 71B	BOURNEMOUTH - 71B
30059	BOURNEMOUTH - 71B	BOURNEMOUTH - 71B	BOURNEMOUTH - 71B	BOURNEMOUTH - 71B	BOURNEMOUTH - 71B	BOURNEMOUTH - 71B	BOURNEMOUTH - 71B
30060	BOURNEMOUTH - 71B	BOURNEMOUTH - 71B	BOURNEMOUTH - 71B	BOURNEMOUTH - 71B	BOURNEMOUTH - 71B	BOURNEMOUTH - 71B	BOURNEMOUTH - 71B
30104	BOURNEMOUTH - 71B	BOURNEMOUTH - 71B	BOURNEMOUTH - 71B	BOURNEMOUTH - 71B	BOURNEMOUTH - 71B	BOURNEMOUTH - 71B	BOURNEMOUTH - 71B
30105	BOURNEMOUTH - 71B	BOURNEMOUTH - 71B	BOURNEMOUTH - 71B	BOURNEMOUTH - 71B	BOURNEMOUTH - 71B	BOURNEMOUTH - 71B	BOURNEMOUTH - 71B
30106	BOURNEMOUTH - 71B	BOURNEMOUTH - 71B	BOURNEMOUTH - 71B	BOURNEMOUTH - 71B	BOURNEMOUTH - 71B	BOURNEMOUTH - 71B	BOURNEMOUTH - 71B
30107	BOURNEMOUTH - 71B	BOURNEMOUTH - 71B	BOURNEMOUTH - 71B	BOURNEMOUTH - 71B	BOURNEMOUTH - 71B	BOURNEMOUTH - 71B	BOURNEMOUTH - 71B
30108	BOURNEMOUTH - 71B	BOURNEMOUTH - 71B	BOURNEMOUTH - 71B	BOURNEMOUTH - 71B	BOURNEMOUTH - 71B	BOURNEMOUTH - 71B	BOURNEMOUTH - 71B
30109	BRIGHTON - 75A	BRIGHTON - 75A	BRIGHTON - 75A	EASTLEIGH - 71A	EASTLEIGH - 71A	EASTLEIGH - 71A	EASTLEIGH - 71A
30110	THREE BRIDGES - 75E	BRIGHTON - 75A	BRIGHTON - 75A	EASTLEIGH - 71A	EASTLEIGH - 71A	EASTLEIGH - 71A	BRIGHTON - 75A
30111	BOURNEMOUTH - 71B	BOURNEMOUTH - 71B	BOURNEMOUTH - 71B	BOURNEMOUTH - 71B	BOURNEMOUTH - 71B	BOURNEMOUTH - 71B	BOURNEMOUTH - 71B
30112	BOURNEMOUTH - 71B	BOURNEMOUTH - 71B	BOURNEMOUTH - 71B	BOURNEMOUTH - 71B	BOURNEMOUTH - 71B	BOURNEMOUTH - 71B	BOURNEMOUTH - 71B
30123	NINE ELMS - 70A	NINE ELMS - 70A	NINE ELMS - 70A	NINE ELMS - 70A	W/D	W/D	W/D
30124	GUILDFORD - 70C	GUILDFORD - 70C	GUILDFORD - 70C	GUILDFORD - 70C	GUILDFORD - 70C	GUILDFORD - 70C	GUILDFORD - 70C
30125	EASTLEIGH - 71A	EASTLEIGH - 71A	EASTLEIGH - 71A	EASTLEIGH - 71A	EASTLEIGH - 71A	EASTLEIGH - 71A	EASTLEIGH - 71A
30127	BOURNEMOUTH - 71B	BOURNEMOUTH - 71B	BOURNEMOUTH - 71B	BOURNEMOUTH - 71B	BOURNEMOUTH - 71B	BOURNEMOUTH - 71B	BOURNEMOUTH - 71B
30128	BOURNEMOUTH - 71B	BOURNEMOUTH - 71B	BOURNEMOUTH - 71B	BOURNEMOUTH - 71B	BOURNEMOUTH - 71B	BOURNEMOUTH - 71B	BOURNEMOUTH - 71B
30129	YEOVIL - 72C	YEOVIL - 72C	YEOVIL - 72C	YEOVIL - 72C	YEOVIL - 72C	YEOVIL - 72C	YEOVIL - 72C
30130	FELTHAM - 70B	FELTHAM - 70B	EASTLEIGH - 71A	EASTLEIGH - 71A	EASTLEIGH - 71A	EASTLEIGH - 71A	EASTLEIGH - 71A
30131	YEOVIL - 72C	YEOVIL - 72C	YEOVIL - 72C	YEOVIL - 72C	YEOVIL - 72C	YEOVIL - 72C	YEOVIL - 72C
30132	NINE ELMS - 70A	NINE ELMS - 70A	GUILDFORD - 70C	GUILDFORD - 70C	GUILDFORD - 70C	GUILDFORD - 70C	GUILDFORD - 70C
30133	NINE ELMS - 70A	NINE ELMS - 70A	NINE ELMS - 70A	NINE ELMS - 70A	NINE ELMS - 70A	NINE ELMS - 70A	NINE ELMS - 70A
30241	NINE ELMS - 70A	NINE ELMS - 70A	NINE ELMS - 70A	NINE ELMS - 70A	NINE ELMS - 70A	NINE ELMS - 70A	NINE ELMS - 70A
30242	NINE ELMS - 70A	W/D	W/D	W/D	W/D	W/D	W/D
30243	FELTHAM - 70B	W/D	W/D	W/D	W/D	W/D	W/D
30245	NINE ELMS - 70A	NINE ELMS - 70A	NINE ELMS - 70A	NINE ELMS - 70A	NINE ELMS - 70A	NINE ELMS - 70A	NINE ELMS - 70A
30246	GUILDFORD - 70C	GUILDFORD - 70C	GUILDFORD - 70C	GUILDFORD - 70C	GUILDFORD - 70C	GUILDFORD - 70C	GUILDFORD - 70C
30247	BARNSTAPLE - 72E	BARNSTAPLE - 72E	BARNSTAPLE - 72E	BARNSTAPLE - 72E	BARNSTAPLE - 72E	BARNSTAPLE - 72E	BARNSTAPLE - 72E
30248	NINE ELMS - 70A	NINE ELMS - 70A	NINE ELMS - 70A	NINE ELMS - 70A	NINE ELMS - 70A	NINE ELMS - 70A	NINE ELMS - 70A
30249	NINE ELMS - 70A	NINE ELMS - 70A	NINE ELMS - 70A	NINE ELMS - 70A	NINE ELMS - 70A	NINE ELMS - 70A	NINE ELMS - 70A
30251	BARNSTAPLE - 72E	BARNSTAPLE - 72E	BARNSTAPLE - 72E	BARNSTAPLE - 72E	BARNSTAPLE - 72E	BARNSTAPLE - 72E	BARNSTAPLE - 72E
30252	BARNSTAPLE - 72E	BARNSTAPLE - 72E	W/D	W/D	W/D	W/D	W/D
30253	BARNSTAPLE - 72E	BARNSTAPLE - 72E	BARNSTAPLE - 72E	BARNSTAPLE - 72E	BARNSTAPLE - 72E	BARNSTAPLE - 72E	BARNSTAPLE - 72E
30254	BARNSTAPLE - 72E	BARNSTAPLE - 72E	BARNSTAPLE - 72E	BARNSTAPLE - 72E	BARNSTAPLE - 72E	BARNSTAPLE - 72E	BARNSTAPLE - 72E
30255	BARNSTAPLE - 72E	BARNSTAPLE - 72E	BARNSTAPLE - 72E	BARNSTAPLE - 72E	BARNSTAPLE - 72E	BARNSTAPLE - 72E	BARNSTAPLE - 72E
30256	EXMOUTHJCN - 72A	EXMOUTHJCN - 72A	EXMOUTHJCN - 72A	W/D	W/D	W/D	W/D
30318	BOURNEMOUTH - 71B	BOURNEMOUTH - 71B	BOURNEMOUTH - 71B	BOURNEMOUTH - 71B	BOURNEMOUTH - 71B	BOURNEMOUTH - 71B	BOURNEMOUTH - 71B
30319	BOURNEMOUTH - 71B	BOURNEMOUTH - 71B	BOURNEMOUTH - 71B	BOURNEMOUTH - 71B	BOURNEMOUTH - 71B	BOURNEMOUTH - 71B	BOURNEMOUTH - 71B
30320	NINE ELMS - 70A	NINE ELMS - 70A	NINE ELMS - 70A	NINE ELMS - 70A	NINE ELMS - 70A	NINE ELMS - 70A	NINE ELMS - 70A
30321	NINE ELMS - 70A	NINE ELMS - 70A	NINE ELMS - 70A	NINE ELMS - 70A	NINE ELMS - 70A	NINE ELMS - 70A	NINE ELMS - 70A
30322	EASTLEIGH - 71A	EASTLEIGH - 71A	W/D	W/D	W/D	W/D	W/D
30323	EASTLEIGH - 71A	EASTLEIGH - 71A	EASTLEIGH - 71A	EASTLEIGH - 71A	EASTLEIGH - 71A	EASTLEIGH - 71A	EASTLEIGH - 71A
30324	BOURNEMOUTH - 71B	BOURNEMOUTH - 71B	BOURNEMOUTH - 71B	BOURNEMOUTH - 71B	BOURNEMOUTH - 71B	BOURNEMOUTH - 71B	W/D
30328	EASTLEIGH - 71A	EASTLEIGH - 71A	EASTLEIGH - 71A	EASTLEIGH - 71A	EASTLEIGH - 71A	EASTLEIGH - 71A	EASTLEIGH - 71A
30356	FRATTON - 70F	FRATTON - 70F	W/D	W/D	W/D	W/D	W/D
30357	FRATTON - 70F	FRATTON - 70F	FRATTON - 70F	FRATTON - 70F	FRATTON - 70F	FRATTON - 70F	FRATTON - 70F
30374	EXMOUTHJCN - 72A	EXMOUTHJCN - 72A	EXMOUTHJCN - 72A	EXMOUTHJCN - 72A	EXMOUTHJCN - 72A	EXMOUTHJCN - 72A	W/D
30375	EASTLEIGH - 71A	EASTLEIGH - 71A	EASTLEIGH - 71A	BARNSTAPLE - 72E	BARNSTAPLE - 72E	BARNSTAPLE - 72E	BARNSTAPLE - 72E
30376	EASTLEIGH - 71A	EASTLEIGH - 71A	W/D	W/D	W/D	W/D	W/D
30377	EASTLEIGH - 71A	EASTLEIGH - 71A	EASTLEIGH - 71A	FRATTON - 70F	FRATTON - 70F	FRATTON - 70F	FRATTON - 70F
30378	EXMOUTHJCN - 72A	EXMOUTHJCN - 72A	EXMOUTHJCN - 72A	GUILDFORD - 70C	GUILDFORD - 70C	GUILDFORD - 70C	GUILDFORD - 70C
30379	EASTLEIGH - 71A	EASTLEIGH - 71A	EASTLEIGH - 71A	EASTLEIGH - 71A	EASTLEIGH - 71A	EASTLEIGH - 71A	EASTLEIGH - 71A
30479	EASTLEIGH - 71A	EASTLEIGH - 71A	EASTLEIGH - 71A	EASTLEIGH - 71A	EASTLEIGH - 71A	EASTLEIGH - 71A	EASTLEIGH - 71A
30480	EASTLEIGH - 71A	EASTLEIGH - 71A	EASTLEIGH - 71A	EASTLEIGH - 71A	EASTLEIGH - 71A	EASTLEIGH - 71A	EASTLEIGH - 71A
30481	EASTLEIGH - 71A	EASTLEIGH - 71A	EASTLEIGH - 71A	W/D	W/D	W/D	W/D
30667	EXMOUTHJCN - 72A	EXMOUTHJCN - 72A	EXMOUTHJCN - 72A	EXMOUTHJCN - 72A	EXMOUTHJCN - 72A	EXMOUTHJCN - 72A	EXMOUTHJCN - 72A
30668	EXMOUTHJCN - 72A	EXMOUTHJCN - 72A	EXMOUTHJCN - 72A	EXMOUTHJCN - 72A	EXMOUTHJCN - 72A	EXMOUTHJCN - 72A	EXMOUTHJCN - 72A
30669	EXMOUTHJCN - 72A	EXMOUTHJCN - 72A	EXMOUTHJCN - 72A	EXMOUTHJCN - 72A	EXMOUTHJCN - 72A	EXMOUTHJCN - 72A	EXMOUTHJCN - 72A
30670	EXMOUTHJCN - 72A	EXMOUTHJCN - 72A	EXMOUTHJCN - 72A	EXMOUTHJCN - 72A	EXMOUTHJCN - 72A	EXMOUTHJCN - 72A	EXMOUTHJCN - 72A
30671	BARNSTAPLE - 72E	BARNSTAPLE - 72E	BARNSTAPLE - 72E	BARNSTAPLE - 72E	W/D	W/D	W/D
30673	SALISBURY - 72B	SALISBURY - 72B	SALISBURY - 72B	SALISBURY - 72B	SALISBURY - 72B	SALISBURY - 72B	SALISBURY - 72B
30674	SALISBURY - 72B	SALISBURY - 72B	SALISBURY - 72B	SALISBURY - 72B	SALISBURY - 72B	SALISBURY - 72B	SALISBURY - 72B
30676	EXMOUTHJCN - 72A	EXMOUTHJCN - 72A	EXMOUTHJCN - 72A	EXMOUTHJCN - 72A	EXMOUTHJCN - 72A	EXMOUTHJCN - 72A	EXMOUTHJCN - 72A

loco	Dec-59	Feb-60	Mar-60	Apr-60	Jul-60	Aug-60	Sep-60	Nov-60
				M7 0-4-4T (1897)				
30021	EXMOUTH JCN - 72A	EXMOUTH JCN - 72A	EXMOUTH JCN - 72A	EXMOUTH JCN - 72A	EXMOUTH JCN - 72A	EXMOUTH JCN - 72A	EXMOUTH JCN - 72A	EXMOUTH JCN - 72A
30023	FRATTON - 70F	FRATTON - 70F	FRATTON - 70F	FRATTON - 70F	FRATTON - 70F	FRATTON - 70F	BARNSTAPLE - 72E	BARNSTAPLE - 72E
30024	EXMOUTH JCN - 72A	EXMOUTH JCN - 72A	EXMOUTH JCN - 72A	EXMOUTH JCN - 72A	EXMOUTH JCN - 72A	EXMOUTH JCN - 72A	EXMOUTH JCN - 72A	EXMOUTH JCN - 72A
30025	SALISBURY - 72B	SALISBURY - 72B	SALISBURY - 72B	SALISBURY - 72B	SALISBURY - 72B	SALISBURY - 72B	SALISBURY - 72B	SALISBURY - 72B
30028	EASTLEIGH - 71A	EASTLEIGH - 71A	EASTLEIGH - 71A	EASTLEIGH - 71A	EASTLEIGH - 71A	EASTLEIGH - 71A	EASTLEIGH - 71A	EASTLEIGH - 71A
30029	EASTLEIGH - 71A	EASTLEIGH - 71A	EASTLEIGH - 71A	EASTLEIGH - 71A	EASTLEIGH - 71A	EASTLEIGH - 71A	EASTLEIGH - 71A	EASTLEIGH - 71A
30031	FELTHAM - 70B	FELTHAM - 70B	FELTHAM - 70B	FELTHAM - 70B	FELTHAM - 70B	FELTHAM - 70B	FELTHAM - 70B	FELTHAM - 70B
30032	FELTHAM - 70B	FELTHAM - 70B	FELTHAM - 70B	FELTHAM - 70B	FELTHAM - 70B	FELTHAM - 70B	FELTHAM - 70B	FELTHAM - 70B
30033	BARNSTAPLE - 72E	BARNSTAPLE - 72E	BARNSTAPLE - 72E	BARNSTAPLE - 72E	BARNSTAPLE - 72E	BARNSTAPLE - 72E	SALISBURY - 72B	SALISBURY - 72B
30034	PLYMOUTH - 83H	PLYMOUTH - 83H	PLYMOUTH - 83H	PLYMOUTH - 83H	PLYMOUTH - 83H	PLYMOUTH - 83H	PLYMOUTH - 83H	PLYMOUTH - 83H
30035	PLYMOUTH - 83H	EASTLEIGH - 71A	EASTLEIGH - 71A	EASTLEIGH - 71A	EASTLEIGH - 71A	EASTLEIGH - 71A	EASTLEIGH - 71A	EASTLEIGH - 71A
30036	PLYMOUTH - 83H	PLYMOUTH - 83H	PLYMOUTH - 83H	PLYMOUTH - 83H	PLYMOUTH - 83H	PLYMOUTH - 83H	PLYMOUTH - 83H	PLYMOUTH - 83H
30039	EASTLEIGH - 71A	EASTLEIGH - 71A	NINE ELMS - 70A	NINE ELMS - 70A	NINE ELMS - 70A	NINE ELMS - 70A	NINE ELMS - 70A	NINE ELMS - 70A
30040	BOURNEMOUTH - 71B	BOURNEMOUTH - 71B	BOURNEMOUTH - 71B	BOURNEMOUTH - 71B	BOURNEMOUTH - 71B	BOURNEMOUTH - 71B	BOURNEMOUTH - 71B	BOURNEMOUTH - 71B
30043	FELTHAM - 70B	FELTHAM - 70B	FELTHAM - 70B	FELTHAM - 70B	FELTHAM - 70B	FELTHAM - 70B	FELTHAM - 70B	FELTHAM - 70B
30044	EXMOUTH JCN - 72A	EXMOUTH JCN - 72A	EXMOUTH JCN - 72A	EXMOUTH JCN - 72A	EXMOUTH JCN - 72A	EXMOUTH JCN - 72A	EXMOUTH JCN - 72A	EXMOUTH JCN - 72A
30045	EXMOUTH JCN - 72A	EXMOUTH JCN - 72A	EXMOUTH JCN - 72A	EXMOUTH JCN - 72A	EXMOUTH JCN - 72A	EXMOUTH JCN - 72A	EXMOUTH JCN - 72A	EXMOUTH JCN - 72A
30047	BRIGHTON - 75A	W/D	W/D	W/D	W/D	W/D	W/D	W/D
30048	EXMOUTH JCN - 72A	EXMOUTH JCN - 72A	EXMOUTH JCN - 72A	EXMOUTH JCN - 72A	EXMOUTH JCN - 72A	EXMOUTH JCN - 72A	EXMOUTH JCN - 72A	EXMOUTH JCN - 72A
30049	BRIGHTON - 75A	BRIGHTON - 75A	BRIGHTON - 75A	BRIGHTON - 75A	BRIGHTON - 75A	BRIGHTON - 75A	BRIGHTON - 75A	BRIGHTON - 75A
30050	BRIGHTON - 75A	BRIGHTON - 75A	BRIGHTON - 75A	BRIGHTON - 75A	BRIGHTON - 75A	BRIGHTON - 75A	BRIGHTON - 75A	BRIGHTON - 75A
30051	BRIGHTON - 75A	BRIGHTON - 75A	BRIGHTON - 75A	BRIGHTON - 75A	BRIGHTON - 75A	BRIGHTON - 75A	BRIGHTON - 75A	BRIGHTON - 75A
30052	THREE BRIDGES - 75E	THREE BRIDGES - 75E	THREE BRIDGES - 75E	THREE BRIDGES - 75E	BRIGHTON - 75A	BRIGHTON - 75A	BRIGHTON - 75A	BRIGHTON - 75A
30053	EASTLEIGH - 71A	BRIGHTON - 75A	BRIGHTON - 75A	BRIGHTON - 75A	BRIGHTON - 75A	BRIGHTON - 75A	BRIGHTON - 75A	BRIGHTON - 75A
30055	THREE BRIDGES - 75E	THREE BRIDGES - 75E	THREE BRIDGES - 75E	THREE BRIDGES - 75E	THREE BRIDGES - 75E	THREE BRIDGES - 75E	THREE BRIDGES - 75E	THREE BRIDGES - 75E
30056	BRIGHTON - 75A	BRIGHTON - 75A	BRIGHTON - 75A	BRIGHTON - 75A	BRIGHTON - 75A	BRIGHTON - 75A	BRIGHTON - 75A	BRIGHTON - 75A
30057	EASTLEIGH - 71A	EASTLEIGH - 71A	EASTLEIGH - 71A	EASTLEIGH - 71A	EASTLEIGH - 71A	EASTLEIGH - 71A	EASTLEIGH - 71A	EASTLEIGH - 71A
30058	BOURNEMOUTH - 71B	BOURNEMOUTH - 71B	BOURNEMOUTH - 71B	BOURNEMOUTH - 71B	BOURNEMOUTH - 71B	BOURNEMOUTH - 71B	W/D	W/D
30059	BOURNEMOUTH - 71B	BOURNEMOUTH - 71B	BOURNEMOUTH - 71B	BOURNEMOUTH - 71B	BOURNEMOUTH - 71B	BOURNEMOUTH - 71B	BOURNEMOUTH - 71B	BOURNEMOUTH - 71B
30060	BOURNEMOUTH - 71B	BOURNEMOUTH - 71B	BOURNEMOUTH - 71B	BOURNEMOUTH - 71B	BOURNEMOUTH - 71B	BOURNEMOUTH - 71B	BOURNEMOUTH - 71B	BOURNEMOUTH - 71B
30104	BOURNEMOUTH - 71B	BOURNEMOUTH - 71B	BOURNEMOUTH - 71B	BOURNEMOUTH - 71B	BOURNEMOUTH - 71B	BOURNEMOUTH - 71B	BOURNEMOUTH - 71B	BOURNEMOUTH - 71B
30105	BOURNEMOUTH - 71B	BOURNEMOUTH - 71B	BOURNEMOUTH - 71B	BOURNEMOUTH - 71B	BOURNEMOUTH - 71B	BOURNEMOUTH - 71B	BOURNEMOUTH - 71B	BOURNEMOUTH - 71B
30106	BOURNEMOUTH - 71B	BOURNEMOUTH - 71B	BOURNEMOUTH - 71B	BOURNEMOUTH - 71B	BOURNEMOUTH - 71B	BOURNEMOUTH - 71B	BOURNEMOUTH - 71B	W/D
30107	BOURNEMOUTH - 71B	BOURNEMOUTH - 71B	BOURNEMOUTH - 71B	BOURNEMOUTH - 71B	BOURNEMOUTH - 71B	BOURNEMOUTH - 71B	BOURNEMOUTH - 71B	BOURNEMOUTH - 71B
30108	BOURNEMOUTH - 71B	BOURNEMOUTH - 71B	BOURNEMOUTH - 71B	BOURNEMOUTH - 71B	BOURNEMOUTH - 71B	BOURNEMOUTH - 71B	BOURNEMOUTH - 71B	BOURNEMOUTH - 71B
30109	THREE BRIDGES - 75E	THREE BRIDGES - 75E	THREE BRIDGES - 75E	THREE BRIDGES - 75E	THREE BRIDGES - 75E	THREE BRIDGES - 75E	THREE BRIDGES - 75E	THREE BRIDGES - 75E
30110	BRIGHTON - 75A	BRIGHTON - 75A	BRIGHTON - 75A	BRIGHTON - 75A	BRIGHTON - 75A	BRIGHTON - 75A	BRIGHTON - 75A	BRIGHTON - 75A
30111	BOURNEMOUTH - 71B	BOURNEMOUTH - 71B	BOURNEMOUTH - 71B	BOURNEMOUTH - 71B	BOURNEMOUTH - 71B	BOURNEMOUTH - 71B	BOURNEMOUTH - 71B	BOURNEMOUTH - 71B
30112	BOURNEMOUTH - 71B	BOURNEMOUTH - 71B	BOURNEMOUTH - 71B	BOURNEMOUTH - 71B	BOURNEMOUTH - 71B	BOURNEMOUTH - 71B	BOURNEMOUTH - 71B	BOURNEMOUTH - 71B
30124	GUILDFORD - 70C	GUILDFORD - 70C	GUILDFORD - 70C	GUILDFORD - 70C	GUILDFORD - 70C	GUILDFORD - 70C	GUILDFORD - 70C	GUILDFORD - 70C
30125	EASTLEIGH - 71A	EASTLEIGH - 71A	EASTLEIGH - 71A	EASTLEIGH - 71A	EASTLEIGH - 71A	EASTLEIGH - 71A	EXMOUTH JCN - 72A	EXMOUTH JCN - 72A
30127	BOURNEMOUTH - 71B	BOURNEMOUTH - 71B	BOURNEMOUTH - 71B	BOURNEMOUTH - 71B	BOURNEMOUTH - 71B	BOURNEMOUTH - 71B	BOURNEMOUTH - 71B	BOURNEMOUTH - 71B
30128	BOURNEMOUTH - 71B	BOURNEMOUTH - 71B	BOURNEMOUTH - 71B	BOURNEMOUTH - 71B	BOURNEMOUTH - 71B	BOURNEMOUTH - 71B	BOURNEMOUTH - 71B	BOURNEMOUTH - 71B
30129	YEOVIL - 72C	YEOVIL - 72C	YEOVIL - 72C	YEOVIL - 72C	YEOVIL - 72C	YEOVIL - 72C	YEOVIL - 72C	YEOVIL - 72C
30131	YEOVIL - 72C	YEOVIL - 72C	YEOVIL - 72C	YEOVIL - 72C	YEOVIL - 72C	YEOVIL - 72C	YEOVIL - 72C	YEOVIL - 72C
30132	GUILDFORD - 70C	GUILDFORD - 70C	GUILDFORD - 70C	GUILDFORD - 70C	GUILDFORD - 70C	GUILDFORD - 70C	GUILDFORD - 70C	GUILDFORD - 70C
30133	NINE ELMS - 70A	NINE ELMS - 70A	EASTLEIGH - 71A	EASTLEIGH - 71A	EASTLEIGH - 71A	EASTLEIGH - 71A	EASTLEIGH - 71A	EASTLEIGH - 71A
30241	NINE ELMS - 70A	NINE ELMS - 70A	NINE ELMS - 70A	NINE ELMS - 70A	NINE ELMS - 70A	NINE ELMS - 70A	NINE ELMS - 70A	NINE ELMS - 70A
30245	NINE ELMS - 70A	NINE ELMS - 70A	NINE ELMS - 70A	NINE ELMS - 70A	NINE ELMS - 70A	NINE ELMS - 70A	NINE ELMS - 70A	NINE ELMS - 70A
30246	GUILDFORD - 70C	GUILDFORD - 70C	GUILDFORD - 70C	GUILDFORD - 70C	GUILDFORD - 70C	GUILDFORD - 70C	GUILDFORD - 70C	GUILDFORD - 70C
30247	BARNSTAPLE - 72E	BARNSTAPLE - 72E	BARNSTAPLE - 72E	BARNSTAPLE - 72E	BARNSTAPLE - 72E	BARNSTAPLE - 72E	BARNSTAPLE - 72E	BARNSTAPLE - 72E
30248	NINE ELMS - 70A	NINE ELMS - 70A	NINE ELMS - 70A	NINE ELMS - 70A	NINE ELMS - 70A	NINE ELMS - 70A	NINE ELMS - 70A	NINE ELMS - 70A
30249	NINE ELMS - 70A	NINE ELMS - 70A	NINE ELMS - 70A	NINE ELMS - 70A	NINE ELMS - 70A	NINE ELMS - 70A	NINE ELMS - 70A	NINE ELMS - 70A
30251	BARNSTAPLE - 72E	BARNSTAPLE - 72E	BARNSTAPLE - 72E	BARNSTAPLE - 72E	BARNSTAPLE - 72E	BARNSTAPLE - 72E	BARNSTAPLE - 72E	BARNSTAPLE - 72E
30253	BARNSTAPLE - 72E	BARNSTAPLE - 72E	BARNSTAPLE - 72E	BARNSTAPLE - 72E	BARNSTAPLE - 72E	BARNSTAPLE - 72E	BARNSTAPLE - 72E	BARNSTAPLE - 72E
30254	BARNSTAPLE - 72E	BARNSTAPLE - 72E	BARNSTAPLE - 72E	BARNSTAPLE - 72E	BARNSTAPLE - 72E	BARNSTAPLE - 72E	BARNSTAPLE - 72E	BARNSTAPLE - 72E
30255	BARNSTAPLE - 72E	BARNSTAPLE - 72E	BARNSTAPLE - 72E	BARNSTAPLE - 72E	BARNSTAPLE - 72E	BARNSTAPLE - 72E	W/D	W/D
30319	BOURNEMOUTH - 71B	W/D	W/D	W/D	W/D	W/D	W/D	W/D
30320	NINE ELMS - 70A	NINE ELMS - 70A	NINE ELMS - 70A	NINE ELMS - 70A	NINE ELMS - 70A	NINE ELMS - 70A	NINE ELMS - 70A	NINE ELMS - 70A
30321	NINE ELMS - 70A	NINE ELMS - 70A	NINE ELMS - 70A	NINE ELMS - 70A	NINE ELMS - 70A	NINE ELMS - 70A	NINE ELMS - 70A	NINE ELMS - 70A
30328	EASTLEIGH - 71A	TONBRIDGE - 73J	TONBRIDGE - 73J	TONBRIDGE - 73J	TONBRIDGE - 73J	BRIGHTON - 75A	BRIGHTON - 75A	BRIGHTON - 75A
30357	EASTLEIGH - 71A	EASTLEIGH - 71A	EASTLEIGH - 71A	EASTLEIGH - 71A	EASTLEIGH - 71A	EASTLEIGH - 71A	EASTLEIGH - 71A	EASTLEIGH - 71A
30375	EASTLEIGH - 71A	EASTLEIGH - 71A	EASTLEIGH - 71A	EASTLEIGH - 71A	EASTLEIGH - 71A	EASTLEIGH - 71A	EASTLEIGH - 71A	EASTLEIGH - 71A
30377	EASTLEIGH - 71A	EASTLEIGH - 71A	EASTLEIGH - 71A	EASTLEIGH - 71A	EASTLEIGH - 71A	EASTLEIGH - 71A	EASTLEIGH - 71A	EASTLEIGH - 71A
30378	GUILDFORD - 70C	GUILDFORD - 70C	GUILDFORD - 70C	GUILDFORD - 70C	GUILDFORD - 70C	GUILDFORD - 70C	GUILDFORD - 70C	GUILDFORD - 70C
30379	EASTLEIGH - 71A	TONBRIDGE - 73J	TONBRIDGE - 73J	TONBRIDGE - 73J	TONBRIDGE - 73J	BRIGHTON - 75A	BRIGHTON - 75A	BRIGHTON - 75A
30479	EASTLEIGH - 71A	EASTLEIGH - 71A	EASTLEIGH - 71A	EASTLEIGH - 71A	EASTLEIGH - 71A	EASTLEIGH - 71A	EASTLEIGH - 71A	EASTLEIGH - 71A
30480	EASTLEIGH - 71A	EASTLEIGH - 71A	EASTLEIGH - 71A	EASTLEIGH - 71A	EASTLEIGH - 71A	EASTLEIGH - 71A	EASTLEIGH - 71A	EASTLEIGH - 71A
30667	EXMOUTH JCN - 72A	EXMOUTH JCN - 72A	EXMOUTH JCN - 72A	EXMOUTH JCN - 72A	EXMOUTH JCN - 72A	EXMOUTH JCN - 72A	EXMOUTH JCN - 72A	EXMOUTH JCN - 72A
30668	EXMOUTH JCN - 72A	EXMOUTH JCN - 72A	EXMOUTH JCN - 72A	EXMOUTH JCN - 72A	EXMOUTH JCN - 72A	EXMOUTH JCN - 72A	EXMOUTH JCN - 72A	EXMOUTH JCN - 72A
30669	EXMOUTH JCN - 72A	EXMOUTH JCN - 72A	EXMOUTH JCN - 72A	EXMOUTH JCN - 72A	EXMOUTH JCN - 72A	EXMOUTH JCN - 72A	EXMOUTH JCN - 72A	EXMOUTH JCN - 72A
30670	EXMOUTH JCN - 72A	EXMOUTH JCN - 72A	EXMOUTH JCN - 72A	EXMOUTH JCN - 72A	EXMOUTH JCN - 72A	EXMOUTH JCN - 72A	EXMOUTH JCN - 72A	EXMOUTH JCN - 72A
30673	SALISBURY - 72B	SALISBURY - 72B	SALISBURY - 72B	SALISBURY - 72B	SALISBURY - 72B	W/D	W/D	W/D
30674	SALISBURY - 72B	SALISBURY - 72B	SALISBURY - 72B	SALISBURY - 72B	SALISBURY - 72B	SALISBURY - 72B	SALISBURY - 72B	SALISBURY - 72B
30676	EXMOUTH JCN - 72A	EXMOUTH JCN - 72A	EXMOUTH JCN - 72A	EXMOUTH JCN - 72A	EXMOUTH JCN - 72A	EXMOUTH JCN - 72A	EXMOUTH JCN - 72A	EXMOUTH JCN - 72A

The high level of capital investment in electrification precluded the need for modern 2-6-4T locomotives and the 0-4-4T survived rather longer on the Southern than might otherwise have been the case. Most of the M7 class remained at LSWR sheds - a few saw service on the LBSCR in the Brighton area - and in spite of the introduction of BR standard engines remained a regular sight on shunting and empty carriage duties between at a variety of locations as far flung as Waterloo and Ilfracombe. 30110 of Guildford stands at Havant with an empty motor-train in 1955.

loco	May-49	Jun-49	Aug-49	Sep-49	Dec-49	Feb-50	Mar-50
				R 0-4-4T (1891)			
31658	GILLINGHAM - 73D	GILLINGHAM - 73D	GILLINGHAM - 73D	GILLINGHAM - 73D	GILLINGHAM - 73D	GILLINGHAM - 73D	GILLINGHAM - 73D
31659	GILLINGHAM - 73D	GILLINGHAM - 73D	GILLINGHAM - 73D	GILLINGHAM - 73D	GILLINGHAM - 73D	GILLINGHAM - 73D	GILLINGHAM - 73D
31660	ASHFORD - 74A	ASHFORD - 74A	ASHFORD - 74A	ASHFORD - 74A	ASHFORD - 74A	ASHFORD - 74A	ASHFORD - 74A
31661	FAVERSHAM - 73E	FAVERSHAM - 73E	FAVERSHAM - 73E	FAVERSHAM - 73E	FAVERSHAM - 73E	FAVERSHAM - 73E	FAVERSHAM - 73E
31662	GILLINGHAM - 73D	GILLINGHAM - 73D	GILLINGHAM - 73D	GILLINGHAM - 73D	GILLINGHAM - 73D	GILLINGHAM - 73D	GILLINGHAM - 73D
31663	GILLINGHAM - 73D	GILLINGHAM - 73D	GILLINGHAM - 73D	GILLINGHAM - 73D	GILLINGHAM - 73D	GILLINGHAM - 73D	GILLINGHAM - 73D
31665	GILLINGHAM - 73D	GILLINGHAM - 73D	GILLINGHAM - 73D	GILLINGHAM - 73D	GILLINGHAM - 73D	GILLINGHAM - 73D	GILLINGHAM - 73D
31666	GILLINGHAM - 73D	GILLINGHAM - 73D	GILLINGHAM - 73D	GILLINGHAM - 73D	GILLINGHAM - 73D	GILLINGHAM - 73D	GILLINGHAM - 73D
31667	TONBRIDGE - 74D	TONBRIDGE - 74D	TONBRIDGE - 74D	TONBRIDGE - 74D	TONBRIDGE - 74D	TONBRIDGE - 74D	TONBRIDGE - 74D
31670	TONBRIDGE - 74D	TONBRIDGE - 74D	TONBRIDGE - 74D	TONBRIDGE - 74D	TONBRIDGE - 74D	TONBRIDGE - 74D	TONBRIDGE - 74D
31671	TONBRIDGE - 74D	TONBRIDGE - 74D	TONBRIDGE - 74D	TONBRIDGE - 74D	TONBRIDGE - 74D	TONBRIDGE - 74D	TONBRIDGE - 74D
31672	TONBRIDGE - 74D	TONBRIDGE - 74D	TONBRIDGE - 74D	TONBRIDGE - 74D	W/D	W/D	W/D
31673	FAVERSHAM - 73E	FAVERSHAM - 73E	FAVERSHAM - 73E	FAVERSHAM - 73E	FAVERSHAM - 73E	FAVERSHAM - 73E	FAVERSHAM - 73E
31674	FAVERSHAM - 73E	FAVERSHAM - 73E	FAVERSHAM - 73E	FAVERSHAM - 73E	FAVERSHAM - 73E	FAVERSHAM - 73E	FAVERSHAM - 73E
31675	TONBRIDGE - 74D	TONBRIDGE - 74D	TONBRIDGE - 74D	TONBRIDGE - 74D	TONBRIDGE - 74D	TONBRIDGE - 74D	TONBRIDGE - 74D
				'0415' 4-4-2T (1882)			
30582	EXMOUTH JCN - 72A	EXMOUTH JCN - 72A	EXMOUTH JCN - 72A	EXMOUTH JCN - 72A	EXMOUTH JCN - 72A	EXMOUTH JCN - 72A	EXMOUTH JCN - 72A
30583	EXMOUTH JCN - 72A	EXMOUTH JCN - 72A	EXMOUTH JCN - 72A	EXMOUTH JCN - 72A	EXMOUTH JCN - 72A	EXMOUTH JCN - 72A	EXMOUTH JCN - 72A
30584	EXMOUTH JCN - 72A	EXMOUTH JCN - 72A	EXMOUTH JCN - 72A	EXMOUTH JCN - 72A	EXMOUTH JCN - 72A	EXMOUTH JCN - 72A	EXMOUTH JCN - 72A
				I1X 4-4-2T (1906/25)			
32002	B.ARMS - 73B	B.ARMS - 73B	B.ARMS - 73B	B.ARMS - 73B	B.ARMS - 73B	B.ARMS - 73B	B.ARMS - 73B
32005	EASTBOURNE - 75G	EASTBOURNE - 75G	EASTBOURNE - 75G	EASTBOURNE - 75G	EASTBOURNE - 75G	EASTBOURNE - 75G	EASTBOURNE - 75G
32008	BOGNOR REGIS	BOGNOR REGIS	BOGNOR REGIS	BOGNOR REGIS	BOGNOR REGIS	BOGNOR REGIS	BOGNOR REGIS
32009	EASTBOURNE - 75G	EASTBOURNE - 75G	EASTBOURNE - 75G	EASTBOURNE - 75G	EASTBOURNE - 75G	EASTBOURNE - 75G	EASTBOURNE - 75G
32595	EASTBOURNE - 75G	EASTBOURNE - 75G	EASTBOURNE - 75G	EASTBOURNE - 75G	EASTBOURNE - 75G	EASTBOURNE - 75G	EASTBOURNE - 75G
32596	BOGNOR REGIS	BOGNOR REGIS	BOGNOR REGIS	BOGNOR REGIS	BOGNOR REGIS	BOGNOR REGIS	BOGNOR REGIS
32602	B.ARMS - 73B	B.ARMS - 73B	B.ARMS - 73B	B.ARMS - 73B	B.ARMS - 73B	B.ARMS - 73B	B.ARMS - 73B
32603	EASTBOURNE - 75G	EASTBOURNE - 75G	EASTBOURNE - 75G	EASTBOURNE - 75G	EASTBOURNE - 75G	EASTBOURNE - 75G	EASTBOURNE - 75G
				I3 4-4-2T (1907)			
32021	T.WELLS - 75F	T.WELLS - 75F	T.WELLS - 75F	T.WELLS - 75F	T.WELLS - 75F	T.WELLS - 75F	T.WELLS - 75F
32022	T.WELLS - 75F	T.WELLS - 75F	T.WELLS - 75F	T.WELLS - 75F	T.WELLS - 75F	T.WELLS - 75F	T.WELLS - 75F
32023	T.WELLS - 75F	T.WELLS - 75F	T.WELLS - 75F	T.WELLS - 75F	T.WELLS - 75F	T.WELLS - 75F	T.WELLS - 75F
32025	T.WELLS - 75F	T.WELLS - 75F	T.WELLS - 75F	T.WELLS - 75F	T.WELLS - 75F	W/D	W/D
32026	T.WELLS - 75F	T.WELLS - 75F	T.WELLS - 75F	T.WELLS - 75F	T.WELLS - 75F	T.WELLS - 75F	T.WELLS - 75F
32027	T.WELLS - 75F	T.WELLS - 75F	T.WELLS - 75F	T.WELLS - 75F	T.WELLS - 75F	T.WELLS - 75F	T.WELLS - 75F
32028	T.WELLS - 75F	T.WELLS - 75F	T.WELLS - 75F	T.WELLS - 75F	T.WELLS - 75F	T.WELLS - 75F	T.WELLS - 75F
32029	T.WELLS - 75F	T.WELLS - 75F	T.WELLS - 75F	T.WELLS - 75F	T.WELLS - 75F	T.WELLS - 75F	T.WELLS - 75F
32030	EASTBOURNE - 75G	EASTBOURNE - 75G	EASTBOURNE - 75G	EASTBOURNE - 75G	EASTBOURNE - 75G	EASTBOURNE - 75G	EASTBOURNE - 75G
32075	B.ARMS - 73B	B.ARMS - 73B	B.ARMS - 73B	B.ARMS - 73B	T.WELLS - 75F	T.WELLS - 75F	T.WELLS - 75F
32076	BRIGHTON - 75A	BRIGHTON - 75A	BRIGHTON - 75A	BRIGHTON - 75A	BRIGHTON - 75A	BRIGHTON - 75A	BRIGHTON - 75A
32077	EASTBOURNE - 75G	EASTBOURNE - 75G	EASTBOURNE - 75G	EASTBOURNE - 75G	EASTBOURNE - 75G	EASTBOURNE - 75G	EASTBOURNE - 75G
32078	THREE BRIDGES - 75E	THREE BRIDGES - 75E	THREE BRIDGES - 75E	THREE BRIDGES - 75E	THREE BRIDGES - 75E	THREE BRIDGES - 75E	THREE BRIDGES - 75E
32079	THREE BRIDGES - 75E	THREE BRIDGES - 75E	THREE BRIDGES - 75E	THREE BRIDGES - 75E	THREE BRIDGES - 75E	THREE BRIDGES - 75E	THREE BRIDGES - 75E
32080	BRIGHTON - 75A	BRIGHTON - 75A	BRIGHTON - 75A	BRIGHTON - 75A	BRIGHTON - 75A	BRIGHTON - 75A	W/D
32081	EASTBOURNE - 75G	EASTBOURNE - 75G	EASTBOURNE - 75G	EASTBOURNE - 75G	EASTBOURNE - 75G	EASTBOURNE - 75G	EASTBOURNE - 75G
32082	T.WELLS - 75F	T.WELLS - 75F	T.WELLS - 75F	T.WELLS - 75F	T.WELLS - 75F	T.WELLS - 75F	T.WELLS - 75F
32083	EASTBOURNE - 75G	EASTBOURNE - 75G	EASTBOURNE - 75G	EASTBOURNE - 75G	EASTBOURNE - 75G	EASTBOURNE - 75G	EASTBOURNE - 75G
32084	THREE BRIDGES - 75E	THREE BRIDGES - 75E	THREE BRIDGES - 75E	THREE BRIDGES - 75E	THREE BRIDGES - 75E	THREE BRIDGES - 75E	THREE BRIDGES - 75E
32085	THREE BRIDGES - 75E	THREE BRIDGES - 75E	THREE BRIDGES - 75E	THREE BRIDGES - 75E	THREE BRIDGES - 75E	THREE BRIDGES - 75E	THREE BRIDGES - 75E
32086	BRIGHTON - 75A	BRIGHTON - 75A	BRIGHTON - 75A	BRIGHTON - 75A	BRIGHTON - 75A	BRIGHTON - 75A	BRIGHTON - 75A
32087	T.WELLS - 75F	T.WELLS - 75F	T.WELLS - 75F	T.WELLS - 75F	T.WELLS - 75F	T.WELLS - 75F	T.WELLS - 75F
32088	BRIGHTON - 75A	BRIGHTON - 75A	BRIGHTON - 75A	BRIGHTON - 75A	BRIGHTON - 75A	BRIGHTON - 75A	BRIGHTON - 75A
32089	EASTBOURNE - 75G	EASTBOURNE - 75G	EASTBOURNE - 75G	EASTBOURNE - 75G	EASTBOURNE - 75G	EASTBOURNE - 75G	EASTBOURNE - 75G
32090	T.WELLS - 75F	T.WELLS - 75F	T.WELLS - 75F	T.WELLS - 75F	T.WELLS - 75F	T.WELLS - 75F	T.WELLS - 75F
32091	THREE BRIDGES - 75E	THREE BRIDGES - 75E	THREE BRIDGES - 75E	THREE BRIDGES - 75E	THREE BRIDGES - 75E	THREE BRIDGES - 75E	THREE BRIDGES - 75E
				H1 4-4-2 (1905)			
32037	BRIGHTON - 75A(N)	BRIGHTON - 75A(N)	BRIGHTON - 75A(N)	BRIGHTON - 75A(N)	BRIGHTON - 75A(N)	BRIGHTON - 75A(N)	BRIGHTON - 75A(N)
32038	BRIGHTON - 75A(N)	BRIGHTON - 75A(N)	BRIGHTON - 75A(N)	BRIGHTON - 75A(N)	BRIGHTON - 75A(N)	BRIGHTON - 75A(N)	BRIGHTON - 75A(N)
32039	BRIGHTON - 75A	BRIGHTON - 75A	BRIGHTON - 75A	BRIGHTON - 75A	BRIGHTON - 75A	BRIGHTON - 75A	BRIGHTON - 75A
				H2 4-4-2 (1911)			
32421	BRIGHTON - 75A	BRIGHTON - 75A	BRIGHTON - 75A	BRIGHTON - 75A	BRIGHTON - 75A	BRIGHTON - 75A	BRIGHTON - 75A
32422	BRIGHTON - 75A	BRIGHTON - 75A	BRIGHTON - 75A	BRIGHTON - 75A	BRIGHTON - 75A	BRIGHTON - 75A	BRIGHTON - 75A
32424	BRIGHTON - 75A	BRIGHTON - 75A	BRIGHTON - 75A	BRIGHTON - 75A	BRIGHTON - 75A	BRIGHTON - 75A	BRIGHTON - 75A
32425	BRIGHTON - 75A(N)	BRIGHTON - 75A(N)	BRIGHTON - 75A(N)	BRIGHTON - 75A(N)	BRIGHTON - 75A(N)	BRIGHTON - 75A(N)	BRIGHTON - 75A(N)
32426	BRIGHTON - 75A(N)	BRIGHTON - 75A(N)	BRIGHTON - 75A(N)	BRIGHTON - 75A(N)	BRIGHTON - 75A(N)	BRIGHTON - 75A(N)	BRIGHTON - 75A(N)
				B1 4-4-0 (1910)			
31217	READING (SR) - 70E	READING (SR) - 70E	READING (SR) - 70E	READING (SR) - 70E	READING (SR) - 70E	READING (SR) - 70E	READING (SR) - 70E
31443	READING (SR) - 70E	READING (SR) - 70E	READING (SR) - 70E	READING (SR) - 70E	READING (SR) - 70E	READING (SR) - 70E	READING (SR) - 70E
31446	READING (SR) - 70E	READING (SR) - 70E	W/D	W/D	W/D	W/D	W/D
31448	READING (SR) - 70E	READING (SR) - 70E	READING (SR) - 70E	W/D	W/D	W/D	W/D
31451	READING (SR) - 70E	READING (SR) - 70E	READING (SR) - 70E	READING (SR) - 70E	W/D	W/D	W/D
31452	READING (SR) - 70E	READING (SR) - 70E	READING (SR) - 70E	READING (SR) - 70E	READING (SR) - 70E	READING (SR) - 70E	READING (SR) - 70E
31455	READING (SR) - 70E	W/D	W/D	W/D	W/D	W/D	W/D
				B4 4-4-0 (1899)			
32054	EASTBOURNE - 75G	EASTBOURNE - 75G	EASTBOURNE - 75G	EASTBOURNE - 75G	EASTBOURNE - 75G	EASTBOURNE - 75G	EASTBOURNE - 75G
32062	EASTBOURNE - 75G	EASTBOURNE - 75G	EASTBOURNE - 75G	EASTBOURNE - 75G	EASTBOURNE - 75G	EASTBOURNE - 75G	EASTBOURNE - 75G
32063	EASTBOURNE - 75G	EASTBOURNE - 75G	EASTBOURNE - 75G	EASTBOURNE - 75G	EASTBOURNE - 75G	EASTBOURNE - 75G	EASTBOURNE - 75G
32068	EASTBOURNE - 75G	EASTBOURNE - 75G	EASTBOURNE - 75G	EASTBOURNE - 75G	EASTBOURNE - 75G	EASTBOURNE - 75G	EASTBOURNE - 75G
32074	BOGNOR REGIS	BOGNOR REGIS	BOGNOR REGIS	BOGNOR REGIS	BOGNOR REGIS	BOGNOR REGIS	W/D
				B4X 4-4-0 (1922)			
32043	EASTBOURNE - 75G	EASTBOURNE - 75G	EASTBOURNE - 75G	EASTBOURNE - 75G	EASTBOURNE - 75G	EASTBOURNE - 75G	EASTBOURNE - 75G
32045	B.ARMS - 73B	B.ARMS - 73B	B.ARMS - 73B	B.ARMS - 73B	B.ARMS - 73B	B.ARMS - 73B	B.ARMS - 73B
32050	B.ARMS - 73B	B.ARMS - 73B	B.ARMS - 73B	B.ARMS - 73B	B.ARMS - 73B	B.ARMS - 73B	B.ARMS - 73B
32052	B.ARMS - 73B	B.ARMS - 73B	B.ARMS - 73B	B.ARMS - 73B	B.ARMS - 73B	B.ARMS - 73B	B.ARMS - 73B
32055	EASTBOURNE - 75G	EASTBOURNE - 75G	EASTBOURNE - 75G	EASTBOURNE - 75G	EASTBOURNE - 75G	EASTBOURNE - 75G	EASTBOURNE - 75G
32056	REDHILL - 75B	REDHILL - 75B	REDHILL - 75B	REDHILL - 75B	REDHILL - 75B	REDHILL - 75B	REDHILL - 75B
32060	EASTBOURNE - 75G	EASTBOURNE - 75G	EASTBOURNE - 75G	EASTBOURNE - 75G	EASTBOURNE - 75G	EASTBOURNE - 75G	EASTBOURNE - 75G
32067	B.ARMS - 73B	B.ARMS - 73B	B.ARMS - 73B	B.ARMS - 73B	B.ARMS - 73B	B.ARMS - 73B	B.ARMS - 73B
32070	B.ARMS - 73B	B.ARMS - 73B	B.ARMS - 73B	B.ARMS - 73B	B.ARMS - 73B	B.ARMS - 73B	B.ARMS - 73B
32071	REDHILL - 75B	REDHILL - 75B	REDHILL - 75B	REDHILL - 75B	REDHILL - 75B	REDHILL - 75B	REDHILL - 75B
32072	REDHILL - 75B	REDHILL - 75B	REDHILL - 75B	REDHILL - 75B	REDHILL - 75B	REDHILL - 75B	REDHILL - 75B
32073	REDHILL - 75B	REDHILL - 75B	REDHILL - 75B	REDHILL - 75B	REDHILL - 75B	REDHILL - 75B	REDHILL - 75B

loco	Apr-50	Sep-50	Oct-50	Nov-50	Dec-50	Mar-51	Apr-51
R 0-4-4T (1891)							
31658	GILLINGHAM - 73D	GILLINGHAM - 73D	GILLINGHAM - 73D	GILLINGHAM - 73D	GILLINGHAM - 73D	GILLINGHAM - 73D	GILLINGHAM - 73D
31659	GILLINGHAM - 73D	GILLINGHAM - 73D	GILLINGHAM - 73D	GILLINGHAM - 73D	GILLINGHAM - 73D	GILLINGHAM - 73D	GILLINGHAM - 73D
31660	ASHFORD - 74A	STEWARTS LANE - 73A	STEWARTS LANE - 73A	STEWARTS LANE - 73A	STEWARTS LANE - 73A	STEWARTS LANE - 73A	STEWARTS LANE - 73A
31661	FAVERSHAM - 73E	FAVERSHAM - 73E	FAVERSHAM - 73E	FAVERSHAM - 73E	FAVERSHAM - 73E	FAVERSHAM - 73E	FAVERSHAM - 73E
31662	GILLINGHAM - 73D	GILLINGHAM - 73D	GILLINGHAM - 73D	GILLINGHAM - 73D	GILLINGHAM - 73D	GILLINGHAM - 73D	GILLINGHAM - 73D
31663	GILLINGHAM - 73D	GILLINGHAM - 73D	GILLINGHAM - 73D	GILLINGHAM - 73D	GILLINGHAM - 73D	GILLINGHAM - 73D	GILLINGHAM - 73D
31665	GILLINGHAM - 73D	GILLINGHAM - 73D	GILLINGHAM - 73D	GILLINGHAM - 73D	GILLINGHAM - 73D	GILLINGHAM - 73D	GILLINGHAM - 73D
31666	GILLINGHAM - 73D	GILLINGHAM - 73D	GILLINGHAM - 73D	GILLINGHAM - 73D	GILLINGHAM - 73D	GILLINGHAM - 73D	GILLINGHAM - 73D
31667	TONBRIDGE - 74D	TONBRIDGE - 74D	TONBRIDGE - 74D	TONBRIDGE - 74D	TONBRIDGE - 74D	TONBRIDGE - 74D	W/D
31670	TONBRIDGE - 74D	TONBRIDGE - 74D	TONBRIDGE - 74D	TONBRIDGE - 74D	TONBRIDGE - 74D	TONBRIDGE - 74D	W/D
31671	TONBRIDGE - 74D	TONBRIDGE - 74D	TONBRIDGE - 74D	TONBRIDGE - 74D	TONBRIDGE - 74D	TONBRIDGE - 74D	TONBRIDGE - 74D
31673	DOVER - 74C	DOVER - 74C	DOVER - 74C	DOVER - 74C	DOVER - 74C	DOVER - 74C	DOVER - 74C
31674	FAVERSHAM - 73E	FAVERSHAM - 73E	FAVERSHAM - 73E	FAVERSHAM - 73E	FAVERSHAM - 73E	FAVERSHAM - 73E	FAVERSHAM - 73E
31675	TONBRIDGE - 74D	TONBRIDGE - 74D	TONBRIDGE - 74D	TONBRIDGE - 74D	TONBRIDGE - 74D	TONBRIDGE - 74D	TONBRIDGE - 74D
'0415' 4-4-2T (1882)							
30582	EXMOUTH JCN - 72A	EXMOUTH JCN - 72A	EXMOUTH JCN - 72A	EXMOUTH JCN - 72A	EXMOUTH JCN - 72A	EXMOUTH JCN - 72A	EXMOUTH JCN - 72A
30583	EXMOUTH JCN - 72A	EXMOUTH JCN - 72A	EXMOUTH JCN - 72A	EXMOUTH JCN - 72A	EXMOUTH JCN - 72A	EXMOUTH JCN - 72A	EXMOUTH JCN - 72A
30584	EXMOUTH JCN - 72A	EXMOUTH JCN - 72A	EXMOUTH JCN - 72A	EXMOUTH JCN - 72A	EXMOUTH JCN - 72A	EXMOUTH JCN - 72A	EXMOUTH JCN - 72A
I1X 4-4-2T (1906/25)							
32002	BOGNOR REGIS	THREE BRIDGES - 75E	BRIGHTON - 75A	BRIGHTON - 75A	BRIGHTON - 75A	BRIGHTON - 75A	BRIGHTON - 75A
32005	EASTBOURNE - 75G	BRIGHTON - 75A	BRIGHTON - 75A	BRIGHTON - 75A	BRIGHTON - 75A	BRIGHTON - 75A	BRIGHTON - 75A
32008	BOGNOR REGIS	B.ARMS - 73B(NX)	B.ARMS - 73B(NX)	B.ARMS - 73B(NX)	B.ARMS - 73B(NX)	B.ARMS - 73B(NX)	B.ARMS - 73B(NX)
32009	EASTBOURNE - 75G	EASTBOURNE - 75G	EASTBOURNE - 75G	EASTBOURNE - 75G	EASTBOURNE - 75G	EASTBOURNE - 75G	W/D
32595	EASTBOURNE - 75G	BRIGHTON - 75A	BRIGHTON - 75A	BRIGHTON - 75A	BRIGHTON - 75A	BRIGHTON - 75A	BRIGHTON - 75A
32596	BOGNOR REGIS	B.ARMS - 73B(NX)	B.ARMS - 73B(NX)	B.ARMS - 73B(NX)	B.ARMS - 73B(NX)	B.ARMS - 73B(NX)	B.ARMS - 73B(NX)
32602	B.ARMS - 73B	B.ARMS - 73B	B.ARMS - 73B	B.ARMS - 73B	B.ARMS - 73B	B.ARMS - 73B	B.ARMS - 73B
32603	EASTBOURNE - 75G	EASTBOURNE - 75G	EASTBOURNE - 75G	EASTBOURNE - 75G	EASTBOURNE - 75G	EASTBOURNE - 75G	W/D
I3 4-4-2T (1907)							
32021	T.WELLS - 75F	T.WELLS - 75F	T.WELLS - 75F	T.WELLS - 75F	T.WELLS - 75F	T.WELLS - 75F	THREE BRIDGES - 75E
32022	T.WELLS - 75F	T.WELLS - 75F	T.WELLS - 75F	T.WELLS - 75F	T.WELLS - 75F	T.WELLS - 75F	W/D
32023	T.WELLS - 75F	T.WELLS - 75F	T.WELLS - 75F	T.WELLS - 75F	T.WELLS - 75F	T.WELLS - 75F	T.WELLS - 75F
32026	T.WELLS - 75F	T.WELLS - 75F	T.WELLS - 75F	T.WELLS - 75F	T.WELLS - 75F	T.WELLS - 75F	T.WELLS - 75F
32027	T.WELLS - 75F	T.WELLS - 75F	T.WELLS - 75F	T.WELLS - 75F	W/D	W/D	W/D
32028	T.WELLS - 75F	T.WELLS - 75F	T.WELLS - 75F	T.WELLS - 75F	T.WELLS - 75F	T.WELLS - 75F	T.WELLS - 75F
32029	T.WELLS - 75F	T.WELLS - 75F	EASTBOURNE - 75G	THREE BRIDGES - 75E	T.WELLS - 75F	W/D	W/D
32030	EASTBOURNE - 75G	EASTBOURNE - 75G	EASTBOURNE - 75G	EASTBOURNE - 75G	EASTBOURNE - 75G	EASTBOURNE - 75G	EASTBOURNE - 75G
32075	T.WELLS - 75F	T.WELLS - 75F	T.WELLS - 75F	T.WELLS - 75F	T.WELLS - 75F	T.WELLS - 75F	T.WELLS - 75F
32076	BRIGHTON - 75A	BRIGHTON - 75A	BRIGHTON - 75A	BRIGHTON - 75A	W/D	W/D	W/D
32077	EASTBOURNE - 75G	EASTBOURNE - 75G	EASTBOURNE - 75G	EASTBOURNE - 75G	EASTBOURNE - 75G	W/D	W/D
32078	THREE BRIDGES - 75E	THREE BRIDGES - 75E	THREE BRIDGES - 75E	THREE BRIDGES - 75E	W/D	W/D	W/D
32079	THREE BRIDGES - 75E	THREE BRIDGES - 75E	THREE BRIDGES - 75E	W/D	W/D	W/D	
32081	EASTBOURNE - 75G	EASTBOURNE - 75G	EASTBOURNE - 75G	EASTBOURNE - 75G	THREE BRIDGES - 75E	THREE BRIDGES - 75E	THREE BRIDGES - 75E
32082	T.WELLS - 75F	EASTBOURNE - 75G	THREE BRIDGES - 75E	THREE BRIDGES - 75E	THREE BRIDGES - 75E	THREE BRIDGES - 75E	THREE BRIDGES - 75E
32083	EASTBOURNE - 75G	EASTBOURNE - 75G	EASTBOURNE - 75G	EASTBOURNE - 75G	EASTBOURNE - 75G	EASTBOURNE - 75G	EASTBOURNE - 75G
32084	THREE BRIDGES - 75E	THREE BRIDGES - 75E	THREE BRIDGES - 75E	THREE BRIDGES - 75E	THREE BRIDGES - 75E	W/D	W/D
32085	THREE BRIDGES - 75E						
32086	BRIGHTON - 75A	BRIGHTON - 75A	BRIGHTON - 75A	BRIGHTON - 75A	BRIGHTON - 75A	BRIGHTON - 75A	BRIGHTON - 75A
32087	T.WELLS - 75F	T.WELLS - 75F	T.WELLS - 75F	W/D	W/D	W/D	W/D
32088	BRIGHTON - 75A	BRIGHTON - 75A	BRIGHTON - 75A	W/D	W/D	W/D	W/D
32089	EASTBOURNE - 75G	EASTBOURNE - 75G	EASTBOURNE - 75G	EASTBOURNE - 75G	EASTBOURNE - 75G	EASTBOURNE - 75G	W/D
32090	T.WELLS - 75F	T.WELLS - 75F	THREE BRIDGES - 75E	W/D	W/D	W/D	W/D
32091	THREE BRIDGES - 75E	THREE BRIDGES - 75E	THREE BRIDGES - 75E	THREE BRIDGES - 75E	THREE BRIDGES - 75E	THREE BRIDGES - 75E	THREE BRIDGES - 75E
H1 4-4-2 (1905)							
32037	BRIGHTON - 75A(N)	BRIGHTON - 75A(N)	BRIGHTON - 75A(N)	BRIGHTON - 75A(N)	BRIGHTON - 75A(N)	BRIGHTON - 75A(N)	BRIGHTON - 75A(N)
32038	EASTBOURNE - 75G	BRIGHTON - 75A(N)	BRIGHTON - 75A(N)	BRIGHTON - 75A(N)	BRIGHTON - 75A(N)	BRIGHTON - 75A(N)	BRIGHTON - 75A(N)
32039	BRIGHTON - 75A	BRIGHTON - 75A	BRIGHTON - 75A	BRIGHTON - 75A	BRIGHTON - 75A	W/D	W/D
H2 4-4-2 (1911)							
32421	BRIGHTON - 75A	BRIGHTON - 75A	BRIGHTON - 75A(N)	BRIGHTON - 75A(N)	BRIGHTON - 75A(N)	BRIGHTON - 75A(N)	BRIGHTON - 75A(N)
32422	BRIGHTON - 75A	BRIGHTON - 75A	BRIGHTON - 75A(N)	BRIGHTON - 75A(N)	BRIGHTON - 75A(N)	BRIGHTON - 75A(N)	BRIGHTON - 75A(N)
32424	BRIGHTON - 75A	BRIGHTON - 75A	BRIGHTON - 75A(N)	BRIGHTON - 75A(N)	BRIGHTON - 75A(N)	BRIGHTON - 75A(N)	BRIGHTON - 75A(N)
32425	BRIGHTON - 75A(N)	BRIGHTON - 75A(N)	BRIGHTON - 75A(N)	BRIGHTON - 75A	BRIGHTON - 75A	BRIGHTON - 75A	BRIGHTON - 75A
32426	BRIGHTON - 75A(N)	BRIGHTON - 75A(N)	BRIGHTON - 75A(N)	BRIGHTON - 75A	BRIGHTON - 75A	BRIGHTON - 75A	BRIGHTON - 75A
B1 4-4-0 (1910)							
31217	READING (SR) - 70E	W/D					
31443	READING (SR) - 70E	READING (SR) - 70E	READING (SR) - 70E	READING (SR) - 70E	READING (SR) - 70E	W/D	W/D
31452	READING (SR) - 70E	W/D					
B4 4-4-0 (1899)							
32054	EASTBOURNE - 75G	EASTBOURNE - 75G	EASTBOURNE - 75G	EASTBOURNE - 75G	EASTBOURNE - 75G	EASTBOURNE - 75G	EASTBOURNE - 75G
32062	EASTBOURNE - 75G	EASTBOURNE - 75G	EASTBOURNE - 75G	EASTBOURNE - 75G	EASTBOURNE - 75G	EASTBOURNE - 75G	W/D
32063	EASTBOURNE - 75G	EASTBOURNE - 75G	EASTBOURNE - 75G	EASTBOURNE - 75G	EASTBOURNE - 75G	EASTBOURNE - 75G	EASTBOURNE - 75G
B4X 4-4-0 (1922)							
32043	EASTBOURNE - 75G	EASTBOURNE - 75G	EASTBOURNE - 75G	EASTBOURNE - 75G	EASTBOURNE - 75G	EASTBOURNE - 75G	EASTBOURNE - 75G
32045	B.ARMS - 73B	BASINGSTOKE - 70D	BASINGSTOKE - 70D	BASINGSTOKE - 70D	BASINGSTOKE - 70D	BASINGSTOKE - 70D	BASINGSTOKE - 70D
32050	B.ARMS - 73B	B.ARMS - 73B	B.ARMS - 73B	B.ARMS - 73B	B.ARMS - 73B	B.ARMS - 73B	B.ARMS - 73B
32052	B.ARMS - 73B	BASINGSTOKE - 70D	BASINGSTOKE - 70D	BASINGSTOKE - 70D	BASINGSTOKE - 70D	BASINGSTOKE - 70D	BASINGSTOKE - 70D
32055	EASTBOURNE - 75G	EASTBOURNE - 75G	EASTBOURNE - 75G	EASTBOURNE - 75G	EASTBOURNE - 75G	EASTBOURNE - 75G	EASTBOURNE - 75G
32056	B.ARMS - 73B	B.ARMS - 73B	B.ARMS - 73B	B.ARMS - 73B	B.ARMS - 73B	B.ARMS - 73B	B.ARMS - 73B
32060	EASTBOURNE - 75G	EASTBOURNE - 75G	EASTBOURNE - 75G	EASTBOURNE - 75G	EASTBOURNE - 75G	EASTBOURNE - 75G	EASTBOURNE - 75G
32067	B.ARMS - 73B	BASINGSTOKE - 70D	BASINGSTOKE - 70D	BASINGSTOKE - 70D	BASINGSTOKE - 70D	BASINGSTOKE - 70D	BASINGSTOKE - 70D
32070	B.ARMS - 73B	B.ARMS - 73B	B.ARMS - 73B	B.ARMS - 73B	B.ARMS - 73B	B.ARMS - 73B	B.ARMS - 73B
32071	EASTBOURNE - 75G	EASTBOURNE - 75G	EASTBOURNE - 75G	EASTBOURNE - 75G	EASTBOURNE - 75G	EASTBOURNE - 75G	EASTBOURNE - 75G
32072	EASTBOURNE - 75G	EASTBOURNE - 75G	EASTBOURNE - 75G	EASTBOURNE - 75G	EASTBOURNE - 75G	EASTBOURNE - 75G	EASTBOURNE - 75G
32073	EASTBOURNE - 75G	EASTBOURNE - 75G	EASTBOURNE - 75G	EASTBOURNE - 75G	EASTBOURNE - 75G	EASTBOURNE - 75G	EASTBOURNE - 75G

loco	Jun-51	Jul-51	Sep-51	Dec-51	Jan-52	Mar-52	Jun-52
				R 0-4-4T (1891)			
31658	GILLINGHAM - 73D	GILLINGHAM - 73D	GILLINGHAM - 73D	GILLINGHAM - 73D	GILLINGHAM - 73D	GILLINGHAM - 73D	GILLINGHAM - 73D
31659	GILLINGHAM - 73D	GILLINGHAM - 73D	W/D	W/D	W/D	W/D	W/D
31660	STEWARTS LANE - 73A	STEWARTS LANE - 73A	STEWARTS LANE - 73A	GILLINGHAM - 73D	GILLINGHAM - 73D	GILLINGHAM - 73D	GILLINGHAM - 73D
31661	FAVERSHAM - 73E	FAVERSHAM - 73E	FAVERSHAM - 73E	FAVERSHAM - 73E	FAVERSHAM - 73E	FAVERSHAM - 73E	FAVERSHAM - 73E
31662	GILLINGHAM - 73D	GILLINGHAM - 73D	GILLINGHAM - 73D	GILLINGHAM - 73D	GILLINGHAM - 73D	GILLINGHAM - 73D	GILLINGHAM - 73D
31663	GILLINGHAM - 73D	GILLINGHAM - 73D	GILLINGHAM - 73D	GILLINGHAM - 73D	GILLINGHAM - 73D	GILLINGHAM - 73D	GILLINGHAM - 73D
31665	TONBRIDGE - 74D	TONBRIDGE - 74D	TONBRIDGE - 74D	TONBRIDGE - 74D	TONBRIDGE - 74D	TONBRIDGE - 74D	TONBRIDGE - 74D
31666	GILLINGHAM - 73D	GILLINGHAM - 73D	GILLINGHAM - 73D	GILLINGHAM - 73D	GILLINGHAM - 73D	GILLINGHAM - 73D	GILLINGHAM - 73D
31671	TONBRIDGE - 74D	TONBRIDGE - 74D	TONBRIDGE - 74D	TONBRIDGE - 74D	TONBRIDGE - 74D	TONBRIDGE - 74D	TONBRIDGE - 74D
31673	DOVER - 74C	DOVER - 74C	DOVER - 74C	DOVER - 74C	DOVER - 74C	DOVER - 74C	DOVER - 74C
31674	FAVERSHAM - 73E	FAVERSHAM - 73E	FAVERSHAM - 73E	FAVERSHAM - 73E	FAVERSHAM - 73E	FAVERSHAM - 73E	
31675	TONBRIDGE - 74D	TONBRIDGE - 74D	TONBRIDGE - 74D	TONBRIDGE - 74D	TONBRIDGE - 74D	TONBRIDGE - 74D	TONBRIDGE - 74D
				'0415' 4-4-2T (1882)			
30582	EXMOUTH JCN - 72A	EXMOUTH JCN - 72A	EXMOUTH JCN - 72A	EXMOUTH JCN - 72A	EXMOUTH JCN - 72A	EXMOUTH JCN - 72A	EXMOUTH JCN - 72A
30583	EXMOUTH JCN - 72A	EXMOUTH JCN - 72A	EXMOUTH JCN - 72A	EXMOUTH JCN - 72A	EXMOUTH JCN - 72A	EXMOUTH JCN - 72A	EXMOUTH JCN - 72A
30584	EXMOUTH JCN - 72A	EXMOUTH JCN - 72A	EXMOUTH JCN - 72A	EXMOUTH JCN - 72A	EXMOUTH JCN - 72A	EXMOUTH JCN - 72A	EXMOUTH JCN - 72A
				IIX 4-4-2T (1906/25)			
32002	BRIGHTON - 75A	W/D	W/D	W/D	W/D	W/D	W/D
				B3 4-4-2T (1907)			
32021	THREE BRIDGES - 75E	THREE BRIDGES - 75E	W/D	W/D	W/D	W/D	W/D
32023	BRIGHTON - 75A	W/D	W/D	W/D	W/D	W/D	W/D
32026	T.WELLS - 75F	T.WELLS - 75F	W/D	W/D	W/D	W/D	W/D
32028	T.WELLS - 75F	T.WELLS - 75F	W/D	W/D	W/D	W/D	W/D
32030	EASTBOURNE - 75G	EASTBOURNE - 75G	W/D	W/D	W/D	W/D	W/D
32075	T.WELLS - 75F	T.WELLS - 75F	THREE BRIDGES - 75E	W/D	W/D	W/D	W/D
32081	THREE BRIDGES - 75E	THREE BRIDGES - 75E	W/D	W/D	W/D	W/D	W/D
32086	BRIGHTON - 75A	BRIGHTON - 75A	W/D	W/D	W/D	W/D	W/D
32091	THREE BRIDGES - 75E	THREE BRIDGES - 75E	THREE BRIDGES - 75E	THREE BRIDGES - 75E	BRIGHTON - 75A	BRIGHTON - 75A	W/D
				H1 4-4-2 (1905)			
32037	BRIGHTON - 75A(N)	W/D	W/D	W/D	W/D	W/D	W/D
32038	BRIGHTON - 75A(N)	W/D	W/D	W/D	W/D	W/D	W/D
				H2 4-4-2 (1911)			
32421	BRIGHTON - 75A (N)	BRIGHTON - 75A (N)	BRIGHTON - 75A (N)	BRIGHTON - 75A (N)	BRIGHTON - 75A (N)	BRIGHTON - 75A (N)	BRIGHTON - 75A (N)
32422	BRIGHTON - 75A (N)	BRIGHTON - 75A (N)	BRIGHTON - 75A	BRIGHTON - 75A	BRIGHTON - 75A	BRIGHTON - 75A	BRIGHTON - 75A
32424	BRIGHTON - 75A (N)	BRIGHTON - 75A (N)	BRIGHTON - 75A (N)	BRIGHTON - 75A (N)	BRIGHTON - 75A (N)	BRIGHTON - 75A (N)	BRIGHTON - 75A (N)
32425	BRIGHTON - 75A	BRIGHTON - 75A	BRIGHTON - 75A(N)	BRIGHTON - 75A(N)	BRIGHTON - 75A(N)	BRIGHTON - 75A(N)	BRIGHTON - 75A
32426	BRIGHTON - 75A	BRIGHTON - 75A	BRIGHTON - 75A	BRIGHTON - 75A	BRIGHTON - 75A	BRIGHTON - 75A	BRIGHTON - 75A
				B4X 4-4-0 (1922)			
32043	EASTBOURNE - 75G	EASTBOURNE - 75G	EASTBOURNE - 75G	W/D	W/D	W/D	W/D
32045	BASINGSTOKE - 70D	BASINGSTOKE - 70D	B.ARMS - 73B	W/D	W/D	W/D	W/D
32050	B.ARMS - 73B	B.ARMS - 73B	B.ARMS - 73B	W/D	W/D	W/D	W/D
32052	BASINGSTOKE - 70D	BASINGSTOKE - 70D	EASTBOURNE - 75G	W/D	W/D	W/D	W/D
32055	EASTBOURNE - 75G	EASTBOURNE - 75G	EASTBOURNE - 75G	W/D	W/D	W/D	W/D
32056	B.ARMS - 73B	B.ARMS - 73B	B.ARMS - 73B	W/D	W/D	W/D	W/D
32060	EASTBOURNE - 75G	EASTBOURNE - 75G	EASTBOURNE - 75G	W/D	W/D	W/D	W/D
32067	BASINGSTOKE - 70D	BASINGSTOKE - 70D	W/D	W/D	W/D	W/D	W/D
32070	B.ARMS - 73B	B.ARMS - 73B	W/D	W/D	W/D	W/D	W/D
32071	EASTBOURNE - 75G	EASTBOURNE - 75G	EASTBOURNE - 75G	W/D	W/D	W/D	W/D
32072	EASTBOURNE - 75G	EASTBOURNE - 75G	EASTBOURNE - 75G	W/D	W/D	W/D	W/D
32073	EASTBOURNE - 75G	EASTBOURNE - 75G	W/D	W/D	W/D	W/D	W/D

loco	Sep-52	Dec-52	Mar-53	May-53	Jul-53	Sep-53	Nov-53
				R 0-4-4T (1891)			
31658	GILLINGHAM - 73D	W/D	W/D	W/D	W/D	W/D	W/D
31660	GILLINGHAM - 73D	GILLINGHAM - 73D	FAVERSHAM - 73E	FAVERSHAM - 73E	FAVERSHAM - 73E	GILLINGHAM - 73D	W/D
31661	FAVERSHAM - 73E	FAVERSHAM - 73E	ASHFORD - 74A	ASHFORD - 74A	DOVER - 74C	DOVER - 74C	DOVER - 74C
31662	GILLINGHAM - 73D	GILLINGHAM - 73D	GILLINGHAM - 73D	GILLINGHAM - 73D	GILLINGHAM - 73D	W/D	W/D
31663	GILLINGHAM - 73D	GILLINGHAM - 73D	FAVERSHAM - 73E	GILLINGHAM - 73D	W/D	W/D	W/D
31666	GILLINGHAM - 73D	GILLINGHAM - 73D	GILLINGHAM - 73D	GILLINGHAM - 73D	GILLINGHAM - 73D	GILLINGHAM - 73D	GILLINGHAM - 73D
31671	TONBRIDGE - 74D	TONBRIDGE - 74D	FAVERSHAM - 73E	FAVERSHAM - 73E	FAVERSHAM - 73E	FAVERSHAM - 73E	FAVERSHAM - 73E
31675	TONBRIDGE - 74D	W/D	W/D	W/D	W/D	W/D	W/D
				'0415' 4-4-2T (1882)			
30582	EXMOUTH JCN - 72A	EXMOUTH JCN - 72A	EXMOUTH JCN - 72A	EXMOUTH JCN - 72A	EXMOUTH JCN - 72A	EXMOUTH JCN - 72A	EXMOUTH JCN - 72A
30583	EXMOUTH JCN - 72A	EXMOUTH JCN - 72A	EXMOUTH JCN - 72A	EXMOUTH JCN - 72A	EXMOUTH JCN - 72A	EXMOUTH JCN - 72A	EXMOUTH JCN - 72A
30584	EXMOUTH JCN - 72A	EXMOUTH JCN - 72A	EXMOUTH JCN - 72A	EXMOUTH JCN - 72A	EXMOUTH JCN - 72A	EXMOUTH JCN - 72A	EXMOUTH JCN - 72A
				H2 4-4-2 (1911)			
32421	BRIGHTON - 75A (N)	BRIGHTON - 75A	BRIGHTON - 75A	BRIGHTON - 75A	BRIGHTON - 75A	BRIGHTON - 75A	BRIGHTON - 75A
32422	BRIGHTON - 75A (N)	BRIGHTON - 75A	BRIGHTON - 75A	BRIGHTON - 75A (N)	BRIGHTON - 75A (N)	BRIGHTON - 75A (N)	BRIGHTON - 75A (N)
32424	BRIGHTON - 75A (N)	BRIGHTON - 75A (N)	BRIGHTON - 75A (N)	BRIGHTON - 75A (N)	BRIGHTON - 75A (N)	BRIGHTON - 75A (N)	BRIGHTON - 75A (N)
32425	BRIGHTON - 75A	BRIGHTON - 75A	BRIGHTON - 75A	BRIGHTON - 75A	BRIGHTON - 75A	BRIGHTON - 75A	BRIGHTON - 75A
32426	BRIGHTON - 75A (N)	BRIGHTON - 75A	BRIGHTON - 75A	BRIGHTON - 75A	BRIGHTON - 75A	BRIGHTON - 75A	BRIGHTON - 75A

loco	Jan-54	Mar-54	May-54	Jun-54	Aug-54	Oct-54	Dec-54
				R 0-4-4T (1891)			
31661	DOVER - 74C	DOVER - 74C	DOVER - 74C	DOVER - 74C	DOVER - 74C	DOVER - 74C	DOVER - 74C
31666	GILLINGHAM - 73D	GILLINGHAM - 73D	GILLINGHAM - 73D	GILLINGHAM - 73D	GILLINGHAM - 73D	GILLINGHAM - 73D	GILLINGHAM - 73D
31671	FAVERSHAM - 73E	FAVERSHAM - 73E	FAVERSHAM - 73E	FAVERSHAM - 73E	GILLINGHAM - 73D	W/D	W/D
				'0415' 4-4-2T (1882)			
30582	EXMOUTH JCN - 72A	EXMOUTH JCN - 72A	EXMOUTH JCN - 72A	EXMOUTH JCN - 72A	EXMOUTH JCN - 72A	EXMOUTH JCN - 72A	EXMOUTH JCN - 72A
30583	EXMOUTH JCN - 72A	EXMOUTH JCN - 72A	EXMOUTH JCN - 72A	EXMOUTH JCN - 72A	EXMOUTH JCN - 72A	EXMOUTH JCN - 72A	EXMOUTH JCN - 72A
30584	EXMOUTH JCN - 72A	EXMOUTH JCN - 72A	EXMOUTH JCN - 72A	EXMOUTH JCN - 72A	EXMOUTH JCN - 72A	EXMOUTH JCN - 72A	EXMOUTH JCN - 72A
				H2 4-4-2 (1911)			
32421	BRIGHTON - 75A	BRIGHTON - 75A	BRIGHTON - 75A	BRIGHTON - 75A	BRIGHTON - 75A	BRIGHTON - 75A	BRIGHTON - 75A
32422	BRIGHTON - 75A (N)	BRIGHTON - 75A (N)	BRIGHTON - 75A (N)	BRIGHTON - 75A (N)	BRIGHTON - 75A (N)	BRIGHTON - 75A (N)	BRIGHTON - 75A
32424	BRIGHTON - 75A (N)	BRIGHTON - 75A (N)	BRIGHTON - 75A (N)	BRIGHTON - 75A (N)	BRIGHTON - 75A (N)	BRIGHTON - 75A (N)	BRIGHTON - 75A (N)
32425	BRIGHTON - 75A	BRIGHTON - 75A	BRIGHTON - 75A	BRIGHTON - 75A	BRIGHTON - 75A	BRIGHTON - 75A(N)	BRIGHTON - 75A
32426	BRIGHTON - 75A	BRIGHTON - 75A	BRIGHTON - 75A	BRIGHTON - 75A	BRIGHTON - 75A	BRIGHTON - 75A	BRIGHTON - 75A

loco	Feb-55	Apr-55	Jun-55	Aug-55	Sep-55	Nov-55	Dec-55
			R 0-4-4T (1891)				
31666	GILLINGHAM - 73D	GILLINGHAM - 73D	GILLINGHAM - 73D	GILLINGHAM - 73D	GILLINGHAM - 73D	GILLINGHAM - 73D	GILLINGHAM - 73D
			'0415' 4-4-2T (1882)				
30582	EXMOUTH JCN - 72A	EXMOUTH JCN - 72A	EXMOUTH JCN - 72A	EXMOUTH JCN - 72A	EXMOUTH JCN - 72A	EXMOUTH JCN - 72A	EXMOUTH JCN - 72A
30583	EXMOUTH JCN - 72A	EXMOUTH JCN - 72A	EXMOUTH JCN - 72A	EXMOUTH JCN - 72A	EXMOUTH JCN - 72A	EXMOUTH JCN - 72A	EXMOUTH JCN - 72A
30584	EXMOUTH JCN - 72A	EXMOUTH JCN - 72A	EXMOUTH JCN - 72A	EXMOUTH JCN - 72A	EXMOUTH JCN - 72A	EXMOUTH JCN - 72A	EXMOUTH JCN - 72A
			H2 4-4-2 (1911)				
32421	BRIGHTON - 75A	BRIGHTON - 75A	BRIGHTON - 75A	BRIGHTON - 75A	BRIGHTON - 75A	BRIGHTON - 75A	BRIGHTON - 75A
32422	BRIGHTON - 75A(N)	BRIGHTON - 75A(N)	BRIGHTON - 75A(N)	BRIGHTON - 75A	BRIGHTON - 75A (N)	BRIGHTON - 75A (N)	BRIGHTON - 75A (N)
32424	BRIGHTON - 75A(N)	BRIGHTON - 75A(N)	BRIGHTON - 75A	BRIGHTON - 75A	BRIGHTON - 75A	BRIGHTON - 75A	BRIGHTON - 75A
32425	BRIGHTON - 75A(N)	BRIGHTON - 75A(N)	BRIGHTON - 75A(N)	BRIGHTON - 75A	BRIGHTON - 75A	BRIGHTON - 75A	BRIGHTON - 75A
32426	BRIGHTON - 75A	BRIGHTON - 75A	BRIGHTON - 75A	BRIGHTON - 75A	BRIGHTON - 75A (N)	BRIGHTON - 75A (N)	BRIGHTON - 75A

loco	Jan-56	Apr-56	May-56	Aug-56	Oct-56	Nov-56	Jan-57
			'0415' 4-4-2T (1882)				
30582	EXMOUTH JCN - 72A	EXMOUTH JCN - 72A	EXMOUTH JCN - 72A	EXMOUTH JCN - 72A	EXMOUTH JCN - 72A	EXMOUTH JCN - 72A	EXMOUTH JCN - 72A
30583	EXMOUTH JCN - 72A	EXMOUTH JCN - 72A	EXMOUTH JCN - 72A	EXMOUTH JCN - 72A	EXMOUTH JCN - 72A	EXMOUTH JCN - 72A	EXMOUTH JCN - 72A
30584	EXMOUTH JCN - 72A	EXMOUTH JCN - 72A	EXMOUTH JCN - 72A	EXMOUTH JCN - 72A	EXMOUTH JCN - 72A	EXMOUTH JCN - 72A	EXMOUTH JCN - 72A
			H2 4-4-2 (1911)				
32421	BRIGHTON - 75A	BRIGHTON - 75A	BRIGHTON - 75A	W/D	W/D	W/D	W/D
32422	BRIGHTON - 75A (N)	BRIGHTON - 75A (N)	BRIGHTON - 75A (N)	BRIGHTON - 75A (N)	W/D	W/D	W/D
32424	BRIGHTON - 75A	BRIGHTON - 75A	BRIGHTON - 75A	BRIGHTON - 75A	BRIGHTON - 75A	BRIGHTON - 75A	BRIGHTON - 75A
32425	BRIGHTON - 75A	BRIGHTON - 75A	BRIGHTON - 75A	BRIGHTON - 75A	W/D	W/D	W/D
32426	BRIGHTON - 75A	BRIGHTON - 75A	BRIGHTON - 75A	W/D	W/D	W/D	W/D

loco	Mar-57	Jun-57	Jul-57	Oct-57	Jan-58	Feb-58	Mar-58
			'0415' 4-4-2T (1882)				
30582	EXMOUTH JCN - 72A	EXMOUTH JCN - 72A	EXMOUTH JCN - 72A	EXMOUTH JCN - 72A	EXMOUTH JCN - 72A	EXMOUTH JCN - 72A	EXMOUTH JCN - 72A
30583	EXMOUTH JCN - 72A	EXMOUTH JCN - 72A	EXMOUTH JCN - 72A	EXMOUTH JCN - 72A	EXMOUTH JCN - 72A	EXMOUTH JCN - 72A	EXMOUTH JCN - 72A
30584	EXMOUTH JCN - 72A	EXMOUTH JCN - 72A	EXMOUTH JCN - 72A	EXMOUTH JCN - 72A	EXMOUTH JCN - 72A	EXMOUTH JCN - 72A	EXMOUTH JCN - 72A
			H2 4-4-2 (1911)				
32424	BRIGHTON - 75A	BRIGHTON - 75A	BRIGHTON - 75A	BRIGHTON - 75A	BRIGHTON - 75A	BRIGHTON - 75A	BRIGHTON - 75A

loco	May-58	Oct-58	Mar-59	Jun-59	Jul-59	Aug-59	Oct-59
			'0415' 4-4-2T (1882)				
30582	EXMOUTH JCN - 72A	EXMOUTH JCN - 72A	EXMOUTH JCN - 72A	EXMOUTH JCN - 72A	EXMOUTH JCN - 72A	EXMOUTH JCN - 72A	EXMOUTH JCN - 72A
30583	EXMOUTH JCN - 72A	EXMOUTH JCN - 72A	EXMOUTH JCN - 72A	EXMOUTH JCN - 72A	EXMOUTH JCN - 72A	EXMOUTH JCN - 72A	EXMOUTH JCN - 72A
30584	EXMOUTH JCN - 72A	EXMOUTH JCN - 72A	EXMOUTH JCN - 72A	EXMOUTH JCN - 72A	EXMOUTH JCN - 72A	EXMOUTH JCN - 72A	EXMOUTH JCN - 72A

loco	Dec-59	Feb-60	Mar-60	Apr-60	Jul-60	Aug-60	Sep-60	Nov-60
				'0415' 4-4-2T (1882)				
30582	EXMOUTH JCN - 72A	EXMOUTH JCN - 72A	EXMOUTH JCN - 72A	EXMOUTH JCN - 72A	EXMOUTH JCN - 72A	EXMOUTH JCN - 72A	EXMOUTH JCN - 72A	EXMOUTH JCN - 72A
30583	EXMOUTH JCN - 72A	EXMOUTH JCN - 72A	EXMOUTH JCN - 72A	EXMOUTH JCN - 72A	EXMOUTH JCN - 72A	EXMOUTH JCN - 72A	EXMOUTH JCN - 72A	EXMOUTH JCN - 72A
30584	EXMOUTH JCN - 72A	EXMOUTH JCN - 72A	EXMOUTH JCN - 72A	EXMOUTH JCN - 72A	EXMOUTH JCN - 72A	EXMOUTH JCN - 72A	EXMOUTH JCN - 72A	EXMOUTH JCN - 72A

The Brighton Atlantics outlived their Great Northern forebears by a good half decade, existing mainly on the Victoria - Newhaven boat trains and - Brighton having appalling troubles with its Pacifics - deputising so frequently for a 4-6-2 on the through Brighton - Bournemouth express that for a time in 1956 an Atlantic was actually diagrammed for the duty. Booked into the working on 3rd September 1955, 32421 'South Foreland' is seen away from Brighton shed by the outside foreman.

D 4-4-0 (1901)

loco	May-49	Jun-49	Aug-49	Sep-49	Dec-49	Feb-50	Mar-50
31057	TONBRIDGE - 74D	TONBRIDGE - 74D	TONBRIDGE - 74D	READING (SR) - 70E	READING (SR) - 70E	READING (SR) - 70E	READING (SR) - 70E
31075	TONBRIDGE - 74D	READING (SR) - 70E	READING (SR) - 70E	READING (SR) - 70E	READING (SR) - 70E	READING (SR) - 70E	READING (SR) - 70E
31092	GILLINGHAM - 73D	GILLINGHAM - 73D	GILLINGHAM - 73D	GILLINGHAM - 73D	GILLINGHAM - 73D	GILLINGHAM - 73D	GILLINGHAM - 73D
31477	ASHFORD - 74A	ASHFORD - 74A	ASHFORD - 74A	ASHFORD - 74A	ASHFORD - 74A	ASHFORD - 74A	ASHFORD - 74A
31488	TONBRIDGE - 74D	TONBRIDGE - 74D	TONBRIDGE - 74D	TONBRIDGE - 74D	TONBRIDGE - 74D	TONBRIDGE - 74D	TONBRIDGE - 74D
31490	TONBRIDGE - 74D	TONBRIDGE - 74D	TONBRIDGE - 74D	TONBRIDGE - 74D	TONBRIDGE - 74D	TONBRIDGE - 74D	TONBRIDGE - 74D
31493	GILLINGHAM - 73D	GILLINGHAM - 73D	GILLINGHAM - 73D	GILLINGHAM - 73D	GILLINGHAM - 73D	ST LEONARDS - 74E	ST LEONARDS - 74E
31496	GILLINGHAM - 73D	GILLINGHAM - 73D	GILLINGHAM - 73D	GILLINGHAM - 73D	GILLINGHAM - 73D	GILLINGHAM - 73D	GILLINGHAM - 73D
31501	FAVERSHAM - 73E	FAVERSHAM - 73E	FAVERSHAM - 73E	FAVERSHAM - 73E	FAVERSHAM - 73E	FAVERSHAM - 73E	FAVERSHAM - 73E
31549	ASHFORD - 74A	ASHFORD - 74A	ASHFORD - 74A	ASHFORD - 74A	ASHFORD - 74A	ASHFORD - 74A	ASHFORD - 74A
31574	ASHFORD - 74A	ASHFORD - 74A	ASHFORD - 74A	ASHFORD - 74A	ASHFORD - 74A	ASHFORD - 74A	ASHFORD - 74A
31577	ASHFORD - 74A	ASHFORD - 74A	ASHFORD - 74A	ASHFORD - 74A	ASHFORD - 74A	ASHFORD - 74A	ASHFORD - 74A
31586	TONBRIDGE - 74D	TONBRIDGE - 74D	TONBRIDGE - 74D	TONBRIDGE - 74D	TONBRIDGE - 74D	TONBRIDGE - 74D	TONBRIDGE - 74D
31591	TONBRIDGE - 74D	TONBRIDGE - 74D	TONBRIDGE - 74D	TONBRIDGE - 74D	TONBRIDGE - 74D	TONBRIDGE - 74D	TONBRIDGE - 74D
31728	REDHILL - 75B	REDHILL - 75B	REDHILL - 75B	REDHILL - 75B	REDHILL - 75B	REDHILL - 75B	REDHILL - 75B
31729	GILLINGHAM - 73D	GILLINGHAM - 73D	GILLINGHAM - 73D	GILLINGHAM - 73D	GILLINGHAM - 73D	GILLINGHAM - 73D	GILLINGHAM - 73D
31730	TONBRIDGE - 74D	TONBRIDGE - 74D	TONBRIDGE - 74D	TONBRIDGE - 74D	TONBRIDGE - 74D	TONBRIDGE - 74D	TONBRIDGE - 74D
31731	TONBRIDGE - 74D	TONBRIDGE - 74D	TONBRIDGE - 74D	TONBRIDGE - 74D	TONBRIDGE - 74D	TONBRIDGE - 74D	TONBRIDGE - 74D
31732	HITHER GREEN - 73C	HITHER GREEN - 73C	HITHER GREEN - 73C	HITHER GREEN - 73C	HITHER GREEN - 73C	HITHER GREEN - 73C	HITHER GREEN - 73C
31733	TONBRIDGE - 74D	TONBRIDGE - 74D	TONBRIDGE - 74D	TONBRIDGE - 74D	TONBRIDGE - 74D	TONBRIDGE - 74D	TONBRIDGE - 74D
31734	TONBRIDGE - 74D	TONBRIDGE - 74D	TONBRIDGE - 74D	TONBRIDGE - 74D	TONBRIDGE - 74D	TONBRIDGE - 74D	TONBRIDGE - 74D
31737	ST LEONARDS - 74E	ST LEONARDS - 74E	ST LEONARDS - 74E	ST LEONARDS - 74E	ST LEONARDS - 74E	ST LEONARDS - 74E	ST LEONARDS - 74E
31738	ST LEONARDS - 74E	ST LEONARDS - 74E	ST LEONARDS - 74E	ST LEONARDS - 74E	ST LEONARDS - 74E	ST LEONARDS - 74E	ST LEONARDS - 74E
31740	TONBRIDGE - 74D	TONBRIDGE - 74D	READING (SR) - 70E	READING (SR) - 70E	READING (SR) - 70E	READING (SR) - 70E	READING (SR) - 70E
31744	ST LEONARDS - 74E	ST LEONARDS - 74E	ST LEONARDS - 74E	ST LEONARDS - 74E	ST LEONARDS - 74E	ST LEONARDS - 74E	ST LEONARDS - 74E
31746	TONBRIDGE - 74D	TONBRIDGE - 74D	TONBRIDGE - 74D	TONBRIDGE - 74D	TONBRIDGE - 74D	TONBRIDGE - 74D	TONBRIDGE - 74D
31748	ASHFORD - 74A	ASHFORD - 74A	ASHFORD - 74A	ASHFORD - 74A	ASHFORD - 74A	ASHFORD - 74A	ASHFORD - 74A
31750	TONBRIDGE - 74D	TONBRIDGE - 74D	TONBRIDGE - 74D	TONBRIDGE - 74D	TONBRIDGE - 74D	TONBRIDGE - 74D	TONBRIDGE - 74D

D1 4-4-0 (1921)

loco	May-49	Jun-49	Aug-49	Sep-49	Dec-49	Feb-50	Mar-50
31145	STEWARTS LANE - 73A	STEWARTS LANE - 73A	STEWARTS LANE - 73A	STEWARTS LANE - 73A	STEWARTS LANE - 73A	STEWARTS LANE - 73A	STEWARTS LANE - 73A
31246	TONBRIDGE - 74D	TONBRIDGE - 74D	TONBRIDGE - 74D	TONBRIDGE - 74D	TONBRIDGE - 74D	TONBRIDGE - 74D	TONBRIDGE - 74D
31247	DOVER - 74C	DOVER - 74C	DOVER - 74C	DOVER - 74C	DOVER - 74C	DOVER - 74C	DOVER - 74C
31470	DOVER - 74C	DOVER - 74C	DOVER - 74C	DOVER - 74C	DOVER - 74C	DOVER - 74C	DOVER - 74C
31487	FAVERSHAM - 73E	FAVERSHAM - 73E	FAVERSHAM - 73E	FAVERSHAM - 73E	FAVERSHAM - 73E	FAVERSHAM - 73E	FAVERSHAM - 73E
31489	FAVERSHAM - 73E	FAVERSHAM - 73E	FAVERSHAM - 73E	FAVERSHAM - 73E	FAVERSHAM - 73E	FAVERSHAM - 73E	FAVERSHAM - 73E
31492	GILLINGHAM - 73D	GILLINGHAM - 73D	GILLINGHAM - 73D	GILLINGHAM - 73D	GILLINGHAM - 73D	GILLINGHAM - 73D	GILLINGHAM - 73D
31494	GILLINGHAM - 73D	GILLINGHAM - 73D	GILLINGHAM - 73D	GILLINGHAM - 73D	GILLINGHAM - 73D	GILLINGHAM - 73D	GILLINGHAM - 73D
31502	FAVERSHAM - 73E	FAVERSHAM - 73E	FAVERSHAM - 73E	FAVERSHAM - 73E	FAVERSHAM - 73E	FAVERSHAM - 73E	FAVERSHAM - 73E
31505	FAVERSHAM - 73E	FAVERSHAM - 73E	FAVERSHAM - 73E	FAVERSHAM - 73E	FAVERSHAM - 73E	FAVERSHAM - 73E	FAVERSHAM - 73E
31509	FAVERSHAM - 73E	FAVERSHAM - 73E	FAVERSHAM - 73E	FAVERSHAM - 73E	FAVERSHAM - 73E	FAVERSHAM - 73E	TONBRIDGE - 74D
31545	DOVER - 74C	DOVER - 74C	DOVER - 74C	DOVER - 74C	DOVER - 74C	DOVER - 74C	DOVER - 74C
31727	FAVERSHAM - 73E	FAVERSHAM - 73E	FAVERSHAM - 73E	FAVERSHAM - 73E	FAVERSHAM - 73E	FAVERSHAM - 73E	FAVERSHAM - 73E
31735	STEWARTS LANE - 73A	STEWARTS LANE - 73A	STEWARTS LANE - 73A	DOVER - 74C	DOVER - 74C	DOVER - 74C	DOVER - 74C
31736	DOVER - 74C	DOVER - 74C	DOVER - 74C	DOVER - 74C	DOVER - 74C	DOVER - 74C	DOVER - 74C
31739	FAVERSHAM - 73E	FAVERSHAM - 73E	FAVERSHAM - 73E	FAVERSHAM - 73E	FAVERSHAM - 73E	FAVERSHAM - 73E	FAVERSHAM - 73E
31741	FAVERSHAM - 73E	FAVERSHAM - 73E	FAVERSHAM - 73E	FAVERSHAM - 73E	FAVERSHAM - 73E	FAVERSHAM - 73E	FAVERSHAM - 73E
31743	TONBRIDGE - 74D	STEWARTS LANE - 73A	STEWARTS LANE - 73A	STEWARTS LANE - 73A	STEWARTS LANE - 73A	STEWARTS LANE - 73A	STEWARTS LANE - 73A
31745	TONBRIDGE - 74D	TONBRIDGE - 74D	TONBRIDGE - 74D	TONBRIDGE - 74D	TONBRIDGE - 74D	TONBRIDGE - 74D	TONBRIDGE - 74D
31749	STEWARTS LANE - 73A	STEWARTS LANE - 73A	STEWARTS LANE - 73A	STEWARTS LANE - 73A	STEWARTS LANE - 73A	STEWARTS LANE - 73A	STEWARTS LANE - 73A

D15 4-4-0 (1912)

loco	May-49	Jun-49	Aug-49	Sep-49	Dec-49	Feb-50	Mar-50
30463	EASTLEIGH - 71A	EASTLEIGH - 71A	EASTLEIGH - 71A	EASTLEIGH - 71A	EASTLEIGH - 71A	EASTLEIGH - 71A	EASTLEIGH - 71A
30464	EASTLEIGH - 71A	EASTLEIGH - 71A	EASTLEIGH - 71A	EASTLEIGH - 71A	EASTLEIGH - 71A	EASTLEIGH - 71A	EASTLEIGH - 71A
30465	EASTLEIGH - 71A	EASTLEIGH - 71A	EASTLEIGH - 71A	EASTLEIGH - 71A	EASTLEIGH - 71A	EASTLEIGH - 71A	EASTLEIGH - 71A
30466	EASTLEIGH - 71A	EASTLEIGH - 71A	EASTLEIGH - 71A	EASTLEIGH - 71A	EASTLEIGH - 71A	EASTLEIGH - 71A	EASTLEIGH - 71A
30467	EASTLEIGH - 71A	EASTLEIGH - 71A	EASTLEIGH - 71A	EASTLEIGH - 71A	EASTLEIGH - 71A	EASTLEIGH - 71A	EASTLEIGH - 71A
30468	EASTLEIGH - 71A	EASTLEIGH - 71A	EASTLEIGH - 71A	EASTLEIGH - 71A	EASTLEIGH - 71A	EASTLEIGH - 71A	EASTLEIGH - 71A
30469	EASTLEIGH - 71A	EASTLEIGH - 71A	EASTLEIGH - 71A	EASTLEIGH - 71A	EASTLEIGH - 71A	EASTLEIGH - 71A	EASTLEIGH - 71A
30470	EASTLEIGH - 71A	EASTLEIGH - 71A	EASTLEIGH - 71A	EASTLEIGH - 71A	EASTLEIGH - 71A	EASTLEIGH - 71A	EASTLEIGH - 71A
30471	EASTLEIGH - 71A	EASTLEIGH - 71A	EASTLEIGH - 71A	EASTLEIGH - 71A	EASTLEIGH - 71A	EASTLEIGH - 71A	EASTLEIGH - 71A
30472	EASTLEIGH - 71A	EASTLEIGH - 71A	EASTLEIGH - 71A	EASTLEIGH - 71A	EASTLEIGH - 71A	EASTLEIGH - 71A	EASTLEIGH - 71A

E 4-4-0 (1905)

loco	May-49	Jun-49	Aug-49	Sep-49	Dec-49	Feb-50	Mar-50
31036	B ARMS - 73B	B ARMS - 73B	B ARMS - 73B	B ARMS - 73B	B ARMS - 73B	B ARMS - 73B	B ARMS - 73B
31157	B ARMS - 73B	B ARMS - 73B	B ARMS - 73B	B ARMS - 73B	B ARMS - 73B	B ARMS - 73B	B ARMS - 73B
31159	B ARMS - 73B	B ARMS - 73B	B ARMS - 73B	B ARMS - 73B	B ARMS - 73B	B ARMS - 73B	B ARMS - 73B
31166	B ARMS - 73B	B ARMS - 73B	B ARMS - 73B	B ARMS - 73B	B ARMS - 73B	B ARMS - 73B	B ARMS - 73B
31175	B ARMS - 73B	B ARMS - 73B	B ARMS - 73B	B ARMS - 73B	B ARMS - 73B	B ARMS - 73B	B ARMS - 73B
31176	B ARMS - 73B	B ARMS - 73B	B ARMS - 73B	B ARMS - 73B	B ARMS - 73B	B ARMS - 73B	B ARMS - 73B
31273	B ARMS - 73B	FAVERSHAM - 73E	FAVERSHAM - 73E	FAVERSHAM - 73E	FAVERSHAM - 73E	FAVERSHAM - 73E	FAVERSHAM - 73E
31275	B ARMS - 73B	B ARMS - 73B	B ARMS - 73B	B ARMS - 73B	B ARMS - 73B	B ARMS - 73B	B ARMS - 73B
31315	B ARMS - 73B	B ARMS - 73B	B ARMS - 73B	B ARMS - 73B	B ARMS - 73B	B ARMS - 73B	B ARMS - 73B
31491	B ARMS - 73B	B ARMS - 73B	B ARMS - 73B	B ARMS - 73B	B ARMS - 73B	B ARMS - 73B	B ARMS - 73B
31514	ASHFORD - 74A	ASHFORD - 74A	ASHFORD - 74A	ASHFORD - 74A	ASHFORD - 74A	ASHFORD - 74A	ASHFORD - 74A
31515	STEWARTS LANE - 73A	STEWARTS LANE - 73A	STEWARTS LANE - 73A	STEWARTS LANE - 73A	STEWARTS LANE - 73A	READING (SR) - 70E	READING (SR) - 70E
31516	ASHFORD - 74A	ASHFORD - 74A	ASHFORD - 74A	ASHFORD - 74A	ASHFORD - 74A	GILLINGHAM - 73D	GILLINGHAM - 73D
31547	B ARMS - 73B	B ARMS - 73B	B ARMS - 73B	B ARMS - 73B	B ARMS - 73B	B ARMS - 73B	B ARMS - 73B
31587	HITHER GREEN - 73C	HITHER GREEN - 73C	HITHER GREEN - 73C	HITHER GREEN - 73C	HITHER GREEN - 73C	HITHER GREEN - 73C	HITHER GREEN - 73C

E1 4-4-0 (1919)

loco	May-49	Jun-49	Aug-49	Sep-49	Dec-49	Feb-50	Mar-50
31019	STEWARTS LANE - 73A	STEWARTS LANE - 73A	STEWARTS LANE - 73A	STEWARTS LANE - 73A	STEWARTS LANE - 73A	STEWARTS LANE - 73A	STEWARTS LANE - 73A
31067	STEWARTS LANE - 73A	STEWARTS LANE - 73A	STEWARTS LANE - 73A	STEWARTS LANE - 73A	STEWARTS LANE - 73A	STEWARTS LANE - 73A	STEWARTS LANE - 73A
31160	B ARMS - 73B	B ARMS - 73B	B ARMS - 73B	B ARMS - 73B	B ARMS - 73B	B ARMS - 73B	B ARMS - 73B
31163	B ARMS - 73B	W/D	W/D	W/D	W/D	W/D	W/D
31165	B ARMS - 73B	B ARMS - 73B	B ARMS - 73B	B ARMS - 73B	B ARMS - 73B	B ARMS - 73B	B ARMS - 73B
31179	B ARMS - 73B	B ARMS - 73B	B ARMS - 73B	B ARMS - 73B	B ARMS - 73B	B ARMS - 73B	B ARMS - 73B
31497	STEWARTS LANE - 73A	B ARMS - 73B	B ARMS - 73B	B ARMS - 73B	B ARMS - 73B	B ARMS - 73B	B ARMS - 73B
31504	STEWARTS LANE - 73A	STEWARTS LANE - 73A	STEWARTS LANE - 73A	STEWARTS LANE - 73A	STEWARTS LANE - 73A	STEWARTS LANE - 73A	STEWARTS LANE - 73A
31506	STEWARTS LANE - 73A	STEWARTS LANE - 73A	STEWARTS LANE - 73A	STEWARTS LANE - 73A	STEWARTS LANE - 73A	STEWARTS LANE - 73A	STEWARTS LANE - 73A
31507	B ARMS - 73B	B ARMS - 73B	B ARMS - 73B	B ARMS - 73B	B ARMS - 73B	B ARMS - 73B	B ARMS - 73B
31511	STEWARTS LANE - 73A	B ARMS - 73B	B ARMS - 73B	B ARMS - 73B	B ARMS - 73B	B ARMS - 73B	B ARMS - 73B

loco	Apr-50	Sep-50	Oct-50	Nov-50	Dec-50	Mar-51	Apr-51
D 4-4-0 (1901)

D 4-4-0 (1901)

loco	Apr-50	Sep-50	Oct-50	Nov-50	Dec-50	Mar-51	Apr-51
31057	READING (SR) - 70E	READING (SR) - 70E	READING (SR) - 70E	READING (SR) - 70E	READING (SR) - 70E	READING (SR) - 70E	W/D
31075	READING (SR) - 70E	READING (SR) - 70E	READING (SR) - 70E	READING (SR) - 70E	READING (SR) - 70E	READING (SR) - 70E	READING (SR) - 70E
31092	GILLINGHAM - 73D	GILLINGHAM - 73D	GILLINGHAM - 73D	GILLINGHAM - 73D	GILLINGHAM - 73D	GILLINGHAM - 73D	GILLINGHAM - 73D
31477	ASHFORD - 74A	ASHFORD - 74A	ASHFORD - 74A	ASHFORD - 74A	W/D	W/D	W/D
31488	TONBRIDGE - 74D	B.ARMS - 73B	B.ARMS - 73B	B.ARMS - 73B	B.ARMS - 73B	B.ARMS - 73B	B.ARMS - 73B
31490	TONBRIDGE - 74D	B.ARMS - 73B	B.ARMS - 73B	B.ARMS - 73B	B.ARMS - 73B	B.ARMS - 73B	B.ARMS - 73B
31493	ST LEONARDS - 74E	ST LEONARDS - 74E	ST LEONARDS - 74E	ST LEONARDS - 74E	ST LEONARDS - 74E	ST LEONARDS - 74E	ST LEONARDS - 74E
31496	GILLINGHAM - 73D	TONBRIDGE - 74D	TONBRIDGE - 74D	TONBRIDGE - 74D	ST LEONARDS - 74E	ST LEONARDS - 74E	ST LEONARDS - 74E
31501	FAVERSHAM - 73E	FAVERSHAM - 73E	FAVERSHAM - 73E	FAVERSHAM - 73E	FAVERSHAM - 73E	FAVERSHAM - 73E	FAVERSHAM - 73E
31549	ASHFORD - 74A	TONBRIDGE - 74D	TONBRIDGE - 74D	TONBRIDGE - 74D	TONBRIDGE - 74D	TONBRIDGE - 74D	TONBRIDGE - 74D
31574	ASHFORD - 74A	ASHFORD - 74A	ASHFORD - 74A	ASHFORD - 74A	ASHFORD - 74A	ASHFORD - 74A	ASHFORD - 74A
31577	ASHFORD - 74A	ASHFORD - 74A	ASHFORD - 74A	ASHFORD - 74A	ASHFORD - 74A	ASHFORD - 74A	ASHFORD - 74A
31586	TONBRIDGE - 74D	FAVERSHAM - 73E	FAVERSHAM - 73E	FAVERSHAM - 73E	FAVERSHAM - 73E	FAVERSHAM - 73E	FAVERSHAM - 73E
31591	B.ARMS - 73B	B.ARMS - 73B	B.ARMS - 73B	B.ARMS - 73B	B.ARMS - 73B	B.ARMS - 73B	B.ARMS - 73B
31728	B.ARMS - 73B	TONBRIDGE - 74D	TONBRIDGE - 74D	TONBRIDGE - 74D	TONBRIDGE - 74D	TONBRIDGE - 74D	TONBRIDGE - 74D
31729	GILLINGHAM - 73D	GILLINGHAM - 73D	GILLINGHAM - 73D	GILLINGHAM - 73D	TONBRIDGE - 74D	TONBRIDGE - 74D	TONBRIDGE - 74D
31730	TONBRIDGE - 74D	TONBRIDGE - 74D	TONBRIDGE - 74D	TONBRIDGE - 74D	TONBRIDGE - 74D	W/D	W/D
31731	TONBRIDGE - 74D	TONBRIDGE - 74D	TONBRIDGE - 74D	TONBRIDGE - 74D	TONBRIDGE - 74D	TONBRIDGE - 74D	TONBRIDGE - 74D
31732	HITHER GREEN - 73C	HITHER GREEN - 73C	HITHER GREEN - 73C	HITHER GREEN - 73C	TONBRIDGE - 74D	TONBRIDGE - 74D	TONBRIDGE - 74D
31733	B.ARMS - 73B	TONBRIDGE - 74D	TONBRIDGE - 74D	TONBRIDGE - 74D	TONBRIDGE - 74D	TONBRIDGE - 74D	TONBRIDGE - 74D
31734	TONBRIDGE - 74D	FAVERSHAM - 73E	FAVERSHAM - 73E	FAVERSHAM - 73E	FAVERSHAM - 73E	FAVERSHAM - 73E	FAVERSHAM - 73E
31737	DOVER - 74C	DOVER - 74C	DOVER - 74C	DOVER - 74C	DOVER - 74C	DOVER - 74C	READING (SR) - 70E
31738	ST LEONARDS - 74E	ST LEONARDS - 74E	W/D	W/D	W/D	W/D	W/D
31740	READING (SR) - 70E	READING (SR) - 70E	READING (SR) - 70E	READING (SR) - 70E	READING (SR) - 70E	W/D	W/D
31744	ST LEONARDS - 74E	READING (SR) - 70E	READING (SR) - 70E	READING (SR) - 70E	READING (SR) - 70E	READING (SR) - 70E	READING (SR) - 70E
31746	TONBRIDGE - 74D	B.ARMS - 73B	B.ARMS - 73B	B.ARMS - 73B	B.ARMS - 73B	B.ARMS - 73B	B.ARMS - 73B
31748	ASHFORD - 74A	ASHFORD - 74A	ASHFORD - 74A	RAMSGATE - 74B	FAVERSHAM - 73E	W/D	W/D
31750	STEWARTS LANE - 73A	READING (SR) - 70E	READING (SR) - 70E	READING (SR) - 70E	READING (SR) - 70E	READING (SR) - 70E	READING (SR) - 70E

D1 4-4-0 (1921)

loco	Apr-50	Sep-50	Oct-50	Nov-50	Dec-50	Mar-51	Apr-51
31145	STEWARTS LANE - 73A	STEWARTS LANE - 73A	STEWARTS LANE - 73A	STEWARTS LANE - 73A	STEWARTS LANE - 73A	STEWARTS LANE - 73A	STEWARTS LANE - 73A
31246	TONBRIDGE - 74D	TONBRIDGE - 74D	TONBRIDGE - 74D	TONBRIDGE - 74D	DOVER - 74C	DOVER - 74C	DOVER - 74C
31247	DOVER - 74C	DOVER - 74C	DOVER - 74C	DOVER - 74C	DOVER - 74C	DOVER - 74C	DOVER - 74C
31470	DOVER - 74C	DOVER - 74C	DOVER - 74C	DOVER - 74C	DOVER - 74C	DOVER - 74C	DOVER - 74C
31487	STEWARTS LANE - 73A	STEWARTS LANE - 73A	STEWARTS LANE - 73A	STEWARTS LANE - 73A	FAVERSHAM - 73E	FAVERSHAM - 73E	FAVERSHAM - 73E
31489	FAVERSHAM - 73E	FAVERSHAM - 73E	FAVERSHAM - 73E	FAVERSHAM - 73E	FAVERSHAM - 73E	FAVERSHAM - 73E	FAVERSHAM - 73E
31492	GILLINGHAM - 73D	GILLINGHAM - 73D	GILLINGHAM - 73D	GILLINGHAM - 73D	GILLINGHAM - 73D	GILLINGHAM - 73D	GILLINGHAM - 73D
31494	GILLINGHAM - 73D	GILLINGHAM - 73D	GILLINGHAM - 73D	GILLINGHAM - 73D	FAVERSHAM - 73E	FAVERSHAM - 73E	FAVERSHAM - 73E
31502	FAVERSHAM - 73E	FAVERSHAM - 73E	FAVERSHAM - 73E	FAVERSHAM - 73E	FAVERSHAM - 73E	W/D	W/D
31505	FAVERSHAM - 73E	FAVERSHAM - 73E	FAVERSHAM - 73E	FAVERSHAM - 73E	FAVERSHAM - 73E	FAVERSHAM - 73E	FAVERSHAM - 73E
31509	TONBRIDGE - 74D	TONBRIDGE - 74D	TONBRIDGE - 74D	TONBRIDGE - 74D	TONBRIDGE - 74D	TONBRIDGE - 74D	FAVERSHAM - 73E
31545	DOVER - 74C	DOVER - 74C	DOVER - 74C	DOVER - 74C	TONBRIDGE - 74D	TONBRIDGE - 74D	FAVERSHAM - 73E
31727	FAVERSHAM - 73E	FAVERSHAM - 73E	FAVERSHAM - 73E	FAVERSHAM - 73E	FAVERSHAM - 73E	FAVERSHAM - 73E	TONBRIDGE - 74D
31735	DOVER - 74C	DOVER - 74C	DOVER - 74C	DOVER - 74C	GILLINGHAM - 73D	GILLINGHAM - 73D	TONBRIDGE - 74D
31736	DOVER - 74C	ASHFORD - 74A	ASHFORD - 74A	ASHFORD - 74A	W/D	W/D	W/D
31739	FAVERSHAM - 73E	FAVERSHAM - 73E	FAVERSHAM - 73E	FAVERSHAM - 73E	FAVERSHAM - 73E	FAVERSHAM - 73E	FAVERSHAM - 73E
31741	FAVERSHAM - 73E	FAVERSHAM - 73E	FAVERSHAM - 73E	FAVERSHAM - 73E	FAVERSHAM - 73E	FAVERSHAM - 73E	FAVERSHAM - 73E
31743	STEWARTS LANE - 73A	STEWARTS LANE - 73A	STEWARTS LANE - 73A	STEWARTS LANE - 73A	STEWARTS LANE - 73A	STEWARTS LANE - 73A	STEWARTS LANE - 73A
31745	TONBRIDGE - 74D	TONBRIDGE - 74D	TONBRIDGE - 74D	TONBRIDGE - 74D	STEWARTS LANE - 73A	W/D	W/D
31749	STEWARTS LANE - 73A	STEWARTS LANE - 73A	STEWARTS LANE - 73A	STEWARTS LANE - 73A	STEWARTS LANE - 73A	STEWARTS LANE - 73A	STEWARTS LANE - 73A

D15 4-4-0 (1912)

loco	Apr-50	Sep-50	Oct-50	Nov-50	Dec-50	Mar-51	Apr-51
30463	EASTLEIGH - 71A	EASTLEIGH - 71A	EASTLEIGH - 71A	EASTLEIGH - 71A	EASTLEIGH - 71A	EASTLEIGH - 71A	EASTLEIGH - 71A
30464	EASTLEIGH - 71A	EASTLEIGH - 71A	EASTLEIGH - 71A	EASTLEIGH - 71A	EASTLEIGH - 71A	EASTLEIGH - 71A	EASTLEIGH - 71A
30465	EASTLEIGH - 71A	EASTLEIGH - 71A	EASTLEIGH - 71A	EASTLEIGH - 71A	EASTLEIGH - 71A	EASTLEIGH - 71A	EASTLEIGH - 71A
30466	EASTLEIGH - 71A	EASTLEIGH - 71A	EASTLEIGH - 71A	EASTLEIGH - 71A	EASTLEIGH - 71A	EASTLEIGH - 71A	EASTLEIGH - 71A
30467	EASTLEIGH - 71A	EASTLEIGH - 71A	EASTLEIGH - 71A	EASTLEIGH - 71A	EASTLEIGH - 71A	EASTLEIGH - 71A	EASTLEIGH - 71A
30468	EASTLEIGH - 71A	EASTLEIGH - 71A	EASTLEIGH - 71A	EASTLEIGH - 71A	EASTLEIGH - 71A	EASTLEIGH - 71A	EASTLEIGH - 71A
30469	EASTLEIGH - 71A	EASTLEIGH - 71A	EASTLEIGH - 71A	EASTLEIGH - 71A	EASTLEIGH - 71A	EASTLEIGH - 71A	EASTLEIGH - 71A
30470	EASTLEIGH - 71A	EASTLEIGH - 71A	EASTLEIGH - 71A	EASTLEIGH - 71A	EASTLEIGH - 71A	EASTLEIGH - 71A	EASTLEIGH - 71A
30471	EASTLEIGH - 71A	EASTLEIGH - 71A	EASTLEIGH - 71A	EASTLEIGH - 71A	EASTLEIGH - 71A	EASTLEIGH - 71A	EASTLEIGH - 71A
30472	EASTLEIGH - 71A	EASTLEIGH - 71A	EASTLEIGH - 71A	EASTLEIGH - 71A	EASTLEIGH - 71A	EASTLEIGH - 71A	EASTLEIGH - 71A

E 4-4-0 (1905)

loco	Apr-50	Sep-50	Oct-50	Nov-50	Dec-50	Mar-51	Apr-51
31036	B.ARMS - 73B	B.ARMS - 73B	B.ARMS - 73B	B.ARMS - 73B	B.ARMS - 73B	W/D	W/D
31157	FAVERSHAM - 73E	FAVERSHAM - 73E	FAVERSHAM - 73E	FAVERSHAM - 73E	FAVERSHAM - 73E	W/D	W/D
31159	B.ARMS - 73B	HITHER GREEN - 73C	HITHER GREEN - 73C	HITHER GREEN - 73C	HITHER GREEN - 73C	HITHER GREEN - 73C	HITHER GREEN - 73C
31166	B.ARMS - 73B	B.ARMS - 73B	B.ARMS - 73B	B.ARMS - 73B	B.ARMS - 73B	B.ARMS - 73B	B.ARMS - 73B
31175	B.ARMS - 73B	B.ARMS - 73B	B.ARMS - 73B	B.ARMS - 73B	B.ARMS - 73B	B.ARMS - 73B	B.ARMS - 73B
31176	B.ARMS - 73B	B.ARMS - 73B	B.ARMS - 73B	B.ARMS - 73B	B.ARMS - 73B	B.ARMS - 73B	B.ARMS - 73B
31273	B.ARMS - 73B	B.ARMS - 73B	B.ARMS - 73B	B.ARMS - 73B	B.ARMS - 73B	B.ARMS - 73B	B.ARMS - 73B
31275	B.ARMS - 73B	B.ARMS - 73B	B.ARMS - 73B	B.ARMS - 73B	B.ARMS - 73B	W/D	W/D
31315	B.ARMS - 73B	B.ARMS - 73B	B.ARMS - 73B	B.ARMS - 73B	B.ARMS - 73B	B.ARMS - 73B	B.ARMS - 73B
31491	B.ARMS - 73B	B.ARMS - 73B	B.ARMS - 73B	B.ARMS - 73B	B.ARMS - 73B	B.ARMS - 73B	B.ARMS - 73B
31514	ASHFORD - 74A	ASHFORD - 74A	ASHFORD - 74A	ASHFORD - 74A	ASHFORD - 74A	ASHFORD - 74A	ASHFORD - 74A
31515	READING (SR) - 70E	READING (SR) - 70E	READING (SR) - 70E	READING (SR) - 70E	READING (SR) - 70E	READING (SR) - 70E	READING (SR) - 70E
31516	GILLINGHAM - 73D	GILLINGHAM - 73D	GILLINGHAM - 73D	GILLINGHAM - 73D	ASHFORD - 74A	ASHFORD - 74A	ASHFORD - 74A
31547	B.ARMS - 73B	B.ARMS - 73B	B.ARMS - 73B	B.ARMS - 73B	W/D	W/D	W/D
31587	B.ARMS - 73B	ST LEONARDS - 74E	ST LEONARDS - 74E	ST LEONARDS - 74E	ST LEONARDS - 74E	ST LEONARDS - 74E	ST LEONARDS - 74E

E1 4-4-0 (1919)

loco	Apr-50	Sep-50	Oct-50	Nov-50	Dec-50	Mar-51	Apr-51
31019	STEWARTS LANE - 73A	STEWARTS LANE - 73A	STEWARTS LANE - 73A	STEWARTS LANE - 73A	STEWARTS LANE - 73A	STEWARTS LANE - 73A	STEWARTS LANE - 73A
31067	STEWARTS LANE - 73A	STEWARTS LANE - 73A	STEWARTS LANE - 73A	STEWARTS LANE - 73A	STEWARTS LANE - 73A	STEWARTS LANE - 73A	STEWARTS LANE - 73A
31160	B.ARMS - 73B	B.ARMS - 73B	B.ARMS - 73B	B.ARMS - 73B	B.ARMS - 73B	B.ARMS - 73B	B.ARMS - 73B
31165	STEWARTS LANE - 73A	STEWARTS LANE - 73A	STEWARTS LANE - 73A	STEWARTS LANE - 73A	B.ARMS - 73B	B.ARMS - 73B	B.ARMS - 73B
31179	B.ARMS - 73B	B.ARMS - 73B	B.ARMS - 73B	B.ARMS - 73B	W/D	W/D	W/D
31497	STEWARTS LANE - 73A	B.ARMS - 73B	B.ARMS - 73B	B.ARMS - 73B	B.ARMS - 73B	B.ARMS - 73B	B.ARMS - 73B
31504	STEWARTS LANE - 73A	STEWARTS LANE - 73A	STEWARTS LANE - 73A	STEWARTS LANE - 73A	STEWARTS LANE - 73A	STEWARTS LANE - 73A	STEWARTS LANE - 73A
31506	STEWARTS LANE - 73A	STEWARTS LANE - 73A	STEWARTS LANE - 73A	STEWARTS LANE - 73A	STEWARTS LANE - 73A	STEWARTS LANE - 73A	STEWARTS LANE - 73A
31507	B.ARMS - 73B	B.ARMS - 73B	B.ARMS - 73B	B.ARMS - 73B	B.ARMS - 73B	B.ARMS - 73B	B.ARMS - 73B
31511	B.ARMS - 73B	B.ARMS - 73B	B.ARMS - 73B	B.ARMS - 73B	W/D	W/D	W/D

loco	Jun-51	Jul-51	Sep-51	Dec-51	Jan-52	Mar-52	Jun-52
				D 4-4-0 (1901)			
31075	READING (SR) - 70E	READING (SR) - 70E	READING (SR) - 70E	READING (SR) - 70E	READING (SR) - 70E	READING (SR) - 70E	READING (SR) - 70E
31488	GILLINGHAM - 73D	GILLINGHAM - 73D	GILLINGHAM - 73D	READING (SR) - 70E	READING (SR) - 70E	READING (SR) - 70E	READING (SR) - 70E
31490	B.ARMS - 73B	B.ARMS - 73B	W/D	W/D	W/D	W/D	W/D
31493	ST LEONARDS - 74E	ST LEONARDS - 74E	ST LEONARDS - 74E	ST LEONARDS - 74E	ST LEONARDS - 74E	ST LEONARDS - 74E	ST LEONARDS - 74E
31496	ST LEONARDS - 74E	ST LEONARDS - 74E	ST LEONARDS - 74E	ST LEONARDS - 74E	ST LEONARDS - 74E	ST LEONARDS - 74E	ST LEONARDS - 74E
31501	FAVERSHAM - 73E	FAVERSHAM - 73E	FAVERSHAM - 73E	HITHER GREEN - 73C	GILLINGHAM - 73D	GILLINGHAM - 73D	GILLINGHAM - 73D
31549	TONBRIDGE - 74D	TONBRIDGE - 74D	TONBRIDGE - 74D	TONBRIDGE - 74D	TONBRIDGE - 74D	TONBRIDGE - 74D	TONBRIDGE - 74D
31574	ASHFORD - 74A	ASHFORD - 74A	ASHFORD - 74A	ASHFORD - 74A	ASHFORD - 74A	ASHFORD - 74A	ASHFORD - 74A
31577	ASHFORD - 74A	REDHILL - 75B	REDHILL - 75B	ASHFORD - 74A	ASHFORD - 74A	ASHFORD - 74A	ASHFORD - 74A
31586	GILLINGHAM - 73D	REDHILL - 75B	TONBRIDGE - 74D	REDHILL - 75B	REDHILL - 75B	REDHILL - 75B	REDHILL - 75B
31591	FAVERSHAM - 73E	REDHILL - 75B	REDHILL - 75B	REDHILL - 75B	REDHILL - 75B	REDHILL - 75B	REDHILL - 75B
31728	TONBRIDGE - 74D	TONBRIDGE - 74D	TONBRIDGE - 74D	TONBRIDGE - 74D	TONBRIDGE - 74D	TONBRIDGE - 74D	TONBRIDGE - 74D
31729	TONBRIDGE - 74D	TONBRIDGE - 74D	TONBRIDGE - 74D	TONBRIDGE - 74D	TONBRIDGE - 74D	TONBRIDGE - 74D	TONBRIDGE - 74D
31732	TONBRIDGE - 74D	TONBRIDGE - 74D	W/D	W/D	W/D	W/D	W/D
31733	TONBRIDGE - 74D	TONBRIDGE - 74D	TONBRIDGE - 74D	TONBRIDGE - 74D	TONBRIDGE - 74D	TONBRIDGE - 74D	TONBRIDGE - 74D
31734	FAVERSHAM - 73E	FAVERSHAM - 73E	FAVERSHAM - 73E	FAVERSHAM - 73E	FAVERSHAM - 73E	FAVERSHAM - 73E	FAVERSHAM - 73E
31737	READING (SR) - 70E	READING (SR) - 70E	READING (SR) - 70E	READING (SR) - 70E	READING (SR) - 70E	READING (SR) - 70E	READING (SR) - 70E
31744	READING (SR) - 70E	READING (SR) - 70E	READING (SR) - 70E	READING (SR) - 70E	READING (SR) - 70E	READING (SR) - 70E	READING (SR) - 70E
31746	B.ARMS - 73B	B.ARMS - 73B	B.ARMS - 73B	B.ARMS - 73B	B.ARMS - 73B	B.ARMS - 73B	B.ARMS - 73B
31750	READING (SR) - 70E	READING (SR) - 70E	READING (SR) - 70E	READING (SR) - 70E	READING (SR) - 70E		
				D1 4-4-0 (1921)			
31145	DOVER - 74C	DOVER - 74C	DOVER - 74C	DOVER - 74C	DOVER - 74C	DOVER - 74C	DOVER - 74C
31246	DOVER - 74C	DOVER - 74C	DOVER - 74C	DOVER - 74C	DOVER - 74C	DOVER - 74C	DOVER - 74C
31247	DOVER - 74C	DOVER - 74C	DOVER - 74C	DOVER - 74C	DOVER - 74C	DOVER - 74C	DOVER - 74C
31470	DOVER - 74C	DOVER - 74C	DOVER - 74C	DOVER - 74C	DOVER - 74C	DOVER - 74C	DOVER - 74C
31487	FAVERSHAM - 73E	FAVERSHAM - 73E	FAVERSHAM - 73E	FAVERSHAM - 73E	FAVERSHAM - 73E	FAVERSHAM - 73E	FAVERSHAM - 73E
31489	FAVERSHAM - 73E	FAVERSHAM - 73E	FAVERSHAM - 73E	FAVERSHAM - 73E	FAVERSHAM - 73E	FAVERSHAM - 73E	FAVERSHAM - 73E
31492	GILLINGHAM - 73D	GILLINGHAM - 73D	GILLINGHAM - 73D	GILLINGHAM - 73D	GILLINGHAM - 73D	GILLINGHAM - 73D	GILLINGHAM - 73D
31494	FAVERSHAM - 73E	FAVERSHAM - 73E	FAVERSHAM - 73E	FAVERSHAM - 73E	FAVERSHAM - 73E	FAVERSHAM - 73E	FAVERSHAM - 73E
31505	ASHFORD - 74A	ASHFORD - 74A	ASHFORD - 74A	B.ARMS - 73B	B.ARMS - 73B	B.ARMS - 73B	FAVERSHAM - 73E
31509	FAVERSHAM - 73E	FAVERSHAM - 73E	FAVERSHAM - 73E	GILLINGHAM - 73D	GILLINGHAM - 73D	GILLINGHAM - 73D	GILLINGHAM - 73D
31545	FAVERSHAM - 73E	FAVERSHAM - 73E	FAVERSHAM - 73E	GILLINGHAM - 73D	GILLINGHAM - 73D	GILLINGHAM - 73D	GILLINGHAM - 73D
31727	TONBRIDGE - 74D	TONBRIDGE - 74D	TONBRIDGE - 74D	TONBRIDGE - 74D	TONBRIDGE - 74D	TONBRIDGE - 74D	TONBRIDGE - 74D
31735	ASHFORD - 74A	ASHFORD - 74A	ASHFORD - 74A	ASHFORD - 74A	ASHFORD - 74A	ASHFORD - 74A	TONBRIDGE - 74D
31739	FAVERSHAM - 73E	FAVERSHAM - 73E	TONBRIDGE - 74D	TONBRIDGE - 74D	TONBRIDGE - 74D	TONBRIDGE - 74D	TONBRIDGE - 74D
31741	FAVERSHAM - 73E	FAVERSHAM - 73E	FAVERSHAM - 73E	FAVERSHAM - 73E	FAVERSHAM - 73E	FAVERSHAM - 73E	FAVERSHAM - 73E
31743	STEWARTS LANE - 73A	STEWARTS LANE - 73A	STEWARTS LANE - 73A	STEWARTS LANE - 73A	STEWARTS LANE - 73A	STEWARTS LANE - 73A	STEWARTS LANE - 73A
31749	STEWARTS LANE - 73A	STEWARTS LANE - 73A	STEWARTS LANE - 73A	STEWARTS LANE - 73A	STEWARTS LANE - 73A	STEWARTS LANE - 73A	STEWARTS LANE - 73A
				D15 4-4-0 (1912)			
30463	EASTLEIGH - 71A	EASTLEIGH - 71A	EASTLEIGH - 71A	W/D	W/D	W/D	W/D
30464	EASTLEIGH - 71A	EASTLEIGH - 71A	EASTLEIGH - 71A	EASTLEIGH - 71A	EASTLEIGH - 71A	EASTLEIGH - 71A	EASTLEIGH - 71A
30465	EASTLEIGH - 71A	EASTLEIGH - 71A	EASTLEIGH - 71A	EASTLEIGH - 71A	EASTLEIGH - 71A	EASTLEIGH - 71A	EASTLEIGH - 71A
30466	EASTLEIGH - 71A	EASTLEIGH - 71A	EASTLEIGH - 71A	EASTLEIGH - 71A	EASTLEIGH - 71A	EASTLEIGH - 71A	EASTLEIGH - 71A
30467	EASTLEIGH - 71A	EASTLEIGH - 71A	EASTLEIGH - 71A	EASTLEIGH - 71A	EASTLEIGH - 71A	EASTLEIGH - 71A	EASTLEIGH - 71A
30468	EASTLEIGH - 71A	EASTLEIGH - 71A	EASTLEIGH - 71A	EASTLEIGH - 71A	EASTLEIGH - 71A	W/D	W/D
30469	EASTLEIGH - 71A	EASTLEIGH - 71A	EASTLEIGH - 71A	EASTLEIGH - 71A	W/D	W/D	W/D
30470	EASTLEIGH - 71A	EASTLEIGH - 71A	EASTLEIGH - 71A	EASTLEIGH - 71A	EASTLEIGH - 71A	EASTLEIGH - 71A	EASTLEIGH - 71A
30471	EASTLEIGH - 71A	EASTLEIGH - 71A	EASTLEIGH - 71A	EASTLEIGH - 71A	EASTLEIGH - 71A	EASTLEIGH - 71A	EASTLEIGH - 71A
30472	EASTLEIGH - 71A	EASTLEIGH - 71A	EASTLEIGH - 71A	EASTLEIGH - 71A	EASTLEIGH - 71A	W/D	W/D
				E 4-4-0 (1905)			
31159	HITHER GREEN - 73C	HITHER GREEN - 73C	HITHER GREEN - 73C	W/D	W/D	W/D	W/D
31166	B.ARMS - 73B	B.ARMS - 73B	B.ARMS - 73B	B.ARMS - 73B	B.ARMS - 73B	FAVERSHAM - 73E	FAVERSHAM - 73E
31175	B.ARMS - 73B	B.ARMS - 73B	W/D	W/D	W/D	W/D	W/D
31176	B.ARMS - 73B	B.ARMS - 73B	W/D				
31273	B.ARMS - 73B	B.ARMS - 73B	B.ARMS - 73B	W/D	W/D	W/D	W/D
31315	B.ARMS - 73B	B.ARMS - 73B	B.ARMS - 73B	B.ARMS - 73B	B.ARMS - 73B	FAVERSHAM - 73E	FAVERSHAM - 73E
31491	B.ARMS - 73B	READING (SR) - 70E	READING (SR) - 70E	REDHILL - 75B	REDHILL - 75B	REDHILL - 75B	REDHILL - 75B
31514	ASHFORD - 74A	ASHFORD - 74A	ASHFORD - 74A	W/D	W/D	W/D	W/D
31515	READING (SR) - 70E	W/D	W/D	W/D	W/D	W/D	W/D
31516	ASHFORD - 74A	ASHFORD - 74A	W/D	W/D	W/D	W/D	W/D
31587	ST LEONARDS - 74E	W/D	W/D	W/D	W/D	W/D	W/D
				E1 4-4-0 (1919)			
31019	STEWARTS LANE - 73A	STEWARTS LANE - 73A	STEWARTS LANE - 73A	STEWARTS LANE - 73A	STEWARTS LANE - 73A	STEWARTS LANE - 73A	STEWARTS LANE - 73A
31067	STEWARTS LANE - 73A	STEWARTS LANE - 73A	STEWARTS LANE - 73A	STEWARTS LANE - 73A	STEWARTS LANE - 73A	STEWARTS LANE - 73A	STEWARTS LANE - 73A
31160	B.ARMS - 73B	B.ARMS - 73B	B.ARMS - 73B	B.ARMS - 73B	B.ARMS - 73B	B.ARMS - 73B	B.ARMS - 73B
31165	B.ARMS - 73B	B.ARMS - 73B	B.ARMS - 73B	B.ARMS - 73B	B.ARMS - 73B	B.ARMS - 73B	B.ARMS - 73B
31497	B.ARMS - 73B	B.ARMS - 73B	B.ARMS - 73B	B.ARMS - 73B	B.ARMS - 73B	B.ARMS - 73B	B.ARMS - 73B
31504	STEWARTS LANE - 73A	STEWARTS LANE - 73A	STEWARTS LANE - 73A	STEWARTS LANE - 73A	STEWARTS LANE - 73A	STEWARTS LANE - 73A	STEWARTS LANE - 73A
31506	STEWARTS LANE - 73A	STEWARTS LANE - 73A	STEWARTS LANE - 73A	STEWARTS LANE - 73A	STEWARTS LANE - 73A	STEWARTS LANE - 73A	STEWARTS LANE - 73A
31507	B.ARMS - 73B	B.ARMS - 73B	B.ARMS - 73B	B.ARMS - 73B	B.ARMS - 73B	B.ARMS - 73B	B.ARMS - 73B

loco	Sep-52	Dec-52	Mar-53	May-53	Jul-53	Sep-53	Nov-53
				D 4-4-0 (1901)			
31075	READING (SR) - 70E	READING (SR) - 70E	READING (SR) - 70E	READING (SR) - 70E	READING (SR) - 70E	READING (SR) - 70E	READING (SR) - 70E
31488	READING (SR) - 70E	READING (SR) - 70E	READING (SR) - 70E	READING (SR) - 70E	READING (SR) - 70E	READING (SR) - 70E	READING (SR) - 70E
31493	ST LEONARDS - 74E	ST LEONARDS - 74E	ST LEONARDS - 74E	ST LEONARDS - 74E	ST LEONARDS - 74E	ST LEONARDS - 74E	ST LEONARDS - 74E
31496	ST LEONARDS - 74E	ST LEONARDS - 74E	ST LEONARDS - 74E	READING (SR) - 70E	READING (SR) - 70E	READING (SR) - 70E	READING (SR) - 70E
31501	GILLINGHAM - 73D	GILLINGHAM - 73D	W/D	W/D	W/D	W/D	W/D
31549	TONBRIDGE - 74D	TONBRIDGE - 74D	TONBRIDGE - 74D	TONBRIDGE - 74D	TONBRIDGE - 74D	TONBRIDGE - 74D	TONBRIDGE - 74D
31574	ASHFORD - 74A	ASHFORD - 74A	ASHFORD - 74A	ASHFORD - 74A	ASHFORD - 74A	ASHFORD - 74A	ASHFORD - 74A
31577	ASHFORD - 74A	ASHFORD - 74A	ASHFORD - 74A	ASHFORD - 74A	ASHFORD - 74A	ASHFORD - 74A	ASHFORD - 74A
31586	REDHILL - 75B	REDHILL - 75B	REDHILL - 75B	READING (SR) - 70E	READING (SR) - 70E	READING (SR) - 70E	READING (SR) - 70E
31591	REDHILL - 75B	REDHILL - 75B	REDHILL - 75B	REDHILL - 75B	REDHILL - 75B	REDHILL - 75B	REDHILL - 75B
31728	TONBRIDGE - 74D	TONBRIDGE - 74D	TONBRIDGE - 74D	W/D	W/D	W/D	W/D
31729	TONBRIDGE - 74D	TONBRIDGE - 74D	TONBRIDGE - 74D	TONBRIDGE - 74D	TONBRIDGE - 74D	TONBRIDGE - 74D	TONBRIDGE - 74D
31733	TONBRIDGE - 74D	TONBRIDGE - 74D	TONBRIDGE - 74D	TONBRIDGE - 74D	TONBRIDGE - 74D	TONBRIDGE - 74D	W/D
31734	FAVERSHAM - 73E	FAVERSHAM - 73E	FAVERSHAM - 73E	FAVERSHAM - 73E	FAVERSHAM - 73E	FAVERSHAM - 73E	FAVERSHAM - 73E
31737	READING (SR) - 70E	READING (SR) - 70E	READING (SR) - 70E	READING (SR) - 70E	READING (SR) - 70E	READING (SR) - 70E	READING (SR) - 70E
31744	READING (SR) - 70E	READING (SR) - 70E	READING (SR) - 70E	W/D	W/D	W/D	W/D
31746	B ARMS - 73B	B ARMS - 73B	B ARMS - 73B	B ARMS - 73B	B ARMS - 73B	B ARMS - 73B	B ARMS - 73B
31750	READING (SR) - 70E	READING (SR) - 70E	W/D	W/D	W/D	W/D	W/D
				D1 4-4-0 (1921)			
31145	DOVER - 74C	DOVER - 74C	DOVER - 74C	DOVER - 74C	DOVER - 74C	DOVER - 74C	DOVER - 74C
31246	DOVER - 74C	DOVER - 74C	DOVER - 74C	DOVER - 74C	DOVER - 74C	DOVER - 74C	DOVER - 74C
31247	DOVER - 74C	FAVERSHAM - 73E	FAVERSHAM - 73E	FAVERSHAM - 73E	FAVERSHAM - 73E	FAVERSHAM - 73E	FAVERSHAM - 73E
31470	DOVER - 74C	DOVER - 74C	DOVER - 74C	DOVER - 74C	DOVER - 74C	FAVERSHAM - 73E	FAVERSHAM - 73E
31487	FAVERSHAM - 73E	FAVERSHAM - 73E	FAVERSHAM - 73E	FAVERSHAM - 73E	FAVERSHAM - 73E	FAVERSHAM - 73E	FAVERSHAM - 73E
31489	FAVERSHAM - 73E	FAVERSHAM - 73E	FAVERSHAM - 73E	FAVERSHAM - 73E	FAVERSHAM - 73E	FAVERSHAM - 73E	FAVERSHAM - 73E
31492	GILLINGHAM - 73D	GILLINGHAM - 73D	GILLINGHAM - 73D	GILLINGHAM - 73D	GILLINGHAM - 73D	GILLINGHAM - 73D	GILLINGHAM - 73D
31494	FAVERSHAM - 73E	FAVERSHAM - 73E	FAVERSHAM - 73E	FAVERSHAM - 73E	FAVERSHAM - 73E	FAVERSHAM - 73E	FAVERSHAM - 73E
31505	FAVERSHAM - 73E	FAVERSHAM - 73E	FAVERSHAM - 73E	FAVERSHAM - 73E	FAVERSHAM - 73E	FAVERSHAM - 73E	FAVERSHAM - 73E
31509	GILLINGHAM - 73D	GILLINGHAM - 73D	GILLINGHAM - 73D	STEWARTS LANE - 73A	STEWARTS LANE - 73A	STEWARTS LANE - 73A	STEWARTS LANE - 73A
31545	GILLINGHAM - 73D	GILLINGHAM - 73D	GILLINGHAM - 73D	STEWARTS LANE - 73A	STEWARTS LANE - 73A	STEWARTS LANE - 73A	STEWARTS LANE - 73A
31727	TONBRIDGE - 74D	TONBRIDGE - 74D	TONBRIDGE - 74D	TONBRIDGE - 74D	TONBRIDGE - 74D	TONBRIDGE - 74D	TONBRIDGE - 74D
31735	TONBRIDGE - 74D	TONBRIDGE - 74D	REDHILL - 75B	REDHILL - 75B	REDHILL - 75B	REDHILL - 75B	REDHILL - 75B
31739	TONBRIDGE - 74D	TONBRIDGE - 74D	REDHILL - 75B	REDHILL - 75B	REDHILL - 75B	REDHILL - 75B	REDHILL - 75B
31741	FAVERSHAM - 73E	FAVERSHAM - 73E	FAVERSHAM - 73E	FAVERSHAM - 73E	FAVERSHAM - 73E	FAVERSHAM - 73E	B ARMS - 73B
31743	STEWARTS LANE - 73A	STEWARTS LANE - 73A	B ARMS - 73B	B ARMS - 73B	B ARMS - 73B	B ARMS - 73B	B ARMS - 73B
31749	STEWARTS LANE - 73A	STEWARTS LANE - 73A	REDHILL - 75B	REDHILL - 75B	REDHILL - 75B	REDHILL - 75B	REDHILL - 75B
				D15 4-4-0 (1912)			
30464	EASTLEIGH - 71A	EASTLEIGH - 71A	EASTLEIGH - 71A	EASTLEIGH - 71A	EASTLEIGH - 71A	EASTLEIGH - 71A	EASTLEIGH - 71A
30465	EASTLEIGH - 71A	EASTLEIGH - 71A	EASTLEIGH - 71A	EASTLEIGH - 71A	EASTLEIGH - 71A	EASTLEIGH - 71A	FRATTON - 71D
30467	EASTLEIGH - 71A	EASTLEIGH - 71A	EASTLEIGH - 71A	EASTLEIGH - 71A	EASTLEIGH - 71A	EASTLEIGH - 71A	EASTLEIGH - 71A
30470	EASTLEIGH - 71A	W/D	W/D	W/D	W/D	W/D	W/D
30471	EASTLEIGH - 71A	EASTLEIGH - 71A	EASTLEIGH - 71A	EASTLEIGH - 71A	EASTLEIGH - 71A	NINE ELMS - 70A	NINE ELMS - 70A
				E 4-4-0 (1905)			
31166	FAVERSHAM - 73E	FAVERSHAM - 73E	FAVERSHAM - 73E	FAVERSHAM - 73E	FAVERSHAM - 73E	FAVERSHAM - 73E	TONBRIDGE - 74D
31315	FAVERSHAM - 73E	FAVERSHAM - 73E	FAVERSHAM - 73E	STEWARTS LANE - 73A	STEWARTS LANE - 73A	STEWARTS LANE - 73A	STEWARTS LANE - 73A
31491	REDHILL - 75B	REDHILL - 75B	W/D	W/D	W/D	W/D	W/D
				E1 4-4-0 (1919)			
31019	STEWARTS LANE - 73A	STEWARTS LANE - 73A	STEWARTS LANE - 73A	STEWARTS LANE - 73A	STEWARTS LANE - 73A	STEWARTS LANE - 73A	STEWARTS LANE - 73A
31067	STEWARTS LANE - 73A	STEWARTS LANE - 73A	STEWARTS LANE - 73A	STEWARTS LANE - 73A	STEWARTS LANE - 73A	STEWARTS LANE - 73A	STEWARTS LANE - 73A
31160	B ARMS - 73B	B ARMS - 73B	B ARMS - 73B	B ARMS - 73B	B ARMS - 73B	B ARMS - 73B	B ARMS - 73B
31165	B ARMS - 73B	B ARMS - 73B	STEWARTS LANE - 73A	B ARMS - 73B	B ARMS - 73B	B ARMS - 73B	B ARMS - 73B
31497	B ARMS - 73B	B ARMS - 73B	B ARMS - 73B	B ARMS - 73B	B ARMS - 73B	B ARMS - 73B	B ARMS - 73B
31504	STEWARTS LANE - 73A	STEWARTS LANE - 73A	STEWARTS LANE - 73A	STEWARTS LANE - 73A	STEWARTS LANE - 73A	STEWARTS LANE - 73A	STEWARTS LANE - 73A
31506	STEWARTS LANE - 73A	STEWARTS LANE - 73A	STEWARTS LANE - 73A	STEWARTS LANE - 73A	STEWARTS LANE - 73A	STEWARTS LANE - 73A	STEWARTS LANE - 73A
31507	B ARMS - 73B	B ARMS - 73B	B ARMS - 73B	B ARMS - 73B	B ARMS - 73B	B ARMS - 73B	B ARMS - 73B

For most of its life D1 4-4-0 31545 had been a country-based engine, working from Ramsgate and Dover sheds, but in 1953 it was moved to Stewarts Lane for the 07.00 Cannon Street - Dartford - Ramsgate, returning with the 19.35 to Holborn Viaduct via Maidstone East. Although a Saturdays-only turn - on weekdays the working was booked to an N 2-6-0 - it was a long duty requiring the engine to be in traffic for almost twenty-four hours. On other days of the week the 4-4-0 was used for special traffic requirements and is seen leaving Stewarts Lane on a thick foggy day in 1956. The engine remained at Stewarts Lane until made redundant by electrification in 1959 after which it was placed in store at Feltham - although nominally allocated to Nine Elms - until being withdrawn in March 1961.

loco	Jan-54	Mar-54	May-54	Jun-54	Aug-54	Oct-54	Dec-54
				D 4-4-0 (1901)			
31075	READING (SR) - 70E	READING (SR) - 70E	READING (SR) - 70E	READING (SR) - 70E	GUILDFORD - 70C	GUILDFORD - 70C	REDHILL - 75B
31488	READING (SR) - 70E	READING (SR) - 70E	READING (SR) - 70E	READING (SR) - 70E	READING (SR) - 70E	READING (SR) - 70E	READING (SR) - 70E
31496	READING (SR) - 70E	READING (SR) - 70E	GUILDFORD - 70C	GUILDFORD - 70C	GUILDFORD - 70C	GUILDFORD - 70C	GUILDFORD - 70C
31549	TONBRIDGE - 74D	TONBRIDGE - 74D	TONBRIDGE - 74D	TONBRIDGE - 74D	TONBRIDGE - 74D	TONBRIDGE - 74D	TONBRIDGE - 74D
31574	ASHFORD - 74A	ASHFORD - 74A	ASHFORD - 74A	ASHFORD - 74A	ASHFORD - 74A	ASHFORD - 74A	ASHFORD - 74A
31577	ASHFORD - 74A	ASHFORD - 74A	ASHFORD - 74A	ASHFORD - 74A	ASHFORD - 74A	ASHFORD - 74A	ASHFORD - 74A
31586	READING (SR) - 70E	READING (SR) - 70E	GUILDFORD - 70C	GUILDFORD - 70C	GUILDFORD - 70C	GUILDFORD - 70C	GUILDFORD - 70C
31591	THREE BRIDGES - 75E	THREE BRIDGES - 75E	THREE BRIDGES - 75E	THREE BRIDGES - 75E	THREE BRIDGES - 75E	THREE BRIDGES - 75E	REDHILL - 75B
31729	TONBRIDGE - 74D	TONBRIDGE - 74D					
31734	FAVERSHAM - 73E	FAVERSHAM - 73E	FAVERSHAM - 73E	FAVERSHAM - 73E	FAVERSHAM - 73E	FAVERSHAM - 73E	FAVERSHAM - 73E
31737	READING (SR) - 70E	READING (SR) - 70E	TONBRIDGE - 74D	TONBRIDGE - 74D	TONBRIDGE - 74D	TONBRIDGE - 74D	TONBRIDGE - 74D
31746	B ARMS - 73B	B ARMS - 73B	GUILDFORD - 70C	GUILDFORD - 70C	GUILDFORD - 70C	GUILDFORD - 70C	W/D
				D1 4-4-0 (1921)			
31145	DOVER - 74C	DOVER - 74C	DOVER - 74C	DOVER - 74C	DOVER - 74C	DOVER - 74C	DOVER - 74C
31246	DOVER - 74C	DOVER - 74C	DOVER - 74C	DOVER - 74C	DOVER - 74C	DOVER - 74C	DOVER - 74C
31247	FAVERSHAM - 73E	FAVERSHAM - 73E	FAVERSHAM - 73E	FAVERSHAM - 73E	FAVERSHAM - 73E	DOVER - 74C	DOVER - 74C
31470	FAVERSHAM - 73E	FAVERSHAM - 73E	FAVERSHAM - 73E	FAVERSHAM - 73E	FAVERSHAM - 73E	FAVERSHAM - 73E	FAVERSHAM - 73E
31487	FAVERSHAM - 73E	FAVERSHAM - 73E	FAVERSHAM - 73E	FAVERSHAM - 73E	FAVERSHAM - 73E	FAVERSHAM - 73E	FAVERSHAM - 73E
31489	FAVERSHAM - 73E	FAVERSHAM - 73E	FAVERSHAM - 73E	FAVERSHAM - 73E	FAVERSHAM - 73E	FAVERSHAM - 73E	FAVERSHAM - 73E
31492	GILLINGHAM - 73D	GILLINGHAM - 73D	GILLINGHAM - 73D	GILLINGHAM - 73D	GILLINGHAM - 73D	GILLINGHAM - 73D	GILLINGHAM - 73D
31494	FAVERSHAM - 73E	FAVERSHAM - 73E	FAVERSHAM - 73E	FAVERSHAM - 73E	FAVERSHAM - 73E	FAVERSHAM - 73E	FAVERSHAM - 73E
31505	FAVERSHAM - 73E	FAVERSHAM - 73E	FAVERSHAM - 73E	GILLINGHAM - 73D	GILLINGHAM - 73D	GILLINGHAM - 73D	GILLINGHAM - 73D
31509	GILLINGHAM - 73D	GILLINGHAM - 73D	GILLINGHAM - 73D	GILLINGHAM - 73D	GILLINGHAM - 73D	GILLINGHAM - 73D	GILLINGHAM - 73D
31545	STEWARTS LANE - 73A	STEWARTS LANE - 73A	STEWARTS LANE - 73A	STEWARTS LANE - 73A	STEWARTS LANE - 73A	STEWARTS LANE - 73A	STEWARTS LANE - 73A
31727	TONBRIDGE - 74D	TONBRIDGE - 74D	TONBRIDGE - 74D	TONBRIDGE - 74D	TONBRIDGE - 74D	TONBRIDGE - 74D	TONBRIDGE - 74D
31735	REDHILL - 75B	REDHILL - 75B	B ARMS - 73B	B ARMS - 73B	B ARMS - 73B	B ARMS - 73B	B ARMS - 73B
31739	REDHILL - 75B	REDHILL - 75B	REDHILL - 75B	REDHILL - 75B	REDHILL - 75B	REDHILL - 75B	REDHILL - 75B
31741	B ARMS - 73B	B ARMS - 73B	B ARMS - 73B	B ARMS - 73B	B ARMS - 73B	B ARMS - 73B	B ARMS - 73B
31743	B ARMS - 73B	B ARMS - 73B	B ARMS - 73B	B ARMS - 73B	B ARMS - 73B	B ARMS - 73B	B ARMS - 73B
31749	REDHILL - 75B	REDHILL - 75B	STEWARTS LANE - 73A	STEWARTS LANE - 73A	STEWARTS LANE - 73A	STEWARTS LANE - 73A	STEWARTS LANE - 73A
				D15 4-4-0 (1912)			
30464	EASTLEIGH - 71A	EASTLEIGH - 71A	EASTLEIGH - 71A	NINE ELMS - 70A	NINE ELMS - 70A	W/D	W/D
30465	FRATTON - 71D	FRATTON - 71D	FRATTON - 71D	NINE ELMS - 70A	NINE ELMS - 70A	NINE ELMS - 70A	NINE ELMS - 70A
30467	EASTLEIGH - 71A	EASTLEIGH - 71A	EASTLEIGH - 71A	NINE ELMS - 70A	NINE ELMS - 70A	NINE ELMS - 70A	NINE ELMS - 70A
30471	FRATTON - 71D	W/D	W/D	W/D	W/D	W/D	W/D
				E 4-4-0 (1905)			
31166	TONBRIDGE - 74D	TONBRIDGE - 74D	TONBRIDGE - 74D	TONBRIDGE - 74D	TONBRIDGE - 74D	TONBRIDGE - 74D	TONBRIDGE - 74D
31315	REDHILL - 75B	W/D	W/D	W/D	W/D	W/D	W/D
				E1 4-4-0 (1919)			
31019	STEWARTS LANE - 73A	STEWARTS LANE - 73A	STEWARTS LANE - 73A	STEWARTS LANE - 73A	STEWARTS LANE - 73A	STEWARTS LANE - 73A	STEWARTS LANE - 73A
31067	STEWARTS LANE - 73A	STEWARTS LANE - 73A	STEWARTS LANE - 73A	STEWARTS LANE - 73A	STEWARTS LANE - 73A	STEWARTS LANE - 73A	STEWARTS LANE - 73A
31160	B ARMS - 73B	B ARMS - 73B	B ARMS - 73B	B ARMS - 73B	B ARMS - 73B	B ARMS - 73B	B ARMS - 73B
31165	B ARMS - 73B	B ARMS - 73B	B ARMS - 73B	B ARMS - 73B	B ARMS - 73B	B ARMS - 73B	B ARMS - 73B
31497	B ARMS - 73B	B ARMS - 73B	B ARMS - 73B	B ARMS - 73B	B ARMS - 73B	B ARMS - 73B	B ARMS - 73B
31504	STEWARTS LANE - 73A	STEWARTS LANE - 73A	STEWARTS LANE - 73A	STEWARTS LANE - 73A	STEWARTS LANE - 73A	STEWARTS LANE - 73A	STEWARTS LANE - 73A
31506	STEWARTS LANE - 73A	STEWARTS LANE - 73A	STEWARTS LANE - 73A	STEWARTS LANE - 73A	STEWARTS LANE - 73A	STEWARTS LANE - 73A	STEWARTS LANE - 73A
31507	B ARMS - 73B	B ARMS - 73B	B ARMS - 73B	B ARMS - 73B	B ARMS - 73B	B ARMS - 73B	B ARMS - 73B

loco	Feb-55	Apr-55	Jun-55	Aug-55	Sep-55	Nov-55	Dec-55
				D 4-4-0 (1901)			
31075	GUILDFORD - 70C	GUILDFORD - 70C	GUILDFORD - 70C	GUILDFORD - 70C	GUILDFORD - 70C	GUILDFORD - 70C	GUILDFORD - 70C
31488	READING (SR) - 70E	READING (SR) - 70E	READING (SR) - 70E	READING (SR) - 70E	GUILDFORD - 70C	GUILDFORD - 70C	GUILDFORD - 70C
31496	GUILDFORD - 70C	GUILDFORD - 70C	GUILDFORD - 70C	W/D	W/D	W/D	W/D
31549	TONBRIDGE - 74D	TONBRIDGE - 74D	TONBRIDGE - 74D	TONBRIDGE - 74D	GUILDFORD - 70C	GUILDFORD - 70C	GUILDFORD - 70C
31574	ASHFORD - 74A	ASHFORD - 74A	ASHFORD - 74A	ASHFORD - 74A	GUILDFORD - 70C	GUILDFORD - 70C	GUILDFORD - 70C
31577	ASHFORD - 74A	ASHFORD - 74A	ASHFORD - 74A	ASHFORD - 74A	GUILDFORD - 70C	GUILDFORD - 70C	GUILDFORD - 70C
31586	GUILDFORD - 70C	GUILDFORD - 70C	GUILDFORD - 70C	W/D	W/D	W/D	W/D
31591	GUILDFORD - 70C	GUILDFORD - 70C	W/D	W/D	W/D	W/D	W/D
31734	FAVERSHAM - 73E	FAVERSHAM - 73E	FAVERSHAM - 73E	FAVERSHAM - 73E	TONBRIDGE - 74D	W/D	W/D
31737	TONBRIDGE - 74D	TONBRIDGE - 74D	TONBRIDGE - 74D	TONBRIDGE - 74D	TONBRIDGE - 74D	TONBRIDGE - 74D	GUILDFORD - 70C
				D1 4-4-0 (1921)			
31145	DOVER - 74C	DOVER - 74C	DOVER - 74C	DOVER - 74C	DOVER - 74C	DOVER - 74C	DOVER - 74C
31246	DOVER - 74C	DOVER - 74C	DOVER - 74C	DOVER - 74C	DOVER - 74C	TONBRIDGE - 74D	TONBRIDGE - 74D
31247	DOVER - 74C	DOVER - 74C	DOVER - 74C	DOVER - 74C	DOVER - 74C	DOVER - 74C	DOVER - 74C
31470	FAVERSHAM - 73E	FAVERSHAM - 73E	FAVERSHAM - 73E	FAVERSHAM - 73E	FAVERSHAM - 73E	FAVERSHAM - 73E	TONBRIDGE - 74D
31487	FAVERSHAM - 73E	FAVERSHAM - 73E	FAVERSHAM - 73E	FAVERSHAM - 73E	FAVERSHAM - 73E	FAVERSHAM - 73E	TONBRIDGE - 74D
31489	FAVERSHAM - 73E	FAVERSHAM - 73E	FAVERSHAM - 73E	FAVERSHAM - 73E	FAVERSHAM - 73E	FAVERSHAM - 73E	TONBRIDGE - 74D
31492	GILLINGHAM - 73D	GILLINGHAM - 73D	GILLINGHAM - 73D	GILLINGHAM - 73D	GILLINGHAM - 73D	GILLINGHAM - 73D	TONBRIDGE - 74D
31494	FAVERSHAM - 73E	FAVERSHAM - 73E	FAVERSHAM - 73E	FAVERSHAM - 73E	FAVERSHAM - 73E	FAVERSHAM - 73E	FAVERSHAM - 73E
31505	GILLINGHAM - 73D	GILLINGHAM - 73D	FAVERSHAM - 73E	FAVERSHAM - 73E	ASHFORD - 74A	ASHFORD - 74A	FAVERSHAM - 73E
31509	GILLINGHAM - 73D	GILLINGHAM - 73D	FAVERSHAM - 73E	FAVERSHAM - 73E	FAVERSHAM - 73E	FAVERSHAM - 73E	FAVERSHAM - 73E
31545	STEWARTS LANE - 73A	STEWARTS LANE - 73A	STEWARTS LANE - 73A	STEWARTS LANE - 73A	STEWARTS LANE - 73A	STEWARTS LANE - 73A	STEWARTS LANE - 73A
31727	TONBRIDGE - 74D	TONBRIDGE - 74D	TONBRIDGE - 74D	TONBRIDGE - 74D	TONBRIDGE - 74D	TONBRIDGE - 74D	TONBRIDGE - 74D
31735	B ARMS - 73B	B ARMS - 73B	B ARMS - 73B	B ARMS - 73B	B ARMS - 73B	B ARMS - 73B	B ARMS - 73B
31739	REDHILL - 75B	REDHILL - 75B	REDHILL - 75B	REDHILL - 75B	B ARMS - 73B	B ARMS - 73B	B ARMS - 73B
31741	B ARMS - 73B	B ARMS - 73B	B ARMS - 73B	B ARMS - 73B	B ARMS - 73B	B ARMS - 73B	B ARMS - 73B
31743	B ARMS - 73B	B ARMS - 73B	B ARMS - 73B	B ARMS - 73B	B ARMS - 73B	B ARMS - 73B	B ARMS - 73B
31749	STEWARTS LANE - 73A	STEWARTS LANE - 73A	STEWARTS LANE - 73A	STEWARTS LANE - 73A	STEWARTS LANE - 73A	STEWARTS LANE - 73A	STEWARTS LANE - 73A
				D15 4-4-0 (1912)			
30465	NINE ELMS - 70A	NINE ELMS - 70A	NINE ELMS - 70A	NINE ELMS - 70A	NINE ELMS - 70A	EASTLEIGH - 71A	EASTLEIGH - 71A
30467	NINE ELMS - 70A	NINE ELMS - 70A	NINE ELMS - 70A	W/D	W/D	W/D	W/D
				E 4-4-0 (1905)			
31166	TONBRIDGE - 74D	TONBRIDGE - 74D	W/D	W/D	W/D	W/D	W/D
				E1 4-4-0 (1919)			
31019	STEWARTS LANE - 73A	STEWARTS LANE - 73A	STEWARTS LANE - 73A	STEWARTS LANE - 73A	STEWARTS LANE - 73A	STEWARTS LANE - 73A	STEWARTS LANE - 73A
31067	STEWARTS LANE - 73A	STEWARTS LANE - 73A	STEWARTS LANE - 73A	STEWARTS LANE - 73A	STEWARTS LANE - 73A	STEWARTS LANE - 73A	STEWARTS LANE - 73A
31160	B ARMS - 73B	B ARMS - 73B	B ARMS - 73B	B ARMS - 73B	B ARMS - 73B	B ARMS - 73B	B ARMS - 73B
31165	B ARMS - 73B	B ARMS - 73B	B ARMS - 73B	B ARMS - 73B	B ARMS - 73B	B ARMS - 73B	B ARMS - 73B
31497	B ARMS - 73B	B ARMS - 73B	B ARMS - 73B	B ARMS - 73B	B ARMS - 73B	B ARMS - 73B	B ARMS - 73B
31504	STEWARTS LANE - 73A	STEWARTS LANE - 73A	STEWARTS LANE - 73A	STEWARTS LANE - 73A	STEWARTS LANE - 73A	STEWARTS LANE - 73A	STEWARTS LANE - 73A
31506	STEWARTS LANE - 73A	STEWARTS LANE - 73A	STEWARTS LANE - 73A	STEWARTS LANE - 73A	STEWARTS LANE - 73A	STEWARTS LANE - 73A	STEWARTS LANE - 73A
31507	B ARMS - 73B	B ARMS - 73B	B ARMS - 73B	B ARMS - 73B	B ARMS - 73B	B ARMS - 73B	B ARMS - 73B

loco	Jan-56	Apr-56	May-56	Aug-56	Oct-56	Nov-56	Jan-57
				D 4-4-0 (1901)			
31075	GUILDFORD - 70C	GUILDFORD - 70C	GUILDFORD - 70C	GUILDFORD - 70C	GUILDFORD - 70C	W/D	W/D
31549	GUILDFORD - 70C	GUILDFORD - 70C	GUILDFORD - 70C	GUILDFORD - 70C	W/D	W/D	W/D
31574	GUILDFORD - 70C	GUILDFORD - 70C	GUILDFORD - 70C	GUILDFORD - 70C	W/D	W/D	W/D
31577	GUILDFORD - 70C	GUILDFORD - 70C	GUILDFORD - 70C	GUILDFORD - 70C	GUILDFORD - 70C	W/D	W/D
31737	GUILDFORD - 70C	GUILDFORD - 70C	GUILDFORD - 70C	GUILDFORD - 70C	W/D	W/D	W/D
				D1 4-4-0 (1921)			
31145	DOVER - 74C	DOVER - 74C	DOVER - 74C	DOVER - 74C	DOVER - 74C	GUILDFORD - 70C	GUILDFORD - 70C
31246	TONBRIDGE - 74D	TONBRIDGE - 74D	TONBRIDGE - 74D	TONBRIDGE - 74D	TONBRIDGE - 74D	ASHFORD - 74A	ASHFORD - 74A
31247	DOVER - 74C	DOVER - 74C	DOVER - 74C	DOVER - 74C	DOVER - 74C	GUILDFORD - 70C	GUILDFORD - 70C
31470	TONBRIDGE - 74D	TONBRIDGE - 74D	TONBRIDGE - 74D	TONBRIDGE - 74D	TONBRIDGE - 74D	TONBRIDGE - 74D	TONBRIDGE - 74D
31487	TONBRIDGE - 74D	TONBRIDGE - 74D	TONBRIDGE - 74D	TONBRIDGE - 74D	TONBRIDGE - 74D	TONBRIDGE - 74D	TONBRIDGE - 74D
31489	TONBRIDGE - 74D	TONBRIDGE - 74D	TONBRIDGE - 74D	TONBRIDGE - 74D	TONBRIDGE - 74D	TONBRIDGE - 74D	TONBRIDGE - 74D
31492	TONBRIDGE - 74D	TONBRIDGE - 74D	TONBRIDGE - 74D	TONBRIDGE - 74D	TONBRIDGE - 74D	TONBRIDGE - 74D	TONBRIDGE - 74D
31494	FAVERSHAM - 73E	FAVERSHAM - 73E	FAVERSHAM - 73E	FAVERSHAM - 73E	FAVERSHAM - 73E	FAVERSHAM - 73E	FAVERSHAM - 73E
31505	FAVERSHAM - 73E	FAVERSHAM - 73E	FAVERSHAM - 73E	FAVERSHAM - 73E	FAVERSHAM - 73E	FAVERSHAM - 73E	FAVERSHAM - 73E
31509	FAVERSHAM - 73E	FAVERSHAM - 73E	FAVERSHAM - 73E	FAVERSHAM - 73E	FAVERSHAM - 73E	FAVERSHAM - 73E	FAVERSHAM - 73E
31545	STEWARTS LANE - 73A	STEWARTS LANE - 73A	STEWARTS LANE - 73A	STEWARTS LANE - 73A	STEWARTS LANE - 73A	STEWARTS LANE - 73A	STEWARTS LANE - 73A
31727	TONBRIDGE - 74D	TONBRIDGE - 74D	TONBRIDGE - 74D	TONBRIDGE - 74D	TONBRIDGE - 74D	ASHFORD - 74A	ASHFORD - 74A
31735	B.ARMS - 73B	B.ARMS - 73B	B.ARMS - 73B	B.ARMS - 73B	B.ARMS - 73B	B.ARMS - 73B	B.ARMS - 73B
31739	B.ARMS - 73B	B.ARMS - 73B	B.ARMS - 73B	B.ARMS - 73B	B.ARMS - 73B	B.ARMS - 73B	B.ARMS - 73B
31741	B.ARMS - 73B	B.ARMS - 73B	B.ARMS - 73B	B.ARMS - 73B	B.ARMS - 73B	B.ARMS - 73B	B.ARMS - 73B
31743	B.ARMS - 73B	B.ARMS - 73B	B.ARMS - 73B	B.ARMS - 73B	B.ARMS - 73B	B.ARMS - 73B	B.ARMS - 73B
31749	STEWARTS LANE - 73A	STEWARTS LANE - 73A	STEWARTS LANE - 73A	STEWARTS LANE - 73A	STEWARTS LANE - 73A	STEWARTS LANE - 73A	STEWARTS LANE - 73A
				E1 4-4-0 (1919)			
31019	STEWARTS LANE - 73A	STEWARTS LANE - 73A	STEWARTS LANE - 73A	STEWARTS LANE - 73A	STEWARTS LANE - 73A	STEWARTS LANE - 73A	STEWARTS LANE - 73A
31067	STEWARTS LANE - 73A	STEWARTS LANE - 73A	STEWARTS LANE - 73A	STEWARTS LANE - 73A	STEWARTS LANE - 73A	STEWARTS LANE - 73A	STEWARTS LANE - 73A
31160	B.ARMS - 73B	B.ARMS - 73B	B.ARMS - 73B	B.ARMS - 73B	B.ARMS - 73B	B.ARMS - 73B	B.ARMS - 73B
31165	B.ARMS - 73B	B.ARMS - 73B	B.ARMS - 73B	B.ARMS - 73B	B.ARMS - 73B	B.ARMS - 73B	B.ARMS - 73B
31497	B.ARMS - 73B	B.ARMS - 73B	B.ARMS - 73B	B.ARMS - 73B	B.ARMS - 73B	B.ARMS - 73B	B.ARMS - 73B
31504	STEWARTS LANE - 73A	STEWARTS LANE - 73A	STEWARTS LANE - 73A	STEWARTS LANE - 73A	STEWARTS LANE - 73A	STEWARTS LANE - 73A	STEWARTS LANE - 73A
31506	STEWARTS LANE - 73A	STEWARTS LANE - 73A	STEWARTS LANE - 73A	STEWARTS LANE - 73A	STEWARTS LANE - 73A	STEWARTS LANE - 73A	STEWARTS LANE - 73A
31507	B.ARMS - 73B	B.ARMS - 73B	B.ARMS - 73B	B.ARMS - 73B	B.ARMS - 73B	B.ARMS - 73B	B.ARMS - 73B

loco	Mar-57	Jun-57	Jul-57	Oct-57	Jan-58	Feb-58	Mar-58
				D1 4-4-0 (1921)			
31145	GUILDFORD - 70C	GUILDFORD - 70C	GUILDFORD - 70C	GUILDFORD - 70C	GUILDFORD - 70C	B.ARMS - 73B	B.ARMS - 73B
31246	ASHFORD - 74A	ASHFORD - 74A	ASHFORD - 74A	ASHFORD - 74A	ASHFORD - 74A	ASHFORD - 74A	ASHFORD - 74A
31247	GUILDFORD - 70C	GUILDFORD - 70C	GUILDFORD - 70C	GUILDFORD - 70C	GUILDFORD - 70C	B.ARMS - 73B	B.ARMS - 73B
31470	TONBRIDGE - 74D	TONBRIDGE - 74D	TONBRIDGE - 74D	TONBRIDGE - 74D	TONBRIDGE - 74D	TONBRIDGE - 74D	TONBRIDGE - 74D
31487	TONBRIDGE - 74D	TONBRIDGE - 74D	TONBRIDGE - 74D	TONBRIDGE - 74D	TONBRIDGE - 74D	TONBRIDGE - 74D	TONBRIDGE - 74D
31489	TONBRIDGE - 74D	TONBRIDGE - 74D	TONBRIDGE - 74D	TONBRIDGE - 74D	TONBRIDGE - 74D	TONBRIDGE - 74D	TONBRIDGE - 74D
31492	TONBRIDGE - 74D	TONBRIDGE - 74D	TONBRIDGE - 74D	TONBRIDGE - 74D	TONBRIDGE - 74D	TONBRIDGE - 74D	TONBRIDGE - 74D
31494	FAVERSHAM - 73E	FAVERSHAM - 73E	FAVERSHAM - 73E	FAVERSHAM - 73E	FAVERSHAM - 73E	FAVERSHAM - 73E	FAVERSHAM - 73E
31505	FAVERSHAM - 73E	FAVERSHAM - 73E	FAVERSHAM - 73E	FAVERSHAM - 73E	FAVERSHAM - 73E	FAVERSHAM - 73E	FAVERSHAM - 73E
31509	FAVERSHAM - 73E	FAVERSHAM - 73E	FAVERSHAM - 73E	FAVERSHAM - 73E	FAVERSHAM - 73E	FAVERSHAM - 73E	FAVERSHAM - 73E
31545	STEWARTS LANE - 73A	STEWARTS LANE - 73A	STEWARTS LANE - 73A	STEWARTS LANE - 73A	STEWARTS LANE - 73A	STEWARTS LANE - 73A	STEWARTS LANE - 73A
31727	ASHFORD - 74A	ASHFORD - 74A	ASHFORD - 74A	ASHFORD - 74A	ASHFORD - 74A	ASHFORD - 74A	ASHFORD - 74A
31735	B.ARMS - 73B	B.ARMS - 73B	B.ARMS - 73B	B.ARMS - 73B	B.ARMS - 73B	B.ARMS - 73B	B.ARMS - 73B
31739	B.ARMS - 73B	B.ARMS - 73B	B.ARMS - 73B	B.ARMS - 73B	B.ARMS - 73B	B.ARMS - 73B	B.ARMS - 73B
31741	B.ARMS - 73B	B.ARMS - 73B	B.ARMS - 73B	B.ARMS - 73B	B.ARMS - 73B	B.ARMS - 73B	B.ARMS - 73B
31743	B.ARMS - 73B	B.ARMS - 73B	B.ARMS - 73B	B.ARMS - 73B	B.ARMS - 73B	B.ARMS - 73B	B.ARMS - 73B
31749	STEWARTS LANE - 73A	STEWARTS LANE - 73A	STEWARTS LANE - 73A	STEWARTS LANE - 73A	STEWARTS LANE - 73A	STEWARTS LANE - 73A	STEWARTS LANE - 73A
				E1 4-4-0 (1919)			
31019	STEWARTS LANE - 73A	STEWARTS LANE - 73A	STEWARTS LANE - 73A	STEWARTS LANE - 73A	STEWARTS LANE - 73A	STEWARTS LANE - 73A	STEWARTS LANE - 73A
31067	STEWARTS LANE - 73A	STEWARTS LANE - 73A	STEWARTS LANE - 73A	STEWARTS LANE - 73A	STEWARTS LANE - 73A	STEWARTS LANE - 73A	STEWARTS LANE - 73A
31160	B.ARMS - 73B	B.ARMS - 73B	B.ARMS - 73B	B.ARMS - 73B	B.ARMS - 73B	B.ARMS - 73B	B.ARMS - 73B
31165	B.ARMS - 73B	B.ARMS - 73B	B.ARMS - 73B	B.ARMS - 73B	B.ARMS - 73B	B.ARMS - 73B	B.ARMS - 73B
31497	B.ARMS - 73B	B.ARMS - 73B	B.ARMS - 73B	B.ARMS - 73B	B.ARMS - 73B	B.ARMS - 73B	B.ARMS - 73B
31504	STEWARTS LANE - 73A	STEWARTS LANE - 73A	STEWARTS LANE - 73A	STEWARTS LANE - 73A	STEWARTS LANE - 73A	W/D	W/D
31506	STEWARTS LANE - 73A	STEWARTS LANE - 73A	STEWARTS LANE - 73A	STEWARTS LANE - 73A	STEWARTS LANE - 73A	STEWARTS LANE - 73A	STEWARTS LANE - 73A
31507	B.ARMS - 73B	B.ARMS - 73B	B.ARMS - 73B	B.ARMS - 73B	B.ARMS - 73B	B.ARMS - 73B	B.ARMS - 73B

loco	May-58	Oct-58	Mar-59	Jun-59	Jul-59	Aug-59	Oct-59
				D1 4-4-0 (1921)			
31145	B.ARMS - 73B	STEWARTS LANE - 73A	STEWARTS LANE - 73A	NINE ELMS - 70A	NINE ELMS - 70A	NINE ELMS - 70A	NINE ELMS - 70A
31246	ASHFORD - 74A	ASHFORD - 73F	ASHFORD - 73F	NINE ELMS - 70A	NINE ELMS - 70A	NINE ELMS - 70A	NINE ELMS - 70A
31247	B.ARMS - 73B	B.ARMS - 73B	B.ARMS - 73B	NINE ELMS - 70A	NINE ELMS - 70A	NINE ELMS - 70A	NINE ELMS - 70A
31470	TONBRIDGE - 74D	TONBRIDGE - 73J	TONBRIDGE - 73J	TONBRIDGE - 73J	W/D	W/D	W/D
31487	TONBRIDGE - 74D	TONBRIDGE - 73J	TONBRIDGE - 73J	TONBRIDGE - 73J	TONBRIDGE - 73J	TONBRIDGE - 73J	TONBRIDGE - 73J
31489	TONBRIDGE - 74D	TONBRIDGE - 73J	TONBRIDGE - 73J	TONBRIDGE - 73J	TONBRIDGE - 73J	TONBRIDGE - 73J	TONBRIDGE - 73J
31492	TONBRIDGE - 74D	TONBRIDGE - 73J	TONBRIDGE - 73J	TONBRIDGE - 73J	TONBRIDGE - 73J	TONBRIDGE - 73J	TONBRIDGE - 73J
31494	FAVERSHAM - 73E	FAVERSHAM - 73E	FAVERSHAM - 73E	NINE ELMS - 70A	NINE ELMS - 70A	NINE ELMS - 70A	NINE ELMS - 70A
31505	FAVERSHAM - 73E	FAVERSHAM - 73E	FAVERSHAM - 73E	NINE ELMS - 70A	NINE ELMS - 70A	NINE ELMS - 70A	NINE ELMS - 70A
31509	FAVERSHAM - 73E	FAVERSHAM - 73E	FAVERSHAM - 73E	NINE ELMS - 70A	NINE ELMS - 70A	NINE ELMS - 70A	NINE ELMS - 70A
31545	STEWARTS LANE - 73A	STEWARTS LANE - 73A	STEWARTS LANE - 73A	NINE ELMS - 70A	NINE ELMS - 70A	NINE ELMS - 70A	NINE ELMS - 70A
31727	ASHFORD - 74A	ASHFORD - 73F	ASHFORD - 73F	NINE ELMS - 70A	NINE ELMS - 70A	NINE ELMS - 70A	NINE ELMS - 70A
31735	B.ARMS - 73B	B.ARMS - 73B	B.ARMS - 73B	NINE ELMS - 70A	NINE ELMS - 70A	EASTLEIGH - 71A	EASTLEIGH - 71A
31739	B.ARMS - 73B	B.ARMS - 73B	B.ARMS - 73B	B.ARMS - 73B	B.ARMS - 73B	B.ARMS - 73B	B.ARMS - 73B
31741	B.ARMS - 73B	B.ARMS - 73B	B.ARMS - 73B	B.ARMS - 73B	B.ARMS - 73B	B.ARMS - 73B	W/D
31743	B.ARMS - 73B	B.ARMS - 73B	B.ARMS - 73B	B.ARMS - 73B	B.ARMS - 73B	B.ARMS - 73B	B.ARMS - 73B
31749	STEWARTS LANE - 73A	STEWARTS LANE - 73A	STEWARTS LANE - 73A	B.ARMS - 73B	B.ARMS - 73B	B.ARMS - 73B	B.ARMS - 73B
				E1 4-4-0 (1919)			
31019	STEWARTS LANE - 73A	STEWARTS LANE - 73A	STEWARTS LANE - 73A	NINE ELMS - 70A	SALISBURY - 72B	SALISBURY - 72B	SALISBURY - 72B
31067	STEWARTS LANE - 73A	STEWARTS LANE - 73A	STEWARTS LANE - 73A	NINE ELMS - 70A	SALISBURY - 72B	SALISBURY - 72B	SALISBURY - 72B
31160	B.ARMS - 73B	B.ARMS - 73B	B.ARMS - 73B	B.ARMS - 73B	B.ARMS - 73B	B.ARMS - 73B	B.ARMS - 73B
31165	B.ARMS - 73B	B.ARMS - 73B	B.ARMS - 73B	W/D	W/D	W/D	W/D
31497	B.ARMS - 73B	B.ARMS - 73B	B.ARMS - 73B	NINE ELMS - 70A	SALISBURY - 72B	SALISBURY - 72B	SALISBURY - 72B
31506	STEWARTS LANE - 73A	W/D	W/D	W/D	W/D	W/D	W/D
31507	B.ARMS - 73B	B.ARMS - 73B	B.ARMS - 73B	NINE ELMS - 70A	SALISBURY - 72B	SALISBURY - 72B	SALISBURY - 72B

loco	Dec-59	Feb-60	Mar-60	Apr-60	Jul-60	Aug-60	Sep-60	Nov-60
				D1 4-4-0 (1921)				
31145	NINE ELMS - 70A	NINE ELMS - 70A	NINE ELMS - 70A	NINE ELMS - 70A	NINE ELMS - 70A	NINE ELMS - 70A	NINE ELMS - 70A	NINE ELMS - 70A
31246	NINE ELMS - 70A	NINE ELMS - 70A	NINE ELMS - 70A	NINE ELMS - 70A	NINE ELMS - 70A	NINE ELMS - 70A	NINE ELMS - 70A	NINE ELMS - 70A
31247	NINE ELMS - 70A	NINE ELMS - 70A	NINE ELMS - 70A	NINE ELMS - 70A	NINE ELMS - 70A	NINE ELMS - 70A	NINE ELMS - 70A	NINE ELMS - 70A
31487	TONBRIDGE - 73J	TONBRIDGE - 73J	TONBRIDGE - 73J	TONBRIDGE - 73J	B.ARMS - 73B	B.ARMS - 73B	B.ARMS - 73B	B.ARMS - 73B
31489	TONBRIDGE - 73J	TONBRIDGE - 73J	TONBRIDGE - 73J	TONBRIDGE - 73J	B.ARMS - 73B	B.ARMS - 73B	B.ARMS - 73B	B.ARMS - 73B
31492	TONBRIDGE - 73J	W/D	W/D	W/D	W/D	W/D	W/D	W/D
31494	NINE ELMS - 70A	NINE ELMS - 70A	NINE ELMS - 70A	NINE ELMS - 70A	NINE ELMS - 70A	NINE ELMS - 70A	W/D	W/D
31505	NINE ELMS - 70A	NINE ELMS - 70A	NINE ELMS - 70A	NINE ELMS - 70A	NINE ELMS - 70A	NINE ELMS - 70A	NINE ELMS - 70A	NINE ELMS - 70A
31509	NINE ELMS - 70A	NINE ELMS - 70A	NINE ELMS - 70A	W/D	W/D	W/D	W/D	W/D
31545	NINE ELMS - 70A	NINE ELMS - 70A	NINE ELMS - 70A	NINE ELMS - 70A	NINE ELMS - 70A	NINE ELMS - 70A	NINE ELMS - 70A	NINE ELMS - 70A
31727	NINE ELMS - 70A	NINE ELMS - 70A	NINE ELMS - 70A	NINE ELMS - 70A	NINE ELMS - 70A	NINE ELMS - 70A	NINE ELMS - 70A	NINE ELMS - 70A
31735	EASTLEIGH - 71A	EASTLEIGH - 71A	EASTLEIGH - 71A	EASTLEIGH - 71A	EASTLEIGH - 71A	EASTLEIGH - 71A	EASTLEIGH - 71A	EASTLEIGH - 71A
31739	B.ARMS - 73B	B.ARMS - 73B	B.ARMS - 73B	B.ARMS - 73B	B.ARMS - 73B	B.ARMS - 73B	B.ARMS - 73B	B.ARMS - 73B
31743	B.ARMS - 73B	W/D	W/D	W/D	W/D	W/D	W/D	W/D
31749	B.ARMS - 73B	B.ARMS - 73B	B.ARMS - 73B	B.ARMS - 73B	B.ARMS - 73B	B.ARMS - 73B	B.ARMS - 73B	B.ARMS - 73B
				E1 4-4-0 (1919)				
31019	SALISBURY - 72B	SALISBURY - 72B	SALISBURY - 72B	STEWARTS LANE - 73A	STEWARTS LANE - 73A	STEWARTS LANE - 73A	STEWARTS LANE - 73A	STEWARTS LANE - 73A
31067	SALISBURY - 72B	SALISBURY - 72B	SALISBURY - 72B	STEWARTS LANE - 73A	STEWARTS LANE - 73A	STEWARTS LANE - 73A	STEWARTS LANE - 73A	STEWARTS LANE - 73A
31160	B.ARMS - 73B	B.ARMS - 73B	B.ARMS - 73B	B.ARMS - 73B	B.ARMS - 73B	B.ARMS - 73B	B.ARMS - 73B	B.ARMS - 73B
31497	SALISBURY - 72B	SALISBURY - 72B	SALISBURY - 72B	B.ARMS - 73B	B.ARMS - 73B	B.ARMS - 73B	B.ARMS - 73B	W/D
31507	SALISBURY - 72B	SALISBURY - 72B	SALISBURY - 72B	B.ARMS - 73B	B.ARMS - 73B	B.ARMS - 73B	B.ARMS - 73B	B.ARMS - 73B

Beset with route availability restrictions the SECR - and the Chatham section in particular- was limited to 4-4-0 locomotives for several years after the grouping and as an alternative to the 4-4-2 or 4-6-0 types becoming widespread elsewhere, produced a family of 4-4-0 engines which launched an era of motive power standardisation on services to Ramsgate and Dover together with many secondary services in Kent.

Eventually the grouping brought in its train a programme of engineering works which at length permitted the use of 4-6-0 locomotives but although the subsequent introduction of King Arthur 4-6-0's and Schools 4-4-0's eliminated the SECR classes from many of the more important services, the 4-4-0's were retained as useful reserves for the summer season as well as for ordinary use on trains operating to and from Holborn Viaduct which remained prohibited to 4-6-0 types.

Nationalisation found the four classes in their original areas and much in demand for seasonal passenger traffic togeter with the several morning newspaper trains which continued to use Holborn Viaduct as their London terminus. In addition they shared many of the stopping services in Kent with the LM 2-6-4 and 2-6-2 tanks and right up to the electrification of 1959, an E1 4-4-0 was the usual power for the late morning stopping service between Cannon Street and Ramsgate via Chatham.

With the arrival of the LMS 2MT 2-6-2T's in Kent in 1951, withdrawal of the SECR 4-4-0's became inevitable and the autumn of that year saw the near elimination of the E class with the D class being transferred to the Redhill - Reading line in 1955 and being taken out of traffic by the end of 1956. The D1 and E1 locomotives were reduced more slowly and many survived the electrification of 1959.

The D15 4-4-0's had been the principal motive power on the Waterloo - Bournemouth services until displaced a few years after the grouping by N15 4-6-0's. The class survived nationalisation but there was little main line work available for them and their final years were spent at Eastleigh working services on the Portsmouth - Salisbury axis until being made redundant by new BR4 2-6-0's. Withdrawals commenced in late 1951 but was staggered over a number of years until the last survivor disappeared at the end of 1955. The last regular working for the class had been in 1952 with the 16.40 Plymouth - Eastleigh from Salisbury although they made frequent appearances on the Portsmouth - Salisbury road after the working had been taken over by a 2-6-0. In a surprise move the three survivors were transferred to Nine Elms for the summer of 1954 in order to provide power for the summer Saturday Waterloo - Lymington boat trains.

loco	May-49	Jun-49	Aug-49	Sep-49	Dec-49	Feb-50	Mar-50
				K10 4-4-0 (1901)			
30137	EASTLEIGH - 71A	EASTLEIGH - 71A	EASTLEIGH - 71A	W/D	W/D	W/D	W/D
30140	EASTLEIGH - 71A	EASTLEIGH - 71A	EASTLEIGH - 71A	EASTLEIGH - 71A	EASTLEIGH - 71A	W/D	W/D
30141	GUILDFORD - 70C	GUILDFORD - 70C	GUILDFORD - 70C	GUILDFORD - 70C	W/D	W/D	W/D
30142	FRATTON - 71D	FRATTON - 71D	FRATTON - 71D	FRATTON - 71D	FRATTON - 71D	W/D	W/D
30144	FELTHAM - 70B	FELTHAM - 70B	W/D	W/D	W/D	W/D	W/D
30151	EASTLEIGH - 71A	EASTLEIGH - 71A	EASTLEIGH - 71A	EASTLEIGH - 71A	EASTLEIGH - 71A	EASTLEIGH - 71A	W/D
30329	EASTLEIGH - 71A	EASTLEIGH - 71A	EASTLEIGH - 71A	EASTLEIGH - 71A	EASTLEIGH - 71A	EASTLEIGH - 71A	EASTLEIGH - 71A
30341	EASTLEIGH - 71A	EASTLEIGH - 71A	EASTLEIGH - 71A	EASTLEIGH - 71A	W/D	W/D	W/D
30345	EASTLEIGH - 71A	EASTLEIGH - 71A	EASTLEIGH - 71A	W/D	W/D	W/D	W/D
30380	NINE ELMS - 70A	W/D	W/D	W/D	W/D	W/D	W/D
30382	GUILDFORD - 70C	GUILDFORD - 70C	GUILDFORD - 70C	GUILDFORD - 70C	GUILDFORD - 70C	GUILDFORD - 70C	GUILDFORD - 70C
30383	FELTHAM - 70B	FELTHAM - 70B	FELTHAM - 70B	FELTHAM - 70B	FELTHAM - 70B	FELTHAM - 70B	FELTHAM - 70B
30384	FELTHAM - 70B	FELTHAM - 70B	FELTHAM - 70B	FELTHAM - 70B	FELTHAM - 70B	FELTHAM - 70B	FELTHAM - 70B
30386	NINE ELMS - 70A	NINE ELMS - 70A	NINE ELMS - 70A	W/D	W/D	W/D	W/D
30389	YEOVIL - 72C	YEOVIL - 72C	YEOVIL - 72C	YEOVIL - 72C	YEOVIL - 72C	YEOVIL - 72C	YEOVIL - 72C
30390	NINE ELMS - 70A	NINE ELMS - 70A	NINE ELMS - 70A	NINE ELMS - 70A	NINE ELMS - 70A	NINE ELMS - 70A	NINE ELMS - 70A
30391	NINE ELMS - 70A	NINE ELMS - 70A	NINE ELMS - 70A	NINE ELMS - 70A	W/D	W/D	W/D
				L 4-4-0 (1914)			
31760	TONBRIDGE - 74D	TONBRIDGE - 74D	TONBRIDGE - 74D	TONBRIDGE - 74D	TONBRIDGE - 74D	TONBRIDGE - 74D	TONBRIDGE - 74D
31761	STEWARTS LANE - 73A	STEWARTS LANE - 73A	TONBRIDGE - 74D	TONBRIDGE - 74D	TONBRIDGE - 74D	TONBRIDGE - 74D	TONBRIDGE - 74D
31762	TONBRIDGE - 74D	TONBRIDGE - 74D	STEWARTS LANE - 73A	STEWARTS LANE - 73A	STEWARTS LANE - 73A	STEWARTS LANE - 73A	STEWARTS LANE - 73A
31763	TONBRIDGE - 74D	TONBRIDGE - 74D	TONBRIDGE - 74D	TONBRIDGE - 74D	TONBRIDGE - 74D	ASHFORD - 74A	ASHFORD - 74A
31764	TONBRIDGE - 74D	TONBRIDGE - 74D	STEWARTS LANE - 73A	STEWARTS LANE - 73A	STEWARTS LANE - 73A	STEWARTS LANE - 73A	STEWARTS LANE - 73A
31765	TONBRIDGE - 74D	TONBRIDGE - 74D	TONBRIDGE - 74D	TONBRIDGE - 74D	TONBRIDGE - 74D	TONBRIDGE - 74D	TONBRIDGE - 74D
31766	ST LEONARDS - 74E	ST LEONARDS - 74E	ST LEONARDS - 74E	ST LEONARDS - 74E	ST LEONARDS - 74E	ST LEONARDS - 74E	ST LEONARDS - 74E
31767	STEWARTS LANE - 73A	STEWARTS LANE - 73A	TONBRIDGE - 74D	TONBRIDGE - 74D	TONBRIDGE - 74D	TONBRIDGE - 74D	TONBRIDGE - 74D
31768	ST LEONARDS - 74E	ST LEONARDS - 74E	ST LEONARDS - 74E	ST LEONARDS - 74E	ST LEONARDS - 74E	ST LEONARDS - 74E	ST LEONARDS - 74E
31769	ST LEONARDS - 74E	ST LEONARDS - 74E	ST LEONARDS - 74E	ST LEONARDS - 74E	ST LEONARDS - 74E	ST LEONARDS - 74E	ST LEONARDS - 74E
31770	ASHFORD - 74A	ASHFORD - 74A	ASHFORD - 74A	ASHFORD - 74A	ASHFORD - 74A	ASHFORD - 74A	ASHFORD - 74A
31771	ASHFORD - 74A	ASHFORD - 74A	ASHFORD - 74A	ASHFORD - 74A	ASHFORD - 74A	ASHFORD - 74A	ASHFORD - 74A
31772	RAMSGATE - 74B	RAMSGATE - 74B	RAMSGATE - 74B	ASHFORD - 74A	ASHFORD - 74A	ASHFORD - 74A	ASHFORD - 74A
31773	ASHFORD - 74A	ASHFORD - 74A	ASHFORD - 74A	ASHFORD - 74A	ASHFORD - 74A	ASHFORD - 74A	ASHFORD - 74A
31774	ASHFORD - 74A	ASHFORD - 74A	ASHFORD - 74A	ASHFORD - 74A	ASHFORD - 74A	ASHFORD - 74A	ASHFORD - 74A
31775	ASHFORD - 74A	ASHFORD - 74A	ASHFORD - 74A	ASHFORD - 74A	ASHFORD - 74A	ASHFORD - 74A	ASHFORD - 74A
31776	RAMSGATE - 74B	RAMSGATE - 74B	RAMSGATE - 74B	RAMSGATE - 74B	RAMSGATE - 74B	RAMSGATE - 74B	RAMSGATE - 74B
31777	RAMSGATE - 74B	RAMSGATE - 74B	RAMSGATE - 74B	RAMSGATE - 74B	RAMSGATE - 74B	RAMSGATE - 74B	RAMSGATE - 74B
31778	RAMSGATE - 74B	RAMSGATE - 74B	RAMSGATE - 74B	TONBRIDGE - 74D	TONBRIDGE - 74D	TONBRIDGE - 74D	TONBRIDGE - 74D
31779	RAMSGATE - 74B	RAMSGATE - 74B	RAMSGATE - 74B	TONBRIDGE - 74D	TONBRIDGE - 74D	TONBRIDGE - 74D	TONBRIDGE - 74D
31780	RAMSGATE - 74B	RAMSGATE - 74B	RAMSGATE - 74B	RAMSGATE - 74B	RAMSGATE - 74B	RAMSGATE - 74B	RAMSGATE - 74B
31781	RAMSGATE - 74B	RAMSGATE - 74B	RAMSGATE - 74B	RAMSGATE - 74B	RAMSGATE - 74B	RAMSGATE - 74B	RAMSGATE - 74B
				L1 4-4-0 (1926)			
31753	DOVER - 74C	DOVER - 74C	DOVER - 74C	DOVER - 74C	DOVER - 74C	DOVER - 74C	DOVER - 74C
31754	DOVER - 74C	DOVER - 74C	DOVER - 74C	DOVER - 74C	DOVER - 74C	DOVER - 74C	DOVER - 74C
31755	DOVER - 74C	DOVER - 74C	DOVER - 74C	STEWARTS LANE - 73A	STEWARTS LANE - 73A	B ARMS - 73B	B ARMS - 73B
31756	DOVER - 74C	DOVER - 74C	DOVER - 74C	STEWARTS LANE - 73A	STEWARTS LANE - 73A	STEWARTS LANE - 73A	STEWARTS LANE - 73A
31757	DOVER - 74C	DOVER - 74C	DOVER - 74C	DOVER - 74C	DOVER - 74C	DOVER - 74C	DOVER - 74C
31758	B ARMS - 73B	B ARMS - 73B	B ARMS - 73B	B ARMS - 73B	B ARMS - 73B	B ARMS - 73B	B ARMS - 73B
31759	DOVER - 74C	DOVER - 74C	DOVER - 74C	DOVER - 74C	DOVER - 74C	DOVER - 74C	DOVER - 74C
31782	B ARMS - 73B	B ARMS - 73B	B ARMS - 73B	B ARMS - 73B	B ARMS - 73B	B ARMS - 73B	B ARMS - 73B
31783	B ARMS - 73B	B ARMS - 73B	B ARMS - 73B	B ARMS - 73B	B ARMS - 73B	B ARMS - 73B	B ARMS - 73B
31784	B ARMS - 73B	B ARMS - 73B	B ARMS - 73B	B ARMS - 73B	B ARMS - 73B	B ARMS - 73B	B ARMS - 73B
31785	B ARMS - 73B	B ARMS - 73B	B ARMS - 73B	B ARMS - 73B	B ARMS - 73B	B ARMS - 73B	B ARMS - 73B
31786	B ARMS - 73B	B ARMS - 73B	B ARMS - 73B	B ARMS - 73B	B ARMS - 73B	B ARMS - 73B	B ARMS - 73B
31787	B ARMS - 73B	B ARMS - 73B	B ARMS - 73B	B ARMS - 73B	B ARMS - 73B	B ARMS - 73B	B ARMS - 73B
31788	B ARMS - 73B	B ARMS - 73B	B ARMS - 73B	B ARMS - 73B	B ARMS - 73B	B ARMS - 73B	B ARMS - 73B
31789	B ARMS - 73B	B ARMS - 73B	B ARMS - 73B	B ARMS - 73B	B ARMS - 73B	B ARMS - 73B	B ARMS - 73B
				L11 4-4-0 (1903)			
30134	YEOVIL - 72C	YEOVIL - 72C	YEOVIL - 72C	YEOVIL - 72C	YEOVIL - 72C	YEOVIL - 72C	YEOVIL - 72C
30148	EASTLEIGH - 71A	EASTLEIGH - 71A	EASTLEIGH - 71A	EASTLEIGH - 71A	EASTLEIGH - 71A	EASTLEIGH - 71A	EASTLEIGH - 71A
30154	EASTLEIGH - 71A	EASTLEIGH - 71A	EASTLEIGH - 71A	EASTLEIGH - 71A	EASTLEIGH - 71A	EASTLEIGH - 71A	EASTLEIGH - 71A
30155	EASTLEIGH - 71A	EASTLEIGH - 71A	EASTLEIGH - 71A	EASTLEIGH - 71A	EASTLEIGH - 71A	EASTLEIGH - 71A	EASTLEIGH - 71A
30156	FRATTON - 71D	FRATTON - 71D	FRATTON - 71D	FRATTON - 71D	FRATTON - 71D	EASTLEIGH - 71A	EASTLEIGH - 71A
30157	EASTLEIGH - 71A	EASTLEIGH - 71A	EASTLEIGH - 71A	EASTLEIGH - 71A	EASTLEIGH - 71A	EASTLEIGH - 71A	EASTLEIGH - 71A
30158	FELTHAM - 70B	GUILDFORD - 70C	GUILDFORD - 70C	GUILDFORD - 70C	GUILDFORD - 70C	GUILDFORD - 70C	GUILDFORD - 70C
30159	EASTLEIGH - 71A	EASTLEIGH - 71A	EASTLEIGH - 71A	EASTLEIGH - 71A	EASTLEIGH - 71A	EASTLEIGH - 71A	EASTLEIGH - 71A
30161	DORCHESTER - 71C	DORCHESTER - 71C	DORCHESTER - 71C	DORCHESTER - 71C	EASTLEIGH - 71A	EASTLEIGH - 71A	W/D
30163	YEOVIL - 72C	YEOVIL - 72C	YEOVIL - 72C	YEOVIL - 72C	NINE ELMS - 70A	NINE ELMS - 70A	NINE ELMS - 70A
30164	FRATTON - 71D	FRATTON - 71D	FRATTON - 71D	FELTHAM - 70B	FELTHAM - 70B	FELTHAM - 70B	FELTHAM - 70B
30165	EASTLEIGH - 71A	EASTLEIGH - 71A	EASTLEIGH - 71A	EASTLEIGH - 71A	EASTLEIGH - 71A	EASTLEIGH - 71A	EASTLEIGH - 71A
30166	EASTLEIGH - 71A	EASTLEIGH - 71A	EASTLEIGH - 71A	EASTLEIGH - 71A	EASTLEIGH - 71A	EASTLEIGH - 71A	EASTLEIGH - 71A
30167	FELTHAM - 70B	FELTHAM - 70B	FELTHAM - 70B	W/D	W/D	W/D	W/D
30168	GUILDFORD - 70C	GUILDFORD - 70C	GUILDFORD - 70C	GUILDFORD - 70C	GUILDFORD - 70C	GUILDFORD - 70C	W/D
30169	EASTLEIGH - 71A	EASTLEIGH - 71A	W/D	W/D	W/D	W/D	W/D
30170	FRATTON - 71D	FRATTON - 71D	FRATTON - 71D	FRATTON - 71D	FRATTON - 71D	FRATTON - 71D	FRATTON - 71D
30171	EASTLEIGH - 71A	EASTLEIGH - 71A	EASTLEIGH - 71A	EASTLEIGH - 71A	EASTLEIGH - 71A	EASTLEIGH - 71A	EASTLEIGH - 71A
30172	FRATTON - 71D	FRATTON - 71D	FRATTON - 71D	FRATTON - 71D	FRATTON - 71D	FRATTON - 71D	FRATTON - 71D
30173	BOURNEMOUTH - 71B	BOURNEMOUTH - 71B	BOURNEMOUTH - 71B	BOURNEMOUTH - 71B	BOURNEMOUTH - 71B	EASTLEIGH - 71A	EASTLEIGH - 71A
30174	FELTHAM - 70B	FELTHAM - 70B	FELTHAM - 70B	FELTHAM - 70B	FELTHAM - 70B	FELTHAM - 70B	FELTHAM - 70B
30175	EASTLEIGH - 71A	EASTLEIGH - 71A	EASTLEIGH - 71A	EASTLEIGH - 71A	EASTLEIGH - 71A	EASTLEIGH - 71A	EASTLEIGH - 71A
30405	EASTLEIGH - 71A	EASTLEIGH - 71A	EASTLEIGH - 71A	EASTLEIGH - 71A	EASTLEIGH - 71A	EASTLEIGH - 71A	EASTLEIGH - 71A
30406	NINE ELMS - 70A	NINE ELMS - 70A	NINE ELMS - 70A	NINE ELMS - 70A	NINE ELMS - 70A	NINE ELMS - 70A	NINE ELMS - 70A
30407	YEOVIL - 72C	YEOVIL - 72C	YEOVIL - 72C	YEOVIL - 72C	YEOVIL - 72C	YEOVIL - 72C	YEOVIL - 72C
30408	EXMOUTH JCN - 72A	EXMOUTH JCN - 72A	EXMOUTH JCN - 72A	EXMOUTH JCN - 72A	EXMOUTH JCN - 72A	EXMOUTH JCN - 72A	EXMOUTH JCN - 72A
30409	EXMOUTH JCN - 72A	EXMOUTH JCN - 72A	EXMOUTH JCN - 72A	EXMOUTH JCN - 72A	EXMOUTH JCN - 72A	EXMOUTH JCN - 72A	EXMOUTH JCN - 72A
30410	EASTLEIGH - 71A	EASTLEIGH - 71A	EASTLEIGH - 71A	EASTLEIGH - 71A	W/D	W/D	W/D
30411	EASTLEIGH - 71A	EASTLEIGH - 71A	EASTLEIGH - 71A	EASTLEIGH - 71A	EASTLEIGH - 71A	EASTLEIGH - 71A	EASTLEIGH - 71A
30412	YEOVIL - 72C	YEOVIL - 72C	YEOVIL - 72C	YEOVIL - 72C	YEOVIL - 72C	YEOVIL - 72C	YEOVIL - 72C
30413	DORCHESTER - 71C	EASTLEIGH - 71A	EASTLEIGH - 71A	EASTLEIGH - 71A	EASTLEIGH - 71A	EASTLEIGH - 71A	EASTLEIGH - 71A
30414	FRATTON - 71D	FRATTON - 71D	FRATTON - 71D	FRATTON - 71D	FRATTON - 71D	FRATTON - 71D	FRATTON - 71D
30435	NINE ELMS - 70A	NINE ELMS - 70A	NINE ELMS - 70A	NINE ELMS - 70A	W/D	W/D	W/D
30436	EXMOUTH JCN - 72A	EXMOUTH JCN - 72A	EXMOUTH JCN - 72A	EXMOUTH JCN - 72A	EXMOUTH JCN - 72A	EXMOUTH JCN - 72A	EXMOUTH JCN - 72A
30437	EASTLEIGH - 71A	EASTLEIGH - 71A	EASTLEIGH - 71A	EASTLEIGH - 71A	EASTLEIGH - 71A	EASTLEIGH - 71A	EASTLEIGH - 71A
30438	GUILDFORD - 70C	GUILDFORD - 70C	GUILDFORD - 70C	GUILDFORD - 70C	GUILDFORD - 70C	GUILDFORD - 70C	GUILDFORD - 70C
30439	EXMOUTH JCN - 72A	EXMOUTH JCN - 72A	EXMOUTH JCN - 72A	EXMOUTH JCN - 72A	EXMOUTH JCN - 72A	EXMOUTH JCN - 72A	EXMOUTH JCN - 72A
30440	YEOVIL - 72C	YEOVIL - 72C	YEOVIL - 72C	YEOVIL - 72C	YEOVIL - 72C	YEOVIL - 72C	YEOVIL - 72C
30441	FRATTON - 71D	FRATTON - 71D	FRATTON - 71D	FRATTON - 71D	FRATTON - 71D	FRATTON - 71D	FRATTON - 71D
30442	NINE ELMS - 70A	NINE ELMS - 70A	NINE ELMS - 70A	NINE ELMS - 70A	NINE ELMS - 70A	EASTLEIGH - 71A	EASTLEIGH - 71A

loco	Apr-50	Sep-50	Oct-50	Nov-50	Dec-50	Mar-51	Apr-51
			K10 4-4-0 (1901)				
30382	GUILDFORD - 70C	W/D					
30384	FELTHAM - 70B	FELTHAM - 70B	GUILDFORD - 70C	GUILDFORD - 70C	GUILDFORD - 70C	GUILDFORD - 70C	YEOVIL - 72C
30389	YEOVIL - 72C	YEOVIL - 72C	YEOVIL - 72C	YEOVIL - 72C	YEOVIL - 72C	YEOVIL - 72C	YEOVIL - 72C
30390	NINE ELMS - 70A	NINE ELMS - 70A	NINE ELMS - 70A	W/D	W/D	W/D	W/D
			L 4-4-0 (1914)				
31760	TONBRIDGE - 74D	TONBRIDGE - 74D	TONBRIDGE - 74D	TONBRIDGE - 74D	TONBRIDGE - 74D	TONBRIDGE - 74D	TONBRIDGE - 74D
31761	TONBRIDGE - 74D	TONBRIDGE - 74D	TONBRIDGE - 74D	TONBRIDGE - 74D	TONBRIDGE - 74D	TONBRIDGE - 74D	TONBRIDGE - 74D
31762	STEWARTS LANE - 73A	STEWARTS LANE - 73A	STEWARTS LANE - 73A	STEWARTS LANE - 73A	TONBRIDGE - 74D	TONBRIDGE - 74D	TONBRIDGE - 74D
31763	ASHFORD - 74A	ASHFORD - 74A	ASHFORD - 74A	ASHFORD - 74A	TONBRIDGE - 74D	TONBRIDGE - 74D	TONBRIDGE - 74D
31764	ASHFORD - 74A	STEWARTS LANE - 73A	STEWARTS LANE - 73A	STEWARTS LANE - 73A	TONBRIDGE - 74D	TONBRIDGE - 74D	TONBRIDGE - 74D
31765	TONBRIDGE - 74D	TONBRIDGE - 74D	TONBRIDGE - 74D	TONBRIDGE - 74D	TONBRIDGE - 74D	TONBRIDGE - 74D	TONBRIDGE - 74D
31766	ST LEONARDS - 74E	ST LEONARDS - 74E	ST LEONARDS - 74E	ST LEONARDS - 74E	ST LEONARDS - 74E	ST LEONARDS - 74E	ST LEONARDS - 74E
31767	B ARMS - 73B	STEWARTS LANE - 73A	STEWARTS LANE - 73A	STEWARTS LANE - 73A	ST LEONARDS - 74E	ST LEONARDS - 74E	ST LEONARDS - 74E
31768	ST LEONARDS - 74E	ST LEONARDS - 74E	ST LEONARDS - 74E	ST LEONARDS - 74E	ST LEONARDS - 74E	ST LEONARDS - 74E	ST LEONARDS - 74E
31769	ST LEONARDS - 74E	ST LEONARDS - 74E	ST LEONARDS - 74E	ST LEONARDS - 74E	ST LEONARDS - 74E	ST LEONARDS - 74E	ST LEONARDS - 74E
31770	ASHFORD - 74A	ASHFORD - 74A	ASHFORD - 74A	ASHFORD - 74A	ASHFORD - 74A	ASHFORD - 74A	ASHFORD - 74A
31771	ASHFORD - 74A	ASHFORD - 74A	ASHFORD - 74A	ASHFORD - 74A	ASHFORD - 74A	ASHFORD - 74A	ASHFORD - 74A
31772	ASHFORD - 74A	ASHFORD - 74A	ASHFORD - 74A	ASHFORD - 74A	ASHFORD - 74A	ASHFORD - 74A	ASHFORD - 74A
31773	ASHFORD - 74A	ASHFORD - 74A	ASHFORD - 74A	ASHFORD - 74A	ASHFORD - 74A	ASHFORD - 74A	ASHFORD - 74A
31774	ASHFORD - 74A	ASHFORD - 74A	ASHFORD - 74A	ASHFORD - 74A	ASHFORD - 74A	ASHFORD - 74A	ASHFORD - 74A
31775	ASHFORD - 74A	ASHFORD - 74A	ASHFORD - 74A	ASHFORD - 74A	ASHFORD - 74A	ASHFORD - 74A	ASHFORD - 74A
31776	RAMSGATE - 74B	RAMSGATE - 74B	RAMSGATE - 74B	RAMSGATE - 74B	RAMSGATE - 74B	RAMSGATE - 74B	RAMSGATE - 74B
31777	RAMSGATE - 74B	RAMSGATE - 74B	RAMSGATE - 74B	RAMSGATE - 74B	RAMSGATE - 74B	ASHFORD - 74A	ASHFORD - 74A
31778	TONBRIDGE - 74D	TONBRIDGE - 74D	TONBRIDGE - 74D	TONBRIDGE - 74D	RAMSGATE - 74B	RAMSGATE - 74B	RAMSGATE - 74B
31779	TONBRIDGE - 74D	TONBRIDGE - 74D	TONBRIDGE - 74D	TONBRIDGE - 74D	RAMSGATE - 74B	RAMSGATE - 74B	RAMSGATE - 74B
31780	RAMSGATE - 74B	RAMSGATE - 74B	RAMSGATE - 74B	RAMSGATE - 74B	RAMSGATE - 74B	RAMSGATE - 74B	RAMSGATE - 74B
31781	RAMSGATE - 74B	RAMSGATE - 74B	RAMSGATE - 74B	RAMSGATE - 74B	RAMSGATE - 74B	RAMSGATE - 74B	RAMSGATE - 74B
			L1 4-4-0 (1926)				
31753	DOVER - 74C	DOVER - 74C	DOVER - 74C	DOVER - 74C	DOVER - 74C	DOVER - 74C	DOVER - 74C
31754	DOVER - 74C	DOVER - 74C	DOVER - 74C	DOVER - 74C	DOVER - 74C	DOVER - 74C	DOVER - 74C
31755	B ARMS - 73B	DOVER - 74C	DOVER - 74C	DOVER - 74C	DOVER - 74C	DOVER - 74C	DOVER - 74C
31756	DOVER - 74C	DOVER - 74C	DOVER - 74C	DOVER - 74C	DOVER - 74C	DOVER - 74C	DOVER - 74C
31757	DOVER - 74C	DOVER - 74C	DOVER - 74C	DOVER - 74C	DOVER - 74C	DOVER - 74C	DOVER - 74C
31758	B ARMS - 73B	B ARMS - 73B	B ARMS - 73B	B ARMS - 73B	B ARMS - 73B	B ARMS - 73B	B ARMS - 73B
31759	DOVER - 74C	B ARMS - 73B	B ARMS - 73B	B ARMS - 73B	B ARMS - 73B	B ARMS - 73B	B ARMS - 73B
31782	B ARMS - 73B	B ARMS - 73B	B ARMS - 73B	B ARMS - 73B	B ARMS - 73B	B ARMS - 73B	B ARMS - 73B
31783	B ARMS - 73B	B ARMS - 73B	B ARMS - 73B	B ARMS - 73B	B ARMS - 73B	B ARMS - 73B	B ARMS - 73B
31784	B ARMS - 73B	B ARMS - 73B	B ARMS - 73B	B ARMS - 73B	B ARMS - 73B	B ARMS - 73B	B ARMS - 73B
31785	B ARMS - 73B	B ARMS - 73B	B ARMS - 73B	B ARMS - 73B	B ARMS - 73B	B ARMS - 73B	B ARMS - 73B
31786	B ARMS - 73B	B ARMS - 73B	B ARMS - 73B	B ARMS - 73B	B ARMS - 73B	B ARMS - 73B	B ARMS - 73B
31787	B ARMS - 73B	B ARMS - 73B	B ARMS - 73B	B ARMS - 73B	B ARMS - 73B	B ARMS - 73B	B ARMS - 73B
31788	B ARMS - 73B	B ARMS - 73B	RAMSGATE - 74B	RAMSGATE - 74B	B ARMS - 73B	B ARMS - 73B	B ARMS - 73B
31789	B ARMS - 73B	B ARMS - 73B	RAMSGATE - 74B	RAMSGATE - 74B	B ARMS - 73B	B ARMS - 73B	B ARMS - 73B
			L11 4-4-0 (1903)				
30134	YEOVIL - 72C	YEOVIL - 72C	YEOVIL - 72C	YEOVIL - 72C	YEOVIL - 72C	W/D	W/D
30148	EASTLEIGH - 71A	EASTLEIGH - 71A	EASTLEIGH - 71A	EASTLEIGH - 71A	EASTLEIGH - 71A	EASTLEIGH - 71A	EASTLEIGH - 71A
30154	EASTLEIGH - 71A	EASTLEIGH - 71A	EASTLEIGH - 71A	EASTLEIGH - 71A	EASTLEIGH - 71A	EASTLEIGH - 71A	W/D
30155	EASTLEIGH - 71A	EASTLEIGH - 71A	EASTLEIGH - 71A	EASTLEIGH - 71A	EASTLEIGH - 71A	EASTLEIGH - 71A	W/D
30156	EASTLEIGH - 71A	EASTLEIGH - 71A	EASTLEIGH - 71A	EASTLEIGH - 71A	EASTLEIGH - 71A	EASTLEIGH - 71A	W/D
30157	EASTLEIGH - 71A	EASTLEIGH - 71A	EASTLEIGH - 71A	EASTLEIGH - 71A	EASTLEIGH - 71A	EASTLEIGH - 71A	EASTLEIGH - 71A
30158	GUILDFORD - 70C	GUILDFORD - 70C	GUILDFORD - 70C	W/D	W/D	W/D	W/D
30159	EASTLEIGH - 71A	EASTLEIGH - 71A	EASTLEIGH - 71A	EASTLEIGH - 71A	EASTLEIGH - 71A	W/D	W/D
30163	NINE ELMS - 70A	NINE ELMS - 70A	NINE ELMS - 70A	NINE ELMS - 70A	NINE ELMS - 70A	NINE ELMS - 70A	NINE ELMS - 70A
30164	FELTHAM - 70B	FELTHAM - 70B	FELTHAM - 70B	FELTHAM - 70B	FELTHAM - 70B	FELTHAM - 70B	FELTHAM - 70B
30165	EASTLEIGH - 71A	NINE ELMS - 70A	NINE ELMS - 70A	NINE ELMS - 70A	NINE ELMS - 70A	NINE ELMS - 70A	W/D
30166	EASTLEIGH - 71A						
30170	FRATTON - 71D	FRATTON - 71D	FRATTON - 71D	FRATTON - 71D	FRATTON - 71D	FRATTON - 71D	FRATTON - 71D
30171	EASTLEIGH - 71A	EASTLEIGH - 71A	EASTLEIGH - 71A	EASTLEIGH - 71A	EASTLEIGH - 71A	EASTLEIGH - 71A	EASTLEIGH - 71A
30172	FRATTON - 71D	FRATTON - 71D	FRATTON - 71D	FRATTON - 71D	FRATTON - 71D	FRATTON - 71D	FRATTON - 71D
30173	EASTLEIGH - 71A	EASTLEIGH - 71A	EASTLEIGH - 71A	EASTLEIGH - 71A	EASTLEIGH - 71A	EASTLEIGH - 71A	W/D
30174	FELTHAM - 70B	FELTHAM - 70B	FELTHAM - 70B	FELTHAM - 70B	FELTHAM - 70B	FELTHAM - 70B	FELTHAM - 70B
30175	EASTLEIGH - 71A	EASTLEIGH - 71A	EASTLEIGH - 71A	EASTLEIGH - 71A	EASTLEIGH - 71A	EASTLEIGH - 71A	EASTLEIGH - 71A
30405	NINE ELMS - 70A	NINE ELMS - 70A	NINE ELMS - 70A	NINE ELMS - 70A	W/D	W/D	W/D
30406	NINE ELMS - 70A	NINE ELMS - 70A	NINE ELMS - 70A	NINE ELMS - 70A	NINE ELMS - 70A	NINE ELMS - 70A	NINE ELMS - 70A
30407	YEOVIL - 72C	YEOVIL - 72C	YEOVIL - 72C	W/D	W/D	W/D	W/D
30408	EXMOUTH JCN - 72A	EXMOUTH JCN - 72A	EXMOUTH JCN - 72A	EXMOUTH JCN - 72A	EXMOUTH JCN - 72A	W/D	W/D
30409	EXMOUTH JCN - 72A	EXMOUTH JCN - 72A	EXMOUTH JCN - 72A	EXMOUTH JCN - 72A	EXMOUTH JCN - 72A	EXMOUTH JCN - 72A	EXMOUTH JCN - 72A
30411	EASTLEIGH - 71A	EASTLEIGH - 71A	EASTLEIGH - 71A	EASTLEIGH - 71A	EASTLEIGH - 71A	EASTLEIGH - 71A	EASTLEIGH - 71A
30412	YEOVIL - 72C	YEOVIL - 72C	YEOVIL - 72C	W/D	W/D	W/D	W/D
30413	EASTLEIGH - 71A	EASTLEIGH - 71A	EASTLEIGH - 71A	NINE ELMS - 70A	NINE ELMS - 70A	W/D	W/D
30414	FELTHAM - 70B	FELTHAM - 70B	EASTLEIGH - 71A	EASTLEIGH - 71A	EASTLEIGH - 71A	YEOVIL - 72C	W/D
30436	GUILDFORD - 70C	GUILDFORD - 70C	GUILDFORD - 70C	GUILDFORD - 70C	GUILDFORD - 70C	GUILDFORD - 70C	GUILDFORD - 70C
30437	EASTLEIGH - 71A	EASTLEIGH - 71A	EASTLEIGH - 71A	EASTLEIGH - 71A	EASTLEIGH - 71A	EASTLEIGH - 71A	EASTLEIGH - 71A
30438	FELTHAM - 70B	FELTHAM - 70B	FELTHAM - 70B	FELTHAM - 70B	FELTHAM - 70B	FELTHAM - 70B	FELTHAM - 70B
30441	FRATTON - 71D	FRATTON - 71D	FRATTON - 71D	FRATTON - 71D	FRATTON - 71D	FRATTON - 71D	W/D
30442	EASTLEIGH - 71A	EASTLEIGH - 71A	EASTLEIGH - 71A	EASTLEIGH - 71A	EASTLEIGH - 71A	EASTLEIGH - 71A	EASTLEIGH - 71A

loco	Jun-51	Jul-51	Sep-51	Dec-51	Jan-52	Mar-52	Jun-52
K10 4-4-0 (1901)							
30389 YEOVIL - 72C	W/D	W/D	W/D	W/D	W/D	W/D	
L 4-4-0 (1914)							
31760 TONBRIDGE - 74D	TONBRIDGE - 74D	TONBRIDGE - 74D	TONBRIDGE - 74D	TONBRIDGE - 74D	TONBRIDGE - 74D	TONBRIDGE - 74D
31761 TONBRIDGE - 74D	TONBRIDGE - 74D	TONBRIDGE - 74D	TONBRIDGE - 74D	TONBRIDGE - 74D	TONBRIDGE - 74D	TONBRIDGE - 74D
31762 TONBRIDGE - 74D	TONBRIDGE - 74D	TONBRIDGE - 74D	TONBRIDGE - 74D	TONBRIDGE - 74D	TONBRIDGE - 74D	TONBRIDGE - 74D
31763 TONBRIDGE - 74D	TONBRIDGE - 74D	TONBRIDGE - 74D	TONBRIDGE - 74D	TONBRIDGE - 74D	TONBRIDGE - 74D	TONBRIDGE - 74D
31764 TONBRIDGE - 74D	TONBRIDGE - 74D	TONBRIDGE - 74D	TONBRIDGE - 74D	TONBRIDGE - 74D	TONBRIDGE - 74D	TONBRIDGE - 74D
31765 TONBRIDGE - 74D	TONBRIDGE - 74D	TONBRIDGE - 74D	TONBRIDGE - 74D	TONBRIDGE - 74D	TONBRIDGE - 74D	TONBRIDGE - 74D
31766 ST LEONARDS - 74E	ST LEONARDS - 74E	ST LEONARDS - 74E	ST LEONARDS - 74E	ST LEONARDS - 74E	ST LEONARDS - 74E	TONBRIDGE - 74D
31767 ST LEONARDS - 74E	ST LEONARDS - 74E	ST LEONARDS - 74E	ST LEONARDS - 74E	ST LEONARDS - 74E	ST LEONARDS - 74E	ST LEONARDS - 74E
31768 ST LEONARDS - 74E	ST LEONARDS - 74E	ST LEONARDS - 74E	ST LEONARDS - 74E	ST LEONARDS - 74E	ST LEONARDS - 74E	ST LEONARDS - 74E
31769 ST LEONARDS - 74E	ST LEONARDS - 74E	ST LEONARDS - 74E	ST LEONARDS - 74E	ST LEONARDS - 74E	ST LEONARDS - 74E	ASHFORD - 74A
31770 ASHFORD - 74A	ASHFORD - 74A	ASHFORD - 74A	EASTLEIGH - 71A	EASTLEIGH - 71A	EASTLEIGH - 71A	ASHFORD - 74A
31771 ASHFORD - 74A	ASHFORD - 74A	ASHFORD - 74A	ASHFORD - 74A	EASTLEIGH - 71A	EASTLEIGH - 71A	ASHFORD - 74A
31772 ASHFORD - 74A	ASHFORD - 74A	ASHFORD - 74A	ASHFORD - 74A	EASTLEIGH - 71A	EASTLEIGH - 71A	ASHFORD - 74A
31773 ASHFORD - 74A	ASHFORD - 74A	ASHFORD - 74A	ASHFORD - 74A	EASTLEIGH - 71A	EASTLEIGH - 71A	ASHFORD - 74A
31774 ASHFORD - 74A	ASHFORD - 74A	ASHFORD - 74A	ASHFORD - 74A	EASTLEIGH - 71A	EASTLEIGH - 71A	EASTLEIGH - 71A
31775 ASHFORD - 74A	ASHFORD - 74A	ASHFORD - 74A	ASHFORD - 74A	EASTLEIGH - 71A	EASTLEIGH - 71A	EASTLEIGH - 71A
31776 RAMSGATE - 74B	RAMSGATE - 74B	ASHFORD - 74A	ASHFORD - 74A	EASTLEIGH - 71A	EASTLEIGH - 71A	EASTLEIGH - 71A
31777 ASHFORD - 74A	ASHFORD - 74A	ASHFORD - 74A	ASHFORD - 74A	EASTLEIGH - 71A	EASTLEIGH - 71A	EASTLEIGH - 71A
31778 RAMSGATE - 74B	RAMSGATE - 74B	ASHFORD - 74A	RAMSGATE - 74B	EASTLEIGH - 71A	EASTLEIGH - 71A	EASTLEIGH - 71A
31779 RAMSGATE - 74B	RAMSGATE - 74B	RAMSGATE - 74B	RAMSGATE - 74B	EASTLEIGH - 71A	EASTLEIGH - 71A	RAMSGATE - 74B
31780 RAMSGATE - 74B	RAMSGATE - 74B	RAMSGATE - 74B	RAMSGATE - 74B	RAMSGATE - 74B	RAMSGATE - 74B	RAMSGATE - 74B
31781 RAMSGATE - 74B	RAMSGATE - 74B	B ARMS - 73B	B ARMS - 73B	B ARMS - 73B	B ARMS - 73B	B ARMS - 73B
L1 4-4-0 (1926)							
31753 DOVER - 74C	DOVER - 74C	DOVER - 74C	DOVER - 74C	DOVER - 74C	DOVER - 74C	DOVER - 74C
31754 DOVER - 74C	DOVER - 74C	DOVER - 74C	DOVER - 74C	DOVER - 74C	DOVER - 74C	DOVER - 74C
31755 DOVER - 74C	DOVER - 74C	DOVER - 74C	DOVER - 74C	ASHFORD - 74A	ASHFORD - 74A	DOVER - 74C
31756 DOVER - 74C	DOVER - 74C	DOVER - 74C	DOVER - 74C	ASHFORD - 74A	ASHFORD - 74A	DOVER - 74C
31757 DOVER - 74C	DOVER - 74C	DOVER - 74C	DOVER - 74C	ASHFORD - 74A	ASHFORD - 74A	DOVER - 74C
31758 STEWARTS LANE - 73A	STEWARTS LANE - 73A	STEWARTS LANE - 73A	STEWARTS LANE - 73A	ASHFORD - 74A	ASHFORD - 74A	STEWARTS LANE - 73A
31759 STEWARTS LANE - 73A	STEWARTS LANE - 73A	STEWARTS LANE - 73A	STEWARTS LANE - 73A	ASHFORD - 74A	ASHFORD - 74A	STEWARTS LANE - 73A
31782 B ARMS - 73B	B ARMS - 73B	B ARMS - 73B	B ARMS - 73B	RAMSGATE - 74B	RAMSGATE - 74B	B ARMS - 73B
31783 B ARMS - 73B	B ARMS - 73B	B ARMS - 73B	B ARMS - 73B	RAMSGATE - 74B	RAMSGATE - 74B	B ARMS - 73B
31784 B ARMS - 73B	B ARMS - 73B	B ARMS - 73B	B ARMS - 73B	ASHFORD - 74A	ASHFORD - 74A	B ARMS - 73B
31785 B ARMS - 73B	B ARMS - 73B	B ARMS - 73B	B ARMS - 73B	ASHFORD - 74A	ASHFORD - 74A	B ARMS - 73B
31786 B ARMS - 73B	B ARMS - 73B	B ARMS - 73B	B ARMS - 73B	B ARMS - 73B	B ARMS - 73B	B ARMS - 73B
31787 B ARMS - 73B	B ARMS - 73B	B ARMS - 73B	B ARMS - 73B	B ARMS - 73B	B ARMS - 73B	B ARMS - 73B
31788 B ARMS - 73B	B ARMS - 73B	B ARMS - 73B	B ARMS - 73B	B ARMS - 73B	B ARMS - 73B	B ARMS - 73B
31789 B ARMS - 73B	B ARMS - 73B	B ARMS - 73B	B ARMS - 73B	B ARMS - 73B	B ARMS - 73B	B ARMS - 73B
L11 4-4-0 (1903)							
30148 EASTLEIGH - 71A	EASTLEIGH - 71A	EASTLEIGH - 71A	EASTLEIGH - 71A	EASTLEIGH - 71A	W/D	W/D
30157 EASTLEIGH - 71A	EASTLEIGH - 71A	EASTLEIGH - 71A	EASTLEIGH - 71A	EASTLEIGH - 71A	W/D	W/D
30163 NINE ELMS - 70A	NINE ELMS - 70A	NINE ELMS - 70A	W/D	W/D	W/D	W/D
30164 FELTHAM - 70B	FELTHAM - 70B	W/D	W/D	W/D	W/D	W/D
30170 FRATTON - 71D	FRATTON - 71D	FRATTON - 71D	FRATTON - 71D	FRATTON - 71D	W/D	W/D
30171 EASTLEIGH - 71A	EASTLEIGH - 71A	W/D	W/D	W/D	W/D	W/D
30172 FRATTON - 71D	FRATTON - 71D	FRATTON - 71D	FRATTON - 71D	FRATTON - 71D	W/D	W/D
30174 FELTHAM - 70B	FELTHAM - 70B	W/D	W/D	W/D	W/D	W/D
30175 EASTLEIGH - 71A	EASTLEIGH - 71A	EASTLEIGH - 71A	W/D	W/D	W/D	W/D
30411 EASTLEIGH - 71A	EASTLEIGH - 71A	EASTLEIGH - 71A	EASTLEIGH - 71A	EASTLEIGH - 71A	EASTLEIGH - 71A	W/D
30436 GUILDFORD - 70C	W/D	W/D	W/D	W/D	W/D	W/D
30437 EASTLEIGH - 71A	EASTLEIGH - 71A	EASTLEIGH - 71A	EASTLEIGH - 71A	EASTLEIGH - 71A	EASTLEIGH - 71A	W/D
30438 FELTHAM - 70B	YEOVIL - 72C	W/D	W/D	W/D	W/D	W/D
30442 EASTLEIGH - 71A	EASTLEIGH - 71A	EASTLEIGH - 71A	W/D	W/D	W/D	W/D

For years the L class 4-4-0's had been associated with the Charing Cross - Hastings trains until the arrival of the Schools 4-4-0's in 1930 engines saw them dispersed to sheds in East Kent. In late 1955 a number were allocated to Faversham to become a useful stand-by for the many Kent Coast relief trains that Ramsgate was unable to cover and in addition handled a two-day cyclic diagram which involved working to Tonbridge via Margate, Canterbury West, Ashford, Rye and Hastings, where the engine remained overnight before returning with the 16.12 Tonbridge - Faversham via Paddock Wood and Ashford. The Faversham 4-4-0's did not have regular bookings to London although 31765 was caught at Stewarts Lane, having worked up from the coast to Victoria in 1956.

loco	Sep-52	Dec-52	Mar-53	May-53	Jul-53	Sep-53	Nov-53
			L 4-4-0 (1914)				
31760	TONBRIDGE - 74D	TONBRIDGE - 74D	TONBRIDGE - 74D	TONBRIDGE - 74D	TONBRIDGE - 74D	TONBRIDGE - 74D	TONBRIDGE - 74D
31761	TONBRIDGE - 74D	TONBRIDGE - 74D	TONBRIDGE - 74D	TONBRIDGE - 74D	TONBRIDGE - 74D	TONBRIDGE - 74D	TONBRIDGE - 74D
31762	TONBRIDGE - 74D	TONBRIDGE - 74D	TONBRIDGE - 74D	TONBRIDGE - 74D	TONBRIDGE - 74D	TONBRIDGE - 74D	TONBRIDGE - 74D
31763	TONBRIDGE - 74D	TONBRIDGE - 74D	TONBRIDGE - 74D	TONBRIDGE - 74D	TONBRIDGE - 74D	TONBRIDGE - 74D	TONBRIDGE - 74D
31764	TONBRIDGE - 74D	TONBRIDGE - 74D	TONBRIDGE - 74D	TONBRIDGE - 74D	TONBRIDGE - 74D	TONBRIDGE - 74D	TONBRIDGE - 74D
31765	TONBRIDGE - 74D	TONBRIDGE - 74D	TONBRIDGE - 74D	TONBRIDGE - 74D	TONBRIDGE - 74D	TONBRIDGE - 74D	TONBRIDGE - 74D
31766	TONBRIDGE - 74D	TONBRIDGE - 74D	TONBRIDGE - 74D	TONBRIDGE - 74D	TONBRIDGE - 74D	TONBRIDGE - 74D	TONBRIDGE - 74D
31767	ST LEONARDS - 74E	ST LEONARDS - 74E	ST LEONARDS - 74E	ST LEONARDS - 74E	ST LEONARDS - 74E	ST LEONARDS - 74E	ST LEONARDS - 74E
31768	ST LEONARDS - 74E	ST LEONARDS - 74E	ST LEONARDS - 74E	ST LEONARDS - 74E	ST LEONARDS - 74E	ST LEONARDS - 74E	ST LEONARDS - 74E
31769	ASHFORD - 74A	ST LEONARDS - 74E	ST LEONARDS - 74E	ST LEONARDS - 74E	ST LEONARDS - 74E	ST LEONARDS - 74E	ST LEONARDS - 74E
31770	TONBRIDGE - 74D	TONBRIDGE - 74D	TONBRIDGE - 74D	TONBRIDGE - 74D	TONBRIDGE - 74D	TONBRIDGE - 74D	TONBRIDGE - 74D
31771	TONBRIDGE - 74D	TONBRIDGE - 74D	TONBRIDGE - 74D	TONBRIDGE - 74D	TONBRIDGE - 74D	TONBRIDGE - 74D	TONBRIDGE - 74D
31772	ASHFORD - 74A	ASHFORD - 74A	ASHFORD - 74A	ASHFORD - 74A	ASHFORD - 74A	ASHFORD - 74A	ASHFORD - 74A
31773	TONBRIDGE - 74D	TONBRIDGE - 74D	TONBRIDGE - 74D	TONBRIDGE - 74D	TONBRIDGE - 74D	TONBRIDGE - 74D	TONBRIDGE - 74D
31774	EASTLEIGH - 71A	ASHFORD - 74A	ASHFORD - 74A	ASHFORD - 74A	ASHFORD - 74A	ASHFORD - 74A	ASHFORD - 74A
31775	EASTLEIGH - 71A	ASHFORD - 74A	ASHFORD - 74A	ASHFORD - 74A	ASHFORD - 74A	ASHFORD - 74A	ASHFORD - 74A
31776	EASTLEIGH - 71A	ASHFORD - 74A	ASHFORD - 74A	ASHFORD - 74A	ASHFORD - 74A	ASHFORD - 74A	ASHFORD - 74A
31777	EASTLEIGH - 71A	ASHFORD - 74A	ASHFORD - 74A	ASHFORD - 74A	ASHFORD - 74A	ASHFORD - 74A	ASHFORD - 74A
31778	EASTLEIGH - 71A	ASHFORD - 74A	ASHFORD - 74A	ASHFORD - 74A	ASHFORD - 74A	ASHFORD - 74A	ASHFORD - 74A
31779	RAMSGATE - 74B	RAMSGATE - 74B	RAMSGATE - 74B	RAMSGATE - 74B	RAMSGATE - 74B	RAMSGATE - 74B	RAMSGATE - 74B
31780	RAMSGATE - 74B	RAMSGATE - 74B	RAMSGATE - 74B	RAMSGATE - 74B	RAMSGATE - 74B	RAMSGATE - 74B	RAMSGATE - 74B
31781	B.ARMS - 73B	B.ARMS - 73B	B.ARMS - 73B	B.ARMS - 73B	B.ARMS - 73B	B.ARMS - 73B	
			L1 4-4-0 (1926)				
31753	DOVER - 74C	DOVER - 74C	DOVER - 74C	DOVER - 74C	DOVER - 74C	DOVER - 74C	DOVER - 74C
31754	DOVER - 74C	DOVER - 74C	DOVER - 74C	DOVER - 74C	DOVER - 74C	DOVER - 74C	DOVER - 74C
31755	DOVER - 74C	DOVER - 74C	DOVER - 74C	DOVER - 74C	DOVER - 74C	DOVER - 74C	DOVER - 74C
31756	RAMSGATE - 74B	RAMSGATE - 74B	RAMSGATE - 74B	RAMSGATE - 74B	RAMSGATE - 74B	ASHFORD - 74A	ASHFORD - 74A
31757	RAMSGATE - 74B	RAMSGATE - 74B	RAMSGATE - 74B	RAMSGATE - 74B	RAMSGATE - 74B	ASHFORD - 74A	ASHFORD - 74A
31758	STEWARTS LANE - 73A	STEWARTS LANE - 73A	STEWARTS LANE - 73A	GILLINGHAM - 73D	GILLINGHAM - 73D	ASHFORD - 74A	ASHFORD - 74A
31759	STEWARTS LANE - 73A	STEWARTS LANE - 73A	STEWARTS LANE - 73A	GILLINGHAM - 73D	GILLINGHAM - 73D	ASHFORD - 74A	ASHFORD - 74A
31782	B.ARMS - 73B	B.ARMS - 73B	B.ARMS - 73B	B.ARMS - 73B	B.ARMS - 73B	ASHFORD - 74A	ASHFORD - 74A
31783	B.ARMS - 73B	B.ARMS - 73B	B.ARMS - 73B	B.ARMS - 73B	B.ARMS - 73B	B.ARMS - 73B	B.ARMS - 73B
31784	B.ARMS - 73B	B.ARMS - 73B	B.ARMS - 73B	B.ARMS - 73B	B.ARMS - 73B	B.ARMS - 73B	B.ARMS - 73B
31785	STEWARTS LANE - 73A	ASHFORD - 74A	ASHFORD - 74A	ASHFORD - 74A	ASHFORD - 74A	ASHFORD - 74A	ASHFORD - 74A
31786	STEWARTS LANE - 73A	EASTLEIGH - 71A	EASTLEIGH - 71A	EASTLEIGH - 71A	EASTLEIGH - 71A	EASTLEIGH - 71A	EASTLEIGH - 71A
31787	STEWARTS LANE - 73A	EASTLEIGH - 71A	EASTLEIGH - 71A	EASTLEIGH - 71A	EASTLEIGH - 71A	EASTLEIGH - 71A	EASTLEIGH - 71A
31788	STEWARTS LANE - 73A	EASTLEIGH - 71A	EASTLEIGH - 71A	EASTLEIGH - 71A	EASTLEIGH - 71A	EASTLEIGH - 71A	EASTLEIGH - 71A
31789	STEWARTS LANE - 73A	EASTLEIGH - 71A	EASTLEIGH - 71A	EASTLEIGH - 71A	EASTLEIGH - 71A	EASTLEIGH - 71A	EASTLEIGH - 71A

loco	Jan-54	Mar-54	May-54	Jun-54	Aug-54	Oct-54	Dec-54
			L 4-4-0 (1914)				
31760	TONBRIDGE - 74D	TONBRIDGE - 74D	TONBRIDGE - 74D	TONBRIDGE - 74D	TONBRIDGE - 74D	TONBRIDGE - 74D	TONBRIDGE - 74D
31761	TONBRIDGE - 74D	TONBRIDGE - 74D	TONBRIDGE - 74D	TONBRIDGE - 74D	TONBRIDGE - 74D	TONBRIDGE - 74D	TONBRIDGE - 74D
31762	TONBRIDGE - 74D	TONBRIDGE - 74D	TONBRIDGE - 74D	TONBRIDGE - 74D	TONBRIDGE - 74D	TONBRIDGE - 74D	TONBRIDGE - 74D
31763	TONBRIDGE - 74D	TONBRIDGE - 74D	TONBRIDGE - 74D	TONBRIDGE - 74D	TONBRIDGE - 74D	TONBRIDGE - 74D	TONBRIDGE - 74D
31764	TONBRIDGE - 74D	TONBRIDGE - 74D	TONBRIDGE - 74D	TONBRIDGE - 74D	TONBRIDGE - 74D	ST LEONARDS - 74E	ST LEONARDS - 74E
31765	TONBRIDGE - 74D	TONBRIDGE - 74D	TONBRIDGE - 74D	TONBRIDGE - 74D	TONBRIDGE - 74D	TONBRIDGE - 74D	TONBRIDGE - 74D
31766	TONBRIDGE - 74D	TONBRIDGE - 74D	TONBRIDGE - 74D	TONBRIDGE - 74D	TONBRIDGE - 74D	TONBRIDGE - 74D	TONBRIDGE - 74D
31767	ST LEONARDS - 74E	ST LEONARDS - 74E	ST LEONARDS - 74E	ST LEONARDS - 74E	ST LEONARDS - 74E	ST LEONARDS - 74E	ST LEONARDS - 74E
31768	ST LEONARDS - 74E	ST LEONARDS - 74E	ST LEONARDS - 74E	ST LEONARDS - 74E	ST LEONARDS - 74E	ST LEONARDS - 74E	ST LEONARDS - 74E
31769	ST LEONARDS - 74E	ST LEONARDS - 74E	ST LEONARDS - 74E	ST LEONARDS - 74E	ST LEONARDS - 74E	ST LEONARDS - 74E	ST LEONARDS - 74E
31770	TONBRIDGE - 74D	TONBRIDGE - 74D	TONBRIDGE - 74D	TONBRIDGE - 74D	TONBRIDGE - 74D	TONBRIDGE - 74D	TONBRIDGE - 74D
31771	TONBRIDGE - 74D	TONBRIDGE - 74D	TONBRIDGE - 74D	TONBRIDGE - 74D	TONBRIDGE - 74D	TONBRIDGE - 74D	TONBRIDGE - 74D
31772	ASHFORD - 74A	ASHFORD - 74A	ASHFORD - 74A	ASHFORD - 74A	ASHFORD - 74A	ASHFORD - 74A	ASHFORD - 74A
31773	TONBRIDGE - 74D	TONBRIDGE - 74D	TONBRIDGE - 74D	TONBRIDGE - 74D	TONBRIDGE - 74D	TONBRIDGE - 74D	TONBRIDGE - 74D
31774	ASHFORD - 74A	ASHFORD - 74A	ASHFORD - 74A	ASHFORD - 74A	ASHFORD - 74A	ASHFORD - 74A	ASHFORD - 74A
31775	ASHFORD - 74A	ASHFORD - 74A	ASHFORD - 74A	ASHFORD - 74A	ASHFORD - 74A	ASHFORD - 74A	ASHFORD - 74A
31776	ASHFORD - 74A	ASHFORD - 74A	ASHFORD - 74A	ASHFORD - 74A	ASHFORD - 74A	ASHFORD - 74A	ASHFORD - 74A
31777	ASHFORD - 74A	ASHFORD - 74A	ASHFORD - 74A	ASHFORD - 74A	ASHFORD - 74A	ASHFORD - 74A	ASHFORD - 74A
31778	ASHFORD - 74A	ASHFORD - 74A	ASHFORD - 74A	ASHFORD - 74A	ASHFORD - 74A	ASHFORD - 74A	ASHFORD - 74A
31779	RAMSGATE - 74B	RAMSGATE - 74B	RAMSGATE - 74B	RAMSGATE - 74B	RAMSGATE - 74B	RAMSGATE - 74B	RAMSGATE - 74B
31780	RAMSGATE - 74B	RAMSGATE - 74B	RAMSGATE - 74B	RAMSGATE - 74B	RAMSGATE - 74B	RAMSGATE - 74B	RAMSGATE - 74B
31781	B.ARMS - 73B	B.ARMS - 73B	B.ARMS - 73B	B.ARMS - 73B	B.ARMS - 73B	B.ARMS - 73B	B.ARMS - 73B
			L1 4-4-0 (1926)				
31753	DOVER - 74C	DOVER - 74C	DOVER - 74C	DOVER - 74C	DOVER - 74C	DOVER - 74C	DOVER - 74C
31754	DOVER - 74C	DOVER - 74C	DOVER - 74C	DOVER - 74C	DOVER - 74C	DOVER - 74C	DOVER - 74C
31755	DOVER - 74C	DOVER - 74C	DOVER - 74C	DOVER - 74C	DOVER - 74C	DOVER - 74C	DOVER - 74C
31756	ASHFORD - 74A	ASHFORD - 74A	ASHFORD - 74A	ASHFORD - 74A	ASHFORD - 74A	ASHFORD - 74A	ASHFORD - 74A
31757	ASHFORD - 74A	ASHFORD - 74A	ASHFORD - 74A	ASHFORD - 74A	ASHFORD - 74A	ASHFORD - 74A	ASHFORD - 74A
31758	ASHFORD - 74A	ASHFORD - 74A	ASHFORD - 74A	ASHFORD - 74A	ASHFORD - 74A	ASHFORD - 74A	ASHFORD - 74A
31759	ASHFORD - 74A	ASHFORD - 74A	ASHFORD - 74A	ASHFORD - 74A	ASHFORD - 74A	ASHFORD - 74A	ASHFORD - 74A
31782	ASHFORD - 74A	ASHFORD - 74A	ASHFORD - 74A	ASHFORD - 74A	ASHFORD - 74A	ASHFORD - 74A	ASHFORD - 74A
31783	B.ARMS - 73B	B.ARMS - 73B	B.ARMS - 73B	B.ARMS - 73B	B.ARMS - 73B	B.ARMS - 73B	B.ARMS - 73B
31784	B.ARMS - 73B	B.ARMS - 73B	B.ARMS - 73B	B.ARMS - 73B	B.ARMS - 73B	B.ARMS - 73B	B.ARMS - 73B
31785	B.ARMS - 73B	B.ARMS - 73B	B.ARMS - 73B	B.ARMS - 73B	B.ARMS - 73B	B.ARMS - 73B	B.ARMS - 73B
31786	EASTLEIGH - 71A	EASTLEIGH - 71A	EASTLEIGH - 71A	B.ARMS - 73B	B.ARMS - 73B	B.ARMS - 73B	B.ARMS - 73B
31787	EASTLEIGH - 71A	EASTLEIGH - 71A	EASTLEIGH - 71A	B.ARMS - 73B	B.ARMS - 73B	B.ARMS - 73B	B.ARMS - 73B
31788	EASTLEIGH - 71A	EASTLEIGH - 71A	EASTLEIGH - 71A	B.ARMS - 73B	B.ARMS - 73B	B.ARMS - 73B	B.ARMS - 73B
31789	EASTLEIGH - 71A	EASTLEIGH - 71A	EASTLEIGH - 71A	B.ARMS - 73B	B.ARMS - 73B	B.ARMS - 73B	B.ARMS - 73B

loco	Feb-55	Apr-55	Jun-55	Aug-55	Sep-55	Nov-55	Dec-55
			L 4-4-0 (1914)				
31760	TONBRIDGE - 74D	TONBRIDGE - 74D	TONBRIDGE - 74D	TONBRIDGE - 74D	TONBRIDGE - 74D	TONBRIDGE - 74D	TONBRIDGE - 74D
31761	TONBRIDGE - 74D	TONBRIDGE - 74D	TONBRIDGE - 74D	TONBRIDGE - 74D	TONBRIDGE - 74D	TONBRIDGE - 74D	TONBRIDGE - 74D
31762	TONBRIDGE - 74D	TONBRIDGE - 74D	TONBRIDGE - 74D	TONBRIDGE - 74D	TONBRIDGE - 74D	TONBRIDGE - 74D	TONBRIDGE - 74D
31763	TONBRIDGE - 74D	TONBRIDGE - 74D	TONBRIDGE - 74D	TONBRIDGE - 74D	TONBRIDGE - 74D	TONBRIDGE - 74D	TONBRIDGE - 74D
31764	ST LEONARDS - 74E	ST LEONARDS - 74E	ST LEONARDS - 74E	ST LEONARDS - 74E	RAMSGATE - 74B	RAMSGATE - 74B	RAMSGATE - 74B
31765	TONBRIDGE - 74D	TONBRIDGE - 74D	TONBRIDGE - 74D	TONBRIDGE - 74D	TONBRIDGE - 74D	TONBRIDGE - 74D	FAVERSHAM - 73E
31766	TONBRIDGE - 74D	TONBRIDGE - 74D	TONBRIDGE - 74D	TONBRIDGE - 74D	TONBRIDGE - 74D	TONBRIDGE - 74D	FAVERSHAM - 73E
31767	ST LEONARDS - 74E	ST LEONARDS - 74E	ST LEONARDS - 74E	ST LEONARDS - 74E	ST LEONARDS - 74E	ST LEONARDS - 74E	FAVERSHAM - 73E
31768	ST LEONARDS - 74E	ST LEONARDS - 74E	ST LEONARDS - 74E	ST LEONARDS - 74E	ST LEONARDS - 74E	ST LEONARDS - 74E	FAVERSHAM - 73E
31769	ST LEONARDS - 74E	ST LEONARDS - 74E	ST LEONARDS - 74E	ST LEONARDS - 74E	RAMSGATE - 74B	RAMSGATE - 74B	RAMSGATE - 74B
31770	TONBRIDGE - 74D	TONBRIDGE - 74D	TONBRIDGE - 74D	TONBRIDGE - 74D	TONBRIDGE - 74D	TONBRIDGE - 74D	TONBRIDGE - 74D
31771	TONBRIDGE - 74D	TONBRIDGE - 74D	TONBRIDGE - 74D	TONBRIDGE - 74D	TONBRIDGE - 74D	TONBRIDGE - 74D	TONBRIDGE - 74D
31772	ASHFORD - 74A	ASHFORD - 74A	ASHFORD - 74A	ASHFORD - 74A	ASHFORD - 74A	ASHFORD - 74A	ASHFORD - 74A
31773	TONBRIDGE - 74D	TONBRIDGE - 74D	TONBRIDGE - 74D	TONBRIDGE - 74D	TONBRIDGE - 74D	TONBRIDGE - 74D	TONBRIDGE - 74D
31774	ASHFORD - 74A	ASHFORD - 74A	ASHFORD - 74A	ASHFORD - 74A	ASHFORD - 74A	ASHFORD - 74A	ASHFORD - 74A
31775	ASHFORD - 74A	ASHFORD - 74A	ASHFORD - 74A	ASHFORD - 74A	ASHFORD - 74A	ASHFORD - 74A	ASHFORD - 74A
31776	ASHFORD - 74A	ASHFORD - 74A	ASHFORD - 74A	ASHFORD - 74A	ASHFORD - 74A	ASHFORD - 74A	ASHFORD - 74A
31777	ASHFORD - 74A	ASHFORD - 74A	ASHFORD - 74A	ASHFORD - 74A	ASHFORD - 74A	ASHFORD - 74A	ASHFORD - 74A
31778	ASHFORD - 74A	ASHFORD - 74A	ASHFORD - 74A	ASHFORD - 74A	ASHFORD - 74A	ASHFORD - 74A	ASHFORD - 74A
31779	RAMSGATE - 74B	RAMSGATE - 74B	RAMSGATE - 74B	RAMSGATE - 74B	RAMSGATE - 74B	RAMSGATE - 74B	RAMSGATE - 74B
31780	RAMSGATE - 74B	RAMSGATE - 74B	RAMSGATE - 74B	RAMSGATE - 74B	RAMSGATE - 74B	RAMSGATE - 74B	RAMSGATE - 74B
31781	B.ARMS - 73B	B.ARMS - 73B	B.ARMS - 73B	B.ARMS - 73B	B.ARMS - 73B	B.ARMS - 73B	B.ARMS - 73B
			L1 4-4-0 (1926)				
31753	DOVER - 74C	DOVER - 74C	DOVER - 74C	DOVER - 74C	DOVER - 74C	DOVER - 74C	DOVER - 74C
31754	DOVER - 74C	DOVER - 74C	DOVER - 74C	DOVER - 74C	DOVER - 74C	DOVER - 74C	DOVER - 74C
31755	DOVER - 74C	DOVER - 74C	DOVER - 74C	DOVER - 74C	DOVER - 74C	DOVER - 74C	DOVER - 74C
31756	ASHFORD - 74A	ASHFORD - 74A	ASHFORD - 74A	ASHFORD - 74A	ASHFORD - 74A	ASHFORD - 74A	ASHFORD - 74A
31757	ASHFORD - 74A	ASHFORD - 74A	ASHFORD - 74A	ASHFORD - 74A	ASHFORD - 74A	ASHFORD - 74A	ASHFORD - 74A
31758	ASHFORD - 74A	ASHFORD - 74A	ASHFORD - 74A	ASHFORD - 74A	ASHFORD - 74A	ASHFORD - 74A	ASHFORD - 74A
31759	ASHFORD - 74A	ASHFORD - 74A	ASHFORD - 74A	ASHFORD - 74A	ASHFORD - 74A	ASHFORD - 74A	ASHFORD - 74A
31782	ASHFORD - 74A	ASHFORD - 74A	ASHFORD - 74A	ASHFORD - 74A	ASHFORD - 74A	ASHFORD - 74A	ASHFORD - 74A
31783	B.ARMS - 73B	B.ARMS - 73B	B.ARMS - 73B	B.ARMS - 73B	B.ARMS - 73B	B.ARMS - 73B	B.ARMS - 73B
31784	B.ARMS - 73B	B.ARMS - 73B	B.ARMS - 73B	B.ARMS - 73B	B.ARMS - 73B	B.ARMS - 73B	B.ARMS - 73B
31785	B.ARMS - 73B	B.ARMS - 73B	GILLINGHAM - 73D	GILLINGHAM - 73D	GILLINGHAM - 73D	GILLINGHAM - 73D	GILLINGHAM - 73D
31786	B.ARMS - 73B	B.ARMS - 73B	GILLINGHAM - 73D	GILLINGHAM - 73D	GILLINGHAM - 73D	GILLINGHAM - 73D	GILLINGHAM - 73D
31787	B.ARMS - 73B	B.ARMS - 73B	GILLINGHAM - 73D	GILLINGHAM - 73D	GILLINGHAM - 73D	GILLINGHAM - 73D	GILLINGHAM - 73D
31788	B.ARMS - 73B	B.ARMS - 73B	DOVER - 74C	DOVER - 74C	DOVER - 74C	DOVER - 74C	DOVER - 74C
31789	B.ARMS - 73B	B.ARMS - 73B	DOVER - 74C	DOVER - 74C	DOVER - 74C	DOVER - 74C	DOVER - 74C

loco	Jan-56	Apr-56	May-56	Aug-56	Oct-56	Nov-56	Jan-57
			L 4-4-0 (1914)				
31760	TONBRIDGE - 74D	TONBRIDGE - 74D	TONBRIDGE - 74D	TONBRIDGE - 74D	TONBRIDGE - 74D	TONBRIDGE - 74D	TONBRIDGE - 74D
31761	TONBRIDGE - 74D	TONBRIDGE - 74D	TONBRIDGE - 74D	TONBRIDGE - 74D	TONBRIDGE - 74D	W/D	W/D
31762	TONBRIDGE - 74D	TONBRIDGE - 74D	TONBRIDGE - 74D	TONBRIDGE - 74D	TONBRIDGE - 74D	TONBRIDGE - 74D	TONBRIDGE - 74D
31763	TONBRIDGE - 74D	TONBRIDGE - 74D	TONBRIDGE - 74D	TONBRIDGE - 74D	TONBRIDGE - 74D	TONBRIDGE - 74D	TONBRIDGE - 74D
31764	RAMSGATE - 74B	RAMSGATE - 74B	RAMSGATE - 74B	RAMSGATE - 74B	RAMSGATE - 74B	RAMSGATE - 74B	RAMSGATE - 74B
31765	FAVERSHAM - 73E	FAVERSHAM - 73E	FAVERSHAM - 73E	FAVERSHAM - 73E	FAVERSHAM - 73E	FAVERSHAM - 73E	FAVERSHAM - 73E
31766	FAVERSHAM - 73E	FAVERSHAM - 73E	FAVERSHAM - 73E	FAVERSHAM - 73E	FAVERSHAM - 73E	FAVERSHAM - 73E	FAVERSHAM - 73E
31767	FAVERSHAM - 73E	FAVERSHAM - 73E	FAVERSHAM - 73E	FAVERSHAM - 73E	FAVERSHAM - 73E	FAVERSHAM - 73E	FAVERSHAM - 73E
31768	FAVERSHAM - 73E	FAVERSHAM - 73E	FAVERSHAM - 73E	FAVERSHAM - 73E	FAVERSHAM - 73E	FAVERSHAM - 73E	FAVERSHAM - 73E
31769	RAMSGATE - 74B	W/D	W/D	W/D	W/D	W/D	W/D
31770	TONBRIDGE - 74D	TONBRIDGE - 74D	TONBRIDGE - 74D	TONBRIDGE - 74D	TONBRIDGE - 74D	TONBRIDGE - 74D	TONBRIDGE - 74D
31771	TONBRIDGE - 74D	TONBRIDGE - 74D	TONBRIDGE - 74D	TONBRIDGE - 74D	TONBRIDGE - 74D	TONBRIDGE - 74D	TONBRIDGE - 74D
31772	ASHFORD - 74A	ASHFORD - 74A	ASHFORD - 74A	ASHFORD - 74A	ASHFORD - 74A	ASHFORD - 74A	ASHFORD - 74A
31773	TONBRIDGE - 74D	TONBRIDGE - 74D	TONBRIDGE - 74D	TONBRIDGE - 74D	TONBRIDGE - 74D	TONBRIDGE - 74D	TONBRIDGE - 74D
31774	ASHFORD - 74A	ASHFORD - 74A	ASHFORD - 74A	ASHFORD - 74A	ASHFORD - 74A	ASHFORD - 74A	ASHFORD - 74A
31775	ASHFORD - 74A	ASHFORD - 74A	ASHFORD - 74A	ASHFORD - 74A	ASHFORD - 74A	ASHFORD - 74A	ASHFORD - 74A
31776	ASHFORD - 74A	ASHFORD - 74A	BRIGHTON - 75A	BRIGHTON - 75A	BRIGHTON - 75A	BRIGHTON - 75A	BRIGHTON - 75A
31777	ASHFORD - 74A	ASHFORD - 74A	BRIGHTON - 75A	BRIGHTON - 75A	BRIGHTON - 75A	BRIGHTON - 75A	BRIGHTON - 75A
31778	ASHFORD - 74A	ASHFORD - 74A	BRIGHTON - 75A	BRIGHTON - 75A	BRIGHTON - 75A	BRIGHTON - 75A	BRIGHTON - 75A
31779	RAMSGATE - 74B	RAMSGATE - 74B	RAMSGATE - 74B	RAMSGATE - 74B	RAMSGATE - 74B	RAMSGATE - 74B	RAMSGATE - 74B
31780	RAMSGATE - 74B	RAMSGATE - 74B	RAMSGATE - 74B	RAMSGATE - 74B	RAMSGATE - 74B	RAMSGATE - 74B	RAMSGATE - 74B
31781	B.ARMS - 73B	B.ARMS - 73B	B.ARMS - 73B	B.ARMS - 73B	B.ARMS - 73B	B.ARMS - 73B	B.ARMS - 73B
			L1 4-4-0 (1926)				
31753	DOVER - 74C	DOVER - 74C	DOVER - 74C	DOVER - 74C	DOVER - 74C	DOVER - 74C	DOVER - 74C
31754	DOVER - 74C	DOVER - 74C	DOVER - 74C	DOVER - 74C	DOVER - 74C	DOVER - 74C	DOVER - 74C
31755	DOVER - 74C	DOVER - 74C	DOVER - 74C	DOVER - 74C	DOVER - 74C	DOVER - 74C	DOVER - 74C
31756	ASHFORD - 74A	ASHFORD - 74A	ASHFORD - 74A	ASHFORD - 74A	ASHFORD - 74A	ASHFORD - 74A	ASHFORD - 74A
31757	ASHFORD - 74A	ASHFORD - 74A	ASHFORD - 74A	ASHFORD - 74A	ASHFORD - 74A	ASHFORD - 74A	ASHFORD - 74A
31758	ASHFORD - 74A	ASHFORD - 74A	ASHFORD - 74A	ASHFORD - 74A	ASHFORD - 74A	ASHFORD - 74A	ASHFORD - 74A
31759	ASHFORD - 74A	ASHFORD - 74A	ASHFORD - 74A	ASHFORD - 74A	ASHFORD - 74A	ASHFORD - 74A	ASHFORD - 74A
31782	ASHFORD - 74A	ASHFORD - 74A	ASHFORD - 74A	ASHFORD - 74A	ASHFORD - 74A	ASHFORD - 74A	ASHFORD - 74A
31783	B.ARMS - 73B	B.ARMS - 73B	B.ARMS - 73B	B.ARMS - 73B	B.ARMS - 73B	B.ARMS - 73B	B.ARMS - 73B
31784	B.ARMS - 73B	B.ARMS - 73B	B.ARMS - 73B	B.ARMS - 73B	B.ARMS - 73B	B.ARMS - 73B	B.ARMS - 73B
31785	GILLINGHAM - 73D	GILLINGHAM - 73D	GILLINGHAM - 73D	GILLINGHAM - 73D	GILLINGHAM - 73D	GILLINGHAM - 73D	GILLINGHAM - 73D
31786	GILLINGHAM - 73D	GILLINGHAM - 73D	GILLINGHAM - 73D	GILLINGHAM - 73D	GILLINGHAM - 73D	GILLINGHAM - 73D	GILLINGHAM - 73D
31787	GILLINGHAM - 73D	GILLINGHAM - 73D	GILLINGHAM - 73D	GILLINGHAM - 73D	GILLINGHAM - 73D	GILLINGHAM - 73D	GILLINGHAM - 73D
31788	DOVER - 74C	DOVER - 74C	DOVER - 74C	DOVER - 74C	DOVER - 74C	DOVER - 74C	DOVER - 74C
31789	DOVER - 74C	DOVER - 74C	DOVER - 74C	DOVER - 74C	DOVER - 74C	DOVER - 74C	DOVER - 74C

loco	Mar-57	Jun-57	Jul-57	Oct-57	Jan-58	Feb-58	Mar-58
				L 4-4-0 (1914)			
31760	TONBRIDGE - 74D	TONBRIDGE - 74D	TONBRIDGE - 74D	TONBRIDGE - 74D	TONBRIDGE - 74D	TONBRIDGE - 74D	TONBRIDGE - 74D
31762	TONBRIDGE - 74D	TONBRIDGE - 74D	TONBRIDGE - 74D	TONBRIDGE - 74D	TONBRIDGE - 74D	TONBRIDGE - 74D	TONBRIDGE - 74D
31763	TONBRIDGE - 74D	TONBRIDGE - 74D	TONBRIDGE - 74D	TONBRIDGE - 74D	TONBRIDGE - 74D	TONBRIDGE - 74D	TONBRIDGE - 74D
31764	RAMSGATE - 74B	RAMSGATE - 74B	RAMSGATE - 74B	RAMSGATE - 74B	RAMSGATE - 74B	RAMSGATE - 74B	RAMSGATE - 74B
31765	FAVERSHAM - 73E	FAVERSHAM - 73E	FAVERSHAM - 73E	FAVERSHAM - 73E	FAVERSHAM - 73E	FAVERSHAM - 73E	FAVERSHAM - 73E
31766	FAVERSHAM - 73E	FAVERSHAM - 73E	FAVERSHAM - 73E	FAVERSHAM - 73E	FAVERSHAM - 73E	FAVERSHAM - 73E	FAVERSHAM - 73E
31767	FAVERSHAM - 73E	FAVERSHAM - 73E	FAVERSHAM - 73E	FAVERSHAM - 73E	FAVERSHAM - 73E	FAVERSHAM - 73E	FAVERSHAM - 73E
31768	FAVERSHAM - 73E	FAVERSHAM - 73E	FAVERSHAM - 73E	FAVERSHAM - 73E	FAVERSHAM - 73E	FAVERSHAM - 73E	FAVERSHAM - 73E
31770	TONBRIDGE - 74D	TONBRIDGE - 74D	TONBRIDGE - 74D	TONBRIDGE - 74D	TONBRIDGE - 74D	TONBRIDGE - 74D	TONBRIDGE - 74D
31771	TONBRIDGE - 74D	TONBRIDGE - 74D	TONBRIDGE - 74D	TONBRIDGE - 74D	TONBRIDGE - 74D	TONBRIDGE - 74D	TONBRIDGE - 74D
31772	ASHFORD - 74A	TONBRIDGE - 74D	TONBRIDGE - 74D	TONBRIDGE - 74D	TONBRIDGE - 74D	TONBRIDGE - 74D	TONBRIDGE - 74D
31773	TONBRIDGE - 74D	ST LEONARDS - 74E	ST LEONARDS - 74E	ST LEONARDS - 74E	ST LEONARDS - 74E	ST LEONARDS - 74E	ST LEONARDS - 74E
31774	ASHFORD - 74A	ST LEONARDS - 74E	ST LEONARDS - 74E	ST LEONARDS - 74E	ST LEONARDS - 74E	ST LEONARDS - 74E	ST LEONARDS - 74E
31775	ASHFORD - 74A	ST LEONARDS - 74E	ST LEONARDS - 74E	ST LEONARDS - 74E	ST LEONARDS - 74E	ST LEONARDS - 74E	ST LEONARDS - 74E
31776	BRIGHTON - 75A	BRIGHTON - 75A	BRIGHTON - 75A	BRIGHTON - 75A	BRIGHTON - 75A	BRIGHTON - 75A	BRIGHTON - 75A
31777	BRIGHTON - 75A	BRIGHTON - 75A	BRIGHTON - 75A	BRIGHTON - 75A	BRIGHTON - 75A	BRIGHTON - 75A	BRIGHTON - 75A
31778	BRIGHTON - 75A	BRIGHTON - 75A	BRIGHTON - 75A	BRIGHTON - 75A	BRIGHTON - 75A	BRIGHTON - 75A	BRIGHTON - 75A
31779	RAMSGATE - 74B	RAMSGATE - 74B	RAMSGATE - 74B	RAMSGATE - 74B	RAMSGATE - 74B	RAMSGATE - 74B	RAMSGATE - 74B
31780	RAMSGATE - 74B	RAMSGATE - 74B	RAMSGATE - 74B	RAMSGATE - 74B	RAMSGATE - 74B	RAMSGATE - 74B	RAMSGATE - 74B
31781	B.ARMS - 73B	B.ARMS - 73B	B.ARMS - 73B	B.ARMS - 73B	B.ARMS - 73B	B.ARMS - 73B	B.ARMS - 73B
				L1 4-4-0 (1926)			
31753	DOVER - 74C	DOVER - 74C	DOVER - 74C	DOVER - 74C	DOVER - 74C	DOVER - 74C	DOVER - 74C
31754	DOVER - 74C	DOVER - 74C	DOVER - 74C	DOVER - 74C	DOVER - 74C	DOVER - 74C	DOVER - 74C
31755	DOVER - 74C	DOVER - 74C	DOVER - 74C	DOVER - 74C	DOVER - 74C	DOVER - 74C	DOVER - 74C
31756	ASHFORD - 74A	ASHFORD - 74A	ASHFORD - 74A	ASHFORD - 74A	ASHFORD - 74A	ASHFORD - 74A	ASHFORD - 74A
31757	ASHFORD - 74A	ASHFORD - 74A	ASHFORD - 74A	ASHFORD - 74A	ASHFORD - 74A	ASHFORD - 74A	ASHFORD - 74A
31758	ASHFORD - 74A	ASHFORD - 74A	ASHFORD - 74A	ASHFORD - 74A	ASHFORD - 74A	ASHFORD - 74A	ASHFORD - 74A
31759	ASHFORD - 74A	ASHFORD - 74A	ASHFORD - 74A	ASHFORD - 74A	ASHFORD - 74A	ASHFORD - 74A	ASHFORD - 74A
31782	ASHFORD - 74A	ASHFORD - 74A	ASHFORD - 74A	ASHFORD - 74A	ASHFORD - 74A	ASHFORD - 74A	ASHFORD - 74A
31783	B.ARMS - 73B	B.ARMS - 73B	B.ARMS - 73B	B.ARMS - 73B	B.ARMS - 73B	B.ARMS - 73B	B.ARMS - 73B
31784	B.ARMS - 73B	B.ARMS - 73B	B.ARMS - 73B	B.ARMS - 73B	B.ARMS - 73B	B.ARMS - 73B	B.ARMS - 73B
31785	GILLINGHAM - 73D	GILLINGHAM - 73D	GILLINGHAM - 73D	GILLINGHAM - 73D	GILLINGHAM - 73D	GILLINGHAM - 73D	GILLINGHAM - 73D
31786	GILLINGHAM - 73D	GILLINGHAM - 73D	GILLINGHAM - 73D	GILLINGHAM - 73D	GILLINGHAM - 73D	GILLINGHAM - 73D	GILLINGHAM - 73D
31787	GILLINGHAM - 73D	GILLINGHAM - 73D	GILLINGHAM - 73D	GILLINGHAM - 73D	GILLINGHAM - 73D	GILLINGHAM - 73D	GILLINGHAM - 73D
31788	DOVER - 74C	DOVER - 74C	DOVER - 74C	DOVER - 74C	DOVER - 74C	DOVER - 74C	DOVER - 74C
31789	DOVER - 74C	DOVER - 74C	DOVER - 74C	DOVER - 74C	DOVER - 74C	DOVER - 74C	DOVER - 74C

loco	May-58	Oct-58	Mar-59	Jun-59	Jul-59	Aug-59	Oct-59
				L 4-4-0 (1914)			
31760	TONBRIDGE - 74D	TONBRIDGE - 73J	TONBRIDGE - 73J	NINE ELMS - 70A	NINE ELMS - 70A	NINE ELMS - 70A	NINE ELMS - 70A
31762	TONBRIDGE - 74D	TONBRIDGE - 73J	TONBRIDGE - 73J	NINE ELMS - 70A	NINE ELMS - 70A	NINE ELMS - 70A	NINE ELMS - 70A
31763	TONBRIDGE - 74D	TONBRIDGE - 73J	TONBRIDGE - 73J	NINE ELMS - 70A	NINE ELMS - 70A	NINE ELMS - 70A	NINE ELMS - 70A
31764	RAMSGATE - 74B	RAMSGATE - 73G	RAMSGATE - 73G	NINE ELMS - 70A	NINE ELMS - 70A	NINE ELMS - 70A	NINE ELMS - 70A
31765	FAVERSHAM - 73E	FAVERSHAM - 73E	FAVERSHAM - 73E	NINE ELMS - 70A	NINE ELMS - 70A	NINE ELMS - 70A	NINE ELMS - 70A
31766	FAVERSHAM - 73E	FAVERSHAM - 73E	FAVERSHAM - 73E	NINE ELMS - 70A	NINE ELMS - 70A	NINE ELMS - 70A	NINE ELMS - 70A
31767	FAVERSHAM - 73E	FAVERSHAM - 73E	W/D	W/D	W/D	W/D	W/D
31768	FAVERSHAM - 73E	FAVERSHAM - 73E	FAVERSHAM - 73E	NINE ELMS - 70A	NINE ELMS - 70A	NINE ELMS - 70A	NINE ELMS - 70A
31770	TONBRIDGE - 74D	TONBRIDGE - 73J	TONBRIDGE - 73J	NINE ELMS - 70A	NINE ELMS - 70A	NINE ELMS - 70A	NINE ELMS - 70A
31771	TONBRIDGE - 74D	TONBRIDGE - 73J	TONBRIDGE - 73J	NINE ELMS - 70A	NINE ELMS - 70A	NINE ELMS - 70A	NINE ELMS - 70A
31772	TONBRIDGE - 74D	TONBRIDGE - 73J	W/D	W/D	W/D	W/D	W/D
31773	TONBRIDGE - 74D	TONBRIDGE - 73J	TONBRIDGE - 73J	NINE ELMS - 70A	NINE ELMS - 70A	W/D	W/D
31774	TONBRIDGE - 74D	TONBRIDGE - 73J	W/D	W/D	W/D	W/D	W/D
31775	RAMSGATE - 74B	RAMSGATE - 73G	RAMSGATE - 73G	NINE ELMS - 70A	NINE ELMS - 70A	NINE ELMS - 70A	W/D
31776	BRIGHTON - 75A	BRIGHTON - 75A	BRIGHTON - 75A	NINE ELMS - 70A	NINE ELMS - 70A	NINE ELMS - 70A	NINE ELMS - 70A
31777	BRIGHTON - 75A	BRIGHTON - 75A	BRIGHTON - 75A	NINE ELMS - 70A	NINE ELMS - 70A	NINE ELMS - 70A	W/D
31778	BRIGHTON - 75A	BRIGHTON - 75A	BRIGHTON - 75A	NINE ELMS - 70A	NINE ELMS - 70A	W/D	W/D
31779	RAMSGATE - 74B	RAMSGATE - 73G	RAMSGATE - 73G	NINE ELMS - 70A	W/D	W/D	W/D
31780	RAMSGATE - 74B	RAMSGATE - 73G	RAMSGATE - 73G	NINE ELMS - 70A	NINE ELMS - 70A	NINE ELMS - 70A	NINE ELMS - 70A
31781	B.ARMS - 73B	B.ARMS - 73B	B.ARMS - 73B	NINE ELMS - 70A	W/D	W/D	W/D
				L1 4-4-0 (1926)			
31753	DOVER - 74C	DOVER - 73H	DOVER - 73H	NINE ELMS - 70A	NINE ELMS - 70A	NINE ELMS - 70A	NINE ELMS - 70A
31754	DOVER - 74C	DOVER - 73H	DOVER - 73H	NINE ELMS - 70A	NINE ELMS - 70A	NINE ELMS - 70A	NINE ELMS - 70A
31755	DOVER - 74C	DOVER - 73H	DOVER - 73H	NINE ELMS - 70A	NINE ELMS - 70A	W/D	W/D
31756	ASHFORD - 74A	ASHFORD - 73F	ASHFORD - 73F	NINE ELMS - 70A	NINE ELMS - 70A	NINE ELMS - 70A	NINE ELMS - 70A
31757	ASHFORD - 74A	ASHFORD - 73F	ASHFORD - 73F	NINE ELMS - 70A	NINE ELMS - 70A	NINE ELMS - 70A	NINE ELMS - 70A
31758	ASHFORD - 74A	ASHFORD - 73F	ASHFORD - 73F	NINE ELMS - 70A	NINE ELMS - 70A	NINE ELMS - 70A	W/D
31759	ASHFORD - 74A	ASHFORD - 73F	ASHFORD - 73F	NINE ELMS - 70A	NINE ELMS - 70A	NINE ELMS - 70A	NINE ELMS - 70A
31782	ASHFORD - 74A	ASHFORD - 73F	ASHFORD - 73F	NINE ELMS - 70A	NINE ELMS - 70A	NINE ELMS - 70A	NINE ELMS - 70A
31783	B.ARMS - 73B	B.ARMS - 73B	B.ARMS - 73B	NINE ELMS - 70A	NINE ELMS - 70A	NINE ELMS - 70A	NINE ELMS - 70A
31784	B.ARMS - 73B	B.ARMS - 73B	B.ARMS - 73B	NINE ELMS - 70A	NINE ELMS - 70A	NINE ELMS - 70A	NINE ELMS - 70A
31785	GILLINGHAM - 73D	GILLINGHAM - 73D	GILLINGHAM - 73D	NINE ELMS - 70A	NINE ELMS - 70A	NINE ELMS - 70A	NINE ELMS - 70A
31786	GILLINGHAM - 73D	GILLINGHAM - 73D	GILLINGHAM - 73D	NINE ELMS - 70A	NINE ELMS - 70A	NINE ELMS - 70A	NINE ELMS - 70A
31787	GILLINGHAM - 73D	GILLINGHAM - 73D	GILLINGHAM - 73D	NINE ELMS - 70A	NINE ELMS - 70A	NINE ELMS - 70A	NINE ELMS - 70A
31788	DOVER - 74C	DOVER - 73H	DOVER - 73H	NINE ELMS - 70A	NINE ELMS - 70A	NINE ELMS - 70A	NINE ELMS - 70A
31789	DOVER - 74C	DOVER - 73H	DOVER - 73H	NINE ELMS - 70A	NINE ELMS - 70A	NINE ELMS - 70A	NINE ELMS - 70A

L 4-4-0 (1914)

loco	Dec-59	Feb-60	Mar-60	Apr-60	Jul-60	Aug-60	Sep-60	Nov-60
31760	NINE ELMS - 70A	NINE ELMS - 70A	NINE ELMS - 70A	NINE ELMS - 70A	NINE ELMS - 70A	NINE ELMS - 70A	NINE ELMS - 70A	NINE ELMS - 70A
31762	NINE ELMS - 70A	W/D	W/D	W/D	W/D	W/D	W/D	W/D
31763	NINE ELMS - 70A	NINE ELMS - 70A	NINE ELMS - 70A	W/D	W/D	W/D	W/D	W/D
31764	NINE ELMS - 70A	NINE ELMS - 70A	NINE ELMS - 70A	NINE ELMS - 70A	NINE ELMS - 70A	NINE ELMS - 70A	NINE ELMS - 70A	NINE ELMS - 70A
31765	NINE ELMS - 70A	NINE ELMS - 70A	NINE ELMS - 70A	NINE ELMS - 70A	NINE ELMS - 70A	NINE ELMS - 70A	NINE ELMS - 70A	NINE ELMS - 70A
31766	NINE ELMS - 70A	NINE ELMS - 70A	NINE ELMS - 70A	NINE ELMS - 70A	NINE ELMS - 70A	NINE ELMS - 70A	NINE ELMS - 70A	NINE ELMS - 70A
31768	NINE ELMS - 70A	NINE ELMS - 70A	NINE ELMS - 70A	NINE ELMS - 70A	NINE ELMS - 70A	NINE ELMS - 70A	NINE ELMS - 70A	NINE ELMS - 70A
31771	NINE ELMS - 70A	NINE ELMS - 70A	NINE ELMS - 70A	NINE ELMS - 70A	NINE ELMS - 70A	NINE ELMS - 70A	NINE ELMS - 70A	NINE ELMS - 70A
31776	NINE ELMS - 70A	NINE ELMS - 70A	NINE ELMS - 70A	NINE ELMS - 70A	NINE ELMS - 70A	NINE ELMS - 70A	NINE ELMS - 70A	NINE ELMS - 70A
31780	NINE ELMS - 70A	NINE ELMS - 70A	NINE ELMS - 70A	NINE ELMS - 70A	NINE ELMS - 70A	NINE ELMS - 70A	NINE ELMS - 70A	NINE ELMS - 70A

L1 4-4-0 (1926)

loco	Dec-59	Feb-60	Mar-60	Apr-60	Jul-60	Aug-60	Sep-60	Nov-60
31753	NINE ELMS - 70A	NINE ELMS - 70A	NINE ELMS - 70A	NINE ELMS - 70A	NINE ELMS - 70A	NINE ELMS - 70A	NINE ELMS - 70A	NINE ELMS - 70A
31754	NINE ELMS - 70A	NINE ELMS - 70A	NINE ELMS - 70A	NINE ELMS - 70A	NINE ELMS - 70A	NINE ELMS - 70A	NINE ELMS - 70A	NINE ELMS - 70A
31756	NINE ELMS - 70A	TONBRIDGE - 73J	TONBRIDGE - 73J	TONBRIDGE - 73J	NINE ELMS - 70A	NINE ELMS - 70A	NINE ELMS - 70A	NINE ELMS - 70A
31757	NINE ELMS - 70A	NINE ELMS - 70A	NINE ELMS - 70A	NINE ELMS - 70A	NINE ELMS - 70A	NINE ELMS - 70A	NINE ELMS - 70A	NINE ELMS - 70A
31759	NINE ELMS - 70A	NINE ELMS - 70A	NINE ELMS - 70A	NINE ELMS - 70A	NINE ELMS - 70A	NINE ELMS - 70A	NINE ELMS - 70A	NINE ELMS - 70A
31782	NINE ELMS - 70A	NINE ELMS - 70A	NINE ELMS - 70A	NINE ELMS - 70A	NINE ELMS - 70A	NINE ELMS - 70A	NINE ELMS - 70A	NINE ELMS - 70A
31783	NINE ELMS - 70A	TONBRIDGE - 73J	TONBRIDGE - 73J	TONBRIDGE - 73J	NINE ELMS - 70A	NINE ELMS - 70A	NINE ELMS - 70A	NINE ELMS - 70A
31784	NINE ELMS - 70A	W/D	W/D	W/D	W/D	W/D	W/D	W/D
31785	NINE ELMS - 70A	W/D	W/D	W/D	W/D	W/D	W/D	W/D
31786	NINE ELMS - 70A	NINE ELMS - 70A	NINE ELMS - 70A	NINE ELMS - 70A	NINE ELMS - 70A	NINE ELMS - 70A	NINE ELMS - 70A	NINE ELMS - 70A
31787	NINE ELMS - 70A	NINE ELMS - 70A	NINE ELMS - 70A	NINE ELMS - 70A	NINE ELMS - 70A	NINE ELMS - 70A	NINE ELMS - 70A	NINE ELMS - 70A
31788	NINE ELMS - 70A	W/D	W/D	W/D	W/D	W/D	W/D	W/D
31789	NINE ELMS - 70A	NINE ELMS - 70A	NINE ELMS - 70A	NINE ELMS - 70A	NINE ELMS - 70A	NINE ELMS - 70A	NINE ELMS - 70A	NINE ELMS - 70A

Well before Urie, Maunsell and Bulleid had provided the Southern Railway with a large fleet of six-coupled engines there was little work left for the smaller LSWR 4-4-0 classes, survival being due to war requirements rather than ordinary needs and few survived nationalisation for very long. L11 (30)347 is pictured in Southern Railway days when they were used mainly for piloting or station shunting.

This section gives a clear demonstration of the differing fortunes of LSWR and SECR 4-4-0's after the war. Other than the T9 and, to a lesser extent, the D15's the LSWR classes had very little work left for them after the arrival of the Bulleid Pacifics and by 1951 both the K10 and L11 locomotives had become extinct. The SECR L and L1 4-4-0's retained a considerable workload even though much of the express traffic in Kent had been taken over by 4-6-0's and - in the case of the L class which had been the standard engine on the Charing Cross - Hastings run - the Schools 4-4-0's.

Much of the work performed by the L and L1 engines during the 1950's was on the numerous stopping trains which ran from Tonbridge, Ashford and Faversham in connection with London services although a Bricklayers Arms L1 retained the 16.32 Cannon Street - Ramsgate business express via Chatham until electrification. Another interesting duty for the L1'a was the piloting of the up and down Night Ferry between Dover and Victoria; an L1 from Dover being used to assist a Bullied light Pacific. The L class were regular performers on the stopping trains between Tonbridge and Hastings.

In late 1951 a number of L 4-4-0's were allocated to Eastleigh to alleviate a suspected power shortage. They were not particularly well received and in December 1952 were replaced by four L1's which remained there until mid-1954.

Other than two L locomotives withdrawn in 1956, the two classes remained intact until 1959 when electrification forced the withdrawal of some and the wholesale transfer to Nine Elms - where they had very little regular work - of the remainder.

loco	May-49	Jun-49	Aug-49	Sep-49	Dec-49	Feb-50	Mar-50
				L12 4-4-0 (1904/15)			
30415	BOURNEMOUTH - 71B	BOURNEMOUTH - 71B	BOURNEMOUTH - 71B	BOURNEMOUTH - 71B	BOURNEMOUTH - 71B	BOURNEMOUTH - 71B	BOURNEMOUTH - 71B
30416	GUILDFORD - 70C	GUILDFORD - 70C	GUILDFORD - 70C	GUILDFORD - 70C	GUILDFORD - 70C	GUILDFORD - 70C	GUILDFORD - 70C
30417	FRATTON - 71D	FRATTON - 71D	FRATTON - 71D	GUILDFORD - 70C	GUILDFORD - 70C	GUILDFORD - 70C	GUILDFORD - 70C
30418	BASINGSTOKE - 70D	BASINGSTOKE - 70D	BASINGSTOKE - 70D	BASINGSTOKE - 70D	BASINGSTOKE - 70D	BASINGSTOKE - 70D	BASINGSTOKE - 70D
30419	GUILDFORD - 70C	GUILDFORD - 70C	GUILDFORD - 70C	GUILDFORD - 70C	GUILDFORD - 70C	GUILDFORD - 70C	GUILDFORD - 70C
30420	GUILDFORD - 70C	GUILDFORD - 70C	GUILDFORD - 70C	GUILDFORD - 70C	GUILDFORD - 70C	GUILDFORD - 70C	GUILDFORD - 70C
30421	SALISBURY - 72B	SALISBURY - 72B	SALISBURY - 72B	SALISBURY - 72B	SALISBURY - 72B	SALISBURY - 72B	SALISBURY - 72B
30422	EASTLEIGH - 71A	EASTLEIGH - 71A	EASTLEIGH - 71A	EASTLEIGH - 71A	EASTLEIGH - 71A	EASTLEIGH - 71A	EASTLEIGH - 71A
30423	EASTLEIGH - 71A	EASTLEIGH - 71A	EASTLEIGH - 71A	EASTLEIGH - 71A	EASTLEIGH - 71A	EASTLEIGH - 71A	EASTLEIGH - 71A
30424	DORCHESTER - 71C	DORCHESTER - 71C	DORCHESTER - 71C	DORCHESTER - 71C	DORCHESTER - 71C	DORCHESTER - 71C	DORCHESTER - 71C
30425	FRATTON - 71D	GUILDFORD - 70C	GUILDFORD - 70C	GUILDFORD - 70C	GUILDFORD - 70C	GUILDFORD - 70C	GUILDFORD - 70C
30426	BASINGSTOKE - 70D	BASINGSTOKE - 70D	BASINGSTOKE - 70D	BASINGSTOKE - 70D	BASINGSTOKE - 70D	BASINGSTOKE - 70D	BASINGSTOKE - 70D
30427	NINE ELMS - 70A	NINE ELMS - 70A	NINE ELMS - 70A	NINE ELMS - 70A	NINE ELMS - 70A	NINE ELMS - 70A	NINE ELMS - 70A
30428	EASTLEIGH - 71A	EASTLEIGH - 71A	EASTLEIGH - 71A	EASTLEIGH - 71A	EASTLEIGH - 71A	EASTLEIGH - 71A	EASTLEIGH - 71A
30429	EASTLEIGH - 71A	EASTLEIGH - 71A	EASTLEIGH - 71A	EASTLEIGH - 71A	EASTLEIGH - 71A	EASTLEIGH - 71A	EASTLEIGH - 71A
30430	EASTLEIGH - 71A	BASINGSTOKE - 70D	BASINGSTOKE - 70D	BASINGSTOKE - 70D	BASINGSTOKE - 70D	BASINGSTOKE - 70D	BASINGSTOKE - 70D
30431	NINE ELMS - 70A	BASINGSTOKE - 70D	BASINGSTOKE - 70D	BASINGSTOKE - 70D	BASINGSTOKE - 70D	BASINGSTOKE - 70D	BASINGSTOKE - 70D
30432	EASTLEIGH - 71A	EASTLEIGH - 71A	EASTLEIGH - 71A	EASTLEIGH - 71A	EASTLEIGH - 71A	EASTLEIGH - 71A	EASTLEIGH - 71A
30433	EASTLEIGH - 71A	EASTLEIGH - 71A	EASTLEIGH - 71A	EASTLEIGH - 71A	EASTLEIGH - 71A	EASTLEIGH - 71A	EASTLEIGH - 71A
30434	GUILDFORD - 70C	GUILDFORD - 70C	GUILDFORD - 70C	GUILDFORD - 70C	GUILDFORD - 70C	GUILDFORD - 70C	GUILDFORD - 70C
				S11 4-4-0 (1903/20)			
30395	FRATTON - 71D	FRATTON - 71D	FRATTON - 71D	FRATTON - 71D	FRATTON - 71D	FRATTON - 71D	FRATTON - 71D
30396	FRATTON - 71D	FRATTON - 71D	FRATTON - 71D	FRATTON - 71D	FRATTON - 71D	FRATTON - 71D	FRATTON - 71D
30397	FRATTON - 71D	FRATTON - 71D	FRATTON - 71D	FRATTON - 71D	FRATTON - 71D	FRATTON - 71D	FRATTON - 71D
30398	BOURNEMOUTH - 71B	BOURNEMOUTH - 71B	BOURNEMOUTH - 71B	BOURNEMOUTH - 71B	BOURNEMOUTH - 71B	BOURNEMOUTH - 71B	BOURNEMOUTH - 71B
30399	FRATTON - 71D	FRATTON - 71D	FRATTON - 71D	FRATTON - 71D	FRATTON - 71D	FRATTON - 71D	FRATTON - 71D
30400	FRATTON - 71D	FRATTON - 71D	FRATTON - 71D	FRATTON - 71D	FRATTON - 71D	FRATTON - 71D	FRATTON - 71D
30401	FRATTON - 71D	FRATTON - 71D	FRATTON - 71D	FRATTON - 71D	FRATTON - 71D	FRATTON - 71D	FRATTON - 71D
30402	FRATTON - 71D	FRATTON - 71D	FRATTON - 71D	FRATTON - 71D	FRATTON - 71D	FRATTON - 71D	FRATTON - 71D
30403	BOURNEMOUTH - 71B	BOURNEMOUTH - 71B	BOURNEMOUTH - 71B	BOURNEMOUTH - 71B	BOURNEMOUTH - 71B	BOURNEMOUTH - 71B	BOURNEMOUTH - 71B
30404	FRATTON - 71D	FRATTON - 71D	FRATTON - 71D	FRATTON - 71D	FRATTON - 71D	FRATTON - 71D	FRATTON - 71D
				T9 4-4-0 (1899/1922)			
30113	FRATTON - 71D	FRATTON - 71D	FRATTON - 71D	FRATTON - 71D	FRATTON - 71D	FRATTON - 71D	FRATTON - 71D
30114	FRATTON - 71D	FRATTON - 71D	FRATTON - 71D	FRATTON - 71D	FRATTON - 71D	FRATTON - 71D	FRATTON - 71D
30115	FRATTON - 71D	FRATTON - 71D	FRATTON - 71D	FRATTON - 71D	FRATTON - 71D	FRATTON - 71D	FRATTON - 71D
30116	FRATTON - 71D	FRATTON - 71D	FRATTON - 71D	FRATTON - 71D	FRATTON - 71D	DORCHESTER - 71C	DORCHESTER - 71C
30117	FRATTON - 71D	FRATTON - 71D	FRATTON - 71D	FRATTON - 71D	FRATTON - 71D	YEOVIL - 72C	YEOVIL - 72C
30118	FRATTON - 71D	FRATTON - 71D	FRATTON - 71D	FRATTON - 71D	FRATTON - 71D	FRATTON - 71D	FRATTON - 71D
30119	NINE ELMS - 70A	NINE ELMS - 70A	NINE ELMS - 70A	NINE ELMS - 70A	NINE ELMS - 70A	NINE ELMS - 70A	NINE ELMS - 70A
30120	EASTLEIGH - 71A	EASTLEIGH - 71A	EASTLEIGH - 71A	EASTLEIGH - 71A	EASTLEIGH - 71A	EASTLEIGH - 71A	EASTLEIGH - 71A
30121	EASTLEIGH - 71A	EASTLEIGH - 71A	EASTLEIGH - 71A	EASTLEIGH - 71A	EASTLEIGH - 71A	EASTLEIGH - 71A	EASTLEIGH - 71A
30122	SALISBURY - 72B	SALISBURY - 72B	SALISBURY - 72B	SALISBURY - 72B	SALISBURY - 72B	SALISBURY - 72B	SALISBURY - 72B
30280	FRATTON - 71D	FRATTON - 71D	FRATTON - 71D	FRATTON - 71D	FRATTON - 71D	FRATTON - 71D	FRATTON - 71D
30281	STEWARTS LANE - 73A	STEWARTS LANE - 73A	GUILDFORD - 70C	GUILDFORD - 70C	GUILDFORD - 70C	GUILDFORD - 70C	GUILDFORD - 70C
30282	STEWARTS LANE - 73A	STEWARTS LANE - 73A	STEWARTS LANE - 73A	STEWARTS LANE - 73A	STEWARTS LANE - 73A	STEWARTS LANE - 73A	STEWARTS LANE - 73A
30283	EXMOUTH JCN - 72A	EXMOUTH JCN - 72A	EXMOUTH JCN - 72A	EXMOUTH JCN - 72A	EXMOUTH JCN - 72A	EXMOUTH JCN - 72A	EXMOUTH JCN - 72A
30284	DORCHESTER - 71C	DORCHESTER - 71C	DORCHESTER - 71C	DORCHESTER - 71C	DORCHESTER - 71C	DORCHESTER - 71C	DORCHESTER - 71C
30285	FRATTON - 71D	FRATTON - 71D	FRATTON - 71D	FRATTON - 71D	FRATTON - 71D	FRATTON - 71D	FRATTON - 71D
30286	EASTLEIGH - 71A	EASTLEIGH - 71A	EASTLEIGH - 71A	EASTLEIGH - 71A	EASTLEIGH - 71A	EASTLEIGH - 71A	EASTLEIGH - 71A
30287	FRATTON - 71D	FRATTON - 71D	FRATTON - 71D	EASTLEIGH - 71A	EASTLEIGH - 71A	EASTLEIGH - 71A	EASTLEIGH - 71A
30288	SALISBURY - 72B	SALISBURY - 72B	SALISBURY - 72B	SALISBURY - 72B	SALISBURY - 72B	SALISBURY - 72B	SALISBURY - 72B
30289	SALISBURY - 72B	SALISBURY - 72B	SALISBURY - 72B	SALISBURY - 72B	SALISBURY - 72B	SALISBURY - 72B	SALISBURY - 72B
30300	DORCHESTER - 71C	DORCHESTER - 71C	DORCHESTER - 71C	DORCHESTER - 71C	DORCHESTER - 71C	DORCHESTER - 71C	DORCHESTER - 71C
30301	STEWARTS LANE - 73A	STEWARTS LANE - 73A	GUILDFORD - 70C	GUILDFORD - 70C	YEOVIL - 72C	YEOVIL - 72C	YEOVIL - 72C
30302	EASTLEIGH - 71A	EASTLEIGH - 71A	EASTLEIGH - 71A	EASTLEIGH - 71A	EASTLEIGH - 71A	BASINGSTOKE - 70D	BASINGSTOKE - 70D
30303	FRATTON - 71D	FRATTON - 71D	FRATTON - 71D	FRATTON - 71D	FRATTON - 71D	FRATTON - 71D	FRATTON - 71D
30304	STEWARTS LANE - 73A	STEWARTS LANE - 73A	STEWARTS LANE - 73A	STEWARTS LANE - 73A	STEWARTS LANE - 73A	STEWARTS LANE - 73A	STEWARTS LANE - 73A
30305	FRATTON - 71D	FRATTON - 71D	FRATTON - 71D	FRATTON - 71D	FRATTON - 71D	FRATTON - 71D	FRATTON - 71D
30307	BASINGSTOKE - 70D	YEOVIL - 72C	YEOVIL - 72C	YEOVIL - 72C	YEOVIL - 72C	YEOVIL - 72C	YEOVIL - 72C
30310	FRATTON - 71D	FRATTON - 71D	FRATTON - 71D	FRATTON - 71D	FRATTON - 71D	FRATTON - 71D	FRATTON - 71D
30311	STEWARTS LANE - 73A	STEWARTS LANE - 73A	STEWARTS LANE - 73A	STEWARTS LANE - 73A	STEWARTS LANE - 73A	STEWARTS LANE - 73A	STEWARTS LANE - 73A
30312	STEWARTS LANE - 73A	STEWARTS LANE - 73A	STEWARTS LANE - 73A	STEWARTS LANE - 73A	STEWARTS LANE - 73A	STEWARTS LANE - 73A	STEWARTS LANE - 73A
30313	EASTLEIGH - 71A	EASTLEIGH - 71A	EASTLEIGH - 71A	EASTLEIGH - 71A	EASTLEIGH - 71A	EASTLEIGH - 71A	EASTLEIGH - 71A
30314	FRATTON - 71D	FRATTON - 71D	FRATTON - 71D	FRATTON - 71D	FRATTON - 71D	FRATTON - 71D	FRATTON - 71D
30336	EASTLEIGH - 71A	EASTLEIGH - 71A	EASTLEIGH - 71A	EASTLEIGH - 71A	EASTLEIGH - 71A	EASTLEIGH - 71A	EASTLEIGH - 71A
30337	YEOVIL - 72C	YEOVIL - 72C	YEOVIL - 72C	YEOVIL - 72C	YEOVIL - 72C	YEOVIL - 72C	YEOVIL - 72C
30338	EASTLEIGH - 71A	EASTLEIGH - 71A	EASTLEIGH - 71A	EASTLEIGH - 71A	EASTLEIGH - 71A	DORCHESTER - 71C	DORCHESTER - 71C
30702	EXMOUTH JCN - 72A	EXMOUTH JCN - 72A	EXMOUTH JCN - 72A	EXMOUTH JCN - 72A	EXMOUTH JCN - 72A	EXMOUTH JCN - 72A	EXMOUTH JCN - 72A
30703	WADEBRIDGE - 72F	WADEBRIDGE - 72F	EXMOUTH JCN - 72A	EXMOUTH JCN - 72A	EXMOUTH JCN - 72A	EXMOUTH JCN - 72A	EXMOUTH JCN - 72A
30704	FRATTON - 71D	FRATTON - 71D	FRATTON - 71D	FRATTON - 71D	FRATTON - 71D	YEOVIL - 72C	YEOVIL - 72C
30705	EASTLEIGH - 71A	EASTLEIGH - 71A	EASTLEIGH - 71A	EASTLEIGH - 71A	EASTLEIGH - 71A	EASTLEIGH - 71A	EASTLEIGH - 71A
30706	BASINGSTOKE - 70D	YEOVIL - 72C	YEOVIL - 72C	YEOVIL - 72C	YEOVIL - 72C	YEOVIL - 72C	YEOVIL - 72C
30707	EASTLEIGH - 71A	EXMOUTH JCN - 72A	EXMOUTH JCN - 72A	EXMOUTH JCN - 72A	EXMOUTH JCN - 72A	EXMOUTH JCN - 72A	EXMOUTH JCN - 72A
30708	GUILDFORD - 70C	GUILDFORD - 70C	GUILDFORD - 70C	GUILDFORD - 70C	GUILDFORD - 70C	GUILDFORD - 70C	GUILDFORD - 70C
30709	SALISBURY - 72B	SALISBURY - 72B	SALISBURY - 72B	SALISBURY - 72B	SALISBURY - 72B	SALISBURY - 72B	SALISBURY - 72B
30710	YEOVIL - 72C	YEOVIL - 72C	YEOVIL - 72C	YEOVIL - 72C	YEOVIL - 72C	YEOVIL - 72C	YEOVIL - 72C
30711	EASTLEIGH - 71A	EASTLEIGH - 71A	EASTLEIGH - 71A	EASTLEIGH - 71A	EASTLEIGH - 71A	EASTLEIGH - 71A	EASTLEIGH - 71A
30712	YEOVIL - 72C	YEOVIL - 72C	YEOVIL - 72C	YEOVIL - 72C	YEOVIL - 72C	BASINGSTOKE - 70D	BASINGSTOKE - 70D
30713	EASTLEIGH - 71A	EASTLEIGH - 71A	EASTLEIGH - 71A	EASTLEIGH - 71A	EASTLEIGH - 71A	EASTLEIGH - 71A	EASTLEIGH - 71A
30714	YEOVIL - 72C	YEOVIL - 72C	YEOVIL - 72C	YEOVIL - 72C	YEOVIL - 72C	YEOVIL - 72C	YEOVIL - 72C
30715	SALISBURY - 72B	SALISBURY - 72B	SALISBURY - 72B	SALISBURY - 72B	SALISBURY - 72B	SALISBURY - 72B	SALISBURY - 72B
30716	EXMOUTH JCN - 72A	EXMOUTH JCN - 72A	WADEBRIDGE - 72F	WADEBRIDGE - 72F	EXMOUTH JCN - 72A	EXMOUTH JCN - 72A	EXMOUTH JCN - 72A
30717	WADEBRIDGE - 72F	WADEBRIDGE - 72F	WADEBRIDGE - 72F	WADEBRIDGE - 72F	EXMOUTH JCN - 72A	EXMOUTH JCN - 72A	EXMOUTH JCN - 72A
30718	NINE ELMS - 70A	NINE ELMS - 70A	NINE ELMS - 70A	NINE ELMS - 70A	NINE ELMS - 70A	NINE ELMS - 70A	NINE ELMS - 70A
30719	BOURNEMOUTH - 71B	BOURNEMOUTH - 71B	BOURNEMOUTH - 71B	BOURNEMOUTH - 71B	BOURNEMOUTH - 71B	BOURNEMOUTH - 71B	BOURNEMOUTH - 71B
30721	DORCHESTER - 71C	DORCHESTER - 71C	DORCHESTER - 71C	DORCHESTER - 71C	DORCHESTER - 71C	DORCHESTER - 71C	DORCHESTER - 71C
30722	EASTLEIGH - 71A	EASTLEIGH - 71A	EASTLEIGH - 71A	EASTLEIGH - 71A	EASTLEIGH - 71A	EASTLEIGH - 71A	EASTLEIGH - 71A
30723	EXMOUTH JCN - 72A	EXMOUTH JCN - 72A	EXMOUTH JCN - 72A	EXMOUTH JCN - 72A	EXMOUTH JCN - 72A	EXMOUTH JCN - 72A	EXMOUTH JCN - 72A
30724	EXMOUTH JCN - 72A	EXMOUTH JCN - 72A	EXMOUTH JCN - 72A	EXMOUTH JCN - 72A	EXMOUTH JCN - 72A	EXMOUTH JCN - 72A	EXMOUTH JCN - 72A
30725	EXMOUTH JCN - 72A	EXMOUTH JCN - 72A	EXMOUTH JCN - 72A	EXMOUTH JCN - 72A	EXMOUTH JCN - 72A	EXMOUTH JCN - 72A	EXMOUTH JCN - 72A
30726	STEWARTS LANE - 73A	STEWARTS LANE - 73A	STEWARTS LANE - 73A	STEWARTS LANE - 73A	STEWARTS LANE - 73A	STEWARTS LANE - 73A	STEWARTS LANE - 73A
30727	SALISBURY - 72B	SALISBURY - 72B	SALISBURY - 72B	SALISBURY - 72B	SALISBURY - 72B	SALISBURY - 72B	SALISBURY - 72B
30728	BOURNEMOUTH - 71B	BOURNEMOUTH - 71B	BOURNEMOUTH - 71B	BOURNEMOUTH - 71B	BOURNEMOUTH - 71B	BOURNEMOUTH - 71B	BOURNEMOUTH - 71B
30729	STEWARTS LANE - 73A	STEWARTS LANE - 73A	STEWARTS LANE - 73A	STEWARTS LANE - 73A	STEWARTS LANE - 73A	STEWARTS LANE - 73A	STEWARTS LANE - 73A
30730	EXMOUTH JCN - 72A	EXMOUTH JCN - 72A	EXMOUTH JCN - 72A	EXMOUTH JCN - 72A	EXMOUTH JCN - 72A	EXMOUTH JCN - 72A	EXMOUTH JCN - 72A
30731	FRATTON - 71D	FRATTON - 71D	FRATTON - 71D	FRATTON - 71D	FRATTON - 71D	FRATTON - 71D	FRATTON - 71D
30732	GUILDFORD - 70C	GUILDFORD - 70C	GUILDFORD - 70C	GUILDFORD - 70C	GUILDFORD - 70C	GUILDFORD - 70C	GUILDFORD - 70C
30733	BOURNEMOUTH - 71B	BOURNEMOUTH - 71B	BOURNEMOUTH - 71B	BOURNEMOUTH - 71B	BOURNEMOUTH - 71B	BOURNEMOUTH - 71B	BOURNEMOUTH - 71B

loco	Apr-50	Sep-50	Oct-50	Nov-50	Dec-50	Mar-51	Apr-51
				L12 4-4-0 (1904/15)			
30415	EASTLEIGH - 71A	DORCHESTER - 71C	DORCHESTER - 71C	DORCHESTER - 71C	DORCHESTER - 71C	DORCHESTER - 71C	DORCHESTER - 71C
30416	GUILDFORD - 70C	GUILDFORD - 70C	GUILDFORD - 70C	GUILDFORD - 70C	GUILDFORD - 70C	GUILDFORD - 70C	GUILDFORD - 70C
30417	FRATTON - 71D	FRATTON - 71D	FRATTON - 71D	FRATTON - 71D	FRATTON - 71D	FRATTON - 71D	FRATTON - 71D
30418	BASINGSTOKE - 70D	BASINGSTOKE - 70D	BASINGSTOKE - 70D	BASINGSTOKE - 70D	FRATTON - 71D	FRATTON - 71D	FRATTON - 71D
30419	FRATTON - 71D	FRATTON - 71D	FRATTON - 71D	FRATTON - 71D	FRATTON - 71D	FRATTON - 71D	FRATTON - 71D
30420	GUILDFORD - 70C	GUILDFORD - 70C	GUILDFORD - 70C	GUILDFORD - 70C	EASTLEIGH - 71A	EASTLEIGH - 71A	EASTLEIGH - 71A
30421	SALISBURY - 72B	SALISBURY - 72B	SALISBURY - 72B	EASTLEIGH - 71A	EASTLEIGH - 71A	EASTLEIGH - 71A	EASTLEIGH - 71A
30422	EASTLEIGH - 71A	EASTLEIGH - 71A	EASTLEIGH - 71A	EASTLEIGH - 71A	EASTLEIGH - 71A	EASTLEIGH - 71A	EASTLEIGH - 71A
30423	EASTLEIGH - 71A	EASTLEIGH - 71A	EASTLEIGH - 71A	EASTLEIGH - 71A	EASTLEIGH - 71A	EASTLEIGH - 71A	EASTLEIGH - 71A
30424	DORCHESTER - 71C	DORCHESTER - 71C	GUILDFORD - 70C	GUILDFORD - 70C	EASTLEIGH - 71A	EASTLEIGH - 71A	EASTLEIGH - 71A
30425	GUILDFORD - 70C	GUILDFORD - 70C	GUILDFORD - 70C	GUILDFORD - 70C	EASTLEIGH - 71A	EASTLEIGH - 71A	EASTLEIGH - 71A
30426	BASINGSTOKE - 70D	FRATTON - 71D	FRATTON - 71D	FRATTON - 71D	FRATTON - 71D	FRATTON - 71D	FRATTON - 71D
30427	NINE ELMS - 70A	FRATTON - 71D	FRATTON - 71D	FRATTON - 71D	FRATTON - 71D	FRATTON - 71D	FRATTON - 71D
30428	GUILDFORD - 70C	GUILDFORD - 70C	GUILDFORD - 70C	GUILDFORD - 70C	EASTLEIGH - 71A	EASTLEIGH - 71A	W/D
30429	EASTLEIGH - 71A	EASTLEIGH - 71A	EASTLEIGH - 71A	EASTLEIGH - 71A	BASINGSTOKE - 70D	BASINGSTOKE - 70D	BASINGSTOKE - 70D
30430	EASTLEIGH - 71A	EASTLEIGH - 71A	EASTLEIGH - 71A	EASTLEIGH - 71A	EASTLEIGH - 71A	W/D	W/D
30431	EASTLEIGH - 71A	EASTLEIGH - 71A	EASTLEIGH - 71A	EASTLEIGH - 71A	EASTLEIGH - 71A	EASTLEIGH - 71A	EASTLEIGH - 71A
30432	EASTLEIGH - 71A	EASTLEIGH - 71A	EASTLEIGH - 71A	GUILDFORD - 70C	GUILDFORD - 70C	GUILDFORD - 70C	GUILDFORD - 70C
30433	EASTLEIGH - 71A	EASTLEIGH - 71A	EASTLEIGH - 71A	GUILDFORD - 70C	GUILDFORD - 70C	GUILDFORD - 70C	GUILDFORD - 70C
30434	EASTLEIGH - 71A	EASTLEIGH - 71A	EASTLEIGH - 71A	EASTLEIGH - 71A	EASTLEIGH - 71A	EASTLEIGH - 71A	EASTLEIGH - 71A
				S11 4-4-0 (1903/20)			
30395	FRATTON - 71D	FRATTON - 71D	FRATTON - 71D	FRATTON - 71D	FRATTON - 71D	FRATTON - 71D	FRATTON - 71D
30396	FRATTON - 71D	FRATTON - 71D	FRATTON - 71D	FRATTON - 71D	FRATTON - 71D	FRATTON - 71D	FRATTON - 71D
30397	FRATTON - 71D	FRATTON - 71D	FRATTON - 71D	FRATTON - 71D	BASINGSTOKE - 70D	BASINGSTOKE - 70D	BASINGSTOKE - 70D
30398	BOURNEMOUTH - 71B	BOURNEMOUTH - 71B	BOURNEMOUTH - 71B	BOURNEMOUTH - 71B	BOURNEMOUTH - 71B	BOURNEMOUTH - 71B	BOURNEMOUTH - 71B
30399	FRATTON - 71D	DORCHESTER - 71C	DORCHESTER - 71C	DORCHESTER - 71C	DORCHESTER - 71C	DORCHESTER - 71C	DORCHESTER - 71C
30400	FRATTON - 71D	FRATTON - 71D	FRATTON - 71D	FRATTON - 71D	GUILDFORD - 70C	GUILDFORD - 70C	GUILDFORD - 70C
30401	EASTLEIGH - 71A	EASTLEIGH - 71A	EASTLEIGH - 71A	EASTLEIGH - 71A	GUILDFORD - 70C	GUILDFORD - 70C	GUILDFORD - 70C
30402	FRATTON - 71D	FRATTON - 71D	FRATTON - 71D	FRATTON - 71D	FRATTON - 71D	W/D	W/D
30403	BOURNEMOUTH - 71B	BOURNEMOUTH - 71B	BOURNEMOUTH - 71B	BOURNEMOUTH - 71B	BOURNEMOUTH - 71B	BOURNEMOUTH - 71B	BOURNEMOUTH - 71B
30404	FRATTON - 71D	BOURNEMOUTH - 71B	BOURNEMOUTH - 71B	BOURNEMOUTH - 71B	BOURNEMOUTH - 71B	BOURNEMOUTH - 71B	BOURNEMOUTH - 71B
				T9 4-4-0 (1899/1922)			
30113	FRATTON - 71D	FRATTON - 71D	FRATTON - 71D	FRATTON - 71D	FRATTON - 71D	FRATTON - 71D	FRATTON - 71D
30114	FRATTON - 71D	FRATTON - 71D	FRATTON - 71D	FRATTON - 71D	FRATTON - 71D	FRATTON - 71D	FRATTON - 71D
30115	FRATTON - 71D	DORCHESTER - 71C	DORCHESTER - 71C	DORCHESTER - 71C	DORCHESTER - 71C	DORCHESTER - 71C	DORCHESTER - 71C
30116	DORCHESTER - 71C	DORCHESTER - 71C	DORCHESTER - 71C	DORCHESTER - 71C	DORCHESTER - 71C	DORCHESTER - 71C	W/D
30117	YEOVIL - 72C	YEOVIL - 72C	YEOVIL - 72C	YEOVIL - 72C	YEOVIL - 72C	YEOVIL - 72C	YEOVIL - 72C
30118	FRATTON - 71D	FRATTON - 71D	FRATTON - 71D	FRATTON - 71D	FRATTON - 71D	FRATTON - 71D	FRATTON - 71D
30119	NINE ELMS - 70A	NINE ELMS - 70A	NINE ELMS - 70A	NINE ELMS - 70A	NINE ELMS - 70A	NINE ELMS - 70A	NINE ELMS - 70A
30120	EASTLEIGH - 71A	FRATTON - 71D	FRATTON - 71D	FRATTON - 71D	FRATTON - 71D	FRATTON - 71D	FRATTON - 71D
30121	EASTLEIGH - 71A	EASTLEIGH - 71A	EASTLEIGH - 71A	EASTLEIGH - 71A	EASTLEIGH - 71A	EASTLEIGH - 71A	W/D
30122	SALISBURY - 72B	SALISBURY - 72B	SALISBURY - 72B	SALISBURY - 72B	YEOVIL - 72C	YEOVIL - 72C	W/D
30280	FRATTON - 71D	FRATTON - 71D	FRATTON - 71D	FRATTON - 71D	FRATTON - 71D	FRATTON - 71D	W/D
30281	GUILDFORD - 70C	GUILDFORD - 70C	GUILDFORD - 70C	GUILDFORD - 70C	EASTLEIGH - 71A	EASTLEIGH - 71A	EASTLEIGH - 71A
30282	FELTHAM - 70B	EASTLEIGH - 71A	EASTLEIGH - 71A	EASTLEIGH - 71A	EASTLEIGH - 71A	EASTLEIGH - 71A	EASTLEIGH - 71A
30283	EXMOUTH JCN - 72A	EXMOUTH JCN - 72A	EXMOUTH JCN - 72A	EXMOUTH JCN - 72A	EASTLEIGH - 71A	EASTLEIGH - 71A	EASTLEIGH - 71A
30284	DORCHESTER - 71C	DORCHESTER - 71C	DORCHESTER - 71C	DORCHESTER - 71C	DORCHESTER - 71C	DORCHESTER - 71C	DORCHESTER - 71C
30285	FRATTON - 71D	FRATTON - 71D	FRATTON - 71D	FRATTON - 71D	FRATTON - 71D	FRATTON - 71D	FRATTON - 71D
30286	EASTLEIGH - 71A	EASTLEIGH - 71A	EASTLEIGH - 71A	EASTLEIGH - 71A	EASTLEIGH - 71A	EASTLEIGH - 71A	W/D
30287	EASTLEIGH - 71A	EASTLEIGH - 71A	EASTLEIGH - 71A	EASTLEIGH - 71A	EASTLEIGH - 71A	EASTLEIGH - 71A	EASTLEIGH - 71A
30288	SALISBURY - 72B	SALISBURY - 72B	SALISBURY - 72B	SALISBURY - 72B	EASTLEIGH - 71A	EASTLEIGH - 71A	EASTLEIGH - 71A
30289	SALISBURY - 72B	SALISBURY - 72B	SALISBURY - 72B	SALISBURY - 72B	EASTLEIGH - 71A	EASTLEIGH - 71A	EASTLEIGH - 71A
30300	EASTLEIGH - 71A	EASTLEIGH - 71A	EASTLEIGH - 71A	SALISBURY - 72B	SALISBURY - 72B	SALISBURY - 72B	SALISBURY - 72B
30301	SALISBURY - 72B	SALISBURY - 72B	SALISBURY - 72B	SALISBURY - 72B	SALISBURY - 72B	SALISBURY - 72B	SALISBURY - 72B
30302	BASINGSTOKE - 70D	BASINGSTOKE - 70D	BASINGSTOKE - 70D	BASINGSTOKE - 70D	SALISBURY - 72B	SALISBURY - 72B	SALISBURY - 72B
30303	FRATTON - 71D	FRATTON - 71D	FRATTON - 71D	FRATTON - 71D	FRATTON - 71D	FRATTON - 71D	W/D
30304	EASTLEIGH - 71A	EASTLEIGH - 71A	EASTLEIGH - 71A	EASTLEIGH - 71A	SALISBURY - 72B	SALISBURY - 72B	SALISBURY - 72B
30305	FRATTON - 71D	FRATTON - 71D	FRATTON - 71D	FRATTON - 71D	FRATTON - 71D	FRATTON - 71D	W/D
30307	YEOVIL - 72C	DORCHESTER - 71C	DORCHESTER - 71C	DORCHESTER - 71C	DORCHESTER - 71C	DORCHESTER - 71C	DORCHESTER - 71C
30310	FRATTON - 71D	FRATTON - 71D	FRATTON - 71D	FRATTON - 71D	FRATTON - 71D	FRATTON - 71D	FRATTON - 71D
30311	FELTHAM - 70B	FELTHAM - 70B	GUILDFORD - 70C	GUILDFORD - 70C	GUILDFORD - 70C	GUILDFORD - 70C	GUILDFORD - 70C
30312	GUILDFORD - 70C	GUILDFORD - 70C	GUILDFORD - 70C	GUILDFORD - 70C	GUILDFORD - 70C	GUILDFORD - 70C	GUILDFORD - 70C
30313	EASTLEIGH - 71A	EASTLEIGH - 71A	EASTLEIGH - 71A	EASTLEIGH - 71A	EASTLEIGH - 71A	EASTLEIGH - 71A	EASTLEIGH - 71A
30314	FRATTON - 71D	FRATTON - 71D	FRATTON - 71D	FRATTON - 71D	FRATTON - 71D	FRATTON - 71D	FRATTON - 71D
30336	EASTLEIGH - 71A	GUILDFORD - 70C	GUILDFORD - 70C	GUILDFORD - 70C	GUILDFORD - 70C	GUILDFORD - 70C	GUILDFORD - 70C
30337	YEOVIL - 72C	YEOVIL - 72C	YEOVIL - 72C	YEOVIL - 72C	YEOVIL - 72C	YEOVIL - 72C	YEOVIL - 72C
30338	DORCHESTER - 71C	DORCHESTER - 71C	DORCHESTER - 71C	DORCHESTER - 71C	DORCHESTER - 71C	DORCHESTER - 71C	DORCHESTER - 71C
30702	EXMOUTH JCN - 72A	EXMOUTH JCN - 72A	EXMOUTH JCN - 72A	EXMOUTH JCN - 72A	EXMOUTH JCN - 72A	EXMOUTH JCN - 72A	EXMOUTH JCN - 72A
30703	EXMOUTH JCN - 72A	EXMOUTH JCN - 72A	EXMOUTH JCN - 72A	EXMOUTH JCN - 72A	EXMOUTH JCN - 72A	EXMOUTH JCN - 72A	EXMOUTH JCN - 72A
30704	YEOVIL - 72C	YEOVIL - 72C	YEOVIL - 72C	YEOVIL - 72C	EXMOUTH JCN - 72A	EXMOUTH JCN - 72A	EXMOUTH JCN - 72A
30705	EASTLEIGH - 71A	EASTLEIGH - 71A	EASTLEIGH - 71A	EASTLEIGH - 71A	EASTLEIGH - 71A	EASTLEIGH - 71A	EASTLEIGH - 71A
30706	SALISBURY - 72B	EXMOUTH JCN - 72A	EXMOUTH JCN - 72A	EXMOUTH JCN - 72A	EXMOUTH JCN - 72A	EXMOUTH JCN - 72A	EXMOUTH JCN - 72A
30707	EXMOUTH JCN - 72A	EXMOUTH JCN - 72A	EXMOUTH JCN - 72A	EXMOUTH JCN - 72A	EXMOUTH JCN - 72A	EXMOUTH JCN - 72A	EXMOUTH JCN - 72A
30708	GUILDFORD - 70C	EASTLEIGH - 71A	EASTLEIGH - 71A	EASTLEIGH - 71A	EASTLEIGH - 71A	EASTLEIGH - 71A	EASTLEIGH - 71A
30709	SALISBURY - 72B	SALISBURY - 72B	SALISBURY - 72B	SALISBURY - 72B	SALISBURY - 72B	SALISBURY - 72B	SALISBURY - 72B
30710	GUILDFORD - 70C	GUILDFORD - 70C	GUILDFORD - 70C	GUILDFORD - 70C	GUILDFORD - 70C	GUILDFORD - 70C	GUILDFORD - 70C
30711	EASTLEIGH - 71A	EASTLEIGH - 71A	EASTLEIGH - 71A	EASTLEIGH - 71A	EASTLEIGH - 71A	EASTLEIGH - 71A	EASTLEIGH - 71A
30712	BASINGSTOKE - 70D	BASINGSTOKE - 70D	BASINGSTOKE - 70D	BASINGSTOKE - 70D	EXMOUTH JCN - 72A	EXMOUTH JCN - 72A	EXMOUTH JCN - 72A
30713	EASTLEIGH - 71A	EASTLEIGH - 71A	EASTLEIGH - 71A	EASTLEIGH - 71A	EASTLEIGH - 71A	EASTLEIGH - 71A	W/D
30714	YEOVIL - 72C	YEOVIL - 72C	EXMOUTH JCN - 72A	EXMOUTH JCN - 72A	EXMOUTH JCN - 72A	EXMOUTH JCN - 72A	W/D
30715	SALISBURY - 72B	EXMOUTH JCN - 72A	EXMOUTH JCN - 72A	EXMOUTH JCN - 72A	EXMOUTH JCN - 72A	EXMOUTH JCN - 72A	EXMOUTH JCN - 72A
30716	EXMOUTH JCN - 72A	EXMOUTH JCN - 72A	EXMOUTH JCN - 72A	EXMOUTH JCN - 72A	EXMOUTH JCN - 72A	EXMOUTH JCN - 72A	EXMOUTH JCN - 72A
30717	EXMOUTH JCN - 72A	EXMOUTH JCN - 72A	EXMOUTH JCN - 72A	EXMOUTH JCN - 72A	EXMOUTH JCN - 72A	EXMOUTH JCN - 72A	EXMOUTH JCN - 72A
30718	NINE ELMS - 70A	NINE ELMS - 70A	NINE ELMS - 70A	NINE ELMS - 70A	NINE ELMS - 70A	NINE ELMS - 70A	NINE ELMS - 70A
30719	SALISBURY - 72B	SALISBURY - 72B	SALISBURY - 72B	SALISBURY - 72B	SALISBURY - 72B	SALISBURY - 72B	SALISBURY - 72B
30721	EASTLEIGH - 71A	EASTLEIGH - 71A	EASTLEIGH - 71A	EASTLEIGH - 71A	EASTLEIGH - 71A	EASTLEIGH - 71A	EASTLEIGH - 71A
30722	EASTLEIGH - 71A	EASTLEIGH - 71A	EASTLEIGH - 71A	EASTLEIGH - 71A	EASTLEIGH - 71A	EASTLEIGH - 71A	W/D
30723	EXMOUTH JCN - 72A	EXMOUTH JCN - 72A	EXMOUTH JCN - 72A	EXMOUTH JCN - 72A	EXMOUTH JCN - 72A	EXMOUTH JCN - 72A	EXMOUTH JCN - 72A
30724	SALISBURY - 72B	SALISBURY - 72B	SALISBURY - 72B	SALISBURY - 72B	SALISBURY - 72B	SALISBURY - 72B	SALISBURY - 72B
30725	EXMOUTH JCN - 72A	SALISBURY - 72B	SALISBURY - 72B	SALISBURY - 72B	SALISBURY - 72B	SALISBURY - 72B	SALISBURY - 72B
30726	FRATTON - 71D	FRATTON - 71D	EASTLEIGH - 71A	EASTLEIGH - 71A	EASTLEIGH - 71A	EASTLEIGH - 71A	EASTLEIGH - 71A
30727	SALISBURY - 72B	SALISBURY - 72B	SALISBURY - 72B	SALISBURY - 72B	SALISBURY - 72B	SALISBURY - 72B	SALISBURY - 72B
30728	BOURNEMOUTH - 71B	BOURNEMOUTH - 71B	BOURNEMOUTH - 71B	BOURNEMOUTH - 71B	BOURNEMOUTH - 71B	BOURNEMOUTH - 71B	BOURNEMOUTH - 71B
30729	EASTLEIGH - 71A	EASTLEIGH - 71A	EASTLEIGH - 71A	EASTLEIGH - 71A	EASTLEIGH - 71A	EASTLEIGH - 71A	EASTLEIGH - 71A
30730	EXMOUTH JCN - 72A	SALISBURY - 72B	SALISBURY - 72B	SALISBURY - 72B	BOURNEMOUTH - 71B	BOURNEMOUTH - 71B	BOURNEMOUTH - 71B
30731	FRATTON - 71D	FRATTON - 71D	FRATTON - 71D	FRATTON - 71D	FRATTON - 71D	FRATTON - 71D	FRATTON - 71D
30732	FELTHAM - 70B	FELTHAM - 70B	FELTHAM - 70B	FELTHAM - 70B	FELTHAM - 70B	FELTHAM - 70B	FELTHAM - 70B
30733	BOURNEMOUTH - 71B	FRATTON - 71D	FRATTON - 71D	BOURNEMOUTH - 71B	BOURNEMOUTH - 71B	BOURNEMOUTH - 71B	BOURNEMOUTH - 71B

loco	Jun-51	Jul-51	Sep-51	Dec-51	Jan-52	Mar-52	Jun-52
			L12 4-4-0 (1904/15)				
30415	FRATTON - 71D	FRATTON - 71D	FRATTON - 71D	FRATTON - 71D	FRATTON - 71D	FRATTON - 71D	FRATTON - 71D
30417	FRATTON - 71D	FRATTON - 71D	FRATTON - 71D	W/D	W/D	W/D	W/D
30419	FRATTON - 71D	FRATTON - 71D	FRATTON - 71D	W/D	W/D	W/D	W/D
30420	EASTLEIGH - 71A	EASTLEIGH - 71A	W/D	W/D	W/D	W/D	W/D
30421	EASTLEIGH - 71A	EASTLEIGH - 71A	W/D	W/D	W/D	W/D	W/D
30422	EASTLEIGH - 71A	EASTLEIGH - 71A	W/D	W/D	W/D	W/D	W/D
30423	EASTLEIGH - 71A	W/D	W/D	W/D	W/D	W/D	W/D
30424	EASTLEIGH - 71A	W/D	W/D	W/D	W/D	W/D	W/D
30425	EASTLEIGH - 71A	EASTLEIGH - 71A	W/D	W/D	W/D	W/D	W/D
30426	FRATTON - 71D	FRATTON - 71D	EASTLEIGH - 71A	W/D	W/D	W/D	W/D
30427	FRATTON - 71D	FRATTON - 71D	EASTLEIGH - 71A	W/D	W/D	W/D	W/D
30429	BASINGSTOKE - 70D	BASINGSTOKE - 70D	W/D	W/D	W/D	W/D	W/D
30431	EASTLEIGH - 71A	EASTLEIGH - 71A	W/D	W/D	W/D	W/D	W/D
30432	GUILDFORD - 70C	GUILDFORD - 70C	W/D	W/D	W/D	W/D	W/D
30433	GUILDFORD - 70C	GUILDFORD - 70C	GUILDFORD - 70C	W/D	W/D	W/D	W/D
30434	EASTLEIGH - 71A	EASTLEIGH - 71A	EASTLEIGH - 71A	EASTLEIGH - 71A	EASTLEIGH - 71A	EASTLEIGH - 71A	EASTLEIGH - 71A
			S11 4-4-0 (1903/20)				
30395	FRATTON - 71D	FRATTON - 71D	W/D	W/D	W/D	W/D	W/D
30396	FRATTON - 71D	FRATTON - 71D	DORCHESTER - 71C	W/D	W/D	W/D	W/D
30397	BASINGSTOKE - 70D	BASINGSTOKE - 70D	BASINGSTOKE - 70D	W/D	W/D	W/D	W/D
30398	BOURNEMOUTH - 71B	BOURNEMOUTH - 71B	BASINGSTOKE - 70D	W/D	W/D	W/D	W/D
30399	DORCHESTER - 71C	DORCHESTER - 71C	GUILDFORD - 70C	W/D	W/D	W/D	W/D
30400	GUILDFORD - 70C	GUILDFORD - 70C	GUILDFORD - 70C	GUILDFORD - 70C	GUILDFORD - 70C	GUILDFORD - 70C	GUILDFORD - 70C
30401	GUILDFORD - 70C	GUILDFORD - 70C	W/D	W/D	W/D	W/D	W/D
30403	BOURNEMOUTH - 71B	BOURNEMOUTH - 71B	W/D	W/D	W/D	W/D	W/D
30404	BOURNEMOUTH - 71B	BOURNEMOUTH - 71B	W/D	W/D	W/D	W/D	W/D
			T9 4-4-0 (1899/1922)				
30117	DORCHESTER - 71C	DORCHESTER - 71C	DORCHESTER - 71C	DORCHESTER - 71C	DORCHESTER - 71C	DORCHESTER - 71C	DORCHESTER - 71C
30119	DORCHESTER - 71C	DORCHESTER - 71C	DORCHESTER - 71C	DORCHESTER - 71C	DORCHESTER - 71C	DORCHESTER - 71C	DORCHESTER - 71C
30120	DORCHESTER - 71C	DORCHESTER - 71C	DORCHESTER - 71C	DORCHESTER - 71C	DORCHESTER - 71C	DORCHESTER - 71C	DORCHESTER - 71C
30281	EASTLEIGH - 71A	EASTLEIGH - 71A	EASTLEIGH - 71A	W/D	W/D	W/D	W/D
30282	EASTLEIGH - 71A	EASTLEIGH - 71A	EASTLEIGH - 71A	EASTLEIGH - 71A	EASTLEIGH - 71A	EASTLEIGH - 71A	EASTLEIGH - 71A
30283	EASTLEIGH - 71A	EASTLEIGH - 71A	EASTLEIGH - 71A	EASTLEIGH - 71A	EASTLEIGH - 71A	EASTLEIGH - 71A	EASTLEIGH - 71A
30284	DORCHESTER - 71C	DORCHESTER - 71C	DORCHESTER - 71C	DORCHESTER - 71C	DORCHESTER - 71C	DORCHESTER - 71C	DORCHESTER - 71C
30285	FRATTON - 71D	FRATTON - 71D	FRATTON - 71D	EASTLEIGH - 71A	EASTLEIGH - 71A	EASTLEIGH - 71A	EASTLEIGH - 71A
30287	EASTLEIGH - 71A	EASTLEIGH - 71A	EASTLEIGH - 71A	EASTLEIGH - 71A	EASTLEIGH - 71A	EASTLEIGH - 71A	EASTLEIGH - 71A
30288	EASTLEIGH - 71A	EASTLEIGH - 71A	EASTLEIGH - 71A	EASTLEIGH - 71A	EASTLEIGH - 71A	EASTLEIGH - 71A	EASTLEIGH - 71A
30289	EASTLEIGH - 71A	EASTLEIGH - 71A	EASTLEIGH - 71A	EASTLEIGH - 71A	EASTLEIGH - 71A	EASTLEIGH - 71A	EASTLEIGH - 71A
30300	SALISBURY - 72B	SALISBURY - 72B	SALISBURY - 72B	EASTLEIGH - 71A	EASTLEIGH - 71A	EASTLEIGH - 71A	EASTLEIGH - 71A
30301	SALISBURY - 72B	SALISBURY - 72B	SALISBURY - 72B	SALISBURY - 72B	SALISBURY - 72B	SALISBURY - 72B	SALISBURY - 72B
30302	SALISBURY - 72B	SALISBURY - 72B	SALISBURY - 72B	SALISBURY - 72B	SALISBURY - 72B	SALISBURY - 72B	SALISBURY - 72B
30304	SALISBURY - 72B	SALISBURY - 72B	SALISBURY - 72B	SALISBURY - 72B	SALISBURY - 72B	SALISBURY - 72B	SALISBURY - 72B
30307	FRATTON - 71D	FRATTON - 71D	FRATTON - 71D	GUILDFORD - 70C	GUILDFORD - 70C	GUILDFORD - 70C	GUILDFORD - 70C
30310	FRATTON - 71D	FRATTON - 71D	GUILDFORD - 70C	GUILDFORD - 70C	GUILDFORD - 70C	GUILDFORD - 70C	GUILDFORD - 70C
30311	GUILDFORD - 70C	GUILDFORD - 70C	GUILDFORD - 70C	GUILDFORD - 70C	GUILDFORD - 70C	GUILDFORD - 70C	W/D
30312	GUILDFORD - 70C	GUILDFORD - 70C	GUILDFORD - 70C	GUILDFORD - 70C	GUILDFORD - 70C	W/D	W/D
30313	GUILDFORD - 70C	GUILDFORD - 70C	GUILDFORD - 70C	GUILDFORD - 70C	GUILDFORD - 70C	GUILDFORD - 70C	GUILDFORD - 70C
30336	GUILDFORD - 70C	GUILDFORD - 70C	GUILDFORD - 70C	GUILDFORD - 70C	GUILDFORD - 70C	GUILDFORD - 70C	GUILDFORD - 70C
30337	YEOVIL - 72C	YEOVIL - 72C	YEOVIL - 72C	GUILDFORD - 70C	GUILDFORD - 70C	GUILDFORD - 70C	GUILDFORD - 70C
30338	DORCHESTER - 71C	DORCHESTER - 71C	DORCHESTER - 71C	GUILDFORD - 70C	GUILDFORD - 70C	GUILDFORD - 70C	GUILDFORD - 70C
30702	EXMOUTH JCN - 72A	EXMOUTH JCN - 72A	EXMOUTH JCN - 72A	EXMOUTH JCN - 72A	EXMOUTH JCN - 72A	EXMOUTH JCN - 72A	SALISBURY - 72B
30703	SALISBURY - 72B	SALISBURY - 72B	SALISBURY - 72B	SALISBURY - 72B	SALISBURY - 72B	SALISBURY - 72B	SALISBURY - 72B
30704	EXMOUTH JCN - 72A	EXMOUTH JCN - 72A	W/D	W/D	W/D	W/D	W/D
30705	SALISBURY - 72B	SALISBURY - 72B	SALISBURY - 72B	BASINGSTOKE - 70D	BASINGSTOKE - 70D	BASINGSTOKE - 70D	BASINGSTOKE - 70D
30706	EXMOUTH JCN - 72A	EXMOUTH JCN - 72A	EXMOUTH JCN - 72A	EXMOUTH JCN - 72A	EXMOUTH JCN - 72A	EXMOUTH JCN - 72A	EXMOUTH JCN - 72A
30707	EXMOUTH JCN - 72A	EXMOUTH JCN - 72A	EXMOUTH JCN - 72A	YEOVIL - 72C	YEOVIL - 72C	YEOVIL - 72C	BASINGSTOKE - 70D
30708	EASTLEIGH - 71A	EASTLEIGH - 71A	EXMOUTH JCN - 72A	BASINGSTOKE - 70D	BASINGSTOKE - 70D	BASINGSTOKE - 70D	BASINGSTOKE - 70D
30709	SALISBURY - 72B	SALISBURY - 72B	EXMOUTH JCN - 72A	EXMOUTH JCN - 72A	EXMOUTH JCN - 72A	EXMOUTH JCN - 72A	EXMOUTH JCN - 72A
30710	GUILDFORD - 70C	GUILDFORD - 70C	GUILDFORD - 70C	GUILDFORD - 70C	GUILDFORD - 70C	GUILDFORD - 70C	GUILDFORD - 70C
30711	EASTLEIGH - 71A	EASTLEIGH - 71A	EXMOUTH JCN - 72A	EXMOUTH JCN - 72A	EXMOUTH JCN - 72A	EXMOUTH JCN - 72A	EXMOUTH JCN - 72A
30712	EXMOUTH JCN - 72A	EXMOUTH JCN - 72A	EXMOUTH JCN - 72A	EXMOUTH JCN - 72A	EXMOUTH JCN - 72A	EXMOUTH JCN - 72A	EXMOUTH JCN - 72A
30715	EXMOUTH JCN - 72A	EXMOUTH JCN - 72A	EXMOUTH JCN - 72A	EXMOUTH JCN - 72A	EXMOUTH JCN - 72A	EXMOUTH JCN - 72A	EXMOUTH JCN - 72A
30716	EXMOUTH JCN - 72A	EXMOUTH JCN - 72A	EXMOUTH JCN - 72A	EXMOUTH JCN - 72A	EXMOUTH JCN - 72A	EXMOUTH JCN - 72A	EXMOUTH JCN - 72A
30717	EXMOUTH JCN - 72A	EXMOUTH JCN - 72A	EXMOUTH JCN - 72A	EXMOUTH JCN - 72A	EXMOUTH JCN - 72A	EXMOUTH JCN - 72A	BARNSTAPLE - 72E
30718	NINE ELMS - 70A	NINE ELMS - 70A	NINE ELMS - 70A	NINE ELMS - 70A	NINE ELMS - 70A	NINE ELMS - 70A	NINE ELMS - 70A
30719	NINE ELMS - 70A	NINE ELMS - 70A	NINE ELMS - 70A	NINE ELMS - 70A	NINE ELMS - 70A	NINE ELMS - 70A	NINE ELMS - 70A
30721	EASTLEIGH - 71A	EASTLEIGH - 71A	EASTLEIGH - 71A	EASTLEIGH - 71A	EASTLEIGH - 71A	EASTLEIGH - 71A	EASTLEIGH - 71A
30724	SALISBURY - 72B	SALISBURY - 72B	NINE ELMS - 70A	NINE ELMS - 70A	NINE ELMS - 70A	NINE ELMS - 70A	NINE ELMS - 70A
30725	SALISBURY - 72B	SALISBURY - 72B	NINE ELMS - 70A	NINE ELMS - 70A	NINE ELMS - 70A	NINE ELMS - 70A	FRATTON - 71D
30726	EASTLEIGH - 71A	EASTLEIGH - 71A	BASINGSTOKE - 70D	BASINGSTOKE - 70D	BASINGSTOKE - 70D	BASINGSTOKE - 70D	FRATTON - 71D
30727	SALISBURY - 72B	SALISBURY - 72B	BOURNEMOUTH - 71B	BOURNEMOUTH - 71B	BOURNEMOUTH - 71B	BOURNEMOUTH - 71B	BOURNEMOUTH - 71B
30728	BOURNEMOUTH - 71B	BOURNEMOUTH - 71B	BOURNEMOUTH - 71B	BOURNEMOUTH - 71B	BOURNEMOUTH - 71B	BOURNEMOUTH - 71B	BOURNEMOUTH - 71B
30729	BOURNEMOUTH - 71B	BOURNEMOUTH - 71B	BOURNEMOUTH - 71B	BOURNEMOUTH - 71B	BOURNEMOUTH - 71B	BOURNEMOUTH - 71B	BOURNEMOUTH - 71B
30730	BOURNEMOUTH - 71B	BOURNEMOUTH - 71B	BOURNEMOUTH - 71B	FRATTON - 71D	FRATTON - 71D	FRATTON - 71D	FRATTON - 71D
30732	FELTHAM - 70B	FRATTON - 71D	FRATTON - 71D	FRATTON - 71D	FRATTON - 71D	FRATTON - 71D	FRATTON - 71D
30733	BOURNEMOUTH - 71B	BOURNEMOUTH - 71B	BOURNEMOUTH - 71B	FELTHAM - 70B	FRATTON - 71D	W/D	W/D

Sitting in a sea of ash with the contents of its smokebox on the buffer beam, T9 4-4-0 (30)722 waits at Eastleigh in 1949 for reconversion from oil-burning. The engine was an early withdrawal and was one of nine taken out of service in the Spring of 1951. Its last years were spent at Eastleigh MPD working passenger services to Portsmouth and Salisbury. Sixteen of the class survived into the 1960's with nine remaining active on the Plymouth and Padstow routes from Exeter.

loco	Sep-52	Dec-52	Mar-53	May-53	Jul-53	Sep-53	Nov-53
			L12 4-4-0 (1904/15)				
30415	FRATTON - 71D	FRATTON - 71D	W/D	W/D	W/D	W/D	W/D
30434	EASTLEIGH - 71A	EASTLEIGH - 71A	EASTLEIGH - 71A	EASTLEIGH - 71A	EASTLEIGH - 71A	EASTLEIGH - 71A	EASTLEIGH - 71A
			S11 4-4-0 (1903/20)				
30400	GUILDFORD - 70C	GUILDFORD - 70C	GUILDFORD - 70C	GUILDFORD - 70C	GUILDFORD - 70C	GUILDFORD - 70C	GUILDFORD - 70C
			T9 4-4-0 (1899/1922)				
30117	DORCHESTER - 71C	DORCHESTER - 71C	DORCHESTER - 71C	DORCHESTER - 71C	DORCHESTER - 71C	EASTLEIGH - 71A	EASTLEIGH - 71A
30119	DORCHESTER - 71C	W/D	W/D	W/D	W/D	W/D	W/D
30120	DORCHESTER - 71C	DORCHESTER - 71C	DORCHESTER - 71C	DORCHESTER - 71C	DORCHESTER - 71C	EASTLEIGH - 71A	EASTLEIGH - 71A
30282	EASTLEIGH - 71A	EASTLEIGH - 71A	EASTLEIGH - 71A	EASTLEIGH - 71A	EASTLEIGH - 71A	EASTLEIGH - 71A	EASTLEIGH - 71A
30283	EASTLEIGH - 71A	EASTLEIGH - 71A	EASTLEIGH - 71A	EASTLEIGH - 71A	EASTLEIGH - 71A	EASTLEIGH - 71A	EASTLEIGH - 71A
30284	DORCHESTER - 71C	DORCHESTER - 71C	DORCHESTER - 71C	DORCHESTER - 71C	DORCHESTER - 71C	DORCHESTER - 71C	DORCHESTER - 71C
30285	EASTLEIGH - 71A	EASTLEIGH - 71A	EASTLEIGH - 71A	EASTLEIGH - 71A	EASTLEIGH - 71A	EASTLEIGH - 71A	EASTLEIGH - 71A
30287	EASTLEIGH - 71A	EASTLEIGH - 71A	EASTLEIGH - 71A	EASTLEIGH - 71A	EASTLEIGH - 71A	EASTLEIGH - 71A	EASTLEIGH - 71A
30288	EASTLEIGH - 71A	EASTLEIGH - 71A	EASTLEIGH - 71A	EASTLEIGH - 71A	EASTLEIGH - 71A	EASTLEIGH - 71A	EASTLEIGH - 71A
30289	EASTLEIGH - 71A	EASTLEIGH - 71A	EASTLEIGH - 71A	EASTLEIGH - 71A	EASTLEIGH - 71A	EASTLEIGH - 71A	EASTLEIGH - 71A
30300	EASTLEIGH - 71A	EASTLEIGH - 71A	EASTLEIGH - 71A	EASTLEIGH - 71A	EASTLEIGH - 71A	EASTLEIGH - 71A	EASTLEIGH - 71A
30301	SALISBURY - 72B	SALISBURY - 72B	SALISBURY - 72B	SALISBURY - 72B	SALISBURY - 72B	SALISBURY - 72B	SALISBURY - 72B
30304	SALISBURY - 72B	SALISBURY - 72B	SALISBURY - 72B	SALISBURY - 72B	SALISBURY - 72B	SALISBURY - 72B	SALISBURY - 72B
30307	SALISBURY - 72B	W/D	W/D	W/D	W/D	W/D	W/D
30310	GUILDFORD - 70C	GUILDFORD - 70C	GUILDFORD - 70C	GUILDFORD - 70C	GUILDFORD - 70C	GUILDFORD - 70C	EASTLEIGH - 71A
30313	GUILDFORD - 70C	GUILDFORD - 70C	GUILDFORD - 70C	GUILDFORD - 70C	GUILDFORD - 70C	GUILDFORD - 70C	GUILDFORD - 70C
30336	GUILDFORD - 70C	GUILDFORD - 70C	W/D	W/D	W/D	W/D	W/D
30337	GUILDFORD - 70C	GUILDFORD - 70C	GUILDFORD - 70C	GUILDFORD - 70C	GUILDFORD - 70C	GUILDFORD - 70C	GUILDFORD - 70C
30338	GUILDFORD - 70C	GUILDFORD - 70C	GUILDFORD - 70C	GUILDFORD - 70C	GUILDFORD - 70C	GUILDFORD - 70C	GUILDFORD - 70C
30702	SALISBURY - 72B	SALISBURY - 72B	SALISBURY - 72B	SALISBURY - 72B	SALISBURY - 72B	SALISBURY - 72B	SALISBURY - 72B
30705	BASINGSTOKE - 70D	BASINGSTOKE - 70D	BASINGSTOKE - 70D	BASINGSTOKE - 70D	BASINGSTOKE - 70D	BASINGSTOKE - 70D	BASINGSTOKE - 70D
30706	EXMOUTH JCN - 72A	EXMOUTH JCN - 72A	EXMOUTH JCN - 72A	EXMOUTH JCN - 72A	EXMOUTH JCN - 72A	EXMOUTH JCN - 72A	EXMOUTH JCN - 72A
30707	EXMOUTH JCN - 72A	EXMOUTH JCN - 72A	YEOVIL - 72C	YEOVIL - 72C	YEOVIL - 72C	YEOVIL - 72C	YEOVIL - 72C
30708	EXMOUTH JCN - 72A	EXMOUTH JCN - 72A	EXMOUTH JCN - 72A	EXMOUTH JCN - 72A	EXMOUTH JCN - 72A	EXMOUTH JCN - 72A	EXMOUTH JCN - 72A
30709	EXMOUTH JCN - 72A	EXMOUTH JCN - 72A	EXMOUTH JCN - 72A	EXMOUTH JCN - 72A	EXMOUTH JCN - 72A	EXMOUTH JCN - 72A	EXMOUTH JCN - 72A
30710	GUILDFORD - 70C	GUILDFORD - 70C	GUILDFORD - 70C	GUILDFORD - 70C	GUILDFORD - 70C	GUILDFORD - 70C	GUILDFORD - 70C
30711	EXMOUTH JCN - 72A	EXMOUTH JCN - 72A	EXMOUTH JCN - 72A	EXMOUTH JCN - 72A	EXMOUTH JCN - 72A	EXMOUTH JCN - 72A	EXMOUTH JCN - 72A
30712	EXMOUTH JCN - 72A	EXMOUTH JCN - 72A	EXMOUTH JCN - 72A	EXMOUTH JCN - 72A	EXMOUTH JCN - 72A	EXMOUTH JCN - 72A	EXMOUTH JCN - 72A
30715	EXMOUTH JCN - 72A	EXMOUTH JCN - 72A	EXMOUTH JCN - 72A	EXMOUTH JCN - 72A	EXMOUTH JCN - 72A	EXMOUTH JCN - 72A	EXMOUTH JCN - 72A
30716	EXMOUTH JCN - 72A	EXMOUTH JCN - 72A	EXMOUTH JCN - 72A	EXMOUTH JCN - 72A	EXMOUTH JCN - 72A	EXMOUTH JCN - 72A	EXMOUTH JCN - 72A
30717	EXMOUTH JCN - 72A	EXMOUTH JCN - 72A	EXMOUTH JCN - 72A	EXMOUTH JCN - 72A	EXMOUTH JCN - 72A	EXMOUTH JCN - 72A	EXMOUTH JCN - 72A
30718	NINE ELMS - 70A	NINE ELMS - 70A	NINE ELMS - 70A	NINE ELMS - 70A	NINE ELMS - 70A	NINE ELMS - 70A	NINE ELMS - 70A
30719	NINE ELMS - 70A	NINE ELMS - 70A	NINE ELMS - 70A	NINE ELMS - 70A	NINE ELMS - 70A	NINE ELMS - 70A	NINE ELMS - 70A
30721	SALISBURY - 72B	SALISBURY - 72B	SALISBURY - 72B	SALISBURY - 72B	SALISBURY - 72B	SALISBURY - 72B	SALISBURY - 72B
30724	BASINGSTOKE - 70D	BASINGSTOKE - 70D	BASINGSTOKE - 70D	BASINGSTOKE - 70D	BASINGSTOKE - 70D	BASINGSTOKE - 70D	BASINGSTOKE - 70D
30725	FRATTON - 71D	W/D	W/D	W/D	W/D	W/D	W/D
30726	FRATTON - 71D	FRATTON - 71D	FRATTON - 71D	FRATTON - 71D	FRATTON - 71D	FRATTON - 71D	FRATTON - 71D
30727	BOURNEMOUTH - 71B	BOURNEMOUTH - 71B	BOURNEMOUTH - 71B	BOURNEMOUTH - 71B	BOURNEMOUTH - 71B	BOURNEMOUTH - 71B	BOURNEMOUTH - 71B
30728	BOURNEMOUTH - 71B	BOURNEMOUTH - 71B	BOURNEMOUTH - 71B	BOURNEMOUTH - 71B	BOURNEMOUTH - 71B	BOURNEMOUTH - 71B	BOURNEMOUTH - 71B
30729	BOURNEMOUTH - 71B	BOURNEMOUTH - 71B	BOURNEMOUTH - 71B	BOURNEMOUTH - 71B	BOURNEMOUTH - 71B	BOURNEMOUTH - 71B	BOURNEMOUTH - 71B
30730	FRATTON - 71D	FRATTON - 71D	FRATTON - 71D	FRATTON - 71D	FRATTON - 71D	FRATTON - 71D	FRATTON - 71D
30732	FRATTON - 71D	GUILDFORD - 70C	FRATTON - 71D	FRATTON - 71D	FRATTON - 71D	FRATTON - 71D	FRATTON - 71D

loco	Jan-54	Mar-54	May-54	Jun-54	Aug-54	Oct-54	Dec-54
			L12 4-4-0 (1904/15)				
30434	EASTLEIGH - 71A	EASTLEIGH - 71A	EASTLEIGH - 71A	EASTLEIGH - 71A	EASTLEIGH - 71A	EASTLEIGH - 71A	GUILDFORD - 70C
			S11 4-4-0 (1903/20)				
30400	GUILDFORD - 70C	GUILDFORD - 70C	GUILDFORD - 70C	GUILDFORD - 70C	GUILDFORD - 70C	W/D	W/D
			T9 4-4-0 (1899/1922)				
30117	EASTLEIGH - 71A	EASTLEIGH - 71A	EASTLEIGH - 71A	EASTLEIGH - 71A	EASTLEIGH - 71A	EASTLEIGH - 71A	EASTLEIGH - 71A
30120	EASTLEIGH - 71A	EASTLEIGH - 71A	EASTLEIGH - 71A	EASTLEIGH - 71A	EASTLEIGH - 71A	EASTLEIGH - 71A	EASTLEIGH - 71A
30282	EASTLEIGH - 71A	W/D	W/D	W/D	W/D	W/D	W/D
30283	EASTLEIGH - 71A	EASTLEIGH - 71A	EASTLEIGH - 71A	EASTLEIGH - 71A	EASTLEIGH - 71A	EASTLEIGH - 71A	EASTLEIGH - 71A
30284	DORCHESTER - 71C	DORCHESTER - 71C	DORCHESTER - 71C	DORCHESTER - 71C	DORCHESTER - 71C	DORCHESTER - 71C	DORCHESTER - 71C
30285	EASTLEIGH - 71A	EASTLEIGH - 71A	EASTLEIGH - 71A	EASTLEIGH - 71A	EASTLEIGH - 71A	EASTLEIGH - 71A	EASTLEIGH - 71A
30287	EASTLEIGH - 71A	EASTLEIGH - 71A	EASTLEIGH - 71A	EASTLEIGH - 71A	EASTLEIGH - 71A	EASTLEIGH - 71A	EASTLEIGH - 71A
30288	EASTLEIGH - 71A	EASTLEIGH - 71A	EASTLEIGH - 71A	EASTLEIGH - 71A	EASTLEIGH - 71A	EASTLEIGH - 71A	EASTLEIGH - 71A
30289	EASTLEIGH - 71A	EASTLEIGH - 71A	EASTLEIGH - 71A	EASTLEIGH - 71A	EASTLEIGH - 71A	EASTLEIGH - 71A	EASTLEIGH - 71A
30300	EASTLEIGH - 71A	EASTLEIGH - 71A	EASTLEIGH - 71A	EASTLEIGH - 71A	EASTLEIGH - 71A	EASTLEIGH - 71A	EASTLEIGH - 71A
30301	SALISBURY - 72B	SALISBURY - 72B	SALISBURY - 72B	SALISBURY - 72B	SALISBURY - 72B	SALISBURY - 72B	SALISBURY - 72B
30304	SALISBURY - 72B	SALISBURY - 72B	SALISBURY - 72B	SALISBURY - 72B	SALISBURY - 72B	SALISBURY - 72B	SALISBURY - 72B
30310	EASTLEIGH - 71A	EASTLEIGH - 71A	EASTLEIGH - 71A	EASTLEIGH - 71A	SALISBURY - 72B	EASTLEIGH - 71A	EASTLEIGH - 71A
30313	GUILDFORD - 70C	GUILDFORD - 70C	GUILDFORD - 70C	GUILDFORD - 70C	GUILDFORD - 70C	GUILDFORD - 70C	GUILDFORD - 70C
30337	GUILDFORD - 70C	GUILDFORD - 70C	GUILDFORD - 70C	GUILDFORD - 70C	SALISBURY - 72B	SALISBURY - 72B	SALISBURY - 72B
30338	GUILDFORD - 70C	GUILDFORD - 70C	NINE ELMS - 70A	NINE ELMS - 70A	NINE ELMS - 70A	NINE ELMS - 70A	NINE ELMS - 70A
30702	SALISBURY - 72B	SALISBURY - 72B	SALISBURY - 72B	SALISBURY - 72B	SALISBURY - 72B	SALISBURY - 72B	SALISBURY - 72B
30705	BASINGSTOKE - 70D	BASINGSTOKE - 70D	BASINGSTOKE - 70D	BASINGSTOKE - 70D	BASINGSTOKE - 70D	BASINGSTOKE - 70D	BASINGSTOKE - 70D
30706	EXMOUTH JCN - 72A	EXMOUTH JCN - 72A	EXMOUTH JCN - 72A	EXMOUTH JCN - 72A	EXMOUTH JCN - 72A	YEOVIL - 72C	BOURNEMOUTH - 71B
30707	YEOVIL - 72C	YEOVIL - 72C	YEOVIL - 72C	YEOVIL - 72C	YEOVIL - 72C	BOURNEMOUTH - 71B	YEOVIL - 72C
30708	EXMOUTH JCN - 72A	EXMOUTH JCN - 72A	EXMOUTH JCN - 72A	EXMOUTH JCN - 72A	EXMOUTH JCN - 72A	EXMOUTH JCN - 72A	EXMOUTH JCN - 72A
30709	EXMOUTH JCN - 72A	EXMOUTH JCN - 72A	EXMOUTH JCN - 72A	EXMOUTH JCN - 72A	EXMOUTH JCN - 72A	EXMOUTH JCN - 72A	EXMOUTH JCN - 72A
30710	GUILDFORD - 70C	GUILDFORD - 70C	GUILDFORD - 70C	GUILDFORD - 70C	GUILDFORD - 70C	GUILDFORD - 70C	GUILDFORD - 70C
30711	EXMOUTH JCN - 72A	EXMOUTH JCN - 72A	EXMOUTH JCN - 72A	EXMOUTH JCN - 72A	EXMOUTH JCN - 72A	EXMOUTH JCN - 72A	EXMOUTH JCN - 72A
30712	EXMOUTH JCN - 72A	EXMOUTH JCN - 72A	EXMOUTH JCN - 72A	EXMOUTH JCN - 72A	EXMOUTH JCN - 72A	EXMOUTH JCN - 72A	EXMOUTH JCN - 72A
30715	EXMOUTH JCN - 72A	EXMOUTH JCN - 72A	EXMOUTH JCN - 72A	EXMOUTH JCN - 72A	EXMOUTH JCN - 72A	EXMOUTH JCN - 72A	EXMOUTH JCN - 72A
30716	EXMOUTH JCN - 72A	EXMOUTH JCN - 72A	EXMOUTH JCN - 72A	EXMOUTH JCN - 72A	EXMOUTH JCN - 72A	EXMOUTH JCN - 72A	EXMOUTH JCN - 72A
30717	EXMOUTH JCN - 72A	EXMOUTH JCN - 72A	EXMOUTH JCN - 72A	EXMOUTH JCN - 72A	EXMOUTH JCN - 72A	EXMOUTH JCN - 72A	EXMOUTH JCN - 72A
30718	NINE ELMS - 70A	NINE ELMS - 70A	NINE ELMS - 70A	NINE ELMS - 70A	NINE ELMS - 70A	NINE ELMS - 70A	NINE ELMS - 70A
30719	NINE ELMS - 70A	NINE ELMS - 70A	NINE ELMS - 70A	NINE ELMS - 70A	NINE ELMS - 70A	NINE ELMS - 70A	NINE ELMS - 70A
30721	SALISBURY - 72B	SALISBURY - 72B	SALISBURY - 72B	SALISBURY - 72B	SALISBURY - 72B	SALISBURY - 72B	BASINGSTOKE - 70D
30724	BASINGSTOKE - 70D	BASINGSTOKE - 70D	BASINGSTOKE - 70D	BASINGSTOKE - 70D	BASINGSTOKE - 70D	BASINGSTOKE - 70D	BASINGSTOKE - 70D
30726	FRATTON - 71D	FRATTON - 71D	FRATTON - 71D	FRATTON - 71D	FRATTON - 71D	FRATTON - 70F	FRATTON - 70F
30727	BOURNEMOUTH - 71B	BOURNEMOUTH - 71B	BOURNEMOUTH - 71B	BOURNEMOUTH - 71B	BOURNEMOUTH - 71B	BOURNEMOUTH - 71B	BOURNEMOUTH - 71B
30728	BOURNEMOUTH - 71B	BOURNEMOUTH - 71B	BOURNEMOUTH - 71B	BOURNEMOUTH - 71B	BOURNEMOUTH - 71B	BOURNEMOUTH - 71B	BOURNEMOUTH - 71B
30729	BOURNEMOUTH - 71B	BOURNEMOUTH - 71B	BOURNEMOUTH - 71B	FRATTON - 71D	FRATTON - 71D	FRATTON - 70F	FRATTON - 70F
30730	FRATTON - 71D	FRATTON - 71D	FRATTON - 71D	FRATTON - 71D	FRATTON - 71D	FRATTON - 70F	FRATTON - 70F
30732	FRATTON - 71D	FRATTON - 71D	FRATTON - 71D	FRATTON - 71D	FRATTON - 71D	FRATTON - 70F	FRATTON - 70F

T9 4-4-0 (1899/1922)

loco	Feb-55	Apr-55	Jun-55	Aug-55	Sep-55	Nov-55	Dec-55
30117	EASTLEIGH - 71A	EASTLEIGH - 71A	EASTLEIGH - 71A	EASTLEIGH - 71A	EASTLEIGH - 71A	EASTLEIGH - 71A	EASTLEIGH - 71A
30120	EASTLEIGH - 71A	EASTLEIGH - 71A	EASTLEIGH - 71A	EASTLEIGH - 71A	EASTLEIGH - 71A	EASTLEIGH - 71A	EASTLEIGH - 71A
30283	EASTLEIGH - 71A	EASTLEIGH - 71A	EASTLEIGH - 71A	EASTLEIGH - 71A	EASTLEIGH - 71A	EASTLEIGH - 71A	EASTLEIGH - 71A
30284	DORCHESTER - 71C	DORCHESTER - 71C	DORCHESTER - 71C	DORCHESTER - 71C	DORCHESTER - 71C	DORCHESTER - 71C	DORCHESTER - 71C
30285	EASTLEIGH - 71A	EASTLEIGH - 71A	EASTLEIGH - 71A	EASTLEIGH - 71A	EASTLEIGH - 71A	EASTLEIGH - 71A	EASTLEIGH - 71A
30287	EASTLEIGH - 71A	EASTLEIGH - 71A	EASTLEIGH - 71A	EASTLEIGH - 71A	EASTLEIGH - 71A	EASTLEIGH - 71A	EASTLEIGH - 71A
30288	EASTLEIGH - 71A	EASTLEIGH - 71A	EASTLEIGH - 71A	EASTLEIGH - 71A	EASTLEIGH - 71A	EASTLEIGH - 71A	EASTLEIGH - 71A
30289	EASTLEIGH - 71A	EASTLEIGH - 71A	EASTLEIGH - 71A	EASTLEIGH - 71A	EASTLEIGH - 71A	EASTLEIGH - 71A	EASTLEIGH - 71A
30300	EASTLEIGH - 71A	EASTLEIGH - 71A	EASTLEIGH - 71A	EASTLEIGH - 71A	EASTLEIGH - 71A	EASTLEIGH - 71A	EASTLEIGH - 71A
30301	SALISBURY - 72B	SALISBURY - 72B	SALISBURY - 72B	SALISBURY - 72B	SALISBURY - 72B	SALISBURY - 72B	SALISBURY - 72B
30304	SALISBURY - 72B	SALISBURY - 72B	SALISBURY - 72B	SALISBURY - 72B	SALISBURY - 72B	SALISBURY - 72B	SALISBURY - 72B
30310	EASTLEIGH - 71A	EASTLEIGH - 71A	EASTLEIGH - 71A	EASTLEIGH - 71A	EASTLEIGH - 71A	EASTLEIGH - 71A	EASTLEIGH - 71A
30313	SALISBURY - 72B	SALISBURY - 72B	SALISBURY - 72B	SALISBURY - 72B	SALISBURY - 72B	SALISBURY - 72B	SALISBURY - 72B
30337	FRATTON - 70F	FRATTON - 70F	FRATTON - 70F	FRATTON - 70F	FRATTON - 70F	FRATTON - 70F	FRATTON - 70F
30338	NINE ELMS - 70A	NINE ELMS - 70A	NINE ELMS - 70A	NINE ELMS - 70A	NINE ELMS - 70A	NINE ELMS - 70A	NINE ELMS - 70A
30702	SALISBURY - 72B	SALISBURY - 72B	SALISBURY - 72B	SALISBURY - 72B	SALISBURY - 72B	SALISBURY - 72B	SALISBURY - 72B
30705	BASINGSTOKE - 70D	BASINGSTOKE - 70D	BASINGSTOKE - 70D	BASINGSTOKE - 70D	BASINGSTOKE - 70D	BASINGSTOKE - 70D	BASINGSTOKE - 70D
30706	BOURNEMOUTH - 71B	BOURNEMOUTH - 71B	BOURNEMOUTH - 71B	BOURNEMOUTH - 71B	BOURNEMOUTH - 71B	BOURNEMOUTH - 71B	BOURNEMOUTH - 71B
30707	EASTLEIGH - 71A	EASTLEIGH - 71A	EASTLEIGH - 71A	EASTLEIGH - 71A	EASTLEIGH - 71A	EASTLEIGH - 71A	EASTLEIGH - 71A
30708	EXMOUTH JCN - 72A	EXMOUTH JCN - 72A	EXMOUTH JCN - 72A	EXMOUTH JCN - 72A	EXMOUTH JCN - 72A	EXMOUTH JCN - 72A	EXMOUTH JCN - 72A
30709	EXMOUTH JCN - 72A	EXMOUTH JCN - 72A	EXMOUTH JCN - 72A	EXMOUTH JCN - 72A	EXMOUTH JCN - 72A	EXMOUTH JCN - 72A	EXMOUTH JCN - 72A
30710	GUILDFORD - 70C	GUILDFORD - 70C	GUILDFORD - 70C	GUILDFORD - 70C	GUILDFORD - 70C	GUILDFORD - 70C	GUILDFORD - 70C
30711	EXMOUTH JCN - 72A	EXMOUTH JCN - 72A	EXMOUTH JCN - 72A	EXMOUTH JCN - 72A	EXMOUTH JCN - 72A	EXMOUTH JCN - 72A	EXMOUTH JCN - 72A
30712	EXMOUTH JCN - 72A	EXMOUTH JCN - 72A	EXMOUTH JCN - 72A	EXMOUTH JCN - 72A	EXMOUTH JCN - 72A	EXMOUTH JCN - 72A	EXMOUTH JCN - 72A
30715	EXMOUTH JCN - 72A	EXMOUTH JCN - 72A	EXMOUTH JCN - 72A	EXMOUTH JCN - 72A	EXMOUTH JCN - 72A	EXMOUTH JCN - 72A	EXMOUTH JCN - 72A
30717	EXMOUTH JCN - 72A	EXMOUTH JCN - 72A	EXMOUTH JCN - 72A	EXMOUTH JCN - 72A	EXMOUTH JCN - 72A	EXMOUTH JCN - 72A	EXMOUTH JCN - 72A
30718	NINE ELMS - 70A	NINE ELMS - 70A	NINE ELMS - 70A	NINE ELMS - 70A	NINE ELMS - 70A	NINE ELMS - 70A	NINE ELMS - 70A
30719	NINE ELMS - 70A	NINE ELMS - 70A	NINE ELMS - 70A	NINE ELMS - 70A	NINE ELMS - 70A	NINE ELMS - 70A	NINE ELMS - 70A
30721	SALISBURY - 72B	SALISBURY - 72B	SALISBURY - 72B	SALISBURY - 72B	SALISBURY - 72B	SALISBURY - 72B	SALISBURY - 72B
30724	BASINGSTOKE - 70D	BASINGSTOKE - 70D	BASINGSTOKE - 70D	BASINGSTOKE - 70D	BASINGSTOKE - 70D	BASINGSTOKE - 70D	BASINGSTOKE - 70D
30726	FRATTON - 70F	FRATTON - 70F	FRATTON - 70F	FRATTON - 70F	FRATTON - 70F	FRATTON - 70F	FRATTON - 70F
30727	EASTLEIGH - 71A	EASTLEIGH - 71A	EASTLEIGH - 71A	EASTLEIGH - 71A	BOURNEMOUTH - 71B	BOURNEMOUTH - 71B	BOURNEMOUTH - 71B
30728	BOURNEMOUTH - 71B	BOURNEMOUTH - 71B	BOURNEMOUTH - 71B	BOURNEMOUTH - 71B	BOURNEMOUTH - 71B	BOURNEMOUTH - 71B	BOURNEMOUTH - 71B
30729	FRATTON - 70F	FRATTON - 70F	FRATTON - 70F	FRATTON - 70F	FRATTON - 70F	FRATTON - 70F	FRATTON - 70F
30730	FRATTON - 70F	FRATTON - 70F	FRATTON - 70F	FRATTON - 70F	FRATTON - 70F	FRATTON - 70F	FRATTON - 70F
30732	FRATTON - 70F	FRATTON - 70F	FRATTON - 70F	FRATTON - 70F	FRATTON - 70F	FRATTON - 70F	FRATTON - 70F

T9 4-4-0 (1899/1922)

loco	Jan-56	Apr-56	May-56	Aug-56	Oct-56	Nov-56	Jan-57
30117	EASTLEIGH - 71A	EASTLEIGH - 71A	EASTLEIGH - 71A	EASTLEIGH - 71A	EASTLEIGH - 71A	EASTLEIGH - 71A	EASTLEIGH - 71A
30120	EASTLEIGH - 71A	EASTLEIGH - 71A	EASTLEIGH - 71A	EASTLEIGH - 71A	EASTLEIGH - 71A	EASTLEIGH - 71A	EASTLEIGH - 71A
30283	EASTLEIGH - 71A	EASTLEIGH - 71A	EASTLEIGH - 71A	EASTLEIGH - 71A	EASTLEIGH - 71A	EASTLEIGH - 71A	EASTLEIGH - 71A
30284	DORCHESTER - 71C	DORCHESTER - 71C	DORCHESTER - 71C	DORCHESTER - 71C	DORCHESTER - 71C	DORCHESTER - 71C	DORCHESTER - 71C
30285	EASTLEIGH - 71A	EASTLEIGH - 71A	EASTLEIGH - 71A	EASTLEIGH - 71A	EASTLEIGH - 71A	EASTLEIGH - 71A	EASTLEIGH - 71A
30287	EASTLEIGH - 71A	EASTLEIGH - 71A	EASTLEIGH - 71A	EASTLEIGH - 71A	EASTLEIGH - 71A	EASTLEIGH - 71A	EASTLEIGH - 71A
30288	EASTLEIGH - 71A	EASTLEIGH - 71A	EASTLEIGH - 71A	EASTLEIGH - 71A	EASTLEIGH - 71A	EASTLEIGH - 71A	EASTLEIGH - 71A
30289	EASTLEIGH - 71A	EASTLEIGH - 71A	EASTLEIGH - 71A	EASTLEIGH - 71A	EASTLEIGH - 71A	EASTLEIGH - 71A	EASTLEIGH - 71A
30300	EASTLEIGH - 71A	EASTLEIGH - 71A	EASTLEIGH - 71A	EASTLEIGH - 71A	EASTLEIGH - 71A	EASTLEIGH - 71A	EASTLEIGH - 71A
30301	SALISBURY - 72B	SALISBURY - 72B	SALISBURY - 72B	SALISBURY - 72B	SALISBURY - 72B	SALISBURY - 72B	SALISBURY - 72B
30304	SALISBURY - 72B	SALISBURY - 72B	SALISBURY - 72B	SALISBURY - 72B	SALISBURY - 72B	SALISBURY - 72B	SALISBURY - 72B
30310	EASTLEIGH - 71A	EASTLEIGH - 71A	EASTLEIGH - 71A	EASTLEIGH - 71A	EASTLEIGH - 71A	EASTLEIGH - 71A	EASTLEIGH - 71A
30313	SALISBURY - 72B	SALISBURY - 72B	SALISBURY - 72B	SALISBURY - 72B	SALISBURY - 72B	SALISBURY - 72B	SALISBURY - 72B
30337	FRATTON - 70F	FRATTON - 70F	FRATTON - 70F	FRATTON - 70F	FRATTON - 70F	GUILDFORD - 70C	GUILDFORD - 70C
30338	NINE ELMS - 70A	NINE ELMS - 70A	NINE ELMS - 70A	NINE ELMS - 70A	NINE ELMS - 70A	NINE ELMS - 70A	NINE ELMS - 70A
30702	SALISBURY - 72B	SALISBURY - 72B	SALISBURY - 72B	SALISBURY - 72B	SALISBURY - 72B	SALISBURY - 72B	SALISBURY - 72B
30705	BASINGSTOKE - 70D	BASINGSTOKE - 70D	BASINGSTOKE - 70D	BASINGSTOKE - 70D	BASINGSTOKE - 70D	GUILDFORD - 70C	GUILDFORD - 70C
30706	BOURNEMOUTH - 71B	BOURNEMOUTH - 71B	BOURNEMOUTH - 71B	BOURNEMOUTH - 71B	BOURNEMOUTH - 71B	BOURNEMOUTH - 71B	BOURNEMOUTH - 71B
30707	EASTLEIGH - 71A	EASTLEIGH - 71A	EASTLEIGH - 71A	EASTLEIGH - 71A	EASTLEIGH - 71A	EASTLEIGH - 71A	EASTLEIGH - 71A
30708	EXMOUTH JCN - 72A	EXMOUTH JCN - 72A	EXMOUTH JCN - 72A	EXMOUTH JCN - 72A	EXMOUTH JCN - 72A	EXMOUTH JCN - 72A	EXMOUTH JCN - 72A
30709	EXMOUTH JCN - 72A	EXMOUTH JCN - 72A	EXMOUTH JCN - 72A	EXMOUTH JCN - 72A	EXMOUTH JCN - 72A	EXMOUTH JCN - 72A	EXMOUTH JCN - 72A
30710	GUILDFORD - 70C	GUILDFORD - 70C	GUILDFORD - 70C	GUILDFORD - 70C	GUILDFORD - 70C	GUILDFORD - 70C	GUILDFORD - 70C
30711	EXMOUTH JCN - 72A	EXMOUTH JCN - 72A	EXMOUTH JCN - 72A	EXMOUTH JCN - 72A	EXMOUTH JCN - 72A	EXMOUTH JCN - 72A	EXMOUTH JCN - 72A
30712	EXMOUTH JCN - 72A	EXMOUTH JCN - 72A	EXMOUTH JCN - 72A	EXMOUTH JCN - 72A	EXMOUTH JCN - 72A	EXMOUTH JCN - 72A	EXMOUTH JCN - 72A
30715	EXMOUTH JCN - 72A	EXMOUTH JCN - 72A	EXMOUTH JCN - 72A	EXMOUTH JCN - 72A	EXMOUTH JCN - 72A	EXMOUTH JCN - 72A	EXMOUTH JCN - 72A
30717	EXMOUTH JCN - 72A	EXMOUTH JCN - 72A	EXMOUTH JCN - 72A	EXMOUTH JCN - 72A	EXMOUTH JCN - 72A	EXMOUTH JCN - 72A	EXMOUTH JCN - 72A
30718	NINE ELMS - 70A	NINE ELMS - 70A	NINE ELMS - 70A	NINE ELMS - 70A	NINE ELMS - 70A	NINE ELMS - 70A	NINE ELMS - 70A
30719	NINE ELMS - 70A	NINE ELMS - 70A	NINE ELMS - 70A	NINE ELMS - 70A	NINE ELMS - 70A	NINE ELMS - 70A	NINE ELMS - 70A
30721	SALISBURY - 72B	SALISBURY - 72B	SALISBURY - 72B	SALISBURY - 72B	SALISBURY - 72B	SALISBURY - 72B	SALISBURY - 72B
30724	BASINGSTOKE - 70D	BASINGSTOKE - 70D	BASINGSTOKE - 70D	BASINGSTOKE - 70D	BASINGSTOKE - 70D	BASINGSTOKE - 70D	BASINGSTOKE - 70D
30726	FRATTON - 70F	FRATTON - 70F	FRATTON - 70F	FRATTON - 70F	FRATTON - 70F	FRATTON - 70F	FRATTON - 70F
30727	BOURNEMOUTH - 71B	BOURNEMOUTH - 71B	BOURNEMOUTH - 71B	BOURNEMOUTH - 71B	BOURNEMOUTH - 71B	BOURNEMOUTH - 71B	BOURNEMOUTH - 71B
30728	BOURNEMOUTH - 71B	BOURNEMOUTH - 71B	BOURNEMOUTH - 71B	W/D	W/D	W/D	W/D
30729	FRATTON - 70F	FRATTON - 70F	FRATTON - 70F	FRATTON - 70F	FRATTON - 70F	FRATTON - 70F	FRATTON - 70F
30730	FRATTON - 70F	FRATTON - 70F	FRATTON - 70F	FRATTON - 70F	FRATTON - 70F	FRATTON - 70F	FRATTON - 70F
30732	FRATTON - 70F	FRATTON - 70F	FRATTON - 70F	FRATTON - 70F	FRATTON - 70F	FRATTON - 70F	FRATTON - 70F

During the first twenty-five years of the twentieth century whilst the LSWR were experiencing troubles in developing a successful 4-6-0, considerable reliance was placed upon the T9 4-4-0's - it was said that they kept the railway together during this period - and it was fitting therefore that class remained generally immune from the slaughter which overtook most of the other LSWR 4-4-0's during the early 1950's. The T9's did not however remain at large on the main line out of Waterloo and to find them in any sort of numbers it was necessary to travel to the secondary lines of the system such as the Portsmouth - Southampton route, local services radiating from Eastleigh and, almost until the end of steam, west of Exeter on the Plymouth and Padstow lines.

T9 4-4-0 (1899/1922)

loco	Mar-57	Jun-57	Jul-57	10.57	Jan-58	Feb-58	Mar-58
30117	EASTLEIGH - 71A	EASTLEIGH - 71A	EASTLEIGH - 71A	EASTLEIGH - 71A	EASTLEIGH - 71A	EASTLEIGH - 71A	EASTLEIGH - 71A
30120	EASTLEIGH - 71A	EASTLEIGH - 71A	EASTLEIGH - 71A	EASTLEIGH - 71A	EASTLEIGH - 71A	EASTLEIGH - 71A	EASTLEIGH - 71A
30283	EASTLEIGH - 71A	EASTLEIGH - 71A	EASTLEIGH - 71A	EASTLEIGH - 71A	W/D	W/D	W/D
30284	DORCHESTER - 71C	DORCHESTER - 71C	DORCHESTER - 71C	DORCHESTER - 71C	DORCHESTER - 71C	DORCHESTER - 71C	DORCHESTER - 71C
30285	EASTLEIGH - 71A	EASTLEIGH - 71A	EASTLEIGH - 71A	EASTLEIGH - 71A	EASTLEIGH - 71A	EASTLEIGH - 71A	EASTLEIGH - 71A
30287	EASTLEIGH - 71A	EASTLEIGH - 71A	EASTLEIGH - 71A	EASTLEIGH - 71A	EASTLEIGH - 71A	EASTLEIGH - 71A	EASTLEIGH - 71A
30288	EASTLEIGH - 71A	EASTLEIGH - 71A	EASTLEIGH - 71A	EASTLEIGH - 71A	EASTLEIGH - 71A	EASTLEIGH - 71A	EASTLEIGH - 71A
30289	EASTLEIGH - 71A	EASTLEIGH - 71A	EASTLEIGH - 71A	EASTLEIGH - 71A	EASTLEIGH - 71A	EASTLEIGH - 71A	EASTLEIGH - 71A
30300	EASTLEIGH - 71A	EASTLEIGH - 71A	EASTLEIGH - 71A	EASTLEIGH - 71A	EASTLEIGH - 71A	EASTLEIGH - 71A	EASTLEIGH - 71A
30301	SALISBURY - 72B	SALISBURY - 72B	SALISBURY - 72B	SALISBURY - 72B	SALISBURY - 72B	SALISBURY - 72B	SALISBURY - 72B
30304	SALISBURY - 72B	SALISBURY - 72B	SALISBURY - 72B	W/D	W/D	W/D	W/D
30310	EASTLEIGH - 71A	EASTLEIGH - 71A	EASTLEIGH - 71A	BOURNEMOUTH - 71B	BOURNEMOUTH - 71B	BOURNEMOUTH - 71B	BOURNEMOUTH - 71B
30313	SALISBURY - 72B	SALISBURY - 72B	SALISBURY - 72B	SALISBURY - 72B	SALISBURY - 72B	SALISBURY - 72B	SALISBURY - 72B
30337	GUILDFORD - 70C	GUILDFORD - 70C	GUILDFORD - 70C	GUILDFORD - 70C	GUILDFORD - 70C	GUILDFORD - 70C	GUILDFORD - 70C
30338	NINE ELMS - 70A	NINE ELMS - 70A	NINE ELMS - 70A	NINE ELMS - 70A	NINE ELMS - 70A	NINE ELMS - 70A	NINE ELMS - 70A
30702	SALISBURY - 72B	SALISBURY - 72B	SALISBURY - 72B	SALISBURY - 72B	SALISBURY - 72B	SALISBURY - 72B	SALISBURY - 72B
30705	GUILDFORD - 70C	GUILDFORD - 70C	GUILDFORD - 70C	GUILDFORD - 70C	W/D	W/D	W/D
30706	BOURNEMOUTH - 71B	BOURNEMOUTH - 71B	BOURNEMOUTH - 71B	BOURNEMOUTH - 71B	BOURNEMOUTH - 71B	BOURNEMOUTH - 71B	BOURNEMOUTH - 71B
30707	EASTLEIGH - 71A	EASTLEIGH - 71A	BOURNEMOUTH - 71B	BOURNEMOUTH - 71B	BOURNEMOUTH - 71B	BOURNEMOUTH - 71B	BOURNEMOUTH - 71B
30708	EXMOUTH JCN - 72A	EXMOUTH JCN - 72A	EXMOUTH JCN - 72A	EXMOUTH JCN - 72A	W/D	W/D	W/D
30709	EXMOUTH JCN - 72A	EXMOUTH JCN - 72A	EXMOUTH JCN - 72A	EXMOUTH JCN - 72A	EXMOUTH JCN - 72A	EXMOUTH JCN - 72A	EXMOUTH JCN - 72A
30710	GUILDFORD - 70C	GUILDFORD - 70C	GUILDFORD - 70C	GUILDFORD - 70C	GUILDFORD - 70C	GUILDFORD - 70C	GUILDFORD - 70C
30711	EXMOUTH JCN - 72A	EXMOUTH JCN - 72A	EXMOUTH JCN - 72A	EXMOUTH JCN - 72A	EXMOUTH JCN - 72A	EXMOUTH JCN - 72A	EXMOUTH JCN - 72A
30712	EXMOUTH JCN - 72A	EXMOUTH JCN - 72A	EXMOUTH JCN - 72A	EXMOUTH JCN - 72A	EXMOUTH JCN - 72A	EXMOUTH JCN - 72A	EXMOUTH JCN - 72A
30715	EXMOUTH JCN - 72A	EXMOUTH JCN - 72A	EXMOUTH JCN - 72A	EXMOUTH JCN - 72A	EXMOUTH JCN - 72A	EXMOUTH JCN - 72A	EXMOUTH JCN - 72A
30717	EXMOUTH JCN - 72A	EXMOUTH JCN - 72A	EXMOUTH JCN - 72A	EXMOUTH JCN - 72A	EXMOUTH JCN - 72A	EXMOUTH JCN - 72A	EXMOUTH JCN - 72A
30718	NINE ELMS - 70A	NINE ELMS - 70A	NINE ELMS - 70A	NINE ELMS - 70A	NINE ELMS - 70A	NINE ELMS - 70A	NINE ELMS - 70A
30719	NINE ELMS - 70A	NINE ELMS - 70A	NINE ELMS - 70A	NINE ELMS - 70A	NINE ELMS - 70A	NINE ELMS - 70A	NINE ELMS - 70A
30721	SALISBURY - 72B	SALISBURY - 72B	SALISBURY - 72B	SALISBURY - 72B	W/D	W/D	W/D
30724	BASINGSTOKE - 70D	BASINGSTOKE - 70D	BASINGSTOKE - 70D	BASINGSTOKE - 70D	BASINGSTOKE - 70D	BASINGSTOKE - 70D	BASINGSTOKE - 70D
30726	FRATTON - 70F	FRATTON - 70F	FRATTON - 70F	FRATTON - 70F	FRATTON - 70F	FRATTON - 70F	FRATTON - 70F
30727	BOURNEMOUTH - 71B	BOURNEMOUTH - 71B	BOURNEMOUTH - 71B	BOURNEMOUTH - 71B	BOURNEMOUTH - 71B	BOURNEMOUTH - 71B	BOURNEMOUTH - 71B
30729	FRATTON - 70F	FRATTON - 70F	FRATTON - 70F	FRATTON - 70F	FRATTON - 70F	FRATTON - 70F	FRATTON - 70F
30730	FRATTON - 70F	FRATTON - 70F	FRATTON - 70F	W/D	W/D	W/D	W/D
30732	FRATTON - 70F	FRATTON - 70F	FRATTON - 70F	FRATTON - 70F	FRATTON - 70F	FRATTON - 70F	FRATTON - 70F

T9 4-4-0 (1899/1922)

loco	May-58	Oct-58	Mar-59	Jun-59	Jul-59	Aug-59	Oct-59
30117	EASTLEIGH - 71A	EASTLEIGH - 71A	EASTLEIGH - 71A	EASTLEIGH - 71A	EASTLEIGH - 71A	EASTLEIGH - 71A	EASTLEIGH - 71A
30120	EASTLEIGH - 71A	EASTLEIGH - 71A	EASTLEIGH - 71A	EASTLEIGH - 71A	EASTLEIGH - 71A	EASTLEIGH - 71A	EASTLEIGH - 71A
30285	EASTLEIGH - 71A	W/D	W/D	W/D	W/D	W/D	W/D
30287	EASTLEIGH - 71A	EASTLEIGH - 71A	EASTLEIGH - 71A	EASTLEIGH - 71A	EASTLEIGH - 71A	EASTLEIGH - 71A	EASTLEIGH - 71A
30288	EASTLEIGH - 71A	EASTLEIGH - 71A	EASTLEIGH - 71A	EASTLEIGH - 71A	EASTLEIGH - 71A	EASTLEIGH - 71A	EASTLEIGH - 71A
30289	EASTLEIGH - 71A	EASTLEIGH - 71A	EASTLEIGH - 71A	EASTLEIGH - 71A	EASTLEIGH - 71A	EASTLEIGH - 71A	EASTLEIGH - 71A
30300	EASTLEIGH - 71A	EASTLEIGH - 71A	EASTLEIGH - 71A	EASTLEIGH - 71A	EASTLEIGH - 71A	EASTLEIGH - 71A	EASTLEIGH - 71A
30301	SALISBURY - 72B	SALISBURY - 72B	SALISBURY - 72B	SALISBURY - 72B	SALISBURY - 72B	SALISBURY - 72B	W/D
30310	BOURNEMOUTH - 71B	BOURNEMOUTH - 71B	BOURNEMOUTH - 71B	W/D	W/D	W/D	W/D
30313	SALISBURY - 72B	SALISBURY - 72B	SALISBURY - 72B	SALISBURY - 72B	SALISBURY - 72B	EXMOUTH JCN - 72A	EXMOUTH JCN - 72A
30337	GUILDFORD - 70C	GUILDFORD - 70C	W/D	W/D	W/D	W/D	W/D
30338	NINE ELMS - 70A	NINE ELMS - 70A	NINE ELMS - 70A	EXMOUTH JCN - 72A	EXMOUTH JCN - 72A	EXMOUTH JCN - 72A	EXMOUTH JCN - 72A
30702	SALISBURY - 72B	SALISBURY - 72B	EXMOUTH JCN - 72A	EXMOUTH JCN - 72A	EXMOUTH JCN - 72A	EXMOUTH JCN - 72A	W/D
30706	BOURNEMOUTH - 71B	BOURNEMOUTH - 71B	BOURNEMOUTH - 71B	W/D	W/D	W/D	W/D
30707	BOURNEMOUTH - 71B	BOURNEMOUTH - 71B	BOURNEMOUTH - 71B	BOURNEMOUTH - 71B	BOURNEMOUTH - 71B	BOURNEMOUTH - 71B	BOURNEMOUTH - 71B
30709	EXMOUTH JCN - 72A	EXMOUTH JCN - 72A	EXMOUTH JCN - 72A	EXMOUTH JCN - 72A	EXMOUTH JCN - 72A	EXMOUTH JCN - 72A	EXMOUTH JCN - 72A
30710	GUILDFORD - 70C	GUILDFORD - 70C	W/D	W/D	W/D	W/D	W/D
30711	EXMOUTH JCN - 72A	EXMOUTH JCN - 72A	EXMOUTH JCN - 72A	EXMOUTH JCN - 72A	EXMOUTH JCN - 72A	EXMOUTH JCN - 72A	EXMOUTH JCN - 72A
30712	EXMOUTH JCN - 72A	EXMOUTH JCN - 72A	W/D	W/D	W/D	W/D	W/D
30715	EXMOUTH JCN - 72A	EXMOUTH JCN - 72A	EXMOUTH JCN - 72A	EXMOUTH JCN - 72A	EXMOUTH JCN - 72A	EXMOUTH JCN - 72A	EXMOUTH JCN - 72A
30717	EXMOUTH JCN - 72A	EXMOUTH JCN - 72A	EXMOUTH JCN - 72A	EXMOUTH JCN - 72A	EXMOUTH JCN - 72A	EXMOUTH JCN - 72A	EXMOUTH JCN - 72A
30718	NINE ELMS - 70A	NINE ELMS - 70A	NINE ELMS - 70A	EXMOUTH JCN - 72A	EXMOUTH JCN - 72A	EXMOUTH JCN - 72A	EXMOUTH JCN - 72A
30719	NINE ELMS - 70A	NINE ELMS - 70A	NINE ELMS - 70A	EXMOUTH JCN - 72A	EXMOUTH JCN - 72A	EXMOUTH JCN - 72A	EXMOUTH JCN - 72A
30724	BASINGSTOKE - 70D	BASINGSTOKE - 70D	GUILDFORD - 70C	W/D	W/D	W/D	W/D
30726	EXMOUTH JCN - 72A	EXMOUTH JCN - 72A	EXMOUTH JCN - 72A	EXMOUTH JCN - 72A	EXMOUTH JCN - 72A	EXMOUTH JCN - 72A	W/D
30727	BOURNEMOUTH - 71B	W/D	W/D	W/D	W/D	W/D	W/D
30729	SALISBURY - 72B	SALISBURY - 72B	SALISBURY - 72B	SALISBURY - 72B	SALISBURY - 72B	SALISBURY - 72B	SALISBURY - 72B
30732	FRATTON - 70F	FRATTON - 70F	FRATTON - 70F	EASTLEIGH - 71A	EASTLEIGH - 71A	EASTLEIGH - 71A	W/D

T9 4-4-0 (1899/1922)

loco	Dec-59	Feb-60	Mar-60	Apr-60	Jul-60	Aug-60	Sep-60	Nov-60
30117	EASTLEIGH - 71A	EASTLEIGH - 71A	EASTLEIGH - 71A	EASTLEIGH - 71A	EASTLEIGH - 71A	EASTLEIGH - 71A	EASTLEIGH - 71A	EASTLEIGH - 71A
30120	EASTLEIGH - 71A	EASTLEIGH - 71A	EASTLEIGH - 71A	EASTLEIGH - 71A	EASTLEIGH - 71A	EASTLEIGH - 71A	EASTLEIGH - 71A	EASTLEIGH - 71A
30287	EASTLEIGH - 71A	EASTLEIGH - 71A	EASTLEIGH - 71A	EASTLEIGH - 71A	EASTLEIGH - 71A	EASTLEIGH - 71A	EASTLEIGH - 71A	EASTLEIGH - 71A
30288	EASTLEIGH - 71A	EASTLEIGH - 71A	EASTLEIGH - 71A	EASTLEIGH - 71A	EASTLEIGH - 71A	EASTLEIGH - 71A	EASTLEIGH - 71A	EASTLEIGH - 71A
30300	EASTLEIGH - 71A	EASTLEIGH - 71A	EASTLEIGH - 71A	EASTLEIGH - 71A	EASTLEIGH - 71A	EASTLEIGH - 71A	EASTLEIGH - 71A	EASTLEIGH - 71A
30313	EXMOUTH JCN - 72A	EXMOUTH JCN - 72A	EXMOUTH JCN - 72A	EXMOUTH JCN - 72A	EXMOUTH JCN - 72A	EXMOUTH JCN - 72A	EXMOUTH JCN - 72A	EXMOUTH JCN - 72A
30338	EXMOUTH JCN - 72A	EXMOUTH JCN - 72A	EXMOUTH JCN - 72A	EXMOUTH JCN - 72A	EXMOUTH JCN - 72A	EXMOUTH JCN - 72A	EXMOUTH JCN - 72A	EXMOUTH JCN - 72A
30707	BOURNEMOUTH - 71B	BOURNEMOUTH - 71B	BOURNEMOUTH - 71B	BOURNEMOUTH - 71B	BOURNEMOUTH - 71B	BOURNEMOUTH - 71B	BOURNEMOUTH - 71B	BOURNEMOUTH - 71B
30709	EXMOUTH JCN - 72A	EXMOUTH JCN - 72A	EXMOUTH JCN - 72A	EXMOUTH JCN - 72A	EXMOUTH JCN - 72A	EXMOUTH JCN - 72A	EXMOUTH JCN - 72A	EXMOUTH JCN - 72A
30715	EXMOUTH JCN - 72A	EXMOUTH JCN - 72A	EXMOUTH JCN - 72A	EXMOUTH JCN - 72A	EXMOUTH JCN - 72A	EXMOUTH JCN - 72A	EXMOUTH JCN - 72A	EXMOUTH JCN - 72A
30717	EXMOUTH JCN - 72A	EXMOUTH JCN - 72A	EXMOUTH JCN - 72A	EXMOUTH JCN - 72A	EXMOUTH JCN - 72A	EXMOUTH JCN - 72A	EXMOUTH JCN - 72A	EXMOUTH JCN - 72A
30718	EXMOUTH JCN - 72A	EXMOUTH JCN - 72A	EXMOUTH JCN - 72A	EXMOUTH JCN - 72A	EXMOUTH JCN - 72A	EXMOUTH JCN - 72A	EXMOUTH JCN - 72A	EXMOUTH JCN - 72A
30719	EXMOUTH JCN - 72A	EXMOUTH JCN - 72A	EXMOUTH JCN - 72A	EXMOUTH JCN - 72A	EXMOUTH JCN - 72A	EXMOUTH JCN - 72A	EXMOUTH JCN - 72A	EXMOUTH JCN - 72A
30729	SALISBURY - 72B	SALISBURY - 72B	SALISBURY - 72B	EXMOUTH JCN - 72A	EXMOUTH JCN - 72A	EXMOUTH JCN - 72A	EXMOUTH JCN - 72A	EXMOUTH JCN - 72A

T9 4-4-0 30726 of Stewarts Lane leaves Eastleigh works in 1949; the paint shops still uncertain as to what to apply to the tender. At the time there was considerable doubt about how to display ownership and in the case of 30726 Eastleigh has taken the sensible course of doing nothing. Early the following year 30726 was transferred to Fratton for working passenger services between Portsmouth and Salisbury until being displaced by diesel multiple-units which started to appear in 1957. In May 1958 the engine was moved to Exmouth Junction - the last T9 stronghold - and operated on the Plymouth and Padstow routes until its withdrawal in the autumn of 1959.

In the aftermath of the Bulleid revolution there was little need for 4-4-0 locomotives and apart from the T9's, which were found work in the Portsmouth and Exeter divisions, the type disappeared quietly from the LSWR scene. The fate of the L12 4-4-0's followed this pattern; the twenty locomotives being taken out of traffic between early 1951 and Christmas 1954 with no less than fourteen being withdrawn in a cull at the end of 1951. 30434, the last survivor, is seen at Eastleigh in 1954, a few weeks before the end.

			V 4-4-0 (1930)				
30900	ST LEONARDS - 74E	ST LEONARDS - 74E	ST LEONARDS - 74E	ST LEONARDS - 74E	ST LEONARDS - 74E	ST LEONARDS - 74E	ST LEONARDS - 74E
30901	ST LEONARDS - 74E	ST LEONARDS - 74E	ST LEONARDS - 74E	ST LEONARDS - 74E	ST LEONARDS - 74E	ST LEONARDS - 74E	ST LEONARDS - 74E
30902	ST LEONARDS - 74E	ST LEONARDS - 74E	ST LEONARDS - 74E	ST LEONARDS - 74E	ST LEONARDS - 74E	ST LEONARDS - 74E	ST LEONARDS - 74E
30903	ST LEONARDS - 74E	ST LEONARDS - 74E	ST LEONARDS - 74E	ST LEONARDS - 74E	ST LEONARDS - 74E	ST LEONARDS - 74E	ST LEONARDS - 74E
30904	ST LEONARDS - 74E	ST LEONARDS - 74E	ST LEONARDS - 74E	ST LEONARDS - 74E	ST LEONARDS - 74E	ST LEONARDS - 74E	ST LEONARDS - 74E
30905	ST LEONARDS - 74E	ST LEONARDS - 74E	ST LEONARDS - 74E	ST LEONARDS - 74E	ST LEONARDS - 74E	ST LEONARDS - 74E	ST LEONARDS - 74E
30906	ST LEONARDS - 74E	ST LEONARDS - 74E	ST LEONARDS - 74E	ST LEONARDS - 74E	ST LEONARDS - 74E	ST LEONARDS - 74E	ST LEONARDS - 74E
30907	ST LEONARDS - 74E	ST LEONARDS - 74E	ST LEONARDS - 74E	ST LEONARDS - 74E	ST LEONARDS - 74E	ST LEONARDS - 74E	ST LEONARDS - 74E
30908	ST LEONARDS - 74E	ST LEONARDS - 74E	ST LEONARDS - 74E	ST LEONARDS - 74E	ST LEONARDS - 74E	ST LEONARDS - 74E	ST LEONARDS - 74E
30909	ST LEONARDS - 74E	ST LEONARDS - 74E	ST LEONARDS - 74E	ST LEONARDS - 74E	ST LEONARDS - 74E	ST LEONARDS - 74E	ST LEONARDS - 74E
30910	ST LEONARDS - 74E	ST LEONARDS - 74E	ST LEONARDS - 74E	ST LEONARDS - 74E	ST LEONARDS - 74E	ST LEONARDS - 74E	ST LEONARDS - 74E
30911	RAMSGATE - 74B	RAMSGATE - 74B	RAMSGATE - 74B	RAMSGATE - 74B	RAMSGATE - 74B	RAMSGATE - 74B	DOVER - 74C
30912	RAMSGATE - 74B	RAMSGATE - 74B	RAMSGATE - 74B	RAMSGATE - 74B	RAMSGATE - 74B	RAMSGATE - 74B	RAMSGATE - 74B
30913	RAMSGATE - 74B	RAMSGATE - 74B	RAMSGATE - 74B	RAMSGATE - 74B	RAMSGATE - 74B	RAMSGATE - 74B	RAMSGATE - 74B
30914	RAMSGATE - 74B	RAMSGATE - 74B	RAMSGATE - 74B	RAMSGATE - 74B	RAMSGATE - 74B	RAMSGATE - 74B	RAMSGATE - 74B
30915	RAMSGATE - 74B	RAMSGATE - 74B	RAMSGATE - 74B	B ARMS - 73B	B ARMS - 73B	B ARMS - 73B	B ARMS - 73B
30916	RAMSGATE - 74B	RAMSGATE - 74B	RAMSGATE - 74B	RAMSGATE - 74B	RAMSGATE - 74B	RAMSGATE - 74B	RAMSGATE - 74B
30917	RAMSGATE - 74B	RAMSGATE - 74B	RAMSGATE - 74B	RAMSGATE - 74B	RAMSGATE - 74B	RAMSGATE - 74B	RAMSGATE - 74B
30918	RAMSGATE - 74B	RAMSGATE - 74B	RAMSGATE - 74B	RAMSGATE - 74B	RAMSGATE - 74B	RAMSGATE - 74B	RAMSGATE - 74B
30919	RAMSGATE - 74B	RAMSGATE - 74B	RAMSGATE - 74B	RAMSGATE - 74B	RAMSGATE - 74B	RAMSGATE - 74B	RAMSGATE - 74B
30920	B ARMS - 73B	B ARMS - 73B	B ARMS - 73B	B ARMS - 73B	B ARMS - 73B	B ARMS - 73B	B ARMS - 73B
30921	B ARMS - 73B	B ARMS - 73B	B ARMS - 73B	B ARMS - 73B	B ARMS - 73B	B ARMS - 73B	B ARMS - 73B
30922	B ARMS - 73B	B ARMS - 73B	B ARMS - 73B	B ARMS - 73B	B ARMS - 73B	B ARMS - 73B	B ARMS - 73B
30923	B ARMS - 73B	B ARMS - 73B	B ARMS - 73B	B ARMS - 73B	B ARMS - 73B	B ARMS - 73B	B ARMS - 73B
30924	DOVER - 74C	DOVER - 74C	DOVER - 74C	DOVER - 74C	DOVER - 74C	DOVER - 74C	DOVER - 74C
30925	DOVER - 74C	DOVER - 74C	DOVER - 74C	DOVER - 74C	DOVER - 74C	DOVER - 74C	DOVER - 74C
30926	DOVER - 74C	DOVER - 74C	DOVER - 74C	DOVER - 74C	RAMSGATE - 74B	RAMSGATE - 74B	RAMSGATE - 74B
30927	DOVER - 74C	DOVER - 74C	DOVER - 74C	DOVER - 74C	DOVER - 74C	DOVER - 74C	DOVER - 74C
30928	B ARMS - 73B	B ARMS - 73B	B ARMS - 73B	B ARMS - 73B	B ARMS - 73B	B ARMS - 73B	B ARMS - 73B
30929	B ARMS - 73B	B ARMS - 73B	B ARMS - 73B	B ARMS - 73B	RAMSGATE - 74B	RAMSGATE - 74B	RAMSGATE - 74B
30930	B ARMS - 73B	B ARMS - 73B	B ARMS - 73B	B ARMS - 73B	B ARMS - 73B	B ARMS - 73B	B ARMS - 73B
30931	B ARMS - 73B	B ARMS - 73B	B ARMS - 73B	B ARMS - 73B	B ARMS - 73B	B ARMS - 73B	B ARMS - 73B
30932	B ARMS - 73B	B ARMS - 73B	B ARMS - 73B	ST LEONARDS - 74E	ST LEONARDS - 74E	ST LEONARDS - 74E	ST LEONARDS - 74E
30933	B ARMS - 73B	B ARMS - 73B	B ARMS - 73B	B ARMS - 73B	B ARMS - 73B	B ARMS - 73B	B ARMS - 73B
30934	B ARMS - 73B	B ARMS - 73B	B ARMS - 73B	B ARMS - 73B	B ARMS - 73B	B ARMS - 73B	B ARMS - 73B
30935	B ARMS - 73B	B ARMS - 73B	B ARMS - 73B	ST LEONARDS - 74E	ST LEONARDS - 74E	ST LEONARDS - 74E	ST LEONARDS - 74E
30936	B ARMS - 73B	B ARMS - 73B	B ARMS - 73B	B ARMS - 73B	B ARMS - 73B	B ARMS - 73B	B ARMS - 73B
30937	B ARMS - 73B	B ARMS - 73B	B ARMS - 73B	B ARMS - 73B	B ARMS - 73B	B ARMS - 73B	B ARMS - 73B
30938	B ARMS - 73B	B ARMS - 73B	B ARMS - 73B	B ARMS - 73B	B ARMS - 73B	B ARMS - 73B	B ARMS - 73B
30939	B ARMS - 73B	B ARMS - 73B	B ARMS - 73B	B ARMS - 73B	B ARMS - 73B	B ARMS - 73B	B ARMS - 73B
			01 0-6-0 (1903)				
31007	GILLINGHAM - 73D	GILLINGHAM - 73D	GILLINGHAM - 73D	GILLINGHAM - 73D	GILLINGHAM - 73D	GILLINGHAM - 73D	GILLINGHAM - 73D
31039	GILLINGHAM - 73D	GILLINGHAM - 73D	W/D	W/D	W/D	W/D	W/D
31041	ASHFORD - 74A	ASHFORD - 74A	ASHFORD - 74A	ASHFORD - 74A	ASHFORD - 74A	ASHFORD - 74A	ASHFORD - 74A
31044	GILLINGHAM - 73D	GILLINGHAM - 73D	GILLINGHAM - 73D	GILLINGHAM - 73D	GILLINGHAM - 73D	GILLINGHAM - 73D	GILLINGHAM - 73D
31048	TONBRIDGE - 74D	TONBRIDGE - 74D	TONBRIDGE - 74D	TONBRIDGE - 74D	TONBRIDGE - 74D	TONBRIDGE - 74D	TONBRIDGE - 74D
31064	GILLINGHAM - 73D	GILLINGHAM - 73D	GILLINGHAM - 73D	GILLINGHAM - 73D	GILLINGHAM - 73D	GILLINGHAM - 73D	GILLINGHAM - 73D
31065	DOVER - 74C	DOVER - 74C	DOVER - 74C	DOVER - 74C	DOVER - 74C	DOVER - 74C	DOVER - 74C
31066	GILLINGHAM - 73D	GILLINGHAM - 73D	GILLINGHAM - 73D	GILLINGHAM - 73D	GILLINGHAM - 73D	GILLINGHAM - 73D	GILLINGHAM - 73D
31080	RAMSGATE - 74B	RAMSGATE - 74B	RAMSGATE - 74B	W/D	W/D	W/D	W/D
31093	DOVER - 74C	DOVER - 74C	DOVER - 74C	DOVER - 74C	DOVER - 74C	DOVER - 74C	DOVER - 74C
31108	DOVER - 74C	DOVER - 74C	DOVER - 74C	DOVER - 74C	DOVER - 74C	DOVER - 74C	DOVER - 74C
31123	ASHFORD - 74A	ASHFORD - 74A	ASHFORD - 74A	ASHFORD - 74A	ASHFORD - 74A	W/D	W/D
31238	GILLINGHAM - 73D	GILLINGHAM - 73D	W/D	W/D	W/D	W/D	W/D
31248	GILLINGHAM - 73D	GILLINGHAM - 73D	GILLINGHAM - 73D	GILLINGHAM - 73D	GILLINGHAM - 73D	GILLINGHAM - 73D	GILLINGHAM - 73D
31258	HITHER GREEN - 73C	HITHER GREEN - 73C	HITHER GREEN - 73C	HITHER GREEN - 73C	HITHER GREEN - 73C	HITHER GREEN - 73C	HITHER GREEN - 73C
31316	RAMSGATE - 74B	W/D	W/D	W/D	W/D	W/D	W/D
31369	FAVERSHAM - 73E	FAVERSHAM - 73E	FAVERSHAM - 73E	FAVERSHAM - 73E	FAVERSHAM - 73E	FAVERSHAM - 73E	FAVERSHAM - 73E
31370	TONBRIDGE - 74D	TONBRIDGE - 74D	TONBRIDGE - 74D	TONBRIDGE - 74D	TONBRIDGE - 74D	TONBRIDGE - 74D	TONBRIDGE - 74D
31373	DOVER - 74C	DOVER - 74C	DOVER - 74C	DOVER - 74C	DOVER - 74C	DOVER - 74C	DOVER - 74C
31374	GILLINGHAM - 73D	GILLINGHAM - 73D	GILLINGHAM - 73D	W/D	W/D	W/D	W/D
31377	HITHER GREEN - 73C	HITHER GREEN - 73C	HITHER GREEN - 73C	HITHER GREEN - 73C	HITHER GREEN - 73C	W/D	W/D
31379	FAVERSHAM - 73E	FAVERSHAM - 73E	FAVERSHAM - 73E	FAVERSHAM - 73E	FAVERSHAM - 73E	FAVERSHAM - 73E	FAVERSHAM - 73E
31380	GILLINGHAM - 73D	GILLINGHAM - 73D	GILLINGHAM - 73D	GILLINGHAM - 73D	W/D	W/D	W/D
31381	DOVER - 74C	DOVER - 74C	DOVER - 74C	DOVER - 74C	DOVER - 74C	DOVER - 74C	DOVER - 74C
31383	DOVER - 74C	DOVER - 74C	DOVER - 74C	DOVER - 74C	DOVER - 74C	DOVER - 74C	DOVER - 74C
31384	GILLINGHAM - 73D	GILLINGHAM - 73D	GILLINGHAM - 73D	GILLINGHAM - 73D	W/D	W/D	W/D
31385	HITHER GREEN - 73C	HITHER GREEN - 73C	HITHER GREEN - 73C	W/D	W/D	W/D	W/D
31390	ASHFORD - 74A	ASHFORD - 74A	ASHFORD - 74A	ASHFORD - 74A	ASHFORD - 74A	ASHFORD - 74A	ASHFORD - 74A
31391	GILLINGHAM - 73D	GILLINGHAM - 73D	GILLINGHAM - 73D	GILLINGHAM - 73D	GILLINGHAM - 73D	GILLINGHAM - 73D	GILLINGHAM - 73D
31395	B ARMS - 73B	B ARMS - 73B	B ARMS - 73B	B ARMS - 73B	B ARMS - 73B	B ARMS - 73B	B ARMS - 73B
31398	B ARMS - 73B	B ARMS - 73B	B ARMS - 73B	B ARMS - 73B	B ARMS - 73B	B ARMS - 73B	B ARMS - 73B
31425	B ARMS - 73B	B ARMS - 73B	B ARMS - 73B	B ARMS - 73B	DOVER - 74C	DOVER - 74C	DOVER - 74C
31429	B ARMS - 73B	B ARMS - 73B	B ARMS - 73B	W/D	W/D	W/D	W/D
31430	GILLINGHAM - 73D	GILLINGHAM - 73D	GILLINGHAM - 73D	GILLINGHAM - 73D	GILLINGHAM - 73D	GILLINGHAM - 73D	GILLINGHAM - 73D
31432	TONBRIDGE - 74D	TONBRIDGE - 74D	TONBRIDGE - 74D	TONBRIDGE - 74D	TONBRIDGE - 74D	GILLINGHAM - 73D	GILLINGHAM - 73D
31434	ASHFORD - 74A	ASHFORD - 74A	ASHFORD - 74A	ASHFORD - 74A	ASHFORD - 74A	ASHFORD - 74A	ASHFORD - 74A
			'0395' 0-6-0 (1881)				
30564	EXMOUTH JCN - 72A	EXMOUTH JCN - 72A	EXMOUTH JCN - 72A	EXMOUTH JCN - 72A	EXMOUTH JCN - 72A	EXMOUTH JCN - 72A	EXMOUTH JCN - 72A
30565	GUILDFORD - 70C	GUILDFORD - 70C	GUILDFORD - 70C	GUILDFORD - 70C	GUILDFORD - 70C	GUILDFORD - 70C	GUILDFORD - 70C
30566	EASTLEIGH - 71A	EASTLEIGH - 71A	EASTLEIGH - 71A	EASTLEIGH - 71A	EASTLEIGH - 71A	EASTLEIGH - 71A	EASTLEIGH - 71A
30567	FELTHAM - 70B	FELTHAM - 70B	FELTHAM - 70B	FELTHAM - 70B	FELTHAM - 70B	FELTHAM - 70B	FELTHAM - 70B
30568	GUILDFORD - 70C	GUILDFORD - 70C	GUILDFORD - 70C	GUILDFORD - 70C	GUILDFORD - 70C	GUILDFORD - 70C	GUILDFORD - 70C
30569	FELTHAM - 70B	FELTHAM - 70B	FELTHAM - 70B	FELTHAM - 70B	FELTHAM - 70B	FELTHAM - 70B	FELTHAM - 70B
30570	FELTHAM - 70B	FELTHAM - 70B	FELTHAM - 70B	FELTHAM - 70B	FELTHAM - 70B	FELTHAM - 70B	FELTHAM - 70B
30571	EASTLEIGH - 71A	EASTLEIGH - 71A	EASTLEIGH - 71A	EASTLEIGH - 71A	EASTLEIGH - 71A	EASTLEIGH - 71A	EASTLEIGH - 71A
30572	FELTHAM - 70B	FELTHAM - 70B	FELTHAM - 70B	FELTHAM - 70B	FELTHAM - 70B	FELTHAM - 70B	FELTHAM - 70B
30573	FELTHAM - 70B	FELTHAM - 70B	FELTHAM - 70B	FELTHAM - 70B	FELTHAM - 70B	FELTHAM - 70B	FELTHAM - 70B
30574	GUILDFORD - 70C	GUILDFORD - 70C	GUILDFORD - 70C	GUILDFORD - 70C	GUILDFORD - 70C	GUILDFORD - 70C	GUILDFORD - 70C
30575	GUILDFORD - 70C	GUILDFORD - 70C	GUILDFORD - 70C	GUILDFORD - 70C	GUILDFORD - 70C	GUILDFORD - 70C	GUILDFORD - 70C
30576	GUILDFORD - 70C	GUILDFORD - 70C	GUILDFORD - 70C	GUILDFORD - 70C	GUILDFORD - 70C	GUILDFORD - 70C	GUILDFORD - 70C
30577	SALISBURY - 72B	SALISBURY - 72B	SALISBURY - 72B	SALISBURY - 72B	SALISBURY - 72B	SALISBURY - 72B	SALISBURY - 72B
30578	GUILDFORD - 70C	GUILDFORD - 70C	GUILDFORD - 70C	GUILDFORD - 70C	GUILDFORD - 70C	GUILDFORD - 70C	GUILDFORD - 70C
30579	FELTHAM - 70B	FELTHAM - 70B	FELTHAM - 70B	FELTHAM - 70B	FELTHAM - 70B	FELTHAM - 70B	FELTHAM - 70B
30580	GUILDFORD - 70C	GUILDFORD - 70C	GUILDFORD - 70C	GUILDFORD - 70C	GUILDFORD - 70C	GUILDFORD - 70C	GUILDFORD - 70C
30581	EASTLEIGH - 71A	EASTLEIGH - 71A	EASTLEIGH - 71A	EASTLEIGH - 71A	EASTLEIGH - 71A	EASTLEIGH - 71A	EASTLEIGH - 71A

loco	Apr-50	Sep-50	Oct-50	Nov-50	Dec-50	Mar-51	Apr-51
				V 4-4-0 (1930)			
30900	ST LEONARDS - 74E	ST LEONARDS - 74E	ST LEONARDS - 74E	ST LEONARDS - 74E	ST LEONARDS - 74E	ST LEONARDS - 74E	ST LEONARDS - 74E
30901	ST LEONARDS - 74E	ST LEONARDS - 74E	ST LEONARDS - 74E	ST LEONARDS - 74E	ST LEONARDS - 74E	ST LEONARDS - 74E	ST LEONARDS - 74E
30902	ST LEONARDS - 74E	ST LEONARDS - 74E	ST LEONARDS - 74E	ST LEONARDS - 74E	ST LEONARDS - 74E	ST LEONARDS - 74E	ST LEONARDS - 74E
30903	ST LEONARDS - 74E	ST LEONARDS - 74E	ST LEONARDS - 74E	ST LEONARDS - 74E	ST LEONARDS - 74E	ST LEONARDS - 74E	ST LEONARDS - 74E
30904	ST LEONARDS - 74E	ST LEONARDS - 74E	ST LEONARDS - 74E	ST LEONARDS - 74E	ST LEONARDS - 74E	ST LEONARDS - 74E	ST LEONARDS - 74E
30905	ST LEONARDS - 74E	ST LEONARDS - 74E	ST LEONARDS - 74E	ST LEONARDS - 74E	ST LEONARDS - 74E	ST LEONARDS - 74E	ST LEONARDS - 74E
30906	B.ARMS - 73B	ST LEONARDS - 74E	ST LEONARDS - 74E	ST LEONARDS - 74E	ST LEONARDS - 74E	ST LEONARDS - 74E	ST LEONARDS - 74E
30907	ST LEONARDS - 74E	ST LEONARDS - 74E	ST LEONARDS - 74E	ST LEONARDS - 74E	ST LEONARDS - 74E	ST LEONARDS - 74E	ST LEONARDS - 74E
30908	B.ARMS - 73B	B.ARMS - 73B	B.ARMS - 73B	ST LEONARDS - 74E	ST LEONARDS - 74E	ST LEONARDS - 74E	ST LEONARDS - 74E
30909	ST LEONARDS - 74E	ST LEONARDS - 74E	ST LEONARDS - 74E	ST LEONARDS - 74E	ST LEONARDS - 74E	ST LEONARDS - 74E	ST LEONARDS - 74E
30910	ST LEONARDS - 74E	ST LEONARDS - 74E	ST LEONARDS - 74E	ST LEONARDS - 74E	ST LEONARDS - 74E	ST LEONARDS - 74E	ST LEONARDS - 74E
30911	DOVER - 74C	RAMSGATE - 74B	RAMSGATE - 74B	RAMSGATE - 74B	RAMSGATE - 74B	ST LEONARDS - 74E	ST LEONARDS - 74E
30912	RAMSGATE - 74B	RAMSGATE - 74B	RAMSGATE - 74B	RAMSGATE - 74B	RAMSGATE - 74B	ST LEONARDS - 74E	ST LEONARDS - 74E
30913	RAMSGATE - 74B	RAMSGATE - 74B	RAMSGATE - 74B	RAMSGATE - 74B	RAMSGATE - 74B	RAMSGATE - 74B	RAMSGATE - 74B
30914	RAMSGATE - 74B	RAMSGATE - 74B	RAMSGATE - 74B	RAMSGATE - 74B	RAMSGATE - 74B	RAMSGATE - 74B	RAMSGATE - 74B
30915	B.ARMS - 73B	RAMSGATE - 74B	RAMSGATE - 74B	RAMSGATE - 74B	RAMSGATE - 74B	RAMSGATE - 74B	RAMSGATE - 74B
30916	RAMSGATE - 74B	RAMSGATE - 74B	RAMSGATE - 74B	RAMSGATE - 74B	RAMSGATE - 74B	RAMSGATE - 74B	RAMSGATE - 74B
30917	RAMSGATE - 74B	RAMSGATE - 74B	RAMSGATE - 74B	RAMSGATE - 74B	RAMSGATE - 74B	RAMSGATE - 74B	RAMSGATE - 74B
30918	RAMSGATE - 74B	RAMSGATE - 74B	RAMSGATE - 74B	RAMSGATE - 74B	RAMSGATE - 74B	RAMSGATE - 74B	RAMSGATE - 74B
30919	B.ARMS - 73B	B.ARMS - 73B	B.ARMS - 73B	B.ARMS - 73B	B.ARMS - 73B	RAMSGATE - 74B	RAMSGATE - 74B
30920	B.ARMS - 73B	B.ARMS - 73B	B.ARMS - 73B	B.ARMS - 73B	B.ARMS - 73B	RAMSGATE - 74B	RAMSGATE - 74B
30921	B.ARMS - 73B	B.ARMS - 73B	B.ARMS - 73B	B.ARMS - 73B	B.ARMS - 73B	RAMSGATE - 74B	RAMSGATE - 74B
30922	B.ARMS - 73B	B.ARMS - 73B	ST LEONARDS - 74E	ST LEONARDS - 74E	DOVER - 74C	DOVER - 74C	DOVER - 74C
30923	B.ARMS - 73B	B.ARMS - 73B	ST LEONARDS - 74E	ST LEONARDS - 74E	DOVER - 74C	DOVER - 74C	DOVER - 74C
30924	DOVER - 74C	DOVER - 74C	DOVER - 74C	DOVER - 74C	DOVER - 74C	DOVER - 74C	DOVER - 74C
30925	DOVER - 74C	DOVER - 74C	DOVER - 74C	DOVER - 74C	DOVER - 74C	DOVER - 74C	DOVER - 74C
30926	RAMSGATE - 74B	DOVER - 74C	RAMSGATE - 74B	RAMSGATE - 74B	RAMSGATE - 74B	RAMSGATE - 74B	RAMSGATE - 74B
30927	DOVER - 74C	DOVER - 74C	DOVER - 74C	DOVER - 74C	DOVER - 74C	DOVER - 74C	DOVER - 74C
30928	B.ARMS - 73B	B.ARMS - 73B	B.ARMS - 73B	B.ARMS - 73B	B.ARMS - 73B	B.ARMS - 73B	B.ARMS - 73B
30929	RAMSGATE - 74B	B.ARMS - 73B	B.ARMS - 73B	B.ARMS - 73B	B.ARMS - 73B	B.ARMS - 73B	B.ARMS - 73B
30930	B.ARMS - 73B	B.ARMS - 73B	B.ARMS - 73B	B.ARMS - 73B	B.ARMS - 73B	B.ARMS - 73B	B.ARMS - 73B
30931	B.ARMS - 73B	B.ARMS - 73B	B.ARMS - 73B	B.ARMS - 73B	B.ARMS - 73B	B.ARMS - 73B	B.ARMS - 73B
30932	ST LEONARDS - 74E	B.ARMS - 73B	B.ARMS - 73B	B.ARMS - 73B	B.ARMS - 73B	B.ARMS - 73B	B.ARMS - 73B
30933	B.ARMS - 73B	B.ARMS - 73B	B.ARMS - 73B	B.ARMS - 73B	B.ARMS - 73B	B.ARMS - 73B	B.ARMS - 73B
30934	B.ARMS - 73B	B.ARMS - 73B	B.ARMS - 73B	B.ARMS - 73B	B.ARMS - 73B	B.ARMS - 73B	B.ARMS - 73B
30935	ST LEONARDS - 74E	ST LEONARDS - 74E	ST LEONARDS - 74E	ST LEONARDS - 74E	ST LEONARDS - 74E	ST LEONARDS - 74E	ST LEONARDS - 74E
30936	B.ARMS - 73B	B.ARMS - 73B	B.ARMS - 73B	B.ARMS - 73B	B.ARMS - 73B	B.ARMS - 73B	B.ARMS - 73B
30937	B.ARMS - 73B	B.ARMS - 73B	B.ARMS - 73B	B.ARMS - 73B	B.ARMS - 73B	B.ARMS - 73B	B.ARMS - 73B
30938	B.ARMS - 73B	B.ARMS - 73B	B.ARMS - 73B	B.ARMS - 73B	B.ARMS - 73B	B.ARMS - 73B	B.ARMS - 73B
30939	B.ARMS - 73B	B.ARMS - 73B	B.ARMS - 73B	B.ARMS - 73B	B.ARMS - 73B	B.ARMS - 73B	B.ARMS - 73B
				01 0-6-0 (1903)			
31041	ASHFORD - 74A	ASHFORD - 74A	ASHFORD - 74A	ASHFORD - 74A	ASHFORD - 74A	ASHFORD - 74A	W/D
31044	B.ARMS - 73B	B.ARMS - 73B	B.ARMS - 73B	B.ARMS - 73B	B.ARMS - 73B	B.ARMS - 73B	B.ARMS - 73B
31048	DOVER - 74C	DOVER - 74C	ASHFORD - 74A	ASHFORD - 74A	ASHFORD - 74A	ASHFORD - 74A	ASHFORD - 74A
31064	B.ARMS - 73B	B.ARMS - 73B(NC)	B.ARMS - 73B(NC)	B.ARMS - 73B(NC)	B.ARMS - 73B(NC)	B.ARMS - 73B(NC)	B.ARMS - 73B(NC)
31065	RAMSGATE - 74B	RAMSGATE - 74B	RAMSGATE - 74B	RAMSGATE - 74B	RAMSGATE - 74B	RAMSGATE - 74B	RAMSGATE - 74B
31066	B.ARMS - 73B	B.ARMS - 73B(NC)	B.ARMS - 73B(NC)	B.ARMS - 73B(NC)	B.ARMS - 73B(NC)	B.ARMS - 73B(NC)	B.ARMS - 73B(NC)
31093	RAMSGATE - 74B	RAMSGATE - 74B	RAMSGATE - 74B	RAMSGATE - 74B	RAMSGATE - 74B	RAMSGATE - 74B	W/D
31108	DOVER - 74C	DOVER - 74C	DOVER - 74C	DOVER - 74C	DOVER - 74C	DOVER - 74C	DOVER - 74C
31248	HITHER GREEN - 73C	HITHER GREEN - 73C	HITHER GREEN - 73C	HITHER GREEN - 73C	HITHER GREEN - 73C	HITHER GREEN - 73C	HITHER GREEN - 73C
31258	HITHER GREEN - 73C	HITHER GREEN - 73C	HITHER GREEN - 73C	HITHER GREEN - 73C	HITHER GREEN - 73C	HITHER GREEN - 73C	HITHER GREEN - 73C
31369	FAVERSHAM - 73E	FAVERSHAM - 73E	FAVERSHAM - 73E	FAVERSHAM - 73E	FAVERSHAM - 73E	FAVERSHAM - 73E	FAVERSHAM - 73E
31370	ASHFORD - 74A	ASHFORD - 74A	ASHFORD - 74A	ASHFORD - 74A	ASHFORD - 74A	ASHFORD - 74A	ASHFORD - 74A
31373	DOVER - 74C	DOVER - 74C	DOVER - 74C	DOVER - 74C	DOVER - 74C	DOVER - 74C	DOVER - 74C
31379	ASHFORD - 74A	ASHFORD - 74A	ASHFORD - 74A	ASHFORD - 74A	ASHFORD - 74A	ASHFORD - 74A	W/D
31381	DOVER - 74C	DOVER - 74C	DOVER - 74C	DOVER - 74C	DOVER - 74C	DOVER - 74C	W/D
31383	DOVER - 74C	DOVER - 74C	DOVER - 74C	DOVER - 74C	DOVER - 74C	DOVER - 74C	W/D
31390	RAMSGATE - 74B	RAMSGATE - 74B	RAMSGATE - 74B	RAMSGATE - 74B	RAMSGATE - 74B	RAMSGATE - 74B	W/D
31391	HITHER GREEN - 73C	HITHER GREEN - 73C	HITHER GREEN - 73C	HITHER GREEN - 73C	HITHER GREEN - 73C	HITHER GREEN - 73C	HITHER GREEN - 73C
31395	B.ARMS - 73B	B.ARMS - 73B(NX)	B.ARMS - 73B(NX)	B.ARMS - 73B(NX)	B.ARMS - 73B(NX)	B.ARMS - 73B(NX)	B.ARMS - 73B(NX)
31425	DOVER - 74C	DOVER - 74C	DOVER - 74C	DOVER - 74C	DOVER - 74C	DOVER - 74C	DOVER - 74C
31430	DOVER - 74C	DOVER - 74C	DOVER - 74C	DOVER - 74C	DOVER - 74C	DOVER - 74C	DOVER - 74C
31432	HITHER GREEN - 73C	HITHER GREEN - 73C	HITHER GREEN - 73C	HITHER GREEN - 73C	HITHER GREEN - 73C	HITHER GREEN - 73C	HITHER GREEN - 73C
31434	ASHFORD - 74A	DOVER - 74C	DOVER - 74C	DOVER - 74C	DOVER - 74C	DOVER - 74C	DOVER - 74C
				'0395' 0-6-0 (1881)			
30564	EXMOUTH JCN - 72A	EXMOUTH JCN - 72A	EXMOUTH JCN - 72A	EXMOUTH JCN - 72A	EXMOUTH JCN - 72A	EXMOUTH JCN - 72A	EXMOUTH JCN - 72A
30565	GUILDFORD - 70C	GUILDFORD - 70C	EASTLEIGH - 71A	EASTLEIGH - 71A	EASTLEIGH - 71A	EASTLEIGH - 71A	EASTLEIGH - 71A
30566	EASTLEIGH - 71A	EASTLEIGH - 71A	EASTLEIGH - 71A	EASTLEIGH - 71A	EASTLEIGH - 71A	EASTLEIGH - 71A	EASTLEIGH - 71A
30567	FELTHAM - 70B	FELTHAM - 70B	FELTHAM - 70B	FELTHAM - 70B	FELTHAM - 70B	FELTHAM - 70B	FELTHAM - 70B
30568	GUILDFORD - 70C	GUILDFORD - 70C	GUILDFORD - 70C	GUILDFORD - 70C	GUILDFORD - 70C	GUILDFORD - 70C	GUILDFORD - 70C
30569	FELTHAM - 70B	FELTHAM - 70B	FELTHAM - 70B	FELTHAM - 70B	FELTHAM - 70B	FELTHAM - 70B	FELTHAM - 70B
30570	FELTHAM - 70B	FELTHAM - 70B	FELTHAM - 70B	FELTHAM - 70B	FELTHAM - 70B	FELTHAM - 70B	FELTHAM - 70B
30571	EASTLEIGH - 71A	EASTLEIGH - 71A	EASTLEIGH - 71A	EASTLEIGH - 71A	EASTLEIGH - 71A	EASTLEIGH - 71A	EASTLEIGH - 71A
30572	FELTHAM - 70B	FELTHAM - 70B	FELTHAM - 70B	FELTHAM - 70B	FELTHAM - 70B	FELTHAM - 70B	FELTHAM - 70B
30573	FELTHAM - 70B	FELTHAM - 70B	FELTHAM - 70B	FELTHAM - 70B	FELTHAM - 70B	FELTHAM - 70B	FELTHAM - 70B
30574	GUILDFORD - 70C	GUILDFORD - 70C	GUILDFORD - 70C	GUILDFORD - 70C	GUILDFORD - 70C	GUILDFORD - 70C	GUILDFORD - 70C
30575	GUILDFORD - 70C	GUILDFORD - 70C	GUILDFORD - 70C	GUILDFORD - 70C	GUILDFORD - 70C	GUILDFORD - 70C	GUILDFORD - 70C
30576	GUILDFORD - 70C	GUILDFORD - 70C	GUILDFORD - 70C	GUILDFORD - 70C	W/D	W/D	W/D
30577	SALISBURY - 72B	SALISBURY - 72B	SALISBURY - 72B	GUILDFORD - 70C	GUILDFORD - 70C	GUILDFORD - 70C	GUILDFORD - 70C
30578	GUILDFORD - 70C	GUILDFORD - 70C	GUILDFORD - 70C	GUILDFORD - 70C	GUILDFORD - 70C	GUILDFORD - 70C	GUILDFORD - 70C
30579	FELTHAM - 70B	FELTHAM - 70B	FELTHAM - 70B	FELTHAM - 70B	FELTHAM - 70B	FELTHAM - 70B	FELTHAM - 70B
30580	GUILDFORD - 70C	GUILDFORD - 70C	GUILDFORD - 70C	GUILDFORD - 70C	EXMOUTH JCN - 72A	EXMOUTH JCN - 72A	EXMOUTH JCN - 72A
30581	EXMOUTH JCN - 72A	EXMOUTH JCN - 72A	EXMOUTH JCN - 72A	EXMOUTH JCN - 72A	EXMOUTH JCN - 72A	EXMOUTH JCN - 72A	EXMOUTH JCN - 72A

loco	Jun-51	Jul-51	Sep-51	Dec-51	Jan-52	Mar-52	Jun-52
				V 4-4-0 (1930)			
30900	ST LEONARDS - 74E	ST LEONARDS - 74E	ST LEONARDS - 74E	ST LEONARDS - 74E	ST LEONARDS - 74E	ST LEONARDS - 74E	ST LEONARDS - 74E
30901	ST LEONARDS - 74E	ST LEONARDS - 74E	ST LEONARDS - 74E	ST LEONARDS - 74E	ST LEONARDS - 74E	ST LEONARDS - 74E	ST LEONARDS - 74E
30902	ST LEONARDS - 74E	ST LEONARDS - 74E	ST LEONARDS - 74E	ST LEONARDS - 74E	ST LEONARDS - 74E	ST LEONARDS - 74E	ST LEONARDS - 74E
30903	ST LEONARDS - 74E	ST LEONARDS - 74E	ST LEONARDS - 74E	ST LEONARDS - 74E	ST LEONARDS - 74E	ST LEONARDS - 74E	ST LEONARDS - 74E
30904	ST LEONARDS - 74E	ST LEONARDS - 74E	ST LEONARDS - 74E	ST LEONARDS - 74E	ST LEONARDS - 74E	ST LEONARDS - 74E	ST LEONARDS - 74E
30905	ST LEONARDS - 74E	ST LEONARDS - 74E	ST LEONARDS - 74E	ST LEONARDS - 74E	ST LEONARDS - 74E	ST LEONARDS - 74E	ST LEONARDS - 74E
30906	ST LEONARDS - 74E	ST LEONARDS - 74E	ST LEONARDS - 74E	ST LEONARDS - 74E	ST LEONARDS - 74E	ST LEONARDS - 74E	ST LEONARDS - 74E
30907	ST LEONARDS - 74E	ST LEONARDS - 74E	ST LEONARDS - 74E	ST LEONARDS - 74E	ST LEONARDS - 74E	ST LEONARDS - 74E	ST LEONARDS - 74E
30908	ST LEONARDS - 74E	ST LEONARDS - 74E	ST LEONARDS - 74E	ST LEONARDS - 74E	ST LEONARDS - 74E	ST LEONARDS - 74E	ST LEONARDS - 74E
30909	ST LEONARDS - 74E	ST LEONARDS - 74E	ST LEONARDS - 74E	ST LEONARDS - 74E	ST LEONARDS - 74E	ST LEONARDS - 74E	ST LEONARDS - 74E
30910	ST LEONARDS - 74E	ST LEONARDS - 74E	ST LEONARDS - 74E	RAMSGATE - 74B	RAMSGATE - 74B	ST LEONARDS - 74E	ST LEONARDS - 74E
30911	ST LEONARDS - 74E	ST LEONARDS - 74E	ST LEONARDS - 74E	RAMSGATE - 74B	RAMSGATE - 74B	ST LEONARDS - 74E	RAMSGATE - 74B
30912	ST LEONARDS - 74E	ST LEONARDS - 74E	ST LEONARDS - 74E	RAMSGATE - 74B	RAMSGATE - 74B	ST LEONARDS - 74E	RAMSGATE - 74B
30913	RAMSGATE - 74B	RAMSGATE - 74B	RAMSGATE - 74B	RAMSGATE - 74B	RAMSGATE - 74B	RAMSGATE - 74B	RAMSGATE - 74B
30914	RAMSGATE - 74B	RAMSGATE - 74B	RAMSGATE - 74B	RAMSGATE - 74B	RAMSGATE - 74B	RAMSGATE - 74B	RAMSGATE - 74B
30915	RAMSGATE - 74B	RAMSGATE - 74B	RAMSGATE - 74B	RAMSGATE - 74B	RAMSGATE - 74B	RAMSGATE - 74B	RAMSGATE - 74B
30916	RAMSGATE - 74B	RAMSGATE - 74B	RAMSGATE - 74B	RAMSGATE - 74B	RAMSGATE - 74B	RAMSGATE - 74B	RAMSGATE - 74B
30917	RAMSGATE - 74B	RAMSGATE - 74B	RAMSGATE - 74B	RAMSGATE - 74B	RAMSGATE - 74B	RAMSGATE - 74B	RAMSGATE - 74B
30918	RAMSGATE - 74B	RAMSGATE - 74B	RAMSGATE - 74B	RAMSGATE - 74B	RAMSGATE - 74B	RAMSGATE - 74B	DOVER - 74C
30919	RAMSGATE - 74B	RAMSGATE - 74B	RAMSGATE - 74B	RAMSGATE - 74B	RAMSGATE - 74B	RAMSGATE - 74B	RAMSGATE - 74B
30920	RAMSGATE - 74B	RAMSGATE - 74B	RAMSGATE - 74B	RAMSGATE - 74B	RAMSGATE - 74B	RAMSGATE - 74B	RAMSGATE - 74B
30921	RAMSGATE - 74B	RAMSGATE - 74B	DOVER - 74C	DOVER - 74C	DOVER - 74C	DOVER - 74C	DOVER - 74C
30922	DOVER - 74C	DOVER - 74C	BRIGHTON - 75A(N)	BRIGHTON - 75A(N)	STEWARTS LANE - 73A	STEWARTS LANE - 73A	STEWARTS LANE - 73A
30923	DOVER - 74C	DOVER - 74C	DOVER - 74C	B ARMS - 73B	B ARMS - 73B	DOVER - 74C	DOVER - 74C
30924	DOVER - 74C	DOVER - 74C	DOVER - 74C	B ARMS - 73B	B ARMS - 73B	DOVER - 74C	B ARMS - 73B
30925	DOVER - 74C	DOVER - 74C	DOVER - 74C	DOVER - 74C	DOVER - 74C	DOVER - 74C	DOVER - 74C
30926	RAMSGATE - 74B	RAMSGATE - 74B	RAMSGATE - 74B	RAMSGATE - 74B	RAMSGATE - 74B	RAMSGATE - 74B	RAMSGATE - 74B
30927	DOVER - 74C	DOVER - 74C	DOVER - 74C	DOVER - 74C	DOVER - 74C	DOVER - 74C	DOVER - 74C
30928	B ARMS - 73B	B ARMS - 73B	B ARMS - 73B	B ARMS - 73B	B ARMS - 73B	B ARMS - 73B	B ARMS - 73B
30929	B ARMS - 73B	B ARMS - 73B	B ARMS - 73B	B ARMS - 73B	B ARMS - 73B	B ARMS - 73B	B ARMS - 73B
30930	B ARMS - 73B	B ARMS - 73B	B ARMS - 73B	B ARMS - 73B	B ARMS - 73B	B ARMS - 73B	B ARMS - 73B
30931	B ARMS - 73B	B ARMS - 73B	B ARMS - 73B	B ARMS - 73B	B ARMS - 73B	B ARMS - 73B	B ARMS - 73B
30932	B ARMS - 73B	B ARMS - 73B	B ARMS - 73B	B ARMS - 73B	B ARMS - 73B	B ARMS - 73B	B ARMS - 73B
30933	B ARMS - 73B	B ARMS - 73B	B ARMS - 73B	B ARMS - 73B	B ARMS - 73B	B ARMS - 73B	B ARMS - 73B
30934	B ARMS - 73B	B ARMS - 73B	B ARMS - 73B	B ARMS - 73B	B ARMS - 73B	B ARMS - 73B	B ARMS - 73B
30935	ST LEONARDS - 74E	ST LEONARDS - 74E	ST LEONARDS - 74E	ST LEONARDS - 74E	ST LEONARDS - 74E	ST LEONARDS - 74E	ST LEONARDS - 74E
30936	B ARMS - 73B	B ARMS - 73B	B ARMS - 73B	B ARMS - 73B	B ARMS - 73B	B ARMS - 73B	B ARMS - 73B
30937	B ARMS - 73B	B ARMS - 73B	B ARMS - 73B	B ARMS - 73B	B ARMS - 73B	B ARMS - 73B	B ARMS - 73B
30938	B ARMS - 73B	B ARMS - 73B	B ARMS - 73B	B ARMS - 73B	B ARMS - 73B	B ARMS - 73B	B ARMS - 73B
30939	B ARMS - 73B	B ARMS - 73B	B ARMS - 73B	B ARMS - 73B	B ARMS - 73B	B ARMS - 73B	B ARMS - 73B
				01 0-6-0 (1903)			
31048	ASHFORD - 74A	ASHFORD - 74A	ASHFORD - 74A	ASHFORD - 74A	ASHFORD - 74A	ASHFORD - 74A	ASHFORD - 74A
31064	B ARMS - 73B(NC)	ASHFORD - 74A	ASHFORD - 74A	ASHFORD - 74A	ASHFORD - 74A	ASHFORD - 74A	ASHFORD - 74A
31065	RAMSGATE - 74B	ASHFORD - 74A	ASHFORD - 74A	ASHFORD - 74A	ASHFORD - 74A	ASHFORD - 74A	ASHFORD - 74A
31108	DOVER - 74C	W/D	W/D	W/D	W/D	W/D	W/D
31258	HITHER GREEN - 73C	DOVER - 74C	DOVER - 74C	DOVER - 74C	DOVER - 74C	DOVER - 74C	DOVER - 74C
31369	FAVERSHAM - 73E	DOVER - 74C	W/D	W/D	W/D	W/D	W/D
31370	ASHFORD - 74A	ASHFORD - 74A	ASHFORD - 74A	ASHFORD - 74A	ASHFORD - 74A	ASHFORD - 74A	ASHFORD - 74A
31373	DOVER - 74C	W/D	W/D	W/D	W/D	W/D	W/D
31425	DOVER - 74C	DOVER - 74C	DOVER - 74C	DOVER - 74C	DOVER - 74C	DOVER - 74C	DOVER - 74C
31430	DOVER - 74C	DOVER - 74C	DOVER - 74C	DOVER - 74C	DOVER - 74C	DOVER - 74C	DOVER - 74C
31434	DOVER - 74C	DOVER - 74C	DOVER - 74C	DOVER - 74C	DOVER - 74C	DOVER - 74C	DOVER - 74C
				'0395' 0-6-0 (1881)			
30564	EXMOUTH JCN - 72A	EXMOUTH JCN - 72A	EXMOUTH JCN - 72A	EXMOUTH JCN - 72A	EXMOUTH JCN - 72A	EXMOUTH JCN - 72A	EXMOUTH JCN - 72A
30565	EASTLEIGH - 71A	EASTLEIGH - 71A	EASTLEIGH - 71A	EASTLEIGH - 71A	EASTLEIGH - 71A	EASTLEIGH - 71A	EASTLEIGH - 71A
30566	EASTLEIGH - 71A	EASTLEIGH - 71A	EASTLEIGH - 71A	EASTLEIGH - 71A	EASTLEIGH - 71A	EASTLEIGH - 71A	EASTLEIGH - 71A
30567	FELTHAM - 70B	FELTHAM - 70B	FELTHAM - 70B	FELTHAM - 70B	FELTHAM - 70B	FELTHAM - 70B	FELTHAM - 70B
30568	GUILDFORD - 70C	GUILDFORD - 70C	GUILDFORD - 70C	GUILDFORD - 70C	GUILDFORD - 70C	GUILDFORD - 70C	GUILDFORD - 70C
30569	FELTHAM - 70B	FELTHAM - 70B	FELTHAM - 70B	FELTHAM - 70B	FELTHAM - 70B	FELTHAM - 70B	FELTHAM - 70B
30570	FELTHAM - 70B	FELTHAM - 70B	FELTHAM - 70B	FELTHAM - 70B	FELTHAM - 70B	FELTHAM - 70B	FELTHAM - 70B
30571	FELTHAM - 70B	FELTHAM - 70B	FELTHAM - 70B	FELTHAM - 70B	FELTHAM - 70B	FELTHAM - 70B	FELTHAM - 70B
30572	FELTHAM - 70B	FELTHAM - 70B	FELTHAM - 70B	FELTHAM - 70B	FELTHAM - 70B	FELTHAM - 70B	FELTHAM - 70B
30573	FELTHAM - 70B	FELTHAM - 70B	FELTHAM - 70B	FELTHAM - 70B	FELTHAM - 70B	FELTHAM - 70B	FELTHAM - 70B
30574	GUILDFORD - 70C	GUILDFORD - 70C	GUILDFORD - 70C	GUILDFORD - 70C	GUILDFORD - 70C	GUILDFORD - 70C	GUILDFORD - 70C
30575	GUILDFORD - 70C	GUILDFORD - 70C	GUILDFORD - 70C	GUILDFORD - 70C	GUILDFORD - 70C	GUILDFORD - 70C	GUILDFORD - 70C
30577	GUILDFORD - 70C	GUILDFORD - 70C	GUILDFORD - 70C	GUILDFORD - 70C	GUILDFORD - 70C	GUILDFORD - 70C	GUILDFORD - 70C
30578	GUILDFORD - 70C	GUILDFORD - 70C	GUILDFORD - 70C	GUILDFORD - 70C	GUILDFORD - 70C	GUILDFORD - 70C	GUILDFORD - 70C
30579	FELTHAM - 70B	FELTHAM - 70B	FELTHAM - 70B	FELTHAM - 70B	FELTHAM - 70B	FELTHAM - 70B	FELTHAM - 70B
30580	EXMOUTH JCN - 72A	EXMOUTH JCN - 72A	EXMOUTH JCN - 72A	EXMOUTH JCN - 72A	EXMOUTH JCN - 72A	EXMOUTH JCN - 72A	EXMOUTH JCN - 72A
30581	EXMOUTH JCN - 72A	EXMOUTH JCN - 72A	EXMOUTH JCN - 72A	EXMOUTH JCN - 72A	EXMOUTH JCN - 72A	EXMOUTH JCN - 72A	EXMOUTH JCN - 72A

'0395' 0-6-0 30565 at Eastleigh in 1949

loco	Sep-52	Dec-52	Mar-53	May-53	Jul-53	Sep-53	Nov-53
				V 4-4-0 (1930)			
30900	ST LEONARDS - 74E	ST LEONARDS - 74E	ST LEONARDS - 74E	ST LEONARDS - 74E	ST LEONARDS - 74E	ST LEONARDS - 74E	ST LEONARDS - 74E
30901	ST LEONARDS - 74E	ST LEONARDS - 74E	ST LEONARDS - 74E	ST LEONARDS - 74E	ST LEONARDS - 74E	ST LEONARDS - 74E	ST LEONARDS - 74E
30902	ST LEONARDS - 74E	ST LEONARDS - 74E	ST LEONARDS - 74E	ST LEONARDS - 74E	ST LEONARDS - 74E	ST LEONARDS - 74E	ST LEONARDS - 74E
30903	ST LEONARDS - 74E	ST LEONARDS - 74E	ST LEONARDS - 74E	ST LEONARDS - 74E	ST LEONARDS - 74E	ST LEONARDS - 74E	ST LEONARDS - 74E
30904	ST LEONARDS - 74E	ST LEONARDS - 74E	ST LEONARDS - 74E	ST LEONARDS - 74E	ST LEONARDS - 74E	ST LEONARDS - 74E	ST LEONARDS - 74E
30905	ST LEONARDS - 74E	ST LEONARDS - 74E	ST LEONARDS - 74E	ST LEONARDS - 74E	ST LEONARDS - 74E	ST LEONARDS - 74E	ST LEONARDS - 74E
30906	ST LEONARDS - 74E	ST LEONARDS - 74E	ST LEONARDS - 74E	ST LEONARDS - 74E	ST LEONARDS - 74E	ST LEONARDS - 74E	ST LEONARDS - 74E
30907	ST LEONARDS - 74E	ST LEONARDS - 74E	ST LEONARDS - 74E	ST LEONARDS - 74E	ST LEONARDS - 74E	ST LEONARDS - 74E	ST LEONARDS - 74E
30908	ST LEONARDS - 74E	ST LEONARDS - 74E	ST LEONARDS - 74E	ST LEONARDS - 74E	ST LEONARDS - 74E	ST LEONARDS - 74E	ST LEONARDS - 74E
30909	ST LEONARDS - 74E	ST LEONARDS - 74E	ST LEONARDS - 74E	ST LEONARDS - 74E	ST LEONARDS - 74E	ST LEONARDS - 74E	ST LEONARDS - 74E
30910	ST LEONARDS - 74E	ST LEONARDS - 74E	ST LEONARDS - 74E	ST LEONARDS - 74E	ST LEONARDS - 74E	ST LEONARDS - 74E	ST LEONARDS - 74E
30911	RAMSGATE - 74B	RAMSGATE - 74B	RAMSGATE - 74B	RAMSGATE - 74B	RAMSGATE - 74B	RAMSGATE - 74B	RAMSGATE - 74B
30912	RAMSGATE - 74B	RAMSGATE - 74B	RAMSGATE - 74B	RAMSGATE - 74B	RAMSGATE - 74B	RAMSGATE - 74B	RAMSGATE - 74B
30913	RAMSGATE - 74B	RAMSGATE - 74B	RAMSGATE - 74B	RAMSGATE - 74B	RAMSGATE - 74B	RAMSGATE - 74B	RAMSGATE - 74B
30914	RAMSGATE - 74B	RAMSGATE - 74B	RAMSGATE - 74B	RAMSGATE - 74B	RAMSGATE - 74B	RAMSGATE - 74B	RAMSGATE - 74B
30915	STEWARTS LANE - 73A	STEWARTS LANE - 73A	STEWARTS LANE - 73A	STEWARTS LANE - 73A	STEWARTS LANE - 73A	STEWARTS LANE - 73A	STEWARTS LANE - 73A
30916	RAMSGATE - 74B	RAMSGATE - 74B	RAMSGATE - 74B	RAMSGATE - 74B	RAMSGATE - 74B	RAMSGATE - 74B	RAMSGATE - 74B
30917	RAMSGATE - 74B	RAMSGATE - 74B	RAMSGATE - 74B	RAMSGATE - 74B	RAMSGATE - 74B	RAMSGATE - 74B	RAMSGATE - 74B
30918	DOVER - 74C	DOVER - 74C	RAMSGATE - 74B	DOVER - 74C	DOVER - 74C	DOVER - 74C	DOVER - 74C
30919	RAMSGATE - 74B	DOVER - 74C	DOVER - 74C	DOVER - 74C	DOVER - 74C	DOVER - 74C	DOVER - 74C
30920	RAMSGATE - 74B	DOVER - 74C	DOVER - 74C	DOVER - 74C	DOVER - 74C	DOVER - 74C	DOVER - 74C
30921	DOVER - 74C	DOVER - 74C	DOVER - 74C	DOVER - 74C	DOVER - 74C	DOVER - 74C	DOVER - 74C
30922	RAMSGATE - 74B	RAMSGATE - 74B	RAMSGATE - 74B	RAMSGATE - 74B	RAMSGATE - 74B	RAMSGATE - 74B	RAMSGATE - 74B
30923	DOVER - 74C	DOVER - 74C	DOVER - 74C	DOVER - 74C	DOVER - 74C	DOVER - 74C	DOVER - 74C
30924	B ARMS - 73B	B ARMS - 73B	B ARMS - 73B	B ARMS - 73B	B ARMS - 73B	B ARMS - 73B	B ARMS - 73B
30925	DOVER - 74C	DOVER - 74C	DOVER - 74C	DOVER - 74C	DOVER - 74C	DOVER - 74C	DOVER - 74C
30926	RAMSGATE - 74B	RAMSGATE - 74B	RAMSGATE - 74B	RAMSGATE - 74B	RAMSGATE - 74B	RAMSGATE - 74B	RAMSGATE - 74B
30927	DOVER - 74C	DOVER - 74C	DOVER - 74C	DOVER - 74C	DOVER - 74C	DOVER - 74C	DOVER - 74C
30928	B ARMS - 73B	B ARMS - 73B	B ARMS - 73B	B ARMS - 73B	B ARMS - 73B	B ARMS - 73B	B ARMS - 73B
30929	B ARMS - 73B	B ARMS - 73B	B ARMS - 73B	B ARMS - 73B	B ARMS - 73B	B ARMS - 73B	B ARMS - 73B
30930	B ARMS - 73B	B ARMS - 73B	B ARMS - 73B	B ARMS - 73B	B ARMS - 73B	B ARMS - 73B	B ARMS - 73B
30931	B ARMS - 73B	B ARMS - 73B	B ARMS - 73B	B ARMS - 73B	B ARMS - 73B	B ARMS - 73B	B ARMS - 73B
30932	B ARMS - 73B	B ARMS - 73B	B ARMS - 73B	B ARMS - 73B	B ARMS - 73B	B ARMS - 73B	B ARMS - 73B
30933	B ARMS - 73B	B ARMS - 73B	B ARMS - 73B	B ARMS - 73B	B ARMS - 73B	B ARMS - 73B	B ARMS - 73B
30934	B ARMS - 73B	B ARMS - 73B	B ARMS - 73B	B ARMS - 73B	B ARMS - 73B	B ARMS - 73B	B ARMS - 73B
30935	ST LEONARDS - 74E	ST LEONARDS - 74E	ST LEONARDS - 74E	ST LEONARDS - 74E	ST LEONARDS - 74E	ST LEONARDS - 74E	ST LEONARDS - 74E
30936	B ARMS - 73B	B ARMS - 73B	B ARMS - 73B	B ARMS - 73B	B ARMS - 73B	B ARMS - 73B	B ARMS - 73B
30937	B ARMS - 73B	B ARMS - 73B	B ARMS - 73B	B ARMS - 73B	B ARMS - 73B	B ARMS - 73B	B ARMS - 73B
30938	B ARMS - 73B	B ARMS - 73B	B ARMS - 73B	B ARMS - 73B	B ARMS - 73B	B ARMS - 73B	B ARMS - 73B
30939	B ARMS - 73B	B ARMS - 73B	B ARMS - 73B	B ARMS - 73B	B ARMS - 73B	B ARMS - 73B	B ARMS - 73B
				01 0-6-0 (1903)			
31048	ASHFORD - 74A	ASHFORD - 74A	ASHFORD - 74A	ASHFORD - 74A	ASHFORD - 74A	ASHFORD - 74A	ASHFORD - 74A
31064	ASHFORD - 74A	ASHFORD - 74A	ASHFORD - 74A	ASHFORD - 74A	ASHFORD - 74A	ASHFORD - 74A	ASHFORD - 74A
31065	ASHFORD - 74A	ASHFORD - 74A	ASHFORD - 74A	ASHFORD - 74A	ASHFORD - 74A	ASHFORD - 74A	ASHFORD - 74A
31258	DOVER - 74C	DOVER - 74C	DOVER - 74C	DOVER - 74C	DOVER - 74C	DOVER - 74C	DOVER - 74C
31370	ASHFORD - 74A	ASHFORD - 74A	ASHFORD - 74A	ASHFORD - 74A	ASHFORD - 74A	ASHFORD - 74A	ASHFORD - 74A
31425	DOVER - 74C	DOVER - 74C	DOVER - 74C	DOVER - 74C	DOVER - 74C	DOVER - 74C	DOVER - 74C
31430	DOVER - 74C	DOVER - 74C	DOVER - 74C	DOVER - 74C	DOVER - 74C	DOVER - 74C	DOVER - 74C
31434	DOVER - 74C	DOVER - 74C	DOVER - 74C	DOVER - 74C	DOVER - 74C	DOVER - 74C	DOVER - 74C
				'0395' 0-6-0 (1881)			
30564	EXMOUTH JCN - 72A	EXMOUTH JCN - 72A	EXMOUTH JCN - 72A	EXMOUTH JCN - 72A	EXMOUTH JCN - 72A	EXMOUTH JCN - 72A	EXMOUTH JCN - 72A
30565	EASTLEIGH - 71A	EASTLEIGH - 71A	W/D	W/D	W/D	W/D	W/D
30566	EASTLEIGH - 71A	EASTLEIGH - 71A	EASTLEIGH - 71A	EASTLEIGH - 71A	EASTLEIGH - 71A	EASTLEIGH - 71A	EASTLEIGH - 71A
30567	FELTHAM - 70B	FELTHAM - 70B	FELTHAM - 70B	FELTHAM - 70B	FELTHAM - 70B	FELTHAM - 70B	FELTHAM - 70B
30568	GUILDFORD - 70C	GUILDFORD - 70C	GUILDFORD - 70C	GUILDFORD - 70C	GUILDFORD - 70C	GUILDFORD - 70C	GUILDFORD - 70C
30569	FELTHAM - 70B	FELTHAM - 70B	FELTHAM - 70B	FELTHAM - 70B	FELTHAM - 70B	FELTHAM - 70B	FELTHAM - 70B
30570	FELTHAM - 70B	FELTHAM - 70B	FELTHAM - 70B	FELTHAM - 70B	FELTHAM - 70B	FELTHAM - 70B	FELTHAM - 70B
30571	FELTHAM - 70B	FELTHAM - 70B	FELTHAM - 70B	FELTHAM - 70B	W/D	W/D	W/D
30572	FELTHAM - 70B	FELTHAM - 70B	FELTHAM - 70B	FELTHAM - 70B	FELTHAM - 70B	FELTHAM - 70B	FELTHAM - 70B
30573	FELTHAM - 70B	FELTHAM - 70B	FELTHAM - 70B	FELTHAM - 70B	FELTHAM - 70B	FELTHAM - 70B	FELTHAM - 70B
30574	GUILDFORD - 70C	GUILDFORD - 70C	GUILDFORD - 70C	GUILDFORD - 70C	GUILDFORD - 70C	GUILDFORD - 70C	GUILDFORD - 70C
30575	GUILDFORD - 70C	EXMOUTH JCN - 72A	EXMOUTH JCN - 72A	EXMOUTH JCN - 72A	EXMOUTH JCN - 72A	EXMOUTH JCN - 72A	EXMOUTH JCN - 72A
30577	GUILDFORD - 70C	GUILDFORD - 70C	GUILDFORD - 70C	GUILDFORD - 70C	GUILDFORD - 70C	GUILDFORD - 70C	GUILDFORD - 70C
30578	GUILDFORD - 70C	GUILDFORD - 70C	GUILDFORD - 70C	GUILDFORD - 70C	GUILDFORD - 70C	GUILDFORD - 70C	GUILDFORD - 70C
30579	FELTHAM - 70B	FELTHAM - 70B	FELTHAM - 70B	FELTHAM - 70B	FELTHAM - 70B	FELTHAM - 70B	FELTHAM - 70B
30580	EXMOUTH JCN - 72A	EXMOUTH JCN - 72A	EXMOUTH JCN - 72A	EXMOUTH JCN - 72A	EXMOUTH JCN - 72A	EXMOUTH JCN - 72A	EXMOUTH JCN - 72A
30581	EXMOUTH JCN - 72A	EXMOUTH JCN - 72A	W/D	W/D	W/D	W/D	W/D

With little originating mineral traffic the LSWR had only a limited need for a general goods 0-6-0 and made do with the 0395 and 700 classes, both of which survived the 1950's. The 0395 'Jumbo' 0-6-0's spent most of their later years on short trip workings, mainly in the Woking area, and for most of the 1950's one could regularly by seen on the Woking - Farnborough goods workings whilst others worked similar short workings from Feltham.

The SECR on the other hand had a considerable volume of mineral traffic in East Kent, the restricted sidings of which kept O1 0-6-0's in work until replaced by diesel shunters. Other traffic on which the class was employed included the large number of local goods trips in the London area although much of this work was gradually handed over to the C class 0-6-0.

The Schools 4-4-0's were four-coupled locomotives with six-coupled operating characteristics and, other than a brief but successful spell on the Waterloo - Bournemouth services during the 1930's, spent most of their working lives on the SECR section. Taking over from the L class 4-4-0's they enjoyed a monopoly of the Charing Cross - Hastings workings but also shared the route to Ramsgate via Ashford and Deal with King Arthur and WC Pacifics. Ramsgate-based members of the class also performed, side by side with the King Arthur's, on LCDR services to Victoria via Chatham.

The first change to their post-war routine came in the summer of 1957 when, following the introduction of multiple-units between Charing Cross and Hastings, five members of the class were moved to the LSWR section at Nine Elms; the number being gradually increased as more multiple units became available. Two engines were also sent to Brighton in the spring of 1958 to take over from West Country Pacifics the working of the morning express to Bournemouth.

Although withdrawal was delayed until the completion of electrification in Kent in 1962, the final years of the class were spent on irregular light duties on all three divisions of the Southern, any permanent niche that might have been found for the class being eliminated by the numbers of rebuilt Pacifics and standard engines that had been drafted in during the second half of the 1950's. Hopes that something of a renaissance would occur with their return to the South Western proved ill founded and, apart from taking over some of the N15X 4-6-0 duties at Basingstoke, most of their workings were of a secondary or seasonal nature although on occasions members of the class found themselves as far west as Exeter on relief services from Waterloo.

loco	Jan-54	Mar-54	May-54	Jun-54	Aug-54	Oct-54	Dec-54
			V 4-4-0 (1930)				
30900	ST LEONARDS - 74E	ST LEONARDS - 74E	ST LEONARDS - 74E	ST LEONARDS - 74E	ST LEONARDS - 74E	ST LEONARDS - 74E	ST LEONARDS - 74E
30901	ST LEONARDS - 74E	ST LEONARDS - 74E	ST LEONARDS - 74E	ST LEONARDS - 74E	ST LEONARDS - 74E	ST LEONARDS - 74E	ST LEONARDS - 74E
30902	ST LEONARDS - 74E	ST LEONARDS - 74E	ST LEONARDS - 74E	ST LEONARDS - 74E	ST LEONARDS - 74E	ST LEONARDS - 74E	ST LEONARDS - 74E
30903	ST LEONARDS - 74E	ST LEONARDS - 74E	ST LEONARDS - 74E	ST LEONARDS - 74E	ST LEONARDS - 74E	ST LEONARDS - 74E	ST LEONARDS - 74E
30904	ST LEONARDS - 74E	ST LEONARDS - 74E	ST LEONARDS - 74E	ST LEONARDS - 74E	ST LEONARDS - 74E	ST LEONARDS - 74E	ST LEONARDS - 74E
30905	ST LEONARDS - 74E	ST LEONARDS - 74E	ST LEONARDS - 74E	ST LEONARDS - 74E	ST LEONARDS - 74E	ST LEONARDS - 74E	ST LEONARDS - 74E
30906	ST LEONARDS - 74E	ST LEONARDS - 74E	ST LEONARDS - 74E	ST LEONARDS - 74E	ST LEONARDS - 74E	ST LEONARDS - 74E	ST LEONARDS - 74E
30907	ST LEONARDS - 74E	ST LEONARDS - 74E	ST LEONARDS - 74E	ST LEONARDS - 74E	ST LEONARDS - 74E	ST LEONARDS - 74E	ST LEONARDS - 74E
30908	ST LEONARDS - 74E	ST LEONARDS - 74E	ST LEONARDS - 74E	ST LEONARDS - 74E	ST LEONARDS - 74E	ST LEONARDS - 74E	ST LEONARDS - 74E
30909	ST LEONARDS - 74E	ST LEONARDS - 74E	ST LEONARDS - 74E	ST LEONARDS - 74E	ST LEONARDS - 74E	ST LEONARDS - 74E	ST LEONARDS - 74E
30910	ST LEONARDS - 74E	ST LEONARDS - 74E	ST LEONARDS - 74E	ST LEONARDS - 74E	ST LEONARDS - 74E	ST LEONARDS - 74E	ST LEONARDS - 74E
30911	RAMSGATE - 74B	RAMSGATE - 74B	RAMSGATE - 74B	RAMSGATE - 74B	RAMSGATE - 74B	RAMSGATE - 74B	RAMSGATE - 74B
30912	RAMSGATE - 74B	RAMSGATE - 74B	RAMSGATE - 74B	RAMSGATE - 74B	RAMSGATE - 74B	RAMSGATE - 74B	RAMSGATE - 74B
30913	RAMSGATE - 74B	RAMSGATE - 74B	RAMSGATE - 74B	RAMSGATE - 74B	RAMSGATE - 74B	RAMSGATE - 74B	RAMSGATE - 74B
30914	RAMSGATE - 74B	RAMSGATE - 74B	RAMSGATE - 74B	RAMSGATE - 74B	RAMSGATE - 74B	RAMSGATE - 74B	RAMSGATE - 74B
30915	STEWARTS LANE - 73A	STEWARTS LANE - 73A	STEWARTS LANE - 73A	STEWARTS LANE - 73A	STEWARTS LANE - 73A	STEWARTS LANE - 73A	STEWARTS LANE - 73A
30916	RAMSGATE - 74B	RAMSGATE - 74B	RAMSGATE - 74B	RAMSGATE - 74B	RAMSGATE - 74B	RAMSGATE - 74B	RAMSGATE - 74B
30917	RAMSGATE - 74B	RAMSGATE - 74B	RAMSGATE - 74B	RAMSGATE - 74B	RAMSGATE - 74B	RAMSGATE - 74B	RAMSGATE - 74B
30918	DOVER - 74C	DOVER - 74C	DOVER - 74C	RAMSGATE - 74B	RAMSGATE - 74B	RAMSGATE - 74B	RAMSGATE - 74B
30919	DOVER - 74C	DOVER - 74C	DOVER - 74C	DOVER - 74C	DOVER - 74C	DOVER - 74C	DOVER - 74C
30920	DOVER - 74C	DOVER - 74C	DOVER - 74C	DOVER - 74C	DOVER - 74C	DOVER - 74C	DOVER - 74C
30921	DOVER - 74C	DOVER - 74C	DOVER - 74C	DOVER - 74C	DOVER - 74C	DOVER - 74C	DOVER - 74C
30922	RAMSGATE - 74B	RAMSGATE - 74B	RAMSGATE - 74B	RAMSGATE - 74B	RAMSGATE - 74B	RAMSGATE - 74B	RAMSGATE - 74B
30923	DOVER - 74C	DOVER - 74C	DOVER - 74C	DOVER - 74C	DOVER - 74C	DOVER - 74C	DOVER - 74C
30924	B ARMS - 73B	B ARMS - 73B	B ARMS - 73B	B ARMS - 73B	B ARMS - 73B	B ARMS - 73B	B ARMS - 73B
30925	B ARMS - 73B	B ARMS - 73B	B ARMS - 73B	B ARMS - 73B	B ARMS - 73B	B ARMS - 73B	B ARMS - 73B
30926	B ARMS - 73B	B ARMS - 73B	B ARMS - 73B	B ARMS - 73B	B ARMS - 73B	B ARMS - 73B	B ARMS - 73B
30927	DOVER - 74C	DOVER - 74C	DOVER - 74C	DOVER - 74C	DOVER - 74C	DOVER - 74C	DOVER - 74C
30928	B ARMS - 73B	B ARMS - 73B	B ARMS - 73B	B ARMS - 73B	B ARMS - 73B	B ARMS - 73B	B ARMS - 73B
30929	B ARMS - 73B	B ARMS - 73B	B ARMS - 73B	B ARMS - 73B	B ARMS - 73B	B ARMS - 73B	B ARMS - 73B
30930	B ARMS - 73B	B ARMS - 73B	B ARMS - 73B	B ARMS - 73B	B ARMS - 73B	B ARMS - 73B	B ARMS - 73B
30931	B ARMS - 73B	B ARMS - 73B	B ARMS - 73B	B ARMS - 73B	B ARMS - 73B	B ARMS - 73B	B ARMS - 73B
30932	B ARMS - 73B	B ARMS - 73B	B ARMS - 73B	B ARMS - 73B	B ARMS - 73B	B ARMS - 73B	B ARMS - 73B
30933	B ARMS - 73B	B ARMS - 73B	B ARMS - 73B	B ARMS - 73B	B ARMS - 73B	B ARMS - 73B	B ARMS - 73B
30934	B ARMS - 73B	B ARMS - 73B	B ARMS - 73B	B ARMS - 73B	B ARMS - 73B	B ARMS - 73B	B ARMS - 73B
30935	B ARMS - 73B	B ARMS - 73B	B ARMS - 73B	B ARMS - 73B	B ARMS - 73B	B ARMS - 73B	B ARMS - 73B
30936	B ARMS - 73B	B ARMS - 73B	B ARMS - 73B	B ARMS - 73B	B ARMS - 73B	B ARMS - 73B	B ARMS - 73B
30937	B ARMS - 73B	B ARMS - 73B	B ARMS - 73B	B ARMS - 73B	B ARMS - 73B	B ARMS - 73B	B ARMS - 73B
30938	B ARMS - 73B	B ARMS - 73B	B ARMS - 73B	B ARMS - 73B	B ARMS - 73B	B ARMS - 73B	B ARMS - 73B
30939	B ARMS - 73B	B ARMS - 73B	B ARMS - 73B	B ARMS - 73B	B ARMS - 73B	B ARMS - 73B	B ARMS - 73B
			01 0-6-0 (1903)				
31048	ASHFORD - 74A	ASHFORD - 74A	ASHFORD - 74A	ASHFORD - 74A	ASHFORD - 74A	ASHFORD - 74A	ASHFORD - 74A
31064	ASHFORD - 74A	ASHFORD - 74A	ASHFORD - 74A	ASHFORD - 74A	ASHFORD - 74A	ASHFORD - 74A	ASHFORD - 74A
31065	ASHFORD - 74A	ASHFORD - 74A	ASHFORD - 74A	DOVER - 74C	DOVER - 74C	DOVER - 74C	DOVER - 74C
31258	DOVER - 74C	DOVER - 74C	DOVER - 74C	DOVER - 74C	DOVER - 74C	DOVER - 74C	DOVER - 74C
31370	ASHFORD - 74A	ASHFORD - 74A	ASHFORD - 74A	ASHFORD - 74A	ASHFORD - 74A	ASHFORD - 74A	ASHFORD - 74A
31425	DOVER - 74C	DOVER - 74C	DOVER - 74C	DOVER - 74C	DOVER - 74C	DOVER - 74C	DOVER - 74C
31430	DOVER - 74C	DOVER - 74C	DOVER - 74C	DOVER - 74C	DOVER - 74C	DOVER - 74C	DOVER - 74C
31434	DOVER - 74C	DOVER - 74C	DOVER - 74C	DOVER - 74C	DOVER - 74C	DOVER - 74C	DOVER - 74C
			'0395' 0-6-0 (1881)				
30564	EXMOUTH JCN - 72A	EXMOUTH JCN - 72A	EXMOUTH JCN - 72A	EXMOUTH JCN - 72A	EXMOUTH JCN - 72A	EXMOUTH JCN - 72A	EXMOUTH JCN - 72A
30566	EASTLEIGH - 71A	EASTLEIGH - 71A	EASTLEIGH - 71A	EASTLEIGH - 71A	EASTLEIGH - 71A	EASTLEIGH - 71A	EASTLEIGH - 71A
30567	FELTHAM - 70B	FELTHAM - 70B	FELTHAM - 70B	FELTHAM - 70B	FELTHAM - 70B	FELTHAM - 70B	FELTHAM - 70B
30568	GUILDFORD - 70C	GUILDFORD - 70C	GUILDFORD - 70C	GUILDFORD - 70C	GUILDFORD - 70C	GUILDFORD - 70C	GUILDFORD - 70C
30569	FELTHAM - 70B	FELTHAM - 70B	FELTHAM - 70B	FELTHAM - 70B	FELTHAM - 70B	FELTHAM - 70B	FELTHAM - 70B
30570	FELTHAM - 70B	FELTHAM - 70B	FELTHAM - 70B	FELTHAM - 70B	FELTHAM - 70B	FELTHAM - 70B	FELTHAM - 70B
30572	FELTHAM - 70B	FELTHAM - 70B	FELTHAM - 70B	FELTHAM - 70B	FELTHAM - 70B	FELTHAM - 70B	FELTHAM - 70B
30573	FELTHAM - 70B	FELTHAM - 70B	FELTHAM - 70B	FELTHAM - 70B	FELTHAM - 70B	FELTHAM - 70B	FELTHAM - 70B
30574	GUILDFORD - 70C	GUILDFORD - 70C	GUILDFORD - 70C	GUILDFORD - 70C	GUILDFORD - 70C	GUILDFORD - 70C	GUILDFORD - 70C
30575	EXMOUTH JCN - 72A	EXMOUTH JCN - 72A	EXMOUTH JCN - 72A	EXMOUTH JCN - 72A	EXMOUTH JCN - 72A	EXMOUTH JCN - 72A	GUILDFORD - 70C
30577	GUILDFORD - 70C	GUILDFORD - 70C	GUILDFORD - 70C	GUILDFORD - 70C	GUILDFORD - 70C	GUILDFORD - 70C	GUILDFORD - 70C
30578	GUILDFORD - 70C	GUILDFORD - 70C	GUILDFORD - 70C	GUILDFORD - 70C	GUILDFORD - 70C	GUILDFORD - 70C	GUILDFORD - 70C
30579	FELTHAM - 70B	FELTHAM - 70B	FELTHAM - 70B	FELTHAM - 70B	FELTHAM - 70B	FELTHAM - 70B	FELTHAM - 70B
30580	EXMOUTH JCN - 72A	EXMOUTH JCN - 72A	EXMOUTH JCN - 72A	EXMOUTH JCN - 72A	EXMOUTH JCN - 72A	EXMOUTH JCN - 72A	GUILDFORD - 70C

'0395' 0-6-0 30578 of Guildford stands ex works at Eastleigh in 1949 with no-one quite clear what to put on the tender side. The Guildford batch of these engines were probably more familiar to enthusiasts during the 1950's than other examples; one of the three engines in daily work running up the main line from Woking each morning with a pick-up goods for Farnborough and working the afternoon trip from Brookwood to Woking later in the day. The other two Guildford 0395's spend their days shunting Woking yard.

V 4-4-0 (1930)

loco	Feb-55	Apr-55	Jun-55	Aug-55	Sep-55	Nov-55	Dec-55
30900	ST LEONARDS - 74E	ST LEONARDS - 74E	ST LEONARDS - 74E	ST LEONARDS - 74E	ST LEONARDS - 74E	ST LEONARDS - 74E	ST LEONARDS - 74E
30901	ST LEONARDS - 74E	ST LEONARDS - 74E	ST LEONARDS - 74E	ST LEONARDS - 74E	ST LEONARDS - 74E	ST LEONARDS - 74E	ST LEONARDS - 74E
30902	ST LEONARDS - 74E	ST LEONARDS - 74E	ST LEONARDS - 74E	ST LEONARDS - 74E	ST LEONARDS - 74E	ST LEONARDS - 74E	ST LEONARDS - 74E
30903	ST LEONARDS - 74E	ST LEONARDS - 74E	ST LEONARDS - 74E	ST LEONARDS - 74E	ST LEONARDS - 74E	ST LEONARDS - 74E	ST LEONARDS - 74E
30904	ST LEONARDS - 74E	ST LEONARDS - 74E	ST LEONARDS - 74E	ST LEONARDS - 74E	ST LEONARDS - 74E	ST LEONARDS - 74E	ST LEONARDS - 74E
30905	ST LEONARDS - 74E	ST LEONARDS - 74E	ST LEONARDS - 74E	ST LEONARDS - 74E	ST LEONARDS - 74E	ST LEONARDS - 74E	ST LEONARDS - 74E
30906	ST LEONARDS - 74E	ST LEONARDS - 74E	ST LEONARDS - 74E	ST LEONARDS - 74E	ST LEONARDS - 74E	ST LEONARDS - 74E	ST LEONARDS - 74E
30907	ST LEONARDS - 74E	ST LEONARDS - 74E	ST LEONARDS - 74E	ST LEONARDS - 74E	ST LEONARDS - 74E	ST LEONARDS - 74E	ST LEONARDS - 74E
30908	ST LEONARDS - 74E	ST LEONARDS - 74E	ST LEONARDS - 74E	ST LEONARDS - 74E	ST LEONARDS - 74E	ST LEONARDS - 74E	ST LEONARDS - 74E
30909	ST LEONARDS - 74E	ST LEONARDS - 74E	ST LEONARDS - 74E	ST LEONARDS - 74E	ST LEONARDS - 74E	ST LEONARDS - 74E	ST LEONARDS - 74E
30910	ST LEONARDS - 74E	ST LEONARDS - 74E	ST LEONARDS - 74E	ST LEONARDS - 74E	ST LEONARDS - 74E	ST LEONARDS - 74E	ST LEONARDS - 74E
30911	RAMSGATE - 74B	RAMSGATE - 74B	RAMSGATE - 74B	RAMSGATE - 74B	RAMSGATE - 74B	RAMSGATE - 74B	RAMSGATE - 74B
30912	RAMSGATE - 74B	RAMSGATE - 74B	RAMSGATE - 74B	RAMSGATE - 74B	ASHFORD - 74A	ASHFORD - 74A	ASHFORD - 74A
30913	RAMSGATE - 74B	RAMSGATE - 74B	RAMSGATE - 74B	RAMSGATE - 74B	RAMSGATE - 74B	RAMSGATE - 74B	RAMSGATE - 74B
30914	RAMSGATE - 74B	RAMSGATE - 74B	RAMSGATE - 74B	RAMSGATE - 74B	RAMSGATE - 74B	RAMSGATE - 74B	RAMSGATE - 74B
30915	STEWARTS LANE - 73A	STEWARTS LANE - 73A	STEWARTS LANE - 73A	STEWARTS LANE - 73A	STEWARTS LANE - 73A	STEWARTS LANE - 73A	STEWARTS LANE - 73A
30916	RAMSGATE - 74B	RAMSGATE - 74B	RAMSGATE - 74B	RAMSGATE - 74B	RAMSGATE - 74B	RAMSGATE - 74B	RAMSGATE - 74B
30917	RAMSGATE - 74B	RAMSGATE - 74B	RAMSGATE - 74B	RAMSGATE - 74B	RAMSGATE - 74B	RAMSGATE - 74B	RAMSGATE - 74B
30918	RAMSGATE - 74B	RAMSGATE - 74B	RAMSGATE - 74B	RAMSGATE - 74B	RAMSGATE - 74B	RAMSGATE - 74B	RAMSGATE - 74B
30919	DOVER - 74C	DOVER - 74C	DOVER - 74C	DOVER - 74C	DOVER - 74C	DOVER - 74C	DOVER - 74C
30920	DOVER - 74C	ST LEONARDS - 74E	ST LEONARDS - 74E	ST LEONARDS - 74E	ST LEONARDS - 74E	ST LEONARDS - 74E	ST LEONARDS - 74E
30921	DOVER - 74C	DOVER - 74C	DOVER - 74C	DOVER - 74C	DOVER - 74C	DOVER - 74C	DOVER - 74C
30922	RAMSGATE - 74B	RAMSGATE - 74B	RAMSGATE - 74B	RAMSGATE - 74B	RAMSGATE - 74B	RAMSGATE - 74B	RAMSGATE - 74B
30923	DOVER - 74C	DOVER - 74C	DOVER - 74C	DOVER - 74C	DOVER - 74C	DOVER - 74C	DOVER - 74C
30924	B ARMS - 73B	B ARMS - 73B	B ARMS - 73B	B ARMS - 73B	B ARMS - 73B	B ARMS - 73B	B ARMS - 73B
30925	B ARMS - 73B	B ARMS - 73B	B ARMS - 73B	B ARMS - 73B	B ARMS - 73B	B ARMS - 73B	B ARMS - 73B
30926	B ARMS - 73B	B ARMS - 73B	B ARMS - 73B	B ARMS - 73B	B ARMS - 73B	B ARMS - 73B	B ARMS - 73B
30927	DOVER - 74C	DOVER - 74C	DOVER - 74C	DOVER - 74C	B ARMS - 73B	B ARMS - 73B	B ARMS - 73B
30928	B ARMS - 73B	B ARMS - 73B	B ARMS - 73B	B ARMS - 73B	B ARMS - 73B	B ARMS - 73B	B ARMS - 73B
30929	B ARMS - 73B	B ARMS - 73B	B ARMS - 73B	B ARMS - 73B	B ARMS - 73B	B ARMS - 73B	B ARMS - 73B
30930	B ARMS - 73B	B ARMS - 73B	B ARMS - 73B	B ARMS - 73B	B ARMS - 73B	ST LEONARDS - 74E	ST LEONARDS - 74E
30931	B ARMS - 73B	B ARMS - 73B	B ARMS - 73B	B ARMS - 73B	B ARMS - 73B	B ARMS - 73B	B ARMS - 73B
30932	B ARMS - 73B	B ARMS - 73B	B ARMS - 73B	B ARMS - 73B	B ARMS - 73B	B ARMS - 73B	B ARMS - 73B
30933	B ARMS - 73B	B ARMS - 73B	B ARMS - 73B	B ARMS - 73B	B ARMS - 73B	B ARMS - 73B	B ARMS - 73B
30934	B ARMS - 73B	B ARMS - 73B	B ARMS - 73B	B ARMS - 73B	B ARMS - 73B	B ARMS - 73B	B ARMS - 73B
30935	B ARMS - 73B	B ARMS - 73B	B ARMS - 73B	B ARMS - 73B	B ARMS - 73B	B ARMS - 73B	B ARMS - 73B
30936	B ARMS - 73B	B ARMS - 73B	B ARMS - 73B	B ARMS - 73B	B ARMS - 73B	B ARMS - 73B	B ARMS - 73B
30937	B ARMS - 73B	B ARMS - 73B	B ARMS - 73B	B ARMS - 73B	B ARMS - 73B	B ARMS - 73B	B ARMS - 73B
30938	B ARMS - 73B	B ARMS - 73B	B ARMS - 73B	B ARMS - 73B	B ARMS - 73B	B ARMS - 73B	B ARMS - 73B
30939	B ARMS - 73B	B ARMS - 73B	B ARMS - 73B	B ARMS - 73B	B ARMS - 73B	B ARMS - 73B	B ARMS - 73B

01 0-6-0 (1903)

loco	Feb-55	Apr-55	Jun-55	Aug-55	Sep-55	Nov-55	Dec-55
31048	ASHFORD - 74A	ASHFORD - 74A	ASHFORD - 74A	ASHFORD - 74A	ASHFORD - 74A	ASHFORD - 74A	ASHFORD - 74A
31064	ASHFORD - 74A	ASHFORD - 74A	ASHFORD - 74A	ASHFORD - 74A	ASHFORD - 74A	ASHFORD - 74A	ASHFORD - 74A
31065	DOVER - 74C	DOVER - 74C	DOVER - 74C	DOVER - 74C	DOVER - 74C	DOVER - 74C	DOVER - 74C
31258	DOVER - 74C	DOVER - 74C	DOVER - 74C	DOVER - 74C	DOVER - 74C	DOVER - 74C	DOVER - 74C
31370	ASHFORD - 74A	ASHFORD - 74A	ASHFORD - 74A	ASHFORD - 74A	ASHFORD - 74A	ASHFORD - 74A	ASHFORD - 74A
31425	DOVER - 74C	DOVER - 74C	DOVER - 74C	DOVER - 74C	DOVER - 74C	DOVER - 74C	DOVER - 74C
31430	DOVER - 74C	DOVER - 74C	DOVER - 74C	DOVER - 74C	DOVER - 74C	DOVER - 74C	DOVER - 74C
31434	DOVER - 74C	DOVER - 74C	DOVER - 74C	DOVER - 74C	DOVER - 74C		

'0395' 0-6-0 (1881)

loco	Feb-55	Apr-55	Jun-55	Aug-55	Sep-55	Nov-55	Dec-55
30564	EXMOUTH JCN - 72A	EXMOUTH JCN - 72A	EXMOUTH JCN - 72A	EXMOUTH JCN - 72A	EXMOUTH JCN - 72A	EXMOUTH JCN - 72A	EXMOUTH JCN - 72A
30566	EASTLEIGH - 71A	EASTLEIGH - 71A	EASTLEIGH - 71A	EASTLEIGH - 71A	EASTLEIGH - 71A	EASTLEIGH - 71A	EASTLEIGH - 71A
30567	FELTHAM - 70B	FELTHAM - 70B	FELTHAM - 70B	FELTHAM - 70B	FELTHAM - 70B	FELTHAM - 70B	FELTHAM - 70B
30568	GUILDFORD - 70C	GUILDFORD - 70C	GUILDFORD - 70C	GUILDFORD - 70C	FELTHAM - 70B	FELTHAM - 70B	FELTHAM - 70B
30569	FELTHAM - 70B	FELTHAM - 70B	FELTHAM - 70B	FELTHAM - 70B	FELTHAM - 70B	FELTHAM - 70B	FELTHAM - 70B
30570	FELTHAM - 70B	FELTHAM - 70B	FELTHAM - 70B	FELTHAM - 70B	FELTHAM - 70B	FELTHAM - 70B	FELTHAM - 70B
30572	FELTHAM - 70B	FELTHAM - 70B	FELTHAM - 70B	FELTHAM - 70B	FELTHAM - 70B	FELTHAM - 70B	FELTHAM - 70B
30573	FELTHAM - 70B	FELTHAM - 70B	FELTHAM - 70B	FELTHAM - 70B	FELTHAM - 70B	FELTHAM - 70B	FELTHAM - 70B
30574	GUILDFORD - 70C	GUILDFORD - 70C	GUILDFORD - 70C	GUILDFORD - 70C	GUILDFORD - 70C	GUILDFORD - 70C	GUILDFORD - 70C
30575	GUILDFORD - 70C	GUILDFORD - 70C	GUILDFORD - 70C	GUILDFORD - 70C	GUILDFORD - 70C	GUILDFORD - 70C	GUILDFORD - 70C
30577	GUILDFORD - 70C	GUILDFORD - 70C	GUILDFORD - 70C	GUILDFORD - 70C	GUILDFORD - 70C	GUILDFORD - 70C	GUILDFORD - 70C
30578	GUILDFORD - 70C	GUILDFORD - 70C	GUILDFORD - 70C	GUILDFORD - 70C	GUILDFORD - 70C	GUILDFORD - 70C	GUILDFORD - 70C
30579	FELTHAM - 70B	FELTHAM - 70B	FELTHAM - 70B	FELTHAM - 70B	FELTHAM - 70B	FELTHAM - 70B	FELTHAM - 70B
30580	GUILDFORD - 70C	GUILDFORD - 70C	GUILDFORD - 70C	GUILDFORD - 70C	GUILDFORD - 70C	GUILDFORD - 70C	GUILDFORD - 70C

The 01 0-6-0's survived into the electric age because of the difficulties in replacing them with diesel traction on the steeply graded and tightly curved Tilmanstone colliery branch at Shepherdswell. During most of the 1950's there were seven daily departures from Tilmanstone, the services being worked by a pair of 0395 engines from Dover shed. 31258, one of the last engines to be in traffic, stands on Dover MPD in 1958.

loco	Jan-56	Apr-56	May-56	Aug-56	Oct-56	Nov-56	Jan-57
				V 4-4-0 (1930)			
30900	ST LEONARDS - 74E	ST LEONARDS - 74E	ST LEONARDS - 74E	ST LEONARDS - 74E	ST LEONARDS - 74E	ST LEONARDS - 74E	ST LEONARDS - 74E
30901	ST LEONARDS - 74E	ST LEONARDS - 74E	ST LEONARDS - 74E	ST LEONARDS - 74E	ST LEONARDS - 74E	ST LEONARDS - 74E	ST LEONARDS - 74E
30902	ST LEONARDS - 74E	ST LEONARDS - 74E	ST LEONARDS - 74E	ST LEONARDS - 74E	ST LEONARDS - 74E	ST LEONARDS - 74E	ST LEONARDS - 74E
30903	ST LEONARDS - 74E	ST LEONARDS - 74E	ST LEONARDS - 74E	ST LEONARDS - 74E	ST LEONARDS - 74E	ST LEONARDS - 74E	ST LEONARDS - 74E
30904	ST LEONARDS - 74E	ST LEONARDS - 74E	ST LEONARDS - 74E	ST LEONARDS - 74E	ST LEONARDS - 74E	ST LEONARDS - 74E	ST LEONARDS - 74E
30905	ST LEONARDS - 74E	ST LEONARDS - 74E	ST LEONARDS - 74E	ST LEONARDS - 74E	ST LEONARDS - 74E	ST LEONARDS - 74E	ST LEONARDS - 74E
30906	ST LEONARDS - 74E	ST LEONARDS - 74E	ST LEONARDS - 74E	ST LEONARDS - 74E	ST LEONARDS - 74E	ST LEONARDS - 74E	ST LEONARDS - 74E
30907	ST LEONARDS - 74E	ST LEONARDS - 74E	ST LEONARDS - 74E	ST LEONARDS - 74E	ST LEONARDS - 74E	ST LEONARDS - 74E	ST LEONARDS - 74E
30908	ST LEONARDS - 74E	ST LEONARDS - 74E	ST LEONARDS - 74E	ST LEONARDS - 74E	ST LEONARDS - 74E	ST LEONARDS - 74E	ST LEONARDS - 74E
30909	ST LEONARDS - 74E	ST LEONARDS - 74E	ST LEONARDS - 74E	ST LEONARDS - 74E	ST LEONARDS - 74E	ST LEONARDS - 74E	ST LEONARDS - 74E
30910	ST LEONARDS - 74E	ST LEONARDS - 74E	ST LEONARDS - 74E	ST LEONARDS - 74E	ST LEONARDS - 74E	ST LEONARDS - 74E	ST LEONARDS - 74E
30911	RAMSGATE - 74B	RAMSGATE - 74B	RAMSGATE - 74B	RAMSGATE - 74B	RAMSGATE - 74B	RAMSGATE - 74B	RAMSGATE - 74B
30912	ASHFORD - 74A	ASHFORD - 74A	RAMSGATE - 74B	RAMSGATE - 74B	RAMSGATE - 74B	RAMSGATE - 74B	RAMSGATE - 74B
30913	RAMSGATE - 74B	RAMSGATE - 74B	RAMSGATE - 74B	RAMSGATE - 74B	RAMSGATE - 74B	RAMSGATE - 74B	RAMSGATE - 74B
30914	RAMSGATE - 74B	RAMSGATE - 74B	RAMSGATE - 74B	RAMSGATE - 74B	RAMSGATE - 74B	RAMSGATE - 74B	RAMSGATE - 74B
30915	STEWARTS LANE - 73A	STEWARTS LANE - 73A	STEWARTS LANE - 73A	STEWARTS LANE - 73A	STEWARTS LANE - 73A	RAMSGATE - 74B	RAMSGATE - 74B
30916	RAMSGATE - 74B	RAMSGATE - 74B	RAMSGATE - 74B	RAMSGATE - 74B	RAMSGATE - 74B	RAMSGATE - 74B	RAMSGATE - 74B
30917	RAMSGATE - 74B	RAMSGATE - 74B	RAMSGATE - 74B	RAMSGATE - 74B	RAMSGATE - 74B	RAMSGATE - 74B	RAMSGATE - 74B
30918	RAMSGATE - 74B	RAMSGATE - 74B	RAMSGATE - 74B	RAMSGATE - 74B	RAMSGATE - 74B	RAMSGATE - 74B	RAMSGATE - 74B
30919	DOVER - 74C	DOVER - 74C	DOVER - 74C	DOVER - 74C	DOVER - 74C	DOVER - 74C	DOVER - 74C
30920	ST LEONARDS - 74E	ST LEONARDS - 74E	ST LEONARDS - 74E	ST LEONARDS - 74E	ST LEONARDS - 74E	ST LEONARDS - 74E	ST LEONARDS - 74E
30921	DOVER - 74C	DOVER - 74C	DOVER - 74C	DOVER - 74C	DOVER - 74C	DOVER - 74C	DOVER - 74C
30922	RAMSGATE - 74B	RAMSGATE - 74B	RAMSGATE - 74B	RAMSGATE - 74B	RAMSGATE - 74B	RAMSGATE - 74B	RAMSGATE - 74B
30923	DOVER - 74C	DOVER - 74C	DOVER - 74C	DOVER - 74C	DOVER - 74C	ST LEONARDS - 74E	ST LEONARDS - 74E
30924	B.ARMS - 73B	B.ARMS - 73B	B.ARMS - 73B	B.ARMS - 73B	B.ARMS - 73B	B.ARMS - 73B	B.ARMS - 73B
30925	B.ARMS - 73B	B.ARMS - 73B	B.ARMS - 73B	B.ARMS - 73B	B.ARMS - 73B	B.ARMS - 73B	B.ARMS - 73B
30926	B.ARMS - 73B	B.ARMS - 73B	B.ARMS - 73B	B.ARMS - 73B	B.ARMS - 73B	B.ARMS - 73B	B.ARMS - 73B
30927	B.ARMS - 73B	B.ARMS - 73B	B.ARMS - 73B	B.ARMS - 73B	B.ARMS - 73B	B.ARMS - 73B	B.ARMS - 73B
30928	B.ARMS - 73B	B.ARMS - 73B	B.ARMS - 73B	B.ARMS - 73B	B.ARMS - 73B	B.ARMS - 73B	B.ARMS - 73B
30929	B.ARMS - 73B	B.ARMS - 73B	B.ARMS - 73B	B.ARMS - 73B	B.ARMS - 73B	B.ARMS - 73B	B.ARMS - 73B
30930	ST LEONARDS - 74E	ST LEONARDS - 74E	ST LEONARDS - 74E	ST LEONARDS - 74E	ST LEONARDS - 74E	ST LEONARDS - 74E	ST LEONARDS - 74E
30931	B.ARMS - 73B	B.ARMS - 73B	B.ARMS - 73B	B.ARMS - 73B	B.ARMS - 73B	B.ARMS - 73B	B.ARMS - 73B
30932	B.ARMS - 73B	B.ARMS - 73B	B.ARMS - 73B	B.ARMS - 73B	B.ARMS - 73B	B.ARMS - 73B	B.ARMS - 73B
30933	B.ARMS - 73B	B.ARMS - 73B	B.ARMS - 73B	B.ARMS - 73B	B.ARMS - 73B	B.ARMS - 73B	B.ARMS - 73B
30934	B.ARMS - 73B	B.ARMS - 73B	B.ARMS - 73B	B.ARMS - 73B	B.ARMS - 73B	B.ARMS - 73B	B.ARMS - 73B
30935	B.ARMS - 73B	B.ARMS - 73B	B.ARMS - 73B	B.ARMS - 73B	B.ARMS - 73B	B.ARMS - 73B	B.ARMS - 73B
30936	B.ARMS - 73B	B.ARMS - 73B	B.ARMS - 73B	B.ARMS - 73B	B.ARMS - 73B	B.ARMS - 73B	B.ARMS - 73B
30937	B.ARMS - 73B	B.ARMS - 73B	B.ARMS - 73B	B.ARMS - 73B	B.ARMS - 73B	B.ARMS - 73B	B.ARMS - 73B
30938	B.ARMS - 73B	B.ARMS - 73B	B.ARMS - 73B	B.ARMS - 73B	B.ARMS - 73B	B.ARMS - 73B	B.ARMS - 73B
30939	B.ARMS - 73B	B.ARMS - 73B	B.ARMS - 73B	B.ARMS - 73B	B.ARMS - 73B	B.ARMS - 73B	B.ARMS - 73B
				01 0-6-0 (1903)			
31048	ASHFORD - 74A	ASHFORD - 74A	ASHFORD - 74A	ASHFORD - 74A	ASHFORD - 74A	ASHFORD - 74A	ASHFORD - 74A
31064	ASHFORD - 74A	ASHFORD - 74A	ASHFORD - 74A	ASHFORD - 74A	ASHFORD - 74A	ASHFORD - 74A	ASHFORD - 74A
31065	DOVER - 74C	DOVER - 74C	DOVER - 74C	DOVER - 74C	DOVER - 74C	DOVER - 74C	DOVER - 74C
31258	DOVER - 74C	DOVER - 74C	DOVER - 74C	DOVER - 74C	DOVER - 74C	DOVER - 74C	DOVER - 74C
31370	ASHFORD - 74A	ASHFORD - 74A	ASHFORD - 74A	ASHFORD - 74A	ASHFORD - 74A	ASHFORD - 74A	ASHFORD - 74A
31425	DOVER - 74C	DOVER - 74C	DOVER - 74C	DOVER - 74C	DOVER - 74C	DOVER - 74C	DOVER - 74C
31430	DOVER - 74C	DOVER - 74C	DOVER - 74C	DOVER - 74C	DOVER - 74C	DOVER - 74C	DOVER - 74C
31434	DOVER - 74C	DOVER - 74C	DOVER - 74C	DOVER - 74C	DOVER - 74C	DOVER - 74C	DOVER - 74C
				'0395' 0-6-0 (1881)			
30564	EXMOUTH JCN - 72A	EXMOUTH JCN - 72A	EXMOUTH JCN - 72A	EXMOUTH JCN - 72A	EXMOUTH JCN - 72A	EXMOUTH JCN - 72A	EXMOUTH JCN - 72A
30566	EASTLEIGH - 71A	EASTLEIGH - 71A	EASTLEIGH - 71A	EASTLEIGH - 71A	EASTLEIGH - 71A	EASTLEIGH - 71A	EASTLEIGH - 71A
30567	FELTHAM - 70B	FELTHAM - 70B	FELTHAM - 70B	FELTHAM - 70B	FELTHAM - 70B	FELTHAM - 70B	FELTHAM - 70B
30568	FELTHAM - 70B	FELTHAM - 70B	FELTHAM - 70B	FELTHAM - 70B	FELTHAM - 70B	FELTHAM - 70B	FELTHAM - 70B
30569	FELTHAM - 70B	FELTHAM - 70B	FELTHAM - 70B	FELTHAM - 70B	FELTHAM - 70B	FELTHAM - 70B	FELTHAM - 70B
30570	FELTHAM - 70B	FELTHAM - 70B	FELTHAM - 70B	FELTHAM - 70B	FELTHAM - 70B	FELTHAM - 70B	W/D
30572	FELTHAM - 70B	FELTHAM - 70B	FELTHAM - 70B	FELTHAM - 70B	FELTHAM - 70B	FELTHAM - 70B	W/D
30573	FELTHAM - 70B	FELTHAM - 70B	FELTHAM - 70B	FELTHAM - 70B	FELTHAM - 70B	W/D	W/D
30574	GUILDFORD - 70C	GUILDFORD - 70C	GUILDFORD - 70C	GUILDFORD - 70C	GUILDFORD - 70C	GUILDFORD - 70C	GUILDFORD - 70C
30575	GUILDFORD - 70C	GUILDFORD - 70C	GUILDFORD - 70C	GUILDFORD - 70C	GUILDFORD - 70C	GUILDFORD - 70C	GUILDFORD - 70C
30578	GUILDFORD - 70C	GUILDFORD - 70C	GUILDFORD - 70C	GUILDFORD - 70C	GUILDFORD - 70C	GUILDFORD - 70C	GUILDFORD - 70C
30580	GUILDFORD - 70C	GUILDFORD - 70C	GUILDFORD - 70C	GUILDFORD - 70C	GUILDFORD - 70C	GUILDFORD - 70C	GUILDFORD - 70C

A Schools 4-4-0 calls at Paddock Wood with the 16.10 Ashford - Charing Cross stopping train on 27th May 1959.

loco	Mar-57	Jun-57	Jul-57	Oct-57	Jan-58	Feb-58	Mar-58
			V 4-4-0 (1930)				
30900 ST LEONARDS - 74E	ST LEONARDS - 74E	ST LEONARDS - 74E	ST LEONARDS - 74E	ST LEONARDS - 74E	ST LEONARDS - 74E	ST LEONARDS - 74E
30901 ST LEONARDS - 74E	ST LEONARDS - 74E	ST LEONARDS - 74E	ST LEONARDS - 74E	ST LEONARDS - 74E	ST LEONARDS - 74E	ST LEONARDS - 74E
30902 ST LEONARDS - 74E	ST LEONARDS - 74E	ST LEONARDS - 74E	ST LEONARDS - 74E	ST LEONARDS - 74E	ST LEONARDS - 74E	ST LEONARDS - 74E
30903 ST LEONARDS - 74E	NINE ELMS - 70A	NINE ELMS - 70A	NINE ELMS - 70A	NINE ELMS - 70A	NINE ELMS - 70A	NINE ELMS - 70A
30904 ST LEONARDS - 74E	NINE ELMS - 70A	NINE ELMS - 70A	NINE ELMS - 70A	NINE ELMS - 70A	NINE ELMS - 70A	NINE ELMS - 70A
30905 ST LEONARDS - 74E	NINE ELMS - 70A	NINE ELMS - 70A	NINE ELMS - 70A	NINE ELMS - 70A	NINE ELMS - 70A	NINE ELMS - 70A
30906 ST LEONARDS - 74E	NINE ELMS - 70A	NINE ELMS - 70A	NINE ELMS - 70A	NINE ELMS - 70A	NINE ELMS - 70A	NINE ELMS - 70A
30907 ST LEONARDS - 74E	NINE ELMS - 70A	NINE ELMS - 70A	NINE ELMS - 70A	NINE ELMS - 70A	NINE ELMS - 70A	NINE ELMS - 70A
30908 ST LEONARDS - 74E	STEWARTS LANE - 73A	STEWARTS LANE - 73A	STEWARTS LANE - 73A	STEWARTS LANE - 73A	STEWARTS LANE - 73A	STEWARTS LANE - 73A
30909 ST LEONARDS - 74E	STEWARTS LANE - 73A	STEWARTS LANE - 73A	STEWARTS LANE - 73A	STEWARTS LANE - 73A	STEWARTS LANE - 73A	STEWARTS LANE - 73A
30910 ST LEONARDS - 74E	RAMSGATE - 74B	RAMSGATE - 74B	RAMSGATE - 74B	RAMSGATE - 74B	RAMSGATE - 74B	RAMSGATE - 74B
30911 RAMSGATE - 74B	RAMSGATE - 74B	RAMSGATE - 74B	RAMSGATE - 74B	RAMSGATE - 74B	RAMSGATE - 74B	RAMSGATE - 74B
30912 RAMSGATE - 74B	RAMSGATE - 74B	RAMSGATE - 74B	RAMSGATE - 74B	RAMSGATE - 74B	RAMSGATE - 74B	RAMSGATE - 74B
30913 RAMSGATE - 74B	RAMSGATE - 74B	RAMSGATE - 74B	RAMSGATE - 74B	RAMSGATE - 74B	RAMSGATE - 74B	RAMSGATE - 74B
30914 RAMSGATE - 74B	RAMSGATE - 74B	RAMSGATE - 74B	RAMSGATE - 74B	RAMSGATE - 74B	RAMSGATE - 74B	RAMSGATE - 74B
30915 STEWARTS LANE - 73A	STEWARTS LANE - 73A	STEWARTS LANE - 73A	STEWARTS LANE - 73A	STEWARTS LANE - 73A	STEWARTS LANE - 73A	STEWARTS LANE - 73A
30916 RAMSGATE - 74B	RAMSGATE - 74B	RAMSGATE - 74B	RAMSGATE - 74B	RAMSGATE - 74B	RAMSGATE - 74B	RAMSGATE - 74B
30917 RAMSGATE - 74B	RAMSGATE - 74B	RAMSGATE - 74B	RAMSGATE - 74B	RAMSGATE - 74B	RAMSGATE - 74B	RAMSGATE - 74B
30918 RAMSGATE - 74B	RAMSGATE - 74B	RAMSGATE - 74B	RAMSGATE - 74B	RAMSGATE - 74B	RAMSGATE - 74B	RAMSGATE - 74B
30919 DOVER - 74C	RAMSGATE - 74B	RAMSGATE - 74B	RAMSGATE - 74B	RAMSGATE - 74B	RAMSGATE - 74B	RAMSGATE - 74B
30920 ST LEONARDS - 74E	RAMSGATE - 74B	RAMSGATE - 74B	RAMSGATE - 74B	RAMSGATE - 74B	RAMSGATE - 74B	RAMSGATE - 74B
30921 DOVER - 74C	RAMSGATE - 74B	RAMSGATE - 74B	RAMSGATE - 74B	RAMSGATE - 74B	RAMSGATE - 74B	RAMSGATE - 74B
30922 RAMSGATE - 74B	RAMSGATE - 74B	RAMSGATE - 74B	RAMSGATE - 74B	RAMSGATE - 74B	RAMSGATE - 74B	RAMSGATE - 74B
30923 ST LEONARDS - 74E	B ARMS - 73B	B ARMS - 73B	B ARMS - 73B	B ARMS - 73B	B ARMS - 73B	B ARMS - 73B
30924 B ARMS - 73B	B ARMS - 73B	B ARMS - 73B	B ARMS - 73B	B ARMS - 73B	B ARMS - 73B	B ARMS - 73B
30925 B ARMS - 73B	B ARMS - 73B	B ARMS - 73B	B ARMS - 73B	B ARMS - 73B	B ARMS - 73B	B ARMS - 73B
30926 B ARMS - 73B	B ARMS - 73B	B ARMS - 73B	B ARMS - 73B	B ARMS - 73B	B ARMS - 73B	B ARMS - 73B
30927 B ARMS - 73B	B ARMS - 73B	B ARMS - 73B	B ARMS - 73B	B ARMS - 73B	B ARMS - 73B	B ARMS - 73B
30928 B ARMS - 73B	B ARMS - 73B	B ARMS - 73B	B ARMS - 73B	B ARMS - 73B	B ARMS - 73B	B ARMS - 73B
30929 B ARMS - 73B	B ARMS - 73B	B ARMS - 73B	B ARMS - 73B	B ARMS - 73B	B ARMS - 73B	B ARMS - 73B
30930 ST LEONARDS - 74E	B ARMS - 73B	B ARMS - 73B	B ARMS - 73B	B ARMS - 73B	B ARMS - 73B	B ARMS - 73B
30931 B ARMS - 73B	B ARMS - 73B	B ARMS - 73B	B ARMS - 73B	B ARMS - 73B	B ARMS - 73B	B ARMS - 73B
30932 B ARMS - 73B	B ARMS - 73B	B ARMS - 73B	B ARMS - 73B	B ARMS - 73B	B ARMS - 73B	B ARMS - 73B
30933 B ARMS - 73B	B ARMS - 73B	B ARMS - 73B	B ARMS - 73B	B ARMS - 73B	B ARMS - 73B	B ARMS - 73B
30934 B ARMS - 73B	B ARMS - 73B	B ARMS - 73B	B ARMS - 73B	B ARMS - 73B	B ARMS - 73B	B ARMS - 73B
30935 B ARMS - 73B	B ARMS - 73B	B ARMS - 73B	B ARMS - 73B	B ARMS - 73B	B ARMS - 73B	B ARMS - 73B
30936 B ARMS - 73B	B ARMS - 73B	B ARMS - 73B	B ARMS - 73B	B ARMS - 73B	B ARMS - 73B	B ARMS - 73B
30937 B ARMS - 73B	B ARMS - 73B	B ARMS - 73B	B ARMS - 73B	B ARMS - 73B	B ARMS - 73B	B ARMS - 73B
30938 B ARMS - 73B	B ARMS - 73B	B ARMS - 73B	B ARMS - 73B	B ARMS - 73B	B ARMS - 73B	B ARMS - 73B
30939 B ARMS - 73B	B ARMS - 73B	B ARMS - 73B	B ARMS - 73B	B ARMS - 73B	B ARMS - 73B	B ARMS - 73B
			01 0-6-0 (1903)				
31048 ASHFORD - 74A	STEWARTS LANE - 73A	STEWARTS LANE - 73A	STEWARTS LANE - 73A	STEWARTS LANE - 73A	STEWARTS LANE - 73A	STEWARTS LANE - 73A
31064 ASHFORD - 74A	STEWARTS LANE - 73A	STEWARTS LANE - 73A	STEWARTS LANE - 73A	STEWARTS LANE - 73A	STEWARTS LANE - 73A	STEWARTS LANE - 73A
31065 DOVER - 74C	DOVER - 74C	DOVER - 74C	DOVER - 74C	DOVER - 74C	DOVER - 74C	DOVER - 74C
31258 DOVER - 74C	ASHFORD - 74A	DOVER - 74C	DOVER - 74C	DOVER - 74C	DOVER - 74C	DOVER - 74C
31370 ASHFORD - 74A	ASHFORD - 74A	ASHFORD - 74A	ASHFORD - 74A	ASHFORD - 74A	ASHFORD - 74A	ASHFORD - 74A
31425 DOVER - 74C	DOVER - 74C	DOVER - 74C	DOVER - 74C	DOVER - 74C	DOVER - 74C	DOVER - 74C
31430 DOVER - 74C	DOVER - 74C	DOVER - 74C	DOVER - 74C	DOVER - 74C	DOVER - 74C	DOVER - 74C
31434 DOVER - 74C	DOVER - 74C	DOVER - 74C	DOVER - 74C	DOVER - 74C	DOVER - 74C	DOVER - 74C
			'0395' 0-6-0 (1881)				
30564 EXMOUTH JCN - 72A	EXMOUTH JCN - 72A	EXMOUTH JCN - 72A	EXMOUTH JCN - 72A	EXMOUTH JCN - 72A	EXMOUTH JCN - 72A	W/D
30566 EASTLEIGH - 71A	EASTLEIGH - 71A	EASTLEIGH - 71A	EASTLEIGH - 71A	EASTLEIGH - 71A	EASTLEIGH - 71A	EASTLEIGH - 71A
30567 FELTHAM - 70B	FELTHAM - 70B	FELTHAM - 70B	FELTHAM - 70B	FELTHAM - 70B	FELTHAM - 70B	FELTHAM - 70B
30568 FELTHAM - 70B	FELTHAM - 70B	FELTHAM - 70B	FELTHAM - 70B	FELTHAM - 70B	FELTHAM - 70B	W/D
30569 FELTHAM - 70B	FELTHAM - 70B	FELTHAM - 70B	FELTHAM - 70B	FELTHAM - 70B	FELTHAM - 70B	W/D
30575 GUILDFORD - 70C	GUILDFORD - 70C	GUILDFORD - 70C	GUILDFORD - 70C	GUILDFORD - 70C	GUILDFORD - 70C	GUILDFORD - 70C
30578 GUILDFORD - 70C	GUILDFORD - 70C	GUILDFORD - 70C	W/D			W/D
30580 GUILDFORD - 70C	W/D	W/D	W/D	W/D	W/D	W/D

Morning shadows obscur much that is to be seen on Brighton MPD as Schools 4-4-0 30911 'Dover' backs off the shed to work the 09.40 to Bournemouth in September 1961. For many years 30911 had been a Ramsgate engine but was moved after the 1959 electrification firstly to Nine Elms, where little work could be found for it, and subsequently, at the end of 1960, to Brighton where it, and other members of the class, took over some of the west coast workings to Salisbury and Bournemouth.

loco	May-58	Oct-58	Mar-59	Jun-59	Jul-59	Aug-59	Oct-59
			V 4-4-0 (1930)				
30900	BRIGHTON - 75A	BRIGHTON - 75A	BRIGHTON - 75A	BRIGHTON - 75A	BRIGHTON - 75A	BRIGHTON - 75A	BRIGHTON - 75A
30901	BRIGHTON - 75A	BRIGHTON - 75A	BRIGHTON - 75A	BRIGHTON - 75A	BRIGHTON - 75A	BRIGHTON - 75A	BRIGHTON - 75A
30902	NINE ELMS - 70A	NINE ELMS - 70A	NINE ELMS - 70A	NINE ELMS - 70A	NINE ELMS - 70A	NINE ELMS - 70A	NINE ELMS - 70A
30903	NINE ELMS - 70A	NINE ELMS - 70A	NINE ELMS - 70A	NINE ELMS - 70A	NINE ELMS - 70A	NINE ELMS - 70A	NINE ELMS - 70A
30904	BASINGSTOKE - 70D	BASINGSTOKE - 70D	BASINGSTOKE - 70D	BASINGSTOKE - 70D	BASINGSTOKE - 70D	BASINGSTOKE - 70D	BASINGSTOKE - 70D
30905	BASINGSTOKE - 70D	BASINGSTOKE - 70D	BASINGSTOKE - 70D	BASINGSTOKE - 70D	BASINGSTOKE - 70D	BASINGSTOKE - 70D	BASINGSTOKE - 70D
30906	NINE ELMS - 70A	NINE ELMS - 70A	NINE ELMS - 70A	NINE ELMS - 70A	NINE ELMS - 70A	NINE ELMS - 70A	NINE ELMS - 70A
30907	NINE ELMS - 70A	NINE ELMS - 70A	NINE ELMS - 70A	NINE ELMS - 70A	NINE ELMS - 70A	NINE ELMS - 70A	NINE ELMS - 70A
30908	STEWARTS LANE - 73A	STEWARTS LANE - 73A	STEWARTS LANE - 73A	BASINGSTOKE - 70D	BASINGSTOKE - 70D	BASINGSTOKE - 70D	BASINGSTOKE - 70D
30909	STEWARTS LANE - 73A	STEWARTS LANE - 73A	STEWARTS LANE - 73A	NINE ELMS - 70A	NINE ELMS - 70A	NINE ELMS - 70A	NINE ELMS - 70A
30910	RAMSGATE - 74B	RAMSGATE - 73G	RAMSGATE - 73G	NINE ELMS - 70A	NINE ELMS - 70A	NINE ELMS - 70A	NINE ELMS - 70A
30911	RAMSGATE - 74B	RAMSGATE - 73G	RAMSGATE - 73G	NINE ELMS - 70A	NINE ELMS - 70A	NINE ELMS - 70A	NINE ELMS - 70A
30912	RAMSGATE - 74B	RAMSGATE - 73G	RAMSGATE - 73G	NINE ELMS - 70A	NINE ELMS - 70A	NINE ELMS - 70A	NINE ELMS - 70A
30913	RAMSGATE - 74B	RAMSGATE - 73G	RAMSGATE - 73G	NINE ELMS - 70A	NINE ELMS - 70A	NINE ELMS - 70A	NINE ELMS - 70A
30914	RAMSGATE - 74B	RAMSGATE - 73G	RAMSGATE - 73G	BRIGHTON - 75A	BRIGHTON - 75A	BRIGHTON - 75A	BRIGHTON - 75A
30915	STEWARTS LANE - 73A	STEWARTS LANE - 73A	STEWARTS LANE - 73A	BRIGHTON - 75A	BRIGHTON - 75A	BRIGHTON - 75A	BRIGHTON - 75A
30916	RAMSGATE - 74B	RAMSGATE - 73G	RAMSGATE - 73G	NINE ELMS - 70A	BRIGHTON - 75A	BRIGHTON - 75A	BRIGHTON - 75A
30917	RAMSGATE - 74B	RAMSGATE - 73G	RAMSGATE - 73G	NINE ELMS - 70A	BRIGHTON - 75A	BRIGHTON - 75A	BRIGHTON - 75A
30918	RAMSGATE - 74B	RAMSGATE - 73G	RAMSGATE - 73G	NINE ELMS - 70A	NINE ELMS - 70A	NINE ELMS - 70A	NINE ELMS - 70A
30919	RAMSGATE - 74B	RAMSGATE - 73G	RAMSGATE - 73G	NINE ELMS - 70A	NINE ELMS - 70A	NINE ELMS - 70A	NINE ELMS - 70A
30920	RAMSGATE - 74B	RAMSGATE - 73G	RAMSGATE - 73G	STEWARTS LANE - 73A	STEWARTS LANE - 73A	STEWARTS LANE - 73A	STEWARTS LANE - 73A
30921	RAMSGATE - 74B	RAMSGATE - 73G	RAMSGATE - 73G	STEWARTS LANE - 73A	STEWARTS LANE - 73A	STEWARTS LANE - 73A	STEWARTS LANE - 73A
30922	RAMSGATE - 74B	RAMSGATE - 73G	RAMSGATE - 73G	STEWARTS LANE - 73A	STEWARTS LANE - 73A	STEWARTS LANE - 73A	STEWARTS LANE - 73A
30923	B ARMS - 73B	B ARMS - 73B	BASINGSTOKE - 70D	STEWARTS LANE - 73A	STEWARTS LANE - 73A	STEWARTS LANE - 73A	STEWARTS LANE - 73A
30924	B ARMS - 73B	B ARMS - 73B	B ARMS - 73B	B ARMS - 73B	B ARMS - 73B	B ARMS - 73B	B ARMS - 73B
30925	B ARMS - 73B	B ARMS - 73B	B ARMS - 73B	B ARMS - 73B	B ARMS - 73B	B ARMS - 73B	B ARMS - 73B
30926	B ARMS - 73B	B ARMS - 73B	B ARMS - 73B	B ARMS - 73B	B ARMS - 73B	B ARMS - 73B	B ARMS - 73B
30927	B ARMS - 73B	B ARMS - 73B	B ARMS - 73B	B ARMS - 73B	B ARMS - 73B	B ARMS - 73B	B ARMS - 73B
30928	B ARMS - 73B	B ARMS - 73B	B ARMS - 73B	B ARMS - 73B	B ARMS - 73B	B ARMS - 73B	B ARMS - 73B
30929	B ARMS - 73B	B ARMS - 73B	B ARMS - 73B	B ARMS - 73B	B ARMS - 73B	B ARMS - 73B	B ARMS - 73B
30930	B ARMS - 73B	B ARMS - 73B	B ARMS - 73B	B ARMS - 73B	B ARMS - 73B	B ARMS - 73B	B ARMS - 73B
30931	B ARMS - 73B	B ARMS - 73B	B ARMS - 73B	B ARMS - 73B	B ARMS - 73B	B ARMS - 73B	B ARMS - 73B
30932	B ARMS - 73B	B ARMS - 73B	B ARMS - 73B	ASHFORD - 73F	ASHFORD - 73F	ASHFORD - 73F	ASHFORD - 73F
30933	B ARMS - 73B	B ARMS - 73B	B ARMS - 73B	ASHFORD - 73F	ASHFORD - 73F	ASHFORD - 73F	ASHFORD - 73F
30934	B ARMS - 73B	B ARMS - 73B	B ARMS - 73B	ASHFORD - 73F	ASHFORD - 73F	ASHFORD - 73F	ASHFORD - 73F
30935	B ARMS - 73B	B ARMS - 73B	B ARMS - 73B	ASHFORD - 73F	ASHFORD - 73F	ASHFORD - 73F	ASHFORD - 73F
30936	B ARMS - 73B	B ARMS - 73B	B ARMS - 73B	ASHFORD - 73F	ASHFORD - 73F	ASHFORD - 73F	ASHFORD - 73F
30937	STEWARTS LANE - 73A	STEWARTS LANE - 73A	STEWARTS LANE - 73A	ASHFORD - 73F	ASHFORD - 73F	ASHFORD - 73F	ASHFORD - 73F
30938	STEWARTS LANE - 73A	STEWARTS LANE - 73A	STEWARTS LANE - 73A	DOVER - 73H		DOVER - 73H	DOVER - 73H
30939	STEWARTS LANE - 73A	STEWARTS LANE - 73A	STEWARTS LANE - 73A	DOVER - 73H	DOVER - 73H	DOVER - 73H	DOVER - 73H
			01 0-6-0 (1903)				
31048	STEWARTS LANE - 73A	STEWARTS LANE - 73A	STEWARTS LANE - 73A	NINE ELMS - 70A	NINE ELMS - 70A	NINE ELMS - 70A	NINE ELMS - 70A
31065	DOVER - 74C	DOVER - 73H	DOVER - 73H	DOVER - 73H	DOVER - 73H	DOVER - 73H	DOVER - 73H
31258	DOVER - 74C	DOVER - 73H	DOVER - 73H	DOVER - 73H	DOVER - 73H	DOVER - 73H	DOVER - 73H
31370	ASHFORD - 74A	STEWARTS LANE - 73A	STEWARTS LANE - 73A	NINE ELMS - 70A	NINE ELMS - 70A	NINE ELMS - 70A	NINE ELMS - 70A
31425	DOVER - 74C	DOVER - 73H	DOVER - 73H	DOVER - 73H	DOVER - 73H	DOVER - 73H	W/D
31430	DOVER - 74C	DOVER - 73H	DOVER - 73H	W/D			W/D
31434	DOVER - 74C	DOVER - 73H	DOVER - 73H	DOVER - 73H	DOVER - 73H		W/D
			'0395' 0-6-0 (1881)				
30566	EASTLEIGH - 71A	EASTLEIGH - 71A	W/D				W/D
30567	FELTHAM - 70B	FELTHAM - 70B	FELTHAM - 70B	FELTHAM - 70B	FELTHAM - 70B	FELTHAM - 70B	W/D
30575	GUILDFORD - 70C	GUILDFORD - 70C	W/D				W/D

The association that the Schools 4-4-0's had with the Hastings service overshadows the work they did on other parts of the Southern and it tends to be forgotten that they worked a good proportion of the Charing Cross - Ramsgate trains, side by side with light Pacifics. The class also had a handful of jobs on the Chatham main line, a Ramsgate Schools being booked to work the 20.35 Victoria - Ramsgate each evening. In the above view 30921 'Shrewsbury', which had been a Ramsgate engine until a few weeks prior to the photograph, is prepared at Ramsgate in place of the usual BR5 4-6-0 for the 15.22 to Victoria via Herne Bay on 27th May 1959. 30921 at the time was a Stewarts Lane engine

loco	Dec-59	Feb-60	Mar-60	Apr-60	Jul-60	Aug-60	Sep-60	Nov-60
V 4-4-0 (1930)								
30900 BRIGHTON - 75A	BRIGHTON - 75A	BRIGHTON - 75A	BRIGHTON - 75A	BRIGHTON - 75A	BRIGHTON - 75A	BRIGHTON - 75A	BRIGHTON - 75A
30901 BRIGHTON - 75A	BRIGHTON - 75A	BRIGHTON - 75A	BRIGHTON - 75A	BRIGHTON - 75A	BRIGHTON - 75A	BRIGHTON - 75A	BRIGHTON - 75A
30902 NINE ELMS - 70A	NINE ELMS - 70A	NINE ELMS - 70A	BRIGHTON - 75A	BRIGHTON - 75A	BRIGHTON - 75A	BRIGHTON - 75A	NINE ELMS - 70A
30903 NINE ELMS - 70A	GUILDFORD - 70C	GUILDFORD - 70C	GUILDFORD - 70C	GUILDFORD - 70C	GUILDFORD - 70C	GUILDFORD - 70C	GUILDFORD - 70C
30904 BASINGSTOKE - 70D	BASINGSTOKE - 70D	BASINGSTOKE - 70D	BASINGSTOKE - 70D	BASINGSTOKE - 70D	BASINGSTOKE - 70D	BASINGSTOKE - 70D	BASINGSTOKE - 70D
30905 BASINGSTOKE - 70D	BASINGSTOKE - 70D	BASINGSTOKE - 70D	BASINGSTOKE - 70D	BASINGSTOKE - 70D	BASINGSTOKE - 70D	BASINGSTOKE - 70D	BASINGSTOKE - 70D
30906 NINE ELMS - 70A	GUILDFORD - 70C	GUILDFORD - 70C	GUILDFORD - 70C	GUILDFORD - 70C	GUILDFORD - 70C	GUILDFORD - 70C	GUILDFORD - 70C
30907 NINE ELMS - 70A	NINE ELMS - 70A	NINE ELMS - 70A	NINE ELMS - 70A	NINE ELMS - 70A	NINE ELMS - 70A	NINE ELMS - 70A	BRIGHTON - 75A
30908 BASINGSTOKE - 70D	BASINGSTOKE - 70D	BASINGSTOKE - 70D	BASINGSTOKE - 70D	BASINGSTOKE - 70D	BASINGSTOKE - 70D	BASINGSTOKE - 70D	BASINGSTOKE - 70D
30909 NINE ELMS - 70A	GUILDFORD - 70C	GUILDFORD - 70C	GUILDFORD - 70C	GUILDFORD - 70C	GUILDFORD - 70C	GUILDFORD - 70C	GUILDFORD - 70C
30910 NINE ELMS - 70A	NINE ELMS - 70A	NINE ELMS - 70A	NINE ELMS - 70A	NINE ELMS - 70A	NINE ELMS - 70A	NINE ELMS - 70A	NINE ELMS - 70A
30911 NINE ELMS - 70A	NINE ELMS - 70A	NINE ELMS - 70A	NINE ELMS - 70A	NINE ELMS - 70A	NINE ELMS - 70A	NINE ELMS - 70A	BRIGHTON - 75A
30912 NINE ELMS - 70A	NINE ELMS - 70A	NINE ELMS - 70A	NINE ELMS - 70A	NINE ELMS - 70A	NINE ELMS - 70A	NINE ELMS - 70A	NINE ELMS - 70A
30913 NINE ELMS - 70A	NINE ELMS - 70A	NINE ELMS - 70A	NINE ELMS - 70A	NINE ELMS - 70A	NINE ELMS - 70A	NINE ELMS - 70A	NINE ELMS - 70A
30914 BRIGHTON - 75A	BRIGHTON - 75A	BRIGHTON - 75A	REDHILL - 75B	REDHILL - 75B	REDHILL - 75B	REDHILL - 75B	REDHILL - 75B
30915 BRIGHTON - 75A	BRIGHTON - 75A	BRIGHTON - 75A	REDHILL - 75B	REDHILL - 75B	REDHILL - 75B	REDHILL - 75B	REDHILL - 75B
30916 BRIGHTON - 75A	BRIGHTON - 75A	BRIGHTON - 75A	REDHILL - 75B	REDHILL - 75B	REDHILL - 75B	REDHILL - 75B	REDHILL - 75B
30917 BRIGHTON - 75A	BRIGHTON - 75A	BRIGHTON - 75A	BRIGHTON - 75A	BRIGHTON - 75A	BRIGHTON - 75A	BRIGHTON - 75A	BRIGHTON - 75A
30918 NINE ELMS - 70A	NINE ELMS - 70A	NINE ELMS - 70A	NINE ELMS - 70A	NINE ELMS - 70A	NINE ELMS - 70A	NINE ELMS - 70A	NINE ELMS - 70A
30919 NINE ELMS - 70A	NINE ELMS - 70A	NINE ELMS - 70A	BRIGHTON - 75A	BRIGHTON - 75A	BRIGHTON - 75A	BRIGHTON - 75A	BRIGHTON - 75A
30920 STEWARTS LANE - 73A	STEWARTS LANE - 73A	STEWARTS LANE - 73A	STEWARTS LANE - 73A	STEWARTS LANE - 73A	STEWARTS LANE - 73A	STEWARTS LANE - 73A	STEWARTS LANE - 73A
30921 STEWARTS LANE - 73A	STEWARTS LANE - 73A	STEWARTS LANE - 73A	STEWARTS LANE - 73A	STEWARTS LANE - 73A	STEWARTS LANE - 73A	STEWARTS LANE - 73A	STEWARTS LANE - 73A
30922 STEWARTS LANE - 73A	STEWARTS LANE - 73A	STEWARTS LANE - 73A	STEWARTS LANE - 73A	STEWARTS LANE - 73A	STEWARTS LANE - 73A	STEWARTS LANE - 73A	STEWARTS LANE - 73A
30923 STEWARTS LANE - 73A	STEWARTS LANE - 73A	STEWARTS LANE - 73A	STEWARTS LANE - 73A	STEWARTS LANE - 73A	STEWARTS LANE - 73A	STEWARTS LANE - 73A	STEWARTS LANE - 73A
30924 B.ARMS - 73B	B.ARMS - 73B	B.ARMS - 73B	B.ARMS - 73B	B.ARMS - 73B	B.ARMS - 73B	B.ARMS - 73B	B.ARMS - 73B
30925 B.ARMS - 73B	B.ARMS - 73B	B.ARMS - 73B	B.ARMS - 73B	B.ARMS - 73B	B.ARMS - 73B	B.ARMS - 73B	B.ARMS - 73B
30926 B.ARMS - 73B	B.ARMS - 73B	B.ARMS - 73B	B.ARMS - 73B	B.ARMS - 73B	B.ARMS - 73B	B.ARMS - 73B	B.ARMS - 73B
30927 B.ARMS - 73B	B.ARMS - 73B	B.ARMS - 73B	B.ARMS - 73B	B.ARMS - 73B	B.ARMS - 73B	B.ARMS - 73B	B.ARMS - 73B
30928 B.ARMS - 73B	B.ARMS - 73B	B.ARMS - 73B	B.ARMS - 73B	B.ARMS - 73B	B.ARMS - 73B	B.ARMS - 73B	B.ARMS - 73B
30929 B.ARMS - 73B	B.ARMS - 73B	B.ARMS - 73B	B.ARMS - 73B	B.ARMS - 73B	B.ARMS - 73B	B.ARMS - 73B	B.ARMS - 73B
30930 B.ARMS - 73B	B.ARMS - 73B	B.ARMS - 73B	B.ARMS - 73B	B.ARMS - 73B	B.ARMS - 73B	B.ARMS - 73B	B.ARMS - 73B
30931 B.ARMS - 73B	B.ARMS - 73B	B.ARMS - 73B	B.ARMS - 73B	B.ARMS - 73B	B.ARMS - 73B	B.ARMS - 73B	B.ARMS - 73B
30932 ASHFORD - 73F	ASHFORD - 73F	ASHFORD - 73F	ASHFORD - 73F	ASHFORD - 73F	ASHFORD - 73F	ASHFORD - 73F	ASHFORD - 73F
30933 ASHFORD - 73F	ASHFORD - 73F	ASHFORD - 73F	ASHFORD - 73F	ASHFORD - 73F	ASHFORD - 73F	ASHFORD - 73F	ASHFORD - 73F
30934 ASHFORD - 73F	ASHFORD - 73F	ASHFORD - 73F	ASHFORD - 73F	ASHFORD - 73F	ASHFORD - 73F	ASHFORD - 73F	ASHFORD - 73F
30935 ASHFORD - 73F	ASHFORD - 73F	ASHFORD - 73F	ASHFORD - 73F	ASHFORD - 73F	ASHFORD - 73F	ASHFORD - 73F	ASHFORD - 73F
30936 ASHFORD - 73F	ASHFORD - 73F	ASHFORD - 73F	ASHFORD - 73F	ASHFORD - 73F	ASHFORD - 73F	ASHFORD - 73F	ASHFORD - 73F
30937 ASHFORD - 73F	ASHFORD - 73F	ASHFORD - 73F	ASHFORD - 73F	ASHFORD - 73F	ASHFORD - 73F	ASHFORD - 73F	ASHFORD - 73F
30938 DOVER - 73H	DOVER - 73H	DOVER - 73H	DOVER - 73H	ASHFORD - 73F	ASHFORD - 73F	ASHFORD - 73F	ASHFORD - 73F
30939 DOVER - 73H	DOVER - 73H	DOVER - 73H	DOVER - 73H	ASHFORD - 73F	ASHFORD - 73F	ASHFORD - 73F	ASHFORD - 73F
01 0-6-0 (1903)								
31048 NINE ELMS - 70A	DOVER - 73H	DOVER - 73H	DOVER - 73H	DOVER - 73H	DOVER - 73H	DOVER - 73H	W/D
31065 DOVER - 73H	DOVER - 73H	DOVER - 73H	DOVER - 73H	DOVER - 73H	DOVER - 73H	DOVER - 73H	DOVER - 73H
31258 DOVER - 73H	DOVER - 73H	DOVER - 73H	DOVER - 73H	DOVER - 73H	DOVER - 73H	DOVER - 73H	DOVER - 73H
31370 NINE ELMS - 70A	W/D	W/D	W/D	W/D	W/D	W/D	W/D

Schools 4-4-0 30931 'King's Wimbledon', the first of the class to appear in lined black livery, stands at Bricklayers Arms on 22nd October 1948.

loco	May-49	Jun-49	Aug-49	Sep-49	Dec-49	Feb-50	Mar-50
				C 0-6-0 (1900)			
31004	RAMSGATE - 74B	RAMSGATE - 74B	RAMSGATE - 74B	RAMSGATE - 74B	RAMSGATE - 74B	RAMSGATE - 74B	RAMSGATE - 74B
31018	HITHER GREEN - 73C	HITHER GREEN - 73C	HITHER GREEN - 73C	HITHER GREEN - 73C	HITHER GREEN - 73C	HITHER GREEN - 73C	HITHER GREEN - 73C
31033	B.ARMS - 73B	B.ARMS - 73B	B.ARMS - 73B	B.ARMS - 73B	B.ARMS - 73B	B.ARMS - 73B	B.ARMS - 73B
31037	ST LEONARDS - 74E	ST LEONARDS - 74E	ST LEONARDS - 74E	ST LEONARDS - 74E	ST LEONARDS - 74E	ST LEONARDS - 74E	ST LEONARDS - 74E
31038	ST LEONARDS - 74E	ST LEONARDS - 74E	ST LEONARDS - 74E	ST LEONARDS - 74E	ST LEONARDS - 74E	ST LEONARDS - 74E	ST LEONARDS - 74E
31054	HITHER GREEN - 73C	HITHER GREEN - 73C	HITHER GREEN - 73C	HITHER GREEN - 73C	HITHER GREEN - 73C	HITHER GREEN - 73C	HITHER GREEN - 73C
31059	HITHER GREEN - 73C	HITHER GREEN - 73C	HITHER GREEN - 73C	HITHER GREEN - 73C	HITHER GREEN - 73C	HITHER GREEN - 73C	HITHER GREEN - 73C
31061	HITHER GREEN - 73C	HITHER GREEN - 73C	HITHER GREEN - 73C	HITHER GREEN - 73C	HITHER GREEN - 73C	HITHER GREEN - 73C	HITHER GREEN - 73C
31063	TONBRIDGE - 74D	TONBRIDGE - 74D	TONBRIDGE - 74D	TONBRIDGE - 74D	TONBRIDGE - 74D	TONBRIDGE - 74D	TONBRIDGE - 74D
31068	HITHER GREEN - 73C	HITHER GREEN - 73C	HITHER GREEN - 73C	HITHER GREEN - 73C	HITHER GREEN - 73C	HITHER GREEN - 73C	HITHER GREEN - 73C
31071	HITHER GREEN - 73C	HITHER GREEN - 73C	HITHER GREEN - 73C	HITHER GREEN - 73C	HITHER GREEN - 73C	HITHER GREEN - 73C	HITHER GREEN - 73C
31086	GUILDFORD - 70C	GUILDFORD - 70C	GUILDFORD - 70C	GUILDFORD - 70C	GUILDFORD - 70C	GUILDFORD - 70C	GUILDFORD - 70C
31090	GUILDFORD - 70C	GUILDFORD - 70C	GUILDFORD - 70C	GUILDFORD - 70C	GUILDFORD - 70C	GUILDFORD - 70C	GUILDFORD - 70C
31102	B.ARMS - 73B	B.ARMS - 73B	B.ARMS - 73B	B.ARMS - 73B	B.ARMS - 73B	B.ARMS - 73B	B.ARMS - 73B
31112	GILLINGHAM - 73D	GILLINGHAM - 73D	GILLINGHAM - 73D	GILLINGHAM - 73D	GILLINGHAM - 73D	GILLINGHAM - 73D	GILLINGHAM - 73D
31113	HITHER GREEN - 73C	HITHER GREEN - 73C	HITHER GREEN - 73C	HITHER GREEN - 73C	HITHER GREEN - 73C	HITHER GREEN - 73C	HITHER GREEN - 73C
31150	HITHER GREEN - 73C	HITHER GREEN - 73C	HITHER GREEN - 73C	HITHER GREEN - 73C	HITHER GREEN - 73C	HITHER GREEN - 73C	HITHER GREEN - 73C
31191	HITHER GREEN - 73C	HITHER GREEN - 73C	HITHER GREEN - 73C	HITHER GREEN - 73C	HITHER GREEN - 73C	HITHER GREEN - 73C	HITHER GREEN - 73C
31218	ASHFORD - 74A	ASHFORD - 74A	ASHFORD - 74A	ASHFORD - 74A	ASHFORD - 74A	ASHFORD - 74A	ASHFORD - 74A
31219	TONBRIDGE - 74D	TONBRIDGE - 74D	TONBRIDGE - 74D	TONBRIDGE - 74D	TONBRIDGE - 74D	TONBRIDGE - 74D	TONBRIDGE - 74D
31221	GUILDFORD - 70C	GUILDFORD - 70C	GUILDFORD - 70C	GUILDFORD - 70C	GUILDFORD - 70C	GUILDFORD - 70C	GUILDFORD - 70C
31223	B.ARMS - 73B	B.ARMS - 73B	B.ARMS - 73B	B.ARMS - 73B	B.ARMS - 73B	B.ARMS - 73B	B.ARMS - 73B
31225	GUILDFORD - 70C	GUILDFORD - 70C	GUILDFORD - 70C	GUILDFORD - 70C	GUILDFORD - 70C	GUILDFORD - 70C	GUILDFORD - 70C
31227	GUILDFORD - 70C	GUILDFORD - 70C	GUILDFORD - 70C	GUILDFORD - 70C	GUILDFORD - 70C	GUILDFORD - 70C	GUILDFORD - 70C
31229	FAVERSHAM - 73E	FAVERSHAM - 73E	FAVERSHAM - 73E	FAVERSHAM - 73E	FAVERSHAM - 73E	FAVERSHAM - 73E	FAVERSHAM - 73E
31234	GILLINGHAM - 73D	GILLINGHAM - 73D	GILLINGHAM - 73D	GILLINGHAM - 73D	GILLINGHAM - 73D	STEWARTS LANE - 73A	STEWARTS LANE - 73A
31242	FAVERSHAM - 73E	FAVERSHAM - 73E	FAVERSHAM - 73E	FAVERSHAM - 73E	FAVERSHAM - 73E	FAVERSHAM - 73E	FAVERSHAM - 73E
31243	HITHER GREEN - 73C	HITHER GREEN - 73C	HITHER GREEN - 73C	HITHER GREEN - 73C	HITHER GREEN - 73C	HITHER GREEN - 73C	HITHER GREEN - 73C
31244	TONBRIDGE - 74D	TONBRIDGE - 74D	TONBRIDGE - 74D	TONBRIDGE - 74D	TONBRIDGE - 74D	TONBRIDGE - 74D	TONBRIDGE - 74D
31245	HITHER GREEN - 73C	HITHER GREEN - 73C	HITHER GREEN - 73C	HITHER GREEN - 73C	HITHER GREEN - 73C	HITHER GREEN - 73C	HITHER GREEN - 73C
31252	DOVER - 74C	DOVER - 74C	DOVER - 74C	DOVER - 74C	RAMSGATE - 74B	RAMSGATE - 74B	RAMSGATE - 74B
31253	HITHER GREEN - 73C	HITHER GREEN - 73C	HITHER GREEN - 73C	HITHER GREEN - 73C	HITHER GREEN - 73C	B.ARMS - 73B	B.ARMS - 73B
31255	DOVER - 74C	DOVER - 74C	DOVER - 74C	DOVER - 74C	DOVER - 74C	DOVER - 74C	DOVER - 74C
31256	GILLINGHAM - 73D	GILLINGHAM - 73D	GILLINGHAM - 73D	GILLINGHAM - 73D	GILLINGHAM - 73D	GILLINGHAM - 73D	GILLINGHAM - 73D
31257	HITHER GREEN - 73C	HITHER GREEN - 73C	W/D	W/D	W/D	W/D	W/D
31260	FAVERSHAM - 73E	FAVERSHAM - 73E	FAVERSHAM - 73E	FAVERSHAM - 73E	FAVERSHAM - 73E	ASHFORD - 74A	ASHFORD - 74A
31267	GILLINGHAM - 73D	GILLINGHAM - 73D	GILLINGHAM - 73D	GILLINGHAM - 73D	GILLINGHAM - 73D	GILLINGHAM - 73D	GILLINGHAM - 73D
31268	ASHFORD - 74A	ASHFORD - 74A	ASHFORD - 74A	ASHFORD - 74A	ASHFORD - 74A	FAVERSHAM - 73E	FAVERSHAM - 73E
31270	HITHER GREEN - 73C	HITHER GREEN - 73C	HITHER GREEN - 73C	HITHER GREEN - 73C	HITHER GREEN - 73C	HITHER GREEN - 73C	HITHER GREEN - 73C
31271	ASHFORD - 74A	ASHFORD - 74A	ASHFORD - 74A	ASHFORD - 74A	ASHFORD - 74A	ASHFORD - 74A	ASHFORD - 74A
31272	TONBRIDGE - 74D	TONBRIDGE - 74D	TONBRIDGE - 74D	TONBRIDGE - 74D	TONBRIDGE - 74D	TONBRIDGE - 74D	TONBRIDGE - 74D
31277	TONBRIDGE - 74D	TONBRIDGE - 74D	TONBRIDGE - 74D	TONBRIDGE - 74D	TONBRIDGE - 74D	TONBRIDGE - 74D	TONBRIDGE - 74D
31280	B.ARMS - 73B	B.ARMS - 73B	B.ARMS - 73B	B.ARMS - 73B	B.ARMS - 73B	B.ARMS - 73B	B.ARMS - 73B
31287	B.ARMS - 73B	B.ARMS - 73B	B.ARMS - 73B	B.ARMS - 73B	B.ARMS - 73B	B.ARMS - 73B	B.ARMS - 73B
31291	DOVER - 74C	DOVER - 74C	DOVER - 74C	DOVER - 74C	DOVER - 74C	DOVER - 74C	DOVER - 74C
31293	GUILDFORD - 70C	GUILDFORD - 70C	GUILDFORD - 70C	GUILDFORD - 70C	GUILDFORD - 70C	GUILDFORD - 70C	GUILDFORD - 70C
31294	GUILDFORD - 70C	GUILDFORD - 70C	GUILDFORD - 70C	GUILDFORD - 70C	GUILDFORD - 70C	GUILDFORD - 70C	GUILDFORD - 70C
31297	B.ARMS - 73B	B.ARMS - 73B	B.ARMS - 73B	B.ARMS - 73B	B.ARMS - 73B	B.ARMS - 73B	B.ARMS - 73B
31298	HITHER GREEN - 73C	HITHER GREEN - 73C	HITHER GREEN - 73C	HITHER GREEN - 73C	RAMSGATE - 74B	RAMSGATE - 74B	RAMSGATE - 74B
31317	GILLINGHAM - 73D	GILLINGHAM - 73D	GILLINGHAM - 73D	GILLINGHAM - 73D	GILLINGHAM - 73D	GILLINGHAM - 73D	GILLINGHAM - 73D
31461	TONBRIDGE - 74D	TONBRIDGE - 74D	TONBRIDGE - 74D	TONBRIDGE - 74D	TONBRIDGE - 74D	TONBRIDGE - 74D	TONBRIDGE - 74D
31480	HITHER GREEN - 73C	HITHER GREEN - 73C	HITHER GREEN - 73C	HITHER GREEN - 73C	HITHER GREEN - 73C	HITHER GREEN - 73C	HITHER GREEN - 73C
31481	FAVERSHAM - 73E	FAVERSHAM - 73E	FAVERSHAM - 73E	FAVERSHAM - 73E	FAVERSHAM - 73E	FAVERSHAM - 73E	FAVERSHAM - 73E
31486	HITHER GREEN - 73C	HITHER GREEN - 73C	HITHER GREEN - 73C	HITHER GREEN - 73C	HITHER GREEN - 73C	HITHER GREEN - 73C	HITHER GREEN - 73C
31495	FAVERSHAM - 73E	FAVERSHAM - 73E	FAVERSHAM - 73E	FAVERSHAM - 73E	FAVERSHAM - 73E	FAVERSHAM - 73E	FAVERSHAM - 73E
31498	GILLINGHAM - 73D	GILLINGHAM - 73D	GILLINGHAM - 73D	GILLINGHAM - 73D	GILLINGHAM - 73D	GILLINGHAM - 73D	GILLINGHAM - 73D
31508	GUILDFORD - 70C	GUILDFORD - 70C	GUILDFORD - 70C	GUILDFORD - 70C	GUILDFORD - 70C	GUILDFORD - 70C	GUILDFORD - 70C
31510	GILLINGHAM - 73D	GILLINGHAM - 73D	GILLINGHAM - 73D	GILLINGHAM - 73D	GILLINGHAM - 73D	GILLINGHAM - 73D	GILLINGHAM - 73D
31513	TONBRIDGE - 74D	TONBRIDGE - 74D	TONBRIDGE - 74D	TONBRIDGE - 74D	TONBRIDGE - 74D	GUILDFORD - 70C	GUILDFORD - 70C
31572	TONBRIDGE - 74D	TONBRIDGE - 74D	TONBRIDGE - 74D	TONBRIDGE - 74D	TONBRIDGE - 74D	GUILDFORD - 70C	GUILDFORD - 70C
31573	GILLINGHAM - 73D	GILLINGHAM - 73D	GILLINGHAM - 73D	GILLINGHAM - 73D	GILLINGHAM - 73D	GILLINGHAM - 73D	GILLINGHAM - 73D
31575	STEWARTS LANE - 73A	STEWARTS LANE - 73A	STEWARTS LANE - 73A	STEWARTS LANE - 73A	STEWARTS LANE - 73A	STEWARTS LANE - 73A	STEWARTS LANE - 73A
31576	STEWARTS LANE - 73A	STEWARTS LANE - 73A	STEWARTS LANE - 73A	STEWARTS LANE - 73A	STEWARTS LANE - 73A	STEWARTS LANE - 73A	STEWARTS LANE - 73A
31578	STEWARTS LANE - 73A	STEWARTS LANE - 73A	STEWARTS LANE - 73A	STEWARTS LANE - 73A	STEWARTS LANE - 73A	STEWARTS LANE - 73A	STEWARTS LANE - 73A
31579	GILLINGHAM - 73D	GILLINGHAM - 73D	GILLINGHAM - 73D	GILLINGHAM - 73D	GILLINGHAM - 73D	GILLINGHAM - 73D	GILLINGHAM - 73D
31580	TONBRIDGE - 74D	TONBRIDGE - 74D	TONBRIDGE - 74D	TONBRIDGE - 74D	TONBRIDGE - 74D	TONBRIDGE - 74D	TONBRIDGE - 74D
31581	HITHER GREEN - 73C	HITHER GREEN - 73C	HITHER GREEN - 73C	HITHER GREEN - 73C	HITHER GREEN - 73C	HITHER GREEN - 73C	HITHER GREEN - 73C
31582	STEWARTS LANE - 73A	STEWARTS LANE - 73A	STEWARTS LANE - 73A	STEWARTS LANE - 73A	STEWARTS LANE - 73A	STEWARTS LANE - 73A	STEWARTS LANE - 73A
31583	GILLINGHAM - 73D	GILLINGHAM - 73D	GILLINGHAM - 73D	GILLINGHAM - 73D	GILLINGHAM - 73D	GILLINGHAM - 73D	GILLINGHAM - 73D
31584	B.ARMS - 73B	B.ARMS - 73B	B.ARMS - 73B	B.ARMS - 73B	B.ARMS - 73B	B.ARMS - 73B	B.ARMS - 73B
31585	GILLINGHAM - 73D	GILLINGHAM - 73D	GILLINGHAM - 73D	GILLINGHAM - 73D	GILLINGHAM - 73D	GILLINGHAM - 73D	GILLINGHAM - 73D
31588	GILLINGHAM - 73D	GILLINGHAM - 73D	GILLINGHAM - 73D	GILLINGHAM - 73D	GILLINGHAM - 73D	GILLINGHAM - 73D	GILLINGHAM - 73D
31589	ASHFORD - 74A	ASHFORD - 74A	ASHFORD - 74A	ASHFORD - 74A	ASHFORD - 74A	ASHFORD - 74A	ASHFORD - 74A
31590	TONBRIDGE - 74D	TONBRIDGE - 74D	TONBRIDGE - 74D	TONBRIDGE - 74D	TONBRIDGE - 74D	TONBRIDGE - 74D	TONBRIDGE - 74D
31592	RAMSGATE - 74B	RAMSGATE - 74B	RAMSGATE - 74B	RAMSGATE - 74B	RAMSGATE - 74B	RAMSGATE - 74B	RAMSGATE - 74B
31593	TONBRIDGE - 74D	TONBRIDGE - 74D	TONBRIDGE - 74D	TONBRIDGE - 74D	TONBRIDGE - 74D	TONBRIDGE - 74D	TONBRIDGE - 74D
31681	STEWARTS LANE - 73A	STEWARTS LANE - 73A	STEWARTS LANE - 73A	STEWARTS LANE - 73A	STEWARTS LANE - 73A	STEWARTS LANE - 73A	STEWARTS LANE - 73A
31682	GILLINGHAM - 73D	GILLINGHAM - 73D	GILLINGHAM - 73D	GILLINGHAM - 73D	GILLINGHAM - 73D	GILLINGHAM - 73D	GILLINGHAM - 73D
31683	STEWARTS LANE - 73A	STEWARTS LANE - 73A	STEWARTS LANE - 73A	STEWARTS LANE - 73A	STEWARTS LANE - 73A	STEWARTS LANE - 73A	STEWARTS LANE - 73A
31684	GILLINGHAM - 73D	GILLINGHAM - 73D	GILLINGHAM - 73D	GILLINGHAM - 73D	GILLINGHAM - 73D	GILLINGHAM - 73D	GILLINGHAM - 73D
31686	TONBRIDGE - 74D	TONBRIDGE - 74D	TONBRIDGE - 74D	TONBRIDGE - 74D	TONBRIDGE - 74D	TONBRIDGE - 74D	TONBRIDGE - 74D
31687	B.ARMS - 73B	B.ARMS - 73B	B.ARMS - 73B	B.ARMS - 73B	B.ARMS - 73B	B.ARMS - 73B	B.ARMS - 73B
31688	GILLINGHAM - 73D	GILLINGHAM - 73D	GILLINGHAM - 73D	GILLINGHAM - 73D	GILLINGHAM - 73D	GILLINGHAM - 73D	GILLINGHAM - 73D
31689	HITHER GREEN - 73C	HITHER GREEN - 73C	HITHER GREEN - 73C	HITHER GREEN - 73C	HITHER GREEN - 73C	HITHER GREEN - 73C	HITHER GREEN - 73C
31690	RAMSGATE - 74B	RAMSGATE - 74B	RAMSGATE - 74B	RAMSGATE - 74B	RAMSGATE - 74B	RAMSGATE - 74B	RAMSGATE - 74B
31691	FAVERSHAM - 73E	FAVERSHAM - 73E	FAVERSHAM - 73E	FAVERSHAM - 73E	FAVERSHAM - 73E	FAVERSHAM - 73E	FAVERSHAM - 73E
31692	FAVERSHAM - 73E	FAVERSHAM - 73E	FAVERSHAM - 73E	FAVERSHAM - 73E	FAVERSHAM - 73E	FAVERSHAM - 73E	FAVERSHAM - 73E
31693	B.ARMS - 73B	B.ARMS - 73B	B.ARMS - 73B	B.ARMS - 73B	B.ARMS - 73B	B.ARMS - 73B	B.ARMS - 73B
31694	HITHER GREEN - 73C	HITHER GREEN - 73C	HITHER GREEN - 73C	HITHER GREEN - 73C	HITHER GREEN - 73C	HITHER GREEN - 73C	HITHER GREEN - 73C
31695	HITHER GREEN - 73C	HITHER GREEN - 73C	HITHER GREEN - 73C	HITHER GREEN - 73C	HITHER GREEN - 73C	HITHER GREEN - 73C	HITHER GREEN - 73C
31711	ASHFORD - 74A	ASHFORD - 74A	ASHFORD - 74A	ASHFORD - 74A	ASHFORD - 74A	ASHFORD - 74A	ASHFORD - 74A
31712	STEWARTS LANE - 73A	STEWARTS LANE - 73A	STEWARTS LANE - 73A	STEWARTS LANE - 73A	STEWARTS LANE - 73A	GILLINGHAM - 73D	GILLINGHAM - 73D
31713	GILLINGHAM - 73D	GILLINGHAM - 73D	GILLINGHAM - 73D	GILLINGHAM - 73D	GILLINGHAM - 73D	GILLINGHAM - 73D	GILLINGHAM - 73D
31714	STEWARTS LANE - 73A	STEWARTS LANE - 73A	STEWARTS LANE - 73A	STEWARTS LANE - 73A	STEWARTS LANE - 73A	STEWARTS LANE - 73A	STEWARTS LANE - 73A
31715	FAVERSHAM - 73E	FAVERSHAM - 73E	FAVERSHAM - 73E	FAVERSHAM - 73E	FAVERSHAM - 73E	FAVERSHAM - 73E	FAVERSHAM - 73E
31716	STEWARTS LANE - 73A	STEWARTS LANE - 73A	STEWARTS LANE - 73A	STEWARTS LANE - 73A	STEWARTS LANE - 73A	STEWARTS LANE - 73A	STEWARTS LANE - 73A
31717	STEWARTS LANE - 73A	STEWARTS LANE - 73A	STEWARTS LANE - 73A	STEWARTS LANE - 73A	STEWARTS LANE - 73A	STEWARTS LANE - 73A	STEWARTS LANE - 73A
31718	STEWARTS LANE - 73A	STEWARTS LANE - 73A	STEWARTS LANE - 73A	STEWARTS LANE - 73A	STEWARTS LANE - 73A	STEWARTS LANE - 73A	STEWARTS LANE - 73A
31719	STEWARTS LANE - 73A	STEWARTS LANE - 73A	STEWARTS LANE - 73A	STEWARTS LANE - 73A	STEWARTS LANE - 73A	STEWARTS LANE - 73A	STEWARTS LANE - 73A
31720	HITHER GREEN - 73C	HITHER GREEN - 73C	HITHER GREEN - 73C	HITHER GREEN - 73C	HITHER GREEN - 73C	HITHER GREEN - 73C	HITHER GREEN - 73C
31721	ASHFORD - 74A	ASHFORD - 74A	ASHFORD - 74A	ASHFORD - 74A	ASHFORD - 74A	ASHFORD - 74A	ASHFORD - 74A
31722	STEWARTS LANE - 73A	STEWARTS LANE - 73A	STEWARTS LANE - 73A	STEWARTS LANE - 73A	STEWARTS LANE - 73A	STEWARTS LANE - 73A	STEWARTS LANE - 73A
31723	B.ARMS - 73B	B.ARMS - 73B	B.ARMS - 73B	B.ARMS - 73B	B.ARMS - 73B	B.ARMS - 73B	B.ARMS - 73B
31724	B.ARMS - 73B	B.ARMS - 73B	B.ARMS - 73B	B.ARMS - 73B	B.ARMS - 73B	B.ARMS - 73B	B.ARMS - 73B
31725	B.ARMS - 73B	B.ARMS - 73B	B.ARMS - 73B	B.ARMS - 73B	B.ARMS - 73B	B.ARMS - 73B	B.ARMS - 73B

loco	Apr-50	Sep-50	Oct-50	Nov-50	Dec-50	Mar-51	Apr-51
				C 0-6-0 (1900)			
31004	RAMSGATE - 74B	RAMSGATE - 74B	RAMSGATE - 74B	RAMSGATE - 74B	RAMSGATE - 74B	RAMSGATE - 74B	RAMSGATE - 74B
31018	HITHER GREEN - 73C	HITHER GREEN - 73C	HITHER GREEN - 73C	HITHER GREEN - 73C	HITHER GREEN - 73C	HITHER GREEN - 73C	HITHER GREEN - 73C
31033	B.ARMS - 73B	B.ARMS - 73B	B.ARMS - 73B	B.ARMS - 73B	B.ARMS - 73B	B.ARMS - 73B	B.ARMS - 73B
31037	ST LEONARDS - 74E	ST LEONARDS - 74E	ST LEONARDS - 74E	ST LEONARDS - 74E	ST LEONARDS - 74E	ST LEONARDS - 74E	ST LEONARDS - 74E
31038	ST LEONARDS - 74E	ST LEONARDS - 74E	ST LEONARDS - 74E	ST LEONARDS - 74E	ST LEONARDS - 74E	ST LEONARDS - 74E	ST LEONARDS - 74E
31054	HITHER GREEN - 73C	HITHER GREEN - 73C	HITHER GREEN - 73C	HITHER GREEN - 73C	HITHER GREEN - 73C	HITHER GREEN - 73C	HITHER GREEN - 73C
31059	HITHER GREEN - 73C	HITHER GREEN - 73C	HITHER GREEN - 73C	HITHER GREEN - 73C	HITHER GREEN - 73C	HITHER GREEN - 73C	HITHER GREEN - 73C
31061	HITHER GREEN - 73C	HITHER GREEN - 73C	HITHER GREEN - 73C	HITHER GREEN - 73C	HITHER GREEN - 73C	HITHER GREEN - 73C	HITHER GREEN - 73C
31063	DOVER - 74C	DOVER - 74C	DOVER - 74C	DOVER - 74C	DOVER - 74C	DOVER - 74C	DOVER - 74C
31068	B.ARMS - 73B	B.ARMS - 73B	B.ARMS - 73B	B.ARMS - 73B	B.ARMS - 73B	B.ARMS - 73B	B.ARMS - 73B
31071	B.ARMS - 73B	B.ARMS - 73B	B.ARMS - 73B	B.ARMS - 73B	B.ARMS - 73B	B.ARMS - 73B	B.ARMS - 73B
31086	GILLINGHAM - 73D	GILLINGHAM - 73D	GILLINGHAM - 73D	GILLINGHAM - 73D	GILLINGHAM - 73D	GILLINGHAM - 73D	GILLINGHAM - 73D
31090	GILLINGHAM - 73D	GILLINGHAM - 73D	GILLINGHAM - 73D	GILLINGHAM - 73D	GILLINGHAM - 73D	GILLINGHAM - 73D	GILLINGHAM - 73D
31102	B.ARMS - 73B	B.ARMS - 73B	B.ARMS - 73B	B.ARMS - 73B	B.ARMS - 73B	B.ARMS - 73B	B.ARMS - 73B
31112	GILLINGHAM - 73D	GILLINGHAM - 73D	GILLINGHAM - 73D	GILLINGHAM - 73D	GILLINGHAM - 73D	GILLINGHAM - 73D	GILLINGHAM - 73D
31113	DOVER - 74C	DOVER - 74C	DOVER - 74C	DOVER - 74C	DOVER - 74C	DOVER - 74C	DOVER - 74C
31150	HITHER GREEN - 73C	HITHER GREEN - 73C	HITHER GREEN - 73C	HITHER GREEN - 73C	HITHER GREEN - 73C	HITHER GREEN - 73C	HITHER GREEN - 73C
31191	DOVER - 74C	DOVER - 74C	DOVER - 74C	DOVER - 74C	DOVER - 74C	DOVER - 74C	DOVER - 74C
31218	ASHFORD - 74A	ASHFORD - 74A	ASHFORD - 74A	ASHFORD - 74A	ASHFORD - 74A	ASHFORD - 74A	ASHFORD - 74A
31219	TONBRIDGE - 74D	TONBRIDGE - 74D	TONBRIDGE - 74D	TONBRIDGE - 74D	TONBRIDGE - 74D	TONBRIDGE - 74D	TONBRIDGE - 74D
31221	GILLINGHAM - 73D	GILLINGHAM - 73D	GILLINGHAM - 73D	GILLINGHAM - 73D	GILLINGHAM - 73D	GILLINGHAM - 73D	GILLINGHAM - 73D
31223	GILLINGHAM - 73D	GILLINGHAM - 73D	GILLINGHAM - 73D	GILLINGHAM - 73D	GILLINGHAM - 73D	GILLINGHAM - 73D	GILLINGHAM - 73D
31225	GILLINGHAM - 73D	GILLINGHAM - 73D	GILLINGHAM - 73D	GILLINGHAM - 73D	GILLINGHAM - 73D	GILLINGHAM - 73D	GILLINGHAM - 73D
31227	B.ARMS - 73B	B.ARMS - 73B	B.ARMS - 73B	B.ARMS - 73B	B.ARMS - 73B	B.ARMS - 73B	B.ARMS - 73B
31229	FAVERSHAM - 73E	FAVERSHAM - 73E	FAVERSHAM - 73E	FAVERSHAM - 73E	FAVERSHAM - 73E	FAVERSHAM - 73E	FAVERSHAM - 73E
31234	STEWARTS LANE - 73A	STEWARTS LANE - 73A	STEWARTS LANE - 73A	STEWARTS LANE - 73A	STEWARTS LANE - 73A	STEWARTS LANE - 73A	STEWARTS LANE - 73A
31242	FAVERSHAM - 73E	FAVERSHAM - 73E	FAVERSHAM - 73E	FAVERSHAM - 73E	FAVERSHAM - 73E	FAVERSHAM - 73E	FAVERSHAM - 73E
31243	DOVER - 74C	DOVER - 74C	DOVER - 74C	DOVER - 74C	DOVER - 74C	DOVER - 74C	DOVER - 74C
31244	TONBRIDGE - 74D	TONBRIDGE - 74D	TONBRIDGE - 74D	TONBRIDGE - 74D	TONBRIDGE - 74D	TONBRIDGE - 74D	TONBRIDGE - 74D
31245	HITHER GREEN - 73C	HITHER GREEN - 73C	HITHER GREEN - 73C	HITHER GREEN - 73C	HITHER GREEN - 73C	HITHER GREEN - 73C	HITHER GREEN - 73C
31252	RAMSGATE - 74B	RAMSGATE - 74B	RAMSGATE - 74B	RAMSGATE - 74B	RAMSGATE - 74B	RAMSGATE - 74B	RAMSGATE - 74B
31253	B.ARMS - 73B	B.ARMS - 73B	B.ARMS - 73B	B.ARMS - 73B	B.ARMS - 73B	B.ARMS - 73B	B.ARMS - 73B
31255	DOVER - 74C	GILLINGHAM - 73D	GILLINGHAM - 73D	GILLINGHAM - 73D	GILLINGHAM - 73D	GILLINGHAM - 73D	GILLINGHAM - 73D
31256	GILLINGHAM - 73D	GILLINGHAM - 73D	GILLINGHAM - 73D	GILLINGHAM - 73D	GILLINGHAM - 73D	GILLINGHAM - 73D	GILLINGHAM - 73D
31260	ASHFORD - 74A	ASHFORD - 74A	ASHFORD - 74A	ASHFORD - 74A	ASHFORD - 74A	ASHFORD - 74A	ASHFORD - 74A
31267	GILLINGHAM - 73D	GILLINGHAM - 73D	GILLINGHAM - 73D	GILLINGHAM - 73D	GILLINGHAM - 73D	GILLINGHAM - 73D	GILLINGHAM - 73D
31268	FAVERSHAM - 73E	FAVERSHAM - 73E	FAVERSHAM - 73E	FAVERSHAM - 73E	FAVERSHAM - 73E	FAVERSHAM - 73E	FAVERSHAM - 73E
31270	HITHER GREEN - 73C	HITHER GREEN - 73C	HITHER GREEN - 73C	HITHER GREEN - 73C	HITHER GREEN - 73C	HITHER GREEN - 73C	HITHER GREEN - 73C
31271	ASHFORD - 74A	ASHFORD - 74A	ASHFORD - 74A	ASHFORD - 74A	ASHFORD - 74A	ASHFORD - 74A	ASHFORD - 74A
31272	TONBRIDGE - 74D	TONBRIDGE - 74D	TONBRIDGE - 74D	TONBRIDGE - 74D	TONBRIDGE - 74D	TONBRIDGE - 74D	TONBRIDGE - 74D
31277	TONBRIDGE - 74D	TONBRIDGE - 74D	TONBRIDGE - 74D	TONBRIDGE - 74D	TONBRIDGE - 74D	TONBRIDGE - 74D	TONBRIDGE - 74D
31280	B.ARMS - 73B	B.ARMS - 73B	B.ARMS - 73B	B.ARMS - 73B	B.ARMS - 73B	B.ARMS - 73B	B.ARMS - 73B
31287	GILLINGHAM - 73D	GILLINGHAM - 73D	GILLINGHAM - 73D	GILLINGHAM - 73D	GILLINGHAM - 73D	GILLINGHAM - 73D	GILLINGHAM - 73D
31291	DOVER - 74C	DOVER - 74C	DOVER - 74C	DOVER - 74C	DOVER - 74C	DOVER - 74C	DOVER - 74C
31293	B.ARMS - 73B	B.ARMS - 73B	B.ARMS - 73B	B.ARMS - 73B	B.ARMS - 73B	B.ARMS - 73B	B.ARMS - 73B
31294	B.ARMS - 73B	B.ARMS - 73B	B.ARMS - 73B	B.ARMS - 73B	B.ARMS - 73B	B.ARMS - 73B	B.ARMS - 73B
31297	B.ARMS - 73B	B.ARMS - 73B	B.ARMS - 73B	B.ARMS - 73B	B.ARMS - 73B	B.ARMS - 73B	B.ARMS - 73B
31298	RAMSGATE - 74B	RAMSGATE - 74B	RAMSGATE - 74B	RAMSGATE - 74B	RAMSGATE - 74B	RAMSGATE - 74B	RAMSGATE - 74B
31317	GILLINGHAM - 73D	GILLINGHAM - 73D	GILLINGHAM - 73D	GILLINGHAM - 73D	GILLINGHAM - 73D	GILLINGHAM - 73D	GILLINGHAM - 73D
31461	TONBRIDGE - 74D	TONBRIDGE - 74D	TONBRIDGE - 74D	TONBRIDGE - 74D	TONBRIDGE - 74D	TONBRIDGE - 74D	TONBRIDGE - 74D
31480	HITHER GREEN - 73C	HITHER GREEN - 73C	HITHER GREEN - 73C	HITHER GREEN - 73C	HITHER GREEN - 73C	HITHER GREEN - 73C	HITHER GREEN - 73C
31481	FAVERSHAM - 73E	FAVERSHAM - 73E	FAVERSHAM - 73E	FAVERSHAM - 73E	FAVERSHAM - 73E	FAVERSHAM - 73E	FAVERSHAM - 73E
31486	HITHER GREEN - 73C	HITHER GREEN - 73C	HITHER GREEN - 73C	HITHER GREEN - 73C	HITHER GREEN - 73C	HITHER GREEN - 73C	HITHER GREEN - 73C
31495	FAVERSHAM - 73E	FAVERSHAM - 73E	FAVERSHAM - 73E	FAVERSHAM - 73E	FAVERSHAM - 73E	FAVERSHAM - 73E	FAVERSHAM - 73E
31498	GILLINGHAM - 73D	GILLINGHAM - 73D	GILLINGHAM - 73D	GILLINGHAM - 73D	GILLINGHAM - 73D	GILLINGHAM - 73D	GILLINGHAM - 73D
31508	B.ARMS - 73B	B.ARMS - 73B	B.ARMS - 73B	B.ARMS - 73B	B.ARMS - 73B	B.ARMS - 73B	B.ARMS - 73B
31510	GILLINGHAM - 73D	GILLINGHAM - 73D	GILLINGHAM - 73D	GILLINGHAM - 73D	GILLINGHAM - 73D	GILLINGHAM - 73D	GILLINGHAM - 73D
31513	ASHFORD - 74A	ASHFORD - 74A	ASHFORD - 74A	ASHFORD - 74A	ASHFORD - 74A	ASHFORD - 74A	ASHFORD - 74A
31572	ASHFORD - 74A	ASHFORD - 74A	ASHFORD - 74A	ASHFORD - 74A	ASHFORD - 74A	ASHFORD - 74A	ASHFORD - 74A
31573	GILLINGHAM - 73D	GILLINGHAM - 73D	GILLINGHAM - 73D	GILLINGHAM - 73D	GILLINGHAM - 73D	GILLINGHAM - 73D	GILLINGHAM - 73D
31575	STEWARTS LANE - 73A	STEWARTS LANE - 73A	STEWARTS LANE - 73A	STEWARTS LANE - 73A	STEWARTS LANE - 73A	STEWARTS LANE - 73A	STEWARTS LANE - 73A
31576	STEWARTS LANE - 73A	STEWARTS LANE - 73A	STEWARTS LANE - 73A	STEWARTS LANE - 73A	STEWARTS LANE - 73A	STEWARTS LANE - 73A	STEWARTS LANE - 73A
31578	STEWARTS LANE - 73A	STEWARTS LANE - 73A	STEWARTS LANE - 73A	STEWARTS LANE - 73A	STEWARTS LANE - 73A	STEWARTS LANE - 73A	STEWARTS LANE - 73A
31579	GILLINGHAM - 73D	GILLINGHAM - 73D	GILLINGHAM - 73D	GILLINGHAM - 73D	GILLINGHAM - 73D	GILLINGHAM - 73D	GILLINGHAM - 73D
31580	TONBRIDGE - 74D	TONBRIDGE - 74D	TONBRIDGE - 74D	TONBRIDGE - 74D	TONBRIDGE - 74D	TONBRIDGE - 74D	TONBRIDGE - 74D
31581	HITHER GREEN - 73C	HITHER GREEN - 73C	HITHER GREEN - 73C	HITHER GREEN - 73C	HITHER GREEN - 73C	HITHER GREEN - 73C	HITHER GREEN - 73C
31582	STEWARTS LANE - 73A	STEWARTS LANE - 73A	STEWARTS LANE - 73A	STEWARTS LANE - 73A	STEWARTS LANE - 73A	STEWARTS LANE - 73A	STEWARTS LANE - 73A
31583	GILLINGHAM - 73D	GILLINGHAM - 73D	GILLINGHAM - 73D	GILLINGHAM - 73D	GILLINGHAM - 73D	GILLINGHAM - 73D	GILLINGHAM - 73D
31584	B.ARMS - 73B	B.ARMS - 73B	B.ARMS - 73B	B.ARMS - 73B	B.ARMS - 73B	B.ARMS - 73B	B.ARMS - 73B
31585	GILLINGHAM - 73D	GILLINGHAM - 73D	GILLINGHAM - 73D	GILLINGHAM - 73D	GILLINGHAM - 73D	GILLINGHAM - 73D	GILLINGHAM - 73D
31588	GILLINGHAM - 73D	GILLINGHAM - 73D	GILLINGHAM - 73D	GILLINGHAM - 73D	GILLINGHAM - 73D	GILLINGHAM - 73D	GILLINGHAM - 73D
31589	ASHFORD - 74A	ASHFORD - 74A	ASHFORD - 74A	ASHFORD - 74A	ASHFORD - 74A	ASHFORD - 74A	ASHFORD - 74A
31590	TONBRIDGE - 74D	TONBRIDGE - 74D	TONBRIDGE - 74D	TONBRIDGE - 74D	TONBRIDGE - 74D	TONBRIDGE - 74D	TONBRIDGE - 74D
31592	RAMSGATE - 74B	RAMSGATE - 74B	RAMSGATE - 74B	RAMSGATE - 74B	RAMSGATE - 74B	RAMSGATE - 74B	RAMSGATE - 74B
31593	TONBRIDGE - 74D	TONBRIDGE - 74D	TONBRIDGE - 74D	TONBRIDGE - 74D	TONBRIDGE - 74D	TONBRIDGE - 74D	TONBRIDGE - 74D
31681	STEWARTS LANE - 73A	STEWARTS LANE - 73A	STEWARTS LANE - 73A	STEWARTS LANE - 73A	STEWARTS LANE - 73A	STEWARTS LANE - 73A	STEWARTS LANE - 73A
31682	GILLINGHAM - 73D	GILLINGHAM - 73D	GILLINGHAM - 73D	GILLINGHAM - 73D	GILLINGHAM - 73D	GILLINGHAM - 73D	GILLINGHAM - 73D
31683	STEWARTS LANE - 73A	STEWARTS LANE - 73A	STEWARTS LANE - 73A	STEWARTS LANE - 73A	STEWARTS LANE - 73A	STEWARTS LANE - 73A	STEWARTS LANE - 73A
31684	GILLINGHAM - 73D	TONBRIDGE - 74D	TONBRIDGE - 74D	TONBRIDGE - 74D	TONBRIDGE - 74D	TONBRIDGE - 74D	TONBRIDGE - 74D
31686	TONBRIDGE - 74D	TONBRIDGE - 74D	TONBRIDGE - 74D	TONBRIDGE - 74D	TONBRIDGE - 74D	TONBRIDGE - 74D	TONBRIDGE - 74D
31687	B.ARMS - 73B	B.ARMS - 73B	B.ARMS - 73B	B.ARMS - 73B	B.ARMS - 73B	B.ARMS - 73B	B.ARMS - 73B
31688	GILLINGHAM - 73D	GILLINGHAM - 73D	GILLINGHAM - 73D	GILLINGHAM - 73D	GILLINGHAM - 73D	GILLINGHAM - 73D	GILLINGHAM - 73D
31689	HITHER GREEN - 73C	HITHER GREEN - 73C	HITHER GREEN - 73C	HITHER GREEN - 73C	HITHER GREEN - 73C	HITHER GREEN - 73C	HITHER GREEN - 73C
31690	RAMSGATE - 74B	RAMSGATE - 74B	RAMSGATE - 74B	RAMSGATE - 74B	RAMSGATE - 74B	RAMSGATE - 74B	RAMSGATE - 74B
31691	FAVERSHAM - 73E	FAVERSHAM - 73E	FAVERSHAM - 73E	FAVERSHAM - 73E	FAVERSHAM - 73E	FAVERSHAM - 73E	FAVERSHAM - 73E
31692	FAVERSHAM - 73E	FAVERSHAM - 73E	FAVERSHAM - 73E	FAVERSHAM - 73E	FAVERSHAM - 73E	FAVERSHAM - 73E	FAVERSHAM - 73E
31693	GILLINGHAM - 73D	GILLINGHAM - 73D	GILLINGHAM - 73D	GILLINGHAM - 73D	GILLINGHAM - 73D	GILLINGHAM - 73D	GILLINGHAM - 73D
31694	HITHER GREEN - 73C	HITHER GREEN - 73C	HITHER GREEN - 73C	HITHER GREEN - 73C	HITHER GREEN - 73C	HITHER GREEN - 73C	HITHER GREEN - 73C
31695	HITHER GREEN - 73C	HITHER GREEN - 73C	HITHER GREEN - 73C	HITHER GREEN - 73C	HITHER GREEN - 73C	HITHER GREEN - 73C	HITHER GREEN - 73C
31711	ASHFORD - 74A	ASHFORD - 74A	ASHFORD - 74A	ASHFORD - 74A	ASHFORD - 74A	ASHFORD - 74A	ASHFORD - 74A
31712	GILLINGHAM - 73D	GILLINGHAM - 73D	GILLINGHAM - 73D	GILLINGHAM - 73D	GILLINGHAM - 73D	GILLINGHAM - 73D	GILLINGHAM - 73D
31713	GILLINGHAM - 73D	GILLINGHAM - 73D	GILLINGHAM - 73D	GILLINGHAM - 73D	GILLINGHAM - 73D	GILLINGHAM - 73D	GILLINGHAM - 73D
31714	STEWARTS LANE - 73A	STEWARTS LANE - 73A	STEWARTS LANE - 73A	STEWARTS LANE - 73A	STEWARTS LANE - 73A	STEWARTS LANE - 73A	STEWARTS LANE - 73A
31715	FAVERSHAM - 73E	FAVERSHAM - 73E	FAVERSHAM - 73E	FAVERSHAM - 73E	FAVERSHAM - 73E	FAVERSHAM - 73E	FAVERSHAM - 73E
31716	STEWARTS LANE - 73A	STEWARTS LANE - 73A	STEWARTS LANE - 73A	STEWARTS LANE - 73A	STEWARTS LANE - 73A	STEWARTS LANE - 73A	STEWARTS LANE - 73A
31717	STEWARTS LANE - 73A	STEWARTS LANE - 73A	STEWARTS LANE - 73A	STEWARTS LANE - 73A	STEWARTS LANE - 73A	STEWARTS LANE - 73A	STEWARTS LANE - 73A
31718	STEWARTS LANE - 73A	STEWARTS LANE - 73A	STEWARTS LANE - 73A	STEWARTS LANE - 73A	STEWARTS LANE - 73A	STEWARTS LANE - 73A	STEWARTS LANE - 73A
31719	STEWARTS LANE - 73A	STEWARTS LANE - 73A	STEWARTS LANE - 73A	STEWARTS LANE - 73A	STEWARTS LANE - 73A	STEWARTS LANE - 73A	STEWARTS LANE - 73A
31720	HITHER GREEN - 73C	HITHER GREEN - 73C	HITHER GREEN - 73C	HITHER GREEN - 73C	HITHER GREEN - 73C	HITHER GREEN - 73C	HITHER GREEN - 73C
31721	ASHFORD - 74A	ASHFORD - 74A	ASHFORD - 74A	ASHFORD - 74A	ASHFORD - 74A	ASHFORD - 74A	ASHFORD - 74A
31722	STEWARTS LANE - 73A	STEWARTS LANE - 73A	STEWARTS LANE - 73A	STEWARTS LANE - 73A	STEWARTS LANE - 73A	STEWARTS LANE - 73A	STEWARTS LANE - 73A
31723	B.ARMS - 73B	B.ARMS - 73B	B.ARMS - 73B	B.ARMS - 73B	B.ARMS - 73B	B.ARMS - 73B	B.ARMS - 73B
31724	GILLINGHAM - 73D	GILLINGHAM - 73D	GILLINGHAM - 73D	GILLINGHAM - 73D	GILLINGHAM - 73D	GILLINGHAM - 73D	GILLINGHAM - 73D
31725	B.ARMS - 73B	B.ARMS - 73B	B.ARMS - 73B	B.ARMS - 73B	B.ARMS - 73B	B.ARMS - 73B	B.ARMS - 73B

C 0-6-0 (1900)

loco	Jun-51	Jul-51	Sep-51	Dec-51	Jan-52	Mar-52	Jun-52
31004	RAMSGATE - 74B	RAMSGATE - 74B	RAMSGATE - 74B	RAMSGATE - 74B	RAMSGATE - 74B	RAMSGATE - 74B	RAMSGATE - 74B
31018	HITHER GREEN - 73C	HITHER GREEN - 73C	HITHER GREEN - 73C	HITHER GREEN - 73C	HITHER GREEN - 73C	HITHER GREEN - 73C	HITHER GREEN - 73C
31033	B.ARMS - 73B	B.ARMS - 73B	B.ARMS - 73B	B.ARMS - 73B	B.ARMS - 73B	B.ARMS - 73B	B.ARMS - 73B
31037	ST LEONARDS - 74E	ST LEONARDS - 74E	ST LEONARDS - 74E	ST LEONARDS - 74E	ST LEONARDS - 74E	ST LEONARDS - 74E	ST LEONARDS - 74E
31038	ST LEONARDS - 74E	ST LEONARDS - 74E	ST LEONARDS - 74E	ST LEONARDS - 74E	ST LEONARDS - 74E	ST LEONARDS - 74E	TONBRIDGE - 74D
31054	HITHER GREEN - 73C	HITHER GREEN - 73C	HITHER GREEN - 73C	HITHER GREEN - 73C	HITHER GREEN - 73C	HITHER GREEN - 73C	HITHER GREEN - 73C
31059	HITHER GREEN - 73C	HITHER GREEN - 73C	HITHER GREEN - 73C	HITHER GREEN - 73C	HITHER GREEN - 73C	HITHER GREEN - 73C	HITHER GREEN - 73C
31061	HITHER GREEN - 73C	HITHER GREEN - 73C	HITHER GREEN - 73C	HITHER GREEN - 73C	HITHER GREEN - 73C	HITHER GREEN - 73C	HITHER GREEN - 73C
31063	HITHER GREEN - 73C	HITHER GREEN - 73C	HITHER GREEN - 73C	HITHER GREEN - 73C	HITHER GREEN - 73C	HITHER GREEN - 73C	HITHER GREEN - 73C
31068	B.ARMS - 73B	B.ARMS - 73B	B.ARMS - 73B	B.ARMS - 73B	B.ARMS - 73B	B.ARMS - 73B	B.ARMS - 73B
31071	B.ARMS - 73B	B.ARMS - 73B	B.ARMS - 73B	B.ARMS - 73B	B.ARMS - 73B	B.ARMS - 73B	B.ARMS - 73B
31086	GILLINGHAM - 73D	GILLINGHAM - 73D	GILLINGHAM - 73D	GILLINGHAM - 73D	GILLINGHAM - 73D	GILLINGHAM - 73D	GILLINGHAM - 73D
31090	GILLINGHAM - 73D	GILLINGHAM - 73D	GILLINGHAM - 73D	GILLINGHAM - 73D	GILLINGHAM - 73D	GILLINGHAM - 73D	GILLINGHAM - 73D
31102	B.ARMS - 73B	B.ARMS - 73B	B.ARMS - 73B	B.ARMS - 73B	B.ARMS - 73B	B.ARMS - 73B	B.ARMS - 73B
31112	GILLINGHAM - 73D	GILLINGHAM - 73D	GILLINGHAM - 73D	GILLINGHAM - 73D	GILLINGHAM - 73D	GILLINGHAM - 73D	GILLINGHAM - 73D
31113	DOVER - 74C	DOVER - 74C	DOVER - 74C	DOVER - 74C	DOVER - 74C	DOVER - 74C	DOVER - 74C
31150	DOVER - 74C	DOVER - 74C	DOVER - 74C	DOVER - 74C	DOVER - 74C	DOVER - 74C	DOVER - 74C
31191	DOVER - 74C	DOVER - 74C	DOVER - 74C	DOVER - 74C	DOVER - 74C	DOVER - 74C	DOVER - 74C
31218	ASHFORD - 74A	ASHFORD - 74A	ASHFORD - 74A	ASHFORD - 74A	ASHFORD - 74A	ASHFORD - 74A	ASHFORD - 74A
31219	TONBRIDGE - 74D	TONBRIDGE - 74D	TONBRIDGE - 74D	TONBRIDGE - 74D	TONBRIDGE - 74D	TONBRIDGE - 74D	TONBRIDGE - 74D
31221	GILLINGHAM - 73D	GILLINGHAM - 73D	GILLINGHAM - 73D	GILLINGHAM - 73D	GILLINGHAM - 73D	GILLINGHAM - 73D	GILLINGHAM - 73D
31223	GILLINGHAM - 73D	GILLINGHAM - 73D	GILLINGHAM - 73D	GILLINGHAM - 73D	GILLINGHAM - 73D	GILLINGHAM - 73D	GILLINGHAM - 73D
31225	GILLINGHAM - 73D	GILLINGHAM - 73D	HITHER GREEN - 73C	HITHER GREEN - 73C	HITHER GREEN - 73C	HITHER GREEN - 73C	GILLINGHAM - 73D
31227	B.ARMS - 73B	B.ARMS - 73B	B.ARMS - 73B	B.ARMS - 73B	B.ARMS - 73B	B.ARMS - 73B	B.ARMS - 73B
31229	FAVERSHAM - 73E	FAVERSHAM - 73E	FAVERSHAM - 73E	FAVERSHAM - 73E	FAVERSHAM - 73E	FAVERSHAM - 73E	FAVERSHAM - 73E
31234	STEWARTS LANE - 73A	STEWARTS LANE - 73A	STEWARTS LANE - 73A	STEWARTS LANE - 73A	STEWARTS LANE - 73A	STEWARTS LANE - 73A	STEWARTS LANE - 73A
31242	FAVERSHAM - 73E	FAVERSHAM - 73E	FAVERSHAM - 73E	FAVERSHAM - 73E	FAVERSHAM - 73E	FAVERSHAM - 73E	FAVERSHAM - 73E
31243	DOVER - 74C	DOVER - 74C	DOVER - 74C	DOVER - 74C	DOVER - 74C	DOVER - 74C	DOVER - 74C
31244	TONBRIDGE - 74D	TONBRIDGE - 74D	TONBRIDGE - 74D	TONBRIDGE - 74D	TONBRIDGE - 74D	TONBRIDGE - 74D	TONBRIDGE - 74D
31245	HITHER GREEN - 73C	HITHER GREEN - 73C	HITHER GREEN - 73C	HITHER GREEN - 73C	HITHER GREEN - 73C	HITHER GREEN - 73C	RAMSGATE - 74B
31252	RAMSGATE - 74B	RAMSGATE - 74B	RAMSGATE - 74B	RAMSGATE - 74B	RAMSGATE - 74B	RAMSGATE - 74B	RAMSGATE - 74B
31253	FAVERSHAM - 73E	FAVERSHAM - 73E	FAVERSHAM - 73E	FAVERSHAM - 73E	FAVERSHAM - 73E	FAVERSHAM - 73E	FAVERSHAM - 73E
31255	FAVERSHAM - 73E	FAVERSHAM - 73E	FAVERSHAM - 73E	FAVERSHAM - 73E	FAVERSHAM - 73E	FAVERSHAM - 73E	FAVERSHAM - 73E
31256	FAVERSHAM - 73E	FAVERSHAM - 73E	FAVERSHAM - 73E	FAVERSHAM - 73E	FAVERSHAM - 73E	FAVERSHAM - 73E	FAVERSHAM - 73E
31260	ASHFORD - 74A	TONBRIDGE - 74D	FAVERSHAM - 73E	FAVERSHAM - 73E	FAVERSHAM - 73E	FAVERSHAM - 73E	FAVERSHAM - 73E
31267	GILLINGHAM - 73D	GILLINGHAM - 73D	GILLINGHAM - 73D	GILLINGHAM - 73D	GILLINGHAM - 73D	GILLINGHAM - 73D	GILLINGHAM - 73D
31268	FAVERSHAM - 73E	FAVERSHAM - 73E	FAVERSHAM - 73E	FAVERSHAM - 73E	FAVERSHAM - 73E	FAVERSHAM - 73E	FAVERSHAM - 73E
31270	HITHER GREEN - 73C	HITHER GREEN - 73C	HITHER GREEN - 73C	HITHER GREEN - 73C	HITHER GREEN - 73C	HITHER GREEN - 73C	HITHER GREEN - 73C
31271	ASHFORD - 74A	ASHFORD - 74A	ASHFORD - 74A	ASHFORD - 74A	ASHFORD - 74A	ASHFORD - 74A	RAMSGATE - 74B
31272	TONBRIDGE - 74D	TONBRIDGE - 74D	TONBRIDGE - 74D	TONBRIDGE - 74D	TONBRIDGE - 74D	TONBRIDGE - 74D	TONBRIDGE - 74D
31277	TONBRIDGE - 74D	TONBRIDGE - 74D	TONBRIDGE - 74D	TONBRIDGE - 74D	TONBRIDGE - 74D	TONBRIDGE - 74D	TONBRIDGE - 74D
31280	B.ARMS - 73B	B.ARMS - 73B	B.ARMS - 73B	B.ARMS - 73B	B.ARMS - 73B	B.ARMS - 73B	B.ARMS - 73B
31287	GILLINGHAM - 73D	GILLINGHAM - 73D	GILLINGHAM - 73D	GILLINGHAM - 73D	GILLINGHAM - 73D	GILLINGHAM - 73D	GILLINGHAM - 73D
31291	B.ARMS - 73B	B.ARMS - 73B	B.ARMS - 73B	B.ARMS - 73B	B.ARMS - 73B	B.ARMS - 73B	B.ARMS - 73B
31293	B.ARMS - 73B	B.ARMS - 73B	B.ARMS - 73B	B.ARMS - 73B	B.ARMS - 73B	B.ARMS - 73B	B.ARMS - 73B
31294	B.ARMS - 73B	B.ARMS - 73B	B.ARMS - 73B	B.ARMS - 73B	B.ARMS - 73B	B.ARMS - 73B	B.ARMS - 73B
31297	B.ARMS - 73B	B.ARMS - 73B	B.ARMS - 73B	B.ARMS - 73B	B.ARMS - 73B	B.ARMS - 73B	B.ARMS - 73B
31298	RAMSGATE - 74B	RAMSGATE - 74B	RAMSGATE - 74B	RAMSGATE - 74B	RAMSGATE - 74B	RAMSGATE - 74B	RAMSGATE - 74B
31317	DOVER - 74C	DOVER - 74C	DOVER - 74C	DOVER - 74C	DOVER - 74C	DOVER - 74C	DOVER - 74C
31461	TONBRIDGE - 74D	FAVERSHAM - 73E	FAVERSHAM - 73E	FAVERSHAM - 73E	FAVERSHAM - 73E	FAVERSHAM - 73E	FAVERSHAM - 73E
31480	HITHER GREEN - 73C	HITHER GREEN - 73C	HITHER GREEN - 73C	HITHER GREEN - 73C	HITHER GREEN - 73C	HITHER GREEN - 73C	HITHER GREEN - 73C
31481	FAVERSHAM - 73E	FAVERSHAM - 73E	FAVERSHAM - 73E	FAVERSHAM - 73E	FAVERSHAM - 73E	FAVERSHAM - 73E	FAVERSHAM - 73E
31486	HITHER GREEN - 73C	HITHER GREEN - 73C	HITHER GREEN - 73C	HITHER GREEN - 73C	HITHER GREEN - 73C	HITHER GREEN - 73C	HITHER GREEN - 73C
31495	FAVERSHAM - 73E	FAVERSHAM - 73E	FAVERSHAM - 73E	FAVERSHAM - 73E	FAVERSHAM - 73E	FAVERSHAM - 73E	FAVERSHAM - 73E
31498	GILLINGHAM - 73D	GILLINGHAM - 73D	GILLINGHAM - 73D	GILLINGHAM - 73D	GILLINGHAM - 73D	GILLINGHAM - 73D	GILLINGHAM - 73D
31508	B.ARMS - 73B	B.ARMS - 73B	B.ARMS - 73B	B.ARMS - 73B	B.ARMS - 73B	B.ARMS - 73B	B.ARMS - 73B
31510	GILLINGHAM - 73D	GILLINGHAM - 73D	GILLINGHAM - 73D	GILLINGHAM - 73D	GILLINGHAM - 73D	GILLINGHAM - 73D	GILLINGHAM - 73D
31513	ASHFORD - 74A	ASHFORD - 74A	ASHFORD - 74A	ASHFORD - 74A	ASHFORD - 74A	ASHFORD - 74A	ASHFORD - 74A
31572	ASHFORD - 74A	ASHFORD - 74A	ASHFORD - 74A	ASHFORD - 74A	ASHFORD - 74A	ASHFORD - 74A	ASHFORD - 74A
31573	GILLINGHAM - 73D	GILLINGHAM - 73D	GILLINGHAM - 73D	GILLINGHAM - 73D	GILLINGHAM - 73D	GILLINGHAM - 73D	GILLINGHAM - 73D
31575	STEWARTS LANE - 73A	STEWARTS LANE - 73A	STEWARTS LANE - 73A	STEWARTS LANE - 73A	STEWARTS LANE - 73A	STEWARTS LANE - 73A	STEWARTS LANE - 73A
31576	STEWARTS LANE - 73A	STEWARTS LANE - 73A	STEWARTS LANE - 73A	STEWARTS LANE - 73A	STEWARTS LANE - 73A	STEWARTS LANE - 73A	STEWARTS LANE - 73A
31578	STEWARTS LANE - 73A	STEWARTS LANE - 73A	STEWARTS LANE - 73A	STEWARTS LANE - 73A	STEWARTS LANE - 73A	STEWARTS LANE - 73A	STEWARTS LANE - 73A
31579	GILLINGHAM - 73D	GILLINGHAM - 73D	GILLINGHAM - 73D	GILLINGHAM - 73D	GILLINGHAM - 73D	GILLINGHAM - 73D	GILLINGHAM - 73D
31580	TONBRIDGE - 74D	STEWARTS LANE - 73A	STEWARTS LANE - 73A	STEWARTS LANE - 73A	STEWARTS LANE - 73A	STEWARTS LANE - 73A	STEWARTS LANE - 73A
31581	HITHER GREEN - 73C	STEWARTS LANE - 73A	STEWARTS LANE - 73A	STEWARTS LANE - 73A	STEWARTS LANE - 73A	STEWARTS LANE - 73A	STEWARTS LANE - 73A
31582	STEWARTS LANE - 73A	STEWARTS LANE - 73A	STEWARTS LANE - 73A	STEWARTS LANE - 73A	STEWARTS LANE - 73A	STEWARTS LANE - 73A	STEWARTS LANE - 73A
31583	GILLINGHAM - 73D	STEWARTS LANE - 73A	STEWARTS LANE - 73A	STEWARTS LANE - 73A	STEWARTS LANE - 73A	STEWARTS LANE - 73A	STEWARTS LANE - 73A
31584	B.ARMS - 73B	STEWARTS LANE - 73A	STEWARTS LANE - 73A	STEWARTS LANE - 73A	STEWARTS LANE - 73A	STEWARTS LANE - 73A	STEWARTS LANE - 73A
31585	GILLINGHAM - 73D	GILLINGHAM - 73D	TONBRIDGE - 74D	TONBRIDGE - 74D	TONBRIDGE - 74D	TONBRIDGE - 74D	TONBRIDGE - 74D
31588	GILLINGHAM - 73D	GILLINGHAM - 73D	GILLINGHAM - 73D	GILLINGHAM - 73D	GILLINGHAM - 73D	GILLINGHAM - 73D	GILLINGHAM - 73D
31589	ASHFORD - 74A	TONBRIDGE - 74D	TONBRIDGE - 74D	ASHFORD - 74A	ASHFORD - 74A	ASHFORD - 74A	ASHFORD - 74A
31590	TONBRIDGE - 74D	TONBRIDGE - 74D	TONBRIDGE - 74D	TONBRIDGE - 74D	TONBRIDGE - 74D	TONBRIDGE - 74D	TONBRIDGE - 74D
31592	RAMSGATE - 74B	RAMSGATE - 74B	RAMSGATE - 74B	RAMSGATE - 74B	RAMSGATE - 74B	RAMSGATE - 74B	RAMSGATE - 74B
31593	TONBRIDGE - 74D	TONBRIDGE - 74D	GILLINGHAM - 73D	GILLINGHAM - 73D	GILLINGHAM - 73D	GILLINGHAM - 73D	GILLINGHAM - 73D
31681	STEWARTS LANE - 73A	STEWARTS LANE - 73A	STEWARTS LANE - 73A	STEWARTS LANE - 73A	STEWARTS LANE - 73A	STEWARTS LANE - 73A	STEWARTS LANE - 73A
31682	GILLINGHAM - 73D	GILLINGHAM - 73D	GILLINGHAM - 73D	GILLINGHAM - 73D	GILLINGHAM - 73D	GILLINGHAM - 73D	GILLINGHAM - 73D
31683	STEWARTS LANE - 73A	STEWARTS LANE - 73A	STEWARTS LANE - 73A	STEWARTS LANE - 73A	STEWARTS LANE - 73A	STEWARTS LANE - 73A	STEWARTS LANE - 73A
31684	TONBRIDGE - 74D	TONBRIDGE - 74D	GILLINGHAM - 73D	GILLINGHAM - 73D	GILLINGHAM - 73D	GILLINGHAM - 73D	GILLINGHAM - 73D
31686	TONBRIDGE - 74D	TONBRIDGE - 74D	GILLINGHAM - 73D	GILLINGHAM - 73D	GILLINGHAM - 73D	GILLINGHAM - 73D	HITHER GREEN - 73C
31687	HITHER GREEN - 73C	HITHER GREEN - 73C	HITHER GREEN - 73C	HITHER GREEN - 73C	HITHER GREEN - 73C	HITHER GREEN - 73C	HITHER GREEN - 73C
31688	HITHER GREEN - 73C	HITHER GREEN - 73C	HITHER GREEN - 73C	HITHER GREEN - 73C	HITHER GREEN - 73C	HITHER GREEN - 73C	HITHER GREEN - 73C
31689	HITHER GREEN - 73C	HITHER GREEN - 73C	HITHER GREEN - 73C	HITHER GREEN - 73C	HITHER GREEN - 73C	HITHER GREEN - 73C	HITHER GREEN - 73C
31690	RAMSGATE - 74B	RAMSGATE - 74B	RAMSGATE - 74B	RAMSGATE - 74B	RAMSGATE - 74B	RAMSGATE - 74B	HITHER GREEN - 73C
31691	FAVERSHAM - 73E	HITHER GREEN - 73C	HITHER GREEN - 73C	HITHER GREEN - 73C	HITHER GREEN - 73C	HITHER GREEN - 73C	HITHER GREEN - 73C
31692	FAVERSHAM - 73E	HITHER GREEN - 73C	HITHER GREEN - 73C	HITHER GREEN - 73C	HITHER GREEN - 73C	HITHER GREEN - 73C	HITHER GREEN - 73C
31693	GILLINGHAM - 73D	HITHER GREEN - 73C	HITHER GREEN - 73C	HITHER GREEN - 73C	HITHER GREEN - 73C	HITHER GREEN - 73C	HITHER GREEN - 73C
31694	HITHER GREEN - 73C	HITHER GREEN - 73C	HITHER GREEN - 73C	HITHER GREEN - 73C	HITHER GREEN - 73C	HITHER GREEN - 73C	HITHER GREEN - 73C
31695	HITHER GREEN - 73C	HITHER GREEN - 73C	HITHER GREEN - 73C	HITHER GREEN - 73C	HITHER GREEN - 73C	HITHER GREEN - 73C	HITHER GREEN - 73C
31711	ASHFORD - 74A	ASHFORD - 74A	ASHFORD - 74A	ASHFORD - 74A	ASHFORD - 74A	ASHFORD - 74A	ASHFORD - 74A
31712	GILLINGHAM - 73D	GILLINGHAM - 73D	GILLINGHAM - 73D	GILLINGHAM - 73D	GILLINGHAM - 73D	GILLINGHAM - 73D	GILLINGHAM - 73D
31713	GILLINGHAM - 73D	GILLINGHAM - 73D	GILLINGHAM - 73D	GILLINGHAM - 73D	GILLINGHAM - 73D	GILLINGHAM - 73D	GILLINGHAM - 73D
31714	STEWARTS LANE - 73A	FAVERSHAM - 73E	FAVERSHAM - 73E	FAVERSHAM - 73E	FAVERSHAM - 73E	FAVERSHAM - 73E	FAVERSHAM - 73E
31715	FAVERSHAM - 73E	FAVERSHAM - 73E	FAVERSHAM - 73E	FAVERSHAM - 73E	FAVERSHAM - 73E	FAVERSHAM - 73E	FAVERSHAM - 73E
31716	STEWARTS LANE - 73A	TONBRIDGE - 74D	TONBRIDGE - 74D	TONBRIDGE - 74D	TONBRIDGE - 74D	TONBRIDGE - 74D	TONBRIDGE - 74D
31717	STEWARTS LANE - 73A	TONBRIDGE - 74D	TONBRIDGE - 74D	TONBRIDGE - 74D	TONBRIDGE - 74D	TONBRIDGE - 74D	TONBRIDGE - 74D
31718	STEWARTS LANE - 73A	STEWARTS LANE - 73A	STEWARTS LANE - 73A	STEWARTS LANE - 73A	STEWARTS LANE - 73A	STEWARTS LANE - 73A	STEWARTS LANE - 73A
31719	STEWARTS LANE - 73A	STEWARTS LANE - 73A	STEWARTS LANE - 73A	STEWARTS LANE - 73A	STEWARTS LANE - 73A	STEWARTS LANE - 73A	STEWARTS LANE - 73A
31720	HITHER GREEN - 73C	HITHER GREEN - 73C	HITHER GREEN - 73C	HITHER GREEN - 73C	HITHER GREEN - 73C	HITHER GREEN - 73C	HITHER GREEN - 73C
31721	ASHFORD - 74A	ASHFORD - 74A	ASHFORD - 74A	ASHFORD - 74A	ASHFORD - 74A	ASHFORD - 74A	ASHFORD - 74A
31722	STEWARTS LANE - 73A	STEWARTS LANE - 73A	STEWARTS LANE - 73A	STEWARTS LANE - 73A	STEWARTS LANE - 73A	STEWARTS LANE - 73A	STEWARTS LANE - 73A
31723	B.ARMS - 73B	B.ARMS - 73B	B.ARMS - 73B	B.ARMS - 73B	B.ARMS - 73B	B.ARMS - 73B	B.ARMS - 73B
31724	GILLINGHAM - 73D	GILLINGHAM - 73D	GILLINGHAM - 73D	GILLINGHAM - 73D	GILLINGHAM - 73D	GILLINGHAM - 73D	GILLINGHAM - 73D
31725	B.ARMS - 73B	B.ARMS - 73B	B.ARMS - 73B	B.ARMS - 73B	B.ARMS - 73B	B.ARMS - 73B	B.ARMS - 73B

loco	Sep-52	Dec-52	Mar-53	May-53	Jul-53	Sep-53	Nov-53
				C 0-6-0 (1900)			
31004	RAMSGATE - 74B	RAMSGATE - 74B	RAMSGATE - 74B	RAMSGATE - 74B	RAMSGATE - 74B	RAMSGATE - 74B	RAMSGATE - 74B
31018	HITHER GREEN - 73C	HITHER GREEN - 73C	HITHER GREEN - 73C	HITHER GREEN - 73C	HITHER GREEN - 73C	HITHER GREEN - 73C	HITHER GREEN - 73C
31033	B.ARMS - 73B	B.ARMS - 73B	B.ARMS - 73B	B.ARMS - 73B	B.ARMS - 73B	B.ARMS - 73B	B.ARMS - 73B
31037	ST LEONARDS - 74E	FAVERSHAM - 73E	FAVERSHAM - 73E	FAVERSHAM - 73E	FAVERSHAM - 73E	FAVERSHAM - 73E	FAVERSHAM - 73E
31038	TONBRIDGE - 74D	TONBRIDGE - 74D	TONBRIDGE - 74D	TONBRIDGE - 74D	TONBRIDGE - 74D	TONBRIDGE - 74D	TONBRIDGE - 74D
31054	HITHER GREEN - 73C	HITHER GREEN - 73C	HITHER GREEN - 73C	HITHER GREEN - 73C	HITHER GREEN - 73C	HITHER GREEN - 73C	HITHER GREEN - 73C
31059	HITHER GREEN - 73C	HITHER GREEN - 73C	HITHER GREEN - 73C	HITHER GREEN - 73C	HITHER GREEN - 73C	HITHER GREEN - 73C	HITHER GREEN - 73C
31061	HITHER GREEN - 73C	HITHER GREEN - 73C	HITHER GREEN - 73C	HITHER GREEN - 73C	HITHER GREEN - 73C	HITHER GREEN - 73C	HITHER GREEN - 73C
31063	HITHER GREEN - 73C	HITHER GREEN - 73C	HITHER GREEN - 73C	HITHER GREEN - 73C	HITHER GREEN - 73C	HITHER GREEN - 73C	HITHER GREEN - 73C
31068	B.ARMS - 73B	B.ARMS - 73B	B.ARMS - 73B	B.ARMS - 73B	B.ARMS - 73B	B.ARMS - 73B	B.ARMS - 73B
31071	B.ARMS - 73B	B.ARMS - 73B	B.ARMS - 73B	B.ARMS - 73B	B.ARMS - 73B	B.ARMS - 73B	B.ARMS - 73B
31086	GILLINGHAM - 73D	GILLINGHAM - 73D	GILLINGHAM - 73D	GILLINGHAM - 73D	GILLINGHAM - 73D	GILLINGHAM - 73D	GILLINGHAM - 73D
31090	GILLINGHAM - 73D	GILLINGHAM - 73D	GILLINGHAM - 73D	GILLINGHAM - 73D	W/D	W/D	W/D
31102	B.ARMS - 73B	B.ARMS - 73B	B.ARMS - 73B	B.ARMS - 73B	B.ARMS - 73B	B.ARMS - 73B	B.ARMS - 73B
31112	GILLINGHAM - 73D	GILLINGHAM - 73D	GILLINGHAM - 73D	GILLINGHAM - 73D	GILLINGHAM - 73D	GILLINGHAM - 73D	GILLINGHAM - 73D
31113	DOVER - 74C	DOVER - 74C	DOVER - 74C	DOVER - 74C	DOVER - 74C	DOVER - 74C	DOVER - 74C
31150	DOVER - 74C	DOVER - 74C	DOVER - 74C	DOVER - 74C	DOVER - 74C	DOVER - 74C	DOVER - 74C
31191	DOVER - 74C	DOVER - 74C	DOVER - 74C	DOVER - 74C	DOVER - 74C	DOVER - 74C	DOVER - 74C
31218	ASHFORD - 74A	ASHFORD - 74A	ASHFORD - 74A	ASHFORD - 74A	ASHFORD - 74A	ASHFORD - 74A	ASHFORD - 74A
31219	TONBRIDGE - 74D	TONBRIDGE - 74D	TONBRIDGE - 74D	TONBRIDGE - 74D	TONBRIDGE - 74D	TONBRIDGE - 74D	TONBRIDGE - 74D
31221	GILLINGHAM - 73D	GILLINGHAM - 73D	GILLINGHAM - 73D	GILLINGHAM - 73D	GILLINGHAM - 73D	GILLINGHAM - 73D	GILLINGHAM - 73D
31223	GILLINGHAM - 73D	GILLINGHAM - 73D	GILLINGHAM - 73D	GILLINGHAM - 73D	GILLINGHAM - 73D	GILLINGHAM - 73D	GILLINGHAM - 73D
31225	GILLINGHAM - 73D	GILLINGHAM - 73D	GILLINGHAM - 73D	GILLINGHAM - 73D	GILLINGHAM - 73D	GILLINGHAM - 73D	GILLINGHAM - 73D
31227	B.ARMS - 73B	B.ARMS - 73B	B.ARMS - 73B	B.ARMS - 73B	B.ARMS - 73B	B.ARMS - 73B	B.ARMS - 73B
31229	FAVERSHAM - 73E	FAVERSHAM - 73E	FAVERSHAM - 73E	FAVERSHAM - 73E	FAVERSHAM - 73E	FAVERSHAM - 73E	FAVERSHAM - 73E
31234	STEWARTS LANE - 73A	STEWARTS LANE - 73A	STEWARTS LANE - 73A	GILLINGHAM - 73D	W/D	W/D	W/D
31242	FAVERSHAM - 73E	FAVERSHAM - 73E	FAVERSHAM - 73E	FAVERSHAM - 73E	FAVERSHAM - 73E	FAVERSHAM - 73E	FAVERSHAM - 73E
31243	DOVER - 74C	DOVER - 74C	DOVER - 74C	DOVER - 74C	DOVER - 74C	DOVER - 74C	DOVER - 74C
31244	TONBRIDGE - 74D	TONBRIDGE - 74D	TONBRIDGE - 74D	TONBRIDGE - 74D	TONBRIDGE - 74D	TONBRIDGE - 74D	TONBRIDGE - 74D
31245	RAMSGATE - 74B	RAMSGATE - 74B	RAMSGATE - 74B	RAMSGATE - 74B	RAMSGATE - 74B	RAMSGATE - 74B	RAMSGATE - 74B
31252	RAMSGATE - 74B	RAMSGATE - 74B	RAMSGATE - 74B	RAMSGATE - 74B	RAMSGATE - 74B	RAMSGATE - 74B	RAMSGATE - 74B
31253	FAVERSHAM - 73E	FAVERSHAM - 73E	FAVERSHAM - 73E	FAVERSHAM - 73E	FAVERSHAM - 73E	FAVERSHAM - 73E	FAVERSHAM - 73E
31255	FAVERSHAM - 73E	FAVERSHAM - 73E	FAVERSHAM - 73E	FAVERSHAM - 73E	FAVERSHAM - 73E	FAVERSHAM - 73E	FAVERSHAM - 73E
31256	FAVERSHAM - 73E	FAVERSHAM - 73E	FAVERSHAM - 73E	FAVERSHAM - 73E	FAVERSHAM - 73E	FAVERSHAM - 73E	FAVERSHAM - 73E
31260	FAVERSHAM - 73E	FAVERSHAM - 73E	FAVERSHAM - 73E	W/D	W/D	W/D	W/D
31267	GILLINGHAM - 73D	GILLINGHAM - 73D	GILLINGHAM - 73D	GILLINGHAM - 73D	GILLINGHAM - 73D	GILLINGHAM - 73D	GILLINGHAM - 73D
31268	FAVERSHAM - 73E	FAVERSHAM - 73E	FAVERSHAM - 73E	FAVERSHAM - 73E	FAVERSHAM - 73E	FAVERSHAM - 73E	FAVERSHAM - 73E
31270	HITHER GREEN - 73C	HITHER GREEN - 73C	HITHER GREEN - 73C	HITHER GREEN - 73C	HITHER GREEN - 73C	HITHER GREEN - 73C	HITHER GREEN - 73C
31271	RAMSGATE - 74B	RAMSGATE - 74B	RAMSGATE - 74B	RAMSGATE - 74B	RAMSGATE - 74B	RAMSGATE - 74B	RAMSGATE - 74B
31272	TONBRIDGE - 74D	TONBRIDGE - 74D	TONBRIDGE - 74D	TONBRIDGE - 74D	TONBRIDGE - 74D	TONBRIDGE - 74D	TONBRIDGE - 74D
31277	TONBRIDGE - 74D	TONBRIDGE - 74D	TONBRIDGE - 74D	TONBRIDGE - 74D	TONBRIDGE - 74D	TONBRIDGE - 74D	TONBRIDGE - 74D
31280	B.ARMS - 73B	B.ARMS - 73B	B.ARMS - 73B	B.ARMS - 73B	B.ARMS - 73B	B.ARMS - 73B	B.ARMS - 73B
31287	GILLINGHAM - 73D	GILLINGHAM - 73D	GILLINGHAM - 73D	GILLINGHAM - 73D	GILLINGHAM - 73D	GILLINGHAM - 73D	GILLINGHAM - 73D
31291	B.ARMS - 73B	B.ARMS - 73B	B.ARMS - 73B	W/D	W/D	W/D	W/D
31293	B.ARMS - 73B	B.ARMS - 73B	B.ARMS - 73B	B.ARMS - 73B	B.ARMS - 73B	B.ARMS - 73B	B.ARMS - 73B
31294	B.ARMS - 73B	B.ARMS - 73B	B.ARMS - 73B	B.ARMS - 73B	B.ARMS - 73B	B.ARMS - 73B	B.ARMS - 73B
31297	B.ARMS - 73B	B.ARMS - 73B	B.ARMS - 73B	B.ARMS - 73B	B.ARMS - 73B	B.ARMS - 73B	B.ARMS - 73B
31298	RAMSGATE - 74B	RAMSGATE - 74B	RAMSGATE - 74B	RAMSGATE - 74B	RAMSGATE - 74B	RAMSGATE - 74B	RAMSGATE - 74B
31317	DOVER - 74C	DOVER - 74C	DOVER - 74C	DOVER - 74C	DOVER - 74C	DOVER - 74C	DOVER - 74C
31461	FAVERSHAM - 73E	FAVERSHAM - 73E	FAVERSHAM - 73E	FAVERSHAM - 73E	FAVERSHAM - 73E	STEWARTS LANE - 73A	STEWARTS LANE - 73A
31480	HITHER GREEN - 73C	HITHER GREEN - 73C	HITHER GREEN - 73C	HITHER GREEN - 73C	HITHER GREEN - 73C	HITHER GREEN - 73C	HITHER GREEN - 73C
31481	FAVERSHAM - 73E	FAVERSHAM - 73E	FAVERSHAM - 73E	FAVERSHAM - 73E	FAVERSHAM - 73E	FAVERSHAM - 73E	FAVERSHAM - 73E
31486	HITHER GREEN - 73C	HITHER GREEN - 73C	HITHER GREEN - 73C	W/D	W/D	W/D	W/D
31495	FAVERSHAM - 73E	FAVERSHAM - 73E	FAVERSHAM - 73E	FAVERSHAM - 73E	FAVERSHAM - 73E	FAVERSHAM - 73E	FAVERSHAM - 73E
31498	GILLINGHAM - 73D	GILLINGHAM - 73D	GILLINGHAM - 73D	GILLINGHAM - 73D	GILLINGHAM - 73D	GILLINGHAM - 73D	GILLINGHAM - 73D
31508	B.ARMS - 73B	B.ARMS - 73B	B.ARMS - 73B	B.ARMS - 73B	B.ARMS - 73B	B.ARMS - 73B	B.ARMS - 73B
31510	GILLINGHAM - 73D	GILLINGHAM - 73D	GILLINGHAM - 73D	GILLINGHAM - 73D	GILLINGHAM - 73D	GILLINGHAM - 73D	GILLINGHAM - 73D
31513	ASHFORD - 74A	ASHFORD - 74A	ASHFORD - 74A	ASHFORD - 74A	ASHFORD - 74A	ASHFORD - 74A	ASHFORD - 74A
31572	ASHFORD - 74A	ASHFORD - 74A	ASHFORD - 74A	ASHFORD - 74A	ASHFORD - 74A	ASHFORD - 74A	ASHFORD - 74A
31573	GILLINGHAM - 73D	GILLINGHAM - 73D	GILLINGHAM - 73D	GILLINGHAM - 73D	GILLINGHAM - 73D	GILLINGHAM - 73D	GILLINGHAM - 73D
31575	STEWARTS LANE - 73A	STEWARTS LANE - 73A	STEWARTS LANE - 73A	STEWARTS LANE - 73A	STEWARTS LANE - 73A	STEWARTS LANE - 73A	STEWARTS LANE - 73A
31576	STEWARTS LANE - 73A	STEWARTS LANE - 73A	STEWARTS LANE - 73A	STEWARTS LANE - 73A	STEWARTS LANE - 73A	STEWARTS LANE - 73A	STEWARTS LANE - 73A
31578	STEWARTS LANE - 73A	STEWARTS LANE - 73A	STEWARTS LANE - 73A	STEWARTS LANE - 73A	STEWARTS LANE - 73A	STEWARTS LANE - 73A	STEWARTS LANE - 73A
31579	GILLINGHAM - 73D	GILLINGHAM - 73D	GILLINGHAM - 73D	GILLINGHAM - 73D	GILLINGHAM - 73D	GILLINGHAM - 73D	GILLINGHAM - 73D
31580	STEWARTS LANE - 73A	STEWARTS LANE - 73A	STEWARTS LANE - 73A	STEWARTS LANE - 73A	W/D	W/D	W/D
31581	STEWARTS LANE - 73A	STEWARTS LANE - 73A	STEWARTS LANE - 73A	STEWARTS LANE - 73A	STEWARTS LANE - 73A	STEWARTS LANE - 73A	STEWARTS LANE - 73A
31582	STEWARTS LANE - 73A	STEWARTS LANE - 73A	STEWARTS LANE - 73A	STEWARTS LANE - 73A	STEWARTS LANE - 73A	STEWARTS LANE - 73A	STEWARTS LANE - 73A
31583	STEWARTS LANE - 73A	STEWARTS LANE - 73A	STEWARTS LANE - 73A	STEWARTS LANE - 73A	STEWARTS LANE - 73A	STEWARTS LANE - 73A	STEWARTS LANE - 73A
31584	STEWARTS LANE - 73A	STEWARTS LANE - 73A	STEWARTS LANE - 73A	STEWARTS LANE - 73A	STEWARTS LANE - 73A	STEWARTS LANE - 73A	STEWARTS LANE - 73A
31585	TONBRIDGE - 74D	TONBRIDGE - 74D	TONBRIDGE - 74D	TONBRIDGE - 74D	TONBRIDGE - 74D	TONBRIDGE - 74D	TONBRIDGE - 74D
31588	GILLINGHAM - 73D	GILLINGHAM - 73D	GILLINGHAM - 73D	GILLINGHAM - 73D	GILLINGHAM - 73D	GILLINGHAM - 73D	GILLINGHAM - 73D
31589	ASHFORD - 74A	ASHFORD - 74A	ASHFORD - 74A	ASHFORD - 74A	ASHFORD - 74A	ASHFORD - 74A	ASHFORD - 74A
31590	TONBRIDGE - 74D	TONBRIDGE - 74D	TONBRIDGE - 74D	TONBRIDGE - 74D	TONBRIDGE - 74D	TONBRIDGE - 74D	TONBRIDGE - 74D
31592	RAMSGATE - 74B	RAMSGATE - 74B	RAMSGATE - 74B	RAMSGATE - 74B	RAMSGATE - 74B	RAMSGATE - 74B	RAMSGATE - 74B
31593	GILLINGHAM - 73D	GILLINGHAM - 73D	GILLINGHAM - 73D	GILLINGHAM - 73D	GILLINGHAM - 73D	GILLINGHAM - 73D	GILLINGHAM - 73D
31681	STEWARTS LANE - 73A	STEWARTS LANE - 73A	STEWARTS LANE - 73A	STEWARTS LANE - 73A	STEWARTS LANE - 73A	STEWARTS LANE - 73A	STEWARTS LANE - 73A
31682	GILLINGHAM - 73D	GILLINGHAM - 73D	GILLINGHAM - 73D	GILLINGHAM - 73D	GILLINGHAM - 73D	GILLINGHAM - 73D	GILLINGHAM - 73D
31683	STEWARTS LANE - 73A	STEWARTS LANE - 73A	STEWARTS LANE - 73A	STEWARTS LANE - 73A	STEWARTS LANE - 73A	STEWARTS LANE - 73A	STEWARTS LANE - 73A
31684	GILLINGHAM - 73D	GILLINGHAM - 73D	GILLINGHAM - 73D	GILLINGHAM - 73D	GILLINGHAM - 73D	GILLINGHAM - 73D	GILLINGHAM - 73D
31686	HITHER GREEN - 73C	HITHER GREEN - 73C	HITHER GREEN - 73C	HITHER GREEN - 73C	HITHER GREEN - 73C	HITHER GREEN - 73C	HITHER GREEN - 73C
31687	HITHER GREEN - 73C	HITHER GREEN - 73C	HITHER GREEN - 73C	HITHER GREEN - 73C	HITHER GREEN - 73C	HITHER GREEN - 73C	HITHER GREEN - 73C
31688	HITHER GREEN - 73C	HITHER GREEN - 73C	HITHER GREEN - 73C	HITHER GREEN - 73C	HITHER GREEN - 73C	HITHER GREEN - 73C	HITHER GREEN - 73C
31689	HITHER GREEN - 73C	HITHER GREEN - 73C	HITHER GREEN - 73C	HITHER GREEN - 73C	HITHER GREEN - 73C	HITHER GREEN - 73C	HITHER GREEN - 73C
31690	HITHER GREEN - 73C	HITHER GREEN - 73C	HITHER GREEN - 73C	HITHER GREEN - 73C	HITHER GREEN - 73C	HITHER GREEN - 73C	HITHER GREEN - 73C
31691	HITHER GREEN - 73C	HITHER GREEN - 73C	HITHER GREEN - 73C	HITHER GREEN - 73C	HITHER GREEN - 73C	HITHER GREEN - 73C	HITHER GREEN - 73C
31692	HITHER GREEN - 73C	HITHER GREEN - 73C	HITHER GREEN - 73C	HITHER GREEN - 73C	HITHER GREEN - 73C	HITHER GREEN - 73C	HITHER GREEN - 73C
31693	HITHER GREEN - 73C	HITHER GREEN - 73C	HITHER GREEN - 73C	HITHER GREEN - 73C	HITHER GREEN - 73C	HITHER GREEN - 73C	HITHER GREEN - 73C
31694	HITHER GREEN - 73C	HITHER GREEN - 73C	HITHER GREEN - 73C	HITHER GREEN - 73C	HITHER GREEN - 73C	HITHER GREEN - 73C	HITHER GREEN - 73C
31695	HITHER GREEN - 73C	HITHER GREEN - 73C	HITHER GREEN - 73C	HITHER GREEN - 73C	HITHER GREEN - 73C	HITHER GREEN - 73C	HITHER GREEN - 73C
31711	ASHFORD - 74A	ASHFORD - 74A	ASHFORD - 74A	ASHFORD - 74A	ASHFORD - 74A	ASHFORD - 74A	ASHFORD - 74A
31712	GILLINGHAM - 73D	GILLINGHAM - 73D	GILLINGHAM - 73D	GILLINGHAM - 73D	GILLINGHAM - 73D	GILLINGHAM - 73D	GILLINGHAM - 73D
31713	GILLINGHAM - 73D	GILLINGHAM - 73D	GILLINGHAM - 73D	GILLINGHAM - 73D	GILLINGHAM - 73D	GILLINGHAM - 73D	GILLINGHAM - 73D
31714	FAVERSHAM - 73E	FAVERSHAM - 73E	FAVERSHAM - 73E	FAVERSHAM - 73E	FAVERSHAM - 73E	FAVERSHAM - 73E	FAVERSHAM - 73E
31715	FAVERSHAM - 73E	FAVERSHAM - 73E	FAVERSHAM - 73E	FAVERSHAM - 73E	FAVERSHAM - 73E	FAVERSHAM - 73E	FAVERSHAM - 73E
31716	TONBRIDGE - 74D	TONBRIDGE - 74D	TONBRIDGE - 74D	TONBRIDGE - 74D	TONBRIDGE - 74D	TONBRIDGE - 74D	TONBRIDGE - 74D
31717	TONBRIDGE - 74D	TONBRIDGE - 74D	TONBRIDGE - 74D	TONBRIDGE - 74D	TONBRIDGE - 74D	TONBRIDGE - 74D	TONBRIDGE - 74D
31718	STEWARTS LANE - 73A	STEWARTS LANE - 73A	STEWARTS LANE - 73A	STEWARTS LANE - 73A	STEWARTS LANE - 73A	STEWARTS LANE - 73A	STEWARTS LANE - 73A
31719	STEWARTS LANE - 73A	STEWARTS LANE - 73A	STEWARTS LANE - 73A	STEWARTS LANE - 73A	STEWARTS LANE - 73A	STEWARTS LANE - 73A	STEWARTS LANE - 73A
31720	HITHER GREEN - 73C	HITHER GREEN - 73C	HITHER GREEN - 73C	HITHER GREEN - 73C	HITHER GREEN - 73C	HITHER GREEN - 73C	HITHER GREEN - 73C
31721	ASHFORD - 74A	ST LEONARDS - 74E	ST LEONARDS - 74E	ST LEONARDS - 74E	ST LEONARDS - 74E	ST LEONARDS - 74E	ST LEONARDS - 74E
31722	STEWARTS LANE - 73A	STEWARTS LANE - 73A	STEWARTS LANE - 73A	STEWARTS LANE - 73A	STEWARTS LANE - 73A	STEWARTS LANE - 73A	STEWARTS LANE - 73A
31723	B.ARMS - 73B	B.ARMS - 73B	B.ARMS - 73B	B.ARMS - 73B	B.ARMS - 73B	B.ARMS - 73B	B.ARMS - 73B
31724	GILLINGHAM - 73D	GILLINGHAM - 73D	GILLINGHAM - 73D	GILLINGHAM - 73D	GILLINGHAM - 73D	GILLINGHAM - 73D	GILLINGHAM - 73D
31725	B.ARMS - 73B	B.ARMS - 73B	B.ARMS - 73B	B.ARMS - 73B	B.ARMS - 73B	B.ARMS - 73B	B.ARMS - 73B

loco	Jan-54	Mar-54	May-54	Jun-54	Aug-54	Oct-54	Dec-54
				C 0-6-0 (1900)			
31004 RAMSGATE - 74B	RAMSGATE - 74B	RAMSGATE - 74B	RAMSGATE - 74B	RAMSGATE - 74B	RAMSGATE - 74B	RAMSGATE - 74B
31018 HITHER GREEN - 73C	HITHER GREEN - 73C	HITHER GREEN - 73C	HITHER GREEN - 73C	HITHER GREEN - 73C	HITHER GREEN - 73C	HITHER GREEN - 73C
31033 B ARMS - 73B	B ARMS - 73B	B ARMS - 73B	B ARMS - 73B	B ARMS - 73B	B ARMS - 73B	B ARMS - 73B
31037 ASHFORD - 74A	ASHFORD - 74A	ASHFORD - 74A	ASHFORD - 74A	ASHFORD - 74A	ASHFORD - 74A	ASHFORD - 74A
31038 TONBRIDGE - 74D	W/D	W/D	W/D	W/D	W/D	W/D
31054 HITHER GREEN - 73C	HITHER GREEN - 73C	HITHER GREEN - 73C	HITHER GREEN - 73C	HITHER GREEN - 73C	HITHER GREEN - 73C	HITHER GREEN - 73C
31059 HITHER GREEN - 73C	HITHER GREEN - 73C	HITHER GREEN - 73C	HITHER GREEN - 73C	HITHER GREEN - 73C	HITHER GREEN - 73C	HITHER GREEN - 73C
31061 HITHER GREEN - 73C	HITHER GREEN - 73C	HITHER GREEN - 73C	HITHER GREEN - 73C	HITHER GREEN - 73C	HITHER GREEN - 73C	HITHER GREEN - 73C
31063 HITHER GREEN - 73C	HITHER GREEN - 73C	HITHER GREEN - 73C	HITHER GREEN - 73C	HITHER GREEN - 73C	HITHER GREEN - 73C	HITHER GREEN - 73C
31068 B ARMS - 73B	B ARMS - 73B	B ARMS - 73B	B ARMS - 73B	B ARMS - 73B	B ARMS - 73B	B ARMS - 73B
31071 B ARMS - 73B	B ARMS - 73B	B ARMS - 73B	B ARMS - 73B	B ARMS - 73B	B ARMS - 73B	B ARMS - 73B
31086 GILLINGHAM - 73D	GILLINGHAM - 73D	GILLINGHAM - 73D	GILLINGHAM - 73D	GILLINGHAM - 73D	GILLINGHAM - 73D	GILLINGHAM - 73D
31102 B ARMS - 73B	B ARMS - 73B	B ARMS - 73B	B ARMS - 73B	B ARMS - 73B	B ARMS - 73B	B ARMS - 73B
31112 GILLINGHAM - 73D	GILLINGHAM - 73D	GILLINGHAM - 73D	GILLINGHAM - 73D	GILLINGHAM - 73D	GILLINGHAM - 73D	GILLINGHAM - 73D
31113 DOVER - 74C	DOVER - 74C	DOVER - 74C	DOVER - 74C	DOVER - 74C	DOVER - 74C	DOVER - 74C
31150 DOVER - 74C	DOVER - 74C	DOVER - 74C	DOVER - 74C	DOVER - 74C	DOVER - 74C	DOVER - 74C
31191 DOVER - 74C	DOVER - 74C	DOVER - 74C	DOVER - 74C	DOVER - 74C	DOVER - 74C	DOVER - 74C
31218 ASHFORD - 74A	ASHFORD - 74A	ASHFORD - 74A	ASHFORD - 74A	ASHFORD - 74A	ASHFORD - 74A	ASHFORD - 74A
31219 ASHFORD - 74A	ASHFORD - 74A	ASHFORD - 74A	ASHFORD - 74A	ASHFORD - 74A	ASHFORD - 74A	ASHFORD - 74A
31221 STEWARTS LANE - 73A	STEWARTS LANE - 73A	STEWARTS LANE - 73A	STEWARTS LANE - 73A	STEWARTS LANE - 73A	ASHFORD - 74A	ASHFORD - 74A
31223 ASHFORD - 74A	ASHFORD - 74A	ASHFORD - 74A	ASHFORD - 74A	ASHFORD - 74A	ASHFORD - 74A	ASHFORD - 74A
31225 B ARMS - 73B	B ARMS - 73B	B ARMS - 73B	B ARMS - 73B	B ARMS - 73B	B ARMS - 73B	B ARMS - 73B
31227 B ARMS - 73B	B ARMS - 73B	B ARMS - 73B	B ARMS - 73B	B ARMS - 73B	B ARMS - 73B	B ARMS - 73B
31229 FAVERSHAM - 73E	FAVERSHAM - 73E	FAVERSHAM - 73E	FAVERSHAM - 73E	FAVERSHAM - 73E	FAVERSHAM - 73E	FAVERSHAM - 73E
31242 B ARMS - 73B	GILLINGHAM - 73D	GILLINGHAM - 73D	GILLINGHAM - 73D	GILLINGHAM - 73D	GILLINGHAM - 73D	GILLINGHAM - 73D
31243 DOVER - 74C	DOVER - 74C	DOVER - 74C	DOVER - 74C	DOVER - 74C	DOVER - 74C	DOVER - 74C
31244 TONBRIDGE - 74D	TONBRIDGE - 74D	TONBRIDGE - 74D	TONBRIDGE - 74D	TONBRIDGE - 74D	TONBRIDGE - 74D	TONBRIDGE - 74D
31245 RAMSGATE - 74B	RAMSGATE - 74B	RAMSGATE - 74B	RAMSGATE - 74B	RAMSGATE - 74B	RAMSGATE - 74B	RAMSGATE - 74B
31252 RAMSGATE - 74B	RAMSGATE - 74B	RAMSGATE - 74B	RAMSGATE - 74B	RAMSGATE - 74B	RAMSGATE - 74B	RAMSGATE - 74B
31253 FAVERSHAM - 73E	FAVERSHAM - 73E	FAVERSHAM - 73E	FAVERSHAM - 73E	FAVERSHAM - 73E	FAVERSHAM - 73E	GUILDFORD - 70C
31255 FAVERSHAM - 73E	FAVERSHAM - 73E	FAVERSHAM - 73E	FAVERSHAM - 73E	FAVERSHAM - 73E	FAVERSHAM - 73E	FAVERSHAM - 73E
31256 FAVERSHAM - 73E	FAVERSHAM - 73E	FAVERSHAM - 73E	FAVERSHAM - 73E	FAVERSHAM - 73E	FAVERSHAM - 73E	FAVERSHAM - 73E
31267 B ARMS - 73B	B ARMS - 73B	B ARMS - 73B	B ARMS - 73B	B ARMS - 73B	B ARMS - 73B	B ARMS - 73B
31268 FAVERSHAM - 73E	FAVERSHAM - 73E	FAVERSHAM - 73E	FAVERSHAM - 73E	FAVERSHAM - 73E	FAVERSHAM - 73E	FAVERSHAM - 73E
31270 HITHER GREEN - 73C	HITHER GREEN - 73C	HITHER GREEN - 73C	HITHER GREEN - 73C	HITHER GREEN - 73C	HITHER GREEN - 73C	HITHER GREEN - 73C
31271 RAMSGATE - 74B	RAMSGATE - 74B	RAMSGATE - 74B	RAMSGATE - 74B	RAMSGATE - 74B	RAMSGATE - 74B	RAMSGATE - 74B
31272 TONBRIDGE - 74D	TONBRIDGE - 74D	TONBRIDGE - 74D	TONBRIDGE - 74D	TONBRIDGE - 74D	TONBRIDGE - 74D	TONBRIDGE - 74D
31277 TONBRIDGE - 74D	TONBRIDGE - 74D	TONBRIDGE - 74D	TONBRIDGE - 74D	TONBRIDGE - 74D	TONBRIDGE - 74D	TONBRIDGE - 74D
31280 B ARMS - 73B	B ARMS - 73B	B ARMS - 73B	B ARMS - 73B	B ARMS - 73B	B ARMS - 73B	B ARMS - 73B
31287 GILLINGHAM - 73D	GILLINGHAM - 73D	GILLINGHAM - 73D	GILLINGHAM - 73D	GILLINGHAM - 73D	GILLINGHAM - 73D	GILLINGHAM - 73D
31293 B ARMS - 73B	B ARMS - 73B	B ARMS - 73B	B ARMS - 73B	B ARMS - 73B	B ARMS - 73B	B ARMS - 73B
31294 B ARMS - 73B	B ARMS - 73B	B ARMS - 73B	B ARMS - 73B	B ARMS - 73B	B ARMS - 73B	B ARMS - 73B
31297 B ARMS - 73B	B ARMS - 73B	B ARMS - 73B	B ARMS - 73B	B ARMS - 73B	B ARMS - 73B	B ARMS - 73B
31298 RAMSGATE - 74B	RAMSGATE - 74B	RAMSGATE - 74B	RAMSGATE - 74B	RAMSGATE - 74B	RAMSGATE - 74B	RAMSGATE - 74B
31317 DOVER - 74C	DOVER - 74C	DOVER - 74C	DOVER - 74C	DOVER - 74C	DOVER - 74C	DOVER - 74C
31461 STEWARTS LANE - 73A	STEWARTS LANE - 73A	STEWARTS LANE - 73A	STEWARTS LANE - 73A	STEWARTS LANE - 73A	STEWARTS LANE - 73A	STEWARTS LANE - 73A
31480 HITHER GREEN - 73C	HITHER GREEN - 73C	HITHER GREEN - 73C	HITHER GREEN - 73C	HITHER GREEN - 73C	HITHER GREEN - 73C	HITHER GREEN - 73C
31481 FAVERSHAM - 73E	FAVERSHAM - 73E	FAVERSHAM - 73E	FAVERSHAM - 73E	FAVERSHAM - 73E	FAVERSHAM - 73E	FAVERSHAM - 73E
31495 FAVERSHAM - 73E	FAVERSHAM - 73E	FAVERSHAM - 73E	FAVERSHAM - 73E	FAVERSHAM - 73E	FAVERSHAM - 73E	FAVERSHAM - 73E
31498 HITHER GREEN - 73C	HITHER GREEN - 73C	HITHER GREEN - 73C	HITHER GREEN - 73C	HITHER GREEN - 73C	HITHER GREEN - 73C	HITHER GREEN - 73C
31508 FAVERSHAM - 73E	GILLINGHAM - 73D	GILLINGHAM - 73D	GILLINGHAM - 73D	GILLINGHAM - 73D	GILLINGHAM - 73D	GILLINGHAM - 73D
31510 GILLINGHAM - 73D	GILLINGHAM - 73D	GILLINGHAM - 73D	GILLINGHAM - 73D	GILLINGHAM - 73D	GILLINGHAM - 73D	GILLINGHAM - 73D
31513 ASHFORD - 74A	ASHFORD - 74A	ASHFORD - 74A	ASHFORD - 74A	ASHFORD - 74A	ASHFORD - 74A	ASHFORD - 74A
31572 ASHFORD - 74A	W/D	W/D	W/D	W/D	W/D	W/D
31573 GILLINGHAM - 73D	GILLINGHAM - 73D	GILLINGHAM - 73D	GILLINGHAM - 73D	GILLINGHAM - 73D	GILLINGHAM - 73D	GILLINGHAM - 73D
31575 STEWARTS LANE - 73A	STEWARTS LANE - 73A	STEWARTS LANE - 73A	STEWARTS LANE - 73A	STEWARTS LANE - 73A	STEWARTS LANE - 73A	STEWARTS LANE - 73A
31576 STEWARTS LANE - 73A	STEWARTS LANE - 73A	STEWARTS LANE - 73A	STEWARTS LANE - 73A	STEWARTS LANE - 73A	STEWARTS LANE - 73A	STEWARTS LANE - 73A
31578 STEWARTS LANE - 73A	STEWARTS LANE - 73A	STEWARTS LANE - 73A	STEWARTS LANE - 73A	STEWARTS LANE - 73A	STEWARTS LANE - 73A	STEWARTS LANE - 73A
31579 GILLINGHAM - 73D	GILLINGHAM - 73D	GILLINGHAM - 73D	GILLINGHAM - 73D	GILLINGHAM - 73D	GILLINGHAM - 73D	GILLINGHAM - 73D
31581 STEWARTS LANE - 73A	STEWARTS LANE - 73A	STEWARTS LANE - 73A	STEWARTS LANE - 73A	STEWARTS LANE - 73A	STEWARTS LANE - 73A	STEWARTS LANE - 73A
31582 STEWARTS LANE - 73A	STEWARTS LANE - 73A	STEWARTS LANE - 73A	STEWARTS LANE - 73A	STEWARTS LANE - 73A	STEWARTS LANE - 73A	STEWARTS LANE - 73A
31583 STEWARTS LANE - 73A	STEWARTS LANE - 73A	STEWARTS LANE - 73A	STEWARTS LANE - 73A	STEWARTS LANE - 73A	STEWARTS LANE - 73A	STEWARTS LANE - 73A
31584 STEWARTS LANE - 73A	STEWARTS LANE - 73A	STEWARTS LANE - 73A	STEWARTS LANE - 73A	STEWARTS LANE - 73A	STEWARTS LANE - 73A	STEWARTS LANE - 73A
31585 TONBRIDGE - 74D	TONBRIDGE - 74D	TONBRIDGE - 74D	TONBRIDGE - 74D	TONBRIDGE - 74D	TONBRIDGE - 74D	TONBRIDGE - 74D
31588 GILLINGHAM - 73D	GILLINGHAM - 73D	GILLINGHAM - 73D	GILLINGHAM - 73D	GILLINGHAM - 73D	GILLINGHAM - 73D	GILLINGHAM - 73D
31589 ASHFORD - 74A	ASHFORD - 74A	ASHFORD - 74A	ASHFORD - 74A	ASHFORD - 74A	ASHFORD - 74A	ASHFORD - 74A
31590 TONBRIDGE - 74D	TONBRIDGE - 74D	TONBRIDGE - 74D	TONBRIDGE - 74D	TONBRIDGE - 74D	TONBRIDGE - 74D	TONBRIDGE - 74D
31592 RAMSGATE - 74B	RAMSGATE - 74B	RAMSGATE - 74B	RAMSGATE - 74B	RAMSGATE - 74B	RAMSGATE - 74B	RAMSGATE - 74B
31593 GILLINGHAM - 73D	GILLINGHAM - 73D	GILLINGHAM - 73D	GILLINGHAM - 73D	GILLINGHAM - 73D	GILLINGHAM - 73D	GUILDFORD - 70C
31681 STEWARTS LANE - 73A	STEWARTS LANE - 73A	STEWARTS LANE - 73A	STEWARTS LANE - 73A	STEWARTS LANE - 73A	STEWARTS LANE - 73A	STEWARTS LANE - 73A
31682 GILLINGHAM - 73D	GILLINGHAM - 73D	GILLINGHAM - 73D	GILLINGHAM - 73D	GILLINGHAM - 73D	GILLINGHAM - 73D	GILLINGHAM - 73D
31683 STEWARTS LANE - 73A	STEWARTS LANE - 73A	STEWARTS LANE - 73A	STEWARTS LANE - 73A	STEWARTS LANE - 73A	STEWARTS LANE - 73A	STEWARTS LANE - 73A
31684 GILLINGHAM - 73D	GILLINGHAM - 73D	GILLINGHAM - 73D	GILLINGHAM - 73D	GILLINGHAM - 73D	GILLINGHAM - 73D	GILLINGHAM - 73D
31686 HITHER GREEN - 73C	HITHER GREEN - 73C	HITHER GREEN - 73C	HITHER GREEN - 73C	HITHER GREEN - 73C	HITHER GREEN - 73C	HITHER GREEN - 73C
31687 HITHER GREEN - 73C	HITHER GREEN - 73C	HITHER GREEN - 73C	HITHER GREEN - 73C	HITHER GREEN - 73C	HITHER GREEN - 73C	HITHER GREEN - 73C
31688 HITHER GREEN - 73C	HITHER GREEN - 73C	HITHER GREEN - 73C	HITHER GREEN - 73C	HITHER GREEN - 73C	HITHER GREEN - 73C	HITHER GREEN - 73C
31689 HITHER GREEN - 73C	HITHER GREEN - 73C	HITHER GREEN - 73C	HITHER GREEN - 73C	HITHER GREEN - 73C	HITHER GREEN - 73C	HITHER GREEN - 73C
31690 HITHER GREEN - 73C	HITHER GREEN - 73C	HITHER GREEN - 73C	HITHER GREEN - 73C	HITHER GREEN - 73C	HITHER GREEN - 73C	HITHER GREEN - 73C
31691 HITHER GREEN - 73C	HITHER GREEN - 73C	HITHER GREEN - 73C	HITHER GREEN - 73C	HITHER GREEN - 73C	HITHER GREEN - 73C	HITHER GREEN - 73C
31692 HITHER GREEN - 73C	HITHER GREEN - 73C	HITHER GREEN - 73C	HITHER GREEN - 73C	HITHER GREEN - 73C	HITHER GREEN - 73C	HITHER GREEN - 73C
31693 HITHER GREEN - 73C	HITHER GREEN - 73C	HITHER GREEN - 73C	HITHER GREEN - 73C	HITHER GREEN - 73C	HITHER GREEN - 73C	HITHER GREEN - 73C
31694 HITHER GREEN - 73C	HITHER GREEN - 73C	HITHER GREEN - 73C	HITHER GREEN - 73C	HITHER GREEN - 73C	HITHER GREEN - 73C	HITHER GREEN - 73C
31695 HITHER GREEN - 73C	HITHER GREEN - 73C	HITHER GREEN - 73C	HITHER GREEN - 73C	HITHER GREEN - 73C	HITHER GREEN - 73C	HITHER GREEN - 73C
31711 GILLINGHAM - 73D	GILLINGHAM - 73D	GILLINGHAM - 73D	GILLINGHAM - 73D	GILLINGHAM - 73D	GILLINGHAM - 73D	GILLINGHAM - 73D
31712 GILLINGHAM - 73D	GILLINGHAM - 73D	GILLINGHAM - 73D	GILLINGHAM - 73D	GILLINGHAM - 73D	GILLINGHAM - 73D	GILLINGHAM - 73D
31713 GILLINGHAM - 73D	GILLINGHAM - 73D	GILLINGHAM - 73D	GILLINGHAM - 73D	GILLINGHAM - 73D	GILLINGHAM - 73D	GILLINGHAM - 73D
31714 FAVERSHAM - 73E	FAVERSHAM - 73E	FAVERSHAM - 73E	FAVERSHAM - 73E	FAVERSHAM - 73E	FAVERSHAM - 73E	FAVERSHAM - 73E
31715 FAVERSHAM - 73E	FAVERSHAM - 73E	FAVERSHAM - 73E	FAVERSHAM - 73E	FAVERSHAM - 73E	FAVERSHAM - 73E	FAVERSHAM - 73E
31716 TONBRIDGE - 74D	TONBRIDGE - 74D	TONBRIDGE - 74D	TONBRIDGE - 74D	TONBRIDGE - 74D	TONBRIDGE - 74D	TONBRIDGE - 74D
31717 TONBRIDGE - 74D	TONBRIDGE - 74D	TONBRIDGE - 74D	TONBRIDGE - 74D	TONBRIDGE - 74D	TONBRIDGE - 74D	TONBRIDGE - 74D
31718 STEWARTS LANE - 73A	STEWARTS LANE - 73A	STEWARTS LANE - 73A	STEWARTS LANE - 73A	STEWARTS LANE - 73A	STEWARTS LANE - 73A	STEWARTS LANE - 73A
31719 STEWARTS LANE - 73A	STEWARTS LANE - 73A	STEWARTS LANE - 73A	STEWARTS LANE - 73A	STEWARTS LANE - 73A	STEWARTS LANE - 73A	STEWARTS LANE - 73A
31720 FAVERSHAM - 73E	FAVERSHAM - 73E	FAVERSHAM - 73E	FAVERSHAM - 73E	FAVERSHAM - 73E	FAVERSHAM - 73E	FAVERSHAM - 73E
31721 ST LEONARDS - 74E	ST LEONARDS - 74E	ST LEONARDS - 74E	ST LEONARDS - 74E	ST LEONARDS - 74E	ST LEONARDS - 74E	ST LEONARDS - 74E
31722 STEWARTS LANE - 73A	STEWARTS LANE - 73A	STEWARTS LANE - 73A	STEWARTS LANE - 73A	STEWARTS LANE - 73A	STEWARTS LANE - 73A	STEWARTS LANE - 73A
31723 B ARMS - 73B	B ARMS - 73B	B ARMS - 73B	B ARMS - 73B	B ARMS - 73B	B ARMS - 73B	B ARMS - 73B
31724 GILLINGHAM - 73D	GILLINGHAM - 73D	GILLINGHAM - 73D	GILLINGHAM - 73D	GILLINGHAM - 73D	GILLINGHAM - 73D	THREE BRIDGES - 75E
31725 B ARMS - 73B	B ARMS - 73B	B ARMS - 73B	B ARMS - 73B	B ARMS - 73B	B ARMS - 73B	HORSHAM - 75D

C 0-6-0 (1900)

loco	Feb-55	Apr-55	Jun-55	Aug-55	Sep-55	Nov-55	Dec-55
31004	RAMSGATE - 74B	RAMSGATE - 74B	RAMSGATE - 74B	RAMSGATE - 74B	RAMSGATE - 74B	RAMSGATE - 74B	RAMSGATE - 74B
31018	HITHER GREEN - 73C	HITHER GREEN - 73C	HITHER GREEN - 73C	HITHER GREEN - 73C	HITHER GREEN - 73C	HITHER GREEN - 73C	HITHER GREEN - 73C
31033	B ARMS - 73B	B ARMS - 73B	B ARMS - 73B	B ARMS - 73B	B ARMS - 73B	B ARMS - 73B	B ARMS - 73B
31037	ASHFORD - 74A	ASHFORD - 74A	ASHFORD - 74A	ASHFORD - 74A	ASHFORD - 74A	ASHFORD - 74A	ASHFORD - 74A
31054	HITHER GREEN - 73C	HITHER GREEN - 73C	HITHER GREEN - 73C	HITHER GREEN - 73C	HITHER GREEN - 73C	HITHER GREEN - 73C	HITHER GREEN - 73C
31059	HITHER GREEN - 73C	HITHER GREEN - 73C	HITHER GREEN - 73C	HITHER GREEN - 73C	HITHER GREEN - 73C	HITHER GREEN - 73C	HITHER GREEN - 73C
31061	HITHER GREEN - 73C	HITHER GREEN - 73C	HITHER GREEN - 73C	HITHER GREEN - 73C	HITHER GREEN - 73C	HITHER GREEN - 73C	HITHER GREEN - 73C
31063	HITHER GREEN - 73C	HITHER GREEN - 73C	HITHER GREEN - 73C	HITHER GREEN - 73C	HITHER GREEN - 73C	HITHER GREEN - 73C	HITHER GREEN - 73C
31068	B ARMS - 73B	B ARMS - 73B	B ARMS - 73B	B ARMS - 73B	B ARMS - 73B	B ARMS - 73B	B ARMS - 73B
31071	B ARMS - 73B	B ARMS - 73B	B ARMS - 73B	B ARMS - 73B	B ARMS - 73B	B ARMS - 73B	B ARMS - 73B
31086	GILLINGHAM - 73D	GILLINGHAM - 73D	GILLINGHAM - 73D	GILLINGHAM - 73D	GILLINGHAM - 73D	GILLINGHAM - 73D	GILLINGHAM - 73D
31102	B ARMS - 73B	B ARMS - 73B	B ARMS - 73B	B ARMS - 73B	B ARMS - 73B	B ARMS - 73B	B ARMS - 73B
31112	GILLINGHAM - 73D	GILLINGHAM - 73D	GILLINGHAM - 73D	GILLINGHAM - 73D	GILLINGHAM - 73D	GILLINGHAM - 73D	GILLINGHAM - 73D
31113	DOVER - 74C	DOVER - 74C	DOVER - 74C	DOVER - 74C	DOVER - 74C	DOVER - 74C	DOVER - 74C
31150	DOVER - 74C	DOVER - 74C	DOVER - 74C	DOVER - 74C	DOVER - 74C	DOVER - 74C	DOVER - 74C
31191	DOVER - 74C	DOVER - 74C	DOVER - 74C	DOVER - 74C	DOVER - 74C	DOVER - 74C	DOVER - 74C
31218	ASHFORD - 74A	ASHFORD - 74A	ASHFORD - 74A	ASHFORD - 74A	ASHFORD - 74A	ASHFORD - 74A	ASHFORD - 74A
31219	ASHFORD - 74A	ASHFORD - 74A	ASHFORD - 74A	ASHFORD - 74A	ASHFORD - 74A	ASHFORD - 74A	ASHFORD - 74A
31221	ASHFORD - 74A	ASHFORD - 74A	ASHFORD - 74A	ASHFORD - 74A	ASHFORD - 74A	ASHFORD - 74A	ASHFORD - 74A
31223	ASHFORD - 74A	ASHFORD - 74A	ASHFORD - 74A	ASHFORD - 74A	ASHFORD - 74A	ASHFORD - 74A	ASHFORD - 74A
31225	B ARMS - 73B	B ARMS - 73B	W/D	W/D	W/D	W/D	W/D
31227	B ARMS - 73B	B ARMS - 73B	B ARMS - 73B	B ARMS - 73B	B ARMS - 73B	B ARMS - 73B	B ARMS - 73B
31229	FAVERSHAM - 73E	FAVERSHAM - 73E	FAVERSHAM - 73E	FAVERSHAM - 73E	FAVERSHAM - 73E	FAVERSHAM - 73E	FAVERSHAM - 73E
31242	GILLINGHAM - 73D	GILLINGHAM - 73D	FAVERSHAM - 73E	FAVERSHAM - 73E	FAVERSHAM - 73E	FAVERSHAM - 73E	FAVERSHAM - 73E
31243	DOVER - 74C	DOVER - 74C	DOVER - 74C	DOVER - 74C	DOVER - 74C	DOVER - 74C	DOVER - 74C
31244	TONBRIDGE - 74D	TONBRIDGE - 74D	TONBRIDGE - 74D	TONBRIDGE - 74D	TONBRIDGE - 74D	TONBRIDGE - 74D	TONBRIDGE - 74D
31245	RAMSGATE - 74B	RAMSGATE - 74B	RAMSGATE - 74B	RAMSGATE - 74B	RAMSGATE - 74B	RAMSGATE - 74B	RAMSGATE - 74B
31252	RAMSGATE - 74B	RAMSGATE - 74B	RAMSGATE - 74B	RAMSGATE - 74B	RAMSGATE - 74B	RAMSGATE - 74B	RAMSGATE - 74B
31253	GUILDFORD - 70C	STEWARTS LANE - 73A	STEWARTS LANE - 73A	STEWARTS LANE - 73A	STEWARTS LANE - 73A	STEWARTS LANE - 73A	STEWARTS LANE - 73A
31255	FAVERSHAM - 73E	FAVERSHAM - 73E	FAVERSHAM - 73E	FAVERSHAM - 73E	FAVERSHAM - 73E	FAVERSHAM - 73E	FAVERSHAM - 73E
31256	FAVERSHAM - 73E	FAVERSHAM - 73E	FAVERSHAM - 73E	FAVERSHAM - 73E	FAVERSHAM - 73E	FAVERSHAM - 73E	FAVERSHAM - 73E
31267	B ARMS - 73B	B ARMS - 73B	B ARMS - 73B	B ARMS - 73B	B ARMS - 73B	B ARMS - 73B	B ARMS - 73B
31268	FAVERSHAM - 73E	FAVERSHAM - 73E	FAVERSHAM - 73E	FAVERSHAM - 73E	FAVERSHAM - 73E	FAVERSHAM - 73E	FAVERSHAM - 73E
31270	HITHER GREEN - 73C	HITHER GREEN - 73C	HITHER GREEN - 73C	HITHER GREEN - 73C	HITHER GREEN - 73C	HITHER GREEN - 73C	HITHER GREEN - 73C
31271	RAMSGATE - 74B	RAMSGATE - 74B	RAMSGATE - 74B	RAMSGATE - 74B	RAMSGATE - 74B	RAMSGATE - 74B	RAMSGATE - 74B
31272	TONBRIDGE - 74D	TONBRIDGE - 74D	TONBRIDGE - 74D	TONBRIDGE - 74D	TONBRIDGE - 74D	TONBRIDGE - 74D	TONBRIDGE - 74D
31277	TONBRIDGE - 74D	TONBRIDGE - 74D	TONBRIDGE - 74D	W/D	W/D	W/D	W/D
31280	B ARMS - 73B	B ARMS - 73B	B ARMS - 73B	B ARMS - 73B	B ARMS - 73B	B ARMS - 73B	B ARMS - 73B
31287	GILLINGHAM - 73D	GILLINGHAM - 73D	GILLINGHAM - 73D	GILLINGHAM - 73D	GILLINGHAM - 73D	GILLINGHAM - 73D	GILLINGHAM - 73D
31293	B ARMS - 73B	B ARMS - 73B	B ARMS - 73B	B ARMS - 73B	B ARMS - 73B	B ARMS - 73B	B ARMS - 73B
31294	B ARMS - 73B	B ARMS - 73B	B ARMS - 73B	B ARMS - 73B	W/D	W/D	W/D
31297	B ARMS - 73B	B ARMS - 73B	B ARMS - 73B	B ARMS - 73B	B ARMS - 73B	B ARMS - 73B	B ARMS - 73B
31298	RAMSGATE - 74B	RAMSGATE - 74B	RAMSGATE - 74B	RAMSGATE - 74B	RAMSGATE - 74B	RAMSGATE - 74B	RAMSGATE - 74B
31317	DOVER - 74C	DOVER - 74C	DOVER - 74C	DOVER - 74C	DOVER - 74C	DOVER - 74C	DOVER - 74C
31461	STEWARTS LANE - 73A	STEWARTS LANE - 73A	STEWARTS LANE - 73A	STEWARTS LANE - 73A	STEWARTS LANE - 73A	STEWARTS LANE - 73A	STEWARTS LANE - 73A
31480	HITHER GREEN - 73C	HITHER GREEN - 73C	HITHER GREEN - 73C	HITHER GREEN - 73C	HITHER GREEN - 73C	HITHER GREEN - 73C	HITHER GREEN - 73C
31481	FAVERSHAM - 73E	FAVERSHAM - 73E	FAVERSHAM - 73E	FAVERSHAM - 73E	FAVERSHAM - 73E	FAVERSHAM - 73E	FAVERSHAM - 73E
31495	FAVERSHAM - 73E	FAVERSHAM - 73E	FAVERSHAM - 73E	FAVERSHAM - 73E	FAVERSHAM - 73E	FAVERSHAM - 73E	FAVERSHAM - 73E
31498	HITHER GREEN - 73C	HITHER GREEN - 73C	HITHER GREEN - 73C	HITHER GREEN - 73C	HITHER GREEN - 73C	HITHER GREEN - 73C	HITHER GREEN - 73C
31508	GILLINGHAM - 73D	GILLINGHAM - 73D	GILLINGHAM - 73D	GILLINGHAM - 73D	GILLINGHAM - 73D	GILLINGHAM - 73D	GILLINGHAM - 73D
31510	GILLINGHAM - 73D	GILLINGHAM - 73D	GILLINGHAM - 73D	GILLINGHAM - 73D	GILLINGHAM - 73D	GILLINGHAM - 73D	GILLINGHAM - 73D
31573	GILLINGHAM - 73D	GILLINGHAM - 73D	GILLINGHAM - 73D	GILLINGHAM - 73D	GILLINGHAM - 73D	GILLINGHAM - 73D	GILLINGHAM - 73D
31575	STEWARTS LANE - 73A	STEWARTS LANE - 73A	STEWARTS LANE - 73A	STEWARTS LANE - 73A	STEWARTS LANE - 73A	STEWARTS LANE - 73A	STEWARTS LANE - 73A
31576	STEWARTS LANE - 73A	STEWARTS LANE - 73A	STEWARTS LANE - 73A	STEWARTS LANE - 73A	STEWARTS LANE - 73A	STEWARTS LANE - 73A	STEWARTS LANE - 73A
31578	STEWARTS LANE - 73A	STEWARTS LANE - 73A	STEWARTS LANE - 73A	STEWARTS LANE - 73A	STEWARTS LANE - 73A	STEWARTS LANE - 73A	STEWARTS LANE - 73A
31579	GILLINGHAM - 73D	GILLINGHAM - 73D	GILLINGHAM - 73D	GILLINGHAM - 73D	GILLINGHAM - 73D	GILLINGHAM - 73D	GILLINGHAM - 73D
31581	STEWARTS LANE - 73A	STEWARTS LANE - 73A	STEWARTS LANE - 73A	STEWARTS LANE - 73A	STEWARTS LANE - 73A	STEWARTS LANE - 73A	STEWARTS LANE - 73A
31582	STEWARTS LANE - 73A	STEWARTS LANE - 73A	STEWARTS LANE - 73A	STEWARTS LANE - 73A	STEWARTS LANE - 73A	STEWARTS LANE - 73A	STEWARTS LANE - 73A
31583	STEWARTS LANE - 73A	STEWARTS LANE - 73A	STEWARTS LANE - 73A	STEWARTS LANE - 73A	TONBRIDGE - 74D	TONBRIDGE - 74D	TONBRIDGE - 74D
31584	STEWARTS LANE - 73A	STEWARTS LANE - 73A	STEWARTS LANE - 73A	STEWARTS LANE - 73A	STEWARTS LANE - 73A	STEWARTS LANE - 73A	STEWARTS LANE - 73A
31585	TONBRIDGE - 74D	TONBRIDGE - 74D	TONBRIDGE - 74D	TONBRIDGE - 74D	TONBRIDGE - 74D	TONBRIDGE - 74D	TONBRIDGE - 74D
31588	GILLINGHAM - 73D	GILLINGHAM - 73D	GILLINGHAM - 73D	GILLINGHAM - 73D	GILLINGHAM - 73D	GILLINGHAM - 73D	GILLINGHAM - 73D
31589	ASHFORD - 74A	ASHFORD - 74A	ASHFORD - 74A	ASHFORD - 74A	ASHFORD - 74A	ASHFORD - 74A	ASHFORD - 74A
31590	TONBRIDGE - 74D	TONBRIDGE - 74D	TONBRIDGE - 74D	TONBRIDGE - 74D	TONBRIDGE - 74D	TONBRIDGE - 74D	TONBRIDGE - 74D
31592	RAMSGATE - 74B	RAMSGATE - 74B	RAMSGATE - 74B	RAMSGATE - 74B	RAMSGATE - 74B	RAMSGATE - 74B	RAMSGATE - 74B
31593	GUILDFORD - 70C	ASHFORD - 74A	ASHFORD - 74A	ASHFORD - 74A	ASHFORD - 74A	ASHFORD - 74A	ASHFORD - 74A
31681	STEWARTS LANE - 73A	STEWARTS LANE - 73A	STEWARTS LANE - 73A	STEWARTS LANE - 73A	STEWARTS LANE - 73A	STEWARTS LANE - 73A	STEWARTS LANE - 73A
31682	GILLINGHAM - 73D	GILLINGHAM - 73D	GILLINGHAM - 73D	GILLINGHAM - 73D	GILLINGHAM - 73D	GILLINGHAM - 73D	GILLINGHAM - 73D
31683	STEWARTS LANE - 73A	STEWARTS LANE - 73A	STEWARTS LANE - 73A	STEWARTS LANE - 73A	STEWARTS LANE - 73A	STEWARTS LANE - 73A	STEWARTS LANE - 73A
31684	GILLINGHAM - 73D	GILLINGHAM - 73D	GILLINGHAM - 73D	GILLINGHAM - 73D	GILLINGHAM - 73D	GILLINGHAM - 73D	GILLINGHAM - 73D
31686	HITHER GREEN - 73C	HITHER GREEN - 73C	HITHER GREEN - 73C	HITHER GREEN - 73C	HITHER GREEN - 73C	HITHER GREEN - 73C	HITHER GREEN - 73C
31687	HITHER GREEN - 73C	W/D	W/D	W/D	W/D	W/D	W/D
31688	HITHER GREEN - 73C	HITHER GREEN - 73C	HITHER GREEN - 73C	HITHER GREEN - 73C	HITHER GREEN - 73C	HITHER GREEN - 73C	HITHER GREEN - 73C
31689	HITHER GREEN - 73C	HITHER GREEN - 73C	HITHER GREEN - 73C	HITHER GREEN - 73C	HITHER GREEN - 73C	HITHER GREEN - 73C	HITHER GREEN - 73C
31690	HITHER GREEN - 73C	HITHER GREEN - 73C	HITHER GREEN - 73C	HITHER GREEN - 73C	HITHER GREEN - 73C	HITHER GREEN - 73C	HITHER GREEN - 73C
31691	HITHER GREEN - 73C	HITHER GREEN - 73C	HITHER GREEN - 73C	HITHER GREEN - 73C	HITHER GREEN - 73C	HITHER GREEN - 73C	HITHER GREEN - 73C
31692	HITHER GREEN - 73C	HITHER GREEN - 73C	HITHER GREEN - 73C	HITHER GREEN - 73C	HITHER GREEN - 73C	HITHER GREEN - 73C	HITHER GREEN - 73C
31693	HITHER GREEN - 73C	HITHER GREEN - 73C	HITHER GREEN - 73C	HITHER GREEN - 73C	HITHER GREEN - 73C	HITHER GREEN - 73C	HITHER GREEN - 73C
31694	HITHER GREEN - 73C	HITHER GREEN - 73C	HITHER GREEN - 73C	HITHER GREEN - 73C	HITHER GREEN - 73C	HITHER GREEN - 73C	HITHER GREEN - 73C
31695	HITHER GREEN - 73C	HITHER GREEN - 73C	HITHER GREEN - 73C	HITHER GREEN - 73C	HITHER GREEN - 73C	HITHER GREEN - 73C	HITHER GREEN - 73C
31711	GILLINGHAM - 73D	GILLINGHAM - 73D	GILLINGHAM - 73D	GILLINGHAM - 73D	GILLINGHAM - 73D	GILLINGHAM - 73D	GILLINGHAM - 73D
31712	GILLINGHAM - 73D	GILLINGHAM - 73D	GILLINGHAM - 73D	GILLINGHAM - 73D	GILLINGHAM - 73D	GILLINGHAM - 73D	GILLINGHAM - 73D
31713	GILLINGHAM - 73D	W/D	W/D	W/D	W/D	W/D	W/D
31714	FAVERSHAM - 73E	FAVERSHAM - 73E	FAVERSHAM - 73E	FAVERSHAM - 73E	FAVERSHAM - 73E	FAVERSHAM - 73E	FAVERSHAM - 73E
31715	FAVERSHAM - 73E	FAVERSHAM - 73E	FAVERSHAM - 73E	FAVERSHAM - 73E	FAVERSHAM - 73E	FAVERSHAM - 73E	FAVERSHAM - 73E
31716	TONBRIDGE - 74D	TONBRIDGE - 74D	TONBRIDGE - 74D	TONBRIDGE - 74D	TONBRIDGE - 74D	TONBRIDGE - 74D	TONBRIDGE - 74D
31717	TONBRIDGE - 74D	TONBRIDGE - 74D	TONBRIDGE - 74D	TONBRIDGE - 74D	TONBRIDGE - 74D	TONBRIDGE - 74D	TONBRIDGE - 74D
31718	STEWARTS LANE - 73A	STEWARTS LANE - 73A	STEWARTS LANE - 73A	STEWARTS LANE - 73A	W/D	W/D	W/D
31719	STEWARTS LANE - 73A	STEWARTS LANE - 73A	STEWARTS LANE - 73A	STEWARTS LANE - 73A	STEWARTS LANE - 73A	STEWARTS LANE - 73A	STEWARTS LANE - 73A
31720	FAVERSHAM - 73E	FAVERSHAM - 73E	FAVERSHAM - 73E	FAVERSHAM - 73E	FAVERSHAM - 73E	FAVERSHAM - 73E	FAVERSHAM - 73E
31721	ST LEONARDS - 74E	ST LEONARDS - 74E	ST LEONARDS - 74E	ST LEONARDS - 74E	ST LEONARDS - 74E	ST LEONARDS - 74E	ST LEONARDS - 74E
31722	STEWARTS LANE - 73A	STEWARTS LANE - 73A	STEWARTS LANE - 73A	STEWARTS LANE - 73A	STEWARTS LANE - 73A	STEWARTS LANE - 73A	STEWARTS LANE - 73A
31723	B ARMS - 73B	B ARMS - 73B	B ARMS - 73B	B ARMS - 73B	B ARMS - 73B	B ARMS - 73B	B ARMS - 73B
31724	BRIGHTON - 75A	BRIGHTON - 75A	BRIGHTON - 75A	BRIGHTON - 75A	BRIGHTON - 75A	BRIGHTON - 75A	BRIGHTON - 75A
31725	BRIGHTON - 75A	BRIGHTON - 75A	BRIGHTON - 75A	BRIGHTON - 75A	BRIGHTON - 75A	BRIGHTON - 75A	BRIGHTON - 75A

loco	Jan-56	Apr-56	May-56	Aug-56	Oct-56	Nov-56	Jan-57
				C 0-6-0 (1900)			
31004	RAMSGATE - 74B	RAMSGATE - 74B	RAMSGATE - 74B	RAMSGATE - 74B	RAMSGATE - 74B	RAMSGATE - 74B	RAMSGATE - 74B
31018	HITHER GREEN - 73C	HITHER GREEN - 73C	HITHER GREEN - 73C	HITHER GREEN - 73C	HITHER GREEN - 73C	HITHER GREEN - 73C	HITHER GREEN - 73C
31033	B.ARMS - 73B	B.ARMS - 73B	B.ARMS - 73B	B.ARMS - 73B	B.ARMS - 73B	B.ARMS - 73B	B.ARMS - 73B
31037	ASHFORD - 74A	ASHFORD - 74A	ASHFORD - 74A	ASHFORD - 74A	ASHFORD - 74A	ASHFORD - 74A	ASHFORD - 74A
31054	HITHER GREEN - 73C	HITHER GREEN - 73C	HITHER GREEN - 73C	HITHER GREEN - 73C	HITHER GREEN - 73C	HITHER GREEN - 73C	HITHER GREEN - 73C
31059	HITHER GREEN - 73C	HITHER GREEN - 73C	HITHER GREEN - 73C	HITHER GREEN - 73C	HITHER GREEN - 73C	HITHER GREEN - 73C	HITHER GREEN - 73C
31061	HITHER GREEN - 73C	HITHER GREEN - 73C	HITHER GREEN - 73C	HITHER GREEN - 73C	HITHER GREEN - 73C	HITHER GREEN - 73C	HITHER GREEN - 73C
31063	HITHER GREEN - 73C	W/D	W/D	W/D	W/D	W/D	W/D
31068	B.ARMS - 73B	B.ARMS - 73B	B.ARMS - 73B	B.ARMS - 73B	B.ARMS - 73B	B.ARMS - 73B	B.ARMS - 73B
31071	B.ARMS - 73B	B.ARMS - 73B	B.ARMS - 73B	B.ARMS - 73B	B.ARMS - 73B	B.ARMS - 73B	B.ARMS - 73B
31086	GILLINGHAM - 73D	GILLINGHAM - 73D	GILLINGHAM - 73D	GILLINGHAM - 73D	GILLINGHAM - 73D	GILLINGHAM - 73D	GILLINGHAM - 73D
31102	B.ARMS - 73B	B.ARMS - 73B	B.ARMS - 73B	B.ARMS - 73B	B.ARMS - 73B	B.ARMS - 73B	B.ARMS - 73B
31112	GILLINGHAM - 73D	GILLINGHAM - 73D	GILLINGHAM - 73D	GILLINGHAM - 73D	GILLINGHAM - 73D	GILLINGHAM - 73D	GILLINGHAM - 73D
31113	DOVER - 74C	DOVER - 74C	DOVER - 74C	DOVER - 74C	DOVER - 74C	DOVER - 74C	DOVER - 74C
31150	DOVER - 74C	DOVER - 74C	DOVER - 74C	DOVER - 74C	DOVER - 74C	DOVER - 74C	DOVER - 74C
31191	DOVER - 74C	DOVER - 74C	DOVER - 74C	DOVER - 74C	DOVER - 74C	DOVER - 74C	DOVER - 74C
31218	ASHFORD - 74A	ASHFORD - 74A	ASHFORD - 74A	ASHFORD - 74A	ASHFORD - 74A	ASHFORD - 74A	ASHFORD - 74A
31219	ASHFORD - 74A	ASHFORD - 74A	ASHFORD - 74A	ASHFORD - 74A	ASHFORD - 74A	ASHFORD - 74A	ASHFORD - 74A
31221	ASHFORD - 74A	ASHFORD - 74A	ASHFORD - 74A	ASHFORD - 74A	ASHFORD - 74A	ASHFORD - 74A	ASHFORD - 74A
31223	ASHFORD - 74A	ASHFORD - 74A	ASHFORD - 74A	ASHFORD - 74A	ASHFORD - 74A	ASHFORD - 74A	ASHFORD - 74A
31227	B.ARMS - 73B	B.ARMS - 73B	B.ARMS - 73B	B.ARMS - 73B	B.ARMS - 73B	B.ARMS - 73B	B.ARMS - 73B
31229	FAVERSHAM - 73E	FAVERSHAM - 73E	FAVERSHAM - 73E	FAVERSHAM - 73E	FAVERSHAM - 73E	FAVERSHAM - 73E	FAVERSHAM - 73E
31242	FAVERSHAM - 73E	FAVERSHAM - 73E	FAVERSHAM - 73E	FAVERSHAM - 73E	FAVERSHAM - 73E	FAVERSHAM - 73E	FAVERSHAM - 73E
31243	DOVER - 74C	DOVER - 74C	DOVER - 74C	DOVER - 74C	DOVER - 74C	DOVER - 74C	DOVER - 74C
31244	TONBRIDGE - 74D	TONBRIDGE - 74D	TONBRIDGE - 74D	TONBRIDGE - 74D	TONBRIDGE - 74D	TONBRIDGE - 74D	TONBRIDGE - 74D
31245	RAMSGATE - 74B	RAMSGATE - 74B	RAMSGATE - 74B	RAMSGATE - 74B	RAMSGATE - 74B	RAMSGATE - 74B	RAMSGATE - 74B
31252	RAMSGATE - 74B	RAMSGATE - 74B	RAMSGATE - 74B	RAMSGATE - 74B	RAMSGATE - 74B	RAMSGATE - 74B	RAMSGATE - 74B
31253	STEWARTS LANE - 73A	STEWARTS LANE - 73A	STEWARTS LANE - 73A	STEWARTS LANE - 73A	STEWARTS LANE - 73A	STEWARTS LANE - 73A	STEWARTS LANE - 73A
31255	FAVERSHAM - 73E	FAVERSHAM - 73E	FAVERSHAM - 73E	FAVERSHAM - 73E	FAVERSHAM - 73E	FAVERSHAM - 73E	FAVERSHAM - 73E
31256	FAVERSHAM - 73E	FAVERSHAM - 73E	FAVERSHAM - 73E	FAVERSHAM - 73E	FAVERSHAM - 73E	FAVERSHAM - 73E	FAVERSHAM - 73E
31267	B.ARMS - 73B	B.ARMS - 73B	B.ARMS - 73B	B.ARMS - 73B	B.ARMS - 73B	B.ARMS - 73B	B.ARMS - 73B
31268	FAVERSHAM - 73E	FAVERSHAM - 73E	FAVERSHAM - 73E	FAVERSHAM - 73E	FAVERSHAM - 73E	FAVERSHAM - 73E	FAVERSHAM - 73E
31270	HITHER GREEN - 73C	HITHER GREEN - 73C	HITHER GREEN - 73C	HITHER GREEN - 73C	HITHER GREEN - 73C	HITHER GREEN - 73C	HITHER GREEN - 73C
31271	RAMSGATE - 74B	RAMSGATE - 74B	RAMSGATE - 74B	RAMSGATE - 74B	RAMSGATE - 74B	RAMSGATE - 74B	RAMSGATE - 74B
31272	TONBRIDGE - 74D	TONBRIDGE - 74D	TONBRIDGE - 74D	TONBRIDGE - 74D	TONBRIDGE - 74D	TONBRIDGE - 74D	TONBRIDGE - 74D
31280	B.ARMS - 73B	B.ARMS - 73B	B.ARMS - 73B	B.ARMS - 73B	B.ARMS - 73B	B.ARMS - 73B	B.ARMS - 73B
31287	GILLINGHAM - 73D	GILLINGHAM - 73D	GILLINGHAM - 73D	GILLINGHAM - 73D	GILLINGHAM - 73D	GILLINGHAM - 73D	GILLINGHAM - 73D
31293	B.ARMS - 73B	B.ARMS - 73B	B.ARMS - 73B	B.ARMS - 73B	B.ARMS - 73B	B.ARMS - 73B	B.ARMS - 73B
31297	B.ARMS - 73B	B.ARMS - 73B	B.ARMS - 73B	B.ARMS - 73B	B.ARMS - 73B	B.ARMS - 73B	B.ARMS - 73B
31298	RAMSGATE - 74B	RAMSGATE - 74B	RAMSGATE - 74B	RAMSGATE - 74B	RAMSGATE - 74B	RAMSGATE - 74B	RAMSGATE - 74B
31317	DOVER - 74C	DOVER - 74C	DOVER - 74C	DOVER - 74C	DOVER - 74C	DOVER - 74C	DOVER - 74C
31461	STEWARTS LANE - 73A	STEWARTS LANE - 73A	STEWARTS LANE - 73A	STEWARTS LANE - 73A	STEWARTS LANE - 73A	STEWARTS LANE - 73A	STEWARTS LANE - 73A
31480	HITHER GREEN - 73C	HITHER GREEN - 73C	HITHER GREEN - 73C	HITHER GREEN - 73C	HITHER GREEN - 73C	HITHER GREEN - 73C	HITHER GREEN - 73C
31481	FAVERSHAM - 73E	FAVERSHAM - 73E	FAVERSHAM - 73E	FAVERSHAM - 73E	FAVERSHAM - 73E	FAVERSHAM - 73E	FAVERSHAM - 73E
31495	FAVERSHAM - 73E	FAVERSHAM - 73E	FAVERSHAM - 73E	FAVERSHAM - 73E	FAVERSHAM - 73E	FAVERSHAM - 73E	FAVERSHAM - 73E
31498	HITHER GREEN - 73C	HITHER GREEN - 73C	HITHER GREEN - 73C	HITHER GREEN - 73C	HITHER GREEN - 73C	HITHER GREEN - 73C	ST LEONARDS - 74E
31508	GILLINGHAM - 73D	GILLINGHAM - 73D	GILLINGHAM - 73D	GILLINGHAM - 73D	GILLINGHAM - 73D	GILLINGHAM - 73D	GILLINGHAM - 73D
31510	GILLINGHAM - 73D	GILLINGHAM - 73D	GILLINGHAM - 73D	GILLINGHAM - 73D	GILLINGHAM - 73D	GILLINGHAM - 73D	GILLINGHAM - 73D
31573	GILLINGHAM - 73D	GILLINGHAM - 73D	GILLINGHAM - 73D	GILLINGHAM - 73D	GILLINGHAM - 73D	GILLINGHAM - 73D	GILLINGHAM - 73D
31575	STEWARTS LANE - 73A	STEWARTS LANE - 73A	STEWARTS LANE - 73A	STEWARTS LANE - 73A	STEWARTS LANE - 73A	STEWARTS LANE - 73A	STEWARTS LANE - 73A
31576	STEWARTS LANE - 73A	STEWARTS LANE - 73A	STEWARTS LANE - 73A	STEWARTS LANE - 73A	STEWARTS LANE - 73A	STEWARTS LANE - 73A	STEWARTS LANE - 73A
31578	STEWARTS LANE - 73A	STEWARTS LANE - 73A	STEWARTS LANE - 73A	STEWARTS LANE - 73A	STEWARTS LANE - 73A	STEWARTS LANE - 73A	STEWARTS LANE - 73A
31579	GILLINGHAM - 73D	GILLINGHAM - 73D	GILLINGHAM - 73D	GILLINGHAM - 73D	GILLINGHAM - 73D	GILLINGHAM - 73D	GILLINGHAM - 73D
31581	STEWARTS LANE - 73A	STEWARTS LANE - 73A	STEWARTS LANE - 73A	STEWARTS LANE - 73A	STEWARTS LANE - 73A	STEWARTS LANE - 73A	STEWARTS LANE - 73A
31582	STEWARTS LANE - 73A	STEWARTS LANE - 73A	STEWARTS LANE - 73A	STEWARTS LANE - 73A	STEWARTS LANE - 73A	STEWARTS LANE - 73A	STEWARTS LANE - 73A
31583	TONBRIDGE - 74D	TONBRIDGE - 74D	TONBRIDGE - 74D	TONBRIDGE - 74D	TONBRIDGE - 74D	TONBRIDGE - 74D	TONBRIDGE - 74D
31584	STEWARTS LANE - 73A	STEWARTS LANE - 73A	STEWARTS LANE - 73A	STEWARTS LANE - 73A	STEWARTS LANE - 73A	STEWARTS LANE - 73A	STEWARTS LANE - 73A
31585	TONBRIDGE - 74D	TONBRIDGE - 74D	TONBRIDGE - 74D	TONBRIDGE - 74D	TONBRIDGE - 74D	TONBRIDGE - 74D	TONBRIDGE - 74D
31588	GILLINGHAM - 73D	GILLINGHAM - 73D	GILLINGHAM - 73D	GILLINGHAM - 73D	GILLINGHAM - 73D	GILLINGHAM - 73D	GILLINGHAM - 73D
31589	ASHFORD - 74A	ASHFORD - 74A	ASHFORD - 74A	ASHFORD - 74A	ASHFORD - 74A	ASHFORD - 74A	ASHFORD - 74A
31590	TONBRIDGE - 74D	TONBRIDGE - 74D	TONBRIDGE - 74D	TONBRIDGE - 74D	TONBRIDGE - 74D	TONBRIDGE - 74D	TONBRIDGE - 74D
31592	RAMSGATE - 74B	RAMSGATE - 74B	RAMSGATE - 74B	RAMSGATE - 74B	RAMSGATE - 74B	RAMSGATE - 74B	RAMSGATE - 74B
31593	ASHFORD - 74A	ASHFORD - 74A	ASHFORD - 74A	ASHFORD - 74A	ASHFORD - 74A	ASHFORD - 74A	ASHFORD - 74A
31681	STEWARTS LANE - 73A	STEWARTS LANE - 73A	STEWARTS LANE - 73A	STEWARTS LANE - 73A	STEWARTS LANE - 73A	STEWARTS LANE - 73A	STEWARTS LANE - 73A
31682	GILLINGHAM - 73D	GILLINGHAM - 73D	GILLINGHAM - 73D	GILLINGHAM - 73D	GILLINGHAM - 73D	GILLINGHAM - 73D	GILLINGHAM - 73D
31683	STEWARTS LANE - 73A	STEWARTS LANE - 73A	STEWARTS LANE - 73A	STEWARTS LANE - 73A	STEWARTS LANE - 73A	STEWARTS LANE - 73A	STEWARTS LANE - 73A
31684	GILLINGHAM - 73D	GILLINGHAM - 73D	GILLINGHAM - 73D	GILLINGHAM - 73D	GILLINGHAM - 73D	GILLINGHAM - 73D	GILLINGHAM - 73D
31686	HITHER GREEN - 73C	HITHER GREEN - 73C	HITHER GREEN - 73C	HITHER GREEN - 73C	HITHER GREEN - 73C	HITHER GREEN - 73C	HITHER GREEN - 73C
31688	HITHER GREEN - 73C	HITHER GREEN - 73C	HITHER GREEN - 73C	HITHER GREEN - 73C	HITHER GREEN - 73C	HITHER GREEN - 73C	HITHER GREEN - 73C
31689	HITHER GREEN - 73C	HITHER GREEN - 73C	HITHER GREEN - 73C	HITHER GREEN - 73C	HITHER GREEN - 73C	HITHER GREEN - 73C	HITHER GREEN - 73C
31690	HITHER GREEN - 73C	HITHER GREEN - 73C	HITHER GREEN - 73C	HITHER GREEN - 73C	HITHER GREEN - 73C	HITHER GREEN - 73C	HITHER GREEN - 73C
31691	HITHER GREEN - 73C	HITHER GREEN - 73C	HITHER GREEN - 73C	HITHER GREEN - 73C	HITHER GREEN - 73C	HITHER GREEN - 73C	HITHER GREEN - 73C
31692	HITHER GREEN - 73C	HITHER GREEN - 73C	HITHER GREEN - 73C	HITHER GREEN - 73C	HITHER GREEN - 73C	HITHER GREEN - 73C	HITHER GREEN - 73C
31693	HITHER GREEN - 73C	HITHER GREEN - 73C	HITHER GREEN - 73C	HITHER GREEN - 73C	HITHER GREEN - 73C	HITHER GREEN - 73C	HITHER GREEN - 73C
31694	HITHER GREEN - 73C	HITHER GREEN - 73C	HITHER GREEN - 73C	HITHER GREEN - 73C	HITHER GREEN - 73C	HITHER GREEN - 73C	HITHER GREEN - 73C
31695	HITHER GREEN - 73C	HITHER GREEN - 73C	HITHER GREEN - 73C	HITHER GREEN - 73C	HITHER GREEN - 73C	HITHER GREEN - 73C	HITHER GREEN - 73C
31711	GILLINGHAM - 73D	GILLINGHAM - 73D	GILLINGHAM - 73D	GILLINGHAM - 73D	GILLINGHAM - 73D	GILLINGHAM - 73D	W/D
31712	GILLINGHAM - 73D	GILLINGHAM - 73D	GILLINGHAM - 73D	GILLINGHAM - 73D	GILLINGHAM - 73D	GILLINGHAM - 73D	GILLINGHAM - 73D
31714	FAVERSHAM - 73E	FAVERSHAM - 73E	FAVERSHAM - 73E	FAVERSHAM - 73E	FAVERSHAM - 73E	FAVERSHAM - 73E	FAVERSHAM - 73E
31715	FAVERSHAM - 73E	FAVERSHAM - 73E	FAVERSHAM - 73E	FAVERSHAM - 73E	FAVERSHAM - 73E	FAVERSHAM - 73E	FAVERSHAM - 73E
31716	TONBRIDGE - 74D	TONBRIDGE - 74D	TONBRIDGE - 74D	TONBRIDGE - 74D	TONBRIDGE - 74D	TONBRIDGE - 74D	TONBRIDGE - 74D
31717	TONBRIDGE - 74D	TONBRIDGE - 74D	TONBRIDGE - 74D	TONBRIDGE - 74D	TONBRIDGE - 74D	NORWOOD JCN - 75C	B.ARMS - 73B
31719	STEWARTS LANE - 73A	STEWARTS LANE - 73A	STEWARTS LANE - 73A	STEWARTS LANE - 73A	STEWARTS LANE - 73A	NORWOOD JCN - 75C	STEWARTS LANE - 73A
31720	FAVERSHAM - 73E	FAVERSHAM - 73E	FAVERSHAM - 73E	FAVERSHAM - 73E	FAVERSHAM - 73E	FAVERSHAM - 73E	FAVERSHAM - 73E
31721	ST LEONARDS - 74E	ST LEONARDS - 74E	ST LEONARDS - 74E	ST LEONARDS - 74E	ST LEONARDS - 74E	HITHER GREEN - 73C	HITHER GREEN - 73C
31722	STEWARTS LANE - 73A	STEWARTS LANE - 73A	STEWARTS LANE - 73A	STEWARTS LANE - 73A	STEWARTS LANE - 73A	GUILDFORD - 70C	GUILDFORD - 70C
31723	B.ARMS - 73B	B.ARMS - 73B	B.ARMS - 73B	B.ARMS - 73B	B.ARMS - 73B	GUILDFORD - 70C	GUILDFORD - 70C
31724	BRIGHTON - 75A	BRIGHTON - 75A	HITHER GREEN - 73C	HITHER GREEN - 73C	HITHER GREEN - 73C	BRIGHTON - 75A	BRIGHTON - 75A
31725	BRIGHTON - 75A	BRIGHTON - 75A	HITHER GREEN - 73C	HITHER GREEN - 73C	HITHER GREEN - 73C	BRIGHTON - 75A	BRIGHTON - 75A

loco	Mar-57	Jun-57	Jul-57	Oct-57	Jan-58	Feb-58	Mar-58
				C 0-6-0 (1900)			
31004	RAMSGATE - 74B	RAMSGATE - 74B	RAMSGATE - 74B	RAMSGATE - 74B	RAMSGATE - 74B	RAMSGATE - 74B	RAMSGATE - 74B
31018	HITHER GREEN - 73C	HITHER GREEN - 73C	HITHER GREEN - 73C	HITHER GREEN - 73C	HITHER GREEN - 73C	HITHER GREEN - 73C	HITHER GREEN - 73C
31033	B ARMS - 73B	B ARMS - 73B	B ARMS - 73B	B ARMS - 73B	B ARMS - 73B	B ARMS - 73B	B ARMS - 73B
31037	ASHFORD - 74A	STEWARTS LANE - 73A	STEWARTS LANE - 73A	GILLINGHAM - 73D	GILLINGHAM - 73D	GILLINGHAM - 73D	GILLINGHAM - 73D
31054	HITHER GREEN - 73C	HITHER GREEN - 73C	HITHER GREEN - 73C	HITHER GREEN - 73C	HITHER GREEN - 73C	HITHER GREEN - 73C	HITHER GREEN - 73C
31059	HITHER GREEN - 73C	HITHER GREEN - 73C	HITHER GREEN - 73C	HITHER GREEN - 73C	HITHER GREEN - 73C	W/D	W/D
31061	HITHER GREEN - 73C	HITHER GREEN - 73C	HITHER GREEN - 73C	HITHER GREEN - 73C	HITHER GREEN - 73C	HITHER GREEN - 73C	HITHER GREEN - 73C
31068	B ARMS - 73B	B ARMS - 73B	B ARMS - 73B	B ARMS - 73B	B ARMS - 73B	B ARMS - 73B	B ARMS - 73B
31071	B ARMS - 73B	B ARMS - 73B	B ARMS - 73B	B ARMS - 73B	B ARMS - 73B	B ARMS - 73B	B ARMS - 73B
31086	GILLINGHAM - 73D	GILLINGHAM - 73D	GILLINGHAM - 73D	GILLINGHAM - 73D	GILLINGHAM - 73D	GILLINGHAM - 73D	GILLINGHAM - 73D
31102	B ARMS - 73B	B ARMS - 73B	B ARMS - 73B	B ARMS - 73B	B ARMS - 73B	B ARMS - 73B	B ARMS - 73B
31112	GILLINGHAM - 73D	GILLINGHAM - 73D	GILLINGHAM - 73D	GILLINGHAM - 73D	GILLINGHAM - 73D	GILLINGHAM - 73D	GILLINGHAM - 73D
31113	DOVER - 74C	DOVER - 74C	DOVER - 74C	DOVER - 74C	DOVER - 74C	DOVER - 74C	DOVER - 74C
31150	DOVER - 74C	DOVER - 74C	DOVER - 74C	DOVER - 74C	DOVER - 74C	DOVER - 74C	DOVER - 74C
31191	DOVER - 74C	DOVER - 74C	DOVER - 74C	DOVER - 74C	DOVER - 74C	DOVER - 74C	DOVER - 74C
31218	ASHFORD - 74A	ASHFORD - 74A	ASHFORD - 74A	ASHFORD - 74A	ASHFORD - 74A	ASHFORD - 74A	ASHFORD - 74A
31219	ASHFORD - 74A	ASHFORD - 74A	ASHFORD - 74A	ASHFORD - 74A	ASHFORD - 74A	ASHFORD - 74A	ASHFORD - 74A
31221	ASHFORD - 74A	ASHFORD - 74A	ASHFORD - 74A	ASHFORD - 74A	ASHFORD - 74A	ASHFORD - 74A	ASHFORD - 74A
31223	ASHFORD - 74A	ASHFORD - 74A	ASHFORD - 74A	ASHFORD - 74A	ASHFORD - 74A	ASHFORD - 74A	ASHFORD - 74A
31227	B ARMS - 73B	B ARMS - 73B	B ARMS - 73B	B ARMS - 73B	B ARMS - 73B	B ARMS - 73B	B ARMS - 73B
31229	FAVERSHAM - 73E	FAVERSHAM - 73E	FAVERSHAM - 73E	FAVERSHAM - 73E	FAVERSHAM - 73E	FAVERSHAM - 73E	FAVERSHAM - 73E
31242	FAVERSHAM - 73E	FAVERSHAM - 73E	FAVERSHAM - 73E	FAVERSHAM - 73E	FAVERSHAM - 73E	FAVERSHAM - 73E	FAVERSHAM - 73E
31243	DOVER - 74C	DOVER - 74C	DOVER - 74C	DOVER - 74C	DOVER - 74C	DOVER - 74C	DOVER - 74C
31244	TONBRIDGE - 74D	TONBRIDGE - 74D	TONBRIDGE - 74D	TONBRIDGE - 74D	TONBRIDGE - 74D	TONBRIDGE - 74D	TONBRIDGE - 74D
31245	RAMSGATE - 74B	RAMSGATE - 74B	RAMSGATE - 74B	RAMSGATE - 74B	RAMSGATE - 74B	RAMSGATE - 74B	RAMSGATE - 74B
31252	RAMSGATE - 74B	RAMSGATE - 74B	RAMSGATE - 74B	RAMSGATE - 74B	RAMSGATE - 74B	RAMSGATE - 74B	RAMSGATE - 74B
31253	STEWARTS LANE - 73A	STEWARTS LANE - 73A	STEWARTS LANE - 73A	HITHER GREEN - 73C	HITHER GREEN - 73C	HITHER GREEN - 73C	HITHER GREEN - 73C
31255	FAVERSHAM - 73E	FAVERSHAM - 73E	FAVERSHAM - 73E	FAVERSHAM - 73E	FAVERSHAM - 73E	FAVERSHAM - 73E	FAVERSHAM - 73E
31256	FAVERSHAM - 73E	FAVERSHAM - 73E	FAVERSHAM - 73E	FAVERSHAM - 73E	FAVERSHAM - 73E	FAVERSHAM - 73E	FAVERSHAM - 73E
31267	B ARMS - 73B	B ARMS - 73B	B ARMS - 73B	B ARMS - 73B	B ARMS - 73B	B ARMS - 73B	B ARMS - 73B
31268	FAVERSHAM - 73E	FAVERSHAM - 73E	FAVERSHAM - 73E	FAVERSHAM - 73E	FAVERSHAM - 73E	FAVERSHAM - 73E	FAVERSHAM - 73E
31270	HITHER GREEN - 73C	HITHER GREEN - 73C	HITHER GREEN - 73C	HITHER GREEN - 73C	HITHER GREEN - 73C	HITHER GREEN - 73C	HITHER GREEN - 73C
31271	RAMSGATE - 74B	RAMSGATE - 74B	RAMSGATE - 74B	RAMSGATE - 74B	RAMSGATE - 74B	RAMSGATE - 74B	RAMSGATE - 74B
31272	TONBRIDGE - 74D	TONBRIDGE - 74D	TONBRIDGE - 74D	TONBRIDGE - 74D	TONBRIDGE - 74D	TONBRIDGE - 74D	TONBRIDGE - 74D
31280	TONBRIDGE - 74D	TONBRIDGE - 74D	TONBRIDGE - 74D	TONBRIDGE - 74D	TONBRIDGE - 74D	TONBRIDGE - 74D	TONBRIDGE - 74D
31287	HITHER GREEN - 73C	HITHER GREEN - 73C	HITHER GREEN - 73C	HITHER GREEN - 73C	HITHER GREEN - 73C	HITHER GREEN - 73C	HITHER GREEN - 73C
31293	B ARMS - 73B	B ARMS - 73B	B ARMS - 73B	B ARMS - 73B	B ARMS - 73B	B ARMS - 73B	B ARMS - 73B
31297	B ARMS - 73B	GILLINGHAM - 73D	GILLINGHAM - 73D	GILLINGHAM - 73D	GILLINGHAM - 73D	GILLINGHAM - 73D	GILLINGHAM - 73D
31298	RAMSGATE - 74B	FAVERSHAM - 73E	FAVERSHAM - 73E	FAVERSHAM - 73E	FAVERSHAM - 73E	FAVERSHAM - 73E	FAVERSHAM - 73E
31317	DOVER - 74C	STEWARTS LANE - 73A	STEWARTS LANE - 73A	STEWARTS LANE - 73A	STEWARTS LANE - 73A	STEWARTS LANE - 73A	STEWARTS LANE - 73A
31461	B ARMS - 73B	B ARMS - 73B	B ARMS - 73B	B ARMS - 73B	B ARMS - 73B	B ARMS - 73B	B ARMS - 73B
31480	B ARMS - 73B	B ARMS - 73B	B ARMS - 73B	B ARMS - 73B	B ARMS - 73B	B ARMS - 73B	B ARMS - 73B
31481	FAVERSHAM - 73E	FAVERSHAM - 73E	FAVERSHAM - 73E	FAVERSHAM - 73E	FAVERSHAM - 73E	FAVERSHAM - 73E	FAVERSHAM - 73E
31495	FAVERSHAM - 73E	FAVERSHAM - 73E	FAVERSHAM - 73E	FAVERSHAM - 73E	FAVERSHAM - 73E	FAVERSHAM - 73E	FAVERSHAM - 73E
31498	ST LEONARDS - 74E	ST LEONARDS - 74E	ST LEONARDS - 74E	ST LEONARDS - 74E	ST LEONARDS - 74E	ST LEONARDS - 74E	ST LEONARDS - 74E
31508	GILLINGHAM - 73D	GILLINGHAM - 73D	GILLINGHAM - 73D	W/D	W/D	W/D	W/D
31510	GILLINGHAM - 73D	GILLINGHAM - 73D	GILLINGHAM - 73D	GILLINGHAM - 73D	GILLINGHAM - 73D	GILLINGHAM - 73D	GILLINGHAM - 73D
31573	GILLINGHAM - 73D	GILLINGHAM - 73D	GILLINGHAM - 73D	HITHER GREEN - 73C	HITHER GREEN - 73C	HITHER GREEN - 73C	HITHER GREEN - 73C
31575	STEWARTS LANE - 73A	STEWARTS LANE - 73A	STEWARTS LANE - 73A	STEWARTS LANE - 73A	STEWARTS LANE - 73A	STEWARTS LANE - 73A	STEWARTS LANE - 73A
31576	STEWARTS LANE - 73A	STEWARTS LANE - 73A	STEWARTS LANE - 73A	GILLINGHAM - 73D	GILLINGHAM - 73D	GILLINGHAM - 73D	GILLINGHAM - 73D
31578	STEWARTS LANE - 73A	STEWARTS LANE - 73A	STEWARTS LANE - 73A	STEWARTS LANE - 73A	STEWARTS LANE - 73A	STEWARTS LANE - 73A	STEWARTS LANE - 73A
31579	GILLINGHAM - 73D	GILLINGHAM - 73D	GILLINGHAM - 73D	GILLINGHAM - 73D	GILLINGHAM - 73D	GILLINGHAM - 73D	GILLINGHAM - 73D
31581	STEWARTS LANE - 73A	STEWARTS LANE - 73A	STEWARTS LANE - 73A	STEWARTS LANE - 73A	STEWARTS LANE - 73A	STEWARTS LANE - 73A	STEWARTS LANE - 73A
31582	STEWARTS LANE - 73A	STEWARTS LANE - 73A	STEWARTS LANE - 73A	STEWARTS LANE - 73A	STEWARTS LANE - 73A	STEWARTS LANE - 73A	STEWARTS LANE - 73A
31583	STEWARTS LANE - 73A	STEWARTS LANE - 73A	STEWARTS LANE - 73A	STEWARTS LANE - 73A	STEWARTS LANE - 73A	STEWARTS LANE - 73A	STEWARTS LANE - 73A
31584	STEWARTS LANE - 73A	STEWARTS LANE - 73A	STEWARTS LANE - 73A	STEWARTS LANE - 73A	STEWARTS LANE - 73A	STEWARTS LANE - 73A	STEWARTS LANE - 73A
31585	TONBRIDGE - 74D	TONBRIDGE - 74D	TONBRIDGE - 74D	TONBRIDGE - 74D	TONBRIDGE - 74D	TONBRIDGE - 74D	TONBRIDGE - 74D
31588	GILLINGHAM - 73D	GILLINGHAM - 73D	GILLINGHAM - 73D	GILLINGHAM - 73D	GILLINGHAM - 73D	GILLINGHAM - 73D	GILLINGHAM - 73D
31589	ASHFORD - 74A	ASHFORD - 74A	ASHFORD - 74A	ASHFORD - 74A	ASHFORD - 74A	ASHFORD - 74A	ASHFORD - 74A
31590	TONBRIDGE - 74D	TONBRIDGE - 74D	TONBRIDGE - 74D	TONBRIDGE - 74D	TONBRIDGE - 74D	TONBRIDGE - 74D	TONBRIDGE - 74D
31592	RAMSGATE - 74B	RAMSGATE - 74B	RAMSGATE - 74B	RAMSGATE - 74B	RAMSGATE - 74B	RAMSGATE - 74B	RAMSGATE - 74B
31593	ASHFORD - 74A	ASHFORD - 74A	ASHFORD - 74A	ASHFORD - 74A	ASHFORD - 74A	W/D	W/D
31681	STEWARTS LANE - 73A	STEWARTS LANE - 73A	STEWARTS LANE - 73A	STEWARTS LANE - 73A	STEWARTS LANE - 73A	STEWARTS LANE - 73A	STEWARTS LANE - 73A
31682	GILLINGHAM - 73D	GILLINGHAM - 73D	GILLINGHAM - 73D	GILLINGHAM - 73D	GILLINGHAM - 73D	GILLINGHAM - 73D	GILLINGHAM - 73D
31683	STEWARTS LANE - 73A	STEWARTS LANE - 73A	STEWARTS LANE - 73A	STEWARTS LANE - 73A	STEWARTS LANE - 73A	STEWARTS LANE - 73A	STEWARTS LANE - 73A
31684	GILLINGHAM - 73D	GILLINGHAM - 73D	GILLINGHAM - 73D	GILLINGHAM - 73D	GILLINGHAM - 73D	GILLINGHAM - 73D	GILLINGHAM - 73D
31686	HITHER GREEN - 73C	HITHER GREEN - 73C	HITHER GREEN - 73C	HITHER GREEN - 73C	HITHER GREEN - 73C	HITHER GREEN - 73C	HITHER GREEN - 73C
31688	HITHER GREEN - 73C	HITHER GREEN - 73C	HITHER GREEN - 73C	HITHER GREEN - 73C	HITHER GREEN - 73C	HITHER GREEN - 73C	HITHER GREEN - 73C
31689	HITHER GREEN - 73C	HITHER GREEN - 73C	HITHER GREEN - 73C	HITHER GREEN - 73C	HITHER GREEN - 73C	HITHER GREEN - 73C	HITHER GREEN - 73C
31690	HITHER GREEN - 73C	HITHER GREEN - 73C	HITHER GREEN - 73C	HITHER GREEN - 73C	HITHER GREEN - 73C	HITHER GREEN - 73C	HITHER GREEN - 73C
31691	HITHER GREEN - 73C	HITHER GREEN - 73C	HITHER GREEN - 73C	HITHER GREEN - 73C	HITHER GREEN - 73C	HITHER GREEN - 73C	HITHER GREEN - 73C
31692	HITHER GREEN - 73C	HITHER GREEN - 73C	HITHER GREEN - 73C	HITHER GREEN - 73C	HITHER GREEN - 73C	HITHER GREEN - 73C	HITHER GREEN - 73C
31693	HITHER GREEN - 73C	HITHER GREEN - 73C	HITHER GREEN - 73C	HITHER GREEN - 73C	HITHER GREEN - 73C	HITHER GREEN - 73C	HITHER GREEN - 73C
31694	HITHER GREEN - 73C	HITHER GREEN - 73C	HITHER GREEN - 73C	HITHER GREEN - 73C	HITHER GREEN - 73C	HITHER GREEN - 73C	HITHER GREEN - 73C
31695	HITHER GREEN - 73C	HITHER GREEN - 73C	HITHER GREEN - 73C	HITHER GREEN - 73C	HITHER GREEN - 73C	HITHER GREEN - 73C	HITHER GREEN - 73C
31714	FAVERSHAM - 73E	FAVERSHAM - 73E	FAVERSHAM - 73E	FAVERSHAM - 73E	FAVERSHAM - 73E	FAVERSHAM - 73E	FAVERSHAM - 73E
31715	FAVERSHAM - 73E	FAVERSHAM - 73E	FAVERSHAM - 73E	FAVERSHAM - 73E	FAVERSHAM - 73E	FAVERSHAM - 73E	FAVERSHAM - 73E
31716	TONBRIDGE - 74D	TONBRIDGE - 74D	TONBRIDGE - 74D	TONBRIDGE - 74D	TONBRIDGE - 74D	TONBRIDGE - 74D	TONBRIDGE - 74D
31717	B ARMS - 73B	B ARMS - 73B	B ARMS - 73B	B ARMS - 73B	B ARMS - 73B	B ARMS - 73B	B ARMS - 73B
31719	STEWARTS LANE - 73A	STEWARTS LANE - 73A	STEWARTS LANE - 73A	STEWARTS LANE - 73A	STEWARTS LANE - 73A	STEWARTS LANE - 73A	STEWARTS LANE - 73A
31720	FAVERSHAM - 73E	FAVERSHAM - 73E	FAVERSHAM - 73E	FAVERSHAM - 73E	FAVERSHAM - 73E	FAVERSHAM - 73E	FAVERSHAM - 73E
31721	HITHER GREEN - 73C	HITHER GREEN - 73C	HITHER GREEN - 73C	HITHER GREEN - 73C	HITHER GREEN - 73C	HITHER GREEN - 73C	HITHER GREEN - 73C
31722	GUILDFORD - 70C	GUILDFORD - 70C	GUILDFORD - 70C	GUILDFORD - 70C	GUILDFORD - 70C	GUILDFORD - 70C	GUILDFORD - 70C
31723	GUILDFORD - 70C	GUILDFORD - 70C	GUILDFORD - 70C	GUILDFORD - 70C	GUILDFORD - 70C	GUILDFORD - 70C	GUILDFORD - 70C
31724	BRIGHTON - 75A	HITHER GREEN - 73C	HITHER GREEN - 73C	BRIGHTON - 75A	BRIGHTON - 75A	BRIGHTON - 75A	BRIGHTON - 75A
31725	BRIGHTON - 75A	HITHER GREEN - 73C	HITHER GREEN - 73C	BRIGHTON - 75A	BRIGHTON - 75A	BRIGHTON - 75A	BRIGHTON - 75A

loco	May-58	Oct-58	Mar-59	Jun-59	Jul-59	Aug-59	Oct-59
				C 0-6-0 (1900)			
31004	RAMSGATE - 74B	RAMSGATE - 73G	RAMSGATE - 73G	NINE ELMS - 70A	NINE ELMS - 70A	NINE ELMS - 70A	NINE ELMS - 70A
31018	HITHER GREEN - 73C	HITHER GREEN - 73C	W/D	W/D	W/D	W/D	W/D
31033	B ARMS - 73B	B ARMS - 73B	B ARMS - 73B	B ARMS - 73B	FELTHAM - 70B	FELTHAM - 70B	FELTHAM - 70B
31037	GILLINGHAM - 73D	GILLINGHAM - 73D	GILLINGHAM - 73D	NINE ELMS - 70A	GUILDFORD - 70C	GUILDFORD - 70C	GUILDFORD - 70C
31054	HITHER GREEN - 73C	HITHER GREEN - 73C	HITHER GREEN - 73C	NINE ELMS - 70A	GUILDFORD - 70C	GUILDFORD - 70C	GUILDFORD - 70C
31061	HITHER GREEN - 73C	HITHER GREEN - 73C	HITHER GREEN - 73C	NINE ELMS - 70A	NINE ELMS - 70A	NINE ELMS - 70A	NINE ELMS - 70A
31068	B ARMS - 73B	B ARMS - 73B	B ARMS - 73B	B ARMS - 73B	B ARMS - 73B	B ARMS - 73B	B ARMS - 73B
31071	B ARMS - 73B	B ARMS - 73B	B ARMS - 73B	B ARMS - 73B	B ARMS - 73B	B ARMS - 73B	W/D
31086	GILLINGHAM - 73D	GILLINGHAM - 73D	GILLINGHAM - 73D	GILLINGHAM - 73D	GILLINGHAM - 73D	GILLINGHAM - 73D	GILLINGHAM - 73D
31102	B ARMS - 73B	B ARMS - 73B	B ARMS - 73B	B ARMS - 73B	B ARMS - 73B	B ARMS - 73B	B ARMS - 73B
31112	GILLINGHAM - 73D	GILLINGHAM - 73D	GILLINGHAM - 73D	NINE ELMS - 70A	NINE ELMS - 70A	DOVER - 73H	DOVER - 73H
31113	DOVER - 74C	DOVER - 73H	DOVER - 73H	DOVER - 73H	DOVER - 73H	DOVER - 73H	DOVER - 73H
31150	DOVER - 74C	DOVER - 73H	DOVER - 73H	DOVER - 73H	DOVER - 73H	DOVER - 73H	DOVER - 73H
31191	DOVER - 74C	DOVER - 73H	DOVER - 73H	DOVER - 73H	DOVER - 73H	DOVER - 73H	W/D
31218	ASHFORD - 74A	ASHFORD - 73F	ASHFORD - 73F	ASHFORD - 73F	ASHFORD - 73F	ASHFORD - 73F	ASHFORD - 73F
31219	ASHFORD - 74A	ASHFORD - 73F	ASHFORD - 73F	ASHFORD - 73F	ASHFORD - 73F	ASHFORD - 73F	W/D
31221	ASHFORD - 74A	ASHFORD - 73F	ASHFORD - 73F	ASHFORD - 73F	ASHFORD - 73F	W/D	W/D
31223	ASHFORD - 74A	ASHFORD - 73F	ASHFORD - 73F	ASHFORD - 73F	ASHFORD - 73F	ASHFORD - 73F	ASHFORD - 73F
31227	B ARMS - 73B	B ARMS - 73B	B ARMS - 73B	NINE ELMS - 70A	NINE ELMS - 70A	NINE ELMS - 70A	NINE ELMS - 70A
31229	FAVERSHAM - 73E	FAVERSHAM - 73E	FAVERSHAM - 73E	NINE ELMS - 70A	NINE ELMS - 70A	NINE ELMS - 70A	NINE ELMS - 70A
31242	FAVERSHAM - 73E	FAVERSHAM - 73E	FAVERSHAM - 73E	NINE ELMS - 70A	NINE ELMS - 70A	NINE ELMS - 70A	NINE ELMS - 70A
31243	DOVER - 74C	DOVER - 73H	DOVER - 73H	DOVER - 73H	DOVER - 73H	DOVER - 73H	W/D
31244	TONBRIDGE - 74D	TONBRIDGE - 73J	TONBRIDGE - 73J	TONBRIDGE - 73J	TONBRIDGE - 73J	TONBRIDGE - 73J	TONBRIDGE - 73J
31245	RAMSGATE - 74B	RAMSGATE - 73G	RAMSGATE - 73G	NINE ELMS - 70A	NINE ELMS - 70A	W/D	W/D
31252	RAMSGATE - 74B	RAMSGATE - 73G	RAMSGATE - 73G	NINE ELMS - 70A	W/D	W/D	W/D
31253	HITHER GREEN - 73C	HITHER GREEN - 73C	HITHER GREEN - 73C	HITHER GREEN - 73C	HITHER GREEN - 73C	HITHER GREEN - 73C	W/D
31255	FAVERSHAM - 73E	FAVERSHAM - 73E	FAVERSHAM - 73E	ASHFORD - 73F	ASHFORD - 73F	ASHFORD - 73F	ASHFORD - 73F
31256	FAVERSHAM - 73E	FAVERSHAM - 73E	FAVERSHAM - 73E	ASHFORD - 73F	ASHFORD - 73F	ASHFORD - 73F	ASHFORD - 73F
31267	B ARMS - 73B	B ARMS - 73B	B ARMS - 73B	B ARMS - 73B	B ARMS - 73B	B ARMS - 73B	B ARMS - 73B
31268	FAVERSHAM - 73E	FAVERSHAM - 73E	FAVERSHAM - 73E	NINE ELMS - 70A	NINE ELMS - 70A	NINE ELMS - 70A	NINE ELMS - 70A
31270	HITHER GREEN - 73C	HITHER GREEN - 73C	HITHER GREEN - 73C	HITHER GREEN - 73C	W/D	W/D	W/D
31271	RAMSGATE - 74B	RAMSGATE - 73G	RAMSGATE - 73G	NINE ELMS - 70A	NINE ELMS - 70A	NINE ELMS - 70A	NINE ELMS - 70A
31272	TONBRIDGE - 74D	TONBRIDGE - 73J	TONBRIDGE - 73J	TONBRIDGE - 73J	TONBRIDGE - 73J	W/D	W/D
31280	TONBRIDGE - 74D	TONBRIDGE - 73J	TONBRIDGE - 73J	TONBRIDGE - 73J	TONBRIDGE - 73J	TONBRIDGE - 73J	TONBRIDGE - 73J
31287	HITHER GREEN - 73C	HITHER GREEN - 73C	HITHER GREEN - 73C	HITHER GREEN - 73C	HITHER GREEN - 73C	HITHER GREEN - 73C	HITHER GREEN - 73C
31293	B ARMS - 73B	B ARMS - 73B	B ARMS - 73B	B ARMS - 73B	B ARMS - 73B	B ARMS - 73B	B ARMS - 73B
31297	GILLINGHAM - 73D	GILLINGHAM - 73D	GILLINGHAM - 73D	NINE ELMS - 70A	NINE ELMS - 70A	NINE ELMS - 70A	W/D
31298	FAVERSHAM - 73E	FAVERSHAM - 73E	FAVERSHAM - 73E	NINE ELMS - 70A	NINE ELMS - 70A	NINE ELMS - 70A	NINE ELMS - 70A
31317	STEWARTS LANE - 73A	STEWARTS LANE - 73A	STEWARTS LANE - 73A	STEWARTS LANE - 73A	STEWARTS LANE - 73A	STEWARTS LANE - 73A	STEWARTS LANE - 73A
31461	B ARMS - 73B	W/D	W/D	W/D	W/D	W/D	W/D
31480	B ARMS - 73B	B ARMS - 73B	B ARMS - 73B	B ARMS - 73B	B ARMS - 73B	B ARMS - 73B	B ARMS - 73B
31481	FAVERSHAM - 73E	FAVERSHAM - 73E	FAVERSHAM - 73E	NINE ELMS - 70A	NINE ELMS - 70A	DOVER - 73H	DOVER - 73H
31495	FAVERSHAM - 73E	FAVERSHAM - 73E	FAVERSHAM - 73E	NINE ELMS - 70A	NINE ELMS - 70A	NINE ELMS - 70A	NINE ELMS - 70A
31498	HITHER GREEN - 73C	HITHER GREEN - 73C	HITHER GREEN - 73C	HITHER GREEN - 73C	HITHER GREEN - 73C	HITHER GREEN - 73C	HITHER GREEN - 73C
31510	GILLINGHAM - 73D	GILLINGHAM - 73D	GILLINGHAM - 73D	NINE ELMS - 70A	NINE ELMS - 70A	NINE ELMS - 70A	NINE ELMS - 70A
31573	HITHER GREEN - 73C	HITHER GREEN - 73C	HITHER GREEN - 73C	HITHER GREEN - 73C	HITHER GREEN - 73C	HITHER GREEN - 73C	HITHER GREEN - 73C
31575	STEWARTS LANE - 73A	STEWARTS LANE - 73A	STEWARTS LANE - 73A	STEWARTS LANE - 73A	STEWARTS LANE - 73A	STEWARTS LANE - 73A	STEWARTS LANE - 73A
31576	GILLINGHAM - 73D	GILLINGHAM - 73D	GILLINGHAM - 73D	NINE ELMS - 70A	NINE ELMS - 70A	NINE ELMS - 70A	NINE ELMS - 70A
31578	STEWARTS LANE - 73A	STEWARTS LANE - 73A	STEWARTS LANE - 73A	STEWARTS LANE - 73A	STEWARTS LANE - 73A	STEWARTS LANE - 73A	STEWARTS LANE - 73A
31579	GILLINGHAM - 73D	GILLINGHAM - 73D	GILLINGHAM - 73D	NINE ELMS - 70A	NINE ELMS - 70A	NINE ELMS - 70A	NINE ELMS - 70A
31581	STEWARTS LANE - 73A	STEWARTS LANE - 73A	STEWARTS LANE - 73A	STEWARTS LANE - 73A	STEWARTS LANE - 73A	STEWARTS LANE - 73A	STEWARTS LANE - 73A
31583	STEWARTS LANE - 73A	STEWARTS LANE - 73A	STEWARTS LANE - 73A	STEWARTS LANE - 73A	STEWARTS LANE - 73A	STEWARTS LANE - 73A	STEWARTS LANE - 73A
31584	STEWARTS LANE - 73A	STEWARTS LANE - 73A	STEWARTS LANE - 73A	STEWARTS LANE - 73A	STEWARTS LANE - 73A	STEWARTS LANE - 73A	STEWARTS LANE - 73A
31585	TONBRIDGE - 74D	TONBRIDGE - 73J	W/D	W/D	W/D	W/D	W/D
31588	GILLINGHAM - 73D	GILLINGHAM - 73D	GILLINGHAM - 73D	GILLINGHAM - 73D	GILLINGHAM - 73D	GILLINGHAM - 73D	GILLINGHAM - 73D
31589	ASHFORD - 74A	ASHFORD - 73F	ASHFORD - 73F	ASHFORD - 73F	ASHFORD - 73F	ASHFORD - 73F	ASHFORD - 73F
31590	TONBRIDGE - 74D	TONBRIDGE - 73J	TONBRIDGE - 73J	TONBRIDGE - 73J	TONBRIDGE - 73J	TONBRIDGE - 73J	TONBRIDGE - 73J
31592	RAMSGATE - 74B	RAMSGATE - 73G	RAMSGATE - 73G	NINE ELMS - 70A	NINE ELMS - 70A	NINE ELMS - 70A	NINE ELMS - 70A
31681	STEWARTS LANE - 73A	STEWARTS LANE - 73A	W/D	W/D	W/D	W/D	W/D
31682	GILLINGHAM - 73D	GILLINGHAM - 73D	GILLINGHAM - 73D	NINE ELMS - 70A	NINE ELMS - 70A	NINE ELMS - 70A	NINE ELMS - 70A
31683	STEWARTS LANE - 73A	STEWARTS LANE - 73A	STEWARTS LANE - 73A	NINE ELMS - 70A	W/D	W/D	W/D
31684	GILLINGHAM - 73D	GILLINGHAM - 73D	GILLINGHAM - 73D	NINE ELMS - 70A	NINE ELMS - 70A	NINE ELMS - 70A	TONBRIDGE - 73J
31686	HITHER GREEN - 73C	HITHER GREEN - 73C	HITHER GREEN - 73C	HITHER GREEN - 73C	HITHER GREEN - 73C	HITHER GREEN - 73C	HITHER GREEN - 73C
31688	HITHER GREEN - 73C	HITHER GREEN - 73C	HITHER GREEN - 73C	HITHER GREEN - 73C	HITHER GREEN - 73C	HITHER GREEN - 73C	HITHER GREEN - 73C
31689	HITHER GREEN - 73C	HITHER GREEN - 73C	HITHER GREEN - 73C	HITHER GREEN - 73C	HITHER GREEN - 73C	HITHER GREEN - 73C	HITHER GREEN - 73C
31690	HITHER GREEN - 73C	HITHER GREEN - 73C	HITHER GREEN - 73C	HITHER GREEN - 73C	HITHER GREEN - 73C	HITHER GREEN - 73C	HITHER GREEN - 73C
31691	HITHER GREEN - 73C	HITHER GREEN - 73C	HITHER GREEN - 73C	HITHER GREEN - 73C	HITHER GREEN - 73C	HITHER GREEN - 73C	HITHER GREEN - 73C
31692	HITHER GREEN - 73C	HITHER GREEN - 73C	HITHER GREEN - 73C	HITHER GREEN - 73C	HITHER GREEN - 73C	HITHER GREEN - 73C	HITHER GREEN - 73C
31693	HITHER GREEN - 73C	HITHER GREEN - 73C	HITHER GREEN - 73C	HITHER GREEN - 73C	HITHER GREEN - 73C	HITHER GREEN - 73C	HITHER GREEN - 73C
31694	HITHER GREEN - 73C	HITHER GREEN - 73C	HITHER GREEN - 73C	HITHER GREEN - 73C	HITHER GREEN - 73C	HITHER GREEN - 73C	HITHER GREEN - 73C
31695	HITHER GREEN - 73C	HITHER GREEN - 73C	HITHER GREEN - 73C	HITHER GREEN - 73C	HITHER GREEN - 73C	HITHER GREEN - 73C	HITHER GREEN - 73C
31714	FAVERSHAM - 73E	FAVERSHAM - 73E	FAVERSHAM - 73E	STEWARTS LANE - 73A	STEWARTS LANE - 73A	STEWARTS LANE - 73A	STEWARTS LANE - 73A
31715	FAVERSHAM - 73E	FAVERSHAM - 73E	FAVERSHAM - 73E	STEWARTS LANE - 73A	STEWARTS LANE - 73A	STEWARTS LANE - 73A	STEWARTS LANE - 73A
31716	TONBRIDGE - 74D	TONBRIDGE - 73J	TONBRIDGE - 73J	TONBRIDGE - 73J	TONBRIDGE - 73J	TONBRIDGE - 73J	TONBRIDGE - 73J
31717	B ARMS - 73B	B ARMS - 73B	B ARMS - 73B	B ARMS - 73B	B ARMS - 73B	B ARMS - 73B	B ARMS - 73B
31719	STEWARTS LANE - 73A	STEWARTS LANE - 73A	STEWARTS LANE - 73A	STEWARTS LANE - 73A	STEWARTS LANE - 73A	STEWARTS LANE - 73A	STEWARTS LANE - 73A
31720	FAVERSHAM - 73E	FAVERSHAM - 73E	FAVERSHAM - 73E	NINE ELMS - 70A	NINE ELMS - 70A	NINE ELMS - 70A	DOVER - 73H
31721	HITHER GREEN - 73C	HITHER GREEN - 73C	HITHER GREEN - 73C	HITHER GREEN - 73C	HITHER GREEN - 73C	HITHER GREEN - 73C	HITHER GREEN - 73C
31722	GUILDFORD - 70C	GUILDFORD - 70C	GUILDFORD - 70C	GUILDFORD - 70C	GUILDFORD - 70C	GUILDFORD - 70C	GUILDFORD - 70C
31723	GUILDFORD - 70C	GUILDFORD - 70C	GUILDFORD - 70C	GUILDFORD - 70C	GUILDFORD - 70C	GUILDFORD - 70C	GUILDFORD - 70C
31724	HITHER GREEN - 73C	HITHER GREEN - 73C	HITHER GREEN - 73C	HITHER GREEN - 73C	HITHER GREEN - 73C	HITHER GREEN - 73C	HITHER GREEN - 73C
31725	HITHER GREEN - 73C	HITHER GREEN - 73C	HITHER GREEN - 73C	HITHER GREEN - 73C	HITHER GREEN - 73C	HITHER GREEN - 73C	HITHER GREEN - 73C

loco	Dec-59	Feb-60	Mar-60	Apr-60	Jul-60	Aug-60	Sep-60	Nov-60
				C 0-6-0 (1900)				
31004 NINE ELMS - 70A	DOVER - 73H	DOVER - 73H	DOVER - 73H	DOVER - 73H	DOVER - 73H	DOVER - 73H	DOVER - 73H	
31033 FELTHAM - 70B	FELTHAM - 70B	W/D	W/D	W/D	W/D	W/D	W/D	
31037 GUILDFORD - 70C	GUILDFORD - 70C	GUILDFORD - 70C	GUILDFORD - 70C	GUILDFORD - 70C	GUILDFORD - 70C	GUILDFORD - 70C	GUILDFORD - 70C	
31054 GUILDFORD - 70C	GUILDFORD - 70C	GUILDFORD - 70C	GUILDFORD - 70C	GUILDFORD - 70C	W/D	W/D	W/D	
31061 NINE ELMS - 70A	TONBRIDGE - 73J	TONBRIDGE - 73J	TONBRIDGE - 73J	FELTHAM - 70B	FELTHAM - 70B	FELTHAM - 70B	FELTHAM - 70B	
31068 B ARMS - 73B	B ARMS - 73B	B ARMS - 73B	B ARMS - 73B	B ARMS - 73B	B ARMS - 73B	B ARMS - 73B	B ARMS - 73B	
31086 GILLINGHAM - 73D	GILLINGHAM - 73D	GILLINGHAM - 73D	GILLINGHAM - 73D	GILLINGHAM - 73D	GILLINGHAM - 73D	GILLINGHAM - 73D	W/D	
31102 B ARMS - 73B	B ARMS - 73B	B ARMS - 73B	B ARMS - 73B	W/D	W/D	W/D	W/D	
31112 DOVER - 73H	DOVER - 73H	DOVER - 73H	DOVER - 73H	DOVER - 73H	DOVER - 73H	DOVER - 73H	DOVER - 73H	
31113 DOVER - 73H	DOVER - 73H	DOVER - 73H	DOVER - 73H	FELTHAM - 70B	FELTHAM - 70B	FELTHAM - 70B	FELTHAM - 70B	
31150 DOVER - 73H	DOVER - 73H	DOVER - 73H	DOVER - 73H	FELTHAM - 70B	FELTHAM - 70B	FELTHAM - 70B	FELTHAM - 70B	
31218 ASHFORD - 73F	ASHFORD - 73F	ASHFORD - 73F	ASHFORD - 73F	ASHFORD - 73F	ASHFORD - 73F	ASHFORD - 73F	ASHFORD - 73F	
31223 ASHFORD - 73F	ASHFORD - 73F	ASHFORD - 73F	ASHFORD - 73F	W/D	W/D	W/D	W/D	
31229 NINE ELMS - 70A	STEWARTS LANE - 73A	STEWARTS LANE - 73A	STEWARTS LANE - 73A	B ARMS - 73B	B ARMS - 73B	B ARMS - 73B	B ARMS - 73B	
31242 NINE ELMS - 70A	NINE ELMS - 70A	NINE ELMS - 70A	NINE ELMS - 70A	NINE ELMS - 70A	NINE ELMS - 70A	NINE ELMS - 70A	NINE ELMS - 70A	
31244 TONBRIDGE - 73J	TONBRIDGE - 73J	TONBRIDGE - 73J	TONBRIDGE - 73J	TONBRIDGE - 73J	TONBRIDGE - 73J	TONBRIDGE - 73J	TONBRIDGE - 73J	
31255 ASHFORD - 73F	ASHFORD - 73F	ASHFORD - 73F	ASHFORD - 73F	ASHFORD - 73F	ASHFORD - 73F	ASHFORD - 73F	ASHFORD - 73F	
31256 ASHFORD - 73F	ASHFORD - 73F	ASHFORD - 73F	ASHFORD - 73F	ASHFORD - 73F	ASHFORD - 73F	ASHFORD - 73F	ASHFORD - 73F	
31267 B ARMS - 73B	B ARMS - 73B	B ARMS - 73B	B ARMS - 73B	B ARMS - 73B	B ARMS - 73B	B ARMS - 73B	B ARMS - 73B	
31268 NINE ELMS - 70A	HITHER GREEN - 73C	HITHER GREEN - 73C	HITHER GREEN - 73C	HITHER GREEN - 73C	HITHER GREEN - 73C	HITHER GREEN - 73C	HITHER GREEN - 73C	
31271 NINE ELMS - 70A	NINE ELMS - 70A	NINE ELMS - 70A	NINE ELMS - 70A	NINE ELMS - 70A	NINE ELMS - 70A	NINE ELMS - 70A	NINE ELMS - 70A	
31280 TONBRIDGE - 73J	TONBRIDGE - 73J	TONBRIDGE - 73J	TONBRIDGE - 73J	TONBRIDGE - 73J	TONBRIDGE - 73J	NORWOOD JCN - 75C	BRIGHTON - 75A	
31287 HITHER GREEN - 73C	HITHER GREEN - 73C	HITHER GREEN - 73C	HITHER GREEN - 73C	HITHER GREEN - 73C	HITHER GREEN - 73C	HITHER GREEN - 73C	W/D	
31293 B ARMS - 73B	B ARMS - 73B	B ARMS - 73B	B ARMS - 73B	B ARMS - 73B	B ARMS - 73B	B ARMS - 73B	B ARMS - 73B	
31298 NINE ELMS - 70A	HITHER GREEN - 73C	HITHER GREEN - 73C	HITHER GREEN - 73C	HITHER GREEN - 73C	HITHER GREEN - 73C	HITHER GREEN - 73C	HITHER GREEN - 73C	
31317 STEWARTS LANE - 73A	STEWARTS LANE - 73A	STEWARTS LANE - 73A	STEWARTS LANE - 73A	STEWARTS LANE - 73A	STEWARTS LANE - 73A	STEWARTS LANE - 73A	STEWARTS LANE - 73A	
31480 B ARMS - 73B	B ARMS - 73B	B ARMS - 73B	B ARMS - 73B	B ARMS - 73B	B ARMS - 73B	B ARMS - 73B	B ARMS - 73B	
31481 DOVER - 73H	DOVER - 73H	DOVER - 73H	DOVER - 73H	FELTHAM - 70B	FELTHAM - 70B	FELTHAM - 70B	FELTHAM - 70B	
31495 NINE ELMS - 70A	NINE ELMS - 70A	NINE ELMS - 70A	NINE ELMS - 70A	NINE ELMS - 70A	NINE ELMS - 70A	NINE ELMS - 70A	NINE ELMS - 70A	
31498 HITHER GREEN - 73C	HITHER GREEN - 73C	HITHER GREEN - 73C	HITHER GREEN - 73C	FELTHAM - 70B	FELTHAM - 70B	FELTHAM - 70B	FELTHAM - 70B	
31510 NINE ELMS - 70A	NINE ELMS - 70A	NINE ELMS - 70A	NINE ELMS - 70A	NINE ELMS - 70A	NINE ELMS - 70A	NINE ELMS - 70A	NINE ELMS - 70A	
31573 HITHER GREEN - 73C	HITHER GREEN - 73C	HITHER GREEN - 73C	HITHER GREEN - 73C	FELTHAM - 70B	FELTHAM - 70B	FELTHAM - 70B	FELTHAM - 70B	
31575 STEWARTS LANE - 73A	STEWARTS LANE - 73A	STEWARTS LANE - 73A	STEWARTS LANE - 73A	STEWARTS LANE - 73A	STEWARTS LANE - 73A	STEWARTS LANE - 73A	STEWARTS LANE - 73A	
31578 STEWARTS LANE - 73A	STEWARTS LANE - 73A	STEWARTS LANE - 73A	STEWARTS LANE - 73A	STEWARTS LANE - 73A	STEWARTS LANE - 73A	STEWARTS LANE - 73A	STEWARTS LANE - 73A	
31579 NINE ELMS - 70A	HITHER GREEN - 73C	HITHER GREEN - 73C	HITHER GREEN - 73C	FELTHAM - 70B	FELTHAM - 70B	FELTHAM - 70B	FELTHAM - 70B	
31581 STEWARTS LANE - 73A	STEWARTS LANE - 73A	W/D	W/D	W/D	W/D	W/D	W/D	
31583 STEWARTS LANE - 73A	STEWARTS LANE - 73A	STEWARTS LANE - 73A	STEWARTS LANE - 73A	STEWARTS LANE - 73A	STEWARTS LANE - 73A	STEWARTS LANE - 73A	STEWARTS LANE - 73A	
31584 STEWARTS LANE - 73A	STEWARTS LANE - 73A	STEWARTS LANE - 73A	STEWARTS LANE - 73A	STEWARTS LANE - 73A	STEWARTS LANE - 73A	STEWARTS LANE - 73A	STEWARTS LANE - 73A	
31588 GILLINGHAM - 73D	GILLINGHAM - 73D	GILLINGHAM - 73D	GILLINGHAM - 73D	GILLINGHAM - 73D	GILLINGHAM - 73D	GILLINGHAM - 73D	GILLINGHAM - 73D	
31589 ASHFORD - 73F	ASHFORD - 73F	ASHFORD - 73F	ASHFORD - 73F	ASHFORD - 73F	ASHFORD - 73F	ASHFORD - 73F	ASHFORD - 73F	
31590 TONBRIDGE - 73J	TONBRIDGE - 73J	TONBRIDGE - 73J	TONBRIDGE - 73J	TONBRIDGE - 73J	TONBRIDGE - 73J	TONBRIDGE - 73J	TONBRIDGE - 73J	
31592 NINE ELMS - 70A	TONBRIDGE - 73J	TONBRIDGE - 73J	TONBRIDGE - 73J	TONBRIDGE - 73J	TONBRIDGE - 73J	TONBRIDGE - 73J	TONBRIDGE - 73J	
31682 NINE ELMS - 70A	HITHER GREEN - 73C	HITHER GREEN - 73C	HITHER GREEN - 73C	HITHER GREEN - 73C	HITHER GREEN - 73C	HITHER GREEN - 73C	HITHER GREEN - 73C	
31684 TONBRIDGE - 73J	TONBRIDGE - 73J	TONBRIDGE - 73J	TONBRIDGE - 73J	TONBRIDGE - 73J	TONBRIDGE - 73J	TONBRIDGE - 73J	TONBRIDGE - 73J	
31686 HITHER GREEN - 73C	HITHER GREEN - 73C	HITHER GREEN - 73C	HITHER GREEN - 73C	HITHER GREEN - 73C	HITHER GREEN - 73C	HITHER GREEN - 73C	HITHER GREEN - 73C	
31688 HITHER GREEN - 73C	W/D	W/D	W/D	W/D	W/D	W/D	W/D	
31689 HITHER GREEN - 73C	HITHER GREEN - 73C	HITHER GREEN - 73C	HITHER GREEN - 73C	HITHER GREEN - 73C	HITHER GREEN - 73C	HITHER GREEN - 73C	HITHER GREEN - 73C	
31690 HITHER GREEN - 73C	HITHER GREEN - 73C	HITHER GREEN - 73C	HITHER GREEN - 73C	HITHER GREEN - 73C	HITHER GREEN - 73C	HITHER GREEN - 73C	HITHER GREEN - 73C	
31691 HITHER GREEN - 73C	HITHER GREEN - 73C	HITHER GREEN - 73C	HITHER GREEN - 73C	HITHER GREEN - 73C	HITHER GREEN - 73C	HITHER GREEN - 73C	HITHER GREEN - 73C	
31692 HITHER GREEN - 73C	HITHER GREEN - 73C	HITHER GREEN - 73C	W/D	W/D	W/D	W/D	W/D	
31693 HITHER GREEN - 73C	HITHER GREEN - 73C	HITHER GREEN - 73C	HITHER GREEN - 73C	B ARMS - 73B	B ARMS - 73B	B ARMS - 73B	B ARMS - 73B	
31694 HITHER GREEN - 73C	HITHER GREEN - 73C	HITHER GREEN - 73C	HITHER GREEN - 73C	B ARMS - 73B	B ARMS - 73B	B ARMS - 73B	B ARMS - 73B	
31695 HITHER GREEN - 73C	HITHER GREEN - 73C	HITHER GREEN - 73C	HITHER GREEN - 73C	HITHER GREEN - 73C	HITHER GREEN - 73C	HITHER GREEN - 73C	HITHER GREEN - 73C	
31714 STEWARTS LANE - 73A	STEWARTS LANE - 73A	STEWARTS LANE - 73A	STEWARTS LANE - 73A	STEWARTS LANE - 73A	STEWARTS LANE - 73A	STEWARTS LANE - 73A	STEWARTS LANE - 73A	
31715 STEWARTS LANE - 73A	STEWARTS LANE - 73A	STEWARTS LANE - 73A	STEWARTS LANE - 73A	STEWARTS LANE - 73A	STEWARTS LANE - 73A	STEWARTS LANE - 73A	STEWARTS LANE - 73A	
31716 TONBRIDGE - 73J	TONBRIDGE - 73J	TONBRIDGE - 73J	TONBRIDGE - 73J	TONBRIDGE - 73J	TONBRIDGE - 73J	TONBRIDGE - 73J	TONBRIDGE - 73J	
31717 B ARMS - 73B	B ARMS - 73B	B ARMS - 73B	B ARMS - 73B	B ARMS - 73B	B ARMS - 73B	B ARMS - 73B	B ARMS - 73B	
31719 STEWARTS LANE - 73A	STEWARTS LANE - 73A	STEWARTS LANE - 73A	STEWARTS LANE - 73A	STEWARTS LANE - 73A	STEWARTS LANE - 73A	STEWARTS LANE - 73A	STEWARTS LANE - 73A	
31720 DOVER - 73H	DOVER - 73H	DOVER - 73H	DOVER - 73H	DOVER - 73H	DOVER - 73H	DOVER - 73H	DOVER - 73H	
31721 HITHER GREEN - 73C	HITHER GREEN - 73C	HITHER GREEN - 73C	HITHER GREEN - 73C	HITHER GREEN - 73C	HITHER GREEN - 73C	HITHER GREEN - 73C	HITHER GREEN - 73C	
31722 GUILDFORD - 70C	GUILDFORD - 70C	GUILDFORD - 70C	GUILDFORD - 70C	GUILDFORD - 70C	GUILDFORD - 70C	GUILDFORD - 70C	GUILDFORD - 70C	
31723 GUILDFORD - 70C	GUILDFORD - 70C	GUILDFORD - 70C	GUILDFORD - 70C	GUILDFORD - 70C	GUILDFORD - 70C	GUILDFORD - 70C	GUILDFORD - 70C	
31724 BRIGHTON - 75A	BRIGHTON - 75A	BRIGHTON - 75A	BRIGHTON - 75A	BRIGHTON - 75A	BRIGHTON - 75A	BRIGHTON - 75A	BRIGHTON - 75A	
31725 BRIGHTON - 75A	BRIGHTON - 75A	BRIGHTON - 75A	BRIGHTON - 75A	BRIGHTON - 75A	W/D	W/D	W/D	

The C class 0-6-0 was not only the standard goods engine of the SECR but one of the best investments made by the railway, the last survivor of the 109 strong class remaining in traffic - albeit as a departmental engine for the final five years - until 1967.

Their duties on the SECR section - their visits to foreign metals were infrequent - encompassed almost all the divisions' goods traffic other than long distance workings which tended to be worked by 2-6-0's or King Arthur 4-6-0's. There was scarcely a section of line in Kent that did not receive a daily visit from a C 0-6-0 and they were as familiar a sight on the banks of the Medway, working between Hoo Junction and Maidstone, as they were on the numerous freight trips that connected the London suburban stations with the main yards at Hither Green and Herne Hill.

Apart from one engine, withdrawn in 1947, scrapping did not commence until 1953 although even then the numbers of engines taken out of traffic was minimal until 1959 when the pace accelerated following electrification of the LCDR. Even so, more than half the original class survived into the 1960's.

loco	May-49	Jun-49	Aug-49	Sep-49	Dec-49	Feb-50	Mar-50
				'700' 0-6-0 (1897)			
30306	EASTLEIGH - 71A	EASTLEIGH - 71A	EASTLEIGH - 71A	EASTLEIGH - 71A	EASTLEIGH - 71A	EASTLEIGH - 71A	EASTLEIGH - 71A
30308	GUILDFORD - 70C	GUILDFORD - 70C	GUILDFORD - 70C	GUILDFORD - 70C	GUILDFORD - 70C	GUILDFORD - 70C	GUILDFORD - 70C
30309	FELTHAM - 70B	FELTHAM - 70B	FELTHAM - 70B	FELTHAM - 70B	FELTHAM - 70B	FELTHAM - 70B	FELTHAM - 70B
30315	SALISBURY - 72B	SALISBURY - 72B	SALISBURY - 72B	SALISBURY - 72B	SALISBURY - 72B	SALISBURY - 72B	SALISBURY - 72B
30316	EASTLEIGH - 71A	EASTLEIGH - 71A	EASTLEIGH - 71A	EASTLEIGH - 71A	EASTLEIGH - 71A	EASTLEIGH - 71A	EASTLEIGH - 71A
30317	SALISBURY - 72B	SALISBURY - 72B	SALISBURY - 72B	SALISBURY - 72B	SALISBURY - 72B	SALISBURY - 72B	SALISBURY - 72B
30325	GUILDFORD - 70C	GUILDFORD - 70C	GUILDFORD - 70C	GUILDFORD - 70C	GUILDFORD - 70C	GUILDFORD - 70C	GUILDFORD - 70C
30326	GUILDFORD - 70C	GUILDFORD - 70C	GUILDFORD - 70C	GUILDFORD - 70C	GUILDFORD - 70C	GUILDFORD - 70C	GUILDFORD - 70C
30327	GUILDFORD - 70C	GUILDFORD - 70C	GUILDFORD - 70C	GUILDFORD - 70C	GUILDFORD - 70C	GUILDFORD - 70C	GUILDFORD - 70C
30339	NINE ELMS - 70A	NINE ELMS - 70A	NINE ELMS - 70A	NINE ELMS - 70A	NINE ELMS - 70A	NINE ELMS - 70A	NINE ELMS - 70A
30346	FELTHAM - 70B	FELTHAM - 70B	FELTHAM - 70B	FELTHAM - 70B	FELTHAM - 70B	FELTHAM - 70B	FELTHAM - 70B
30350	EASTLEIGH - 71A	EASTLEIGH - 71A	EASTLEIGH - 71A	EASTLEIGH - 71A	EASTLEIGH - 71A	EASTLEIGH - 71A	EASTLEIGH - 71A
30352	FELTHAM - 70B	FELTHAM - 70B	FELTHAM - 70B	FELTHAM - 70B	FELTHAM - 70B	FELTHAM - 70B	FELTHAM - 70B
30355	SALISBURY - 72B	SALISBURY - 72B	SALISBURY - 72B	SALISBURY - 72B	SALISBURY - 72B	SALISBURY - 72B	SALISBURY - 72B
30368	BASINGSTOKE - 70D	BASINGSTOKE - 70D	BASINGSTOKE - 70D	BASINGSTOKE - 70D	BASINGSTOKE - 70D	BASINGSTOKE - 70D	BASINGSTOKE - 70D
30687	FELTHAM - 70B	FELTHAM - 70B	FELTHAM - 70B	FELTHAM - 70B	FELTHAM - 70B	FELTHAM - 70B	FELTHAM - 70B
30688	FELTHAM - 70B	FELTHAM - 70B	FELTHAM - 70B	FELTHAM - 70B	FELTHAM - 70B	FELTHAM - 70B	FELTHAM - 70B
30689	FELTHAM - 70B	FELTHAM - 70B	FELTHAM - 70B	FELTHAM - 70B	FELTHAM - 70B	FELTHAM - 70B	FELTHAM - 70B
30690	SALISBURY - 72B	SALISBURY - 72B	SALISBURY - 72B	SALISBURY - 72B	SALISBURY - 72B	SALISBURY - 72B	SALISBURY - 72B
30691	SALISBURY - 72B	SALISBURY - 72B	SALISBURY - 72B	SALISBURY - 72B	SALISBURY - 72B	SALISBURY - 72B	SALISBURY - 72B
30692	NINE ELMS - 70A	NINE ELMS - 70A	NINE ELMS - 70A	NINE ELMS - 70A	NINE ELMS - 70A	NINE ELMS - 70A	NINE ELMS - 70A
30693	BASINGSTOKE - 70D	BASINGSTOKE - 70D	BASINGSTOKE - 70D	BASINGSTOKE - 70D	BASINGSTOKE - 70D	BASINGSTOKE - 70D	BASINGSTOKE - 70D
30694	NINE ELMS - 70A	NINE ELMS - 70A	NINE ELMS - 70A	NINE ELMS - 70A	NINE ELMS - 70A	NINE ELMS - 70A	NINE ELMS - 70A
30695	BOURNEMOUTH - 71B	BOURNEMOUTH - 71B	BOURNEMOUTH - 71B	BOURNEMOUTH - 71B	BOURNEMOUTH - 71B	BOURNEMOUTH - 71B	BOURNEMOUTH - 71B
30696	BOURNEMOUTH - 71B	BOURNEMOUTH - 71B	BOURNEMOUTH - 71B	BOURNEMOUTH - 71B	FELTHAM - 70B	FELTHAM - 70B	FELTHAM - 70B
30697	FELTHAM - 70B	FELTHAM - 70B	FELTHAM - 70B	FELTHAM - 70B	FELTHAM - 70B	FELTHAM - 70B	FELTHAM - 70B
30698	FELTHAM - 70B	FELTHAM - 70B	FELTHAM - 70B	FELTHAM - 70B	FELTHAM - 70B	FELTHAM - 70B	FELTHAM - 70B
30699	NINE ELMS - 70A	NINE ELMS - 70A	NINE ELMS - 70A	NINE ELMS - 70A	NINE ELMS - 70A	NINE ELMS - 70A	NINE ELMS - 70A
30700	BOURNEMOUTH - 71B	BOURNEMOUTH - 71B	BOURNEMOUTH - 71B	BOURNEMOUTH - 71B	EASTLEIGH - 71A	EASTLEIGH - 71A	EASTLEIGH - 71A
30701	NINE ELMS - 70A	NINE ELMS - 70A	NINE ELMS - 70A	NINE ELMS - 70A	NINE ELMS - 70A	NINE ELMS - 70A	NINE ELMS - 70A
				C2 0-6-0 (1893)			
32436	THREE BRIDGES - 75E	THREE BRIDGES - 75E	THREE BRIDGES - 75E	THREE BRIDGES - 75E	THREE BRIDGES - 75E	W/D	W/D
32533	BRIGHTON - 75A(N)	BRIGHTON - 75A(N)	BRIGHTON - 75A(N)	BRIGHTON - 75A(N)	BRIGHTON - 75A(N)	BRIGHTON - 75A(N)	W/D
				C2X 0-6-0 (1908)			
32434	EASTBOURNE - 75G	EASTBOURNE - 75G	EASTBOURNE - 75G	EASTBOURNE - 75G	EASTBOURNE - 75G	EASTBOURNE - 75G	EASTBOURNE - 75G
32437	BRIGHTON - 75A(N)	BRIGHTON - 75A(N)	BRIGHTON - 75A(N)	BRIGHTON - 75A(N)	BRIGHTON - 75A(N)	BRIGHTON - 75A(N)	BRIGHTON - 75A(N)
32438	BRIGHTON - 75A	BRIGHTON - 75A	BRIGHTON - 75A	BRIGHTON - 75A	BRIGHTON - 75A	BRIGHTON - 75A	BRIGHTON - 75A
32440	NORWOOD JCN - 75C	NORWOOD JCN - 75C	NORWOOD JCN - 75C	NORWOOD JCN - 75C	NORWOOD JCN - 75C	NORWOOD JCN - 75C	NORWOOD JCN - 75C
32441	THREE BRIDGES - 75E	THREE BRIDGES - 75E	THREE BRIDGES - 75E	THREE BRIDGES - 75E	THREE BRIDGES - 75E	THREE BRIDGES - 75E	THREE BRIDGES - 75E
32442	B ARMS - 73B	B ARMS - 73B	B ARMS - 73B	B ARMS - 73B	B ARMS - 73B	B ARMS - 73B	B ARMS - 73B
32443	BRIGHTON - 75A	BRIGHTON - 75A	BRIGHTON - 75A	BRIGHTON - 75A	BRIGHTON - 75A	BRIGHTON - 75A	BRIGHTON - 75A
32444	NORWOOD JCN - 75C	NORWOOD JCN - 75C	NORWOOD JCN - 75C	NORWOOD JCN - 75C	NORWOOD JCN - 75C	NORWOOD JCN - 75C	NORWOOD JCN - 75C
32445	THREE BRIDGES - 75E	THREE BRIDGES - 75E	THREE BRIDGES - 75E	THREE BRIDGES - 75E	THREE BRIDGES - 75E	THREE BRIDGES - 75E	THREE BRIDGES - 75E
32446	B ARMS - 73B	B ARMS - 73B	B ARMS - 73B	B ARMS - 73B	B ARMS - 73B	B ARMS - 73B	B ARMS - 73B
32447	NORWOOD JCN - 75C	NORWOOD JCN - 75C	NORWOOD JCN - 75C	NORWOOD JCN - 75C	NORWOOD JCN - 75C	NORWOOD JCN - 75C	NORWOOD JCN - 75C
32448	B ARMS - 73B	B ARMS - 73B	B ARMS - 73B	B ARMS - 73B	B ARMS - 73B	B ARMS - 73B	B ARMS - 73B
32449	REDHILL - 75B	REDHILL - 75B	REDHILL - 75B	REDHILL - 75B	REDHILL - 75B	REDHILL - 75B	REDHILL - 75B
32450	REDHILL - 75B	REDHILL - 75B	REDHILL - 75B	REDHILL - 75B	REDHILL - 75B	REDHILL - 75B	REDHILL - 75B
32451	THREE BRIDGES - 75E	THREE BRIDGES - 75E	THREE BRIDGES - 75E	THREE BRIDGES - 75E	THREE BRIDGES - 75E	THREE BRIDGES - 75E	THREE BRIDGES - 75E
32521	HORSHAM - 75D	HORSHAM - 75D	HORSHAM - 75D	HORSHAM - 75D	HORSHAM - 75D	HORSHAM - 75D	HORSHAM - 75D
32522	THREE BRIDGES - 75E	THREE BRIDGES - 75E	THREE BRIDGES - 75E	THREE BRIDGES - 75E	THREE BRIDGES - 75E	THREE BRIDGES - 75E	THREE BRIDGES - 75E
32523	BRIGHTON - 75A	BRIGHTON - 75A	BRIGHTON - 75A	BRIGHTON - 75A	BRIGHTON - 75A	BRIGHTON - 75A	BRIGHTON - 75A
32524	B ARMS - 73B	B ARMS - 73B	B ARMS - 73B	B ARMS - 73B	B ARMS - 73B	B ARMS - 73B	B ARMS - 73B
32525	B ARMS - 73B	B ARMS - 73B	B ARMS - 73B	B ARMS - 73B	B ARMS - 73B	B ARMS - 73B	B ARMS - 73B
32526	NORWOOD JCN - 75C	NORWOOD JCN - 75C	NORWOOD JCN - 75C	NORWOOD JCN - 75C	NORWOOD JCN - 75C	NORWOOD JCN - 75C	NORWOOD JCN - 75C
32527	THREE BRIDGES - 75E	THREE BRIDGES - 75E	THREE BRIDGES - 75E	THREE BRIDGES - 75E	THREE BRIDGES - 75E	THREE BRIDGES - 75E	THREE BRIDGES - 75E
32528	BRIGHTON - 75A	BRIGHTON - 75A	BRIGHTON - 75A	BRIGHTON - 75A	BRIGHTON - 75A	BRIGHTON - 75A	BRIGHTON - 75A
32529	THREE BRIDGES - 75E	THREE BRIDGES - 75E	THREE BRIDGES - 75E	THREE BRIDGES - 75E	THREE BRIDGES - 75E	THREE BRIDGES - 75E	THREE BRIDGES - 75E
32532	THREE BRIDGES - 75E	THREE BRIDGES - 75E	THREE BRIDGES - 75E	THREE BRIDGES - 75E	THREE BRIDGES - 75E	THREE BRIDGES - 75E	THREE BRIDGES - 75E
32534	EASTBOURNE - 75G	EASTBOURNE - 75G	EASTBOURNE - 75G	EASTBOURNE - 75G	EASTBOURNE - 75G	EASTBOURNE - 75G	EASTBOURNE - 75G
32535	NORWOOD JCN - 75C	NORWOOD JCN - 75C	NORWOOD JCN - 75C	NORWOOD JCN - 75C	NORWOOD JCN - 75C	NORWOOD JCN - 75C	NORWOOD JCN - 75C
32536	NORWOOD JCN - 75C	NORWOOD JCN - 75C	NORWOOD JCN - 75C	NORWOOD JCN - 75C	NORWOOD JCN - 75C	NORWOOD JCN - 75C	NORWOOD JCN - 75C
32537	HORSHAM - 75D	HORSHAM - 75D	HORSHAM - 75D	HORSHAM - 75D	HORSHAM - 75D	HORSHAM - 75D	HORSHAM - 75D
32538	EASTBOURNE - 75G	EASTBOURNE - 75G	EASTBOURNE - 75G	EASTBOURNE - 75G	EASTBOURNE - 75G	EASTBOURNE - 75G	EASTBOURNE - 75G
32539	BRIGHTON - 75A	BRIGHTON - 75A	BRIGHTON - 75A	BRIGHTON - 75A	BRIGHTON - 75A	BRIGHTON - 75A	BRIGHTON - 75A
32540	REDHILL - 75B	REDHILL - 75B	REDHILL - 75B	REDHILL - 75B	REDHILL - 75B	REDHILL - 75B	REDHILL - 75B
32541	REDHILL - 75B	REDHILL - 75B	REDHILL - 75B	REDHILL - 75B	REDHILL - 75B	REDHILL - 75B	REDHILL - 75B
32543	BRIGHTON - 75A	BRIGHTON - 75A	BRIGHTON - 75A	BRIGHTON - 75A	BRIGHTON - 75A	BRIGHTON - 75A	BRIGHTON - 75A
32544	NORWOOD JCN - 75C	NORWOOD JCN - 75C	NORWOOD JCN - 75C	NORWOOD JCN - 75C	NORWOOD JCN - 75C	NORWOOD JCN - 75C	NORWOOD JCN - 75C
32545	THREE BRIDGES - 75E	THREE BRIDGES - 75E	THREE BRIDGES - 75E	THREE BRIDGES - 75E	THREE BRIDGES - 75E	THREE BRIDGES - 75E	THREE BRIDGES - 75E
32546	NORWOOD JCN - 75C	NORWOOD JCN - 75C	NORWOOD JCN - 75C	NORWOOD JCN - 75C	NORWOOD JCN - 75C	NORWOOD JCN - 75C	NORWOOD JCN - 75C
32547	NORWOOD JCN - 75C	NORWOOD JCN - 75C	NORWOOD JCN - 75C	NORWOOD JCN - 75C	NORWOOD JCN - 75C	NORWOOD JCN - 75C	NORWOOD JCN - 75C
32548	HORSHAM - 75D	HORSHAM - 75D	HORSHAM - 75D	HORSHAM - 75D	HORSHAM - 75D	HORSHAM - 75D	HORSHAM - 75D
32549	B ARMS - 73B	B ARMS - 73B	B ARMS - 73B	B ARMS - 73B	B ARMS - 73B	B ARMS - 73B	B ARMS - 73B
32550	HORSHAM - 75D	HORSHAM - 75D	HORSHAM - 75D	HORSHAM - 75D	HORSHAM - 75D	HORSHAM - 75D	HORSHAM - 75D
32551	B ARMS - 73B	B ARMS - 73B	B ARMS - 73B	B ARMS - 73B	B ARMS - 73B	B ARMS - 73B	B ARMS - 73B
32552	THREE BRIDGES - 75E	THREE BRIDGES - 75E	THREE BRIDGES - 75E	THREE BRIDGES - 75E	THREE BRIDGES - 75E	THREE BRIDGES - 75E	THREE BRIDGES - 75E
32553	THREE BRIDGES - 75E	THREE BRIDGES - 75E	THREE BRIDGES - 75E	THREE BRIDGES - 75E	THREE BRIDGES - 75E	THREE BRIDGES - 75E	THREE BRIDGES - 75E
32554	B ARMS - 73B	B ARMS - 73B	B ARMS - 73B	B ARMS - 73B	B ARMS - 73B	B ARMS - 73B	B ARMS - 73B
				C3 0-6-0 (1906)			
32300	FRATTON - 71D	FRATTON - 71D	FRATTON - 71D	FRATTON - 71D	FRATTON - 71D	FRATTON - 71D	FRATTON - 71D
32301	FRATTON - 71D	FRATTON - 71D	FRATTON - 71D	FRATTON - 71D	FRATTON - 71D	FRATTON - 71D	FRATTON - 71D
32302	HORSHAM - 75D	HORSHAM - 75D	HORSHAM - 75D	HORSHAM - 75D	HORSHAM - 75D	HORSHAM - 75D	HORSHAM - 75D
32303	FRATTON - 71D	FRATTON - 71D	FRATTON - 71D	FRATTON - 71D	FRATTON - 71D	FRATTON - 71D	FRATTON - 71D
32306	FRATTON - 71D	FRATTON - 71D	FRATTON - 71D	FRATTON - 71D	FRATTON - 71D	FRATTON - 71D	FRATTON - 71D

'700' 0-6-0 (1897)

loco	Apr-50	Sep-50	Oct-50	Nov-50	Dec-50	Mar-51	Apr-51
30306	EASTLEIGH - 71A	EASTLEIGH - 71A	EASTLEIGH - 71A	EASTLEIGH - 71A	EASTLEIGH - 71A	EASTLEIGH - 71A	EASTLEIGH - 71A
30308	GUILDFORD - 70C	GUILDFORD - 70C	GUILDFORD - 70C	GUILDFORD - 70C	GUILDFORD - 70C	GUILDFORD - 70C	GUILDFORD - 70C
30309	FELTHAM - 70B	FELTHAM - 70B	FELTHAM - 70B	FELTHAM - 70B	FELTHAM - 70B	FELTHAM - 70B	FELTHAM - 70B
30315	SALISBURY - 72B	SALISBURY - 72B	SALISBURY - 72B	SALISBURY - 72B	SALISBURY - 72B	SALISBURY - 72B	SALISBURY - 72B
30316	EASTLEIGH - 71A	EASTLEIGH - 71A	EASTLEIGH - 71A	EASTLEIGH - 71A	EASTLEIGH - 71A	EASTLEIGH - 71A	EASTLEIGH - 71A
30317	SALISBURY - 72B	SALISBURY - 72B	SALISBURY - 72B	SALISBURY - 72B	SALISBURY - 72B	SALISBURY - 72B	SALISBURY - 72B
30325	GUILDFORD - 70C	GUILDFORD - 70C	GUILDFORD - 70C	GUILDFORD - 70C	GUILDFORD - 70C	GUILDFORD - 70C	GUILDFORD - 70C
30326	GUILDFORD - 70C	GUILDFORD - 70C	GUILDFORD - 70C	GUILDFORD - 70C	GUILDFORD - 70C	GUILDFORD - 70C	GUILDFORD - 70C
30327	GUILDFORD - 70C	GUILDFORD - 70C	GUILDFORD - 70C	GUILDFORD - 70C	GUILDFORD - 70C	GUILDFORD - 70C	GUILDFORD - 70C
30339	NINE ELMS - 70A	NINE ELMS - 70A	NINE ELMS - 70A	NINE ELMS - 70A	NINE ELMS - 70A	NINE ELMS - 70A	NINE ELMS - 70A
30346	FELTHAM - 70B	FELTHAM - 70B	FELTHAM - 70B	FELTHAM - 70B	FELTHAM - 70B	FELTHAM - 70B	FELTHAM - 70B
30350	EASTLEIGH - 71A	EASTLEIGH - 71A	EASTLEIGH - 71A	EASTLEIGH - 71A	EASTLEIGH - 71A	EASTLEIGH - 71A	EASTLEIGH - 71A
30352	FELTHAM - 70B	FELTHAM - 70B	FELTHAM - 70B	FELTHAM - 70B	FELTHAM - 70B	FELTHAM - 70B	FELTHAM - 70B
30355	SALISBURY - 72B	SALISBURY - 72B	SALISBURY - 72B	BASINGSTOKE - 70D	GUILDFORD - 70C	GUILDFORD - 70C	GUILDFORD - 70C
30368	BASINGSTOKE - 70D	BASINGSTOKE - 70D	BASINGSTOKE - 70D	BASINGSTOKE - 70D	BASINGSTOKE - 70D	BASINGSTOKE - 70D	BASINGSTOKE - 70D
30687	FELTHAM - 70B	FELTHAM - 70B	FELTHAM - 70B	FELTHAM - 70B	FELTHAM - 70B	FELTHAM - 70B	FELTHAM - 70B
30688	FELTHAM - 70B	FELTHAM - 70B	FELTHAM - 70B	FELTHAM - 70B	FELTHAM - 70B	FELTHAM - 70B	FELTHAM - 70B
30689	FELTHAM - 70B	FELTHAM - 70B	FELTHAM - 70B	FELTHAM - 70B	FELTHAM - 70B	FELTHAM - 70B	FELTHAM - 70B
30690	SALISBURY - 72B	SALISBURY - 72B	SALISBURY - 72B	SALISBURY - 72B	SALISBURY - 72B	SALISBURY - 72B	SALISBURY - 72B
30691	SALISBURY - 72B	SALISBURY - 72B	SALISBURY - 72B	SALISBURY - 72B	SALISBURY - 72B	SALISBURY - 72B	SALISBURY - 72B
30692	NINE ELMS - 70A	NINE ELMS - 70A	NINE ELMS - 70A	NINE ELMS - 70A	NINE ELMS - 70A	NINE ELMS - 70A	NINE ELMS - 70A
30693	BASINGSTOKE - 70D	BASINGSTOKE - 70D	BASINGSTOKE - 70D	BASINGSTOKE - 70D	BASINGSTOKE - 70D	BASINGSTOKE - 70D	FELTHAM - 70B
30694	NINE ELMS - 70A	NINE ELMS - 70A	NINE ELMS - 70A	NINE ELMS - 70A	NINE ELMS - 70A	NINE ELMS - 70A	NINE ELMS - 70A
30695	BOURNEMOUTH - 71B	BOURNEMOUTH - 71B	BOURNEMOUTH - 71B	BOURNEMOUTH - 71B	BOURNEMOUTH - 71B	BOURNEMOUTH - 71B	BOURNEMOUTH - 71B
30696	FELTHAM - 70B	FELTHAM - 70B	FELTHAM - 70B	FELTHAM - 70B	FELTHAM - 70B	FELTHAM - 70B	FELTHAM - 70B
30697	FELTHAM - 70B	FELTHAM - 70B	FELTHAM - 70B	FELTHAM - 70B	FELTHAM - 70B	FELTHAM - 70B	FELTHAM - 70B
30698	FELTHAM - 70B	FELTHAM - 70B	FELTHAM - 70B	FELTHAM - 70B	FELTHAM - 70B	FELTHAM - 70B	FELTHAM - 70B
30699	NINE ELMS - 70A	NINE ELMS - 70A	NINE ELMS - 70A	NINE ELMS - 70A	NINE ELMS - 70A	NINE ELMS - 70A	NINE ELMS - 70A
30700	EASTLEIGH - 71A	EASTLEIGH - 71A	EASTLEIGH - 71A	EASTLEIGH - 71A	EASTLEIGH - 71A	EASTLEIGH - 71A	EASTLEIGH - 71A
30701	NINE ELMS - 70A	NINE ELMS - 70A	NINE ELMS - 70A	NINE ELMS - 70A	NINE ELMS - 70A	NINE ELMS - 70A	NINE ELMS - 70A

C2X 0-6-0 (1908)

loco	Apr-50	Sep-50	Oct-50	Nov-50	Dec-50	Mar-51	Apr-51
32434	EASTBOURNE - 75G	EASTBOURNE - 75G	BRIGHTON - 75A	BRIGHTON - 75A	BRIGHTON - 75A	EASTBOURNE - 75G	EASTBOURNE - 75G
32437	BRIGHTON - 75A(N)	BRIGHTON - 75A (N)	BRIGHTON - 75A (N)	BRIGHTON - 75A (N)	BRIGHTON - 75A (N)	BRIGHTON - 75A (N)	BRIGHTON - 75A (N)
32438	BRIGHTON - 75A	BRIGHTON - 75A	BRIGHTON - 75A	BRIGHTON - 75A	BRIGHTON - 75A	BRIGHTON - 75A	BRIGHTON - 75A
32440	NORWOOD JCN - 75C	NORWOOD JCN - 75C	NORWOOD JCN - 75C	NORWOOD JCN - 75C	NORWOOD JCN - 75C	NORWOOD JCN - 75C	NORWOOD JCN - 75C
32441	THREE BRIDGES - 75E	THREE BRIDGES - 75E	THREE BRIDGES - 75E	THREE BRIDGES - 75E	THREE BRIDGES - 75E	THREE BRIDGES - 75E	THREE BRIDGES - 75E
32442	B ARMS - 73B	B ARMS - 73B	B ARMS - 73B	B ARMS - 73B	B ARMS - 73B	B ARMS - 73B	B ARMS - 73B
32443	BRIGHTON - 75A	BRIGHTON - 75A	BRIGHTON - 75A	BRIGHTON - 75A	BRIGHTON - 75A	BRIGHTON - 75A	BRIGHTON - 75A
32444	NORWOOD JCN - 75C	NORWOOD JCN - 75C	NORWOOD JCN - 75C	NORWOOD JCN - 75C	NORWOOD JCN - 75C	NORWOOD JCN - 75C	NORWOOD JCN - 75C
32445	THREE BRIDGES - 75E	THREE BRIDGES - 75E	THREE BRIDGES - 75E	THREE BRIDGES - 75E	THREE BRIDGES - 75E	THREE BRIDGES - 75E	THREE BRIDGES - 75E
32446	B ARMS - 73B	B ARMS - 73B	B ARMS - 73B	B ARMS - 73B	B ARMS - 73B	B ARMS - 73B	B ARMS - 73B
32447	NORWOOD JCN - 75C	NORWOOD JCN - 75C	NORWOOD JCN - 75C	NORWOOD JCN - 75C	NORWOOD JCN - 75C	NORWOOD JCN - 75C	NORWOOD JCN - 75C
32448	B ARMS - 73B	B ARMS - 73B	B ARMS - 73B	B ARMS - 73B	B ARMS - 73B	B ARMS - 73B	B ARMS - 73B
32449	REDHILL - 75B	REDHILL - 75B	REDHILL - 75B	REDHILL - 75B	REDHILL - 75B	REDHILL - 75B	REDHILL - 75B
32450	REDHILL - 75B	REDHILL - 75B	REDHILL - 75B	REDHILL - 75B	REDHILL - 75B	REDHILL - 75B	REDHILL - 75B
32451	THREE BRIDGES - 75E	THREE BRIDGES - 75E	THREE BRIDGES - 75E	THREE BRIDGES - 75E	THREE BRIDGES - 75E	THREE BRIDGES - 75E	THREE BRIDGES - 75E
32521	HORSHAM - 75D	HORSHAM - 75D	HORSHAM - 75D	HORSHAM - 75D	HORSHAM - 75D	HORSHAM - 75D	HORSHAM - 75D
32522	THREE BRIDGES - 75E	THREE BRIDGES - 75E	THREE BRIDGES - 75E	THREE BRIDGES - 75E	THREE BRIDGES - 75E	THREE BRIDGES - 75E	THREE BRIDGES - 75E
32523	BRIGHTON - 75A	BRIGHTON - 75A	BRIGHTON - 75A	BRIGHTON - 75A	BRIGHTON - 75A	BRIGHTON - 75A	BRIGHTON - 75A
32524	B ARMS - 73B	B ARMS - 73B	B ARMS - 73B	B ARMS - 73B	B ARMS - 73B	B ARMS - 73B	B ARMS - 73B
32525	B ARMS - 73B	B ARMS - 73B	B ARMS - 73B	B ARMS - 73B	B ARMS - 73B	B ARMS - 73B	B ARMS - 73B
32526	NORWOOD JCN - 75C	NORWOOD JCN - 75C	NORWOOD JCN - 75C	NORWOOD JCN - 75C	NORWOOD JCN - 75C	NORWOOD JCN - 75C	NORWOOD JCN - 75C
32527	THREE BRIDGES - 75E	THREE BRIDGES - 75E	THREE BRIDGES - 75E	THREE BRIDGES - 75E	THREE BRIDGES - 75E	THREE BRIDGES - 75E	THREE BRIDGES - 75E
32528	BRIGHTON - 75A	BRIGHTON - 75A	BRIGHTON - 75A	BRIGHTON - 75A	BRIGHTON - 75A	BRIGHTON - 75A	BRIGHTON - 75A
32529	THREE BRIDGES - 75E	THREE BRIDGES - 75E	THREE BRIDGES - 75E	THREE BRIDGES - 75E	THREE BRIDGES - 75E	THREE BRIDGES - 75E	THREE BRIDGES - 75E
32532	THREE BRIDGES - 75E	THREE BRIDGES - 75E	THREE BRIDGES - 75E	THREE BRIDGES - 75E	THREE BRIDGES - 75E	THREE BRIDGES - 75E	THREE BRIDGES - 75E
32534	EASTBOURNE - 75G	EASTBOURNE - 75G	BRIGHTON - 75A	BRIGHTON - 75A	BRIGHTON - 75A	BRIGHTON - 75A	BRIGHTON - 75A
32535	NORWOOD JCN - 75C	NORWOOD JCN - 75C	NORWOOD JCN - 75C	NORWOOD JCN - 75C	NORWOOD JCN - 75C	NORWOOD JCN - 75C	NORWOOD JCN - 75C
32536	NORWOOD JCN - 75C	NORWOOD JCN - 75C	NORWOOD JCN - 75C	NORWOOD JCN - 75C	NORWOOD JCN - 75C	NORWOOD JCN - 75C	NORWOOD JCN - 75C
32537	HORSHAM - 75D	HORSHAM - 75D	HORSHAM - 75D	BRIGHTON - 75A(N)	BRIGHTON - 75A(N)	BRIGHTON - 75A(N)	BRIGHTON - 75A(N)
32538	EASTBOURNE - 75G	EASTBOURNE - 75G	BRIGHTON - 75A	BRIGHTON - 75A	BRIGHTON - 75A	EASTBOURNE - 75G	EASTBOURNE - 75G
32539	BRIGHTON - 75A	BRIGHTON - 75A	BRIGHTON - 75A	HORSHAM - 75D	HORSHAM - 75D	HORSHAM - 75D	HORSHAM - 75D
32540	REDHILL - 75B	REDHILL - 75B	REDHILL - 75B	REDHILL - 75B	REDHILL - 75B	REDHILL - 75B	REDHILL - 75B
32541	REDHILL - 75B	REDHILL - 75B	REDHILL - 75B	REDHILL - 75B	REDHILL - 75B	REDHILL - 75B	REDHILL - 75B
32543	BRIGHTON - 75A	BRIGHTON - 75A	BRIGHTON - 75A	BRIGHTON - 75A	BRIGHTON - 75A	BRIGHTON - 75A	BRIGHTON - 75A
32544	NORWOOD JCN - 75C	HORSHAM - 75D	HORSHAM - 75D	HORSHAM - 75D	HORSHAM - 75D	HORSHAM - 75D	HORSHAM - 75D
32545	THREE BRIDGES - 75E	THREE BRIDGES - 75E	THREE BRIDGES - 75E	THREE BRIDGES - 75E	THREE BRIDGES - 75E	THREE BRIDGES - 75E	THREE BRIDGES - 75E
32546	NORWOOD JCN - 75C	NORWOOD JCN - 75C	NORWOOD JCN - 75C	NORWOOD JCN - 75C	NORWOOD JCN - 75C	NORWOOD JCN - 75C	NORWOOD JCN - 75C
32547	NORWOOD JCN - 75C	NORWOOD JCN - 75C	NORWOOD JCN - 75C	NORWOOD JCN - 75C	NORWOOD JCN - 75C	NORWOOD JCN - 75C	NORWOOD JCN - 75C
32548	HORSHAM - 75D	HORSHAM - 75D	HORSHAM - 75D	HORSHAM - 75D	HORSHAM - 75D	FRATTON - 71D	FRATTON - 71D
32549	B ARMS - 73B	B ARMS - 73B	B ARMS - 73B	B ARMS - 73B	B ARMS - 73B	B ARMS - 73B	B ARMS - 73B
32550	HORSHAM - 75D	REDHILL - 75B	REDHILL - 75B	REDHILL - 75B	REDHILL - 75B	REDHILL - 75B	REDHILL - 75B
32551	B ARMS - 73B	B ARMS - 73B	B ARMS - 73B	B ARMS - 73B	B ARMS - 73B	B ARMS - 73B	B ARMS - 73B
32552	THREE BRIDGES - 75E	THREE BRIDGES - 75E	THREE BRIDGES - 75E	THREE BRIDGES - 75E	THREE BRIDGES - 75E	THREE BRIDGES - 75E	THREE BRIDGES - 75E
32553	THREE BRIDGES - 75E	THREE BRIDGES - 75E	THREE BRIDGES - 75E	THREE BRIDGES - 75E	THREE BRIDGES - 75E	THREE BRIDGES - 75E	THREE BRIDGES - 75E
32554	B ARMS - 73B	B ARMS - 73B	B ARMS - 73B	B ARMS - 73B	B ARMS - 73B	B ARMS - 73B	B ARMS - 73B

C3 0-6-0 (1906)

loco	Apr-50	Sep-50	Oct-50	Nov-50	Dec-50	Mar-51	Apr-51
32300	FRATTON - 71D	FRATTON - 71D	FRATTON - 71D	FRATTON - 71D	FRATTON - 71D	FRATTON - 71D	FRATTON - 71D
32301	FRATTON - 71D	FRATTON - 71D	FRATTON - 71D	FRATTON - 71D	FRATTON - 71D	W/D	W/D
32302	HORSHAM - 75D	HORSHAM - 75D	HORSHAM - 75D	FRATTON - 71D	FRATTON - 71D	FRATTON - 71D	FRATTON - 71D
32303	FRATTON - 71D	FRATTON - 71D	FRATTON - 71D	FRATTON - 71D	FRATTON - 71D	FRATTON - 71D	FRATTON - 71D
32306	FRATTON - 71D	FRATTON - 71D	FRATTON - 71D	FRATTON - 71D	FRATTON - 71D	FRATTON - 71D	FRATTON - 71D

loco	Jun-51	Jul-51	Sep-51	Dec-51	Jan-52	Mar-52	Jun-52
'700' 0-6-0 (1897)							
30306	EASTLEIGH - 71A	EASTLEIGH - 71A	EASTLEIGH - 71A	EASTLEIGH - 71A	EASTLEIGH - 71A	EASTLEIGH - 71A	EASTLEIGH - 71A
30308	GUILDFORD - 70C	GUILDFORD - 70C	GUILDFORD - 70C	GUILDFORD - 70C	GUILDFORD - 70C	GUILDFORD - 70C	GUILDFORD - 70C
30309	FELTHAM - 70B	FELTHAM - 70B	FELTHAM - 70B	FELTHAM - 70B	FELTHAM - 70B	FELTHAM - 70B	FELTHAM - 70B
30315	SALISBURY - 72B	SALISBURY - 72B	SALISBURY - 72B	SALISBURY - 72B	SALISBURY - 72B	SALISBURY - 72B	SALISBURY - 72B
30316	EASTLEIGH - 71A	EASTLEIGH - 71A	EASTLEIGH - 71A	EASTLEIGH - 71A	EASTLEIGH - 71A	EASTLEIGH - 71A	EASTLEIGH - 71A
30317	SALISBURY - 72B	SALISBURY - 72B	SALISBURY - 72B	SALISBURY - 72B	SALISBURY - 72B	SALISBURY - 72B	SALISBURY - 72B
30325	GUILDFORD - 70C	GUILDFORD - 70C	GUILDFORD - 70C	GUILDFORD - 70C	GUILDFORD - 70C	GUILDFORD - 70C	GUILDFORD - 70C
30326	GUILDFORD - 70C	GUILDFORD - 70C	GUILDFORD - 70C	GUILDFORD - 70C	GUILDFORD - 70C	GUILDFORD - 70C	GUILDFORD - 70C
30327	GUILDFORD - 70C	GUILDFORD - 70C	GUILDFORD - 70C	GUILDFORD - 70C	GUILDFORD - 70C	GUILDFORD - 70C	GUILDFORD - 70C
30339	NINE ELMS - 70A	NINE ELMS - 70A	NINE ELMS - 70A	NINE ELMS - 70A	NINE ELMS - 70A	NINE ELMS - 70A	NINE ELMS - 70A
30346	FELTHAM - 70B	FELTHAM - 70B	FELTHAM - 70B	FELTHAM - 70B	FELTHAM - 70B	FELTHAM - 70B	FELTHAM - 70B
30350	EASTLEIGH - 71A	EASTLEIGH - 71A	EASTLEIGH - 71A	EASTLEIGH - 71A	EASTLEIGH - 71A	EASTLEIGH - 71A	EASTLEIGH - 71A
30352	FELTHAM - 70B	FELTHAM - 70B	FELTHAM - 70B	FELTHAM - 70B	FELTHAM - 70B	FELTHAM - 70B	FELTHAM - 70B
30355	GUILDFORD - 70C	GUILDFORD - 70C	GUILDFORD - 70C	GUILDFORD - 70C	GUILDFORD - 70C	GUILDFORD - 70C	GUILDFORD - 70C
30368	BASINGSTOKE - 70D	BASINGSTOKE - 70D	BASINGSTOKE - 70D	BASINGSTOKE - 70D	BASINGSTOKE - 70D	BASINGSTOKE - 70D	BASINGSTOKE - 70D
30687	FELTHAM - 70B	FELTHAM - 70B	FELTHAM - 70B	FELTHAM - 70B	FELTHAM - 70B	FELTHAM - 70B	FELTHAM - 70B
30688	FELTHAM - 70B	FELTHAM - 70B	FELTHAM - 70B	FELTHAM - 70B	FELTHAM - 70B	FELTHAM - 70B	FELTHAM - 70B
30689	FELTHAM - 70B	FELTHAM - 70B	FELTHAM - 70B	FELTHAM - 70B	FELTHAM - 70B	FELTHAM - 70B	FELTHAM - 70B
30690	SALISBURY - 72B	SALISBURY - 72B	SALISBURY - 72B	SALISBURY - 72B	SALISBURY - 72B	SALISBURY - 72B	SALISBURY - 72B
30691	SALISBURY - 72B	SALISBURY - 72B	SALISBURY - 72B	SALISBURY - 72B	SALISBURY - 72B	SALISBURY - 72B	SALISBURY - 72B
30692	NINE ELMS - 70A	NINE ELMS - 70A	NINE ELMS - 70A	NINE ELMS - 70A	NINE ELMS - 70A	NINE ELMS - 70A	NINE ELMS - 70A
30693	FELTHAM - 70B	BOURNEMOUTH - 71B	GUILDFORD - 70C	GUILDFORD - 70C	GUILDFORD - 70C	GUILDFORD - 70C	GUILDFORD - 70C
30694	NINE ELMS - 70A	NINE ELMS - 70A	NINE ELMS - 70A	NINE ELMS - 70A	NINE ELMS - 70A	NINE ELMS - 70A	NINE ELMS - 70A
30695	BOURNEMOUTH - 71B	BOURNEMOUTH - 71B	BOURNEMOUTH - 71B	BOURNEMOUTH - 71B	BOURNEMOUTH - 71B	BOURNEMOUTH - 71B	BOURNEMOUTH - 71B
30696	FELTHAM - 70B	FELTHAM - 70B	FELTHAM - 70B	FELTHAM - 70B	FELTHAM - 70B	FELTHAM - 70B	FELTHAM - 70B
30697	FELTHAM - 70B	FELTHAM - 70B	FELTHAM - 70B	FELTHAM - 70B	FELTHAM - 70B	FELTHAM - 70B	FELTHAM - 70B
30698	FELTHAM - 70B	FELTHAM - 70B	FELTHAM - 70B	FELTHAM - 70B	FELTHAM - 70B	FELTHAM - 70B	FELTHAM - 70B
30699	NINE ELMS - 70A	NINE ELMS - 70A	NINE ELMS - 70A	NINE ELMS - 70A	NINE ELMS - 70A	NINE ELMS - 70A	NINE ELMS - 70A
30700	EASTLEIGH - 71A	EASTLEIGH - 71A	EASTLEIGH - 71A	EASTLEIGH - 71A	EASTLEIGH - 71A	EASTLEIGH - 71A	EASTLEIGH - 71A
30701	NINE ELMS - 70A	NINE ELMS - 70A	NINE ELMS - 70A	NINE ELMS - 70A	NINE ELMS - 70A	NINE ELMS - 70A	NINE ELMS - 70A
C2X 0-6-0 (1908)							
32434	EASTBOURNE - 75G	EASTBOURNE - 75G	EASTBOURNE - 75G	EASTBOURNE - 75G	EASTBOURNE - 75G	EASTBOURNE - 75G	EASTBOURNE - 75G
32437	BRIGHTON - 75A (N)	BRIGHTON - 75A (N)	BRIGHTON - 75A (N)	BRIGHTON - 75A (N)	BRIGHTON - 75A (N)	BRIGHTON - 75A (N)	BRIGHTON - 75A (N)
32438	BRIGHTON - 75A	BRIGHTON - 75A	BRIGHTON - 75A	BRIGHTON - 75A	BRIGHTON - 75A	BRIGHTON - 75A	BRIGHTON - 75A
32440	NORWOOD JCN - 75C	NORWOOD JCN - 75C	NORWOOD JCN - 75C	NORWOOD JCN - 75C	NORWOOD JCN - 75C	NORWOOD JCN - 75C	NORWOOD JCN - 75C
32441	THREE BRIDGES - 75E	THREE BRIDGES - 75E	THREE BRIDGES - 75E	THREE BRIDGES - 75E	THREE BRIDGES - 75E	THREE BRIDGES - 75E	THREE BRIDGES - 75E
32442	B.ARMS - 73B	B.ARMS - 73B	B.ARMS - 73B	B.ARMS - 73B	B.ARMS - 73B	B.ARMS - 73B	B.ARMS - 73B
32443	BRIGHTON - 75A	NORWOOD JCN - 75C	NORWOOD JCN - 75C	NORWOOD JCN - 75C	NORWOOD JCN - 75C	NORWOOD JCN - 75C	NORWOOD JCN - 75C
32444	NORWOOD JCN - 75C	NORWOOD JCN - 75C	NORWOOD JCN - 75C	NORWOOD JCN - 75C	NORWOOD JCN - 75C	NORWOOD JCN - 75C	NORWOOD JCN - 75C
32445	THREE BRIDGES - 75E	THREE BRIDGES - 75E	THREE BRIDGES - 75E	THREE BRIDGES - 75E	THREE BRIDGES - 75E	THREE BRIDGES - 75E	THREE BRIDGES - 75E
32446	B.ARMS - 73B	B.ARMS - 73B	B.ARMS - 73B	B.ARMS - 73B	B.ARMS - 73B	B.ARMS - 73B	B.ARMS - 73B
32447	NORWOOD JCN - 75C	NORWOOD JCN - 75C	NORWOOD JCN - 75C	NORWOOD JCN - 75C	NORWOOD JCN - 75C	NORWOOD JCN - 75C	NORWOOD JCN - 75C
32448	B.ARMS - 73B	B.ARMS - 73B	B.ARMS - 73B	B.ARMS - 73B	B.ARMS - 73B	B.ARMS - 73B	B.ARMS - 73B
32449	REDHILL - 75B	REDHILL - 75B	REDHILL - 75B	REDHILL - 75B	REDHILL - 75B	REDHILL - 75B	REDHILL - 75B
32450	REDHILL - 75B	REDHILL - 75B	REDHILL - 75B	REDHILL - 75B	REDHILL - 75B	REDHILL - 75B	REDHILL - 75B
32451	THREE BRIDGES - 75E	THREE BRIDGES - 75E	THREE BRIDGES - 75E	THREE BRIDGES - 75E	THREE BRIDGES - 75E	THREE BRIDGES - 75E	THREE BRIDGES - 75E
32521	HORSHAM - 75D	HORSHAM - 75D	HORSHAM - 75D	HORSHAM - 75D	HORSHAM - 75D	HORSHAM - 75D	HORSHAM - 75D
32522	THREE BRIDGES - 75E	THREE BRIDGES - 75E	THREE BRIDGES - 75E	THREE BRIDGES - 75E	THREE BRIDGES - 75E	THREE BRIDGES - 75E	THREE BRIDGES - 75E
32523	BRIGHTON - 75A	BRIGHTON - 75A	BRIGHTON - 75A	BRIGHTON - 75A	BRIGHTON - 75A	BRIGHTON - 75A	BRIGHTON - 75A
32524	B.ARMS - 73B	B.ARMS - 73B	B.ARMS - 73B	B.ARMS - 73B	B.ARMS - 73B	B.ARMS - 73B	B.ARMS - 73B
32525	B.ARMS - 73B	B.ARMS - 73B	B.ARMS - 73B	B.ARMS - 73B	B.ARMS - 73B	B.ARMS - 73B	B.ARMS - 73B
32526	NORWOOD JCN - 75C	NORWOOD JCN - 75C	NORWOOD JCN - 75C	NORWOOD JCN - 75C	NORWOOD JCN - 75C	NORWOOD JCN - 75C	NORWOOD JCN - 75C
32527	THREE BRIDGES - 75E	THREE BRIDGES - 75E	THREE BRIDGES - 75E	THREE BRIDGES - 75E	THREE BRIDGES - 75E	THREE BRIDGES - 75E	THREE BRIDGES - 75E
32528	BRIGHTON - 75A	BRIGHTON - 75A	BRIGHTON - 75A	BRIGHTON - 75A	BRIGHTON - 75A	BRIGHTON - 75A	BRIGHTON - 75A
32529	THREE BRIDGES - 75E	THREE BRIDGES - 75E	THREE BRIDGES - 75E	THREE BRIDGES - 75E	THREE BRIDGES - 75E	THREE BRIDGES - 75E	THREE BRIDGES - 75E
32532	THREE BRIDGES - 75E	THREE BRIDGES - 75E	THREE BRIDGES - 75E	THREE BRIDGES - 75E	THREE BRIDGES - 75E	THREE BRIDGES - 75E	THREE BRIDGES - 75E
32534	BRIGHTON - 75A	BRIGHTON - 75A	BRIGHTON - 75A	BRIGHTON - 75A	BRIGHTON - 75A	BRIGHTON - 75A	BRIGHTON - 75A
32535	NORWOOD JCN - 75C	NORWOOD JCN - 75C	NORWOOD JCN - 75C	NORWOOD JCN - 75C	NORWOOD JCN - 75C	NORWOOD JCN - 75C	NORWOOD JCN - 75C
32536	NORWOOD JCN - 75C	NORWOOD JCN - 75C	NORWOOD JCN - 75C	NORWOOD JCN - 75C	NORWOOD JCN - 75C	NORWOOD JCN - 75C	NORWOOD JCN - 75C
32537	BRIGHTON - 75A(N)	BRIGHTON - 75A(N)	BRIGHTON - 75A(N)	BRIGHTON - 75A(N)	BRIGHTON - 75A(N)	BRIGHTON - 75A(N)	BRIGHTON - 75A(N)
32538	EASTBOURNE - 75G	EASTBOURNE - 75G	EASTBOURNE - 75G	EASTBOURNE - 75G	EASTBOURNE - 75G	EASTBOURNE - 75G	EASTBOURNE - 75G
32539	HORSHAM - 75D	HORSHAM - 75D	HORSHAM - 75D	HORSHAM - 75D	HORSHAM - 75D	HORSHAM - 75D	HORSHAM - 75D
32540	REDHILL - 75B	REDHILL - 75B	REDHILL - 75B	REDHILL - 75B	REDHILL - 75B	REDHILL - 75B	REDHILL - 75B
32541	REDHILL - 75B	REDHILL - 75B	REDHILL - 75B	REDHILL - 75B	REDHILL - 75B	REDHILL - 75B	REDHILL - 75B
32543	BRIGHTON - 75A	BRIGHTON - 75A	BRIGHTON - 75A	BRIGHTON - 75A	BRIGHTON - 75A	BRIGHTON - 75A	BRIGHTON - 75A
32544	HORSHAM - 75D	HORSHAM - 75D	HORSHAM - 75D	HORSHAM - 75D	HORSHAM - 75D	HORSHAM - 75D	HORSHAM - 75D
32545	THREE BRIDGES - 75E	THREE BRIDGES - 75E	THREE BRIDGES - 75E	THREE BRIDGES - 75E	THREE BRIDGES - 75E	THREE BRIDGES - 75E	THREE BRIDGES - 75E
32546	NORWOOD JCN - 75C	NORWOOD JCN - 75C	NORWOOD JCN - 75C	NORWOOD JCN - 75C	NORWOOD JCN - 75C	NORWOOD JCN - 75C	NORWOOD JCN - 75C
32547	NORWOOD JCN - 75C	NORWOOD JCN - 75C	NORWOOD JCN - 75C	NORWOOD JCN - 75C	NORWOOD JCN - 75C	NORWOOD JCN - 75C	NORWOOD JCN - 75C
32548	FRATTON - 71D	FRATTON - 71D	FRATTON - 71D	FRATTON - 71D	FRATTON - 71D	FRATTON - 71D	FRATTON - 71D
32549	FRATTON - 71D	FRATTON - 71D	FRATTON - 71D	FRATTON - 71D	FRATTON - 71D	FRATTON - 71D	FRATTON - 71D
32550	FRATTON - 71D	FRATTON - 71D	FRATTON - 71D	FRATTON - 71D	FRATTON - 71D	FRATTON - 71D	FRATTON - 71D
32551	T.WELLS - 75F	T.WELLS - 75F	T.WELLS - 75F	T.WELLS - 75F	T.WELLS - 75F	T.WELLS - 75F	T.WELLS - 75F
32552	THREE BRIDGES - 75E	THREE BRIDGES - 75E	THREE BRIDGES - 75E	THREE BRIDGES - 75E	THREE BRIDGES - 75E	THREE BRIDGES - 75E	THREE BRIDGES - 75E
32553	THREE BRIDGES - 75E	THREE BRIDGES - 75E	THREE BRIDGES - 75E	THREE BRIDGES - 75E	THREE BRIDGES - 75E	THREE BRIDGES - 75E	THREE BRIDGES - 75E
32554	B.ARMS - 73B	B.ARMS - 73B	B.ARMS - 73B	B.ARMS - 73B	B.ARMS - 73B	B.ARMS - 73B	B.ARMS - 73B
C3 0-6-0 (1906)							
32300	FRATTON - 71D	W/D	W/D	W/D	W/D	W/D	W/D
32302	FRATTON - 71D	FRATTON - 71D	FRATTON - 71D	FRATTON - 71D	W/D	W/D	W/D
32303	FRATTON - 71D	FRATTON - 71D	W/D	W/D	W/D	W/D	W/D
32306	FRATTON - 71D	FRATTON - 71D	FRATTON - 71D	W/D	W/D	W/D	W/D

loco	Sep-52	Dec-52	Mar-53	May-53	Jul-53	Sep-53	Nov-53
				'700' 0-6-0 (1897)			
30306	EASTLEIGH - 71A	EASTLEIGH - 71A	EASTLEIGH - 71A	EASTLEIGH - 71A	EASTLEIGH - 71A	EASTLEIGH - 71A	EASTLEIGH - 71A
30308	GUILDFORD - 70C	GUILDFORD - 70C	GUILDFORD - 70C	GUILDFORD - 70C	GUILDFORD - 70C	GUILDFORD - 70C	GUILDFORD - 70C
30309	FELTHAM - 70B	FELTHAM - 70B	FELTHAM - 70B	FELTHAM - 70B	FELTHAM - 70B	FELTHAM - 70B	FELTHAM - 70B
30315	SALISBURY - 72B	SALISBURY - 72B	SALISBURY - 72B	SALISBURY - 72B	SALISBURY - 72B	SALISBURY - 72B	SALISBURY - 72B
30316	EASTLEIGH - 71A	EASTLEIGH - 71A	EASTLEIGH - 71A	EASTLEIGH - 71A	EASTLEIGH - 71A	EASTLEIGH - 71A	EASTLEIGH - 71A
30317	SALISBURY - 72B	SALISBURY - 72B	SALISBURY - 72B	SALISBURY - 72B	SALISBURY - 72B	SALISBURY - 72B	SALISBURY - 72B
30325	GUILDFORD - 70C	GUILDFORD - 70C	GUILDFORD - 70C	GUILDFORD - 70C	GUILDFORD - 70C	GUILDFORD - 70C	GUILDFORD - 70C
30326	GUILDFORD - 70C	GUILDFORD - 70C	GUILDFORD - 70C	GUILDFORD - 70C	GUILDFORD - 70C	GUILDFORD - 70C	GUILDFORD - 70C
30327	GUILDFORD - 70C	GUILDFORD - 70C	GUILDFORD - 70C	GUILDFORD - 70C	GUILDFORD - 70C	GUILDFORD - 70C	GUILDFORD - 70C
30339	NINE ELMS - 70A	NINE ELMS - 70A	NINE ELMS - 70A	NINE ELMS - 70A	NINE ELMS - 70A	NINE ELMS - 70A	NINE ELMS - 70A
30346	FELTHAM - 70B	FELTHAM - 70B	FELTHAM - 70B	FELTHAM - 70B	FELTHAM - 70B	FELTHAM - 70B	FELTHAM - 70B
30350	EASTLEIGH - 71A	EASTLEIGH - 71A	EASTLEIGH - 71A	EASTLEIGH - 71A	EASTLEIGH - 71A	EASTLEIGH - 71A	GUILDFORD - 70C
30352	FELTHAM - 70B	FELTHAM - 70B	FELTHAM - 70B	FELTHAM - 70B	FELTHAM - 70B	FELTHAM - 70B	FELTHAM - 70B
30355	GUILDFORD - 70C	GUILDFORD - 70C	GUILDFORD - 70C	GUILDFORD - 70C	GUILDFORD - 70C	GUILDFORD - 70C	GUILDFORD - 70C
30368	BASINGSTOKE - 70D	BASINGSTOKE - 70D	BASINGSTOKE - 70D	BASINGSTOKE - 70D	BASINGSTOKE - 70D	BASINGSTOKE - 70D	BASINGSTOKE - 70D
30687	FELTHAM - 70B	FELTHAM - 70B	FELTHAM - 70B	FELTHAM - 70B	FELTHAM - 70B	FELTHAM - 70B	FELTHAM - 70B
30688	FELTHAM - 70B	FELTHAM - 70B	FELTHAM - 70B	FELTHAM - 70B	FELTHAM - 70B	FELTHAM - 70B	FELTHAM - 70B
30689	FELTHAM - 70B	FELTHAM - 70B	FELTHAM - 70B	FELTHAM - 70B	FELTHAM - 70B	FELTHAM - 70B	FELTHAM - 70B
30690	SALISBURY - 72B	SALISBURY - 72B	SALISBURY - 72B	SALISBURY - 72B	SALISBURY - 72B	SALISBURY - 72B	SALISBURY - 72B
30691	SALISBURY - 72B	SALISBURY - 72B	SALISBURY - 72B	SALISBURY - 72B	SALISBURY - 72B	SALISBURY - 72B	SALISBURY - 72B
30692	NINE ELMS - 70A	NINE ELMS - 70A	NINE ELMS - 70A	NINE ELMS - 70A	NINE ELMS - 70A	NINE ELMS - 70A	NINE ELMS - 70A
30693	GUILDFORD - 70C	GUILDFORD - 70C	GUILDFORD - 70C	GUILDFORD - 70C	GUILDFORD - 70C	GUILDFORD - 70C	GUILDFORD - 70C
30694	NINE ELMS - 70A	NINE ELMS - 70A	NINE ELMS - 70A	NINE ELMS - 70A	NINE ELMS - 70A	NINE ELMS - 70A	NINE ELMS - 70A
30695	BOURNEMOUTH - 71B	BOURNEMOUTH - 71B	BOURNEMOUTH - 71B	BOURNEMOUTH - 71B	BOURNEMOUTH - 71B	BOURNEMOUTH - 71B	BOURNEMOUTH - 71B
30696	FELTHAM - 70B	FELTHAM - 70B	FELTHAM - 70B	FELTHAM - 70B	FELTHAM - 70B	FELTHAM - 70B	FELTHAM - 70B
30697	FELTHAM - 70B	FELTHAM - 70B	FELTHAM - 70B	FELTHAM - 70B	FELTHAM - 70B	NINE ELMS - 70A	NINE ELMS - 70A
30698	FELTHAM - 70B	FELTHAM - 70B	FELTHAM - 70B	FELTHAM - 70B	FELTHAM - 70B	NINE ELMS - 70A	NINE ELMS - 70A
30699	NINE ELMS - 70A	NINE ELMS - 70A	NINE ELMS - 70A	NINE ELMS - 70A	NINE ELMS - 70A	NINE ELMS - 70A	NINE ELMS - 70A
30700	EASTLEIGH - 71A	EASTLEIGH - 71A	EASTLEIGH - 71A	EASTLEIGH - 71A	EASTLEIGH - 71A	EASTLEIGH - 71A	EASTLEIGH - 71A
30701	NINE ELMS - 70A	NINE ELMS - 70A	NINE ELMS - 70A	NINE ELMS - 70A	NINE ELMS - 70A	NINE ELMS - 70A	NINE ELMS - 70A
				C2X 0-6-0 (1908)			
32434	EASTBOURNE - 75G	EASTBOURNE - 75G	EASTBOURNE - 75G	EASTBOURNE - 75G	EASTBOURNE - 75G	EASTBOURNE - 75G	EASTBOURNE - 75G
32437	BRIGHTON - 75A (N)	BRIGHTON - 75A (N)	BRIGHTON - 75A (N)	BRIGHTON - 75A (N)	BRIGHTON - 75A (N)	BRIGHTON - 75A (N)	BRIGHTON - 75A (N)
32438	BRIGHTON - 75A	BRIGHTON - 75A	BRIGHTON - 75A	BRIGHTON - 75A	BRIGHTON - 75A	BRIGHTON - 75A	BRIGHTON - 75A
32440	NORWOOD JCN - 75C	NORWOOD JCN - 75C	NORWOOD JCN - 75C	NORWOOD JCN - 75C	NORWOOD JCN - 75C	NORWOOD JCN - 75C	NORWOOD JCN - 75C
32441	THREE BRIDGES - 75E	THREE BRIDGES - 75E	THREE BRIDGES - 75E	THREE BRIDGES - 75E	THREE BRIDGES - 75E	THREE BRIDGES - 75E	THREE BRIDGES - 75E
32442	B.ARMS - 73B	B.ARMS - 73B	B.ARMS - 73B	B.ARMS - 73B	B.ARMS - 73B	B.ARMS - 73B	B.ARMS - 73B
32443	NORWOOD JCN - 75C	NORWOOD JCN - 75C	NORWOOD JCN - 75C	NORWOOD JCN - 75C	NORWOOD JCN - 75C	NORWOOD JCN - 75C	NORWOOD JCN - 75C
32444	NORWOOD JCN - 75C	NORWOOD JCN - 75C	NORWOOD JCN - 75C	NORWOOD JCN - 75C	NORWOOD JCN - 75C	NORWOOD JCN - 75C	NORWOOD JCN - 75C
32445	THREE BRIDGES - 75E	THREE BRIDGES - 75E	THREE BRIDGES - 75E	THREE BRIDGES - 75E	THREE BRIDGES - 75E	THREE BRIDGES - 75E	THREE BRIDGES - 75E
32446	B.ARMS - 73B	B.ARMS - 73B	B.ARMS - 73B	B.ARMS - 73B	B.ARMS - 73B	B.ARMS - 73B	B.ARMS - 73B
32447	NORWOOD JCN - 75C	NORWOOD JCN - 75C	NORWOOD JCN - 75C	NORWOOD JCN - 75C	NORWOOD JCN - 75C	NORWOOD JCN - 75C	NORWOOD JCN - 75C
32448	B.ARMS - 73B	B.ARMS - 73B	B.ARMS - 73B	B.ARMS - 73B	B.ARMS - 73B	B.ARMS - 73B	B.ARMS - 73B
32449	REDHILL - 75B	REDHILL - 75B	REDHILL - 75B	REDHILL - 75B	REDHILL - 75B	REDHILL - 75B	REDHILL - 75B
32450	REDHILL - 75B	REDHILL - 75B	REDHILL - 75B	REDHILL - 75B	REDHILL - 75B	REDHILL - 75B	REDHILL - 75B
32451	THREE BRIDGES - 75E	THREE BRIDGES - 75E	THREE BRIDGES - 75E	THREE BRIDGES - 75E	THREE BRIDGES - 75E	THREE BRIDGES - 75E	THREE BRIDGES - 75E
32521	HORSHAM - 75D	HORSHAM - 75D	HORSHAM - 75D	HORSHAM - 75D	HORSHAM - 75D	HORSHAM - 75D	HORSHAM - 75D
32522	THREE BRIDGES - 75E	THREE BRIDGES - 75E	THREE BRIDGES - 75E	THREE BRIDGES - 75E	THREE BRIDGES - 75E	THREE BRIDGES - 75E	THREE BRIDGES - 75E
32523	BRIGHTON - 75A	BRIGHTON - 75A	BRIGHTON - 75A	BRIGHTON - 75A	BRIGHTON - 75A	BRIGHTON - 75A	BRIGHTON - 75A
32524	B.ARMS - 73B	B.ARMS - 73B	B.ARMS - 73B	B.ARMS - 73B	B.ARMS - 73B	B.ARMS - 73B	B.ARMS - 73B
32525	B.ARMS - 73B	B.ARMS - 73B	B.ARMS - 73B	B.ARMS - 73B	B.ARMS - 73B	B.ARMS - 73B	B.ARMS - 73B
32526	NORWOOD JCN - 75C	NORWOOD JCN - 75C	NORWOOD JCN - 75C	NORWOOD JCN - 75C	NORWOOD JCN - 75C	NORWOOD JCN - 75C	NORWOOD JCN - 75C
32527	THREE BRIDGES - 75E	THREE BRIDGES - 75E	THREE BRIDGES - 75E	THREE BRIDGES - 75E	THREE BRIDGES - 75E	THREE BRIDGES - 75E	THREE BRIDGES - 75E
32528	BRIGHTON - 75A	BRIGHTON - 75A	BRIGHTON - 75A	BRIGHTON - 75A	BRIGHTON - 75A	BRIGHTON - 75A	BRIGHTON - 75A
32529	THREE BRIDGES - 75E	THREE BRIDGES - 75E	THREE BRIDGES - 75E	THREE BRIDGES - 75E	THREE BRIDGES - 75E	THREE BRIDGES - 75E	THREE BRIDGES - 75E
32532	THREE BRIDGES - 75E	THREE BRIDGES - 75E	THREE BRIDGES - 75E	THREE BRIDGES - 75E	THREE BRIDGES - 75E	THREE BRIDGES - 75E	THREE BRIDGES - 75E
32534	BRIGHTON - 75A	BRIGHTON - 75A	BRIGHTON - 75A	BRIGHTON - 75A	BRIGHTON - 75A	BRIGHTON - 75A	BRIGHTON - 75A
32535	NORWOOD JCN - 75C	NORWOOD JCN - 75C	NORWOOD JCN - 75C	NORWOOD JCN - 75C	NORWOOD JCN - 75C	NORWOOD JCN - 75C	NORWOOD JCN - 75C
32536	NORWOOD JCN - 75C	NORWOOD JCN - 75C	NORWOOD JCN - 75C	NORWOOD JCN - 75C	NORWOOD JCN - 75C	NORWOOD JCN - 75C	NORWOOD JCN - 75C
32537	BRIGHTON - 75A(N)	BRIGHTON - 75A(N)	BRIGHTON - 75A(N)	BRIGHTON - 75A(N)	BRIGHTON - 75A(N)	BRIGHTON - 75A(N)	BRIGHTON - 75A(N)
32538	THREE BRIDGES - 75E	THREE BRIDGES - 75E	THREE BRIDGES - 75E	THREE BRIDGES - 75E	THREE BRIDGES - 75E	THREE BRIDGES - 75E	THREE BRIDGES - 75E
32539	HORSHAM - 75D	HORSHAM - 75D	HORSHAM - 75D	HORSHAM - 75D	HORSHAM - 75D	HORSHAM - 75D	HORSHAM - 75D
32540	REDHILL - 75B	REDHILL - 75B	REDHILL - 75B	REDHILL - 75B	REDHILL - 75B	REDHILL - 75B	REDHILL - 75B
32541	HORSHAM - 75D	HORSHAM - 75D	HORSHAM - 75D	HORSHAM - 75D	HORSHAM - 75D	HORSHAM - 75D	HORSHAM - 75D
32543	NORWOOD JCN - 75C	NORWOOD JCN - 75C	NORWOOD JCN - 75C	NORWOOD JCN - 75C	NORWOOD JCN - 75C	NORWOOD JCN - 75C	NORWOOD JCN - 75C
32544	HORSHAM - 75D	HORSHAM - 75D	HORSHAM - 75D	HORSHAM - 75D	HORSHAM - 75D	HORSHAM - 75D	HORSHAM - 75D
32545	THREE BRIDGES - 75E	THREE BRIDGES - 75E	THREE BRIDGES - 75E	THREE BRIDGES - 75E	THREE BRIDGES - 75E	THREE BRIDGES - 75E	THREE BRIDGES - 75E
32546	NORWOOD JCN - 75C	NORWOOD JCN - 75C	NORWOOD JCN - 75C	NORWOOD JCN - 75C	NORWOOD JCN - 75C	NORWOOD JCN - 75C	NORWOOD JCN - 75C
32547	NORWOOD JCN - 75C	NORWOOD JCN - 75C	NORWOOD JCN - 75C	NORWOOD JCN - 75C	NORWOOD JCN - 75C	NORWOOD JCN - 75C	NORWOOD JCN - 75C
32548	FRATTON - 71D	FRATTON - 71D	FRATTON - 71D	FRATTON - 71D	FRATTON - 71D	FRATTON - 71D	FRATTON - 71D
32549	FRATTON - 71D	FRATTON - 71D	FRATTON - 71D	FRATTON - 71D	FRATTON - 71D	FRATTON - 71D	FRATTON - 71D
32550	FRATTON - 71D	FRATTON - 71D	FRATTON - 71D	FRATTON - 71D	FRATTON - 71D	FRATTON - 71D	FRATTON - 71D
32551	T.WELLS - 75F	T.WELLS - 75F	T.WELLS - 75F	T.WELLS - 75F	T.WELLS - 75F	T.WELLS - 75F	T.WELLS - 75F
32552	THREE BRIDGES - 75E	THREE BRIDGES - 75E	THREE BRIDGES - 75E	THREE BRIDGES - 75E	THREE BRIDGES - 75E	THREE BRIDGES - 75E	THREE BRIDGES - 75E
32553	THREE BRIDGES - 75E	THREE BRIDGES - 75E	THREE BRIDGES - 75E	THREE BRIDGES - 75E	THREE BRIDGES - 75E	THREE BRIDGES - 75E	THREE BRIDGES - 75E
32554	B.ARMS - 73B	B.ARMS - 73B	B.ARMS - 73B	B.ARMS - 73B	B.ARMS - 73B	B.ARMS - 73B	B.ARMS - 73B

loco	Jan-54	Mar-54	May-54	Jun-54	Aug-54	Oct-54	Dec-54
			'700' 0-6-0 (1897)				
30306	EASTLEIGH - 71A	EASTLEIGH - 71A	EASTLEIGH - 71A	EASTLEIGH - 71A	EASTLEIGH - 71A	EASTLEIGH - 71A	EASTLEIGH - 71A
30308	GUILDFORD - 70C	GUILDFORD - 70C	GUILDFORD - 70C	GUILDFORD - 70C	GUILDFORD - 70C	GUILDFORD - 70C	GUILDFORD - 70C
30309	FELTHAM - 70B	FELTHAM - 70B	FELTHAM - 70B	FELTHAM - 70B	FELTHAM - 70B	FELTHAM - 70B	SALISBURY - 72B
30315	SALISBURY - 72B	SALISBURY - 72B	SALISBURY - 72B	SALISBURY - 72B	SALISBURY - 72B	SALISBURY - 72B	EXMOUTH JCN - 72A
30316	EASTLEIGH - 71A	EASTLEIGH - 71A	EASTLEIGH - 71A	EASTLEIGH - 71A	EASTLEIGH - 71A	EASTLEIGH - 71A	EASTLEIGH - 71A
30317	SALISBURY - 72B	SALISBURY - 72B	SALISBURY - 72B	SALISBURY - 72B	SALISBURY - 72B	SALISBURY - 72B	SALISBURY - 72B
30325	GUILDFORD - 70C	GUILDFORD - 70C	GUILDFORD - 70C	GUILDFORD - 70C	GUILDFORD - 70C	GUILDFORD - 70C	GUILDFORD - 70C
30326	GUILDFORD - 70C	GUILDFORD - 70C	GUILDFORD - 70C	GUILDFORD - 70C	GUILDFORD - 70C	GUILDFORD - 70C	GUILDFORD - 70C
30327	GUILDFORD - 70C	GUILDFORD - 70C	GUILDFORD - 70C	GUILDFORD - 70C	GUILDFORD - 70C	GUILDFORD - 70C	SALISBURY - 72B
30339	NINE ELMS - 70A	NINE ELMS - 70A	NINE ELMS - 70A	NINE ELMS - 70A	NINE ELMS - 70A	NINE ELMS - 70A	NINE ELMS - 70A
30346	FELTHAM - 70B	FELTHAM - 70B	FELTHAM - 70B	FELTHAM - 70B	FELTHAM - 70B	FELTHAM - 70B	FELTHAM - 70B
30350	GUILDFORD - 70C	GUILDFORD - 70C	GUILDFORD - 70C	GUILDFORD - 70C	GUILDFORD - 70C	GUILDFORD - 70C	GUILDFORD - 70C
30352	FELTHAM - 70B	FELTHAM - 70B	FELTHAM - 70B	FELTHAM - 70B	FELTHAM - 70B	FELTHAM - 70B	FELTHAM - 70B
30355	GUILDFORD - 70C	GUILDFORD - 70C	GUILDFORD - 70C	GUILDFORD - 70C	GUILDFORD - 70C	GUILDFORD - 70C	GUILDFORD - 70C
30368	BASINGSTOKE - 70D	BASINGSTOKE - 70D	BASINGSTOKE - 70D	BASINGSTOKE - 70D	BASINGSTOKE - 70D	BASINGSTOKE - 70D	BASINGSTOKE - 70D
30687	FELTHAM - 70B	FELTHAM - 70B	FELTHAM - 70B	FELTHAM - 70B	FELTHAM - 70B	FELTHAM - 70B	FELTHAM - 70B
30688	FELTHAM - 70B	FELTHAM - 70B	FELTHAM - 70B	FELTHAM - 70B	FELTHAM - 70B	FELTHAM - 70B	FELTHAM - 70B
30689	FELTHAM - 70B	FELTHAM - 70B	FELTHAM - 70B	FELTHAM - 70B	FELTHAM - 70B	FELTHAM - 70B	FELTHAM - 70B
30690	SALISBURY - 72B	SALISBURY - 72B	SALISBURY - 72B	SALISBURY - 72B	SALISBURY - 72B	BOURNEMOUTH - 71B	BOURNEMOUTH - 71B
30691	SALISBURY - 72B	SALISBURY - 72B	SALISBURY - 72B	SALISBURY - 72B	SALISBURY - 72B	SALISBURY - 72B	EXMOUTH JCN - 72A
30692	NINE ELMS - 70A	NINE ELMS - 70A	NINE ELMS - 70A	NINE ELMS - 70A	NINE ELMS - 70A	NINE ELMS - 70A	NINE ELMS - 70A
30693	GUILDFORD - 70C	GUILDFORD - 70C	GUILDFORD - 70C	GUILDFORD - 70C	GUILDFORD - 70C	GUILDFORD - 70C	GUILDFORD - 70C
30694	NINE ELMS - 70A	NINE ELMS - 70A	NINE ELMS - 70A	NINE ELMS - 70A	NINE ELMS - 70A	NINE ELMS - 70A	NINE ELMS - 70A
30695	BOURNEMOUTH - 71B	BOURNEMOUTH - 71B	BOURNEMOUTH - 71B	BOURNEMOUTH - 71B	BOURNEMOUTH - 71B	BOURNEMOUTH - 71B	BOURNEMOUTH - 71B
30696	FELTHAM - 70B	FELTHAM - 70B	FELTHAM - 70B	FELTHAM - 70B	FELTHAM - 70B	FELTHAM - 70B	FELTHAM - 70B
30697	NINE ELMS - 70A	NINE ELMS - 70A	NINE ELMS - 70A	NINE ELMS - 70A	NINE ELMS - 70A	NINE ELMS - 70A	NINE ELMS - 70A
30698	NINE ELMS - 70A	NINE ELMS - 70A	NINE ELMS - 70A	NINE ELMS - 70A	NINE ELMS - 70A	NINE ELMS - 70A	NINE ELMS - 70A
30699	NINE ELMS - 70A	NINE ELMS - 70A	NINE ELMS - 70A	NINE ELMS - 70A	NINE ELMS - 70A	NINE ELMS - 70A	NINE ELMS - 70A
30700	EASTLEIGH - 71A	EASTLEIGH - 71A	EASTLEIGH - 71A	EASTLEIGH - 71A	EASTLEIGH - 71A	EASTLEIGH - 71A	EASTLEIGH - 71A
30701	NINE ELMS - 70A	NINE ELMS - 70A	NINE ELMS - 70A	NINE ELMS - 70A	NINE ELMS - 70A	NINE ELMS - 70A	NINE ELMS - 70A
			C2X 0-6-0 (1908)				
32434	EASTBOURNE - 75G	EASTBOURNE - 75G	EASTBOURNE - 75G	EASTBOURNE - 75G	EASTBOURNE - 75G	EASTBOURNE - 75G	EASTBOURNE - 75G
32437	BRIGHTON - 75A (N)	BRIGHTON - 75A (N)	BRIGHTON - 75A (N)	BRIGHTON - 75A (N)	BRIGHTON - 75A (N)	BRIGHTON - 75A (N)	BRIGHTON - 75A (N)
32438	BRIGHTON - 75A	BRIGHTON - 75A	BRIGHTON - 75A	BRIGHTON - 75A	BRIGHTON - 75A	BRIGHTON - 75A	BRIGHTON - 75A
32440	NORWOOD JCN - 75C	NORWOOD JCN - 75C	NORWOOD JCN - 75C	NORWOOD JCN - 75C	NORWOOD JCN - 75C	NORWOOD JCN - 75C	NORWOOD JCN - 75C
32441	THREE BRIDGES - 75E	THREE BRIDGES - 75E	THREE BRIDGES - 75E	THREE BRIDGES - 75E	THREE BRIDGES - 75E	THREE BRIDGES - 75E	THREE BRIDGES - 75E
32442	B.ARMS - 73B	B.ARMS - 73B	B.ARMS - 73B	B.ARMS - 73B	B.ARMS - 73B	B.ARMS - 73B	B.ARMS - 73B
32443	NORWOOD JCN - 75C	NORWOOD JCN - 75C	NORWOOD JCN - 75C	NORWOOD JCN - 75C	NORWOOD JCN - 75C	NORWOOD JCN - 75C	NORWOOD JCN - 75C
32444	NORWOOD JCN - 75C	NORWOOD JCN - 75C	NORWOOD JCN - 75C	NORWOOD JCN - 75C	NORWOOD JCN - 75C	NORWOOD JCN - 75C	NORWOOD JCN - 75C
32445	THREE BRIDGES - 75E	THREE BRIDGES - 75E	THREE BRIDGES - 75E	THREE BRIDGES - 75E	THREE BRIDGES - 75E	THREE BRIDGES - 75E	THREE BRIDGES - 75E
32446	B.ARMS - 73B	B.ARMS - 73B	B.ARMS - 73B	B.ARMS - 73B	B.ARMS - 73B	B.ARMS - 73B	B.ARMS - 73B
32447	NORWOOD JCN - 75C	NORWOOD JCN - 75C	NORWOOD JCN - 75C	NORWOOD JCN - 75C	NORWOOD JCN - 75C	NORWOOD JCN - 75C	NORWOOD JCN - 75C
32448	B.ARMS - 73B	B.ARMS - 73B	B.ARMS - 73B	B.ARMS - 73B	B.ARMS - 73B	B.ARMS - 73B	B.ARMS - 73B
32449	REDHILL - 75B	REDHILL - 75B	REDHILL - 75B	REDHILL - 75B	REDHILL - 75B	REDHILL - 75B	REDHILL - 75B
32450	REDHILL - 75B	REDHILL - 75B	REDHILL - 75B	REDHILL - 75B	REDHILL - 75B	REDHILL - 75B	REDHILL - 75B
32451	THREE BRIDGES - 75E	THREE BRIDGES - 75E	THREE BRIDGES - 75E	THREE BRIDGES - 75E	THREE BRIDGES - 75E	THREE BRIDGES - 75E	THREE BRIDGES - 75E
32521	HORSHAM - 75D	HORSHAM - 75D	HORSHAM - 75D	HORSHAM - 75D	HORSHAM - 75D	HORSHAM - 75D	HORSHAM - 75D
32522	THREE BRIDGES - 75E	THREE BRIDGES - 75E	THREE BRIDGES - 75E	THREE BRIDGES - 75E	THREE BRIDGES - 75E	THREE BRIDGES - 75E	THREE BRIDGES - 75E
32523	BRIGHTON - 75A	BRIGHTON - 75A	BRIGHTON - 75A	BRIGHTON - 75A	BRIGHTON - 75A	BRIGHTON - 75A	BRIGHTON - 75A
32524	B.ARMS - 73B	B.ARMS - 73B	B.ARMS - 73B	B.ARMS - 73B	B.ARMS - 73B	B.ARMS - 73B	B.ARMS - 73B
32525	B.ARMS - 73B	B.ARMS - 73B	B.ARMS - 73B	B.ARMS - 73B	B.ARMS - 73B	B.ARMS - 73B	B.ARMS - 73B
32526	NORWOOD JCN - 75C	NORWOOD JCN - 75C	NORWOOD JCN - 75C	NORWOOD JCN - 75C	NORWOOD JCN - 75C	NORWOOD JCN - 75C	B.ARMS - 73B
32527	THREE BRIDGES - 75E	THREE BRIDGES - 75E	THREE BRIDGES - 75E	THREE BRIDGES - 75E	THREE BRIDGES - 75E	THREE BRIDGES - 75E	B.ARMS - 73B
32528	BRIGHTON - 75A	BRIGHTON - 75A	BRIGHTON - 75A	BRIGHTON - 75A	BRIGHTON - 75A	BRIGHTON - 75A	BRIGHTON - 75A
32529	THREE BRIDGES - 75E	THREE BRIDGES - 75E	THREE BRIDGES - 75E	THREE BRIDGES - 75E	THREE BRIDGES - 75E	THREE BRIDGES - 75E	THREE BRIDGES - 75E
32532	THREE BRIDGES - 75E	THREE BRIDGES - 75E	THREE BRIDGES - 75E	THREE BRIDGES - 75E	THREE BRIDGES - 75E	THREE BRIDGES - 75E	THREE BRIDGES - 75E
32534	BRIGHTON - 75A	BRIGHTON - 75A	BRIGHTON - 75A	BRIGHTON - 75A	BRIGHTON - 75A	BRIGHTON - 75A	BRIGHTON - 75A
32535	NORWOOD JCN - 75C	NORWOOD JCN - 75C	NORWOOD JCN - 75C	NORWOOD JCN - 75C	NORWOOD JCN - 75C	NORWOOD JCN - 75C	NORWOOD JCN - 75C
32536	NORWOOD JCN - 75C	NORWOOD JCN - 75C	NORWOOD JCN - 75C	NORWOOD JCN - 75C	NORWOOD JCN - 75C	NORWOOD JCN - 75C	NORWOOD JCN - 75C
32537	BRIGHTON - 75A(N)	BRIGHTON - 75A(N)	BRIGHTON - 75A(N)	BRIGHTON - 75A(N)	BRIGHTON - 75A(N)	BRIGHTON - 75A(N)	BRIGHTON - 75A(N)
32538	THREE BRIDGES - 75E	THREE BRIDGES - 75E	THREE BRIDGES - 75E	THREE BRIDGES - 75E	THREE BRIDGES - 75E	THREE BRIDGES - 75E	THREE BRIDGES - 75E
32539	HORSHAM - 75D	HORSHAM - 75D	HORSHAM - 75D	HORSHAM - 75D	HORSHAM - 75D	HORSHAM - 75D	HORSHAM - 75D
32540	REDHILL - 75B	REDHILL - 75B	REDHILL - 75B	REDHILL - 75B	REDHILL - 75B	REDHILL - 75B	REDHILL - 75B
32541	HORSHAM - 75D	HORSHAM - 75D	HORSHAM - 75D	HORSHAM - 75D	HORSHAM - 75D	HORSHAM - 75D	HORSHAM - 75D
32543	NORWOOD JCN - 75C	NORWOOD JCN - 75C	NORWOOD JCN - 75C	NORWOOD JCN - 75C	NORWOOD JCN - 75C	NORWOOD JCN - 75C	NORWOOD JCN - 75C
32544	HORSHAM - 75D	HORSHAM - 75D	HORSHAM - 75D	HORSHAM - 75D	HORSHAM - 75D	HORSHAM - 75D	HORSHAM - 75D
32545	THREE BRIDGES - 75E	THREE BRIDGES - 75E	THREE BRIDGES - 75E	THREE BRIDGES - 75E	THREE BRIDGES - 75E	THREE BRIDGES - 75E	THREE BRIDGES - 75E
32546	NORWOOD JCN - 75C	NORWOOD JCN - 75C	NORWOOD JCN - 75C	NORWOOD JCN - 75C	NORWOOD JCN - 75C	NORWOOD JCN - 75C	NORWOOD JCN - 75C
32547	NORWOOD JCN - 75C	NORWOOD JCN - 75C	NORWOOD JCN - 75C	NORWOOD JCN - 75C	NORWOOD JCN - 75C	NORWOOD JCN - 75C	NORWOOD JCN - 75C
32548	FRATTON - 71D	FRATTON - 71D	FRATTON - 71D	FRATTON - 71D	FRATTON - 71D	FRATTON - 70F	FRATTON - 70F
32549	FRATTON - 71D	FRATTON - 71D	FRATTON - 71D	FRATTON - 71D	FRATTON - 71D	FRATTON - 70F	FRATTON - 70F
32550	FRATTON - 71D	FRATTON - 71D	FRATTON - 71D	FRATTON - 71D	FRATTON - 71D	FRATTON - 70F	FRATTON - 70F
32551	T.WELLS - 75F	T.WELLS - 75F	T.WELLS - 75F	T.WELLS - 75F	T.WELLS - 75F	T.WELLS - 75F	T.WELLS - 75F
32552	THREE BRIDGES - 75E	THREE BRIDGES - 75E	THREE BRIDGES - 75E	THREE BRIDGES - 75E	THREE BRIDGES - 75E	THREE BRIDGES - 75E	THREE BRIDGES - 75E
32553	THREE BRIDGES - 75E	THREE BRIDGES - 75E	THREE BRIDGES - 75E	THREE BRIDGES - 75E	THREE BRIDGES - 75E	THREE BRIDGES - 75E	THREE BRIDGES - 75E
32554	B.ARMS - 73B	B.ARMS - 73B	B.ARMS - 73B	B.ARMS - 73B	B.ARMS - 73B	B.ARMS - 73B	B.ARMS - 73B

loco	Feb-55	Apr-55	Jun-55	Aug-55	Sep-55	Nov-55	Dec-55
			'700' 0-6-0 (1897)				
30306	EASTLEIGH - 71A	EASTLEIGH - 71A	EASTLEIGH - 71A	EASTLEIGH - 71A	EASTLEIGH - 71A	EASTLEIGH - 71A	EASTLEIGH - 71A
30308	GUILDFORD - 70C	GUILDFORD - 70C	GUILDFORD - 70C	GUILDFORD - 70C	GUILDFORD - 70C	GUILDFORD - 70C	GUILDFORD - 70C
30309	SALISBURY - 72B	SALISBURY - 72B	SALISBURY - 72B	SALISBURY - 72B	SALISBURY - 72B	SALISBURY - 72B	SALISBURY - 72B
30315	EXMOUTH JCN - 72A	EXMOUTH JCN - 72A	EXMOUTH JCN - 72A	EXMOUTH JCN - 72A	EXMOUTH JCN - 72A	EXMOUTH JCN - 72A	EXMOUTH JCN - 72A
30316	EASTLEIGH - 71A	EASTLEIGH - 71A	EASTLEIGH - 71A	EASTLEIGH - 71A	EASTLEIGH - 71A	EASTLEIGH - 71A	EASTLEIGH - 71A
30317	SALISBURY - 72B	SALISBURY - 72B	SALISBURY - 72B	SALISBURY - 72B	SALISBURY - 72B	SALISBURY - 72B	SALISBURY - 72B
30325	GUILDFORD - 70C	GUILDFORD - 70C	GUILDFORD - 70C	GUILDFORD - 70C	GUILDFORD - 70C	GUILDFORD - 70C	GUILDFORD - 70C
30326	GUILDFORD - 70C	GUILDFORD - 70C	GUILDFORD - 70C	GUILDFORD - 70C	GUILDFORD - 70C	GUILDFORD - 70C	GUILDFORD - 70C
30327	SALISBURY - 72B	SALISBURY - 72B	SALISBURY - 72B	SALISBURY - 72B	SALISBURY - 72B	SALISBURY - 72B	SALISBURY - 72B
30339	NINE ELMS - 70A	NINE ELMS - 70A	NINE ELMS - 70A	NINE ELMS - 70A	NINE ELMS - 70A	NINE ELMS - 70A	NINE ELMS - 70A
30346	FELTHAM - 70B	FELTHAM - 70B	FELTHAM - 70B	FELTHAM - 70B	FELTHAM - 70B	FELTHAM - 70B	FELTHAM - 70B
30350	GUILDFORD - 70C	GUILDFORD - 70C	GUILDFORD - 70C	GUILDFORD - 70C	GUILDFORD - 70C	GUILDFORD - 70C	GUILDFORD - 70C
30352	FELTHAM - 70B	FELTHAM - 70B	FELTHAM - 70B	FELTHAM - 70B	FELTHAM - 70B	FELTHAM - 70B	FELTHAM - 70B
30355	GUILDFORD - 70C	GUILDFORD - 70C	GUILDFORD - 70C	GUILDFORD - 70C	GUILDFORD - 70C	GUILDFORD - 70C	GUILDFORD - 70C
30368	BASINGSTOKE - 70D	BASINGSTOKE - 70D	BASINGSTOKE - 70D	BASINGSTOKE - 70D	BASINGSTOKE - 70D	BASINGSTOKE - 70D	BASINGSTOKE - 70D
30687	FELTHAM - 70B	FELTHAM - 70B	FELTHAM - 70B	FELTHAM - 70B	FELTHAM - 70B	FELTHAM - 70B	FELTHAM - 70B
30688	FELTHAM - 70B	FELTHAM - 70B	FELTHAM - 70B	FELTHAM - 70B	FELTHAM - 70B	FELTHAM - 70B	FELTHAM - 70B
30689	FELTHAM - 70B	FELTHAM - 70B	FELTHAM - 70B	FELTHAM - 70B	FELTHAM - 70B	FELTHAM - 70B	FELTHAM - 70B
30690	BOURNEMOUTH - 71B	BOURNEMOUTH - 71B	BOURNEMOUTH - 71B	BOURNEMOUTH - 71B	BOURNEMOUTH - 71B	BOURNEMOUTH - 71B	BOURNEMOUTH - 71B
30691	EXMOUTH JCN - 72A	EXMOUTH JCN - 72A	EXMOUTH JCN - 72A	EXMOUTH JCN - 72A	EXMOUTH JCN - 72A	EXMOUTH JCN - 72A	EXMOUTH JCN - 72A
30692	NINE ELMS - 70A	NINE ELMS - 70A	NINE ELMS - 70A	NINE ELMS - 70A	NINE ELMS - 70A	NINE ELMS - 70A	NINE ELMS - 70A
30693	GUILDFORD - 70C	GUILDFORD - 70C	GUILDFORD - 70C	GUILDFORD - 70C	GUILDFORD - 70C	GUILDFORD - 70C	GUILDFORD - 70C
30694	NINE ELMS - 70A	NINE ELMS - 70A	NINE ELMS - 70A	NINE ELMS - 70A	NINE ELMS - 70A	NINE ELMS - 70A	NINE ELMS - 70A
30695	BOURNEMOUTH - 71B	BOURNEMOUTH - 71B	BOURNEMOUTH - 71B	BOURNEMOUTH - 71B	BOURNEMOUTH - 71B	BOURNEMOUTH - 71B	BOURNEMOUTH - 71B
30696	FELTHAM - 70B	FELTHAM - 70B	FELTHAM - 70B	FELTHAM - 70B	FELTHAM - 70B	FELTHAM - 70B	FELTHAM - 70B
30697	NINE ELMS - 70A	GUILDFORD - 70C	GUILDFORD - 70C	GUILDFORD - 70C	GUILDFORD - 70C	GUILDFORD - 70C	GUILDFORD - 70C
30698	NINE ELMS - 70A	NINE ELMS - 70A	NINE ELMS - 70A	NINE ELMS - 70A	GUILDFORD - 70C	GUILDFORD - 70C	GUILDFORD - 70C
30699	NINE ELMS - 70A	NINE ELMS - 70A	NINE ELMS - 70A	NINE ELMS - 70A	NINE ELMS - 70A	NINE ELMS - 70A	NINE ELMS - 70A
30700	EASTLEIGH - 71A	GUILDFORD - 70C	GUILDFORD - 70C	GUILDFORD - 70C	GUILDFORD - 70C	GUILDFORD - 70C	GUILDFORD - 70C
30701	NINE ELMS - 70A	NINE ELMS - 70A	NINE ELMS - 70A	NINE ELMS - 70A	NINE ELMS - 70A	NINE ELMS - 70A	NINE ELMS - 70A
			C2X 0-6-0 (1908)				
32434	EASTBOURNE - 75G	EASTBOURNE - 75G	EASTBOURNE - 75G	EASTBOURNE - 75G	EASTBOURNE - 75G	EASTBOURNE - 75G	EASTBOURNE - 75G
32437	BRIGHTON - 75A (N)	BRIGHTON - 75A (N)	BRIGHTON - 75A (N)	BRIGHTON - 75A (N)	BRIGHTON - 75A (N)	BRIGHTON - 75A (N)	BRIGHTON - 75A (N)
32438	BRIGHTON - 75A	BRIGHTON - 75A	BRIGHTON - 75A	BRIGHTON - 75A	BRIGHTON - 75A	BRIGHTON - 75A	BRIGHTON - 75A
32440	NORWOOD JCN - 75C	NORWOOD JCN - 75C	NORWOOD JCN - 75C	NORWOOD JCN - 75C	NORWOOD JCN - 75C	NORWOOD JCN - 75C	NORWOOD JCN - 75C
32441	THREE BRIDGES - 75E	THREE BRIDGES - 75E	THREE BRIDGES - 75E	THREE BRIDGES - 75E	THREE BRIDGES - 75E	THREE BRIDGES - 75E	THREE BRIDGES - 75E
32442	B.ARMS - 73B	B.ARMS - 73B	B.ARMS - 73B	B.ARMS - 73B	B.ARMS - 73B	B.ARMS - 73B	B.ARMS - 73B
32443	NORWOOD JCN - 75C	NORWOOD JCN - 75C	NORWOOD JCN - 75C	NORWOOD JCN - 75C	NORWOOD JCN - 75C	NORWOOD JCN - 75C	NORWOOD JCN - 75C
32444	NORWOOD JCN - 75C	NORWOOD JCN - 75C	NORWOOD JCN - 75C	NORWOOD JCN - 75C	NORWOOD JCN - 75C	NORWOOD JCN - 75C	NORWOOD JCN - 75C
32445	THREE BRIDGES - 75E	THREE BRIDGES - 75E	THREE BRIDGES - 75E	THREE BRIDGES - 75E	THREE BRIDGES - 75E	THREE BRIDGES - 75E	THREE BRIDGES - 75E
32446	B.ARMS - 73B	B.ARMS - 73B	B.ARMS - 73B	B.ARMS - 73B	B.ARMS - 73B	B.ARMS - 73B	B.ARMS - 73B
32447	NORWOOD JCN - 75C	NORWOOD JCN - 75C	NORWOOD JCN - 75C	NORWOOD JCN - 75C	NORWOOD JCN - 75C	NORWOOD JCN - 75C	NORWOOD JCN - 75C
32448	B.ARMS - 73B	B.ARMS - 73B	B.ARMS - 73B	B.ARMS - 73B	REDHILL - 75B	REDHILL - 75B	REDHILL - 75B
32449	REDHILL - 75B	REDHILL - 75B	REDHILL - 75B	REDHILL - 75B	REDHILL - 75B	REDHILL - 75B	REDHILL - 75B
32450	REDHILL - 75B	REDHILL - 75B	REDHILL - 75B	REDHILL - 75B	REDHILL - 75B	REDHILL - 75B	REDHILL - 75B
32451	THREE BRIDGES - 75E	THREE BRIDGES - 75E	THREE BRIDGES - 75E	THREE BRIDGES - 75E	REDHILL - 75B	REDHILL - 75B	REDHILL - 75B
32521	HORSHAM - 75D	HORSHAM - 75D	HORSHAM - 75D	HORSHAM - 75D	HORSHAM - 75D	B.ARMS - 73B	B.ARMS - 73B
32522	THREE BRIDGES - 75E	THREE BRIDGES - 75E	THREE BRIDGES - 75E	THREE BRIDGES - 75E	THREE BRIDGES - 75E	THREE BRIDGES - 75E	THREE BRIDGES - 75E
32523	BRIGHTON - 75A	BRIGHTON - 75A	BRIGHTON - 75A	BRIGHTON - 75A	BRIGHTON - 75A	BRIGHTON - 75A	BRIGHTON - 75A
32524	B.ARMS - 73B	B.ARMS - 73B	B.ARMS - 73B	B.ARMS - 73B	B.ARMS - 73B	B.ARMS - 73B	B.ARMS - 73B
32525	B.ARMS - 73B	B.ARMS - 73B	B.ARMS - 73B	B.ARMS - 73B	B.ARMS - 73B	B.ARMS - 73B	B.ARMS - 73B
32526	B.ARMS - 73B	B.ARMS - 73B	B.ARMS - 73B	B.ARMS - 73B	THREE BRIDGES - 75E	THREE BRIDGES - 75E	THREE BRIDGES - 75E
32527	B.ARMS - 73B	B.ARMS - 73B	B.ARMS - 73B	B.ARMS - 73B	THREE BRIDGES - 75E	THREE BRIDGES - 75E	THREE BRIDGES - 75E
32528	BRIGHTON - 75A	THREE BRIDGES - 75E	THREE BRIDGES - 75E	THREE BRIDGES - 75E	BRIGHTON - 75A	BRIGHTON - 75A	BRIGHTON - 75A
32529	THREE BRIDGES - 75E	THREE BRIDGES - 75E	THREE BRIDGES - 75E	THREE BRIDGES - 75E	THREE BRIDGES - 75E	THREE BRIDGES - 75E	THREE BRIDGES - 75E
32532	THREE BRIDGES - 75E	THREE BRIDGES - 75E	THREE BRIDGES - 75E	THREE BRIDGES - 75E	THREE BRIDGES - 75E	THREE BRIDGES - 75E	THREE BRIDGES - 75E
32534	BRIGHTON - 75A	BRIGHTON - 75A	BRIGHTON - 75A	BRIGHTON - 75A	BRIGHTON - 75A	BRIGHTON - 75A	BRIGHTON - 75A
32535	NORWOOD JCN - 75C	NORWOOD JCN - 75C	NORWOOD JCN - 75C	NORWOOD JCN - 75C	NORWOOD JCN - 75C	NORWOOD JCN - 75C	NORWOOD JCN - 75C
32536	NORWOOD JCN - 75C	NORWOOD JCN - 75C	NORWOOD JCN - 75C	NORWOOD JCN - 75C	B.ARMS - 73B	THREE BRIDGES - 75E	THREE BRIDGES - 75E
32537	BRIGHTON - 75A(N)	BRIGHTON - 75A(N)	BRIGHTON - 75A(N)	BRIGHTON - 75A(N)	B.ARMS - 73B	B.ARMS - 73B	B.ARMS - 73B
32538	THREE BRIDGES - 75E	THREE BRIDGES - 75E	THREE BRIDGES - 75E	THREE BRIDGES - 75E	B.ARMS - 73B	B.ARMS - 73B	B.ARMS - 73B
32539	HORSHAM - 75D	HORSHAM - 75D	HORSHAM - 75D	HORSHAM - 75D	B.ARMS - 73B	B.ARMS - 73B	B.ARMS - 73B
32540	REDHILL - 75B	REDHILL - 75B	REDHILL - 75B	REDHILL - 75B	BRIGHTON - 75A	BRIGHTON - 75A	BRIGHTON - 75A
32541	HORSHAM - 75D	HORSHAM - 75D	HORSHAM - 75D	HORSHAM - 75D	HORSHAM - 75D	HORSHAM - 75D	HORSHAM - 75D
32543	NORWOOD JCN - 75C	NORWOOD JCN - 75C	NORWOOD JCN - 75C	NORWOOD JCN - 75C	NORWOOD JCN - 75C	NORWOOD JCN - 75C	NORWOOD JCN - 75C
32544	HORSHAM - 75D	HORSHAM - 75D	HORSHAM - 75D	HORSHAM - 75D	HORSHAM - 75D	HORSHAM - 75D	HORSHAM - 75D
32545	THREE BRIDGES - 75E	THREE BRIDGES - 75E	THREE BRIDGES - 75E	THREE BRIDGES - 75E	THREE BRIDGES - 75E	THREE BRIDGES - 75E	THREE BRIDGES - 75E
32546	NORWOOD JCN - 75C	NORWOOD JCN - 75C	NORWOOD JCN - 75C	NORWOOD JCN - 75C	NORWOOD JCN - 75C	NORWOOD JCN - 75C	NORWOOD JCN - 75C
32547	NORWOOD JCN - 75C	NORWOOD JCN - 75C	NORWOOD JCN - 75C	NORWOOD JCN - 75C	NORWOOD JCN - 75C	NORWOOD JCN - 75C	NORWOOD JCN - 75C
32548	FRATTON - 70F	FRATTON - 70F	FRATTON - 70F	FRATTON - 70F	FRATTON - 70F	FRATTON - 70F	FRATTON - 70F
32549	FRATTON - 70F	FRATTON - 70F	FRATTON - 70F	FRATTON - 70F	FRATTON - 70F	FRATTON - 70F	FRATTON - 70F
32550	FRATTON - 70F	FRATTON - 70F	FRATTON - 70F	FRATTON - 70F	FRATTON - 70F	FRATTON - 70F	FRATTON - 70F
32551	T.WELLS - 75F	T.WELLS - 75F	T.WELLS - 75F	T.WELLS - 75F	T.WELLS - 75F	T.WELLS - 75F	T.WELLS - 75F
32552	THREE BRIDGES - 75E	THREE BRIDGES - 75E	THREE BRIDGES - 75E	THREE BRIDGES - 75E	THREE BRIDGES - 75E	THREE BRIDGES - 75E	THREE BRIDGES - 75E
32553	THREE BRIDGES - 75E	THREE BRIDGES - 75E	THREE BRIDGES - 75E	THREE BRIDGES - 75E	THREE BRIDGES - 75E	THREE BRIDGES - 75E	THREE BRIDGES - 75E
32554	B.ARMS - 73B	B.ARMS - 73B	B.ARMS - 73B	B.ARMS - 73B	B.ARMS - 73B	B.ARMS - 73B	B.ARMS - 73B

loco	Jan-56	Apr-56	May-56	Aug-56	Oct-56	Nov-56	Jan-57
				'700' 0-6-0 (1897)			
30306	EASTLEIGH - 71A	EASTLEIGH - 71A	EASTLEIGH - 71A	EASTLEIGH - 71A	EASTLEIGH - 71A	BOURNEMOUTH - 71B	BOURNEMOUTH - 71B
30308	GUILDFORD - 70C	GUILDFORD - 70C	GUILDFORD - 70C	GUILDFORD - 70C	GUILDFORD - 70C	GUILDFORD - 70C	GUILDFORD - 70C
30309	SALISBURY - 72B	SALISBURY - 72B	SALISBURY - 72B	SALISBURY - 72B	SALISBURY - 72B	SALISBURY - 72B	SALISBURY - 72B
30315	EXMOUTH JCN - 72A	EXMOUTH JCN - 72A	EXMOUTH JCN - 72A	EXMOUTH JCN - 72A	EXMOUTH JCN - 72A	EXMOUTH JCN - 72A	EXMOUTH JCN - 72A
30316	EASTLEIGH - 71A	EASTLEIGH - 71A	EASTLEIGH - 71A	EASTLEIGH - 71A	EASTLEIGH - 71A	EASTLEIGH - 71A	EASTLEIGH - 71A
30317	SALISBURY - 72B	SALISBURY - 72B	SALISBURY - 72B	SALISBURY - 72B	SALISBURY - 72B	SALISBURY - 72B	SALISBURY - 72B
30325	GUILDFORD - 70C	GUILDFORD - 70C	GUILDFORD - 70C	GUILDFORD - 70C	GUILDFORD - 70C	GUILDFORD - 70C	GUILDFORD - 70C
30326	GUILDFORD - 70C	GUILDFORD - 70C	GUILDFORD - 70C	GUILDFORD - 70C	GUILDFORD - 70C	GUILDFORD - 70C	GUILDFORD - 70C
30327	SALISBURY - 72B	SALISBURY - 72B	SALISBURY - 72B	SALISBURY - 72B	SALISBURY - 72B	SALISBURY - 72B	SALISBURY - 72B
30339	NINE ELMS - 70A	NINE ELMS - 70A	NINE ELMS - 70A	NINE ELMS - 70A	NINE ELMS - 70A	NINE ELMS - 70A	NINE ELMS - 70A
30346	FELTHAM - 70B	FELTHAM - 70B	FELTHAM - 70B	FELTHAM - 70B	FELTHAM - 70B	FELTHAM - 70B	FELTHAM - 70B
30350	GUILDFORD - 70C	GUILDFORD - 70C	GUILDFORD - 70C	GUILDFORD - 70C	GUILDFORD - 70C	GUILDFORD - 70C	GUILDFORD - 70C
30352	FELTHAM - 70B	FELTHAM - 70B	FELTHAM - 70B	FELTHAM - 70B	FELTHAM - 70B	FELTHAM - 70B	FELTHAM - 70B
30355	GUILDFORD - 70C	GUILDFORD - 70C	GUILDFORD - 70C	GUILDFORD - 70C	GUILDFORD - 70C	GUILDFORD - 70C	GUILDFORD - 70C
30368	BASINGSTOKE - 70D	BASINGSTOKE - 70D	BASINGSTOKE - 70D	BASINGSTOKE - 70D	BASINGSTOKE - 70D	BASINGSTOKE - 70D	BASINGSTOKE - 70D
30687	FELTHAM - 70B	FELTHAM - 70B	FELTHAM - 70B	FELTHAM - 70B	FELTHAM - 70B	FELTHAM - 70B	FELTHAM - 70B
30688	FELTHAM - 70B	FELTHAM - 70B	FELTHAM - 70B	FELTHAM - 70B	FELTHAM - 70B	FELTHAM - 70B	FELTHAM - 70B
30689	FELTHAM - 70B	FELTHAM - 70B	FELTHAM - 70B	FELTHAM - 70B	FELTHAM - 70B	FELTHAM - 70B	FELTHAM - 70B
30690	BOURNEMOUTH - 71B	BOURNEMOUTH - 71B	BOURNEMOUTH - 71B	BOURNEMOUTH - 71B	BOURNEMOUTH - 71B	BOURNEMOUTH - 71B	BOURNEMOUTH - 71B
30691	EXMOUTH JCN - 72A	EXMOUTH JCN - 72A	EXMOUTH JCN - 72A	EXMOUTH JCN - 72A	EXMOUTH JCN - 72A	EXMOUTH JCN - 72A	EXMOUTH JCN - 72A
30692	NINE ELMS - 70A	NINE ELMS - 70A	NINE ELMS - 70A	NINE ELMS - 70A	NINE ELMS - 70A	NINE ELMS - 70A	NINE ELMS - 70A
30693	GUILDFORD - 70C	GUILDFORD - 70C	GUILDFORD - 70C	GUILDFORD - 70C	GUILDFORD - 70C	GUILDFORD - 70C	GUILDFORD - 70C
30694	NINE ELMS - 70A	NINE ELMS - 70A	NINE ELMS - 70A	NINE ELMS - 70A	NINE ELMS - 70A	NINE ELMS - 70A	NINE ELMS - 70A
30695	BOURNEMOUTH - 71B	BOURNEMOUTH - 71B	BOURNEMOUTH - 71B	BOURNEMOUTH - 71B	BOURNEMOUTH - 71B	BOURNEMOUTH - 71B	BOURNEMOUTH - 71B
30696	FELTHAM - 70B	FELTHAM - 70B	FELTHAM - 70B	FELTHAM - 70B	FELTHAM - 70B	FELTHAM - 70B	FELTHAM - 70B
30697	GUILDFORD - 70C	GUILDFORD - 70C	GUILDFORD - 70C	GUILDFORD - 70C	GUILDFORD - 70C	GUILDFORD - 70C	GUILDFORD - 70C
30698	GUILDFORD - 70C	GUILDFORD - 70C	GUILDFORD - 70C	GUILDFORD - 70C	GUILDFORD - 70C	GUILDFORD - 70C	GUILDFORD - 70C
30699	NINE ELMS - 70A	NINE ELMS - 70A	NINE ELMS - 70A	NINE ELMS - 70A	NINE ELMS - 70A	NINE ELMS - 70A	NINE ELMS - 70A
30700	GUILDFORD - 70C	GUILDFORD - 70C	GUILDFORD - 70C	GUILDFORD - 70C	GUILDFORD - 70C	GUILDFORD - 70C	GUILDFORD - 70C
30701	NINE ELMS - 70A	NINE ELMS - 70A	NINE ELMS - 70A	NINE ELMS - 70A	NINE ELMS - 70A	NINE ELMS - 70A	NINE ELMS - 70A
				C2X 0-6-0 (1908)			
32434	EASTBOURNE - 75G	EASTBOURNE - 75G	EASTBOURNE - 75G	EASTBOURNE - 75G	EASTBOURNE - 75G	EASTBOURNE - 75G	EASTBOURNE - 75G
32437	BRIGHTON - 75A (N)	BRIGHTON - 75A (N)	BRIGHTON - 75A (N)	BRIGHTON - 75A (N)	BRIGHTON - 75A (N)	BRIGHTON - 75A (N)	BRIGHTON - 75A (N)
32438	BRIGHTON - 75A	BRIGHTON - 75A	BRIGHTON - 75A	BRIGHTON - 75A	BRIGHTON - 75A	THREE BRIDGES - 75E	THREE BRIDGES - 75E
32440	NORWOOD JCN - 75C	NORWOOD JCN - 75C	NORWOOD JCN - 75C	NORWOOD JCN - 75C	NORWOOD JCN - 75C	NORWOOD JCN - 75C	NORWOOD JCN - 75C
32441	THREE BRIDGES - 75E	THREE BRIDGES - 75E	THREE BRIDGES - 75E	THREE BRIDGES - 75E	THREE BRIDGES - 75E	THREE BRIDGES - 75E	THREE BRIDGES - 75E
32442	B.ARMS - 73B	B.ARMS - 73B	B.ARMS - 73B	B.ARMS - 73B	B.ARMS - 73B	B.ARMS - 73B	B.ARMS - 73B
32443	NORWOOD JCN - 75C	NORWOOD JCN - 75C	NORWOOD JCN - 75C	NORWOOD JCN - 75C	NORWOOD JCN - 75C	NORWOOD JCN - 75C	TONBRIDGE - 74D
32444	NORWOOD JCN - 75C	NORWOOD JCN - 75C	NORWOOD JCN - 75C	NORWOOD JCN - 75C	NORWOOD JCN - 75C	NORWOOD JCN - 75C	NORWOOD JCN - 75C
32445	THREE BRIDGES - 75E	THREE BRIDGES - 75E	THREE BRIDGES - 75E	THREE BRIDGES - 75E	THREE BRIDGES - 75E	THREE BRIDGES - 75E	THREE BRIDGES - 75E
32446	B.ARMS - 73B	B.ARMS - 73B	B.ARMS - 73B	B.ARMS - 73B	B.ARMS - 73B	B.ARMS - 73B	B.ARMS - 73B
32447	NORWOOD JCN - 75C	NORWOOD JCN - 75C	NORWOOD JCN - 75C	NORWOOD JCN - 75C	NORWOOD JCN - 75C	NORWOOD JCN - 75C	NORWOOD JCN - 75C
32448	REDHILL - 75B	REDHILL - 75B	REDHILL - 75B	REDHILL - 75B	REDHILL - 75B	STEWARTS LANE - 73A	NORWOOD JCN - 75C
32449	REDHILL - 75B	REDHILL - 75B	REDHILL - 75B	REDHILL - 75B	REDHILL - 75B	BRIGHTON - 75A	BRIGHTON - 75A
32450	REDHILL - 75B	REDHILL - 75B	REDHILL - 75B	REDHILL - 75B	REDHILL - 75B	REDHILL - 75B	REDHILL - 75B
32451	REDHILL - 75B	REDHILL - 75B	REDHILL - 75B	REDHILL - 75B	REDHILL - 75B	REDHILL - 75B	REDHILL - 75B
32521	B.ARMS - 73B	B.ARMS - 73B	B.ARMS - 73B	B.ARMS - 73B	B.ARMS - 73B	BRIGHTON - 75A	BRIGHTON - 75A
32522	THREE BRIDGES - 75E	THREE BRIDGES - 75E	THREE BRIDGES - 75E	THREE BRIDGES - 75E	THREE BRIDGES - 75E	THREE BRIDGES - 75E	THREE BRIDGES - 75E
32523	BRIGHTON - 75A	BRIGHTON - 75A	BRIGHTON - 75A	BRIGHTON - 75A	BRIGHTON - 75A	BRIGHTON - 75A	BRIGHTON - 75A
32524	B.ARMS - 73B	B.ARMS - 73B	B.ARMS - 73B	B.ARMS - 73B	B.ARMS - 73B	B.ARMS - 73B	B.ARMS - 73B
32525	B.ARMS - 73B	B.ARMS - 73B	B.ARMS - 73B	B.ARMS - 73B	B.ARMS - 73B	B.ARMS - 73B	B.ARMS - 73B
32526	THREE BRIDGES - 75E	THREE BRIDGES - 75E	THREE BRIDGES - 75E	THREE BRIDGES - 75E	THREE BRIDGES - 75E	THREE BRIDGES - 75E	THREE BRIDGES - 75E
32527	THREE BRIDGES - 75E	THREE BRIDGES - 75E	THREE BRIDGES - 75E	THREE BRIDGES - 75E	THREE BRIDGES - 75E	THREE BRIDGES - 75E	THREE BRIDGES - 75E
32528	BRIGHTON - 75A	BRIGHTON - 75A	BRIGHTON - 75A	BRIGHTON - 75A	BRIGHTON - 75A	BRIGHTON - 75A	BRIGHTON - 75A
32529	THREE BRIDGES - 75E	THREE BRIDGES - 75E	THREE BRIDGES - 75E	THREE BRIDGES - 75E	THREE BRIDGES - 75E	THREE BRIDGES - 75E	THREE BRIDGES - 75E
32532	THREE BRIDGES - 75E	THREE BRIDGES - 75E	THREE BRIDGES - 75E	THREE BRIDGES - 75E	THREE BRIDGES - 75E	THREE BRIDGES - 75E	THREE BRIDGES - 75E
32534	BRIGHTON - 75A	BRIGHTON - 75A	BRIGHTON - 75A	BRIGHTON - 75A	BRIGHTON - 75A	BRIGHTON - 75A	BRIGHTON - 75A
32535	NORWOOD JCN - 75C	NORWOOD JCN - 75C	NORWOOD JCN - 75C	NORWOOD JCN - 75C	NORWOOD JCN - 75C	NORWOOD JCN - 75C	NORWOOD JCN - 75C
32536	THREE BRIDGES - 75E	THREE BRIDGES - 75E	THREE BRIDGES - 75E	THREE BRIDGES - 75E	THREE BRIDGES - 75E	BRIGHTON - 75A	THREE BRIDGES - 75E
32537	B.ARMS - 73B	B.ARMS - 73B	B.ARMS - 73B	B.ARMS - 73B	B.ARMS - 73B	B.ARMS - 73B	B.ARMS - 73B
32538	B.ARMS - 73B	B.ARMS - 73B	B.ARMS - 73B	B.ARMS - 73B	B.ARMS - 73B	B.ARMS - 73B	B.ARMS - 73B
32539	B.ARMS - 73B	B.ARMS - 73B	B.ARMS - 73B	B.ARMS - 73B	B.ARMS - 73B	B.ARMS - 73B	B.ARMS - 73B
32540	BRIGHTON - 75A	BRIGHTON - 75A	BRIGHTON - 75A	BRIGHTON - 75A	BRIGHTON - 75A	BRIGHTON - 75A	BRIGHTON - 75A
32541	HORSHAM - 75D	HORSHAM - 75D	HORSHAM - 75D	HORSHAM - 75D	HORSHAM - 75D	HORSHAM - 75D	HORSHAM - 75D
32543	NORWOOD JCN - 75C	NORWOOD JCN - 75C	NORWOOD JCN - 75C	NORWOOD JCN - 75C	NORWOOD JCN - 75C	NORWOOD JCN - 75C	NORWOOD JCN - 75C
32544	HORSHAM - 75D	HORSHAM - 75D	HORSHAM - 75D	HORSHAM - 75D	HORSHAM - 75D	HORSHAM - 75D	HORSHAM - 75D
32545	THREE BRIDGES - 75E	THREE BRIDGES - 75E	THREE BRIDGES - 75E	THREE BRIDGES - 75E	THREE BRIDGES - 75E	THREE BRIDGES - 75E	THREE BRIDGES - 75E
32546	NORWOOD JCN - 75C	NORWOOD JCN - 75C	NORWOOD JCN - 75C	NORWOOD JCN - 75C	NORWOOD JCN - 75C	NORWOOD JCN - 75C	NORWOOD JCN - 75C
32547	NORWOOD JCN - 75C	NORWOOD JCN - 75C	NORWOOD JCN - 75C	NORWOOD JCN - 75C	NORWOOD JCN - 75C	NORWOOD JCN - 75C	NORWOOD JCN - 75C
32548	FRATTON - 70F	FRATTON - 70F	FRATTON - 70F	FRATTON - 70F	FRATTON - 70F	FRATTON - 70F	FRATTON - 70F
32549	FRATTON - 70F	FRATTON - 70F	FRATTON - 70F	FRATTON - 70F	FRATTON - 70F	FRATTON - 70F	FRATTON - 70F
32550	FRATTON - 70F	FRATTON - 70F	FRATTON - 70F	FRATTON - 70F	FRATTON - 70F	FRATTON - 70F	FRATTON - 70F
32551	T.WELLS - 75F	T.WELLS - 75F	T.WELLS - 75F	T.WELLS - 75F	T.WELLS - 75F	T.WELLS - 75F	T.WELLS - 75F
32552	THREE BRIDGES - 75E	THREE BRIDGES - 75E	THREE BRIDGES - 75E	THREE BRIDGES - 75E	THREE BRIDGES - 75E	THREE BRIDGES - 75E	THREE BRIDGES - 75E
32553	THREE BRIDGES - 75E	THREE BRIDGES - 75E	THREE BRIDGES - 75E	THREE BRIDGES - 75E	THREE BRIDGES - 75E	THREE BRIDGES - 75E	THREE BRIDGES - 75E
32554	B.ARMS - 73B	B.ARMS - 73B	B.ARMS - 73B	B.ARMS - 73B	B.ARMS - 73B	B.ARMS - 73B	B.ARMS - 73B

loco	Mar-57	Jun-57	Jul-57	Oct-57	Jan-58	Feb-58	Mar-58
				'700' 0-6-0 (1897)			
30306	EASTLEIGH - 71A	EASTLEIGH - 71A	EASTLEIGH - 71A	EASTLEIGH - 71A	EASTLEIGH - 71A	EASTLEIGH - 71A	EASTLEIGH - 71A
30308	GUILDFORD - 70C	GUILDFORD - 70C	GUILDFORD - 70C	GUILDFORD - 70C	GUILDFORD - 70C	GUILDFORD - 70C	GUILDFORD - 70C
30309	SALISBURY - 72B	SALISBURY - 72B	SALISBURY - 72B	SALISBURY - 72B	SALISBURY - 72B	SALISBURY - 72B	SALISBURY - 72B
30315	EXMOUTH JCN - 72A	EXMOUTH JCN - 72A	EXMOUTH JCN - 72A	EXMOUTH JCN - 72A	EXMOUTH JCN - 72A	EXMOUTH JCN - 72A	SALISBURY - 72B
30316	EASTLEIGH - 71A	EASTLEIGH - 71A	EASTLEIGH - 71A	EASTLEIGH - 71A	EASTLEIGH - 71A	EASTLEIGH - 71A	EASTLEIGH - 71A
30317	SALISBURY - 72B	SALISBURY - 72B	SALISBURY - 72B	SALISBURY - 72B	SALISBURY - 72B	SALISBURY - 72B	EXMOUTH JCN - 72A
30325	GUILDFORD - 70C	GUILDFORD - 70C	GUILDFORD - 70C	GUILDFORD - 70C	GUILDFORD - 70C	GUILDFORD - 70C	GUILDFORD - 70C
30326	GUILDFORD - 70C	GUILDFORD - 70C	GUILDFORD - 70C	GUILDFORD - 70C	GUILDFORD - 70C	GUILDFORD - 70C	GUILDFORD - 70C
30327	SALISBURY - 72B	SALISBURY - 72B	SALISBURY - 72B	SALISBURY - 72B	SALISBURY - 72B	SALISBURY - 72B	SALISBURY - 72B
30339	NINE ELMS - 70A	NINE ELMS - 70A	NINE ELMS - 70A	NINE ELMS - 70A	NINE ELMS - 70A	NINE ELMS - 70A	NINE ELMS - 70A
30346	FELTHAM - 70B	FELTHAM - 70B	FELTHAM - 70B	FELTHAM - 70B	FELTHAM - 70B	FELTHAM - 70B	FELTHAM - 70B
30350	GUILDFORD - 70C	GUILDFORD - 70C	GUILDFORD - 70C	GUILDFORD - 70C	GUILDFORD - 70C	GUILDFORD - 70C	GUILDFORD - 70C
30352	FELTHAM - 70B	FELTHAM - 70B	FELTHAM - 70B	FELTHAM - 70B	FELTHAM - 70B	FELTHAM - 70B	FELTHAM - 70B
30355	GUILDFORD - 70C	GUILDFORD - 70C	GUILDFORD - 70C	GUILDFORD - 70C	GUILDFORD - 70C	GUILDFORD - 70C	GUILDFORD - 70C
30368	BASINGSTOKE - 70D	BASINGSTOKE - 70D	BASINGSTOKE - 70D	BASINGSTOKE - 70D	BASINGSTOKE - 70D	BASINGSTOKE - 70D	BASINGSTOKE - 70D
30687	FELTHAM - 70B	FELTHAM - 70B	FELTHAM - 70B	FELTHAM - 70B	FELTHAM - 70B	FELTHAM - 70B	FELTHAM - 70B
30688	FELTHAM - 70B	FELTHAM - 70B	FELTHAM - 70B	W/D	W/D	W/D	W/D
30689	FELTHAM - 70B	FELTHAM - 70B	FELTHAM - 70B	FELTHAM - 70B	FELTHAM - 70B	FELTHAM - 70B	FELTHAM - 70B
30690	BOURNEMOUTH - 71B	BOURNEMOUTH - 71B	BOURNEMOUTH - 71B	BOURNEMOUTH - 71B	BOURNEMOUTH - 71B	BOURNEMOUTH - 71B	BOURNEMOUTH - 71B
30691	EXMOUTH JCN - 72A	EXMOUTH JCN - 72A	EXMOUTH JCN - 72A	EXMOUTH JCN - 72A	EXMOUTH JCN - 72A	EXMOUTH JCN - 72A	EXMOUTH JCN - 72A
30692	NINE ELMS - 70A	NINE ELMS - 70A	NINE ELMS - 70A	NINE ELMS - 70A	NINE ELMS - 70A	NINE ELMS - 70A	NINE ELMS - 70A
30693	GUILDFORD - 70C	GUILDFORD - 70C	GUILDFORD - 70C	GUILDFORD - 70C	GUILDFORD - 70C	GUILDFORD - 70C	GUILDFORD - 70C
30694	NINE ELMS - 70A	NINE ELMS - 70A	NINE ELMS - 70A	NINE ELMS - 70A	NINE ELMS - 70A	NINE ELMS - 70A	NINE ELMS - 70A
30695	BOURNEMOUTH - 71B	BOURNEMOUTH - 71B	BOURNEMOUTH - 71B	BOURNEMOUTH - 71B	BOURNEMOUTH - 71B	BOURNEMOUTH - 71B	BOURNEMOUTH - 71B
30696	FELTHAM - 70B	FELTHAM - 70B	FELTHAM - 70B	FELTHAM - 70B	FELTHAM - 70B	FELTHAM - 70B	FELTHAM - 70B
30697	GUILDFORD - 70C	GUILDFORD - 70C	GUILDFORD - 70C	GUILDFORD - 70C	GUILDFORD - 70C	GUILDFORD - 70C	GUILDFORD - 70C
30698	GUILDFORD - 70C	GUILDFORD - 70C	GUILDFORD - 70C	GUILDFORD - 70C	GUILDFORD - 70C	GUILDFORD - 70C	GUILDFORD - 70C
30699	NINE ELMS - 70A	NINE ELMS - 70A	NINE ELMS - 70A	NINE ELMS - 70A	NINE ELMS - 70A	NINE ELMS - 70A	NINE ELMS - 70A
30700	GUILDFORD - 70C	GUILDFORD - 70C	GUILDFORD - 70C	GUILDFORD - 70C	GUILDFORD - 70C	GUILDFORD - 70C	GUILDFORD - 70C
30701	NINE ELMS - 70A	NINE ELMS - 70A	NINE ELMS - 70A	NINE ELMS - 70A	NINE ELMS - 70A	NINE ELMS - 70A	NINE ELMS - 70A
				C2X 0-6-0 (1908)			
32437	BRIGHTON - 75A (N)	BRIGHTON - 75A (N)	BRIGHTON - 75A (N)	BRIGHTON - 75A (N)	BRIGHTON - 75A (N)	BRIGHTON - 75A (N)	FELTHAM - 70B
32438	THREE BRIDGES - 75E	THREE BRIDGES - 75E	THREE BRIDGES - 75E	THREE BRIDGES - 75E	THREE BRIDGES - 75E	THREE BRIDGES - 75E	FELTHAM - 70B
32440	NORWOOD JCN - 75C	NORWOOD JCN - 75C	NORWOOD JCN - 75C	NORWOOD JCN - 75C	NORWOOD JCN - 75C	NORWOOD JCN - 75C	NORWOOD JCN - 75C
32441	THREE BRIDGES - 75E	THREE BRIDGES - 75E	THREE BRIDGES - 75E	THREE BRIDGES - 75E	THREE BRIDGES - 75E	THREE BRIDGES - 75E	THREE BRIDGES - 75E
32442	B.ARMS - 73B	B.ARMS - 73B	B.ARMS - 73B	B.ARMS - 73B	B.ARMS - 73B	B.ARMS - 73B	B.ARMS - 73B
32443	TONBRIDGE - 74D	TONBRIDGE - 74D	TONBRIDGE - 74D	THREE BRIDGES - 75E	NORWOOD JCN - 75C	NORWOOD JCN - 75C	NORWOOD JCN - 75C
32444	NORWOOD JCN - 75C	NORWOOD JCN - 75C	NORWOOD JCN - 75C	NORWOOD JCN - 75C	NORWOOD JCN - 75C	NORWOOD JCN - 75C	NORWOOD JCN - 75C
32445	THREE BRIDGES - 75E	THREE BRIDGES - 75E	THREE BRIDGES - 75E	THREE BRIDGES - 75E	THREE BRIDGES - 75E	THREE BRIDGES - 75E	THREE BRIDGES - 75E
32446	B.ARMS - 73B	B.ARMS - 73B	B.ARMS - 73B	B.ARMS - 73B	B.ARMS - 73B	B.ARMS - 73B	B.ARMS - 73B
32447	NORWOOD JCN - 75C	NORWOOD JCN - 75C	NORWOOD JCN - 75C	NORWOOD JCN - 75C	NORWOOD JCN - 75C	NORWOOD JCN - 75C	NORWOOD JCN - 75C
32448	NORWOOD JCN - 75C	NORWOOD JCN - 75C	NORWOOD JCN - 75C	NORWOOD JCN - 75C	NORWOOD JCN - 75C	NORWOOD JCN - 75C	NORWOOD JCN - 75C
32449	BRIGHTON - 75A	BRIGHTON - 75A	BRIGHTON - 75A	BRIGHTON - 75A	BRIGHTON - 75A	BRIGHTON - 75A	BRIGHTON - 75A
32450	REDHILL - 75B	REDHILL - 75B	REDHILL - 75B	REDHILL - 75B	REDHILL - 75B	REDHILL - 75B	REDHILL - 75B
32451	REDHILL - 75B	REDHILL - 75B	REDHILL - 75B	REDHILL - 75B	REDHILL - 75B	REDHILL - 75B	REDHILL - 75B
32521	BRIGHTON - 75A	BRIGHTON - 75A	BRIGHTON - 75A	BRIGHTON - 75A	BRIGHTON - 75A	BRIGHTON - 75A	NORWOOD JCN - 75C
32522	THREE BRIDGES - 75E	THREE BRIDGES - 75E	THREE BRIDGES - 75E	THREE BRIDGES - 75E	THREE BRIDGES - 75E	THREE BRIDGES - 75E	THREE BRIDGES - 75E
32523	THREE BRIDGES - 75E	THREE BRIDGES - 75E	THREE BRIDGES - 75E	THREE BRIDGES - 75E	THREE BRIDGES - 75E	THREE BRIDGES - 75E	THREE BRIDGES - 75E
32524	B.ARMS - 73B	B.ARMS - 73B	B.ARMS - 73B	B.ARMS - 73B	B.ARMS - 73B	W/D	W/D
32525	B.ARMS - 73B	B.ARMS - 73B	B.ARMS - 73B	B.ARMS - 73B	B.ARMS - 73B	B.ARMS - 73B	B.ARMS - 73B
32526	HORSHAM - 75D	HORSHAM - 75D	HORSHAM - 75D	HORSHAM - 75D	HORSHAM - 75D	HORSHAM - 75D	HORSHAM - 75D
32527	THREE BRIDGES - 75E	THREE BRIDGES - 75E	THREE BRIDGES - 75E	THREE BRIDGES - 75E	THREE BRIDGES - 75E	THREE BRIDGES - 75E	THREE BRIDGES - 75E
32528	BRIGHTON - 75A	BRIGHTON - 75A	BRIGHTON - 75A	BRIGHTON - 75A	BRIGHTON - 75A	BRIGHTON - 75A	BRIGHTON - 75A
32529	THREE BRIDGES - 75E	THREE BRIDGES - 75E	THREE BRIDGES - 75E	THREE BRIDGES - 75E	THREE BRIDGES - 75E	THREE BRIDGES - 75E	THREE BRIDGES - 75E
32534	BRIGHTON - 75A	BRIGHTON - 75A	BRIGHTON - 75A	BRIGHTON - 75A	BRIGHTON - 75A	BRIGHTON - 75A	BRIGHTON - 75A
32535	NORWOOD JCN - 75C	NORWOOD JCN - 75C	NORWOOD JCN - 75C	NORWOOD JCN - 75C	NORWOOD JCN - 75C	NORWOOD JCN - 75C	NORWOOD JCN - 75C
32536	THREE BRIDGES - 75E	THREE BRIDGES - 75E	THREE BRIDGES - 75E	THREE BRIDGES - 75E	THREE BRIDGES - 75E	THREE BRIDGES - 75E	THREE BRIDGES - 75E
32537	B.ARMS - 73B	W/D	W/D	W/D	W/D	W/D	W/D
32538	B.ARMS - 73B	B.ARMS - 73B	B.ARMS - 73B	B.ARMS - 73B	B.ARMS - 73B	B.ARMS - 73B	B.ARMS - 73B
32539	B.ARMS - 73B	B.ARMS - 73B	B.ARMS - 73B	B.ARMS - 73B	B.ARMS - 73B	B.ARMS - 73B	B.ARMS - 73B
32540	BRIGHTON - 75A	BRIGHTON - 75A	BRIGHTON - 75A	BRIGHTON - 75A	BRIGHTON - 75A	BRIGHTON - 75A	W/D
32541	HORSHAM - 75D	HORSHAM - 75D	HORSHAM - 75D	HORSHAM - 75D	HORSHAM - 75D	HORSHAM - 75D	HORSHAM - 75D
32543	NORWOOD JCN - 75C	NORWOOD JCN - 75C	NORWOOD JCN - 75C	NORWOOD JCN - 75C	NORWOOD JCN - 75C	NORWOOD JCN - 75C	NORWOOD JCN - 75C
32544	HORSHAM - 75D	HORSHAM - 75D	HORSHAM - 75D	HORSHAM - 75D	HORSHAM - 75D	HORSHAM - 75D	HORSHAM - 75D
32545	THREE BRIDGES - 75E	THREE BRIDGES - 75E	THREE BRIDGES - 75E	THREE BRIDGES - 75E	THREE BRIDGES - 75E	THREE BRIDGES - 75E	THREE BRIDGES - 75E
32546	NORWOOD JCN - 75C	NORWOOD JCN - 75C	NORWOOD JCN - 75C	NORWOOD JCN - 75C	NORWOOD JCN - 75C	NORWOOD JCN - 75C	NORWOOD JCN - 75C
32547	NORWOOD JCN - 75C	NORWOOD JCN - 75C	NORWOOD JCN - 75C	NORWOOD JCN - 75C	NORWOOD JCN - 75C	NORWOOD JCN - 75C	NORWOOD JCN - 75C
32548	FRATTON - 70F	FRATTON - 70F	FRATTON - 70F	FRATTON - 70F	FRATTON - 70F	FRATTON - 70F	FRATTON - 70F
32549	FRATTON - 70F	FRATTON - 70F	FRATTON - 70F	FRATTON - 70F	FRATTON - 70F	FRATTON - 70F	FRATTON - 70F
32550	FRATTON - 70F	FRATTON - 70F	FRATTON - 70F	FRATTON - 70F	FRATTON - 70F	FRATTON - 70F	FRATTON - 70F
32551	T.WELLS - 75F	T.WELLS - 75F	T.WELLS - 75F	T.WELLS - 75F	T.WELLS - 75F	T.WELLS - 75F	T.WELLS - 75F
32552	THREE BRIDGES - 75E	THREE BRIDGES - 75E	THREE BRIDGES - 75E	THREE BRIDGES - 75E	THREE BRIDGES - 75E	THREE BRIDGES - 75E	THREE BRIDGES - 75E
32553	THREE BRIDGES - 75E	THREE BRIDGES - 75E	THREE BRIDGES - 75E	THREE BRIDGES - 75E	THREE BRIDGES - 75E	THREE BRIDGES - 75E	THREE BRIDGES - 75E
32554	B.ARMS - 73B	B.ARMS - 73B	B.ARMS - 73B	B.ARMS - 73B	B.ARMS - 73B	B.ARMS - 73B	B.ARMS - 73B

loco	May-58	Oct-58	Mar-59	Jun-59	Jul-59	Aug-59	Oct-59
				'700' 0-6-0 (1897)			
30306	EASTLEIGH-71A	EASTLEIGH-71A	EASTLEIGH-71A	EASTLEIGH-71A	EASTLEIGH-71A	EASTLEIGH-71A	EASTLEIGH-71A
30308	GUILDFORD-70C	GUILDFORD-70C	GUILDFORD-70C	GUILDFORD-70C	GUILDFORD-70C	GUILDFORD-70C	GUILDFORD-70C
30309	SALISBURY-72B	SALISBURY-72B	SALISBURY-72B	SALISBURY-72B	SALISBURY-72B	SALISBURY-72B	SALISBURY-72B
30315	SALISBURY-72B	SALISBURY-72B	SALISBURY-72B	SALISBURY-72B	SALISBURY-72B	SALISBURY-72B	SALISBURY-72B
30316	EASTLEIGH-71A	EASTLEIGH-71A	EASTLEIGH-71A	EASTLEIGH-71A	EASTLEIGH-71A	EASTLEIGH-71A	EASTLEIGH-71A
30317	EXMOUTH JCN-72A	EXMOUTH JCN-72A	EXMOUTH JCN-72A	EXMOUTH JCN-72A	EXMOUTH JCN-72A	EXMOUTH JCN-72A	EXMOUTH JCN-72A
30325	GUILDFORD-70C	GUILDFORD-70C	GUILDFORD-70C	GUILDFORD-70C	GUILDFORD-70C	GUILDFORD-70C	GUILDFORD-70C
30326	GUILDFORD-70C	GUILDFORD-70C	GUILDFORD-70C	GUILDFORD-70C	GUILDFORD-70C	GUILDFORD-70C	GUILDFORD-70C
30327	SALISBURY-72B	SALISBURY-72B	EXMOUTH JCN-72A	EXMOUTH JCN-72A	EXMOUTH JCN-72A	EXMOUTH JCN-72A	EXMOUTH JCN-72A
30339	NINE ELMS-70A	NINE ELMS-70A	NINE ELMS-70A	NINE ELMS-70A	NINE ELMS-70A	NINE ELMS-70A	NINE ELMS-70A
30346	FELTHAM-70B	FELTHAM-70B	FELTHAM-70B	FELTHAM-70B	FELTHAM-70B	FELTHAM-70B	FELTHAM-70B
30350	GUILDFORD-70C	GUILDFORD-70C	GUILDFORD-70C	GUILDFORD-70C	GUILDFORD-70C	GUILDFORD-70C	GUILDFORD-70C
30352	FELTHAM-70B	FELTHAM-70B	FELTHAM-70B	FELTHAM-70B	WD	WD	WD
30355	GUILDFORD-70C	GUILDFORD-70C	GUILDFORD-70C	GUILDFORD-70C	GUILDFORD-70C	GUILDFORD-70C	GUILDFORD-70C
30368	BASINGSTOKE-70D	BASINGSTOKE-70D	BASINGSTOKE-70D	BASINGSTOKE-70D	BASINGSTOKE-70D	BASINGSTOKE-70D	BASINGSTOKE-70D
30687	FELTHAM-70B	FELTHAM-70B	FELTHAM-70B	FELTHAM-70B	FELTHAM-70B	FELTHAM-70B	FELTHAM-70B
30689	FELTHAM-70B	FELTHAM-70B	FELTHAM-70B	FELTHAM-70B	FELTHAM-70B	FELTHAM-70B	FELTHAM-70B
30690	BOURNEMOUTH-71B	BOURNEMOUTH-71B	BOURNEMOUTH-71B	BOURNEMOUTH-71B	BOURNEMOUTH-71B	BOURNEMOUTH-71B	BOURNEMOUTH-71B
30691	EXMOUTH JCN-72A	EXMOUTH JCN-72A	EXMOUTH JCN-72A	SALISBURY-72B	SALISBURY-72B	SALISBURY-72B	SALISBURY-72B
30692	NINE ELMS-70A	NINE ELMS-70A	SALISBURY-72B	GUILDFORD-70C	GUILDFORD-70C	GUILDFORD-70C	GUILDFORD-70C
30693	GUILDFORD-70C	GUILDFORD-70C	GUILDFORD-70C	GUILDFORD-70C	GUILDFORD-70C	GUILDFORD-70C	GUILDFORD-70C
30694	NINE ELMS-70A	NINE ELMS-70A	NINE ELMS-70A	NINE ELMS-70A	NINE ELMS-70A	NINE ELMS-70A	NINE ELMS-70A
30695	BOURNEMOUTH-71B	BOURNEMOUTH-71B	BOURNEMOUTH-71B	BOURNEMOUTH-71B	BOURNEMOUTH-71B	BOURNEMOUTH-71B	BOURNEMOUTH-71B
30696	FELTHAM-70B	FELTHAM-70B	FELTHAM-70B	FELTHAM-70B	FELTHAM-70B	FELTHAM-70B	FELTHAM-70B
30697	GUILDFORD-70C	GUILDFORD-70C	GUILDFORD-70C	GUILDFORD-70C	GUILDFORD-70C	GUILDFORD-70C	GUILDFORD-70C
30698	GUILDFORD-70C	GUILDFORD-70C	GUILDFORD-70C	GUILDFORD-70C	GUILDFORD-70C	GUILDFORD-70C	GUILDFORD-70C
30699	NINE ELMS-70A	NINE ELMS-70A	NINE ELMS-70A	NINE ELMS-70A	NINE ELMS-70A	NINE ELMS-70A	NINE ELMS-70A
30700	GUILDFORD-70C	GUILDFORD-70C	GUILDFORD-70C	GUILDFORD-70C	GUILDFORD-70C	GUILDFORD-70C	GUILDFORD-70C
30701	NINE ELMS-70A	NINE ELMS-70A	NINE ELMS-70A	NINE ELMS-70A	NINE ELMS-70A	NINE ELMS-70A	NINE ELMS-70A
				C2X 0-6-0 (1908)			
32437	FELTHAM-70B	FELTHAM-70B	FELTHAM-70B	FELTHAM-70B	WD	WD	WD
32438	FELTHAM-70B	FELTHAM-70B	FELTHAM-70B	FELTHAM-70B	FELTHAM-70B	FELTHAM-70B	FELTHAM-70B
32440	NORWOOD JCN-75C	WD	WD	WD	WD	WD	WD
32441	THREE BRIDGES-75E	THREE BRIDGES-75E	THREE BRIDGES-75E	THREE BRIDGES-75E	THREE BRIDGES-75E	THREE BRIDGES-75E	THREE BRIDGES-75E
32442	B.ARMS-73B	B.ARMS-73B	B.ARMS-73B	B.ARMS-73B	B.ARMS-73B	B.ARMS-73B	B.ARMS-73B
32443	NORWOOD JCN-75C	NORWOOD JCN-75C	NORWOOD JCN-75C	NORWOOD JCN-75C	NORWOOD JCN-75C	NORWOOD JCN-75C	NORWOOD JCN-75C
32444	NORWOOD JCN-75C	THREE BRIDGES-75E	THREE BRIDGES-75E	THREE BRIDGES-75E	THREE BRIDGES-75E	THREE BRIDGES-75E	THREE BRIDGES-75E
32445	THREE BRIDGES-75E	THREE BRIDGES-75E	THREE BRIDGES-75E	THREE BRIDGES-75E	THREE BRIDGES-75E	THREE BRIDGES-75E	THREE BRIDGES-75E
32446	B.ARMS-73B	B.ARMS-73B	B.ARMS-73B	B.ARMS-73B	B.ARMS-73B	B.ARMS-73B	B.ARMS-73B
32447	NORWOOD JCN-75C	NORWOOD JCN-75C	NORWOOD JCN-75C	NORWOOD JCN-75C	NORWOOD JCN-75C	NORWOOD JCN-75C	NORWOOD JCN-75C
32448	NORWOOD JCN-75C	NORWOOD JCN-75C	NORWOOD JCN-75C	NORWOOD JCN-75C	NORWOOD JCN-75C	NORWOOD JCN-75C	NORWOOD JCN-75C
32449	BRIGHTON-75A	BRIGHTON-75A	BRIGHTON-75A	BRIGHTON-75A	BRIGHTON-75A	BRIGHTON-75A	BRIGHTON-75A
32450	REDHILL-75B	REDHILL-75B	REDHILL-75B	REDHILL-75B	REDHILL-75B	REDHILL-75B	REDHILL-75B
32451	REDHILL-75B	REDHILL-75B	REDHILL-75B	REDHILL-75B	REDHILL-75B	REDHILL-75B	REDHILL-75B
32521	NORWOOD JCN-75C	NORWOOD JCN-75C	NORWOOD JCN-75C	NORWOOD JCN-75C	NORWOOD JCN-75C	NORWOOD JCN-75C	NORWOOD JCN-75C
32522	THREE BRIDGES-75E	THREE BRIDGES-75E	THREE BRIDGES-75E	THREE BRIDGES-75E	THREE BRIDGES-75E	THREE BRIDGES-75E	THREE BRIDGES-75E
32523	THREE BRIDGES-75E	THREE BRIDGES-75E	THREE BRIDGES-75E	THREE BRIDGES-75E	THREE BRIDGES-75E	THREE BRIDGES-75E	THREE BRIDGES-75E
32525	B.ARMS-73B	B.ARMS-73B	B.ARMS-73B	B.ARMS-73B	B.ARMS-73B	B.ARMS-73B	B.ARMS-73B
32526	HORSHAM-75D	HORSHAM-75D	HORSHAM-75D	HORSHAM-75D	THREE BRIDGES-75E	THREE BRIDGES-75E	THREE BRIDGES-75E
32527	THREE BRIDGES-75E	THREE BRIDGES-75E	THREE BRIDGES-75E	THREE BRIDGES-75E	BRIGHTON-75A	BRIGHTON-75A	BRIGHTON-75A
32528	BRIGHTON-75A	BRIGHTON-75A	BRIGHTON-75A	BRIGHTON-75A	THREE BRIDGES-75E	THREE BRIDGES-75E	WD
32529	THREE BRIDGES-75E	THREE BRIDGES-75E	THREE BRIDGES-75E	THREE BRIDGES-75E	THREE BRIDGES-75E	THREE BRIDGES-75E	THREE BRIDGES-75E
32532	THREE BRIDGES-75E	BRIGHTON-75A	BRIGHTON-75A	BRIGHTON-75A	BRIGHTON-75A	BRIGHTON-75A	BRIGHTON-75A
32534	BRIGHTON-75A						
32535	NORWOOD JCN-75C	NORWOOD JCN-75C	NORWOOD JCN-75C	NORWOOD JCN-75C	NORWOOD JCN-75C	NORWOOD JCN-75C	NORWOOD JCN-75C
32536	THREE BRIDGES-75E	THREE BRIDGES-75E	THREE BRIDGES-75E	THREE BRIDGES-75E	THREE BRIDGES-75E	THREE BRIDGES-75E	THREE BRIDGES-75E
32538	B.ARMS-73B	B.ARMS-73B	B.ARMS-73B	B.ARMS-73B	B.ARMS-73B	B.ARMS-73B	B.ARMS-73B
32539	B.ARMS-73B	B.ARMS-73B	B.ARMS-73B	B.ARMS-73B	B.ARMS-73B	B.ARMS-73B	B.ARMS-73B
32541	HORSHAM-75D	HORSHAM-75D	HORSHAM-75D	HORSHAM-75D	THREE BRIDGES-75E	THREE BRIDGES-75E	NORWOOD JCN-75C
32543	NORWOOD JCN-75C	NORWOOD JCN-75C	NORWOOD JCN-75C	NORWOOD JCN-75C	NORWOOD JCN-75C	NORWOOD JCN-75C	NORWOOD JCN-75C
32544	HORSHAM-75D	HORSHAM-75D	HORSHAM-75D	HORSHAM-75D	HORSHAM-75D	HORSHAM-75D	HORSHAM-75D
32545	THREE BRIDGES-75E	THREE BRIDGES-75E	THREE BRIDGES-75E	THREE BRIDGES-75E	THREE BRIDGES-75E	THREE BRIDGES-75E	THREE BRIDGES-75E
32546	NORWOOD JCN-75C	NORWOOD JCN-75C	NORWOOD JCN-75C	NORWOOD JCN-75C	NORWOOD JCN-75C	NORWOOD JCN-75C	NORWOOD JCN-75C
32547	NORWOOD JCN-75C	NORWOOD JCN-75C	NORWOOD JCN-75C	NORWOOD JCN-75C	NORWOOD JCN-75C	NORWOOD JCN-75C	NORWOOD JCN-75C
32548	FRATTON-70F	FRATTON-70F	FRATTON-70F	FRATTON-70F	FRATTON-70F	FRATTON-70F	FRATTON-70F
32549	FRATTON-70F	FRATTON-70F	FRATTON-70F	FRATTON-70F	FRATTON-70F	FRATTON-70F	FRATTON-70F
32550	FRATTON-70F	FRATTON-70F	FRATTON-70F	FRATTON-70F	FRATTON-70F	FRATTON-70F	FRATTON-70F
32551	T.WELLS-75F	T.WELLS-75F	T.WELLS-75F	T.WELLS-75F	T.WELLS-75F	T.WELLS-75F	T.WELLS-75F
32552	THREE BRIDGES-75E	THREE BRIDGES-75E	THREE BRIDGES-75E	THREE BRIDGES-75E	THREE BRIDGES-75E	THREE BRIDGES-75E	THREE BRIDGES-75E
32553	THREE BRIDGES-75E	THREE BRIDGES-75E	THREE BRIDGES-75E	THREE BRIDGES-75E	B.ARMS-73B	B.ARMS-73B	THREE BRIDGES-75E
32554	B.ARMS-73B	B.ARMS-73B	B.ARMS-73B	B.ARMS-73B	B.ARMS-73B	B.ARMS-73B	B.ARMS-73B

loco	Dec-59	Feb-60	Mar-60	Apr-60	Jul-60	Aug-60	Sep-60	Nov-60
'700' 0-6-0 (1897)								
30306	EASTLEIGH - 71A	EASTLEIGH - 71A	EASTLEIGH - 71A	EASTLEIGH - 71A	EASTLEIGH - 71A	EASTLEIGH - 71A	EASTLEIGH - 71A	EASTLEIGH - 71A
30308	GUILDFORD - 70C	GUILDFORD - 70C	GUILDFORD - 70C	GUILDFORD - 70C	GUILDFORD - 70C	GUILDFORD - 70C	GUILDFORD - 70C	GUILDFORD - 70C
30309	SALISBURY - 72B	SALISBURY - 72B	SALISBURY - 72B	SALISBURY - 72B	SALISBURY - 72B	SALISBURY - 72B	SALISBURY - 72B	SALISBURY - 72B
30315	SALISBURY - 72B	SALISBURY - 72B	SALISBURY - 72B	SALISBURY - 72B	SALISBURY - 72B	SALISBURY - 72B	SALISBURY - 72B	SALISBURY - 72B
30316	EASTLEIGH - 71A	EASTLEIGH - 71A	EASTLEIGH - 71A	EASTLEIGH - 71A	EASTLEIGH - 71A	EASTLEIGH - 71A	EASTLEIGH - 71A	EASTLEIGH - 71A
30317	EXMOUTH JCN - 72A	EXMOUTH JCN - 72A	EXMOUTH JCN - 72A	EXMOUTH JCN - 72A	EXMOUTH JCN - 72A	EXMOUTH JCN - 72A	EXMOUTH JCN - 72A	EXMOUTH JCN - 72A
30325	GUILDFORD - 70C	GUILDFORD - 70C	GUILDFORD - 70C	GUILDFORD - 70C	GUILDFORD - 70C	GUILDFORD - 70C	GUILDFORD - 70C	GUILDFORD - 70C
30326	GUILDFORD - 70C	GUILDFORD - 70C	GUILDFORD - 70C	GUILDFORD - 70C	GUILDFORD - 70C	GUILDFORD - 70C	GUILDFORD - 70C	GUILDFORD - 70C
30327	EXMOUTH JCN - 72A	EXMOUTH JCN - 72A	EXMOUTH JCN - 72A	EXMOUTH JCN - 72A	EXMOUTH JCN - 72A	EXMOUTH JCN - 72A	EXMOUTH JCN - 72A	EXMOUTH JCN - 72A
30339	NINE ELMS - 70A	NINE ELMS - 70A	NINE ELMS - 70A	NINE ELMS - 70A	NINE ELMS - 70A	NINE ELMS - 70A	NINE ELMS - 70A	NINE ELMS - 70A
30346	FELTHAM - 70B	FELTHAM - 70B	FELTHAM - 70B	FELTHAM - 70B	FELTHAM - 70B	FELTHAM - 70B	FELTHAM - 70B	FELTHAM - 70B
30350	GUILDFORD - 70C	GUILDFORD - 70C	GUILDFORD - 70C	GUILDFORD - 70C	GUILDFORD - 70C	GUILDFORD - 70C	GUILDFORD - 70C	GUILDFORD - 70C
30355	GUILDFORD - 70C	GUILDFORD - 70C	GUILDFORD - 70C	GUILDFORD - 70C	GUILDFORD - 70C	GUILDFORD - 70C	GUILDFORD - 70C	GUILDFORD - 70C
30368	BASINGSTOKE - 70D	BASINGSTOKE - 70D	BASINGSTOKE - 70D	BASINGSTOKE - 70D	BASINGSTOKE - 70D	BASINGSTOKE - 70D	BASINGSTOKE - 70D	BASINGSTOKE - 70D
30687	FELTHAM - 70B	FELTHAM - 70B	FELTHAM - 70B	FELTHAM - 70B	FELTHAM - 70B	FELTHAM - 70B	W/D	W/D
30689	FELTHAM - 70B	FELTHAM - 70B	FELTHAM - 70B	FELTHAM - 70B	FELTHAM - 70B	FELTHAM - 70B	FELTHAM - 70B	FELTHAM - 70B
30690	BOURNEMOUTH - 71B	BOURNEMOUTH - 71B	BOURNEMOUTH - 71B	BOURNEMOUTH - 71B	BOURNEMOUTH - 71B	BOURNEMOUTH - 71B	BOURNEMOUTH - 71B	BOURNEMOUTH - 71B
30691	EXMOUTH JCN - 72A	EXMOUTH JCN - 72A	EXMOUTH JCN - 72A	EXMOUTH JCN - 72A	EXMOUTH JCN - 72A	EXMOUTH JCN - 72A	EXMOUTH JCN - 72A	EXMOUTH JCN - 72A
30692	SALISBURY - 72B	SALISBURY - 72B	SALISBURY - 72B	SALISBURY - 72B	SALISBURY - 72B	SALISBURY - 72B	SALISBURY - 72B	SALISBURY - 72B
30693	GUILDFORD - 70C	GUILDFORD - 70C	GUILDFORD - 70C	GUILDFORD - 70C	GUILDFORD - 70C	GUILDFORD - 70C	GUILDFORD - 70C	GUILDFORD - 70C
30694	NINE ELMS - 70A	NINE ELMS - 70A	NINE ELMS - 70A	NINE ELMS - 70A	NINE ELMS - 70A	NINE ELMS - 70A	NINE ELMS - 70A	NINE ELMS - 70A
30695	BOURNEMOUTH - 71B	BOURNEMOUTH - 71B	BOURNEMOUTH - 71B	BOURNEMOUTH - 71B	BOURNEMOUTH - 71B	BOURNEMOUTH - 71B	BOURNEMOUTH - 71B	BOURNEMOUTH - 71B
30696	FELTHAM - 70B	FELTHAM - 70B	FELTHAM - 70B	FELTHAM - 70B	FELTHAM - 70B	FELTHAM - 70B	FELTHAM - 70B	FELTHAM - 70B
30697	GUILDFORD - 70C	GUILDFORD - 70C	GUILDFORD - 70C	GUILDFORD - 70C	GUILDFORD - 70C	GUILDFORD - 70C	GUILDFORD - 70C	GUILDFORD - 70C
30698	GUILDFORD - 70C	GUILDFORD - 70C	GUILDFORD - 70C	GUILDFORD - 70C	GUILDFORD - 70C	GUILDFORD - 70C	GUILDFORD - 70C	GUILDFORD - 70C
30699	NINE ELMS - 70A	NINE ELMS - 70A	NINE ELMS - 70A	NINE ELMS - 70A	NINE ELMS - 70A	NINE ELMS - 70A	NINE ELMS - 70A	NINE ELMS - 70A
30700	GUILDFORD - 70C	GUILDFORD - 70C	GUILDFORD - 70C	GUILDFORD - 70C	GUILDFORD - 70C	GUILDFORD - 70C	GUILDFORD - 70C	GUILDFORD - 70C
30701	NINE ELMS - 70A	NINE ELMS - 70A	NINE ELMS - 70A	NINE ELMS - 70A	NINE ELMS - 70A	NINE ELMS - 70A	NINE ELMS - 70A	NINE ELMS - 70A
C2X 0-6-0 (1908)								
32438	FELTHAM - 70B	FELTHAM - 70B	FELTHAM - 70B	FELTHAM - 70B	FELTHAM - 70B	FELTHAM - 70B	STEWARTS LANE - 73A	STEWARTS LANE - 73A
32441	THREE BRIDGES - 75E	THREE BRIDGES - 75E	THREE BRIDGES - 75E	THREE BRIDGES - 75E	THREE BRIDGES - 75E	THREE BRIDGES - 75E	THREE BRIDGES - 75E	THREE BRIDGES - 75E
32442	B.ARMS - 73B	W/D	W/D	W/D	W/D	W/D	W/D	W/D
32443	NORWOOD JCN - 75C	NORWOOD JCN - 75C	NORWOOD JCN - 75C	NORWOOD JCN - 75C	NORWOOD JCN - 75C	NORWOOD JCN - 75C	W/D	W/D
32444	NORWOOD JCN - 75C	NORWOOD JCN - 75C	NORWOOD JCN - 75C	NORWOOD JCN - 75C	W/D	W/D	W/D	W/D
32445	THREE BRIDGES - 75E	THREE BRIDGES - 75E	THREE BRIDGES - 75E	THREE BRIDGES - 75E	THREE BRIDGES - 75E	THREE BRIDGES - 75E	THREE BRIDGES - 75E	THREE BRIDGES - 75E
32446	B.ARMS - 73B	B.ARMS - 73B	B.ARMS - 73B	B.ARMS - 73B	B.ARMS - 73B	B.ARMS - 73B	B.ARMS - 73B	W/D
32447	NORWOOD JCN - 75C	W/D	W/D	W/D	W/D	W/D	W/D	W/D
32448	NORWOOD JCN - 75C	NORWOOD JCN - 75C	NORWOOD JCN - 75C	NORWOOD JCN - 75C	NORWOOD JCN - 75C	NORWOOD JCN - 75C	NORWOOD JCN - 75C	NORWOOD JCN - 75C
32449	BRIGHTON - 75A	BRIGHTON - 75A	BRIGHTON - 75A	BRIGHTON - 75A	BRIGHTON - 75A	BRIGHTON - 75A	BRIGHTON - 75A	BRIGHTON - 75A
32450	REDHILL - 75B	REDHILL - 75B	REDHILL - 75B	REDHILL - 75B	REDHILL - 75B	REDHILL - 75B	REDHILL - 75B	NORWOOD JCN - 75C
32451	REDHILL - 75B	REDHILL - 75B	REDHILL - 75B	REDHILL - 75B	REDHILL - 75B	REDHILL - 75B	REDHILL - 75B	REDHILL - 75B
32521	NORWOOD JCN - 75C	NORWOOD JCN - 75C	NORWOOD JCN - 75C	NORWOOD JCN - 75C	NORWOOD JCN - 75C	NORWOOD JCN - 75C	NORWOOD JCN - 75C	NORWOOD JCN - 75C
32522	THREE BRIDGES - 75E	THREE BRIDGES - 75E	THREE BRIDGES - 75E	THREE BRIDGES - 75E	THREE BRIDGES - 75E	THREE BRIDGES - 75E	THREE BRIDGES - 75E	THREE BRIDGES - 75E
32523	THREE BRIDGES - 75E	THREE BRIDGES - 75E	THREE BRIDGES - 75E	THREE BRIDGES - 75E	THREE BRIDGES - 75E	THREE BRIDGES - 75E	THREE BRIDGES - 75E	THREE BRIDGES - 75E
32525	B.ARMS - 73B	B.ARMS - 73B	B.ARMS - 73B	B.ARMS - 73B	B.ARMS - 73B	B.ARMS - 73B	B.ARMS - 73B	B.ARMS - 73B
32526	THREE BRIDGES - 75E	W/D	W/D	W/D	W/D	W/D	W/D	W/D
32527	THREE BRIDGES - 75E	THREE BRIDGES - 75E	THREE BRIDGES - 75E	THREE BRIDGES - 75E	THREE BRIDGES - 75E	THREE BRIDGES - 75E	THREE BRIDGES - 75E	W/D
32528	BRIGHTON - 75A	BRIGHTON - 75A	BRIGHTON - 75A	BRIGHTON - 75A	BRIGHTON - 75A	BRIGHTON - 75A	BRIGHTON - 75A	BRIGHTON - 75A
32532	THREE BRIDGES - 75E	THREE BRIDGES - 75E	THREE BRIDGES - 75E	THREE BRIDGES - 75E	W/D	W/D	W/D	W/D
32534	BRIGHTON - 75A	BRIGHTON - 75A	BRIGHTON - 75A	BRIGHTON - 75A	BRIGHTON - 75A	BRIGHTON - 75A	BRIGHTON - 75A	BRIGHTON - 75A
32535	NORWOOD JCN - 75C	NORWOOD JCN - 75C	NORWOOD JCN - 75C	NORWOOD JCN - 75C	NORWOOD JCN - 75C	NORWOOD JCN - 75C	NORWOOD JCN - 75C	NORWOOD JCN - 75C
32536	THREE BRIDGES - 75E	THREE BRIDGES - 75E	THREE BRIDGES - 75E	THREE BRIDGES - 75E	THREE BRIDGES - 75E	THREE BRIDGES - 75E	THREE BRIDGES - 75E	THREE BRIDGES - 75E
32538	B.ARMS - 73B	B.ARMS - 73B	B.ARMS - 73B	B.ARMS - 73B	B.ARMS - 73B	B.ARMS - 73B	B.ARMS - 73B	B.ARMS - 73B
32539	B.ARMS - 73B	B.ARMS - 73B	B.ARMS - 73B	B.ARMS - 73B	B.ARMS - 73B	B.ARMS - 73B	B.ARMS - 73B	B.ARMS - 73B
32541	NORWOOD JCN - 75C	NORWOOD JCN - 75C	NORWOOD JCN - 75C	NORWOOD JCN - 75C	NORWOOD JCN - 75C	NORWOOD JCN - 75C	NORWOOD JCN - 75C	NORWOOD JCN - 75C
32543	NORWOOD JCN - 75C	NORWOOD JCN - 75C	NORWOOD JCN - 75C	NORWOOD JCN - 75C	NORWOOD JCN - 75C	NORWOOD JCN - 75C	W/D	W/D
32544	HORSHAM - 75D	HORSHAM - 75D	HORSHAM - 75D	HORSHAM - 75D	HORSHAM - 75D	HORSHAM - 75D	HORSHAM - 75D	HORSHAM - 75D
32545	THREE BRIDGES - 75E	THREE BRIDGES - 75E	THREE BRIDGES - 75E	THREE BRIDGES - 75E	THREE BRIDGES - 75E	THREE BRIDGES - 75E	THREE BRIDGES - 75E	THREE BRIDGES - 75E
32546	NORWOOD JCN - 75C	NORWOOD JCN - 75C	NORWOOD JCN - 75C	NORWOOD JCN - 75C	NORWOOD JCN - 75C	NORWOOD JCN - 75C	NORWOOD JCN - 75C	NORWOOD JCN - 75C
32547	NORWOOD JCN - 75C	NORWOOD JCN - 75C	NORWOOD JCN - 75C	NORWOOD JCN - 75C	NORWOOD JCN - 75C	NORWOOD JCN - 75C	NORWOOD JCN - 75C	NORWOOD JCN - 75C
32548	NORWOOD JCN - 75C	NORWOOD JCN - 75C	NORWOOD JCN - 75C	NORWOOD JCN - 75C	NORWOOD JCN - 75C	NORWOOD JCN - 75C	NORWOOD JCN - 75C	NORWOOD JCN - 75C
32549	NORWOOD JCN - 75C	NORWOOD JCN - 75C	NORWOOD JCN - 75C	NORWOOD JCN - 75C	NORWOOD JCN - 75C	NORWOOD JCN - 75C	NORWOOD JCN - 75C	NORWOOD JCN - 75C
32550	NORWOOD JCN - 75C	NORWOOD JCN - 75C	NORWOOD JCN - 75C	NORWOOD JCN - 75C	NORWOOD JCN - 75C	NORWOOD JCN - 75C	NORWOOD JCN - 75C	NORWOOD JCN - 75C
32551	T.WELLS - 75F	W/D	W/D	W/D	W/D	W/D	W/D	W/D
32552	THREE BRIDGES - 75E	THREE BRIDGES - 75E	THREE BRIDGES - 75E	THREE BRIDGES - 75E	THREE BRIDGES - 75E	THREE BRIDGES - 75E	THREE BRIDGES - 75E	THREE BRIDGES - 75E
32553	THREE BRIDGES - 75E	THREE BRIDGES - 75E	THREE BRIDGES - 75E	THREE BRIDGES - 75E	THREE BRIDGES - 75E	THREE BRIDGES - 75E	THREE BRIDGES - 75E	THREE BRIDGES - 75E
32554	B.ARMS - 73B	W/D	W/D	W/D	W/D	W/D	W/D	W/D

Although the K class 2-6-0's stole the goods limelight on the Brighton section, a high proportion of traffic remained in the hands of the C2X 'Large Vulcans' 0-6-0's and almost two-thirds of the class survived into the 1960's. 32440, a long term resident of Norwood Junction until being taken out of traffic in the autumn of 1958, moves onto the head shunt at Brighton MPD in 1955 whilst being prepared for a main line goods working.

loco	May-49	Jun-49	Aug-49	Sep-49	Dec-49	Feb-50	Mar-50
				Q 0-6-0 (1938)			
30530	EASTLEIGH - 71A	EASTLEIGH - 71A	EASTLEIGH - 71A	EASTLEIGH - 71A	EASTLEIGH - 71A	EASTLEIGH - 71A	EASTLEIGH - 71A
30531	HORSHAM - 75D	HORSHAM - 75D	HORSHAM - 75D	HORSHAM - 75D	HORSHAM - 75D	HORSHAM - 75D	HORSHAM - 75D
30532	EASTLEIGH - 71A	EASTLEIGH - 71A	EASTLEIGH - 71A	EASTLEIGH - 71A	EASTLEIGH - 71A	EASTLEIGH - 71A	EASTLEIGH - 71A
30533	NORWOOD JCN - 75C	NORWOOD JCN - 75C	NORWOOD JCN - 75C	NORWOOD JCN - 75C	NORWOOD JCN - 75C	NORWOOD JCN - 75C	NORWOOD JCN - 75C
30534	T.WELLS - 75F	T.WELLS - 75F	T.WELLS - 75F	T.WELLS - 75F	T.WELLS - 75F	T.WELLS - 75F	T.WELLS - 75F
30535	EASTLEIGH - 71A	EASTLEIGH - 71A	EASTLEIGH - 71A	EASTLEIGH - 71A	EASTLEIGH - 71A	EASTLEIGH - 71A	EASTLEIGH - 71A
30536	EASTLEIGH - 71A	EASTLEIGH - 71A	EASTLEIGH - 71A	EASTLEIGH - 71A	EASTLEIGH - 71A	EASTLEIGH - 71A	EASTLEIGH - 71A
30537	NORWOOD JCN - 75C	NORWOOD JCN - 75C	NORWOOD JCN - 75C	NORWOOD JCN - 75C	NORWOOD JCN - 75C	NORWOOD JCN - 75C	NORWOOD JCN - 75C
30538	NORWOOD JCN - 75C	NORWOOD JCN - 75C	NORWOOD JCN - 75C	NORWOOD JCN - 75C	NORWOOD JCN - 75C	NORWOOD JCN - 75C	NORWOOD JCN - 75C
30539	NORWOOD JCN - 75C	NORWOOD JCN - 75C	NORWOOD JCN - 75C	NORWOOD JCN - 75C	NORWOOD JCN - 75C	NORWOOD JCN - 75C	NORWOOD JCN - 75C
30540	THREE BRIDGES - 75E	THREE BRIDGES - 75E	THREE BRIDGES - 75E	THREE BRIDGES - 75E	THREE BRIDGES - 75E	THREE BRIDGES - 75E	THREE BRIDGES - 75E
30541	THREE BRIDGES - 75E	THREE BRIDGES - 75E	THREE BRIDGES - 75E	THREE BRIDGES - 75E	THREE BRIDGES - 75E	THREE BRIDGES - 75E	THREE BRIDGES - 75E
30542	T.WELLS - 75F	T.WELLS - 75F	T.WELLS - 75F	T.WELLS - 75F	T.WELLS - 75F	T.WELLS - 75F	T.WELLS - 75F
30543	T.WELLS - 75F	T.WELLS - 75F	T.WELLS - 75F	T.WELLS - 75F	T.WELLS - 75F	T.WELLS - 75F	T.WELLS - 75F
30544	T.WELLS - 75F	T.WELLS - 75F	T.WELLS - 75F	T.WELLS - 75F	T.WELLS - 75F	T.WELLS - 75F	T.WELLS - 75F
30545	HORSHAM - 75D	HORSHAM - 75D	HORSHAM - 75D	HORSHAM - 75D	HORSHAM - 75D	HORSHAM - 75D	HORSHAM - 75D
30546	HORSHAM - 75D	HORSHAM - 75D	HORSHAM - 75D	HORSHAM - 75D	HORSHAM - 75D	HORSHAM - 75D	HORSHAM - 75D
30547	NORWOOD JCN - 75C	NORWOOD JCN - 75C	NORWOOD JCN - 75C	NORWOOD JCN - 75C	NORWOOD JCN - 75C	NORWOOD JCN - 75C	NORWOOD JCN - 75C
30548	BOURNEMOUTH - 71B	BOURNEMOUTH - 71B	BOURNEMOUTH - 71B	BOURNEMOUTH - 71B	BOURNEMOUTH - 71B	BOURNEMOUTH - 71B	BOURNEMOUTH - 71B
30549	BOURNEMOUTH - 71B	BOURNEMOUTH - 71B	BOURNEMOUTH - 71B	BOURNEMOUTH - 71B	BOURNEMOUTH - 71B	BOURNEMOUTH - 71B	BOURNEMOUTH - 71B
				Q1 0-6-0 (1942)			
33001	GUILDFORD - 70C	GUILDFORD - 70C	GUILDFORD - 70C	GUILDFORD - 70C	GUILDFORD - 70C	GUILDFORD - 70C	GUILDFORD - 70C
33002	GUILDFORD - 70C	GUILDFORD - 70C	GUILDFORD - 70C	GUILDFORD - 70C	GUILDFORD - 70C	GUILDFORD - 70C	GUILDFORD - 70C
33003	GUILDFORD - 70C	GUILDFORD - 70C	GUILDFORD - 70C	GUILDFORD - 70C	GUILDFORD - 70C	GUILDFORD - 70C	GUILDFORD - 70C
33004	GUILDFORD - 70C	GUILDFORD - 70C	GUILDFORD - 70C	GUILDFORD - 70C	GUILDFORD - 70C	GUILDFORD - 70C	GUILDFORD - 70C
33005	GUILDFORD - 70C	GUILDFORD - 70C	GUILDFORD - 70C	GUILDFORD - 70C	GUILDFORD - 70C	GUILDFORD - 70C	GUILDFORD - 70C
33006	GUILDFORD - 70C	GUILDFORD - 70C	GUILDFORD - 70C	GUILDFORD - 70C	GUILDFORD - 70C	FELTHAM - 70B	FELTHAM - 70B
33007	GUILDFORD - 70C	GUILDFORD - 70C	GUILDFORD - 70C	GUILDFORD - 70C	GUILDFORD - 70C	FELTHAM - 70B	FELTHAM - 70B
33008	FELTHAM - 70B	FELTHAM - 70B	FELTHAM - 70B	FELTHAM - 70B	FELTHAM - 70B	FELTHAM - 70B	FELTHAM - 70B
33009	FELTHAM - 70B	FELTHAM - 70B	FELTHAM - 70B	FELTHAM - 70B	FELTHAM - 70B	FELTHAM - 70B	FELTHAM - 70B
33010	FELTHAM - 70B	FELTHAM - 70B	FELTHAM - 70B	FELTHAM - 70B	FELTHAM - 70B	FELTHAM - 70B	FELTHAM - 70B
33011	FELTHAM - 70B	FELTHAM - 70B	FELTHAM - 70B	FELTHAM - 70B	FELTHAM - 70B	FELTHAM - 70B	FELTHAM - 70B
33012	FELTHAM - 70B	FELTHAM - 70B	FELTHAM - 70B	FELTHAM - 70B	FELTHAM - 70B	FELTHAM - 70B	FELTHAM - 70B
33013	FELTHAM - 70B	FELTHAM - 70B	FELTHAM - 70B	FELTHAM - 70B	FELTHAM - 70B	FELTHAM - 70B	FELTHAM - 70B
33014	EASTLEIGH - 71A	EASTLEIGH - 71A	EASTLEIGH - 71A	EASTLEIGH - 71A	EASTLEIGH - 71A	EASTLEIGH - 71A	EASTLEIGH - 71A
33015	EASTLEIGH - 71A	EASTLEIGH - 71A	EASTLEIGH - 71A	EASTLEIGH - 71A	EASTLEIGH - 71A	EASTLEIGH - 71A	EASTLEIGH - 71A
33016	EASTLEIGH - 71A	EASTLEIGH - 71A	EASTLEIGH - 71A	EASTLEIGH - 71A	EASTLEIGH - 71A	EASTLEIGH - 71A	EASTLEIGH - 71A
33017	EASTLEIGH - 71A	EASTLEIGH - 71A	EASTLEIGH - 71A	EASTLEIGH - 71A	EASTLEIGH - 71A	EASTLEIGH - 71A	EASTLEIGH - 71A
33018	EASTLEIGH - 71A	EASTLEIGH - 71A	EASTLEIGH - 71A	EASTLEIGH - 71A	EASTLEIGH - 71A	EASTLEIGH - 71A	EASTLEIGH - 71A
33019	EASTLEIGH - 71A	EASTLEIGH - 71A	EASTLEIGH - 71A	EASTLEIGH - 71A	EASTLEIGH - 71A	EASTLEIGH - 71A	EASTLEIGH - 71A
33020	EASTLEIGH - 71A	EASTLEIGH - 71A	EASTLEIGH - 71A	EASTLEIGH - 71A	EASTLEIGH - 71A	EASTLEIGH - 71A	EASTLEIGH - 71A
33021	EASTLEIGH - 71A	EASTLEIGH - 71A	EASTLEIGH - 71A	EASTLEIGH - 71A	EASTLEIGH - 71A	EASTLEIGH - 71A	EASTLEIGH - 71A
33022	EASTLEIGH - 71A	EASTLEIGH - 71A	EASTLEIGH - 71A	EASTLEIGH - 71A	EASTLEIGH - 71A	EASTLEIGH - 71A	EASTLEIGH - 71A
33023	EASTLEIGH - 71A	EASTLEIGH - 71A	EASTLEIGH - 71A	EASTLEIGH - 71A	EASTLEIGH - 71A	EASTLEIGH - 71A	EASTLEIGH - 71A
33024	EASTLEIGH - 71A	EASTLEIGH - 71A	EASTLEIGH - 71A	EASTLEIGH - 71A	EASTLEIGH - 71A	EASTLEIGH - 71A	EASTLEIGH - 71A
33025	EASTLEIGH - 71A	EASTLEIGH - 71A	EASTLEIGH - 71A	EASTLEIGH - 71A	EASTLEIGH - 71A	EASTLEIGH - 71A	EASTLEIGH - 71A
33026	TONBRIDGE - 74D	TONBRIDGE - 74D	TONBRIDGE - 74D	TONBRIDGE - 74D	TONBRIDGE - 74D	TONBRIDGE - 74D	TONBRIDGE - 74D
33027	TONBRIDGE - 74D	TONBRIDGE - 74D	TONBRIDGE - 74D	TONBRIDGE - 74D	TONBRIDGE - 74D	TONBRIDGE - 74D	TONBRIDGE - 74D
33028	TONBRIDGE - 74D	TONBRIDGE - 74D	TONBRIDGE - 74D	TONBRIDGE - 74D	TONBRIDGE - 74D	TONBRIDGE - 74D	TONBRIDGE - 74D
33029	TONBRIDGE - 74D	TONBRIDGE - 74D	TONBRIDGE - 74D	TONBRIDGE - 74D	TONBRIDGE - 74D	TONBRIDGE - 74D	TONBRIDGE - 74D
33030	TONBRIDGE - 74D	TONBRIDGE - 74D	TONBRIDGE - 74D	TONBRIDGE - 74D	TONBRIDGE - 74D	TONBRIDGE - 74D	TONBRIDGE - 74D
33031	TONBRIDGE - 74D	TONBRIDGE - 74D	TONBRIDGE - 74D	TONBRIDGE - 74D	TONBRIDGE - 74D	TONBRIDGE - 74D	TONBRIDGE - 74D
33032	TONBRIDGE - 74D	TONBRIDGE - 74D	TONBRIDGE - 74D	TONBRIDGE - 74D	TONBRIDGE - 74D	TONBRIDGE - 74D	TONBRIDGE - 74D
33033	TONBRIDGE - 74D	TONBRIDGE - 74D	TONBRIDGE - 74D	TONBRIDGE - 74D	TONBRIDGE - 74D	TONBRIDGE - 74D	TONBRIDGE - 74D
33034	TONBRIDGE - 74D	TONBRIDGE - 74D	TONBRIDGE - 74D	TONBRIDGE - 74D	TONBRIDGE - 74D	TONBRIDGE - 74D	TONBRIDGE - 74D
33035	TONBRIDGE - 74D	TONBRIDGE - 74D	TONBRIDGE - 74D	TONBRIDGE - 74D	TONBRIDGE - 74D	TONBRIDGE - 74D	TONBRIDGE - 74D
33036	STEWARTS LANE - 73A	STEWARTS LANE - 73A	STEWARTS LANE - 73A	STEWARTS LANE - 73A	STEWARTS LANE - 73A	TONBRIDGE - 74D	TONBRIDGE - 74D
33037	STEWARTS LANE - 73A	STEWARTS LANE - 73A	STEWARTS LANE - 73A	STEWARTS LANE - 73A	STEWARTS LANE - 73A	TONBRIDGE - 74D	TONBRIDGE - 74D
33038	STEWARTS LANE - 73A	STEWARTS LANE - 73A	STEWARTS LANE - 73A	STEWARTS LANE - 73A	STEWARTS LANE - 73A	TONBRIDGE - 74D	TONBRIDGE - 74D
33039	STEWARTS LANE - 73A	STEWARTS LANE - 73A	STEWARTS LANE - 73A	STEWARTS LANE - 73A	STEWARTS LANE - 73A	STEWARTS LANE - 73A	STEWARTS LANE - 73A
33040	STEWARTS LANE - 73A	STEWARTS LANE - 73A	STEWARTS LANE - 73A	STEWARTS LANE - 73A	STEWARTS LANE - 73A	STEWARTS LANE - 73A	STEWARTS LANE - 73A
				W 2-6-4T (1931)			
31911	HITHER GREEN - 73C	HITHER GREEN - 73C	HITHER GREEN - 73C	HITHER GREEN - 73C	HITHER GREEN - 73C	HITHER GREEN - 73C	HITHER GREEN - 73C
31912	STEWARTS LANE - 73A	STEWARTS LANE - 73A	STEWARTS LANE - 73A	STEWARTS LANE - 73A	STEWARTS LANE - 73A	STEWARTS LANE - 73A	STEWARTS LANE - 73A
31913	HITHER GREEN - 73C	HITHER GREEN - 73C	HITHER GREEN - 73C	HITHER GREEN - 73C	HITHER GREEN - 73C	HITHER GREEN - 73C	HITHER GREEN - 73C
31914	STEWARTS LANE - 73A	STEWARTS LANE - 73A	STEWARTS LANE - 73A	STEWARTS LANE - 73A	STEWARTS LANE - 73A	STEWARTS LANE - 73A	STEWARTS LANE - 73A
31915	STEWARTS LANE - 73A	STEWARTS LANE - 73A	STEWARTS LANE - 73A	STEWARTS LANE - 73A	STEWARTS LANE - 73A	STEWARTS LANE - 73A	STEWARTS LANE - 73A
31916	NORWOOD JCN - 75C	NORWOOD JCN - 75C	NORWOOD JCN - 75C	NORWOOD JCN - 75C	NORWOOD JCN - 75C	NORWOOD JCN - 75C	NORWOOD JCN - 75C
31917	NORWOOD JCN - 75C	NORWOOD JCN - 75C	NORWOOD JCN - 75C	NORWOOD JCN - 75C	NORWOOD JCN - 75C	NORWOOD JCN - 75C	NORWOOD JCN - 75C
31918	NORWOOD JCN - 75C	NORWOOD JCN - 75C	NORWOOD JCN - 75C	NORWOOD JCN - 75C	NORWOOD JCN - 75C	NORWOOD JCN - 75C	NORWOOD JCN - 75C
31919	NORWOOD JCN - 75C	NORWOOD JCN - 75C	NORWOOD JCN - 75C	NORWOOD JCN - 75C	NORWOOD JCN - 75C	NORWOOD JCN - 75C	NORWOOD JCN - 75C
31920	NORWOOD JCN - 75C	NORWOOD JCN - 75C	NORWOOD JCN - 75C	NORWOOD JCN - 75C	NORWOOD JCN - 75C	NORWOOD JCN - 75C	NORWOOD JCN - 75C
31921	HITHER GREEN - 73C	HITHER GREEN - 73C	HITHER GREEN - 73C	HITHER GREEN - 73C	HITHER GREEN - 73C	HITHER GREEN - 73C	HITHER GREEN - 73C
31922	HITHER GREEN - 73C	HITHER GREEN - 73C	HITHER GREEN - 73C	HITHER GREEN - 73C	HITHER GREEN - 73C	HITHER GREEN - 73C	HITHER GREEN - 73C
31923	HITHER GREEN - 73C	HITHER GREEN - 73C	HITHER GREEN - 73C	HITHER GREEN - 73C	HITHER GREEN - 73C	HITHER GREEN - 73C	HITHER GREEN - 73C
31924	HITHER GREEN - 73C	HITHER GREEN - 73C	HITHER GREEN - 73C	HITHER GREEN - 73C	HITHER GREEN - 73C	HITHER GREEN - 73C	HITHER GREEN - 73C
31925	HITHER GREEN - 73C	HITHER GREEN - 73C	HITHER GREEN - 73C	HITHER GREEN - 73C	HITHER GREEN - 73C	HITHER GREEN - 73C	HITHER GREEN - 73C
				Z 0-8-0T (1929)			
30950	HITHER GREEN - 73C	HITHER GREEN - 73C	HITHER GREEN - 73C	EASTLEIGH - 71A	EASTLEIGH - 71A	EASTLEIGH - 71A	EASTLEIGH - 71A
30951	HITHER GREEN - 73C	HITHER GREEN - 73C	GILLINGHAM - 73D	GILLINGHAM - 73D	GILLINGHAM - 73D	GILLINGHAM - 73D	GILLINGHAM - 73D
30952	EASTLEIGH - 71A	EASTLEIGH - 71A	EASTLEIGH - 71A	EASTLEIGH - 71A	EASTLEIGH - 71A	EASTLEIGH - 71A	EASTLEIGH - 71A
30953	HITHER GREEN - 73C	HITHER GREEN - 73C	ASHFORD - 74A	ASHFORD - 74A	ASHFORD - 74A	ASHFORD - 74A	ASHFORD - 74A
30954	EXMOUTH JCN - 72A	EXMOUTH JCN - 72A	EXMOUTH JCN - 72A	EXMOUTH JCN - 72A	EXMOUTH JCN - 72A	EXMOUTH JCN - 72A	EXMOUTH JCN - 72A
30955	HITHER GREEN - 73C	HITHER GREEN - 73C	HITHER GREEN - 73C	FELTHAM - 70B	NINE ELMS - 70A	NINE ELMS - 70A	NINE ELMS - 70A
30956	EASTLEIGH - 71A	EASTLEIGH - 71A	EASTLEIGH - 71A	EASTLEIGH - 71A	EASTLEIGH - 71A	EASTLEIGH - 71A	EASTLEIGH - 71A
30957	SALISBURY - 72B	SALISBURY - 72B	SALISBURY - 72B	SALISBURY - 72B	SALISBURY - 72B	SALISBURY - 72B	SALISBURY - 72B
				J1 4-6-2T (1910)			
32325	T.WELLS - 75F	T.WELLS - 75F	T.WELLS - 75F	T.WELLS - 75F	T.WELLS - 75F	T.WELLS - 75F	T.WELLS - 75F
				J2 4-6-2T (1912)			
32326	T.WELLS - 75F	T.WELLS - 75F	T.WELLS - 75F	T.WELLS - 75F	T.WELLS - 75F	T.WELLS - 75F	T.WELLS - 75F
				J 0-6-4T (1913)			
31595	ASHFORD - 74A	ASHFORD - 74A	ASHFORD - 74A	ASHFORD - 74A	ASHFORD - 74A	ASHFORD - 74A	ASHFORD - 74A
31596	ASHFORD - 74A	ASHFORD - 74A	ASHFORD - 74A	ASHFORD - 74A	ASHFORD - 74A	ASHFORD - 74A	ASHFORD - 74A
31597	ASHFORD - 74A	ASHFORD - 74A	ASHFORD - 74A	ASHFORD - 74A	ASHFORD - 74A	ASHFORD - 74A	ASHFORD - 74A
31598	ASHFORD - 74A	ASHFORD - 74A	ASHFORD - 74A	ASHFORD - 74A	ASHFORD - 74A	ASHFORD - 74A	ASHFORD - 74A
31599	ASHFORD - 74A	ASHFORD - 74A	ASHFORD - 74A	ASHFORD - 74A	W/D	W/D	W/D
				H16 4-6-2T (1921)			
30516	FELTHAM - 70B	FELTHAM - 70B	FELTHAM - 70B	FELTHAM - 70B	FELTHAM - 70B	FELTHAM - 70B	FELTHAM - 70B
30517	FELTHAM - 70B	FELTHAM - 70B	FELTHAM - 70B	FELTHAM - 70B	FELTHAM - 70B	FELTHAM - 70B	FELTHAM - 70B
30518	FELTHAM - 70B	FELTHAM - 70B	FELTHAM - 70B	FELTHAM - 70B	FELTHAM - 70B	FELTHAM - 70B	FELTHAM - 70B
30519	FELTHAM - 70B	FELTHAM - 70B	FELTHAM - 70B	FELTHAM - 70B	FELTHAM - 70B	FELTHAM - 70B	FELTHAM - 70B
30520	FELTHAM - 70B	FELTHAM - 70B	FELTHAM - 70B	FELTHAM - 70B	FELTHAM - 70B	FELTHAM - 70B	FELTHAM - 70B

loco	Apr-50	Sep-50	Oct-50	Nov-50	Dec-50	Mar-51	Apr-51
Q 0-6-0 (1938)							
30530	EASTLEIGH - 71A	EASTLEIGH - 71A	EASTLEIGH - 71A	EASTLEIGH - 71A	EASTLEIGH - 71A	EASTLEIGH - 71A	EASTLEIGH - 71A
30531	HORSHAM - 75D	EASTLEIGH - 71A	EASTLEIGH - 71A	EASTLEIGH - 71A	EASTLEIGH - 71A	EASTLEIGH - 71A	EASTLEIGH - 71A
30532	EASTLEIGH - 71A	EASTLEIGH - 71A	EASTLEIGH - 71A	EASTLEIGH - 71A	EASTLEIGH - 71A	EASTLEIGH - 71A	EASTLEIGH - 71A
30533	NORWOOD JCN - 75C	NORWOOD JCN - 75C	NORWOOD JCN - 75C	NORWOOD JCN - 75C	NORWOOD JCN - 75C	NORWOOD JCN - 75C	NORWOOD JCN - 75C
30534	T.WELLS - 75F	NORWOOD JCN - 75C	NORWOOD JCN - 75C	NORWOOD JCN - 75C	NORWOOD JCN - 75C	NORWOOD JCN - 75C	NORWOOD JCN - 75C
30535	EASTLEIGH - 71A	EASTLEIGH - 71A	EASTLEIGH - 71A	EASTLEIGH - 71A	EASTLEIGH - 71A	EASTLEIGH - 71A	EASTLEIGH - 71A
30536	EASTLEIGH - 71A	EASTLEIGH - 71A	EASTLEIGH - 71A	EASTLEIGH - 71A	EASTLEIGH - 71A	EASTLEIGH - 71A	EASTLEIGH - 71A
30537	NORWOOD JCN - 75C	NORWOOD JCN - 75C	NORWOOD JCN - 75C	NORWOOD JCN - 75C	NORWOOD JCN - 75C	NORWOOD JCN - 75C	NORWOOD JCN - 75C
30538	NORWOOD JCN - 75C	NORWOOD JCN - 75C	NORWOOD JCN - 75C	NORWOOD JCN - 75C	NORWOOD JCN - 75C	NORWOOD JCN - 75C	NORWOOD JCN - 75C
30539	NORWOOD JCN - 75C	NORWOOD JCN - 75C	NORWOOD JCN - 75C	NORWOOD JCN - 75C	NORWOOD JCN - 75C	NORWOOD JCN - 75C	NORWOOD JCN - 75C
30540	THREE BRIDGES - 75E	THREE BRIDGES - 75E	THREE BRIDGES - 75E	THREE BRIDGES - 75E	THREE BRIDGES - 75E	THREE BRIDGES - 75E	THREE BRIDGES - 75E
30541	THREE BRIDGES - 75E	THREE BRIDGES - 75E	THREE BRIDGES - 75E	THREE BRIDGES - 75E	THREE BRIDGES - 75E	THREE BRIDGES - 75E	THREE BRIDGES - 75E
30542	T.WELLS - 75F	EASTLEIGH - 71A	EASTLEIGH - 71A	EASTLEIGH - 71A	EASTLEIGH - 71A	EASTLEIGH - 71A	EASTLEIGH - 71A
30543	T.WELLS - 75F	EASTLEIGH - 71A	EASTLEIGH - 71A	EASTLEIGH - 71A	EASTLEIGH - 71A	EASTLEIGH - 71A	EASTLEIGH - 71A
30544	T.WELLS - 75F	EASTLEIGH - 71A	EASTLEIGH - 71A	EASTLEIGH - 71A	EASTLEIGH - 71A	EASTLEIGH - 71A	EASTLEIGH - 71A
30545	HORSHAM - 75D	HORSHAM - 75D	HORSHAM - 75D	HORSHAM - 75D	HORSHAM - 75D	HORSHAM - 75D	HORSHAM - 75D
30546	HORSHAM - 75D	HORSHAM - 75D	HORSHAM - 75D	HORSHAM - 75D	HORSHAM - 75D	HORSHAM - 75D	HORSHAM - 75D
30547	NORWOOD JCN - 75C	NORWOOD JCN - 75C	NORWOOD JCN - 75C	NORWOOD JCN - 75C	NORWOOD JCN - 75C	NORWOOD JCN - 75C	NORWOOD JCN - 75C
30548	BOURNEMOUTH - 71B	BOURNEMOUTH - 71B	BOURNEMOUTH - 71B	BOURNEMOUTH - 71B	BOURNEMOUTH - 71B	BOURNEMOUTH - 71B	BOURNEMOUTH - 71B
30549	BOURNEMOUTH - 71B	BOURNEMOUTH - 71B	BOURNEMOUTH - 71B	BOURNEMOUTH - 71B	BOURNEMOUTH - 71B	BOURNEMOUTH - 71B	BOURNEMOUTH - 71B
Q1 0-6-0 (1942)							
33001	GUILDFORD - 70C	GUILDFORD - 70C	GUILDFORD - 70C	GUILDFORD - 70C	GUILDFORD - 70C	GUILDFORD - 70C	GUILDFORD - 70C
33002	GUILDFORD - 70C	GUILDFORD - 70C	GUILDFORD - 70C	GUILDFORD - 70C	GUILDFORD - 70C	GUILDFORD - 70C	GUILDFORD - 70C
33003	GUILDFORD - 70C	GUILDFORD - 70C	GUILDFORD - 70C	GUILDFORD - 70C	GUILDFORD - 70C	GUILDFORD - 70C	GUILDFORD - 70C
33004	GUILDFORD - 70C	GUILDFORD - 70C	GUILDFORD - 70C	GUILDFORD - 70C	GUILDFORD - 70C	GUILDFORD - 70C	GUILDFORD - 70C
33005	GUILDFORD - 70C	GUILDFORD - 70C	GUILDFORD - 70C	GUILDFORD - 70C	GUILDFORD - 70C	GUILDFORD - 70C	GUILDFORD - 70C
33006	FELTHAM - 70B	FELTHAM - 70B	FELTHAM - 70B	FELTHAM - 70B	FELTHAM - 70B	FELTHAM - 70B	FELTHAM - 70B
33007	FELTHAM - 70B	FELTHAM - 70B	FELTHAM - 70B	FELTHAM - 70B	FELTHAM - 70B	FELTHAM - 70B	FELTHAM - 70B
33008	FELTHAM - 70B	FELTHAM - 70B	FELTHAM - 70B	FELTHAM - 70B	FELTHAM - 70B	FELTHAM - 70B	FELTHAM - 70B
33009	FELTHAM - 70B	FELTHAM - 70B	FELTHAM - 70B	FELTHAM - 70B	FELTHAM - 70B	FELTHAM - 70B	FELTHAM - 70B
33010	FELTHAM - 70B	FELTHAM - 70B	FELTHAM - 70B	FELTHAM - 70B	FELTHAM - 70B	FELTHAM - 70B	FELTHAM - 70B
33011	FELTHAM - 70B	FELTHAM - 70B	FELTHAM - 70B	FELTHAM - 70B	FELTHAM - 70B	FELTHAM - 70B	FELTHAM - 70B
33012	FELTHAM - 70B	FELTHAM - 70B	FELTHAM - 70B	FELTHAM - 70B	FELTHAM - 70B	FELTHAM - 70B	FELTHAM - 70B
33013	FELTHAM - 70B	FELTHAM - 70B	FELTHAM - 70B	FELTHAM - 70B	FELTHAM - 70B	FELTHAM - 70B	FELTHAM - 70B
33014	EASTLEIGH - 71A	GUILDFORD - 70C	GUILDFORD - 70C	GUILDFORD - 70C	GUILDFORD - 70C	GUILDFORD - 70C	GUILDFORD - 70C
33015	EASTLEIGH - 71A	GUILDFORD - 70C	GUILDFORD - 70C	GUILDFORD - 70C	GUILDFORD - 70C	GUILDFORD - 70C	GUILDFORD - 70C
33016	EASTLEIGH - 71A	GUILDFORD - 70C	GUILDFORD - 70C	GUILDFORD - 70C	GUILDFORD - 70C	GUILDFORD - 70C	GUILDFORD - 70C
33017	EASTLEIGH - 71A	EASTLEIGH - 71A	EASTLEIGH - 71A	EASTLEIGH - 71A	EASTLEIGH - 71A	EASTLEIGH - 71A	EASTLEIGH - 71A
33018	EASTLEIGH - 71A	EASTLEIGH - 71A	EASTLEIGH - 71A	EASTLEIGH - 71A	EASTLEIGH - 71A	EASTLEIGH - 71A	EASTLEIGH - 71A
33019	EASTLEIGH - 71A	EASTLEIGH - 71A	EASTLEIGH - 71A	EASTLEIGH - 71A	EASTLEIGH - 71A	EASTLEIGH - 71A	EASTLEIGH - 71A
33020	EASTLEIGH - 71A	EASTLEIGH - 71A	EASTLEIGH - 71A	EASTLEIGH - 71A	EASTLEIGH - 71A	EASTLEIGH - 71A	EASTLEIGH - 71A
33021	EASTLEIGH - 71A	EASTLEIGH - 71A	EASTLEIGH - 71A	EASTLEIGH - 71A	EASTLEIGH - 71A	EASTLEIGH - 71A	EASTLEIGH - 71A
33022	EASTLEIGH - 71A	EASTLEIGH - 71A	EASTLEIGH - 71A	EASTLEIGH - 71A	EASTLEIGH - 71A	EASTLEIGH - 71A	EASTLEIGH - 71A
33023	EASTLEIGH - 71A	EASTLEIGH - 71A	EASTLEIGH - 71A	EASTLEIGH - 71A	EASTLEIGH - 71A	EASTLEIGH - 71A	EASTLEIGH - 71A
33024	EASTLEIGH - 71A	EASTLEIGH - 71A	EASTLEIGH - 71A	EASTLEIGH - 71A	EASTLEIGH - 71A	EASTLEIGH - 71A	EASTLEIGH - 71A
33025	EASTLEIGH - 71A	EASTLEIGH - 71A	EASTLEIGH - 71A	EASTLEIGH - 71A	EASTLEIGH - 71A	EASTLEIGH - 71A	EASTLEIGH - 71A
33026	TONBRIDGE - 74D	TONBRIDGE - 74D	TONBRIDGE - 74D	GILLINGHAM - 73D	GILLINGHAM - 73D	GILLINGHAM - 73D	GILLINGHAM - 73D
33027	TONBRIDGE - 74D	TONBRIDGE - 74D	TONBRIDGE - 74D	TONBRIDGE - 74D	TONBRIDGE - 74D	TONBRIDGE - 74D	TONBRIDGE - 74D
33028	TONBRIDGE - 74D	TONBRIDGE - 74D	TONBRIDGE - 74D	TONBRIDGE - 74D	TONBRIDGE - 74D	TONBRIDGE - 74D	TONBRIDGE - 74D
33029	TONBRIDGE - 74D	TONBRIDGE - 74D	TONBRIDGE - 74D	TONBRIDGE - 74D	TONBRIDGE - 74D	TONBRIDGE - 74D	TONBRIDGE - 74D
33030	TONBRIDGE - 74D	TONBRIDGE - 74D	TONBRIDGE - 74D	TONBRIDGE - 74D	TONBRIDGE - 74D	TONBRIDGE - 74D	TONBRIDGE - 74D
33031	TONBRIDGE - 74D	TONBRIDGE - 74D	TONBRIDGE - 74D	TONBRIDGE - 74D	TONBRIDGE - 74D	TONBRIDGE - 74D	TONBRIDGE - 74D
33032	TONBRIDGE - 74D	TONBRIDGE - 74D	TONBRIDGE - 74D	TONBRIDGE - 74D	TONBRIDGE - 74D	TONBRIDGE - 74D	TONBRIDGE - 74D
33033	TONBRIDGE - 74D	TONBRIDGE - 74D	TONBRIDGE - 74D	TONBRIDGE - 74D	TONBRIDGE - 74D	TONBRIDGE - 74D	TONBRIDGE - 74D
33034	TONBRIDGE - 74D	TONBRIDGE - 74D	TONBRIDGE - 74D	TONBRIDGE - 74D	TONBRIDGE - 74D	TONBRIDGE - 74D	TONBRIDGE - 74D
33035	TONBRIDGE - 74D	TONBRIDGE - 74D	TONBRIDGE - 74D	TONBRIDGE - 74D	TONBRIDGE - 74D	TONBRIDGE - 74D	TONBRIDGE - 74D
33036	TONBRIDGE - 74D	TONBRIDGE - 74D	TONBRIDGE - 74D	TONBRIDGE - 74D	TONBRIDGE - 74D	TONBRIDGE - 74D	TONBRIDGE - 74D
33037	TONBRIDGE - 74D	TONBRIDGE - 74D	TONBRIDGE - 74D	TONBRIDGE - 74D	TONBRIDGE - 74D	TONBRIDGE - 74D	TONBRIDGE - 74D
33038	TONBRIDGE - 74D	TONBRIDGE - 74D	TONBRIDGE - 74D	TONBRIDGE - 74D	TONBRIDGE - 74D	TONBRIDGE - 74D	TONBRIDGE - 74D
33039	TONBRIDGE - 74D	TONBRIDGE - 74D	TONBRIDGE - 74D	TONBRIDGE - 74D	TONBRIDGE - 74D	TONBRIDGE - 74D	TONBRIDGE - 74D
33040	TONBRIDGE - 74D	TONBRIDGE - 74D	TONBRIDGE - 74D	TONBRIDGE - 74D	TONBRIDGE - 74D	TONBRIDGE - 74D	TONBRIDGE - 74D
W 2-6-4T (1931)							
31911	HITHER GREEN - 73C	HITHER GREEN - 73C	HITHER GREEN - 73C	HITHER GREEN - 73C	HITHER GREEN - 73C	HITHER GREEN - 73C	HITHER GREEN - 73C
31912	STEWARTS LANE - 73A	STEWARTS LANE - 73A	STEWARTS LANE - 73A	STEWARTS LANE - 73A	STEWARTS LANE - 73A	STEWARTS LANE - 73A	STEWARTS LANE - 73A
31913	HITHER GREEN - 73C	HITHER GREEN - 73C	HITHER GREEN - 73C	HITHER GREEN - 73C	HITHER GREEN - 73C	HITHER GREEN - 73C	HITHER GREEN - 73C
31914	STEWARTS LANE - 73A	STEWARTS LANE - 73A	STEWARTS LANE - 73A	STEWARTS LANE - 73A	STEWARTS LANE - 73A	STEWARTS LANE - 73A	STEWARTS LANE - 73A
31915	STEWARTS LANE - 73A	STEWARTS LANE - 73A	STEWARTS LANE - 73A	STEWARTS LANE - 73A	STEWARTS LANE - 73A	STEWARTS LANE - 73A	STEWARTS LANE - 73A
31916	NORWOOD JCN - 75C	NORWOOD JCN - 75C	NORWOOD JCN - 75C	NORWOOD JCN - 75C	NORWOOD JCN - 75C	NORWOOD JCN - 75C	NORWOOD JCN - 75C
31917	NORWOOD JCN - 75C	NORWOOD JCN - 75C	NORWOOD JCN - 75C	NORWOOD JCN - 75C	NORWOOD JCN - 75C	NORWOOD JCN - 75C	NORWOOD JCN - 75C
31918	NORWOOD JCN - 75C	NORWOOD JCN - 75C	NORWOOD JCN - 75C	NORWOOD JCN - 75C	NORWOOD JCN - 75C	NORWOOD JCN - 75C	NORWOOD JCN - 75C
31919	NORWOOD JCN - 75C	NORWOOD JCN - 75C	NORWOOD JCN - 75C	NORWOOD JCN - 75C	NORWOOD JCN - 75C	NORWOOD JCN - 75C	NORWOOD JCN - 75C
31920	NORWOOD JCN - 75C	NORWOOD JCN - 75C	NORWOOD JCN - 75C	NORWOOD JCN - 75C	NORWOOD JCN - 75C	NORWOOD JCN - 75C	NORWOOD JCN - 75C
31921	HITHER GREEN - 73C	HITHER GREEN - 73C	HITHER GREEN - 73C	HITHER GREEN - 73C	HITHER GREEN - 73C	HITHER GREEN - 73C	HITHER GREEN - 73C
31922	HITHER GREEN - 73C	HITHER GREEN - 73C	HITHER GREEN - 73C	HITHER GREEN - 73C	HITHER GREEN - 73C	HITHER GREEN - 73C	HITHER GREEN - 73C
31923	HITHER GREEN - 73C	HITHER GREEN - 73C	HITHER GREEN - 73C	HITHER GREEN - 73C	HITHER GREEN - 73C	HITHER GREEN - 73C	HITHER GREEN - 73C
31924	HITHER GREEN - 73C	HITHER GREEN - 73C	HITHER GREEN - 73C	HITHER GREEN - 73C	HITHER GREEN - 73C	HITHER GREEN - 73C	HITHER GREEN - 73C
31925	HITHER GREEN - 73C	HITHER GREEN - 73C	HITHER GREEN - 73C	HITHER GREEN - 73C	HITHER GREEN - 73C	HITHER GREEN - 73C	HITHER GREEN - 73C
Z 0-8-0T (1929)							
30950	EASTLEIGH - 71A	EASTLEIGH - 71A	EASTLEIGH - 71A	EASTLEIGH - 71A	EASTLEIGH - 71A	EASTLEIGH - 71A	EASTLEIGH - 71A
30951	GILLINGHAM - 73D	GILLINGHAM - 73D	GILLINGHAM - 73D	GILLINGHAM - 73D	GILLINGHAM - 73D	GILLINGHAM - 73D	GILLINGHAM - 73D
30952	EASTLEIGH - 71A	EASTLEIGH - 71A	EASTLEIGH - 71A	EASTLEIGH - 71A	EASTLEIGH - 71A	EASTLEIGH - 71A	EASTLEIGH - 71A
30953	ASHFORD - 74A	ASHFORD - 74A	ASHFORD - 74A	ASHFORD - 74A	ASHFORD - 74A	ASHFORD - 74A	ASHFORD - 74A
30954	EXMOUTH JCN - 72A	EXMOUTH JCN - 72A	EXMOUTH JCN - 72A	EXMOUTH JCN - 72A	EXMOUTH JCN - 72A	EXMOUTH JCN - 72A	EXMOUTH JCN - 72A
30955	NINE ELMS - 70A	NINE ELMS - 70A	NINE ELMS - 70A	NINE ELMS - 70A	NINE ELMS - 70A	NINE ELMS - 70A	NINE ELMS - 70A
30956	EASTLEIGH - 71A	EASTLEIGH - 71A	EASTLEIGH - 71A	EASTLEIGH - 71A	EASTLEIGH - 71A	EASTLEIGH - 71A	EASTLEIGH - 71A
30957	SALISBURY - 72B	SALISBURY - 72B	SALISBURY - 72B	SALISBURY - 72B	SALISBURY - 72B	SALISBURY - 72B	SALISBURY - 72B
J1 4-6-2T (1910)							
32325	T.WELLS - 75F	T.WELLS - 75F	BRIGHTON - 75A	BRIGHTON - 75A	BRIGHTON - 75A	BRIGHTON - 75A	BRIGHTON - 75A
32326	T.WELLS - 75F	T.WELLS - 75F	BRIGHTON - 75A	BRIGHTON - 75A	BRIGHTON - 75A	BRIGHTON - 75A	BRIGHTON - 75A
J2 4-6-2T (1912)							
31595	ASHFORD - 74A	ASHFORD - 74A	ASHFORD - 74A	ASHFORD - 74A	ASHFORD - 74A	ASHFORD - 74A	W/D
31596	ASHFORD - 74A	ASHFORD - 74A	ASHFORD - 74A	ASHFORD - 74A	ASHFORD - 74A	ASHFORD - 74A	ASHFORD - 74A
31597	ASHFORD - 74A	ASHFORD - 74A	ASHFORD - 74A	W/D	W/D	W/D	W/D
31598	ASHFORD - 74A	ASHFORD - 74A	ASHFORD - 74A	ASHFORD - 74A	W/D	W/D	W/D
H16 4-6-2T (1921)							
30516	FELTHAM - 70B	FELTHAM - 70B	FELTHAM - 70B	FELTHAM - 70B	FELTHAM - 70B	FELTHAM - 70B	FELTHAM - 70B
30517	FELTHAM - 70B	FELTHAM - 70B	FELTHAM - 70B	FELTHAM - 70B	FELTHAM - 70B	FELTHAM - 70B	FELTHAM - 70B
30518	FELTHAM - 70B	FELTHAM - 70B	FELTHAM - 70B	FELTHAM - 70B	FELTHAM - 70B	FELTHAM - 70B	FELTHAM - 70B
30519	FELTHAM - 70B	FELTHAM - 70B	FELTHAM - 70B	FELTHAM - 70B	FELTHAM - 70B	FELTHAM - 70B	FELTHAM - 70B
30520	FELTHAM - 70B	FELTHAM - 70B	FELTHAM - 70B	FELTHAM - 70B	FELTHAM - 70B	FELTHAM - 70B	FELTHAM - 70B

loco	Jun-51	Jul-51	Sep-51	Dec-51	Jan-52	Mar-52	Jun-52
				Q 0-6-0 (1938)			
30530	EASTLEIGH - 71A	EASTLEIGH - 71A	EASTLEIGH - 71A	EASTLEIGH - 71A	EASTLEIGH - 71A	EASTLEIGH - 71A	EASTLEIGH - 71A
30531	EASTLEIGH - 71A	EASTLEIGH - 71A	EASTLEIGH - 71A	EASTLEIGH - 71A	EASTLEIGH - 71A	EASTLEIGH - 71A	EASTLEIGH - 71A
30532	EASTLEIGH - 71A	EASTLEIGH - 71A	EASTLEIGH - 71A	EASTLEIGH - 71A	EASTLEIGH - 71A	EASTLEIGH - 71A	EASTLEIGH - 71A
30533	NORWOOD JCN - 75C	NORWOOD JCN - 75C	NORWOOD JCN - 75C	NORWOOD JCN - 75C	NORWOOD JCN - 75C	NORWOOD JCN - 75C	NORWOOD JCN - 75C
30534	NORWOOD JCN - 75C	NORWOOD JCN - 75C	NORWOOD JCN - 75C	NORWOOD JCN - 75C	NORWOOD JCN - 75C	NORWOOD JCN - 75C	NORWOOD JCN - 75C
30535	EASTLEIGH - 71A	EASTLEIGH - 71A	EASTLEIGH - 71A	EASTLEIGH - 71A	EASTLEIGH - 71A	EASTLEIGH - 71A	EASTLEIGH - 71A
30536	EASTLEIGH - 71A	EASTLEIGH - 71A	EASTLEIGH - 71A	EASTLEIGH - 71A	EASTLEIGH - 71A	EASTLEIGH - 71A	EASTLEIGH - 71A
30537	NORWOOD JCN - 75C	NORWOOD JCN - 75C	NORWOOD JCN - 75C	NORWOOD JCN - 75C	NORWOOD JCN - 75C	NORWOOD JCN - 75C	NORWOOD JCN - 75C
30538	NORWOOD JCN - 75C	NORWOOD JCN - 75C	NORWOOD JCN - 75C	NORWOOD JCN - 75C	NORWOOD JCN - 75C	NORWOOD JCN - 75C	NORWOOD JCN - 75C
30539	NORWOOD JCN - 75C	NORWOOD JCN - 75C	NORWOOD JCN - 75C	NORWOOD JCN - 75C	NORWOOD JCN - 75C	NORWOOD JCN - 75C	NORWOOD JCN - 75C
30540	THREE BRIDGES - 75E	THREE BRIDGES - 75E	THREE BRIDGES - 75E	THREE BRIDGES - 75E	THREE BRIDGES - 75E	THREE BRIDGES - 75E	THREE BRIDGES - 75E
30541	THREE BRIDGES - 75E	THREE BRIDGES - 75E	THREE BRIDGES - 75E	THREE BRIDGES - 75E	THREE BRIDGES - 75E	THREE BRIDGES - 75E	THREE BRIDGES - 75E
30542	EASTLEIGH - 71A	EASTLEIGH - 71A	EASTLEIGH - 71A	EASTLEIGH - 71A	EASTLEIGH - 71A	EASTLEIGH - 71A	EASTLEIGH - 71A
30543	EASTLEIGH - 71A	EASTLEIGH - 71A	EASTLEIGH - 71A	EASTLEIGH - 71A	EASTLEIGH - 71A	EASTLEIGH - 71A	EASTLEIGH - 71A
30544	EASTLEIGH - 71A	EASTLEIGH - 71A	EASTLEIGH - 71A	EASTLEIGH - 71A	EASTLEIGH - 71A	THREE BRIDGES - 75E	THREE BRIDGES - 75E
30545	HORSHAM - 75D	HORSHAM - 75D	HORSHAM - 75D	HORSHAM - 75D	HORSHAM - 75D	HORSHAM - 75D	HORSHAM - 75D
30546	HORSHAM - 75D	HORSHAM - 75D	HORSHAM - 75D	HORSHAM - 75D	HORSHAM - 75D	HORSHAM - 75D	HORSHAM - 75D
30547	NORWOOD JCN - 75C	NORWOOD JCN - 75C	NORWOOD JCN - 75C	NORWOOD JCN - 75C	NORWOOD JCN - 75C	NORWOOD JCN - 75C	NORWOOD JCN - 75C
30548	BOURNEMOUTH - 71B	BOURNEMOUTH - 71B	BOURNEMOUTH - 71B	BOURNEMOUTH - 71B	BOURNEMOUTH - 71B	BOURNEMOUTH - 71B	BOURNEMOUTH - 71B
30549	BOURNEMOUTH - 71B	BOURNEMOUTH - 71B	BOURNEMOUTH - 71B	BOURNEMOUTH - 71B	BOURNEMOUTH - 71B	BOURNEMOUTH - 71B	BOURNEMOUTH - 71B
				Q1 0-6-0 (1942)			
33001	GUILDFORD - 70C	GUILDFORD - 70C	GUILDFORD - 70C	GUILDFORD - 70C	GUILDFORD - 70C	GUILDFORD - 70C	GUILDFORD - 70C
33002	GUILDFORD - 70C	GUILDFORD - 70C	GUILDFORD - 70C	GUILDFORD - 70C	GUILDFORD - 70C	GUILDFORD - 70C	GUILDFORD - 70C
33003	GUILDFORD - 70C	GUILDFORD - 70C	GUILDFORD - 70C	GUILDFORD - 70C	GUILDFORD - 70C	GUILDFORD - 70C	GUILDFORD - 70C
33004	GUILDFORD - 70C	GUILDFORD - 70C	GUILDFORD - 70C	GUILDFORD - 70C	GUILDFORD - 70C	GUILDFORD - 70C	GUILDFORD - 70C
33005	GUILDFORD - 70C	GUILDFORD - 70C	GUILDFORD - 70C	GUILDFORD - 70C	GUILDFORD - 70C	GUILDFORD - 70C	GUILDFORD - 70C
33006	FELTHAM - 70B	FELTHAM - 70B	FELTHAM - 70B	FELTHAM - 70B	FELTHAM - 70B	FELTHAM - 70B	FELTHAM - 70B
33007	FELTHAM - 70B	FELTHAM - 70B	FELTHAM - 70B	FELTHAM - 70B	FELTHAM - 70B	FELTHAM - 70B	FELTHAM - 70B
33008	FELTHAM - 70B	FELTHAM - 70B	FELTHAM - 70B	FELTHAM - 70B	FELTHAM - 70B	FELTHAM - 70B	FELTHAM - 70B
33009	FELTHAM - 70B	FELTHAM - 70B	FELTHAM - 70B	FELTHAM - 70B	FELTHAM - 70B	FELTHAM - 70B	FELTHAM - 70B
33010	FELTHAM - 70B	FELTHAM - 70B	FELTHAM - 70B	FELTHAM - 70B	FELTHAM - 70B	FELTHAM - 70B	FELTHAM - 70B
33011	FELTHAM - 70B	FELTHAM - 70B	FELTHAM - 70B	FELTHAM - 70B	FELTHAM - 70B	FELTHAM - 70B	FELTHAM - 70B
33012	FELTHAM - 70B	FELTHAM - 70B	FELTHAM - 70B	FELTHAM - 70B	FELTHAM - 70B	FELTHAM - 70B	FELTHAM - 70B
33013	FELTHAM - 70B	FELTHAM - 70B	FELTHAM - 70B	FELTHAM - 70B	FELTHAM - 70B	FELTHAM - 70B	FELTHAM - 70B
33014	GUILDFORD - 70C	HITHER GREEN - 73C	HITHER GREEN - 73C	HITHER GREEN - 73C	HITHER GREEN - 73C	HITHER GREEN - 73C	HITHER GREEN - 73C
33015	GUILDFORD - 70C	HITHER GREEN - 73C	HITHER GREEN - 73C	HITHER GREEN - 73C	HITHER GREEN - 73C	HITHER GREEN - 73C	HITHER GREEN - 73C
33016	FRATTON - 71D	FRATTON - 71D	FRATTON - 71D	FRATTON - 71D	EASTLEIGH - 71A	EASTLEIGH - 71A	EASTLEIGH - 71A
33017	EASTLEIGH - 71A	EASTLEIGH - 71A	EASTLEIGH - 71A	EASTLEIGH - 71A	EASTLEIGH - 71A	EASTLEIGH - 71A	EASTLEIGH - 71A
33018	EASTLEIGH - 71A	EASTLEIGH - 71A	EASTLEIGH - 71A	EASTLEIGH - 71A	EASTLEIGH - 71A	EASTLEIGH - 71A	EASTLEIGH - 71A
33019	EASTLEIGH - 71A	EASTLEIGH - 71A	EASTLEIGH - 71A	EASTLEIGH - 71A	EASTLEIGH - 71A	EASTLEIGH - 71A	EASTLEIGH - 71A
33020	EASTLEIGH - 71A	EASTLEIGH - 71A	EASTLEIGH - 71A	EASTLEIGH - 71A	EASTLEIGH - 71A	EASTLEIGH - 71A	EASTLEIGH - 71A
33021	EASTLEIGH - 71A	EASTLEIGH - 71A	EASTLEIGH - 71A	EASTLEIGH - 71A	EASTLEIGH - 71A	EASTLEIGH - 71A	EASTLEIGH - 71A
33022	EASTLEIGH - 71A	EASTLEIGH - 71A	EASTLEIGH - 71A	EASTLEIGH - 71A	EASTLEIGH - 71A	EASTLEIGH - 71A	EASTLEIGH - 71A
33023	EASTLEIGH - 71A	EASTLEIGH - 71A	EASTLEIGH - 71A	EASTLEIGH - 71A	EASTLEIGH - 71A	EASTLEIGH - 71A	EASTLEIGH - 71A
33024	EASTLEIGH - 71A	EASTLEIGH - 71A	EASTLEIGH - 71A	EASTLEIGH - 71A	EASTLEIGH - 71A	EASTLEIGH - 71A	EASTLEIGH - 71A
33025	EASTLEIGH - 71A	EASTLEIGH - 71A	EASTLEIGH - 71A	EASTLEIGH - 71A	EASTLEIGH - 71A	EASTLEIGH - 71A	EASTLEIGH - 71A
33026	GILLINGHAM - 73D	GILLINGHAM - 73D	TONBRIDGE - 74D	TONBRIDGE - 74D	TONBRIDGE - 74D	TONBRIDGE - 74D	TONBRIDGE - 74D
33027	TONBRIDGE - 74D	TONBRIDGE - 74D	TONBRIDGE - 74D	TONBRIDGE - 74D	TONBRIDGE - 74D	TONBRIDGE - 74D	TONBRIDGE - 74D
33028	TONBRIDGE - 74D	TONBRIDGE - 74D	TONBRIDGE - 74D	TONBRIDGE - 74D	TONBRIDGE - 74D	TONBRIDGE - 74D	TONBRIDGE - 74D
33029	TONBRIDGE - 74D	TONBRIDGE - 74D	TONBRIDGE - 74D	TONBRIDGE - 74D	TONBRIDGE - 74D	TONBRIDGE - 74D	TONBRIDGE - 74D
33030	TONBRIDGE - 74D	TONBRIDGE - 74D	TONBRIDGE - 74D	TONBRIDGE - 74D	TONBRIDGE - 74D	TONBRIDGE - 74D	TONBRIDGE - 74D
33031	TONBRIDGE - 74D	TONBRIDGE - 74D	TONBRIDGE - 74D	TONBRIDGE - 74D	TONBRIDGE - 74D	TONBRIDGE - 74D	TONBRIDGE - 74D
33032	TONBRIDGE - 74D	TONBRIDGE - 74D	TONBRIDGE - 74D	TONBRIDGE - 74D	TONBRIDGE - 74D	TONBRIDGE - 74D	TONBRIDGE - 74D
33033	TONBRIDGE - 74D	TONBRIDGE - 74D	TONBRIDGE - 74D	TONBRIDGE - 74D	TONBRIDGE - 74D	TONBRIDGE - 74D	TONBRIDGE - 74D
33034	TONBRIDGE - 74D	TONBRIDGE - 74D	TONBRIDGE - 74D	TONBRIDGE - 74D	TONBRIDGE - 74D	TONBRIDGE - 74D	TONBRIDGE - 74D
33035	TONBRIDGE - 74D	TONBRIDGE - 74D	TONBRIDGE - 74D	TONBRIDGE - 74D	TONBRIDGE - 74D	TONBRIDGE - 74D	TONBRIDGE - 74D
33036	TONBRIDGE - 74D	STEWARTS LANE - 73A	STEWARTS LANE - 73A	STEWARTS LANE - 73A	STEWARTS LANE - 73A	STEWARTS LANE - 73A	STEWARTS LANE - 73A
33037	TONBRIDGE - 74D	STEWARTS LANE - 73A	STEWARTS LANE - 73A	STEWARTS LANE - 73A	STEWARTS LANE - 73A	STEWARTS LANE - 73A	STEWARTS LANE - 73A
33038	TONBRIDGE - 74D	STEWARTS LANE - 73A	STEWARTS LANE - 73A	STEWARTS LANE - 73A	STEWARTS LANE - 73A	STEWARTS LANE - 73A	STEWARTS LANE - 73A
33039	TONBRIDGE - 74D	TONBRIDGE - 74D	TONBRIDGE - 74D	TONBRIDGE - 74D	TONBRIDGE - 74D	TONBRIDGE - 74D	TONBRIDGE - 74D
33040	TONBRIDGE - 74D	TONBRIDGE - 74D	TONBRIDGE - 74D	TONBRIDGE - 74D	TONBRIDGE - 74D	TONBRIDGE - 74D	TONBRIDGE - 74D
				W 2-6-4T (1931)			
31911	HITHER GREEN - 73C	HITHER GREEN - 73C	HITHER GREEN - 73C	HITHER GREEN - 73C	HITHER GREEN - 73C	HITHER GREEN - 73C	HITHER GREEN - 73C
31912	STEWARTS LANE - 73A	STEWARTS LANE - 73A	STEWARTS LANE - 73A	STEWARTS LANE - 73A	STEWARTS LANE - 73A	STEWARTS LANE - 73A	STEWARTS LANE - 73A
31913	HITHER GREEN - 73C	HITHER GREEN - 73C	HITHER GREEN - 73C	HITHER GREEN - 73C	HITHER GREEN - 73C	HITHER GREEN - 73C	HITHER GREEN - 73C
31914	STEWARTS LANE - 73A	STEWARTS LANE - 73A	STEWARTS LANE - 73A	STEWARTS LANE - 73A	STEWARTS LANE - 73A	STEWARTS LANE - 73A	STEWARTS LANE - 73A
31915	STEWARTS LANE - 73A	STEWARTS LANE - 73A	HITHER GREEN - 73C	HITHER GREEN - 73C	HITHER GREEN - 73C	HITHER GREEN - 73C	HITHER GREEN - 73C
31916	NORWOOD JCN - 75C	NORWOOD JCN - 75C	NORWOOD JCN - 75C	NORWOOD JCN - 75C	NORWOOD JCN - 75C	NORWOOD JCN - 75C	NORWOOD JCN - 75C
31917	NORWOOD JCN - 75C	NORWOOD JCN - 75C	NORWOOD JCN - 75C	NORWOOD JCN - 75C	NORWOOD JCN - 75C	NORWOOD JCN - 75C	NORWOOD JCN - 75C
31918	NORWOOD JCN - 75C	NORWOOD JCN - 75C	NORWOOD JCN - 75C	NORWOOD JCN - 75C	NORWOOD JCN - 75C	NORWOOD JCN - 75C	NORWOOD JCN - 75C
31919	NORWOOD JCN - 75C	NORWOOD JCN - 75C	NORWOOD JCN - 75C	NORWOOD JCN - 75C	NORWOOD JCN - 75C	NORWOOD JCN - 75C	NORWOOD JCN - 75C
31920	NORWOOD JCN - 75C	NORWOOD JCN - 75C	NORWOOD JCN - 75C	NORWOOD JCN - 75C	NORWOOD JCN - 75C	NORWOOD JCN - 75C	NORWOOD JCN - 75C
31921	HITHER GREEN - 73C	HITHER GREEN - 73C	HITHER GREEN - 73C	HITHER GREEN - 73C	HITHER GREEN - 73C	HITHER GREEN - 73C	HITHER GREEN - 73C
31922	HITHER GREEN - 73C	HITHER GREEN - 73C	HITHER GREEN - 73C	HITHER GREEN - 73C	HITHER GREEN - 73C	HITHER GREEN - 73C	HITHER GREEN - 73C
31923	HITHER GREEN - 73C	HITHER GREEN - 73C	HITHER GREEN - 73C	HITHER GREEN - 73C	HITHER GREEN - 73C	HITHER GREEN - 73C	HITHER GREEN - 73C
31924	HITHER GREEN - 73C	HITHER GREEN - 73C	HITHER GREEN - 73C	HITHER GREEN - 73C	HITHER GREEN - 73C	HITHER GREEN - 73C	HITHER GREEN - 73C
31925	HITHER GREEN - 73C	HITHER GREEN - 73C	HITHER GREEN - 73C	HITHER GREEN - 73C	HITHER GREEN - 73C	HITHER GREEN - 73C	HITHER GREEN - 73C
				Z 0-8-0T (1929)			
30950	EASTLEIGH - 71A	EASTLEIGH - 71A	EASTLEIGH - 71A	EASTLEIGH - 71A	EASTLEIGH - 71A	EASTLEIGH - 71A	EASTLEIGH - 71A
30951	GILLINGHAM - 73D	GILLINGHAM - 73D	GILLINGHAM - 73D	GILLINGHAM - 73D	GILLINGHAM - 73D	GILLINGHAM - 73D	GILLINGHAM - 73D
30952	EASTLEIGH - 71A	EASTLEIGH - 71A	EASTLEIGH - 71A	EASTLEIGH - 71A	EASTLEIGH - 71A	EASTLEIGH - 71A	EASTLEIGH - 71A
30953	ASHFORD - 74A	ASHFORD - 74A	ASHFORD - 74A	ASHFORD - 74A	ASHFORD - 74A	ASHFORD - 74A	ASHFORD - 74A
30954	EXMOUTH JCN - 72A	EXMOUTH JCN - 72A	EXMOUTH JCN - 72A	EXMOUTH JCN - 72A	EXMOUTH JCN - 72A	EXMOUTH JCN - 72A	EXMOUTH JCN - 72A
30955	NINE ELMS - 70A	NINE ELMS - 70A	NINE ELMS - 70A	NINE ELMS - 70A	ASHFORD - 74A	ASHFORD - 74A	EASTLEIGH - 71A
30956	EASTLEIGH - 71A	EASTLEIGH - 71A	EASTLEIGH - 71A	EASTLEIGH - 71A	EASTLEIGH - 71A	EASTLEIGH - 71A	EASTLEIGH - 71A
30957	SALISBURY - 72B	SALISBURY - 72B	SALISBURY - 72B	SALISBURY - 72B	SALISBURY - 72B	SALISBURY - 72B	SALISBURY - 72B
				J2 4-6-2T (1912)			
31596	ASHFORD - 74A	ASHFORD - 74A	W/D	W/D	W/D	W/D	W/D
				H16 4-6-2T (1921)			
30516	FELTHAM - 70B	FELTHAM - 70B	FELTHAM - 70B	FELTHAM - 70B	FELTHAM - 70B	FELTHAM - 70B	FELTHAM - 70B
30517	FELTHAM - 70B	FELTHAM - 70B	FELTHAM - 70B	FELTHAM - 70B	FELTHAM - 70B	FELTHAM - 70B	FELTHAM - 70B
30518	FELTHAM - 70B	FELTHAM - 70B	FELTHAM - 70B	FELTHAM - 70B	FELTHAM - 70B	FELTHAM - 70B	FELTHAM - 70B
30519	FELTHAM - 70B	FELTHAM - 70B	FELTHAM - 70B	FELTHAM - 70B	FELTHAM - 70B	FELTHAM - 70B	FELTHAM - 70B
30520	FELTHAM - 70B	FELTHAM - 70B	FELTHAM - 70B	FELTHAM - 70B	FELTHAM - 70B	FELTHAM - 70B	FELTHAM - 70B

loco	Sep-52	Dec-52	Mar-53	May-53	Jul-53	Sep-53	Nov-53
				Q 0-6-0 (1938)			
30530	EASTLEIGH - 71A	EASTLEIGH - 71A	EASTLEIGH - 71A	EASTLEIGH - 71A	EASTLEIGH - 71A	EASTLEIGH - 71A	EASTLEIGH - 71A
30531	EASTLEIGH - 71A	EASTLEIGH - 71A	EASTLEIGH - 71A	EASTLEIGH - 71A	EASTLEIGH - 71A	EASTLEIGH - 71A	EASTLEIGH - 71A
30532	EASTLEIGH - 71A	EASTLEIGH - 71A	EASTLEIGH - 71A	EASTLEIGH - 71A	EASTLEIGH - 71A	EASTLEIGH - 71A	EASTLEIGH - 71A
30533	NORWOOD JCN - 75C	NORWOOD JCN - 75C	NORWOOD JCN - 75C	NORWOOD JCN - 75C	NORWOOD JCN - 75C	NORWOOD JCN - 75C	NORWOOD JCN - 75C
30534	NORWOOD JCN - 75C	NORWOOD JCN - 75C	NORWOOD JCN - 75C	NORWOOD JCN - 75C	NORWOOD JCN - 75C	NORWOOD JCN - 75C	NORWOOD JCN - 75C
30535	EASTLEIGH - 71A	EASTLEIGH - 71A	EASTLEIGH - 71A	EASTLEIGH - 71A	EASTLEIGH - 71A	EASTLEIGH - 71A	EASTLEIGH - 71A
30536	EASTLEIGH - 71A	EASTLEIGH - 71A	EASTLEIGH - 71A	EASTLEIGH - 71A	EASTLEIGH - 71A	EASTLEIGH - 71A	EASTLEIGH - 71A
30537	NORWOOD JCN - 75C	NORWOOD JCN - 75C	NORWOOD JCN - 75C	NORWOOD JCN - 75C	NORWOOD JCN - 75C	NORWOOD JCN - 75C	NORWOOD JCN - 75C
30538	NORWOOD JCN - 75C	NORWOOD JCN - 75C	NORWOOD JCN - 75C	NORWOOD JCN - 75C	NORWOOD JCN - 75C	NORWOOD JCN - 75C	NORWOOD JCN - 75C
30539	NORWOOD JCN - 75C	NORWOOD JCN - 75C	NORWOOD JCN - 75C	NORWOOD JCN - 75C	NORWOOD JCN - 75C	NORWOOD JCN - 75C	NORWOOD JCN - 75C
30540	THREE BRIDGES - 75E	THREE BRIDGES - 75E	THREE BRIDGES - 75E	THREE BRIDGES - 75E	THREE BRIDGES - 75E	THREE BRIDGES - 75E	THREE BRIDGES - 75E
30541	THREE BRIDGES - 75E	THREE BRIDGES - 75E	THREE BRIDGES - 75E	THREE BRIDGES - 75E	THREE BRIDGES - 75E	BOURNEMOUTH - 71B	BOURNEMOUTH - 71B
30542	EASTLEIGH - 71A	EASTLEIGH - 71A	EASTLEIGH - 71A	EASTLEIGH - 71A	EASTLEIGH - 71A	EASTLEIGH - 71A	EASTLEIGH - 71A
30543	EASTLEIGH - 71A	EASTLEIGH - 71A	EASTLEIGH - 71A	EASTLEIGH - 71A	EASTLEIGH - 71A	EASTLEIGH - 71A	EASTLEIGH - 71A
30544	THREE BRIDGES - 75E	THREE BRIDGES - 75E	THREE BRIDGES - 75E	THREE BRIDGES - 75E	THREE BRIDGES - 75E	HORSHAM - 75D	HORSHAM - 75D
30545	HORSHAM - 75D	HORSHAM - 75D	HORSHAM - 75D	HORSHAM - 75D	HORSHAM - 75D	HORSHAM - 75D	HORSHAM - 75D
30546	HORSHAM - 75D	HORSHAM - 75D	HORSHAM - 75D	HORSHAM - 75D	HORSHAM - 75D	HORSHAM - 75D	HORSHAM - 75D
30547	NORWOOD JCN - 75C	NORWOOD JCN - 75C	NORWOOD JCN - 75C	NORWOOD JCN - 75C	NORWOOD JCN - 75C	NORWOOD JCN - 75C	NORWOOD JCN - 75C
30548	BOURNEMOUTH - 71B	BOURNEMOUTH - 71B	BOURNEMOUTH - 71B	BOURNEMOUTH - 71B	BOURNEMOUTH - 71B	BOURNEMOUTH - 71B	BOURNEMOUTH - 71B
30549	BOURNEMOUTH - 71B	BOURNEMOUTH - 71B	BOURNEMOUTH - 71B	BOURNEMOUTH - 71B	BOURNEMOUTH - 71B	BOURNEMOUTH - 71B	BOURNEMOUTH - 71B
				Q1 0-6-0 (1942)			
33001	GUILDFORD - 70C	GUILDFORD - 70C	GUILDFORD - 70C	GUILDFORD - 70C	GUILDFORD - 70C	GUILDFORD - 70C	GUILDFORD - 70C
33002	GUILDFORD - 70C	GUILDFORD - 70C	GUILDFORD - 70C	GUILDFORD - 70C	GUILDFORD - 70C	GUILDFORD - 70C	GUILDFORD - 70C
33003	GUILDFORD - 70C	GUILDFORD - 70C	GUILDFORD - 70C	GUILDFORD - 70C	GUILDFORD - 70C	GUILDFORD - 70C	GUILDFORD - 70C
33004	GUILDFORD - 70C	GUILDFORD - 70C	FAVERSHAM - 73E	FAVERSHAM - 73E	FAVERSHAM - 73E	FAVERSHAM - 73E	FAVERSHAM - 73E
33005	GUILDFORD - 70C	GUILDFORD - 70C	FAVERSHAM - 73E	GUILDFORD - 70C	GUILDFORD - 70C	GUILDFORD - 70C	GUILDFORD - 70C
33006	FELTHAM - 70B	FELTHAM - 70B	FELTHAM - 70B	FELTHAM - 70B	FELTHAM - 70B	FELTHAM - 70B	FELTHAM - 70B
33007	FELTHAM - 70B	FELTHAM - 70B	HITHER GREEN - 73C	FELTHAM - 70B	FELTHAM - 70B	FELTHAM - 70B	FELTHAM - 70B
33008	FELTHAM - 70B	FELTHAM - 70B	FELTHAM - 70B	FELTHAM - 70B	FELTHAM - 70B	FELTHAM - 70B	FELTHAM - 70B
33009	FELTHAM - 70B	FELTHAM - 70B	HITHER GREEN - 73C	FELTHAM - 70B	FELTHAM - 70B	FELTHAM - 70B	FELTHAM - 70B
33010	FELTHAM - 70B	FELTHAM - 70B	FELTHAM - 70B	FELTHAM - 70B	FELTHAM - 70B	FELTHAM - 70B	FELTHAM - 70B
33011	FELTHAM - 70B	FELTHAM - 70B	HITHER GREEN - 73C	FELTHAM - 70B	FELTHAM - 70B	FELTHAM - 70B	FELTHAM - 70B
33012	FELTHAM - 70B	FELTHAM - 70B	FELTHAM - 70B	FELTHAM - 70B	FELTHAM - 70B	FELTHAM - 70B	FELTHAM - 70B
33013	FELTHAM - 70B	FELTHAM - 70B	FELTHAM - 70B	FELTHAM - 70B	FELTHAM - 70B	FELTHAM - 70B	FELTHAM - 70B
33014	HITHER GREEN - 73C	HITHER GREEN - 73C	HITHER GREEN - 73C	HITHER GREEN - 73C	HITHER GREEN - 73C	HITHER GREEN - 73C	HITHER GREEN - 73C
33015	HITHER GREEN - 73C	HITHER GREEN - 73C	HITHER GREEN - 73C	HITHER GREEN - 73C	HITHER GREEN - 73C	HITHER GREEN - 73C	HITHER GREEN - 73C
33016	EASTLEIGH - 71A	EASTLEIGH - 71A	FAVERSHAM - 73E	FAVERSHAM - 73E	FAVERSHAM - 73E	FAVERSHAM - 73E	FAVERSHAM - 73E
33017	EASTLEIGH - 71A	EASTLEIGH - 71A	EASTLEIGH - 71A	EASTLEIGH - 71A	EASTLEIGH - 71A	EASTLEIGH - 71A	EASTLEIGH - 71A
33018	EASTLEIGH - 71A	EASTLEIGH - 71A	RAMSGATE - 74B	GUILDFORD - 70C	GUILDFORD - 70C	HITHER GREEN - 73C	HITHER GREEN - 73C
33019	EASTLEIGH - 71A	EASTLEIGH - 71A	RAMSGATE - 74B	RAMSGATE - 74B	GUILDFORD - 70C	GUILDFORD - 70C	GUILDFORD - 70C
33020	EASTLEIGH - 71A	EASTLEIGH - 71A	EASTLEIGH - 71A	EASTLEIGH - 71A	EASTLEIGH - 71A	EASTLEIGH - 71A	EASTLEIGH - 71A
33021	EASTLEIGH - 71A	EASTLEIGH - 71A	EASTLEIGH - 71A	EASTLEIGH - 71A	EASTLEIGH - 71A	EASTLEIGH - 71A	EASTLEIGH - 71A
33022	EASTLEIGH - 71A	EASTLEIGH - 71A	RAMSGATE - 74B	RAMSGATE - 74B	RAMSGATE - 74B	GUILDFORD - 70C	GUILDFORD - 70C
33023	EASTLEIGH - 71A	EASTLEIGH - 71A	EASTLEIGH - 71A	EASTLEIGH - 71A	EASTLEIGH - 71A	EASTLEIGH - 71A	EASTLEIGH - 71A
33024	EASTLEIGH - 71A	EASTLEIGH - 71A	EASTLEIGH - 71A	EASTLEIGH - 71A	EASTLEIGH - 71A	EASTLEIGH - 71A	TONBRIDGE - 74D
33025	EASTLEIGH - 71A	EASTLEIGH - 71A	EASTLEIGH - 71A	EASTLEIGH - 71A	EASTLEIGH - 71A	EASTLEIGH - 71A	EASTLEIGH - 71A
33026	TONBRIDGE - 74D	TONBRIDGE - 74D	TONBRIDGE - 74D	TONBRIDGE - 74D	TONBRIDGE - 74D	FELTHAM - 70B	FELTHAM - 70B
33027	TONBRIDGE - 74D	TONBRIDGE - 74D	TONBRIDGE - 74D	TONBRIDGE - 74D	TONBRIDGE - 74D	FELTHAM - 70B	FELTHAM - 70B
33028	TONBRIDGE - 74D	TONBRIDGE - 74D	TONBRIDGE - 74D	TONBRIDGE - 74D	TONBRIDGE - 74D	TONBRIDGE - 74D	TONBRIDGE - 74D
33029	TONBRIDGE - 74D	TONBRIDGE - 74D	TONBRIDGE - 74D	TONBRIDGE - 74D	TONBRIDGE - 74D	TONBRIDGE - 74D	TONBRIDGE - 74D
33030	TONBRIDGE - 74D	TONBRIDGE - 74D	TONBRIDGE - 74D	TONBRIDGE - 74D	TONBRIDGE - 74D	TONBRIDGE - 74D	TONBRIDGE - 74D
33031	TONBRIDGE - 74D	TONBRIDGE - 74D	TONBRIDGE - 74D	TONBRIDGE - 74D	TONBRIDGE - 74D	TONBRIDGE - 74D	TONBRIDGE - 74D
33032	TONBRIDGE - 74D	TONBRIDGE - 74D	TONBRIDGE - 74D	TONBRIDGE - 74D	TONBRIDGE - 74D	TONBRIDGE - 74D	TONBRIDGE - 74D
33033	TONBRIDGE - 74D	TONBRIDGE - 74D	TONBRIDGE - 74D	TONBRIDGE - 74D	TONBRIDGE - 74D	TONBRIDGE - 74D	TONBRIDGE - 74D
33034	TONBRIDGE - 74D	TONBRIDGE - 74D	TONBRIDGE - 74D	TONBRIDGE - 74D	TONBRIDGE - 74D	TONBRIDGE - 74D	TONBRIDGE - 74D
33035	TONBRIDGE - 74D	TONBRIDGE - 74D	TONBRIDGE - 74D	TONBRIDGE - 74D	TONBRIDGE - 74D	TONBRIDGE - 74D	TONBRIDGE - 74D
33036	TONBRIDGE - 74D	TONBRIDGE - 74D	TONBRIDGE - 74D	TONBRIDGE - 74D	TONBRIDGE - 74D	TONBRIDGE - 74D	TONBRIDGE - 74D
33037	HITHER GREEN - 73C	HITHER GREEN - 73C	HITHER GREEN - 73C	HITHER GREEN - 73C	HITHER GREEN - 73C	HITHER GREEN - 73C	HITHER GREEN - 73C
33038	EASTLEIGH - 71A	EASTLEIGH - 71A	EASTLEIGH - 71A	EASTLEIGH - 71A	EASTLEIGH - 71A	EASTLEIGH - 71A	EASTLEIGH - 71A
33039	TONBRIDGE - 74D	TONBRIDGE - 74D	TONBRIDGE - 74D	TONBRIDGE - 74D	TONBRIDGE - 74D	TONBRIDGE - 74D	TONBRIDGE - 74D
33040	TONBRIDGE - 74D	TONBRIDGE - 74D	TONBRIDGE - 74D	TONBRIDGE - 74D	TONBRIDGE - 74D	TONBRIDGE - 74D	TONBRIDGE - 74D
				W 2-6-4T (1931)			
31911	HITHER GREEN - 73C	HITHER GREEN - 73C	HITHER GREEN - 73C	HITHER GREEN - 73C	HITHER GREEN - 73C	HITHER GREEN - 73C	HITHER GREEN - 73C
31912	STEWARTS LANE - 73A	STEWARTS LANE - 73A	STEWARTS LANE - 73A	STEWARTS LANE - 73A	HITHER GREEN - 73C	HITHER GREEN - 73C	HITHER GREEN - 73C
31913	HITHER GREEN - 73C	HITHER GREEN - 73C	HITHER GREEN - 73C	HITHER GREEN - 73C	HITHER GREEN - 73C	HITHER GREEN - 73C	HITHER GREEN - 73C
31914	STEWARTS LANE - 73A	STEWARTS LANE - 73A	STEWARTS LANE - 73A	STEWARTS LANE - 73A	STEWARTS LANE - 73A	STEWARTS LANE - 73A	STEWARTS LANE - 73A
31915	HITHER GREEN - 73C	HITHER GREEN - 73C	HITHER GREEN - 73C	HITHER GREEN - 73C	HITHER GREEN - 73C	HITHER GREEN - 73C	HITHER GREEN - 73C
31916	NORWOOD JCN - 75C	NORWOOD JCN - 75C	HITHER GREEN - 73C	HITHER GREEN - 73C	HITHER GREEN - 73C	HITHER GREEN - 73C	HITHER GREEN - 73C
31917	NORWOOD JCN - 75C	NORWOOD JCN - 75C	NORWOOD JCN - 75C	NORWOOD JCN - 75C	NORWOOD JCN - 75C	NORWOOD JCN - 75C	NORWOOD JCN - 75C
31918	NORWOOD JCN - 75C	NORWOOD JCN - 75C	NORWOOD JCN - 75C	NORWOOD JCN - 75C	NORWOOD JCN - 75C	NORWOOD JCN - 75C	NORWOOD JCN - 75C
31919	NORWOOD JCN - 75C	NORWOOD JCN - 75C	NORWOOD JCN - 75C	NORWOOD JCN - 75C	NORWOOD JCN - 75C	NORWOOD JCN - 75C	NORWOOD JCN - 75C
31920	NORWOOD JCN - 75C	NORWOOD JCN - 75C	NORWOOD JCN - 75C	NORWOOD JCN - 75C	NORWOOD JCN - 75C	NORWOOD JCN - 75C	NORWOOD JCN - 75C
31921	HITHER GREEN - 73C	HITHER GREEN - 73C	HITHER GREEN - 73C	HITHER GREEN - 73C	HITHER GREEN - 73C	HITHER GREEN - 73C	HITHER GREEN - 73C
31922	HITHER GREEN - 73C	HITHER GREEN - 73C	HITHER GREEN - 73C	HITHER GREEN - 73C	HITHER GREEN - 73C	HITHER GREEN - 73C	HITHER GREEN - 73C
31923	HITHER GREEN - 73C	HITHER GREEN - 73C	HITHER GREEN - 73C	HITHER GREEN - 73C	HITHER GREEN - 73C	HITHER GREEN - 73C	HITHER GREEN - 73C
31924	HITHER GREEN - 73C	HITHER GREEN - 73C	HITHER GREEN - 73C	HITHER GREEN - 73C	HITHER GREEN - 73C	HITHER GREEN - 73C	HITHER GREEN - 73C
31925	HITHER GREEN - 73C	HITHER GREEN - 73C	HITHER GREEN - 73C	HITHER GREEN - 73C	HITHER GREEN - 73C	HITHER GREEN - 73C	HITHER GREEN - 73C
				Z 0-8-0T (1929)			
30950	EASTLEIGH - 71A	EASTLEIGH - 71A	BRIGHTON - 75A	BRIGHTON - 75A	BRIGHTON - 75A	BRIGHTON - 75A	BRIGHTON - 75A
30951	GILLINGHAM - 73D	GILLINGHAM - 73D	THREE BRIDGES - 75E	THREE BRIDGES - 75E	THREE BRIDGES - 75E	THREE BRIDGES - 75E	THREE BRIDGES - 75E
30952	EASTLEIGH - 71A	EASTLEIGH - 71A	DOVER - 74C	DOVER - 74C	DOVER - 74C	EASTLEIGH - 71A	EASTLEIGH - 71A
30953	ASHFORD - 74A	ASHFORD - 74A	ASHFORD - 74A	ASHFORD - 74A	ASHFORD - 74A	ASHFORD - 74A	ASHFORD - 74A
30954	EXMOUTH JCN - 72A	EXMOUTH JCN - 72A	EXMOUTH JCN - 72A	EXMOUTH JCN - 72A	EXMOUTH JCN - 72A	EXMOUTH JCN - 72A	EXMOUTH JCN - 72A
30955	EASTLEIGH - 71A	EASTLEIGH - 71A	EASTLEIGH - 71A	EASTLEIGH - 71A	EASTLEIGH - 71A	EASTLEIGH - 71A	EASTLEIGH - 71A
30956	EASTLEIGH - 71A	EASTLEIGH - 71A	EASTLEIGH - 71A	EASTLEIGH - 71A	EASTLEIGH - 71A	EASTLEIGH - 71A	EASTLEIGH - 71A
30957	SALISBURY - 72B	SALISBURY - 72B	SALISBURY - 72B	SALISBURY - 72B	SALISBURY - 72B	SALISBURY - 72B	SALISBURY - 72B
				H16 4-6-2T (1921)			
30516	FELTHAM - 70B	FELTHAM - 70B	FELTHAM - 70B	FELTHAM - 70B	FELTHAM - 70B	FELTHAM - 70B	FELTHAM - 70B
30517	FELTHAM - 70B	FELTHAM - 70B	FELTHAM - 70B	FELTHAM - 70B	FELTHAM - 70B	FELTHAM - 70B	FELTHAM - 70B
30518	FELTHAM - 70B	FELTHAM - 70B	FELTHAM - 70B	FELTHAM - 70B	FELTHAM - 70B	FELTHAM - 70B	FELTHAM - 70B
30519	FELTHAM - 70B	FELTHAM - 70B	FELTHAM - 70B	FELTHAM - 70B	FELTHAM - 70B	FELTHAM - 70B	FELTHAM - 70B
30520	FELTHAM - 70B	FELTHAM - 70B	FELTHAM - 70B	FELTHAM - 70B	FELTHAM - 70B	FELTHAM - 70B	FELTHAM - 70B

loco	Jan-54	Mar-54	May-54	Jun-54	Aug-54	Oct-54	Dec-54
				Q 0-6-0 (1938)			
30530	EASTLEIGH - 71A	EASTLEIGH - 71A	EASTLEIGH - 71A	EASTLEIGH - 71A	EASTLEIGH - 71A	EASTLEIGH - 71A	EASTLEIGH - 71A
30531	EASTLEIGH - 71A	EASTLEIGH - 71A	EASTLEIGH - 71A	EASTLEIGH - 71A	EASTLEIGH - 71A	EASTLEIGH - 71A	EASTLEIGH - 71A
30532	EASTLEIGH - 71A	EASTLEIGH - 71A	EASTLEIGH - 71A	EASTLEIGH - 71A	EASTLEIGH - 71A	EASTLEIGH - 71A	EASTLEIGH - 71A
30533	NORWOOD JCN - 75C	NORWOOD JCN - 75C	NORWOOD JCN - 75C	NORWOOD JCN - 75C	NORWOOD JCN - 75C	NORWOOD JCN - 75C	NORWOOD JCN - 75C
30534	NORWOOD JCN - 75C	NORWOOD JCN - 75C	NORWOOD JCN - 75C	NORWOOD JCN - 75C	NORWOOD JCN - 75C	NORWOOD JCN - 75C	NORWOOD JCN - 75C
30535	EASTLEIGH - 71A	EASTLEIGH - 71A	EASTLEIGH - 71A	EASTLEIGH - 71A	EASTLEIGH - 71A	EASTLEIGH - 71A	EASTLEIGH - 71A
30536	EASTLEIGH - 71A	EASTLEIGH - 71A	EASTLEIGH - 71A	EASTLEIGH - 71A	EASTLEIGH - 71A	EASTLEIGH - 71A	EASTLEIGH - 71A
30537	NORWOOD JCN - 75C	NORWOOD JCN - 75C	NORWOOD JCN - 75C	STEWARTS LANE - 73A	STEWARTS LANE - 73A	NORWOOD JCN - 75C	NORWOOD JCN - 75C
30538	NORWOOD JCN - 75C	NORWOOD JCN - 75C	NORWOOD JCN - 75C	STEWARTS LANE - 73A	STEWARTS LANE - 73A	NORWOOD JCN - 75C	NORWOOD JCN - 75C
30539	NORWOOD JCN - 75C	NORWOOD JCN - 75C	NORWOOD JCN - 75C	NORWOOD JCN - 75C	NORWOOD JCN - 75C	NORWOOD JCN - 75C	NORWOOD JCN - 75C
30540	THREE BRIDGES - 75E	THREE BRIDGES - 75E	THREE BRIDGES - 75E	THREE BRIDGES - 75E	THREE BRIDGES - 75E	THREE BRIDGES - 75E	THREE BRIDGES - 75E
30541	BOURNEMOUTH - 71B	BOURNEMOUTH - 71B	BOURNEMOUTH - 71B	BOURNEMOUTH - 71B	BOURNEMOUTH - 71B	BOURNEMOUTH - 71B	BOURNEMOUTH - 71B
30542	EASTLEIGH - 71A	EASTLEIGH - 71A	EASTLEIGH - 71A	EASTLEIGH - 71A	EASTLEIGH - 71A	EASTLEIGH - 71A	EASTLEIGH - 71A
30543	EASTLEIGH - 71A	EASTLEIGH - 71A	EASTLEIGH - 71A	EASTLEIGH - 71A	EASTLEIGH - 71A	EASTLEIGH - 71A	EASTLEIGH - 71A
30544	HORSHAM - 75D	HORSHAM - 75D	HORSHAM - 75D	HORSHAM - 75D	HORSHAM - 75D	HORSHAM - 75D	HORSHAM - 75D
30545	HORSHAM - 75D	HORSHAM - 75D	HORSHAM - 75D	HORSHAM - 75D	HORSHAM - 75D	HORSHAM - 75D	HORSHAM - 75D
30546	HORSHAM - 75D	HORSHAM - 75D	HORSHAM - 75D	HORSHAM - 75D	HORSHAM - 75D	HORSHAM - 75D	HORSHAM - 75D
30547	NORWOOD JCN - 75C	NORWOOD JCN - 75C	NORWOOD JCN - 75C	NORWOOD JCN - 75C	NORWOOD JCN - 75C	NORWOOD JCN - 75C	NORWOOD JCN - 75C
30548	BOURNEMOUTH - 71B	BOURNEMOUTH - 71B	BOURNEMOUTH - 71B	BOURNEMOUTH - 71B	BOURNEMOUTH - 71B	BOURNEMOUTH - 71B	BOURNEMOUTH - 71B
30549	BOURNEMOUTH - 71B	BOURNEMOUTH - 71B	BOURNEMOUTH - 71B	BOURNEMOUTH - 71B	BOURNEMOUTH - 71B	BOURNEMOUTH - 71B	BOURNEMOUTH - 71B
				Q1 0-6-0 (1942)			
33001	GUILDFORD - 70C	GUILDFORD - 70C	GUILDFORD - 70C	GUILDFORD - 70C	GUILDFORD - 70C	GUILDFORD - 70C	GUILDFORD - 70C
33002	GUILDFORD - 70C	GUILDFORD - 70C	GUILDFORD - 70C	GUILDFORD - 70C	GUILDFORD - 70C	GUILDFORD - 70C	GUILDFORD - 70C
33003	GUILDFORD - 70C	GUILDFORD - 70C	GUILDFORD - 70C	GUILDFORD - 70C	GUILDFORD - 70C	GUILDFORD - 70C	GUILDFORD - 70C
33004	FAVERSHAM - 73E	FAVERSHAM - 73E	FAVERSHAM - 73E	FAVERSHAM - 73E	FAVERSHAM - 73E	FAVERSHAM - 73E	FAVERSHAM - 73E
33005	GUILDFORD - 70C	GUILDFORD - 70C	GUILDFORD - 70C	GUILDFORD - 70C	GUILDFORD - 70C	GUILDFORD - 70C	GUILDFORD - 70C
33006	FELTHAM - 70B	FELTHAM - 70B	FELTHAM - 70B	FELTHAM - 70B	FELTHAM - 70B	FELTHAM - 70B	FELTHAM - 70B
33007	FELTHAM - 70B	FELTHAM - 70B	FELTHAM - 70B	FELTHAM - 70B	FELTHAM - 70B	FELTHAM - 70B	FELTHAM - 70B
33008	FELTHAM - 70B	FELTHAM - 70B	FELTHAM - 70B	FELTHAM - 70B	FELTHAM - 70B	FELTHAM - 70B	FELTHAM - 70B
33009	FELTHAM - 70B	FELTHAM - 70B	FELTHAM - 70B	FELTHAM - 70B	FELTHAM - 70B	FELTHAM - 70B	FELTHAM - 70B
33010	FELTHAM - 70B	FELTHAM - 70B	FELTHAM - 70B	FELTHAM - 70B	FELTHAM - 70B	FELTHAM - 70B	FELTHAM - 70B
33011	FELTHAM - 70B	FELTHAM - 70B	FELTHAM - 70B	FELTHAM - 70B	FELTHAM - 70B	FELTHAM - 70B	FELTHAM - 70B
33012	FELTHAM - 70B	FELTHAM - 70B	FELTHAM - 70B	FELTHAM - 70B	FELTHAM - 70B	FELTHAM - 70B	FELTHAM - 70B
33013	FELTHAM - 70B	FELTHAM - 70B	FELTHAM - 70B	FELTHAM - 70B	FELTHAM - 70B	FELTHAM - 70B	FELTHAM - 70B
33014	HITHER GREEN - 73C	HITHER GREEN - 73C	HITHER GREEN - 73C	HITHER GREEN - 73C	HITHER GREEN - 73C	HITHER GREEN - 73C	HITHER GREEN - 73C
33015	HITHER GREEN - 73C	HITHER GREEN - 73C	HITHER GREEN - 73C	NORWOOD JCN - 75C	NORWOOD JCN - 75C	STEWARTS LANE - 73A	STEWARTS LANE - 73A
33016	FAVERSHAM - 73E	FAVERSHAM - 73E	NORWOOD JCN - 75C	NORWOOD JCN - 75C	NORWOOD JCN - 75C	FELTHAM - 70B	FELTHAM - 70B
33017	EASTLEIGH - 71A	EASTLEIGH - 71A	BRIGHTON - 75A	BRIGHTON - 75A	BRIGHTON - 75A	STEWARTS LANE - 73A	STEWARTS LANE - 73A
33018	HITHER GREEN - 73C	HITHER GREEN - 73C	NORWOOD JCN - 75C	NORWOOD JCN - 75C	NORWOOD JCN - 75C	FELTHAM - 70B	FELTHAM - 70B
33019	GUILDFORD - 70C	GUILDFORD - 70C	GUILDFORD - 70C	GUILDFORD - 70C	GUILDFORD - 70C	GUILDFORD - 70C	GUILDFORD - 70C
33020	EASTLEIGH - 71A	EASTLEIGH - 71A	EASTLEIGH - 71A	EASTLEIGH - 71A	EASTLEIGH - 71A	EASTLEIGH - 71A	EASTLEIGH - 71A
33021	EASTLEIGH - 71A	EASTLEIGH - 71A	EASTLEIGH - 71A	EASTLEIGH - 71A	EASTLEIGH - 71A	EASTLEIGH - 71A	EASTLEIGH - 71A
33022	GUILDFORD - 70C	GUILDFORD - 70C	GUILDFORD - 70C	GUILDFORD - 70C	GUILDFORD - 70C	GUILDFORD - 70C	GUILDFORD - 70C
33023	EASTLEIGH - 71A	EASTLEIGH - 71A	EASTLEIGH - 71A	EASTLEIGH - 71A	EASTLEIGH - 71A	EASTLEIGH - 71A	EASTLEIGH - 71A
33024	TONBRIDGE - 74D	TONBRIDGE - 74D	TONBRIDGE - 74D	TONBRIDGE - 74D	TONBRIDGE - 74D	TONBRIDGE - 74D	TONBRIDGE - 74D
33025	EASTLEIGH - 71A	EASTLEIGH - 71A	EASTLEIGH - 71A	NINE ELMS - 70A	GUILDFORD - 70C	GUILDFORD - 70C	GUILDFORD - 70C
33026	FELTHAM - 70B	FELTHAM - 70B	FELTHAM - 70B	FELTHAM - 70B	FELTHAM - 70B	FELTHAM - 70B	FELTHAM - 70B
33027	FELTHAM - 70B	FELTHAM - 70B	FELTHAM - 70B	FELTHAM - 70B	FELTHAM - 70B	FELTHAM - 70B	FELTHAM - 70B
33028	TONBRIDGE - 74D	TONBRIDGE - 74D	TONBRIDGE - 74D	TONBRIDGE - 74D	TONBRIDGE - 74D	TONBRIDGE - 74D	TONBRIDGE - 74D
33029	TONBRIDGE - 74D	TONBRIDGE - 74D	TONBRIDGE - 74D	TONBRIDGE - 74D	TONBRIDGE - 74D	TONBRIDGE - 74D	TONBRIDGE - 74D
33030	TONBRIDGE - 74D	TONBRIDGE - 74D	TONBRIDGE - 74D	TONBRIDGE - 74D	TONBRIDGE - 74D	TONBRIDGE - 74D	TONBRIDGE - 74D
33031	TONBRIDGE - 74D	TONBRIDGE - 74D	TONBRIDGE - 74D	TONBRIDGE - 74D	TONBRIDGE - 74D	TONBRIDGE - 74D	TONBRIDGE - 74D
33032	TONBRIDGE - 74D	TONBRIDGE - 74D	TONBRIDGE - 74D	TONBRIDGE - 74D	TONBRIDGE - 74D	TONBRIDGE - 74D	TONBRIDGE - 74D
33033	TONBRIDGE - 74D	TONBRIDGE - 74D	TONBRIDGE - 74D	TONBRIDGE - 74D	TONBRIDGE - 74D	TONBRIDGE - 74D	TONBRIDGE - 74D
33034	TONBRIDGE - 74D	TONBRIDGE - 74D	TONBRIDGE - 74D	TONBRIDGE - 74D	TONBRIDGE - 74D	TONBRIDGE - 74D	TONBRIDGE - 74D
33035	TONBRIDGE - 74D	TONBRIDGE - 74D	TONBRIDGE - 74D	TONBRIDGE - 74D	TONBRIDGE - 74D	TONBRIDGE - 74D	TONBRIDGE - 74D
33036	TONBRIDGE - 74D	TONBRIDGE - 74D	TONBRIDGE - 74D	TONBRIDGE - 74D	TONBRIDGE - 74D	TONBRIDGE - 74D	TONBRIDGE - 74D
33037	HITHER GREEN - 73C	HITHER GREEN - 73C	BRIGHTON - 75A	BRIGHTON - 75A	BRIGHTON - 75A	HITHER GREEN - 73C	HITHER GREEN - 73C
33038	EASTLEIGH - 71A	EASTLEIGH - 71A	EASTLEIGH - 71A	NORWOOD JCN - 75C	NORWOOD JCN - 75C	STEWARTS LANE - 73A	STEWARTS LANE - 73A
33039	TONBRIDGE - 74D	TONBRIDGE - 74D	TONBRIDGE - 74D	TONBRIDGE - 74D	TONBRIDGE - 74D	TONBRIDGE - 74D	TONBRIDGE - 74D
33040	TONBRIDGE - 74D	TONBRIDGE - 74D	TONBRIDGE - 74D	TONBRIDGE - 74D	TONBRIDGE - 74D	TONBRIDGE - 74D	TONBRIDGE - 74D
				W 2-6-4T (1931)			
31911	HITHER GREEN - 73C	HITHER GREEN - 73C	HITHER GREEN - 73C	HITHER GREEN - 73C	HITHER GREEN - 73C	HITHER GREEN - 73C	HITHER GREEN - 73C
31912	HITHER GREEN - 73C	HITHER GREEN - 73C	HITHER GREEN - 73C	HITHER GREEN - 73C	HITHER GREEN - 73C	HITHER GREEN - 73C	HITHER GREEN - 73C
31913	HITHER GREEN - 73C	HITHER GREEN - 73C	HITHER GREEN - 73C	HITHER GREEN - 73C	HITHER GREEN - 73C	HITHER GREEN - 73C	HITHER GREEN - 73C
31914	STEWARTS LANE - 73A	STEWARTS LANE - 73A	STEWARTS LANE - 73A	STEWARTS LANE - 73A	STEWARTS LANE - 73A	STEWARTS LANE - 73A	STEWARTS LANE - 73A
31915	HITHER GREEN - 73C	HITHER GREEN - 73C	HITHER GREEN - 73C	HITHER GREEN - 73C	HITHER GREEN - 73C	HITHER GREEN - 73C	HITHER GREEN - 73C
31916	HITHER GREEN - 73C	HITHER GREEN - 73C	HITHER GREEN - 73C	HITHER GREEN - 73C	HITHER GREEN - 73C	HITHER GREEN - 73C	HITHER GREEN - 73C
31917	NORWOOD JCN - 75C	NORWOOD JCN - 75C	NORWOOD JCN - 75C	NORWOOD JCN - 75C	NORWOOD JCN - 75C	NORWOOD JCN - 75C	NORWOOD JCN - 75C
31918	NORWOOD JCN - 75C	NORWOOD JCN - 75C	NORWOOD JCN - 75C	NORWOOD JCN - 75C	NORWOOD JCN - 75C	NORWOOD JCN - 75C	NORWOOD JCN - 75C
31919	NORWOOD JCN - 75C	NORWOOD JCN - 75C	NORWOOD JCN - 75C	NORWOOD JCN - 75C	NORWOOD JCN - 75C	NORWOOD JCN - 75C	NORWOOD JCN - 75C
31920	NORWOOD JCN - 75C	NORWOOD JCN - 75C	NORWOOD JCN - 75C	NORWOOD JCN - 75C	NORWOOD JCN - 75C	NORWOOD JCN - 75C	NORWOOD JCN - 75C
31921	HITHER GREEN - 73C	HITHER GREEN - 73C	HITHER GREEN - 73C	HITHER GREEN - 73C	STEWARTS LANE - 73A	STEWARTS LANE - 73A	STEWARTS LANE - 73A
31922	HITHER GREEN - 73C	HITHER GREEN - 73C	HITHER GREEN - 73C	HITHER GREEN - 73C	HITHER GREEN - 73C	HITHER GREEN - 73C	HITHER GREEN - 73C
31923	HITHER GREEN - 73C	HITHER GREEN - 73C	HITHER GREEN - 73C	HITHER GREEN - 73C	HITHER GREEN - 73C	HITHER GREEN - 73C	HITHER GREEN - 73C
31924	HITHER GREEN - 73C	HITHER GREEN - 73C	HITHER GREEN - 73C	HITHER GREEN - 73C	HITHER GREEN - 73C	HITHER GREEN - 73C	HITHER GREEN - 73C
31925	HITHER GREEN - 73C	HITHER GREEN - 73C	HITHER GREEN - 73C	HITHER GREEN - 73C	HITHER GREEN - 73C	HITHER GREEN - 73C	HITHER GREEN - 73C
				Z 0-8-0T (1929)			
30950	BRIGHTON - 75A	BRIGHTON - 75A	BRIGHTON - 75A	BRIGHTON - 75A	BRIGHTON - 75A	TONBRIDGE - 74D	TONBRIDGE - 74D
30951	THREE BRIDGES - 75E	THREE BRIDGES - 75E	THREE BRIDGES - 75E	THREE BRIDGES - 75E	THREE BRIDGES - 75E	THREE BRIDGES - 75E	THREE BRIDGES - 75E
30952	EASTLEIGH - 71A	EASTLEIGH - 71A	EASTLEIGH - 71A	ASHFORD - 74A	ASHFORD - 74A	ASHFORD - 74A	ASHFORD - 74A
30953	ASHFORD - 74A	ASHFORD - 74A	ASHFORD - 74A	ASHFORD - 74A	ASHFORD - 74A	ASHFORD - 74A	TEMPLECOMBE - 71H
30954	EXMOUTH JCN - 72A	EXMOUTH JCN - 72A	EXMOUTH JCN - 72A	EXMOUTH JCN - 72A	EXMOUTH JCN - 72A	EXMOUTH JCN - 72A	EXMOUTH JCN - 72A
30955	EASTLEIGH - 71A	EASTLEIGH - 71A	EASTLEIGH - 71A	EASTLEIGH - 71A	BRIGHTON - 75A	BRIGHTON - 75A	ASHFORD - 74A
30956	EASTLEIGH - 71A	EASTLEIGH - 71A	EASTLEIGH - 71A	EASTLEIGH - 71A	BRIGHTON - 75A	BRIGHTON - 75A	BRIGHTON - 75A
30957	SALISBURY - 72B	SALISBURY - 72B	SALISBURY - 72B	SALISBURY - 72B	SALISBURY - 72B	SALISBURY - 72B	SALISBURY - 72B
				H16 4-6-2T (1921)			
30516	FELTHAM - 70B	FELTHAM - 70B	FELTHAM - 70B	FELTHAM - 70B	FELTHAM - 70B	FELTHAM - 70B	FELTHAM - 70B
30517	FELTHAM - 70B	FELTHAM - 70B	FELTHAM - 70B	FELTHAM - 70B	FELTHAM - 70B	FELTHAM - 70B	FELTHAM - 70B
30518	FELTHAM - 70B	FELTHAM - 70B	FELTHAM - 70B	FELTHAM - 70B	FELTHAM - 70B	FELTHAM - 70B	FELTHAM - 70B
30519	FELTHAM - 70B	FELTHAM - 70B	FELTHAM - 70B	FELTHAM - 70B	FELTHAM - 70B	FELTHAM - 70B	FELTHAM - 70B
30520	FELTHAM - 70B	FELTHAM - 70B	FELTHAM - 70B	FELTHAM - 70B	FELTHAM - 70B	FELTHAM - 70B	FELTHAM - 70B

loco	Feb-55	Apr-55	Jun-55	Aug-55	Sep-55	Nov-55	Dec-55
				Q 0-6-0 (1938)			
30530	EASTLEIGH - 71A	EASTLEIGH - 71A	EASTLEIGH - 71A	EASTLEIGH - 71A	EASTLEIGH - 71A	EASTLEIGH - 71A	EASTLEIGH - 71A
30531	EASTLEIGH - 71A	EASTLEIGH - 71A	EASTLEIGH - 71A	EASTLEIGH - 71A	EASTLEIGH - 71A	EASTLEIGH - 71A	EASTLEIGH - 71A
30532	EASTLEIGH - 71A	EASTLEIGH - 71A	EASTLEIGH - 71A	EASTLEIGH - 71A	EASTLEIGH - 71A	EASTLEIGH - 71A	EASTLEIGH - 71A
30533	NORWOOD JCN - 75C	NORWOOD JCN - 75C	NORWOOD JCN - 75C	NORWOOD JCN - 75C	NORWOOD JCN - 75C	NORWOOD JCN - 75C	NORWOOD JCN - 75C
30534	NORWOOD JCN - 75C	NORWOOD JCN - 75C	NORWOOD JCN - 75C	NORWOOD JCN - 75C	NORWOOD JCN - 75C	NORWOOD JCN - 75C	NORWOOD JCN - 75C
30535	EASTLEIGH - 71A	EASTLEIGH - 71A	EASTLEIGH - 71A	EASTLEIGH - 71A	EASTLEIGH - 71A	EASTLEIGH - 71A	EASTLEIGH - 71A
30536	EASTLEIGH - 71A	EASTLEIGH - 71A	EASTLEIGH - 71A	EASTLEIGH - 71A	EASTLEIGH - 71A	EASTLEIGH - 71A	EASTLEIGH - 71A
30537	NORWOOD JCN - 75C	NORWOOD JCN - 75C	NORWOOD JCN - 75C	NORWOOD JCN - 75C	NORWOOD JCN - 75C	NORWOOD JCN - 75C	NORWOOD JCN - 75C
30538	NORWOOD JCN - 75C	NORWOOD JCN - 75C	NORWOOD JCN - 75C	NORWOOD JCN - 75C	NORWOOD JCN - 75C	NORWOOD JCN - 75C	NORWOOD JCN - 75C
30539	NORWOOD JCN - 75C	NORWOOD JCN - 75C	NORWOOD JCN - 75C	NORWOOD JCN - 75C	BOURNEMOUTH - 71B	BOURNEMOUTH - 71B	BOURNEMOUTH - 71B
30540	THREE BRIDGES - 75E	THREE BRIDGES - 75E	THREE BRIDGES - 75E	THREE BRIDGES - 75E	THREE BRIDGES - 75E	THREE BRIDGES - 75E	THREE BRIDGES - 75E
30541	BOURNEMOUTH - 71B	BOURNEMOUTH - 71B	BOURNEMOUTH - 71B	BOURNEMOUTH - 71B	BOURNEMOUTH - 71B	BOURNEMOUTH - 71B	BOURNEMOUTH - 71B
30542	EASTLEIGH - 71A	EASTLEIGH - 71A	EASTLEIGH - 71A	EASTLEIGH - 71A	EASTLEIGH - 71A	EASTLEIGH - 71A	EASTLEIGH - 71A
30543	EASTLEIGH - 71A	EASTLEIGH - 71A	EASTLEIGH - 71A	EASTLEIGH - 71A	EASTLEIGH - 71A	EASTLEIGH - 71A	EASTLEIGH - 71A
30544	HORSHAM - 75D	HORSHAM - 75D	HORSHAM - 75D	HORSHAM - 75D	HORSHAM - 75D	HORSHAM - 75D	HORSHAM - 75D
30545	HORSHAM - 75D	HORSHAM - 75D	HORSHAM - 75D	HORSHAM - 75D	HORSHAM - 75D	HORSHAM - 75D	HORSHAM - 75D
30546	HORSHAM - 75D	HORSHAM - 75D	HORSHAM - 75D	HORSHAM - 75D	HORSHAM - 75D	HORSHAM - 75D	HORSHAM - 75D
30547	NORWOOD JCN - 75C	NORWOOD JCN - 75C	NORWOOD JCN - 75C	NORWOOD JCN - 75C	HORSHAM - 75D	HORSHAM - 75D	HORSHAM - 75D
30548	BOURNEMOUTH - 71B	BOURNEMOUTH - 71B	BOURNEMOUTH - 71B	BOURNEMOUTH - 71B	BOURNEMOUTH - 71B	BOURNEMOUTH - 71B	BOURNEMOUTH - 71B
30549	BOURNEMOUTH - 71B	BOURNEMOUTH - 71B	BOURNEMOUTH - 71B	BOURNEMOUTH - 71B	NORWOOD JCN - 75C	NORWOOD JCN - 75C	NORWOOD JCN - 75C
				Q1 0-6-0 (1942)			
33001	GUILDFORD - 70C	GUILDFORD - 70C	GUILDFORD - 70C	GUILDFORD - 70C	GUILDFORD - 70C	GUILDFORD - 70C	GUILDFORD - 70C
33002	GUILDFORD - 70C	GUILDFORD - 70C	GUILDFORD - 70C	GUILDFORD - 70C	GUILDFORD - 70C	GUILDFORD - 70C	GUILDFORD - 70C
33003	GUILDFORD - 70C	GUILDFORD - 70C	GUILDFORD - 70C	GUILDFORD - 70C	GUILDFORD - 70C	GUILDFORD - 70C	GUILDFORD - 70C
33004	FAVERSHAM - 73E	FAVERSHAM - 73E	FAVERSHAM - 73E	FAVERSHAM - 73E	FAVERSHAM - 73E	FAVERSHAM - 73E	FAVERSHAM - 73E
33005	GUILDFORD - 70C	GUILDFORD - 70C	GUILDFORD - 70C	GUILDFORD - 70C	GUILDFORD - 70C	GUILDFORD - 70C	GUILDFORD - 70C
33006	FELTHAM - 70B	FELTHAM - 70B	FELTHAM - 70B	FELTHAM - 70B	FELTHAM - 70B	FELTHAM - 70B	FELTHAM - 70B
33007	FELTHAM - 70B	FELTHAM - 70B	FELTHAM - 70B	FELTHAM - 70B	FELTHAM - 70B	FELTHAM - 70B	FELTHAM - 70B
33008	FELTHAM - 70B	FELTHAM - 70B	FELTHAM - 70B	FELTHAM - 70B	FELTHAM - 70B	FELTHAM - 70B	FELTHAM - 70B
33009	FELTHAM - 70B	FELTHAM - 70B	FELTHAM - 70B	FELTHAM - 70B	FELTHAM - 70B	FELTHAM - 70B	FELTHAM - 70B
33010	FELTHAM - 70B	FELTHAM - 70B	FELTHAM - 70B	FELTHAM - 70B	FELTHAM - 70B	FELTHAM - 70B	FELTHAM - 70B
33011	FELTHAM - 70B	FELTHAM - 70B	FELTHAM - 70B	FELTHAM - 70B	FELTHAM - 70B	FELTHAM - 70B	FELTHAM - 70B
33012	FELTHAM - 70B	FELTHAM - 70B	FELTHAM - 70B	FELTHAM - 70B	FELTHAM - 70B	FELTHAM - 70B	FELTHAM - 70B
33013	FELTHAM - 70B	FELTHAM - 70B	FELTHAM - 70B	FELTHAM - 70B	FELTHAM - 70B	FELTHAM - 70B	FELTHAM - 70B
33014	HITHER GREEN - 73C	HITHER GREEN - 73C	HITHER GREEN - 73C	HITHER GREEN - 73C	HITHER GREEN - 73C	HITHER GREEN - 73C	HITHER GREEN - 73C
33015	NINE ELMS - 70A	NINE ELMS - 70A	NINE ELMS - 70A	NINE ELMS - 70A	NINE ELMS - 70A	NINE ELMS - 70A	NINE ELMS - 70A
33016	FELTHAM - 70B	FELTHAM - 70B	FELTHAM - 70B	FELTHAM - 70B	FELTHAM - 70B	FELTHAM - 70B	FELTHAM - 70B
33017	NINE ELMS - 70A	NINE ELMS - 70A	NINE ELMS - 70A	NINE ELMS - 70A	NINE ELMS - 70A	NINE ELMS - 70A	NINE ELMS - 70A
33018	FELTHAM - 70B	FELTHAM - 70B	FELTHAM - 70B	FELTHAM - 70B	FELTHAM - 70B	FELTHAM - 70B	FELTHAM - 70B
33019	GUILDFORD - 70C	GUILDFORD - 70C	GUILDFORD - 70C	GUILDFORD - 70C	GUILDFORD - 70C	GUILDFORD - 70C	GUILDFORD - 70C
33020	EASTLEIGH - 71A	EASTLEIGH - 71A	EASTLEIGH - 71A	EASTLEIGH - 71A	EASTLEIGH - 71A	EASTLEIGH - 71A	EASTLEIGH - 71A
33021	EASTLEIGH - 71A	EASTLEIGH - 71A	EASTLEIGH - 71A	EASTLEIGH - 71A	EASTLEIGH - 71A	EASTLEIGH - 71A	EASTLEIGH - 71A
33022	GUILDFORD - 70C	GUILDFORD - 70C	GUILDFORD - 70C	GUILDFORD - 70C	GUILDFORD - 70C	GUILDFORD - 70C	GUILDFORD - 70C
33023	EASTLEIGH - 71A	EASTLEIGH - 71A	EASTLEIGH - 71A	EASTLEIGH - 71A	EASTLEIGH - 71A	EASTLEIGH - 71A	EASTLEIGH - 71A
33024	TONBRIDGE - 74D	TONBRIDGE - 74D	TONBRIDGE - 74D	TONBRIDGE - 74D	TONBRIDGE - 74D	TONBRIDGE - 74D	TONBRIDGE - 74D
33025	GUILDFORD - 70C	GUILDFORD - 70C	GUILDFORD - 70C	GUILDFORD - 70C	GUILDFORD - 70C	GUILDFORD - 70C	GUILDFORD - 70C
33026	FELTHAM - 70B	FELTHAM - 70B	FELTHAM - 70B	FELTHAM - 70B	FELTHAM - 70B	FELTHAM - 70B	FELTHAM - 70B
33027	FELTHAM - 70B	FELTHAM - 70B	FELTHAM - 70B	FELTHAM - 70B	FELTHAM - 70B	FELTHAM - 70B	FELTHAM - 70B
33028	TONBRIDGE - 74D	TONBRIDGE - 74D	TONBRIDGE - 74D	TONBRIDGE - 74D	TONBRIDGE - 74D	TONBRIDGE - 74D	TONBRIDGE - 74D
33029	TONBRIDGE - 74D	TONBRIDGE - 74D	TONBRIDGE - 74D	TONBRIDGE - 74D	TONBRIDGE - 74D	TONBRIDGE - 74D	TONBRIDGE - 74D
33030	TONBRIDGE - 74D	TONBRIDGE - 74D	TONBRIDGE - 74D	TONBRIDGE - 74D	TONBRIDGE - 74D	TONBRIDGE - 74D	TONBRIDGE - 74D
33031	TONBRIDGE - 74D	TONBRIDGE - 74D	TONBRIDGE - 74D	TONBRIDGE - 74D	TONBRIDGE - 74D	TONBRIDGE - 74D	TONBRIDGE - 74D
33032	TONBRIDGE - 74D	TONBRIDGE - 74D	TONBRIDGE - 74D	TONBRIDGE - 74D	TONBRIDGE - 74D	TONBRIDGE - 74D	TONBRIDGE - 74D
33033	TONBRIDGE - 74D	TONBRIDGE - 74D	TONBRIDGE - 74D	TONBRIDGE - 74D	TONBRIDGE - 74D	TONBRIDGE - 74D	TONBRIDGE - 74D
33034	TONBRIDGE - 74D	TONBRIDGE - 74D	TONBRIDGE - 74D	TONBRIDGE - 74D	TONBRIDGE - 74D	TONBRIDGE - 74D	TONBRIDGE - 74D
33035	TONBRIDGE - 74D	TONBRIDGE - 74D	TONBRIDGE - 74D	TONBRIDGE - 74D	TONBRIDGE - 74D	TONBRIDGE - 74D	TONBRIDGE - 74D
33036	TONBRIDGE - 74D	TONBRIDGE - 74D	TONBRIDGE - 74D	TONBRIDGE - 74D	TONBRIDGE - 74D	TONBRIDGE - 74D	TONBRIDGE - 74D
33037	HITHER GREEN - 73C	HITHER GREEN - 73C	HITHER GREEN - 73C	HITHER GREEN - 73C	HITHER GREEN - 73C	HITHER GREEN - 73C	HITHER GREEN - 73C
33038	NINE ELMS - 70A	NINE ELMS - 70A	NINE ELMS - 70A	NINE ELMS - 70A	NINE ELMS - 70A	NINE ELMS - 70A	NINE ELMS - 70A
33039	TONBRIDGE - 74D	TONBRIDGE - 74D	TONBRIDGE - 74D	TONBRIDGE - 74D	TONBRIDGE - 74D	TONBRIDGE - 74D	TONBRIDGE - 74D
33040	TONBRIDGE - 74D	TONBRIDGE - 74D	TONBRIDGE - 74D	TONBRIDGE - 74D	TONBRIDGE - 74D	TONBRIDGE - 74D	TONBRIDGE - 74D
				W 2-6-4T (1931)			
31911	HITHER GREEN - 73C	HITHER GREEN - 73C	HITHER GREEN - 73C	HITHER GREEN - 73C	HITHER GREEN - 73C	HITHER GREEN - 73C	HITHER GREEN - 73C
31912	HITHER GREEN - 73C	HITHER GREEN - 73C	HITHER GREEN - 73C	HITHER GREEN - 73C	HITHER GREEN - 73C	HITHER GREEN - 73C	HITHER GREEN - 73C
31913	HITHER GREEN - 73C	HITHER GREEN - 73C	HITHER GREEN - 73C	HITHER GREEN - 73C	HITHER GREEN - 73C	HITHER GREEN - 73C	HITHER GREEN - 73C
31914	STEWARTS LANE - 73A	STEWARTS LANE - 73A	STEWARTS LANE - 73A	STEWARTS LANE - 73A	STEWARTS LANE - 73A	STEWARTS LANE - 73A	STEWARTS LANE - 73A
31915	HITHER GREEN - 73C	HITHER GREEN - 73C	HITHER GREEN - 73C	HITHER GREEN - 73C	HITHER GREEN - 73C	HITHER GREEN - 73C	HITHER GREEN - 73C
31916	HITHER GREEN - 73C	HITHER GREEN - 73C	HITHER GREEN - 73C	HITHER GREEN - 73C	HITHER GREEN - 73C	HITHER GREEN - 73C	HITHER GREEN - 73C
31917	NORWOOD JCN - 75C	NORWOOD JCN - 75C	NORWOOD JCN - 75C	NORWOOD JCN - 75C	NORWOOD JCN - 75C	NORWOOD JCN - 75C	NORWOOD JCN - 75C
31918	NORWOOD JCN - 75C	NORWOOD JCN - 75C	NORWOOD JCN - 75C	NORWOOD JCN - 75C	NORWOOD JCN - 75C	NORWOOD JCN - 75C	NORWOOD JCN - 75C
31919	NORWOOD JCN - 75C	NORWOOD JCN - 75C	NORWOOD JCN - 75C	NORWOOD JCN - 75C	NORWOOD JCN - 75C	NORWOOD JCN - 75C	NORWOOD JCN - 75C
31920	NORWOOD JCN - 75C	NORWOOD JCN - 75C	NORWOOD JCN - 75C	NORWOOD JCN - 75C	NORWOOD JCN - 75C	NORWOOD JCN - 75C	NORWOOD JCN - 75C
31921	STEWARTS LANE - 73A	STEWARTS LANE - 73A	STEWARTS LANE - 73A	STEWARTS LANE - 73A	STEWARTS LANE - 73A	STEWARTS LANE - 73A	STEWARTS LANE - 73A
31922	HITHER GREEN - 73C	HITHER GREEN - 73C	HITHER GREEN - 73C	HITHER GREEN - 73C	HITHER GREEN - 73C	HITHER GREEN - 73C	HITHER GREEN - 73C
31923	HITHER GREEN - 73C	HITHER GREEN - 73C	HITHER GREEN - 73C	HITHER GREEN - 73C	HITHER GREEN - 73C	HITHER GREEN - 73C	HITHER GREEN - 73C
31924	HITHER GREEN - 73C	HITHER GREEN - 73C	HITHER GREEN - 73C	HITHER GREEN - 73C	HITHER GREEN - 73C	HITHER GREEN - 73C	HITHER GREEN - 73C
31925	HITHER GREEN - 73C	HITHER GREEN - 73C	HITHER GREEN - 73C	HITHER GREEN - 73C	HITHER GREEN - 73C	HITHER GREEN - 73C	HITHER GREEN - 73C
				Z 0-8-0T (1929)			
30950	TONBRIDGE - 74D	TONBRIDGE - 74D	TONBRIDGE - 74D	TONBRIDGE - 74D	TONBRIDGE - 74D	ASHFORD - 74A	ASHFORD - 74A
30951	THREE BRIDGES - 75E	THREE BRIDGES - 75E	THREE BRIDGES - 75E	THREE BRIDGES - 75E	THREE BRIDGES - 75E	ASHFORD - 74A	ASHFORD - 74A
30952	ASHFORD - 74A	ASHFORD - 74A	ASHFORD - 74A	ASHFORD - 74A	ASHFORD - 74A	ASHFORD - 74A	ASHFORD - 74A
30953	TEMPLECOMBE - 71H	TEMPLECOMBE - 71H	TEMPLECOMBE - 71H	TEMPLECOMBE - 71H	TEMPLECOMBE - 71H	TEMPLECOMBE - 71H	TEMPLECOMBE - 71H
30954	EXMOUTH JCN - 72A	EXMOUTH JCN - 72A	EXMOUTH JCN - 72A	EXMOUTH JCN - 72A	EXMOUTH JCN - 72A	EXMOUTH JCN - 72A	EXMOUTH JCN - 72A
30955	ASHFORD - 74A	ASHFORD - 74A	ASHFORD - 74A	ASHFORD - 74A	ASHFORD - 74A	ASHFORD - 74A	ASHFORD - 74A
30956	BRIGHTON - 75A	BRIGHTON - 75A	BRIGHTON - 75A	EXMOUTH JCN - 72A	SALISBURY - 72B	SALISBURY - 72B	SALISBURY - 72B
30957	SALISBURY - 72B	SALISBURY - 72B	SALISBURY - 72B	SALISBURY - 72B	SALISBURY - 72B	SALISBURY - 72B	SALISBURY - 72B
				H16 4-6-2T (1921)			
30516	FELTHAM - 70B	FELTHAM - 70B	FELTHAM - 70B	FELTHAM - 70B	FELTHAM - 70B	FELTHAM - 70B	FELTHAM - 70B
30517	FELTHAM - 70B	FELTHAM - 70B	FELTHAM - 70B	FELTHAM - 70B	FELTHAM - 70B	FELTHAM - 70B	FELTHAM - 70B
30518	FELTHAM - 70B	FELTHAM - 70B	FELTHAM - 70B	FELTHAM - 70B	FELTHAM - 70B	FELTHAM - 70B	FELTHAM - 70B
30519	FELTHAM - 70B	FELTHAM - 70B	FELTHAM - 70B	FELTHAM - 70B	FELTHAM - 70B	FELTHAM - 70B	FELTHAM - 70B
30520	FELTHAM - 70B	FELTHAM - 70B	FELTHAM - 70B	FELTHAM - 70B	FELTHAM - 70B	FELTHAM - 70B	FELTHAM - 70B

loco	Jan-56	Apr-56	May-56	Aug-56	Oct-56	Nov-56	Jan-57
			Q 0-6-0 (1938)				
30530	EASTLEIGH - 71A	EASTLEIGH - 71A	EASTLEIGH - 71A	EASTLEIGH - 71A	EASTLEIGH - 71A	EASTLEIGH - 71A	EASTLEIGH - 71A
30531	EASTLEIGH - 71A	EASTLEIGH - 71A	EASTLEIGH - 71A	EASTLEIGH - 71A	EASTLEIGH - 71A	EASTLEIGH - 71A	EASTLEIGH - 71A
30532	EASTLEIGH - 71A	EASTLEIGH - 71A	EASTLEIGH - 71A	EASTLEIGH - 71A	EASTLEIGH - 71A	EASTLEIGH - 71A	EASTLEIGH - 71A
30533	NORWOOD JCN - 75C	NORWOOD JCN - 75C	NORWOOD JCN - 75C	NORWOOD JCN - 75C	NORWOOD JCN - 75C	NORWOOD JCN - 75C	NORWOOD JCN - 75C
30534	NORWOOD JCN - 75C	NORWOOD JCN - 75C	NORWOOD JCN - 75C	NORWOOD JCN - 75C	NORWOOD JCN - 75C	NORWOOD JCN - 75C	NORWOOD JCN - 75C
30535	EASTLEIGH - 71A	EASTLEIGH - 71A	EASTLEIGH - 71A	EASTLEIGH - 71A	EASTLEIGH - 71A	EASTLEIGH - 71A	EASTLEIGH - 71A
30536	EASTLEIGH - 71A	EASTLEIGH - 71A	EASTLEIGH - 71A	EASTLEIGH - 71A	EASTLEIGH - 71A	EASTLEIGH - 71A	EASTLEIGH - 71A
30537	NORWOOD JCN - 75C	NORWOOD JCN - 75C	NORWOOD JCN - 75C	NORWOOD JCN - 75C	NORWOOD JCN - 75C	NORWOOD JCN - 75C	NORWOOD JCN - 75C
30538	NORWOOD JCN - 75C	NORWOOD JCN - 75C	NORWOOD JCN - 75C	NORWOOD JCN - 75C	NORWOOD JCN - 75C	NORWOOD JCN - 75C	NORWOOD JCN - 75C
30539	BOURNEMOUTH - 71B	BOURNEMOUTH - 71B	BOURNEMOUTH - 71B	BOURNEMOUTH - 71B	BOURNEMOUTH - 71B	BOURNEMOUTH - 71B	BOURNEMOUTH - 71B
30540	THREE BRIDGES - 75E	THREE BRIDGES - 75E	THREE BRIDGES - 75E	THREE BRIDGES - 75E	THREE BRIDGES - 75E	THREE BRIDGES - 75E	THREE BRIDGES - 75E
30541	BOURNEMOUTH - 71B	BOURNEMOUTH - 71B	BOURNEMOUTH - 71B	BOURNEMOUTH - 71B	BOURNEMOUTH - 71B	BOURNEMOUTH - 71B	BOURNEMOUTH - 71B
30542	EASTLEIGH - 71A	EASTLEIGH - 71A	EASTLEIGH - 71A	EASTLEIGH - 71A	EASTLEIGH - 71A	EASTLEIGH - 71A	EASTLEIGH - 71A
30543	EASTLEIGH - 71A	EASTLEIGH - 71A	EASTLEIGH - 71A	EASTLEIGH - 71A	EASTLEIGH - 71A	EASTLEIGH - 71A	EASTLEIGH - 71A
30544	HORSHAM - 75D	HORSHAM - 75D	HORSHAM - 75D	HORSHAM - 75D	HORSHAM - 75D	HORSHAM - 75D	HORSHAM - 75D
30545	HORSHAM - 75D	HORSHAM - 75D	HORSHAM - 75D	HORSHAM - 75D	HORSHAM - 75D	HORSHAM - 75D	HORSHAM - 75D
30546	HORSHAM - 75D	HORSHAM - 75D	HORSHAM - 75D	HORSHAM - 75D	HORSHAM - 75D	HORSHAM - 75D	HORSHAM - 75D
30547	HORSHAM - 75D	HORSHAM - 75D	HORSHAM - 75D	HORSHAM - 75D	HORSHAM - 75D	HORSHAM - 75D	HORSHAM - 75D
30548	BOURNEMOUTH - 71B	BOURNEMOUTH - 71B	BOURNEMOUTH - 71B	BOURNEMOUTH - 71B	BOURNEMOUTH - 71B	BOURNEMOUTH - 71B	BOURNEMOUTH - 71B
30549	NORWOOD JCN - 75C	NORWOOD JCN - 75C	NORWOOD JCN - 75C	NORWOOD JCN - 75C	NORWOOD JCN - 75C	NORWOOD JCN - 75C	NORWOOD JCN - 75C
			Q1 0-6-0 (1942)				
33001	GUILDFORD - 70C	GUILDFORD - 70C	GUILDFORD - 70C	GUILDFORD - 70C	GUILDFORD - 70C	GUILDFORD - 70C	GUILDFORD - 70C
33002	GUILDFORD - 70C	GUILDFORD - 70C	GUILDFORD - 70C	GUILDFORD - 70C	GUILDFORD - 70C	GUILDFORD - 70C	GUILDFORD - 70C
33003	GUILDFORD - 70C	GUILDFORD - 70C	GUILDFORD - 70C	GUILDFORD - 70C	GUILDFORD - 70C	GUILDFORD - 70C	GUILDFORD - 70C
33004	FAVERSHAM - 73E	FAVERSHAM - 73E	FAVERSHAM - 73E	FAVERSHAM - 73E	FAVERSHAM - 73E	FAVERSHAM - 73E	FAVERSHAM - 73E
33005	GUILDFORD - 70C	GUILDFORD - 70C	GUILDFORD - 70C	GUILDFORD - 70C	GUILDFORD - 70C	GUILDFORD - 70C	GUILDFORD - 70C
33006	FELTHAM - 70B	FELTHAM - 70B	FELTHAM - 70B	FELTHAM - 70B	FELTHAM - 70B	FELTHAM - 70B	FELTHAM - 70B
33007	FELTHAM - 70B	FELTHAM - 70B	FELTHAM - 70B	FELTHAM - 70B	FELTHAM - 70B	FELTHAM - 70B	FELTHAM - 70B
33008	FELTHAM - 70B	FELTHAM - 70B	FELTHAM - 70B	FELTHAM - 70B	FELTHAM - 70B	FELTHAM - 70B	FELTHAM - 70B
33009	FELTHAM - 70B	FELTHAM - 70B	FELTHAM - 70B	FELTHAM - 70B	FELTHAM - 70B	FELTHAM - 70B	FELTHAM - 70B
33010	FELTHAM - 70B	FELTHAM - 70B	FELTHAM - 70B	FELTHAM - 70B	FELTHAM - 70B	FELTHAM - 70B	FELTHAM - 70B
33011	FELTHAM - 70B	FELTHAM - 70B	FELTHAM - 70B	FELTHAM - 70B	FELTHAM - 70B	FELTHAM - 70B	FELTHAM - 70B
33012	FELTHAM - 70B	FELTHAM - 70B	FELTHAM - 70B	FELTHAM - 70B	FELTHAM - 70B	FELTHAM - 70B	FELTHAM - 70B
33013	FELTHAM - 70B	FELTHAM - 70B	FELTHAM - 70B	FELTHAM - 70B	FELTHAM - 70B	FELTHAM - 70B	FELTHAM - 70B
33014	HITHER GREEN - 73C	HITHER GREEN - 73C	HITHER GREEN - 73C	HITHER GREEN - 73C	HITHER GREEN - 73C	HITHER GREEN - 73C	HITHER GREEN - 73C
33015	NINE ELMS - 70A	NINE ELMS - 70A	NINE ELMS - 70A	NINE ELMS - 70A	NINE ELMS - 70A	NINE ELMS - 70A	NINE ELMS - 70A
33016	FELTHAM - 70B	FELTHAM - 70B	FELTHAM - 70B	FELTHAM - 70B	FELTHAM - 70B	FELTHAM - 70B	FELTHAM - 70B
33017	NINE ELMS - 70A	NINE ELMS - 70A	NINE ELMS - 70A	NINE ELMS - 70A	NINE ELMS - 70A	NINE ELMS - 70A	NINE ELMS - 70A
33018	FELTHAM - 70B	FELTHAM - 70B	FELTHAM - 70B	FELTHAM - 70B	FELTHAM - 70B	FELTHAM - 70B	FELTHAM - 70B
33019	GUILDFORD - 70C	GUILDFORD - 70C	GUILDFORD - 70C	GUILDFORD - 70C	GUILDFORD - 70C	GUILDFORD - 70C	GUILDFORD - 70C
33020	EASTLEIGH - 71A	EASTLEIGH - 71A	EASTLEIGH - 71A	EASTLEIGH - 71A	EASTLEIGH - 71A	EASTLEIGH - 71A	EASTLEIGH - 71A
33021	EASTLEIGH - 71A	EASTLEIGH - 71A	EASTLEIGH - 71A	EASTLEIGH - 71A	EASTLEIGH - 71A	EASTLEIGH - 71A	EASTLEIGH - 71A
33022	GUILDFORD - 70C	GUILDFORD - 70C	GUILDFORD - 70C	GUILDFORD - 70C	GUILDFORD - 70C	GUILDFORD - 70C	GUILDFORD - 70C
33023	EASTLEIGH - 71A	EASTLEIGH - 71A	EASTLEIGH - 71A	EASTLEIGH - 71A	EASTLEIGH - 71A	EASTLEIGH - 71A	EASTLEIGH - 71A
33024	TONBRIDGE - 74D	TONBRIDGE - 74D	TONBRIDGE - 74D	TONBRIDGE - 74D	TONBRIDGE - 74D	TONBRIDGE - 74D	TONBRIDGE - 74D
33025	GUILDFORD - 70C	GUILDFORD - 70C	GUILDFORD - 70C	GUILDFORD - 70C	GUILDFORD - 70C	GUILDFORD - 70C	GUILDFORD - 70C
33026	FELTHAM - 70B	FELTHAM - 70B	FELTHAM - 70B	FELTHAM - 70B	FELTHAM - 70B	FELTHAM - 70B	FELTHAM - 70B
33027	FELTHAM - 70B	FELTHAM - 70B	FELTHAM - 70B	FELTHAM - 70B	FELTHAM - 70B	FELTHAM - 70B	FELTHAM - 70B
33028	TONBRIDGE - 74D	TONBRIDGE - 74D	TONBRIDGE - 74D	TONBRIDGE - 74D	TONBRIDGE - 74D	TONBRIDGE - 74D	TONBRIDGE - 74D
33029	TONBRIDGE - 74D	TONBRIDGE - 74D	TONBRIDGE - 74D	TONBRIDGE - 74D	TONBRIDGE - 74D	TONBRIDGE - 74D	TONBRIDGE - 74D
33030	TONBRIDGE - 74D	TONBRIDGE - 74D	TONBRIDGE - 74D	TONBRIDGE - 74D	TONBRIDGE - 74D	TONBRIDGE - 74D	TONBRIDGE - 74D
33031	TONBRIDGE - 74D	TONBRIDGE - 74D	TONBRIDGE - 74D	TONBRIDGE - 74D	TONBRIDGE - 74D	TONBRIDGE - 74D	TONBRIDGE - 74D
33032	TONBRIDGE - 74D	TONBRIDGE - 74D	TONBRIDGE - 74D	TONBRIDGE - 74D	TONBRIDGE - 74D	TONBRIDGE - 74D	TONBRIDGE - 74D
33033	TONBRIDGE - 74D	TONBRIDGE - 74D	TONBRIDGE - 74D	TONBRIDGE - 74D	TONBRIDGE - 74D	TONBRIDGE - 74D	TONBRIDGE - 74D
33034	TONBRIDGE - 74D	TONBRIDGE - 74D	TONBRIDGE - 74D	TONBRIDGE - 74D	TONBRIDGE - 74D	TONBRIDGE - 74D	TONBRIDGE - 74D
33035	TONBRIDGE - 74D	TONBRIDGE - 74D	TONBRIDGE - 74D	TONBRIDGE - 74D	TONBRIDGE - 74D	TONBRIDGE - 74D	TONBRIDGE - 74D
33036	TONBRIDGE - 74D	TONBRIDGE - 74D	TONBRIDGE - 74D	TONBRIDGE - 74D	TONBRIDGE - 74D	TONBRIDGE - 74D	TONBRIDGE - 74D
33037	HITHER GREEN - 73C	HITHER GREEN - 73C	HITHER GREEN - 73C	HITHER GREEN - 73C	HITHER GREEN - 73C	HITHER GREEN - 73C	HITHER GREEN - 73C
33038	NINE ELMS - 70A	NINE ELMS - 70A	NINE ELMS - 70A	NINE ELMS - 70A	NINE ELMS - 70A	NINE ELMS - 70A	NINE ELMS - 70A
33039	TONBRIDGE - 74D	TONBRIDGE - 74D	TONBRIDGE - 74D	TONBRIDGE - 74D	TONBRIDGE - 74D	TONBRIDGE - 74D	TONBRIDGE - 74D
33040	TONBRIDGE - 74D	TONBRIDGE - 74D	TONBRIDGE - 74D	TONBRIDGE - 74D	TONBRIDGE - 74D	TONBRIDGE - 74D	TONBRIDGE - 74D
			W 2-6-4T (1931)				
31911	HITHER GREEN - 73C	HITHER GREEN - 73C	HITHER GREEN - 73C	HITHER GREEN - 73C	HITHER GREEN - 73C	HITHER GREEN - 73C	HITHER GREEN - 73C
31912	HITHER GREEN - 73C	HITHER GREEN - 73C	HITHER GREEN - 73C	HITHER GREEN - 73C	HITHER GREEN - 73C	HITHER GREEN - 73C	HITHER GREEN - 73C
31913	HITHER GREEN - 73C	HITHER GREEN - 73C	HITHER GREEN - 73C	HITHER GREEN - 73C	HITHER GREEN - 73C	HITHER GREEN - 73C	HITHER GREEN - 73C
31914	STEWARTS LANE - 73A	STEWARTS LANE - 73A	STEWARTS LANE - 73A	STEWARTS LANE - 73A	STEWARTS LANE - 73A	STEWARTS LANE - 73A	STEWARTS LANE - 73A
31915	HITHER GREEN - 73C	HITHER GREEN - 73C	HITHER GREEN - 73C	HITHER GREEN - 73C	HITHER GREEN - 73C	HITHER GREEN - 73C	HITHER GREEN - 73C
31916	HITHER GREEN - 73C	HITHER GREEN - 73C	HITHER GREEN - 73C	HITHER GREEN - 73C	HITHER GREEN - 73C	HITHER GREEN - 73C	HITHER GREEN - 73C
31917	NORWOOD JCN - 75C	NORWOOD JCN - 75C	NORWOOD JCN - 75C	NORWOOD JCN - 75C	NORWOOD JCN - 75C	NORWOOD JCN - 75C	NORWOOD JCN - 75C
31918	NORWOOD JCN - 75C	NORWOOD JCN - 75C	NORWOOD JCN - 75C	NORWOOD JCN - 75C	NORWOOD JCN - 75C	NORWOOD JCN - 75C	NORWOOD JCN - 75C
31919	NORWOOD JCN - 75C	NORWOOD JCN - 75C	NORWOOD JCN - 75C	NORWOOD JCN - 75C	NORWOOD JCN - 75C	NORWOOD JCN - 75C	NORWOOD JCN - 75C
31920	NORWOOD JCN - 75C	NORWOOD JCN - 75C	NORWOOD JCN - 75C	NORWOOD JCN - 75C	NORWOOD JCN - 75C	NORWOOD JCN - 75C	NORWOOD JCN - 75C
31921	STEWARTS LANE - 73A	STEWARTS LANE - 73A	STEWARTS LANE - 73A	STEWARTS LANE - 73A	STEWARTS LANE - 73A	STEWARTS LANE - 73A	STEWARTS LANE - 73A
31922	HITHER GREEN - 73C	HITHER GREEN - 73C	HITHER GREEN - 73C	HITHER GREEN - 73C	HITHER GREEN - 73C	HITHER GREEN - 73C	HITHER GREEN - 73C
31923	HITHER GREEN - 73C	HITHER GREEN - 73C	HITHER GREEN - 73C	HITHER GREEN - 73C	HITHER GREEN - 73C	HITHER GREEN - 73C	HITHER GREEN - 73C
31924	HITHER GREEN - 73C	HITHER GREEN - 73C	HITHER GREEN - 73C	HITHER GREEN - 73C	HITHER GREEN - 73C	HITHER GREEN - 73C	HITHER GREEN - 73C
31925	HITHER GREEN - 73C	HITHER GREEN - 73C	HITHER GREEN - 73C	HITHER GREEN - 73C	HITHER GREEN - 73C	HITHER GREEN - 73C	HITHER GREEN - 73C
			Z 0-8-0T (1929)				
30950	ASHFORD - 74A	EXMOUTH JCN - 72A	EXMOUTH JCN - 72A	EXMOUTH JCN - 72A	EXMOUTH JCN - 72A	EXMOUTH JCN - 72A	EXMOUTH JCN - 72A
30951	ASHFORD - 74A	ASHFORD - 74A	ASHFORD - 74A	ASHFORD - 74A	ASHFORD - 74A	ASHFORD - 74A	ASHFORD - 74A
30952	ASHFORD - 74A	ASHFORD - 74A	ASHFORD - 74A	ASHFORD - 74A	ASHFORD - 74A	ASHFORD - 74A	ASHFORD - 74A
30953	TEMPLECOMBE - 71H	TEMPLECOMBE - 71H	TEMPLECOMBE - 71H	TEMPLECOMBE - 71H	TEMPLECOMBE - 71H	TEMPLECOMBE - 71H	TEMPLECOMBE - 71H
30954	EXMOUTH JCN - 72A	EXMOUTH JCN - 72A	EXMOUTH JCN - 72A	EXMOUTH JCN - 72A	EXMOUTH JCN - 72A	SALISBURY - 72B	SALISBURY - 72B
30955	ASHFORD - 74A	ASHFORD - 74A	ASHFORD - 74A	ASHFORD - 74A	ASHFORD - 74A	ASHFORD - 74A	ASHFORD - 74A
30956	SALISBURY - 72B	EXMOUTH JCN - 72A	EXMOUTH JCN - 72A	EXMOUTH JCN - 72A	EXMOUTH JCN - 72A	EXMOUTH JCN - 72A	EXMOUTH JCN - 72A
30957	SALISBURY - 72B	SALISBURY - 72B	SALISBURY - 72B	SALISBURY - 72B	SALISBURY - 72B	SALISBURY - 72B	SALISBURY - 72B
			H16 4-6-2T (1921)				
30516	FELTHAM - 70B	FELTHAM - 70B	FELTHAM - 70B	FELTHAM - 70B	FELTHAM - 70B	FELTHAM - 70B	FELTHAM - 70B
30517	FELTHAM - 70B	FELTHAM - 70B	FELTHAM - 70B	FELTHAM - 70B	FELTHAM - 70B	FELTHAM - 70B	FELTHAM - 70B
30518	FELTHAM - 70B	FELTHAM - 70B	FELTHAM - 70B	FELTHAM - 70B	FELTHAM - 70B	FELTHAM - 70B	FELTHAM - 70B
30519	FELTHAM - 70B	FELTHAM - 70B	FELTHAM - 70B	FELTHAM - 70B	FELTHAM - 70B	FELTHAM - 70B	FELTHAM - 70B
30520	FELTHAM - 70B	FELTHAM - 70B	FELTHAM - 70B	FELTHAM - 70B	FELTHAM - 70B	FELTHAM - 70B	FELTHAM - 70B

loco	Mar-57	Jun-57	Jul-57	Oct-57	Jan-58	Feb-58	Mar-58
				Q 0-6-0 (1938)			
30530	EASTLEIGH - 71A	EASTLEIGH - 71A	EASTLEIGH - 71A	EASTLEIGH - 71A	EASTLEIGH - 71A	EASTLEIGH - 71A	EASTLEIGH - 71A
30531	EASTLEIGH - 71A	EASTLEIGH - 71A	EASTLEIGH - 71A	EASTLEIGH - 71A	EASTLEIGH - 71A	EASTLEIGH - 71A	EASTLEIGH - 71A
30532	EASTLEIGH - 71A	EASTLEIGH - 71A	EASTLEIGH - 71A	EASTLEIGH - 71A	EASTLEIGH - 71A	EASTLEIGH - 71A	EASTLEIGH - 71A
30533	NORWOOD JCN - 75C	NORWOOD JCN - 75C	NORWOOD JCN - 75C	NORWOOD JCN - 75C	NORWOOD JCN - 75C	NORWOOD JCN - 75C	NORWOOD JCN - 75C
30534	NORWOOD JCN - 75C	NORWOOD JCN - 75C	NORWOOD JCN - 75C	NORWOOD JCN - 75C	NORWOOD JCN - 75C	NORWOOD JCN - 75C	NORWOOD JCN - 75C
30535	EASTLEIGH - 71A	EASTLEIGH - 71A	EASTLEIGH - 71A	EASTLEIGH - 71A	EASTLEIGH - 71A	EASTLEIGH - 71A	EASTLEIGH - 71A
30536	EASTLEIGH - 71A	EASTLEIGH - 71A	EASTLEIGH - 71A	EASTLEIGH - 71A	EASTLEIGH - 71A	EASTLEIGH - 71A	EASTLEIGH - 71A
30537	NORWOOD JCN - 75C	NORWOOD JCN - 75C	NORWOOD JCN - 75C	NORWOOD JCN - 75C	NORWOOD JCN - 75C	NORWOOD JCN - 75C	NORWOOD JCN - 75C
30538	NORWOOD JCN - 75C	NORWOOD JCN - 75C	NORWOOD JCN - 75C	NORWOOD JCN - 75C	NORWOOD JCN - 75C	NORWOOD JCN - 75C	NORWOOD JCN - 75C
30539	BOURNEMOUTH - 71B	BOURNEMOUTH - 71B	BOURNEMOUTH - 71B	BOURNEMOUTH - 71B	BOURNEMOUTH - 71B	BOURNEMOUTH - 71B	BOURNEMOUTH - 71B
30540	THREE BRIDGES - 75E	THREE BRIDGES - 75E	THREE BRIDGES - 75E	THREE BRIDGES - 75E	THREE BRIDGES - 75E	THREE BRIDGES - 75E	THREE BRIDGES - 75E
30541	BOURNEMOUTH - 71B	BOURNEMOUTH - 71B	BOURNEMOUTH - 71B	BOURNEMOUTH - 71B	BOURNEMOUTH - 71B	BOURNEMOUTH - 71B	BOURNEMOUTH - 71B
30542	EASTLEIGH - 71A	EASTLEIGH - 71A	EASTLEIGH - 71A	EASTLEIGH - 71A	EASTLEIGH - 71A	EASTLEIGH - 71A	EASTLEIGH - 71A
30543	EASTLEIGH - 71A	EASTLEIGH - 71A	EASTLEIGH - 71A	EASTLEIGH - 71A	EASTLEIGH - 71A	EASTLEIGH - 71A	EASTLEIGH - 71A
30544	HORSHAM - 75D	HORSHAM - 75D	HORSHAM - 75D	HORSHAM - 75D	HORSHAM - 75D	HORSHAM - 75D	HORSHAM - 75D
30545	HORSHAM - 75D	HORSHAM - 75D	HORSHAM - 75D	HORSHAM - 75D	HORSHAM - 75D	HORSHAM - 75D	HORSHAM - 75D
30546	HORSHAM - 75D	HORSHAM - 75D	HORSHAM - 75D	HORSHAM - 75D	HORSHAM - 75D	HORSHAM - 75D	HORSHAM - 75D
30547	HORSHAM - 75D	HORSHAM - 75D	HORSHAM - 75D	HORSHAM - 75D	HORSHAM - 75D	HORSHAM - 75D	HORSHAM - 75D
30548	BOURNEMOUTH - 71B	BOURNEMOUTH - 71B	BOURNEMOUTH - 71B	BOURNEMOUTH - 71B	BOURNEMOUTH - 71B	BOURNEMOUTH - 71B	BOURNEMOUTH - 71B
30549	NORWOOD JCN - 75C	NORWOOD JCN - 75C	NORWOOD JCN - 75C	NORWOOD JCN - 75C	NORWOOD JCN - 75C	NORWOOD JCN - 75C	NORWOOD JCN - 75C
				Q1 0-6-0 (1942)			
33001	GUILDFORD - 70C	GUILDFORD - 70C	GUILDFORD - 70C	GUILDFORD - 70C	GUILDFORD - 70C	GUILDFORD - 70C	GUILDFORD - 70C
33002	GUILDFORD - 70C	GUILDFORD - 70C	GUILDFORD - 70C	GUILDFORD - 70C	GUILDFORD - 70C	GUILDFORD - 70C	GUILDFORD - 70C
33003	GUILDFORD - 70C	GUILDFORD - 70C	GUILDFORD - 70C	GUILDFORD - 70C	GUILDFORD - 70C	GUILDFORD - 70C	GUILDFORD - 70C
33004	FAVERSHAM - 73E	FAVERSHAM - 73E	FAVERSHAM - 73E	FAVERSHAM - 73E	FAVERSHAM - 73E	FAVERSHAM - 73E	FAVERSHAM - 73E
33005	GUILDFORD - 70C	GUILDFORD - 70C	GUILDFORD - 70C	GUILDFORD - 70C	GUILDFORD - 70C	GUILDFORD - 70C	GUILDFORD - 70C
33006	FELTHAM - 70B	FELTHAM - 70B	FELTHAM - 70B	FELTHAM - 70B	FELTHAM - 70B	FELTHAM - 70B	FELTHAM - 70B
33007	FELTHAM - 70B	FELTHAM - 70B	FELTHAM - 70B	FELTHAM - 70B	FELTHAM - 70B	FELTHAM - 70B	FELTHAM - 70B
33008	FELTHAM - 70B	FELTHAM - 70B	FELTHAM - 70B	FELTHAM - 70B	FELTHAM - 70B	FELTHAM - 70B	FELTHAM - 70B
33009	FELTHAM - 70B	FELTHAM - 70B	FELTHAM - 70B	FELTHAM - 70B	FELTHAM - 70B	FELTHAM - 70B	FELTHAM - 70B
33010	FELTHAM - 70B	FELTHAM - 70B	FELTHAM - 70B	FELTHAM - 70B	FELTHAM - 70B	FELTHAM - 70B	FELTHAM - 70B
33011	FELTHAM - 70B	FELTHAM - 70B	FELTHAM - 70B	FELTHAM - 70B	FELTHAM - 70B	FELTHAM - 70B	FELTHAM - 70B
33012	FELTHAM - 70B	FELTHAM - 70B	FELTHAM - 70B	FELTHAM - 70B	FELTHAM - 70B	FELTHAM - 70B	FELTHAM - 70B
33013	FELTHAM - 70B	FELTHAM - 70B	FELTHAM - 70B	FELTHAM - 70B	FELTHAM - 70B	FELTHAM - 70B	FELTHAM - 70B
33014	HITHER GREEN - 73C	HITHER GREEN - 73C	HITHER GREEN - 73C	HITHER GREEN - 73C	HITHER GREEN - 73C	HITHER GREEN - 73C	HITHER GREEN - 73C
33015	NINE ELMS - 70A	NINE ELMS - 70A	NINE ELMS - 70A	NINE ELMS - 70A	NINE ELMS - 70A	NINE ELMS - 70A	NINE ELMS - 70A
33016	FELTHAM - 70B	FELTHAM - 70B	FELTHAM - 70B	FELTHAM - 70B	FELTHAM - 70B	FELTHAM - 70B	FELTHAM - 70B
33017	NINE ELMS - 70A	NINE ELMS - 70A	NINE ELMS - 70A	NINE ELMS - 70A	NINE ELMS - 70A	NINE ELMS - 70A	NINE ELMS - 70A
33018	FELTHAM - 70B	FELTHAM - 70B	FELTHAM - 70B	FELTHAM - 70B	FELTHAM - 70B	FELTHAM - 70B	FELTHAM - 70B
33019	GUILDFORD - 70C	GUILDFORD - 70C	GUILDFORD - 70C	GUILDFORD - 70C	GUILDFORD - 70C	GUILDFORD - 70C	GUILDFORD - 70C
33020	EASTLEIGH - 71A	EASTLEIGH - 71A	EASTLEIGH - 71A	EASTLEIGH - 71A	EASTLEIGH - 71A	EASTLEIGH - 71A	EASTLEIGH - 71A
33021	EASTLEIGH - 71A	EASTLEIGH - 71A	EASTLEIGH - 71A	EASTLEIGH - 71A	EASTLEIGH - 71A	EASTLEIGH - 71A	EASTLEIGH - 71A
33022	GUILDFORD - 70C	GUILDFORD - 70C	GUILDFORD - 70C	GUILDFORD - 70C	GUILDFORD - 70C	GUILDFORD - 70C	GUILDFORD - 70C
33023	EASTLEIGH - 71A	EASTLEIGH - 71A	EASTLEIGH - 71A	EASTLEIGH - 71A	EASTLEIGH - 71A	EASTLEIGH - 71A	EASTLEIGH - 71A
33024	TONBRIDGE - 74D	TONBRIDGE - 74D	TONBRIDGE - 74D	TONBRIDGE - 74D	TONBRIDGE - 74D	TONBRIDGE - 74D	TONBRIDGE - 74D
33025	GUILDFORD - 70C	GUILDFORD - 70C	GUILDFORD - 70C	GUILDFORD - 70C	GUILDFORD - 70C	GUILDFORD - 70C	GUILDFORD - 70C
33026	FELTHAM - 70B	FELTHAM - 70B	FELTHAM - 70B	FELTHAM - 70B	FELTHAM - 70B	FELTHAM - 70B	FELTHAM - 70B
33027	FELTHAM - 70B	FELTHAM - 70B	FELTHAM - 70B	FELTHAM - 70B	FELTHAM - 70B	FELTHAM - 70B	FELTHAM - 70B
33028	TONBRIDGE - 74D	TONBRIDGE - 74D	TONBRIDGE - 74D	TONBRIDGE - 74D	TONBRIDGE - 74D	TONBRIDGE - 74D	TONBRIDGE - 74D
33029	TONBRIDGE - 74D	TONBRIDGE - 74D	TONBRIDGE - 74D	TONBRIDGE - 74D	TONBRIDGE - 74D	TONBRIDGE - 74D	TONBRIDGE - 74D
33030	TONBRIDGE - 74D	TONBRIDGE - 74D	TONBRIDGE - 74D	TONBRIDGE - 74D	TONBRIDGE - 74D	TONBRIDGE - 74D	TONBRIDGE - 74D
33031	TONBRIDGE - 74D	TONBRIDGE - 74D	TONBRIDGE - 74D	TONBRIDGE - 74D	TONBRIDGE - 74D	TONBRIDGE - 74D	TONBRIDGE - 74D
33032	TONBRIDGE - 74D	TONBRIDGE - 74D	TONBRIDGE - 74D	TONBRIDGE - 74D	TONBRIDGE - 74D	TONBRIDGE - 74D	TONBRIDGE - 74D
33033	TONBRIDGE - 74D	TONBRIDGE - 74D	TONBRIDGE - 74D	TONBRIDGE - 74D	TONBRIDGE - 74D	TONBRIDGE - 74D	TONBRIDGE - 74D
33034	TONBRIDGE - 74D	TONBRIDGE - 74D	TONBRIDGE - 74D	TONBRIDGE - 74D	TONBRIDGE - 74D	TONBRIDGE - 74D	TONBRIDGE - 74D
33035	TONBRIDGE - 74D	TONBRIDGE - 74D	TONBRIDGE - 74D	TONBRIDGE - 74D	TONBRIDGE - 74D	TONBRIDGE - 74D	TONBRIDGE - 74D
33036	TONBRIDGE - 74D	TONBRIDGE - 74D	TONBRIDGE - 74D	TONBRIDGE - 74D	TONBRIDGE - 74D	TONBRIDGE - 74D	TONBRIDGE - 74D
33037	HITHER GREEN - 73C	HITHER GREEN - 73C	HITHER GREEN - 73C	HITHER GREEN - 73C	HITHER GREEN - 73C	HITHER GREEN - 73C	HITHER GREEN - 73C
33038	NINE ELMS - 70A	NINE ELMS - 70A	NINE ELMS - 70A	NINE ELMS - 70A	NINE ELMS - 70A	NINE ELMS - 70A	NINE ELMS - 70A
33039	TONBRIDGE - 74D	TONBRIDGE - 74D	HITHER GREEN - 73C	HITHER GREEN - 73C	HITHER GREEN - 73C	HITHER GREEN - 73C	HITHER GREEN - 73C
33040	TONBRIDGE - 74D	TONBRIDGE - 74D	HITHER GREEN - 73C	HITHER GREEN - 73C	HITHER GREEN - 73C	HITHER GREEN - 73C	HITHER GREEN - 73C
				W 2-6-4T (1931)			
31911	HITHER GREEN - 73C	HITHER GREEN - 73C	HITHER GREEN - 73C	HITHER GREEN - 73C	HITHER GREEN - 73C	HITHER GREEN - 73C	HITHER GREEN - 73C
31912	HITHER GREEN - 73C	HITHER GREEN - 73C	HITHER GREEN - 73C	HITHER GREEN - 73C	HITHER GREEN - 73C	HITHER GREEN - 73C	HITHER GREEN - 73C
31913	HITHER GREEN - 73C	HITHER GREEN - 73C	HITHER GREEN - 73C	HITHER GREEN - 73C	HITHER GREEN - 73C	HITHER GREEN - 73C	HITHER GREEN - 73C
31914	STEWARTS LANE - 73A	STEWARTS LANE - 73A	STEWARTS LANE - 73A	STEWARTS LANE - 73A	STEWARTS LANE - 73A	STEWARTS LANE - 73A	STEWARTS LANE - 73A
31915	HITHER GREEN - 73C	HITHER GREEN - 73C	HITHER GREEN - 73C	HITHER GREEN - 73C	HITHER GREEN - 73C	HITHER GREEN - 73C	HITHER GREEN - 73C
31916	HITHER GREEN - 73C	HITHER GREEN - 73C	HITHER GREEN - 73C	HITHER GREEN - 73C	HITHER GREEN - 73C	HITHER GREEN - 73C	HITHER GREEN - 73C
31917	NORWOOD JCN - 75C	NORWOOD JCN - 75C	NORWOOD JCN - 75C	NORWOOD JCN - 75C	NORWOOD JCN - 75C	NORWOOD JCN - 75C	NORWOOD JCN - 75C
31918	NORWOOD JCN - 75C	NORWOOD JCN - 75C	NORWOOD JCN - 75C	NORWOOD JCN - 75C	NORWOOD JCN - 75C	NORWOOD JCN - 75C	NORWOOD JCN - 75C
31919	NORWOOD JCN - 75C	NORWOOD JCN - 75C	NORWOOD JCN - 75C	NORWOOD JCN - 75C	NORWOOD JCN - 75C	NORWOOD JCN - 75C	NORWOOD JCN - 75C
31920	NORWOOD JCN - 75C	NORWOOD JCN - 75C	NORWOOD JCN - 75C	NORWOOD JCN - 75C	NORWOOD JCN - 75C	NORWOOD JCN - 75C	NORWOOD JCN - 75C
31921	STEWARTS LANE - 73A	STEWARTS LANE - 73A	STEWARTS LANE - 73A	STEWARTS LANE - 73A	STEWARTS LANE - 73A	STEWARTS LANE - 73A	STEWARTS LANE - 73A
31922	HITHER GREEN - 73C	HITHER GREEN - 73C	HITHER GREEN - 73C	HITHER GREEN - 73C	HITHER GREEN - 73C	HITHER GREEN - 73C	HITHER GREEN - 73C
31923	HITHER GREEN - 73C	HITHER GREEN - 73C	HITHER GREEN - 73C	HITHER GREEN - 73C	HITHER GREEN - 73C	HITHER GREEN - 73C	HITHER GREEN - 73C
31924	HITHER GREEN - 73C	HITHER GREEN - 73C	HITHER GREEN - 73C	HITHER GREEN - 73C	HITHER GREEN - 73C	HITHER GREEN - 73C	HITHER GREEN - 73C
31925	HITHER GREEN - 73C	HITHER GREEN - 73C	HITHER GREEN - 73C	HITHER GREEN - 73C	HITHER GREEN - 73C	HITHER GREEN - 73C	HITHER GREEN - 73C
				Z 0-8-0T (1929)			
30950	EXMOUTH JCN - 72A	EXMOUTH JCN - 72A	EXMOUTH JCN - 72A	EXMOUTH JCN - 72A	EXMOUTH JCN - 72A	EXMOUTH JCN - 72A	EXMOUTH JCN - 72A
30951	ASHFORD - 74A	ASHFORD - 74A	ASHFORD - 74A	ASHFORD - 74A	ASHFORD - 74A	ASHFORD - 74A	ASHFORD - 74A
30952	ASHFORD - 74A	ASHFORD - 74A	ASHFORD - 74A	ASHFORD - 74A	ASHFORD - 74A	ASHFORD - 74A	ASHFORD - 74A
30953	SALISBURY - 72B	SALISBURY - 72B	TEMPLECOMBE - 71H	TEMPLECOMBE - 71H	TEMPLECOMBE - 71H	TEMPLECOMBE - 82G	TEMPLECOMBE - 82G
30954	TEMPLECOMBE - 71H	TEMPLECOMBE - 71H	SALISBURY - 72B	SALISBURY - 72B	SALISBURY - 72B	SALISBURY - 72B	SALISBURY - 72B
30955	ASHFORD - 74A	ASHFORD - 74A	ASHFORD - 74A	ASHFORD - 74A	ASHFORD - 74A	ASHFORD - 74A	ASHFORD - 74A
30956	EXMOUTH JCN - 72A	EXMOUTH JCN - 72A	EXMOUTH JCN - 72A	EXMOUTH JCN - 72A	EXMOUTH JCN - 72A	EXMOUTH JCN - 72A	EXMOUTH JCN - 72A
30957	SALISBURY - 72B	SALISBURY - 72B	SALISBURY - 72B	SALISBURY - 72B	SALISBURY - 72B	SALISBURY - 72B	SALISBURY - 72B
				H16 4-6-2T (1921)			
30516	FELTHAM - 70B	FELTHAM - 70B	FELTHAM - 70B	FELTHAM - 70B	FELTHAM - 70B	FELTHAM - 70B	FELTHAM - 70B
30517	FELTHAM - 70B	FELTHAM - 70B	FELTHAM - 70B	FELTHAM - 70B	FELTHAM - 70B	FELTHAM - 70B	FELTHAM - 70B
30518	FELTHAM - 70B	FELTHAM - 70B	FELTHAM - 70B	FELTHAM - 70B	FELTHAM - 70B	FELTHAM - 70B	FELTHAM - 70B
30519	FELTHAM - 70B	FELTHAM - 70B	FELTHAM - 70B	FELTHAM - 70B	FELTHAM - 70B	FELTHAM - 70B	FELTHAM - 70B
30520	FELTHAM - 70B	FELTHAM - 70B	FELTHAM - 70B	FELTHAM - 70B	FELTHAM - 70B	FELTHAM - 70B	FELTHAM - 70B

loco	May-58	Oct-58	Mar-59	Jun-59	Jul-59	Aug-59	Oct-59
				Q 0-6-0 (1938)			
30530	EASTLEIGH - 71A	EASTLEIGH - 71A	EASTLEIGH - 71A	EASTLEIGH - 71A	EASTLEIGH - 71A	EASTLEIGH - 71A	EASTLEIGH - 71A
30531	EASTLEIGH - 71A	EASTLEIGH - 71A	EASTLEIGH - 71A	EASTLEIGH - 71A	EASTLEIGH - 71A	EASTLEIGH - 71A	EASTLEIGH - 71A
30532	EASTLEIGH - 71A	EASTLEIGH - 71A	EASTLEIGH - 71A	EASTLEIGH - 71A	EASTLEIGH - 71A	EASTLEIGH - 71A	EASTLEIGH - 71A
30533	NORWOOD JCN - 75C	NORWOOD JCN - 75C	NORWOOD JCN - 75C	NORWOOD JCN - 75C	NORWOOD JCN - 75C	NORWOOD JCN - 75C	NORWOOD JCN - 75C
30534	NORWOOD JCN - 75C	NORWOOD JCN - 75C	NORWOOD JCN - 75C	NORWOOD JCN - 75C	NORWOOD JCN - 75C	NORWOOD JCN - 75C	NORWOOD JCN - 75C
30535	EASTLEIGH - 71A	EASTLEIGH - 71A	EASTLEIGH - 71A	EASTLEIGH - 71A	EASTLEIGH - 71A	EASTLEIGH - 71A	EASTLEIGH - 71A
30536	EASTLEIGH - 71A	EASTLEIGH - 71A	EASTLEIGH - 71A	EASTLEIGH - 71A	EASTLEIGH - 71A	EASTLEIGH - 71A	EASTLEIGH - 71A
30537	NORWOOD JCN - 75C	NORWOOD JCN - 75C	NORWOOD JCN - 75C	NORWOOD JCN - 75C	NORWOOD JCN - 75C	NORWOOD JCN - 75C	NORWOOD JCN - 75C
30538	NORWOOD JCN - 75C	NORWOOD JCN - 75C	NORWOOD JCN - 75C	NORWOOD JCN - 75C	NORWOOD JCN - 75C	NORWOOD JCN - 75C	NORWOOD JCN - 75C
30539	BOURNEMOUTH - 71B	BOURNEMOUTH - 71B	BOURNEMOUTH - 71B	BOURNEMOUTH - 71B	BOURNEMOUTH - 71B	BOURNEMOUTH - 71B	BOURNEMOUTH - 71B
30540	THREE BRIDGES - 75E	THREE BRIDGES - 75E	THREE BRIDGES - 75E	THREE BRIDGES - 75E	THREE BRIDGES - 75E	THREE BRIDGES - 75E	THREE BRIDGES - 75E
30541	BOURNEMOUTH - 71B	BOURNEMOUTH - 71B	BOURNEMOUTH - 71B	BOURNEMOUTH - 71B	BOURNEMOUTH - 71B	BOURNEMOUTH - 71B	BOURNEMOUTH - 71B
30542	EASTLEIGH - 71A	EASTLEIGH - 71A	EASTLEIGH - 71A	EASTLEIGH - 71A	EASTLEIGH - 71A	EASTLEIGH - 71A	EASTLEIGH - 71A
30543	EASTLEIGH - 71A	EASTLEIGH - 71A	EASTLEIGH - 71A	EASTLEIGH - 71A	EASTLEIGH - 71A	EASTLEIGH - 71A	EASTLEIGH - 71A
30544	HORSHAM - 75D	HORSHAM - 75D	HORSHAM - 75D	HORSHAM - 75D	THREE BRIDGES - 75E	THREE BRIDGES - 75E	THREE BRIDGES - 75E
30545	HORSHAM - 75D	HORSHAM - 75D	HORSHAM - 75D	HORSHAM - 75D	THREE BRIDGES - 75E	THREE BRIDGES - 75E	THREE BRIDGES - 75E
30546	HORSHAM - 75D	HORSHAM - 75D	HORSHAM - 75D	HORSHAM - 75D	THREE BRIDGES - 75E	THREE BRIDGES - 75E	THREE BRIDGES - 75E
30547	HORSHAM - 75D	HORSHAM - 75D	HORSHAM - 75D	HORSHAM - 75D	THREE BRIDGES - 75E	THREE BRIDGES - 75E	THREE BRIDGES - 75E
30548	BOURNEMOUTH - 71B	BOURNEMOUTH - 71B	BOURNEMOUTH - 71B	BOURNEMOUTH - 71B	BOURNEMOUTH - 71B	BOURNEMOUTH - 71B	BOURNEMOUTH - 71B
30549	NORWOOD JCN - 75C	NORWOOD JCN - 75C	NORWOOD JCN - 75C	NORWOOD JCN - 75C	NORWOOD JCN - 75C	NORWOOD JCN - 75C	NORWOOD JCN - 75C
				Q1 0-6-0 (1942)			
33001	GUILDFORD - 70C	GUILDFORD - 70C	GUILDFORD - 70C	TONBRIDGE - 73J	TONBRIDGE - 73J	TONBRIDGE - 73J	TONBRIDGE - 73J
33002	GUILDFORD - 70C	GUILDFORD - 70C	GUILDFORD - 70C	TONBRIDGE - 73J	TONBRIDGE - 73J	TONBRIDGE - 73J	TONBRIDGE - 73J
33003	GUILDFORD - 70C	GUILDFORD - 70C	GUILDFORD - 70C	TONBRIDGE - 73J	TONBRIDGE - 73J	TONBRIDGE - 73J	TONBRIDGE - 73J
33004	FAVERSHAM - 73E	FAVERSHAM - 73E	FAVERSHAM - 73E	TONBRIDGE - 73J	TONBRIDGE - 73J	TONBRIDGE - 73J	TONBRIDGE - 73J
33005	GUILDFORD - 70C	GUILDFORD - 70C	GUILDFORD - 70C	GUILDFORD - 70C	GUILDFORD - 70C	GUILDFORD - 70C	GUILDFORD - 70C
33006	FELTHAM - 70B	FELTHAM - 70B	FELTHAM - 70B	FELTHAM - 70B	FELTHAM - 70B	FELTHAM - 70B	FELTHAM - 70B
33007	FELTHAM - 70B	FELTHAM - 70B	FELTHAM - 70B	FELTHAM - 70B	FELTHAM - 70B	FELTHAM - 70B	FELTHAM - 70B
33008	FELTHAM - 70B	FELTHAM - 70B	FELTHAM - 70B	FELTHAM - 70B	FELTHAM - 70B	FELTHAM - 70B	FELTHAM - 70B
33009	FELTHAM - 70B	FELTHAM - 70B	FELTHAM - 70B	FELTHAM - 70B	FELTHAM - 70B	FELTHAM - 70B	FELTHAM - 70B
33010	FELTHAM - 70B	FELTHAM - 70B	FELTHAM - 70B	FELTHAM - 70B	FELTHAM - 70B	FELTHAM - 70B	FELTHAM - 70B
33011	FELTHAM - 70B	FELTHAM - 70B	FELTHAM - 70B	FELTHAM - 70B	FELTHAM - 70B	FELTHAM - 70B	FELTHAM - 70B
33012	FELTHAM - 70B	FELTHAM - 70B	FELTHAM - 70B	FELTHAM - 70B	FELTHAM - 70B	FELTHAM - 70B	FELTHAM - 70B
33013	FELTHAM - 70B	FELTHAM - 70B	FELTHAM - 70B	FELTHAM - 70B	FELTHAM - 70B	FELTHAM - 70B	FELTHAM - 70B
33014	HITHER GREEN - 73C	HITHER GREEN - 73C	HITHER GREEN - 73C	TONBRIDGE - 73J	TONBRIDGE - 73J	TONBRIDGE - 73J	TONBRIDGE - 73J
33015	NINE ELMS - 70A	NINE ELMS - 70A	NINE ELMS - 70A	NINE ELMS - 70A	NINE ELMS - 70A	NINE ELMS - 70A	NINE ELMS - 70A
33016	FELTHAM - 70B	FELTHAM - 70B	FELTHAM - 70B	FELTHAM - 70B	FELTHAM - 70B	FELTHAM - 70B	FELTHAM - 70B
33017	NINE ELMS - 70A	NINE ELMS - 70A	NINE ELMS - 70A	NINE ELMS - 70A	NINE ELMS - 70A	NINE ELMS - 70A	NINE ELMS - 70A
33018	FELTHAM - 70B	FELTHAM - 70B	FELTHAM - 70B	FELTHAM - 70B	FELTHAM - 70B	FELTHAM - 70B	FELTHAM - 70B
33019	GUILDFORD - 70C	GUILDFORD - 70C	GUILDFORD - 70C	GUILDFORD - 70C	GUILDFORD - 70C	GUILDFORD - 70C	GUILDFORD - 70C
33020	EASTLEIGH - 71A	EASTLEIGH - 71A	EASTLEIGH - 71A	EASTLEIGH - 71A	EASTLEIGH - 71A	EASTLEIGH - 71A	EASTLEIGH - 71A
33021	EASTLEIGH - 71A	EASTLEIGH - 71A	EASTLEIGH - 71A	EASTLEIGH - 71A	EASTLEIGH - 71A	EASTLEIGH - 71A	EASTLEIGH - 71A
33022	GUILDFORD - 70C	GUILDFORD - 70C	GUILDFORD - 70C	GUILDFORD - 70C	GUILDFORD - 70C	GUILDFORD - 70C	GUILDFORD - 70C
33023	EASTLEIGH - 71A	EASTLEIGH - 71A	EASTLEIGH - 71A	EASTLEIGH - 71A	EASTLEIGH - 71A	EASTLEIGH - 71A	EASTLEIGH - 71A
33024	TONBRIDGE - 74D	TONBRIDGE - 73J	TONBRIDGE - 73J	TONBRIDGE - 73J	TONBRIDGE - 73J	TONBRIDGE - 73J	TONBRIDGE - 73J
33025	GUILDFORD - 70C	GUILDFORD - 70C	GUILDFORD - 70C	GUILDFORD - 70C	GUILDFORD - 70C	GUILDFORD - 70C	GUILDFORD - 70C
33026	FELTHAM - 70B	FELTHAM - 70B	FELTHAM - 70B	FELTHAM - 70B	FELTHAM - 70B	FELTHAM - 70B	FELTHAM - 70B
33027	FELTHAM - 70B	FELTHAM - 70B	FELTHAM - 70B	FELTHAM - 70B	FELTHAM - 70B	FELTHAM - 70B	FELTHAM - 70B
33028	TONBRIDGE - 74D	TONBRIDGE - 73J	TONBRIDGE - 73J	TONBRIDGE - 73J	TONBRIDGE - 73J	TONBRIDGE - 73J	TONBRIDGE - 73J
33029	TONBRIDGE - 74D	TONBRIDGE - 73J	TONBRIDGE - 73J	TONBRIDGE - 73J	TONBRIDGE - 73J	TONBRIDGE - 73J	TONBRIDGE - 73J
33030	TONBRIDGE - 74D	TONBRIDGE - 73J	TONBRIDGE - 73J	TONBRIDGE - 73J	TONBRIDGE - 73J	TONBRIDGE - 73J	TONBRIDGE - 73J
33031	TONBRIDGE - 74D	TONBRIDGE - 73J	TONBRIDGE - 73J	TONBRIDGE - 73J	TONBRIDGE - 73J	TONBRIDGE - 73J	TONBRIDGE - 73J
33032	TONBRIDGE - 74D	TONBRIDGE - 73J	TONBRIDGE - 73J	TONBRIDGE - 73J	TONBRIDGE - 73J	TONBRIDGE - 73J	TONBRIDGE - 73J
33033	TONBRIDGE - 74D	TONBRIDGE - 73J	TONBRIDGE - 73J	TONBRIDGE - 73J	TONBRIDGE - 73J	TONBRIDGE - 73J	TONBRIDGE - 73J
33034	TONBRIDGE - 74D	TONBRIDGE - 73J	TONBRIDGE - 73J	TONBRIDGE - 73J	TONBRIDGE - 73J	TONBRIDGE - 73J	TONBRIDGE - 73J
33035	TONBRIDGE - 74D	TONBRIDGE - 73J	TONBRIDGE - 73J	TONBRIDGE - 73J	TONBRIDGE - 73J	TONBRIDGE - 73J	TONBRIDGE - 73J
33036	TONBRIDGE - 74D	TONBRIDGE - 73J	TONBRIDGE - 73J	TONBRIDGE - 73J	TONBRIDGE - 73J	TONBRIDGE - 73J	TONBRIDGE - 73J
33037	HITHER GREEN - 73C	HITHER GREEN - 73C	HITHER GREEN - 73C	TONBRIDGE - 73J	TONBRIDGE - 73J	TONBRIDGE - 73J	TONBRIDGE - 73J
33038	NINE ELMS - 70A	NINE ELMS - 70A	NINE ELMS - 70A	NINE ELMS - 70A	NINE ELMS - 70A	NINE ELMS - 70A	NINE ELMS - 70A
33039	HITHER GREEN - 73C	HITHER GREEN - 73C	HITHER GREEN - 73C	TONBRIDGE - 73J	TONBRIDGE - 73J	TONBRIDGE - 73J	TONBRIDGE - 73J
33040	HITHER GREEN - 73C	HITHER GREEN - 73C	HITHER GREEN - 73C	TONBRIDGE - 73J	TONBRIDGE - 73J	TONBRIDGE - 73J	TONBRIDGE - 73J
				W 2-6-4T (1931)			
31911	HITHER GREEN - 73C	HITHER GREEN - 73C	HITHER GREEN - 73C	HITHER GREEN - 73C	HITHER GREEN - 73C	HITHER GREEN - 73C	HITHER GREEN - 73C
31912	HITHER GREEN - 73C	HITHER GREEN - 73C	HITHER GREEN - 73C	HITHER GREEN - 73C	HITHER GREEN - 73C	HITHER GREEN - 73C	HITHER GREEN - 73C
31913	HITHER GREEN - 73C	HITHER GREEN - 73C	HITHER GREEN - 73C	HITHER GREEN - 73C	HITHER GREEN - 73C	HITHER GREEN - 73C	HITHER GREEN - 73C
31914	STEWARTS LANE - 73A	STEWARTS LANE - 73A	STEWARTS LANE - 73A	STEWARTS LANE - 73A	STEWARTS LANE - 73A	STEWARTS LANE - 73A	STEWARTS LANE - 73A
31915	HITHER GREEN - 73C	HITHER GREEN - 73C	HITHER GREEN - 73C	HITHER GREEN - 73C	HITHER GREEN - 73C	HITHER GREEN - 73C	HITHER GREEN - 73C
31916	HITHER GREEN - 73C	HITHER GREEN - 73C	HITHER GREEN - 73C	HITHER GREEN - 73C	HITHER GREEN - 73C	HITHER GREEN - 73C	HITHER GREEN - 73C
31917	NORWOOD JCN - 75C	NORWOOD JCN - 75C	NORWOOD JCN - 75C	NORWOOD JCN - 75C	NORWOOD JCN - 75C	NORWOOD JCN - 75C	NORWOOD JCN - 75C
31918	NORWOOD JCN - 75C	NORWOOD JCN - 75C	NORWOOD JCN - 75C	NORWOOD JCN - 75C	NORWOOD JCN - 75C	NORWOOD JCN - 75C	NORWOOD JCN - 75C
31919	NORWOOD JCN - 75C	NORWOOD JCN - 75C	NORWOOD JCN - 75C	NORWOOD JCN - 75C	NORWOOD JCN - 75C	NORWOOD JCN - 75C	NORWOOD JCN - 75C
31920	NORWOOD JCN - 75C	NORWOOD JCN - 75C	NORWOOD JCN - 75C	NORWOOD JCN - 75C	NORWOOD JCN - 75C	NORWOOD JCN - 75C	NORWOOD JCN - 75C
31921	STEWARTS LANE - 73A	STEWARTS LANE - 73A	STEWARTS LANE - 73A	STEWARTS LANE - 73A	STEWARTS LANE - 73A	STEWARTS LANE - 73A	STEWARTS LANE - 73A
31922	HITHER GREEN - 73C	HITHER GREEN - 73C	HITHER GREEN - 73C	HITHER GREEN - 73C	HITHER GREEN - 73C	HITHER GREEN - 73C	HITHER GREEN - 73C
31923	HITHER GREEN - 73C	HITHER GREEN - 73C	HITHER GREEN - 73C	HITHER GREEN - 73C	HITHER GREEN - 73C	HITHER GREEN - 73C	HITHER GREEN - 73C
31924	HITHER GREEN - 73C	HITHER GREEN - 73C	HITHER GREEN - 73C	HITHER GREEN - 73C	HITHER GREEN - 73C	HITHER GREEN - 73C	HITHER GREEN - 73C
31925	HITHER GREEN - 73C	HITHER GREEN - 73C	HITHER GREEN - 73C	HITHER GREEN - 73C	HITHER GREEN - 73C	HITHER GREEN - 73C	HITHER GREEN - 73C
				Z 0-8-0T (1929)			
30950	EXMOUTH JCN - 72A	EXMOUTH JCN - 72A	EXMOUTH JCN - 72A	EXMOUTH JCN - 72A	EXMOUTH JCN - 72A	EXMOUTH JCN - 72A	EXMOUTH JCN - 72A
30951	ASHFORD - 74A	ASHFORD - 73F	ASHFORD - 73F	EXMOUTH JCN - 72A	EXMOUTH JCN - 72A	EXMOUTH JCN - 72A	EXMOUTH JCN - 72A
30952	ASHFORD - 74A	ASHFORD - 73F	ASHFORD - 73F	EXMOUTH JCN - 72A	EXMOUTH JCN - 72A	EXMOUTH JCN - 72A	EXMOUTH JCN - 72A
30953	TEMPLECOMBE - 82G	TEMPLECOMBE - 82G	EXMOUTH JCN - 72A	EXMOUTH JCN - 72A	EXMOUTH JCN - 72A	EXMOUTH JCN - 72A	EXMOUTH JCN - 72A
30954	SALISBURY - 72B	SALISBURY - 72B	SALISBURY - 72B	EXMOUTH JCN - 72A	EXMOUTH JCN - 72A	EXMOUTH JCN - 72A	EXMOUTH JCN - 72A
30955	ASHFORD - 74A	EXMOUTH JCN - 72A	EXMOUTH JCN - 72A	EXMOUTH JCN - 72A	EXMOUTH JCN - 72A	EXMOUTH JCN - 72A	EXMOUTH JCN - 72A
30956	EXMOUTH JCN - 72A	EXMOUTH JCN - 72A	EXMOUTH JCN - 72A	EXMOUTH JCN - 72A	EXMOUTH JCN - 72A	EXMOUTH JCN - 72A	EXMOUTH JCN - 72A
30957	SALISBURY - 72B	SALISBURY - 72B	SALISBURY - 72B	SALISBURY - 72B	SALISBURY - 72B	SALISBURY - 72B	SALISBURY - 72B
				H16 4-6-2T (1921)			
30516	FELTHAM - 70B	FELTHAM - 70B	FELTHAM - 70B	FELTHAM - 70B	FELTHAM - 70B	FELTHAM - 70B	FELTHAM - 70B
30517	FELTHAM - 70B	FELTHAM - 70B	FELTHAM - 70B	FELTHAM - 70B	FELTHAM - 70B	FELTHAM - 70B	FELTHAM - 70B
30518	FELTHAM - 70B	FELTHAM - 70B	FELTHAM - 70B	FELTHAM - 70B	FELTHAM - 70B	FELTHAM - 70B	FELTHAM - 70B
30519	FELTHAM - 70B	FELTHAM - 70B	FELTHAM - 70B	FELTHAM - 70B	FELTHAM - 70B	FELTHAM - 70B	FELTHAM - 70B
30520	FELTHAM - 70B	FELTHAM - 70B	FELTHAM - 70B	FELTHAM - 70B	FELTHAM - 70B	FELTHAM - 70B	FELTHAM - 70B

loco	Dec-59	Feb-60	Mar-60	Apr-60	Jul-60	Aug-60	Sep-60	Nov-60
Q 0-6-0 (1938)								
30530	EASTLEIGH - 71A	EASTLEIGH - 71A	EASTLEIGH - 71A	EASTLEIGH - 71A	EASTLEIGH - 71A	EASTLEIGH - 71A	EASTLEIGH - 71A	EASTLEIGH - 71A
30531	EASTLEIGH - 71A	EASTLEIGH - 71A	EASTLEIGH - 71A	EASTLEIGH - 71A	EASTLEIGH - 71A	EASTLEIGH - 71A	EASTLEIGH - 71A	EASTLEIGH - 71A
30532	EASTLEIGH - 71A	EASTLEIGH - 71A	EASTLEIGH - 71A	EASTLEIGH - 71A	EASTLEIGH - 71A	EASTLEIGH - 71A	EASTLEIGH - 71A	EASTLEIGH - 71A
30533	NORWOOD JCN - 75C	NORWOOD JCN - 75C	NORWOOD JCN - 75C	NORWOOD JCN - 75C	NORWOOD JCN - 75C	NORWOOD JCN - 75C	NORWOOD JCN - 75C	NORWOOD JCN - 75C
30534	NORWOOD JCN - 75C	NORWOOD JCN - 75C	NORWOOD JCN - 75C	NORWOOD JCN - 75C	NORWOOD JCN - 75C	NORWOOD JCN - 75C	NORWOOD JCN - 75C	NORWOOD JCN - 75C
30535	EASTLEIGH - 71A	EASTLEIGH - 71A	EASTLEIGH - 71A	EASTLEIGH - 71A	EASTLEIGH - 71A	EASTLEIGH - 71A	EASTLEIGH - 71A	EASTLEIGH - 71A
30536	EASTLEIGH - 71A	EASTLEIGH - 71A	EASTLEIGH - 71A	EASTLEIGH - 71A	EASTLEIGH - 71A	EASTLEIGH - 71A	EASTLEIGH - 71A	EASTLEIGH - 71A
30537	NORWOOD JCN - 75C	NORWOOD JCN - 75C	NORWOOD JCN - 75C	NORWOOD JCN - 75C	NORWOOD JCN - 75C	NORWOOD JCN - 75C	NORWOOD JCN - 75C	NORWOOD JCN - 75C
30538	NORWOOD JCN - 75C	NORWOOD JCN - 75C	NORWOOD JCN - 75C	NORWOOD JCN - 75C	NORWOOD JCN - 75C	NORWOOD JCN - 75C	NORWOOD JCN - 75C	NORWOOD JCN - 75C
30539	BOURNEMOUTH - 71B	BOURNEMOUTH - 71B	BOURNEMOUTH - 71B	BOURNEMOUTH - 71B	BOURNEMOUTH - 71B	BOURNEMOUTH - 71B	BOURNEMOUTH - 71B	BOURNEMOUTH - 71B
30540	THREE BRIDGES - 75E	THREE BRIDGES - 75E	THREE BRIDGES - 75E	THREE BRIDGES - 75E	THREE BRIDGES - 75E	THREE BRIDGES - 75E	THREE BRIDGES - 75E	THREE BRIDGES - 75E
30541	BOURNEMOUTH - 71B	BOURNEMOUTH - 71B	BOURNEMOUTH - 71B	BOURNEMOUTH - 71B	BOURNEMOUTH - 71B	BOURNEMOUTH - 71B	BOURNEMOUTH - 71B	BOURNEMOUTH - 71B
30542	EASTLEIGH - 71A	EASTLEIGH - 71A	EASTLEIGH - 71A	EASTLEIGH - 71A	EASTLEIGH - 71A	EASTLEIGH - 71A	EASTLEIGH - 71A	EASTLEIGH - 71A
30543	EASTLEIGH - 71A	EASTLEIGH - 71A	EASTLEIGH - 71A	EASTLEIGH - 71A	EASTLEIGH - 71A	EASTLEIGH - 71A	EASTLEIGH - 71A	EASTLEIGH - 71A
30544	THREE BRIDGES - 75E	THREE BRIDGES - 75E	THREE BRIDGES - 75E	THREE BRIDGES - 75E	THREE BRIDGES - 75E	THREE BRIDGES - 75E	THREE BRIDGES - 75E	THREE BRIDGES - 75E
30545	THREE BRIDGES - 75E	THREE BRIDGES - 75E	THREE BRIDGES - 75E	THREE BRIDGES - 75E	THREE BRIDGES - 75E	THREE BRIDGES - 75E	THREE BRIDGES - 75E	THREE BRIDGES - 75E
30546	THREE BRIDGES - 75E	THREE BRIDGES - 75E	THREE BRIDGES - 75E	THREE BRIDGES - 75E	THREE BRIDGES - 75E	THREE BRIDGES - 75E	THREE BRIDGES - 75E	THREE BRIDGES - 75E
30547	THREE BRIDGES - 75E	THREE BRIDGES - 75E	THREE BRIDGES - 75E	THREE BRIDGES - 75E	THREE BRIDGES - 75E	THREE BRIDGES - 75E	THREE BRIDGES - 75E	THREE BRIDGES - 75E
30548	BOURNEMOUTH - 71B	BOURNEMOUTH - 71B	BOURNEMOUTH - 71B	BOURNEMOUTH - 71B	BOURNEMOUTH - 71B	BOURNEMOUTH - 71B	BOURNEMOUTH - 71B	BOURNEMOUTH - 71B
30549	NORWOOD JCN - 75C	NORWOOD JCN - 75C	NORWOOD JCN - 75C	NORWOOD JCN - 75C	NORWOOD JCN - 75C	NORWOOD JCN - 75C	NORWOOD JCN - 75C	NORWOOD JCN - 75C
Q1 0-6-0 (1942)								
33001	TONBRIDGE - 73J	TONBRIDGE - 73J	TONBRIDGE - 73J	TONBRIDGE - 73J	TONBRIDGE - 73J	TONBRIDGE - 73J	TONBRIDGE - 73J	TONBRIDGE - 73J
33002	TONBRIDGE - 73J	TONBRIDGE - 73J	TONBRIDGE - 73J	TONBRIDGE - 73J	TONBRIDGE - 73J	TONBRIDGE - 73J	TONBRIDGE - 73J	TONBRIDGE - 73J
33003	TONBRIDGE - 73J	TONBRIDGE - 73J	TONBRIDGE - 73J	TONBRIDGE - 73J	TONBRIDGE - 73J	TONBRIDGE - 73J	TONBRIDGE - 73J	TONBRIDGE - 73J
33004	TONBRIDGE - 73J	TONBRIDGE - 73J	TONBRIDGE - 73J	TONBRIDGE - 73J	TONBRIDGE - 73J	TONBRIDGE - 73J	TONBRIDGE - 73J	TONBRIDGE - 73J
33005	GUILDFORD - 70C	GUILDFORD - 70C	GUILDFORD - 70C	GUILDFORD - 70C	GUILDFORD - 70C	GUILDFORD - 70C	GUILDFORD - 70C	GUILDFORD - 70C
33006	FELTHAM - 70B	FELTHAM - 70B	FELTHAM - 70B	FELTHAM - 70B	FELTHAM - 70B	FELTHAM - 70B	FELTHAM - 70B	FELTHAM - 70B
33007	FELTHAM - 70B	FELTHAM - 70B	FELTHAM - 70B	FELTHAM - 70B	FELTHAM - 70B	FELTHAM - 70B	FELTHAM - 70B	FELTHAM - 70B
33008	FELTHAM - 70B	FELTHAM - 70B	FELTHAM - 70B	FELTHAM - 70B	FELTHAM - 70B	FELTHAM - 70B	FELTHAM - 70B	FELTHAM - 70B
33009	FELTHAM - 70B	FELTHAM - 70B	FELTHAM - 70B	FELTHAM - 70B	FELTHAM - 70B	FELTHAM - 70B	FELTHAM - 70B	FELTHAM - 70B
33010	FELTHAM - 70B	FELTHAM - 70B	FELTHAM - 70B	FELTHAM - 70B	FELTHAM - 70B	FELTHAM - 70B	FELTHAM - 70B	FELTHAM - 70B
33011	FELTHAM - 70B	FELTHAM - 70B	FELTHAM - 70B	FELTHAM - 70B	FELTHAM - 70B	FELTHAM - 70B	FELTHAM - 70B	FELTHAM - 70B
33012	FELTHAM - 70B	FELTHAM - 70B	FELTHAM - 70B	FELTHAM - 70B	FELTHAM - 70B	FELTHAM - 70B	FELTHAM - 70B	FELTHAM - 70B
33013	FELTHAM - 70B	FELTHAM - 70B	FELTHAM - 70B	FELTHAM - 70B	FELTHAM - 70B	FELTHAM - 70B	FELTHAM - 70B	FELTHAM - 70B
33014	TONBRIDGE - 73J	TONBRIDGE - 73J	TONBRIDGE - 73J	TONBRIDGE - 73J	TONBRIDGE - 73J	TONBRIDGE - 73J	TONBRIDGE - 73J	TONBRIDGE - 73J
33015	NINE ELMS - 70A	NINE ELMS - 70A	NINE ELMS - 70A	NINE ELMS - 70A	NINE ELMS - 70A	NINE ELMS - 70A	NINE ELMS - 70A	NINE ELMS - 70A
33016	FELTHAM - 70B	FELTHAM - 70B	FELTHAM - 70B	FELTHAM - 70B	FELTHAM - 70B	FELTHAM - 70B	FELTHAM - 70B	FELTHAM - 70B
33017	NINE ELMS - 70A	NINE ELMS - 70A	NINE ELMS - 70A	NINE ELMS - 70A	NINE ELMS - 70A	NINE ELMS - 70A	NINE ELMS - 70A	NINE ELMS - 70A
33018	FELTHAM - 70B	FELTHAM - 70B	FELTHAM - 70B	FELTHAM - 70B	FELTHAM - 70B	FELTHAM - 70B	FELTHAM - 70B	FELTHAM - 70B
33019	GUILDFORD - 70C	GUILDFORD - 70C	GUILDFORD - 70C	GUILDFORD - 70C	GUILDFORD - 70C	GUILDFORD - 70C	GUILDFORD - 70C	GUILDFORD - 70C
33020	EASTLEIGH - 71A	EASTLEIGH - 71A	EASTLEIGH - 71A	EASTLEIGH - 71A	EASTLEIGH - 71A	EASTLEIGH - 71A	EASTLEIGH - 71A	EASTLEIGH - 71A
33021	EASTLEIGH - 71A	EASTLEIGH - 71A	EASTLEIGH - 71A	EASTLEIGH - 71A	EASTLEIGH - 71A	EASTLEIGH - 71A	EASTLEIGH - 71A	EASTLEIGH - 71A
33022	GUILDFORD - 70C	GUILDFORD - 70C	GUILDFORD - 70C	GUILDFORD - 70C	GUILDFORD - 70C	GUILDFORD - 70C	GUILDFORD - 70C	GUILDFORD - 70C
33023	EASTLEIGH - 71A	EASTLEIGH - 71A	EASTLEIGH - 71A	EASTLEIGH - 71A	EASTLEIGH - 71A	EASTLEIGH - 71A	EASTLEIGH - 71A	EASTLEIGH - 71A
33024	TONBRIDGE - 73J	TONBRIDGE - 73J	TONBRIDGE - 73J	TONBRIDGE - 73J	TONBRIDGE - 73J	TONBRIDGE - 73J	TONBRIDGE - 73J	TONBRIDGE - 73J
33025	GUILDFORD - 70C	GUILDFORD - 70C	GUILDFORD - 70C	GUILDFORD - 70C	GUILDFORD - 70C	GUILDFORD - 70C	GUILDFORD - 70C	GUILDFORD - 70C
33026	FELTHAM - 70B	FELTHAM - 70B	FELTHAM - 70B	FELTHAM - 70B	FELTHAM - 70B	FELTHAM - 70B	FELTHAM - 70B	FELTHAM - 70B
33027	FELTHAM - 70B	FELTHAM - 70B	FELTHAM - 70B	FELTHAM - 70B	FELTHAM - 70B	FELTHAM - 70B	FELTHAM - 70B	FELTHAM - 70B
33028	TONBRIDGE - 73J	TONBRIDGE - 73J	TONBRIDGE - 73J	TONBRIDGE - 73J	TONBRIDGE - 73J	TONBRIDGE - 73J	TONBRIDGE - 73J	TONBRIDGE - 73J
33029	TONBRIDGE - 73J	TONBRIDGE - 73J	TONBRIDGE - 73J	TONBRIDGE - 73J	TONBRIDGE - 73J	TONBRIDGE - 73J	TONBRIDGE - 73J	TONBRIDGE - 73J
33030	TONBRIDGE - 73J	TONBRIDGE - 73J	TONBRIDGE - 73J	TONBRIDGE - 73J	TONBRIDGE - 73J	TONBRIDGE - 73J	TONBRIDGE - 73J	TONBRIDGE - 73J
33031	TONBRIDGE - 73J	TONBRIDGE - 73J	TONBRIDGE - 73J	TONBRIDGE - 73J	TONBRIDGE - 73J	TONBRIDGE - 73J	TONBRIDGE - 73J	TONBRIDGE - 73J
33032	TONBRIDGE - 73J	TONBRIDGE - 73J	TONBRIDGE - 73J	TONBRIDGE - 73J	TONBRIDGE - 73J	TONBRIDGE - 73J	TONBRIDGE - 73J	TONBRIDGE - 73J
33033	TONBRIDGE - 73J	TONBRIDGE - 73J	TONBRIDGE - 73J	TONBRIDGE - 73J	TONBRIDGE - 73J	TONBRIDGE - 73J	TONBRIDGE - 73J	TONBRIDGE - 73J
33034	TONBRIDGE - 73J	TONBRIDGE - 73J	TONBRIDGE - 73J	TONBRIDGE - 73J	TONBRIDGE - 73J	TONBRIDGE - 73J	TONBRIDGE - 73J	TONBRIDGE - 73J
33035	TONBRIDGE - 73J	TONBRIDGE - 73J	TONBRIDGE - 73J	TONBRIDGE - 73J	TONBRIDGE - 73J	TONBRIDGE - 73J	TONBRIDGE - 73J	TONBRIDGE - 73J
33036	TONBRIDGE - 73J	TONBRIDGE - 73J	TONBRIDGE - 73J	TONBRIDGE - 73J	TONBRIDGE - 73J	TONBRIDGE - 73J	TONBRIDGE - 73J	TONBRIDGE - 73J
33037	TONBRIDGE - 73J	TONBRIDGE - 73J	TONBRIDGE - 73J	TONBRIDGE - 73J	TONBRIDGE - 73J	TONBRIDGE - 73J	TONBRIDGE - 73J	TONBRIDGE - 73J
33038	NINE ELMS - 70A	NINE ELMS - 70A	NINE ELMS - 70A	NINE ELMS - 70A	NINE ELMS - 70A	NINE ELMS - 70A	NINE ELMS - 70A	NINE ELMS - 70A
33039	TONBRIDGE - 73J	TONBRIDGE - 73J	TONBRIDGE - 73J	TONBRIDGE - 73J	TONBRIDGE - 73J	TONBRIDGE - 73J	TONBRIDGE - 73J	TONBRIDGE - 73J
33040	TONBRIDGE - 73J	TONBRIDGE - 73J	TONBRIDGE - 73J	TONBRIDGE - 73J	TONBRIDGE - 73J	TONBRIDGE - 73J	TONBRIDGE - 73J	TONBRIDGE - 73J
W 2-6-4T (1931)								
31911	HITHER GREEN - 73C	HITHER GREEN - 73C	HITHER GREEN - 73C	HITHER GREEN - 73C	HITHER GREEN - 73C	HITHER GREEN - 73C	HITHER GREEN - 73C	HITHER GREEN - 73C
31912	HITHER GREEN - 73C	HITHER GREEN - 73C	HITHER GREEN - 73C	HITHER GREEN - 73C	HITHER GREEN - 73C	HITHER GREEN - 73C	HITHER GREEN - 73C	HITHER GREEN - 73C
31913	HITHER GREEN - 73C	HITHER GREEN - 73C	HITHER GREEN - 73C	HITHER GREEN - 73C	HITHER GREEN - 73C	HITHER GREEN - 73C	HITHER GREEN - 73C	HITHER GREEN - 73C
31914	STEWARTS LANE - 73A	STEWARTS LANE - 73A	STEWARTS LANE - 73A	STEWARTS LANE - 73A	STEWARTS LANE - 73A	STEWARTS LANE - 73A	STEWARTS LANE - 73A	NORWOOD JCN - 75C
31915	HITHER GREEN - 73C	HITHER GREEN - 73C	HITHER GREEN - 73C	HITHER GREEN - 73C	HITHER GREEN - 73C	HITHER GREEN - 73C	HITHER GREEN - 73C	NORWOOD JCN - 75C
31916	HITHER GREEN - 73C	HITHER GREEN - 73C	HITHER GREEN - 73C	HITHER GREEN - 73C	HITHER GREEN - 73C	HITHER GREEN - 73C	HITHER GREEN - 73C	HITHER GREEN - 73C
31917	NORWOOD JCN - 75C	NORWOOD JCN - 75C	NORWOOD JCN - 75C	NORWOOD JCN - 75C	NORWOOD JCN - 75C	NORWOOD JCN - 75C	NORWOOD JCN - 75C	NORWOOD JCN - 75C
31918	NORWOOD JCN - 75C	NORWOOD JCN - 75C	NORWOOD JCN - 75C	NORWOOD JCN - 75C	NORWOOD JCN - 75C	NORWOOD JCN - 75C	NORWOOD JCN - 75C	NORWOOD JCN - 75C
31919	NORWOOD JCN - 75C	NORWOOD JCN - 75C	NORWOOD JCN - 75C	NORWOOD JCN - 75C	NORWOOD JCN - 75C	NORWOOD JCN - 75C	NORWOOD JCN - 75C	NORWOOD JCN - 75C
31920	NORWOOD JCN - 75C	NORWOOD JCN - 75C	NORWOOD JCN - 75C	NORWOOD JCN - 75C	NORWOOD JCN - 75C	NORWOOD JCN - 75C	NORWOOD JCN - 75C	NORWOOD JCN - 75C
31921	STEWARTS LANE - 73A	STEWARTS LANE - 73A	STEWARTS LANE - 73A	STEWARTS LANE - 73A	STEWARTS LANE - 73A	STEWARTS LANE - 73A	STEWARTS LANE - 73A	NORWOOD JCN - 75C
31922	HITHER GREEN - 73C	HITHER GREEN - 73C	HITHER GREEN - 73C	HITHER GREEN - 73C	HITHER GREEN - 73C	HITHER GREEN - 73C	HITHER GREEN - 73C	HITHER GREEN - 73C
31923	HITHER GREEN - 73C	HITHER GREEN - 73C	HITHER GREEN - 73C	HITHER GREEN - 73C	HITHER GREEN - 73C	HITHER GREEN - 73C	HITHER GREEN - 73C	HITHER GREEN - 73C
31924	HITHER GREEN - 73C	HITHER GREEN - 73C	HITHER GREEN - 73C	HITHER GREEN - 73C	HITHER GREEN - 73C	HITHER GREEN - 73C	HITHER GREEN - 73C	HITHER GREEN - 73C
31925	HITHER GREEN - 73C	HITHER GREEN - 73C	HITHER GREEN - 73C	HITHER GREEN - 73C	HITHER GREEN - 73C	HITHER GREEN - 73C	HITHER GREEN - 73C	HITHER GREEN - 73C
Z 0-8-0T (1929)								
30950	EXMOUTH JCN - 72A	EXMOUTH JCN - 72A	EXMOUTH JCN - 72A	EXMOUTH JCN - 72A	EXMOUTH JCN - 72A	EXMOUTH JCN - 72A	EXMOUTH JCN - 72A	EXMOUTH JCN - 72A
30951	EXMOUTH JCN - 72A	EXMOUTH JCN - 72A	EXMOUTH JCN - 72A	EXMOUTH JCN - 72A	EXMOUTH JCN - 72A	EXMOUTH JCN - 72A	EXMOUTH JCN - 72A	EXMOUTH JCN - 72A
30952	EXMOUTH JCN - 72A	EXMOUTH JCN - 72A	EXMOUTH JCN - 72A	EXMOUTH JCN - 72A	EXMOUTH JCN - 72A	EXMOUTH JCN - 72A	EXMOUTH JCN - 72A	EXMOUTH JCN - 72A
30953	EXMOUTH JCN - 72A	EXMOUTH JCN - 72A	EXMOUTH JCN - 72A	EXMOUTH JCN - 72A	EXMOUTH JCN - 72A	EXMOUTH JCN - 72A	EXMOUTH JCN - 72A	EXMOUTH JCN - 72A
30954	EXMOUTH JCN - 72A	EXMOUTH JCN - 72A	EXMOUTH JCN - 72A	EXMOUTH JCN - 72A	EXMOUTH JCN - 72A	EXMOUTH JCN - 72A	EXMOUTH JCN - 72A	EXMOUTH JCN - 72A
30955	EXMOUTH JCN - 72A	EXMOUTH JCN - 72A	EXMOUTH JCN - 72A	EXMOUTH JCN - 72A	EXMOUTH JCN - 72A	EXMOUTH JCN - 72A	EXMOUTH JCN - 72A	EXMOUTH JCN - 72A
30956	EXMOUTH JCN - 72A	EXMOUTH JCN - 72A	EXMOUTH JCN - 72A	EXMOUTH JCN - 72A	EXMOUTH JCN - 72A	EXMOUTH JCN - 72A	EXMOUTH JCN - 72A	EXMOUTH JCN - 72A
30957	SALISBURY - 72B	SALISBURY - 72B	SALISBURY - 72B	SALISBURY - 72B	SALISBURY - 72B	SALISBURY - 72B	SALISBURY - 72B	SALISBURY - 72B
H16 4-6-2T (1921)								
30516	FELTHAM - 70B	EASTLEIGH - 71A	EASTLEIGH - 71A	EASTLEIGH - 71A	EASTLEIGH - 71A	EASTLEIGH - 71A	EASTLEIGH - 71A	EASTLEIGH - 71A
30517	FELTHAM - 70B	EASTLEIGH - 71A	EASTLEIGH - 71A	EASTLEIGH - 71A	EASTLEIGH - 71A	EASTLEIGH - 71A	EASTLEIGH - 71A	EASTLEIGH - 71A
30518	FELTHAM - 70B	FELTHAM - 70B	FELTHAM - 70B	FELTHAM - 70B	FELTHAM - 70B	FELTHAM - 70B	FELTHAM - 70B	FELTHAM - 70B
30519	FELTHAM - 70B	FELTHAM - 70B	FELTHAM - 70B	FELTHAM - 70B	FELTHAM - 70B	FELTHAM - 70B	FELTHAM - 70B	FELTHAM - 70B
30520	FELTHAM - 70B	FELTHAM - 70B	FELTHAM - 70B	FELTHAM - 70B	FELTHAM - 70B	FELTHAM - 70B	FELTHAM - 70B	FELTHAM - 70B

The H16 4-6-2T's were more common at Feltham than Waterloo but one of the class had a daily working into the terminus where it spent four hours on empty stock duties to and from Clapham Junction. 30520, having finished its stint at Waterloo, looks into Nine Elms prior to working the 14.13 goods to Feltham.

Although the Q and Q1 0-6-0's were an attempt by the Southern to modernise its fleet of ageing 0-6-0's, neither class had much effect on the numbers of '700' and C class engines. The Q class of 1938 were essentially Brighton section engines, being used on short distance goods workings at both ends of the LBSCR, although a number were allocated to the South Western for services between Eastleigh and Bournemouth.

The curious looking Q1 engines tended to be used more on secondary than trunk routes and were familiar sights on local goods workings in the vicinity of Tonbridge and Guildford. They were uncommon on the LSWR main line although they could be seen in small numbers at Salisbury, working in via Romsey from the Brighton area.

The W class 2-6-4 tanks were something of a curiosity since their introduction came only a short time after the Southern had abandoned plans to make the 2-6-4T its standard passenger engine and rebuilt a large number of such engines as 2-6-0 tender engines. Unlike the earlier locomotives, however, the W class was prohibited from working passenger services and their entire lives were spent on yard to yard transfer goods workings from the London marshalling yards of the former SECR and LBSCR.

The Z 0-8-0T's were built, to a great extent, from spare LBSCR components at Brighton works, the class of eight engines being used in the larger yards outside London for shunting. Ousted from their traditional duties by diesel 0-6-0's, the Z's were gradually concentrated at Exmouth Junction as replacements for the E1R 0-6-2T bankers.

The J1 and J2 Pacific tanks were the remnants of the LBSCR's principal express fleet but had been made redundant by the electrification projects of the 1930's and put out to grass at Tunbridge Wells West, working services to Victoria and Eastbourne in the company of I3 4-4-2T's. Their post-nationalisation career was short-lived - as was that of the 4-4-2T's - and the arrival of LMS 2-6-4T's from 1950 onwards saw both engines withdrawn in June 1951.

The J class 0-6-4 tanks represented an abortive attempt to provide additional power for the semi-fast SECR trains out of Charing Cross; the five engines of the class being quickly displaced by the new breed of 4-4-0's and 2-6-0's. Thereafter much of their time was spent at Ashford working local services to Ramsgate and Margate until being made redundant in the early 1950's by the influx of LMS 2-6-4 tanks.

The opening of Feltham marshalling yard in 1921 caused a complete revision of goods services to and from the London yards of neighbouring railways and it was with these revised workings in mind that the five H16 4-6-2T's were introduced. Their duties did not vary significantly except that one of the Feltham duties included an element of empty stock working between Waterloo and Clapham Junction - a duty that gave rise to much speculation regarding the possible broadening of duties although in fact the visit to Waterloo was a perfectly routine aspect of operations.

loco	May-49	Jun-49	Aug-49	Sep-49	Dec-49	Feb-50	Mar-50
				E1/R 0-6-2T (1927)			
32094	BARNSTAPLE - 72E	BARNSTAPLE - 72E	BARNSTAPLE - 72E	BARNSTAPLE - 72E	PLYMOUTH - 72D	PLYMOUTH - 72D	PLYMOUTH - 72D
32095	BARNSTAPLE - 72E	BARNSTAPLE - 72E	BARNSTAPLE - 72E	BARNSTAPLE - 72E	BARNSTAPLE - 72E	BARNSTAPLE - 72E	BARNSTAPLE - 72E
32096	BARNSTAPLE - 72E	BARNSTAPLE - 72E	BARNSTAPLE - 72E	BARNSTAPLE - 72E	BARNSTAPLE - 72E	BARNSTAPLE - 72E	BARNSTAPLE - 72E
32124	EXMOUTH JCN - 72A	EXMOUTH JCN - 72A	EXMOUTH JCN - 72A	EXMOUTH JCN - 72A	EXMOUTH JCN - 72A	EXMOUTH JCN - 72A	EXMOUTH JCN - 72A
32135	EXMOUTH JCN - 72A	EXMOUTH JCN - 72A	EXMOUTH JCN - 72A	EXMOUTH JCN - 72A	EXMOUTH JCN - 72A	EXMOUTH JCN - 72A	EXMOUTH JCN - 72A
32608	BARNSTAPLE - 72E	BARNSTAPLE - 72E	BARNSTAPLE - 72E	BARNSTAPLE - 72E	BARNSTAPLE - 72E	BARNSTAPLE - 72E	BARNSTAPLE - 72E
32610	BARNSTAPLE - 72E	BARNSTAPLE - 72E	BARNSTAPLE - 72E	BARNSTAPLE - 72E	BARNSTAPLE - 72E	BARNSTAPLE - 72E	BARNSTAPLE - 72E
32695	EXMOUTH JCN - 72A	EXMOUTH JCN - 72A	EXMOUTH JCN - 72A	EXMOUTH JCN - 72A	EXMOUTH JCN - 72A	EXMOUTH JCN - 72A	EXMOUTH JCN - 72A
32696	BARNSTAPLE - 72E	BARNSTAPLE - 72E	BARNSTAPLE - 72E	BARNSTAPLE - 72E	BARNSTAPLE - 72E	BARNSTAPLE - 72E	BARNSTAPLE - 72E
32697	EXMOUTH JCN - 72A	EXMOUTH JCN - 72A	EXMOUTH JCN - 72A	EXMOUTH JCN - 72A	EXMOUTH JCN - 72A	EXMOUTH JCN - 72A	EXMOUTH JCN - 72A
				E3 0-6-2T (1894)			
32165	B ARMS - 73B	B ARMS - 73B	B ARMS - 73B	B ARMS - 73B	B ARMS - 73B	B ARMS - 73B	B ARMS - 73B
32166	B ARMS - 73B	B ARMS - 73B	B ARMS - 73B	B ARMS - 73B	B ARMS - 73B	B ARMS - 73B	B ARMS - 73B
32167	TONBRIDGE - 74D	TONBRIDGE - 74D	TONBRIDGE - 74D	TONBRIDGE - 74D	TONBRIDGE - 74D	TONBRIDGE - 74D	TONBRIDGE - 74D
32168	B ARMS - 73B	B ARMS - 73B	B ARMS - 73B	B ARMS - 73B	B ARMS - 73B	B ARMS - 73B	B ARMS - 73B
32169	TONBRIDGE - 74D	TONBRIDGE - 74D	TONBRIDGE - 74D	TONBRIDGE - 74D	TONBRIDGE - 74D	TONBRIDGE - 74D	TONBRIDGE - 74D
32170	B ARMS - 73B	B ARMS - 73B	B ARMS - 73B	B ARMS - 73B	B ARMS - 73B	B ARMS - 73B	B ARMS - 73B
32453	B ARMS - 73B	B ARMS - 73B	B ARMS - 73B	B ARMS - 73B	B ARMS - 73B	B ARMS - 73B	B ARMS - 73B
32454	B ARMS - 73B	B ARMS - 73B	B ARMS - 73B	B ARMS - 73B	B ARMS - 73B	TONBRIDGE - 74D	TONBRIDGE - 74D
32455	BRIGHTON - 75A	BRIGHTON - 75A	BRIGHTON - 75A	BRIGHTON - 75A	BRIGHTON - 75A	BRIGHTON - 75A	BRIGHTON - 75A
32456	TONBRIDGE - 74D	TONBRIDGE - 74D	TONBRIDGE - 74D	TONBRIDGE - 74D	TONBRIDGE - 74D	TONBRIDGE - 74D	TONBRIDGE - 74D
32458	B ARMS - 73B	B ARMS - 73B	B ARMS - 73B	B ARMS - 73B	B ARMS - 73B	B ARMS - 73B	B ARMS - 73B
32459	B ARMS - 73B	B ARMS - 73B	B ARMS - 73B	B ARMS - 73B	B ARMS - 73B	B ARMS - 73B	B ARMS - 73B
32460	B ARMS - 73B	B ARMS - 73B	B ARMS - 73B	B ARMS - 73B	B ARMS - 73B	B ARMS - 73B	B ARMS - 73B
32461	B ARMS - 73B	B ARMS - 73B	B ARMS - 73B	B ARMS - 73B	B ARMS - 73B	B ARMS - 73B	B ARMS - 73B
32462	B ARMS - 73B	B ARMS - 73B	B ARMS - 73B	B ARMS - 73B	B ARMS - 73B	B ARMS - 73B	B ARMS - 73B
				E4 0-6-2T (1897)			
32463	B ARMS - 73B	B ARMS - 73B	B ARMS - 73B	B ARMS - 73B	B ARMS - 73B	B ARMS - 73B	B ARMS - 73B
32464	HORSHAM - 75D	HORSHAM - 75D	HORSHAM - 75D	HORSHAM - 75D	HORSHAM - 75D	HORSHAM - 75D	HORSHAM - 75D
32465	THREE BRIDGES - 75E	THREE BRIDGES - 75E	THREE BRIDGES - 75E	THREE BRIDGES - 75E	THREE BRIDGES - 75E	THREE BRIDGES - 75E	THREE BRIDGES - 75E
32467	B ARMS - 73B	B ARMS - 73B	B ARMS - 73B	B ARMS - 73B	B ARMS - 73B	B ARMS - 73B	B ARMS - 73B
32468	NINE ELMS - 70A	NINE ELMS - 70A	NINE ELMS - 70A	NINE ELMS - 70A	NINE ELMS - 70A	NINE ELMS - 70A	NINE ELMS - 70A
32469	B ARMS - 73B	B ARMS - 73B	B ARMS - 73B	B ARMS - 73B	B ARMS - 73B	B ARMS - 73B	B ARMS - 73B
32470	BRIGHTON - 75A	BRIGHTON - 75A	BRIGHTON - 75A	BRIGHTON - 75A	BRIGHTON - 75A	BRIGHTON - 75A	BRIGHTON - 75A
32471	BRIGHTON - 75A	BRIGHTON - 75A	BRIGHTON - 75A	BRIGHTON - 75A	BRIGHTON - 75A	BRIGHTON - 75A	BRIGHTON - 75A
32472	B ARMS - 73B	B ARMS - 73B	B ARMS - 73B	B ARMS - 73B	B ARMS - 73B	B ARMS - 73B	B ARMS - 73B
32473	NORWOOD JCN - 75C	NORWOOD JCN - 75C	NORWOOD JCN - 75C	NORWOOD JCN - 75C	NORWOOD JCN - 75C	NORWOOD JCN - 75C	NORWOOD JCN - 75C
32474	B ARMS - 73B	B ARMS - 73B	B ARMS - 73B	B ARMS - 73B	B ARMS - 73B	B ARMS - 73B	B ARMS - 73B
32475	BRIGHTON - 75A(N)	BRIGHTON - 75A(N)	BRIGHTON - 75A(N)	BRIGHTON - 75A(N)	BRIGHTON - 75A(N)	BRIGHTON - 75A(N)	BRIGHTON - 75A(N)
32476	NORWOOD JCN - 75C	NORWOOD JCN - 75C	NORWOOD JCN - 75C	NORWOOD JCN - 75C	NORWOOD JCN - 75C	NORWOOD JCN - 75C	NORWOOD JCN - 75C
32479	NORWOOD JCN - 75C	NORWOOD JCN - 75C	NORWOOD JCN - 75C	NORWOOD JCN - 75C	NORWOOD JCN - 75C	NORWOOD JCN - 75C	NORWOOD JCN - 75C
32480	THREE BRIDGES - 75E	THREE BRIDGES - 75E	THREE BRIDGES - 75E	THREE BRIDGES - 75E	THREE BRIDGES - 75E	THREE BRIDGES - 75E	THREE BRIDGES - 75E
32481	B ARMS - 73B	B ARMS - 73B	B ARMS - 73B	B ARMS - 73B	B ARMS - 73B	B ARMS - 73B	B ARMS - 73B
32482	BRIGHTON - 75A(N)	HORSHAM - 75D	HORSHAM - 75D	HORSHAM - 75D	HORSHAM - 75D	HORSHAM - 75D	HORSHAM - 75D
32484	THREE BRIDGES - 75E	THREE BRIDGES - 75E	THREE BRIDGES - 75E	THREE BRIDGES - 75E	THREE BRIDGES - 75E	THREE BRIDGES - 75E	THREE BRIDGES - 75E
32485	EASTBOURNE - 75G	EASTBOURNE - 75G	EASTBOURNE - 75G	EASTBOURNE - 75G	EASTBOURNE - 75G	EASTBOURNE - 75G	EASTBOURNE - 75G
32486	BRIGHTON - 75A	BRIGHTON - 75A	BRIGHTON - 75A	BRIGHTON - 75A	BRIGHTON - 75A	BRIGHTON - 75A	BRIGHTON - 75A
32487	READING (SR) - 70E	READING (SR) - 70E	READING (SR) - 70E	READING (SR) - 70E	READING (SR) - 70E	FRATTON - 71D	FRATTON - 71D
32488	TONBRIDGE - 74D	TONBRIDGE - 74D	TONBRIDGE - 74D	TONBRIDGE - 74D	TONBRIDGE - 74D	TONBRIDGE - 74D	TONBRIDGE - 74D
32490	BASINGSTOKE - 70D	BASINGSTOKE - 70D	BASINGSTOKE - 70D	BASINGSTOKE - 70D	BASINGSTOKE - 70D	BASINGSTOKE - 70D	GUILDFORD - 70C
32491	BRIGHTON - 75A	BRIGHTON - 75A	BRIGHTON - 75A	BRIGHTON - 75A	BRIGHTON - 75A	BRIGHTON - 75A	BRIGHTON - 75A
32492	EASTLEIGH - 71A	EASTLEIGH - 71A	EASTLEIGH - 71A	EASTLEIGH - 71A	EASTLEIGH - 71A	EASTLEIGH - 71A	EASTLEIGH - 71A
32493	NINE ELMS - 70A	NINE ELMS - 70A	NINE ELMS - 70A	NINE ELMS - 70A	NINE ELMS - 70A	NINE ELMS - 70A	NINE ELMS - 70A
32494	BRIGHTON - 75A(N)	BRIGHTON - 75A(N)	BRIGHTON - 75A(N)	BRIGHTON - 75A(N)	BRIGHTON - 75A(N)	BRIGHTON - 75A(N)	BRIGHTON - 75A(N)
32495	NORWOOD JCN - 75C	NORWOOD JCN - 75C	NORWOOD JCN - 75C	NORWOOD JCN - 75C	NORWOOD JCN - 75C	NORWOOD JCN - 75C	NORWOOD JCN - 75C
32496	HORSHAM - 75D	BRIGHTON - 75A(N)	BRIGHTON - 75A(N)	THREE BRIDGES - 75E	THREE BRIDGES - 75E	THREE BRIDGES - 75E	THREE BRIDGES - 75E
32497	THREE BRIDGES - 75E	THREE BRIDGES - 75E	THREE BRIDGES - 75E	THREE BRIDGES - 75E	THREE BRIDGES - 75E	THREE BRIDGES - 75E	THREE BRIDGES - 75E
32498	NORWOOD JCN - 75C	NORWOOD JCN - 75C	NORWOOD JCN - 75C	NORWOOD JCN - 75C	NORWOOD JCN - 75C	NORWOOD JCN - 75C	NORWOOD JCN - 75C
32499	B ARMS - 73B	B ARMS - 73B	B ARMS - 73B	B ARMS - 73B	B ARMS - 73B	B ARMS - 73B	B ARMS - 73B
32500	NINE ELMS - 70A	NINE ELMS - 70A	NINE ELMS - 70A	NINE ELMS - 70A	NINE ELMS - 70A	NINE ELMS - 70A	NINE ELMS - 70A
32501	HORSHAM - 75D	HORSHAM - 75D	HORSHAM - 75D	HORSHAM - 75D	HORSHAM - 75D	HORSHAM - 75D	HORSHAM - 75D
32502	NORWOOD JCN - 75C	NORWOOD JCN - 75C	NORWOOD JCN - 75C	NORWOOD JCN - 75C	NORWOOD JCN - 75C	NORWOOD JCN - 75C	NORWOOD JCN - 75C
32503	TONBRIDGE - 74D	TONBRIDGE - 74D	TONBRIDGE - 74D	TONBRIDGE - 74D	TONBRIDGE - 74D	TONBRIDGE - 74D	TONBRIDGE - 74D
32504	BRIGHTON - 75A(N)	BRIGHTON - 75A(N)	BRIGHTON - 75A(N)	BRIGHTON - 75A(N)	BRIGHTON - 75A(N)	BRIGHTON - 75A(N)	BRIGHTON - 75A(N)
32505	BRIGHTON - 75A	BRIGHTON - 75A	BRIGHTON - 75A	BRIGHTON - 75A	BRIGHTON - 75A	BRIGHTON - 75A	BRIGHTON - 75A
32506	NORWOOD JCN - 75C	NORWOOD JCN - 75C	NORWOOD JCN - 75C	NORWOOD JCN - 75C	NORWOOD JCN - 75C	NORWOOD JCN - 75C	NORWOOD JCN - 75C
32507	REDHILL - 75B	REDHILL - 75B	REDHILL - 75B	REDHILL - 75B	REDHILL - 75B	REDHILL - 75B	REDHILL - 75B
32508	BRIGHTON - 75A(N)	BRIGHTON - 75A(N)	BRIGHTON - 75A(N)	BRIGHTON - 75A(N)	BRIGHTON - 75A(N)	BRIGHTON - 75A(N)	BRIGHTON - 75A(N)
32509	BRIGHTON - 75A	BRIGHTON - 75A	BRIGHTON - 75A	BRIGHTON - 75A	BRIGHTON - 75A	BRIGHTON - 75A	BRIGHTON - 75A
32510	EASTLEIGH - 71A	EASTLEIGH - 71A	EASTLEIGH - 71A	EASTLEIGH - 71A	EASTLEIGH - 71A	EASTLEIGH - 71A	EASTLEIGH - 71A
32511	HORSHAM - 75D	HORSHAM - 75D	HORSHAM - 75D	HORSHAM - 75D	HORSHAM - 75D	HORSHAM - 75D	HORSHAM - 75D
32512	T.WELLS - 75F	T.WELLS - 75F	T.WELLS - 75F	T.WELLS - 75F	T.WELLS - 75F	T.WELLS - 75F	T.WELLS - 75F
32513	BRIGHTON - 75A	BRIGHTON - 75A	BRIGHTON - 75A	BRIGHTON - 75A	BRIGHTON - 75A	BRIGHTON - 75A	BRIGHTON - 75A
32514	BRIGHTON - 75A	BRIGHTON - 75A	BRIGHTON - 75A	BRIGHTON - 75A	BRIGHTON - 75A	BRIGHTON - 75A	BRIGHTON - 75A
32515	HORSHAM - 75D	HORSHAM - 75D	HORSHAM - 75D	HORSHAM - 75D	HORSHAM - 75D	HORSHAM - 75D	HORSHAM - 75D
32516	THREE BRIDGES - 75E	THREE BRIDGES - 75E	THREE BRIDGES - 75E	THREE BRIDGES - 75E	THREE BRIDGES - 75E	THREE BRIDGES - 75E	THREE BRIDGES - 75E
32517	REDHILL - 75B	REDHILL - 75B	REDHILL - 75B	REDHILL - 75B	REDHILL - 75B	REDHILL - 75B	REDHILL - 75B
32518	EASTBOURNE - 75G	EASTBOURNE - 75G	EASTBOURNE - 75G	EASTBOURNE - 75G	EASTBOURNE - 75G	EASTBOURNE - 75G	EASTBOURNE - 75G
32519	THREE BRIDGES - 75E	THREE BRIDGES - 75E	THREE BRIDGES - 75E	THREE BRIDGES - 75E	THREE BRIDGES - 75E	THREE BRIDGES - 75E	THREE BRIDGES - 75E
32520	THREE BRIDGES - 75E	THREE BRIDGES - 75E	THREE BRIDGES - 75E	THREE BRIDGES - 75E	THREE BRIDGES - 75E	THREE BRIDGES - 75E	THREE BRIDGES - 75E
32556	HORSHAM - 75D	HORSHAM - 75D	HORSHAM - 75D	HORSHAM - 75D	HORSHAM - 75D	HORSHAM - 75D	HORSHAM - 75D
32557	EASTLEIGH - 71A	EASTLEIGH - 71A	EASTLEIGH - 71A	EASTLEIGH - 71A	EASTLEIGH - 71A	EASTLEIGH - 71A	EASTLEIGH - 71A
32558	EASTLEIGH - 71A	EASTLEIGH - 71A	EASTLEIGH - 71A	EASTLEIGH - 71A	EASTLEIGH - 71A	EASTLEIGH - 71A	EASTLEIGH - 71A
32559	EASTLEIGH - 71A	EASTLEIGH - 71A	EASTLEIGH - 71A	EASTLEIGH - 71A	EASTLEIGH - 71A	EASTLEIGH - 71A	EASTLEIGH - 71A
32560	REDHILL - 75B	REDHILL - 75B	REDHILL - 75B	REDHILL - 75B	REDHILL - 75B	REDHILL - 75B	REDHILL - 75B
32561	REDHILL - 75B	REDHILL - 75B	REDHILL - 75B	REDHILL - 75B	REDHILL - 75B	REDHILL - 75B	REDHILL - 75B
32562	EASTLEIGH - 71A	EASTLEIGH - 71A	EASTLEIGH - 71A	EASTLEIGH - 71A	EASTLEIGH - 71A	EASTLEIGH - 71A	EASTLEIGH - 71A
32563	EASTLEIGH - 71A	EASTLEIGH - 71A	EASTLEIGH - 71A	EASTLEIGH - 71A	EASTLEIGH - 71A	EASTLEIGH - 71A	EASTLEIGH - 71A
32564	B ARMS - 73B	B ARMS - 73B	B ARMS - 73B	B ARMS - 73B	B ARMS - 73B	B ARMS - 73B	B ARMS - 73B
32565	B ARMS - 73B	B ARMS - 73B	B ARMS - 73B	B ARMS - 73B	B ARMS - 73B	B ARMS - 73B	B ARMS - 73B
32566	BRIGHTON - 75A	BRIGHTON - 75A	BRIGHTON - 75A	BRIGHTON - 75A	BRIGHTON - 75A	BRIGHTON - 75A	BRIGHTON - 75A
32577	BRIGHTON - 75A	BRIGHTON - 75A	BRIGHTON - 75A	BRIGHTON - 75A	BRIGHTON - 75A	BRIGHTON - 75A	BRIGHTON - 75A
32578	NORWOOD JCN - 75C	NORWOOD JCN - 75C	NORWOOD JCN - 75C	NORWOOD JCN - 75C	NORWOOD JCN - 75C	NORWOOD JCN - 75C	NORWOOD JCN - 75C
32579	EASTLEIGH - 71A	EASTLEIGH - 71A	EASTLEIGH - 71A	EASTLEIGH - 71A	EASTLEIGH - 71A	EASTLEIGH - 71A	EASTLEIGH - 71A
32580	TONBRIDGE - 74D	TONBRIDGE - 74D	TONBRIDGE - 74D	TONBRIDGE - 74D	TONBRIDGE - 74D	TONBRIDGE - 74D	TONBRIDGE - 74D
32581	TONBRIDGE - 74D	TONBRIDGE - 74D	TONBRIDGE - 74D	TONBRIDGE - 74D	TONBRIDGE - 74D	TONBRIDGE - 74D	TONBRIDGE - 74D
32582	T.WELLS - 75F	T.WELLS - 75F	T.WELLS - 75F	T.WELLS - 75F	T.WELLS - 75F	T.WELLS - 75F	T.WELLS - 75F

loco	Apr-50	Sep-50	Oct-50	Nov-50	Dec-50	Mar-51	Apr-51
				E1/R 0-6-2T (1927)			
32094	PLYMOUTH - 72D	PLYMOUTH - 72D	PLYMOUTH - 72D	PLYMOUTH - 72D	PLYMOUTH - 72D	PLYMOUTH - 72D	PLYMOUTH - 72D
32095	BARNSTAPLE - 72E	BARNSTAPLE - 72E	BARNSTAPLE - 72E	BARNSTAPLE - 72E	BARNSTAPLE - 72E	BARNSTAPLE - 72E	BARNSTAPLE - 72E
32096	BARNSTAPLE - 72E	BARNSTAPLE - 72E	BARNSTAPLE - 72E	BARNSTAPLE - 72E	BARNSTAPLE - 72E	BARNSTAPLE - 72E	BARNSTAPLE - 72E
32124	EXMOUTH JCN - 72A	EXMOUTH JCN - 72A	EXMOUTH JCN - 72A	EXMOUTH JCN - 72A	EXMOUTH JCN - 72A	EXMOUTH JCN - 72A	EXMOUTH JCN - 72A
32135	EXMOUTH JCN - 72A	EXMOUTH JCN - 72A	EXMOUTH JCN - 72A	EXMOUTH JCN - 72A	EXMOUTH JCN - 72A	EXMOUTH JCN - 72A	EXMOUTH JCN - 72A
32608	BARNSTAPLE - 72E	BARNSTAPLE - 72E	BARNSTAPLE - 72E	BARNSTAPLE - 72E	BARNSTAPLE - 72E	BARNSTAPLE - 72E	BARNSTAPLE - 72E
32610	BARNSTAPLE - 72E	BARNSTAPLE - 72E	BARNSTAPLE - 72E	BARNSTAPLE - 72E	BARNSTAPLE - 72E	BARNSTAPLE - 72E	BARNSTAPLE - 72E
32695	EXMOUTH JCN - 72A	EXMOUTH JCN - 72A	EXMOUTH JCN - 72A	EXMOUTH JCN - 72A	EXMOUTH JCN - 72A	EXMOUTH JCN - 72A	EXMOUTH JCN - 72A
32696	BARNSTAPLE - 72E	BARNSTAPLE - 72E	BARNSTAPLE - 72E	BARNSTAPLE - 72E	BARNSTAPLE - 72E	BARNSTAPLE - 72E	BARNSTAPLE - 72E
32697	EXMOUTH JCN - 72A	EXMOUTH JCN - 72A	EXMOUTH JCN - 72A	EXMOUTH JCN - 72A	EXMOUTH JCN - 72A	EXMOUTH JCN - 72A	EXMOUTH JCN - 72A
				E3 0-6-2T (1894)			
32165	B ARMS - 73B	B ARMS - 73B	B ARMS - 73B	B ARMS - 73B	B ARMS - 73B	B ARMS - 73B	B ARMS - 73B
32166	B ARMS - 73B	B ARMS - 73B	B ARMS - 73B	B ARMS - 73B	B ARMS - 73B	B ARMS - 73B	B ARMS - 73B
32167	TONBRIDGE - 74D	TONBRIDGE - 74D	TONBRIDGE - 74D	TONBRIDGE - 74D	TONBRIDGE - 74D	TONBRIDGE - 74D	TONBRIDGE - 74D
32168	B ARMS - 73B	B ARMS - 73B	B ARMS - 73B	B ARMS - 73B	B ARMS - 73B	B ARMS - 73B	B ARMS - 73B
32169	TONBRIDGE - 74D	TONBRIDGE - 74D	TONBRIDGE - 74D	TONBRIDGE - 74D	TONBRIDGE - 74D	BRIGHTON - 75A(N)	BRIGHTON - 75A(N)
32170	B ARMS - 73B	B ARMS - 73B	B ARMS - 73B	B ARMS - 73B	B ARMS - 73B	B ARMS - 73B	BRIGHTON - 75A
32453	B ARMS - 73B	B ARMS - 73B	B ARMS - 73B	B ARMS - 73B	B ARMS - 73B	B ARMS - 73B	B ARMS - 73B
32454	TONBRIDGE - 74D	TONBRIDGE - 74D	TONBRIDGE - 74D	TONBRIDGE - 74D	TONBRIDGE - 74D	TONBRIDGE - 74D	TONBRIDGE - 74D
32455	BRIGHTON - 75A	BRIGHTON - 75A	BRIGHTON - 75A	TONBRIDGE - 74D	B ARMS - 73B	B ARMS - 73B	B ARMS - 73B
32456	TONBRIDGE - 74D	TONBRIDGE - 74D	TONBRIDGE - 74D	TONBRIDGE - 74D	TONBRIDGE - 74D	TONBRIDGE - 74D	TONBRIDGE - 74D
32458	B ARMS - 73B	B ARMS - 73B	B ARMS - 73B	B ARMS - 73B	B ARMS - 73B	B ARMS - 73B	B ARMS - 73B
32459	B ARMS - 73B	B ARMS - 73B	B ARMS - 73B	B ARMS - 73B	B ARMS - 73B	B ARMS - 73B	B ARMS - 73B
32460	B ARMS - 73B	B ARMS - 73B	B ARMS - 73B	B ARMS - 73B	B ARMS - 73B	B ARMS - 73B	B ARMS - 73B
32461	B ARMS - 73B	B ARMS - 73B	B ARMS - 73B	B ARMS - 73B	B ARMS - 73B	B ARMS - 73B	B ARMS - 73B
32462	B ARMS - 73B	B ARMS - 73B	B ARMS - 73B	B ARMS - 73B	B ARMS - 73B	B ARMS - 73B	B ARMS - 73B
				E4 0-6-2T (1897)			
32463	B ARMS - 73B	B ARMS - 73B	B ARMS - 73B	B ARMS - 73B	B ARMS - 73B	B ARMS - 73B	B ARMS - 73B
32464	HORSHAM - 75D	HORSHAM - 75D	HORSHAM - 75D	HORSHAM - 75D	HORSHAM - 75D	HORSHAM - 75D	HORSHAM - 75D
32465	THREE BRIDGES - 75E	THREE BRIDGES - 75E	THREE BRIDGES - 75E	THREE BRIDGES - 75E	THREE BRIDGES - 75E	THREE BRIDGES - 75E	THREE BRIDGES - 75E
32467	B ARMS - 73B	B ARMS - 73B	B ARMS - 73B	B ARMS - 73B	B ARMS - 73B	B ARMS - 73B	B ARMS - 73B
32468	NINE ELMS - 70A	NINE ELMS - 70A	NINE ELMS - 70A	NINE ELMS - 70A	NINE ELMS - 70A	NINE ELMS - 70A	NINE ELMS - 70A
32469	B ARMS - 73B	B ARMS - 73B	B ARMS - 73B	B ARMS - 73B	B ARMS - 73B	B ARMS - 73B	B ARMS - 73B
32470	BRIGHTON - 75A	BRIGHTON - 75A	BRIGHTON - 75A	BRIGHTON - 75A	BRIGHTON - 75A	BRIGHTON - 75A	BRIGHTON - 75A
32471	BRIGHTON - 75A	BRIGHTON - 75A	BRIGHTON - 75A	BRIGHTON - 75A	BRIGHTON - 75A	BRIGHTON - 75A	BRIGHTON - 75A
32472	B ARMS - 73B	B ARMS - 73B	B ARMS - 73B	B ARMS - 73B	B ARMS - 73B	B ARMS - 73B	B ARMS - 73B
32473	NORWOOD JCN - 75C	NORWOOD JCN - 75C	B ARMS - 73B	B ARMS - 73B	B ARMS - 73B	B ARMS - 73B	B ARMS - 73B
32474	B ARMS - 73B	B ARMS - 73B	B ARMS - 73B	B ARMS - 73B	B ARMS - 73B	B ARMS - 73B	B ARMS - 73B
32475	BRIGHTON - 75A(N)	BRIGHTON - 75A(N)	BRIGHTON - 75A(N)	BRIGHTON - 75A(N)	BRIGHTON - 75A(N)	BRIGHTON - 75A(N)	BRIGHTON - 75A(N)
32476	NORWOOD JCN - 75C	NORWOOD JCN - 75C	NORWOOD JCN - 75C	NORWOOD JCN - 75C	NORWOOD JCN - 75C	NORWOOD JCN - 75C	NORWOOD JCN - 75C
32479	NORWOOD JCN - 75C	NORWOOD JCN - 75C	NORWOOD JCN - 75C	NORWOOD JCN - 75C	NORWOOD JCN - 75C	NORWOOD JCN - 75C	NORWOOD JCN - 75C
32480	THREE BRIDGES - 75E	THREE BRIDGES - 75E	THREE BRIDGES - 75E	THREE BRIDGES - 75E	THREE BRIDGES - 75E	THREE BRIDGES - 75E	THREE BRIDGES - 75E
32481	B ARMS - 73B	B ARMS - 73B	B ARMS - 73B	B ARMS - 73B	B ARMS - 73B	B ARMS - 73B	B ARMS - 73B
32482	HORSHAM - 75D	HORSHAM - 75D	HORSHAM - 75D	HORSHAM - 75D	HORSHAM - 75D	HORSHAM - 75D	HORSHAM - 75D
32484	THREE BRIDGES - 75E	THREE BRIDGES - 75E	THREE BRIDGES - 75E	THREE BRIDGES - 75E	THREE BRIDGES - 75E	THREE BRIDGES - 75E	THREE BRIDGES - 75E
32485	EASTBOURNE - 75G	EASTBOURNE - 75G	EASTBOURNE - 75G	EASTBOURNE - 75G	EASTBOURNE - 75G	EASTBOURNE - 75G	EASTBOURNE - 75G
32486	BRIGHTON - 75A	BRIGHTON - 75A	BRIGHTON - 75A	BRIGHTON - 75A	BRIGHTON - 75A	BRIGHTON - 75A	BRIGHTON - 75A
32487	FRATTON - 71D	FRATTON - 71D	FRATTON - 71D	GUILDFORD - 70C	GUILDFORD - 70C	GUILDFORD - 70C	GUILDFORD - 70C
32488	TONBRIDGE - 74D	TONBRIDGE - 74D	TONBRIDGE - 74D	TONBRIDGE - 74D	TONBRIDGE - 74D	TONBRIDGE - 74D	TONBRIDGE - 74D
32490	GUILDFORD - 70C	GUILDFORD - 70C	GUILDFORD - 70C	GUILDFORD - 70C	GUILDFORD - 70C	GUILDFORD - 70C	GUILDFORD - 70C
32491	EASTLEIGH - 71A	EASTLEIGH - 71A	EASTLEIGH - 71A	EASTLEIGH - 71A	EASTLEIGH - 71A	EASTLEIGH - 71A	EASTLEIGH - 71A
32492	EASTLEIGH - 71A	EASTLEIGH - 71A	EASTLEIGH - 71A	EASTLEIGH - 71A	EASTLEIGH - 71A	EASTLEIGH - 71A	EASTLEIGH - 71A
32493	NINE ELMS - 70A	NINE ELMS - 70A	NINE ELMS - 70A	NINE ELMS - 70A	NINE ELMS - 70A	NINE ELMS - 70A	NINE ELMS - 70A
32494	BRIGHTON - 75A(N)	BRIGHTON - 75A(N)	BRIGHTON - 75A(N)	BRIGHTON - 75A(N)	BRIGHTON - 75A(N)	BRIGHTON - 75A(N)	BRIGHTON - 75A(N)
32495	NORWOOD JCN - 75C	NORWOOD JCN - 75C	NORWOOD JCN - 75C	NORWOOD JCN - 75C	NORWOOD JCN - 75C	NORWOOD JCN - 75C	NORWOOD JCN - 75C
32496	THREE BRIDGES - 75E	THREE BRIDGES - 75E	THREE BRIDGES - 75E	BRIGHTON - 75A(N)	BRIGHTON - 75A(N)	BRIGHTON - 75A(N)	BRIGHTON - 75A(N)
32497	THREE BRIDGES - 75E	THREE BRIDGES - 75E	THREE BRIDGES - 75E	THREE BRIDGES - 75E	THREE BRIDGES - 75E	THREE BRIDGES - 75E	THREE BRIDGES - 75E
32498	NORWOOD JCN - 75C	NORWOOD JCN - 75C	NINE ELMS - 70A	NINE ELMS - 70A	NINE ELMS - 70A	NINE ELMS - 70A	NINE ELMS - 70A
32499	B ARMS - 73B	B ARMS - 73B	NINE ELMS - 70A	NINE ELMS - 70A	NINE ELMS - 70A	NINE ELMS - 70A	NINE ELMS - 70A
32500	NINE ELMS - 70A	NINE ELMS - 70A	NINE ELMS - 70A	NINE ELMS - 70A	NINE ELMS - 70A	NINE ELMS - 70A	NINE ELMS - 70A
32501	HORSHAM - 75D	HORSHAM - 75D	HORSHAM - 75D	NINE ELMS - 70A	NINE ELMS - 70A	NINE ELMS - 70A	NINE ELMS - 70A
32502	NORWOOD JCN - 75C	NORWOOD JCN - 75C	NORWOOD JCN - 75C	NINE ELMS - 70A	NINE ELMS - 70A	NINE ELMS - 70A	NINE ELMS - 70A
32503	TONBRIDGE - 74D	TONBRIDGE - 74D	TONBRIDGE - 74D	TONBRIDGE - 74D	TONBRIDGE - 74D	TONBRIDGE - 74D	TONBRIDGE - 74D
32504	BRIGHTON - 75A(N)	BRIGHTON - 75A(N)	BRIGHTON - 75A(N)	BRIGHTON - 75A(N)	BRIGHTON - 75A(N)	BRIGHTON - 75A(N)	BRIGHTON - 75A(N)
32505	BRIGHTON - 75A	BRIGHTON - 75A	BRIGHTON - 75A	BRIGHTON - 75A	BRIGHTON - 75A	BRIGHTON - 75A	BRIGHTON - 75A
32506	NORWOOD JCN - 75C	NORWOOD JCN - 75C	NORWOOD JCN - 75C	NORWOOD JCN - 75C	NORWOOD JCN - 75C	NORWOOD JCN - 75C	NORWOOD JCN - 75C
32507	REDHILL - 75B	REDHILL - 75B	REDHILL - 75B	REDHILL - 75B	REDHILL - 75B	REDHILL - 75B	REDHILL - 75B
32508	BRIGHTON - 75A(N)	BRIGHTON - 75A(N)	BRIGHTON - 75A(N)	BRIGHTON - 75A(N)	BRIGHTON - 75A(N)	BRIGHTON - 75A(N)	BRIGHTON - 75A(N)
32509	BRIGHTON - 75A	BRIGHTON - 75A	BRIGHTON - 75A	BRIGHTON - 75A	BRIGHTON - 75A	BRIGHTON - 75A	BRIGHTON - 75A
32510	EASTLEIGH - 71A	EASTLEIGH - 71A	EASTLEIGH - 71A	EASTLEIGH - 71A	EASTLEIGH - 71A	EASTLEIGH - 71A	EASTLEIGH - 71A
32511	HORSHAM - 75D	HORSHAM - 75D	HORSHAM - 75D	HORSHAM - 75D	HORSHAM - 75D	HORSHAM - 75D	HORSHAM - 75D
32512	T.WELLS - 75F	T.WELLS - 75F	REDHILL - 75B	REDHILL - 75B	REDHILL - 75B	REDHILL - 75B	REDHILL - 75B
32513	BRIGHTON - 75A	BRIGHTON - 75A	BRIGHTON - 75A	BRIGHTON - 75A	BRIGHTON - 75A	BRIGHTON - 75A	BRIGHTON - 75A
32514	BRIGHTON - 75A	BRIGHTON - 75A	BRIGHTON - 75A	BRIGHTON - 75A	BRIGHTON - 75A	BRIGHTON - 75A	BRIGHTON - 75A
32515	HORSHAM - 75D	HORSHAM - 75D	HORSHAM - 75D	HORSHAM - 75D	HORSHAM - 75D	HORSHAM - 75D	HORSHAM - 75D
32516	THREE BRIDGES - 75E	THREE BRIDGES - 75E	THREE BRIDGES - 75E	THREE BRIDGES - 75E	THREE BRIDGES - 75E	THREE BRIDGES - 75E	THREE BRIDGES - 75E
32517	REDHILL - 75B	REDHILL - 75B	REDHILL - 75B	REDHILL - 75B	REDHILL - 75B	REDHILL - 75B	REDHILL - 75B
32518	EASTBOURNE - 75G	EASTBOURNE - 75G	EASTBOURNE - 75G	EASTBOURNE - 75G	EASTBOURNE - 75G	EASTBOURNE - 75G	EASTBOURNE - 75G
32519	THREE BRIDGES - 75E	THREE BRIDGES - 75E	THREE BRIDGES - 75E	THREE BRIDGES - 75E	THREE BRIDGES - 75E	THREE BRIDGES - 75E	THREE BRIDGES - 75E
32520	THREE BRIDGES - 75E	THREE BRIDGES - 75E	THREE BRIDGES - 75E	THREE BRIDGES - 75E	THREE BRIDGES - 75E	THREE BRIDGES - 75E	THREE BRIDGES - 75E
32556	HORSHAM - 75D	HORSHAM - 75D	HORSHAM - 75D	HORSHAM - 75D	HORSHAM - 75D	HORSHAM - 75D	HORSHAM - 75D
32557	EASTLEIGH - 71A	EASTLEIGH - 71A	EASTLEIGH - 71A	EASTLEIGH - 71A	EASTLEIGH - 71A	EASTLEIGH - 71A	EASTLEIGH - 71A
32558	EASTLEIGH - 71A	EASTLEIGH - 71A	EASTLEIGH - 71A	EASTLEIGH - 71A	EASTLEIGH - 71A	EASTLEIGH - 71A	EASTLEIGH - 71A
32559	EASTLEIGH - 71A	EASTLEIGH - 71A	EASTLEIGH - 71A	EASTLEIGH - 71A	EASTLEIGH - 71A	EASTLEIGH - 71A	EASTLEIGH - 71A
32560	REDHILL - 75B	REDHILL - 75B	REDHILL - 75B	REDHILL - 75B	REDHILL - 75B	REDHILL - 75B	REDHILL - 75B
32561	REDHILL - 75B	REDHILL - 75B	REDHILL - 75B	REDHILL - 75B	REDHILL - 75B	REDHILL - 75B	REDHILL - 75B
32562	EASTLEIGH - 71A	EASTLEIGH - 71A	EASTLEIGH - 71A	EASTLEIGH - 71A	EASTLEIGH - 71A	EASTLEIGH - 71A	EASTLEIGH - 71A
32563	EASTLEIGH - 71A	EASTLEIGH - 71A	EASTLEIGH - 71A	EASTLEIGH - 71A	EASTLEIGH - 71A	EASTLEIGH - 71A	EASTLEIGH - 71A
32564	B ARMS - 73B	B ARMS - 73B	B ARMS - 73B	B ARMS - 73B	B ARMS - 73B	B ARMS - 73B	B ARMS - 73B
32565	B ARMS - 73B	B ARMS - 73B	B ARMS - 73B	B ARMS - 73B	B ARMS - 73B	B ARMS - 73B	B ARMS - 73B
32566	BRIGHTON - 75A	BRIGHTON - 75A	BRIGHTON - 75A	BRIGHTON - 75A	BRIGHTON - 75A	BRIGHTON - 75A	BRIGHTON - 75A
32577	BRIGHTON - 75A	BRIGHTON - 75A	BRIGHTON - 75A	BRIGHTON - 75A	BRIGHTON - 75A	BRIGHTON - 75A	BRIGHTON - 75A
32578	NORWOOD JCN - 75C	NORWOOD JCN - 75C	NORWOOD JCN - 75C	NORWOOD JCN - 75C	NORWOOD JCN - 75C	NORWOOD JCN - 75C	NORWOOD JCN - 75C
32579	EASTLEIGH - 71A	EASTLEIGH - 71A	EASTLEIGH - 71A	EASTLEIGH - 71A	EASTLEIGH - 71A	EASTLEIGH - 71A	EASTLEIGH - 71A
32580	TONBRIDGE - 74D	HORSHAM - 75D	HORSHAM - 75D	HORSHAM - 75D	HORSHAM - 75D	HORSHAM - 75D	HORSHAM - 75D
32581	TONBRIDGE - 74D	HORSHAM - 75D	HORSHAM - 75D	HORSHAM - 75D	HORSHAM - 75D	HORSHAM - 75D	HORSHAM - 75D
32582	T.WELLS - 75F	T.WELLS - 75F	READING (SR) - 70E	THREE BRIDGES - 75E	THREE BRIDGES - 75E	T.WELLS - 75F	T.WELLS - 75F

loco	Jun-51	Jul-51	Sep-51	Dec-51	Jan-52	Mar-52	Jun-52
				E1/R 0-6-2T (1927)			
32094	PLYMOUTH - 72D	PLYMOUTH - 72D	PLYMOUTH - 72D	PLYMOUTH - 72D	PLYMOUTH - 72D	PLYMOUTH - 72D	PLYMOUTH - 72D
32095	BARNSTAPLE - 72E	BARNSTAPLE - 72E	BARNSTAPLE - 72E	BARNSTAPLE - 72E	BARNSTAPLE - 72E	BARNSTAPLE - 72E	BARNSTAPLE - 72E
32096	BARNSTAPLE - 72E	BARNSTAPLE - 72E	BARNSTAPLE - 72E	BARNSTAPLE - 72E	BARNSTAPLE - 72E	BARNSTAPLE - 72E	BARNSTAPLE - 72E
32124	EXMOUTH JCN - 72A	EXMOUTH JCN - 72A	EXMOUTH JCN - 72A	EXMOUTH JCN - 72A	EXMOUTH JCN - 72A	EXMOUTH JCN - 72A	EXMOUTH JCN - 72A
32135	EXMOUTH JCN - 72A	EXMOUTH JCN - 72A	EXMOUTH JCN - 72A	EXMOUTH JCN - 72A	EXMOUTH JCN - 72A	EXMOUTH JCN - 72A	EXMOUTH JCN - 72A
32608	BARNSTAPLE - 72E	BARNSTAPLE - 72E	BARNSTAPLE - 72E	BARNSTAPLE - 72E	BARNSTAPLE - 72E	BARNSTAPLE - 72E	BARNSTAPLE - 72E
32610	BARNSTAPLE - 72E	BARNSTAPLE - 72E	BARNSTAPLE - 72E	BARNSTAPLE - 72E	BARNSTAPLE - 72E	BARNSTAPLE - 72E	BARNSTAPLE - 72E
32695	EXMOUTH JCN - 72A	EXMOUTH JCN - 72A	EXMOUTH JCN - 72A	EXMOUTH JCN - 72A	EXMOUTH JCN - 72A	EXMOUTH JCN - 72A	EXMOUTH JCN - 72A
32696	BARNSTAPLE - 72E	BARNSTAPLE - 72E	BARNSTAPLE - 72E	BARNSTAPLE - 72E	BARNSTAPLE - 72E	BARNSTAPLE - 72E	BARNSTAPLE - 72E
32697	EXMOUTH JCN - 72A	EXMOUTH JCN - 72A	EXMOUTH JCN - 72A	EXMOUTH JCN - 72A	EXMOUTH JCN - 72A	EXMOUTH JCN - 72A	EXMOUTH JCN - 72A
				E3 0-6-2T (1894)			
32165	B ARMS - 73B	B ARMS - 73B	B ARMS - 73B	B ARMS - 73B	B ARMS - 73B	B ARMS - 73B	B ARMS - 73B
32166	B ARMS - 73B	B ARMS - 73B	B ARMS - 73B	B ARMS - 73B	B ARMS - 73B	B ARMS - 73B	BRIGHTON - 75A
32167	TONBRIDGE - 74D	TONBRIDGE - 74D	TONBRIDGE - 74D	TONBRIDGE - 74D	BRIGHTON - 75A	BRIGHTON - 75A	BRIGHTON - 75A
32168	BRIGHTON - 75A	BRIGHTON - 75A	BRIGHTON - 75A	BRIGHTON - 75A	BRIGHTON - 75A	BRIGHTON - 75A	BRIGHTON - 75A
32169	BRIGHTON - 75A(N)	BRIGHTON - 75A(N)	BRIGHTON - 75A(N)	BRIGHTON - 75A(N)	BRIGHTON - 75A(N)	BRIGHTON - 75A(N)	BRIGHTON - 75A(N)
32170	BRIGHTON - 75A	BRIGHTON - 75A	BRIGHTON - 75A	BRIGHTON - 75A	BRIGHTON - 75A	BRIGHTON - 75A	BRIGHTON - 75A
32453	B ARMS - 73B	B ARMS - 73B	B ARMS - 73B	B ARMS - 73B	B ARMS - 73B	B ARMS - 73B	B ARMS - 73B
32454	TONBRIDGE - 74D	TONBRIDGE - 74D	TONBRIDGE - 74D	TONBRIDGE - 74D	TONBRIDGE - 74D	TONBRIDGE - 74D	TONBRIDGE - 74D
32455	B ARMS - 73B	B ARMS - 73B	B ARMS - 73B	B ARMS - 73B	B ARMS - 73B	B ARMS - 73B	B ARMS - 73B
32456	TONBRIDGE - 74D	TONBRIDGE - 74D	TONBRIDGE - 74D	TONBRIDGE - 74D	TONBRIDGE - 74D	TONBRIDGE - 74D	TONBRIDGE - 74D
32458	B ARMS - 73B	B ARMS - 73B	B ARMS - 73B	B ARMS - 73B	B ARMS - 73B	B ARMS - 73B	B ARMS - 73B
32459	B ARMS - 73B	B ARMS - 73B	B ARMS - 73B	B ARMS - 73B	B ARMS - 73B	B ARMS - 73B	B ARMS - 73B
32460	B ARMS - 73B	B ARMS - 73B	B ARMS - 73B	B ARMS - 73B	B ARMS - 73B	B ARMS - 73B	B ARMS - 73B
32461	B ARMS - 73B	B ARMS - 73B	B ARMS - 73B	B ARMS - 73B	B ARMS - 73B	B ARMS - 73B	B ARMS - 73B
32462	B ARMS - 73B	B ARMS - 73B	B ARMS - 73B	B ARMS - 73B	B ARMS - 73B	B ARMS - 73B	B ARMS - 73B
				E4 0-6-2T (1897)			
32463	B ARMS - 73B	B ARMS - 73B	HORSHAM - 75D	HORSHAM - 75D	HORSHAM - 75D	HORSHAM - 75D	HORSHAM - 75D
32464	HORSHAM - 75D	HORSHAM - 75D	HORSHAM - 75D	HORSHAM - 75D	HORSHAM - 75D	HORSHAM - 75D	HORSHAM - 75D
32465	THREE BRIDGES - 75E	THREE BRIDGES - 75E	HORSHAM - 75D	HORSHAM - 75D	HORSHAM - 75D	HORSHAM - 75D	HORSHAM - 75D
32467	B ARMS - 73B	B ARMS - 73B	HORSHAM - 75D	HORSHAM - 75D	HORSHAM - 75D	HORSHAM - 75D	HORSHAM - 75D
32468	NINE ELMS - 70A	NINE ELMS - 70A	NINE ELMS - 70A	HORSHAM - 75D	HORSHAM - 75D	HORSHAM - 75D	HORSHAM - 75D
32469	B ARMS - 73B	B ARMS - 73B	B ARMS - 73B	HORSHAM - 75D	HORSHAM - 75D	HORSHAM - 75D	HORSHAM - 75D
32470	BRIGHTON - 75A	BRIGHTON - 75A	BRIGHTON - 75A	HORSHAM - 75D	HORSHAM - 75D	HORSHAM - 75D	HORSHAM - 75D
32471	BRIGHTON - 75A	BRIGHTON - 75A	BRIGHTON - 75A	BRIGHTON - 75A	B ARMS - 73B	B ARMS - 73B	B ARMS - 73B
32472	B ARMS - 73B	B ARMS - 73B	B ARMS - 73B	B ARMS - 73B	B ARMS - 73B	B ARMS - 73B	B ARMS - 73B
32473	B ARMS - 73B	B ARMS - 73B	B ARMS - 73B	B ARMS - 73B	B ARMS - 73B	B ARMS - 73B	B ARMS - 73B
32474	B ARMS - 73B	B ARMS - 73B	B ARMS - 73B	B ARMS - 73B	B ARMS - 73B	B ARMS - 73B	B ARMS - 73B
32475	BRIGHTON - 75A(N)	BRIGHTON - 75A(N)	BRIGHTON - 75A(N)	BRIGHTON - 75A(N)	BRIGHTON - 75A(N)	BRIGHTON - 75A(N)	BRIGHTON - 75A(N)
32476	NORWOOD JCN - 75C	NORWOOD JCN - 75C	NORWOOD JCN - 75C	NORWOOD JCN - 75C	NORWOOD JCN - 75C	NORWOOD JCN - 75C	NORWOOD JCN - 75C
32479	NORWOOD JCN - 75C	NORWOOD JCN - 75C	NORWOOD JCN - 75C	NORWOOD JCN - 75C	FRATTON - 71D	FRATTON - 71D	FRATTON - 71D
32480	THREE BRIDGES - 75E	THREE BRIDGES - 75E	THREE BRIDGES - 75E	THREE BRIDGES - 75E	THREE BRIDGES - 75E	THREE BRIDGES - 75E	THREE BRIDGES - 75E
32481	B ARMS - 73B	B ARMS - 73B	THREE BRIDGES - 75E	THREE BRIDGES - 75E	THREE BRIDGES - 75E	THREE BRIDGES - 75E	THREE BRIDGES - 75E
32482	HORSHAM - 75D	HORSHAM - 75D	THREE BRIDGES - 75E	THREE BRIDGES - 75E	THREE BRIDGES - 75E	THREE BRIDGES - 75E	THREE BRIDGES - 75E
32484	THREE BRIDGES - 75E	THREE BRIDGES - 75E	THREE BRIDGES - 75E	THREE BRIDGES - 75E	THREE BRIDGES - 75E	THREE BRIDGES - 75E	THREE BRIDGES - 75E
32485	EASTBOURNE - 75G	EASTBOURNE - 75G	EASTBOURNE - 75G	EASTBOURNE - 75G	EASTBOURNE - 75G	EASTBOURNE - 75G	EASTBOURNE - 75G
32486	BRIGHTON - 75A	BRIGHTON - 75A	BRIGHTON - 75A	BRIGHTON - 75A	BRIGHTON - 75A	EASTLEIGH - 71A	SALISBURY - 72B
32487	GUILDFORD - 70C	GUILDFORD - 70C	GUILDFORD - 70C	GUILDFORD - 70C	GUILDFORD - 70C	GUILDFORD - 70C	GUILDFORD - 70C
32488	TONBRIDGE - 74D	TONBRIDGE - 74D	TONBRIDGE - 74D	TONBRIDGE - 74D	TONBRIDGE - 74D	TONBRIDGE - 74D	TONBRIDGE - 74D
32490	GUILDFORD - 70C	GUILDFORD - 70C	GUILDFORD - 70C	GUILDFORD - 70C	GUILDFORD - 70C	GUILDFORD - 70C	GUILDFORD - 70C
32491	EASTLEIGH - 71A	EASTLEIGH - 71A	EASTLEIGH - 71A	EASTLEIGH - 71A	EASTLEIGH - 71A	EASTLEIGH - 71A	EASTLEIGH - 71A
32492	EASTLEIGH - 71A	EASTLEIGH - 71A	EASTLEIGH - 71A	EASTLEIGH - 71A	EASTLEIGH - 71A	EASTLEIGH - 71A	EASTLEIGH - 71A
32493	NINE ELMS - 70A	NINE ELMS - 70A	NINE ELMS - 70A	NINE ELMS - 70A	NINE ELMS - 70A	NINE ELMS - 70A	NINE ELMS - 70A
32494	BRIGHTON - 75A(N)	BRIGHTON - 75A(N)	BRIGHTON - 75A(N)	BRIGHTON - 75A(N)	BRIGHTON - 75A(N)	BRIGHTON - 75A(N)	BRIGHTON - 75A(N)
32495	NORWOOD JCN - 75C	NORWOOD JCN - 75C	NORWOOD JCN - 75C	NORWOOD JCN - 75C	FRATTON - 71D	FRATTON - 71D	FRATTON - 71D
32496	BRIGHTON - 75A(N)	BRIGHTON - 75A(N)	BRIGHTON - 75A(N)	BRIGHTON - 75A(N)	BRIGHTON - 75A(N)	BRIGHTON - 75A(N)	BRIGHTON - 75A(N)
32497	THREE BRIDGES - 75E	THREE BRIDGES - 75E	NINE ELMS - 70A	NINE ELMS - 70A	NINE ELMS - 70A	NINE ELMS - 70A	NINE ELMS - 70A
32498	NINE ELMS - 70A	NINE ELMS - 70A	NINE ELMS - 70A	NINE ELMS - 70A	NINE ELMS - 70A	NINE ELMS - 70A	NINE ELMS - 70A
32499	NINE ELMS - 70A	NINE ELMS - 70A	NINE ELMS - 70A	NINE ELMS - 70A	NINE ELMS - 70A	NINE ELMS - 70A	NINE ELMS - 70A
32500	NINE ELMS - 70A	NINE ELMS - 70A	NINE ELMS - 70A	NINE ELMS - 70A	NINE ELMS - 70A	NINE ELMS - 70A	NINE ELMS - 70A
32501	NINE ELMS - 70A	NINE ELMS - 70A	READING (SR) - 70E	READING (SR) - 70E	READING (SR) - 70E	READING (SR) - 70E	READING (SR) - 70E
32502	NINE ELMS - 70A	NINE ELMS - 70A	NINE ELMS - 70A	NINE ELMS - 70A	NINE ELMS - 70A	NINE ELMS - 70A	NINE ELMS - 70A
32503	TONBRIDGE - 74D	TONBRIDGE - 74D	TONBRIDGE - 74D	TONBRIDGE - 74D	TONBRIDGE - 74D	TONBRIDGE - 74D	TONBRIDGE - 74D
32504	BRIGHTON - 75A(N)	BRIGHTON - 75A(N)	BRIGHTON - 75A(N)	BRIGHTON - 75A(N)	BRIGHTON - 75A(N)	BRIGHTON - 75A(N)	BRIGHTON - 75A(N)
32505	BRIGHTON - 75A	BRIGHTON - 75A	BRIGHTON - 75A	FRATTON - 71D	FRATTON - 71D	FRATTON - 71D	FRATTON - 71D
32506	SALISBURY - 72B	SALISBURY - 72B	SALISBURY - 72B	SALISBURY - 72B	SALISBURY - 72B	SALISBURY - 72B	SALISBURY - 72B
32507	REDHILL - 75B	REDHILL - 75B	REDHILL - 75B	REDHILL - 75B	REDHILL - 75B	REDHILL - 75B	REDHILL - 75B
32508	BRIGHTON - 75A(N)	BRIGHTON - 75A(N)	BRIGHTON - 75A	BRIGHTON - 75A	BRIGHTON - 75A	BRIGHTON - 75A	BRIGHTON - 75A
32509	BRIGHTON - 75A	BRIGHTON - 75A	BRIGHTON - 75A	FRATTON - 71D	FRATTON - 71D	FRATTON - 71D	FRATTON - 71D
32510	EASTLEIGH - 71A	EASTLEIGH - 71A	EASTLEIGH - 71A	EASTLEIGH - 71A	EASTLEIGH - 71A	EASTLEIGH - 71A	EASTLEIGH - 71A
32511	HORSHAM - 75D	HORSHAM - 75D	HORSHAM - 75D	HORSHAM - 75D	HORSHAM - 75D	HORSHAM - 75D	HORSHAM - 75D
32512	REDHILL - 75B	REDHILL - 75B	REDHILL - 75B	REDHILL - 75B	REDHILL - 75B	REDHILL - 75B	REDHILL - 75B
32513	BRIGHTON - 75A	BRIGHTON - 75A	BRIGHTON - 75A	BRIGHTON - 75A	BRIGHTON - 75A	BRIGHTON - 75A	BRIGHTON - 75A
32514	BRIGHTON - 75A	BRIGHTON - 75A	BRIGHTON - 75A	BRIGHTON - 75A	BRIGHTON - 75A	BRIGHTON - 75A	BRIGHTON - 75A
32515	HORSHAM - 75D	HORSHAM - 75D	HORSHAM - 75D	HORSHAM - 75D	BRIGHTON - 75A	BRIGHTON - 75A	BRIGHTON - 75A
32516	THREE BRIDGES - 75E	THREE BRIDGES - 75E	THREE BRIDGES - 75E	THREE BRIDGES - 75E	THREE BRIDGES - 75E	THREE BRIDGES - 75E	THREE BRIDGES - 75E
32517	REDHILL - 75B	REDHILL - 75B	REDHILL - 75B	EASTBOURNE - 75G	EASTBOURNE - 75G	EASTBOURNE - 75G	EASTBOURNE - 75G
32518	EASTBOURNE - 75G	EASTBOURNE - 75G	EASTBOURNE - 75G	EASTBOURNE - 75G	EASTBOURNE - 75G	EASTBOURNE - 75G	EASTBOURNE - 75G
32519	THREE BRIDGES - 75E	THREE BRIDGES - 75E	THREE BRIDGES - 75E	THREE BRIDGES - 75E	THREE BRIDGES - 75E	THREE BRIDGES - 75E	THREE BRIDGES - 75E
32520	THREE BRIDGES - 75E	THREE BRIDGES - 75E	THREE BRIDGES - 75E	THREE BRIDGES - 75E	THREE BRIDGES - 75E	THREE BRIDGES - 75E	THREE BRIDGES - 75E
32556	HORSHAM - 75D	HORSHAM - 75D	HORSHAM - 75D	EASTLEIGH - 71A	EASTLEIGH - 71A	EASTLEIGH - 71A	EASTLEIGH - 71A
32557	EASTLEIGH - 71A	EASTLEIGH - 71A	EASTLEIGH - 71A	EASTLEIGH - 71A	EASTLEIGH - 71A	EASTLEIGH - 71A	EASTLEIGH - 71A
32558	EASTLEIGH - 71A	EASTLEIGH - 71A	EASTLEIGH - 71A	EASTLEIGH - 71A	EASTLEIGH - 71A	EASTLEIGH - 71A	EASTLEIGH - 71A
32559	EASTLEIGH - 71A	EASTLEIGH - 71A	EASTLEIGH - 71A	EASTLEIGH - 71A	EASTLEIGH - 71A	EASTLEIGH - 71A	EASTLEIGH - 71A
32560	REDHILL - 75B	REDHILL - 75B	REDHILL - 75B	REDHILL - 75B	REDHILL - 75B	REDHILL - 75B	REDHILL - 75B
32561	REDHILL - 75B	REDHILL - 75B	REDHILL - 75B	REDHILL - 75B	REDHILL - 75B	REDHILL - 75B	REDHILL - 75B
32562	EASTLEIGH - 71A	EASTLEIGH - 71A	EASTLEIGH - 71A	EASTLEIGH - 71A	EASTLEIGH - 71A	EASTLEIGH - 71A	EASTLEIGH - 71A
32563	EASTLEIGH - 71A	EASTLEIGH - 71A	EASTLEIGH - 71A	EASTLEIGH - 71A	EASTLEIGH - 71A	EASTLEIGH - 71A	EASTLEIGH - 71A
32564	B ARMS - 73B	B ARMS - 73B	B ARMS - 73B	B ARMS - 73B	B ARMS - 73B	B ARMS - 73B	B ARMS - 73B
32565	B ARMS - 73B	B ARMS - 73B	B ARMS - 73B	B ARMS - 73B	B ARMS - 73B	B ARMS - 73B	B ARMS - 73B
32566	BRIGHTON - 75A	BRIGHTON - 75A	BRIGHTON - 75A	BRIGHTON - 75A	BRIGHTON - 75A	BRIGHTON - 75A	BRIGHTON - 75A
32577	BRIGHTON - 75A	BRIGHTON - 75A	BRIGHTON - 75A	BRIGHTON - 75A	BRIGHTON - 75A	BRIGHTON - 75A	BRIGHTON - 75A
32578	NORWOOD JCN - 75C	NORWOOD JCN - 75C	NORWOOD JCN - 75C	TONBRIDGE - 74D	TONBRIDGE - 74D	TONBRIDGE - 74D	TONBRIDGE - 74D
32579	EASTLEIGH - 71A	EASTLEIGH - 71A	EASTLEIGH - 71A	EASTLEIGH - 71A	EASTLEIGH - 71A	EASTLEIGH - 71A	EASTLEIGH - 71A
32580	HORSHAM - 75D	HORSHAM - 75D	HORSHAM - 75D	HORSHAM - 75D	HORSHAM - 75D	HORSHAM - 75D	HORSHAM - 75D
32581	T.WELLS - 75F	T.WELLS - 75F	T.WELLS - 75F	T.WELLS - 75F	T.WELLS - 75F	T.WELLS - 75F	T.WELLS - 75F
32582	T.WELLS - 75F	T.WELLS - 75F	T.WELLS - 75F	T.WELLS - 75F	T.WELLS - 75F	T.WELLS - 75F	T.WELLS - 75F

loco	Sep-52	Dec-52	Mar-53	May-53	Jul-53	Sep-53	Nov-53
			E1/R 0-6-2T (1927)				
32094	PLYMOUTH - 72D	PLYMOUTH - 72D	PLYMOUTH - 72D	PLYMOUTH - 72D	PLYMOUTH - 72D	PLYMOUTH - 72D	PLYMOUTH - 72D
32095	BARNSTAPLE - 72E	BARNSTAPLE - 72E	BARNSTAPLE - 72E	BARNSTAPLE - 72E	BARNSTAPLE - 72E	PLYMOUTH - 72D	PLYMOUTH - 72D
32096	BARNSTAPLE - 72E	BARNSTAPLE - 72E	BARNSTAPLE - 72E	BARNSTAPLE - 72E	BARNSTAPLE - 72E	BARNSTAPLE - 72E	BARNSTAPLE - 72E
32124	EXMOUTH JCN - 72A	EXMOUTH JCN - 72A	EXMOUTH JCN - 72A	EXMOUTH JCN - 72A	EXMOUTH JCN - 72A	EXMOUTH JCN - 72A	EXMOUTH JCN - 72A
32135	EXMOUTH JCN - 72A	EXMOUTH JCN - 72A	EXMOUTH JCN - 72A	EXMOUTH JCN - 72A	EXMOUTH JCN - 72A	EXMOUTH JCN - 72A	EXMOUTH JCN - 72A
32608	BARNSTAPLE - 72E	BARNSTAPLE - 72E	BARNSTAPLE - 72E	BARNSTAPLE - 72E	BARNSTAPLE - 72E	BARNSTAPLE - 72E	BARNSTAPLE - 72E
32610	BARNSTAPLE - 72E	BARNSTAPLE - 72E	BARNSTAPLE - 72E	BARNSTAPLE - 72E	BARNSTAPLE - 72E	BARNSTAPLE - 72E	BARNSTAPLE - 72E
32695	EXMOUTH JCN - 72A	EXMOUTH JCN - 72A	EXMOUTH JCN - 72A	EXMOUTH JCN - 72A	EXMOUTH JCN - 72A	EXMOUTH JCN - 72A	EXMOUTH JCN - 72A
32696	BARNSTAPLE - 72E	BARNSTAPLE - 72E	BARNSTAPLE - 72E	BARNSTAPLE - 72E	BARNSTAPLE - 72E	BARNSTAPLE - 72E	BARNSTAPLE - 72E
32697	EXMOUTH JCN - 72A	EXMOUTH JCN - 72A	EXMOUTH JCN - 72A	EXMOUTH JCN - 72A	EXMOUTH JCN - 72A	EXMOUTH JCN - 72A	EXMOUTH JCN - 72A
			E3 0-6-2T (1894)				
32165	B.ARMS - 73B	BRIGHTON - 75A	BRIGHTON - 75A	BRIGHTON - 75A	BRIGHTON - 75A	BRIGHTON - 75A	BRIGHTON - 75A
32166	BRIGHTON - 75A	BRIGHTON - 75A	BRIGHTON - 75A	BRIGHTON - 75A	BRIGHTON - 75A	BRIGHTON - 75A	BRIGHTON - 75A
32167	BRIGHTON - 75A	BRIGHTON - 75A	BRIGHTON - 75A	BRIGHTON - 75A	BRIGHTON - 75A	BRIGHTON - 75A	BRIGHTON - 75A
32168	BRIGHTON - 75A	BRIGHTON - 75A	BRIGHTON - 75A	BRIGHTON - 75A	BRIGHTON - 75A	BRIGHTON - 75A	READING (SR) - 70E
32169	BRIGHTON - 75A(N)	BRIGHTON - 75A(N)	BRIGHTON - 75A(N)	BRIGHTON - 75A(N)	BRIGHTON - 75A(N)	BRIGHTON - 75A(N)	BRIGHTON - 75A(N)
32170	BRIGHTON - 75A	BRIGHTON - 75A	BRIGHTON - 75A	BRIGHTON - 75A	BRIGHTON - 75A	BRIGHTON - 75A	BRIGHTON - 75A
32453	EASTLEIGH - 71A	B.ARMS - 73B	B.ARMS - 73B	B.ARMS - 73B	B.ARMS - 73B	B.ARMS - 73B	B.ARMS - 73B
32454	TONBRIDGE - 74D	TONBRIDGE - 74D	TONBRIDGE - 74D	TONBRIDGE - 74D	TONBRIDGE - 74D	TONBRIDGE - 74D	TONBRIDGE - 74D
32455	B.ARMS - 73B	B.ARMS - 73B	B.ARMS - 73B	B.ARMS - 73B	B.ARMS - 73B	B.ARMS - 73B	B.ARMS - 73B
32456	TONBRIDGE - 74D	TONBRIDGE - 74D	TONBRIDGE - 74D	TONBRIDGE - 74D	TONBRIDGE - 74D	TONBRIDGE - 74D	TONBRIDGE - 74D
32458	B.ARMS - 73B	B.ARMS - 73B	B.ARMS - 73B	B.ARMS - 73B	B.ARMS - 73B	B.ARMS - 73B	B.ARMS - 73B
32459	B.ARMS - 73B	B.ARMS - 73B	B.ARMS - 73B	B.ARMS - 73B	B.ARMS - 73B	B.ARMS - 73B	B.ARMS - 73B
32460	EASTLEIGH - 71A	B.ARMS - 73B	B.ARMS - 73B	B.ARMS - 73B	B.ARMS - 73B	B.ARMS - 73B	B.ARMS - 73B
32461	B.ARMS - 73B	B.ARMS - 73B	B.ARMS - 73B	B.ARMS - 73B	B.ARMS - 73B	B.ARMS - 73B	B.ARMS - 73B
32462	B.ARMS - 73B	B.ARMS - 73B	B.ARMS - 73B	B.ARMS - 73B	B.ARMS - 73B	B.ARMS - 73B	B.ARMS - 73B
			E4 0-6-2T (1897)				
32463	HORSHAM - 75D	HORSHAM - 75D	HORSHAM - 75D	HORSHAM - 75D	HORSHAM - 75D	HORSHAM - 75D	HORSHAM - 75D
32464	HORSHAM - 75D	HORSHAM - 75D	HORSHAM - 75D	HORSHAM - 75D	HORSHAM - 75D	HORSHAM - 75D	HORSHAM - 75D
32465	HORSHAM - 75D	HORSHAM - 75D	HORSHAM - 75D	HORSHAM - 75D	HORSHAM - 75D	HORSHAM - 75D	HORSHAM - 75D
32467	HORSHAM - 75D	HORSHAM - 75D	HORSHAM - 75D	HORSHAM - 75D	HORSHAM - 75D	HORSHAM - 75D	HORSHAM - 75D
32468	HORSHAM - 75D	HORSHAM - 75D	HORSHAM - 75D	HORSHAM - 75D	HORSHAM - 75D	HORSHAM - 75D	HORSHAM - 75D
32469	HORSHAM - 75D	HORSHAM - 75D	HORSHAM - 75D	HORSHAM - 75D	HORSHAM - 75D	HORSHAM - 75D	HORSHAM - 75D
32470	HORSHAM - 75D	HORSHAM - 75D	HORSHAM - 75D	HORSHAM - 75D	HORSHAM - 75D	HORSHAM - 75D	HORSHAM - 75D
32471	B.ARMS - 73B	B.ARMS - 73B	B.ARMS - 73B	B.ARMS - 73B	B.ARMS - 73B	B.ARMS - 73B	B.ARMS - 73B
32472	B.ARMS - 73B	B.ARMS - 73B	B.ARMS - 73B	B.ARMS - 73B	B.ARMS - 73B	B.ARMS - 73B	B.ARMS - 73B
32473	B.ARMS - 73B	B.ARMS - 73B	B.ARMS - 73B	B.ARMS - 73B	B.ARMS - 73B	B.ARMS - 73B	B.ARMS - 73B
32474	B.ARMS - 73B	B.ARMS - 73B	B.ARMS - 73B	B.ARMS - 73B	B.ARMS - 73B	B.ARMS - 73B	B.ARMS - 73B
32475	BRIGHTON - 75A(N)	BRIGHTON - 75A(N)	BRIGHTON - 75A(N)	BRIGHTON - 75A(N)	BRIGHTON - 75A(N)	BRIGHTON - 75A(N)	BRIGHTON - 75A(N)
32476	NORWOOD JCN - 75C	NORWOOD JCN - 75C	NORWOOD JCN - 75C	NORWOOD JCN - 75C	NORWOOD JCN - 75C	NINE ELMS - 70A	NINE ELMS - 70A
32479	FRATTON - 71D	FRATTON - 71D	FRATTON - 71D	FRATTON - 71D	FRATTON - 71D	FRATTON - 71D	FRATTON - 71D
32480	THREE BRIDGES - 75E	THREE BRIDGES - 75E	THREE BRIDGES - 75E	THREE BRIDGES - 75E	THREE BRIDGES - 75E	THREE BRIDGES - 75E	THREE BRIDGES - 75E
32481	THREE BRIDGES - 75E	THREE BRIDGES - 75E	THREE BRIDGES - 75E	THREE BRIDGES - 75E	THREE BRIDGES - 75E	THREE BRIDGES - 75E	THREE BRIDGES - 75E
32482	THREE BRIDGES - 75E	THREE BRIDGES - 75E	THREE BRIDGES - 75E	THREE BRIDGES - 75E	THREE BRIDGES - 75E	THREE BRIDGES - 75E	THREE BRIDGES - 75E
32484	THREE BRIDGES - 75E	THREE BRIDGES - 75E	THREE BRIDGES - 75E	THREE BRIDGES - 75E	THREE BRIDGES - 75E	THREE BRIDGES - 75E	THREE BRIDGES - 75E
32485	BRIGHTON - 75A	BRIGHTON - 75A	BRIGHTON - 75A	BRIGHTON - 75A	BRIGHTON - 75A	BRIGHTON - 75A	BRIGHTON - 75A
32486	SALISBURY - 72B	SALISBURY - 72B	SALISBURY - 72B	SALISBURY - 72B	SALISBURY - 72B	SALISBURY - 72B	SALISBURY - 72B
32487	GUILDFORD - 70C	GUILDFORD - 70C	GUILDFORD - 70C	GUILDFORD - 70C	GUILDFORD - 70C	GUILDFORD - 70C	GUILDFORD - 70C
32488	TONBRIDGE - 74D	TONBRIDGE - 74D	TONBRIDGE - 74D	TONBRIDGE - 74D	TONBRIDGE - 74D	TONBRIDGE - 74D	TONBRIDGE - 74D
32490	GUILDFORD - 70C	GUILDFORD - 70C	GUILDFORD - 70C	GUILDFORD - 70C	GUILDFORD - 70C	GUILDFORD - 70C	GUILDFORD - 70C
32491	EASTLEIGH - 71A	EASTLEIGH - 71A	EASTLEIGH - 71A	EASTLEIGH - 71A	EASTLEIGH - 71A	EASTLEIGH - 71A	EASTLEIGH - 71A
32492	EASTLEIGH - 71A	EASTLEIGH - 71A	EASTLEIGH - 71A	EASTLEIGH - 71A	EASTLEIGH - 71A	EASTLEIGH - 71A	EASTLEIGH - 71A
32493	NINE ELMS - 70A	NINE ELMS - 70A	NINE ELMS - 70A	NINE ELMS - 70A	NINE ELMS - 70A	NINE ELMS - 70A	NINE ELMS - 70A
32494	BRIGHTON - 75A(N)	BRIGHTON - 75A(N)	BRIGHTON - 75A(N)	BRIGHTON - 75A(N)	BRIGHTON - 75A(N)	BRIGHTON - 75A(N)	BRIGHTON - 75A(N)
32495	FRATTON - 71D	FRATTON - 71D	FRATTON - 71D	FRATTON - 71D	FRATTON - 71D	FRATTON - 71D	FRATTON - 71D
32496	BRIGHTON - 75A(N)	BRIGHTON - 75A(N)	BRIGHTON - 75A(N)	BRIGHTON - 75A(N)	BRIGHTON - 75A(N)	BRIGHTON - 75A(N)	BRIGHTON - 75A(N)
32497	NINE ELMS - 70A	NINE ELMS - 70A	NINE ELMS - 70A	NINE ELMS - 70A	NINE ELMS - 70A	NINE ELMS - 70A	NINE ELMS - 70A
32498	NINE ELMS - 70A	NINE ELMS - 70A	NINE ELMS - 70A	NINE ELMS - 70A	NINE ELMS - 70A	NINE ELMS - 70A	NINE ELMS - 70A
32499	NINE ELMS - 70A	NINE ELMS - 70A	NINE ELMS - 70A	NINE ELMS - 70A	NINE ELMS - 70A	NINE ELMS - 70A	NINE ELMS - 70A
32500	NINE ELMS - 70A	NINE ELMS - 70A	NINE ELMS - 70A	NINE ELMS - 70A	NINE ELMS - 70A	NINE ELMS - 70A	NINE ELMS - 70A
32501	READING (SR) - 70E	READING (SR) - 70E	READING (SR) - 70E	READING (SR) - 70E	READING (SR) - 70E	READING (SR) - 70E	READING (SR) - 70E
32502	NINE ELMS - 70A	NINE ELMS - 70A	NINE ELMS - 70A	NINE ELMS - 70A	NINE ELMS - 70A	NINE ELMS - 70A	NINE ELMS - 70A
32503	TONBRIDGE - 74D	TONBRIDGE - 74D	TONBRIDGE - 74D	TONBRIDGE - 74D	TONBRIDGE - 74D	TONBRIDGE - 74D	TONBRIDGE - 74D
32504	BRIGHTON - 75A(N)	BRIGHTON - 75A(N)	BRIGHTON - 75A(N)	BRIGHTON - 75A(N)	BRIGHTON - 75A(N)	BRIGHTON - 75A(N)	BRIGHTON - 75A(N)
32505	FRATTON - 71D	FRATTON - 71D	FRATTON - 71D	FRATTON - 71D	FRATTON - 71D	FRATTON - 71D	FRATTON - 71D
32506	SALISBURY - 72B	SALISBURY - 72B	SALISBURY - 72B	SALISBURY - 72B	SALISBURY - 72B	SALISBURY - 72B	SALISBURY - 72B
32507	REDHILL - 75B	REDHILL - 75B	REDHILL - 75B	REDHILL - 75B	REDHILL - 75B	REDHILL - 75B	REDHILL - 75B
32508	BRIGHTON - 75A	BRIGHTON - 75A	BRIGHTON - 75A	BRIGHTON - 75A	BRIGHTON - 75A	BRIGHTON - 75A	BRIGHTON - 75A
32509	FRATTON - 71D	FRATTON - 71D	FRATTON - 71D	FRATTON - 71D	FRATTON - 71D	FRATTON - 71D	FRATTON - 71D
32510	EASTLEIGH - 71A	EASTLEIGH - 71A	EASTLEIGH - 71A	EASTLEIGH - 71A	EASTLEIGH - 71A	EASTLEIGH - 71A	EASTLEIGH - 71A
32511	HORSHAM - 75D	HORSHAM - 75D	HORSHAM - 75D	HORSHAM - 75D	HORSHAM - 75D	HORSHAM - 75D	HORSHAM - 75D
32512	REDHILL - 75B	REDHILL - 75B	REDHILL - 75B	REDHILL - 75B	REDHILL - 75B	REDHILL - 75B	REDHILL - 75B
32513	BRIGHTON - 75A	BRIGHTON - 75A	BRIGHTON - 75A	BRIGHTON - 75A	BRIGHTON - 75A	BRIGHTON - 75A	BRIGHTON - 75A
32514	BRIGHTON - 75A	BRIGHTON - 75A	BRIGHTON - 75A	BRIGHTON - 75A	BRIGHTON - 75A	BRIGHTON - 75A	BRIGHTON - 75A
32515	BRIGHTON - 75A	BRIGHTON - 75A	BRIGHTON - 75A	BRIGHTON - 75A	BRIGHTON - 75A	BRIGHTON - 75A	BRIGHTON - 75A
32516	THREE BRIDGES - 75E	THREE BRIDGES - 75E	THREE BRIDGES - 75E	THREE BRIDGES - 75E	THREE BRIDGES - 75E	THREE BRIDGES - 75E	THREE BRIDGES - 75E
32517	T.WELLS - 75F	T.WELLS - 75F	T.WELLS - 75F	T.WELLS - 75F	T.WELLS - 75F	T.WELLS - 75F	T.WELLS - 75F
32518	BRIGHTON - 75A	BRIGHTON - 75A	BRIGHTON - 75A	BRIGHTON - 75A	BRIGHTON - 75A	BRIGHTON - 75A	BRIGHTON - 75A
32519	THREE BRIDGES - 75E	THREE BRIDGES - 75E	THREE BRIDGES - 75E	THREE BRIDGES - 75E	THREE BRIDGES - 75E	THREE BRIDGES - 75E	THREE BRIDGES - 75E
32520	THREE BRIDGES - 75E	THREE BRIDGES - 75E	THREE BRIDGES - 75E	THREE BRIDGES - 75E	THREE BRIDGES - 75E	THREE BRIDGES - 75E	THREE BRIDGES - 75E
32556	EASTLEIGH - 71A	EASTLEIGH - 71A	EASTLEIGH - 71A	EASTLEIGH - 71A	EASTLEIGH - 71A	EASTLEIGH - 71A	EASTLEIGH - 71A
32557	EASTLEIGH - 71A	EASTLEIGH - 71A	EASTLEIGH - 71A	EASTLEIGH - 71A	EASTLEIGH - 71A	EASTLEIGH - 71A	EASTLEIGH - 71A
32558	EASTLEIGH - 71A	EASTLEIGH - 71A	EASTLEIGH - 71A	EASTLEIGH - 71A	EASTLEIGH - 71A	EASTLEIGH - 71A	EASTLEIGH - 71A
32559	EASTLEIGH - 71A	EASTLEIGH - 71A	EASTLEIGH - 71A	EASTLEIGH - 71A	EASTLEIGH - 71A	EASTLEIGH - 71A	EASTLEIGH - 71A
32560	REDHILL - 75B	REDHILL - 75B	REDHILL - 75B	REDHILL - 75B	REDHILL - 75B	REDHILL - 75B	REDHILL - 75B
32561	REDHILL - 75B	REDHILL - 75B	REDHILL - 75B	REDHILL - 75B	REDHILL - 75B	REDHILL - 75B	REDHILL - 75B
32562	EASTLEIGH - 71A	EASTLEIGH - 71A	EASTLEIGH - 71A	EASTLEIGH - 71A	EASTLEIGH - 71A	EASTLEIGH - 71A	EASTLEIGH - 71A
32563	EASTLEIGH - 71A	EASTLEIGH - 71A	EASTLEIGH - 71A	EASTLEIGH - 71A	EASTLEIGH - 71A	EASTLEIGH - 71A	EASTLEIGH - 71A
32564	B.ARMS - 73B	B.ARMS - 73B	B.ARMS - 73B	B.ARMS - 73B	B.ARMS - 73B	B.ARMS - 73B	B.ARMS - 73B
32565	B.ARMS - 73B	B.ARMS - 73B	B.ARMS - 73B	B.ARMS - 73B	B.ARMS - 73B	B.ARMS - 73B	B.ARMS - 73B
32566	BRIGHTON - 75A	BRIGHTON - 75A	BRIGHTON - 75A	BRIGHTON - 75A	BRIGHTON - 75A	BRIGHTON - 75A	BRIGHTON - 75A
32577	BRIGHTON - 75A	BRIGHTON - 75A	BRIGHTON - 75A	BRIGHTON - 75A	BRIGHTON - 75A	BRIGHTON - 75A	BRIGHTON - 75A
32578	TONBRIDGE - 74D	TONBRIDGE - 74D	TONBRIDGE - 74D	TONBRIDGE - 74D	TONBRIDGE - 74D	TONBRIDGE - 74D	TONBRIDGE - 74D
32579	EASTLEIGH - 71A	EASTLEIGH - 71A	EASTLEIGH - 71A	EASTLEIGH - 71A	EASTLEIGH - 71A	EASTLEIGH - 71A	EASTLEIGH - 71A
32580	HORSHAM - 75D	HORSHAM - 75D	HORSHAM - 75D	HORSHAM - 75D	HORSHAM - 75D	HORSHAM - 75D	HORSHAM - 75D
32581	T.WELLS - 75F	T.WELLS - 75F	T.WELLS - 75F	T.WELLS - 75F	T.WELLS - 75F	T.WELLS - 75F	T.WELLS - 75F
32582	T.WELLS - 75F	T.WELLS - 75F	T.WELLS - 75F	T.WELLS - 75F	T.WELLS - 75F	T.WELLS - 75F	T.WELLS - 75F

loco	Jan-54	Mar-54	May-54	Jun-54	Aug-54	Oct-54	Dec-54
			E1/R 0-6-2T (1927)				
32094	P LYMOUTH - 72D	P LYMOUTH - 72D	P LYMOUTH - 72D	P LYMOUTH - 72D	P LYMOUTH - 72D	P LYMOUTH - 72D	P LYMOUTH - 72D
32095	P LYMOUTH - 72D	P LYMOUTH - 72D	P LYMOUTH - 72D	P LYMOUTH - 72D	P LYMOUTH - 72D	P LYMOUTH - 72D	P LYMOUTH - 72D
32096	BARNSTAPLE - 72E	BARNSTAPLE - 72E	BARNSTAPLE - 72E	BARNSTAPLE - 72E	BARNSTAPLE - 72E	BARNSTAPLE - 72E	BARNSTAPLE - 72E
32124	EXMOUTH JCN - 72A	EXMOUTH JCN - 72A	EXMOUTH JCN - 72A	EXMOUTH JCN - 72A	EXMOUTH JCN - 72A	EXMOUTH JCN - 72A	EXMOUTH JCN - 72A
32135	EXMOUTH JCN - 72A	EXMOUTH JCN - 72A	EXMOUTH JCN - 72A	EXMOUTH JCN - 72A	EXMOUTH JCN - 72A	EXMOUTH JCN - 72A	EXMOUTH JCN - 72A
32608	BARNSTAPLE - 72E	BARNSTAPLE - 72E	BARNSTAPLE - 72E	BARNSTAPLE - 72E	BARNSTAPLE - 72E	BARNSTAPLE - 72E	BARNSTAPLE - 72E
32610	BARNSTAPLE - 72E	BARNSTAPLE - 72E	BARNSTAPLE - 72E	BARNSTAPLE - 72E	BARNSTAPLE - 72E	BARNSTAPLE - 72E	BARNSTAPLE - 72E
32695	EXMOUTH JCN - 72A	EXMOUTH JCN - 72A	EXMOUTH JCN - 72A	EXMOUTH JCN - 72A	EXMOUTH JCN - 72A	EXMOUTH JCN - 72A	EXMOUTH JCN - 72A
32696	BARNSTAPLE - 72E	BARNSTAPLE - 72E	BARNSTAPLE - 72E	BARNSTAPLE - 72E	BARNSTAPLE - 72E	BARNSTAPLE - 72E	BARNSTAPLE - 72E
32697	EXMOUTH JCN - 72A	EXMOUTH JCN - 72A	EXMOUTH JCN - 72A	EXMOUTH JCN - 72A	EXMOUTH JCN - 72A	EXMOUTH JCN - 72A	EXMOUTH JCN - 72A
			E3 0-6-2T (1894)				
32165	BRIGHTON - 75A	BRIGHTON - 75A	BRIGHTON - 75A	BRIGHTON - 75A	BRIGHTON - 75A	BRIGHTON - 75A	BRIGHTON - 75A
32166	BRIGHTON - 75A	BRIGHTON - 75A	BRIGHTON - 75A	BRIGHTON - 75A	BRIGHTON - 75A	BRIGHTON - 75A	BRIGHTON - 75A
32167	BRIGHTON - 75A	BRIGHTON - 75A	BRIGHTON - 75A	BRIGHTON - 75A	BRIGHTON - 75A	BRIGHTON - 75A	BRIGHTON - 75A
32168	READING (SR) - 70E	READING (SR) - 70E	READING (SR) - 70E	READING (SR) - 70E	READING (SR) - 70E	READING (SR) - 70E	READING (SR) - 70E
32169	BRIGHTON - 75A(N)	BRIGHTON - 75A(N)	BRIGHTON - 75A(N)	BRIGHTON - 75A(N)	BRIGHTON - 75A(N)	BRIGHTON - 75A(N)	BRIGHTON - 75A(N)
32170	BRIGHTON - 75A	BRIGHTON - 75A	BRIGHTON - 75A	BRIGHTON - 75A	BRIGHTON - 75A	BRIGHTON - 75A	BRIGHTON - 75A
32453	B.ARMS - 73B	B.ARMS - 73B	B.ARMS - 73B	B.ARMS - 73B	B.ARMS - 73B	B.ARMS - 73B	B.ARMS - 73B
32454	TONBRIDGE - 74D	TONBRIDGE - 74D	TONBRIDGE - 74D	TONBRIDGE - 74D	TONBRIDGE - 74D	TONBRIDGE - 74D	TONBRIDGE - 74D
32455	B.ARMS - 73B	B.ARMS - 73B	B.ARMS - 73B	B.ARMS - 73B	STEWARTS LANE - 73A	STEWARTS LANE - 73A	STEWARTS LANE - 73A
32456	TONBRIDGE - 74D	TONBRIDGE - 74D	TONBRIDGE - 74D	TONBRIDGE - 74D	TONBRIDGE - 74D	TONBRIDGE - 74D	TONBRIDGE - 74D
32458	B.ARMS - 73B	B.ARMS - 73B	B.ARMS - 73B	B.ARMS - 73B	B.ARMS - 73B	B.ARMS - 73B	B.ARMS - 73B
32459	B.ARMS - 73B	B.ARMS - 73B	B.ARMS - 73B	B.ARMS - 73B	B.ARMS - 73B	B.ARMS - 73B	B.ARMS - 73B
32460	B.ARMS - 73B	B.ARMS - 73B	B.ARMS - 73B	B.ARMS - 73B	B.ARMS - 73B	B.ARMS - 73B	B.ARMS - 73B
32461	B.ARMS - 73B	B.ARMS - 73B	B.ARMS - 73B	B.ARMS - 73B	B.ARMS - 73B	B.ARMS - 73B	B.ARMS - 73B
32462	B.ARMS - 73B	B.ARMS - 73B	B.ARMS - 73B	B.ARMS - 73B	B.ARMS - 73B	B.ARMS - 73B	B.ARMS - 73B
			E4 0-6-2T (1897)				
32463	HORSHAM - 75D	HORSHAM - 75D	HORSHAM - 75D	HORSHAM - 75D	HORSHAM - 75D	HORSHAM - 75D	HORSHAM - 75D
32464	HORSHAM - 75D	HORSHAM - 75D	HORSHAM - 75D	HORSHAM - 75D	HORSHAM - 75D	HORSHAM - 75D	HORSHAM - 75D
32465	HORSHAM - 75D	HORSHAM - 75D	HORSHAM - 75D	HORSHAM - 75D	HORSHAM - 75D	HORSHAM - 75D	HORSHAM - 75D
32467	HORSHAM - 75D	HORSHAM - 75D	HORSHAM - 75D	HORSHAM - 75D	HORSHAM - 75D	HORSHAM - 75D	HORSHAM - 75D
32468	HORSHAM - 75D	HORSHAM - 75D	HORSHAM - 75D	HORSHAM - 75D	HORSHAM - 75D	HORSHAM - 75D	HORSHAM - 75D
32469	HORSHAM - 75D	HORSHAM - 75D	HORSHAM - 75D	HORSHAM - 75D	HORSHAM - 75D	HORSHAM - 75D	HORSHAM - 75D
32470	HORSHAM - 75D	HORSHAM - 75D	HORSHAM - 75D	HORSHAM - 75D	HORSHAM - 75D	HORSHAM - 75D	HORSHAM - 75D
32471	B.ARMS - 73B	B.ARMS - 73B	B.ARMS - 73B	B.ARMS - 73B	B.ARMS - 73B	B.ARMS - 73B	B.ARMS - 73B
32472	B.ARMS - 73B	B.ARMS - 73B	B.ARMS - 73B	B.ARMS - 73B	B.ARMS - 73B	B.ARMS - 73B	B.ARMS - 73B
32473	B.ARMS - 73B	B.ARMS - 73B	B.ARMS - 73B	B.ARMS - 73B	B.ARMS - 73B	B.ARMS - 73B	B.ARMS - 73B
32474	B.ARMS - 73B	B.ARMS - 73B	B.ARMS - 73B	B.ARMS - 73B	B.ARMS - 73B	B.ARMS - 73B	B.ARMS - 73B
32475	BRIGHTON - 75A(N)	BRIGHTON - 75A(N)	BRIGHTON - 75A(N)	BRIGHTON - 75A(N)	BRIGHTON - 75A(N)	BRIGHTON - 75A(N)	BRIGHTON - 75A(N)
32476	NINE ELMS - 70A	NINE ELMS - 70A	NINE ELMS - 70A	NINE ELMS - 70A	NINE ELMS - 70A	NINE ELMS - 70A	NINE ELMS - 70A
32479	FRATTON - 71D	FRATTON - 71D	FRATTON - 71D	FRATTON - 71D	FRATTON - 71D	FRATTON - 70F	FRATTON - 70F
32480	THREE BRIDGES - 75E	THREE BRIDGES - 75E	THREE BRIDGES - 75E	THREE BRIDGES - 75E	THREE BRIDGES - 75E	THREE BRIDGES - 75E	THREE BRIDGES - 75E
32481	THREE BRIDGES - 75E	THREE BRIDGES - 75E	THREE BRIDGES - 75E	THREE BRIDGES - 75E	THREE BRIDGES - 75E	THREE BRIDGES - 75E	THREE BRIDGES - 75E
32482	THREE BRIDGES - 75E	THREE BRIDGES - 75E	THREE BRIDGES - 75E	THREE BRIDGES - 75E	THREE BRIDGES - 75E	BRIGHTON - 75A	BRIGHTON - 75A
32484	THREE BRIDGES - 75E	THREE BRIDGES - 75E	THREE BRIDGES - 75E	THREE BRIDGES - 75E	THREE BRIDGES - 75E	THREE BRIDGES - 75E	NORWOOD JCN - 75C
32485	BRIGHTON - 75A	BRIGHTON - 75A	BRIGHTON - 75A	BRIGHTON - 75A	BRIGHTON - 75A	BRIGHTON - 75A	BRIGHTON - 75A
32486	SALISBURY - 72B	SALISBURY - 72B	SALISBURY - 72B	SALISBURY - 72B	SALISBURY - 72B	SALISBURY - 72B	SALISBURY - 72B
32487	GUILDFORD - 70C	GUILDFORD - 70C	GUILDFORD - 70C	GUILDFORD - 70C	GUILDFORD - 70C	GUILDFORD - 70C	GUILDFORD - 70C
32488	TONBRIDGE - 74D	TONBRIDGE - 74D	TONBRIDGE - 74D	TONBRIDGE - 74D	TONBRIDGE - 74D	TONBRIDGE - 74D	TONBRIDGE - 74D
32490	GUILDFORD - 70C	GUILDFORD - 70C	GUILDFORD - 70C	GUILDFORD - 70C	GUILDFORD - 70C	GUILDFORD - 70C	GUILDFORD - 70C
32491	EASTLEIGH - 71A	EASTLEIGH - 71A	EASTLEIGH - 71A	EASTLEIGH - 71A	EASTLEIGH - 71A	EASTLEIGH - 71A	EASTLEIGH - 71A
32492	EASTLEIGH - 71A	EASTLEIGH - 71A	EASTLEIGH - 71A	EASTLEIGH - 71A	EASTLEIGH - 71A	EASTLEIGH - 71A	EASTLEIGH - 71A
32493	NINE ELMS - 70A	NINE ELMS - 70A	NINE ELMS - 70A	NINE ELMS - 70A	NINE ELMS - 70A	NINE ELMS - 70A	NINE ELMS - 70A
32494	BRIGHTON - 75A(N)	BRIGHTON - 75A(N)	BRIGHTON - 75A(N)	BRIGHTON - 75A(N)	BRIGHTON - 75A(N)	BRIGHTON - 75A(N)	BRIGHTON - 75A(N)
32495	FRATTON - 71D	FRATTON - 71D	FRATTON - 71D	FRATTON - 71D	FRATTON - 71D	FRATTON - 70F	FRATTON - 70F
32496	BRIGHTON - 75A(N)	BRIGHTON - 75A(N)	BRIGHTON - 75A(N)	BRIGHTON - 75A(N)	BRIGHTON - 75A(N)	BRIGHTON - 75A(N)	BRIGHTON - 75A(N)
32497	NINE ELMS - 70A	NINE ELMS - 70A	NINE ELMS - 70A	NINE ELMS - 70A	NINE ELMS - 70A	NINE ELMS - 70A	NINE ELMS - 70A
32498	NINE ELMS - 70A	NINE ELMS - 70A	NINE ELMS - 70A	NINE ELMS - 70A	NINE ELMS - 70A	NINE ELMS - 70A	NINE ELMS - 70A
32499	NINE ELMS - 70A	NINE ELMS - 70A	NINE ELMS - 70A	NINE ELMS - 70A	NINE ELMS - 70A	NINE ELMS - 70A	NINE ELMS - 70A
32500	NINE ELMS - 70A	NINE ELMS - 70A	NINE ELMS - 70A	NINE ELMS - 70A	NINE ELMS - 70A	NINE ELMS - 70A	NINE ELMS - 70A
32501	READING (SR) - 70E	READING (SR) - 70E	READING (SR) - 70E	READING (SR) - 70E	READING (SR) - 70E	READING (SR) - 70E	READING (SR) - 70E
32502	NINE ELMS - 70A	NINE ELMS - 70A	READING (SR) - 70E	READING (SR) - 70E	READING (SR) - 70E	READING (SR) - 70E	READING (SR) - 70E
32503	TONBRIDGE - 74D	TONBRIDGE - 74D	TONBRIDGE - 74D	TONBRIDGE - 74D	TONBRIDGE - 74D	TONBRIDGE - 74D	TONBRIDGE - 74D
32504	BRIGHTON - 75A(N)	BRIGHTON - 75A(N)	BRIGHTON - 75A(N)	BRIGHTON - 75A(N)	BRIGHTON - 75A(N)	BRIGHTON - 75A(N)	BRIGHTON - 75A(N)
32505	FRATTON - 71D	FRATTON - 71D	FRATTON - 71D	FRATTON - 71D	FRATTON - 71D	FRATTON - 70F	FRATTON - 70F
32506	SALISBURY - 72B	SALISBURY - 72B	SALISBURY - 72B	SALISBURY - 72B	SALISBURY - 72B	SALISBURY - 72B	SALISBURY - 72B
32507	REDHILL - 75B	REDHILL - 75B	REDHILL - 75B	REDHILL - 75B	REDHILL - 75B	REDHILL - 75B	REDHILL - 75B
32508	BRIGHTON - 75A	BRIGHTON - 75A	BRIGHTON - 75A	BRIGHTON - 75A	BRIGHTON - 75A	BRIGHTON - 75A	BRIGHTON - 75A
32509	FRATTON - 71D	FRATTON - 71D	FRATTON - 71D	FRATTON - 71D	FRATTON - 71D	FRATTON - 70F	FRATTON - 70F
32510	EASTLEIGH - 71A	EASTLEIGH - 71A	EASTLEIGH - 71A	EASTLEIGH - 71A	EASTLEIGH - 71A	EASTLEIGH - 71A	EASTLEIGH - 71A
32511	HORSHAM - 75D	HORSHAM - 75D	HORSHAM - 75D	HORSHAM - 75D	HORSHAM - 75D	HORSHAM - 75D	HORSHAM - 75D
32512	REDHILL - 75B	REDHILL - 75B	REDHILL - 75B	REDHILL - 75B	REDHILL - 75B	REDHILL - 75B	REDHILL - 75B
32513	BRIGHTON - 75A	BRIGHTON - 75A	BRIGHTON - 75A	BRIGHTON - 75A	BRIGHTON - 75A	BRIGHTON - 75A	BRIGHTON - 75A
32514	BRIGHTON - 75A	BRIGHTON - 75A	BRIGHTON - 75A	BRIGHTON - 75A	BRIGHTON - 75A	BRIGHTON - 75A	BRIGHTON - 75A
32515	BRIGHTON - 75A	BRIGHTON - 75A	BRIGHTON - 75A	BRIGHTON - 75A	BRIGHTON - 75A	BRIGHTON - 75A	BRIGHTON - 75A
32516	THREE BRIDGES - 75E	THREE BRIDGES - 75E	THREE BRIDGES - 75E	THREE BRIDGES - 75E	THREE BRIDGES - 75E	THREE BRIDGES - 75E	THREE BRIDGES - 75E
32517	T.WELLS - 75F	T.WELLS - 75F	T.WELLS - 75F	T.WELLS - 75F	T.WELLS - 75F	T.WELLS - 75F	T.WELLS - 75F
32518	BRIGHTON - 75A	BRIGHTON - 75A	BRIGHTON - 75A	BRIGHTON - 75A	BRIGHTON - 75A	BRIGHTON - 75A	BRIGHTON - 75A
32519	THREE BRIDGES - 75E	THREE BRIDGES - 75E	THREE BRIDGES - 75E	THREE BRIDGES - 75E	THREE BRIDGES - 75E	THREE BRIDGES - 75E	THREE BRIDGES - 75E
32520	THREE BRIDGES - 75E	THREE BRIDGES - 75E	THREE BRIDGES - 75E	THREE BRIDGES - 75E	THREE BRIDGES - 75E	THREE BRIDGES - 75E	THREE BRIDGES - 75E
32556	EASTLEIGH - 71A	EASTLEIGH - 71A	EASTLEIGH - 71A	EASTLEIGH - 71A	EASTLEIGH - 71A	EASTLEIGH - 71A	EASTLEIGH - 71A
32557	EASTLEIGH - 71A	EASTLEIGH - 71A	EASTLEIGH - 71A	EASTLEIGH - 71A	EASTLEIGH - 71A	EASTLEIGH - 71A	EASTLEIGH - 71A
32558	DORCHESTER - 71C	DORCHESTER - 71C	DORCHESTER - 71C	DORCHESTER - 71C	DORCHESTER - 71C	DORCHESTER - 71C	DORCHESTER - 71C
32559	EASTLEIGH - 71A	EASTLEIGH - 71A	EASTLEIGH - 71A	EASTLEIGH - 71A	EASTLEIGH - 71A	EASTLEIGH - 71A	EASTLEIGH - 71A
32560	REDHILL - 75B	REDHILL - 75B	REDHILL - 75B	REDHILL - 75B	REDHILL - 75B	REDHILL - 75B	REDHILL - 75B
32561	REDHILL - 75B	REDHILL - 75B	REDHILL - 75B	REDHILL - 75B	REDHILL - 75B	REDHILL - 75B	REDHILL - 75B
32562	EASTLEIGH - 71A	EASTLEIGH - 71A	EASTLEIGH - 71A	EASTLEIGH - 71A	EASTLEIGH - 71A	EASTLEIGH - 71A	EASTLEIGH - 71A
32563	EASTLEIGH - 71A	EASTLEIGH - 71A	EASTLEIGH - 71A	EASTLEIGH - 71A	EASTLEIGH - 71A	EASTLEIGH - 71A	EASTLEIGH - 71A
32564	B.ARMS - 73B	B.ARMS - 73B	B.ARMS - 73B	B.ARMS - 73B	B.ARMS - 73B	B.ARMS - 73B	B.ARMS - 73B
32565	B.ARMS - 73B	B.ARMS - 73B	B.ARMS - 73B	B.ARMS - 73B	B.ARMS - 73B	B.ARMS - 73B	B.ARMS - 73B
32566	BRIGHTON - 75A	BRIGHTON - 75A	BRIGHTON - 75A	BRIGHTON - 75A	BRIGHTON - 75A	BRIGHTON - 75A	BRIGHTON - 75A
32577	BRIGHTON - 75A	BRIGHTON - 75A	BRIGHTON - 75A	BRIGHTON - 75A	BRIGHTON - 75A	BRIGHTON - 75A	BRIGHTON - 75A
32578	TONBRIDGE - 74D	TONBRIDGE - 74D	TONBRIDGE - 74D	TONBRIDGE - 74D	TONBRIDGE - 74D	TONBRIDGE - 74D	ST LEONARDS - 74E
32579	EASTLEIGH - 71A	EASTLEIGH - 71A	EASTLEIGH - 71A	EASTLEIGH - 71A	EASTLEIGH - 71A	EASTLEIGH - 71A	EASTLEIGH - 71A
32580	HORSHAM - 75D	HORSHAM - 75D	HORSHAM - 75D	HORSHAM - 75D	HORSHAM - 75D	HORSHAM - 75D	HORSHAM - 75D
32581	T.WELLS - 75F	T.WELLS - 75F	T.WELLS - 75F	T.WELLS - 75F	T.WELLS - 75F	T.WELLS - 75F	T.WELLS - 75F
32582	T.WELLS - 75F	T.WELLS - 75F	T.WELLS - 75F	T.WELLS - 75F	T.WELLS - 75F	T.WELLS - 75F	T.WELLS - 75F

loco	Feb-55	Apr-55	Jun-55	Aug-55	Sep-55	Nov-55	Dec-55
				E1/R 0-6-2T (1927)			
32094	PLYMOUTH - 72D	W/D	W/D	W/D	W/D	W/D	W/D
32095	PLYMOUTH - 72D	PLYMOUTH - 72D	PLYMOUTH - 72D	PLYMOUTH - 72D	PLYMOUTH - 72D	PLYMOUTH - 72D	PLYMOUTH - 72D
32096	BARNSTAPLE - 72E	BARNSTAPLE - 72E	BARNSTAPLE - 72E	PLYMOUTH - 72D	PLYMOUTH - 72D	PLYMOUTH - 72D	PLYMOUTH - 72D
32124	EXMOUTH JCN - 72A	EXMOUTH JCN - 72A	EXMOUTH JCN - 72A	EXMOUTH JCN - 72A	EXMOUTH JCN - 72A	EXMOUTH JCN - 72A	EXMOUTH JCN - 72A
32135	EXMOUTH JCN - 72A	EXMOUTH JCN - 72A	EXMOUTH JCN - 72A	EXMOUTH JCN - 72A	EXMOUTH JCN - 72A	EXMOUTH JCN - 72A	EXMOUTH JCN - 72A
32608	BARNSTAPLE - 72E	BARNSTAPLE - 72E	BARNSTAPLE - 72E	BARNSTAPLE - 72E	BARNSTAPLE - 72E	BARNSTAPLE - 72E	BARNSTAPLE - 72E
32610	BARNSTAPLE - 72E	BARNSTAPLE - 72E	BARNSTAPLE - 72E	BARNSTAPLE - 72E	BARNSTAPLE - 72E	BARNSTAPLE - 72E	BARNSTAPLE - 72E
32695	EXMOUTH JCN - 72A	EXMOUTH JCN - 72A	EXMOUTH JCN - 72A	EXMOUTH JCN - 72A	EXMOUTH JCN - 72A	EXMOUTH JCN - 72A	EXMOUTH JCN - 72A
32696	BARNSTAPLE - 72E	BARNSTAPLE - 72E	BARNSTAPLE - 72E	BARNSTAPLE - 72E	BARNSTAPLE - 72E	BARNSTAPLE - 72E	BARNSTAPLE - 72E
32697	EXMOUTH JCN - 72A	EXMOUTH JCN - 72A	EXMOUTH JCN - 72A	EXMOUTH JCN - 72A	EXMOUTH JCN - 72A	EXMOUTH JCN - 72A	EXMOUTH JCN - 72A
				E3 0-6-2T (1894)			
32165	BRIGHTON - 75A	HORSHAM - 75D	HORSHAM - 75D	HORSHAM - 75D	HORSHAM - 75D	HORSHAM - 75D	HORSHAM - 75D
32166	BRIGHTON - 75A	HORSHAM - 75D	HORSHAM - 75D	HORSHAM - 75D	HORSHAM - 75D	HORSHAM - 75D	HORSHAM - 75D
32167	BRIGHTON - 75A	BRIGHTON - 75A	BRIGHTON - 75A	BRIGHTON - 75A	W/D	W/D	W/D
32168	READING (SR) - 70E	READING (SR) - 70E	READING (SR) - 70E	READING (SR) - 70E	READING (SR) - 70E	READING (SR) - 70E	READING (SR) - 70E
32169	BRIGHTON - 75A	BRIGHTON - 75A	BRIGHTON - 75A	W/D	W/D	W/D	W/D
32170	BRIGHTON - 75A	HORSHAM - 75D	HORSHAM - 75D	HORSHAM - 75D	HORSHAM - 75D	HORSHAM - 75D	HORSHAM - 75D
32453	B.ARMS - 73B	B.ARMS - 73B	B.ARMS - 73B	W/D	W/D	W/D	W/D
32454	TONBRIDGE - 74D	TONBRIDGE - 74D	TONBRIDGE - 74D	TONBRIDGE - 74D	TONBRIDGE - 74D	TONBRIDGE - 74D	TONBRIDGE - 74D
32455	STEWARTS LANE - 73A	STEWARTS LANE - 73A	STEWARTS LANE - 73A	STEWARTS LANE - 73A	STEWARTS LANE - 73A	STEWARTS LANE - 73A	STEWARTS LANE - 73A
32456	TONBRIDGE - 74D	TONBRIDGE - 74D	TONBRIDGE - 74D	TONBRIDGE - 74D	TONBRIDGE - 74D	TONBRIDGE - 74D	TONBRIDGE - 74D
32458	B.ARMS - 73B	B.ARMS - 73B	B.ARMS - 73B	B.ARMS - 73B	B.ARMS - 73B	B.ARMS - 73B	B.ARMS - 73B
32459	B.ARMS - 73B	B.ARMS - 73B	B.ARMS - 73B	B.ARMS - 73B	B.ARMS - 73B	B.ARMS - 73B	B.ARMS - 73B
32460	B.ARMS - 73B	B.ARMS - 73B	B.ARMS - 73B	B.ARMS - 73B	B.ARMS - 73B	B.ARMS - 73B	B.ARMS - 73B
32461	B.ARMS - 73B	B.ARMS - 73B	B.ARMS - 73B	B.ARMS - 73B	B.ARMS - 73B	B.ARMS - 73B	B.ARMS - 73B
32462	B.ARMS - 73B	B.ARMS - 73B	B.ARMS - 73B	B.ARMS - 73B	B.ARMS - 73B	B.ARMS - 73B	B.ARMS - 73B
				E4 0-6-2T (1897)			
32463	HORSHAM - 75D	HORSHAM - 75D	HORSHAM - 75D	HORSHAM - 75D	HORSHAM - 75D	HORSHAM - 75D	HORSHAM - 75D
32464	HORSHAM - 75D	HORSHAM - 75D	HORSHAM - 75D	HORSHAM - 75D	HORSHAM - 75D	HORSHAM - 75D	HORSHAM - 75D
32465	HORSHAM - 75D	W/D	W/D	W/D	W/D	W/D	W/D
32467	HORSHAM - 75D	HORSHAM - 75D	HORSHAM - 75D	HORSHAM - 75D	BRIGHTON - 75A	BRIGHTON - 75A	BRIGHTON - 75A
32468	BRIGHTON - 75A	BRIGHTON - 75A	BRIGHTON - 75A	BRIGHTON - 75A	BRIGHTON - 75A	BRIGHTON - 75A	BRIGHTON - 75A
32469	HORSHAM - 75D	HORSHAM - 75D	HORSHAM - 75D	HORSHAM - 75D	HORSHAM - 75D	HORSHAM - 75D	HORSHAM - 75D
32470	HORSHAM - 75D	HORSHAM - 75D	HORSHAM - 75D	HORSHAM - 75D	HORSHAM - 75D	HORSHAM - 75D	HORSHAM - 75D
32471	B.ARMS - 73B	B.ARMS - 73B	B.ARMS - 73B	B.ARMS - 73B	B.ARMS - 73B	B.ARMS - 73B	B.ARMS - 73B
32472	B.ARMS - 73B	B.ARMS - 73B	B.ARMS - 73B	B.ARMS - 73B	B.ARMS - 73B	B.ARMS - 73B	B.ARMS - 73B
32473	B.ARMS - 73B	B.ARMS - 73B	B.ARMS - 73B	B.ARMS - 73B	B.ARMS - 73B	B.ARMS - 73B	B.ARMS - 73B
32474	B.ARMS - 73B	B.ARMS - 73B	B.ARMS - 73B	B.ARMS - 73B	B.ARMS - 73B	B.ARMS - 73B	B.ARMS - 73B
32475	BRIGHTON - 75A(N)	BRIGHTON - 75A(N)	BRIGHTON - 75A(N)	BRIGHTON - 75A(N)	BRIGHTON - 75A	BRIGHTON - 75A	BRIGHTON - 75A
32476	NINE ELMS - 70A	NINE ELMS - 70A	NINE ELMS - 70A	NINE ELMS - 70A	NINE ELMS - 70A	NINE ELMS - 70A	NINE ELMS - 70A
32479	FRATTON - 70F	FRATTON - 70F	FRATTON - 70F	FRATTON - 70F	FRATTON - 70F	FRATTON - 70F	FRATTON - 70F
32480	THREE BRIDGES - 75E	THREE BRIDGES - 75E	THREE BRIDGES - 75E	THREE BRIDGES - 75E	THREE BRIDGES - 75E	THREE BRIDGES - 75E	THREE BRIDGES - 75E
32481	BRIGHTON - 75A	BRIGHTON - 75A	BRIGHTON - 75A	BRIGHTON - 75A	BRIGHTON - 75A	BRIGHTON - 75A	BRIGHTON - 75A
32482	BRIGHTON - 75A	BRIGHTON - 75A	BRIGHTON - 75A	BRIGHTON - 75A	BRIGHTON - 75A	W/D	W/D
32484	THREE BRIDGES - 75E	THREE BRIDGES - 75E	THREE BRIDGES - 75E	THREE BRIDGES - 75E	BRIGHTON - 75A	BRIGHTON - 75A	BRIGHTON - 75A
32485	BRIGHTON - 75A	BRIGHTON - 75A	BRIGHTON - 75A	BRIGHTON - 75A	BRIGHTON - 75A	BRIGHTON - 75A	BRIGHTON - 75A
32486	SALISBURY - 72B	SALISBURY - 72B	SALISBURY - 72B	SALISBURY - 72B	SALISBURY - 72B	SALISBURY - 72B	SALISBURY - 72B
32487	GUILDFORD - 70C	GUILDFORD - 70C	GUILDFORD - 70C	GUILDFORD - 70C	GUILDFORD - 70C	GUILDFORD - 70C	GUILDFORD - 70C
32488	TONBRIDGE - 74D	TONBRIDGE - 74D	TONBRIDGE - 74D	TONBRIDGE - 74D	TONBRIDGE - 74D	TONBRIDGE - 74D	TONBRIDGE - 74D
32490	GUILDFORD - 70C	GUILDFORD - 70C	GUILDFORD - 70C	GUILDFORD - 70C	GUILDFORD - 70C	GUILDFORD - 70C	W/D
32491	EASTLEIGH - 71A	EASTLEIGH - 71A	EASTLEIGH - 71A	EASTLEIGH - 71A	NINE ELMS - 70A	NINE ELMS - 70A	NINE ELMS - 70A
32492	EASTLEIGH - 71A	EASTLEIGH - 71A	EASTLEIGH - 71A	EASTLEIGH - 71A	NINE ELMS - 70A	NINE ELMS - 70A	NINE ELMS - 70A
32493	NINE ELMS - 70A	NINE ELMS - 70A	NINE ELMS - 70A	NINE ELMS - 70A	NINE ELMS - 70A	NINE ELMS - 70A	NINE ELMS - 70A
32494	BRIGHTON - 75A(N)	BRIGHTON - 75A(N)	BRIGHTON - 75A(N)	BRIGHTON - 75A(N)	BRIGHTON - 75A	BRIGHTON - 75A	BRIGHTON - 75A
32495	FRATTON - 70F	FRATTON - 70F	FRATTON - 70F	FRATTON - 70F	NINE ELMS - 70A	NINE ELMS - 70A	FRATTON - 70F
32496	BRIGHTON - 75A(N)	BRIGHTON - 75A(N)	BRIGHTON - 75A(N)	BRIGHTON - 75A(N)	BRIGHTON - 75A	W/D	W/D
32497	NINE ELMS - 70A	NINE ELMS - 70A	NINE ELMS - 70A	NINE ELMS - 70A	NINE ELMS - 70A	NINE ELMS - 70A	NINE ELMS - 70A
32498	NINE ELMS - 70A	NINE ELMS - 70A	NINE ELMS - 70A	NINE ELMS - 70A	NINE ELMS - 70A	NINE ELMS - 70A	NINE ELMS - 70A
32499	NINE ELMS - 70A	NINE ELMS - 70A	NINE ELMS - 70A	NINE ELMS - 70A	NINE ELMS - 70A	NINE ELMS - 70A	NINE ELMS - 70A
32500	NINE ELMS - 70A	NINE ELMS - 70A	NINE ELMS - 70A	NINE ELMS - 70A	NINE ELMS - 70A	NINE ELMS - 70A	NINE ELMS - 70A
32501	READING (SR) - 70E	READING (SR) - 70E	READING (SR) - 70E	W/D	W/D	W/D	W/D
32502	BASINGSTOKE - 70D	BASINGSTOKE - 70D	BASINGSTOKE - 70D	BASINGSTOKE - 70D	BASINGSTOKE - 70D	BASINGSTOKE - 70D	BASINGSTOKE - 70D
32503	TONBRIDGE - 74D	TONBRIDGE - 74D	TONBRIDGE - 74D	TONBRIDGE - 74D	BRIGHTON - 75A	BRIGHTON - 75A	BRIGHTON - 75A
32504	BRIGHTON - 75A(N)	BRIGHTON - 75A(N)	BRIGHTON - 75A(N)	BRIGHTON - 75A(N)	BRIGHTON - 75A	BRIGHTON - 75A	BRIGHTON - 75A
32505	FRATTON - 70F	FRATTON - 70F	FRATTON - 70F	FRATTON - 70F	GUILDFORD - 70C	GUILDFORD - 70C	GUILDFORD - 70C
32506	SALISBURY - 72B	SALISBURY - 72B	SALISBURY - 72B	SALISBURY - 72B	GUILDFORD - 70C	GUILDFORD - 70C	GUILDFORD - 70C
32507	REDHILL - 75B	REDHILL - 75B	REDHILL - 75B	REDHILL - 75B	REDHILL - 75B	REDHILL - 75B	REDHILL - 75B
32508	BRIGHTON - 75A(N)	BRIGHTON - 75A(N)	BRIGHTON - 75A(N)	BRIGHTON - 75A(N)	BRIGHTON - 75A	BRIGHTON - 75A	BRIGHTON - 75A
32509	FRATTON - 70F	FRATTON - 70F	FRATTON - 70F	FRATTON - 70F	FRATTON - 70F	FRATTON - 70F	FRATTON - 70F
32510	EASTLEIGH - 71A	EASTLEIGH - 71A	EASTLEIGH - 71A	EASTLEIGH - 71A	EASTLEIGH - 71A	EASTLEIGH - 71A	EASTLEIGH - 71A
32511	HORSHAM - 75D	HORSHAM - 75D	HORSHAM - 75D	HORSHAM - 75D	HORSHAM - 75D	HORSHAM - 75D	HORSHAM - 75D
32512	REDHILL - 75B	REDHILL - 75B	REDHILL - 75B	REDHILL - 75B	BRIGHTON - 75A	BRIGHTON - 75A	BRIGHTON - 75A
32513	BRIGHTON - 75A	BRIGHTON - 75A	BRIGHTON - 75A	BRIGHTON - 75A	BRIGHTON - 75A	BRIGHTON - 75A	BRIGHTON - 75A
32514	BRIGHTON - 75A	BRIGHTON - 75A	BRIGHTON - 75A	BRIGHTON - 75A	BRIGHTON - 75A	BRIGHTON - 75A	BRIGHTON - 75A
32515	BRIGHTON - 75A	BRIGHTON - 75A	BRIGHTON - 75A	BRIGHTON - 75A	BRIGHTON - 75A	BRIGHTON - 75A	BRIGHTON - 75A
32516	THREE BRIDGES - 75E	BRIGHTON - 75A	BRIGHTON - 75A	BRIGHTON - 75A	W/D	W/D	W/D
32517	T.WELLS - 75F	T.WELLS - 75F	T.WELLS - 75F	T.WELLS - 75F	T.WELLS - 75F	T.WELLS - 75F	T.WELLS - 75F
32518	BRIGHTON - 75A	BRIGHTON - 75A	W/D	W/D	W/D	W/D	W/D
32519	THREE BRIDGES - 75E	THREE BRIDGES - 75E	THREE BRIDGES - 75E	THREE BRIDGES - 75E	THREE BRIDGES - 75E	THREE BRIDGES - 75E	THREE BRIDGES - 75E
32520	THREE BRIDGES - 75E	THREE BRIDGES - 75E	THREE BRIDGES - 75E	THREE BRIDGES - 75E	THREE BRIDGES - 75E	THREE BRIDGES - 75E	THREE BRIDGES - 75E
32556	EASTLEIGH - 71A	EASTLEIGH - 71A	EASTLEIGH - 71A	EASTLEIGH - 71A	EASTLEIGH - 71A	EASTLEIGH - 71A	EASTLEIGH - 71A
32557	EASTLEIGH - 71A	EASTLEIGH - 71A	EASTLEIGH - 71A	EASTLEIGH - 71A	EASTLEIGH - 71A	EASTLEIGH - 71A	EASTLEIGH - 71A
32558	DORCHESTER - 71C	DORCHESTER - 71C	EASTLEIGH - 71A	EASTLEIGH - 71A	EASTLEIGH - 71A	EASTLEIGH - 71A	EASTLEIGH - 71A
32559	EASTLEIGH - 71A	EASTLEIGH - 71A	EASTLEIGH - 71A	EASTLEIGH - 71A	EASTLEIGH - 71A	EASTLEIGH - 71A	EASTLEIGH - 71A
32560	REDHILL - 75B	REDHILL - 75B	REDHILL - 75B	REDHILL - 75B	REDHILL - 75B	REDHILL - 75B	REDHILL - 75B
32561	REDHILL - 75B	REDHILL - 75B	REDHILL - 75B	REDHILL - 75B	REDHILL - 75B	REDHILL - 75B	REDHILL - 75B
32562	EASTLEIGH - 71A	EASTLEIGH - 71A	EASTLEIGH - 71A	EASTLEIGH - 71A	EASTLEIGH - 71A	EASTLEIGH - 71A	EASTLEIGH - 71A
32563	EASTLEIGH - 71A	EASTLEIGH - 71A	EASTLEIGH - 71A	EASTLEIGH - 71A	EASTLEIGH - 71A	EASTLEIGH - 71A	EASTLEIGH - 71A
32564	B.ARMS - 73B	B.ARMS - 73B	B.ARMS - 73B	B.ARMS - 73B	B.ARMS - 73B	B.ARMS - 73B	B.ARMS - 73B
32565	B.ARMS - 73B	B.ARMS - 73B	B.ARMS - 73B	B.ARMS - 73B	B.ARMS - 73B	B.ARMS - 73B	B.ARMS - 73B
32566	BRIGHTON - 75A	BRIGHTON - 75A	BRIGHTON - 75A	BRIGHTON - 75A	BRIGHTON - 75A	BRIGHTON - 75A	BRIGHTON - 75A
32577	BRIGHTON - 75A	BRIGHTON - 75A	BRIGHTON - 75A	BRIGHTON - 75A	BRIGHTON - 75A	BRIGHTON - 75A	BRIGHTON - 75A
32578	TONBRIDGE - 74D	TONBRIDGE - 74D	TONBRIDGE - 74D	TONBRIDGE - 74D	TONBRIDGE - 74D	TONBRIDGE - 74D	TONBRIDGE - 74D
32579	EASTLEIGH - 71A	EASTLEIGH - 71A	EASTLEIGH - 71A	EASTLEIGH - 71A	EASTLEIGH - 71A	EASTLEIGH - 71A	EASTLEIGH - 71A
32580	TONBRIDGE - 74D	TONBRIDGE - 74D	TONBRIDGE - 74D	TONBRIDGE - 74D	TONBRIDGE - 74D	TONBRIDGE - 74D	TONBRIDGE - 74D
32581	T.WELLS - 75F	T.WELLS - 75F	T.WELLS - 75F	T.WELLS - 75F	T.WELLS - 75F	T.WELLS - 75F	T.WELLS - 75F
32582	T.WELLS - 75F	T.WELLS - 75F	T.WELLS - 75F	T.WELLS - 75F	T.WELLS - 75F	T.WELLS - 75F	T.WELLS - 75F

loco	Jan-56	Apr-56	May-56	Aug-56	Oct-56	Nov-56	Jan-57
				E1/R 0-6-2T (1927)			
32095	PLYMOUTH - 72D	PLYMOUTH - 72D	PLYMOUTH - 72D	PLYMOUTH - 72D	PLYMOUTH - 72D	W/D	W/D
32096	PLYMOUTH - 72D	PLYMOUTH - 72D	PLYMOUTH - 72D	PLYMOUTH - 72D	PLYMOUTH - 72D	W/D	W/D
32124	EXMOUTH JCN - 72A	EXMOUTH JCN - 72A	EXMOUTH JCN - 72A	EXMOUTH JCN - 72A	EXMOUTH JCN - 72A	EXMOUTH JCN - 72A	EXMOUTH JCN - 72A
32135	EXMOUTH JCN - 72A	EXMOUTH JCN - 72A	EXMOUTH JCN - 72A	EXMOUTH JCN - 72A	EXMOUTH JCN - 72A	EXMOUTH JCN - 72A	EXMOUTH JCN - 72A
32608	BARNSTAPLE - 72E	BARNSTAPLE - 72E	BARNSTAPLE - 72E	BARNSTAPLE - 72E	BARNSTAPLE - 72E	BARNSTAPLE - 72E	BARNSTAPLE - 72E
32610	BARNSTAPLE - 72E	W/D	W/D	W/D	W/D	W/D	W/D
32695	EXMOUTH JCN - 72A	EXMOUTH JCN - 72A	EXMOUTH JCN - 72A	EXMOUTH JCN - 72A	EXMOUTH JCN - 72A	EXMOUTH JCN - 72A	EXMOUTH JCN - 72A
32697	EXMOUTH JCN - 72A	EXMOUTH JCN - 72A	EXMOUTH JCN - 72A	EXMOUTH JCN - 72A	EXMOUTH JCN - 72A	EXMOUTH JCN - 72A	EXMOUTH JCN - 72A
				E3 0-6-2T (1894)			
32165	HORSHAM - 75D	HORSHAM - 75D	HORSHAM - 75D	HORSHAM - 75D	HORSHAM - 75D	BRIGHTON - 75A	BRIGHTON - 75A
32166	HORSHAM - 75D	HORSHAM - 75D	HORSHAM - 75D	HORSHAM - 75D	HORSHAM - 75D	BRIGHTON - 75A	BRIGHTON - 75A
32170	READING (SR) - 70E	READING (SR) - 70E	READING (SR) - 70E	READING (SR) - 70E	READING (SR) - 70E	READING (SR) - 70E	READING (SR) - 70E
32454	TONBRIDGE - 74D	TONBRIDGE - 74D	TONBRIDGE - 74D	TONBRIDGE - 74D	TONBRIDGE - 74D	TONBRIDGE - 74D	TONBRIDGE - 74D
32455	STEWARTS LANE - 73A	STEWARTS LANE - 73A	STEWARTS LANE - 73A	STEWARTS LANE - 73A	STEWARTS LANE - 73A	STEWARTS LANE - 73A	STEWARTS LANE - 73A
32456	TONBRIDGE - 74D	TONBRIDGE - 74D	TONBRIDGE - 74D	TONBRIDGE - 74D	TONBRIDGE - 74D	TONBRIDGE - 74D	TONBRIDGE - 74D
32458	B.ARMS - 73B	B.ARMS - 73B	B.ARMS - 73B	B.ARMS - 73B	B.ARMS - 73B	B.ARMS - 73B	B.ARMS - 73B
32459	B.ARMS - 73B	B.ARMS - 73B	B.ARMS - 73B	B.ARMS - 73B	B.ARMS - 73B	B.ARMS - 73B	B.ARMS - 73B
32460	B.ARMS - 73B	W/D	W/D	W/D	W/D	W/D	W/D
32461	B.ARMS - 73B	B.ARMS - 73B	B.ARMS - 73B	B.ARMS - 73B	B.ARMS - 73B	B.ARMS - 73B	B.ARMS - 73B
32462	B.ARMS - 73B	B.ARMS - 73B	B.ARMS - 73B	B.ARMS - 73B	B.ARMS - 73B	B.ARMS - 73B	B.ARMS - 73B
				E4 0-6-2T (1897)			
32463	HORSHAM - 75D	HORSHAM - 75D	HORSHAM - 75D	HORSHAM - 75D	HORSHAM - 75D	HORSHAM - 75D	HORSHAM - 75D
32467	BRIGHTON - 75A	BRIGHTON - 75A	BRIGHTON - 75A	BRIGHTON - 75A	BRIGHTON - 75A	BRIGHTON - 75A	BRIGHTON - 75A
32468	BRIGHTON - 75A	BRIGHTON - 75A	BRIGHTON - 75A	BRIGHTON - 75A	BRIGHTON - 75A	BRIGHTON - 75A	BRIGHTON - 75A
32469	HORSHAM - 75D	HORSHAM - 75D	HORSHAM - 75D	HORSHAM - 75D	HORSHAM - 75D	HORSHAM - 75D	HORSHAM - 75D
32470	HORSHAM - 75D	HORSHAM - 75D	HORSHAM - 75D	HORSHAM - 75D	HORSHAM - 75D	HORSHAM - 75D	HORSHAM - 75D
32471	B.ARMS - 73B	B.ARMS - 73B	B.ARMS - 73B	B.ARMS - 73B	B.ARMS - 73B	B.ARMS - 73B	B.ARMS - 73B
32472	B.ARMS - 73B	B.ARMS - 73B	B.ARMS - 73B	B.ARMS - 73B	B.ARMS - 73B	B.ARMS - 73B	B.ARMS - 73B
32473	B.ARMS - 73B	B.ARMS - 73B	B.ARMS - 73B	B.ARMS - 73B	B.ARMS - 73B	B.ARMS - 73B	B.ARMS - 73B
32474	B.ARMS - 73B	B.ARMS - 73B	B.ARMS - 73B	B.ARMS - 73B	B.ARMS - 73B	B.ARMS - 73B	B.ARMS - 73B
32475	BRIGHTON - 75A	BRIGHTON - 75A	BRIGHTON - 75A	BRIGHTON - 75A	BRIGHTON - 75A	BRIGHTON - 75A	BRIGHTON - 75A
32476	NINE ELMS - 70A	NINE ELMS - 70A	NINE ELMS - 70A	NINE ELMS - 70A	NINE ELMS - 70A	NINE ELMS - 70A	NINE ELMS - 70A
32479	FRATTON - 70F	FRATTON - 70F	FRATTON - 70F	FRATTON - 70F	FRATTON - 70F	FRATTON - 70F	FRATTON - 70F
32480	THREE BRIDGES - 75E	THREE BRIDGES - 75E	THREE BRIDGES - 75E	THREE BRIDGES - 75E	THREE BRIDGES - 75E	HORSHAM - 75D	HORSHAM - 75D
32481	BRIGHTON - 75A	BRIGHTON - 75A	BRIGHTON - 75A	BRIGHTON - 75A	BRIGHTON - 75A	BRIGHTON - 75A	BRIGHTON - 75A
32484	BRIGHTON - 75A	BRIGHTON - 75A	BRIGHTON - 75A	BRIGHTON - 75A	BRIGHTON - 75A	BRIGHTON - 75A	BRIGHTON - 75A
32485	BRIGHTON - 75A	BRIGHTON - 75A	BRIGHTON - 75A	BRIGHTON - 75A	BRIGHTON - 75A	BRIGHTON - 75A	BRIGHTON - 75A
32486	SALISBURY - 72B	SALISBURY - 72B	SALISBURY - 72B	SALISBURY - 72B	SALISBURY - 72B	NINE ELMS - 70A	NINE ELMS - 70A
32487	GUILDFORD - 70C	GUILDFORD - 70C	GUILDFORD - 70C	GUILDFORD - 70C	GUILDFORD - 70C	GUILDFORD - 70C	GUILDFORD - 70C
32488	TONBRIDGE - 74D	TONBRIDGE - 74D	TONBRIDGE - 74D	TONBRIDGE - 74D	TONBRIDGE - 74D	TONBRIDGE - 74D	TONBRIDGE - 74D
32491	BASINGSTOKE - 70D	BASINGSTOKE - 70D	BASINGSTOKE - 70D	BASINGSTOKE - 70D	BASINGSTOKE - 70D	EASTLEIGH - 71A	EASTLEIGH - 71A
32492	NINE ELMS - 70A	NINE ELMS - 70A	NINE ELMS - 70A	NINE ELMS - 70A	NINE ELMS - 70A	NINE ELMS - 70A	NINE ELMS - 70A
32493	NINE ELMS - 70A	NINE ELMS - 70A	NINE ELMS - 70A	NINE ELMS - 70A	NINE ELMS - 70A	NINE ELMS - 70A	NINE ELMS - 70A
32494	BRIGHTON - 75A	BRIGHTON - 75A	BRIGHTON - 75A	BRIGHTON - 75A	BRIGHTON - 75A	BRIGHTON - 75A	BRIGHTON - 75A
32495	FRATTON - 70F	FRATTON - 70F	FRATTON - 70F	FRATTON - 70F	FRATTON - 70F	FRATTON - 70F	FRATTON - 70F
32497	NINE ELMS - 70A	NINE ELMS - 70A	NINE ELMS - 70A	NINE ELMS - 70A	NINE ELMS - 70A	NINE ELMS - 70A	NINE ELMS - 70A
32498	NINE ELMS - 70A	NINE ELMS - 70A	NINE ELMS - 70A	NINE ELMS - 70A	NINE ELMS - 70A	NINE ELMS - 70A	NINE ELMS - 70A
32499	NINE ELMS - 70A	NINE ELMS - 70A	NINE ELMS - 70A	NINE ELMS - 70A	NINE ELMS - 70A	NINE ELMS - 70A	NINE ELMS - 70A
32500	NINE ELMS - 70A	NINE ELMS - 70A	NINE ELMS - 70A	NINE ELMS - 70A	NINE ELMS - 70A	NINE ELMS - 70A	NINE ELMS - 70A
32502	BASINGSTOKE - 70D	BASINGSTOKE - 70D	BASINGSTOKE - 70D	BASINGSTOKE - 70D	BASINGSTOKE - 70D	BRIGHTON - 75A	BRIGHTON - 75A
32503	BRIGHTON - 75A	BRIGHTON - 75A	BRIGHTON - 75A	BRIGHTON - 75A	BRIGHTON - 75A	BRIGHTON - 75A	BRIGHTON - 75A
32504	BRIGHTON - 75A	BRIGHTON - 75A	BRIGHTON - 75A	BRIGHTON - 75A	BRIGHTON - 75A	BRIGHTON - 75A	BRIGHTON - 75A
32505	GUILDFORD - 70C	GUILDFORD - 70C	GUILDFORD - 70C	GUILDFORD - 70C	GUILDFORD - 70C	GUILDFORD - 70C	GUILDFORD - 70C
32506	GUILDFORD - 70C	GUILDFORD - 70C	GUILDFORD - 70C	GUILDFORD - 70C	GUILDFORD - 70C	GUILDFORD - 70C	GUILDFORD - 70C
32507	REDHILL - 75B	REDHILL - 75B	REDHILL - 75B	REDHILL - 75B	REDHILL - 75B	REDHILL - 75B	REDHILL - 75B
32508	BRIGHTON - 75A	BRIGHTON - 75A	BRIGHTON - 75A	BRIGHTON - 75A	BRIGHTON - 75A	BRIGHTON - 75A	BRIGHTON - 75A
32509	FRATTON - 70F	FRATTON - 70F	FRATTON - 70F	FRATTON - 70F	FRATTON - 70F	FRATTON - 70F	FRATTON - 70F
32510	EASTLEIGH - 71A	EASTLEIGH - 71A	EASTLEIGH - 71A	EASTLEIGH - 71A	EASTLEIGH - 71A	EASTLEIGH - 71A	EASTLEIGH - 71A
32511	HORSHAM - 75D	HORSHAM - 75D	HORSHAM - 75D	HORSHAM - 75D	W/D	W/D	W/D
32512	BRIGHTON - 75A	BRIGHTON - 75A	BRIGHTON - 75A	BRIGHTON - 75A	BRIGHTON - 75A	BRIGHTON - 75A	BRIGHTON - 75A
32514	BRIGHTON - 75A	BRIGHTON - 75A	BRIGHTON - 75A	BRIGHTON - 75A	W/D	W/D	W/D
32515	BRIGHTON - 75A	BRIGHTON - 75A	BRIGHTON - 75A	BRIGHTON - 75A	BRIGHTON - 75A	BRIGHTON - 75A	BRIGHTON - 75A
32517	T.WELLS - 75F	T.WELLS - 75F	T.WELLS - 75F	T.WELLS - 75F	T.WELLS - 75F	T.WELLS - 75F	T.WELLS - 75F
32519	THREE BRIDGES - 75E	THREE BRIDGES - 75E	THREE BRIDGES - 75E	THREE BRIDGES - 75E	THREE BRIDGES - 75E	THREE BRIDGES - 75E	THREE BRIDGES - 75E
32520	THREE BRIDGES - 75E	THREE BRIDGES - 75E	THREE BRIDGES - 75E	THREE BRIDGES - 75E	THREE BRIDGES - 75E	THREE BRIDGES - 75E	W/D
32556	EASTLEIGH - 71A	EASTLEIGH - 71A	EASTLEIGH - 71A	EASTLEIGH - 71A	EASTLEIGH - 71A	EASTLEIGH - 71A	EASTLEIGH - 71A
32557	EASTLEIGH - 71A	EASTLEIGH - 71A	EASTLEIGH - 71A	EASTLEIGH - 71A	EASTLEIGH - 71A	EASTLEIGH - 71A	EASTLEIGH - 71A
32558	EASTLEIGH - 71A	EASTLEIGH - 71A	EASTLEIGH - 71A	EASTLEIGH - 71A	EASTLEIGH - 71A	W/D	W/D
32559	EASTLEIGH - 71A	EASTLEIGH - 71A	EASTLEIGH - 71A	EASTLEIGH - 71A	EASTLEIGH - 71A	EASTLEIGH - 71A	EASTLEIGH - 71A
32560	REDHILL - 75B	REDHILL - 75B	REDHILL - 75B	REDHILL - 75B	REDHILL - 75B	REDHILL - 75B	REDHILL - 75B
32561	REDHILL - 75B	W/D	W/D	W/D	W/D	W/D	W/D
32562	EASTLEIGH - 71A	EASTLEIGH - 71A	BRIGHTON - 75A	BRIGHTON - 75A	BRIGHTON - 75A	BRIGHTON - 75A	BRIGHTON - 75A
32563	NINE ELMS - 70A	NINE ELMS - 70A	NINE ELMS - 70A	NINE ELMS - 70A	NINE ELMS - 70A	NINE ELMS - 70A	NINE ELMS - 70A
32564	B.ARMS - 73B	B.ARMS - 73B	B.ARMS - 73B	B.ARMS - 73B	B.ARMS - 73B	B.ARMS - 73B	B.ARMS - 73B
32565	B.ARMS - 73B	B.ARMS - 73B	B.ARMS - 73B	B.ARMS - 73B	B.ARMS - 73B	B.ARMS - 73B	B.ARMS - 73B
32566	BRIGHTON - 75A	BRIGHTON - 75A	BRIGHTON - 75A	BRIGHTON - 75A	BRIGHTON - 75A	BRIGHTON - 75A	BRIGHTON - 75A
32577	BRIGHTON - 75A	BRIGHTON - 75A	BRIGHTON - 75A	BRIGHTON - 75A	BRIGHTON - 75A	BRIGHTON - 75A	BRIGHTON - 75A
32578	TONBRIDGE - 74D	TONBRIDGE - 74D	TONBRIDGE - 74D	TONBRIDGE - 74D	TONBRIDGE - 74D	TONBRIDGE - 74D	TONBRIDGE - 74D
32579	EASTLEIGH - 71A	EASTLEIGH - 71A	EASTLEIGH - 71A	EASTLEIGH - 71A	EASTLEIGH - 71A	EASTLEIGH - 71A	EASTLEIGH - 71A
32580	TONBRIDGE - 74D	TONBRIDGE - 74D	TONBRIDGE - 74D	TONBRIDGE - 74D	TONBRIDGE - 74D	TONBRIDGE - 74D	TONBRIDGE - 74D
32581	T.WELLS - 75F	T.WELLS - 75F	T.WELLS - 75F	T.WELLS - 75F	T.WELLS - 75F	T.WELLS - 75F	T.WELLS - 75F
32582	T.WELLS - 75F	T.WELLS - 75F	T.WELLS - 75F	T.WELLS - 75F	W/D	W/D	W/D

loco	Mar-57	Jun-57	Jul-57	Oct-57	Jan-58	Feb-58	Mar-58
				E1/R 0-6-2T (1927)			
32124	EXMOUTH JCN - 72A	EXMOUTH JCN - 72A	EXMOUTH JCN - 72A	EXMOUTH JCN - 72A	EXMOUTH JCN - 72A	EXMOUTH JCN - 72A	EXMOUTH JCN - 72A
32135	EXMOUTH JCN - 72A	EXMOUTH JCN - 72A	EXMOUTH JCN - 72A	EXMOUTH JCN - 72A	EXMOUTH JCN - 72A	EXMOUTH JCN - 72A	EXMOUTH JCN - 72A
32608	BARNSTAPLE - 72E	W/D	W/D	W/D	W/D	W/D	W/D
32697	EXMOUTH JCN - 72A	EXMOUTH JCN - 72A	EXMOUTH JCN - 72A	EXMOUTH JCN - 72A	EXMOUTH JCN - 72A	EXMOUTH JCN - 72A	EXMOUTH JCN - 72A
				E3 0-6-2T (1894)			
32165	BRIGHTON - 75A	BRIGHTON - 75A	BRIGHTON - 75A	BRIGHTON - 75A	BRIGHTON - 75A	BRIGHTON - 75A	BRIGHTON - 75A
32166	BRIGHTON - 75A	BRIGHTON - 75A	BRIGHTON - 75A	BRIGHTON - 75A	BRIGHTON - 75A	BRIGHTON - 75A	BRIGHTON - 75A
32170	B.ARMS - 73B	B.ARMS - 73B	W/D	W/D	W/D	W/D	W/D
32454	B.ARMS - 73B	B.ARMS - 73B	B.ARMS - 73B	B.ARMS - 73B	B.ARMS - 73B	B.ARMS - 73B	W/D
32455	STEWARTS LANE - 73A	STEWARTS LANE - 73A	STEWARTS LANE - 73A	STEWARTS LANE - 73A	STEWARTS LANE - 73A	W/D	W/D
32456	TONBRIDGE - 74D	TONBRIDGE - 74D	TONBRIDGE - 74D	TONBRIDGE - 74D	TONBRIDGE - 74D	TONBRIDGE - 74D	TONBRIDGE - 74D
32459	B.ARMS - 73B	W/D	W/D	W/D	W/D	W/D	W/D
32462	B.ARMS - 73B	W/D	W/D	W/D	W/D	W/D	W/D
				E4 0-6-2T (1897)			
32463	HORSHAM - 75D	HORSHAM - 75D	HORSHAM - 75D	HORSHAM - 75D	HORSHAM - 75D	HORSHAM - 75D	HORSHAM - 75D
32467	BRIGHTON - 75A	BRIGHTON - 75A	BRIGHTON - 75A	BRIGHTON - 75A	BRIGHTON - 75A	BRIGHTON - 75A	BRIGHTON - 75A
32468	BRIGHTON - 75A	BRIGHTON - 75A	BRIGHTON - 75A	BRIGHTON - 75A	BRIGHTON - 75A	BRIGHTON - 75A	BRIGHTON - 75A
32469	HORSHAM - 75D	HORSHAM - 75D	HORSHAM - 75D	HORSHAM - 75D	HORSHAM - 75D	HORSHAM - 75D	HORSHAM - 75D
32470	HORSHAM - 75D	HORSHAM - 75D	HORSHAM - 75D	HORSHAM - 75D	HORSHAM - 75D	HORSHAM - 75D	HORSHAM - 75D
32471	B.ARMS - 73B	B.ARMS - 73B	B.ARMS - 73B	B.ARMS - 73B	B.ARMS - 73B	B.ARMS - 73B	B.ARMS - 73B
32472	B.ARMS - 73B	B.ARMS - 73B	B.ARMS - 73B	B.ARMS - 73B	B.ARMS - 73B	B.ARMS - 73B	B.ARMS - 73B
32473	B.ARMS - 73B	B.ARMS - 73B	B.ARMS - 73B	B.ARMS - 73B	B.ARMS - 73B	B.ARMS - 73B	B.ARMS - 73B
32474	B.ARMS - 73B	B.ARMS - 73B	B.ARMS - 73B	B.ARMS - 73B	B.ARMS - 73B	B.ARMS - 73B	B.ARMS - 73B
32475	BRIGHTON - 75A	BRIGHTON - 75A	BRIGHTON - 75A	BRIGHTON - 75A	BRIGHTON - 75A	BRIGHTON - 75A	BRIGHTON - 75A
32476	NINE ELMS - 70A	W/D	W/D	W/D	W/D	W/D	W/D
32479	FRATTON - 70F	FRATTON - 70F	FRATTON - 70F	FRATTON - 70F	FRATTON - 70F	FRATTON - 70F	FRATTON - 70F
32480	HORSHAM - 75D	HORSHAM - 75D	HORSHAM - 75D	HORSHAM - 75D	HORSHAM - 75D	HORSHAM - 75D	BRIGHTON - 75A
32481	BRIGHTON - 75A	BRIGHTON - 75A	BRIGHTON - 75A	BRIGHTON - 75A	BRIGHTON - 75A	BRIGHTON - 75A	W/D
32484	BRIGHTON - 75A	BRIGHTON - 75A	BRIGHTON - 75A	BRIGHTON - 75A	BRIGHTON - 75A	BRIGHTON - 75A	BRIGHTON - 75A
32485	BRIGHTON - 75A	BRIGHTON - 75A	BRIGHTON - 75A	BRIGHTON - 75A	W/D	W/D	W/D
32486	NINE ELMS - 70A	NINE ELMS - 70A	NINE ELMS - 70A	NINE ELMS - 70A	NINE ELMS - 70A	NINE ELMS - 70A	NINE ELMS - 70A
32487	GUILDFORD - 70C	GUILDFORD - 70C	GUILDFORD - 70C	GUILDFORD - 70C	GUILDFORD - 70C	NINE ELMS - 70A	NINE ELMS - 70A
32488	TONBRIDGE - 74D	W/D	W/D	W/D	W/D	W/D	W/D
32491	EASTLEIGH - 71A	EASTLEIGH - 71A	EASTLEIGH - 71A	EASTLEIGH - 71A	EASTLEIGH - 71A	EASTLEIGH - 71A	EASTLEIGH - 71A
32492	NINE ELMS - 70A	W/D	W/D	W/D	W/D	W/D	W/D
32493	NINE ELMS - 70A	NINE ELMS - 70A	NINE ELMS - 70A	NINE ELMS - 70A	NINE ELMS - 70A	W/D	W/D
32494	BRIGHTON - 75A	BRIGHTON - 75A	BRIGHTON - 75A	BRIGHTON - 75A	BRIGHTON - 75A	BRIGHTON - 75A	BRIGHTON - 75A
32495	FRATTON - 70F	FRATTON - 70F	FRATTON - 70F	FRATTON - 70F	FRATTON - 70F	FRATTON - 70F	FRATTON - 70F
32497	NINE ELMS - 70A	NINE ELMS - 70A	NINE ELMS - 70A	NINE ELMS - 70A	NINE ELMS - 70A	NINE ELMS - 70A	NINE ELMS - 70A
32498	NINE ELMS - 70A	NINE ELMS - 70A	NINE ELMS - 70A	NINE ELMS - 70A	NINE ELMS - 70A	NINE ELMS - 70A	NINE ELMS - 70A
32499	NINE ELMS - 70A	W/D	W/D	W/D	W/D	W/D	W/D
32500	NINE ELMS - 70A	NINE ELMS - 70A	NINE ELMS - 70A	NINE ELMS - 70A	NINE ELMS - 70A	NINE ELMS - 70A	NINE ELMS - 70A
32502	BRIGHTON - 75A	BRIGHTON - 75A	BRIGHTON - 75A	BRIGHTON - 75A	BRIGHTON - 75A	W/D	W/D
32503	BRIGHTON - 75A	BRIGHTON - 75A	BRIGHTON - 75A	BRIGHTON - 75A	BRIGHTON - 75A	BRIGHTON - 75A	BRIGHTON - 75A
32504	BRIGHTON - 75A	BRIGHTON - 75A	BRIGHTON - 75A	BRIGHTON - 75A	BRIGHTON - 75A	BRIGHTON - 75A	BRIGHTON - 75A
32505	GUILDFORD - 70C	GUILDFORD - 70C	GUILDFORD - 70C	GUILDFORD - 70C	GUILDFORD - 70C	GUILDFORD - 70C	GUILDFORD - 70C
32506	GUILDFORD - 70C	GUILDFORD - 70C	GUILDFORD - 70C	GUILDFORD - 70C	GUILDFORD - 70C	GUILDFORD - 70C	GUILDFORD - 70C
32507	REDHILL - 75B	REDHILL - 75B	REDHILL - 75B	REDHILL - 75B	REDHILL - 75B	REDHILL - 75B	BRIGHTON - 75A
32508	BRIGHTON - 75A	BRIGHTON - 75A	BRIGHTON - 75A	BRIGHTON - 75A	BRIGHTON - 75A	BRIGHTON - 75A	BRIGHTON - 75A
32509	FRATTON - 70F	FRATTON - 70F	FRATTON - 70F	FRATTON - 70F	FRATTON - 70F	FRATTON - 70F	FRATTON - 70F
32510	EASTLEIGH - 71A	EASTLEIGH - 71A	EASTLEIGH - 71A	EASTLEIGH - 71A	EASTLEIGH - 71A	EASTLEIGH - 71A	EASTLEIGH - 71A
32512	BRIGHTON - 75A	BRIGHTON - 75A	BRIGHTON - 75A	BRIGHTON - 75A	BRIGHTON - 75A	BRIGHTON - 75A	BRIGHTON - 75A
32515	BRIGHTON - 75A	BRIGHTON - 75A	BRIGHTON - 75A	BRIGHTON - 75A	BRIGHTON - 75A	BRIGHTON - 75A	BRIGHTON - 75A
32517	T.WELLS - 75F	T.WELLS - 75F	T.WELLS - 75F	T.WELLS - 75F	T.WELLS - 75F	T.WELLS - 75F	T.WELLS - 75F
32519	THREE BRIDGES - 75E	THREE BRIDGES - 75E	THREE BRIDGES - 75E	THREE BRIDGES - 75E	THREE BRIDGES - 75E	THREE BRIDGES - 75E	BRIGHTON - 75A
32556	EASTLEIGH - 71A	EASTLEIGH - 71A	EASTLEIGH - 71A	EASTLEIGH - 71A	EASTLEIGH - 71A	EASTLEIGH - 71A	EASTLEIGH - 71A
32557	EASTLEIGH - 71A	EASTLEIGH - 71A	EASTLEIGH - 71A	EASTLEIGH - 71A	EASTLEIGH - 71A	EASTLEIGH - 71A	EASTLEIGH - 71A
32559	EASTLEIGH - 71A	EASTLEIGH - 71A	EASTLEIGH - 71A	EASTLEIGH - 71A	EASTLEIGH - 71A	EASTLEIGH - 71A	EASTLEIGH - 71A
32560	REDHILL - 75B	REDHILL - 75B	REDHILL - 75B	NINE ELMS - 70A	NINE ELMS - 70A	NINE ELMS - 70A	NINE ELMS - 70A
32562	BRIGHTON - 75A	BRIGHTON - 75A	BRIGHTON - 75A	BRIGHTON - 75A	BRIGHTON - 75A	BRIGHTON - 75A	BRIGHTON - 75A
32563	NINE ELMS - 70A	NINE ELMS - 70A	NINE ELMS - 70A	NINE ELMS - 70A	NINE ELMS - 70A	NINE ELMS - 70A	NINE ELMS - 70A
32564	B.ARMS - 73B	B.ARMS - 73B	B.ARMS - 73B	B.ARMS - 73B	B.ARMS - 73B	B.ARMS - 73B	B.ARMS - 73B
32565	B.ARMS - 73B	B.ARMS - 73B	B.ARMS - 73B	B.ARMS - 73B	B.ARMS - 73B	B.ARMS - 73B	B.ARMS - 73B
32566	BRIGHTON - 75A	BRIGHTON - 75A	BRIGHTON - 75A	BRIGHTON - 75A	BRIGHTON - 75A	BRIGHTON - 75A	BRIGHTON - 75A
32577	BRIGHTON - 75A	BRIGHTON - 75A	BRIGHTON - 75A	BRIGHTON - 75A	BRIGHTON - 75A	BRIGHTON - 75A	BRIGHTON - 75A
32578	TONBRIDGE - 74D	TONBRIDGE - 74D	TONBRIDGE - 74D	TONBRIDGE - 74D	TONBRIDGE - 74D	TONBRIDGE - 74D	TONBRIDGE - 74D
32579	EASTLEIGH - 71A	EASTLEIGH - 71A	EASTLEIGH - 71A	EASTLEIGH - 71A	EASTLEIGH - 71A	EASTLEIGH - 71A	EASTLEIGH - 71A
32580	TONBRIDGE - 74D	TONBRIDGE - 74D	TONBRIDGE - 74D	TONBRIDGE - 74D	TONBRIDGE - 74D	TONBRIDGE - 74D	TONBRIDGE - 74D
32581	T.WELLS - 75F	T.WELLS - 75F	T.WELLS - 75F	T.WELLS - 75F	T.WELLS - 75F	T.WELLS - 75F	T.WELLS - 75F

loco	May-58	Oct-58	Mar-59	Jun-59	Jul-59	Aug-59	Oct-59
				E1/R 0-6-2T (1927)			
32124	EXMOUTH JCN - 72A	EXMOUTH JCN - 72A	W/D	W/D	W/D	W/D	W/D
32135	EXMOUTH JCN - 72A	EXMOUTH JCN - 72A	EXMOUTH JCN - 72A	W/D	W/D	W/D	W/D
32697	EXMOUTH JCN - 72A	EXMOUTH JCN - 72A	EXMOUTH JCN - 72A	EXMOUTH JCN - 72A	EXMOUTH JCN - 72A	EXMOUTH JCN - 72A	EXMOUTH JCN - 72A
				E3 0-6-2T (1894)			
32165	BRIGHTON - 75A	BRIGHTON - 75A	NORWOOD JCN - 75C	NORWOOD JCN - 75C	NORWOOD JCN - 75C	NORWOOD JCN - 75C	NORWOOD JCN - 75C
32166	BRIGHTON - 75A	BRIGHTON - 75A	NORWOOD JCN - 75C	NORWOOD JCN - 75C	NORWOOD JCN - 75C	NORWOOD JCN - 75C	W/D
32456	TONBRIDGE - 74D	TONBRIDGE - 73J	TONBRIDGE - 73J	TONBRIDGE - 73J	NORWOOD JCN - 75C	W/D	W/D
				E4 0-6-2T (1897)			
32463	HORSHAM - 75D	HORSHAM - 75D	HORSHAM - 75D	HORSHAM - 75D	THREE BRIDGES - 75E	THREE BRIDGES - 75E	W/D
32468	BRIGHTON - 75A	BRIGHTON - 75A	BRIGHTON - 75A	BRIGHTON - 75A	BRIGHTON - 75A	BRIGHTON - 75A	BRIGHTON - 75A
32469	HORSHAM - 75D	HORSHAM - 75D	HORSHAM - 75D	HORSHAM - 75D	THREE BRIDGES - 75E	THREE BRIDGES - 75E	THREE BRIDGES - 75E
32470	HORSHAM - 75D	HORSHAM - 75D	HORSHAM - 75D	HORSHAM - 75D	THREE BRIDGES - 75E	THREE BRIDGES - 75E	THREE BRIDGES - 75E
32471	B.ARMS - 73B	B.ARMS - 73B	B.ARMS - 73B	B.ARMS - 73B	B.ARMS - 73B	B.ARMS - 73B	W/D
32472	B.ARMS - 73B	B.ARMS - 73B	B.ARMS - 73B	B.ARMS - 73B	B.ARMS - 73B	B.ARMS - 73B	B.ARMS - 73B
32473	B.ARMS - 73B	B.ARMS - 73B	B.ARMS - 73B	B.ARMS - 73B	B.ARMS - 73B	B.ARMS - 73B	B.ARMS - 73B
32474	B.ARMS - 73B	B.ARMS - 73B	B.ARMS - 73B	B.ARMS - 73B	B.ARMS - 73B	B.ARMS - 73B	B.ARMS - 73B
32475	BRIGHTON - 75A	BRIGHTON - 75A	BRIGHTON - 75A	BRIGHTON - 75A	BRIGHTON - 75A	BRIGHTON - 75A	BRIGHTON - 75A
32479	FRATTON - 70F	FRATTON - 70F	FRATTON - 70F	FRATTON - 70F	FRATTON - 70F	FRATTON - 70F	FRATTON - 70F
32480	BRIGHTON - 75A	BRIGHTON - 75A	BRIGHTON - 75A	W/D	W/D	W/D	W/D
32484	BRIGHTON - 75A	BRIGHTON - 75A	BRIGHTON - 75A	BRIGHTON - 75A	BRIGHTON - 75A	BRIGHTON - 75A	BRIGHTON - 75A
32486	NINE ELMS - 70A	NINE ELMS - 70A	W/D	W/D	W/D	W/D	W/D
32487	NINE ELMS - 70A	NINE ELMS - 70A	NINE ELMS - 70A	NINE ELMS - 70A	NINE ELMS - 70A	NINE ELMS - 70A	NINE ELMS - 70A
32491	EASTLEIGH - 71A	EASTLEIGH - 71A	EASTLEIGH - 71A	EASTLEIGH - 71A	EASTLEIGH - 71A	EASTLEIGH - 71A	EASTLEIGH - 71A
32494	BRIGHTON - 75A	BRIGHTON - 75A	BRIGHTON - 75A	BRIGHTON - 75A	BRIGHTON - 75A	BRIGHTON - 75A	W/D
32495	FRATTON - 70F	FRATTON - 70F	FRATTON - 70F	FRATTON - 70F	FRATTON - 70F	FRATTON - 70F	FRATTON - 70F
32497	NINE ELMS - 70A	NINE ELMS - 70A	NINE ELMS - 70A	NINE ELMS - 70A	NINE ELMS - 70A	NINE ELMS - 70A	NINE ELMS - 70A
32498	NINE ELMS - 70A	NINE ELMS - 70A	NINE ELMS - 70A	NINE ELMS - 70A	NINE ELMS - 70A	NINE ELMS - 70A	NINE ELMS - 70A
32500	NINE ELMS - 70A	NINE ELMS - 70A	NINE ELMS - 70A	NINE ELMS - 70A	NINE ELMS - 70A	NINE ELMS - 70A	NINE ELMS - 70A
32503	BRIGHTON - 75A	BRIGHTON - 75A	BRIGHTON - 75A	BRIGHTON - 75A	BRIGHTON - 75A	BRIGHTON - 75A	BRIGHTON - 75A
32504	BRIGHTON - 75A	BRIGHTON - 75A	BRIGHTON - 75A	BRIGHTON - 75A	BRIGHTON - 75A	BRIGHTON - 75A	BRIGHTON - 75A
32505	GUILDFORD - 70C	GUILDFORD - 70C	GUILDFORD - 70C	GUILDFORD - 70C	GUILDFORD - 70C	GUILDFORD - 70C	GUILDFORD - 70C
32506	GUILDFORD - 70C	GUILDFORD - 70C	GUILDFORD - 70C	GUILDFORD - 70C	GUILDFORD - 70C	GUILDFORD - 70C	GUILDFORD - 70C
32507	BRIGHTON - 75A	BRIGHTON - 75A	BRIGHTON - 75A	W/D	W/D	W/D	W/D
32508	BRIGHTON - 75A	BRIGHTON - 75A	BRIGHTON - 75A	BRIGHTON - 75A	BRIGHTON - 75A	BRIGHTON - 75A	BRIGHTON - 75A
32509	FRATTON - 70F	FRATTON - 70F	FRATTON - 70F	FRATTON - 70F	FRATTON - 70F	FRATTON - 70F	FRATTON - 70F
32510	EASTLEIGH - 71A	EASTLEIGH - 71A	EASTLEIGH - 71A	EASTLEIGH - 71A	EASTLEIGH - 71A	EASTLEIGH - 71A	EASTLEIGH - 71A
32512	BRIGHTON - 75A	BRIGHTON - 75A	BRIGHTON - 75A	BRIGHTON - 75A	BRIGHTON - 75A	BRIGHTON - 75A	BRIGHTON - 75A
32515	BRIGHTON - 75A	BRIGHTON - 75A	BRIGHTON - 75A	BRIGHTON - 75A	BRIGHTON - 75A	BRIGHTON - 75A	BRIGHTON - 75A
32517	T.WELLS - 75F	T.WELLS - 75F	T.WELLS - 75F	T.WELLS - 75F	W/D	W/D	W/D
32519	BRIGHTON - 75A	BRIGHTON - 75A	BRIGHTON - 75A	BRIGHTON - 75A	BRIGHTON - 75A	BRIGHTON - 75A	W/D
32556	EASTLEIGH - 71A	EASTLEIGH - 71A	EASTLEIGH - 71A	EASTLEIGH - 71A	EASTLEIGH - 71A	EASTLEIGH - 71A	EASTLEIGH - 71A
32557	B.ARMS - 73B	B.ARMS - 73B	B.ARMS - 73B	B.ARMS - 73B	B.ARMS - 73B	B.ARMS - 73B	B.ARMS - 73B
32559	EASTLEIGH - 71A	EASTLEIGH - 71A	EASTLEIGH - 71A	EASTLEIGH - 71A	EASTLEIGH - 71A	EASTLEIGH - 71A	EASTLEIGH - 71A
32560	NINE ELMS - 70A	W/D	W/D	W/D	W/D	W/D	W/D
32562	BRIGHTON - 75A	BRIGHTON - 75A	BRIGHTON - 75A	BRIGHTON - 75A	BRIGHTON - 75A	BRIGHTON - 75A	BRIGHTON - 75A
32563	NINE ELMS - 70A	NINE ELMS - 70A	NINE ELMS - 70A	NINE ELMS - 70A	NINE ELMS - 70A	NINE ELMS - 70A	NINE ELMS - 70A
32564	B.ARMS - 73B	B.ARMS - 73B	B.ARMS - 73B	B.ARMS - 73B	B.ARMS - 73B	B.ARMS - 73B	B.ARMS - 73B
32565	B.ARMS - 73B	B.ARMS - 73B	B.ARMS - 73B	B.ARMS - 73B	B.ARMS - 73B	B.ARMS - 73B	B.ARMS - 73B
32566	BRIGHTON - 75A	BRIGHTON - 75A	BRIGHTON - 75A	W/D	W/D	W/D	W/D
32577	BRIGHTON - 75A	BRIGHTON - 75A	BRIGHTON - 75A	BRIGHTON - 75A	BRIGHTON - 75A	BRIGHTON - 75A	W/D
32578	TONBRIDGE - 74D	TONBRIDGE - 73J	TONBRIDGE - 73J	TONBRIDGE - 73J	TONBRIDGE - 73J	TONBRIDGE - 73J	TONBRIDGE - 73J
32579	EASTLEIGH - 71A	EASTLEIGH - 71A	EASTLEIGH - 71A	EASTLEIGH - 71A	EASTLEIGH - 71A	EASTLEIGH - 71A	EASTLEIGH - 71A
32580	TONBRIDGE - 74D	TONBRIDGE - 73J	TONBRIDGE - 73J	TONBRIDGE - 73J	TONBRIDGE - 73J	TONBRIDGE - 73J	BRIGHTON - 75A
32581	T.WELLS - 75F	T.WELLS - 75F	T.WELLS - 75F	T.WELLS - 75F	T.WELLS - 75F	T.WELLS - 75F	T.WELLS - 75F

In common with the Great Northern, the LBSCR was a great believer in the 0-6-2T which provided an intermediate design between the 0-6-0T, generally considered unsuitable on grounds of stability for passenger work, and the 4-4-2T. Not only did the Brighton built large numbers of 0-6-2T's - over one hundred and thirty - but many survived into the 1960's, outliving by a considerable margin the more modern four and six-coupled express tanks that the company introduced during the Edwardian decade.

Their longevity owed much to their mixed traffic status together with an ability to work in minor sidings where the use of larger engines would have called for expensive permanent way modifications whilst in addition they continued throughout the fifties to do useful service on a range of branch passenger services, in particular over the rural lines radiating from Brighton.

There were rather more 0-6-2T's than the Brighton system actually needed after nationalisation and although the elderly E3 class clung on to life, there was little work for the class and in fact none was regularly allocated to the class during the 1950's. The later E4 series continued in everyday use throughout the decade and could be found well away from their home metals, several examples being transferred to the LSWR for shunting at Nine Elms, Eastleigh and Basingstoke. As late as 1956 Brighton and Newhaven sheds combined were allocating no less than seven of the class to daily duties whilst they were particularly active on the Horsham route.

The E1R class although having an LBSCR pedigree were actually post-grouping engines, built by the Southern Railway for work in the West Country. Most of the class were employed on banking duties between St David's and Central stations, Exeter, and from Ilfracombe to Mortehoe. Ironically they were replaced on the latter duties by LSWR 0-4-4T's made redundant from the Barnstaple - Torrington branch by LMS Ivatt 2-6-2T's.

loco	Dec-59	Feb-60	Mar-60	Apr-60	Jul-60	Aug-60	Sep-60	Nov-60
				E4 0-6-2T (1897)				
32468	BRIGHTON - 75A	BRIGHTON - 75A	BRIGHTON - 75A	BRIGHTON - 75A	BRIGHTON - 75A	BRIGHTON - 75A	BRIGHTON - 75A	BRIGHTON - 75A
32469	THREE BRIDGES - 75E	THREE BRIDGES - 75E	THREE BRIDGES - 75E	THREE BRIDGES - 75E	THREE BRIDGES - 75E	THREE BRIDGES - 75E	THREE BRIDGES - 75E	THREE BRIDGES - 75E
32470	THREE BRIDGES - 75E	THREE BRIDGES - 75E	THREE BRIDGES - 75E	THREE BRIDGES - 75E	THREE BRIDGES - 75E	THREE BRIDGES - 75E	THREE BRIDGES - 75E	THREE BRIDGES - 75E
32472	B.ARMS - 73B	B.ARMS - 73B	B.ARMS - 73B	B.ARMS - 73B	NINE ELMS - 70A	NINE ELMS - 70A	NINE ELMS - 70A	NINE ELMS - 70A
32473	B.ARMS - 73B	B.ARMS - 73B	B.ARMS - 73B	B.ARMS - 73B	NINE ELMS - 70A	NINE ELMS - 70A	NINE ELMS - 70A	NINE ELMS - 70A
32474	B.ARMS - 73B	B.ARMS - 73B	B.ARMS - 73B	B.ARMS - 73B	B.ARMS - 73B	B.ARMS - 73B	B.ARMS - 73B	B.ARMS - 73B
32475	BRIGHTON - 75A	BRIGHTON - 75A	BRIGHTON - 75A	BRIGHTON - 75A	BRIGHTON - 75A	BRIGHTON - 75A	BRIGHTON - 75A	BRIGHTON - 75A
32479	NORWOOD JCN - 75C	NORWOOD JCN - 75C	BRIGHTON - 75A	BRIGHTON - 75A	BRIGHTON - 75A	BRIGHTON - 75A	BRIGHTON - 75A	BRIGHTON - 75A
32484	BRIGHTON - 75A	BRIGHTON - 75A	BRIGHTON - 75A	BRIGHTON - 75A	BRIGHTON - 75A	BRIGHTON - 75A	W/D	W/D
32487	NINE ELMS - 70A	NINE ELMS - 70A	NINE ELMS - 70A	NINE ELMS - 70A	NINE ELMS - 70A	NINE ELMS - 70A	NINE ELMS - 70A	NINE ELMS - 70A
32491	EASTLEIGH - 71A	EASTLEIGH - 71A	EASTLEIGH - 71A	EASTLEIGH - 71A	EASTLEIGH - 71A	EASTLEIGH - 71A	EASTLEIGH - 71A	EASTLEIGH - 71A
32495	NORWOOD JCN - 75C	NORWOOD JCN - 75C	BRIGHTON - 75A	BRIGHTON - 75A	BRIGHTON - 75A	BRIGHTON - 75A	W/D	W/D
32498	NINE ELMS - 70A	NINE ELMS - 70A	NINE ELMS - 70A	NINE ELMS - 70A	NINE ELMS - 70A	NINE ELMS - 70A	NINE ELMS - 70A	NINE ELMS - 70A
32500	NINE ELMS - 70A	NINE ELMS - 70A	NINE ELMS - 70A	NINE ELMS - 70A	NINE ELMS - 70A	NINE ELMS - 70A	NINE ELMS - 70A	NINE ELMS - 70A
32503	BRIGHTON - 75A	BRIGHTON - 75A	BRIGHTON - 75A	BRIGHTON - 75A	BRIGHTON - 75A	BRIGHTON - 75A	BRIGHTON - 75A	BRIGHTON - 75A
32504	BRIGHTON - 75A	BRIGHTON - 75A	BRIGHTON - 75A	BRIGHTON - 75A	BRIGHTON - 75A	BRIGHTON - 75A	BRIGHTON - 75A	BRIGHTON - 75A
32505	GUILDFORD - 70C	GUILDFORD - 70C	GUILDFORD - 70C	NINE ELMS - 70A	NINE ELMS - 70A	NINE ELMS - 70A	NINE ELMS - 70A	NINE ELMS - 70A
32506	GUILDFORD - 70C	GUILDFORD - 70C	GUILDFORD - 70C	NINE ELMS - 70A	NINE ELMS - 70A	NINE ELMS - 70A	NINE ELMS - 70A	NINE ELMS - 70A
32508	BRIGHTON - 75A	W/D	W/D	W/D	W/D	W/D	W/D	W/D
32509	NORWOOD JCN - 75C	NORWOOD JCN - 75C	T.WELLS - 75F	T.WELLS - 75F	T.WELLS - 75F	T.WELLS - 75F	T.WELLS - 75F	T.WELLS - 75F
32510	EASTLEIGH - 71A	EASTLEIGH - 71A	EASTLEIGH - 71A	EASTLEIGH - 71A	EASTLEIGH - 71A	EASTLEIGH - 71A	EASTLEIGH - 71A	EASTLEIGH - 71A
32512	BRIGHTON - 75A	BRIGHTON - 75A	BRIGHTON - 75A	BRIGHTON - 75A	BRIGHTON - 75A	BRIGHTON - 75A	BRIGHTON - 75A	BRIGHTON - 75A
32515	BRIGHTON - 75A	BRIGHTON - 75A	BRIGHTON - 75A	BRIGHTON - 75A	BRIGHTON - 75A	BRIGHTON - 75A	BRIGHTON - 75A	BRIGHTON - 75A
32556	EASTLEIGH - 71A	EASTLEIGH - 71A	EASTLEIGH - 71A	EASTLEIGH - 71A	EASTLEIGH - 71A	EASTLEIGH - 71A	EASTLEIGH - 71A	EASTLEIGH - 71A
32557	B.ARMS - 73B	B.ARMS - 73B	B.ARMS - 73B	B.ARMS - 73B	B.ARMS - 73B	B.ARMS - 73B	B.ARMS - 73B	B.ARMS - 73B
32559	EASTLEIGH - 71A	EASTLEIGH - 71A	EASTLEIGH - 71A	EASTLEIGH - 71A	W/D	W/D	W/D	W/D
32562	BRIGHTON - 75A	BRIGHTON - 75A	BRIGHTON - 75A	BRIGHTON - 75A	BRIGHTON - 75A	W/D	W/D	W/D
32563	NINE ELMS - 70A	NINE ELMS - 70A	NINE ELMS - 70A	NINE ELMS - 70A	NINE ELMS - 70A	NINE ELMS - 70A	NINE ELMS - 70A	NINE ELMS - 70A
32564	B.ARMS - 73B	THREE BRIDGES - 75E	THREE BRIDGES - 75E	THREE BRIDGES - 75E	THREE BRIDGES - 75E	THREE BRIDGES - 75E	THREE BRIDGES - 75E	THREE BRIDGES - 75E
32565	B.ARMS - 73B	B.ARMS - 73B	B.ARMS - 73B	B.ARMS - 73B	B.ARMS - 73B	B.ARMS - 73B	B.ARMS - 73B	B.ARMS - 73B
32578	TONBRIDGE - 73J	TONBRIDGE - 73J	TONBRIDGE - 73J	TONBRIDGE - 73J	TONBRIDGE - 73J	BRIGHTON - 75A	BRIGHTON - 75A	BRIGHTON - 75A
32580	BRIGHTON - 75A	BRIGHTON - 75A	BRIGHTON - 75A	BRIGHTON - 75A	BRIGHTON - 75A	BRIGHTON - 75A	BRIGHTON - 75A	BRIGHTON - 75A
32581	T.WELLS - 75F	T.WELLS - 75F	T.WELLS - 75F	T.WELLS - 75F	T.WELLS - 75F	T.WELLS - 75F	T.WELLS - 75F	T.WELLS - 75F

The West of England seemed unlikely territory for engines of Brighton ancestry to be found but the banking duties at Exeter and Ilfracombe called for engines with particular qualities and after considering the '757' 0-6-2T's, the Southern produced an enlarged version of the LBSCR E1 0-6-0T in 1927 and used them for the next thirty years in banking trains between Exeter St David's and Central and from Ilfracombe to Braunton. The Exmouth Junction E1/R's were made redundant in the 1950's by the Z class 0-8-0T's whilst those at Barnstaple were ousted by M7 0-4-4T's which in turn had been replaced by LMS 2-6-2T's on the Torrington branch. An unkempt 32096 stands unattended at Barnstaple in 1949.

loco	May-49	Jun-49	Aug-49	Sep-49	Dec-49	Feb-50	Mar-50
				E4X 0-6-2T (1909)			
32466	NORWOOD JCN - 75C	NORWOOD JCN - 75C	NORWOOD JCN - 75C	NORWOOD JCN - 75C	NORWOOD JCN - 75C	NORWOOD JCN - 75C	NORWOOD JCN - 75C
32477	NORWOOD JCN - 75C	NORWOOD JCN - 75C	NORWOOD JCN - 75C	NORWOOD JCN - 75C	NORWOOD JCN - 75C	NORWOOD JCN - 75C	NORWOOD JCN - 75C
32478	NORWOOD JCN - 75C	NORWOOD JCN - 75C	NORWOOD JCN - 75C	NORWOOD JCN - 75C	NORWOOD JCN - 75C	NORWOOD JCN - 75C	NORWOOD JCN - 75C
32489	NORWOOD JCN - 75C	NORWOOD JCN - 75C	NORWOOD JCN - 75C	NORWOOD JCN - 75C	NORWOOD JCN - 75C	NORWOOD JCN - 75C	NORWOOD JCN - 75C
				E5 0-6-2T (1902)			
32399	HORSHAM - 75D	HORSHAM - 75D	HORSHAM - 75D	HORSHAM - 75D	HORSHAM - 75D	HORSHAM - 75D	HORSHAM - 75D
32400	BRIGHTON - 75A	BRIGHTON - 75A	BRIGHTON - 75A	BRIGHTON - 75A	BRIGHTON - 75A	BRIGHTON - 75A	BRIGHTON - 75A
32402	EASTBOURNE - 75G	EASTBOURNE - 75G	EASTBOURNE - 75G	EASTBOURNE - 75G	EASTBOURNE - 75G	EASTBOURNE - 75G	EASTBOURNE - 75G
32404	EASTLEIGH - 71A	EASTLEIGH - 71A	EASTLEIGH - 71A	EASTLEIGH - 71A	EASTLEIGH - 71A	EASTLEIGH - 71A	EASTBOURNE - 75G
32405	THREE BRIDGES - 75E	THREE BRIDGES - 75E	THREE BRIDGES - 75E	THREE BRIDGES - 75E	THREE BRIDGES - 75E	THREE BRIDGES - 75E	THREE BRIDGES - 75E
32406	EASTBOURNE - 75G	EASTBOURNE - 75G	EASTBOURNE - 75G	EASTBOURNE - 75G	EASTBOURNE - 75G	EASTBOURNE - 75G	EASTBOURNE - 75G
32567	BRIGHTON - 75A	BRIGHTON - 75A	BRIGHTON - 75A	BRIGHTON - 75A	W/D	W/D	W/D
32568	B.ARMS - 73B	B.ARMS - 73B	B.ARMS - 73B	B.ARMS - 73B	B.ARMS - 73B	B.ARMS - 73B	B.ARMS - 73B
32571	THREE BRIDGES - 75E	THREE BRIDGES - 75E	THREE BRIDGES - 75E	THREE BRIDGES - 75E	THREE BRIDGES - 75E	THREE BRIDGES - 75E	THREE BRIDGES - 75E
32573	HORSHAM - 75D	THREE BRIDGES - 75E	THREE BRIDGES - 75E	THREE BRIDGES - 75E	THREE BRIDGES - 75E	THREE BRIDGES - 75E	THREE BRIDGES - 75E
32574	EASTBOURNE - 75G	EASTBOURNE - 75G	EASTBOURNE - 75G	EASTBOURNE - 75G	EASTBOURNE - 75G	EASTBOURNE - 75G	EASTBOURNE - 75G
32575	EASTBOURNE - 75G	EASTBOURNE - 75G	EASTBOURNE - 75G	EASTBOURNE - 75G	EASTBOURNE - 75G	EASTBOURNE - 75G	EASTBOURNE - 75G
32583	BRIGHTON - 75A	BRIGHTON - 75A	BRIGHTON - 75A	BRIGHTON - 75A	BRIGHTON - 75A	BRIGHTON - 75A	BRIGHTON - 75A
32584	HORSHAM - 75D	HORSHAM - 75D	HORSHAM - 75D	HORSHAM - 75D	HORSHAM - 75D	HORSHAM - 75D	HORSHAM - 75D
32585	THREE BRIDGES - 75E	THREE BRIDGES - 75E	THREE BRIDGES - 75E	THREE BRIDGES - 75E	THREE BRIDGES - 75E	THREE BRIDGES - 75E	THREE BRIDGES - 75E
32587	BRIGHTON - 75A	BRIGHTON - 75A	BRIGHTON - 75A	BRIGHTON - 75A	BRIGHTON - 75A	BRIGHTON - 75A	BRIGHTON - 75A
32588	EASTBOURNE - 75G	EASTBOURNE - 75G	EASTBOURNE - 75G	EASTBOURNE - 75G	EASTBOURNE - 75G	EASTBOURNE - 75G	EASTBOURNE - 75G
32590	REDHILL - 75B	REDHILL - 75B	REDHILL - 75B	REDHILL - 75B	REDHILL - 75B	REDHILL - 75B	REDHILL - 75B
32591	BRIGHTON - 75A	BRIGHTON - 75A	BRIGHTON - 75A	BRIGHTON - 75A	BRIGHTON - 75A	BRIGHTON - 75A	BRIGHTON - 75A
32592	REDHILL - 75B	REDHILL - 75B	REDHILL - 75B	REDHILL - 75B	REDHILL - 75B	REDHILL - 75B	REDHILL - 75B
32593	EASTBOURNE - 75G	EASTBOURNE - 75G	EASTBOURNE - 75G	EASTBOURNE - 75G	EASTBOURNE - 75G	EASTBOURNE - 75G	EASTBOURNE - 75G
32594	BRIGHTON - 75A	BRIGHTON - 75A	BRIGHTON - 75A	BRIGHTON - 75A	BRIGHTON - 75A	BRIGHTON - 75A	BRIGHTON - 75A
				E5X 0-6-2T (1911)			
32401	HORSHAM - 75D	HORSHAM - 75D	HORSHAM - 75D	HORSHAM - 75D	HORSHAM - 75D	HORSHAM - 75D	HORSHAM - 75D
32570	HORSHAM - 75D	HORSHAM - 75D	HORSHAM - 75D	HORSHAM - 75D	HORSHAM - 75D	HORSHAM - 75D	HORSHAM - 75D
32576	BRIGHTON - 75A	BRIGHTON - 75A	BRIGHTON - 75A	BRIGHTON - 75A	BRIGHTON - 75A	BRIGHTON - 75A	BRIGHTON - 75A
32586	REDHILL - 75B	REDHILL - 75B	REDHILL - 75B	REDHILL - 75B	REDHILL - 75B	REDHILL - 75B	REDHILL - 75B
				E6 0-6-2T (1904)			
32408	B.ARMS - 73B	B.ARMS - 73B	B.ARMS - 73B	B.ARMS - 73B	B.ARMS - 73B	B.ARMS - 73B	B.ARMS - 73B
32409	NORWOOD JCN - 75C	NORWOOD JCN - 75C	NORWOOD JCN - 75C	NORWOOD JCN - 75C	NORWOOD JCN - 75C	NORWOOD JCN - 75C	NORWOOD JCN - 75C
32410	B.ARMS - 73B	B.ARMS - 73B	B.ARMS - 73B	B.ARMS - 73B	B.ARMS - 73B	B.ARMS - 73B	B.ARMS - 73B
32412	B.ARMS - 73B	B.ARMS - 73B	B.ARMS - 73B	B.ARMS - 73B	B.ARMS - 73B	B.ARMS - 73B	B.ARMS - 73B
32413	B.ARMS - 73B	B.ARMS - 73B	B.ARMS - 73B	B.ARMS - 73B	B.ARMS - 73B	B.ARMS - 73B	B.ARMS - 73B
32414	NORWOOD JCN - 75C	NORWOOD JCN - 75C	NORWOOD JCN - 75C	NORWOOD JCN - 75C	NORWOOD JCN - 75C	NORWOOD JCN - 75C	NORWOOD JCN - 75C
32415	B.ARMS - 73B	B.ARMS - 73B	B.ARMS - 73B	B.ARMS - 73B	B.ARMS - 73B	B.ARMS - 73B	B.ARMS - 73B
32416	NORWOOD JCN - 75C	NORWOOD JCN - 75C	NORWOOD JCN - 75C	NORWOOD JCN - 75C	NORWOOD JCN - 75C	NORWOOD JCN - 75C	NORWOOD JCN - 75C
32417	NORWOOD JCN - 75C	NORWOOD JCN - 75C	NORWOOD JCN - 75C	NORWOOD JCN - 75C	NORWOOD JCN - 75C	NORWOOD JCN - 75C	NORWOOD JCN - 75C
32418	NORWOOD JCN - 75C	NORWOOD JCN - 75C	NORWOOD JCN - 75C	NORWOOD JCN - 75C	NORWOOD JCN - 75C	NORWOOD JCN - 75C	NORWOOD JCN - 75C
				E6X 0-6-2T (1911)			
32407	NORWOOD JCN - 75C	NORWOOD JCN - 75C	NORWOOD JCN - 75C	NORWOOD JCN - 75C	NORWOOD JCN - 75C	NORWOOD JCN - 75C	NORWOOD JCN - 75C
32411	NORWOOD JCN - 75C	NORWOOD JCN - 75C	NORWOOD JCN - 75C	NORWOOD JCN - 75C	NORWOOD JCN - 75C	NORWOOD JCN - 75C	NORWOOD JCN - 75C
				KES 0-8-0T (1905)			
30949	NINE ELMS - 70A	NINE ELMS - 70A	NINE ELMS - 70A	NINE ELMS - 70A	NINE ELMS - 70A	NINE ELMS - 70A	NINE ELMS - 70A
				G16 4-8-0T (1921)			
30492	FELTHAM - 70B	FELTHAM - 70B	FELTHAM - 70B	FELTHAM - 70B	FELTHAM - 70B	FELTHAM - 70B	FELTHAM - 70B
30493	FELTHAM - 70B	FELTHAM - 70B	FELTHAM - 70B	FELTHAM - 70B	FELTHAM - 70B	FELTHAM - 70B	FELTHAM - 70B
30494	FELTHAM - 70B	FELTHAM - 70B	FELTHAM - 70B	FELTHAM - 70B	FELTHAM - 70B	FELTHAM - 70B	FELTHAM - 70B
30495	FELTHAM - 70B	FELTHAM - 70B	FELTHAM - 70B	FELTHAM - 70B	FELTHAM - 70B	FELTHAM - 70B	FELTHAM - 70B
				K 2-6-0 (1913)			
32337	BRIGHTON - 75A(N)	BRIGHTON - 75A(N)	BRIGHTON - 75A(N)	BRIGHTON - 75A(N)	BRIGHTON - 75A(N)	BRIGHTON - 75A(N)	BRIGHTON - 75A(N)
32338	FRATTON - 71D	FRATTON - 71D	FRATTON - 71D	FRATTON - 71D	FRATTON - 71D	FRATTON - 71D	FRATTON - 71D
32339	BRIGHTON - 75A	BRIGHTON - 75A	BRIGHTON - 75A	BRIGHTON - 75A	BRIGHTON - 75A	BRIGHTON - 75A	BRIGHTON - 75A
32340	FRATTON - 71D	FRATTON - 71D	FRATTON - 71D	FRATTON - 71D	FRATTON - 71D	FRATTON - 71D	FRATTON - 71D
32341	BRIGHTON - 75A	BRIGHTON - 75A	BRIGHTON - 75A	BRIGHTON - 75A	BRIGHTON - 75A	BRIGHTON - 75A	BRIGHTON - 75A
32342	BRIGHTON - 75A	BRIGHTON - 75A	BRIGHTON - 75A	BRIGHTON - 75A	BRIGHTON - 75A	BRIGHTON - 75A	BRIGHTON - 75A
32343	BRIGHTON - 75A	BRIGHTON - 75A	BRIGHTON - 75A	BRIGHTON - 75A	BRIGHTON - 75A	BRIGHTON - 75A	BRIGHTON - 75A
32344	BRIGHTON - 75A	BRIGHTON - 75A	BRIGHTON - 75A	BRIGHTON - 75A	BRIGHTON - 75A	BRIGHTON - 75A	BRIGHTON - 75A
32345	BRIGHTON - 75A	BRIGHTON - 75A	BRIGHTON - 75A	BRIGHTON - 75A	BRIGHTON - 75A	BRIGHTON - 75A	BRIGHTON - 75A
32346	THREE BRIDGES - 75E	THREE BRIDGES - 75E	THREE BRIDGES - 75E	THREE BRIDGES - 75E	THREE BRIDGES - 75E	THREE BRIDGES - 75E	THREE BRIDGES - 75E
32347	THREE BRIDGES - 75E	THREE BRIDGES - 75E	THREE BRIDGES - 75E	THREE BRIDGES - 75E	THREE BRIDGES - 75E	THREE BRIDGES - 75E	THREE BRIDGES - 75E
32348	EASTBOURNE - 75G	EASTBOURNE - 75G	EASTBOURNE - 75G	EASTBOURNE - 75G	EASTBOURNE - 75G	EASTBOURNE - 75G	EASTBOURNE - 75G
32349	EASTBOURNE - 75G	EASTBOURNE - 75G	EASTBOURNE - 75G	EASTBOURNE - 75G	EASTBOURNE - 75G	EASTBOURNE - 75G	EASTBOURNE - 75G
32350	THREE BRIDGES - 75E	THREE BRIDGES - 75E	THREE BRIDGES - 75E	THREE BRIDGES - 75E	THREE BRIDGES - 75E	THREE BRIDGES - 75E	THREE BRIDGES - 75E
32351	THREE BRIDGES - 75E	THREE BRIDGES - 75E	THREE BRIDGES - 75E	THREE BRIDGES - 75E	THREE BRIDGES - 75E	THREE BRIDGES - 75E	THREE BRIDGES - 75E
32352	THREE BRIDGES - 75E	THREE BRIDGES - 75E	THREE BRIDGES - 75E	THREE BRIDGES - 75E	THREE BRIDGES - 75E	THREE BRIDGES - 75E	THREE BRIDGES - 75E
32353	THREE BRIDGES - 75E	THREE BRIDGES - 75E	THREE BRIDGES - 75E	THREE BRIDGES - 75E	THREE BRIDGES - 75E	THREE BRIDGES - 75E	THREE BRIDGES - 75E
				U 2-6-0 (R/B 2-6-4T) 1928			
31790	YEOVIL - 72C	YEOVIL - 72C	YEOVIL - 72C	YEOVIL - 72C	YEOVIL - 72C	YEOVIL - 72C	YEOVIL - 72C
31791	YEOVIL - 72C	YEOVIL - 72C	YEOVIL - 72C	YEOVIL - 72C	YEOVIL - 72C	YEOVIL - 72C	YEOVIL - 72C
31792	YEOVIL - 72C	YEOVIL - 72C	YEOVIL - 72C	YEOVIL - 72C	YEOVIL - 72C	YEOVIL - 72C	YEOVIL - 72C
31793	YEOVIL - 72C	YEOVIL - 72C	YEOVIL - 72C	YEOVIL - 72C	YEOVIL - 72C	YEOVIL - 72C	YEOVIL - 72C
31794	YEOVIL - 72C	YEOVIL - 72C	YEOVIL - 72C	YEOVIL - 72C	YEOVIL - 72C	YEOVIL - 72C	YEOVIL - 72C
31795	YEOVIL - 72C	YEOVIL - 72C	YEOVIL - 72C	YEOVIL - 72C	YEOVIL - 72C	YEOVIL - 72C	YEOVIL - 72C
31796	BOURNEMOUTH - 71B	BOURNEMOUTH - 71B	BOURNEMOUTH - 71B	BOURNEMOUTH - 71B	BOURNEMOUTH - 71B	BOURNEMOUTH - 71B	BOURNEMOUTH - 71B
31797	READING (SR) - 70E	READING (SR) - 70E	READING (SR) - 70E	READING (SR) - 70E	READING (SR) - 70E	READING (SR) - 70E	READING (SR) - 70E
31798	GUILDFORD - 70C	GUILDFORD - 70C	GUILDFORD - 70C	GUILDFORD - 70C	GUILDFORD - 70C	GUILDFORD - 70C	GUILDFORD - 70C
31799	GUILDFORD - 70C	GUILDFORD - 70C	GUILDFORD - 70C	GUILDFORD - 70C	GUILDFORD - 70C	GUILDFORD - 70C	GUILDFORD - 70C
31800	GUILDFORD - 70C	GUILDFORD - 70C	GUILDFORD - 70C	GUILDFORD - 70C	GUILDFORD - 70C	GUILDFORD - 70C	GUILDFORD - 70C
31801	GUILDFORD - 70C	GUILDFORD - 70C	GUILDFORD - 70C	GUILDFORD - 70C	GUILDFORD - 70C	GUILDFORD - 70C	GUILDFORD - 70C
31802	GUILDFORD - 70C	GUILDFORD - 70C	GUILDFORD - 70C	GUILDFORD - 70C	GUILDFORD - 70C	GUILDFORD - 70C	GUILDFORD - 70C
31803	GUILDFORD - 70C	GUILDFORD - 70C	GUILDFORD - 70C	GUILDFORD - 70C	GUILDFORD - 70C	GUILDFORD - 70C	GUILDFORD - 70C
31804	GUILDFORD - 70C	GUILDFORD - 70C	GUILDFORD - 70C	GUILDFORD - 70C	GUILDFORD - 70C	GUILDFORD - 70C	GUILDFORD - 70C
31805	GUILDFORD - 70C	GUILDFORD - 70C	GUILDFORD - 70C	GUILDFORD - 70C	GUILDFORD - 70C	FRATTON - 71D	FRATTON - 71D
31806	GUILDFORD - 70C	GUILDFORD - 70C	STEWARTS LANE - 73A	NINE ELMS - 70A	FAVERSHAM - 73E	FAVERSHAM - 73E	FAVERSHAM - 73E
31807	FRATTON - 71D	FRATTON - 71D	STEWARTS LANE - 73A	NINE ELMS - 70A	NINE ELMS - 70A	NINE ELMS - 70A	NINE ELMS - 70A
31808	FAVERSHAM - 73E	FAVERSHAM - 73E	FAVERSHAM - 73E	FAVERSHAM - 73E	FAVERSHAM - 73E	FAVERSHAM - 73E	FAVERSHAM - 73E
31809	FRATTON - 71D	FRATTON - 71D	FRATTON - 71D	FRATTON - 71D	FRATTON - 71D	FRATTON - 71D	FRATTON - 71D

loco	Apr-50	Sep-50	Oct-50	Nov-50	Dec-50	Mar-51	Apr-51
E4X 0-6-2T (1909)							
32466	NORWOOD JCN - 75C	NORWOOD JCN - 75C	NORWOOD JCN - 75C	NORWOOD JCN - 75C	NORWOOD JCN - 75C	NORWOOD JCN - 75C	NORWOOD JCN - 75C
32477	NORWOOD JCN - 75C	NORWOOD JCN - 75C	NORWOOD JCN - 75C	NORWOOD JCN - 75C	NORWOOD JCN - 75C	NORWOOD JCN - 75C	NORWOOD JCN - 75C
32478	NORWOOD JCN - 75C	NORWOOD JCN - 75C	NORWOOD JCN - 75C	NORWOOD JCN - 75C	NORWOOD JCN - 75C	NORWOOD JCN - 75C	NORWOOD JCN - 75C
32489	NORWOOD JCN - 75C	NORWOOD JCN - 75C	NORWOOD JCN - 75C	NORWOOD JCN - 75C	NORWOOD JCN - 75C	NORWOOD JCN - 75C	NORWOOD JCN - 75C
E5 0-6-2T (1902)							
32399	HORSHAM - 75D	HORSHAM - 75D	HORSHAM - 75D	HORSHAM - 75D	HORSHAM - 75D	HORSHAM - 75D	HORSHAM - 75D
32400	BRIGHTON - 75A	BRIGHTON - 75A	BRIGHTON - 75A	BRIGHTON - 75A	BRIGHTON - 75A	BRIGHTON - 75A	BRIGHTON - 75A
32402	EASTBOURNE - 75G	EASTBOURNE - 75G	BRIGHTON - 75A	EASTBOURNE - 75G	EASTBOURNE - 75G	W/D	W/D
32404	EASTBOURNE - 75G	EASTBOURNE - 75G	EASTBOURNE - 75G	EASTBOURNE - 75G	EASTBOURNE - 75G	EASTBOURNE - 75G	EASTBOURNE - 75G
32405	EASTBOURNE - 75G	EASTBOURNE - 75G	EASTBOURNE - 75G	EASTBOURNE - 75G	EASTBOURNE - 75G	EASTBOURNE - 75G	EASTBOURNE - 75G
32406	EASTBOURNE - 75G	EASTBOURNE - 75G	EASTBOURNE - 75G	EASTBOURNE - 75G	EASTBOURNE - 75G	EASTBOURNE - 75G	EASTBOURNE - 75G
32568	B.ARMS - 73B	HORSHAM - 75D	HORSHAM - 75D	HORSHAM - 75D	HORSHAM - 75D	HORSHAM - 75D	HORSHAM - 75D
32571	THREE BRIDGES - 75E	THREE BRIDGES - 75E	THREE BRIDGES - 75E	THREE BRIDGES - 75E	THREE BRIDGES - 75E	THREE BRIDGES - 75E	THREE BRIDGES - 75E
32573	BRIGHTON - 75A	BRIGHTON - 75A	BRIGHTON - 75A	BRIGHTON - 75A	BRIGHTON - 75A	BRIGHTON - 75A	BRIGHTON - 75A
32574	EASTBOURNE - 75G	EASTBOURNE - 75G	EASTBOURNE - 75G	EASTBOURNE - 75G	EASTBOURNE - 75G	EASTBOURNE - 75G	EASTBOURNE - 75G
32575	BRIGHTON - 75A	BRIGHTON - 75A	BRIGHTON - 75A	BRIGHTON - 75A	BRIGHTON - 75A	BRIGHTON - 75A	BRIGHTON - 75A
32583	BRIGHTON - 75A	BRIGHTON - 75A	BRIGHTON - 75A	BRIGHTON - 75A	BRIGHTON - 75A	BRIGHTON - 75A	BRIGHTON - 75A
32584	HORSHAM - 75D	THREE BRIDGES - 75E	THREE BRIDGES - 75E	THREE BRIDGES - 75E	W/D	W/D	W/D
32585	THREE BRIDGES - 75E	B.ARMS - 73B(NX)	B.ARMS - 73B(NX)	B.ARMS - 73B(NX)	B.ARMS - 73B(NX)	B.ARMS - 73B(NX)	B.ARMS - 73B(NX)
32587	BRIGHTON - 75A	B.ARMS - 73B(NX)	B.ARMS - 73B(NX)	B.ARMS - 73B(NX)	B.ARMS - 73B(NX)	B.ARMS - 73B(NX)	B.ARMS - 73B(NX)
32588	EASTBOURNE - 75G	EASTBOURNE - 75G	EASTBOURNE - 75G	EASTBOURNE - 75G	EASTBOURNE - 75G	EASTBOURNE - 75G	EASTBOURNE - 75G
32590	B.ARMS - 73B	B.ARMS - 73B	B.ARMS - 73B	B.ARMS - 73B	B.ARMS - 73B	B.ARMS - 73B	BASINGSTOKE - 70D
32591	EASTBOURNE - 75G	EASTBOURNE - 75G	EASTBOURNE - 75G	EASTBOURNE - 75G	EASTBOURNE - 75G	EASTBOURNE - 75G	EASTBOURNE - 75G
32592	REDHILL - 75B	REDHILL - 75B	REDHILL - 75B	REDHILL - 75B	REDHILL - 75B	REDHILL - 75B	REDHILL - 75B
32593	EASTBOURNE - 75G	EASTBOURNE - 75G	EASTBOURNE - 75G	EASTBOURNE - 75G	EASTBOURNE - 75G	EASTBOURNE - 75G	EASTBOURNE - 75G
32594	BRIGHTON - 75A	BRIGHTON - 75A	BRIGHTON - 75A	BRIGHTON - 75A	BRIGHTON - 75A	W/D	W/D
E5X 0-6-2T (1911)							
32401	HORSHAM - 75D	HORSHAM - 75D	HORSHAM - 75D	HORSHAM - 75D	HORSHAM - 75D	HORSHAM - 75D	HORSHAM - 75D
32570	HORSHAM - 75D	HORSHAM - 75D	HORSHAM - 75D	HORSHAM - 75D	HORSHAM - 75D	HORSHAM - 75D	HORSHAM - 75D
32576	BRIGHTON - 75A	BRIGHTON - 75A	BRIGHTON - 75A	BRIGHTON - 75A	BRIGHTON - 75A	BRIGHTON - 75A	HORSHAM - 75D
32586	EASTBOURNE - 75G	HORSHAM - 75D	HORSHAM - 75D	HORSHAM - 75D	HORSHAM - 75D	HORSHAM - 75D	HORSHAM - 75D
E6 0-6-2T (1904)							
32408	B.ARMS - 73B	B.ARMS - 73B	B.ARMS - 73B	B.ARMS - 73B	B.ARMS - 73B	B.ARMS - 73B	B.ARMS - 73B
32409	NORWOOD JCN - 75C	NORWOOD JCN - 75C	EASTLEIGH - 71A	EASTLEIGH - 71A	EASTLEIGH - 71A	EASTLEIGH - 71A	EASTLEIGH - 71A
32410	B.ARMS - 73B	B.ARMS - 73B	B.ARMS - 73B	B.ARMS - 73B	B.ARMS - 73B	B.ARMS - 73B	B.ARMS - 73B
32412	B.ARMS - 73B	B.ARMS - 73B	EASTLEIGH - 71A	EASTLEIGH - 71A	EASTLEIGH - 71A	EASTLEIGH - 71A	EASTLEIGH - 71A
32413	B.ARMS - 73B	B.ARMS - 73B	B.ARMS - 73B	B.ARMS - 73B	B.ARMS - 73B	B.ARMS - 73B	B.ARMS - 73B
32414	NORWOOD JCN - 75C	NORWOOD JCN - 75C	NORWOOD JCN - 75C	NORWOOD JCN - 75C	NORWOOD JCN - 75C	NORWOOD JCN - 75C	NORWOOD JCN - 75C
32415	B.ARMS - 73B	B.ARMS - 73B	B.ARMS - 73B	B.ARMS - 73B	B.ARMS - 73B	B.ARMS - 73B	B.ARMS - 73B
32416	NORWOOD JCN - 75C	NORWOOD JCN - 75C	EASTLEIGH - 71A	EASTLEIGH - 71A	EASTLEIGH - 71A	EASTLEIGH - 71A	EASTLEIGH - 71A
32417	NORWOOD JCN - 75C	NORWOOD JCN - 75C	NORWOOD JCN - 75C	NORWOOD JCN - 75C	NORWOOD JCN - 75C	NORWOOD JCN - 75C	NORWOOD JCN - 75C
32418	NORWOOD JCN - 75C	NORWOOD JCN - 75C	NORWOOD JCN - 75C	NORWOOD JCN - 75C	NORWOOD JCN - 75C	NORWOOD JCN - 75C	NORWOOD JCN - 75C
E6X 0-6-2T (1911)							
32407	NORWOOD JCN - 75C	NORWOOD JCN - 75C	NORWOOD JCN - 75C	NORWOOD JCN - 75C	NORWOOD JCN - 75C	NORWOOD JCN - 75C	NORWOOD JCN - 75C
32411	NORWOOD JCN - 75C	NORWOOD JCN - 75C	NORWOOD JCN - 75C	NORWOOD JCN - 75C	NORWOOD JCN - 75C	NORWOOD JCN - 75C	NORWOOD JCN - 75C
G16 4-8-0T (1921)							
30492	FELTHAM - 70B	FELTHAM - 70B	FELTHAM - 70B	FELTHAM - 70B	FELTHAM - 70B	FELTHAM - 70B	FELTHAM - 70B
30493	FELTHAM - 70B	FELTHAM - 70B	FELTHAM - 70B	FELTHAM - 70B	FELTHAM - 70B	FELTHAM - 70B	FELTHAM - 70B
30494	FELTHAM - 70B	FELTHAM - 70B	FELTHAM - 70B	FELTHAM - 70B	FELTHAM - 70B	FELTHAM - 70B	FELTHAM - 70B
30495	FELTHAM - 70B	FELTHAM - 70B	FELTHAM - 70B	FELTHAM - 70B	FELTHAM - 70B	FELTHAM - 70B	FELTHAM - 70B
K 2-6-0 (1913)							
32337	BRIGHTON - 75A(N)	BRIGHTON - 75A(N)	EASTBOURNE - 75G	BRIGHTON - 75A	BRIGHTON - 75A	BRIGHTON - 75A	BRIGHTON - 75A
32338	FRATTON - 71D	FRATTON - 71D	FRATTON - 71D	FRATTON - 71D	BRIGHTON - 75A	BRIGHTON - 75A	BRIGHTON - 75A
32339	BRIGHTON - 75A	BRIGHTON - 75A	BRIGHTON - 75A	BRIGHTON - 75A	BRIGHTON - 75A	BRIGHTON - 75A	BRIGHTON - 75A
32340	FRATTON - 71D	FRATTON - 71D	FRATTON - 71D	FRATTON - 71D	BRIGHTON - 75A	BRIGHTON - 75A	BRIGHTON - 75A
32341	BRIGHTON - 75A	BRIGHTON - 75A	BRIGHTON - 75A	BRIGHTON - 75A	BRIGHTON - 75A	BRIGHTON - 75A	BRIGHTON - 75A
32342	BRIGHTON - 75A	BRIGHTON - 75A	BRIGHTON - 75A	BRIGHTON - 75A	BRIGHTON - 75A	BRIGHTON - 75A	BRIGHTON - 75A
32343	BRIGHTON - 75A	BRIGHTON - 75A	BRIGHTON - 75A	BRIGHTON - 75A	BRIGHTON - 75A	BRIGHTON - 75A	BRIGHTON - 75A
32344	BRIGHTON - 75A	BRIGHTON - 75A	BRIGHTON - 75A	BRIGHTON - 75A	BRIGHTON - 75A	BRIGHTON - 75A	BRIGHTON - 75A
32345	BRIGHTON - 75A	BRIGHTON - 75A	BRIGHTON - 75A	BRIGHTON - 75A	BRIGHTON - 75A	BRIGHTON - 75A	BRIGHTON - 75A
32346	THREE BRIDGES - 75E	BRIGHTON - 75A	BRIGHTON - 75A	BRIGHTON - 75A	BRIGHTON - 75A	BRIGHTON - 75A	BRIGHTON - 75A
32347	THREE BRIDGES - 75E	BRIGHTON - 75A	THREE BRIDGES - 75E	THREE BRIDGES - 75E	THREE BRIDGES - 75E	BRIGHTON - 75A(N)	BRIGHTON - 75A(N)
32348	EASTBOURNE - 75G	EASTBOURNE - 75G	THREE BRIDGES - 75E	BRIGHTON - 75A	BRIGHTON - 75A	THREE BRIDGES - 75E	THREE BRIDGES - 75E
32349	EASTBOURNE - 75G	BRIGHTON - 75A	THREE BRIDGES - 75E	THREE BRIDGES - 75E	THREE BRIDGES - 75E	THREE BRIDGES - 75E	THREE BRIDGES - 75E
32350	THREE BRIDGES - 75E	THREE BRIDGES - 75E	THREE BRIDGES - 75E	THREE BRIDGES - 75E	THREE BRIDGES - 75E	THREE BRIDGES - 75E	THREE BRIDGES - 75E
32351	THREE BRIDGES - 75E	THREE BRIDGES - 75E	THREE BRIDGES - 75E	THREE BRIDGES - 75E	THREE BRIDGES - 75E	THREE BRIDGES - 75E	THREE BRIDGES - 75E
32352	THREE BRIDGES - 75E	THREE BRIDGES - 75E	THREE BRIDGES - 75E	THREE BRIDGES - 75E	THREE BRIDGES - 75E	THREE BRIDGES - 75E	THREE BRIDGES - 75E
32353	THREE BRIDGES - 75E	THREE BRIDGES - 75E	THREE BRIDGES - 75E	THREE BRIDGES - 75E	THREE BRIDGES - 75E	THREE BRIDGES - 75E	THREE BRIDGES - 75E
U 2-6-0 (R/B 2-6-4T) 1928							
31790	YEOVIL - 72C	YEOVIL - 72C	YEOVIL - 72C	YEOVIL - 72C	YEOVIL - 72C	YEOVIL - 72C	YEOVIL - 72C
31791	YEOVIL - 72C	YEOVIL - 72C	YEOVIL - 72C	YEOVIL - 72C	YEOVIL - 72C	YEOVIL - 72C	YEOVIL - 72C
31792	YEOVIL - 72C	YEOVIL - 72C	YEOVIL - 72C	YEOVIL - 72C	YEOVIL - 72C	YEOVIL - 72C	YEOVIL - 72C
31793	GUILDFORD - 70C	STEWARTS LANE - 73A	READING (SR) - 70E	YEOVIL - 72C	YEOVIL - 72C	YEOVIL - 72C	YEOVIL - 72C
31794	READING (SR) - 70E	READING (SR) - 70E	READING (SR) - 70E	READING (SR) - 70E	YEOVIL - 72C	YEOVIL - 72C	YEOVIL - 72C
31795	SALISBURY - 72B	BOURNEMOUTH - 71B	BOURNEMOUTH - 71B	BOURNEMOUTH - 71B	BOURNEMOUTH - 71B	BOURNEMOUTH - 71B	BOURNEMOUTH - 71B
31796	READING (SR) - 70E	READING (SR) - 70E	READING (SR) - 70E	READING (SR) - 70E	READING (SR) - 70E	READING (SR) - 70E	READING (SR) - 70E
31797	READING (SR) - 70E	READING (SR) - 70E	READING (SR) - 70E	READING (SR) - 70E	READING (SR) - 70E	READING (SR) - 70E	GUILDFORD - 70C
31798	GUILDFORD - 70C	GUILDFORD - 70C	GUILDFORD - 70C	GUILDFORD - 70C	GUILDFORD - 70C	GUILDFORD - 70C	GUILDFORD - 70C
31799	READING (SR) - 70E	READING (SR) - 70E	READING (SR) - 70E	READING (SR) - 70E	READING (SR) - 70E	READING (SR) - 70E	GUILDFORD - 70C
31800	GUILDFORD - 70C	GUILDFORD - 70C	GUILDFORD - 70C	GUILDFORD - 70C	GUILDFORD - 70C	GUILDFORD - 70C	GUILDFORD - 70C
31801	GUILDFORD - 70C	GUILDFORD - 70C	GUILDFORD - 70C	GUILDFORD - 70C	GUILDFORD - 70C	GUILDFORD - 70C	GUILDFORD - 70C
31802	GUILDFORD - 70C	GUILDFORD - 70C	GUILDFORD - 70C	GUILDFORD - 70C	GUILDFORD - 70C	GUILDFORD - 70C	GUILDFORD - 70C
31803	GUILDFORD - 70C	STEWARTS LANE - 73A	STEWARTS LANE - 73A	GUILDFORD - 70C	GUILDFORD - 70C	GUILDFORD - 70C	HITHER GREEN - 73C
31804	GUILDFORD - 70C	GUILDFORD - 70C	GUILDFORD - 70C	GUILDFORD - 70C	GUILDFORD - 70C	GUILDFORD - 70C	HITHER GREEN - 73C
31805	FRATTON - 71D	FRATTON - 71D	FRATTON - 71D	FRATTON - 71D	FRATTON - 71D	FRATTON - 71D	FRATTON - 71D
31806	FAVERSHAM - 73E	FAVERSHAM - 73E	FAVERSHAM - 73E	FAVERSHAM - 73E	FAVERSHAM - 73E	FAVERSHAM - 73E	FAVERSHAM - 73E
31807	NINE ELMS - 70A	NINE ELMS - 70A	NINE ELMS - 70A	NINE ELMS - 70A	FRATTON - 71D	FRATTON - 71D	FRATTON - 71D
31808	FAVERSHAM - 73E	FAVERSHAM - 73E	FAVERSHAM - 73E	FAVERSHAM - 73E	FAVERSHAM - 73E	FAVERSHAM - 73E	FAVERSHAM - 73E
31809	FRATTON - 71D	FRATTON - 71D	FRATTON - 71D	FRATTON - 71D	FRATTON - 71D	FRATTON - 71D	FRATTON - 71D

loco	Jun-51	Jul-51	Sep-51	Dec-51	Jan-52	Mar-52	Jun-52
E4X 0-6-2T (1909)							
32466 NORWOOD JCN - 75C	NORWOOD JCN - 75C	NORWOOD JCN - 75C	NORWOOD JCN - 75C	NORWOOD JCN - 75C	NORWOOD JCN - 75C	NORWOOD JCN - 75C
32477 NORWOOD JCN - 75C	NORWOOD JCN - 75C	NORWOOD JCN - 75C	NORWOOD JCN - 75C	NORWOOD JCN - 75C	NORWOOD JCN - 75C	NORWOOD JCN - 75C
32478 NORWOOD JCN - 75C	NORWOOD JCN - 75C	NORWOOD JCN - 75C	NORWOOD JCN - 75C	NORWOOD JCN - 75C	NORWOOD JCN - 75C	NORWOOD JCN - 75C
32489 NORWOOD JCN - 75C	NORWOOD JCN - 75C	NORWOOD JCN - 75C	NORWOOD JCN - 75C	NORWOOD JCN - 75C	NORWOOD JCN - 75C	NORWOOD JCN - 75C
E5 0-6-2T (1902)							
32399 HORSHAM - 75D	HORSHAM - 75D	HORSHAM - 75D	HORSHAM - 75D	HORSHAM - 75D	THREE BRIDGES - 75E	THREE BRIDGES - 75E
32400 BRIGHTON - 75A	BRIGHTON - 75A	BRIGHTON - 75A	W/D	W/D	W/D	W/D
32404 EASTBOURNE - 75G	EASTBOURNE - 75G	EASTBOURNE - 75G	W/D	W/D	W/D	W/D
32405 EASTBOURNE - 75G	EASTBOURNE - 75G	EASTBOURNE - 75G	W/D	W/D	W/D	W/D
32406 EASTBOURNE - 75G	EASTBOURNE - 75G	W/D	W/D	W/D	W/D	W/D
32568 HORSHAM - 75D	HORSHAM - 75D	HORSHAM - 75D	HORSHAM - 75D	HORSHAM - 75D	HORSHAM - 75D	HORSHAM - 75D
32571 THREE BRIDGES - 75E	THREE BRIDGES - 75E	THREE BRIDGES - 75E	THREE BRIDGES - 75E	THREE BRIDGES - 75E	THREE BRIDGES - 75E	THREE BRIDGES - 75E
32573 BRIGHTON - 75A	BRIGHTON - 75A	HORSHAM - 75D	BRIGHTON - 75A	BRIGHTON - 75A	BRIGHTON - 75A	BRIGHTON - 75A
32575 BRIGHTON - 75A	BRIGHTON - 75A	BRIGHTON - 75A	W/D	W/D	W/D	W/D
32583 BRIGHTON - 75A	BRIGHTON - 75A	HORSHAM - 75D	BRIGHTON - 75A	BRIGHTON - 75A	BRIGHTON - 75A	BRIGHTON - 75A
32585 B.ARMS - 73B(NX)	B.ARMS - 73B(NX)	B.ARMS - 73B(NX)	EASTBOURNE - 75G	EASTBOURNE - 75G	EASTBOURNE - 75G	EASTBOURNE - 75G
32587 B.ARMS - 73B(NX)	B.ARMS - 73B(NX)	T.WELLS - 75F	T.WELLS - 75F	T.WELLS - 75F	T.WELLS - 75F	BRIGHTON - 75A
32588 EASTBOURNE - 75G	EASTBOURNE - 75G	EASTBOURNE - 75G	EASTBOURNE - 75G	EASTBOURNE - 75G	EASTBOURNE - 75G	EASTBOURNE - 75G
32590 BASINGSTOKE - 70D	BASINGSTOKE - 70D	W/D	W/D	W/D	W/D	W/D
32591 EASTBOURNE - 75G	EASTBOURNE - 75G	BASINGSTOKE - 70D	BASINGSTOKE - 70D	BASINGSTOKE - 70D	BASINGSTOKE - 70D	BASINGSTOKE - 70D
32592 REDHILL - 75B	REDHILL - 75B	BASINGSTOKE - 70D	BASINGSTOKE - 70D	BASINGSTOKE - 70D	BASINGSTOKE - 70D	BASINGSTOKE - 70D
32593 EASTBOURNE - 75G	EASTBOURNE - 75G	DOVER - 74C	DOVER - 74C	DOVER - 74C	DOVER - 74C	DOVER - 74C
E5X 0-6-2T (1911)							
32401 HORSHAM - 75D	HORSHAM - 75D	HORSHAM - 75D	HORSHAM - 75D	HORSHAM - 75D	HORSHAM - 75D	BRIGHTON - 75A
32570 HORSHAM - 75D	HORSHAM - 75D	HORSHAM - 75D	B.ARMS - 73B	HORSHAM - 75D	HORSHAM - 75D	HORSHAM - 75D
32576 HORSHAM - 75D	HORSHAM - 75D	HORSHAM - 75D	BRIGHTON - 75A	HORSHAM - 75D	HORSHAM - 75D	HORSHAM - 75D
32586 HORSHAM - 75D	HORSHAM - 75D	HORSHAM - 75D	HORSHAM - 75D	HORSHAM - 75D	HORSHAM - 75D	BRIGHTON - 75A
E6 0-6-2T (1904)							
32408 B.ARMS - 73B	B.ARMS - 73B	B.ARMS - 73B	B.ARMS - 73B	B.ARMS - 73B	B.ARMS - 73B	B.ARMS - 73B
32409 EASTLEIGH - 71A	EASTLEIGH - 71A	EASTLEIGH - 71A	EASTLEIGH - 71A	EASTLEIGH - 71A	EASTLEIGH - 71A	EASTLEIGH - 71A
32410 B.ARMS - 73B	B.ARMS - 73B	B.ARMS - 73B	B.ARMS - 73B	B.ARMS - 73B	B.ARMS - 73B	B.ARMS - 73B
32412 EASTLEIGH - 71A	EASTLEIGH - 71A	EASTLEIGH - 71A	EASTLEIGH - 71A	EASTLEIGH - 71A	EASTLEIGH - 71A	EASTLEIGH - 71A
32413 B.ARMS - 73B	B.ARMS - 73B	B.ARMS - 73B	B.ARMS - 73B	B.ARMS - 73B	B.ARMS - 73B	B.ARMS - 73B
32414 NORWOOD JCN - 75C	NORWOOD JCN - 75C	NORWOOD JCN - 75C	NORWOOD JCN - 75C	NORWOOD JCN - 75C	NORWOOD JCN - 75C	NORWOOD JCN - 75C
32415 B.ARMS - 73B	B.ARMS - 73B	B.ARMS - 73B	B.ARMS - 73B	B.ARMS - 73B	B.ARMS - 73B	B.ARMS - 73B
32416 EASTLEIGH - 71A	EASTLEIGH - 71A	EASTLEIGH - 71A	EASTLEIGH - 71A	EASTLEIGH - 71A	EASTLEIGH - 71A	EASTLEIGH - 71A
32417 NORWOOD JCN - 75C	NORWOOD JCN - 75C	NORWOOD JCN - 75C	NORWOOD JCN - 75C	NORWOOD JCN - 75C	NORWOOD JCN - 75C	NORWOOD JCN - 75C
32418 NORWOOD JCN - 75C	NORWOOD JCN - 75C	NORWOOD JCN - 75C	NORWOOD JCN - 75C	NORWOOD JCN - 75C	NORWOOD JCN - 75C	NORWOOD JCN - 75C
E6X 0-6-2T (1911)							
32407 NORWOOD JCN - 75C	NORWOOD JCN - 75C	NORWOOD JCN - 75C	NORWOOD JCN - 75C	NORWOOD JCN - 75C	NORWOOD JCN - 75C	NORWOOD JCN - 75C
32411 NORWOOD JCN - 75C	NORWOOD JCN - 75C	NORWOOD JCN - 75C	NORWOOD JCN - 75C	NORWOOD JCN - 75C	NORWOOD JCN - 75C	NORWOOD JCN - 75C
G16 4-8-0T (1921)							
30492 FELTHAM - 70B	FELTHAM - 70B	FELTHAM - 70B	FELTHAM - 70B	FELTHAM - 70B	FELTHAM - 70B	FELTHAM - 70B
30493 FELTHAM - 70B	FELTHAM - 70B	FELTHAM - 70B	FELTHAM - 70B	FELTHAM - 70B	FELTHAM - 70B	FELTHAM - 70B
30494 FELTHAM - 70B	FELTHAM - 70B	FELTHAM - 70B	FELTHAM - 70B	FELTHAM - 70B	FELTHAM - 70B	FELTHAM - 70B
30495 FELTHAM - 70B	FELTHAM - 70B	FELTHAM - 70B	FELTHAM - 70B	FELTHAM - 70B	FELTHAM - 70B	FELTHAM - 70B
K 2-6-0 (1913)							
32337 BRIGHTON - 75A	BRIGHTON - 75A	BRIGHTON - 75A	BRIGHTON - 75A	BRIGHTON - 75A	BRIGHTON - 75A	BRIGHTON - 75A
32338 BRIGHTON - 75A	BRIGHTON - 75A	BRIGHTON - 75A	BRIGHTON - 75A	BRIGHTON - 75A	BRIGHTON - 75A	BRIGHTON - 75A
32339 BRIGHTON - 75A	BRIGHTON - 75A	BRIGHTON - 75A	BRIGHTON - 75A	BRIGHTON - 75A	BRIGHTON - 75A	BRIGHTON - 75A
32340 BRIGHTON - 75A	BRIGHTON - 75A	BRIGHTON - 75A	BRIGHTON - 75A	BRIGHTON - 75A	BRIGHTON - 75A	BRIGHTON - 75A
32341 BRIGHTON - 75A	BRIGHTON - 75A	BRIGHTON - 75A	BRIGHTON - 75A	BRIGHTON - 75A	BRIGHTON - 75A	BRIGHTON - 75A
32342 BRIGHTON - 75A	BRIGHTON - 75A	BRIGHTON - 75A	BRIGHTON - 75A	BRIGHTON - 75A	BRIGHTON - 75A	BRIGHTON - 75A
32343 BRIGHTON - 75A	BRIGHTON - 75A	BRIGHTON - 75A	BRIGHTON - 75A	BRIGHTON - 75A	BRIGHTON - 75A	BRIGHTON - 75A
32344 BRIGHTON - 75A	BRIGHTON - 75A	BRIGHTON - 75A	BRIGHTON - 75A	BRIGHTON - 75A	BRIGHTON - 75A	BRIGHTON - 75A
32345 BRIGHTON - 75A	BRIGHTON - 75A	BRIGHTON - 75A	BRIGHTON - 75A	BRIGHTON - 75A	BRIGHTON - 75A	BRIGHTON - 75A
32346 BRIGHTON - 75A	B.ARMS - 73B	BRIGHTON - 75A	BRIGHTON - 75A	BRIGHTON - 75A	BRIGHTON - 75A	BRIGHTON - 75A
32347 BRIGHTON - 75A(N)	B.ARMS - 73B	BRIGHTON - 75A	BRIGHTON - 75A	BRIGHTON - 75A	THREE BRIDGES - 75E	THREE BRIDGES - 75E
32348 THREE BRIDGES - 75E	B.ARMS - 73B	THREE BRIDGES - 75E	THREE BRIDGES - 75E	THREE BRIDGES - 75E	THREE BRIDGES - 75E	THREE BRIDGES - 75E
32349 THREE BRIDGES - 75E	FRATTON - 71D	FRATTON - 71D	FRATTON - 71D	FRATTON - 71D	FRATTON - 71D	FRATTON - 71D
32350 THREE BRIDGES - 75E	THREE BRIDGES - 75E	THREE BRIDGES - 75E	THREE BRIDGES - 75E	THREE BRIDGES - 75E	THREE BRIDGES - 75E	THREE BRIDGES - 75E
32351 THREE BRIDGES - 75E	THREE BRIDGES - 75E	THREE BRIDGES - 75E	THREE BRIDGES - 75E	THREE BRIDGES - 75E	THREE BRIDGES - 75E	THREE BRIDGES - 75E
32352 THREE BRIDGES - 75E	THREE BRIDGES - 75E	THREE BRIDGES - 75E	THREE BRIDGES - 75E	THREE BRIDGES - 75E	THREE BRIDGES - 75E	THREE BRIDGES - 75E
32353 THREE BRIDGES - 75E	THREE BRIDGES - 75E	THREE BRIDGES - 75E	THREE BRIDGES - 75E	THREE BRIDGES - 75E	THREE BRIDGES - 75E	THREE BRIDGES - 75E
U 2-6-0 (R/B 2-6-4T) 1928							
31790 YEOVIL - 72C	YEOVIL - 72C	YEOVIL - 72C	YEOVIL - 72C	YEOVIL - 72C	YEOVIL - 72C	YEOVIL - 72C
31791 YEOVIL - 72C	YEOVIL - 72C	YEOVIL - 72C	YEOVIL - 72C	YEOVIL - 72C	YEOVIL - 72C	YEOVIL - 72C
31792 YEOVIL - 72C	YEOVIL - 72C	YEOVIL - 72C	YEOVIL - 72C	YEOVIL - 72C	YEOVIL - 72C	YEOVIL - 72C
31793 YEOVIL - 72C	YEOVIL - 72C	YEOVIL - 72C	YEOVIL - 72C	YEOVIL - 72C	YEOVIL - 72C	YEOVIL - 72C
31794 YEOVIL - 72C	YEOVIL - 72C	YEOVIL - 72C	YEOVIL - 72C	YEOVIL - 72C	YEOVIL - 72C	YEOVIL - 72C
31795 BOURNEMOUTH - 71B	BOURNEMOUTH - 71B	BOURNEMOUTH - 71B	YEOVIL - 72C	YEOVIL - 72C	YEOVIL - 72C	YEOVIL - 72C
31796 READING (SR) - 70E	READING (SR) - 70E	READING (SR) - 70E	YEOVIL - 72C	YEOVIL - 72C	YEOVIL - 72C	YEOVIL - 72C
31797 GUILDFORD - 70C	GUILDFORD - 70C	GUILDFORD - 70C	GUILDFORD - 70C	GUILDFORD - 70C	GUILDFORD - 70C	GUILDFORD - 70C
31798 GUILDFORD - 70C	GUILDFORD - 70C	GUILDFORD - 70C	GUILDFORD - 70C	GUILDFORD - 70C	GUILDFORD - 70C	GUILDFORD - 70C
31799 GUILDFORD - 70C	GUILDFORD - 70C	GUILDFORD - 70C	GUILDFORD - 70C	GUILDFORD - 70C	GUILDFORD - 70C	GUILDFORD - 70C
31800 GUILDFORD - 70C	GUILDFORD - 70C	GUILDFORD - 70C	GUILDFORD - 70C	GUILDFORD - 70C	GUILDFORD - 70C	GUILDFORD - 70C
31801 GUILDFORD - 70C	GUILDFORD - 70C	GUILDFORD - 70C	GUILDFORD - 70C	GUILDFORD - 70C	GUILDFORD - 70C	GUILDFORD - 70C
31802 GUILDFORD - 70C	GUILDFORD - 70C	GUILDFORD - 70C	GUILDFORD - 70C	GUILDFORD - 70C	GUILDFORD - 70C	GUILDFORD - 70C
31803 HITHER GREEN - 73C	HITHER GREEN - 73C	HITHER GREEN - 73C	HITHER GREEN - 73C	HITHER GREEN - 73C	HITHER GREEN - 73C	HITHER GREEN - 73C
31804 HITHER GREEN - 73C	HITHER GREEN - 73C	HITHER GREEN - 73C	HITHER GREEN - 73C	HITHER GREEN - 73C	HITHER GREEN - 73C	HITHER GREEN - 73C
31805 FRATTON - 71D	FRATTON - 71D	FRATTON - 71D	FRATTON - 71D	EASTLEIGH - 71A	EASTLEIGH - 71A	EASTLEIGH - 71A
31806 FAVERSHAM - 73E	FAVERSHAM - 73E	FAVERSHAM - 73E	FAVERSHAM - 73E	FAVERSHAM - 73E	FAVERSHAM - 73E	FAVERSHAM - 73E
31807 FRATTON - 71D	FRATTON - 71D	FRATTON - 71D	FRATTON - 71D	FRATTON - 71D	FRATTON - 71D	FRATTON - 71D
31808 FAVERSHAM - 73E	FAVERSHAM - 73E	FAVERSHAM - 73E	FAVERSHAM - 73E	FAVERSHAM - 73E	EASTLEIGH - 71A	EASTLEIGH - 71A
31809 FRATTON - 71D	FRATTON - 71D	FRATTON - 71D	FRATTON - 71D	FRATTON - 71D	FRATTON - 71D	FRATTON - 71D

loco	Sep-52	Dec-52	Mar-53	May-53	Jul-53	Sep-53	Nov-53
				E4X 0-6-2T (1909)			
32466	NORWOOD JCN - 75C	NORWOOD JCN - 75C	NORWOOD JCN - 75C	NORWOOD JCN - 75C	NORWOOD JCN - 75C	NORWOOD JCN - 75C	NORWOOD JCN - 75C
32477	NORWOOD JCN - 75C	NORWOOD JCN - 75C	NORWOOD JCN - 75C	NORWOOD JCN - 75C	NORWOOD JCN - 75C	NORWOOD JCN - 75C	NORWOOD JCN - 75C
32478	NORWOOD JCN - 75C	NORWOOD JCN - 75C	NORWOOD JCN - 75C	NORWOOD JCN - 75C	NORWOOD JCN - 75C	NORWOOD JCN - 75C	NORWOOD JCN - 75C
32489	NORWOOD JCN - 75C	NORWOOD JCN - 75C	NORWOOD JCN - 75C	NORWOOD JCN - 75C	NORWOOD JCN - 75C	NORWOOD JCN - 75C	NORWOOD JCN - 75C
				E5 0-6-2T (1902)			
32399	THREE BRIDGES - 75E	THREE BRIDGES - 75E	THREE BRIDGES - 75E	BASINGSTOKE - 70D	W/D	W/D	W/D
32568	HORSHAM - 75D	HORSHAM - 75D	HORSHAM - 75D	HORSHAM - 75D	HORSHAM - 75D	BASINGSTOKE - 70D	BASINGSTOKE - 70D
32571	THREE BRIDGES - 75E	THREE BRIDGES - 75E	REDHILL - 75B	REDHILL - 75B	THREE BRIDGES - 75E	THREE BRIDGES - 75E	THREE BRIDGES - 75E
32573	BRIGHTON - 75A	BRIGHTON - 75A	BRIGHTON - 75A	BRIGHTON - 75A	W/D	W/D	W/D
32583	BRIGHTON - 75A	BRIGHTON - 75A	BRIGHTON - 75A	BRIGHTON - 75A	BRIGHTON - 75A	BRIGHTON - 75A	BRIGHTON - 75A
32585	BRIGHTON - 75A	BRIGHTON - 75A	BRIGHTON - 75A	BRIGHTON - 75A	BRIGHTON - 75A	BRIGHTON - 75A	BRIGHTON - 75A
32587	BRIGHTON - 75A	BRIGHTON - 75A	BRIGHTON - 75A	BRIGHTON - 75A	BRIGHTON - 75A	BRIGHTON - 75A	BRIGHTON - 75A
32588	BRIGHTON - 75A	BRIGHTON - 75A	BRIGHTON - 75A	BRIGHTON - 75A	BRIGHTON - 75A	BRIGHTON - 75A	W/D
32591	BASINGSTOKE - 70D	BASINGSTOKE - 70D	BASINGSTOKE - 70D	BASINGSTOKE - 70D	BASINGSTOKE - 70D	BASINGSTOKE - 70D	BASINGSTOKE - 70D
32592	BASINGSTOKE - 70D	BASINGSTOKE - 70D	BASINGSTOKE - 70D	W/D	W/D	W/D	W/D
32593	DOVER - 74C	DOVER - 74C	DOVER - 74C		DOVER - 74C	DOVER - 74C	DOVER - 74C
				E5X 0-6-2T (1911)			
32401	BRIGHTON - 75A	BRIGHTON - 75A	BRIGHTON - 75A	BRIGHTON - 75A	BRIGHTON - 75A	BRIGHTON - 75A	BRIGHTON - 75A
32570	HORSHAM - 75D	HORSHAM - 75D	HORSHAM - 75D	HORSHAM - 75D	HORSHAM - 75D	HORSHAM - 75D	HORSHAM - 75D
32576	HORSHAM - 75D	HORSHAM - 75D	HORSHAM - 75D	HORSHAM - 75D	HORSHAM - 75D	HORSHAM - 75D	HORSHAM - 75D
32586	BRIGHTON - 75A	BRIGHTON - 75A	BRIGHTON - 75A	BRIGHTON - 75A	BRIGHTON - 75A	BRIGHTON - 75A	BRIGHTON - 75A
				E6 0-6-2T (1904)			
32408	B ARMS - 73B	B ARMS - 73B	B ARMS - 73B	B ARMS - 73B	B ARMS - 73B	B ARMS - 73B	B ARMS - 73B
32409	EASTLEIGH - 71A	EASTLEIGH - 71A	EASTLEIGH - 71A	EASTLEIGH - 71A	EASTLEIGH - 71A	EASTLEIGH - 71A	EASTLEIGH - 71A
32410	B ARMS - 73B	B ARMS - 73B	B ARMS - 73B	B ARMS - 73B	B ARMS - 73B	B ARMS - 73B	B ARMS - 73B
32412	EASTLEIGH - 71A	EASTLEIGH - 71A	EASTLEIGH - 71A	EASTLEIGH - 71A	EASTLEIGH - 71A	B ARMS - 73B	B ARMS - 73B
32413	B ARMS - 73B	B ARMS - 73B	B ARMS - 73B	B ARMS - 73B	EASTLEIGH - 71A	NORWOOD JCN - 75C	NORWOOD JCN - 75C
32414	NORWOOD JCN - 75C	NORWOOD JCN - 75C	NORWOOD JCN - 75C	NORWOOD JCN - 75C	NORWOOD JCN - 75C	NORWOOD JCN - 75C	NORWOOD JCN - 75C
32415	B ARMS - 73B	B ARMS - 73B	B ARMS - 73B	B ARMS - 73B	B ARMS - 73B	B ARMS - 73B	B ARMS - 73B
32416	EASTLEIGH - 71A	EASTLEIGH - 71A	EASTLEIGH - 71A	EASTLEIGH - 71A	EASTLEIGH - 71A	NORWOOD JCN - 75C	NORWOOD JCN - 75C
32417	NORWOOD JCN - 75C	NORWOOD JCN - 75C	NORWOOD JCN - 75C	NORWOOD JCN - 75C	NORWOOD JCN - 75C	NORWOOD JCN - 75C	NORWOOD JCN - 75C
32418	NORWOOD JCN - 75C	NORWOOD JCN - 75C	NORWOOD JCN - 75C	NORWOOD JCN - 75C	NORWOOD JCN - 75C	NORWOOD JCN - 75C	NORWOOD JCN - 75C
				E6X 0-6-2T (1911)			
32407	NORWOOD JCN - 75C	NORWOOD JCN - 75C	NORWOOD JCN - 75C	NORWOOD JCN - 75C	NORWOOD JCN - 75C	NORWOOD JCN - 75C	NORWOOD JCN - 75C
32411	NORWOOD JCN - 75C	NORWOOD JCN - 75C	NORWOOD JCN - 75C	NORWOOD JCN - 75C	NORWOOD JCN - 75C	NORWOOD JCN - 75C	NORWOOD JCN - 75C
				G16 4-8-0T (1921)			
30492	FELTHAM - 70B	FELTHAM - 70B	FELTHAM - 70B	FELTHAM - 70B	FELTHAM - 70B	FELTHAM - 70B	FELTHAM - 70B
30493	FELTHAM - 70B	FELTHAM - 70B	FELTHAM - 70B	FELTHAM - 70B	FELTHAM - 70B	FELTHAM - 70B	FELTHAM - 70B
30494	FELTHAM - 70B	FELTHAM - 70B	FELTHAM - 70B	FELTHAM - 70B	FELTHAM - 70B	FELTHAM - 70B	FELTHAM - 70B
30495	FELTHAM - 70B	FELTHAM - 70B	FELTHAM - 70B	FELTHAM - 70B	FELTHAM - 70B	FELTHAM - 70B	FELTHAM - 70B
				K 2-6-0 (1913)			
32337	BRIGHTON - 75A	BRIGHTON - 75A	BRIGHTON - 75A	BRIGHTON - 75A	BRIGHTON - 75A	BRIGHTON - 75A	BRIGHTON - 75A
32338	BRIGHTON - 75A	BRIGHTON - 75A	BRIGHTON - 75A	BRIGHTON - 75A	BRIGHTON - 75A	BRIGHTON - 75A	BRIGHTON - 75A
32339	BRIGHTON - 75A	BRIGHTON - 75A	BRIGHTON - 75A	BRIGHTON - 75A	BRIGHTON - 75A	BRIGHTON - 75A	BRIGHTON - 75A
32340	BRIGHTON - 75A	BRIGHTON - 75A	BRIGHTON - 75A	BRIGHTON - 75A	BRIGHTON - 75A	BRIGHTON - 75A	BRIGHTON - 75A
32341	BRIGHTON - 75A	BRIGHTON - 75A	BRIGHTON - 75A	BRIGHTON - 75A	BRIGHTON - 75A	BRIGHTON - 75A	BRIGHTON - 75A
32342	BRIGHTON - 75A	BRIGHTON - 75A	BRIGHTON - 75A	BRIGHTON - 75A	BRIGHTON - 75A	BRIGHTON - 75A	BRIGHTON - 75A
32343	BRIGHTON - 75A	BRIGHTON - 75A	BRIGHTON - 75A	BRIGHTON - 75A	BRIGHTON - 75A	BRIGHTON - 75A	BRIGHTON - 75A
32344	BRIGHTON - 75A	BRIGHTON - 75A	BRIGHTON - 75A	BRIGHTON - 75A	BRIGHTON - 75A	BRIGHTON - 75A	BRIGHTON - 75A
32345	BRIGHTON - 75A	BRIGHTON - 75A	BRIGHTON - 75A	BRIGHTON - 75A	BRIGHTON - 75A	BRIGHTON - 75A	BRIGHTON - 75A
32346	BRIGHTON - 75A	BRIGHTON - 75A	BRIGHTON - 75A	BRIGHTON - 75A	BRIGHTON - 75A	BRIGHTON - 75A	BRIGHTON - 75A
32347	THREE BRIDGES - 75E	THREE BRIDGES - 75E	THREE BRIDGES - 75E	THREE BRIDGES - 75E	THREE BRIDGES - 75E	THREE BRIDGES - 75E	THREE BRIDGES - 75E
32348	THREE BRIDGES - 75E	THREE BRIDGES - 75E	THREE BRIDGES - 75E	THREE BRIDGES - 75E	THREE BRIDGES - 75E	THREE BRIDGES - 75E	THREE BRIDGES - 75E
32349	FRATTON - 71D	FRATTON - 71D	FRATTON - 71D	FRATTON - 71D	FRATTON - 71D	FRATTON - 71D	FRATTON - 71D
32350	THREE BRIDGES - 75E	THREE BRIDGES - 75E	THREE BRIDGES - 75E	THREE BRIDGES - 75E	THREE BRIDGES - 75E	THREE BRIDGES - 75E	THREE BRIDGES - 75E
32351	THREE BRIDGES - 75E	THREE BRIDGES - 75E	THREE BRIDGES - 75E	THREE BRIDGES - 75E	THREE BRIDGES - 75E	THREE BRIDGES - 75E	THREE BRIDGES - 75E
32352	THREE BRIDGES - 75E	THREE BRIDGES - 75E	THREE BRIDGES - 75E	THREE BRIDGES - 75E	THREE BRIDGES - 75E	THREE BRIDGES - 75E	THREE BRIDGES - 75E
32353	THREE BRIDGES - 75E	THREE BRIDGES - 75E	THREE BRIDGES - 75E	THREE BRIDGES - 75E	THREE BRIDGES - 75E	THREE BRIDGES - 75E	THREE BRIDGES - 75E
				U 2-6-0 (R/B 2-6-4T) 1928			
31790	YEOVIL - 72C	YEOVIL - 72C	YEOVIL - 72C	YEOVIL - 72C	YEOVIL - 72C	YEOVIL - 72C	YEOVIL - 72C
31791	YEOVIL - 72C	YEOVIL - 72C	YEOVIL - 72C	YEOVIL - 72C	YEOVIL - 72C	YEOVIL - 72C	YEOVIL - 72C
31792	YEOVIL - 72C	YEOVIL - 72C	YEOVIL - 72C	YEOVIL - 72C	YEOVIL - 72C	YEOVIL - 72C	YEOVIL - 72C
31793	YEOVIL - 72C	YEOVIL - 72C	YEOVIL - 72C	YEOVIL - 72C	YEOVIL - 72C	YEOVIL - 72C	YEOVIL - 72C
31794	YEOVIL - 72C	YEOVIL - 72C	YEOVIL - 72C	YEOVIL - 72C	YEOVIL - 72C	YEOVIL - 72C	YEOVIL - 72C
31795	YEOVIL - 72C	YEOVIL - 72C	YEOVIL - 72C	YEOVIL - 72C	YEOVIL - 72C	YEOVIL - 72C	YEOVIL - 72C
31796	YEOVIL - 72C	YEOVIL - 72C	YEOVIL - 72C	YEOVIL - 72C	YEOVIL - 72C	YEOVIL - 72C	YEOVIL - 72C
31797	GUILDFORD - 70C	GUILDFORD - 70C	GUILDFORD - 70C	GUILDFORD - 70C	GUILDFORD - 70C	GUILDFORD - 70C	GUILDFORD - 70C
31798	GUILDFORD - 70C	GUILDFORD - 70C	GUILDFORD - 70C	GUILDFORD - 70C	GUILDFORD - 70C	GUILDFORD - 70C	GUILDFORD - 70C
31799	GUILDFORD - 70C	GUILDFORD - 70C	GUILDFORD - 70C	GUILDFORD - 70C	GUILDFORD - 70C	GUILDFORD - 70C	GUILDFORD - 70C
31800	GUILDFORD - 70C	GUILDFORD - 70C	GUILDFORD - 70C	GUILDFORD - 70C	GUILDFORD - 70C	GUILDFORD - 70C	GUILDFORD - 70C
31801	GUILDFORD - 70C	GUILDFORD - 70C	GUILDFORD - 70C	GUILDFORD - 70C	GUILDFORD - 70C	EASTLEIGH - 71A	EASTLEIGH - 71A
31802	GUILDFORD - 70C	GUILDFORD - 70C	GUILDFORD - 70C	GUILDFORD - 70C	GUILDFORD - 70C	GUILDFORD - 70C	GUILDFORD - 70C
31803	HITHER GREEN - 73C	HITHER GREEN - 73C	HITHER GREEN - 73C	HITHER GREEN - 73C	HITHER GREEN - 73C	HITHER GREEN - 73C	HITHER GREEN - 73C
31804	HITHER GREEN - 73C	HITHER GREEN - 73C	HITHER GREEN - 73C	HITHER GREEN - 73C	HITHER GREEN - 73C	HITHER GREEN - 73C	HITHER GREEN - 73C
31805	EASTLEIGH - 71A	EASTLEIGH - 71A	REDHILL - 75B	REDHILL - 75B	REDHILL - 75B	REDHILL - 75B	REDHILL - 75B
31806	FAVERSHAM - 73E	FAVERSHAM - 73E	FAVERSHAM - 73E	FAVERSHAM - 73E	FAVERSHAM - 73E	FAVERSHAM - 73E	FAVERSHAM - 73E
31807	FRATTON - 71D	FRATTON - 71D	FRATTON - 71D	FRATTON - 71D	FRATTON - 71D	FRATTON - 71D	FRATTON - 71D
31808	FRATTON - 71D	FRATTON - 71D	FRATTON - 71D	FRATTON - 71D	FRATTON - 71D	FRATTON - 71D	FRATTON - 71D
31809	FRATTON - 71D	FRATTON - 71D	FRATTON - 71D	FRATTON - 71D	FRATTON - 71D	FRATTON - 71D	FRATTON - 71D

loco	Jan-54	Mar-54	May-54	Jun-54	Aug-54	Oct-54	Dec-54
			E4X 0-6-2T (1909)				
32466	NORWOOD JCN - 75C	NORWOOD JCN - 75C	NORWOOD JCN - 75C	NORWOOD JCN - 75C	NORWOOD JCN - 75C	NORWOOD JCN - 75C	NORWOOD JCN - 75C
32477	NORWOOD JCN - 75C	NORWOOD JCN - 75C	NORWOOD JCN - 75C	NORWOOD JCN - 75C	NORWOOD JCN - 75C	NORWOOD JCN - 75C	NORWOOD JCN - 75C
32478	NORWOOD JCN - 75C	NORWOOD JCN - 75C	NORWOOD JCN - 75C	NORWOOD JCN - 75C	NORWOOD JCN - 75C	NORWOOD JCN - 75C	NORWOOD JCN - 75C
32489	NORWOOD JCN - 75C	NORWOOD JCN - 75C	NORWOOD JCN - 75C	NORWOOD JCN - 75C	NORWOOD JCN - 75C	NORWOOD JCN - 75C	NORWOOD JCN - 75C
			E5 0-6-2T (1902)				
32568	BASINGSTOKE - 70D	BASINGSTOKE - 70D	BASINGSTOKE - 70D	BASINGSTOKE - 70D	BASINGSTOKE - 70D	BASINGSTOKE - 70D	BASINGSTOKE - 70D
32571	THREE BRIDGES - 75E	THREE BRIDGES - 75E	THREE BRIDGES - 75E	NORWOOD JCN - 75C	NORWOOD JCN - 75C	NORWOOD JCN - 75C	NORWOOD JCN - 75C
32583	BRIGHTON - 75A	BRIGHTON - 75A	BRIGHTON - 75A	BRIGHTON - 75A	BRIGHTON - 75A	BRIGHTON - 75A	BASINGSTOKE - 70D
32585	BRIGHTON - 75A	BRIGHTON - 75A	BRIGHTON - 75A	W/D	W/D	W/D	W/D
32587	BRIGHTON - 75A	BRIGHTON - 75A	BRIGHTON - 75A	BRIGHTON - 75A	BASINGSTOKE - 70D	W/D	W/D
32591	BASINGSTOKE - 70D	BASINGSTOKE - 70D	BASINGSTOKE - 70D	BASINGSTOKE - 70D	BASINGSTOKE - 70D	BASINGSTOKE - 70D	W/D
32593	DOVER - 74C	DOVER - 74C	DOVER - 74C	DOVER - 74C	DOVER - 74C	DOVER - 74C	DOVER - 74C
			E5X 0-6-2T (1911)				
32401	BRIGHTON - 75A	BRIGHTON - 75A	BRIGHTON - 75A	BRIGHTON - 75A	W/D	W/D	W/D
32570	HORSHAM - 75D	HORSHAM - 75D	HORSHAM - 75D	HORSHAM - 75D	HORSHAM - 75D	HORSHAM - 75D	HORSHAM - 75D
32576	HORSHAM - 75D	HORSHAM - 75D	HORSHAM - 75D	HORSHAM - 75D	HORSHAM - 75D	HORSHAM - 75D	HORSHAM - 75D
32586	BRIGHTON - 75A	BRIGHTON - 75A	BRIGHTON - 75A	BRIGHTON - 75A	BRIGHTON - 75A	BRIGHTON - 75A	BRIGHTON - 75A
			E6 0-6-2T (1904)				
32408	B ARMS - 73B	B ARMS - 73B	B ARMS - 73B	B ARMS - 73B	B ARMS - 73B	B ARMS - 73B	B ARMS - 73B
32409	EASTLEIGH - 71A	EASTLEIGH - 71A	EASTLEIGH - 71A	EASTLEIGH - 71A	EASTLEIGH - 71A	EASTLEIGH - 71A	EASTLEIGH - 71A
32410	B ARMS - 73B	B ARMS - 73B	B ARMS - 73B	B ARMS - 73B	B ARMS - 73B	B ARMS - 73B	B ARMS - 73B
32412	B ARMS - 73B	B ARMS - 73B	B ARMS - 73B	B ARMS - 73B	B ARMS - 73B	B ARMS - 73B	B ARMS - 73B
32413	NORWOOD JCN - 75C	NORWOOD JCN - 75C	NORWOOD JCN - 75C	NORWOOD JCN - 75C	NORWOOD JCN - 75C	NORWOOD JCN - 75C	NORWOOD JCN - 75C
32414	NORWOOD JCN - 75C	NORWOOD JCN - 75C	NORWOOD JCN - 75C	NORWOOD JCN - 75C	NORWOOD JCN - 75C	NORWOOD JCN - 75C	NORWOOD JCN - 75C
32415	B ARMS - 73B	B ARMS - 73B	B ARMS - 73B	B ARMS - 73B	B ARMS - 73B	B ARMS - 73B	B ARMS - 73B
32416	NORWOOD JCN - 75C	NORWOOD JCN - 75C	NORWOOD JCN - 75C	NORWOOD JCN - 75C	NORWOOD JCN - 75C	NORWOOD JCN - 75C	NORWOOD JCN - 75C
32417	NORWOOD JCN - 75C	NORWOOD JCN - 75C	NORWOOD JCN - 75C	NORWOOD JCN - 75C	NORWOOD JCN - 75C	NORWOOD JCN - 75C	NORWOOD JCN - 75C
32418	NORWOOD JCN - 75C	NORWOOD JCN - 75C	NORWOOD JCN - 75C	NORWOOD JCN - 75C	NORWOOD JCN - 75C	NORWOOD JCN - 75C	NORWOOD JCN - 75C
			E6X 0-6-2T (1911)				
32407	NORWOOD JCN - 75C	NORWOOD JCN - 75C	NORWOOD JCN - 75C	NORWOOD JCN - 75C	NORWOOD JCN - 75C	NORWOOD JCN - 75C	NORWOOD JCN - 75C
32411	NORWOOD JCN - 75C	NORWOOD JCN - 75C	NORWOOD JCN - 75C	NORWOOD JCN - 75C	NORWOOD JCN - 75C	NORWOOD JCN - 75C	NORWOOD JCN - 75C
			G16 4-8-0T (1921)				
30492	FELTHAM - 70B	FELTHAM - 70B	FELTHAM - 70B	FELTHAM - 70B	FELTHAM - 70B	FELTHAM - 70B	FELTHAM - 70B
30493	FELTHAM - 70B	FELTHAM - 70B	FELTHAM - 70B	FELTHAM - 70B	FELTHAM - 70B	FELTHAM - 70B	FELTHAM - 70B
30494	FELTHAM - 70B	FELTHAM - 70B	FELTHAM - 70B	FELTHAM - 70B	FELTHAM - 70B	FELTHAM - 70B	FELTHAM - 70B
30495	FELTHAM - 70B	FELTHAM - 70B	FELTHAM - 70B	FELTHAM - 70B	FELTHAM - 70B	FELTHAM - 70B	FELTHAM - 70B
			K 2-6-0 (1913)				
32337	BRIGHTON - 75A	BRIGHTON - 75A	BRIGHTON - 75A	BRIGHTON - 75A	BRIGHTON - 75A	BRIGHTON - 75A	FRATTON - 70F
32338	BRIGHTON - 75A	BRIGHTON - 75A	BRIGHTON - 75A	BRIGHTON - 75A	BRIGHTON - 75A	BRIGHTON - 75A	BRIGHTON - 75A
32339	BRIGHTON - 75A	BRIGHTON - 75A	BRIGHTON - 75A	BRIGHTON - 75A	BRIGHTON - 75A	BRIGHTON - 75A	BRIGHTON - 75A
32340	BRIGHTON - 75A	BRIGHTON - 75A	BRIGHTON - 75A	BRIGHTON - 75A	BRIGHTON - 75A	BRIGHTON - 75A	BRIGHTON - 75A
32341	BRIGHTON - 75A	BRIGHTON - 75A	BRIGHTON - 75A	BRIGHTON - 75A	BRIGHTON - 75A	BRIGHTON - 75A	BRIGHTON - 75A
32342	BRIGHTON - 75A	BRIGHTON - 75A	BRIGHTON - 75A	BRIGHTON - 75A	BRIGHTON - 75A	BRIGHTON - 75A	BRIGHTON - 75A
32343	BRIGHTON - 75A	BRIGHTON - 75A	BRIGHTON - 75A	BRIGHTON - 75A	BRIGHTON - 75A	FRATTON - 70F	BRIGHTON - 75A
32344	BRIGHTON - 75A	BRIGHTON - 75A	BRIGHTON - 75A	BRIGHTON - 75A	THREE BRIDGES - 75E	THREE BRIDGES - 75E	THREE BRIDGES - 75E
32345	BRIGHTON - 75A	BRIGHTON - 75A	BRIGHTON - 75A	BRIGHTON - 75A	BRIGHTON - 75A	BRIGHTON - 75A	BRIGHTON - 75A
32346	BRIGHTON - 75A	BRIGHTON - 75A	BRIGHTON - 75A	BRIGHTON - 75A	BRIGHTON - 75A	BRIGHTON - 75A	BRIGHTON - 75A
32347	THREE BRIDGES - 75E	THREE BRIDGES - 75E	THREE BRIDGES - 75E	THREE BRIDGES - 75E	THREE BRIDGES - 75E	THREE BRIDGES - 75E	THREE BRIDGES - 75E
32348	THREE BRIDGES - 75E	THREE BRIDGES - 75E	THREE BRIDGES - 75E	THREE BRIDGES - 75E	THREE BRIDGES - 75E	THREE BRIDGES - 75E	THREE BRIDGES - 75E
32349	FRATTON - 71D	FRATTON - 71D	FRATTON - 71D	FRATTON - 71D	FRATTON - 71D	FRATTON - 70F	FRATTON - 70F
32350	THREE BRIDGES - 75E	THREE BRIDGES - 75E	THREE BRIDGES - 75E	THREE BRIDGES - 75E	THREE BRIDGES - 75E	THREE BRIDGES - 75E	THREE BRIDGES - 75E
32351	THREE BRIDGES - 75E	THREE BRIDGES - 75E	THREE BRIDGES - 75E	THREE BRIDGES - 75E	THREE BRIDGES - 75E	THREE BRIDGES - 75E	THREE BRIDGES - 75E
32352	THREE BRIDGES - 75E	THREE BRIDGES - 75E	THREE BRIDGES - 75E	THREE BRIDGES - 75E	THREE BRIDGES - 75E	THREE BRIDGES - 75E	THREE BRIDGES - 75E
32353	THREE BRIDGES - 75E	THREE BRIDGES - 75E	THREE BRIDGES - 75E	THREE BRIDGES - 75E	THREE BRIDGES - 75E	THREE BRIDGES - 75E	THREE BRIDGES - 75E
			U 2-6-0 (R/B 2-6-4T) 1928				
31790	YEOVIL- 72C	YEOVIL- 72C	YEOVIL- 72C	YEOVIL- 72C	YEOVIL- 72C	YEOVIL- 72C	YEOVIL- 72C
31791	YEOVIL- 72C	YEOVIL- 72C	YEOVIL- 72C	YEOVIL- 72C	YEOVIL- 72C	YEOVIL- 72C	YEOVIL- 72C
31792	YEOVIL- 72C	YEOVIL- 72C	YEOVIL- 72C	YEOVIL- 72C	YEOVIL- 72C	YEOVIL- 72C	YEOVIL- 72C
31793	YEOVIL- 72C	YEOVIL- 72C	YEOVIL- 72C	YEOVIL- 72C	YEOVIL- 72C	YEOVIL- 72C	YEOVIL- 72C
31794	YEOVIL- 72C	YEOVIL- 72C	YEOVIL- 72C	YEOVIL- 72C	YEOVIL- 72C	YEOVIL- 72C	YEOVIL- 72C
31795	YEOVIL- 72C	YEOVIL- 72C	YEOVIL- 72C	YEOVIL- 72C	YEOVIL- 72C	YEOVIL- 72C	YEOVIL- 72C
31796	YEOVIL- 72C	YEOVIL- 72C	YEOVIL- 72C	YEOVIL- 72C	YEOVIL- 72C	YEOVIL- 72C	YEOVIL- 72C
31797	GUILDFORD - 70C	GUILDFORD - 70C	GUILDFORD - 70C	GUILDFORD - 70C	GUILDFORD - 70C	GUILDFORD - 70C	GUILDFORD - 70C
31798	GUILDFORD - 70C	GUILDFORD - 70C	GUILDFORD - 70C	GUILDFORD - 70C	GUILDFORD - 70C	GUILDFORD - 70C	GUILDFORD - 70C
31799	GUILDFORD - 70C	GUILDFORD - 70C	GUILDFORD - 70C	GUILDFORD - 70C	GUILDFORD - 70C	GUILDFORD - 70C	GUILDFORD - 70C
31800	GUILDFORD - 70C	GUILDFORD - 70C	GUILDFORD - 70C	GUILDFORD - 70C	GUILDFORD - 70C	GUILDFORD - 70C	GUILDFORD - 70C
31801	EASTLEIGH - 71A	EASTLEIGH - 71A	EASTLEIGH - 71A	EASTLEIGH - 71A	EASTLEIGH - 71A	EASTLEIGH - 71A	EASTLEIGH - 71A
31802	GUILDFORD - 70C	GUILDFORD - 70C	GUILDFORD - 70C	FAVERSHAM - 73E	FAVERSHAM - 73E	FAVERSHAM - 73E	FAVERSHAM - 73E
31803	HITHER GREEN - 73C	HITHER GREEN - 73C	HITHER GREEN - 73C	HITHER GREEN - 73C	HITHER GREEN - 73C	HITHER GREEN - 73C	HITHER GREEN - 73C
31804	HITHER GREEN - 73C	HITHER GREEN - 73C	HITHER GREEN - 73C	HITHER GREEN - 73C	HITHER GREEN - 73C	HITHER GREEN - 73C	HITHER GREEN - 73C
31805	REDHILL- 75B	REDHILL- 75B	REDHILL- 75B	REDHILL- 75B	REDHILL- 75B	REDHILL- 75B	REDHILL- 75B
31806	FAVERSHAM - 73E	FAVERSHAM - 73E	FAVERSHAM - 73E	FAVERSHAM - 73E	FAVERSHAM - 73E	NINE ELMS - 70A	NINE ELMS - 70A
31807	FRATTON - 71D	FRATTON - 71D	FRATTON - 71D	FRATTON - 71D	FRATTON - 71D	FRATTON - 70F	FRATTON - 70F
31808	FRATTON - 71D	FRATTON - 71D	FRATTON - 71D	FRATTON - 71D	FRATTON - 71D	FRATTON - 70F	FRATTON - 70F
31809	FRATTON - 71D	FRATTON - 71D	FRATTON - 71D	FRATTON - 71D	FRATTON - 71D	FRATTON - 70F	FRATTON - 70F

loco	Feb-55	Apr-55	Jun-55	Aug-55	Sep-55	Nov-55	Dec-55
			E4X 0-6-2T (1909)				
32466	NORWOOD JCN - 75C	NORWOOD JCN - 75C	NORWOOD JCN - 75C	NORWOOD JCN - 75C	NORWOOD JCN - 75C	NORWOOD JCN - 75C	NORWOOD JCN - 75C
32477	NORWOOD JCN - 75C	NORWOOD JCN - 75C	NORWOOD JCN - 75C	NORWOOD JCN - 75C	NORWOOD JCN - 75C	NORWOOD JCN - 75C	NORWOOD JCN - 75C
32478	NORWOOD JCN - 75C	NORWOOD JCN - 75C	NORWOOD JCN - 75C	NORWOOD JCN - 75C	NORWOOD JCN - 75C	NORWOOD JCN - 75C	NORWOOD JCN - 75C
32489	NORWOOD JCN - 75C	NORWOOD JCN - 75C	W/D	W/D	W/D	W/D	W/D
			E5 0-6-2T (1902)				
32571	NORWOOD JCN - 75C	NORWOOD JCN - 75C	NORWOOD JCN - 75C	NORWOOD JCN - 75C	NORWOOD JCN - 75C	NORWOOD JCN - 75C	NORWOOD JCN - 75C
32583	BASINGSTOKE - 70D	BASINGSTOKE - 70D	BASINGSTOKE - 70D	BASINGSTOKE - 70D	BASINGSTOKE - 70D	BASINGSTOKE - 70D	BASINGSTOKE - 70D
32593	DOVER - 74C	DOVER - 74C	DOVER - 74C	DOVER - 74C	DOVER - 74C	DOVER - 74C	DOVER - 74C
			E5X 0-6-2T (1911)				
32570	BRIGHTON - 75A	BRIGHTON - 75A	BRIGHTON - 75A	BRIGHTON - 75A	BRIGHTON - 75A	BRIGHTON - 75A	BRIGHTON - 75A
32576	BRIGHTON - 75A	BRIGHTON - 75A	W/D	W/D	W/D	W/D	W/D
32586	BRIGHTON - 75A	W/D	W/D	W/D	W/D	W/D	W/D
			E6 0-6-2T (1904)				
32408	B ARMS - 73B	B ARMS - 73B	B ARMS - 73B	B ARMS - 73B	B ARMS - 73B	B ARMS - 73B	B ARMS - 73B
32409	EASTLEIGH - 71A	EASTLEIGH - 71A	EASTLEIGH - 71A	EASTLEIGH - 71A	EASTLEIGH - 71A	EASTLEIGH - 71A	EASTLEIGH - 71A
32410	B ARMS - 73B	B ARMS - 73B	B ARMS - 73B	B ARMS - 73B	B ARMS - 73B	B ARMS - 73B	B ARMS - 73B
32412	B ARMS - 73B	B ARMS - 73B	B ARMS - 73B	B ARMS - 73B	B ARMS - 73B	B ARMS - 73B	B ARMS - 73B
32413	NORWOOD JCN - 75C	NORWOOD JCN - 75C	NORWOOD JCN - 75C	NORWOOD JCN - 75C	NORWOOD JCN - 75C	NORWOOD JCN - 75C	NORWOOD JCN - 75C
32414	NORWOOD JCN - 75C	NORWOOD JCN - 75C	NORWOOD JCN - 75C	NORWOOD JCN - 75C	NORWOOD JCN - 75C	NORWOOD JCN - 75C	NORWOOD JCN - 75C
32415	B ARMS - 73B	B ARMS - 73B	B ARMS - 73B	B ARMS - 73B	B ARMS - 73B	B ARMS - 73B	B ARMS - 73B
32416	NORWOOD JCN - 75C	NORWOOD JCN - 75C	NORWOOD JCN - 75C	NORWOOD JCN - 75C	NORWOOD JCN - 75C	NORWOOD JCN - 75C	NORWOOD JCN - 75C
32417	NORWOOD JCN - 75C	NORWOOD JCN - 75C	NORWOOD JCN - 75C	NORWOOD JCN - 75C	NORWOOD JCN - 75C	NORWOOD JCN - 75C	NORWOOD JCN - 75C
32418	NORWOOD JCN - 75C	NORWOOD JCN - 75C	NORWOOD JCN - 75C	NORWOOD JCN - 75C	NORWOOD JCN - 75C	NORWOOD JCN - 75C	NORWOOD JCN - 75C
			E6X 0-6-2T (1911)				
32407	NORWOOD JCN - 75C	NORWOOD JCN - 75C	NORWOOD JCN - 75C	NORWOOD JCN - 75C	NORWOOD JCN - 75C	NORWOOD JCN - 75C	NORWOOD JCN - 75C
32411	NORWOOD JCN - 75C	NORWOOD JCN - 75C	NORWOOD JCN - 75C	NORWOOD JCN - 75C	NORWOOD JCN - 75C	NORWOOD JCN - 75C	NORWOOD JCN - 75C
			G16 4-8-0T (1921)				
30492	FELTHAM - 70B	FELTHAM - 70B	FELTHAM - 70B	FELTHAM - 70B	FELTHAM - 70B	FELTHAM - 70B	FELTHAM - 70B
30493	FELTHAM - 70B	FELTHAM - 70B	FELTHAM - 70B	FELTHAM - 70B	FELTHAM - 70B	FELTHAM - 70B	FELTHAM - 70B
30494	FELTHAM - 70B	FELTHAM - 70B	FELTHAM - 70B	FELTHAM - 70B	FELTHAM - 70B	FELTHAM - 70B	FELTHAM - 70B
30495	FELTHAM - 70B	FELTHAM - 70B	FELTHAM - 70B	FELTHAM - 70B	FELTHAM - 70B	FELTHAM - 70B	FELTHAM - 70B
			K 2-6-0 (1913)				
32337	FRATTON - 70F	FRATTON - 70F	FRATTON - 70F	FRATTON - 70F	FRATTON - 70F	FRATTON - 70F	FRATTON - 70F
32338	BRIGHTON - 75A	BRIGHTON - 75A	BRIGHTON - 75A	BRIGHTON - 75A	BRIGHTON - 75A	BRIGHTON - 75A	BRIGHTON - 75A
32339	BRIGHTON - 75A	BRIGHTON - 75A	BRIGHTON - 75A	BRIGHTON - 75A	BRIGHTON - 75A	BRIGHTON - 75A	BRIGHTON - 75A
32340	BRIGHTON - 75A	BRIGHTON - 75A	BRIGHTON - 75A	BRIGHTON - 75A	BRIGHTON - 75A	BRIGHTON - 75A	BRIGHTON - 75A
32341	BRIGHTON - 75A	BRIGHTON - 75A	BRIGHTON - 75A	BRIGHTON - 75A	BRIGHTON - 75A	BRIGHTON - 75A	BRIGHTON - 75A
32342	BRIGHTON - 75A	BRIGHTON - 75A	BRIGHTON - 75A	BRIGHTON - 75A	BRIGHTON - 75A	BRIGHTON - 75A	BRIGHTON - 75A
32343	BRIGHTON - 75A	BRIGHTON - 75A	BRIGHTON - 75A	BRIGHTON - 75A	BRIGHTON - 75A	BRIGHTON - 75A	BRIGHTON - 75A
32344	THREE BRIDGES - 75E	THREE BRIDGES - 75E	THREE BRIDGES - 75E	THREE BRIDGES - 75E	THREE BRIDGES - 75E	THREE BRIDGES - 75E	THREE BRIDGES - 75E
32345	BRIGHTON - 75A	BRIGHTON - 75A	BRIGHTON - 75A	BRIGHTON - 75A	BRIGHTON - 75A	BRIGHTON - 75A	BRIGHTON - 75A
32346	BRIGHTON - 75A	BRIGHTON - 75A	BRIGHTON - 75A	BRIGHTON - 75A	BRIGHTON - 75A	BRIGHTON - 75A	BRIGHTON - 75A
32347	THREE BRIDGES - 75E	THREE BRIDGES - 75E	THREE BRIDGES - 75E	THREE BRIDGES - 75E	THREE BRIDGES - 75E	THREE BRIDGES - 75E	THREE BRIDGES - 75E
32348	THREE BRIDGES - 75E	THREE BRIDGES - 75E	THREE BRIDGES - 75E	THREE BRIDGES - 75E	THREE BRIDGES - 75E	THREE BRIDGES - 75E	THREE BRIDGES - 75E
32349	FRATTON - 70F	FRATTON - 70F	FRATTON - 70F	FRATTON - 70F	FRATTON - 70F	FRATTON - 70F	FRATTON - 70F
32350	THREE BRIDGES - 75E	THREE BRIDGES - 75E	THREE BRIDGES - 75E	THREE BRIDGES - 75E	THREE BRIDGES - 75E	THREE BRIDGES - 75E	THREE BRIDGES - 75E
32351	THREE BRIDGES - 75E	THREE BRIDGES - 75E	THREE BRIDGES - 75E	THREE BRIDGES - 75E	THREE BRIDGES - 75E	THREE BRIDGES - 75E	THREE BRIDGES - 75E
32352	THREE BRIDGES - 75E	THREE BRIDGES - 75E	THREE BRIDGES - 75E	THREE BRIDGES - 75E	THREE BRIDGES - 75E	THREE BRIDGES - 75E	THREE BRIDGES - 75E
32353	THREE BRIDGES - 75E	THREE BRIDGES - 75E	THREE BRIDGES - 75E	THREE BRIDGES - 75E	THREE BRIDGES - 75E	THREE BRIDGES - 75E	THREE BRIDGES - 75E
			U 2-6-0 (R/B 2-6-4T) 1928				
31790	YEOVIL - 72C	YEOVIL - 72C	YEOVIL - 72C	YEOVIL - 72C	YEOVIL - 72C	YEOVIL - 72C	YEOVIL - 72C
31791	YEOVIL - 72C	YEOVIL - 72C	YEOVIL - 72C	YEOVIL - 72C	YEOVIL - 72C	YEOVIL - 72C	YEOVIL - 72C
31792	YEOVIL - 72C	YEOVIL - 72C	YEOVIL - 72C	YEOVIL - 72C	YEOVIL - 72C	YEOVIL - 72C	YEOVIL - 72C
31793	YEOVIL - 72C	YEOVIL - 72C	YEOVIL - 72C	YEOVIL - 72C	YEOVIL - 72C	YEOVIL - 72C	YEOVIL - 72C
31794	YEOVIL - 72C	YEOVIL - 72C	YEOVIL - 72C	YEOVIL - 72C	YEOVIL - 72C	YEOVIL - 72C	YEOVIL - 72C
31795	YEOVIL - 72C	YEOVIL - 72C	YEOVIL - 72C	YEOVIL - 72C	YEOVIL - 72C	YEOVIL - 72C	YEOVIL - 72C
31796	YEOVIL - 72C	YEOVIL - 72C	YEOVIL - 72C	YEOVIL - 72C	YEOVIL - 72C	YEOVIL - 72C	YEOVIL - 72C
31797	GUILDFORD - 70C	GUILDFORD - 70C	GUILDFORD - 70C	GUILDFORD - 70C	GUILDFORD - 70C	GUILDFORD - 70C	GUILDFORD - 70C
31798	GUILDFORD - 70C	GUILDFORD - 70C	GUILDFORD - 70C	GUILDFORD - 70C	GUILDFORD - 70C	GUILDFORD - 70C	GUILDFORD - 70C
31799	GUILDFORD - 70C	GUILDFORD - 70C	GUILDFORD - 70C	GUILDFORD - 70C	GUILDFORD - 70C	GUILDFORD - 70C	GUILDFORD - 70C
31800	GUILDFORD - 70C	GUILDFORD - 70C	GUILDFORD - 70C	GUILDFORD - 70C	GUILDFORD - 70C	GUILDFORD - 70C	GUILDFORD - 70C
31801	EASTLEIGH - 71A	EASTLEIGH - 71A	EASTLEIGH - 71A	EASTLEIGH - 71A	EASTLEIGH - 71A	EASTLEIGH - 71A	EASTLEIGH - 71A
31802	FAVERSHAM - 73E	FAVERSHAM - 73E	EASTLEIGH - 71A	EASTLEIGH - 71A	EASTLEIGH - 71A	EASTLEIGH - 71A	EASTLEIGH - 71A
31803	HITHER GREEN - 73C	HITHER GREEN - 73C	EASTLEIGH - 71A	EASTLEIGH - 71A	EASTLEIGH - 71A	EASTLEIGH - 71A	EASTLEIGH - 71A
31804	HITHER GREEN - 73C	HITHER GREEN - 73C	EASTLEIGH - 71A	EASTLEIGH - 71A	EASTLEIGH - 71A	EASTLEIGH - 71A	EASTLEIGH - 71A
31805	REDHILL - 75B	REDHILL - 75B	REDHILL - 75B	REDHILL - 75B	REDHILL - 75B	REDHILL - 75B	REDHILL - 75B
31806	NINE ELMS - 70A	NINE ELMS - 70A	BASINGSTOKE - 70D	BASINGSTOKE - 70D	BASINGSTOKE - 70D	BASINGSTOKE - 70D	BASINGSTOKE - 70D
31807	FRATTON - 70F	FRATTON - 70F	FRATTON - 70F	FRATTON - 70F	FRATTON - 70F	FRATTON - 70F	FRATTON - 70F
31808	FRATTON - 70F	FRATTON - 70F	FRATTON - 70F	FRATTON - 70F	FRATTON - 70F	FRATTON - 70F	FRATTON - 70F
31809	FRATTON - 70F	FRATTON - 70F	FRATTON - 70F	FRATTON - 70F	FRATTON - 70F	FRATTON - 70F	FRATTON - 70F

In spite of belonging to the first main line to be electrified, the K 2-6-0's proved to be survivors and the class remained intact until as late as 1962 working the principal goods services of the Brighton section until being withdrawn.

loco	Jan-56	Apr-56	May-56	Aug-56	Oct-56	Nov-56	Jan-57
E4X 0-6-2T (1909)							
32466	NORWOOD JCN - 75C	NORWOOD JCN - 75C	NORWOOD JCN - 75C	NORWOOD JCN - 75C	NORWOOD JCN - 75C	NORWOOD JCN - 75C	NORWOOD JCN - 75C
32477	NORWOOD JCN - 75C	NORWOOD JCN - 75C	NORWOOD JCN - 75C	NORWOOD JCN - 75C	NORWOOD JCN - 75C	NORWOOD JCN - 75C	NORWOOD JCN - 75C
32478	NORWOOD JCN - 75C	NORWOOD JCN - 75C	NORWOOD JCN - 75C	NORWOOD JCN - 75C	W/D	W/D	W/D
E6 0-6-2T (1904)							
32408	B ARMS - 73B	B ARMS - 73B	B ARMS - 73B	B ARMS - 73B	B ARMS - 73B	B ARMS - 73B	B ARMS - 73B
32409	EASTLEIGH - 71A	EASTLEIGH - 71A	EASTLEIGH - 71A	EASTLEIGH - 71A	EASTLEIGH - 71A	EASTLEIGH - 71A	EASTLEIGH - 71A
32410	B ARMS - 73B	B ARMS - 73B	B ARMS - 73B	B ARMS - 73B	B ARMS - 73B	B ARMS - 73B	B ARMS - 73B
32412	B ARMS - 73B	B ARMS - 73B	B ARMS - 73B	B ARMS - 73B	B ARMS - 73B	B ARMS - 73B	B ARMS - 73B
32413	NORWOOD JCN - 75C	NORWOOD JCN - 75C	NORWOOD JCN - 75C	NORWOOD JCN - 75C	NORWOOD JCN - 75C	NORWOOD JCN - 75C	NORWOOD JCN - 75C
32414	NORWOOD JCN - 75C	NORWOOD JCN - 75C	NORWOOD JCN - 75C	NORWOOD JCN - 75C	NORWOOD JCN - 75C	NORWOOD JCN - 75C	NORWOOD JCN - 75C
32415	B ARMS - 73B	B ARMS - 73B	B ARMS - 73B	B ARMS - 73B	B ARMS - 73B	B ARMS - 73B	B ARMS - 73B
32416	NORWOOD JCN - 75C	NORWOOD JCN - 75C	NORWOOD JCN - 75C	NORWOOD JCN - 75C	NORWOOD JCN - 75C	NORWOOD JCN - 75C	NORWOOD JCN - 75C
32417	NORWOOD JCN - 75C	NORWOOD JCN - 75C	NORWOOD JCN - 75C	NORWOOD JCN - 75C	NORWOOD JCN - 75C	NORWOOD JCN - 75C	NORWOOD JCN - 75C
32418	NORWOOD JCN - 75C	NORWOOD JCN - 75C	NORWOOD JCN - 75C	NORWOOD JCN - 75C	NORWOOD JCN - 75C	NORWOOD JCN - 75C	NORWOOD JCN - 75C
E6X 0-6-2T (1911)							
32407	NORWOOD JCN - 75C	NORWOOD JCN - 75C	NORWOOD JCN - 75C	NORWOOD JCN - 75C	NORWOOD JCN - 75C	NORWOOD JCN - 75C	NORWOOD JCN - 75C
32411	NORWOOD JCN - 75C	NORWOOD JCN - 75C	NORWOOD JCN - 75C	NORWOOD JCN - 75C	NORWOOD JCN - 75C	NORWOOD JCN - 75C	NORWOOD JCN - 75C
G16 4-8-0T (1921)							
30492	FELTHAM - 70B	FELTHAM - 70B	FELTHAM - 70B	FELTHAM - 70B	FELTHAM - 70B	FELTHAM - 70B	FELTHAM - 70B
30493	FELTHAM - 70B	FELTHAM - 70B	FELTHAM - 70B	FELTHAM - 70B	FELTHAM - 70B	FELTHAM - 70B	FELTHAM - 70B
30494	FELTHAM - 70B	FELTHAM - 70B	FELTHAM - 70B	FELTHAM - 70B	FELTHAM - 70B	FELTHAM - 70B	FELTHAM - 70B
30495	FELTHAM - 70B	FELTHAM - 70B	FELTHAM - 70B	FELTHAM - 70B	FELTHAM - 70B	FELTHAM - 70B	FELTHAM - 70B
K 2-6-0 (1913)							
32337	FRATTON - 70F	FRATTON - 70F	FRATTON - 70F	FRATTON - 70F	FRATTON - 70F	FRATTON - 70F	FRATTON - 70F
32338	BRIGHTON - 75A	BRIGHTON - 75A	BRIGHTON - 75A	BRIGHTON - 75A	BRIGHTON - 75A	BRIGHTON - 75A	BRIGHTON - 75A
32339	BRIGHTON - 75A	BRIGHTON - 75A	BRIGHTON - 75A	BRIGHTON - 75A	BRIGHTON - 75A	BRIGHTON - 75A	BRIGHTON - 75A
32340	BRIGHTON - 75A	BRIGHTON - 75A	BRIGHTON - 75A	BRIGHTON - 75A	BRIGHTON - 75A	BRIGHTON - 75A	BRIGHTON - 75A
32341	BRIGHTON - 75A	BRIGHTON - 75A	BRIGHTON - 75A	BRIGHTON - 75A	BRIGHTON - 75A	BRIGHTON - 75A	BRIGHTON - 75A
32342	BRIGHTON - 75A	BRIGHTON - 75A	BRIGHTON - 75A	BRIGHTON - 75A	BRIGHTON - 75A	BRIGHTON - 75A	BRIGHTON - 75A
32343	BRIGHTON - 75A	BRIGHTON - 75A	BRIGHTON - 75A	BRIGHTON - 75A	BRIGHTON - 75A	BRIGHTON - 75A	BRIGHTON - 75A
32344	THREE BRIDGES - 75E	THREE BRIDGES - 75E	THREE BRIDGES - 75E	THREE BRIDGES - 75E	THREE BRIDGES - 75E	THREE BRIDGES - 75E	THREE BRIDGES - 75E
32345	BRIGHTON - 75A	BRIGHTON - 75A	BRIGHTON - 75A	BRIGHTON - 75A	BRIGHTON - 75A	BRIGHTON - 75A	BRIGHTON - 75A
32346	BRIGHTON - 75A	BRIGHTON - 75A	BRIGHTON - 75A	BRIGHTON - 75A	BRIGHTON - 75A	BRIGHTON - 75A	BRIGHTON - 75A
32347	THREE BRIDGES - 75E	THREE BRIDGES - 75E	THREE BRIDGES - 75E	THREE BRIDGES - 75E	THREE BRIDGES - 75E	THREE BRIDGES - 75E	THREE BRIDGES - 75E
32348	THREE BRIDGES - 75E	THREE BRIDGES - 75E	THREE BRIDGES - 75E	THREE BRIDGES - 75E	THREE BRIDGES - 75E	THREE BRIDGES - 75E	THREE BRIDGES - 75E
32349	FRATTON - 70F	FRATTON - 70F	FRATTON - 70F	FRATTON - 70F	FRATTON - 70F	FRATTON - 70F	FRATTON - 70F
32350	THREE BRIDGES - 75E	THREE BRIDGES - 75E	THREE BRIDGES - 75E	THREE BRIDGES - 75E	THREE BRIDGES - 75E	THREE BRIDGES - 75E	THREE BRIDGES - 75E
32351	THREE BRIDGES - 75E	THREE BRIDGES - 75E	THREE BRIDGES - 75E	THREE BRIDGES - 75E	THREE BRIDGES - 75E	THREE BRIDGES - 75E	THREE BRIDGES - 75E
32352	THREE BRIDGES - 75E	THREE BRIDGES - 75E	THREE BRIDGES - 75E	THREE BRIDGES - 75E	THREE BRIDGES - 75E	THREE BRIDGES - 75E	THREE BRIDGES - 75E
32353	THREE BRIDGES - 75E	THREE BRIDGES - 75E	THREE BRIDGES - 75E	THREE BRIDGES - 75E	THREE BRIDGES - 75E	THREE BRIDGES - 75E	THREE BRIDGES - 75E
U 2-6-0 (R/B 2-6-4T) 1928							
31790	YEOVIL - 72C	YEOVIL - 72C	YEOVIL - 72C	YEOVIL - 72C	YEOVIL - 72C	YEOVIL - 72C	YEOVIL - 72C
31791	YEOVIL - 72C	YEOVIL - 72C	YEOVIL - 72C	YEOVIL - 72C	YEOVIL - 72C	YEOVIL - 72C	YEOVIL - 72C
31792	YEOVIL - 72C	YEOVIL - 72C	YEOVIL - 72C	YEOVIL - 72C	YEOVIL - 72C	YEOVIL - 72C	YEOVIL - 72C
31793	YEOVIL - 72C	YEOVIL - 72C	YEOVIL - 72C	YEOVIL - 72C	YEOVIL - 72C	YEOVIL - 72C	YEOVIL - 72C
31794	YEOVIL - 72C	YEOVIL - 72C	YEOVIL - 72C	YEOVIL - 72C	YEOVIL - 72C	YEOVIL - 72C	YEOVIL - 72C
31795	YEOVIL - 72C	YEOVIL - 72C	YEOVIL - 72C	YEOVIL - 72C	YEOVIL - 72C	YEOVIL - 72C	YEOVIL - 72C
31796	YEOVIL - 72C	YEOVIL - 72C	YEOVIL - 72C	YEOVIL - 72C	YEOVIL - 72C	YEOVIL - 72C	YEOVIL - 72C
31797	GUILDFORD - 70C	GUILDFORD - 70C	GUILDFORD - 70C	GUILDFORD - 70C	GUILDFORD - 70C	GUILDFORD - 70C	GUILDFORD - 70C
31798	GUILDFORD - 70C	GUILDFORD - 70C	GUILDFORD - 70C	GUILDFORD - 70C	GUILDFORD - 70C	GUILDFORD - 70C	GUILDFORD - 70C
31799	GUILDFORD - 70C	GUILDFORD - 70C	GUILDFORD - 70C	GUILDFORD - 70C	GUILDFORD - 70C	GUILDFORD - 70C	GUILDFORD - 70C
31800	GUILDFORD - 70C	GUILDFORD - 70C	GUILDFORD - 70C	GUILDFORD - 70C	GUILDFORD - 70C	GUILDFORD - 70C	GUILDFORD - 70C
31801	EASTLEIGH - 71A	EASTLEIGH - 71A	EASTLEIGH - 71A	EASTLEIGH - 71A	EASTLEIGH - 71A	EASTLEIGH - 71A	EASTLEIGH - 71A
31802	EASTLEIGH - 71A	EASTLEIGH - 71A	EASTLEIGH - 71A	EASTLEIGH - 71A	EASTLEIGH - 71A	EASTLEIGH - 71A	EASTLEIGH - 71A
31803	EASTLEIGH - 71A	EASTLEIGH - 71A	EASTLEIGH - 71A	EASTLEIGH - 71A	EASTLEIGH - 71A	EASTLEIGH - 71A	EASTLEIGH - 71A
31804	EASTLEIGH - 71A	EASTLEIGH - 71A	EXMOUTH JCN - 72A	EXMOUTH JCN - 72A	EXMOUTH JCN - 72A	EXMOUTH JCN - 72A	FRATTON - 70F
31805	REDHILL - 75B	REDHILL - 75B	REDHILL - 75B	REDHILL - 75B	REDHILL - 75B	REDHILL - 75B	REDHILL - 75B
31806	BASINGSTOKE - 70D	BASINGSTOKE - 70D	BASINGSTOKE - 70D	BASINGSTOKE - 70D	BASINGSTOKE - 70D	BASINGSTOKE - 70D	BASINGSTOKE - 70D
31807	FRATTON - 70F	FRATTON - 70F	FRATTON - 70F	FRATTON - 70F	FRATTON - 70F	FRATTON - 70F	FRATTON - 70F
31808	FRATTON - 70F	FRATTON - 70F	FRATTON - 70F	FRATTON - 70F	FRATTON - 70F	FRATTON - 70F	FRATTON - 70F
31809	FRATTON - 70F	FRATTON - 70F	FRATTON - 70F	FRATTON - 70F	FRATTON - 70F	FRATTON - 70F	FRATTON - 70F

The E5X 0-6-2T's were very handsome engines but being outclassed by the imported LM and BR 2-6-4 tanks, had very little work to perform. At one point all four engines were allocated to Horsham yet not one of the thirteen daily diagrams from that shed included work for an E5X. 32586 stands with E3 0-6-2T 32169 at Eastleigh in 1951.

loco	Mar-57	Jun-57	Jul-57	Oct-57	Jan-58	Feb-58	Mar-58
E4X 0-6-2T (1909)							
32466	NORWOOD JCN - 75C	NORWOOD JCN - 75C	NORWOOD JCN - 75C	NORWOOD JCN - 75C	NORWOOD JCN - 75C	NORWOOD JCN - 75C	NORWOOD JCN - 75C
32477	NORWOOD JCN - 75C	NORWOOD JCN - 75C	NORWOOD JCN - 75C	NORWOOD JCN - 75C	NORWOOD JCN - 75C	NORWOOD JCN - 75C	NORWOOD JCN - 75C
E6 0-6-2T (1904)							
32408	B ARMS - 73B	B ARMS - 73B	B ARMS - 73B		B ARMS - 73B	B ARMS - 73B	B ARMS - 73B
32409	EASTLEIGH - 71A	EASTLEIGH - 71A	EASTLEIGH - 71A	EASTLEIGH - 71A	W/D	W/D	W/D
32410	B ARMS - 73B	B ARMS - 73B	B ARMS - 73B	B ARMS - 73B	B ARMS - 73B	B ARMS - 73B	B ARMS - 73B
32412	B ARMS - 73B	B ARMS - 73B	B ARMS - 73B	W/D	W/D	W/D	W/D
32413	NORWOOD JCN - 75C	NORWOOD JCN - 75C	NORWOOD JCN - 75C	NORWOOD JCN - 75C	B ARMS - 73B	NORWOOD JCN - 75C	NORWOOD JCN - 75C
32414	NORWOOD JCN - 75C	NORWOOD JCN - 75C	NORWOOD JCN - 75C	NORWOOD JCN - 75C	B ARMS - 73B	B ARMS - 73B	B ARMS - 73B
32415	B ARMS - 73B	B ARMS - 73B	B ARMS - 73B	B ARMS - 73B	B ARMS - 73B	B ARMS - 73B	B ARMS - 73B
32416	NORWOOD JCN - 75C	NORWOOD JCN - 75C	NORWOOD JCN - 75C	NORWOOD JCN - 75C	NORWOOD JCN - 75C	NORWOOD JCN - 75C	NORWOOD JCN - 75C
32417	NORWOOD JCN - 75C	NORWOOD JCN - 75C	NORWOOD JCN - 75C	B ARMS - 73B	B ARMS - 73B	B ARMS - 73B	B ARMS - 73B
32418	NORWOOD JCN - 75C	NORWOOD JCN - 75C	NORWOOD JCN - 75C	NORWOOD JCN - 75C	NORWOOD JCN - 75C	NORWOOD JCN - 75C	NORWOOD JCN - 75C
E6X 0-6-2T (1911)							
32407	NORWOOD JCN - 75C	NORWOOD JCN - 75C	NORWOOD JCN - 75C	NORWOOD JCN - 75C	W/D	W/D	W/D
32411	NORWOOD JCN - 75C	NORWOOD JCN - 75C	NORWOOD JCN - 75C	NORWOOD JCN - 75C	NORWOOD JCN - 75C	NORWOOD JCN - 75C	NORWOOD JCN - 75C
G16 4-8-0T (1921)							
30492	FELTHAM - 70B	FELTHAM - 70B	FELTHAM - 70B	FELTHAM - 70B	FELTHAM - 70B	FELTHAM - 70B	FELTHAM - 70B
30493	FELTHAM - 70B	FELTHAM - 70B	FELTHAM - 70B	FELTHAM - 70B	FELTHAM - 70B	FELTHAM - 70B	FELTHAM - 70B
30494	FELTHAM - 70B	FELTHAM - 70B	FELTHAM - 70B	FELTHAM - 70B	FELTHAM - 70B	FELTHAM - 70B	FELTHAM - 70B
30495	FELTHAM - 70B	FELTHAM - 70B	FELTHAM - 70B	FELTHAM - 70B	FELTHAM - 70B	FELTHAM - 70B	FELTHAM - 70B
K 2-6-0 (1913)							
32337	FRATTON - 70F	FRATTON - 70F	FRATTON - 70F	FRATTON - 70F	FRATTON - 70F	FRATTON - 70F	FRATTON - 70F
32338	BRIGHTON - 75A	BRIGHTON - 75A	BRIGHTON - 75A	BRIGHTON - 75A	BRIGHTON - 75A	BRIGHTON - 75A	BRIGHTON - 75A
32339	BRIGHTON - 75A	BRIGHTON - 75A	BRIGHTON - 75A	BRIGHTON - 75A	BRIGHTON - 75A	BRIGHTON - 75A	BRIGHTON - 75A
32340	BRIGHTON - 75A	BRIGHTON - 75A	BRIGHTON - 75A	BRIGHTON - 75A	BRIGHTON - 75A	BRIGHTON - 75A	BRIGHTON - 75A
32341	BRIGHTON - 75A	BRIGHTON - 75A	BRIGHTON - 75A	BRIGHTON - 75A	BRIGHTON - 75A	BRIGHTON - 75A	BRIGHTON - 75A
32342	BRIGHTON - 75A	BRIGHTON - 75A	BRIGHTON - 75A	BRIGHTON - 75A	BRIGHTON - 75A	BRIGHTON - 75A	BRIGHTON - 75A
32343	BRIGHTON - 75A	BRIGHTON - 75A	BRIGHTON - 75A	BRIGHTON - 75A	BRIGHTON - 75A	BRIGHTON - 75A	BRIGHTON - 75A
32344	THREE BRIDGES - 75E	THREE BRIDGES - 75E	THREE BRIDGES - 75E	THREE BRIDGES - 75E	THREE BRIDGES - 75E	THREE BRIDGES - 75E	THREE BRIDGES - 75E
32345	BRIGHTON - 75A	BRIGHTON - 75A	BRIGHTON - 75A	BRIGHTON - 75A	BRIGHTON - 75A	BRIGHTON - 75A	BRIGHTON - 75A
32346	BRIGHTON - 75A	BRIGHTON - 75A	BRIGHTON - 75A	BRIGHTON - 75A	BRIGHTON - 75A	BRIGHTON - 75A	BRIGHTON - 75A
32347	THREE BRIDGES - 75E	THREE BRIDGES - 75E	THREE BRIDGES - 75E	THREE BRIDGES - 75E	THREE BRIDGES - 75E	THREE BRIDGES - 75E	THREE BRIDGES - 75E
32348	THREE BRIDGES - 75E	THREE BRIDGES - 75E	THREE BRIDGES - 75E	THREE BRIDGES - 75E	THREE BRIDGES - 75E	THREE BRIDGES - 75E	THREE BRIDGES - 75E
32349	FRATTON - 70F	FRATTON - 70F	FRATTON - 70F	FRATTON - 70F	FRATTON - 70F	FRATTON - 70F	FRATTON - 70F
32350	THREE BRIDGES - 75E	THREE BRIDGES - 75E	THREE BRIDGES - 75E	THREE BRIDGES - 75E	THREE BRIDGES - 75E	THREE BRIDGES - 75E	THREE BRIDGES - 75E
32351	THREE BRIDGES - 75E	THREE BRIDGES - 75E	THREE BRIDGES - 75E	THREE BRIDGES - 75E	THREE BRIDGES - 75E	THREE BRIDGES - 75E	THREE BRIDGES - 75E
32352	THREE BRIDGES - 75E	THREE BRIDGES - 75E	THREE BRIDGES - 75E	THREE BRIDGES - 75E	THREE BRIDGES - 75E	THREE BRIDGES - 75E	THREE BRIDGES - 75E
32353	THREE BRIDGES - 75E	THREE BRIDGES - 75E	THREE BRIDGES - 75E	THREE BRIDGES - 75E	THREE BRIDGES - 75E	THREE BRIDGES - 75E	THREE BRIDGES - 75E
U 2-6-0 (R/B 2-6-4T) 1928							
31790	YEOVIL - 72C	YEOVIL - 72C	YEOVIL - 72C	YEOVIL - 72C	YEOVIL - 72C	YEOVIL - 72C	YEOVIL - 72C
31791	YEOVIL - 72C	YEOVIL - 72C	YEOVIL - 72C	YEOVIL - 72C	YEOVIL - 72C	YEOVIL - 72C	YEOVIL - 72C
31792	YEOVIL - 72C	YEOVIL - 72C	YEOVIL - 72C	YEOVIL - 72C	YEOVIL - 72C	YEOVIL - 72C	YEOVIL - 72C
31793	YEOVIL - 72C	YEOVIL - 72C	YEOVIL - 72C	YEOVIL - 72C	YEOVIL - 72C	YEOVIL - 72C	YEOVIL - 72C
31794	YEOVIL - 72C	YEOVIL - 72C	YEOVIL - 72C	YEOVIL - 72C	YEOVIL - 72C	YEOVIL - 72C	YEOVIL - 72C
31795	YEOVIL - 72C	YEOVIL - 72C	YEOVIL - 72C	YEOVIL - 72C	YEOVIL - 72C	YEOVIL - 72C	YEOVIL - 72C
31796	YEOVIL - 72C	YEOVIL - 72C	YEOVIL - 72C	YEOVIL - 72C	YEOVIL - 72C	YEOVIL - 72C	YEOVIL - 72C
31797	GUILDFORD - 70C	GUILDFORD - 70C	GUILDFORD - 70C	GUILDFORD - 70C	GUILDFORD - 70C	GUILDFORD - 70C	GUILDFORD - 70C
31798	GUILDFORD - 70C	GUILDFORD - 70C	GUILDFORD - 70C	GUILDFORD - 70C	GUILDFORD - 70C	GUILDFORD - 70C	GUILDFORD - 70C
31799	GUILDFORD - 70C	GUILDFORD - 70C	GUILDFORD - 70C	GUILDFORD - 70C	GUILDFORD - 70C	GUILDFORD - 70C	GUILDFORD - 70C
31800	GUILDFORD - 70C	GUILDFORD - 70C	GUILDFORD - 70C	GUILDFORD - 70C	GUILDFORD - 70C	GUILDFORD - 70C	GUILDFORD - 70C
31801	EASTLEIGH - 71A	EASTLEIGH - 71A	EASTLEIGH - 71A	EASTLEIGH - 71A	EASTLEIGH - 71A	EASTLEIGH - 71A	EASTLEIGH - 71A
31802	EASTLEIGH - 71A	EASTLEIGH - 71A	EASTLEIGH - 71A	EASTLEIGH - 71A	EASTLEIGH - 71A	EASTLEIGH - 71A	EASTLEIGH - 71A
31803	EASTLEIGH - 71A	EASTLEIGH - 71A	EASTLEIGH - 71A	EASTLEIGH - 71A	EASTLEIGH - 71A	EASTLEIGH - 71A	EASTLEIGH - 71A
31804	FRATTON - 70F	FRATTON - 70F	FRATTON - 70F	FRATTON - 70F	FRATTON - 70F	FRATTON - 70F	FRATTON - 70F
31805	REDHILL - 75B	REDHILL - 75B	REDHILL - 75B	REDHILL - 75B	REDHILL - 75B	REDHILL - 75B	REDHILL - 75B
31806	BASINGSTOKE - 70D	BASINGSTOKE - 70D	BASINGSTOKE - 70D	BASINGSTOKE - 70D	BASINGSTOKE - 70D	BASINGSTOKE - 70D	BASINGSTOKE - 70D
31807	FRATTON - 70F	FRATTON - 70F	FRATTON - 70F	FRATTON - 70F	FRATTON - 70F	FRATTON - 70F	FRATTON - 70F
31808	FRATTON - 70F	FRATTON - 70F	FRATTON - 70F	FRATTON - 70F	FRATTON - 70F	FRATTON - 70F	FRATTON - 70F
31809	FRATTON - 70F	FRATTON - 70F	FRATTON - 70F	FRATTON - 70F	FRATTON - 70F	FRATTON - 70F	FRATTON - 70F

The four E4X 0-6-2T's were produced in an attempt to improve the E4 class through the fitting of a larger boiler and although the rebuilt engines were never returned to their original state, the difference in performance was insufficient to justify any further modifications. Unlike the original engines which worked both passenger and goods services, the rebuilds were allocated to Norwood Junction where one of the class shunted the down yard and another worked local goods services to Coulsden and Waddon Marsh. Eventually the arrival of diesel shunters at Norwood saw to their extinction.

The E5 0-6-2T's were another - and more successful - development of the E4 class designed for duties on the longer distance stopping trains between London and the South Coast. Although surviving to nationalisation in large numbers - only two were withdrawn by the Southern Railway - many of the class were in poor mechanical order and fell prey to the post-nationalisation influx of LMS and BR standard tanks. A small number found their way to Basingstoke where they found ready acceptance as yard shunters whilst another was sent to Dover MPD as a static shed heater. As with the E4 class, four E5 0-6-2T's were reboilered to become E5X's.

The E6 0-6-2T's were an improved freight version of the E5 class and remained on goods workings for the span of their lives, operating chiefly in the London (LBSCR) area although several were allocated to Eastleigh for workings on the Totton - Fawley branch. Originally it was intended to produce two of the engines as 0-8-0T's for shunting the yards at Brighton and London but at the last minute the order was rescinded since weight restrictions would have prevented the eight coupled engines from being able to work on the main line. Two of the class however were reboilered and classified E6X.

The G16 4-8-0T's were essentially eight coupled versions of the H16 4-6-2T class for use as hump shunters in the up and down yards at Feltham, two of the four engines working 24-hour shifts at a time. They were eventually replaced with 350hp diesel shunting 0-6-0's.

loco	May-58	Oct-58	Mar-59	Jun-59	Jul-59	Aug-59	Oct-59
			E4X 0-6-2T (1909)				
32466	NORWOOD JCN - 75C	NORWOOD JCN - 75C	W/D	W/D	W/D	W/D	W/D
32477	NORWOOD JCN - 75C	NORWOOD JCN - 75C	W/D	W/D	W/D	W/D	W/D
			E6 0-6-2T (1904)				
32408	B ARMS - 73B	B ARMS - 73B	B ARMS - 73B	B ARMS - 73B	B ARMS - 73B	B ARMS - 73B	B ARMS - 73B
32410	B ARMS - 73B	B ARMS - 73B	B ARMS - 73B	B ARMS - 73B	B ARMS - 73B	B ARMS - 73B	B ARMS - 73B
32413	NORWOOD JCN - 75C	NORWOOD JCN - 75C	W/D	W/D	W/D	W/D	W/D
32415	B ARMS - 73B	B ARMS - 73B	B ARMS - 73B	B ARMS - 73B	B ARMS - 73B	B ARMS - 73B	B ARMS - 73B
32416	NORWOOD JCN - 75C	NORWOOD JCN - 75C	NORWOOD JCN - 75C	NORWOOD JCN - 75C	B ARMS - 73B	B ARMS - 73B	B ARMS - 73B
32417	B ARMS - 73B	B ARMS - 73B	B ARMS - 73B	B ARMS - 73B	B ARMS - 73B	B ARMS - 73B	B ARMS - 73B
32418	B ARMS - 73B	B ARMS - 73B	B ARMS - 73B	B ARMS - 73B	B ARMS - 73B	B ARMS - 73B	B ARMS - 73B
			E6X 0-6-2T (1911)				
32411	NORWOOD JCN - 75C	NORWOOD JCN - 75C	W/D	W/D	W/D	W/D	W/D
			G16 4-8-0T (1921)				
30492	FELTHAM - 70B	FELTHAM - 70B	W/D	W/D	W/D	W/D	W/D
30493	FELTHAM - 70B	FELTHAM - 70B	FELTHAM - 70B	FELTHAM - 70B	FELTHAM - 70B	FELTHAM - 70B	FELTHAM - 70B
30494	FELTHAM - 70B	FELTHAM - 70B	FELTHAM - 70B	FELTHAM - 70B	FELTHAM - 70B	FELTHAM - 70B	FELTHAM - 70B
30495	FELTHAM - 70B	FELTHAM - 70B	FELTHAM - 70B	FELTHAM - 70B	FELTHAM - 70B	FELTHAM - 70B	FELTHAM - 70B
			K 2-6-0 (1913)				
32337	FRATTON - 70F	FRATTON - 70F	FRATTON - 70F	FRATTON - 70F	FRATTON - 70F	FRATTON - 70F	FRATTON - 70F
32338	BRIGHTON - 75A	BRIGHTON - 75A	BRIGHTON - 75A	BRIGHTON - 75A	BRIGHTON - 75A	BRIGHTON - 75A	BRIGHTON - 75A
32339	BRIGHTON - 75A	BRIGHTON - 75A	BRIGHTON - 75A	BRIGHTON - 75A	BRIGHTON - 75A	BRIGHTON - 75A	BRIGHTON - 75A
32340	BRIGHTON - 75A	BRIGHTON - 75A	BRIGHTON - 75A	BRIGHTON - 75A	BRIGHTON - 75A	BRIGHTON - 75A	BRIGHTON - 75A
32341	BRIGHTON - 75A	BRIGHTON - 75A	BRIGHTON - 75A	BRIGHTON - 75A	BRIGHTON - 75A	BRIGHTON - 75A	BRIGHTON - 75A
32342	BRIGHTON - 75A	BRIGHTON - 75A	BRIGHTON - 75A	BRIGHTON - 75A	BRIGHTON - 75A	BRIGHTON - 75A	BRIGHTON - 75A
32343	BRIGHTON - 75A	BRIGHTON - 75A	BRIGHTON - 75A	BRIGHTON - 75A	BRIGHTON - 75A	BRIGHTON - 75A	BRIGHTON - 75A
32344	THREE BRIDGES - 75E	THREE BRIDGES - 75E	THREE BRIDGES - 75E	THREE BRIDGES - 75E	THREE BRIDGES - 75E	THREE BRIDGES - 75E	THREE BRIDGES - 75E
32345	BRIGHTON - 75A	BRIGHTON - 75A	BRIGHTON - 75A	BRIGHTON - 75A	BRIGHTON - 75A	BRIGHTON - 75A	BRIGHTON - 75A
32346	BRIGHTON - 75A	BRIGHTON - 75A	BRIGHTON - 75A	BRIGHTON - 75A	BRIGHTON - 75A	BRIGHTON - 75A	BRIGHTON - 75A
32347	THREE BRIDGES - 75E	THREE BRIDGES - 75E	THREE BRIDGES - 75E	THREE BRIDGES - 75E	THREE BRIDGES - 75E	THREE BRIDGES - 75E	THREE BRIDGES - 75E
32348	THREE BRIDGES - 75E	THREE BRIDGES - 75E	THREE BRIDGES - 75E	THREE BRIDGES - 75E	THREE BRIDGES - 75E	THREE BRIDGES - 75E	THREE BRIDGES - 75E
32349	FRATTON - 70F	FRATTON - 70F	FRATTON - 70F	FRATTON - 70F	FRATTON - 70F	FRATTON - 70F	FRATTON - 70F
32350	THREE BRIDGES - 75E	THREE BRIDGES - 75E	THREE BRIDGES - 75E	THREE BRIDGES - 75E	THREE BRIDGES - 75E	THREE BRIDGES - 75E	THREE BRIDGES - 75E
32351	THREE BRIDGES - 75E	THREE BRIDGES - 75E	THREE BRIDGES - 75E	THREE BRIDGES - 75E	THREE BRIDGES - 75E	THREE BRIDGES - 75E	THREE BRIDGES - 75E
32352	THREE BRIDGES - 75E	THREE BRIDGES - 75E	THREE BRIDGES - 75E	THREE BRIDGES - 75E	THREE BRIDGES - 75E	THREE BRIDGES - 75E	THREE BRIDGES - 75E
32353	THREE BRIDGES - 75E	THREE BRIDGES - 75E	THREE BRIDGES - 75E	THREE BRIDGES - 75E	THREE BRIDGES - 75E	THREE BRIDGES - 75E	THREE BRIDGES - 75E
			U 2-6-0 (R/B 2-6-4T) 1928				
31790	YEOVIL - 72C	EXMOUTH JCN - 72A	EXMOUTH JCN - 72A	YEOVIL - 72C	YEOVIL - 72C	YEOVIL - 72C	YEOVIL - 72C
31791	YEOVIL - 72C	EXMOUTH JCN - 72A	EXMOUTH JCN - 72A	YEOVIL - 72C	YEOVIL - 72C	YEOVIL - 72C	YEOVIL - 72C
31792	YEOVIL - 72C	EASTLEIGH - 71A	EASTLEIGH - 71A	EASTLEIGH - 71A	EASTLEIGH - 71A	EASTLEIGH - 71A	EASTLEIGH - 71A
31793	YEOVIL - 72C	EASTLEIGH - 71A	EASTLEIGH - 71A	EASTLEIGH - 71A	EASTLEIGH - 71A	EASTLEIGH - 71A	EASTLEIGH - 71A
31794	YEOVIL - 72C	EASTLEIGH - 71A	EASTLEIGH - 71A	EASTLEIGH - 71A	EASTLEIGH - 71A	EASTLEIGH - 71A	EASTLEIGH - 71A
31795	YEOVIL - 72C	EASTLEIGH - 71A	EASTLEIGH - 71A	EASTLEIGH - 71A	EASTLEIGH - 71A	EASTLEIGH - 71A	EASTLEIGH - 71A
31796	YEOVIL - 72C	EASTLEIGH - 71A	EASTLEIGH - 71A	EASTLEIGH - 71A	EASTLEIGH - 71A	EASTLEIGH - 71A	EASTLEIGH - 71A
31797	GUILDFORD - 70C	GUILDFORD - 70C	GUILDFORD - 70C	GUILDFORD - 70C	GUILDFORD - 70C	GUILDFORD - 70C	GUILDFORD - 70C
31798	GUILDFORD - 70C	GUILDFORD - 70C	GUILDFORD - 70C	GUILDFORD - 70C	GUILDFORD - 70C	GUILDFORD - 70C	GUILDFORD - 70C
31799	GUILDFORD - 70C	GUILDFORD - 70C	GUILDFORD - 70C	GUILDFORD - 70C	GUILDFORD - 70C	GUILDFORD - 70C	GUILDFORD - 70C
31800	GUILDFORD - 70C	GUILDFORD - 70C	GUILDFORD - 70C	GUILDFORD - 70C	GUILDFORD - 70C	GUILDFORD - 70C	GUILDFORD - 70C
31801	EASTLEIGH - 71A	EASTLEIGH - 71A	EASTLEIGH - 71A	EASTLEIGH - 71A	EASTLEIGH - 71A	EASTLEIGH - 71A	EASTLEIGH - 71A
31802	EASTLEIGH - 71A	EASTLEIGH - 71A	EASTLEIGH - 71A	EASTLEIGH - 71A	EASTLEIGH - 71A	EASTLEIGH - 71A	EASTLEIGH - 71A
31803	EASTLEIGH - 71A	EASTLEIGH - 71A	EASTLEIGH - 71A	EASTLEIGH - 71A	EASTLEIGH - 71A	EASTLEIGH - 71A	EASTLEIGH - 71A
31804	FRATTON - 70F	FRATTON - 70F	FRATTON - 70F	FRATTON - 70F	FRATTON - 70F	FRATTON - 70F	FRATTON - 70F
31805	REDHILL - 75B	REDHILL - 75B	REDHILL - 75B	REDHILL - 75B	REDHILL - 75B	REDHILL - 75B	REDHILL - 75B
31806	BASINGSTOKE - 70D	BASINGSTOKE - 70D	BASINGSTOKE - 70D	BASINGSTOKE - 70D	BASINGSTOKE - 70D	BASINGSTOKE - 70D	BASINGSTOKE - 70D
31807	FRATTON - 70F	FRATTON - 70F	GUILDFORD - 70C	GUILDFORD - 70C	GUILDFORD - 70C	GUILDFORD - 70C	GUILDFORD - 70C
31808	FRATTON - 70F	FRATTON - 70F	EASTLEIGH - 71A	EASTLEIGH - 71A	EASTLEIGH - 71A	EASTLEIGH - 71A	EASTLEIGH - 71A
31809	FRATTON - 70F	FRATTON - 70F	FRATTON - 70F	FRATTON - 70F	FRATTON - 70F	FRATTON - 70F	FRATTON - 70F

The K class 2-6-0's were arguably the most successful engines produced by the LBSCR and were largely unaffected by the electrification projects of the inter-war years which made no provision for goods traffic. During the 1950's most of their work was based on Three Bridges and Brighton from which points they worked all over the southern parts of the LBSCR. Their use on passenger services was by no means unknown - a number of local workings between Brighton and Horsham were booked to the class - and such employment included seasonal express traffic on the east coast route between Brighton and Eastbourne. One of the class could usually be found at Fratton where it was used to work the daily Chichester - Eastleigh goods.

Historically the U class - or a section of it - was amongst the most interesting of all Southern classes since they started life as what was intended to be the standard 2-6-4 express passenger tank for services between London and the coastal points of the SECR and LBSCR. Starting shortly after the end of the Great War, the project was blighted by reports of instability and the scheme came to an end in 1927 when (31)800 derailed at high speed with the 17.00 Cannon Street - Ramsgate, resulting in the loss of thirteen lives.

It was subsequently determined that the state of the permanent way rather than the engines was the prime cause of the accident but in view of the adverse publicity attracted tohether with difficulties with water consumption on the longer runs, the 2-6-4T's were rebuilt as 2-6-0 mixed-traffic tender engines.

Except when called upon for seasonal passenger traffic the U class spent most of their time on goods traffic, usually operating on secondary rather than the main lines although the Yeovil contingent played a part in the working of stopping trains west of Salisbury. Another regular exception was the use of the Faversham-based engine which for much of the 1950's was regularly booked to work the 17.21 Cannon Street - Dover express via Chatham: one of the services the original 2-6-4T's were intended for.

loco	Dec-59	Feb-60	Mar-60	Apr-60	Jul-60	Aug-60	Sep-60	Nov-60
E6 0-6-2T (1904)								
32408	B.ARMS - 73B	B.ARMS - 73B	B.ARMS - 73B	B.ARMS - 73B	B.ARMS - 73B	B.ARMS - 73B	B.ARMS - 73B	B.ARMS - 73B
32410	B.ARMS - 73B	DOVER - 73H	DOVER - 73H	DOVER - 73H	DOVER - 73H	DOVER - 73H	DOVER - 73H	DOVER - 73H
32415	B.ARMS - 73B	DOVER - 73H	DOVER - 73H	DOVER - 73H	DOVER - 73H	DOVER - 73H	DOVER - 73H	DOVER - 73H
32416	B.ARMS - 73T	B.ARMS - 73B	B.ARMS - 73B	B.ARMS - 73B	B.ARMS - 73B	B.ARMS - 73B	B.ARMS - 73B	B.ARMS - 73B
32417	B.ARMS - 73B	B.ARMS - 73B	B.ARMS - 73B	B.ARMS - 73B	B.ARMS - 73B	B.ARMS - 73B	B.ARMS - 73B	B.ARMS - 73B
32418	B.ARMS - 73B	B.ARMS - 73B	B.ARMS - 73B	B.ARMS - 73B	B.ARMS - 73B	B.ARMS - 73B	B.ARMS - 73B	B.ARMS - 73B
G16 4-8-0T (1921)								
30494	FELTHAM - 70B	FELTHAM - 70B	FELTHAM - 70B	FELTHAM - 70B	FELTHAM - 70B	FELTHAM - 70B	FELTHAM - 70B	FELTHAM - 70B
30495	FELTHAM - 70B	FELTHAM - 70B	FELTHAM - 70B	FELTHAM - 70B	FELTHAM - 70B	FELTHAM - 70B	FELTHAM - 70B	FELTHAM - 70B
K 2-6-0 (1913)								
32337	THREE BRIDGES - 75E	THREE BRIDGES - 75E	THREE BRIDGES - 75E	THREE BRIDGES - 75E	THREE BRIDGES - 75E	THREE BRIDGES - 75E	BRIGHTON - 75A	BRIGHTON - 75A
32338	BRIGHTON - 75A	BRIGHTON - 75A	BRIGHTON - 75A	BRIGHTON - 75A	BRIGHTON - 75A	BRIGHTON - 75A	BRIGHTON - 75A	BRIGHTON - 75A
32339	BRIGHTON - 75A	BRIGHTON - 75A	BRIGHTON - 75A	BRIGHTON - 75A	BRIGHTON - 75A	BRIGHTON - 75A	BRIGHTON - 75A	BRIGHTON - 75A
32340	BRIGHTON - 75A	BRIGHTON - 75A	BRIGHTON - 75A	BRIGHTON - 75A	BRIGHTON - 75A	BRIGHTON - 75A	BRIGHTON - 75A	BRIGHTON - 75A
32341	BRIGHTON - 75A	BRIGHTON - 75A	BRIGHTON - 75A	BRIGHTON - 75A	BRIGHTON - 75A	BRIGHTON - 75A	BRIGHTON - 75A	BRIGHTON - 75A
32342	BRIGHTON - 75A	BRIGHTON - 75A	BRIGHTON - 75A	BRIGHTON - 75A	BRIGHTON - 75A	BRIGHTON - 75A	BRIGHTON - 75A	BRIGHTON - 75A
32343	BRIGHTON - 75A	BRIGHTON - 75A	BRIGHTON - 75A	BRIGHTON - 75A	BRIGHTON - 75A	BRIGHTON - 75A	BRIGHTON - 75A	BRIGHTON - 75A
32344	THREE BRIDGES - 75E	THREE BRIDGES - 75E	THREE BRIDGES - 75E	THREE BRIDGES - 75E	THREE BRIDGES - 75E	THREE BRIDGES - 75E	BRIGHTON - 75A	BRIGHTON - 75A
32345	BRIGHTON - 75A	BRIGHTON - 75A	BRIGHTON - 75A	BRIGHTON - 75A	BRIGHTON - 75A	BRIGHTON - 75A	BRIGHTON - 75A	BRIGHTON - 75A
32346	BRIGHTON - 75A	BRIGHTON - 75A	BRIGHTON - 75A	BRIGHTON - 75A	BRIGHTON - 75A	BRIGHTON - 75A	BRIGHTON - 75A	BRIGHTON - 75A
32347	THREE BRIDGES - 75E	THREE BRIDGES - 75E	THREE BRIDGES - 75E	THREE BRIDGES - 75E	THREE BRIDGES - 75E	THREE BRIDGES - 75E	THREE BRIDGES - 75E	THREE BRIDGES - 75E
32348	THREE BRIDGES - 75E	THREE BRIDGES - 75E	THREE BRIDGES - 75E	THREE BRIDGES - 75E	THREE BRIDGES - 75E	THREE BRIDGES - 75E	THREE BRIDGES - 75E	THREE BRIDGES - 75E
32349	THREE BRIDGES - 75E	THREE BRIDGES - 75E	THREE BRIDGES - 75E	THREE BRIDGES - 75E	THREE BRIDGES - 75E	THREE BRIDGES - 75E	THREE BRIDGES - 75E	THREE BRIDGES - 75E
32350	THREE BRIDGES - 75E	THREE BRIDGES - 75E	THREE BRIDGES - 75E	THREE BRIDGES - 75E	THREE BRIDGES - 75E	THREE BRIDGES - 75E	THREE BRIDGES - 75E	THREE BRIDGES - 75E
32351	THREE BRIDGES - 75E	THREE BRIDGES - 75E	THREE BRIDGES - 75E	THREE BRIDGES - 75E	THREE BRIDGES - 75E	THREE BRIDGES - 75E	THREE BRIDGES - 75E	THREE BRIDGES - 75E
32352	THREE BRIDGES - 75E	THREE BRIDGES - 75E	THREE BRIDGES - 75E	THREE BRIDGES - 75E	THREE BRIDGES - 75E	THREE BRIDGES - 75E	THREE BRIDGES - 75E	THREE BRIDGES - 75E
32353	THREE BRIDGES - 75E	THREE BRIDGES - 75E	THREE BRIDGES - 75E	THREE BRIDGES - 75E	THREE BRIDGES - 75E	THREE BRIDGES - 75E	THREE BRIDGES - 75E	THREE BRIDGES - 75E
U 2-6-0 (R/B 2-6-4T) 1928								
31790	YEOVIL - 72C	GUILDFORD - 70C	GUILDFORD - 70C	GUILDFORD - 70C	GUILDFORD - 70C	GUILDFORD - 70C	EASTLEIGH - 71A	EASTLEIGH - 71A
31791	YEOVIL - 72C	EASTLEIGH - 71A	EASTLEIGH - 71A	EASTLEIGH - 71A	EASTLEIGH - 71A	EASTLEIGH - 71A	EASTLEIGH - 71A	EASTLEIGH - 71A
31792	EASTLEIGH - 71A	YEOVIL - 72C	YEOVIL - 72C	YEOVIL - 72C	YEOVIL - 72C	YEOVIL - 72C	YEOVIL - 72C	YEOVIL - 72C
31793	EASTLEIGH - 71A	EASTLEIGH - 71A	EASTLEIGH - 71A	EASTLEIGH - 71A	EASTLEIGH - 71A	EASTLEIGH - 71A	EASTLEIGH - 71A	EASTLEIGH - 71A
31794	EASTLEIGH - 71A	EASTLEIGH - 71A	EASTLEIGH - 71A	EASTLEIGH - 71A	EASTLEIGH - 71A	EASTLEIGH - 71A	EASTLEIGH - 71A	EASTLEIGH - 71A
31795	EASTLEIGH - 71A	EASTLEIGH - 71A	EASTLEIGH - 71A	EASTLEIGH - 71A	EASTLEIGH - 71A	EASTLEIGH - 71A	EASTLEIGH - 71A	EASTLEIGH - 71A
31796	EASTLEIGH - 71A	EASTLEIGH - 71A	EASTLEIGH - 71A	EASTLEIGH - 71A	EASTLEIGH - 71A	EASTLEIGH - 71A	EASTLEIGH - 71A	EASTLEIGH - 71A
31797	GUILDFORD - 70C	GUILDFORD - 70C	GUILDFORD - 70C	GUILDFORD - 70C	GUILDFORD - 70C	GUILDFORD - 70C	GUILDFORD - 70C	GUILDFORD - 70C
31798	GUILDFORD - 70C	YEOVIL - 72C	YEOVIL - 72C	YEOVIL - 72C	YEOVIL - 72C	YEOVIL - 72C	YEOVIL - 72C	YEOVIL - 72C
31799	GUILDFORD - 70C	REDHILL - 75B	REDHILL - 75B	REDHILL - 75B	REDHILL - 75B	REDHILL - 75B	REDHILL - 75B	REDHILL - 75B
31800	GUILDFORD - 70C	GUILDFORD - 70C	GUILDFORD - 70C	GUILDFORD - 70C	GUILDFORD - 70C	GUILDFORD - 70C	GUILDFORD - 70C	GUILDFORD - 70C
31801	EASTLEIGH - 71A	EASTLEIGH - 71A	EASTLEIGH - 71A	EASTLEIGH - 71A	EASTLEIGH - 71A	EASTLEIGH - 71A	EASTLEIGH - 71A	EASTLEIGH - 71A
31802	EASTLEIGH - 71A	YEOVIL - 72C	YEOVIL - 72C	YEOVIL - 72C	YEOVIL - 72C	YEOVIL - 72C	YEOVIL - 72C	YEOVIL - 72C
31803	EASTLEIGH - 71A	EASTLEIGH - 71A	EASTLEIGH - 71A	EASTLEIGH - 71A	EASTLEIGH - 71A	EASTLEIGH - 71A	EASTLEIGH - 71A	EASTLEIGH - 71A
31804	EASTLEIGH - 71A	EASTLEIGH - 71A	EASTLEIGH - 71A	EASTLEIGH - 71A	EASTLEIGH - 71A	EASTLEIGH - 71A	EASTLEIGH - 71A	EASTLEIGH - 71A
31805	GUILDFORD - 70C	YEOVIL - 72C	YEOVIL - 72C	YEOVIL - 72C	YEOVIL - 72C	YEOVIL - 72C	YEOVIL - 72C	YEOVIL - 72C
31806	BASINGSTOKE - 70D	BASINGSTOKE - 70D	BASINGSTOKE - 70D	BASINGSTOKE - 70D	BASINGSTOKE - 70D	BASINGSTOKE - 70D	BASINGSTOKE - 70D	BASINGSTOKE - 70D
31807	GUILDFORD - 70C	REDHILL - 75B	REDHILL - 75B	REDHILL - 75B	REDHILL - 75B	REDHILL - 75B	REDHILL - 75B	REDHILL - 75B
31808	EASTLEIGH - 71A	EASTLEIGH - 71A	EASTLEIGH - 71A	EASTLEIGH - 71A	EASTLEIGH - 71A	EASTLEIGH - 71A	EASTLEIGH - 71A	EASTLEIGH - 71A
31809	EASTLEIGH - 71A	EASTLEIGH - 71A	EASTLEIGH - 71A	EASTLEIGH - 71A	EASTLEIGH - 71A	EASTLEIGH - 71A	EASTLEIGH - 71A	EASTLEIGH - 71A

Almost a permanent feature of Yeovil MPD, U 2-6-0 31792 waits for the right away at Salisbury with a stopping service for Yeovil Town. 31792 was a rebuild of a K class 2-6-4T, 'River Arun', and had started its career on the LBSCR in 1925, initially working from Brighton but on being displaced by the N15 4-6-0's, from Eastbourne where with nine other 2-6-4T's it took over the services to Victoria from B4X 4-4-0's. Water capacity proved to be a handicap on such long runs and in 1926 the 4-4-0's returned to Eastbourne with the 2-6-4T's being moved to Redhill for work on the SECR Reading branch. A year later all the K class were taken out of traffic and rebuilt as U class 2-6-0's, 792 reappearing in July 1928 and being allocated once again to Eastbourne for the Victoria expresses. In 1933 electrification prompted another move and 792 was reallocated to Yeovil where it remained for no less than twenty seven years.

loco	May-49	Jun-49	Aug-49	Sep-49	Dec-49	Feb-50	Mar-50
				N 2-6-0 (1917)			
31400	ASHFORD - 74A	ASHFORD - 74A	ASHFORD - 74A	ASHFORD - 74A	ASHFORD - 74A	ASHFORD - 74A	ASHFORD - 74A
31401	ASHFORD - 74A	ASHFORD - 74A	ASHFORD - 74A	ASHFORD - 74A	ASHFORD - 74A	ASHFORD - 74A	ASHFORD - 74A
31402	ASHFORD - 74A	ASHFORD - 74A	ASHFORD - 74A	ASHFORD - 74A	ASHFORD - 74A	ASHFORD - 74A	ASHFORD - 74A
31403	ASHFORD - 74A	ASHFORD - 74A	ASHFORD - 74A	ASHFORD - 74A	ASHFORD - 74A	ASHFORD - 74A	ASHFORD - 74A
31404	ASHFORD - 74A	ASHFORD - 74A	ASHFORD - 74A	ASHFORD - 74A	ASHFORD - 74A	ASHFORD - 74A	ASHFORD - 74A
31405	ASHFORD - 74A	ASHFORD - 74A	ASHFORD - 74A	ASHFORD - 74A	ASHFORD - 74A	ASHFORD - 74A	ASHFORD - 74A
31406	STEWARTS LANE - 73A	STEWARTS LANE - 73A	STEWARTS LANE - 73A	STEWARTS LANE - 73A	STEWARTS LANE - 73A	ASHFORD - 74A	ASHFORD - 74A
31407	EXMOUTH JCN - 72A	EXMOUTH JCN - 72A	EXMOUTH JCN - 72A	EXMOUTH JCN - 72A	EXMOUTH JCN - 72A	EXMOUTH JCN - 72A	EXMOUTH JCN - 72A
31408	EXMOUTH JCN - 72A	EXMOUTH JCN - 72A	EXMOUTH JCN - 72A	EXMOUTH JCN - 72A	EXMOUTH JCN - 72A	EXMOUTH JCN - 72A	EXMOUTH JCN - 72A
31409	EXMOUTH JCN - 72A	EXMOUTH JCN - 72A	EXMOUTH JCN - 72A	EXMOUTH JCN - 72A	EXMOUTH JCN - 72A	STEWARTS LANE - 73A	STEWARTS LANE - 73A
31410	STEWARTS LANE - 73A	STEWARTS LANE - 73A	STEWARTS LANE - 73A	STEWARTS LANE - 73A	STEWARTS LANE - 73A	STEWARTS LANE - 73A	STEWARTS LANE - 73A
31411	STEWARTS LANE - 73A	STEWARTS LANE - 73A	STEWARTS LANE - 73A	STEWARTS LANE - 73A	STEWARTS LANE - 73A	STEWARTS LANE - 73A	STEWARTS LANE - 73A
31412	STEWARTS LANE - 73A	STEWARTS LANE - 73A	STEWARTS LANE - 73A	STEWARTS LANE - 73A	STEWARTS LANE - 73A	STEWARTS LANE - 73A	STEWARTS LANE - 73A
31413	STEWARTS LANE - 73A	STEWARTS LANE - 73A	STEWARTS LANE - 73A	STEWARTS LANE - 73A	STEWARTS LANE - 73A	STEWARTS LANE - 73A	STEWARTS LANE - 73A
31414	STEWARTS LANE - 73A	STEWARTS LANE - 73A	STEWARTS LANE - 73A	STEWARTS LANE - 73A	STEWARTS LANE - 73A	STEWARTS LANE - 73A	STEWARTS LANE - 73A
31810	STEWARTS LANE - 73A	STEWARTS LANE - 73A	STEWARTS LANE - 73A	STEWARTS LANE - 73A	STEWARTS LANE - 73A	STEWARTS LANE - 73A	STEWARTS LANE - 73A
31811	STEWARTS LANE - 73A	STEWARTS LANE - 73A	STEWARTS LANE - 73A	STEWARTS LANE - 73A	STEWARTS LANE - 73A	STEWARTS LANE - 73A	STEWARTS LANE - 73A
31812	STEWARTS LANE - 73A	STEWARTS LANE - 73A	STEWARTS LANE - 73A	STEWARTS LANE - 73A	STEWARTS LANE - 73A	STEWARTS LANE - 73A	STEWARTS LANE - 73A
31813	STEWARTS LANE - 73A	STEWARTS LANE - 73A	STEWARTS LANE - 73A	STEWARTS LANE - 73A	STEWARTS LANE - 73A	STEWARTS LANE - 73A	STEWARTS LANE - 73A
31814	STEWARTS LANE - 73A	STEWARTS LANE - 73A	STEWARTS LANE - 73A	STEWARTS LANE - 73A	STEWARTS LANE - 73A	STEWARTS LANE - 73A	STEWARTS LANE - 73A
31815	STEWARTS LANE - 73A	STEWARTS LANE - 73A	STEWARTS LANE - 73A	STEWARTS LANE - 73A	STEWARTS LANE - 73A	STEWARTS LANE - 73A	STEWARTS LANE - 73A
31816	STEWARTS LANE - 73A	STEWARTS LANE - 73A	STEWARTS LANE - 73A	STEWARTS LANE - 73A	STEWARTS LANE - 73A	STEWARTS LANE - 73A	STEWARTS LANE - 73A
31817	REDHILL - 75B	REDHILL - 75B	REDHILL - 75B	REDHILL - 75B	REDHILL - 75B	REDHILL - 75B	REDHILL - 75B
31818	REDHILL - 75B	REDHILL - 75B	REDHILL - 75B	REDHILL - 75B	REDHILL - 75B	REDHILL - 75B	REDHILL - 75B
31819	DOVER - 74C	DOVER - 74C	DOVER - 74C	DOVER - 74C	DOVER - 74C	DOVER - 74C	DOVER - 74C
31820	DOVER - 74C	DOVER - 74C	DOVER - 74C	DOVER - 74C	DOVER - 74C	DOVER - 74C	DOVER - 74C
31821	DOVER - 74C	DOVER - 74C	DOVER - 74C	DOVER - 74C	DOVER - 74C	DOVER - 74C	DOVER - 74C
31823	DOVER - 74C	DOVER - 74C	DOVER - 74C	DOVER - 74C	DOVER - 74C	DOVER - 74C	DOVER - 74C
31824	B ARMS - 73B	B ARMS - 73B	B ARMS - 73B	B ARMS - 73B	B ARMS - 73B	B ARMS - 73B	B ARMS - 73B
31825	B ARMS - 73B	B ARMS - 73B	B ARMS - 73B	B ARMS - 73B	B ARMS - 73B	B ARMS - 73B	B ARMS - 73B
31826	B ARMS - 73B	B ARMS - 73B	B ARMS - 73B	B ARMS - 73B	B ARMS - 73B	B ARMS - 73B	B ARMS - 73B
31827	EASTLEIGH - 71A	EASTLEIGH - 71A	EASTLEIGH - 71A	EASTLEIGH - 71A	EASTLEIGH - 71A	B ARMS - 73B	B ARMS - 73B
31828	EXMOUTH JCN - 72A	EXMOUTH JCN - 72A	EXMOUTH JCN - 72A	EXMOUTH JCN - 72A	EXMOUTH JCN - 72A	STEWARTS LANE - 73A	STEWARTS LANE - 73A
31829	EASTLEIGH - 71A	EASTLEIGH - 71A	EASTLEIGH - 71A	EASTLEIGH - 71A	EASTLEIGH - 71A	EASTLEIGH - 71A	EASTLEIGH - 71A
31830	ASHFORD - 74A	ASHFORD - 74A	ASHFORD - 74A	ASHFORD - 74A	ASHFORD - 74A	FAVERSHAM - 73E	FAVERSHAM - 73E
31831	EXMOUTH JCN - 72A	EXMOUTH JCN - 72A	EXMOUTH JCN - 72A	EXMOUTH JCN - 72A	EXMOUTH JCN - 72A	REDHILL - 75B	REDHILL - 75B
31832	EXMOUTH JCN - 72A	EXMOUTH JCN - 72A	EXMOUTH JCN - 72A	EXMOUTH JCN - 72A	EXMOUTH JCN - 72A	EXMOUTH JCN - 72A	EXMOUTH JCN - 72A
31833	EXMOUTH JCN - 72A	EXMOUTH JCN - 72A	EXMOUTH JCN - 72A	EXMOUTH JCN - 72A	EXMOUTH JCN - 72A	EXMOUTH JCN - 72A	EXMOUTH JCN - 72A
31834	EXMOUTH JCN - 72A	EXMOUTH JCN - 72A	EXMOUTH JCN - 72A	EXMOUTH JCN - 72A	EXMOUTH JCN - 72A	EXMOUTH JCN - 72A	EXMOUTH JCN - 72A
31835	EXMOUTH JCN - 72A	EXMOUTH JCN - 72A	EXMOUTH JCN - 72A	EXMOUTH JCN - 72A	EXMOUTH JCN - 72A	EXMOUTH JCN - 72A	EXMOUTH JCN - 72A
31836	SALISBURY - 72B	SALISBURY - 72B	SALISBURY - 72B	SALISBURY - 72B	SALISBURY - 72B	SALISBURY - 72B	SALISBURY - 72B
31837	EXMOUTH JCN - 72A	EXMOUTH JCN - 72A	EXMOUTH JCN - 72A	EXMOUTH JCN - 72A	EXMOUTH JCN - 72A	EXMOUTH JCN - 72A	EXMOUTH JCN - 72A
31838	EXMOUTH JCN - 72A	EXMOUTH JCN - 72A	EXMOUTH JCN - 72A	EXMOUTH JCN - 72A	EXMOUTH JCN - 72A	EXMOUTH JCN - 72A	EXMOUTH JCN - 72A
31839	EXMOUTH JCN - 72A	EXMOUTH JCN - 72A	EXMOUTH JCN - 72A	EXMOUTH JCN - 72A	EXMOUTH JCN - 72A	EXMOUTH JCN - 72A	EXMOUTH JCN - 72A
31840	EXMOUTH JCN - 72A	EXMOUTH JCN - 72A	EXMOUTH JCN - 72A	EXMOUTH JCN - 72A	EXMOUTH JCN - 72A	EXMOUTH JCN - 72A	EXMOUTH JCN - 72A
31841	EXMOUTH JCN - 72A	EXMOUTH JCN - 72A	EXMOUTH JCN - 72A	EXMOUTH JCN - 72A	EXMOUTH JCN - 72A	EXMOUTH JCN - 72A	EXMOUTH JCN - 72A
31842	BARNSTAPLE - 72E	BARNSTAPLE - 72E	BARNSTAPLE - 72E	BARNSTAPLE - 72E	BARNSTAPLE - 72E	BARNSTAPLE - 72E	BARNSTAPLE - 72E
31843	ASHFORD - 74A	REDHILL - 75B	REDHILL - 75B	REDHILL - 75B	REDHILL - 75B	REDHILL - 75B	REDHILL - 75B
31844	ASHFORD - 74A	REDHILL - 75B	REDHILL - 75B	REDHILL - 75B	REDHILL - 75B	REDHILL - 75B	REDHILL - 75B
31845	EXMOUTH JCN - 72A	EXMOUTH JCN - 72A	EXMOUTH JCN - 72A	EXMOUTH JCN - 72A	EXMOUTH JCN - 72A	EXMOUTH JCN - 72A	EXMOUTH JCN - 72A
31846	SALISBURY - 72B	SALISBURY - 72B	SALISBURY - 72B	SALISBURY - 72B	SALISBURY - 72B	SALISBURY - 72B	SALISBURY - 72B
31847	EXMOUTH JCN - 72A	EXMOUTH JCN - 72A	EXMOUTH JCN - 72A	EXMOUTH JCN - 72A	EXMOUTH JCN - 72A	EXMOUTH JCN - 72A	EXMOUTH JCN - 72A
31848	REDHILL - 75B	REDHILL - 75B	REDHILL - 75B	REDHILL - 75B	REDHILL - 75B	REDHILL - 75B	REDHILL - 75B
31849	REDHILL - 75B	REDHILL - 75B	REDHILL - 75B	REDHILL - 75B	REDHILL - 75B	REDHILL - 75B	REDHILL - 75B
31850	FAVERSHAM - 73E	FAVERSHAM - 73E	FAVERSHAM - 73E	FAVERSHAM - 73E	FAVERSHAM - 73E	FAVERSHAM - 73E	FAVERSHAM - 73E
31851	REDHILL - 75B	REDHILL - 75B	REDHILL - 75B	REDHILL - 75B	REDHILL - 75B	REDHILL - 75B	REDHILL - 75B
31852	REDHILL - 75B	REDHILL - 75B	REDHILL - 75B	REDHILL - 75B	REDHILL - 75B	REDHILL - 75B	REDHILL - 75B
31853	EXMOUTH JCN - 72A	EXMOUTH JCN - 72A	EXMOUTH JCN - 72A	EXMOUTH JCN - 72A	EXMOUTH JCN - 72A	EXMOUTH JCN - 72A	EXMOUTH JCN - 72A
31854	FAVERSHAM - 73E	FAVERSHAM - 73E	FAVERSHAM - 73E	FAVERSHAM - 73E	FAVERSHAM - 73E	FAVERSHAM - 73E	FAVERSHAM - 73E
31855	EXMOUTH JCN - 72A	EXMOUTH JCN - 72A	EXMOUTH JCN - 72A	EXMOUTH JCN - 72A	EXMOUTH JCN - 72A	EXMOUTH JCN - 72A	EXMOUTH JCN - 72A
31856	EXMOUTH JCN - 72A	EXMOUTH JCN - 72A	EXMOUTH JCN - 72A	EXMOUTH JCN - 72A	EXMOUTH JCN - 72A	EXMOUTH JCN - 72A	EXMOUTH JCN - 72A
31857	READING (SR) - 70E	READING (SR) - 70E	READING (SR) - 70E	READING (SR) - 70E	READING (SR) - 70E	READING (SR) - 70E	READING (SR) - 70E
31858	REDHILL - 75B	REDHILL - 75B	REDHILL - 75B	REDHILL - 75B	REDHILL - 75B	REDHILL - 75B	REDHILL - 75B
31859	REDHILL - 75B	REDHILL - 75B	REDHILL - 75B	REDHILL - 75B	REDHILL - 75B	REDHILL - 75B	REDHILL - 75B
31860	READING (SR) - 70E	READING (SR) - 70E	READING (SR) - 70E	READING (SR) - 70E	READING (SR) - 70E	READING (SR) - 70E	READING (SR) - 70E
31861	READING (SR) - 70E	READING (SR) - 70E	READING (SR) - 70E	READING (SR) - 70E	READING (SR) - 70E	READING (SR) - 70E	READING (SR) - 70E
31862	REDHILL - 75B	REDHILL - 75B	REDHILL - 75B	REDHILL - 75B	REDHILL - 75B	REDHILL - 75B	REDHILL - 75B
31863	REDHILL - 75B	REDHILL - 75B	REDHILL - 75B	REDHILL - 75B	REDHILL - 75B	REDHILL - 75B	REDHILL - 75B
31864	REDHILL - 75B	REDHILL - 75B	REDHILL - 75B	REDHILL - 75B	REDHILL - 75B	REDHILL - 75B	REDHILL - 75B
31865	B ARMS - 73B	B ARMS - 73B	B ARMS - 73B	B ARMS - 73B	B ARMS - 73B	REDHILL - 75B	REDHILL - 75B
31866	EASTLEIGH - 71A	EASTLEIGH - 71A	EASTLEIGH - 71A	EASTLEIGH - 71A	EASTLEIGH - 71A	EASTLEIGH - 71A	EASTLEIGH - 71A
31867	EASTLEIGH - 71A	EASTLEIGH - 71A	EASTLEIGH - 71A	EASTLEIGH - 71A	EASTLEIGH - 71A	EASTLEIGH - 71A	EASTLEIGH - 71A
31868	READING (SR) - 70E	READING (SR) - 70E	READING (SR) - 70E	READING (SR) - 70E	READING (SR) - 70E	READING (SR) - 70E	READING (SR) - 70E
31869	EXMOUTH JCN - 72A	EXMOUTH JCN - 72A	EXMOUTH JCN - 72A	EXMOUTH JCN - 72A	EXMOUTH JCN - 72A	EXMOUTH JCN - 72A	EXMOUTH JCN - 72A
31870	FRATTON - 71D	FRATTON - 71D	FRATTON - 71D	FRATTON - 71D	FRATTON - 71D	FRATTON - 71D	FRATTON - 71D
31871	EXMOUTH JCN - 72A	EXMOUTH JCN - 72A	EXMOUTH JCN - 72A	EXMOUTH JCN - 72A	PLYMOUTH - 72D	PLYMOUTH - 72D	PLYMOUTH - 72D
31872	SALISBURY - 72B	SALISBURY - 72B	SALISBURY - 72B	SALISBURY - 72B	SALISBURY - 72B	SALISBURY - 72B	SALISBURY - 72B
31873	SALISBURY - 72B	SALISBURY - 72B	SALISBURY - 72B	SALISBURY - 72B	SALISBURY - 72B	SALISBURY - 72B	SALISBURY - 72B
31874	EXMOUTH JCN - 72A	EXMOUTH JCN - 72A	EXMOUTH JCN - 72A	EXMOUTH JCN - 72A	EXMOUTH JCN - 72A	EXMOUTH JCN - 72A	EXMOUTH JCN - 72A
31875	EXMOUTH JCN - 72A	EXMOUTH JCN - 72A	EXMOUTH JCN - 72A	EXMOUTH JCN - 72A	EXMOUTH JCN - 72A	EXMOUTH JCN - 72A	EXMOUTH JCN - 72A
				N1 2-6-0 (1922)			
31822	ST LEONARDS - 74E	ST LEONARDS - 74E	ST LEONARDS - 74E	ST LEONARDS - 74E	ST LEONARDS - 74E	ST LEONARDS - 74E	ST LEONARDS - 74E
31876	ST LEONARDS - 74E	ST LEONARDS - 74E	ST LEONARDS - 74E	ST LEONARDS - 74E	ST LEONARDS - 74E	ST LEONARDS - 74E	ST LEONARDS - 74E
31877	HITHER GREEN - 73C	HITHER GREEN - 73C	HITHER GREEN - 73C	HITHER GREEN - 73C	HITHER GREEN - 73C	HITHER GREEN - 73C	HITHER GREEN - 73C
31878	HITHER GREEN - 73C	HITHER GREEN - 73C	HITHER GREEN - 73C	HITHER GREEN - 73C	HITHER GREEN - 73C	HITHER GREEN - 73C	HITHER GREEN - 73C
31879	HITHER GREEN - 73C	HITHER GREEN - 73C	HITHER GREEN - 73C	HITHER GREEN - 73C	HITHER GREEN - 73C	HITHER GREEN - 73C	HITHER GREEN - 73C
31880	HITHER GREEN - 73C	HITHER GREEN - 73C	HITHER GREEN - 73C	HITHER GREEN - 73C	HITHER GREEN - 73C	HITHER GREEN - 73C	HITHER GREEN - 73C

loco	Apr-50	Sep-50	Oct-50	Nov-50	Dec-50	Mar-51	Apr-51
				N 2-6-0 (1917)			
31400	ASHFORD - 74A	ASHFORD - 74A	ASHFORD - 74A	ASHFORD - 74A	ASHFORD - 74A	ASHFORD - 74A	ASHFORD - 74A
31401	ASHFORD - 74A	ASHFORD - 74A	ASHFORD - 74A	ASHFORD - 74A	ASHFORD - 74A	ASHFORD - 74A	ASHFORD - 74A
31402	ASHFORD - 74A	ASHFORD - 74A	ASHFORD - 74A	ASHFORD - 74A	ASHFORD - 74A	ASHFORD - 74A	ASHFORD - 74A
31403	ASHFORD - 74A	ASHFORD - 74A	ASHFORD - 74A	ASHFORD - 74A	ASHFORD - 74A	ASHFORD - 74A	ASHFORD - 74A
31404	ASHFORD - 74A	ASHFORD - 74A	ASHFORD - 74A	ASHFORD - 74A	ASHFORD - 74A	ASHFORD - 74A	ASHFORD - 74A
31405	ASHFORD - 74A	ASHFORD - 74A	ASHFORD - 74A	ASHFORD - 74A	ASHFORD - 74A	ASHFORD - 74A	ASHFORD - 74A
31406	ASHFORD - 74A	ASHFORD - 74A	ASHFORD - 74A	ASHFORD - 74A	ASHFORD - 74A	ASHFORD - 74A	ASHFORD - 74A
31407	EXMOUTH J CN - 72A	EXMOUTH J CN - 72A	EXMOUTH J CN - 72A	EXMOUTH J CN - 72A	ASHFORD - 74A	ASHFORD - 74A	ASHFORD - 74A
31408	EXMOUTH J CN - 72A	EXMOUTH J CN - 72A	EXMOUTH J CN - 72A	EXMOUTH J CN - 72A	ASHFORD - 74A	ASHFORD - 74A	ASHFORD - 74A
31409	STEWARTS LANE - 73A	STEWARTS LANE - 73A	STEWARTS LANE - 73A	STEWARTS LANE - 73A	STEWARTS LANE - 73A	STEWARTS LANE - 73A	STEWARTS LANE - 73A
31410	STEWARTS LANE - 73A	STEWARTS LANE - 73A	STEWARTS LANE - 73A	STEWARTS LANE - 73A	STEWARTS LANE - 73A	STEWARTS LANE - 73A	STEWARTS LANE - 73A
31411	STEWARTS LANE - 73A	STEWARTS LANE - 73A	STEWARTS LANE - 73A	STEWARTS LANE - 73A	STEWARTS LANE - 73A	STEWARTS LANE - 73A	STEWARTS LANE - 73A
31412	STEWARTS LANE - 73A	STEWARTS LANE - 73A	STEWARTS LANE - 73A	STEWARTS LANE - 73A	STEWARTS LANE - 73A	STEWARTS LANE - 73A	STEWARTS LANE - 73A
31413	STEWARTS LANE - 73A	STEWARTS LANE - 73A	STEWARTS LANE - 73A	STEWARTS LANE - 73A	STEWARTS LANE - 73A	STEWARTS LANE - 73A	STEWARTS LANE - 73A
31414	STEWARTS LANE - 73A	STEWARTS LANE - 73A	STEWARTS LANE - 73A	STEWARTS LANE - 73A	STEWARTS LANE - 73A	STEWARTS LANE - 73A	STEWARTS LANE - 73A
31810	STEWARTS LANE - 73A	STEWARTS LANE - 73A	STEWARTS LANE - 73A	STEWARTS LANE - 73A	STEWARTS LANE - 73A	STEWARTS LANE - 73A	STEWARTS LANE - 73A
31811	STEWARTS LANE - 73A	STEWARTS LANE - 73A	STEWARTS LANE - 73A	STEWARTS LANE - 73A	STEWARTS LANE - 73A	STEWARTS LANE - 73A	STEWARTS LANE - 73A
31812	STEWARTS LANE - 73A	STEWARTS LANE - 73A	STEWARTS LANE - 73A	STEWARTS LANE - 73A	STEWARTS LANE - 73A	STEWARTS LANE - 73A	STEWARTS LANE - 73A
31813	STEWARTS LANE - 73A	STEWARTS LANE - 73A	STEWARTS LANE - 73A	STEWARTS LANE - 73A	STEWARTS LANE - 73A	STEWARTS LANE - 73A	STEWARTS LANE - 73A
31814	STEWARTS LANE - 73A	STEWARTS LANE - 73A	STEWARTS LANE - 73A	STEWARTS LANE - 73A	STEWARTS LANE - 73A	STEWARTS LANE - 73A	STEWARTS LANE - 73A
31815	STEWARTS LANE - 73A	STEWARTS LANE - 73A	STEWARTS LANE - 73A	STEWARTS LANE - 73A	STEWARTS LANE - 73A	STEWARTS LANE - 73A	STEWARTS LANE - 73A
31816	STEWARTS LANE - 73A	STEWARTS LANE - 73A	STEWARTS LANE - 73A	STEWARTS LANE - 73A	STEWARTS LANE - 73A	STEWARTS LANE - 73A	STEWARTS LANE - 73A
31817	STEWARTS LANE - 73A	STEWARTS LANE - 73A	STEWARTS LANE - 73A	STEWARTS LANE - 73A	STEWARTS LANE - 73A	STEWARTS LANE - 73A	STEWARTS LANE - 73A
31818	STEWARTS LANE - 73A	STEWARTS LANE - 73A	STEWARTS LANE - 73A	STEWARTS LANE - 73A	STEWARTS LANE - 73A	STEWARTS LANE - 73A	STEWARTS LANE - 73A
31819	DOVER - 74C	DOVER - 74C	DOVER - 74C	DOVER - 74C	DOVER - 74C	DOVER - 74C	DOVER - 74C
31820	DOVER - 74C	DOVER - 74C	DOVER - 74C	DOVER - 74C	DOVER - 74C	DOVER - 74C	DOVER - 74C
31821	DOVER - 74C	DOVER - 74C	DOVER - 74C	DOVER - 74C	DOVER - 74C	DOVER - 74C	DOVER - 74C
31823	DOVER - 74C	DOVER - 74C	DOVER - 74C	DOVER - 74C	DOVER - 74C	DOVER - 74C	DOVER - 74C
31824	B.ARMS - 73B	B.ARMS - 73B	B.ARMS - 73B	B.ARMS - 73B	B.ARMS - 73B	B.ARMS - 73B	B.ARMS - 73B
31825	B.ARMS - 73B	B.ARMS - 73B	B.ARMS - 73B	B.ARMS - 73B	B.ARMS - 73B	B.ARMS - 73B	B.ARMS - 73B
31826	B.ARMS - 73B	B.ARMS - 73B	B.ARMS - 73B	B.ARMS - 73B	B.ARMS - 73B	B.ARMS - 73B	B.ARMS - 73B
31827	B.ARMS - 73B	B.ARMS - 73B	B.ARMS - 73B	B.ARMS - 73B	B.ARMS - 73B	B.ARMS - 73B	B.ARMS - 73B
31828	EASTLEIGH - 71A	EASTLEIGH - 71A	EASTLEIGH - 71A	EXMOUTH J CN - 72A	EXMOUTH J CN - 72A	EXMOUTH J CN - 72A	EXMOUTH J CN - 72A
31829	EASTLEIGH - 71A	EXMOUTH J CN - 72A	EXMOUTH J CN - 72A	EXMOUTH J CN - 72A	EXMOUTH J CN - 72A	EXMOUTH J CN - 72A	EXMOUTH J CN - 72A
31830	FAVERSHAM - 73E	EXMOUTH J CN - 72A	EXMOUTH J CN - 72A	EXMOUTH J CN - 72A	EXMOUTH J CN - 72A	EXMOUTH J CN - 72A	EXMOUTH J CN - 72A
31831	REDHILL - 75B	EXMOUTH J CN - 72A	EXMOUTH J CN - 72A	EXMOUTH J CN - 72A	EXMOUTH J CN - 72A	EXMOUTH J CN - 72A	EXMOUTH J CN - 72A
31832	EXMOUTH J CN - 72A	EXMOUTH J CN - 72A	EXMOUTH J CN - 72A	EXMOUTH J CN - 72A	EXMOUTH J CN - 72A	EXMOUTH J CN - 72A	EXMOUTH J CN - 72A
31833	EXMOUTH J CN - 72A	EXMOUTH J CN - 72A	EXMOUTH J CN - 72A	EXMOUTH J CN - 72A	EXMOUTH J CN - 72A	EXMOUTH J CN - 72A	EXMOUTH J CN - 72A
31834	EXMOUTH J CN - 72A	EXMOUTH J CN - 72A	EXMOUTH J CN - 72A	EXMOUTH J CN - 72A	EXMOUTH J CN - 72A	EXMOUTH J CN - 72A	EXMOUTH J CN - 72A
31835	EXMOUTH J CN - 72A	EXMOUTH J CN - 72A	EXMOUTH J CN - 72A	EXMOUTH J CN - 72A	EXMOUTH J CN - 72A	EXMOUTH J CN - 72A	EXMOUTH J CN - 72A
31836	SALISBURY - 72B	SALISBURY - 72B	SALISBURY - 72B	EXMOUTH J CN - 72A	EXMOUTH J CN - 72A	EXMOUTH J CN - 72A	EXMOUTH J CN - 72A
31837	EXMOUTH J CN - 72A	EXMOUTH J CN - 72A	EXMOUTH J CN - 72A	EXMOUTH J CN - 72A	EXMOUTH J CN - 72A	EXMOUTH J CN - 72A	EXMOUTH J CN - 72A
31838	EXMOUTH J CN - 72A	EXMOUTH J CN - 72A	EXMOUTH J CN - 72A	EXMOUTH J CN - 72A	EXMOUTH J CN - 72A	EXMOUTH J CN - 72A	EXMOUTH J CN - 72A
31839	EXMOUTH J CN - 72A	EXMOUTH J CN - 72A	EXMOUTH J CN - 72A	EXMOUTH J CN - 72A	EXMOUTH J CN - 72A	EXMOUTH J CN - 72A	EXMOUTH J CN - 72A
31840	EXMOUTH J CN - 72A	EXMOUTH J CN - 72A	EXMOUTH J CN - 72A	EXMOUTH J CN - 72A	EXMOUTH J CN - 72A	EXMOUTH J CN - 72A	EXMOUTH J CN - 72A
31841	EXMOUTH J CN - 72A	EXMOUTH J CN - 72A	EXMOUTH J CN - 72A	EXMOUTH J CN - 72A	EXMOUTH J CN - 72A	EXMOUTH J CN - 72A	EXMOUTH J CN - 72A
31842	BARNSTAPLE - 72E	BARNSTAPLE - 72E	BARNSTAPLE - 72E	BARNSTAPLE - 72E	BARNSTAPLE - 72E	BARNSTAPLE - 72E	BARNSTAPLE - 72E
31843	REDHILL - 75B	REDHILL - 75B	REDHILL - 75B	REDHILL - 75B	EXMOUTH J CN - 72A	EXMOUTH J CN - 72A	EXMOUTH J CN - 72A
31844	REDHILL - 75B	REDHILL - 75B	REDHILL - 75B	REDHILL - 75B	EXMOUTH J CN - 72A	EXMOUTH J CN - 72A	EXMOUTH J CN - 72A
31845	EXMOUTH J CN - 72A	EXMOUTH J CN - 72A	EXMOUTH J CN - 72A	EXMOUTH J CN - 72A	EXMOUTH J CN - 72A	EXMOUTH J CN - 72A	EXMOUTH J CN - 72A
31846	SALISBURY - 72B	SALISBURY - 72B	SALISBURY - 72B	EXMOUTH J CN - 72A	EXMOUTH J CN - 72A	EXMOUTH J CN - 72A	EXMOUTH J CN - 72A
31847	EXMOUTH J CN - 72A	EXMOUTH J CN - 72A	EXMOUTH J CN - 72A	EXMOUTH J CN - 72A	EXMOUTH J CN - 72A	EXMOUTH J CN - 72A	EXMOUTH J CN - 72A
31848	REDHILL - 75B	REDHILL - 75B	REDHILL - 75B	REDHILL - 75B	REDHILL - 75B	REDHILL - 75B	EXMOUTH J CN - 72A
31849	REDHILL - 75B	REDHILL - 75B	REDHILL - 75B	REDHILL - 75B	REDHILL - 75B	REDHILL - 75B	EXMOUTH J CN - 72A
31850	FAVERSHAM - 73E	FAVERSHAM - 73E	FAVERSHAM - 73E	FAVERSHAM - 73E	FAVERSHAM - 73E	FAVERSHAM - 73E	FAVERSHAM - 73E
31851	REDHILL - 75B	REDHILL - 75B	REDHILL - 75B	REDHILL - 75B	REDHILL - 75B	REDHILL - 75B	EXMOUTH J CN - 72A
31852	REDHILL - 75B	REDHILL - 75B	REDHILL - 75B	REDHILL - 75B	REDHILL - 75B	REDHILL - 75B	EXMOUTH J CN - 72A
31853	EXMOUTH J CN - 72A	EXMOUTH J CN - 72A	EXMOUTH J CN - 72A	EXMOUTH J CN - 72A	EXMOUTH J CN - 72A	EXMOUTH J CN - 72A	EXMOUTH J CN - 72A
31854	FAVERSHAM - 73E	FAVERSHAM - 73E	FAVERSHAM - 73E	FAVERSHAM - 73E	FAVERSHAM - 73E	FAVERSHAM - 73E	FAVERSHAM - 73E
31855	EXMOUTH J CN - 72A	EXMOUTH J CN - 72A	EXMOUTH J CN - 72A	EXMOUTH J CN - 72A	EXMOUTH J CN - 72A	EXMOUTH J CN - 72A	EXMOUTH J CN - 72A
31856	EXMOUTH J CN - 72A	EXMOUTH J CN - 72A	EXMOUTH J CN - 72A	EXMOUTH J CN - 72A	EXMOUTH J CN - 72A	EXMOUTH J CN - 72A	EXMOUTH J CN - 72A
31857	REDHILL - 75B	REDHILL - 75B	REDHILL - 75B	REDHILL - 75B	REDHILL - 75B	REDHILL - 75B	REDHILL - 75B
31858	REDHILL - 75B	REDHILL - 75B	REDHILL - 75B	REDHILL - 75B	REDHILL - 75B	REDHILL - 75B	REDHILL - 75B
31859	STEWARTS LANE - 73A	STEWARTS LANE - 73A	STEWARTS LANE - 73A	RAMSGATE - 74B	RAMSGATE - 74B	RAMSGATE - 74B	RAMSGATE - 74B
31860	STEWARTS LANE - 73A	ASHFORD - 74A	ASHFORD - 74A	ASHFORD - 74A	ASHFORD - 74A	ASHFORD - 74A	ASHFORD - 74A
31861	STEWARTS LANE - 73A	ASHFORD - 74A	ASHFORD - 74A	ASHFORD - 74A	ASHFORD - 74A	ASHFORD - 74A	ASHFORD - 74A
31862	REDHILL - 75B	REDHILL - 75B	REDHILL - 75B	REDHILL - 75B	REDHILL - 75B	REDHILL - 75B	REDHILL - 75B
31863	REDHILL - 75B	REDHILL - 75B	REDHILL - 75B	REDHILL - 75B	REDHILL - 75B	REDHILL - 75B	REDHILL - 75B
31864	REDHILL - 75B	REDHILL - 75B	REDHILL - 75B	REDHILL - 75B	REDHILL - 75B	REDHILL - 75B	REDHILL - 75B
31865	REDHILL - 75B	REDHILL - 75B	REDHILL - 75B	REDHILL - 75B	REDHILL - 75B	REDHILL - 75B	REDHILL - 75B
31866	EASTLEIGH - 71A	EASTLEIGH - 71A	EASTLEIGH - 71A	EXMOUTH J CN - 72A	EXMOUTH J CN - 72A	EXMOUTH J CN - 72A	REDHILL - 75B
31867	EASTLEIGH - 71A	EASTLEIGH - 71A	EASTLEIGH - 71A	EXMOUTH J CN - 72A	EXMOUTH J CN - 72A	EXMOUTH J CN - 72A	REDHILL - 75B
31868	FAVERSHAM - 73E	FAVERSHAM - 73E	FAVERSHAM - 73E	FAVERSHAM - 73E	FAVERSHAM - 73E	FAVERSHAM - 73E	REDHILL - 75B
31869	EXMOUTH J CN - 72A	EXMOUTH J CN - 72A	EXMOUTH J CN - 72A	EXMOUTH J CN - 72A	EXMOUTH J CN - 72A	EXMOUTH J CN - 72A	REDHILL - 75B
31870	FRATTON - 71D	FRATTON - 71D	FRATTON - 71D	BRIGHTON - 75A	FRATTON - 71D	FRATTON - 71D	FRATTON - 71D
31871	PLYMOUTH - 72D	PLYMOUTH - 72D	PLYMOUTH - 72D	BRIGHTON - 75A	FRATTON - 71D	FRATTON - 71D	FRATTON - 71D
31872	SALISBURY - 72B	SALISBURY - 72B	SALISBURY - 72B	SALISBURY - 72B	SALISBURY - 72B	SALISBURY - 72B	SALISBURY - 72B
31873	SALISBURY - 72B	SALISBURY - 72B	SALISBURY - 72B	SALISBURY - 72B	SALISBURY - 72B	SALISBURY - 72B	SALISBURY - 72B
31874	EXMOUTH J CN - 72A	EXMOUTH J CN - 72A	EXMOUTH J CN - 72A	SALISBURY - 72B	SALISBURY - 72B	SALISBURY - 72B	SALISBURY - 72B
31875	EXMOUTH J CN - 72A	EXMOUTH J CN - 72A	EXMOUTH J CN - 72A	SALISBURY - 72B	SALISBURY - 72B	SALISBURY - 72B	SALISBURY - 72B
				N1 2-6-0 (1922)			
31822	ST LEONARDS - 74E	HITHER GREEN - 73C	HITHER GREEN - 73C	HITHER GREEN - 73C	HITHER GREEN - 73C	HITHER GREEN - 73C	HITHER GREEN - 73C
31876	ST LEONARDS - 74E	HITHER GREEN - 73C	HITHER GREEN - 73C	HITHER GREEN - 73C	HITHER GREEN - 73C	HITHER GREEN - 73C	HITHER GREEN - 73C
31877	HITHER GREEN - 73C	HITHER GREEN - 73C	HITHER GREEN - 73C	HITHER GREEN - 73C	HITHER GREEN - 73C	HITHER GREEN - 73C	HITHER GREEN - 73C
31878	HITHER GREEN - 73C	HITHER GREEN - 73C	HITHER GREEN - 73C	HITHER GREEN - 73C	HITHER GREEN - 73C	HITHER GREEN - 73C	HITHER GREEN - 73C
31879	HITHER GREEN - 73C	HITHER GREEN - 73C	HITHER GREEN - 73C	HITHER GREEN - 73C	HITHER GREEN - 73C	HITHER GREEN - 73C	HITHER GREEN - 73C
31880	HITHER GREEN - 73C	HITHER GREEN - 73C	HITHER GREEN - 73C	HITHER GREEN - 73C	HITHER GREEN - 73C	HITHER GREEN - 73C	HITHER GREEN - 73C

loco	Jun-51	Jul-51	Sep-51	Dec-51	Jan-52	Mar-52	Jun-52
				N 2-6-0 (1917)			
31400	ASHFORD - 74A	ASHFORD - 74A	ASHFORD - 74A	ASHFORD - 74A	ASHFORD - 74A	ASHFORD - 74A	ASHFORD - 74A
31401	ASHFORD - 74A	ASHFORD - 74A	ASHFORD - 74A	ASHFORD - 74A	ASHFORD - 74A	ASHFORD - 74A	ASHFORD - 74A
31402	ASHFORD - 74A	ASHFORD - 74A	ASHFORD - 74A	ASHFORD - 74A	ASHFORD - 74A	ASHFORD - 74A	ASHFORD - 74A
31403	ASHFORD - 74A	ASHFORD - 74A	ASHFORD - 74A	ASHFORD - 74A	ASHFORD - 74A	ASHFORD - 74A	ASHFORD - 74A
31404	ASHFORD - 74A	ASHFORD - 74A	ASHFORD - 74A	ASHFORD - 74A	ASHFORD - 74A	ASHFORD - 74A	ASHFORD - 74A
31405	ASHFORD - 74A	ASHFORD - 74A	ASHFORD - 74A	ASHFORD - 74A	ASHFORD - 74A	ASHFORD - 74A	ASHFORD - 74A
31406	ASHFORD - 74A	ASHFORD - 74A	ASHFORD - 74A	ASHFORD - 74A	ASHFORD - 74A	ASHFORD - 74A	ASHFORD - 74A
31407	ASHFORD - 74A	ASHFORD - 74A	ASHFORD - 74A	ASHFORD - 74A	ASHFORD - 74A	ASHFORD - 74A	ASHFORD - 74A
31408	ASHFORD - 74A	ASHFORD - 74A	ASHFORD - 74A	ASHFORD - 74A	ASHFORD - 74A	ASHFORD - 74A	ASHFORD - 74A
31409	STEWARTS LANE - 73A	STEWARTS LANE - 73A	STEWARTS LANE - 73A	STEWARTS LANE - 73A	STEWARTS LANE - 73A	STEWARTS LANE - 73A	STEWARTS LANE - 73A
31410	STEWARTS LANE - 73A	STEWARTS LANE - 73A	STEWARTS LANE - 73A	STEWARTS LANE - 73A	STEWARTS LANE - 73A	STEWARTS LANE - 73A	STEWARTS LANE - 73A
31411	STEWARTS LANE - 73A	STEWARTS LANE - 73A	STEWARTS LANE - 73A	STEWARTS LANE - 73A	STEWARTS LANE - 73A	STEWARTS LANE - 73A	STEWARTS LANE - 73A
31412	STEWARTS LANE - 73A	STEWARTS LANE - 73A	STEWARTS LANE - 73A	STEWARTS LANE - 73A	STEWARTS LANE - 73A	STEWARTS LANE - 73A	STEWARTS LANE - 73A
31413	STEWARTS LANE - 73A	STEWARTS LANE - 73A	STEWARTS LANE - 73A	STEWARTS LANE - 73A	STEWARTS LANE - 73A	STEWARTS LANE - 73A	STEWARTS LANE - 73A
31414	STEWARTS LANE - 73A	STEWARTS LANE - 73A	STEWARTS LANE - 73A	STEWARTS LANE - 73A	STEWARTS LANE - 73A	STEWARTS LANE - 73A	STEWARTS LANE - 73A
31810	STEWARTS LANE - 73A	STEWARTS LANE - 73A	STEWARTS LANE - 73A	STEWARTS LANE - 73A	STEWARTS LANE - 73A	STEWARTS LANE - 73A	STEWARTS LANE - 73A
31811	STEWARTS LANE - 73A	STEWARTS LANE - 73A	STEWARTS LANE - 73A	STEWARTS LANE - 73A	STEWARTS LANE - 73A	STEWARTS LANE - 73A	STEWARTS LANE - 73A
31812	STEWARTS LANE - 73A	STEWARTS LANE - 73A	STEWARTS LANE - 73A	STEWARTS LANE - 73A	STEWARTS LANE - 73A	STEWARTS LANE - 73A	STEWARTS LANE - 73A
31813	STEWARTS LANE - 73A	STEWARTS LANE - 73A	STEWARTS LANE - 73A	STEWARTS LANE - 73A	STEWARTS LANE - 73A	STEWARTS LANE - 73A	STEWARTS LANE - 73A
31814	STEWARTS LANE - 73A	STEWARTS LANE - 73A	STEWARTS LANE - 73A	STEWARTS LANE - 73A	STEWARTS LANE - 73A	STEWARTS LANE - 73A	STEWARTS LANE - 73A
31815	STEWARTS LANE - 73A	STEWARTS LANE - 73A	STEWARTS LANE - 73A	GILLINGHAM - 73D	GILLINGHAM - 73D	GILLINGHAM - 73D	GILLINGHAM - 73D
31816	STEWARTS LANE - 73A	STEWARTS LANE - 73A	GILLINGHAM - 73D	GILLINGHAM - 73D	GILLINGHAM - 73D	GILLINGHAM - 73D	GILLINGHAM - 73D
31817	STEWARTS LANE - 73A	DOVER - 74C	DOVER - 74C	DOVER - 74C	DOVER - 74C	DOVER - 74C	DOVER - 74C
31818	STEWARTS LANE - 73A	DOVER - 74C	DOVER - 74C	DOVER - 74C	DOVER - 74C	DOVER - 74C	DOVER - 74C
31819	DOVER - 74C	DOVER - 74C	DOVER - 74C	DOVER - 74C	DOVER - 74C	DOVER - 74C	DOVER - 74C
31820	DOVER - 74C	DOVER - 74C	DOVER - 74C	DOVER - 74C	DOVER - 74C	DOVER - 74C	DOVER - 74C
31821	DOVER - 74C	DOVER - 74C	DOVER - 74C	DOVER - 74C	DOVER - 74C	DOVER - 74C	DOVER - 74C
31823	DOVER - 74C	B.ARMS - 73B	B.ARMS - 73B	B.ARMS - 73B	B.ARMS - 73B	B.ARMS - 73B	B.ARMS - 73B
31824	B.ARMS - 73B	B.ARMS - 73B	B.ARMS - 73B	B.ARMS - 73B	B.ARMS - 73B	B.ARMS - 73B	B.ARMS - 73B
31825	B.ARMS - 73B	B.ARMS - 73B	B.ARMS - 73B	B.ARMS - 73B	B.ARMS - 73B	B.ARMS - 73B	B.ARMS - 73B
31826	B.ARMS - 73B	B.ARMS - 73B	B.ARMS - 73B	B.ARMS - 73B	B.ARMS - 73B	B.ARMS - 73B	B.ARMS - 73B
31827	B.ARMS - 73B	B.ARMS - 73B	B.ARMS - 73B	B.ARMS - 73B	B.ARMS - 73B	B.ARMS - 73B	B.ARMS - 73B
31828	B.ARMS - 73B	B.ARMS - 73B	B.ARMS - 73B	B.ARMS - 73B	B.ARMS - 73B	B.ARMS - 73B	B.ARMS - 73B
31829	B.ARMS - 73B	B.ARMS - 73B	B.ARMS - 73B	B.ARMS - 73B	B.ARMS - 73B	B.ARMS - 73B	B.ARMS - 73B
31830	EXMOUTH J CN - 72A	EXMOUTH J CN - 72A	EXMOUTH J CN - 72A	EXMOUTH J CN - 72A	EXMOUTH J CN - 72A	EXMOUTH J CN - 72A	EXMOUTH J CN - 72A
31831	EXMOUTH J CN - 72A	EXMOUTH J CN - 72A	EXMOUTH J CN - 72A	EXMOUTH J CN - 72A	EXMOUTH J CN - 72A	EXMOUTH J CN - 72A	EXMOUTH J CN - 72A
31832	EXMOUTH J CN - 72A	EXMOUTH J CN - 72A	EXMOUTH J CN - 72A	EXMOUTH J CN - 72A	EXMOUTH J CN - 72A	EXMOUTH J CN - 72A	EXMOUTH J CN - 72A
31833	EXMOUTH J CN - 72A	EXMOUTH J CN - 72A	EXMOUTH J CN - 72A	EXMOUTH J CN - 72A	EXMOUTH J CN - 72A	EXMOUTH J CN - 72A	EXMOUTH J CN - 72A
31834	EXMOUTH J CN - 72A	EXMOUTH J CN - 72A	EXMOUTH J CN - 72A	EXMOUTH J CN - 72A	EXMOUTH J CN - 72A	EXMOUTH J CN - 72A	EXMOUTH J CN - 72A
31835	EXMOUTH J CN - 72A	EXMOUTH J CN - 72A	EXMOUTH J CN - 72A	EXMOUTH J CN - 72A	EXMOUTH J CN - 72A	EXMOUTH J CN - 72A	EXMOUTH J CN - 72A
31836	EXMOUTH J CN - 72A	EXMOUTH J CN - 72A	EXMOUTH J CN - 72A	EXMOUTH J CN - 72A	EXMOUTH J CN - 72A	EXMOUTH J CN - 72A	EXMOUTH J CN - 72A
31837	EXMOUTH J CN - 72A	EXMOUTH J CN - 72A	EXMOUTH J CN - 72A	EXMOUTH J CN - 72A	EXMOUTH J CN - 72A	EXMOUTH J CN - 72A	EXMOUTH J CN - 72A
31838	EXMOUTH J CN - 72A	EXMOUTH J CN - 72A	EXMOUTH J CN - 72A	EXMOUTH J CN - 72A	EXMOUTH J CN - 72A	EXMOUTH J CN - 72A	EXMOUTH J CN - 72A
31839	EXMOUTH J CN - 72A	EXMOUTH J CN - 72A	EXMOUTH J CN - 72A	EXMOUTH J CN - 72A	EXMOUTH J CN - 72A	EXMOUTH J CN - 72A	EXMOUTH J CN - 72A
31840	EXMOUTH J CN - 72A	EXMOUTH J CN - 72A	EXMOUTH J CN - 72A	EXMOUTH J CN - 72A	EXMOUTH J CN - 72A	EXMOUTH J CN - 72A	BARNSTAPLE - 72E
31841	EXMOUTH J CN - 72A	EXMOUTH J CN - 72A	EXMOUTH J CN - 72A	EXMOUTH J CN - 72A	EXMOUTH J CN - 72A	EXMOUTH J CN - 72A	BARNSTAPLE - 72E
31842	BARNSTAPLE - 72E	BARNSTAPLE - 72E	BARNSTAPLE - 72E	BARNSTAPLE - 72E	BARNSTAPLE - 72E	BARNSTAPLE - 72E	BARNSTAPLE - 72E
31843	EXMOUTH J CN - 72A	EXMOUTH J CN - 72A	EXMOUTH J CN - 72A	EXMOUTH J CN - 72A	EXMOUTH J CN - 72A	EXMOUTH J CN - 72A	EXMOUTH J CN - 72A
31844	EXMOUTH J CN - 72A	EXMOUTH J CN - 72A	EXMOUTH J CN - 72A	EXMOUTH J CN - 72A	EXMOUTH J CN - 72A	EXMOUTH J CN - 72A	EXMOUTH J CN - 72A
31845	EXMOUTH J CN - 72A	EXMOUTH J CN - 72A	EXMOUTH J CN - 72A	EXMOUTH J CN - 72A	EXMOUTH J CN - 72A	EXMOUTH J CN - 72A	EXMOUTH J CN - 72A
31846	EXMOUTH J CN - 72A	EXMOUTH J CN - 72A	EXMOUTH J CN - 72A	EXMOUTH J CN - 72A	EXMOUTH J CN - 72A	EXMOUTH J CN - 72A	EXMOUTH J CN - 72A
31847	EXMOUTH J CN - 72A	EXMOUTH J CN - 72A	EXMOUTH J CN - 72A	EXMOUTH J CN - 72A	EXMOUTH J CN - 72A	EXMOUTH J CN - 72A	EXMOUTH J CN - 72A
31848	EXMOUTH J CN - 72A	EXMOUTH J CN - 72A	EXMOUTH J CN - 72A	EXMOUTH J CN - 72A	EXMOUTH J CN - 72A	EXMOUTH J CN - 72A	EXMOUTH J CN - 72A
31849	EXMOUTH J CN - 72A	EXMOUTH J CN - 72A	EXMOUTH J CN - 72A	EXMOUTH J CN - 72A	EXMOUTH J CN - 72A	EXMOUTH J CN - 72A	EXMOUTH J CN - 72A
31850	FAVERSHAM - 73E	FAVERSHAM - 73E	FAVERSHAM - 73E	FAVERSHAM - 73E	FAVERSHAM - 73E	FAVERSHAM - 73E	FAVERSHAM - 73E
31851	EXMOUTH J CN - 72A	EXMOUTH J CN - 72A	FRATTON - 71D	FRATTON - 71D	FRATTON - 71D	FRATTON - 71D	FRATTON - 71D
31852	EXMOUTH J CN - 72A	EXMOUTH J CN - 72A	FRATTON - 71D	FRATTON - 71D	FRATTON - 71D	FRATTON - 71D	FRATTON - 71D
31853	EXMOUTH J CN - 72A	EXMOUTH J CN - 72A	B.ARMS - 73B	B.ARMS - 73B	B.ARMS - 73B	B.ARMS - 73B	B.ARMS - 73B
31854	FAVERSHAM - 73E	FAVERSHAM - 73E	FAVERSHAM - 73E	FAVERSHAM - 73E	FAVERSHAM - 73E	FAVERSHAM - 73E	FAVERSHAM - 73E
31855	EXMOUTH J CN - 72A	EXMOUTH J CN - 72A	B.ARMS - 73B	B.ARMS - 73B	B.ARMS - 73B	B.ARMS - 73B	B.ARMS - 73B
31856	EXMOUTH J CN - 72A	EXMOUTH J CN - 72A	HITHER GREEN - 73C	HITHER GREEN - 73C	HITHER GREEN - 73C	HITHER GREEN - 73C	HITHER GREEN - 73C
31857	REDHILL - 75B	HITHER GREEN - 73C	HITHER GREEN - 73C	HITHER GREEN - 73C	HITHER GREEN - 73C	HITHER GREEN - 73C	HITHER GREEN - 73C
31858	REDHILL - 75B	HITHER GREEN - 73C	HITHER GREEN - 73C	HITHER GREEN - 73C	HITHER GREEN - 73C	HITHER GREEN - 73C	HITHER GREEN - 73C
31859	RAMSGATE - 74B	HITHER GREEN - 73C	HITHER GREEN - 73C	HITHER GREEN - 73C	HITHER GREEN - 73C	HITHER GREEN - 73C	HITHER GREEN - 73C
31860	ASHFORD - 74A	HITHER GREEN - 73C	HITHER GREEN - 73C	HITHER GREEN - 73C	HITHER GREEN - 73C	HITHER GREEN - 73C	HITHER GREEN - 73C
31861	ASHFORD - 74A	HITHER GREEN - 73C	HITHER GREEN - 73C	HITHER GREEN - 73C	HITHER GREEN - 73C	HITHER GREEN - 73C	HITHER GREEN - 73C
31862	REDHILL - 75B	HITHER GREEN - 73C	HITHER GREEN - 73C	HITHER GREEN - 73C	HITHER GREEN - 73C	HITHER GREEN - 73C	HITHER GREEN - 73C
31863	REDHILL - 75B	REDHILL - 75B	REDHILL - 75B	REDHILL - 75B	REDHILL - 75B	REDHILL - 75B	REDHILL - 75B
31864	REDHILL - 75B	REDHILL - 75B	REDHILL - 75B	REDHILL - 75B	REDHILL - 75B	REDHILL - 75B	REDHILL - 75B
31865	REDHILL - 75B	REDHILL - 75B	REDHILL - 75B	REDHILL - 75B	REDHILL - 75B	REDHILL - 75B	REDHILL - 75B
31866	REDHILL - 75B	REDHILL - 75B	REDHILL - 75B	REDHILL - 75B	REDHILL - 75B	REDHILL - 75B	REDHILL - 75B
31867	REDHILL - 75B	REDHILL - 75B	REDHILL - 75B	REDHILL - 75B	REDHILL - 75B	REDHILL - 75B	REDHILL - 75B
31868	REDHILL - 75B	REDHILL - 75B	REDHILL - 75B	REDHILL - 75B	REDHILL - 75B	REDHILL - 75B	REDHILL - 75B
31869	REDHILL - 75B	REDHILL - 75B	REDHILL - 75B	REDHILL - 75B	REDHILL - 75B	REDHILL - 75B	REDHILL - 75B
31870	FRATTON - 71D	FRATTON - 71D	B.ARMS - 73B	B.ARMS - 73B	B.ARMS - 73B	B.ARMS - 73B	B.ARMS - 73B
31871	FRATTON - 71D	FRATTON - 71D	B.ARMS - 73B	B.ARMS - 73B	B.ARMS - 73B	B.ARMS - 73B	B.ARMS - 73B
31872	B.ARMS - 73B	B.ARMS - 73B	B.ARMS - 73B	B.ARMS - 73B	B.ARMS - 73B	B.ARMS - 73B	B.ARMS - 73B
31873	B.ARMS - 73B	B.ARMS - 73B	B.ARMS - 73B	B.ARMS - 73B	B.ARMS - 73B	B.ARMS - 73B	B.ARMS - 73B
31874	HITHER GREEN - 73C	B.ARMS - 73B	B.ARMS - 73B	B.ARMS - 73B	B.ARMS - 73B	B.ARMS - 73B	B.ARMS - 73B
31875	HITHER GREEN - 73C	B.ARMS - 73B	B.ARMS - 73B	B.ARMS - 73B	B.ARMS - 73B	B.ARMS - 73B	B.ARMS - 73B
				N1 2-6-0 (1922)			
31822	HITHER GREEN - 73C	HITHER GREEN - 73C	HITHER GREEN - 73C	HITHER GREEN - 73C	HITHER GREEN - 73C	HITHER GREEN - 73C	HITHER GREEN - 73C
31876	HITHER GREEN - 73C	HITHER GREEN - 73C	HITHER GREEN - 73C	HITHER GREEN - 73C	HITHER GREEN - 73C	HITHER GREEN - 73C	HITHER GREEN - 73C
31877	HITHER GREEN - 73C	HITHER GREEN - 73C	HITHER GREEN - 73C	HITHER GREEN - 73C	HITHER GREEN - 73C	HITHER GREEN - 73C	HITHER GREEN - 73C
31878	HITHER GREEN - 73C	HITHER GREEN - 73C	HITHER GREEN - 73C	HITHER GREEN - 73C	HITHER GREEN - 73C	HITHER GREEN - 73C	HITHER GREEN - 73C
31879	HITHER GREEN - 73C	HITHER GREEN - 73C	HITHER GREEN - 73C	HITHER GREEN - 73C	HITHER GREEN - 73C	HITHER GREEN - 73C	HITHER GREEN - 73C
31880	HITHER GREEN - 73C	HITHER GREEN - 73C	HITHER GREEN - 73C	HITHER GREEN - 73C	HITHER GREEN - 73C	HITHER GREEN - 73C	HITHER GREEN - 73C

loco	Sep-52	Dec-52	Mar-53	May-53	Jul-53	Sep-53	Nov-53
			N 2-6-0 (1917)				
31400	ASHFORD - 74A	ASHFORD - 74A	B.ARMS - 73B	B.ARMS - 73B	B.ARMS - 73B	B.ARMS - 73B	B.ARMS - 73B
31401	ASHFORD - 74A	ASHFORD - 74A	ASHFORD - 74A	ASHFORD - 74A	ASHFORD - 74A	ASHFORD - 74A	ASHFORD - 74A
31402	ASHFORD - 74A	ASHFORD - 74A	ASHFORD - 74A	ASHFORD - 74A	ASHFORD - 74A	ASHFORD - 74A	ASHFORD - 74A
31403	ASHFORD - 74A	ASHFORD - 74A	ASHFORD - 74A	ASHFORD - 74A	ASHFORD - 74A	ASHFORD - 74A	ASHFORD - 74A
31404	ASHFORD - 74A	ASHFORD - 74A	ASHFORD - 74A	ASHFORD - 74A	ASHFORD - 74A	ASHFORD - 74A	ASHFORD - 74A
31405	ASHFORD - 74A	ASHFORD - 74A	ASHFORD - 74A	ASHFORD - 74A	ASHFORD - 74A	ASHFORD - 74A	ASHFORD - 74A
31406	ASHFORD - 74A	ASHFORD - 74A	HITHER GREEN - 73C	HITHER GREEN - 73C	HITHER GREEN - 73C	HITHER GREEN - 73C	HITHER GREEN - 73C
31407	ASHFORD - 74A	ASHFORD - 74A	ASHFORD - 74A	ASHFORD - 74A	ASHFORD - 74A	ASHFORD - 74A	ASHFORD - 74A
31408	ASHFORD - 74A	ASHFORD - 74A	HITHER GREEN - 73C	HITHER GREEN - 73C	HITHER GREEN - 73C	B.ARMS - 73B	B.ARMS - 73B
31409	STEWARTS LANE - 73A	STEWARTS LANE - 73A	STEWARTS LANE - 73A	STEWARTS LANE - 73A	STEWARTS LANE - 73A	STEWARTS LANE - 73A	STEWARTS LANE - 73A
31410	STEWARTS LANE - 73A	STEWARTS LANE - 73A	STEWARTS LANE - 73A	STEWARTS LANE - 73A	STEWARTS LANE - 73A	STEWARTS LANE - 73A	STEWARTS LANE - 73A
31411	STEWARTS LANE - 73A	STEWARTS LANE - 73A	STEWARTS LANE - 73A	STEWARTS LANE - 73A	STEWARTS LANE - 73A	STEWARTS LANE - 73A	STEWARTS LANE - 73A
31412	STEWARTS LANE - 73A	STEWARTS LANE - 73A	STEWARTS LANE - 73A	STEWARTS LANE - 73A	STEWARTS LANE - 73A	STEWARTS LANE - 73A	STEWARTS LANE - 73A
31413	STEWARTS LANE - 73A	STEWARTS LANE - 73A	STEWARTS LANE - 73A	STEWARTS LANE - 73A	STEWARTS LANE - 73A	STEWARTS LANE - 73A	STEWARTS LANE - 73A
31414	STEWARTS LANE - 73A	STEWARTS LANE - 73A	STEWARTS LANE - 73A	STEWARTS LANE - 73A	STEWARTS LANE - 73A	STEWARTS LANE - 73A	STEWARTS LANE - 73A
31810	STEWARTS LANE - 73A	STEWARTS LANE - 73A	STEWARTS LANE - 73A	STEWARTS LANE - 73A	STEWARTS LANE - 73A	STEWARTS LANE - 73A	STEWARTS LANE - 73A
31811	STEWARTS LANE - 73A	STEWARTS LANE - 73A	STEWARTS LANE - 73A	STEWARTS LANE - 73A	STEWARTS LANE - 73A	STEWARTS LANE - 73A	STEWARTS LANE - 73A
31812	STEWARTS LANE - 73A	STEWARTS LANE - 73A	STEWARTS LANE - 73A	STEWARTS LANE - 73A	STEWARTS LANE - 73A	STEWARTS LANE - 73A	STEWARTS LANE - 73A
31813	STEWARTS LANE - 73A	STEWARTS LANE - 73A	STEWARTS LANE - 73A	STEWARTS LANE - 73A	STEWARTS LANE - 73A	SALISBURY - 72B	SALISBURY - 72B
31814	STEWARTS LANE - 73A	STEWARTS LANE - 73A	STEWARTS LANE - 73A	STEWARTS LANE - 73A	STEWARTS LANE - 73A	SALISBURY - 72B	SALISBURY - 72B
31815	GILLINGHAM - 73D	GILLINGHAM - 73D	GILLINGHAM - 73D	GILLINGHAM - 73D	GILLINGHAM - 73D	STEWARTS LANE - 73A	STEWARTS LANE - 73A
31816	GILLINGHAM - 73D	GILLINGHAM - 73D	GILLINGHAM - 73D	GILLINGHAM - 73D	GILLINGHAM - 73D	STEWARTS LANE - 73A	STEWARTS LANE - 73A
31817	DOVER - 74C	DOVER - 74C	DOVER - 74C	DOVER - 74C	DOVER - 74C	DOVER - 74C	DOVER - 74C
31818	DOVER - 74C	DOVER - 74C	DOVER - 74C	DOVER - 74C	DOVER - 74C	DOVER - 74C	DOVER - 74C
31819	DOVER - 74C	DOVER - 74C	DOVER - 74C	DOVER - 74C	DOVER - 74C	DOVER - 74C	DOVER - 74C
31820	DOVER - 74C	DOVER - 74C	DOVER - 74C	DOVER - 74C	DOVER - 74C	DOVER - 74C	DOVER - 74C
31821	DOVER - 74C	DOVER - 74C	DOVER - 74C	DOVER - 74C	DOVER - 74C	DOVER - 74C	DOVER - 74C
31823	B.ARMS - 73B	B.ARMS - 73B	B.ARMS - 73B	B.ARMS - 73B	B.ARMS - 73B	B.ARMS - 73B	B.ARMS - 73B
31824	B.ARMS - 73B	B.ARMS - 73B	B.ARMS - 73B	B.ARMS - 73B	B.ARMS - 73B	B.ARMS - 73B	B.ARMS - 73B
31825	B.ARMS - 73B	B.ARMS - 73B	B.ARMS - 73B	B.ARMS - 73B	B.ARMS - 73B	B.ARMS - 73B	B.ARMS - 73B
31826	B.ARMS - 73B	B.ARMS - 73B	B.ARMS - 73B	B.ARMS - 73B	B.ARMS - 73B	B.ARMS - 73B	B.ARMS - 73B
31827	B.ARMS - 73B	B.ARMS - 73B	B.ARMS - 73B	B.ARMS - 73B	B.ARMS - 73B	B.ARMS - 73B	B.ARMS - 73B
31828	B.ARMS - 73B	B.ARMS - 73B	B.ARMS - 73B	B.ARMS - 73B	B.ARMS - 73B	B.ARMS - 73B	B.ARMS - 73B
31829	B.ARMS - 73B	B.ARMS - 73B	B.ARMS - 73B	B.ARMS - 73B	B.ARMS - 73B	B.ARMS - 73B	B.ARMS - 73B
31830	EXMOUTH JCN - 72A	EXMOUTH JCN - 72A	EXMOUTH JCN - 72A	EXMOUTH JCN - 72A	EXMOUTH JCN - 72A	EXMOUTH JCN - 72A	EXMOUTH JCN - 72A
31831	EXMOUTH JCN - 72A	EXMOUTH JCN - 72A	EXMOUTH JCN - 72A	EXMOUTH JCN - 72A	EXMOUTH JCN - 72A	EXMOUTH JCN - 72A	EXMOUTH JCN - 72A
31832	EXMOUTH JCN - 72A	EXMOUTH JCN - 72A	EXMOUTH JCN - 72A	EXMOUTH JCN - 72A	EXMOUTH JCN - 72A	EXMOUTH JCN - 72A	EXMOUTH JCN - 72A
31833	EXMOUTH JCN - 72A	EXMOUTH JCN - 72A	EXMOUTH JCN - 72A	EXMOUTH JCN - 72A	EXMOUTH JCN - 72A	EXMOUTH JCN - 72A	EXMOUTH JCN - 72A
31834	EXMOUTH JCN - 72A	EXMOUTH JCN - 72A	EXMOUTH JCN - 72A	EXMOUTH JCN - 72A	EXMOUTH JCN - 72A	EXMOUTH JCN - 72A	EXMOUTH JCN - 72A
31835	EXMOUTH JCN - 72A	EXMOUTH JCN - 72A	EXMOUTH JCN - 72A	EXMOUTH JCN - 72A	EXMOUTH JCN - 72A	EXMOUTH JCN - 72A	EXMOUTH JCN - 72A
31836	EXMOUTH JCN - 72A	EXMOUTH JCN - 72A	EXMOUTH JCN - 72A	EXMOUTH JCN - 72A	EXMOUTH JCN - 72A	EXMOUTH JCN - 72A	EXMOUTH JCN - 72A
31837	EXMOUTH JCN - 72A	YEOVIL - 72C	EXMOUTH JCN - 72A	EXMOUTH JCN - 72A	EXMOUTH JCN - 72A	EXMOUTH JCN - 72A	EXMOUTH JCN - 72A
31838	EXMOUTH JCN - 72A	EXMOUTH JCN - 72A	EXMOUTH JCN - 72A	EXMOUTH JCN - 72A	EXMOUTH JCN - 72A	EXMOUTH JCN - 72A	EXMOUTH JCN - 72A
31839	EXMOUTH JCN - 72A	EXMOUTH JCN - 72A	EXMOUTH JCN - 72A	EXMOUTH JCN - 72A	EXMOUTH JCN - 72A	EXMOUTH JCN - 72A	EXMOUTH JCN - 72A
31840	EXMOUTH JCN - 72A	EXMOUTH JCN - 72A	EXMOUTH JCN - 72A	EXMOUTH JCN - 72A	EXMOUTH JCN - 72A	EXMOUTH JCN - 72A	EXMOUTH JCN - 72A
31841	EXMOUTH JCN - 72A	EXMOUTH JCN - 72A	EXMOUTH JCN - 72A	EXMOUTH JCN - 72A	EXMOUTH JCN - 72A	EXMOUTH JCN - 72A	EXMOUTH JCN - 72A
31842	BARNSTAPLE - 72E	EXMOUTH JCN - 72A	EXMOUTH JCN - 72A	EXMOUTH JCN - 72A	EXMOUTH JCN - 72A	EXMOUTH JCN - 72A	EXMOUTH JCN - 72A
31843	BARNSTAPLE - 72E	BARNSTAPLE - 72E	BARNSTAPLE - 72E	BARNSTAPLE - 72E	BARNSTAPLE - 72E	BARNSTAPLE - 72E	BARNSTAPLE - 72E
31844	FRATTON - 71D	FRATTON - 71D	FRATTON - 71D	FRATTON - 71D	FRATTON - 71D	EXMOUTH JCN - 72A	EXMOUTH JCN - 72A
31845	EXMOUTH JCN - 72A	EXMOUTH JCN - 72A	EXMOUTH JCN - 72A	EXMOUTH JCN - 72A	EXMOUTH JCN - 72A	EXMOUTH JCN - 72A	EXMOUTH JCN - 72A
31846	EXMOUTH JCN - 72A	EXMOUTH JCN - 72A	EXMOUTH JCN - 72A	EXMOUTH JCN - 72A	EXMOUTH JCN - 72A	EXMOUTH JCN - 72A	EXMOUTH JCN - 72A
31847	EXMOUTH JCN - 72A	EXMOUTH JCN - 72A	EXMOUTH JCN - 72A	EXMOUTH JCN - 72A	EXMOUTH JCN - 72A	EXMOUTH JCN - 72A	EXMOUTH JCN - 72A
31848	EXMOUTH JCN - 72A	EXMOUTH JCN - 72A	EXMOUTH JCN - 72A	EXMOUTH JCN - 72A	EXMOUTH JCN - 72A	EXMOUTH JCN - 72A	EXMOUTH JCN - 72A
31849	EXMOUTH JCN - 72A	EXMOUTH JCN - 72A	EXMOUTH JCN - 72A	EXMOUTH JCN - 72A	EXMOUTH JCN - 72A	EXMOUTH JCN - 72A	EXMOUTH JCN - 72A
31850	FAVERSHAM - 73E	FAVERSHAM - 73E	FAVERSHAM - 73E	FAVERSHAM - 73E	FAVERSHAM - 73E	FAVERSHAM - 73E	FAVERSHAM - 73E
31851	FRATTON - 71D	FRATTON - 71D	FRATTON - 71D	FRATTON - 71D	FRATTON - 71D	FRATTON - 71D	FRATTON - 71D
31852	FRATTON - 71D	FRATTON - 71D	FELTHAM - 70B	ASHFORD - 74A	ASHFORD - 74A	ASHFORD - 74A	ASHFORD - 74A
31853	B.ARMS - 73B	B.ARMS - 73B	B.ARMS - 73B	B.ARMS - 73B	B.ARMS - 73B	B.ARMS - 73B	B.ARMS - 73B
31854	FAVERSHAM - 73E	FAVERSHAM - 73E	FAVERSHAM - 73E	FAVERSHAM - 73E	FAVERSHAM - 73E	FAVERSHAM - 73E	FAVERSHAM - 73E
31855	B.ARMS - 73B	B.ARMS - 73B	B.ARMS - 73B	B.ARMS - 73B	B.ARMS - 73B	B.ARMS - 73B	B.ARMS - 73B
31856	HITHER GREEN - 73C	HITHER GREEN - 73C	GUILDFORD - 70C	REDHILL - 75B	REDHILL - 75B	REDHILL - 75B	REDHILL - 75B
31857	HITHER GREEN - 73C	HITHER GREEN - 73C	HITHER GREEN - 73C	HITHER GREEN - 73C	HITHER GREEN - 73C	HITHER GREEN - 73C	HITHER GREEN - 73C
31858	HITHER GREEN - 73C	HITHER GREEN - 73C	HITHER GREEN - 73C	HITHER GREEN - 73C	HITHER GREEN - 73C	HITHER GREEN - 73C	HITHER GREEN - 73C
31859	HITHER GREEN - 73C	HITHER GREEN - 73C	HITHER GREEN - 73C	HITHER GREEN - 73C	HITHER GREEN - 73C	HITHER GREEN - 73C	HITHER GREEN - 73C
31860	HITHER GREEN - 73C	HITHER GREEN - 73C	HITHER GREEN - 73C	HITHER GREEN - 73C	HITHER GREEN - 73C	HITHER GREEN - 73C	HITHER GREEN - 73C
31861	HITHER GREEN - 73C	HITHER GREEN - 73C	HITHER GREEN - 73C	HITHER GREEN - 73C	HITHER GREEN - 73C	HITHER GREEN - 73C	HITHER GREEN - 73C
31862	HITHER GREEN - 73C	HITHER GREEN - 73C	GUILDFORD - 70C	REDHILL - 75B	REDHILL - 75B	REDHILL - 75B	REDHILL - 75B
31863	REDHILL - 75B	REDHILL - 75B	FELTHAM - 70B	ASHFORD - 74A	ASHFORD - 74A	ASHFORD - 74A	ASHFORD - 74A
31864	REDHILL - 75B	REDHILL - 75B	FELTHAM - 70B	REDHILL - 75B	REDHILL - 75B	REDHILL - 75B	REDHILL - 75B
31865	REDHILL - 75B	REDHILL - 75B	REDHILL - 75B	REDHILL - 75B	REDHILL - 75B	REDHILL - 75B	REDHILL - 75B
31866	REDHILL - 75B	REDHILL - 75B	REDHILL - 75B	REDHILL - 75B	REDHILL - 75B	REDHILL - 75B	REDHILL - 75B
31867	REDHILL - 75B	REDHILL - 75B	REDHILL - 75B	REDHILL - 75B	REDHILL - 75B	REDHILL - 75B	REDHILL - 75B
31868	REDHILL - 75B	REDHILL - 75B	REDHILL - 75B	REDHILL - 75B	REDHILL - 75B	REDHILL - 75B	REDHILL - 75B
31869	REDHILL - 75B	REDHILL - 75B	REDHILL - 75B	REDHILL - 75B	REDHILL - 75B	REDHILL - 75B	REDHILL - 75B
31870	B.ARMS - 73B	B.ARMS - 73B	B.ARMS - 73B	B.ARMS - 73B	B.ARMS - 73B	B.ARMS - 73B	B.ARMS - 73B
31871	B.ARMS - 73B	B.ARMS - 73B	B.ARMS - 73B	B.ARMS - 73B	B.ARMS - 73B	B.ARMS - 73B	B.ARMS - 73B
31872	B.ARMS - 73B	B.ARMS - 73B	B.ARMS - 73B	B.ARMS - 73B	B.ARMS - 73B	B.ARMS - 73B	B.ARMS - 73B
31873	B.ARMS - 73B	B.ARMS - 73B	B.ARMS - 73B	B.ARMS - 73B	B.ARMS - 73B	B.ARMS - 73B	B.ARMS - 73B
31874	B.ARMS - 73B	B.ARMS - 73B	B.ARMS - 73B	B.ARMS - 73B	B.ARMS - 73B	B.ARMS - 73B	B.ARMS - 73B
31875	B.ARMS - 73B	B.ARMS - 73B	B.ARMS - 73B	B.ARMS - 73B	B.ARMS - 73B	B.ARMS - 73B	B.ARMS - 73B
			N1 2-6-0 (1922)				
31822	HITHER GREEN - 73C	HITHER GREEN - 73C	HITHER GREEN - 73C	HITHER GREEN - 73C	HITHER GREEN - 73C	HITHER GREEN - 73C	HITHER GREEN - 73C
31876	HITHER GREEN - 73C	HITHER GREEN - 73C	HITHER GREEN - 73C	HITHER GREEN - 73C	HITHER GREEN - 73C	HITHER GREEN - 73C	HITHER GREEN - 73C
31877	HITHER GREEN - 73C	HITHER GREEN - 73C	HITHER GREEN - 73C	HITHER GREEN - 73C	HITHER GREEN - 73C	HITHER GREEN - 73C	HITHER GREEN - 73C
31878	HITHER GREEN - 73C	HITHER GREEN - 73C	HITHER GREEN - 73C	HITHER GREEN - 73C	HITHER GREEN - 73C	HITHER GREEN - 73C	HITHER GREEN - 73C
31879	HITHER GREEN - 73C	HITHER GREEN - 73C	HITHER GREEN - 73C	HITHER GREEN - 73C	HITHER GREEN - 73C	HITHER GREEN - 73C	HITHER GREEN - 73C
31880	HITHER GREEN - 73C	HITHER GREEN - 73C	HITHER GREEN - 73C	HITHER GREEN - 73C	HITHER GREEN - 73C	HITHER GREEN - 73C	HITHER GREEN - 73C

				N 2-6-0 (1917)			
31400	B ARMS - 73B	B ARMS - 73B	B ARMS - 73B	B ARMS - 73B	B ARMS - 73B	B ARMS - 73B	B ARMS - 73B
31401	ASHFORD - 74A	ASHFORD - 74A	ASHFORD - 74A	ASHFORD - 74A	ASHFORD - 74A	ASHFORD - 74A	ASHFORD - 74A
31402	ASHFORD - 74A	ASHFORD - 74A	ASHFORD - 74A	ASHFORD - 74A	ASHFORD - 74A	ASHFORD - 74A	ASHFORD - 74A
31403	ASHFORD - 74A	ASHFORD - 74A	ASHFORD - 74A	ASHFORD - 74A	ASHFORD - 74A	ASHFORD - 74A	ASHFORD - 74A
31404	ASHFORD - 74A	ASHFORD - 74A	ASHFORD - 74A	ASHFORD - 74A	ASHFORD - 74A	ASHFORD - 74A	ASHFORD - 74A
31405	ASHFORD - 74A	ASHFORD - 74A	ASHFORD - 74A	ASHFORD - 74A	ASHFORD - 74A	ASHFORD - 74A	ASHFORD - 74A
31406	HITHER GREEN - 73C	HITHER GREEN - 73C	HITHER GREEN - 73C	HITHER GREEN - 73C	HITHER GREEN - 73C	HITHER GREEN - 73C	HITHER GREEN - 73C
31407	ASHFORD - 74A	ASHFORD - 74A	ASHFORD - 74A	ASHFORD - 74A	ASHFORD - 74A	ASHFORD - 74A	ASHFORD - 74A
31408	B ARMS - 73B	B ARMS - 73B	B ARMS - 73B	B ARMS - 73B	B ARMS - 73B	B ARMS - 73B	B ARMS - 73B
31409	STEWARTS LANE - 73A	STEWARTS LANE - 73A	STEWARTS LANE - 73A	STEWARTS LANE - 73A	STEWARTS LANE - 73A	STEWARTS LANE - 73A	STEWARTS LANE - 73A
31410	STEWARTS LANE - 73A	STEWARTS LANE - 73A	STEWARTS LANE - 73A	STEWARTS LANE - 73A	STEWARTS LANE - 73A	STEWARTS LANE - 73A	STEWARTS LANE - 73A
31411	STEWARTS LANE - 73A	STEWARTS LANE - 73A	STEWARTS LANE - 73A	STEWARTS LANE - 73A	STEWARTS LANE - 73A	STEWARTS LANE - 73A	STEWARTS LANE - 73A
31412	STEWARTS LANE - 73A	STEWARTS LANE - 73A	STEWARTS LANE - 73A	STEWARTS LANE - 73A	STEWARTS LANE - 73A	STEWARTS LANE - 73A	STEWARTS LANE - 73A
31413	STEWARTS LANE - 73A	STEWARTS LANE - 73A	STEWARTS LANE - 73A	STEWARTS LANE - 73A	STEWARTS LANE - 73A	STEWARTS LANE - 73A	STEWARTS LANE - 73A
31414	STEWARTS LANE - 73A	STEWARTS LANE - 73A	STEWARTS LANE - 73A	STEWARTS LANE - 73A	STEWARTS LANE - 73A	STEWARTS LANE - 73A	STEWARTS LANE - 73A
31810	STEWARTS LANE - 73A	STEWARTS LANE - 73A	STEWARTS LANE - 73A	STEWARTS LANE - 73A	STEWARTS LANE - 73A	STEWARTS LANE - 73A	STEWARTS LANE - 73A
31811	STEWARTS LANE - 73A	STEWARTS LANE - 73A	STEWARTS LANE - 73A	STEWARTS LANE - 73A	STEWARTS LANE - 73A	STEWARTS LANE - 73A	STEWARTS LANE - 73A
31812	STEWARTS LANE - 73A	STEWARTS LANE - 73A	STEWARTS LANE - 73A	STEWARTS LANE - 73A	STEWARTS LANE - 73A	STEWARTS LANE - 73A	STEWARTS LANE - 73A
31813	SALISBURY - 72B	SALISBURY - 72B	SALISBURY - 72B	SALISBURY - 72B	SALISBURY - 72B	SALISBURY - 72B	SALISBURY - 72B
31814	SALISBURY - 72B	SALISBURY - 72B	SALISBURY - 72B	SALISBURY - 72B	SALISBURY - 72B	SALISBURY - 72B	SALISBURY - 72B
31815	STEWARTS LANE - 73A	STEWARTS LANE - 73A	GILLINGHAM - 73D	GILLINGHAM - 73D	GILLINGHAM - 73D	GILLINGHAM - 73D	GILLINGHAM - 73D
31816	STEWARTS LANE - 73A	STEWARTS LANE - 73A	GILLINGHAM - 73D	GILLINGHAM - 73D	GILLINGHAM - 73D	GILLINGHAM - 73D	GILLINGHAM - 73D
31817	DOVER - 74C	DOVER - 74C	DOVER - 74C	DOVER - 74C	DOVER - 74C	DOVER - 74C	DOVER - 74C
31818	DOVER - 74C	DOVER - 74C	DOVER - 74C	DOVER - 74C	DOVER - 74C	DOVER - 74C	DOVER - 74C
31819	DOVER - 74C	DOVER - 74C	DOVER - 74C	DOVER - 74C	DOVER - 74C	DOVER - 74C	DOVER - 74C
31820	DOVER - 74C	DOVER - 74C	DOVER - 74C	DOVER - 74C	DOVER - 74C	DOVER - 74C	DOVER - 74C
31821	DOVER - 74C	DOVER - 74C	DOVER - 74C	DOVER - 74C	DOVER - 74C	DOVER - 74C	DOVER - 74C
31823	B ARMS - 73B	B ARMS - 73B	B ARMS - 73B	B ARMS - 73B	B ARMS - 73B	B ARMS - 73B	B ARMS - 73B
31824	B ARMS - 73B	B ARMS - 73B	B ARMS - 73B	B ARMS - 73B	B ARMS - 73B	B ARMS - 73B	B ARMS - 73B
31825	B ARMS - 73B	B ARMS - 73B	B ARMS - 73B	B ARMS - 73B	B ARMS - 73B	B ARMS - 73B	B ARMS - 73B
31826	B ARMS - 73B	B ARMS - 73B	B ARMS - 73B	B ARMS - 73B	B ARMS - 73B	B ARMS - 73B	B ARMS - 73B
31827	B ARMS - 73B	B ARMS - 73B	B ARMS - 73B	B ARMS - 73B	B ARMS - 73B	B ARMS - 73B	B ARMS - 73B
31828	B ARMS - 73B	B ARMS - 73B	B ARMS - 73B	B ARMS - 73B	B ARMS - 73B	B ARMS - 73B	B ARMS - 73B
31829	B ARMS - 73B	B ARMS - 73B	B ARMS - 73B	B ARMS - 73B	B ARMS - 73B	B ARMS - 73B	B ARMS - 73B
31830	EXMOUTH J CN - 72A	EXMOUTH J CN - 72A	EXMOUTH J CN - 72A	EXMOUTH J CN - 72A	EXMOUTH J CN - 72A	EXMOUTH J CN - 72A	EXMOUTH J CN - 72A
31831	EXMOUTH J CN - 72A	EXMOUTH J CN - 72A	EXMOUTH J CN - 72A	EXMOUTH J CN - 72A	EXMOUTH J CN - 72A	EXMOUTH J CN - 72A	EXMOUTH J CN - 72A
31832	EXMOUTH J CN - 72A	EXMOUTH J CN - 72A	EXMOUTH J CN - 72A	EXMOUTH J CN - 72A	EXMOUTH J CN - 72A	EXMOUTH J CN - 72A	EXMOUTH J CN - 72A
31833	EXMOUTH J CN - 72A	EXMOUTH J CN - 72A	EXMOUTH J CN - 72A	EXMOUTH J CN - 72A	EXMOUTH J CN - 72A	EXMOUTH J CN - 72A	EXMOUTH J CN - 72A
31834	EXMOUTH J CN - 72A	EXMOUTH J CN - 72A	EXMOUTH J CN - 72A	EXMOUTH J CN - 72A	EXMOUTH J CN - 72A	EXMOUTH J CN - 72A	EXMOUTH J CN - 72A
31835	EXMOUTH J CN - 72A	EXMOUTH J CN - 72A	EXMOUTH J CN - 72A	EXMOUTH J CN - 72A	EXMOUTH J CN - 72A	EXMOUTH J CN - 72A	EXMOUTH J CN - 72A
31836	EXMOUTH J CN - 72A	EXMOUTH J CN - 72A	EXMOUTH J CN - 72A	EXMOUTH J CN - 72A	EXMOUTH J CN - 72A	EXMOUTH J CN - 72A	EXMOUTH J CN - 72A
31837	EXMOUTH J CN - 72A	EXMOUTH J CN - 72A	EXMOUTH J CN - 72A	EXMOUTH J CN - 72A	EXMOUTH J CN - 72A	EXMOUTH J CN - 72A	EXMOUTH J CN - 72A
31838	EXMOUTH J CN - 72A	EXMOUTH J CN - 72A	EXMOUTH J CN - 72A	EXMOUTH J CN - 72A	EXMOUTH J CN - 72A	EXMOUTH J CN - 72A	EXMOUTH J CN - 72A
31839	EXMOUTH J CN - 72A	EXMOUTH J CN - 72A	EXMOUTH J CN - 72A	EXMOUTH J CN - 72A	EXMOUTH J CN - 72A	EXMOUTH J CN - 72A	EXMOUTH J CN - 72A
31840	EXMOUTH J CN - 72A	EXMOUTH J CN - 72A	EXMOUTH J CN - 72A	EXMOUTH J CN - 72A	EXMOUTH J CN - 72A	EXMOUTH J CN - 72A	EXMOUTH J CN - 72A
31841	EXMOUTH J CN - 72A	EXMOUTH J CN - 72A	EXMOUTH J CN - 72A	EXMOUTH J CN - 72A	EXMOUTH J CN - 72A	EXMOUTH J CN - 72A	EXMOUTH J CN - 72A
31842	EXMOUTH J CN - 72A	EXMOUTH J CN - 72A	EXMOUTH J CN - 72A	BARNSTAPLE - 72E	BARNSTAPLE - 72E	BARNSTAPLE - 72E	BARNSTAPLE - 72E
31843	BARNSTAPLE - 72E	BARNSTAPLE - 72E	BARNSTAPLE - 72E	BARNSTAPLE - 72E	BARNSTAPLE - 72E	BARNSTAPLE - 72E	BARNSTAPLE - 72E
31844	EXMOUTH J CN - 72A	EXMOUTH J CN - 72A	EXMOUTH J CN - 72A	EXMOUTH J CN - 72A	EXMOUTH J CN - 72A	EXMOUTH J CN - 72A	EXMOUTH J CN - 72A
31845	EXMOUTH J CN - 72A	EXMOUTH J CN - 72A	EXMOUTH J CN - 72A	EXMOUTH J CN - 72A	EXMOUTH J CN - 72A	EXMOUTH J CN - 72A	EXMOUTH J CN - 72A
31846	EXMOUTH J CN - 72A	EXMOUTH J CN - 72A	EXMOUTH J CN - 72A	EXMOUTH J CN - 72A	EXMOUTH J CN - 72A	EXMOUTH J CN - 72A	EXMOUTH J CN - 72A
31847	EXMOUTH J CN - 72A	EXMOUTH J CN - 72A	EXMOUTH J CN - 72A	EXMOUTH J CN - 72A	EXMOUTH J CN - 72A	EXMOUTH J CN - 72A	EXMOUTH J CN - 72A
31848	EXMOUTH J CN - 72A	EXMOUTH J CN - 72A	EXMOUTH J CN - 72A	EXMOUTH J CN - 72A	EXMOUTH J CN - 72A	EXMOUTH J CN - 72A	EXMOUTH J CN - 72A
31849	EXMOUTH J CN - 72A	EXMOUTH J CN - 72A	EXMOUTH J CN - 72A	EXMOUTH J CN - 72A	EXMOUTH J CN - 72A	EXMOUTH J CN - 72A	EXMOUTH J CN - 72A
31850	FAVERSHAM - 73E	FAVERSHAM - 73E	FAVERSHAM - 73E	FAVERSHAM - 73E	FAVERSHAM - 73E	FAVERSHAM - 73E	FAVERSHAM - 73E
31851	FRATTON - 71D	FRATTON - 71D	FRATTON - 71D	FRATTON - 71D	FRATTON - 71D	FRATTON - 70F	FRATTON - 70F
31852	ASHFORD - 74A	ASHFORD - 74A	ASHFORD - 74A	ASHFORD - 74A	ASHFORD - 74A	ASHFORD - 74A	ASHFORD - 74A
31853	B ARMS - 73B	B ARMS - 73B	B ARMS - 73B	B ARMS - 73B	B ARMS - 73B	B ARMS - 73B	B ARMS - 73B
31854	FAVERSHAM - 73E	FAVERSHAM - 73E	FAVERSHAM - 73E	FAVERSHAM - 73E	FAVERSHAM - 73E	HITHER GREEN - 73C	HITHER GREEN - 73C
31855	B ARMS - 73B	B ARMS - 73B	B ARMS - 73B	HITHER GREEN - 73C	HITHER GREEN - 73C	HITHER GREEN - 73C	HITHER GREEN - 73C
31856	REDHILL - 75B	REDHILL - 75B	REDHILL - 75B	REDHILL - 75B	REDHILL - 75B	REDHILL - 75B	REDHILL - 75B
31857	HITHER GREEN - 73C	HITHER GREEN - 73C	HITHER GREEN - 73C	HITHER GREEN - 73C	HITHER GREEN - 73C	HITHER GREEN - 73C	HITHER GREEN - 73C
31858	HITHER GREEN - 73C	HITHER GREEN - 73C	HITHER GREEN - 73C	HITHER GREEN - 73C	HITHER GREEN - 73C	HITHER GREEN - 73C	HITHER GREEN - 73C
31859	HITHER GREEN - 73C	HITHER GREEN - 73C	HITHER GREEN - 73C	HITHER GREEN - 73C	HITHER GREEN - 73C	HITHER GREEN - 73C	HITHER GREEN - 73C
31860	HITHER GREEN - 73C	HITHER GREEN - 73C	HITHER GREEN - 73C	HITHER GREEN - 73C	HITHER GREEN - 73C	HITHER GREEN - 73C	HITHER GREEN - 73C
31861	HITHER GREEN - 73C	HITHER GREEN - 73C	HITHER GREEN - 73C	HITHER GREEN - 73C	HITHER GREEN - 73C	HITHER GREEN - 73C	HITHER GREEN - 73C
31862	REDHILL - 75B	REDHILL - 75B	REDHILL - 75B	REDHILL - 75B	REDHILL - 75B	REDHILL - 75B	REDHILL - 75B
31863	ASHFORD - 74A	ASHFORD - 74A	ASHFORD - 74A	ASHFORD - 74A	ASHFORD - 74A	ASHFORD - 74A	ASHFORD - 74A
31864	REDHILL - 75B	REDHILL - 75B	REDHILL - 75B	REDHILL - 75B	REDHILL - 75B	REDHILL - 75B	REDHILL - 75B
31865	REDHILL - 75B	REDHILL - 75B	REDHILL - 75B	REDHILL - 75B	REDHILL - 75B	REDHILL - 75B	REDHILL - 75B
31866	REDHILL - 75B	REDHILL - 75B	REDHILL - 75B	REDHILL - 75B	REDHILL - 75B	REDHILL - 75B	REDHILL - 75B
31867	REDHILL - 75B	REDHILL - 75B	REDHILL - 75B	REDHILL - 75B	REDHILL - 75B	REDHILL - 75B	REDHILL - 75B
31868	REDHILL - 75B	REDHILL - 75B	REDHILL - 75B	REDHILL - 75B	REDHILL - 75B	REDHILL - 75B	REDHILL - 75B
31869	REDHILL - 75B	REDHILL - 75B	REDHILL - 75B	REDHILL - 75B	REDHILL - 75B	REDHILL - 75B	REDHILL - 75B
31870	B ARMS - 73B	B ARMS - 73B	B ARMS - 73B	B ARMS - 73B	B ARMS - 73B	B ARMS - 73B	B ARMS - 73B
31871	B ARMS - 73B	B ARMS - 73B	B ARMS - 73B	B ARMS - 73B	B ARMS - 73B	B ARMS - 73B	B ARMS - 73B
31872	B ARMS - 73B	B ARMS - 73B	B ARMS - 73B	B ARMS - 73B	B ARMS - 73B	B ARMS - 73B	B ARMS - 73B
31873	B ARMS - 73B	B ARMS - 73B	B ARMS - 73B	B ARMS - 73B	B ARMS - 73B	B ARMS - 73B	B ARMS - 73B
31874	B ARMS - 73B	B ARMS - 73B	B ARMS - 73B	B ARMS - 73B	B ARMS - 73B	B ARMS - 73B	B ARMS - 73B
31875	B ARMS - 73B	B ARMS - 73B	B ARMS - 73B	B ARMS - 73B	B ARMS - 73B	B ARMS - 73B	B ARMS - 73B
				N 1 2-6-0 (1922)			
31822	HITHER GREEN - 73C	HITHER GREEN - 73C	HITHER GREEN - 73C	HITHER GREEN - 73C	HITHER GREEN - 73C	HITHER GREEN - 73C	HITHER GREEN - 73C
31876	HITHER GREEN - 73C	HITHER GREEN - 73C	HITHER GREEN - 73C	HITHER GREEN - 73C	HITHER GREEN - 73C	HITHER GREEN - 73C	HITHER GREEN - 73C
31877	HITHER GREEN - 73C	HITHER GREEN - 73C	HITHER GREEN - 73C	HITHER GREEN - 73C	HITHER GREEN - 73C	HITHER GREEN - 73C	HITHER GREEN - 73C
31878	HITHER GREEN - 73C	HITHER GREEN - 73C	HITHER GREEN - 73C	HITHER GREEN - 73C	HITHER GREEN - 73C	HITHER GREEN - 73C	HITHER GREEN - 73C
31879	HITHER GREEN - 73C	HITHER GREEN - 73C	HITHER GREEN - 73C	HITHER GREEN - 73C	HITHER GREEN - 73C	HITHER GREEN - 73C	HITHER GREEN - 73C
31880	HITHER GREEN - 73C	HITHER GREEN - 73C	HITHER GREEN - 73C	HITHER GREEN - 73C	HITHER GREEN - 73C	HITHER GREEN - 73C	HITHER GREEN - 73C

loco	Feb-55	Apr-55	Jun-55	Aug-55	Sep-55	Nov-55	Dec-55
				N 2-6-0 (1917)			
31400	B.ARMS - 73B	B.ARMS - 73B	B.ARMS - 73B	B.ARMS - 73B	B.ARMS - 73B	B.ARMS - 73B	B.ARMS - 73B
31401	ASHFORD - 74A	ASHFORD - 74A	ASHFORD - 74A	ASHFORD - 74A	ASHFORD - 74A	ASHFORD - 74A	ASHFORD - 74A
31402	ASHFORD - 74A	ASHFORD - 74A	ASHFORD - 74A	ASHFORD - 74A	ASHFORD - 74A	ASHFORD - 74A	ASHFORD - 74A
31403	ASHFORD - 74A	ASHFORD - 74A	ASHFORD - 74A	ASHFORD - 74A	ASHFORD - 74A	ASHFORD - 74A	ASHFORD - 74A
31404	ASHFORD - 74A	ASHFORD - 74A	ASHFORD - 74A	ASHFORD - 74A	ASHFORD - 74A	ASHFORD - 74A	ASHFORD - 74A
31405	ASHFORD - 74A	ASHFORD - 74A	ASHFORD - 74A	ASHFORD - 74A	ASHFORD - 74A	ASHFORD - 74A	ASHFORD - 74A
31406	HITHER GREEN - 73C	HITHER GREEN - 73C	HITHER GREEN - 73C	HITHER GREEN - 73C	HITHER GREEN - 73C	HITHER GREEN - 73C	HITHER GREEN - 73C
31407	ASHFORD - 74A	ASHFORD - 74A	DOVER - 74C	DOVER - 74C	ASHFORD - 74A	ASHFORD - 74A	ASHFORD - 74A
31408	STEWARTS LANE - 73A	STEWARTS LANE - 73A	STEWARTS LANE - 73A	STEWARTS LANE - 73A	STEWARTS LANE - 73A	STEWARTS LANE - 73A	STEWARTS LANE - 73A
31409	STEWARTS LANE - 73A	STEWARTS LANE - 73A	STEWARTS LANE - 73A	STEWARTS LANE - 73A	STEWARTS LANE - 73A	STEWARTS LANE - 73A	STEWARTS LANE - 73A
31410	STEWARTS LANE - 73A	STEWARTS LANE - 73A	STEWARTS LANE - 73A	STEWARTS LANE - 73A	STEWARTS LANE - 73A	STEWARTS LANE - 73A	STEWARTS LANE - 73A
31411	STEWARTS LANE - 73A	STEWARTS LANE - 73A	STEWARTS LANE - 73A	STEWARTS LANE - 73A	STEWARTS LANE - 73A	STEWARTS LANE - 73A	STEWARTS LANE - 73A
31412	STEWARTS LANE - 73A	STEWARTS LANE - 73A	STEWARTS LANE - 73A	STEWARTS LANE - 73A	STEWARTS LANE - 73A	STEWARTS LANE - 73A	STEWARTS LANE - 73A
31413	STEWARTS LANE - 73A	STEWARTS LANE - 73A	STEWARTS LANE - 73A	STEWARTS LANE - 73A	STEWARTS LANE - 73A	STEWARTS LANE - 73A	STEWARTS LANE - 73A
31414	STEWARTS LANE - 73A	STEWARTS LANE - 73A	STEWARTS LANE - 73A	STEWARTS LANE - 73A	STEWARTS LANE - 73A	STEWARTS LANE - 73A	STEWARTS LANE - 73A
31810	STEWARTS LANE - 73A	STEWARTS LANE - 73A	STEWARTS LANE - 73A	STEWARTS LANE - 73A	STEWARTS LANE - 73A	STEWARTS LANE - 73A	STEWARTS LANE - 73A
31811	STEWARTS LANE - 73A	STEWARTS LANE - 73A	STEWARTS LANE - 73A	STEWARTS LANE - 73A	STEWARTS LANE - 73A	STEWARTS LANE - 73A	STEWARTS LANE - 73A
31812	STEWARTS LANE - 73A	STEWARTS LANE - 73A	STEWARTS LANE - 73A	STEWARTS LANE - 73A	STEWARTS LANE - 73A	STEWARTS LANE - 73A	STEWARTS LANE - 73A
31813	SALISBURY - 72B	SALISBURY - 72B	SALISBURY - 72B	SALISBURY - 72B	SALISBURY - 72B	SALISBURY - 72B	SALISBURY - 72B
31814	SALISBURY - 72B	SALISBURY - 72B	SALISBURY - 72B	SALISBURY - 72B	SALISBURY - 72B	SALISBURY - 72B	SALISBURY - 72B
31815	GILLINGHAM - 73D	GILLINGHAM - 73D	GILLINGHAM - 73D	GILLINGHAM - 73D	GILLINGHAM - 73D	GILLINGHAM - 73D	GILLINGHAM - 73D
31816	GILLINGHAM - 73D	GILLINGHAM - 73D	GILLINGHAM - 73D	GILLINGHAM - 73D	GILLINGHAM - 73D	GILLINGHAM - 73D	GILLINGHAM - 73D
31817	DOVER - 74C	DOVER - 74C	DOVER - 74C	DOVER - 74C	REDHILL - 75B	REDHILL - 75B	REDHILL - 75B
31818	DOVER - 74C	DOVER - 74C	DOVER - 74C	DOVER - 74C	DOVER - 74C	DOVER - 74C	DOVER - 74C
31819	DOVER - 74C	DOVER - 74C	DOVER - 74C	DOVER - 74C	DOVER - 74C	DOVER - 74C	DOVER - 74C
31820	DOVER - 74C	DOVER - 74C	DOVER - 74C	DOVER - 74C	DOVER - 74C	DOVER - 74C	DOVER - 74C
31821	DOVER - 74C	DOVER - 74C	DOVER - 74C	DOVER - 74C	DOVER - 74C	DOVER - 74C	DOVER - 74C
31823	B.ARMS - 73B	B.ARMS - 73B	B.ARMS - 73B	B.ARMS - 73B	B.ARMS - 73B	B.ARMS - 73B	B.ARMS - 73B
31824	B.ARMS - 73B	B.ARMS - 73B	B.ARMS - 73B	B.ARMS - 73B	B.ARMS - 73B	B.ARMS - 73B	B.ARMS - 73B
31825	B.ARMS - 73B	B.ARMS - 73B	B.ARMS - 73B	B.ARMS - 73B	B.ARMS - 73B	B.ARMS - 73B	B.ARMS - 73B
31826	B.ARMS - 73B	B.ARMS - 73B	B.ARMS - 73B	B.ARMS - 73B	B.ARMS - 73B	B.ARMS - 73B	B.ARMS - 73B
31827	B.ARMS - 73B	B.ARMS - 73B	B.ARMS - 73B	B.ARMS - 73B	B.ARMS - 73B	B.ARMS - 73B	B.ARMS - 73B
31828	B.ARMS - 73B	B.ARMS - 73B	B.ARMS - 73B	B.ARMS - 73B	B.ARMS - 73B	B.ARMS - 73B	B.ARMS - 73B
31829	B.ARMS - 73B	B.ARMS - 73B	B.ARMS - 73B	B.ARMS - 73B	B.ARMS - 73B	B.ARMS - 73B	B.ARMS - 73B
31830	EXMOUTH JCN - 72A	EXMOUTH JCN - 72A	EXMOUTH JCN - 72A	EXMOUTH JCN - 72A	EXMOUTH JCN - 72A	EXMOUTH JCN - 72A	EXMOUTH JCN - 72A
31831	EXMOUTH JCN - 72A	EXMOUTH JCN - 72A	EXMOUTH JCN - 72A	EXMOUTH JCN - 72A	EXMOUTH JCN - 72A	EXMOUTH JCN - 72A	EXMOUTH JCN - 72A
31832	EXMOUTH JCN - 72A	EXMOUTH JCN - 72A	EXMOUTH JCN - 72A	EXMOUTH JCN - 72A	EXMOUTH JCN - 72A	EXMOUTH JCN - 72A	EXMOUTH JCN - 72A
31833	EXMOUTH JCN - 72A	EXMOUTH JCN - 72A	EXMOUTH JCN - 72A	EXMOUTH JCN - 72A	EXMOUTH JCN - 72A	EXMOUTH JCN - 72A	EXMOUTH JCN - 72A
31834	EXMOUTH JCN - 72A	EXMOUTH JCN - 72A	EXMOUTH JCN - 72A	EXMOUTH JCN - 72A	EXMOUTH JCN - 72A	EXMOUTH JCN - 72A	EXMOUTH JCN - 72A
31835	EXMOUTH JCN - 72A	EXMOUTH JCN - 72A	EXMOUTH JCN - 72A	EXMOUTH JCN - 72A	EXMOUTH JCN - 72A	EXMOUTH JCN - 72A	EXMOUTH JCN - 72A
31836	EXMOUTH JCN - 72A	EXMOUTH JCN - 72A	EXMOUTH JCN - 72A	EXMOUTH JCN - 72A	EXMOUTH JCN - 72A	EXMOUTH JCN - 72A	EXMOUTH JCN - 72A
31837	EXMOUTH JCN - 72A	EXMOUTH JCN - 72A	EXMOUTH JCN - 72A	EXMOUTH JCN - 72A	EXMOUTH JCN - 72A	EXMOUTH JCN - 72A	EXMOUTH JCN - 72A
31838	EXMOUTH JCN - 72A	EXMOUTH JCN - 72A	EXMOUTH JCN - 72A	EXMOUTH JCN - 72A	EXMOUTH JCN - 72A	EXMOUTH JCN - 72A	EXMOUTH JCN - 72A
31839	EXMOUTH JCN - 72A	EXMOUTH JCN - 72A	EXMOUTH JCN - 72A	EXMOUTH JCN - 72A	EXMOUTH JCN - 72A	EXMOUTH JCN - 72A	EXMOUTH JCN - 72A
31840	EXMOUTH JCN - 72A	EXMOUTH JCN - 72A	EXMOUTH JCN - 72A	EXMOUTH JCN - 72A	EXMOUTH JCN - 72A	EXMOUTH JCN - 72A	EXMOUTH JCN - 72A
31841	EXMOUTH JCN - 72A	EXMOUTH JCN - 72A	EXMOUTH JCN - 72A	EXMOUTH JCN - 72A	EXMOUTH JCN - 72A	EXMOUTH JCN - 72A	EXMOUTH JCN - 72A
31842	EXMOUTH JCN - 72A	EXMOUTH JCN - 72A	BARNSTAPLE - 72E	BARNSTAPLE - 72E	BARNSTAPLE - 72E	BARNSTAPLE - 72E	BARNSTAPLE - 72E
31843	BARNSTAPLE - 72E	BARNSTAPLE - 72E	BARNSTAPLE - 72E	BARNSTAPLE - 72E	BARNSTAPLE - 72E	BARNSTAPLE - 72E	BARNSTAPLE - 72E
31844	EXMOUTH JCN - 72A	EXMOUTH JCN - 72A	EXMOUTH JCN - 72A	EXMOUTH JCN - 72A	EXMOUTH JCN - 72A	EXMOUTH JCN - 72A	EXMOUTH JCN - 72A
31845	EXMOUTH JCN - 72A	EXMOUTH JCN - 72A	EXMOUTH JCN - 72A	EXMOUTH JCN - 72A	EXMOUTH JCN - 72A	EXMOUTH JCN - 72A	EXMOUTH JCN - 72A
31846	EXMOUTH JCN - 72A	EXMOUTH JCN - 72A	EXMOUTH JCN - 72A	EXMOUTH JCN - 72A	EXMOUTH JCN - 72A	EXMOUTH JCN - 72A	EXMOUTH JCN - 72A
31847	EXMOUTH JCN - 72A	EXMOUTH JCN - 72A	EXMOUTH JCN - 72A	EXMOUTH JCN - 72A	EXMOUTH JCN - 72A	EXMOUTH JCN - 72A	EXMOUTH JCN - 72A
31848	EXMOUTH JCN - 72A	EXMOUTH JCN - 72A	EXMOUTH JCN - 72A	EXMOUTH JCN - 72A	EXMOUTH JCN - 72A	ASHFORD - 74A	ASHFORD - 74A
31849	EXMOUTH JCN - 72A	EXMOUTH JCN - 72A	EXMOUTH JCN - 72A	EXMOUTH JCN - 72A	EXMOUTH JCN - 72A	EXMOUTH JCN - 72A	EXMOUTH JCN - 72A
31850	FAVERSHAM - 73E	FAVERSHAM - 73E	FAVERSHAM - 73E	FAVERSHAM - 73E	FAVERSHAM - 73E	FAVERSHAM - 73E	FAVERSHAM - 73E
31851	B.ARMS - 73B	B.ARMS - 73B	B.ARMS - 73B	B.ARMS - 73B	B.ARMS - 73B	B.ARMS - 73B	B.ARMS - 73B
31852	ASHFORD - 74A	ASHFORD - 74A	ASHFORD - 74A	ASHFORD - 74A	ASHFORD - 74A	ASHFORD - 74A	ASHFORD - 74A
31853	B.ARMS - 73B	B.ARMS - 73B	B.ARMS - 73B	B.ARMS - 73B	B.ARMS - 73B	B.ARMS - 73B	B.ARMS - 73B
31854	HITHER GREEN - 73C	HITHER GREEN - 73C	HITHER GREEN - 73C	HITHER GREEN - 73C	HITHER GREEN - 73C	HITHER GREEN - 73C	HITHER GREEN - 73C
31855	HITHER GREEN - 73C	HITHER GREEN - 73C	HITHER GREEN - 73C	HITHER GREEN - 73C	HITHER GREEN - 73C	HITHER GREEN - 73C	HITHER GREEN - 73C
31856	REDHILL - 75B	REDHILL - 75B	REDHILL - 75B	REDHILL - 75B	REDHILL - 75B	REDHILL - 75B	REDHILL - 75B
31857	HITHER GREEN - 73C	HITHER GREEN - 73C	HITHER GREEN - 73C	HITHER GREEN - 73C	HITHER GREEN - 73C	HITHER GREEN - 73C	HITHER GREEN - 73C
31858	HITHER GREEN - 73C	HITHER GREEN - 73C	HITHER GREEN - 73C	HITHER GREEN - 73C	HITHER GREEN - 73C	HITHER GREEN - 73C	HITHER GREEN - 73C
31859	HITHER GREEN - 73C	HITHER GREEN - 73C	HITHER GREEN - 73C	HITHER GREEN - 73C	HITHER GREEN - 73C	HITHER GREEN - 73C	HITHER GREEN - 73C
31860	HITHER GREEN - 73C	HITHER GREEN - 73C	HITHER GREEN - 73C	HITHER GREEN - 73C	HITHER GREEN - 73C	HITHER GREEN - 73C	HITHER GREEN - 73C
31861	HITHER GREEN - 73C	HITHER GREEN - 73C	HITHER GREEN - 73C	HITHER GREEN - 73C	HITHER GREEN - 73C	HITHER GREEN - 73C	HITHER GREEN - 73C
31862	REDHILL - 75B	REDHILL - 75B	REDHILL - 75B	REDHILL - 75B	REDHILL - 75B	REDHILL - 75B	REDHILL - 75B
31863	ASHFORD - 74A	ASHFORD - 74A	ASHFORD - 74A	ASHFORD - 74A	ASHFORD - 74A	ASHFORD - 74A	ASHFORD - 74A
31864	REDHILL - 75B	REDHILL - 75B	REDHILL - 75B	REDHILL - 75B	REDHILL - 75B	REDHILL - 75B	REDHILL - 75B
31865	REDHILL - 75B	REDHILL - 75B	REDHILL - 75B	REDHILL - 75B	REDHILL - 75B	REDHILL - 75B	REDHILL - 75B
31866	REDHILL - 75B	REDHILL - 75B	REDHILL - 75B	REDHILL - 75B	REDHILL - 75B	REDHILL - 75B	REDHILL - 75B
31867	REDHILL - 75B	REDHILL - 75B	REDHILL - 75B	REDHILL - 75B	REDHILL - 75B	REDHILL - 75B	REDHILL - 75B
31868	REDHILL - 75B	REDHILL - 75B	REDHILL - 75B	REDHILL - 75B	REDHILL - 75B	REDHILL - 75B	REDHILL - 75B
31869	REDHILL - 75B	REDHILL - 75B	REDHILL - 75B	REDHILL - 75B	REDHILL - 75B	REDHILL - 75B	REDHILL - 75B
31870	B.ARMS - 73B	B.ARMS - 73B	B.ARMS - 73B	B.ARMS - 73B	B.ARMS - 73B	B.ARMS - 73B	B.ARMS - 73B
31871	B.ARMS - 73B	B.ARMS - 73B	B.ARMS - 73B	B.ARMS - 73B	B.ARMS - 73B	B.ARMS - 73B	B.ARMS - 73B
31872	B.ARMS - 73B	B.ARMS - 73B	B.ARMS - 73B	B.ARMS - 73B	B.ARMS - 73B	B.ARMS - 73B	B.ARMS - 73B
31873	B.ARMS - 73B	B.ARMS - 73B	B.ARMS - 73B	B.ARMS - 73B	B.ARMS - 73B	B.ARMS - 73B	B.ARMS - 73B
31874	B.ARMS - 73B	B.ARMS - 73B	B.ARMS - 73B	B.ARMS - 73B	B.ARMS - 73B	B.ARMS - 73B	B.ARMS - 73B
31875	B.ARMS - 73B	B.ARMS - 73B	B.ARMS - 73B	B.ARMS - 73B	B.ARMS - 73B	B.ARMS - 73B	B.ARMS - 73B
				N1 2-6-0 (1922)			
31822	HITHER GREEN - 73C	HITHER GREEN - 73C	HITHER GREEN - 73C	HITHER GREEN - 73C	HITHER GREEN - 73C	HITHER GREEN - 73C	HITHER GREEN - 73C
31876	HITHER GREEN - 73C	HITHER GREEN - 73C	HITHER GREEN - 73C	HITHER GREEN - 73C	HITHER GREEN - 73C	HITHER GREEN - 73C	HITHER GREEN - 73C
31877	HITHER GREEN - 73C	HITHER GREEN - 73C	HITHER GREEN - 73C	HITHER GREEN - 73C	HITHER GREEN - 73C	HITHER GREEN - 73C	HITHER GREEN - 73C
31878	HITHER GREEN - 73C	HITHER GREEN - 73C	HITHER GREEN - 73C	HITHER GREEN - 73C	HITHER GREEN - 73C	HITHER GREEN - 73C	HITHER GREEN - 73C
31879	HITHER GREEN - 73C	HITHER GREEN - 73C	HITHER GREEN - 73C	HITHER GREEN - 73C	HITHER GREEN - 73C	HITHER GREEN - 73C	HITHER GREEN - 73C
31880	HITHER GREEN - 73C	HITHER GREEN - 73C	HITHER GREEN - 73C	HITHER GREEN - 73C	HITHER GREEN - 73C	HITHER GREEN - 73C	HITHER GREEN - 73C

loco	Jan-56	Apr-56	May-56	Aug-56	Oct-56	Nov-56	Jan-57
				N 2-6-0 (1917)			
31400	B.ARMS - 73B	B.ARMS - 73B	B.ARMS - 73B	B.ARMS - 73B	B.ARMS - 73B	B.ARMS - 73B	B.ARMS - 73B
31401	ASHFORD - 74A	ASHFORD - 74A	ASHFORD - 74A	ASHFORD - 74A	ASHFORD - 74A	ASHFORD - 74A	ASHFORD - 74A
31402	ASHFORD - 74A	ASHFORD - 74A	ASHFORD - 74A	ASHFORD - 74A	ASHFORD - 74A	ASHFORD - 74A	ASHFORD - 74A
31403	ASHFORD - 74A	ASHFORD - 74A	ASHFORD - 74A	ASHFORD - 74A	ASHFORD - 74A	ASHFORD - 74A	ASHFORD - 74A
31404	ASHFORD - 74A	ASHFORD - 74A	ASHFORD - 74A	ASHFORD - 74A	ASHFORD - 74A	ASHFORD - 74A	ASHFORD - 74A
31405	ASHFORD - 74A	ASHFORD - 74A	ASHFORD - 74A	ASHFORD - 74A	ASHFORD - 74A	ASHFORD - 74A	ASHFORD - 74A
31406	HITHER GREEN - 73C	HITHER GREEN - 73C	HITHER GREEN - 73C	HITHER GREEN - 73C	HITHER GREEN - 73C	HITHER GREEN - 73C	HITHER GREEN - 73C
31407	ASHFORD - 74A	ASHFORD - 74A	ASHFORD - 74A	ASHFORD - 74A	ASHFORD - 74A	ASHFORD - 74A	ASHFORD - 74A
31408	STEWARTS LANE - 73A	STEWARTS LANE - 73A	STEWARTS LANE - 73A	STEWARTS LANE - 73A	STEWARTS LANE - 73A	STEWARTS LANE - 73A	STEWARTS LANE - 73A
31409	STEWARTS LANE - 73A	STEWARTS LANE - 73A	STEWARTS LANE - 73A	STEWARTS LANE - 73A	STEWARTS LANE - 73A	STEWARTS LANE - 73A	STEWARTS LANE - 73A
31410	STEWARTS LANE - 73A	STEWARTS LANE - 73A	STEWARTS LANE - 73A	STEWARTS LANE - 73A	STEWARTS LANE - 73A	STEWARTS LANE - 73A	STEWARTS LANE - 73A
31411	STEWARTS LANE - 73A	STEWARTS LANE - 73A	STEWARTS LANE - 73A	STEWARTS LANE - 73A	STEWARTS LANE - 73A	STEWARTS LANE - 73A	STEWARTS LANE - 73A
31412	STEWARTS LANE - 73A	STEWARTS LANE - 73A	STEWARTS LANE - 73A	STEWARTS LANE - 73A	STEWARTS LANE - 73A	STEWARTS LANE - 73A	STEWARTS LANE - 73A
31413	STEWARTS LANE - 73A	STEWARTS LANE - 73A	STEWARTS LANE - 73A	STEWARTS LANE - 73A	STEWARTS LANE - 73A	STEWARTS LANE - 73A	STEWARTS LANE - 73A
31414	STEWARTS LANE - 73A	STEWARTS LANE - 73A	STEWARTS LANE - 73A	STEWARTS LANE - 73A	STEWARTS LANE - 73A	STEWARTS LANE - 73A	STEWARTS LANE - 73A
31810	STEWARTS LANE - 73A	STEWARTS LANE - 73A	STEWARTS LANE - 73A	STEWARTS LANE - 73A	STEWARTS LANE - 73A	STEWARTS LANE - 73A	STEWARTS LANE - 73A
31811	STEWARTS LANE - 73A	STEWARTS LANE - 73A	STEWARTS LANE - 73A	STEWARTS LANE - 73A	STEWARTS LANE - 73A	STEWARTS LANE - 73A	STEWARTS LANE - 73A
31812	STEWARTS LANE - 73A	STEWARTS LANE - 73A	STEWARTS LANE - 73A	STEWARTS LANE - 73A	STEWARTS LANE - 73A	STEWARTS LANE - 73A	STEWARTS LANE - 73A
31813	SALISBURY - 72B	SALISBURY - 72B	SALISBURY - 72B	SALISBURY - 72B	SALISBURY - 72B	SALISBURY - 72B	SALISBURY - 72B
31814	SALISBURY - 72B	SALISBURY - 72B	SALISBURY - 72B	SALISBURY - 72B	SALISBURY - 72B	SALISBURY - 72B	SALISBURY - 72B
31815	GILLINGHAM - 73D	GILLINGHAM - 73D	GILLINGHAM - 73D	GILLINGHAM - 73D	GILLINGHAM - 73D	GILLINGHAM - 73D	GILLINGHAM - 73D
31816	GILLINGHAM - 73D	GILLINGHAM - 73D	GILLINGHAM - 73D	GILLINGHAM - 73D	GILLINGHAM - 73D	GILLINGHAM - 73D	GILLINGHAM - 73D
31817	REDHILL - 75B	REDHILL - 75B	REDHILL - 75B	REDHILL - 75B	REDHILL - 75B	REDHILL - 75B	REDHILL - 75B
31818	DOVER - 74C	DOVER - 74C	DOVER - 74C	DOVER - 74C	DOVER - 74C	DOVER - 74C	DOVER - 74C
31819	DOVER - 74C	DOVER - 74C	DOVER - 74C	DOVER - 74C	DOVER - 74C	DOVER - 74C	DOVER - 74C
31820	DOVER - 74C	DOVER - 74C	DOVER - 74C	DOVER - 74C	DOVER - 74C	DOVER - 74C	DOVER - 74C
31821	DOVER - 74C	DOVER - 74C	DOVER - 74C	DOVER - 74C	DOVER - 74C	DOVER - 74C	DOVER - 74C
31823	B.ARMS - 73B	B.ARMS - 73B	B.ARMS - 73B	B.ARMS - 73B	B.ARMS - 73B	B.ARMS - 73B	B.ARMS - 73B
31824	B.ARMS - 73B	B.ARMS - 73B	B.ARMS - 73B	B.ARMS - 73B	B.ARMS - 73B	B.ARMS - 73B	B.ARMS - 73B
31825	B.ARMS - 73B	B.ARMS - 73B	B.ARMS - 73B	B.ARMS - 73B	B.ARMS - 73B	B.ARMS - 73B	B.ARMS - 73B
31826	B.ARMS - 73B	B.ARMS - 73B	B.ARMS - 73B	B.ARMS - 73B	B.ARMS - 73B	B.ARMS - 73B	B.ARMS - 73B
31827	B.ARMS - 73B	B.ARMS - 73B	B.ARMS - 73B	B.ARMS - 73B	B.ARMS - 73B	B.ARMS - 73B	B.ARMS - 73B
31828	B.ARMS - 73B	B.ARMS - 73B	B.ARMS - 73B	B.ARMS - 73B	B.ARMS - 73B	B.ARMS - 73B	B.ARMS - 73B
31829	B.ARMS - 73B	B.ARMS - 73B	B.ARMS - 73B	B.ARMS - 73B	B.ARMS - 73B	B.ARMS - 73B	B.ARMS - 73B
31830	EXMOUTH JCN - 72A	EXMOUTH JCN - 72A	EXMOUTH JCN - 72A	EXMOUTH JCN - 72A	EXMOUTH JCN - 72A	EXMOUTH JCN - 72A	EXMOUTH JCN - 72A
31831	EXMOUTH JCN - 72A	EXMOUTH JCN - 72A	EXMOUTH JCN - 72A	EXMOUTH JCN - 72A	EXMOUTH JCN - 72A	EXMOUTH JCN - 72A	EXMOUTH JCN - 72A
31832	EXMOUTH JCN - 72A	EXMOUTH JCN - 72A	EXMOUTH JCN - 72A	EXMOUTH JCN - 72A	EXMOUTH JCN - 72A	EXMOUTH JCN - 72A	EXMOUTH JCN - 72A
31833	EXMOUTH JCN - 72A	EXMOUTH JCN - 72A	EXMOUTH JCN - 72A	EXMOUTH JCN - 72A	EXMOUTH JCN - 72A	EXMOUTH JCN - 72A	EXMOUTH JCN - 72A
31834	EXMOUTH JCN - 72A	EXMOUTH JCN - 72A	EXMOUTH JCN - 72A	EXMOUTH JCN - 72A	EXMOUTH JCN - 72A	EXMOUTH JCN - 72A	EXMOUTH JCN - 72A
31835	EXMOUTH JCN - 72A	EXMOUTH JCN - 72A	EXMOUTH JCN - 72A	EXMOUTH JCN - 72A	EXMOUTH JCN - 72A	EXMOUTH JCN - 72A	EXMOUTH JCN - 72A
31836	EXMOUTH JCN - 72A	EXMOUTH JCN - 72A	EXMOUTH JCN - 72A	EXMOUTH JCN - 72A	EXMOUTH JCN - 72A	EXMOUTH JCN - 72A	EXMOUTH JCN - 72A
31837	EXMOUTH JCN - 72A	EXMOUTH JCN - 72A	EXMOUTH JCN - 72A	EXMOUTH JCN - 72A	EXMOUTH JCN - 72A	EXMOUTH JCN - 72A	EXMOUTH JCN - 72A
31838	EXMOUTH JCN - 72A	EXMOUTH JCN - 72A	EXMOUTH JCN - 72A	EXMOUTH JCN - 72A	EXMOUTH JCN - 72A	EXMOUTH JCN - 72A	EXMOUTH JCN - 72A
31839	EXMOUTH JCN - 72A	EXMOUTH JCN - 72A	EXMOUTH JCN - 72A	EXMOUTH JCN - 72A	EXMOUTH JCN - 72A	EXMOUTH JCN - 72A	EXMOUTH JCN - 72A
31840	EXMOUTH JCN - 72A	EXMOUTH JCN - 72A	EXMOUTH JCN - 72A	EXMOUTH JCN - 72A	EXMOUTH JCN - 72A	EXMOUTH JCN - 72A	EXMOUTH JCN - 72A
31841	EXMOUTH JCN - 72A	EXMOUTH JCN - 72A	EXMOUTH JCN - 72A	EXMOUTH JCN - 72A	EXMOUTH JCN - 72A	EXMOUTH JCN - 72A	EXMOUTH JCN - 72A
31842	BARNSTAPLE - 72E	BARNSTAPLE - 72E	BARNSTAPLE - 72E	BARNSTAPLE - 72E	BARNSTAPLE - 72E	EXMOUTH JCN - 72A	EXMOUTH JCN - 72A
31843	BARNSTAPLE - 72E	BARNSTAPLE - 72E	BARNSTAPLE - 72E	BARNSTAPLE - 72E	BARNSTAPLE - 72E	EXMOUTH JCN - 72A	EXMOUTH JCN - 72A
31844	EXMOUTH JCN - 72A	EXMOUTH JCN - 72A	EXMOUTH JCN - 72A	EXMOUTH JCN - 72A	EXMOUTH JCN - 72A	EXMOUTH JCN - 72A	EXMOUTH JCN - 72A
31845	EXMOUTH JCN - 72A	EXMOUTH JCN - 72A	EXMOUTH JCN - 72A	EXMOUTH JCN - 72A	EXMOUTH JCN - 72A	EXMOUTH JCN - 72A	EXMOUTH JCN - 72A
31846	EXMOUTH JCN - 72A	EXMOUTH JCN - 72A	EXMOUTH JCN - 72A	EXMOUTH JCN - 72A	EXMOUTH JCN - 72A	EXMOUTH JCN - 72A	EXMOUTH JCN - 72A
31847	EXMOUTH JCN - 72A	EXMOUTH JCN - 72A	EXMOUTH JCN - 72A	EXMOUTH JCN - 72A	EXMOUTH JCN - 72A	EXMOUTH JCN - 72A	EXMOUTH JCN - 72A
31848	ASHFORD - 74A	ASHFORD - 74A	ASHFORD - 74A	ASHFORD - 74A	ASHFORD - 74A	ASHFORD - 74A	ASHFORD - 74A
31849	EXMOUTH JCN - 72A	EXMOUTH JCN - 72A	EXMOUTH JCN - 72A	EXMOUTH JCN - 72A	EXMOUTH JCN - 72A	EXMOUTH JCN - 72A	EXMOUTH JCN - 72A
31850	FAVERSHAM - 73E	FAVERSHAM - 73E	FAVERSHAM - 73E	FAVERSHAM - 73E	FAVERSHAM - 73E	FAVERSHAM - 73E	FAVERSHAM - 73E
31851	B.ARMS - 73B	B.ARMS - 73B	B.ARMS - 73B	B.ARMS - 73B	B.ARMS - 73B	B.ARMS - 73B	B.ARMS - 73B
31852	ASHFORD - 74A	ASHFORD - 74A	ASHFORD - 74A	ASHFORD - 74A	ASHFORD - 74A	ASHFORD - 74A	ASHFORD - 74A
31853	B.ARMS - 73B	B.ARMS - 73B	B.ARMS - 73B	B.ARMS - 73B	B.ARMS - 73B	B.ARMS - 73B	B.ARMS - 73B
31854	HITHER GREEN - 73C	HITHER GREEN - 73C	HITHER GREEN - 73C	HITHER GREEN - 73C	HITHER GREEN - 73C	HITHER GREEN - 73C	HITHER GREEN - 73C
31855	HITHER GREEN - 73C	HITHER GREEN - 73C	HITHER GREEN - 73C	HITHER GREEN - 73C	HITHER GREEN - 73C	HITHER GREEN - 73C	HITHER GREEN - 73C
31856	REDHILL - 75B	REDHILL - 75B	REDHILL - 75B	REDHILL - 75B	REDHILL - 75B	REDHILL - 75B	REDHILL - 75B
31857	HITHER GREEN - 73C	HITHER GREEN - 73C	HITHER GREEN - 73C	HITHER GREEN - 73C	HITHER GREEN - 73C	HITHER GREEN - 73C	HITHER GREEN - 73C
31858	HITHER GREEN - 73C	HITHER GREEN - 73C	HITHER GREEN - 73C	HITHER GREEN - 73C	HITHER GREEN - 73C	HITHER GREEN - 73C	HITHER GREEN - 73C
31859	HITHER GREEN - 73C	HITHER GREEN - 73C	HITHER GREEN - 73C	HITHER GREEN - 73C	HITHER GREEN - 73C	HITHER GREEN - 73C	HITHER GREEN - 73C
31860	HITHER GREEN - 73C	HITHER GREEN - 73C	HITHER GREEN - 73C	HITHER GREEN - 73C	HITHER GREEN - 73C	HITHER GREEN - 73C	HITHER GREEN - 73C
31861	HITHER GREEN - 73C	HITHER GREEN - 73C	HITHER GREEN - 73C	HITHER GREEN - 73C	HITHER GREEN - 73C	HITHER GREEN - 73C	HITHER GREEN - 73C
31862	REDHILL - 75B	REDHILL - 75B	REDHILL - 75B	REDHILL - 75B	REDHILL - 75B	REDHILL - 75B	REDHILL - 75B
31863	ASHFORD - 74A	ASHFORD - 74A	ASHFORD - 74A	ASHFORD - 74A	ASHFORD - 74A	ASHFORD - 74A	ASHFORD - 74A
31864	REDHILL - 75B	REDHILL - 75B	REDHILL - 75B	REDHILL - 75B	REDHILL - 75B	REDHILL - 75B	REDHILL - 75B
31865	REDHILL - 75B	REDHILL - 75B	REDHILL - 75B	REDHILL - 75B	REDHILL - 75B	REDHILL - 75B	REDHILL - 75B
31866	REDHILL - 75B	REDHILL - 75B	REDHILL - 75B	REDHILL - 75B	REDHILL - 75B	REDHILL - 75B	REDHILL - 75B
31867	REDHILL - 75B	REDHILL - 75B	REDHILL - 75B	REDHILL - 75B	REDHILL - 75B	REDHILL - 75B	REDHILL - 75B
31868	REDHILL - 75B	REDHILL - 75B	REDHILL - 75B	REDHILL - 75B	REDHILL - 75B	REDHILL - 75B	REDHILL - 75B
31869	REDHILL - 75B	REDHILL - 75B	REDHILL - 75B	REDHILL - 75B	REDHILL - 75B	REDHILL - 75B	REDHILL - 75B
31870	B.ARMS - 73B	B.ARMS - 73B	B.ARMS - 73B	B.ARMS - 73B	B.ARMS - 73B	B.ARMS - 73B	B.ARMS - 73B
31871	B.ARMS - 73B	B.ARMS - 73B	B.ARMS - 73B	B.ARMS - 73B	B.ARMS - 73B	B.ARMS - 73B	B.ARMS - 73B
31872	B.ARMS - 73B	B.ARMS - 73B	B.ARMS - 73B	B.ARMS - 73B	B.ARMS - 73B	B.ARMS - 73B	B.ARMS - 73B
31873	B.ARMS - 73B	B.ARMS - 73B	B.ARMS - 73B	B.ARMS - 73B	B.ARMS - 73B	B.ARMS - 73B	B.ARMS - 73B
31874	B.ARMS - 73B	B.ARMS - 73B	B.ARMS - 73B	B.ARMS - 73B	B.ARMS - 73B	B.ARMS - 73B	B.ARMS - 73B
31875	B.ARMS - 73B	B.ARMS - 73B	B.ARMS - 73B	B.ARMS - 73B	B.ARMS - 73B	B.ARMS - 73B	B.ARMS - 73B
				N1 2-6-0 (1922)			
31822	HITHER GREEN - 73C	HITHER GREEN - 73C	HITHER GREEN - 73C	HITHER GREEN - 73C	HITHER GREEN - 73C	HITHER GREEN - 73C	HITHER GREEN - 73C
31876	HITHER GREEN - 73C	HITHER GREEN - 73C	HITHER GREEN - 73C	HITHER GREEN - 73C	HITHER GREEN - 73C	HITHER GREEN - 73C	HITHER GREEN - 73C
31877	HITHER GREEN - 73C	HITHER GREEN - 73C	HITHER GREEN - 73C	HITHER GREEN - 73C	HITHER GREEN - 73C	HITHER GREEN - 73C	HITHER GREEN - 73C
31878	HITHER GREEN - 73C	HITHER GREEN - 73C	HITHER GREEN - 73C	HITHER GREEN - 73C	HITHER GREEN - 73C	HITHER GREEN - 73C	HITHER GREEN - 73C
31879	HITHER GREEN - 73C	HITHER GREEN - 73C	HITHER GREEN - 73C	HITHER GREEN - 73C	HITHER GREEN - 73C	HITHER GREEN - 73C	HITHER GREEN - 73C
31880	HITHER GREEN - 73C	HITHER GREEN - 73C	HITHER GREEN - 73C	HITHER GREEN - 73C	HITHER GREEN - 73C	HITHER GREEN - 73C	HITHER GREEN - 73C

loco	Mar-57	Jun-57	Jul-57	Oct-57	Jan-58	Feb-58	Mar-58
				N 2-6-0 (1917)			
31400	B ARMS - 73B	B ARMS - 73B	B ARMS - 73B	B ARMS - 73B	B ARMS - 73B	B ARMS - 73B	B ARMS - 73B
31401	ASHFORD - 74A	ASHFORD - 74A	ASHFORD - 74A	ASHFORD - 74A	ASHFORD - 74A	ASHFORD - 74A	ASHFORD - 74A
31402	ASHFORD - 74A	ASHFORD - 74A	ASHFORD - 74A	ASHFORD - 74A	ASHFORD - 74A	ASHFORD - 74A	ASHFORD - 74A
31403	ASHFORD - 74A	ASHFORD - 74A	ASHFORD - 74A	ASHFORD - 74A	ASHFORD - 74A	ASHFORD - 74A	ASHFORD - 74A
31404	ASHFORD - 74A	ASHFORD - 74A	ASHFORD - 74A	ASHFORD - 74A	ASHFORD - 74A	ASHFORD - 74A	ASHFORD - 74A
31405	ASHFORD - 74A	ASHFORD - 74A	ASHFORD - 74A	ASHFORD - 74A	ASHFORD - 74A	ASHFORD - 74A	ASHFORD - 74A
31406	HITHER GREEN - 73C	HITHER GREEN - 73C	HITHER GREEN - 73C	HITHER GREEN - 73C	HITHER GREEN - 73C	HITHER GREEN - 73C	HITHER GREEN - 73C
31407	ASHFORD - 74A	ASHFORD - 74A	ASHFORD - 74A	ASHFORD - 74A	ASHFORD - 74A	ASHFORD - 74A	ASHFORD - 74A
31408	STEWARTS LANE - 73A	STEWARTS LANE - 73A	STEWARTS LANE - 73A	STEWARTS LANE - 73A	STEWARTS LANE - 73A	STEWARTS LANE - 73A	STEWARTS LANE - 73A
31409	STEWARTS LANE - 73A	STEWARTS LANE - 73A	STEWARTS LANE - 73A	STEWARTS LANE - 73A	STEWARTS LANE - 73A	STEWARTS LANE - 73A	STEWARTS LANE - 73A
31410	STEWARTS LANE - 73A	STEWARTS LANE - 73A	STEWARTS LANE - 73A	STEWARTS LANE - 73A	STEWARTS LANE - 73A	STEWARTS LANE - 73A	STEWARTS LANE - 73A
31411	STEWARTS LANE - 73A	STEWARTS LANE - 73A	STEWARTS LANE - 73A	STEWARTS LANE - 73A	STEWARTS LANE - 73A	STEWARTS LANE - 73A	STEWARTS LANE - 73A
31412	STEWARTS LANE - 73A	STEWARTS LANE - 73A	STEWARTS LANE - 73A	STEWARTS LANE - 73A	STEWARTS LANE - 73A	STEWARTS LANE - 73A	STEWARTS LANE - 73A
31413	STEWARTS LANE - 73A	STEWARTS LANE - 73A	STEWARTS LANE - 73A	STEWARTS LANE - 73A	STEWARTS LANE - 73A	STEWARTS LANE - 73A	STEWARTS LANE - 73A
31414	STEWARTS LANE - 73A	STEWARTS LANE - 73A	STEWARTS LANE - 73A	STEWARTS LANE - 73A	STEWARTS LANE - 73A	STEWARTS LANE - 73A	STEWARTS LANE - 73A
31810	STEWARTS LANE - 73A	STEWARTS LANE - 73A	STEWARTS LANE - 73A	STEWARTS LANE - 73A	STEWARTS LANE - 73A	STEWARTS LANE - 73A	STEWARTS LANE - 73A
31811	STEWARTS LANE - 73A	STEWARTS LANE - 73A	STEWARTS LANE - 73A	STEWARTS LANE - 73A	STEWARTS LANE - 73A	STEWARTS LANE - 73A	STEWARTS LANE - 73A
31812	STEWARTS LANE - 73A	STEWARTS LANE - 73A	STEWARTS LANE - 73A	STEWARTS LANE - 73A	STEWARTS LANE - 73A	STEWARTS LANE - 73A	STEWARTS LANE - 73A
31813	SALISBURY - 72B	SALISBURY - 72B	SALISBURY - 72B	SALISBURY - 72B	SALISBURY - 72B	SALISBURY - 72B	SALISBURY - 72B
31814	SALISBURY - 72B	SALISBURY - 72B	SALISBURY - 72B	SALISBURY - 72B	SALISBURY - 72B	SALISBURY - 72B	SALISBURY - 72B
31815	GILLINGHAM - 73D	GILLINGHAM - 73D	GILLINGHAM - 73D	GILLINGHAM - 73D	GILLINGHAM - 73D	GILLINGHAM - 73D	GILLINGHAM - 73D
31816	GILLINGHAM - 73D	GILLINGHAM - 73D	GILLINGHAM - 73D	GILLINGHAM - 73D	GILLINGHAM - 73D	GILLINGHAM - 73D	GILLINGHAM - 73D
31817	REDHILL - 75B	REDHILL - 75B	REDHILL - 75B	REDHILL - 75B	REDHILL - 75B	REDHILL - 75B	REDHILL - 75B
31818	DOVER - 74C	DOVER - 74C	DOVER - 74C	DOVER - 74C	DOVER - 74C	DOVER - 74C	DOVER - 74C
31819	DOVER - 74C	DOVER - 74C	DOVER - 74C	DOVER - 74C	DOVER - 74C	DOVER - 74C	DOVER - 74C
31820	DOVER - 74C	DOVER - 74C	DOVER - 74C	DOVER - 74C	DOVER - 74C	DOVER - 74C	DOVER - 74C
31821	DOVER - 74C	DOVER - 74C	DOVER - 74C	DOVER - 74C	DOVER - 74C	DOVER - 74C	DOVER - 74C
31823	B ARMS - 73B	B ARMS - 73B	B ARMS - 73B	B ARMS - 73B	B ARMS - 73B	B ARMS - 73B	B ARMS - 73B
31824	B ARMS - 73B	B ARMS - 73B	B ARMS - 73B	B ARMS - 73B	B ARMS - 73B	B ARMS - 73B	B ARMS - 73B
31825	B ARMS - 73B	B ARMS - 73B	B ARMS - 73B	B ARMS - 73B	B ARMS - 73B	B ARMS - 73B	B ARMS - 73B
31826	B ARMS - 73B	B ARMS - 73B	B ARMS - 73B	B ARMS - 73B	B ARMS - 73B	B ARMS - 73B	B ARMS - 73B
31827	B ARMS - 73B	B ARMS - 73B	B ARMS - 73B	B ARMS - 73B	B ARMS - 73B	B ARMS - 73B	B ARMS - 73B
31828	B ARMS - 73B	B ARMS - 73B	B ARMS - 73B	B ARMS - 73B	B ARMS - 73B	B ARMS - 73B	B ARMS - 73B
31829	B ARMS - 73B	B ARMS - 73B	B ARMS - 73B	B ARMS - 73B	B ARMS - 73B	B ARMS - 73B	B ARMS - 73B
31830	EXMOUTH JCN - 72A	EXMOUTH JCN - 72A	EXMOUTH JCN - 72A	EXMOUTH JCN - 72A	EXMOUTH JCN - 72A	EXMOUTH JCN - 72A	EXMOUTH JCN - 72A
31831	EXMOUTH JCN - 72A	EXMOUTH JCN - 72A	EXMOUTH JCN - 72A	EXMOUTH JCN - 72A	EXMOUTH JCN - 72A	EXMOUTH JCN - 72A	EXMOUTH JCN - 72A
31832	EXMOUTH JCN - 72A	EXMOUTH JCN - 72A	EXMOUTH JCN - 72A	EXMOUTH JCN - 72A	EXMOUTH JCN - 72A	EXMOUTH JCN - 72A	EXMOUTH JCN - 72A
31833	EXMOUTH JCN - 72A	EXMOUTH JCN - 72A	EXMOUTH JCN - 72A	EXMOUTH JCN - 72A	EXMOUTH JCN - 72A	EXMOUTH JCN - 72A	EXMOUTH JCN - 72A
31834	EXMOUTH JCN - 72A	EXMOUTH JCN - 72A	EXMOUTH JCN - 72A	EXMOUTH JCN - 72A	EXMOUTH JCN - 72A	EXMOUTH JCN - 72A	EXMOUTH JCN - 72A
31835	EXMOUTH JCN - 72A	EXMOUTH JCN - 72A	EXMOUTH JCN - 72A	EXMOUTH JCN - 72A	EXMOUTH JCN - 72A	EXMOUTH JCN - 72A	EXMOUTH JCN - 72A
31836	EXMOUTH JCN - 72A	EXMOUTH JCN - 72A	EXMOUTH JCN - 72A	EXMOUTH JCN - 72A	EXMOUTH JCN - 72A	EXMOUTH JCN - 72A	EXMOUTH JCN - 72A
31837	EXMOUTH JCN - 72A	EXMOUTH JCN - 72A	EXMOUTH JCN - 72A	EXMOUTH JCN - 72A	EXMOUTH JCN - 72A	EXMOUTH JCN - 72A	EXMOUTH JCN - 72A
31838	EXMOUTH JCN - 72A	EXMOUTH JCN - 72A	EXMOUTH JCN - 72A	EXMOUTH JCN - 72A	EXMOUTH JCN - 72A	EXMOUTH JCN - 72A	EXMOUTH JCN - 72A
31839	EXMOUTH JCN - 72A	EXMOUTH JCN - 72A	EXMOUTH JCN - 72A	EXMOUTH JCN - 72A	EXMOUTH JCN - 72A	EXMOUTH JCN - 72A	EXMOUTH JCN - 72A
31840	EXMOUTH JCN - 72A	EXMOUTH JCN - 72A	EXMOUTH JCN - 72A	EXMOUTH JCN - 72A	EXMOUTH JCN - 72A	EXMOUTH JCN - 72A	EXMOUTH JCN - 72A
31841	EXMOUTH JCN - 72A	EXMOUTH JCN - 72A	EXMOUTH JCN - 72A	EXMOUTH JCN - 72A	EXMOUTH JCN - 72A	EXMOUTH JCN - 72A	EXMOUTH JCN - 72A
31842	EXMOUTH JCN - 72A	EXMOUTH JCN - 72A	EXMOUTH JCN - 72A	EXMOUTH JCN - 72A	EXMOUTH JCN - 72A	EXMOUTH JCN - 72A	EXMOUTH JCN - 72A
31843	EXMOUTH JCN - 72A	EXMOUTH JCN - 72A	EXMOUTH JCN - 72A	EXMOUTH JCN - 72A	EXMOUTH JCN - 72A	EXMOUTH JCN - 72A	EXMOUTH JCN - 72A
31844	EXMOUTH JCN - 72A	EXMOUTH JCN - 72A	EXMOUTH JCN - 72A	EXMOUTH JCN - 72A	EXMOUTH JCN - 72A	EXMOUTH JCN - 72A	EXMOUTH JCN - 72A
31845	EXMOUTH JCN - 72A	EXMOUTH JCN - 72A	EXMOUTH JCN - 72A	EXMOUTH JCN - 72A	EXMOUTH JCN - 72A	EXMOUTH JCN - 72A	EXMOUTH JCN - 72A
31846	EXMOUTH JCN - 72A	EXMOUTH JCN - 72A	EXMOUTH JCN - 72A	EXMOUTH JCN - 72A	EXMOUTH JCN - 72A	EXMOUTH JCN - 72A	EXMOUTH JCN - 72A
31847	EXMOUTH JCN - 72A	EXMOUTH JCN - 72A	EXMOUTH JCN - 72A	EXMOUTH JCN - 72A	EXMOUTH JCN - 72A	EXMOUTH JCN - 72A	EXMOUTH JCN - 72A
31848	ASHFORD - 74A	ASHFORD - 74A	ASHFORD - 74A	ASHFORD - 74A	ASHFORD - 74A	ASHFORD - 74A	ASHFORD - 74A
31849	EXMOUTH JCN - 72A	EXMOUTH JCN - 72A	EXMOUTH JCN - 72A	EXMOUTH JCN - 72A	EXMOUTH JCN - 72A	EXMOUTH JCN - 72A	EXMOUTH JCN - 72A
31850	FAVERSHAM - 73E	FAVERSHAM - 73E	FAVERSHAM - 73E	FAVERSHAM - 73E	FAVERSHAM - 73E	FAVERSHAM - 73E	FAVERSHAM - 73E
31851	B ARMS - 73B	B ARMS - 73B	B ARMS - 73B	B ARMS - 73B	B ARMS - 73B	B ARMS - 73B	B ARMS - 73B
31852	ASHFORD - 74A	ASHFORD - 74A	ASHFORD - 74A	ASHFORD - 74A	ASHFORD - 74A	ASHFORD - 74A	ASHFORD - 74A
31853	B ARMS - 73B	B ARMS - 73B	B ARMS - 73B	B ARMS - 73B	B ARMS - 73B	B ARMS - 73B	B ARMS - 73B
31854	HITHER GREEN - 73C	HITHER GREEN - 73C	ASHFORD - 74A	ASHFORD - 74A	ASHFORD - 74A	ASHFORD - 74A	ASHFORD - 74A
31855	HITHER GREEN - 73C	HITHER GREEN - 73C	HITHER GREEN - 73C	HITHER GREEN - 73C	HITHER GREEN - 73C	HITHER GREEN - 73C	HITHER GREEN - 73C
31856	REDHILL - 75B	REDHILL - 75B	REDHILL - 75B	REDHILL - 75B	REDHILL - 75B	REDHILL - 75B	REDHILL - 75B
31857	HITHER GREEN - 73C	HITHER GREEN - 73C	HITHER GREEN - 73C	HITHER GREEN - 73C	HITHER GREEN - 73C	HITHER GREEN - 73C	HITHER GREEN - 73C
31858	HITHER GREEN - 73C	HITHER GREEN - 73C	HITHER GREEN - 73C	HITHER GREEN - 73C	HITHER GREEN - 73C	HITHER GREEN - 73C	HITHER GREEN - 73C
31859	HITHER GREEN - 73C	HITHER GREEN - 73C	HITHER GREEN - 73C	HITHER GREEN - 73C	HITHER GREEN - 73C	HITHER GREEN - 73C	HITHER GREEN - 73C
31860	HITHER GREEN - 73C	HITHER GREEN - 73C	HITHER GREEN - 73C	HITHER GREEN - 73C	HITHER GREEN - 73C	HITHER GREEN - 73C	HITHER GREEN - 73C
31861	HITHER GREEN - 73C	HITHER GREEN - 73C	HITHER GREEN - 73C	HITHER GREEN - 73C	HITHER GREEN - 73C	HITHER GREEN - 73C	HITHER GREEN - 73C
31862	REDHILL - 75B	REDHILL - 75B	REDHILL - 75B	REDHILL - 75B	REDHILL - 75B	REDHILL - 75B	REDHILL - 75B
31863	ASHFORD - 74A	ASHFORD - 74A	ASHFORD - 74A	ASHFORD - 74A	ASHFORD - 74A	ASHFORD - 74A	ASHFORD - 74A
31864	REDHILL - 75B	REDHILL - 75B	REDHILL - 75B	REDHILL - 75B	REDHILL - 75B	REDHILL - 75B	REDHILL - 75B
31865	REDHILL - 75B	REDHILL - 75B	REDHILL - 75B	REDHILL - 75B	REDHILL - 75B	REDHILL - 75B	REDHILL - 75B
31866	REDHILL - 75B	REDHILL - 75B	REDHILL - 75B	REDHILL - 75B	REDHILL - 75B	REDHILL - 75B	REDHILL - 75B
31867	REDHILL - 75B	REDHILL - 75B	REDHILL - 75B	REDHILL - 75B	REDHILL - 75B	REDHILL - 75B	REDHILL - 75B
31868	REDHILL - 75B	REDHILL - 75B	REDHILL - 75B	REDHILL - 75B	REDHILL - 75B	REDHILL - 75B	REDHILL - 75B
31869	REDHILL - 75B	REDHILL - 75B	REDHILL - 75B	REDHILL - 75B	REDHILL - 75B	REDHILL - 75B	REDHILL - 75B
31870	B ARMS - 73B	B ARMS - 73B	B ARMS - 73B	B ARMS - 73B	B ARMS - 73B	B ARMS - 73B	B ARMS - 73B
31871	B ARMS - 73B	B ARMS - 73B	B ARMS - 73B	B ARMS - 73B	B ARMS - 73B	B ARMS - 73B	B ARMS - 73B
31872	B ARMS - 73B	B ARMS - 73B	B ARMS - 73B	B ARMS - 73B	B ARMS - 73B	B ARMS - 73B	B ARMS - 73B
31873	B ARMS - 73B	B ARMS - 73B	B ARMS - 73B	B ARMS - 73B	B ARMS - 73B	B ARMS - 73B	B ARMS - 73B
31874	B ARMS - 73B	B ARMS - 73B	B ARMS - 73B	B ARMS - 73B	B ARMS - 73B	B ARMS - 73B	B ARMS - 73B
31875	B ARMS - 73B	B ARMS - 73B	B ARMS - 73B	B ARMS - 73B	B ARMS - 73B	B ARMS - 73B	B ARMS - 73B
				N1 2-6-0 (1922)			
31822	HITHER GREEN - 73C	HITHER GREEN - 73C	HITHER GREEN - 73C	HITHER GREEN - 73C	HITHER GREEN - 73C	HITHER GREEN - 73C	HITHER GREEN - 73C
31876	HITHER GREEN - 73C	HITHER GREEN - 73C	HITHER GREEN - 73C	HITHER GREEN - 73C	HITHER GREEN - 73C	HITHER GREEN - 73C	HITHER GREEN - 73C
31877	HITHER GREEN - 73C	HITHER GREEN - 73C	HITHER GREEN - 73C	HITHER GREEN - 73C	HITHER GREEN - 73C	HITHER GREEN - 73C	HITHER GREEN - 73C
31878	HITHER GREEN - 73C	HITHER GREEN - 73C	HITHER GREEN - 73C	HITHER GREEN - 73C	HITHER GREEN - 73C	HITHER GREEN - 73C	HITHER GREEN - 73C
31879	HITHER GREEN - 73C	HITHER GREEN - 73C	HITHER GREEN - 73C	HITHER GREEN - 73C	HITHER GREEN - 73C	HITHER GREEN - 73C	HITHER GREEN - 73C
31880	HITHER GREEN - 73C	HITHER GREEN - 73C	HITHER GREEN - 73C	HITHER GREEN - 73C	HITHER GREEN - 73C	HITHER GREEN - 73C	HITHER GREEN - 73C

loco	May-58	Oct-58	Mar-59	Jun-59	Jul-59	Aug-59	Oct-59
				N 2-6-0 (1917)			
31400	B.ARMS - 73B	B.ARMS - 73B	B.ARMS - 73B	B.ARMS - 73B	B.ARMS - 73B	B.ARMS - 73B	B.ARMS - 73B
31401	ASHFORD - 74A	ASHFORD - 73F	ASHFORD - 73F	ASHFORD - 73F	ASHFORD - 73F	ASHFORD - 73F	ASHFORD - 73F
31402	ASHFORD - 74A	ASHFORD - 73F	ASHFORD - 73F	ASHFORD - 73F	ASHFORD - 73F	ASHFORD - 73F	ASHFORD - 73F
31403	ASHFORD - 74A	ASHFORD - 73F	ASHFORD - 73F	ASHFORD - 73F	ASHFORD - 73F	ASHFORD - 73F	ASHFORD - 73F
31404	ASHFORD - 74A	ASHFORD - 73F	ASHFORD - 73F	ASHFORD - 73F	ASHFORD - 73F	ASHFORD - 73F	ASHFORD - 73F
31405	ASHFORD - 74A	ASHFORD - 73F	ASHFORD - 73F	ASHFORD - 73F	ASHFORD - 73F	ASHFORD - 73F	ASHFORD - 73F
31406	HITHER GREEN - 73C	HITHER GREEN - 73C	HITHER GREEN - 73C	HITHER GREEN - 73C	HITHER GREEN - 73C	HITHER GREEN - 73C	HITHER GREEN - 73C
31407	ASHFORD - 74A	ASHFORD - 73F	ASHFORD - 73F	ASHFORD - 73F	ASHFORD - 73F	ASHFORD - 73F	ASHFORD - 73F
31408	STEWARTS LANE - 73A	STEWARTS LANE - 73A	STEWARTS LANE - 73A	ASHFORD - 73F	ASHFORD - 73F	ASHFORD - 73F	ASHFORD - 73F
31409	STEWARTS LANE - 73A	STEWARTS LANE - 73A	STEWARTS LANE - 73A	ASHFORD - 73F	ASHFORD - 73F	ASHFORD - 73F	ASHFORD - 73F
31410	STEWARTS LANE - 73A	STEWARTS LANE - 73A	STEWARTS LANE - 73A	STEWARTS LANE - 73A	STEWARTS LANE - 73A	STEWARTS LANE - 73A	STEWARTS LANE - 73A
31411	STEWARTS LANE - 73A	STEWARTS LANE - 73A	STEWARTS LANE - 73A	STEWARTS LANE - 73A	STEWARTS LANE - 73A	STEWARTS LANE - 73A	STEWARTS LANE - 73A
31412	STEWARTS LANE - 73A	STEWARTS LANE - 73A	STEWARTS LANE - 73A	STEWARTS LANE - 73A	STEWARTS LANE - 73A	STEWARTS LANE - 73A	STEWARTS LANE - 73A
31413	STEWARTS LANE - 73A	STEWARTS LANE - 73A	STEWARTS LANE - 73A	DOVER - 73H	DOVER - 73H	DOVER - 73H	DOVER - 73H
31414	STEWARTS LANE - 73A	STEWARTS LANE - 73A	STEWARTS LANE - 73A	DOVER - 73H	DOVER - 73H	DOVER - 73H	DOVER - 73H
31810	STEWARTS LANE - 73A	STEWARTS LANE - 73A	STEWARTS LANE - 73A	DOVER - 73H	DOVER - 73H	DOVER - 73H	DOVER - 73H
31811	STEWARTS LANE - 73A	STEWARTS LANE - 73A	STEWARTS LANE - 73A	GUILDFORD - 70C	GUILDFORD - 70C	GUILDFORD - 70C	GUILDFORD - 70C
31812	STEWARTS LANE - 73A	STEWARTS LANE - 73A	STEWARTS LANE - 73A	GUILDFORD - 70C	GUILDFORD - 70C	GUILDFORD - 70C	GUILDFORD - 70C
31813	SALISBURY - 72B	SALISBURY - 72B	SALISBURY - 72B	SALISBURY - 72B	SALISBURY - 72B	SALISBURY - 72B	SALISBURY - 72B
31814	SALISBURY - 72B	SALISBURY - 72B	SALISBURY - 72B	SALISBURY - 72B	SALISBURY - 72B	SALISBURY - 72B	SALISBURY - 72B
31815	GILLINGHAM - 73D	GILLINGHAM - 73D	GILLINGHAM - 73D	GUILDFORD - 70C	GUILDFORD - 70C	GUILDFORD - 70C	GUILDFORD - 70C
31816	GILLINGHAM - 73D	GILLINGHAM - 73D	GILLINGHAM - 73D	GUILDFORD - 70C	GUILDFORD - 70C	GUILDFORD - 70C	HITHER GREEN - 73C
31817	REDHILL - 75B	REDHILL - 75B	REDHILL - 75B	REDHILL - 75B	REDHILL - 75B	REDHILL - 75B	REDHILL - 75B
31818	DOVER - 74C	DOVER - 73H	DOVER - 73H	DOVER - 73H	DOVER - 73H	DOVER - 73H	DOVER - 73H
31819	DOVER - 74C	DOVER - 73H	DOVER - 73H	DOVER - 73H	DOVER - 73H	DOVER - 73H	DOVER - 73H
31820	DOVER - 74C	DOVER - 73H	DOVER - 73H	DOVER - 73H	DOVER - 73H	DOVER - 73H	DOVER - 73H
31821	DOVER - 74C	DOVER - 73H	DOVER - 73H	DOVER - 73H	DOVER - 73H	DOVER - 73H	DOVER - 73H
31823	B.ARMS - 73B	B.ARMS - 73B	B.ARMS - 73B	B.ARMS - 73B	B.ARMS - 73B	B.ARMS - 73B	B.ARMS - 73B
31824	B.ARMS - 73B	B.ARMS - 73B	B.ARMS - 73B	B.ARMS - 73B	B.ARMS - 73B	B.ARMS - 73B	B.ARMS - 73B
31825	B.ARMS - 73B	B.ARMS - 73B	B.ARMS - 73B	B.ARMS - 73B	B.ARMS - 73B	B.ARMS - 73B	B.ARMS - 73B
31826	B.ARMS - 73B	B.ARMS - 73B	B.ARMS - 73B	B.ARMS - 73B	B.ARMS - 73B	B.ARMS - 73B	B.ARMS - 73B
31827	B.ARMS - 73B	B.ARMS - 73B	B.ARMS - 73B	B.ARMS - 73B	B.ARMS - 73B	B.ARMS - 73B	B.ARMS - 73B
31828	B.ARMS - 73B	B.ARMS - 73B	B.ARMS - 73B	B.ARMS - 73B	B.ARMS - 73B	B.ARMS - 73B	B.ARMS - 73B
31829	B.ARMS - 73B	B.ARMS - 73B	B.ARMS - 73B	B.ARMS - 73B	B.ARMS - 73B	B.ARMS - 73B	B.ARMS - 73B
31830	EXMOUTH J CN - 72A	EXMOUTH J CN - 72A	EXMOUTH J CN - 72A	EXMOUTH J CN - 72A	EXMOUTH J CN - 72A	EXMOUTH J CN - 72A	EXMOUTH J CN - 72A
31831	EXMOUTH J CN - 72A	EXMOUTH J CN - 72A	EXMOUTH J CN - 72A	EXMOUTH J CN - 72A	EXMOUTH J CN - 72A	EXMOUTH J CN - 72A	EXMOUTH J CN - 72A
31832	EXMOUTH J CN - 72A	EXMOUTH J CN - 72A	EXMOUTH J CN - 72A	EXMOUTH J CN - 72A	EXMOUTH J CN - 72A	EXMOUTH J CN - 72A	EXMOUTH J CN - 72A
31833	EXMOUTH J CN - 72A	EXMOUTH J CN - 72A	EXMOUTH J CN - 72A	EXMOUTH J CN - 72A	EXMOUTH J CN - 72A	EXMOUTH J CN - 72A	EXMOUTH J CN - 72A
31834	EXMOUTH J CN - 72A	EXMOUTH J CN - 72A	EXMOUTH J CN - 72A	EXMOUTH J CN - 72A	EXMOUTH J CN - 72A	EXMOUTH J CN - 72A	EXMOUTH J CN - 72A
31835	EXMOUTH J CN - 72A	EXMOUTH J CN - 72A	EXMOUTH J CN - 72A	EXMOUTH J CN - 72A	EXMOUTH J CN - 72A	EXMOUTH J CN - 72A	EXMOUTH J CN - 72A
31836	EXMOUTH J CN - 72A	EXMOUTH J CN - 72A	EXMOUTH J CN - 72A	EXMOUTH J CN - 72A	EXMOUTH J CN - 72A	EXMOUTH J CN - 72A	EXMOUTH J CN - 72A
31837	EXMOUTH J CN - 72A	EXMOUTH J CN - 72A	EXMOUTH J CN - 72A	EXMOUTH J CN - 72A	EXMOUTH J CN - 72A	EXMOUTH J CN - 72A	EXMOUTH J CN - 72A
31838	EXMOUTH J CN - 72A	EXMOUTH J CN - 72A	EXMOUTH J CN - 72A	EXMOUTH J CN - 72A	EXMOUTH J CN - 72A	EXMOUTH J CN - 72A	EXMOUTH J CN - 72A
31839	EXMOUTH J CN - 72A	EXMOUTH J CN - 72A	EXMOUTH J CN - 72A	EXMOUTH J CN - 72A	EXMOUTH J CN - 72A	EXMOUTH J CN - 72A	EXMOUTH J CN - 72A
31840	EXMOUTH J CN - 72A	EXMOUTH J CN - 72A	EXMOUTH J CN - 72A	EXMOUTH J CN - 72A	EXMOUTH J CN - 72A	EXMOUTH J CN - 72A	EXMOUTH J CN - 72A
31841	EXMOUTH J CN - 72A	EXMOUTH J CN - 72A	EXMOUTH J CN - 72A	EXMOUTH J CN - 72A	EXMOUTH J CN - 72A	EXMOUTH J CN - 72A	EXMOUTH J CN - 72A
31842	EXMOUTH J CN - 72A	EXMOUTH J CN - 72A	EXMOUTH J CN - 72A	EXMOUTH J CN - 72A	EXMOUTH J CN - 72A	EXMOUTH J CN - 72A	EXMOUTH J CN - 72A
31843	EXMOUTH J CN - 72A	EXMOUTH J CN - 72A	EXMOUTH J CN - 72A	EXMOUTH J CN - 72A	EXMOUTH J CN - 72A	EXMOUTH J CN - 72A	EXMOUTH J CN - 72A
31844	EXMOUTH J CN - 72A	EXMOUTH J CN - 72A	EXMOUTH J CN - 72A	EXMOUTH J CN - 72A	EXMOUTH J CN - 72A	EXMOUTH J CN - 72A	EXMOUTH J CN - 72A
31845	EXMOUTH J CN - 72A	EXMOUTH J CN - 72A	EXMOUTH J CN - 72A	EXMOUTH J CN - 72A	EXMOUTH J CN - 72A	EXMOUTH J CN - 72A	EXMOUTH J CN - 72A
31846	EXMOUTH J CN - 72A	EXMOUTH J CN - 72A	EXMOUTH J CN - 72A	EXMOUTH J CN - 72A	EXMOUTH J CN - 72A	EXMOUTH J CN - 72A	EXMOUTH J CN - 72A
31847	EXMOUTH J CN - 72A	EXMOUTH J CN - 72A	EXMOUTH J CN - 72A	EXMOUTH J CN - 72A	EXMOUTH J CN - 72A	EXMOUTH J CN - 72A	EXMOUTH J CN - 72A
31848	ASHFORD - 74A	ASHFORD - 73F	ASHFORD - 73F	ASHFORD - 73F	ASHFORD - 73F	ASHFORD - 73F	ASHFORD - 73F
31849	EXMOUTH J CN - 72A	EXMOUTH J CN - 72A	EXMOUTH J CN - 72A	EXMOUTH J CN - 72A	EXMOUTH J CN - 72A	EXMOUTH J CN - 72A	EXMOUTH J CN - 72A
31850	FAVERSHAM - 73E	FAVERSHAM - 73E	FAVERSHAM - 73E	EXMOUTH J CN - 72A	EXMOUTH J CN - 72A	EXMOUTH J CN - 72A	EXMOUTH J CN - 72A
31851	B.ARMS - 73B	B.ARMS - 73B	B.ARMS - 73B	EXMOUTH J CN - 72A	EXMOUTH J CN - 72A	EXMOUTH J CN - 72A	EXMOUTH J CN - 72A
31852	ASHFORD - 74A	ASHFORD - 73F	ASHFORD - 73F	EXMOUTH J CN - 72A	EXMOUTH J CN - 72A	EXMOUTH J CN - 72A	EXMOUTH J CN - 72A
31853	B.ARMS - 73B	B.ARMS - 73B	B.ARMS - 73B	EXMOUTH J CN - 72A	EXMOUTH J CN - 72A	EXMOUTH J CN - 72A	EXMOUTH J CN - 72A
31854	ASHFORD - 74A	ASHFORD - 73F	ASHFORD - 73F	ASHFORD - 73F	ASHFORD - 73F	ASHFORD - 73F	ASHFORD - 73F
31855	HITHER GREEN - 73C	HITHER GREEN - 73C	HITHER GREEN - 73C	HITHER GREEN - 73C	HITHER GREEN - 73C	HITHER GREEN - 73C	HITHER GREEN - 73C
31856	REDHILL - 75B	REDHILL - 75B	REDHILL - 75B	REDHILL - 75B	REDHILL - 75B	REDHILL - 75B	REDHILL - 75B
31857	HITHER GREEN - 73C	HITHER GREEN - 73C	HITHER GREEN - 73C	HITHER GREEN - 73C	HITHER GREEN - 73C	HITHER GREEN - 73C	HITHER GREEN - 73C
31858	HITHER GREEN - 73C	HITHER GREEN - 73C	HITHER GREEN - 73C	HITHER GREEN - 73C	HITHER GREEN - 73C	HITHER GREEN - 73C	GUILDFORD - 70C
31859	HITHER GREEN - 73C	HITHER GREEN - 73C	HITHER GREEN - 73C	HITHER GREEN - 73C	HITHER GREEN - 73C	HITHER GREEN - 73C	HITHER GREEN - 73C
31860	HITHER GREEN - 73C	HITHER GREEN - 73C	HITHER GREEN - 73C	EXMOUTH J CN - 72A	EXMOUTH J CN - 72A	EXMOUTH J CN - 72A	EXMOUTH J CN - 72A
31861	HITHER GREEN - 73C	HITHER GREEN - 73C	HITHER GREEN - 73C	REDHILL - 75B	REDHILL - 75B	REDHILL - 75B	REDHILL - 75B
31862	REDHILL - 75B	REDHILL - 75B	REDHILL - 75B	REDHILL - 75B	REDHILL - 75B	REDHILL - 75B	REDHILL - 75B
31863	ASHFORD - 74A	ASHFORD - 73F	ASHFORD - 73F	ASHFORD - 73F	ASHFORD - 73F	ASHFORD - 73F	ASHFORD - 73F
31864	REDHILL - 75B	REDHILL - 75B	REDHILL - 75B	REDHILL - 75B	REDHILL - 75B	REDHILL - 75B	REDHILL - 75B
31865	REDHILL - 75B	REDHILL - 75B	REDHILL - 75B	REDHILL - 75B	REDHILL - 75B	REDHILL - 75B	REDHILL - 75B
31866	REDHILL - 75B	REDHILL - 75B	REDHILL - 75B	REDHILL - 75B	REDHILL - 75B	REDHILL - 75B	REDHILL - 75B
31867	REDHILL - 75B	REDHILL - 75B	REDHILL - 75B	REDHILL - 75B	REDHILL - 75B	REDHILL - 75B	REDHILL - 75B
31868	REDHILL - 75B	REDHILL - 75B	REDHILL - 75B	REDHILL - 75B	REDHILL - 75B	REDHILL - 75B	REDHILL - 75B
31869	REDHILL - 75B	REDHILL - 75B	REDHILL - 75B	REDHILL - 75B	REDHILL - 75B	REDHILL - 75B	REDHILL - 75B
31870	B.ARMS - 73B	B.ARMS - 73B	B.ARMS - 73B	REDHILL - 75B	REDHILL - 75B	REDHILL - 75B	REDHILL - 75B
31871	B.ARMS - 73B	B.ARMS - 73B	B.ARMS - 73B	REDHILL - 75B	REDHILL - 75B	REDHILL - 75B	REDHILL - 75B
31872	B.ARMS - 73B	B.ARMS - 73B	B.ARMS - 73B	REDHILL - 75B	REDHILL - 75B	REDHILL - 75B	REDHILL - 75B
31873	B.ARMS - 73B	B.ARMS - 73B	B.ARMS - 73B	B.ARMS - 73B	B.ARMS - 73B	B.ARMS - 73B	B.ARMS - 73B
31874	B.ARMS - 73B	B.ARMS - 73B	B.ARMS - 73B	B.ARMS - 73B	B.ARMS - 73B	B.ARMS - 73B	B.ARMS - 73B
31875	B.ARMS - 73B	B.ARMS - 73B	B.ARMS - 73B	B.ARMS - 73B	B.ARMS - 73B	B.ARMS - 73B	B.ARMS - 73B
				N1 2-6-0 (1922)			
31822	HITHER GREEN - 73C	HITHER GREEN - 73C	HITHER GREEN - 73C	TONBRIDGE - 73J	TONBRIDGE - 73J	TONBRIDGE - 73J	TONBRIDGE - 73J
31876	HITHER GREEN - 73C	HITHER GREEN - 73C	HITHER GREEN - 73C	TONBRIDGE - 73J	TONBRIDGE - 73J	TONBRIDGE - 73J	TONBRIDGE - 73J
31877	HITHER GREEN - 73C	HITHER GREEN - 73C	HITHER GREEN - 73C	TONBRIDGE - 73J	TONBRIDGE - 73J	TONBRIDGE - 73J	TONBRIDGE - 73J
31878	HITHER GREEN - 73C	HITHER GREEN - 73C	HITHER GREEN - 73C	TONBRIDGE - 73J	TONBRIDGE - 73J	TONBRIDGE - 73J	TONBRIDGE - 73J
31879	HITHER GREEN - 73C	HITHER GREEN - 73C	HITHER GREEN - 73C	TONBRIDGE - 73J	TONBRIDGE - 73J	TONBRIDGE - 73J	TONBRIDGE - 73J
31880	HITHER GREEN - 73C	HITHER GREEN - 73C	HITHER GREEN - 73C	TONBRIDGE - 73J	TONBRIDGE - 73J	TONBRIDGE - 73J	TONBRIDGE - 73J

loco	Dec-59	Feb-60	Mar-60	Apr-60	Jul-60	Aug-60	Sep-60	Nov-60
				N 2-6-0 (1917)				
31400	B ARMS - 73B	B ARMS - 73B	B ARMS - 73B	B ARMS - 73B	GUILDFORD - 70C	GUILDFORD - 70C	GUILDFORD - 70C	GUILDFORD - 70C
31401	ASHFORD - 73F	ASHFORD - 73F	ASHFORD - 73F	ASHFORD - 73F	GUILDFORD - 70C	GUILDFORD - 70C	GUILDFORD - 70C	GUILDFORD - 70C
31402	ASHFORD - 73F	ASHFORD - 73F	ASHFORD - 73F	ASHFORD - 73F	ASHFORD - 73F	ASHFORD - 73F	ASHFORD - 73F	ASHFORD - 73F
31403	ASHFORD - 73F	ASHFORD - 73F	ASHFORD - 73F	ASHFORD - 73F	ASHFORD - 73F	ASHFORD - 73F	ASHFORD - 73F	ASHFORD - 73F
31404	ASHFORD - 73F	ASHFORD - 73F	ASHFORD - 73F	ASHFORD - 73F	ASHFORD - 73F	ASHFORD - 73F	ASHFORD - 73F	ASHFORD - 73F
31405	ASHFORD - 73F	ASHFORD - 73F	ASHFORD - 73F	ASHFORD - 73F	ASHFORD - 73F	ASHFORD - 73F	ASHFORD - 73F	ASHFORD - 73F
31406	HITHER GREEN - 73C	HITHER GREEN - 73C	HITHER GREEN - 73C	HITHER GREEN - 73C	HITHER GREEN - 73C	HITHER GREEN - 73C	HITHER GREEN - 73C	HITHER GREEN - 73C
31407	ASHFORD - 73F	ASHFORD - 73F	ASHFORD - 73F	ASHFORD - 73F	ASHFORD - 73F	ASHFORD - 73F	ASHFORD - 73F	ASHFORD - 73F
31408	ASHFORD - 73F	ASHFORD - 73F	ASHFORD - 73F	ASHFORD - 73F	ASHFORD - 73F	ASHFORD - 73F	ASHFORD - 73F	ASHFORD - 73F
31409	ASHFORD - 73F	ASHFORD - 73F	ASHFORD - 73F	ASHFORD - 73F	ASHFORD - 73F	ASHFORD - 73F	ASHFORD - 73F	ASHFORD - 73F
31410	STEWARTS LANE - 73A	STEWARTS LANE - 73A	STEWARTS LANE - 73A	STEWARTS LANE - 73A	STEWARTS LANE - 73A	STEWARTS LANE - 73A	STEWARTS LANE - 73A	STEWARTS LANE - 73A
31411	STEWARTS LANE - 73A	STEWARTS LANE - 73A	STEWARTS LANE - 73A	STEWARTS LANE - 73A	STEWARTS LANE - 73A	STEWARTS LANE - 73A	STEWARTS LANE - 73A	STEWARTS LANE - 73A
31412	STEWARTS LANE - 73A	STEWARTS LANE - 73A	STEWARTS LANE - 73A	STEWARTS LANE - 73A	STEWARTS LANE - 73A	STEWARTS LANE - 73A	STEWARTS LANE - 73A	STEWARTS LANE - 73A
31413	DOVER - 73H	DOVER - 73H	DOVER - 73H	DOVER - 73H	DOVER - 73H	DOVER - 73H	DOVER - 73H	DOVER - 73H
31414	DOVER - 73H	DOVER - 73H	DOVER - 73H	DOVER - 73H	DOVER - 73H	DOVER - 73H	DOVER - 73H	DOVER - 73H
31810	DOVER - 73H	DOVER - 73H	DOVER - 73H	DOVER - 73H	DOVER - 73H	DOVER - 73H	DOVER - 73H	DOVER - 73H
31811	GUILDFORD - 70C	GUILDFORD - 70C	GUILDFORD - 70C	GUILDFORD - 70C	GUILDFORD - 70C	GUILDFORD - 70C	GUILDFORD - 70C	GUILDFORD - 70C
31812	GUILDFORD - 70C	GUILDFORD - 70C	GUILDFORD - 70C	GUILDFORD - 70C	GUILDFORD - 70C	GUILDFORD - 70C	GUILDFORD - 70C	GUILDFORD - 70C
31813	SALISBURY - 72B	SALISBURY - 72B	SALISBURY - 72B	SALISBURY - 72B	SALISBURY - 72B	SALISBURY - 72B	SALISBURY - 72B	SALISBURY - 72B
31814	SALISBURY - 72B	SALISBURY - 72B	SALISBURY - 72B	SALISBURY - 72B	SALISBURY - 72B	SALISBURY - 72B	SALISBURY - 72B	SALISBURY - 72B
31815	GUILDFORD - 70C	GUILDFORD - 70C	GUILDFORD - 70C	GUILDFORD - 70C	GUILDFORD - 70C	GUILDFORD - 70C	GUILDFORD - 70C	GUILDFORD - 70C
31816	HITHER GREEN - 73C	HITHER GREEN - 73C	HITHER GREEN - 73C	HITHER GREEN - 73C	HITHER GREEN - 73C	HITHER GREEN - 73C	HITHER GREEN - 73C	HITHER GREEN - 73C
31817	REDHILL - 75B	REDHILL - 75B	REDHILL - 75B	REDHILL - 75B	REDHILL - 75B	REDHILL - 75B	REDHILL - 75B	REDHILL - 75B
31818	DOVER - 73H	DOVER - 73H	DOVER - 73H	DOVER - 73H	DOVER - 73H	DOVER - 73H	DOVER - 73H	DOVER - 73H
31819	DOVER - 73H	DOVER - 73H	DOVER - 73H	DOVER - 73H	DOVER - 73H	DOVER - 73H	DOVER - 73H	DOVER - 73H
31820	DOVER - 73H	DOVER - 73H	DOVER - 73H	DOVER - 73H	DOVER - 73H	DOVER - 73H	DOVER - 73H	DOVER - 73H
31821	DOVER - 73H	DOVER - 73H	DOVER - 73H	DOVER - 73H	DOVER - 73H	DOVER - 73H	DOVER - 73H	DOVER - 73H
31823	B ARMS - 73B	B ARMS - 73B	B ARMS - 73B	B ARMS - 73B	STEWARTS LANE - 73A	STEWARTS LANE - 73A	STEWARTS LANE - 73A	STEWARTS LANE - 73A
31824	B ARMS - 73B	B ARMS - 73B	B ARMS - 73B	B ARMS - 73B	STEWARTS LANE - 73A	STEWARTS LANE - 73A	STEWARTS LANE - 73A	STEWARTS LANE - 73A
31825	B ARMS - 73B	B ARMS - 73B	B ARMS - 73B	B ARMS - 73B	B ARMS - 73B	B ARMS - 73B	B ARMS - 73B	B ARMS - 73B
31826	B ARMS - 73B	B ARMS - 73B	B ARMS - 73B	B ARMS - 73B	B ARMS - 73B	B ARMS - 73B	B ARMS - 73B	B ARMS - 73B
31827	B ARMS - 73B	B ARMS - 73B	B ARMS - 73B	B ARMS - 73B	B ARMS - 73B	B ARMS - 73B	B ARMS - 73B	B ARMS - 73B
31828	B ARMS - 73B	B ARMS - 73B	B ARMS - 73B	B ARMS - 73B	B ARMS - 73B	B ARMS - 73B	B ARMS - 73B	B ARMS - 73B
31829	B ARMS - 73B	B ARMS - 73B	B ARMS - 73B	B ARMS - 73B	B ARMS - 73B	B ARMS - 73B	B ARMS - 73B	B ARMS - 73B
31830	EXMOUTH JCN - 72A	EXMOUTH JCN - 72A	EXMOUTH JCN - 72A	EXMOUTH JCN - 72A	EXMOUTH JCN - 72A	EXMOUTH JCN - 72A	EXMOUTH JCN - 72A	EXMOUTH JCN - 72A
31831	EXMOUTH JCN - 72A	EXMOUTH JCN - 72A	EXMOUTH JCN - 72A	EXMOUTH JCN - 72A	EXMOUTH JCN - 72A	EXMOUTH JCN - 72A	EXMOUTH JCN - 72A	EXMOUTH JCN - 72A
31832	EXMOUTH JCN - 72A	EXMOUTH JCN - 72A	EXMOUTH JCN - 72A	EXMOUTH JCN - 72A	EXMOUTH JCN - 72A	EXMOUTH JCN - 72A	EXMOUTH JCN - 72A	EXMOUTH JCN - 72A
31833	EXMOUTH JCN - 72A	EXMOUTH JCN - 72A	EXMOUTH JCN - 72A	EXMOUTH JCN - 72A	EXMOUTH JCN - 72A	EXMOUTH JCN - 72A	EXMOUTH JCN - 72A	EXMOUTH JCN - 72A
31834	EXMOUTH JCN - 72A	EXMOUTH JCN - 72A	EXMOUTH JCN - 72A	EXMOUTH JCN - 72A	EXMOUTH JCN - 72A	EXMOUTH JCN - 72A	EXMOUTH JCN - 72A	EXMOUTH JCN - 72A
31835	EXMOUTH JCN - 72A	EXMOUTH JCN - 72A	EXMOUTH JCN - 72A	EXMOUTH JCN - 72A	EXMOUTH JCN - 72A	EXMOUTH JCN - 72A	EXMOUTH JCN - 72A	EXMOUTH JCN - 72A
31836	EXMOUTH JCN - 72A	EXMOUTH JCN - 72A	EXMOUTH JCN - 72A	EXMOUTH JCN - 72A	EXMOUTH JCN - 72A	EXMOUTH JCN - 72A	EXMOUTH JCN - 72A	EXMOUTH JCN - 72A
31837	EXMOUTH JCN - 72A	EXMOUTH JCN - 72A	EXMOUTH JCN - 72A	EXMOUTH JCN - 72A	EXMOUTH JCN - 72A	EXMOUTH JCN - 72A	EXMOUTH JCN - 72A	EXMOUTH JCN - 72A
31838	EXMOUTH JCN - 72A	EXMOUTH JCN - 72A	EXMOUTH JCN - 72A	EXMOUTH JCN - 72A	EXMOUTH JCN - 72A	EXMOUTH JCN - 72A	EXMOUTH JCN - 72A	EXMOUTH JCN - 72A
31839	EXMOUTH JCN - 72A	EXMOUTH JCN - 72A	EXMOUTH JCN - 72A	EXMOUTH JCN - 72A	EXMOUTH JCN - 72A	EXMOUTH JCN - 72A	EXMOUTH JCN - 72A	EXMOUTH JCN - 72A
31840	EXMOUTH JCN - 72A	EXMOUTH JCN - 72A	EXMOUTH JCN - 72A	EXMOUTH JCN - 72A	EXMOUTH JCN - 72A	EXMOUTH JCN - 72A	EXMOUTH JCN - 72A	EXMOUTH JCN - 72A
31841	EXMOUTH JCN - 72A	EXMOUTH JCN - 72A	EXMOUTH JCN - 72A	EXMOUTH JCN - 72A	EXMOUTH JCN - 72A	EXMOUTH JCN - 72A	EXMOUTH JCN - 72A	EXMOUTH JCN - 72A
31842	EXMOUTH JCN - 72A	EXMOUTH JCN - 72A	EXMOUTH JCN - 72A	EXMOUTH JCN - 72A	EXMOUTH JCN - 72A	EXMOUTH JCN - 72A	EXMOUTH JCN - 72A	EXMOUTH JCN - 72A
31843	EXMOUTH JCN - 72A	EXMOUTH JCN - 72A	EXMOUTH JCN - 72A	EXMOUTH JCN - 72A	EXMOUTH JCN - 72A	EXMOUTH JCN - 72A	EXMOUTH JCN - 72A	EXMOUTH JCN - 72A
31844	EXMOUTH JCN - 72A	EXMOUTH JCN - 72A	EXMOUTH JCN - 72A	EXMOUTH JCN - 72A	EXMOUTH JCN - 72A	EXMOUTH JCN - 72A	EXMOUTH JCN - 72A	EXMOUTH JCN - 72A
31845	EXMOUTH JCN - 72A	EXMOUTH JCN - 72A	EXMOUTH JCN - 72A	EXMOUTH JCN - 72A	EXMOUTH JCN - 72A	EXMOUTH JCN - 72A	EXMOUTH JCN - 72A	EXMOUTH JCN - 72A
31846	EXMOUTH JCN - 72A	EXMOUTH JCN - 72A	EXMOUTH JCN - 72A	EXMOUTH JCN - 72A	EXMOUTH JCN - 72A	EXMOUTH JCN - 72A	EXMOUTH JCN - 72A	EXMOUTH JCN - 72A
31847	EXMOUTH JCN - 72A	EXMOUTH JCN - 72A	EXMOUTH JCN - 72A	EXMOUTH JCN - 72A	EXMOUTH JCN - 72A	EXMOUTH JCN - 72A	EXMOUTH JCN - 72A	EXMOUTH JCN - 72A
31848	ASHFORD - 73F	ASHFORD - 73F	ASHFORD - 73F	ASHFORD - 73F	ASHFORD - 73F	ASHFORD - 73F	ASHFORD - 73F	ASHFORD - 73F
31849	EXMOUTH JCN - 72A	EXMOUTH JCN - 72A	EXMOUTH JCN - 72A	EXMOUTH JCN - 72A	EXMOUTH JCN - 72A	EXMOUTH JCN - 72A	EXMOUTH JCN - 72A	EXMOUTH JCN - 72A
31850	REDHILL - 75B	REDHILL - 75B	REDHILL - 75B	REDHILL - 75B	REDHILL - 75B	REDHILL - 75B	REDHILL - 75B	REDHILL - 75B
31851	REDHILL - 75B	REDHILL - 75B	REDHILL - 75B	REDHILL - 75B	REDHILL - 75B	REDHILL - 75B	REDHILL - 75B	REDHILL - 75B
31852	REDHILL - 75B	REDHILL - 75B	REDHILL - 75B	REDHILL - 75B	REDHILL - 75B	REDHILL - 75B	REDHILL - 75B	REDHILL - 75B
31853	EXMOUTH JCN - 72A	EXMOUTH JCN - 72A	EXMOUTH JCN - 72A	EXMOUTH JCN - 72A	EXMOUTH JCN - 72A	EXMOUTH JCN - 72A	EXMOUTH JCN - 72A	EXMOUTH JCN - 72A
31854	ASHFORD - 73F	ASHFORD - 73F	ASHFORD - 73F	ASHFORD - 73F	ASHFORD - 73F	ASHFORD - 73F	ASHFORD - 73F	ASHFORD - 73F
31855	HITHER GREEN - 73C	HITHER GREEN - 73C	HITHER GREEN - 73C	HITHER GREEN - 73C	HITHER GREEN - 73C	HITHER GREEN - 73C	HITHER GREEN - 73C	HITHER GREEN - 73C
31856	REDHILL - 75B	REDHILL - 75B	REDHILL - 75B	REDHILL - 75B	REDHILL - 75B	REDHILL - 75B	REDHILL - 75B	REDHILL - 75B
31857	HITHER GREEN - 73C	HITHER GREEN - 73C	HITHER GREEN - 73C	HITHER GREEN - 73C	HITHER GREEN - 73C	HITHER GREEN - 73C	HITHER GREEN - 73C	HITHER GREEN - 73C
31858	GUILDFORD - 70C	GUILDFORD - 70C	GUILDFORD - 70C	GUILDFORD - 70C	GUILDFORD - 70C	GUILDFORD - 70C	GUILDFORD - 70C	GUILDFORD - 70C
31859	HITHER GREEN - 73C	HITHER GREEN - 73C	HITHER GREEN - 73C	HITHER GREEN - 73C	HITHER GREEN - 73C	HITHER GREEN - 73C	HITHER GREEN - 73C	HITHER GREEN - 73C
31860	EXMOUTH JCN - 72A	EXMOUTH JCN - 72A	EXMOUTH JCN - 72A	EXMOUTH JCN - 72A	EXMOUTH JCN - 72A	EXMOUTH JCN - 72A	EXMOUTH JCN - 72A	EXMOUTH JCN - 72A
31861	REDHILL - 75B	REDHILL - 75B	REDHILL - 75B	REDHILL - 75B	REDHILL - 75B	REDHILL - 75B	REDHILL - 75B	REDHILL - 75B
31862	REDHILL - 75B	REDHILL - 75B	REDHILL - 75B	REDHILL - 75B	REDHILL - 75B	REDHILL - 75B	REDHILL - 75B	REDHILL - 75B
31863	ASHFORD - 73F	ASHFORD - 73F	ASHFORD - 73F	ASHFORD - 73F	ASHFORD - 73F	ASHFORD - 73F	ASHFORD - 73F	ASHFORD - 73F
31864	REDHILL - 75B	REDHILL - 75B	REDHILL - 75B	REDHILL - 75B	REDHILL - 75B	REDHILL - 75B	REDHILL - 75B	REDHILL - 75B
31865	REDHILL - 75B	REDHILL - 75B	REDHILL - 75B	REDHILL - 75B	REDHILL - 75B	REDHILL - 75B	REDHILL - 75B	REDHILL - 75B
31866	REDHILL - 75B	REDHILL - 75B	REDHILL - 75B	REDHILL - 75B	REDHILL - 75B	REDHILL - 75B	REDHILL - 75B	REDHILL - 75B
31867	REDHILL - 75B	REDHILL - 75B	REDHILL - 75B	REDHILL - 75B	REDHILL - 75B	REDHILL - 75B	REDHILL - 75B	REDHILL - 75B
31868	REDHILL - 75B	REDHILL - 75B	REDHILL - 75B	REDHILL - 75B	REDHILL - 75B	REDHILL - 75B	REDHILL - 75B	REDHILL - 75B
31869	REDHILL - 75B	REDHILL - 75B	REDHILL - 75B	REDHILL - 75B	REDHILL - 75B	REDHILL - 75B	REDHILL - 75B	REDHILL - 75B
31870	REDHILL - 75B	REDHILL - 75B	REDHILL - 75B	REDHILL - 75B	REDHILL - 75B	REDHILL - 75B	REDHILL - 75B	REDHILL - 75B
31871	REDHILL - 75B	REDHILL - 75B	REDHILL - 75B	REDHILL - 75B	REDHILL - 75B	REDHILL - 75B	REDHILL - 75B	REDHILL - 75B
31872	REDHILL - 75B	REDHILL - 75B	REDHILL - 75B	REDHILL - 75B	REDHILL - 75B	REDHILL - 75B	REDHILL - 75B	REDHILL - 75B
31873	B ARMS - 73B	B ARMS - 73B	B ARMS - 73B	B ARMS - 73B	B ARMS - 73B	B ARMS - 73B	B ARMS - 73B	B ARMS - 73B
31874	B ARMS - 73B	B ARMS - 73B	B ARMS - 73B	B ARMS - 73B	B ARMS - 73B	B ARMS - 73B	B ARMS - 73B	B ARMS - 73B
31875	B ARMS - 73B	B ARMS - 73B	B ARMS - 73B	B ARMS - 73B	B ARMS - 73B	B ARMS - 73B	B ARMS - 73B	B ARMS - 73B
				N1 2-6-0 (1922)				
31822	TONBRIDGE - 73J	TONBRIDGE - 73J	TONBRIDGE - 73J	TONBRIDGE - 73J	TONBRIDGE - 73J	TONBRIDGE - 73J	TONBRIDGE - 73J	TONBRIDGE - 73J
31876	TONBRIDGE - 73J	TONBRIDGE - 73J	TONBRIDGE - 73J	TONBRIDGE - 73J	TONBRIDGE - 73J	TONBRIDGE - 73J	TONBRIDGE - 73J	TONBRIDGE - 73J
31877	TONBRIDGE - 73J	TONBRIDGE - 73J	TONBRIDGE - 73J	TONBRIDGE - 73J	TONBRIDGE - 73J	TONBRIDGE - 73J	TONBRIDGE - 73J	TONBRIDGE - 73J
31878	TONBRIDGE - 73J	TONBRIDGE - 73J	TONBRIDGE - 73J	TONBRIDGE - 73J	TONBRIDGE - 73J	TONBRIDGE - 73J	TONBRIDGE - 73J	TONBRIDGE - 73J
31879	TONBRIDGE - 73J	TONBRIDGE - 73J	TONBRIDGE - 73J	TONBRIDGE - 73J	TONBRIDGE - 73J	TONBRIDGE - 73J	TONBRIDGE - 73J	TONBRIDGE - 73J
31880	TONBRIDGE - 73J	TONBRIDGE - 73J	TONBRIDGE - 73J	TONBRIDGE - 73J	TONBRIDGE - 73J	TONBRIDGE - 73J	TONBRIDGE - 73J	TONBRIDGE - 73J

Few chapters of locomotive history make as rewarding a study as that of the SR 2-6-0's, some of which started life as 2-6-4 tanks whilst others were part of a doubtful scheme for a class of 'national' locomotives of country-wide availability. Construction was as protracted as the history was interesting and N 2-6-0 31413, the penultimate of the class, appeared some seventeen years after the first of the class. Prior to being ousted by Bulleid Pacifics in the late 1940's, 31413 worked at Exmouth Junction and Salisbury before being moved to Stewarts Lane for goods duties over the Brighton section. Its stay at Stewarts Lane was prolonged and lasted until 1959 when it was transferred to Dover for working engineering services over the SECR main line, then in the throes of electrification. 31413's last years were spent at Eastleigh from where it was withdrawn in June 1964. The view shows the engine at Eastleigh immediately after being taken out of traffic.

loco	May-49	Jun-49	Aug-49	Sep-49	Dec-49	Feb-50	Mar-50
U 2-6-0 (1928)							
31610	READING (SR) - 70E	READING (SR) - 70E	READING (SR) - 70E	READING (SR) - 70E	READING (SR) - 70E	READING (SR) - 70E	READING (SR) - 70E
31611	READING (SR) - 70E	READING (SR) - 70E	READING (SR) - 70E	READING (SR) - 70E	READING (SR) - 70E	READING (SR) - 70E	READING (SR) - 70E
31612	SALISBURY - 72B	SALISBURY - 72B	SALISBURY - 72B	SALISBURY - 72B	SALISBURY - 72B	SALISBURY - 72B	SALISBURY - 72B
31613	NINE ELMS - 70A	NINE ELMS - 70A	NINE ELMS - 70A	NINE ELMS - 70A	NINE ELMS - 70A	NINE ELMS - 70A	NINE ELMS - 70A
31614	READING (SR) - 70E	READING (SR) - 70E	READING (SR) - 70E	READING (SR) - 70E	READING (SR) - 70E	READING (SR) - 70E	READING (SR) - 70E
31615	READING (SR) - 70E	READING (SR) - 70E	READING (SR) - 70E	READING (SR) - 70E	READING (SR) - 70E	READING (SR) - 70E	READING (SR) - 70E
31616	NINE ELMS - 70A	NINE ELMS - 70A	NINE ELMS - 70A	NINE ELMS - 70A	NINE ELMS - 70A	YEOVIL - 72C	YEOVIL - 72C
31617	NINE ELMS - 70A	NINE ELMS - 70A	NINE ELMS - 70A	NINE ELMS - 70A	NINE ELMS - 70A	NINE ELMS - 70A	NINE ELMS - 70A
31618	SALISBURY - 72B	SALISBURY - 72B	SALISBURY - 72B	SALISBURY - 72B	SALISBURY - 72B	SALISBURY - 72B	SALISBURY - 72B
31619	NINE ELMS - 70A	NINE ELMS - 70A	STEWARTS LANE - 73A	STEWARTS LANE - 73A	STEWARTS LANE - 73A	STEWARTS LANE - 73A	STEWARTS LANE - 73A
31620	GUILDFORD - 70C	GUILDFORD - 70C	GUILDFORD - 70C	GUILDFORD - 70C	GUILDFORD - 70C	GUILDFORD - 70C	GUILDFORD - 70C
31621	GUILDFORD - 70C	GUILDFORD - 70C	GUILDFORD - 70C	GUILDFORD - 70C	GUILDFORD - 70C	GUILDFORD - 70C	GUILDFORD - 70C
31622	BOURNEMOUTH - 71B	BOURNEMOUTH - 71B	BOURNEMOUTH - 71B	BOURNEMOUTH - 71B	BOURNEMOUTH - 71B	BOURNEMOUTH - 71B	BOURNEMOUTH - 71B
31623	GUILDFORD - 70C	GUILDFORD - 70C	GUILDFORD - 70C	GUILDFORD - 70C	GUILDFORD - 70C	GUILDFORD - 70C	GUILDFORD - 70C
31624	BOURNEMOUTH - 71B	BOURNEMOUTH - 71B	BOURNEMOUTH - 71B	BOURNEMOUTH - 71B	DORCHESTER - 71C	DORCHESTER - 71C	DORCHESTER - 71C
31625	NINE ELMS - 70A	NINE ELMS - 70A	NINE ELMS - 70A	NINE ELMS - 70A	NINE ELMS - 70A	NINE ELMS - 70A	NINE ELMS - 70A
31626	SALISBURY - 72B	SALISBURY - 72B	SALISBURY - 72B	SALISBURY - 72B	SALISBURY - 72B	SALISBURY - 72B	SALISBURY - 72B
31627	BASINGSTOKE - 70D	BASINGSTOKE - 70D	BASINGSTOKE - 70D	BASINGSTOKE - 70D	BASINGSTOKE - 70D	BASINGSTOKE - 70D	BASINGSTOKE - 70D
31628	EXMOUTH JCN - 72A	EXMOUTH JCN - 72A	EXMOUTH JCN - 72A	EXMOUTH JCN - 72A	EXMOUTH JCN - 72A	GUILDFORD - 70C	GUILDFORD - 70C
31629	BASINGSTOKE - 70D	BASINGSTOKE - 70D	BASINGSTOKE - 70D	GUILDFORD - 70C	GUILDFORD - 70C	GUILDFORD - 70C	GUILDFORD - 70C
31630	SALISBURY - 72B	SALISBURY - 72B	SALISBURY - 72B	SALISBURY - 72B	SALISBURY - 72B	SALISBURY - 72B	SALISBURY - 72B
31631	FAVERSHAM - 73E	FAVERSHAM - 73E	FAVERSHAM - 73E	FAVERSHAM - 73E	FAVERSHAM - 73E	FAVERSHAM - 73E	FAVERSHAM - 73E
31632	BASINGSTOKE - 70D	BASINGSTOKE - 70D	BASINGSTOKE - 70D	BASINGSTOKE - 70D	BASINGSTOKE - 70D	GUILDFORD - 70C	GUILDFORD - 70C
31633	BASINGSTOKE - 70D	BASINGSTOKE - 70D	BASINGSTOKE - 70D	BASINGSTOKE - 70D	BASINGSTOKE - 70D	BASINGSTOKE - 70D	BASINGSTOKE - 70D
31634	EXMOUTH JCN - 72A	EXMOUTH JCN - 72A	EXMOUTH JCN - 72A	EXMOUTH JCN - 72A	YEOVIL - 72C	YEOVIL - 72C	YEOVIL - 72C
31635	EXMOUTH JCN - 72A	EXMOUTH JCN - 72A	EXMOUTH JCN - 72A	EXMOUTH JCN - 72A	EXMOUTH JCN - 72A	GUILDFORD - 70C	GUILDFORD - 70C
31636	SALISBURY - 72B	SALISBURY - 72B	SALISBURY - 72B	SALISBURY - 72B	SALISBURY - 72B	YEOVIL - 72C	YEOVIL - 72C
31637	NINE ELMS - 70A	NINE ELMS - 70A	NINE ELMS - 70A	NINE ELMS - 70A	NINE ELMS - 70A	NINE ELMS - 70A	NINE ELMS - 70A
31638	NINE ELMS - 70A	NINE ELMS - 70A	STEWARTS LANE - 73A	STEWARTS LANE - 73A	FAVERSHAM - 73E	FAVERSHAM - 73E	FAVERSHAM - 73E
31639	FAVERSHAM - 73E	FAVERSHAM - 73E	FAVERSHAM - 73E	FAVERSHAM - 73E	FAVERSHAM - 73E	FAVERSHAM - 73E	FAVERSHAM - 73E
U1 2-6-0 (2-6-4T R/B) 1925							
31890	BRIGHTON - 75A	BRIGHTON - 75A	BRIGHTON - 75A	BRIGHTON - 75A	BRIGHTON - 75A	BRIGHTON - 75A	BRIGHTON - 75A
U1 2-6-0 (1925)							
31891	BRIGHTON - 75A	BRIGHTON - 75A	BRIGHTON - 75A	BRIGHTON - 75A	BRIGHTON - 75A	BRIGHTON - 75A	BRIGHTON - 75A
31892	BRIGHTON - 75A	BRIGHTON - 75A	BRIGHTON - 75A	BRIGHTON - 75A	BRIGHTON - 75A	BRIGHTON - 75A	BRIGHTON - 75A
31893	BRIGHTON - 75A	BRIGHTON - 75A	BRIGHTON - 75A	BRIGHTON - 75A	BRIGHTON - 75A	BRIGHTON - 75A	BRIGHTON - 75A
31894	BRIGHTON - 75A	BRIGHTON - 75A	BRIGHTON - 75A	BRIGHTON - 75A	BRIGHTON - 75A	BRIGHTON - 75A	BRIGHTON - 75A
31895	REDHILL - 75B	REDHILL - 75B	REDHILL - 75B	REDHILL - 75B	REDHILL - 75B	REDHILL - 75B	REDHILL - 75B
31896	REDHILL - 75B	REDHILL - 75B	REDHILL - 75B	REDHILL - 75B	REDHILL - 75B	REDHILL - 75B	REDHILL - 75B
31897	REDHILL - 75B	REDHILL - 75B	REDHILL - 75B	REDHILL - 75B	REDHILL - 75B	REDHILL - 75B	REDHILL - 75B
31898	REDHILL - 75B	REDHILL - 75B	REDHILL - 75B	REDHILL - 75B	REDHILL - 75B	REDHILL - 75B	REDHILL - 75B
31899	REDHILL - 75B	REDHILL - 75B	REDHILL - 75B	REDHILL - 75B	REDHILL - 75B	REDHILL - 75B	REDHILL - 75B
31900	BRIGHTON - 75A	BRIGHTON - 75A	BRIGHTON - 75A	BRIGHTON - 75A	BRIGHTON - 75A	BRIGHTON - 75A	BRIGHTON - 75A
31901	B ARMS - 73B	B ARMS - 73B	B ARMS - 73B	B ARMS - 73B	B ARMS - 73B	B ARMS - 73B	B ARMS - 73B
31902	B ARMS - 73B	B ARMS - 73B	B ARMS - 73B	B ARMS - 73B	B ARMS - 73B	B ARMS - 73B	B ARMS - 73B
31903	STEWARTS LANE - 73A	STEWARTS LANE - 73A	STEWARTS LANE - 73A	STEWARTS LANE - 73A	STEWARTS LANE - 73A	STEWARTS LANE - 73A	STEWARTS LANE - 73A
31904	STEWARTS LANE - 73A	STEWARTS LANE - 73A	STEWARTS LANE - 73A	STEWARTS LANE - 73A	BRIGHTON - 75A	BRIGHTON - 75A	REDHILL - 75B
31905	STEWARTS LANE - 73A	STEWARTS LANE - 73A	STEWARTS LANE - 73A	STEWARTS LANE - 73A	STEWARTS LANE - 73A	STEWARTS LANE - 73A	STEWARTS LANE - 73A
31906	STEWARTS LANE - 73A	STEWARTS LANE - 73A	STEWARTS LANE - 73A	STEWARTS LANE - 73A	STEWARTS LANE - 73A	STEWARTS LANE - 73A	STEWARTS LANE - 73A
31907	STEWARTS LANE - 73A	STEWARTS LANE - 73A	STEWARTS LANE - 73A	STEWARTS LANE - 73A	STEWARTS LANE - 73A	STEWARTS LANE - 73A	STEWARTS LANE - 73A
31908	STEWARTS LANE - 73A	STEWARTS LANE - 73A	STEWARTS LANE - 73A	STEWARTS LANE - 73A	STEWARTS LANE - 73A	STEWARTS LANE - 73A	STEWARTS LANE - 73A
31909	STEWARTS LANE - 73A	STEWARTS LANE - 73A	STEWARTS LANE - 73A	STEWARTS LANE - 73A	STEWARTS LANE - 73A	STEWARTS LANE - 73A	STEWARTS LANE - 73A
31910	STEWARTS LANE - 73A	STEWARTS LANE - 73A	STEWARTS LANE - 73A	STEWARTS LANE - 73A	STEWARTS LANE - 73A	STEWARTS LANE - 73A	STEWARTS LANE - 73A
T14 4-6-0 (1911/30)							
30444	NINE ELMS - 70A	NINE ELMS - 70A	NINE ELMS - 70A	NINE ELMS - 70A	NINE ELMS - 70A	NINE ELMS - 70A	W/D
30446	NINE ELMS - 70A	NINE ELMS - 70A	NINE ELMS - 70A	NINE ELMS - 70A	NINE ELMS - 70A	NINE ELMS - 70A	NINE ELMS - 70A
30447	NINE ELMS - 70A	NINE ELMS - 70A	NINE ELMS - 70A	NINE ELMS - 70A	W/D	W/D	W/D
30461	NINE ELMS - 70A	NINE ELMS - 70A	NINE ELMS - 70A	NINE ELMS - 70A	NINE ELMS - 70A	NINE ELMS - 70A	NINE ELMS - 70A
30462	NINE ELMS - 70A	NINE ELMS - 70A	NINE ELMS - 70A	NINE ELMS - 70A	NINE ELMS - 70A	NINE ELMS - 70A	W/D
N15X 4-6-0 (1914/34)							
32327	BASINGSTOKE - 70D	BASINGSTOKE - 70D	BASINGSTOKE - 70D	BASINGSTOKE - 70D	BASINGSTOKE - 70D	BASINGSTOKE - 70D	BASINGSTOKE - 70D
32328	BASINGSTOKE - 70D	BASINGSTOKE - 70D	BASINGSTOKE - 70D	BASINGSTOKE - 70D	BASINGSTOKE - 70D	BASINGSTOKE - 70D	BASINGSTOKE - 70D
32329	BASINGSTOKE - 70D	BASINGSTOKE - 70D	BASINGSTOKE - 70D	BASINGSTOKE - 70D	BASINGSTOKE - 70D	BASINGSTOKE - 70D	BASINGSTOKE - 70D
32330	BASINGSTOKE - 70D	BASINGSTOKE - 70D	BASINGSTOKE - 70D	BASINGSTOKE - 70D	BASINGSTOKE - 70D	BASINGSTOKE - 70D	BASINGSTOKE - 70D
32331	BASINGSTOKE - 70D	BASINGSTOKE - 70D	BASINGSTOKE - 70D	BASINGSTOKE - 70D	BASINGSTOKE - 70D	BASINGSTOKE - 70D	BASINGSTOKE - 70D
32332	BASINGSTOKE - 70D	BASINGSTOKE - 70D	BASINGSTOKE - 70D	BASINGSTOKE - 70D	BASINGSTOKE - 70D	BASINGSTOKE - 70D	BASINGSTOKE - 70D
32333	BASINGSTOKE - 70D	BASINGSTOKE - 70D	BASINGSTOKE - 70D	BASINGSTOKE - 70D	BASINGSTOKE - 70D	BASINGSTOKE - 70D	BASINGSTOKE - 70D
H15 4-6-0 (1907/14)							
30330	SALISBURY - 72B	SALISBURY - 72B	SALISBURY - 72B	SALISBURY - 72B	SALISBURY - 72B	SALISBURY - 72B	SALISBURY - 72B
30331	SALISBURY - 72B	SALISBURY - 72B	SALISBURY - 72B	SALISBURY - 72B	SALISBURY - 72B	FELTHAM - 70B	FELTHAM - 70B
30332	SALISBURY - 72B	SALISBURY - 72B	SALISBURY - 72B	SALISBURY - 72B	SALISBURY - 72B	SALISBURY - 72B	SALISBURY - 72B
30333	SALISBURY - 72B	SALISBURY - 72B	SALISBURY - 72B	SALISBURY - 72B	SALISBURY - 72B	SALISBURY - 72B	SALISBURY - 72B
30334	SALISBURY - 72B	SALISBURY - 72B	SALISBURY - 72B	SALISBURY - 72B	SALISBURY - 72B	FELTHAM - 70B	FELTHAM - 70B
30335	SALISBURY - 72B	SALISBURY - 72B	SALISBURY - 72B	SALISBURY - 72B	SALISBURY - 72B	FELTHAM - 70B	FELTHAM - 70B
H15 4-6-0 (1914)							
30482	NINE ELMS - 70A	NINE ELMS - 70A	NINE ELMS - 70A	NINE ELMS - 70A	NINE ELMS - 70A	NINE ELMS - 70A	NINE ELMS - 70A
30483	NINE ELMS - 70A	NINE ELMS - 70A	NINE ELMS - 70A	NINE ELMS - 70A	NINE ELMS - 70A	NINE ELMS - 70A	NINE ELMS - 70A
30484	NINE ELMS - 70A	NINE ELMS - 70A	NINE ELMS - 70A	NINE ELMS - 70A	NINE ELMS - 70A	NINE ELMS - 70A	NINE ELMS - 70A
30485	NINE ELMS - 70A	NINE ELMS - 70A	NINE ELMS - 70A	NINE ELMS - 70A	NINE ELMS - 70A	NINE ELMS - 70A	NINE ELMS - 70A
30486	NINE ELMS - 70A	NINE ELMS - 70A	NINE ELMS - 70A	NINE ELMS - 70A	NINE ELMS - 70A	NINE ELMS - 70A	NINE ELMS - 70A
30487	NINE ELMS - 70A	NINE ELMS - 70A	NINE ELMS - 70A	NINE ELMS - 70A	NINE ELMS - 70A	NINE ELMS - 70A	NINE ELMS - 70A
30488	NINE ELMS - 70A	NINE ELMS - 70A	NINE ELMS - 70A	NINE ELMS - 70A	NINE ELMS - 70A	NINE ELMS - 70A	NINE ELMS - 70A
30489	NINE ELMS - 70A	NINE ELMS - 70A	NINE ELMS - 70A	NINE ELMS - 70A	NINE ELMS - 70A	NINE ELMS - 70A	NINE ELMS - 70A
30490	NINE ELMS - 70A	NINE ELMS - 70A	NINE ELMS - 70A	NINE ELMS - 70A	NINE ELMS - 70A	NINE ELMS - 70A	NINE ELMS - 70A
30491	NINE ELMS - 70A	NINE ELMS - 70A	NINE ELMS - 70A	NINE ELMS - 70A	NINE ELMS - 70A	NINE ELMS - 70A	NINE ELMS - 70A
H15 4-6-0 (1924)							
30473	EASTLEIGH - 71A	EASTLEIGH - 71A	EASTLEIGH - 71A	EASTLEIGH - 71A	EASTLEIGH - 71A	EASTLEIGH - 71A	EASTLEIGH - 71A
30474	EASTLEIGH - 71A	EASTLEIGH - 71A	EASTLEIGH - 71A	EASTLEIGH - 71A	EASTLEIGH - 71A	EASTLEIGH - 71A	EASTLEIGH - 71A
30475	SALISBURY - 72B	SALISBURY - 72B	SALISBURY - 72B	SALISBURY - 72B	SALISBURY - 72B	SALISBURY - 72B	SALISBURY - 72B
30476	NINE ELMS - 70A	NINE ELMS - 70A	NINE ELMS - 70A	NINE ELMS - 70A	NINE ELMS - 70A	NINE ELMS - 70A	NINE ELMS - 70A
30477	EASTLEIGH - 71A	EASTLEIGH - 71A	EASTLEIGH - 71A	EASTLEIGH - 71A	EASTLEIGH - 71A	EASTLEIGH - 71A	EASTLEIGH - 71A
30478	EASTLEIGH - 71A	EASTLEIGH - 71A	EASTLEIGH - 71A	EASTLEIGH - 71A	EASTLEIGH - 71A	EASTLEIGH - 71A	EASTLEIGH - 71A
30521	EASTLEIGH - 71A	EASTLEIGH - 71A	EASTLEIGH - 71A	EASTLEIGH - 71A	EASTLEIGH - 71A	EASTLEIGH - 71A	EASTLEIGH - 71A
30522	EASTLEIGH - 71A	EASTLEIGH - 71A	EASTLEIGH - 71A	EASTLEIGH - 71A	EASTLEIGH - 71A	EASTLEIGH - 71A	EASTLEIGH - 71A
30523	EASTLEIGH - 71A	EASTLEIGH - 71A	EASTLEIGH - 71A	EASTLEIGH - 71A	EASTLEIGH - 71A	EASTLEIGH - 71A	EASTLEIGH - 71A
30524	EASTLEIGH - 71A	EASTLEIGH - 71A	EASTLEIGH - 71A	EASTLEIGH - 71A	EASTLEIGH - 71A	EASTLEIGH - 71A	EASTLEIGH - 71A

loco	Apr-50	Sep-50	Oct-50	Nov-50	Dec-50	Mar-51	Apr-51
U 2-6-0 (1928)							
31610	READING (SR) - 70E	READING (SR) - 70E	READING (SR) - 70E	READING (SR) - 70E	READING (SR) - 70E	READING (SR) - 70E	READING (SR) - 70E
31611	READING (SR) - 70E	READING (SR) - 70E	READING (SR) - 70E	READING (SR) - 70E	READING (SR) - 70E	READING (SR) - 70E	READING (SR) - 70E
31612	SALISBURY - 72B	SALISBURY - 72B	SALISBURY - 72B	FRATTON - 71D	READING (SR) - 70E	READING (SR) - 70E	READING (SR) - 70E
31613	NINE ELMS - 70A	NINE ELMS - 70A	NINE ELMS - 70A	NINE ELMS - 70A	READING (SR) - 70E	READING (SR) - 70E	READING (SR) - 70E
31614	READING (SR) - 70E	READING (SR) - 70E	READING (SR) - 70E	READING (SR) - 70E	READING (SR) - 70E	READING (SR) - 70E	READING (SR) - 70E
31615	READING (SR) - 70E	READING (SR) - 70E	READING (SR) - 70E	READING (SR) - 70E	READING (SR) - 70E	READING (SR) - 70E	READING (SR) - 70E
31616	HITHER GREEN - 73C	HITHER GREEN - 73C	HITHER GREEN - 73C	HITHER GREEN - 73C	HITHER GREEN - 73C	HITHER GREEN - 73C	READING (SR) - 70E
31617	HITHER GREEN - 73C	HITHER GREEN - 73C	HITHER GREEN - 73C	HITHER GREEN - 73C	HITHER GREEN - 73C	HITHER GREEN - 73C	READING (SR) - 70E
31618	SALISBURY - 72B	SALISBURY - 72B	SALISBURY - 72B	SALISBURY - 72B	SALISBURY - 72B	SALISBURY - 72B	SALISBURY - 72B
31619	NINE ELMS - 70A	NINE ELMS - 70A	NINE ELMS - 70A	NINE ELMS - 70A	NINE ELMS - 70A	NINE ELMS - 70A	NINE ELMS - 70A
31620	GUILDFORD - 70C	GUILDFORD - 70C	GUILDFORD - 70C	GUILDFORD - 70C	GUILDFORD - 70C	GUILDFORD - 70C	GUILDFORD - 70C
31621	GUILDFORD - 70C	GUILDFORD - 70C	GUILDFORD - 70C	GUILDFORD - 70C	GUILDFORD - 70C	GUILDFORD - 70C	GUILDFORD - 70C
31622	BOURNEMOUTH - 71B	BOURNEMOUTH - 71B	BOURNEMOUTH - 71B	BOURNEMOUTH - 71B	BOURNEMOUTH - 71B	BOURNEMOUTH - 71B	BOURNEMOUTH - 71B
31623	GUILDFORD - 70C	STEWARTS LANE - 73A	STEWARTS LANE - 73A	NINE ELMS - 70A	NINE ELMS - 70A	NINE ELMS - 70A	NINE ELMS - 70A
31624	DORCHESTER - 71C	FELTHAM - 70B	FELTHAM - 70B	FELTHAM - 70B	FELTHAM - 70B	FELTHAM - 70B	FELTHAM - 70B
31625	NINE ELMS - 70A	NINE ELMS - 70A	NINE ELMS - 70A	NINE ELMS - 70A	NINE ELMS - 70A	NINE ELMS - 70A	NINE ELMS - 70A
31626	SALISBURY - 72B	SALISBURY - 72B	SALISBURY - 72B	SALISBURY - 72B	SALISBURY - 72B	SALISBURY - 72B	SALISBURY - 72B
31627	GUILDFORD - 70C	GUILDFORD - 70C	GUILDFORD - 70C	GUILDFORD - 70C	GUILDFORD - 70C	GUILDFORD - 70C	GUILDFORD - 70C
31628	GUILDFORD - 70C	GUILDFORD - 70C	GUILDFORD - 70C	GUILDFORD - 70C	GUILDFORD - 70C	GUILDFORD - 70C	GUILDFORD - 70C
31629	GUILDFORD - 70C	GUILDFORD - 70C	GUILDFORD - 70C	GUILDFORD - 70C	GUILDFORD - 70C	GUILDFORD - 70C	GUILDFORD - 70C
31630	GUILDFORD - 70C	GUILDFORD - 70C	GUILDFORD - 70C	GUILDFORD - 70C	GUILDFORD - 70C	GUILDFORD - 70C	GUILDFORD - 70C
31631	FAVERSHAM - 73E	HITHER GREEN - 73C	HITHER GREEN - 73C	HITHER GREEN - 73C	HITHER GREEN - 73C	HITHER GREEN - 73C	HITHER GREEN - 73C
31632	GUILDFORD - 70C	BOURNEMOUTH - 71B	DORCHESTER - 71C	DORCHESTER - 71C	DORCHESTER - 71C	DORCHESTER - 71C	DORCHESTER - 71C
31633	BASINGSTOKE - 70D	BASINGSTOKE - 70D	BASINGSTOKE - 70D	BASINGSTOKE - 70D	BASINGSTOKE - 70D	BASINGSTOKE - 70D	BASINGSTOKE - 70D
31634	YEOVIL - 72C	YEOVIL - 72C	YEOVIL - 72C	YEOVIL - 72C	EXMOUTH JCN - 72A	EXMOUTH JCN - 72A	EXMOUTH JCN - 72A
31635	GUILDFORD - 70C	GUILDFORD - 70C	GUILDFORD - 70C	GUILDFORD - 70C	EXMOUTH JCN - 72A	EXMOUTH JCN - 72A	EXMOUTH JCN - 72A
31636	YEOVIL - 72C	YEOVIL - 72C	YEOVIL - 72C	YEOVIL - 72C	EXMOUTH JCN - 72A	EXMOUTH JCN - 72A	EXMOUTH JCN - 72A
31637	NINE ELMS - 70A	NINE ELMS - 70A	NINE ELMS - 70A	NINE ELMS - 70A	NINE ELMS - 70A	NINE ELMS - 70A	NINE ELMS - 70A
31638	FAVERSHAM - 73E	FAVERSHAM - 73E	FAVERSHAM - 73E	FAVERSHAM - 73E	FAVERSHAM - 73E	FAVERSHAM - 73E	FAVERSHAM - 73E
31639	HITHER GREEN - 73C	HITHER GREEN - 73C	HITHER GREEN - 73C	HITHER GREEN - 73C	HITHER GREEN - 73C	HITHER GREEN - 73C	HITHER GREEN - 73C
U1 2-6-0 (2-6-4T R/B) 1925							
31890	BRIGHTON - 75A	BRIGHTON - 75A	BRIGHTON - 75A	BRIGHTON - 75A	BRIGHTON - 75A	BRIGHTON - 75A	BRIGHTON - 75A
U1 2-6-0 (1925)							
31891	BRIGHTON - 75A	BRIGHTON - 75A	BRIGHTON - 75A	BRIGHTON - 75A	BRIGHTON - 75A	BRIGHTON - 75A	BRIGHTON - 75A
31892	BRIGHTON - 75A	BRIGHTON - 75A	BRIGHTON - 75A	BRIGHTON - 75A	BRIGHTON - 75A	BRIGHTON - 75A	BRIGHTON - 75A
31893	BRIGHTON - 75A	BRIGHTON - 75A	BRIGHTON - 75A	BRIGHTON - 75A	BRIGHTON - 75A	BRIGHTON - 75A	BRIGHTON - 75A
31894	BRIGHTON - 75A	BRIGHTON - 75A	BRIGHTON - 75A	BRIGHTON - 75A	BRIGHTON - 75A	BRIGHTON - 75A	BRIGHTON - 75A
31895	REDHILL - 75B	REDHILL - 75B	REDHILL - 75B	REDHILL - 75B	REDHILL - 75B	BRIGHTON - 75A(N)	BRIGHTON - 75A(N)
31896	REDHILL - 75B	REDHILL - 75B	REDHILL - 75B	REDHILL - 75B	REDHILL - 75B	REDHILL - 75B	REDHILL - 75B
31897	REDHILL - 75B	REDHILL - 75B	REDHILL - 75B	REDHILL - 75B	REDHILL - 75B	REDHILL - 75B	REDHILL - 75B
31898	REDHILL - 75B	REDHILL - 75B	REDHILL - 75B	REDHILL - 75B	REDHILL - 75B	REDHILL - 75B	REDHILL - 75B
31899	REDHILL - 75B	REDHILL - 75B	B ARMS - 73B	B ARMS - 73B	BRIGHTON - 75A	REDHILL - 75B	REDHILL - 75B
31900	BRIGHTON - 75A	REDHILL - 75B	B ARMS - 73B	B ARMS - 73B	BRIGHTON - 75A	REDHILL - 75B	REDHILL - 75B
31901	B ARMS - 73B	B ARMS - 73B	B ARMS - 73B	B ARMS - 73B	B ARMS - 73B	B ARMS - 73B	B ARMS - 73B
31902	B ARMS - 73B	B ARMS - 73B	B ARMS - 73B	B ARMS - 73B	B ARMS - 73B	B ARMS - 73B	B ARMS - 73B
31903	STEWARTS LANE - 73A	STEWARTS LANE - 73A	STEWARTS LANE - 73A	STEWARTS LANE - 73A	B ARMS - 73B	B ARMS - 73B	B ARMS - 73B
31904	REDHILL - 75B	STEWARTS LANE - 73A	STEWARTS LANE - 73A	STEWARTS LANE - 73A	B ARMS - 73B	B ARMS - 73B	B ARMS - 73B
31905	STEWARTS LANE - 73A	STEWARTS LANE - 73A	STEWARTS LANE - 73A	STEWARTS LANE - 73A	STEWARTS LANE - 73A	STEWARTS LANE - 73A	STEWARTS LANE - 73A
31906	STEWARTS LANE - 73A	STEWARTS LANE - 73A	STEWARTS LANE - 73A	STEWARTS LANE - 73A	STEWARTS LANE - 73A	STEWARTS LANE - 73A	STEWARTS LANE - 73A
31907	STEWARTS LANE - 73A	STEWARTS LANE - 73A	STEWARTS LANE - 73A	STEWARTS LANE - 73A	STEWARTS LANE - 73A	STEWARTS LANE - 73A	STEWARTS LANE - 73A
31908	STEWARTS LANE - 73A	STEWARTS LANE - 73A	STEWARTS LANE - 73A	STEWARTS LANE - 73A	STEWARTS LANE - 73A	STEWARTS LANE - 73A	STEWARTS LANE - 73A
31909	STEWARTS LANE - 73A	STEWARTS LANE - 73A	STEWARTS LANE - 73A	STEWARTS LANE - 73A	STEWARTS LANE - 73A	STEWARTS LANE - 73A	STEWARTS LANE - 73A
31910	STEWARTS LANE - 73A	STEWARTS LANE - 73A	STEWARTS LANE - 73A	STEWARTS LANE - 73A	STEWARTS LANE - 73A	STEWARTS LANE - 73A	STEWARTS LANE - 73A
T14 4-6-0 (1911/30)							
30446	NINE ELMS - 70A	NINE ELMS - 70A	NINE ELMS - 70A	NINE ELMS - 70A	NINE ELMS - 70A	NINE ELMS - 70A	W/D
30461	NINE ELMS - 70A	NINE ELMS - 70A	NINE ELMS - 70A	NINE ELMS - 70A	NINE ELMS - 70A	NINE ELMS - 70A	NINE ELMS - 70A
N15X 4-6-0 (1914/34)							
32327	BASINGSTOKE - 70D	BASINGSTOKE - 70D	BASINGSTOKE - 70D	BASINGSTOKE - 70D	BASINGSTOKE - 70D	BASINGSTOKE - 70D	BASINGSTOKE - 70D
32328	BASINGSTOKE - 70D	BASINGSTOKE - 70D	BASINGSTOKE - 70D	BASINGSTOKE - 70D	BASINGSTOKE - 70D	BASINGSTOKE - 70D	BASINGSTOKE - 70D
32329	BASINGSTOKE - 70D	BASINGSTOKE - 70D	BASINGSTOKE - 70D	BASINGSTOKE - 70D	BASINGSTOKE - 70D	BASINGSTOKE - 70D	BASINGSTOKE - 70D
32330	BASINGSTOKE - 70D	BASINGSTOKE - 70D	BASINGSTOKE - 70D	BASINGSTOKE - 70D	BASINGSTOKE - 70D	BASINGSTOKE - 70D	BASINGSTOKE - 70D
32331	BASINGSTOKE - 70D	BASINGSTOKE - 70D	BASINGSTOKE - 70D	BASINGSTOKE - 70D	BASINGSTOKE - 70D	BASINGSTOKE - 70D	BASINGSTOKE - 70D
32332	BASINGSTOKE - 70D	BASINGSTOKE - 70D	BASINGSTOKE - 70D	BASINGSTOKE - 70D	BASINGSTOKE - 70D	BASINGSTOKE - 70D	BASINGSTOKE - 70D
32333	BASINGSTOKE - 70D	BASINGSTOKE - 70D	BASINGSTOKE - 70D	BASINGSTOKE - 70D	BASINGSTOKE - 70D	BASINGSTOKE - 70D	BASINGSTOKE - 70D
H15 4-6-0 (1907/14)							
30330	SALISBURY - 72B	FELTHAM - 70B	SALISBURY - 72B	SALISBURY - 72B	SALISBURY - 72B	SALISBURY - 72B	SALISBURY - 72B
30331	FELTHAM - 70B	FELTHAM - 70B	SALISBURY - 72B	SALISBURY - 72B	SALISBURY - 72B	SALISBURY - 72B	SALISBURY - 72B
30332	SALISBURY - 72B	NINE ELMS - 70A	NINE ELMS - 70A	SALISBURY - 72B	SALISBURY - 72B	SALISBURY - 72B	SALISBURY - 72B
30333	SALISBURY - 72B	NINE ELMS - 70A	NINE ELMS - 70A	SALISBURY - 72B	SALISBURY - 72B	SALISBURY - 72B	SALISBURY - 72B
30334	FELTHAM - 70B	NINE ELMS - 70A	NINE ELMS - 70A	SALISBURY - 72B	SALISBURY - 72B	SALISBURY - 72B	SALISBURY - 72B
30335	FELTHAM - 70B	NINE ELMS - 70A	NINE ELMS - 70A	SALISBURY - 72B	SALISBURY - 72B	SALISBURY - 72B	SALISBURY - 72B
H15 4-6-0 (1914)							
30482	NINE ELMS - 70A	NINE ELMS - 70A	NINE ELMS - 70A	NINE ELMS - 70A	NINE ELMS - 70A	NINE ELMS - 70A	NINE ELMS - 70A
30483	NINE ELMS - 70A	EASTLEIGH - 71A	EASTLEIGH - 71A	EASTLEIGH - 71A	EASTLEIGH - 71A	EASTLEIGH - 71A	EASTLEIGH - 71A
30484	NINE ELMS - 70A	NINE ELMS - 70A	NINE ELMS - 70A	NINE ELMS - 70A	NINE ELMS - 70A	NINE ELMS - 70A	NINE ELMS - 70A
30485	NINE ELMS - 70A	NINE ELMS - 70A	NINE ELMS - 70A	NINE ELMS - 70A	NINE ELMS - 70A	NINE ELMS - 70A	NINE ELMS - 70A
30486	NINE ELMS - 70A	NINE ELMS - 70A	NINE ELMS - 70A	NINE ELMS - 70A	NINE ELMS - 70A	NINE ELMS - 70A	NINE ELMS - 70A
30487	NINE ELMS - 70A	NINE ELMS - 70A	NINE ELMS - 70A	NINE ELMS - 70A	NINE ELMS - 70A	NINE ELMS - 70A	NINE ELMS - 70A
30488	NINE ELMS - 70A	NINE ELMS - 70A	NINE ELMS - 70A	NINE ELMS - 70A	NINE ELMS - 70A	NINE ELMS - 70A	NINE ELMS - 70A
30489	NINE ELMS - 70A	EASTLEIGH - 71A	EASTLEIGH - 71A	EASTLEIGH - 71A	EASTLEIGH - 71A	EASTLEIGH - 71A	EASTLEIGH - 71A
30490	NINE ELMS - 70A	NINE ELMS - 70A	NINE ELMS - 70A	NINE ELMS - 70A	NINE ELMS - 70A	NINE ELMS - 70A	NINE ELMS - 70A
30491	NINE ELMS - 70A	EASTLEIGH - 71A	EASTLEIGH - 71A	EASTLEIGH - 71A	EASTLEIGH - 71A	EASTLEIGH - 71A	EASTLEIGH - 71A
H15 4-6-0 (1924)							
30473	EASTLEIGH - 71A	EASTLEIGH - 71A	EASTLEIGH - 71A	EASTLEIGH - 71A	EASTLEIGH - 71A	EASTLEIGH - 71A	EASTLEIGH - 71A
30474	EASTLEIGH - 71A	EASTLEIGH - 71A	EASTLEIGH - 71A	EASTLEIGH - 71A	EASTLEIGH - 71A	EASTLEIGH - 71A	EASTLEIGH - 71A
30475	EASTLEIGH - 71A	EASTLEIGH - 71A	EASTLEIGH - 71A	EASTLEIGH - 71A	EASTLEIGH - 71A	EASTLEIGH - 71A	EASTLEIGH - 71A
30476	NINE ELMS - 70A	NINE ELMS - 70A	NINE ELMS - 70A	EASTLEIGH - 71A	EASTLEIGH - 71A	EASTLEIGH - 71A	EASTLEIGH - 71A
30477	EASTLEIGH - 71A	EASTLEIGH - 71A	EASTLEIGH - 71A	EASTLEIGH - 71A	EASTLEIGH - 71A	EASTLEIGH - 71A	EASTLEIGH - 71A
30478	EASTLEIGH - 71A	EASTLEIGH - 71A	EASTLEIGH - 71A	EASTLEIGH - 71A	EASTLEIGH - 71A	EASTLEIGH - 71A	EASTLEIGH - 71A
30521	EASTLEIGH - 71A	EASTLEIGH - 71A	EASTLEIGH - 71A	NINE ELMS - 70A	NINE ELMS - 70A	NINE ELMS - 70A	NINE ELMS - 70A
30522	EASTLEIGH - 71A	EASTLEIGH - 71A	EASTLEIGH - 71A	EASTLEIGH - 71A	NINE ELMS - 70A	NINE ELMS - 70A	NINE ELMS - 70A
30523	EASTLEIGH - 71A	EASTLEIGH - 71A	EASTLEIGH - 71A	EASTLEIGH - 71A	NINE ELMS - 70A	NINE ELMS - 70A	NINE ELMS - 70A
30524	EASTLEIGH - 71A	EASTLEIGH - 71A	EASTLEIGH - 71A	EASTLEIGH - 71A	NINE ELMS - 70A	NINE ELMS - 70A	NINE ELMS - 70A

loco	Jun-51	Jul-51	Sep-51	Dec-51	Jan-52	Mar-52	Jun-52
				U 2-6-0 (1928)			
31610 READING (SR) - 70E	READING (SR) - 70E	READING (SR) - 70E	READING (SR) - 70E	READING (SR) - 70E	READING (SR) - 70E	READING (SR) - 70E
31611 READING (SR) - 70E	READING (SR) - 70E	READING (SR) - 70E	READING (SR) - 70E	READING (SR) - 70E	READING (SR) - 70E	READING (SR) - 70E
31612 READING (SR) - 70E	READING (SR) - 70E	READING (SR) - 70E	READING (SR) - 70E	READING (SR) - 70E	READING (SR) - 70E	READING (SR) - 70E
31613 READING (SR) - 70E	READING (SR) - 70E	READING (SR) - 70E	READING (SR) - 70E	READING (SR) - 70E	READING (SR) - 70E	READING (SR) - 70E
31614 READING (SR) - 70E	READING (SR) - 70E	READING (SR) - 70E	READING (SR) - 70E	READING (SR) - 70E	READING (SR) - 70E	READING (SR) - 70E
31615 READING (SR) - 70E	READING (SR) - 70E	READING (SR) - 70E	READING (SR) - 70E	READING (SR) - 70E	READING (SR) - 70E	READING (SR) - 70E
31616 READING (SR) - 70E	READING (SR) - 70E	READING (SR) - 70E	READING (SR) - 70E	READING (SR) - 70E	READING (SR) - 70E	READING (SR) - 70E
31617 READING (SR) - 70E	READING (SR) - 70E	READING (SR) - 70E	READING (SR) - 70E	READING (SR) - 70E	READING (SR) - 70E	READING (SR) - 70E
31618 SALISBURY - 72B	SALISBURY - 72B	READING (SR) - 70E	READING (SR) - 70E	READING (SR) - 70E	READING (SR) - 70E	READING (SR) - 70E
31619 NINE ELMS - 70A	NINE ELMS - 70A	NINE ELMS - 70A	NINE ELMS - 70A	NINE ELMS - 70A	NINE ELMS - 70A	HITHER GREEN - 73C
31620 GUILDFORD - 70C	GUILDFORD - 70C	GUILDFORD - 70C	GUILDFORD - 70C	GUILDFORD - 70C	GUILDFORD - 70C	HITHER GREEN - 73C
31621 GUILDFORD - 70C	GUILDFORD - 70C	BOURNEMOUTH - 71B	NINE ELMS - 70A	NINE ELMS - 70A	NINE ELMS - 70A	HITHER GREEN - 73C
31622 BOURNEMOUTH - 71B	BOURNEMOUTH - 71B	BOURNEMOUTH - 71B	BOURNEMOUTH - 71B	BOURNEMOUTH - 71B	BOURNEMOUTH - 71B	BOURNEMOUTH - 71B
31623 NINE ELMS - 70A	NINE ELMS - 70A	NINE ELMS - 70A	BOURNEMOUTH - 71B	BOURNEMOUTH - 71B	BOURNEMOUTH - 71B	BOURNEMOUTH - 71B
31624 FELTHAM - 70B	FELTHAM - 70B	FELTHAM - 70B	FELTHAM - 70B	FELTHAM - 70B	FELTHAM - 70B	FELTHAM - 70B
31625 NINE ELMS - 70A	NINE ELMS - 70A	NINE ELMS - 70A	NINE ELMS - 70A	NINE ELMS - 70A	NINE ELMS - 70A	NINE ELMS - 70A
31626 SALISBURY - 72B	SALISBURY - 72B	SALISBURY - 72B	SALISBURY - 72B	SALISBURY - 72B	SALISBURY - 72B	SALISBURY - 72B
31627 GUILDFORD - 70C	GUILDFORD - 70C	GUILDFORD - 70C	GUILDFORD - 70C	GUILDFORD - 70C	GUILDFORD - 70C	GUILDFORD - 70C
31628 GUILDFORD - 70C	GUILDFORD - 70C	GUILDFORD - 70C	GUILDFORD - 70C	GUILDFORD - 70C	GUILDFORD - 70C	GUILDFORD - 70C
31629 GUILDFORD - 70C	GUILDFORD - 70C	GUILDFORD - 70C	GUILDFORD - 70C	GUILDFORD - 70C	GUILDFORD - 70C	GUILDFORD - 70C
31630 GUILDFORD - 70C	GUILDFORD - 70C	GUILDFORD - 70C	GUILDFORD - 70C	GUILDFORD - 70C	GUILDFORD - 70C	GUILDFORD - 70C
31631 HITHER GREEN - 73C	REDHILL - 75B	BRIGHTON - 75A	EASTLEIGH - 71A	EASTLEIGH - 71A	EASTLEIGH - 71A	DORCHESTER - 71C
31632 DORCHESTER - 71C	DORCHESTER - 71C	DORCHESTER - 71C	DORCHESTER - 71C	DORCHESTER - 71C	DORCHESTER - 71C	DORCHESTER - 71C
31633 BASINGSTOKE - 70D	BASINGSTOKE - 70D	BASINGSTOKE - 70D	BASINGSTOKE - 70D	BASINGSTOKE - 70D	BASINGSTOKE - 70D	BASINGSTOKE - 70D
31634 BASINGSTOKE - 70D	BASINGSTOKE - 70D	BASINGSTOKE - 70D	BASINGSTOKE - 70D	BASINGSTOKE - 70D	BASINGSTOKE - 70D	BASINGSTOKE - 70D
31635 BOURNEMOUTH - 71B	BOURNEMOUTH - 71B	SALISBURY - 72B	SALISBURY - 72B	SALISBURY - 72B	SALISBURY - 72B	SALISBURY - 72B
31636 SALISBURY - 72B	SALISBURY - 72B	SALISBURY - 72B	SALISBURY - 72B	SALISBURY - 72B	SALISBURY - 72B	SALISBURY - 72B
31637 NINE ELMS - 70A	NINE ELMS - 70A	NINE ELMS - 70A	NINE ELMS - 70A	NINE ELMS - 70A	NINE ELMS - 70A	FAVERSHAM - 73E
31638 FAVERSHAM - 73E	REDHILL - 75B	BRIGHTON - 75A	EASTLEIGH - 71A	EASTLEIGH - 71A	EASTLEIGH - 71A	EASTLEIGH - 71A
31639 HITHER GREEN - 73C	HITHER GREEN - 73C	HITHER GREEN - 73C	HITHER GREEN - 73C	HITHER GREEN - 73C	HITHER GREEN - 73C	YEOVIL - 72C
			U1 2-6-0 (2-6-4T R/B) 1925				
31890 B.ARMS - 73B	B.ARMS - 73B	B.ARMS - 73B	B.ARMS - 73B	B.ARMS - 73B	B.ARMS - 73B	B.ARMS - 73B
			U1 2-6-0 (1925)				
31891 B.ARMS - 73B	B.ARMS - 73B	B.ARMS - 73B	B.ARMS - 73B	B.ARMS - 73B	B.ARMS - 73B	B.ARMS - 73B
31892 B.ARMS - 73B	B.ARMS - 73B	B.ARMS - 73B	B.ARMS - 73B	B.ARMS - 73B	B.ARMS - 73B	STEWARTS LANE - 73A
31893 B.ARMS - 73B	B.ARMS - 73B	B.ARMS - 73B	B.ARMS - 73B	B.ARMS - 73B	B.ARMS - 73B	STEWARTS LANE - 73A
31894 BRIGHTON - 75A	BRIGHTON - 75A	BRIGHTON - 75A	BRIGHTON - 75A	BRIGHTON - 75A	BRIGHTON - 75A	BRIGHTON - 75A
31895 BRIGHTON - 75A(N)	BRIGHTON - 75A(N)	BRIGHTON - 75A(N)	BRIGHTON - 75A(N)	BRIGHTON - 75A(N)	BRIGHTON - 75A(N)	BRIGHTON - 75A(N)
31896 BRIGHTON - 75A	BRIGHTON - 75A	BRIGHTON - 75A	BRIGHTON - 75A	BRIGHTON - 75A	BRIGHTON - 75A	BRIGHTON - 75A
31897 REDHILL - 75B	REDHILL - 75B	REDHILL - 75B	REDHILL - 75B	REDHILL - 75B	REDHILL - 75B	REDHILL - 75B
31898 REDHILL - 75B	REDHILL - 75B	REDHILL - 75B	REDHILL - 75B	REDHILL - 75B	REDHILL - 75B	REDHILL - 75B
31899 REDHILL - 75B	STEWARTS LANE - 73A	HITHER GREEN - 73C	HITHER GREEN - 73C	HITHER GREEN - 73C	HITHER GREEN - 73C	STEWARTS LANE - 73A
31900 REDHILL - 75B	STEWARTS LANE - 73A	HITHER GREEN - 73C	HITHER GREEN - 73C	HITHER GREEN - 73C	HITHER GREEN - 73C	STEWARTS LANE - 73A
31901 STEWARTS LANE - 73A	STEWARTS LANE - 73A	STEWARTS LANE - 73A	STEWARTS LANE - 73A	STEWARTS LANE - 73A	STEWARTS LANE - 73A	STEWARTS LANE - 73A
31902 STEWARTS LANE - 73A	STEWARTS LANE - 73A	STEWARTS LANE - 73A	STEWARTS LANE - 73A	STEWARTS LANE - 73A	STEWARTS LANE - 73A	STEWARTS LANE - 73A
31903 STEWARTS LANE - 73A	STEWARTS LANE - 73A	STEWARTS LANE - 73A	STEWARTS LANE - 73A	STEWARTS LANE - 73A	STEWARTS LANE - 73A	STEWARTS LANE - 73A
31904 STEWARTS LANE - 73A	STEWARTS LANE - 73A	STEWARTS LANE - 73A	STEWARTS LANE - 73A	STEWARTS LANE - 73A	STEWARTS LANE - 73A	STEWARTS LANE - 73A
31905 STEWARTS LANE - 73A	STEWARTS LANE - 73A	STEWARTS LANE - 73A	STEWARTS LANE - 73A	STEWARTS LANE - 73A	STEWARTS LANE - 73A	STEWARTS LANE - 73A
31906 STEWARTS LANE - 73A	STEWARTS LANE - 73A	STEWARTS LANE - 73A	STEWARTS LANE - 73A	STEWARTS LANE - 73A	STEWARTS LANE - 73A	STEWARTS LANE - 73A
31907 STEWARTS LANE - 73A	STEWARTS LANE - 73A	STEWARTS LANE - 73A	STEWARTS LANE - 73A	STEWARTS LANE - 73A	STEWARTS LANE - 73A	NINE ELMS - 70A
31908 STEWARTS LANE - 73A	STEWARTS LANE - 73A	STEWARTS LANE - 73A	STEWARTS LANE - 73A	STEWARTS LANE - 73A	STEWARTS LANE - 73A	NINE ELMS - 70A
31909 STEWARTS LANE - 73A	STEWARTS LANE - 73A	STEWARTS LANE - 73A	STEWARTS LANE - 73A	STEWARTS LANE - 73A	STEWARTS LANE - 73A	NINE ELMS - 70A
31910 STEWARTS LANE - 73A	STEWARTS LANE - 73A	STEWARTS LANE - 73A	STEWARTS LANE - 73A	STEWARTS LANE - 73A	STEWARTS LANE - 73A	NINE ELMS - 70A
			N15X 4-6-0 (1914/34)				
32327 BASINGSTOKE - 70D	BASINGSTOKE - 70D	BASINGSTOKE - 70D	BASINGSTOKE - 70D	BASINGSTOKE - 70D	BASINGSTOKE - 70D	BASINGSTOKE - 70D
32328 BASINGSTOKE - 70D	BASINGSTOKE - 70D	BASINGSTOKE - 70D	BASINGSTOKE - 70D	BASINGSTOKE - 70D	BASINGSTOKE - 70D	BASINGSTOKE - 70D
32329 BASINGSTOKE - 70D	BASINGSTOKE - 70D	BASINGSTOKE - 70D	BASINGSTOKE - 70D	BASINGSTOKE - 70D	BASINGSTOKE - 70D	BASINGSTOKE - 70D
32330 BASINGSTOKE - 70D	BASINGSTOKE - 70D	BASINGSTOKE - 70D	BASINGSTOKE - 70D	BASINGSTOKE - 70D	BASINGSTOKE - 70D	BASINGSTOKE - 70D
32331 BASINGSTOKE - 70D	BASINGSTOKE - 70D	BASINGSTOKE - 70D	BASINGSTOKE - 70D	BASINGSTOKE - 70D	BASINGSTOKE - 70D	BASINGSTOKE - 70D
32332 BASINGSTOKE - 70D	BASINGSTOKE - 70D	BASINGSTOKE - 70D	BASINGSTOKE - 70D	BASINGSTOKE - 70D	BASINGSTOKE - 70D	BASINGSTOKE - 70D
32333 BASINGSTOKE - 70D	BASINGSTOKE - 70D	BASINGSTOKE - 70D	BASINGSTOKE - 70D	BASINGSTOKE - 70D	BASINGSTOKE - 70D	BASINGSTOKE - 70D
			H15 4-6-0 (1907/14)				
30330 SALISBURY - 72B	SALISBURY - 72B	SALISBURY - 72B	SALISBURY - 72B	SALISBURY - 72B	SALISBURY - 72B	SALISBURY - 72B
30331 SALISBURY - 72B	SALISBURY - 72B	SALISBURY - 72B	SALISBURY - 72B	SALISBURY - 72B	SALISBURY - 72B	SALISBURY - 72B
30332 SALISBURY - 72B	SALISBURY - 72B	SALISBURY - 72B	SALISBURY - 72B	SALISBURY - 72B	SALISBURY - 72B	SALISBURY - 72B
30333 SALISBURY - 72B	SALISBURY - 72B	SALISBURY - 72B	SALISBURY - 72B	SALISBURY - 72B	SALISBURY - 72B	SALISBURY - 72B
30334 SALISBURY - 72B	SALISBURY - 72B	SALISBURY - 72B	SALISBURY - 72B	SALISBURY - 72B	SALISBURY - 72B	SALISBURY - 72B
30335 SALISBURY - 72B	SALISBURY - 72B	SALISBURY - 72B	SALISBURY - 72B	SALISBURY - 72B	SALISBURY - 72B	SALISBURY - 72B
			H15 4-6-0 (1914)				
30482 NINE ELMS - 70A	NINE ELMS - 70A	NINE ELMS - 70A	NINE ELMS - 70A	NINE ELMS - 70A	NINE ELMS - 70A	NINE ELMS - 70A
30483 EASTLEIGH - 71A	EASTLEIGH - 71A	EASTLEIGH - 71A	EASTLEIGH - 71A	EASTLEIGH - 71A	EASTLEIGH - 71A	EASTLEIGH - 71A
30484 NINE ELMS - 70A	NINE ELMS - 70A	NINE ELMS - 70A	NINE ELMS - 70A	NINE ELMS - 70A	NINE ELMS - 70A	NINE ELMS - 70A
30485 NINE ELMS - 70A	NINE ELMS - 70A	NINE ELMS - 70A	NINE ELMS - 70A	NINE ELMS - 70A	NINE ELMS - 70A	NINE ELMS - 70A
30486 NINE ELMS - 70A	NINE ELMS - 70A	NINE ELMS - 70A	NINE ELMS - 70A	NINE ELMS - 70A	NINE ELMS - 70A	NINE ELMS - 70A
30487 NINE ELMS - 70A	NINE ELMS - 70A	NINE ELMS - 70A	NINE ELMS - 70A	NINE ELMS - 70A	NINE ELMS - 70A	NINE ELMS - 70A
30488 NINE ELMS - 70A	NINE ELMS - 70A	NINE ELMS - 70A	NINE ELMS - 70A	NINE ELMS - 70A	NINE ELMS - 70A	NINE ELMS - 70A
30489 EASTLEIGH - 71A	EASTLEIGH - 71A	EASTLEIGH - 71A	EASTLEIGH - 71A	EASTLEIGH - 71A	EASTLEIGH - 71A	EASTLEIGH - 71A
30490 NINE ELMS - 70A	NINE ELMS - 70A	NINE ELMS - 70A	NINE ELMS - 70A	NINE ELMS - 70A	NINE ELMS - 70A	NINE ELMS - 70A
30491 EASTLEIGH - 71A	EASTLEIGH - 71A	EASTLEIGH - 71A	EASTLEIGH - 71A	EASTLEIGH - 71A	EASTLEIGH - 71A	EASTLEIGH - 71A
			H15 4-6-0 (1924)				
30473 EASTLEIGH - 71A	EASTLEIGH - 71A	EASTLEIGH - 71A	EASTLEIGH - 71A	EASTLEIGH - 71A	EASTLEIGH - 71A	EASTLEIGH - 71A
30474 EASTLEIGH - 71A	EASTLEIGH - 71A	EASTLEIGH - 71A	EASTLEIGH - 71A	EASTLEIGH - 71A	EASTLEIGH - 71A	EASTLEIGH - 71A
30475 EASTLEIGH - 71A	EASTLEIGH - 71A	EASTLEIGH - 71A	EASTLEIGH - 71A	EASTLEIGH - 71A	EASTLEIGH - 71A	EASTLEIGH - 71A
30476 EASTLEIGH - 71A	EASTLEIGH - 71A	EASTLEIGH - 71A	EASTLEIGH - 71A	EASTLEIGH - 71A	EASTLEIGH - 71A	EASTLEIGH - 71A
30477 EASTLEIGH - 71A	EASTLEIGH - 71A	EASTLEIGH - 71A	EASTLEIGH - 71A	EASTLEIGH - 71A	EASTLEIGH - 71A	EASTLEIGH - 71A
30478 EASTLEIGH - 71A	EASTLEIGH - 71A	EASTLEIGH - 71A	EASTLEIGH - 71A	EASTLEIGH - 71A	EASTLEIGH - 71A	EASTLEIGH - 71A
30521 NINE ELMS - 70A	NINE ELMS - 70A	NINE ELMS - 70A	NINE ELMS - 70A	NINE ELMS - 70A	NINE ELMS - 70A	NINE ELMS - 70A
30522 NINE ELMS - 70A	NINE ELMS - 70A	NINE ELMS - 70A	NINE ELMS - 70A	NINE ELMS - 70A	NINE ELMS - 70A	NINE ELMS - 70A
30523 NINE ELMS - 70A	NINE ELMS - 70A	NINE ELMS - 70A	NINE ELMS - 70A	NINE ELMS - 70A	NINE ELMS - 70A	NINE ELMS - 70A
30524 NINE ELMS - 70A	NINE ELMS - 70A	NINE ELMS - 70A	NINE ELMS - 70A	NINE ELMS - 70A	NINE ELMS - 70A	NINE ELMS - 70A

loco	Sep-52	Dec-52	Mar-53	May-53	Jul-53	Sep-53	Nov-53
				U 2-6-0 (1928)			
31610	READING (SR) - 70E	READING (SR) - 70E	READING (SR) - 70E	READING (SR) - 70E	READING (SR) - 70E	READING (SR) - 70E	READING (SR) - 70E
31611	READING (SR) - 70E	READING (SR) - 70E	READING (SR) - 70E	READING (SR) - 70E	READING (SR) - 70E	READING (SR) - 70E	READING (SR) - 70E
31612	READING (SR) - 70E	READING (SR) - 70E	READING (SR) - 70E	READING (SR) - 70E	READING (SR) - 70E	READING (SR) - 70E	READING (SR) - 70E
31613	READING (SR) - 70E	READING (SR) - 70E	READING (SR) - 70E	READING (SR) - 70E	READING (SR) - 70E	EASTLEIGH - 71A	EASTLEIGH - 71A
31614	READING (SR) - 70E	READING (SR) - 70E	READING (SR) - 70E	READING (SR) - 70E	READING (SR) - 70E	READING (SR) - 70E	READING (SR) - 70E
31615	READING (SR) - 70E	READING (SR) - 70E	READING (SR) - 70E	READING (SR) - 70E	READING (SR) - 70E	READING (SR) - 70E	READING (SR) - 70E
31616	READING (SR) - 70E	READING (SR) - 70E	READING (SR) - 70E	READING (SR) - 70E	READING (SR) - 70E	READING (SR) - 70E	READING (SR) - 70E
31617	READING (SR) - 70E	READING (SR) - 70E	READING (SR) - 70E	READING (SR) - 70E	READING (SR) - 70E	READING (SR) - 70E	READING (SR) - 70E
31618	DORCHESTER - 71C	READING (SR) - 70E	DORCHESTER - 71C	DORCHESTER - 71C	DORCHESTER - 71C	DORCHESTER - 71C	DORCHESTER - 71C
31619	HITHER GREEN - 73C	HITHER GREEN - 73C	HITHER GREEN - 73C	HITHER GREEN - 73C	HITHER GREEN - 73C	READING (SR) - 70E	READING (SR) - 70E
31620	HITHER GREEN - 73C	HITHER GREEN - 73C	HITHER GREEN - 73C	HITHER GREEN - 73C	HITHER GREEN - 73C	EASTLEIGH - 71A	EASTLEIGH - 71A
31621	HITHER GREEN - 73C	HITHER GREEN - 73C	HITHER GREEN - 73C	HITHER GREEN - 73C	HITHER GREEN - 73C	EASTLEIGH - 71A	EASTLEIGH - 71A
31622	BOURNEMOUTH - 71B	BOURNEMOUTH - 71B	BOURNEMOUTH - 71B	BOURNEMOUTH - 71B	BOURNEMOUTH - 71B	DORCHESTER - 71C	DORCHESTER - 71C
31623	BOURNEMOUTH - 71B	BOURNEMOUTH - 71B	DORCHESTER - 71C	DORCHESTER - 71C	DORCHESTER - 71C	DORCHESTER - 71C	DORCHESTER - 71C
31624	FELTHAM - 70B	FELTHAM - 70B	FELTHAM - 70B	FELTHAM - 70B	EASTLEIGH - 71A	GUILDFORD - 70C	GUILDFORD - 70C
31625	NINE ELMS - 70A	NINE ELMS - 70A	NINE ELMS - 70A	NINE ELMS - 70A	EASTLEIGH - 71A	GUILDFORD - 70C	GUILDFORD - 70C
31626	SALISBURY - 72B	SALISBURY - 72B	SALISBURY - 72B	SALISBURY - 72B	EASTLEIGH - 71A	EASTLEIGH - 71A	EASTLEIGH - 71A
31627	GUILDFORD - 70C	GUILDFORD - 70C	GUILDFORD - 70C	GUILDFORD - 70C	GUILDFORD - 70C	GUILDFORD - 70C	GUILDFORD - 70C
31628	GUILDFORD - 70C	GUILDFORD - 70C	GUILDFORD - 70C	GUILDFORD - 70C	GUILDFORD - 70C	GUILDFORD - 70C	GUILDFORD - 70C
31629	GUILDFORD - 70C	GUILDFORD - 70C	GUILDFORD - 70C	GUILDFORD - 70C	GUILDFORD - 70C	GUILDFORD - 70C	GUILDFORD - 70C
31630	GUILDFORD - 70C	GUILDFORD - 70C	GUILDFORD - 70C	GUILDFORD - 70C	GUILDFORD - 70C	GUILDFORD - 70C	GUILDFORD - 70C
31631	DORCHESTER - 71C	DORCHESTER - 71C	DORCHESTER - 71C	DORCHESTER - 71C	DORCHESTER - 71C	DORCHESTER - 71C	DORCHESTER - 71C
31632	DORCHESTER - 71C	DORCHESTER - 71C	DORCHESTER - 71C	DORCHESTER - 71C	DORCHESTER - 71C	DORCHESTER - 71C	DORCHESTER - 71C
31633	BASINGSTOKE - 70D	BASINGSTOKE - 70D	BASINGSTOKE - 70D	BASINGSTOKE - 70D	BASINGSTOKE - 70D	BASINGSTOKE - 70D	BASINGSTOKE - 70D
31634	BASINGSTOKE - 70D	BASINGSTOKE - 70D	BASINGSTOKE - 70D	BASINGSTOKE - 70D	BASINGSTOKE - 70D	BASINGSTOKE - 70D	BASINGSTOKE - 70D
31635	SALISBURY - 72B	SALISBURY - 72B	SALISBURY - 72B	SALISBURY - 72B	SALISBURY - 72B	SALISBURY - 72B	SALISBURY - 72B
31636	SALISBURY - 72B	SALISBURY - 72B	SALISBURY - 72B	SALISBURY - 72B	SALISBURY - 72B	SALISBURY - 72B	SALISBURY - 72B
31637	FAVERSHAM - 73E	FAVERSHAM - 73E	FAVERSHAM - 73E	FAVERSHAM - 73E	FAVERSHAM - 73E	FRATTON - 71D	FRATTON - 71D
31638	EASTLEIGH - 71A	EASTLEIGH - 71A	REDHILL - 75B	REDHILL - 75B	REDHILL - 75B	FRATTON - 71D	FRATTON - 71D
31639	YEOVIL - 72C	YEOVIL - 72C	SALISBURY - 72B	SALISBURY - 72B	SALISBURY - 72B	SALISBURY - 72B	SALISBURY - 72B
			U1 2-6-0 (2-6-4T R/B) 1925				
31890	B.ARMS - 73B	B.ARMS - 73B	B.ARMS - 73B	B.ARMS - 73B	B.ARMS - 73B	B.ARMS - 73B	B.ARMS - 73B
				U1 2-6-0 (1925)			
31891	STEWARTS LANE - 73A	STEWARTS LANE - 73A	STEWARTS LANE - 73A	STEWARTS LANE - 73A	B.ARMS - 73B	B.ARMS - 73B	B.ARMS - 73B
31892	STEWARTS LANE - 73A	STEWARTS LANE - 73A	STEWARTS LANE - 73A	STEWARTS LANE - 73A	STEWARTS LANE - 73A	HITHER GREEN - 73C	HITHER GREEN - 73C
31893	STEWARTS LANE - 73A	STEWARTS LANE - 73A	STEWARTS LANE - 73A	STEWARTS LANE - 73A	STEWARTS LANE - 73A	HITHER GREEN - 73C	HITHER GREEN - 73C
31894	BRIGHTON - 75A	BRIGHTON - 75A	BRIGHTON - 75A	BRIGHTON - 75A	BRIGHTON - 75A	BRIGHTON - 75A	BRIGHTON - 75A
31895	BRIGHTON - 75A(N)	BRIGHTON - 75A(N)	BRIGHTON - 75A(N)	BRIGHTON - 75A(N)	BRIGHTON - 75A(N)	BRIGHTON - 75A(N)	BRIGHTON - 75A(N)
31896	BRIGHTON - 75A	BRIGHTON - 75A	BRIGHTON - 75A	BRIGHTON - 75A	BRIGHTON - 75A	BRIGHTON - 75A	BRIGHTON - 75A
31897	REDHILL - 75B	REDHILL - 75B	REDHILL - 75B	REDHILL - 75B	REDHILL - 75B	REDHILL - 75B	REDHILL - 75B
31898	REDHILL - 75B	REDHILL - 75B	REDHILL - 75B	REDHILL - 75B	REDHILL - 75B	REDHILL - 75B	REDHILL - 75B
31899	STEWARTS LANE - 73A	STEWARTS LANE - 73A	STEWARTS LANE - 73A	STEWARTS LANE - 73A	STEWARTS LANE - 73A	REDHILL - 75B	REDHILL - 75B
31900	STEWARTS LANE - 73A	STEWARTS LANE - 73A	STEWARTS LANE - 73A	STEWARTS LANE - 73A	STEWARTS LANE - 73A	REDHILL - 75B	REDHILL - 75B
31901	STEWARTS LANE - 73A	STEWARTS LANE - 73A	STEWARTS LANE - 73A	STEWARTS LANE - 73A	STEWARTS LANE - 73A	STEWARTS LANE - 73A	STEWARTS LANE - 73A
31902	STEWARTS LANE - 73A	STEWARTS LANE - 73A	STEWARTS LANE - 73A	STEWARTS LANE - 73A	STEWARTS LANE - 73A	STEWARTS LANE - 73A	STEWARTS LANE - 73A
31903	STEWARTS LANE - 73A	STEWARTS LANE - 73A	STEWARTS LANE - 73A	STEWARTS LANE - 73A	STEWARTS LANE - 73A	STEWARTS LANE - 73A	STEWARTS LANE - 73A
31904	STEWARTS LANE - 73A	STEWARTS LANE - 73A	STEWARTS LANE - 73A	STEWARTS LANE - 73A	STEWARTS LANE - 73A	STEWARTS LANE - 73A	STEWARTS LANE - 73A
31905	STEWARTS LANE - 73A	STEWARTS LANE - 73A	STEWARTS LANE - 73A	STEWARTS LANE - 73A	STEWARTS LANE - 73A	STEWARTS LANE - 73A	STEWARTS LANE - 73A
31906	STEWARTS LANE - 73A	STEWARTS LANE - 73A	STEWARTS LANE - 73A	STEWARTS LANE - 73A	STEWARTS LANE - 73A	STEWARTS LANE - 73A	STEWARTS LANE - 73A
31907	NINE ELMS - 70A	NINE ELMS - 70A	NINE ELMS - 70A	NINE ELMS - 70A	NINE ELMS - 70A	NINE ELMS - 70A	NINE ELMS - 70A
31908	NINE ELMS - 70A	NINE ELMS - 70A	NINE ELMS - 70A	NINE ELMS - 70A	NINE ELMS - 70A	NINE ELMS - 70A	NINE ELMS - 70A
31909	NINE ELMS - 70A	NINE ELMS - 70A	NINE ELMS - 70A	NINE ELMS - 70A	NINE ELMS - 70A	NINE ELMS - 70A	NINE ELMS - 70A
31910	NINE ELMS - 70A	NINE ELMS - 70A	NINE ELMS - 70A	NINE ELMS - 70A	NINE ELMS - 70A	NINE ELMS - 70A	NINE ELMS - 70A
				N15X 4-6-0 (1914/34)			
32327	BASINGSTOKE - 70D	BASINGSTOKE - 70D	BASINGSTOKE - 70D	BASINGSTOKE - 70D	BASINGSTOKE - 70D	BASINGSTOKE - 70D	BASINGSTOKE - 70D
32328	BASINGSTOKE - 70D	BASINGSTOKE - 70D	BASINGSTOKE - 70D	BASINGSTOKE - 70D	BASINGSTOKE - 70D	BASINGSTOKE - 70D	BASINGSTOKE - 70D
32329	BASINGSTOKE - 70D	BASINGSTOKE - 70D	BASINGSTOKE - 70D	BASINGSTOKE - 70D	BASINGSTOKE - 70D	BASINGSTOKE - 70D	BASINGSTOKE - 70D
32330	BASINGSTOKE - 70D	BASINGSTOKE - 70D	BASINGSTOKE - 70D	BASINGSTOKE - 70D	BASINGSTOKE - 70D	BASINGSTOKE - 70D	BASINGSTOKE - 70D
32331	BASINGSTOKE - 70D	BASINGSTOKE - 70D	BASINGSTOKE - 70D	BASINGSTOKE - 70D	BASINGSTOKE - 70D	BASINGSTOKE - 70D	BASINGSTOKE - 70D
32332	BASINGSTOKE - 70D	BASINGSTOKE - 70D	BASINGSTOKE - 70D	BASINGSTOKE - 70D	BASINGSTOKE - 70D	BASINGSTOKE - 70D	BASINGSTOKE - 70D
32333	BASINGSTOKE - 70D	BASINGSTOKE - 70D	BASINGSTOKE - 70D	BASINGSTOKE - 70D	BASINGSTOKE - 70D	BASINGSTOKE - 70D	BASINGSTOKE - 70D
				H15 4-6-0 (1907/14)			
30330	SALISBURY - 72B	SALISBURY - 72B	SALISBURY - 72B	SALISBURY - 72B	SALISBURY - 72B	SALISBURY - 72B	SALISBURY - 72B
30331	SALISBURY - 72B	SALISBURY - 72B	SALISBURY - 72B	SALISBURY - 72B	SALISBURY - 72B	SALISBURY - 72B	SALISBURY - 72B
30332	SALISBURY - 72B	SALISBURY - 72B	SALISBURY - 72B	SALISBURY - 72B	SALISBURY - 72B	SALISBURY - 72B	SALISBURY - 72B
30333	SALISBURY - 72B	SALISBURY - 72B	SALISBURY - 72B	SALISBURY - 72B	SALISBURY - 72B	SALISBURY - 72B	SALISBURY - 72B
30334	SALISBURY - 72B	SALISBURY - 72B	SALISBURY - 72B	SALISBURY - 72B	SALISBURY - 72B	SALISBURY - 72B	SALISBURY - 72B
30335	SALISBURY - 72B	SALISBURY - 72B	SALISBURY - 72B	SALISBURY - 72B	SALISBURY - 72B	SALISBURY - 72B	SALISBURY - 72B
				H15 4-6-0 (1914)			
30482	NINE ELMS - 70A	NINE ELMS - 70A	NINE ELMS - 70A	NINE ELMS - 70A	NINE ELMS - 70A	NINE ELMS - 70A	NINE ELMS - 70A
30483	EASTLEIGH - 71A	EASTLEIGH - 71A	EASTLEIGH - 71A	EASTLEIGH - 71A	EASTLEIGH - 71A	EASTLEIGH - 71A	EASTLEIGH - 71A
30484	NINE ELMS - 70A	NINE ELMS - 70A	NINE ELMS - 70A	NINE ELMS - 70A	NINE ELMS - 70A	NINE ELMS - 70A	NINE ELMS - 70A
30485	NINE ELMS - 70A	NINE ELMS - 70A	NINE ELMS - 70A	NINE ELMS - 70A	NINE ELMS - 70A	NINE ELMS - 70A	NINE ELMS - 70A
30486	NINE ELMS - 70A	NINE ELMS - 70A	NINE ELMS - 70A	NINE ELMS - 70A	NINE ELMS - 70A	NINE ELMS - 70A	NINE ELMS - 70A
30487	NINE ELMS - 70A	NINE ELMS - 70A	NINE ELMS - 70A	NINE ELMS - 70A	NINE ELMS - 70A	NINE ELMS - 70A	NINE ELMS - 70A
30488	NINE ELMS - 70A	NINE ELMS - 70A	NINE ELMS - 70A	NINE ELMS - 70A	NINE ELMS - 70A	NINE ELMS - 70A	NINE ELMS - 70A
30489	EASTLEIGH - 71A	EASTLEIGH - 71A	EASTLEIGH - 71A	EASTLEIGH - 71A	EASTLEIGH - 71A	EASTLEIGH - 71A	EASTLEIGH - 71A
30490	NINE ELMS - 70A	NINE ELMS - 70A	NINE ELMS - 70A	NINE ELMS - 70A	NINE ELMS - 70A	NINE ELMS - 70A	NINE ELMS - 70A
30491	EASTLEIGH - 71A	EASTLEIGH - 71A	EASTLEIGH - 71A	EASTLEIGH - 71A	EASTLEIGH - 71A	EASTLEIGH - 71A	EASTLEIGH - 71A
				H15 4-6-0 (1924)			
30473	EASTLEIGH - 71A	EASTLEIGH - 71A	EASTLEIGH - 71A	EASTLEIGH - 71A	EASTLEIGH - 71A	EASTLEIGH - 71A	EASTLEIGH - 71A
30474	EASTLEIGH - 71A	EASTLEIGH - 71A	EASTLEIGH - 71A	EASTLEIGH - 71A	EASTLEIGH - 71A	EASTLEIGH - 71A	EASTLEIGH - 71A
30475	EASTLEIGH - 71A	EASTLEIGH - 71A	EASTLEIGH - 71A	EASTLEIGH - 71A	EASTLEIGH - 71A	EASTLEIGH - 71A	EASTLEIGH - 71A
30476	EASTLEIGH - 71A	EASTLEIGH - 71A	EASTLEIGH - 71A	EASTLEIGH - 71A	EASTLEIGH - 71A	EASTLEIGH - 71A	EASTLEIGH - 71A
30477	EASTLEIGH - 71A	EASTLEIGH - 71A	EASTLEIGH - 71A	EASTLEIGH - 71A	EASTLEIGH - 71A	EASTLEIGH - 71A	EASTLEIGH - 71A
30478	EASTLEIGH - 71A	EASTLEIGH - 71A	EASTLEIGH - 71A	EASTLEIGH - 71A	EASTLEIGH - 71A	EASTLEIGH - 71A	EASTLEIGH - 71A
30521	NINE ELMS - 70A	NINE ELMS - 70A	NINE ELMS - 70A	NINE ELMS - 70A	NINE ELMS - 70A	NINE ELMS - 70A	NINE ELMS - 70A
30522	NINE ELMS - 70A	NINE ELMS - 70A	NINE ELMS - 70A	NINE ELMS - 70A	NINE ELMS - 70A	NINE ELMS - 70A	NINE ELMS - 70A
30523	NINE ELMS - 70A	NINE ELMS - 70A	NINE ELMS - 70A	NINE ELMS - 70A	NINE ELMS - 70A	NINE ELMS - 70A	NINE ELMS - 70A
30524	NINE ELMS - 70A	NINE ELMS - 70A	NINE ELMS - 70A	NINE ELMS - 70A	NINE ELMS - 70A	NINE ELMS - 70A	NINE ELMS - 70A

loco	Jan-54	Mar-54	May-54	Jun-54	Aug-54	Oct-54	Dec-54
				U 2-6-0 (1928)			
31610	READING (SR) - 70E	READING (SR) - 70E	REDHILL - 75B	REDHILL - 75B	REDHILL - 75B	YEOVIL - 72C	YEOVIL - 72C
31611	READING (SR) - 70E	READING (SR) - 70E	REDHILL - 75B	REDHILL - 75B	REDHILL - 75B	REDHILL - 75B	REDHILL - 75B
31612	READING (SR) - 70E	READING (SR) - 70E	REDHILL - 75B	REDHILL - 75B	REDHILL - 75B	REDHILL - 75B	REDHILL - 75B
31613	EASTLEIGH - 71A	EASTLEIGH - 71A	EASTLEIGH - 71A	EASTLEIGH - 71A	EASTLEIGH - 71A	EASTLEIGH - 71A	EASTLEIGH - 71A
31614	READING (SR) - 70E	READING (SR) - 70E	REDHILL - 75B	REDHILL - 75B	REDHILL - 75B	REDHILL - 75B	REDHILL - 75B
31615	READING (SR) - 70E	READING (SR) - 70E	REDHILL - 75B	REDHILL - 75B	REDHILL - 75B	REDHILL - 75B	REDHILL - 75B
31616	READING (SR) - 70E	READING (SR) - 70E	GUILDFORD - 70C	GUILDFORD - 70C	GUILDFORD - 70C	GUILDFORD - 70C	GUILDFORD - 70C
31617	READING (SR) - 70E	READING (SR) - 70E	GUILDFORD - 70C	GUILDFORD - 70C	NINE ELMS - 70A	NINE ELMS - 70A	NINE ELMS - 70A
31618	DORCHESTER - 71C	DORCHESTER - 71C	EASTLEIGH - 71A	EASTLEIGH - 71A	EASTLEIGH - 71A	EASTLEIGH - 71A	EASTLEIGH - 71A
31619	READING (SR) - 70E	READING (SR) - 70E	EASTLEIGH - 71A	EASTLEIGH - 71A	EASTLEIGH - 71A	EASTLEIGH - 71A	EASTLEIGH - 71A
31620	GUILDFORD - 70C	GUILDFORD - 70C	EASTLEIGH - 71A	EASTLEIGH - 71A	EASTLEIGH - 71A	EASTLEIGH - 71A	EASTLEIGH - 71A
31621	EASTLEIGH - 71A	EASTLEIGH - 71A	EASTLEIGH - 71A	EASTLEIGH - 71A	EASTLEIGH - 71A	EASTLEIGH - 71A	EASTLEIGH - 71A
31622	DORCHESTER - 71C	DORCHESTER - 71C	YEOVIL - 72C	YEOVIL - 72C	YEOVIL - 72C	GUILDFORD - 70C	GUILDFORD - 70C
31623	DORCHESTER - 71C	DORCHESTER - 71C	DORCHESTER - 71C	DORCHESTER - 71C	DORCHESTER - 71C	DORCHESTER - 71C	DORCHESTER - 71C
31624	GUILDFORD - 70C	GUILDFORD - 70C	GUILDFORD - 70C	GUILDFORD - 70C	GUILDFORD - 70C	GUILDFORD - 70C	GUILDFORD - 70C
31625	GUILDFORD - 70C	GUILDFORD - 70C	GUILDFORD - 70C	GUILDFORD - 70C	GUILDFORD - 70C	GUILDFORD - 70C	GUILDFORD - 70C
31626	EASTLEIGH - 71A	EASTLEIGH - 71A	EASTLEIGH - 71A	EASTLEIGH - 71A	EASTLEIGH - 71A	EASTLEIGH - 71A	EASTLEIGH - 71A
31627	GUILDFORD - 70C	GUILDFORD - 70C	GUILDFORD - 70C	GUILDFORD - 70C	GUILDFORD - 70C	GUILDFORD - 70C	GUILDFORD - 70C
31628	GUILDFORD - 70C	GUILDFORD - 70C	GUILDFORD - 70C	GUILDFORD - 70C	GUILDFORD - 70C	GUILDFORD - 70C	GUILDFORD - 70C
31629	GUILDFORD - 70C	GUILDFORD - 70C	GUILDFORD - 70C	GUILDFORD - 70C	NINE ELMS - 70A	NINE ELMS - 70A	NINE ELMS - 70A
31630	GUILDFORD - 70C	GUILDFORD - 70C	GUILDFORD - 70C	GUILDFORD - 70C	GUILDFORD - 70C	GUILDFORD - 70C	GUILDFORD - 70C
31631	DORCHESTER - 71C	DORCHESTER - 71C	GUILDFORD - 70C	GUILDFORD - 70C	GUILDFORD - 70C	GUILDFORD - 70C	GUILDFORD - 70C
31632	DORCHESTER - 71C	DORCHESTER - 71C	BASINGSTOKE - 70D	DORCHESTER - 71C	DORCHESTER - 71C	DORCHESTER - 71C	DORCHESTER - 71C
31633	BASINGSTOKE - 70D	BASINGSTOKE - 70D	BASINGSTOKE - 70D	BASINGSTOKE - 70D	BASINGSTOKE - 70D	BASINGSTOKE - 70D	BASINGSTOKE - 70D
31634	BASINGSTOKE - 70D	BASINGSTOKE - 70D	BASINGSTOKE - 70D	BASINGSTOKE - 70D	BASINGSTOKE - 70D	BASINGSTOKE - 70D	BASINGSTOKE - 70D
31635	SALISBURY - 72B	SALISBURY - 72B	SALISBURY - 72B	SALISBURY - 72B	SALISBURY - 72B	SALISBURY - 72B	SALISBURY - 72B
31636	SALISBURY - 72B	SALISBURY - 72B	SALISBURY - 72B	SALISBURY - 72B	SALISBURY - 72B	SALISBURY - 72B	SALISBURY - 72B
31637	FRATTON - 71D	FRATTON - 71D	FRATTON - 71D	FRATTON - 71D	FRATTON - 71D	FRATTON - 70F	FRATTON - 70F
31638	FRATTON - 71D	FRATTON - 71D	FRATTON - 71D	FRATTON - 71D	FRATTON - 71D	FRATTON - 70F	FRATTON - 70F
31639	SALISBURY - 72B	SALISBURY - 72B	SALISBURY - 72B	SALISBURY - 72B	SALISBURY - 72B	SALISBURY - 72B	SALISBURY - 72B
				U1 2-6-0 (2-6-4T R/B) 1925			
31890	B.ARMS - 73B	B.ARMS - 73B	B.ARMS - 73B	B.ARMS - 73B	B.ARMS - 73B	B.ARMS - 73B	B.ARMS - 73B
				U1 2-6-0 (1925)			
31891	B.ARMS - 73B	B.ARMS - 73B	B.ARMS - 73B	B.ARMS - 73B	B.ARMS - 73B	B.ARMS - 73B	B.ARMS - 73B
31892	HITHER GREEN - 73C	HITHER GREEN - 73C	HITHER GREEN - 73C	HITHER GREEN - 73C	HITHER GREEN - 73C	HITHER GREEN - 73C	HITHER GREEN - 73C
31893	HITHER GREEN - 73C	HITHER GREEN - 73C	HITHER GREEN - 73C	HITHER GREEN - 73C	HITHER GREEN - 73C	HITHER GREEN - 73C	HITHER GREEN - 73C
31894	BRIGHTON - 75A	BRIGHTON - 75A	BRIGHTON - 75A	BRIGHTON - 75A	BRIGHTON - 75A	BRIGHTON - 75A	BRIGHTON - 75A
31895	BRIGHTON - 75A(N)	BRIGHTON - 75A(N)	BRIGHTON - 75A(N)	BRIGHTON - 75A(N)	BRIGHTON - 75A(N)	BRIGHTON - 75A(N)	BRIGHTON - 75A(N)
31896	BRIGHTON - 75A	BRIGHTON - 75A	BRIGHTON - 75A	BRIGHTON - 75A	BRIGHTON - 75A	BRIGHTON - 75A	BRIGHTON - 75A
31897	REDHILL - 75B	REDHILL - 75B	REDHILL - 75B	REDHILL - 75B	REDHILL - 75B	REDHILL - 75B	REDHILL - 75B
31898	REDHILL - 75B	REDHILL - 75B	REDHILL - 75B	REDHILL - 75B	REDHILL - 75B	REDHILL - 75B	REDHILL - 75B
31899	REDHILL - 75B	REDHILL - 75B	REDHILL - 75B	REDHILL - 75B	REDHILL - 75B	REDHILL - 75B	REDHILL - 75B
31900	REDHILL - 75B	REDHILL - 75B	REDHILL - 75B	STEWARTS LANE - 73A	STEWARTS LANE - 73A	STEWARTS LANE - 73A	BRIGHTON - 75A
31901	STEWARTS LANE - 73A	STEWARTS LANE - 73A	STEWARTS LANE - 73A	STEWARTS LANE - 73A	STEWARTS LANE - 73A	STEWARTS LANE - 73A	BRIGHTON - 75A
31902	STEWARTS LANE - 73A	STEWARTS LANE - 73A	STEWARTS LANE - 73A	STEWARTS LANE - 73A	STEWARTS LANE - 73A	STEWARTS LANE - 73A	BRIGHTON - 75A
31903	STEWARTS LANE - 73A	STEWARTS LANE - 73A	STEWARTS LANE - 73A	STEWARTS LANE - 73A	STEWARTS LANE - 73A	STEWARTS LANE - 73A	BRIGHTON - 75A
31904	STEWARTS LANE - 73A	STEWARTS LANE - 73A	STEWARTS LANE - 73A	STEWARTS LANE - 73A	STEWARTS LANE - 73A	STEWARTS LANE - 73A	STEWARTS LANE - 73A
31905	STEWARTS LANE - 73A	STEWARTS LANE - 73A	STEWARTS LANE - 73A	STEWARTS LANE - 73A	STEWARTS LANE - 73A	STEWARTS LANE - 73A	STEWARTS LANE - 73A
31906	STEWARTS LANE - 73A	STEWARTS LANE - 73A	STEWARTS LANE - 73A	STEWARTS LANE - 73A	STEWARTS LANE - 73A	NINE ELMS - 70A	STEWARTS LANE - 73A
31907	NINE ELMS - 70A	NINE ELMS - 70A	NINE ELMS - 70A	STEWARTS LANE - 73A	STEWARTS LANE - 73A	NINE ELMS - 70A	STEWARTS LANE - 73A
31908	NINE ELMS - 70A	NINE ELMS - 70A	NINE ELMS - 70A	STEWARTS LANE - 73A	STEWARTS LANE - 73A	TONBRIDGE - 74D	TONBRIDGE - 74D
31909	NINE ELMS - 70A	NINE ELMS - 70A	NINE ELMS - 70A	NINE ELMS - 70A	TONBRIDGE - 74D	TONBRIDGE - 74D	TONBRIDGE - 74D
31910	NINE ELMS - 70A	NINE ELMS - 70A	NINE ELMS - 70A	NINE ELMS - 70A	B.ARMS - 73B	TONBRIDGE - 74D	TONBRIDGE - 74D
				N15X 4-6-0 (1914/34)			
32327	BASINGSTOKE - 70D	BASINGSTOKE - 70D	BASINGSTOKE - 70D	BASINGSTOKE - 70D	BASINGSTOKE - 70D	BASINGSTOKE - 70D	BASINGSTOKE - 70D
32328	BASINGSTOKE - 70D	BASINGSTOKE - 70D	BASINGSTOKE - 70D	BASINGSTOKE - 70D	BASINGSTOKE - 70D	BASINGSTOKE - 70D	BASINGSTOKE - 70D
32329	BASINGSTOKE - 70D	BASINGSTOKE - 70D	BASINGSTOKE - 70D	BASINGSTOKE - 70D	BASINGSTOKE - 70D	BASINGSTOKE - 70D	BASINGSTOKE - 70D
32330	BASINGSTOKE - 70D	BASINGSTOKE - 70D	BASINGSTOKE - 70D	BASINGSTOKE - 70D	BASINGSTOKE - 70D	BASINGSTOKE - 70D	BASINGSTOKE - 70D
32331	BASINGSTOKE - 70D	BASINGSTOKE - 70D	BASINGSTOKE - 70D	BASINGSTOKE - 70D	BASINGSTOKE - 70D	BASINGSTOKE - 70D	BASINGSTOKE - 70D
32332	BASINGSTOKE - 70D	BASINGSTOKE - 70D	BASINGSTOKE - 70D	BASINGSTOKE - 70D	BASINGSTOKE - 70D	BASINGSTOKE - 70D	BASINGSTOKE - 70D
32333	BASINGSTOKE - 70D	BASINGSTOKE - 70D	BASINGSTOKE - 70D	BASINGSTOKE - 70D	BASINGSTOKE - 70D	BASINGSTOKE - 70D	BASINGSTOKE - 70D
				H15 4-6-0 (1907/14)			
30330	SALISBURY - 72B	SALISBURY - 72B	SALISBURY - 72B	SALISBURY - 72B	SALISBURY - 72B	SALISBURY - 72B	SALISBURY - 72B
30331	SALISBURY - 72B	SALISBURY - 72B	SALISBURY - 72B	SALISBURY - 72B	SALISBURY - 72B	SALISBURY - 72B	SALISBURY - 72B
30332	SALISBURY - 72B	SALISBURY - 72B	SALISBURY - 72B	SALISBURY - 72B	SALISBURY - 72B	SALISBURY - 72B	SALISBURY - 72B
30333	SALISBURY - 72B	SALISBURY - 72B	SALISBURY - 72B	SALISBURY - 72B	SALISBURY - 72B	SALISBURY - 72B	SALISBURY - 72B
30334	SALISBURY - 72B	SALISBURY - 72B	SALISBURY - 72B	SALISBURY - 72B	SALISBURY - 72B	SALISBURY - 72B	SALISBURY - 72B
30335	SALISBURY - 72B	SALISBURY - 72B	SALISBURY - 72B	SALISBURY - 72B	SALISBURY - 72B	SALISBURY - 72B	SALISBURY - 72B
				H15 4-6-0 (1914)			
30482	NINE ELMS - 70A	NINE ELMS - 70A	NINE ELMS - 70A	NINE ELMS - 70A	NINE ELMS - 70A	NINE ELMS - 70A	NINE ELMS - 70A
30483	EASTLEIGH - 71A	EASTLEIGH - 71A	EASTLEIGH - 71A	EASTLEIGH - 71A	EASTLEIGH - 71A	EASTLEIGH - 71A	EASTLEIGH - 71A
30484	NINE ELMS - 70A	NINE ELMS - 70A	NINE ELMS - 70A	NINE ELMS - 70A	NINE ELMS - 70A	NINE ELMS - 70A	NINE ELMS - 70A
30485	NINE ELMS - 70A	NINE ELMS - 70A	NINE ELMS - 70A	NINE ELMS - 70A	NINE ELMS - 70A	NINE ELMS - 70A	NINE ELMS - 70A
30486	NINE ELMS - 70A	NINE ELMS - 70A	NINE ELMS - 70A	NINE ELMS - 70A	NINE ELMS - 70A	NINE ELMS - 70A	NINE ELMS - 70A
30487	NINE ELMS - 70A	NINE ELMS - 70A	NINE ELMS - 70A	NINE ELMS - 70A	NINE ELMS - 70A	NINE ELMS - 70A	NINE ELMS - 70A
30488	NINE ELMS - 70A	NINE ELMS - 70A	NINE ELMS - 70A	NINE ELMS - 70A	NINE ELMS - 70A	NINE ELMS - 70A	NINE ELMS - 70A
30489	EASTLEIGH - 71A	EASTLEIGH - 71A	EASTLEIGH - 71A	EASTLEIGH - 71A	EASTLEIGH - 71A	EASTLEIGH - 71A	EASTLEIGH - 71A
30490	NINE ELMS - 70A	NINE ELMS - 70A	NINE ELMS - 70A	NINE ELMS - 70A	NINE ELMS - 70A	NINE ELMS - 70A	NINE ELMS - 70A
30491	EASTLEIGH - 71A	EASTLEIGH - 71A	EASTLEIGH - 71A	EASTLEIGH - 71A	EASTLEIGH - 71A	EASTLEIGH - 71A	EASTLEIGH - 71A
				H15 4-6-0 (1924)			
30473	EASTLEIGH - 71A	EASTLEIGH - 71A	EASTLEIGH - 71A	EASTLEIGH - 71A	EASTLEIGH - 71A	EASTLEIGH - 71A	EASTLEIGH - 71A
30474	EASTLEIGH - 71A	EASTLEIGH - 71A	EASTLEIGH - 71A	EASTLEIGH - 71A	EASTLEIGH - 71A	EASTLEIGH - 71A	EASTLEIGH - 71A
30475	EASTLEIGH - 71A	EASTLEIGH - 71A	EASTLEIGH - 71A	EASTLEIGH - 71A	EASTLEIGH - 71A	EASTLEIGH - 71A	EASTLEIGH - 71A
30476	EASTLEIGH - 71A	EASTLEIGH - 71A	EASTLEIGH - 71A	EASTLEIGH - 71A	EASTLEIGH - 71A	EASTLEIGH - 71A	EASTLEIGH - 71A
30477	EASTLEIGH - 71A	EASTLEIGH - 71A	EASTLEIGH - 71A	EASTLEIGH - 71A	EASTLEIGH - 71A	EASTLEIGH - 71A	EASTLEIGH - 71A
30478	EASTLEIGH - 71A	EASTLEIGH - 71A	EASTLEIGH - 71A	EASTLEIGH - 71A	EASTLEIGH - 71A	EASTLEIGH - 71A	EASTLEIGH - 71A
30521	NINE ELMS - 70A	NINE ELMS - 70A	NINE ELMS - 70A	NINE ELMS - 70A	NINE ELMS - 70A	NINE ELMS - 70A	NINE ELMS - 70A
30522	NINE ELMS - 70A	NINE ELMS - 70A	NINE ELMS - 70A	NINE ELMS - 70A	NINE ELMS - 70A	NINE ELMS - 70A	NINE ELMS - 70A
30523	NINE ELMS - 70A	NINE ELMS - 70A	NINE ELMS - 70A	NINE ELMS - 70A	NINE ELMS - 70A	NINE ELMS - 70A	NINE ELMS - 70A
30524	NINE ELMS - 70A	NINE ELMS - 70A	NINE ELMS - 70A	NINE ELMS - 70A	NINE ELMS - 70A	NINE ELMS - 70A	NINE ELMS - 70A

loco	Feb-55	Apr-55	Jun-55	Aug-55	Sep-55	Nov-55	Dec-55
				U 2-6-0 (1928)			
31610	YEOVIL - 72C	YEOVIL - 72C	YEOVIL - 72C	YEOVIL - 72C	YEOVIL - 72C	YEOVIL - 72C	YEOVIL - 72C
31611	REDHILL - 75B	REDHILL - 75B	BASINGSTOKE - 70D	BASINGSTOKE - 70D	BASINGSTOKE - 70D	BASINGSTOKE - 70D	BASINGSTOKE - 70D
31612	REDHILL - 75B	REDHILL - 75B	FRATTON - 70F	FRATTON - 70F	READING (SR) - 70E	READING (SR) - 70E	READING (SR) - 70E
31613	EASTLEIGH - 71A	EASTLEIGH - 71A	EASTLEIGH - 71A	EASTLEIGH - 71A	EASTLEIGH - 71A	EASTLEIGH - 71A	EASTLEIGH - 71A
31614	REDHILL - 75B	REDHILL - 75B	BOURNEMOUTH - 71B	BOURNEMOUTH - 71B	BOURNEMOUTH - 71B	BOURNEMOUTH - 71B	BOURNEMOUTH - 71B
31615	REDHILL - 75B	REDHILL - 75B	BOURNEMOUTH - 71B	BOURNEMOUTH - 71B	BOURNEMOUTH - 71B	BOURNEMOUTH - 71B	BOURNEMOUTH - 71B
31616	GUILDFORD - 70C	GUILDFORD - 70C	GUILDFORD - 70C	GUILDFORD - 70C	GUILDFORD - 70C	GUILDFORD - 70C	GUILDFORD - 70C
31617	NINE ELMS - 70A	NINE ELMS - 70A	NINE ELMS - 70A	NINE ELMS - 70A	NINE ELMS - 70A	NINE ELMS - 70A	NINE ELMS - 70A
31618	EASTLEIGH - 71A	EASTLEIGH - 71A	EASTLEIGH - 71A	EASTLEIGH - 71A	EASTLEIGH - 71A	EASTLEIGH - 71A	EASTLEIGH - 71A
31619	EASTLEIGH - 71A	EASTLEIGH - 71A	EASTLEIGH - 71A	EASTLEIGH - 71A	EASTLEIGH - 71A	EASTLEIGH - 71A	EASTLEIGH - 71A
31620	EASTLEIGH - 71A	EASTLEIGH - 71A	EASTLEIGH - 71A	EASTLEIGH - 71A	EASTLEIGH - 71A	EASTLEIGH - 71A	EASTLEIGH - 71A
31621	EASTLEIGH - 71A	EASTLEIGH - 71A	NINE ELMS - 70A	NINE ELMS - 70A	NINE ELMS - 70A	NINE ELMS - 70A	NINE ELMS - 70A
31622	GUILDFORD - 70C	GUILDFORD - 70C	GUILDFORD - 70C	GUILDFORD - 70C	GUILDFORD - 70C	GUILDFORD - 70C	GUILDFORD - 70C
31623	DORCHESTER - 71C	DORCHESTER - 71C	DORCHESTER - 71C	DORCHESTER - 71C	DORCHESTER - 71C	DORCHESTER - 71C	DORCHESTER - 71C
31624	GUILDFORD - 70C	GUILDFORD - 70C	GUILDFORD - 70C	GUILDFORD - 70C	GUILDFORD - 70C	GUILDFORD - 70C	GUILDFORD - 70C
31625	GUILDFORD - 70C	GUILDFORD - 70C	GUILDFORD - 70C	GUILDFORD - 70C	GUILDFORD - 70C	GUILDFORD - 70C	GUILDFORD - 70C
31626	YEOVIL - 72C	YEOVIL - 72C	YEOVIL - 72C	YEOVIL - 72C	YEOVIL - 72C	YEOVIL - 72C	YEOVIL - 72C
31627	GUILDFORD - 70C	GUILDFORD - 70C	GUILDFORD - 70C	GUILDFORD - 70C	GUILDFORD - 70C	GUILDFORD - 70C	GUILDFORD - 70C
31628	GUILDFORD - 70C	GUILDFORD - 70C	GUILDFORD - 70C	GUILDFORD - 70C	GUILDFORD - 70C	GUILDFORD - 70C	GUILDFORD - 70C
31629	NINE ELMS - 70A	NINE ELMS - 70A	EASTLEIGH - 71A	EASTLEIGH - 71A	EASTLEIGH - 71A	EASTLEIGH - 71A	EASTLEIGH - 71A
31630	GUILDFORD - 70C	GUILDFORD - 70C	GUILDFORD - 70C	GUILDFORD - 70C	GUILDFORD - 70C	GUILDFORD - 70C	GUILDFORD - 70C
31631	GUILDFORD - 70C	GUILDFORD - 70C	GUILDFORD - 70C	GUILDFORD - 70C	GUILDFORD - 70C	GUILDFORD - 70C	GUILDFORD - 70C
31632	BOURNEMOUTH - 71B	BOURNEMOUTH - 71B	BOURNEMOUTH - 71B	BOURNEMOUTH - 71B	BOURNEMOUTH - 71B	BOURNEMOUTH - 71B	BOURNEMOUTH - 71B
31633	BASINGSTOKE - 70D	BASINGSTOKE - 70D	BASINGSTOKE - 70D	BASINGSTOKE - 70D	BASINGSTOKE - 70D	BASINGSTOKE - 70D	BASINGSTOKE - 70D
31634	BASINGSTOKE - 70D	BASINGSTOKE - 70D	NINE ELMS - 70A	NINE ELMS - 70A	NINE ELMS - 70A	NINE ELMS - 70A	NINE ELMS - 70A
31635	SALISBURY - 72B	SALISBURY - 72B	EASTLEIGH - 71A	EASTLEIGH - 71A	EASTLEIGH - 71A	EASTLEIGH - 71A	EASTLEIGH - 71A
31636	SALISBURY - 72B	SALISBURY - 72B	EASTLEIGH - 71A	EASTLEIGH - 71A	EASTLEIGH - 71A	EASTLEIGH - 71A	EASTLEIGH - 71A
31637	FRATTON - 70F	FRATTON - 70F	FRATTON - 70F	FRATTON - 70F	FRATTON - 70F	FRATTON - 70F	FRATTON - 70F
31638	FRATTON - 70F	FRATTON - 70F	FRATTON - 70F	FRATTON - 70F	FRATTON - 70F	FRATTON - 70F	FRATTON - 70F
31639	SALISBURY - 72B	SALISBURY - 72B	EASTLEIGH - 71A	EASTLEIGH - 71A	EASTLEIGH - 71A	EASTLEIGH - 71A	EASTLEIGH - 71A
			U1 2-6-0 (2-6-4T R/B) 1925				
31890	B.ARMS - 73B	B.ARMS - 73B	B.ARMS - 73B	B.ARMS - 73B	B.ARMS - 73B	B.ARMS - 73B	B.ARMS - 73B
			U1 2-6-0 (1925)				
31891	B.ARMS - 73B	B.ARMS - 73B	B.ARMS - 73B	B.ARMS - 73B	B.ARMS - 73B	B.ARMS - 73B	B.ARMS - 73B
31892	HITHER GREEN - 73C	HITHER GREEN - 73C	FAVERSHAM - 73E	FAVERSHAM - 73E	FAVERSHAM - 73E	FAVERSHAM - 73E	FAVERSHAM - 73E
31893	HITHER GREEN - 73C	HITHER GREEN - 73C	FAVERSHAM - 73E	FAVERSHAM - 73E	FAVERSHAM - 73E	FAVERSHAM - 73E	FAVERSHAM - 73E
31894	BRIGHTON - 75A	BRIGHTON - 75A	STEWARTS LANE - 73A	STEWARTS LANE - 73A	STEWARTS LANE - 73A	STEWARTS LANE - 73A	STEWARTS LANE - 73A
31895	BRIGHTON - 75A(N)	BRIGHTON - 75A(N)	STEWARTS LANE - 73A	STEWARTS LANE - 73A	STEWARTS LANE - 73A	STEWARTS LANE - 73A	STEWARTS LANE - 73A
31896	BRIGHTON - 75A	BRIGHTON - 75A	STEWARTS LANE - 73A	STEWARTS LANE - 73A	STEWARTS LANE - 73A	STEWARTS LANE - 73A	STEWARTS LANE - 73A
31897	REDHILL - 75B	REDHILL - 75B	STEWARTS LANE - 73A	STEWARTS LANE - 73A	STEWARTS LANE - 73A	STEWARTS LANE - 73A	STEWARTS LANE - 73A
31898	REDHILL - 75B	REDHILL - 75B	STEWARTS LANE - 73A	STEWARTS LANE - 73A	STEWARTS LANE - 73A	STEWARTS LANE - 73A	STEWARTS LANE - 73A
31899	REDHILL - 75B	REDHILL - 75B	B.ARMS - 73B	B.ARMS - 73B	B.ARMS - 73B	B.ARMS - 73B	B.ARMS - 73B
31900	BRIGHTON - 75A	BRIGHTON - 75A	B.ARMS - 73B	B.ARMS - 73B	B.ARMS - 73B	B.ARMS - 73B	B.ARMS - 73B
31901	BRIGHTON - 75A	BRIGHTON - 75A	B.ARMS - 73B	B.ARMS - 73B	B.ARMS - 73B	B.ARMS - 73B	B.ARMS - 73B
31902	BRIGHTON - 75A	BRIGHTON - 75A	B.ARMS - 73B	B.ARMS - 73B	B.ARMS - 73B	B.ARMS - 73B	B.ARMS - 73B
31903	BRIGHTON - 75A	BRIGHTON - 75A	FAVERSHAM - 73E	FAVERSHAM - 73E	FAVERSHAM - 73E	FAVERSHAM - 73E	FAVERSHAM - 73E
31904	STEWARTS LANE - 73A	STEWARTS LANE - 73A	STEWARTS LANE - 73A	STEWARTS LANE - 73A	STEWARTS LANE - 73A	STEWARTS LANE - 73A	STEWARTS LANE - 73A
31905	STEWARTS LANE - 73A	STEWARTS LANE - 73A	STEWARTS LANE - 73A	STEWARTS LANE - 73A	STEWARTS LANE - 73A	STEWARTS LANE - 73A	STEWARTS LANE - 73A
31906	STEWARTS LANE - 73A	STEWARTS LANE - 73A	STEWARTS LANE - 73A	STEWARTS LANE - 73A	STEWARTS LANE - 73A	STEWARTS LANE - 73A	STEWARTS LANE - 73A
31907	STEWARTS LANE - 73A	STEWARTS LANE - 73A	STEWARTS LANE - 73A	STEWARTS LANE - 73A	STEWARTS LANE - 73A	STEWARTS LANE - 73A	STEWARTS LANE - 73A
31908	TONBRIDGE - 74D	TONBRIDGE - 74D	TONBRIDGE - 74D	TONBRIDGE - 74D	TONBRIDGE - 74D	TONBRIDGE - 74D	TONBRIDGE - 74D
31909	TONBRIDGE - 74D	TONBRIDGE - 74D	TONBRIDGE - 74D	TONBRIDGE - 74D	TONBRIDGE - 74D	TONBRIDGE - 74D	TONBRIDGE - 74D
31910	TONBRIDGE - 74D	TONBRIDGE - 74D	TONBRIDGE - 74D	TONBRIDGE - 74D	TONBRIDGE - 74D	TONBRIDGE - 74D	TONBRIDGE - 74D
			N15X 4-6-0 (1914/34)				
32327	BASINGSTOKE - 70D	BASINGSTOKE - 70D	BASINGSTOKE - 70D	BASINGSTOKE - 70D	BASINGSTOKE - 70D	BASINGSTOKE - 70D	BASINGSTOKE - 70D
32329	BASINGSTOKE - 70D	BASINGSTOKE - 70D	BASINGSTOKE - 70D	BASINGSTOKE - 70D	BASINGSTOKE - 70D	BASINGSTOKE - 70D	BASINGSTOKE - 70D
32330	BASINGSTOKE - 70D	BASINGSTOKE - 70D	BASINGSTOKE - 70D	W/D	W/D	W/D	W/D
32331	BASINGSTOKE - 70D	BASINGSTOKE - 70D	BASINGSTOKE - 70D	BASINGSTOKE - 70D	BASINGSTOKE - 70D	BASINGSTOKE - 70D	BASINGSTOKE - 70D
32332	BASINGSTOKE - 70D	BASINGSTOKE - 70D	BASINGSTOKE - 70D	BASINGSTOKE - 70D	BASINGSTOKE - 70D	BASINGSTOKE - 70D	BASINGSTOKE - 70D
32333	BASINGSTOKE - 70D	BASINGSTOKE - 70D	BASINGSTOKE - 70D	BASINGSTOKE - 70D	BASINGSTOKE - 70D	BASINGSTOKE - 70D	BASINGSTOKE - 70D
			H15 4-6-0 (1907/14)				
30330	SALISBURY - 72B	SALISBURY - 72B	SALISBURY - 72B	SALISBURY - 72B	SALISBURY - 72B	SALISBURY - 72B	SALISBURY - 72B
30331	SALISBURY - 72B	SALISBURY - 72B	SALISBURY - 72B	SALISBURY - 72B	SALISBURY - 72B	SALISBURY - 72B	SALISBURY - 72B
30332	SALISBURY - 72B	SALISBURY - 72B	SALISBURY - 72B	SALISBURY - 72B	SALISBURY - 72B	SALISBURY - 72B	SALISBURY - 72B
30333	SALISBURY - 72B	SALISBURY - 72B	SALISBURY - 72B	SALISBURY - 72B	SALISBURY - 72B	SALISBURY - 72B	SALISBURY - 72B
30334	SALISBURY - 72B	SALISBURY - 72B	SALISBURY - 72B	SALISBURY - 72B	SALISBURY - 72B	SALISBURY - 72B	SALISBURY - 72B
30335	SALISBURY - 72B	SALISBURY - 72B	SALISBURY - 72B	SALISBURY - 72B	SALISBURY - 72B	SALISBURY - 72B	SALISBURY - 72B
			H15 4-6-0 (1914)				
30482	NINE ELMS - 70A	NINE ELMS - 70A	NINE ELMS - 70A	NINE ELMS - 70A	NINE ELMS - 70A	NINE ELMS - 70A	NINE ELMS - 70A
30483	EASTLEIGH - 71A	EASTLEIGH - 71A	EASTLEIGH - 71A	EASTLEIGH - 71A	EASTLEIGH - 71A	EASTLEIGH - 71A	EASTLEIGH - 71A
30484	NINE ELMS - 70A	NINE ELMS - 70A	NINE ELMS - 70A	NINE ELMS - 70A	NINE ELMS - 70A	NINE ELMS - 70A	NINE ELMS - 70A
30485	NINE ELMS - 70A	W/D	W/D	W/D	W/D	W/D	W/D
30486	NINE ELMS - 70A	NINE ELMS - 70A	NINE ELMS - 70A	NINE ELMS - 70A	NINE ELMS - 70A	NINE ELMS - 70A	NINE ELMS - 70A
30487	NINE ELMS - 70A	NINE ELMS - 70A	NINE ELMS - 70A	NINE ELMS - 70A	NINE ELMS - 70A	NINE ELMS - 70A	NINE ELMS - 70A
30488	NINE ELMS - 70A	NINE ELMS - 70A	NINE ELMS - 70A	NINE ELMS - 70A	NINE ELMS - 70A	NINE ELMS - 70A	NINE ELMS - 70A
30489	EASTLEIGH - 71A	EASTLEIGH - 71A	EASTLEIGH - 71A	EASTLEIGH - 71A	EASTLEIGH - 71A	EASTLEIGH - 71A	EASTLEIGH - 71A
30490	NINE ELMS - 70A	NINE ELMS - 70A	W/D	W/D	W/D	W/D	W/D
30491	EASTLEIGH - 71A	EASTLEIGH - 71A	EASTLEIGH - 71A	EASTLEIGH - 71A	EASTLEIGH - 71A	EASTLEIGH - 71A	EASTLEIGH - 71A
			H15 4-6-0 (1924)				
30473	EASTLEIGH - 71A	EASTLEIGH - 71A	EASTLEIGH - 71A	EASTLEIGH - 71A	EASTLEIGH - 71A	EASTLEIGH - 71A	EASTLEIGH - 71A
30474	EASTLEIGH - 71A	EASTLEIGH - 71A	EASTLEIGH - 71A	EASTLEIGH - 71A	EASTLEIGH - 71A	EASTLEIGH - 71A	EASTLEIGH - 71A
30475	EASTLEIGH - 71A	EASTLEIGH - 71A	EASTLEIGH - 71A	EASTLEIGH - 71A	EASTLEIGH - 71A	EASTLEIGH - 71A	EASTLEIGH - 71A
30476	EASTLEIGH - 71A	EASTLEIGH - 71A	EASTLEIGH - 71A	EASTLEIGH - 71A	EASTLEIGH - 71A	EASTLEIGH - 71A	EASTLEIGH - 71A
30477	EASTLEIGH - 71A	EASTLEIGH - 71A	EASTLEIGH - 71A	EASTLEIGH - 71A	EASTLEIGH - 71A	EASTLEIGH - 71A	EASTLEIGH - 71A
30478	EASTLEIGH - 71A	EASTLEIGH - 71A	NINE ELMS - 70A	NINE ELMS - 70A	NINE ELMS - 70A	NINE ELMS - 70A	NINE ELMS - 70A
30521	NINE ELMS - 70A	NINE ELMS - 70A	NINE ELMS - 70A	NINE ELMS - 70A	NINE ELMS - 70A	NINE ELMS - 70A	NINE ELMS - 70A
30522	NINE ELMS - 70A	NINE ELMS - 70A	NINE ELMS - 70A	NINE ELMS - 70A	NINE ELMS - 70A	NINE ELMS - 70A	NINE ELMS - 70A
30523	NINE ELMS - 70A	NINE ELMS - 70A	NINE ELMS - 70A	NINE ELMS - 70A	NINE ELMS - 70A	NINE ELMS - 70A	NINE ELMS - 70A
30524	NINE ELMS - 70A	NINE ELMS - 70A	NINE ELMS - 70A	NINE ELMS - 70A	NINE ELMS - 70A	NINE ELMS - 70A	NINE ELMS - 70A

loco	Jan-56	Apr-56	May-56	Aug-56	Oct-56	Nov-56	Jan-57
				U 2-6-0 (1928)			
31610 YEOVIL - 72C	YEOVIL - 72C	YEOVIL - 72C	YEOVIL - 72C	YEOVIL - 72C	YEOVIL - 72C	YEOVIL - 72C
31611 BASINGSTOKE - 70D	BASINGSTOKE - 70D	BASINGSTOKE - 70D	BASINGSTOKE - 70D	BASINGSTOKE - 70D	BASINGSTOKE - 70D	BASINGSTOKE - 70D
31612 READING (SR) - 70E	READING (SR) - 70E	READING (SR) - 70E	READING (SR) - 70E	READING (SR) - 70E	GUILDFORD - 70C	GUILDFORD - 70C
31613 EASTLEIGH - 71A	EASTLEIGH - 71A	EASTLEIGH - 71A	EASTLEIGH - 71A	EASTLEIGH - 71A	EASTLEIGH - 71A	EASTLEIGH - 71A
31614 BOURNEMOUTH - 71B	BOURNEMOUTH - 71B	BOURNEMOUTH - 71B	BOURNEMOUTH - 71B	BOURNEMOUTH - 71B	BOURNEMOUTH - 71B	BOURNEMOUTH - 71B
31615 BOURNEMOUTH - 71B	BOURNEMOUTH - 71B	BOURNEMOUTH - 71B	BOURNEMOUTH - 71B	BOURNEMOUTH - 71B	BOURNEMOUTH - 71B	BOURNEMOUTH - 71B
31616 GUILDFORD - 70C	GUILDFORD - 70C	GUILDFORD - 70C	GUILDFORD - 70C	GUILDFORD - 70C	GUILDFORD - 70C	GUILDFORD - 70C
31617 NINE ELMS - 70A	NINE ELMS - 70A	NINE ELMS - 70A	NINE ELMS - 70A	NINE ELMS - 70A	NINE ELMS - 70A	NINE ELMS - 70A
31618 EASTLEIGH - 71A	EASTLEIGH - 71A	EASTLEIGH - 71A	EASTLEIGH - 71A	EASTLEIGH - 71A	EASTLEIGH - 71A	EASTLEIGH - 71A
31619 EASTLEIGH - 71A	EASTLEIGH - 71A	EASTLEIGH - 71A	EASTLEIGH - 71A	EASTLEIGH - 71A	EASTLEIGH - 71A	EASTLEIGH - 71A
31620 EASTLEIGH - 71A	EASTLEIGH - 71A	EASTLEIGH - 71A	EASTLEIGH - 71A	EASTLEIGH - 71A	EASTLEIGH - 71A	EASTLEIGH - 71A
31621 NINE ELMS - 70A	NINE ELMS - 70A	NINE ELMS - 70A	NINE ELMS - 70A	NINE ELMS - 70A	NINE ELMS - 70A	NINE ELMS - 70A
31622 GUILDFORD - 70C	GUILDFORD - 70C	GUILDFORD - 70C	GUILDFORD - 70C	GUILDFORD - 70C	GUILDFORD - 70C	GUILDFORD - 70C
31623 DORCHESTER - 71C	DORCHESTER - 71C	DORCHESTER - 71C	DORCHESTER - 71C	DORCHESTER - 71C	DORCHESTER - 71C	DORCHESTER - 71C
31624 GUILDFORD - 70C	GUILDFORD - 70C	GUILDFORD - 70C	NINE ELMS - 70A	NINE ELMS - 70A	NINE ELMS - 70A	NINE ELMS - 70A
31625 GUILDFORD - 70C	GUILDFORD - 70C	GUILDFORD - 70C	GUILDFORD - 70C	GUILDFORD - 70C	GUILDFORD - 70C	GUILDFORD - 70C
31626 YEOVIL - 72C	YEOVIL - 72C	YEOVIL - 72C	YEOVIL - 72C	YEOVIL - 72C	YEOVIL - 72C	YEOVIL - 72C
31627 GUILDFORD - 70C	GUILDFORD - 70C	GUILDFORD - 70C	GUILDFORD - 70C	GUILDFORD - 70C	GUILDFORD - 70C	GUILDFORD - 70C
31628 GUILDFORD - 70C	GUILDFORD - 70C	GUILDFORD - 70C	GUILDFORD - 70C	GUILDFORD - 70C	GUILDFORD - 70C	GUILDFORD - 70C
31629 EASTLEIGH - 71A	EASTLEIGH - 71A	EASTLEIGH - 71A	EASTLEIGH - 71A	EASTLEIGH - 71A	EASTLEIGH - 71A	EASTLEIGH - 71A
31630 GUILDFORD - 70C	GUILDFORD - 70C	GUILDFORD - 70C	GUILDFORD - 70C	GUILDFORD - 70C	GUILDFORD - 70C	GUILDFORD - 70C
31631 GUILDFORD - 70C	GUILDFORD - 70C	GUILDFORD - 70C	GUILDFORD - 70C	GUILDFORD - 70C	GUILDFORD - 70C	GUILDFORD - 70C
31632 BOURNEMOUTH - 71B	BOURNEMOUTH - 71B	BOURNEMOUTH - 71B	BOURNEMOUTH - 71B	BOURNEMOUTH - 71B	BOURNEMOUTH - 71B	BOURNEMOUTH - 71B
31633 BASINGSTOKE - 70D	BASINGSTOKE - 70D	BASINGSTOKE - 70D	BASINGSTOKE - 70D	BASINGSTOKE - 70D	BASINGSTOKE - 70D	BASINGSTOKE - 70D
31634 NINE ELMS - 70A	NINE ELMS - 70A	NINE ELMS - 70A	NINE ELMS - 70A	NINE ELMS - 70A	NINE ELMS - 70A	NINE ELMS - 70A
31635 EASTLEIGH - 71A	EASTLEIGH - 71A	EXMOUTH JCN - 72A	EXMOUTH JCN - 72A	EXMOUTH JCN - 72A	EXMOUTH JCN - 72A	GUILDFORD - 70C
31636 EASTLEIGH - 71A	EASTLEIGH - 71A	EASTLEIGH - 71A	GUILDFORD - 70C	GUILDFORD - 70C	GUILDFORD - 70C	GUILDFORD - 70C
31637 FRATTON - 70F	FRATTON - 70F	FRATTON - 70F	FRATTON - 70F	FRATTON - 70F	FRATTON - 70F	FRATTON - 70F
31638 FRATTON - 70F	FRATTON - 70F	FRATTON - 70F	FRATTON - 70F	FRATTON - 70F	FRATTON - 70F	FRATTON - 70F
31639 EASTLEIGH - 71A	EASTLEIGH - 71A	EASTLEIGH - 71A	EASTLEIGH - 71A	EASTLEIGH - 71A	EASTLEIGH - 71A	EASTLEIGH - 71A
			U1 2-6-0 (2-6-4T R/B) 1925				
31890 B ARMS - 73B	B ARMS - 73B	B ARMS - 73B	B ARMS - 73B	B ARMS - 73B	B ARMS - 73B	B ARMS - 73B
			U1 2-6-0 (1925)				
31891 B ARMS - 73B	B ARMS - 73B	B ARMS - 73B	B ARMS - 73B	B ARMS - 73B	B ARMS - 73B	B ARMS - 73B
31892 FAVERSHAM - 73E	FAVERSHAM - 73E	FAVERSHAM - 73E	FAVERSHAM - 73E	FAVERSHAM - 73E	FAVERSHAM - 73E	FAVERSHAM - 73E
31893 FAVERSHAM - 73E	FAVERSHAM - 73E	FAVERSHAM - 73E	FAVERSHAM - 73E	FAVERSHAM - 73E	FAVERSHAM - 73E	FAVERSHAM - 73E
31894 STEWARTS LANE - 73A	STEWARTS LANE - 73A	STEWARTS LANE - 73A	STEWARTS LANE - 73A	STEWARTS LANE - 73A	STEWARTS LANE - 73A	STEWARTS LANE - 73A
31895 STEWARTS LANE - 73A	STEWARTS LANE - 73A	STEWARTS LANE - 73A	STEWARTS LANE - 73A	STEWARTS LANE - 73A	STEWARTS LANE - 73A	STEWARTS LANE - 73A
31896 STEWARTS LANE - 73A	STEWARTS LANE - 73A	STEWARTS LANE - 73A	STEWARTS LANE - 73A	STEWARTS LANE - 73A	STEWARTS LANE - 73A	STEWARTS LANE - 73A
31897 STEWARTS LANE - 73A	STEWARTS LANE - 73A	STEWARTS LANE - 73A	STEWARTS LANE - 73A	STEWARTS LANE - 73A	STEWARTS LANE - 73A	STEWARTS LANE - 73A
31898 STEWARTS LANE - 73A	STEWARTS LANE - 73A	STEWARTS LANE - 73A	STEWARTS LANE - 73A	STEWARTS LANE - 73A	STEWARTS LANE - 73A	STEWARTS LANE - 73A
31899 B ARMS - 73B	B ARMS - 73B	B ARMS - 73B	B ARMS - 73B	B ARMS - 73B	B ARMS - 73B	B ARMS - 73B
31900 B ARMS - 73B	B ARMS - 73B	B ARMS - 73B	B ARMS - 73B	B ARMS - 73B	B ARMS - 73B	B ARMS - 73B
31901 B ARMS - 73B	B ARMS - 73B	B ARMS - 73B	B ARMS - 73B	B ARMS - 73B	B ARMS - 73B	B ARMS - 73B
31902 B ARMS - 73B	B ARMS - 73B	B ARMS - 73B	B ARMS - 73B	B ARMS - 73B	B ARMS - 73B	B ARMS - 73B
31903 FAVERSHAM - 73E	FAVERSHAM - 73E	FAVERSHAM - 73E	FAVERSHAM - 73E	FAVERSHAM - 73E	FAVERSHAM - 73E	FAVERSHAM - 73E
31904 STEWARTS LANE - 73A	STEWARTS LANE - 73A	STEWARTS LANE - 73A	STEWARTS LANE - 73A	STEWARTS LANE - 73A	STEWARTS LANE - 73A	STEWARTS LANE - 73A
31905 STEWARTS LANE - 73A	STEWARTS LANE - 73A	STEWARTS LANE - 73A	STEWARTS LANE - 73A	STEWARTS LANE - 73A	STEWARTS LANE - 73A	STEWARTS LANE - 73A
31906 STEWARTS LANE - 73A	STEWARTS LANE - 73A	STEWARTS LANE - 73A	STEWARTS LANE - 73A	STEWARTS LANE - 73A	STEWARTS LANE - 73A	STEWARTS LANE - 73A
31907 STEWARTS LANE - 73A	STEWARTS LANE - 73A	STEWARTS LANE - 73A	STEWARTS LANE - 73A	STEWARTS LANE - 73A	STEWARTS LANE - 73A	STEWARTS LANE - 73A
31908 TONBRIDGE - 74D	TONBRIDGE - 74D	TONBRIDGE - 74D	TONBRIDGE - 74D	TONBRIDGE - 74D	TONBRIDGE - 74D	TONBRIDGE - 74D
31909 TONBRIDGE - 74D	TONBRIDGE - 74D	TONBRIDGE - 74D	TONBRIDGE - 74D	TONBRIDGE - 74D	TONBRIDGE - 74D	TONBRIDGE - 74D
31910 TONBRIDGE - 74D	TONBRIDGE - 74D	TONBRIDGE - 74D	TONBRIDGE - 74D	TONBRIDGE - 74D	TONBRIDGE - 74D	TONBRIDGE - 74D
			N15X 4-6-0 (1914/34)				
32329 BASINGSTOKE - 70D	BASINGSTOKE - 70D	BASINGSTOKE - 70D	W/D	W/D	W/D	W/D
32331 BASINGSTOKE - 70D	BASINGSTOKE - 70D	BASINGSTOKE - 70D	BASINGSTOKE - 70D	BASINGSTOKE - 70D	BASINGSTOKE - 70D	BASINGSTOKE - 70D
32333 BASINGSTOKE - 70D	W/D	W/D	W/D	W/D	W/D	W/D
			H15 4-6-0 (1907/14)				
30330 SALISBURY - 72B	SALISBURY - 72B	SALISBURY - 72B	SALISBURY - 72B	SALISBURY - 72B	SALISBURY - 72B	SALISBURY - 72B
30331 SALISBURY - 72B	SALISBURY - 72B	SALISBURY - 72B	SALISBURY - 72B	SALISBURY - 72B	SALISBURY - 72B	SALISBURY - 72B
30332 SALISBURY - 72B	SALISBURY - 72B	SALISBURY - 72B	SALISBURY - 72B	SALISBURY - 72B	W/D	W/D
30333 SALISBURY - 72B	SALISBURY - 72B	SALISBURY - 72B	SALISBURY - 72B	SALISBURY - 72B	SALISBURY - 72B	SALISBURY - 72B
30334 SALISBURY - 72B	SALISBURY - 72B	SALISBURY - 72B	SALISBURY - 72B	SALISBURY - 72B	SALISBURY - 72B	SALISBURY - 72B
30335 SALISBURY - 72B	SALISBURY - 72B	SALISBURY - 72B	SALISBURY - 72B	SALISBURY - 72B	SALISBURY - 72B	SALISBURY - 72B
			H15 4-6-0 (1914)				
30482 NINE ELMS - 70A	NINE ELMS - 70A	NINE ELMS - 70A	NINE ELMS - 70A	NINE ELMS - 70A	NINE ELMS - 70A	NINE ELMS - 70A
30483 EASTLEIGH - 71A	EASTLEIGH - 71A	EASTLEIGH - 71A	EASTLEIGH - 71A	EASTLEIGH - 71A	EASTLEIGH - 71A	EASTLEIGH - 71A
30484 NINE ELMS - 70A	NINE ELMS - 70A	NINE ELMS - 70A	NINE ELMS - 70A	NINE ELMS - 70A	NINE ELMS - 70A	NINÉ ELMS - 70A
30486 NINE ELMS - 70A	NINE ELMS - 70A	NINE ELMS - 70A	NINE ELMS - 70A	NINE ELMS - 70A	NINE ELMS - 70A	NINE ELMS - 70A
30487 NINE ELMS - 70A	NINE ELMS - 70A	NINE ELMS - 70A	NINE ELMS - 70A	NINE ELMS - 70A	NINE ELMS - 70A	NINE ELMS - 70A
30488 NINE ELMS - 70A	NINE ELMS - 70A	NINE ELMS - 70A	NINE ELMS - 70A	NINE ELMS - 70A	NINE ELMS - 70A	NINE ELMS - 70A
30489 EASTLEIGH - 71A	EASTLEIGH - 71A	EASTLEIGH - 71A	EASTLEIGH - 71A	EASTLEIGH - 71A	EASTLEIGH - 71A	EASTLEIGH - 71A
30491 EASTLEIGH - 71A	EASTLEIGH - 71A	EASTLEIGH - 71A	EASTLEIGH - 71A	EASTLEIGH - 71A	EASTLEIGH - 71A	EASTLEIGH - 71A
			H15 4-6-0 (1924)				
30473 EASTLEIGH - 71A	EASTLEIGH - 71A	EASTLEIGH - 71A	EASTLEIGH - 71A	EASTLEIGH - 71A	EASTLEIGH - 71A	EASTLEIGH - 71A
30474 EASTLEIGH - 71A	EASTLEIGH - 71A	EASTLEIGH - 71A	EASTLEIGH - 71A	EASTLEIGH - 71A	EASTLEIGH - 71A	EASTLEIGH - 71A
30475 EASTLEIGH - 71A	EASTLEIGH - 71A	EASTLEIGH - 71A	EASTLEIGH - 71A	EASTLEIGH - 71A	EASTLEIGH - 71A	EASTLEIGH - 71A
30476 EASTLEIGH - 71A	EASTLEIGH - 71A	EASTLEIGH - 71A	EASTLEIGH - 71A	EASTLEIGH - 71A	EASTLEIGH - 71A	EASTLEIGH - 71A
30477 EASTLEIGH - 71A	EASTLEIGH - 71A	EASTLEIGH - 71A	EASTLEIGH - 71A	EASTLEIGH - 71A	EASTLEIGH - 71A	EASTLEIGH - 71A
30478 NINE ELMS - 70A	NINE ELMS - 70A	NINE ELMS - 70A	NINE ELMS - 70A	NINE ELMS - 70A	NINE ELMS - 70A	NINE ELMS - 70A
30521 NINE ELMS - 70A	NINE ELMS - 70A	NINE ELMS - 70A	NINE ELMS - 70A	NINE ELMS - 70A	NINE ELMS - 70A	NINE ELMS - 70A
30522 NINE ELMS - 70A	NINE ELMS - 70A	NINE ELMS - 70A	NINE ELMS - 70A	NINE ELMS - 70A	NINE ELMS - 70A	NINE ELMS - 70A
30523 NINE ELMS - 70A	NINE ELMS - 70A	NINE ELMS - 70A	NINE ELMS - 70A	NINE ELMS - 70A	NINE ELMS - 70A	NINE ELMS - 70A
30524 NINE ELMS - 70A	NINE ELMS - 70A	NINE ELMS - 70A	NINE ELMS - 70A	NINE ELMS - 70A	NINE ELMS - 70A	NINE ELMS - 70A

loco	Mar-57	Jun-57	Jul-57	Oct-57	Jan-58	Feb-58	Mar-58
				U 2-6-0 (1928)			
31610	YEOVIL - 72C	YEOVIL - 72C	YEOVIL - 72C	YEOVIL - 72C	YEOVIL - 72C	YEOVIL - 72C	YEOVIL - 72C
31611	BASINGSTOKE - 70D	BASINGSTOKE - 70D	BASINGSTOKE - 70D	BASINGSTOKE - 70D	BASINGSTOKE - 70D	BASINGSTOKE - 70D	BASINGSTOKE - 70D
31612	GUILDFORD - 70C	GUILDFORD - 70C	GUILDFORD - 70C	GUILDFORD - 70C	GUILDFORD - 70C	GUILDFORD - 70C	GUILDFORD - 70C
31613	EASTLEIGH - 71A	EASTLEIGH - 71A	EASTLEIGH - 71A	EASTLEIGH - 71A	EASTLEIGH - 71A	EASTLEIGH - 71A	EASTLEIGH - 71A
31614	BOURNEMOUTH - 71B	BOURNEMOUTH - 71B	BOURNEMOUTH - 71B	BOURNEMOUTH - 71B	BOURNEMOUTH - 71B	BOURNEMOUTH - 71B	BOURNEMOUTH - 71B
31615	BOURNEMOUTH - 71B	BOURNEMOUTH - 71B	BOURNEMOUTH - 71B	BOURNEMOUTH - 71B	BOURNEMOUTH - 71B	BOURNEMOUTH - 71B	BOURNEMOUTH - 71B
31616	GUILDFORD - 70C	GUILDFORD - 70C	GUILDFORD - 70C	GUILDFORD - 70C	GUILDFORD - 70C	GUILDFORD - 70C	GUILDFORD - 70C
31617	NINE ELMS - 70A	NINE ELMS - 70A	NINE ELMS - 70A	NINE ELMS - 70A	NINE ELMS - 70A	NINE ELMS - 70A	NINE ELMS - 70A
31618	EASTLEIGH - 71A	EASTLEIGH - 71A	EASTLEIGH - 71A	EASTLEIGH - 71A	EASTLEIGH - 71A	EASTLEIGH - 71A	EASTLEIGH - 71A
31619	EASTLEIGH - 71A	EASTLEIGH - 71A	EASTLEIGH - 71A	EASTLEIGH - 71A	EASTLEIGH - 71A	EASTLEIGH - 71A	EASTLEIGH - 71A
31620	EASTLEIGH - 71A	EASTLEIGH - 71A	EASTLEIGH - 71A	EASTLEIGH - 71A	EASTLEIGH - 71A	EASTLEIGH - 71A	EASTLEIGH - 71A
31621	NINE ELMS - 70A	NINE ELMS - 70A	NINE ELMS - 70A	NINE ELMS - 70A	NINE ELMS - 70A	NINE ELMS - 70A	NINE ELMS - 70A
31622	GUILDFORD - 70C	GUILDFORD - 70C	GUILDFORD - 70C	GUILDFORD - 70C	GUILDFORD - 70C	GUILDFORD - 70C	GUILDFORD - 70C
31623	DORCHESTER - 71C	DORCHESTER - 71C	DORCHESTER - 71C	DORCHESTER - 71C	DORCHESTER - 71C	DORCHESTER - 71C	DORCHESTER - 71C
31624	NINE ELMS - 70A	NINE ELMS - 70A	NINE ELMS - 70A	NINE ELMS - 70A	NINE ELMS - 70A	NINE ELMS - 70A	NINE ELMS - 70A
31625	GUILDFORD - 70C	GUILDFORD - 70C	GUILDFORD - 70C	GUILDFORD - 70C	GUILDFORD - 70C	GUILDFORD - 70C	GUILDFORD - 70C
31626	YEOVIL - 72C	YEOVIL - 72C	YEOVIL - 72C	GUILDFORD - 70C	YEOVIL - 72C	GUILDFORD - 70C	YEOVIL - 72C
31627	GUILDFORD - 70C	GUILDFORD - 70C	GUILDFORD - 70C	GUILDFORD - 70C	GUILDFORD - 70C	GUILDFORD - 70C	GUILDFORD - 70C
31628	GUILDFORD - 70C	GUILDFORD - 70C	GUILDFORD - 70C	GUILDFORD - 70C	GUILDFORD - 70C	GUILDFORD - 70C	GUILDFORD - 70C
31629	EASTLEIGH - 71A	EASTLEIGH - 71A	EASTLEIGH - 71A	EASTLEIGH - 71A	EASTLEIGH - 71A	EASTLEIGH - 71A	EASTLEIGH - 71A
31630	GUILDFORD - 70C	GUILDFORD - 70C	GUILDFORD - 70C	GUILDFORD - 70C	GUILDFORD - 70C	GUILDFORD - 70C	GUILDFORD - 70C
31631	GUILDFORD - 70C	GUILDFORD - 70C	GUILDFORD - 70C	GUILDFORD - 70C	GUILDFORD - 70C	GUILDFORD - 70C	GUILDFORD - 70C
31632	BOURNEMOUTH - 71B	BOURNEMOUTH - 71B	BOURNEMOUTH - 71B	BOURNEMOUTH - 71B	BOURNEMOUTH - 71B	BOURNEMOUTH - 71B	BOURNEMOUTH - 71B
31633	BASINGSTOKE - 70D	BASINGSTOKE - 70D	BASINGSTOKE - 70D	BASINGSTOKE - 70D	BASINGSTOKE - 70D	BASINGSTOKE - 70D	BASINGSTOKE - 70D
31634	NINE ELMS - 70A	NINE ELMS - 70A	NINE ELMS - 70A	NINE ELMS - 70A	NINE ELMS - 70A	NINE ELMS - 70A	NINE ELMS - 70A
31635	GUILDFORD - 70C	GUILDFORD - 70C	GUILDFORD - 70C	GUILDFORD - 70C	GUILDFORD - 70C	GUILDFORD - 70C	GUILDFORD - 70C
31636	GUILDFORD - 70C	GUILDFORD - 70C	GUILDFORD - 70C	GUILDFORD - 70C	GUILDFORD - 70C	GUILDFORD - 70C	GUILDFORD - 70C
31637	FRATTON - 70F	FRATTON - 70F	FRATTON - 70F	FRATTON - 70F	FRATTON - 70F	FRATTON - 70F	FRATTON - 70F
31638	FRATTON - 70F	FRATTON - 70F	FRATTON - 70F	FRATTON - 70F	FRATTON - 70F	FRATTON - 70F	FRATTON - 70F
31639	EASTLEIGH - 71A	EASTLEIGH - 71A	EASTLEIGH - 71A	EASTLEIGH - 71A	EASTLEIGH - 71A	EASTLEIGH - 71A	EASTLEIGH - 71A
				U1 2-6-0 (2-6-4T R/B) 1925			
31890	B ARMS - 73B	B ARMS - 73B	B ARMS - 73B	B ARMS - 73B	B ARMS - 73B	B ARMS - 73B	B ARMS - 73B
				U1 2-6-0 (1925)			
31891	B ARMS - 73B	B ARMS - 73B	B ARMS - 73B	B ARMS - 73B	B ARMS - 73B	B ARMS - 73B	B ARMS - 73B
31892	FAVERSHAM - 73E	FAVERSHAM - 73E	FAVERSHAM - 73E	FAVERSHAM - 73E	FAVERSHAM - 73E	FAVERSHAM - 73E	FAVERSHAM - 73E
31893	FAVERSHAM - 73E	FAVERSHAM - 73E	FAVERSHAM - 73E	FAVERSHAM - 73E	FAVERSHAM - 73E	FAVERSHAM - 73E	FAVERSHAM - 73E
31894	TONBRIDGE - 74D	STEWARTS LANE - 73A	STEWARTS LANE - 73A	STEWARTS LANE - 73A	STEWARTS LANE - 73A	STEWARTS LANE - 73A	STEWARTS LANE - 73A
31895	STEWARTS LANE - 73A	STEWARTS LANE - 73A	STEWARTS LANE - 73A	STEWARTS LANE - 73A	STEWARTS LANE - 73A	STEWARTS LANE - 73A	STEWARTS LANE - 73A
31896	TONBRIDGE - 74D	TONBRIDGE - 74D	TONBRIDGE - 74D	TONBRIDGE - 74D	TONBRIDGE - 74D	TONBRIDGE - 74D	TONBRIDGE - 74D
31897	STEWARTS LANE - 73A	STEWARTS LANE - 73A	STEWARTS LANE - 73A	STEWARTS LANE - 73A	STEWARTS LANE - 73A	STEWARTS LANE - 73A	STEWARTS LANE - 73A
31898	STEWARTS LANE - 73A	STEWARTS LANE - 73A	STEWARTS LANE - 73A	STEWARTS LANE - 73A	STEWARTS LANE - 73A	STEWARTS LANE - 73A	STEWARTS LANE - 73A
31899	B ARMS - 73B	B ARMS - 73B	B ARMS - 73B	B ARMS - 73B	B ARMS - 73B	B ARMS - 73B	B ARMS - 73B
31900	B ARMS - 73B	B ARMS - 73B	B ARMS - 73B	B ARMS - 73B	B ARMS - 73B	B ARMS - 73B	B ARMS - 73B
31901	B ARMS - 73B	B ARMS - 73B	B ARMS - 73B	B ARMS - 73B	B ARMS - 73B	B ARMS - 73B	B ARMS - 73B
31902	B ARMS - 73B	B ARMS - 73B	B ARMS - 73B	B ARMS - 73B	B ARMS - 73B	B ARMS - 73B	B ARMS - 73B
31903	FAVERSHAM - 73E	FAVERSHAM - 73E	FAVERSHAM - 73E	FAVERSHAM - 73E	FAVERSHAM - 73E	FAVERSHAM - 73E	FAVERSHAM - 73E
31904	STEWARTS LANE - 73A	STEWARTS LANE - 73A	STEWARTS LANE - 73A	STEWARTS LANE - 73A	STEWARTS LANE - 73A	STEWARTS LANE - 73A	STEWARTS LANE - 73A
31905	STEWARTS LANE - 73A	STEWARTS LANE - 73A	STEWARTS LANE - 73A	STEWARTS LANE - 73A	STEWARTS LANE - 73A	STEWARTS LANE - 73A	STEWARTS LANE - 73A
31906	STEWARTS LANE - 73A	STEWARTS LANE - 73A	STEWARTS LANE - 73A	STEWARTS LANE - 73A	STEWARTS LANE - 73A	STEWARTS LANE - 73A	STEWARTS LANE - 73A
31907	STEWARTS LANE - 73A	STEWARTS LANE - 73A	STEWARTS LANE - 73A	STEWARTS LANE - 73A	STEWARTS LANE - 73A	STEWARTS LANE - 73A	STEWARTS LANE - 73A
31908	TONBRIDGE - 74D	TONBRIDGE - 74D	TONBRIDGE - 74D	TONBRIDGE - 74D	TONBRIDGE - 74D	TONBRIDGE - 74D	TONBRIDGE - 74D
31909	TONBRIDGE - 74D	TONBRIDGE - 74D	TONBRIDGE - 74D	TONBRIDGE - 74D	TONBRIDGE - 74D	TONBRIDGE - 74D	TONBRIDGE - 74D
31910	TONBRIDGE - 74D	TONBRIDGE - 74D	TONBRIDGE - 74D	TONBRIDGE - 74D	TONBRIDGE - 74D	TONBRIDGE - 74D	TONBRIDGE - 74D
				N15X 4-6-0 (1914/34)			
32331	BASINGSTOKE - 70D	BASINGSTOKE - 70D	W/D	W/D	W/D	W/D	W/D
				H15 4-6-0 (1907/14)			
30330	SALISBURY - 72B	W/D	W/D	W/D	W/D	W/D	W/D
30331	SALISBURY - 72B	SALISBURY - 72B	SALISBURY - 72B	SALISBURY - 72B	SALISBURY - 72B	SALISBURY - 72B	SALISBURY - 72B
30333	SALISBURY - 72B	SALISBURY - 72B	SALISBURY - 72B	SALISBURY - 72B	SALISBURY - 72B	SALISBURY - 72B	SALISBURY - 72B
30334	SALISBURY - 72B	SALISBURY - 72B	SALISBURY - 72B	SALISBURY - 72B	SALISBURY - 72B	SALISBURY - 72B	SALISBURY - 72B
30335	SALISBURY - 72B	SALISBURY - 72B	SALISBURY - 72B	SALISBURY - 72B	SALISBURY - 72B		
				H15 4-6-0 (1914)			
30482	NINE ELMS - 70A	NINE ELMS - 70A	NINE ELMS - 70A	NINE ELMS - 70A	NINE ELMS - 70A	NINE ELMS - 70A	NINE ELMS - 70A
30483	EASTLEIGH - 71A	EASTLEIGH - 71A	W/D	W/D	W/D	W/D	W/D
30484	NINE ELMS - 70A	NINE ELMS - 70A	NINE ELMS - 70A	NINE ELMS - 70A	NINE ELMS - 70A	NINE ELMS - 70A	NINE ELMS - 70A
30486	NINE ELMS - 70A	NINE ELMS - 70A	NINE ELMS - 70A	NINE ELMS - 70A	NINE ELMS - 70A	NINE ELMS - 70A	NINE ELMS - 70A
30487	NINE ELMS - 70A	NINE ELMS - 70A	NINE ELMS - 70A	NINE ELMS - 70A	W/D	W/D	W/D
30488	NINE ELMS - 70A	NINE ELMS - 70A	NINE ELMS - 70A	NINE ELMS - 70A	NINE ELMS - 70A	NINE ELMS - 70A	NINE ELMS - 70A
30489	EASTLEIGH - 71A	EASTLEIGH - 71A	EASTLEIGH - 71A	EASTLEIGH - 71A	EASTLEIGH - 71A	EASTLEIGH - 71A	EASTLEIGH - 71A
30491	EASTLEIGH - 71A	EASTLEIGH - 71A	EASTLEIGH - 71A	EASTLEIGH - 71A	EASTLEIGH - 71A	EASTLEIGH - 71A	EASTLEIGH - 71A
				H15 4-6-0 (1924)			
30473	EASTLEIGH - 71A	EASTLEIGH - 71A	EASTLEIGH - 71A	EASTLEIGH - 71A	EASTLEIGH - 71A	EASTLEIGH - 71A	EASTLEIGH - 71A
30474	EASTLEIGH - 71A	EASTLEIGH - 71A	EASTLEIGH - 71A	EASTLEIGH - 71A	EASTLEIGH - 71A	EASTLEIGH - 71A	EASTLEIGH - 71A
30475	EASTLEIGH - 71A	EASTLEIGH - 71A	EASTLEIGH - 71A	EASTLEIGH - 71A	EASTLEIGH - 71A	EASTLEIGH - 71A	EASTLEIGH - 71A
30476	EASTLEIGH - 71A	EASTLEIGH - 71A	EASTLEIGH - 71A	EASTLEIGH - 71A	EASTLEIGH - 71A	EASTLEIGH - 71A	EASTLEIGH - 71A
30477	EASTLEIGH - 71A	EASTLEIGH - 71A	EASTLEIGH - 71A	EASTLEIGH - 71A	EASTLEIGH - 71A	EASTLEIGH - 71A	EASTLEIGH - 71A
30478	NINE ELMS - 70A	NINE ELMS - 70A	NINE ELMS - 70A	NINE ELMS - 70A	NINE ELMS - 70A	NINE ELMS - 70A	NINE ELMS - 70A
30521	NINE ELMS - 70A	NINE ELMS - 70A	NINE ELMS - 70A	NINE ELMS - 70A	NINE ELMS - 70A	NINE ELMS - 70A	NINE ELMS - 70A
30522	NINE ELMS - 70A	NINE ELMS - 70A	NINE ELMS - 70A	NINE ELMS - 70A	NINE ELMS - 70A	NINE ELMS - 70A	NINE ELMS - 70A
30523	NINE ELMS - 70A	NINE ELMS - 70A	NINE ELMS - 70A	NINE ELMS - 70A	NINE ELMS - 70A	NINE ELMS - 70A	NINE ELMS - 70A
30524	NINE ELMS - 70A	NINE ELMS - 70A	NINE ELMS - 70A	NINE ELMS - 70A	NINE ELMS - 70A	NINE ELMS - 70A	NINE ELMS - 70A

The 2-6-0 classes were used in considerable numbers on the secondary lines of all three sections of the Southern but did not, except at the height of the holiday peak, play a significant role in main line workings. The N class, for example, had a strong presence west of Exeter whilst the U's could be found in large numbers on the Reading - Redhill and between Salisbury - Portsmouth routes.

Several of the Southern's more successful 4-6-0 classes had been rebuilt from earlier engines although none more drastically than the N15X 'Remembrance' class which were an attempt to integrate the LBSCR 4-6-4 express tanks, redundant after electrification, into the N15 class. Rebuilt as 4-6-0 tender engines for use on the LSWR they were not the equal of an N15 and gravitated to Basingstoke where for many years they worked a proportion of the slow trains to London in addition to workings on the Reading branch and to Eastleigh. From the mid-1950's they were replaced by BR standard 4MT locomotives, withdrawal taking place between 1955 and 1957.

loco	May-58	Oct-58	Mar-59	Jun-59	Jul-59	Aug-59	Oct-59
			U 2-6-0 (1928)				
31610	YEOVIL - 72C	YEOVIL - 72C	YEOVIL - 72C	YEOVIL - 72C	YEOVIL - 72C	YEOVIL - 72C	YEOVIL - 72C
31611	BASINGSTOKE - 70D	EASTLEIGH - 71A	BASINGSTOKE - 70D	BASINGSTOKE - 70D	BASINGSTOKE - 70D	BASINGSTOKE - 70D	BASINGSTOKE - 70D
31612	GUILDFORD - 70C	GUILDFORD - 70C	GUILDFORD - 70C	GUILDFORD - 70C	GUILDFORD - 70C	GUILDFORD - 70C	GUILDFORD - 70C
31613	EASTLEIGH - 71A	EASTLEIGH - 71A	YEOVIL - 72C	YEOVIL - 72C	YEOVIL - 72C	YEOVIL - 72C	YEOVIL - 72C
31614	BOURNEMOUTH - 71B	BOURNEMOUTH - 71B	BOURNEMOUTH - 71B	FRATTON - 70F	FRATTON - 70F	FRATTON - 70F	FRATTON - 70F
31615	BOURNEMOUTH - 71B	BOURNEMOUTH - 71B	BOURNEMOUTH - 71B	GUILDFORD - 70C	GUILDFORD - 70C	GUILDFORD - 70C	GUILDFORD - 70C
31616	GUILDFORD - 70C	GUILDFORD - 70C	GUILDFORD - 70C	GUILDFORD - 70C	GUILDFORD - 70C	GUILDFORD - 70C	GUILDFORD - 70C
31617	NINE ELMS - 70A	NINE ELMS - 70A	NINE ELMS - 70A	NINE ELMS - 70A	NINE ELMS - 70A	NINE ELMS - 70A	NINE ELMS - 70A
31618	EASTLEIGH - 71A	EASTLEIGH - 71A	EASTLEIGH - 71A	EASTLEIGH - 71A	EASTLEIGH - 71A	EASTLEIGH - 71A	EASTLEIGH - 71A
31619	EASTLEIGH - 71A	EASTLEIGH - 71A	EASTLEIGH - 71A	EASTLEIGH - 71A	EASTLEIGH - 71A	EASTLEIGH - 71A	EASTLEIGH - 71A
31620	EASTLEIGH - 71A	EASTLEIGH - 71A	EASTLEIGH - 71A	EASTLEIGH - 71A	EASTLEIGH - 71A	EASTLEIGH - 71A	EASTLEIGH - 71A
31621	NINE ELMS - 70A	NINE ELMS - 70A	NINE ELMS - 70A	NINE ELMS - 70A	NINE ELMS - 70A	NINE ELMS - 70A	NINE ELMS - 70A
31622	GUILDFORD - 70C	GUILDFORD - 70C	GUILDFORD - 70C	GUILDFORD - 70C	GUILDFORD - 70C	GUILDFORD - 70C	GUILDFORD - 70C
31623	DORCHESTER - 71C	DORCHESTER - 71C	DORCHESTER - 71C	DORCHESTER - 71C	DORCHESTER - 71C	DORCHESTER - 71C	DORCHESTER - 71C
31624	NINE ELMS - 70A	NINE ELMS - 70A	NINE ELMS - 70A	NINE ELMS - 70A	NINE ELMS - 70A	NINE ELMS - 70A	NINE ELMS - 70A
31625	GUILDFORD - 70C	GUILDFORD - 70C	GUILDFORD - 70C	GUILDFORD - 70C	GUILDFORD - 70C	GUILDFORD - 70C	GUILDFORD - 70C
31626	YEOVIL - 72C	EXMOUTH JCN - 72A	YEOVIL - 72C	YEOVIL - 72C	YEOVIL - 72C	YEOVIL - 72C	YEOVIL - 72C
31627	GUILDFORD - 70C	GUILDFORD - 70C	GUILDFORD - 70C	GUILDFORD - 70C	GUILDFORD - 70C	GUILDFORD - 70C	GUILDFORD - 70C
31628	GUILDFORD - 70C	GUILDFORD - 70C	GUILDFORD - 70C	GUILDFORD - 70C	GUILDFORD - 70C	GUILDFORD - 70C	GUILDFORD - 70C
31629	EASTLEIGH - 71A	EASTLEIGH - 71A	EASTLEIGH - 71A	EASTLEIGH - 71A	EASTLEIGH - 71A	EASTLEIGH - 71A	EASTLEIGH - 71A
31630	GUILDFORD - 70C	GUILDFORD - 70C	GUILDFORD - 70C	GUILDFORD - 70C	GUILDFORD - 70C	GUILDFORD - 70C	GUILDFORD - 70C
31631	GUILDFORD - 70C	GUILDFORD - 70C	GUILDFORD - 70C	GUILDFORD - 70C	GUILDFORD - 70C	GUILDFORD - 70C	GUILDFORD - 70C
31632	BOURNEMOUTH - 71B	BOURNEMOUTH - 71B	BOURNEMOUTH - 71B	EASTLEIGH - 71A	EASTLEIGH - 71A	EASTLEIGH - 71A	EASTLEIGH - 71A
31633	BASINGSTOKE - 70D	EASTLEIGH - 71A	YEOVIL - 72C	YEOVIL - 72C	YEOVIL - 72C	YEOVIL - 72C	YEOVIL - 72C
31634	NINE ELMS - 70A	NINE ELMS - 70A	NINE ELMS - 70A	NINE ELMS - 70A	NINE ELMS - 70A	NINE ELMS - 70A	NINE ELMS - 70A
31635	GUILDFORD - 70C	GUILDFORD - 70C	GUILDFORD - 70C	GUILDFORD - 70C	GUILDFORD - 70C	GUILDFORD - 70C	GUILDFORD - 70C
31636	GUILDFORD - 70C	GUILDFORD - 70C	GUILDFORD - 70C	GUILDFORD - 70C	GUILDFORD - 70C	GUILDFORD - 70C	GUILDFORD - 70C
31637	FRATTON - 70F	FRATTON - 70F	GUILDFORD - 70C	GUILDFORD - 70C	GUILDFORD - 70C	GUILDFORD - 70C	GUILDFORD - 70C
31638	FRATTON - 70F	FRATTON - 70F	FRATTON - 70F	FRATTON - 70F	FRATTON - 70F	FRATTON - 70F	FRATTON - 70F
31639	EASTLEIGH - 71A	EASTLEIGH - 71A	EASTLEIGH - 71A	EASTLEIGH - 71A	EASTLEIGH - 71A	EASTLEIGH - 71A	EASTLEIGH - 71A
			U1 2-6-0 (2-6-4T R/B) 1925				
31890	B.ARMS - 73B	B.ARMS - 73B	B.ARMS - 73B	BRIGHTON - 75A	BRIGHTON - 75A	BRIGHTON - 75A	BRIGHTON - 75A
			U1 2-6-0 (1925)				
31891	B.ARMS - 73B	B.ARMS - 73B	B.ARMS - 73B	BRIGHTON - 75A	BRIGHTON - 75A	BRIGHTON - 75A	BRIGHTON - 75A
31892	FAVERSHAM - 73E	FAVERSHAM - 73E	FAVERSHAM - 73E	FELTHAM - 70B	FELTHAM - 70B	FELTHAM - 70B	FELTHAM - 70B
31893	FAVERSHAM - 73E	FAVERSHAM - 73E	FAVERSHAM - 73E	FELTHAM - 70B	FELTHAM - 70B	FELTHAM - 70B	FELTHAM - 70B
31894	STEWARTS LANE - 73A	STEWARTS LANE - 73A	STEWARTS LANE - 73A	STEWARTS LANE - 73A	STEWARTS LANE - 73A	STEWARTS LANE - 73A	STEWARTS LANE - 73A
31895	STEWARTS LANE - 73A	STEWARTS LANE - 73A	STEWARTS LANE - 73A	STEWARTS LANE - 73A	STEWARTS LANE - 73A	STEWARTS LANE - 73A	STEWARTS LANE - 73A
31896	TONBRIDGE - 74D	TONBRIDGE - 73J	TONBRIDGE - 73J	STEWARTS LANE - 73A	STEWARTS LANE - 73A	STEWARTS LANE - 73A	STEWARTS LANE - 73A
31897	STEWARTS LANE - 73A	STEWARTS LANE - 73A	STEWARTS LANE - 73A	STEWARTS LANE - 73A	STEWARTS LANE - 73A	STEWARTS LANE - 73A	STEWARTS LANE - 73A
31898	STEWARTS LANE - 73A	STEWARTS LANE - 73A	STEWARTS LANE - 73A	STEWARTS LANE - 73A	STEWARTS LANE - 73A	STEWARTS LANE - 73A	STEWARTS LANE - 73A
31899	B.ARMS - 73B	B.ARMS - 73B	B.ARMS - 73B	STEWARTS LANE - 73A	STEWARTS LANE - 73A	STEWARTS LANE - 73A	STEWARTS LANE - 73A
31900	B.ARMS - 73B	B.ARMS - 73B	B.ARMS - 73B	STEWARTS LANE - 73A	STEWARTS LANE - 73A	STEWARTS LANE - 73A	STEWARTS LANE - 73A
31901	B.ARMS - 73B	B.ARMS - 73B	B.ARMS - 73B	TONBRIDGE - 73J	TONBRIDGE - 73J	TONBRIDGE - 73J	TONBRIDGE - 73J
31902	B.ARMS - 73B	B.ARMS - 73B	B.ARMS - 73B	TONBRIDGE - 73J	TONBRIDGE - 73J	TONBRIDGE - 73J	TONBRIDGE - 73J
31903	FAVERSHAM - 73E	FAVERSHAM - 73E	FAVERSHAM - 73E	TONBRIDGE - 73J	TONBRIDGE - 73J	TONBRIDGE - 73J	TONBRIDGE - 73J
31904	STEWARTS LANE - 73A	STEWARTS LANE - 73A	STEWARTS LANE - 73A	TONBRIDGE - 73J	TONBRIDGE - 73J	TONBRIDGE - 73J	TONBRIDGE - 73J
31905	STEWARTS LANE - 73A	STEWARTS LANE - 73A	STEWARTS LANE - 73A	TONBRIDGE - 73J	TONBRIDGE - 73J	TONBRIDGE - 73J	TONBRIDGE - 73J
31906	STEWARTS LANE - 73A	STEWARTS LANE - 73A	STEWARTS LANE - 73A	TONBRIDGE - 73J	TONBRIDGE - 73J	TONBRIDGE - 73J	TONBRIDGE - 73J
31907	STEWARTS LANE - 73A	STEWARTS LANE - 73A	STEWARTS LANE - 73A	TONBRIDGE - 73J	TONBRIDGE - 73J	TONBRIDGE - 73J	TONBRIDGE - 73J
31908	TONBRIDGE - 74D	TONBRIDGE - 73J	TONBRIDGE - 73J	TONBRIDGE - 73J	TONBRIDGE - 73J	TONBRIDGE - 73J	TONBRIDGE - 73J
31909	TONBRIDGE - 74D	TONBRIDGE - 73J	TONBRIDGE - 73J	TONBRIDGE - 73J	TONBRIDGE - 73J	TONBRIDGE - 73J	TONBRIDGE - 73J
31910	TONBRIDGE - 74D	TONBRIDGE - 73J	TONBRIDGE - 73J	TONBRIDGE - 73J	TONBRIDGE - 73J	TONBRIDGE - 73J	TONBRIDGE - 73J
			H15 4-6-0 (1907/14)				
30331	SALISBURY - 72B	SALISBURY - 72B	SALISBURY - 72B	SALISBURY - 72B	SALISBURY - 72B	SALISBURY - 72B	SALISBURY - 72B
30333	SALISBURY - 72B	SALISBURY - 72B	W/D	W/D	W/D	W/D	W/D
30334	SALISBURY - 72B	W/D	W/D	W/D	W/D	W/D	W/D
30335	SALISBURY - 72B	SALISBURY - 72B	SALISBURY - 72B	W/D	W/D	W/D	W/D
			H15 4-6-0 (1914)				
30482	NINE ELMS - 70A	NINE ELMS - 70A	NINE ELMS - 70A	W/D	W/D	W/D	W/D
30484	NINE ELMS - 70A	NINE ELMS - 70A	NINE ELMS - 70A	W/D	W/D	W/D	W/D
30486	NINE ELMS - 70A	NINE ELMS - 70A	NINE ELMS - 70A	NINE ELMS - 70A	W/D	W/D	W/D
30488	NINE ELMS - 70A	NINE ELMS - 70A	NINE ELMS - 70A	NINE ELMS - 70A	NINE ELMS - 70A	NINE ELMS - 70A	NINE ELMS - 70A
30489	EASTLEIGH - 71A	EASTLEIGH - 71A	EASTLEIGH - 71A	EASTLEIGH - 71A	EASTLEIGH - 71A	EASTLEIGH - 71A	EASTLEIGH - 71A
30491	EASTLEIGH - 71A	EASTLEIGH - 71A	EASTLEIGH - 71A	EASTLEIGH - 71A	EASTLEIGH - 71A	EASTLEIGH - 71A	EASTLEIGH - 71A
			H15 4-6-0 (1924)				
30473	EASTLEIGH - 71A	EASTLEIGH - 71A	EASTLEIGH - 71A	EASTLEIGH - 71A	EASTLEIGH - 71A	W/D	W/D
30474	EASTLEIGH - 71A	EASTLEIGH - 71A	EASTLEIGH - 71A	EASTLEIGH - 71A	EASTLEIGH - 71A	EASTLEIGH - 71A	EASTLEIGH - 71A
30475	EASTLEIGH - 71A	EASTLEIGH - 71A	EASTLEIGH - 71A	EASTLEIGH - 71A	EASTLEIGH - 71A	EASTLEIGH - 71A	EASTLEIGH - 71A
30476	EASTLEIGH - 71A	EASTLEIGH - 71A	EASTLEIGH - 71A	EASTLEIGH - 71A	EASTLEIGH - 71A	EASTLEIGH - 71A	EASTLEIGH - 71A
30477	EASTLEIGH - 71A	EASTLEIGH - 71A	EASTLEIGH - 71A	EASTLEIGH - 71A	EASTLEIGH - 71A	W/D	W/D
30478	NINE ELMS - 70A	NINE ELMS - 70A	NINE ELMS - 70A	W/D	W/D	W/D	W/D
30521	NINE ELMS - 70A	NINE ELMS - 70A	NINE ELMS - 70A	NINE ELMS - 70A	NINE ELMS - 70A	NINE ELMS - 70A	NINE ELMS - 70A
30522	NINE ELMS - 70A	NINE ELMS - 70A	NINE ELMS - 70A	SALISBURY - 72B	SALISBURY - 72B	SALISBURY - 72B	SALISBURY - 72B
30523	NINE ELMS - 70A	NINE ELMS - 70A	NINE ELMS - 70A	SALISBURY - 72B	SALISBURY - 72B	SALISBURY - 72B	SALISBURY - 72B
30524	NINE ELMS - 70A	NINE ELMS - 70A	NINE ELMS - 70A	SALISBURY - 72B	SALISBURY - 72B	SALISBURY - 72B	SALISBURY - 72B

Although nominally a mixed traffic design, the H15 4-6-0's spent most of their existence on goods workings, particularly those between London and the Southampton area; the class being divided between Nine Elms, Salisbury and Eastleigh. Although no distinction was made by the operating department between the various H15 'types' (which in reality were three separate classes, one being a rebuild of an early Drummond 4-6-0 series), withdrawals at first effected the older engines, the pace being rather slow at first. In 1959 when the South Western found itself with an ample supply of engines redundant from the LCDR electrification, the rate of withdrawals increased although thirteen examples, including members from each subdivision, survived to see the 1960's.

loco	Dec-59	Feb-60	Mar-60	Apr-60	Jul-60	Aug-60	Sep-60	Nov-60
U 2-6-0 (1928)								
31610	YEOVIL - 72C	GUILDFORD - 70C	GUILDFORD - 70C	GUILDFORD - 70C	GUILDFORD - 70C	GUILDFORD - 70C	GUILDFORD - 70C	GUILDFORD - 70C
31611	BASINGSTOKE - 70D	BASINGSTOKE - 70D	BASINGSTOKE - 70D	BASINGSTOKE - 70D	BASINGSTOKE - 70D	BASINGSTOKE - 70D	BASINGSTOKE - 70D	BASINGSTOKE - 70D
31612	GUILDFORD - 70C	GUILDFORD - 70C	GUILDFORD - 70C	GUILDFORD - 70C	GUILDFORD - 70C	GUILDFORD - 70C	GUILDFORD - 70C	GUILDFORD - 70C
31613	YEOVIL - 72C	EASTLEIGH - 71A	EASTLEIGH - 71A	EASTLEIGH - 71A	EASTLEIGH - 71A	EASTLEIGH - 71A	EASTLEIGH - 71A	EASTLEIGH - 71A
31614	GUILDFORD - 70C	YEOVIL - 72C	YEOVIL - 72C	YEOVIL - 72C	YEOVIL - 72C	YEOVIL - 72C	YEOVIL - 72C	YEOVIL - 72C
31615	GUILDFORD - 70C	GUILDFORD - 70C	GUILDFORD - 70C	GUILDFORD - 70C	GUILDFORD - 70C	GUILDFORD - 70C	GUILDFORD - 70C	GUILDFORD - 70C
31616	GUILDFORD - 70C	REDHILL - 75B	REDHILL - 75B	REDHILL - 75B	REDHILL - 75B	REDHILL - 75B	REDHILL - 75B	REDHILL - 75B
31617	NINE ELMS - 70A	NINE ELMS - 70A	NINE ELMS - 70A	NINE ELMS - 70A	NINE ELMS - 70A	NINE ELMS - 70A	NINE ELMS - 70A	NINE ELMS - 70A
31618	EASTLEIGH - 71A	EASTLEIGH - 71A	EASTLEIGH - 71A	EASTLEIGH - 71A	EASTLEIGH - 71A	EASTLEIGH - 71A	EASTLEIGH - 71A	EASTLEIGH - 71A
31619	EASTLEIGH - 71A	EASTLEIGH - 71A	EASTLEIGH - 71A	EASTLEIGH - 71A	EASTLEIGH - 71A	EASTLEIGH - 71A	EASTLEIGH - 71A	EASTLEIGH - 71A
31620	EASTLEIGH - 71A	EASTLEIGH - 71A	EASTLEIGH - 71A	EASTLEIGH - 71A	EASTLEIGH - 71A	EASTLEIGH - 71A	EASTLEIGH - 71A	EASTLEIGH - 71A
31621	NINE ELMS - 70A	NINE ELMS - 70A	NINE ELMS - 70A	NINE ELMS - 70A	NINE ELMS - 70A	NINE ELMS - 70A	NINE ELMS - 70A	NINE ELMS - 70A
31622	GUILDFORD - 70C	GUILDFORD - 70C	GUILDFORD - 70C	GUILDFORD - 70C	GUILDFORD - 70C	GUILDFORD - 70C	GUILDFORD - 70C	GUILDFORD - 70C
31623	DORCHESTER - 71C	GUILDFORD - 70C	GUILDFORD - 70C	GUILDFORD - 70C	GUILDFORD - 70C	GUILDFORD - 70C	GUILDFORD - 70C	GUILDFORD - 70C
31624	NINE ELMS - 70A	NINE ELMS - 70A	NINE ELMS - 70A	NINE ELMS - 70A	NINE ELMS - 70A	NINE ELMS - 70A	NINE ELMS - 70A	NINE ELMS - 70A
31625	GUILDFORD - 70C	GUILDFORD - 70C	GUILDFORD - 70C	GUILDFORD - 70C	GUILDFORD - 70C	GUILDFORD - 70C	GUILDFORD - 70C	GUILDFORD - 70C
31626	YEOVIL - 72C	EASTLEIGH - 71A	EASTLEIGH - 71A	EASTLEIGH - 71A	EASTLEIGH - 71A	EASTLEIGH - 71A	EASTLEIGH - 71A	EASTLEIGH - 71A
31627	GUILDFORD - 70C	GUILDFORD - 70C	GUILDFORD - 70C	GUILDFORD - 70C	GUILDFORD - 70C	GUILDFORD - 70C	GUILDFORD - 70C	GUILDFORD - 70C
31628	GUILDFORD - 70C	GUILDFORD - 70C	GUILDFORD - 70C	GUILDFORD - 70C	GUILDFORD - 70C	GUILDFORD - 70C	GUILDFORD - 70C	GUILDFORD - 70C
31629	EASTLEIGH - 71A	EASTLEIGH - 71A	EASTLEIGH - 71A	EASTLEIGH - 71A	EASTLEIGH - 71A	EASTLEIGH - 71A	EASTLEIGH - 71A	EASTLEIGH - 71A
31630	GUILDFORD - 70C	GUILDFORD - 70C	GUILDFORD - 70C	GUILDFORD - 70C	GUILDFORD - 70C	GUILDFORD - 70C	GUILDFORD - 70C	GUILDFORD - 70C
31631	GUILDFORD - 70C	GUILDFORD - 70C	GUILDFORD - 70C	GUILDFORD - 70C	GUILDFORD - 70C	GUILDFORD - 70C	GUILDFORD - 70C	GUILDFORD - 70C
31632	EASTLEIGH - 71A	YEOVIL - 72C	YEOVIL - 72C	YEOVIL - 72C	YEOVIL - 72C	YEOVIL - 72C	YEOVIL - 72C	YEOVIL - 72C
31633	YEOVIL - 72C	GUILDFORD - 70C	GUILDFORD - 70C	GUILDFORD - 70C	GUILDFORD - 70C	GUILDFORD - 70C	GUILDFORD - 70C	GUILDFORD - 70C
31634	NINE ELMS - 70A	NINE ELMS - 70A	NINE ELMS - 70A	NINE ELMS - 70A	NINE ELMS - 70A	NINE ELMS - 70A	NINE ELMS - 70A	NINE ELMS - 70A
31635	GUILDFORD - 70C	GUILDFORD - 70C	GUILDFORD - 70C	GUILDFORD - 70C	GUILDFORD - 70C	GUILDFORD - 70C	GUILDFORD - 70C	GUILDFORD - 70C
31636	GUILDFORD - 70C	GUILDFORD - 70C	GUILDFORD - 70C	GUILDFORD - 70C	GUILDFORD - 70C	GUILDFORD - 70C	GUILDFORD - 70C	GUILDFORD - 70C
31637	GUILDFORD - 70C	YEOVIL - 72C	YEOVIL - 72C	YEOVIL - 72C	YEOVIL - 72C	YEOVIL - 72C	YEOVIL - 72C	YEOVIL - 72C
31638	GUILDFORD - 70C	GUILDFORD - 70C	GUILDFORD - 70C	GUILDFORD - 70C	GUILDFORD - 70C	GUILDFORD - 70C	GUILDFORD - 70C	GUILDFORD - 70C
31639	EASTLEIGH - 71A	EASTLEIGH - 71A	EASTLEIGH - 71A	EASTLEIGH - 71A	EASTLEIGH - 71A -	EASTLEIGH - 71A	EASTLEIGH - 71A	EASTLEIGH - 71A
U1 2-6-0 (2-6-4T R/B) 1925								
31890	BRIGHTON - 75A	BRIGHTON - 75A	BRIGHTON - 75A	BRIGHTON - 75A	BRIGHTON - 75A	BRIGHTON - 75A	BRIGHTON - 75A	BRIGHTON - 75A
U1 2-6-0 (1925)								
31891	BRIGHTON - 75A	BRIGHTON - 75A	BRIGHTON - 75A	BRIGHTON - 75A	BRIGHTON - 75A	BRIGHTON - 75A	BRIGHTON - 75A	BRIGHTON - 75A
31892	FELTHAM - 70B	FELTHAM - 70B	FELTHAM - 70B	FELTHAM - 70B	TONBRIDGE - 73J	TONBRIDGE - 73J	TONBRIDGE - 73J	TONBRIDGE - 73J
31893	FELTHAM - 70B	FELTHAM - 70B	FELTHAM - 70B	FELTHAM - 70B	TONBRIDGE - 73J	TONBRIDGE - 73J	TONBRIDGE - 73J	TONBRIDGE - 73J
31894	STEWARTS LANE - 73A	STEWARTS LANE - 73A	STEWARTS LANE - 73A	STEWARTS LANE - 73A	STEWARTS LANE - 73A	STEWARTS LANE - 73A	STEWARTS LANE - 73A	STEWARTS LANE - 73A
31895	STEWARTS LANE - 73A	STEWARTS LANE - 73A	STEWARTS LANE - 73A	STEWARTS LANE - 73A	STEWARTS LANE - 73A	STEWARTS LANE - 73A	STEWARTS LANE - 73A	STEWARTS LANE - 73A
31896	STEWARTS LANE - 73A	STEWARTS LANE - 73A	STEWARTS LANE - 73A	STEWARTS LANE - 73A	STEWARTS LANE - 73A	STEWARTS LANE - 73A	STEWARTS LANE - 73A	STEWARTS LANE - 73A
31897	STEWARTS LANE - 73A	STEWARTS LANE - 73A	STEWARTS LANE - 73A	STEWARTS LANE - 73A	STEWARTS LANE - 73A	STEWARTS LANE - 73A	STEWARTS LANE - 73A	STEWARTS LANE - 73A
31898	STEWARTS LANE - 73A	STEWARTS LANE - 73A	STEWARTS LANE - 73A	STEWARTS LANE - 73A	STEWARTS LANE - 73A	STEWARTS LANE - 73A	STEWARTS LANE - 73A	STEWARTS LANE - 73A
31899	STEWARTS LANE - 73A	STEWARTS LANE - 73A	STEWARTS LANE - 73A	STEWARTS LANE - 73A	STEWARTS LANE - 73A	STEWARTS LANE - 73A	STEWARTS LANE - 73A	STEWARTS LANE - 73A
31900	STEWARTS LANE - 73A	STEWARTS LANE - 73A	STEWARTS LANE - 73A	STEWARTS LANE - 73A	STEWARTS LANE - 73A	STEWARTS LANE - 73A	STEWARTS LANE - 73A	STEWARTS LANE - 73A
31901	TONBRIDGE - 73J	TONBRIDGE - 73J	TONBRIDGE - 73J	TONBRIDGE - 73J	TONBRIDGE - 73J	TONBRIDGE - 73J	TONBRIDGE - 73J	TONBRIDGE - 73J
31902	TONBRIDGE - 73J	TONBRIDGE - 73J	TONBRIDGE - 73J	TONBRIDGE - 73J	TONBRIDGE - 73J	TONBRIDGE - 73J	TONBRIDGE - 73J	TONBRIDGE - 73J
31903	TONBRIDGE - 73J	TONBRIDGE - 73J	TONBRIDGE - 73J	TONBRIDGE - 73J	TONBRIDGE - 73J	TONBRIDGE - 73J	TONBRIDGE - 73J	TONBRIDGE - 73J
31904	TONBRIDGE - 73J	TONBRIDGE - 73J	TONBRIDGE - 73J	TONBRIDGE - 73J	TONBRIDGE - 73J	TONBRIDGE - 73J	TONBRIDGE - 73J	TONBRIDGE - 73J
31905	TONBRIDGE - 73J	TONBRIDGE - 73J	TONBRIDGE - 73J	TONBRIDGE - 73J	TONBRIDGE - 73J	TONBRIDGE - 73J	TONBRIDGE - 73J	TONBRIDGE - 73J
31906	TONBRIDGE - 73J	TONBRIDGE - 73J	TONBRIDGE - 73J	TONBRIDGE - 73J	TONBRIDGE - 73J	TONBRIDGE - 73J	TONBRIDGE - 73J	TONBRIDGE - 73J
31907	TONBRIDGE - 73J	TONBRIDGE - 73J	TONBRIDGE - 73J	TONBRIDGE - 73J	TONBRIDGE - 73J	TONBRIDGE - 73J	TONBRIDGE - 73J	TONBRIDGE - 73J
31908	TONBRIDGE - 73J	TONBRIDGE - 73J	TONBRIDGE - 73J	TONBRIDGE - 73J	TONBRIDGE - 73J	TONBRIDGE - 73J	TONBRIDGE - 73J	TONBRIDGE - 73J
31909	TONBRIDGE - 73J	TONBRIDGE - 73J	TONBRIDGE - 73J	TONBRIDGE - 73J	TONBRIDGE - 73J	TONBRIDGE - 73J	TONBRIDGE - 73J	TONBRIDGE - 73J
31910	TONBRIDGE - 73J	TONBRIDGE - 73J	TONBRIDGE - 73J	TONBRIDGE - 73J	TONBRIDGE - 73J	TONBRIDGE - 73J	TONBRIDGE - 73J	TONBRIDGE - 73J
H15 4-6-0 (1907/14)								
30331	SALISBURY - 72B	SALISBURY - 72B	SALISBURY - 72B	SALISBURY - 72B	SALISBURY - 72B	SALISBURY - 72B	SALISBURY - 72B	SALISBURY - 72B
H15 4-6-0 (1914)								
30488	NINE ELMS - 70A	NINE ELMS - 70A	NINE ELMS - 70A	NINE ELMS - 70A	NINE ELMS - 70A	NINE ELMS - 70A	NINE ELMS - 70A	NINE ELMS - 70A
30489	EASTLEIGH - 71A	EASTLEIGH - 71A	EASTLEIGH - 71A	EASTLEIGH - 71A	EASTLEIGH - 71A	EASTLEIGH - 71A	EASTLEIGH - 71A	EASTLEIGH - 71A
30491	EASTLEIGH - 71A	EASTLEIGH - 71A	EASTLEIGH - 71A	EASTLEIGH - 71A	EASTLEIGH - 71A	EASTLEIGH - 71A	EASTLEIGH - 71A	EASTLEIGH - 71A
H15 4-6-0 (1924)								
30474	EASTLEIGH - 71A	EASTLEIGH - 71A	EASTLEIGH - 71A	EASTLEIGH - 71A	W/D	W/D	W/D	W/D
30475	EASTLEIGH - 71A	EASTLEIGH - 71A	EASTLEIGH - 71A	EASTLEIGH - 71A	EASTLEIGH - 71A	EASTLEIGH - 71A	EASTLEIGH - 71A	EASTLEIGH - 71A
30476	EASTLEIGH - 71A	EASTLEIGH - 71A	EASTLEIGH - 71A	EASTLEIGH - 71A	EASTLEIGH - 71A	EASTLEIGH - 71A	EASTLEIGH - 71A	EASTLEIGH - 71A
30521	NINE ELMS - 70A	NINE ELMS - 70A	NINE ELMS - 70A	NINE ELMS - 70A	NINE ELMS - 70A	NINE ELMS - 70A	NINE ELMS - 70A	NINE ELMS - 70A
30522	SALISBURY - 72B	SALISBURY - 72B	SALISBURY - 72B	SALISBURY - 72B	SALISBURY - 72B	SALISBURY - 72B	SALISBURY - 72B	SALISBURY - 72B
30523	SALISBURY - 72B	SALISBURY - 72B	SALISBURY - 72B	SALISBURY - 72B	SALISBURY - 72B	SALISBURY - 72B	SALISBURY - 72B	SALISBURY - 72B
30524	SALISBURY - 72B	SALISBURY - 72B	SALISBURY - 72B	SALISBURY - 72B	SALISBURY - 72B	SALISBURY - 72B	SALISBURY - 72B	SALISBURY - 72B

Although a common feature of SR operating, the S15 and H15 goods engines were less evident that they might have been since most of their duties involved fast goods services which operated at night. Generally the S15 engines handled freight traffic between London and Exeter whilst the H15's worked between London and Southampton although both classes could be seen, especially in the summer season, on secondary passenger services. H15 4-6-0 30489 of Eastleigh, one of the last survivors, is seen in Southern Railway days.

loco	May-49	Jun-49	Aug-49	Sep-49	Dec-49	Feb-50	Mar-50
S15 4-6-0 (1927)							
30823	EXMOUTH JCN-72A	EXMOUTH JCN-72A	EXMOUTH JCN-72A	EXMOUTH JCN-72A	EXMOUTH JCN-72A	EXMOUTH JCN-72A	EXMOUTH JCN-72A
30824	EXMOUTH JCN-72A	EXMOUTH JCN-72A	EXMOUTH JCN-72A	EXMOUTH JCN-72A	EXMOUTH JCN-72A	EXMOUTH JCN-72A	EXMOUTH JCN-72A
30825	EXMOUTH JCN-72A	EXMOUTH JCN-72A	EXMOUTH JCN-72A	EXMOUTH JCN-72A	EXMOUTH JCN-72A	EXMOUTH JCN-72A	EXMOUTH JCN-72A
30826	EXMOUTH JCN-72A	EXMOUTH JCN-72A	EXMOUTH JCN-72A	EXMOUTH JCN-72A	EXMOUTH JCN-72A	EXMOUTH JCN-72A	EXMOUTH JCN-72A
30827	EXMOUTH JCN-72A	EXMOUTH JCN-72A	EXMOUTH JCN-72A	EXMOUTH JCN-72A	EXMOUTH JCN-72A	SALISBURY-72B	SALISBURY-72B
30828	SALISBURY-72B	SALISBURY-72B	SALISBURY-72B	SALISBURY-72B	SALISBURY-72B	SALISBURY-72B	SALISBURY-72B
30829	SALISBURY-72B	SALISBURY-72B	SALISBURY-72B	SALISBURY-72B	SALISBURY-72B	SALISBURY-72B	SALISBURY-72B
30830	SALISBURY-72B	SALISBURY-72B	SALISBURY-72B	SALISBURY-72B	SALISBURY-72B	SALISBURY-72B	SALISBURY-72B
30831	SALISBURY-72B	SALISBURY-72B	SALISBURY-72B	SALISBURY-72B	SALISBURY-72B	SALISBURY-72B	SALISBURY-72B
30832	SALISBURY-72B	SALISBURY-72B	SALISBURY-72B	SALISBURY-72B	SALISBURY-72B	SALISBURY-72B	SALISBURY-72B
30833	FELTHAM-70B	FELTHAM-70B	FELTHAM-70B	FELTHAM-70B	FELTHAM-70B	FELTHAM-70B	FELTHAM-70B
30834	FELTHAM-70B	FELTHAM-70B	FELTHAM-70B	FELTHAM-70B	FELTHAM-70B	FELTHAM-70B	FELTHAM-70B
30835	FELTHAM-70B	FELTHAM-70B	FELTHAM-70B	FELTHAM-70B	FELTHAM-70B	FELTHAM-70B	FELTHAM-70B
30836	FELTHAM-70B	FELTHAM-70B	FELTHAM-70B	FELTHAM-70B	FELTHAM-70B	FELTHAM-70B	FELTHAM-70B
30837	FELTHAM-70B	FELTHAM-70B	FELTHAM-70B	FELTHAM-70B	FELTHAM-70B		
S15 4-6-0 (1920)							
30496	NINE ELMS-70A	NINE ELMS-70A	NINE ELMS-70A	NINE ELMS-70A	NINE ELMS-70A	FELTHAM-70B	FELTHAM-70B
30497	NINE ELMS-70A	NINE ELMS-70A	NINE ELMS-70A	NINE ELMS-70A	NINE ELMS-70A	FELTHAM-70B	FELTHAM-70B
30498	NINE ELMS-70A	NINE ELMS-70A	NINE ELMS-70A	NINE ELMS-70A	NINE ELMS-70A	FELTHAM-70B	FELTHAM-70B
30499	FELTHAM-70B	FELTHAM-70B	FELTHAM-70B	FELTHAM-70B	FELTHAM-70B	FELTHAM-70B	FELTHAM-70B
30500	FELTHAM-70B	FELTHAM-70B	FELTHAM-70B	FELTHAM-70B	FELTHAM-70B	FELTHAM-70B	FELTHAM-70B
30501	FELTHAM-70B	FELTHAM-70B	FELTHAM-70B	FELTHAM-70B	FELTHAM-70B	FELTHAM-70B	FELTHAM-70B
30502	FELTHAM-70B	FELTHAM-70B	FELTHAM-70B	FELTHAM-70B	FELTHAM-70B	FELTHAM-70B	FELTHAM-70B
30503	FELTHAM-70B	FELTHAM-70B	FELTHAM-70B	FELTHAM-70B	FELTHAM-70B	FELTHAM-70B	FELTHAM-70B
30504	FELTHAM-70B	FELTHAM-70B	FELTHAM-70B	FELTHAM-70B	FELTHAM-70B	FELTHAM-70B	FELTHAM-70B
30505	FELTHAM-70B	FELTHAM-70B	FELTHAM-70B	FELTHAM-70B	FELTHAM-70B	FELTHAM-70B	FELTHAM-70B
30506	FELTHAM-70B	FELTHAM-70B	FELTHAM-70B	FELTHAM-70B	FELTHAM-70B	FELTHAM-70B	FELTHAM-70B
30507	FELTHAM-70B	FELTHAM-70B	FELTHAM-70B	FELTHAM-70B	FELTHAM-70B	FELTHAM-70B	FELTHAM-70B
30508	FELTHAM-70B	FELTHAM-70B	FELTHAM-70B	FELTHAM-70B	FELTHAM-70B	FELTHAM-70B	FELTHAM-70B
30509	FELTHAM-70B	FELTHAM-70B	FELTHAM-70B	FELTHAM-70B	FELTHAM-70B	FELTHAM-70B	FELTHAM-70B
30510	FELTHAM-70B	FELTHAM-70B	FELTHAM-70B	FELTHAM-70B	FELTHAM-70B	FELTHAM-70B	FELTHAM-70B
30511	FELTHAM-70B	FELTHAM-70B	FELTHAM-70B	FELTHAM-70B	FELTHAM-70B	FELTHAM-70B	FELTHAM-70B
30512	FELTHAM-70B	FELTHAM-70B	FELTHAM-70B	FELTHAM-70B	FELTHAM-70B	FELTHAM-70B	FELTHAM-70B
30513	FELTHAM-70B	FELTHAM-70B	FELTHAM-70B	FELTHAM-70B	FELTHAM-70B	FELTHAM-70B	FELTHAM-70B
30514	FELTHAM-70B	FELTHAM-70B	FELTHAM-70B	FELTHAM-70B	FELTHAM-70B	FELTHAM-70B	FELTHAM-70B
30515	FELTHAM-70B	FELTHAM-70B	FELTHAM-70B	FELTHAM-70B	FELTHAM-70B	FELTHAM-70B	FELTHAM-70B
S15 4-6-0 (1936)							
30838	FELTHAM-70B	FELTHAM-70B	FELTHAM-70B	FELTHAM-70B	FELTHAM-70B	FELTHAM-70B	FELTHAM-70B
30839	FELTHAM-70B	FELTHAM-70B	FELTHAM-70B	FELTHAM-70B	FELTHAM-70B	FELTHAM-70B	FELTHAM-70B
30840	FELTHAM-70B	FELTHAM-70B	FELTHAM-70B	FELTHAM-70B	FELTHAM-70B	FELTHAM-70B	FELTHAM-70B
30841	EXMOUTH JCN-72A	EXMOUTH JCN-72A	EXMOUTH JCN-72A	EXMOUTH JCN-72A	EXMOUTH JCN-72A	EXMOUTH JCN-72A	EXMOUTH JCN-72A
30842	EXMOUTH JCN-72A	EXMOUTH JCN-72A	EXMOUTH JCN-72A	EXMOUTH JCN-72A	EXMOUTH JCN-72A	EXMOUTH JCN-72A	EXMOUTH JCN-72A
30843	EXMOUTH JCN-72A	EXMOUTH JCN-72A	EXMOUTH JCN-72A	EXMOUTH JCN-72A	EXMOUTH JCN-72A	EXMOUTH JCN-72A	EXMOUTH JCN-72A
30844	EXMOUTH JCN-72A	EXMOUTH JCN-72A	EXMOUTH JCN-72A	EXMOUTH JCN-72A	EXMOUTH JCN-72A	EXMOUTH JCN-72A	EXMOUTH JCN-72A
30845	EXMOUTH JCN-72A	EXMOUTH JCN-72A	EXMOUTH JCN-72A	EXMOUTH JCN-72A	EXMOUTH JCN-72A	EXMOUTH JCN-72A	EXMOUTH JCN-72A
30846	EXMOUTH JCN-72A	EXMOUTH JCN-72A	EXMOUTH JCN-72A	EXMOUTH JCN-72A	EXMOUTH JCN-72A	EXMOUTH JCN-72A	EXMOUTH JCN-72A
30847	EXMOUTH JCN-72A	EXMOUTH JCN-72A	EXMOUTH JCN-72A	EXMOUTH JCN-72A	EXMOUTH JCN-72A	EXMOUTH JCN-72A	EXMOUTH JCN-72A
N15 4-6-0 (1918)							
30736	BOURNEMOUTH-71B	BOURNEMOUTH-71B	BOURNEMOUTH-71B	BOURNEMOUTH-71B	BOURNEMOUTH-71B	BOURNEMOUTH-71B	BOURNEMOUTH-71B
30737	BOURNEMOUTH-71B	BOURNEMOUTH-71B	BOURNEMOUTH-71B	BOURNEMOUTH-71B	BOURNEMOUTH-71B	BOURNEMOUTH-71B	BOURNEMOUTH-71B
30738	NINE ELMS-70A	NINE ELMS-70A	NINE ELMS-70A	NINE ELMS-70A	NINE ELMS-70A	NINE ELMS-70A	NINE ELMS-70A
30739	NINE ELMS-70A	NINE ELMS-70A	NINE ELMS-70A	NINE ELMS-70A	NINE ELMS-70A	SALISBURY-72B	SALISBURY-72B
30740	BOURNEMOUTH-71B	BOURNEMOUTH-71B	BOURNEMOUTH-71B	BOURNEMOUTH-71B	BOURNEMOUTH-71B	BOURNEMOUTH-71B	BOURNEMOUTH-71B
30741	BASINGSTOKE-70D	BASINGSTOKE-70D	BASINGSTOKE-70D	BASINGSTOKE-70D	BASINGSTOKE-70D	BASINGSTOKE-70D	BASINGSTOKE-70D
30742	NINE ELMS-70A	NINE ELMS-70A	NINE ELMS-70A	NINE ELMS-70A	NINE ELMS-70A	NINE ELMS-70A	NINE ELMS-70A
30743	BOURNEMOUTH-71B	BOURNEMOUTH-71B	BOURNEMOUTH-71B	BOURNEMOUTH-71B	BOURNEMOUTH-71B	BOURNEMOUTH-71B	BOURNEMOUTH-71B
30744	EXMOUTH JCN-72A	NINE ELMS-70A	NINE ELMS-70A	NINE ELMS-70A	NINE ELMS-70A	SALISBURY-72B	SALISBURY-72B
30745	NINE ELMS-70A	NINE ELMS-70A	NINE ELMS-70A	NINE ELMS-70A	NINE ELMS-70A	NINE ELMS-70A	NINE ELMS-70A
30746	BOURNEMOUTH-71B	BOURNEMOUTH-71B	BOURNEMOUTH-71B	BOURNEMOUTH-71B	BOURNEMOUTH-71B	BOURNEMOUTH-71B	BOURNEMOUTH-71B
30747	NINE ELMS-70A	NINE ELMS-70A	NINE ELMS-70A	NINE ELMS-70A	NINE ELMS-70A	NINE ELMS-70A	NINE ELMS-70A
30748	EASTLEIGH-71A	EASTLEIGH-71A	NINE ELMS-70A	NINE ELMS-70A	NINE ELMS-70A	NINE ELMS-70A	NINE ELMS-70A
30749	EASTLEIGH-71A	EASTLEIGH-71A	EASTLEIGH-71A	EASTLEIGH-71A	EASTLEIGH-71A	EASTLEIGH-71A	EASTLEIGH-71A
30750	BOURNEMOUTH-71B	BOURNEMOUTH-71B	BOURNEMOUTH-71B	BOURNEMOUTH-71B	BOURNEMOUTH-71B	BOURNEMOUTH-71B	BOURNEMOUTH-71B
30751	BOURNEMOUTH-71B	BOURNEMOUTH-71B	BOURNEMOUTH-71B	BOURNEMOUTH-71B	BOURNEMOUTH-71B	BOURNEMOUTH-71B	BOURNEMOUTH-71B
30752	BOURNEMOUTH-71B	BOURNEMOUTH-71B	BOURNEMOUTH-71B	BOURNEMOUTH-71B	EASTLEIGH-71A	EASTLEIGH-71A	EASTLEIGH-71A
30753	EASTLEIGH-71A	NINE ELMS-70A	NINE ELMS-70A	NINE ELMS-70A	NINE ELMS-70A	NINE ELMS-70A	NINE ELMS-70A
30754	NINE ELMS-70A	EASTLEIGH-71A	EASTLEIGH-71A	EASTLEIGH-71A	EASTLEIGH-71A	EASTLEIGH-71A	EASTLEIGH-71A
30755	NINE ELMS-70A	NINE ELMS-70A	NINE ELMS-70A	NINE ELMS-70A	NINE ELMS-70A	NINE ELMS-70A	NINE ELMS-70A

Displaced by Bulleid Pacifics from Nine Elms, 30742 'Camelot' moved to Bournemouth in October 1950 and remained there until withdrawal in Summer 1957. During the early 1950's Bournemouth had four daily N15 duties, one of which was a two-day cycle based on Dorchester MPD involving the Bournemouth - York express as far as Oxford. The other services were based at Bournemouth itself and covered the Bournemouth - Birkenhead service to and from Oxford plus a mixture of local passenger and goods services between Southampton and Weymouth. In 1960 the nameplate from 30742 was transferred to BR 5MT 4-6-0 73082.
30742 at Eastleigh in 1954.

loco	Apr-50	Sep-50	Oct-50	Nov-50	Dec-50	Mar-51	Apr-51
				S15 4-6-0 (1927)			
30823	EXMOUTH JCN - 72A	EXMOUTH JCN - 72A	EXMOUTH JCN - 72A	EXMOUTH JCN - 72A	EXMOUTH JCN - 72A	EXMOUTH JCN - 72A	EXMOUTH JCN - 72A
30824	EXMOUTH JCN - 72A	EXMOUTH JCN - 72A	EXMOUTH JCN - 72A	EXMOUTH JCN - 72A	EXMOUTH JCN - 72A	EXMOUTH JCN - 72A	EXMOUTH JCN - 72A
30825	EXMOUTH JCN - 72A	EXMOUTH JCN - 72A	EXMOUTH JCN - 72A	EXMOUTH JCN - 72A	EXMOUTH JCN - 72A	EXMOUTH JCN - 72A	EXMOUTH JCN - 72A
30826	EXMOUTH JCN - 72A	SALISBURY - 72B	SALISBURY - 72B	SALISBURY - 72B	SALISBURY - 72B	SALISBURY - 72B	SALISBURY - 72B
30827	SALISBURY - 72B	SALISBURY - 72B	SALISBURY - 72B	SALISBURY - 72B	SALISBURY - 72B	SALISBURY - 72B	SALISBURY - 72B
30828	SALISBURY - 72B	SALISBURY - 72B	SALISBURY - 72B	SALISBURY - 72B	SALISBURY - 72B	SALISBURY - 72B	SALISBURY - 72B
30829	SALISBURY - 72B	SALISBURY - 72B	SALISBURY - 72B	SALISBURY - 72B	SALISBURY - 72B	SALISBURY - 72B	SALISBURY - 72B
30830	SALISBURY - 72B	SALISBURY - 72B	SALISBURY - 72B	SALISBURY - 72B	SALISBURY - 72B	SALISBURY - 72B	SALISBURY - 72B
30831	SALISBURY - 72B	SALISBURY - 72B	SALISBURY - 72B	SALISBURY - 72B	SALISBURY - 72B	SALISBURY - 72B	SALISBURY - 72B
30832	SALISBURY - 72B	SALISBURY - 72B	SALISBURY - 72B	SALISBURY - 72B	SALISBURY - 72B	SALISBURY - 72B	SALISBURY - 72B
30833	FELTHAM - 70B	FELTHAM - 70B	FELTHAM - 70B	FELTHAM - 70B	FELTHAM - 70B	FELTHAM - 70B	FELTHAM - 70B
30834	FELTHAM - 70B	FELTHAM - 70B	FELTHAM - 70B	FELTHAM - 70B	FELTHAM - 70B	FELTHAM - 70B	FELTHAM - 70B
30835	FELTHAM - 70B	FELTHAM - 70B	FELTHAM - 70B	FELTHAM - 70B	FELTHAM - 70B	FELTHAM - 70B	FELTHAM - 70B
30836	FELTHAM - 70B	FELTHAM - 70B	FELTHAM - 70B	FELTHAM - 70B	FELTHAM - 70B	FELTHAM - 70B	FELTHAM - 70B
30837	FELTHAM - 70B	FELTHAM - 70B	FELTHAM - 70B	FELTHAM - 70B	FELTHAM - 70B	FELTHAM - 70B	FELTHAM - 70B
				S15 4-6-0 (1920)			
30496	FELTHAM - 70B	FELTHAM - 70B	FELTHAM - 70B	FELTHAM - 70B	FELTHAM - 70B	FELTHAM - 70B	FELTHAM - 70B
30497	FELTHAM - 70B	FELTHAM - 70B	FELTHAM - 70B	FELTHAM - 70B	FELTHAM - 70B	FELTHAM - 70B	FELTHAM - 70B
30498	FELTHAM - 70B	FELTHAM - 70B	FELTHAM - 70B	FELTHAM - 70B	FELTHAM - 70B	FELTHAM - 70B	FELTHAM - 70B
30499	FELTHAM - 70B	FELTHAM - 70B	FELTHAM - 70B	FELTHAM - 70B	FELTHAM - 70B	FELTHAM - 70B	FELTHAM - 70B
30500	FELTHAM - 70B	FELTHAM - 70B	FELTHAM - 70B	FELTHAM - 70B	FELTHAM - 70B	FELTHAM - 70B	FELTHAM - 70B
30501	FELTHAM - 70B	FELTHAM - 70B	FELTHAM - 70B	FELTHAM - 70B	FELTHAM - 70B	FELTHAM - 70B	FELTHAM - 70B
30502	FELTHAM - 70B	FELTHAM - 70B	FELTHAM - 70B	FELTHAM - 70B	FELTHAM - 70B	FELTHAM - 70B	FELTHAM - 70B
30503	FELTHAM - 70B	FELTHAM - 70B	FELTHAM - 70B	FELTHAM - 70B	FELTHAM - 70B	FELTHAM - 70B	FELTHAM - 70B
30504	FELTHAM - 70B	FELTHAM - 70B	FELTHAM - 70B	FELTHAM - 70B	FELTHAM - 70B	FELTHAM - 70B	FELTHAM - 70B
30505	FELTHAM - 70B	FELTHAM - 70B	FELTHAM - 70B	FELTHAM - 70B	FELTHAM - 70B	FELTHAM - 70B	FELTHAM - 70B
30506	FELTHAM - 70B	FELTHAM - 70B	FELTHAM - 70B	FELTHAM - 70B	FELTHAM - 70B	FELTHAM - 70B	FELTHAM - 70B
30507	FELTHAM - 70B	FELTHAM - 70B	FELTHAM - 70B	FELTHAM - 70B	FELTHAM - 70B	FELTHAM - 70B	FELTHAM - 70B
30508	FELTHAM - 70B	FELTHAM - 70B	FELTHAM - 70B	FELTHAM - 70B	FELTHAM - 70B	FELTHAM - 70B	FELTHAM - 70B
30509	FELTHAM - 70B	FELTHAM - 70B	FELTHAM - 70B	FELTHAM - 70B	FELTHAM - 70B	FELTHAM - 70B	FELTHAM - 70B
30510	FELTHAM - 70B	FELTHAM - 70B	FELTHAM - 70B	FELTHAM - 70B	FELTHAM - 70B	FELTHAM - 70B	FELTHAM - 70B
30511	FELTHAM - 70B	FELTHAM - 70B	FELTHAM - 70B	FELTHAM - 70B	FELTHAM - 70B	FELTHAM - 70B	FELTHAM - 70B
30512	FELTHAM - 70B	FELTHAM - 70B	FELTHAM - 70B	FELTHAM - 70B	FELTHAM - 70B	FELTHAM - 70B	FELTHAM - 70B
30513	FELTHAM - 70B	FELTHAM - 70B	FELTHAM - 70B	FELTHAM - 70B	FELTHAM - 70B	FELTHAM - 70B	FELTHAM - 70B
30514	FELTHAM - 70B	FELTHAM - 70B	FELTHAM - 70B	FELTHAM - 70B	FELTHAM - 70B	FELTHAM - 70B	FELTHAM - 70B
30515	FELTHAM - 70B	FELTHAM - 70B	FELTHAM - 70B	FELTHAM - 70B	FELTHAM - 70B	FELTHAM - 70B	FELTHAM - 70B
				S15 4-6-0 (1936)			
30838	FELTHAM - 70B	FELTHAM - 70B	FELTHAM - 70B	FELTHAM - 70B	FELTHAM - 70B	FELTHAM - 70B	FELTHAM - 70B
30839	FELTHAM - 70B	FELTHAM - 70B	FELTHAM - 70B	FELTHAM - 70B	FELTHAM - 70B	FELTHAM - 70B	FELTHAM - 70B
30840	FELTHAM - 70B	FELTHAM - 70B	FELTHAM - 70B	FELTHAM - 70B	FELTHAM - 70B	FELTHAM - 70B	FELTHAM - 70B
30841	EXMOUTH JCN - 72A	EXMOUTH JCN - 72A	EXMOUTH JCN - 72A	EXMOUTH JCN - 72A	EXMOUTH JCN - 72A	EXMOUTH JCN - 72A	EXMOUTH JCN - 72A
30842	EXMOUTH JCN - 72A	EXMOUTH JCN - 72A	EXMOUTH JCN - 72A	EXMOUTH JCN - 72A	EXMOUTH JCN - 72A	EXMOUTH JCN - 72A	EXMOUTH JCN - 72A
30843	EXMOUTH JCN - 72A	EXMOUTH JCN - 72A	EXMOUTH JCN - 72A	EXMOUTH JCN - 72A	EXMOUTH JCN - 72A	EXMOUTH JCN - 72A	EXMOUTH JCN - 72A
30844	EXMOUTH JCN - 72A	EXMOUTH JCN - 72A	EXMOUTH JCN - 72A	EXMOUTH JCN - 72A	EXMOUTH JCN - 72A	EXMOUTH JCN - 72A	EXMOUTH JCN - 72A
30845	EXMOUTH JCN - 72A	EXMOUTH JCN - 72A	EXMOUTH JCN - 72A	EXMOUTH JCN - 72A	EXMOUTH JCN - 72A	EXMOUTH JCN - 72A	EXMOUTH JCN - 72A
30846	EXMOUTH JCN - 72A	EXMOUTH JCN - 72A	EXMOUTH JCN - 72A	EXMOUTH JCN - 72A	EXMOUTH JCN - 72A	EXMOUTH JCN - 72A	EXMOUTH JCN - 72A
30847	EXMOUTH JCN - 72A	EXMOUTH JCN - 72A	EXMOUTH JCN - 72A	EXMOUTH JCN - 72A	EXMOUTH JCN - 72A	EXMOUTH JCN - 72A	EXMOUTH JCN - 72A
				N15 4-6-0 (1918)			
30736	BOURNEMOUTH - 71B	BOURNEMOUTH - 71B	BOURNEMOUTH - 71B	BOURNEMOUTH - 71B	BOURNEMOUTH - 71B	BOURNEMOUTH - 71B	BOURNEMOUTH - 71B
30737	BOURNEMOUTH - 71B	BOURNEMOUTH - 71B	BOURNEMOUTH - 71B	BOURNEMOUTH - 71B	BOURNEMOUTH - 71B	BOURNEMOUTH - 71B	BOURNEMOUTH - 71B
30738	NINE ELMS - 70A	FELTHAM - 70B	FELTHAM - 70B	FELTHAM - 70B	BOURNEMOUTH - 71B	BOURNEMOUTH - 71B	BOURNEMOUTH - 71B
30739	SALISBURY - 72B	SALISBURY - 72B	SALISBURY - 72B	BOURNEMOUTH - 71B	BOURNEMOUTH - 71B	BOURNEMOUTH - 71B	BOURNEMOUTH - 71B
30740	BOURNEMOUTH - 71B	BOURNEMOUTH - 71B	BOURNEMOUTH - 71B	BOURNEMOUTH - 71B	BOURNEMOUTH - 71B	BOURNEMOUTH - 71B	BOURNEMOUTH - 71B
30741	SALISBURY - 72B	BOURNEMOUTH - 71B	BOURNEMOUTH - 71B	BOURNEMOUTH - 71B	BOURNEMOUTH - 71B	BOURNEMOUTH - 71B	BOURNEMOUTH - 71B
30742	NINE ELMS - 70A	NINE ELMS - 70A	BOURNEMOUTH - 71B	BOURNEMOUTH - 71B	BOURNEMOUTH - 71B	BOURNEMOUTH - 71B	BOURNEMOUTH - 71B
30743	BOURNEMOUTH - 71B	BOURNEMOUTH - 71B	BOURNEMOUTH - 71B	BOURNEMOUTH - 71B	BOURNEMOUTH - 71B	BOURNEMOUTH - 71B	BOURNEMOUTH - 71B
30744	SALISBURY - 72B	SALISBURY - 72B	SALISBURY - 72B	EASTLEIGH - 71A	BASINGSTOKE - 70D	BASINGSTOKE - 70D	BASINGSTOKE - 70D
30745	NINE ELMS - 70A	NINE ELMS - 70A	BASINGSTOKE - 70D	EASTLEIGH - 71A	BASINGSTOKE - 70D	BASINGSTOKE - 70D	BASINGSTOKE - 70D
30746	BOURNEMOUTH - 71B	BOURNEMOUTH - 71B	BOURNEMOUTH - 71B	BOURNEMOUTH - 71B	BOURNEMOUTH - 71B	BOURNEMOUTH - 71B	BOURNEMOUTH - 71B
30747	NINE ELMS - 70A	NINE ELMS - 70A	NINE ELMS - 70A	NINE ELMS - 70A	NINE ELMS - 70A	NINE ELMS - 70A	NINE ELMS - 70A
30748	NINE ELMS - 70A	SALISBURY - 72B	SALISBURY - 72B	SALISBURY - 72B	SALISBURY - 72B	SALISBURY - 72B	SALISBURY - 72B
30749	EASTLEIGH - 71A	EASTLEIGH - 71A	EASTLEIGH - 71A	EASTLEIGH - 71A	EASTLEIGH - 71A	EASTLEIGH - 71A	EASTLEIGH - 71A
30750	EASTLEIGH - 71A	BOURNEMOUTH - 71B	BOURNEMOUTH - 71B	BOURNEMOUTH - 71B	BOURNEMOUTH - 71B	BOURNEMOUTH - 71B	BOURNEMOUTH - 71B
30751	BOURNEMOUTH - 71B	BOURNEMOUTH - 71B	BOURNEMOUTH - 71B	EASTLEIGH - 71A	EASTLEIGH - 71A	EASTLEIGH - 71A	EASTLEIGH - 71A
30752	EASTLEIGH - 71A	EASTLEIGH - 71A	EASTLEIGH - 71A	EASTLEIGH - 71A	EASTLEIGH - 71A	EASTLEIGH - 71A	EASTLEIGH - 71A
30753	NINE ELMS - 70A	SALISBURY - 72B	SALISBURY - 72B	SALISBURY - 72B	SALISBURY - 72B	SALISBURY - 72B	SALISBURY - 72B
30754	EASTLEIGH - 71A	BOURNEMOUTH - 71B	BOURNEMOUTH - 71B	BOURNEMOUTH - 71B	BOURNEMOUTH - 71B	BOURNEMOUTH - 71B	BOURNEMOUTH - 71B
30755	NINE ELMS - 70A	NINE ELMS - 70A	NINE ELMS - 70A	NINE ELMS - 70A	EASTLEIGH - 71A	EASTLEIGH - 71A	EASTLEIGH - 71A

loco	Jun-51	Jul-51	Sep-51	Dec-51	Jan-52	Mar-52	Jun-52
				S15 4-6-0 (1927)			
30823	SALISBURY-72B	SALISBURY-72B	SALISBURY-72B	SALISBURY-72B	SALISBURY-72B	SALISBURY-72B	SALISBURY-72B
30824	SALISBURY-72B	SALISBURY-72B	SALISBURY-72B	SALISBURY-72B	SALISBURY-72B	SALISBURY-72B	SALISBURY-72B
30825	SALISBURY-72B	SALISBURY-72B	SALISBURY-72B	SALISBURY-72B	SALISBURY-72B	SALISBURY-72B	SALISBURY-72B
30826	SALISBURY-72B	SALISBURY-72B	SALISBURY-72B	SALISBURY-72B	SALISBURY-72B	SALISBURY-72B	SALISBURY-72B
30827	SALISBURY-72B	SALISBURY-72B	SALISBURY-72B	SALISBURY-72B	SALISBURY-72B	SALISBURY-72B	SALISBURY-72B
30828	SALISBURY-72B	SALISBURY-72B	SALISBURY-72B	SALISBURY-72B	SALISBURY-72B	SALISBURY-72B	SALISBURY-72B
30829	SALISBURY-72B	SALISBURY-72B	SALISBURY-72B	SALISBURY-72B	SALISBURY-72B	SALISBURY-72B	SALISBURY-72B
30830	SALISBURY-72B	SALISBURY-72B	SALISBURY-72B	SALISBURY-72B	SALISBURY-72B	SALISBURY-72B	SALISBURY-72B
30831	SALISBURY-72B	SALISBURY-72B	SALISBURY-72B	SALISBURY-72B	SALISBURY-72B	SALISBURY-72B	SALISBURY-72B
30832	SALISBURY-72B	SALISBURY-72B	SALISBURY-72B	SALISBURY-72B	SALISBURY-72B	SALISBURY-72B	SALISBURY-72B
30833	FELTHAM-70B	FELTHAM-70B	FELTHAM-70B	FELTHAM-70B	FELTHAM-70B	FELTHAM-70B	FELTHAM-70B
30834	FELTHAM-70B	FELTHAM-70B	FELTHAM-70B	FELTHAM-70B	FELTHAM-70B	FELTHAM-70B	FELTHAM-70B
30835	FELTHAM-70B	REDHILL-75B	REDHILL-75B	REDHILL-75B	REDHILL-75B	REDHILL-75B	REDHILL-75B
30836	FELTHAM-70B	REDHILL-75B	REDHILL-75B	REDHILL-75B	REDHILL-75B	REDHILL-75B	REDHILL-75B
30837	FELTHAM-70B	REDHILL-75B	REDHILL-75B	REDHILL-75B	REDHILL-75B	REDHILL-75B	REDHILL-75B
				S15 4-6-0 (1920)			
30496	FELTHAM-70B	FELTHAM-70B	FELTHAM-70B	FELTHAM-70B	FELTHAM-70B	FELTHAM-70B	FELTHAM-70B
30497	FELTHAM-70B	FELTHAM-70B	FELTHAM-70B	FELTHAM-70B	FELTHAM-70B	FELTHAM-70B	FELTHAM-70B
30498	FELTHAM-70B	FELTHAM-70B	FELTHAM-70B	FELTHAM-70B	FELTHAM-70B	FELTHAM-70B	FELTHAM-70B
30499	FELTHAM-70B	FELTHAM-70B	FELTHAM-70B	FELTHAM-70B	FELTHAM-70B	FELTHAM-70B	FELTHAM-70B
30500	FELTHAM-70B	FELTHAM-70B	FELTHAM-70B	FELTHAM-70B	FELTHAM-70B	FELTHAM-70B	FELTHAM-70B
30501	FELTHAM-70B	FELTHAM-70B	FELTHAM-70B	FELTHAM-70B	FELTHAM-70B	FELTHAM-70B	FELTHAM-70B
30502	FELTHAM-70B	FELTHAM-70B	FELTHAM-70B	FELTHAM-70B	FELTHAM-70B	FELTHAM-70B	FELTHAM-70B
30503	FELTHAM-70B	FELTHAM-70B	FELTHAM-70B	FELTHAM-70B	FELTHAM-70B	FELTHAM-70B	FELTHAM-70B
30504	FELTHAM-70B	FELTHAM-70B	FELTHAM-70B	FELTHAM-70B	FELTHAM-70B	FELTHAM-70B	FELTHAM-70B
30505	FELTHAM-70B	FELTHAM-70B	FELTHAM-70B	FELTHAM-70B	FELTHAM-70B	FELTHAM-70B	FELTHAM-70B
30506	FELTHAM-70B	FELTHAM-70B	FELTHAM-70B	FELTHAM-70B	FELTHAM-70B	FELTHAM-70B	FELTHAM-70B
30507	FELTHAM-70B	FELTHAM-70B	FELTHAM-70B	FELTHAM-70B	FELTHAM-70B	FELTHAM-70B	FELTHAM-70B
30508	FELTHAM-70B	FELTHAM-70B	FELTHAM-70B	FELTHAM-70B	FELTHAM-70B	FELTHAM-70B	FELTHAM-70B
30509	FELTHAM-70B	FELTHAM-70B	FELTHAM-70B	FELTHAM-70B	FELTHAM-70B	FELTHAM-70B	FELTHAM-70B
30510	FELTHAM-70B	FELTHAM-70B	FELTHAM-70B	FELTHAM-70B	FELTHAM-70B	FELTHAM-70B	FELTHAM-70B
30511	FELTHAM-70B	FELTHAM-70B	FELTHAM-70B	FELTHAM-70B	FELTHAM-70B	FELTHAM-70B	FELTHAM-70B
30512	FELTHAM-70B	FELTHAM-70B	FELTHAM-70B	FELTHAM-70B	FELTHAM-70B	FELTHAM-70B	FELTHAM-70B
30513	FELTHAM-70B	FELTHAM-70B	FELTHAM-70B	FELTHAM-70B	FELTHAM-70B	FELTHAM-70B	FELTHAM-70B
30514	FELTHAM-70B	FELTHAM-70B	FELTHAM-70B	FELTHAM-70B	FELTHAM-70B	FELTHAM-70B	FELTHAM-70B
30515	FELTHAM-70B	FELTHAM-70B	FELTHAM-70B	FELTHAM-70B	FELTHAM-70B	FELTHAM-70B	FELTHAM-70B
				S15 4-6-0 (1936)			
30838	FELTHAM-70B	FELTHAM-70B	FELTHAM-70B	FELTHAM-70B	FELTHAM-70B	FELTHAM-70B	FELTHAM-70B
30839	FELTHAM-70B	FELTHAM-70B	FELTHAM-70B	FELTHAM-70B	FELTHAM-70B	FELTHAM-70B	FELTHAM-70B
30840	FELTHAM-70B	FELTHAM-70B	FELTHAM-70B	FELTHAM-70B	FELTHAM-70B	FELTHAM-70B	FELTHAM-70B
30841	EXMOUTH JCN-72A	EXMOUTH JCN-72A	EXMOUTH JCN-72A	EXMOUTH JCN-72A	EXMOUTH JCN-72A	EXMOUTH JCN-72A	EXMOUTH JCN-72A
30842	EXMOUTH JCN-72A	EXMOUTH JCN-72A	EXMOUTH JCN-72A	EXMOUTH JCN-72A	EXMOUTH JCN-72A	EXMOUTH JCN-72A	EXMOUTH JCN-72A
30843	EXMOUTH JCN-72A	EXMOUTH JCN-72A	EXMOUTH JCN-72A	EXMOUTH JCN-72A	EXMOUTH JCN-72A	EXMOUTH JCN-72A	EXMOUTH JCN-72A
30844	EXMOUTH JCN-72A	EXMOUTH JCN-72A	EXMOUTH JCN-72A	EXMOUTH JCN-72A	EXMOUTH JCN-72A	EXMOUTH JCN-72A	EXMOUTH JCN-72A
30845	EXMOUTH JCN-72A	EXMOUTH JCN-72A	EXMOUTH JCN-72A	EXMOUTH JCN-72A	EXMOUTH JCN-72A	EXMOUTH JCN-72A	EXMOUTH JCN-72A
30846	SALISBURY-72B	SALISBURY-72B	SALISBURY-72B	SALISBURY-72B	SALISBURY-72B	SALISBURY-72B	SALISBURY-72B
30847	SALISBURY-72B	SALISBURY-72B	SALISBURY-72B	SALISBURY-72B	SALISBURY-72B	SALISBURY-72B	SALISBURY-72B
				N15 4-6-0 (1918)			
30736	BOURNEMOUTH-71B	BOURNEMOUTH-71B	BOURNEMOUTH-71B	BOURNEMOUTH-71B	BOURNEMOUTH-71B	BOURNEMOUTH-71B	BOURNEMOUTH-71B
30737	BOURNEMOUTH-71B	BOURNEMOUTH-71B	BOURNEMOUTH-71B	BOURNEMOUTH-71B	BOURNEMOUTH-71B	BOURNEMOUTH-71B	BOURNEMOUTH-71B
30738	BOURNEMOUTH-71B	BOURNEMOUTH-71B	BOURNEMOUTH-71B	BOURNEMOUTH-71B	BOURNEMOUTH-71B	BOURNEMOUTH-71B	BOURNEMOUTH-71B
30739	BOURNEMOUTH-71B	BOURNEMOUTH-71B	BOURNEMOUTH-71B	BOURNEMOUTH-71B	BOURNEMOUTH-71B	BOURNEMOUTH-71B	BOURNEMOUTH-71B
30740	BOURNEMOUTH-71B	BOURNEMOUTH-71B	BOURNEMOUTH-71B	BOURNEMOUTH-71B	BOURNEMOUTH-71B	BOURNEMOUTH-71B	BOURNEMOUTH-71B
30741	BOURNEMOUTH-71B	BOURNEMOUTH-71B	BOURNEMOUTH-71B	BOURNEMOUTH-71B	BOURNEMOUTH-71B	BOURNEMOUTH-71B	BOURNEMOUTH-71B
30742	BOURNEMOUTH-71B	BOURNEMOUTH-71B	BOURNEMOUTH-71B	BOURNEMOUTH-71B	BOURNEMOUTH-71B	BOURNEMOUTH-71B	BOURNEMOUTH-71B
30743	BOURNEMOUTH-71B	BOURNEMOUTH-71B	BOURNEMOUTH-71B	BOURNEMOUTH-71B	BOURNEMOUTH-71B	BOURNEMOUTH-71B	BOURNEMOUTH-71B
30744	FELTHAM-70B	FELTHAM-70B	FELTHAM-70B	NINE ELMS-70A	NINE ELMS-70A	NINE ELMS-70A	NINE ELMS-70A
30745	BASINGSTOKE-70D	BASINGSTOKE-70D	BASINGSTOKE-70D	BASINGSTOKE-70D	BASINGSTOKE-70D	BASINGSTOKE-70D	BASINGSTOKE-70D
30746	BOURNEMOUTH-71B	BOURNEMOUTH-71B	BOURNEMOUTH-71B	BOURNEMOUTH-71B	BOURNEMOUTH-71B	BOURNEMOUTH-71B	BOURNEMOUTH-71B
30747	NINE ELMS-70A	NINE ELMS-70A	NINE ELMS-70A	NINE ELMS-70A	NINE ELMS-70A	NINE ELMS-70A	NINE ELMS-70A
30748	SALISBURY-72B	SALISBURY-72B	SALISBURY-72B	SALISBURY-72B	SALISBURY-72B	SALISBURY-72B	SALISBURY-72B
30749	EASTLEIGH-71A	EASTLEIGH-71A	EASTLEIGH-71A	EASTLEIGH-71A	EASTLEIGH-71A	EASTLEIGH-71A	EASTLEIGH-71A
30750	BOURNEMOUTH-71B	BOURNEMOUTH-71B	BOURNEMOUTH-71B	BOURNEMOUTH-71B	BOURNEMOUTH-71B	BOURNEMOUTH-71B	BOURNEMOUTH-71B
30751	EASTLEIGH-71A	EASTLEIGH-71A	NINE ELMS-70A	NINE ELMS-70A	NINE ELMS-70A	NINE ELMS-70A	NINE ELMS-70A
30752	EASTLEIGH-71A	EASTLEIGH-71A	NINE ELMS-70A	NINE ELMS-70A	NINE ELMS-70A	NINE ELMS-70A	NINE ELMS-70A
30753	SALISBURY-72B	SALISBURY-72B	BASINGSTOKE-70D	NINE ELMS-70A	NINE ELMS-70A	NINE ELMS-70A	BASINGSTOKE-70D
30754	BOURNEMOUTH-71B	BOURNEMOUTH-71B	BASINGSTOKE-70D	NINE ELMS-70A	NINE ELMS-70A	NINE ELMS-70A	BASINGSTOKE-70D
30755	EASTLEIGH-71A	EASTLEIGH-71A	EASTLEIGH-71A	EASTLEIGH-71A	EASTLEIGH-71A	EASTLEIGH-71A	EASTLEIGH-71A

loco	Sep-52	Dec-52	Mar-53	May-53	Jul-53	Sep-53	Nov-53
			S15 4-6-0 (1927)				
30823	SALISBURY - 72B	SALISBURY - 72B	SALISBURY - 72B	SALISBURY - 72B	SALISBURY - 72B	SALISBURY - 72B	SALISBURY - 72B
30824	SALISBURY - 72B	SALISBURY - 72B	SALISBURY - 72B	SALISBURY - 72B	SALISBURY - 72B	SALISBURY - 72B	SALISBURY - 72B
30825	SALISBURY - 72B	SALISBURY - 72B	SALISBURY - 72B	SALISBURY - 72B	SALISBURY - 72B	SALISBURY - 72B	SALISBURY - 72B
30826	SALISBURY - 72B	SALISBURY - 72B	SALISBURY - 72B	SALISBURY - 72B	SALISBURY - 72B	SALISBURY - 72B	SALISBURY - 72B
30827	SALISBURY - 72B	SALISBURY - 72B	SALISBURY - 72B	SALISBURY - 72B	SALISBURY - 72B	SALISBURY - 72B	SALISBURY - 72B
30828	SALISBURY - 72B	SALISBURY - 72B	SALISBURY - 72B	SALISBURY - 72B	SALISBURY - 72B	SALISBURY - 72B	SALISBURY - 72B
30829	SALISBURY - 72B	SALISBURY - 72B	SALISBURY - 72B	SALISBURY - 72B	SALISBURY - 72B	SALISBURY - 72B	SALISBURY - 72B
30830	SALISBURY - 72B	SALISBURY - 72B	SALISBURY - 72B	SALISBURY - 72B	SALISBURY - 72B	SALISBURY - 72B	SALISBURY - 72B
30831	SALISBURY - 72B	SALISBURY - 72B	SALISBURY - 72B	SALISBURY - 72B	SALISBURY - 72B	SALISBURY - 72B	SALISBURY - 72B
30832	SALISBURY - 72B	SALISBURY - 72B	SALISBURY - 72B	SALISBURY - 72B	SALISBURY - 72B	SALISBURY - 72B	SALISBURY - 72B
30833	FELTHAM - 70B	FELTHAM - 70B	FELTHAM - 70B	FELTHAM - 70B	FELTHAM - 70B	FELTHAM - 70B	FELTHAM - 70B
30834	FELTHAM - 70B	FELTHAM - 70B	FELTHAM - 70B	FELTHAM - 70B	FELTHAM - 70B	FELTHAM - 70B	FELTHAM - 70B
30835	REDHILL - 75B	REDHILL - 75B	REDHILL - 75B	REDHILL - 75B	REDHILL - 75B	REDHILL - 75B	REDHILL - 75B
30836	REDHILL - 75B	REDHILL - 75B	REDHILL - 75B	REDHILL - 75B	REDHILL - 75B	REDHILL - 75B	REDHILL - 75B
30837	REDHILL - 75B	REDHILL - 75B	REDHILL - 75B	REDHILL - 75B	REDHILL - 75B	REDHILL - 75B	REDHILL - 75B
			S15 4-6-0 (1920)				
30496	FELTHAM - 70B	FELTHAM - 70B	FELTHAM - 70B	FELTHAM - 70B	FELTHAM - 70B	FELTHAM - 70B	FELTHAM - 70B
30497	FELTHAM - 70B	FELTHAM - 70B	FELTHAM - 70B	FELTHAM - 70B	FELTHAM - 70B	FELTHAM - 70B	FELTHAM - 70B
30498	FELTHAM - 70B	FELTHAM - 70B	FELTHAM - 70B	FELTHAM - 70B	FELTHAM - 70B	FELTHAM - 70B	FELTHAM - 70B
30499	FELTHAM - 70B	FELTHAM - 70B	FELTHAM - 70B	FELTHAM - 70B	FELTHAM - 70B	FELTHAM - 70B	FELTHAM - 70B
30500	FELTHAM - 70B	FELTHAM - 70B	FELTHAM - 70B	FELTHAM - 70B	FELTHAM - 70B	FELTHAM - 70B	FELTHAM - 70B
30501	FELTHAM - 70B	FELTHAM - 70B	FELTHAM - 70B	FELTHAM - 70B	FELTHAM - 70B	FELTHAM - 70B	FELTHAM - 70B
30502	FELTHAM - 70B	FELTHAM - 70B	FELTHAM - 70B	FELTHAM - 70B	FELTHAM - 70B	FELTHAM - 70B	FELTHAM - 70B
30503	FELTHAM - 70B	FELTHAM - 70B	FELTHAM - 70B	FELTHAM - 70B	FELTHAM - 70B	FELTHAM - 70B	FELTHAM - 70B
30504	FELTHAM - 70B	FELTHAM - 70B	FELTHAM - 70B	FELTHAM - 70B	FELTHAM - 70B	FELTHAM - 70B	FELTHAM - 70B
30505	FELTHAM - 70B	FELTHAM - 70B	FELTHAM - 70B	FELTHAM - 70B	FELTHAM - 70B	FELTHAM - 70B	FELTHAM - 70B
30506	FELTHAM - 70B	FELTHAM - 70B	FELTHAM - 70B	FELTHAM - 70B	FELTHAM - 70B	FELTHAM - 70B	FELTHAM - 70B
30507	FELTHAM - 70B	FELTHAM - 70B	FELTHAM - 70B	FELTHAM - 70B	FELTHAM - 70B	FELTHAM - 70B	FELTHAM - 70B
30508	FELTHAM - 70B	FELTHAM - 70B	FELTHAM - 70B	FELTHAM - 70B	FELTHAM - 70B	FELTHAM - 70B	FELTHAM - 70B
30509	FELTHAM - 70B	FELTHAM - 70B	FELTHAM - 70B	FELTHAM - 70B	FELTHAM - 70B	FELTHAM - 70B	FELTHAM - 70B
30510	FELTHAM - 70B	FELTHAM - 70B	FELTHAM - 70B	FELTHAM - 70B	FELTHAM - 70B	FELTHAM - 70B	FELTHAM - 70B
30511	FELTHAM - 70B	FELTHAM - 70B	FELTHAM - 70B	FELTHAM - 70B	FELTHAM - 70B	FELTHAM - 70B	FELTHAM - 70B
30512	FELTHAM - 70B	FELTHAM - 70B	FELTHAM - 70B	FELTHAM - 70B	FELTHAM - 70B	FELTHAM - 70B	FELTHAM - 70B
30513	FELTHAM - 70B	FELTHAM - 70B	FELTHAM - 70B	FELTHAM - 70B	FELTHAM - 70B	FELTHAM - 70B	FELTHAM - 70B
30514	FELTHAM - 70B	FELTHAM - 70B	FELTHAM - 70B	FELTHAM - 70B	FELTHAM - 70B	FELTHAM - 70B	FELTHAM - 70B
30515	FELTHAM - 70B	FELTHAM - 70B	FELTHAM - 70B	FELTHAM - 70B	FELTHAM - 70B	FELTHAM - 70B	FELTHAM - 70B
			S15 4-6-0 (1936)				
30838	FELTHAM - 70B	FELTHAM - 70B	FELTHAM - 70B	FELTHAM - 70B	FELTHAM - 70B	FELTHAM - 70B	FELTHAM - 70B
30839	FELTHAM - 70B	FELTHAM - 70B	FELTHAM - 70B	FELTHAM - 70B	FELTHAM - 70B	FELTHAM - 70B	FELTHAM - 70B
30840	FELTHAM - 70B	FELTHAM - 70B	FELTHAM - 70B	FELTHAM - 70B	FELTHAM - 70B	FELTHAM - 70B	FELTHAM - 70B
30841	EXMOUTH JCN - 72A	EXMOUTH JCN - 72A	EXMOUTH JCN - 72A	EXMOUTH JCN - 72A	EXMOUTH JCN - 72A	EXMOUTH JCN - 72A	EXMOUTH JCN - 72A
30842	EXMOUTH JCN - 72A	EXMOUTH JCN - 72A	EXMOUTH JCN - 72A	EXMOUTH JCN - 72A	EXMOUTH JCN - 72A	EXMOUTH JCN - 72A	EXMOUTH JCN - 72A
30843	EXMOUTH JCN - 72A	EXMOUTH JCN - 72A	EXMOUTH JCN - 72A	EXMOUTH JCN - 72A	EXMOUTH JCN - 72A	EXMOUTH JCN - 72A	EXMOUTH JCN - 72A
30844	EXMOUTH JCN - 72A	EXMOUTH JCN - 72A	EXMOUTH JCN - 72A	EXMOUTH JCN - 72A	EXMOUTH JCN - 72A	EXMOUTH JCN - 72A	EXMOUTH JCN - 72A
30845	EXMOUTH JCN - 72A	EXMOUTH JCN - 72A	EXMOUTH JCN - 72A	EXMOUTH JCN - 72A	EXMOUTH JCN - 72A	EXMOUTH JCN - 72A	EXMOUTH JCN - 72A
30846	SALISBURY - 72B	SALISBURY - 72B	SALISBURY - 72B	SALISBURY - 72B	SALISBURY - 72B	EXMOUTH JCN - 72A	EXMOUTH JCN - 72A
30847	SALISBURY - 72B	SALISBURY - 72B	SALISBURY - 72B	SALISBURY - 72B	SALISBURY - 72B	SALISBURY - 72B	SALISBURY - 72B
			N15 4-6-0 (1918)				
30736	BOURNEMOUTH - 71B	BOURNEMOUTH - 71B	BOURNEMOUTH - 71B	BOURNEMOUTH - 71B	BOURNEMOUTH - 71B	BOURNEMOUTH - 71B	BOURNEMOUTH - 71B
30737	BOURNEMOUTH - 71B	BOURNEMOUTH - 71B	BOURNEMOUTH - 71B	BOURNEMOUTH - 71B	BOURNEMOUTH - 71B	BOURNEMOUTH - 71B	BOURNEMOUTH - 71B
30738	BOURNEMOUTH - 71B	BOURNEMOUTH - 71B	BOURNEMOUTH - 71B	BOURNEMOUTH - 71B	BOURNEMOUTH - 71B	BOURNEMOUTH - 71B	BOURNEMOUTH - 71B
30739	BOURNEMOUTH - 71B	BOURNEMOUTH - 71B	BOURNEMOUTH - 71B	BOURNEMOUTH - 71B	BOURNEMOUTH - 71B	BOURNEMOUTH - 71B	BOURNEMOUTH - 71B
30740	BOURNEMOUTH - 71B	BOURNEMOUTH - 71B	BOURNEMOUTH - 71B	BOURNEMOUTH - 71B	BOURNEMOUTH - 71B	BOURNEMOUTH - 71B	BOURNEMOUTH - 71B
30741	BOURNEMOUTH - 71B	BOURNEMOUTH - 71B	BOURNEMOUTH - 71B	BOURNEMOUTH - 71B	BOURNEMOUTH - 71B	BOURNEMOUTH - 71B	BOURNEMOUTH - 71B
30742	BOURNEMOUTH - 71B	BOURNEMOUTH - 71B	BOURNEMOUTH - 71B	BOURNEMOUTH - 71B	BOURNEMOUTH - 71B	BOURNEMOUTH - 71B	BOURNEMOUTH - 71B
30743	BOURNEMOUTH - 71B	BOURNEMOUTH - 71B	BOURNEMOUTH - 71B	BOURNEMOUTH - 71B	BOURNEMOUTH - 71B	BOURNEMOUTH - 71B	BOURNEMOUTH - 71B
30744	NINE ELMS - 70A	NINE ELMS - 70A	BASINGSTOKE - 70D	NINE ELMS - 70A	NINE ELMS - 70A	NINE ELMS - 70A	NINE ELMS - 70A
30745	BASINGSTOKE - 70D	BASINGSTOKE - 70D	BASINGSTOKE - 70D	BASINGSTOKE - 70D	BASINGSTOKE - 70D	BASINGSTOKE - 70D	BASINGSTOKE - 70D
30746	BOURNEMOUTH - 71B	BOURNEMOUTH - 71B	BOURNEMOUTH - 71B	BOURNEMOUTH - 71B	BOURNEMOUTH - 71B	BOURNEMOUTH - 71B	BOURNEMOUTH - 71B
30747	NINE ELMS - 70A	NINE ELMS - 70A	NINE ELMS - 70A	NINE ELMS - 70A	NINE ELMS - 70A	NINE ELMS - 70A	NINE ELMS - 70A
30748	SALISBURY - 72B	SALISBURY - 72B	SALISBURY - 72B	SALISBURY - 72B	SALISBURY - 72B	SALISBURY - 72B	SALISBURY - 72B
30749	EASTLEIGH - 71A	EASTLEIGH - 71A	EASTLEIGH - 71A	BASINGSTOKE - 70D	BASINGSTOKE - 70D	BASINGSTOKE - 70D	BASINGSTOKE - 70D
30750	BOURNEMOUTH - 71B	BOURNEMOUTH - 71B	BOURNEMOUTH - 71B	BOURNEMOUTH - 71B	BOURNEMOUTH - 71B	BOURNEMOUTH - 71B	BOURNEMOUTH - 71B
30751	NINE ELMS - 70A	NINE ELMS - 70A	NINE ELMS - 70A	NINE ELMS - 70A	NINE ELMS - 70A	NINE ELMS - 70A	NINE ELMS - 70A
30752	NINE ELMS - 70A	NINE ELMS - 70A	NINE ELMS - 70A	NINE ELMS - 70A	NINE ELMS - 70A	NINE ELMS - 70A	NINE ELMS - 70A
30753	BASINGSTOKE - 70D	BASINGSTOKE - 70D	BASINGSTOKE - 70D	BASINGSTOKE - 70D	BASINGSTOKE - 70D	BASINGSTOKE - 70D	BASINGSTOKE - 70D
30754	BASINGSTOKE - 70D	W/D	W/D	W/D	W/D	W/D	W/D
30755	EASTLEIGH - 71A	EASTLEIGH - 71A	EASTLEIGH - 71A	EASTLEIGH - 71A	EASTLEIGH - 71A	EASTLEIGH - 71A	EASTLEIGH - 71A

Other than the H15's, the S15 4-6-0's were the only large goods engine that the Southern possessed and spent most of their lives at Feltham, Salisbury and Exmouth Junction although some of their booked workings included return trips between London and Southampton. One of the few exceptional moves made by the class came in the summer of 1951 when three S15's moved permanently from Feltham to Redhill to work the 01.15 Hoo Junction - Eastleigh between Redhill and Woking and the 17.40 Dover - Reading from Redhill. The third engine remained as a spare.

On the South Western main line their duties included most of the goods trains of note to and from the West of England, usually with a change of engines at Salisbury. It was not unknown for them to be seen on passenger services and in fact one of the Feltham allocation was booked to work an evening train between Waterloo and Basingstoke. The class also tended to monopolise stopping services between Salisbury and Exeter on summer Saturdays in order to release the usual passenger engines for relief express services. All the S15 4-6-0's survived until dieselisation.

In common with the S15 and H15 classes, the N15 King Arthur 4-6-0's comprised several subsections, the earliest of which were the 1918 'Urie' Arthurs. These engines had not at first been the success expected and they remained rather disappointing machines until being rebuilt by the Southern Railway. Once assimilated into the N15 class, no running distinction was drawn between the older and newer member of the type until 1955 when age and the arrival of standard 5MT 4-6-0's saw the gradual withdrawal of the Urie engines, the type becoming extinct in 1959.

loco	Jan-54	Mar-54	May-54	Jun-54	Aug-54	Oct-54	Dec-54
				S15 4-6-0 (1927)			
30823	SALISBURY-72B	SALISBURY-72B	SALISBURY-72B	SALISBURY-72B	SALISBURY-72B	SALISBURY-72B	SALISBURY-72B
30824	SALISBURY-72B	SALISBURY-72B	SALISBURY-72B	SALISBURY-72B	SALISBURY-72B	SALISBURY-72B	SALISBURY-72B
30825	SALISBURY-72B	SALISBURY-72B	SALISBURY-72B	SALISBURY-72B	SALISBURY-72B	SALISBURY-72B	SALISBURY-72B
30826	SALISBURY-72B	SALISBURY-72B	SALISBURY-72B	SALISBURY-72B	SALISBURY-72B	SALISBURY-72B	SALISBURY-72B
30827	SALISBURY-72B	SALISBURY-72B	SALISBURY-72B	SALISBURY-72B	SALISBURY-72B	SALISBURY-72B	SALISBURY-72B
30828	SALISBURY-72B	SALISBURY-72B	SALISBURY-72B	SALISBURY-72B	SALISBURY-72B	SALISBURY-72B	SALISBURY-72B
30829	SALISBURY-72B	SALISBURY-72B	SALISBURY-72B	SALISBURY-72B	SALISBURY-72B	SALISBURY-72B	SALISBURY-72B
30830	SALISBURY-72B	SALISBURY-72B	SALISBURY-72B	SALISBURY-72B	SALISBURY-72B	SALISBURY-72B	SALISBURY-72B
30831	SALISBURY-72B	SALISBURY-72B	SALISBURY-72B	SALISBURY-72B	SALISBURY-72B	SALISBURY-72B	SALISBURY-72B
30832	SALISBURY-72B	SALISBURY-72B	SALISBURY-72B	SALISBURY-72B	SALISBURY-72B	SALISBURY-72B	SALISBURY-72B
30833	FELTHAM-70B	FELTHAM-70B	FELTHAM-70B	FELTHAM-70B	FELTHAM-70B	FELTHAM-70B	FELTHAM-70B
30834	FELTHAM-70B	FELTHAM-70B	FELTHAM-70B	FELTHAM-70B	FELTHAM-70B	FELTHAM-70B	FELTHAM-70B
30835	REDHILL-75B	REDHILL-75B	REDHILL-75B	REDHILL-75B	REDHILL-75B	REDHILL-75B	REDHILL-75B
30836	REDHILL-75B	REDHILL-75B	REDHILL-75B	REDHILL-75B	REDHILL-75B	REDHILL-75B	REDHILL-75B
30837	REDHILL-75B	REDHILL-75B	REDHILL-75B	REDHILL-75B	REDHILL-75B	REDHILL-75B	REDHILL-75B
				S15 4-6-0 (1920)			
30496	FELTHAM-70B	FELTHAM-70B	FELTHAM-70B	FELTHAM-70B	FELTHAM-70B	FELTHAM-70B	FELTHAM-70B
30497	FELTHAM-70B	FELTHAM-70B	FELTHAM-70B	FELTHAM-70B	FELTHAM-70B	FELTHAM-70B	FELTHAM-70B
30498	FELTHAM-70B	FELTHAM-70B	FELTHAM-70B	FELTHAM-70B	FELTHAM-70B	FELTHAM-70B	FELTHAM-70B
30499	FELTHAM-70B	FELTHAM-70B	FELTHAM-70B	FELTHAM-70B	FELTHAM-70B	FELTHAM-70B	FELTHAM-70B
30500	FELTHAM-70B	FELTHAM-70B	FELTHAM-70B	FELTHAM-70B	FELTHAM-70B	FELTHAM-70B	FELTHAM-70B
30501	FELTHAM-70B	FELTHAM-70B	FELTHAM-70B	FELTHAM-70B	FELTHAM-70B	FELTHAM-70B	FELTHAM-70B
30502	FELTHAM-70B	FELTHAM-70B	FELTHAM-70B	FELTHAM-70B	FELTHAM-70B	FELTHAM-70B	FELTHAM-70B
30503	FELTHAM-70B	FELTHAM-70B	FELTHAM-70B	FELTHAM-70B	FELTHAM-70B	FELTHAM-70B	FELTHAM-70B
30504	FELTHAM-70B	FELTHAM-70B	FELTHAM-70B	FELTHAM-70B	FELTHAM-70B	FELTHAM-70B	FELTHAM-70B
30505	FELTHAM-70B	FELTHAM-70B	FELTHAM-70B	FELTHAM-70B	FELTHAM-70B	FELTHAM-70B	FELTHAM-70B
30506	FELTHAM-70B	FELTHAM-70B	FELTHAM-70B	FELTHAM-70B	FELTHAM-70B	FELTHAM-70B	FELTHAM-70B
30507	FELTHAM-70B	FELTHAM-70B	FELTHAM-70B	FELTHAM-70B	FELTHAM-70B	FELTHAM-70B	FELTHAM-70B
30508	FELTHAM-70B	FELTHAM-70B	FELTHAM-70B	FELTHAM-70B	FELTHAM-70B	FELTHAM-70B	FELTHAM-70B
30509	FELTHAM-70B	FELTHAM-70B	FELTHAM-70B	FELTHAM-70B	FELTHAM-70B	FELTHAM-70B	FELTHAM-70B
30510	FELTHAM-70B	FELTHAM-70B	FELTHAM-70B	FELTHAM-70B	FELTHAM-70B	FELTHAM-70B	FELTHAM-70B
30511	FELTHAM-70B	FELTHAM-70B	FELTHAM-70B	FELTHAM-70B	FELTHAM-70B	FELTHAM-70B	FELTHAM-70B
30512	FELTHAM-70B	FELTHAM-70B	FELTHAM-70B	FELTHAM-70B	FELTHAM-70B	FELTHAM-70B	FELTHAM-70B
30513	FELTHAM-70B	FELTHAM-70B	FELTHAM-70B	FELTHAM-70B	FELTHAM-70B	FELTHAM-70B	FELTHAM-70B
30514	FELTHAM-70B	FELTHAM-70B	FELTHAM-70B	FELTHAM-70B	FELTHAM-70B	FELTHAM-70B	FELTHAM-70B
30515	FELTHAM-70B	FELTHAM-70B	FELTHAM-70B	FELTHAM-70B	FELTHAM-70B	FELTHAM-70B	FELTHAM-70B
				S15 4-6-0 (1936)			
30838	FELTHAM-70B	FELTHAM-70B	FELTHAM-70B	FELTHAM-70B	FELTHAM-70B	FELTHAM-70B	FELTHAM-70B
30839	FELTHAM-70B	FELTHAM-70B	FELTHAM-70B	FELTHAM-70B	FELTHAM-70B	FELTHAM-70B	FELTHAM-70B
30840	FELTHAM-70B	FELTHAM-70B	FELTHAM-70B	FELTHAM-70B	FELTHAM-70B	FELTHAM-70B	FELTHAM-70B
30841	EXMOUTH JCN-72A	EXMOUTH JCN-72A	EXMOUTH JCN-72A	EXMOUTH JCN-72A	EXMOUTH JCN-72A	EXMOUTH JCN-72A	EXMOUTH JCN-72A
30842	EXMOUTH JCN-72A	EXMOUTH JCN-72A	EXMOUTH JCN-72A	EXMOUTH JCN-72A	EXMOUTH JCN-72A	EXMOUTH JCN-72A	EXMOUTH JCN-72A
30843	EXMOUTH JCN-72A	EXMOUTH JCN-72A	EXMOUTH JCN-72A	EXMOUTH JCN-72A	EXMOUTH JCN-72A	EXMOUTH JCN-72A	EXMOUTH JCN-72A
30844	EXMOUTH JCN-72A	EXMOUTH JCN-72A	EXMOUTH JCN-72A	EXMOUTH JCN-72A	EXMOUTH JCN-72A	EXMOUTH JCN-72A	EXMOUTH JCN-72A
30845	EXMOUTH JCN-72A	EXMOUTH JCN-72A	EXMOUTH JCN-72A	EXMOUTH JCN-72A	EXMOUTH JCN-72A	EXMOUTH JCN-72A	EXMOUTH JCN-72A
30846	EXMOUTH JCN-72A	EXMOUTH JCN-72A	EXMOUTH JCN-72A	EXMOUTH JCN-72A	EXMOUTH JCN-72A	EXMOUTH JCN-72A	EXMOUTH JCN-72A
30847	SALISBURY-72B	SALISBURY-72B	SALISBURY-72B	SALISBURY-72B	SALISBURY-72B	SALISBURY-72B	SALISBURY-72B
				N15 4-6-0 (1918)			
30736	BOURNEMOUTH-71B	BOURNEMOUTH-71B	BOURNEMOUTH-71B	BOURNEMOUTH-71B	BOURNEMOUTH-71B	BOURNEMOUTH-71B	BOURNEMOUTH-71B
30737	BOURNEMOUTH-71B	BOURNEMOUTH-71B	BOURNEMOUTH-71B	BOURNEMOUTH-71B	BOURNEMOUTH-71B	BOURNEMOUTH-71B	BOURNEMOUTH-71B
30738	BOURNEMOUTH-71B	BOURNEMOUTH-71B	BOURNEMOUTH-71B	BOURNEMOUTH-71B	BOURNEMOUTH-71B	BOURNEMOUTH-71B	BOURNEMOUTH-71B
30739	BOURNEMOUTH-71B	BOURNEMOUTH-71B	BOURNEMOUTH-71B	BOURNEMOUTH-71B	BOURNEMOUTH-71B	BOURNEMOUTH-71B	BOURNEMOUTH-71B
30740	BOURNEMOUTH-71B	BOURNEMOUTH-71B	BOURNEMOUTH-71B	BOURNEMOUTH-71B	BOURNEMOUTH-71B	BOURNEMOUTH-71B	BOURNEMOUTH-71B
30741	BOURNEMOUTH-71B	BOURNEMOUTH-71B	BOURNEMOUTH-71B	BOURNEMOUTH-71B	BOURNEMOUTH-71B	BOURNEMOUTH-71B	BOURNEMOUTH-71B
30742	BOURNEMOUTH-71B	BOURNEMOUTH-71B	BOURNEMOUTH-71B	BOURNEMOUTH-71B	BOURNEMOUTH-71B	BOURNEMOUTH-71B	BOURNEMOUTH-71B
30743	BOURNEMOUTH-71B	BOURNEMOUTH-71B	BOURNEMOUTH-71B	BOURNEMOUTH-71B	BOURNEMOUTH-71B	BOURNEMOUTH-71B	BOURNEMOUTH-71B
30744	NINE ELMS-70A	NINE ELMS-70A	NINE ELMS-70A	NINE ELMS-70A	NINE ELMS-70A	NINE ELMS-70A	NINE ELMS-70A
30745	BASINGSTOKE-70D	BASINGSTOKE-70D	BASINGSTOKE-70D	BASINGSTOKE-70D	BASINGSTOKE-70D	BASINGSTOKE-70D	BASINGSTOKE-70D
30746	BOURNEMOUTH-71B	BOURNEMOUTH-71B	BOURNEMOUTH-71B	BOURNEMOUTH-71B	BOURNEMOUTH-71B	BOURNEMOUTH-71B	BOURNEMOUTH-71B
30747	NINE ELMS-70A	NINE ELMS-70A	NINE ELMS-70A	EASTLEIGH-71A	EASTLEIGH-71A	EASTLEIGH-71A	EASTLEIGH-71A
30748	SALISBURY-72B	SALISBURY-72B	SALISBURY-72B	SALISBURY-72B	SALISBURY-72B	SALISBURY-72B	SALISBURY-72B
30749	BASINGSTOKE-70D	BASINGSTOKE-70D	BASINGSTOKE-70D	BASINGSTOKE-70D	BASINGSTOKE-70D	BASINGSTOKE-70D	BASINGSTOKE-70D
30750	BOURNEMOUTH-71B	BOURNEMOUTH-71B	BOURNEMOUTH-71B	BOURNEMOUTH-71B	BOURNEMOUTH-71B	BOURNEMOUTH-71B	BOURNEMOUTH-71B
30751	NINE ELMS-70A	NINE ELMS-70A	NINE ELMS-70A	NINE ELMS-70A	NINE ELMS-70A	NINE ELMS-70A	NINE ELMS-70A
30752	NINE ELMS-70A	NINE ELMS-70A	NINE ELMS-70A	NINE ELMS-70A	NINE ELMS-70A	NINE ELMS-70A	NINE ELMS-70A
30753	BASINGSTOKE-70D	BASINGSTOKE-70D	BASINGSTOKE-70D	BASINGSTOKE-70D	BASINGSTOKE-70D	BASINGSTOKE-70D	BASINGSTOKE-70D
30755	EASTLEIGH-71A	EASTLEIGH-71A	EASTLEIGH-71A	EASTLEIGH-71A	EASTLEIGH-71A	EASTLEIGH-71A	EASTLEIGH-71A

loco	Feb-55	Apr-55	Jun-55	Aug-55	Sep-55	Nov-55	Dec-55
				S15 4-6-0 (1927)			
30823	SALISBURY-72B	SALISBURY-72B	SALISBURY-72B	SALISBURY-72B	SALISBURY-72B	SALISBURY-72B	SALISBURY-72B
30824	SALISBURY-72B	SALISBURY-72B	SALISBURY-72B	SALISBURY-72B	SALISBURY-72B	SALISBURY-72B	SALISBURY-72B
30825	SALISBURY-72B	SALISBURY-72B	SALISBURY-72B	SALISBURY-72B	SALISBURY-72B	SALISBURY-72B	SALISBURY-72B
30826	SALISBURY-72B	SALISBURY-72B	SALISBURY-72B	SALISBURY-72B	SALISBURY-72B	SALISBURY-72B	SALISBURY-72B
30827	SALISBURY-72B	SALISBURY-72B	SALISBURY-72B	SALISBURY-72B	SALISBURY-72B	SALISBURY-72B	SALISBURY-72B
30828	SALISBURY-72B	SALISBURY-72B	SALISBURY-72B	SALISBURY-72B	SALISBURY-72B	SALISBURY-72B	SALISBURY-72B
30829	SALISBURY-72B	SALISBURY-72B	SALISBURY-72B	SALISBURY-72B	SALISBURY-72B	SALISBURY-72B	SALISBURY-72B
30830	SALISBURY-72B	SALISBURY-72B	SALISBURY-72B	SALISBURY-72B	SALISBURY-72B	SALISBURY-72B	SALISBURY-72B
30831	SALISBURY-72B	SALISBURY-72B	SALISBURY-72B	SALISBURY-72B	SALISBURY-72B	SALISBURY-72B	SALISBURY-72B
30832	SALISBURY-72B	SALISBURY-72B	SALISBURY-72B	SALISBURY-72B	SALISBURY-72B	SALISBURY-72B	SALISBURY-72B
30833	FELTHAM-70B	FELTHAM-70B	FELTHAM-70B	FELTHAM-70B	FELTHAM-70B	FELTHAM-70B	FELTHAM-70B
30834	FELTHAM-70B	FELTHAM-70B	FELTHAM-70B	FELTHAM-70B	FELTHAM-70B	FELTHAM-70B	FELTHAM-70B
30835	REDHILL-75B	REDHILL-75B	REDHILL-75B	REDHILL-75B	REDHILL-75B	REDHILL-75B	REDHILL-75B
30836	REDHILL-75B	REDHILL-75B	REDHILL-75B	REDHILL-75B	REDHILL-75B	REDHILL-75B	REDHILL-75B
30837	REDHILL-75B	REDHILL-75B	REDHILL-75B	REDHILL-75B	REDHILL-75B	REDHILL-75B	REDHILL-75B
				S15 4-6-0 (1920)			
30496	FELTHAM-70B	FELTHAM-70B	FELTHAM-70B	FELTHAM-70B	FELTHAM-70B	FELTHAM-70B	FELTHAM-70B
30497	FELTHAM-70B	FELTHAM-70B	FELTHAM-70B	FELTHAM-70B	FELTHAM-70B	FELTHAM-70B	FELTHAM-70B
30498	FELTHAM-70B	FELTHAM-70B	FELTHAM-70B	FELTHAM-70B	FELTHAM-70B	FELTHAM-70B	FELTHAM-70B
30499	FELTHAM-70B	FELTHAM-70B	FELTHAM-70B	FELTHAM-70B	FELTHAM-70B	FELTHAM-70B	FELTHAM-70B
30500	FELTHAM-70B	FELTHAM-70B	FELTHAM-70B	FELTHAM-70B	FELTHAM-70B	FELTHAM-70B	FELTHAM-70B
30501	FELTHAM-70B	FELTHAM-70B	FELTHAM-70B	FELTHAM-70B	FELTHAM-70B	FELTHAM-70B	FELTHAM-70B
30502	FELTHAM-70B	FELTHAM-70B	FELTHAM-70B	FELTHAM-70B	FELTHAM-70B	FELTHAM-70B	FELTHAM-70B
30503	FELTHAM-70B	FELTHAM-70B	FELTHAM-70B	FELTHAM-70B	FELTHAM-70B	FELTHAM-70B	FELTHAM-70B
30504	FELTHAM-70B	FELTHAM-70B	FELTHAM-70B	FELTHAM-70B	FELTHAM-70B	FELTHAM-70B	FELTHAM-70B
30505	FELTHAM-70B	FELTHAM-70B	FELTHAM-70B	FELTHAM-70B	FELTHAM-70B	FELTHAM-70B	FELTHAM-70B
30506	FELTHAM-70B	FELTHAM-70B	FELTHAM-70B	FELTHAM-70B	FELTHAM-70B	FELTHAM-70B	FELTHAM-70B
30507	FELTHAM-70B	FELTHAM-70B	FELTHAM-70B	FELTHAM-70B	FELTHAM-70B	FELTHAM-70B	FELTHAM-70B
30508	FELTHAM-70B	FELTHAM-70B	FELTHAM-70B	FELTHAM-70B	FELTHAM-70B	FELTHAM-70B	FELTHAM-70B
30509	FELTHAM-70B	FELTHAM-70B	FELTHAM-70B	FELTHAM-70B	FELTHAM-70B	FELTHAM-70B	FELTHAM-70B
30510	FELTHAM-70B	FELTHAM-70B	FELTHAM-70B	FELTHAM-70B	FELTHAM-70B	FELTHAM-70B	FELTHAM-70B
30511	FELTHAM-70B	FELTHAM-70B	FELTHAM-70B	FELTHAM-70B	FELTHAM-70B	FELTHAM-70B	FELTHAM-70B
30512	FELTHAM-70B	FELTHAM-70B	FELTHAM-70B	FELTHAM-70B	FELTHAM-70B	FELTHAM-70B	FELTHAM-70B
30513	FELTHAM-70B	FELTHAM-70B	FELTHAM-70B	FELTHAM-70B	FELTHAM-70B	FELTHAM-70B	FELTHAM-70B
30514	FELTHAM-70B	FELTHAM-70B	FELTHAM-70B	FELTHAM-70B	FELTHAM-70B	FELTHAM-70B	FELTHAM-70B
30515	FELTHAM-70B	FELTHAM-70B	FELTHAM-70B	FELTHAM-70B	FELTHAM-70B	FELTHAM-70B	FELTHAM-70B
				S15 4-6-0 (1936)			
30838	FELTHAM-70B	FELTHAM-70B	FELTHAM-70B	FELTHAM-70B	FELTHAM-70B	FELTHAM-70B	FELTHAM-70B
30839	FELTHAM-70B	FELTHAM-70B	FELTHAM-70B	FELTHAM-70B	FELTHAM-70B	FELTHAM-70B	FELTHAM-70B
30840	FELTHAM-70B	FELTHAM-70B	FELTHAM-70B	FELTHAM-70B	FELTHAM-70B	FELTHAM-70B	FELTHAM-70B
30841	EXMOUTH JCN-72A	EXMOUTH JCN-72A	EXMOUTH JCN-72A	EXMOUTH JCN-72A	EXMOUTH JCN-72A	EXMOUTH JCN-72A	EXMOUTH JCN-72A
30842	EXMOUTH JCN-72A	EXMOUTH JCN-72A	EXMOUTH JCN-72A	EXMOUTH JCN-72A	EXMOUTH JCN-72A	EXMOUTH JCN-72A	EXMOUTH JCN-72A
30843	EXMOUTH JCN-72A	EXMOUTH JCN-72A	EXMOUTH JCN-72A	EXMOUTH JCN-72A	EXMOUTH JCN-72A	EXMOUTH JCN-72A	EXMOUTH JCN-72A
30844	EXMOUTH JCN-72A	EXMOUTH JCN-72A	EXMOUTH JCN-72A	EXMOUTH JCN-72A	EXMOUTH JCN-72A	EXMOUTH JCN-72A	EXMOUTH JCN-72A
30845	EXMOUTH JCN-72A	EXMOUTH JCN-72A	EXMOUTH JCN-72A	EXMOUTH JCN-72A	EXMOUTH JCN-72A	EXMOUTH JCN-72A	EXMOUTH JCN-72A
30846	EXMOUTH JCN-72A	EXMOUTH JCN-72A	EXMOUTH JCN-72A	EXMOUTH JCN-72A	EXMOUTH JCN-72A	EXMOUTH JCN-72A	EXMOUTH JCN-72A
30847	SALISBURY-72B	SALISBURY-72B	SALISBURY-72B	SALISBURY-72B	SALISBURY-72B	SALISBURY-72B	SALISBURY-72B
				N15 4-6-0 (1918)			
30736	BOURNEMOUTH-71B	BOURNEMOUTH-71B	BOURNEMOUTH-71B	BOURNEMOUTH-71B	BOURNEMOUTH-71B	BOURNEMOUTH-71B	BOURNEMOUTH-71B
30737	BOURNEMOUTH-71B	BOURNEMOUTH-71B	BOURNEMOUTH-71B	BOURNEMOUTH-71B	BOURNEMOUTH-71B	BOURNEMOUTH-71B	BOURNEMOUTH-71B
30738	BOURNEMOUTH-71B	BOURNEMOUTH-71B	BOURNEMOUTH-71B	BOURNEMOUTH-71B	BOURNEMOUTH-71B	BOURNEMOUTH-71B	BOURNEMOUTH-71B
30739	BOURNEMOUTH-71B	BOURNEMOUTH-71B	BOURNEMOUTH-71B	BOURNEMOUTH-71B	BOURNEMOUTH-71B	BOURNEMOUTH-71B	BOURNEMOUTH-71B
30740	BOURNEMOUTH-71B	BOURNEMOUTH-71B	BOURNEMOUTH-71B	BOURNEMOUTH-71B	BOURNEMOUTH-71B	BOURNEMOUTH-71B	W/D
30741	BOURNEMOUTH-71B	BOURNEMOUTH-71B	BOURNEMOUTH-71B	BOURNEMOUTH-71B	BOURNEMOUTH-71B	BOURNEMOUTH-71B	BOURNEMOUTH-71B
30742	BOURNEMOUTH-71B	BOURNEMOUTH-71B	BOURNEMOUTH-71B	BOURNEMOUTH-71B	BOURNEMOUTH-71B	BOURNEMOUTH-71B	BOURNEMOUTH-71B
30743	BOURNEMOUTH-71B	BOURNEMOUTH-71B	BOURNEMOUTH-71B	BOURNEMOUTH-71B	W/D	W/D	W/D
30744	NINE ELMS-70A	NINE ELMS-70A	NINE ELMS-70A	NINE ELMS-70A	BASINGSTOKE-70D	BASINGSTOKE-70D	BASINGSTOKE-70D
30745	BASINGSTOKE-70D	BASINGSTOKE-70D	BASINGSTOKE-70D	BASINGSTOKE-70D	BASINGSTOKE-70D	BASINGSTOKE-70D	BASINGSTOKE-70D
30746	BOURNEMOUTH-71B	BOURNEMOUTH-71B	BOURNEMOUTH-71B	BOURNEMOUTH-71B	BOURNEMOUTH-71B	W/D	W/D
30747	EASTLEIGH-71A	EASTLEIGH-71A	EASTLEIGH-71A	EASTLEIGH-71A	EASTLEIGH-71A	EASTLEIGH-71A	EASTLEIGH-71A
30748	SALISBURY-72B	SALISBURY-72B	SALISBURY-72B	SALISBURY-72B	SALISBURY-72B	SALISBURY-72B	SALISBURY-72B
30749	BASINGSTOKE-70D	BASINGSTOKE-70D	BASINGSTOKE-70D	BASINGSTOKE-70D	EASTLEIGH-71A	EASTLEIGH-71A	EASTLEIGH-71A
30750	BOURNEMOUTH-71B	BOURNEMOUTH-71B	BOURNEMOUTH-71B	BOURNEMOUTH-71B	EASTLEIGH-71A	EASTLEIGH-71A	EASTLEIGH-71A
30751	NINE ELMS-70A	NINE ELMS-70A	NINE ELMS-70A	NINE ELMS-70A	NINE ELMS-70A	NINE ELMS-70A	NINE ELMS-70A
30752	NINE ELMS-70A	NINE ELMS-70A	NINE ELMS-70A	NINE ELMS-70A	NINE ELMS-70A	NINE ELMS-70A	W/D
30753	BASINGSTOKE-70D	BASINGSTOKE-70D	BASINGSTOKE-70D	BASINGSTOKE-70D	NINE ELMS-70A	BASINGSTOKE-70D	BASINGSTOKE-70D
30755	EASTLEIGH-71A	EASTLEIGH-71A	EASTLEIGH-71A	EASTLEIGH-71A	EASTLEIGH-71A	EASTLEIGH-71A	EASTLEIGH-71A

loco	Jan-56	Apr-56	May-56	Aug-56	Oct-56	Nov-56	Jan-57
				S15 4-6-0 (1927)			
30823	SALISBURY-72B	SALISBURY-72B	SALISBURY-72B	SALISBURY-72B	SALISBURY-72B	SALISBURY-72B	SALISBURY-72B
30824	SALISBURY-72B	SALISBURY-72B	SALISBURY-72B	SALISBURY-72B	SALISBURY-72B	SALISBURY-72B	SALISBURY-72B
30825	SALISBURY-72B	SALISBURY-72B	SALISBURY-72B	SALISBURY-72B	SALISBURY-72B	SALISBURY-72B	SALISBURY-72B
30826	SALISBURY-72B	SALISBURY-72B	SALISBURY-72B	SALISBURY-72B	SALISBURY-72B	SALISBURY-72B	SALISBURY-72B
30827	SALISBURY-72B	SALISBURY-72B	SALISBURY-72B	SALISBURY-72B	SALISBURY-72B	SALISBURY-72B	SALISBURY-72B
30828	SALISBURY-72B	SALISBURY-72B	SALISBURY-72B	SALISBURY-72B	SALISBURY-72B	SALISBURY-72B	SALISBURY-72B
30829	SALISBURY-72B	SALISBURY-72B	SALISBURY-72B	SALISBURY-72B	SALISBURY-72B	SALISBURY-72B	SALISBURY-72B
30830	SALISBURY-72B	SALISBURY-72B	SALISBURY-72B	SALISBURY-72B	SALISBURY-72B	SALISBURY-72B	SALISBURY-72B
30831	SALISBURY-72B	SALISBURY-72B	SALISBURY-72B	SALISBURY-72B	SALISBURY-72B	SALISBURY-72B	SALISBURY-72B
30832	SALISBURY-72B	SALISBURY-72B	SALISBURY-72B	SALISBURY-72B	SALISBURY-72B	SALISBURY-72B	SALISBURY-72B
30833	FELTHAM-70B	FELTHAM-70B	FELTHAM-70B	FELTHAM-70B	FELTHAM-70B	FELTHAM-70B	FELTHAM-70B
30834	FELTHAM-70B	FELTHAM-70B	FELTHAM-70B	FELTHAM-70B	FELTHAM-70B	FELTHAM-70B	FELTHAM-70B
30835	REDHILL-75B	REDHILL-75B	REDHILL-75B	REDHILL-75B	REDHILL-75B	REDHILL-75B	REDHILL-75B
30836	REDHILL-75B	REDHILL-75B	REDHILL-75B	REDHILL-75B	REDHILL-75B	REDHILL-75B	REDHILL-75B
30837	REDHILL-75B	REDHILL-75B	REDHILL-75B	REDHILL-75B	REDHILL-75B	REDHILL-75B	REDHILL-75B
				S15 4-6-0 (1920)			
30496	FELTHAM-70B	FELTHAM-70B	FELTHAM-70B	FELTHAM-70B	FELTHAM-70B	FELTHAM-70B	FELTHAM-70B
30497	FELTHAM-70B	FELTHAM-70B	FELTHAM-70B	FELTHAM-70B	FELTHAM-70B	FELTHAM-70B	FELTHAM-70B
30498	FELTHAM-70B	FELTHAM-70B	FELTHAM-70B	FELTHAM-70B	FELTHAM-70B	FELTHAM-70B	FELTHAM-70B
30499	FELTHAM-70B	FELTHAM-70B	FELTHAM-70B	FELTHAM-70B	FELTHAM-70B	FELTHAM-70B	FELTHAM-70B
30500	FELTHAM-70B	FELTHAM-70B	FELTHAM-70B	FELTHAM-70B	FELTHAM-70B	FELTHAM-70B	FELTHAM-70B
30501	FELTHAM-70B	FELTHAM-70B	FELTHAM-70B	FELTHAM-70B	FELTHAM-70B	FELTHAM-70B	FELTHAM-70B
30502	FELTHAM-70B	FELTHAM-70B	FELTHAM-70B	FELTHAM-70B	FELTHAM-70B	FELTHAM-70B	FELTHAM-70B
30503	FELTHAM-70B	FELTHAM-70B	FELTHAM-70B	FELTHAM-70B	FELTHAM-70B	FELTHAM-70B	FELTHAM-70B
30504	FELTHAM-70B	FELTHAM-70B	FELTHAM-70B	FELTHAM-70B	FELTHAM-70B	FELTHAM-70B	FELTHAM-70B
30505	FELTHAM-70B	FELTHAM-70B	FELTHAM-70B	FELTHAM-70B	FELTHAM-70B	FELTHAM-70B	FELTHAM-70B
30506	FELTHAM-70B	FELTHAM-70B	FELTHAM-70B	FELTHAM-70B	FELTHAM-70B	FELTHAM-70B	FELTHAM-70B
30507	FELTHAM-70B	FELTHAM-70B	FELTHAM-70B	FELTHAM-70B	FELTHAM-70B	FELTHAM-70B	FELTHAM-70B
30508	FELTHAM-70B	FELTHAM-70B	FELTHAM-70B	FELTHAM-70B	FELTHAM-70B	FELTHAM-70B	FELTHAM-70B
30509	FELTHAM-70B	FELTHAM-70B	FELTHAM-70B	FELTHAM-70B	FELTHAM-70B	FELTHAM-70B	FELTHAM-70B
30510	FELTHAM-70B	FELTHAM-70B	FELTHAM-70B	FELTHAM-70B	FELTHAM-70B	FELTHAM-70B	FELTHAM-70B
30511	FELTHAM-70B	FELTHAM-70B	FELTHAM-70B	FELTHAM-70B	FELTHAM-70B	FELTHAM-70B	FELTHAM-70B
30512	FELTHAM-70B	FELTHAM-70B	FELTHAM-70B	FELTHAM-70B	FELTHAM-70B	FELTHAM-70B	FELTHAM-70B
30513	FELTHAM-70B	FELTHAM-70B	FELTHAM-70B	FELTHAM-70B	FELTHAM-70B	FELTHAM-70B	FELTHAM-70B
30514	FELTHAM-70B	FELTHAM-70B	FELTHAM-70B	FELTHAM-70B	FELTHAM-70B	FELTHAM-70B	FELTHAM-70B
30515	FELTHAM-70B	FELTHAM-70B	FELTHAM-70B	FELTHAM-70B	FELTHAM-70B	FELTHAM-70B	FELTHAM-70B
				S15 4-6-0 (1936)			
30838	FELTHAM-70B	FELTHAM-70B	FELTHAM-70B	FELTHAM-70B	FELTHAM-70B	FELTHAM-70B	FELTHAM-70B
30839	FELTHAM-70B	FELTHAM-70B	FELTHAM-70B	FELTHAM-70B	FELTHAM-70B	FELTHAM-70B	FELTHAM-70B
30840	FELTHAM-70B	FELTHAM-70B	FELTHAM-70B	FELTHAM-70B	FELTHAM-70B	FELTHAM-70B	FELTHAM-70B
30841	EXMOUTH JCN-72A	EXMOUTH JCN-72A	EXMOUTH JCN-72A	EXMOUTH JCN-72A	EXMOUTH JCN-72A	EXMOUTH JCN-72A	EXMOUTH JCN-72A
30842	EXMOUTH JCN-72A	EXMOUTH JCN-72A	EXMOUTH JCN-72A	EXMOUTH JCN-72A	EXMOUTH JCN-72A	EXMOUTH JCN-72A	EXMOUTH JCN-72A
30843	EXMOUTH JCN-72A	EXMOUTH JCN-72A	EXMOUTH JCN-72A	EXMOUTH JCN-72A	EXMOUTH JCN-72A	EXMOUTH JCN-72A	EXMOUTH JCN-72A
30844	EXMOUTH JCN-72A	EXMOUTH JCN-72A	EXMOUTH JCN-72A	EXMOUTH JCN-72A	EXMOUTH JCN-72A	EXMOUTH JCN-72A	EXMOUTH JCN-72A
30845	EXMOUTH JCN-72A	EXMOUTH JCN-72A	EXMOUTH JCN-72A	EXMOUTH JCN-72A	EXMOUTH JCN-72A	EXMOUTH JCN-72A	EXMOUTH JCN-72A
30846	EXMOUTH JCN-72A	EXMOUTH JCN-72A	EXMOUTH JCN-72A	EXMOUTH JCN-72A	EXMOUTH JCN-72A	EXMOUTH JCN-72A	EXMOUTH JCN-72A
30847	SALISBURY-72B	SALISBURY-72B	SALISBURY-72B	SALISBURY-72B	SALISBURY-72B	SALISBURY-72B	SALISBURY-72B
				N15 4-6-0 (1918)			
30736	BOURNEMOUTH-71B	BOURNEMOUTH-71B	BOURNEMOUTH-71B	BOURNEMOUTH-71B	WD	WD	WD
30737	BOURNEMOUTH-71B	BOURNEMOUTH-71B	BOURNEMOUTH-71B	WD	WD	WD	WD
30738	BOURNEMOUTH-71B	BOURNEMOUTH-71B	BOURNEMOUTH-71B	BOURNEMOUTH-71B	BOURNEMOUTH-71B	BOURNEMOUTH-71B	BOURNEMOUTH-71B
30739	BOURNEMOUTH-71B	BOURNEMOUTH-71B	BOURNEMOUTH-71B	BOURNEMOUTH-71B	BOURNEMOUTH-71B	BOURNEMOUTH-71B	BOURNEMOUTH-71B
30742	BOURNEMOUTH-71B	BOURNEMOUTH-71B	BOURNEMOUTH-71B	BOURNEMOUTH-71B	BOURNEMOUTH-71B	BOURNEMOUTH-71B	WD
30747	EASTLEIGH-71A	EASTLEIGH-71A	EASTLEIGH-71A	EASTLEIGH-71A	WD	WD	WD
30748	SALISBURY-72B	SALISBURY-72B	SALISBURY-72B	SALISBURY-72B	SALISBURY-72B	SALISBURY-72B	SALISBURY-72B
30749	EASTLEIGH-71A	EASTLEIGH-71A	BASINGSTOKE-70D	BASINGSTOKE-70D	BASINGSTOKE-70D	BASINGSTOKE-70D	BASINGSTOKE-70D
30750	NINE ELMS-70A	NINE ELMS-70A	NINE ELMS-70A	NINE ELMS-70A	NINE ELMS-70A	NINE ELMS-70A	NINE ELMS-70A
30751	NINE ELMS-70A	NINE ELMS-70A	BASINGSTOKE-70D	BASINGSTOKE-70D	BASINGSTOKE-70D	BASINGSTOKE-70D	BASINGSTOKE-70D
30753	BASINGSTOKE-70D	BASINGSTOKE-70D	BASINGSTOKE-70D	BASINGSTOKE-70D	BASINGSTOKE-70D	BASINGSTOKE-70D	BASINGSTOKE-70D
30755	NINE ELMS-70A	NINE ELMS-70A	BASINGSTOKE-70D	BASINGSTOKE-70D	BASINGSTOKE-70D	BASINGSTOKE-70D	BASINGSTOKE-70D

loco	Mar-57	Jun-57	Jul-57	Oct-57	Jan-58	Feb-58	Mar-58
				S15 4-6-0 (1927)			
30823 SALISBURY - 72B	SALISBURY - 72B	SALISBURY - 72B	SALISBURY - 72B	SALISBURY - 72B	SALISBURY - 72B	SALISBURY - 72B
30824 SALISBURY - 72B	SALISBURY - 72B	SALISBURY - 72B	SALISBURY - 72B	SALISBURY - 72B	SALISBURY - 72B	SALISBURY - 72B
30825 SALISBURY - 72B	SALISBURY - 72B	SALISBURY - 72B	SALISBURY - 72B	SALISBURY - 72B	SALISBURY - 72B	SALISBURY - 72B
30826 SALISBURY - 72B	SALISBURY - 72B	SALISBURY - 72B	SALISBURY - 72B	SALISBURY - 72B	SALISBURY - 72B	SALISBURY - 72B
30827 SALISBURY - 72B	SALISBURY - 72B	SALISBURY - 72B	SALISBURY - 72B	SALISBURY - 72B	SALISBURY - 72B	SALISBURY - 72B
30828 SALISBURY - 72B	SALISBURY - 72B	SALISBURY - 72B	SALISBURY - 72B	SALISBURY - 72B	SALISBURY - 72B	SALISBURY - 72B
30829 SALISBURY - 72B	SALISBURY - 72B	SALISBURY - 72B	SALISBURY - 72B	SALISBURY - 72B	SALISBURY - 72B	SALISBURY - 72B
30830 SALISBURY - 72B	SALISBURY - 72B	SALISBURY - 72B	SALISBURY - 72B	SALISBURY - 72B	SALISBURY - 72B	SALISBURY - 72B
30831 SALISBURY - 72B	SALISBURY - 72B	SALISBURY - 72B	SALISBURY - 72B	SALISBURY - 72B	SALISBURY - 72B	SALISBURY - 72B
30832 SALISBURY - 72B	SALISBURY - 72B	SALISBURY - 72B	SALISBURY - 72B	SALISBURY - 72B	SALISBURY - 72B	SALISBURY - 72B
30833 FELTHAM - 70B	FELTHAM - 70B	FELTHAM - 70B	FELTHAM - 70B	FELTHAM - 70B	FELTHAM - 70B	FELTHAM - 70B
30834 FELTHAM - 70B	FELTHAM - 70B	FELTHAM - 70B	FELTHAM - 70B	FELTHAM - 70B	FELTHAM - 70B	FELTHAM - 70B
30835 REDHILL - 75B	REDHILL - 75B	REDHILL - 75B	REDHILL - 75B	REDHILL - 75B	REDHILL - 75B	REDHILL - 75B
30836 REDHILL - 75B	REDHILL - 75B	REDHILL - 75B	REDHILL - 75B	REDHILL - 75B	REDHILL - 75B	REDHILL - 75B
30837 REDHILL - 75B	REDHILL - 75B	REDHILL - 75B	REDHILL - 75B	REDHILL - 75B	REDHILL - 75B	REDHILL - 75B
				S15 4-6-0 (1920)			
30496 FELTHAM - 70B	FELTHAM - 70B	FELTHAM - 70B	FELTHAM - 70B	FELTHAM - 70B	FELTHAM - 70B	FELTHAM - 70B
30497 FELTHAM - 70B	FELTHAM - 70B	FELTHAM - 70B	FELTHAM - 70B	FELTHAM - 70B	FELTHAM - 70B	FELTHAM - 70B
30498 FELTHAM - 70B	FELTHAM - 70B	FELTHAM - 70B	FELTHAM - 70B	FELTHAM - 70B	FELTHAM - 70B	FELTHAM - 70B
30499 FELTHAM - 70B	FELTHAM - 70B	FELTHAM - 70B	FELTHAM - 70B	FELTHAM - 70B	FELTHAM - 70B	FELTHAM - 70B
30500 FELTHAM - 70B	FELTHAM - 70B	FELTHAM - 70B	FELTHAM - 70B	FELTHAM - 70B	FELTHAM - 70B	FELTHAM - 70B
30501 FELTHAM - 70B	FELTHAM - 70B	FELTHAM - 70B	FELTHAM - 70B	FELTHAM - 70B	FELTHAM - 70B	FELTHAM - 70B
30502 FELTHAM - 70B	FELTHAM - 70B	FELTHAM - 70B	FELTHAM - 70B	FELTHAM - 70B	FELTHAM - 70B	FELTHAM - 70B
30503 FELTHAM - 70B	FELTHAM - 70B	FELTHAM - 70B	FELTHAM - 70B	FELTHAM - 70B	FELTHAM - 70B	FELTHAM - 70B
30504 FELTHAM - 70B	FELTHAM - 70B	FELTHAM - 70B	FELTHAM - 70B	FELTHAM - 70B	FELTHAM - 70B	FELTHAM - 70B
30505 FELTHAM - 70B	FELTHAM - 70B	FELTHAM - 70B	FELTHAM - 70B	FELTHAM - 70B	FELTHAM - 70B	FELTHAM - 70B
30506 FELTHAM - 70B	FELTHAM - 70B	FELTHAM - 70B	FELTHAM - 70B	FELTHAM - 70B	FELTHAM - 70B	FELTHAM - 70B
30507 FELTHAM - 70B	FELTHAM - 70B	FELTHAM - 70B	FELTHAM - 70B	FELTHAM - 70B	FELTHAM - 70B	FELTHAM - 70B
30508 FELTHAM - 70B	FELTHAM - 70B	FELTHAM - 70B	FELTHAM - 70B	FELTHAM - 70B	FELTHAM - 70B	FELTHAM - 70B
30509 FELTHAM - 70B	FELTHAM - 70B	FELTHAM - 70B	FELTHAM - 70B	FELTHAM - 70B	FELTHAM - 70B	FELTHAM - 70B
30510 FELTHAM - 70B	FELTHAM - 70B	FELTHAM - 70B	FELTHAM - 70B	FELTHAM - 70B	FELTHAM - 70B	FELTHAM - 70B
30511 FELTHAM - 70B	FELTHAM - 70B	FELTHAM - 70B	FELTHAM - 70B	FELTHAM - 70B	FELTHAM - 70B	FELTHAM - 70B
30512 FELTHAM - 70B	FELTHAM - 70B	FELTHAM - 70B	FELTHAM - 70B	FELTHAM - 70B	FELTHAM - 70B	FELTHAM - 70B
30513 FELTHAM - 70B	FELTHAM - 70B	FELTHAM - 70B	FELTHAM - 70B	FELTHAM - 70B	FELTHAM - 70B	FELTHAM - 70B
30514 FELTHAM - 70B	FELTHAM - 70B	FELTHAM - 70B	FELTHAM - 70B	FELTHAM - 70B	FELTHAM - 70B	FELTHAM - 70B
30515 FELTHAM - 70B	FELTHAM - 70B	FELTHAM - 70B	FELTHAM - 70B	FELTHAM - 70B	FELTHAM - 70B	FELTHAM - 70B
				S15 4-6-0 (1936)			
30838 FELTHAM - 70B	FELTHAM - 70B	FELTHAM - 70B	FELTHAM - 70B	FELTHAM - 70B	FELTHAM - 70B	FELTHAM - 70B
30839 FELTHAM - 70B	FELTHAM - 70B	FELTHAM - 70B	FELTHAM - 70B	FELTHAM - 70B	FELTHAM - 70B	FELTHAM - 70B
30840 FELTHAM - 70B	FELTHAM - 70B	FELTHAM - 70B	FELTHAM - 70B	FELTHAM - 70B	FELTHAM - 70B	FELTHAM - 70B
30841 EXMOUTH JCN - 72A	EXMOUTH JCN - 72A	EXMOUTH JCN - 72A	EXMOUTH JCN - 72A	EXMOUTH JCN - 72A	EXMOUTH JCN - 72A	EXMOUTH JCN - 72A
30842 EXMOUTH JCN - 72A	EXMOUTH JCN - 72A	EXMOUTH JCN - 72A	EXMOUTH JCN - 72A	EXMOUTH JCN - 72A	EXMOUTH JCN - 72A	EXMOUTH JCN - 72A
30843 EXMOUTH JCN - 72A	EXMOUTH JCN - 72A	EXMOUTH JCN - 72A	EXMOUTH JCN - 72A	EXMOUTH JCN - 72A	EXMOUTH JCN - 72A	EXMOUTH JCN - 72A
30844 EXMOUTH JCN - 72A	EXMOUTH JCN - 72A	EXMOUTH JCN - 72A	EXMOUTH JCN - 72A	EXMOUTH JCN - 72A	EXMOUTH JCN - 72A	EXMOUTH JCN - 72A
30845 EXMOUTH JCN - 72A	EXMOUTH JCN - 72A	EXMOUTH JCN - 72A	EXMOUTH JCN - 72A	EXMOUTH JCN - 72A	EXMOUTH JCN - 72A	EXMOUTH JCN - 72A
30846 EXMOUTH JCN - 72A	EXMOUTH JCN - 72A	EXMOUTH JCN - 72A	EXMOUTH JCN - 72A	EXMOUTH JCN - 72A	EXMOUTH JCN - 72A	EXMOUTH JCN - 72A
30847 SALISBURY - 72B	SALISBURY - 72B	SALISBURY - 72B	SALISBURY - 72B	SALISBURY - 72B	SALISBURY - 72B	SALISBURY - 72B
				N15 4-6-0 (1918)			
30738 BOURNEMOUTH - 71B	BASINGSTOKE - 70D	BASINGSTOKE - 70D	BASINGSTOKE - 70D	BASINGSTOKE - 70D	BASINGSTOKE - 70D	W/D
30739 BOURNEMOUTH - 71B	W/D	W/D	W/D	W/D	W/D	W/D
30748 SALISBURY - 72B	BASINGSTOKE - 70D	BASINGSTOKE - 70D	W/D	W/D	W/D	W/D
30749 BASINGSTOKE - 70D	W/D	W/D	W/D	W/D	W/D	W/D
30750 NINE ELMS - 70A	BASINGSTOKE - 70D	W/D	W/D	W/D	W/D	W/D
30751 BASINGSTOKE - 70D	W/D	W/D	W/D	W/D	W/D	W/D
30755 BASINGSTOKE - 70D	W/D	W/D	W/D	W/D	W/D	W/D

loco	May-58	Oct-58	Mar-59	Jun-59	Jul-59	Aug-59	Oct-59
S15 4-6-0 (1927)							
30823	SALISBURY - 72B	SALISBURY - 72B	SALISBURY - 72B	SALISBURY - 72B	SALISBURY - 72B	SALISBURY - 72B	SALISBURY - 72B
30824	SALISBURY - 72B	SALISBURY - 72B	SALISBURY - 72B	SALISBURY - 72B	SALISBURY - 72B	SALISBURY - 72B	SALISBURY - 72B
30825	SALISBURY - 72B	SALISBURY - 72B	SALISBURY - 72B	SALISBURY - 72B	SALISBURY - 72B	SALISBURY - 72B	SALISBURY - 72B
30826	SALISBURY - 72B	SALISBURY - 72B	SALISBURY - 72B	SALISBURY - 72B	SALISBURY - 72B	SALISBURY - 72B	SALISBURY - 72B
30827	SALISBURY - 72B	SALISBURY - 72B	SALISBURY - 72B	SALISBURY - 72B	SALISBURY - 72B	SALISBURY - 72B	SALISBURY - 72B
30828	SALISBURY - 72B	SALISBURY - 72B	SALISBURY released for passenger	SALISBURY - 72B	SALISBURY - 72B	SALISBURY - 72B	SALISBURY - 72B
30829	SALISBURY - 72B	SALISBURY - 72B	SALISBURY - 72B	SALISBURY - 72B	SALISBURY - 72B	SALISBURY - 72B	SALISBURY - 72B
30830	SALISBURY - 72B	SALISBURY - 72B	SALISBURY - 72B	SALISBURY - 72B	SALISBURY - 72B	SALISBURY - 72B	SALISBURY - 72B
30831	SALISBURY - 72B	SALISBURY - 72B	SALISBURY - 72B	SALISBURY - 72B	SALISBURY - 72B	SALISBURY - 72B	SALISBURY - 72B
30832	SALISBURY - 72B	SALISBURY - 72B	SALISBURY - 72B	SALISBURY - 72B	SALISBURY - 72B	SALISBURY - 72B	SALISBURY - 72B
30833	FELTHAM - 70B	FELTHAM - 70B	FELTHAM - 70B	FELTHAM - 70B	FELTHAM - 70B	FELTHAM - 70B	FELTHAM - 70B
30834	FELTHAM - 70B	FELTHAM - 70B	FELTHAM - 70B	FELTHAM - 70B	FELTHAM - 70B	FELTHAM - 70B	FELTHAM - 70B
30835	REDHILL - 75B	REDHILL - 75B	REDHILL - 75B	REDHILL - 75B	REDHILL - 75B	REDHILL - 75B	REDHILL - 75B
30836	REDHILL - 75B	REDHILL - 75B	REDHILL - 75B	REDHILL - 75B	REDHILL - 75B	REDHILL - 75B	REDHILL - 75B
30837	REDHILL - 75B	REDHILL - 75B	REDHILL - 75B	REDHILL - 75B	REDHILL - 75B	REDHILL - 75B	REDHILL - 75B
S15 4-6-0 (1920)							
30496	FELTHAM - 70B	FELTHAM - 70B	FELTHAM - 70B	FELTHAM - 70B	FELTHAM - 70B	FELTHAM - 70B	FELTHAM - 70B
30497	FELTHAM - 70B	FELTHAM - 70B	FELTHAM - 70B	FELTHAM - 70B	FELTHAM - 70B	FELTHAM - 70B	FELTHAM - 70B
30498	FELTHAM - 70B	FELTHAM - 70B	FELTHAM - 70B	FELTHAM - 70B	FELTHAM - 70B	FELTHAM - 70B	FELTHAM - 70B
30499	FELTHAM - 70B	FELTHAM - 70B	FELTHAM - 70B	FELTHAM - 70B	FELTHAM - 70B	FELTHAM - 70B	FELTHAM - 70B
30500	FELTHAM - 70B	FELTHAM - 70B	FELTHAM - 70B	FELTHAM - 70B	FELTHAM - 70B	FELTHAM - 70B	FELTHAM - 70B
30501	FELTHAM - 70B	FELTHAM - 70B	FELTHAM - 70B	FELTHAM - 70B	FELTHAM - 70B	FELTHAM - 70B	FELTHAM - 70B
30502	FELTHAM - 70B	FELTHAM - 70B	FELTHAM - 70B	FELTHAM - 70B	FELTHAM - 70B	FELTHAM - 70B	FELTHAM - 70B
30503	FELTHAM - 70B	FELTHAM - 70B	FELTHAM - 70B	FELTHAM - 70B	FELTHAM - 70B	FELTHAM - 70B	FELTHAM - 70B
30504	FELTHAM - 70B	FELTHAM - 70B	FELTHAM - 70B	FELTHAM - 70B	FELTHAM - 70B	FELTHAM - 70B	FELTHAM - 70B
30505	FELTHAM - 70B	FELTHAM - 70B	FELTHAM - 70B	FELTHAM - 70B	FELTHAM - 70B	FELTHAM - 70B	FELTHAM - 70B
30506	FELTHAM - 70B	FELTHAM - 70B	FELTHAM - 70B	FELTHAM - 70B	FELTHAM - 70B	FELTHAM - 70B	FELTHAM - 70B
30507	FELTHAM - 70B	FELTHAM - 70B	FELTHAM - 70B	FELTHAM - 70B	FELTHAM - 70B	FELTHAM - 70B	FELTHAM - 70B
30508	FELTHAM - 70B	FELTHAM - 70B	FELTHAM - 70B	FELTHAM - 70B	FELTHAM - 70B	FELTHAM - 70B	FELTHAM - 70B
30509	FELTHAM - 70B	FELTHAM - 70B	FELTHAM - 70B	FELTHAM - 70B	FELTHAM - 70B	FELTHAM - 70B	FELTHAM - 70B
30510	FELTHAM - 70B	FELTHAM - 70B	FELTHAM - 70B	FELTHAM - 70B	FELTHAM - 70B	FELTHAM - 70B	FELTHAM - 70B
30511	FELTHAM - 70B	FELTHAM - 70B	FELTHAM - 70B	FELTHAM - 70B	FELTHAM - 70B	FELTHAM - 70B	FELTHAM - 70B
30512	FELTHAM - 70B	FELTHAM - 70B	FELTHAM - 70B	FELTHAM - 70B	FELTHAM - 70B	FELTHAM - 70B	FELTHAM - 70B
30513	FELTHAM - 70B	FELTHAM - 70B	FELTHAM - 70B	FELTHAM - 70B	FELTHAM - 70B	FELTHAM - 70B	FELTHAM - 70B
30514	FELTHAM - 70B	FELTHAM - 70B	FELTHAM - 70B	FELTHAM - 70B	FELTHAM - 70B	FELTHAM - 70B	FELTHAM - 70B
30515	FELTHAM - 70B	FELTHAM - 70B	FELTHAM - 70B	FELTHAM - 70B	FELTHAM - 70B	FELTHAM - 70B	FELTHAM - 70B
S15 4-6-0 (1936)							
30838	FELTHAM - 70B	FELTHAM - 70B	FELTHAM - 70B	FELTHAM - 70B	FELTHAM - 70B	FELTHAM - 70B	FELTHAM - 70B
30839	FELTHAM - 70B	FELTHAM - 70B	FELTHAM - 70B	FELTHAM - 70B	FELTHAM - 70B	FELTHAM - 70B	FELTHAM - 70B
30840	FELTHAM - 70B	FELTHAM - 70B	FELTHAM - 70B	FELTHAM - 70B	FELTHAM - 70B	FELTHAM - 70B	FELTHAM - 70B
30841	EXMOUTH JCN - 72A	EXMOUTH JCN - 72A	EXMOUTH JCN - 72A	EXMOUTH JCN - 72A	EXMOUTH JCN - 72A	EXMOUTH JCN - 72A	EXMOUTH JCN - 72A
30842	EXMOUTH JCN - 72A	EXMOUTH JCN - 72A	EXMOUTH JCN - 72A	EXMOUTH JCN - 72A	EXMOUTH JCN - 72A	EXMOUTH JCN - 72A	EXMOUTH JCN - 72A
30843	EXMOUTH JCN - 72A	EXMOUTH JCN - 72A	EXMOUTH JCN - 72A	EXMOUTH JCN - 72A	EXMOUTH JCN - 72A	EXMOUTH JCN - 72A	EXMOUTH JCN - 72A
30844	EXMOUTH JCN - 72A	EXMOUTH JCN - 72A	EXMOUTH JCN - 72A	EXMOUTH JCN - 72A	EXMOUTH JCN - 72A	EXMOUTH JCN - 72A	EXMOUTH JCN - 72A
30845	EXMOUTH JCN - 72A	EXMOUTH JCN - 72A	EXMOUTH JCN - 72A	EXMOUTH JCN - 72A	EXMOUTH JCN - 72A	EXMOUTH JCN - 72A	EXMOUTH JCN - 72A
30846	EXMOUTH JCN - 72A	EXMOUTH JCN - 72A	EXMOUTH JCN - 72A	EXMOUTH JCN - 72A	EXMOUTH JCN - 72A	EXMOUTH JCN - 72A	EXMOUTH JCN - 72A
30847	SALISBURY - 72B	SALISBURY - 72B	SALISBURY - 72B	SALISBURY - 72B	REDHILL - 75B	REDHILL - 75B	REDHILL - 75B

Although described as a mixed-traffic class, with so many passenger engines on the books the S15 4-6-0's were more often than not to be found on goods services although summer Saturdays saw quite a number released for passenger duties, especially on stopping trains between Salisbury and Exeter. On 30 June 1964 30839 had been spare at Guildford after working a late morning goods from Woking and was given an Birmingham - Bournemouth relief to work, seen running in to Southampton Central, from Reading as a filling-in turn.

loco	Dec-59	Feb-60	Mar-60	Apr-60	Jul-60	Aug-60	Sep-60	Nov-60
S15 4-6-0 (1927)								
30823	SALISBURY-72B	SALISBURY-72B	SALISBURY-72B	SALISBURY-72B	SALISBURY-72B	SALISBURY-72B	SALISBURY-72B	SALISBURY-72B
30824	SALISBURY-72B	SALISBURY-72B	SALISBURY-72B	SALISBURY-72B	SALISBURY-72B	SALISBURY-72B	SALISBURY-72B	SALISBURY-72B
30825	SALISBURY-72B	SALISBURY-72B	SALISBURY-72B	SALISBURY-72B	SALISBURY-72B	SALISBURY-72B	SALISBURY-72B	SALISBURY-72B
30826	SALISBURY-72B	SALISBURY-72B	SALISBURY-72B	SALISBURY-72B	SALISBURY-72B	SALISBURY-72B	SALISBURY-72B	SALISBURY-72B
30827	SALISBURY-72B	SALISBURY-72B	SALISBURY-72B	SALISBURY-72B	SALISBURY-72B	SALISBURY-72B	SALISBURY-72B	SALISBURY-72B
30828	SALISBURY-72B	SALISBURY-72B	SALISBURY-72B	SALISBURY-72B	SALISBURY-72B	SALISBURY-72B	SALISBURY-72B	SALISBURY-72B
30829	SALISBURY-72B	SALISBURY-72B	SALISBURY-72B	SALISBURY-72B	SALISBURY-72B	SALISBURY-72B	SALISBURY-72B	SALISBURY-72B
30830	SALISBURY-72B	SALISBURY-72B	SALISBURY-72B	SALISBURY-72B	SALISBURY-72B	SALISBURY-72B	SALISBURY-72B	SALISBURY-72B
30831	SALISBURY-72B	SALISBURY-72B	SALISBURY-72B	SALISBURY-72B	SALISBURY-72B	SALISBURY-72B	SALISBURY-72B	SALISBURY-72B
30832	SALISBURY-72B	SALISBURY-72B	SALISBURY-72B	SALISBURY-72B	SALISBURY-72B	SALISBURY-72B	SALISBURY-72B	SALISBURY-72B
30833	FELTHAM-70B	FELTHAM-70B	FELTHAM-70B	FELTHAM-70B	FELTHAM-70B	FELTHAM-70B	FELTHAM-70B	FELTHAM-70B
30834	FELTHAM-70B	FELTHAM-70B	FELTHAM-70B	FELTHAM-70B	FELTHAM-70B	FELTHAM-70B	FELTHAM-70B	FELTHAM-70B
30835	REDHILL-75B	REDHILL-75B	REDHILL-75B	REDHILL-75B	REDHILL-75B	REDHILL-75B	REDHILL-75B	REDHILL-75B
30836	REDHILL-75B	REDHILL-75B	REDHILL-75B	REDHILL-75B	REDHILL-75B	REDHILL-75B	REDHILL-75B	REDHILL-75B
30837	REDHILL-75B	REDHILL-75B	REDHILL-75B	REDHILL-75B	REDHILL-75B	REDHILL-75B	REDHILL-75B	REDHILL-75B
S15 4-6-0 (1920)								
30496	FELTHAM-70B	FELTHAM-70B	FELTHAM-70B	FELTHAM-70B	FELTHAM-70B	FELTHAM-70B	FELTHAM-70B	FELTHAM-70B
30497	FELTHAM-70B	FELTHAM-70B	FELTHAM-70B	FELTHAM-70B	FELTHAM-70B	FELTHAM-70B	FELTHAM-70B	FELTHAM-70B
30498	FELTHAM-70B	FELTHAM-70B	FELTHAM-70B	FELTHAM-70B	FELTHAM-70B	FELTHAM-70B	FELTHAM-70B	FELTHAM-70B
30499	FELTHAM-70B	FELTHAM-70B	FELTHAM-70B	FELTHAM-70B	FELTHAM-70B	FELTHAM-70B	FELTHAM-70B	FELTHAM-70B
30500	FELTHAM-70B	FELTHAM-70B	FELTHAM-70B	FELTHAM-70B	FELTHAM-70B	FELTHAM-70B	FELTHAM-70B	FELTHAM-70B
30501	FELTHAM-70B	FELTHAM-70B	FELTHAM-70B	FELTHAM-70B	FELTHAM-70B	FELTHAM-70B	FELTHAM-70B	FELTHAM-70B
30502	FELTHAM-70B	FELTHAM-70B	FELTHAM-70B	FELTHAM-70B	FELTHAM-70B	FELTHAM-70B	FELTHAM-70B	FELTHAM-70B
30503	FELTHAM-70B	FELTHAM-70B	FELTHAM-70B	FELTHAM-70B	FELTHAM-70B	FELTHAM-70B	FELTHAM-70B	FELTHAM-70B
30504	FELTHAM-70B	FELTHAM-70B	FELTHAM-70B	FELTHAM-70B	FELTHAM-70B	FELTHAM-70B	FELTHAM-70B	FELTHAM-70B
30505	FELTHAM-70B	FELTHAM-70B	FELTHAM-70B	FELTHAM-70B	FELTHAM-70B	FELTHAM-70B	FELTHAM-70B	FELTHAM-70B
30506	FELTHAM-70B	FELTHAM-70B	FELTHAM-70B	FELTHAM-70B	FELTHAM-70B	FELTHAM-70B	FELTHAM-70B	FELTHAM-70B
30507	FELTHAM-70B	FELTHAM-70B	FELTHAM-70B	FELTHAM-70B	FELTHAM-70B	FELTHAM-70B	FELTHAM-70B	FELTHAM-70B
30508	FELTHAM-70B	FELTHAM-70B	FELTHAM-70B	FELTHAM-70B	FELTHAM-70B	FELTHAM-70B	FELTHAM-70B	FELTHAM-70B
30509	FELTHAM-70B	FELTHAM-70B	FELTHAM-70B	FELTHAM-70B	FELTHAM-70B	FELTHAM-70B	FELTHAM-70B	FELTHAM-70B
30510	FELTHAM-70B	FELTHAM-70B	FELTHAM-70B	FELTHAM-70B	FELTHAM-70B	FELTHAM-70B	FELTHAM-70B	FELTHAM-70B
30511	FELTHAM-70B	FELTHAM-70B	FELTHAM-70B	FELTHAM-70B	FELTHAM-70B	FELTHAM-70B	FELTHAM-70B	FELTHAM-70B
30512	FELTHAM-70B	FELTHAM-70B	FELTHAM-70B	FELTHAM-70B	FELTHAM-70B	FELTHAM-70B	FELTHAM-70B	FELTHAM-70B
30513	FELTHAM-70B	FELTHAM-70B	FELTHAM-70B	FELTHAM-70B	FELTHAM-70B	FELTHAM-70B	FELTHAM-70B	FELTHAM-70B
30514	FELTHAM-70B	FELTHAM-70B	FELTHAM-70B	FELTHAM-70B	FELTHAM-70B	FELTHAM-70B	FELTHAM-70B	FELTHAM-70B
30515	FELTHAM-70B	FELTHAM-70B	FELTHAM-70B	FELTHAM-70B	FELTHAM-70B	FELTHAM-70B	FELTHAM-70B	FELTHAM-70B
S15 4-6-0 (1936)								
30838	FELTHAM-70B	FELTHAM-70B	FELTHAM-70B	FELTHAM-70B	FELTHAM-70B	FELTHAM-70B	FELTHAM-70B	FELTHAM-70B
30839	FELTHAM-70B	FELTHAM-70B	FELTHAM-70B	FELTHAM-70B	FELTHAM-70B	FELTHAM-70B	FELTHAM-70B	FELTHAM-70B
30840	FELTHAM-70B	FELTHAM-70B	FELTHAM-70B	FELTHAM-70B	FELTHAM-70B	FELTHAM-70B	FELTHAM-70B	FELTHAM-70B
30841	EXMOUTH JCN-72A	EXMOUTH JCN-72A	EXMOUTH JCN-72A	EXMOUTH JCN-72A	EXMOUTH JCN-72A	EXMOUTH JCN-72A	EXMOUTH JCN-72A	EXMOUTH JCN-72A
30842	EXMOUTH JCN-72A	EXMOUTH JCN-72A	EXMOUTH JCN-72A	EXMOUTH JCN-72A	EXMOUTH JCN-72A	EXMOUTH JCN-72A	EXMOUTH JCN-72A	EXMOUTH JCN-72A
30843	EXMOUTH JCN-72A	EXMOUTH JCN-72A	EXMOUTH JCN-72A	EXMOUTH JCN-72A	EXMOUTH JCN-72A	EXMOUTH JCN-72A	EXMOUTH JCN-72A	EXMOUTH JCN-72A
30844	EXMOUTH JCN-72A	EXMOUTH JCN-72A	EXMOUTH JCN-72A	EXMOUTH JCN-72A	EXMOUTH JCN-72A	EXMOUTH JCN-72A	EXMOUTH JCN-72A	EXMOUTH JCN-72A
30845	EXMOUTH JCN-72A	EXMOUTH JCN-72A	EXMOUTH JCN-72A	EXMOUTH JCN-72A	EXMOUTH JCN-72A	EXMOUTH JCN-72A	EXMOUTH JCN-72A	EXMOUTH JCN-72A
30846	EXMOUTH JCN-72A	EXMOUTH JCN-72A	EXMOUTH JCN-72A	EXMOUTH JCN-72A	EXMOUTH JCN-72A	EXMOUTH JCN-72A	EXMOUTH JCN-72A	EXMOUTH JCN-72A
30847	REDHILL-75B	REDHILL-75B	REDHILL-75B	REDHILL-75B	REDHILL-75B	REDHILL-75B	REDHILL-75B	REDHILL-75B

S15 4-6-0 30837 waits, with its smokebox door hanging open, to enter Eastleigh works in June 1964

N15 4-6-0 (1925)

loco	May-49	Jun-49	Aug-49	Sep-49	Dec-49	Feb-50	Mar-50
30448	SALISBURY - 72B	SALISBURY - 72B	SALISBURY - 72B	SALISBURY - 72B	SALISBURY - 72B	SALISBURY - 72B	SALISBURY - 72B
30449	SALISBURY - 72B	SALISBURY - 72B	SALISBURY - 72B	SALISBURY - 72B	SALISBURY - 72B	SALISBURY - 72B	SALISBURY - 72B
30450	SALISBURY - 72B	SALISBURY - 72B	SALISBURY - 72B	SALISBURY - 72B	SALISBURY - 72B	SALISBURY - 72B	SALISBURY - 72B
30451	SALISBURY - 72B	SALISBURY - 72B	SALISBURY - 72B	BASINGSTOKE - 70D	BASINGSTOKE - 70D	BASINGSTOKE - 70D	BASINGSTOKE - 70D
30452	SALISBURY - 72B	SALISBURY - 72B	SALISBURY - 72B	SALISBURY - 72B	SALISBURY - 72B	SALISBURY - 72B	SALISBURY - 72B
30453	SALISBURY - 72B	SALISBURY - 72B	SALISBURY - 72B	SALISBURY - 72B	SALISBURY - 72B	SALISBURY - 72B	SALISBURY - 72B
30454	SALISBURY - 72B	SALISBURY - 72B	SALISBURY - 72B	SALISBURY - 72B	SALISBURY - 72B	SALISBURY - 72B	SALISBURY - 72B
30455	SALISBURY - 72B	SALISBURY - 72B	SALISBURY - 72B	SALISBURY - 72B	SALISBURY - 72B	SALISBURY - 72B	SALISBURY - 72B
30456	SALISBURY - 72B	SALISBURY - 72B	SALISBURY - 72B	SALISBURY - 72B	SALISBURY - 72B	SALISBURY - 72B	SALISBURY - 72B
30457	BASINGSTOKE - 70D	BASINGSTOKE - 70D	BASINGSTOKE - 70D	SALISBURY - 72B	SALISBURY - 72B	SALISBURY - 72B	SALISBURY - 72B
30763	STEWARTS LANE - 73A	STEWARTS LANE - 73A	STEWARTS LANE - 73A	STEWARTS LANE - 73A	STEWARTS LANE - 73A	STEWARTS LANE - 73A	STEWARTS LANE - 73A
30764	STEWARTS LANE - 73A	STEWARTS LANE - 73A	STEWARTS LANE - 73A	STEWARTS LANE - 73A	STEWARTS LANE - 73A	STEWARTS LANE - 73A	STEWARTS LANE - 73A
30765	STEWARTS LANE - 73A	STEWARTS LANE - 73A	STEWARTS LANE - 73A	STEWARTS LANE - 73A	STEWARTS LANE - 73A	STEWARTS LANE - 73A	STEWARTS LANE - 73A
30766	STEWARTS LANE - 73A	STEWARTS LANE - 73A	STEWARTS LANE - 73A	STEWARTS LANE - 73A	STEWARTS LANE - 73A	STEWARTS LANE - 73A	STEWARTS LANE - 73A
30767	DOVER - 74C	DOVER - 74C	DOVER - 74C	DOVER - 74C	DOVER - 74C	DOVER - 74C	DOVER - 74C
30768	DOVER - 74C	DOVER - 74C	DOVER - 74C	DOVER - 74C	DOVER - 74C	DOVER - 74C	DOVER - 74C
30769	DOVER - 74C	DOVER - 74C	DOVER - 74C	DOVER - 74C	DOVER - 74C	DOVER - 74C	DOVER - 74C
30770	DOVER - 74C	DOVER - 74C	DOVER - 74C	DOVER - 74C	DOVER - 74C	DOVER - 74C	DOVER - 74C
30771	DOVER - 74C	DOVER - 74C	DOVER - 74C	DOVER - 74C	DOVER - 74C	DOVER - 74C	DOVER - 74C
30772	BOURNEMOUTH - 71B	BOURNEMOUTH - 71B	BOURNEMOUTH - 71B	EASTLEIGH - 71A	EASTLEIGH - 71A	EASTLEIGH - 71A	EASTLEIGH - 71A
30773	NINE ELMS - 70A	NINE ELMS - 70A	NINE ELMS - 70A	NINE ELMS - 70A	NINE ELMS - 70A	NINE ELMS - 70A	NINE ELMS - 70A
30774	STEWARTS LANE - 73A	STEWARTS LANE - 73A	STEWARTS LANE - 73A	STEWARTS LANE - 73A	STEWARTS LANE - 73A	STEWARTS LANE - 73A	STEWARTS LANE - 73A
30775	STEWARTS LANE - 73A	STEWARTS LANE - 73A	STEWARTS LANE - 73A	STEWARTS LANE - 73A	STEWARTS LANE - 73A	STEWARTS LANE - 73A	STEWARTS LANE - 73A
30776	STEWARTS LANE - 73A	STEWARTS LANE - 73A	STEWARTS LANE - 73A	STEWARTS LANE - 73A	STEWARTS LANE - 73A	STEWARTS LANE - 73A	STEWARTS LANE - 73A
30777	EASTLEIGH - 71A	EASTLEIGH - 71A	EASTLEIGH - 71A	EASTLEIGH - 71A	EASTLEIGH - 71A	EASTLEIGH - 71A	EASTLEIGH - 71A
30778	STEWARTS LANE - 73A	STEWARTS LANE - 73A	STEWARTS LANE - 73A	STEWARTS LANE - 73A	STEWARTS LANE - 73A	STEWARTS LANE - 73A	STEWARTS LANE - 73A
30779	EASTLEIGH - 71A	EASTLEIGH - 71A	EASTLEIGH - 71A	EASTLEIGH - 71A	EASTLEIGH - 71A	EASTLEIGH - 71A	EASTLEIGH - 71A
30780	NINE ELMS - 70A	NINE ELMS - 70A	NINE ELMS - 70A	NINE ELMS - 70A	NINE ELMS - 70A	NINE ELMS - 70A	NINE ELMS - 70A
30781	DOVER - 74C	DOVER - 74C	DOVER - 74C	DOVER - 74C	DOVER - 74C	DOVER - 74C	DOVER - 74C
30782	NINE ELMS - 70A	NINE ELMS - 70A	NINE ELMS - 70A	NINE ELMS - 70A	NINE ELMS - 70A	NINE ELMS - 70A	NINE ELMS - 70A
30783	NINE ELMS - 70A	NINE ELMS - 70A	NINE ELMS - 70A	NINE ELMS - 70A	NINE ELMS - 70A	EASTLEIGH - 71A	EASTLEIGH - 71A
30784	EASTLEIGH - 71A	EASTLEIGH - 71A	EASTLEIGH - 71A	EASTLEIGH - 71A	EASTLEIGH - 71A	EASTLEIGH - 71A	EASTLEIGH - 71A
30785	EASTLEIGH - 71A	EASTLEIGH - 71A	EASTLEIGH - 71A	EASTLEIGH - 71A	EASTLEIGH - 71A	EASTLEIGH - 71A	EASTLEIGH - 71A
30786	NINE ELMS - 70A	NINE ELMS - 70A	NINE ELMS - 70A	NINE ELMS - 70A	NINE ELMS - 70A	NINE ELMS - 70A	NINE ELMS - 70A
30787	BOURNEMOUTH - 71B	BOURNEMOUTH - 71B	BOURNEMOUTH - 71B	NINE ELMS - 70A	NINE ELMS - 70A	NINE ELMS - 70A	NINE ELMS - 70A
30788	EASTLEIGH - 71A	EASTLEIGH - 71A	EASTLEIGH - 71A	EASTLEIGH - 71A	EASTLEIGH - 71A	EASTLEIGH - 71A	EASTLEIGH - 71A
30789	EASTLEIGH - 71A	EASTLEIGH - 71A	EASTLEIGH - 71A	EASTLEIGH - 71A	EASTLEIGH - 71A	EASTLEIGH - 71A	EASTLEIGH - 71A
30790	EASTLEIGH - 71A	EASTLEIGH - 71A	EASTLEIGH - 71A	EASTLEIGH - 71A	EASTLEIGH - 71A	EASTLEIGH - 71A	EASTLEIGH - 71A
30791	NINE ELMS - 70A	NINE ELMS - 70A	NINE ELMS - 70A	NINE ELMS - 70A	NINE ELMS - 70A	NINE ELMS - 70A	NINE ELMS - 70A
30792	NINE ELMS - 70A	NINE ELMS - 70A	NINE ELMS - 70A	NINE ELMS - 70A	NINE ELMS - 70A	NINE ELMS - 70A	NINE ELMS - 70A

N15 4-6-0 (1926)

loco	May-49	Jun-49	Aug-49	Sep-49	Dec-49	Feb-50	Mar-50
30793	STEWARTS LANE - 73A	STEWARTS LANE - 73A	STEWARTS LANE - 73A	STEWARTS LANE - 73A	ASHFORD - 74A	ASHFORD - 74A	ASHFORD - 74A
30794	STEWARTS LANE - 73A	STEWARTS LANE - 73A	STEWARTS LANE - 73A	STEWARTS LANE - 73A	STEWARTS LANE - 73A	B ARMS - 73B	B ARMS - 73B
30795	STEWARTS LANE - 73A	STEWARTS LANE - 73A	STEWARTS LANE - 73A	STEWARTS LANE - 73A	STEWARTS LANE - 73A	STEWARTS LANE - 73A	B ARMS - 73B
30796	STEWARTS LANE - 73A	STEWARTS LANE - 73A	STEWARTS LANE - 73A	STEWARTS LANE - 73A	STEWARTS LANE - 73A	B ARMS - 73B	B ARMS - 73B
30797	STEWARTS LANE - 73A	STEWARTS LANE - 73A	STEWARTS LANE - 73A	STEWARTS LANE - 73A	STEWARTS LANE - 73A	STEWARTS LANE - 73A	ASHFORD - 74A
30798	B ARMS - 73B	B ARMS - 73B	B ARMS - 73B	B ARMS - 73B	B ARMS - 73B	B ARMS - 73B	B ARMS - 73B
30799	B ARMS - 73B	B ARMS - 73B	B ARMS - 73B	B ARMS - 73B	B ARMS - 73B	B ARMS - 73B	B ARMS - 73B
30800	HITHER GREEN - 73C	HITHER GREEN - 73C	HITHER GREEN - 73C	HITHER GREEN - 73C	HITHER GREEN - 73C	HITHER GREEN - 73C	HITHER GREEN - 73C
30801	ASHFORD - 74A	ASHFORD - 74A	ASHFORD - 74A	ASHFORD - 74A	ASHFORD - 74A	ASHFORD - 74A	ASHFORD - 74A
30802	ASHFORD - 74A	ASHFORD - 74A	ASHFORD - 74A	ASHFORD - 74A	ASHFORD - 74A	ASHFORD - 74A	ASHFORD - 74A
30803	ASHFORD - 74A	ASHFORD - 74A	ASHFORD - 74A	ASHFORD - 74A	ASHFORD - 74A	ASHFORD - 74A	ASHFORD - 74A
30804	ASHFORD - 74A	ASHFORD - 74A	ASHFORD - 74A	ASHFORD - 74A	ASHFORD - 74A	ASHFORD - 74A	ASHFORD - 74A
30805	ASHFORD - 74A	ASHFORD - 74A	ASHFORD - 74A	DOVER - 74C	DOVER - 74C	HITHER GREEN - 73C	HITHER GREEN - 73C
30806	ASHFORD - 74A	ASHFORD - 74A	ASHFORD - 74A	ASHFORD - 74A	ASHFORD - 74A	ASHFORD - 74A	ASHFORD - 74A

LN 4-6-0 (1926)

loco	May-49	Jun-49	Aug-49	Sep-49	Dec-49	Feb-50	Mar-50
30850	EASTLEIGH - 71A	EASTLEIGH - 71A	EASTLEIGH - 71A	EASTLEIGH - 71A	EASTLEIGH - 71A	EASTLEIGH - 71A	EASTLEIGH - 71A
30851	EASTLEIGH - 71A	EASTLEIGH - 71A	EASTLEIGH - 71A	EASTLEIGH - 71A	EASTLEIGH - 71A	EASTLEIGH - 71A	EASTLEIGH - 71A
30852	EASTLEIGH - 71A	EASTLEIGH - 71A	EASTLEIGH - 71A	EASTLEIGH - 71A	EASTLEIGH - 71A	EASTLEIGH - 71A	EASTLEIGH - 71A
30853	EASTLEIGH - 71A	EASTLEIGH - 71A	EASTLEIGH - 71A	EASTLEIGH - 71A	EASTLEIGH - 71A	EASTLEIGH - 71A	EASTLEIGH - 71A
30854	NINE ELMS - 70A	NINE ELMS - 70A	NINE ELMS - 70A	NINE ELMS - 70A	NINE ELMS - 70A	EASTLEIGH - 71A	EASTLEIGH - 71A
30855	NINE ELMS - 70A	NINE ELMS - 70A	NINE ELMS - 70A	NINE ELMS - 70A	NINE ELMS - 70A	EASTLEIGH - 71A	EASTLEIGH - 71A
30856	NINE ELMS - 70A	NINE ELMS - 70A	NINE ELMS - 70A	NINE ELMS - 70A	NINE ELMS - 70A	EASTLEIGH - 71A	EASTLEIGH - 71A
30857	NINE ELMS - 70A	NINE ELMS - 70A	NINE ELMS - 70A	NINE ELMS - 70A	NINE ELMS - 70A	EASTLEIGH - 71A	EASTLEIGH - 71A
30858	NINE ELMS - 70A	NINE ELMS - 70A	NINE ELMS - 70A	NINE ELMS - 70A	NINE ELMS - 70A	NINE ELMS - 70A	NINE ELMS - 70A
30859	NINE ELMS - 70A	NINE ELMS - 70A	NINE ELMS - 70A	NINE ELMS - 70A	NINE ELMS - 70A	NINE ELMS - 70A	NINE ELMS - 70A
30860	NINE ELMS - 70A	NINE ELMS - 70A	NINE ELMS - 70A	NINE ELMS - 70A	NINE ELMS - 70A	NINE ELMS - 70A	NINE ELMS - 70A
30861	BOURNEMOUTH - 71B	BOURNEMOUTH - 71B	BOURNEMOUTH - 71B	BOURNEMOUTH - 71B	BOURNEMOUTH - 71B	BOURNEMOUTH - 71B	BOURNEMOUTH - 71B
30862	BOURNEMOUTH - 71B	BOURNEMOUTH - 71B	BOURNEMOUTH - 71B	BOURNEMOUTH - 71B	BOURNEMOUTH - 71B	BOURNEMOUTH - 71B	BOURNEMOUTH - 71B
30863	BOURNEMOUTH - 71B	BOURNEMOUTH - 71B	BOURNEMOUTH - 71B	BOURNEMOUTH - 71B	BOURNEMOUTH - 71B	BOURNEMOUTH - 71B	BOURNEMOUTH - 71B
30864	BOURNEMOUTH - 71B	BOURNEMOUTH - 71B	BOURNEMOUTH - 71B	BOURNEMOUTH - 71B	BOURNEMOUTH - 71B	BOURNEMOUTH - 71B	BOURNEMOUTH - 71B
30865	BOURNEMOUTH - 71B	BOURNEMOUTH - 71B	BOURNEMOUTH - 71B	BOURNEMOUTH - 71B	BOURNEMOUTH - 71B	BOURNEMOUTH - 71B	BOURNEMOUTH - 71B

loco	Apr-50	Sep-50	Oct-50	Nov-50	Dec-50	Mar-51	Apr-51
			N15 4-6-0 (1925)				
30448	SALISBURY - 72B	SALISBURY - 72B	SALISBURY - 72B	SALISBURY - 72B	SALISBURY - 72B	SALISBURY - 72B	SALISBURY - 72B
30449	SALISBURY - 72B	SALISBURY - 72B	SALISBURY - 72B	SALISBURY - 72B	SALISBURY - 72B	SALISBURY - 72B	SALISBURY - 72B
30450	SALISBURY - 72B	SALISBURY - 72B	SALISBURY - 72B	SALISBURY - 72B	SALISBURY - 72B	SALISBURY - 72B	SALISBURY - 72B
30451	BASINGSTOKE - 70D	BASINGSTOKE - 70D	BASINGSTOKE - 70D	BASINGSTOKE - 70D	BASINGSTOKE - 70D	BASINGSTOKE - 70D	BASINGSTOKE - 70D
30452	SALISBURY - 72B	SALISBURY - 72B	SALISBURY - 72B	SALISBURY - 72B	SALISBURY - 72B	SALISBURY - 72B	SALISBURY - 72B
30453	SALISBURY - 72B	SALISBURY - 72B	SALISBURY - 72B	SALISBURY - 72B	SALISBURY - 72B	SALISBURY - 72B	SALISBURY - 72B
30454	SALISBURY - 72B	SALISBURY - 72B	SALISBURY - 72B	SALISBURY - 72B	SALISBURY - 72B	SALISBURY - 72B	SALISBURY - 72B
30455	SALISBURY - 72B	EXMOUTH JCN - 72A	EXMOUTH JCN - 72A	EXMOUTH JCN - 72A	EXMOUTH JCN - 72A	EXMOUTH JCN - 72A	EXMOUTH JCN - 72A
30456	BASINGSTOKE - 70D	BASINGSTOKE - 70D	BASINGSTOKE - 70D	SALISBURY - 72B	SALISBURY - 72B	EXMOUTH JCN - 72A	EXMOUTH JCN - 72A
30457	EXMOUTH JCN - 72A	EXMOUTH JCN - 72A	EXMOUTH JCN - 72A	EXMOUTH JCN - 72A	EXMOUTH JCN - 72A	EXMOUTH JCN - 72A	EXMOUTH JCN - 72A
30763	STEWARTS LANE - 73A	STEWARTS LANE - 73A	STEWARTS LANE - 73A	STEWARTS LANE - 73A	STEWARTS LANE - 73A	STEWARTS LANE - 73A	STEWARTS LANE - 73A
30764	STEWARTS LANE - 73A	STEWARTS LANE - 73A	STEWARTS LANE - 73A	STEWARTS LANE - 73A	STEWARTS LANE - 73A	STEWARTS LANE - 73A	STEWARTS LANE - 73A
30765	NINE ELMS - 70A	NINE ELMS - 70A	SALISBURY - 72B	NINE ELMS - 70A	STEWARTS LANE - 73A	STEWARTS LANE - 73A	STEWARTS LANE - 73A
30766	STEWARTS LANE - 73A	STEWARTS LANE - 73A	STEWARTS LANE - 73A	STEWARTS LANE - 73A	STEWARTS LANE - 73A	STEWARTS LANE - 73A	STEWARTS LANE - 73A
30767	DOVER - 74C	DOVER - 74C	DOVER - 74C	DOVER - 74C	DOVER - 74C	DOVER - 74C	DOVER - 74C
30768	DOVER - 74C	DOVER - 74C	DOVER - 74C	DOVER - 74C	DOVER - 74C	DOVER - 74C	DOVER - 74C
30769	DOVER - 74C	DOVER - 74C	DOVER - 74C	DOVER - 74C	DOVER - 74C	DOVER - 74C	DOVER - 74C
30770	DOVER - 74C	DOVER - 74C	DOVER - 74C	DOVER - 74C	DOVER - 74C	DOVER - 74C	DOVER - 74C
30771	DOVER - 74C	DOVER - 74C	DOVER - 74C	DOVER - 74C	DOVER - 74C	DOVER - 74C	DOVER - 74C
30772	EASTLEIGH - 71A	EASTLEIGH - 71A	EASTLEIGH - 71A	STEWARTS LANE - 73A	DOVER - 74C	DOVER - 74C	DOVER - 74C
30773	NINE ELMS - 70A	NINE ELMS - 70A	SALISBURY - 72B	STEWARTS LANE - 73A	DOVER - 74C	DOVER - 74C	DOVER - 74C
30774	STEWARTS LANE - 73A	STEWARTS LANE - 73A	STEWARTS LANE - 73A	STEWARTS LANE - 73A	DOVER - 74C	DOVER - 74C	DOVER - 74C
30775	STEWARTS LANE - 73A	STEWARTS LANE - 73A	STEWARTS LANE - 73A	STEWARTS LANE - 73A	STEWARTS LANE - 73A	STEWARTS LANE - 73A	STEWARTS LANE - 73A
30776	STEWARTS LANE - 73A	STEWARTS LANE - 73A	STEWARTS LANE - 73A	STEWARTS LANE - 73A	STEWARTS LANE - 73A	STEWARTS LANE - 73A	STEWARTS LANE - 73A
30777	EASTLEIGH - 71A	EASTLEIGH - 71A	EASTLEIGH - 71A	EASTLEIGH - 71A	NINE ELMS - 70A	NINE ELMS - 70A	NINE ELMS - 70A
30778	STEWARTS LANE - 73A	STEWARTS LANE - 73A	STEWARTS LANE - 73A	EASTLEIGH - 71A	NINE ELMS - 70A	NINE ELMS - 70A	NINE ELMS - 70A
30779	EASTLEIGH - 71A	EASTLEIGH - 71A	EASTLEIGH - 71A	EASTLEIGH - 71A	NINE ELMS - 70A	NINE ELMS - 70A	NINE ELMS - 70A
30780	NINE ELMS - 70A	NINE ELMS - 70A	NINE ELMS - 70A	NINE ELMS - 70A	NINE ELMS - 70A	NINE ELMS - 70A	NINE ELMS - 70A
30781	DOVER - 74C	DOVER - 74C	DOVER - 74C	DOVER - 74C	EASTLEIGH - 71A	NINE ELMS - 70A	EASTLEIGH - 71A
30782	NINE ELMS - 70A	NINE ELMS - 70A	NINE ELMS - 70A	NINE ELMS - 70A	EASTLEIGH - 71A	EASTLEIGH - 71A	EASTLEIGH - 71A
30783	EASTLEIGH - 71A	EASTLEIGH - 71A	EASTLEIGH - 71A	NINE ELMS - 70A	EASTLEIGH - 71A	EASTLEIGH - 71A	EASTLEIGH - 71A
30784	EASTLEIGH - 71A	EASTLEIGH - 71A	EASTLEIGH - 71A	NINE ELMS - 70A	EASTLEIGH - 71A	EASTLEIGH - 71A	EASTLEIGH - 71A
30785	EASTLEIGH - 71A	EASTLEIGH - 71A	EASTLEIGH - 71A	NINE ELMS - 70A	EASTLEIGH - 71A	EASTLEIGH - 71A	EASTLEIGH - 71A
30786	STEWARTS LANE - 73A	STEWARTS LANE - 73A	STEWARTS LANE - 73A	STEWARTS LANE - 73A	STEWARTS LANE - 73A	STEWARTS LANE - 73A	EASTLEIGH - 71A
30787	NINE ELMS - 70A	NINE ELMS - 70A	EASTLEIGH - 71A	NINE ELMS - 70A	EASTLEIGH - 71A	EASTLEIGH - 71A	EASTLEIGH - 71A
30788	EASTLEIGH - 71A	EASTLEIGH - 71A	EASTLEIGH - 71A	NINE ELMS - 70A	EASTLEIGH - 71A	EASTLEIGH - 71A	EASTLEIGH - 71A
30789	EASTLEIGH - 71A	EASTLEIGH - 71A	EASTLEIGH - 71A	BASINGSTOKE - 70D	EASTLEIGH - 71A	EASTLEIGH - 71A	EASTLEIGH - 71A
30790	EASTLEIGH - 71A	EASTLEIGH - 71A	EASTLEIGH - 71A	BASINGSTOKE - 70D	EASTLEIGH - 71A	EASTLEIGH - 71A	EASTLEIGH - 71A
30791	NINE ELMS - 70A	NINE ELMS - 70A	NINE ELMS - 70A	STEWARTS LANE - 73A	NINE ELMS - 70A	STEWARTS LANE - 73A	STEWARTS LANE - 73A
30792	NINE ELMS - 70A	NINE ELMS - 70A	NINE ELMS - 70A	STEWARTS LANE - 73A	NINE ELMS - 70A	NINE ELMS - 70A	NINE ELMS - 70A
			N15 4-6-0 (1926)				
30793	ASHFORD - 74A	STEWARTS LANE - 73A	STEWARTS LANE - 73A	STEWARTS LANE - 73A	STEWARTS LANE - 73A	STEWARTS LANE - 73A	STEWARTS LANE - 73A
30794	B ARMS - 73B	B ARMS - 73B	B ARMS - 73B	B ARMS - 73B	B ARMS - 73B	B ARMS - 73B	B ARMS - 73B
30795	B ARMS - 73B	B ARMS - 73B	B ARMS - 73B	RAMSGATE - 74B	STEWARTS LANE - 73A	STEWARTS LANE - 73A	STEWARTS LANE - 73A
30796	STEWARTS LANE - 73A	STEWARTS LANE - 73A	STEWARTS LANE - 73A	STEWARTS LANE - 73A	STEWARTS LANE - 73A	STEWARTS LANE - 73A	STEWARTS LANE - 73A
30797	ASHFORD - 74A	ASHFORD - 74A	HITHER GREEN - 73C	HITHER GREEN - 73C	B ARMS - 73B	B ARMS - 73B	B ARMS - 73B
30798	B ARMS - 73B	B ARMS - 73B	B ARMS - 73B	B ARMS - 73B	B ARMS - 73B	B ARMS - 73B	B ARMS - 73B
30799	B ARMS - 73B	B ARMS - 73B	B ARMS - 73B	B ARMS - 73B	B ARMS - 73B	B ARMS - 73B	B ARMS - 73B
30800	B ARMS - 73B	HITHER GREEN - 73C	HITHER GREEN - 73C	HITHER GREEN - 73C	HITHER GREEN - 73C	HITHER GREEN - 73C	HITHER GREEN - 73C
30801	ASHFORD - 74A	ASHFORD - 74A	ASHFORD - 74A	ASHFORD - 74A	ASHFORD - 74A	ASHFORD - 74A	ASHFORD - 74A
30802	ASHFORD - 74A	ASHFORD - 74A	ASHFORD - 74A	ASHFORD - 74A	ASHFORD - 74A	ASHFORD - 74A	ASHFORD - 74A
30803	ASHFORD - 74A	ASHFORD - 74A	ASHFORD - 74A	ASHFORD - 74A	ASHFORD - 74A	ASHFORD - 74A	ASHFORD - 74A
30804	ASHFORD - 74A	ASHFORD - 74A	ASHFORD - 74A	ASHFORD - 74A	ASHFORD - 74A	ASHFORD - 74A	ASHFORD - 74A
30805	HITHER GREEN - 73C	ASHFORD - 74A	ASHFORD - 74A	ASHFORD - 74A	ASHFORD - 74A	ASHFORD - 74A	ASHFORD - 74A
30806	DOVER - 74C	DOVER - 74C	DOVER - 74C	DOVER - 74C	HITHER GREEN - 73C	HITHER GREEN - 73C	HITHER GREEN - 73C
			LN 4-6-0 (1926)				
30850	EASTLEIGH - 71A	EASTLEIGH - 71A	EASTLEIGH - 71A	EASTLEIGH - 71A	EASTLEIGH - 71A	EASTLEIGH - 71A	EASTLEIGH - 71A
30851	EASTLEIGH - 71A	EASTLEIGH - 71A	EASTLEIGH - 71A	EASTLEIGH - 71A	EASTLEIGH - 71A	EASTLEIGH - 71A	EASTLEIGH - 71A
30852	EASTLEIGH - 71A	EASTLEIGH - 71A	EASTLEIGH - 71A	EASTLEIGH - 71A	EASTLEIGH - 71A	EASTLEIGH - 71A	EASTLEIGH - 71A
30853	EASTLEIGH - 71A	EASTLEIGH - 71A	EASTLEIGH - 71A	EASTLEIGH - 71A	EASTLEIGH - 71A	EASTLEIGH - 71A	EASTLEIGH - 71A
30854	EASTLEIGH - 71A	EASTLEIGH - 71A	EASTLEIGH - 71A	EASTLEIGH - 71A	EASTLEIGH - 71A	EASTLEIGH - 71A	EASTLEIGH - 71A
30855	EASTLEIGH - 71A	EASTLEIGH - 71A	EASTLEIGH - 71A	EASTLEIGH - 71A	EASTLEIGH - 71A	EASTLEIGH - 71A	EASTLEIGH - 71A
30856	EASTLEIGH - 71A	EASTLEIGH - 71A	EASTLEIGH - 71A	EASTLEIGH - 71A	EASTLEIGH - 71A	EASTLEIGH - 71A	EASTLEIGH - 71A
30857	EASTLEIGH - 71A	EASTLEIGH - 71A	EASTLEIGH - 71A	EASTLEIGH - 71A	EASTLEIGH - 71A	EASTLEIGH - 71A	EASTLEIGH - 71A
30858	NINE ELMS - 70A	NINE ELMS - 70A	NINE ELMS - 70A	NINE ELMS - 70A	NINE ELMS - 70A	NINE ELMS - 70A	NINE ELMS - 70A
30859	NINE ELMS - 70A	NINE ELMS - 70A	NINE ELMS - 70A	NINE ELMS - 70A	NINE ELMS - 70A	NINE ELMS - 70A	NINE ELMS - 70A
30860	NINE ELMS - 70A	NINE ELMS - 70A	NINE ELMS - 70A	NINE ELMS - 70A	NINE ELMS - 70A	NINE ELMS - 70A	NINE ELMS - 70A
30861	BOURNEMOUTH - 71B	BOURNEMOUTH - 71B	BOURNEMOUTH - 71B	BOURNEMOUTH - 71B	BOURNEMOUTH - 71B	BOURNEMOUTH - 71B	BOURNEMOUTH - 71B
30862	BOURNEMOUTH - 71B	BOURNEMOUTH - 71B	BOURNEMOUTH - 71B	BOURNEMOUTH - 71B	BOURNEMOUTH - 71B	BOURNEMOUTH - 71B	BOURNEMOUTH - 71B
30863	BOURNEMOUTH - 71B	BOURNEMOUTH - 71B	BOURNEMOUTH - 71B	BOURNEMOUTH - 71B	BOURNEMOUTH - 71B	BOURNEMOUTH - 71B	BOURNEMOUTH - 71B
30864	BOURNEMOUTH - 71B	BOURNEMOUTH - 71B	BOURNEMOUTH - 71B	BOURNEMOUTH - 71B	BOURNEMOUTH - 71B	BOURNEMOUTH - 71B	BOURNEMOUTH - 71B
30865	BOURNEMOUTH - 71B	BOURNEMOUTH - 71B	BOURNEMOUTH - 71B	BOURNEMOUTH - 71B	BOURNEMOUTH - 71B	BOURNEMOUTH - 71B	BOURNEMOUTH - 71B

The 1925 series of the King Arthur class concluded the long search for a successful express 4-6-0 and for more than twenty years they - and the 1918 series which was rebuilt to conform with the later engines - became the Southern's standard passenger engine working the express traffic of every route out of London except the restricted Charing Cross - Hastings line.

With the possible exception of the Great Western Castle class, it is doubtful if any other company achieved the same degree of passenger motive power standardisation; the N15's being as common in Ramsgate as they were in Exeter.

With the introduction of 140 Bulleid Pacifics during the 1940's it was initially expected that little regular work would remain for the N15's yet they retained a strong presence until the arrival of standard BR 5MT 4-6-0's from 1955 onwards.

The first sheds to lose significant numbers of N15 duties were those at the extremities of the Southern. Ramsgate, which was primarily responsible for the Cannon Street business trains, was an early convert to the light Pacifics as was Exmouth Junction whose share of the West of England expresses was completely taken over by Merchant Navy Pacifics. Stewarts Lane, which handled the Victoria - Ramsgate workings, continued to use N15's on the turns until the arrival of BR 5MT 4-6-0's in late 1955 whilst many of the stopping services from Waterloo to Salisbury and in the Southampton area retained N15's until the last days of the 1950's.

The 1926 series of N15's were produced for LBSCR express services but were made redundant by electrification in less than a decade and moved to the SECR section where they remained until 1959.

Although the early Urie engines disappeared during the 1950's, the Maunsell variants survived the 1950's in good numbers; the first withdrawals not taking place until 1959.

loco	Jun-51	Jul-51	Sep-51	Dec-51	Jan-52	Mar-52	Jun-52
			N15 4-6-0 (1925)				
30448	SALISBURY - 72B	SALISBURY - 72B	SALISBURY - 72B	SALISBURY - 72B	SALISBURY - 72B	SALISBURY - 72B	SALISBURY - 72B
30449	SALISBURY - 72B	SALISBURY - 72B	SALISBURY - 72B	SALISBURY - 72B	SALISBURY - 72B	SALISBURY - 72B	SALISBURY - 72B
30450	SALISBURY - 72B	SALISBURY - 72B	SALISBURY - 72B	SALISBURY - 72B	SALISBURY - 72B	SALISBURY - 72B	SALISBURY - 72B
30451	BASINGSTOKE - 70D	BASINGSTOKE - 70D	BASINGSTOKE - 70D	BASINGSTOKE - 70D	BASINGSTOKE - 70D	BASINGSTOKE - 70D	BASINGSTOKE - 70D
30452	SALISBURY - 72B	SALISBURY - 72B	SALISBURY - 72B	SALISBURY - 72B	SALISBURY - 72B	SALISBURY - 72B	SALISBURY - 72B
30453	SALISBURY - 72B	SALISBURY - 72B	SALISBURY - 72B	SALISBURY - 72B	SALISBURY - 72B	SALISBURY - 72B	SALISBURY - 72B
30454	SALISBURY - 72B	SALISBURY - 72B	SALISBURY - 72B	SALISBURY - 72B	SALISBURY - 72B	SALISBURY - 72B	SALISBURY - 72B
30455	EXMOUTH JCN - 72A	EXMOUTH JCN - 72A	EXMOUTH JCN - 72A	EXMOUTH JCN - 72A	EXMOUTH JCN - 72A	EXMOUTH JCN - 72A	NINE ELMS - 70A
30456	EASTLEIGH - 71A	EASTLEIGH - 71A	EASTLEIGH - 71A	EASTLEIGH - 71A	EASTLEIGH - 71A	EASTLEIGH - 71A	EASTLEIGH - 71A
30457	EASTLEIGH - 71A	EASTLEIGH - 71A	EASTLEIGH - 71A	EASTLEIGH - 71A	EASTLEIGH - 71A	EASTLEIGH - 71A	EASTLEIGH - 71A
30763	STEWARTS LANE - 73A	STEWARTS LANE - 73A	STEWARTS LANE - 73A	STEWARTS LANE - 73A	STEWARTS LANE - 73A	STEWARTS LANE - 73A	STEWARTS LANE - 73A
30764	STEWARTS LANE - 73A	STEWARTS LANE - 73A	STEWARTS LANE - 73A	STEWARTS LANE - 73A	STEWARTS LANE - 73A	STEWARTS LANE - 73A	STEWARTS LANE - 73A
30765	STEWARTS LANE - 73A	STEWARTS LANE - 73A	STEWARTS LANE - 73A	STEWARTS LANE - 73A	STEWARTS LANE - 73A	STEWARTS LANE - 73A	STEWARTS LANE - 73A
30766	STEWARTS LANE - 73A	STEWARTS LANE - 73A	STEWARTS LANE - 73A	STEWARTS LANE - 73A	STEWARTS LANE - 73A	STEWARTS LANE - 73A	STEWARTS LANE - 73A
30767	STEWARTS LANE - 73A	STEWARTS LANE - 73A	STEWARTS LANE - 73A	STEWARTS LANE - 73A	STEWARTS LANE - 73A	STEWARTS LANE - 73A	STEWARTS LANE - 73A
30768	STEWARTS LANE - 73A	STEWARTS LANE - 73A	STEWARTS LANE - 73A	STEWARTS LANE - 73A	STEWARTS LANE - 73A	STEWARTS LANE - 73A	STEWARTS LANE - 73A
30769	STEWARTS LANE - 73A	STEWARTS LANE - 73A	STEWARTS LANE - 73A	STEWARTS LANE - 73A	STEWARTS LANE - 73A	STEWARTS LANE - 73A	STEWARTS LANE - 73A
30770	DOVER - 74C	DOVER - 74C	DOVER - 74C	DOVER - 74C	DOVER - 74C	DOVER - 74C	STEWARTS LANE - 73A
30771	DOVER - 74C	DOVER - 74C	DOVER - 74C	DOVER - 74C	DOVER - 74C	DOVER - 74C	STEWARTS LANE - 73A
30772	DOVER - 74C	DOVER - 74C	DOVER - 74C	DOVER - 74C	DOVER - 74C	DOVER - 74C	STEWARTS LANE - 73A
30773	DOVER - 74C	DOVER - 74C	DOVER - 74C	DOVER - 74C	DOVER - 74C	DOVER - 74C	STEWARTS LANE - 73A
30774	DOVER - 74C	DOVER - 74C	DOVER - 74C	DOVER - 74C	DOVER - 74C	DOVER - 74C	STEWARTS LANE - 73A
30775	STEWARTS LANE - 73A	STEWARTS LANE - 73A	STEWARTS LANE - 73A	STEWARTS LANE - 73A	STEWARTS LANE - 73A	STEWARTS LANE - 73A	STEWARTS LANE - 73A
30776	STEWARTS LANE - 73A	STEWARTS LANE - 73A	STEWARTS LANE - 73A	STEWARTS LANE - 73A	STEWARTS LANE - 73A	STEWARTS LANE - 73A	STEWARTS LANE - 73A
30777	STEWARTS LANE - 73A	STEWARTS LANE - 73A	STEWARTS LANE - 73A	DOVER - 74C	DOVER - 74C	DOVER - 74C	DOVER - 74C
30778	STEWARTS LANE - 73A	STEWARTS LANE - 73A	DOVER - 74C	DOVER - 74C	DOVER - 74C	DOVER - 74C	DOVER - 74C
30779	STEWARTS LANE - 73A	STEWARTS LANE - 73A	DOVER - 74C	DOVER - 74C	DOVER - 74C	DOVER - 74C	DOVER - 74C
30780	EASTLEIGH - 71A	EASTLEIGH - 71A	EASTLEIGH - 71A	EASTLEIGH - 71A	EASTLEIGH - 71A	EASTLEIGH - 71A	EASTLEIGH - 71A
30781	EASTLEIGH - 71A	EASTLEIGH - 71A	EASTLEIGH - 71A	EASTLEIGH - 71A	EASTLEIGH - 71A	EASTLEIGH - 71A	EASTLEIGH - 71A
30782	BOURNEMOUTH - 71B	BOURNEMOUTH - 71B	BOURNEMOUTH - 71B	BOURNEMOUTH - 71B	BOURNEMOUTH - 71B	BOURNEMOUTH - 71B	BOURNEMOUTH - 71B
30783	BOURNEMOUTH - 71B	BOURNEMOUTH - 71B	BOURNEMOUTH - 71B	BOURNEMOUTH - 71B	BOURNEMOUTH - 71B	BOURNEMOUTH - 71B	BOURNEMOUTH - 71B
30784	EASTLEIGH - 71A	EASTLEIGH - 71A	EASTLEIGH - 71A	EASTLEIGH - 71A	EASTLEIGH - 71A	EASTLEIGH - 71A	EASTLEIGH - 71A
30785	EASTLEIGH - 71A	EASTLEIGH - 71A	EASTLEIGH - 71A	EASTLEIGH - 71A	EASTLEIGH - 71A	EASTLEIGH - 71A	EASTLEIGH - 71A
30786	EASTLEIGH - 71A	EASTLEIGH - 71A	EASTLEIGH - 71A	EASTLEIGH - 71A	EASTLEIGH - 71A	EASTLEIGH - 71A	EASTLEIGH - 71A
30787	EASTLEIGH - 71A	EASTLEIGH - 71A	EASTLEIGH - 71A	EASTLEIGH - 71A	EASTLEIGH - 71A	EASTLEIGH - 71A	EASTLEIGH - 71A
30788	EASTLEIGH - 71A	EASTLEIGH - 71A	EASTLEIGH - 71A	EASTLEIGH - 71A	EASTLEIGH - 71A	EASTLEIGH - 71A	EASTLEIGH - 71A
30789	EASTLEIGH - 71A	EASTLEIGH - 71A	EASTLEIGH - 71A	EASTLEIGH - 71A	EASTLEIGH - 71A	EASTLEIGH - 71A	EASTLEIGH - 71A
30790	EASTLEIGH - 71A	EASTLEIGH - 71A	EASTLEIGH - 71A	EASTLEIGH - 71A	EASTLEIGH - 71A	EASTLEIGH - 71A	EASTLEIGH - 71A
30791	STEWARTS LANE - 73A	STEWARTS LANE - 73A	STEWARTS LANE - 73A	STEWARTS LANE - 73A	STEWARTS LANE - 73A	STEWARTS LANE - 73A	STEWARTS LANE - 73A
30792	NINE ELMS - 70A	NINE ELMS - 70A	NINE ELMS - 70A	NINE ELMS - 70A	NINE ELMS - 70A	NINE ELMS - 70A	NINE ELMS - 70A
			N15 4-6-0 (1926)				
30793	STEWARTS LANE - 73A	STEWARTS LANE - 73A	STEWARTS LANE - 73A	STEWARTS LANE - 73A	STEWARTS LANE - 73A	STEWARTS LANE - 73A	STEWARTS LANE - 73A
30794	B ARMS - 73B	B ARMS - 73B	B ARMS - 73B	B ARMS - 73B	B ARMS - 73B	B ARMS - 73B	B ARMS - 73B
30795	STEWARTS LANE - 73A	STEWARTS LANE - 73A	STEWARTS LANE - 73A	STEWARTS LANE - 73A	STEWARTS LANE - 73A	STEWARTS LANE - 73A	STEWARTS LANE - 73A
30796	DOVER - 74C	DOVER - 74C	DOVER - 74C	DOVER - 74C	DOVER - 74C	DOVER - 74C	DOVER - 74C
30797	DOVER - 74C	DOVER - 74C	DOVER - 74C	DOVER - 74C	DOVER - 74C	DOVER - 74C	DOVER - 74C
30798	DOVER - 74C	DOVER - 74C	DOVER - 74C	DOVER - 74C	DOVER - 74C	DOVER - 74C	DOVER - 74C
30799	B ARMS - 73B	B ARMS - 73B	B ARMS - 73B	B ARMS - 73B	B ARMS - 73B	B ARMS - 73B	B ARMS - 73B
30800	HITHER GREEN - 73C	HITHER GREEN - 73C	HITHER GREEN - 73C	HITHER GREEN - 73C	HITHER GREEN - 73C	HITHER GREEN - 73C	HITHER GREEN - 73C
30801	ASHFORD - 74A	ASHFORD - 74A	ASHFORD - 74A	ASHFORD - 74A	ASHFORD - 74A	ASHFORD - 74A	ASHFORD - 74A
30802	ASHFORD - 74A	ASHFORD - 74A	ASHFORD - 74A	ASHFORD - 74A	ASHFORD - 74A	ASHFORD - 74A	ASHFORD - 74A
30803	ASHFORD - 74A	ASHFORD - 74A	ASHFORD - 74A	ASHFORD - 74A	ASHFORD - 74A	ASHFORD - 74A	ASHFORD - 74A
30804	ASHFORD - 74A	ASHFORD - 74A	ASHFORD - 74A	ASHFORD - 74A	ASHFORD - 74A	ASHFORD - 74A	ASHFORD - 74A
30805	ASHFORD - 74A	ASHFORD - 74A	ASHFORD - 74A	ASHFORD - 74A	ASHFORD - 74A	ASHFORD - 74A	ASHFORD - 74A
30806	HITHER GREEN - 73C	HITHER GREEN - 73C	HITHER GREEN - 73C	HITHER GREEN - 73C	HITHER GREEN - 73C	HITHER GREEN - 73C	HITHER GREEN - 73C
			LN 4-6-0 (1926)				
30850	EASTLEIGH - 71A	EASTLEIGH - 71A	EASTLEIGH - 71A	EASTLEIGH - 71A	EASTLEIGH - 71A	EASTLEIGH - 71A	EASTLEIGH - 71A
30851	EASTLEIGH - 71A	EASTLEIGH - 71A	EASTLEIGH - 71A	EASTLEIGH - 71A	EASTLEIGH - 71A	EASTLEIGH - 71A	EASTLEIGH - 71A
30852	EASTLEIGH - 71A	EASTLEIGH - 71A	EASTLEIGH - 71A	EASTLEIGH - 71A	EASTLEIGH - 71A	EASTLEIGH - 71A	EASTLEIGH - 71A
30853	EASTLEIGH - 71A	EASTLEIGH - 71A	EASTLEIGH - 71A	EASTLEIGH - 71A	EASTLEIGH - 71A	EASTLEIGH - 71A	EASTLEIGH - 71A
30854	EASTLEIGH - 71A	EASTLEIGH - 71A	EASTLEIGH - 71A	EASTLEIGH - 71A	EASTLEIGH - 71A	EASTLEIGH - 71A	EASTLEIGH - 71A
30855	EASTLEIGH - 71A	EASTLEIGH - 71A	EASTLEIGH - 71A	EASTLEIGH - 71A	EASTLEIGH - 71A	EASTLEIGH - 71A	EASTLEIGH - 71A
30856	EASTLEIGH - 71A	EASTLEIGH - 71A	EASTLEIGH - 71A	EASTLEIGH - 71A	EASTLEIGH - 71A	EASTLEIGH - 71A	EASTLEIGH - 71A
30857	EASTLEIGH - 71A	EASTLEIGH - 71A	EASTLEIGH - 71A	EASTLEIGH - 71A	EASTLEIGH - 71A	EASTLEIGH - 71A	EASTLEIGH - 71A
30858	NINE ELMS - 70A	NINE ELMS - 70A	NINE ELMS - 70A	NINE ELMS - 70A	NINE ELMS - 70A	NINE ELMS - 70A	NINE ELMS - 70A
30859	NINE ELMS - 70A	NINE ELMS - 70A	NINE ELMS - 70A	NINE ELMS - 70A	NINE ELMS - 70A	NINE ELMS - 70A	NINE ELMS - 70A
30860	NINE ELMS - 70A	NINE ELMS - 70A	NINE ELMS - 70A	NINE ELMS - 70A	NINE ELMS - 70A	NINE ELMS - 70A	NINE ELMS - 70A
30861	BOURNEMOUTH - 71B	BOURNEMOUTH - 71B	BOURNEMOUTH - 71B	BOURNEMOUTH - 71B	BOURNEMOUTH - 71B	BOURNEMOUTH - 71B	BOURNEMOUTH - 71B
30862	BOURNEMOUTH - 71B	BOURNEMOUTH - 71B	BOURNEMOUTH - 71B	BOURNEMOUTH - 71B	BOURNEMOUTH - 71B	BOURNEMOUTH - 71B	BOURNEMOUTH - 71B
30863	BOURNEMOUTH - 71B	BOURNEMOUTH - 71B	BOURNEMOUTH - 71B	BOURNEMOUTH - 71B	BOURNEMOUTH - 71B	BOURNEMOUTH - 71B	BOURNEMOUTH - 71B
30864	BOURNEMOUTH - 71B	BOURNEMOUTH - 71B	BOURNEMOUTH - 71B	BOURNEMOUTH - 71B	BOURNEMOUTH - 71B	BOURNEMOUTH - 71B	BOURNEMOUTH - 71B
30865	BOURNEMOUTH - 71B	BOURNEMOUTH - 71B	BOURNEMOUTH - 71B	BOURNEMOUTH - 71B	BOURNEMOUTH - 71B	BOURNEMOUTH - 71B	BOURNEMOUTH - 71B

The Lord Nelson 4-6-0's - the most powerful SR express engines until the arrival of the Merchant Navy Pacifics - were not the success they might have been and underwent considerable modifications, probably more than any other class, before their performance started to approach expectations. During the 1930's the class had been divided between the principal services of the South Western and the Continental boat trains of the South Eastern. After the war, however, the class was congregated on the South Western where their workings included the night services between London and Dorset, a day express from Waterloo to Bournemouth and a stopping service to Salisbury. Heavily outnumbered by Bulleid Pacifics, as the 1950's progressed the class was gradually concentrated at Eastleigh where a Lord Nelson link was formed to work the numerous Ocean Liner Expresses between Waterloo and Southampton docks.

loco	Sep-52	Dec-52	Mar-53	May-53	Jul-53	Sep-53	Nov-53
N15 4-6-0 (1925)							
30448	SALISBURY - 72B	SALISBURY - 72B	SALISBURY - 72B	SALISBURY - 72B	SALISBURY - 72B	SALISBURY - 72B	SALISBURY - 72B
30449	SALISBURY - 72B	SALISBURY - 72B	SALISBURY - 72B	SALISBURY - 72B	SALISBURY - 72B	SALISBURY - 72B	SALISBURY - 72B
30450	SALISBURY - 72B	SALISBURY - 72B	SALISBURY - 72B	SALISBURY - 72B	SALISBURY - 72B	SALISBURY - 72B	SALISBURY - 72B
30451	BASINGSTOKE - 70D	BASINGSTOKE - 70D	BASINGSTOKE - 70D	BASINGSTOKE - 70D	BASINGSTOKE - 70D	BASINGSTOKE - 70D	BASINGSTOKE - 70D
30452	SALISBURY - 72B	SALISBURY - 72B	SALISBURY - 72B	SALISBURY - 72B	SALISBURY - 72B	SALISBURY - 72B	SALISBURY - 72B
30453	SALISBURY - 72B	SALISBURY - 72B	SALISBURY - 72B	SALISBURY - 72B	SALISBURY - 72B	SALISBURY - 72B	SALISBURY - 72B
30454	SALISBURY - 72B	SALISBURY - 72B	SALISBURY - 72B	SALISBURY - 72B	SALISBURY - 72B	SALISBURY - 72B	SALISBURY - 72B
30455	NINE ELMS - 70A	NINE ELMS - 70A	NINE ELMS - 70A	NINE ELMS - 70A	NINE ELMS - 70A	NINE ELMS - 70A	NINE ELMS - 70A
30456	EASTLEIGH - 71A	EASTLEIGH - 71A	EASTLEIGH - 71A	EASTLEIGH - 71A	EASTLEIGH - 71A	EASTLEIGH - 71A	EASTLEIGH - 71A
30457	EASTLEIGH - 71A	EASTLEIGH - 71A	EASTLEIGH - 71A	EASTLEIGH - 71A	EASTLEIGH - 71A	EASTLEIGH - 71A	EASTLEIGH - 71A
30763	STEWARTS LANE - 73A	STEWARTS LANE - 73A	STEWARTS LANE - 73A	STEWARTS LANE - 73A	STEWARTS LANE - 73A	STEWARTS LANE - 73A	STEWARTS LANE - 73A
30764	STEWARTS LANE - 73A	STEWARTS LANE - 73A	STEWARTS LANE - 73A	STEWARTS LANE - 73A	STEWARTS LANE - 73A	STEWARTS LANE - 73A	STEWARTS LANE - 73A
30765	STEWARTS LANE - 73A	STEWARTS LANE - 73A	STEWARTS LANE - 73A	STEWARTS LANE - 73A	STEWARTS LANE - 73A	STEWARTS LANE - 73A	STEWARTS LANE - 73A
30766	STEWARTS LANE - 73A	STEWARTS LANE - 73A	STEWARTS LANE - 73A	STEWARTS LANE - 73A	STEWARTS LANE - 73A	STEWARTS LANE - 73A	STEWARTS LANE - 73A
30767	STEWARTS LANE - 73A	STEWARTS LANE - 73A	STEWARTS LANE - 73A	STEWARTS LANE - 73A	STEWARTS LANE - 73A	STEWARTS LANE - 73A	STEWARTS LANE - 73A
30768	STEWARTS LANE - 73A	STEWARTS LANE - 73A	STEWARTS LANE - 73A	STEWARTS LANE - 73A	STEWARTS LANE - 73A	STEWARTS LANE - 73A	STEWARTS LANE - 73A
30769	STEWARTS LANE - 73A	STEWARTS LANE - 73A	DOVER - 74C	DOVER - 74C	DOVER - 74C	DOVER - 74C	DOVER - 74C
30770	STEWARTS LANE - 73A	STEWARTS LANE - 73A	STEWARTS LANE - 73A	STEWARTS LANE - 73A	STEWARTS LANE - 73A	STEWARTS LANE - 73A	STEWARTS LANE - 73A
30771	STEWARTS LANE - 73A	STEWARTS LANE - 73A	STEWARTS LANE - 73A	STEWARTS LANE - 73A	STEWARTS LANE - 73A	STEWARTS LANE - 73A	STEWARTS LANE - 73A
30772	STEWARTS LANE - 73A	STEWARTS LANE - 73A	RAMSGATE - 74B	RAMSGATE - 74B	RAMSGATE - 74B	RAMSGATE - 74B	RAMSGATE - 74B
30773	STEWARTS LANE - 73A	STEWARTS LANE - 73A	STEWARTS LANE - 73A	STEWARTS LANE - 73A	STEWARTS LANE - 73A	STEWARTS LANE - 73A	STEWARTS LANE - 73A
30774	STEWARTS LANE - 73A	STEWARTS LANE - 73A	STEWARTS LANE - 73A	STEWARTS LANE - 73A	STEWARTS LANE - 73A	STEWARTS LANE - 73A	STEWARTS LANE - 73A
30775	STEWARTS LANE - 73A	STEWARTS LANE - 73A	STEWARTS LANE - 73A	STEWARTS LANE - 73A	STEWARTS LANE - 73A	STEWARTS LANE - 73A	STEWARTS LANE - 73A
30776	STEWARTS LANE - 73A	STEWARTS LANE - 73A	STEWARTS LANE - 73A	STEWARTS LANE - 73A	STEWARTS LANE - 73A	STEWARTS LANE - 73A	STEWARTS LANE - 73A
30777	DOVER - 74C	DOVER - 74C	DOVER - 74C	DOVER - 74C	DOVER - 74C	DOVER - 74C	DOVER - 74C
30778	DOVER - 74C	DOVER - 74C	DOVER - 74C	DOVER - 74C	DOVER - 74C	DOVER - 74C	DOVER - 74C
30779	DOVER - 74C	DOVER - 74C	DOVER - 74C	DOVER - 74C	DOVER - 74C	DOVER - 74C	DOVER - 74C
30780	EASTLEIGH - 71A	EASTLEIGH - 71A	EASTLEIGH - 71A	EASTLEIGH - 71A	EASTLEIGH - 71A	EASTLEIGH - 71A	EASTLEIGH - 71A
30781	EASTLEIGH - 71A	EASTLEIGH - 71A	EASTLEIGH - 71A	EASTLEIGH - 71A	EASTLEIGH - 71A	EASTLEIGH - 71A	EASTLEIGH - 71A
30782	BOURNEMOUTH - 71B	BOURNEMOUTH - 71B	BOURNEMOUTH - 71B	BOURNEMOUTH - 71B	BOURNEMOUTH - 71B	BOURNEMOUTH - 71B	BOURNEMOUTH - 71B
30783	BOURNEMOUTH - 71B	BOURNEMOUTH - 71B	BOURNEMOUTH - 71B	BOURNEMOUTH - 71B	BOURNEMOUTH - 71B	BOURNEMOUTH - 71B	BOURNEMOUTH - 71B
30784	EASTLEIGH - 71A	EASTLEIGH - 71A	EASTLEIGH - 71A	EASTLEIGH - 71A	EASTLEIGH - 71A	EASTLEIGH - 71A	EASTLEIGH - 71A
30785	EASTLEIGH - 71A	EASTLEIGH - 71A	EASTLEIGH - 71A	EASTLEIGH - 71A	EASTLEIGH - 71A	EASTLEIGH - 71A	EASTLEIGH - 71A
30786	EASTLEIGH - 71A	EASTLEIGH - 71A	EASTLEIGH - 71A	EASTLEIGH - 71A	EASTLEIGH - 71A	EASTLEIGH - 71A	EASTLEIGH - 71A
30787	EASTLEIGH - 71A	EASTLEIGH - 71A	EASTLEIGH - 71A	EASTLEIGH - 71A	EASTLEIGH - 71A	EASTLEIGH - 71A	EASTLEIGH - 71A
30788	EASTLEIGH - 71A	EASTLEIGH - 71A	EASTLEIGH - 71A	EASTLEIGH - 71A	EASTLEIGH - 71A	EASTLEIGH - 71A	EASTLEIGH - 71A
30789	EASTLEIGH - 71A	EASTLEIGH - 71A	EASTLEIGH - 71A	EASTLEIGH - 71A	EASTLEIGH - 71A	EASTLEIGH - 71A	EASTLEIGH - 71A
30790	EASTLEIGH - 71A	EASTLEIGH - 71A	EASTLEIGH - 71A	EASTLEIGH - 71A	EASTLEIGH - 71A	EASTLEIGH - 71A	EASTLEIGH - 71A
30791	STEWARTS LANE - 73A	STEWARTS LANE - 73A	STEWARTS LANE - 73A	STEWARTS LANE - 73A	STEWARTS LANE - 73A	STEWARTS LANE - 73A	STEWARTS LANE - 73A
30792	NINE ELMS - 70A	NINE ELMS - 70A	NINE ELMS - 70A	NINE ELMS - 70A	NINE ELMS - 70A	NINE ELMS - 70A	NINE ELMS - 70A
N15 4-6-0 (1926)							
30793	STEWARTS LANE - 73A	STEWARTS LANE - 73A	STEWARTS LANE - 73A	STEWARTS LANE - 73A	STEWARTS LANE - 73A	STEWARTS LANE - 73A	STEWARTS LANE - 73A
30794	B ARMS - 73B	B ARMS - 73B	B ARMS - 73B	B ARMS - 73B	B ARMS - 73B	B ARMS - 73B	B ARMS - 73B
30795	STEWARTS LANE - 73A	STEWARTS LANE - 73A	STEWARTS LANE - 73A	STEWARTS LANE - 73A	STEWARTS LANE - 73A	STEWARTS LANE - 73A	STEWARTS LANE - 73A
30796	DOVER - 74C	DOVER - 74C	RAMSGATE - 74B	RAMSGATE - 74B	RAMSGATE - 74B	RAMSGATE - 74B	RAMSGATE - 74B
30797	DOVER - 74C	DOVER - 74C	ASHFORD - 74A	ASHFORD - 74A	ASHFORD - 74A	ASHFORD - 74A	ASHFORD - 74A
30798	DOVER - 74C	DOVER - 74C	DOVER - 74C	DOVER - 74C	DOVER - 74C	DOVER - 74C	DOVER - 74C
30799	B ARMS - 73B	B ARMS - 73B	B ARMS - 73B	B ARMS - 73B	B ARMS - 73B	B ARMS - 73B	B ARMS - 73B
30800	HITHER GREEN - 73C	HITHER GREEN - 73C	HITHER GREEN - 73C	HITHER GREEN - 73C	HITHER GREEN - 73C	HITHER GREEN - 73C	HITHER GREEN - 73C
30801	ASHFORD - 74A	ASHFORD - 74A	ASHFORD - 74A	ASHFORD - 74A	ASHFORD - 74A	ASHFORD - 74A	ASHFORD - 74A
30802	ASHFORD - 74A	ASHFORD - 74A	ASHFORD - 74A	ASHFORD - 74A	ASHFORD - 74A	ASHFORD - 74A	ASHFORD - 74A
30803	ASHFORD - 74A	ASHFORD - 74A	ASHFORD - 74A	ASHFORD - 74A	ASHFORD - 74A	ASHFORD - 74A	ASHFORD - 74A
30804	ASHFORD - 74A	ASHFORD - 74A	ASHFORD - 74A	ASHFORD - 74A	ASHFORD - 74A	ASHFORD - 74A	ASHFORD - 74A
30805	ASHFORD - 74A	ASHFORD - 74A	ASHFORD - 74A	ASHFORD - 74A	ASHFORD - 74A	ASHFORD - 74A	ASHFORD - 74A
30806	HITHER GREEN - 73C	HITHER GREEN - 73C	HITHER GREEN - 73C	HITHER GREEN - 73C	HITHER GREEN - 73C	HITHER GREEN - 73C	HITHER GREEN - 73C
LN 4-6-0 (1926)							
30850	EASTLEIGH - 71A	EASTLEIGH - 71A	EASTLEIGH - 71A	EASTLEIGH - 71A	EASTLEIGH - 71A	EASTLEIGH - 71A	EASTLEIGH - 71A
30851	EASTLEIGH - 71A	EASTLEIGH - 71A	EASTLEIGH - 71A	EASTLEIGH - 71A	EASTLEIGH - 71A	EASTLEIGH - 71A	EASTLEIGH - 71A
30852	EASTLEIGH - 71A	EASTLEIGH - 71A	EASTLEIGH - 71A	EASTLEIGH - 71A	EASTLEIGH - 71A	EASTLEIGH - 71A	EASTLEIGH - 71A
30853	EASTLEIGH - 71A	EASTLEIGH - 71A	EASTLEIGH - 71A	EASTLEIGH - 71A	EASTLEIGH - 71A	EASTLEIGH - 71A	EASTLEIGH - 71A
30854	EASTLEIGH - 71A	EASTLEIGH - 71A	EASTLEIGH - 71A	EASTLEIGH - 71A	EASTLEIGH - 71A	EASTLEIGH - 71A	EASTLEIGH - 71A
30855	EASTLEIGH - 71A	EASTLEIGH - 71A	EASTLEIGH - 71A	EASTLEIGH - 71A	EASTLEIGH - 71A	EASTLEIGH - 71A	EASTLEIGH - 71A
30856	EASTLEIGH - 71A	EASTLEIGH - 71A	EASTLEIGH - 71A	EASTLEIGH - 71A	EASTLEIGH - 71A	EASTLEIGH - 71A	EASTLEIGH - 71A
30857	EASTLEIGH - 71A	EASTLEIGH - 71A	EASTLEIGH - 71A	EASTLEIGH - 71A	EASTLEIGH - 71A	EASTLEIGH - 71A	EASTLEIGH - 71A
30858	NINE ELMS - 70A	NINE ELMS - 70A	NINE ELMS - 70A	NINE ELMS - 70A	NINE ELMS - 70A	NINE ELMS - 70A	NINE ELMS - 70A
30859	NINE ELMS - 70A	NINE ELMS - 70A	NINE ELMS - 70A	NINE ELMS - 70A	NINE ELMS - 70A	NINE ELMS - 70A	NINE ELMS - 70A
30860	NINE ELMS - 70A	NINE ELMS - 70A	NINE ELMS - 70A	NINE ELMS - 70A	NINE ELMS - 70A	NINE ELMS - 70A	NINE ELMS - 70A
30861	BOURNEMOUTH - 71B	BOURNEMOUTH - 71B	BOURNEMOUTH - 71B	BOURNEMOUTH - 71B	BOURNEMOUTH - 71B	BOURNEMOUTH - 71B	BOURNEMOUTH - 71B
30862	BOURNEMOUTH - 71B	BOURNEMOUTH - 71B	BOURNEMOUTH - 71B	BOURNEMOUTH - 71B	BOURNEMOUTH - 71B	BOURNEMOUTH - 71B	BOURNEMOUTH - 71B
30863	BOURNEMOUTH - 71B	BOURNEMOUTH - 71B	BOURNEMOUTH - 71B	BOURNEMOUTH - 71B	BOURNEMOUTH - 71B	BOURNEMOUTH - 71B	BOURNEMOUTH - 71B
30864	BOURNEMOUTH - 71B	BOURNEMOUTH - 71B	BOURNEMOUTH - 71B	BOURNEMOUTH - 71B	BOURNEMOUTH - 71B	BOURNEMOUTH - 71B	BOURNEMOUTH - 71B
30865	BOURNEMOUTH - 71B	BOURNEMOUTH - 71B	BOURNEMOUTH - 71B	BOURNEMOUTH - 71B	BOURNEMOUTH - 71B	BOURNEMOUTH - 71B	BOURNEMOUTH - 71B

Framed by the girders of Stewarts Lane MPD, N15 30768 'Sir Balin' is prepared for the 15.35 'Granville' from Victoria to Ramsgate in 1954. This was the only double turn of the day between London and Ramsgate, the engine starting its duty with the 03.30 Newspapers from Victoria and returning with the 09.25 Ramsgate - Victoria. In practice, however, a second engine was in-

loco	Jan-54	Mar-54	May-54	Jun-54	Aug-54	Oct-54	Dec-54
				N15 4-6-0 (1925)			
30448 SALISBURY - 72B	SALISBURY - 72B	SALISBURY - 72B	SALISBURY - 72B	SALISBURY - 72B	SALISBURY - 72B	SALISBURY - 72B
30449 SALISBURY - 72B	SALISBURY - 72B	SALISBURY - 72B	SALISBURY - 72B	SALISBURY - 72B	SALISBURY - 72B	SALISBURY - 72B
30450 SALISBURY - 72B	SALISBURY - 72B	SALISBURY - 72B	SALISBURY - 72B	SALISBURY - 72B	SALISBURY - 72B	SALISBURY - 72B
30451 BASINGSTOKE - 70D	BASINGSTOKE - 70D	BASINGSTOKE - 70D	BASINGSTOKE - 70D	BASINGSTOKE - 70D	BASINGSTOKE - 70D	BASINGSTOKE - 70D
30452 SALISBURY - 72B	SALISBURY - 72B	SALISBURY - 72B	SALISBURY - 72B	SALISBURY - 72B	SALISBURY - 72B	SALISBURY - 72B
30453 SALISBURY - 72B	SALISBURY - 72B	SALISBURY - 72B	SALISBURY - 72B	SALISBURY - 72B	SALISBURY - 72B	SALISBURY - 72B
30454 SALISBURY - 72B	SALISBURY - 72B	SALISBURY - 72B	SALISBURY - 72B	SALISBURY - 72B	SALISBURY - 72B	SALISBURY - 72B
30455 NINE ELMS - 70A	NINE ELMS - 70A	NINE ELMS - 70A	NINE ELMS - 70A	NINE ELMS - 70A	NINE ELMS - 70A	NINE ELMS - 70A
30456 EASTLEIGH - 71A	EASTLEIGH - 71A	EASTLEIGH - 71A	EASTLEIGH - 71A	EASTLEIGH - 71A	NINE ELMS - 70A	NINE ELMS - 70A
30457 EASTLEIGH - 71A	EASTLEIGH - 71A	EASTLEIGH - 71A	EASTLEIGH - 71A	EASTLEIGH - 71A	EASTLEIGH - 71A	EASTLEIGH - 71A
30763 STEWARTS LANE - 73A	STEWARTS LANE - 73A	STEWARTS LANE - 73A	STEWARTS LANE - 73A	STEWARTS LANE - 73A	STEWARTS LANE - 73A	STEWARTS LANE - 73A
30764 STEWARTS LANE - 73A	STEWARTS LANE - 73A	STEWARTS LANE - 73A	STEWARTS LANE - 73A	STEWARTS LANE - 73A	STEWARTS LANE - 73A	STEWARTS LANE - 73A
30765 STEWARTS LANE - 73A	STEWARTS LANE - 73A	STEWARTS LANE - 73A	STEWARTS LANE - 73A	STEWARTS LANE - 73A	STEWARTS LANE - 73A	STEWARTS LANE - 73A
30766 STEWARTS LANE - 73A	STEWARTS LANE - 73A	STEWARTS LANE - 73A	STEWARTS LANE - 73A	STEWARTS LANE - 73A	STEWARTS LANE - 73A	STEWARTS LANE - 73A
30767 STEWARTS LANE - 73A	STEWARTS LANE - 73A	STEWARTS LANE - 73A	STEWARTS LANE - 73A	STEWARTS LANE - 73A	STEWARTS LANE - 73A	STEWARTS LANE - 73A
30768 STEWARTS LANE - 73A	STEWARTS LANE - 73A	STEWARTS LANE - 73A	STEWARTS LANE - 73A	STEWARTS LANE - 73A	STEWARTS LANE - 73A	STEWARTS LANE - 73A
30769 DOVER - 74C	DOVER - 74C	STEWARTS LANE - 73A	STEWARTS LANE - 73A	STEWARTS LANE - 73A	STEWARTS LANE - 73A	STEWARTS LANE - 73A
30770 STEWARTS LANE - 73A	STEWARTS LANE - 73A	STEWARTS LANE - 73A	STEWARTS LANE - 73A	STEWARTS LANE - 73A	STEWARTS LANE - 73A	STEWARTS LANE - 73A
30771 STEWARTS LANE - 73A	STEWARTS LANE - 73A	STEWARTS LANE - 73A	STEWARTS LANE - 73A	STEWARTS LANE - 73A	STEWARTS LANE - 73A	STEWARTS LANE - 73A
30772 RAMSGATE - 74B	RAMSGATE - 74B	RAMSGATE - 74B	RAMSGATE - 74B	HITHER GREEN - 73C	HITHER GREEN - 73C	HITHER GREEN - 73C
30773 STEWARTS LANE - 73A	STEWARTS LANE - 73A	STEWARTS LANE - 73A	STEWARTS LANE - 73A	STEWARTS LANE - 73A	STEWARTS LANE - 73A	STEWARTS LANE - 73A
30774 STEWARTS LANE - 73A	STEWARTS LANE - 73A	STEWARTS LANE - 73A	STEWARTS LANE - 73A	STEWARTS LANE - 73A	STEWARTS LANE - 73A	STEWARTS LANE - 73A
30775 STEWARTS LANE - 73A	STEWARTS LANE - 73A	STEWARTS LANE - 73A	STEWARTS LANE - 73A	STEWARTS LANE - 73A	STEWARTS LANE - 73A	STEWARTS LANE - 73A
30776 STEWARTS LANE - 73A	STEWARTS LANE - 73A	STEWARTS LANE - 73A	STEWARTS LANE - 73A	STEWARTS LANE - 73A	STEWARTS LANE - 73A	STEWARTS LANE - 73A
30777 DOVER - 74C	DOVER - 74C	DOVER - 74C	DOVER - 74C	DOVER - 74C	DOVER - 74C	DOVER - 74C
30778 DOVER - 74C	DOVER - 74C	DOVER - 74C	DOVER - 74C	DOVER - 74C	DOVER - 74C	DOVER - 74C
30779 DOVER - 74C	DOVER - 74C	DOVER - 74C	DOVER - 74C	DOVER - 74C	DOVER - 74C	DOVER - 74C
30780 EASTLEIGH - 71A	EASTLEIGH - 71A	EASTLEIGH - 71A	EASTLEIGH - 71A	EASTLEIGH - 71A	EASTLEIGH - 71A	EASTLEIGH - 71A
30781 EASTLEIGH - 71A	EASTLEIGH - 71A	NINE ELMS - 70A	NINE ELMS - 70A	NINE ELMS - 70A	NINE ELMS - 70A	NINE ELMS - 70A
30782 BOURNEMOUTH - 71B	BOURNEMOUTH - 71B	BOURNEMOUTH - 71B	BOURNEMOUTH - 71B	BOURNEMOUTH - 71B	BOURNEMOUTH - 71B	BOURNEMOUTH - 71B
30783 BOURNEMOUTH - 71B	BOURNEMOUTH - 71B	BOURNEMOUTH - 71B	BOURNEMOUTH - 71B	BOURNEMOUTH - 71B	BOURNEMOUTH - 71B	BOURNEMOUTH - 71B
30784 EASTLEIGH - 71A	EASTLEIGH - 71A	EASTLEIGH - 71A	EASTLEIGH - 71A	EASTLEIGH - 71A	EASTLEIGH - 71A	EASTLEIGH - 71A
30785 EASTLEIGH - 71A	EASTLEIGH - 71A	EASTLEIGH - 71A	EASTLEIGH - 71A	EASTLEIGH - 71A	EASTLEIGH - 71A	EASTLEIGH - 71A
30786 EASTLEIGH - 71A	EASTLEIGH - 71A	EASTLEIGH - 71A	EASTLEIGH - 71A	EASTLEIGH - 71A	EASTLEIGH - 71A	EASTLEIGH - 71A
30787 EASTLEIGH - 71A	EASTLEIGH - 71A	EASTLEIGH - 71A	EASTLEIGH - 71A	EASTLEIGH - 71A	EASTLEIGH - 71A	EASTLEIGH - 71A
30788 EASTLEIGH - 71A	EASTLEIGH - 71A	EASTLEIGH - 71A	EASTLEIGH - 71A	EASTLEIGH - 71A	EASTLEIGH - 71A	EASTLEIGH - 71A
30789 EASTLEIGH - 71A	EASTLEIGH - 71A	EASTLEIGH - 71A	EASTLEIGH - 71A	EASTLEIGH - 71A	EASTLEIGH - 71A	EASTLEIGH - 71A
30790 EASTLEIGH - 71A	EASTLEIGH - 71A	EASTLEIGH - 71A	EASTLEIGH - 71A	EASTLEIGH - 71A	EASTLEIGH - 71A	EASTLEIGH - 71A
30791 STEWARTS LANE - 73A	STEWARTS LANE - 73A	STEWARTS LANE - 73A	STEWARTS LANE - 73A	STEWARTS LANE - 73A	STEWARTS LANE - 73A	STEWARTS LANE - 73A
30792 NINE ELMS - 70A	NINE ELMS - 70A	NINE ELMS - 70A	STEWARTS LANE - 73A	STEWARTS LANE - 73A	STEWARTS LANE - 73A	STEWARTS LANE - 73A
				N15 4-6-0 (1926)			
30793 STEWARTS LANE - 73A	STEWARTS LANE - 73A	STEWARTS LANE - 73A	STEWARTS LANE - 73A	STEWARTS LANE - 73A	STEWARTS LANE - 73A	STEWARTS LANE - 73A
30794 B ARMS - 73B	B ARMS - 73B	B ARMS - 73B	B ARMS - 73B	STEWARTS LANE - 73A	STEWARTS LANE - 73A	STEWARTS LANE - 73A
30795 STEWARTS LANE - 73A	STEWARTS LANE - 73A	STEWARTS LANE - 73A	HITHER GREEN - 73C	STEWARTS LANE - 73A	STEWARTS LANE - 73A	STEWARTS LANE - 73A
30796 RAMSGATE - 74B	RAMSGATE - 74B	DOVER - 74C	DOVER - 74C	DOVER - 74C	DOVER - 74C	DOVER - 74C
30797 ASHFORD - 74A	ASHFORD - 74A	ASHFORD - 74A	ASHFORD - 74A	ASHFORD - 74A	ASHFORD - 74A	ASHFORD - 74A
30798 DOVER - 74C	DOVER - 74C	DOVER - 74C	DOVER - 74C	DOVER - 74C	DOVER - 74C	DOVER - 74C
30799 B ARMS - 73B	B ARMS - 73B	B ARMS - 73B	B ARMS - 73B	B ARMS - 73B	B ARMS - 73B	B ARMS - 73B
30800 HITHER GREEN - 73C	HITHER GREEN - 73C	HITHER GREEN - 73C	HITHER GREEN - 73C	HITHER GREEN - 73C	HITHER GREEN - 73C	HITHER GREEN - 73C
30801 ASHFORD - 74A	ASHFORD - 74A	ASHFORD - 74A	ASHFORD - 74A	ASHFORD - 74A	ASHFORD - 74A	ASHFORD - 74A
30802 ASHFORD - 74A	ASHFORD - 74A	ASHFORD - 74A	ASHFORD - 74A	ASHFORD - 74A	ASHFORD - 74A	ASHFORD - 74A
30803 ASHFORD - 74A	ASHFORD - 74A	ASHFORD - 74A	ASHFORD - 74A	ASHFORD - 74A	ASHFORD - 74A	ASHFORD - 74A
30804 ASHFORD - 74A	ASHFORD - 74A	ASHFORD - 74A	ASHFORD - 74A	ASHFORD - 74A	ASHFORD - 74A	ASHFORD - 74A
30805 ASHFORD - 74A	ASHFORD - 74A	ASHFORD - 74A	ASHFORD - 74A	ASHFORD - 74A	ASHFORD - 74A	ASHFORD - 74A
30806 HITHER GREEN - 73C	HITHER GREEN - 73C	HITHER GREEN - 73C	HITHER GREEN - 73C	HITHER GREEN - 73C	HITHER GREEN - 73C	HITHER GREEN - 73C
				LN 4-6-0 (1926)			
30850 EASTLEIGH - 71A	EASTLEIGH - 71A	EASTLEIGH - 71A	EASTLEIGH - 71A	EASTLEIGH - 71A	EASTLEIGH - 71A	EASTLEIGH - 71A
30851 EASTLEIGH - 71A	EASTLEIGH - 71A	EASTLEIGH - 71A	EASTLEIGH - 71A	EASTLEIGH - 71A	EASTLEIGH - 71A	EASTLEIGH - 71A
30852 EASTLEIGH - 71A	EASTLEIGH - 71A	EASTLEIGH - 71A	EASTLEIGH - 71A	EASTLEIGH - 71A	EASTLEIGH - 71A	EASTLEIGH - 71A
30853 EASTLEIGH - 71A	EASTLEIGH - 71A	EASTLEIGH - 71A	EASTLEIGH - 71A	EASTLEIGH - 71A	EASTLEIGH - 71A	EASTLEIGH - 71A
30854 EASTLEIGH - 71A	EASTLEIGH - 71A	EASTLEIGH - 71A	EASTLEIGH - 71A	EASTLEIGH - 71A	EASTLEIGH - 71A	EASTLEIGH - 71A
30855 EASTLEIGH - 71A	EASTLEIGH - 71A	EASTLEIGH - 71A	EASTLEIGH - 71A	EASTLEIGH - 71A	EASTLEIGH - 71A	EASTLEIGH - 71A
30856 EASTLEIGH - 71A	EASTLEIGH - 71A	EASTLEIGH - 71A	EASTLEIGH - 71A	EASTLEIGH - 71A	EASTLEIGH - 71A	EASTLEIGH - 71A
30857 EASTLEIGH - 71A	EASTLEIGH - 71A	EASTLEIGH - 71A	EASTLEIGH - 71A	EASTLEIGH - 71A	EASTLEIGH - 71A	EASTLEIGH - 71A
30858 NINE ELMS - 70A	NINE ELMS - 70A	NINE ELMS - 70A	NINE ELMS - 70A	NINE ELMS - 70A	NINE ELMS - 70A	NINE ELMS - 70A
30859 NINE ELMS - 70A	NINE ELMS - 70A	NINE ELMS - 70A	NINE ELMS - 70A	NINE ELMS - 70A	NINE ELMS - 70A	NINE ELMS - 70A
30860 NINE ELMS - 70A	NINE ELMS - 70A	NINE ELMS - 70A	NINE ELMS - 70A	NINE ELMS - 70A	NINE ELMS - 70A	NINE ELMS - 70A
30861 BOURNEMOUTH - 71B	BOURNEMOUTH - 71B	BOURNEMOUTH - 71B	BOURNEMOUTH - 71B	BOURNEMOUTH - 71B	BOURNEMOUTH - 71B	BOURNEMOUTH - 71B
30862 BOURNEMOUTH - 71B	BOURNEMOUTH - 71B	BOURNEMOUTH - 71B	BOURNEMOUTH - 71B	BOURNEMOUTH - 71B	BOURNEMOUTH - 71B	BOURNEMOUTH - 71B
30863 BOURNEMOUTH - 71B	BOURNEMOUTH - 71B	BOURNEMOUTH - 71B	BOURNEMOUTH - 71B	BOURNEMOUTH - 71B	BOURNEMOUTH - 71B	BOURNEMOUTH - 71B
30864 BOURNEMOUTH - 71B	BOURNEMOUTH - 71B	DORCHESTER - 71C	DORCHESTER - 71C	DORCHESTER - 71C	BOURNEMOUTH - 71B	BOURNEMOUTH - 71B
30865 BOURNEMOUTH - 71B	BOURNEMOUTH - 71B	DORCHESTER - 71C	DORCHESTER - 71C	DORCHESTER - 71C	BOURNEMOUTH - 71B	BOURNEMOUTH - 71B

variably turned out for the second leg of the diagram: 30768 being a regular on the second part of the turn for several years. Later in the day 30768, beautifully clean, draws forward to run light to Victoria.

A year later the tenure of the N15's came to an end with the arrival of new BR5 4-6-0's which took over the Victoria - Ramsgate workings although a number of King Arthurs, 30768 amongst them, were retained at Stewarts Lane for special workings. 30768, however, continued to be used regularly for the down Granville until electrification in 1959.

loco	Feb-55	Apr-55	Jun-55	Aug-55	Sep-55	Nov-55	Dec-55
				N15 4-6-0 (1925)			
30448	SALISBURY - 72B	SALISBURY - 72B	SALISBURY - 72B	SALISBURY - 72B	SALISBURY - 72B	SALISBURY - 72B	SALISBURY - 72B
30449	SALISBURY - 72B	SALISBURY - 72B	SALISBURY - 72B	SALISBURY - 72B	SALISBURY - 72B	SALISBURY - 72B	SALISBURY - 72B
30450	SALISBURY - 72B	SALISBURY - 72B	SALISBURY - 72B	SALISBURY - 72B	SALISBURY - 72B	SALISBURY - 72B	SALISBURY - 72B
30451	BASINGSTOKE - 70D	BASINGSTOKE - 70D	BASINGSTOKE - 70D	BASINGSTOKE - 70D	BASINGSTOKE - 70D	BASINGSTOKE - 70D	BASINGSTOKE - 70D
30452	SALISBURY - 72B	SALISBURY - 72B	SALISBURY - 72B	SALISBURY - 72B	SALISBURY - 72B	SALISBURY - 72B	SALISBURY - 72B
30453	SALISBURY - 72B	SALISBURY - 72B	SALISBURY - 72B	SALISBURY - 72B	SALISBURY - 72B	SALISBURY - 72B	SALISBURY - 72B
30454	SALISBURY - 72B	SALISBURY - 72B	SALISBURY - 72B	SALISBURY - 72B	SALISBURY - 72B	SALISBURY - 72B	SALISBURY - 72B
30455	NINE ELMS - 70A	NINE ELMS - 70A	NINE ELMS - 70A	NINE ELMS - 70A	NINE ELMS - 70A	NINE ELMS - 70A	NINE ELMS - 70A
30456	NINE ELMS - 70A	NINE ELMS - 70A	NINE ELMS - 70A	NINE ELMS - 70A	NINE ELMS - 70A	NINE ELMS - 70A	NINE ELMS - 70A
30457	EASTLEIGH - 71A	EASTLEIGH - 71A	EASTLEIGH - 71A	EASTLEIGH - 71A	EASTLEIGH - 71A	EASTLEIGH - 71A	EASTLEIGH - 71A
30763	STEWARTS LANE - 73A	STEWARTS LANE - 73A	STEWARTS LANE - 73A	BASINGSTOKE - 70D	BASINGSTOKE - 70D	BASINGSTOKE - 70D	BASINGSTOKE - 70D
30764	STEWARTS LANE - 73A	STEWARTS LANE - 73A	STEWARTS LANE - 73A	BOURNEMOUTH - 71B	BOURNEMOUTH - 71B	BOURNEMOUTH - 71B	BOURNEMOUTH - 71B
30765	STEWARTS LANE - 73A	STEWARTS LANE - 73A	STEWARTS LANE - 73A	BOURNEMOUTH - 71B	BOURNEMOUTH - 71B	BOURNEMOUTH - 71B	BOURNEMOUTH - 71B
30766	STEWARTS LANE - 73A	STEWARTS LANE - 73A	STEWARTS LANE - 73A	STEWARTS LANE - 73A	STEWARTS LANE - 73A	STEWARTS LANE - 73A	STEWARTS LANE - 73A
30767	STEWARTS LANE - 73A	STEWARTS LANE - 73A	STEWARTS LANE - 73A	STEWARTS LANE - 73A	STEWARTS LANE - 73A	STEWARTS LANE - 73A	STEWARTS LANE - 73A
30768	STEWARTS LANE - 73A	STEWARTS LANE - 73A	STEWARTS LANE - 73A	STEWARTS LANE - 73A	STEWARTS LANE - 73A	STEWARTS LANE - 73A	STEWARTS LANE - 73A
30769	STEWARTS LANE - 73A	STEWARTS LANE - 73A	STEWARTS LANE - 73A	STEWARTS LANE - 73A	STEWARTS LANE - 73A	STEWARTS LANE - 73A	STEWARTS LANE - 73A
30770	STEWARTS LANE - 73A	STEWARTS LANE - 73A	STEWARTS LANE - 73A	BASINGSTOKE - 70D	BASINGSTOKE - 70D	BASINGSTOKE - 70D	BASINGSTOKE - 70D
30771	STEWARTS LANE - 73A	STEWARTS LANE - 73A	STEWARTS LANE - 73A	STEWARTS LANE - 73A	BASINGSTOKE - 70D	BASINGSTOKE - 70D	BASINGSTOKE - 70D
30772	HITHER GREEN - 73C	HITHER GREEN - 73C	HITHER GREEN - 73C	HITHER GREEN - 73C	HITHER GREEN - 73C	HITHER GREEN - 73C	HITHER GREEN - 73C
30773	STEWARTS LANE - 73A	STEWARTS LANE - 73A	STEWARTS LANE - 73A	STEWARTS LANE - 73A	NINE ELMS - 70A	NINE ELMS - 70A	NINE ELMS - 70A
30774	STEWARTS LANE - 73A	STEWARTS LANE - 73A	STEWARTS LANE - 73A	NINE ELMS - 70A	NINE ELMS - 70A	NINE ELMS - 70A	NINE ELMS - 70A
30775	STEWARTS LANE - 73A	STEWARTS LANE - 73A	STEWARTS LANE - 73A	STEWARTS LANE - 73A	DOVER - 74C	DOVER - 74C	DOVER - 74C
30776	STEWARTS LANE - 73A	STEWARTS LANE - 73A	STEWARTS LANE - 73A	STEWARTS LANE - 73A	STEWARTS LANE - 73A	STEWARTS LANE - 73A	STEWARTS LANE - 73A
30777	DOVER - 74C	DOVER - 74C	DOVER - 74C	DOVER - 74C	DOVER - 74C	DOVER - 74C	DOVER - 74C
30778	DOVER - 74C	DOVER - 74C	DOVER - 74C	DOVER - 74C	DOVER - 74C	DOVER - 74C	DOVER - 74C
30779	DOVER - 74C	DOVER - 74C	DOVER - 74C	DOVER - 74C	DOVER - 74C	DOVER - 74C	DOVER - 74C
30780	EASTLEIGH - 71A	EASTLEIGH - 71A	EASTLEIGH - 71A	EASTLEIGH - 71A	EASTLEIGH - 71A	EASTLEIGH - 71A	EASTLEIGH - 71A
30781	NINE ELMS - 70A	NINE ELMS - 70A	NINE ELMS - 70A	NINE ELMS - 70A	NINE ELMS - 70A	NINE ELMS - 70A	NINE ELMS - 70A
30782	BOURNEMOUTH - 71B	BOURNEMOUTH - 71B	BOURNEMOUTH - 71B	BOURNEMOUTH - 71B	BOURNEMOUTH - 71B	BOURNEMOUTH - 71B	BOURNEMOUTH - 71B
30783	BOURNEMOUTH - 71B	BOURNEMOUTH - 71B	BOURNEMOUTH - 71B	BOURNEMOUTH - 71B	BOURNEMOUTH - 71B	BOURNEMOUTH - 71B	BOURNEMOUTH - 71B
30784	EASTLEIGH - 71A	EASTLEIGH - 71A	EASTLEIGH - 71A	EASTLEIGH - 71A	EASTLEIGH - 71A	EASTLEIGH - 71A	EASTLEIGH - 71A
30785	EASTLEIGH - 71A	EASTLEIGH - 71A	EASTLEIGH - 71A	EASTLEIGH - 71A	EASTLEIGH - 71A	EASTLEIGH - 71A	EASTLEIGH - 71A
30786	EASTLEIGH - 71A	EASTLEIGH - 71A	EASTLEIGH - 71A	EASTLEIGH - 71A	EASTLEIGH - 71A	EASTLEIGH - 71A	EASTLEIGH - 71A
30787	EASTLEIGH - 71A	EASTLEIGH - 71A	EASTLEIGH - 71A	EASTLEIGH - 71A	EASTLEIGH - 71A	EASTLEIGH - 71A	EASTLEIGH - 71A
30788	EASTLEIGH - 71A	EASTLEIGH - 71A	EASTLEIGH - 71A	EASTLEIGH - 71A	EASTLEIGH - 71A	EASTLEIGH - 71A	EASTLEIGH - 71A
30789	EASTLEIGH - 71A	EASTLEIGH - 71A	EASTLEIGH - 71A	EASTLEIGH - 71A	EASTLEIGH - 71A	EASTLEIGH - 71A	EASTLEIGH - 71A
30790	EASTLEIGH - 71A	EASTLEIGH - 71A	EASTLEIGH - 71A	EASTLEIGH - 71A	EASTLEIGH - 71A	EASTLEIGH - 71A	EASTLEIGH - 71A
30791	STEWARTS LANE - 73A	STEWARTS LANE - 73A	STEWARTS LANE - 73A	STEWARTS LANE - 73A	EASTLEIGH - 71A	EASTLEIGH - 71A	EASTLEIGH - 71A
30792	STEWARTS LANE - 73A	STEWARTS LANE - 73A	STEWARTS LANE - 73A	STEWARTS LANE - 73A	STEWARTS LANE - 73A	STEWARTS LANE - 73A	STEWARTS LANE - 73A
				N15 4-6-0 (1926)			
30793	STEWARTS LANE - 73A	STEWARTS LANE - 73A	STEWARTS LANE - 73A	STEWARTS LANE - 73A	STEWARTS LANE - 73A	STEWARTS LANE - 73A	STEWARTS LANE - 73A
30794	STEWARTS LANE - 73A	STEWARTS LANE - 73A	STEWARTS LANE - 73A	STEWARTS LANE - 73A	STEWARTS LANE - 73A	STEWARTS LANE - 73A	STEWARTS LANE - 73A
30795	STEWARTS LANE - 73A	STEWARTS LANE - 73A	STEWARTS LANE - 73A	STEWARTS LANE - 73A	EASTLEIGH - 71A	EASTLEIGH - 71A	EASTLEIGH - 71A
30796	DOVER - 74C	DOVER - 74C	DOVER - 74C	DOVER - 74C	DOVER - 74C	DOVER - 74C	DOVER - 74C
30797	DOVER - 74C	DOVER - 74C	DOVER - 74C	DOVER - 74C	DOVER - 74C	DOVER - 74C	DOVER - 74C
30798	DOVER - 74C	DOVER - 74C	DOVER - 74C	DOVER - 74C	DOVER - 74C	DOVER - 74C	DOVER - 74C
30799	B ARMS - 73B	B ARMS - 73B	B ARMS - 73B	B ARMS - 73B	B ARMS - 73B	B ARMS - 73B	B ARMS - 73B
30800	HITHER GREEN - 73C	HITHER GREEN - 73C	HITHER GREEN - 73C	HITHER GREEN - 73C	HITHER GREEN - 73C	HITHER GREEN - 73C	HITHER GREEN - 73C
30801	ASHFORD - 74A	ASHFORD - 74A	ASHFORD - 74A	ASHFORD - 74A	ASHFORD - 74A	ASHFORD - 74A	ASHFORD - 74A
30802	ASHFORD - 74A	ASHFORD - 74A	ASHFORD - 74A	ASHFORD - 74A	ASHFORD - 74A	ASHFORD - 74A	ASHFORD - 74A
30803	ASHFORD - 74A	ASHFORD - 74A	ASHFORD - 74A	ASHFORD - 74A	ASHFORD - 74A	ASHFORD - 74A	ASHFORD - 74A
30804	ASHFORD - 74A	ASHFORD - 74A	ASHFORD - 74A	ASHFORD - 74A	ASHFORD - 74A	ASHFORD - 74A	ASHFORD - 74A
30805	ASHFORD - 74A	ASHFORD - 74A	ASHFORD - 74A	ASHFORD - 74A	ASHFORD - 74A	ASHFORD - 74A	ASHFORD - 74A
30806	HITHER GREEN - 73C	HITHER GREEN - 73C	HITHER GREEN - 73C	HITHER GREEN - 73C	HITHER GREEN - 73C	HITHER GREEN - 73C	HITHER GREEN - 73C
				LN 4-6-0 (1926)			
30850	EASTLEIGH - 71A	EASTLEIGH - 71A	EASTLEIGH - 71A	EASTLEIGH - 71A	EASTLEIGH - 71A	EASTLEIGH - 71A	EASTLEIGH - 71A
30851	EASTLEIGH - 71A	EASTLEIGH - 71A	EASTLEIGH - 71A	EASTLEIGH - 71A	EASTLEIGH - 71A	EASTLEIGH - 71A	EASTLEIGH - 71A
30852	EASTLEIGH - 71A	EASTLEIGH - 71A	EASTLEIGH - 71A	EASTLEIGH - 71A	EASTLEIGH - 71A	EASTLEIGH - 71A	EASTLEIGH - 71A
30853	EASTLEIGH - 71A	EASTLEIGH - 71A	EASTLEIGH - 71A	EASTLEIGH - 71A	EASTLEIGH - 71A	EASTLEIGH - 71A	EASTLEIGH - 71A
30854	EASTLEIGH - 71A	EASTLEIGH - 71A	EASTLEIGH - 71A	EASTLEIGH - 71A	EASTLEIGH - 71A	EASTLEIGH - 71A	EASTLEIGH - 71A
30855	EASTLEIGH - 71A	EASTLEIGH - 71A	EASTLEIGH - 71A	EASTLEIGH - 71A	EASTLEIGH - 71A	EASTLEIGH - 71A	EASTLEIGH - 71A
30856	EASTLEIGH - 71A	EASTLEIGH - 71A	EASTLEIGH - 71A	EASTLEIGH - 71A	EASTLEIGH - 71A	EASTLEIGH - 71A	EASTLEIGH - 71A
30857	EASTLEIGH - 71A	EASTLEIGH - 71A	EASTLEIGH - 71A	EASTLEIGH - 71A	EASTLEIGH - 71A	EASTLEIGH - 71A	EASTLEIGH - 71A
30858	NINE ELMS - 70A	NINE ELMS - 70A	NINE ELMS - 70A	NINE ELMS - 70A	NINE ELMS - 70A	NINE ELMS - 70A	NINE ELMS - 70A
30859	NINE ELMS - 70A	NINE ELMS - 70A	NINE ELMS - 70A	NINE ELMS - 70A	NINE ELMS - 70A	NINE ELMS - 70A	NINE ELMS - 70A
30860	NINE ELMS - 70A	NINE ELMS - 70A	NINE ELMS - 70A	NINE ELMS - 70A	NINE ELMS - 70A	NINE ELMS - 70A	NINE ELMS - 70A
30861	BOURNEMOUTH - 71B	BOURNEMOUTH - 71B	BOURNEMOUTH - 71B	BOURNEMOUTH - 71B	BOURNEMOUTH - 71B	BOURNEMOUTH - 71B	BOURNEMOUTH - 71B
30862	BOURNEMOUTH - 71B	BOURNEMOUTH - 71B	BOURNEMOUTH - 71B	BOURNEMOUTH - 71B	BOURNEMOUTH - 71B	BOURNEMOUTH - 71B	BOURNEMOUTH - 71B
30863	BOURNEMOUTH - 71B	BOURNEMOUTH - 71B	BOURNEMOUTH - 71B	BOURNEMOUTH - 71B	BOURNEMOUTH - 71B	BOURNEMOUTH - 71B	BOURNEMOUTH - 71B
30864	BOURNEMOUTH - 71B	BOURNEMOUTH - 71B	BOURNEMOUTH - 71B	BOURNEMOUTH - 71B	BOURNEMOUTH - 71B	BOURNEMOUTH - 71B	BOURNEMOUTH - 71B
30865	BOURNEMOUTH - 71B	BOURNEMOUTH - 71B	BOURNEMOUTH - 71B	BOURNEMOUTH - 71B	BOURNEMOUTH - 71B	BOURNEMOUTH - 71B	BOURNEMOUTH - 71B

| --- | --- | --- | --- | --- | --- | --- | --- |
				N15 4-6-0 (1925)			
30448	SALISBURY - 72B	SALISBURY - 72B	SALISBURY - 72B	SALISBURY - 72B	SALISBURY - 72B	SALISBURY - 72B	SALISBURY - 72B
30449	SALISBURY - 72B	SALISBURY - 72B	SALISBURY - 72B	SALISBURY - 72B	SALISBURY - 72B	SALISBURY - 72B	SALISBURY - 72B
30450	SALISBURY - 72B	SALISBURY - 72B	SALISBURY - 72B	SALISBURY - 72B	SALISBURY - 72B	SALISBURY - 72B	SALISBURY - 72B
30451	BASINGSTOKE - 70D	BASINGSTOKE - 70D	BASINGSTOKE - 70D	BASINGSTOKE - 70D	BASINGSTOKE - 70D	BASINGSTOKE - 70D	BASINGSTOKE - 70D
30452	SALISBURY - 72B	SALISBURY - 72B	SALISBURY - 72B	SALISBURY - 72B	SALISBURY - 72B	SALISBURY - 72B	SALISBURY - 72B
30453	SALISBURY - 72B	SALISBURY - 72B	SALISBURY - 72B	SALISBURY - 72B	SALISBURY - 72B	SALISBURY - 72B	SALISBURY - 72B
30454	SALISBURY - 72B	SALISBURY - 72B	SALISBURY - 72B	SALISBURY - 72B	SALISBURY - 72B	SALISBURY - 72B	SALISBURY - 72B
30455	NINE ELMS - 70A	NINE ELMS - 70A	NINE ELMS - 70A	NINE ELMS - 70A	NINE ELMS - 70A	NINE ELMS - 70A	NINE ELMS - 70A
30456	NINE ELMS - 70A	NINE ELMS - 70A	NINE ELMS - 70A	NINE ELMS - 70A	NINE ELMS - 70A	NINE ELMS - 70A	NINE ELMS - 70A
30457	EASTLEIGH - 71A	EASTLEIGH - 71A	EASTLEIGH - 71A	EASTLEIGH - 71A	EASTLEIGH - 71A	EASTLEIGH - 71A	EASTLEIGH - 71A
30763	BASINGSTOKE - 70D	BASINGSTOKE - 70D	EASTLEIGH - 71A	EASTLEIGH - 71A	EASTLEIGH - 71A	EASTLEIGH - 71A	EASTLEIGH - 71A
30764	BOURNEMOUTH - 71B	BOURNEMOUTH - 71B	BOURNEMOUTH - 71B	BOURNEMOUTH - 71B	BOURNEMOUTH - 71B	BOURNEMOUTH - 71B	BOURNEMOUTH - 71B
30765	BOURNEMOUTH - 71B	BOURNEMOUTH - 71B	BOURNEMOUTH - 71B	BOURNEMOUTH - 71B	BOURNEMOUTH - 71B	BOURNEMOUTH - 71B	BOURNEMOUTH - 71B
30766	STEWARTS LANE - 73A	STEWARTS LANE - 73A	STEWARTS LANE - 73A	STEWARTS LANE - 73A	STEWARTS LANE - 73A	STEWARTS LANE - 73A	STEWARTS LANE - 73A
30767	STEWARTS LANE - 73A	STEWARTS LANE - 73A	STEWARTS LANE - 73A	STEWARTS LANE - 73A	STEWARTS LANE - 73A	STEWARTS LANE - 73A	STEWARTS LANE - 73A
30768	STEWARTS LANE - 73A	STEWARTS LANE - 73A	STEWARTS LANE - 73A	STEWARTS LANE - 73A	STEWARTS LANE - 73A	STEWARTS LANE - 73A	STEWARTS LANE - 73A
30769	STEWARTS LANE - 73A	STEWARTS LANE - 73A	STEWARTS LANE - 73A	STEWARTS LANE - 73A	STEWARTS LANE - 73A	STEWARTS LANE - 73A	STEWARTS LANE - 73A
30770	BASINGSTOKE - 70D	BASINGSTOKE - 70D	EASTLEIGH - 71A	EASTLEIGH - 71A	EASTLEIGH - 71A	EASTLEIGH - 71A	EASTLEIGH - 71A
30771	NINE ELMS - 70A	NINE ELMS - 70A	BOURNEMOUTH - 71B	BOURNEMOUTH - 71B	BOURNEMOUTH - 71B	BOURNEMOUTH - 71B	BOURNEMOUTH - 71B
30772	HITHER GREEN - 73C	HITHER GREEN - 73C	HITHER GREEN - 73C	HITHER GREEN - 73C	HITHER GREEN - 73C	HITHER GREEN - 73C	HITHER GREEN - 73C
30773	NINE ELMS - 70A	NINE ELMS - 70A	NINE ELMS - 70A	NINE ELMS - 70A	NINE ELMS - 70A	NINE ELMS - 70A	NINE ELMS - 70A
30774	NINE ELMS - 70A	NINE ELMS - 70A	NINE ELMS - 70A	NINE ELMS - 70A	NINE ELMS - 70A	NINE ELMS - 70A	NINE ELMS - 70A
30775	DOVER - 74C	DOVER - 74C	DOVER - 74C	DOVER - 74C	DOVER - 74C	DOVER - 74C	DOVER - 74C
30776	STEWARTS LANE - 73A	STEWARTS LANE - 73A	STEWARTS LANE - 73A	STEWARTS LANE - 73A	STEWARTS LANE - 73A	STEWARTS LANE - 73A	STEWARTS LANE - 73A
30777	DOVER - 74C	DOVER - 74C	DOVER - 74C	DOVER - 74C	DOVER - 74C	DOVER - 74C	DOVER - 74C
30778	DOVER - 74C	DOVER - 74C	DOVER - 74C	DOVER - 74C	DOVER - 74C	DOVER - 74C	DOVER - 74C
30779	DOVER - 74C	DOVER - 74C	DOVER - 74C	DOVER - 74C	DOVER - 74C	DOVER - 74C	DOVER - 74C
30780	BASINGSTOKE - 70D	BASINGSTOKE - 70D	BOURNEMOUTH - 71B	BOURNEMOUTH - 71B	BOURNEMOUTH - 71B	BOURNEMOUTH - 71B	BOURNEMOUTH - 71B
30781	BASINGSTOKE - 70D	BASINGSTOKE - 70D	BOURNEMOUTH - 71B	BOURNEMOUTH - 71B	BOURNEMOUTH - 71B	BOURNEMOUTH - 71B	BOURNEMOUTH - 71B
30782	BOURNEMOUTH - 71B	BOURNEMOUTH - 71B	BOURNEMOUTH - 71B	BOURNEMOUTH - 71B	BOURNEMOUTH - 71B	BOURNEMOUTH - 71B	BOURNEMOUTH - 71B
30783	BOURNEMOUTH - 71B	BOURNEMOUTH - 71B	BOURNEMOUTH - 71B	BOURNEMOUTH - 71B	BOURNEMOUTH - 71B	BOURNEMOUTH - 71B	BOURNEMOUTH - 71B
30784	EASTLEIGH - 71A	EASTLEIGH - 71A	EASTLEIGH - 71A	EASTLEIGH - 71A	EASTLEIGH - 71A	EASTLEIGH - 71A	EASTLEIGH - 71A
30785	EASTLEIGH - 71A	EASTLEIGH - 71A	EASTLEIGH - 71A	EASTLEIGH - 71A	EASTLEIGH - 71A	EASTLEIGH - 71A	EASTLEIGH - 71A
30786	EASTLEIGH - 71A	EASTLEIGH - 71A	EASTLEIGH - 71A	EASTLEIGH - 71A	EASTLEIGH - 71A	EASTLEIGH - 71A	EASTLEIGH - 71A
30787	EASTLEIGH - 71A	EASTLEIGH - 71A	EASTLEIGH - 71A	EASTLEIGH - 71A	EASTLEIGH - 71A	EASTLEIGH - 71A	EASTLEIGH - 71A
30788	EASTLEIGH - 71A	EASTLEIGH - 71A	EASTLEIGH - 71A	EASTLEIGH - 71A	EASTLEIGH - 71A	EASTLEIGH - 71A	EASTLEIGH - 71A
30789	EASTLEIGH - 71A	EASTLEIGH - 71A	EASTLEIGH - 71A	EASTLEIGH - 71A	EASTLEIGH - 71A	EASTLEIGH - 71A	EASTLEIGH - 71A
30790	EASTLEIGH - 71A	EASTLEIGH - 71A	EASTLEIGH - 71A	EASTLEIGH - 71A	EASTLEIGH - 71A	EASTLEIGH - 71A	EASTLEIGH - 71A
30791	EASTLEIGH - 71A	EASTLEIGH - 71A	EASTLEIGH - 71A	EASTLEIGH - 71A	EASTLEIGH - 71A	EASTLEIGH - 71A	EASTLEIGH - 71A
30792	STEWARTS LANE - 73A	STEWARTS LANE - 73A	STEWARTS LANE - 73A	STEWARTS LANE - 73A	STEWARTS LANE - 73A	STEWARTS LANE - 73A	STEWARTS LANE - 73A
				N15 4-6-0 (1926)			
30793	STEWARTS LANE - 73A	STEWARTS LANE - 73A	STEWARTS LANE - 73A	STEWARTS LANE - 73A	STEWARTS LANE - 73A	STEWARTS LANE - 73A	STEWARTS LANE - 73A
30794	STEWARTS LANE - 73A	STEWARTS LANE - 73A	STEWARTS LANE - 73A	STEWARTS LANE - 73A	STEWARTS LANE - 73A	STEWARTS LANE - 73A	STEWARTS LANE - 73A
30795	EASTLEIGH - 71A	EASTLEIGH - 71A	STEWARTS LANE - 73A	STEWARTS LANE - 73A	STEWARTS LANE - 73A	STEWARTS LANE - 73A	STEWARTS LANE - 73A
30796	DOVER - 74C	DOVER - 74C	DOVER - 74C	DOVER - 74C	DOVER - 74C	DOVER - 74C	DOVER - 74C
30797	DOVER - 74C	DOVER - 74C	DOVER - 74C	DOVER - 74C	DOVER - 74C	DOVER - 74C	DOVER - 74C
30798	DOVER - 74C	DOVER - 74C	DOVER - 74C	DOVER - 74C	DOVER - 74C	DOVER - 74C	DOVER - 74C
30799	B ARMS - 73B	B ARMS - 73B	B ARMS - 73B	B ARMS - 73B	B ARMS - 73B	B ARMS - 73B	B ARMS - 73B
30800	HITHER GREEN - 73C	HITHER GREEN - 73C	HITHER GREEN - 73C	HITHER GREEN - 73C	HITHER GREEN - 73C	HITHER GREEN - 73C	HITHER GREEN - 73C
30801	ASHFORD - 74A	ASHFORD - 74A	ASHFORD - 74A	ASHFORD - 74A	ASHFORD - 74A	ASHFORD - 74A	ASHFORD - 74A
30802	ASHFORD - 74A	ASHFORD - 74A	ASHFORD - 74A	ASHFORD - 74A	ASHFORD - 74A	ASHFORD - 74A	ASHFORD - 74A
30803	ASHFORD - 74A	ASHFORD - 74A	ASHFORD - 74A	ASHFORD - 74A	ASHFORD - 74A	ASHFORD - 74A	ASHFORD - 74A
30804	ASHFORD - 74A	ASHFORD - 74A	ASHFORD - 74A	ASHFORD - 74A	ASHFORD - 74A	ASHFORD - 74A	ASHFORD - 74A
30805	ASHFORD - 74A	ASHFORD - 74A	ASHFORD - 74A	ASHFORD - 74A	ASHFORD - 74A	ASHFORD - 74A	ASHFORD - 74A
30806	HITHER GREEN - 73C	HITHER GREEN - 73C	HITHER GREEN - 73C	HITHER GREEN - 73C	HITHER GREEN - 73C	HITHER GREEN - 73C	HITHER GREEN - 73C
				LN 4-6-0 (1926)			
30850	EASTLEIGH - 71A	EASTLEIGH - 71A	EASTLEIGH - 71A	EASTLEIGH - 71A	EASTLEIGH - 71A	EASTLEIGH - 71A	EASTLEIGH - 71A
30851	EASTLEIGH - 71A	EASTLEIGH - 71A	EASTLEIGH - 71A	EASTLEIGH - 71A	EASTLEIGH - 71A	EASTLEIGH - 71A	EASTLEIGH - 71A
30852	EASTLEIGH - 71A	EASTLEIGH - 71A	EASTLEIGH - 71A	EASTLEIGH - 71A	EASTLEIGH - 71A	EASTLEIGH - 71A	EASTLEIGH - 71A
30853	EASTLEIGH - 71A	EASTLEIGH - 71A	EASTLEIGH - 71A	EASTLEIGH - 71A	EASTLEIGH - 71A	EASTLEIGH - 71A	EASTLEIGH - 71A
30854	EASTLEIGH - 71A	EASTLEIGH - 71A	EASTLEIGH - 71A	EASTLEIGH - 71A	EASTLEIGH - 71A	EASTLEIGH - 71A	EASTLEIGH - 71A
30855	EASTLEIGH - 71A	EASTLEIGH - 71A	EASTLEIGH - 71A	EASTLEIGH - 71A	EASTLEIGH - 71A	EASTLEIGH - 71A	EASTLEIGH - 71A
30856	EASTLEIGH - 71A	EASTLEIGH - 71A	EASTLEIGH - 71A	EASTLEIGH - 71A	EASTLEIGH - 71A	EASTLEIGH - 71A	EASTLEIGH - 71A
30857	EASTLEIGH - 71A	EASTLEIGH - 71A	EASTLEIGH - 71A	EASTLEIGH - 71A	EASTLEIGH - 71A	EASTLEIGH - 71A	EASTLEIGH - 71A
30858	NINE ELMS - 70A	NINE ELMS - 70A	NINE ELMS - 70A	NINE ELMS - 70A	NINE ELMS - 70A	NINE ELMS - 70A	NINE ELMS - 70A
30859	NINE ELMS - 70A	NINE ELMS - 70A	NINE ELMS - 70A	NINE ELMS - 70A	NINE ELMS - 70A	NINE ELMS - 70A	NINE ELMS - 70A
30860	NINE ELMS - 70A	NINE ELMS - 70A	NINE ELMS - 70A	NINE ELMS - 70A	NINE ELMS - 70A	NINE ELMS - 70A	NINE ELMS - 70A
30861	BOURNEMOUTH - 71B	BOURNEMOUTH - 71B	EASTLEIGH - 71A	EASTLEIGH - 71A	EASTLEIGH - 71A	EASTLEIGH - 71A	EASTLEIGH - 71A
30862	BOURNEMOUTH - 71B	BOURNEMOUTH - 71B	EASTLEIGH - 71A	EASTLEIGH - 71A	EASTLEIGH - 71A	EASTLEIGH - 71A	EASTLEIGH - 71A
30863	BOURNEMOUTH - 71B	BOURNEMOUTH - 71B	EASTLEIGH - 71A	EASTLEIGH - 71A	EASTLEIGH - 71A	EASTLEIGH - 71A	EASTLEIGH - 71A
30864	BOURNEMOUTH - 71B	BOURNEMOUTH - 71B	BOURNEMOUTH - 71B	BOURNEMOUTH - 71B	BOURNEMOUTH - 71B	BOURNEMOUTH - 71B	BOURNEMOUTH - 71B
30865	BOURNEMOUTH - 71B	BOURNEMOUTH - 71B	BOURNEMOUTH - 71B	BOURNEMOUTH - 71B	BOURNEMOUTH - 71B	BOURNEMOUTH - 71B	BOURNEMOUTH - 71B

Left: 30806 'Sir Galleron', seen at Nine Elms in 1960, was one of the more interesting King Arthur's since it was one of a handful allocated to Hither Green - principally a goods depot - in order to allow the shed's staff to take part in the evening peak service and thus retain route knowledge which was useful for working relief trains during the holiday periods. Although two and sometimes three N15's were allocated to Hither Green, there was only one regular duty for the class and this involved working the 17.40 Cannon Street - Dover Priory via Orpington. The Hither Green crew worked only as far as Ashford but the engine continued forward and returned with the 21.35 goods from Dover to Hither Green via Maidstone East. 30806 was at Hither Green from December 1950 until June 1959 and was usually maintained in very good condition. For the last few years of its life the engine was based at Eastleigh.

N15 4-6-0 (1925)

loco	Mar-57	Jun-57	Jul-57	Oct-57	Jan-58	Feb-58	Mar-58
30448	SALISBURY - 72B	SALISBURY - 72B	SALISBURY - 72B	SALISBURY - 72B	SALISBURY - 72B	SALISBURY - 72B	SALISBURY - 72B
30449	SALISBURY - 72B	SALISBURY - 72B	SALISBURY - 72B	SALISBURY - 72B	SALISBURY - 72B	SALISBURY - 72B	SALISBURY - 72B
30450	SALISBURY - 72B	SALISBURY - 72B	SALISBURY - 72B	SALISBURY - 72B	SALISBURY - 72B	SALISBURY - 72B	SALISBURY - 72B
30451	BASINGSTOKE - 70D	BASINGSTOKE - 70D	BASINGSTOKE - 70D	BASINGSTOKE - 70D	BASINGSTOKE - 72B	BASINGSTOKE - 72B	BASINGSTOKE - 70D
30452	SALISBURY - 72B	SALISBURY - 72B	SALISBURY - 72B	SALISBURY - 72B	SALISBURY - 72B	SALISBURY - 72B	SALISBURY - 72B
30453	SALISBURY - 72B	SALISBURY - 72B	SALISBURY - 72B	SALISBURY - 72B	SALISBURY - 72B	SALISBURY - 72B	SALISBURY - 72B
30454	SALISBURY - 72B	SALISBURY - 72B	SALISBURY - 72B	SALISBURY - 72B	SALISBURY - 72B	SALISBURY - 72B	SALISBURY - 72B
30455	NINE ELMS - 70A	NINE ELMS - 70A	NINE ELMS - 70A	BASINGSTOKE - 70D	BASINGSTOKE - 70D	BASINGSTOKE - 70D	BASINGSTOKE - 70D
30456	BASINGSTOKE - 70D	BASINGSTOKE - 70D	BASINGSTOKE - 70D	BASINGSTOKE - 70D	BASINGSTOKE - 70D	BASINGSTOKE - 70D	BASINGSTOKE - 70D
30457	EASTLEIGH - 71A	EASTLEIGH - 71A	EASTLEIGH - 71A	BASINGSTOKE - 70D	BASINGSTOKE - 70D	BASINGSTOKE - 70D	BASINGSTOKE - 70D
30763	EASTLEIGH - 71A	BOURNEMOUTH - 71B	BOURNEMOUTH - 71B	NINE ELMS - 70A	NINE ELMS - 70A	NINE ELMS - 70A	NINE ELMS - 70A
30764	BOURNEMOUTH - 71B	BOURNEMOUTH - 71B	BOURNEMOUTH - 71B	BOURNEMOUTH - 71B	BOURNEMOUTH - 71B	BOURNEMOUTH - 71B	BOURNEMOUTH - 71B
30765	BOURNEMOUTH - 71B	BOURNEMOUTH - 71B	BOURNEMOUTH - 71B	BOURNEMOUTH - 71B	BOURNEMOUTH - 71B	BOURNEMOUTH - 71B	BOURNEMOUTH - 71B
30766	STEWARTS LANE - 73A	STEWARTS LANE - 73A	STEWARTS LANE - 73A	STEWARTS LANE - 73A	STEWARTS LANE - 73A	STEWARTS LANE - 73A	STEWARTS LANE - 73A
30767	STEWARTS LANE - 73A	STEWARTS LANE - 73A	STEWARTS LANE - 73A	STEWARTS LANE - 73A	STEWARTS LANE - 73A	STEWARTS LANE - 73A	STEWARTS LANE - 73A
30768	STEWARTS LANE - 73A	STEWARTS LANE - 73A	STEWARTS LANE - 73A	STEWARTS LANE - 73A	STEWARTS LANE - 73A	STEWARTS LANE - 73A	STEWARTS LANE - 73A
30769	STEWARTS LANE - 73A	STEWARTS LANE - 73A	STEWARTS LANE - 73A	STEWARTS LANE - 73A	STEWARTS LANE - 73A	STEWARTS LANE - 73A	STEWARTS LANE - 73A
30770	EASTLEIGH - 71A	EASTLEIGH - 71A	EASTLEIGH - 71A	EASTLEIGH - 71A	EASTLEIGH - 71A	EASTLEIGH - 71A	EASTLEIGH - 71A
30771	BOURNEMOUTH - 71B	BOURNEMOUTH - 71B	BOURNEMOUTH - 71B	BOURNEMOUTH - 71B	BOURNEMOUTH - 71B	BOURNEMOUTH - 71B	BOURNEMOUTH - 71B
30772	HITHER GREEN - 73C	BOURNEMOUTH - 71B	BOURNEMOUTH - 71B	BOURNEMOUTH - 71B	BOURNEMOUTH - 71B	BOURNEMOUTH - 71B	BOURNEMOUTH - 71B
30773	NINE ELMS - 70A	BOURNEMOUTH - 71B	BOURNEMOUTH - 71B	BOURNEMOUTH - 71B	BOURNEMOUTH - 71B	BOURNEMOUTH - 71B	BOURNEMOUTH - 71B
30774	NINE ELMS - 70A	NINE ELMS - 70A	NINE ELMS - 70A	NINE ELMS - 70A	NINE ELMS - 70A	NINE ELMS - 70A	NINE ELMS - 70A
30775	DOVER - 74C	DOVER - 74C	DOVER - 74C	DOVER - 74C	DOVER - 74C	DOVER - 74C	DOVER - 74C
30776	STEWARTS LANE - 73A	STEWARTS LANE - 73A	STEWARTS LANE - 73A	STEWARTS LANE - 73A	STEWARTS LANE - 73A	STEWARTS LANE - 73A	STEWARTS LANE - 73A
30777	DOVER - 74C	DOVER - 74C	DOVER - 74C	DOVER - 74C	DOVER - 74C	DOVER - 74C	DOVER - 74C
30778	DOVER - 74C	DOVER - 74C	DOVER - 74C	DOVER - 74C	DOVER - 74C	DOVER - 74C	DOVER - 74C
30779	DOVER - 74C	DOVER - 74C	DOVER - 74C	DOVER - 74C	DOVER - 74C	DOVER - 74C	DOVER - 74C
30780	BOURNEMOUTH - 71B	BOURNEMOUTH - 71B	BOURNEMOUTH - 71B	BOURNEMOUTH - 71B	BOURNEMOUTH - 71B	BOURNEMOUTH - 71B	BOURNEMOUTH - 71B
30781	BOURNEMOUTH - 71B	BOURNEMOUTH - 71B	BOURNEMOUTH - 71B	BOURNEMOUTH - 71B	BOURNEMOUTH - 71B	BOURNEMOUTH - 71B	BOURNEMOUTH - 71B
30782	BOURNEMOUTH - 71B	BOURNEMOUTH - 71B	BOURNEMOUTH - 71B	BOURNEMOUTH - 71B	BOURNEMOUTH - 71B	BOURNEMOUTH - 71B	BOURNEMOUTH - 71B
30783	BOURNEMOUTH - 71B	BOURNEMOUTH - 71B	BOURNEMOUTH - 71B	BOURNEMOUTH - 71B	BOURNEMOUTH - 71B	BOURNEMOUTH - 71B	BOURNEMOUTH - 71B
30784	EASTLEIGH - 71A	EASTLEIGH - 71A	EASTLEIGH - 71A	EASTLEIGH - 71A	EASTLEIGH - 71A	EASTLEIGH - 71A	EASTLEIGH - 71A
30785	EASTLEIGH - 71A	EASTLEIGH - 71A	EASTLEIGH - 71A	EASTLEIGH - 71A	EASTLEIGH - 71A	EASTLEIGH - 71A	EASTLEIGH - 71A
30786	EASTLEIGH - 71A	EASTLEIGH - 71A	EASTLEIGH - 71A	EASTLEIGH - 71A	EASTLEIGH - 71A	EASTLEIGH - 71A	EASTLEIGH - 71A
30787	EASTLEIGH - 71A	EASTLEIGH - 71A	EASTLEIGH - 71A	EASTLEIGH - 71A	EASTLEIGH - 71A	EASTLEIGH - 71A	EASTLEIGH - 71A
30788	EASTLEIGH - 71A	EASTLEIGH - 71A	EASTLEIGH - 71A	EASTLEIGH - 71A	EASTLEIGH - 71A	EASTLEIGH - 71A	EASTLEIGH - 71A
30789	EASTLEIGH - 71A	EASTLEIGH - 71A	EASTLEIGH - 71A	EASTLEIGH - 71A	EASTLEIGH - 71A	EASTLEIGH - 71A	EASTLEIGH - 71A
30790	EASTLEIGH - 71A	EASTLEIGH - 71A	EASTLEIGH - 71A	EASTLEIGH - 71A	EASTLEIGH - 71A	EASTLEIGH - 71A	EASTLEIGH - 71A
30791	EASTLEIGH - 71A	EASTLEIGH - 71A	EASTLEIGH - 71A	EASTLEIGH - 71A	EASTLEIGH - 71A	EASTLEIGH - 71A	EASTLEIGH - 71A
30792	STEWARTS LANE - 73A	EASTLEIGH - 71A	EASTLEIGH - 71A	EASTLEIGH - 71A	EASTLEIGH - 71A	EASTLEIGH - 71A	EASTLEIGH - 71A

N15 4-6-0 (1926)

loco	Mar-57	Jun-57	Jul-57	Oct-57	Jan-58	Feb-58	Mar-58
30793	STEWARTS LANE - 73A	STEWARTS LANE - 73A	STEWARTS LANE - 73A	STEWARTS LANE - 73A	STEWARTS LANE - 73A	STEWARTS LANE - 73A	STEWARTS LANE - 73A
30794	STEWARTS LANE - 73A	STEWARTS LANE - 73A	STEWARTS LANE - 73A	STEWARTS LANE - 73A	STEWARTS LANE - 73A	STEWARTS LANE - 73A	STEWARTS LANE - 73A
30795	STEWARTS LANE - 73A	STEWARTS LANE - 73A	STEWARTS LANE - 73A	STEWARTS LANE - 73A	STEWARTS LANE - 73A	STEWARTS LANE - 73A	STEWARTS LANE - 73A
30796	DOVER - 74C	HITHER GREEN - 73C	HITHER GREEN - 73C	HITHER GREEN - 73C	HITHER GREEN - 73C	HITHER GREEN - 73C	HITHER GREEN - 73C
30797	DOVER - 74C	DOVER - 74C	DOVER - 74C	DOVER - 74C	DOVER - 74C	DOVER - 74C	DOVER - 74C
30798	DOVER - 74C	DOVER - 74C	DOVER - 74C	DOVER - 74C	DOVER - 74C	DOVER - 74C	DOVER - 74C
30799	B ARMS - 73B	B ARMS - 73B	B ARMS - 73B	B ARMS - 73B	B ARMS - 73B	B ARMS - 73B	B ARMS - 73B
30800	HITHER GREEN - 73C	HITHER GREEN - 73C	HITHER GREEN - 73C	HITHER GREEN - 73C	HITHER GREEN - 73C	HITHER GREEN - 73C	HITHER GREEN - 73C
30801	ASHFORD - 74A	ASHFORD - 74A	ASHFORD - 74A	ASHFORD - 74A	ASHFORD - 74A	ASHFORD - 74A	ASHFORD - 74A
30802	ASHFORD - 74A	ASHFORD - 74A	ASHFORD - 74A	ASHFORD - 74A	ASHFORD - 74A	ASHFORD - 74A	ASHFORD - 74A
30803	ASHFORD - 74A	ASHFORD - 74A	ASHFORD - 74A	ASHFORD - 74A	ASHFORD - 74A	ASHFORD - 74A	ASHFORD - 74A
30804	ASHFORD - 74A	DOVER - 74C	DOVER - 74C	DOVER - 74C	DOVER - 74C	DOVER - 74C	DOVER - 74C
30805	ASHFORD - 74A	DOVER - 74C	DOVER - 74C	DOVER - 74C	DOVER - 74C	DOVER - 74C	DOVER - 74C
30806	HITHER GREEN - 73C	HITHER GREEN - 73C	HITHER GREEN - 73C	HITHER GREEN - 73C	HITHER GREEN - 73C	HITHER GREEN - 73C	HITHER GREEN - 73C

LN 4-6-0 (1926)

loco	Mar-57	Jun-57	Jul-57	Oct-57	Jan-58	Feb-58	Mar-58
30850	EASTLEIGH - 71A	EASTLEIGH - 71A	EASTLEIGH - 71A	EASTLEIGH - 71A	EASTLEIGH - 71A	EASTLEIGH - 71A	EASTLEIGH - 71A
30851	EASTLEIGH - 71A	EASTLEIGH - 71A	EASTLEIGH - 71A	EASTLEIGH - 71A	EASTLEIGH - 71A	EASTLEIGH - 71A	EASTLEIGH - 71A
30852	EASTLEIGH - 71A	EASTLEIGH - 71A	EASTLEIGH - 71A	EASTLEIGH - 71A	EASTLEIGH - 71A	EASTLEIGH - 71A	EASTLEIGH - 71A
30853	EASTLEIGH - 71A	EASTLEIGH - 71A	EASTLEIGH - 71A	EASTLEIGH - 71A	EASTLEIGH - 71A	EASTLEIGH - 71A	EASTLEIGH - 71A
30854	EASTLEIGH - 71A	EASTLEIGH - 71A	EASTLEIGH - 71A	EASTLEIGH - 71A	EASTLEIGH - 71A	EASTLEIGH - 71A	EASTLEIGH - 71A
30855	EASTLEIGH - 71A	EASTLEIGH - 71A	EASTLEIGH - 71A	EASTLEIGH - 71A	EASTLEIGH - 71A	EASTLEIGH - 71A	EASTLEIGH - 71A
30856	EASTLEIGH - 71A	EASTLEIGH - 71A	EASTLEIGH - 71A	EASTLEIGH - 71A	EASTLEIGH - 71A	EASTLEIGH - 71A	EASTLEIGH - 71A
30857	EASTLEIGH - 71A	EASTLEIGH - 71A	EASTLEIGH - 71A	EASTLEIGH - 71A	EASTLEIGH - 71A	EASTLEIGH - 71A	EASTLEIGH - 71A
30858	NINE ELMS - 70A	NINE ELMS - 70A	NINE ELMS - 70A	NINE ELMS - 70A	NINE ELMS - 70A	NINE ELMS - 70A	NINE ELMS - 70A
30859	NINE ELMS - 70A	NINE ELMS - 70A	NINE ELMS - 70A	NINE ELMS - 70A	NINE ELMS - 70A	NINE ELMS - 70A	NINE ELMS - 70A
30860	NINE ELMS - 70A	NINE ELMS - 70A	NINE ELMS - 70A	NINE ELMS - 70A	NINE ELMS - 70A	NINE ELMS - 70A	NINE ELMS - 70A
30861	EASTLEIGH - 71A	EASTLEIGH - 71A	EASTLEIGH - 71A	EASTLEIGH - 71A	EASTLEIGH - 71A	EASTLEIGH - 71A	EASTLEIGH - 71A
30862	EASTLEIGH - 71A	EASTLEIGH - 71A	EASTLEIGH - 71A	EASTLEIGH - 71A	EASTLEIGH - 71A	EASTLEIGH - 71A	EASTLEIGH - 71A
30863	EASTLEIGH - 71A	EASTLEIGH - 71A	EASTLEIGH - 71A	EASTLEIGH - 71A	EASTLEIGH - 71A	EASTLEIGH - 71A	EASTLEIGH - 71A
30864	BOURNEMOUTH - 71B	BOURNEMOUTH - 71B	BOURNEMOUTH - 71B	BOURNEMOUTH - 71B	BOURNEMOUTH - 71B	BOURNEMOUTH - 71B	BOURNEMOUTH - 71B
30865	BOURNEMOUTH - 71B	BOURNEMOUTH - 71B	BOURNEMOUTH - 71B	BOURNEMOUTH - 71B	BOURNEMOUTH - 71B	BOURNEMOUTH - 71B	BOURNEMOUTH - 71B

73082 CAMELOT
LOCOMOTIVE SOCIETY

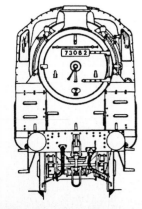

Although it seemed at times as though the N15 King Arthur 4-6-0's would go on forever, in the mid-1950's their replacements arrived in the shape of new BR 5MT 4-6-0's; one batch going to Nine Elms for semi-fast services out of Waterloo and another being allocated to Stewarts Lane as successors to the N15 4-6-0's on the Victoria - Ramsgate expresses. Whilst the Nine Elms engines had only limited opportunities for high speeds, those at Stewarts Lane worked the (almost) hourly non-stop runs between Bromley South and Chatham with the prospect of high speeds on the descent of Sole Street bank. Many instances of speeds in excess of 90 mph were clocked on this section - a stretch of line which had never previously been known for such fireworks.

One of the Stewarts Lane engines was 73082 which, with its nine shedmates, worked the Ramsgate route from 1955 until 1959 when, with the electrification of the LCDR main line, they joined the others at Nine Elms.

Fortunately 73082 survives in the care of the *Camelot Locomotive Society* - appropriately 73082 and other SR standard 5MT's received King Arthur nameplates from 1960 - and an invitation is extended to join the society and take an active interest in the locomotive and its future.

Enquiries to 73082 Camelot Locomotive Society, 54 Latimer Gardens, Pinner, Middlesex. HA5 3RA (0181 429-2795)

loco	May-58	Oct-58	Mar-59	Jun-59	Jul-59	Aug-59	Oct-59
N15 4-6-0 (1925)							
30448	SALISBURY - 72B	SALISBURY - 72B	SALISBURY - 72B	SALISBURY - 72B	SALISBURY - 72B	SALISBURY - 72B	SALISBURY - 72B
30449	SALISBURY - 72B	SALISBURY - 72B	SALISBURY - 72B	SALISBURY - 72B	SALISBURY - 72B	SALISBURY - 72B	SALISBURY - 72B
30450	SALISBURY - 72B	SALISBURY - 72B	SALISBURY - 72B	SALISBURY - 72B	SALISBURY - 72B	SALISBURY - 72B	SALISBURY - 72B
30451	BASINGSTOKE - 70D	BASINGSTOKE - 70D	BASINGSTOKE - 70D	BASINGSTOKE - 70D	BASINGSTOKE - 70D	BASINGSTOKE - 70D	BASINGSTOKE - 70D
30452	SALISBURY - 72B	SALISBURY - 72B	SALISBURY - 72B	SALISBURY - 72B	SALISBURY - 72B	SALISBURY - 72B	W/D
30453	SALISBURY - 72B	SALISBURY - 72B	SALISBURY - 72B	SALISBURY - 72B	SALISBURY - 72B	SALISBURY - 72B	SALISBURY - 72B
30454	SALISBURY - 72B	SALISBURY - 72B	W/D	W/D	W/D	W/D	W/D
30455	BASINGSTOKE - 70D	BASINGSTOKE - 70D	BASINGSTOKE - 70D	W/D	W/D	W/D	W/D
30456	BASINGSTOKE - 70D	BASINGSTOKE - 70D	BASINGSTOKE - 70D	BASINGSTOKE - 70D	BASINGSTOKE - 70D	BASINGSTOKE - 70D	BASINGSTOKE - 70D
30457	NINE ELMS - 70A	NINE ELMS - 70A	NINE ELMS - 70A	NINE ELMS - 70A	NINE ELMS - 70A	NINE ELMS - 70A	NINE ELMS - 70A
30763	NINE ELMS - 70A	NINE ELMS - 70A	NINE ELMS - 70A	NINE ELMS - 70A	NINE ELMS - 70A	NINE ELMS - 70A	NINE ELMS - 70A
30764	BOURNEMOUTH - 71B	BOURNEMOUTH - 71B	BOURNEMOUTH - 71B	BOURNEMOUTH - 71B	BOURNEMOUTH - 71B	BOURNEMOUTH - 71B	BOURNEMOUTH - 71B
30765	BOURNEMOUTH - 71B	BASINGSTOKE - 70D	BASINGSTOKE - 70D	BASINGSTOKE - 70D	BASINGSTOKE - 70D	BASINGSTOKE - 70D	BASINGSTOKE - 70D
30766	STEWARTS LANE - 73A	STEWARTS LANE - 73A	W/D	W/D	W/D	W/D	W/D
30767	STEWARTS LANE - 73A	STEWARTS LANE - 73A	STEWARTS LANE - 73A	EASTLEIGH - 71A	W/D	W/D	W/D
30768	STEWARTS LANE - 73A	STEWARTS LANE - 73A	STEWARTS LANE - 73A	EASTLEIGH - 71A	EASTLEIGH - 71A	EASTLEIGH - 71A	EASTLEIGH - 71A
30769	STEWARTS LANE - 73A	STEWARTS LANE - 73A	STEWARTS LANE - 73A	EASTLEIGH - 71A	EASTLEIGH - 71A	EASTLEIGH - 71A	EASTLEIGH - 71A
30770	EASTLEIGH - 71A	EASTLEIGH - 71A	EASTLEIGH - 71A	EASTLEIGH - 71A	EASTLEIGH - 71A	EASTLEIGH - 71A	EASTLEIGH - 71A
30771	BOURNEMOUTH - 71B	BOURNEMOUTH - 71B	BOURNEMOUTH - 71B	BOURNEMOUTH - 71B	BOURNEMOUTH - 71B	BOURNEMOUTH - 71B	BOURNEMOUTH - 71B
30772	BOURNEMOUTH - 71B	BOURNEMOUTH - 71B	BOURNEMOUTH - 71B	BOURNEMOUTH - 71B	BOURNEMOUTH - 71B	BOURNEMOUTH - 71B	BOURNEMOUTH - 71B
30773	BOURNEMOUTH - 71B	BASINGSTOKE - 70D	BASINGSTOKE - 70D	BASINGSTOKE - 70D	BASINGSTOKE - 70D	BASINGSTOKE - 70D	BASINGSTOKE - 70D
30774	NINE ELMS - 70A	NINE ELMS - 70A	NINE ELMS - 70A	NINE ELMS - 70A	NINE ELMS - 70A	NINE ELMS - 70A	NINE ELMS - 70A
30775	DOVER - 74C	DOVER - 73H	DOVER - 73H	FELTHAM - 70B	FELTHAM - 70B	FELTHAM - 70B	FELTHAM - 70B
30776	STEWARTS LANE - 73A	STEWARTS LANE - 73A	W/D	W/D	W/D	W/D	W/D
30777	DOVER - 74C	DOVER - 73H	DOVER - 73H	FELTHAM - 70B	FELTHAM - 70B	FELTHAM - 70B	FELTHAM - 70B
30778	DOVER - 74C	DOVER - 73H	DOVER - 73H	W/D	W/D	W/D	W/D
30779	DOVER - 74C	DOVER - 73H	DOVER - 73H	DOVER - 73H	W/D	W/D	W/D
30780	BOURNEMOUTH - 71B	BOURNEMOUTH - 71B	BOURNEMOUTH - 71B	BOURNEMOUTH - 71B	W/D	W/D	W/D
30781	BOURNEMOUTH - 71B	BOURNEMOUTH - 71B	BOURNEMOUTH - 71B	BOURNEMOUTH - 71B	BOURNEMOUTH - 71B	BOURNEMOUTH - 71B	BOURNEMOUTH - 71B
30782	BOURNEMOUTH - 71B	BOURNEMOUTH - 71B	BOURNEMOUTH - 71B	BOURNEMOUTH - 71B	BOURNEMOUTH - 71B	BOURNEMOUTH - 71B	BOURNEMOUTH - 71B
30783	BOURNEMOUTH - 71B	BOURNEMOUTH - 71B	BOURNEMOUTH - 71B	BOURNEMOUTH - 71B	BOURNEMOUTH - 71B	BOURNEMOUTH - 71B	BOURNEMOUTH - 71B
30784	EASTLEIGH - 71A	EASTLEIGH - 71A	EASTLEIGH - 71A	EASTLEIGH - 71A	EASTLEIGH - 71A	EASTLEIGH - 71A	W/D
30785	EASTLEIGH - 71A	EASTLEIGH - 71A	EASTLEIGH - 71A	EASTLEIGH - 71A	EASTLEIGH - 71A	EASTLEIGH - 71A	W/D
30786	EASTLEIGH - 71A	EASTLEIGH - 71A	EASTLEIGH - 71A	EASTLEIGH - 71A	EASTLEIGH - 71A	EASTLEIGH - 71A	
30787	EASTLEIGH - 71A	EASTLEIGH - 71A	W/D	W/D	W/D	W/D	W/D
30788	EASTLEIGH - 71A	EASTLEIGH - 71A	EASTLEIGH - 71A	EASTLEIGH - 71A	EASTLEIGH - 71A	EASTLEIGH - 71A	EASTLEIGH - 71A
30789	EASTLEIGH - 71A	EASTLEIGH - 71A	EASTLEIGH - 71A	EASTLEIGH - 71A	EASTLEIGH - 71A	EASTLEIGH - 71A	EASTLEIGH - 71A
30790	EASTLEIGH - 71A	EASTLEIGH - 71A	EASTLEIGH - 71A	EASTLEIGH - 71A	EASTLEIGH - 71A	EASTLEIGH - 71A	EASTLEIGH - 71A
30791	EASTLEIGH - 71A	EASTLEIGH - 71A	EASTLEIGH - 71A	EASTLEIGH - 71A	EASTLEIGH - 71A	EASTLEIGH - 71A	EASTLEIGH - 71A
30792	EASTLEIGH - 71A	EASTLEIGH - 71A	W/D	W/D	W/D	W/D	W/D
N15 4-6-0 (1926)							
30793	STEWARTS LANE - 73A	STEWARTS LANE - 73A	STEWARTS LANE - 73A	FELTHAM - 70B	FELTHAM - 70B	FELTHAM - 70B	FELTHAM - 70B
30794	STEWARTS LANE - 73A	STEWARTS LANE - 73A	BASINGSTOKE - 70D	BASINGSTOKE - 70D	BASINGSTOKE - 70D	BASINGSTOKE - 70D	BASINGSTOKE - 70D
30795	STEWARTS LANE - 73A	STEWARTS LANE - 73A	STEWARTS LANE - 73A	FELTHAM - 70B	FELTHAM - 70B	FELTHAM - 70B	FELTHAM - 70B
30796	HITHER GREEN - 73C	HITHER GREEN - 73C	HITHER GREEN - 73C	SALISBURY - 72B	SALISBURY - 72B	SALISBURY - 72B	SALISBURY - 72B
30797	DOVER - 74C	DOVER - 73H	DOVER - 73H	W/D	W/D	W/D	W/D
30798	DOVER - 74C	DOVER - 73H	DOVER - 73H	SALISBURY - 72B	SALISBURY - 72B	SALISBURY - 72B	SALISBURY - 72B
30799	B.ARMS - 73B	B.ARMS - 73B	B.ARMS - 73B	SALISBURY - 72B	SALISBURY - 72B	SALISBURY - 72B	SALISBURY - 72B
30800	HITHER GREEN - 73C	HITHER GREEN - 73C	HITHER GREEN - 73C	EASTLEIGH - 71A	EASTLEIGH - 71A	EASTLEIGH - 71A	EASTLEIGH - 71A
30801	ASHFORD - 74A	ASHFORD - 73F	ASHFORD - 73F	W/D	W/D	W/D	W/D
30802	STEWARTS LANE - 73A	STEWARTS LANE - 73A	STEWARTS LANE - 73A	EASTLEIGH - 71A	EASTLEIGH - 71A	EASTLEIGH - 71A	EASTLEIGH - 71A
30803	STEWARTS LANE - 73A	STEWARTS LANE - 73A	STEWARTS LANE - 73A	EASTLEIGH - 71A	EASTLEIGH - 71A	EASTLEIGH - 71A	EASTLEIGH - 71A
30804	DOVER - 74C	DOVER - 73H	DOVER - 73H	EASTLEIGH - 71A	EASTLEIGH - 71A	EASTLEIGH - 71A	EASTLEIGH - 71A
30805	DOVER - 74C	DOVER - 73H	DOVER - 73H	EASTLEIGH - 71A	EASTLEIGH - 71A	EASTLEIGH - 71A	EASTLEIGH - 71A
30806	HITHER GREEN - 73C	HITHER GREEN - 73C	HITHER GREEN - 73C	EASTLEIGH - 71A	EASTLEIGH - 71A	EASTLEIGH - 71A	EASTLEIGH - 71A
LN 4-6-0 (1926)							
30850	EASTLEIGH - 71A	EASTLEIGH - 71A	EASTLEIGH - 71A	EASTLEIGH - 71A	EASTLEIGH - 71A	EASTLEIGH - 71A	EASTLEIGH - 71A
30851	EASTLEIGH - 71A	EASTLEIGH - 71A	EASTLEIGH - 71A	EASTLEIGH - 71A	EASTLEIGH - 71A	EASTLEIGH - 71A	EASTLEIGH - 71A
30852	EASTLEIGH - 71A	EASTLEIGH - 71A	EASTLEIGH - 71A	EASTLEIGH - 71A	EASTLEIGH - 71A	EASTLEIGH - 71A	EASTLEIGH - 71A
30853	EASTLEIGH - 71A	EASTLEIGH - 71A	EASTLEIGH - 71A	EASTLEIGH - 71A	EASTLEIGH - 71A	EASTLEIGH - 71A	EASTLEIGH - 71A
30854	EASTLEIGH - 71A	EASTLEIGH - 71A	EASTLEIGH - 71A	EASTLEIGH - 71A	EASTLEIGH - 71A	EASTLEIGH - 71A	EASTLEIGH - 71A
30855	EASTLEIGH - 71A	EASTLEIGH - 71A	EASTLEIGH - 71A	EASTLEIGH - 71A	EASTLEIGH - 71A	EASTLEIGH - 71A	EASTLEIGH - 71A
30856	EASTLEIGH - 71A	EASTLEIGH - 71A	EASTLEIGH - 71A	EASTLEIGH - 71A	EASTLEIGH - 71A	EASTLEIGH - 71A	EASTLEIGH - 71A
30857	EASTLEIGH - 71A	EASTLEIGH - 71A	EASTLEIGH - 71A	EASTLEIGH - 71A	EASTLEIGH - 71A	EASTLEIGH - 71A	EASTLEIGH - 71A
30858	EASTLEIGH - 71A	EASTLEIGH - 71A	EASTLEIGH - 71A	EASTLEIGH - 71A	EASTLEIGH - 71A	EASTLEIGH - 71A	EASTLEIGH - 71A
30859	EASTLEIGH - 71A	EASTLEIGH - 71A	EASTLEIGH - 71A	EASTLEIGH - 71A	EASTLEIGH - 71A	EASTLEIGH - 71A	EASTLEIGH - 71A
30860	BOURNEMOUTH - 71B	BOURNEMOUTH - 71B	BOURNEMOUTH - 71B	BOURNEMOUTH - 71B	BOURNEMOUTH - 71B	BOURNEMOUTH - 71B	BOURNEMOUTH - 71B
30861	EASTLEIGH - 71A	EASTLEIGH - 71A	EASTLEIGH - 71A	EASTLEIGH - 71A	EASTLEIGH - 71A	EASTLEIGH - 71A	EASTLEIGH - 71A
30862	EASTLEIGH - 71A	EASTLEIGH - 71A	EASTLEIGH - 71A	EASTLEIGH - 71A	EASTLEIGH - 71A	EASTLEIGH - 71A	EASTLEIGH - 71A
30863	EASTLEIGH - 71A	EASTLEIGH - 71A	EASTLEIGH - 71A	EASTLEIGH - 71A	EASTLEIGH - 71A	EASTLEIGH - 71A	EASTLEIGH - 71A
30864	BOURNEMOUTH - 71B	BOURNEMOUTH - 71B	BOURNEMOUTH - 71B	BOURNEMOUTH - 71B	BOURNEMOUTH - 71B	BOURNEMOUTH - 71B	BOURNEMOUTH - 71B
30865	BOURNEMOUTH - 71B	BOURNEMOUTH - 71B	BOURNEMOUTH - 71B	BOURNEMOUTH - 71B	BOURNEMOUTH - 71B	BOURNEMOUTH - 71B	BOURNEMOUTH - 71B

Wherever you were on the Southern, Scotland was a long way away and the thirty N15's, 30763-92, built by the North British Co. in Glasgow were regarded by enthusiasts as being quite separate from the rest and christened 'Scotch Arthurs' to distinguish them from the others. Few if any railwaymen were aware of the difference however and the only operating distinction made was between the examples fitted with 6-wheel tenders (30793-805), originally for use on the LBSCR, and the remainder which had eight-wheel high capacity tenders. Scotch Arthur 30785 'Sir Mador de la Porte' stands dead with its smokebox door ajar at Eastleigh in 1954.

loco	Dec-59	Feb-60	Mar-60	Apr-60	Jul-60	Aug-60	Sep-60	Nov-60
N15 4-6-0 (1925)								
30448	SALISBURY - 72B	SALISBURY - 72B	SALISBURY - 72B	SALISBURY - 72B	SALISBURY - 72B	SALISBURY - 72B	W/D	W/D
30450	SALISBURY - 72B	SALISBURY - 72B	SALISBURY - 72B	SALISBURY - 72B	SALISBURY - 72B	SALISBURY - 72B	W/D	W/D
30451	BASINGSTOKE - 70D	BASINGSTOKE - 70D	BASINGSTOKE - 70D	BASINGSTOKE - 70D	BASINGSTOKE - 70D	BASINGSTOKE - 70D	BASINGSTOKE - 70D	BASINGSTOKE - 70D
30453	SALISBURY - 72B	SALISBURY - 72B	SALISBURY - 72B	SALISBURY - 72B	SALISBURY - 72B	SALISBURY - 72B	SALISBURY - 72B	SALISBURY - 72B
30456	BASINGSTOKE - 70D	BASINGSTOKE - 70D	BASINGSTOKE - 70D	BASINGSTOKE - 70D	W/D	W/D	W/D	W/D
30457	NINE ELMS - 70A	NINE ELMS - 70A	NINE ELMS - 70A	NINE ELMS - 70A	NINE ELMS - 70A	NINE ELMS - 70A	NINE ELMS - 70A	NINE ELMS - 70A
30763	NINE ELMS - 70A	NINE ELMS - 70A	NINE ELMS - 70A	NINE ELMS - 70A	NINE ELMS - 70A	NINE ELMS - 70A	W/D	W/D
30764	BOURNEMOUTH - 71B	BOURNEMOUTH - 71B	BOURNEMOUTH - 71B	BOURNEMOUTH - 71B	BOURNEMOUTH - 71B	BOURNEMOUTH - 71B	SALISBURY - 72B	BOURNEMOUTH - 71B
30765	BASINGSTOKE - 70D	BASINGSTOKE - 70D	BASINGSTOKE - 70D	BASINGSTOKE - 70D	BASINGSTOKE - 70D	BASINGSTOKE - 70D	BASINGSTOKE - 70D	BASINGSTOKE - 70D
30768	EASTLEIGH - 71A	EASTLEIGH - 71A	EASTLEIGH - 71A	EASTLEIGH - 71A	EASTLEIGH - 71A	EASTLEIGH - 71A	EASTLEIGH - 71A	EASTLEIGH - 71A
30769	EASTLEIGH - 71A	W/D	W/D	W/D	W/D	W/D	W/D	W/D
30770	EASTLEIGH - 71A	EASTLEIGH - 71A	EASTLEIGH - 71A	EASTLEIGH - 71A	EASTLEIGH - 71A	EASTLEIGH - 71A	EASTLEIGH - 71A	EASTLEIGH - 71A
30771	BOURNEMOUTH - 71B	BOURNEMOUTH - 71B	BOURNEMOUTH - 71B	BOURNEMOUTH - 71B	BOURNEMOUTH - 71B	BOURNEMOUTH - 71B	BOURNEMOUTH - 71B	SALISBURY - 72B
30772	BOURNEMOUTH - 71B	BOURNEMOUTH - 71B	BOURNEMOUTH - 71B	BOURNEMOUTH - 71B	BOURNEMOUTH - 71B	BOURNEMOUTH - 71B	BOURNEMOUTH - 71B	BOURNEMOUTH - 71B
30773	BASINGSTOKE - 70D	BASINGSTOKE - 70D	BASINGSTOKE - 70D	BASINGSTOKE - 70D	BASINGSTOKE - 70D	BASINGSTOKE - 70D	BASINGSTOKE - 70D	BASINGSTOKE - 70D
30774	NINE ELMS - 70A	W/D	W/D	W/D	W/D	W/D	W/D	W/D
30775	FELTHAM - 70B	W/D	W/D	W/D	W/D	W/D	W/D	W/D
30777	FELTHAM - 70B	FELTHAM - 70B	FELTHAM - 70B	FELTHAM - 70B	FELTHAM - 70B	FELTHAM - 70B	BASINGSTOKE - 70D	BASINGSTOKE - 70D
30781	BOURNEMOUTH - 71B	BOURNEMOUTH - 71B	BOURNEMOUTH - 71B	BOURNEMOUTH - 71B	BOURNEMOUTH - 71B	BOURNEMOUTH - 71B	BOURNEMOUTH - 71B	BOURNEMOUTH - 71B
30782	BOURNEMOUTH - 71B	BOURNEMOUTH - 71B	BOURNEMOUTH - 71B	BOURNEMOUTH - 71B	BOURNEMOUTH - 71B	BOURNEMOUTH - 71B	BOURNEMOUTH - 71B	BOURNEMOUTH - 71B
30783	BOURNEMOUTH - 71B	BOURNEMOUTH - 71B	BOURNEMOUTH - 71B	BOURNEMOUTH - 71B	BOURNEMOUTH - 71B	BOURNEMOUTH - 71B	BOURNEMOUTH - 71B	SALISBURY - 72B
30788	EASTLEIGH - 71A	EASTLEIGH - 71A	EASTLEIGH - 71A	EASTLEIGH - 71A	EASTLEIGH - 71A	EASTLEIGH - 71A	EASTLEIGH - 71A	EASTLEIGH - 71A
30790	EASTLEIGH - 71A	EASTLEIGH - 71A	EASTLEIGH - 71A	EASTLEIGH - 71A	EASTLEIGH - 71A	EASTLEIGH - 71A	EASTLEIGH - 71A	EASTLEIGH - 71A
30791	EASTLEIGH - 71A	EASTLEIGH - 71A	EASTLEIGH - 71A	EASTLEIGH - 71A	W/D	W/D	W/D	W/D
N15 4-6-0 (1926)								
30793	FELTHAM - 70B	FELTHAM - 70B	FELTHAM - 70B	FELTHAM - 70B	FELTHAM - 70B	FELTHAM - 70B	FELTHAM - 70B	FELTHAM - 70B
30794	BASINGSTOKE - 70D	BASINGSTOKE - 70D	BASINGSTOKE - 70D	BASINGSTOKE - 70D	BASINGSTOKE - 70D	W/D	W/D	W/D
30795	FELTHAM - 70B	FELTHAM - 70B	FELTHAM - 70B	FELTHAM - 70B	FELTHAM - 70B	FELTHAM - 70B	BASINGSTOKE - 70D	BASINGSTOKE - 70D
30796	SALISBURY - 72B	SALISBURY - 72B	SALISBURY - 72B	SALISBURY - 72B	SALISBURY - 72B	SALISBURY - 72B	SALISBURY - 72B	SALISBURY - 72B
30798	SALISBURY - 72B	SALISBURY - 72B	SALISBURY - 72B	SALISBURY - 72B	SALISBURY - 72B	SALISBURY - 72B	SALISBURY - 72B	SALISBURY - 72B
30799	SALISBURY - 72B	SALISBURY - 72B	SALISBURY - 72B	SALISBURY - 72B	SALISBURY - 72B	SALISBURY - 72B	SALISBURY - 72B	SALISBURY - 72B
30800	EASTLEIGH - 71A	EASTLEIGH - 71A	EASTLEIGH - 71A	EASTLEIGH - 71A	EASTLEIGH - 71A	EASTLEIGH - 71A	EASTLEIGH - 71A	EASTLEIGH - 71A
30802	EASTLEIGH - 71A	EASTLEIGH - 71A	EASTLEIGH - 71A	EASTLEIGH - 71A	EASTLEIGH - 71A	EASTLEIGH - 71A	EASTLEIGH - 71A	EASTLEIGH - 71A
30803	EASTLEIGH - 71A	EASTLEIGH - 71A	EASTLEIGH - 71A	EASTLEIGH - 71A	EASTLEIGH - 71A	EASTLEIGH - 71A	EASTLEIGH - 71A	EASTLEIGH - 71A
30804	EASTLEIGH - 71A	EASTLEIGH - 71A	EASTLEIGH - 71A	EASTLEIGH - 71A	EASTLEIGH - 71A	EASTLEIGH - 71A	EASTLEIGH - 71A	EASTLEIGH - 71A
30806	EASTLEIGH - 71A	EASTLEIGH - 71A	EASTLEIGH - 71A	EASTLEIGH - 71A	EASTLEIGH - 71A	EASTLEIGH - 71A	EASTLEIGH - 71A	EASTLEIGH - 71A
LN 4-6-0 (1926)								
30850	EASTLEIGH - 71A	EASTLEIGH - 71A	EASTLEIGH - 71A	EASTLEIGH - 71A	EASTLEIGH - 71A	EASTLEIGH - 71A	EASTLEIGH - 71A	EASTLEIGH - 71A
30851	EASTLEIGH - 71A	EASTLEIGH - 71A	EASTLEIGH - 71A	EASTLEIGH - 71A	EASTLEIGH - 71A	EASTLEIGH - 71A	EASTLEIGH - 71A	EASTLEIGH - 71A
30852	EASTLEIGH - 71A	EASTLEIGH - 71A	EASTLEIGH - 71A	EASTLEIGH - 71A	EASTLEIGH - 71A	EASTLEIGH - 71A	EASTLEIGH - 71A	EASTLEIGH - 71A
30853	EASTLEIGH - 71A	EASTLEIGH - 71A	EASTLEIGH - 71A	EASTLEIGH - 71A	EASTLEIGH - 71A	EASTLEIGH - 71A	EASTLEIGH - 71A	EASTLEIGH - 71A
30854	EASTLEIGH - 71A	EASTLEIGH - 71A	EASTLEIGH - 71A	EASTLEIGH - 71A	EASTLEIGH - 71A	EASTLEIGH - 71A	EASTLEIGH - 71A	EASTLEIGH - 71A
30855	EASTLEIGH - 71A	EASTLEIGH - 71A	EASTLEIGH - 71A	EASTLEIGH - 71A	EASTLEIGH - 71A	EASTLEIGH - 71A	EASTLEIGH - 71A	EASTLEIGH - 71A
30856	EASTLEIGH - 71A	EASTLEIGH - 71A	EASTLEIGH - 71A	EASTLEIGH - 71A	EASTLEIGH - 71A	EASTLEIGH - 71A	EASTLEIGH - 71A	EASTLEIGH - 71A
30857	EASTLEIGH - 71A	EASTLEIGH - 71A	EASTLEIGH - 71A	EASTLEIGH - 71A	EASTLEIGH - 71A	EASTLEIGH - 71A	EASTLEIGH - 71A	EASTLEIGH - 71A
30858	EASTLEIGH - 71A	EASTLEIGH - 71A	EASTLEIGH - 71A	EASTLEIGH - 71A	EASTLEIGH - 71A	EASTLEIGH - 71A	EASTLEIGH - 71A	EASTLEIGH - 71A
30859	EASTLEIGH - 71A	EASTLEIGH - 71A	EASTLEIGH - 71A	EASTLEIGH - 71A	EASTLEIGH - 71A	EASTLEIGH - 71A	EASTLEIGH - 71A	EASTLEIGH - 71A
30860	EASTLEIGH - 71A	EASTLEIGH - 71A	EASTLEIGH - 71A	EASTLEIGH - 71A	EASTLEIGH - 71A	EASTLEIGH - 71A	EASTLEIGH - 71A	EASTLEIGH - 71A
30861	EASTLEIGH - 71A	EASTLEIGH - 71A	EASTLEIGH - 71A	EASTLEIGH - 71A	EASTLEIGH - 71A	EASTLEIGH - 71A	EASTLEIGH - 71A	EASTLEIGH - 71A
30862	EASTLEIGH - 71A	EASTLEIGH - 71A	EASTLEIGH - 71A	EASTLEIGH - 71A	EASTLEIGH - 71A	EASTLEIGH - 71A	EASTLEIGH - 71A	EASTLEIGH - 71A
30863	EASTLEIGH - 71A	EASTLEIGH - 71A	EASTLEIGH - 71A	EASTLEIGH - 71A	EASTLEIGH - 71A	EASTLEIGH - 71A	EASTLEIGH - 71A	EASTLEIGH - 71A
30864	EASTLEIGH - 71A	EASTLEIGH - 71A	EASTLEIGH - 71A	EASTLEIGH - 71A	EASTLEIGH - 71A	EASTLEIGH - 71A	EASTLEIGH - 71A	EASTLEIGH - 71A
30865	EASTLEIGH - 71A	EASTLEIGH - 71A	EASTLEIGH - 71A	EASTLEIGH - 71A	EASTLEIGH - 71A	EASTLEIGH - 71A	EASTLEIGH - 71A	EASTLEIGH - 71A

Like 30806, 30804 'Sir Cador of Cornwall' was also an interesting engine since it was a long-term resident of Ashford, which did not take a great share of express passenger activity. It had two N15's working a hectic two-day cycle which started with the 07.24 Ashford - Cannon Street business train, returning east to Ramsgate with the 11.44 stopping service via Tonbridge and Canterbury West. In the afternoon the engine worked the 17.17 semi-fast Ramsgate to Charing Cross via Deal and Dover and the 23.50 mail from London Bridge to Deal via Redhill after which it ran light to Dover for the 04.55 'workmans' to Ashford and the 06.43 slow to Tonbridge. In spite of having been in service for more than twenty-four hours, the engine turned and worked back to Ramsgate with the 10.12 slow train to Margate - the N15 being relieved by a C class 0-6-0 at Ramsgate - and finished the working with an afternoon goods from Minster to Ashford.

loco	May-49	Jun-49	Aug-49	Sep-49	Dec-49	Feb-50	Mar-50
			MN 4-6-2 (1941)				
35001	EXMOUTH JCN - 72A	EXMOUTH JCN - 72A	EXMOUTH JCN - 72A	EXMOUTH JCN - 72A	EXMOUTH JCN - 72A	EXMOUTH JCN - 72A	EXMOUTH JCN - 72A
35002	EXMOUTH JCN - 72A	EXMOUTH JCN - 72A	EXMOUTH JCN - 72A	EXMOUTH JCN - 72A	EXMOUTH JCN - 72A	EXMOUTH JCN - 72A	EXMOUTH JCN - 72A
35003	EXMOUTH JCN - 72A	EXMOUTH JCN - 72A	EXMOUTH JCN - 72A	EXMOUTH JCN - 72A	EXMOUTH JCN - 72A	EXMOUTH JCN - 72A	EXMOUTH JCN - 72A
35004	SALISBURY - 72B	SALISBURY - 72B	SALISBURY - 72B	SALISBURY - 72B	SALISBURY - 72B	EXMOUTH JCN - 72A	EXMOUTH JCN - 72A
35005	NINE ELMS - 70A	NINE ELMS - 70A	NINE ELMS - 70A	NINE ELMS - 70A	NINE ELMS - 70A	NINE ELMS - 70A	NINE ELMS - 70A
35006	SALISBURY - 72B	SALISBURY - 72B	SALISBURY - 72B	SALISBURY - 72B	SALISBURY - 72B	SALISBURY - 72B	SALISBURY - 72B
35007	SALISBURY - 72B	SALISBURY - 72B	SALISBURY - 72B	SALISBURY - 72B	SALISBURY - 72B	SALISBURY - 72B	SALISBURY - 72B
35008	SALISBURY - 72B	SALISBURY - 72B	SALISBURY - 72B	SALISBURY - 72B	SALISBURY - 72B	SALISBURY - 72B	SALISBURY - 72B
35009	SALISBURY - 72B	SALISBURY - 72B	SALISBURY - 72B	SALISBURY - 72B	SALISBURY - 72B	SALISBURY - 72B	SALISBURY - 72B
35010	SALISBURY - 72B	SALISBURY - 72B	SALISBURY - 72B	SALISBURY - 72B	SALISBURY - 72B	SALISBURY - 72B	SALISBURY - 72B
35011	NINE ELMS - 70A	NINE ELMS - 70A	NINE ELMS - 70A	NINE ELMS - 70A	NINE ELMS - 70A	NINE ELMS - 70A	NINE ELMS - 70A
35012	NINE ELMS - 70A	NINE ELMS - 70A	NINE ELMS - 70A	NINE ELMS - 70A	NINE ELMS - 70A	NINE ELMS - 70A	NINE ELMS - 70A
35013	NINE ELMS - 70A	NINE ELMS - 70A	NINE ELMS - 70A	NINE ELMS - 70A	NINE ELMS - 70A	NINE ELMS - 70A	NINE ELMS - 70A
35014	NINE ELMS - 70A	NINE ELMS - 70A	NINE ELMS - 70A	NINE ELMS - 70A	NINE ELMS - 70A	NINE ELMS - 70A	NINE ELMS - 70A
35015	NINE ELMS - 70A	NINE ELMS - 70A	NINE ELMS - 70A	NINE ELMS - 70A	NINE ELMS - 70A	NINE ELMS - 70A	NINE ELMS - 70A
35016	NINE ELMS - 70A	NINE ELMS - 70A	NINE ELMS - 70A	NINE ELMS - 70A	NINE ELMS - 70A	NINE ELMS - 70A	NINE ELMS - 70A
35017	NINE ELMS - 70A	NINE ELMS - 70A	NINE ELMS - 70A	NINE ELMS - 70A	NINE ELMS - 70A	NINE ELMS - 70A	NINE ELMS - 70A
35018	NINE ELMS - 70A	NINE ELMS - 70A	NINE ELMS - 70A	NINE ELMS - 70A	NINE ELMS - 70A	NINE ELMS - 70A	NINE ELMS - 70A
35019	NINE ELMS - 70A	NINE ELMS - 70A	NINE ELMS - 70A	NINE ELMS - 70A	NINE ELMS - 70A	NINE ELMS - 70A	NINE ELMS - 70A
35020	NINE ELMS - 70A	NINE ELMS - 70A	NINE ELMS - 70A	NINE ELMS - 70A	NINE ELMS - 70A	NINE ELMS - 70A	NINE ELMS - 70A
35021	EXMOUTH JCN - 72A	EXMOUTH JCN - 72A	EXMOUTH JCN - 72A	EXMOUTH JCN - 72A	EXMOUTH JCN - 72A	EXMOUTH JCN - 72A	EXMOUTH JCN - 72A
35022	EXMOUTH JCN - 72A	EXMOUTH JCN - 72A	EXMOUTH JCN - 72A	EXMOUTH JCN - 72A	EXMOUTH JCN - 72A	EXMOUTH JCN - 72A	EXMOUTH JCN - 72A
35023	EXMOUTH JCN - 72A	EXMOUTH JCN - 72A	EXMOUTH JCN - 72A	EXMOUTH JCN - 72A	EXMOUTH JCN - 72A	EXMOUTH JCN - 72A	EXMOUTH JCN - 72A
35024	EXMOUTH JCN - 72A	EXMOUTH JCN - 72A	EXMOUTH JCN - 72A	EXMOUTH JCN - 72A	EXMOUTH JCN - 72A	EXMOUTH JCN - 72A	EXMOUTH JCN - 72A
35025	BOURNEMOUTH - 71B	BOURNEMOUTH - 71B	BOURNEMOUTH - 71B	BOURNEMOUTH - 71B	BOURNEMOUTH - 71B	BOURNEMOUTH - 71B	BOURNEMOUTH - 71B
35026	BOURNEMOUTH - 71B	BOURNEMOUTH - 71B	BOURNEMOUTH - 71B	BOURNEMOUTH - 71B	BOURNEMOUTH - 71B	BOURNEMOUTH - 71B	BOURNEMOUTH - 71B
35027	BOURNEMOUTH - 71B	BOURNEMOUTH - 71B	BOURNEMOUTH - 71B	BOURNEMOUTH - 71B	BOURNEMOUTH - 71B	BOURNEMOUTH - 71B	BOURNEMOUTH - 71B
35028	BOURNEMOUTH - 71B	BOURNEMOUTH - 71B	BOURNEMOUTH - 71B	BOURNEMOUTH - 71B	DOVER - 74C	DOVER - 74C	DOVER - 74C
35029	BOURNEMOUTH - 71B	BOURNEMOUTH - 71B	BOURNEMOUTH - 71B	BOURNEMOUTH - 71B	DOVER - 74C	DOVER - 74C	DOVER - 74C
35030	BOURNEMOUTH - 71B	BOURNEMOUTH - 71B	BOURNEMOUTH - 71B	BOURNEMOUTH - 71B	DOVER - 74C	DOVER - 74C	DOVER - 74C
			WC 4-6-2 (1945)				
34001	EXMOUTH JCN - 72A	EXMOUTH JCN - 72A	EXMOUTH JCN - 72A	EXMOUTH JCN - 72A	EXMOUTH JCN - 72A	EXMOUTH JCN - 72A	EXMOUTH JCN - 72A
34002	EXMOUTH JCN - 72A	EXMOUTH JCN - 72A	EXMOUTH JCN - 72A	EXMOUTH JCN - 72A	EXMOUTH JCN - 72A	EXMOUTH JCN - 72A	EXMOUTH JCN - 72A
34003	PLYMOUTH - 72D	PLYMOUTH - 72D	PLYMOUTH - 72D	PLYMOUTH - 72D	PLYMOUTH - 72D	PLYMOUTH - 72D	PLYMOUTH - 72D
34004	EXMOUTH JCN - 72A	EXMOUTH JCN - 72A	EXMOUTH JCN - 72A	EXMOUTH JCN - 72A	EXMOUTH JCN - 72A	EXMOUTH JCN - 72A	EXMOUTH JCN - 72A
34005	EXMOUTH JCN - 72A	EXMOUTH JCN - 72A	EXMOUTH JCN - 72A	EXMOUTH JCN - 72A	EXMOUTH JCN - 72A	EXMOUTH JCN - 72A	EXMOUTH JCN - 72A
34006	EXMOUTH JCN - 72A	EXMOUTH JCN - 72A	EXMOUTH JCN - 72A	EXMOUTH JCN - 72A	EXMOUTH JCN - 72A	EXMOUTH JCN - 72A	EXMOUTH JCN - 72A
34007	EXMOUTH JCN - 72A	EXMOUTH JCN - 72A	EXMOUTH JCN - 72A	EXMOUTH JCN - 72A	EXMOUTH JCN - 72A	EXMOUTH JCN - 72A	EXMOUTH JCN - 72A
34008	EXMOUTH JCN - 72A	EXMOUTH JCN - 72A	EXMOUTH JCN - 72A	EXMOUTH JCN - 72A	EXMOUTH JCN - 72A	EXMOUTH JCN - 72A	EXMOUTH JCN - 72A
34009	EXMOUTH JCN - 72A	EXMOUTH JCN - 72A	EXMOUTH JCN - 72A	EXMOUTH JCN - 72A	EXMOUTH JCN - 72A	EXMOUTH JCN - 72A	EXMOUTH JCN - 72A
34010	EXMOUTH JCN - 72A	EXMOUTH JCN - 72A	EXMOUTH JCN - 72A	EXMOUTH JCN - 72A	EXMOUTH JCN - 72A	EXMOUTH JCN - 72A	EXMOUTH JCN - 72A
34011	PLYMOUTH - 72D	PLYMOUTH - 72D	PLYMOUTH - 72D	PLYMOUTH - 72D	PLYMOUTH - 72D	PLYMOUTH - 72D	PLYMOUTH - 72D
34012	PLYMOUTH - 72D	PLYMOUTH - 72D	PLYMOUTH - 72D	PLYMOUTH - 72D	PLYMOUTH - 72D	PLYMOUTH - 72D	PLYMOUTH - 72D
34013	PLYMOUTH - 72D	PLYMOUTH - 72D	PLYMOUTH - 72D	PLYMOUTH - 72D	PLYMOUTH - 72D	PLYMOUTH - 72D	PLYMOUTH - 72D
34014	EXMOUTH JCN - 72A	EXMOUTH JCN - 72A	EXMOUTH JCN - 72A	EXMOUTH JCN - 72A	EXMOUTH JCN - 72A	EXMOUTH JCN - 72A	EXMOUTH JCN - 72A
34015	EXMOUTH JCN - 72A	EXMOUTH JCN - 72A	EXMOUTH JCN - 72A	EXMOUTH JCN - 72A	EXMOUTH JCN - 72A	EXMOUTH JCN - 72A	EXMOUTH JCN - 72A
34016	EXMOUTH JCN - 72A	EXMOUTH JCN - 72A	EXMOUTH JCN - 72A	EXMOUTH JCN - 72A	EXMOUTH JCN - 72A	EXMOUTH JCN - 72A	EXMOUTH JCN - 72A
34017	EXMOUTH JCN - 72A	EXMOUTH JCN - 72A	EXMOUTH JCN - 72A	EXMOUTH JCN - 72A	EXMOUTH JCN - 72A	EXMOUTH JCN - 72A	EXMOUTH JCN - 72A
34018	EXMOUTH JCN - 72A	EXMOUTH JCN - 72A	EXMOUTH JCN - 72A	EXMOUTH JCN - 72A	EXMOUTH JCN - 72A	EXMOUTH JCN - 72A	EXMOUTH JCN - 72A
34019	EXMOUTH JCN - 72A	EXMOUTH JCN - 72A	EXMOUTH JCN - 72A	EXMOUTH JCN - 72A	EXMOUTH JCN - 72A	EXMOUTH JCN - 72A	EXMOUTH JCN - 72A
34020	EXMOUTH JCN - 72A	EXMOUTH JCN - 72A	EXMOUTH JCN - 72A	EXMOUTH JCN - 72A	EXMOUTH JCN - 72A	EXMOUTH JCN - 72A	EXMOUTH JCN - 72A
34021	PLYMOUTH - 72D	PLYMOUTH - 72D	PLYMOUTH - 72D	PLYMOUTH - 72D	PLYMOUTH - 72D	PLYMOUTH - 72D	PLYMOUTH - 72D
34022	NINE ELMS - 70A	NINE ELMS - 70A	NINE ELMS - 70A	NINE ELMS - 70A	NINE ELMS - 70A	SALISBURY - 72B	SALISBURY - 72B
34023	NINE ELMS - 70A	NINE ELMS - 70A	NINE ELMS - 70A	NINE ELMS - 70A	NINE ELMS - 70A	SALISBURY - 72B	SALISBURY - 72B
34024	EXMOUTH JCN - 72A	EXMOUTH JCN - 72A	SALISBURY - 72B	EXMOUTH JCN - 72A	EXMOUTH JCN - 72A	EXMOUTH JCN - 72A	EXMOUTH JCN - 72A
34025	EXMOUTH JCN - 72A	EXMOUTH JCN - 72A	EXMOUTH JCN - 72A	EXMOUTH JCN - 72A	EXMOUTH JCN - 72A	EXMOUTH JCN - 72A	EXMOUTH JCN - 72A
34026	EXMOUTH JCN - 72A	EXMOUTH JCN - 72A	EXMOUTH JCN - 72A	EXMOUTH JCN - 72A	EXMOUTH JCN - 72A	EXMOUTH JCN - 72A	EXMOUTH JCN - 72A
34027	EXMOUTH JCN - 72A	EXMOUTH JCN - 72A	EXMOUTH JCN - 72A	EXMOUTH JCN - 72A	EXMOUTH JCN - 72A	EXMOUTH JCN - 72A	EXMOUTH JCN - 72A
34028	EXMOUTH JCN - 72A	EXMOUTH JCN - 72A	EXMOUTH JCN - 72A	EXMOUTH JCN - 72A	EXMOUTH JCN - 72A	EXMOUTH JCN - 72A	EXMOUTH JCN - 72A
34029	EXMOUTH JCN - 72A	EXMOUTH JCN - 72A	EXMOUTH JCN - 72A	EXMOUTH JCN - 72A	EXMOUTH JCN - 72A	EXMOUTH JCN - 72A	EXMOUTH JCN - 72A
34030	EXMOUTH JCN - 72A	EXMOUTH JCN - 72A	EXMOUTH JCN - 72A	EXMOUTH JCN - 72A	EXMOUTH JCN - 72A	EXMOUTH JCN - 72A	EXMOUTH JCN - 72A

West Country Pacifics continued in the following section

Alone amongst the railways that had never used the Pacific wheel arrangement, the Southern moved very quickly from one extreme to the other during the late 1940's by acquiring no less than 140 examples which, on paper, should have been sufficient for all the regular London-based expresses of the system.

The larger Merchant Navy engines were initially used on the West of England and Wessex services, the engines being divided between Nine Elms, Salisbury, Exmouth Junction and Bournemouth, but in 1949 the decision was taken to transfer a number to the South Eastern in order to take over the heavier Victoria - Dover boat trains. In order to achieve this the Bournemouth allocation of five engines was split between Dover and Stewarts Lane leaving Nine Elms shed to cover the handful of Merchant Navy-worked services to Bournemouth and Weymouth. At the same time the through working of engines between Waterloo and Exeter - which had been tried with the Lord Nelson 4-6-0's in the 1930's - was introduced as a permanent measure.

With only thirty engines in the class difficulties were sometime experienced in distributing them around the system and the need to reconsider the requirements of Bournemouth, where a larger engine than a light Pacific was required for the heaviest services, was met initially by a reduction in the Salisbury allocation and later by the transfer of two engines from Dover. (This last change resulted in the interesting sight of the Night Ferry being booked to a Light Pacific and an L1 4-4-0).

The allocations remained fairly static during the second half of the decade, the principal change arising from the need to increase the number of engines at Bournemouth, whose number eventually rose to eight locomotives. In 1959, when the Victoria - Dover service was electrified, the three South Eastern engines returned to Nine Elms and thereafter the entire class was confined to the Wessex and West of England services from Waterloo.

All thirty engines were completely rebuilt between 1956 and 1959.

loco	Apr-50	Sep-50	Oct-50	Nov-50	Dec-50	Mar-51	Apr-51
			MN 4-6-2 (1941)				
35001	EXMOUTH JCN - 72A	EXMOUTH JCN - 72A	EXMOUTH JCN - 72A	EXMOUTH JCN - 72A	EXMOUTH JCN - 72A	EXMOUTH JCN - 72A	EXMOUTH JCN - 72A
35002	EXMOUTH JCN - 72A	EXMOUTH JCN - 72A	EXMOUTH JCN - 72A	EXMOUTH JCN - 72A	EXMOUTH JCN - 72A	EXMOUTH JCN - 72A	EXMOUTH JCN - 72A
35003	EXMOUTH JCN - 72A	EXMOUTH JCN - 72A	EXMOUTH JCN - 72A	EXMOUTH JCN - 72A	EXMOUTH JCN - 72A	EXMOUTH JCN - 72A	EXMOUTH JCN - 72A
35004	EXMOUTH JCN - 72A	EXMOUTH JCN - 72A	EXMOUTH JCN - 72A	EXMOUTH JCN - 72A	EXMOUTH JCN - 72A	EXMOUTH JCN - 72A	EXMOUTH JCN - 72A
35005	NINE ELMS - 70A	NINE ELMS - 70A	NINE ELMS - 70A	NINE ELMS - 70A	NINE ELMS - 70A	NINE ELMS - 70A	EXMOUTH JCN - 72A
35006	SALISBURY - 72B	SALISBURY - 72B	SALISBURY - 72B	SALISBURY - 72B	SALISBURY - 72B	SALISBURY - 72B	SALISBURY - 72B
35007	SALISBURY - 72B	SALISBURY - 72B	SALISBURY - 72B	SALISBURY - 72B	SALISBURY - 72B	SALISBURY - 72B	SALISBURY - 72B
35008	SALISBURY - 72B	SALISBURY - 72B	SALISBURY - 72B	SALISBURY - 72B	SALISBURY - 72B	SALISBURY - 72B	SALISBURY - 72B
35009	SALISBURY - 72B	SALISBURY - 72B	SALISBURY - 72B	SALISBURY - 72B	SALISBURY - 72B	SALISBURY - 72B	SALISBURY - 72B
35010	NINE ELMS - 70A	NINE ELMS - 70A	NINE ELMS - 70A	NINE ELMS - 70A	NINE ELMS - 70A	NINE ELMS - 70A	NINE ELMS - 70A
35011	NINE ELMS - 70A	NINE ELMS - 70A	NINE ELMS - 70A	NINE ELMS - 70A	NINE ELMS - 70A	NINE ELMS - 70A	NINE ELMS - 70A
35012	NINE ELMS - 70A	NINE ELMS - 70A	NINE ELMS - 70A	NINE ELMS - 70A	NINE ELMS - 70A	NINE ELMS - 70A	NINE ELMS - 70A
35013	NINE ELMS - 70A	NINE ELMS - 70A	NINE ELMS - 70A	NINE ELMS - 70A	NINE ELMS - 70A	NINE ELMS - 70A	NINE ELMS - 70A
35014	NINE ELMS - 70A	NINE ELMS - 70A	NINE ELMS - 70A	NINE ELMS - 70A	NINE ELMS - 70A	NINE ELMS - 70A	NINE ELMS - 70A
35015	NINE ELMS - 70A	NINE ELMS - 70A	NINE ELMS - 70A	NINE ELMS - 70A	NINE ELMS - 70A	NINE ELMS - 70A	NINE ELMS - 70A
35016	NINE ELMS - 70A	NINE ELMS - 70A	NINE ELMS - 70A	NINE ELMS - 70A	NINE ELMS - 70A	NINE ELMS - 70A	NINE ELMS - 70A
35017	NINE ELMS - 70A	NINE ELMS - 70A	NINE ELMS - 70A	NINE ELMS - 70A	NINE ELMS - 70A	NINE ELMS - 70A	NINE ELMS - 70A
35018	NINE ELMS - 70A	NINE ELMS - 70A	NINE ELMS - 70A	NINE ELMS - 70A	NINE ELMS - 70A	NINE ELMS - 70A	NINE ELMS - 70A
35019	NINE ELMS - 70A	NINE ELMS - 70A	NINE ELMS - 70A	NINE ELMS - 70A	NINE ELMS - 70A	NINE ELMS - 70A	NINE ELMS - 70A
35020	NINE ELMS - 70A	NINE ELMS - 70A	NINE ELMS - 70A	NINE ELMS - 70A	NINE ELMS - 70A	NINE ELMS - 70A	NINE ELMS - 70A
35021	EXMOUTH JCN - 72A	EXMOUTH JCN - 72A	EXMOUTH JCN - 72A	EXMOUTH JCN - 72A	EXMOUTH JCN - 72A	EXMOUTH JCN - 72A	NINE ELMS - 70A
35022	EXMOUTH JCN - 72A	EXMOUTH JCN - 72A	EXMOUTH JCN - 72A	EXMOUTH JCN - 72A	EXMOUTH JCN - 72A	EXMOUTH JCN - 72A	EXMOUTH JCN - 72A
35023	EXMOUTH JCN - 72A	EXMOUTH JCN - 72A	EXMOUTH JCN - 72A	EXMOUTH JCN - 72A	EXMOUTH JCN - 72A	EXMOUTH JCN - 72A	EXMOUTH JCN - 72A
35024	EXMOUTH JCN - 72A	EXMOUTH JCN - 72A	EXMOUTH JCN - 72A	EXMOUTH JCN - 72A	EXMOUTH JCN - 72A	EXMOUTH JCN - 72A	EXMOUTH JCN - 72A
35025	STEWARTS LANE - 73A	STEWARTS LANE - 73A	STEWARTS LANE - 73A	STEWARTS LANE - 73A	STEWARTS LANE - 73A	STEWARTS LANE - 73A	STEWARTS LANE - 73A
35026	STEWARTS LANE - 73A	STEWARTS LANE - 73A	STEWARTS LANE - 73A	STEWARTS LANE - 73A	STEWARTS LANE - 73A	STEWARTS LANE - 73A	STEWARTS LANE - 73A
35027	STEWARTS LANE - 73A	STEWARTS LANE - 73A	STEWARTS LANE - 73A	STEWARTS LANE - 73A	STEWARTS LANE - 73A	STEWARTS LANE - 73A	STEWARTS LANE - 73A
35028	STEWARTS LANE - 73A	STEWARTS LANE - 73A	STEWARTS LANE - 73A	STEWARTS LANE - 73A	STEWARTS LANE - 73A	STEWARTS LANE - 73A	STEWARTS LANE - 73A
35029	STEWARTS LANE - 73A	STEWARTS LANE - 73A	STEWARTS LANE - 73A	STEWARTS LANE - 73A	STEWARTS LANE - 73A	STEWARTS LANE - 73A	STEWARTS LANE - 73A
35030	STEWARTS LANE - 73A	STEWARTS LANE - 73A	STEWARTS LANE - 73A	STEWARTS LANE - 73A	STEWARTS LANE - 73A	STEWARTS LANE - 73A	STEWARTS LANE - 73A
			WC 4-6-2 (1945)				
34001	EXMOUTH JCN - 72A	EXMOUTH JCN - 72A	EXMOUTH JCN - 72A	EXMOUTH JCN - 72A	EXMOUTH JCN - 72A	EXMOUTH JCN - 72A	EXMOUTH JCN - 72A
34002	EXMOUTH JCN - 72A	EXMOUTH JCN - 72A	EXMOUTH JCN - 72A	EXMOUTH JCN - 72A	EXMOUTH JCN - 72A	EXMOUTH JCN - 72A	EXMOUTH JCN - 72A
34003	PLYMOUTH - 72D	EXMOUTH JCN - 72A	EXMOUTH JCN - 72A	EXMOUTH JCN - 72A	EXMOUTH JCN - 72A	EXMOUTH JCN - 72A	EXMOUTH JCN - 72A
34004	EXMOUTH JCN - 72A	EXMOUTH JCN - 72A	EXMOUTH JCN - 72A	EXMOUTH JCN - 72A	EXMOUTH JCN - 72A	EXMOUTH JCN - 72A	EXMOUTH JCN - 72A
34005	EXMOUTH JCN - 72A	EXMOUTH JCN - 72A	EXMOUTH JCN - 72A	EXMOUTH JCN - 72A	EXMOUTH JCN - 72A	EXMOUTH JCN - 72A	NINE ELMS - 70A
34006	EXMOUTH JCN - 72A	EXMOUTH JCN - 72A	EXMOUTH JCN - 72A	EXMOUTH JCN - 72A	EXMOUTH JCN - 72A	EXMOUTH JCN - 72A	NINE ELMS - 70A
34007	EXMOUTH JCN - 72A	EXMOUTH JCN - 72A	EXMOUTH JCN - 72A	EXMOUTH JCN - 72A	EXMOUTH JCN - 72A	EXMOUTH JCN - 72A	NINE ELMS - 70A
34008	EXMOUTH JCN - 72A	EXMOUTH JCN - 72A	EXMOUTH JCN - 72A	EXMOUTH JCN - 72A	EXMOUTH JCN - 72A	EXMOUTH JCN - 72A	NINE ELMS - 70A
34009	EXMOUTH JCN - 72A	EXMOUTH JCN - 72A	EXMOUTH JCN - 72A	EXMOUTH JCN - 72A	EXMOUTH JCN - 72A	EXMOUTH JCN - 72A	NINE ELMS - 70A
34010	EXMOUTH JCN - 72A	EXMOUTH JCN - 72A	EXMOUTH JCN - 72A	EXMOUTH JCN - 72A	EXMOUTH JCN - 72A	EXMOUTH JCN - 72A	NINE ELMS - 70A
34011	PLYMOUTH - 72D	PLYMOUTH - 72D	PLYMOUTH - 72D	PLYMOUTH - 72D	PLYMOUTH - 72D	PLYMOUTH - 72D	NINE ELMS - 70A
34012	PLYMOUTH - 72D	PLYMOUTH - 72D	PLYMOUTH - 72D	PLYMOUTH - 72D	PLYMOUTH - 72D	PLYMOUTH - 72D	NINE ELMS - 70A
34013	PLYMOUTH - 72D	PLYMOUTH - 72D	PLYMOUTH - 72D	PLYMOUTH - 72D	PLYMOUTH - 72D	PLYMOUTH - 72D	PLYMOUTH - 72D
34014	EXMOUTH JCN - 72A	EXMOUTH JCN - 72A	EXMOUTH JCN - 72A	EXMOUTH JCN - 72A	EXMOUTH JCN - 72A	EXMOUTH JCN - 72A	EXMOUTH JCN - 72A
34015	EXMOUTH JCN - 72A	EXMOUTH JCN - 72A	EXMOUTH JCN - 72A	EXMOUTH JCN - 72A	EXMOUTH JCN - 72A	EXMOUTH JCN - 72A	EXMOUTH JCN - 72A
34016	EXMOUTH JCN - 72A	EXMOUTH JCN - 72A	EXMOUTH JCN - 72A	EXMOUTH JCN - 72A	EXMOUTH JCN - 72A	EXMOUTH JCN - 72A	EXMOUTH JCN - 72A
34017	EXMOUTH JCN - 72A	EXMOUTH JCN - 72A	EXMOUTH JCN - 72A	EXMOUTH JCN - 72A	EXMOUTH JCN - 72A	EXMOUTH JCN - 72A	NINE ELMS - 70A
34018	EXMOUTH JCN - 72A	EXMOUTH JCN - 72A	EXMOUTH JCN - 72A	EXMOUTH JCN - 72A	EXMOUTH JCN - 72A	EXMOUTH JCN - 72A	NINE ELMS - 70A
34019	EXMOUTH JCN - 72A	EXMOUTH JCN - 72A	EXMOUTH JCN - 72A	EXMOUTH JCN - 72A	EXMOUTH JCN - 72A	EXMOUTH JCN - 72A	NINE ELMS - 70A
34020	EXMOUTH JCN - 72A	EXMOUTH JCN - 72A	EXMOUTH JCN - 72A	EXMOUTH JCN - 72A	EXMOUTH JCN - 72A	EXMOUTH JCN - 72A	NINE ELMS - 70A
34021	PLYMOUTH - 72D	PLYMOUTH - 72D	PLYMOUTH - 72D	EXMOUTH JCN - 72A	EXMOUTH JCN - 72A	EXMOUTH JCN - 72A	NINE ELMS - 70A
34022	SALISBURY - 72B	SALISBURY - 72B	SALISBURY - 72B	SALISBURY - 72B	SALISBURY - 72B	SALISBURY - 72B	NINE ELMS - 70A
34023	SALISBURY - 72B	SALISBURY - 72B	SALISBURY - 72B	SALISBURY - 72B	SALISBURY - 72B	SALISBURY - 72B	NINE ELMS - 70A
34024	EXMOUTH JCN - 72A	EXMOUTH JCN - 72A	EXMOUTH JCN - 72A	EXMOUTH JCN - 72A	EXMOUTH JCN - 72A	EXMOUTH JCN - 72A	NINE ELMS - 70A
34025	EXMOUTH JCN - 72A	EXMOUTH JCN - 72A	EXMOUTH JCN - 72A	EXMOUTH JCN - 72A	EXMOUTH JCN - 72A	EXMOUTH JCN - 72A	NINE ELMS - 70A
34026	EXMOUTH JCN - 72A	EXMOUTH JCN - 72A	EXMOUTH JCN - 72A	EXMOUTH JCN - 72A	EXMOUTH JCN - 72A	EXMOUTH JCN - 72A	NINE ELMS - 70A
34027	EXMOUTH JCN - 72A	EXMOUTH JCN - 72A	EXMOUTH JCN - 72A	EXMOUTH JCN - 72A	EXMOUTH JCN - 72A	EXMOUTH JCN - 72A	NINE ELMS - 70A
34028	EXMOUTH JCN - 72A	EXMOUTH JCN - 72A	EXMOUTH JCN - 72A	EXMOUTH JCN - 72A	EXMOUTH JCN - 72A	EXMOUTH JCN - 72A	NINE ELMS - 70A
34029	EXMOUTH JCN - 72A	EXMOUTH JCN - 72A	EXMOUTH JCN - 72A	EXMOUTH JCN - 72A	EXMOUTH JCN - 72A	EXMOUTH JCN - 72A	NINE ELMS - 70A
34030	EXMOUTH JCN - 72A	EXMOUTH JCN - 72A	EXMOUTH JCN - 72A	EXMOUTH JCN - 72A	EXMOUTH JCN - 72A	EXMOUTH JCN - 72A	NINE ELMS - 70A

West Country Pacifics continued in the following section

Coal piled high and passably clean, Merchant Navy 35023 'Holland-Afrika Line' gets ready to leave Nine Elms on a summer's afternoon in 1954 to work the 18.00 Waterloo - Plymouth express. 35023 was an Exmouth Junction engine and remained there until early 1960 when, as part of a move to increase the number of Pacifics working the Wessex expresses, it was transferred to Bournemouth.

loco	Jun-51	Jul-51	Sep-51	Dec-51	Jan-52	Mar-52	Jun-52
			MN 4-6-2 (1941)				
35001	EXMOUTH JCN - 72A	EXMOUTH JCN - 72A	EXMOUTH JCN - 72A	EXMOUTH JCN - 72A	EXMOUTH JCN - 72A	EXMOUTH JCN - 72A	EXMOUTH JCN - 72A
35002	EXMOUTH JCN - 72A	EXMOUTH JCN - 72A	EXMOUTH JCN - 72A	EXMOUTH JCN - 72A	EXMOUTH JCN - 72A	EXMOUTH JCN - 72A	EXMOUTH JCN - 72A
35003	EXMOUTH JCN - 72A	EXMOUTH JCN - 72A	EXMOUTH JCN - 72A	EXMOUTH JCN - 72A	EXMOUTH JCN - 72A	EXMOUTH JCN - 72A	EXMOUTH JCN - 72A
35004	EXMOUTH JCN - 72A	EXMOUTH JCN - 72A	EXMOUTH JCN - 72A	EXMOUTH JCN - 72A	EXMOUTH JCN - 72A	EXMOUTH JCN - 72A	EXMOUTH JCN - 72A
35005	EXMOUTH JCN - 72A	EXMOUTH JCN - 72A	EXMOUTH JCN - 72A	EXMOUTH JCN - 72A	EXMOUTH JCN - 72A	EXMOUTH JCN - 72A	EXMOUTH JCN - 72A
35006	SALISBURY - 72B	SALISBURY - 72B	SALISBURY - 72B	SALISBURY - 72B	SALISBURY - 72B	SALISBURY - 72B	SALISBURY - 72B
35007	SALISBURY - 72B	SALISBURY - 72B	SALISBURY - 72B	SALISBURY - 72B	SALISBURY - 72B	SALISBURY - 72B	SALISBURY - 72B
35008	SALISBURY - 72B	SALISBURY - 72B	SALISBURY - 72B	SALISBURY - 72B	SALISBURY - 72B	SALISBURY - 72B	SALISBURY - 72B
35009	SALISBURY - 72B	SALISBURY - 72B	SALISBURY - 72B	SALISBURY - 72B	SALISBURY - 72B	SALISBURY - 72B	SALISBURY - 72B
35010	NINE ELMS - 70A	NINE ELMS - 70A	NINE ELMS - 70A	NINE ELMS - 70A	NINE ELMS - 70A	NINE ELMS - 70A	NINE ELMS - 70A
35011	NINE ELMS - 70A	NINE ELMS - 70A	NINE ELMS - 70A	NINE ELMS - 70A	NINE ELMS - 70A	NINE ELMS - 70A	NINE ELMS - 70A
35012	NINE ELMS - 70A	NINE ELMS - 70A	NINE ELMS - 70A	NINE ELMS - 70A	NINE ELMS - 70A	NINE ELMS - 70A	NINE ELMS - 70A
35013	NINE ELMS - 70A	NINE ELMS - 70A	NINE ELMS - 70A	NINE ELMS - 70A	NINE ELMS - 70A	NINE ELMS - 70A	NINE ELMS - 70A
35014	NINE ELMS - 70A	NINE ELMS - 70A	NINE ELMS - 70A	NINE ELMS - 70A	NINE ELMS - 70A	NINE ELMS - 70A	NINE ELMS - 70A
35015	NINE ELMS - 70A	NINE ELMS - 70A	NINE ELMS - 70A	NINE ELMS - 70A	NINE ELMS - 70A	NINE ELMS - 70A	NINE ELMS - 70A
35016	NINE ELMS - 70A	NINE ELMS - 70A	NINE ELMS - 70A	NINE ELMS - 70A	NINE ELMS - 70A	NINE ELMS - 70A	NINE ELMS - 70A
35017	NINE ELMS - 70A	NINE ELMS - 70A	NINE ELMS - 70A	NINE ELMS - 70A	NINE ELMS - 70A	NINE ELMS - 70A	NINE ELMS - 70A
35018	NINE ELMS - 70A	NINE ELMS - 70A	NINE ELMS - 70A	NINE ELMS - 70A	NINE ELMS - 70A	NINE ELMS - 70A	NINE ELMS - 70A
35019	NINE ELMS - 70A	NINE ELMS - 70A	NINE ELMS - 70A	NINE ELMS - 70A	NINE ELMS - 70A	NINE ELMS - 70A	NINE ELMS - 70A
35020	NINE ELMS - 70A	NINE ELMS - 70A	NINE ELMS - 70A	NINE ELMS - 70A	NINE ELMS - 70A	NINE ELMS - 70A	NINE ELMS - 70A
35021	NINE ELMS - 70A	NINE ELMS - 70A	NINE ELMS - 70A	NINE ELMS - 70A	NINE ELMS - 70A	NINE ELMS - 70A	NINE ELMS - 70A
35022	EXMOUTH JCN - 72A	EXMOUTH JCN - 72A	EXMOUTH JCN - 72A	EXMOUTH JCN - 72A	EXMOUTH JCN - 72A	EXMOUTH JCN - 72A	RUGBY PLANT
35023	EXMOUTH JCN - 72A	EXMOUTH JCN - 72A	EXMOUTH JCN - 72A	EXMOUTH JCN - 72A	EXMOUTH JCN - 72A	EXMOUTH JCN - 72A	EXMOUTH JCN - 72A
35024	EXMOUTH JCN - 72A	EXMOUTH JCN - 72A	EXMOUTH JCN - 72A	EXMOUTH JCN - 72A	EXMOUTH JCN - 72A	EXMOUTH JCN - 72A	EXMOUTH JCN - 72A
35025	STEWARTS LANE - 73A	STEWARTS LANE - 73A	STEWARTS LANE - 73A	STEWARTS LANE - 73A	STEWARTS LANE - 73A	EXMOUTH JCN - 72A	EXMOUTH JCN - 72A
35026	STEWARTS LANE - 73A	STEWARTS LANE - 73A	STEWARTS LANE - 73A	STEWARTS LANE - 73A	STEWARTS LANE - 73A	STEWARTS LANE - 73A	STEWARTS LANE - 73A
35027	STEWARTS LANE - 73A	STEWARTS LANE - 73A	STEWARTS LANE - 73A	STEWARTS LANE - 73A	STEWARTS LANE - 73A	STEWARTS LANE - 73A	STEWARTS LANE - 73A
35028	STEWARTS LANE - 73A	STEWARTS LANE - 73A	STEWARTS LANE - 73A	STEWARTS LANE - 73A	STEWARTS LANE - 73A	STEWARTS LANE - 73A	STEWARTS LANE - 73A
35029	STEWARTS LANE - 73A	STEWARTS LANE - 73A	STEWARTS LANE - 73A	STEWARTS LANE - 73A	STEWARTS LANE - 73A	STEWARTS LANE - 73A	STEWARTS LANE - 73A
35030	STEWARTS LANE - 73A	STEWARTS LANE - 73A	STEWARTS LANE - 73A	STEWARTS LANE - 73A	STEWARTS LANE - 73A	STEWARTS LANE - 73A	STEWARTS LANE - 73A
			WC 4-6-2 (1945)				
34001	EXMOUTH JCN - 72A	EXMOUTH JCN - 72A	EXMOUTH JCN - 72A	EXMOUTH JCN - 72A	EXMOUTH JCN - 72A	EXMOUTH JCN - 72A	EXMOUTH JCN - 72A
34002	EXMOUTH JCN - 72A	EXMOUTH JCN - 72A	EXMOUTH JCN - 72A	EXMOUTH JCN - 72A	EXMOUTH JCN - 72A	EXMOUTH JCN - 72A	EXMOUTH JCN - 72A
34003	EXMOUTH JCN - 72A	EXMOUTH JCN - 72A	EXMOUTH JCN - 72A	EXMOUTH JCN - 72A	EXMOUTH JCN - 72A	EXMOUTH JCN - 72A	EXMOUTH JCN - 72A
34004	EXMOUTH JCN - 72A	EXMOUTH JCN - 72A	EXMOUTH JCN - 72A	EXMOUTH JCN - 72A	EXMOUTH JCN - 72A	EXMOUTH JCN - 72A	EXMOUTH JCN - 72A
34005	NINE ELMS - 70A	NINE ELMS - 70A	NINE ELMS - 70A	NINE ELMS - 70A	NINE ELMS - 70A	NINE ELMS - 70A	NINE ELMS - 70A
34006	NINE ELMS - 70A	NINE ELMS - 70A	NINE ELMS - 70A	NINE ELMS - 70A	NINE ELMS - 70A	NINE ELMS - 70A	NINE ELMS - 70A
34007	NINE ELMS - 70A	NINE ELMS - 70A	NINE ELMS - 70A	NINE ELMS - 70A	NINE ELMS - 70A	NINE ELMS - 70A	NINE ELMS - 70A
34008	NINE ELMS - 70A	NINE ELMS - 70A	NINE ELMS - 70A	NINE ELMS - 70A	NINE ELMS - 70A	NINE ELMS - 70A	NINE ELMS - 70A
34009	NINE ELMS - 70A	NINE ELMS - 70A	NINE ELMS - 70A	NINE ELMS - 70A	NINE ELMS - 70A	NINE ELMS - 70A	NINE ELMS - 70A
34010	NINE ELMS - 70A	NINE ELMS - 70A	NINE ELMS - 70A	NINE ELMS - 70A	NINE ELMS - 70A	NINE ELMS - 70A	NINE ELMS - 70A
34011	NINE ELMS - 70A	NINE ELMS - 70A	NINE ELMS - 70A	NINE ELMS - 70A	NINE ELMS - 70A	NINE ELMS - 70A	NINE ELMS - 70A
34012	NINE ELMS - 70A	NINE ELMS - 70A	NINE ELMS - 70A	NINE ELMS - 70A	NINE ELMS - 70A	NINE ELMS - 70A	NINE ELMS - 70A
34013	PLYMOUTH - 72D	PLYMOUTH - 72D	PLYMOUTH - 72D	PLYMOUTH - 72D	PLYMOUTH - 72D	PLYMOUTH - 72D	PLYMOUTH - 72D
34014	EXMOUTH JCN - 72A	EXMOUTH JCN - 72A	EXMOUTH JCN - 72A	EXMOUTH JCN - 72A	EXMOUTH JCN - 72A	EXMOUTH JCN - 72A	EXMOUTH JCN - 72A
34015	EXMOUTH JCN - 72A	EXMOUTH JCN - 72A	EXMOUTH JCN - 72A	EXMOUTH JCN - 72A	EXMOUTH JCN - 72A	EXMOUTH JCN - 72A	EXMOUTH JCN - 72A
34016	EXMOUTH JCN - 72A	EXMOUTH JCN - 72A	EXMOUTH JCN - 72A	EXMOUTH JCN - 72A	EXMOUTH JCN - 72A	EXMOUTH JCN - 72A	EXMOUTH JCN - 72A
34017	EXMOUTH JCN - 72A	EXMOUTH JCN - 72A	EXMOUTH JCN - 72A	EXMOUTH JCN - 72A	EXMOUTH JCN - 72A	EXMOUTH JCN - 72A	EXMOUTH JCN - 72A
34018	NINE ELMS - 70A	NINE ELMS - 70A	NINE ELMS - 70A	NINE ELMS - 70A	NINE ELMS - 70A	NINE ELMS - 70A	NINE ELMS - 70A
34019	NINE ELMS - 70A	NINE ELMS - 70A	NINE ELMS - 70A	NINE ELMS - 70A	NINE ELMS - 70A	NINE ELMS - 70A	NINE ELMS - 70A
34020	NINE ELMS - 70A	NINE ELMS - 70A	NINE ELMS - 70A	NINE ELMS - 70A	NINE ELMS - 70A	NINE ELMS - 70A	NINE ELMS - 70A
34021	NINE ELMS - 70A	NINE ELMS - 70A	EXMOUTH JCN - 72A	EXMOUTH JCN - 72A	EXMOUTH JCN - 72A	EXMOUTH JCN - 72A	EXMOUTH JCN - 72A
34022	NINE ELMS - 70A	NINE ELMS - 70A	NINE ELMS - 70A	NINE ELMS - 70A	NINE ELMS - 70A	NINE ELMS - 70A	NINE ELMS - 70A
34023	NINE ELMS - 70A	NINE ELMS - 70A	EXMOUTH JCN - 72A	EXMOUTH JCN - 72A	EXMOUTH JCN - 72A	EXMOUTH JCN - 72A	EXMOUTH JCN - 72A
34024	NINE ELMS - 70A	NINE ELMS - 70A	NINE ELMS - 70A	NINE ELMS - 70A	NINE ELMS - 70A	NINE ELMS - 70A	NINE ELMS - 70A
34025	NINE ELMS - 70A	NINE ELMS - 70A	NINE ELMS - 70A	NINE ELMS - 70A	NINE ELMS - 70A	NINE ELMS - 70A	NINE ELMS - 70A
34026	NINE ELMS - 70A	NINE ELMS - 70A	NINE ELMS - 70A	NINE ELMS - 70A	NINE ELMS - 70A	NINE ELMS - 70A	NINE ELMS - 70A
34027	NINE ELMS - 70A	NINE ELMS - 70A	NINE ELMS - 70A	NINE ELMS - 70A	NINE ELMS - 70A	NINE ELMS - 70A	NINE ELMS - 70A
34028	NINE ELMS - 70A	NINE ELMS - 70A	NINE ELMS - 70A	NINE ELMS - 70A	NINE ELMS - 70A	NINE ELMS - 70A	NINE ELMS - 70A
34029	NINE ELMS - 70A	NINE ELMS - 70A	NINE ELMS - 70A	NINE ELMS - 70A	NINE ELMS - 70A	NINE ELMS - 70A	NINE ELMS - 70A
34030	NINE ELMS - 70A	NINE ELMS - 70A	NINE ELMS - 70A	NINE ELMS - 70A	NINE ELMS - 70A	NINE ELMS - 70A	NINE ELMS - 70A

West Country Pacifics continued in the following section

35020 'Bibby Line' and a Q1 0-6-0 on Nine Elms in 1960.

loco	Sep-52	Dec-52	Mar-53	May-53	Jul-53	Sep-53	Nov-53
				MN 4-6-2 (1941)			
35001	EXMOUTH JCN - 72A	EXMOUTH JCN - 72A	EXMOUTH JCN - 72A	EXMOUTH JCN - 72A	EXMOUTH JCN - 72A	EXMOUTH JCN - 72A	EXMOUTH JCN - 72A
35002	EXMOUTH JCN - 72A	EXMOUTH JCN - 72A	EXMOUTH JCN - 72A	EXMOUTH JCN - 72A	EXMOUTH JCN - 72A	EXMOUTH JCN - 72A	EXMOUTH JCN - 72A
35003	EXMOUTH JCN - 72A	EXMOUTH JCN - 72A	EXMOUTH JCN - 72A	EXMOUTH JCN - 72A	EXMOUTH JCN - 72A	EXMOUTH JCN - 72A	EXMOUTH JCN - 72AT
35004	EXMOUTH JCN - 72A	EXMOUTH JCN - 72A	EXMOUTH JCN - 72A	EXMOUTH JCN - 72A	EXMOUTH JCN - 72A	EXMOUTH JCN - 72A	EXMOUTH JCN - 72A
35005	EXMOUTH JCN - 72A	EXMOUTH JCN - 72A	EXMOUTH JCN - 72A	EXMOUTH JCN - 72A	EXMOUTH JCN - 72A	EXMOUTH JCN - 72A	EXMOUTH JCN - 72A
35006	SALISBURY - 72B	SALISBURY - 72B	SALISBURY - 72B	SALISBURY - 72B	SALISBURY - 72B	SALISBURY - 72B	SALISBURY - 72B
35007	SALISBURY - 72B	SALISBURY - 72B	SALISBURY - 72B	SALISBURY - 72B	SALISBURY - 72B	SALISBURY - 72B	SALISBURY - 72B
35008	SALISBURY - 72B	SALISBURY - 72B	SALISBURY - 72B	SALISBURY - 72B	SALISBURY - 72B	SALISBURY - 72B	SALISBURY - 72B
35009	SALISBURY - 72B	SALISBURY - 72B	SALISBURY - 72B	SALISBURY - 72B	SALISBURY - 72B	SALISBURY - 72B	SALISBURY - 72B
35010	NINE ELMS - 70A	NINE ELMS - 70A	NINE ELMS - 70A	NINE ELMS - 70A	NINE ELMS - 70A	NINE ELMS - 70A	NINE ELMS - 70A
35011	NINE ELMS - 70A	NINE ELMS - 70A	NINE ELMS - 70A	NINE ELMS - 70A	NINE ELMS - 70A	NINE ELMS - 70A	NINE ELMS - 70A
35012	NINE ELMS - 70A	NINE ELMS - 70A	NINE ELMS - 70A	NINE ELMS - 70A	NINE ELMS - 70A	NINE ELMS - 70A	NINE ELMS - 70A
35013	NINE ELMS - 70A	NINE ELMS - 70A	NINE ELMS - 70A	NINE ELMS - 70A	NINE ELMS - 70A	NINE ELMS - 70A	NINE ELMS - 70A
35014	NINE ELMS - 70A	NINE ELMS - 70A	NINE ELMS - 70A	NINE ELMS - 70A	NINE ELMS - 70A	NINE ELMS - 70A	NINE ELMS - 70A
35015	NINE ELMS - 70A	NINE ELMS - 70A	NINE ELMS - 70A	NINE ELMS - 70A	NINE ELMS - 70A	NINE ELMS - 70A	NINE ELMS - 70A
35016	NINE ELMS - 70A	NINE ELMS - 70A	NINE ELMS - 70A	NINE ELMS - 70A	NINE ELMS - 70A	NINE ELMS - 70A	NINE ELMS - 70A
35017	NINE ELMS - 70A	NINE ELMS - 70A	NINE ELMS - 70A	NINE ELMS - 70A	NINE ELMS - 70A	NINE ELMS - 70A	NINE ELMS - 70A
35018	NINE ELMS - 70A	NINE ELMS - 70A	NINE ELMS - 70A	NINE ELMS - 70A	NINE ELMS - 70A	NINE ELMS - 70A	NINE ELMS - 70A
35019	NINE ELMS - 70A	NINE ELMS - 70A	NINE ELMS - 70A	NINE ELMS - 70A	NINE ELMS - 70A	NINE ELMS - 70A	NINE ELMS - 70A
35020	NINE ELMS - 70A	NINE ELMS - 70A	NINE ELMS - 70A	NINE ELMS - 70A	NINE ELMS - 70A	NINE ELMS - 70A	NINE ELMS - 70A
35021	NINE ELMS - 70A	NINE ELMS - 70A	NINE ELMS - 70A	NINE ELMS - 70A	NINE ELMS - 70A	NINE ELMS - 70A	NINE ELMS - 70A
35022	RUGBY PLANT	RUGBY PLANT	RUGBY PLANT	RUGBY PLANT	RUGBY PLANT	RUGBY PLANT	RUGBY PLANT
35023	EXMOUTH JCN - 72A	EXMOUTH JCN - 72A	EXMOUTH JCN - 72A	EXMOUTH JCN - 72A	EXMOUTH JCN - 72A	EXMOUTH JCN - 72A	EXMOUTH JCN - 72A
35024	EXMOUTH JCN - 72A	EXMOUTH JCN - 72A	EXMOUTH JCN - 72A	EXMOUTH JCN - 72A	EXMOUTH JCN - 72A	EXMOUTH JCN - 72A	EXMOUTH JCN - 72A
35025	EXMOUTH JCN - 72A	EXMOUTH JCN - 72A	EXMOUTH JCN - 72A	EXMOUTH JCN - 72A	EXMOUTH JCN - 72A	EXMOUTH JCN - 72A	EXMOUTH JCN - 72A
35026	STEWARTS LANE - 73A	STEWARTS LANE - 73A	STEWARTS LANE - 73A	STEWARTS LANE - 73A	STEWARTS LANE - 73A	STEWARTS LANE - 73A	STEWARTS LANE - 73A
35027	STEWARTS LANE - 73A	STEWARTS LANE - 73A	STEWARTS LANE - 73A	STEWARTS LANE - 73A	STEWARTS LANE - 73A	STEWARTS LANE - 73A	STEWARTS LANE - 73A
35028	STEWARTS LANE - 73A	STEWARTS LANE - 73A	STEWARTS LANE - 73A	STEWARTS LANE - 73A	STEWARTS LANE - 73A	STEWARTS LANE - 73A	STEWARTS LANE - 73A
35029	STEWARTS LANE - 73A	STEWARTS LANE - 73A	STEWARTS LANE - 73A	STEWARTS LANE - 73A	STEWARTS LANE - 73A	STEWARTS LANE - 73A	STEWARTS LANE - 73A
35030	STEWARTS LANE - 73A	STEWARTS LANE - 73A	STEWARTS LANE - 73A	STEWARTS LANE - 73A	STEWARTS LANE - 73A	STEWARTS LANE - 73A	STEWARTS LANE - 73A
				WC 4-6-2 (1945)			
34001	EXMOUTH JCN - 72A	EXMOUTH JCN - 72A	EXMOUTH JCN - 72A	EXMOUTH JCN - 72A	EXMOUTH JCN - 72A	EXMOUTH JCN - 72A	EXMOUTH JCN - 72A
34002	EXMOUTH JCN - 72A	EXMOUTH JCN - 72A	EXMOUTH JCN - 72A	EXMOUTH JCN - 72A	EXMOUTH JCN - 72A	EXMOUTH JCN - 72A	EXMOUTH JCN - 72A
34003	EXMOUTH JCN - 72A	EXMOUTH JCN - 72A	EXMOUTH JCN - 72A	EXMOUTH JCN - 72A	EXMOUTH JCN - 72A	EXMOUTH JCN - 72A	EXMOUTH JCN - 72A
34004	EXMOUTH JCN - 72A	EXMOUTH JCN - 72A	EXMOUTH JCN - 72A	EXMOUTH JCN - 72A	EXMOUTH JCN - 72A	EXMOUTH JCN - 72A	EXMOUTH JCN - 72A
34005	NINE ELMS - 70A	NINE ELMS - 70A	NINE ELMS - 70A	NINE ELMS - 70A	NINE ELMS - 70A	NINE ELMS - 70A	NINE ELMS - 70A
34006	NINE ELMS - 70A	NINE ELMS - 70A	NINE ELMS - 70A	NINE ELMS - 70A	NINE ELMS - 70A	NINE ELMS - 70A	NINE ELMS - 70A
34007	NINE ELMS - 70A	NINE ELMS - 70A	NINE ELMS - 70A	NINE ELMS - 70A	NINE ELMS - 70A	NINE ELMS - 70A	NINE ELMS - 70A
34008	NINE ELMS - 70A	NINE ELMS - 70A	NINE ELMS - 70A	NINE ELMS - 70A	NINE ELMS - 70A	NINE ELMS - 70A	NINE ELMS - 70A
34009	NINE ELMS - 70A	NINE ELMS - 70A	NINE ELMS - 70A	NINE ELMS - 70A	NINE ELMS - 70A	NINE ELMS - 70A	NINE ELMS - 70A
34010	NINE ELMS - 70A	NINE ELMS - 70A	NINE ELMS - 70A	NINE ELMS - 70A	NINE ELMS - 70A	NINE ELMS - 70A	NINE ELMS - 70A
34011	NINE ELMS - 70A	NINE ELMS - 70A	NINE ELMS - 70A	NINE ELMS - 70A	NINE ELMS - 70A	NINE ELMS - 70A	NINE ELMS - 70A
34012	NINE ELMS - 70A	NINE ELMS - 70A	NINE ELMS - 70A	NINE ELMS - 70A	NINE ELMS - 70A	NINE ELMS - 70A	NINE ELMS - 70A
34013	PLYMOUTH - 72D	PLYMOUTH - 72D	PLYMOUTH - 72D	PLYMOUTH - 72D	PLYMOUTH - 72D	PLYMOUTH - 72D	PLYMOUTH - 72D
34014	EXMOUTH JCN - 72A	EXMOUTH JCN - 72A	EXMOUTH JCN - 72A	EXMOUTH JCN - 72A	EXMOUTH JCN - 72A	EXMOUTH JCN - 72A	EXMOUTH JCN - 72A
34015	EXMOUTH JCN - 72A	EXMOUTH JCN - 72A	EXMOUTH JCN - 72A	EXMOUTH JCN - 72A	EXMOUTH JCN - 72A	EXMOUTH JCN - 72A	EXMOUTH JCN - 72A
34016	EXMOUTH JCN - 72A	EXMOUTH JCN - 72A	EXMOUTH JCN - 72A	EXMOUTH JCN - 72A	EXMOUTH JCN - 72A	EXMOUTH JCN - 72A	EXMOUTH JCN - 72A
34017	EXMOUTH JCN - 72A	EXMOUTH JCN - 72A	EXMOUTH JCN - 72A	EXMOUTH JCN - 72A	EXMOUTH JCN - 72A	EXMOUTH JCN - 72A	EXMOUTH JCN - 72A
34018	NINE ELMS - 70A	NINE ELMS - 70A	NINE ELMS - 70A	NINE ELMS - 70A	NINE ELMS - 70A	NINE ELMS - 70A	NINE ELMS - 70A
34019	NINE ELMS - 70A	NINE ELMS - 70A	NINE ELMS - 70A	NINE ELMS - 70A	NINE ELMS - 70A	NINE ELMS - 70A	NINE ELMS - 70A
34020	NINE ELMS - 70A	NINE ELMS - 70A	NINE ELMS - 70A	NINE ELMS - 70A	NINE ELMS - 70A	NINE ELMS - 70A	NINE ELMS - 70A
34021	EXMOUTH JCN - 72A	EXMOUTH JCN - 72A	EXMOUTH JCN - 72A	EXMOUTH JCN - 72A	EXMOUTH JCN - 72A	EXMOUTH JCN - 72A	EXMOUTH JCN - 72A
34022	NINE ELMS - 70A	NINE ELMS - 70A	NINE ELMS - 70A	NINE ELMS - 70A	NINE ELMS - 70A	NINE ELMS - 70A	NINE ELMS - 70A
34023	EXMOUTH JCN - 72A	EXMOUTH JCN - 72A	EXMOUTH JCN - 72A	EXMOUTH JCN - 72A	EXMOUTH JCN - 72A	NINE ELMS - 70A	NINE ELMS - 70A
34024	NINE ELMS - 70A	NINE ELMS - 70A	NINE ELMS - 70A	NINE ELMS - 70A	NINE ELMS - 70A	NINE ELMS - 70A	NINE ELMS - 70A
34025	NINE ELMS - 70A	NINE ELMS - 70A	NINE ELMS - 70A	NINE ELMS - 70A	NINE ELMS - 70A	NINE ELMS - 70A	NINE ELMS - 70A
34026	NINE ELMS - 70A	NINE ELMS - 70A	NINE ELMS - 70A	NINE ELMS - 70A	NINE ELMS - 70A	NINE ELMS - 70A	NINE ELMS - 70A
34027	NINE ELMS - 70A	NINE ELMS - 70A	NINE ELMS - 70A	NINE ELMS - 70A	NINE ELMS - 70A	NINE ELMS - 70A	NINE ELMS - 70A
34028	NINE ELMS - 70A	NINE ELMS - 70A	NINE ELMS - 70A	NINE ELMS - 70A	NINE ELMS - 70A	NINE ELMS - 70A	NINE ELMS - 70A
34029	NINE ELMS - 70A	NINE ELMS - 70A	NINE ELMS - 70A	NINE ELMS - 70A	NINE ELMS - 70A	NINE ELMS - 70A	NINE ELMS - 70A
34030	NINE ELMS - 70A	NINE ELMS - 70A	NINE ELMS - 70A	NINE ELMS - 70A	NINE ELMS - 70A	NINE ELMS - 70A	NINE ELMS - 70A

West Country Pacifics continued in the following section

Although they rarely came into working contact, the enmity that existed between local traffic railwaymen and the workshop staff at Eastleigh had to be seen to be believed. The perceived truth according to the former was one of four-hour three-day weeks at astronomical rates of overtime: the main source being a local station where the staff conspiratorially recorded the times workshopmen travelled to work and came home again. ("They work a shorter week than our stationmaster......"). True or not, a BR 4MT, a light Pacific and a BR 5MT suggest some measure of productivity in Eastleigh works.

loco	Jan-54	Mar-54	May-54	Jun-54	Aug-54	Oct-54	Dec-54
				MN 4-6-2 (1941)			
35001	EXMOUTH JCN - 72A	EXMOUTH JCN - 72A	EXMOUTH JCN - 72A	EXMOUTH JCN - 72A	EXMOUTH JCN - 72A	EXMOUTH JCN - 72A	EXMOUTH JCN - 72A
35002	EXMOUTH JCN - 72A	EXMOUTH JCN - 72A	BOURNEMOUTH - 71B	EXMOUTH JCN - 72A	EXMOUTH JCN - 72A	EXMOUTH JCN - 72A	EXMOUTH JCN - 72A
35003	EXMOUTH JCN - 72A	EXMOUTH JCN - 72A	EXMOUTH JCN - 72A	EXMOUTH JCN - 72A	EXMOUTH JCN - 72A	EXMOUTH JCN - 72A	EXMOUTH JCN - 72A
35004	EXMOUTH JCN - 72A	EXMOUTH JCN - 72A	EXMOUTH JCN - 72A	EXMOUTH JCN - 72A	EXMOUTH JCN - 72A	EXMOUTH JCN - 72A	EXMOUTH JCN - 72A
35005	EXMOUTH JCN - 72A	NINE ELMS - 70A	NINE ELMS - 70A	NINE ELMS - 70A	NINE ELMS - 70A	NINE ELMS - 70A	NINE ELMS - 70A
35006	SALISBURY - 72B	SALISBURY - 72B	SALISBURY - 72B	SALISBURY - 72B	SALISBURY - 72B	SALISBURY - 72B	SALISBURY - 72B
35007	SALISBURY - 72B	SALISBURY - 72B	SALISBURY - 72B	SALISBURY - 72B	SALISBURY - 72B	SALISBURY - 72B	SALISBURY - 72B
35008	BOURNEMOUTH - 71B	BOURNEMOUTH - 71B	BOURNEMOUTH - 71B	BOURNEMOUTH - 71B	EXMOUTH JCN - 72A	EXMOUTH JCN - 72A	EXMOUTH JCN - 72A
35009	SALISBURY - 72B	SALISBURY - 72B	SALISBURY - 72B	SALISBURY - 72B	SALISBURY - 72B	SALISBURY - 72B	SALISBURY - 72B
35010	NINE ELMS - 70A	NINE ELMS - 70A	NINE ELMS - 70A	NINE ELMS - 70A	NINE ELMS - 70A	NINE ELMS - 70A	NINE ELMS - 70A
35011	BOURNEMOUTH - 71B	BOURNEMOUTH - 71B	NINE ELMS - 70A	NINE ELMS - 70A	NINE ELMS - 70A	NINE ELMS - 70A	NINE ELMS - 70A
35012	BOURNEMOUTH - 71B	BOURNEMOUTH - 71B	NINE ELMS - 70A	NINE ELMS - 70A	NINE ELMS - 70A	NINE ELMS - 70A	NINE ELMS - 70A
35013	NINE ELMS - 70A	EXMOUTH JCN - 72A	EXMOUTH JCN - 72A	EXMOUTH JCN - 72A	EXMOUTH JCN - 72A	EXMOUTH JCN - 72A	EXMOUTH JCN - 72A
35014	NINE ELMS - 70A	NINE ELMS - 70A	NINE ELMS - 70A	NINE ELMS - 70A	BOURNEMOUTH - 71B	BOURNEMOUTH - 71B	BOURNEMOUTH - 71B
35015	NINE ELMS - 70A	NINE ELMS - 70A	NINE ELMS - 70A	NINE ELMS - 70A	NINE ELMS - 70A	NINE ELMS - 70A	NINE ELMS - 70A
35016	NINE ELMS - 70A	NINE ELMS - 70A	NINE ELMS - 70A	NINE ELMS - 70A	NINE ELMS - 70A	NINE ELMS - 70A	NINE ELMS - 70A
35017	NINE ELMS - 70A	NINE ELMS - 70A	NINE ELMS - 70A	NINE ELMS - 70A	NINE ELMS - 70A	NINE ELMS - 70A	NINE ELMS - 70A
35018	NINE ELMS - 70A	NINE ELMS - 70A	NINE ELMS - 70A	NINE ELMS - 70A	NINE ELMS - 70A	NINE ELMS - 70A	NINE ELMS - 70A
35019	NINE ELMS - 70A	NINE ELMS - 70A	NINE ELMS - 70A	NINE ELMS - 70A	NINE ELMS - 70A	NINE ELMS - 70A	NINE ELMS - 70A
35020	NINE ELMS - 70A	NINE ELMS - 70A	NINE ELMS - 70A	NINE ELMS - 70A	NINE ELMS - 70A	NINE ELMS - 70A	NINE ELMS - 70A
35021	NINE ELMS - 70A	NINE ELMS - 70A	NINE ELMS - 70A	NINE ELMS - 70A	NINE ELMS - 70A	NINE ELMS - 70A	NINE ELMS - 70A
35022	RUGBY PLANT	RUGBY PLANT	RUGBY PLANT	BOURNEMOUTH - 71B	BOURNEMOUTH - 71B	BOURNEMOUTH - 71B	BOURNEMOUTH - 71B
35023	EXMOUTH JCN - 72A	EXMOUTH JCN - 72A	EXMOUTH JCN - 72A	EXMOUTH JCN - 72A	EXMOUTH JCN - 72A	EXMOUTH JCN - 72A	EXMOUTH JCN - 72A
35024	EXMOUTH JCN - 72A	EXMOUTH JCN - 72A	EXMOUTH JCN - 72A	EXMOUTH JCN - 72A	EXMOUTH JCN - 72A	EXMOUTH JCN - 72A	EXMOUTH JCN - 72A
35025	EXMOUTH JCN - 72A	EXMOUTH JCN - 72A	EXMOUTH JCN - 72A	NINE ELMS - 70A	NINE ELMS - 70A	NINE ELMS - 70A	NINE ELMS - 70A
35026	STEWARTS LANE - 73A	STEWARTS LANE - 73A	STEWARTS LANE - 73A	STEWARTS LANE - 73A	STEWARTS LANE - 73A	STEWARTS LANE - 73A	STEWARTS LANE - 73A
35027	STEWARTS LANE - 73A	STEWARTS LANE - 73A	STEWARTS LANE - 73A	STEWARTS LANE - 73A	STEWARTS LANE - 73A	STEWARTS LANE - 73A	STEWARTS LANE - 73A
35028	STEWARTS LANE - 73A	STEWARTS LANE - 73A	STEWARTS LANE - 73A	STEWARTS LANE - 73A	STEWARTS LANE - 73A	STEWARTS LANE - 73A	STEWARTS LANE - 73A
35029	STEWARTS LANE - 73A	STEWARTS LANE - 73A	STEWARTS LANE - 73A	STEWARTS LANE - 73A	STEWARTS LANE - 73A	STEWARTS LANE - 73A	STEWARTS LANE - 73A
35030	STEWARTS LANE - 73A	STEWARTS LANE - 73A	STEWARTS LANE - 73A	STEWARTS LANE - 73A	STEWARTS LANE - 73A	STEWARTS LANE - 73A	STEWARTS LANE - 73A
				WC 4-6-2 (1945)			
34001	EXMOUTH JCN - 72A	EXMOUTH JCN - 72A	EXMOUTH JCN - 72A	EXMOUTH JCN - 72A	EXMOUTH JCN - 72A	EXMOUTH JCN - 72A	EXMOUTH JCN - 72A
34002	EXMOUTH JCN - 72A	EXMOUTH JCN - 72A	EXMOUTH JCN - 72A	EXMOUTH JCN - 72A	EXMOUTH JCN - 72A	EXMOUTH JCN - 72A	EXMOUTH JCN - 72A
34003	EXMOUTH JCN - 72A	EXMOUTH JCN - 72A	EXMOUTH JCN - 72A	EXMOUTH JCN - 72A	EXMOUTH JCN - 72A	EXMOUTH JCN - 72A	EXMOUTH JCN - 72A
34004	EXMOUTH JCN - 72A	EXMOUTH JCN - 72A	EXMOUTH JCN - 72A	EXMOUTH JCN - 72A	EXMOUTH JCN - 72A	EXMOUTH JCN - 72A	EXMOUTH JCN - 72A
34005	NINE ELMS - 70A	NINE ELMS - 70A	NINE ELMS - 70A	NINE ELMS - 70A	NINE ELMS - 70A	NINE ELMS - 70A	NINE ELMS - 70A
34006	NINE ELMS - 70A	NINE ELMS - 70A	NINE ELMS - 70A	NINE ELMS - 70A	NINE ELMS - 70A	NINE ELMS - 70A	NINE ELMS - 70A
34007	NINE ELMS - 70A	NINE ELMS - 70A	NINE ELMS - 70A	NINE ELMS - 70A	NINE ELMS - 70A	NINE ELMS - 70A	NINE ELMS - 70A
34008	NINE ELMS - 70A	NINE ELMS - 70A	NINE ELMS - 70A	NINE ELMS - 70A	NINE ELMS - 70A	NINE ELMS - 70A	NINE ELMS - 70A
34009	NINE ELMS - 70A	NINE ELMS - 70A	NINE ELMS - 70A	NINE ELMS - 70A	NINE ELMS - 70A	NINE ELMS - 70A	NINE ELMS - 70A
34010	NINE ELMS - 70A	NINE ELMS - 70A	NINE ELMS - 70A	NINE ELMS - 70A	NINE ELMS - 70A	NINE ELMS - 70A	NINE ELMS - 70A
34011	NINE ELMS - 70A	NINE ELMS - 70A	NINE ELMS - 70A	NINE ELMS - 70A	NINE ELMS - 70A	NINE ELMS - 70A	NINE ELMS - 70A
34012	NINE ELMS - 70A	NINE ELMS - 70A	NINE ELMS - 70A	NINE ELMS - 70A	NINE ELMS - 70A	NINE ELMS - 70A	NINE ELMS - 70A
34013	PLYMOUTH - 72D	PLYMOUTH - 72D	PLYMOUTH - 72D	PLYMOUTH - 72D	PLYMOUTH - 72D	PLYMOUTH - 72D	PLYMOUTH - 72D
34014	EXMOUTH JCN - 72A	EXMOUTH JCN - 72A	EXMOUTH JCN - 72A	EXMOUTH JCN - 72A	EXMOUTH JCN - 72A	EXMOUTH JCN - 72A	EXMOUTH JCN - 72A
34015	EXMOUTH JCN - 72A	EXMOUTH JCN - 72A	EXMOUTH JCN - 72A	EXMOUTH JCN - 72A	EXMOUTH JCN - 72A	EXMOUTH JCN - 72A	EXMOUTH JCN - 72A
34016	EXMOUTH JCN - 72A	EXMOUTH JCN - 72A	EXMOUTH JCN - 72A	EXMOUTH JCN - 72A	EXMOUTH JCN - 72A	EXMOUTH JCN - 72A	EXMOUTH JCN - 72A
34017	EXMOUTH JCN - 72A	STEWARTS LANE - 73A	STEWARTS LANE - 73A	STEWARTS LANE - 73A	STEWARTS LANE - 73A	STEWARTS LANE - 73A	STEWARTS LANE - 73A
34018	NINE ELMS - 70A	NINE ELMS - 70A	NINE ELMS - 70A	NINE ELMS - 70A	NINE ELMS - 70A	NINE ELMS - 70A	NINE ELMS - 70A
34019	NINE ELMS - 70A	NINE ELMS - 70A	NINE ELMS - 70A	NINE ELMS - 70A	NINE ELMS - 70A	NINE ELMS - 70A	NINE ELMS - 70A
34020	NINE ELMS - 70A	NINE ELMS - 70A	NINE ELMS - 70A	NINE ELMS - 70A	NINE ELMS - 70A	NINE ELMS - 70A	NINE ELMS - 70A
34021	EXMOUTH JCN - 72A	EXMOUTH JCN - 72A	EXMOUTH JCN - 72A	EXMOUTH JCN - 72A	EXMOUTH JCN - 72A	EXMOUTH JCN - 72A	EXMOUTH JCN - 72A
34022	NINE ELMS - 70A	NINE ELMS - 70A	NINE ELMS - 70A	NINE ELMS - 70A	NINE ELMS - 70A	NINE ELMS - 70A	NINE ELMS - 70A
34023	EXMOUTH JCN - 72A	EXMOUTH JCN - 72A	EXMOUTH JCN - 72A	EXMOUTH JCN - 72A	EXMOUTH JCN - 72A	EXMOUTH JCN - 72A	EXMOUTH JCN - 72A
34024	NINE ELMS - 70A	NINE ELMS - 70A	NINE ELMS - 70A	NINE ELMS - 70A	NINE ELMS - 70A	NINE ELMS - 70A	NINE ELMS - 70A
34025	NINE ELMS - 70A	NINE ELMS - 70A	NINE ELMS - 70A	NINE ELMS - 70A	NINE ELMS - 70A	EXMOUTH JCN - 72A	EXMOUTH JCN - 72A
34026	NINE ELMS - 70A	NINE ELMS - 70A	NINE ELMS - 70A	NINE ELMS - 70A	NINE ELMS - 70A	NINE ELMS - 70A	NINE ELMS - 70A
34027	NINE ELMS - 70A	NINE ELMS - 70A	NINE ELMS - 70A	NINE ELMS - 70A	NINE ELMS - 70A	NINE ELMS - 70A	NINE ELMS - 70A
34028	NINE ELMS - 70A	NINE ELMS - 70A	NINE ELMS - 70A	NINE ELMS - 70A	NINE ELMS - 70A	NINE ELMS - 70A	NINE ELMS - 70A
34029	NINE ELMS - 70A	NINE ELMS - 70A	NINE ELMS - 70A	NINE ELMS - 70A	NINE ELMS - 70A	NINE ELMS - 70A	NINE ELMS - 70A
34030	NINE ELMS - 70A	NINE ELMS - 70A	NINE ELMS - 70A	NINE ELMS - 70A	NINE ELMS - 70A	NINE ELMS - 70A	NINE ELMS - 70A

West Country Pacifics continued in the following section

Rebuilt Merchant Navy 35021 'New Zealand Line' stands with a group of Light Pacifics on Bournemouth MPD in 1963. 35021 was originally an Exmouth Junction engine but moved to Nine Elms in exchange for 35005 in April 1951 and remained there until being transferred to Bournemouth in the summer of 1957.

MN 4-6-2 (1941)

loco	Feb-55	Apr-55	Jun-55	Aug-55	Sep-55	Nov-55	Dec-55
35001	EXMOUTH JCN - 72A	EXMOUTH JCN - 72A	EXMOUTH JCN - 72A	EXMOUTH JCN - 72A	EXMOUTH JCN - 72A	EXMOUTH JCN - 72A	EXMOUTH JCN - 72A
35002	EXMOUTH JCN - 72A	EXMOUTH JCN - 72A	EXMOUTH JCN - 72A	EXMOUTH JCN - 72A	EXMOUTH JCN - 72A	EXMOUTH JCN - 72A	EXMOUTH JCN - 72A
35003	EXMOUTH JCN - 72A	EXMOUTH JCN - 72A	EXMOUTH JCN - 72A	EXMOUTH JCN - 72A	EXMOUTH JCN - 72A	EXMOUTH JCN - 72A	EXMOUTH JCN - 72A
35004	EXMOUTH JCN - 72A	EXMOUTH JCN - 72A	EXMOUTH JCN - 72A	EXMOUTH JCN - 72A	EXMOUTH JCN - 72A	EXMOUTH JCN - 72A	EXMOUTH JCN - 72A
35005	NINE ELMS - 70A	NINE ELMS - 70A	NINE ELMS - 70A	NINE ELMS - 70A	NINE ELMS - 70A	NINE ELMS - 70A	NINE ELMS - 70A
35006	SALISBURY - 72B	SALISBURY - 72B	SALISBURY - 72B	SALISBURY - 72B	SALISBURY - 72B	SALISBURY - 72B	SALISBURY - 72B
35007	SALISBURY - 72B	SALISBURY - 72B	SALISBURY - 72B	SALISBURY - 72B	SALISBURY - 72B	SALISBURY - 72B	SALISBURY - 72B
35008	EXMOUTH JCN - 72A	EXMOUTH JCN - 72A	EXMOUTH JCN - 72A	EXMOUTH JCN - 72A	EXMOUTH JCN - 72A	EXMOUTH JCN - 72A	EXMOUTH JCN - 72A
35009	SALISBURY - 72B	SALISBURY - 72B	SALISBURY - 72B	SALISBURY - 72B	SALISBURY - 72B	SALISBURY - 72B	SALISBURY - 72B
35010	NINE ELMS - 70A	NINE ELMS - 70A	NINE ELMS - 70A	NINE ELMS - 70A	NINE ELMS - 70A	NINE ELMS - 70A	NINE ELMS - 70A
35011	NINE ELMS - 70A	NINE ELMS - 70A	NINE ELMS - 70A	NINE ELMS - 70A	NINE ELMS - 70A	NINE ELMS - 70A	NINE ELMS - 70A
35012	NINE ELMS - 70A	NINE ELMS - 70A	NINE ELMS - 70A	NINE ELMS - 70A	NINE ELMS - 70A	NINE ELMS - 70A	NINE ELMS - 70A
35013	EXMOUTH JCN - 72A	EXMOUTH JCN - 72A	EXMOUTH JCN - 72A	EXMOUTH JCN - 72A	EXMOUTH JCN - 72A	EXMOUTH JCN - 72A	EXMOUTH JCN - 72A
35014	BOURNEMOUTH - 71B	BOURNEMOUTH - 71B	STEWARTS LANE - 73A	STEWARTS LANE - 73A	STEWARTS LANE - 73A	STEWARTS LANE - 73A	STEWARTS LANE - 73A
35015	NINE ELMS - 70A	NINE ELMS - 70A	NINE ELMS - 70A	NINE ELMS - 70A	NINE ELMS - 70A	NINE ELMS - 70A	NINE ELMS - 70A
35016	NINE ELMS - 70A	NINE ELMS - 70A	NINE ELMS - 70A	NINE ELMS - 70A	NINE ELMS - 70A	NINE ELMS - 70A	NINE ELMS - 70A
35017	NINE ELMS - 70A	NINE ELMS - 70A	NINE ELMS - 70A	NINE ELMS - 70A	NINE ELMS - 70A	NINE ELMS - 70A	NINE ELMS - 70A
35018	NINE ELMS - 70A	NINE ELMS - 70A	NINE ELMS - 70A	NINE ELMS - 70A	NINE ELMS - 70A	NINE ELMS - 70A	NINE ELMS - 70A
35019	NINE ELMS - 70A	NINE ELMS - 70A	NINE ELMS - 70A	NINE ELMS - 70A	NINE ELMS - 70A	NINE ELMS - 70A	NINE ELMS - 70A
35020	NINE ELMS - 70A	NINE ELMS - 70A	NINE ELMS - 70A	NINE ELMS - 70A	NINE ELMS - 70A	NINE ELMS - 70A	NINE ELMS - 70A
35021	NINE ELMS - 70A	NINE ELMS - 70A	NINE ELMS - 70A	NINE ELMS - 70A	NINE ELMS - 70A	NINE ELMS - 70A	NINE ELMS - 70A
35022	BOURNEMOUTH - 71B	BOURNEMOUTH - 71B	BOURNEMOUTH - 71B	BOURNEMOUTH - 71B	BOURNEMOUTH - 71B	BOURNEMOUTH - 71B	BOURNEMOUTH - 71B
35023	EXMOUTH JCN - 72A	EXMOUTH JCN - 72A	EXMOUTH JCN - 72A	EXMOUTH JCN - 72A	EXMOUTH JCN - 72A	EXMOUTH JCN - 72A	EXMOUTH JCN - 72A
35024	EXMOUTH JCN - 72A	EXMOUTH JCN - 72A	EXMOUTH JCN - 72A	EXMOUTH JCN - 72A	EXMOUTH JCN - 72A	EXMOUTH JCN - 72A	EXMOUTH JCN - 72A
35025	NINE ELMS - 70A	NINE ELMS - 70A	NINE ELMS - 70A	NINE ELMS - 70A	NINE ELMS - 70A	NINE ELMS - 70A	NINE ELMS - 70A
35026	STEWARTS LANE - 73A	STEWARTS LANE - 73A	STEWARTS LANE - 73A	STEWARTS LANE - 73A	STEWARTS LANE - 73A	STEWARTS LANE - 73A	STEWARTS LANE - 73A
35027	STEWARTS LANE - 73A	STEWARTS LANE - 73A	BOURNEMOUTH - 71B	BOURNEMOUTH - 71B	BOURNEMOUTH - 71B	BOURNEMOUTH - 71B	BOURNEMOUTH - 71B
35028	STEWARTS LANE - 73A	STEWARTS LANE - 73A	STEWARTS LANE - 73A	STEWARTS LANE - 73A	STEWARTS LANE - 73A	STEWARTS LANE - 73A	STEWARTS LANE - 73A
35029	STEWARTS LANE - 73A	STEWARTS LANE - 73A	NINE ELMS - 70A	NINE ELMS - 70A	NINE ELMS - 70A	NINE ELMS - 70A	NINE ELMS - 70A
35030	STEWARTS LANE - 73A	STEWARTS LANE - 73A	NINE ELMS - 70A	NINE ELMS - 70A	NINE ELMS - 70A	NINE ELMS - 70A	NINE ELMS - 70A

WC 4-6-2 (1945)

loco	Feb-55	Apr-55	Jun-55	Aug-55	Sep-55	Nov-55	Dec-55
34001	EXMOUTH JCN - 72A	EXMOUTH JCN - 72A	EXMOUTH JCN - 72A	EXMOUTH JCN - 72A	EXMOUTH JCN - 72A	EXMOUTH JCN - 72A	EXMOUTH JCN - 72A
34002	EXMOUTH JCN - 72A	EXMOUTH JCN - 72A	EXMOUTH JCN - 72A	EXMOUTH JCN - 72A	EXMOUTH JCN - 72A	EXMOUTH JCN - 72A	EXMOUTH JCN - 72A
34003	EXMOUTH JCN - 72A	EXMOUTH JCN - 72A	EXMOUTH JCN - 72A	EXMOUTH JCN - 72A	EXMOUTH JCN - 72A	EXMOUTH JCN - 72A	EXMOUTH JCN - 72A
34004	EXMOUTH JCN - 72A	EXMOUTH JCN - 72A	EXMOUTH JCN - 72A	EXMOUTH JCN - 72A	EXMOUTH JCN - 72A	EXMOUTH JCN - 72A	EXMOUTH JCN - 72A
34005	NINE ELMS - 70A	NINE ELMS - 70A	NINE ELMS - 70A	NINE ELMS - 70A	NINE ELMS - 70A	NINE ELMS - 70A	NINE ELMS - 70A
34006	NINE ELMS - 70A	NINE ELMS - 70A	NINE ELMS - 70A	NINE ELMS - 70A	NINE ELMS - 70A	NINE ELMS - 70A	NINE ELMS - 70A
34007	NINE ELMS - 70A	NINE ELMS - 70A	NINE ELMS - 70A	NINE ELMS - 70A	NINE ELMS - 70A	NINE ELMS - 70A	NINE ELMS - 70A
34008	NINE ELMS - 70A	NINE ELMS - 70A	NINE ELMS - 70A	NINE ELMS - 70A	NINE ELMS - 70A	NINE ELMS - 70A	NINE ELMS - 70A
34009	NINE ELMS - 70A	NINE ELMS - 70A	NINE ELMS - 70A	NINE ELMS - 70A	NINE ELMS - 70A	NINE ELMS - 70A	NINE ELMS - 70A
34010	NINE ELMS - 70A	NINE ELMS - 70A	NINE ELMS - 70A	NINE ELMS - 70A	NINE ELMS - 70A	NINE ELMS - 70A	NINE ELMS - 70A
34011	NINE ELMS - 70A	NINE ELMS - 70A	NINE ELMS - 70A	NINE ELMS - 70A	NINE ELMS - 70A	NINE ELMS - 70A	NINE ELMS - 70A
34012	NINE ELMS - 70A	NINE ELMS - 70A	NINE ELMS - 70A	NINE ELMS - 70A	NINE ELMS - 70A	NINE ELMS - 70A	NINE ELMS - 70A
34013	PLYMOUTH - 72D	PLYMOUTH - 72D	PLYMOUTH - 72D	PLYMOUTH - 72D	PLYMOUTH - 72D	PLYMOUTH - 72D	PLYMOUTH - 72D
34014	EXMOUTH JCN - 72A	EXMOUTH JCN - 72A	EXMOUTH JCN - 72A	EXMOUTH JCN - 72A	EXMOUTH JCN - 72A	EXMOUTH JCN - 72A	EXMOUTH JCN - 72A
34015	EXMOUTH JCN - 72A	EXMOUTH JCN - 72A	EXMOUTH JCN - 72A	EXMOUTH JCN - 72A	EXMOUTH JCN - 72A	EXMOUTH JCN - 72A	EXMOUTH JCN - 72A
34016	EXMOUTH JCN - 72A	EXMOUTH JCN - 72A	EXMOUTH JCN - 72A	EXMOUTH JCN - 72A	EXMOUTH JCN - 72A	EXMOUTH JCN - 72A	EXMOUTH JCN - 72A
34017	STEWARTS LANE - 73A	STEWARTS LANE - 73A	STEWARTS LANE - 73A	STEWARTS LANE - 73A	STEWARTS LANE - 73A	STEWARTS LANE - 73A	STEWARTS LANE - 73A
34018	NINE ELMS - 70A	NINE ELMS - 70A	NINE ELMS - 70A	NINE ELMS - 70A	NINE ELMS - 70A	NINE ELMS - 70A	NINE ELMS - 70A
34019	NINE ELMS - 70A	NINE ELMS - 70A	NINE ELMS - 70A	NINE ELMS - 70A	NINE ELMS - 70A	NINE ELMS - 70A	NINE ELMS - 70A
34020	NINE ELMS - 70A	NINE ELMS - 70A	NINE ELMS - 70A	NINE ELMS - 70A	NINE ELMS - 70A	NINE ELMS - 70A	NINE ELMS - 70A
34021	EXMOUTH JCN - 72A	EXMOUTH JCN - 72A	EXMOUTH JCN - 72A	EXMOUTH JCN - 72A	EXMOUTH JCN - 72A	NINE ELMS - 70A	EXMOUTH JCN - 72A
34022	NINE ELMS - 70A	NINE ELMS - 70A	NINE ELMS - 70A	NINE ELMS - 70A	NINE ELMS - 70A	NINE ELMS - 70A	NINE ELMS - 70A
34023	EXMOUTH JCN - 72A	EXMOUTH JCN - 72A	EXMOUTH JCN - 72A	EXMOUTH JCN - 72A	EXMOUTH JCN - 72A	EXMOUTH JCN - 72A	EXMOUTH JCN - 72A
34024	NINE ELMS - 70A	NINE ELMS - 70A	NINE ELMS - 70A	NINE ELMS - 70A	NINE ELMS - 70A	NINE ELMS - 70A	NINE ELMS - 70A
34025	EXMOUTH JCN - 72A	EXMOUTH JCN - 72A	EXMOUTH JCN - 72A	EXMOUTH JCN - 72A	EXMOUTH JCN - 72A	EXMOUTH JCN - 72A	EXMOUTH JCN - 72A
34026	NINE ELMS - 70A	NINE ELMS - 70A	NINE ELMS - 70A	NINE ELMS - 70A	NINE ELMS - 70A	NINE ELMS - 70A	NINE ELMS - 70A
34027	NINE ELMS - 70A	NINE ELMS - 70A	NINE ELMS - 70A	NINE ELMS - 70A	NINE ELMS - 70A	NINE ELMS - 70A	NINE ELMS - 70A
34028	NINE ELMS - 70A	NINE ELMS - 70A	NINE ELMS - 70A	NINE ELMS - 70A	NINE ELMS - 70A	NINE ELMS - 70A	NINE ELMS - 70A
34029	EXMOUTH JCN - 72A	EXMOUTH JCN - 72A	EXMOUTH JCN - 72A	EXMOUTH JCN - 72A	EXMOUTH JCN - 72A	EXMOUTH JCN - 72A	EXMOUTH JCN - 72A
34030	NINE ELMS - 70A	NINE ELMS - 70A	NINE ELMS - 70A	NINE ELMS - 70A	NINE ELMS - 70A	NINE ELMS - 70A	NINE ELMS - 70A

West Country Pacifics continued in the following section

Apart from the number series and the nameplate, the only distinguishing feature between the Merchant Navy Pacifics and the West Country class was the marked bulbousness of the former when viewed from the front. In 1954, when the South Eastern possessed an allocation of 8P locomotives, 35030 'Elder Dempster Line' is seen being prepared at Stewarts Lane for the 21.00 Night Ferry from Victoria to Dover Marine.

loco	Jan-56	Apr-56	May-56	Aug-56	Oct-56	Nov-56	Jan-57
			MN 4-6-2 (1941)				
35001	EXMOUTH JCN - 72A	EXMOUTH JCN - 72A	EXMOUTH JCN - 72A	EXMOUTH JCN - 72A	EXMOUTH JCN - 72A	EXMOUTH JCN - 72A	STEWARTS LANE - 73A
35002	EXMOUTH JCN - 72A	EXMOUTH JCN - 72A	EXMOUTH JCN - 72A	EXMOUTH JCN - 72A	EXMOUTH JCN - 72A	EXMOUTH JCN - 72A	EXMOUTH JCN - 72A
35003	EXMOUTH JCN - 72A	EXMOUTH JCN - 72A	EXMOUTH JCN - 72A	EXMOUTH JCN - 72A	EXMOUTH JCN - 72A	EXMOUTH JCN - 72A	EXMOUTH JCN - 72A
35004	EXMOUTH JCN - 72A	EXMOUTH JCN - 72A	EXMOUTH JCN - 72A	EXMOUTH JCN - 72A	EXMOUTH JCN - 72A	EXMOUTH JCN - 72A	EXMOUTH JCN - 72A
35005	NINE ELMS - 70A	NINE ELMS - 70A	NINE ELMS - 70A	NINE ELMS - 70A	NINE ELMS - 70A	NINE ELMS - 70A	NINE ELMS - 70A
35006	SALISBURY - 72B	SALISBURY - 72B	SALISBURY - 72B	SALISBURY - 72B	SALISBURY - 72B	SALISBURY - 72B	SALISBURY - 72B
35007	SALISBURY - 72B	SALISBURY - 72B	SALISBURY - 72B	SALISBURY - 72B	SALISBURY - 72B	SALISBURY - 72B	SALISBURY - 72B
35008	EXMOUTH JCN - 72A	EXMOUTH JCN - 72A	EXMOUTH JCN - 72A	EXMOUTH JCN - 72A	EXMOUTH JCN - 72A	EXMOUTH JCN - 72A	EXMOUTH JCN - 72A
35009	SALISBURY - 72B	SALISBURY - 72B	SALISBURY - 72B	SALISBURY - 72B	SALISBURY - 72B	SALISBURY - 72B	SALISBURY - 72B
35010	BOURNEMOUTH - 71B	BOURNEMOUTH - 71B	BOURNEMOUTH - 71B	BOURNEMOUTH - 71B	BOURNEMOUTH - 71B	BOURNEMOUTH - 71B	R/B
35011	NINE ELMS - 70A	NINE ELMS - 70A	NINE ELMS - 70A	NINE ELMS - 70A	NINE ELMS - 70A	NINE ELMS - 70A	NINE ELMS - 70A
35012	NINE ELMS - 70A	NINE ELMS - 70A	NINE ELMS - 70A	NINE ELMS - 70A	NINE ELMS - 70A	NINE ELMS - 70A	NINE ELMS - 70A
35013	EXMOUTH JCN - 72A	EXMOUTH JCN - 72A	R/B	R/B	R/B	R/B	R/B
35014	STEWARTS LANE - 73A	STEWARTS LANE - 73A	NINE ELMS - 70A	R/B	R/B	R/B	R/B
35015	NINE ELMS - 70A	NINE ELMS - 70A	STEWARTS LANE - 73A	STEWARTS LANE - 73A	STEWARTS LANE - 73A	STEWARTS LANE - 73A	STEWARTS LANE - 73A
35016	NINE ELMS - 70A	NINE ELMS - 70A	NINE ELMS - 70A	NINE ELMS - 70A	NINE ELMS - 70A	NINE ELMS - 70A	NINE ELMS - 70A
35017	NINE ELMS - 70A	NINE ELMS - 70A	NINE ELMS - 70A	NINE ELMS - 70A	NINE ELMS - 70A	NINE ELMS - 70A	NINE ELMS - 70A
35018	NINE ELMS - 70A	R/B	R/B	R/B	R/B	R/B	R/B
35019	NINE ELMS - 70A	NINE ELMS - 70A	NINE ELMS - 70A	NINE ELMS - 70A	NINE ELMS - 70A	NINE ELMS - 70A	NINE ELMS - 70A
35020	NINE ELMS - 70A	R/B	R/B	R/B	R/B	R/B	R/B
35021	NINE ELMS - 70A	NINE ELMS - 70A	NINE ELMS - 70A	NINE ELMS - 70A	NINE ELMS - 70A	NINE ELMS - 70A	NINE ELMS - 70A
35022	BOURNEMOUTH - 71B	BOURNEMOUTH - 71B	BOURNEMOUTH - 71B	R/B	R/B	R/B	R/B
35023	EXMOUTH JCN - 72A	EXMOUTH JCN - 72A	EXMOUTH JCN - 72A	EXMOUTH JCN - 72A	EXMOUTH JCN - 72A	EXMOUTH JCN - 72A	EXMOUTH JCN - 72A
35024	EXMOUTH JCN - 72A	EXMOUTH JCN - 72A	EXMOUTH JCN - 72A	EXMOUTH JCN - 72A	EXMOUTH JCN - 72A	EXMOUTH JCN - 72A	EXMOUTH JCN - 72A
35025	NINE ELMS - 70A	NINE ELMS - 70A	BOURNEMOUTH - 71B	BOURNEMOUTH - 71B	BOURNEMOUTH - 71B	BOURNEMOUTH - 71B	R/B
35026	STEWARTS LANE - 73A	STEWARTS LANE - 73A	STEWARTS LANE - 73A	STEWARTS LANE - 73A	STEWARTS LANE - 73A	STEWARTS LANE - 73A	R/B
35027	BOURNEMOUTH - 71B	BOURNEMOUTH - 71B	BOURNEMOUTH - 71B	BOURNEMOUTH - 71B	BOURNEMOUTH - 71B	BOURNEMOUTH - 71B	BOURNEMOUTH - 71B
35028	STEWARTS LANE - 73A	STEWARTS LANE - 73A	STEWARTS LANE - 73A	STEWARTS LANE - 73A	STEWARTS LANE - 73A	STEWARTS LANE - 73A	STEWARTS LANE - 73A
35029	NINE ELMS - 70A	NINE ELMS - 70A	NINE ELMS - 70A	NINE ELMS - 70A	NINE ELMS - 70A	NINE ELMS - 70A	NINE ELMS - 70A
35030	NINE ELMS - 70A	NINE ELMS - 70A	NINE ELMS - 70A	NINE ELMS - 70A	NINE ELMS - 70A	NINE ELMS - 70A	NINE ELMS - 70A
			MN/R (1956)				
35001							
35002							
35003							
35004							
35005							
35006							
35007							
35008							
35009							
35010							BOURNEMOUTH - 71B
35011							
35012							
35013			EXMOUTH JCN - 72A	EXMOUTH JCN - 72A	EXMOUTH JCN - 72A	EXMOUTH JCN - 72A	EXMOUTH JCN - 72A
35014			NINE ELMS - 70A	NINE ELMS - 70A	NINE ELMS - 70A	NINE ELMS - 70A	NINE ELMS - 70A
35015							
35016							
35017							
35018		NINE ELMS - 70A	NINE ELMS - 70A	NINE ELMS - 70A	NINE ELMS - 70A	NINE ELMS - 70A	NINE ELMS - 70A
35019							
35020		NINE ELMS - 70A	NINE ELMS - 70A	NINE ELMS - 70A	NINE ELMS - 70A	NINE ELMS - 70A	NINE ELMS - 70A
35021							
35022				BOURNEMOUTH - 71B	BOURNEMOUTH - 71B	BOURNEMOUTH - 71B	BOURNEMOUTH - 71B
35023							
35024							
35025							BOURNEMOUTH - 71B
35026							EXMOUTH JCN - 72A
35027							
35028							
35029							
35030							
			WC 4-6-2 (1945)				
34001	EXMOUTH JCN - 72A	EXMOUTH JCN - 72A	EXMOUTH JCN - 72A	EXMOUTH JCN - 72A	EXMOUTH JCN - 72A	EXMOUTH JCN - 72A	EXMOUTH JCN - 72A
34002	EXMOUTH JCN - 72A	EXMOUTH JCN - 72A	EXMOUTH JCN - 72A	EXMOUTH JCN - 72A	EXMOUTH JCN - 72A	EXMOUTH JCN - 72A	EXMOUTH JCN - 72A
34003	EXMOUTH JCN - 72A	EXMOUTH JCN - 72A	EXMOUTH JCN - 72A	EXMOUTH JCN - 72A	EXMOUTH JCN - 72A	EXMOUTH JCN - 72A	EXMOUTH JCN - 72A
34004	EXMOUTH JCN - 72A	EXMOUTH JCN - 72A	EXMOUTH JCN - 72A	EXMOUTH JCN - 72A	EXMOUTH JCN - 72A	EXMOUTH JCN - 72A	EXMOUTH JCN - 72A
34005	NINE ELMS - 70A	NINE ELMS - 70A	NINE ELMS - 70A	NINE ELMS - 70A	NINE ELMS - 70A	NINE ELMS - 70A	NINE ELMS - 70A
34006	NINE ELMS - 70A	NINE ELMS - 70A	NINE ELMS - 70A	NINE ELMS - 70A	NINE ELMS - 70A	NINE ELMS - 70A	NINE ELMS - 70A
34007	NINE ELMS - 70A	NINE ELMS - 70A	NINE ELMS - 70A	NINE ELMS - 70A	NINE ELMS - 70A	NINE ELMS - 70A	NINE ELMS - 70A
34008	NINE ELMS - 70A	NINE ELMS - 70A	NINE ELMS - 70A	NINE ELMS - 70A	NINE ELMS - 70A	NINE ELMS - 70A	NINE ELMS - 70A
34009	NINE ELMS - 70A	NINE ELMS - 70A	NINE ELMS - 70A	NINE ELMS - 70A	NINE ELMS - 70A	NINE ELMS - 70A	NINE ELMS - 70A
34010	NINE ELMS - 70A	NINE ELMS - 70A	NINE ELMS - 70A	NINE ELMS - 70A	NINE ELMS - 70A	NINE ELMS - 70A	NINE ELMS - 70A
34011	NINE ELMS - 70A	NINE ELMS - 70A	NINE ELMS - 70A	NINE ELMS - 70A	NINE ELMS - 70A	NINE ELMS - 70A	NINE ELMS - 70A
34012	NINE ELMS - 70A	NINE ELMS - 70A	NINE ELMS - 70A	NINE ELMS - 70A	NINE ELMS - 70A	NINE ELMS - 70A	NINE ELMS - 70A
34013	PLYMOUTH - 72D	PLYMOUTH - 72D	PLYMOUTH - 72D	PLYMOUTH - 72D	PLYMOUTH - 72D	PLYMOUTH - 72D	PLYMOUTH - 72D
34014	EXMOUTH JCN - 72A	EXMOUTH JCN - 72A	EXMOUTH JCN - 72A	EXMOUTH JCN - 72A	EXMOUTH JCN - 72A	EXMOUTH JCN - 72A	EXMOUTH JCN - 72A
34015	EXMOUTH JCN - 72A	EXMOUTH JCN - 72A	EXMOUTH JCN - 72A	EXMOUTH JCN - 72A	EXMOUTH JCN - 72A	EXMOUTH JCN - 72A	EXMOUTH JCN - 72A
34016	EXMOUTH JCN - 72A	EXMOUTH JCN - 72A	EXMOUTH JCN - 72A	EXMOUTH JCN - 72A	EXMOUTH JCN - 72A	EXMOUTH JCN - 72A	EXMOUTH JCN - 72A
34017	STEWARTS LANE - 73A	STEWARTS LANE - 73A	STEWARTS LANE - 73A	STEWARTS LANE - 73A	STEWARTS LANE - 73A	STEWARTS LANE - 73A	STEWARTS LANE - 73A
34018	NINE ELMS - 70A	NINE ELMS - 70A	NINE ELMS - 70A	NINE ELMS - 70A	NINE ELMS - 70A	NINE ELMS - 70A	NINE ELMS - 70A
34019	NINE ELMS - 70A	NINE ELMS - 70A	NINE ELMS - 70A	NINE ELMS - 70A	NINE ELMS - 70A	NINE ELMS - 70A	NINE ELMS - 70A
34020	NINE ELMS - 70A	NINE ELMS - 70A	BOURNEMOUTH - 71B	BOURNEMOUTH - 71B	BOURNEMOUTH - 71B	BOURNEMOUTH - 71B	BOURNEMOUTH - 71B
34021	EXMOUTH JCN - 72A	EXMOUTH JCN - 72A	BOURNEMOUTH - 71B	BOURNEMOUTH - 71B	BOURNEMOUTH - 71B	BOURNEMOUTH - 71B	BOURNEMOUTH - 71B
34022	NINE ELMS - 70A	NINE ELMS - 70A	BOURNEMOUTH - 71B	BOURNEMOUTH - 71B	BOURNEMOUTH - 71B	BOURNEMOUTH - 71B	BOURNEMOUTH - 71B
34023	EXMOUTH JCN - 72A	EXMOUTH JCN - 72A	EXMOUTH JCN - 72A	EXMOUTH JCN - 72A	EXMOUTH JCN - 72A	EXMOUTH JCN - 72A	EXMOUTH JCN - 72A
34024	EXMOUTH JCN - 72A	EXMOUTH JCN - 72A	EXMOUTH JCN - 72A	EXMOUTH JCN - 72A	EXMOUTH JCN - 72A	EXMOUTH JCN - 72A	EXMOUTH JCN - 72A
34025	EXMOUTH JCN - 72A	EXMOUTH JCN - 72A	EXMOUTH JCN - 72A	EXMOUTH JCN - 72A	EXMOUTH JCN - 72A	EXMOUTH JCN - 72A	EXMOUTH JCN - 72A
34026	NINE ELMS - 70A	NINE ELMS - 70A	NINE ELMS - 70A	NINE ELMS - 70A	NINE ELMS - 70A	NINE ELMS - 70A	NINE ELMS - 70A
34027	NINE ELMS - 70A	NINE ELMS - 70A	NINE ELMS - 70A	NINE ELMS - 70A	NINE ELMS - 70A	NINE ELMS - 70A	NINE ELMS - 70A
34028	NINE ELMS - 70A	NINE ELMS - 70A	NINE ELMS - 70A	NINE ELMS - 70A	NINE ELMS - 70A	NINE ELMS - 70A	NINE ELMS - 70A
34029	EXMOUTH JCN - 72A	EXMOUTH JCN - 72A	EXMOUTH JCN - 72A	EXMOUTH JCN - 72A	EXMOUTH JCN - 72A	EXMOUTH JCN - 72A	EXMOUTH JCN - 72A
34030	NINE ELMS - 70A	NINE ELMS - 70A	NINE ELMS - 70A	NINE ELMS - 70A	NINE ELMS - 70A	NINE ELMS - 70A	NINE ELMS - 70A

West Country Pacifics continued in the following section

loco	Mar-57	Jun-57	Jul-57	Oct-57	Jan-58	Feb-58	Mar-58
				MN 4-6-2 (1941)			
35001	STEWARTS LANE - 73A	STEWARTS LANE - 73A	STEWARTS LANE - 73A	STEWARTS LANE - 73A	STEWARTS LANE - 73A	STEWARTS LANE - 73A	STEWARTS LANE - 73A
35002	EXMOUTH JCN - 72A	EXMOUTH JCN - 72A	EXMOUTH JCN - 72A	EXMOUTH JCN - 72A	EXMOUTH JCN - 72A	EXMOUTH JCN - 72A	EXMOUTH JCN - 72A
35003	EXMOUTH JCN - 72A	EXMOUTH JCN - 72A	EXMOUTH JCN - 72A	EXMOUTH JCN - 72A	EXMOUTH JCN - 72A	EXMOUTH JCN - 72A	EXMOUTH JCN - 72A
35004	SALISBURY - 72B	SALISBURY - 72B	SALISBURY - 72B	SALISBURY - 72B	SALISBURY - 72B	SALISBURY - 72B	SALISBURY - 72B
35005	NINE ELMS - 70A	NINE ELMS - 70A	NINE ELMS - 70A	NINE ELMS - 70A	NINE ELMS - 70A	NINE ELMS - 70A	NINE ELMS - 70A
35006	SALISBURY - 72B	SALISBURY - 72B	SALISBURY - 72B	SALISBURY - 72B	SALISBURY - 72B	SALISBURY - 72B	SALISBURY - 72B
35007	SALISBURY - 72B	SALISBURY - 72B	SALISBURY - 72B	SALISBURY - 72B	SALISBURY - 72B	SALISBURY - 72B	SALISBURY - 72B
35008	EXMOUTH JCN - 72A	R/B	R/B	R/B	R/B	R/B	R/B
35011	NINE ELMS - 70A	EXMOUTH JCN - 72A	EXMOUTH JCN - 72A	EXMOUTH JCN - 72A	EXMOUTH JCN - 72A	EXMOUTH JCN - 72A	EXMOUTH JCN - 72A
35015	STEWARTS LANE - 73A	STEWARTS LANE - 73A	STEWARTS LANE - 73A	STEWARTS LANE - 73A	STEWARTS LANE - 73A	STEWARTS LANE - 73A	STEWARTS LANE - 73A
35016	NINE ELMS - 70A	R/B	R/B	R/B	R/B	R/B	R/B
35019	NINE ELMS - 70A	NINE ELMS - 70A	NINE ELMS - 70A	NINE ELMS - 70A	NINE ELMS - 70A	NINE ELMS - 70A	NINE ELMS - 70A
35021	NINE ELMS - 70A	BOURNEMOUTH - 71B	BOURNEMOUTH - 71B	BOURNEMOUTH - 71B	BOURNEMOUTH - 71B	BOURNEMOUTH - 71B	BOURNEMOUTH - 71B
35024	EXMOUTH JCN - 72A	EXMOUTH JCN - 72A	EXMOUTH JCN - 72A	EXMOUTH JCN - 72A	EXMOUTH JCN - 72A	EXMOUTH JCN - 72A	EXMOUTH JCN - 72A
35027	BOURNEMOUTH - 71B	R/B	R/B	R/B	R/B	R/B	R/B
35028	STEWARTS LANE - 73A	STEWARTS LANE - 73A	STEWARTS LANE - 73A	STEWARTS LANE - 73A	STEWARTS LANE - 73A	STEWARTS LANE - 73A	STEWARTS LANE - 73A
35029	NINE ELMS - 70A	NINE ELMS - 70A	NINE ELMS - 70A	NINE ELMS - 70A	NINE ELMS - 70A	NINE ELMS - 70A	NINE ELMS - 70A
35030	NINE ELMS - 70A	NINE ELMS - 70A	NINE ELMS - 70A	NINE ELMS - 70A	NINE ELMS - 70A	NINE ELMS - 70A	NINE ELMS - 70A
				MN/R (1956)			
35008		EXMOUTH JCN - 72A	EXMOUTH JCN - 72A	EXMOUTH JCN - 72A	EXMOUTH JCN - 72A	EXMOUTH JCN - 72A	EXMOUTH JCN - 72A
35009	EXMOUTH JCN - 72A	EXMOUTH JCN - 72A	EXMOUTH JCN - 72A	EXMOUTH JCN - 72A	EXMOUTH JCN - 72A	EXMOUTH JCN - 72A	EXMOUTH JCN - 72A
35010	BOURNEMOUTH - 71B	BOURNEMOUTH - 71B	BOURNEMOUTH - 71B	BOURNEMOUTH - 71B	BOURNEMOUTH - 71B	BOURNEMOUTH - 71B	BOURNEMOUTH - 71B
35012	NINE ELMS - 70A	NINE ELMS - 70A	NINE ELMS - 70A	NINE ELMS - 70A	NINE ELMS - 70A	NINE ELMS - 70A	NINE ELMS - 70A
35013	EXMOUTH JCN - 72A	EXMOUTH JCN - 72A	EXMOUTH JCN - 72A	EXMOUTH JCN - 72A	EXMOUTH JCN - 72A	EXMOUTH JCN - 72A	EXMOUTH JCN - 72A
35014	NINE ELMS - 70A	NINE ELMS - 70A	NINE ELMS - 70A	NINE ELMS - 70A	NINE ELMS - 70A	NINE ELMS - 70A	NINE ELMS - 70A
35016		NINE ELMS - 70A	NINE ELMS - 70A	NINE ELMS - 70A	NINE ELMS - 70A	NINE ELMS - 70A	NINE ELMS - 70A
35017	NINE ELMS - 70A	NINE ELMS - 70A	NINE ELMS - 70A	NINE ELMS - 70A	NINE ELMS - 70A	NINE ELMS - 70A	NINE ELMS - 70A
35018	NINE ELMS - 70A	NINE ELMS - 70A	NINE ELMS - 70A	NINE ELMS - 70A	NINE ELMS - 70A	NINE ELMS - 70A	NINE ELMS - 70A
35020	NINE ELMS - 70A	NINE ELMS - 70A	NINE ELMS - 70A	NINE ELMS - 70A	NINE ELMS - 70A	NINE ELMS - 70A	NINE ELMS - 70A
35022	BOURNEMOUTH - 71B	BOURNEMOUTH - 71B	BOURNEMOUTH - 71B	BOURNEMOUTH - 71B	BOURNEMOUTH - 71B	BOURNEMOUTH - 71B	BOURNEMOUTH - 71B
35023	EXMOUTH JCN - 72A	EXMOUTH JCN - 72A	EXMOUTH JCN - 72A	EXMOUTH JCN - 72A	EXMOUTH JCN - 72A	EXMOUTH JCN - 72A	EXMOUTH JCN - 72A
35025	BOURNEMOUTH - 71B	BOURNEMOUTH - 71B	BOURNEMOUTH - 71B	BOURNEMOUTH - 71B	BOURNEMOUTH - 71B	BOURNEMOUTH - 71B	BOURNEMOUTH - 71B
35026	EXMOUTH JCN - 72A	BOURNEMOUTH - 71B	BOURNEMOUTH - 71B	BOURNEMOUTH - 71B	BOURNEMOUTH - 71B	BOURNEMOUTH - 71B	BOURNEMOUTH - 71B
35027		BOURNEMOUTH - 71B	BOURNEMOUTH - 71B	BOURNEMOUTH - 71B	BOURNEMOUTH - 71B	BOURNEMOUTH - 71B	BOURNEMOUTH - 71B
				WC 4-6-2 (1945)			
34001	EXMOUTH JCN - 72A	EXMOUTH JCN - 72A	EXMOUTH JCN - 72A	B.ARMS - 73B	R/B	R/B	R/B
34002	EXMOUTH JCN - 72A	EXMOUTH JCN - 72A	EXMOUTH JCN - 72A	EXMOUTH JCN - 72A	EXMOUTH JCN - 72A	EXMOUTH JCN - 72A	EXMOUTH JCN - 72A
34003	EXMOUTH JCN - 72A	EXMOUTH JCN - 72A	EXMOUTH JCN - 72A	R/B	R/B	R/B	R/B
34004	EXMOUTH JCN - 72A	EXMOUTH JCN - 72A	EXMOUTH JCN - 72A	EXMOUTH JCN - 72A	EXMOUTH JCN - 72A	R/B	R/B
34005	NINE ELMS - 70A	R/B	R/B	R/B	R/B	R/B	R/B
34006	NINE ELMS - 70A	NINE ELMS - 70A	NINE ELMS - 70A	NINE ELMS - 70A	NINE ELMS - 70A	NINE ELMS - 70A	NINE ELMS - 70A
34007	NINE ELMS - 70A	NINE ELMS - 70A	NINE ELMS - 70A	NINE ELMS - 70A	NINE ELMS - 70A	NINE ELMS - 70A	NINE ELMS - 70A
34008	NINE ELMS - 70A	NINE ELMS - 70A	NINE ELMS - 70A	NINE ELMS - 70A	NINE ELMS - 70A	NINE ELMS - 70A	NINE ELMS - 70A
34009	NINE ELMS - 70A	NINE ELMS - 70A	NINE ELMS - 70A	NINE ELMS - 70A	NINE ELMS - 70A	NINE ELMS - 70A	NINE ELMS - 70A
34010	NINE ELMS - 70A	NINE ELMS - 70A	NINE ELMS - 70A	NINE ELMS - 70A	NINE ELMS - 70A	NINE ELMS - 70A	NINE ELMS - 70A
34011	NINE ELMS - 70A	NINE ELMS - 70A	NINE ELMS - 70A	NINE ELMS - 70A	NINE ELMS - 70A	NINE ELMS - 70A	NINE ELMS - 70A
34012	NINE ELMS - 70A	NINE ELMS - 70A	NINE ELMS - 70A	NINE ELMS - 70A	R/B	R/B	R/B
34013	PLYMOUTH - 72D	PLYMOUTH - 72D	PLYMOUTH - 72D	R/B	R/B	R/B	R/B
34014	EXMOUTH JCN - 72A	EXMOUTH JCN - 72A	EXMOUTH JCN - 72A	R/B	R/B	R/B	B.ARMS - 73B
34015	EXMOUTH JCN - 72A	EXMOUTH JCN - 72A	EXMOUTH JCN - 72A	EXMOUTH JCN - 72A	EXMOUTH JCN - 72A	EXMOUTH JCN - 72A	EXMOUTH JCN - 72A
34016	EXMOUTH JCN - 72A	EXMOUTH JCN - 72A	EXMOUTH JCN - 72A	EXMOUTH JCN - 72A	EXMOUTH JCN - 72A	RAMSGATE - 74B	R/B
34017	STEWARTS LANE - 73A	STEWARTS LANE - 73A	STEWARTS LANE - 73A	B.ARMS - 73B	R/B	R/B	R/B
34018	NINE ELMS - 70A	NINE ELMS - 70A	NINE ELMS - 70A	NINE ELMS - 70A	NINE ELMS - 70A	NINE ELMS - 70A	NINE ELMS - 70A
34019	NINE ELMS - 70A	NINE ELMS - 70A	NINE ELMS - 70A	NINE ELMS - 70A	NINE ELMS - 70A	NINE ELMS - 70A	NINE ELMS - 70A
34020	BOURNEMOUTH - 71B	BOURNEMOUTH - 71B	BOURNEMOUTH - 71B	BOURNEMOUTH - 71B	BOURNEMOUTH - 71B	BOURNEMOUTH - 71B	BOURNEMOUTH - 71B
34021	BOURNEMOUTH - 71B	BOURNEMOUTH - 71B	BOURNEMOUTH - 71B	R/B	R/B	R/B	R/B
34022	BOURNEMOUTH - 71B	BOURNEMOUTH - 71B	BOURNEMOUTH - 71B	R/B	R/B	R/B	R/B
34023	EXMOUTH JCN - 72A	EXMOUTH JCN - 72A	EXMOUTH JCN - 72A	EXMOUTH JCN - 72A	EXMOUTH JCN - 72A	EXMOUTH JCN - 72A	EXMOUTH JCN - 72A
34024	EXMOUTH JCN - 72A	EXMOUTH JCN - 72A	EXMOUTH JCN - 72A	EXMOUTH JCN - 72A	EXMOUTH JCN - 72A	EXMOUTH JCN - 72A	EXMOUTH JCN - 72A
34025	EXMOUTH JCN - 72A	EXMOUTH JCN - 72A	EXMOUTH JCN - 72A	R/B	R/B	R/B	R/B
34026	NINE ELMS - 70A	NINE ELMS - 70A	NINE ELMS - 70A	NINE ELMS - 70A	NINE ELMS - 70A	R/B	R/B
34027	NINE ELMS - 70A	NINE ELMS - 70A	NINE ELMS - 70A	R/B	R/B	R/B	R/B
34028	NINE ELMS - 70A	NINE ELMS - 70A	NINE ELMS - 70A	NINE ELMS - 70A	NINE ELMS - 70A	NINE ELMS - 70A	NINE ELMS - 70A
34029	EXMOUTH JCN - 72A	EXMOUTH JCN - 72A	EXMOUTH JCN - 72A	EXMOUTH JCN - 72A	EXMOUTH JCN - 72A	EXMOUTH JCN - 72A	EXMOUTH JCN - 72A
34030	NINE ELMS - 70A	NINE ELMS - 70A	NINE ELMS - 70A	NINE ELMS - 70A	NINE ELMS - 70A	NINE ELMS - 70A	NINE ELMS - 70A
				WC/R 4-6-2 (1957)			
34001					B.ARMS - 73B	B.ARMS - 73B	B.ARMS - 73B
34003				B.ARMS - 73B	B.ARMS - 73B	B.ARMS - 73B	B.ARMS - 73B
34004						B.ARMS - 73B	B.ARMS - 73B
34005		STEWARTS LANE - 73A	STEWARTS LANE - 73A	STEWARTS LANE - 73A	B.ARMS - 73B	B.ARMS - 73B	B.ARMS - 73B
34012					NINE ELMS - 70A	B.ARMS - 73B	B.ARMS - 73B
34013				B.ARMS - 73B	B.ARMS - 73B	B.ARMS - 73B	B.ARMS - 73B
34014							B.ARMS - 73B
34017					B.ARMS - 73B	RAMSGATE - 74B	RAMSGATE - 74B
34021					RAMSGATE - 74B	RAMSGATE - 74B	RAMSGATE - 74B
34022					RAMSGATE - 74B	RAMSGATE - 74B	RAMSGATE - 74B
34025				B.ARMS - 73B	B.ARMS - 73B	RAMSGATE - 74B	RAMSGATE - 74B
34026						RAMSGATE - 74B	RAMSGATE - 74B
34027				B.ARMS - 73B	B.ARMS - 73B	RAMSGATE - 74B	RAMSGATE - 74B

West Country Pacifics continued in the following section

loco	May-58	Oct-58	Mar-59	Jun-59	Jul-59	Aug-59	Oct-59
				MN 4-6-2 (1941)			
35001	STEWARTS LANE - 73A	STEWARTS LANE - 73A	STEWARTS LANE - 73A	NINE ELMS - 70A	NINE ELMS - 70A	R/B	R/B
35003	EXMOUTH JCN - 72A	EXMOUTH JCN - 72A	EXMOUTH JCN - 72A	EXMOUTH JCN - 72A	EXMOUTH JCN - 72A	R/B	R/B
35004	SALISBURY - 72B	R/B	R/B	R/B	R/B	R/B	R/B
35005	NINE ELMS - 70A	NINE ELMS - 70A	NINE ELMS - 70A	R/B	R/B	R/B	R/B
35006	SALISBURY - 72B	SALISBURY - 72B	SALISBURY - 72B	SALISBURY - 72B	SALISBURY - 72B	SALISBURY - 72B	R/B
35011	EXMOUTH JCN - 72A	EXMOUTH JCN - 72A	R/B	R/B	R/B	R/B	R/B
35015	STEWARTS LANE - 73A	R/B	R/B	R/B	R/B	R/B	R/B
35019	NINE ELMS - 70A	NINE ELMS - 70A	NINE ELMS - 70A	R/B	R/B	R/B	R/B
35021	BOURNEMOUTH - 71B	BOURNEMOUTH - 71B	BOURNEMOUTH - 71B	R/B	R/B	R/B	R/B
35024	EXMOUTH JCN - 72A	EXMOUTH JCN - 72A	EXMOUTH JCN - 72A	R/B	R/B	R/B	R/B
35028	STEWARTS LANE - 73A	STEWARTS LANE - 73A	STEWARTS LANE - 73A	NINE ELMS - 70A	NINE ELMS - 70A	NINE ELMS - 70A	R/B
35029	NINE ELMS - 70A	NINE ELMS - 70A	NINE ELMS - 70A	NINE ELMS - 70A	NINE ELMS - 70A	NINE ELMS - 70A	R/B
				MN/R (1956)			
35001						NINE ELMS - 70A	NINE ELMS - 70A
35002	BOURNEMOUTH - 71B	BOURNEMOUTH - 71B	BOURNEMOUTH - 71B	BOURNEMOUTH - 71B	BOURNEMOUTH - 71B	BOURNEMOUTH - 71B	BOURNEMOUTH - 71B
35003						EXMOUTH JCN - 72A	EXMOUTH JCN - 72A
35004		SALISBURY - 72B	SALISBURY - 72B	SALISBURY - 72B	SALISBURY - 72B	SALISBURY - 72B	SALISBURY - 72B
35005				NINE ELMS - 70A	NINE ELMS - 70A	NINE ELMS - 70A	NINE ELMS - 70A
35006							SALISBURY - 72B
35007	SALISBURY - 72B	SALISBURY - 72B	SALISBURY - 72B	SALISBURY - 72B	SALISBURY - 72B	SALISBURY - 72B	SALISBURY - 72B
35008	EXMOUTH JCN - 72A	EXMOUTH JCN - 72A	EXMOUTH JCN - 72A	EXMOUTH JCN - 72A	EXMOUTH JCN - 72A	EXMOUTH JCN - 72A	EXMOUTH JCN - 72A
35009	EXMOUTH JCN - 72A	EXMOUTH JCN - 72A	EXMOUTH JCN - 72A	EXMOUTH JCN - 72A	EXMOUTH JCN - 72A	EXMOUTH JCN - 72A	EXMOUTH JCN - 72A
35010	BOURNEMOUTH - 71B	BOURNEMOUTH - 71B	BOURNEMOUTH - 71B	BOURNEMOUTH - 71B	BOURNEMOUTH - 71B	BOURNEMOUTH - 71B	BOURNEMOUTH - 71B
35011		EXMOUTH JCN - 72A	EXMOUTH JCN - 72A	EXMOUTH JCN - 72A	EXMOUTH JCN - 72A	EXMOUTH JCN - 72A	EXMOUTH JCN - 72A
35012	NINE ELMS - 70A	NINE ELMS - 70A	NINE ELMS - 70A	NINE ELMS - 70A	NINE ELMS - 70A	NINE ELMS - 70A	NINE ELMS - 70A
35013	EXMOUTH JCN - 72A	EXMOUTH JCN - 72A	EXMOUTH JCN - 72A	EXMOUTH JCN - 72A	EXMOUTH JCN - 72A	EXMOUTH JCN - 72A	EXMOUTH JCN - 72A
35014	NINE ELMS - 70A	NINE ELMS - 70A	NINE ELMS - 70A	NINE ELMS - 70A	NINE ELMS - 70A	NINE ELMS - 70A	NINE ELMS - 70A
35015		STEWARTS LANE - 73A	STEWARTS LANE - 73A	NINE ELMS - 70A	NINE ELMS - 70A	NINE ELMS - 70A	NINE ELMS - 70A
35016	NINE ELMS - 70A	NINE ELMS - 70A	NINE ELMS - 70A	NINE ELMS - 70A	NINE ELMS - 70A	NINE ELMS - 70A	NINE ELMS - 70A
35017	NINE ELMS - 70A	NINE ELMS - 70A	NINE ELMS - 70A	NINE ELMS - 70A	NINE ELMS - 70A	NINE ELMS - 70A	NINE ELMS - 70A
35018	NINE ELMS - 70A	NINE ELMS - 70A	NINE ELMS - 70A	NINE ELMS - 70A	NINE ELMS - 70A	NINE ELMS - 70A	NINE ELMS - 70A
35019				NINE ELMS - 70A	NINE ELMS - 70A	NINE ELMS - 70A	NINE ELMS - 70A
35020	NINE ELMS - 70A	NINE ELMS - 70A	NINE ELMS - 70A	NINE ELMS - 70A	NINE ELMS - 70A	NINE ELMS - 70A	NINE ELMS - 70A
35021				BOURNEMOUTH - 71B	BOURNEMOUTH - 71B	BOURNEMOUTH - 71B	BOURNEMOUTH - 71B
35022	BOURNEMOUTH - 71B	BOURNEMOUTH - 71B	BOURNEMOUTH - 71B	BOURNEMOUTH - 71B	BOURNEMOUTH - 71B	BOURNEMOUTH - 71B	BOURNEMOUTH - 71B
35023	EXMOUTH JCN - 72A	EXMOUTH JCN - 72A	EXMOUTH JCN - 72A	EXMOUTH JCN - 72A	EXMOUTH JCN - 72A	EXMOUTH JCN - 72A	EXMOUTH JCN - 72A
35024				EXMOUTH JCN - 72A	EXMOUTH JCN - 72A	EXMOUTH JCN - 72A	EXMOUTH JCN - 72A
35025	BOURNEMOUTH - 71B	BOURNEMOUTH - 71B	BOURNEMOUTH - 71B	BOURNEMOUTH - 71B	BOURNEMOUTH - 71B	BOURNEMOUTH - 71B	BOURNEMOUTH - 71B
35026	BOURNEMOUTH - 71B	BOURNEMOUTH - 71B	BOURNEMOUTH - 71B	BOURNEMOUTH - 71B	BOURNEMOUTH - 71B	BOURNEMOUTH - 71B	BOURNEMOUTH - 71B
35027	BOURNEMOUTH - 71B	BOURNEMOUTH - 71B	BOURNEMOUTH - 71B	BOURNEMOUTH - 71B	BOURNEMOUTH - 71B	BOURNEMOUTH - 71B	BOURNEMOUTH - 71B
35028							NINE ELMS - 70A
35029							NINE ELMS - 70A
35030	NINE ELMS - 70A	NINE ELMS - 70A	NINE ELMS - 70A	NINE ELMS - 70A	NINE ELMS - 70A	NINE ELMS - 70A	NINE ELMS - 70A
				WC 4-6-2 (1945)			
34002	EXMOUTH JCN - 72A	EXMOUTH JCN - 72A	EXMOUTH JCN - 72A	EXMOUTH JCN - 72A	EXMOUTH JCN - 72A	EXMOUTH JCN - 72A	EXMOUTH JCN - 72A
34006	NINE ELMS - 70A	NINE ELMS - 70A	NINE ELMS - 70A	NINE ELMS - 70A	NINE ELMS - 70A	NINE ELMS - 70A	NINE ELMS - 70A
34007	NINE ELMS - 70A	NINE ELMS - 70A	NINE ELMS - 70A	NINE ELMS - 70A	NINE ELMS - 70A	NINE ELMS - 70A	NINE ELMS - 70A
34008	NINE ELMS - 70A	BRIGHTON - 75A	BRIGHTON - 75A	BRIGHTON - 75A	BRIGHTON - 75A	BRIGHTON - 75A	BRIGHTON - 75A
34009	NINE ELMS - 70A	NINE ELMS - 70A	NINE ELMS - 70A	NINE ELMS - 70A	NINE ELMS - 70A	NINE ELMS - 70A	NINE ELMS - 70A
34010	NINE ELMS - 70A	NINE ELMS - 70A	R/B	R/B	R/B	R/B	R/B
34011	NINE ELMS - 70A	NINE ELMS - 70A	EXMOUTH JCN - 72A	EXMOUTH JCN - 72A	EXMOUTH JCN - 72A	EXMOUTH JCN - 72A	EXMOUTH JCN - 72A
34015	EXMOUTH JCN - 72A	EXMOUTH JCN - 72A	EXMOUTH JCN - 72A	EXMOUTH JCN - 72A	EXMOUTH JCN - 72A	EXMOUTH JCN - 72A	EXMOUTH JCN - 72A
34018	NINE ELMS - 70A	R/B	R/B	R/B	R/B	R/B	R/B
34019	NINE ELMS - 70A	BRIGHTON - 75A	BRIGHTON - 75A	BRIGHTON - 75A	BRIGHTON - 75A	BRIGHTON - 75A	BRIGHTON - 75A
34020	BOURNEMOUTH - 71B	BOURNEMOUTH - 71B	BOURNEMOUTH - 71B	BOURNEMOUTH - 71B	BOURNEMOUTH - 71B	BOURNEMOUTH - 71B	BOURNEMOUTH - 71B
34023	EXMOUTH JCN - 72A	EXMOUTH JCN - 72A	EXMOUTH JCN - 72A	EXMOUTH JCN - 72A	EXMOUTH JCN - 72A	EXMOUTH JCN - 72A	EXMOUTH JCN - 72A
34024	EXMOUTH JCN - 72A	EXMOUTH JCN - 72A	EXMOUTH JCN - 72A	EXMOUTH JCN - 72A	EXMOUTH JCN - 72A	EXMOUTH JCN - 72A	EXMOUTH JCN - 72A
34028	NINE ELMS - 70A	R/B	R/B	R/B	R/B	R/B	R/B
34029	EXMOUTH JCN - 72A	EXMOUTH JCN - 72A	R/B	R/B	R/B	R/B	R/B
34030	NINE ELMS - 70A	NINE ELMS - 70A	NINE ELMS - 70A	NINE ELMS - 70A	NINE ELMS - 70A	NINE ELMS - 70A	NINE ELMS - 70A
				WC/R 4-6-2 (1957)			
34001	B.ARMS - 73B	B.ARMS - 73B	B.ARMS - 73B	B.ARMS - 73B	B.ARMS - 73B	B.ARMS - 73B	B.ARMS - 73B
34003	B.ARMS - 73B	B.ARMS - 73B	B.ARMS - 73B	B.ARMS - 73B	B.ARMS - 73B	B.ARMS - 73B	B.ARMS - 73B
34004	B.ARMS - 73B	B.ARMS - 73B	B.ARMS - 73B	B.ARMS - 73B	B.ARMS - 73B	B.ARMS - 73B	B.ARMS - 73B
34005	B.ARMS - 73B	B.ARMS - 73B	B.ARMS - 73B	B.ARMS - 73B	B.ARMS - 73B	B.ARMS - 73B	B.ARMS - 73B
34010		NINE ELMS - 70A	NINE ELMS - 70A	NINE ELMS - 70A	NINE ELMS - 70A	NINE ELMS - 70A	NINE ELMS - 70A
34012	B.ARMS - 73B	B.ARMS - 73B	B.ARMS - 73B	B.ARMS - 73B	B.ARMS - 73B	B.ARMS - 73B	B.ARMS - 73B
34013	B.ARMS - 73B	B.ARMS - 73B	B.ARMS - 73B	B.ARMS - 73B	B.ARMS - 73B	B.ARMS - 73B	B.ARMS - 73B
34014	B.ARMS - 73B	B.ARMS - 73B	B.ARMS - 73B	B.ARMS - 73B	B.ARMS - 73B	B.ARMS - 73B	B.ARMS - 73B
34016	RAMSGATE - 74B	RAMSGATE - 73G	RAMSGATE - 73G	B.ARMS - 73B	B.ARMS - 73B	B.ARMS - 73B	B.ARMS - 73B
34017	RAMSGATE - 74B	RAMSGATE - 73G	RAMSGATE - 73G	B.ARMS - 73B	B.ARMS - 73B	B.ARMS - 73B	B.ARMS - 73B
34018		NINE ELMS - 70A	NINE ELMS - 70A	NINE ELMS - 70A	NINE ELMS - 70A	NINE ELMS - 70A	NINE ELMS - 70A
34021	RAMSGATE - 74B	RAMSGATE - 73G	RAMSGATE - 73G	B.ARMS - 73B	B.ARMS - 73B	B.ARMS - 73B	B.ARMS - 73B
34022	RAMSGATE - 74B	RAMSGATE - 73G	RAMSGATE - 73G	B.ARMS - 73B	B.ARMS - 73B	B.ARMS - 73B	B.ARMS - 73B
34025	RAMSGATE - 74B	RAMSGATE - 73G	RAMSGATE - 73G	B.ARMS - 73B	B.ARMS - 73B	B.ARMS - 73B	B.ARMS - 73B
34026	RAMSGATE - 74B	RAMSGATE - 73G	RAMSGATE - 73G	B.ARMS - 73B	B.ARMS - 73B	B.ARMS - 73B	B.ARMS - 73B
34027	RAMSGATE - 74B	RAMSGATE - 73G	RAMSGATE - 73G	B.ARMS - 73B	B.ARMS - 73B	B.ARMS - 73B	B.ARMS - 73B
34028		NINE ELMS - 70A	BOURNEMOUTH - 71B	BOURNEMOUTH - 71B	BOURNEMOUTH - 71B	BOURNEMOUTH - 71B	BOURNEMOUTH - 71B
34029			NINE ELMS - 70A	BOURNEMOUTH - 71B	BOURNEMOUTH - 71B	BOURNEMOUTH - 71B	BOURNEMOUTH - 71B

West Country Pacifics continued in the following section

loco	Dec-59	Feb-60	Mar-60	Apr-60	Jul-60	Aug-60	Sep-60	Nov-60
MN/R (1956)								
35001	NINE ELMS - 70A	NINE ELMS - 70A	NINE ELMS - 70A	NINE ELMS - 70A	NINE ELMS - 70A	NINE ELMS - 70A	NINE ELMS - 70A	NINE ELMS - 70A
35002	BOURNEMOUTH - 71B	BOURNEMOUTH - 71B	BOURNEMOUTH - 71B	BOURNEMOUTH - 71B	BOURNEMOUTH - 71B	BOURNEMOUTH - 71B	BOURNEMOUTH - 71B	NINE ELMS - 70A
35003	EXMOUTH JCN - 72A	EXMOUTH JCN - 72A	EXMOUTH JCN - 72A	EXMOUTH JCN - 72A	EXMOUTH JCN - 72A	EXMOUTH JCN - 72A	EXMOUTH JCN - 72A	EXMOUTH JCN - 72A
35004	SALISBURY - 72B	SALISBURY - 72B	SALISBURY - 72B	SALISBURY - 72B	SALISBURY - 72B	SALISBURY - 72B	SALISBURY - 72B	SALISBURY - 72B
35005	BOURNEMOUTH - 71B	BOURNEMOUTH - 71B	BOURNEMOUTH - 71B	BOURNEMOUTH - 71B	BOURNEMOUTH - 71B	BOURNEMOUTH - 71B	BOURNEMOUTH - 71B	BOURNEMOUTH - 71B
35006	SALISBURY - 72B	SALISBURY - 72B	SALISBURY - 72B	SALISBURY - 72B	SALISBURY - 72B	SALISBURY - 72B	SALISBURY - 72B	SALISBURY - 72B
35007	SALISBURY - 72B	SALISBURY - 72B	SALISBURY - 72B	SALISBURY - 72B	SALISBURY - 72B	SALISBURY - 72B	SALISBURY - 72B	SALISBURY - 72B
35008	EXMOUTH JCN - 72A	BOURNEMOUTH - 71B	BOURNEMOUTH - 71B	BOURNEMOUTH - 71B	BOURNEMOUTH - 71B	BOURNEMOUTH - 71B	BOURNEMOUTH - 71B	BOURNEMOUTH - 71B
35009	EXMOUTH JCN - 72A	EXMOUTH JCN - 72A	EXMOUTH JCN - 72A	EXMOUTH JCN - 72A	EXMOUTH JCN - 72A	EXMOUTH JCN - 72A	EXMOUTH JCN - 72A	EXMOUTH JCN - 72A
35010	BOURNEMOUTH - 71B	EXMOUTH JCN - 72A	EXMOUTH JCN - 72A	EXMOUTH JCN - 72A	EXMOUTH JCN - 72A	EXMOUTH JCN - 72A	EXMOUTH JCN - 72A	EXMOUTH JCN - 72A
35011	EXMOUTH JCN - 72A	BOURNEMOUTH - 71B	BOURNEMOUTH - 71B	BOURNEMOUTH - 71B	BOURNEMOUTH - 71B	BOURNEMOUTH - 71B	BOURNEMOUTH - 71B	BOURNEMOUTH - 71B
35012	NINE ELMS - 70A	NINE ELMS - 70A	NINE ELMS - 70A	NINE ELMS - 70A	NINE ELMS - 70A	NINE ELMS - 70A	NINE ELMS - 70A	NINE ELMS - 70A
35013	EXMOUTH JCN - 72A	EXMOUTH JCN - 72A	EXMOUTH JCN - 72A	EXMOUTH JCN - 72A	EXMOUTH JCN - 72A	EXMOUTH JCN - 72A	EXMOUTH JCN - 72A	EXMOUTH JCN - 72A
35014	NINE ELMS - 70A	NINE ELMS - 70A	NINE ELMS - 70A	NINE ELMS - 70A	NINE ELMS - 70A	NINE ELMS - 70A	NINE ELMS - 70A	NINE ELMS - 70A
35015	NINE ELMS - 70A	NINE ELMS - 70A	NINE ELMS - 70A	NINE ELMS - 70A	NINE ELMS - 70A	NINE ELMS - 70A	NINE ELMS - 70A	NINE ELMS - 70A
35016	NINE ELMS - 70A	NINE ELMS - 70A	NINE ELMS - 70A	NINE ELMS - 70A	NINE ELMS - 70A	NINE ELMS - 70A	NINE ELMS - 70A	NINE ELMS - 70A
35017	NINE ELMS - 70A	NINE ELMS - 70A	NINE ELMS - 70A	NINE ELMS - 70A	NINE ELMS - 70A	NINE ELMS - 70A	NINE ELMS - 70A	NINE ELMS - 70A
35018	NINE ELMS - 70A	NINE ELMS - 70A	NINE ELMS - 70A	NINE ELMS - 70A	NINE ELMS - 70A	NINE ELMS - 70A	NINE ELMS - 70A	BOURNEMOUTH - 71B
35019	NINE ELMS - 70A	NINE ELMS - 70A	NINE ELMS - 70A	NINE ELMS - 70A	NINE ELMS - 70A	NINE ELMS - 70A	NINE ELMS - 70A	NINE ELMS - 70A
35020	NINE ELMS - 70A	NINE ELMS - 70A	NINE ELMS - 70A	NINE ELMS - 70A	NINE ELMS - 70A	NINE ELMS - 70A	NINE ELMS - 70A	NINE ELMS - 70A
35021	BOURNEMOUTH - 71B	BOURNEMOUTH - 71B	BOURNEMOUTH - 71B	BOURNEMOUTH - 71B	BOURNEMOUTH - 71B	BOURNEMOUTH - 71B	BOURNEMOUTH - 71B	BOURNEMOUTH - 71B
35022	BOURNEMOUTH - 71B	EXMOUTH JCN - 72A	EXMOUTH JCN - 72A	EXMOUTH JCN - 72A	EXMOUTH JCN - 72A	EXMOUTH JCN - 72A	EXMOUTH JCN - 72A	EXMOUTH JCN - 72A
35023	EXMOUTH JCN - 72A	BOURNEMOUTH - 71B	BOURNEMOUTH - 71B	BOURNEMOUTH - 71B	BOURNEMOUTH - 71B	BOURNEMOUTH - 71B	BOURNEMOUTH - 71B	BOURNEMOUTH - 71B
35024	EXMOUTH JCN - 72A	EXMOUTH JCN - 72A	EXMOUTH JCN - 72A	EXMOUTH JCN - 72A	EXMOUTH JCN - 72A	EXMOUTH JCN - 72A	EXMOUTH JCN - 72A	EXMOUTH JCN - 72A
35025	BOURNEMOUTH - 71B	EXMOUTH JCN - 72A	EXMOUTH JCN - 72A	EXMOUTH JCN - 72A	EXMOUTH JCN - 72A	EXMOUTH JCN - 72A	EXMOUTH JCN - 72A	EXMOUTH JCN - 72A
35026	BOURNEMOUTH - 71B	BOURNEMOUTH - 71B	BOURNEMOUTH - 71B	BOURNEMOUTH - 71B	BOURNEMOUTH - 71B	BOURNEMOUTH - 71B	BOURNEMOUTH - 71B	BOURNEMOUTH - 71B
35027	BOURNEMOUTH - 71B	BOURNEMOUTH - 71B	BOURNEMOUTH - 71B	BOURNEMOUTH - 71B	BOURNEMOUTH - 71B	BOURNEMOUTH - 71B	BOURNEMOUTH - 71B	BOURNEMOUTH - 71B
35028	NINE ELMS - 70A	NINE ELMS - 70A	NINE ELMS - 70A	NINE ELMS - 70A	NINE ELMS - 70A	NINE ELMS - 70A	NINE ELMS - 70A	NINE ELMS - 70A
35029	NINE ELMS - 70A	NINE ELMS - 70A	NINE ELMS - 70A	NINE ELMS - 70A	NINE ELMS - 70A	NINE ELMS - 70A	NINE ELMS - 70A	NINE ELMS - 70A
35030	NINE ELMS - 70A	NINE ELMS - 70A	NINE ELMS - 70A	NINE ELMS - 70A	NINE ELMS - 70A	NINE ELMS - 70A	NINE ELMS - 70A	NINE ELMS - 70A
WC 4-6-2 (1945)								
34002	EXMOUTH JCN - 72A	EXMOUTH JCN - 72A	EXMOUTH JCN - 72A	EXMOUTH JCN - 72A	EXMOUTH JCN - 72Ā	EXMOUTH JCN - 72A	EXMOUTH JCN - 72A	EXMOUTH JCN - 72A
34006	NINE ELMS - 70A	NINE ELMS - 70A	NINE ELMS - 70A	NINE ELMS - 70A	NINE ELMS - 70A	NINE ELMS - 70A	NINE ELMS - 70A	NINE ELMS - 70A
34007	NINE ELMS - 70A	NINE ELMS - 70A	NINE ELMS - 70A	NINE ELMS - 70A	NINE ELMS - 70A	NINE ELMS - 70A	NINE ELMS - 70A	NINE ELMS - 70A
34008	BRIGHTON - 75A	BRIGHTON - 75A	BRIGHTON - 75A	BRIGHTON - 75A	R/B	R/B	R/B	R/B
34009	NINE ELMS - 70A	NINE ELMS - 70A	NINE ELMS - 70A	NINE ELMS - 70A	NINE ELMS - 70A	NINE ELMS - 70A	NINE ELMS - 70A	NINE ELMS - 70A
34011	EXMOUTH JCN - 72A	EXMOUTH JCN - 72A	EXMOUTH JCN - 72A	EXMOUTH JCN - 72A	EXMOUTH JCN - 72A	EXMOUTH JCN - 72A	EXMOUTH JCN - 72A	EXMOUTH JCN - 72A
34015	EXMOUTH JCN - 72A	EXMOUTH JCN - 72A	EXMOUTH JCN - 72A	EXMOUTH JCN - 72A	EXMOUTH JCN - 72A	EXMOUTH JCN - 72A	EXMOUTH JCN - 72A	EXMOUTH JCN - 72A
34019	BRIGHTON - 75A	BRIGHTON - 75A	BRIGHTON - 75A	BRIGHTON - 75A	BRIGHTON - 75A	BRIGHTON - 75A	BRIGHTON - 75A	BRIGHTON - 75A
34020	BOURNEMOUTH - 71B	BOURNEMOUTH - 71B	BOURNEMOUTH - 71B	BOURNEMOUTH - 71B	BOURNEMOUTH - 71B	BOURNEMOUTH - 71B	BOURNEMOUTH - 71B	BOURNEMOUTH - 71B
34023	EXMOUTH JCN - 72A	EXMOUTH JCN - 72A	EXMOUTH JCN - 72A	EXMOUTH JCN - 72A	EXMOUTH JCN - 72A	EXMOUTH JCN - 72A	EXMOUTH JCN - 72A	EXMOUTH JCN - 72A
34024	EXMOUTH JCN - 72A	EXMOUTH JCN - 72A	EXMOUTH JCN - 72A	EXMOUTH JCN - 72A	EXMOUTH JCN - 72A	EXMOUTH JCN - 72A	EXMOUTH JCN - 72A	EXMOUTH JCN - 72A
34030	NINE ELMS - 70A	NINE ELMS - 70A	NINE ELMS - 70A	NINE ELMS - 70A	NINE ELMS - 70A	NINE ELMS - 70A	NINE ELMS - 70A	NINE ELMS - 70A
WC/R 4-6-2 (1957)								
34001	B ARMS - 73B	B ARMS - 73B	B ARMS - 73B	B ARMS - 73B	B ARMS - 73B	B ARMS - 73B	B ARMS - 73B	B ARMS - 73B
34003	B ARMS - 73B	B ARMS - 73B	B ARMS - 73B	B ARMS - 73B	B ARMS - 73B	B ARMS - 73B	B ARMS - 73B	B ARMS - 73B
34004	B ARMS - 73B	B ARMS - 73B	B ARMS - 73B	B ARMS - 73B	B ARMS - 73B	B ARMS - 73B	B ARMS - 73B	B ARMS - 73B
34005	B ARMS - 73B	B ARMS - 73B	B ARMS - 73B	B ARMS - 73B	B ARMS - 73B	B ARMS - 73B	B ARMS - 73B	B ARMS - 73B
34008					BRIGHTON - 75A	BRIGHTON - 75A	BRIGHTON - 75A	BRIGHTON - 75A
34010	NINE ELMS - 70A	NINE ELMS - 70A	NINE ELMS - 70A	NINE ELMS - 70A	NINE ELMS - 70A	NINE ELMS - 70A	NINE ELMS - 70A	NINE ELMS - 70A
34012	B ARMS - 73B	B ARMS - 73B	B ARMS - 73B	B ARMS - 73B	B ARMS - 73B	B ARMS - 73B	B ARMS - 73B	B ARMS - 73B
34013	B ARMS - 73B	B ARMS - 73B	B ARMS - 73B	B ARMS - 73B	B ARMS - 73B	B ARMS - 73B	B ARMS - 73B	B ARMS - 73B
34014	B ARMS - 73B	B ARMS - 73B	B ARMS - 73B	B ARMS - 73B	B ARMS - 73B	B ARMS - 73B	B ARMS - 73B	B ARMS - 73B
34016	B ARMS - 73B	B ARMS - 73B	B ARMS - 73B	B ARMS - 73B	B ARMS - 73B	B ARMS - 73B	B ARMS - 73B	B ARMS - 73B
34017	B ARMS - 73B	B ARMS - 73B	B ARMS - 73B	B ARMS - 73B	B ARMS - 73B	B ARMS - 73B	B ARMS - 73B	B ARMS - 73B
34018	NINE ELMS - 70A	NINE ELMS - 70A	NINE ELMS - 70A	NINE ELMS - 70A	NINE ELMS - 70A	NINE ELMS - 70A	NINE ELMS - 70A	NINE ELMS - 70A
34021	B ARMS - 73B	B ARMS - 73B	B ARMS - 73B	B ARMS - 73B	B ARMS - 73B	B ARMS - 73B	B ARMS - 73B	B ARMS - 73B
34022	B ARMS - 73B	B ARMS - 73B	B ARMS - 73B	B ARMS - 73B	B ARMS - 73B	B ARMS - 73B	B ARMS - 73B	B ARMS - 73B
34025	B ARMS - 73B	B ARMS - 73B	B ARMS - 73B	B ARMS - 73B	B ARMS - 73B	B ARMS - 73B	B ARMS - 73B	B ARMS - 73B
34026	B ARMS - 73B	B ARMS - 73B	B ARMS - 73B	B ARMS - 73B	B ARMS - 73B	B ARMS - 73B	SALISBURY - 72B	B ARMS - 73B
34027	B ARMS - 73B	B ARMS - 73B	B ARMS - 73B	B ARMS - 73B	B ARMS - 73B	B ARMS - 73B	B ARMS - 73B	B ARMS - 73B
34028	BOURNEMOUTH - 71B	BOURNEMOUTH - 71B	BOURNEMOUTH - 71B	BOURNEMOUTH - 71B	BOURNEMOUTH - 71B	BOURNEMOUTH - 71B	BOURNEMOUTH - 71B	BOURNEMOUTH - 71B
34029	BOURNEMOUTH - 71B	BOURNEMOUTH - 71B	BOURNEMOUTH - 71B	BOURNEMOUTH - 71B	BOURNEMOUTH - 71B	BOURNEMOUTH - 71B	BOURNEMOUTH - 71B	BOURNEMOUTH - 71B

West Country Pacifics continued in the following section

Rebuilt in mid-1958, 35015 'Rotterdam Lloyd' moves away from the pit roads at Nine Elms in 1960. Much of its time was spent on the South Western at Nine Elms but from May 1956 until the summer of 1959 it worked from Stewarts Lane on the Victoria - Dover Continental Boat services.

loco	May-49	Jun-49	Aug-49	Sep-49	Dec-49	Feb-50	Mar-50
				WC 4-6-2 (1945)			
34031	STEWARTS LANE - 73A	STEWARTS LANE - 73A	STEWARTS LANE - 73A	STEWARTS LANE - 73A	EXMOUTH JCN - 72A	EXMOUTH JCN - 72A	EXMOUTH JCN - 72A
34032	SALISBURY - 72B	SALISBURY - 72B	SALISBURY - 72B	SALISBURY - 72B	SALISBURY - 72B	SALISBURY - 72B	SALISBURY - 72B
34033	STEWARTS LANE - 73A	STEWARTS LANE - 73A	STEWARTS LANE - 73A	STEWARTS LANE - 73A	EXMOUTH JCN - 72A	EXMOUTH JCN - 72A	EXMOUTH JCN - 72A
34034	SALISBURY - 72B	SALISBURY - 72B	SALISBURY - 72B	SALISBURY - 72B	SALISBURY - 72B	SALISBURY - 72B	SALISBURY - 72B
34035	SALISBURY - 72B	SALISBURY - 72B	SALISBURY - 72B	SALISBURY - 72B	SALISBURY - 72B	BRIGHTON - 75A	BRIGHTON - 75A
34036	EASTLEIGH - 71A	EASTLEIGH - 71A	EASTLEIGH - 71A	EASTLEIGH - 71A	EASTLEIGH - 71A	BRIGHTON - 75A	BRIGHTON - 75A
34037	BRIGHTON - 75A	BRIGHTON - 75A	BRIGHTON - 75A	BRIGHTON - 75A	BRIGHTON - 75A	BRIGHTON - 75A	BRIGHTON - 75A
34038	BRIGHTON - 75A	BRIGHTON - 75A	BRIGHTON - 75A	BRIGHTON - 75A	BRIGHTON - 75A	BRIGHTON - 75A	BRIGHTON - 75A
34039	BRIGHTON - 75A	BRIGHTON - 75A	BRIGHTON - 75A	BRIGHTON - 75A	BRIGHTON - 75A	BRIGHTON - 75A	BRIGHTON - 75A
34040	BRIGHTON - 75A	BRIGHTON - 75A	BRIGHTON - 75A	BRIGHTON - 75A	BRIGHTON - 75A	BRIGHTON - 75A	BRIGHTON - 75A
34041	EXMOUTH JCN - 72A	EXMOUTH JCN - 72A	EXMOUTH JCN - 72A	EXMOUTH JCN - 72A	EXMOUTH JCN - 72A	BRIGHTON - 75A	BRIGHTON - 75A
34042	SALISBURY - 72B	SALISBURY - 72B	SALISBURY - 72B	SALISBURY - 72B	SALISBURY - 72B	SALISBURY - 72B	SALISBURY - 72B
34043	EXMOUTH JCN - 72A	EXMOUTH JCN - 72A	EXMOUTH JCN - 72A	EXMOUTH JCN - 72A	EXMOUTH JCN - 72A	SALISBURY - 72B	SALISBURY - 72B
34044	EXMOUTH JCN - 72A	EXMOUTH JCN - 72A	EXMOUTH JCN - 72A	EXMOUTH JCN - 72A	EXMOUTH JCN - 72A	EXMOUTH JCN - 72A	EXMOUTH JCN - 72A
34045	EXMOUTH JCN - 72A	EXMOUTH JCN - 72A	EXMOUTH JCN - 72A	EXMOUTH JCN - 72A	EXMOUTH JCN - 72A	EXMOUTH JCN - 72A	EXMOUTH JCN - 72A
34046	EXMOUTH JCN - 72A	EXMOUTH JCN - 72A	EXMOUTH JCN - 72A	EXMOUTH JCN - 72A	EXMOUTH JCN - 72A	EXMOUTH JCN - 72A	EXMOUTH JCN - 72A
34047	EXMOUTH JCN - 72A	EXMOUTH JCN - 72A	EXMOUTH JCN - 72A	EXMOUTH JCN - 72A	EXMOUTH JCN - 72A	EXMOUTH JCN - 72A	EXMOUTH JCN - 72A
34048	EXMOUTH JCN - 72A	EXMOUTH JCN - 72A	EXMOUTH JCN - 72A	EXMOUTH JCN - 72A	EXMOUTH JCN - 72A	EXMOUTH JCN - 72A	EXMOUTH JCN - 72A
34049	SALISBURY - 72B	SALISBURY - 72B	SALISBURY - 72B	SALISBURY - 72B	SALISBURY - 72B	SALISBURY - 72B	SALISBURY - 72B
34050	SALISBURY - 72B	SALISBURY - 72B	SALISBURY - 72B	SALISBURY - 72B	SALISBURY - 72B	SALISBURY - 72B	SALISBURY - 72B
34051	SALISBURY - 72B	SALISBURY - 72B	SALISBURY - 72B	SALISBURY - 72B	SALISBURY - 72B	SALISBURY - 72B	SALISBURY - 72B
34052	SALISBURY - 72B	SALISBURY - 72B	SALISBURY - 72B	SALISBURY - 72B	SALISBURY - 72B	SALISBURY - 72B	SALISBURY - 72B
34053	SALISBURY - 72B	SALISBURY - 72B	SALISBURY - 72B	SALISBURY - 72B	SALISBURY - 72B	SALISBURY - 72B	SALISBURY - 72B
34054	SALISBURY - 72B	SALISBURY - 72B	SALISBURY - 72B	SALISBURY - 72B	SALISBURY - 72B	SALISBURY - 72B	SALISBURY - 72B
34055	SALISBURY - 72B	SALISBURY - 72B	STEWARTS LANE - 73A	SALISBURY - 72B	SALISBURY - 72B	SALISBURY - 72B	SALISBURY - 72B
34056	RAMSGATE - 74B	STEWARTS LANE - 73A	STEWARTS LANE - 73A	STEWARTS LANE - 73A	NINE ELMS - 70A	NINE ELMS - 70A	NINE ELMS - 70A
34057	STEWARTS LANE - 73A	STEWARTS LANE - 73A	STEWARTS LANE - 73A	STEWARTS LANE - 73A	NINE ELMS - 70A	NINE ELMS - 70A	NINE ELMS - 70A
34058	NINE ELMS - 70A	NINE ELMS - 70A	STEWARTS LANE - 73A	NINE ELMS - 70A	NINE ELMS - 70A	NINE ELMS - 70A	NINE ELMS - 70A
34059	NINE ELMS - 70A	NINE ELMS - 70A	NINE ELMS - 70A	NINE ELMS - 70A	NINE ELMS - 70A	NINE ELMS - 70A	NINE ELMS - 70A
34060	NINE ELMS - 70A	NINE ELMS - 70A	NINE ELMS - 70A	NINE ELMS - 70A	NINE ELMS - 70A	NINE ELMS - 70A	NINE ELMS - 70A
34061	NINE ELMS - 70A	NINE ELMS - 70A	NINE ELMS - 70A	NINE ELMS - 70A	NINE ELMS - 70A	NINE ELMS - 70A	NINE ELMS - 70A
34062	STEWARTS LANE - 73A	STEWARTS LANE - 73A	STEWARTS LANE - 73A	STEWARTS LANE - 73A	STEWARTS LANE - 73A	STEWARTS LANE - 73A	STEWARTS LANE - 73A
34063	STEWARTS LANE - 73A	STEWARTS LANE - 73A	STEWARTS LANE - 73A	STEWARTS LANE - 73A	STEWARTS LANE - 73A	STEWARTS LANE - 73A	STEWARTS LANE - 73A
34064	STEWARTS LANE - 73A	STEWARTS LANE - 73A	STEWARTS LANE - 73A	STEWARTS LANE - 73A	STEWARTS LANE - 73A	STEWARTS LANE - 73A	STEWARTS LANE - 73A
34065	STEWARTS LANE - 73A	STEWARTS LANE - 73A	STEWARTS LANE - 73A	STEWARTS LANE - 73A	STEWARTS LANE - 73A	STEWARTS LANE - 73A	STEWARTS LANE - 73A
34066	RAMSGATE - 74B	RAMSGATE - 74B	RAMSGATE - 74B	RAMSGATE - 74B	STEWARTS LANE - 73A	STEWARTS LANE - 73A	STEWARTS LANE - 73A
34067	RAMSGATE - 74B	RAMSGATE - 74B	RAMSGATE - 74B	RAMSGATE - 74B	STEWARTS LANE - 73A	STEWARTS LANE - 73A	STEWARTS LANE - 73A
34068	RAMSGATE - 74B	RAMSGATE - 74B	RAMSGATE - 74B	RAMSGATE - 74B	STEWARTS LANE - 73A	STEWARTS LANE - 73A	STEWARTS LANE - 73A
34069	RAMSGATE - 74B	RAMSGATE - 74B	RAMSGATE - 74B	RAMSGATE - 74B	STEWARTS LANE - 73A	STEWARTS LANE - 73A	STEWARTS LANE - 73A
34070	RAMSGATE - 74B	RAMSGATE - 74B	RAMSGATE - 74B	RAMSGATE - 74B	STEWARTS LANE - 73A	STEWARTS LANE - 73A	STEWARTS LANE - 73A
34071	DOVER - 74C	DOVER - 74C	DOVER - 74C	DOVER - 74C	STEWARTS LANE - 73A	STEWARTS LANE - 73A	STEWARTS LANE - 73A
34072	DOVER - 74C	DOVER - 74C	DOVER - 74C	DOVER - 74C	DOVER - 74C	DOVER - 74C	DOVER - 74C
34073	DOVER - 74C	DOVER - 74C	DOVER - 74C	DOVER - 74C	DOVER - 74C	DOVER - 74C	DOVER - 74C
34074	STEWARTS LANE - 73A	STEWARTS LANE - 73A	STEWARTS LANE - 73A	STEWARTS LANE - 73A	STEWARTS LANE - 73A	STEWARTS LANE - 73A	STEWARTS LANE - 73A
34075	STEWARTS LANE - 73A	STEWARTS LANE - 73A	STEWARTS LANE - 73A	STEWARTS LANE - 73A	STEWARTS LANE - 73A	STEWARTS LANE - 73A	STEWARTS LANE - 73A
34076	STEWARTS LANE - 73A	STEWARTS LANE - 73A	STEWARTS LANE - 73A	STEWARTS LANE - 73A	STEWARTS LANE - 73A	STEWARTS LANE - 73A	STEWARTS LANE - 73A
34077	STEWARTS LANE - 73A	STEWARTS LANE - 73A	STEWARTS LANE - 73A	STEWARTS LANE - 73A	RAMSGATE - 74B	RAMSGATE - 74B	RAMSGATE - 74B
34078	RAMSGATE - 74B	RAMSGATE - 74B	RAMSGATE - 74B	RAMSGATE - 74B	RAMSGATE - 74B	RAMSGATE - 74B	RAMSGATE - 74B
34079	RAMSGATE - 74B	RAMSGATE - 74B	RAMSGATE - 74B	RAMSGATE - 74B	RAMSGATE - 74B	RAMSGATE - 74B	RAMSGATE - 74B
34080	RAMSGATE - 74B	RAMSGATE - 74B	RAMSGATE - 74B	RAMSGATE - 74B	RAMSGATE - 74B	RAMSGATE - 74B	RAMSGATE - 74B
34081	RAMSGATE - 74B	RAMSGATE - 74B	RAMSGATE - 74B	RAMSGATE - 74B	RAMSGATE - 74B	RAMSGATE - 74B	RAMSGATE - 74B
34082	RAMSGATE - 74B	RAMSGATE - 74B	RAMSGATE - 74B	RAMSGATE - 74B	RAMSGATE - 74B	RAMSGATE - 74B	RAMSGATE - 74B
34083	STEWARTS LANE - 73A	STEWARTS LANE - 73A	STEWARTS LANE - 73A	STEWARTS LANE - 73A	STEWARTS LANE - 73A	STEWARTS LANE - 73A	STEWARTS LANE - 73A
34084	STEWARTS LANE - 73A	STEWARTS LANE - 73A	STEWARTS LANE - 73A	STEWARTS LANE - 73A	STEWARTS LANE - 73A	STEWARTS LANE - 73A	STEWARTS LANE - 73A
34085	STEWARTS LANE - 73A	STEWARTS LANE - 73A	STEWARTS LANE - 73A	STEWARTS LANE - 73A	STEWARTS LANE - 73A	STEWARTS LANE - 73A	STEWARTS LANE - 73A
34086	RAMSGATE - 74B	RAMSGATE - 74B	RAMSGATE - 74B	RAMSGATE - 74B	RAMSGATE - 74B	RAMSGATE - 74B	RAMSGATE - 74B
34087	RAMSGATE - 74B	RAMSGATE - 74B	RAMSGATE - 74B	RAMSGATE - 74B	RAMSGATE - 74B	RAMSGATE - 74B	RAMSGATE - 74B
34088	RAMSGATE - 74B	RAMSGATE - 74B	RAMSGATE - 74B	RAMSGATE - 74B	RAMSGATE - 74B	RAMSGATE - 74B	RAMSGATE - 74B
34089	RAMSGATE - 74B	RAMSGATE - 74B	RAMSGATE - 74B	RAMSGATE - 74B	RAMSGATE - 74B	RAMSGATE - 74B	RAMSGATE - 74B
34090	RAMSGATE - 74B	RAMSGATE - 74B	RAMSGATE - 74B	RAMSGATE - 74B	RAMSGATE - 74B	RAMSGATE - 74B	RAMSGATE - 74B
34091				STEWARTS LANE - 73A	STEWARTS LANE - 73A	STEWARTS LANE - 73A	STEWARTS LANE - 73A
34092				STEWARTS LANE - 73A	STEWARTS LANE - 73A	STEWARTS LANE - 73A	STEWARTS LANE - 73A
34093					BOURNEMOUTH - 71B	BOURNEMOUTH - 71B	BOURNEMOUTH - 71B
34094					BOURNEMOUTH - 71B	BOURNEMOUTH - 71B	BOURNEMOUTH - 71B
34095					BOURNEMOUTH - 71B	BOURNEMOUTH - 71B	BOURNEMOUTH - 71B
34096					RAMSGATE - 74B	RAMSGATE - 74B	RAMSGATE - 74B
34097					RAMSGATE - 74B	RAMSGATE - 74B	RAMSGATE - 74B
34098					RAMSGATE - 74B	RAMSGATE - 74B	RAMSGATE - 74B
34099					RAMSGATE - 74B	RAMSGATE - 74B	RAMSGATE - 74B
34100					RAMSGATE - 74B	RAMSGATE - 74B	RAMSGATE - 74B
34101							STEWARTS LANE - 73A
34102							
34103							STEWARTS LANE - 73A
34104							
34105							BOURNEMOUTH - 71B
34106							
34107							
34108							
34109							
34110							

loco	Apr-50	Sep-50	Oct-50	Nov-50	Dec-50	Mar-51	Apr-51
				WC 4-6-2 (1945)			
34031	EXMOUTH JCN - 72A	EXMOUTH JCN - 72A	EXMOUTH JCN - 72A	NINE ELMS - 70A	NINE ELMS - 70A	NINE ELMS - 70A	NINE ELMS - 70A
34032	EXMOUTH JCN - 72A	SALISBURY - 72B	SALISBURY - 72B	SALISBURY - 72B	SALISBURY - 72B	SALISBURY - 72B	SALISBURY - 72B
34033	SALISBURY - 72B	STEWARTS LANE - 73A	STEWARTS LANE - 73A	STEWARTS LANE - 73A	STEWARTS LANE - 73A	STEWARTS LANE - 73A	STEWARTS LANE - 73A
34034	SALISBURY - 72B	STEWARTS LANE - 73A	EXMOUTH JCN - 72A	EXMOUTH JCN - 72A	PLYMOUTH - 72D	PLYMOUTH - 72D	PLYMOUTH - 72D
34035	BRIGHTON - 75A	STEWARTS LANE - 73A	BRIGHTON - 75A	PLYMOUTH - 72D	PLYMOUTH - 72D	PLYMOUTH - 72D	PLYMOUTH - 72D
34036	BRIGHTON - 75A	BRIGHTON - 75A	BRIGHTON - 75A	PLYMOUTH - 72D	PLYMOUTH - 72D	PLYMOUTH - 72D	PLYMOUTH - 72D
34037	BRIGHTON - 75A	BRIGHTON - 75A	BRIGHTON - 75A	BRIGHTON - 75A	BRIGHTON - 75A	BRIGHTON - 75A	BRIGHTON - 75A
34038	BRIGHTON - 75A	BRIGHTON - 75A	BRIGHTON - 75A	BRIGHTON - 75A	BRIGHTON - 75A	BRIGHTON - 75A	BRIGHTON - 75A
34039	BRIGHTON - 75A	BRIGHTON - 75A	BRIGHTON - 75A	BRIGHTON - 75A	BRIGHTON - 75A	BRIGHTON - 75A	BRIGHTON - 75A
34040	BRIGHTON - 75A	BRIGHTON - 75A	BRIGHTON - 75A	BRIGHTON - 75A	BRIGHTON - 75A	BRIGHTON - 75A	BRIGHTON - 75A
34041	BRIGHTON - 75A	BRIGHTON - 75A	BRIGHTON - 75A	BRIGHTON - 75A	BRIGHTON - 75A	BRIGHTON - 75A	BRIGHTON - 75A
34042	SALISBURY - 72B	SALISBURY - 72B	SALISBURY - 72B	SALISBURY - 72B	SALISBURY - 72B	SALISBURY - 72B	SALISBURY - 72B
34043	SALISBURY - 72B	SALISBURY - 72B	SALISBURY - 72B	SALISBURY - 72B	SALISBURY - 72B	SALISBURY - 72B	SALISBURY - 72B
34044	EXMOUTH JCN - 72A	EXMOUTH JCN - 72A	EXMOUTH JCN - 72A	EXMOUTH JCN - 72A	EXMOUTH JCN - 72A	EXMOUTH JCN - 72A	EXMOUTH JCN - 72A
34045	EXMOUTH JCN - 72A	EXMOUTH JCN - 72A	EXMOUTH JCN - 72A	EXMOUTH JCN - 72A	EXMOUTH JCN - 72A	EXMOUTH JCN - 72A	EXMOUTH JCN - 72A
34046	EXMOUTH JCN - 72A	EXMOUTH JCN - 72A	EXMOUTH JCN - 72A	EXMOUTH JCN - 72A	EXMOUTH JCN - 72A	EXMOUTH JCN - 72A	EXMOUTH JCN - 72A
34047	EXMOUTH JCN - 72A	EXMOUTH JCN - 72A	EXMOUTH JCN - 72A	EXMOUTH JCN - 72A	EXMOUTH JCN - 72A	EXMOUTH JCN - 72A	EXMOUTH JCN - 72A
34048	EXMOUTH JCN - 72A	EXMOUTH JCN - 72A	EXMOUTH JCN - 72A	EXMOUTH JCN - 72A	EXMOUTH JCN - 72A	EXMOUTH JCN - 72A	EXMOUTH JCN - 72A
34049	NINE ELMS - 70A	NINE ELMS - 70A	NINE ELMS - 70A	NINE ELMS - 70A	NINE ELMS - 70A	NINE ELMS - 70A	EXMOUTH JCN - 72A
34050	NINE ELMS - 70A	NINE ELMS - 70A	NINE ELMS - 70A	NINE ELMS - 70A	NINE ELMS - 70A	NINE ELMS - 70A	EXMOUTH JCN - 72A
34051	NINE ELMS - 70A	NINE ELMS - 70A	NINE ELMS - 70A	NINE ELMS - 70A	NINE ELMS - 70A	NINE ELMS - 70A	EXMOUTH JCN - 72A
34052	NINE ELMS - 70A	NINE ELMS - 70A	NINE ELMS - 70A	NINE ELMS - 70A	NINE ELMS - 70A	NINE ELMS - 70A	EXMOUTH JCN - 72A
34053	NINE ELMS - 70A	NINE ELMS - 70A	NINE ELMS - 70A	NINE ELMS - 70A	NINE ELMS - 70A	NINE ELMS - 70A	EXMOUTH JCN - 72A
34054	NINE ELMS - 70A	NINE ELMS - 70A	NINE ELMS - 70A	NINE ELMS - 70A	NINE ELMS - 70A	NINE ELMS - 70A	EXMOUTH JCN - 72A
34055	NINE ELMS - 70A	NINE ELMS - 70A	NINE ELMS - 70A	NINE ELMS - 70A	NINE ELMS - 70A	NINE ELMS - 70A	EXMOUTH JCN - 72A
34056	NINE ELMS - 70A	NINE ELMS - 70A	NINE ELMS - 70A	NINE ELMS - 70A	NINE ELMS - 70A	NINE ELMS - 70A	EXMOUTH JCN - 72A
34057	NINE ELMS - 70A	NINE ELMS - 70A	NINE ELMS - 70A	NINE ELMS - 70A	NINE ELMS - 70A	NINE ELMS - 70A	EXMOUTH JCN - 72A
34058	NINE ELMS - 70A	NINE ELMS - 70A	NINE ELMS - 70A	NINE ELMS - 70A	NINE ELMS - 70A	NINE ELMS - 70A	EXMOUTH JCN - 72A
34059	NINE ELMS - 70A	NINE ELMS - 70A	NINE ELMS - 70A	NINE ELMS - 70A	NINE ELMS - 70A	NINE ELMS - 70A	EXMOUTH JCN - 72A
34060	NINE ELMS - 70A	NINE ELMS - 70A	NINE ELMS - 70A	NINE ELMS - 70A	NINE ELMS - 70A	NINE ELMS - 70A	NINE ELMS - 70A
34061	NINE ELMS - 70A	NINE ELMS - 70A	NINE ELMS - 70A	NINE ELMS - 70A	NINE ELMS - 70A	NINE ELMS - 70A	NINE ELMS - 70A
34062	NINE ELMS - 70A	NINE ELMS - 70A	NINE ELMS - 70A	NINE ELMS - 70A	NINE ELMS - 70A	NINE ELMS - 70A	NINE ELMS - 70A
34063	NINE ELMS - 70A	NINE ELMS - 70A	NINE ELMS - 70A	NINE ELMS - 70A	NINE ELMS - 70A	NINE ELMS - 70A	NINE ELMS - 70A
34064	NINE ELMS - 70A	NINE ELMS - 70A	NINE ELMS - 70A	NINE ELMS - 70A	NINE ELMS - 70A	NINE ELMS - 70A	NINE ELMS - 70A
34065	NINE ELMS - 70A	NINE ELMS - 70A	NINE ELMS - 70A	NINE ELMS - 70A	NINE ELMS - 70A	NINE ELMS - 70A	NINE ELMS - 70A
34066	STEWARTS LANE - 73A	STEWARTS LANE - 73A	STEWARTS LANE - 73A	STEWARTS LANE - 73A	STEWARTS LANE - 73A	STEWARTS LANE - 73A	STEWARTS LANE - 73A
34067	STEWARTS LANE - 73A	STEWARTS LANE - 73A	STEWARTS LANE - 73A	STEWARTS LANE - 73A	STEWARTS LANE - 73A	STEWARTS LANE - 73A	STEWARTS LANE - 73A
34068	STEWARTS LANE - 73A	STEWARTS LANE - 73A	STEWARTS LANE - 73A	STEWARTS LANE - 73A	STEWARTS LANE - 73A	STEWARTS LANE - 73A	STEWARTS LANE - 73A
34069	STEWARTS LANE - 73A	STEWARTS LANE - 73A	STEWARTS LANE - 73A	STEWARTS LANE - 73A	STEWARTS LANE - 73A	STEWARTS LANE - 73A	STEWARTS LANE - 73A
34070	STEWARTS LANE - 73A	STEWARTS LANE - 73A	STEWARTS LANE - 73A	STEWARTS LANE - 73A	STEWARTS LANE - 73A	STEWARTS LANE - 73A	STEWARTS LANE - 73A
34071	STEWARTS LANE - 73A	STEWARTS LANE - 73A	STEWARTS LANE - 73A	STEWARTS LANE - 73A	STEWARTS LANE - 73A	STEWARTS LANE - 73A	STEWARTS LANE - 73A
34072	DOVER - 74C	DOVER - 74C	DOVER - 74C	DOVER - 74C	DOVER - 74C	DOVER - 74C	DOVER - 74C
34073	DOVER - 74C	DOVER - 74C	DOVER - 74C	DOVER - 74C	DOVER - 74C	DOVER - 74C	DOVER - 74C
34074	STEWARTS LANE - 73A	DOVER - 74C	STEWARTS LANE - 73A	STEWARTS LANE - 73A	DOVER - 74C	DOVER - 74C	DOVER - 74C
34075	STEWARTS LANE - 73A	DOVER - 74C	STEWARTS LANE - 73A	STEWARTS LANE - 73A	DOVER - 74C	DOVER - 74C	DOVER - 74C
34076	STEWARTS LANE - 73A	STEWARTS LANE - 73A	STEWARTS LANE - 73A	STEWARTS LANE - 73A	STEWARTS LANE - 73A	STEWARTS LANE - 73A	STEWARTS LANE - 73A
34077	RAMSGATE - 74B	RAMSGATE - 74B	RAMSGATE - 74B	RAMSGATE - 74B	RAMSGATE - 74B	RAMSGATE - 74B	RAMSGATE - 74B
34078	RAMSGATE - 74B	RAMSGATE - 74B	RAMSGATE - 74B	RAMSGATE - 74B	RAMSGATE - 74B	RAMSGATE - 74B	RAMSGATE - 74B
34079	RAMSGATE - 74B	RAMSGATE - 74B	RAMSGATE - 74B	RAMSGATE - 74B	RAMSGATE - 74B	RAMSGATE - 74B	RAMSGATE - 74B
34080	RAMSGATE - 74B	RAMSGATE - 74B	RAMSGATE - 74B	RAMSGATE - 74B	RAMSGATE - 74B	RAMSGATE - 74B	RAMSGATE - 74B
34081	RAMSGATE - 74B	RAMSGATE - 74B	RAMSGATE - 74B	RAMSGATE - 74B	RAMSGATE - 74B	RAMSGATE - 74B	RAMSGATE - 74B
34082	RAMSGATE - 74B	RAMSGATE - 74B	RAMSGATE - 74B	RAMSGATE - 74B	RAMSGATE - 74B	RAMSGATE - 74B	RAMSGATE - 74B
34083	STEWARTS LANE - 73A	STEWARTS LANE - 73A	STEWARTS LANE - 73A	STEWARTS LANE - 73A	STEWARTS LANE - 73A	STEWARTS LANE - 73A	STEWARTS LANE - 73A
34084	STEWARTS LANE - 73A	STEWARTS LANE - 73A	STEWARTS LANE - 73A	STEWARTS LANE - 73A	STEWARTS LANE - 73A	STEWARTS LANE - 73A	STEWARTS LANE - 73A
34085	STEWARTS LANE - 73A	STEWARTS LANE - 73A	STEWARTS LANE - 73A	STEWARTS LANE - 73A	STEWARTS LANE - 73A	STEWARTS LANE - 73A	STEWARTS LANE - 73A
34086	RAMSGATE - 74B	RAMSGATE - 74B	RAMSGATE - 74B	RAMSGATE - 74B	RAMSGATE - 74B	RAMSGATE - 74B	RAMSGATE - 74B
34087	RAMSGATE - 74B	RAMSGATE - 74B	RAMSGATE - 74B	RAMSGATE - 74B	RAMSGATE - 74B	RAMSGATE - 74B	RAMSGATE - 74B
34088	RAMSGATE - 74B	RAMSGATE - 74B	RAMSGATE - 74B	RAMSGATE - 74B	RAMSGATE - 74B	RAMSGATE - 74B	RAMSGATE - 74B
34089	RAMSGATE - 74B	RAMSGATE - 74B	RAMSGATE - 74B	RAMSGATE - 74B	RAMSGATE - 74B	RAMSGATE - 74B	RAMSGATE - 74B
34090	RAMSGATE - 74B	RAMSGATE - 74B	RAMSGATE - 74B	RAMSGATE - 74B	RAMSGATE - 74B	RAMSGATE - 74B	RAMSGATE - 74B
34091	STEWARTS LANE - 73A	STEWARTS LANE - 73A	STEWARTS LANE - 73A	STEWARTS LANE - 73A	STEWARTS LANE - 73A	STEWARTS LANE - 73A	STEWARTS LANE - 73A
34092	STEWARTS LANE - 73A	STEWARTS LANE - 73A	STEWARTS LANE - 73A	STEWARTS LANE - 73A	STEWARTS LANE - 73A	STEWARTS LANE - 73A	STEWARTS LANE - 73A
34093	BOURNEMOUTH - 71B	BOURNEMOUTH - 71B	BOURNEMOUTH - 71B	BOURNEMOUTH - 71B	BOURNEMOUTH - 71B	BOURNEMOUTH - 71B	BOURNEMOUTH - 71B
34094	BOURNEMOUTH - 71B	BOURNEMOUTH - 71B	BOURNEMOUTH - 71B	BOURNEMOUTH - 71B	BOURNEMOUTH - 71B	BOURNEMOUTH - 71B	BOURNEMOUTH - 71B
34095	BOURNEMOUTH - 71B	BOURNEMOUTH - 71B	BOURNEMOUTH - 71B	BOURNEMOUTH - 71B	BOURNEMOUTH - 71B	BOURNEMOUTH - 71B	BOURNEMOUTH - 71B
34096	RAMSGATE - 74B	RAMSGATE - 74B	RAMSGATE - 74B	RAMSGATE - 74B	RAMSGATE - 74B	RAMSGATE - 74B	RAMSGATE - 74B
34097	RAMSGATE - 74B	RAMSGATE - 74B	RAMSGATE - 74B	RAMSGATE - 74B	RAMSGATE - 74B	RAMSGATE - 74B	RAMSGATE - 74B
34098	RAMSGATE - 74B	RAMSGATE - 74B	RAMSGATE - 74B	RAMSGATE - 74B	RAMSGATE - 74B	RAMSGATE - 74B	RAMSGATE - 74B
34099	RAMSGATE - 74B	RAMSGATE - 74B	RAMSGATE - 74B	RAMSGATE - 74B	RAMSGATE - 74B	RAMSGATE - 74B	RAMSGATE - 74B
34100	RAMSGATE - 74B	RAMSGATE - 74B	RAMSGATE - 74B	RAMSGATE - 74B	RAMSGATE - 74B	RAMSGATE - 74B	RAMSGATE - 74B
34101	STEWARTS LANE - 73A	STEWARTS LANE - 73A	STEWARTS LANE - 73A	STEWARTS LANE - 73A	STEWARTS LANE - 73A	STEWARTS LANE - 73A	STEWARTS LANE - 73A
34102	STEWARTS LANE - 73A	STEWARTS LANE - 73A	STEWARTS LANE - 73A	STEWARTS LANE - 73A	STEWARTS LANE - 73A	STEWARTS LANE - 73A	STEWARTS LANE - 73A
34103	STEWARTS LANE - 73A	STEWARTS LANE - 73A	STEWARTS LANE - 73A	STEWARTS LANE - 73A	STEWARTS LANE - 73A	STEWARTS LANE - 73A	STEWARTS LANE - 73A
34104	STEWARTS LANE - 73A	STEWARTS LANE - 73A	STEWARTS LANE - 73A	STEWARTS LANE - 73A	STEWARTS LANE - 73A	STEWARTS LANE - 73A	STEWARTS LANE - 73A
34105	BOURNEMOUTH - 71B	BOURNEMOUTH - 71B	BOURNEMOUTH - 71B	BOURNEMOUTH - 71B	BOURNEMOUTH - 71B	BOURNEMOUTH - 71B	BOURNEMOUTH - 71B
34106	BOURNEMOUTH - 71B	BOURNEMOUTH - 71B	BOURNEMOUTH - 71B	BOURNEMOUTH - 71B	BOURNEMOUTH - 71B	BOURNEMOUTH - 71B	BOURNEMOUTH - 71B
34107	BOURNEMOUTH - 71B	BOURNEMOUTH - 71B	BOURNEMOUTH - 71B	BOURNEMOUTH - 71B	BOURNEMOUTH - 71B	BOURNEMOUTH - 71B	BOURNEMOUTH - 71B
34108	BOURNEMOUTH - 71B	BOURNEMOUTH - 71B	BOURNEMOUTH - 71B	BOURNEMOUTH - 71B	BOURNEMOUTH - 71B	BOURNEMOUTH - 71B	BOURNEMOUTH - 71B
34109	BOURNEMOUTH - 71B	BOURNEMOUTH - 71B	BOURNEMOUTH - 71B	BOURNEMOUTH - 71B	BOURNEMOUTH - 71B	BOURNEMOUTH - 71B	BOURNEMOUTH - 71B
34110					BOURNEMOUTH - 71B	BOURNEMOUTH - 71B	BOURNEMOUTH - 71B

loco	Jun-51	Jul-51	Sep-51	Dec-51	Jan-52	Mar-52	Jun-52
				WC 4-6-2 (1945)			
34031	NINE ELMS - 70A	NINE ELMS - 70A	EXMOUTH J CN - 72A	EXMOUTH J CN - 72A	EXMOUTH J CN - 72A	EXMOUTH J CN - 72A	EXMOUTH J CN - 72A
34032	SALISBURY - 72B	SALISBURY - 72B	SALISBURY - 72B	SALISBURY - 72B	SALISBURY - 72B	SALISBURY - 72B	SALISBURY - 72B
34033	STEWARTS LANE - 73A	STEWARTS LANE - 73A	PLYMOUTH - 72D	EXMOUTH J CN - 72A	EXMOUTH J CN - 72A	EXMOUTH J CN - 72A	EXMOUTH J CN - 72A
34034	PLYMOUTH - 72D	PLYMOUTH - 72D	PLYMOUTH - 72D	PLYMOUTH - 72D	PLYMOUTH - 72D	EXMOUTH J CN - 72A	EXMOUTH J CN - 72A
34035	PLYMOUTH - 72D	PLYMOUTH - 72D	PLYMOUTH - 72D	PLYMOUTH - 72D	PLYMOUTH - 72D	PLYMOUTH - 72D	PLYMOUTH - 72D
34036	PLYMOUTH - 72D	PLYMOUTH - 72D	PLYMOUTH - 72D	PLYMOUTH - 72D	PLYMOUTH - 72D	PLYMOUTH - 72D	PLYMOUTH - 72D
34037	BRIGHTON - 75A	BRIGHTON - 75A	BRIGHTON - 75A	BRIGHTON - 75A	BRIGHTON - 75A	BRIGHTON - 75A	BRIGHTON - 75A
34038	BRIGHTON - 75A	BRIGHTON - 75A	BRIGHTON - 75A	BRIGHTON - 75A	BRIGHTON - 75A	BRIGHTON - 75A	BRIGHTON - 75A
34039	BRIGHTON - 75A	BRIGHTON - 75A	TO ER	TO ER	TO ER	BRIGHTON - 75A	BRIGHTON - 75A
34040	BOURNEMOUTH - 71B	BOURNEMOUTH - 71B	BOURNEMOUTH - 71B	BOURNEMOUTH - 71B	BOURNEMOUTH - 71B	BOURNEMOUTH - 71B	BATH (S&D) - 71G
34041	BOURNEMOUTH - 71B	BOURNEMOUTH - 71B	BOURNEMOUTH - 71B	BATH (S&D) - 71G	BATH (S&D) - 71G	BATH (S&D) - 71G	BATH (S&D) - 71G
34042	BOURNEMOUTH - 71B	BOURNEMOUTH - 71B	BOURNEMOUTH - 71B	BATH (S&D) - 71G	BATH (S&D) - 71G	BATH (S&D) - 71G	BATH (S&D) - 71G
34043	SALISBURY - 72B	SALISBURY - 72B	SALISBURY - 72B	SALISBURY - 72B	SALISBURY - 72B	SALISBURY - 72B	BOURNEMOUTH - 71B
34044	EXMOUTH J CN - 72A	EXMOUTH J CN - 72A	EXMOUTH J CN - 72A	BOURNEMOUTH - 71B	BOURNEMOUTH - 71B	BOURNEMOUTH - 71B	BOURNEMOUTH - 71B
34045	BRIGHTON - 75A	BRIGHTON - 75A	BRIGHTON - 75A	BRIGHTON - 75A	BRIGHTON - 75A	BRIGHTON - 75A	BRIGHTON - 75A
34046	BRIGHTON - 75A	BRIGHTON - 75A	BRIGHTON - 75A	BRIGHTON - 75A	BRIGHTON - 75A	BRIGHTON - 75A	BRIGHTON - 75A
34047	BRIGHTON - 75A	BRIGHTON - 75A	BRIGHTON - 75A	BRIGHTON - 75A	BRIGHTON - 75A	BRIGHTON - 75A	BRIGHTON - 75A
34048	BRIGHTON - 75A	BRIGHTON - 75A	BRIGHTON - 75A	BRIGHTON - 75A	BRIGHTON - 75A	BRIGHTON - 75A	BRIGHTON - 75A
34049	EXMOUTH J CN - 72A	EXMOUTH J CN - 72A	EXMOUTH J CN - 72A	EXMOUTH J CN - 72A	EXMOUTH J CN - 72A	EXMOUTH J CN - 72A	EXMOUTH J CN - 72A
34050	SALISBURY - 72B	SALISBURY - 72B	SALISBURY - 72B	SALISBURY - 72B	SALISBURY - 72B	SALISBURY - 72B	SALISBURY - 72B
34051	SALISBURY - 72B	SALISBURY - 72B	SALISBURY - 72B	SALISBURY - 72B	SALISBURY - 72B	SALISBURY - 72B	SALISBURY - 72B
34052	SALISBURY - 72B	SALISBURY - 72B	SALISBURY - 72B	SALISBURY - 72B	SALISBURY - 72B	SALISBURY - 72B	SALISBURY - 72B
34053	SALISBURY - 72B	SALISBURY - 72B	SALISBURY - 72B	SALISBURY - 72B	SALISBURY - 72B	SALISBURY - 72B	SALISBURY - 72B
34054	EXMOUTH J CN - 72A	EXMOUTH J CN - 72A	EXMOUTH J CN - 72A	EXMOUTH J CN - 72A	EXMOUTH J CN - 72A	EXMOUTH J CN - 72A	SALISBURY - 72B
34055	EXMOUTH J CN - 72A	EXMOUTH J CN - 72A	EXMOUTH J CN - 72A	EXMOUTH J CN - 72A	EXMOUTH J CN - 72A	EXMOUTH J CN - 72A	SALISBURY - 72B
34056	EXMOUTH J CN - 72A	EXMOUTH J CN - 72A	EXMOUTH J CN - 72A	EXMOUTH J CN - 72A	EXMOUTH J CN - 72A	EXMOUTH J CN - 72A	EXMOUTH J CN - 72A
34057	EXMOUTH J CN - 72A	EXMOUTH J CN - 72A	TO ER	TO ER	TO ER	TO ER	EXMOUTH J CN - 72A
34058	EXMOUTH J CN - 72A	EXMOUTH J CN - 72A	EXMOUTH J CN - 72A	EXMOUTH J CN - 72A	EXMOUTH J CN - 72A	EXMOUTH J CN - 72A	EXMOUTH J CN - 72A
34059	EXMOUTH J CN - 72A	EXMOUTH J CN - 72A	EXMOUTH J CN - 72A	EXMOUTH J CN - 72A	EXMOUTH J CN - 72A	EXMOUTH J CN - 72A	EXMOUTH J CN - 72A
34060	NINE ELMS - 70A	NINE ELMS - 70A	NINE ELMS - 70A	NINE ELMS - 70A	NINE ELMS - 70A	NINE ELMS - 70A	NINE ELMS - 70A
34061	NINE ELMS - 70A	NINE ELMS - 70A	NINE ELMS - 70A	NINE ELMS - 70A	NINE ELMS - 70A	NINE ELMS - 70A	NINE ELMS - 70A
34062	NINE ELMS - 70A	NINE ELMS - 70A	NINE ELMS - 70A	NINE ELMS - 70A	NINE ELMS - 70A	NINE ELMS - 70A	NINE ELMS - 70A
34063	NINE ELMS - 70A	NINE ELMS - 70A	NINE ELMS - 70A	NINE ELMS - 70A	NINE ELMS - 70A	NINE ELMS - 70A	NINE ELMS - 70A
34064	NINE ELMS - 70A	NINE ELMS - 70A	NINE ELMS - 70A	NINE ELMS - 70A	NINE ELMS - 70A	NINE ELMS - 70A	NINE ELMS - 70A
34065	NINE ELMS - 70A	NINE ELMS - 70A	TO ER	TO ER	TO ER	TO ER	NINE ELMS - 70A
34066	STEWARTS LANE - 73A	STEWARTS LANE - 73A	STEWARTS LANE - 73A	STEWARTS LANE - 73A	STEWARTS LANE - 73A	STEWARTS LANE - 73A	STEWARTS LANE - 73A
34067	STEWARTS LANE - 73A	STEWARTS LANE - 73A	STEWARTS LANE - 73A	STEWARTS LANE - 73A	STEWARTS LANE - 73A	STEWARTS LANE - 73A	STEWARTS LANE - 73A
34068	STEWARTS LANE - 73A	STEWARTS LANE - 73A	STEWARTS LANE - 73A	STEWARTS LANE - 73A	STEWARTS LANE - 73A	STEWARTS LANE - 73A	STEWARTS LANE - 73A
34069	STEWARTS LANE - 73A	STEWARTS LANE - 73A	STEWARTS LANE - 73A	STEWARTS LANE - 73A	STEWARTS LANE - 73A	STEWARTS LANE - 73A	STEWARTS LANE - 73A
34070	STEWARTS LANE - 73A	STEWARTS LANE - 73A	STEWARTS LANE - 73A	STEWARTS LANE - 73A	STEWARTS LANE - 73A	STEWARTS LANE - 73A	STEWARTS LANE - 73A
34071	STEWARTS LANE - 73A	STEWARTS LANE - 73A	STEWARTS LANE - 73A	STEWARTS LANE - 73A	STEWARTS LANE - 73A	STEWARTS LANE - 73A	STEWARTS LANE - 73A
34072	DOVER - 74C	DOVER - 74C	DOVER - 74C	DOVER - 74C	DOVER - 74C	DOVER - 74C	DOVER - 74C
34073	DOVER - 74C	DOVER - 74C	DOVER - 74C	DOVER - 74C	DOVER - 74C	DOVER - 74C	DOVER - 74C
34074	DOVER - 74C	DOVER - 74C	DOVER - 74C	DOVER - 74C	DOVER - 74C	DOVER - 74C	DOVER - 74C
34075	DOVER - 74C	DOVER - 74C	DOVER - 74C	DOVER - 74C	DOVER - 74C	DOVER - 74C	RAMSGATE - 74B
34076	STEWARTS LANE - 73A	STEWARTS LANE - 73A	STEWARTS LANE - 73A	STEWARTS LANE - 73A	STEWARTS LANE - 73A	TO ER	RAMSGATE - 74B
34077	RAMSGATE - 74B	RAMSGATE - 74B	RAMSGATE - 74B	RAMSGATE - 74B	RAMSGATE - 74B	RAMSGATE - 74B	RAMSGATE - 74B
34078	RAMSGATE - 74B	RAMSGATE - 74B	RAMSGATE - 74B	RAMSGATE - 74B	RAMSGATE - 74B	RAMSGATE - 74B	RAMSGATE - 74B
34079	RAMSGATE - 74B	RAMSGATE - 74B	RAMSGATE - 74B	RAMSGATE - 74B	RAMSGATE - 74B	RAMSGATE - 74B	RAMSGATE - 74B
34080	RAMSGATE - 74B	RAMSGATE - 74B	RAMSGATE - 74B	RAMSGATE - 74B	RAMSGATE - 74B	RAMSGATE - 74B	RAMSGATE - 74B
34081	RAMSGATE - 74B	RAMSGATE - 74B	RAMSGATE - 74B	RAMSGATE - 74B	RAMSGATE - 74B	RAMSGATE - 74B	RAMSGATE - 74B
34082	RAMSGATE - 74B	RAMSGATE - 74B	RAMSGATE - 74B	RAMSGATE - 74B	RAMSGATE - 74B	RAMSGATE - 74B	RAMSGATE - 74B
34083	STEWARTS LANE - 73A	STEWARTS LANE - 73A	STEWARTS LANE - 73A	STEWARTS LANE - 73A	STEWARTS LANE - 73A	STEWARTS LANE - 73A	STEWARTS LANE - 73A
34084	STEWARTS LANE - 73A	STEWARTS LANE - 73A	STEWARTS LANE - 73A	STEWARTS LANE - 73A	STEWARTS LANE - 73A	STEWARTS LANE - 73A	STEWARTS LANE - 73A
34085	STEWARTS LANE - 73A	STEWARTS LANE - 73A	STEWARTS LANE - 73A	STEWARTS LANE - 73A	STEWARTS LANE - 73A	STEWARTS LANE - 73A	STEWARTS LANE - 73A
34086	RAMSGATE - 74B	RAMSGATE - 74B	RAMSGATE - 74B	RAMSGATE - 74B	RAMSGATE - 74B	RAMSGATE - 74B	RAMSGATE - 74B
34087	RAMSGATE - 74B	RAMSGATE - 74B	RAMSGATE - 74B	RAMSGATE - 74B	RAMSGATE - 74B	RAMSGATE - 74B	RAMSGATE - 74B
34088	RAMSGATE - 74B	RAMSGATE - 74B	RAMSGATE - 74B	RAMSGATE - 74B	RAMSGATE - 74B	RAMSGATE - 74B	RAMSGATE - 74B
34089	RAMSGATE - 74B	RAMSGATE - 74B	RAMSGATE - 74B	RAMSGATE - 74B	RAMSGATE - 74B	RAMSGATE - 74B	RAMSGATE - 74B
34090	RAMSGATE - 74B	RAMSGATE - 74B	RAMSGATE - 74B	RAMSGATE - 74B	RAMSGATE - 74B	RAMSGATE - 74B	RAMSGATE - 74B
34091	STEWARTS LANE - 73A	STEWARTS LANE - 73A	STEWARTS LANE - 73A	STEWARTS LANE - 73A	STEWARTS LANE - 73A	STEWARTS LANE - 73A	STEWARTS LANE - 73A
34092	STEWARTS LANE - 73A	STEWARTS LANE - 73A	STEWARTS LANE - 73A	STEWARTS LANE - 73A	STEWARTS LANE - 73A	STEWARTS LANE - 73A	STEWARTS LANE - 73A
34093	BOURNEMOUTH - 71B	BOURNEMOUTH - 71B	BOURNEMOUTH - 71B	BOURNEMOUTH - 71B	BOURNEMOUTH - 71B	BOURNEMOUTH - 71B	BOURNEMOUTH - 71B
34094	BOURNEMOUTH - 71B	BOURNEMOUTH - 71B	BOURNEMOUTH - 71B	BOURNEMOUTH - 71B	BOURNEMOUTH - 71B	BOURNEMOUTH - 71B	BOURNEMOUTH - 71B
34095	BOURNEMOUTH - 71B	BOURNEMOUTH - 71B	BOURNEMOUTH - 71B	BOURNEMOUTH - 71B	BOURNEMOUTH - 71B	BOURNEMOUTH - 71B	BOURNEMOUTH - 71B
34096	RAMSGATE - 74B	RAMSGATE - 74B	RAMSGATE - 74B	RAMSGATE - 74B	RAMSGATE - 74B	RAMSGATE - 74B	RAMSGATE - 74B
34097	RAMSGATE - 74B	RAMSGATE - 74B	RAMSGATE - 74B	RAMSGATE - 74B	RAMSGATE - 74B	RAMSGATE - 74B	RAMSGATE - 74B
34098	RAMSGATE - 74B	RAMSGATE - 74B	RAMSGATE - 74B	RAMSGATE - 74B	RAMSGATE - 74B	RAMSGATE - 74B	RAMSGATE - 74B
34099	RAMSGATE - 74B	RAMSGATE - 74B	RAMSGATE - 74B	RAMSGATE - 74B	RAMSGATE - 74B	RAMSGATE - 74B	RAMSGATE - 74B
34100	RAMSGATE - 74B	RAMSGATE - 74B	RAMSGATE - 74B	RAMSGATE - 74B	RAMSGATE - 74B	RAMSGATE - 74B	RAMSGATE - 74B
34101	STEWARTS LANE - 73A	STEWARTS LANE - 73A	STEWARTS LANE - 73A	STEWARTS LANE - 73A	STEWARTS LANE - 73A	STEWARTS LANE - 73A	STEWARTS LANE - 73A
34102	STEWARTS LANE - 73A	STEWARTS LANE - 73A	STEWARTS LANE - 73A	STEWARTS LANE - 73A	STEWARTS LANE - 73A	STEWARTS LANE - 73A	STEWARTS LANE - 73A
34103	STEWARTS LANE - 73A	STEWARTS LANE - 73A	STEWARTS LANE - 73A	STEWARTS LANE - 73A	STEWARTS LANE - 73A	STEWARTS LANE - 73A	STEWARTS LANE - 73A
34104	STEWARTS LANE - 73A	STEWARTS LANE - 73A	STEWARTS LANE - 73A	STEWARTS LANE - 73A	STEWARTS LANE - 73A	STEWARTS LANE - 73A	STEWARTS LANE - 73A
34105	BOURNEMOUTH - 71B	BOURNEMOUTH - 71B	BOURNEMOUTH - 71B	BOURNEMOUTH - 71B	BOURNEMOUTH - 71B	BOURNEMOUTH - 71B	BOURNEMOUTH - 71B
34106	BOURNEMOUTH - 71B	BOURNEMOUTH - 71B	BOURNEMOUTH - 71B	BOURNEMOUTH - 71B	BOURNEMOUTH - 71B	BOURNEMOUTH - 71B	BOURNEMOUTH - 71B
34107	BOURNEMOUTH - 71B	BOURNEMOUTH - 71B	BOURNEMOUTH - 71B	BOURNEMOUTH - 71B	BOURNEMOUTH - 71B	BOURNEMOUTH - 71B	BOURNEMOUTH - 71B
34108	BOURNEMOUTH - 71B	BOURNEMOUTH - 71B	BOURNEMOUTH - 71B	BOURNEMOUTH - 71B	BOURNEMOUTH - 71B	BOURNEMOUTH - 71B	BOURNEMOUTH - 71B
34109	BOURNEMOUTH - 71B	BOURNEMOUTH - 71B	BOURNEMOUTH - 71B	BOURNEMOUTH - 71B	BOURNEMOUTH - 71B	BOURNEMOUTH - 71B	BOURNEMOUTH - 71B
34110	BOURNEMOUTH - 71B	BOURNEMOUTH - 71B	BOURNEMOUTH - 71B	BOURNEMOUTH - 71B	BOURNEMOUTH - 71B	BOURNEMOUTH - 71B	BOURNEMOUTH - 71B

loco	Sep-52	Dec-52	Mar-53	May-53	Jul-53	Sep-53	Nov-53
			WC 4-6-2 (1945)				
34031	EXMOUTH JCN - 72A	EXMOUTH JCN - 72A	EXMOUTH JCN - 72A	EXMOUTH JCN - 72A	EXMOUTH JCN - 72A	EXMOUTH JCN - 72A	EXMOUTH JCN - 72A
34032	SALISBURY - 72B	SALISBURY - 72B	SALISBURY - 72B	SALISBURY - 72B	SALISBURY - 72B	SALISBURY - 72B	SALISBURY - 72B
34033	EXMOUTH JCN - 72A	EXMOUTH JCN - 72A	EXMOUTH JCN - 72A	EXMOUTH JCN - 72A	EXMOUTH JCN - 72A	EXMOUTH JCN - 72A	EXMOUTH JCN - 72A
34034	EXMOUTH JCN - 72A	EXMOUTH JCN - 72A	EXMOUTH JCN - 72A	EXMOUTH JCN - 72A	EXMOUTH JCN - 72A	EXMOUTH JCN - 72A	EXMOUTH JCN - 72A
34035	PLYMOUTH - 72D	PLYMOUTH - 72D	PLYMOUTH - 72D	PLYMOUTH - 72D	PLYMOUTH - 72D	PLYMOUTH - 72D	PLYMOUTH - 72D
34036	PLYMOUTH - 72D	PLYMOUTH - 72D	PLYMOUTH - 72D	PLYMOUTH - 72D	PLYMOUTH - 72D	PLYMOUTH - 72D	PLYMOUTH - 72D
34037	BRIGHTON - 75A	BRIGHTON - 75A	BRIGHTON - 75A	BRIGHTON - 75A	BRIGHTON - 75A	BRIGHTON - 75A	BRIGHTON - 75A
34038	BRIGHTON - 75A	BRIGHTON - 75A	BRIGHTON - 75A	BRIGHTON - 75A	BRIGHTON - 75A	BRIGHTON - 75A	BRIGHTON - 75A
34039	BRIGHTON - 75A	BRIGHTON - 75A	BRIGHTON - 75A	BRIGHTON - 75A	BRIGHTON - 75A	BRIGHTON - 75A	BRIGHTON - 75A
34040	BATH(S&D) - 71G	BATH(S&D) - 71G	BATH(S&D) - 71G	BATH(S&D) - 71G	BATH(S&D) - 71G	BATH(S&D) - 71G	BATH(S&D) - 71G
34041	BATH(S&D) - 71G	BATH(S&D) - 71G	BATH(S&D) - 71G	BATH(S&D) - 71G	BATH(S&D) - 71G	BATH(S&D) - 71G	BATH(S&D) - 71G
34042	BATH(S&D) - 71G	BATH(S&D) - 71G	BATH(S&D) - 71G	BATH(S&D) - 71G	BATH(S&D) - 71G	BATH(S&D) - 71G	BATH(S&D) - 71G
34043	BOURNEMOUTH - 71B	BOURNEMOUTH - 71B	BOURNEMOUTH - 71B	BOURNEMOUTH - 71B	BOURNEMOUTH - 71B	BOURNEMOUTH - 71B	BOURNEMOUTH - 71B
34044	BOURNEMOUTH - 71B	BOURNEMOUTH - 71B	BOURNEMOUTH - 71B	BOURNEMOUTH - 71B	BOURNEMOUTH - 71B	BOURNEMOUTH - 71B	BOURNEMOUTH - 71B
34045	BRIGHTON - 75A	BRIGHTON - 75A	BRIGHTON - 75A	BRIGHTON - 75A	BRIGHTON - 75A	BRIGHTON - 75A	BRIGHTON - 75A
34046	BRIGHTON - 75A	BRIGHTON - 75A	BRIGHTON - 75A	BRIGHTON - 75A	BRIGHTON - 75A	BRIGHTON - 75A	BRIGHTON - 75A
34047	BRIGHTON - 75A	BRIGHTON - 75A	BRIGHTON - 75A	BRIGHTON - 75A	BRIGHTON - 75A	BRIGHTON - 75A	BRIGHTON - 75A
34048	BRIGHTON - 75A	BRIGHTON - 75A	BRIGHTON - 75A	BRIGHTON - 75A	BRIGHTON - 75A	BRIGHTON - 75A	BRIGHTON - 75A
34049	EXMOUTH JCN - 72A	EXMOUTH JCN - 72A	EXMOUTH JCN - 72A	EXMOUTH JCN - 72A	EXMOUTH JCN - 72A	EXMOUTH JCN - 72A	EXMOUTH JCN - 72A
34050	SALISBURY - 72B	SALISBURY - 72B	SALISBURY - 72B	SALISBURY - 72B	SALISBURY - 72B	SALISBURY - 72B	SALISBURY - 72B
34051	SALISBURY - 72B	SALISBURY - 72B	SALISBURY - 72B	SALISBURY - 72B	SALISBURY - 72B	SALISBURY - 72B	SALISBURY - 72B
34052	SALISBURY - 72B	SALISBURY - 72B	SALISBURY - 72B	SALISBURY - 72B	SALISBURY - 72B	SALISBURY - 72B	SALISBURY - 72B
34053	SALISBURY - 72B	SALISBURY - 72B	SALISBURY - 72B	SALISBURY - 72B	SALISBURY - 72B	SALISBURY - 72B	SALISBURY - 72B
34054	SALISBURY - 72B	SALISBURY - 72B	SALISBURY - 72B	SALISBURY - 72B	SALISBURY - 72B	SALISBURY - 72B	SALISBURY - 72B
34055	SALISBURY - 72B	SALISBURY - 72B	SALISBURY - 72B	SALISBURY - 72B	SALISBURY - 72B	SALISBURY - 72B	SALISBURY - 72B
34056	EXMOUTH JCN - 72A	EXMOUTH JCN - 72A	EXMOUTH JCN - 72A	EXMOUTH JCN - 72A	EXMOUTH JCN - 72A	EXMOUTH JCN - 72A	EXMOUTH JCN - 72A
34057	EXMOUTH JCN - 72A	EXMOUTH JCN - 72A	EXMOUTH JCN - 72A	EXMOUTH JCN - 72A	EXMOUTH JCN - 72A	EXMOUTH JCN - 72A	EXMOUTH JCN - 72A
34058	EXMOUTH JCN - 72A	EXMOUTH JCN - 72A	EXMOUTH JCN - 72A	EXMOUTH JCN - 72A	EXMOUTH JCN - 72A	EXMOUTH JCN - 72A	EXMOUTH JCN - 72A
34059	EXMOUTH JCN - 72A	EXMOUTH JCN - 72A	EXMOUTH JCN - 72A	EXMOUTH JCN - 72A	EXMOUTH JCN - 72A	EXMOUTH JCN - 72A	EXMOUTH JCN - 72A
34060	NINE ELMS - 70A	NINE ELMS - 70A	NINE ELMS - 70A	NINE ELMS - 70A	NINE ELMS - 70A	NINE ELMS - 70A	NINE ELMS - 70A
34061	NINE ELMS - 70A	NINE ELMS - 70A	NINE ELMS - 70A	NINE ELMS - 70A	NINE ELMS - 70A	NINE ELMS - 70A	NINE ELMS - 70A
34062	NINE ELMS - 70A	NINE ELMS - 70A	NINE ELMS - 70A	NINE ELMS - 70A	NINE ELMS - 70A	NINE ELMS - 70A	NINE ELMS - 70A
34063	NINE ELMS - 70A	NINE ELMS - 70A	NINE ELMS - 70A	NINE ELMS - 70A	NINE ELMS - 70A	NINE ELMS - 70A	NINE ELMS - 70A
34064	NINE ELMS - 70A	NINE ELMS - 70A	NINE ELMS - 70A	NINE ELMS - 70A	NINE ELMS - 70A	NINE ELMS - 70A	NINE ELMS - 70A
34065	NINE ELMS - 70A	NINE ELMS - 70A	NINE ELMS - 70A	NINE ELMS - 70A	NINE ELMS - 70A	NINE ELMS - 70A	NINE ELMS - 70A
34066	STEWARTS LANE - 73A	STEWARTS LANE - 73A	STEWARTS LANE - 73A	STEWARTS LANE - 73A	STEWARTS LANE - 73A	STEWARTS LANE - 73A	STEWARTS LANE - 73A
34067	STEWARTS LANE - 73A	STEWARTS LANE - 73A	STEWARTS LANE - 73A	STEWARTS LANE - 73A	STEWARTS LANE - 73A	STEWARTS LANE - 73A	STEWARTS LANE - 73A
34068	STEWARTS LANE - 73A	STEWARTS LANE - 73A	STEWARTS LANE - 73A	STEWARTS LANE - 73A	STEWARTS LANE - 73A	STEWARTS LANE - 73A	STEWARTS LANE - 73A
34069	STEWARTS LANE - 73A	STEWARTS LANE - 73A	STEWARTS LANE - 73A	STEWARTS LANE - 73A	STEWARTS LANE - 73A	STEWARTS LANE - 73A	STEWARTS LANE - 73A
34070	STEWARTS LANE - 73A	STEWARTS LANE - 73A	STEWARTS LANE - 73A	STEWARTS LANE - 73A	STEWARTS LANE - 73A	STEWARTS LANE - 73A	STEWARTS LANE - 73A
34071	STEWARTS LANE - 73A	STEWARTS LANE - 73A	STEWARTS LANE - 73A	STEWARTS LANE - 73A	STEWARTS LANE - 73A	STEWARTS LANE - 73A	STEWARTS LANE - 73A
34072	DOVER - 74C	DOVER - 74C	DOVER - 74C	DOVER - 74C	DOVER - 74C	DOVER - 74C	DOVER - 74C
34073	DOVER - 74C	DOVER - 74C	DOVER - 74C	DOVER - 74C	DOVER - 74C	DOVER - 74C	DOVER - 74C
34074	DOVER - 74C	DOVER - 74C	DOVER - 74C	DOVER - 74C	DOVER - 74C	DOVER - 74C	DOVER - 74C
34075	RAMSGATE - 74B	RAMSGATE - 74B	RAMSGATE - 74B	RAMSGATE - 74B	RAMSGATE - 74B	RAMSGATE - 74B	RAMSGATE - 74B
34076	RAMSGATE - 74B	RAMSGATE - 74B	RAMSGATE - 74B	RAMSGATE - 74B	RAMSGATE - 74B	RAMSGATE - 74B	RAMSGATE - 74B
34077	RAMSGATE - 74B	RAMSGATE - 74B	RAMSGATE - 74B	RAMSGATE - 74B	RAMSGATE - 74B	RAMSGATE - 74B	RAMSGATE - 74B
34078	RAMSGATE - 74B	RAMSGATE - 74B	RAMSGATE - 74B	RAMSGATE - 74B	RAMSGATE - 74B	RAMSGATE - 74B	RAMSGATE - 74B
34079	RAMSGATE - 74B	RAMSGATE - 74B	RAMSGATE - 74B	RAMSGATE - 74B	RAMSGATE - 74B	RAMSGATE - 74B	RAMSGATE - 74B
34080	RAMSGATE - 74B	RAMSGATE - 74B	RAMSGATE - 74B	RAMSGATE - 74B	RAMSGATE - 74B	RAMSGATE - 74B	RAMSGATE - 74B
34081	RAMSGATE - 74B	RAMSGATE - 74B	RAMSGATE - 74B	RAMSGATE - 74B	RAMSGATE - 74B	RAMSGATE - 74B	RAMSGATE - 74B
34082	RAMSGATE - 74B	RAMSGATE - 74B	RAMSGATE - 74B	RAMSGATE - 74B	RAMSGATE - 74B	RAMSGATE - 74B	RAMSGATE - 74B
34083	STEWARTS LANE - 73A	STEWARTS LANE - 73A	STEWARTS LANE - 73A	STEWARTS LANE - 73A	STEWARTS LANE - 73A	STEWARTS LANE - 73A	STEWARTS LANE - 73A
34084	STEWARTS LANE - 73A	STEWARTS LANE - 73A	STEWARTS LANE - 73A	STEWARTS LANE - 73A	STEWARTS LANE - 73A	STEWARTS LANE - 73A	STEWARTS LANE - 73A
34085	STEWARTS LANE - 73A	STEWARTS LANE - 73A	STEWARTS LANE - 73A	STEWARTS LANE - 73A	STEWARTS LANE - 73A	STEWARTS LANE - 73A	STEWARTS LANE - 73A
34086	RAMSGATE - 74B	RAMSGATE - 74B	RAMSGATE - 74B	RAMSGATE - 74B	RAMSGATE - 74B	RAMSGATE - 74B	RAMSGATE - 74B
34087	RAMSGATE - 74B	RAMSGATE - 74B	RAMSGATE - 74B	RAMSGATE - 74B	RAMSGATE - 74B	RAMSGATE - 74B	RAMSGATE - 74B
34088	RAMSGATE - 74B	RAMSGATE - 74B	RAMSGATE - 74B	RAMSGATE - 74B	RAMSGATE - 74B	RAMSGATE - 74B	RAMSGATE - 74B
34089	RAMSGATE - 74B	RAMSGATE - 74B	RAMSGATE - 74B	RAMSGATE - 74B	RAMSGATE - 74B	RAMSGATE - 74B	RAMSGATE - 74B
34090	RAMSGATE - 74B	RAMSGATE - 74B	RAMSGATE - 74B	RAMSGATE - 74B	RAMSGATE - 74B	RAMSGATE - 74B	RAMSGATE - 74B
34091	STEWARTS LANE - 73A	STEWARTS LANE - 73A	STEWARTS LANE - 73A	STEWARTS LANE - 73A	STEWARTS LANE - 73A	STEWARTS LANE - 73A	STEWARTS LANE - 73A
34092	STEWARTS LANE - 73A	STEWARTS LANE - 73A	STEWARTS LANE - 73A	STEWARTS LANE - 73A	STEWARTS LANE - 73A	STEWARTS LANE - 73A	STEWARTS LANE - 73A
34093	BOURNEMOUTH - 71B	BOURNEMOUTH - 71B	BOURNEMOUTH - 71B	BOURNEMOUTH - 71B	BOURNEMOUTH - 71B	BOURNEMOUTH - 71B	BOURNEMOUTH - 71B
34094	BOURNEMOUTH - 71B	BOURNEMOUTH - 71B	BOURNEMOUTH - 71B	BOURNEMOUTH - 71B	BOURNEMOUTH - 71B	BOURNEMOUTH - 71B	BOURNEMOUTH - 71B
34095	BOURNEMOUTH - 71B	BOURNEMOUTH - 71B	BOURNEMOUTH - 71B	BOURNEMOUTH - 71B	BOURNEMOUTH - 71B	BOURNEMOUTH - 71B	BOURNEMOUTH - 71B
34096	RAMSGATE - 74B	RAMSGATE - 74B	RAMSGATE - 74B	RAMSGATE - 74B	RAMSGATE - 74B	RAMSGATE - 74B	RAMSGATE - 74B
34097	RAMSGATE - 74B	RAMSGATE - 74B	RAMSGATE - 74B	RAMSGATE - 74B	RAMSGATE - 74B	RAMSGATE - 74B	RAMSGATE - 74B
34098	RAMSGATE - 74B	RAMSGATE - 74B	RAMSGATE - 74B	RAMSGATE - 74B	RAMSGATE - 74B	RAMSGATE - 74B	RAMSGATE - 74B
34099	RAMSGATE - 74B	RAMSGATE - 74B	RAMSGATE - 74B	RAMSGATE - 74B	RAMSGATE - 74B	RAMSGATE - 74B	RAMSGATE - 74B
34100	RAMSGATE - 74B	RAMSGATE - 74B	RAMSGATE - 74B	RAMSGATE - 74B	RAMSGATE - 74B	RAMSGATE - 74B	RAMSGATE - 74B
34101	STEWARTS LANE - 73A	STEWARTS LANE - 73A	STEWARTS LANE - 73A	STEWARTS LANE - 73A	STEWARTS LANE - 73A	STEWARTS LANE - 73A	STEWARTS LANE - 73A
34102	STEWARTS LANE - 73A	STEWARTS LANE - 73A	STEWARTS LANE - 73A	STEWARTS LANE - 73A	STEWARTS LANE - 73A	STEWARTS LANE - 73A	STEWARTS LANE - 73A
34103	STEWARTS LANE - 73A	STEWARTS LANE - 73A	STEWARTS LANE - 73A	STEWARTS LANE - 73A	STEWARTS LANE - 73A	STEWARTS LANE - 73A	STEWARTS LANE - 73A
34104	STEWARTS LANE - 73A	STEWARTS LANE - 73A	STEWARTS LANE - 73A	STEWARTS LANE - 73A	STEWARTS LANE - 73A	STEWARTS LANE - 73A	STEWARTS LANE - 73A
34105	BOURNEMOUTH - 71B	BOURNEMOUTH - 71B	BOURNEMOUTH - 71B	BOURNEMOUTH - 71B	BOURNEMOUTH - 71B	BOURNEMOUTH - 71B	BOURNEMOUTH - 71B
34106	BOURNEMOUTH - 71B	BOURNEMOUTH - 71B	BOURNEMOUTH - 71B	BOURNEMOUTH - 71B	BOURNEMOUTH - 71B	BOURNEMOUTH - 71B	BOURNEMOUTH - 71B
34107	BOURNEMOUTH - 71B	BOURNEMOUTH - 71B	BOURNEMOUTH - 71B	BOURNEMOUTH - 71B	BOURNEMOUTH - 71B	BOURNEMOUTH - 71B	BOURNEMOUTH - 71B
34108	BOURNEMOUTH - 71B	BOURNEMOUTH - 71B	BOURNEMOUTH - 71B	BOURNEMOUTH - 71B	BOURNEMOUTH - 71B	BOURNEMOUTH - 71B	BOURNEMOUTH - 71B
34109	BOURNEMOUTH - 71B	BOURNEMOUTH - 71B	BOURNEMOUTH - 71B	BOURNEMOUTH - 71B	BOURNEMOUTH - 71B	BOURNEMOUTH - 71B	BOURNEMOUTH - 71B
34110	BOURNEMOUTH - 71B	BOURNEMOUTH - 71B	BOURNEMOUTH - 71B	BOURNEMOUTH - 71B	BOURNEMOUTH - 71B	BOURNEMOUTH - 71B	BOURNEMOUTH - 71B

loco	Jan-54	Mar-54	May-54	Jun-54	Aug-54	Oct-54	Dec-54
				WC 4-6-2 (1945)			
34031	EXMOUTH JCN- 72A	EXMOUTH JCN- 72A	EXMOUTH JCN- 72A	EXMOUTH JCN- 72A	EXMOUTH JCN- 72A	EXMOUTH JCN- 72A	EXMOUTH JCN- 72A
34032	SALISBURY- 72B	SALISBURY- 72B	SALISBURY- 72B	SALISBURY- 72B	SALISBURY- 72B	SALISBURY- 72B	SALISBURY- 72B
34033	EXMOUTH JCN- 72A	EXMOUTH JCN- 72A	EXMOUTH JCN- 72A	EXMOUTH JCN- 72A	EXMOUTH JCN- 72A	EXMOUTH JCN- 72A	EXMOUTH JCN- 72A
34034	EXMOUTH JCN- 72A	EXMOUTH JCN- 72A	EXMOUTH JCN- 72A	EXMOUTH JCN- 72A	EXMOUTH JCN- 72A	EXMOUTH JCN- 72A	EXMOUTH JCN- 72A
34035	PLYMOUTH- 72D	PLYMOUTH- 72D	PLYMOUTH- 72D	PLYMOUTH- 72D	PLYMOUTH- 72D	PLYMOUTH- 72D	PLYMOUTH- 72D
34036	PLYMOUTH- 72D	PLYMOUTH- 72D	PLYMOUTH- 72D	PLYMOUTH- 72D	PLYMOUTH- 72D	PLYMOUTH- 72D	PLYMOUTH- 72D
34037	BRIGHTON- 75A	BRIGHTON- 75A	BRIGHTON- 75A	BRIGHTON- 75A	BRIGHTON- 75A	BRIGHTON- 75A	BRIGHTON- 75A
34038	BRIGHTON- 75A	BRIGHTON- 75A	BRIGHTON- 75A	BRIGHTON- 75A	BRIGHTON- 75A	BRIGHTON- 75A	BRIGHTON- 75A
34039	BRIGHTON- 75A	BRIGHTON- 75A	BRIGHTON- 75A	BRIGHTON- 75A	BRIGHTON- 75A	BRIGHTON- 75A	BRIGHTON- 75A
34040	BATH(S&D)- 71G	BATH(S&D)- 71G	BATH(S&D)- 71G	BATH(S&D)- 71G	BATH(S&D)- 71G	EASTLEIGH- 71A	EASTLEIGH- 71A
34041	BATH(S&D)- 71G	BATH(S&D)- 71G	BATH(S&D)- 71G	BATH(S&D)- 71G	BATH(S&D)- 71G	EASTLEIGH- 71A	EASTLEIGH- 71A
34042	BATH(S&D)- 71G	BATH(S&D)- 71G	BATH(S&D)- 71G	BATH(S&D)- 71G	BATH(S&D)- 71G	EASTLEIGH- 71A	EASTLEIGH- 71A
34043	BOURNEMOUTH- 71B	BOURNEMOUTH- 71B	BOURNEMOUTH- 71B	BOURNEMOUTH- 71B	BOURNEMOUTH- 71B	BOURNEMOUTH- 71B	BOURNEMOUTH- 71B
34044	BOURNEMOUTH- 71B	BOURNEMOUTH- 71B	BOURNEMOUTH- 71B	BOURNEMOUTH- 71B	BOURNEMOUTH- 71B	BOURNEMOUTH- 71B	BOURNEMOUTH- 71B
34045	BRIGHTON- 75A	BRIGHTON- 75A	BRIGHTON- 75A	BRIGHTON- 75A	BRIGHTON- 75A	BRIGHTON- 75A	BRIGHTON- 75A
34046	BRIGHTON- 75A	BRIGHTON- 75A	BRIGHTON- 75A	BRIGHTON- 75A	BRIGHTON- 75A	BRIGHTON- 75A	BRIGHTON- 75A
34047	BRIGHTON- 75A	BRIGHTON- 75A	BRIGHTON- 75A	BRIGHTON- 75A	BRIGHTON- 75A	BRIGHTON- 75A	BRIGHTON- 75A
34048	BRIGHTON- 75A	BRIGHTON- 75A	BRIGHTON- 75A	BRIGHTON- 75A	BRIGHTON- 75A	BRIGHTON- 75A	BRIGHTON- 75A
34049	EXMOUTH JCN- 72A	EXMOUTH JCN- 72A	EXMOUTH JCN- 72A	EXMOUTH JCN- 72A	EXMOUTH JCN- 72A	SALISBURY- 72B	SALISBURY- 72B
34050	SALISBURY- 72B	SALISBURY- 72B	SALISBURY- 72B	SALISBURY- 72B	SALISBURY- 72B	SALISBURY- 72B	SALISBURY- 72B
34051	SALISBURY- 72B	SALISBURY- 72B	SALISBURY- 72B	SALISBURY- 72B	SALISBURY- 72B	SALISBURY- 72B	SALISBURY- 72B
34052	SALISBURY- 72B	SALISBURY- 72B	SALISBURY- 72B	SALISBURY- 72B	SALISBURY- 72B	SALISBURY- 72B	SALISBURY- 72B
34053	SALISBURY- 72B	SALISBURY- 72B	SALISBURY- 72B	SALISBURY- 72B	SALISBURY- 72B	SALISBURY- 72B	SALISBURY- 72B
34054	SALISBURY- 72B	SALISBURY- 72B	SALISBURY- 72B	SALISBURY- 72B	SALISBURY- 72B	SALISBURY- 72B	SALISBURY- 72B
34055	SALISBURY- 72B	SALISBURY- 72B	SALISBURY- 72B	SALISBURY- 72B	SALISBURY- 72B	SALISBURY- 72B	SALISBURY- 72B
34056	EXMOUTH JCN- 72A	EXMOUTH JCN- 72A	EXMOUTH JCN- 72A	EXMOUTH JCN- 72A	EXMOUTH JCN- 72A	SALISBURY- 72B	EXMOUTH JCN- 72A
34057	EXMOUTH JCN- 72A	EXMOUTH JCN- 72A	EXMOUTH JCN- 72A	EXMOUTH JCN- 72A	EXMOUTH JCN- 72A	SALISBURY- 72B	EXMOUTH JCN- 72A
34058	EXMOUTH JCN- 72A	EXMOUTH JCN- 72A	EXMOUTH JCN- 72A	EXMOUTH JCN- 72A	EXMOUTH JCN- 72A	EXMOUTH JCN- 72A	EXMOUTH JCN- 72A
34059	EXMOUTH JCN- 72A	EXMOUTH JCN- 72A	EXMOUTH JCN- 72A	EXMOUTH JCN- 72A	EXMOUTH JCN- 72A	EXMOUTH JCN- 72A	EXMOUTH JCN- 72A
34060	NINE ELMS - 70A	NINE ELMS - 70A	NINE ELMS - 70A	NINE ELMS - 70A	NINE ELMS - 70A	NINE ELMS - 70A	NINE ELMS - 70A
34061	NINE ELMS - 70A	NINE ELMS - 70A	NINE ELMS - 70A	EXMOUTH JCN- 72A	EXMOUTH JCN- 72A	EXMOUTH JCN- 72A	EXMOUTH JCN- 72A
34062	NINE ELMS - 70A	NINE ELMS - 70A	NINE ELMS - 70A	NINE ELMS - 70A	NINE ELMS - 70A	NINE ELMS - 70A	NINE ELMS - 70A
34063	NINE ELMS - 70A	NINE ELMS - 70A	NINE ELMS - 70A	NINE ELMS - 70A	NINE ELMS - 70A	NINE ELMS - 70A	NINE ELMS - 70A
34064	NINE ELMS - 70A	NINE ELMS - 70A	NINE ELMS - 70A	NINE ELMS - 70A	NINE ELMS - 70A	NINE ELMS - 70A	NINE ELMS - 70A
34065	NINE ELMS - 70A	NINE ELMS - 70A	NINE ELMS - 70A	STEWARTS LANE - 73A	STEWARTS LANE - 73A	STEWARTS LANE - 73A	STEWARTS LANE - 73A
34066	STEWARTS LANE - 73A	STEWARTS LANE - 73A	STEWARTS LANE - 73A	STEWARTS LANE - 73A	STEWARTS LANE - 73A	STEWARTS LANE - 73A	STEWARTS LANE - 73A
34067	STEWARTS LANE - 73A	STEWARTS LANE - 73A	STEWARTS LANE - 73A	STEWARTS LANE - 73A	STEWARTS LANE - 73A	STEWARTS LANE - 73A	STEWARTS LANE - 73A
34068	STEWARTS LANE - 73A	STEWARTS LANE - 73A	STEWARTS LANE - 73A	STEWARTS LANE - 73A	STEWARTS LANE - 73A	STEWARTS LANE - 73A	STEWARTS LANE - 73A
34069	STEWARTS LANE - 73A	EXMOUTH JCN- 72A	EXMOUTH JCN- 72A	EXMOUTH JCN- 72A	EXMOUTH JCN- 72A	EXMOUTH JCN- 72A	EXMOUTH JCN- 72A
34070	STEWARTS LANE - 73A	STEWARTS LANE - 73A	STEWARTS LANE - 73A	STEWARTS LANE - 73A	STEWARTS LANE - 73A	STEWARTS LANE - 73A	STEWARTS LANE - 73A
34071	STEWARTS LANE - 73A	STEWARTS LANE - 73A	STEWARTS LANE - 73A	STEWARTS LANE - 73A	STEWARTS LANE - 73A	STEWARTS LANE - 73A	STEWARTS LANE - 73A
34072	DOVER - 74C	DOVER - 74C	DOVER - 74C	DOVER - 74C	DOVER - 74C	DOVER - 74C	DOVER - 74C
34073	DOVER - 74C	DOVER - 74C	DOVER - 74C	DOVER - 74C	DOVER - 74C	DOVER - 74C	DOVER - 74C
34074	DOVER - 74C	DOVER - 74C	DOVER - 74C	DOVER - 74C	DOVER - 74C	DOVER - 74C	DOVER - 74C
34075	RAMSGATE- 74B	RAMSGATE- 74B	RAMSGATE- 74B	RAMSGATE- 74B	RAMSGATE- 74B	RAMSGATE- 74B	RAMSGATE- 74B
34076	RAMSGATE- 74B	RAMSGATE- 74B	RAMSGATE- 74B	RAMSGATE- 74B	RAMSGATE- 74B	RAMSGATE- 74B	RAMSGATE- 74B
34077	RAMSGATE- 74B	RAMSGATE- 74B	RAMSGATE- 74B	RAMSGATE- 74B	RAMSGATE- 74B	RAMSGATE- 74B	RAMSGATE- 74B
34078	RAMSGATE- 74B	RAMSGATE- 74B	RAMSGATE- 74B	RAMSGATE- 74B	RAMSGATE- 74B	RAMSGATE- 74B	RAMSGATE- 74B
34079	RAMSGATE- 74B	RAMSGATE- 74B	RAMSGATE- 74B	RAMSGATE- 74B	RAMSGATE- 74B	RAMSGATE- 74B	RAMSGATE- 74B
34080	RAMSGATE- 74B	RAMSGATE- 74B	RAMSGATE- 74B	RAMSGATE- 74B	RAMSGATE- 74B	RAMSGATE- 74B	RAMSGATE- 74B
34081	RAMSGATE- 74B	RAMSGATE- 74B	RAMSGATE- 74B	RAMSGATE- 74B	RAMSGATE- 74B	RAMSGATE- 74B	RAMSGATE- 74B
34082	RAMSGATE- 74B	RAMSGATE- 74B	RAMSGATE- 74B	RAMSGATE- 74B	RAMSGATE- 74B	RAMSGATE- 74B	RAMSGATE- 74B
34083	STEWARTS LANE - 73A	STEWARTS LANE - 73A	STEWARTS LANE - 73A	STEWARTS LANE - 73A	STEWARTS LANE - 73A	STEWARTS LANE - 73A	STEWARTS LANE - 73A
34084	STEWARTS LANE - 73A	STEWARTS LANE - 73A	STEWARTS LANE - 73A	STEWARTS LANE - 73A	STEWARTS LANE - 73A	STEWARTS LANE - 73A	STEWARTS LANE - 73A
34085	STEWARTS LANE - 73A	STEWARTS LANE - 73A	STEWARTS LANE - 73A	STEWARTS LANE - 73A	STEWARTS LANE - 73A	STEWARTS LANE - 73A	STEWARTS LANE - 73A
34086	RAMSGATE- 74B	RAMSGATE- 74B	RAMSGATE- 74B	RAMSGATE- 74B	RAMSGATE- 74B	RAMSGATE- 74B	RAMSGATE- 74B
34087	RAMSGATE- 74B	RAMSGATE- 74B	RAMSGATE- 74B	RAMSGATE- 74B	RAMSGATE- 74B	STEWARTS LANE - 73A	STEWARTS LANE - 73A
34088	RAMSGATE- 74B	RAMSGATE- 74B	RAMSGATE- 74B	RAMSGATE- 74B	RAMSGATE- 74B	STEWARTS LANE - 73A	STEWARTS LANE - 73A
34089	RAMSGATE- 74B	RAMSGATE- 74B	RAMSGATE- 74B	RAMSGATE- 74B	RAMSGATE- 74B	STEWARTS LANE - 73A	STEWARTS LANE - 73A
34090	RAMSGATE- 74B	RAMSGATE- 74B	RAMSGATE- 74B	RAMSGATE- 74B	RAMSGATE- 74B	RAMSGATE- 74B	RAMSGATE- 74B
34091	STEWARTS LANE - 73A	STEWARTS LANE - 73A	STEWARTS LANE - 73A	STEWARTS LANE - 73A	STEWARTS LANE - 73A	STEWARTS LANE - 73A	STEWARTS LANE - 73A
34092	STEWARTS LANE - 73A	STEWARTS LANE - 73A	STEWARTS LANE - 73A	STEWARTS LANE - 73A	STEWARTS LANE - 73A	STEWARTS LANE - 73A	STEWARTS LANE - 73A
34093	BOURNEMOUTH- 71B	BOURNEMOUTH- 71B	BOURNEMOUTH- 71B	BOURNEMOUTH- 71B	BOURNEMOUTH- 71B	BOURNEMOUTH- 71B	BOURNEMOUTH- 71B
34094	BOURNEMOUTH- 71B	BOURNEMOUTH- 71B	BOURNEMOUTH- 71B	BOURNEMOUTH- 71B	BOURNEMOUTH- 71B	BOURNEMOUTH- 71B	BOURNEMOUTH- 71B
34095	BOURNEMOUTH- 71B	BOURNEMOUTH- 71B	BOURNEMOUTH- 71B	BOURNEMOUTH- 71B	BOURNEMOUTH- 71B	BOURNEMOUTH- 71B	BOURNEMOUTH- 71B
34096	RAMSGATE- 74B	RAMSGATE- 74B	RAMSGATE- 74B	RAMSGATE- 74B	RAMSGATE- 74B	RAMSGATE- 74B	RAMSGATE- 74B
34097	RAMSGATE- 74B	RAMSGATE- 74B	RAMSGATE- 74B	RAMSGATE- 74B	RAMSGATE- 74B	RAMSGATE- 74B	RAMSGATE- 74B
34098	RAMSGATE- 74B	RAMSGATE- 74B	RAMSGATE- 74B	RAMSGATE- 74B	RAMSGATE- 74B	RAMSGATE- 74B	RAMSGATE- 74B
34099	RAMSGATE- 74B	RAMSGATE- 74B	RAMSGATE- 74B	RAMSGATE- 74B	RAMSGATE- 74B	RAMSGATE- 74B	RAMSGATE- 74B
34100	RAMSGATE- 74B	RAMSGATE- 74B	RAMSGATE- 74B	RAMSGATE- 74B	RAMSGATE- 74B	RAMSGATE- 74B	RAMSGATE- 74B
34101	STEWARTS LANE - 73A	STEWARTS LANE - 73A	STEWARTS LANE - 73A	STEWARTS LANE - 73A	STEWARTS LANE - 73A	STEWARTS LANE - 73A	STEWARTS LANE - 73A
34102	STEWARTS LANE - 73A	STEWARTS LANE - 73A	STEWARTS LANE - 73A	STEWARTS LANE - 73A	STEWARTS LANE - 73A	STEWARTS LANE - 73A	STEWARTS LANE - 73A
34103	STEWARTS LANE - 73A	STEWARTS LANE - 73A	STEWARTS LANE - 73A	STEWARTS LANE - 73A	STEWARTS LANE - 73A	STEWARTS LANE - 73A	STEWARTS LANE - 73A
34104	STEWARTS LANE - 73A	STEWARTS LANE - 73A	STEWARTS LANE - 73A	STEWARTS LANE - 73A	STEWARTS LANE - 73A	STEWARTS LANE - 73A	STEWARTS LANE - 73A
34105	BOURNEMOUTH- 71B	BOURNEMOUTH- 71B	BOURNEMOUTH- 71B	BOURNEMOUTH- 71B	BOURNEMOUTH- 71B	BOURNEMOUTH- 71B	BOURNEMOUTH- 71B
34106	BOURNEMOUTH- 71B	BOURNEMOUTH- 71B	BOURNEMOUTH- 71B	BOURNEMOUTH- 71B	BOURNEMOUTH- 71B	BOURNEMOUTH- 71B	BOURNEMOUTH- 71B
34107	BOURNEMOUTH- 71B	BOURNEMOUTH- 71B	BOURNEMOUTH- 71B	BOURNEMOUTH- 71B	BOURNEMOUTH- 71B	BOURNEMOUTH- 71B	BOURNEMOUTH- 71B
34108	BOURNEMOUTH- 71B	BOURNEMOUTH- 71B	BOURNEMOUTH- 71B	BOURNEMOUTH- 71B	BOURNEMOUTH- 71B	BOURNEMOUTH- 71B	BOURNEMOUTH- 71B
34109	BOURNEMOUTH- 71B	BOURNEMOUTH- 71B	BOURNEMOUTH- 71B	BOURNEMOUTH- 71B	BOURNEMOUTH- 71B	BOURNEMOUTH- 71B	BOURNEMOUTH- 71B
34110	BOURNEMOUTH- 71B	BOURNEMOUTH- 71B	BOURNEMOUTH- 71B	BOURNEMOUTH- 71B	BOURNEMOUTH- 71B	BOURNEMOUTH- 71B	BOURNEMOUTH- 71B

loco	Feb-55	Apr-55	Jun-55	Aug-55	Sep-55	Nov-55	Dec-55
				WC 4-6-2 (1945)			
34031	EXMOUTH J CN-72A	EXMOUTH J CN-72A	EXMOUTH J CN-72A	EXMOUTH J CN-72A	EXMOUTH J CN-72A	EXMOUTH J CN-72A	EXMOUTH J CN-72A
34032	EXMOUTH J CN-72A	EXMOUTH J CN-72A	EXMOUTH J CN-72A	EXMOUTH J CN-72A	EXMOUTH J CN-72A	EXMOUTH J CN-72A	EXMOUTH J CN-72A
34033	EXMOUTH J CN-72A	EXMOUTH J CN-72A	EXMOUTH J CN-72A	EXMOUTH J CN-72A	EXMOUTH J CN-72A	EXMOUTH J CN-72A	EXMOUTH J CN-72A
34034	EXMOUTH J CN-72A	EXMOUTH J CN-72A	EXMOUTH J CN-72A	EXMOUTH J CN-72A	EXMOUTH J CN-72A	EXMOUTH J CN-72A	EXMOUTH J CN-72A
34035	PLYMOUTH-72D	PLYMOUTH-72D	PLYMOUTH-72D	PLYMOUTH-72D	PLYMOUTH-72D	PLYMOUTH-72D	PLYMOUTH-72D
34036	PLYMOUTH-72D	PLYMOUTH-72D	PLYMOUTH-72D	PLYMOUTH-72D	PLYMOUTH-72D	PLYMOUTH-72D	PLYMOUTH-72D
34037	BRIGHTON-75A	BRIGHTON-75A	BRIGHTON-75A	BRIGHTON-75A	BRIGHTON-75A	BRIGHTON-75A	BRIGHTON-75A
34038	BRIGHTON-75A	BRIGHTON-75A	BRIGHTON-75A	BRIGHTON-75A	BRIGHTON-75A	BRIGHTON-75A	BRIGHTON-75A
34039	BRIGHTON-75A	BRIGHTON-75A	BRIGHTON-75A	BRIGHTON-75A	BRIGHTON-75A	BRIGHTON-75A	BRIGHTON-75A
34040	EASTLEIGH-71A	EASTLEIGH-71A	EASTLEIGH-71A	EASTLEIGH-71A	EASTLEIGH-71A	EASTLEIGH-71A	EASTLEIGH-71A
34041	EASTLEIGH-71A	EASTLEIGH-71A	EASTLEIGH-71A	EASTLEIGH-71A	EASTLEIGH-71A	EASTLEIGH-71A	EASTLEIGH-71A
34042	EASTLEIGH-71A	EASTLEIGH-71A	EASTLEIGH-71A	EASTLEIGH-71A	EASTLEIGH-71A	EASTLEIGH-71A	EASTLEIGH-71A
34043	BOURNEMOUTH-71B	BOURNEMOUTH-71B	BOURNEMOUTH-71B	BOURNEMOUTH-71B	BOURNEMOUTH-71B	BOURNEMOUTH-71B	BOURNEMOUTH-71B
34044	BOURNEMOUTH-71B	BOURNEMOUTH-71B	BOURNEMOUTH-71B	BOURNEMOUTH-71B	BOURNEMOUTH-71B	BOURNEMOUTH-71B	BOURNEMOUTH-71B
34045	BRIGHTON-75A	BRIGHTON-75A	BRIGHTON-75A	BRIGHTON-75A	BRIGHTON-75A	BRIGHTON-75A	BRIGHTON-75A
34046	BRIGHTON-75A	BRIGHTON-75A	BRIGHTON-75A	BRIGHTON-75A	BRIGHTON-75A	BRIGHTON-75A	BRIGHTON-75A
34047	BRIGHTON-75A	BRIGHTON-75A	BRIGHTON-75A	BRIGHTON-75A	BRIGHTON-75A	BRIGHTON-75A	BRIGHTON-75A
34048	BRIGHTON-75A	BRIGHTON-75A	BRIGHTON-75A	BRIGHTON-75A	BRIGHTON-75A	BRIGHTON-75A	BRIGHTON-75A
34049	SALISBURY-72B	SALISBURY-72B	SALISBURY-72B	SALISBURY-72B	SALISBURY-72B	SALISBURY-72B	SALISBURY-72B
34050	SALISBURY-72B	SALISBURY-72B	SALISBURY-72B	SALISBURY-72B	SALISBURY-72B	SALISBURY-72B	SALISBURY-72B
34051	SALISBURY-72B	SALISBURY-72B	SALISBURY-72B	SALISBURY-72B	SALISBURY-72B	SALISBURY-72B	SALISBURY-72B
34052	SALISBURY-72B	SALISBURY-72B	SALISBURY-72B	SALISBURY-72B	SALISBURY-72B	SALISBURY-72B	SALISBURY-72B
34053	SALISBURY-72B	SALISBURY-72B	SALISBURY-72B	SALISBURY-72B	SALISBURY-72B	SALISBURY-72B	SALISBURY-72B
34054	SALISBURY-72B	SALISBURY-72B	SALISBURY-72B	SALISBURY-72B	SALISBURY-72B	SALISBURY-72B	SALISBURY-72B
34055	SALISBURY-72B	SALISBURY-72B	SALISBURY-72B	SALISBURY-72B	SALISBURY-72B	SALISBURY-72B	SALISBURY-72B
34056	EXMOUTH J CN-72A	EXMOUTH J CN-72A	EXMOUTH J CN-72A	EXMOUTH J CN-72A	EXMOUTH J CN-72A	EXMOUTH J CN-72A	EXMOUTH J CN-72A
34057	EXMOUTH J CN-72A	EXMOUTH J CN-72A	EXMOUTH J CN-72A	EXMOUTH J CN-72A	EXMOUTH J CN-72A	EXMOUTH J CN-72A	EXMOUTH J CN-72A
34058	EXMOUTH J CN-72A	EXMOUTH J CN-72A	EXMOUTH J CN-72A	EXMOUTH J CN-72A	EXMOUTH J CN-72A	EXMOUTH J CN-72A	EXMOUTH J CN-72A
34059	EXMOUTH J CN-72A	EXMOUTH J CN-72A	EXMOUTH J CN-72A	EXMOUTH J CN-72A	SALISBURY-72B	SALISBURY-72B	SALISBURY-72B
34060	NINE ELMS-70A	NINE ELMS-70A	NINE ELMS-70A	NINE ELMS-70A	NINE ELMS-70A	NINE ELMS-70A	NINE ELMS-70A
34061	EXMOUTH J CN-72A	EXMOUTH J CN-72A	EXMOUTH J CN-72A	EXMOUTH J CN-72A	EXMOUTH J CN-72A	EXMOUTH J CN-72A	EXMOUTH J CN-72A
34062	NINE ELMS-70A	NINE ELMS-70A	NINE ELMS-70A	NINE ELMS-70A	NINE ELMS-70A	NINE ELMS-70A	NINE ELMS-70A
34063	NINE ELMS-70A	NINE ELMS-70A	NINE ELMS-70A	NINE ELMS-70A	NINE ELMS-70A	NINE ELMS-70A	NINE ELMS-70A
34064	NINE ELMS-70A	NINE ELMS-70A	NINE ELMS-70A	NINE ELMS-70A	NINE ELMS-70A	NINE ELMS-70A	NINE ELMS-70A
34065	STEWARTS LANE-73A	STEWARTS LANE-73A	NINE ELMS-70A	NINE ELMS-70A	NINE ELMS-70A	NINE ELMS-70A	NINE ELMS-70A
34066	STEWARTS LANE-73A	STEWARTS LANE-73A	STEWARTS LANE-73A	STEWARTS LANE-73A	STEWARTS LANE-73A	STEWARTS LANE-73A	STEWARTS LANE-73A
34067	STEWARTS LANE-73A	STEWARTS LANE-73A	STEWARTS LANE-73A	STEWARTS LANE-73A	STEWARTS LANE-73A	STEWARTS LANE-73A	STEWARTS LANE-73A
34068	STEWARTS LANE-73A	STEWARTS LANE-73A	STEWARTS LANE-73A	STEWARTS LANE-73A	STEWARTS LANE-73A	STEWARTS LANE-73A	STEWARTS LANE-73A
34069	EXMOUTH J CN-72A	EXMOUTH J CN-72A	EXMOUTH J CN-72A	EXMOUTH J CN-72A	EXMOUTH J CN-72A	EXMOUTH J CN-72A	EXMOUTH J CN-72A
34070	STEWARTS LANE-73A	STEWARTS LANE-73A	DOVER-74C	DOVER-74C	DOVER-74C	DOVER-74C	DOVER-74C
34071	STEWARTS LANE-73A	STEWARTS LANE-73A	DOVER-74C	DOVER-74C	DOVER-74C	DOVER-74C	DOVER-74C
34072	DOVER-74C	DOVER-74C	DOVER-74C	DOVER-74C	DOVER-74C	DOVER-74C	DOVER-74C
34073	DOVER-74C	DOVER-74C	DOVER-74C	DOVER-74C	DOVER-74C	DOVER-74C	DOVER-74C
34074	DOVER-74C	DOVER-74C	DOVER-74C	DOVER-74C	DOVER-74C	DOVER-74C	DOVER-74C
34075	RAMSGATE-74B	RAMSGATE-74B	RAMSGATE-74B	RAMSGATE-74B	RAMSGATE-74B	RAMSGATE-74B	RAMSGATE-74B
34076	RAMSGATE-74B	RAMSGATE-74B	RAMSGATE-74B	RAMSGATE-74B	RAMSGATE-74B	RAMSGATE-74B	RAMSGATE-74B
34077	RAMSGATE-74B	RAMSGATE-74B	RAMSGATE-74B	RAMSGATE-74B	RAMSGATE-74B	RAMSGATE-74B	RAMSGATE-74B
34078	RAMSGATE-74B	RAMSGATE-74B	RAMSGATE-74B	RAMSGATE-74B	RAMSGATE-74B	RAMSGATE-74B	RAMSGATE-74B
34079	RAMSGATE-74B	RAMSGATE-74B	RAMSGATE-74B	RAMSGATE-74B	RAMSGATE-74B	RAMSGATE-74B	RAMSGATE-74B
34080	RAMSGATE-74B	RAMSGATE-74B	RAMSGATE-74B	RAMSGATE-74B	RAMSGATE-74B	RAMSGATE-74B	RAMSGATE-74B
34081	RAMSGATE-74B	RAMSGATE-74B	RAMSGATE-74B	RAMSGATE-74B	RAMSGATE-74B	RAMSGATE-74B	RAMSGATE-74B
34082	RAMSGATE-74B	RAMSGATE-74B	RAMSGATE-74B	RAMSGATE-74B	RAMSGATE-74B	RAMSGATE-74B	RAMSGATE-74B
34083	STEWARTS LANE-73A	STEWARTS LANE-73A	STEWARTS LANE-73A	STEWARTS LANE-73A	STEWARTS LANE-73A	STEWARTS LANE-73A	STEWARTS LANE-73A
34084	STEWARTS LANE-73A	STEWARTS LANE-73A	STEWARTS LANE-73A	STEWARTS LANE-73A	STEWARTS LANE-73A	STEWARTS LANE-73A	STEWARTS LANE-73A
34085	STEWARTS LANE-73A	STEWARTS LANE-73A	STEWARTS LANE-73A	STEWARTS LANE-73A	STEWARTS LANE-73A	STEWARTS LANE-73A	STEWARTS LANE-73A
34086	RAMSGATE-74B	RAMSGATE-74B	RAMSGATE-74B	RAMSGATE-74B	RAMSGATE-74B	RAMSGATE-74B	RAMSGATE-74B
34087	STEWARTS LANE-73A	STEWARTS LANE-73A	STEWARTS LANE-73A	STEWARTS LANE-73A	STEWARTS LANE-73A	STEWARTS LANE-73A	STEWARTS LANE-73A
34088	STEWARTS LANE-73A	STEWARTS LANE-73A	STEWARTS LANE-73A	STEWARTS LANE-73A	STEWARTS LANE-73A	STEWARTS LANE-73A	STEWARTS LANE-73A
34089	STEWARTS LANE-73A	STEWARTS LANE-73A	STEWARTS LANE-73A	STEWARTS LANE-73A	STEWARTS LANE-73A	STEWARTS LANE-73A	STEWARTS LANE-73A
34090	RAMSGATE-74B	RAMSGATE-74B	RAMSGATE-74B	RAMSGATE-74B	STEWARTS LANE-73A	STEWARTS LANE-73A	STEWARTS LANE-73A
34091	STEWARTS LANE-73A	STEWARTS LANE-73A	STEWARTS LANE-73A	STEWARTS LANE-73A	STEWARTS LANE-73A	STEWARTS LANE-73A	STEWARTS LANE-73A
34092	STEWARTS LANE-73A	STEWARTS LANE-73A	STEWARTS LANE-73A	STEWARTS LANE-73A	STEWARTS LANE-73A	STEWARTS LANE-73A	STEWARTS LANE-73A
34093	BOURNEMOUTH-71B	BOURNEMOUTH-71B	BOURNEMOUTH-71B	BOURNEMOUTH-71B	BOURNEMOUTH-71B	BOURNEMOUTH-71B	BOURNEMOUTH-71B
34094	BOURNEMOUTH-71B	BOURNEMOUTH-71B	BOURNEMOUTH-71B	BOURNEMOUTH-71B	BOURNEMOUTH-71B	BOURNEMOUTH-71B	BOURNEMOUTH-71B
34095	BOURNEMOUTH-71B	BOURNEMOUTH-71B	BOURNEMOUTH-71B	BOURNEMOUTH-71B	BOURNEMOUTH-71B	BOURNEMOUTH-71B	BOURNEMOUTH-71B
34096	RAMSGATE-74B	RAMSGATE-74B	RAMSGATE-74B	RAMSGATE-74B	RAMSGATE-74B	RAMSGATE-74B	RAMSGATE-74B
34097	RAMSGATE-74B	RAMSGATE-74B	RAMSGATE-74B	RAMSGATE-74B	RAMSGATE-74B	RAMSGATE-74B	RAMSGATE-74B
34098	RAMSGATE-74B	RAMSGATE-74B	RAMSGATE-74B	RAMSGATE-74B	RAMSGATE-74B	RAMSGATE-74B	RAMSGATE-74B
34099	RAMSGATE-74B	RAMSGATE-74B	RAMSGATE-74B	RAMSGATE-74B	RAMSGATE-74B	RAMSGATE-74B	RAMSGATE-74B
34100	RAMSGATE-74B	RAMSGATE-74B	RAMSGATE-74B	RAMSGATE-74B	RAMSGATE-74B	RAMSGATE-74B	RAMSGATE-74B
34101	STEWARTS LANE-73A	STEWARTS LANE-73A	STEWARTS LANE-73A	STEWARTS LANE-73A	STEWARTS LANE-73A	STEWARTS LANE-73A	STEWARTS LANE-73A
34102	STEWARTS LANE-73A	STEWARTS LANE-73A	STEWARTS LANE-73A	STEWARTS LANE-73A	STEWARTS LANE-73A	STEWARTS LANE-73A	STEWARTS LANE-73A
34103	STEWARTS LANE-73A	STEWARTS LANE-73A	STEWARTS LANE-73A	STEWARTS LANE-73A	STEWARTS LANE-73A	STEWARTS LANE-73A	STEWARTS LANE-73A
34104	STEWARTS LANE-73A	STEWARTS LANE-73A	STEWARTS LANE-73A	STEWARTS LANE-73A	STEWARTS LANE-73A	STEWARTS LANE-73A	STEWARTS LANE-73A
34105	BOURNEMOUTH-71B	BOURNEMOUTH-71B	BOURNEMOUTH-71B	BOURNEMOUTH-71B	BOURNEMOUTH-71B	BOURNEMOUTH-71B	BOURNEMOUTH-71B
34106	BOURNEMOUTH-71B	BOURNEMOUTH-71B	BOURNEMOUTH-71B	BOURNEMOUTH-71B	BOURNEMOUTH-71B	BOURNEMOUTH-71B	BOURNEMOUTH-71B
34107	BOURNEMOUTH-71B	BOURNEMOUTH-71B	BOURNEMOUTH-71B	BOURNEMOUTH-71B	BOURNEMOUTH-71B	BOURNEMOUTH-71B	BOURNEMOUTH-71B
34108	BOURNEMOUTH-71B	BOURNEMOUTH-71B	BOURNEMOUTH-71B	BOURNEMOUTH-71B	BOURNEMOUTH-71B	BOURNEMOUTH-71B	BOURNEMOUTH-71B
34109	BOURNEMOUTH-71B	BOURNEMOUTH-71B	BOURNEMOUTH-71B	BOURNEMOUTH-71B	BOURNEMOUTH-71B	BOURNEMOUTH-71B	BOURNEMOUTH-71B
34110	BOURNEMOUTH-71B	BOURNEMOUTH-71B	BOURNEMOUTH-71B	BOURNEMOUTH-71B	BOURNEMOUTH-71B	BOURNEMOUTH-71B	BOURNEMOUTH-71B

loco	Jan-56	Apr-56	May-56	Aug-56	Oct-56	Nov-56	Jan-57
				WC 4-6-2 (1945)			
34031	EXMOUTH JCN-72A	EXMOUTH JCN-72A	EXMOUTH JCN-72A	EXMOUTH JCN-72A	EXMOUTH JCN-72A	EXMOUTH JCN-72A	EXMOUTH JCN-72A
34032	EXMOUTH JCN-72A	EXMOUTH JCN-72A	EXMOUTH JCN-72A	EXMOUTH JCN-72A	EXMOUTH JCN-72A	EXMOUTH JCN-72A	EXMOUTH JCN-72A
34033	EXMOUTH JCN-72A	EXMOUTH JCN-72A	EXMOUTH JCN-72A	EXMOUTH JCN-72A	EXMOUTH JCN-72A	EXMOUTH JCN-72A	EXMOUTH JCN-72A
34034	EXMOUTH JCN-72A	EXMOUTH JCN-72A	EXMOUTH JCN-72A	EXMOUTH JCN-72A	EXMOUTH JCN-72A	EXMOUTH JCN-72A	EXMOUTH JCN-72A
34035	PLYMOUTH-72D	PLYMOUTH-72D	PLYMOUTH-72D	PLYMOUTH-72D	PLYMOUTH-72D	PLYMOUTH-72D	PLYMOUTH-72D
34036	PLYMOUTH-72D	PLYMOUTH-72D	PLYMOUTH-72D	PLYMOUTH-72D	PLYMOUTH-72D	PLYMOUTH-72D	PLYMOUTH-72D
34037	BRIGHTON-75A	BRIGHTON-75A	BRIGHTON-75A	BRIGHTON-75A	BRIGHTON-75A	BRIGHTON-75A	BRIGHTON-75A
34038	BRIGHTON-75A	BRIGHTON-75A	BRIGHTON-75A	BRIGHTON-75A	BRIGHTON-75A	BRIGHTON-75A	BRIGHTON-75A
34039	BRIGHTON-75A	BRIGHTON-75A	BRIGHTON-75A	BRIGHTON-75A	BRIGHTON-75A	BRIGHTON-75A	BRIGHTON-75A
34040	EASTLEIGH-71A	EASTLEIGH-71A	EASTLEIGH-71A	EASTLEIGH-71A	EASTLEIGH-71A	EASTLEIGH-71A	EASTLEIGH-71A
34041	EASTLEIGH-71A	EASTLEIGH-71A	EASTLEIGH-71A	EASTLEIGH-71A	EASTLEIGH-71A	EASTLEIGH-71A	EASTLEIGH-71A
34042	EASTLEIGH-71A	EASTLEIGH-71A	EASTLEIGH-71A	EASTLEIGH-71A	EASTLEIGH-71A	EASTLEIGH-71A	EASTLEIGH-71A
34043	BOURNEMOUTH-71B	BOURNEMOUTH-71B	BOURNEMOUTH-71B	BOURNEMOUTH-71B	BOURNEMOUTH-71B	BOURNEMOUTH-71B	BOURNEMOUTH-71B
34044	BOURNEMOUTH-71B	BOURNEMOUTH-71B	BOURNEMOUTH-71B	BOURNEMOUTH-71B	BOURNEMOUTH-71B	BOURNEMOUTH-71B	BOURNEMOUTH-71B
34045	BRIGHTON-75A	BRIGHTON-75A	BRIGHTON-75A	BRIGHTON-75A	BRIGHTON-75A	BRIGHTON-75A	BRIGHTON-75A
34046	BRIGHTON-75A	BRIGHTON-75A	BRIGHTON-75A	BRIGHTON-75A	BRIGHTON-75A	BRIGHTON-75A	BRIGHTON-75A
34047	BRIGHTON-75A	BRIGHTON-75A	BRIGHTON-75A	BRIGHTON-75A	BRIGHTON-75A	BRIGHTON-75A	BRIGHTON-75A
34048	BRIGHTON-75A	BRIGHTON-75A	BRIGHTON-75A	BRIGHTON-75A	BRIGHTON-75A	BRIGHTON-75A	BRIGHTON-75A
34049	SALISBURY-72B	SALISBURY-72B	SALISBURY-72B	SALISBURY-72B	SALISBURY-72B	SALISBURY-72B	SALISBURY-72B
34050	SALISBURY-72B	SALISBURY-72B	SALISBURY-72B	SALISBURY-72B	SALISBURY-72B	SALISBURY-72B	SALISBURY-72B
34051	SALISBURY-72B	SALISBURY-72B	SALISBURY-72B	SALISBURY-72B	SALISBURY-72B	SALISBURY-72B	SALISBURY-72B
34052	SALISBURY-72B	SALISBURY-72B	SALISBURY-72B	SALISBURY-72B	SALISBURY-72B	SALISBURY-72B	SALISBURY-72B
34053	SALISBURY-72B	SALISBURY-72B	SALISBURY-72B	SALISBURY-72B	SALISBURY-72B	SALISBURY-72B	SALISBURY-72B
34054	SALISBURY-72B	SALISBURY-72B	SALISBURY-72B	SALISBURY-72B	SALISBURY-72B	SALISBURY-72B	SALISBURY-72B
34055	SALISBURY-72B	SALISBURY-72B	SALISBURY-72B	SALISBURY-72B	SALISBURY-72B	SALISBURY-72B	SALISBURY-72B
34056	EXMOUTH JCN-72A	EXMOUTH JCN-72A	EXMOUTH JCN-72A	EXMOUTH JCN-72A	EXMOUTH JCN-72A	EXMOUTH JCN-72A	EXMOUTH JCN-72A
34057	EXMOUTH JCN-72A	EXMOUTH JCN-72A	EXMOUTH JCN-72A	EXMOUTH JCN-72A	EXMOUTH JCN-72A	EXMOUTH JCN-72A	EXMOUTH JCN-72A
34058	EXMOUTH JCN-72A	EXMOUTH JCN-72A	EXMOUTH JCN-72A	EXMOUTH JCN-72A	EXMOUTH JCN-72A	EXMOUTH JCN-72A	EXMOUTH JCN-72A
34059	SALISBURY-72B	SALISBURY-72B	SALISBURY-72B	SALISBURY-72B	SALISBURY-72B	SALISBURY-72B	SALISBURY-72B
34060	NINE ELMS-70A	NINE ELMS-70A	NINE ELMS-70A	NINE ELMS-70A	NINE ELMS-70A	NINE ELMS-70A	NINE ELMS-70A
34061	EXMOUTH JCN-72A	EXMOUTH JCN-72A	EXMOUTH JCN-72A	EXMOUTH JCN-72A	EXMOUTH JCN-72A	EXMOUTH JCN-72A	EXMOUTH JCN-72A
34062	NINE ELMS-70A	NINE ELMS-70A	NINE ELMS-70A	NINE ELMS-70A	NINE ELMS-70A	NINE ELMS-70A	NINE ELMS-70A
34063	NINE ELMS-70A	NINE ELMS-70A	NINE ELMS-70A	NINE ELMS-70A	NINE ELMS-70A	NINE ELMS-70A	NINE ELMS-70A
34064	NINE ELMS-70A	NINE ELMS-70A	NINE ELMS-70A	NINE ELMS-70A	NINE ELMS-70A	NINE ELMS-70A	NINE ELMS-70A
34065	NINE ELMS-70A	NINE ELMS-70A	NINE ELMS-70A	NINE ELMS-70A	NINE ELMS-70A	NINE ELMS-70A	NINE ELMS-70A
34066	STEWARTS LANE-73A	STEWARTS LANE-73A	STEWARTS LANE-73A	STEWARTS LANE-73A	STEWARTS LANE-73A	STEWARTS LANE-73A	STEWARTS LANE-73A
34067	STEWARTS LANE-73A	STEWARTS LANE-73A	STEWARTS LANE-73A	STEWARTS LANE-73A	STEWARTS LANE-73A	STEWARTS LANE-73A	STEWARTS LANE-73A
34068	STEWARTS LANE-73A	STEWARTS LANE-73A	STEWARTS LANE-73A	STEWARTS LANE-73A	STEWARTS LANE-73A	STEWARTS LANE-73A	STEWARTS LANE-73A
34069	EXMOUTH JCN-72A	EXMOUTH JCN-72A	EXMOUTH JCN-72A	EXMOUTH JCN-72A	EXMOUTH JCN-72A	EXMOUTH JCN-72A	EXMOUTH JCN-72A
34070	DOVER-74C	DOVER-74C	DOVER-74C	DOVER-74C	DOVER-74C	DOVER-74C	DOVER-74C
34071	DOVER-74C	DOVER-74C	DOVER-74C	DOVER-74C	DOVER-74C	DOVER-74C	DOVER-74C
34072	DOVER-74C	DOVER-74C	DOVER-74C	DOVER-74C	DOVER-74C	DOVER-74C	DOVER-74C
34073	DOVER-74C	DOVER-74C	DOVER-74C	DOVER-74C	DOVER-74C	DOVER-74C	DOVER-74C
34074	DOVER-74C	DOVER-74C	DOVER-74C	DOVER-74C	DOVER-74C	DOVER-74C	DOVER-74C
34075	RAMSGATE-74B	RAMSGATE-74B	RAMSGATE-74B	RAMSGATE-74B	RAMSGATE-74B	RAMSGATE-74B	RAMSGATE-74B
34076	RAMSGATE-74B	RAMSGATE-74B	RAMSGATE-74B	RAMSGATE-74B	RAMSGATE-74B	RAMSGATE-74B	RAMSGATE-74B
34077	RAMSGATE-74B	RAMSGATE-74B	RAMSGATE-74B	RAMSGATE-74B	RAMSGATE-74B	RAMSGATE-74B	RAMSGATE-74B
34078	RAMSGATE-74B	RAMSGATE-74B	RAMSGATE-74B	RAMSGATE-74B	RAMSGATE-74B	RAMSGATE-74B	RAMSGATE-74B
34079	RAMSGATE-74B	RAMSGATE-74B	RAMSGATE-74B	RAMSGATE-74B	RAMSGATE-74B	RAMSGATE-74B	RAMSGATE-74B
34080	RAMSGATE-74B	RAMSGATE-74B	RAMSGATE-74B	RAMSGATE-74B	RAMSGATE-74B	RAMSGATE-74B	RAMSGATE-74B
34081	RAMSGATE-74B	RAMSGATE-74B	RAMSGATE-74B	RAMSGATE-74B	RAMSGATE-74B	RAMSGATE-74B	RAMSGATE-74B
34082	RAMSGATE-74B	RAMSGATE-74B	RAMSGATE-74B	RAMSGATE-74B	RAMSGATE-74B	RAMSGATE-74B	RAMSGATE-74B
34083	STEWARTS LANE-73A	STEWARTS LANE-73A	STEWARTS LANE-73A	STEWARTS LANE-73A	STEWARTS LANE-73A	STEWARTS LANE-73A	STEWARTS LANE-73A
34084	STEWARTS LANE-73A	STEWARTS LANE-73A	STEWARTS LANE-73A	STEWARTS LANE-73A	STEWARTS LANE-73A	STEWARTS LANE-73A	STEWARTS LANE-73A
34085	STEWARTS LANE-73A	STEWARTS LANE-73A	STEWARTS LANE-73A	STEWARTS LANE-73A	STEWARTS LANE-73A	STEWARTS LANE-73A	STEWARTS LANE-73A
34086	RAMSGATE-74B	RAMSGATE-74B	RAMSGATE-74B	RAMSGATE-74B	RAMSGATE-74B	RAMSGATE-74B	RAMSGATE-74B
34087	STEWARTS LANE-73A	STEWARTS LANE-73A	STEWARTS LANE-73A	STEWARTS LANE-73A	STEWARTS LANE-73A	STEWARTS LANE-73A	STEWARTS LANE-73A
34088	STEWARTS LANE-73A	STEWARTS LANE-73A	STEWARTS LANE-73A	STEWARTS LANE-73A	STEWARTS LANE-73A	STEWARTS LANE-73A	STEWARTS LANE-73A
34089	STEWARTS LANE-73A	STEWARTS LANE-73A	STEWARTS LANE-73A	STEWARTS LANE-73A	STEWARTS LANE-73A	STEWARTS LANE-73A	STEWARTS LANE-73A
34090	STEWARTS LANE-73A	STEWARTS LANE-73A	STEWARTS LANE-73A	STEWARTS LANE-73A	STEWARTS LANE-73A	STEWARTS LANE-73A	STEWARTS LANE-73A
34091	STEWARTS LANE-73A	STEWARTS LANE-73A	STEWARTS LANE-73A	STEWARTS LANE-73A	STEWARTS LANE-73A	STEWARTS LANE-73A	STEWARTS LANE-73A
34092	STEWARTS LANE-73A	STEWARTS LANE-73A	STEWARTS LANE-73A	STEWARTS LANE-73A	STEWARTS LANE-73A	STEWARTS LANE-73A	STEWARTS LANE-73A
34093	BOURNEMOUTH-71B	BOURNEMOUTH-71B	BOURNEMOUTH-71B	BOURNEMOUTH-71B	BOURNEMOUTH-71B	BOURNEMOUTH-71B	BOURNEMOUTH-71B
34094	BOURNEMOUTH-71B	BOURNEMOUTH-71B	BOURNEMOUTH-71B	BOURNEMOUTH-71B	BOURNEMOUTH-71B	BOURNEMOUTH-71B	BOURNEMOUTH-71B
34095	NINE ELMS-70A	NINE ELMS-70A	NINE ELMS-70A	NINE ELMS-70A	NINE ELMS-70A	NINE ELMS-70A	NINE ELMS-70A
34096	RAMSGATE-74B	RAMSGATE-74B	RAMSGATE-74B	RAMSGATE-74B	RAMSGATE-74B	RAMSGATE-74B	RAMSGATE-74B
34097	RAMSGATE-74B	RAMSGATE-74B	RAMSGATE-74B	RAMSGATE-74B	RAMSGATE-74B	RAMSGATE-74B	RAMSGATE-74B
34098	RAMSGATE-74B	RAMSGATE-74B	RAMSGATE-74B	RAMSGATE-74B	RAMSGATE-74B	RAMSGATE-74B	RAMSGATE-74B
34099	RAMSGATE-74B	RAMSGATE-74B	RAMSGATE-74B	RAMSGATE-74B	RAMSGATE-74B	RAMSGATE-74B	RAMSGATE-74B
34100	RAMSGATE-74B	RAMSGATE-74B	RAMSGATE-74B	RAMSGATE-74B	RAMSGATE-74B	RAMSGATE-74B	RAMSGATE-74B
34101	STEWARTS LANE-73A	STEWARTS LANE-73A	STEWARTS LANE-73A	STEWARTS LANE-73A	STEWARTS LANE-73A	STEWARTS LANE-73A	STEWARTS LANE-73A
34102	STEWARTS LANE-73A	STEWARTS LANE-73A	STEWARTS LANE-73A	STEWARTS LANE-73A	STEWARTS LANE-73A	STEWARTS LANE-73A	STEWARTS LANE-73A
34103	STEWARTS LANE-73A	STEWARTS LANE-73A	STEWARTS LANE-73A	STEWARTS LANE-73A	STEWARTS LANE-73A	DOVER-74C	DOVER-74C
34104	STEWARTS LANE-73A	STEWARTS LANE-73A	STEWARTS LANE-73A	STEWARTS LANE-73A	STEWARTS LANE-73A	DOVER-74C	DOVER-74C
34105	BOURNEMOUTH-71B	BOURNEMOUTH-71B	BOURNEMOUTH-71B	BOURNEMOUTH-71B	BOURNEMOUTH-71B	BOURNEMOUTH-71B	BOURNEMOUTH-71B
34106	BOURNEMOUTH-71B	BOURNEMOUTH-71B	BOURNEMOUTH-71B	BOURNEMOUTH-71B	BOURNEMOUTH-71B	BOURNEMOUTH-71B	BOURNEMOUTH-71B
34107	BOURNEMOUTH-71B	BOURNEMOUTH-71B	BOURNEMOUTH-71B	BOURNEMOUTH-71B	BOURNEMOUTH-71B	BOURNEMOUTH-71B	BOURNEMOUTH-71B
34108	BOURNEMOUTH-71B	BOURNEMOUTH-71B	BOURNEMOUTH-71B	BOURNEMOUTH-71B	BOURNEMOUTH-71B	BOURNEMOUTH-71B	BOURNEMOUTH-71B
34109	BOURNEMOUTH-71B	BOURNEMOUTH-71B	BOURNEMOUTH-71B	BOURNEMOUTH-71B	BOURNEMOUTH-71B	BOURNEMOUTH-71B	BOURNEMOUTH-71B
34110	BOURNEMOUTH-71B	BOURNEMOUTH-71B	BOURNEMOUTH-71B	BOURNEMOUTH-71B	BOURNEMOUTH-71B	BOURNEMOUTH-71B	BOURNEMOUTH-71B

loco	Mar-57	Jun-57	Jul-57	Oct-57	Jan-58	Feb-58	Mar-58
				WC 4-6-2 (1945)			
34031	EXMOUTH JCN - 72A	EXMOUTH JCN - 72A	EXMOUTH JCN - 72A	EXMOUTH JCN - 72A	EXMOUTH JCN - 72A	EXMOUTH JCN - 72A	EXMOUTH JCN - 72A
34032	EXMOUTH JCN - 72A	EXMOUTH JCN - 72A	EXMOUTH JCN - 72A	EXMOUTH JCN - 72A	EXMOUTH JCN - 72A	EXMOUTH JCN - 72A	EXMOUTH JCN - 72A
34033	EXMOUTH JCN - 72A	EXMOUTH JCN - 72A	EXMOUTH JCN - 72A	EXMOUTH JCN - 72A	EXMOUTH JCN - 72A	EXMOUTH JCN - 72A	EXMOUTH JCN - 72A
34034	EXMOUTH JCN - 72A	EXMOUTH JCN - 72A	EXMOUTH JCN - 72A	EXMOUTH JCN - 72A	EXMOUTH JCN - 72A	EXMOUTH JCN - 72A	EXMOUTH JCN - 72A
34035	PLYMOUTH - 72D	PLYMOUTH - 72D	PLYMOUTH - 72D	PLYMOUTH - 72D	EXMOUTH JCN - 72A	EXMOUTH JCN - 72A	EXMOUTH JCN - 72A
34036	PLYMOUTH - 72D	PLYMOUTH - 72D	PLYMOUTH - 72D	PLYMOUTH - 72D	EXMOUTH JCN - 72A	EXMOUTH JCN - 72A	EXMOUTH JCN - 72A
34037	BRIGHTON - 75A	BRIGHTON - 75A	BRIGHTON - 75A	BRIGHTON - 75A	EXMOUTH JCN - 72A	RAMSGATE - 74B	R/B
34038	BRIGHTON - 75A	BRIGHTON - 75A	BRIGHTON - 75A	BRIGHTON - 75A	EXMOUTH JCN - 72A	EXMOUTH JCN - 72A	EXMOUTH JCN - 72A
34039	BRIGHTON - 75A	BRIGHTON - 75A	BRIGHTON - 75A	BRIGHTON - 75A	BRIGHTON - 75A	BRIGHTON - 75A	BRIGHTON - 75A
34040	EASTLEIGH - 71A	EASTLEIGH - 71A	EASTLEIGH - 71A	EASTLEIGH - 71A	EASTLEIGH - 71A	EASTLEIGH - 71A	EASTLEIGH - 71A
34041	EASTLEIGH - 71A	EASTLEIGH - 71A	EASTLEIGH - 71A	EASTLEIGH - 71A	EASTLEIGH - 71A	EASTLEIGH - 71A	EASTLEIGH - 71A
34042	EASTLEIGH - 71A	EASTLEIGH - 71A	EASTLEIGH - 71A	EASTLEIGH - 71A	EASTLEIGH - 71A	EASTLEIGH - 71A	EASTLEIGH - 71A
34043	BOURNEMOUTH - 71B	BOURNEMOUTH - 71B	BOURNEMOUTH - 71B	BOURNEMOUTH - 71B	BOURNEMOUTH - 71B	BOURNEMOUTH - 71B	BOURNEMOUTH - 71B
34044	BOURNEMOUTH - 71B	BOURNEMOUTH - 71B	BOURNEMOUTH - 71B	BOURNEMOUTH - 71B	BOURNEMOUTH - 71B	BOURNEMOUTH - 71B	BOURNEMOUTH - 71B
34045	BRIGHTON - 75A	BRIGHTON - 75A	BRIGHTON - 75A	BRIGHTON - 75A	BRIGHTON - 75A	BRIGHTON - 75A	BRIGHTON - 75A
34046	BRIGHTON - 75A	BRIGHTON - 75A	BRIGHTON - 75A	BRIGHTON - 75A	BRIGHTON - 75A	BRIGHTON - 75A	BRIGHTON - 75A
34047	BRIGHTON - 75A	BRIGHTON - 75A	BRIGHTON - 75A	BRIGHTON - 75A	BRIGHTON - 75A	BRIGHTON - 75A	BRIGHTON - 75A
34048	BRIGHTON - 75A	BRIGHTON - 75A	BRIGHTON - 75A	BRIGHTON - 75A	BRIGHTON - 75A	BRIGHTON - 75A	BRIGHTON - 75A
34049	SALISBURY - 72B	SALISBURY - 72B	SALISBURY - 72B	SALISBURY - 72B	SALISBURY - 72B	SALISBURY - 72B	SALISBURY - 72B
34050	SALISBURY - 72B	SALISBURY - 72B	SALISBURY - 72B	SALISBURY - 72B	SALISBURY - 72B	SALISBURY - 72B	SALISBURY - 72B
34051	SALISBURY - 72B	SALISBURY - 72B	SALISBURY - 72B	SALISBURY - 72B	SALISBURY - 72B	SALISBURY - 72B	SALISBURY - 72B
34052	SALISBURY - 72B	SALISBURY - 72B	SALISBURY - 72B	SALISBURY - 72B	SALISBURY - 72B	SALISBURY - 72B	SALISBURY - 72B
34053	SALISBURY - 72B	SALISBURY - 72B	SALISBURY - 72B	SALISBURY - 72B	SALISBURY - 72B	SALISBURY - 72B	SALISBURY - 72B
34054	SALISBURY - 72B	SALISBURY - 72B	SALISBURY - 72B	SALISBURY - 72B	SALISBURY - 72B	SALISBURY - 72B	SALISBURY - 72B
34055	SALISBURY - 72B	SALISBURY - 72B	SALISBURY - 72B	SALISBURY - 72B	SALISBURY - 72B	SALISBURY - 72B	SALISBURY - 72B
34056	EXMOUTH JCN - 72A	EXMOUTH JCN - 72A	EXMOUTH JCN - 72A	EXMOUTH JCN - 72A	EXMOUTH JCN - 72A	EXMOUTH JCN - 72A	EXMOUTH JCN - 72A
34057	EXMOUTH JCN - 72A	EXMOUTH JCN - 72A	EXMOUTH JCN - 72A	EXMOUTH JCN - 72A	EXMÓUTH JCN - 72A	EXMOUTH JCN - 72A	EXMOUTH JCN - 72A
34058	EXMOUTH JCN - 72A	EXMOUTH JCN - 72A	EXMOUTH JCN - 72A	EXMOUTH JCN - 72A	EXMOUTH JCN - 72A	EXMOUTH JCN - 72A	EXMOUTH JCN - 72A
34059	SALISBURY - 72B	SALISBURY - 72B	SALISBURY - 72B	SALISBURY - 72B	SALISBURY - 72B	SALISBURY - 72B	SALISBURY - 72B
34060	NINE ELMS - 70A	NINE ELMS - 70A	NINE ELMS - 70A	NINE ELMS - 70A	NINE ELMS - 70A	NINE ELMS - 70A	NINE ELMS - 70A
34061	EXMOUTH JCN - 72A	EXMOUTH JCN - 72A	EXMOUTH JCN - 72A	EXMOUTH JCN - 72A	EXMOUTH JCN - 72A	EXMOUTH JCN - 72A	EXMOUTH JCN - 72A
34062	NINE ELMS - 70A	NINE ELMS - 70A	NINE ELMS - 70A	NINE ELMS - 70A	NINE ELMS - 70A	NINE ELMS - 70A	NINE ELMS - 70A
34063	NINE ELMS - 70A	NINE ELMS - 70A	NINE ELMS - 70A	NINE ELMS - 70A	NINE ELMS - 70A	NINE ELMS - 70A	NINE ELMS - 70A
34064	NINE ELMS - 70A	NINE ELMS - 70A	NINE ELMS - 70A	NINE ELMS - 70A	NINE ELMS - 70A	NINE ELMS - 70A	NINE ELMS - 70A
34065	NINE ELMS - 70A	NINE ELMS - 70A	NINE ELMS - 70A	NINE ELMS - 70A	NINE ELMS - 70A	NINE ELMS - 70A	NINE ELMS - 70A
34066	STEWARTS LANE - 73A	STEWARTS LANE - 73A	STEWARTS LANE - 73A	STEWARTS LANE - 73A	STEWARTS LANE - 73A	STEWARTS LANE - 73A	STEWARTS LANE - 73A
34067	STEWARTS LANE - 73A	STEWARTS LANE - 73A	STEWARTS LANE - 73A	STEWARTS LANE - 73A	STEWARTS LANE - 73A	STEWARTS LANE - 73A	STEWARTS LANE - 73A
34068	STEWARTS LANE - 73A	STEWARTS LANE - 73A	STEWARTS LANE - 73A	STEWARTS LANE - 73A	STEWARTS LANE - 73A	STEWARTS LANE - 73A	STEWARTS LANE - 73A
34069	EXMOUTH JCN - 72A	EXMOUTH JCN - 72A	EXMOUTH JCN - 72A	EXMOUTH JCN - 72A	EXMOUTH JCN - 72A	EXMOUTH JCN - 72A	EXMOUTH JCN - 72A
34070	DOVER - 74C	DOVER - 74C	DOVER - 74C	DOVER - 74C	DOVER - 74C	DOVER - 74C	DOVER - 74C
34071	DOVER - 74C	DOVER - 74C	DOVER - 74C	DOVER - 74C	DOVER - 74C	DOVER - 74C	DOVER - 74C
34072	DOVER - 74C	DOVER - 74C	DOVER - 74C	DOVER - 74C	DOVER - 74C	EXMOUTH JCN - 72A	EXMOUTH JCN - 72A
34073	DOVER - 74C	DOVER - 74C	DOVER - 74C	DOVER - 74C	DOVER - 74C	DOVER - 74C	DOVER - 74C
34074	DOVER - 74C	DOVER - 74C	DOVER - 74C	DOVER - 74C	DOVER - 74C	DOVER - 74C	EXMOUTH JCN - 72A
34075	RAMSGATE - 74B	RAMSGATE - 74B	RAMSGATE - 74B	EXMOUTH JCN - 72A	EXMOUTH JCN - 72A	EXMOUTH JCN - 72A	EXMOUTH JCN - 72A
34076	RAMSGATE - 74B	RAMSGATE - 74B	RAMSGATE - 74B	EXMOUTH JCN - 72A	EXMOUTH JCN - 72A	EXMOUTH JCN - 72A	EXMOUTH JCN - 72A
34077	RAMSGATE - 74B	RAMSGATE - 74B	RAMSGATE - 74B	RAMSGATE - 74B	STEWARTS LANE - 73A	STEWARTS LANE - 73A	STEWARTS LANE - 73A
34078	RAMSGATE - 74B	RAMSGATE - 74B	RAMSGATE - 74B	RAMSGATE - 74B	RAMSGATE - 74B	RAMSGATE - 74B	RAMSGATE - 74B
34079	RAMSGATE - 74B	RAMSGATE - 74B	RAMSGATE - 74B	RAMSGATE - 74B	RAMSGATE - 74B	EXMOUTH JCN - 72A	EXMOUTH JCN - 72A
34080	RAMSGATE - 74B	RAMSGATE - 74B	RAMSGATE - 74B	RAMSGATE - 74B	EXMOUTH JCN - 72A	EXMOUTH JCN - 72A	EXMOUTH JCN - 72A
34081	RAMSGATE - 74B	RAMSGATE - 74B	RAMSGATE - 74B	EXMOUTH JCN - 72A	EXMOUTH JCN - 72A	EXMOUTH JCN - 72A	EXMOUTH JCN - 72A
34082	RAMSGATE - 74B	RAMSGATE - 74B	RAMSGATE - 74B	RAMSGATE - 74B	STEWARTS LANE - 73A	STEWARTS LANE - 73A	DOVER - 74C
34083	STEWARTS LANE - 73A	STEWARTS LANE - 73A	STEWARTS LANE - 73A	STEWARTS LANE - 73A	STEWARTS LANE - 73A	DOVER - 74C	DOVER - 74C
34084	STEWARTS LANE - 73A	STEWARTS LANE - 73A	STEWARTS LANE - 73A	STEWARTS LANE - 73A	STEWARTS LANE - 73A	STEWARTS LANE - 73A	DOVER - 74C
34085	STEWARTS LANE - 73A	STEWARTS LANE - 73A	STEWARTS LANE - 73A	STEWARTS LANE - 73A	STEWARTS LANE - 73A	DOVER - 74C	STEWARTS LANE - 73A
34086	RAMSGATE - 74B	RAMSGATE - 74B	RAMSGATE - 74B	EXMOUTH JCN - 72A	EXMOUTH JCN - 72A	DOVER - 74C	STEWARTS LANE - 73A
34087	STEWARTS LANE - 73A	STEWARTS LANE - 73A	STEWARTS LANE - 73A	STEWARTS LANE - 73A	STEWARTS LANE - 73A	STEWARTS LANE - 73A	STEWARTS LANE - 73A
34088	STEWARTS LANE - 73A	STEWARTS LANE - 73A	STEWARTS LANE - 73A	STEWARTS LANE - 73A	STEWARTS LANE - 73A	STEWARTS LANE - 73A	STEWARTS LANE - 73A
34089	STEWARTS LANE - 73A	STEWARTS LANE - 73A	STEWARTS LANE - 73A	STEWARTS LANE - 73A	STEWARTS LANE - 73A	STEWARTS LANE - 73A	STEWARTS LANE - 73A
34090	STEWARTS LANE - 73A	NINE ELMS - 70A	NINE ELMS - 70A	NINE ELMS - 70A	NINE ELMS - 70A	NINE ELMS - 70A	NINE ELMS - 70A
34091	STEWARTS LANE - 73A	STEWARTS LANE - 73A	STEWARTS LANE - 73A	STEWARTS LANE - 73A	STEWARTS LANE - 73A	STEWARTS LANE - 73A	STEWARTS LANE - 73A
34092	STEWARTS LANE - 73A	STEWARTS LANE - 73A	STEWARTS LANE - 73A	STEWARTS LANE - 73A	STEWARTS LANE - 73A	STEWARTS LANE - 73A	STEWARTS LANE - 73A
34093	BOURNEMOUTH - 71B	BOURNEMOUTH - 71B	BOURNEMOUTH - 71B	BOURNEMOUTH - 71B	BOURNEMOUTH - 71B	BOURNEMOUTH - 71B	BOURNEMOUTH - 71B
34094	BOURNEMOUTH - 71B	BOURNEMOUTH - 71B	BOURNEMOUTH - 71B	BOURNEMOUTH - 71B	BOURNEMOUTH - 71B	NINE ELMS - 70A	NINE ELMS - 70A
34095	NINE ELMS - 70A	NINE ELMS - 70A	NINE ELMS - 70A	NINE ELMS - 70A	NINE ELMS - 70A	NINE ELMS - 70A	NINE ELMS - 70A
34096	RAMSGATE - 74B	RAMSGATE - 74B	RAMSGATE - 74B	RAMSGATE - 74B	EXMOUTH JCN - 72A	EXMOUTH JCN - 72A	EXMOUTH JCN - 72A
34097	RAMSGATE - 74B	RAMSGATE - 74B	RAMSGATE - 74B	RAMSGATE - 74B	RAMSGATE - 74B	BOURNEMOUTH - 71B	BOURNEMOUTH - 71B
34098	RAMSGATE - 74B	RAMSGATE - 74B	RAMSGATE - 74B	RAMSGATE - 74B	RAMSGATE - 74B	BOURNEMOUTH - 71B	BOURNEMOUTH - 71B
34099	RAMSGATE - 74B	RAMSGATE - 74B	RAMSGATE - 74B	RAMSGATE - 74B	RAMSGATE - 74B	BOURNEMOUTH - 71B	BOURNEMOUTH - 71B
34100	RAMSGATE - 74B	RAMSGATE - 74B	RAMSGATE - 74B	RAMSGATE - 74B	RAMSGATE - 74B	STEWARTS LANE - 73A	STEWARTS LANE - 73A
34101	STEWARTS LANE - 73A	STEWARTS LANE - 73A	STEWARTS LANE - 73A	STEWARTS LANE - 73A	STEWARTS LANE - 73A	BOURNEMOUTH - 71B	BOURNEMOUTH - 71B
34102	STEWARTS LANE - 73A	STEWARTS LANE - 73A	STEWARTS LANE - 73A	STEWARTS LANE - 73A	STEWARTS LANE - 73A	BOURNEMOUTH - 71B	BOURNEMOUTH - 71B
34103	DOVER - 74C	DOVER - 74C	DOVER - 74C	DOVER - 74C	DOVER - 74C	DOVER - 74C	DOVER - 74C
34104	DOVER - 74C	DOVER - 74C	DOVER - 74C	DOVER - 74C	DOVER - 74C	EXMOUTH JCN - 72A	EXMOUTH JCN - 72A
34105	BOURNEMOUTH - 71B	BOURNEMOUTH - 71B	BOURNEMOUTH - 71B	BOURNEMOUTH - 71B	BOURNEMOUTH - 71B	BOURNEMOUTH - 71B	BOURNEMOUTH - 71B
34106	BOURNEMOUTH - 71B	BOURNEMOUTH - 71B	BOURNEMOUTH - 71B	BOURNEMOUTH - 71B	BOURNEMOUTH - 71B	EXMOUTH JCN - 72A	EXMOUTH JCN - 72A
34107	BOURNEMOUTH - 71B	BOURNEMOUTH - 71B	BOURNEMOUTH - 71B	BOURNEMOUTH - 71B	BOURNEMOUTH - 71B	BOURNEMOUTH - 71B	BOURNEMOUTH - 71B
34108	BOURNEMOUTH - 71B	BOURNEMOUTH - 71B	BOURNEMOUTH - 71B	BOURNEMOUTH - 71B	BOURNEMOUTH - 71B	EXMOUTH JCN - 72A	EXMOUTH JCN - 72A
34109	BOURNEMOUTH - 71B	BOURNEMOUTH - 71B	BOURNEMOUTH - 71B	BOURNEMOUTH - 71B	BOURNEMOUTH - 71B	EXMOUTH JCN - 72A	EXMOUTH JCN - 72A
34110	BOURNEMOUTH - 71B	BOURNEMOUTH - 71B	BOURNEMOUTH - 71B	BOURNEMOUTH - 71B	BOURNEMOUTH - 71B	BOURNEMOUTH - 71B	BOURNEMOUTH - 71B
				WC/R (1957)			
34037							RAMSGATE - 74B

loco	May-58	Oct-58	Mar-59	Jun-59	Jul-59	Aug-59	Oct-59
				WC 4-6-2 (1945)			
34031	EXMOUTH JCN - 72A	EXMOUTH JCN - 72A	R/B				
34032	EXMOUTH JCN - 72A	EXMOUTH JCN - 72A	EXMOUTH JCN - 72A	EXMOUTH JCN - 72A	EXMOUTH JCN - 72A	EXMOUTH JCN - 72A	EXMOUTH JCN - 72A
34033	EXMOUTH JCN - 72A	EXMOUTH JCN - 72A	EXMOUTH JCN - 72A	EXMOUTH JCN - 72A	EXMOUTH JCN - 72A	EXMOUTH JCN - 72A	EXMOUTH JCN - 72A
34034	EXMOUTH JCN - 72A	EXMOUTH JCN - 72A	EXMOUTH JCN - 72A	EXMOUTH JCN - 72A	EXMOUTH JCN - 72A	EXMOUTH JCN - 72A	EXMOUTH JCN - 72A
34035	EXMOUTH JCN - 72A	EXMOUTH JCN - 72A	EXMOUTH JCN - 72A	EXMOUTH JCN - 72A	EXMOUTH JCN - 72A	EXMOUTH JCN - 72A	EXMOUTH JCN - 72A
34036	EXMOUTH JCN - 72A	EXMOUTH JCN - 72A	EXMOUTH JCN - 72A	EXMOUTH JCN - 72A	EXMOUTH JCN - 72A	EXMOUTH JCN - 72A	EXMOUTH JCN - 72A
34038	EXMOUTH JCN - 72A	EXMOUTH JCN - 72A	EXMOUTH JCN - 72A	EXMOUTH JCN - 72A	EXMOUTH JCN - 72A	EXMOUTH JCN - 72A	EXMOUTH JCN - 72A
34039	BRIGHTON - 75A	BRIGHTON - 75A	R/B				
34040	EASTLEIGH - 71A	EASTLEIGH - 71A	EASTLEIGH - 71A	EASTLEIGH - 71A	EASTLEIGH - 71A	EASTLEIGH - 71A	EASTLEIGH - 71A
34041	EASTLEIGH - 71A	EASTLEIGH - 71A	EASTLEIGH - 71A	EASTLEIGH - 71A	EASTLEIGH - 71A	EASTLEIGH - 71A	EASTLEIGH - 71A
34042	EASTLEIGH - 71A	EASTLEIGH - 71A	R/B				
34043	BOURNEMOUTH - 71B	BOURNEMOUTH - 71B	BOURNEMOUTH - 71B	BOURNEMOUTH - 71B	BOURNEMOUTH - 71B	BOURNEMOUTH - 71B	BOURNEMOUTH - 71B
34044	BOURNEMOUTH - 71B	BOURNEMOUTH - 71B	BOURNEMOUTH - 71B	BOURNEMOUTH - 71B	BOURNEMOUTH - 71B	BOURNEMOUTH - 71B	BOURNEMOUTH - 71B
34045	BRIGHTON - 75A	R/B					
34046	BRIGHTON - 75A	BRIGHTON - 75A	R/B				
34047	BRIGHTON - 75A	NINE ELMS - 70A	R/B				
34048	BRIGHTON - 75A	BRIGHTON - 75A	R/B				
34049	SALISBURY - 72B	SALISBURY - 72B	SALISBURY - 72B	SALISBURY - 72B	SALISBURY - 72B	SALISBURY - 72B	SALISBURY - 72B
34050	SALISBURY - 72B	R/B					
34051	SALISBURY - 72B	SALISBURY - 72B	SALISBURY - 72B	SALISBURY - 72B	SALISBURY - 72B	SALISBURY - 72B	SALISBURY - 72B
34052	SALISBURY - 72B	R/B					
34053	SALISBURY - 72B	SALISBURY - 72B	R/B				
34054	SALISBURY - 72B	SALISBURY - 72B	SALISBURY - 72B	SALISBURY - 72B	SALISBURY - 72B	SALISBURY - 72B	SALISBURY - 72B
34055	SALISBURY - 72B	SALISBURY - 72B	SALISBURY - 72B	SALISBURY - 72B	SALISBURY - 72B	SALISBURY - 72B	SALISBURY - 72B
34056	EXMOUTH JCN - 72A	EXMOUTH JCN - 72A	EXMOUTH JCN - 72A	EXMOUTH JCN - 72A	EXMOUTH JCN - 72A	EXMOUTH JCN - 72A	EXMOUTH JCN - 72A
34057	EXMOUTH JCN - 72A	EXMOUTH JCN - 72A	EXMOUTH JCN - 72A	EXMOUTH JCN - 72A	EXMOUTH JCN - 72A	EXMOUTH JCN - 72A	EXMOUTH JCN - 72A
34058	EXMOUTH JCN - 72A	EXMOUTH JCN - 72A	EXMOUTH JCN - 72A	EXMOUTH JCN - 72A	EXMOUTH JCN - 72A	EXMOUTH JCN - 72A	EXMOUTH JCN - 72A
34059	SALISBURY - 72B	SALISBURY - 72B	SALISBURY - 72B	SALISBURY - 72B	SALISBURY - 72B	SALISBURY - 72B	SALISBURY - 72B
34060	NINE ELMS - 70A	NINE ELMS - 70A	NINE ELMS - 70A	NINE ELMS - 70A	NINE ELMS - 70A	NINE ELMS - 70A	NINE ELMS - 70A
34061	EXMOUTH JCN - 72A	EXMOUTH JCN - 72A	EXMOUTH JCN - 72A	EXMOUTH JCN - 72A	EXMOUTH JCN - 72A	EXMOUTH JCN - 72A	EXMOUTH JCN - 72A
34062	NINE ELMS - 70A	NINE ELMS - 70A	R/B				
34063	NINE ELMS - 70A	NINE ELMS - 70A	EXMOUTH JCN - 72A	EXMOUTH JCN - 72A	EXMOUTH JCN - 72A	EXMOUTH JCN - 72A	EXMOUTH JCN - 72A
34064	NINE ELMS - 70A	NINE ELMS - 70A	NINE ELMS - 70A	EXMOUTH JCN - 72A	EXMOUTH JCN - 72A	EXMOUTH JCN - 72A	EXMOUTH JCN - 72A
34065	NINE ELMS - 70A	NINE ELMS - 70A	NINE ELMS - 70A	EXMOUTH JCN - 72A	EXMOUTH JCN - 72A	EXMOUTH JCN - 72A	EXMOUTH JCN - 72A
34066	STEWARTS LANE - 73A	STEWARTS LANE - 73A	STEWARTS LANE - 73A	STEWARTS LANE - 73A	STEWARTS LANE - 73A	STEWARTS LANE - 73A	STEWARTS LANE - 73A
34067	STEWARTS LANE - 73A	STEWARTS LANE - 73A	STEWARTS LANE - 73A	STEWARTS LANE - 73A	STEWARTS LANE - 73A	STEWARTS LANE - 73A	STEWARTS LANE - 73A
34068	STEWARTS LANE - 73A	STEWARTS LANE - 73A	STEWARTS LANE - 73A	STEWARTS LANE - 73A	STEWARTS LANE - 73A	STEWARTS LANE - 73A	STEWARTS LANE - 73A
34069	EXMOUTH JCN - 72A	EXMOUTH JCN - 72A	EXMOUTH JCN - 72A	EXMOUTH JCN - 72A	EXMOUTH JCN - 72A	EXMOUTH JCN - 72A	EXMOUTH JCN - 72A
34070	DOVER - 74C	DOVER - 73H	DOVER - 73H	DOVER - 73H	DOVER - 73H	DOVER - 73H	DOVER - 73H
34071	DOVER - 74C	DOVER - 73H	DOVER - 73H	DOVER - 73H	DOVER - 73H	DOVER - 73H	DOVER - 73H
34072	EXMOUTH JCN - 72A	EXMOUTH JCN - 72A	EXMOUTH JCN - 72A	EXMOUTH JCN - 72A	EXMOUTH JCN - 72A	EXMOUTH JCN - 72A	EXMOUTH JCN - 72A
34073	DOVER - 74C	DOVER - 73H	DOVER - 73H	DOVER - 73H	DOVER - 73H	DOVER - 73H	DOVER - 73H
34074	EXMOUTH JCN - 72A	EXMOUTH JCN - 72A	EXMOUTH JCN - 72A	EXMOUTH JCN - 72A	EXMOUTH JCN - 72A	EXMOUTH JCN - 72A	EXMOUTH JCN - 72A
34075	EXMOUTH JCN - 72A	EXMOUTH JCN - 72A	EXMOUTH JCN - 72A	EXMOUTH JCN - 72A	EXMOUTH JCN - 72A	EXMOUTH JCN - 72A	EXMOUTH JCN - 72A
34076	EXMOUTH JCN - 72A	EXMOUTH JCN - 72A	EXMOUTH JCN - 72A	EXMOUTH JCN - 72A	EXMOUTH JCN - 72A	EXMOUTH JCN - 72A	EXMOUTH JCN - 72A
34077	STEWARTS LANE - 73A	STEWARTS LANE - 73A	STEWARTS LANE - 73A	STEWARTS LANE - 73A	STEWARTS LANE - 73A	STEWARTS LANE - 73A	STEWARTS LANE - 73A
34078	RAMSGATE - 74B	RAMSGATE - 73G	RAMSGATE - 73G	B ARMS - 73B	B ARMS - 73B	B ARMS - 73B	B ARMS - 73B
34079	EXMOUTH JCN - 72A	EXMOUTH JCN - 72A	EXMOUTH JCN - 72A	EXMOUTH JCN - 72A	EXMOUTH JCN - 72A	EXMOUTH JCN - 72A	EXMOUTH JCN - 72A
34080	EXMOUTH JCN - 72A	EXMOUTH JCN - 72A	EXMOUTH JCN - 72A	EXMOUTH JCN - 72A	EXMOUTH JCN - 72A	EXMOUTH JCN - 72A	EXMOUTH JCN - 72A
34081	EXMOUTH JCN - 72A	EXMOUTH JCN - 72A	EXMOUTH JCN - 72A	EXMOUTH JCN - 72A	EXMOUTH JCN - 72A	EXMOUTH JCN - 72A	EXMOUTH JCN - 72A
34082	DOVER - 74C	DOVER - 73H	DOVER - 73H	DOVER - 73H	DOVER - 73H	DOVER - 73H	DOVER - 73H
34083	DOVER - 74C	DOVER - 73H	DOVER - 73H	DOVER - 73H	DOVER - 73H	DOVER - 73H	DOVER - 73H
34084	DOVER - 74C	DOVER - 73H	DOVER - 73H	DOVER - 73H	DOVER - 73H	DOVER - 73H	DOVER - 73H
34085	STEWARTS LANE - 73A	STEWARTS LANE - 73A	STEWARTS LANE - 73A	STEWARTS LANE - 73A	STEWARTS LANE - 73A	STEWARTS LANE - 73A	STEWARTS LANE - 73A
34086	STEWARTS LANE - 73A	STEWARTS LANE - 73A	STEWARTS LANE - 73A	STEWARTS LANE - 73A	STEWARTS LANE - 73A	STEWARTS LANE - 73A	STEWARTS LANE - 73A
34087	STEWARTS LANE - 73A	STEWARTS LANE - 73A	STEWARTS LANE - 73A	STEWARTS LANE - 73A	STEWARTS LANE - 73A	STEWARTS LANE - 73A	STEWARTS LANE - 73A
34088	STEWARTS LANE - 73A	STEWARTS LANE - 73A	STEWARTS LANE - 73A	STEWARTS LANE - 73A	STEWARTS LANE - 73A	STEWARTS LANE - 73A	STEWARTS LANE - 73A
34089	STEWARTS LANE - 73A	STEWARTS LANE - 73A	STEWARTS LANE - 73A	STEWARTS LANE - 73A	STEWARTS LANE - 73A	STEWARTS LANE - 73A	STEWARTS LANE - 73A
34090	NINE ELMS - 70A	NINE ELMS - 70A	NINE ELMS - 70A	NINE ELMS - 70A	NINE ELMS - 70A	NINE ELMS - 70A	NINE ELMS - 70A
34091	STEWARTS LANE - 73A	STEWARTS LANE - 73A	STEWARTS LANE - 73A	STEWARTS LANE - 73A	STEWARTS LANE - 73A	STEWARTS LANE - 73A	STEWARTS LANE - 73A
34092	STEWARTS LANE - 73A	STEWARTS LANE - 73A	STEWARTS LANE - 73A	STEWARTS LANE - 73A	STEWARTS LANE - 73A	STEWARTS LANE - 73A	STEWARTS LANE - 73A
34093	NINE ELMS - 70A	NINE ELMS - 70A	NINE ELMS - 70A	NINE ELMS - 70A	NINE ELMS - 70A	NINE ELMS - 70A	NINE ELMS - 70A
34094	NINE ELMS - 70A	NINE ELMS - 70A	NINE ELMS - 70A	NINE ELMS - 70A	NINE ELMS - 70A	NINE ELMS - 70A	NINE ELMS - 70A
34095	NINE ELMS - 70A	NINE ELMS - 70A	NINE ELMS - 70A	NINE ELMS - 70A	NINE ELMS - 70A	NINE ELMS - 70A	NINE ELMS - 70A
34096	EXMOUTH JCN - 72A	EXMOUTH JCN - 72A	EXMOUTH JCN - 72A	EXMOUTH JCN - 72A	EXMOUTH JCN - 72A	EXMOUTH JCN - 72A	EXMOUTH JCN - 72A
34097	BOURNEMOUTH - 71B	BOURNEMOUTH - 71B	BRIGHTON - 75A	BRIGHTON - 75A	BRIGHTON - 75A	BRIGHTON - 75A	BRIGHTON - 75A
34098	BOURNEMOUTH - 71B	BOURNEMOUTH - 71B	BRIGHTON - 75A	BRIGHTON - 75A	BRIGHTON - 75A	BRIGHTON - 75A	BRIGHTON - 75A
34099	BOURNEMOUTH - 71B	BOURNEMOUTH - 71B	BRIGHTON - 75A	BRIGHTON - 75A	BRIGHTON - 75A	BRIGHTON - 75A	BRIGHTON - 75A
34100	STEWARTS LANE - 73A	STEWARTS LANE - 73A	STEWARTS LANE - 73A	STEWARTS LANE - 73A	STEWARTS LANE - 73A	STEWARTS LANE - 73A	STEWARTS LANE - 73A
34101	STEWARTS LANE - 73A	STEWARTS LANE - 73A	STEWARTS LANE - 73A	STEWARTS LANE - 73A	STEWARTS LANE - 73A	STEWARTS LANE - 73A	STEWARTS LANE - 73A
34102	BOURNEMOUTH - 71B	BOURNEMOUTH - 71B	BOURNEMOUTH - 71B	BOURNEMOUTH - 71B	BOURNEMOUTH - 71B	BOURNEMOUTH - 71B	BOURNEMOUTH - 71B
34103	DOVER - 74C	DOVER - 73H	DOVER - 73H	DOVER - 73H	DOVER - 73H	DOVER - 73H	DOVER - 73H
34104	EXMOUTH JCN - 72A	EXMOUTH JCN - 72A	EXMOUTH JCN - 72A	EXMOUTH JCN - 72A	EXMOUTH JCN - 72A	EXMOUTH JCN - 72A	EXMOUTH JCN - 72A
34105	BOURNEMOUTH - 71B	BOURNEMOUTH - 71B	BOURNEMOUTH - 71B	BOURNEMOUTH - 71B	BOURNEMOUTH - 71B	BOURNEMOUTH - 71B	BOURNEMOUTH - 71B
34106	EXMOUTH JCN - 72A	EXMOUTH JCN - 72A	EXMOUTH JCN - 72A	EXMOUTH JCN - 72A	EXMOUTH JCN - 72A	EXMOUTH JCN - 72A	EXMOUTH JCN - 72A
34107	BOURNEMOUTH - 71B	BOURNEMOUTH - 71B	BOURNEMOUTH - 71B	EXMOUTH JCN - 72A	EXMOUTH JCN - 72A	EXMOUTH JCN - 72A	EXMOUTH JCN - 72A
34108	EXMOUTH JCN - 72A	EXMOUTH JCN - 72A	EXMOUTH JCN - 72A	EXMOUTH JCN - 72A	EXMOUTH JCN - 72A	EXMOUTH JCN - 72A	EXMOUTH JCN - 72A
34109	EXMOUTH JCN - 72A	EXMOUTH JCN - 72A	EXMOUTH JCN - 72A	EXMOUTH JCN - 72A	EXMOUTH JCN - 72A	EXMOUTH JCN - 72A	EXMOUTH JCN - 72A
34110	BOURNEMOUTH - 71B	BOURNEMOUTH - 71B	EXMOUTH JCN - 72A	EXMOUTH JCN - 72A	EXMOUTH JCN - 72A	EXMOUTH JCN - 72A	EXMOUTH JCN - 72A
				WC/R (1957)			
34031			NINE ELMS - 70A	NINE ELMS - 70A	NINE ELMS - 70A	NINE ELMS - 70A	NINE ELMS - 70A
34037	RAMSGATE - 74B	RAMSGATE - 73G	RAMSGATE - 73G	B ARMS - 73B	B ARMS - 73B	B ARMS - 73B	B ARMS - 73B
34039			BOURNEMOUTH - 71B	BOURNEMOUTH - 71B	BOURNEMOUTH - 71B	BOURNEMOUTH - 71B	BOURNEMOUTH - 71B
34042			EASTLEIGH - 71A	EASTLEIGH - 71A	EASTLEIGH - 71A	EASTLEIGH - 71A	EASTLEIGH - 71A
34045		NINE ELMS - 70A	BOURNEMOUTH - 71B	BOURNEMOUTH - 71B	BOURNEMOUTH - 71B	BOURNEMOUTH - 71B	BOURNEMOUTH - 71B
34046			BOURNEMOUTH - 71B	BOURNEMOUTH - 71B	BOURNEMOUTH - 71B	BOURNEMOUTH - 71B	BOURNEMOUTH - 71B
34047			NINE ELMS - 70A	BOURNEMOUTH - 71B	BOURNEMOUTH - 71B	BOURNEMOUTH - 71B	BOURNEMOUTH - 71B
34048			BOURNEMOUTH - 71B	BOURNEMOUTH - 71B	BOURNEMOUTH - 71B	BOURNEMOUTH - 71B	BOURNEMOUTH - 71B
34050		SALISBURY - 72B	SALISBURY - 72B	SALISBURY - 72B	SALISBURY - 72B	SALISBURY - 72B	SALISBURY - 72B
34052		SALISBURY - 72B	SALISBURY - 72B	SALISBURY - 72B	SALISBURY - 72B	SALISBURY - 72B	SALISBURY - 72B
34053			SALISBURY - 72B	SALISBURY - 72B	SALISBURY - 72B	SALISBURY - 72B	SALISBURY - 72B
34062			NINE ELMS - 70A	NINE ELMS - 70A	NINE ELMS - 70A	NINE ELMS - 70A	NINE ELMS - 70A

loco	Dec-59	Feb-60	Mar-60	Apr-60	Jul-60	Aug-60	Sep-60	Nov-60
				WC 4-6-2 (1945)				
34032	EXMOUTH JCN - 72A	EXMOUTH JCN - 72A	EXMOUTH JCN - 72A	EXMOUTH JCN - 72A	EXMOUTH JCN - 72A	EXMOUTH JCN - 72A	EXMOUTH JCN - 72A	R/B
34033	EXMOUTH JCN - 72A	EXMOUTH JCN - 72A	EXMOUTH JCN - 72A	EXMOUTH JCN - 72A	EXMOUTH JCN - 72A	EXMOUTH JCN - 72A	EXMOUTH JCN - 72A	EXMOUTH JCN - 72A
34034	EXMOUTH JCN - 72A	EXMOUTH JCN - 72A	EXMOUTH JCN - 72A	EXMOUTH JCN - 72A	EXMOUTH JCN - 72A	EXMOUTH JCN - 72A	EXMOUTH JCN - 72A	R/B
34035	EXMOUTH JCN - 72A	EXMOUTH JCN - 72A	EXMOUTH JCN - 72A	EXMOUTH JCN - 72A	EXMOUTH JCN - 72A	EXMOUTH JCN - 72A	EXMOUTH JCN - 72A	EXMOUTH JCN - 72A
34036	EXMOUTH JCN - 72A	EXMOUTH JCN - 72A	EXMOUTH JCN - 72A	EXMOUTH JCN - 72A	EXMOUTH JCN - 72A	R/B		
34038	EXMOUTH JCN - 72A	EXMOUTH JCN - 72A	EXMOUTH JCN - 72A	EXMOUTH JCN - 72A	EXMOUTH JCN - 72A	EXMOUTH JCN - 72A	EXMOUTH JCN - 72A	BRIGHTON - 75A
34040	EASTLEIGH - 71A	EASTLEIGH - 71A	EASTLEIGH - 71A	EASTLEIGH - 71A	EASTLEIGH - 71A	EASTLEIGH - 71A	EASTLEIGH - 71A	R/B
34041	EASTLEIGH - 71A	EASTLEIGH - 71A	EASTLEIGH - 71A	EASTLEIGH - 71A	EASTLEIGH - 71A	EASTLEIGH - 71A	EASTLEIGH - 71A	EASTLEIGH - 71A
34043	BOURNEMOUTH - 71B	BOURNEMOUTH - 71B	BOURNEMOUTH - 71B	BOURNEMOUTH - 71B	BOURNEMOUTH - 71B	BOURNEMOUTH - 71B	BOURNEMOUTH - 71B	BOURNEMOUTH - 71B
34044	BOURNEMOUTH - 71B	BOURNEMOUTH - 71B	BOURNEMOUTH - 71B	BOURNEMOUTH - 71B	R/B			
34049	SALISBURY - 72B	SALISBURY - 72B	SALISBURY - 72B	SALISBURY - 72B	SALISBURY - 72B	SALISBURY - 72B	SALISBURY - 72B	SALISBURY - 72B
34051	SALISBURY - 72B	SALISBURY - 72B	SALISBURY - 72B	SALISBURY - 72B	SALISBURY - 72B	SALISBURY - 72B	SALISBURY - 72B	SALISBURY - 72B
34054	SALISBURY - 72B	SALISBURY - 72B	SALISBURY - 72B	SALISBURY - 72B	SALISBURY - 72B	SALISBURY - 72B	SALISBURY - 72B	SALISBURY - 72B
34055	SALISBURY - 72B	BRIGHTON - 75A	BRIGHTON - 75A	BRIGHTON - 75A	BRIGHTON - 75A	BRIGHTON - 75A	BRIGHTON - 75A	BRIGHTON - 75A
34056	EXMOUTH JCN - 72A	EXMOUTH JCN - 72A	EXMOUTH JCN - 72A	EXMOUTH JCN - 72A	EXMOUTH JCN - 72A	EXMOUTH JCN - 72A	EXMOUTH JCN - 72A	EXMOUTH JCN - 72A
34057	EXMOUTH JCN - 72A	EXMOUTH JCN - 72A	EXMOUTH JCN - 72A	EXMOUTH JCN - 72A	EXMOUTH JCN - 72A	EXMOUTH JCN - 72A	EXMOUTH JCN - 72A	BRIGHTON - 75A
34058	EXMOUTH JCN - 72A	EXMOUTH JCN - 72A	EXMOUTH JCN - 72A	EXMOUTH JCN - 72A	EXMOUTH JCN - 72A	EXMOUTH JCN - 72A	EXMOUTH JCN - 72A	R/B
34059	SALISBURY - 72B	SALISBURY - 72B	R/B					
34060	NINE ELMS - 70A	NINE ELMS - 70A	NINE ELMS - 70A	NINE ELMS - 70A	NINE ELMS - 70A	NINE ELMS - 70A	NINE ELMS - 70A	R/B
34061	EXMOUTH JCN - 72A	EXMOUTH JCN - 72A	EXMOUTH JCN - 72A	EXMOUTH JCN - 72A	EXMOUTH JCN - 72A	EXMOUTH JCN - 72A	EXMOUTH JCN - 72A	DOVER - 73H
34063	EXMOUTH JCN - 72A	EXMOUTH JCN - 72A	EXMOUTH JCN - 72A	EXMOUTH JCN - 72A	EXMOUTH JCN - 72A	EXMOUTH JCN - 72A	EXMOUTH JCN - 72A	EXMOUTH JCN - 72A
34064	EXMOUTH JCN - 72A	EXMOUTH JCN - 72A	EXMOUTH JCN - 72A	EXMOUTH JCN - 72A	EXMOUTH JCN - 72A	EXMOUTH JCN - 72A	EXMOUTH JCN - 72A	EXMOUTH JCN - 72A
34065	EXMOUTH JCN - 72A	EXMOUTH JCN - 72A	EXMOUTH JCN - 72A	EXMOUTH JCN - 72A	EXMOUTH JCN - 72A	EXMOUTH JCN - 72A	EXMOUTH JCN - 72A	EXMOUTH JCN - 72A
34066	STEWARTS LANE - 73A	STEWARTS LANE - 73A	STEWARTS LANE - 73A	STEWARTS LANE - 73A	STEWARTS LANE - 73A	STEWARTS LANE - 73A	STEWARTS LANE - 73A	STEWARTS LANE - 73A
34067	STEWARTS LANE - 73A	STEWARTS LANE - 73A	STEWARTS LANE - 73A	STEWARTS LANE - 73A	STEWARTS LANE - 73A	STEWARTS LANE - 73A	STEWARTS LANE - 73A	STEWARTS LANE - 73A
34068	STEWARTS LANE - 73A	STEWARTS LANE - 73A	STEWARTS LANE - 73A	STEWARTS LANE - 73A	STEWARTS LANE - 73A	STEWARTS LANE - 73A	STEWARTS LANE - 73A	STEWARTS LANE - 73A
34069	EXMOUTH JCN - 72A	EXMOUTH JCN - 72A	EXMOUTH JCN - 72A	EXMOUTH JCN - 72A	EXMOUTH JCN - 72A	EXMOUTH JCN - 72A	EXMOUTH JCN - 72A	EXMOUTH JCN - 72A
34070	DOVER - 73H	DOVER - 73H	DOVER - 73H	DOVER - 73H	DOVER - 73H	DOVER - 73H	DOVER - 73H	DOVER - 73H
34071	DOVER - 73H	DOVER - 73H	DOVER - 73H	DOVER - 73H	R/B			
34072	EXMOUTH JCN - 72A	EXMOUTH JCN - 72A	EXMOUTH JCN - 72A	EXMOUTH JCN - 72A	EXMOUTH JCN - 72A	EXMOUTH JCN - 72A	EXMOUTH JCN - 72A	EXMOUTH JCN - 72A
34073	DOVER - 73H	DOVER - 73H	DOVER - 73H	DOVER - 73H	DOVER - 73H	DOVER - 73H	DOVER - 73H	DOVER - 73H
34074	EXMOUTH JCN - 72A	EXMOUTH JCN - 72A	EXMOUTH JCN - 72A	EXMOUTH JCN - 72A	EXMOUTH JCN - 72A	EXMOUTH JCN - 72A	EXMOUTH JCN - 72A	EXMOUTH JCN - 72A
34075	EXMOUTH JCN - 72A	EXMOUTH JCN - 72A	EXMOUTH JCN - 72A	EXMOUTH JCN - 72A	EXMOUTH JCN - 72A	EXMOUTH JCN - 72A	EXMOUTH JCN - 72A	EXMOUTH JCN - 72A
34076	EXMOUTH JCN - 72A	EXMOUTH JCN - 72A	EXMOUTH JCN - 72A	EXMOUTH JCN - 72A	EXMOUTH JCN - 72A	EXMOUTH JCN - 72A	EXMOUTH JCN - 72A	EXMOUTH JCN - 72A
34077	STEWARTS LANE - 73A	STEWARTS LANE - 73A	STEWARTS LANE - 73A	STEWARTS LANE - 73A	STEWARTS LANE - 73A	R/B		
34078	B ARMS - 73B	B ARMS - 73B	B ARMS - 73B	B ARMS - 73B	B ARMS - 73B	B ARMS - 73B	B ARMS - 73B	B ARMS - 73B
34079	EXMOUTH JCN - 72A	EXMOUTH JCN - 72A	EXMOUTH JCN - 72A	EXMOUTH JCN - 72A	EXMOUTH JCN - 72A	EXMOUTH JCN - 72A	EXMOUTH JCN - 72A	EXMOUTH JCN - 72A
34080	EXMOUTH JCN - 72A	EXMOUTH JCN - 72A	EXMOUTH JCN - 72A	EXMOUTH JCN - 72A	EXMOUTH JCN - 72A	EXMOUTH JCN - 72A	EXMOUTH JCN - 72A	EXMOUTH JCN - 72A
34081	EXMOUTH JCN - 72A	EXMOUTH JCN - 72A	EXMOUTH JCN - 72A	EXMOUTH JCN - 72A	EXMOUTH JCN - 72A	EXMOUTH JCN - 72A	EXMOUTH JCN - 72A	EXMOUTH JCN - 72A
34082	DOVER - 73H	DOVER - 73H	DOVER - 73H	R/B				
34083	DOVER - 73H	DOVER - 73H	DOVER - 73H	DOVER - 73H	DOVER - 73H	DOVER - 73H	DOVER - 73H	DOVER - 73H
34084	DOVER - 73H	DOVER - 73H	DOVER - 73H	DOVER - 73H	DOVER - 73H	DOVER - 73H	DOVER - 73H	EXMOUTH JCN - 72A
34085	STEWARTS LANE - 73A	STEWARTS LANE - 73A	STEWARTS LANE - 73A	STEWARTS LANE - 73A	R/B			
34086	STEWARTS LANE - 73A	STEWARTS LANE - 73A	STEWARTS LANE - 73A	STEWARTS LANE - 73A	STEWARTS LANE - 73A	STEWARTS LANE - 73A	STEWARTS LANE - 73A	STEWARTS LANE - 73A
34087	STEWARTS LANE - 73A	STEWARTS LANE - 73A	STEWARTS LANE - 73A	STEWARTS LANE - 73A	STEWARTS LANE - 73A	STEWARTS LANE - 73A	STEWARTS LANE - 73A	STEWARTS LANE - 73A
34088	STEWARTS LANE - 73A	STEWARTS LANE - 73A	STEWARTS LANE - 73A	R/B				
34089	STEWARTS LANE - 73A	STEWARTS LANE - 73A	STEWARTS LANE - 73A	STEWARTS LANE - 73A	STEWARTS LANE - 73A	STEWARTS LANE - 73A	STEWARTS LANE - 73A	R/B
34090	NINE ELMS - 70A	NINE ELMS - 70A	NINE ELMS - 70A	NINE ELMS - 70A	NINE ELMS - 70A	R/B		
34091	STEWARTS LANE - 73A	STEWARTS LANE - 73A	STEWARTS LANE - 73A	STEWARTS LANE - 73A	STEWARTS LANE - 73A	STEWARTS LANE - 73A	STEWARTS LANE - 73A	STEWARTS LANE - 73A
34092	STEWARTS LANE - 73A	STEWARTS LANE - 73A	STEWARTS LANE - 73A	STEWARTS LANE - 73A	STEWARTS LANE - 73A	STEWARTS LANE - 73A	STEWARTS LANE - 73A	STEWARTS LANE - 73A
34093	NINE ELMS - 70A	NINE ELMS - 70A	NINE ELMS - 70A	NINE ELMS - 70A	R/B			
34094	NINE ELMS - 70A	NINE ELMS - 70A	NINE ELMS - 70A	NINE ELMS - 70A	NINE ELMS - 70A	NINE ELMS - 70A	NINE ELMS - 70A	NINE ELMS - 70A
34095	NINE ELMS - 70A	NINE ELMS - 70A	NINE ELMS - 70A	NINE ELMS - 70A	NINE ELMS - 70A	NINE ELMS - 70A	NINE ELMS - 70A	NINE ELMS - 70A
34096	EXMOUTH JCN - 72A	EXMOUTH JCN - 72A	EXMOUTH JCN - 72A	EXMOUTH JCN - 72A	EXMOUTH JCN - 72A	EXMOUTH JCN - 72A	EXMOUTH JCN - 72A	EXMOUTH JCN - 72A
34097	BRIGHTON - 75A	BRIGHTON - 75A	BRIGHTON - 75A	BRIGHTON - 75A	BRIGHTON - 75A	BRIGHTON - 75A	BRIGHTON - 75A	EXMOUTH JCN - 72A
34098	BRIGHTON - 75A	BRIGHTON - 75A	BRIGHTON - 75A	BRIGHTON - 75A	BRIGHTON - 75A	BRIGHTON - 75A	BRIGHTON - 75A	EXMOUTH JCN - 72A
34099	BRIGHTON - 75A	SALISBURY - 72B	SALISBURY - 72B	SALISBURY - 72B	SALISBURY - 72B	SALISBURY - 72B	SALISBURY - 72B	SALISBURY - 72B
34100	STEWARTS LANE - 73A	STEWARTS LANE - 73A	STEWARTS LANE - 73A	STEWARTS LANE - 73A	STEWARTS LANE - 73A	STEWARTS LANE - 73A	R/B	
34101	STEWARTS LANE - 73A	STEWARTS LANE - 73A	STEWARTS LANE - 73A	STEWARTS LANE - 73A	STEWARTS LANE - 73A	STEWARTS LANE - 73A	R/B	
34102	BOURNEMOUTH - 71B	BOURNEMOUTH - 71B	BOURNEMOUTH - 71B	BOURNEMOUTH - 71B	BOURNEMOUTH - 71B	BOURNEMOUTH - 71B	BOURNEMOUTH - 71B	BOURNEMOUTH - 71B
34103	DOVER - 73H	DOVER - 73H	DOVER - 73H	DOVER - 73H	DOVER - 73H	DOVER - 73H	DOVER - 73H	DOVER - 73H
34104	EXMOUTH JCN - 72A	EXMOUTH JCN - 72A	EXMOUTH JCN - 72A	EXMOUTH JCN - 72A	EXMOUTH JCN - 72A	EXMOUTH JCN - 72A	EXMOUTH JCN - 72A	EXMOUTH JCN - 72A
34105	BOURNEMOUTH - 71B	BOURNEMOUTH - 71B	BOURNEMOUTH - 71B	BOURNEMOUTH - 71B	BOURNEMOUTH - 71B	BOURNEMOUTH - 71B	BOURNEMOUTH - 71B	BOURNEMOUTH - 71B
34106	EXMOUTH JCN - 72A	EXMOUTH JCN - 72A	EXMOUTH JCN - 72A	EXMOUTH JCN - 72A	EXMOUTH JCN - 72A	EXMOUTH JCN - 72A	EXMOUTH JCN - 72A	EXMOUTH JCN - 72A
34107	EXMOUTH JCN - 72A	EXMOUTH JCN - 72A	EXMOUTH JCN - 72A	EXMOUTH JCN - 72A	EXMOUTH JCN - 72A	EXMOUTH JCN - 72A	EXMOUTH JCN - 72A	EXMOUTH JCN - 72A
34108	EXMOUTH JCN - 72A	EXMOUTH JCN - 72A	EXMOUTH JCN - 72A	EXMOUTH JCN - 72A	EXMOUTH JCN - 72A	EXMOUTH JCN - 72A	EXMOUTH JCN - 72A	EXMOUTH JCN - 72A
34109	EXMOUTH JCN - 72A	EXMOUTH JCN - 72A	EXMOUTH JCN - 72A	EXMOUTH JCN - 72A	EXMOUTH JCN - 72A	EXMOUTH JCN - 72A	EXMOUTH JCN - 72A	EXMOUTH JCN - 72A
34110	EXMOUTH JCN - 72A	EXMOUTH JCN - 72A	EXMOUTH JCN - 72A	EXMOUTH JCN - 72A	EXMOUTH JCN - 72A	EXMOUTH JCN - 72A	EXMOUTH JCN - 72A	EXMOUTH JCN - 72A
				WC/R (1957)				
34031	NINE ELMS - 70A	NINE ELMS - 70A	NINE ELMS - 70A	NINE ELMS - 70A	NINE ELMS - 70A	NINE ELMS - 70A	NINE ELMS - 70A	NINE ELMS - 70A
34032								EXMOUTH JCN - 72A
34034								EXMOUTH JCN - 72A
34036						EXMOUTH JCN - 72A	EXMOUTH JCN - 72A	EXMOUTH JCN - 72A
34037	B ARMS - 73B	B ARMS - 73B	B ARMS - 73B	B ARMS - 73B	B ARMS - 73B	B ARMS - 73B	B ARMS - 73B	B ARMS - 73B
34039	BOURNEMOUTH - 71B	BOURNEMOUTH - 71B	BOURNEMOUTH - 71B	BOURNEMOUTH - 71B	BOURNEMOUTH - 71B	BOURNEMOUTH - 71B	BOURNEMOUTH - 71B	BOURNEMOUTH - 71B
34040								EASTLEIGH - 71A
34042	EASTLEIGH - 71A	EASTLEIGH - 71A	EASTLEIGH - 71A	EASTLEIGH - 71A	EASTLEIGH - 71A	EASTLEIGH - 71A	EASTLEIGH - 71A	EASTLEIGH - 71A
34044					BOURNEMOUTH - 71B	BOURNEMOUTH - 71B	BOURNEMOUTH - 71B	BOURNEMOUTH - 71B
34045	BOURNEMOUTH - 71B	BOURNEMOUTH - 71B	BOURNEMOUTH - 71B	BOURNEMOUTH - 71B	BOURNEMOUTH - 71B	BOURNEMOUTH - 71B	BOURNEMOUTH - 71B	BOURNEMOUTH - 71B
34046	BOURNEMOUTH - 71B	BOURNEMOUTH - 71B	BOURNEMOUTH - 71B	BOURNEMOUTH - 71B	BOURNEMOUTH - 71B	BOURNEMOUTH - 71B	BOURNEMOUTH - 71B	BOURNEMOUTH - 71B
34047	BOURNEMOUTH - 71B	BOURNEMOUTH - 71B	BOURNEMOUTH - 71B	BOURNEMOUTH - 71B	BOURNEMOUTH - 71B	BOURNEMOUTH - 71B	BOURNEMOUTH - 71B	BOURNEMOUTH - 71B
34048	BOURNEMOUTH - 71B	SALISBURY - 72B	SALISBURY - 72B	SALISBURY - 72B	SALISBURY - 72B	SALISBURY - 72B	SALISBURY - 72B	SALISBURY - 72B
34050	SALISBURY - 72B	SALISBURY - 72B	SALISBURY - 72B	SALISBURY - 72B	SALISBURY - 72B	SALISBURY - 72B	SALISBURY - 72B	B ARMS - 73B
34052	SALISBURY - 72B	SALISBURY - 72B	SALISBURY - 72B	SALISBURY - 72B	SALISBURY - 72B	SALISBURY - 72B	SALISBURY - 72B	SALISBURY - 72B
34053	SALISBURY - 72B	BOURNEMOUTH - 71B	BOURNEMOUTH - 71B	BOURNEMOUTH - 71B	BOURNEMOUTH - 71B	BOURNEMOUTH - 71B	BOURNEMOUTH - 71B	BOURNEMOUTH - 71B
34058								EXMOUTH JCN - 72A
34059			SALISBURY - 72B	SALISBURY - 72B	SALISBURY - 72B	SALISBURY - 72B	SALISBURY - 72B	SALISBURY - 72B
34060								NINE ELMS - 70A
34062	NINE ELMS - 70A	NINE ELMS - 70A	NINE ELMS - 70A	NINE ELMS - 70A	NINE ELMS - 70A	NINE ELMS - 70A	NINE ELMS - 70A	NINE ELMS - 70A
34071					DOVER - 73H	DOVER - 73H	DOVER - 73H	DOVER - 73H
34077						STEWARTS LANE - 73A	STEWARTS LANE - 73A	STEWARTS LANE - 73A
34082				DOVER - 73H	DOVER - 73H	DOVER - 73H	DOVER - 73H	DOVER - 73H
34085					STEWARTS LANE - 73A	STEWARTS LANE - 73A	STEWARTS LANE - 73A	STEWARTS LANE - 73A
34088				STEWARTS LANE - 73A	STEWARTS LANE - 73A	STEWARTS LANE - 73A	STEWARTS LANE - 73A	STEWARTS LANE - 73A
34089								STEWARTS LANE - 73A
34090						NINE ELMS - 70A	NINE ELMS - 70A	NINE ELMS - 70A
34093					NINE ELMS - 70A	NINE ELMS - 70A	NINE ELMS - 70A	NINE ELMS - 70A
34100							STEWARTS LANE - 73A	STEWARTS LANE - 73A
34101							STEWARTS LANE - 73A	STEWARTS LANE - 73A

In spite of its name, 34092 'City of Wells' spent most of its days working in Kent, operating from Stewarts Lane on the Dover Boat trains and it was not until 1962, following the electrification of the SECR main lines, that it could be seen on the lines from Waterloo. It was never rebuilt and is seen standing with a down express at Southampton in 1964.

The fireman of 34021 'Dartmoor' sits waiting to be called back off the table and onto a shed road at Bournemouth MPD. Although losing its Merchant Navy allocation for a time during the 1950's, Bournemouth was always a focal point for Pacific operations since it not only provided power for its own expresses but also those of Weymouth which until 1958 was a Great Western depot with no provision for Southern trains. Many of the principal Weymouth - Waterloo services were worked by Bournemouth engines which worked to and from Weymouth on stopping trains. It was not until well into the sixties that Weymouth acquired a Southern allocation for its Waterloo services.

loco	May-49	Jun-49	Aug-49	Sep-49	Dec-49	Feb-50	Mar-50
Electric							
20001	SELHURST	SELHURST	SELHURST	SELHURST	SELHURST	SELHURST	SELHURST
20002	SELHURST	SELHURST	SELHURST	SELHURST	SELHURST	SELHURST	SELHURST
20003	SELHURST	SELHURST	SELHURST	SELHURST	SELHURST	SELHURST	SELHURST

loco	Apr-50	Sep-50	Oct-50	Nov-50	Dec-50	Mar-51	Apr-51
LMS 2MT 2-6-2T (1946)							
41240		BATH (S&D)-71G	BATH (S&D)-71G	BATH (S&D)-71G	BATH (S&D)-71G	BATH (S&D)-71G	BATH (S&D)-71G
41241		BATH (S&D)-71G	BATH (S&D)-71G	BATH (S&D)-71G	BATH (S&D)-71G	BATH (S&D)-71G	BATH (S&D)-71G
41242		BATH (S&D)-71G	BATH (S&D)-71G	BATH (S&D)-71G	BATH (S&D)-71G	BATH (S&D)-71G	BATH (S&D)-71G
41243		BATH (S&D)-71G	BATH (S&D)-71G	BATH (S&D)-71G	BATH (S&D)-71G	BATH (S&D)-71G	BATH (S&D)-71G
LMS 4MT 2-6-4T (1948)							
42066		RAMSGATE-74B	RAMSGATE-74B	RAMSGATE-74B	RAMSGATE-74B	RAMSGATE-74B	RAMSGATE-74B
42067		RAMSGATE-74B	RAMSGATE-74B	RAMSGATE-74B	RAMSGATE-74B	RAMSGATE-74B	RAMSGATE-74B
42068			RAMSGATE-74B	RAMSGATE-74B	RAMSGATE-74B	RAMSGATE-74B	RAMSGATE-74B
42069			RAMSGATE-74B	RAMSGATE-74B	RAMSGATE-74B	RAMSGATE-74B	RAMSGATE-74B
42070				STEWARTS LANE-73A	RAMSGATE-74B	RAMSGATE-74B	RAMSGATE-74B
42071				STEWARTS LANE-73A	ASHFORD-74A	ASHFORD-74A	ASHFORD-74A
42072				STEWARTS LANE-73A	ASHFORD-74A	ASHFORD-74A	ASHFORD-74A
42073				STEWARTS LANE-73A	ASHFORD-74A	ASHFORD-74A	ASHFORD-74A
42074				STEWARTS LANE-73A	ASHFORD-74A	ASHFORD-74A	ASHFORD-74A
42075					DOVER-74C	DOVER-74C	DOVER-74C
42076					DOVER-74C	DOVER-74C	DOVER-74C
42077					DOVER-74C	DOVER-74C	DOVER-74C
42078					DOVER-74C	DOVER-74C	DOVER-74C
42079					DOVER-74C	DOVER-74C	DOVER-74C
42080					STEWARTS LANE-73A	STEWARTS LANE-73A	STEWARTS LANE-73A
42081					STEWARTS LANE-73A	STEWARTS LANE-73A	STEWARTS LANE-73A
42082					STEWARTS LANE-73A	STEWARTS LANE-73A	STEWARTS LANE-73A
42083					STEWARTS LANE-73A	STEWARTS LANE-73A	STEWARTS LANE-73A
42084						STEWARTS LANE-73A	STEWARTS LANE-73A
42085						BRIGHTON-75A	BRIGHTON-75A
42086							BRIGHTON-75A
42087							BRIGHTON-75A
42088							BRIGHTON-75A
42089							BRIGHTON-75A
42090							BRIGHTON-75A
42091							BRIGHTON-75A
42096		T.WELLS-75F	T.WELLS-75F	T.WELLS-75F	T.WELLS-75F	T.WELLS-75F	T.WELLS-75F
42097		T.WELLS-75F	T.WELLS-75F	T.WELLS-75F	T.WELLS-75F	T.WELLS-75F	T.WELLS-75F
42098		T.WELLS-75F	T.WELLS-75F	T.WELLS-75F	T.WELLS-75F	T.WELLS-75F	T.WELLS-75F
42099		T.WELLS-75F	T.WELLS-75F	T.WELLS-75F	T.WELLS-75F	T.WELLS-75F	T.WELLS-75F
42100		T.WELLS-75F	T.WELLS-75F	T.WELLS-75F	T.WELLS-75F	T.WELLS-75F	T.WELLS-75F
42101		T.WELLS-75F	T.WELLS-75F	T.WELLS-75F	T.WELLS-75F	T.WELLS-75F	T.WELLS-75F
42102			T.WELLS-75F	T.WELLS-75F	T.WELLS-75F	T.WELLS-75F	T.WELLS-75F
42103			T.WELLS-75F	T.WELLS-75F	T.WELLS-75F	T.WELLS-75F	T.WELLS-75F
42104			T.WELLS-75F	T.WELLS-75F	T.WELLS-75F	T.WELLS-75F	T.WELLS-75F
42105			T.WELLS-75F	T.WELLS-75F	T.WELLS-75F	T.WELLS-75F	T.WELLS-75F
42106		RAMSGATE-74B	RAMSGATE-74B	T.WELLS-75F	T.WELLS-75F	T.WELLS-75F	T.WELLS-75F
Electric							
20001	SELHURST	SELHURST	SELHURST	SELHURST	SELHURST	SELHURST	SELHURST
20002	SELHURST	SELHURST	SELHURST	SELHURST	SELHURST	SELHURST	SELHURST
20003	SELHURST	SELHURST	SELHURST	SELHURST	SELHURST	SELHURST	SELHURST

Tunbridge Wells West provided a sanctuary of steam in the otherwise electrified LBSCR. Most of the shed's allocation consisted of BR and LMS 2-6-4T's for the hourly service to and from Victoria but a number of Ivatt 2MT 2-6-2's were used for the occasional services across to Eastbourne. Most of the engines seen at the West were regulars and 41301, seen on 1st September 1952, may have been a welcome sight for local enthusiasts as it was a Bricklayers Arms locomotive and usually confined to empty stock workings at Cannon Street, Victoria and Charing Cross.

loco	Jun-51	Jul-51	Sep-51	Dec-51	Jan-52	Mar-52	Jun-52
			LMS 2MT 2-6-2T (1946)				
41240	BATH (S&D) - 71G	BATH (S&D) - 71G	BATH (S&D) - 71G	BATH (S&D) - 71G	BATH (S&D) - 71G	BATH (S&D) - 71G	BATH (S&D) - 71G
41241	BATH (S&D) - 71G	BATH (S&D) - 71G	BATH (S&D) - 71G	BATH (S&D) - 71G	BATH (S&D) - 71G	BATH (S&D) - 71G	BATH (S&D) - 71G
41242	BATH (S&D) - 71G	BATH (S&D) - 71G	BATH (S&D) - 71G	BATH (S&D) - 71G	BATH (S&D) - 71G	BATH (S&D) - 71G	BATH (S&D) - 71G
41243	BATH (S&D) - 71G	BATH (S&D) - 71G	BATH (S&D) - 71G	BATH (S&D) - 71G	BATH (S&D) - 71G	BATH (S&D) - 71G	BATH (S&D) - 71G
41290			STEWARTS LANE - 73A	STEWARTS LANE - 73A	STEWARTS LANE - 73A	STEWARTS LANE - 73A	STEWARTS LANE - 73A
41291			EASTBOURNE - 75G	EASTBOURNE - 75G	EASTBOURNE - 75G	EASTBOURNE - 75G	STEWARTS LANE - 73A
41292				STEWARTS LANE - 73A	STEWARTS LANE - 73A	STEWARTS LANE - 73A	STEWARTS LANE - 73A
41293				STEWARTS LANE - 73A	STEWARTS LANE - 73A	STEWARTS LANE - 73A	EASTLEIGH - 71A
41294				STEWARTS LANE - 73A	STEWARTS LANE - 73A	STEWARTS LANE - 73A	STEWARTS LANE - 73A
41295				B.ARMS - 73B	B.ARMS - 73B	B.ARMS - 73B	STEWARTS LANE - 73A
41296				THREE BRIDGES - 75E	THREE BRIDGES - 75E	THREE BRIDGES - 75E	STEWARTS LANE - 73A
41297				THREE BRIDGES - 75E	THREE BRIDGES - 75E	THREE BRIDGES - 75E	STEWARTS LANE - 73A
41298				B.ARMS - 73B	B.ARMS - 73B	B.ARMS - 73B	B.ARMS - 73B
41299				B.ARMS - 73B	B.ARMS - 73B	B.ARMS - 73B	B.ARMS - 73B
41300				B.ARMS - 73B	B.ARMS - 73B	B.ARMS - 73B	B.ARMS - 73B
41301				B.ARMS - 73B	B.ARMS - 73B	B.ARMS - 73B	B.ARMS - 73B
41302				B.ARMS - 73B	B.ARMS - 73B	B.ARMS - 73B	B.ARMS - 73B
41303				B.ARMS - 73B	B.ARMS - 73B	B.ARMS - 73B	B.ARMS - 73B
41304				THREE BRIDGES - 75E	THREE BRIDGES - 75E	THREE BRIDGES - 75E	EASTLEIGH - 71A
41304				THREE BRIDGES - 75E	THREE BRIDGES - 75E	THREE BRIDGES - 75E	THREE BRIDGES - 75E
41305				THREE BRIDGES - 75E	THREE BRIDGES - 75E	THREE BRIDGES - 75E	EASTLEIGH - 71A
41306				THREE BRIDGES - 75E	THREE BRIDGES - 75E	THREE BRIDGES - 75E	THREE BRIDGES - 75E
41307				THREE BRIDGES - 75E	THREE BRIDGES - 75E	THREE BRIDGES - 75E	THREE BRIDGES - 75E
41308				FAVERSHAM - 73E	FAVERSHAM - 73E	FAVERSHAM - 73E	FAVERSHAM - 73E
41309				FAVERSHAM - 73E	FAVERSHAM - 73E	FAVERSHAM - 73E	FAVERSHAM - 73E
41310				FAVERSHAM - 73E	FAVERSHAM - 73E	FAVERSHAM - 73E	FAVERSHAM - 73E
41311				FAVERSHAM - 73E	FAVERSHAM - 73E	FAVERSHAM - 73E	FAVERSHAM - 73E
41312				FAVERSHAM - 73E	FAVERSHAM - 73E	FAVERSHAM - 73E	FAVERSHAM - 73E
41313				BRIGHTON - 75A	BRIGHTON - 75A	BRIGHTON - 75A	EXMOUTH JCN - 72A
41314				BRIGHTON - 75A	BRIGHTON - 75A	BRIGHTON - 75A	EXMOUTH JCN - 72A
41315				BRIGHTON - 75A	BRIGHTON - 75A	BRIGHTON - 75A	EXMOUTH JCN - 72A
41316				EASTBOURNE - 75G	EASTBOURNE - 75G	EASTBOURNE - 75G	EASTBOURNE - 75G
41317				EASTBOURNE - 75G	EASTBOURNE - 75G	EASTBOURNE - 75G	EASTBOURNE - 75G
41318				EASTBOURNE - 75G	EASTBOURNE - 75G	EASTBOURNE - 75G	T.WELLS - 75F
41319				EASTBOURNE - 75G	EASTBOURNE - 75G	EASTBOURNE - 75G	T.WELLS - 75F
			LMS 4MT 2-6-4T (1948)				
42066	RAMSGATE - 74B	RAMSGATE - 74B	RAMSGATE - 74B	RAMSGATE - 74B	RAMSGATE - 74B	RAMSGATE - 74B	THREE BRIDGES - 75E
42067	RAMSGATE - 74B	RAMSGATE - 74B	RAMSGATE - 74B	RAMSGATE - 74B	RAMSGATE - 74B	RAMSGATE - 74B	RAMSGATE - 74B
42068	RAMSGATE - 74B	RAMSGATE - 74B	RAMSGATE - 74B	RAMSGATE - 74B	RAMSGATE - 74B	RAMSGATE - 74B	RAMSGATE - 74B
42069	RAMSGATE - 74B	RAMSGATE - 74B	RAMSGATE - 74B	RAMSGATE - 74B	RAMSGATE - 74B	RAMSGATE - 74B	RAMSGATE - 74B
42070	RAMSGATE - 74B	RAMSGATE - 74B	RAMSGATE - 74B	RAMSGATE - 74B	RAMSGATE - 74B	RAMSGATE - 74B	RAMSGATE - 74B
42071	ASHFORD - 74A	ASHFORD - 74A	RAMSGATE - 74B	RAMSGATE - 74B	RAMSGATE - 74B	RAMSGATE - 74B	RAMSGATE - 74B
42072	ASHFORD - 74A	ASHFORD - 74A	RAMSGATE - 74B	RAMSGATE - 74B	RAMSGATE - 74B	RAMSGATE - 74B	RAMSGATE - 74B
42073	ASHFORD - 74A	ASHFORD - 74A	DOVER - 74C	DOVER - 74C	DOVER - 74C	DOVER - 74C	DOVER - 74C
42074	ASHFORD - 74A	ASHFORD - 74A	DOVER - 74C	DOVER - 74C	DOVER - 74C	DOVER - 74C	DOVER - 74C
42075	DOVER - 74C	DOVER - 74C	DOVER - 74C	DOVER - 74C	DOVER - 74C	DOVER - 74C	DOVER - 74C
42076	DOVER - 74C	DOVER - 74C	DOVER - 74C	DOVER - 74C	DOVER - 74C	DOVER - 74C	DOVER - 74C
42077	DOVER - 74C	DOVER - 74C	DOVER - 74C	DOVER - 74C	DOVER - 74C	DOVER - 74C	DOVER - 74C
42078	DOVER - 74C	DOVER - 74C	DOVER - 74C	DOVER - 74C	DOVER - 74C	DOVER - 74C	DOVER - 74C
42079	DOVER - 74C	DOVER - 74C	DOVER - 74C	DOVER - 74C	DOVER - 74C	DOVER - 74C	DOVER - 74C
42080	STEWARTS LANE - 73A	STEWARTS LANE - 73A	STEWARTS LANE - 73A	STEWARTS LANE - 73A	STEWARTS LANE - 73A	STEWARTS LANE - 73A	STEWARTS LANE - 73A
42081	STEWARTS LANE - 73A	STEWARTS LANE - 73A	STEWARTS LANE - 73A	STEWARTS LANE - 73A	STEWARTS LANE - 73A	STEWARTS LANE - 73A	STEWARTS LANE - 73A
42082	STEWARTS LANE - 73A	STEWARTS LANE - 73A	STEWARTS LANE - 73A	STEWARTS LANE - 73A	STEWARTS LANE - 73A	STEWARTS LANE - 73A	STEWARTS LANE - 73A
42083	STEWARTS LANE - 73A	STEWARTS LANE - 73A	STEWARTS LANE - 73A	STEWARTS LANE - 73A	STEWARTS LANE - 73A	TO NER	TO NER
42084	STEWARTS LANE - 73A	STEWARTS LANE - 73A	STEWARTS LANE - 73A	STEWARTS LANE - 73A	STEWARTS LANE - 73A	TO NER	TO NER
42085	BRIGHTON - 75A	BRIGHTON - 75A	BRIGHTON - 75A	BRIGHTON - 75A	BRIGHTON - 75A	TO NER	TO NER
42086	BRIGHTON - 75A	BRIGHTON - 75A	BRIGHTON - 75A	BRIGHTON - 75A	BRIGHTON - 75A	BRIGHTON - 75A	BRIGHTON - 75A
42087	BRIGHTON - 75A	BRIGHTON - 75A	BRIGHTON - 75A	BRIGHTON - 75A	BRIGHTON - 75A	BRIGHTON - 75A	BRIGHTON - 75A
42088	BRIGHTON - 75A	BRIGHTON - 75A	BRIGHTON - 75A	BRIGHTON - 75A	BRIGHTON - 75A	BRIGHTON - 75A	BRIGHTON - 75A
42089	BRIGHTON - 75A	BRIGHTON - 75A	BRIGHTON - 75A	BRIGHTON - 75A	BRIGHTON - 75A	STEWARTS LANE - 73A	STEWARTS LANE - 73A
42090	BRIGHTON - 75A	BRIGHTON - 75A	BRIGHTON - 75A	BRIGHTON - 75A	BRIGHTON - 75A	BRIGHTON - 75A	STEWARTS LANE - 73A
42091	BRIGHTON - 75A	BRIGHTON - 75A	BRIGHTON - 75A	BRIGHTON - 75A	BRIGHTON - 75A	STEWARTS LANE - 73A	STEWARTS LANE - 73A
42092	BRIGHTON - 75A	BRIGHTON - 75A	BRIGHTON - 75A	BRIGHTON - 75A	BRIGHTON - 75A	THREE BRIDGES - 75E	THREE BRIDGES - 75E
42093	BRIGHTON - 75A	BRIGHTON - 75A	BRIGHTON - 75A	BRIGHTON - 75A	BRIGHTON - 75A	BRIGHTON - 75A	THREE BRIDGES - 75E
42094	RAMSGATE - 74B	RAMSGATE - 74B	ASHFORD - 74A	ASHFORD - 74A	ASHFORD - 74A	ASHFORD - 74A	ASHFORD - 74A
42095	T.WELLS - 75F	T.WELLS - 75F	ASHFORD - 74A	ASHFORD - 74A	ASHFORD - 74A	ASHFORD - 74A	ASHFORD - 74A
42096	T.WELLS - 75F	T.WELLS - 75F	ASHFORD - 74A	ASHFORD - 74A	ASHFORD - 74A	ASHFORD - 74A	ASHFORD - 74A
42097	T.WELLS - 75F	T.WELLS - 75F	ASHFORD - 74A	ASHFORD - 74A	ASHFORD - 74A	ASHFORD - 74A	ASHFORD - 74A
42098	T.WELLS - 75F	T.WELLS - 75F	ASHFORD - 74A	ASHFORD - 74A	ASHFORD - 74A	ASHFORD - 74A	ASHFORD - 74A
42099	T.WELLS - 75F	T.WELLS - 75F	EXMOUTH JCN - 72A	EXMOUTH JCN - 72A	THREE BRIDGES - 75E	T.WELLS - 75F	T.WELLS - 75F
42100	T.WELLS - 75F	T.WELLS - 75F	T.WELLS - 75F	T.WELLS - 75F	T.WELLS - 75F	T.WELLS - 75F	T.WELLS - 75F
42101	T.WELLS - 75F	T.WELLS - 75F	T.WELLS - 75F	T.WELLS - 75F	T.WELLS - 75F	T.WELLS - 75F	T.WELLS - 75F
42102	T.WELLS - 75F	T.WELLS - 75F	T.WELLS - 75F	EXMOUTH JCN - 72A	THREE BRIDGES - 75E	T.WELLS - 75F	T.WELLS - 75F
42103	T.WELLS - 75F	T.WELLS - 75F	EXMOUTH JCN - 72A	EXMOUTH JCN - 72A	BRIGHTON - 75A	BRIGHTON - 75A	BRIGHTON - 75A
42104	T.WELLS - 75F	T.WELLS - 75F	T.WELLS - 75F	T.WELLS - 75F	T.WELLS - 75F	T.WELLS - 75F	BRIGHTON - 75A
42105	T.WELLS - 75F	T.WELLS - 75F	EXMOUTH JCN - 72A	EXMOUTH JCN - 72A	BRIGHTON - 75A	BRIGHTON - 75A	BRIGHTON - 75A
42106	T.WELLS - 75F	T.WELLS - 75F	T.WELLS - 75F	T.WELLS - 75F	T.WELLS - 75F	T.WELLS - 75F	BRIGHTON - 75A
			Electric				
20001	SELHURST	SELHURST	SELHURST	SELHURST	SELHURST	SELHURST	SELHURST
20002	SELHURST	SELHURST	SELHURST	SELHURST	SELHURST	SELHURST	SELHURST
20003	SELHURST	SELHURST	SELHURST	SELHURST	SELHURST	SELHURST	SELHURST
			DIESEL				
10201				NINE ELMS - 70A	NINE ELMS - 70A	NINE ELMS - 70A	NINE ELMS - 70A
10202				NINE ELMS - 70A	NINE ELMS - 70A	NINE ELMS - 70A	NINE ELMS - 70A

loco	Sep-52	Dec-52	Mar-53	May-53	Jul-53	Sep-53	Nov-53
				LMS 2MT 2-6-2T (1946)			
41240	BATH (S&D) - 71G	BATH (S&D) - 71G	BATH (S&D) - 71G	BATH (S&D) - 71G	BATH (S&D) - 71G	BATH (S&D) - 71G	TO LMR
41241	BATH (S&D) - 71G	BATH (S&D) - 71G	BATH (S&D) - 71G	BATH (S&D) - 71G	BATH (S&D) - 71G	BATH (S&D) - 71G	BATH (S&D) - 71G
41242	BATH (S&D) - 71G	BATH (S&D) - 71G	BATH (S&D) - 71G	BATH (S&D) - 71G	BATH (S&D) - 71G	BATH (S&D) - 71G	BATH (S&D) - 71G
41243	BATH (S&D) - 71G	BATH (S&D) - 71G	BATH (S&D) - 71G	BATH (S&D) - 71G	BATH (S&D) - 71G	BATH (S&D) - 71G	BATH (S&D) - 71G
41248					TEMPLECOMBE - 71H	TEMPLECOMBE - 71H	TEMPLECOMBE - 71H
41249					TEMPLECOMBE - 71H	TEMPLECOMBE - 71H	TEMPLECOMBE - 71H
41290	STEWARTS LANE - 73A	STEWARTS LANE - 73A	STEWARTS LANE - 73A	STEWARTS LANE - 73A	STEWARTS LANE - 73A	STEWARTS LANE - 73A	STEWARTS LANE - 73A
41291	STEWARTS LANE - 73A	STEWARTS LANE - 73A	STEWARTS LANE - 73A	STEWARTS LANE - 73A	STEWARTS LANE - 73A	STEWARTS LANE - 73A	STEWARTS LANE - 73A
41292	STEWARTS LANE - 73A	STEWARTS LANE - 73A	STEWARTS LANE - 73A	STEWARTS LANE - 73A	STEWARTS LANE - 73A	STEWARTS LANE - 73A	STEWARTS LANE - 73A
41293	EASTLEIGH - 71A	EASTLEIGH - 71A	EASTLEIGH - 71A	EASTLEIGH - 71A	EASTLEIGH - 71A	EASTLEIGH - 71A	EASTLEIGH - 71A
41294	STEWARTS LANE - 73A	STEWARTS LANE - 73A	STEWARTS LANE - 73A	STEWARTS LANE - 73A	STEWARTS LANE - 73A	STEWARTS LANE - 73A	STEWARTS LANE - 73A
41295	STEWARTS LANE - 73A	STEWARTS LANE - 73A	STEWARTS LANE - 73A	STEWARTS LANE - 73A	STEWARTS LANE - 73A	STEWARTS LANE - 73A	STEWARTS LANE - 73A
41296	STEWARTS LANE - 73A	STEWARTS LANE - 73A	STEWARTS LANE - 73A	STEWARTS LANE - 73A	STEWARTS LANE - 73A	STEWARTS LANE - 73A	STEWARTS LANE - 73A
41297	STEWARTS LANE - 73A	STEWARTS LANE - 73A	T.WELLS - 75F	T.WELLS - 75F	T.WELLS - 75F	T.WELLS - 75F	T.WELLS - 75F
41298	B.ARMS - 73B	B.ARMS - 73B	B.ARMS - 73B	B.ARMS - 73B	BARNSTAPLE - 72E	BARNSTAPLE - 72E	BARNSTAPLE - 72E
41299	B.ARMS - 73B	B.ARMS - 73B	B.ARMS - 73B	B.ARMS - 73B	B.ARMS - 73B	B.ARMS - 73B	B.ARMS - 73B
41300	B.ARMS - 73B	B.ARMS - 73B	B.ARMS - 73B	B.ARMS - 73B	B.ARMS - 73B	B.ARMS - 73B	B.ARMS - 73B
41301	B.ARMS - 73B	B.ARMS - 73B	B.ARMS - 73B	B.ARMS - 73B	B.ARMS - 73B	B.ARMS - 73B	B.ARMS - 73B
41302	B.ARMS - 73B	B.ARMS - 73B	B.ARMS - 73B	B.ARMS - 73B	B.ARMS - 73B	B.ARMS - 73B	B.ARMS - 73B
41303	B.ARMS - 73B	B.ARMS - 73B	FAVERSHAM - 73E	FAVERSHAM - 73E	FAVERSHAM - 73E	FAVERSHAM - 73E	FAVERSHAM - 73E
41304	EASTLEIGH - 71A	EASTLEIGH - 71A	EASTLEIGH - 71A	EASTLEIGH - 71A	EASTLEIGH - 71A	EASTLEIGH - 71A	EASTLEIGH - 71A
41304	THREE BRIDGES - 75E	THREE BRIDGES - 75E	THREE BRIDGES - 75E	THREE BRIDGES - 75E	THREE BRIDGES - 75E	THREE BRIDGES - 75E	THREE BRIDGES - 75E
41305	EASTLEIGH - 71A	EASTLEIGH - 71A	EASTLEIGH - 71A	EASTLEIGH - 71A	EASTLEIGH - 71A	EASTLEIGH - 71A	EASTLEIGH - 71A
41306	THREE BRIDGES - 75E	THREE BRIDGES - 75E	THREE BRIDGES - 75E	THREE BRIDGES - 75E	THREE BRIDGES - 75E	THREE BRIDGES - 75E	THREE BRIDGES - 75E
41307	THREE BRIDGES - 75E	THREE BRIDGES - 75E	THREE BRIDGES - 75E	THREE BRIDGES - 75E	THREE BRIDGES - 75E	THREE BRIDGES - 75E	THREE BRIDGES - 75E
41308	FAVERSHAM - 73E	FAVERSHAM - 73E	FAVERSHAM - 73E	FAVERSHAM - 73E	FAVERSHAM - 73E	FAVERSHAM - 73E	FAVERSHAM - 73E
41309	FAVERSHAM - 73E	FAVERSHAM - 73E	FAVERSHAM - 73E	FAVERSHAM - 73E	FAVERSHAM - 73E	FAVERSHAM - 73E	FAVERSHAM - 73E
41310	FAVERSHAM - 73E	FAVERSHAM - 73E	FAVERSHAM - 73E	FAVERSHAM - 73E	FAVERSHAM - 73E	FAVERSHAM - 73E	FAVERSHAM - 73E
41311	FAVERSHAM - 73E	FAVERSHAM - 73E	FAVERSHAM - 73E	FAVERSHAM - 73E	FAVERSHAM - 73E	FAVERSHAM - 73E	FAVERSHAM - 73E
41312	FAVERSHAM - 73E	FAVERSHAM - 73E	FAVERSHAM - 73E	FAVERSHAM - 73E	FAVERSHAM - 73E	FAVERSHAM - 73E	FAVERSHAM - 73E
41313	EXMOUTH JCN - 72A	EXMOUTH JCN - 72A	EXMOUTH JCN - 72A	EXMOUTH JCN - 72A	EXMOUTH JCN - 72A	EXMOUTH JCN - 72A	EXMOUTH JCN - 72A
41314	EXMOUTH JCN - 72A	EXMOUTH JCN - 72A	EXMOUTH JCN - 72A	EXMOUTH JCN - 72A	EXMOUTH JCN - 72A	EXMOUTH JCN - 72A	EXMOUTH JCN - 72A
41315	EXMOUTH JCN - 72A	EXMOUTH JCN - 72A	PLYMOUTH - 72D	PLYMOUTH - 72D	PLYMOUTH - 72D	PLYMOUTH - 72D	PLYMOUTH - 72D
41316	T.WELLS - 75F	T.WELLS - 75F	T.WELLS - 75F	T.WELLS - 75F	T.WELLS - 75F	T.WELLS - 75F	T.WELLS - 75F
41317	T.WELLS - 75F	T.WELLS - 75F	T.WELLS - 75F	T.WELLS - 75F	T.WELLS - 75F	T.WELLS - 75F	T.WELLS - 75F
41318	T.WELLS - 75F	T.WELLS - 75F	T.WELLS - 75F	T.WELLS - 75F	T.WELLS - 75F	T.WELLS - 75F	T.WELLS - 75F
41319	T.WELLS - 75F	T.WELLS - 75F	T.WELLS - 75F	T.WELLS - 75F	T.WELLS - 75F	T.WELLS - 75F	T.WELLS - 75F
				LMS 4MT 2-6-4T (1948)			
42066	THREE BRIDGES - 75E	THREE BRIDGES - 75E	THREE BRIDGES - 75E	THREE BRIDGES - 75E	THREE BRIDGES - 75E	THREE BRIDGES - 75E	THREE BRIDGES - 75E
42067	RAMSGATE - 74B	RAMSGATE - 74B	RAMSGATE - 74B	RAMSGATE - 74B	RAMSGATE - 74B	RAMSGATE - 74B	RAMSGATE - 74B
42068	RAMSGATE - 74B	RAMSGATE - 74B	BRIGHTON - 75A	RAMSGATE - 74B	RAMSGATE - 74B	RAMSGATE - 74B	REDHILL - 75B
42069	ASHFORD - 74A	ASHFORD - 74A	ASHFORD - 74A	ASHFORD - 74A	ASHFORD - 74A	ASHFORD - 74A	ASHFORD - 74A
42070	RAMSGATE - 74B	RAMSGATE - 74B	RAMSGATE - 74B	RAMSGATE - 74B	RAMSGATE - 74B	RAMSGATE - 74B	RAMSGATE - 74B
42071	RAMSGATE - 74B	RAMSGATE - 74B	RAMSGATE - 74B	RAMSGATE - 74B	RAMSGATE - 74B	RAMSGATE - 74B	RAMSGATE - 74B
42072	RAMSGATE - 74B	RAMSGATE - 74B	RAMSGATE - 74B	RAMSGATE - 74B	RAMSGATE - 74B	RAMSGATE - 74B	RAMSGATE - 74B
42073	ASHFORD - 74A	ASHFORD - 74A	ASHFORD - 74A	ASHFORD - 74A	ASHFORD - 74A	ASHFORD - 74A	ASHFORD - 74A
42074	DOVER - 74C	DOVER - 74C	DOVER - 74C	DOVER - 74C	DOVER - 74C	DOVER - 74C	DOVER - 74C
42075	DOVER - 74C	DOVER - 74C	BRIGHTON - 75A	BRIGHTON - 75A	BRIGHTON - 75A	BRIGHTON - 75A	BRIGHTON - 75A
42076	DOVER - 74C	DOVER - 74C	DOVER - 74C	DOVER - 74C	DOVER - 74C	DOVER - 74C	DOVER - 74C
42077	DOVER - 74C	DOVER - 74C	BRIGHTON - 75A	BRIGHTON - 75A	BRIGHTON - 75A	BRIGHTON - 75A	REDHILL - 75B
42078	DOVER - 74C	DOVER - 74C	DOVER - 74C	DOVER - 74C	DOVER - 74C	DOVER - 74C	DOVER - 74C
42079	DOVER - 74C	DOVER - 74C	DOVER - 74C	DOVER - 74C	DOVER - 74C	DOVER - 74C	DOVER - 74C
42080	STEWARTS LANE - 73A	STEWARTS LANE - 73A	STEWARTS LANE - 73A	STEWARTS LANE - 73A	STEWARTS LANE - 73A	STEWARTS LANE - 73A	STEWARTS LANE - 73A
42081	STEWARTS LANE - 73A	STEWARTS LANE - 73A	STEWARTS LANE - 73A	STEWARTS LANE - 73A	STEWARTS LANE - 73A	STEWARTS LANE - 73A	STEWARTS LANE - 73A
42082	STEWARTS LANE - 73A	STEWARTS LANE - 73A	BRIGHTON - 75A	BRIGHTON - 75A	BRIGHTON - 75A	BRIGHTON - 75A	BRIGHTON - 75A
42086	BRIGHTON - 75A	BRIGHTON - 75A	BRIGHTON - 75A	BRIGHTON - 75A	BRIGHTON - 75A	BRIGHTON - 75A	BRIGHTON - 75A
42087	BRIGHTON - 75A	BRIGHTON - 75A	BRIGHTON - 75A	BRIGHTON - 75A	BRIGHTON - 75A	BRIGHTON - 75A	BRIGHTON - 75A
42088	BRIGHTON - 75A	BRIGHTON - 75A	BRIGHTON - 75A	BRIGHTON - 75A	BRIGHTON - 75A	BRIGHTON - 75A	BRIGHTON - 75A
42089	STEWARTS LANE - 73A	STEWARTS LANE - 73A	STEWARTS LANE - 73A	STEWARTS LANE - 73A	STEWARTS LANE - 73A	STEWARTS LANE - 73A	STEWARTS LANE - 73A
42090	STEWARTS LANE - 73A	STEWARTS LANE - 73A	STEWARTS LANE - 73A	STEWARTS LANE - 73A	STEWARTS LANE - 73A	STEWARTS LANE - 73A	STEWARTS LANE - 73A
42091	STEWARTS LANE - 73A	STEWARTS LANE - 73A	STEWARTS LANE - 73A	STEWARTS LANE - 73A	STEWARTS LANE - 73A	STEWARTS LANE - 73A	STEWARTS LANE - 73A
42092	THREE BRIDGES - 75E	THREE BRIDGES - 75E	THREE BRIDGES - 75E	THREE BRIDGES - 75E	THREE BRIDGES - 75E	THREE BRIDGES - 75E	THREE BRIDGES - 75E
42093	THREE BRIDGES - 75E	THREE BRIDGES - 75E	THREE BRIDGES - 75E	THREE BRIDGES - 75E	THREE BRIDGES - 75E	THREE BRIDGES - 75E	THREE BRIDGES - 75E
42094	ASHFORD - 74A	ASHFORD - 74A	ASHFORD - 74A	ASHFORD - 74A	ASHFORD - 74A	ASHFORD - 74A	ASHFORD - 74A
42095	ASHFORD - 74A	ASHFORD - 74A	ASHFORD - 74A	ASHFORD - 74A	ASHFORD - 74A	ASHFORD - 74A	ASHFORD - 74A
42096	ASHFORD - 74A	ASHFORD - 74A	ASHFORD - 74A	ASHFORD - 74A	ASHFORD - 74A	ASHFORD - 74A	ASHFORD - 74A
42097	ASHFORD - 74A	ASHFORD - 74A	ASHFORD - 74A	ASHFORD - 74A	ASHFORD - 74A	ASHFORD - 74A	ASHFORD - 74A
42098	ASHFORD - 74A	ASHFORD - 74A	ASHFORD - 74A	ASHFORD - 74A	ASHFORD - 74A	ASHFORD - 74A	ASHFORD - 74A
42099	T.WELLS - 75F	T.WELLS - 75F	T.WELLS - 75F	T.WELLS - 75F	T.WELLS - 75F	T.WELLS - 75F	T.WELLS - 75F
42100	T.WELLS - 75F	T.WELLS - 75F	T.WELLS - 75F	T.WELLS - 75F	T.WELLS - 75F	T.WELLS - 75F	T.WELLS - 75F
42101	T.WELLS - 75F	T.WELLS - 75F	T.WELLS - 75F	T.WELLS - 75F	T.WELLS - 75F	T.WELLS - 75F	T.WELLS - 75F
42102	T.WELLS - 75F	T.WELLS - 75F	T.WELLS - 75F	T.WELLS - 75F	T.WELLS - 75F	T.WELLS - 75F	T.WELLS - 75F
42103	BRIGHTON - 75A	BRIGHTON - 75A	BRIGHTON - 75A	BRIGHTON - 75A	BRIGHTON - 75A	BRIGHTON - 75A	BRIGHTON - 75A
42104	BRIGHTON - 75A	BRIGHTON - 75A	BRIGHTON - 75A	BRIGHTON - 75A	BRIGHTON - 75A	BRIGHTON - 75A	BRIGHTON - 75A
42105	BRIGHTON - 75A	BRIGHTON - 75A	BRIGHTON - 75A	BRIGHTON - 75A	BRIGHTON - 75A	BRIGHTON - 75A	BRIGHTON - 75A
42106	BRIGHTON - 75A	BRIGHTON - 75A	BRIGHTON - 75A	BRIGHTON - 75A	BRIGHTON - 75A	BRIGHTON - 75A	BRIGHTON - 75A
				Electric			
20001	SELHURST	SELHURST	SELHURST	SELHURST	SELHURST	SELHURST	SELHURST
20002	SELHURST	SELHURST	SELHURST	SELHURST	SELHURST	SELHURST	SELHURST
20003	SELHURST	SELHURST	SELHURST	SELHURST	SELHURST	SELHURST	SELHURST
				DIESEL			
10800	NORWOOD JCN - 75C	NORWOOD JCN - 75C	NORWOOD JCN - 75C	NORWOOD JCN - 75C	NORWOOD JCN - 75C	NORWOOD JCN - 75C	NORWOOD JCN - 75C
10000			FROM LMR	NINE ELMS - 70A	NINE ELMS - 70A	NINE ELMS - 70A	NINE ELMS - 70A
10001			FROM LMR	NINE ELMS - 70A	NINE ELMS - 70A	NINE ELMS - 70A	NINE ELMS - 70A
10201	NINE ELMS - 70A	NINE ELMS - 70A	NINE ELMS - 70A	NINE ELMS - 70A	NINE ELMS - 70A	NINE ELMS - 70A	NINE ELMS - 70A
10202	NINE ELMS - 70A	NINE ELMS - 70A	NINE ELMS - 70A	NINE ELMS - 70A	NINE ELMS - 70A	NINE ELMS - 70A	NINE ELMS - 70A

loco	Jan-54	Mar-54	May-54	Jun-54	Aug-54	Oct-54	Dec-54
			LMS 2MT 2-6-2T (1946)				
41241	BATH (S&D) - 71G	BATH (S&D) - 71G	BATH (S&D) - 71G	BATH (S&D) - 71G	BATH (S&D) - 71G	BATH (S&D) - 71G	BATH (S&D) - 71G
41242	BATH (S&D) - 71G	BATH (S&D) - 71G	BATH (S&D) - 71G	BATH (S&D) - 71G	BATH (S&D) - 71G	BATH (S&D) - 71G	BATH (S&D) - 71G
41243	BATH (S&D) - 71G	BATH (S&D) - 71G	BATH (S&D) - 71G	BATH (S&D) - 71G	BATH (S&D) - 71G	BATH (S&D) - 71G	BATH (S&D) - 71G
41248	TEMPLECOMBE - 71H	TEMPLECOMBE - 71H	TEMPLECOMBE - 71H	TEMPLECOMBE - 71H	TEMPLECOMBE - 71H	TEMPLECOMBE - 71H	TEMPLECOMBE - 71H
41249	TEMPLECOMBE - 71H	TEMPLECOMBE - 71H	TEMPLECOMBE - 71H	TEMPLECOMBE - 71H	TEMPLECOMBE - 71H	TEMPLECOMBE - 71H	TEMPLECOMBE - 71H
41290	STEWARTS LANE - 73A	STEWARTS LANE - 73A	STEWARTS LANE - 73A	STEWARTS LANE - 73A	STEWARTS LANE - 73A	STEWARTS LANE - 73A	STEWARTS LANE - 73A
41291	STEWARTS LANE - 73A	STEWARTS LANE - 73A	STEWARTS LANE - 73A	STEWARTS LANE - 73A	STEWARTS LANE - 73A	STEWARTS LANE - 73A	STEWARTS LANE - 73A
41292	STEWARTS LANE - 73A	STEWARTS LANE - 73A	STEWARTS LANE - 73A	STEWARTS LANE - 73A	STEWARTS LANE - 73A	STEWARTS LANE - 73A	STEWARTS LANE - 73A
41293	EASTLEIGH - 71A	EASTLEIGH - 71A	EASTLEIGH - 71A	EASTLEIGH - 71A	EASTLEIGH - 71A	EASTLEIGH - 71A	EASTLEIGH - 71A
41294	STEWARTS LANE - 73A	STEWARTS LANE - 73A	STEWARTS LANE - 73A	STEWARTS LANE - 73A	STEWARTS LANE - 73A	STEWARTS LANE - 73A	STEWARTS LANE - 73A
41295	STEWARTS LANE - 73A	STEWARTS LANE - 73A	STEWARTS LANE - 73A	STEWARTS LANE - 73A	BARNSTAPLE - 72E	BARNSTAPLE - 72E	BARNSTAPLE - 72E
41296	STEWARTS LANE - 73A	STEWARTS LANE - 73A	STEWARTS LANE - 73A	STEWARTS LANE - 73A	EXMOUTH JCN - 72A	EXMOUTH JCN - 72A	EXMOUTH JCN - 72A
41297	T.WELLS - 75F	T.WELLS - 75F	T.WELLS - 75F	T.WELLS - 75F	T.WELLS - 75F	T.WELLS - 75F	T.WELLS - 75F
41298	BARNSTAPLE - 72E	BARNSTAPLE - 72E	BARNSTAPLE - 72E	BARNSTAPLE - 72E	BARNSTAPLE - 72E	BARNSTAPLE - 72E	BARNSTAPLE - 72E
41299	B.ARMS - 73B	B.ARMS - 73B	B.ARMS - 73B	B.ARMS - 73B	B.ARMS - 73B	B.ARMS - 73B	B.ARMS - 73B
41300	B.ARMS - 73B	B.ARMS - 73B	B.ARMS - 73B	B.ARMS - 73B	B.ARMS - 73B	B.ARMS - 73B	B.ARMS - 73B
41301	B.ARMS - 73B	B.ARMS - 73B	B.ARMS - 73B	B.ARMS - 73B	B.ARMS - 73B	B.ARMS - 73B	B.ARMS - 73B
41302	B.ARMS - 73B	B.ARMS - 73B	B.ARMS - 73B	B.ARMS - 73B	B.ARMS - 73B	B.ARMS - 73B	B.ARMS - 73B
41303	FAVERSHAM - 73E	FAVERSHAM - 73E	FAVERSHAM - 73E	FAVERSHAM - 73E	FAVERSHAM - 73E	FAVERSHAM - 73E	FAVERSHAM - 73E
41304	EASTLEIGH - 71A	EASTLEIGH - 71A	EASTLEIGH - 71A	EASTLEIGH - 71A	EASTLEIGH - 71A	EASTLEIGH - 71A	EASTLEIGH - 71A
41304	THREE BRIDGES - 75E	THREE BRIDGES - 75E	THREE BRIDGES - 75E	THREE BRIDGES - 75E	THREE BRIDGES - 75E	THREE BRIDGES - 75E	THREE BRIDGES - 75E
41305	EASTLEIGH - 71A	EASTLEIGH - 71A	EASTLEIGH - 71A	EASTLEIGH - 71A	EASTLEIGH - 71A	EASTLEIGH - 71A	EASTLEIGH - 71A
41306	THREE BRIDGES - 75E	THREE BRIDGES - 75E	THREE BRIDGES - 75E	THREE BRIDGES - 75E	THREE BRIDGES - 75E	THREE BRIDGES - 75E	THREE BRIDGES - 75E
41307	THREE BRIDGES - 75E	THREE BRIDGES - 75E	THREE BRIDGES - 75E	THREE BRIDGES - 75E	THREE BRIDGES - 75E	THREE BRIDGES - 75E	THREE BRIDGES - 75E
41308	FAVERSHAM - 73E	FAVERSHAM - 73E	FAVERSHAM - 73E	FAVERSHAM - 73E	FAVERSHAM - 73E	FAVERSHAM - 73E	FAVERSHAM - 73E
41309	FAVERSHAM - 73E	FAVERSHAM - 73E	FAVERSHAM - 73E	FAVERSHAM - 73E	FAVERSHAM - 73E	FAVERSHAM - 73E	FAVERSHAM - 73E
41310	FAVERSHAM - 73E	FAVERSHAM - 73E	FAVERSHAM - 73E	FAVERSHAM - 73E	FAVERSHAM - 73E	FAVERSHAM - 73E	FAVERSHAM - 73E
41311	FAVERSHAM - 73E	FAVERSHAM - 73E	FAVERSHAM - 73E	FAVERSHAM - 73E	FAVERSHAM - 73E	FAVERSHAM - 73E	FAVERSHAM - 73E
41312	FAVERSHAM - 73E	FAVERSHAM - 73E	FAVERSHAM - 73E	FAVERSHAM - 73E	FAVERSHAM - 73E	FAVERSHAM - 73E	FAVERSHAM - 73E
41313	EXMOUTH JCN - 72A	EXMOUTH JCN - 72A	EXMOUTH JCN - 72A	EXMOUTH JCN - 72A	EXMOUTH JCN - 72A	EXMOUTH JCN - 72A	EXMOUTH JCN - 72A
41314	EXMOUTH JCN - 72A	EXMOUTH JCN - 72A	EXMOUTH JCN - 72A	EXMOUTH JCN - 72A	EXMOUTH JCN - 72A	EXMOUTH JCN - 72A	EXMOUTH JCN - 72A
41315	PLYMOUTH - 72D	PLYMOUTH - 72D	PLYMOUTH - 72D	PLYMOUTH - 72D	PLYMOUTH - 72D	PLYMOUTH - 72D	PLYMOUTH - 72D
41316	T.WELLS - 75F	T.WELLS - 75F	T.WELLS - 75F	T.WELLS - 75F	T.WELLS - 75F	T.WELLS - 75F	T.WELLS - 75F
41317	T.WELLS - 75F	T.WELLS - 75F	T.WELLS - 75F	T.WELLS - 75F	T.WELLS - 75F	T.WELLS - 75F	T.WELLS - 75F
41318	T.WELLS - 75F	T.WELLS - 75F	T.WELLS - 75F	T.WELLS - 75F	T.WELLS - 75F	T.WELLS - 75F	T.WELLS - 75F
41319	T.WELLS - 75F	T.WELLS - 75F	T.WELLS - 75F	T.WELLS - 75F	T.WELLS - 75F	T.WELLS - 75F	T.WELLS - 75F
			LMS 4MT 2-6-4T (1948)				
42066	THREE BRIDGES - 75E	THREE BRIDGES - 75E	THREE BRIDGES - 75E	THREE BRIDGES - 75E	THREE BRIDGES - 75E	THREE BRIDGES - 75E	THREE BRIDGES - 75E
42067	RAMSGATE - 74B	RAMSGATE - 74B	RAMSGATE - 74B	RAMSGATE - 74B	RAMSGATE - 74B	RAMSGATE - 74B	RAMSGATE - 74B
42068	RAMSGATE - 74B	RAMSGATE - 74B	RAMSGATE - 74B	RAMSGATE - 74B	RAMSGATE - 74B	RAMSGATE - 74B	RAMSGATE - 74B
42069	ASHFORD - 74A	ASHFORD - 74A	ASHFORD - 74A	ASHFORD - 74A	ASHFORD - 74A	ASHFORD - 74A	ASHFORD - 74A
42070	RAMSGATE - 74B	RAMSGATE - 74B	RAMSGATE - 74B	RAMSGATE - 74B	RAMSGATE - 74B	RAMSGATE - 74B	RAMSGATE - 74B
42071	RAMSGATE - 74B	RAMSGATE - 74B	RAMSGATE - 74B	RAMSGATE - 74B	RAMSGATE - 74B	RAMSGATE - 74B	RAMSGATE - 74B
42072	RAMSGATE - 74B	RAMSGATE - 74B	RAMSGATE - 74B	RAMSGATE - 74B	RAMSGATE - 74B	TO NER	TO NER
42073	ASHFORD - 74A	ASHFORD - 74A	ASHFORD - 74A	ASHFORD - 74A	ASHFORD - 74A	TO NER	TO NER
42074	DOVER - 74C	DOVER - 74C	DOVER - 74C	DOVER - 74C	DOVER - 74C	DOVER - 74C	DOVER - 74C
42075	BRIGHTON - 75A	BRIGHTON - 75A	BRIGHTON - 75A	BRIGHTON - 75A	BRIGHTON - 75A	BRIGHTON - 75A	BRIGHTON - 75A
42076	DOVER - 74C	DOVER - 74C	DOVER - 74C	DOVER - 74C	DOVER - 74C	DOVER - 74C	DOVER - 74C
42077	DOVER - 74C	DOVER - 74C	DOVER - 74C	DOVER - 74C	DOVER - 74C	DOVER - 74C	DOVER - 74C
42078	DOVER - 74C	DOVER - 74C	DOVER - 74C	DOVER - 74C	DOVER - 74C	DOVER - 74C	DOVER - 74C
42079	DOVER - 74C	DOVER - 74C	DOVER - 74C	DOVER - 74C	DOVER - 74C	DOVER - 74C	DOVER - 74C
42080	STEWARTS LANE - 73A	STEWARTS LANE - 73A	STEWARTS LANE - 73A	STEWARTS LANE - 73A	STEWARTS LANE - 73A	STEWARTS LANE - 73A	STEWARTS LANE - 73A
42081	STEWARTS LANE - 73A	STEWARTS LANE - 73A	STEWARTS LANE - 73A	STEWARTS LANE - 73A	STEWARTS LANE - 73A	STEWARTS LANE - 73A	STEWARTS LANE - 73A
42082	BRIGHTON - 75A	BRIGHTON - 75A	BRIGHTON - 75A	BRIGHTON - 75A	BRIGHTON - 75A	BRIGHTON - 75A	BRIGHTON - 75A
42086	BRIGHTON - 75A	BRIGHTON - 75A	BRIGHTON - 75A	BRIGHTON - 75A	BRIGHTON - 75A	BRIGHTON - 75A	BRIGHTON - 75A
42087	BRIGHTON - 75A	BRIGHTON - 75A	BRIGHTON - 75A	BRIGHTON - 75A	BRIGHTON - 75A	BRIGHTON - 75A	BRIGHTON - 75A
42088	BRIGHTON - 75A	BRIGHTON - 75A	BRIGHTON - 75A	BRIGHTON - 75A	BRIGHTON - 75A	BRIGHTON - 75A	STEWARTS LANE - 73A
42089	STEWARTS LANE - 73A	STEWARTS LANE - 73A	STEWARTS LANE - 73A	STEWARTS LANE - 73A	STEWARTS LANE - 73A	STEWARTS LANE - 73A	STEWARTS LANE - 73A
42090	STEWARTS LANE - 73A	STEWARTS LANE - 73A	STEWARTS LANE - 73A	STEWARTS LANE - 73A	STEWARTS LANE - 73A	STEWARTS LANE - 73A	STEWARTS LANE - 73A
42091	STEWARTS LANE - 73A	STEWARTS LANE - 73A	STEWARTS LANE - 73A	STEWARTS LANE - 73A	STEWARTS LANE - 73A	STEWARTS LANE - 73A	STEWARTS LANE - 73A
42092	THREE BRIDGES - 75E	THREE BRIDGES - 75E	THREE BRIDGES - 75E	THREE BRIDGES - 75E	THREE BRIDGES - 75E	THREE BRIDGES - 75E	THREE BRIDGES - 75E
42093	THREE BRIDGES - 75E	THREE BRIDGES - 75E	THREE BRIDGES - 75E	THREE BRIDGES - 75E	THREE BRIDGES - 75E	THREE BRIDGES - 75E	TO NER
42094	ASHFORD - 74A	ASHFORD - 74A	ASHFORD - 74A	ASHFORD - 74A	ASHFORD - 74A	ASHFORD - 74A	TO NER
42095	ASHFORD - 74A	ASHFORD - 74A	ASHFORD - 74A	ASHFORD - 74A	ASHFORD - 74A	ASHFORD - 74A	ASHFORD - 74A
42096	ASHFORD - 74A	ASHFORD - 74A	ASHFORD - 74A	ASHFORD - 74A	ASHFORD - 74A	ASHFORD - 74A	ASHFORD - 74A
42097	ASHFORD - 74A	ASHFORD - 74A	ASHFORD - 74A	ASHFORD - 74A	ASHFORD - 74A	ASHFORD - 74A	ASHFORD - 74A
42098	ASHFORD - 74A	ASHFORD - 74A	ASHFORD - 74A	ASHFORD - 74A	ASHFORD - 74A	ASHFORD - 74A	ASHFORD - 74A
42099	T.WELLS - 75F	T.WELLS - 75F	T.WELLS - 75F	T.WELLS - 75F	T.WELLS - 75F	T.WELLS - 75F	T.WELLS - 75F
42100	T.WELLS - 75F	T.WELLS - 75F	T.WELLS - 75F	T.WELLS - 75F	T.WELLS - 75F	T.WELLS - 75F	T.WELLS - 75F
42101	T.WELLS - 75F	T.WELLS - 75F	T.WELLS - 75F	T.WELLS - 75F	T.WELLS - 75F	T.WELLS - 75F	T.WELLS - 75F
42102	T.WELLS - 75F	T.WELLS - 75F	T.WELLS - 75F	T.WELLS - 75F	T.WELLS - 75F	T.WELLS - 75F	T.WELLS - 75F
42103	BRIGHTON - 75A	BRIGHTON - 75A	BRIGHTON - 75A	BRIGHTON - 75A	BRIGHTON - 75A	BRIGHTON - 75A	BRIGHTON - 75A
42104	BRIGHTON - 75A	BRIGHTON - 75A	BRIGHTON - 75A	BRIGHTON - 75A	BRIGHTON - 75A	BRIGHTON - 75A	BRIGHTON - 75A
42105	BRIGHTON - 75A	BRIGHTON - 75A	BRIGHTON - 75A	BRIGHTON - 75A	BRIGHTON - 75A	BRIGHTON - 75A	BRIGHTON - 75A
42106	BRIGHTON - 75A	BRIGHTON - 75A	BRIGHTON - 75A	BRIGHTON - 75A	BRIGHTON - 75A	BRIGHTON - 75A	BRIGHTON - 75A
			Electric				
20001	SELHURST	SELHURST	SELHURST	SELHURST	SELHURST	SELHURST	SELHURST
20002	SELHURST	SELHURST	SELHURST	SELHURST	SELHURST	SELHURST	SELHURST
20003	SELHURST	SELHURST	SELHURST	SELHURST	SELHURST	SELHURST	SELHURST
			DIESEL				
10800	NORWOOD JCN - 75C	NORWOOD JCN - 75C	NORWOOD JCN - 75C	NORWOOD JCN - 75C	NORWOOD JCN - 75C	NORWOOD JCN - 75C	NORWOOD JCN - 75C
10000	NINE ELMS - 70A	NINE ELMS - 70A	NINE ELMS - 70A	NINE ELMS - 70A	NINE ELMS - 70A	NINE ELMS - 70A	NINE ELMS - 70A
10001	NINE ELMS - 70A	NINE ELMS - 70A	NINE ELMS - 70A	NINE ELMS - 70A	NINE ELMS - 70A	NINE ELMS - 70A	NINE ELMS - 70A
10201	NINE ELMS - 70A	NINE ELMS - 70A	NINE ELMS - 70A	NINE ELMS - 70A	NINE ELMS - 70A	NINE ELMS - 70A	NINE ELMS - 70A
10202	NINE ELMS - 70A	NINE ELMS - 70A	NINE ELMS - 70A	NINE ELMS - 70A	NINE ELMS - 70A	NINE ELMS - 70A	NINE ELMS - 70A
10203			NINE ELMS - 70A	NINE ELMS - 70A	NINE ELMS - 70A	NINE ELMS - 70A	NINE ELMS - 70A

loco	Feb-55	Apr-55	Jun-55	Aug-55	Sep-55	Nov-55	Dec-55
LMS 2MT 2-6-2T (1946)							
41241	BATH(S&D) - 71G	BATH(S&D) - 71G	BATH(S&D) - 71G	BATH(S&D) - 71G	BATH(S&D) - 71G	BATH(S&D) - 71G	BATH(S&D) - 71G
41242	BATH(S&D) - 71G	BATH(S&D) - 71G	BATH(S&D) - 71G	BATH(S&D) - 71G	BATH(S&D) - 71G	BATH(S&D) - 71G	BATH(S&D) - 71G
41243	BATH(S&D) - 71G	BATH(S&D) - 71G	BATH(S&D) - 71G	BATH(S&D) - 71G	BATH(S&D) - 71G	BATH(S&D) - 71G	BATH(S&D) - 71G
41248	TEMPLECOMBE - 71H	TEMPLECOMBE - 71H	TEMPLECOMBE - 71H	TEMPLECOMBE - 71H	TEMPLECOMBE - 71H	TEMPLECOMBE - 71H	TEMPLECOMBE - 71H
41249	TEMPLECOMBE - 71H	TEMPLECOMBE - 71H	TEMPLECOMBE - 71H	TEMPLECOMBE - 71H	TEMPLECOMBE - 71H	TEMPLECOMBE - 71H	TEMPLECOMBE - 71H
41290	STEWARTS LANE - 73A	STEWARTS LANE - 73A	STEWARTS LANE - 73A	STEWARTS LANE - 73A	STEWARTS LANE - 73A	STEWARTS LANE - 73A	STEWARTS LANE - 73A
41291	STEWARTS LANE - 73A	STEWARTS LANE - 73A	STEWARTS LANE - 73A	STEWARTS LANE - 73A	STEWARTS LANE - 73A	STEWARTS LANE - 73A	STEWARTS LANE - 73A
41292	STEWARTS LANE - 73A	STEWARTS LANE - 73A	STEWARTS LANE - 73A	STEWARTS LANE - 73A	STEWARTS LANE - 73A	STEWARTS LANE - 73A	STEWARTS LANE - 73A
41293	EASTLEIGH - 71A	EASTLEIGH - 71A	EASTLEIGH - 71A	EASTLEIGH - 71A	EASTLEIGH - 71A	EASTLEIGH - 71A	EASTLEIGH - 71A
41294	ASHFORD - 74A	ASHFORD - 74A	ASHFORD - 74A	ASHFORD - 74A	ASHFORD - 74A	ASHFORD - 74A	ASHFORD - 74A
41295	BARNSTAPLE - 72E	BARNSTAPLE - 72E	BARNSTAPLE - 72E	BARNSTAPLE - 72E	BARNSTAPLE - 72E	BARNSTAPLE - 72E	BARNSTAPLE - 72E
41296	STEWARTS LANE - 73A	STEWARTS LANE - 73A	STEWARTS LANE - 73A	STEWARTS LANE - 73A	STEWARTS LANE - 73A	STEWARTS LANE - 73A	STEWARTS LANE - 73A
41297	T.WELLS - 75F	T.WELLS - 75F	EXMOUTH JCN - 72A	EXMOUTH JCN - 72A	BARNSTAPLE - 72E	BARNSTAPLE - 72E	BARNSTAPLE - 72E
41298	BARNSTAPLE - 72E	BARNSTAPLE - 72E	BARNSTAPLE - 72E	BARNSTAPLE - 72E	BARNSTAPLE - 72E	BARNSTAPLE - 72E	BARNSTAPLE - 72E
41299	B.ARMS - 73B	B.ARMS - 73B	B.ARMS - 73B	B.ARMS - 73B	B.ARMS - 73B	B.ARMS - 73B	B.ARMS - 73B
41300	B.ARMS - 73B	B.ARMS - 73B	B.ARMS - 73B	B.ARMS - 73B	B.ARMS - 73B	B.ARMS - 73B	B.ARMS - 73B
41301	B.ARMS - 73B	B.ARMS - 73B	B.ARMS - 73B	B.ARMS - 73B	B.ARMS - 73B	B.ARMS - 73B	B.ARMS - 73B
41302	B.ARMS - 73B	B.ARMS - 73B	B.ARMS - 73B	B.ARMS - 73B	B.ARMS - 73B	B.ARMS - 73B	B.ARMS - 73B
41303	ASHFORD - 74A	ASHFORD - 74A	ASHFORD - 74A	ASHFORD - 74A	ASHFORD - 74A	ASHFORD - 74A	ASHFORD - 74A
41304	EASTLEIGH - 71A	EASTLEIGH - 71A	EASTLEIGH - 71A	EASTLEIGH - 71A	EASTLEIGH - 71A	EASTLEIGH - 71A	EASTLEIGH - 71A
41304	THREE BRIDGES - 75E	THREE BRIDGES - 75E	THREE BRIDGES - 75E	THREE BRIDGES - 75E	THREE BRIDGES - 75E	THREE BRIDGES - 75E	THREE BRIDGES - 75E
41305	EASTLEIGH - 71A	EASTLEIGH - 71A	EASTLEIGH - 71A	EASTLEIGH - 71A	EASTLEIGH - 71A	EASTLEIGH - 71A	EASTLEIGH - 71A
41306	THREE BRIDGES - 75E	THREE BRIDGES - 75E	EXMOUTH JCN - 72A	EXMOUTH JCN - 72A	EXMOUTH JCN - 72A	EXMOUTH JCN - 72A	EXMOUTH JCN - 72A
41307	THREE BRIDGES - 75E	THREE BRIDGES - 75E	EXMOUTH JCN - 72A	EXMOUTH JCN - 72A	EXMOUTH JCN - 72A	EXMOUTH JCN - 72A	EXMOUTH JCN - 72A
41308	FAVERSHAM - 73E	FAVERSHAM - 73E	FAVERSHAM - 73E	FAVERSHAM - 73E	FAVERSHAM - 73E	FAVERSHAM - 73E	FAVERSHAM - 73E
41309	FAVERSHAM - 73E	FAVERSHAM - 73E	FAVERSHAM - 73E	FAVERSHAM - 73E	FAVERSHAM - 73E	FAVERSHAM - 73E	FAVERSHAM - 73E
41310	FAVERSHAM - 73E	FAVERSHAM - 73E	FAVERSHAM - 73E	FAVERSHAM - 73E	FAVERSHAM - 73E	FAVERSHAM - 73E	FAVERSHAM - 73E
41311	FAVERSHAM - 73E	FAVERSHAM - 73E	FAVERSHAM - 73E	FAVERSHAM - 73E	FAVERSHAM - 73E	FAVERSHAM - 73E	FAVERSHAM - 73E
41312	FAVERSHAM - 73E	FAVERSHAM - 73E	FAVERSHAM - 73E	FAVERSHAM - 73E	FAVERSHAM - 73E	FAVERSHAM - 73E	FAVERSHAM - 73E
41313	THREE BRIDGES - 75E	THREE BRIDGES - 75E	FAVERSHAM - 73E	FAVERSHAM - 73E	FAVERSHAM - 73E	FAVERSHAM - 73E	FAVERSHAM - 73E
41314	B.ARMS - 73B	B.ARMS - 73B	B.ARMS - 73B	B.ARMS - 73B	B.ARMS - 73B	B.ARMS - 73B	B.ARMS - 73B
41315	PLYMOUTH - 72D	PLYMOUTH - 72D	PLYMOUTH - 72D	PLYMOUTH - 72D	PLYMOUTH - 72D	PLYMOUTH - 72D	PLYMOUTH - 72D
41316	T.WELLS - 75F	T.WELLS - 75F	ASHFORD - 74A	ASHFORD - 74A	ASHFORD - 74A	ASHFORD - 74A	ASHFORD - 74A
41317	T.WELLS - 75F	T.WELLS - 75F	ASHFORD - 74A	ASHFORD - 74A	ASHFORD - 74A	ASHFORD - 74A	ASHFORD - 74A
41318	T.WELLS - 75F	T.WELLS - 75F	T.WELLS - 75F	T.WELLS - 75F	T.WELLS - 75F	T.WELLS - 75F	T.WELLS - 75F
41319	T.WELLS - 75F	T.WELLS - 75F	T.WELLS - 75F	T.WELLS - 75F	T.WELLS - 75F	T.WELLS - 75F	T.WELLS - 75F
LMS 4MT 2-6-4T (1948)							
42066	THREE BRIDGES - 75E	THREE BRIDGES - 75E	THREE BRIDGES - 75E	THREE BRIDGES - 75E	THREE BRIDGES - 75E	THREE BRIDGES - 75E	THREE BRIDGES - 75E
42067	RAMSGATE - 74B	RAMSGATE - 74B	BRIGHTON - 75A	BRIGHTON - 75A	BRIGHTON - 75A	BRIGHTON - 75A	BRIGHTON - 75A
42068	RAMSGATE - 74B	RAMSGATE - 74B	RAMSGATE - 74B	RAMSGATE - 74B	RAMSGATE - 74B	RAMSGATE - 74B	RAMSGATE - 74B
42069	ASHFORD - 74A	ASHFORD - 74A	THREE BRIDGES - 75E	THREE BRIDGES - 75E	THREE BRIDGES - 75E	THREE BRIDGES - 75E	THREE BRIDGES - 75E
42070	RAMSGATE - 74B	RAMSGATE - 74B	RAMSGATE - 74B	RAMSGATE - 74B	RAMSGATE - 74B	RAMSGATE - 74B	RAMSGATE - 74B
42071	RAMSGATE - 74B	RAMSGATE - 74B	RAMSGATE - 74B	RAMSGATE - 74B	RAMSGATE - 74B	RAMSGATE - 74B	RAMSGATE - 74B
42074	DOVER - 74C	DOVER - 74C	T.WELLS - 75F	T.WELLS - 75F	T.WELLS - 75F	T.WELLS - 75F	T.WELLS - 75F
42075	BRIGHTON - 75A	BRIGHTON - 75A	BRIGHTON - 75A	BRIGHTON - 75A	BRIGHTON - 75A	BRIGHTON - 75A	BRIGHTON - 75A
42076	DOVER - 74C	DOVER - 74C	DOVER - 74C	DOVER - 74C	DOVER - 74C	DOVER - 74C	DOVER - 74C
42077	DOVER - 74C	DOVER - 74C	DOVER - 74C	DOVER - 74C	DOVER - 74C	DOVER - 74C	DOVER - 74C
42078	DOVER - 74C	DOVER - 74C	DOVER - 74C	DOVER - 74C	DOVER - 74C	DOVER - 74C	DOVER - 74C
42079	DOVER - 74C	DOVER - 74C	DOVER - 74C	DOVER - 74C	DOVER - 74C	DOVER - 74C	DOVER - 74C
42080	STEWARTS LANE - 73A	STEWARTS LANE - 73A	STEWARTS LANE - 73A	STEWARTS LANE - 73A	STEWARTS LANE - 73A	STEWARTS LANE - 73A	STEWARTS LANE - 73A
42081	STEWARTS LANE - 73A	STEWARTS LANE - 73A	STEWARTS LANE - 73A	STEWARTS LANE - 73A	STEWARTS LANE - 73A	STEWARTS LANE - 73A	STEWARTS LANE - 73A
42082	BRIGHTON - 75A	BRIGHTON - 75A	BRIGHTON - 75A	BRIGHTON - 75A	BRIGHTON - 75A	BRIGHTON - 75A	BRIGHTON - 75A
42086	THREE BRIDGES - 75E	THREE BRIDGES - 75E	THREE BRIDGES - 75E	THREE BRIDGES - 75E	THREE BRIDGES - 75E	THREE BRIDGES - 75E	THREE BRIDGES - 75E
42087	BRIGHTON - 75A	BRIGHTON - 75A	BRIGHTON - 75A	BRIGHTON - 75A	BRIGHTON - 75A	BRIGHTON - 75A	BRIGHTON - 75A
42088	STEWARTS LANE - 73A	STEWARTS LANE - 73A	STEWARTS LANE - 73A	STEWARTS LANE - 73A	STEWARTS LANE - 73A	STEWARTS LANE - 73A	STEWARTS LANE - 73A
42089	STEWARTS LANE - 73A	STEWARTS LANE - 73A	STEWARTS LANE - 73A	STEWARTS LANE - 73A	STEWARTS LANE - 73A	STEWARTS LANE - 73A	STEWARTS LANE - 73A
42090	STEWARTS LANE - 73A	STEWARTS LANE - 73A	STEWARTS LANE - 73A	STEWARTS LANE - 73A	STEWARTS LANE - 73A	STEWARTS LANE - 73A	STEWARTS LANE - 73A
42091	STEWARTS LANE - 73A	STEWARTS LANE - 73A	STEWARTS LANE - 73A	STEWARTS LANE - 73A	STEWARTS LANE - 73A	STEWARTS LANE - 73A	STEWARTS LANE - 73A
42092	THREE BRIDGES - 75E	THREE BRIDGES - 75E	THREE BRIDGES - 75E	THREE BRIDGES - 75E	THREE BRIDGES - 75E	THREE BRIDGES - 75E	THREE BRIDGES - 75E
42095	ASHFORD - 74A	ASHFORD - 74A	ASHFORD - 74A	ASHFORD - 74A	ASHFORD - 74A	ASHFORD - 74A	ASHFORD - 74A
42096	ASHFORD - 74A	ASHFORD - 74A	ASHFORD - 74A	ASHFORD - 74A	ASHFORD - 74A	ASHFORD - 74A	ASHFORD - 74A
42097	ASHFORD - 74A	ASHFORD - 74A	ASHFORD - 74A	ASHFORD - 74A	ASHFORD - 74A	ASHFORD - 74A	ASHFORD - 74A
42098	ASHFORD - 74A	ASHFORD - 74A	ASHFORD - 74A	ASHFORD - 74A	ASHFORD - 74A	ASHFORD - 74A	ASHFORD - 74A
42099	T.WELLS - 75F	T.WELLS - 75F	T.WELLS - 75F	T.WELLS - 75F	T.WELLS - 75F	T.WELLS - 75F	T.WELLS - 75F
42100	T.WELLS - 75F	T.WELLS - 75F	T.WELLS - 75F	T.WELLS - 75F	T.WELLS - 75F	T.WELLS - 75F	T.WELLS - 75F
42101	T.WELLS - 75F	T.WELLS - 75F	T.WELLS - 75F	T.WELLS - 75F	T.WELLS - 75F	T.WELLS - 75F	T.WELLS - 75F
42102	T.WELLS - 75F	T.WELLS - 75F	T.WELLS - 75F	T.WELLS - 75F	T.WELLS - 75F	T.WELLS - 75F	T.WELLS - 75F
42103	BRIGHTON - 75A	BRIGHTON - 75A	BRIGHTON - 75A	BRIGHTON - 75A	BRIGHTON - 75A	BRIGHTON - 75A	BRIGHTON - 75A
42104	BRIGHTON - 75A	BRIGHTON - 75A	BRIGHTON - 75A	BRIGHTON - 75A	BRIGHTON - 75A	BRIGHTON - 75A	BRIGHTON - 75A
42105	BRIGHTON - 75A	BRIGHTON - 75A	BRIGHTON - 75A	BRIGHTON - 75A	BRIGHTON - 75A	BRIGHTON - 75A	BRIGHTON - 75A
42106	BRIGHTON - 75A	BRIGHTON - 75A	BRIGHTON - 75A	BRIGHTON - 75A	BRIGHTON - 75A	BRIGHTON - 75A	BRIGHTON - 75A
Electric							
20001	SELHURST	SELHURST	SELHURST	SELHURST	SELHURST	SELHURST	SELHURST
20002	SELHURST	SELHURST	SELHURST	SELHURST	SELHURST	SELHURST	SELHURST
20003	SELHURST	SELHURST	SELHURST	SELHURST	SELHURST	SELHURST	SELHURST
DIESEL							
10800	NORWOOD JCN - 75C	TO LMR					
10000	NINE ELMS - 70A	TO LMR					
10001	TO LMR						
10201	NINE ELMS - 70A	TO LMR					
10202	NINE ELMS - 70A	TO LMR					
10203	NINE ELMS - 70A	NINE ELMS - 70A	NINE ELMS - 70A	TO LMR			

LMS 2MT 2-6-2T (1946)

loco	Jan-56	Apr-56	May-56	Aug-56	Oct-56	Nov-56	Jan-57
41241	BATH (S&D) - 71G	BATH (S&D) - 71G	BATH (S&D) - 71G	BATH (S&D) - 71G	BATH (S&D) - 71G	BATH (S&D) - 71G	BATH (S&D) - 71G
41242	BATH (S&D) - 71G	BATH (S&D) - 71G	BATH (S&D) - 71G	BATH (S&D) - 71G	BATH (S&D) - 71G	BATH (S&D) - 71G	BATH (S&D) - 71G
41243	BATH (S&D) - 71G	BATH (S&D) - 71G	BATH (S&D) - 71G	BATH (S&D) - 71G	BATH (S&D) - 71G	BATH (S&D) - 71G	BATH (S&D) - 71G
41248	TEMPLECOMBE - 71H	TEMPLECOMBE - 71H	TEMPLECOMBE - 71H	TEMPLECOMBE - 71H	TEMPLECOMBE - 71H	TEMPLECOMBE - 71H	TEMPLECOMBE - 71H
41249	TEMPLECOMBE - 71H	TEMPLECOMBE - 71H	TEMPLECOMBE - 71H	TEMPLECOMBE - 71H	TEMPLECOMBE - 71H	TEMPLECOMBE - 71H	TEMPLECOMBE - 71H
41290	STEWARTS LANE - 73A	STEWARTS LANE - 73A	STEWARTS LANE - 73A	STEWARTS LANE - 73A	STEWARTS LANE - 73A	STEWARTS LANE - 73A	STEWARTS LANE - 73A
41291	STEWARTS LANE - 73A	STEWARTS LANE - 73A	STEWARTS LANE - 73A	STEWARTS LANE - 73A	STEWARTS LANE - 73A	STEWARTS LANE - 73A	STEWARTS LANE - 73A
41292	STEWARTS LANE - 73A	STEWARTS LANE - 73A	STEWARTS LANE - 73A	STEWARTS LANE - 73A	STEWARTS LANE - 73A	STEWARTS LANE - 73A	STEWARTS LANE - 73A
41293	EASTLEIGH - 71A	EASTLEIGH - 71A	EASTLEIGH - 71A	EASTLEIGH - 71A	EASTLEIGH - 71A	EASTLEIGH - 71A	EASTLEIGH - 71A
41294	ASHFORD - 74A	ASHFORD - 74A	ASHFORD - 74A	ASHFORD - 74A	ASHFORD - 74A	ASHFORD - 74A	ASHFORD - 74A
41295	BARNSTAPLE - 72E	BARNSTAPLE - 72E	BARNSTAPLE - 72E	BARNSTAPLE - 72E	BARNSTAPLE - 72E	BARNSTAPLE - 72E	BARNSTAPLE - 72E
41296	STEWARTS LANE - 73A	STEWARTS LANE - 73A	STEWARTS LANE - 73A	STEWARTS LANE - 73A	STEWARTS LANE - 73A	BARNSTAPLE - 72E	BARNSTAPLE - 72E
41297	BARNSTAPLE - 72E	BARNSTAPLE - 72E	BARNSTAPLE - 72E	BARNSTAPLE - 72E	BARNSTAPLE - 72E	BARNSTAPLE - 72E	BARNSTAPLE - 72E
41298	BARNSTAPLE - 72E	BARNSTAPLE - 72E	BARNSTAPLE - 72E	BARNSTAPLE - 72E	BARNSTAPLE - 72E	BARNSTAPLE - 72E	BARNSTAPLE - 72E
41299	B.ARMS - 73B	B.ARMS - 73B	B.ARMS - 73B	B.ARMS - 73B	B.ARMS - 73B	B.ARMS - 73B	B.ARMS - 73B
41300	B.ARMS - 73B	B.ARMS - 73B	B.ARMS - 73B	B.ARMS - 73B	B.ARMS - 73B	B.ARMS - 73B	B.ARMS - 73B
41301	B.ARMS - 73B	B.ARMS - 73B	RAMSGATE - 74B	RAMSGATE - 74B	RAMSGATE - 74B	RAMSGATE - 74B	RAMSGATE - 74B
41302	B.ARMS - 73B	B.ARMS - 73B	B.ARMS - 73B	B.ARMS - 73B	B.ARMS - 73B	B.ARMS - 73B	PLYMOUTH - 72D
41303	ASHFORD - 74A	ASHFORD - 74A	ASHFORD - 74A	ASHFORD - 74A	ASHFORD - 74A	ASHFORD - 74A	ASHFORD - 74A
41304	EASTLEIGH - 71A	EASTLEIGH - 71A	EASTLEIGH - 71A	EASTLEIGH - 71A	EASTLEIGH - 71A	EASTLEIGH - 71A	EASTLEIGH - 71A
41304	THREE BRIDGES - 75E	THREE BRIDGES - 75E	RAMSGATE - 74B	RAMSGATE - 74B	RAMSGATE - 74B	RAMSGATE - 74B	RAMSGATE - 74B
41305	EASTLEIGH - 71A	EASTLEIGH - 71A	EASTLEIGH - 71A	EASTLEIGH - 71A	EASTLEIGH - 71A	EASTLEIGH - 71A	EASTLEIGH - 71A
41306	EXMOUTH JCN - 72A	EXMOUTH JCN - 72A	EXMOUTH JCN - 72A	EXMOUTH JCN - 72A	EXMOUTH JCN - 72A	EXMOUTH JCN - 72A	EXMOUTH JCN - 72A
41307	EXMOUTH JCN - 72A	EXMOUTH JCN - 72A	EXMOUTH JCN - 72A	EXMOUTH JCN - 72A	EXMOUTH JCN - 72A	EXMOUTH JCN - 72A	EXMOUTH JCN - 72A
41308	FAVERSHAM - 73E	FAVERSHAM - 73E	FAVERSHAM - 73E	FAVERSHAM - 73E	FAVERSHAM - 73E	FAVERSHAM - 73E	FAVERSHAM - 73E
41309	FAVERSHAM - 73E	FAVERSHAM - 73E	FAVERSHAM - 73E	FAVERSHAM - 73E	FAVERSHAM - 73E	FAVERSHAM - 73E	FAVERSHAM - 73E
41310	FAVERSHAM - 73E	FAVERSHAM - 73E	FAVERSHAM - 73E	FAVERSHAM - 73E	FAVERSHAM - 73E	FAVERSHAM - 73E	FAVERSHAM - 73E
41311	FAVERSHAM - 73E	FAVERSHAM - 73E	FAVERSHAM - 73E	FAVERSHAM - 73E	FAVERSHAM - 73E	FAVERSHAM - 73E	FAVERSHAM - 73E
41312	FAVERSHAM - 73E	FAVERSHAM - 73E	FAVERSHAM - 73E	FAVERSHAM - 73E	FAVERSHAM - 73E	FAVERSHAM - 73E	FAVERSHAM - 73E
41313	FAVERSHAM - 73E	FAVERSHAM - 73E	FAVERSHAM - 73E	FAVERSHAM - 73E	FAVERSHAM - 73E	FAVERSHAM - 73E	FAVERSHAM - 73E
41314	B.ARMS - 73B	B.ARMS - 73B	B.ARMS - 73B	B.ARMS - 73B	B.ARMS - 73B	PLYMOUTH - 72D	B.ARMS - 73B
41315	PLYMOUTH - 72D	PLYMOUTH - 72D	PLYMOUTH - 72D	PLYMOUTH - 72D	PLYMOUTH - 72D	PLYMOUTH - 72D	PLYMOUTH - 72D
41316	ASHFORD - 74A	ASHFORD - 74A	ASHFORD - 74A	ASHFORD - 74A	ASHFORD - 74A	PLYMOUTH - 72D	PLYMOUTH - 72D
41317	ASHFORD - 74A	ASHFORD - 74A	ASHFORD - 74A	ASHFORD - 74A	ASHFORD - 74A	ASHFORD - 74A	ASHFORD - 74A
41318	T.WELLS - 75F	T.WELLS - 75F	RAMSGATE - 74B	RAMSGATE - 74B	RAMSGATE - 74B	RAMSGATE - 74B	RAMSGATE - 74B
41319	T.WELLS - 75F	T.WELLS - 75F	RAMSGATE - 74B	RAMSGATE - 74B	RAMSGATE - 74B	RAMSGATE - 74B	RAMSGATE - 74B

LMS 4MT 2-6-4T (1948)

loco	Jan-56	Apr-56	May-56	Aug-56	Oct-56	Nov-56	Jan-57
42066	THREE BRIDGES - 75E	THREE BRIDGES - 75E	THREE BRIDGES - 75E	THREE BRIDGES - 75E	THREE BRIDGES - 75E	THREE BRIDGES - 75E	THREE BRIDGES - 75E
42067	BRIGHTON - 75A	BRIGHTON - 75A	BRIGHTON - 75A	BRIGHTON - 75A	BRIGHTON - 75A	THREE BRIDGES - 75E	THREE BRIDGES - 75E
42068	RAMSGATE - 74B	RAMSGATE - 74B	BRIGHTON - 75A	BRIGHTON - 75A	BRIGHTON - 75A	THREE BRIDGES - 75E	THREE BRIDGES - 75E
42069	THREE BRIDGES - 75E	THREE BRIDGES - 75E	THREE BRIDGES - 75E	THREE BRIDGES - 75E	THREE BRIDGES - 75E	THREE BRIDGES - 75E	THREE BRIDGES - 75E
42070	RAMSGATE - 74B	RAMSGATE - 74B	BRIGHTON - 75A	BRIGHTON - 75A	BRIGHTON - 75A	THREE BRIDGES - 75E	THREE BRIDGES - 75E
42071	RAMSGATE - 74B	RAMSGATE - 74B	BRIGHTON - 75A	BRIGHTON - 75A	BRIGHTON - 75A	THREE BRIDGES - 75E	THREE BRIDGES - 75E
42074	T.WELLS - 75F	T.WELLS - 75F	T.WELLS - 75F	T.WELLS - 75F	T.WELLS - 75F	RAMSGATE - 74B	RAMSGATE - 74B
42075	BRIGHTON - 75A	BRIGHTON - 75A	BRIGHTON - 75A	BRIGHTON - 75A	BRIGHTON - 75A	DOVER - 74C	DOVER - 74C
42076	DOVER - 74C	DOVER - 74C	DOVER - 74C	DOVER - 74C	DOVER - 74C	DOVER - 74C	DOVER - 74C
42077	DOVER - 74C	DOVER - 74C	DOVER - 74C	DOVER - 74C	DOVER - 74C	DOVER - 74C	DOVER - 74C
42078	DOVER - 74C	DOVER - 74C	DOVER - 74C	DOVER - 74C	DOVER - 74C	DOVER - 74C	DOVER - 74C
42079	DOVER - 74C	DOVER - 74C	DOVER - 74C	DOVER - 74C	DOVER - 74C	DOVER - 74C	DOVER - 74C
42080	STEWARTS LANE - 73A	STEWARTS LANE - 73A	STEWARTS LANE - 73A	STEWARTS LANE - 73A	STEWARTS LANE - 73A	STEWARTS LANE - 73A	STEWARTS LANE - 73A
42081	STEWARTS LANE - 73A	STEWARTS LANE - 73A	STEWARTS LANE - 73A	STEWARTS LANE - 73A	STEWARTS LANE - 73A	STEWARTS LANE - 73A	STEWARTS LANE - 73A
42082	BRIGHTON - 75A	BRIGHTON - 75A	BRIGHTON - 75A	BRIGHTON - 75A	BRIGHTON - 75A	BRIGHTON - 75A	BRIGHTON - 75A
42086	THREE BRIDGES - 75E	THREE BRIDGES - 75E	THREE BRIDGES - 75E	THREE BRIDGES - 75E	THREE BRIDGES - 75E	STEWARTS LANE - 73A	STEWARTS LANE - 73A
42087	BRIGHTON - 75A	BRIGHTON - 75A	T.WELLS - 75F	T.WELLS - 75F	T.WELLS - 75F	STEWARTS LANE - 73A	STEWARTS LANE - 73A
42088	STEWARTS LANE - 73A	STEWARTS LANE - 73A	STEWARTS LANE - 73A	STEWARTS LANE - 73A	STEWARTS LANE - 73A	STEWARTS LANE - 73A	STEWARTS LANE - 73A
42089	STEWARTS LANE - 73A	STEWARTS LANE - 73A	STEWARTS LANE - 73A	STEWARTS LANE - 73A	STEWARTS LANE - 73A	STEWARTS LANE - 73A	STEWARTS LANE - 73A
42090	STEWARTS LANE - 73A	STEWARTS LANE - 73A	STEWARTS LANE - 73A	STEWARTS LANE - 73A	STEWARTS LANE - 73A	STEWARTS LANE - 73A	STEWARTS LANE - 73A
42091	STEWARTS LANE - 73A	STEWARTS LANE - 73A	STEWARTS LANE - 73A	STEWARTS LANE - 73A	STEWARTS LANE - 73A	STEWARTS LANE - 73A	STEWARTS LANE - 73A
42092	THREE BRIDGES - 75E	THREE BRIDGES - 75E	THREE BRIDGES - 75E	THREE BRIDGES - 75E	THREE BRIDGES - 75E	ASHFORD - 74A	ASHFORD - 74A
42095	ASHFORD - 74A	ASHFORD - 74A	ASHFORD - 74A	ASHFORD - 74A	ASHFORD - 74A	ASHFORD - 74A	ASHFORD - 74A
42096	ASHFORD - 74A	ASHFORD - 74A	ASHFORD - 74A	ASHFORD - 74A	ASHFORD - 74A	ASHFORD - 74A	ASHFORD - 74A
42097	ASHFORD - 74A	ASHFORD - 74A	ASHFORD - 74A	ASHFORD - 74A	ASHFORD - 74A	ASHFORD - 74A	ASHFORD - 74A
42098	ASHFORD - 74A	ASHFORD - 74A	ASHFORD - 74A	ASHFORD - 74A	ASHFORD - 74A	ASHFORD - 74A	ASHFORD - 74A
42099	T.WELLS - 75F	T.WELLS - 75F	T.WELLS - 75F	T.WELLS - 75F	T.WELLS - 75F	ASHFORD - 74A	ASHFORD - 74A
42100	T.WELLS - 75F	T.WELLS - 75F	T.WELLS - 75F	T.WELLS - 75F	T.WELLS - 75F	ASHFORD - 74A	ASHFORD - 74A
42101	T.WELLS - 75F	T.WELLS - 75F	T.WELLS - 75F	T.WELLS - 75F	T.WELLS - 75F	T.WELLS - 75F	T.WELLS - 75F
42102	T.WELLS - 75F	T.WELLS - 75F	T.WELLS - 75F	T.WELLS - 75F	T.WELLS - 75F	T.WELLS - 75F	T.WELLS - 75F
42103	BRIGHTON - 75A	BRIGHTON - 75A	BRIGHTON - 75A	BRIGHTON - 75A	BRIGHTON - 75A	BRIGHTON - 75A	BRIGHTON - 75A
42104	BRIGHTON - 75A	BRIGHTON - 75A	BRIGHTON - 75A	T.WELLS - 75F	T.WELLS - 75F	T.WELLS - 75F	T.WELLS - 75F
42105	BRIGHTON - 75A	BRIGHTON - 75A	T.WELLS - 75F	T.WELLS - 75F	T.WELLS - 75F	T.WELLS - 75F	T.WELLS - 75F
42106	BRIGHTON - 75A	BRIGHTON - 75A	BRIGHTON - 75A	BRIGHTON - 75A	BRIGHTON - 75A	T.WELLS - 75F	T.WELLS - 75F

Electric

loco	Jan-56	Apr-56	May-56	Aug-56	Oct-56	Nov-56	Jan-57
20001	SELHURST	SELHURST	SELHURST	SELHURST	SELHURST	SELHURST	SELHURST
20002	SELHURST	SELHURST	SELHURST	SELHURST	SELHURST	SELHURST	SELHURST
20003	SELHURST	SELHURST	SELHURST	SELHURST	SELHURST	SELHURST	SELHURST

Although the three SR electric locomotives are popularly associated with the Victoria - Newhaven boat trains, in fact only one of the trio was ever involved in passenger work whilst all three were heavily involved in goods traffic. One engine would be occupied with the boat trains and, between workings, head an express goods from New Cross Gate to Lewes and back whilst the second would be occupied with general goods services between Chichester and Horsham. The third engine worked a night goods from Horsham to Fratton and then joined the second engine by working in the Horsham and Chichester areas.

For maintenance purposes the engines were allocated to Selhurst although in practice they remained in traffic continuously, returning only to Selhurst when mechanical attention was due. The use of three engines for diagrams - 100% availability - was probably unique on British Railways. Their workings changed very little over the years and even after the electrification of Kent in 1959 they remained wedded to the LBSCR system.

loco	Mar-57	Jun-57	Jul-57	Oct-57	Jan-58	Feb-58	Mar-58
				LMS 2MT 2-6-2T (1946)			
41241	BATH (S&D) - 71G	BATH (S&D) - 71G	BATH (S&D) - 71G	BATH (S&D) - 71G	BATH (S&D) - 71G	BATH (S&D) - 82F	BATH (S&D) - 82F
41242	BATH (S&D) - 71G	BATH (S&D) - 71G	BATH (S&D) - 71G	BATH (S&D) - 71G	BATH (S&D) - 71G	BATH (S&D) - 82F	BATH (S&D) - 82F
41243	BATH (S&D) - 71G	BATH (S&D) - 71G	BATH (S&D) - 71G	BATH (S&D) - 71G	BATH (S&D) - 71G	BATH (S&D) - 82F	BATH (S&D) - 82F
41248	TEMPLECOMBE - 71H	TEMPLECOMBE - 71H	TEMPLECOMBE - 71H	TEMPLECOMBE - 71H	TEMPLECOMBE - 71H	TEMPLECOMBE - 82G	TEMPLECOMBE - 82G
41249	TEMPLECOMBE - 71H	TEMPLECOMBE - 71H	TEMPLECOMBE - 71H	TEMPLECOMBE - 71H	TEMPLECOMBE - 71H	TEMPLECOMBE - 82G	TEMPLECOMBE - 82G
41290	STEWARTS LANE - 73A	STEWARTS LANE - 73A	STEWARTS LANE - 73A	STEWARTS LANE - 73A	STEWARTS LANE - 73A	STEWARTS LANE - 73A	STEWARTS LANE - 73A
41291	STEWARTS LANE - 73A	STEWARTS LANE - 73A	STEWARTS LANE - 73A	STEWARTS LANE - 73A	STEWARTS LANE - 73A	STEWARTS LANE - 73A	STEWARTS LANE - 73A
41292	STEWARTS LANE - 73A	STEWARTS LANE - 73A	STEWARTS LANE - 73A	STEWARTS LANE - 73A	STEWARTS LANE - 73A	STEWARTS LANE - 73A	STEWARTS LANE - 73A
41293	EASTLEIGH - 71A	EASTLEIGH - 71A	EASTLEIGH - 71A	EASTLEIGH - 71A	EASTLEIGH - 71A	EASTLEIGH - 71A	EASTLEIGH - 71A
41294	ASHFORD - 74A	BARNSTAPLE - 72E	BARNSTAPLE - 72E	BARNSTAPLE - 72E	BARNSTAPLE - 72E	BARNSTAPLE - 72E	BARNSTAPLE - 72E
41295	BARNSTAPLE - 72E	BARNSTAPLE - 72E	BARNSTAPLE - 72E	BARNSTAPLE - 72E	BARNSTAPLE - 72E	BARNSTAPLE - 72E	BARNSTAPLE - 72E
41296	HIGHBRIDGE - 71J	HIGHBRIDGE - 71J	HIGHBRIDGE - 71J	HIGHBRIDGE - 71J	HIGHBRIDGE - 71J	HIGHBRIDGE - 71J	HIGHBRIDGE - 71J
41297	BARNSTAPLE - 72E	BARNSTAPLE - 72E	BARNSTAPLE - 72E	BARNSTAPLE - 72E	BARNSTAPLE - 72E	BARNSTAPLE - 72E	BARNSTAPLE - 72E
41298	BARNSTAPLE - 72E	BARNSTAPLE - 72E	BARNSTAPLE - 72E	BARNSTAPLE - 72E	BARNSTAPLE - 72E	BARNSTAPLE - 72E	BARNSTAPLE - 72E
41299	B.ARMS - 73B	B.ARMS - 73B	B.ARMS - 73B	B.ARMS - 73B	B.ARMS - 73B	B.ARMS - 73B	B.ARMS - 73B
41300	B.ARMS - 73B	B.ARMS - 73B	B.ARMS - 73B	B.ARMS - 73B	B.ARMS - 73B	B.ARMS - 73B	B.ARMS - 73B
41301	RAMSGATE - 74B	B.ARMS - 73B	B.ARMS - 73B	B.ARMS - 73B	B.ARMS - 73B	B.ARMS - 73B	B.ARMS - 73B
41302	PLYMOUTH - 72D	PLYMOUTH - 72D	PLYMOUTH - 72D	PLYMOUTH - 72D	PLYMOUTH - 72D	PLYMOUTH - 83H	PLYMOUTH - 83H
41303	ASHFORD - 74A	B.ARMS - 73B	B.ARMS - 73B	B.ARMS - 73B	B.ARMS - 73B	B.ARMS - 73B	B.ARMS - 73B
41304	HIGHBRIDGE - 71J	HIGHBRIDGE - 71J	HIGHBRIDGE - 71J	HIGHBRIDGE - 71J	HIGHBRIDGE - 71J	HIGHBRIDGE - 71J	HIGHBRIDGE - 71J
41304	RAMSGATE - 74B	RAMSGATE - 74B	RAMSGATE - 74B	RAMSGATE - 74B	RAMSGATE - 74B	RAMSGATE - 74B	RAMSGATE - 74B
41305	EASTLEIGH - 71A	EASTLEIGH - 71A	EASTLEIGH - 71A	EASTLEIGH - 71A	EASTLEIGH - 71A	EASTLEIGH - 71A	EASTLEIGH - 71A
41306	EXMOUTH JCN - 72A	EXMOUTH JCN - 72A	EXMOUTH JCN - 72A	EXMOUTH JCN - 72A	EXMOUTH JCN - 72A	EXMOUTH JCN - 72A	EXMOUTH JCN - 72A
41307	EXMOUTH JCN - 72A	EXMOUTH JCN - 72A	EXMOUTH JCN - 72A	EXMOUTH JCN - 72A	EXMOUTH JCN - 72A	EXMOUTH JCN - 72A	EXMOUTH JCN - 72A
41308	FAVERSHAM - 73E	FAVERSHAM - 73E	FAVERSHAM - 73E	FAVERSHAM - 73E	FAVERSHAM - 73E	FAVERSHAM - 73E	FAVERSHAM - 73E
41309	FAVERSHAM - 73E	FAVERSHAM - 73E	FAVERSHAM - 73E	FAVERSHAM - 73E	FAVERSHAM - 73E	FAVERSHAM - 73E	FAVERSHAM - 73E
41310	FAVERSHAM - 73E	FAVERSHAM - 73E	FAVERSHAM - 73E	FAVERSHAM - 73E	FAVERSHAM - 73E	FAVERSHAM - 73E	FAVERSHAM - 73E
41311	FAVERSHAM - 73E	FAVERSHAM - 73E	FAVERSHAM - 73E	FAVERSHAM - 73E	FAVERSHAM - 73E	FAVERSHAM - 73E	FAVERSHAM - 73E
41312	FAVERSHAM - 73E	FAVERSHAM - 73E	FAVERSHAM - 73E	FAVERSHAM - 73E	FAVERSHAM - 73E	FAVERSHAM - 73E	FAVERSHAM - 73E
41313	FAVERSHAM - 73E	FAVERSHAM - 73E	FAVERSHAM - 73E	FAVERSHAM - 73E	FAVERSHAM - 73E	FAVERSHAM - 73E	FAVERSHAM - 73E
41314	B.ARMS - 73B	BARNSTAPLE - 72E	BARNSTAPLE - 72E	BARNSTAPLE - 72E	BARNSTAPLE - 72E	BARNSTAPLE - 72E	BARNSTAPLE - 72E
41315	PLYMOUTH - 72D	PLYMOUTH - 72D	PLYMOUTH - 72D	PLYMOUTH - 72D	PLYMOUTH - 72D	PLYMOUTH - 83H	PLYMOUTH - 83H
41316	PLYMOUTH - 72D	PLYMOUTH - 72D	PLYMOUTH - 72D	PLYMOUTH - 72D	PLYMOUTH - 72D	PLYMOUTH - 83H	PLYMOUTH - 83H
41317	ASHFORD - 74A	PLYMOUTH - 72D	PLYMOUTH - 72D	PLYMOUTH - 72D	PLYMOUTH - 72D	PLYMOUTH - 83H	PLYMOUTH - 83H
41318	RAMSGATE - 74B	EXMOUTH JCN - 72A	EXMOUTH JCN - 72A	EXMOUTH JCN - 72A	EXMOUTH JCN - 72A	EXMOUTH JCN - 72A	EXMOUTH JCN - 72A
41319	RAMSGATE - 74B	THREE BRIDGES - 75E	THREE BRIDGES - 75E	THREE BRIDGES - 75E	THREE BRIDGES - 75E	THREE BRIDGES - 75E	THREE BRIDGES - 75E
				LMS 4MT 2-6-4T (1948)			
42066	THREE BRIDGES - 75E	THREE BRIDGES - 75E	THREE BRIDGES - 75E	THREE BRIDGES - 75E	THREE BRIDGES - 75E	THREE BRIDGES - 75E	THREE BRIDGES - 75E
42067	THREE BRIDGES - 75E	THREE BRIDGES - 75E	THREE BRIDGES - 75E	THREE BRIDGES - 75E	THREE BRIDGES - 75E	THREE BRIDGES - 75E	THREE BRIDGES - 75E
42068	THREE BRIDGES - 75E	THREE BRIDGES - 75E	THREE BRIDGES - 75E	THREE BRIDGES - 75E	THREE BRIDGES - 75E	THREE BRIDGES - 75E	THREE BRIDGES - 75E
42069	THREE BRIDGES - 75E	THREE BRIDGES - 75E	THREE BRIDGES - 75E	THREE BRIDGES - 75E	THREE BRIDGES - 75E	THREE BRIDGES - 75E	THREE BRIDGES - 75E
42070	THREE BRIDGES - 75E	THREE BRIDGES - 75E	THREE BRIDGES - 75E	THREE BRIDGES - 75E	THREE BRIDGES - 75E	THREE BRIDGES - 75E	THREE BRIDGES - 75E
42071	THREE BRIDGES - 75E	THREE BRIDGES - 75E	THREE BRIDGES - 75E	THREE BRIDGES - 75E	THREE BRIDGES - 75E	THREE BRIDGES - 75E	THREE BRIDGES - 75E
42074	RAMSGATE - 74B	STEWARTS LANE - 73A	STEWARTS LANE - 73A	STEWARTS LANE - 73A	STEWARTS LANE - 73A	STEWARTS LANE - 73A	THREE BRIDGES - 75E
42075	DOVER - 74C	DOVER - 74C	DOVER - 74C	DOVER - 74C	DOVER - 74C	DOVER - 74C	DOVER - 74C
42076	DOVER - 74C	DOVER - 74C	DOVER - 74C	DOVER - 74C	DOVER - 74C	DOVER - 74C	DOVER - 74C
42077	DOVER - 74C	DOVER - 74C	DOVER - 74C	DOVER - 74C	DOVER - 74C	DOVER - 74C	DOVER - 74C
42078	DOVER - 74C	DOVER - 74C	DOVER - 74C	DOVER - 74C	DOVER - 74C	DOVER - 74C	DOVER - 74C
42079	DOVER - 74C	DOVER - 74C	DOVER - 74C	DOVER - 74C	DOVER - 74C	DOVER - 74C	DOVER - 74C
42080	STEWARTS LANE - 73A	STEWARTS LANE - 73A	STEWARTS LANE - 73A	STEWARTS LANE - 73A	STEWARTS LANE - 73A	STEWARTS LANE - 73A	STEWARTS LANE - 73A
42081	STEWARTS LANE - 73A	STEWARTS LANE - 73A	STEWARTS LANE - 73A	STEWARTS LANE - 73A	STEWARTS LANE - 73A	STEWARTS LANE - 73A	STEWARTS LANE - 73A
42082	BRIGHTON - 75A	BRIGHTON - 75A	BRIGHTON - 75A	BRIGHTON - 75A	BRIGHTON - 75A	BRIGHTON - 75A	BRIGHTON - 75A
42086	STEWARTS LANE - 73A	STEWARTS LANE - 73A	STEWARTS LANE - 73A	STEWARTS LANE - 73A	STEWARTS LANE - 73A	STEWARTS LANE - 73A	B.ARMS - 73B
42087	STEWARTS LANE - 73A	STEWARTS LANE - 73A	STEWARTS LANE - 73A	STEWARTS LANE - 73A	STEWARTS LANE - 73A	STEWARTS LANE - 73A	STEWARTS LANE - 73A
42088	STEWARTS LANE - 73A	STEWARTS LANE - 73A	STEWARTS LANE - 73A	STEWARTS LANE - 73A	STEWARTS LANE - 73A	STEWARTS LANE - 73A	STEWARTS LANE - 73A
42089	STEWARTS LANE - 73A	STEWARTS LANE - 73A	STEWARTS LANE - 73A	STEWARTS LANE - 73A	STEWARTS LANE - 73A	STEWARTS LANE - 73A	STEWARTS LANE - 73A
42090	STEWARTS LANE - 73A	STEWARTS LANE - 73A	STEWARTS LANE - 73A	STEWARTS LANE - 73A	STEWARTS LANE - 73A	STEWARTS LANE - 73A	STEWARTS LANE - 73A
42091	STEWARTS LANE - 73A	STEWARTS LANE - 73A	STEWARTS LANE - 73A	STEWARTS LANE - 73A	STEWARTS LANE - 73A	STEWARTS LANE - 73A	STEWARTS LANE - 73A
42092	ASHFORD - 74A	ASHFORD - 74A	ASHFORD - 74A	ASHFORD - 74A	ASHFORD - 74A	ASHFORD - 74A	ASHFORD - 74A
42095	ASHFORD - 74A	ASHFORD - 74A	ASHFORD - 74A	ASHFORD - 74A	ASHFORD - 74A	ASHFORD - 74A	ASHFORD - 74A
42096	ASHFORD - 74A	ASHFORD - 74A	ASHFORD - 74A	ASHFORD - 74A	ASHFORD - 74A	ASHFORD - 74A	ASHFORD - 74A
42097	ASHFORD - 74A	ASHFORD - 74A	ASHFORD - 74A	ASHFORD - 74A	ASHFORD - 74A	ASHFORD - 74A	ASHFORD - 74A
42098	ASHFORD - 74A	ASHFORD - 74A	ASHFORD - 74A	ASHFORD - 74A	ASHFORD - 74A	ASHFORD - 74A	ASHFORD - 74A
42099	ASHFORD - 74A	ASHFORD - 74A	ASHFORD - 74A	ASHFORD - 74A	ASHFORD - 74A	ASHFORD - 74A	ASHFORD - 74A
42100	ASHFORD - 74A	ASHFORD - 74A	ASHFORD - 74A	ASHFORD - 74A	ASHFORD - 74A	ASHFORD - 74A	ASHFORD - 74A
42101	T.WELLS - 75F	T.WELLS - 75F	T.WELLS - 75F	T.WELLS - 75F	T.WELLS - 75F	T.WELLS - 75F	T.WELLS - 75F
42102	T.WELLS - 75F	T.WELLS - 75F	T.WELLS - 75F	T.WELLS - 75F	T.WELLS - 75F	T.WELLS - 75F	T.WELLS - 75F
42103	BRIGHTON - 75A	BRIGHTON - 75A	BRIGHTON - 75A	BRIGHTON - 75A	BRIGHTON - 75A	BRIGHTON - 75A	BRIGHTON - 75A
42104	T.WELLS - 75F	T.WELLS - 75F	T.WELLS - 75F	T.WELLS - 75F	T.WELLS - 75F	T.WELLS - 75F	T.WELLS - 75F
42105	T.WELLS - 75F	T.WELLS - 75F	T.WELLS - 75F	T.WELLS - 75F	T.WELLS - 75F	T.WELLS - 75F	T.WELLS - 75F
42106	STEWARTS LANE - 73A	STEWARTS LANE - 73A	STEWARTS LANE - 73A	STEWARTS LANE - 73A	STEWARTS LANE - 73A	STEWARTS LANE - 73A	T.WELLS - 75F
				Electric			
20001	SELHURST	SELHURST	SELHURST	SELHURST	SELHURST	SELHURST	SELHURST
20002	SELHURST	SELHURST	SELHURST	SELHURST	SELHURST	SELHURST	SELHURST
20003	SELHURST	SELHURST	SELHURST	SELHURST	SELHURST	SELHURST	SELHURST

The Southern, alone of the four companies, did not pursued any large passenger tank designs, partly because of its experiences with the 2-6-4T's in the 1920's but chiefly because its inter-wars electrification programmes which made available a sufficiency of suburban locomotives for rural local workings.

By the time of nationalisation many of these older engines were in need of replacement and, under the aegis of an authority remote from the memories of 1927, a large number of LMS designed passenger tanks were introduced to the system. The first arrivals were a batch of 2-6-4T's allocated to the Tunbridge Wells - Victoria workings, the only steam worked suburban service from London, as replacement for the LBSCR 4-4-2T's but very quickly further examples were added, most working on sections of the Brighton section. Additional batches were subsequently allocated to Ashford and Dover, taking over many local workings in East Kent and the Maidstone branch in particular.

Ivatt 2-6-2 tanks arrived at the same time as the 2-6-4T's but were initially confined to the Somerset & Dorset section before multiplying to cover empty stock workings in the London area, the Sheerness branch and the Brighton district of the LBSCR. A small number was allocated to the West of England for working the Exeter - Exmouth services and, with Plymouth-based engines, the Callington branch.

The workings of both classes remained largely static until 1959 electrification when the 2-6-4 tanks were exchanged en masse for BR 4MT 2-6-4T's whilst the smaller engines, no longer required in Kent, were moved to the West Country taking over most of the duties that had hitherto been worked by M7 and O2 0-4-4T's.

loco	May-58	Oct-58	Mar-59	Jun-59	Jul-59	Aug-59	Oct-59
			LMS 2MT 2-6-2T (1946)				
41241	BATH (S&D) - 82F	BATH (S&D) - 82F	BATH (S&D) - 82F	BATH (S&D) - 82F	BATH (S&D) - 82F	BATH (S&D) - 82F	BATH (S&D) - 82F
41242	BATH (S&D) - 82F	BATH (S&D) - 82F	BATH (S&D) - 82F	BATH (S&D) - 82F	BATH (S&D) - 82F	BATH (S&D) - 82F	BATH (S&D) - 82F
41243	BATH (S&D) - 82F	BATH (S&D) - 82F	BATH (S&D) - 82F	BATH (S&D) - 82F	BATH (S&D) - 82F	BATH (S&D) - 82F	BATH (S&D) - 82F
41248	TEMPLECOMBE - 82G	TEMPLECOMBE - 82G	TEMPLECOMBE - 82G	TEMPLECOMBE - 82G	TEMPLECOMBE - 82G	TEMPLECOMBE - 82G	TEMPLECOMBE - 82G
41249	TEMPLECOMBE - 82G	TEMPLECOMBE - 82G	TEMPLECOMBE - 82G	TEMPLECOMBE - 82G	TEMPLECOMBE - 82G	TEMPLECOMBE - 82G	TEMPLECOMBE - 82G
41290	STEWARTS LANE - 73A	STEWARTS LANE - 73A	STEWARTS LANE - 73A	STEWARTS LANE - 73A	STEWARTS LANE - 73A	STEWARTS LANE - 73A	STEWARTS LANE - 73A
41291	STEWARTS LANE - 73A	STEWARTS LANE - 73A	STEWARTS LANE - 73A	STEWARTS LANE - 73A	STEWARTS LANE - 73A	STEWARTS LANE - 73A	STEWARTS LANE - 73A
41292	STEWARTS LANE - 73A	STEWARTS LANE - 73A	STEWARTS LANE - 73A	STEWARTS LANE - 73A	STEWARTS LANE - 73A	STEWARTS LANE - 73A	STEWARTS LANE - 73A
41293	EASTLEIGH - 71A	EASTLEIGH - 71A	EASTLEIGH - 71A	EASTLEIGH - 71A	EASTLEIGH - 71A	EASTLEIGH - 71A	EASTLEIGH - 71A
41294	BARNSTAPLE - 72E	BARNSTAPLE - 72E	BARNSTAPLE - 72E	BARNSTAPLE - 72E	BARNSTAPLE - 72E	BARNSTAPLE - 72E	BARNSTAPLE - 72E
41295	BARNSTAPLE - 72E	BARNSTAPLE - 72E	BARNSTAPLE - 72E	BARNSTAPLE - 72E	BARNSTAPLE - 72E	BARNSTAPLE - 72E	BARNSTAPLE - 72E
41296	HIGHBRIDGE - 71J	HIGHBRIDGE - 71J	HIGHBRIDGE - 71J	TO WR	TO WR	TO WR	TO WR
41297	BARNSTAPLE - 72E	BARNSTAPLE - 72E	BARNSTAPLE - 72E	BARNSTAPLE - 72E	BARNSTAPLE - 72E	BARNSTAPLE - 72E	BARNSTAPLE - 72E
41298	BARNSTAPLE - 72E	BARNSTAPLE - 72E	BARNSTAPLE - 72E	BARNSTAPLE - 72E	BARNSTAPLE - 72E	BARNSTAPLE - 72E	BARNSTAPLE - 72E
41299	B ARMS - 73B	B ARMS - 73B	B ARMS - 73B	B ARMS - 73B	B ARMS - 73B	B ARMS - 73B	B ARMS - 73B
41300	B ARMS - 73B	B ARMS - 73B	B ARMS - 73B	B ARMS - 73B	B ARMS - 73B	B ARMS - 73B	B ARMS - 73B
41301	B ARMS - 73B	B ARMS - 73B	B ARMS - 73B	B ARMS - 73B	B ARMS - 73B	B ARMS - 73B	B ARMS - 73B
41302	PLYMOUTH - 83H	PLYMOUTH - 83H	PLYMOUTH - 83H	PLYMOUTH - 83H	PLYMOUTH - 83H	PLYMOUTH - 83H	PLYMOUTH - 83H
41303	B ARMS - 73B	B ARMS - 73B	B ARMS - 73B	B ARMS - 73B	B ARMS - 73B	B ARMS - 73B	B ARMS - 73B
41304	HIGHBRIDGE - 71J	HIGHBRIDGE - 71J	HIGHBRIDGE - 71J	HIGHBRIDGE - 71J	HIGHBRIDGE - 71J	HIGHBRIDGE - 71J	HIGHBRIDGE - 71J
41304	RAMSGATE - 74B	RAMSGATE - 73G	RAMSGATE - 73G	TO WR	TO WR	TO WR	TO WR
41305	EASTLEIGH - 71A	EASTLEIGH - 71A	EASTLEIGH - 71A	EASTLEIGH - 71A	EASTLEIGH - 71A	EASTLEIGH - 71A	EASTLEIGH - 71A
41306	EXMOUTH JCN - 72A	EXMOUTH JCN - 72A	EXMOUTH JCN - 72A	EXMOUTH JCN - 72A	EXMOUTH JCN - 72A	EXMOUTH JCN - 72A	EXMOUTH JCN - 72A
41307	EXMOUTH JCN - 72A	EXMOUTH JCN - 72A	EXMOUTH JCN - 72A	EXMOUTH JCN - 72A	EXMOUTH JCN - 72A	EXMOUTH JCN - 72A	EXMOUTH JCN - 72A
41308	FAVERSHAM - 73E	FAVERSHAM - 73E	FAVERSHAM - 73E	ASHFORD - 73F	ASHFORD - 73F	ASHFORD - 73F	ASHFORD - 73F
41309	FAVERSHAM - 73E	FAVERSHAM - 73E	FAVERSHAM - 73E	ASHFORD - 73F	ASHFORD - 73F	ASHFORD - 73F	ASHFORD - 73F
41310	FAVERSHAM - 73E	FAVERSHAM - 73E	FAVERSHAM - 73E	ASHFORD - 73F	ASHFORD - 73F	ASHFORD - 73F	ASHFORD - 73F
41311	FAVERSHAM - 73E	FAVERSHAM - 73E	FAVERSHAM - 73E	ASHFORD - 73F	ASHFORD - 73F	ASHFORD - 73F	ASHFORD - 73F
41312	FAVERSHAM - 73E	FAVERSHAM - 73E	FAVERSHAM - 73E	ASHFORD - 73F	ASHFORD - 73F	ASHFORD - 73F	ASHFORD - 73F
41313	FAVERSHAM - 73E	FAVERSHAM - 73E	FAVERSHAM - 73E	ASHFORD - 73F	ASHFORD - 73F	ASHFORD - 73F	ASHFORD - 73F
41314	BARNSTAPLE - 72E	BARNSTAPLE - 72E	BARNSTAPLE - 72E	BARNSTAPLE - 72E	BARNSTAPLE - 72E	BARNSTAPLE - 72E	BARNSTAPLE - 72E
41315	PLYMOUTH - 83H	PLYMOUTH - 83H	PLYMOUTH - 83H	PLYMOUTH - 83H	PLYMOUTH - 83H	PLYMOUTH - 83H	PLYMOUTH - 83H
41316	PLYMOUTH - 83H	PLYMOUTH - 83H	PLYMOUTH - 83H	PLYMOUTH - 83H	PLYMOUTH - 83H	PLYMOUTH - 83H	PLYMOUTH - 83H
41317	PLYMOUTH - 83H	PLYMOUTH - 83H	PLYMOUTH - 83H	PLYMOUTH - 83H	PLYMOUTH - 83H	PLYMOUTH - 83H	PLYMOUTH - 83H
41318	EXMOUTH JCN - 72A	EXMOUTH JCN - 72A	EXMOUTH JCN - 72A	EXMOUTH JCN - 72A	EXMOUTH JCN - 72A	EXMOUTH JCN - 72A	EXMOUTH JCN - 72A
41319	THREE BRIDGES - 75E	T.WELLS - 75F	T.WELLS - 75F	T.WELLS - 75F	EASTLEIGH - 71A	EASTLEIGH - 71A	EASTLEIGH - 71A
			LMS 4MT 2-6-4T (1948)				
42066	THREE BRIDGES - 75E	THREE BRIDGES - 75E	BRIGHTON - 75A	BRIGHTON - 75A	BRIGHTON - 75A	BRIGHTON - 75A	BRIGHTON - 75A
42067	THREE BRIDGES - 75E	THREE BRIDGES - 75E	BRIGHTON - 75A	BRIGHTON - 75A	BRIGHTON - 75A	BRIGHTON - 75A	BRIGHTON - 75A
42068	THREE BRIDGES - 75E	THREE BRIDGES - 75E	THREE BRIDGES - 75E	THREE BRIDGES - 75E	THREE BRIDGES - 75E	THREE BRIDGES - 75E	THREE BRIDGES - 75E
42069	THREE BRIDGES - 75E	THREE BRIDGES - 75E	THREE BRIDGES - 75E	THREE BRIDGES - 75E	THREE BRIDGES - 75E	THREE BRIDGES - 75E	THREE BRIDGES - 75E
42070	THREE BRIDGES - 75E	THREE BRIDGES - 75E	THREE BRIDGES - 75E	THREE BRIDGES - 75E	THREE BRIDGES - 75E	THREE BRIDGES - 75E	THREE BRIDGES - 75E
42071	THREE BRIDGES - 75E	THREE BRIDGES - 75E	THREE BRIDGES - 75E	THREE BRIDGES - 75E	THREE BRIDGES - 75E	THREE BRIDGES - 75E	THREE BRIDGES - 75E
42074	THREE BRIDGES - 75E	THREE BRIDGES - 75E	DOVER - 73H	DOVER - 73H	DOVER - 73H	DOVER - 73H	DOVER - 73H
42075	DOVER - 74C	DOVER - 73H	DOVER - 73H	DOVER - 73H	DOVER - 73H	DOVER - 73H	DOVER - 73H
42076	DOVER - 74C	DOVER - 73H	DOVER - 73H	DOVER - 73H	DOVER - 73H	DOVER - 73H	DOVER - 73H
42077	DOVER - 74C	DOVER - 73H	DOVER - 73H	DOVER - 73H	DOVER - 73H	DOVER - 73H	DOVER - 73H
42078	DOVER - 74C	DOVER - 73H	DOVER - 73H	DOVER - 73H	DOVER - 73H	DOVER - 73H	DOVER - 73H
42079	DOVER - 74C	DOVER - 73H	DOVER - 73H	DOVER - 73H	DOVER - 73H	DOVER - 73H	ASHFORD - 73F
42080	STEWARTS LANE - 73A	STEWARTS LANE - 73A	STEWARTS LANE - 73A	STEWARTS LANE - 73A	STEWARTS LANE - 73A	STEWARTS LANE - 73A	STEWARTS LANE - 73A
42081	STEWARTS LANE - 73A	STEWARTS LANE - 73A	STEWARTS LANE - 73A	STEWARTS LANE - 73A	STEWARTS LANE - 73A	STEWARTS LANE - 73A	STEWARTS LANE - 73A
42082	BRIGHTON - 75A	BRIGHTON - 75A	BRIGHTON - 75A	BRIGHTON - 75A	BRIGHTON - 75A	BRIGHTON - 75A	BRIGHTON - 75A
42086	B ARMS - 73B	B ARMS - 73B	B ARMS - 73B	B ARMS - 73B	B ARMS - 73B	B ARMS - 73B	B ARMS - 73B
42087	STEWARTS LANE - 73A	STEWARTS LANE - 73A	STEWARTS LANE - 73A	STEWARTS LANE - 73A	T.WELLS - 75F	T.WELLS - 75F	T.WELLS - 75F
42088	STEWARTS LANE - 73A	STEWARTS LANE - 73A	STEWARTS LANE - 73A	STEWARTS LANE - 73A	STEWARTS LANE - 73A	STEWARTS LANE - 73A	STEWARTS LANE - 73A
42089	STEWARTS LANE - 73A	STEWARTS LANE - 73A	STEWARTS LANE - 73A	STEWARTS LANE - 73A	STEWARTS LANE - 73A	STEWARTS LANE - 73A	STEWARTS LANE - 73A
42090	STEWARTS LANE - 73A	STEWARTS LANE - 73A	STEWARTS LANE - 73A	STEWARTS LANE - 73A	STEWARTS LANE - 73A	STEWARTS LANE - 73A	STEWARTS LANE - 73A
42091	STEWARTS LANE - 73A	STEWARTS LANE - 73A	STEWARTS LANE - 73A	STEWARTS LANE - 73A	STEWARTS LANE - 73A	STEWARTS LANE - 73A	STEWARTS LANE - 73A
42092	DOVER - 74C	DOVER - 73H	DOVER - 73H	DOVER - 73H	DOVER - 73H	DOVER - 73H	ASHFORD - 73F
42095	DOVER - 74C	DOVER - 73H	DOVER - 73H	DOVER - 73H	DOVER - 73H	DOVER - 73H	ASHFORD - 73F
42096	ASHFORD - 74A	ASHFORD - 73F	ASHFORD - 73F	ASHFORD - 73F	ASHFORD - 73F	ASHFORD - 73F	ASHFORD - 73F
42097	ASHFORD - 74A	ASHFORD - 73F	ASHFORD - 73F	ASHFORD - 73F	ASHFORD - 73F	ASHFORD - 73F	ASHFORD - 73F
42098	ASHFORD - 74A	ASHFORD - 73F	ASHFORD - 73F	ASHFORD - 73F	ASHFORD - 73F	ASHFORD - 73F	ASHFORD - 73F
42099	ASHFORD - 74A	ASHFORD - 73F	ASHFORD - 73F	ASHFORD - 73F	ASHFORD - 73F	ASHFORD - 73F	ASHFORD - 73F
42100	ASHFORD - 74A	ASHFORD - 73F	ASHFORD - 73F	ASHFORD - 73F	ASHFORD - 73F	ASHFORD - 73F	ASHFORD - 73F
42101	T.WELLS - 75F	T.WELLS - 75F	T.WELLS - 75F	T.WELLS - 75F	T.WELLS - 75F	T.WELLS - 75F	T.WELLS - 75F
42102	T.WELLS - 75F	T.WELLS - 75F	T.WELLS - 75F	T.WELLS - 75F	T.WELLS - 75F	T.WELLS - 75F	T.WELLS - 75F
42103	BRIGHTON - 75A	BRIGHTON - 75A	BRIGHTON - 75A	BRIGHTON - 75A	BRIGHTON - 75A	BRIGHTON - 75A	BRIGHTON - 75A
42104	T.WELLS - 75F	T.WELLS - 75F	T.WELLS - 75F	T.WELLS - 75F	T.WELLS - 75F	T.WELLS - 75F	T.WELLS - 75F
42105	T.WELLS - 75F	T.WELLS - 75F	T.WELLS - 75F	T.WELLS - 75F	T.WELLS - 75F	T.WELLS - 75F	T.WELLS - 75F
42106	T.WELLS - 75F	T.WELLS - 75F	T.WELLS - 75F	T.WELLS - 75F	T.WELLS - 75F	T.WELLS - 75F	T.WELLS - 75F
			Electric				
20001	SELHURST	SELHURST	SELHURST	SELHURST	SELHURST	SELHURST	SELHURST
20002	SELHURST	SELHURST	SELHURST	SELHURST	SELHURST	SELHURST	SELHURST
20003	SELHURST	SELHURST	SELHURST	SELHURST	SELHURST	SELHURST	SELHURST

Quite why the Southern, with 140 new Pacifics, should have been the chosen region for most of the early diesels - especially when the London Midland was so short of large passenger engines - remains a mystery but nevertheless in early 1953 the two 1600hp LMS diesels joined the pair of 1750hp SR locomotives, all four engines working amended Merchant Navy diagrams to Bournemouth and Exeter from Waterloo. The small 800hp 10800 also came from the LMR to work on the LBSCR from Norwood Junction and a fifth engine was added in 1954 with the appearance of 2000hp 10203.

Even allowing for the novel nature of main line diesels at the time, none of the quintet covered themselves in glory and the failure rate of 10800 in particular was a talking point for years. A notable use of the main line engines was on Christmas days when one would work the only service between Waterloo and Exeter: the advantage over a Pacific being that the diesel was (theoretically) better suited to the tight turn-round at Exeter. Before leaving the region some runs were made by the SR locomotives on the continental boat trains between Victoria and Dover but in early 1955 all five engines were transferred to the Midland Region, 10201 and 10202 to work between Derby and St Pancras and the remainder on the West Coast main line.

loco	Dec-59	Feb-60	Mar-60	Apr-60	Jul-60	Aug-60	Sep-60	Nov-60
				LMS 2MT 2-6-2T (1946)				
41241	BATH (S&D) - 82F	BATH (S&D) - 82F	BATH (S&D) - 82F	BATH (S&D) - 82F	BATH (S&D) - 82F	BATH (S&D) - 82F	BATH (S&D) - 82F	BATH (S&D) - 82F
41242	BATH (S&D) - 82F	BATH (S&D) - 82F	BATH (S&D) - 82F	BATH (S&D) - 82F	BATH (S&D) - 82F	BATH (S&D) - 82F	BATH (S&D) - 82F	BATH (S&D) - 82F
41243	BATH (S&D) - 82F	BATH (S&D) - 82F	BATH (S&D) - 82F	BATH (S&D) - 82F	BATH (S&D) - 82F	BATH (S&D) - 82F	BATH (S&D) - 82F	BATH (S&D) - 82F
41248	TEMPLECOMBE - 82G	TEMPLECOMBE - 82G	TEMPLECOMBE - 82G	TEMPLECOMBE - 82G	TEMPLECOMBE - 82G	TEMPLECOMBE - 82G	TEMPLECOMBE - 82G	TEMPLECOMBE - 82G
41249	TEMPLECOMBE - 82G	TEMPLECOMBE - 82G	TEMPLECOMBE - 82G	TEMPLECOMBE - 82G	TEMPLECOMBE - 82G	TEMPLECOMBE - 82G	TEMPLECOMBE - 82G	TEMPLECOMBE - 82G
41290	STEWARTS LANE - 73A	STEWARTS LANE - 73A	STEWARTS LANE - 73A	STEWARTS LANE - 73A	STEWARTS LANE - 73A	STEWARTS LANE - 73A	STEWARTS LANE - 73A	STEWARTS LANE - 73A
41291	STEWARTS LANE - 73A	STEWARTS LANE - 73A	STEWARTS LANE - 73A	STEWARTS LANE - 73A	STEWARTS LANE - 73A	STEWARTS LANE - 73A	STEWARTS LANE - 73A	STEWARTS LANE - 73A
41292	STEWARTS LANE - 73A	STEWARTS LANE - 73A	STEWARTS LANE - 73A	STEWARTS LANE - 73A	STEWARTS LANE - 73A	STEWARTS LANE - 73A	STEWARTS LANE - 73A	STEWARTS LANE - 73A
41293	EASTLEIGH - 71A	EASTLEIGH - 71A	EASTLEIGH - 71A	EASTLEIGH - 71A	EASTLEIGH - 71A	EASTLEIGH - 71A	EASTLEIGH - 71A	EASTLEIGH - 71A
41294	BARNSTAPLE - 72E	BARNSTAPLE - 72E	BARNSTAPLE - 72E	BARNSTAPLE - 72E	BARNSTAPLE - 72E	BARNSTAPLE - 72E	BARNSTAPLE - 72E	BARNSTAPLE - 72E
41295	BARNSTAPLE - 72E	BARNSTAPLE - 72E	BARNSTAPLE - 72E	BARNSTAPLE - 72E	BARNSTAPLE - 72E	BARNSTAPLE - 72E	BARNSTAPLE - 72E	BARNSTAPLE - 72E
41297	BARNSTAPLE - 72E	BARNSTAPLE - 72E	BARNSTAPLE - 72E	BARNSTAPLE - 72E	BARNSTAPLE - 72E	BARNSTAPLE - 72E	BARNSTAPLE - 72E	BARNSTAPLE - 72E
41298	BARNSTAPLE - 72E	BARNSTAPLE - 72E	BARNSTAPLE - 72E	BARNSTAPLE - 72E	BARNSTAPLE - 72E	BARNSTAPLE - 72E	BARNSTAPLE - 72E	BARNSTAPLE - 72E
41299	B ARMS - 73B	B ARMS - 73B	B ARMS - 73B	B ARMS - 73B	B ARMS - 73B	B ARMS - 73B	B ARMS - 73B	B ARMS - 73B
41300	B ARMS - 73B	B ARMS - 73B	B ARMS - 73B	B ARMS - 73B	B ARMS - 73B	B ARMS - 73B	B ARMS - 73B	B ARMS - 73B
41301	B ARMS - 73B	B ARMS - 73B	B ARMS - 73B	B ARMS - 73B	B ARMS - 73B	B ARMS - 73B	B ARMS - 73B	B ARMS - 73B
41302	PLYMOUTH - 83H	PLYMOUTH - 83H	PLYMOUTH - 83H	PLYMOUTH - 83H	PLYMOUTH - 83H	PLYMOUTH - 83H	PLYMOUTH - 83H	PLYMOUTH - 83H
41303	B ARMS - 73B	B ARMS - 73B	B ARMS - 73B	B ARMS - 73B	B ARMS - 73B	B ARMS - 73B	B ARMS - 73B	B ARMS - 73B
41304	HIGHBRIDGE - 71J	HIGHBRIDGE - 71J	HIGHBRIDGE - 71J	HIGHBRIDGE - 71J	HIGHBRIDGE - 71J	HIGHBRIDGE - 71J	HIGHBRIDGE - 71J	HIGHBRIDGE - 71J
41305	EASTLEIGH - 71A	EASTLEIGH - 71A	EASTLEIGH - 71A	EASTLEIGH - 71A	EASTLEIGH - 71A	EASTLEIGH - 71A	EASTLEIGH - 71A	EASTLEIGH - 71A
41306	EXMOUTH JCN - 72A	EXMOUTH JCN - 72A	EXMOUTH JCN - 72A	EXMOUTH JCN - 72A	EXMOUTH JCN - 72A	EXMOUTH JCN - 72A	EXMOUTH JCN - 72A	EXMOUTH JCN - 72A
41307	EXMOUTH JCN - 72A	EXMOUTH JCN - 72A	EXMOUTH JCN - 72A	EXMOUTH JCN - 72A	EXMOUTH JCN - 72A	EXMOUTH JCN - 72A	EXMOUTH JCN - 72A	EXMOUTH JCN - 72A
41308	ASHFORD - 73F	EXMOUTH JCN - 72A	EXMOUTH JCN - 72A	EXMOUTH JCN - 72A	EXMOUTH JCN - 72A	EXMOUTH JCN - 72A	EXMOUTH JCN - 72A	EXMOUTH JCN - 72A
41309	ASHFORD - 73F	EXMOUTH JCN - 72A	EXMOUTH JCN - 72A	EXMOUTH JCN - 72A	EXMOUTH JCN - 72A	EXMOUTH JCN - 72A	EXMOUTH JCN - 72A	EXMOUTH JCN - 72A
41310	ASHFORD - 73F	TO WR	TO WR	TO WR	TO WR	TO WR	TO WR	TO WR
41311	ASHFORD - 73F	EASTLEIGH - 71A	EASTLEIGH - 71A	EASTLEIGH - 71A	EASTLEIGH - 71A	EASTLEIGH - 71A	EASTLEIGH - 71A	EASTLEIGH - 71A
41312	ASHFORD - 73F	BARNSTAPLE - 72E	BARNSTAPLE - 72E	BARNSTAPLE - 72E	BARNSTAPLE - 72E	BARNSTAPLE - 72E	BARNSTAPLE - 72E	BARNSTAPLE - 72E
41313	ASHFORD - 73F	BARNSTAPLE - 72E	BARNSTAPLE - 72E	BARNSTAPLE - 72E	BARNSTAPLE - 72E	BARNSTAPLE - 72E	BARNSTAPLE - 72E	BARNSTAPLE - 72E
41314	BARNSTAPLE - 72E	BARNSTAPLE - 72E	BARNSTAPLE - 72E	BARNSTAPLE - 72E	BARNSTAPLE - 72E	BARNSTAPLE - 72E	BARNSTAPLE - 72E	BARNSTAPLE - 72E
41315	PLYMOUTH - 83H	PLYMOUTH - 83H	PLYMOUTH - 83H	PLYMOUTH - 83H	PLYMOUTH - 83H	PLYMOUTH - 83H	PLYMOUTH - 83H	PLYMOUTH - 83H
41316	PLYMOUTH - 83H	PLYMOUTH - 83H	PLYMOUTH - 83H	PLYMOUTH - 83H	PLYMOUTH - 83H	PLYMOUTH - 83H	PLYMOUTH - 83H	PLYMOUTH - 83H
41317	PLYMOUTH - 83H	PLYMOUTH - 83H	PLYMOUTH - 83H	PLYMOUTH - 83H	PLYMOUTH - 83H	PLYMOUTH - 83H	PLYMOUTH - 83H	PLYMOUTH - 83H
41318	EXMOUTH JCN - 72A	EXMOUTH JCN - 72A	EXMOUTH JCN - 72A	EXMOUTH JCN - 72A	EXMOUTH JCN - 72A	EXMOUTH JCN - 72A	EXMOUTH JCN - 72A	EXMOUTH JCN - 72A
41319	EASTLEIGH - 71A	EASTLEIGH - 71A	EASTLEIGH - 71A	EASTLEIGH - 71A	EASTLEIGH - 71A	EASTLEIGH - 71A	EASTLEIGH - 71A	EASTLEIGH - 71A
				LMS 4MT 2-6-4T (1948)				
42066	TO LMR							
42067	TO LMR							
42068	TO LMR							
42069	TO LMR							
42070	TO LMR							
42071	TO LMR							
42072	TO NER							
42073	TO NER							
42074	TO LMR							
42075	TO LMR							
42076	TO LMR							
42077	TO LMR							
42078	TO LMR							
42079	TO LMR							
42080	TO LMR							
42081	TO LMR							
42082	TO LMR							
42083	TO NER							
42084	TO NER							
42085	TO NER							
42086	TO LMR							
42087	TO LMR							
42088	TO LMR							
42089	TO LMR							
42090	TO LMR							
42091	TO LMR							
42092	TO LMR							
42093	TO NER							
42094	TO NER							
42095	TO LMR							
42096	TO LMR							
42097	TO LMR							
42098	TO LMR							
42099	TO LMR							
42100	TO LMR							
42101	TO LMR							
42102	TO LMR							
42103	TO LMR							
42104	TO LMR							
42105	TO LMR							
42106	TO LMR							
				Electric				
20001	SELHURST	SELHURST	SELHURST	SELHURST	SELHURST	SELHURST	SELHURST	SELHURST
20002	SELHURST	SELHURST	SELHURST	SELHURST	SELHURST	SELHURST	SELHURST	SELHURST
20003	SELHURST	SELHURST	SELHURST	SELHURST	SELHURST	SELHURST	SELHURST	SELHURST

loco	Jun-51	Jul-51	Sep-51	Dec-51	Jan-52	Mar-52	Jun-52
BR3 2-6-2T							
82010							EXMOUTH JCN - 72A
82011							EXMOUTH JCN - 72A
82012							EXMOUTH JCN - 72A
82013							EXMOUTH JCN - 72A
82014							EXMOUTH JCN - 72A
82015							EXMOUTH JCN - 72A
82016							EXMOUTH JCN - 72A
82017							EXMOUTH JCN - 72A
82018							EXMOUTH JCN - 72A
82019							EXMOUTH JCN - 72A
BR4 2-6-4T							
80010		T.WELLS - 75F	T.WELLS - 75F	T.WELLS - 75F	T.WELLS - 75F	T.WELLS - 75F	T.WELLS - 75F
80011		T.WELLS - 75F	T.WELLS - 75F	T.WELLS - 75F	T.WELLS - 75F	T.WELLS - 75F	T.WELLS - 75F
80012			T.WELLS - 75F	T.WELLS - 75F	T.WELLS - 75F	T.WELLS - 75F	T.WELLS - 75F
80013			T.WELLS - 75F	T.WELLS - 75F	T.WELLS - 75F	T.WELLS - 75F	T.WELLS - 75F
80014			T.WELLS - 75F	T.WELLS - 75F	T.WELLS - 75F	T.WELLS - 75F	T.WELLS - 75F
80015			T.WELLS - 75F	T.WELLS - 75F	T.WELLS - 75F	T.WELLS - 75F	T.WELLS - 75F
80016			T.WELLS - 75F	T.WELLS - 75F	T.WELLS - 75F	BRIGHTON - 75A	BRIGHTON - 75A
80017			T.WELLS - 75F	T.WELLS - 75F	BRIGHTON - 75A	EASTBOURNE - 75G	EASTBOURNE - 75G
80018			T.WELLS - 75F	T.WELLS - 75F	BRIGHTON - 75A	EASTBOURNE - 75G	EASTBOURNE - 75G
80019				T.WELLS - 75F	BRIGHTON - 75A	BRIGHTON - 75A	EASTBOURNE - 75G
80031						BRIGHTON - 75A	BRIGHTON - 75A
80032						BRIGHTON - 75A	BRIGHTON - 75A
80032						BRIGHTON - 75A	BRIGHTON - 75A
80033						BRIGHTON - 75A	BRIGHTON - 75A
80033						BRIGHTON - 75A	BRIGHTON - 75A
BR7 4-6-2 (1951)							
70004	STEWARTS LANE - 73A	STEWARTS LANE - 73A	STEWARTS LANE - 73A	STEWARTS LANE - 73A	STEWARTS LANE - 73A	STEWARTS LANE - 73A	STEWARTS LANE - 73A
70014	NINE ELMS - 70A	STEWARTS LANE - 73A	STEWARTS LANE - 73A	STEWARTS LANE - 73A	STEWARTS LANE - 73A	STEWARTS LANE - 73A	STEWARTS LANE - 73A

loco	Sep-52	Dec-52	Mar-53	May-53	Jul-53	Sep-53	Nov-53
BR3 2-6-2T							
82010	EXMOUTH JCN - 72A	EXMOUTH JCN - 72A	EXMOUTH JCN - 72A	EXMOUTH JCN - 72A	EXMOUTH JCN - 72A	EXMOUTH JCN - 72A	EXMOUTH JCN - 72A
82011	EXMOUTH JCN - 72A	EXMOUTH JCN - 72A	EXMOUTH JCN - 72A	EXMOUTH JCN - 72A	EXMOUTH JCN - 72A	EXMOUTH JCN - 72A	EXMOUTH JCN - 72A
82012	EXMOUTH JCN - 72A	EXMOUTH JCN - 72A	EASTLEIGH - 71A	EASTLEIGH - 71A	EASTLEIGH - 71A	EASTLEIGH - 71A	EASTLEIGH - 71A
82013	EXMOUTH JCN - 72A	EXMOUTH JCN - 72A	EXMOUTH JCN - 72A	EXMOUTH JCN - 72A	EXMOUTH JCN - 72A	EXMOUTH JCN - 72A	EASTLEIGH - 71A
82014	EASTLEIGH - 71A	EASTLEIGH - 71A	EASTLEIGH - 71A	EASTLEIGH - 71A	EASTLEIGH - 71A	EASTLEIGH - 71A	EASTLEIGH - 71A
82015	EASTLEIGH - 71A	EASTLEIGH - 71A	EASTLEIGH - 71A	EASTLEIGH - 71A	EASTLEIGH - 71A	EASTLEIGH - 71A	EASTLEIGH - 71A
82016	EASTLEIGH - 71A	EASTLEIGH - 71A	EASTLEIGH - 71A	EASTLEIGH - 71A	EASTLEIGH - 71A	EASTLEIGH - 71A	EASTLEIGH - 71A
82017	EXMOUTH JCN - 72A	EXMOUTH JCN - 72A	EXMOUTH JCN - 72A	EXMOUTH JCN - 72A	EXMOUTH JCN - 72A	EXMOUTH JCN - 72A	EXMOUTH JCN - 72A
82018	EXMOUTH JCN - 72A	EXMOUTH JCN - 72A	EXMOUTH JCN - 72A	EXMOUTH JCN - 72A	EXMOUTH JCN - 72A	EXMOUTH JCN - 72A	EXMOUTH JCN - 72A
82019	EXMOUTH JCN - 72A	EXMOUTH JCN - 72A	EXMOUTH JCN - 72A	EXMOUTH JCN - 72A	EXMOUTH JCN - 72A	EXMOUTH JCN - 72A	EXMOUTH JCN - 72A
BR4 2-6-4T							
80010	T.WELLS - 75F	T.WELLS - 75F	T.WELLS - 75F	T.WELLS - 75F	T.WELLS - 75F	T.WELLS - 75F	T.WELLS - 75F
80011	T.WELLS - 75F	T.WELLS - 75F	T.WELLS - 75F	T.WELLS - 75F	T.WELLS - 75F	T.WELLS - 75F	T.WELLS - 75F
80012	T.WELLS - 75F	T.WELLS - 75F	T.WELLS - 75F	T.WELLS - 75F	T.WELLS - 75F	T.WELLS - 75F	T.WELLS - 75F
80013	T.WELLS - 75F	T.WELLS - 75F	T.WELLS - 75F	T.WELLS - 75F	T.WELLS - 75F	T.WELLS - 75F	T.WELLS - 75F
80014	T.WELLS - 75F	T.WELLS - 75F	T.WELLS - 75F	T.WELLS - 75F	T.WELLS - 75F	T.WELLS - 75F	T.WELLS - 75F
80015	T.WELLS - 75F	T.WELLS - 75F	T.WELLS - 75F	T.WELLS - 75F	T.WELLS - 75F	T.WELLS - 75F	T.WELLS - 75F
80016	BRIGHTON - 75A	BRIGHTON - 75A	BRIGHTON - 75A	BRIGHTON - 75A	BRIGHTON - 75A	BRIGHTON - 75A	BRIGHTON - 75A
80017	T.WELLS - 75F	T.WELLS - 75F	T.WELLS - 75F	T.WELLS - 75F	T.WELLS - 75F	T.WELLS - 75F	T.WELLS - 75F
80018	REDHILL - 75B	REDHILL - 75B	T.WELLS - 75F	T.WELLS - 75F	T.WELLS - 75F	T.WELLS - 75F	T.WELLS - 75F
80019	REDHILL - 75B	REDHILL - 75B	BRIGHTON - 75A	BRIGHTON - 75A	BRIGHTON - 75A	BRIGHTON - 75A	BRIGHTON - 75A
80031	BRIGHTON - 75A	BRIGHTON - 75A	BRIGHTON - 75A	BRIGHTON - 75A	BRIGHTON - 75A	BRIGHTON - 75A	BRIGHTON - 75A
80032	BRIGHTON - 75A	BRIGHTON - 75A	BRIGHTON - 75A	BRIGHTON - 75A	BRIGHTON - 75A	BRIGHTON - 75A	BRIGHTON - 75A
80032	BRIGHTON - 75A	BRIGHTON - 75A	BRIGHTON - 75A	BRIGHTON - 75A	BRIGHTON - 75A	BRIGHTON - 75A	BRIGHTON - 75A
80033	BRIGHTON - 75A	BRIGHTON - 75A	BRIGHTON - 75A	BRIGHTON - 75A	BRIGHTON - 75A	BRIGHTON - 75A	BRIGHTON - 75A
80033	BRIGHTON - 75A	BRIGHTON - 75A	BRIGHTON - 75A	BRIGHTON - 75A	BRIGHTON - 75A	BRIGHTON - 75A	BRIGHTON - 75A
BR4 2-6-0							
76005		EASTLEIGH - 71A	EASTLEIGH - 71A	EASTLEIGH - 71A	EASTLEIGH - 71A	EASTLEIGH - 71A	EASTLEIGH - 71A
76006		EASTLEIGH - 71A	EASTLEIGH - 71A	EASTLEIGH - 71A	EASTLEIGH - 71A	EASTLEIGH - 71A	EASTLEIGH - 71A
76007			EASTLEIGH - 71A	EASTLEIGH - 71A	EASTLEIGH - 71A	EASTLEIGH - 71A	EASTLEIGH - 71A
76008			EASTLEIGH - 71A	EASTLEIGH - 71A	EASTLEIGH - 71A	EASTLEIGH - 71A	EASTLEIGH - 71A
76009			EASTLEIGH - 71A	EASTLEIGH - 71A	EASTLEIGH - 71A	EASTLEIGH - 71A	EASTLEIGH - 71A
76010			EASTLEIGH - 71A	EASTLEIGH - 71A	EASTLEIGH - 71A	EASTLEIGH - 71A	EASTLEIGH - 71A
76011			EASTLEIGH - 71A	EASTLEIGH - 71A	EASTLEIGH - 71A	EASTLEIGH - 71A	EASTLEIGH - 71A
76012			EASTLEIGH - 71A	EASTLEIGH - 71A	EASTLEIGH - 71A	EASTLEIGH - 71A	EASTLEIGH - 71A
76013			EASTLEIGH - 71A	EASTLEIGH - 71A	EASTLEIGH - 71A	EASTLEIGH - 71A	EASTLEIGH - 71A
76014			EASTLEIGH - 71A	EASTLEIGH - 71A	EASTLEIGH - 71A	EASTLEIGH - 71A	EASTLEIGH - 71A
76015				EASTLEIGH - 71A	EASTLEIGH - 71A	EASTLEIGH - 71A	EASTLEIGH - 71A
76016					EASTLEIGH - 71A	EASTLEIGH - 71A	EASTLEIGH - 71A
76017					EASTLEIGH - 71A	EASTLEIGH - 71A	EASTLEIGH - 71A
76019					EASTLEIGH - 71A	EASTLEIGH - 71A	EASTLEIGH - 71A
76025						EASTLEIGH - 71A	EASTLEIGH - 71A
76026							EASTLEIGH - 71A
76027							EASTLEIGH - 71A
76028							EASTLEIGH - 71A
76029							EASTLEIGH - 71A
BR5 4-6-0							
73003			FROM LMR	NINE ELMS - 70A	TO LMR		
73015			FROM LMR	NINE ELMS - 70A	TO LMR		
73017			FROM LMR	NINE ELMS - 70A	TO LMR		
BR7 4-6-2 (1951)							
70004	STEWARTS LANE - 73A	STEWARTS LANE - 73A	STEWARTS LANE - 73A	STEWARTS LANE - 73A	STEWARTS LANE - 73A	STEWARTS LANE - 73A	STEWARTS LANE - 73A
70014	STEWARTS LANE - 73A	STEWARTS LANE - 73A	STEWARTS LANE - 73A	STEWARTS LANE - 73A	STEWARTS LANE - 73A	STEWARTS LANE - 73A	STEWARTS LANE - 73A
70017			FROM WR	SALISBURY - 72B	TO WR		
70023			FROM WR	SALISBURY - 72B	TO WR		
70024			FROM WR	EXMOUTH JCN - 72A	TO WR		
70028			FROM WR	EXMOUTH JCN - 72A	TO WR		
70029			FROM WR	EXMOUTH JCN - 72A	TO WR		
70030			FROM LMR	DOVER - 74C	TO LMR		
70034			FROM LMR	STEWARTS LANE - 73A	TO LMR		

loco	Jan-54	Mar-54	May-54	Jun-54	Aug-54	Oct-54	Dec-54
				BR3 2-6-2T			
82010	EXMOUTH JCN - 72A	EXMOUTH JCN - 72A	EXMOUTH JCN - 72A	EXMOUTH JCN - 72A	EXMOUTH JCN - 72A	EXMOUTH JCN - 72A	EXMOUTH JCN - 72A
82011	EXMOUTH JCN - 72A	EXMOUTH JCN - 72A	EXMOUTH JCN - 72A	EXMOUTH JCN - 72A	EXMOUTH JCN - 72A	EXMOUTH JCN - 72A	EXMOUTH JCN - 72A
82012	EASTLEIGH - 71A	EASTLEIGH - 71A	EASTLEIGH - 71A	EASTLEIGH - 71A	EASTLEIGH - 71A	EASTLEIGH - 71A	EASTLEIGH - 71A
82013	EXMOUTH JCN - 72A	EXMOUTH JCN - 72A	EXMOUTH JCN - 72A	EXMOUTH JCN - 72A	EXMOUTH JCN - 72A	EXMOUTH JCN - 72A	EXMOUTH JCN - 72A
82014	EASTLEIGH - 71A	EASTLEIGH - 71A	EASTLEIGH - 71A	EASTLEIGH - 71A	EASTLEIGH - 71A	EASTLEIGH - 71A	EASTLEIGH - 71A
82015	EASTLEIGH - 71A	EASTLEIGH - 71A	EASTLEIGH - 71A	EASTLEIGH - 71A	EASTLEIGH - 71A	EASTLEIGH - 71A	EASTLEIGH - 71A
82016	EASTLEIGH - 71A	EASTLEIGH - 71A	EASTLEIGH - 71A	EASTLEIGH - 71A	EASTLEIGH - 71A	EASTLEIGH - 71A	EASTLEIGH - 71A
82017	EXMOUTH JCN - 72A	EXMOUTH JCN - 72A	EXMOUTH JCN - 72A	EXMOUTH JCN - 72A	EXMOUTH JCN - 72A	EXMOUTH JCN - 72A	EXMOUTH JCN - 72A
82018	EXMOUTH JCN - 72A	EXMOUTH JCN - 72A	EXMOUTH JCN - 72A	EXMOUTH JCN - 72A	EXMOUTH JCN - 72A	EXMOUTH JCN - 72A	EXMOUTH JCN - 72A
82019	EXMOUTH JCN - 72A	EXMOUTH JCN - 72A	EXMOUTH JCN - 72A	EXMOUTH JCN - 72A	EXMOUTH JCN - 72A	EXMOUTH JCN - 72A	EXMOUTH JCN - 72A
82022						EXMOUTH JCN - 72A	EXMOUTH JCN - 72A
82023						EXMOUTH JCN - 72A	EXMOUTH JCN - 72A
82024					EXMOUTH JCN - 72A	EXMOUTH JCN - 72A	EXMOUTH JCN - 72A
82024						EXMOUTH JCN - 72A	EXMOUTH JCN - 72A
82025					EXMOUTH JCN - 72A	EXMOUTH JCN - 72A	EXMOUTH JCN - 72A
				BR4 2-6-4T			
80010	T.WELLS - 75F	T.WELLS - 75F	T.WELLS - 75F	T.WELLS - 75F	T.WELLS - 75F	T.WELLS - 75F	T.WELLS - 75F
80011	T.WELLS - 75F	T.WELLS - 75F	T.WELLS - 75F	T.WELLS - 75F	T.WELLS - 75F	T.WELLS - 75F	T.WELLS - 75F
80012	T.WELLS - 75F	T.WELLS - 75F	T.WELLS - 75F	T.WELLS - 75F	T.WELLS - 75F	T.WELLS - 75F	T.WELLS - 75F
80013	T.WELLS - 75F	T.WELLS - 75F	T.WELLS - 75F	T.WELLS - 75F	T.WELLS - 75F	T.WELLS - 75F	T.WELLS - 75F
80014	T.WELLS - 75F	T.WELLS - 75F	T.WELLS - 75F	T.WELLS - 75F	T.WELLS - 75F	T.WELLS - 75F	T.WELLS - 75F
80015	T.WELLS - 75F	T.WELLS - 75F	T.WELLS - 75F	T.WELLS - 75F	T.WELLS - 75F	T.WELLS - 75F	T.WELLS - 75F
80016	BRIGHTON - 75A	BRIGHTON - 75A	BRIGHTON - 75A	BRIGHTON - 75A	BRIGHTON - 75A	BRIGHTON - 75A	BRIGHTON - 75A
80017	T.WELLS - 75F	T.WELLS - 75F	T.WELLS - 75F	T.WELLS - 75F	T.WELLS - 75F	T.WELLS - 75F	T.WELLS - 75F
80018	T.WELLS - 75F	T.WELLS - 75F	T.WELLS - 75F	T.WELLS - 75F	T.WELLS - 75F	T.WELLS - 75F	T.WELLS - 75F
80019	BRIGHTON - 75A	BRIGHTON - 75A	BRIGHTON - 75A	BRIGHTON - 75A	BRIGHTON - 75A	BRIGHTON - 75A	BRIGHTON - 75A
80031	BRIGHTON - 75A	BRIGHTON - 75A	BRIGHTON - 75A	BRIGHTON - 75A	BRIGHTON - 75A	BRIGHTON - 75A	BRIGHTON - 75A
80032	BRIGHTON - 75A	BRIGHTON - 75A	BRIGHTON - 75A	BRIGHTON - 75A	BRIGHTON - 75A	BRIGHTON - 75A	BRIGHTON - 75A
80032	BRIGHTON - 75A	BRIGHTON - 75A	BRIGHTON - 75A	BRIGHTON - 75A	BRIGHTON - 75A	BRIGHTON - 75A	BRIGHTON - 75A
80033	BRIGHTON - 75A	BRIGHTON - 75A	BRIGHTON - 75A	BRIGHTON - 75A	BRIGHTON - 75A	BRIGHTON - 75A	BRIGHTON - 75A
80033	BRIGHTON - 75A	BRIGHTON - 75A	BRIGHTON - 75A	BRIGHTON - 75A	BRIGHTON - 75A	BRIGHTON - 75A	BRIGHTON - 75A
				BR4 2-6-0			
76005	EASTLEIGH - 71A	EASTLEIGH - 71A	DORCHESTER - 71C	DORCHESTER - 71C	DORCHESTER - 71C	DORCHESTER - 71C	DORCHESTER - 71C
76006	EASTLEIGH - 71A	EASTLEIGH - 71A	DORCHESTER - 71C	DORCHESTER - 71C	DORCHESTER - 71C	DORCHESTER - 71C	DORCHESTER - 71C
76007	EASTLEIGH - 71A	EASTLEIGH - 71A	EASTLEIGH - 71A	EASTLEIGH - 71A	EASTLEIGH - 71A	EASTLEIGH - 71A	EASTLEIGH - 71A
76008	EASTLEIGH - 71A	EASTLEIGH - 71A	EASTLEIGH - 71A	EASTLEIGH - 71A	EASTLEIGH - 71A	EASTLEIGH - 71A	EASTLEIGH - 71A
76009	EASTLEIGH - 71A	EASTLEIGH - 71A	EASTLEIGH - 71A	EASTLEIGH - 71A	EASTLEIGH - 71A	EASTLEIGH - 71A	EASTLEIGH - 71A
76010	EASTLEIGH - 71A	EASTLEIGH - 71A	EASTLEIGH - 71A	EASTLEIGH - 71A	EASTLEIGH - 71A	EASTLEIGH - 71A	EASTLEIGH - 71A
76011	EASTLEIGH - 71A	EASTLEIGH - 71A	EASTLEIGH - 71A	EASTLEIGH - 71A	EASTLEIGH - 71A	EASTLEIGH - 71A	EASTLEIGH - 71A
76012	EASTLEIGH - 71A	EASTLEIGH - 71A	EASTLEIGH - 71A	EASTLEIGH - 71A	EASTLEIGH - 71A	EASTLEIGH - 71A	EASTLEIGH - 71A
76013	EASTLEIGH - 71A	EASTLEIGH - 71A	EASTLEIGH - 71A	EASTLEIGH - 71A	EASTLEIGH - 71A	EASTLEIGH - 71A	EASTLEIGH - 71A
76014	EASTLEIGH - 71A	EASTLEIGH - 71A	EASTLEIGH - 71A	EASTLEIGH - 71A	EASTLEIGH - 71A	EASTLEIGH - 71A	EASTLEIGH - 71A
76015	EASTLEIGH - 71A	EASTLEIGH - 71A	EASTLEIGH - 71A	EASTLEIGH - 71A	EASTLEIGH - 71A	EASTLEIGH - 71A	EASTLEIGH - 71A
76016	EASTLEIGH - 71A	EASTLEIGH - 71A	EASTLEIGH - 71A	EASTLEIGH - 71A	EASTLEIGH - 71A	EASTLEIGH - 71A	EASTLEIGH - 71A
76017	EASTLEIGH - 71A	EASTLEIGH - 71A	EASTLEIGH - 71A	EASTLEIGH - 71A	EASTLEIGH - 71A	EASTLEIGH - 71A	EASTLEIGH - 71A
76019	EASTLEIGH - 71A	EASTLEIGH - 71A	EASTLEIGH - 71A	EASTLEIGH - 71A	EASTLEIGH - 71A	EASTLEIGH - 71A	EASTLEIGH - 71A
76025	EASTLEIGH - 71A	EASTLEIGH - 71A	EASTLEIGH - 71A	EASTLEIGH - 71A	EASTLEIGH - 71A	EASTLEIGH - 71A	EASTLEIGH - 71A
76026	EASTLEIGH - 71A	EASTLEIGH - 71A	EASTLEIGH - 71A	EASTLEIGH - 71A	EASTLEIGH - 71A	EASTLEIGH - 71A	EASTLEIGH - 71A
76027	EASTLEIGH - 71A	EASTLEIGH - 71A	EASTLEIGH - 71A	EASTLEIGH - 71A	EASTLEIGH - 71A	EASTLEIGH - 71A	EASTLEIGH - 71A
76028	EASTLEIGH - 71A	EASTLEIGH - 71A	EASTLEIGH - 71A	EASTLEIGH - 71A	EASTLEIGH - 71A	EASTLEIGH - 71A	EASTLEIGH - 71A
76029	EASTLEIGH - 71A	EASTLEIGH - 71A	EASTLEIGH - 71A	EASTLEIGH - 71A	EASTLEIGH - 71A	EASTLEIGH - 71A	EASTLEIGH - 71A
				BR5 4-6-0			
73050				BATH (S&D) - 71G	BATH (S&D) - 71G	BATH (S&D) - 71G	BATH (S&D) - 71G
73051				BATH (S&D) - 71G	BATH (S&D) - 71G	BATH (S&D) - 71G	BATH (S&D) - 71G
				BR7 4-6-2 (1951)			
70004	STEWARTS LANE - 73A	STEWARTS LANE - 73A	STEWARTS LANE - 73A	STEWARTS LANE - 73A	STEWARTS LANE - 73A	STEWARTS LANE - 73A	STEWARTS LANE - 73A
70014	STEWARTS LANE - 73A	STEWARTS LANE - 73A	STEWARTS LANE - 73A	STEWARTS LANE - 73A	STEWARTS LANE - 73A	STEWARTS LANE - 73A	STEWARTS LANE - 73A

A 1956 midday at Stewarts Lane and Britannia 70014 'Iron Duke' is prepared for the 13.00 Continental express to Folkestone Junction (where the train will be handed over to a brace of R1 0-6-0's). After reaching Folkestone the engine worked empty stock to Dover Marine and returned to London with the 16.58 Golden Arrow to Victoria. In the Autumn of 1958 70014 was moved to Trafford Park as part of a scheme to provide class 7 power for the Manchester - St Pancras expresses.

loco	Feb-55	Apr-55	Jun-55	Aug-55	Sep-55	Nov-55	Dec-55
				BR3 2-6-2T			
82010	EXMOUTH JCN - 72A	EXMOUTH JCN - 72A	EXMOUTH JCN - 72A	EXMOUTH JCN - 72A	EXMOUTH JCN - 72A	EXMOUTH JCN - 72A	EXMOUTH JCN - 72A
82011	EXMOUTH JCN - 72A	EXMOUTH JCN - 72A	EXMOUTH JCN - 72A	EXMOUTH JCN - 72A	EXMOUTH JCN - 72A	EXMOUTH JCN - 72A	EXMOUTH JCN - 72A
82012	EASTLEIGH - 71A	EASTLEIGH - 71A	EASTLEIGH - 71A	EASTLEIGH - 71A	EASTLEIGH - 71A	EASTLEIGH - 71A	EASTLEIGH - 71A
82013	EXMOUTH JCN - 72A	EXMOUTH JCN - 72A	EXMOUTH JCN - 72A	EXMOUTH JCN - 72A	EXMOUTH JCN - 72A	EXMOUTH JCN - 72A	EXMOUTH JCN - 72A
82014	EASTLEIGH - 71A	EASTLEIGH - 71A	EASTLEIGH - 71A	EASTLEIGH - 71A	EASTLEIGH - 71A	EASTLEIGH - 71A	EASTLEIGH - 71A
82015	EASTLEIGH - 71A	EASTLEIGH - 71A	EASTLEIGH - 71A	EASTLEIGH - 71A	EASTLEIGH - 71A	EASTLEIGH - 71A	EASTLEIGH - 71A
82016	EASTLEIGH - 71A	EASTLEIGH - 71A	EASTLEIGH - 71A	EASTLEIGH - 71A	EASTLEIGH - 71A	EASTLEIGH - 71A	EASTLEIGH - 71A
82017	EXMOUTH JCN - 72A	EXMOUTH JCN - 72A	EXMOUTH JCN - 72A	EXMOUTH JCN - 72A	EXMOUTH JCN - 72A	EXMOUTH JCN - 72A	EXMOUTH JCN - 72A
82018	EXMOUTH JCN - 72A	EXMOUTH JCN - 72A	EXMOUTH JCN - 72A	EXMOUTH JCN - 72A	EXMOUTH JCN - 72A	EXMOUTH JCN - 72A	EXMOUTH JCN - 72A
82019	EXMOUTH JCN - 72A	EXMOUTH JCN - 72A	EXMOUTH JCN - 72A	EXMOUTH JCN - 72A	EXMOUTH JCN - 72A	EXMOUTH JCN - 72A	EXMOUTH JCN - 72A
82022	EXMOUTH JCN - 72A	EXMOUTH JCN - 72A	EXMOUTH JCN - 72A	EXMOUTH JCN - 72A	EXMOUTH JCN - 72A	EXMOUTH JCN - 72A	EXMOUTH JCN - 72A
82023	EXMOUTH JCN - 72A	EXMOUTH JCN - 72A	EXMOUTH JCN - 72A	EXMOUTH JCN - 72A	EXMOUTH JCN - 72A	EXMOUTH JCN - 72A	EXMOUTH JCN - 72A
82024	EXMOUTH JCN - 72A	EXMOUTH JCN - 72A	EXMOUTH JCN - 72A	EXMOUTH JCN - 72A	EXMOUTH JCN - 72A	EXMOUTH JCN - 72A	EXMOUTH JCN - 72A
82024	EXMOUTH JCN - 72A	EXMOUTH JCN - 72A	EXMOUTH JCN - 72A	EXMOUTH JCN - 72A	EXMOUTH JCN - 72A	EXMOUTH JCN - 72A	EXMOUTH JCN - 72A
82025	EXMOUTH JCN - 72A	EXMOUTH JCN - 72A	EXMOUTH JCN - 72A	EXMOUTH JCN - 72A	EXMOUTH JCN - 72A	EXMOUTH JCN - 72A	EXMOUTH JCN - 72A
				BR4 2-6-4T			
80010	T.WELLS - 75F	T.WELLS - 75F	T.WELLS - 75F	T.WELLS - 75F	T.WELLS - 75F	T.WELLS - 75F	T.WELLS - 75F
80011	T.WELLS - 75F	T.WELLS - 75F	T.WELLS - 75F	T.WELLS - 75F	T.WELLS - 75F	T.WELLS - 75F	T.WELLS - 75F
80012	T.WELLS - 75F	T.WELLS - 75F	T.WELLS - 75F	T.WELLS - 75F	T.WELLS - 75F	T.WELLS - 75F	T.WELLS - 75F
80013	T.WELLS - 75F	T.WELLS - 75F	T.WELLS - 75F	T.WELLS - 75F	T.WELLS - 75F	T.WELLS - 75F	T.WELLS - 75F
80014	T.WELLS - 75F	T.WELLS - 75F	T.WELLS - 75F	T.WELLS - 75F	T.WELLS - 75F	T.WELLS - 75F	T.WELLS - 75F
80015	T.WELLS - 75F	T.WELLS - 75F	T.WELLS - 75F	T.WELLS - 75F	T.WELLS - 75F	T.WELLS - 75F	T.WELLS - 75F
80016	BRIGHTON - 75A	BRIGHTON - 75A	BRIGHTON - 75A	BRIGHTON - 75A	BRIGHTON - 75A	BRIGHTON - 75A	BRIGHTON - 75A
80017	T.WELLS - 75F	T.WELLS - 75F	T.WELLS - 75F	T.WELLS - 75F	T.WELLS - 75F	T.WELLS - 75F	T.WELLS - 75F
80018	T.WELLS - 75F	T.WELLS - 75F	T.WELLS - 75F	T.WELLS - 75F	T.WELLS - 75F	T.WELLS - 75F	T.WELLS - 75F
80019	BRIGHTON - 75A	BRIGHTON - 75A	BRIGHTON - 75A	BRIGHTON - 75A	BRIGHTON - 75A	BRIGHTON - 75A	BRIGHTON - 75A
80031	BRIGHTON - 75A	BRIGHTON - 75A	BRIGHTON - 75A	BRIGHTON - 75A	BRIGHTON - 75A	BRIGHTON - 75A	BRIGHTON - 75A
80032	BRIGHTON - 75A	BRIGHTON - 75A	BRIGHTON - 75A	BRIGHTON - 75A	BRIGHTON - 75A	BRIGHTON - 75A	BRIGHTON - 75A
80032	BRIGHTON - 75A	BRIGHTON - 75A	BRIGHTON - 75A	BRIGHTON - 75A	BRIGHTON - 75A	BRIGHTON - 75A	BRIGHTON - 75A
80033	BRIGHTON - 75A	BRIGHTON - 75A	BRIGHTON - 75A	BRIGHTON - 75A	BRIGHTON - 75A	BRIGHTON - 75A	BRIGHTON - 75A
80033	BRIGHTON - 75A	BRIGHTON - 75A	BRIGHTON - 75A	BRIGHTON - 75A	BRIGHTON - 75A	BRIGHTON - 75A	BRIGHTON - 75A
				BR4 2-6-0			
76005	EASTLEIGH - 71A	EASTLEIGH - 71A	SALISBURY - 72B	SALISBURY - 72B	SALISBURY - 72B	SALISBURY - 72B	SALISBURY - 72B
76006	EASTLEIGH - 71A	EASTLEIGH - 71A	SALISBURY - 72B	SALISBURY - 72B	SALISBURY - 72B	SALISBURY - 72B	SALISBURY - 72B
76007	EASTLEIGH - 71A	EASTLEIGH - 71A	EASTLEIGH - 71A	SALISBURY - 72B	SALISBURY - 72B	SALISBURY - 72B	EASTLEIGH - 71A
76008	EASTLEIGH - 71A	EASTLEIGH - 71A	SALISBURY - 72B	SALISBURY - 72B	SALISBURY - 72B	SALISBURY - 72B	SALISBURY - 72B
76009	EASTLEIGH - 71A	EASTLEIGH - 71A	EASTLEIGH - 71A	EASTLEIGH - 71A	EASTLEIGH - 71A	EASTLEIGH - 71A	EASTLEIGH - 71A
76010	EASTLEIGH - 71A	EASTLEIGH - 71A	EASTLEIGH - 71A	EASTLEIGH - 71A	EASTLEIGH - 71A	EASTLEIGH - 71A	EASTLEIGH - 71A
76011	EASTLEIGH - 71A	EASTLEIGH - 71A	EASTLEIGH - 71A	EASTLEIGH - 71A	EASTLEIGH - 71A	EASTLEIGH - 71A	EASTLEIGH - 71A
76012	EASTLEIGH - 71A	EASTLEIGH - 71A	EASTLEIGH - 71A	EASTLEIGH - 71A	EASTLEIGH - 71A	EASTLEIGH - 71A	EASTLEIGH - 71A
76013	EASTLEIGH - 71A	EASTLEIGH - 71A	EASTLEIGH - 71A	EASTLEIGH - 71A	EASTLEIGH - 71A	EASTLEIGH - 71A	EASTLEIGH - 71A
76014	EASTLEIGH - 71A	EASTLEIGH - 71A	EASTLEIGH - 71A	EASTLEIGH - 71A	EASTLEIGH - 71A	EASTLEIGH - 71A	EASTLEIGH - 71A
76015	EASTLEIGH - 71A	EASTLEIGH - 71A	EASTLEIGH - 71A	EASTLEIGH - 71A	EASTLEIGH - 71A	EASTLEIGH - 71A	EASTLEIGH - 71A
76016	EASTLEIGH - 71A	EASTLEIGH - 71A	EASTLEIGH - 71A	EASTLEIGH - 71A	EASTLEIGH - 71A	EASTLEIGH - 71A	EASTLEIGH - 71A
76017	EASTLEIGH - 71A	EASTLEIGH - 71A	EASTLEIGH - 71A	EASTLEIGH - 71A	EASTLEIGH - 71A	EASTLEIGH - 71A	EASTLEIGH - 71A
76019	EASTLEIGH - 71A	EASTLEIGH - 71A	EASTLEIGH - 71A	EASTLEIGH - 71A	EASTLEIGH - 71A	EASTLEIGH - 71A	EASTLEIGH - 71A
76025	EASTLEIGH - 71A	EASTLEIGH - 71A	EASTLEIGH - 71A	EASTLEIGH - 71A	EASTLEIGH - 71A	EASTLEIGH - 71A	EASTLEIGH - 71A
76026	EASTLEIGH - 71A	EASTLEIGH - 71A	EASTLEIGH - 71A	EASTLEIGH - 71A	EASTLEIGH - 71A	EASTLEIGH - 71A	EASTLEIGH - 71A
76027	EASTLEIGH - 71A	EASTLEIGH - 71A	EASTLEIGH - 71A	EASTLEIGH - 71A	EASTLEIGH - 71A	EASTLEIGH - 71A	EASTLEIGH - 71A
76028	EASTLEIGH - 71A	EASTLEIGH - 71A	EASTLEIGH - 71A	EASTLEIGH - 71A	EASTLEIGH - 71A	EASTLEIGH - 71A	EASTLEIGH - 71A
76029	EASTLEIGH - 71A	EASTLEIGH - 71A	EASTLEIGH - 71A	EASTLEIGH - 71A	EASTLEIGH - 71A	EASTLEIGH - 71A	EASTLEIGH - 71A
76053		REDHILL - 75B	REDHILL - 75B	REDHILL - 75B	REDHILL - 75B	REDHILL - 75B	REDHILL - 75B
76054		REDHILL - 75B	REDHILL - 75B	REDHILL - 75B	REDHILL - 75B	REDHILL - 75B	REDHILL - 75B
76055		REDHILL - 75B	REDHILL - 75B	REDHILL - 75B	REDHILL - 75B	REDHILL - 75B	REDHILL - 75B
76056			REDHILL - 75B	REDHILL - 75B	REDHILL - 75B	REDHILL - 75B	REDHILL - 75B
76057			REDHILL - 75B	REDHILL - 75B	REDHILL - 75B	REDHILL - 75B	REDHILL - 75B
76058			REDHILL - 75B	REDHILL - 75B	REDHILL - 75B	REDHILL - 75B	REDHILL - 75B
76059			REDHILL - 75B	REDHILL - 75B	REDHILL - 75B	REDHILL - 75B	REDHILL - 75B
76060			REDHILL - 75B	REDHILL - 75B	REDHILL - 75B	REDHILL - 75B	REDHILL - 75B
76061				REDHILL - 75B	REDHILL - 75B	REDHILL - 75B	REDHILL - 75B
76062				REDHILL - 75B	REDHILL - 75B	REDHILL - 75B	REDHILL - 75B
				BR4 4-6-0			
75065				DOVER - 74C	DOVER - 74C	DOVER - 74C	DOVER - 74C
75066				DOVER - 74C	DOVER - 74C	DOVER - 74C	DOVER - 74C
75067					DOVER - 74C	DOVER - 74C	DOVER - 74C
75068					DOVER - 74C	DOVER - 74C	DOVER - 74C
75069					DOVER - 74C	DOVER - 74C	DOVER - 74C
75070						EXMOUTH JCN - 72A	EXMOUTH JCN - 72A
75071						EXMOUTH JCN - 72A	EXMOUTH JCN - 72A
75072						EXMOUTH JCN - 72A	EXMOUTH JCN - 72A
75073						EXMOUTH JCN - 72A	EXMOUTH JCN - 72A
75074						EXMOUTH JCN - 72A	EXMOUTH JCN - 72A
75075						EXMOUTH JCN - 72A	EXMOUTH JCN - 72A
75076							EXMOUTH JCN - 72A
				BR5 4-6-0			
73047				BATH(S&D) - 71G	BATH(S&D) - 71G	BATH(S&D) - 71G	BATH(S&D) - 71G
73049				BATH(S&D) - 71G	BATH(S&D) - 71G	BATH(S&D) - 71G	BATH(S&D) - 71G
73050	BATH(S&D) - 71G	BATH(S&D) - 71G	BATH(S&D) - 71G	BATH(S&D) - 71G	BATH(S&D) - 71G	BATH(S&D) - 71G	BATH(S&D) - 71G
73051	BATH(S&D) - 71G	BATH(S&D) - 71G	BATH(S&D) - 71G	BATH(S&D) - 71G	BATH(S&D) - 71G	BATH(S&D) - 71G	BATH(S&D) - 71G
73073		BATH(S&D) - 71G	BATH(S&D) - 71G	BATH(S&D) - 71G	BATH(S&D) - 71G	BATH(S&D) - 71G	BATH(S&D) - 71G
73074		BATH(S&D) - 71G	BATH(S&D) - 71G	BATH(S&D) - 71G	BATH(S&D) - 71G	BATH(S&D) - 71G	BATH(S&D) - 71G
73080			STEWARTS LANE - 73A	STEWARTS LANE - 73A	STEWARTS LANE - 73A	STEWARTS LANE - 73A	STEWARTS LANE - 73A
73081			STEWARTS LANE - 73A	STEWARTS LANE - 73A	STEWARTS LANE - 73A	STEWARTS LANE - 73A	STEWARTS LANE - 73A
73082			STEWARTS LANE - 73A	STEWARTS LANE - 73A	STEWARTS LANE - 73A	STEWARTS LANE - 73A	STEWARTS LANE - 73A
73083			STEWARTS LANE - 73A	STEWARTS LANE - 73A	STEWARTS LANE - 73A	STEWARTS LANE - 73A	STEWARTS LANE - 73A
73084				STEWARTS LANE - 73A	STEWARTS LANE - 73A	STEWARTS LANE - 73A	STEWARTS LANE - 73A
73085				STEWARTS LANE - 73A	STEWARTS LANE - 73A	STEWARTS LANE - 73A	STEWARTS LANE - 73A
73086				STEWARTS LANE - 73A	STEWARTS LANE - 73A	STEWARTS LANE - 73A	STEWARTS LANE - 73A
73087				STEWARTS LANE - 73A	STEWARTS LANE - 73A	STEWARTS LANE - 73A	STEWARTS LANE - 73A
73088				STEWARTS LANE - 73A	STEWARTS LANE - 73A	STEWARTS LANE - 73A	STEWARTS LANE - 73A
73089					STEWARTS LANE - 73A	STEWARTS LANE - 73A	STEWARTS LANE - 73A
73110						NINE ELMS - 70A	NINE ELMS - 70A
73111						NINE ELMS - 70A	NINE ELMS - 70A
73112						NINE ELMS - 70A	NINE ELMS - 70A
73113						NINE ELMS - 70A	NINE ELMS - 70A
73114						NINE ELMS - 70A	NINE ELMS - 70A
73114						NINE ELMS - 70A	NINE ELMS - 70A
73115						NINE ELMS - 70A	NINE ELMS - 70A
73116						NINE ELMS - 70A	NINE ELMS - 70A
73117						NINE ELMS - 70A	NINE ELMS - 70A
73118							NINE ELMS - 70A
73119							NINE ELMS - 70A
				BR7 4-6-2 (1951)			
70004	STEWARTS LANE - 73A	STEWARTS LANE - 73A	STEWARTS LANE - 73A	STEWARTS LANE - 73A	STEWARTS LANE - 73A	STEWARTS LANE - 73A	STEWARTS LANE - 73A
70014	STEWARTS LANE - 73A	STEWARTS LANE - 73A	STEWARTS LANE - 73A	STEWARTS LANE - 73A	STEWARTS LANE - 73A	STEWARTS LANE - 73A	STEWARTS LANE - 73A

loco	Jan-56	Apr-56	May-56	Aug-56	Oct-56	Nov-56	Jan-57
BR2 2-6-2T							
84020							FROM LMR
BR3 2-6-2T							
82010	EXMOUTH JCN - 72A	EXMOUTH JCN - 72A	EXMOUTH JCN - 72A	EXMOUTH JCN - 72A	EXMOUTH JCN - 72A	EXMOUTH JCN - 72A	EXMOUTH JCN - 72A
82011	EXMOUTH JCN - 72A	EXMOUTH JCN - 72A	EXMOUTH JCN - 72A	EXMOUTH JCN - 72A	EXMOUTH JCN - 72A	EXMOUTH JCN - 72A	EXMOUTH JCN - 72A
82012	EASTLEIGH - 71A	EASTLEIGH - 71A	EASTLEIGH - 71A	EASTLEIGH - 71A	EASTLEIGH - 71A	EASTLEIGH - 71A	EASTLEIGH - 71A
82013	EXMOUTH JCN - 72A	EXMOUTH JCN - 72A	EXMOUTH JCN - 72A	EXMOUTH JCN - 72A	EXMOUTH JCN - 72A	EXMOUTH JCN - 72A	EXMOUTH JCN - 72A
82014	EASTLEIGH - 71A	EASTLEIGH - 71A	EASTLEIGH - 71A	EASTLEIGH - 71A	EASTLEIGH - 71A	EASTLEIGH - 71A	EASTLEIGH - 71A
82015	EASTLEIGH - 71A	EASTLEIGH - 71A	EASTLEIGH - 71A	EASTLEIGH - 71A	EASTLEIGH - 71A	EASTLEIGH - 71A	EASTLEIGH - 71A
82016	EASTLEIGH - 71A	EASTLEIGH - 71A	EASTLEIGH - 71A	EASTLEIGH - 71A	EASTLEIGH - 71A	EASTLEIGH - 71A	EASTLEIGH - 71A
82017	EXMOUTH JCN - 72A	EXMOUTH JCN - 72A	EXMOUTH JCN - 72A	EXMOUTH JCN - 72A	EXMOUTH JCN - 72A	EXMOUTH JCN - 72A	EXMOUTH JCN - 72A
82018	EXMOUTH JCN - 72A	EXMOUTH JCN - 72A	EXMOUTH JCN - 72A	EXMOUTH JCN - 72A	EXMOUTH JCN - 72A	EXMOUTH JCN - 72A	EXMOUTH JCN - 72A
82019	EXMOUTH JCN - 72A	EXMOUTH JCN - 72A	EXMOUTH JCN - 72A	EXMOUTH JCN - 72A	EXMOUTH JCN - 72A	EXMOUTH JCN - 72A	EXMOUTH JCN - 72A
82022	EXMOUTH JCN - 72A	EXMOUTH JCN - 72A	EXMOUTH JCN - 72A	EXMOUTH JCN - 72A	EXMOUTH JCN - 72A	EXMOUTH JCN - 72A	EXMOUTH JCN - 72A
82023	EXMOUTH JCN - 72A	EXMOUTH JCN - 72A	EXMOUTH JCN - 72A	EXMOUTH JCN - 72A	EXMOUTH JCN - 72A	EXMOUTH JCN - 72A	EXMOUTH JCN - 72A
82024	EXMOUTH JCN - 72A	EXMOUTH JCN - 72A	EXMOUTH JCN - 72A	EXMOUTH JCN - 72A	EXMOUTH JCN - 72A	EXMOUTH JCN - 72A	EXMOUTH JCN - 72A
82024	EXMOUTH JCN - 72A	EXMOUTH JCN - 72A	EXMOUTH JCN - 72A	EXMOUTH JCN - 72A	EXMOUTH JCN - 72A	EXMOUTH JCN - 72A	EXMOUTH JCN - 72A
82025	EXMOUTH JCN - 72A	EXMOUTH JCN - 72A	EXMOUTH JCN - 72A	EXMOUTH JCN - 72A	EXMOUTH JCN - 72A	EXMOUTH JCN - 72A	EXMOUTH JCN - 72A
BR4 2-6-4T							
80010	T.WELLS - 75F	T.WELLS - 75F	T.WELLS - 75F	T.WELLS - 75F	T.WELLS - 75F	BRIGHTON - 75A	BRIGHTON - 75A
80011	T.WELLS - 75F	T.WELLS - 75F	T.WELLS - 75F	T.WELLS - 75F	T.WELLS - 75F	BRIGHTON - 75A	BRIGHTON - 75A
80012	T.WELLS - 75F	T.WELLS - 75F	T.WELLS - 75F	T.WELLS - 75F	T.WELLS - 75F	T.WELLS - 75F	T.WELLS - 75F
80013	T.WELLS - 75F	T.WELLS - 75F	T.WELLS - 75F	T.WELLS - 75F	T.WELLS - 75F	T.WELLS - 75F	T.WELLS - 75F
80014	T.WELLS - 75F	T.WELLS - 75F	T.WELLS - 75F	T.WELLS - 75F	T.WELLS - 75F	T.WELLS - 75F	T.WELLS - 75F
80015	T.WELLS - 75F	T.WELLS - 75F	BRIGHTON - 75A	BRIGHTON - 75A	BRIGHTON - 75A	T.WELLS - 75F	T.WELLS - 75F
80016	BRIGHTON - 75A	BRIGHTON - 75A	BRIGHTON - 75A	BRIGHTON - 75A	BRIGHTON - 75A	T.WELLS - 75F	T.WELLS - 75F
80017	T.WELLS - 75F	T.WELLS - 75F	BRIGHTON - 75A	BRIGHTON - 75A	BRIGHTON - 75A	T.WELLS - 75F	T.WELLS - 75F
80018	T.WELLS - 75F	T.WELLS - 75F	BRIGHTON - 75A	BRIGHTON - 75A	BRIGHTON - 75A	T.WELLS - 75F	T.WELLS - 75F
80019	BRIGHTON - 75A	BRIGHTON - 75A	BRIGHTON - 75A	BRIGHTON - 75A	BRIGHTON - 75A	T.WELLS - 75F	T.WELLS - 75F
80031	BRIGHTON - 75A	BRIGHTON - 75A	BRIGHTON - 75A	BRIGHTON - 75A	BRIGHTON - 75A	BRIGHTON - 75A	BRIGHTON - 75A
80032	BRIGHTON - 75A	BRIGHTON - 75A	BRIGHTON - 75A	BRIGHTON - 75A	BRIGHTON - 75A	BRIGHTON - 75A	BRIGHTON - 75A
80032	BRIGHTON - 75A	BRIGHTON - 75A	BRIGHTON - 75A	BRIGHTON - 75A	BRIGHTON - 75A	BRIGHTON - 75A	BRIGHTON - 75A
80033	BRIGHTON - 75A	BRIGHTON - 75A	BRIGHTON - 75A	BRIGHTON - 75A	BRIGHTON - 75A	BRIGHTON - 75A	BRIGHTON - 75A
80033	BRIGHTON - 75A	BRIGHTON - 75A	BRIGHTON - 75A	BRIGHTON - 75A	BRIGHTON - 75A	BRIGHTON - 75A	BRIGHTON - 75A
80145					BRIGHTON - 75A	BRIGHTON - 75A	BRIGHTON - 75A
80146						BRIGHTON - 75A	BRIGHTON - 75A
80147						BRIGHTON - 75A	BRIGHTON - 75A
80148						BRIGHTON - 75A	BRIGHTON - 75A
80149						BRIGHTON - 75A	BRIGHTON - 75A
80150						BRIGHTON - 75A	BRIGHTON - 75A
80151						BRIGHTON - 75A	BRIGHTON - 75A
80152						BRIGHTON - 75A	BRIGHTON - 75A
80153						BRIGHTON - 75A	BRIGHTON - 75A
80154						BRIGHTON - 75A	BRIGHTON - 75A

Although only 45-strong, the BR standard 3MT 2-6-2T's were widely dispersed with examples being allocated as far apart as Darlington, Wrexham, Newton Abbot and South Wales. The Southern contingent were for the most part allocated to Exmouth Junction for the Exeter - Exmouth branch although a small number were based at Eastleigh. In the last few years of steam the Southern 3MT's were brought up to Nine Elms as replacements for M7 0-4-4T's on empty stock workings between Waterloo and Clapham Junction.

loco	Jan-56	Apr-56	May-56	Aug-56	Oct-56	Nov-56	Jan-57
				BR4 2-6-0			
76005	SALISBURY-72B	SALISBURY-72B	SALISBURY-72B	SALISBURY-72B	SALISBURY-72B	SALISBURY-72B	SALISBURY-72B
76006	SALISBURY-72B	SALISBURY-72B	SALISBURY-72B	SALISBURY-72B	SALISBURY-72B	SALISBURY-72B	SALISBURY-72B
76007	EASTLEIGH-71A	EASTLEIGH-71A	EASTLEIGH-71A	EASTLEIGH-71A	EASTLEIGH-71A	EASTLEIGH-71A	EASTLEIGH-71A
76008	SALISBURY-72B	SALISBURY-72B	SALISBURY-72B	SALISBURY-72B	SALISBURY-72B	SALISBURY-72B	SALISBURY-72B
76009	EASTLEIGH-71A	EASTLEIGH-71A	EASTLEIGH-71A	REDHILL-75B	REDHILL-75B	REDHILL-75B	EASTLEIGH-71A
76010	EASTLEIGH-71A	EASTLEIGH-71A	EASTLEIGH-71A	EASTLEIGH-71A	EASTLEIGH-71A	EASTLEIGH-71A	EASTLEIGH-71A
76011	EASTLEIGH-71A	EASTLEIGH-71A	EASTLEIGH-71A	EASTLEIGH-71A	EASTLEIGH-71A	EASTLEIGH-71A	EASTLEIGH-71A
76012	EASTLEIGH-71A	EASTLEIGH-71A	EASTLEIGH-71A	EASTLEIGH-71A	EASTLEIGH-71A	EASTLEIGH-71A	EASTLEIGH-71A
76013	EASTLEIGH-71A	EASTLEIGH-71A	EASTLEIGH-71A	EASTLEIGH-71A	EASTLEIGH-71A	EASTLEIGH-71A	EASTLEIGH-71A
76014	EASTLEIGH-71A	EASTLEIGH-71A	EASTLEIGH-71A	REDHILL-75B	REDHILL-75B	REDHILL-75B	EASTLEIGH-71A
76015	EASTLEIGH-71A	EASTLEIGH-71A	EASTLEIGH-71A	EASTLEIGH-71A	EASTLEIGH-71A	EASTLEIGH-71A	EASTLEIGH-71A
76016	EASTLEIGH-71A	EASTLEIGH-71A	EASTLEIGH-71A	EASTLEIGH-71A	EASTLEIGH-71A	EASTLEIGH-71A	EASTLEIGH-71A
76017	EASTLEIGH-71A	EASTLEIGH-71A	EASTLEIGH-71A	EASTLEIGH-71A	EASTLEIGH-71A	EASTLEIGH-71A	EASTLEIGH-71A
76019	EASTLEIGH-71A	EASTLEIGH-71A	EASTLEIGH-71A	EASTLEIGH-71A	EASTLEIGH-71A	EASTLEIGH-71A	EASTLEIGH-71A
76025	EASTLEIGH-71A	EASTLEIGH-71A	EASTLEIGH-71A	EASTLEIGH-71A	EASTLEIGH-71A	EASTLEIGH-71A	EASTLEIGH-71A
76026	EASTLEIGH-71A	EASTLEIGH-71A	EASTLEIGH-71A	EASTLEIGH-71A	EASTLEIGH-71A	EASTLEIGH-71A	EASTLEIGH-71A
76027	EASTLEIGH-71A	EASTLEIGH-71A	EASTLEIGH-71A	EASTLEIGH-71A	EASTLEIGH-71A	EASTLEIGH-71A	EASTLEIGH-71A
76028	EASTLEIGH-71A	EASTLEIGH-71A	EASTLEIGH-71A	EASTLEIGH-71A	EASTLEIGH-71A	EASTLEIGH-71A	EASTLEIGH-71A
76029	EASTLEIGH-71A	EASTLEIGH-71A	EASTLEIGH-71A	EASTLEIGH-71A	EASTLEIGH-71A	EASTLEIGH-71A	EASTLEIGH-71A
76053	REDHILL-75B	REDHILL-75B	REDHILL-75B	REDHILL-75B	REDHILL-75B	REDHILL-75B	REDHILL-75B
76054	REDHILL-75B	REDHILL-75B	REDHILL-75B	REDHILL-75B	REDHILL-75B	REDHILL-75B	REDHILL-75B
76055	REDHILL-75B	REDHILL-75B	REDHILL-75B	REDHILL-75B	REDHILL-75B	REDHILL-75B	REDHILL-75B
76056	REDHILL-75B	REDHILL-75B	REDHILL-75B	REDHILL-75B	REDHILL-75B	REDHILL-75B	REDHILL-75B
76057	REDHILL-75B	REDHILL-75B	REDHILL-75B	REDHILL-75B	REDHILL-75B	REDHILL-75B	REDHILL-75B
76058	REDHILL-75B	REDHILL-75B	REDHILL-75B	REDHILL-75B	REDHILL-75B	REDHILL-75B	REDHILL-75B
76059	REDHILL-75B	REDHILL-75B	REDHILL-75B	REDHILL-75B	REDHILL-75B	REDHILL-75B	REDHILL-75B
76060	REDHILL-75B	REDHILL-75B	REDHILL-75B	REDHILL-75B	REDHILL-75B	REDHILL-75B	REDHILL-75B
76061	REDHILL-75B	REDHILL-75B	REDHILL-75B	REDHILL-75B	REDHILL-75B	REDHILL-75B	REDHILL-75B
76062	REDHILL-75B	REDHILL-75B	REDHILL-75B	REDHILL-75B	REDHILL-75B	REDHILL-75B	REDHILL-75B
76063				EASTLEIGH-71A	EASTLEIGH-71A	EASTLEIGH-71A	EASTLEIGH-71A
76064				EASTLEIGH-71A	EASTLEIGH-71A	EASTLEIGH-71A	EASTLEIGH-71A
76065				EASTLEIGH-71A	EASTLEIGH-71A	EASTLEIGH-71A	EASTLEIGH-71A
76066				EASTLEIGH-71A	EASTLEIGH-71A	EASTLEIGH-71A	EASTLEIGH-71A
76067				EASTLEIGH-71A	EASTLEIGH-71A	EASTLEIGH-71A	EASTLEIGH-71A
76068				EASTLEIGH-71A	EASTLEIGH-71A	EASTLEIGH-71A	EASTLEIGH-71A
76069				EASTLEIGH-71A	EASTLEIGH-71A	EASTLEIGH-71A	EASTLEIGH-71A
				BR4 4-6-0			
75065	DOVER-74C	DOVER-74C	DOVER-74C	DOVER-74C	DOVER-74C	DOVER-74C	DOVER-74C
75066	DOVER-74C	DOVER-74C	DOVER-74C	DOVER-74C	DOVER-74C	DOVER-74C	DOVER-74C
75067	DOVER-74C	DOVER-74C	DOVER-74C	DOVER-74C	DOVER-74C	DOVER-74C	DOVER-74C
75068	DOVER-74C	DOVER-74C	DOVER-74C	DOVER-74C	DOVER-74C	DOVER-74C	DOVER-74C
75069	DOVER-74C	DOVER-74C	DOVER-74C	DOVER-74C	DOVER-74C	DOVER-74C	DOVER-74C
75070	EXMOUTH JCN-72A	EXMOUTH JCN-72A	BATH(S&D)-71G	BATH(S&D)-71G	BATH(S&D)-71G	BATH(S&D)-71G	BATH(S&D)-71G
75071	EXMOUTH JCN-72A	EXMOUTH JCN-72A	BATH(S&D)-71G	BATH(S&D)-71G	BATH(S&D)-71G	BATH(S&D)-71G	BATH(S&D)-71G
75072	EXMOUTH JCN-72A	EXMOUTH JCN-72A	BATH(S&D)-71G	BATH(S&D)-71G	BATH(S&D)-71G	BATH(S&D)-71G	BATH(S&D)-71G
75073	EXMOUTH JCN-72A	EXMOUTH JCN-72A	EASTLEIGH-71A	EASTLEIGH-71A	EASTLEIGH-71A	EASTLEIGH-71A	EASTLEIGH-71A
75074	EXMOUTH JCN-72A	EXMOUTH JCN-72A	EASTLEIGH-71A	EASTLEIGH-71A	EASTLEIGH-71A	EASTLEIGH-71A	EASTLEIGH-71A
75075	EXMOUTH JCN-72A	EXMOUTH JCN-72A	BASINGSTOKE-70D	BASINGSTOKE-70D	BASINGSTOKE-70D	BASINGSTOKE-70D	BASINGSTOKE-70D
75076	EXMOUTH JCN-72A	EXMOUTH JCN-72A	BASINGSTOKE-70D	BASINGSTOKE-70D	BASINGSTOKE-70D	BASINGSTOKE-70D	BASINGSTOKE-70D
75077			BASINGSTOKE-70D	BASINGSTOKE-70D	BASINGSTOKE-70D	BASINGSTOKE-70D	BASINGSTOKE-70D
75078			BASINGSTOKE-70D	BASINGSTOKE-70D	BASINGSTOKE-70D	BASINGSTOKE-70D	BASINGSTOKE-70D
75079			BASINGSTOKE-70D	BASINGSTOKE-70D	BASINGSTOKE-70D	BASINGSTOKE-70D	BASINGSTOKE-70D
				BR5 4-6-0			
73047	BATH(S&D)-71G	BATH(S&D)-71G	BATH(S&D)-71G	BATH(S&D)-71G	BATH(S&D)-71G	BATH(S&D)-71G	BATH(S&D)-71G
73049	BATH(S&D)-71G	BATH(S&D)-71G	BATH(S&D)-71G	BATH(S&D)-71G	BATH(S&D)-71G	BATH(S&D)-71G	BATH(S&D)-71G
73050	BATH(S&D)-71G	BATH(S&D)-71G	BATH(S&D)-71G	BATH(S&D)-71G	BATH(S&D)-71G	BATH(S&D)-71G	BATH(S&D)-71G
73051	BATH(S&D)-71G	BATH(S&D)-71G	BATH(S&D)-71G	BATH(S&D)-71G	BATH(S&D)-71G	BATH(S&D)-71G	BATH(S&D)-71G
73073	BATH(S&D)-71G	BATH(S&D)-71G	BATH(S&D)-71G	BATH(S&D)-71G	BATH(S&D)-71G	BATH(S&D)-71G	BATH(S&D)-71G
73074	BATH(S&D)-71G	BATH(S&D)-71G	BATH(S&D)-71G	BATH(S&D)-71G	BATH(S&D)-71G	BATH(S&D)-71G	BATH(S&D)-71G
73080	STEWARTS LANE-73A	STEWARTS LANE-73A	STEWARTS LANE-73A	STEWARTS LANE-73A	STEWARTS LANE-73A	STEWARTS LANE-73A	STEWARTS LANE-73A
73081	STEWARTS LANE-73A	STEWARTS LANE-73A	STEWARTS LANE-73A	STEWARTS LANE-73A	STEWARTS LANE-73A	STEWARTS LANE-73A	STEWARTS LANE-73A
73082	STEWARTS LANE-73A	STEWARTS LANE-73A	STEWARTS LANE-73A	STEWARTS LANE-73A	STEWARTS LANE-73A	STEWARTS LANE-73A	STEWARTS LANE-73A
73083	STEWARTS LANE-73A	STEWARTS LANE-73A	STEWARTS LANE-73A	STEWARTS LANE-73A	STEWARTS LANE-73A	STEWARTS LANE-73A	STEWARTS LANE-73A
73084	STEWARTS LANE-73A	STEWARTS LANE-73A	STEWARTS LANE-73A	STEWARTS LANE-73A	STEWARTS LANE-73A	STEWARTS LANE-73A	STEWARTS LANE-73A
73085	STEWARTS LANE-73A	STEWARTS LANE-73A	STEWARTS LANE-73A	STEWARTS LANE-73A	STEWARTS LANE-73A	STEWARTS LANE-73A	STEWARTS LANE-73A
73086	STEWARTS LANE-73A	STEWARTS LANE-73A	STEWARTS LANE-73A	STEWARTS LANE-73A	STEWARTS LANE-73A	STEWARTS LANE-73A	STEWARTS LANE-73A
73087	STEWARTS LANE-73A	STEWARTS LANE-73A	STEWARTS LANE-73A	BATH(S&D)-71G	EASTLEIGH-71A	EASTLEIGH-71A	EASTLEIGH-71A
73088	STEWARTS LANE-73A	STEWARTS LANE-73A	STEWARTS LANE-73A	STEWARTS LANE-73A	STEWARTS LANE-73A	STEWARTS LANE-73A	STEWARTS LANE-73A
73089	STEWARTS LANE-73A	STEWARTS LANE-73A	STEWARTS LANE-73A	STEWARTS LANE-73A	STEWARTS LANE-73A	STEWARTS LANE-73A	STEWARTS LANE-73A
73110	NINE ELMS-70A	NINE ELMS-70A	NINE ELMS-70A	NINE ELMS-70A	NINE ELMS-70A	NINE ELMS-70A	NINE ELMS-70A
73111	NINE ELMS-70A	NINE ELMS-70A	NINE ELMS-70A	NINE ELMS-70A	NINE ELMS-70A	NINE ELMS-70A	NINE ELMS-70A
73112	NINE ELMS-70A	NINE ELMS-70A	NINE ELMS-70A	NINE ELMS-70A	NINE ELMS-70A	NINE ELMS-70A	NINE ELMS-70A
73113	NINE ELMS-70A	NINE ELMS-70A	NINE ELMS-70A	NINE ELMS-70A	NINE ELMS-70A	NINE ELMS-70A	NINE ELMS-70A
73114	NINE ELMS-70A	NINE ELMS-70A	NINE ELMS-70A	NINE ELMS-70A	NINE ELMS-70A	NINE ELMS-70A	NINE ELMS-70A
73114	NINE ELMS-70A	NINE ELMS-70A	NINE ELMS-70A	NINE ELMS-70A	NINE ELMS-70A	NINE ELMS-70A	NINE ELMS-70A
73115	NINE ELMS-70A	NINE ELMS-70A	NINE ELMS-70A	NINE ELMS-70A	NINE ELMS-70A	NINE ELMS-70A	NINE ELMS-70A
73116	NINE ELMS-70A	NINE ELMS-70A	NINE ELMS-70A	BATH(S&D)-71G	EASTLEIGH-71A	EASTLEIGH-71A	EASTLEIGH-71A
73117	NINE ELMS-70A	NINE ELMS-70A	NINE ELMS-70A	NINE ELMS-70A	NINE ELMS-70A	NINE ELMS-70A	NINE ELMS-70A
73118	NINE ELMS-70A	NINE ELMS-70A	NINE ELMS-70A	NINE ELMS-70A	NINE ELMS-70A	NINE ELMS-70A	NINE ELMS-70A
73119	NINE ELMS-70A	NINE ELMS-70A	NINE ELMS-70A	NINE ELMS-70A	NINE ELMS-70A	NINE ELMS-70A	NINE ELMS-70A
				BR7 4-6-2 (1951)			
70004	STEWARTS LANE-73A	STEWARTS LANE-73A	STEWARTS LANE-73A	STEWARTS LANE-73A	STEWARTS LANE-73A	STEWARTS LANE-73A	STEWARTS LANE-73A
70014	STEWARTS LANE-73A	STEWARTS LANE-73A	STEWARTS LANE-73A	STEWARTS LANE-73A	STEWARTS LANE-73A	STEWARTS LANE-73A	STEWARTS LANE-73A

loco	Mar-57	Jun-57	Jul-57	Oct-57	Jan-58	Feb-58	Mar-58
BR4 2-6-0							
76005	SALISBURY-72B	SALISBURY-72B	SALISBURY-72B	SALISBURY-72B	SALISBURY-72B	SALISBURY-72B	SALISBURY-72B
76006	SALISBURY-72B	SALISBURY-72B	SALISBURY-72B	SALISBURY-72B	SALISBURY-72B	SALISBURY-72B	SALISBURY-72B
76007	EASTLEIGH-71A	EASTLEIGH-71A	EASTLEIGH-71A	EASTLEIGH-71A	EASTLEIGH-71A	EASTLEIGH-71A	EASTLEIGH-71A
76008	SALISBURY-72B	SALISBURY-72B	SALISBURY-72B	SALISBURY-72B	SALISBURY-72B	SALISBURY-72B	SALISBURY-72B
76009	EASTLEIGH-71A	EASTLEIGH-71A	EASTLEIGH-71A	EASTLEIGH-71A	EASTLEIGH-71A	EASTLEIGH-71A	EASTLEIGH-71A
76010	EASTLEIGH-71A	EASTLEIGH-71A	EASTLEIGH-71A	EASTLEIGH-71A	EASTLEIGH-71A	EASTLEIGH-71A	EASTLEIGH-71A
76011	EASTLEIGH-71A	EASTLEIGH-71A	EASTLEIGH-71A	EASTLEIGH-71A	EASTLEIGH-71A	EASTLEIGH-71A	EASTLEIGH-71A
76012	EASTLEIGH-71A	EASTLEIGH-71A	EASTLEIGH-71A	EASTLEIGH-71A	EASTLEIGH-71A	EASTLEIGH-71A	EASTLEIGH-71A
76013	EASTLEIGH-71A	EASTLEIGH-71A	EASTLEIGH-71A	EASTLEIGH-71A	EASTLEIGH-71A	EASTLEIGH-71A	EASTLEIGH-71A
76014	EASTLEIGH-71A	EASTLEIGH-71A	EASTLEIGH-71A	EASTLEIGH-71A	EASTLEIGH-71A	EASTLEIGH-71A	EASTLEIGH-71A
76015	EASTLEIGH-71A	EASTLEIGH-71A	EASTLEIGH-71A	EASTLEIGH-71A	EASTLEIGH-71A	EASTLEIGH-71A	EASTLEIGH-71A
76016	EASTLEIGH-71A	EASTLEIGH-71A	EASTLEIGH-71A	EASTLEIGH-71A	EASTLEIGH-71A	EASTLEIGH-71A	EASTLEIGH-71A
76017	EASTLEIGH-71A	EASTLEIGH-71A	EASTLEIGH-71A	EASTLEIGH-71A	EASTLEIGH-71A	EASTLEIGH-71A	EASTLEIGH-71A
76019	EASTLEIGH-71A	EASTLEIGH-71A	EASTLEIGH-71A	EASTLEIGH-71A	EASTLEIGH-71A	EASTLEIGH-71A	EASTLEIGH-71A
76025	EASTLEIGH-71A	EASTLEIGH-71A	EASTLEIGH-71A	EASTLEIGH-71A	EASTLEIGH-71A	EASTLEIGH-71A	EASTLEIGH-71A
76026	EASTLEIGH-71A	EASTLEIGH-71A	EASTLEIGH-71A	EASTLEIGH-71A	EASTLEIGH-71A	EASTLEIGH-71A	EASTLEIGH-71A
76027	EASTLEIGH-71A	EASTLEIGH-71A	EASTLEIGH-71A	EASTLEIGH-71A	EASTLEIGH-71A	EASTLEIGH-71A	EASTLEIGH-71A
76028	EASTLEIGH-71A	EASTLEIGH-71A	EASTLEIGH-71A	EASTLEIGH-71A	EASTLEIGH-71A	EASTLEIGH-71A	EASTLEIGH-71A
76029	EASTLEIGH-71A	EASTLEIGH-71A	EASTLEIGH-71A	EASTLEIGH-71A	EASTLEIGH-71A	EASTLEIGH-71A	EASTLEIGH-71A
76053	REDHILL-75B	REDHILL-75B	REDHILL-75B	REDHILL-75B	REDHILL-75B	REDHILL-75B	REDHILL-75B
76054	REDHILL-75B	REDHILL-75B	REDHILL-75B	REDHILL-75B	REDHILL-75B	REDHILL-75B	REDHILL-75B
76055	REDHILL-75B	REDHILL-75B	REDHILL-75B	REDHILL-75B	REDHILL-75B	REDHILL-75B	REDHILL-75B
76056	REDHILL-75B	REDHILL-75B	REDHILL-75B	REDHILL-75B	REDHILL-75B	REDHILL-75B	REDHILL-75B
76057	REDHILL-75B	REDHILL-75B	REDHILL-75B	REDHILL-75B	REDHILL-75B	REDHILL-75B	REDHILL-75B
76058	REDHILL-75B	REDHILL-75B	REDHILL-75B	REDHILL-75B	REDHILL-75B	REDHILL-75B	REDHILL-75B
76059	REDHILL-75B	REDHILL-75B	REDHILL-75B	REDHILL-75B	REDHILL-75B	REDHILL-75B	REDHILL-75B
76060	REDHILL-75B	REDHILL-75B	REDHILL-75B	REDHILL-75B	REDHILL-75B	REDHILL-75B	REDHILL-75B
76061	REDHILL-75B	REDHILL-75B	REDHILL-75B	REDHILL-75B	REDHILL-75B	REDHILL-75B	REDHILL-75B
76062	REDHILL-75B	REDHILL-75B	REDHILL-75B	REDHILL-75B	REDHILL-75B	REDHILL-75B	REDHILL-75B
76063	EASTLEIGH-71A	EASTLEIGH-71A	EASTLEIGH-71A	EASTLEIGH-71A	EASTLEIGH-71A	EASTLEIGH-71A	EASTLEIGH-71A
76064	EASTLEIGH-71A	EASTLEIGH-71A	EASTLEIGH-71A	EASTLEIGH-71A	EASTLEIGH-71A	EASTLEIGH-71A	EASTLEIGH-71A
76065	EASTLEIGH-71A	EASTLEIGH-71A	EASTLEIGH-71A	EASTLEIGH-71A	EASTLEIGH-71A	EASTLEIGH-71A	EASTLEIGH-71A
76066	EASTLEIGH-71A	EASTLEIGH-71A	EASTLEIGH-71A	EASTLEIGH-71A	EASTLEIGH-71A	EASTLEIGH-71A	EASTLEIGH-71A
76067	EASTLEIGH-71A	EASTLEIGH-71A	EASTLEIGH-71A	EASTLEIGH-71A	EASTLEIGH-71A	EASTLEIGH-71A	EASTLEIGH-71A
76068	EASTLEIGH-71A	EASTLEIGH-71A	EASTLEIGH-71A	EASTLEIGH-71A	EASTLEIGH-71A	EASTLEIGH-71A	EASTLEIGH-71A
76069	EASTLEIGH-71A	EASTLEIGH-71A	EASTLEIGH-71A	EASTLEIGH-71A	EASTLEIGH-71A	EASTLEIGH-71A	EASTLEIGH-71A
BR4 4-6-0							
75065	DOVER-74C	DOVER-74C	DOVER-74C	DOVER-74C	DOVER-74C	DOVER-74C	DOVER-74C
75066	DOVER-74C	DOVER-74C	DOVER-74C	DOVER-74C	DOVER-74C	DOVER-74C	DOVER-74C
75067	DOVER-74C	DOVER-74C	DOVER-74C	DOVER-74C	DOVER-74C	DOVER-74C	DOVER-74C
75068	DOVER-74C	DOVER-74C	DOVER-74C	DOVER-74C	DOVER-74C	DOVER-74C	DOVER-74C
75069	DOVER-74C	DOVER-74C	DOVER-74C	DOVER-74C	DOVER-74C	DOVER-74C	DOVER-74C
75070	EASTLEIGH-71A	EASTLEIGH-71A	EASTLEIGH-71A	EASTLEIGH-71A	EASTLEIGH-71A	EASTLEIGH-71A	EASTLEIGH-71A
75071	BATH(S&D)-71G	BATH(S&D)-71G	BATH(S&D)-71G	BATH(S&D)-71G	BATH(S&D)-71G	BATH(S&D)-82F	BATH(S&D)-82F
75072	BATH(S&D)-71G	BATH(S&D)-71G	BATH(S&D)-71G	BATH(S&D)-71G	BATH(S&D)-71G	BATH(S&D)-82F	BATH(S&D)-82F
75073	BATH(S&D)-71G	BATH(S&D)-71G	BATH(S&D)-71G	BATH(S&D)-71G	BATH(S&D)-71G	BATH(S&D)-82F	BATH(S&D)-82F
75074	EASTLEIGH-71A	EASTLEIGH-71A	EASTLEIGH-71A	BASINGSTOKE-70D	BASINGSTOKE-70D	BASINGSTOKE-70D	BASINGSTOKE-70D
75075	BASINGSTOKE-70D	BASINGSTOKE-70D	BASINGSTOKE-70D	BASINGSTOKE-70D	BASINGSTOKE-70D	BASINGSTOKE-70D	BASINGSTOKE-70D
75076	BASINGSTOKE-70D	BASINGSTOKE-70D	BASINGSTOKE-70D	BASINGSTOKE-70D	BASINGSTOKE-70D	BASINGSTOKE-70D	BASINGSTOKE-70D
75077	BASINGSTOKE-70D	BASINGSTOKE-70D	BASINGSTOKE-70D	BASINGSTOKE-70D	BASINGSTOKE-70D	BASINGSTOKE-70D	BASINGSTOKE-70D
75078	BASINGSTOKE-70D	BASINGSTOKE-70D	BASINGSTOKE-70D	BASINGSTOKE-70D	BASINGSTOKE-70D	BASINGSTOKE-70D	BASINGSTOKE-70D
75079	BASINGSTOKE-70D	BASINGSTOKE-70D	BASINGSTOKE-70D	BASINGSTOKE-70D	BASINGSTOKE-70D	BASINGSTOKE-70D	BASINGSTOKE-70D
BR5 4-6-0							
73047	BATH(S&D)-71G	BATH(S&D)-71G	BATH(S&D)-71G	BATH(S&D)-71G	BATH(S&D)-71G	BATH(S&D)-82F	BATH(S&D)-82F
73049	BATH(S&D)-71G	BATH(S&D)-71G	BATH(S&D)-71G	BATH(S&D)-71G	BATH(S&D)-71G	BATH(S&D)-82F	BATH(S&D)-82F
73050	BATH(S&D)-71G	BATH(S&D)-71G	BATH(S&D)-71G	BATH(S&D)-71G	BATH(S&D)-71G	BATH(S&D)-82F	BATH(S&D)-82F
73051	BATH(S&D)-71G	BATH(S&D)-71G	BATH(S&D)-71G	BATH(S&D)-71G	BATH(S&D)-71G	BATH(S&D)-82F	BATH(S&D)-82F
73073	BATH(S&D)-71G	BATH(S&D)-71G	BATH(S&D)-71G	BATH(S&D)-71G	BATH(S&D)-71G	BATH(S&D)-82F	BATH(S&D)-82F
73074	BATH(S&D)-71G	BATH(S&D)-71G	BATH(S&D)-71G	BATH(S&D)-71G	BATH(S&D)-71G	BATH(S&D)-82F	BATH(S&D)-82F
73080	STEWARTS LANE-73A	STEWARTS LANE-73A	STEWARTS LANE-73A	STEWARTS LANE-73A	STEWARTS LANE-73A	STEWARTS LANE-73A	STEWARTS LANE-73A
73081	STEWARTS LANE-73A	STEWARTS LANE-73A	STEWARTS LANE-73A	STEWARTS LANE-73A	STEWARTS LANE-73A	STEWARTS LANE-73A	STEWARTS LANE-73A
73082	STEWARTS LANE-73A	STEWARTS LANE-73A	STEWARTS LANE-73A	STEWARTS LANE-73A	STEWARTS LANE-73A	STEWARTS LANE-73A	STEWARTS LANE-73A
73083	STEWARTS LANE-73A	STEWARTS LANE-73A	STEWARTS LANE-73A	STEWARTS LANE-73A	STEWARTS LANE-73A	STEWARTS LANE-73A	STEWARTS LANE-73A
73084	STEWARTS LANE-73A	STEWARTS LANE-73A	STEWARTS LANE-73A	STEWARTS LANE-73A	STEWARTS LANE-73A	STEWARTS LANE-73A	STEWARTS LANE-73A
73085	STEWARTS LANE-73A	STEWARTS LANE-73A	STEWARTS LANE-73A	STEWARTS LANE-73A	STEWARTS LANE-73A	STEWARTS LANE-73A	STEWARTS LANE-73A
73086	STEWARTS LANE-73A	STEWARTS LANE-73A	STEWARTS LANE-73A	STEWARTS LANE-73A	STEWARTS LANE-73A	STEWARTS LANE-73A	STEWARTS LANE-73A
73087	EASTLEIGH-71A	EASTLEIGH-71A	BATH(S&D)-71G	STEWARTS LANE-73A	STEWARTS LANE-73A	STEWARTS LANE-73A	STEWARTS LANE-73A
73088	STEWARTS LANE-73A	STEWARTS LANE-73A	STEWARTS LANE-73A	STEWARTS LANE-73A	STEWARTS LANE-73A	STEWARTS LANE-73A	STEWARTS LANE-73A
73089	STEWARTS LANE-73A	STEWARTS LANE-73A	STEWARTS LANE-73A	STEWARTS LANE-73A	STEWARTS LANE-73A	STEWARTS LANE-73A	STEWARTS LANE-73A
73110	NINE ELMS-70A	NINE ELMS-70A	NINE ELMS-70A	NINE ELMS-70A	NINE ELMS-70A	NINE ELMS-70A	NINE ELMS-70A
73111	NINE ELMS-70A	NINE ELMS-70A	NINE ELMS-70A	NINE ELMS-70A	NINE ELMS-70A	NINE ELMS-70A	NINE ELMS-70A
73112	NINE ELMS-70A	NINE ELMS-70A	NINE ELMS-70A	NINE ELMS-70A	NINE ELMS-70A	NINE ELMS-70A	NINE ELMS-70A
73113	NINE ELMS-70A	NINE ELMS-70A	NINE ELMS-70A	NINE ELMS-70A	NINE ELMS-70A	NINE ELMS-70A	NINE ELMS-70A
73114	NINE ELMS-70A	NINE ELMS-70A	NINE ELMS-70A	NINE ELMS-70A	NINE ELMS-70A	NINE ELMS-70A	NINE ELMS-70A
73114	NINE ELMS-70A	NINE ELMS-70A	NINE ELMS-70A	NINE ELMS-70A	NINE ELMS-70A	NINE ELMS-70A	NINE ELMS-70A
73115	NINE ELMS-70A	NINE ELMS-70A	NINE ELMS-70A	NINE ELMS-70A	NINE ELMS-70A	NINE ELMS-70A	NINE ELMS-70A
73116	EASTLEIGH-71A	EASTLEIGH-71A	BATH(S&D)-71G	NINE ELMS-70A	NINE ELMS-70A	NINE ELMS-70A	NINE ELMS-70A
73117	NINE ELMS-70A	NINE ELMS-70A	NINE ELMS-70A	NINE ELMS-70A	NINE ELMS-70A	NINE ELMS-70A	NINE ELMS-70A
73118	NINE ELMS-70A	NINE ELMS-70A	NINE ELMS-70A	NINE ELMS-70A	NINE ELMS-70A	NINE ELMS-70A	NINE ELMS-70A
73119	NINE ELMS-70A	NINE ELMS-70A	NINE ELMS-70A	NINE ELMS-70A	NINE ELMS-70A	NINE ELMS-70A	NINE ELMS-70A
BR7 4-6-2 (1951)							
70004	STEWARTS LANE-73A	STEWARTS LANE-73A	STEWARTS LANE-73A	STEWARTS LANE-73A	STEWARTS LANE-73A	STEWARTS LANE-73A	STEWARTS LANE-73A
70014	STEWARTS LANE-73A	STEWARTS LANE-73A	STEWARTS LANE-73A	STEWARTS LANE-73A	STEWARTS LANE-73A	STEWARTS LANE-73A	STEWARTS LANE-73A

loco	Mar-57	Jun-57	Jul-57	Oct-57	Jan-58	Feb-58	Mar-58
				BR2 2-6-2T			
84020	ASHFORD - 74A	ASHFORD - 74A	ASHFORD - 74A	ASHFORD - 74A	ASHFORD - 74A	ASHFORD - 74A	ASHFORD - 74A
84021		ASHFORD - 74A	ASHFORD - 74A	ASHFORD - 74A	ASHFORD - 74A	ASHFORD - 74A	ASHFORD - 74A
84022		ASHFORD - 74A	ASHFORD - 74A	ASHFORD - 74A	ASHFORD - 74A	ASHFORD - 74A	ASHFORD - 74A
84023		ASHFORD - 74A	ASHFORD - 74A	ASHFORD - 74A	ASHFORD - 74A	ASHFORD - 74A	ASHFORD - 74A
84024		ASHFORD - 74A	ASHFORD - 74A	ASHFORD - 74A	ASHFORD - 74A	ASHFORD - 74A	ASHFORD - 74A
84025		RAMSGATE - 74B	RAMSGATE - 74B	RAMSGATE - 74B	RAMSGATE - 74B	RAMSGATE - 74B	RAMSGATE - 74B
84026		RAMSGATE - 74B	RAMSGATE - 74B	RAMSGATE - 74B	RAMSGATE - 74B	RAMSGATE - 74B	RAMSGATE - 74B
84027		RAMSGATE - 74B	RAMSGATE - 74B	RAMSGATE - 74B	RAMSGATE - 74B	RAMSGATE - 74B	RAMSGATE - 74B
84028		RAMSGATE - 74B	RAMSGATE - 74B	RAMSGATE - 74B	RAMSGATE - 74B	RAMSGATE - 74B	RAMSGATE - 74B
84029		RAMSGATE - 74B	RAMSGATE - 74B	RAMSGATE - 74B	RAMSGATE - 74B	RAMSGATE - 74B	RAMSGATE - 74B
				BR3 2-6-2T			
82010	EXMOUTH JCN - 72A	EXMOUTH JCN - 72A	EXMOUTH JCN - 72A	EXMOUTH JCN - 72A	EXMOUTH JCN - 72A	EXMOUTH JCN - 72A	EXMOUTH JCN - 72A
82011	EXMOUTH JCN - 72A	EXMOUTH JCN - 72A	EXMOUTH JCN - 72A	EXMOUTH JCN - 72A	EXMOUTH JCN - 72A	EXMOUTH JCN - 72A	EXMOUTH JCN - 72A
82012	EASTLEIGH - 71A	EASTLEIGH - 71A	EASTLEIGH - 71A	EASTLEIGH - 71A	EASTLEIGH - 71A	EASTLEIGH - 71A	EASTLEIGH - 71A
82013	EXMOUTH JCN - 72A	EXMOUTH JCN - 72A	EXMOUTH JCN - 72A	EXMOUTH JCN - 72A	EXMOUTH JCN - 72A	EXMOUTH JCN - 72A	EXMOUTH JCN - 72A
82014	EASTLEIGH - 71A	EASTLEIGH - 71A	EASTLEIGH - 71A	EASTLEIGH - 71A	EASTLEIGH - 71A	EASTLEIGH - 71A	EASTLEIGH - 71A
82015	EASTLEIGH - 71A	EASTLEIGH - 71A	EASTLEIGH - 71A	EASTLEIGH - 71A	EASTLEIGH - 71A	EASTLEIGH - 71A	EASTLEIGH - 71A
82016	EASTLEIGH - 71A	EASTLEIGH - 71A	EASTLEIGH - 71A	EASTLEIGH - 71A	EASTLEIGH - 71A	EASTLEIGH - 71A	EASTLEIGH - 71A
82017	EXMOUTH JCN - 72A	EXMOUTH JCN - 72A	EXMOUTH JCN - 72A	EXMOUTH JCN - 72A	EXMOUTH JCN - 72A	EXMOUTH JCN - 72A	EXMOUTH JCN - 72A
82018	EXMOUTH JCN - 72A	EXMOUTH JCN - 72A	EXMOUTH JCN - 72A	EXMOUTH JCN - 72A	EXMOUTH JCN - 72A	EXMOUTH JCN - 72A	EXMOUTH JCN - 72A
82019	EXMOUTH JCN - 72A	EXMOUTH JCN - 72A	EXMOUTH JCN - 72A	EXMOUTH JCN - 72A	EXMOUTH JCN - 72A	EXMOUTH JCN - 72A	EXMOUTH JCN - 72A
82022	EXMOUTH JCN - 72A	EXMOUTH JCN - 72A	EXMOUTH JCN - 72A	EXMOUTH JCN - 72A	EXMOUTH JCN - 72A	EXMOUTH JCN - 72A	EXMOUTH JCN - 72A
82023	EXMOUTH JCN - 72A	EXMOUTH JCN - 72A	EXMOUTH JCN - 72A	EXMOUTH JCN - 72A	EXMOUTH JCN - 72A	EXMOUTH JCN - 72A	EXMOUTH JCN - 72A
82024	EXMOUTH JCN - 72A	EXMOUTH JCN - 72A	EXMOUTH JCN - 72A	EXMOUTH JCN - 72A	EXMOUTH JCN - 72A	EXMOUTH JCN - 72A	EXMOUTH JCN - 72A
82024	EXMOUTH JCN - 72A	EXMOUTH JCN - 72A	EXMOUTH JCN - 72A	EXMOUTH JCN - 72A	EXMOUTH JCN - 72A	EXMOUTH JCN - 72A	EXMOUTH JCN - 72A
82025	EXMOUTH JCN - 72A	EXMOUTH JCN - 72A	EXMOUTH JCN - 72A	EXMOUTH JCN - 72A	EXMOUTH JCN - 72A	EXMOUTH JCN - 72A	EXMOUTH JCN - 72A
				BR4 2-6-4T			
80010	BRIGHTON - 75A	BRIGHTON - 75A	BRIGHTON - 75A	BRIGHTON - 75A	BRIGHTON - 75A	BRIGHTON - 75A	BRIGHTON - 75A
80011	BRIGHTON - 75A	BRIGHTON - 75A	BRIGHTON - 75A	BRIGHTON - 75A	BRIGHTON - 75A	BRIGHTON - 75A	BRIGHTON - 75A
80012	T.WELLS - 75F	T.WELLS - 75F	T.WELLS - 75F	T.WELLS - 75F	T.WELLS - 75F	T.WELLS - 75F	BRIGHTON - 75A
80013	T.WELLS - 75F	T.WELLS - 75F	T.WELLS - 75F	T.WELLS - 75F	T.WELLS - 75F	T.WELLS - 75F	T.WELLS - 75F
80014	T.WELLS - 75F	T.WELLS - 75F	T.WELLS - 75F	T.WELLS - 75F	T.WELLS - 75F	T.WELLS - 75F	T.WELLS - 75F
80015	T.WELLS - 75F	T.WELLS - 75F	T.WELLS - 75F	T.WELLS - 75F	T.WELLS - 75F	T.WELLS - 75F	T.WELLS - 75F
80016	T.WELLS - 75F	T.WELLS - 75F	T.WELLS - 75F	T.WELLS - 75F	T.WELLS - 75F	T.WELLS - 75F	T.WELLS - 75F
80017	T.WELLS - 75F	T.WELLS - 75F	T.WELLS - 75F	T.WELLS - 75F	T.WELLS - 75F	T.WELLS - 75F	T.WELLS - 75F
80018	T.WELLS - 75F	T.WELLS - 75F	T.WELLS - 75F	T.WELLS - 75F	T.WELLS - 75F	T.WELLS - 75F	T.WELLS - 75F
80019	T.WELLS - 75F	T.WELLS - 75F	T.WELLS - 75F	T.WELLS - 75F	T.WELLS - 75F	T.WELLS - 75F	T.WELLS - 75F
80031	BRIGHTON - 75A	BRIGHTON - 75A	BRIGHTON - 75A	BRIGHTON - 75A	BRIGHTON - 75A	BRIGHTON - 75A	BRIGHTON - 75A
80032	BRIGHTON - 75A	BRIGHTON - 75A	BRIGHTON - 75A	BRIGHTON - 75A	BRIGHTON - 75A	BRIGHTON - 75A	BRIGHTON - 75A
80032	BRIGHTON - 75A	BRIGHTON - 75A	BRIGHTON - 75A	BRIGHTON - 75A	BRIGHTON - 75A	BRIGHTON - 75A	BRIGHTON - 75A
80033	BRIGHTON - 75A	BRIGHTON - 75A	BRIGHTON - 75A	BRIGHTON - 75A	BRIGHTON - 75A	BRIGHTON - 75A	BRIGHTON - 75A
80033	BRIGHTON - 75A	BRIGHTON - 75A	BRIGHTON - 75A	BRIGHTON - 75A	BRIGHTON - 75A	BRIGHTON - 75A	BRIGHTON - 75A
80145	BRIGHTON - 75A	BRIGHTON - 75A	BRIGHTON - 75A	BRIGHTON - 75A	BRIGHTON - 75A	BRIGHTON - 75A	BRIGHTON - 75A
80146	BRIGHTON - 75A	BRIGHTON - 75A	BRIGHTON - 75A	BRIGHTON - 75A	BRIGHTON - 75A	BRIGHTON - 75A	BRIGHTON - 75A
80147	BRIGHTON - 75A	BRIGHTON - 75A	BRIGHTON - 75A	BRIGHTON - 75A	BRIGHTON - 75A	BRIGHTON - 75A	BRIGHTON - 75A
80148	BRIGHTON - 75A	BRIGHTON - 75A	BRIGHTON - 75A	BRIGHTON - 75A	BRIGHTON - 75A	BRIGHTON - 75A	BRIGHTON - 75A
80149	BRIGHTON - 75A	BRIGHTON - 75A	BRIGHTON - 75A	BRIGHTON - 75A	BRIGHTON - 75A	BRIGHTON - 75A	BRIGHTON - 75A
80150	BRIGHTON - 75A	BRIGHTON - 75A	BRIGHTON - 75A	BRIGHTON - 75A	BRIGHTON - 75A	BRIGHTON - 75A	BRIGHTON - 75A
80151	BRIGHTON - 75A	BRIGHTON - 75A	BRIGHTON - 75A	BRIGHTON - 75A	BRIGHTON - 75A	BRIGHTON - 75A	BRIGHTON - 75A
80152	BRIGHTON - 75A	BRIGHTON - 75A	BRIGHTON - 75A	BRIGHTON - 75A	BRIGHTON - 75A	BRIGHTON - 75A	BRIGHTON - 75A
80153	BRIGHTON - 75A	BRIGHTON - 75A	BRIGHTON - 75A	BRIGHTON - 75A	BRIGHTON - 75A	BRIGHTON - 75A	BRIGHTON - 75A
80154	BRIGHTON - 75A	BRIGHTON - 75A	BRIGHTON - 75A	BRIGHTON - 75A	BRIGHTON - 75A	BRIGHTON - 75A	BRIGHTON - 75A

BR 5MT 4-6-0 73081 'Excalibur' of Nine Elms stands at Southampton Central with a Waterloo service; the fireman getting ready for the long climb up Micheldever bank. 73081 had originally been a Stewarts Lane engine and had spent from 1955 to 1959 working the Victoria - Ramsgate expresses after which it was sent to Nine Elms as a King Arthur replacement. In their early days on the semi-fast trains from Waterloo the Standard 5MT's could easily better the express electric timing of 27 minutes to Woking and in their final years on the Bournemouth and Weymouth expresses they put up performances far beyond those normally expected of a class 5 locomotive.

loco	May-58	Oct-58	Mar-59	Jun-59	Jul-59	Aug-59	Oct-59
				BR4 2-6-0			
76005	SALISBURY - 72B	SALISBURY - 72B	SALISBURY - 72B	SALISBURY - 72B	SALISBURY - 72B	SALISBURY - 72B	SALISBURY - 72B
76006	SALISBURY - 72B	SALISBURY - 72B	SALISBURY - 72B	SALISBURY - 72B	SALISBURY - 72B	SALISBURY - 72B	SALISBURY - 72B
76007	SALISBURY - 72B	SALISBURY - 72B	SALISBURY - 72B	SALISBURY - 72B	SALISBURY - 72B	SALISBURY - 72B	SALISBURY - 72B
76008	SALISBURY - 72B	SALISBURY - 72B	SALISBURY - 72B	SALISBURY - 72B	SALISBURY - 72B	SALISBURY - 72B	SALISBURY - 72B
76009	EASTLEIGH - 71A	YEOVIL - 72C	SALISBURY - 72B	SALISBURY - 72B	SALISBURY - 72B	SALISBURY - 72B	SALISBURY - 72B
76010	EASTLEIGH - 71A	YEOVIL - 72C	EASTLEIGH - 71A	EASTLEIGH - 71A	EASTLEIGH - 71A	EASTLEIGH - 71A	EASTLEIGH - 71A
76011	EASTLEIGH - 71A	YEOVIL - 72C	EASTLEIGH - 71A	EASTLEIGH - 71A	EASTLEIGH - 71A	EASTLEIGH - 71A	EASTLEIGH - 71A
76012	EASTLEIGH - 71A	EASTLEIGH - 71A	EASTLEIGH - 71A	EASTLEIGH - 71A	EASTLEIGH - 71A	EASTLEIGH - 71A	EASTLEIGH - 71A
76013	EASTLEIGH - 71A	EASTLEIGH - 71A	EASTLEIGH - 71A	EASTLEIGH - 71A	EASTLEIGH - 71A	EASTLEIGH - 71A	EASTLEIGH - 71A
76014	EASTLEIGH - 71A	EASTLEIGH - 71A	EASTLEIGH - 71A	EASTLEIGH - 71A	EASTLEIGH - 71A	EASTLEIGH - 71A	EASTLEIGH - 71A
76015	EASTLEIGH - 71A	EASTLEIGH - 71A	EASTLEIGH - 71A	EASTLEIGH - 71A	EASTLEIGH - 71A	EASTLEIGH - 71A	EASTLEIGH - 71A
76016	EASTLEIGH - 71A	EASTLEIGH - 71A	EASTLEIGH - 71A	EASTLEIGH - 71A	EASTLEIGH - 71A	EASTLEIGH - 71A	EASTLEIGH - 71A
76017	EASTLEIGH - 71A	EASTLEIGH - 71A	EASTLEIGH - 71A	EASTLEIGH - 71A	EASTLEIGH - 71A	EASTLEIGH - 71A	EASTLEIGH - 71A
76019	EASTLEIGH - 71A	EASTLEIGH - 71A	EASTLEIGH - 71A	EASTLEIGH - 71A	EASTLEIGH - 71A	EASTLEIGH - 71A	EASTLEIGH - 71A
76025	EASTLEIGH - 71A	EASTLEIGH - 71A	EASTLEIGH - 71A	EASTLEIGH - 71A	EASTLEIGH - 71A	EASTLEIGH - 71A	EASTLEIGH - 71A
76026	EASTLEIGH - 71A	EASTLEIGH - 71A	EASTLEIGH - 71A	EASTLEIGH - 71A	EASTLEIGH - 71A	EASTLEIGH - 71A	EASTLEIGH - 71A
76027	EASTLEIGH - 71A	EASTLEIGH - 71A	EASTLEIGH - 71A	EASTLEIGH - 71A	EASTLEIGH - 71A	EASTLEIGH - 71A	EASTLEIGH - 71A
76028	EASTLEIGH - 71A	EASTLEIGH - 71A	EASTLEIGH - 71A	EASTLEIGH - 71A	EASTLEIGH - 71A	EASTLEIGH - 71A	EASTLEIGH - 71A
76029	EASTLEIGH - 71A	EASTLEIGH - 71A	EASTLEIGH - 71A	EASTLEIGH - 71A	EASTLEIGH - 71A	EASTLEIGH - 71A	EASTLEIGH - 71A
76053	REDHILL - 75B	REDHILL - 75B	REDHILL - 75B	REDHILL - 75B	REDHILL - 75B	REDHILL - 75B	REDHILL - 75B
76054	REDHILL - 75B	REDHILL - 75B	REDHILL - 75B	REDHILL - 75B	REDHILL - 75B	REDHILL - 75B	REDHILL - 75B
76055	REDHILL - 75B	REDHILL - 75B	REDHILL - 75B	REDHILL - 75B	REDHILL - 75B	REDHILL - 75B	REDHILL - 75B
76056	REDHILL - 75B	REDHILL - 75B	REDHILL - 75B	REDHILL - 75B	REDHILL - 75B	REDHILL - 75B	REDHILL - 75B
76057	REDHILL - 75B	REDHILL - 75B	REDHILL - 75B	REDHILL - 75B	REDHILL - 75B	REDHILL - 75B	REDHILL - 75B
76058	REDHILL - 75B	REDHILL - 75B	REDHILL - 75B	REDHILL - 75B	REDHILL - 75B	REDHILL - 75B	REDHILL - 75B
76059	REDHILL - 75B	REDHILL - 75B	REDHILL - 75B	SALISBURY - 72B	SALISBURY - 72B	SALISBURY - 72B	SALISBURY - 72B
76060	REDHILL - 75B	REDHILL - 75B	REDHILL - 75B	SALISBURY - 72B	SALISBURY - 72B	SALISBURY - 72B	SALISBURY - 72B
76061	REDHILL - 75B	REDHILL - 75B	REDHILL - 75B	EASTLEIGH - 71A	EASTLEIGH - 71A	EASTLEIGH - 71A	EASTLEIGH - 71A
76062	REDHILL - 75B	REDHILL - 75B	REDHILL - 75B	EASTLEIGH - 71A	EASTLEIGH - 71A	EASTLEIGH - 71A	EASTLEIGH - 71A
76063	EASTLEIGH - 71A	EASTLEIGH - 71A	EASTLEIGH - 71A	EASTLEIGH - 71A	EASTLEIGH - 71A	EASTLEIGH - 71A	EASTLEIGH - 71A
76064	EASTLEIGH - 71A	EASTLEIGH - 71A	EASTLEIGH - 71A	EASTLEIGH - 71A	EASTLEIGH - 71A	EASTLEIGH - 71A	EASTLEIGH - 71A
76065	EASTLEIGH - 71A	EASTLEIGH - 71A	EASTLEIGH - 71A	EASTLEIGH - 71A	EASTLEIGH - 71A	EASTLEIGH - 71A	EASTLEIGH - 71A
76066	EASTLEIGH - 71A	EASTLEIGH - 71A	EASTLEIGH - 71A	EASTLEIGH - 71A	EASTLEIGH - 71A	EASTLEIGH - 71A	EASTLEIGH - 71A
76067	EASTLEIGH - 71A	EASTLEIGH - 71A	EASTLEIGH - 71A	EASTLEIGH - 71A	EASTLEIGH - 71A	EASTLEIGH - 71A	EASTLEIGH - 71A
76068	EASTLEIGH - 71A	EASTLEIGH - 71A	EASTLEIGH - 71A	EASTLEIGH - 71A	EASTLEIGH - 71A	EASTLEIGH - 71A	EASTLEIGH - 71A
76069	EASTLEIGH - 71A	EASTLEIGH - 71A	EASTLEIGH - 71A	EASTLEIGH - 71A	EASTLEIGH - 71A	EASTLEIGH - 71A	EASTLEIGH - 71A
				BR4 4-6-0			
75065	DOVER - 74C	DOVER - 73H	DOVER - 73H	EASTLEIGH - 71A	EASTLEIGH - 71A	EASTLEIGH - 71A	EASTLEIGH - 71A
75066	DOVER - 74C	DOVER - 73H	DOVER - 73H	EASTLEIGH - 71A	EASTLEIGH - 71A	EASTLEIGH - 71A	EASTLEIGH - 71A
75067	DOVER - 74C	DOVER - 73H	DOVER - 73H	EASTLEIGH - 71A	EASTLEIGH - 71A	EASTLEIGH - 71A	EASTLEIGH - 71A
75068	DOVER - 74C	DOVER - 73H	DOVER - 73H	EASTLEIGH - 71A	EASTLEIGH - 71A	EASTLEIGH - 71A	EASTLEIGH - 71A
75069	DOVER - 74C	DOVER - 73H	DOVER - 73H	EASTLEIGH - 71A	EASTLEIGH - 71A	EASTLEIGH - 71A	EASTLEIGH - 71A
75070	EASTLEIGH - 71A	EASTLEIGH - 71A	BRIGHTON - 75A	BRIGHTON - 75A	BRIGHTON - 75A	BRIGHTON - 75A	BRIGHTON - 75A
75071	BATH (S&D) - 82F	BATH (S&D) - 82F	BATH (S&D) - 82F	BATH (S&D) - 82F	BATH (S&D) - 82F	BATH (S&D) - 82F	BATH (S&D) - 82F
75072	BATH (S&D) - 82F	BATH (S&D) - 82F	BATH (S&D) - 82F	BATH (S&D) - 82F	BATH (S&D) - 82F	BATH (S&D) - 82F	BATH (S&D) - 82F
75073	BATH (S&D) - 82F	BATH (S&D) - 82F	BATH (S&D) - 82F	BATH (S&D) - 82F	BATH (S&D) - 82F	BATH (S&D) - 82F	BATH (S&D) - 82F
75074	BASINGSTOKE - 70D	BASINGSTOKE - 70D	STEWARTS LANE - 73A	STEWARTS LANE - 73A	STEWARTS LANE - 73A	STEWARTS LANE - 73A	STEWARTS LANE - 73A
75075	BASINGSTOKE - 70D	BASINGSTOKE - 70D	THREE BRIDGES - 75E	THREE BRIDGES - 75E	THREE BRIDGES - 75E	THREE BRIDGES - 75E	THREE BRIDGES - 75E
75076	BASINGSTOKE - 70D	BASINGSTOKE - 70D	BASINGSTOKE - 70D	BASINGSTOKE - 70D	BASINGSTOKE - 70D	BASINGSTOKE - 70D	BASINGSTOKE - 70D
75077	BASINGSTOKE - 70D	BASINGSTOKE - 70D	BASINGSTOKE - 70D	BASINGSTOKE - 70D	BASINGSTOKE - 70D	BASINGSTOKE - 70D	BASINGSTOKE - 70D
75078	BASINGSTOKE - 70D	BASINGSTOKE - 70D	BASINGSTOKE - 70D	BASINGSTOKE - 70D	BASINGSTOKE - 70D	BASINGSTOKE - 70D	BASINGSTOKE - 70D
75079	BASINGSTOKE - 70D	BASINGSTOKE - 70D	BASINGSTOKE - 70D	BASINGSTOKE - 70D	BASINGSTOKE - 70D	BASINGSTOKE - 70D	BASINGSTOKE - 70D
				BR5 4-6-0			
73017		WEYMOUTH - 71G	WEYMOUTH - 71G	WEYMOUTH - 71G	WEYMOUTH - 71G	WEYMOUTH - 71G	WEYMOUTH - 71G
73018		WEYMOUTH - 71G	WEYMOUTH - 71G	WEYMOUTH - 71G	WEYMOUTH - 71G	WEYMOUTH - 71G	WEYMOUTH - 71G
73020		WEYMOUTH - 71G	WEYMOUTH - 71G	WEYMOUTH - 71G	WEYMOUTH - 71G	WEYMOUTH - 71G	WEYMOUTH - 71G
73022		WEYMOUTH - 71G	WEYMOUTH - 71G	WEYMOUTH - 71G	WEYMOUTH - 71G	WEYMOUTH - 71G	WEYMOUTH - 71G
73029		WEYMOUTH - 71G	WEYMOUTH - 71G	WEYMOUTH - 71G	WEYMOUTH - 71G	WEYMOUTH - 71G	WEYMOUTH - 71G
73041				NINE ELMS - 70A	NINE ELMS - 70A	NINE ELMS - 70A	NINE ELMS - 70A
73042				NINE ELMS - 70A	NINE ELMS - 70A	NINE ELMS - 70A	NINE ELMS - 70A
73047	BATH (S&D) - 82F	BATH (S&D) - 82F	BATH (S&D) - 82F	BATH (S&D) - 82F	BATH (S&D) - 82F	BATH (S&D) - 82F	BATH (S&D) - 82F
73049	BATH (S&D) - 82F	BATH (S&D) - 82F	BATH (S&D) - 82F	BATH (S&D) - 82F	BATH (S&D) - 82F	BATH (S&D) - 82F	BATH (S&D) - 82F
73050	BATH (S&D) - 82F	BATH (S&D) - 82F	BATH (S&D) - 82F	BATH (S&D) - 82F	BATH (S&D) - 82F	BATH (S&D) - 82F	BATH (S&D) - 82F
73051	BATH (S&D) - 82F	BATH (S&D) - 82F	BATH (S&D) - 82F	BATH (S&D) - 82F	BATH (S&D) - 82F	BATH (S&D) - 82F	BATH (S&D) - 82F
73073	BATH (S&D) - 82F	BATH (S&D) - 82F	BATH (S&D) - 82F	BATH (S&D) - 82F	BATH (S&D) - 82F	BATH (S&D) - 82F	BATH (S&D) - 82F
73074	BATH (S&D) - 82F	BATH (S&D) - 82F	BATH (S&D) - 82F	BATH (S&D) - 82F	BATH (S&D) - 82F	BATH (S&D) - 82F	BATH (S&D) - 82F
73080	STEWARTS LANE - 73A	STEWARTS LANE - 73A	STEWARTS LANE - 73A	NINE ELMS - 70A	NINE ELMS - 70A	NINE ELMS - 70A	NINE ELMS - 70A
73081	STEWARTS LANE - 73A	STEWARTS LANE - 73A	STEWARTS LANE - 73A	NINE ELMS - 70A	NINE ELMS - 70A	NINE ELMS - 70A	NINE ELMS - 70A
73082	STEWARTS LANE - 73A	STEWARTS LANE - 73A	STEWARTS LANE - 73A	NINE ELMS - 70A	NINE ELMS - 70A	NINE ELMS - 70A	NINE ELMS - 70A
73083	STEWARTS LANE - 73A	STEWARTS LANE - 73A	STEWARTS LANE - 73A	NINE ELMS - 70A	NINE ELMS - 70A	NINE ELMS - 70A	NINE ELMS - 70A
73084	STEWARTS LANE - 73A	STEWARTS LANE - 73A	STEWARTS LANE - 73A	NINE ELMS - 70A	NINE ELMS - 70A	NINE ELMS - 70A	NINE ELMS - 70A
73085	STEWARTS LANE - 73A	STEWARTS LANE - 73A	STEWARTS LANE - 73A	NINE ELMS - 70A	NINE ELMS - 70A	NINE ELMS - 70A	NINE ELMS - 70A
73086	STEWARTS LANE - 73A	STEWARTS LANE - 73A	STEWARTS LANE - 73A	NINE ELMS - 70A	NINE ELMS - 70A	NINE ELMS - 70A	NINE ELMS - 70A
73087	TO WR	NINE ELMS - 70A	NINE ELMS - 70A	NINE ELMS - 70A	NINE ELMS - 70A	NINE ELMS - 70A	NINE ELMS - 70A
73088	STEWARTS LANE - 73A	NINE ELMS - 70A	NINE ELMS - 70A	NINE ELMS - 70A	NINE ELMS - 70A	NINE ELMS - 70A	NINE ELMS - 70A
73089	NINE ELMS - 70A	NINE ELMS - 70A	NINE ELMS - 70A	NINE ELMS - 70A	NINE ELMS - 70A	NINE ELMS - 70A	NINE ELMS - 70A
73110	NINE ELMS - 70A	NINE ELMS - 70A	NINE ELMS - 70A	NINE ELMS - 70A	NINE ELMS - 70A	NINE ELMS - 70A	NINE ELMS - 70A
73111	NINE ELMS - 70A	NINE ELMS - 70A	NINE ELMS - 70A	NINE ELMS - 70A	NINE ELMS - 70A	NINE ELMS - 70A	NINE ELMS - 70A
73112	NINE ELMS - 70A	NINE ELMS - 70A	NINE ELMS - 70A	NINE ELMS - 70A	NINE ELMS - 70A	NINE ELMS - 70A	NINE ELMS - 70A
73113	NINE ELMS - 70A	NINE ELMS - 70A	NINE ELMS - 70A	NINE ELMS - 70A	NINE ELMS - 70A	NINE ELMS - 70A	NINE ELMS - 70A
73114	NINE ELMS - 70A	NINE ELMS - 70A	NINE ELMS - 70A	NINE ELMS - 70A	NINE ELMS - 70A	NINE ELMS - 70A	NINE ELMS - 70A
73114	NINE ELMS - 70A	NINE ELMS - 70A	NINE ELMS - 70A	NINE ELMS - 70A	NINE ELMS - 70A	NINE ELMS - 70A	NINE ELMS - 70A
73115	NINE ELMS - 70A	NINE ELMS - 70A	NINE ELMS - 70A	NINE ELMS - 70A	NINE ELMS - 70A	NINE ELMS - 70A	NINE ELMS - 70A
73116	NINE ELMS - 70A	NINE ELMS - 70A	NINE ELMS - 70A	NINE ELMS - 70A	NINE ELMS - 70A	NINE ELMS - 70A	NINE ELMS - 70A
73117	NINE ELMS - 70A	NINE ELMS - 70A	NINE ELMS - 70A	NINE ELMS - 70A	NINE ELMS - 70A	NINE ELMS - 70A	NINE ELMS - 70A
73118	NINE ELMS - 70A	NINE ELMS - 70A	NINE ELMS - 70A	NINE ELMS - 70A	NINE ELMS - 70A	NINE ELMS - 70A	NINE ELMS - 70A
73119	NINE ELMS - 70A	NINE ELMS - 70A	NINE ELMS - 70A	NINE ELMS - 70A	NINE ELMS - 70A	NINE ELMS - 70A	NINE ELMS - 70A
				BR7 4-6-2 (1951)			
70004	STEWARTS LANE - 73A	TO LMR					
70014	STEWARTS LANE - 73A	TO LMR					

loco	May-58	Oct-58	Mar-59	Jun-59	Jul-59	Aug-59	Oct-59
BR2 2-6-2T							
84020	ASHFORD - 74A	ASHFORD - 73F	ASHFORD - 73F	ASHFORD - 73F	ASHFORD - 73F	ASHFORD - 73F	ASHFORD - 73F
84021	ASHFORD - 74A	ASHFORD - 73F	ASHFORD - 73F	ASHFORD - 73F	ASHFORD - 73F	ASHFORD - 73F	ASHFORD - 73F
84022	ASHFORD - 74A	ASHFORD - 73F	ASHFORD - 73F	ASHFORD - 73F	ASHFORD - 73F	ASHFORD - 73F	ASHFORD - 73F
84023	ASHFORD - 74A	ASHFORD - 73F	ASHFORD - 73F	ASHFORD - 73F	ASHFORD - 73F	ASHFORD - 73F	ASHFORD - 73F
84024	ASHFORD - 74A	ASHFORD - 73F	ASHFORD - 73F	ASHFORD - 73F	ASHFORD - 73F	ASHFORD - 73F	ASHFORD - 73F
84025	RAMSGATE - 74B	RAMSGATE - 73G	RAMSGATE - 73G	ASHFORD - 73F	ASHFORD - 73F	ASHFORD - 73F	ASHFORD - 73F
84026	RAMSGATE - 74B	RAMSGATE - 73G	RAMSGATE - 73G	ASHFORD - 73F	ASHFORD - 73F	ASHFORD - 73F	ASHFORD - 73F
84027	RAMSGATE - 74B	RAMSGATE - 73G	RAMSGATE - 73G	ASHFORD - 73F	ASHFORD - 73F	ASHFORD - 73F	ASHFORD - 73F
84028	RAMSGATE - 74B	RAMSGATE - 73G	RAMSGATE - 73G	ASHFORD - 73F	ASHFORD - 73F	ASHFORD - 73F	ASHFORD - 73F
84029	RAMSGATE - 74B	RAMSGATE - 73G	RAMSGATE - 73G	ASHFORD - 73F	ASHFORD - 73F	ASHFORD - 73F	ASHFORD - 73F
BR3 2-6-2T							
82010	EXMOUTH JCN - 72A	EXMOUTH JCN - 72A	EXMOUTH JCN - 72A	EXMOUTH JCN - 72A	EXMOUTH JCN - 72A	EXMOUTH JCN - 72A	EXMOUTH JCN - 72A
82011	EXMOUTH JCN - 72A	EXMOUTH JCN - 72A	EXMOUTH JCN - 72A	EXMOUTH JCN - 72A	EXMOUTH JCN - 72A	EXMOUTH JCN - 72A	EXMOUTH JCN - 72A
82012	EASTLEIGH - 71A	EASTLEIGH - 71A	EASTLEIGH - 71A	EASTLEIGH - 71A	EASTLEIGH - 71A	EASTLEIGH - 71A	EASTLEIGH - 71A
82013	EXMOUTH JCN - 72A	EXMOUTH JCN - 72A	EXMOUTH JCN - 72A	EXMOUTH JCN - 72A	EXMOUTH JCN - 72A	EXMOUTH JCN - 72A	EXMOUTH JCN - 72A
82014	EASTLEIGH - 71A	EASTLEIGH - 71A	EASTLEIGH - 71A	EASTLEIGH - 71A	EASTLEIGH - 71A	EASTLEIGH - 71A	EASTLEIGH - 71A
82015	EASTLEIGH - 71A	EASTLEIGH - 71A	EASTLEIGH - 71A	EASTLEIGH - 71A	EASTLEIGH - 71A	EASTLEIGH - 71A	EASTLEIGH - 71A
82016	EASTLEIGH - 71A	EASTLEIGH - 71A	EASTLEIGH - 71A	EASTLEIGH - 71A	EASTLEIGH - 71A	EASTLEIGH - 71A	EASTLEIGH - 71A
82017	EXMOUTH JCN - 72A	EXMOUTH JCN - 72A	EXMOUTH JCN - 72A	EXMOUTH JCN - 72A	EXMOUTH JCN - 72A	EXMOUTH JCN - 72A	EXMOUTH JCN - 72A
82018	EXMOUTH JCN - 72A	EXMOUTH JCN - 72A	EXMOUTH JCN - 72A	EXMOUTH JCN - 72A	EXMOUTH JCN - 72A	EXMOUTH JCN - 72A	EXMOUTH JCN - 72A
82019	EXMOUTH JCN - 72A	EXMOUTH JCN - 72A	EXMOUTH JCN - 72A	EXMOUTH JCN - 72A	EXMOUTH JCN - 72A	EXMOUTH JCN - 72A	EXMOUTH JCN - 72A
82022	EXMOUTH JCN - 72A	EXMOUTH JCN - 72A	EXMOUTH JCN - 72A	EXMOUTH JCN - 72A	EXMOUTH JCN - 72A	EXMOUTH JCN - 72A	EXMOUTH JCN - 72A
82023	EXMOUTH JCN - 72A	EXMOUTH JCN - 72A	EXMOUTH JCN - 72A	EXMOUTH JCN - 72A	EXMOUTH JCN - 72A	EXMOUTH JCN - 72A	EXMOUTH JCN - 72A
82024	EXMOUTH JCN - 72A	EXMOUTH JCN - 72A	EXMOUTH JCN - 72A	EXMOUTH JCN - 72A	EXMOUTH JCN - 72A	EXMOUTH JCN - 72A	EXMOUTH JCN - 72A
82024	EXMOUTH JCN - 72A	EXMOUTH JCN - 72A	EXMOUTH JCN - 72A	EXMOUTH JCN - 72A	EXMOUTH JCN - 72A	EXMOUTH JCN - 72A	EXMOUTH JCN - 72A
82025	EXMOUTH JCN - 72A	EXMOUTH JCN - 72A	EXMOUTH JCN - 72A	EXMOUTH JCN - 72A	EXMOUTH JCN - 72A	EXMOUTH JCN - 72A	EXMOUTH JCN - 72A
BR4 2-6-4T							
80010	BRIGHTON - 75A	BRIGHTON - 75A	THREE BRIDGES - 75E	THREE BRIDGES - 75E	THREE BRIDGES - 75E	THREE BRIDGES - 75E	THREE BRIDGES - 75E
80011	BRIGHTON - 75A	BRIGHTON - 75A	THREE BRIDGES - 75E	THREE BRIDGES - 75E	THREE BRIDGES - 75E	THREE BRIDGES - 75E	THREE BRIDGES - 75E
80012	BRIGHTON - 75A	BRIGHTON - 75A	THREE BRIDGES - 75E	THREE BRIDGES - 75E	THREE BRIDGES - 75E	THREE BRIDGES - 75E	THREE BRIDGES - 75E
80013	T.WELLS - 75F	T.WELLS - 75F	BRIGHTON - 75A	BRIGHTON - 75A	BRIGHTON - 75A	BRIGHTON - 75A	BRIGHTON - 75A
80014	T.WELLS - 75F	T.WELLS - 75F	T.WELLS - 75F	T.WELLS - 75F	T.WELLS - 75F	T.WELLS - 75F	T.WELLS - 75F
80015	T.WELLS - 75F	T.WELLS - 75F	T.WELLS - 75F	T.WELLS - 75F	T.WELLS - 75F	T.WELLS - 75F	T.WELLS - 75F
80016	T.WELLS - 75F	T.WELLS - 75F	T.WELLS - 75F	T.WELLS - 75F	T.WELLS - 75F	T.WELLS - 75F	T.WELLS - 75F
80017	T.WELLS - 75F	T.WELLS - 75F	T.WELLS - 75F	T.WELLS - 75F	T.WELLS - 75F	T.WELLS - 75F	T.WELLS - 75F
80018	T.WELLS - 75F	T.WELLS - 75F	T.WELLS - 75F	T.WELLS - 75F	T.WELLS - 75F	T.WELLS - 75F	T.WELLS - 75F
80019	T.WELLS - 75F	T.WELLS - 75F	T.WELLS - 75F	T.WELLS - 75F	T.WELLS - 75F	T.WELLS - 75F	T.WELLS - 75F
80031	BRIGHTON - 75A	BRIGHTON - 75A	BRIGHTON - 75A	BRIGHTON - 75A	BRIGHTON - 75A	BRIGHTON - 75A	BRIGHTON - 75A
80032	BRIGHTON - 75A	BRIGHTON - 75A	BRIGHTON - 75A	BRIGHTON - 75A	BRIGHTON - 75A	BRIGHTON - 75A	BRIGHTON - 75A
80032	BRIGHTON - 75A	BRIGHTON - 75A	BRIGHTON - 75A	BRIGHTON - 75A	BRIGHTON - 75A	BRIGHTON - 75A	BRIGHTON - 75A
80033	BRIGHTON - 75A	BRIGHTON - 75A	BRIGHTON - 75A	BRIGHTON - 75A	BRIGHTON - 75A	BRIGHTON - 75A	BRIGHTON - 75A
80033	BRIGHTON - 75A	BRIGHTON - 75A	BRIGHTON - 75A	BRIGHTON - 75A	BRIGHTON - 75A	BRIGHTON - 75A	BRIGHTON - 75A
80145	BRIGHTON - 75A	BRIGHTON - 75A	BRIGHTON - 75A	BRIGHTON - 75A	BRIGHTON - 75A	BRIGHTON - 75A	BRIGHTON - 75A
80146	BRIGHTON - 75A	BRIGHTON - 75A	BRIGHTON - 75A	BRIGHTON - 75A	BRIGHTON - 75A	BRIGHTON - 75A	BRIGHTON - 75A
80147	BRIGHTON - 75A	BRIGHTON - 75A	BRIGHTON - 75A	BRIGHTON - 75A	BRIGHTON - 75A	BRIGHTON - 75A	BRIGHTON - 75A
80148	BRIGHTON - 75A	BRIGHTON - 75A	BRIGHTON - 75A	BRIGHTON - 75A	BRIGHTON - 75A	BRIGHTON - 75A	BRIGHTON - 75A
80149	BRIGHTON - 75A	BRIGHTON - 75A	BRIGHTON - 75A	BRIGHTON - 75A	BRIGHTON - 75A	BRIGHTON - 75A	BRIGHTON - 75A
80150	BRIGHTON - 75A	BRIGHTON - 75A	BRIGHTON - 75A	BRIGHTON - 75A	BRIGHTON - 75A	BRIGHTON - 75A	BRIGHTON - 75A
80151	BRIGHTON - 75A	BRIGHTON - 75A	BRIGHTON - 75A	BRIGHTON - 75A	BRIGHTON - 75A	BRIGHTON - 75A	BRIGHTON - 75A
80152	BRIGHTON - 75A	BRIGHTON - 75A	BRIGHTON - 75A	BRIGHTON - 75A	BRIGHTON - 75A	BRIGHTON - 75A	BRIGHTON - 75A
80153	BRIGHTON - 75A	BRIGHTON - 75A	BRIGHTON - 75A	BRIGHTON - 75A	BRIGHTON - 75A	BRIGHTON - 75A	BRIGHTON - 75A
80154	BRIGHTON - 75A	BRIGHTON - 75A	BRIGHTON - 75A	BRIGHTON - 75A	BRIGHTON - 75A	BRIGHTON - 75A	BRIGHTON - 75A

BR 4MT 2-6-0 76009 passes Southampton Central with a special goods from Southampton Docks to Salisbury in June 1964. These engines arrived at Eastleigh in late 1952 as a replacement for D15 4-4-0's and performed a considerable amount of work on the Portsmouth - Salisbury route although they never succeeded in ousting the T9 4-4-0's. They were not regularly seen on the LSWR main line until the last years of steam when they took over from SR 2-6-0's the working of the two early morning stopping trains from Woking to Southampton.

loco	Dec-59	Feb-60	Mar-60	Apr-60	Jul-60	Aug-60	Sep-60	Nov-60
BR4 2-6-0								
76005	SALISBURY - 72B	SALISBURY - 72B	SALISBURY - 72B	SALISBURY - 72B	SALISBURY - 72B	SALISBURY - 72B	SALISBURY - 72B	SALISBURY - 72B
76006	SALISBURY - 72B	EASTLEIGH - 71A	EASTLEIGH - 71A	EASTLEIGH - 71A	EASTLEIGH - 71A	EASTLEIGH - 71A	EASTLEIGH - 71A	EASTLEIGH - 71A
76007	SALISBURY - 72B	SALISBURY - 72B	SALISBURY - 72B	SALISBURY - 72B	SALISBURY - 72B	SALISBURY - 72B	SALISBURY - 72B	SALISBURY - 72B
76008	SALISBURY - 72B	SALISBURY - 72B	SALISBURY - 72B	SALISBURY - 72B	SALISBURY - 72B	SALISBURY - 72B	SALISBURY - 72B	SALISBURY - 72B
76009	SALISBURY - 72B	EASTLEIGH - 71A	EASTLEIGH - 71A	EASTLEIGH - 71A	EASTLEIGH - 71A	EASTLEIGH - 71A	EASTLEIGH - 71A	EASTLEIGH - 71A
76010	EASTLEIGH - 71A	EASTLEIGH - 71A	EASTLEIGH - 71A	EASTLEIGH - 71A	EASTLEIGH - 71A	EASTLEIGH - 71A	EASTLEIGH - 71A	EASTLEIGH - 71A
76011	EASTLEIGH - 71A	EASTLEIGH - 71A	EASTLEIGH - 71A	EASTLEIGH - 71A	EASTLEIGH - 71A	EASTLEIGH - 71A	EASTLEIGH - 71A	EASTLEIGH - 71A
76012	EASTLEIGH - 71A	EASTLEIGH - 71A	EASTLEIGH - 71A	EASTLEIGH - 71A	EASTLEIGH - 71A	EASTLEIGH - 71A	EASTLEIGH - 71A	EASTLEIGH - 71A
76013	EASTLEIGH - 71A	EASTLEIGH - 71A	EASTLEIGH - 71A	EASTLEIGH - 71A	EASTLEIGH - 71A	EASTLEIGH - 71A	EASTLEIGH - 71A	EASTLEIGH - 71A
76014	EASTLEIGH - 71A	EASTLEIGH - 71A	EASTLEIGH - 71A	EASTLEIGH - 71A	EASTLEIGH - 71A	EASTLEIGH - 71A	EASTLEIGH - 71A	EASTLEIGH - 71A
76015	EASTLEIGH - 71A	EASTLEIGH - 71A	EASTLEIGH - 71A	EASTLEIGH - 71A	EASTLEIGH - 71A	EASTLEIGH - 71A	EASTLEIGH - 71A	EASTLEIGH - 71A
76016	EASTLEIGH - 71A	EASTLEIGH - 71A	EASTLEIGH - 71A	EASTLEIGH - 71A	EASTLEIGH - 71A	EASTLEIGH - 71A	EASTLEIGH - 71A	EASTLEIGH - 71A
76017	EASTLEIGH - 71A	SALISBURY - 72B	SALISBURY - 72B	SALISBURY - 72B	SALISBURY - 72B	SALISBURY - 72B	SALISBURY - 72B	SALISBURY - 72B
76019	EASTLEIGH - 71A	EASTLEIGH - 71A	EASTLEIGH - 71A	EASTLEIGH - 71A	EASTLEIGH - 71A	EASTLEIGH - 71A	EASTLEIGH - 71A	EASTLEIGH - 71A
76025	EASTLEIGH - 71A	EASTLEIGH - 71A	EASTLEIGH - 71A	EASTLEIGH - 71A	EASTLEIGH - 71A	EASTLEIGH - 71A	EASTLEIGH - 71A	EASTLEIGH - 71A
76026	EASTLEIGH - 71A	EASTLEIGH - 71A	EASTLEIGH - 71A	EASTLEIGH - 71A	EASTLEIGH - 71A	EASTLEIGH - 71A	EASTLEIGH - 71A	EASTLEIGH - 71A
76027	EASTLEIGH - 71A	EASTLEIGH - 71A	EASTLEIGH - 71A	EASTLEIGH - 71A	EASTLEIGH - 71A	EASTLEIGH - 71A	EASTLEIGH - 71A	EASTLEIGH - 71A
76028	EASTLEIGH - 71A	EASTLEIGH - 71A	EASTLEIGH - 71A	EASTLEIGH - 71A	EASTLEIGH - 71A	EASTLEIGH - 71A	EASTLEIGH - 71A	EASTLEIGH - 71A
76029	EASTLEIGH - 71A	EASTLEIGH - 71A	EASTLEIGH - 71A	EASTLEIGH - 71A	EASTLEIGH - 71A	EASTLEIGH - 71A	EASTLEIGH - 71A	EASTLEIGH - 71A
76053	REDHILL - 75B	REDHILL - 75B	REDHILL - 75B	SALISBURY - 72B	SALISBURY - 72B	SALISBURY - 72B	SALISBURY - 72B	SALISBURY - 72B
76054	REDHILL - 75B	REDHILL - 75B	REDHILL - 75B	SALISBURY - 72B	SALISBURY - 72B	SALISBURY - 72B	SALISBURY - 72B	SALISBURY - 72B
76055	REDHILL - 75B	REDHILL - 75B	REDHILL - 75B	SALISBURY - 72B	SALISBURY - 72B	SALISBURY - 72B	SALISBURY - 72B	SALISBURY - 72B
76056	BOURNEMOUTH - 71B	BOURNEMOUTH - 71B	BOURNEMOUTH - 71B	BOURNEMOUTH - 71B	BOURNEMOUTH - 71B	BOURNEMOUTH - 71B	BOURNEMOUTH - 71B	BOURNEMOUTH - 71B
76057	BOURNEMOUTH - 71B	BOURNEMOUTH - 71B	BOURNEMOUTH - 71B	BOURNEMOUTH - 71B	BOURNEMOUTH - 71B	BOURNEMOUTH - 71B	BOURNEMOUTH - 71B	BOURNEMOUTH - 71B
76058	BOURNEMOUTH - 71B	BOURNEMOUTH - 71B	BOURNEMOUTH - 71B	BOURNEMOUTH - 71B	BOURNEMOUTH - 71B	BOURNEMOUTH - 71B	BOURNEMOUTH - 71B	BOURNEMOUTH - 71B
76059	SALISBURY - 72B	EASTLEIGH - 71A	EASTLEIGH - 71A	EASTLEIGH - 71A	EASTLEIGH - 71A	EASTLEIGH - 71A	EASTLEIGH - 71A	EASTLEIGH - 71A
76060	SALISBURY - 72B	EASTLEIGH - 71A	EASTLEIGH - 71A	EASTLEIGH - 71A	EASTLEIGH - 71A	EASTLEIGH - 71A	EASTLEIGH - 71A	EASTLEIGH - 71A
76061	EASTLEIGH - 71A	EASTLEIGH - 71A	EASTLEIGH - 71A	EASTLEIGH - 71A	EASTLEIGH - 71A	EASTLEIGH - 71A	EASTLEIGH - 71A	EASTLEIGH - 71A
76062	EASTLEIGH - 71A	EASTLEIGH - 71A	EASTLEIGH - 71A	EASTLEIGH - 71A	EASTLEIGH - 71A	EASTLEIGH - 71A	EASTLEIGH - 71A	EASTLEIGH - 71A
76063	EASTLEIGH - 71A	EASTLEIGH - 71A	EASTLEIGH - 71A	EASTLEIGH - 71A	EASTLEIGH - 71A	EASTLEIGH - 71A	EASTLEIGH - 71A	EASTLEIGH - 71A
76064	EASTLEIGH - 71A	EASTLEIGH - 71A	EASTLEIGH - 71A	EASTLEIGH - 71A	EASTLEIGH - 71A	EASTLEIGH - 71A	EASTLEIGH - 71A	EASTLEIGH - 71A
76065	EASTLEIGH - 71A	EASTLEIGH - 71A	EASTLEIGH - 71A	EASTLEIGH - 71A	EASTLEIGH - 71A	EASTLEIGH - 71A	EASTLEIGH - 71A	EASTLEIGH - 71A
76066	EASTLEIGH - 71A	SALISBURY - 72B	SALISBURY - 72B	SALISBURY - 72B	SALISBURY - 72B	SALISBURY - 72B	SALISBURY - 72B	SALISBURY - 72B
76067	EASTLEIGH - 71A	SALISBURY - 72B	SALISBURY - 72B	SALISBURY - 72B	SALISBURY - 72B	SALISBURY - 72B	SALISBURY - 72B	SALISBURY - 72B
76068	EASTLEIGH - 71A	EASTLEIGH - 71A	EASTLEIGH - 71A	EASTLEIGH - 71A	EASTLEIGH - 71A	EASTLEIGH - 71A	EASTLEIGH - 71A	EASTLEIGH - 71A
76069	EASTLEIGH - 71A	EASTLEIGH - 71A	EASTLEIGH - 71A	EASTLEIGH - 71A	EASTLEIGH - 71A	EASTLEIGH - 71A	EASTLEIGH - 71A	EASTLEIGH - 71A
BR4 4-6-0								
75065	EASTLEIGH - 71A	EASTLEIGH - 71A	EASTLEIGH - 71A	EASTLEIGH - 71A	EASTLEIGH - 71A	EASTLEIGH - 71A	EASTLEIGH - 71A	EASTLEIGH - 71A
75066	EASTLEIGH - 71A	EASTLEIGH - 71A	EASTLEIGH - 71A	EASTLEIGH - 71A	EASTLEIGH - 71A	EASTLEIGH - 71A	EASTLEIGH - 71A	EASTLEIGH - 71A
75067	EASTLEIGH - 71A	EASTLEIGH - 71A	EASTLEIGH - 71A	EASTLEIGH - 71A	EASTLEIGH - 71A	EASTLEIGH - 71A	EASTLEIGH - 71A	EASTLEIGH - 71A
75068	EASTLEIGH - 71A	EASTLEIGH - 71A	EASTLEIGH - 71A	EASTLEIGH - 71A	EASTLEIGH - 71A	EASTLEIGH - 71A	EASTLEIGH - 71A	EASTLEIGH - 71A
75069	STEWARTS LANE - 73A	STEWARTS LANE - 73A	STEWARTS LANE - 73A	STEWARTS LANE - 73A	STEWARTS LANE - 73A	STEWARTS LANE - 73A	STEWARTS LANE - 73A	STEWARTS LANE - 73A
75070	BRIGHTON - 75A	THREE BRIDGES - 75E	THREE BRIDGES - 75E	THREE BRIDGES - 75E	THREE BRIDGES - 75E	THREE BRIDGES - 75E	THREE BRIDGES - 75E	THREE BRIDGES - 75E
75071	BATH (S&D) - 82F	BATH (S&D) - 82F	BATH (S&D) - 82F	BATH (S&D) - 82F	BATH (S&D) - 82F	BATH (S&D) - 82F	BATH (S&D) - 82F	BATH (S&D) - 82F
75072	BATH (S&D) - 82F	BATH (S&D) - 82F	BATH (S&D) - 82F	BATH (S&D) - 82F	BATH (S&D) - 82F	BATH (S&D) - 82F	BATH (S&D) - 82F	BATH (S&D) - 82F
75073	BATH (S&D) - 82F	BATH (S&D) - 82F	BATH (S&D) - 82F	BATH (S&D) - 82F	BATH (S&D) - 82F	BATH (S&D) - 82F	BATH (S&D) - 82F	BATH (S&D) - 82F
75074	STEWARTS LANE - 73A	STEWARTS LANE - 73A	STEWARTS LANE - 73A	STEWARTS LANE - 73A	STEWARTS LANE - 73A	STEWARTS LANE - 73A	STEWARTS LANE - 73A	STEWARTS LANE - 73A
75075	THREE BRIDGES - 75E	THREE BRIDGES - 75E	THREE BRIDGES - 75E	THREE BRIDGES - 75E	THREE BRIDGES - 75E	THREE BRIDGES - 75E	THREE BRIDGES - 75E	THREE BRIDGES - 75E
75076	BASINGSTOKE - 70D	BASINGSTOKE - 70D	BASINGSTOKE - 70D	BASINGSTOKE - 70D	BASINGSTOKE - 70D	BASINGSTOKE - 70D	BASINGSTOKE - 70D	BASINGSTOKE - 70D
75077	BASINGSTOKE - 70D	BASINGSTOKE - 70D	BASINGSTOKE - 70D	BASINGSTOKE - 70D	BASINGSTOKE - 70D	BASINGSTOKE - 70D	BASINGSTOKE - 70D	BASINGSTOKE - 70D
75078	BASINGSTOKE - 70D	BASINGSTOKE - 70D	BASINGSTOKE - 70D	BASINGSTOKE - 70D	BASINGSTOKE - 70D	BASINGSTOKE - 70D	BASINGSTOKE - 70D	BASINGSTOKE - 70D
75079	BASINGSTOKE - 70D	BASINGSTOKE - 70D	BASINGSTOKE - 70D	BASINGSTOKE - 70D	BASINGSTOKE - 70D	BASINGSTOKE - 70D	BASINGSTOKE - 70D	BASINGSTOKE - 70D
BR5 4-6-0								
73017	WEYMOUTH - 71G	WEYMOUTH - 71G	WEYMOUTH - 71G	WEYMOUTH - 71G	WEYMOUTH - 71G	WEYMOUTH - 71G	WEYMOUTH - 71G	WEYMOUTH - 71G
73018	WEYMOUTH - 71G	WEYMOUTH - 71G	WEYMOUTH - 71G	WEYMOUTH - 71G	WEYMOUTH - 71G	WEYMOUTH - 71G	WEYMOUTH - 71G	WEYMOUTH - 71G
73020	WEYMOUTH - 71G	WEYMOUTH - 71G	WEYMOUTH - 71G	WEYMOUTH - 71G	WEYMOUTH - 71G	WEYMOUTH - 71G	WEYMOUTH - 71G	WEYMOUTH - 71G
73022	WEYMOUTH - 71G	WEYMOUTH - 71G	WEYMOUTH - 71G	WEYMOUTH - 71G	WEYMOUTH - 71G	WEYMOUTH - 71G	WEYMOUTH - 71G	WEYMOUTH - 71G
73029	WEYMOUTH - 71G	WEYMOUTH - 71G	WEYMOUTH - 71G	WEYMOUTH - 71G	WEYMOUTH - 71G	WEYMOUTH - 71G	WEYMOUTH - 71G	WEYMOUTH - 71G
73041	WEYMOUTH - 71G	WEYMOUTH - 71G	WEYMOUTH - 71G	WEYMOUTH - 71G	WEYMOUTH - 71G	WEYMOUTH - 71G	WEYMOUTH - 71G	WEYMOUTH - 71G
73042	WEYMOUTH - 71G	WEYMOUTH - 71G	WEYMOUTH - 71G	WEYMOUTH - 71G	WEYMOUTH - 71G	WEYMOUTH - 71G	WEYMOUTH - 71G	WEYMOUTH - 71G
73047	BATH (S&D) - 82F	BATH (S&D) - 82F	BATH (S&D) - 82F	BATH (S&D) - 82F	BATH (S&D) - 82F	BATH (S&D) - 82F	BATH (S&D) - 82F	BATH (S&D) - 82F
73049	BATH (S&D) - 82F	BATH (S&D) - 82F	BATH (S&D) - 82F	BATH (S&D) - 82F	BATH (S&D) - 82F	BATH (S&D) - 82F	BATH (S&D) - 82F	BATH (S&D) - 82F
73050	BATH (S&D) - 82F	BATH (S&D) - 82F	BATH (S&D) - 82F	BATH (S&D) - 82F	BATH (S&D) - 82F	BATH (S&D) - 82F	BATH (S&D) - 82F	BATH (S&D) - 82F
73051	BATH (S&D) - 82F	BATH (S&D) - 82F	BATH (S&D) - 82F	BATH (S&D) - 82F	BATH (S&D) - 82F	BATH (S&D) - 82F	BATH (S&D) - 82F	BATH (S&D) - 82F
73073	BATH (S&D) - 82F	BATH (S&D) - 82F	BATH (S&D) - 82F	BATH (S&D) - 82F	BATH (S&D) - 82F	BATH (S&D) - 82F	BATH (S&D) - 82F	BATH (S&D) - 82F
73074	BATH (S&D) - 82F	BATH (S&D) - 82F	BATH (S&D) - 82F	BATH (S&D) - 82F	BATH (S&D) - 82F	BATH (S&D) - 82F	BATH (S&D) - 82F	BATH (S&D) - 82F
73080	WEYMOUTH - 71G	WEYMOUTH - 71G	WEYMOUTH - 71G	WEYMOUTH - 71G	WEYMOUTH - 71G	WEYMOUTH - 71G	WEYMOUTH - 71G	WEYMOUTH - 71G
73081	NINE ELMS - 70A	NINE ELMS - 70A	NINE ELMS - 70A	NINE ELMS - 70A	NINE ELMS - 70A	NINE ELMS - 70A	NINE ELMS - 70A	NINE ELMS - 70A
73082	NINE ELMS - 70A	NINE ELMS - 70A	NINE ELMS - 70A	NINE ELMS - 70A	NINE ELMS - 70A	NINE ELMS - 70A	NINE ELMS - 70A	NINE ELMS - 70A
73083	NINE ELMS - 70A	NINE ELMS - 70A	NINE ELMS - 70A	NINE ELMS - 70A	NINE ELMS - 70A	NINE ELMS - 70A	NINE ELMS - 70A	NINE ELMS - 70A
73084	NINE ELMS - 70A	NINE ELMS - 70A	NINE ELMS - 70A	NINE ELMS - 70A	NINE ELMS - 70A	NINE ELMS - 70A	NINE ELMS - 70A	NINE ELMS - 70A
73085	NINE ELMS - 70A	NINE ELMS - 70A	NINE ELMS - 70A	NINE ELMS - 70A	NINE ELMS - 70A	NINE ELMS - 70A	NINE ELMS - 70A	NINE ELMS - 70A
73086	NINE ELMS - 70A	NINE ELMS - 70A	NINE ELMS - 70A	NINE ELMS - 70A	NINE ELMS - 70A	NINE ELMS - 70A	NINE ELMS - 70A	NINE ELMS - 70A
73087	NINE ELMS - 70A	NINE ELMS - 70A	NINE ELMS - 70A	NINE ELMS - 70A	NINE ELMS - 70A	NINE ELMS - 70A	NINE ELMS - 70A	NINE ELMS - 70A
73088	NINE ELMS - 70A	NINE ELMS - 70A	NINE ELMS - 70A	NINE ELMS - 70A	NINE ELMS - 70A	NINE ELMS - 70A	NINE ELMS - 70A	NINE ELMS - 70A
73089	NINE ELMS - 70A	NINE ELMS - 70A	NINE ELMS - 70A	NINE ELMS - 70A	NINE ELMS - 70A	NINE ELMS - 70A	NINE ELMS - 70A	NINE ELMS - 70A
73110	NINE ELMS - 70A	NINE ELMS - 70A	NINE ELMS - 70A	NINE ELMS - 70A	NINE ELMS - 70A	NINE ELMS - 70A	NINE ELMS - 70A	NINE ELMS - 70A
73111	NINE ELMS - 70A	NINE ELMS - 70A	NINE ELMS - 70A	NINE ELMS - 70A	NINE ELMS - 70A	NINE ELMS - 70A	NINE ELMS - 70A	NINE ELMS - 70A
73112	NINE ELMS - 70A	NINE ELMS - 70A	NINE ELMS - 70A	NINE ELMS - 70A	NINE ELMS - 70A	NINE ELMS - 70A	NINE ELMS - 70A	NINE ELMS - 70A
73113	NINE ELMS - 70A	NINE ELMS - 70A	NINE ELMS - 70A	NINE ELMS - 70A	NINE ELMS - 70A	NINE ELMS - 70A	NINE ELMS - 70A	NINE ELMS - 70A
73114	NINE ELMS - 70A	NINE ELMS - 70A	NINE ELMS - 70A	NINE ELMS - 70A	NINE ELMS - 70A	NINE ELMS - 70A	NINE ELMS - 70A	NINE ELMS - 70A
73114	NINE ELMS - 70A	NINE ELMS - 70A	NINE ELMS - 70A	NINE ELMS - 70A	NINE ELMS - 70A	NINE ELMS - 70A	NINE ELMS - 70A	NINE ELMS - 70A
73115	NINE ELMS - 70A	NINE ELMS - 70A	NINE ELMS - 70A	NINE ELMS - 70A	NINE ELMS - 70A	NINE ELMS - 70A	NINE ELMS - 70A	NINE ELMS - 70A
73116	NINE ELMS - 70A	NINE ELMS - 70A	NINE ELMS - 70A	NINE ELMS - 70A	NINE ELMS - 70A	NINE ELMS - 70A	NINE ELMS - 70A	NINE ELMS - 70A
73117	NINE ELMS - 70A	NINE ELMS - 70A	NINE ELMS - 70A	NINE ELMS - 70A	NINE ELMS - 70A	NINE ELMS - 70A	NINE ELMS - 70A	NINE ELMS - 70A
73118	NINE ELMS - 70A	NINE ELMS - 70A	NINE ELMS - 70A	NINE ELMS - 70A	NINE ELMS - 70A	NINE ELMS - 70A	NINE ELMS - 70A	NINE ELMS - 70A
73119	NINE ELMS - 70A	NINE ELMS - 70A	NINE ELMS - 70A	NINE ELMS - 70A	NINE ELMS - 70A	NINE ELMS - 70A	NINE ELMS - 70A	NINE ELMS - 70A

loco	Dec-59	Feb-60	Mar-60	Apr-60	Jul-60	Aug-60	Sep-60	Nov-60
BR2 2-6-2T								
84020	ASHFORD-73F	ASHFORD-73F	ASHFORD-73F	ASHFORD-73F	ASHFORD-73F	ASHFORD-73F	ASHFORD-73F	ASHFORD-73F
84021	ASHFORD-73F	ASHFORD-73F	ASHFORD-73F	ASHFORD-73F	ASHFORD-73F	ASHFORD-73F	ASHFORD-73F	ASHFORD-73F
84022	ASHFORD-73F	ASHFORD-73F	ASHFORD-73F	ASHFORD-73F	ASHFORD-73F	ASHFORD-73F	ASHFORD-73F	ASHFORD-73F
84023	ASHFORD-73F	ASHFORD-73F	ASHFORD-73F	ASHFORD-73F	ASHFORD-73F	ASHFORD-73F	ASHFORD-73F	ASHFORD-73F
84024	ASHFORD-73F	ASHFORD-73F	ASHFORD-73F	ASHFORD-73F	ASHFORD-73F	ASHFORD-73F	ASHFORD-73F	
84025	ASHFORD-73F	ASHFORD-73F	ASHFORD-73F	ASHFORD-73F	ASHFORD-73F	ASHFORD-73F	ASHFORD-73F	ASHFORD-73F
84026	ASHFORD-73F	ASHFORD-73F	ASHFORD-73F	ASHFORD-73F	ASHFORD-73F	ASHFORD-73F	ASHFORD-73F	ASHFORD-73F
84027	ASHFORD-73F	ASHFORD-73F	ASHFORD-73F	ASHFORD-73F	ASHFORD-73F	ASHFORD-73F	ASHFORD-73F	ASHFORD-73F
84028	ASHFORD-73F	ASHFORD-73F	ASHFORD-73F	ASHFORD-73F	ASHFORD-73F	ASHFORD-73F	ASHFORD-73F	ASHFORD-73F
84029	ASHFORD-73F	ASHFORD-73F	ASHFORD-73F	ASHFORD-73F	ASHFORD-73F	ASHFORD-73F	ASHFORD-73F	ASHFORD-73F
BR3 2-6-2T								
82010	EXMOUTH JCN-72A	EXMOUTH JCN-72A	EXMOUTH JCN-72A	EXMOUTH JCN-72A	EXMOUTH JCN-72A	EXMOUTH JCN-72A	EXMOUTH JCN-72A	EXMOUTH JCN-72A
82011	EXMOUTH JCN-72A	EXMOUTH JCN-72A	EXMOUTH JCN-72A	EXMOUTH JCN-72A	EXMOUTH JCN-72A	EXMOUTH JCN-72A	EXMOUTH JCN-72A	EXMOUTH JCN-72A
82012	EASTLEIGH-71A	EASTLEIGH-71A	EASTLEIGH-71A	EASTLEIGH-71A	EASTLEIGH-71A	EASTLEIGH-71A	EASTLEIGH-71A	EASTLEIGH-71A
82013	EXMOUTH JCN-72A	EXMOUTH JCN-72A	EXMOUTH JCN-72A	EXMOUTH JCN-72A	EXMOUTH JCN-72A	EXMOUTH JCN-72A	EXMOUTH JCN-72A	EXMOUTH JCN-72A
82014	EASTLEIGH-71A	EASTLEIGH-71A	EASTLEIGH-71A	EASTLEIGH-71A	EASTLEIGH-71A	EASTLEIGH-71A	EASTLEIGH-71A	EASTLEIGH-71A
82015	EASTLEIGH-71A	EASTLEIGH-71A	EASTLEIGH-71A	EASTLEIGH-71A	EASTLEIGH-71A	EASTLEIGH-71A	EASTLEIGH-71A	EASTLEIGH-71A
82016	EASTLEIGH-71A	EASTLEIGH-71A	EASTLEIGH-71A	EASTLEIGH-71A	EASTLEIGH-71A	EASTLEIGH-71A	EASTLEIGH-71A	EASTLEIGH-71A
82017	EXMOUTH JCN-72A	EXMOUTH JCN-72A	EXMOUTH JCN-72A	EXMOUTH JCN-72A	EXMOUTH JCN-72A	EXMOUTH JCN-72A	EXMOUTH JCN-72A	EXMOUTH JCN-72A
82018	EXMOUTH JCN-72A	EXMOUTH JCN-72A	EXMOUTH JCN-72A	EXMOUTH JCN-72A	EXMOUTH JCN-72A	EXMOUTH JCN-72A	EXMOUTH JCN-72A	EXMOUTH JCN-72A
82019	EXMOUTH JCN-72A	EXMOUTH JCN-72A	EXMOUTH JCN-72A	EXMOUTH JCN-72A	EXMOUTH JCN-72A	EXMOUTH JCN-72A	EXMOUTH JCN-72A	EXMOUTH JCN-72A
82022	EXMOUTH JCN-72A	EXMOUTH JCN-72A	EXMOUTH JCN-72A	EXMOUTH JCN-72A	EXMOUTH JCN-72A	EXMOUTH JCN-72A	EXMOUTH JCN-72A	EXMOUTH JCN-72A
82023	EXMOUTH JCN-72A	EXMOUTH JCN-72A	EXMOUTH JCN-72A	EXMOUTH JCN-72A	EXMOUTH JCN-72A	EXMOUTH JCN-72A	EXMOUTH JCN-72A	EXMOUTH JCN-72A
82024	EXMOUTH JCN-72A	EXMOUTH JCN-72A	EXMOUTH JCN-72A	EXMOUTH JCN-72A	EXMOUTH JCN-72A	EXMOUTH JCN-72A	EXMOUTH JCN-72A	EXMOUTH JCN-72A
82024	EXMOUTH JCN-72A	EXMOUTH JCN-72A	EXMOUTH JCN-72A	EXMOUTH JCN-72A	EXMOUTH JCN-72A	EXMOUTH JCN-72A	EXMOUTH JCN-72A	EXMOUTH JCN-72A
82025	EXMOUTH JCN-72A	EXMOUTH JCN-72A	EXMOUTH JCN-72A	EXMOUTH JCN-72A	EXMOUTH JCN-72A	EXMOUTH JCN-72A	EXMOUTH JCN-72A	EXMOUTH JCN-72A
BR4 2-6-4T								
80010	THREE BRIDGES-75E	THREE BRIDGES-75E	THREE BRIDGES-75E	THREE BRIDGES-75E	THREE BRIDGES-75E	THREE BRIDGES-75E	THREE BRIDGES-75E	THREE BRIDGES-75E
80011	THREE BRIDGES-75E	THREE BRIDGES-75E	THREE BRIDGES-75E	THREE BRIDGES-75E	THREE BRIDGES-75E	THREE BRIDGES-75E	THREE BRIDGES-75E	THREE BRIDGES-75E
80012	THREE BRIDGES-75E	THREE BRIDGES-75E	THREE BRIDGES-75E	THREE BRIDGES-75E	THREE BRIDGES-75E	THREE BRIDGES-75E	THREE BRIDGES-75E	THREE BRIDGES-75E
80013	BRIGHTON-75A	BRIGHTON-75A	BRIGHTON-75A	BRIGHTON-75A	BRIGHTON-75A	BRIGHTON-75A	BRIGHTON-75A	BRIGHTON-75A
80014	T.WELLS-75F	T.WELLS-75F	T.WELLS-75F	T.WELLS-75F	T.WELLS-75F	T.WELLS-75F	T.WELLS-75F	T.WELLS-75F
80015	T.WELLS-75F	T.WELLS-75F	T.WELLS-75F	T.WELLS-75F	T.WELLS-75F	T.WELLS-75F	T.WELLS-75F	T.WELLS-75F
80016	T.WELLS-75F	T.WELLS-75F	T.WELLS-75F	T.WELLS-75F	T.WELLS-75F	T.WELLS-75F	T.WELLS-75F	T.WELLS-75F
80017	T.WELLS-75F	T.WELLS-75F	T.WELLS-75F	T.WELLS-75F	T.WELLS-75F	T.WELLS-75F	T.WELLS-75F	T.WELLS-75F
80018	T.WELLS-75F	T.WELLS-75F	T.WELLS-75F	T.WELLS-75F	T.WELLS-75F	T.WELLS-75F	T.WELLS-75F	T.WELLS-75F
80019	T.WELLS-75F	T.WELLS-75F	T.WELLS-75F	T.WELLS-75F	T.WELLS-75F	T.WELLS-75F	T.WELLS-75F	T.WELLS-75F
80031	BRIGHTON-75A	BRIGHTON-75A	BRIGHTON-75A	BRIGHTON-75A	BRIGHTON-75A	BRIGHTON-75A	BRIGHTON-75A	BRIGHTON-75A
80032	BRIGHTON-75A	BRIGHTON-75A	BRIGHTON-75A	BRIGHTON-75A	BRIGHTON-75A	BRIGHTON-75A	BRIGHTON-75A	BRIGHTON-75A
80032	BRIGHTON-75A	BRIGHTON-75A	BRIGHTON-75A	BRIGHTON-75A	BRIGHTON-75A	BRIGHTON-75A	BRIGHTON-75A	BRIGHTON-75A
80033	BRIGHTON-75A	BRIGHTON-75A	BRIGHTON-75A	BRIGHTON-75A	BRIGHTON-75A	BRIGHTON-75A	BRIGHTON-75A	BRIGHTON-75A
80033	BRIGHTON-75A	BRIGHTON-75A	BRIGHTON-75A	BRIGHTON-75A	BRIGHTON-75A	BRIGHTON-75A	BRIGHTON-75A	BRIGHTON-75A
80034	ASHFORD-73F	ASHFORD-73F	ASHFORD-73F	ASHFORD-73F	ASHFORD-73F	ASHFORD-73F	ASHFORD-73F	ASHFORD-73F
80035	ASHFORD-73F	ASHFORD-73F	ASHFORD-73F	ASHFORD-73F	ASHFORD-73F	ASHFORD-73F	ASHFORD-73F	ASHFORD-73F
80036	ASHFORD-73F	ASHFORD-73F	ASHFORD-73F	ASHFORD-73F	ASHFORD-73F	ASHFORD-73F	ASHFORD-73F	ASHFORD-73F
80037	ASHFORD-73F	ASHFORD-73F	ASHFORD-73F	ASHFORD-73F	ASHFORD-73F	ASHFORD-73F	ASHFORD-73F	ASHFORD-73F
80038	ASHFORD-73F	ASHFORD-73F	ASHFORD-73F	ASHFORD-73F	ASHFORD-73F	ASHFORD-73F	ASHFORD-73F	ASHFORD-73F
80039	ASHFORD-73F	ASHFORD-73F	ASHFORD-73F	ASHFORD-73F	ASHFORD-73F	ASHFORD-73F	ASHFORD-73F	ASHFORD-73F
80040	ASHFORD-73F	ASHFORD-73F	ASHFORD-73F	ASHFORD-73F	ASHFORD-73F	ASHFORD-73F	ASHFORD-73F	ASHFORD-73F
80041	ASHFORD-73F	ASHFORD-73F	ASHFORD-73F	ASHFORD-73F	ASHFORD-73F	ASHFORD-73F	ASHFORD-73F	ASHFORD-73F
80042	ASHFORD-73F	ASHFORD-73F	ASHFORD-73F	ASHFORD-73F	ASHFORD-73F	ASHFORD-73F	ASHFORD-73F	ASHFORD-73F
80043	DOVER-73H	ASHFORD-73F	ASHFORD-73F	ASHFORD-73F	ASHFORD-73F	ASHFORD-73F	ASHFORD-73F	ASHFORD-73F
80059	DOVER-73H	ASHFORD-73F	ASHFORD-73F	ASHFORD-73F	ASHFORD-73F	ASHFORD-73F	ASHFORD-73F	ASHFORD-73F
80064	DOVER-73H	ASHFORD-73F	ASHFORD-73F	ASHFORD-73F	ASHFORD-73F	ASHFORD-73F	ASHFORD-73F	ASHFORD-73F
80065	DOVER-73H	ASHFORD-73F	ASHFORD-73F	ASHFORD-73F	ASHFORD-73F	ASHFORD-73F	ASHFORD-73F	ASHFORD-73F
80066	STEWARTS LANE-73A	ASHFORD-73F	ASHFORD-73F	ASHFORD-73F	ASHFORD-73F	ASHFORD-73F	ASHFORD-73F	ASHFORD-73F
80067	STEWARTS LANE-73A	STEWARTS LANE-73A	STEWARTS LANE-73A	STEWARTS LANE-73A	STEWARTS LANE-73A	STEWARTS LANE-73A	STEWARTS LANE-73A	STEWARTS LANE-73A
80068	STEWARTS LANE-73A	STEWARTS LANE-73A	STEWARTS LANE-73A	STEWARTS LANE-73A	STEWARTS LANE-73A	STEWARTS LANE-73A	STEWARTS LANE-73A	STEWARTS LANE-73A
80081	STEWARTS LANE-73A	STEWARTS LANE-73A	STEWARTS LANE-73A	STEWARTS LANE-73A	STEWARTS LANE-73A	STEWARTS LANE-73A	STEWARTS LANE-73A	STEWARTS LANE-73A
80082	B.ARMS-73B	B.ARMS-73B	B.ARMS-73B	B.ARMS-73B	B.ARMS-73B	B.ARMS-73B	B.ARMS-73B	B.ARMS-73B
80083	B.ARMS-73B	B.ARMS-73B	B.ARMS-73B	B.ARMS-73B	B.ARMS-73B	B.ARMS-73B	B.ARMS-73B	B.ARMS-73B
80084	B.ARMS-73B	B.ARMS-73B	B.ARMS-73B	B.ARMS-73B	B.ARMS-73B	B.ARMS-73B	B.ARMS-73B	B.ARMS-73B
80085	B.ARMS-73B	B.ARMS-73B	B.ARMS-73B	B.ARMS-73B	B.ARMS-73B	B.ARMS-73B	B.ARMS-73B	B.ARMS-73B
80087	THREE BRIDGES-75E	ASHFORD-73F	ASHFORD-73F	ASHFORD-73F	ASHFORD-73F	ASHFORD-73F	ASHFORD-73F	ASHFORD-73F
80088	THREE BRIDGES-75E	THREE BRIDGES-75E	THREE BRIDGES-75E	THREE BRIDGES-75E	THREE BRIDGES-75E	THREE BRIDGES-75E	THREE BRIDGES-75E	THREE BRIDGES-75E
80089	THREE BRIDGES-75E	THREE BRIDGES-75E	THREE BRIDGES-75E	THREE BRIDGES-75E	THREE BRIDGES-75E	THREE BRIDGES-75E	THREE BRIDGES-75E	THREE BRIDGES-75E
80094	THREE BRIDGES-75E	THREE BRIDGES-75E	THREE BRIDGES-75E	THREE BRIDGES-75E	THREE BRIDGES-75E	THREE BRIDGES-75E	THREE BRIDGES-75E	THREE BRIDGES-75E
80095	T.WELLS-75F	T.WELLS-75F	T.WELLS-75F	T.WELLS-75F	T.WELLS-75F	T.WELLS-75F	T.WELLS-75F	T.WELLS-75F
80137	T.WELLS-75F	T.WELLS-75F	T.WELLS-75F	T.WELLS-75F	T.WELLS-75F	T.WELLS-75F	T.WELLS-75F	T.WELLS-75F
80138	T.WELLS-75F	T.WELLS-75F	T.WELLS-75F	T.WELLS-75F	T.WELLS-75F	T.WELLS-75F	T.WELLS-75F	T.WELLS-75F
80139	T.WELLS-75F	T.WELLS-75F	T.WELLS-75F	T.WELLS-75F	T.WELLS-75F	T.WELLS-75F	T.WELLS-75F	T.WELLS-75F
80140	T.WELLS-75F	T.WELLS-75F	T.WELLS-75F	T.WELLS-75F	T.WELLS-75F	T.WELLS-75F	T.WELLS-75F	T.WELLS-75F
80141	T.WELLS-75F	T.WELLS-75F	T.WELLS-75F	T.WELLS-75F	T.WELLS-75F	T.WELLS-75F	T.WELLS-75F	T.WELLS-75F
80142	T.WELLS-75F	T.WELLS-75F	T.WELLS-75F	T.WELLS-75F	T.WELLS-75F	T.WELLS-75F	T.WELLS-75F	T.WELLS-75F
80143	BRIGHTON-75A	BRIGHTON-75A	BRIGHTON-75A	BRIGHTON-75A	BRIGHTON-75A	BRIGHTON-75A	BRIGHTON-75A	BRIGHTON-75A
80144	BRIGHTON-75A	BRIGHTON-75A	BRIGHTON-75A	BRIGHTON-75A	BRIGHTON-75A	BRIGHTON-75A	BRIGHTON-75A	BRIGHTON-75A
80145	BRIGHTON-75A	BRIGHTON-75A	BRIGHTON-75A	BRIGHTON-75A	BRIGHTON-75A	BRIGHTON-75A	BRIGHTON-75A	BRIGHTON-75A
80146	BRIGHTON-75A	BRIGHTON-75A	BRIGHTON-75A	BRIGHTON-75A	BRIGHTON-75A	BRIGHTON-75A	BRIGHTON-75A	BRIGHTON-75A
80147	BRIGHTON-75A	BRIGHTON-75A	BRIGHTON-75A	BRIGHTON-75A	BRIGHTON-75A	BRIGHTON-75A	BRIGHTON-75A	BRIGHTON-75A
80148	BRIGHTON-75A	BRIGHTON-75A	BRIGHTON-75A	BRIGHTON-75A	BRIGHTON-75A	BRIGHTON-75A	BRIGHTON-75A	BRIGHTON-75A
80149	BRIGHTON-75A	BRIGHTON-75A	BRIGHTON-75A	BRIGHTON-75A	BRIGHTON-75A	BRIGHTON-75A	BRIGHTON-75A	BRIGHTON-75A
80150	BRIGHTON-75A	BRIGHTON-75A	BRIGHTON-75A	BRIGHTON-75A	BRIGHTON-75A	BRIGHTON-75A	BRIGHTON-75A	BRIGHTON-75A
80151	BRIGHTON-75A	BRIGHTON-75A	BRIGHTON-75A	BRIGHTON-75A	BRIGHTON-75A	BRIGHTON-75A	BRIGHTON-75A	BRIGHTON-75A
80152	BRIGHTON-75A	BRIGHTON-75A	BRIGHTON-75A	BRIGHTON-75A	BRIGHTON-75A	BRIGHTON-75A	BRIGHTON-75A	BRIGHTON-75A
80153	BRIGHTON-75A	BRIGHTON-75A	BRIGHTON-75A	BRIGHTON-75A	BRIGHTON-75A	BRIGHTON-75A	BRIGHTON-75A	BRIGHTON-75A
80154	BRIGHTON-75A	BRIGHTON-75A	BRIGHTON-75A	BRIGHTON-75A	BRIGHTON-75A	BRIGHTON-75A	BRIGHTON-75A	BRIGHTON-75A

loco	May-49	Jun-49	Aug-49	Sep-49	Dec-49	Feb-50	Mar-50
			2-8-0 WD				
90107 BRIGHTON - 75A	BRIGHTON - 75A	BRIGHTON - 75A	BRIGHTON - 75A	BRIGHTON - 75A	BRIGHTON - 75A	BRIGHTON - 75A
90127 FELTHAM - 70B	FELTHAM - 70B	FELTHAM - 70B	FELTHAM - 70B	FELTHAM - 70B	FELTHAM - 70B	FELTHAM - 70B
90142 FELTHAM - 70B	FELTHAM - 70B	FELTHAM - 70B	FELTHAM - 70B	FELTHAM - 70B	FELTHAM - 70B	FELTHAM - 70B
90164 B.ARMS - 73B	B.ARMS - 73B	B.ARMS - 73B	B.ARMS - 73B	B.ARMS - 73B	B.ARMS - 73B	B.ARMS - 73B
90181 B.ARMS - 73B	B.ARMS - 73B	B.ARMS - 73B	B.ARMS - 73B	B.ARMS - 73B	B.ARMS - 73B	B.ARMS - 73B
90194 B.ARMS - 73B	B.ARMS - 73B	B.ARMS - 73B	B.ARMS - 73B	B.ARMS - 73B	B.ARMS - 73B	B.ARMS - 73B
90213 B.ARMS - 73B	B.ARMS - 73B	B.ARMS - 73B	B.ARMS - 73B	B.ARMS - 73B	B.ARMS - 73B	B.ARMS - 73B
90216 B.ARMS - 73B	B.ARMS - 73B	B.ARMS - 73B	B.ARMS - 73B	B.ARMS - 73B	B.ARMS - 73B	B.ARMS - 73B
90226 B.ARMS - 73B	B.ARMS - 73B	B.ARMS - 73B	B.ARMS - 73B	B.ARMS - 73B	B.ARMS - 73B	B.ARMS - 73B
90234 B.ARMS - 73B	B.ARMS - 73B	B.ARMS - 73B	B.ARMS - 73B	B.ARMS - 73B	B.ARMS - 73B	B.ARMS - 73B
90247 BRIGHTON - 75A	BRIGHTON - 75A	BRIGHTON - 75A	BRIGHTON - 75A	BRIGHTON - 75A	BRIGHTON - 75A	BRIGHTON - 75A
90254 B.ARMS - 73B	B.ARMS - 73B	B.ARMS - 73B	B.ARMS - 73B	B.ARMS - 73B	B.ARMS - 73B	B.ARMS - 73B
90257 FELTHAM - 70B	FELTHAM - 70B	FELTHAM - 70B	FELTHAM - 70B	FELTHAM - 70B	FELTHAM - 70B	FELTHAM - 70B
90267 FELTHAM - 70B	FELTHAM - 70B	FELTHAM - 70B	FELTHAM - 70B	FELTHAM - 70B	FELTHAM - 70B	FELTHAM - 70B
90308 FELTHAM - 70B	FELTHAM - 70B	FELTHAM - 70B	FELTHAM - 70B	FELTHAM - 70B	FELTHAM - 70B	FELTHAM - 70B
90317 REDHILL - 75B	REDHILL - 75B	REDHILL - 75B	REDHILL - 75B	REDHILL - 75B	REDHILL - 75B	REDHILL - 75B
90332 HITHER GREEN - 73C	HITHER GREEN - 73C	HITHER GREEN - 73C	HITHER GREEN - 73C	HITHER GREEN - 73C	HITHER GREEN - 73C	HITHER GREEN - 73C
90345 B.ARMS - 73B	BRIGHTON - 75A	BRIGHTON - 75A	BRIGHTON - 75A	BRIGHTON - 75A	BRIGHTON - 75A	BRIGHTON - 75A
90347 BRIGHTON - 75A	BRIGHTON - 75A	BRIGHTON - 75A	BRIGHTON - 75A	BRIGHTON - 75A	BRIGHTON - 75A	BRIGHTON - 75A
90354 BRIGHTON - 75A	BRIGHTON - 75A	BRIGHTON - 75A	BRIGHTON - 75A	BRIGHTON - 75A	BRIGHTON - 75A	BRIGHTON - 75A
90360 REDHILL - 75B	REDHILL - 75B	REDHILL - 75B	REDHILL - 75B	REDHILL - 75B	REDHILL - 75B	REDHILL - 75B
90375 B.ARMS - 73B	B.ARMS - 73B	B.ARMS - 73B	B.ARMS - 73B	B.ARMS - 73B	B.ARMS - 73B	B.ARMS - 73B
90389 HITHER GREEN - 73C	HITHER GREEN - 73C	HITHER GREEN - 73C	HITHER GREEN - 73C	HITHER GREEN - 73C	HITHER GREEN - 73C	HITHER GREEN - 73C
90390 HITHER GREEN - 73C	HITHER GREEN - 73C	HITHER GREEN - 73C	HITHER GREEN - 73C	HITHER GREEN - 73C	HITHER GREEN - 73C	HITHER GREEN - 73C
90408 B.ARMS - 73B	B.ARMS - 73B	B.ARMS - 73B	B.ARMS - 73B	B.ARMS - 73B	B.ARMS - 73B	B.ARMS - 73B
90523 FELTHAM - 70B	FELTHAM - 70B	FELTHAM - 70B	FELTHAM - 70B	FELTHAM - 70B	FELTHAM - 70B	FELTHAM - 70B
90527 FELTHAM - 70B	FELTHAM - 70B	FELTHAM - 70B	FELTHAM - 70B	FELTHAM - 70B	FELTHAM - 70B	FELTHAM - 70B
90530 FELTHAM - 70B	FELTHAM - 70B	FELTHAM - 70B	FELTHAM - 70B	FELTHAM - 70B	FELTHAM - 70B	FELTHAM - 70B
90533 B.ARMS - 73B	B.ARMS - 73B	B.ARMS - 73B	B.ARMS - 73B	B.ARMS - 73B	B.ARMS - 73B	B.ARMS - 73B
90543 FELTHAM - 70B	FELTHAM - 70B	FELTHAM - 70B	FELTHAM - 70B	FELTHAM - 70B	FELTHAM - 70B	FELTHAM - 70B
90552 B.ARMS - 73B	B.ARMS - 73B	B.ARMS - 73B	B.ARMS - 73B	B.ARMS - 73B	B.ARMS - 73B	B.ARMS - 73B
90556 HITHER GREEN - 73C	HITHER GREEN - 73C	HITHER GREEN - 73C	HITHER GREEN - 73C	HITHER GREEN - 73C	HITHER GREEN - 73C	HITHER GREEN - 73C
90558 B.ARMS - 73B	B.ARMS - 73B	B.ARMS - 73B	B.ARMS - 73B	B.ARMS - 73B	B.ARMS - 73B	B.ARMS - 73B
90562 FELTHAM - 70B	FELTHAM - 70B	FELTHAM - 70B	FELTHAM - 70B	FELTHAM - 70B	FELTHAM - 70B	FELTHAM - 70B
90564 B.ARMS - 73B	B.ARMS - 73B	B.ARMS - 73B	B.ARMS - 73B	B.ARMS - 73B	B.ARMS - 73B	B.ARMS - 73B
90566 HITHER GREEN - 73C	HITHER GREEN - 73C	HITHER GREEN - 73C	HITHER GREEN - 73C	HITHER GREEN - 73C	HITHER GREEN - 73C	HITHER GREEN - 73C
90570 FELTHAM - 70B	FELTHAM - 70B	FELTHAM - 70B	FELTHAM - 70B	FELTHAM - 70B	FELTHAM - 70B	FELTHAM - 70B
90578 FELTHAM - 70B	FELTHAM - 70B	FELTHAM - 70B	FELTHAM - 70B	FELTHAM - 70B	FELTHAM - 70B	FELTHAM - 70B
90604 FELTHAM - 70B	FELTHAM - 70B	FELTHAM - 70B	FELTHAM - 70B	FELTHAM - 70B	FELTHAM - 70B	FELTHAM - 70B
90619 B.ARMS - 73B	B.ARMS - 73B	B.ARMS - 73B	B.ARMS - 73B	B.ARMS - 73B	B.ARMS - 73B	B.ARMS - 73B
90622 B.ARMS - 73B	ASHFORD - 74A	ASHFORD - 74A	ASHFORD - 74A	ASHFORD - 74A	ASHFORD - 74A	ASHFORD - 74A
90641 REDHILL - 75B	REDHILL - 75B	REDHILL - 75B	REDHILL - 75B	REDHILL - 75B	REDHILL - 75B	REDHILL - 75B
90650 B.ARMS - 73B	ASHFORD - 74A	ASHFORD - 74A	ASHFORD - 74A	ASHFORD - 74A	ASHFORD - 74A	ASHFORD - 74A
90655 HITHER GREEN - 73C	HITHER GREEN - 73C	HITHER GREEN - 73C	HITHER GREEN - 73C	HITHER GREEN - 73C	HITHER GREEN - 73C	HITHER GREEN - 73C
90669 HITHER GREEN - 73C	HITHER GREEN - 73C	HITHER GREEN - 73C	HITHER GREEN - 73C	HITHER GREEN - 73C	HITHER GREEN - 73C	HITHER GREEN - 73C
90671 HITHER GREEN - 73C	HITHER GREEN - 73C	HITHER GREEN - 73C	HITHER GREEN - 73C	HITHER GREEN - 73C	HITHER GREEN - 73C	HITHER GREEN - 73C
90675 FELTHAM - 70B	FELTHAM - 70B	FELTHAM - 70B	FELTHAM - 70B	FELTHAM - 70B	FELTHAM - 70B	FELTHAM - 70B
90678 HITHER GREEN - 73C	HITHER GREEN - 73C	HITHER GREEN - 73C	HITHER GREEN - 73C	HITHER GREEN - 73C	HITHER GREEN - 73C	HITHER GREEN - 73C
90702 HITHER GREEN - 73C	HITHER GREEN - 73C	HITHER GREEN - 73C	HITHER GREEN - 73C	HITHER GREEN - 73C	HITHER GREEN - 73C	HITHER GREEN - 73C
90718 HITHER GREEN - 73C	HITHER GREEN - 73C	HITHER GREEN - 73C	HITHER GREEN - 73C	HITHER GREEN - 73C	HITHER GREEN - 73C	HITHER GREEN - 73C

Showpiece of the new order, the Britannia Pacifics were distributed as widely as possible throughout the five regions with the Southern receiving two for working the Golden Arrow continental express between Victoria and Dover, working on which they remained - other than a very occasional trip to Bournemouth from Waterloo - until moved to the Midland Division of the LMR in 1958. For a very short period in 1953 when the Bulleid Pacifics were withdrawn for axle examinations they were joined by seven other members of the class.

Shortly after the arrival of the Britannia Pacifics, further standard engines reached the Southern in the shape of 4MT 2-6-4T's which supplemented the LM 2-6-4T's on the LBSCR, working from Victoria to Tunbridge Wells and branch services on the South Coast. This remained the extent of the class until 1959 when the regions LM 2-6-4T's were exchanged for the BR variety, the latter then being allocated to SECR workings at Ashford and in the London area until the completion of electrification in 1962.

The 2-6-4 tanks did not, until very late in the day, operate on the South Western but instead a number of the smaller 3MT 2-6-2T's were sent to Exmouth Junction to replace the M7 0-4-4T's on the restricted Exeter - Exmouth branch. A small allocation was also received by Eastleigh for duties on the Fawley branch.

Ten of the smallest standard tanks were despatched to the SECR in 1957 - rather hurriedly since 84020 had no sooner arrived at Bedford when a set of men had to specially booked on duty the following Sunday to take it south - and were shared between Ramsgate and Ashford for working local services via Deal and Canterbury West. On electrification of the LCDR, all ten were gathered at Ashford.

loco	Apr-50	Sep-50	Oct-50	Nov-50	Dec-50	Mar-51	Apr-51	Jun-51
				2-8-0 WD				
90107	HITHER GREEN - 73C	HITHER GREEN - 73C	HITHER GREEN - 73C	HITHER GREEN - 73C	HITHER GREEN - 73C	HITHER GREEN - 73C	HITHER GREEN - 73C	HITHER GREEN - 73C
90127	HITHER GREEN - 73C	HITHER GREEN - 73C	HITHER GREEN - 73C	HITHER GREEN - 73C	HITHER GREEN - 73C	HITHER GREEN - 73C	HITHER GREEN - 73C	HITHER GREEN - 73C
90142	HITHER GREEN - 73C	HITHER GREEN - 73C	HITHER GREEN - 73C	HITHER GREEN - 73C	HITHER GREEN - 73C	HITHER GREEN - 73C	HITHER GREEN - 73C	HITHER GREEN - 73C
90164	B.ARMS - 73B	B.ARMS - 73B	B.ARMS - 73B	B.ARMS - 73B	B.ARMS - 73B	B.ARMS - 73B	B.ARMS - 73B	B.ARMS - 73B
90181	B.ARMS - 73B							
90194	B.ARMS - 73B	B.ARMS - 73B	B.ARMS - 73B	B.ARMS - 73B	B.ARMS - 73B	B.ARMS - 73B	B.ARMS - 73B	B.ARMS - 73B
90213	HITHER GREEN - 73C	HITHER GREEN - 73C	HITHER GREEN - 73C	HITHER GREEN - 73C	HITHER GREEN - 73C	HITHER GREEN - 73C	HITHER GREEN - 73C	HITHER GREEN - 73C
90216	B.ARMS - 73B	B.ARMS - 73B	B.ARMS - 73B	B.ARMS - 73B	B.ARMS - 73B	B.ARMS - 73B	B.ARMS - 73B	B.ARMS - 73B
90226	B.ARMS - 73B	B.ARMS - 73B	B.ARMS - 73B	B.ARMS - 73B	B.ARMS - 73B	B.ARMS - 73B	B.ARMS - 73B	B.ARMS - 73B
90234	B.ARMS - 73B	B.ARMS - 73B	B.ARMS - 73B	B.ARMS - 73B	B.ARMS - 73B	B.ARMS - 73B	B.ARMS - 73B	B.ARMS - 73B
90247	BRIGHTON - 75A	BRIGHTON - 75A	BRIGHTON - 75A	BRIGHTON - 75A	HITHER GREEN - 73C	HITHER GREEN - 73C	HITHER GREEN - 73C	HITHER GREEN - 73C
90254	B.ARMS - 73B	B.ARMS - 73B	B.ARMS - 73B	B.ARMS - 73B	B.ARMS - 73B	B.ARMS - 73B	B.ARMS - 73B	B.ARMS - 73B
90257	FELTHAM - 70B	FELTHAM - 70B	FELTHAM - 70B	FELTHAM - 70B	FELTHAM - 70B	TO LMR	TO LMR	TO LMR
90267	FELTHAM - 70B	HITHER GREEN - 73C	HITHER GREEN - 73C	HITHER GREEN - 73C	HITHER GREEN - 73C	HITHER GREEN - 73C	HITHER GREEN - 73C	HITHER GREEN - 73C
90308	FELTHAM - 70B							
90317	REDHILL - 75B	REDHILL - 75B	REDHILL - 75B	REDHILL - 75B	REDHILL - 75B	REDHILL - 75B	REDHILL - 75B	REDHILL - 75B
90332	HITHER GREEN - 73C							
90345	BRIGHTON - 75A							
90347	BRIGHTON - 75A							
90354	BRIGHTON - 75A	BRIGHTON - 75A	BRIGHTON - 75A	BRIGHTON - 75A	REDHILL - 75B	REDHILL - 75B	REDHILL - 75B	REDHILL - 75B
90360	REDHILL - 75B	REDHILL - 75B	REDHILL - 75B	REDHILL - 75B	REDHILL - 75B	REDHILL - 75B	REDHILL - 75B	REDHILL - 75B
90375	B.ARMS - 73B	REDHILL - 75B	REDHILL - 75B	REDHILL - 75B	REDHILL - 75B	REDHILL - 75B	REDHILL - 75B	REDHILL - 75B
90389	HITHER GREEN - 73C	HITHER GREEN - 73C	HITHER GREEN - 73C	HITHER GREEN - 73C	HITHER GREEN - 73C	HITHER GREEN - 73C	HITHER GREEN - 73C	HITHER GREEN - 73C
90390	HITHER GREEN - 73C	HITHER GREEN - 73C	HITHER GREEN - 73C	HITHER GREEN - 73C	HITHER GREEN - 73C	HITHER GREEN - 73C	HITHER GREEN - 73C	HITHER GREEN - 73C
90408	B.ARMS - 73B	B.ARMS - 73B	B.ARMS - 73B	B.ARMS - 73B	B.ARMS - 73B	B.ARMS - 73B	B.ARMS - 73B	B.ARMS - 73B
90523	FELTHAM - 70B							
90527	FELTHAM - 70B							
90530	FELTHAM - 70B							
90533	B.ARMS - 73B	B.ARMS - 73B	B.ARMS - 73B	B.ARMS - 73B	B.ARMS - 73B	B.ARMS - 73B	B.ARMS - 73B	B.ARMS - 73B
90543	FELTHAM - 70B							
90552	B.ARMS - 73B	B.ARMS - 73B	B.ARMS - 73B	B.ARMS - 73B	B.ARMS - 73B	B.ARMS - 73B	B.ARMS - 73B	B.ARMS - 73B
90556	HITHER GREEN - 73C	HITHER GREEN - 73C	HITHER GREEN - 73C	HITHER GREEN - 73C	HITHER GREEN - 73C	HITHER GREEN - 73C	HITHER GREEN - 73C	HITHER GREEN - 73C
90558	B.ARMS - 73B	B.ARMS - 73B	B.ARMS - 73B	B.ARMS - 73B	B.ARMS - 73B	B.ARMS - 73B	B.ARMS - 73B	B.ARMS - 73B
90562	FELTHAM - 70B	FELTHAM - 70B	FELTHAM - 70B	FELTHAM - 70B	FELTHAM - 70B	TO LMR	TO LMR	TO LMR
90564	B.ARMS - 73B	B.ARMS - 73B	B.ARMS - 73B	B.ARMS - 73B	B.ARMS - 73B	B.ARMS - 73B	B.ARMS - 73B	B.ARMS - 73B
90566	HITHER GREEN - 73C	HITHER GREEN - 73C	HITHER GREEN - 73C	HITHER GREEN - 73C	HITHER GREEN - 73C	HITHER GREEN - 73C	HITHER GREEN - 73C	HITHER GREEN - 73C
90570	FELTHAM - 70B	FELTHAM - 70B	FELTHAM - 70B	FELTHAM - 70B	FELTHAM - 70B	FELTHAM - 70B	FELTHAM - 70B	FELTHAM - 70B
90578	FELTHAM - 70B							
90604	FELTHAM - 70B	FELTHAM - 70B	FELTHAM - 70B	FELTHAM - 70B	FELTHAM - 70B	FELTHAM - 70B	FELTHAM - 70B	FELTHAM - 70B
90619	B.ARMS - 73B							
90622	ASHFORD - 74A							
90641	REDHILL - 75B	REDHILL - 75B	REDHILL - 75B	REDHILL - 75B	REDHILL - 75B	REDHILL - 75B	REDHILL - 75B	REDHILL - 75B
90650	ASHFORD - 74A							
90655	HITHER GREEN - 73C							
90669	HITHER GREEN - 73C	HITHER GREEN - 73C	HITHER GREEN - 73C	HITHER GREEN - 73C	HITHER GREEN - 73C	HITHER GREEN - 73C	HITHER GREEN - 73C	HITHER GREEN - 73C
90671	HITHER GREEN - 73C	HITHER GREEN - 73C	HITHER GREEN - 73C	HITHER GREEN - 73C	HITHER GREEN - 73C	HITHER GREEN - 73C	HITHER GREEN - 73C	HITHER GREEN - 73C
90675	FELTHAM - 70B							
90678	HITHER GREEN - 73C	HITHER GREEN - 73C	HITHER GREEN - 73C	HITHER GREEN - 73C	HITHER GREEN - 73C	HITHER GREEN - 73C	TO LMR	TO LMR
90702	HITHER GREEN - 73C	HITHER GREEN - 73C	HITHER GREEN - 73C	HITHER GREEN - 73C	HITHER GREEN - 73C	HITHER GREEN - 73C	HITHER GREEN - 73C	HITHER GREEN - 73C
90718	HITHER GREEN - 73C	HITHER GREEN - 73C	HITHER GREEN - 73C	HITHER GREEN - 73C	HITHER GREEN - 73C	HITHER GREEN - 73C	HITHER GREEN - 73C	HITHER GREEN - 73C

Other than the two Britannia Pacifics, three classes of standard tender engine were sent to the Southern: the 4MT 2-6-0's and the 4MT and 5MT 4-6-0's.

The first to arrive were the 2-6-0's, the first of which went to Eastleigh in December 1952 with the object, never completely realised, of replacing D15 and T9 4-4-0's on the Portsmouth - Salisbury duties. Other examples were later allocated to Salisbury and Redhill, the latter taking over much of the passenger work on the Reading line and relegating the N 2-6-0's to goods work until 1959 when the standard engines were reallocated to the South Western with three going to Bournemouth.

The first batch of 4MT 4-6-0's was initially divided between Dover, where they worked parcels trains to London, and Exmouth Junction although the latter were very quickly moved to Basingstoke, Bath and Eastleigh after which the allocation remained relatively static for the remainder of the decade.

Apart from the loan of three engines during 1953, the first standard 5MT 4-6-0's to arrive were located at Bath for Somerset and Dorset services to Bournemouth, the first allocations to the Southern proper coming in 1955 when ten of the class were sent to Stewarts Lane to take over the Victoria - Ramsgate services from the N15 4-6-0's. Later in the same year eleven were allocated to Nine Elms to relieve the King Arthur's of some of the stopping services between Waterloo and Salisbury.

The next additions, five engines, came in 1958 with the acquisition of Weymouth MPD from the Western Region, the allocations then remained static until the summer of 1959 when the Stewarts Lane engines, ousted by electrification, were sent to Nine Elms.

The Austerity 2-8-0's were not engines obviously suited to the Southern which had no originating mineral traffic, and although considerable numbers were allocated to a wide variety of sheds, by the middle of 1951 all had been sent away to other parts of BR.

	May-49	Jun-49	Aug-49	Sep-49	Dec-49
Norwood Jcn	9	11	11	11	11
Hither Green				5	8
TOTAL	9	11	11	16	19

	Feb-50	Mar-50	Apr-50	Sep-50	Oct-50	Nov-50	Dec-50
Norwood Jcn	11	11	18	18	18	18	18
Hither Green	8	8	8	8	8	8	9
TOTAL	19	19	26	26	26	26	27

	Mar-51	Apr-51	Jun-51	Jul-51	Sep-51	Dec-51
Norwood Jcn	11	11	20	20	18	19
Hither Green	9	11	10	11	12	16
TOTAL	20	22	30	31	30	35

	Jan-52	Mar-52	Jun-52	Sep-52	Dec-52
Norwood Jcn	18	19	20	4	4
Hither Green	16	15	14	10	15
Feltham		1	1	1	2
TOTAL	34	35	35	15	21

	Mar-53	May-53	Jul-53	Sep-53	Nov-53
Norwood Jcn	3	3	3	3	3
Hither Green	13	13	13	12	13
Feltham	1	1	1	1	1
Eastleigh	3	3	3	3	3
Southampton				1	
TOTAL	20	20	20	20	20

	Jan-54	Mar-54	May-54	Jun-54	Aug-54	Oct-54	Dec-54
Norwood Jcn	3	3	7	7	7	4	6
Hither Green	14	14	14	14	14	14	14
Feltham	4	4	4	4	4	4	4
Eastleigh	3	3	5	5	5	8	8
TOTAL	24	24	30	30	30 *	30	32

	Feb-55	Apr-55	Jun-55	Aug-55	Sep-55	Nov-55	Dec-55
Norwood Jcn	10	9	13	12	12	12	13
Hither Green	14	15	16	14	14	14	14
Feltham	4	4	4	4	4	4	4
Eastleigh	9	10	11	11	11	11	11
Brighton	3	7	7	7	7	7	7
Ashford			1	4	4	4	3
TOTAL	40	45	52	52	52	52	52

	Jan-56	Apr-56	May-56	Aug-56	Oct-56	Nov-56
Norwood Jcn	10	10	10	10	11	11
Hither Green	16	16	16	16	16	22
Feltham	4	4	4	4	4	4
Eastleigh	12	12	12	12	12	12
Brighton	7	7	7	7	7	7
Ashford	3	3	3	3	3	3
TOTAL	52	52	52	52	53	59

	Jan-57	Mar-57	Jun-57	Jul-57	Oct-57
Norwood Jcn	11	11	11	11	14
Hither Green	22	22	27	35	33
Feltham	4	4	4	4	4
Eastleigh	12	11	11	11	11
Brighton	7	7	8	8	8
Ashford	3	3	3	3	5
Dover					1
Plymouth					4
Guildford					2
TOTAL	59	58	64	72	82

	Jan-58	Feb-58	Mar-58	May-58	Oct-58
Norwood Jcn	14	13	13	13	13
Hither Green	33	32	32	32	32
Feltham	4	4	4	4	4
Eastleigh	11	10	10	11	11
Brighton	8	8	8	8	8
Ashford	5	11	11	11	11
Dover	1	1	1	1	1
Plymouth	4	4	4	4	4
Guildford	2	1	1	1	1
Yeovil PM		1	1	1	1
TOTAL	82	85	85	86	86

	Mar-59	Jun-59	Jul-59	Aug-59	Oct-59	Dec-59
Norwood Jcn	14	14	14	13	13	16
Hither Green	33	33	33	33	34	33
Feltham	4	4	4	4	4	4
Eastleigh	17	17	17	17	17	17
Bournemouth				1	1	1
Brighton	9	9	9	9	9	9
Ashford	11	11	11	12	12	12
Dover	1	1	1	1	1	1
Faversham		5	5	5	5	6
Plymouth	4	4	4	4	4	4
Guildford	1	1	1	1	1	1
Yeovil PM	1		1	1	1	
TOTAL	95	99	100	101	102	104

	Feb-60	Mar-60	Apr-60	Jul-60	Aug-60	Sep-60	Nov-60
Norwood Jcn	18	18	19	21	21	23	24
Hither Green	33	34	35	36	36	34	33
Feltham	4	5	5	5	5	6	6
Eastleigh	17	17	18	19	19	18	18
Bournemouth	1	1	1	1	1	1	1
Brighton	11	12	12	12	12	12	12
Ashford	12	13	13	16	16	16	16
Dover	1	1	2	1	1	1	1
Faversham	6	6	6	6	6	6	6
Plymouth	4	4	4	4	4	4	4
Guildford	1	1	2	2	2	2	2
Yeovil PM							
Salisbury	1	1	1	1	1	1	1
TOTAL	109	113	118	124	124	124	124

When the early diesel shunters appeared they were made to resemble steam engines - in the case of Eastleigh-based D2085 seen shunting at Canute Road, Southampton - down to the chimney.